CANADA

MINNESOTA
Fargo
Duluth
L. Superior

MICHIGAN
L. Huron

MAINE
Augusta

Burlington
Montpelier
VT.
N.H.
Concord
Portland

Manchester

St. Paul
Minneapolis
WISCONSIN
Wisconsin R.
L. Michigan
L. Ontario
L. Erie
NEW YORK
Albany
Boston
MASS.
Providence
R.I.

Sioux Falls
Milwaukee
Madison
Lansing
Detroit
Buffalo
Hartford
CONN.

IOWA
Chicago
Gary
Cleveland
PENNSYLVANIA
Alleghany R.
Harrisburg
Newark
New York
Trenton
NEW JERSEY
Philadelphia

Omaha
Des Moines
Illinois R.
Wabash R.
OHIO
Wheeling
Pittsburgh
Baltimore
MD.
Dover
DELAWARE

Lincoln
ILLINOIS
Springfield
INDIANA
Indianapolis
Columbus
Cincinnati
WEST VIRGINIA
Potomac
Annapolis
WASHINGTON D.C.

Missouri R.
Topeka
Kansas City
St. Louis
Frankfort
Louisville
Charleston
Richmond
VIRGINIA
Norfolk

Jefferson City
MISSOURI
Ohio R.
KENTUCKY
Cumberland R.
Roanoke R.

Arkansas R.
Nashville
Knoxville
Raleigh
NORTH CAROLINA
Cape Fear R.

Oklahoma City
Canadian R.
ARKANSAS
Little Rock
Memphis
TENNESSEE
Charlotte
APPALACHIAN MOUNTAINS
SOUTH CAROLINA
Columbia

Mississippi R.
Tennessee R.
Chattahoochee R.
Santee R.
Charleston

Dallas
Birmingham
MISSISSIPPI
Jackson
ALABAMA
Montgomery
Altamaha R.
GEORGIA
Atlanta

Fort Worth
Sabine R.
LOUISIANA
Red R.
Alabama R.

Brazos R.
Trinity R.
Baton Rouge
New Orleans
Tallahassee
Jacksonville

Houston
Colorado R.
Gulf of Mexico

FLORIDA

Miami

Atlantic Ocean

St. Lawrence R.
Hudson R.

BAHAMAS

CUBA

PUERTO RICO
Atlantic Ocean
67°
66°
San Juan
Ponce
18°
Caribbean Sea
0   50
Miles

Elevation

Feet	Meters
9,843	3,000
6,562	2,000
3,281	1,000
1,640	500
656	200
0	0
Below sea level	Below sea level

0   200   400
Miles

95°   90°   85°   80°   75°

America's History

FOURTH EDITION

America's History

James A. Henretta
University of Maryland

David Brody
University of California, Davis

Susan Ware
Radcliffe College

Marilynn S. Johnson
Boston College

Bedford / St. Martin's
Boston • New York

For Bedford/St. Martin's

Executive Editor: Katherine E. Kurzman
Senior Developmental Editor: Elizabeth M. Welch
Senior Production Editor: Shuli Traub
Senior Production Supervisor: Joe Ford
Senior Marketing Manager: Charles Cavaliere
Art Director: Lucy Krikorian
Text and Cover Design: Wanda Kossak
Advisory Editor for Cartography: Michael P. Conzen, University of Chicago
Copy Editors: Alice Vigliani/Patricia Herbst
Indexer: Melanie Belkin
Photo Research: Pembroke Herbert and Sandi Rygiel/Picture Research Consultants & Archives
Cover Art: Library of Congress
Composition: TSI Graphics
Printing and Binding: RR Donnelley & Sons Company

President: Charles H. Christensen
Editorial Director: Joan E. Feinberg
Director of Editing, Design, and Production: Marcia Cohen
Managing Editor: Erica T. Appel

Library of Congress Catalog Card Number: 99-62280

For information, write: Bedford/St. Martin's, 75 Arlington Street, Boston, MA 02116 (617-426-7440)

ISBN: 0-312-19396-3

Credits
Credits and copyrights are continued at the back of the book on pages C-1–C-3, which constitute an extension of the copyright page.

For our families

Preface for Instructors

The year 2000 is an auspicious time to be publishing the fourth edition of *America's History*. There's nothing like a new millennium to get the historical juices flowing, even in the most unsuspecting student. She is going to pause before some monumental development and say, "Whoa, wait a minute, how did that happen?" It might be the crowd of students in the library, online, peering into computer screens; or, on so many campuses, the glorious multi-ethnic, multi-racial mix of her classmates; or, on TV, news of more U.S. aid to Russia (formerly of President Reagan's Evil Empire). How did that happen?

This question is the very substance of historical inquiry. And in asking it, the student is thinking historically. In *America's History* we aspire to satisfy that student's curiosity. We try to ask the right questions—the big ones and the not-so-big ones—and then write narrative history that illuminates the answers. The story, we hope, tells not only what happened, but *why*. We exclude no student from our potential audience of readers. How could we, when we hold the conviction that every student, bar none, is curious about his or her past?

From the very inception of *America's History*, we set out to write a democratic history, one that would convey the experiences of ordinary people even as it recorded the accomplishments of the great and powerful. Throughout the book, we focus not only on the marvelous diversity of peoples who became American but also on the institutions—political, economic, social, and cultural—that forged a common national identity. And we present political and social history in an integrated way, using each perspective to make better sense of the other. In our discussion of government and politics, diplomacy and war, we show how they affected—and were affected by—ethnic groups and economic conditions, intellectual beliefs and social changes, and the religious and moral values of the times. Just as

important, we place the American experience in a global context. We trace aspects of American society to their origins in European and African cultures, consider the American Industrial Revolution within the framework of the world economy, and plot the foreign relations of the United States as part of an ever-shifting international system of imperial expansion, financial exchange, and diplomatic alliances.

In emphasizing the global context, however, we had something more in mind. We wanted to remind students that America has never existed alone in the world; that other societies have experienced developments comparable to our own; and that, knowing this, we can better understand what was distinctive and particular to the American experience. At opportune junctures, we pause along the way for a comparative discussion, as, for example, in this fourth edition, about the abolition of slavery in different nineteenth-century plantation economies. This enables us to explain why, in the universal struggle by emancipated slaves for economic freedom, the freedmen of the American South became sharecrop tenants in a market economy and not, as in the Caribbean, gang laborers or subsistence farmers. The operative word is *explain* and, insofar as we can make it so, explaining the past is what we intend *America's History* to do. The challenge is to write a text that has explanatory power and yet is immediately accessible to every student who enrolls in the survey course.

Organization

──────────★──────────

This means first of all grounding *America's History* in a clear chronology and a strong conceptual framework. Each half of the nation's history is divided into three parts, with each part corresponding to a distinct phase of development. Each part begins at a crucial turning point, such as the American Revolution or the Cold War, and emphasizes the dynamic forces that unleashed it and that symbolized the era. We want to show how people of all classes and groups make their own history, but also how people's choices are influenced and constrained by circumstances: the customs and institutions inherited from the past and the distribution of power in the present. We are writing narrative history, but harnessed to historical argument—not simply a retelling of "this happened, then that happened."

To aid student comprehension, each part begins with a two-page overview: first, a **thematic timeline** highlights the key developments in government, economy, society, culture, and diplomacy; then these themes are fleshed out in a corresponding **part essay.** Each part essay focuses on the crucial engines of historical change—in some eras, primarily economic; in others, political or diplomatic—that created new conditions of life and transformed social relations. The part organization, encapsulated in the thematic timelines and opening essays, helps students understand the major themes and periods of American history, to see that individual historical facts acquire significance as part of a larger pattern of development.

The individual chapters are similarly constructed with student comprehension in mind. A **chapter outline** gives readers an overview of the text discussion, followed by a **thematic introduction** that orients them to the main issues and ideas of the chapter. We reiterate the themes in an analytic **chapter summary,** which is paired with a **chapter timeline** that reminds students of important events. The **suggested readings** that conclude each chapter are annotated for students and, to facilitate research, divided into sections corresponding to the main sections of the chapter.

Features

The fourth edition of *America's History* contains a wealth of special features, offered not with an eye to embellishing the book but as essential components of the text's pedagogical mission. Each chapter includes two **American Voices**—excerpts from letters, diaries, autobiographies, and public testimony that convey the experiences of ordinary Americans in their own words. One-third of these personal documents are new to this edition, including Philip Fithian on "Sadism under Slavery," Black Hawk on "A Sacred Reverence for Our Lands," and Anne Moody on "'We Would Like to Be Served.'" Entirely new are the **Voices from Abroad**—first-person testimony in every chapter by a foreign vis-

itor or observer that casts the American experience in a different light. Recognizing the centrality of technology in American life, we have doubled the number of **New Technology** essays, in which we describe key technical innovations and their impact on American history. New subjects include folk medicine, the battleship, and the biotech revolution. We retain our well-received **American Lives** feature—incisive biographies in every chapter of important, representative American figures of the time. Among the new Lives in this edition are the Shawnee prophet Tenskwatawa, the World War I propaganda chief George Creel, the black New Dealer Mary McLeod Bethune, and the architect of Cold War containment, George Kennan.

America's History has always been noted for its rich illustration program. In this edition, a new full-color design complements our special effort to enlarge many of the pictures and maps for better clarity and impact. Over one-third of the pictures are new to this edition, selected to reflect changes in the text and to underscore book themes. Ten new maps, mainly political in content, bring the number of maps to over 125, covering every aspect of American life that can be captured geographically.

Taken together, these documents and illustrations provide instructors with a trove of teaching materials, and students with a chance to enter the life of the past and see it from within.

Textual Changes

Of all the reasons for a new edition, of course, the most compelling is to improve the text itself—a task we have found to be never finished and yet, to our surprise, always gratifying. In this fourth edition, rather special considerations have spurred us on. Whenever authorial responsibility shifts, there is bound to be much rewriting. Elliot Brownlee, one of our original number, retires with this edition, and his section has been taken over by James Henretta (Chapters 10–14) and David Brody (Chapter 15). As a result, James Henretta now authors all of Volume 1 save the final chapter, while David Brody writes Chapters 15–21, Susan Ware Chapters 22–26 and 31, and Lynn Johnson Chapters 27–30.

We have also reduced the number of chapters from 33 to 31 to correspond more closely to the weeks of the academic calendar. In Part Three, former Chapters 13 (on sectionalism) and 14 (on the crisis of the Union) have been combined, with much of Chapter 13's discussion of southern society, Northeast industrialization, and the West shifted to earlier chapters. In Part Six, former Chapter 30 (on the politics of the 1960s) has been incorporated into the surrounding chapters. Structural changes of this magnitude have a bracing effect, and we are hopeful that by being forced to think hard about how to organize materials, we have come up with a stronger periodization and a clearer thematic development.

We also decided to cut text discussion by ten percent, in part to accommodate a richer array of features, but also to achieve a leaner, more sharply delineated narrative. In this, we were instructed by our experience in writing the Concise version of *America's History* that appeared in 1999. Brevity, we have learned all over again, is the best antidote to imprecise language and shoddy thinking. As textbook authors, we have always contended that if written with enough clarity and skill, the introductory survey text could be made accessible to students at all levels without simplifying the story or skimping on explanation. In this fourth edition, we have enlisted the power of brevity to get us ever closer to that goal.

The revising process is also an opportunity to incorporate new scholarship into our text. In this edition we have expanded the treatment of native Americans in the colonial era, and we have been more attentive to the appearance of a distinctive southern social order before 1820. Our treatment of the coming of the Industrial Revolution shifts the emphasis from industrialization as such to the extension of markets, in keeping with new scholarship on the Market Revolution. Chapter 11 on antebellum reform now stresses the religious roots and impulses common to communalism, women's rights, and abolitionism. We have drawn on recent Reconstruction scholarship that sees the transition from slavery to freedom in large part as a battle over labor systems, and that reveals the gender dimensions of the black struggle for racial equality, including most notably the political role of black women after disfranchisement in the late nineteenth century. We have continued our efforts to incorporate the West into the nation's historical narrative, relying on the new western history for insight into the interactions among environment, peoples, and economic development. In our coverage of the 1930s, we have linked the discussion of popular culture and movies more explicitly to the impact of the depression, and we have expanded our coverage of Mexican Americans during World War II and postwar decades. In our look at the modern era, more attention is given to the role of religion in American life and politics, and in our discussion of diplomacy our treatment of the Cold War is informed by recent scholarship drawing on hitherto closed Soviet and U.S. archives.

Finally, in deference to the new millennium, Susan Ware closes this fourth edition with the epilogue "America and the World at 2000: How Historians Interpret Contemporary Events and Their Legacy for the Future."

In seeking her own bearings at the millennium, Ware invites the student to enter the historian's world—to participate with her in the act of interpretation that lies behind every historical text, including this one.

Supplements

Readers of *America's History* often cite its ancillary package as a key to the book's success in the classroom. Hence we have revised and expanded with care our array of print and electronic ancillaries for students and teachers. We are especially pleased to welcome in the **Bedford Series in History and Culture** a new collection of potential supplements.

For Students

Documents Collection—Volume 1 by David L. Carlton (Vanderbilt University), Volume 2 by Samuel T. McSeveney (Vanderbilt University). This affordable two-volume Documents Collection offers students over 350 primary-source readings on topics covered in *America's History*, arranged to match the organization of the textbook. One-quarter of the documents in the collection are new, giving emphasis to contested issues in American history that will spark critical thinking and class discussions. Sets of documents highlight different perspectives on the same issue, while added attention has been given to America in the context of the larger world. Each document is preceded by a brief introduction and followed by questions for further thought.

Student Guide—Volume 1 by Timothy R. Mahoney (University of Nebraska); Volume 2 by Albert Berger (University of North Dakota). The two-volume Student Guide serves as a personal aid to students in their study of *America's History*, paralleling the textbook chapter by chapter to help them identify key ideas and assess their own grasp of the material. Each chapter in the Student Guide opens with all-new learning objectives that identify key themes for students to look for as they read, and a chapter summary that helps them determine whether they have mastered the primary concepts. The chapter timelines from the textbook appear with annotations, providing further framework for students' review. Newly expanded chapter glossaries include terms specific to each chapter as well as broader historical concepts that have changed in meaning over time. A set of exercises on the maps, art, and special features in the text encourage critical thinking, while identification and multiple-choice questions allow students to test their knowledge of the material. Guides to studying the part introductions (thematic timelines and corresponding part essays) in the textbook and a set of questions for each part help students understand the major themes in each period of American history. Finally, two new essays—"Doing History" and "What History Is"—set the study of *America's History* in a broader context and offer an understanding of the purpose and the techniques of the discipline.

Bedford/St. Martin's History Website—Developed by a group of scholars from Columbia University and New York University, the Bedford/St. Martin's History Website allows students to crystallize their knowledge of the themes and discussions in American history and to develop their own critical-thinking skills through a technological medium. Interactive chapter quizzes, map exercises, and primary-source research modules give students a means of reviewing what they have learned in *America's History* and of making meaningful connections between individual events in American history and larger trends. A prominently placed Research Room provides students with a collection of important documents from American history; an organized and annotated set of links to major libraries, history research centers, and American history sites; and a tutorial to help students evaluate historical sources critically for content and reliability. An unabridged online version of Scott Hovey's *Using* the Bedford Series in History and Culture *in the United States History Survey* can also help instructors integrate primary documents into their course syllabi, lectures, and class discussion.

The Bedford Series in History and Culture—Any of the volumes from this highly acclaimed series of brief, inexpensive, document-based supplements can be packaged with *America's History* at a reduced price. More than forty titles include *The Sovereignty and Goodness of God, The Interesting Narrative of the Life of Olaudah Equiano, The Autobiography of Benjamin Franklin, Narrative of the Life of Frederick Douglass, The Souls of Black Folk, Plunkitt of Tammany Hall*, and many more.

For Instructors

Instructor's Resource Manual—by Bradley T. Gericke (United States Military Academy). The *Instructor's Resource Manual*, provided free of charge with adoption of the textbook, offers an extensive collection of tools to aid both the first-time and the experienced teacher in structuring and customizing the American history course. Paralleling the textbook organization, this guide includes for each chapter in the text an all-new set of instructional objectives, a new annotated chapter outline to guide lectures, a chapter summary,

and an expanded version of the chapter timeline that gives greater detail about each entry. Lecture strategies and ideas for class discussion offer possible approaches to teaching each chapter and cover potentially difficult topics and how to present them; also included are suggestions for teaching the special boxed features in the textbook. A set of exercises for students includes questions about maps, graphs, and pictures in the textbook, and suggested writing assignments include topics involving the boxed features. The manual also reproduces the part introductions from the text and offers part instructional objectives to help instructors tie together larger sections of the book for students.

In addition to the chapter-by-chapter guidelines, the *Instructor's Resource Manual* features a set of fifteen updated historiographic essays on particular topics intended either as background for the instructor or for use with students. An expanded set of special primary-source modules on significant themes in American history allows instructors to customize their courses by emphasizing certain topics or perspectives in assignments or class discussions. Retained modules have been updated with new documents to represent more fully African Americans, Latino Americans, native Americans, women, the South, and constitutional history. All-new modules address religious history, military history, economic history, the presidency, and the West. A new essay about writing history can be photocopied and shared with students, while an updated and extensive list of suggested films is arranged by chapter and gives full detail for instructors wishing to use other media in the classroom. Finally, a new essay on using computers in the teaching of history keeps instructors abreast of the rapidly changing arena of electronic resources.

Test Bank—by James Miller. A fully updated Test Bank offers over 120 exercises for each chapter, allowing instructors to pick and choose from a collection of multiple-choice, fill-in, and map questions and short and long essay questions. To aid instructors in customizing their tests to suit their classes, every question is labeled by topic according to the chapter headings and includes a textbook page number that allows instructors to direct students to a particular page for correct answers. The multiple-choice questions are also labeled for instructors by difficulty level, and the correct answers are included. The Test Bank is available in bound paper format, with perforated pages for easy removal, or in Macintosh and Windows formats on disk.

Transparencies—A newly expanded set of over 150 full-color acetate transparencies, free to adopters, includes all maps and many tables, graphs, and images from the text.

CD-ROM with Presentation Manager Pro—For teachers who wish to use electronic media in the classroom, this new CD-ROM includes images, maps, graphs, and tables from *America's History* as well as sound recordings and a collection of supplementary images, in an easy-to-use format that allows instructors to customize their own presentations. The CD-ROM may be used with Presentation Manager Pro or with PowerPoint.

Using the Bedford Series in History and Culture *in the United States History Survey*—by Scott Hovey. Recognizing that many instructors use a survey text in conjunction with supplements, Bedford/St. Martin's has made the Bedford series volumes available at a discount to adopters of *America's History*. This short guide gives practical suggestions for using more than forty volumes from the **Bedford Series in History and Culture** with a core text. The guide not only supplies links between the text and the supplements but also provides ideas for starting discussions focused on a single primary-source volume.

Acknowledgments

———————★———————

We are extremely grateful to the following scholars and teachers who reported on their experiences with the third edition or reviewed manuscript chapters of the fourth edition. Their comments often challenged us to rethink or justify our interpretations and always provided a check on accuracy down to the smallest detail.

Ruth M. Alexander, Colorado State University
Robin F. Bachin, University of Miami
Albert I. Berger, University of North Dakota
Neal A. Brooks, Essex Community College (Maryland)
Thomas Bryan, Alvin Community College
Markus C. Cachia-Riedl, University of California, Berkeley
Kay J. Carr, Southern Illinois University at Carbondale
Myles L. Clowers, San Diego City College
John P. Daly, Louisiana Tech University
Bradley T. Gericke, United States Military Academy
Nita S. Howard, Clovis Community College
Jen A. Huntley-Smith, University of Nevada—Reno
Davis D. Joyce, East Central University (Oklahoma)
Norman D. Love, El Paso Community College

John R. McKivigan, West Virginia University
Samuel T. McSeveney, Vanderbilt University
M. Catherine Miller, Texas Tech University
Charles K. Piehl, Mankato State University
Edwin G. Quattlebaum III, Phillips Academy
Steven D. Reschly, Truman State University
Leonard Riforgiato, Penn State University—Shenango
Howard B. Rock, Florida International University
Peter H. Shattuck, California State University—Sacramento
Emily J. Teipe, Fullerton College
Suzanne R. Thurman, Mesa State College
Ken L. Weatherbie, Del Mar College
Arthur J. Worrall, Colorado State University

As the authors of *America's History*, we know better than anyone how much of this book is the work of other hands and other minds. We are grateful to R. Jackson Wilson, who served as intellectual midwife at the project's birth, and to David Follmer, who in various guises as our editor, publisher, and agent has from the outset been a partner in our endeavors. We are equally appreciative of the help given us during our years at Worth Publishers by three very special people: Bob Worth, Paul Shensa, and our indefatigable editor, Jennifer Sutherland.

At Bedford/St. Martin's, Elizabeth Welch has held us to the highest standards of clarity and accuracy as she masterfully edited our text. Charles Christensen, Joan Feinberg, and Katherine Kurzman have been generous in providing the resources we needed to produce the fourth edition. Special thanks are due to many other individuals: Pembroke Herbert and her staff at Picture Research Associates; editor John Elliott; our senior project editor, Shuli Traub; the fine copyeditors who worked closely with us—Patricia Herbst and Alice Vigliani; editorial assistants Becky Anderson, Gretchen Boger, and Regan Park; our senior marketing manager, Charles Cavaliere; and senior production supervisor Joe Ford. We also want to express our thanks for the valuable assistance provided by John Cashman, Patricia Deveneau, Scott Hovey, and Lawrence Peskin.

From the very beginning we have considered this book as a joint intellectual venture and with each edition our collaborative effort has grown. We are proud to acknowledge our collective authorship of *America's History*.

James A. Henretta
David Brody
Susan Ware
Marilynn S. Johnson

Presenting *America's History:*
An Introduction for Students

★

I
TS TITLE REVEALS a lot about this book. From the very inception of *America's History*, the authors were determined to write a democratic history, one that would convey the experiences of ordinary people just as it recorded the accomplishments of the famous and powerful. They wanted to show the remarkable diversity of peoples who became American, and they wanted to show how broad historical forces and institutions—political, economic, social, and cultural—have influenced people's choices and forged a common national identity. In keeping with their inclusive vision of U.S. history, the authors sought also to place the American experience in a global context, to reveal the interactions between America and the wider world that have helped to shape the United States.

Broader in scope and richer in information and ideas than many texts, *America's History* nonetheless explains the past clearly and compellingly for all students of the U.S. survey. For explaining America's history—telling not only what happened but why it happened and why it matters—is what the authors set out to do. By reading this introduction, you will discover how they constructed their book and how to gain the most from it.

Part and Chapter Structure

There are many ways to tell the multifaceted story of America's past. Even if the basic information remains the same, historians understand causes and effects differently, consider different facts as more or less important, and—because social, cultural, and political developments often have rhythms and timelines of their own—even tell parts of the story in a different order. The authors of *America's History* intend to explain major social, cultural, and economic developments as clearly as political and diplomatic ones. Hence they have given careful thought to the structure of their book, so that its very organization might make clear all the main themes and developments of American history.

The thirty-one chapters in the text are grouped into six parts, with each part corresponding to a distinct historical period, or phase of development. Each part begins at a crucial turning point, such as the American Revolution or the Cold War, and chapters within each part explore the central historical forces—the engines of change—that shaped each period. This part organization, encapsulated in the part introductions, will help you to place individual events into historical context and to understand the major themes and periods of American history.

Part Introductions

Each part opens with a two-page overview intended to serve as a road map for the chapters ahead. First, a **thematic timeline** highlights the key developments in government, diplomacy, the economy, society, and culture that characterized the period. By reading the timelines vertically, you will see the principal developments in each of these categories over the course of the part; by reading them horizontally you will see what was happening on all those fronts at a specific time.

Second, a **part essay** that faces the timeline discusses the themes labeled in the timeline. By reading each part timeline and essay, you will gain a firm grasp on the main ideas and topics developed in the following chapters. Too, the part introductions double as useful review aids in preparation for tests and exams.

THEMATIC TIMELINE

	Government	Diplomacy	Economy	Society	Culture
	Creating Republican Institutions	**European Entanglements**	**Expansion of Commerce and Manufacturing**	**Defining Liberty and Equality**	**Pluralism and National Identity**
1775	State constitutions written	Independence declared (1776) French alliance (1778)	Wartime expansion of manufacturing	Slavery emancipation in the North Judith Sargent Murray, "On the Equality of the Sexes" (1779)	Paine's *Common Sense* calls for a republic
1780	Articles of Confederation ratified (1781) Legislative supremacy in states Philadelphia convention drafts U.S. Constitution (1787)	Treaty of Paris (1783) British trade restrictions in West Indies	Bank of North America (1781) Commercial recession (1783–1789) Western land speculation	Virginia Statute of Religious Freedom (1786) Idea of republican motherhood	Land ordinances create a national domain in the West German settlers preserve own language Webster defines American English
1790	Bill of Rights (1791) First national parties;	Wars of the French Revolution	First Bank of the United States (1792–1812)	Sedition Act limits freedom of the press (1798)	Indians form Western Confederacy

Tᴀᴇ Aᴍᴇʀɪᴄᴀɴ ᴡᴀʀ is over, the Philadelphia Patriot Benjamin Rush declared in 1787, "but this is far from being the case with the *American revolution.* On the contrary, nothing but the first act of the great drama is closed. It remains yet to establish and perfect our new forms of government." The job was even greater than Rush imagined, for the republican revolution of 1776 challenged nearly all the values and institutions of the colonial social order, forcing changes not only in politics but also in economic, religious, and cultural life.

Government. The first and most fundamental task was to devise a republican system of government. In 1775 no one in America knew how the new state governments should be organized and if there should be a

foundations for a strong national economy. Beginning in the 1780s merchants financed a banking system and organized a rural-based system of manufacturing, while state governments used charters and legal incentives to assist their efforts and provide improved transportation. During these years southern planters carried slavery westward to Alabama and Mississippi and grew rich by exporting a new crop—cotton—to markets in Europe and the North. Simultaneously northern farm families settled lands in the West, produced raw materials such as leather and wool for the burgeoning manufacturing enterprises, and undertook additional labor as handicraft workers. As a result of these efforts, by 1820 the young American republic had begun to achieve economic as well as political independence.

Chapter Introductions

Just as the part introductions highlight central themes and topics in both graphic and narrative form, each chapter opens with two expressions of its main ideas and topics. To start, a **chapter outline** consisting of the main headings and subheadings of the chapter introduces you to subject matter and organization even before you begin to read. Next, a **thematic introduction** picks up from the outline to forecast the main issues and ideas of the chapter.

Chapter Headings

America's History contains a lot of information important for you to learn and remember. To help you navigate each chapter successfully, the authors employ three levels of headings—main headings to announce major topics and themes, subheadings to identify different aspects of the main topic, and sub-subheadings to divide subsections into related but distinct categories. The size and design of each heading indicate its level, with main headings the largest and most visually arresting and sub-subheadings the smallest and least prominent. As you read the chapter, consider the headings as signposts to main and contributing ideas and topics.

American Neutrality, 1939–1941
The Road to War
The Attack on Pearl Harbor

Organizing for Victory
Mobilizing for Defense
Mobilizing the American Fighting Force
Workers and the War Effort
Civil Rights during Wartime
Politics in Wartime

Life on the Home Front
"For the Duration"
Japanese Relocation

Fighting and Winning the War
Wartime Aims and Strategies
The War in Europe

ON A SUNDAY night in October 1938 the actor Orson Welles's "Mercury Theater of the Air" broadcast a modern version of *The War of the Worlds* (1898) by the British writer H. G. Wells. The fictional news bulletins, interspersed with simulated on-the-spot reports, convinced many people that Martians had landed near Princeton, New Jersey, and were invading the countryside. Even though the broadcast included four announcements that the radio program was a dramatization, some people fled their homes. No one doubted the power of radio anymore.

One reason that so many people believed in Orson Welles's fictional invasion may have been that in September 1938, radio programs had been interrupted repeatedly by ominous news bulletins about a possible European war. Even the September 30 reports of the Munich agreement among Britain, France, and Germany, which prevented war for another year, did not ease people's fears of imminent catastrophe. In the late 1930s popular culture reflected America's connection to international events, an involvement that the coming of World War II would intensify. When radios announced on December 7, 1941, that the Japanese had attacked Pearl Harbor, Americans realized that this news flash was not a hoax.

Class, Culture, and the Second Party System

———— ★ ————

The rise of the Democrats and Jackson's tumultuous presidency sparked the creation in the mid-1830s of a second national party—the Whigs. For the next two decades Whigs and Democrats dominated American politics, forming what historians call the Second Party System. Many evangelical Protestants became Whigs, whereas most Catholics and non-evangelical Protestants joined the Democrats. The two parties competed fiercely for votes, debating issues of economic policy, class power, and moral reform and offering Americans a clear choice between political programs.

The Whigs and Their Outlook

The Whig Party began in Congress in 1834, when opponents of Jackson banded together to protest his policies and high-handed actions. They took the name *Whigs* to identify themselves with the pre-Revolutionary American and British parties—also called Whigs—that had opposed the arbitrary actions of King George III and previous monarchs. The congressional Whigs labeled Jackson as "King Andrew I," accusing him of acting like an American monarch and violating the Constitution through "executive usurpation." By creating a "spoils system" and increasing presidential authority, they charged, Jackson had undermined government by elected legislators, the true representatives of the sovereign people.

Initially, the congressional Whigs were led by Senators Webster of Massachusetts, Clay of Kentucky, and Calhoun of South Carolina, who were united primarily by their opposition to Jackson. Webster and Clay also held a similar economic outlook, for Webster spoke on behalf of New England's business elite while Clay represented merchants and traders in the Ohio and Mississippi Valleys. Both men advocated a national program of economic development; this placed them at odds with Calhoun, now the most prominent defender of the interests of the white planters of the South. Having broken with Jackson over nullification, however, Calhoun had little choice but to join the Whigs regardless of his reservations about their economic policies.

Whig Ideology. During the election of 1836 the Whigs elaborated their plan for the nation's future, formulating a party platform and seeking votes among evangelical Protestants and upwardly mobile middle- and working-

Chapter Conclusions

Each chapter ends with a **chapter summary** that revisits central issues and themes. A paired **chapter timeline** lists key events and dates. Together, the summary and timeline provide a quick review of the main developments discussed in the chapter and the specific events that shaped those developments.

Suggested Readings

The final page of each chapter provides a comprehensive list of Suggested Readings, each entry succinctly described by the text authors. If you want to learn more about a certain subject or need to find secondary sources for research, these up-to-date bibliographies will direct you toward interesting and important scholarship. To help you find easily works on a particular subject, the Suggested Readings are organized under headings that correspond to the main sections of the chapter.

Summary

★

A new chapter in American reform began at the start of the twentieth century. For decades the problems resulting from industrialization and urban growth had been mounting. Now, after 1900, reform began to dominate the nation's public life. The unifying element in progressivism was a common intellectual outlook, highly principled and idealistic as to goals, and confident of the human capacity to find the means.

Beyond this shared outlook, progressives broke up into diverse and often conflicting groups. Political reformers included business groups concerned chiefly with improving the efficiency of city government. Other progressives, such as Robert La Follette, opposed privilege and wanted to democratize the political process. Both groups worked to enhance their power at the expense of entrenched party machines.

T I M E L I N E

1889	Jane Addams and Ellen Gates Starr found Hull House
1893	Panic of 1893 starts depression of the 1890s
1899	National Consumers' League founded
1900	Robert M. La Follette elected Wisconsin governor
	Commission form of city government first appears, in Galveston, Texas
1901	President McKinley assassinated; Theodore Roosevelt succeeds him
1902	President Roosevelt settles national anthracite strike
1903	National Women's Trade Union League founded
1904	Supreme Court dissolves the Northern Securities Company

Suggested Readings

★

Western history has become a bitterly contested ground in recent years. The fountainhead of the voluminous traditional scholarship is Frederick Jackson Turner's famous essay "The Significance of the Frontier in American History" (1893), reprinted in Ray A. Billington, ed., *Frontier and Section: Selected Essays of Frederick Jackson Turner* (1961). The "new" western history is critical of Turnerian scholarship for being "Eurocentric"—for seeing western history only through the eyes of frontiersmen and settlers—and for masking the rapacious and environmentally destructive underside of western settlement. Patricia N. Limerick's skillfully argued *The Legacy of Conquest: The Unbroken Past of the American West* (1987) opened the debate. Richard White, *"It's Your Misfortune and None of My Own": A New History of the American West* (1991), provides the fullest synthesis of the new scholarship. For an authoritative, balanced treatment of the main themes of western history, see the essays in Clyde A. Milner II *et al.*, *The Oxford History of the American West* (1994). On women's experience—another primary concern of the new western history—the starting point is Susan Armitage and Elizabeth Jameson, eds., *The Women's West* (1987). There are incisive environmental essays in Donald Worster, *Under Western Skies: Nature and History in the American West* (1992).

The Great Plains

The classic book, stressing the settlers' adaptation to climate and environment, is Walter P. Webb, *The Great Plains* (1931). There is an excellent chapter on the ecological history of the southern plains in Donald Worster, *The Great Plains* (1979). Robert M. Utley, *The Indian Frontier of the American West, 1846–1890* (1984), is a good introduction; Robert H. Lowie, *Indians of the Great Plains* (1954), is a classic anthropological study. On the religious life of the Plains Indians, see Howard L. Harrod, *Renewing the World: Plains Indian Religion and Morality* (1987). The assault on Indian culture is recounted in Fredrick E. Hoxie, *A Final Promise: The Campaign to Assimilate the Indians, 1880–1920* (1984). On phases of plains settlement, see Oscar Winther, *The Transportation Frontier: The Trans-Mississippi West, 1865–1890* (1964); Lewis Atherton, *The Cattle Kings* (1964); Gilbert Fite, *The Farmer's Frontier, 1865–1900* (1966); and Mary W. M. Hargreaves, *Dry-Farming*

Illustration Program

America's History contains an unusually rich assortment of pictures, maps, graphs, and tables, all carefully chosen to extend or to reinforce the text. To help you appreciate the historical significance of each illustration, explanatory captions link the images to chapter discussion.

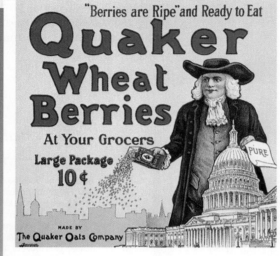

Quaker Oats

Like crackers, sugar, and other nonperishable foods, oatmeal had traditionally been marketed to consumers in bulk from barrels. In 1882 the grain merchant Henry P. Cowell completed the first continuous-process mill for oatmeal, cutting production costs and greatly increasing output. He also hit on the idea of selling oatmeal in boxes of standard size and weight to a national market. Broadsides showing the Quaker Oats man soon appeared in every American town, advertising a product

Pictures

Historians value the art and artifacts of a period much as they value its written documents—as primary sources, or historical evidence for what people thought and did in the past. The over 500 images in *America's History* are all contemporaneous with the period under discussion; that is, people living at that time created the art and artifacts reproduced. Thus you can examine each picture for clues to the period, much as you would study a printed historical document.

MAP 13.6
The California Gold Rush, 1849–1857
Traveling from all parts of the world—Europe, China, and Australia, as well as the eastern United States—hundreds of thousands of bonanza seekers converged on the California goldfields. Miners traveling by sea landed at San Francisco, which became an instant metropolis, and then stocked up on food and supplies at Stockton and Sacramento. By the mid-1850s the seaborne boom was over; almost as many people departed from San Francisco each year as had arrived to seek their fortune.

Maps

Maps in *America's History* show much more than a visual representation of the land— each conveys information that is significantly dependent on *place*. The over 125 maps in your book cover every aspect of American life that can be captured geographically, from military campaigns and political shifts to territorial expansion and changes in ethnic and religious distribution. Study each map and its caption critically, remembering that maps extend as well as reinforce the text. (For a complete listing of maps, see p. xxxvii.)

Graphs

Like maps, graphs reveal some historical patterns more clearly and vividly than words alone can. The many graphs in *America's History* show how specific data can add up to large social, economic, cultural, and political trends. Study them in conjunction with the text to understand key developments in greater depth and to learn how historians support their arguments with statistical evidence. (For a complete listing of graphs, see p. xxxix.)

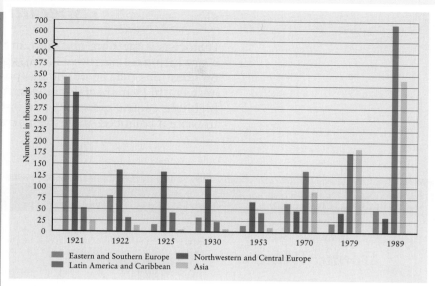

FIGURE 23.1
American Immigration after World War I
Legislation reflecting nativism slowed the influx of immigrants after 1920, as did the dislocations brought on by depression and war in the 1930s and 1940s. Note the higher rate of non-European immigration since the 1970s.

Tables

Tables present factual information, often involving dates or quantities, in rows and columns for easy comparison. By looking at the information presented, you can usually identify an increase or decrease over time, a contrast or similarity between different places, and other progressions or developments. (For a complete listing of tables, see p. xxxix.)

TABLE 5.2

Patriot Resistance, 1762–1775

British Action	Date	Patriot Response
Revenue Act	1762	Merchants complain privately
Proclamation Line	1763	Land speculators voice discontent
Sugar Act	1764	Protests by merchants and Massachusetts House
Stamp Act	1765	Riots by Sons of Liberty Stamp Act Congress First nonimportation movement
Quartering Act	1765	New York Assembly refuses to implement until 1767
Townshend Duties	1767	Second nonimportation movement Harassment of pro-British merchants
Troops occupy Boston	1768	Boston Massacre of 1770
Gaspée affair	1772	Committees of Correspondence created
Tea Act	1773	Widespread resistance Boston Tea Party
Coercive Acts and Quebec Act	1774	First Continental Congress Third nonimportation movement
British raids on Lexington and Concord	1775	Armed resistance by Minutemen Second Continental Congress

Special Features

History is something one does, not just something one reads. Behind every historical narrative is the historian's act of interpretation, focused on questions that he or she has posed, researched, and sought to answer. In four special features, the authors of *America's History* highlight central questions and issues they have explored in their effort to write a balanced, inclusive narrative of the nation's history.

AMERICAN VOICES

ISAAC NELSON
Atomic Witness

★

*I*saac Nelson, a naval veteran of World War II, returned to his hometown of Cedar City, Utah, in 1945 and went to work for a nearby hardware company. Like many other residents of southern Utah, he and his wife Oleta lived downwind from the Nevada Test Site, where the U.S. government detonated 126 atomic bombs into the atmosphere between 1951 and 1963.

After 1951 they were going to start the testing in Nevada, and everybody was really excited, and thought maybe we'd get a part to play in it and show our patriotism. We wanted to help out what little we could. My wife and I and a hundred or so residents of Cedar drove out to see the first one. We huddled up, our blankets around us because it was cold, so early in the morning before daylight, and we were chattering like chipmunks, so excited! Pretty soon,

would go out and ooh and aah just like a bunch of hicks. We was never warned that there was any danger involved in going out and being under these fallout clouds all the time I lived here. . . .

Along about 1955 a cloud came over Cedar, and my wife and I, the kids and the neighbors stood outside looking at it and talking about it. Later on towards evening, my wife, her skin, her hands, arms, neck, face, legs, anything that was exposed just turned a beet red. . . . She got a severe headache, and nausea, diarrhea, really miserable. We drove out to the hospital, and the doctor said, "Well it looks like sunburn, but then it doesn't." Her headache persisted for several months, and the diarrhea and nausea for a few weeks.

Four weeks after that I was sittin' in the front room reading the paper and she'd gone into the bathroom to wash her hair. All at once she let out the most ungodly scream, and I run in there and there's about half her hair layin' in the washbasin! You can imagine a woman with beautiful, raven-black hair, so black it would glint green in the sunlight just like a raven's wing. . . . She was in a state of panic. . . . After that she kept getting weaker, and listless, and she didn't even have any desire to go out

American Voices

Each chapter contains two primary-source excerpts drawn from letters, diaries, autobiographies, public testimony, and other documents that convey the experience of ordinary Americans in their own words. Individually each feature provides a firsthand account of an event or development central to the chapter; together the excerpts reveal the rich diversity of the American people. (For a complete listing of "American Voices," see p. xli.)

Voices from Abroad

Despite its geographic distance from other parts of the world, America has always been influenced by events and traditions elsewhere. To illuminate what is comparable in the American experience and what is distinctive, first-person testimony in every chapter by a foreign observer casts America's history in a global perspective. (For a complete listing of "Voices from Abroad," see p. xliii.)

VOICES FROM ABROAD

ALEXIS DE TOCQUEVILLE
Law and Lawyers in the United States

★

A French aristocrat and lawyer, Alexis de Tocqueville came to the United States to study its innovative prison system but ended up writing Democracy in America (1835), a comprehensive and astute analysis of its dynamic society. Here Tocqueville argues that the raw vigor of American democracy was restrained by the ingrained conservatism of men of the law, who dominated the political system.

The political activity that pervades the United States must be seen in order to be understood. No sooner do you set foot upon American ground than you are stunned by a kind of tumult . . . everything is in motion around you; here the people of one quarter of a town meet to decide upon the building of a

security against the excesses of democracy. This effect seems to me to result from a general cause, which it is useful to investigate. . . . Men who have made a special study of the laws derive from [that] occupation certain habits of order, a taste for formalities, and a kind of instinctive regard for the regular connection of ideas, which naturally render them very hostile to the revolutionary spirit and the unreflecting passions of the multitude. . . .

[Moreover,] the government of democracy is favorable to the political power of lawyers; for when the wealthy, the noble, and the prince are excluded from the government, the lawyers take possession of it, in their own right, as it were, since they are the only men of information and sagacity, beyond the sphere of the people, who can be the object of popular choice. . . .

The people in democratic states do not mistrust the members of the legal profession, because it is known that they are interested to serve the popular cause. . . . Lawyers belong to the people by birth and interest, and to the aristocracy by habit and taste; they may be looked upon as the connecting link between the two great classes of society. . . . When the American people are intoxicated by passion or

American Lives

The authors want to show how people of all classes and groups shape their own history, but also how people's choices are influenced and constrained by circumstances: the customs and institutions inherited from the past and the distribution of power in the present. Incisive biographies in every chapter demonstrate how influential Americans confronted the major issues of their times. (For a complete listing of "American Lives," see p. xli.)

(For a complete listing of "American Lives," see p. xli.)

AMERICAN LIVES

Mary McLeod Bethune: Black Braintruster

★

THE NEW DEAL brought many remarkable people to Washington, but few had traveled as far as Mary McLeod Bethune. As the Reverend Adam Clayton Powell Sr. wrote to her in 1935 when she received the prestigious Spingarn Medal from the National Association for the Advancement of Colored People, "It is a long way from the rice and cotton fields of South Carolina to this distinguished recognition, but you have made it in such a short span of years that I am afraid you are going to be arrested for breaking the speed limit." In terms of her contributions to black history, Mary McLeod Bethune deserves to be remembered alongside such luminaries as Frederick Douglass, W. E. B. Du Bois, and Martin Luther King Jr.

Born on July 10, 1875, near Mayesville, South Carolina, Mary was the fifteenth of seventeen children born to Sam and Patsy McLeod, former slaves liberated after the Civil War. She was educated at the Scotia Seminary in Concord, North Carolina, and the Bible Institute for Home and Foreign Missions in Chicago (later the Moody Bible Institute) in preparation for her chosen career as a missionary. Turning from her original plan to go to Africa, she redirected her missionary [...] the field [...] expanded educational opportunities for Afric[...]

Mary McLeod Bethune
This 1943 painting by Betsy Graves Reyneau captures the strength and dignity of one of the twentieth century's most important African Americans. Behind Bethune is a picture of the first building at the Daytona Literary and Industrial School for Training of Negro Girls, which later became Bethune-Cookman College.
National Portrait Gallery, Smithsonian Institution/Art Resource, NY.

NEW TECHNOLOGY

The Biotech Revolution

★

WAS ZACHARY TAYLOR poisoned? Did Abraham Lincoln have a rare disease called Marfan's syndrome? Were Tzar Nicholas II and his family executed during the Bolshevik Revolution in 1918? Was the Vietnam serviceman buried in Arlington Cemetery's Tomb of the Unknowns really Air Force Lieutenant Michael Blassie? Recent advances in DNA testing, part of the dramatic growth in biotechnology in the 1980s and 1990s, mean that these historical questions, plus a host of contemporary ones, can be answered. With promises of breakthroughs in medicine (gene therapy and cancer research), the environment (genetically altered microorganisms for pollution cleanup), and agriculture (genetically engineered foods), biotechnology offers the possibility not just to understand but also to manipulate the processes of life.

The essence of biotechnology is exploiting genes, a process revolutionized by the 1953 discovery of DNA by scientists James Watson and Francis Crick. DNA (deoxyribonucleic acid) is the molecule that carries the genetic blueprint of all living things; genes are DNA chains made up of hundreds or some-

New Technology

Recognizing the centrality of technology in American history, the authors pause twice in each part to consider revolutionary changes in technology that were central to the economic and cultural life of that period. (For a complete listing of "New Technology," see p. xliii.)

(For a complete listing of "New Technology," see p. xliii.)

Appendices

A rich collection of important documents, historical data, and research resources follows the chapters for your reference.

Documents

In addition to the complete texts of the Declaration of Independence, the Articles of Confederation, and the Constitution, this section provides annotations to the twenty-seven constitutional amendments that explain when and why each amendment was adopted. Six amendments that did not make it into the final document are discussed as well.

Amendment III [1791]

No soldier shall, in time of peace, be quartered in any house without the consent of the owner, nor in time of war, but in a manner to be prescribed by law.

★ ★ ★

The Third Amendment was extremely important to the framers of the Constitution, but today it is nearly forgotten. American colonists were especially outraged that they were forced to quarter British troops in the years before and during the American Revolution. The philosophy of the Third Amendment has been viewed by some justices and scholars as the foundation of the modern constitutional right to privacy.

No person shall be held to an infamous crime, unless on a grand jury, except in cases ari or in the militia, when in actu lic danger; nor shall any pe offence to be twice put in jeop compelled in any criminal ca self, nor be deprived of life, l process of law; nor shall priva use without just compensatio

★

The Fifth Amendment protects authority in the prosecution of the state, first, from charging a without a grand jury hearing t cient evidence to support the c

The American Nation

This section includes such cornerstone facts of American political history as the admission of states into the Union, results of presidential elections, and a record of the Supreme Court justices.

Admission of States into the Union

State	Date of Admission		State	Date of Admission		State
1. Delaware	December 7, 1787		18. Louisiana	April 30, 1812		35. West `
2. Pennsylvania	December 12, 1787		19. Indiana	December 11, 1816		36. Nevac
3. New Jersey	December 18, 1787		20. Mississippi	December 10, 1817		37. Nebra
4. Georgia	January 2, 1788		21. Illinois	December 3, 1818		38. Color
5. Connecticut	January 9, 1788		22. Alabama	December 14, 1819		39. North
6. Massachusetts	February 6, 1788		23. Maine	March 15, 1820		40. South
7. Maryland	April 28, 1788		24. Missouri	August 10, 1821		41. Monta
8. South Carolina	May 23, 1788		25. Arkansas	June 15, 1836		42. Washi
9. New Hampshire	June 21, 1788		26. Michigan	January 26, 1837		43. Idaho

The American People

Numerous charts, graphs, and tables on issues such as population size, racial and ethnic composition, life expectancy, immigration trends, and changing labor patterns serve as a demographic survey of the American people.

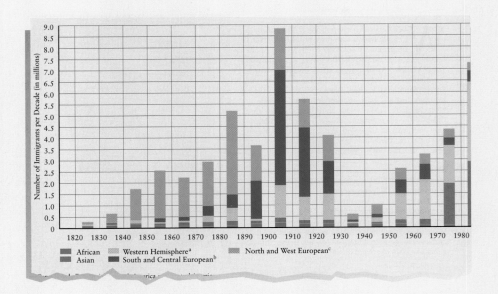

African   Western Hemisphere[a]   North and West European[c]
Asian   South and Central European[b]

Internet Resources

This section directs you to a variety of sources for further research—a list of internet sites that are major gateways to information on American history.

American Memory: Historical Collection from the National Digital Library Program. <http://rs6.loc.gov/amhome.html> An Internet site that features digitized primary source materials from the Library of Congress, among them African American pamphlets, Civil War photographs, documents from the Continental Congress and the Constitutional Convention of 1774–1790, materials on woman suffrage, and oral histories.

Decisions of the U.S. Supreme Court. <http://supct.law.cornell.edu/supct/#historic> This database can be used to search for information on various Supreme Court cases. Although the site primarily covers cases that occurred after 1990, there is information on some earlier historic cases. The justices' opinions, as originally written, are also included.

Directory of Scholarly and Professional Electronic Conferences. <http://n2h2.com/KOVAKS/> A good place to find out what electronic conversations are going on in a scholarly discipline. Includes a good search facility and instructions on how to connect to e-mail discussion lists, newsgroups, and

A central place to com native American history

Index of Resources f edu/history/index.html> sites of interest to histo eral topic. Some links information, but most a start an exploration of I

Internet Archives tory.hanover.edu/texts.h purpose of this site is t students and faculty. / cally, and by subject, the primary-document link sources on each subject

Internet Resources) <http://www.libraries.rut A good place to begin r

Index

An unusually comprehensive index allows you to locate information in the text quickly and easily. The index, intended to double as a review aid for tests and exams, cites illustrations, maps, and figures as well as narrative discussion.

Website

In addition to the many print supplements described in the Preface, *America's History* has a website that provides further guidance to the text. Located at http://www.bedfordstmartins.com/henretta.htm, the website includes quizzes on each chapter with explanations of correct and incorrect answers, interactive map exercises, and exercises on how to use primary sources and to research history topics online. Use it to extend your reading of the text and your own discovery of America's history.

Contents in Brief

Contents

Maps, Figures, and Tables

Maps

Special Features

Voices from Abroad

New Technology

About the Authors

JAMES A. HENRETTA is Priscilla Alden Burke Professor of American History at the University of Maryland, College Park. He received his undergraduate education at Swarthmore College and his Ph.D. from Harvard University. He has taught at the University of Sussex, England; Princeton University; UCLA; and Boston University; as a Fulbright lecturer in Australia at the University of New England; and in 1991–1992 at Oxford University as the Harmsworth Professor of American History. His publications include *The Evolution of American Society, 1700–1815: An Interdisciplinary Analysis; "Salutary Neglect": Colonial Administration under the Duke of Newcastle; Evolution and Revolution: American Society, 1600–1820; The Origins of American Capitalism;* and important articles in early American and social history. He is currently working on a study of the *Transformation of the Liberal State in America, 1800–1970.*

DAVID BRODY is Professor Emeritus of History at the University of California, Davis. He received his B.A., M.A., and Ph.D. from Harvard University. He has taught at the University of Warwick in England, at Moscow State University in the former Soviet Union, and at Sydney University in Australia. He is the author of *Steelworkers in America; Workers in Industrial America: Essays on the 20th Century Struggle;* and *In Labor's Cause: Main Themes on the History of the American Worker.* He has been awarded fellowships from the Social Science Research Council, the Guggenheim Foundation, and the National Endowment for the Humanities. He is past president (1991–1992) of the Pacific Coast Branch of the American Historical Association. His current research is on industrial labor during the Great Depression.

SUSAN WARE specializes in twentieth-century U.S. history and the history of American women. She is affiliated with Radcliffe College, where she is editing the next volume of the noted biographical dictionary *Notable American Women.* Ware received her undergraduate degree from Wellesley College and her Ph.D. from Harvard University and from 1986 to 1995 taught in the history department at New York University. Her publications include *Beyond Suffrage: Women in the New Deal; Holding Their Own: American Women in the 1930s; Partner and I: Molly Dewson, Feminism, and New Deal Politics; Modern American Women: A Documentary History; Still Missing: Amelia Earhart and the Search for Modern Feminism;* and *Letter to the World: Seven Women Who Shaped the American Century.* She has served on the national advisory boards of the Franklin and Eleanor Roosevelt Institute and the Schlesinger Library of Radcliffe College, and has been a historical consultant to numerous documentary film projects. She is currently writing a biography of radio talk show pioneer Mary Margaret McBride.

MARILYNN S. JOHNSON is Associate Professor of History at Boston College, where she teaches U.S. social history and the history of the American West. She received her B.A. from Stanford University and her M.A. and Ph.D. from New York University. She is the author of *The Second Gold Rush: Oakland and the East Bay in World War II* and is currently working on a study of urban police violence in the late nineteenth and twentieth centuries. She has been a fellow of the American Council of Learned Societies and has served on the editorial board of *Pacific Historical Review.* Her articles and reviews have appeared in the *American Historical Review,* the *Journal of American History,* the *Journal of Urban History, Pacific Historical Review, Labor History,* and other scholarly publications.

America's History

Part One

★

The Creation of American Society, 1450–1775

THEMATIC TIMELINE

	Economy	Society	Government	Religion	Culture
	From Staple Crops to Internal Growth	Ethnic, Racial, and Class Divisions	From Monarchy to Republic	From Hierarchy to Pluralism	The Creation of American Identity
1450	Native American subsistence economy Europeans fish off North American coast	Sporadic warfare among Indian peoples Spanish conquest of Mexico (1519–1521)	Rise of monarchical nation-states in Europe	Protestant Reformation begins (1517)	Diverse native American cultures in eastern Woodlands
1600	First staple crops: furs and tobacco	English-Indian warfare African servitude begins in Virginia (1619)	James I rules by "divine right" in England Virginia House of Burgesses (1619)	Persecuted English Puritans and Catholics migrate to America	Puritans implant Calvinism, education, and freehold ideal
1640	New England trade with sugar islands Mercantilist regulations: first Navigation Act (1651)	White indentured servitude in Chesapeake Indians retreat inland	Puritan Revolution Stuart restoration (1660) Bacon's rebellion (1675)	Religious liberty in Rhode Island	Aristocratic aspirations in Chesapeake
1680	Tobacco trade stagnates Rice cultivation expands	Indian slavery in Carolinas Ethnic rebellion in New York (1689)	Dominion of New England (1686–1689) Glorious Revolution (1688–1689)	Rise of toleration	Emergence of African American language and culture
1720	Mature subsistence economy in North Imports from Britain increase	Scots-Irish and German migration Growing rural inequality	Rise of the representative assembly Challenge to "deferential" policies	German and Scots-Irish Pietists in mid-Atlantic region Great Awakening	Expansion of colleges, newspapers, and magazines Franklin and the American Enlightenment
1760	Trade boycotts encourage domestic manufacturing	Uprisings by tenants and backcountry farmers Artisan protests	Ideas of popular sovereignty Battles of Lexington and Concord (1775)	Evangelical Baptists Quebec Act allows Catholicism (1774)	Emergence of "American" identity Innovations in political theory

SOCIETIES ARE MADE, not born. They are the creation of decades, even centuries, of human endeavor and experience. The first American societies were formed by hunting and gathering peoples who migrated to the Western Hemisphere from Asia many centuries ago. Over many generations these migrants—the native Americans—came to live in a wide variety of environments and cultures. In much of North America they developed kin-based societies that relied on farming and hunting. But in the lower Mississippi valley, native Americans developed a hierarchical social order similar to that of the great Indian civilizations of Mesoamerica. The coming of Europeans and their diseases tore the fabric of most native American cultures into shreds. Native Americans increasingly confronted a *new* American society, one dominated by men and women of European origins.

The Europeans who settled America sought to transplant their traditional societies to the new world—their farming practices, their social hierarchies, their culture and heritage, and their religious ideas. But in learning to live in the new land, the Europeans who came to England's North American colonies eventually created societies that were distinctly different from those of their homelands.

Economy. First, many settlers compiled an impressive record of economic achievement. Traditional Europe was made up of poor and unequal societies periodically racked by famine. But in the bountiful natural environment of North America, plenty replaced poverty, and the settlers created a bustling economy and prosperous communities of independent farm families. Indeed, the northern mainland colonies became the "best poor man's country" for migrants from the British Isles and Germany.

Society. Second, some of the new settlements became places of oppressive captivity for Africans. Hundreds of thousands of Africans, from many peoples, were transported in chains to the West Indies and the southern mainland colonies and forced to labor as slaves on tobacco and rice plantations. Slowly and with great effort, they and their descendants created an African American culture within a social order dominated by Europeans.

Government. Third, whites in the emerging American societies created an increasingly free and competitive political system. The first English settlers transplanted authoritarian institutions, and the English government continued to manage their lives. But after 1689 traditional controls gradually gave way to governments based in part on representative assemblies. Eventually, the growth of self-rule would lead to demands for political independence from England.

Religion. Fourth, the American experience profoundly changed religious institutions and values. Many migrants came to America in the wake of Europe's Protestant Reformation to practice their religion without interference, and the society they created became increasingly religious, especially after the evangelical revivals of the 1740s. By this time many Americans had rejected the harshest tenets of Calvinism (a strict Protestant faith), and others had embraced the rationalist view of the European Enlightenment. As a result, American Protestant Christianity became increasingly tolerant, democratic, and optimistic.

Culture. Fifth, the new American society was marked by change in the family and local community. The first English settlers lived in patriarchal families ruled by dominant fathers and in communities controlled by men of high status. By 1750, however, many American fathers no longer strictly managed their children's lives. And as communities became more diverse and open, many men—and some women—began to enjoy greater personal independence. This new American society was increasingly pluralistic, composed of migrants from varied backgrounds: English, Scots, Scots-Irish, Dutch, Germans, and West Africans as well as many native American peoples. Distinct regional cultures developed in New England, the mid-Atlantic colonies, and the Chesapeake and Carolina areas. An American identity—based on the English language, British legal and political institutions, and shared experiences—emerged very slowly.

The story of the colonial experience is thus both tragic and exciting. The settlers created a new American world but one that warred with native Americans and condemned most African Americans to bondage even as it offered Europeans rich opportunities for economic security, political freedom, and spiritual fulfillment.

Chapter 1

Worlds Collide: Europe and the Americas, *1450–1620*

IN A.D. 1450 the peoples of Europe and the Americas lived in separate worlds, unaware of each other's existence. An estimated 70 million native Americans, the descendants of migrants from Asia, populated the vast continents of the Western Hemisphere. They were divided into scores of language groups and hundreds of distinct societies, each with its own culture. Many native American peoples lived in large and well-organized empires, but many also resided in smaller agricultural societies in which kinship and community formed the primary bonds of government.

Across the Atlantic Ocean another 70 million people inhabited the much less extensive lands of Western Europe. Unlike native Americans, Europeans shared a common religious heritage, but they too were divided by language and territorial boundaries, and most of them lived in poor agricultural communities. A small class of armed aristocrats, the feudal nobility, ruled over a mass of illiterate peasants. Except for the city-states of Italy, which had established themselves as vibrant centers of trade, European society had little potential for sustained economic growth.

Around 1450 some Europeans, hungry for the trade and riches of Asia, began to venture far from their native shores. Within a few decades Christopher Columbus, an Italian navigator in the service of Spain, encountered the lands and peoples of the Americas, setting off a collision of European and native American cultures that changed the course of world history. The subsequent arrival in the Western Hemisphere of Africans—by 1500 in the West Indies and by 1550 in Brazil—added another dimension to the unfolding story.

The "Four Huron Nations" Wampum, 1611
In 1611 the Huron people presented Samuel de Champlain, the governor of the French colony of Quebec, with this belt of wampum, a highly prized gift of sea shells. The four persons depicted in the belt (far right) represent the four Huron nations, who were united in a Confederacy. The Huron intended the belt to signify an alliance with the French, so each figure holds a lozenge-shaped object (see detail), a symbol of union between peoples.
Musée de l'Homme, Paris.

By 1620 both Europe and the Americas had changed significantly, in no small measure because of the penetration of Portuguese and Dutch merchants into the trade of Asia and the conquest by Spanish adventurers of the native American empires of the Western Hemisphere. The Age of Exploration fueled economic activity in Europe and stimulated the rise of England. Tragically, it also brought disease and death to native Americans, forced migration and slavery on thousands of West Africans, and brought landless poverty to many English peasants.

How did Europeans become leaders in world trade and extend their influence across the Atlantic? What was the character of the native Americans' life and culture, and what made their societies vulnerable to conquest by European adventurers? And what led to the transatlantic trade in enslaved Africans? Finally, how did England, an insignificant nation in 1492, acquire the political will and economic resources to establish colonies in North America by the 1620s? In the answers to these questions lie the origins of the United States.

the Bering Strait to be exposed. These first "migrants" were not consciously migrating but were following herds of caribou and other wild game.

Most anthropologists believe that this migratory stream continued for about 20,000 years, until about 10,000 B.C., when the glaciers melted and the rising ocean waters submerged the land bridge. Following wild herds and looking for edible plants and fresh water, some of these Asian migrants moved eastward. Crossing the northern Rocky Mountains, they traversed an ice-free corridor along the eastern side of the mountains from present-day Alaska to Montana, and from there they spread out in all directions. By 8000 B.C., when the glaciers finally retreated, groups of hunter-gatherers were already established throughout the hemisphere, from the tip of South America to the Atlantic coast of North America. Then the people of the Western Hemisphere were cut off from the rest of the world for over 9,500 years.

Until 3000 B.C. the first Americans lived as hunter-gatherers. Using flint and jasper they developed distinctive tools and weapons, fashioning sharp "fluted" points that they attached to spears and used to hunt

Native American Worls

———— ★ ————

When the Europeans arrived in the Western Hemisphere, most native Americans—probably 45 million—lived in Mesoamerica (the area that stretches from present-day Mexico to Panama) and the Caribbean, another 15 million resided in lands to the north (present-day United States and Canada), and the rest lived in Peru and other parts of South America. Some Indians lived in simple hunter-gatherer or agricultural communities, but the majority resided in richer and more complex societies ruled by warrior-kings and priests. In Mesoamerica and Peru, Indian peoples created civilizations whose art, religion, society, and economy were as complex as those of Europe and the Mediterranean.

The First Americans

The first people who lived in the Western Hemisphere were migrants whose ancestors came from various regions of Asia. Some might have come by water to South America, but most probably came by land to North America. Strong archaeological evidence suggests that during the last Ice Age, which began about 30,000 years ago, large family-based groups of hunter-gatherers moved to the Western Hemisphere from northeastern Asia. They traveled from Siberia to Alaska, both of which consisted of ice-free tundra, across a wide land bridge formed when glaciation caused the sea level to become lower and dry land at

Gold Piece from Peru
Skilled Inca artisans created gold jewelry of striking beauty. Note the intricate detail on the headdress and the stylized treatment of the face.
Dunbarton Oaks Research Library and Collections, Washington, DC.

big-game species such as the mammoths and mastodons. As these species declined in numbers because of ecological changes brought by the end of the Ice Age, early native peoples turned for subsistence to smaller animals, fish, and wild plants and berries.

Then some native American peoples began to develop horticulture, most notably in the area of present-day Mexico. These inventive farmers planted avocados, chili peppers, and cotton, and learned how to breed maize, or Indian corn, as well as tomatoes, potatoes, and manioc (a rapidly growing but not very nutritious root crop)—foods that would eventually enhance the diet of the entire world. Over the centuries the Indian peoples bred maize into a much larger, extremely nutritious plant that was hardier, had more varieties, and produced a higher yield per acre than wheat, barley, or rye, the staple cereals of Europe. They also learned to cultivate beans and squash and plant them in the same fields as their corn, creating a mix of crops that provided a diet rich in calories and essential amino acids. This mix also preserved soil fertility, promoting inten-

sive farming and high yields. The resulting agricultural surplus laid the foundation for the development of populous and wealthy societies with complex civilizations in Mexico, Peru, and the Mississippi Valley.

The Maya and the Aztec

The flowering of civilization in Mesoamerica began among the Mayan peoples of the Yucatan peninsula of Mexico and the neighboring rain forests of the area known today as Guatemala (see Map 1.1). The Maya built large religious centers, urban communities with elaborate systems of water storage and irrigation. By A.D. 300 the Mayan city of Tikal had at least 20,000 inhabitants, mostly farmers who worked the nearby fields and whose labor was used to build huge stone temples. An elite class claiming descent from the gods ruled Mayan society, living in splendor on goods and taxes extracted from peasant families. Drawing on traditions that stretched back to the Olmec people, who had lived along the Gulf of Mexico around 700 B.C., skilled Mayan artisans decorated

Celebrating a New Mayan Ruler, A.D. 790
This brilliantly colored depiction of Mayan lords paying homage to the newborn heir to the kingdom of Bonampak is the best surviving example of Mayan painting. The wealthy nobles wear pendants and necklaces of carved jade and sport elaborate head-dresses. Note their receding foreheads, a Mayan mark of beauty achieved by shaping the skulls of infants.
Doug Stern and Enrico Feroelli/National Geographic Society Image Collection.

temples and palaces with art depicting warrior-gods and complex religious rituals. Mayan astronomers created a calendar that recorded historical events and predicted eclipses of the sun and the moon with remarkable accuracy. Most fascinating of all, perhaps, was Mayan hieroglyphic writing, which recorded the royal lineage of the various city-states and noteworthy events, including wars and famines.

Beginning around A.D. 800, Mayan civilization declined for reasons that are unclear. Some evidence suggests that a two-century-long dry period caused a decline in population and an economic crisis that prompted overtaxed peasants to desert the temple cities and retreat into the countryside. By A.D. 900 many religious centers had been abandoned and their temples desecrated by fleeing peasants. Some Mayan emigrants who fled this chaos may have carried their advanced technology and culture into the Mississippi River Valley of North America. Other Mayan city-states remained vibrant until the Spanish invasion in the sixteenth century.

As the Mayan empire flourished in the Yucatan, a second major Mesoamerican civilization developed in the central Valley of Mexico around the city of Teotihuacán. The Teotihuacán people were headed by an elite of religious leaders and military officials who ruled over a vast assemblage of farmers and artisans. The farmers developed an innovative agricultural system known as *chinampas*—small, intensively cultivated islands that were constructed on a network of natural and artificial lakes. Teotihuacán artisans were no less inventive than the farmers, working in stone, pottery, cloth, leather, and especially obsidian (hard volcanic glass used for sharp-edged weapons and tools).

At its zenith about A.D. 500 Teotihuacán had more than 100 temples, about 4,000 apartment buildings, and a population of at least 100,000. It also boasted the Pyramid of the Sun, a huge religious monument that was as large at its base as the great pyramid of Cheops in Egypt. By A.D. 800 Teotihuacán had also declined, probably because of a long-term drop in rainfall and recurrent invasions by seminomadic peoples. Eventually the militant Aztec from the deserts of northern Mexico took control of Teotihuacán and created an even more extensive empire.

Upon entering the Valley of Mexico, the Aztec settled on an island in Lake Texcoco. There, in A.D. 1325, the Aztec began to build a new city, Tenochtitlán (present-day Mexico City). They learned the settled ways of the resident peoples, mastered their complex irrigation systems, and established an elaborate culture with a hierarchical social order. Priests and warrior nobles ruled over twenty clans of free Aztec commoners who farmed communally owned land, and the nobles used huge numbers of non-Aztec slaves and serfs to labor on their private estates.

The Aztec remained an aggressive tribe and used brute military force to extend their rule, ultimately subjugating most of central Mexico. Their rulers demanded both economic and human tribute from scores of subject tribes, causing the gruesome sacrifice of untold thousands of men and women to their patron deity, Huitzilopochtli, the god of the sun and war. According to Aztec beliefs, such sacrifices were necessary to keep the sun moving across the sky. Aztec merchants, organized in a guild whose membership was hereditary, created far-flung trading routes and imported furs, gold, textiles, food, and obsidian. By A.D. 1500 Tenochtitlán had grown into a great metropolis with splendid palaces and temples and over 200,000 inhabitants. The Aztec's wealth, strong institutions, and military power posed a formidable challenge to any adversary, at home or from afar.

The Indians North of the Rio Grande

In A.D. 1500, as many as 15 million native Americans were living north of the Rio Grande, in habitats as diverse as the dry lands of the Southwest and the densely forested lands east of the Mississippi River (Map 1.1). Like the Mesoamericans, these peoples were descendants of the hunter-gatherers who had crossed the land bridge from Asia—an epic journey that was kept alive from one generation to the next in stories and legends. A tale of the Tuscarora Indians, who occupied the area of present-day North Carolina about this time, tells of a famine in the old world and a journey over ice toward where "the sun rises," a long trek that finally brought their ancestors to a lush forest with abundant food and game, where they settled.

Most of these native Americans were organized in self-governing tribes composed of *clans*, groups of related families that had a common identity and a real or legendary common ancestor. They were led by local chiefs who, aided by the clan elders, led ceremonies and regulated personal life. Elders encouraged individuals to share food and other scarce goods, promoting a social ethic of reciprocity rather than one of accumulation. Elders banned marriage between members of the same clan, a rule that helped prevent inbreeding; they also granted families use-rights over certain planting grounds and hunting areas, since the concept of private ownership of land was virtually unknown in Indian tribal culture. Clan leaders also resolved personal feuds, disciplined individuals who violated customs, and decided whether or not to go to war. However, their power was far less than that of the Mayan and Aztec nobles, because their kinship-based system of government was locally based and worked by consensus, not by coercion. Over the centuries a number of these Indian peoples rose to prominence, exerting influence over their immediate neighbors through conquest and over a much wider area through trade.

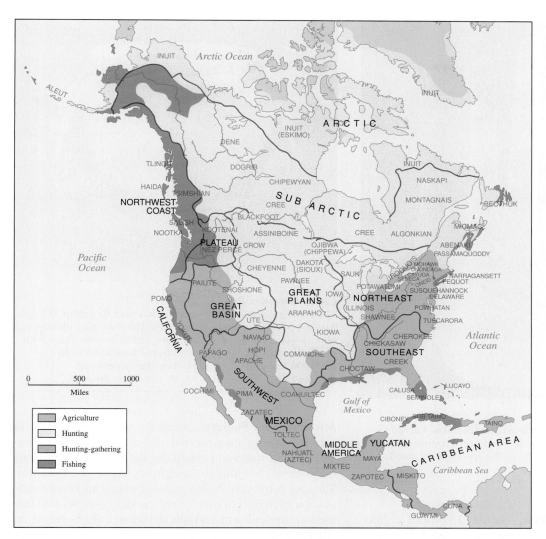

MAP 1.1
Native American Peoples, 1492
Native Americans populated the entire Western Hemisphere at the time of Columbus's
arrival, having learned how to live in many environments. They created diverse cultures
that ranged from the centralized agriculture-based empires of the Maya and the Aztec to
seminomadic tribes of hunter-gatherers. The sheer diversity among Indians—of culture,
language, tribal identity—inhibited united resistance to the European invaders.

The Adena and Hopewell Cultures. The earliest
expansive Indian culture was that devised by the Adena
and Hopewell peoples who lived in the well-watered
forests and valleys of the area of present-day Ohio. As
early as 500 B.C. the Adena had begun to erect large burial mounds in the Ohio River Valley, and their burial
practices and religious ideas gradually spread across
northeastern North America. Building on this foundation, by A.D. 100 the Hopewell people had created an
even more elaborate and influential culture in both the
Ohio and Illinois valleys. The Hopewell increased their
food supply by domesticating plants, which allowed
clans to settle in large villages. Near those settlements
they built elaborate ceremonial centers and numerous
burial mounds, surrounding them with extensive circu-

lar, rectangular, or octagonal earthworks that in some
cases still survive. An artistic people, the Hopewell
imported raw materials from distant territories and
fashioned them into handsome ornaments: copper
beaten into elaborate designs, beautiful crystals of
quartz, mica cut into the shapes of serpents and human
hands, and stone pipes carved to represent frogs,
hawks, bears, and other animals. Like the Adena, they
buried this art with their dead and exchanged it with
other peoples. Indeed, through their trade in seeds,
scarce minerals, and craft products, the Hopewell's cultural influence spread as far as the areas of present-day
Wisconsin and Louisiana. For unknown reasons, their
elaborate trading network gradually collapsed around
A.D. 400.

Hopewell Art
The Hopewell people had a rich artistic tradition. Carved objects, such as this elegant mica hand, were commonly placed in burial mounds as gifts to the spirits of the dead.
Ohio Historical Society.

Casas Grandes Pot
The artistically and architecturally talented Mogollon and Anasazi peoples of Arizona and New Mexico took utilitarian objects—such as this ordinary pot—and decorated them with black-on-white designs. Their cultures flourished from A.D. 1000 to 1250, after which they slowly declined.
Amerind Foundation, Dragoon, AZ. Photo by Robin Stancliff.

The Southwestern Tribes. As the Hopewell culture declined in the East, three important native American cultures—known as the Pueblo peoples because of the design of their houses—developed along the river valleys of the Southwest. By A.D. 600 farmers of the Hohokam culture in the area of present-day Arizona were using irrigation to grow two crops a year, fashioning pottery with red-on-buff designs, and, under Mesoamerican influence, building ball courts and low platform mounds for religious worship. To the east, in the Mimbres Valley of New Mexico, the Mogollon peoples developed a distinctive black-on-white pottery and, after A.D. 1000, large multiroom stone structures. The Anasazi of northern Arizona and New Mexico fully developed this architecture, building elaborate residential-ceremonial villages in steep cliffs as well as devising an elaborate ceremonial road system and various astronomical devices. All three peoples fell into decline after A.D. 1250 as long periods of drought and invasions by the nomadic Navajo and Apache disrupted their precarious system of food production. But the descendants of these Pueblo peoples—including the Zuni and Hopi—later built strong but smaller and more dispersed village societies.

Mississippian Society. Around A.D. 800 a new burst of creative energy transformed the culture of the Mississippi Valley, inspired perhaps by the farming technology introduced by Mayan emigrants from the war-torn Yucatan peninsula. New strains of maize and beans provided a protein-rich diet for the resident peoples and created an agricultural surplus. A robust culture based on small fortified temple cities and a class-divided society gradually emerged. By A.D. 1150 the largest city, Cahokia (near present-day St. Louis), had a population of 10,000 and more than 100 temple mounds. As in the societies of Mesoamerica, the tribute paid by peasant cultivators supported a privileged class of nobles and priests who patronized skilled artisans. However, by A.D. 1350 Mississippian civilization was in rapid decline, undermined by urban diseases such as tuberculosis and warfare between city-states over access to the fertile soils of the river valleys.

The values and institutions of Mississippian civilization endured for centuries among the Natchez and other peoples of the region and accounted in part for their fierce resistance to Spanish and French invaders. In 1700 French traders and priests described Natchez society as being rigidly divided among four classes: a hereditary caste of Suns, two intermediate groups of Nobles and Honored People, and a bottom class of peasants, called Stinkards. Undoubtedly influenced by Mesoamerican rituals, the Natchez practiced human sacrifice; the death of a Great Sun called for the sacrifice of his wives and the enlargement of a ceremonial mound to bury their remains (see American Voices,

FATHER LE PETITE
The Customs of the Natchez

———★———

Beliefs and institutions from the earlier Mississippian culture (A.D. 800–1350) lasted for centuries among the Natchez, who lived in the area of present-day Mississippi. This letter was written around 1730 by Father le Petite, one of the hundreds of Jesuits who lived among the Indians in the French colonies of Louisiana and Canada and wrote detailed accounts of what they saw. Here, Father le Petite accurately describes many Indian customs but misinterprets the rules governing the succession of the chief, which simply followed the normal practice of descent and inheritance in a matrilineal society.

My Reverend Father, The peace of Our Lord.

This Nation of Savages inhabits one of the most beautiful and fertile countries in the World, and is the only one on this continent which appears to have any regular worship. Their Religion in certain points is very similar to that of the ancient Romans. They have a Temple filled with Idols, which are different figures of men and of animals, and for which they have the most profound veneration. Their Temple in shape resembles an earthen oven, a hundred feet in circumference. They enter it by a little door about four feet high, and not more than three in breadth. Above on the outside are three figures of eagles made of wood, and painted red, yellow, and white. Before the door is a kind of shed with folding-doors, where the Guardian of the Temple is lodged; all around it runs a circle of palisades [pointed wooden stakes], on which are seen exposed the skulls of all the heads which their Warriors had brought back from the battles in which they had been engaged with the enemies of their Nation. . . .

The Sun is the principal object of veneration to these people; as they cannot conceive of anything which can be above this heavenly body, nothing else appears to them more worthy of their homage. It is for the same reason that the great Chief of this Nation, who knows nothing on the earth more dignified than himself, takes the title of brother of the Sun, and the credulity of the people maintains him in the despotic authority which he claims. To enable them better to converse together, they raise a mound of artificial soil, on which they build his cabin, which is of the same construction as the Temple.

The old men prescribe the Laws for the rest of the people, and one of their principles is . . . the immortality of the soul, and when they leave this world they go, they say, to live in another, there to be recompensed or punished.

In former times the Nation of the *Natchez* was very large. It counted sixty Villages and eight hundred Suns or Princes; now it is reduced to six little Villages and eleven Suns. [Its] Government is hereditary; it is not, however, the son of the reigning Chief who succeeds his father, but the son of his sister, or the first Princess of the blood. This policy is founded on the knowledge they have of the licentiousness of their women. They are not sure, they say, that the children of the chief's wife may be of the blood Royal, whereas the son of the sister of the great Chief must be, at least on the side of the mother.

———

Source: Reuben Gold Thwaites, ed., *The Jesuit Relations and Allied Documents* (Cleveland: Murrow Brothers, 1900), vol. 68: 121–135.

"Father le Petite: The Customs of the Natchez," above). Other Mesoamerican practices persisted among some tribes in Florida and also among the Choctaw, who regarded a mound in the area of present-day Winston County, Mississippi, as *ishki chito*, the "great mother." There, according to a Choctaw legend, "the Great Spirit created the first Choctaws, and through a hole or cave, they crawled forth into the light of day." Class divisions marked all peoples who spoke Muskhogean languages, such as the Creeks and the Chickasaw, as well as the Iroquoian-speaking Cherokee. Because of the hierarchical social order and cultural achievements of these southeastern peoples, eighteenth-century British settlers would call them the Civilized Tribes.

For the rest of eastern North America, the most important legacy of the Mississippian civilization was its agricultural practices, including the use of flint hoes and superior strains of corn, beans, and squash. This new horticultural technology produced a more reliable and abundant food supply, permitting the tribes of the eastern region to enjoy a more fixed and stable way of life after A.D. 1000. As better nutrition improved health and lengthened the life span, communities expanded and developed more complex cultures.

The Eastern Woodland Peoples.   Although advances in farming raised living standards, on the eve of European contact the native peoples of eastern North America enjoyed few material comforts and their societies remained small and divided by language—five major language groups containing some sixty-eight dialects. Most of the coastal Indians who lived north of the Chesapeake Bay, such as the Pequot and the Delaware, spoke Algonquian dialects. The Five Iroquois Nations—the Mohawk, Oneida, Onondaga, Cayuga, and Seneca—that dominated the region between the Hudson River and the Great Lakes spoke Iroquoian languages. Indians along the southern Atlantic coast, such as the Creeks and the Choctaw, were primarily Muskhogean and Sioux speakers, whereas most of the tribes living in the area of present-day Florida used varieties of the Timucuan and Calusan tongues.

Each of these Indian peoples claimed its own territory but did not live in permanent settlements. Instead, bands of people moved about, using different parts of their domain on a seasonal basis. Some tribes built semipermanent villages of domed wigwams covered with thatch or, among the Iroquois, multifamily longhouses of wood frames and bark or skin coverings. They situated these settlements near their cultivated fields, where the tribe lived from April to October. Using flint-tipped hoes the women planted corn, squash, and beans; the community celebrated the agricultural cycle with religious ceremonies such as the Iroquois green corn and strawberry festivals. After the harvest these peoples broke into groups consisting of three or four families, with the men hunting together for large game.

In this way the eastern Woodland peoples adapted Mesoamerican advances in food production to their tribal structures and values. In Mesoamerica (and the Mississippian culture) peasant men as well as peasant women worked in the fields, but among eastern Woodland peoples men remained hunters while farming became women's work. As Indian women perfected their skills as horticulturalists, they came to provide the bulk of their society's food supply (see New Technology, "Indian Women and Agriculture," pp. 14–15). Among many tribes, women's role in food production greatly enhanced their authority; indeed, among the Iroquois of New York, it helped to produce a matrilineal-based clan and inheritance system. In those tribes, use-rights to land and other property passed from mother to daughter (rather than from father to son, as in patrilineal European societies), and the senior women of each clan chose the (male) clan chief.

This combination of hunting, gathering, and simple hoe agriculture provided the eastern Woodland peoples with an adequate supply of food but with few other amenities. They did not make intensive use of the environment, and their populations did not grow rapidly. Consequently these peoples, unlike the native Americans in Mesoamerica, did not live in densely populated communities with elaborate religious sites nor did they trade extensively with other peoples. Instead, each group's economic life depended primarily on the climate and natural resources of its territory. For example, the short growing season along the St. Lawrence River diminished the importance of horticulture for northern Algonquians, such as the Abenaki and Passamaquoddy of the area of present-day Maine, who lived by hunting wild animals, fishing, and gathering wild grasses, nuts, and berries. By contrast, the more southerly Algonquians, such as the Delaware and the Powhatan, depended on farming by women for most of their food. In some cases, foraging peoples traded furs for the foodstuffs grown by the farming groups. Even before the arrival of the Europeans, a long-distance trade in *wampum* (shell money) and furs linked the distant communities of Long Island and Maine.

Despite the relatively settled existence of the Woodland peoples, they remained small societies and were divided by language and by ancient rivalries. Neither their social organization nor their historical experience prepared them to deal collectively with the European invaders.

Traditional European Society, 1450–1550

————————★————————

In A.D. 1450 few observers would have predicted that the European peoples would become the overlords of the Western Hemisphere. A thousand years after the decline of the western Roman empire, Europe remained a relatively backward society. Most Europeans, like most native Americans, were exploited peasants or poor farmers who had little knowledge of the wider world. Their lives and those of their descendants who would migrate to the Americas were shaped by the cultural and religious values of the traditional rural world.

The Peasantry

There were only a few large cities in Western Europe before A.D. 1550—only Paris, London, and Naples had 100,000 residents and thus equaled the size of Teotihuacán at its zenith. More than 90 percent of the population lived in small, relatively isolated rural communities separated from each other by rolling hills or dense forests. The primitive state of transportation reinforced this isolation. Because peasant villages were linked only by rough dirt roads and ox-drawn carts, travel was slow and cumbersome at best and virtually impossible in heavy rain or deep snow. Since there were few merchants, most peasant families exchanged surplus grain or meat with their relatives and neighbors and bartered their produce for the services of local artisans: millers, weavers, blacksmiths, and roof thatchers.

The Seasonal Cycle. As among the native Americans, nearly all aspects of European peasant life followed a seasonal pattern. The agricultural year began in March or April when the ground thawed and dried, allowing the villagers to begin the exhausting work of spring plowing and planting. During these busy spring months men also sheared the thick winter wool of their sheep, which the women washed and began to spin into yarn. In June peasants cut the first crop of hay and stored it as winter fodder for their livestock. In the summer life became more relaxed. Families could mend their fences or repair their barns and houses. Fall brought the strenuous harvest, but once the crops were in, people celebrated with solemn feasts of thanksgiving and riotous bouts of merrymaking. As winter approached, peasants slaughtered excess livestock and salted or smoked the meat. During the cold months they completed the tasks of threshing grain and weaving textiles and had time to visit friends and relatives in nearby villages.

Life and death also followed a seasonal pattern (Figure 1.1). Many rural folk died in January and February, victims of the cold and of viral diseases. August and September were even more dangerous months, as infants and old people succumbed to epidemics of fly-borne dysentery. More mysteriously, in European villages (and later in rural British America), the greatest numbers of babies were born in February and March,

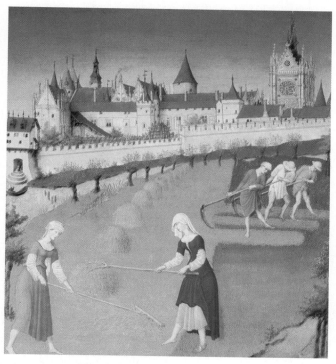

An Idealized Medieval World
In this illustration from a medieval manuscript, well-dressed peasants labor effortlessly in a field of hay. However, the walled town with its moat suggests the warfare of the era while the size and majesty of the urban dwellings and cathedral testify to the power of the nobility and the church over the lives of ordinary men and women.
Musée Conde/Giraudon/Art Resource.

with a smaller peak in September and October. The precise causes of this pattern are unknown. Religious practices, such as the abstention from sexual intercourse by devout Christians during the eight weeks of Lent, might have affected the number of conceptions. Even more likely, fluctuations in the food supply or in women's

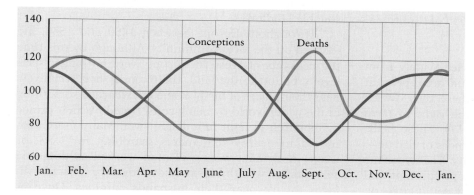

Note: If equal numbers died or were conceived in each month, there would be a horizontal line at 100.

FIGURE 1.1
The Yearly Rhythm of Rural Life
The annual cycle of nature profoundly affected life in the traditional world. Deaths were about 20 percent above normal in February and September. Summer was the healthiest season, with the fewest deaths and the greatest number of successful conceptions (as measured by births nine months later).

Indian Women and Agriculture

———— ★ ————

CORN WAS THE dietary staple of most native Americans, and its cultivation shaped their vision of the natural world. The Agawam Indians of Massachusetts began their year with the month of Squannikesas, a word that meant "when they set Indian corn," and subsequent months had names that referred to the weeding, hilling, and ripening of corn. To appease the spirit forces in nature and ensure a bountiful harvest, the Seneca Indians of New York held a corn-planting ceremony. They asked the Thunderers, "our grandfathers," to water their crops and beseeched the Sun, "our older brother," not to burn them.

Among the eastern Woodland tribes, growing corn was women's work. Indian women prepared the ground with wooden hoes tipped with bone, flint, or clamshells. According to a Dutch traveler, they made "heaps like molehills, each about two and a half feet from the others," and planted "in each heap five or six grains." As the tall, slender plants appeared, the women piled on more dirt to support the roots. They also "put in each hill three or four Brazilian [kidney] beans. When they grow up, they interlace with the corn, which reaches to a height of from five to six feet; and they keep the ground free of weeds."

The planting together of corn and beans represented a significant technological advance, dramatically increasing total yields and improving human nutrition. The beans fixed nitrogen in the soil, preserving fertility, and conserved moisture, preventing erosion. Beans and corn provided a diet rich in vegetable proteins. By intensively cultivating two acres, an Indian woman could typically harvest sixty bushels of shelled corn—half the calories required by five persons for a year.

This economic contribution enhanced the political influence of women in some tribes, especially those in which names and inheritance rights passed through women (matrilinealism). Thus, among the matrilineal Iroquois, women chose the clan leaders. To preserve their status, women jealously guarded their productive role. A Quaker missionary reported as late as 1809 that "if a man took hold of a hoe to use it, the Women would get down his gun by way of derision & laugh and say such a Warrior is a timid woman."

In seventeenth-century America, English farmers appropriated Indian corn technology and made it part of their own culture. Now Protestant ministers (as well as Indian shamans) prayed for a bountiful harvest of corn. After clearing their fields of tree stumps, English farmers plowed furrows at three-foot intervals from north to south. Then they cut east-west furrows, heaping up the soil into Indian-

work patterns might have altered a woman's ability to carry a child to full term. One thing is certain—this seasonal pattern of births does not exist in modern urban societies, so it must have been a reflection of traditional rural life.

The Peasant's Lot. Peasant life varied widely from one region of Europe to another. In some areas peasant families lived in compact villages, where they owned or leased small dwellings and had the right to farm strips of land in the surrounding fields. These fields were "open"—that is, not divided by fences or hedges—making cooperative farming a necessity. Each year the male householders decided which crops to plant and how many cows and sheep each family could graze on the commonly used meadows. In other regions families owned or leased enclosed farms and managed their own affairs. Everywhere, most peasants yearned to control the land, either owning it as independent farmers or leasing it on a long-term, low-rent basis from a reasonable landlord.

Throughout Europe between 1450 and 1550, life focused on the local community. Although by this time the peasants of Western Europe were no longer serfs legally bound to the land, the majority lived relatively near their places of birth. Some men learned something of the wider world by being conscripted by their prince or monarch to fight in a distant war. Many more men moved to nearby settlements searching for work or wives. And many young women worked as domestic servants for wealthy farmers or moved to adjacent villages to live near their husbands' families. Once or twice in their lives, ordinary peasants might make a pilgrimage to a famous religious shrine or cathedral, such

Timucuan Women at Work in the Field
In this stylized—and inaccurate—engraving by De Bry, a visiting European artist, Timucuan men in Florida break up the soil while women plant beans and maize. In fact, Indians did not use plows (and so there should be no furrows), and though men removed trees and brush from fields, they did not usually wield hoes.
Courtesy of the John Carter Brown Library at Brown University.

style cornhills at the intersecting points. English planting methods were less labor-intensive than Indian techniques and far less productive, averaging from ten to fifteen bushels per acre, not thirty.

Equally significant, among European settlers the men—not women—planted, tended, and harvested the crop. In combination with patrilineal naming and inheritance practices, the dominance of men in agriculture confined colonial women to a subordinate role in economic and political life.

Among Europeans as well as Indians, corn soon became the premier crop, and with good reason. As a Welsh migrant to Pennsylvania noted, corn "produced more increase than any other Graine whatsoever." Pigs and chickens ate its kernels, and cows munched its stalks and leaves. Ground into flour and made into bread, cakes, or porridge, corn became the dietary staple of poor people in the northern English colonies and of white tenant farmers and enslaved blacks in the South and in the West Indies.

as Canterbury in England or Chartres in France. But these events were extraordinary. Most men and women lived hard, unvarying lives as agricultural workers.

In this preindustrial society, mere survival required unceasing labor. Other than water- or wind-powered mills for grinding grain, raw muscle was the major source of energy. Horses and oxen strained to break the soil with primitive wooden plows, while workers harvested hay, wheat, rye, and barley with hand sickles. Because of the lack of high-quality seeds, chemical fertilizers, and pesticides, output was very small—less than one-tenth of present-day yields.

Consequently, for most peasants the margin of existence was thin, and this scarcity corroded family relations. Most married women bore six or more children, but a majority of them died before the age of twenty-one, usually from epidemic diseases. Famine also

struck from time to time, the result of a local drought or hailstorm. In those difficult years, observers noted, malnourished mothers fed their babies sparingly, calling them "greedy and gluttonous," and many newborn girls were "helped to die" so that their older brothers would have enough to eat.

Hierarchy and Authority

In the traditional European social order, as in the Aztec and Mayan empires, authority came from above. Rulers, priests, and local officials intruded into the lives of the peasantry and regulated their affairs.

The Ruling Orders. Kings and princes owned vast tracts of land and lived in splendor off the labor of the dependent peasants. Monarchs sought to extend their

An Artisan Family
Work was slow and output limited in the preindustrial world, and survival required the efforts of all family members. Here a fifteenth-century French woodworker planes a panel of wood while his wife twists flax fibers into linen yarn for the family's clothes and their son fashions a basket out of reeds.
Giraudon/Art Resource, NY.

power by levying royal taxes, creating law courts, and conscripting men for military service. Yet most kings and princes were far from supreme, given the power of the nobles, each of whom also owned large estates and controlled the labor of hundreds of peasant families. Collectively, these noblemen had the power to challenge royal authority. They had their own legislative institutions, such as the French *parlements* and the English House of Lords, and enjoyed special privileges, such as the right to a trial before a jury of their own (noble) peers. Because nobles had direct control over the peasantry, monarchs had little choice but to appoint them as local judges and militia officers. Such legacies of the medieval feudal order, when most kings were dependent on the nobility, worked against the formation of strong centralized states that had the capacity for overseas expansion.

Family and Community.   Just as kings and nobles ruled the polity, the men in peasant families ruled their women and children. The man was the head of the house in European societies, his power justified by the teachings of the Christian Church. As one English clergyman put it, "The woman is a weak creature not embued with like strength and constancy of mind"; law and custom consequently "subjected her to the power of man." Upon marriage, an English woman assumed her husband's surname and usually moved to his village. She was required (under the threat of legally sanctioned physical "correction") to submit to her husband's orders. Moreover, she surrendered to her husband the legal right to all her property, including her clothes. Upon his death she was legally entitled only to a *dower*, defined by custom and law as the use during her lifetime of one-third of the family's land and goods.

Fathers controlled the lives of children with equal authority. Landowning peasants in Western Europe normally retained legal control of farms until their physical strength ebbed. Only then, after age fifty, did they provide land to sons and livestock or furnishings to daughters, thereby permitting their children to marry. Consequently most young men and women worked for their fathers until their middle or late twenties, enduring years of emotional domination and sexual deprivation. When they finally did marry, it was often to someone not to their liking, since most marriages were arranged, with parents choosing partners of comparable wealth and status to protect the family's economic position.

Within the family, children were not born equal: their social position depended on their sex and birth order. In many regions cultural rules dictated that a father bestow most of his land on his oldest son (a system known as primogeniture). That son became the new patriarch, responsible for the welfare of his siblings. Custom called for landless brothers and sisters to work on their property-owning brother's farm in return for food and shelter. But as the European population began to rise after A.D. 1500, the size of most peasant holdings declined, forcing many younger children to join the ranks of the roaming poor who were condemned to desperate lives on the edge of respectable society.

In this harsh world most individuals had to submit to the discipline of superiors or to the village community, which strictly regulated behavior for the common good. For example, in many parts of Germany village authorities granted marriage licenses only to couples with enough property to support a family. Officials also imposed limits on what could be charged for the basic necessities of life: a loaf of bread, a sack of flour or grain. Fearful of change, they made tradition the measure of existence. "After a thing had been practiced for so long that it becomes a Custom," an English clergyman proclaimed, "that Custom is Law." In such a society few men—and even fewer women—had much personal freedom or individual identity.

Hierarchy and authority prevailed in the traditional European social order both because of the power of established institutions and because, in a difficult and unpredictable world, they offered ordinary people a measure of security. These values, which migrants carried with them to America, would shape the character of family life and the social order there well into the eighteenth century.

The Power of Religion

The Roman Catholic Church preserved Latin, the language of the Roman Empire and of classical scholarship, and because of its widespread influence, served as one of the great unifying forces in Western European society. The pope, as head of the Catholic Church, directed a vast hierarchy of cardinals, bishops, and priests. The clergy carried Church teachings into every village and hamlet, providing peasants and rulers throughout the continent with a common understanding of God, the world, and human history. Equally important, the Church provided another bulwark of authority and discipline, using moral authority and the threat of eternal damnation to enforce social order.

Religion in Daily Life. Christian doctrine penetrated deeply into the everyday lives of peasants. Over the centuries the Church had adopted a religious calendar that followed the traditional agricultural cycle and gradually transformed pagan festivals into Christian holy days. Thus the winter solstice, which for pagans marked the return of the sun and the victory of light over darkness, became the feast of Christmas—marking the birth of Christ. Likewise the feast of Easter, celebrating Christ's resurrection from the dead, gave a new meaning to the pagans' spring fertility festivals. Christian and pagan

Christ's Crucifixion
This graphic portrayal of Christ's death on the cross, by the German painter Grünewald, reminded believers of the reality of death and the need for repentance. Grünewald painted this crucifixion scene between 1509 and 1515 for a monastery church in Isenheim, Germany.
Musée Unterlinden, Colmar-Giraudon/Art Resource.

traditions blended again in the autumn months as ancient harvest celebrations gradually evolved into holy days of thanksgiving.

This merging of the sacred and the agricultural cycle endowed all worldly events with meaning. Few Christians believed that events occurred by chance; they were seen as the result of God's will. To avert famine and plague, peasants turned to priests for spiritual guidance and offered prayers to Christ and the saints. God's presence in the world was renewed continually through the sacrament of Holy Communion. According to Catholic doctrine, priests had the power to change sacramental bread and wine into the body and blood of Christ. By consuming the bread of the Host, peasants—along with priests and aristocrats—could partake of the divine.

The Church taught that there was another supernatural force at large in the world: Satan. According to Christian beliefs, Satan constantly challenged God by tempting people into evil. If prophets spread unusual doctrines, they were surely the tools of Satan. If a devout Christian fell mysteriously ill, the sickness might be the result of an evil spell cast by a witch in league with Satan. Fear of Satan's wiles justified periodic campaigns against witchcraft and purges of heretics—men and women who questioned the Church's doctrine and practices.

The Crusades. As the Catholic Church consolidated its power in Europe, popes and priests urged their followers to crush all those who held other religious beliefs. Muslims—followers of the Islamic religion—became a prime target. After the death in A.D. 632 of the prophet Muhammad, the founder of Islam, the newly converted peoples of his homeland of Arabia set out to conquer the world in the name of the new religion. By persuasion and military force, they spread the Islamic faith and Arab civilization far beyond its homeland—into sub-Saharan Africa, India, and Indonesia and deep into Spain and the Balkan region of Eastern Europe. Between 1095 and 1272 successive armies of Christians, led by the flower of the nobility, embarked on a series of great Crusades against Muslim "infidels." They halted Arab advances into southern Europe and invaded Palestine, seeking to expel Muslims from the Holy Land where Christ had lived.

The Crusades had some success in their military mission, gaining control of much of Palestine for nearly 200 years, but their spiritual impact on Europe was more profound, strengthening the Christian identity of its population. The resulting religious fervor contributed to the persecution—and forced conversion—of Jews in many European countries. England expelled most of those who retained their Jewish identity in 1290, and France did the same in 1306. Jewish refugees went mostly to Germany, the great center of European Jewry, only to be driven farther east, to Poland, throughout the next century.

The Crusades also broadened the intellectual and economic horizons of the privileged classes of Western Europe, bringing them into contact with the advanced civilizations of the Middle East and Asia. A fresh wind blew through Europe, resulting in marked changes in that continent's commercial interests and military power—changes that in turn would cause slower but equally significant alterations in its traditional agricultural society.

Europe and the World, 1450–1550

Around 1450 Europeans shook off the lethargy of their traditional agricultural society with a major revival of learning and cultural life—the Renaissance (from the French word for "rebirth"). Inspired by new knowledge and a new optimism, the rulers of Portugal and Spain commissioned Italian navigators to find new trade routes to India and China. These maritime adventurers soon brought Europeans into direct contact with the peoples of Africa, Asia, and the Americas, thereby beginning a new era in world history.

The Renaissance

The Crusades had exposed Europeans to the highly developed civilizations of the Arab world. Stimulated by these contacts, first Italy and then other European societies experienced the cultural flowering known as the Renaissance. Arab traders had access to the fabulous treasures of the East: luxurious Chinese silks, brilliant Indian cottons, precious stones, and exotic spices, including pepper, nutmeg, ginger, and cloves. Arab inventors had developed magnetic compasses, water-powered mills, and mechanical clocks, and from their trading contacts in China they had learned the properties and uses of gunpowder. In great cultural centers such as Alexandria and Cairo in Egypt, Arab scholars carried on the legacy of Christian Byzantine civilization, which had preserved the great achievements of the Greeks and Romans in religion, medicine, philosophy, mathematics, astronomy, and geography. Arab learning gradually filtered into Europe from Córdoba and other cities in southern Spain, which had been conquered by Arab Muslims. Muslim scholars translated Aristotle, Ptolemy, and other ancient writers into Latin, reacquainting the peoples of Europe with their own classical heritage.

Merchants from the Italian city-states of Venice, Genoa, and Pisa played a key role in the Renaissance. They dispatched ships to Alexandria, Beirut, and other eastern Mediterranean ports, where they purchased

The Spice Trade
This illustration from a French manuscript (c. 1380) shows workers in Malabar (near Calicut on the western coast of India) harvesting pepper for the spice trade. The white-skinned man is meant to be Marco Polo, one of the few Europeans to visit India or China during the Middle Ages.
Bibliothèque Nationale.

goods from China, India, Persia, and Arabia and sold them throughout Europe. The enormous profits from this commerce created a wealthy class of merchants, bankers, and textile manufacturers who conducted trade, lent vast sums of money, and spurred technological innovation in silk and wool production. This moneyed elite ruled the republican city-states of Italy, and in *The Discourses* (1510), Niccolò Machiavelli articulated its political culture of *civic humanism*—an ideology that celebrated public virtue and service to the state and that would profoundly influence European and American conceptions of government.

In what was to become the fashion of the age, wealthy Italian families became patrons of the arts and sciences, subsidizing a remarkable array of artistic and intellectual projects. Perhaps no other age in European history has produced such a flowering of artistic genius. Michelangelo Buonarroti, Andrea Palladio, and Filippo Brunelleschi designed and built great architectural masterpieces, while Leonardo da Vinci and Raphael Santi produced magnificent religious paintings, creating styles and setting standards that have endured into the modern era.

The Renaissance did not directly affect the average European peasant, but it had a profound impact on the upper classes. The artists and intellectuals of the Renaissance were optimistic in their view of human nature—they were humanists who celebrated individual potential. Whereas traditional paintings had depicted (often grimly) religious themes and symbols, Renaissance works of art and literature showed real men (and a few women) with complex personalities and creative talents. Those who embraced the psychology of the Renaissance saw themselves not as prisoners of blind fate or victims of the forces of nature but as complex individuals with the capacity to change the world.

The idea that the world could be shaped by human ingenuity was particularly appealing to Renaissance rulers, who were eager to shape it to their own benefit. In *The Prince* (1513), Machiavelli provided unsentimental advice on how monarchs could increase their political power. Machiavelli's hero in this treatise was the Italian ruler Cesare Borgia, but he was inspired by the state-building activities of the ambitious monarchs of France and Western Europe.

Astronomers at Istanbul, 1581
Arab and Turkish scholars transmitted ancient texts and learning to Europeans in the Middle Ages. Their contribution to geographical and astronomical knowledge continued throughout the sixteenth century, the great European Age of Discovery.
Ergun Cagutay, Istanbul.

Renaissance Architecture
In this depiction of the "Ideal City," the Renaissance painter Piero della Francesca uses columned buildings to recall the classical world of Greece and Rome. The symmetrical design reflects the impulse to create a world of ordered beauty.
Scala/Art Resource.

Portugal Penetrates Africa and Asia

It was Portugal, a small Atlantic country of only 1.5 million people, that led the way in the great surge of European expansion. Portugal boasted political stability, a tradition of seafaring, and a fleet of merchant ships. It also had a prince, Henry the Navigator (1394–1460), who was determined to find a new ocean route to the wealth of Asia. Henry was a multifaceted individual, at once a Christian warrior and a Renaissance humanist. As a general of the Crusading Order of Christ he had fought the Muslims in North Africa, an experience that reinforced his desire to extend the bounds of Christendom—and Portuguese power. As a humanist, Henry patronized Renaissance thinkers and relied on Arab and Italian geographers for the latest knowledge about the shape and size of the continents. Imbued with the spirit of the Renaissance, he tried to fulfill the mission assigned by astrologers to one born under his sign: "to engage in great and noble conquests and to attempt the discovery of things hidden from other men."

African Slavery. Because Arab and Italian merchants dominated trade in the Mediterranean Sea, Henry sought an alternate oceanic route to the wealth of Asia. In the 1420s he established a center for exploration and ocean mapping near Lisbon and sent out ships to sail along the African coast. His seamen soon discovered and settled the islands of Madeira and the Azores. By 1435 Portuguese sea captains were roaming the coast of West Africa, seeking ivory and gold in exchange for Portuguese salt, wine, and fish. By the 1440s they were trading in humans as well, the first

These monarchs—among them France's Louis XI (r. 1461–1483), England's Henry VII (r. 1485–1509), and Spain's Ferdinand (r. 1479–1516) and Isabella (r. 1474–1504)—created royal law courts and bureaucracies to reduce the power of the landed classes, and formed alliances with commercial interests to build strong and prosperous national states. They allowed merchants to trade throughout their realms and granted privileges to artisan guilds, thereby encouraging both foreign trade and domestic manufacturing. In return, they extracted taxes from towns and loans from merchants to support their armies and officials. The alliance of monarchs, merchants, and royal bureaucrats challenged the primacy of the agrarian nobility. Indeed, the increasing wealth and power of the monarchical nation-state propelled Europe into its first age of expansion.

MAP 1.2

Europeans Seek Control of World Trade, 1460–1560

For centuries the Mediterranean Sea was the meeting point for the commerce of Europe, northern Africa, and southern Asia. Beginning in the 1490s, Portuguese, Spanish, and Dutch adventurers and merchants opened up new trade routes, challenging the primacy of the Muslim-dominated Mediterranean.

Europeans to engage in the African slave trade. For centuries Arab merchants had conducted a brisk overland trade in slaves, buying sub-Saharan Africans captured during local conflicts and selling them throughout the Mediterranean region. At first the Portuguese transported enslaved West Africans to sugar-growing estates in Madeira and the Azores. Later they would carry hundreds of thousands of slaves to toil and die on sugar plantations in the West Indies and in its colony of Brazil—a Portuguese possession under the terms of an agreement with Spain, the Treaty of Tordesillas (1494).

The Portuguese Maritime Empire. After Henry's death in 1460 Portuguese adventurers continued to look for a direct ocean route to Asia, sailing far to the south along the Atlantic coast of Africa. In 1488 Bartholomew Días rounded the Cape of Good Hope, the southern tip of Africa; ten years later Vasco da Gama sailed up the eastern coast of Africa and across the Indian Ocean to India (Map 1.2). Although the Arab, Indian, and Jewish merchants who controlled the trade along India's Malabar Coast shunned da Gama as a dangerous commercial rival, he acquired a highly profitable cargo of cinnamon and pepper, which were used to flavor and preserve meat. To capture control of trade along the Indian coast for Portugal, da Gama returned to India in 1502 with twenty-one caravels, small but well-armed vessels that could sail close to the wind, enabling them to outmaneuver and defeat the Arab fleets. The plunder-hungry Portuguese burned cities and seized the property of rival traders.

Soon the Portuguese government set up fortified trading posts for its merchants at key points around the Indian Ocean and opened trade routes from Africa to Indonesia and up the coast of Asia to China and Japan. Portuguese merchants could undersell Arab traders because their ships held more and traveled faster than overland caravans. In a momentous transition, Portuguese replaced Arabs as the leaders in both world commerce and the trade in African slaves.

Spain and America

Spain quickly followed Portugal's example. As Renaissance rulers, King Ferdinand of Aragon and Queen Isabella of Castile saw national unity and commerce as the keys to power and prosperity. Married in their teens in an arranged match, the young rulers (r. 1474–1516) had combined their kingdoms. Initially they devoted their energies and resources to the *reconquista*, the centuries-long campaign to oust the Muslims from their realm. In 1492 their armies reconquered Granada, the last outpost of Islam in Western Europe. Continuing their effort to use the Catholic religion to build a sense of "Spanishness," Ferdinand and Isabella launched a brutal Inquisition against suspected Christian heretics and expelled or forcibly converted thousands of Jews. Simultaneously they sought new opportunities for trade and empire.

Because Portugal controlled the southern, or African, approach to Asia, Isabella and Ferdinand listened with interest to proposals for an alternate, western route to the riches of the East. The main advocate for such a route was Christopher Columbus, a forceful Genoese sea captain who was determined to become rich and famous. Columbus was familiar with the findings of Italian geographers who had rediscovered the maps of the ancient Greeks and had reached the mistaken conclusion that Europe, Africa, and Asia covered more than half the earth's surface. Using these calculations (in part because they suited his purposes), Columbus argued that the Atlantic Ocean, long feared by Arab sailors as an endless "green sea of darkness," was little more than a narrow channel of water separating Europe from Asia. Ultimately convincing Ferdinand and Isabella of his point of view, Columbus won their support and the financial backing of Spanish merchants.

Columbus set sail with three small ships on August 3, 1492. An ambitious man, he wanted not only to discover a new trading route to China but to find and rule the "islands and mainland in the Ocean Sea." So he insisted that his monarch-patrons give him the titles of viceroy and governor as well as admiral. On October 12, 1492, after a voyage of 3,000 miles, Columbus landed at one of the islands of the present-day Bahamas. Regardless of his original intentions, the Italian adventurer had "discovered" for Europeans the lands of the Western Hemisphere.

Believing he had reached Asia—"the Indies," in fifteenth-century parlance—Columbus called the native inhabitants Indians and the islands the West Indies. Although he was surprised by the crude living conditions of the natives, Columbus expected them to be quickly "delivered and converted to our holy faith"; with ceremony and solemnity he claimed the lands for Spain and for Christendom (see Voices from Abroad, "Christopher Columbus: First Impressions of Native Americans," p. 23). He then explored the Caribbean islands (so-called after one of the native peoples), demanding gold from the local Taino, Arawak, and Carib settlements. Buoyed by the natives' stories of rivers of gold lying "to the west," Columbus left forty men on the island of Hispaniola and returned triumphantly to Spain, taking several Tainos to display to Isabella and Ferdinand.

Although Columbus brought back no gold or valuable goods, the Spanish monarchs were sufficiently impressed by this discovery to support three more voyages over the next twelve years (see Map 1.3). During those expeditions Columbus established a repressive regime on Hispaniola, forcing Indians to labor on the estates of Spanish landlords or pay them tribute. He also began the transatlantic slave trade, carrying hundreds of Indians from Hispaniola to bondage in Europe and importing slaves from Africa to work as artisans and farmers in the new Spanish settlements in the Caribbean. However, he failed to find either golden treasures or great kingdoms, and his death in 1506 went virtually unrecognized. Ignoring Columbus, a German geographer gave the new continents the name of a Florentine merchant, Amerigo Vespucci, who had traveled to South America around 1500 and called it a *nuevo mundo*, a New World. For its part, the Spanish Crown was determined to make it a Spanish world.

The Conquest

Although Columbus had found no gold, rumors of riches to the west encouraged Spanish adventurers to follow in his footsteps. Most of these men were not explorers or merchants but hardened veterans of the wars of the *reconquista* against the Muslims. The Spanish Crown catered to their desires to get rich, licensing some of them as *adelantados* (entrepreneurs or proprietors) and offering them plunder, landed estates in America, and titles of nobility in return for conquering the native peoples. These military chieftains used military force to subdue the Arawak and Caribs and brought death to as many as a million Tainos on the

CHRISTOPHER COLUMBUS

First Impressions of Native Americans

───────★───────

As a well-traveled mariner, Columbus knew the world and its peoples. But he was clearly puzzled by the first "Indians" he encountered on the islands: their lack of clothes and iron weapons, skin color, and painted bodies surprised him. To maintain his belief that he had reached Asia, he told himself that there must be a more advanced civilization on the mainland. This selection is taken from the journal kept by Columbus during his voyage.

Because I knew that they were a people to be delivered and converted to our holy faith rather by love than by force, [I] gave to some among them some red caps and some glass beads, which they hung around their necks, and many other things of little value. At this they were greatly pleased and became so entirely our friends that it was a wonder to see. . . .

They all go naked as their mothers bore them, and the women also, although I saw only one very young girl. . . . Their hair is coarse almost like the hairs of a horse's tail and short; they wear their hair down over their eyebrows, except for a few strands behind, which they wear long and never cut. Some of them are painted black, and they are the colour of the people of the Canaries, neither black nor white, and some of them are painted white and red. . . .

They do not bear arms or know them, for I showed to them swords and they took them by the blade and cut themselves through ignorance. They have no iron. Their spears are certain reeds, without iron, and some of these have a fish hook at the end, while others are pointed in various ways. . . . I saw some who bore marks of wounds on their bodies . . . and they indicated to me that people came from other islands, which are near, and wished to capture them, and they defended themselves. And I believed and still believe that they come here from the mainland to take them for slaves. They should be good servants and of quick intelligence, . . . and I believe that they would easily be made Christians, for it appeared to me that they had no creed.

Source: The Journal of Christopher Columbus, trans. Cecil Jane, rev. and annotated by L. A. Vigneras (London: Hakluyt Society, 1960), 39–41.

---

island of Hispaniola, mostly through the inadvertent spread of European diseases. Then they began to penetrate the mainland in search of gold and other booty.

Disappointment and death greeted some adventurers, such as Juan Ponce de León, who went searching for gold and slaves along the coast of Florida in 1513 and gave the peninsula its name; in 1521 his attempt to conquer and settle the new land was cut short by an arrow from a Calusa Indian. Other Spaniards won fame rather than fortune: Vasco Núñez de Balboa crossed the Isthmus of Darien (Panama) in 1513, becoming the first European to see the Pacific Ocean.

Some Spanish adventurers fulfilled their fondest dreams. Between 1519 and 1535 a few thousand Spaniards seized control of the powerful Aztec empire in the Mexican highlands, the Mayan settlements in the Yucatan peninsula, and the rich Inca civilization in the mountains of Peru. Within a generation these adventurers and their monarch, King Charles I (r. 1516–1556), had become masters of the wealthiest and most populous regions of the Western Hemisphere (Map 1.3).

The Fall of the Aztec Empire. The first great success of the Spanish *conquistadors* (conquerors) came against the Aztec empire. In 1519 Hernando Cortés landed on the Mexican coast with 600 men and marched toward the Aztec capital of Tenochtitlán. Fortuitously for the Spaniards, Cortés arrived in the very year in which Aztec mythology had predicted the return of the god Quetzalcoatl to his earthly kingdom. Believing that Cortés might be the returning god, Moctezuma, the Aztec ruler, acted indecisively. After the failure of an ambush against the conquistadors, he allowed Cortés to proceed without challenge to Tenochtitlán and received the Spaniard with great ceremony, only to become his captive.

When Moctezuma's forces attempted to expel Cortés and his men, they were confronted by European military technology. The sight of the Spaniards in full armor, with cannon that shook the heavens, made a deep impression on the Aztecs, who had learned how to purify gold and fashion it into ornate religious objects but did not produce iron tools or weapons. Moreover they had no

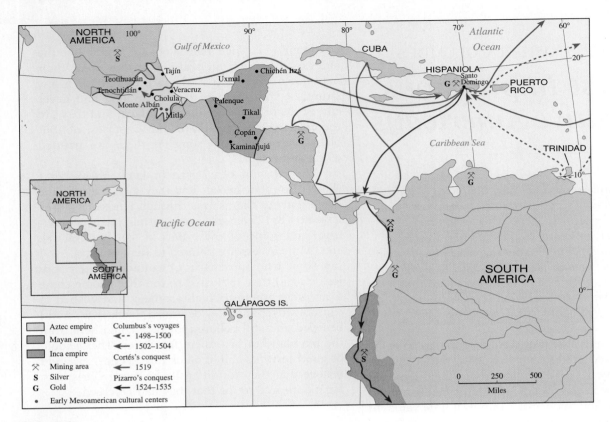

MAP 1.3

The Spanish Conquest

The Spanish first invaded the islands of the Caribbean. Rumors of a magnificent golden civilization led to Cortés's invasion of the Aztec empire in 1519. By 1535 other Spanish conquistadors had conquered the Mayan temple cities and the Inca empire in Peru, completing one of the great conquests in world history.

wheeled carts or cavalry, for horses, once abundant in the Western Hemisphere, had died out thousands of years earlier. Aztec warriors, fighting on foot with flint- or obsidian-tipped spears and arrows, were no match in small-group combat for Spanish conquistadors, seated high on their horses, protected by heavy armor, and wielding steel swords (see American Voices, "Aztec Elders Describe the Spanish Conquest," p. 26).

Still, the vast population of the Aztec empire, which numbered in the millions, could easily have crushed the European invaders if the Indian peoples had remained united. But Cortés astutely exploited the widespread resentment against the Aztecs on the part of various Indian peoples, who had been forced for decades to pay tribute in goods and provide human victims for sacrifice. By forming military alliances and raising thousands of troops from the subject peoples who suffered under Aztec rule, Cortés created a powerful army. Moctezuma's empire collapsed, the victim not of superior Spanish military technology but of a vast internal rebellion of Indian peoples.

As the Spanish sought to impose their dominion over these peoples, they had a silent and extraordinarily powerful ally—disease. Separated from the peoples of Eurasia

for thousands of years, the Indian inhabitants of the Western Hemisphere did not have immunities to common European diseases. Smallpox, influenza, and measles ravaged the native American peoples, killing tens of thousands of warriors and their families, depriving the people of leaders, and sapping the morale of the survivors. Exploiting this demographic weakness, Cortés quickly extended Spanish rule over the entire Valley of Mexico. His lieutenants subdued the rest of the highland peoples and then moved against the Maya in the Yucatan peninsula, eventually conquering them as well (see American Lives, "Cortés and Malinche: The Dynamics of Conquest," pp. 28–29).

The End of the Inca Empire. In the late 1520s Francisco Pizarro, another conquistador, embarked on a long expedition to the mountains of Peru, home of the rich and powerful Inca empire. Starting around A.D. 1440 as a small chiefdom centered on the Andean valley of Cuzco, some 9,000 feet above sea level, the Incas had quickly extended their control over lands stretching 2,000 miles along the Pacific coast of South America. In order to govern this far-flung empire, the Inca rulers built 24,000 miles of roads and dozens of carefully

A Premonition of Disaster
In the 1570s Fray Diego Durán, a Spanish Dominican monk, recorded the history of the Aztec peoples. This leaf from his manuscript captures the moment when Moctezuma first hears of the arrival of white-skinned strangers on the coast of his country. The watercolor shows the comet that Moctezuma reportedly saw plunging to earth, an event that according to Aztec belief was a harbinger of disaster.
Library of Congress.

placed administrative centers, which were constructed of finely crafted stone. A semidivine Inca king ruled the empire, assisted by a hierarchical bureaucracy staffed by noblemen, many of whom were his relatives.

Despite its size and wealth, the Inca empire, like the Aztec, succumbed to the Spanish invaders. By the time Pizarro reached Peru, the Inca king and one-half of the population had already died from European diseases, which had been spread by Indian traders and travelers. Weakened militarily and emotionally by this abrupt loss of people, and fighting among themselves over succession to the throne, the Inca nobility was easy prey for Pizarro and his army. In little more than a decade the Spanish had conquered the wealthiest and most populous regions of the Western Hemisphere.

Seeking fame and fortune, other Spanish adventurers explored large sections of the southern and western United States (Map 2.1). But despite many years and thousands of miles of exploration, these explorers found no gold and few other riches, so for the next two centuries Spanish settlement was limited primarily to Mesoamerica and the northern and western coasts of South America.

The Legacy of the Conquest. By dramatically reducing the size of the native population, the Spanish invasion and European diseases changed life forever throughout the Western Hemisphere. Within a single generation, virtually all the Indian residents of Hispaniola—an estimated 1 million people—were wiped out by disease and warfare. Elsewhere the story was almost as tragic. In 1500 probably 45 million Indians lived in Mesoamerica; by 1650 that region had only 3 million native Americans. The population of Peru plummeted from 9 million in 1530 to fewer than half a million a century later. In the present-day United States, diseases introduced by the early Spanish expeditions may have inflicted equally catastrophic losses on the Pueblo peoples of the Southwest and the Mississippian chiefdoms of present-day Florida and the Southeast.

Aztec Elders Describe the Spanish Conquest

———————★———————

During the 1550s Friar Bernardino de Sahagún published the Florentine Codex: General History of New Spain. According to Sahagún, the authors of the Codex were Aztec elders who lived through the Spanish conquest. Here the elders describe their reaction to the invading Europeans and the devastating impact of smallpox. They told their stories to Sahagún in a repetitive style, using the conventions of Aztec oral histories, and he translated them into Spanish.

Moctezuma enjoyed no sleep, no food, no one spoke to him. Whatsoever he did, it was as if he were in torment. Ofttimes it was as if he sighed, became weak, felt weak. . . . Wherefore he said, "What will now befall us? Who indeed stands [in charge]? Alas, until now, I. In great torment is my heart; as if it were washed in chili water it indeed burns.". . . And when he had so heard what the messengers reported, he was terrified, he was astounded. . . . Especially did it cause him to faint away when he heard how the gun, at [the Spaniards'] command, discharged: how it resounded as if it thundered when it went off. It indeed bereft one of strength; it shut off one's ears. And when it discharged, something like a round pebble came forth from within. Fire went showering forth; sparks went blazing forth. And its smoke smelled very foul; it had a fetid odor which verily wounded the head. And when [the shot] struck a mountain, it was as if it were destroyed, dissolved . . . as if someone blew it away.

All iron was their war array. In iron they clothed themselves. With iron they covered their heads. Iron were their swords. Iron were their crossbows. Iron were their shields. Iron were their lances. And those which bore them upon their backs, their deer [horses], were as tall as roof terraces.

And their bodies were everywhere covered; only their faces appeared. They were very white; they had chalky faces; they had yellow hair, though the hair of some was black. . . . And when Moctezuma so heard, he was much terrified. It was as if he fainted away. His heart saddened; his heart failed him. . . .

[Soon] there came to be prevalent a great sickness, a plague. It was in Tepeilhuitl that it originated, that there spread over the people a great destruction of men. Some it indeed covered [with pustules]; they were spread everywhere, on one's face, on one's head, on one's breast. There was indeed perishing; many indeed died of it. No longer could they walk; they only lay in their abodes, in their beds. No longer could they move. . . . And when they bestirred themselves, much did they cry out. There was much perishing. Like a covering, covering-like, were the pustules. Indeed, many people died of them, and many just died of hunger. There was death from hunger; there was no one to take care of another; there was no one to attend to another.

Source: Friar Bernardino de Sahagún, *Florentine Codex: General History of New Spain*, trans. Arthur J. O. Anderson and Charles E. Dibble (Salt Lake City: University of Utah Press, 1975), book 12:17–20, 26, 83.

Moreover, Spanish overlords ruthlessly exploited the surviving native Americans of Mesoamerica, forcing them to work on vast plantations to raise crops for local consumption and tend cattle whose hides were exported to Europe. The Spaniards also altered the natural environment by introducing the grain crops of wheat and rapidly growing grasses used for cattle feed; over time, these European plants replaced the native flora. Horses, first brought over by Cortés, gradually increased in number throughout the Western Hemisphere and in the following centuries dramatically changed the way of life of many Indian peoples, especially on the Great Plains of the United States.

The Spanish invasion of the Americas had a significant impact on life in Europe and Africa as well. In a process of transfer known as the Columbian Exchange, the food products of the Western Hemisphere—maize, tomatoes, potatoes, manioc—became available to the peoples of other continents, increasing agricultural yields and stimulating the growth of population. Similarly, the crops—and human diseases—of African and Eurasian lands became part of the lives of residents of the Americas. Nor was that all. The gold and silver that had honored Aztec gods flowed into the countinghouses of Spain and into the treasury of its monarchs, making that nation the most powerful in Europe for more than a century.

By 1550 the once magnificent civilizations of Mexico and Peru lay in ruins, and the surviving native Americans had lost much of their cultural identity. Spanish priests suppressed the natives' traditional gods and imposed Catholic beliefs; as early as 1531 an Indian convert reported a vision of a dark-skinned Virgin Mary later known as the Virgin of Guadalupe. Indian numbers continued to decline over the next century, as no fewer than 500,000 Spanish migrants crossed the Atlantic and settled on the lands once occupied by the native peoples. The cultural impact of this migration was immense, in part because nearly 90 percent of the settlers were men. As the migrants took Indian women as wives or mistresses, the Spanish colonies developed a large *mestizo* (mixed-race) population with a culture that combined Spanish and Indian values and practices. Around 1800, at the end of the colonial era, Spanish America had about 17 million people: 7.5 million Indians, 3.2 million Europeans, 1 million enslaved Africans, and 5.5 million people of mixed race and mixed cultural heritage.

Resisting assimilation, many of the Indian peoples retreated into highlands and mountains and preserved their traditional agriculture and values. In the centuries to come, their descendants, unlike the inhabitants of Africa and India, would never have the numbers or the power to oust the descendants of the European invaders; these natives lived on as subordinate and largely impoverished peoples. Today, only a single Indian tongue, Guarani in Paraguay, is a recognized national language, and no native American state has representation in the United Nations. For the original Americans, the consequences of the Spanish intrusion in 1492 were tragic and irreversible.

The Protestant Reformation and the Rise of England, 1500–1620

Religious fervor had played an important role in the expansionary policies of Portugal and Spain, but in 1517 a major schism divided the Christian peoples of Europe, plunging the continent into religious wars that lasted for decades. Simultaneously, gold and silver from America set off a great inflation, which altered traditional European society. England in particular was reshaped by these forces. Inflation—a threefold rise in prices in less than a century—along with the enclosure of open fields and religious persecution, disrupted the lives of the peasantry, laying the foundation for a vast transatlantic migration. At the same time, English monarchs assisted the expansion of shipping and trade, creating the maritime resources required to establish overseas colonies.

The Protestant Movement

Over the centuries the Catholic Church had become a large and wealthy institution, controlling vast resources throughout Europe. Renaissance popes and cardinals were among the leading patrons of the arts, but some also misused the Church's wealth. Pope Leo X (1513–1521) was the most notorious, receiving half a million ducats a year—a sum equal to the income of 30,000 peasants—by selling money-making religious offices to greedy priests. In England, Cardinal Thomas Wolsey set an equally poor example by giving dozens of church positions to his relatives. Ordinary priests and monks sometimes used their authority to obtain economic or sexual favors. These abuses ignited a smoldering anticlericalism. One English reformer denounced the clergy as a "gang of scoundrels" who should be "rid of their vices or stripped of their authority," but he was ignored. Other reformers, such as Jan Hus of Bohemia, were tried and executed as heretics.

Martin Luther's Attack on Church Doctrine. In 1517 Martin Luther, a German monk and professor at the university in Wittenberg, publicly challenged church leaders by nailing his famous Ninety-five Theses to the door of the castle church. That widely reprinted document condemned the sale of *indulgences*—church certificates that pardoned a sinner from punishments in the afterlife. Luther argued that indulgences were worthless; redemption could come only from God through grace, not from the church for a fee. When Luther refused to recant his views, he was excommunicated by the pope. Moreover, he was threatened with punishment by King Charles I of Spain, who was also the head of the Holy Roman Empire, which embraced most of Germany (see Map 1.4 and Table 1.1). Northern German princes, who were resisting the emperor's authority for political reasons, embraced Luther's teachings and protected him from arrest, thus allowing his Protestant movement to flourish.

Luther broadened his attack against Roman Catholic doctrine, stating positions that differed from orthodox beliefs in three major respects. First, Luther rejected the doctrine that Christians could win salvation through good deeds ("justification by works"), arguing that people could be saved only through grace ("justification by faith"), which came as a gift from God. Second, he downplayed the role of clergymen as mediators between God and the people, proclaiming, "Our baptism consecrates us all without exception and makes us all priests." Third, Luther said that Christians must look to the Bible, not to church doctrine, as the ultimate authority in matters of faith. So that every believer could read the Bible, he translated it from Latin into German. Embracing Luther's views, most princes in northern Germany broke from Rome, in part because they wanted the power to appoint bishops and control the Church's property.

Cortés and Malinche: The Dynamics of Conquest

★

Malinche and Cortés
In this Aztec pictograph (c. 1540), Cortés is shown with his Nahuatl-speaking interpreter, mistress, and advisor, Malinche (or Mariana in Spanish). Signifying her dual identity as an Indian and a European, Malinche wears native clothes while holding up the Christian rosary.
Bibliothèque Nationale.

Hernando Cortés conquered an empire and destroyed a civilization, an achievement that was both magnificent and tragic. The immensity of his dual triumph was partly accidental, owing to the rebellion of the non-Aztec peoples and the extraordinarily devastating impact of European diseases, but it also reflected the ambition and vision of the man. Unlike most other gold-hungry Spanish adventurers, Cortés had a sense of politics and of history. Once he learned from the Maya, in whose territory he first landed, of the existence of Moctezuma and his kingdom, Cortés's priority became the pursuit of power rather than of plunder. As Bernal Díaz del Castillo, one of his commanders, reported in the *History of the Conquest of New Spain*, Cortés immediately declared his intention "to serve God and the king" by subjugating the Aztec king and his great empire.

Could this be done? Six hundred Spanish troops might plunder the lands at the far reaches of an empire of millions, but what chance did they stand against an Aztec army of tens of thousands? The odds of conquering the empire were so low that a less audacious man would not even have tried. But Cortés was no ordinary man. A person of great presence—intelligent and unscrupulous, courageous yet prudent, decisive yet flexible —the Spanish chieftain inspired fear and respect among his enemies and unthinking loyalty among his followers, who time and again risked their lives at his command. No one was more loyal to Cortés—and, at crucial points in the conquest of Mexico, more important—than the native woman known as La Malinche, who became his interpreter and mistress. Had he not conquered her affections, he might have failed to conquer the Aztec empire.

As a child, the girl who became Malinche was called Malinali, the name of the twelfth month in the Nahuatl language spoken by the Aztec and other Mexican peoples. Her father was the local lord of Painala, a village near the Gulf of Mexico in the far southern reaches of the Aztec empire, and her mother was the ruler of Xatipan, a small nearby settlement. As the daughter of minor nobles, Malinali lived in comfort and no doubt developed the sense of confidence that would serve her so well in the future. But she lived her adolescent years as a mere slave. Following the death of her father and the remarriage of her mother, Malinali was sold into bondage by her mother and stepfather, who wanted to enhance the succession rights of their newly born son. Owned first by merchants, she ended up as an enslaved worker in the Mayan settlement of Potonchan on the Gulf of

Mexico. There, in March 1519 and now about seventeen years old, Malinali had her rendezvous with destiny.

Initially the confrontation between Europeans and native Americans took place with gestures and misunderstandings, for the two peoples could not comprehend each other's language and therefore could not convey their intentions, values, and ways of life. But Cortés was lucky, for his expedition had chanced upon Father Gerónimo de Aguilar, a shipwrecked Spanish priest who had lived for a decade as a slave among the Maya and knew their language. And he was doubly lucky when the Maya of Potonchan, whom he had defeated in battle, presented him with twenty slave women, one of whom was Malinali. Cortés treated these women as servants and concubines, assigning them to his commanders; and because Malinali was "of pleasing appearance and sharp-witted and outward-going" (according to Díaz del Castillo), she was given to his chief lieutenant, Alonso Puertocarrero. Learning that the young woman could speak Nahuatl, Cortés soon took her as his own. At his command she conversed with Nahuatl-speaking peoples and then used Mayan to convey what she had learned to Aguilar, who translated it into Spanish. The process was cumbersome, but it worked. Now Cortés could negotiate directly with both Moctezuma's officials and the leaders of the non-Aztec peoples whose help he needed to conquer the empire.

Of Malinali's motives in providing aid to the Spanish invaders there is no record. Like other Mexican peoples, including Moctezuma, at first she may have viewed Cortés as a returning god. Or, like his Spanish followers, she may have been dazzled by his powerful presence and personality. Or, quite likely, Malinali may have calculated that Cortés was her best hope for escaping slavery and reclaiming a noble status. Whatever the reasons, Malinali's loyalty to her new master was complete and unbending. Rejecting an opportunity to desert the Spanish on their march to the Aztec capital of Tenochtitlán in 1519, she risked her life by warning Cortés of a surprise attack by the Cholulans. In 1520 she stood by him when the Spanish cause seemed lost following the disastrous retreat from Tenochtitlán. And in 1524 and 1525 she helped him survive a catastrophic military campaign in the jungles of present-day Honduras.

There is no question about Malinali's importance to the Spanish cause. As Bernal Díaz del Castillo concluded, "without her we never should have understood the Mexican language and, upon the whole, [would] have been unable to surmount many difficulties." The Aztecs likewise acknowledged her eminence; they called her Malinche, addressing her with respect by adding the suffix -che to her original name, and they often referred to Cortés as "the captain of Malinche," defining the Spaniard in terms of the interpreter through whom he spoke.

Yet there is no evidence that Cortés felt indebted to Malinche or developed a deep emotional bond with the young woman. In 1522 or 1523 she bore him a son (whom he named Martin after his father), but by then he had enjoyed many other mistresses, including the daughters of Moctezuma, and in succeeding years sired numerous illegitimate children by other Mexican women. Moreover, in 1525 Cortés again gave the services of Malinali, now known by the respectful Spanish name of Doña Marina, to one of his commanders, Juan Jaramillo, with whom she lived in marriage until her death in 1551. A mere native woman was not what the great conqueror had in mind as a wife for himself. To solidify his achievement and lay the foundation for a great family dynasty, Cortés won entry into the ranks of the Spanish nobility in 1528, taking as his wife Juana, daughter of the Count of Aguilar and a niece of the Duke of Béjar, one of the richest and most politically powerful men in Spain. After living with Juana in Mexico for a decade Cortés returned to his native land, where he died in 1647 at the age of sixty-two, a respected and colossally wealthy man.

Malinche fared less well than her former master not only in life but also in death. Because she was among the first native women to bear mixed-race (mestizo) children, Malinche has sometimes been celebrated as the symbolic mother of the post-Conquest Mexican people. More often, she has seemed to subsequent generations of Mexicans as a traitor to her people, a mere instrument in the hands of greedy invaders who subjugated a society and destroyed a civilization. Within the dynamics of sexual and military conquest, both views are correct.

TABLE 1.1

Spanish Monarchs, 1474–1598

Monarch	Dates of Reign	Achievements
Ferdinand and Isabella	1474–1516	Expelled Muslims from Spain; dispatched Columbus
Charles I	1516–1556	Holy Roman Emperor, 1519–1556
Philip II	1556–1598	Attacked Protestantism; mounted Spanish Armada

Social Revolution. Peasants as well as princes heeded Luther's attack on authority and, to his dismay, mounted protests of their own. In 1524 some German peasants rebelled against their manorial lords and were ruthlessly suppressed. Fearing social revolution, Luther urged obedience to established political institutions. Ten years later a more radical group of Protestants called Anabaptists (because they rejected the baptism of infants) seized control of the German city of Münster. The Münster Anabaptists established polygamy, abolished most rights to private property, and placed political power in the hands of "Saints"—those who felt God had saved them through grace. The Catholic and Lutheran princes of Germany joined together to quell the Münster Anabaptists, who became a symbol to conservatives of the dangers of permitting a variety of religious opinions. Fearing such social revolutions, most rulers in southern Europe did not contest the authority of the pope or the validity of Catholic doctrine.

For his part, Charles I of Spain unleashed a generation of warfare by dispatching armies to Germany to restore Catholicism and his political authority as Holy Roman Emperor. But he failed to preserve either his faith or his empire. In 1555 the Peace of Augsburg ended the fighting by allowing princes to decide whether their subjects were to be Catholic or Protestant. Most rulers in the south of Germany installed Catholicism as the official religion, whereas those in the north made Lutheranism—Luther's formulation of Protestantism—the state creed (Map 1.4).

The Teachings of John Calvin. A more rigorous form of Protestant doctrine and practice was established in Geneva, Switzerland, under the leadership of the French theologian John Calvin. Even more than Luther, Calvin stressed the omnipotence of God and the corruption of human nature. His *Institutes of the Christian Religion* (1536) depicts God as an awe-inspiring and absolute sovereign who governed the "wills of men so as to move precisely to that end directed by him." Calvin preached the doctrine of *predestination*, the idea that God had chosen certain people for salvation even before they were born and condemned the rest of humanity to eternal damnation. In Geneva he set up a model Christian community, eliminating bishops and placing spiritual power in the hands of ministers chosen by the members of each congregation. Calvinist clergy and pious laymen attempted to remake the city into a disciplined religious community by prohibiting frivolity and luxury and imposing religious discipline on the entire society.

Despite widespread persecution by princes who wanted to suppress minority religions in the name of national unity, Calvinists won converts all over Europe. Between 1550 and 1650 Calvinism became the creed of the Huguenots in France, the Protestant Reformed churches in Belgium and Holland, and the Presbyterians and Puritans in Scotland and England (see Map 1.4).

Protestantism in England. In England, King Henry VIII (r. 1509–1547) initially opposed the spread of Protestantism. But when the pope denied his request for an annulment of his marriage to Catherine of Aragon, who had failed to provide him with a male heir, Henry broke with Rome and made himself the head of a national Church of England (which promptly granted his divorce). Henry confiscated the vast properties of the Catholic monasteries and distributed them to his supporters, but he made few changes in church organization; spiritual authority still flowed downward in hierarchical fashion, from bishops to priests to laity. And he retained most Catholic doctrines and rituals. But after the reign of his daughter Queen Mary (r. 1553–1558), who briefly restored Catholicism as the state religion and executed 300 Protestant clergymen (gaining the nickname "Bloody Mary"), there was growing sentiment in England against Catholic beliefs and practices.

Henry's younger daughter, Queen Elizabeth I (r. 1558–1603), sought a religious settlement that would satisfy Protestants of different outlooks. Accepting the general Protestant emphasis on bringing religion closer to the people, the queen specified that church services be conducted in English rather than in Latin. More important, she approved a declaration of church doctrine, the Thirty-nine Articles, that could be interpreted as accepting both the Lutheran doctrine of salvation by grace and the Calvinist belief in predestination. To mollify traditionalists and attract Catholics to the Church of England, Elizabeth retained the hierarchy of bishops and the ritual of Holy Communion.

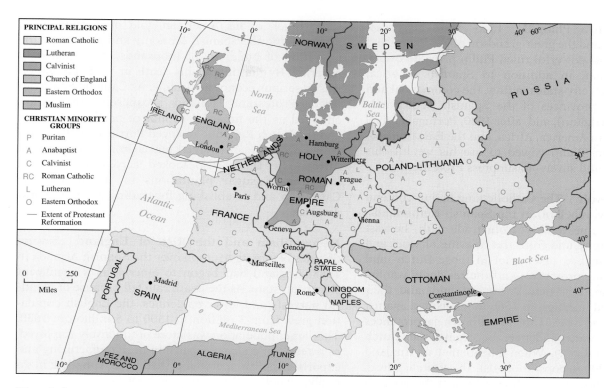

MAP 1.4
Religious Diversity in Europe, 1600
By 1600 Europe was permanently divided. Catholicism remained dominant in the south, but Lutheran princes and monarchs ruled northern Europe, and Calvinism had strongholds in Switzerland, Holland, and Scotland. Radical sects were persecuted by legally established Protestant churches as well as by Catholic clergy and monarchs. These religious conflicts encouraged the migration of minority sects to America.

Presbyterians and Puritans. Elizabeth's compromises angered radical Protestants, who condemned the power of bishops as "anti-Christian and devilish and contrary to the Scriptures." They demanded major changes in church organization and practice. Many of these reformers took inspiration from the Presbyterian system pioneered in Calvin's Geneva and developed fully by John Knox for the Church of Scotland; in Scotland, local congregations elected lay elders (presbyters) who assisted ministers in running the church. By 1600, 500 ministers in the Church of England wanted to eliminate bishops and install a presbyterian form of church government.

By this time other radical English Protestants were calling themselves "unspotted lambs of the Lord" or (embracing a term initially devised to insult them) "Puritans." To a greater extent than most Protestants, these men and women wanted to "purify" the Church of England of "false" teachings and practices. Puritans despised elaborately robed priests and gaudy statue-filled churches that appealed to people's emotions and love of show. Following radical Calvinist principles, Puritans condemned such displays as idolatrous. They also denounced many traditional rites, such as communion, as superstition, arguing that it was impossible for priests to change bread and wine into Christ's body and blood.

Believing that true spirituality and genuine religious knowledge came through the mind, Puritans organized their services around carefully argued sermons on ethics or dogma. They also placed special emphasis on the idea of a "calling," the duty to serve God in one's work. To ensure that all men and women had access to God's commands, these reformers encouraged everyone to read the Bible, thus promoting widespread literacy. Finally, most Puritans wanted authority over spiritual and financial matters to rest primarily with the local congregation—the laity—not with bishops or Presbyterian synods (church councils).

These radical Protestant doctrines commanded the support of a substantial minority of English Protestants, and carried across the Atlantic by a stream of Puritan migrants, they would play a major role in American history.

The Dutch and the English Challenge Spain

Luther's challenge to Catholicism in 1517 came just two years before Cortés conquered the Aztec empire, and the two events remained linked. Gold and silver from Mexico and Peru made Catholic Spain the wealthiest nation in Europe and King Philip II (r. 1556–1598), the successor to Charles I and the great-grandson of Ferdinand and Isabella, its most powerful ruler. Philip presided over a vast empire that, in addition to Spanish America, included wealthy city-states in Italy, the commercial and manufacturing provinces of the Spanish Netherlands (Holland and Belgium), and, after 1580, Portugal and all its possessions in America, Africa, and the East Indies. A devout Catholic, Philip vowed to use his wealth—his American gold and silver—to suppress Protestantism.

The Dutch Revolt.   The Catholic king had to contend with a religious rebellion in the Spanish Netherlands, which had become wealthy from trade with the vast Portuguese empire and from the weaving of wool and linen. Calvinism had taken root in those Dutch- and Flemish-speaking provinces, and the residents wanted to protect both their new Protestant faith and their ancient political liberties. In 1566 they revolted against Spanish rule, and in 1581 the seven northern provinces declared their independence, becoming the Dutch Republic (or Holland). When Elizabeth I of England dispatched 6,000 troops to assist the Dutch cause, Philip found a new enemy. In 1588 he sent the Spanish Armada—130 ships and 30,000 men—to invade Elizabeth's nation, planning to reimpose Catholicism in England and wipe out Calvinism in Holland. But the Armada failed utterly, as English ships and a fierce storm destroyed the Spanish fleet.

This military disaster was only the most obvious sign of Spain's troubles. During his long reign, Philip spent much of his American gold on foreign wars, undermining the Spanish economy and prompting the migration of hundreds of thousands of Spaniards to America. By the time of his death in 1598, his nation was in serious economic decline. As Catholic Spain faltered, Protestant Holland prospered. Amsterdam emerged as the financial capital of northern Europe, and the Dutch Republic replaced Portugal as the dominant European commercial power in Asia and coastal Africa. The Dutch also looked across the Atlantic, investing in sugar plantations in Brazil and the Caribbean and establishing fur-trading posts in North America.

Mercantilism and the Rise of England.   Several decades before its triumph over the Spanish Armada in 1588, England had begun to emerge as a significant European state. As the death rate fell because of plentiful harvests and fewer epidemics, the English population grew from 3 million in 1500 to 5 million in 1630. This larger population was more productively employed, as a result of a sharp expansion in manufacturing and exports. English merchants had long supplied high-quality wool to European weavers; beginning around 1500, they expanded their exports and created a domestic system of textile production. In this *outwork* (or *putting-out*) system, merchants bought wool and provided it to landless families. The women of these families carded and spun the wool into yarn, and they and their husbands wove it into cloth. The merchants then sold the finished product in English and foreign markets.

A Dutch Merchant Family
This painting by the Dutch artist Cornelius de Zeeuw captures the prosperity and the severe Calvinist ethos of Holland in the sixteenth century as well as the character of the traditional patriarchal family, with its rigid hierarchy of gender and age.
Rijksmuseum, Amsterdam.

The English government helped merchant capitalists expand the production of textiles and other goods in various ways. A new Poor Law in 1601 eliminated or reduced welfare payments, forcing poor people to work rather than rely on public assistance. Other legislation set low wage rates for workers, enabling manufacturers to produce inexpensive goods. To increase the export of these products, Elizabeth I awarded bonuses to manufacturers who sold goods in foreign markets. Moreover, the English government negotiated commercial treaties with foreign governments and granted special privileges to merchant groups. To encourage trade with Russia, Elizabeth provided the Muscovy Company with a monopoly on the export of English cloth to that market. Her government granted similar exclusive charters to the Levant Company (Turkey) in 1581, the Guinea Company (Africa) in 1588, and the East India Company in 1600.

This system of state-supported manufacturing and trade soon became known as *mercantilism*. Its prime purpose was to increase both the wealth of the emergent nation-states of Europe and the power of their monarchs. Mercantilist-minded leaders like Elizabeth encouraged merchants to invest in domestic manufacturing, thereby increasing exports and reducing imports, in order to give England a favorable balance of trade. The queen and her advisors wanted gold and silver to flow into the country to pay for English manufactures, stimulating further economic expansion and national wealth. Increased trade would also enrich the merchant community, an ally in the monarch's struggle against the landed nobility, and produce higher revenues from import duties, thereby swelling the royal treasury. These policies worked. By 1600 England was almost ready to challenge Holland's dominant position in world trade and Spain's colonial monopoly in the Western Hemisphere.

The Social Causes of English Colonization

England's monarchs and ministers of state had long been interested in America. As early as 1497, they had dispatched John Cabot to explore the coasts of Newfoundland and Nova Scotia, establishing an English claim to the region. But for the next half-century England was too weak in number, wealth, and military power to do more than send fishing fleets across the Atlantic. By 1550 the expansion of foreign exports and domestic manufacturing had created an ample supply of merchant shipping and financial capital, two key prerequisites for overseas expansion. But a successful colonization movement developed only as major economic and religious upheavals profoundly disrupted the traditional world of English rural life and provided a large body of willing settlers.

The Price Revolution. An underlying cause of economic turmoil in England was the massive impact on European prices of the gold and silver imported from Spanish America. This vast supply of gold and silver doubled the money supply and sparked a major economic transition—known today as the Price Revolution. Because people had more gold and silver to spend, they were willing to bid up the price of goods; between 1530 and 1600 the price of a bushel of wheat tripled. Also encouraging the rise of prices was the growth in Europe's population, which increased more quickly than the output of goods. More people with more money trying to buy a relatively fixed supply of goods meant sharply higher prices (Figure 1.2).

In England, the nobility were among the first casualties of the Price Revolution. Aristocrats had customarily rented out their estates on long leases for fixed rents, gaining a secure income and plenty of leisure. As one English nobleman put it, "We eat and drink and rise up to play and this is to live like a gentleman." Then inflation struck. In two generations the price of goods tripled, but the nobility's income from the rents on its farmlands barely increased. Many nobles could no longer live in luxury.

As the wealth and status of the aristocracy declined, that of the gentry and the yeomanry rose. The *gentry* (substantial landholders who lacked the titles

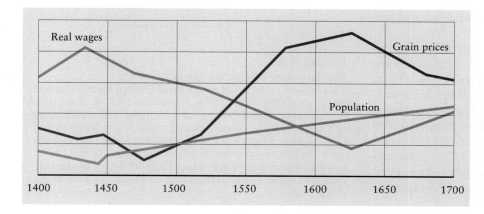

FIGURE 1.2
Inflation and Living Standards in Europe
The influx of Spanish gold and silver was the main cause of the great inflation in grain prices, but increased demand (from a constantly growing population) also played a role. Higher prices cut real wages, resulting in lower living standards.

and legal privileges of the aristocracy) had smaller but more efficiently managed estates than the nobility. They kept pace with inflation by renting land on short leases at higher rates. *Yeomen*, described by a European traveler as "middle people of a condition between gentlemen and peasants," owned small amounts of land that they worked with family help. Since their labor costs remained constant, the yeomen's sale of wheat—which now brought two or three times its traditional price—yielded increasing profits, which they used to build substantial houses and provide land for their children.

Economics influenced politics. As aristocrats lost wealth, their branch of Parliament, the House of Lords, declined in relative influence. Simultaneously, members of the rising gentry entered the House of Commons, the political voice of the propertied classes. Supported by yeomen voters, the gentry demanded new rights and powers for the Commons, such as control of taxation. Thus the Price Revolution encouraged the rise of governing institutions in which rich commoners and small property owners had a voice, a development with profound consequences for American political history.

Peasants and Enclosures. Peasants and farm laborers made up three-fourths of the population of England, and their lives, too, were transformed by the great inflation and by mercantilist policies. Many of these rural folk lived in open-field settlements, owning or leasing a house plot in the village center and holding the right to farm strips in the large surrounding fields. As the rise of domestic manufacturing after 1500 heightened the demand for wool, profit-minded landlords and wool merchants persuaded Parliament to pass *enclosure* acts. These acts allowed owners to fence in open fields and put sheep to graze on them. Thereby dispossessed from their customary right to farm the land, many peasant families lived on the brink of poverty—spinning and weaving wool or working as wage laborers on large estates. Wealthy men had "taken farms into their hands," an observer noted in 1600, "and rent them to those that will give most, whereby the peasantry of England is decayed and become servants to gentlemen."

English agriculture thus became increasingly capitalistic, with a few families owning the land and many other families working for them (Figure 1.3). These changes in English rural life set the stage for a substantial migration to America. As land prices continued to rise, thousands of yeomen families worried about preserving their new prosperity and looked across the Atlantic for land for their children. The enclosure movement created an even greater number of impoverished peasants who were willing to go to America as indentured servants.

Investment in Colonization. And now there were enterprising men—landed gentlemen and merchants alike—ready to establish permanent English settlements in America. The first attempts at colonization, all failures, occurred in the 1580s. Sir Humphrey Gilbert began a settlement in Newfoundland that quickly collapsed for lack of financing, and Sir Ferdinando Gorges's colony along the coast of Maine foundered because of inadequate supplies and the harsh climate. Sir Walter Raleigh was more persistent, mounting three expeditions to North Carolina. But Raleigh's enterprise also ended in disaster when a group of settlers at Roanoke vanished over the winter. When a ship carrying supplies reached Roanoke the following year, the 100 men, women, and children were gone without a trace or an apparent cause, a "lost" colony whose fate remains unknown.

After these setbacks, merchants replaced minor gentry as the leaders of the colonization movement. To provide adequate funding, the merchants organized *joint-stock companies*, which sold shares of stock in their company to many investors. A royally chartered joint-stock venture, the Virginia Company of London, founded the first permanent English settlement in America at Jamestown (Virginia) in 1607 (see Chapter 2). The

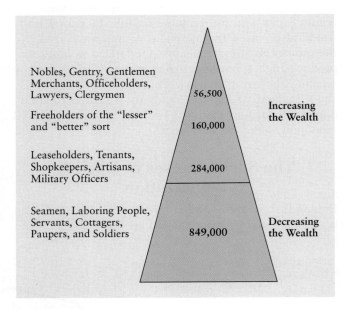

FIGURE 1.3
The Structure of English Society, 1688
This famous table of the structure of English society, devised by Gregory King in the 1680s, shows the result of centuries of aristocratic rule and of the enclosure movement. The majority of English families (some 849,000, according to King) lacked land or other productive resources and therefore, he thought, were "Decreasing the Wealth of the Kingdom." In fact, the labor of the propertyless produced a good deal of the wealth owned by those 500,500 families at the middle and top of the social scale.

investors hoped to grow rich, like the Spanish, by finding gold and exploiting the labor of the natives to mine it. Subsequently, they would prosper by transporting tens of thousands of English indentured servants to the new colony to grow tobacco.

Religious Emigration. While English merchants promoted settlement in Virginia, thousands of English men and women contemplated migration to America to escape a new wave of religious conflict. Elizabeth's successor, King James I (r. 1603–1625), had rejected most of the religious reforms proposed by Puritans and Presbyterians and bitterly resented their challenge to royal authority. The representative institutions of church government favored by Presbyterians, the king remarked, "agreeth as well with a monarchy as God with the Devil." James wanted to exercise absolute power, not share political and religious authority with Parliament and Presbyterian synods. In his essay entitled *The True Laws of Free Monarchy* (r. 1601), James argued that kings drew their authority directly from God and thus had a "divine right" to rule. As for the Puritans, who wished to place authority over religious appointments in the hands of the lay congregation, James had only contempt. The king threatened to "harry them out of the land, or else do worse."

Radical Protestants took the king at his word and began to flee, first to the Dutch Republic and then to New England and the West Indies. Although James I was sympathetic to Catholicism, fear of religious persecution in England also caused English Catholics to look toward America, where they would ultimately settle in Maryland. Fleeing poverty or hoping for greater prosperity, thousands of other settlers accompanied these religious refugees.

The English Legacy to America. Indeed, the economic and religious transformation of England between 1550 and 1620 greatly influenced the character of its North American settlements. Because the English aristocracy was on the decline and played a small role in colonization, the American settlements were not dominated by a legally privileged nobility. Rather, the increasing importance of English merchants enhanced their role in overseas expansion and resulted in the rapid creation of a transatlantic trading economy. Similarly, the enclosure movement produced a vast group of landless peasants, whose emigration as indentured servants shaped the social character of early Virginia and other settlements. Finally, as a result of the influence of Calvinism on English Protestantism, many migrants carried radical forms of Christianity to America and made the New England colonies into bastions of Puritanism.

These migrations would also spark a new collision between the European and native American worlds. Just as the intrusion of the Spanish into Mesoamerica around 1500 had forever changed the history of that region, the coming of the English—and Dutch and French—to eastern North America a century later would produce a similar spectacle of disease and war and cultural conflict.

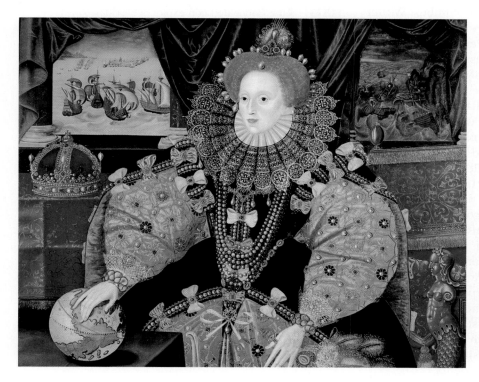

Elizabeth I (r. 1558–1603)
Attired in richly decorated clothes that symbolize her power, Queen Elizabeth I relishes the destruction of the Spanish Armada (pictured in background) and proclaims her nation's imperial ambitions. The queen's hand rests on a globe, asserting England's claims in the Western Hemisphere.
Woburn Abbey Collection, by permission of the Marquess of Tavistock and the Trustees of the Bedford Estates.

Summary

★

The first inhabitants of the Western Hemisphere were hunter-gatherers from Asia who migrated some 30,000 years ago. Their descendants settled throughout North and South America, establishing a great variety of cultures. In Mesoamerica, the Mayan and Aztec peoples created populous agricultural societies with highly sophisticated systems of art, religion, and politics, while the Inca established an empire along the western coast of South America. In North America, the peoples of the Hopewell and Mississippian cultures created elaborate ceremonial and urban sites, as did the Pueblo peoples of the Southwest. However, in 1500 most North American Indians lived in small-scale, self-governing communities of foragers, hunters, and horticulturalists.

The Europeans who invaded America came from a traditional agricultural society in which a privileged elite ruled a mass of peasants. Christianity provided unity to European civilization and gave emotional richness and meaning to life. Church and state alike endorsed values of hierarchy and authority, demanding that people submit to strict discipline as the price of survival in a world of scarcity. These values strongly influenced American life well into the eighteenth century.

The Crusades opened the eyes of Europeans to the learning of the Arab Muslim world, and the Italian Renaissance and the emergence of monarchical nation-states changed Europe from a static to a dynamic society. Portugal sent explorers and merchants to Africa and Asia, and Spain undertook the conquest of the "new world" found in 1492 by Christopher Columbus. Within a generation, Spanish conquistadors had pillaged the wealthy civilizations of Mexico and Peru. The coming of Europeans—and their diseases, horses, government, and religion—brought death to millions of native Americans and changed forever the lives of those who survived.

The influx of gold and silver from America disrupted traditional European society, which was already reeling from the religious wars unleashed by the Protestant Reformation. Warfare and the Price Revolution undermined Catholic Spain while assisting the rise of Holland, France, and England. In England, monarchs used mercantilist policies to promote domestic manufacturing, foreign trade, and colonization, while the enclosure movement and religious conflicts laid the social basis for a mass migration to America. The migrants carried both traditional and modern ideas and institutions across the Atlantic—a contrast between old and new that was sharpened in America. In England's Chesapeake colonies a new form of aristocratic rule would emerge, based first on white indentured servitude and then on African slavery, while in New England the settlers would establish a yeoman society that had few European antecedents.

TIMELINE

30,000– Settlement of eastern North America
10,000
B.C.

3000– Cultivation of crops begins in Mesoamerica
2000
B.C.

100– Flourishing of Hopewell culture
400

300 Rise of Mayan civilization

500 Zenith of Teotihuacán civilization

600 Emergence of Pueblo cultures

700– Spread of Arab Muslim civilization
1100

800– Development of Mississippian culture
1350

1095– Crusades link Europe with Arab Muslim learning
1272

1325 Aztecs establish their capital at Tenochtitlán

1400– Italian Renaissance
1550

1440s Portugal enters trade in African slaves

1492 Christopher Columbus's first voyage to America

1513 Juan Ponce de León explores Florida

1517 Martin Luther begins Protestant Reformation

1519– Hernando Cortés conquers Aztec empire
1521

1531– Francisco Pizarro vanquishes Incas in Peru
1538

1534 Henry VIII establishes Church of England

1536 John Calvin's *Institutes of the Christian Religion*

1550– Price Revolution
1630
English mercantilism

Enclosure movement

1556– Philip II, king of Spain
1598

1558– Elizabeth I, queen of England
1603

1560s English Puritan movement begins

1603– James I, first Stuart king of England
1625

Suggested Readings

★

One of the few works that covers the history of the various European and native American peoples is Eric Wolf, *Europe and the People without History* (1982). See also Alfred W. Crosby Jr., *Ecological Imperialism: The Biological Expansion of Europe, 900–1900* (1986); Robert R. Reynolds, *Europe Emerges: Transition toward an Industrial World-Wide Society, 600–1750* (1961); G. V. Scammell, *The World Encompassed: The First European Maritime Empires* (1981); and Roger Schlesinger, *In the Wake of Columbus: The Impact of the New World on Europe, 1492–1650* (1996).

Native American Worlds

Brian M. Fagan, *The Great Journey; The People of Ancient America* (1987), synthesizes recent scholarship on prehistoric American Indians, and his *Kingdoms of Gold, Kingdoms of Jade: The Americas before Columbus* (1991) does the same for the Mesoamerican peoples. See also Stuart J. Fiedel, *Prehistory of the Americas* (1992); Inga Clendinnen, *Aztecs: An Interpretation* (1991); John S. Henderson, *The World of the Maya* (1981); David Carrasco, *Quetzalcoatl and the Irony of Empire* (1982); and R. Tom Zuidema, *Inca Civilization in Cuzco* (1992). Two fine supplements are Michael Coe et al., *Atlas of Ancient America* (1986), and Manuel Lucena Salmoral, *America in 1492* (1991), a photographic survey of dress, artifacts, and architecture.

On the impact of European diseases, see Henry F. Dobyns, *Their Numbers Became Thinned: Native American Population Dynamics in Eastern North America* (1983), and William M. Denevan, *The Native Population of the Americas in 1492* (1992).

On North America, consult Alvin M. Josephy Jr., ed., *America in 1492* (1993); Linda S. Cordell, *Ancient Pueblo Peoples* (1994); Bruce D. Smith, ed., *The Mississippian Emergence* (1990); Carl Waldman and Molly Braun, *Atlas of the North American Indian* (1985); and Robert Silverberg, *Mound Builders of Ancient America: The Archaeology of a Myth* (1968). Roger Kennedy, *Hidden Cities* (1994), surveys the early Indian civilizations of the Mississippi Valley, and Samuel W. Wilson, ed., *The Indigenous People of the Caribbean* (1997), offers important essays on that topic.

Traditional European Society, 1450–1550

Barbara W. Tuchman, *A Distant Mirror: The Calamitous Fourteenth Century* (1978), presents a vivid portrait of the late medieval world. Two wide-ranging studies of subsequent developments are George Huppert, *After the Black Death: A Social History of Modern Europe* (1986), and Henry Kamen, *European Society, 1500–1700* (1984). Illuminating specialized studies include Peter Burke, *Popular Culture in Early Modern Europe* (1978); Pierre Goubert, *The French Peasantry in the Seventeenth Century* (1986); B. H. Slicher Van Bath, *The Agrarian History of Western Europe, A.D. 500–1850* (1963); and Emanuel Le Roy Ladurie, *The Peasants of Languedoc* (1974).

See also Joel Mokyr, *The Lever of Riches: Technological Creativity and Economic Progress* (1990), and E. P. Thompson, *Customs in Common: Studies in Traditional Popular Culture* (1991).

Europe and the World, 1450–1550

The preconditions for European expansion are treated in James D. Tracy, ed., *Rise of Merchant Empires: Long Distance Trade in the Early Modern World, 1350–1750* (1990).

Paul H. Chapman, *The Norse Discovery of America* (1981), and Boies Penrose, *Travel and Discovery in the Renaissance, 1420–1620* (1952), illuminate the growth of geographical knowledge. For the expansion of Portugal and Spain peoples, see Bailey W. Diffie and George Winius, *Foundations of the Portuguese Empire, 1415–1580* (1977), and Henry Kamen, *Crisis and Change in Early Modern Spain* (1993). A good short biography of Columbus and his times is Felipe Fernández-Armesto, *Columbus* (1991).

For the Spanish and Portuguese colonial empires, see Charles R. Boxer, *The Portuguese Seaborne Empire* (1969), and James Lockhard and Stuart B. Schwartz, *Early Latin America: Colonial Spanish America and Brazil* (1984). Fine accounts of the Spanish conquest include the memorable firsthand report by Bernal Díaz del Castillo, *The Discovery and Conquest of Mexico* (edited by I. A. Leonard, 1956); Leon Portilla, *Broken Spears: The Aztec Account of the Conquest of Mexico* (1962); and Hugh Thomas, *Conquest: Montezuma, Cortés and the Fall of Old Mexico* (1994). The impact on native society in New Spain is portrayed in Daniel T. Reff, *Disease, Depopulation, and Culture Change in Northwestern New Spain, 1518–1764* (1991). Susan E. Ramírez, *The World Upside Down: Cross-Cultural Contact and Conflict in Sixteenth-Century Peru* (1996), offers a close analysis of Inca life after the conquest.

The Protestant Reformation and the Rise of England, 1500–1620

On the European Reformation, consult William J. Bouwsma, *John Calvin* (1987), and De Lamar Jensen, *Reformation Europe: Age of Reform and Revolution* (1981). For developments in England, see Patrick Collinson, *The Religion of the Protestants: The Church in English Society, 1559–1625* (1982), and Susan Doran and Christopher Durston, *Princes, Pastors, and People: The Church and Religion in England, 1529–1689* (1991).

On the decline of Spain, consult Henry Kamen, *Spain: A Society in Conflict, 1479–1714*, 2nd ed. (1991), and John Lynch, *The Hispanic World in Crisis and Change, 1598–1700* (1992), which also traces the growing economic independence of New Spain.

A brilliant and forceful portrait of English preindustrial society is offered by Peter Laslett, *The World We Have Lost* (3rd ed., 1984). Other important works are Keith Wrightson, *English Society, 1580–1680* (1982), and Lawrence Stone, *The Crisis of the Aristocracy* (1965). On the movement of people, see Ida Altman and James Horn, eds., *"To Make America": European Emigration in the Early Modern Period* (1991).

Chapter 2

The Invasion and Settlement of North America, 1550–1700

ESTABLISHING COLONIES IN distant lands was not for the faint of heart. First came a long voyage in small ships over uncharted waters. Then the migrants, weakened by weeks of travel, spoiled food, and shipboard diseases, faced the challenge of life in an alien land inhabited by potentially hostile peoples. The risks were great and the rewards uncertain, yet tens of thousands of Europeans crossed the Atlantic during the seventeenth century, driven by poverty and persecution at home or drawn by the lures of the New World: land, wealth, and—as one group of pious English settlers put it—the prospect of advancing the "gospell of the Kingdome of Christ in those remote parts."

Whatever the motives of individual migrants, European statesmen and diplomats considered the settlers instruments of national power: their tasks were to subdue the native peoples, set up colonies, and export gold and valuable crops to the homeland. By 1565 Spain had sent settlers and soldiers north of the Rio Grande and had established a permanent presence in Florida. For the next century and a half, Spain tried—unsuccessfully—to exclude other European nations from the continent of North America.

By the early 1600s France, Holland, and England had established permanent settlements in North America. Small numbers of French settlers and fur traders moved down the St. Lawrence River Valley, while Dutch merchants set up trading posts along the Hudson River. Migrants from England founded two tiny colonies along the Atlantic coast—Jamestown and Plymouth—and were soon joined by tens of thousands of English men and women who settled in the Chesapeake Bay region and in New England.

"America"

This late sixteenth-century or early seventeenth-century Spanish ceramic tile was part of a series that represented the four known continents. The scene is an allegorical portrayal of the New World—the Indian king represents the American continents, now under the guidance of Spanish conquistadors.

For native Americans, European invasion and settlement were nothing short of catastrophic. Whether they came as missionaries, fur traders, or settlers, the new arrivals spread havoc. European diseases and religious conversion threatened Indian peoples with the loss of their lives and age-old cultures. And European-style warfare—waged for land and conquest rather than primarily to demonstrate courage and prowess (as among the eastern Woodland peoples)—depleted the thin ranks of Indian warriors; as the Narragansett of Rhode Island protested, all-out military conflict "slays too many men." The first century of cultural contact foretold the course of North American history: the advance of the invaders and the dispossession of the Indian peoples.

Imperial Conflicts and Rival Colonial Models

———————★———————

The Spanish colonial regime established in Mesoamerica imposed authoritarian controls over the native peoples. Government officials and private landlords in New Spain forced the Indians to convert to Catholicism and to work digging gold and farming large estates. This coercive handling of the native peoples was much less effective in the sparsely populated lands north of the Rio Grande, where other Europeans founded different types of colonies and interacted in different ways with the Indians (Table 2.1). In the fur-trading empires

created by the French and the Dutch, the native peoples retained their lands and political autonomy, whereas in the quickly growing colonies settled by the English, Indians were simply not welcome as laborers, farmers, and trappers, and were pushed ever farther to the west. Despite the differing goals of these colonial regimes—the exploitation of native labor by the Spanish, the collection of furs by the French and Dutch, the creation of farming communities by the English—nearly everywhere the Indian peoples eventually rose in revolt.

New Spain: Colonization and Conversion

Spain sent military adventurers to explore and conquer the lands north of the Rio Grande and counted on the Catholic Church to convert the resident peoples and ensure their loyalty.

The Northern Frontier. Spanish penetration of the vast lands north of the Rio Grande began in 1540 when Francisco Vásquez de Coronado searched for the fabled seven cities of Cíbola, said to lie north of present-day Albuquerque and to be capped with golden towers (Map 2.1). Traveling over well-worn Indian trails, in 1541 Coronado's expedition of 300 Spanish adventurers and 1,000 Indian allies reached and captured the alleged Cíbola, which turned out to be a poor Zuni pueblo of 100 families. Refusing to abandon his quest, Coronado dispatched expeditions that discovered the Grand Canyon in Arizona and explored much of the Rio Grande Valley in New Mexico, where in 1542 they encountered the

TABLE 2.1

European Colonies in North America before 1660

	Date	First Settlement	Type	Religion	Chief Export or Economic Activity
New France	1608	Quebec	Royal	Catholic	Furs
New Netherland	1613	New Amsterdam	Corporate	Dutch Reformed	Furs
New Sweden	1628	Fort Christina	Corporate	Lutheran	Furs; farming
English Colonies					
Virginia	1607	Jamestown	Corporate (Merchant)	Anglican	Tobacco
Plymouth	1620	Plymouth	Corporate (Religious)	Separatist-Puritan	Mixed farming; livestock
Massachusetts Bay	1630	Boston	Corporate (Religious)	Puritan	Mixed farming
Maryland	1634	St. Mary's	Proprietary	Catholic	Tobacco; grain
Connecticut	1635	Hartford	Corporate (Religious)	Puritan	Mixed farming; livestock
Rhode Island	1636	Providence	Corporate (Religious)	Separatist-Puritan	Mixed farming; livestock

MAP 2.1
New Spain Looks North, 1513–1610
The quest for gold drew Spanish adventurers deep into North America. Hernando de Soto
and Francisco Vásquez de Coronado led wide-ranging expeditions in the 1540s, but the
first permanent settlement to the north of New Spain came only in 1565, at St. Augustine
in present-day Florida. A generation later, following the explorations of Juan de Oñate,
the Spanish founded Santa Fe in New Mexico.

Pueblo people for the first time. Coronado himself drove eastward, pursuing more empty rumors and eventually reaching the grasslands of present-day central Kansas.

Simultaneously, Hernando de Soto, who was also driven by visions of gold and glory, embarked from Florida on a mission of conquest and plunder. Between 1539 and 1543 de Soto's force of 600 adventurers cut a bloody swath across the densely populated Southeast, doing battle with the chiefdoms of Mississippian culture: the Apalachee of northern Florida, the Cofitachequi of South Carolina, and the Coosa of northern Alabama (see Map 2.1). De Soto suffered heavy losses and had little to show for it. He found caches of freshwater pearls but—like Coronado—no gold, so for the next two decades Spain largely ignored the northern regions.

In the 1560s officials in New Spain again turned their attention to the distant lands of North America. Operating from temporary bases on the mainland and in the West Indies, roving English privateers were plundering Spanish possessions, and French adventurers

were attacking Spanish treasure ships, halving the Spanish Crown's revenue. Equally ominous for the Spanish, in 1564 French Protestants began a settlement along the St. John River in Florida, which Spain had claimed a half-century earlier. In response King Philip II ordered the military adventurer Pedro Menéndez de Avilés to find the Frenchmen and "cast them out by the best means"; Menéndez's troops promptly massacred 300 members of what he called the "evil Lutheran sect."

To safeguard Florida from new incursions by other European powers, in 1565 Menéndez established a fort at St. Augustine, the first permanent European settlement in the future United States, and six other bases, the most important at Santa Elena on Port Royal Sound in present-day South Carolina (see Map 2.1). From there he sent expeditions into the interior and to the Bahía de Santa María (Chesapeake Bay), where in 1571 Spanish priests of the Society of Jesus (Jesuits) founded a short-lived mission (see American Lives, "Luis de Velasco/Opechancanough/Massatamohtnock: A Case of Possible Multiple Identities," pp. 42–43).

Luis de Velasco/ Opechancanough/ Massatamohtnock: A Case of Possible Multiple Identities

———————★———————

LONG BEFORE THE Chesapeake Bay took its present name, it was known as the Bahía de Santa María (the Bay of Saint Mary), claimed by Spain and part of the giant colony of Florida that stretched from present-day Texas to Newfoundland. And long before the first English adventurers set foot in the colony they called Virginia, Spanish Jesuits established a mission there (in 1571) at Ajacán; they came to convert the local Algonquian inhabitants— the Powhatan people—to the Catholic faith.

For eighty years, from the 1560s to the 1640s, this land would be contested ground, as Spanish conquistadors, English adventurers, and native chiefs vied with each other for control of the land and its people. Strong but not conclusive evidence suggests that the life of one man spanned this eighty-year struggle and shaped its course. The Spanish knew him as Don Luis de Velasco, a young Indian *cacique* (chief) who had lived in Spain for a time and become a pious convert to the Catholic faith. A generation later the English probably encountered the same man as Opechancanough, a local chief, "the King of the Pamaunches" (Pamunkey) and an astute negotiator who seemed to favor interracial peace. Finally, when Opechancanough succeeded his elder brother as the *Powhatan*, or main chief, in 1621, he assumed a new name, Massatamohtnock, and a new role: a diplomat-warrior who led two Indian uprisings.

Spanish Catholic convert, pacific leader and diplomat, zealous native American patriot: Was this a case of several individuals or was there only one man? If so, what accounts for his multiple identities? A confused response to contradictory cultural pressures? Simple deception?

This puzzle has its origins in 1561, when two vessels commanded by the Spanish mariner and adventurer Pedro Menéndez de Avilés sailed into the Bahía de Santa María. Like other conquistadors Menéndez came looking for gold and plunder, but he also sought good harbors for naval garrisons that would protect Spanish treasure ships from pirates. Menéndez went away without riches but took with him the seventeen-year-old son of a local chief, an Indian youth "of fine presence and bearing," whom he promised to take to Europe "that the King of Spain, his lord, might see him." King Philip II was equally impressed by the imposing stature of the young *cacique*, who stood more than six feet tall, and by his intelligence, for he granted the young Indian an allowance and had Dominican friars teach him the Spanish language and the principles of the Catholic faith.

Three years later the young man was in Mexico, where he acquired a new patron, Don Luis de Velasco, the viceroy of New Spain, who became his godfather and gave the Indian his own name. Anxious to return to his people, in 1566 the Indian Don Luis accompanied an expedition to the Bahía de Santa María that was blown off course, and he found himself once again in Spain. Now taught by Jesuits, a contemporary chronicler noted, "he was made ready and they gave him the holy sacraments of the altar and Confirmation." For his part, the Indian Don Luis convinced the Jesuit father Juan Baptista de Segura of his "plan and determination . . . of converting his parents, relatives, and countrymen to the faith of Jesus Christ, and baptizing them and making them Christians as he was."

Thus it was that the young Christianized Indian and eight Jesuit missionaries landed in 1571 in Ajacán, five miles from the later site of Jamestown. Once restored to the land of his childhood, Don Luis readopted its customs, taking a number of wives. Publicly chastised for adultery by Father Segura, he took refuge in his native village. When three missionaries came to fetch him, Don Luis had them killed with a "shower of arrows"; then, according to one account, he murdered Father Segura and the rest of the Jesuits by his own hand. This massacre brought quick retribution. In 1572 Menéndez personally led a punitive expedition that resulted in the deaths of dozens of Indians, but his former protégé escaped his wrath.

At this point the historical record becomes cloudy, but there is strong circumstantial evidence that suggests that the young *cacique*, Don Luis, now took the name of Opechancanough and became chief of the Pamunkey people. Both chiefs are described in

John Smith and Chief Opechancanough
The powerful Indian chief Opechancanough towers over John Smith in this engraving of their confrontation in 1609 over English access to Indian supplies of food.
Library of Congress.

the records as imposing in size, much taller than most Indians and most Europeans. And there is a chronological fit between their lives. When Don Luis returned to America in 1571, he was about twenty-seven years old; in 1621, when Opechancanough succeeded Powhatan as chief, he was an elderly man. Finally, there is the translation of Opechancanough's name: "He whose soul is white"—perhaps a reference to his life as a Christian Indian or his remorse about Father Segura's fate.

As Spanish dreams of an eastern North American empire faded in the face of fierce native American resistance, England dispatched its own adventurers to search for gold and promote "the Christian religion to such People as yet live in Darkness." Opechancanough first confronted the new invaders in December 1607, when he captured Captain John Smith but spared his life. Two years later, after Smith grabbed

Opechancanough "by the long lock of his head; and with my pistol at his breast . . . made him fill our bark with twenty tuns of corn," the chief did not seek revenge. Instead, for the next decade, the Pamunkey leader pursued a complicated diplomatic strategy: he "stood aloof" from the English and "would not be drawn to any Treaty." In particular, he strongly resisted proposals to take Indian children from their parents so that they might be "brought upp in Christianytie." At the same time, Opechancanough promoted interracial peace by accepting the marriage of his niece Pocahontas to John Rolfe and by arranging a treaty between the English and a Chesapeake tribe. The chief's allegiance may have been divided between two worlds: an Algonquian in culture and outlook, but also a person whose soul was "white."

Then, in 1621, this man assumed a new identity, taking the name Massatamohtnock. And he took up a new cause. The number of English migrants had greatly increased, leading many Algonquians to believe that the English would soon take up "all their lands and would drive them out the country." To prevent this, the aging Massatamohtnock played a double game. While assuring Governor Wyatt of Virginia that "the Skye should sooner falle than Peace be broken, on his parte," he secretly mobilized the Pamunkey and more than two dozen other Indian peoples. In 1622 these tribes launched a surprise attack that took the lives of 347 English men, women, and children. Urging the chief of the Potomacks to continue the onslaught, Massatamohtnock declared his goal: "before the end of two Moons there should not be an Englishman in all their Countries."

Finally defeated in the late 1620s when the English systematically burned Indian cornfields, the old chief reappeared in 1644, orchestrating another surprise assault that took the lives of "near five hundred Christians." Now a hundred years old, "so decrepit that he was not able to walk alone but was carried about by his men," Massatamohtnock was captured by the English and taken to Jamestown. There, an English official reported, an angry soldier "basely shot him through the back . . . of which wound he died."

The absence of Algonquian sources makes it unlikely that we will ever know the complete history or the real motives of this remarkable man. But the violent treatment Don Luis meted out to Father Segura, and the resistance Massatamohtnock unleashed in 1622 and 1644 suggest that ultimately he defined himself as an Indian patriot, a resolute enemy of the European invaders and their Christian religion.

However, attacks by the Calusa and Timucuan peoples soon destroyed most of these Spanish outposts, prompting Menéndez to condemn the Indians as an "infamous people, Sodomites, sacrificers to the devil . . . [who should be] given as slaves."

The English met these Spanish efforts with new initiatives of their own. During the 1570s Sir Walter Raleigh dispatched settlers to North Carolina (see Chapter 1), and the English sea captain Sir Francis Drake sailed around the tip of South America and plundered a rich Spanish bullion fleet in the Pacific. After landing in California, which he claimed for England, Drake sailed west to Asia. Circumnavigating the globe, he returned to England with £600,000 in bullion (equal to about $30 million in 1999), twenty times the annual income of the wealthiest aristocrat. A decade later the intrepid Drake sacked the important port city of Cartagena (in present-day Colombia) and nearly wiped out St. Augustine in Florida.

The Settlement of New Mexico.   These military set-backs prompted the Spanish Crown to adopt a new set of policies, concentrating their defensive forces in Florida and Cuba in the east and seeking to win native American allies in the west. The Comprehensive Orders for New Discoveries, issued in 1573, placed the "pacification" of the northern lands primarily in the hands of missionaries rather than military adventurers. Franciscan friars promptly established missions in the Pueblo world visited by Coronado two generations before, naming the area Nuevo México.

The friars built their missions and churches near existing Indian pueblos and villages and often learned the Indian languages. But for the Franciscans, religious conversion and cultural assimilation went hand in hand. They introduced European agricultural practices and encouraged the Indians to talk, cook, dress, and walk like Spaniards. They smashed the religious idols of the native Americans and, to win their allegiance to the Christian god, dazzled them with rich vestments, gold crosses, and silver chalices. Sexual sinners and spirit worshipers were punished, usually by whipping. Most native Americans tolerated the Franciscans out of fear of military reprisals or in hopes of learning their spiritual secrets. But when Christian prayers failed to prevent European diseases and soldiers from devastating their communities, many Indians returned to their ancestral religions.

Despite its religious emphasis, Spanish rule was hardly benevolent. The survival of the Franciscan missions depended on Indian workers, who grew the crops and carried them to market—often on their backs. Authorities in New Spain granted huge tracts of land in New Mexico to well-connected Spanish settlers, or *encomenderos,* and gave them the right to collect tribute from the natives, usually in goods but often through a system of forced labor known as *repartimiento.* Other

Conversion in New Mexico
Franciscan friars introduced Catholicism to the Indian peoples north of the Rio Grande, assisted by nuns of various religious orders. This 1631 engraving shows one of those nuns, María de Jesús de Agreda, preaching to a nomadic people (*los chichimecos*) in New Mexico.
Nettie Lee Benson Latin American Collection, University of Texas at Austin.

Indians, usually Pueblo women and children captured by nomadic tribes, were ransomed by Spanish landowners and forced to work for them as slaves. Monks and settlers alike ignored the Spanish laws that regulated the use of Indian labor.

The harsh treatment of the natives prompted a series of small uprisings and two major rebellions. The first revolt took place in 1598, when Juan de Oñate led an expedition of 500 soldiers and settlers into New Mexico to establish a fort and a trading villa. Oñate's men seized corn and clothing from the Pueblo peoples and murdered or raped those who resisted. When Indians of the Acoma pueblo killed 11 Spanish soldiers, the remaining troops looted the pueblo and massacred 500 men and 300 women and children. Faced by now-hostile Indian peoples, most of the settlers withdrew (see American Voices, "A Franciscan Reflects on Spain's Policies in New Mexico," p. 45).

A Franciscan Reflects on Spain's Policies in New Mexico

———————— ★ ————————

New Spain extended its empire north of the Rio Grande through military force and religious conversion. Spanish conquistadors, such as Juan de Oñate, had different interests and goals from those of the Franciscan friars, and the two groups came into conflict. However, these two agents of Spanish expansionism often cooperated. The friars called on troops stationed in military forts (presidios) *to induce local Indians to remain at the missions and protect them from attacks by nomadic Indian peoples. This plea from a Franciscan to the viceroy of New Spain endorses the limited use of military force even as it condemns past excesses.*

The first and foremost difficulty, from which have sprung all the evils and the ruin of this land, is the fact that this conquest was entrusted to a man of such limited resources as Don Juan de Oñate. The result was that soon after he entered the land, his people began to perpetrate many offenses against the natives and to plunder their pueblos of the corn they had gathered for their own sustenance; here corn is God, for they have nothing else with which to support themselves. Because of this situation and because the Spaniards asked the natives for blankets as tribute, even before teaching them the meaning of God, the Indians began to get restless, abandon their pueblos, and take to the mountains. Your lordship must not believe that the Indians part willingly with their corn, or the blankets with which they cover themselves; on the contrary, this extortion is done by threats and force of arms, the soldiers burning some of the houses and killing the Indians. This was the cause of the Acoma war [of 1598], as I have clearly established after questioning friars, captains, and soldiers. And the war which was recently waged against the Jumanas started the same way. In these conflicts, more than eight hundred men, women, and children were killed, and three pueblos burned.

I do not hesitate to say that his majesty could have discovered this land with fifty well-armed Christian men, giving them the necessary things for this purpose, and that what these fifty men might discover could be placed under the royal crown and the conquest effected in a Christian manner without outraging or killing these poor Indians, who think that we are all evil and that the king who sent us here is ineffective and a tyrant. By so doing we would satisfy the wishes of our mother church, which, not without long consideration and forethought and illuminated by the Holy Spirit, entrusted these conquests and the conversions of souls to the kings of Castile, our lords, acknowledging in them the means, Christianity, and holiness for an undertaking as heroic as is that of winning souls for God.

Because of these matters (and others that I am not telling), we cannot preach the gospel now, for it is despised by these people on account of our great offenses and the harm we have done them. At the same time it is not desirable to abandon this land, either for the service of God or the conscience of his majesty since many souls have already been baptized. Besides, this place where we are now established is a good stepping stone and site from which to explore this whole land.

___

Source: G. P. Hammond and Agapito Rey, *Don Juan de Oñate, Colonizer of New Mexico, 1595–1628* (Albuquerque: University of New Mexico Press, 1953), part 2:692–695.

Over the next decade Spanish settlers and missionaries slowly moved up the Rio Grande. In 1610 they founded the town of Sante Fe and soon reestablished the missions and the system of forced labor. Over the years Spanish demands for tribute took their toll on the Pueblo peoples, as did raids by Navajos and Apache. By 1680 many pueblos in New Mexico were threatened with extinction. Led by Popé, an Indian *shaman* (priest), the peoples of two dozen pueblos came together to mount a second major rebellion, killing over 400 Spaniards and forcing the remaining 2,000 colonists to flee 300 miles down the Rio Grande to El Paso. Enraged by the way they had been mistreated, the Pueblo rebels desecrated Catholic churches and tortured and killed twenty-one missionaries. Reconquered a decade later, the Indians rebelled again in 1696, only to be subdued once more.

Finally the two sides arranged a compromise. The Pueblo peoples agreed to accept Spanish political rule and settlers; in return they received the right to practice their own religion, freedom from forced labor, and Spanish military assistance against attacks by nomadic Indians.

Spain had managed to maintain its northern empire but only with great difficulty. And it had largely failed to achieve its goals of religious conversion and cultural assimilation. Taken aback by the costs of expansion, Spanish officials decided not to undertake the settlement of the distant region of California, delaying until 1769 the permanent European occupation of that area. For the time being, Florida and New Mexico stood as the defensive outposts of Spain's American empire.

New France: Furs and Souls

Far to the northeast the French likewise tried to convert the native peoples to Catholicism but, because they relied on priests rather than soldiers, in a much less coercive fashion. In the 1530s Jacques Cartier had claimed the lands bordered by the Gulf of St. Lawrence for France, but the first permanent settlement wasn't established until 1608, with the founding of Quebec by Samuel de Champlain (see Map 2.2). To safeguard the new settlement, Champlain entered into an alliance with the Huron, trading with them for furs and providing them with weapons to resist the powerful Iroquois peoples of New York.

In 1628 the small settlement came under the control of the Company of New France, a merchant-run joint-stock enterprise founded by Cardinal Richelieu, a leading French statesman and a strong advocate of colonization. The Company received a monopoly on the fur trade and title to all the lands of New France. In return the Company was required to dispatch 4,000 settlers to the new colony and to provide them with supplies and priests.

However, relatively few French men and women migrated to America. Unlike the English peasantry, which after 1550 was gradually dispossessed of its lands, most French cultivators held strong legal rights to their property and thus successfully resisted the enclosure of common fields. Moreover, for military reasons the French government wanted an ample supply of young men at home, so it offered few incentives to emigrate. French monarchs also barred Huguenots (French Protestants) from settling in Quebec, fearing that they might disrupt the colony. Finally, nearly 70 percent of the 67,000 men and women who actually migrated to Quebec between 1608 and 1763 eventually returned to France, their hopes for prosperity as farmers in the fertile lands along the St. Lawrence River dashed by short growing seasons and long, bitter winters.

Because farming prospects were so much more favorable in France, New France did not develop as a settler colony. In 1698 its European population was only 15,200, whereas there were 100,000 settlers in the English colonies. Instead, the French settlement became a vast fur-trading enterprise, and French explorers traveled deep into the continent to seek new suppliers and claim new lands. In 1673 Jacques Marquette, a priest of the Society of Jesus (Jesuits), journeyed west with the fur trader Louis Joliet, reaching the Mississippi River in present-day Wisconsin and then traveling as far south as Arkansas. Exploration of the majestic river was completed in 1681 by Robert de La Salle, who sought fortune as well as fame. As a French priest noted with disgust, La Salle's expedition hoped "to buy all the Furs and Skins of the remotest Savages, who, as they thought, did not know their Value; and so enrich themselves in one single voyage." To honor the French monarch Louis XIV, La Salle named the region Louisiana; soon it included the thriving port of New Orleans on the Gulf of Mexico.

Despite their small numbers, French traders and explorers had a disastrous impact on native Americans living near the Great Lakes. By introducing European diseases, they unwittingly triggered epidemics that wiped out 25 to 90 percent of the native population, and by providing a market for deerskins and beaver pelts, they set in motion a devastating series of wars between Indian peoples for control of the fur trade.

The Iroquois of New York profited the most from these wars. Since the 1550s the Iroquois had been organized in large towns of 500 to 2,000 persons and were united in a great "longhouse" confederation, the Five Nations. In the 1640s they embarked on a decades-long series of wars to control the lucrative trade in furs. Becoming what one historian has called an "engine of destruction," the Five Nations virtually destroyed two western Iroquois tribes, the Eries and the Neutrals; forced the Iroquois-speaking Huron to move north of the Great Lakes; and pushed a dozen Algonquin-speaking peoples—including Ottawas, Fox, Sauks, Kickapoos, Miamis, and Illinois—out of their traditional lands north of the Ohio River. The Algonquian refugees crowded into a newly formed multitribal region west of Lake Michigan (present-day Wisconsin) and, to protect themselves against the powerful Iroquois, in the 1670s allied themselves with the French, who also feared the Five Nations. By 1701 Algonquian-French attacks had so weakened the Iroquois that they agreed to the Grand Settlement, promising neutrality in French-British warfare and abandoning efforts to dominate the western Indian peoples.

While French traders amassed furs, French priests sought converts among both the dispossessed Huron and the belligerent Iroquois. Between 1625 and 1763 hundreds of Jesuit priests lived among the Indians and, to a greater extent than the Spanish Franciscans, came to understand their values. One Jesuit, Father Paul Ragueneau, reported a Huron belief that "our souls have desires which are inborn and concealed, yet are made known by means of dreams"; drawing upon this Indian concept of an invisible spiritual world, he explained Christian doctrines of grace and an eternal afterlife. Indians at first welcomed the "Black Robes" as *manitou*, powerful spiritual beings with magical secrets, such as the ability to forge iron. But native peoples grew skeptical when prayers to the Christian god did not protect them from disease, famine, and enemy attack. A Peoria chief charged that their priest's "fables are good only in his own country; we have our own, which do not make us die as his do."

Nonetheless, the French missionaries won more converts than the Spanish Franciscans, in part because they did not use Indians for forced labor and protected them from the dangers of alcohol by preventing brandy from becoming a bargaining item in the French fur trade (as rum had become in the English trade in pelts). The French Jesuits gained other converts by showing how Christian principles could address Indian concerns. For example, in the 1690s some young native American women in Illinois embraced the cult of the Virgin Mary, in part to use its emphasis on chastity to reassert Algonquian beliefs that unmarried women were "masters of their own body," as a tribal elder put it. Yet many Indians who had the choice found it more satisfying to hold on to their traditional values than to adopt Catholic beliefs. Thus, despite its success as a fur-trading venture, New France failed as a settler colony and had only mixed success as a missionary enterprise.

New Netherland: Commerce

Unlike the French and Spanish, the Dutch in North America had little interest in religious conversion. Their eyes were fastened on commerce, for the Dutch

New Amsterdam, 1639
This early Dutch map of the entrance to New York harbor provides a bird's-eye view of the windmills, farms, and Indian villages of Manhattan Island and the surrounding countryside. The map key lists the names and location of all the farms in the area. The map, the earliest known depiction of Manhattan and its vicinity, was likely used by the Dutch West India Company to promote settlement in the growing Dutch community.
Library of Congress.

Republic was the trading hub of Europe. In 1609, Henry Hudson, an Englishman employed by the Dutch East India Company, found and named the Hudson River in the area of present-day New York. A few years later the Dutch established fur-trading posts on Manhattan Island and at Fort Nassau (Albany). In 1621 the Dutch government chartered a new joint-stock enterprise, the West India Company, intending to use it to plunder the Portuguese plantations in Brazil and the Spanish colonies in the Caribbean. But it also gave the company a monopoly over the slave trade in West Africa and exclusive authority to establish outposts in America. Taking over the fur posts along the Hudson, the West India Company set up new trading stations in the areas of present-day Connecticut, New Jersey, Delaware, and Pennsylvania. In 1624 its director, Peter Minuit, "purchased" all of Manhattan Island from the Indians and founded the town of New Amsterdam as the capital of a new colony: New Netherland.

New Netherland attracted few Dutch settlers, for Holland was enjoying great economic prosperity and the small size of these wilderness outposts made them vulnerable to invasion from New England or New France. To encourage migration, the West India Company granted huge estates along the Hudson River to wealthy Dutchmen, stipulating that each proprietor, or *patroon*, settle fifty tenants on his land within four years or the estate would revert to the company. Among all the patroons, only Kiliaen Van Rensselaer, a diamond merchant, brought over enough peasant-tenants to retain his vast American holding, the manor of Rensselaerswyck. Consequently, the population in Dutch North America remained small, reaching only 1,500 at the time of the English conquest in 1664.

Although New Netherland failed as a settler colony, it flourished briefly as a fur-trading enterprise, albeit a bloody one. In the 1640s Governor William Kieft embarked on an expansionist policy, dispatching armed Dutch bands to seize prime farming land from the neighboring Algonquian peoples and take over their trading network, in which corn and wampum from Long Island were exchanged for furs from Maine. Threatened by the Dutch guns supplied to their traditional Iroquois enemies, the Algonquians responded with force. By the end of "Kieft's War" (1643–1646), more than two hundred Dutch residents and a thousand Indians had been killed, many in brutal massacres of women, children, and elderly men. In the wake of this disaster the Dutch West India Company largely ignored its crippled North American settlement, concentrating instead on the profitable importation of African slaves to its sugar plantations in Brazil.

Moreover, Dutch officials in New Amsterdam ruled shortsightedly. Governor Peter Stuyvesant rejected the demands of English Puritans on Long Island for a representative system of government, and his arbitrary deci-sions alienated other groups in the colony's increasingly diverse population, which now included a significant number of English and Swedish migrants. As a result, in 1664, during an Anglo-Dutch war, the population of New Amsterdam offered little resistance to an English invasion and subsequently accepted English rule. For the rest of the century the renamed towns of New York and Albany remained small fur-trading centers, Dutch-English outposts in a region still dominated by native Americans; in Albany, Mohawk remained the language of business until the 1720s.

The First English Model: Tobacco and Settlers

The first successful English colony in North America was, like those of its French and Dutch rivals, an economic venture. In 1606 the ambitious merchant stockholders of the Virginia Company of London received a charter from James I that granted them the right to exploit the riches of North America from the area of present-day North Carolina to southern New York. The company's directors had chosen the name Virginia both to honor the memory of Elizabeth I, the "Virgin Queen" who had died in 1603, and to enhance their chances of obtaining a charter. As an additional inducement, they promised to "propagate the *Christian* religion" among "infidels and Savages." Charter in hand, the company's directors were able to raise funds from no fewer than 56 London commercial firms and 659 individual investors. Their goal was to find and exploit rich and populous Indian peoples.

The "Starving Time." In 1607 the company dispatched an expedition to Virginia to found a trading outpost, not a settler colony. Only men and boys—not families—were aboard the three small ships that set sail from London. The company retained ownership of all the land in Virginia and appointed a governor and a small council to direct the migrants, who were its employees, or "servants." The company expected them to procure their own food and ship anything of value—gold, exotic crops, and Indian merchandise—back to England.

The traders were unprepared for the challenges they would face. Some were young gentlemen with personal ties to the shareholders of the Virginia Company but no experience in living off the land; as a critical observer noted, they were nothing more than a bunch of "unruly Sparks, packed off by their Friends to escape worse Destinies at home." The rest were cynical adventurers bent on conquering the Indians for their gold or turning a quick profit from trade. Like the company's directors, they expected to find established towns with ample supplies of food and labor, and Indians with gold to trade for English cloth and tinware.

Carolina Indians, 1585
The artist John White was one of the first English settlers in Sir Walter Raleigh's colony on Roanoke Island, and his watercolors provide a rich visual record of native American life. Here the Indians who resided near present-day Albemarle Sound in North Carolina are harvesting a protein-rich diet of fish from its shallow waters.

Arriving in Virginia after a hazardous four-month voyage, the newcomers settled on a swampy peninsula on a river. They named both their new home (Jamestown) and the waterway (James River) after the new king, James I. The traders found forty Algonquin-speaking Indian peoples, among them the Monacan and the Chickahominy, who willingly exchanged corn for English goods but had little else to offer and no interest in working for them. And the traders were not much interested in working for themselves, at least not in planting crops and raising food. All they wanted, as one of them said, was to "dig gold, refine gold, load gold."

But there was no gold and not much food. Of the 120 Englishmen who embarked on the expedition, only 38 were still alive after nine months in America, the rest having fallen victim to malnutrition and disease. Only

the determination of Governor John Smith, a soldier of fortune who managed the infant colony like a dictator, saved the enterprise from total collapse. When Smith left, starvation loomed. As of 1611, the Virginia Company had sent 1,200 servants to Jamestown, but fewer than half had survived. "Our men were destroyed with cruell diseases, as Swellings, Fluxes, Burning Fevers, and by warres," one of the leaders reported, "but for the most part they died of meere famine." Desperate for food, survivors raided Indian villages, provoking hostility. The new governor, Thomas West, made things worse by demanding that the native Americans acknowledge the sovereignty of James I.

Powhatan, the leading chief of a loose confederation of some two dozen Indian tribes, was prepared to extend privileges to the English traders if they would support him against his Indian rivals. But faced with food seizures and West's haughty demands, the chief accused the English of coming "not to trade but to invade my people and possess my country." Nevertheless, Powhatan, whom Smith had described as a "grave majestical man," accepted the presence of the English, giving his daughter Pocahontas in marriage to the adventurer John Rolfe in 1614.

Settlers and Indians. Rolfe had come to Virginia in 1610, and he played a leading role in the colony until his death in 1622. Importing seeds from the West Indies, Rolfe began to cultivate tobacco, which was already popular in England as a result of supplies from Spanish America. Soon tobacco, cultivated primarily by hundreds of poor white English laborers, became the basis of economic life in Virginia. Then in 1619, as Rolfe noted, "a Dutch man of warre . . . sold us twenty Negars." Those black workers were the first Africans in British North America.

As hopes for the Indian trade declined and the level of tobacco exports rose, the Virginia Company devised new policies that created a settler colony. To encourage migration, in 1617 the company allowed individual settlers to own land. It granted 100 acres to every freeman in Virginia and established a *headright* system by which every incoming head of a household had a right to 50 acres of land and 50 additional acres for every adult family member or servant. The company also approved a system of representative government. The House of Burgesses, which first convened in Jamestown in 1619, had the authority to make laws and levy taxes, although its legislative acts could be vetoed by the governor or nullified by the company. By 1622 these incentives of land ownership and local self-government had attracted about 4,500 new English recruits. Unlike the fur-trading outposts of the French and the Dutch and the authoritarian Spanish settlements in Mesoamerica, Virginia was on the verge of becoming a self-governing settler colony.

Then disaster struck. As land-hungry settlers poured into Virginia in the late 1610s, they continued to die from disease, and equally grave, they sparked all-out war with the resident Indians. As English farmers occupied lands that the native Americans had cleared and were still using, Opechancanough, Powhatan's brother and successor, grew increasingly alarmed (see *American Lives*, p. 00). After forming an alliance with other Chesapeake tribes, in 1622 Opechancanough launched a surprise attack, killing nearly a third of the white population and vowing to drive the rest into the ocean. The English retaliated by burning the Indians' cornfields to deprive them of food, a strategy that secured the safety of the colony by the late 1620s.

MAP 2.2
Eastern North America in 1660
Four European nations had permanent settlements in eastern North America by 1660, but only England had substantial numbers of settlers—some 25,000 in New England and another 15,000 in Virginia and Maryland. Even so, the English settlements hugged the coastline, leaving most of the land in the hands of native American peoples.

The cost of the war was high for both sides. The Virginia adventurers had dreamed of gold and instead found death—first by starvation and then by the sword. By killing so many settlers and burning their property, the Indians crippled the colony's economy and threatened the Virginia Company with bankruptcy. But native American losses were even worse. The time of coexistence was past. As one English militiaman put it, "[we now felt we could] by right of Warre, and law of Nations, invade the Country, and destroy them who sought to destroy us; whereby wee shall enjoy their cultivated places . . . possessing the fruits of others' labour." By 1630 Virginia had 4,000 English residents, lured by the hope of growing rich by planting tobacco.

Just as Indian gold and labor attracted tens of thousands of Spanish migrants to New Spain, so Indian tobacco and lands would soon draw 100,000 English settlers to the Chesapeake region (Map 2.2). However, in the Chesapeake colonies—and in other English settlements in North America—there were more women migrants than in New Spain and much less sexual interaction between the European invaders and the Indian peoples. Consequently, in British North America, many fewer English-Indian marriages or sexual liaisons took place, and the *mestizo* population remained small.

The Chesapeake Experience

The English colonies in the Chesapeake Bay region were an economic success for some but a social and moral disaster for many more. Settlers forcefully dispossessed Indians of their lands, and prominent families ruthlessly exploited the labor of white indentured servants and, after 1670, enslaved laborers from Africa, pursuing their dreams of wealth by ruling the society through deceit and force of arms.

Settling the Tobacco Colonies

Distressed by the Indian uprising of 1622 that had almost destroyed the fledgling colony in Virginia, James I dissolved the Virginia Company, accusing its directors of mismanagement. In 1624 the king created a new royal colony in Virginia. Under the terms of the charter, the king and his ministers appointed the governor and a small advisory council. The monarch retained the elected House of Burgesses, but its legislation now required ratification by the king's Privy Council. James also legally established the Church of England in Virginia, so that all property owners had to pay taxes to support the clergy. These institutions—a royal governor, an elected assembly, and an established Anglican Church—became the model for royal colonies throughout English America.

Catholics in Maryland. A second tobacco-growing settler colony developed in neighboring Maryland, but it had very different roots. Maryland was owned by an aristocrat, Cecilius Calvert, who carried the title Lord Baltimore. In 1632 King Charles I (r. 1625–1649), the successor to James I, gave Baltimore a charter that made him the *proprietor* of the territory bordering the vast Chesapeake Bay. Baltimore could sell, lease, or give away this land as he wished. He also had the authority to appoint public officials and to found churches and appoint ministers. Baltimore wanted Maryland to become a refuge from persecution for his fellow English Catholics. He therefore advocated a policy of religious toleration in order to minimize conflict between Catholics and Protestants, instructing the governor (his brother, Leonard Calvert) to allow "no scandall nor offence to be given to any of the Protestants" and to "cause All Acts of Romane Catholicque Religion to be done as privately as may be."

The settlement of Maryland began in 1634. Twenty gentlemen (mostly Catholics) and 200 artisans and laborers (mostly Protestants) established St. Mary's City overlooking the mouth of the Potomac River. The population grew quickly, for the Calvert family carefully planned and supervised the colony's development, hiring skilled artisans and offering ample grants of land to wealthy migrants. The booming European market for tobacco ensured the economic success of the young colony.

However, political and religious conflict soon threatened Maryland's stability. When Governor Leonard Calvert tried to govern without the "Advice, Assent, and Approbation" of the freemen of the colony, as the charter specified, a representative assembly elected by the freemen insisted on the right to initiate legislation, which Lord Baltimore grudgingly granted. Armed uprisings by Protestant settlers also threatened Maryland's religious mission as a refuge for Catholics. To protect his coreligionists, who remained a minority in the colony, Lord Baltimore managed to persuade the assembly to enact a Toleration Act (1649) that granted religious freedom to all Christians and temporarily ended religious conflict in the colony.

Tobacco and Disease. After 1630 tobacco and disease became the primary factors shaping the history of the Chesapeake colonies. Indians had long used tobacco leaves as a medicine and a stimulant. By the 1620s well-to-do English men and women had learned to crave tobacco and the nicotine it contained—smoking, chewing, and snorting it with abandon. Initially James I condemned the use of this "vile Weed,"

The Tobacco Economy
Most poor farmers raised tobacco, for it grew well in small fields and was easy to process. But larger plantations, such as the one pictured here, used indentured servants and slaves to grow and process the crop. The workers cured the tobacco stalks by hanging them for several months in a well-ventilated shed; then they stripped the leaves and packed them tightly into large plantation-made barrels, or "hogsheads," for shipment to Europe.
Library of Congress.

warning prophetically that its "black stinking fumes" would be "baleful to the nose, harmful to the brain, and dangerous to the lungs." But the king's attitude changed as revenues from a tobacco duty, or import tax, filled the royal treasury.

European demand for tobacco set off a forty-year economic boom in the Chesapeake region, and thousands of profit-hungry migrants flocked to the area. "All our riches for the present do consist in tobacco," a

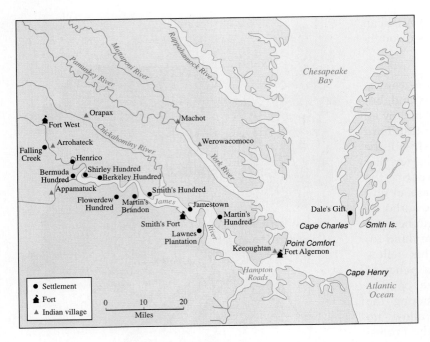

MAP 2.3
River Plantations in Virginia, c. 1640
The first migrants settled in widely dispersed plantations along the James River. The growth of the tobacco economy reinforced this pattern as wealthy planter-merchants traded with English ship captains from their riverfront plantations. Consequently, few substantial towns or trading centers developed in the Chesapeake region.

happy planter remarked in 1630. Exports rose from about 3 million pounds in 1640 to 10 million pounds in 1660. Planters moved up the river valleys, establishing large farms (plantations) that were distant from one another but easy to reach by water (Map 2.3). The scarcity of towns in Virginia produced a much weaker sense of community than that which existed in the open-field villages of rural England.

Unfortunately, mosquitoes as well as tobacco flourished in the mild Chesapeake climate, and they quickly spread malaria, a virus that weakened people's resistance to other diseases. Because the virus attacks red blood cells, pregnant women were especially vulnerable to the effects of malaria; they had less strength to withstand the rigors of childbirth, and their weakened immune systems could not resist birth-related infections. Many women died after bearing a first or second child, so settler families were small. Indeed, malaria, smallpox, fever, and dysentery took such a toll that even though more than 15,000 settlers arrived in Virginia between 1622 and 1640, the population rose only from 2,000 to 8,000.

For most of the seventeenth century, life in the Chesapeake colonies remained harsh and short (Figure 2.1). Most men never married because there were few women. The marriages that did take place often ended abruptly with an early death. Rarely did both parents survive to see their children grow to adulthood. As a result, unmarried young men and orphaned children accounted for a substantial portion of the population, making Chesapeake society very different from that in England.

The precarious state of life partially undermined the traditional authority of men within the family. Because

men expected their male relatives to die young, many Chesapeake husbands deviated from custom and named their wives as the executors of their wills. Those wills also enhanced the position of widows (in relation to child-heirs) by giving them the use of more of the family property than was strictly required by law. Frequently a man's will permitted his widow to retain an ample legacy even if she remarried, as most women did. In fact, women who survived the rigors of life in the Chesapeake region often improved their social position and legal privileges through inheritance and remarriage.

Servants and Masters

Despite the dangers, the prospect of owning land and growing rich continued to lure migrants to the Chesapeake region. By 1700 over 80,000 English settlers had moved to Virginia and another 20,000 had arrived in Maryland—and the overwhelming majority, perhaps 90 percent, came as indentured servants. English shipping registers provide insight into the background of these servants. Three-quarters of the 5,000 indentured migrants who departed from the western English port of Bristol were men, mostly under twenty-five years of age; some had traveled hundreds of miles searching for work. Once in Bristol, these penniless wanderers were persuaded by merchants and sea captains to sign labor contracts called *indentures* and embark for the Chesapeake. The indentures bound them to work in return for room and board for a period of four or five years (or, in the case of younger servants, until age twenty-one). Upon reaching Virginia or Maryland, the merchants signed over the contracts to local planters in return for cash or tobacco.

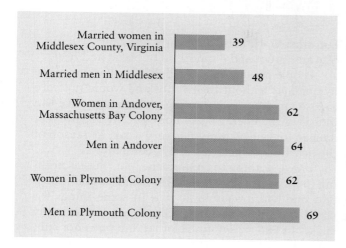

Married women in Middlesex County, Virginia	39
Married men in Middlesex	48
Women in Andover, Massachusetts Bay Colony	62
Men in Andover	64
Women in Plymouth Colony	62
Men in Plymouth Colony	69

FIGURE 2.1
Average Life Expectancy at Age Twenty in Virginia and New England, 1640–1700
Malaria and other diseases brought early death to English migrants in the Chesapeake region, producing a society filled with orphaned children. Settlers in New England lived into their sixties, often transmitting their customs and values to their grandchildren.

For merchants, servants represented valuable cargo because their indentures fetched high prices in the labor-starved Chesapeake. For plantation owners, indentured servants were an incredible bargain. During the first decade of the tobacco boom (when the crop sold for 6 pence a pound), a male servant could produce tobacco worth five times his purchase price in a single year. Furthermore, servants were counted as household members, so planters in Virginia received a bonus; through the headright system, created in 1617 to encourage migration, masters received 50 acres of land for each servant they imported.

Most masters ruled their servants with an iron hand, beating them for bad behavior and withholding permission to marry. If a servant ran away or became pregnant, a master went to court to extend the term of service. Female servants were especially vulnerable to abuse. As a Virginia law of 1692 stated, "dissolute masters have gotten their maids with child; and yet claim the benefit of their service." Planters could get rid of uncooperative servants by selling their contracts to new masters. One Englishman remarked in disgust that in Virginia, "servants were sold up and down like horses."

For most indentured servants this ordeal did not provide the escape from poverty they had sought (see Voices from Abroad, "Richard Frethorne: Hard Times in Early Virginia," p. 54). Half the men died before receiving their freedom, and another quarter remained poor. The remaining quarter got some benefit from their ordeal, acquiring property and respectability. If they survived, female servants generally fared better

because, one planter noted, men in the Chesapeake had grown "very sensible of the Misfortune of Wanting Wives." Many such servants married their masters or other well-established men. By migrating to the Chesapeake, these few—and very fortunate—men and women escaped a life of landless poverty in England.

The Seeds of Revolt

During a few boom years of the 1620s tobacco sold for 24 pence a pound, bringing high profits. Then a rapid expansion of production created a supply of tobacco that was greater than the demand, and the price dropped steadily—to 6 pence a pound in 1630 and 4 pence a decade later. Political decisions made in England encouraged a further decline, so that by 1660 tobacco was fetching about 2 pence a pound. As the economic boom in the Chesapeake turned into a "bust," longstanding social conflicts flared up in political turmoil.

The Navigation Acts. In 1651, in an effort to exclude Dutch ships and traders from England's overseas possessions, Parliament passed an Act of Trade and Navigation. Revised and extended in 1660 and 1663, the Navigation Acts permitted only English or colonial-owned ships to enter American ports. They also required the colonists to ship certain "enumerated articles," including tobacco, only to England. Thus Chesapeake planters could no longer legally trade with Dutch merchants, who traditionally paid the highest prices for tobacco. Moreover, the English monarchs continually raised the import duty on tobacco in order to increase royal revenues. Those duties, collected from merchants who passed on the cost to consumers, kept the price of tobacco high in England and stifled the growth of the market. By the 1670s, planters received only one penny a pound for their crop.

Nonetheless, the number of planters in Virginia and Maryland grew and tobacco exports continued to increase, from 20 million pounds annually in the 1670s to 41 million pounds between 1690 and 1720. But profit margins remained thin and the Chesapeake—always a graveyard for indentured servants—ceased even to be a land in which a few lucky men and women could hope for upward social mobility. Each year a typical small freeholder family grew about 1,800 pounds of marketable tobacco. Taxes (often paid in tobacco) amounted to 200 pounds of the crop, and clothes accounted for another 800, leaving only about 800 pounds to be sold or bartered for supplies and equipment. Many freeholders fell into debt and had to sell their land. Even harder hit were newly freed indentured servants, who were entitled to fifty acres of land. Low tobacco prices in Virginia made it nearly impossible for them to borrow the money to buy tools and seed and

RICHARD FRETHORNE

Hard Times in Early Virginia

— ★ —

The lot of an indentured servant in Virginia was always hard, especially before 1630, when food was scarce and Indians were a constant danger. In 1623 Richard Frethorne wrote a letter to his parents, begging them to buy out the remaining years of his labor contract so that he could return to England. Richard Frethorne's fate is unknown, but documentary evidence indicates that more than half of the English men and women who went to Virginia as indentured servants died during their four years of service.

Loving and kind father and mother . . . this is to let you understand that I your child am in a most heavy case by reason of the nature of the country . . . it causes much sickness, as the scurvy and the bloody flux [severe dysentery], and diverse other diseases, which make the body very poor and weak, and when we are sick there is nothing to comfort us. For since I came out of the ship, I never ate anything but peas and loblollie [gruel]. As for deer or venison I never saw any since I came into this land. There is indeed some fowl, but we are not allowed to go and get it, but must work hard both early and late for a mess of water gruel and a mouthful of bread and beef.

People cry out day and night, Oh that they were in England without their limbs and would not care to lose any limb to be in England again . . . we live in fear of the enemy every hour. . . . We are in great danger, for our plantation is very weak, by reason of the dearth, and sickness of our company. . . .

I have nothing to comfort me, nor there is nothing to be gotten here but sickness and death, except that one had money to lay out in some things for profit; but I have nothing at all, no not a shirt to my back, but two rags nor no clothes, but one poor suit, nor but one pair of shoes . . . my cloak is stolen by one of my own fellows, and to his dying hours would not tell me what he did with it, but some of my fellows saw him have butter and beef out of a ship, which my cloak [no] doubt paid for. . . .

I am not half, a quarter, so strong as I was in England, and all is for want of victuals, for I do protest unto you, that I have eaten more in a day at home than [is] allowed me here for a week. . . . Good father, do not forget me, but have mercy and pity my miserable case. I know if you did but see me you would weep. . . . The answer of this letter will be life or death to me; therefore, good father, send as soon as you can. . . .

Source: Susan M. Kingsbury, ed., *The Records of the Virginia Company of London* (Washington, DC: Library of Congress, 1935), 4:58–60.

---

become independent farmers. Instead, most former servants had to sign new labor contracts or become wage workers or tenant farmers.

Increasing Social Divisions. Declining tobacco prices increased the power of the wealthy planter-landlords and merchants who had dominated Virginia from as early as the 1630s. The landowners prospered by dividing their ample estates into small plots and leasing them to the growing population of former servants. They also profited by lending money at high rates of interest to hard-pressed yeomen families. Some well-to-do planters became commercial middlemen, setting up small retail stores or charging a commission for storing the tobacco of their poorer neighbors and selling it to English merchants. In Virginia this elite of planter-merchants was able to accumulate nearly half the surveyed land in the colony by soliciting large land grants from royal governors and claiming headright shares (of fifty acres per person) for fictitious migrants. In Maryland wealthy planters controlled labor with equal success; in one county they owned about 40 percent of the work force through the indenture system.

Social discord intensified as these aggressive entrepreneurs confronted a growing number of young landless laborers, and it reached a breaking point during the corrupt regime of Governor William Berkeley. Berkeley first served as governor of Virginia between 1642 and 1652, and he won fame in 1644 by quelling the second Indian revolt led by Opechancanough (see American Lives, pp. 42–43). Serving as governor again beginning in 1660, he made large land grants to himself and to members of his council, who exempted their own lands from taxation and appointed friends as

Green Spring
Governor Berkeley ran Virginia from his country estate at Green Spring, which, as this watercolor by Benjamin Latrobe suggests, was large but architecturally undistinguished. The wooden outbuildings housed equipment and the indentured servants who worked as farm laborers.
Maryland Historical Society.

county judges and local magistrates. Berkeley was a calculating politician who suppressed dissent in the House of Burgesses by assigning land grants to friendly legislators and appointing their relatives to the posts of sheriff, tax collector, and justice of the peace. Once his favorites were in power, the governor refused to hold new elections.

Political protests erupted when the corrupt Burgesses changed the voting system to exclude landless freemen, who constituted half the adult white male population. Property-holding yeomen retained the vote, and they blamed Berkeley and his faction for falling tobacco prices, rising taxes, and political corruption. The Virginia elite—unlike the English aristocracy and gentry—was too newly formed and crudely ambitious to command the respect of the lower orders. Social and political unrest began to reach the boiling point.

Bacon's Rebellion

In the summer of 1675 a new Indian conflict sparked a social revolution. The Indians in Virginia were no longer a threat to the colony, for their numbers had dwindled from about 30,000 in 1607 to a mere 2,000 in 1675. But they lived on treaty-guaranteed frontier lands coveted by westward-looking English settlers. Because most wealthy planters lived in the coastal districts and wanted

to retain their labor force, they opposed armed expansion into Indian territory, as did the planter-merchants who traded with the native Americans for furs. But poor freeholders and aspiring tenants who wanted cheap land insisted that the Indians be expelled or exterminated.

Fighting broke out when Virginia militiamen crossed the Potomac River into Maryland and murdered thirty Indians. Defying orders from Governor Berkeley, a larger force of 1,000 militiamen then surrounded a fortified Susquehannock village and killed four chiefs. The outraged Susquehannock retaliated by killing eighty whites in raids on outlying plantations. Berkeley did not want war, which would disrupt the fur trade controlled by his merchant-allies, and proposed a defensive military policy; he asked the House of Burgesses in March 1676 to raise money for a series of forts to protect the frontier plantations. Western settlers dismissed this strategy as useless—a plot by coastal planters and merchants to impose high taxes on the yeomen and, in the words of one freeman, to take "all our tobacco into their own hands."

Nathaniel Bacon, a wealthy young man who had recently arrived from England and settled on a frontier estate, emerged as the leader of the dissident whites. Although Bacon was only twenty-eight years old, he commanded the respect of his neighbors because of his high status—Berkeley had made him a member of the governor's council—and forceful personality. When Berkeley refused to grant Bacon a military commission, Bacon marched his frontiersmen against the Indians anyway, slaughtering some of the peaceful Doeg people and triggering a political upheaval. Condemning the frontiersmen as "rebels and mutineers," Berkeley expelled Bacon from the council and placed him under arrest. Then, realizing the rebel leader's military power, the governor reinstated him, agreed to legislative elections, and accepted the far-reaching political reforms that curbed the powers of the governor and the council and restored voting rights to landless freemen.

These much-needed reforms did not end the rebellion. Bacon was bitter at Berkeley, and the poor farmers and indentured servants in his army were resentful of exploitation by the political elite and eager to flaunt their power. Backed by 400 armed men, Bacon seized control of the colony and issued a Manifesto and Declaration of the People, demanding the death or removal of all Indians and an end to the rule of wealthy "parasites." "The poverty of the country," Bacon proclaimed, "is such that all the power and sway is got into the hands of the rich." In the bloody civil war that followed, Bacon's army burned Jamestown to the ground and plundered the plantations of Berkeley's allies. When Bacon died suddenly from dysentery in October 1676, the governor took his revenge, dispersing the rebel army, seizing the estates of well-to-do rebels, and hanging twenty-three men.

Bacon's rebellion was a pivotal event in Virginia's history. Although planter-merchants continued to dominate the colony, they limited the governor's authority and found public positions for substantial and politically ambitious property owners like Bacon; in addition, they appeased members of the lower social orders by cutting their taxes and supporting the expansion of English settlement onto Indian lands.

The uprising also contributed to the emergence of a new labor system: African slavery. The number of slaves in the Chesapeake had grown, albeit slowly, to 2 percent of the population in 1650 and 5 percent in 1670 because of a scarcity of English indentured servants and a surge in the Atlantic slave trade (see Chapter 3). Following Bacon's rebellion, expansion of the slave system was fueled by the elite's desire to forestall another uprising by freed white servants. Thus in All Hallows Parish in Maryland, enslaved Africans made up 10 percent of the population in 1675; by 1700 they accounted for no less than 35 percent. To maintain their privileged position, the leaders of Maryland and Virginia committed themselves and their descendants to a social system based on the exploitation of enslaved blacks.

went about the mundane tasks of creating a society, they addressed ethical and religious issues, giving a moral dimension to the way subsequent generations of Americans would think about their history.

The Puritan Migration

Puritans came to New England in two separate migrations. The first to arrive were a group of Separatists, who in 1620 began to settle the Plymouth colony.

Plymouth Colony. The Separatists differed from other Puritans because they had separated completely from the Church of England, founding independent congregations. To escape the control of bishops and other religious authorities, some Separatists had left England in the 1610s and settled among like-minded Dutch Calvinists in Holland. Subsequently, thirty-five of them decided to migrate to America in order to maintain their English identity and, as one of them put it, to advance the true "gospell of the Kingdome of Christ in those remote parts of the world." Their journey would be a holy migration, a "pilgrimage"—so they became known as Pilgrims. Led by William Bradford and joined by sixty-seven Separatist Puritans from England, in

Puritan New England

★

Puritanism had arisen in England primarily as a religious movement, an attempt to "purify" a corrupt church. But, because of the upheavals that were shaking English society, many Puritans were worried about the economic future of their families. Consequently, the Puritan migration to America was motivated both by a moral effort to preserve the pure Christian faith and by a worldly desire to acquire land and financial security. This blend of idealism and realism gave a distinctive character to the Puritans' experiment. Whereas in Virginia the adventurers simply seized Indian lands and greedily occupied as much as they could, in New England the Puritan leaders treated the issue of taking Indian territory as a moral problem that had to be resolved through debate.

Puritan New England was distinctive in its social character as well. New Spain and Jamestown were populated initially by unruly male adventurers, and New France and New Netherland by commercial-minded fur traders. By contrast the Puritan settlements were populated by women and children as well as men—families who would farm the land for their livelihood. In a conscious effort to create a more just agricultural society, the Puritans distributed land among themselves in a relatively equal fashion. Thus, even as the Puritans

New England Domestic Architecture
Well-to-do Puritans affirmed their commitment to America by building well-constructed dwellings. Most late-seventeenth-century houses were built of wood and had plain symmetrical facades and substantial central chimneys to preserve heat during the cold New England winters.
Paul Rocheleau.

1620 the Pilgrims sailed to America aboard the *Mayflower*.

Before their departure, the Pilgrims had organized themselves into a joint-stock corporation and secured financial backing from sympathetic Puritan merchants. Their stated intention was to settle in the territory granted to the Virginia Company, but by accident or design they landed on the coast of New England (Map 2.4). There, outside the jurisdiction of Virginia and lacking a charter from King James I, they created their own covenant of government, the Mayflower Compact, to "combine ourselves together into a civill body politick." This document, which was signed by the forty-one adult men on board the *Mayflower*, was the first "constitution" adopted by European settlers in North America. It translated into political terms the

Separatists' longstanding belief in the autonomy of each religious congregation. Although they recognized the sovereignty of the king over their domain, the settlers wanted to govern themselves, so they ruled themselves through a system of agreed-upon laws and regulations.

The first winter in America tested the Pilgrims' conviction. In Plymouth, as in Jamestown, hunger and disease took a heavy toll; of the 102 people who arrived in November, only half survived until the spring. Thereafter the Plymouth colony—unlike Virginia—became a healthy and thriving community, in part because the cold climate inhibited the spread of mosquito-borne diseases. Equally important, the Pilgrims' religious discipline and sense of community established an emphasis on work and responsibility. Unlike the gold-hungry

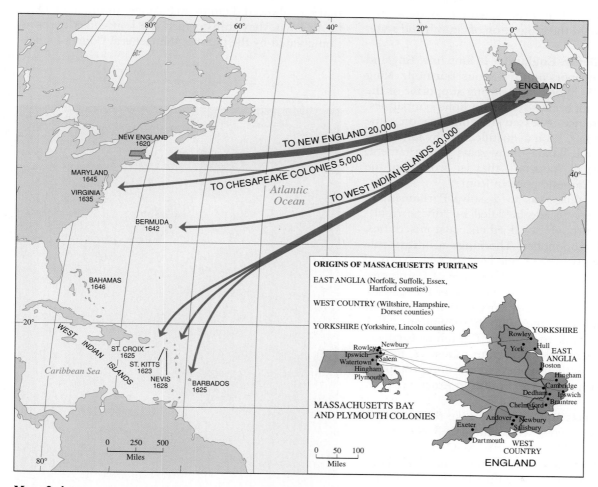

MAP 2.4
The Puritan Migration to America, 1620–1640
Nearly 50,000 Puritans left England between 1620 and 1640. In New England, migrants from the three major areas of English Puritanism—Yorkshire, East Anglia, and the West Country—commonly settled among those from their own region. They named American communities after their English towns of origin and transplanted regional customs, such as the open-field agriculture practiced in Rowley in Yorkshire and Rowley in Massachusetts Bay.

adventurers in Virginia, the New England migrants quickly built solid houses and planted ample crops. Their numbers grew rapidly to 3,000 by 1640.

As their colony increased in number and size, the Pilgrims continued their political innovations. Rather than rule their expanding domain from the original settlement at Plymouth, they created ten new towns with extensive powers of self-government. In 1636 they established a legal code that set up a colonywide system of representative government and guaranteed various political rights. Following their interpretation of the Bible, the Pilgrims also limited the power of the state over religion. As Separatists, they had declared that their churches would not be under the authority of the bishops of the Church of England; now they declared that each congregation should be completely self-governing, free from control by the political magistrates within Plymouth itself. By denying their own secular leaders control over spiritual matters, the Pilgrims anticipated the separation of church and state.

Religious Conflict in England. Meanwhile, England was plunging deeper into religious turmoil. King Charles I (r. 1625–1649) was a strong supporter of the Church of England; because of his Catholic sympathies, he used his influence to lessen the emphasis on some Protestant doctrines, such as justification by faith. The Puritans, who had gained many seats in Parliament, accused the king of "popery"—that is, promoting the teachings of the Catholic pope in Rome.

Charles's response was to dissolve Parliament in 1629. For the next decade he ruled by "divine right," raising money through royal edicts, customs duties, and the sale of monopolies. The king's arbitrary rule struck at the dignity of the landed gentry, who expected to exercise authority through the House of Commons. The merchant community, a stronghold of Puritanism, was also displeased as higher tariffs ate away at their profits. Then, in 1633, the king chose William Laud, who loathed Puritans, to head the Church of England. Laud removed hundreds of Puritan ministers, forcing Anglican rituals on their congregations and prompting thousands of Puritans to seek refuge in America.

The Massachusetts Bay Colony. Like the settlers at Plymouth, the Puritans who established the neighboring colony of Massachusetts Bay envisioned a reformed Christian society, a genuinely "new" England. However, rather than break with the Church of England, the Puritans hoped to reform the church from within (hence they were "non-Separatists"). In fact, many Puritans saw themselves as central actors in a great drama, a "saving remnant" chosen by God to preserve the true faith in America. The Lord "has sifted a whole nation," a Puritan minister declared, "that he might send choice grain over into this Wilderness."

In 1630, 900 Puritans boarded eleven ships and sailed across the Atlantic under the leadership of John Winthrop, a well-educated and highly regarded country squire and lawyer. Like many other Puritans, Winthrop believed that England was morally corrupt and "overburdened with people." He sought land and opportunity for his children and a place in history for his people. "We must consider that we shall be as a City upon a Hill," Winthrop told his fellow passengers aboard the ship *Arbella*. "The eyes of all people are upon us."

Landing near Boston, the Puritans established the Massachusetts Bay colony. Over the next decade about 10,000 Puritans migrated to the new settlement, along with 10,000 others fleeing hard times in England (see Map 2.4). Having fled from the arbitrary rule of Archbishop Laud, the Puritans wanted to govern themselves. Therefore Winthrop and his associates carried with them the corporate charter granted by the king that had allowed them to do business in England. Once in America, they transformed the joint-stock corporation created by the charter, the General Court of stock-

Governor John Winthrop
This portrait, painted in the style of the Flemish artist Anthony Van Dyke, captures the gravity and intensity of Winthrop, whose policies of religious orthodoxy and elite rule shaped the early history of the Massachusetts Bay colony.
Courtesy, American Antiquarian Society.

holders, into a framework of government. Like the migrants to Plymouth, the Puritans created representative political institutions that were locally based, with the governor as well as the assembly and council elected by the colony's freemen. Unlike the separatist-minded Pilgrims, they insisted on linking church and state. To ensure rule by the godly, the Massachusetts Bay Puritans limited the right to vote and hold office to men who were members of an approved Puritan congregation. Rejecting the religious toleration of the Pilgrims, they established Puritanism as the state-supported religion and barred members of other faiths from conducting services.

Massachusetts Bay thus became a religious commonwealth, with the Bible as its legal as well as spiritual guide. For example, following a biblical rule, Puritans there divided inheritances among all children in a given family, with a double portion going to the oldest son. "Where there is no Law," the colony's government advised local magistrates, they should rule "as near the law of God as they can."

Religion and Society, 1630–1670

Taking advantage of their isolation in the "wilderness" of America, the Puritans in Plymouth and Massachusetts Bay set about recreating the "true" Christian church. Disposing of elaborate Catholic features such as bishops and intricate rituals, they followed what they believed to be the practice of the first Christians, devising a simple church structure controlled by the laity, or the ordinary members of the congregation—hence their name, *Congregationalists.*

The Elect.   Influenced by John Calvin (see Chapter 1), most Puritans embraced predestination, the belief that God had decided—or "predestined"—the fates of all people before they were born; a few "elect" men and women were saved and would go to heaven and the rest were condemned to damnation in hell. This doctrine was harsh, for it seemed to deny people any control over their salvation. Moreover, it sharply divided society between church members (the Elect or Saints, as they were called) and the rest of the population. Because the Saints set extraordinarily high standards for church membership, rigorously examining those who applied, they always constituted a minority of the population of New England.

Being a Saint was not easy, for few Puritans were certain that God had really chosen them to be among the Elect. "I have seen Persons Quaking on their Death Beds, and their very beds therewith Shaking under them," the minister Cotton Mather reported, their deathbed utterances testifying to their terror regarding their fate: "O! The wrath of a Dreadful God, Makes me Tremble; I Tremble, I Tremble, at that wrath."

Changing Images of Death
Death—sudden and arbitrary—was a constant presence in the preindustrial world. Pre-1700 New England gravestones often depicted death as a frightening skull, warning sinners to repent of their sins. After 1700 a smiling cherub adorned many gravestones, suggesting a more optimistic view of the afterlife. Peabody and Essex Museum.

Puritans dealt with the uncertainties of divine election in a variety of ways. There was not a single "orthodox" doctrine but rather a range of beliefs. Some congregations stressed the transforming effect of the conversion experience. They believed that when God infused a soul with grace, the person was literally "born again" and *knew* that salvation was at hand. Other Puritans emphasized "preparation," the idea that years of spiritual guidance and church discipline would result in redemption. Many of these "preparationists" followed the Dutch Protestant theologian Jacobus Arminius in conceiving of God as a more reasonable and merciful deity than the one portrayed by Calvin. If a person expressed "the merest desire to be saved," declared one Arminian-influenced Puritan minister,

God would bestow His saving grace. Still other Puritans believed that God had entered into a *covenant*, or contract, with them, promising to treat them as a divinely "chosen people" as long as they ordered their lives in accordance with His laws.

Roger Williams and Anne Hutchinson.   To remain in God's favor, the Puritan magistrates of Massachusetts Bay felt they must purge their society of those who held extremely controversial beliefs. One target was Roger Williams, who in 1634 had become minister of the Puritan church in Salem, Massachusetts. Williams condemned the legal establishment of Congregationalism in Massachusetts Bay, declaring his preference for the Pilgrims' separation of church and state in the Plymouth colony. He taught that political magistrates should have authority over only the "bodies, goods, and outward estates of men," not their spiritual lives. Moreover, Williams questioned the Puritans' right to seize (rather than buy) Indian lands. In response, the Puritan magistrates banished him from Massachusetts Bay in 1635.

Williams and his followers resettled in Rhode Island in 1636, founding the town of Providence on land acquired from the Narragansett Indians. Other religious dissidents founded nearby Portsmouth and Newport. In 1644 these towns obtained a corporate charter from the English Parliament that granted them full authority "to rule themselves," and they chose to follow the example of the Pilgrims. In Rhode Island as in Plymouth, there was no legally established church; every congregation was autonomous, and individual men and women could worship God as they pleased.

Puritan magistrates also felt threatened by Anne Hutchinson, the wife of a merchant and the mother of seven children who worked as a midwife. Hutchinson held weekly prayer meetings in her house—often attended by as many as sixty women and, later, by some men as well—at which she questioned the teachings of certain Boston clergymen, saying that they placed undue emphasis on church laws and good behavior. In words that recalled Martin Luther's rejection of indulgences, Hutchinson argued that salvation was not something that people could earn through good deeds; there was no "covenant of works." Instead, salvation was bestowed by God through the "covenant of grace." Moreover, Hutchinson stressed the importance of revelation: the direct communication of truth by God to the individual believer. Since this doctrine diminished the role of ministers and, indeed, of all established authority, Puritan magistrates found it heretical.

The magistrates also resented Hutchinson because of her sex. Like other Christians, Puritans believed in the equality of souls: both men and women could be saved. When it came to matters concerning the governance of church and state, however, women were seen as being clearly inferior to men. As the Pilgrim minister John Robinson put it, women "are debarred by their sex from ordinary prophesying, and from any other dealing in the church wherein they take authority over the man." Puritan women could never be ministers, lay preachers, or even voting members of the congregation.

In 1637 the Massachusetts Bay magistrates put Hutchinson on trial for heresy as an *antinomian*, a person who believes that inward grace or truth frees an individual from the rules of the church. In dramatic courtroom testimony, Hutchinson defended her views with great skill and tenacity, and even Winthrop admitted that she was "a woman of fierce and haughty courage." But the judges found her guilty and berated her for not attending to "her household affairs, and such things as belong to women." Banished, she followed Roger Williams into exile in Rhode Island and eventually settled in New York, where she was killed in an Indian raid in 1643. Puritan magistrates noted Hutchinson's death with grim satisfaction, interpreting it as a sign of God's approval of their enforcement of religious orthodoxy.

The coercive policies of the magistrates, along with the desire for better land, prompted some Puritans to leave Massachusetts Bay. In 1636 Thomas Hooker, who had originally settled near Boston, led a hundred settlers to the Connecticut River Valley, where they established the town of Hartford (see Map 2.5). Other Bay colony residents followed, settling along the river at Wethersfield and Windsor. In 1639 the Connecticut Puritans adopted the Fundamental Orders, a plan of government that included a representative assembly and a popularly elected governor. A royal charter from King Charles II in 1662 bestowed self-government on these Connecticut towns, whose population had grown to almost 5,000, and joined them to another Puritan settlement at New Haven. Connecticut was patterned after Massachusetts Bay, with a firm union of church and state and a congregational system of church government, but voting rights were extended to most property-owning men—not just church members.

Puritan Triumph and Decline.   As Puritans established themselves in America, England fell into a religious war. When Archbishop Laud imposed a Church of England prayer book on the Calvinist Presbyterians in Scotland, who dissented from many of its teachings, a Scottish army invaded England. In 1642 thousands of English Puritans also took up arms against King Charles I, demanding greater authority for Parliament and an end to arbitrary royal rule. After four years of civil war the Presbyterian-Puritan forces, led by Oliver Cromwell, were victorious. In 1649 a Puritan-dominated Parliament executed Charles, proclaimed a republican Commonwealth, and eliminated bishops by imposing a Presbyterian system of governance on the Church of England.

The Puritan triumph was short-lived. Popular support for the Commonwealth quickly ebbed, especially when Cromwell took dictatorial control of the government in 1653. After Cromwell's death a repentant Parliament summoned Charles I's son, Charles II, to the throne. In 1660 the monarchy was restored and bishops reclaimed their authority in the Church of England. For many Puritans, the accession of Charles II represented the victory of the Antichrist—the false prophet described in the last book of the New Testament.

American Puritans were equally grim. They had left England to preserve the true church and had high hopes that the Puritan Revolution would allow them to reform the Church of England according to their principles. Hundreds had returned to the home country to fight in the victorious war, and now they were bitterly disappointed by the failure of the Puritan Commonwealth. Nor could they take solace from events in New England, for Puritans there were experiencing grave doubts about their religious mission, which one minister had described as a holy "errand into the wilderness," in part because the second generation seemed to have lost the intense spirit of the original migrants. Many younger Puritans had been baptized as infants but, perhaps intimidated by the religious zeal of their parents, had not experienced conversion and become full church members. Ministers pointed out that their "deadness of soul" threatened to end the Puritan experiment, since the unconverted could not present their own children for baptism. Never more than a bare majority, the Saints had imposed their religious vision out of determination, not numbers. If Puritans became a small minority, they might well lose control of the colony.

To keep the churches vigorous, Puritan ministers devised the Halfway Covenant in 1662. This covenant altered Calvinist theology by making salvation more predictable, indeed almost hereditary. Under its terms, the children of all baptized Puritans could be presented for baptism and thus become "halfway" members. Not conversion but *birth* became the key to Puritan identity. For example, the First Church of Milford, Connecticut, had 962 members in the period 1639–1770. No fewer than 693 of these Puritan Saints (72 percent) were members of the thirty-six families who had established the original congregation.

The Halfway Covenant introduced a new phase of the Puritan experiment. Puritans had come to America to preserve the "pure" Christian church; many of them half expected to return in triumph to a Europe ready to receive the true gospel. With that sacred mission dashed by the Restoration in England, Puritan ministers instead exhorted their congregations to create in the American wilderness a new society based on high moral and intellectual principles.

A Millers House and Mill Burnt etc.

Divine Retribution
As this illustration from *Divine Examples of God's Severe Judgments upon Sabbath-Breakers* (1671) reminded Puritans, they could be held immediately accountable for their every worldly action.
Houghton Library, Harvard University.

The Puritan Imagination and Witchcraft

Like the native Americans they encountered in New England, the Puritans thought that the physical world was full of supernatural forces. This belief in "spirits" stemmed in part from Christian teachings, such as the Catholic belief in supernatural miracles and the Protestant faith in the power of invisible "grace" to enter one's heart. Devout Christians saw signs of God's (or Satan's) power in blazing stars, deformed births, and other unusual events. Noting that "more Ministers' Houses than others proportionably had been smitten with Lightning," Cotton Mather, a prominent Massachusetts minister, wondered "what the meaning of God should be in it."

The Puritans' respect for spiritual "forces" also reflected Europe's pagan heritage. Many seventeenth-century European Christians still believed that elements of the natural world—animals, streams, trees—contained spiritual forces that had to be acknowledged. For example, when Samuel Sewall, who was a highly educated man and a Saint, moved into a new house, he tried to fend off evil spirits by driving a metal pin into the floor. Thousands of other Puritans followed pagan astrological charts printed in farmers' almanacs. These charts correlated the movements of the planets and stars with signs of the zodiac. Farmers consulted the charts when determining the best times to plant crops, when marrying off their children, and when making other important decisions.

Zealous ministers attacked many of these beliefs and practices as a return to "superstition" and condemned "cunning" individuals who claimed to have special powers as healers or prophets. Many ordinary Christians regarded folk doctors or conjurers as "wizards" or "witches" who acted at the command of Satan. Between 1647 and 1662 civil authorities in Massachusetts and Connecticut hanged fourteen people for witchcraft, mostly older women who, their accusers claimed, were "double-tongued," "had an unruly spirit," or in some way challenged prevailing customs. As in Europe, most of those executed were women because they were assumed to be more susceptible than men to the wiles of the Devil.

The most dramatic episode of witch-hunting took place in Salem, Massachusetts, in 1692 (see Map 2.5). The causes were complex and involved group rivalries and deception. Poor and resentful farmers in rural Salem Village apparently sought to retaliate against certain wealthier church members who lived near the seaport of Salem Town by bringing charges of witchcraft against the church members' families and friends. Things got out of hand when judges allowed the introduction of uncorroborated testimony by adolescent girls that they had been tormented by invisible beings. Frightened by these tales and fearful of satanic witches, Massachusetts authorities arrested 175 people and executed 20, 19 of them women. Fear and suspicion spread into the neighboring village of Andover. Its people "were much addicted to sorcery," claimed one observer, and "there were forty men in it that could raise the Devil as well as any astrologer."

The Salem episode marked a turning point in the spiritual history of New England. The intense religiosity of the first two generations of Puritans was dealt a blow by popular revulsion against the mass executions at Salem; there would be no more legal prosecutions for witchcraft. The European Enlightenment, a major intellectual movement that began around 1675, also promoted a more rational view of the world. Increasingly, educated people explained accidents and sudden deaths through theories about natural laws, not through religion, satanism, astrology, or witchcraft. For example, in contrast to Cotton Mather (who died in 1728), well-read men of the next generation—such as Benjamin Franklin—would conceive of lightning as a natural phenomenon rather than a supernatural sign.

A Yeoman Society, 1670–1700

In creating New England communities, Puritans consciously avoided the worst features of traditional Europe. They did not wish to live in a society dominated by a few wealthy landowners or under a distant govern-

An Affluent Puritan Woman
This well-known painting (c. 1671) of Elizabeth Freake and her daughter, Mary, is perhaps the finest portrait of a seventeenth-century American and suggests the growing prosperity of the Boston merchant community.
Worcester Art Museum.

ment that levied oppressive taxes. Rather, they implemented policies that created self-governing communities composed primarily of property-owning families.

Property ownership was an essential ingredient in the Puritans' conception of a God-fearing "just society." New England governments relied primarily on land-distribution policies to fashion a new social order of independent landowning families. The General Courts of Massachusetts Bay and Connecticut did not adopt the Chesapeake headright system, which favored wealthy planters by awarding them land for importing servants. Nor, except in a few instances, did the New England governments bestow thousands of acres of land on politically well-connected individuals. Instead, they gave the title to a township—usually measuring about 6 miles by 10 miles—to a group of male settlers, or proprietors. The title was given in *fee simple*, which meant that the proprietors and their heirs held the land outright, free from manorial obligations or feudal dues owed to a noble landlord; they could bequeath the land to their children or sell, lease, or rent their properties to later arrivals.

The proprietors of the towns distributed the land among themselves, usually taking into account an individual's present wealth and status. Like most seventeenth-century Europeans, Puritans believed that inequality and hierarchy were natural and inevitable. "God had Ordained different degrees and orders of men," proclaimed the wealthy Boston merchant John Saffin, "some to be Masters and Commanders, others to be Subjects, and to be commanded." Consequently, town proprietors normally bestowed the largest plots of land on men of high social status. For example, Edward Johnson came to New England from Kent, where he had been a man of "rank and quality." Johnson became well known on both sides of the Atlantic as the author of the *Wonder-Working Providence of Zion's Saviour*, a prophetic tract published in 1650, but he prospered in Massachusetts Bay primarily because, as a gentleman, he was able to claim a large land grant in Woburn. However, all proprietors received enough land to support their families, laying the foundation for a society composed primarily of independent *yeomen* farmers (Map 2.5).

All men—both proprietors and later arrivals—had a voice in the town meeting, the main institution of government in these communities. New England towns controlled virtually all local affairs, giving them much more political power than most peasant villages in Europe. Each year the town meeting chose selectmen to manage town affairs. It also enacted ordinances regarding fencing, lot sizes, and road building, and regulated the use of common fields for grazing livestock and cutting firewood. Most important, it levied and collected taxes, ensuring local control of the town's economic resources.

Gradually the towns emerged as the most powerful force in the colony-wide government. Beginning in 1634, each town in the Massachusetts Bay colony elected its own representatives to the General Court. As the number of towns increased, the General Court gained authority at the expense of the governor and magistrates and firmly established a tradition of local rule that remained strong into the twenty-first century.

The general economic equality in the farming communities of New England gradually declined. Initially the larger proprietors owned sizable farms of 500 or 600 acres, enough land to divide among all their sons (usually three or four). Smallholders were less fortunate and could provide land for only some of their sons, the rest of whom became propertyless laborers or migrated elsewhere. Newcomers to the town lacked the rights of proprietors and were the least well off, for they had to buy land or work as tenants or laborers. By 1702, in Windsor, Connecticut, landless sons and newcomers accounted for no less than 30 percent of the male taxpayers. It would take years of saving or migration to a new town for these men and their families to become freeholders.

Despite these inequalities, nearly all New Englanders had an opportunity to acquire property, and even those at the bottom of the social scale enjoyed some economic security. For example, when he died in the 1690s,

Nathaniel Fish was one of the poorest men in Barnstable, Massachusetts, yet he owned a two-room cottage, eight acres of land, an ox, and a cow. For him and thousands of other settlers, New England had proven itself to be the promised land, a new world of opportunity.

The Indians' New World

Native Americans on the eastern seaboard were also living in a new world, but for them it was a bleak, dangerous, and conflict-ridden place. They responded to European invasion and settlement in a variety of ways. Some Indian peoples, like the Pequots, resisted the invaders by force. Others coped with devastating epidemics of European diseases by merging and intermarrying with other tribes. Still others retreated westward to the Appalachian Mountains in order to preserve their traditional culture.

Puritans and Pequots

The Puritans' conception of themselves as God's chosen people shaped their relations with native Americans. Initially they felt obliged to justify their intrusion into the Indians' domain. "By what right or warrant can we enter into the land of the Savages," they asked themselves while still in England, "and take away their rightfull inheritance from them and plant ourselves in their places?" An answer to this question was provided by John Winthrop, who suggested that a disastrous smallpox epidemic that killed hundreds of Indians in 1633 was in fact a mark of divine favor. "If God were not pleased with our inheriting these parts," he asked, "Why doth he still make roome for us by diminishing them as we increase?"

For a second justification the Puritans turned to the Book of Genesis, which instructed them to "be fruitful, and multiply, and replenish the earth, and subdue it." From this, the magistrates of Massachusetts Bay argued that because the Indians had not "subdued" most of their land by plowing or fencing it, they had no "just right" to it.

Believing that God was on their side and filled with moral righteousness, the Puritans often treated native Americans with a brutality equal to that of the Spanish conquistadors and Nathaniel Bacon's frontiersmen. In 1636 Pequot warriors attacked Puritan farmers who had begun to intrude onto their lands in the Connecticut River Valley. As sporadic violence escalated into war, Puritan militiamen and their Indian allies led a surprise attack on a Pequot village and massacred about 500 men, women, and children. "God laughed at the Enemies of his People," one soldier boasted, "filling the Place with Dead Bodies." The survivors were ruthlessly

MAP 2.5
Settlement Patterns in New England, 1630–1700

Initially, most Puritan towns were compact; families lived close to one another in the
nucleated village center and traveled daily to the surrounding fields. In 1640 this pattern
was apparent in Wethersfield, which was situated on the broad plains of the Connecticut
River Valley. The rugged geography of eastern Massachusetts encouraged a more dispersed form of settlement. By 1692 many residents of Andover lived outside the village
center, on their own farms.

tracked down and sold into slavery in the Caribbean. In the end the Pequot people were virtually exterminated.

Like most Europeans, English Puritans viewed the Indians as "savages," culturally inferior people who did not deserve civilized treatment. But the Puritans were not racist as the term is understood today. To them, native Americans were neither genetically inferior nor members of a different race—they were simply white people with sun-darkened skins. Not race but sin accounted for the Indians' degenerate condition, according to the Puritans. "Probably the devil" delivered these "miserable savages" to America, wrote the Puritan minister Cotton Mather, "in hopes that the gospel of the Lord Jesus Christ would never come here to destroy or disturb his absolute empire over them."

This understanding of Indian history inspired attempts at conversion. John Eliot, a Puritan minister, translated the Bible into Algonquin and undertook missions to Indians outside Boston and on Cape Cod. Because Puritans demanded that Indians conform to English customs and master Puritan theology, only a few native Americans became full members of Puritan congregations. However, the Puritans created "praying towns" that, like the Spanish Franciscans' missions in New Mexico, represented an attempt to control the Indian population. Within a generation more than a thousand Indians lived under Puritan supervision in fourteen special mission towns. They were forbidden to practice their native religion, required to conform to the laws of Massachusetts, and initially denied the right to own the land on which they lived. This Puritan Christianization effort, in combination with European diseases and military force, gradually subdued most of the Algonquian peoples who lived along the seacoast of New England, guaranteeing—at least temporarily—the safety of the white population.

Metacom (King Philip), Chief of the Wampanoag
The Indian uprising of 1675 left an indelible mark on the historical memory of New England. This painting from the 1850s, done on semitransparent cloth and lit from behind for dramatic effect, was used by traveling performers to tell the story of King Philip's war.
Shelburne Museum.

Metacom's War

By the 1670s the white population of New England had increased to 55,000 but the number of native Americans had rapidly declined. An estimated 120,000 Indians lived in the region in 1570, but only 70,000 in 1620 and a mere 16,000 in 1670. Like Opechancanough in Virginia and Popé in New Mexico, Metacom, leader of the Wampanoag tribe in central Massachusetts, concluded that only united resistance could stop the relentless advance of the Puritans, whose towns now stretched along the Massachusetts coast and deep into the Connecticut River Valley (see Map 2.5).

In 1675 Metacom, whom the Puritans called King Philip, forged a military alliance with the Narragansett and Nipmuck peoples of Rhode Island and southern Massachusetts, and attacked white settlements throughout New England. Bitter fighting continued into 1676, ending only when Mohawks hired by the Massachusetts

government ambushed and killed Metacom (and then carried his severed head to Boston). The war was a deadly affair. The Indians burned 20 percent of the English towns in Massachusetts and Rhode Island and killed 5 percent of the adult white population (see American Voices, "Mary Rowlandson: A Captivity Narrative," p. 66). But their own losses—from famine and disease as well as from battle—were much larger: as much as 4,000, or 25 percent, of the already diminished Indian population. To ensure their triumph, Puritans sold hundreds of Indians—including Metacom's wife and nine-year-old son—into slavery in the West Indies.

Subsequently, most New England Indians accepted their change in status. Some survived as small, dependent groups, living in poverty on the margins of white society. Many others intermarried with the members of other New England tribes, blending their languages and

MARY ROWLANDSON
A Captivity Narrative

★

Mary Rowlandson, a minister's wife in Lancaster, Massachusetts, was one of many settlers taken captive by the Indians during Metacom's war. Mrs. Rowlandson spent twelve weeks in captivity, traveling constantly, until her family ransomed her for the considerable sum of £20. Her account of this adventure, The Sovereignty and Goodness of God, *published in 1682, became one of the most popular prose works of its time.*

On the tenth of February 1675, came the Indians with great numbers upon Lancaster: their first coming was about sunrising; hearing the noise of some guns, we looked out; several houses were burning, and the smoke ascending to heaven. . . . [T]he Indians laid hold of us, pulling me one way, and the children another, and said, "Come go along with us"; I told them they would kill me: they answered, if I were willing to go along with them, they would not hurt me. . . .

The first week of my being among them I hardly ate any thing; the second week I found my stomach grow very faint for want of something; and yet it was very hard to get down their filthy trash; but the third week . . . they were sweet and savory to my taste. I was at this time knitting a pair of white cotton stockings for my [Indian] mistress; and had not yet wrought upon a sabbath day. When the sabbath came they bade me go to work. I told them it was the sabbath-day, and desired them to let me rest, and told them I would do as much tomorrow; to which they answered me they would break my face. . . .

During my abode in this place, [King] Philip spake to me to make a shirt for his boy, which I did, for which he gave me a shilling. I offered the money to my master, but he bade me keep it; and with it I bought a piece of horse flesh. Afterwards he asked me to make a cap for his boy, for which he invited me to dinner. I went, and he gave me a pancake, about as big as two fingers. It was made of parched wheat, beaten, and fried in bear's grease, but I thought I never tasted pleasanter meat in my life. . . .

Hearing that my son was come to this place, I went to see him. . . . He told me also, that awhile before, his master (together with other Indians) were going to the French for powder; but by the way the Mohawks met with them, and killed four of their company, which made the rest turn back again, for which I desire that myself and he may bless the Lord; for it might have been worse with him, had he been sold to the French, than it proved to be in his remaining with the Indians. . . .

My master had three squaws, living sometimes with one, and sometimes with another one. . . . [It] was Weetamoo with whom I had lived and served all this while. A severe and proud dame she was, bestowing every day in dressing herself near as much time as any of the gentry of the land: powdering her hair, and painting her face, going with necklaces, with jewels in her ears, and bracelets upon her hands. When she had dressed herself, her work was to make girdles of wampom and beads. . . .

On Tuesday morning they called their general court (as they call it) to consult and determine, whether I should go home or no. And they all as one man did seemingly consent to it, that I should go home. . . .

Source: C. H. Lincoln, ed., *Original Narratives of Early American History: Narratives of Indian Wars, 1675–1699,* vol. 14 (New York: Barnes and Noble, 1952).

---

rituals to create new Indian cultures. In either event, these native Americans suffered a double tragedy, losing both their land and their traditional way of life.

The Fur Trade and the Inland Peoples

Until well after 1700 the Indian peoples who lived near the Appalachian Mountains and in the great forested areas beyond remained independent, but only a few were not affected by the European invaders. Traders introduced European diseases as well as brandy and rum, so that epidemics and drunkenness sapped the vitality of some peoples. Moreover, as native Americans exchanged furs for iron utensils and cloth blankets, they made fewer flint hoes, clay pots, and skin garments—gradually losing their traditional artisan skills. After two or three generations some eastern Indians had come to rely on European manufacturers for many basic goods.

Algonquian Beaver Bowl
In part because of the importance to the fur trade, the beaver played a significant role in native American cultural life. This beaver-shaped bowl, carved from the root of an ash tree, was the work of an eighteenth-century Algonquian artisan in present-day Ohio or Illinois.
Peabody Museum, Harvard University. Photograph by Hillel Burger.

Ætatis suæ 21. Aᵒ 1616.

An English View of Pocahontas
By depicting the Indian princess Pocahontas as a well-dressed European woman, the artist casts her as a symbol of peaceful assimilation to English culture. In actuality, marriages between white men (often fur traders) and Indian women usually created bilingual families that absorbed elements from both cultures.
National Portrait Gallery, Smithsonian Institution/Art Resource, NY.

To the west of the Appalachians, traditional skills remained strong because the traders' canoes could carry only small quantities of imported goods.

The greatest threat to the traditional way of life of the inland peoples was the fur trade. Eager for European manufactures, Indian families and villages began to claim exclusive hunting and trapping rights over certain areas, undermining clan unity. More important, as early as the 1640s conflict between tribes increased as well because rival bands of hunter-warriors competed to control the trade in furs. As the population of fur-bearing animals dwindled, these struggles for pelts grew more frequent and more violent. Wars between the Iroquois of New York and their western neighbors devastated the Indian cultures to the west of the Appalachian Mountains. The wars also altered tribal politics because commitment to warfare increased the influence of those who made war, gradually shifting the balance of power from cautious elders to headstrong young warriors.

The fur trade also transformed the Indians' relationship with the natural world. Native Americans were animists, believing that everything—animals, trees, rocks—had a living spirit that demanded respect. Each clan in a tribe venerated an animal as its *totem*, or symbol, often considering themselves descendants of that animal. Tribesmen could hunt totem animals—fox, deer, beaver—only if they followed certain customs. As they skinned beaver for clothing or butchered deer for food, Indians thanked the spirit of the animal, and a principal guardian spirit, a "master of animals," by offering prayers or burning tobacco and respectfully burying the carcass and entrails.

In bringing about the deaths of millions of beaver, the European fur trade altered the ecology of eastern North America, for beaver dams no longer controlled the flow of creeks and streams. It brought spiritual upheaval to the Indians as well. Warriors now hunted ceaselessly in order to trade with the French in Quebec and the English in New York. As they killed more and more deer and beaver, the Indians sensed the displeasure of the spirits in nature. The epidemics that swept through their communities confirmed their fears: the spirits of the animals were taking their revenge. The Micmac warriors of Nova Scotia confessed that they no longer knew "whether the beavers are among our friends or our enemies."

America had become a new world for Indians as well as Europeans. All the invaders—Dutch and French fur traders no less than Spanish conquistadors and English settlers—had undermined traditional native American societies, leaving their members to fashion new ways of life.

Summary
★

Beginning in 1565, first Spain and then England, France, and Holland established permanent settlements in North America. Spain claimed most of the continent, but its empire consisted primarily of a few military garrisons and Franciscan missions in the areas of present-day Florida and New Mexico. Both soldiers and friars exploited the labor of the native peoples, prompting Indian revolts that by 1700 had temporarily expelled most Spaniards from New Mexico. In Quebec, the French attempted to create an agricultural colony, but the fur trade became the lifeblood of New France and of the Dutch colony of New Netherland. Fur traders and Jesuit priests explored the North American continent, extending France's influence among the native peoples of the Mississippi Valley. The English came primarily as settlers, and their relentless quest for land led to war with the Indian peoples.

The English created two very different types of colonies in North America. Settlers in the Chesapeake region created a plantation society that raised tobacco for export to Europe. Wealthy planters and corrupt officials controlled Chesapeake society, dominating freeholding farm families, propertyless freemen, and white indentured servants. The pursuit of self-interest by Governor Berkeley and his faction in Virginia and economic hardship prompted Nathaniel Bacon's unsuccessful rebellion of 1675–1676. Subsequently, planters in Virginia and Maryland made some concessions to white freeholders and turned increasingly to slave labor from Africa, creating full-blown slave societies.

The English migrants who settled in New England grew rapidly in number and raised crops mostly for their own consumption. Reacting against the religious hierarchy and economic hardships they had experienced in England, Puritan settlers created a society based on widespread ownership of land and independent, self-governing churches and towns. At first Puritan magistrates enforced religious orthodoxy, banishing Roger Williams, Anne Hutchinson, and other religious dissidents, but eventually they conceded extensive power to the lay members of local Congregational churches, thereby ensuring political stability.

Wherever Europeans intruded, the native peoples died from new epidemic diseases and went to war to defend their lands. The Pueblo peoples rose in major revolts in 1598 and 1680, the Chesapeake Indians nearly wiped out the Virginia colony in 1622, and Metacom's forces dealt New England a devastating blow in 1675–1676. By 1700, however, many native American peoples along the Atlantic seaboard had been nearly annihilated by disease and warfare.

TIMELINE

1539–1543	Coronado and de Soto explore northern lands
1565	Spain establishes St. Augustine, Florida
1598	Acoma rebellion in New Mexico
1603–1625	King James I of England
1607	English adventurers settle Jamestown, Virginia
1608	Samuel de Champlain founds Quebec
1613	Dutch set up fur-trading post on Manhattan Island
1619	First Africans arrive in the Chesapeake region
	Virginia House of Burgesses convened
1620	Pilgrims found Plymouth colony
1620–1660	Tobacco boom in Chesapeake colonies
1621	Dutch West India Company chartered
1622	Opechancanough's uprising
1624	Virginia becomes a royal colony
1625–1649	King Charles I of England
1630	Puritans found Massachusetts Bay colony
1634	Maryland settled
1636–1637	Pequot war
	Roger Williams and Anne Hutchinson banished
1640s	Puritan revolution in England
	Iroquois go to war over fur trade
1651	First Navigation Act
1660	Restoration of English monarchy
	Poor tobacco market begins
1664	English conquer New Netherland
1675–1676	Bacon's rebellion
	Metacom's uprising
	Expansion of African slavery in the Chesapeake region
1680	Popé's rebellion in New Mexico
1692	Salem witchcraft trials

Suggested Readings

David Weber, *The Spanish Frontier in North America* (1992), and Richard White, *The Middle Ground: Indians, Empires, and Republics in the Great Lakes Region, 1650–1815* (1991), are important studies. For a useful overview, see Colin Calloway, *New Worlds for All: Indians, Europeans, and the Remaking of Early America* (1997).

Imperial Conflicts and Rival Colonial Models

For a discussion of Spain's northern empire in America, see Ramón Gutiérrez, *When Jesus Came, the Corn Mothers Went Away: Marriage, Sexuality, and Power in New Mexico, 1500–1846* (1991). The French threat to Spain's domain is traced by Robert S. Weddle, *The French Thorn: Rival Explorers in the Spanish Sea, 1682–1762* (1991), and Daniel H. Usner Jr., *Indians, Settlers, and Slaves in a Frontier Exchange Economy: The Lower Mississippi Valley before 1783* (1991).

The best general studies of French Canada are by W. J. Eccles: *The Canadian Frontier, 1534–1760* (1983), and *France in America*, rev. ed. (1990). French interaction with native Americans is covered by Bruce G. Trigger, *The Children of Aataentsic: A History of the Huron People to 1660* (1976); Daniel K. Richter, *The Ordeal of the Long House: The Peoples of the Iroquois League in the Era of European Colonization* (1992); and Patricia O. Dickason, *Canada's First Nations: A History of the Founding Peoples from Earliest Times* (1992).

For a discussion of English expansion, see Kenneth Andrews, *Trade, Plunder, and Settlement: Maritime Enterprise and the Genesis of the British Empire, 1480–1630* (1984); Nicholas Canny, *Kingdom and Colony: Ireland in the Atlantic World, 1560–1800* (1988); A. L. Rowse, *Sir Walter Raleigh* (1962); David B. Quinn, *England and the Discovery of America, 1481–1620* (1974); and Karen O. Kupperman, *Roanoke* (1984). The interaction of the English and Dutch with native Americans can be followed in Gary B. Nash, *Red, White, and Black: The Peoples of Early America* (1982), and James Axtell, *The Invasion Within: The Contest of Cultures in Colonial North America* (1985).

The Chesapeake Experience

Alden Vaughan, *American Genesis: Captain John Smith and the Founding of Virginia* (1975), covers the earliest years, while Edmund S. Morgan, *American Slavery, American Freedom: The Ordeal of Colonial Virginia* (1975), provides a brilliant analysis of the rest of the colonial period. Important essays appear in Thad W. Tate and David L. Ammerman, eds., *The Chesapeake in the Seventeenth Century* (1979), and Lois Green Carr, Philip D. Morgan, and Jean B. Russo, *Colonial Chesapeake Society* (1989). Other significant studies include Lois Green Carr et al., *Robert Cole's World: Agriculture and Society in Early Maryland* (1991); Kathleen Brown, *Good Wives, Nasty Wenches, and Anxious Patriarchs: Gender, Race, and Power in Colonial Virginia* (1996); and James Horn, *Adapting to a New World: English Society in the Seventeenth-Century Chesapeake* (1994). For a discussion of political institutions, see David W. Jordan, *Foundations of Representative Government in Maryland, 1632–1715* (1988).

Puritan New England

For the Puritan migration, see Edmund Morgan, *The Puritan Dilemma: The Story of John Winthrop* (1955); David Grayson Allen, *In English Ways: The Movement of Societies and the Transferral of English Local Law and Custom to Massachusetts Bay in the Seventeenth Century* (1981); and David Cressy, *Coming Over: Migration and Communication between England and New England in the Seventeenth Century* (1987).

Puritanism as an intellectual movement is best explored in the works of Perry Miller; see especially *The New England Mind: The Seventeenth Century* (1939). Charles Hambrick-Stowe, *The Practice of Piety: Puritan Devotional Disciplines* (1982), discusses the emotional dimension of Puritanism, while David D. Hall, *World of Wonder, Days of Judgment: Popular Religious Belief in Early New England* (1989), explores its supernatural aspects.

For a discussion of dissent in early New England, consult Philip Gura, *A Glimpse of Sion's Glory: Puritan Radicalism in New England, 1620–1660* (1984); Edwin S. Gaustad, *Liberty of Conscience: Roger Williams in America* (1991); Amy Schrager Lang, *Prophetic Woman: Anne Hutchinson and the Problem of Dissent in the Literature of New England* (1987); Paul Boyer and Steven Nissenbaum, *Salem Possessed: The Social Origins of Witchcraft* (1974); and Carol F. Karlsen, *The Devil in the Shape of a Woman: Witchcraft in New England* (1987).

Community studies that describe the lives of ordinary New England men and women include John Demos, *The Little Commonwealth: Family Life in Plymouth Colony* (1971), and Kenneth A. Lockridge, *A New England Town . . . Dedham, Massachusetts, 1636–1736* (1970). See also John Demos, *The Unredeemed Captive: A Family Story from Early America* (1994), and Daniel Vickers, *Farmers and Fishermen: Two Centuries of Work in Essex County, Massachusetts, 1630–1850* (1994).

The Indians' New World

James H. Merrell, *The Indians' New World: Catawbas and Their Neighbors from European Contact through the Era of Removal* (1989), is a path-breaking study. For a discussion of warfare in New England, see Alfred Cave, *The Pequot War* (1996), and Russell Bourne, *Red King's Rebellion* (1991), a study of Metacom's war. See also Karen Ordahl Kupperman, *Settling with the Indians: The Meeting of English and Indian Cultures in America, 1580–1640* (1981); Bernard Sheehan, *Savagism and Civility: Indians and Englishmen in Colonial Virginia* (1980); and Daniel K. Richter and James H. Merrell, *Beyond the Covenant Chain: The Iroquois and Their Neighbors in Indian North America* (1987). Two ecological studies are Calvin Martin, *Keepers of the Game: Indian-Animal Relations and the Fur Trade* (1978), and William Cronon, *Changes in the Land: Indians, Colonists, and the Ecology of New England* (1983).

The British Empire in America, 1660–1750

BY 1660 ENGLISH traders and settlers had pushed aside the native Americans and founded two clusters of colonies along the eastern coast of North America. The pace of settlement quickened as British officials encouraged the migration of tens of thousands of English men and women to New England and the Chesapeake. By 1720 there were 450,000 settlers on the mainland, and by 1750 no less than 1.2 million.

As the colonial settlements grew in numbers, they became crucial parts of a transatlantic system of trade. The mercantilist Navigation Acts encouraged the expansion of commerce and the production of valuable export crops in America, bringing great profits to British merchants and manufacturers. Even more wealth poured into Britain from its plantations in the West Indies, where a vast labor force of enslaved Africans grew sugar for sale in Europe. As a British imperialist commented in 1745, the colonial empire "was a magnificent superstructure of American commerce and British naval power on an African foundation."

The British Empire was the product of calculated policy, not chance. To protect its increasingly valuable colonies from European rivals—the Dutch in New Netherland, the French in Quebec and the West Indies, and the Spanish in Florida—Britain expanded its navy and repeatedly went to war. No less than trade, imperial warfare was a crucial ingredient of mercantilism and a predominant theme of the century between 1660 and 1750.

These years also witnessed a long struggle over imperial administrative control. Many English men and women had fled to America to escape religious

Power and Race in the Chesapeake
Lord Baltimore holds a map of his proprietary colony of Maryland in this 1670 painting by Gerard Soest. The colony will soon belong to his grandson Cecil Calvert, who, attended by an African servant, points to his magnificent inheritance.
Enoch Pratt Free Library of Baltimore.

persecution and wanted to govern themselves. But the home government wished to profit from their products and commerce, so it tried to control their trade and subordinate their local political institutions to imperial direction. Although Britain's attempts to manage American politics were never completely successful, its economic policies worked remarkably well, creating a prosperous empire and elevating Britain to the rank of an important European power.

The Politics of Empire, 1660–1713

——————★——————

In the first decades of settlement, the Chesapeake and New England colonies were governed in a haphazard fashion. Taking advantage of the upheaval produced by civil war in England between 1640 and 1660, local cliques of Puritan magistrates and tobacco-growing planters governed as they wished. Subsequently, royal bureaucrats struggled to impose order on the unruly American settlements and to mobilize the settlers and friendly Indians against rival European nations.

The Restoration Colonies

In 1660 Charles II returned from exile, ending the republican commonwealth and restoring the monarchy. Like King James I, Charles II (r. 1660–1685) supported the Anglican Church and believed in the divine right of kings to govern as they wished. A robust and vigorous man, he offended Puritans and many of his other subjects by marrying a Portuguese Catholic princess and presiding over a sexually permissive court.

Charles was also a generous and extravagant king who was always in debt. To pay his creditors and reward the aristocrats who supported his return to power, he gave away millions of acres of land in America. In 1663 he gave the Carolinas, an area long claimed by Spain and populated by thousands of Indians, to eight aristocratic friends. In 1664 he granted all the territory between the Delaware and Connecticut Rivers, including the recently conquered Dutch province of New Netherland, to his brother James, the duke of York. James took possession of New Netherland, renaming it New York after himself, and bestowed ownership of the adjacent lands on two of the Carolina proprietors, who established the province of New Jersey (Table 3.1).

In one of the great land grabs in history, a few English aristocrats had won title to vast provinces. Like Lord Baltimore's province of Maryland, the new colonies created by Charles II were proprietorships. The proprietors owned all the land and could rule as they wished as long as the laws in their colonies conformed broadly to those of England. Most proprietors tried to create a traditional social order presided over by a gentry class and regulated by the legally established Church of England.

The Carolinas. This traditionalist vision provided a background for the Fundamental Constitutions of Carolina, which the proprietors promulgated in 1669. It called for the creation of a manorial system in which a powerful nobility would control a mass of serfs bound to the land. However, the reality in North Carolina turned out to be far different from this vision. The first settlers, mostly poor families from Virginia, refused to

TABLE 3.1

English Colonies in North America, 1660–1750

	Date	Type	Religion	Status in 1775	Chief Export or Economic Activity
Carolinas	1663	Proprietary	Church of England	Royal	
North	1691				Mixed farming; naval stores
South	1691				Rice; indigo
New Jersey	1664	Proprietary	Church of England	Royal	Wheat
New York	1664	Proprietary	Church of England	Royal	Wheat
Pennsylvania	1681	Proprietary	No established church	Proprietary	Wheat
Georgia	1732	Trustees	Church of England	Royal	Rice
New Hampshire (separated from Massachusetts)	1739	Royal	Congregationalist	Royal	Mixed farming; lumber; naval stores
Nova Scotia	1749	Royal	Church of England	Royal	Fishing; mixed farming; naval stores

work on large manors and chose to live on modest farms, raising grain and tobacco. Indeed, farmers in Albemarle County, angered by taxes on their tobacco exports and by the annual *quitrents* (small payments required as an acknowledgment of the lordship of the proprietors), rebelled in 1677. Led by John Culpepper, a farmer, they deposed the governor and forced the proprietors to abandon most of their financial claims.

The colonists of South Carolina, many of whom had come from Barbados (by then an overcrowded sugar-producing island), refused to accept either the Fundamental Constitutions or the payment of quitrents. Rather, they imposed their own design on the colony, bringing enslaved Africans from Barbados and using them to raise cattle and food crops for export to the West Indies. The South Carolinians also established a lucrative trade with native Americans, exchanging English manufactured goods for furs and Indian slaves. The demand for Indian slaves motivated adventurers to launch slave-raiding attacks on Franciscan missions in Florida, raising the threat of war with Spain and, in 1715, prompting a brutal war with the resident Yamasee people. South Carolina remained an ill-governed, violence-ridden frontier settlement until the 1720s.

William Penn and Pennsylvania. In dramatic contrast to the Carolinas, the proprietary colony of Pennsylvania pursued a pacifistic policy toward native Americans and soon became a prosperous and well-governed society. In 1681 Charles II bestowed the colony on William Penn in payment of a large debt owed to Penn's father, Admiral William Penn. Born to wealth and seemingly destined for courtly pursuits, the younger Penn chose to live a very different life, converting to the Society of Friends (Quakers), a radical Protestant sect, and using his prestige to spread its influence. His pamphlet *No Cross, No Crown* (1677) offered an articulate defense of the Quakers' belief in religious liberty. He designed Pennsylvania as a refuge for Quakers, who were persecuted in England because they refused to serve in the army and would not pay taxes to support the Church of England.

Like the Puritans in New England, the Quakers wanted to restore the simplicity and spirituality of early Christianity. But Quakers were not like Puritans or other Calvinists, who restricted salvation to a small elect. Rather, they followed the teachings of leaders such as the English visionary George Fox and his associate, Margaret Fell, who argued that everyone could be saved because God had imbued each person with an inner "light" of grace or understanding. Equally important, Quakers believed that women as well as men should take an active role in church life, and many women served as influential leaders.

 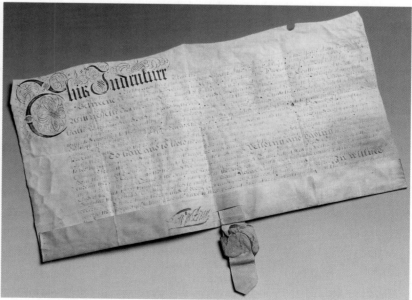

William Penn, Quaker Proprietor
As a member of the Society of Friends, Penn dressed in a plain and simple style, as this portrait shows. However, as a result of his proprietorship, the young Quaker was a wealthy man, the sole owner of millions of acres of land. This 1685 indenture, or contract, authorizes the sale of 500 acres of Penn's land along the Delaware River to John Dwight, a "gentleman" of Fulham in England.
Historical Society of Pennsylvania; Jonathan Horne.

The principal Quaker religious institution—the weekly meeting for worship—was designed to help members discover the inner light. The meetings were not led by a minister and did not center on a sermon. Instead, Friends encouraged anyone, man or woman, who felt the promptings of the inner light to speak. "Nearest the front by the wall are two benches," a traveler reported after a visit to a Philadelphia meetinghouse. "In these pews sit those of both sexes who either are already accustomed to preach or expect to be inspired by the Holy Ghost."

Penn's Frame of Government (1681) for the new province was a radical document for its time. It not only guaranteed political liberty and religious freedom but also allowed Christians of all denominations to vote and hold office. During the 1680s thousands of Quakers, primarily farmers and artisans from northwestern England, settled along the Delaware River in or near the city of Philadelphia, which Penn himself planned. The proprietor sold them land at low prices and in fee simple (making them the absolute owners), and, to attract other Protestants to settle in the colony, advertised its merits in pamphlets translated into Dutch and German. In 1683 migrants from the German province of Saxony founded Germantown (just outside Philadelphia) and were soon joined by thousands of other Germans, attracted by fertile land and the prospect of freedom from religious warfare and persecution.

In 1682 James, duke of York, gave Penn the colony of Delaware, originally a Swedish settlement that had been conquered first by the Dutch and then, in 1664, by the English. The Quaker leader incorporated the Delaware settlements into Pennsylvania as the Lower Counties, and after 1703 he allowed the inhabitants to select their own representative assembly. Ethnic diversity, pacifism, and freedom of conscience made Penn-sylvania and Delaware the most open and democratic of all the colonies created during this period.

From Mercantilism to Dominion

Since the 1560s, Elizabeth I and her successors had used mercantilist subsidies and regulations to stimulate domestic manufacturing and foreign trade. Beginning in the 1650s, English officials extended these policies to the colonies in America, where they created a generation of political controversy.

The Navigation Acts. The prime stimulus for these economic controls came from Dutch merchants, who were growing rich by trading with English plantation owners in Virginia and the West Indies. To keep the commerce of these colonies in English hands, in 1651 Parliament passed a Navigation Act. The act stipulated that all goods imported into England or its American settlements be carried on ships registered in England, Ireland, or the colonies.

Upon ascending the throne in 1660, Charles II extended this mercantilist policy. He created a new committee, the Lords of Trade and Plantations, and charged it with formulating policies for the colonies. He also had Parliament pass new Navigation Acts in 1660 and 1663. These acts strengthened the ban on foreign merchants trading with the colonies and stipulated that American sugar, tobacco, and indigo (a deep-blue dye) be shipped only to England. To provide even more business for English merchants, the acts required that all exports to America from European countries pass through England. To enforce these laws, the Revenue Act of 1673 created a staff of customs officials and, to pay their salaries, imposed a "plantation duty" on sugar and tobacco exported from the colonies (Table 3.2).

TABLE 3.2

Navigation Acts, 1651–1751

	Date	Purpose	Result
Act of 1651	1651	Cut Dutch trade	Mostly ignored
Act of 1660	1660	Ban foreign shipping; enumerated goods only to England	Partially obeyed
Act of 1663	1663	Require European imports to pass only through England	Partially obeyed
Staple Act	1663	Require enumerated goods and European imports to pass through England	Mostly obeyed
Revenue Act	1673	Impose "plantation duty"; create customs system	Mostly obeyed
Act of 1696	1696	Prevent frauds; create Vice-Admiralty Courts	Mostly obeyed
Woolen Act	1699	Prevent export or intercolonial sale of textiles	Partially obeyed
Hat Act	1732	Prevent export or intercolonial sale of hats	Partially obeyed
Molasses Act	1733	Cut American imports of molasses from French West Indies	Extensively violated
Iron Act	1750	Prevent manufacture of finished iron products	Extensively violated
Currency Act	1751	End use of paper currency as legal tender in New England	Mostly obeyed

The English government backed these mercantilist measures with military force. "What we want," the duke of Albemarle bluntly declared, "is more of the trade the Dutch now have." In three commercial wars between 1652 and 1674 the English navy drove the Dutch from New Netherland and brought an end to Dutch supremacy in the West African slave trade. Meanwhile, English merchants expanded their fleets and dominated Atlantic commerce.

Unaccustomed to the regulation of their trade, the colonial governments and settlers—especially those in Puritan New England—resisted these mercantilist policies as burdensome and intrusive. They wanted to send their goods to the markets where they fetched the best return, and to buy manufactures from the cheapest suppliers (primarily the Dutch). Edmund Randolph, an English customs official in Massachusetts Bay, reported that the colony's Puritan-dominated government took "no notice of the laws of trade." Instead, it welcomed foreign merchants, imported molasses from the French-controlled sugar islands, and claimed that its royal charter exempted it from most of the new regulations. Outraged, Randolph called for English troops to "reduce Massachusetts to obedience."

Responding to Randolph's plea, the Lords of Trade and Plantations launched a punitive legal campaign against the Puritan colony. In 1679 the Lords denied the claim of Massachusetts Bay to the adjoining province of New Hampshire; instead, they created a separate colony with a royal governor. Then the Lords brought the Puritan colony under direct English control. In 1684 they persuaded an English court to annul the charter of Massachusetts Bay on the grounds that its government had virtually outlawed the Church of England and intentionally violated the Navigation Acts.

The Dominion of New England. The accession to the throne of James II (r. 1685–1688) prompted the Lords of Trade to undertake a widespread reform of the colonial system. James was an admirer of France's despotic King Louis XIV and a firm believer in the divine right of monarchs. Strongly backed by the king, the Lords eliminated many of the existing American colonial governments. In 1686 they revoked the corporate charters of Connecticut and Rhode Island and merged these colonies with the Massachusetts Bay and Plymouth colonies to form a new royal province, the Dominion of New England (Map 3.1). Two years later the Lords added New York and New Jersey to the Dominion, creating a massive colony that stretched from the Delaware River to Maine.

The Dominion of New England created an authoritarian administrative system. Previous mercantilist policies had regulated the trade of the colonies while respecting the autonomy of their representative assemblies. But as the name implied, the new colony was to

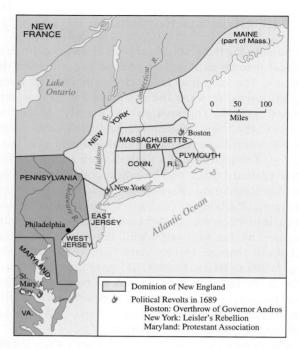

MAP 3.1
The Dominion of New England, 1686–1689
The Dominion created a vast new royal colony stretching nearly 500 miles along the Atlantic coast. After the Glorious Revolution in England, revolts in Boston and New York City ousted royal officials, effectively ending the Dominion. In Maryland a Protestant Association mounted a third revolt, deposing the Catholic proprietary governor.

be the king's own "dominion," an American version of the harsh system of rule that the Crown had already imposed on the conquered province of Ireland. In Ireland, there were no representative institutions, and garrisons of English soldiers dotted the landscape, enforcing the edicts of royally appointed English governors and magistrates.

To create a similar system in America, James II appointed Sir Edmund Andros, a former military officer, as governor of the Dominion and empowered him to abolish the existing legislative assemblies and rule by decree. Taking up residence in Massachusetts, Andros attacked all the main institutions of Puritan society. He advocated public worship in the Church of England, offending Puritan Congregationalists, and banned town meetings, angering villagers who prized local self-rule. Even worse, the new governor challenged all land titles granted under the original Massachusetts charter. Andros offered to provide new deeds, but only if the colonists would agree to pay an annual quitrent. When the Puritans protested to the king about this assault on their way of life, James rejected their petitions and refused to restore the old charter.

The Glorious Revolution of 1688

Fortunately for the colonists, James II angered English political leaders as much as Andros had offended the Puritans. The king had revoked the charters of many English towns, rejected the advice of Parliament, and aroused popular opposition by openly practicing Roman Catholicism. Dissent reached crisis proportions in 1688, when James's Spanish Catholic wife gave birth to a son. The prospect of a Catholic heir to the English throne ignited a quick and bloodless coup known as the Glorious Revolution. Backed by popular protests and the army, Protestant parliamentary leaders forced James into exile and enthroned Mary, his Protestant daughter by his first wife, and her Dutch husband, William of Orange. Queen Mary II (r. 1689–1694) and King William III (r. 1689–1701) gave up the Stuarts' claim to divine right and agreed to rule as constitutional monarchs. They accepted a Declaration of Rights that limited royal prerogatives and expanded personal liberties and parliamentary powers.

The coup leaders felt a need to justify their substitution of one monarch for another. English philosopher John Locke provided that justification in his *Two Treatises on Government* (1690), which rejected divine right theories of monarchical rule and argued that the legitimacy of government rests on the consent of the governed. Locke also maintained that individuals have inalienable natural rights to life, liberty, and property. This celebration of individual rights and representative government had a lasting influence in America, where many political leaders wanted to expand the powers of the colonial assemblies. More immediately, the Glorious Revolution sparked rebellions by colonists in Maryland, Massachusetts, and New York.

The ouster of James II renewed the longstanding religious conflict between Protestants and Catholics in Maryland. Since 1660, tobacco prices had been falling, threatening the livelihoods of smallholders, tenant farmers, and former indentured servants, most of whom were Protestants. They resented the rising taxes and the high fees imposed by wealthy proprietary officials, who were primarily Catholics. In 1689 Protestants in Maryland rose in rebellion, forcibly removing the officials appointed by the Catholic Lord Baltimore. To quiet the Protestant rebels, the Lords of Trade promptly suspended Baltimore's proprietorship, imposed royal government, and established the Church of England as the colony's official church. This arrangement lasted until 1715, when Benedict Calvert, the fourth Lord Baltimore, converted to the Anglican faith and the Crown restored the proprietorship to the Calvert family.

When the news of James II's ouster reached Boston in April 1689, Puritan leaders carried out a revolution of their own. They seized Governor Andros, sent him back to England, and demanded restoration of the charter of 1629. William and Mary and their advisors agreed to break up the Dominion of New England, but they refused to restore complete power to the Puritans. Instead, the monarchs created the new colony of Massachusetts (which included Plymouth and Maine) and gave it a royal form of government. According to the new Massachusetts charter of 1692, the Crown had the power to appoint the governor (as well as the naval officers who were charged with enforcing customs regulations), and members of the Church of England had the right to worship in public. The charter restored the Massachusetts assembly but stipulated that its members be elected by *all* male property owners (not just Puritan church members). These measures ended the old system of Puritan rule and gave Massachusetts a representative system of government that worked well for the next seventy years.

In New York, which had been added to the Dominion of New England in 1688, the Glorious Revolution produced great turmoil, in part because the colony was divided along the lines of class and ethnicity. After England had conquered New Netherland in 1664, James II (as duke of York) had imposed strict authoritarian rule, prohibiting representative institutions. However, he had not expelled the Dutch residents and most of them remained in the colony; in 1689 nearly 60 percent of the taxpayers in New York City were Dutch artisans and shopkeepers.

As proud Protestants from Holland, New York's Dutch residents welcomed Queen Mary and her Dutch husband to the English throne. In 1689 they joined with English settlers on Long Island to oust Francis Nicholson—the lieutenant governor of the Dominion and an alleged Catholic sympathizer—and the other "Popish Doggs & Divells," as the Protestant rebels called them, appointed by James II. They replaced Nicholson with Jacob Leisler, a migrant German soldier who had married into a prominent Dutch merchant family.

At first Leisler found supporters among all classes and ethnic groups. But when he freed debtors from prison and championed a more democratic town-meeting form of government, most wealthy merchants (who had traditionally controlled the city government) turned against him. Merchant Nicholas Bayard accused Leisler of being a "Masaniello," referring to a fishmonger who in 1647 had led a popular revolt in Naples, Italy. In 1691 a newly appointed royal governor took control of New York from Leisler, restored the representative assembly, and supported the wealthy classes against the Dutch artisans. He had Leisler indicted for treason, and the former governor was convicted by an English jury, hanged, and then decapitated—a fate reserved for those found guilty of committing treason. Subsequently, a new merchant-dominated Board of Aldermen passed ordinances that lowered artisans' wages, extending the unrest. Conflict between the Leislerian and anti-Leislerian factions continued until the 1710s.

A Prosperous Dutch Farmstead
Many Dutch farmers in the Hudson River Valley prospered because of easy access to market and their exploitation of black slaves. To record his success, Martin Van Bergen of Leeds, New York, had this mural painted over his mantelpiece.
New-York State Historical Association.

The Glorious Revolution of 1688–1689 began a new phase in imperial history. In America, the uprisings in Boston and in New York toppled the authoritarian institutions of the Dominion of New England and restored representative political institutions. In England, the new constitutional monarchy gave effective control of the affairs of state to representatives of the propertied classes. These men promoted an empire based on commerce by curbing royal monopolies (such as the East India and Royal African companies) and by giving free rein to enterprising merchants and financiers who developed the American colonies as a source of trade. Equally important, the renewed commitment of England to the cause of Protestantism helped to spark a new series of wars with the Catholic monarchs of France and Spain.

Imperial Wars and Native Peoples

Beginning in 1689, England and France fought a century-long series of wars to determine which nation would be dominant in Western Europe. These wars quickly spilled over into the Western Hemisphere, where they affected not only the English and French settlers but also colonists from Spain and many Indian peoples (Table 3.3). Using Indian allies, England fought to enlarge its settlements along the eastern coast of North America, while France made similar alliances with native peoples and extended its claims of dominion to include the entire Mississippi Valley. Spain assumed a defensive posture north of the Rio Grande, strengthening its borderland settlements to protect its treasure fleets and the rich silver and gold mines of New Spain.

TABLE 3.3

English Wars, 1650–1750

	Date	Purpose	Result
Anglo-Dutch	1652–1654	Develop commercial markets	Stalemate
Anglo-Dutch	1664	Acquire markets—conquest	England takes New Amsterdam
Anglo-Dutch	1673	Develop commercial markets	England makes maritime gains
King William's (War of the League of Augsburg)	1689–1697	Maintain European balance of power	Stalemate in North America
Queen Anne's (War of the Spanish Succession)	1702–1713	Maintain European balance of power	British get Hudson Bay and Nova Scotia
Jenkins' Ear	1739	Expand markets in Spanish America	Stalemate
King George's (War of Austrian Succession)	1740–1748	Maintain European balance of power	Capture and return of Louisbourg (on Cape Breton Island)

European Strategy and Indian Alliances. The first of these European conflicts to have an impact in the Western Hemisphere was the War of the League of Augsburg, known in America as King William's War. During this conflict, which lasted from 1689 to 1697, New England troops and their Iroquois allies fought against French troops and their Algonquian allies, mostly in Indian territory. French and Indian forces destroyed the frontier town of Schenectady, New York, in 1690, while Massachusetts troops captured Port Royal, the capital of Acadia (present-day Nova Scotia in Canada). In 1697 the Treaty of Ryswick ended the war, restoring prewar boundaries in North America and confirming French control of the western half of the rich sugar island of Santo Domingo (present-day Haiti).

Five years later, the War of the Spanish Succession (1702–1713) again pitted England (part of Great Britain following the union in 1707 of England and Scotland) against France, which was now allied with Spain. In this conflict, which Americans called Queen Anne's War, the British protected their growing settlements in the Carolinas by launching an attack against Spanish Florida. An English expedition from South Carolina burned the town of St. Augustine but failed to capture the fort. Then, in 1704, the Carolinians armed Creek and Chickasaw warriors and other Indians who had fled from forced labor at the Spanish missions. This Indian army destroyed the remaining Franciscan missions in northern Florida, attacked the Spanish settlement at Pensacola, and massacred the Apalachee who were allied with Spain. To preserve control of Florida and protect Havana in nearby Cuba, the Spanish reinforced St. Augustine and launched unsuccessful attacks against Charleston, South Carolina.

Indian warriors played a significant role in Queen Anne's War, both in the Carolinas and Florida and along the boundary between Quebec and New England. To halt the expansion of Puritan settlements, French officials provided supplies and arms to the Abenaki, who destroyed English settlements along the coast of Maine. In 1704 an expedition of pro-French Iroquois warriors attacked the western Massachusetts town of Deerfield, where they killed 48 residents and carried 112 into captivity. The New England colonists responded to these raids by launching attacks against French settlements, joining with British troops to seize Port Royal in Acadia.

The New York frontier remained quiet during Queen Anne's War because France and Britain did not want to disrupt the lucrative fur trade. In addition, most members of the powerful Iroquois peoples—the Five Nations, as the English and Dutch called them because of their strong political organization—had adopted a new policy of "aggressive neutrality." In the 1670s, in response to an alliance between the French and the Huron, the Five Nations—the Mohawk, Oneida, Onondaga, Cayuga, and Seneca—had entered into a "covenant chain" of alliances with the English governors of New York and the Algonquian tribes of New England. However, during King William's War these alliances resulted in a devastating struggle over the fur trade, prompting most members of the Five Nations to favor a policy of neutrality. After 1701 the Iroquois and their Algonquian allies exploited their central location by trading with the English and the French but refusing to fight for either side. The leader of the Delaware tribe, Teedyuscung, explained this strategy by showing his people a pictorial message from the Iroquois: "You see a Square in the Middle, meaning the Lands of the Indians; and at one End, the Figure of a Man, indicating the English; and at the other End, another, meaning the French. Let us join together to defend our land against both."

Lacking the active Indian allies, neither the British nor French could prevail in Queen Anne's War. Following the failure in 1710 of a large British-American expedition against the French stronghold at Quebec, there was little fighting in America. However, as a result of victories in Europe, Britain won important territorial and commercial concessions in the Treaty of Utrecht (1713) that ended the war. From France, Britain obtained Newfoundland, Acadia (Nova Scotia), the Hudson Bay region of northern Canada, and access to the Indian trade in the Great Lakes region (see Map 4.4). From Spain, Britain acquired the strategic fortress of Gibraltar at the entrance to the Mediterranean Sea and commercial privileges in Spanish America.

To protect its increasingly vulnerable empire in America, Spain bolstered its presence in Florida and the Southwest. Beginning in 1718 with the foundation of San Antonio, it established permanent settlements in Texas to protect the silver mines in northern New Spain. Spanish expansion into Texas was strongly opposed by the town-dwelling Caddo Indians, one of whose confederacies, the Kingdom of Tejas, would give the region its name. During the 1690s the Caddo had expelled the Spanish Franciscans from its lands, blaming them for a fatal smallpox epidemic. Now in 1718 they renewed their opposition to the Spanish intruders, refusing to have Franciscans baptize them (believing "that the [holy] water kills them") and turning to the French in Louisiana for firearms and trade goods. Like the Iroquois of New York, the Caddo peoples had learned how to turn European imperial rivalries and warfare to their own advantage.

Britain's American Empire. The Treaty of Utrecht brought peace to eastern North America for more than a generation, giving the British government the opportunity to reform its diverse and haphazardly governed empire. Some of its American colonies produced crops for export and were commercially tied to England; others were settlements of religious dissidents who wanted to be left alone. Some colonies had corporate charters, others were proprietary ventures, and still others had royal governors.

In 1696 Parliament had attempted to establish a uniform system of government by creating a Board of Trade (to replace the Lords of Trade and Plantations) and staffing it with rising politicians and experienced bureaucrats. But the Board lacked the political power to impose direct Crown control over the proprietary and charter colonies and install royal governors appointed by the king. Parliament had just overthrown a power-hungry monarch (James II) at home, and English politicians were unwilling to increase the Crown's power in America.

Consequently, in 1713 the British empire continued to be governed in a haphazard fashion (Map 3.2). There were royal governments in the great staple-producing tobacco and sugar colonies of Virginia and the West

BRITISH COLONIES			
☐ Royal	■ Proprietary	■ Corporate	
	Population	Average Annual	Exports
	White Black	Exports, 1698-1717	per white (shillings)*
West Indian Islands	27,000 122,000	£700,000	538s.
Southern Mainland	114,000 37,000	£220,000	39s.
Northern Mainland	177,000 3,000	£135,000	15s.
*(20 shillings = 1£, 1 pound = about $3.60.)			

MAP 3.2
Britain's American Empire, 1713
Britain's West Indian possessions were small—mere dots on the Caribbean Sea. However, in 1713 they were by far the most valuable parts of the empire. Their sugar crops brought wealth to English merchants, trade to the northern colonies, and a brutal life (and early death) to enslaved African workers.

Indies, and also in Massachusetts, New York, and New Jersey. In these royal colonies, the Crown appointed the governors, and property owners elected an assembly to represent their interests. Connecticut and Rhode Island remained virtually independent colonies operating under charters granted by Charles I and Charles II. They were bound by the Navigation Acts and their laws were subject to review by the Privy Council in London, but they elected their own governors and all other local officials. Other colonies—North and South Carolina, Maryland, and Pennsylvania—remained proprietorships, with assemblies elected by the property-owning residents, and governors appointed by the proprietors, who also owned all ungranted land.

In 1713, as in 1660, the British settlements in North America resembled a patchwork quilt, its colors and textures representing corporate, proprietary, and royal colonies. Those colonies, however, were no longer small religious settlements or weak and disease-ridden plantations. Rather, they were rapidly growing agricultural societies that had become important parts of a thriving commercial empire. The first British Empire was coming of age.

The Imperial Slave Economy

——————★——————

Beginning around 1550, European merchants and migrants created a new type of agricultural economy, which historians call the South Atlantic system. Using land seized from native Americans and the labor of enslaved Africans, the migrants established plantations in Brazil and the West Indies on which they raised sugar, tobacco, and other valuable crops, which the merchants then brought to markets in Europe. After 1700 this transoceanic trade in American products (and African slaves) increased dramatically in scale and changed the history of four continents. It sapped the human resources of West Africa, set off a commercial revolution in Europe, and populated North America and South America with a score of racially mixed societies. This slave-based economy also provided markets for farmers in England's northern mainland colonies and stimulated the growth of seaports and merchant communities there.

The African Background

West Africa is a vast and diverse region that stretches along 2,000 miles of coastline from present-day Senegal to Cameroon and includes the modern states of Liberia, the Ivory Coast, Ghana, and Nigeria. To the south along another 1,200 miles of that coast lie Gabon, the two

An African King
This striking bronze plaque, c. 1550–1680, from Benin, an important kingdom in West Central Africa, depicts a mounted king, his attendants, and (probably) his children.
Metropolitan Museum of Art. The Michael C. Rockefeller Collection.

Congo republics, and Angola, also important sources of the transatlantic trade in slaves. In 1500 a thick expanse of tropical rain forest covered much of the coast, but a series of great rivers—the Senegal, Gambia, Volta, Niger, and Congo—provided relatively easy access to the woodlands, plains, and savanna (vast grasslands) of the interior (Map 3.3).

Most West Africans farmed small plots and lived in extended families in small villages. Normally, men cleared the land and women planted and harvested the crops. On the plains of the savanna in the interior, farmers raised millet and cotton and herded livestock, whereas the coastal forest peoples grew yams and harvested oil-rich palm nuts. Forest dwellers exchanged kola nuts, a mild stimulant, for the textiles and leather goods produced by savanna dwellers. Similarly, salt produced along the seacoast was traded for iron or gold mined in the hills of the interior.

Political and Social Organization. Most West Africans spoke related languages, but they represented hundreds of distinct cultural and political groups. A majority of the people lived in hierarchical, socially stratified societies ruled by princes. For example, the

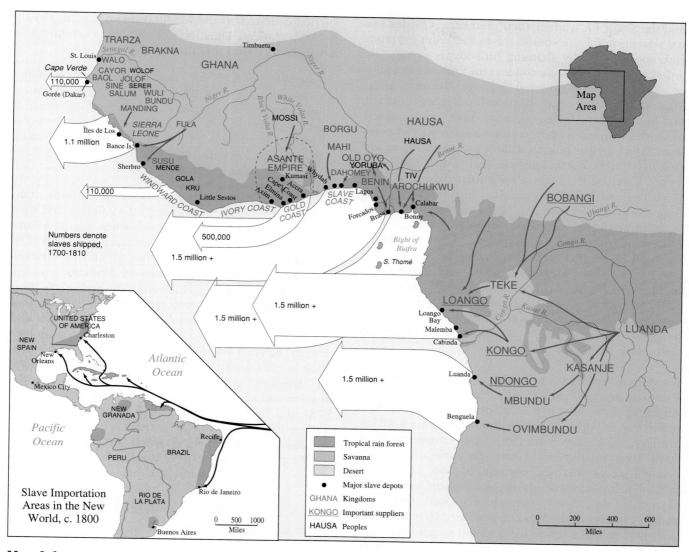

MAP 3.3

Africa in the Eighteenth Century

The tropical rain forest region of West Africa was home to scores of peoples and dozens of kingdoms. Some kingdoms, such as Dahomey, became aggressive slavers, taking tens of thousands of war captives and funneling them to the seacoast, where they were purchased by European traders. About 15 percent of enslaved Africans died on the transatlantic voyage, the feared "middle passage"; most of the survivors labored on sugar plantations in Brazil and the British and French West Indies (Table 3.4).

Akan peoples of Ghana were organized in states ruled by kings whose authority was limited by a council of ministers. The Wolof kings of Senegambia were much more powerful. Warrior-rulers with armies of soldier-slaves, they appointed local chiefs and grew rich from tax revenues and levies imposed on merchants and conquered peoples. Women of the royal Wolof clans exercised considerable power as well, collecting tribute from various villages and judging cases of adultery.

Other West Africans resided in stateless societies organized by family and lineage (much like those of the Woodland Indians of eastern North America—see Chapter 1). Thus the Tiv people who lived along the Niger River created a relatively egalitarian society in which land was available to all; chiefs and elders administered justice but could neither impose taxes and rents nor control individual laborers. Other West Africans lived in communities managed by a village council.

In addition to these political institutions, most African peoples had important voluntary associations. These groups helped to unify the society by spanning lineage and clan loyalties in stateless cultures and checking the powers of rulers in princely states. The most important organizations were the *Poro* for men and the *Sande* for women; their members provided sexual education for the young, conducted adult initiation ceremonies, and, by shaming individuals or officials, enforced codes of public conduct and private morality.

Spiritual beliefs varied greatly. Although some West Africans had been converted to the Muslim faith and believed in a single god, most recognized a variety of deities ranging from a remote creator-god who seldom interfered in human affairs to numerous spirits that lived in the earth, animals, and plants. According to the latter belief, male blacksmiths (who had mastered the secrets of iron making) and female potters (who had transformed the basic elements of earth, water, and fire) were able to capture these spiritual powers in amulets, which people wore to protect themselves against evil forces. Africans also paid homage to their ancestors, who were believed to inhabit a spiritual world from which they could intercede on behalf of their descendants. Attempting to give themselves an aura of divinity, many royal families in West Africa created elaborate ceremonies honoring their ancestors.

European Traders and African Society. At first European traders had a positive impact on life in West Africa by introducing new plants and animals. Portuguese merchants carried coconuts from East Africa, oranges and lemons from the Mediterranean, and pigs from Western Europe. From the Americas traders brought sweet potatoes, peanuts, papaya, pineapples, and tobacco. American maize (or corn) and cassava (or manioc, a root crop) gradually displaced millet and yams as staples in the West African diet; in many areas their higher yields promoted population growth.

The first Portuguese merchants also expanded existing trade networks, thereby stimulating the African economy. European iron bars and metal products joined kola nuts and salt moving inland; grain, gold, ivory, and cotton textiles flowed to the coast to provision European ships. This inland trade remained in the hands of Africans in part because of disease; Europeans who lived in West Africa were readily stricken by yellow fever, malaria, and dysentery, and their death rate was higher than 50 percent a year.

However, European merchants soon joined in the long-established trade in human beings. Unfree status had existed for many centuries in West Africa. Some people were held in bondage as security for debts; others were sold into servitude by their kin, often in return for food in times of famine; still others were war captives. Although they were treated as property and exploited as agricultural laborers, slaves in West Africa usually retained some rights, such as the ability to marry, and their children were often free.

A small proportion of unfree West Africans were "trade slaves," sold from one kingdom to another or carried overland to the Mediterranean region, mostly by Arab traders. Thus, one of the first Portuguese in Senegambia found that the Wolof king

supports himself by raids which result in many slaves from his own as well as neighboring countries. He employs these slaves in cultivating the land allotted to him: but he also sells many to the Azanaghi [Arab] merchants in return for horses and other goods, and also to the Christians, since they have begun to trade with these blacks.

The demand for labor on sugar plantations managed by Europeans on islands in the Atlantic and then in the Americas gradually transformed the scale and nature of West African slavery. Between 1440 and 1550 Portuguese traders carried a few thousand Africans each year to sugar plantations in Madeira and the Canary Islands. Then, between 1550 and 1700, Portuguese and Dutch merchants annually transported about 10,000 Africans across the Atlantic to Brazil and the Caribbean—about a million slaves in all. Subsequently, English and French merchants took over this trade in human beings and vastly expanded it, developing slave-catching systems that extended far into the interior and that were managed by Africans. Between 1700 and 1810 European merchants carried about 7 million Africans—800,000 in the 1780s alone—to toil and die in the Americas, primarily on sugar estates in the West Indies (see Map 3.3 and Table 3.4).

The South Atlantic System

Sugar was the cornerstone of the South Atlantic system. Before 1500, Europeans had few sources of sweeteners—primarily honey and fruit juices. The cultivation of sugarcane, and later the sugar beet, changed the diet of Europe and the world. Once people had tasted sweetness, they craved it. They added sugar to tea and coffee, pies and cakes, and ate it straight in the form of candy. (By 1900 sugar accounted for 20 percent of the calories consumed by people throughout the world.)

Imitating Dutch and Portuguese planters in Brazil, English and French merchants developed sugar plantations in the West Indies, beginning in Barbados around 1650. By 1700 they were investing heavily in the Leeward Islands and Jamaica; by 1750 Jamaica had 700 large sugar plantations worked by more than 105,000 enslaved Africans.

Sugar production was complex and expensive. It required fertile land, many laborers to plant and cut the cane, and heavy equipment to process the cane into raw sugar and molasses. Because only wealthy merchants or landowners had the capital to outfit a plantation, a planter-merchant elite came to dominate the sugar industry. Successful planters earned 8 to 10 percent annually on their investment, double the rate of return on government bonds. Their enrichment led the Scottish economist Adam Smith to declare in *The Wealth of Nations* (1776) that sugar was the most profitable crop in either Europe or America.

The South Atlantic system brought wealth to the entire English economy. Most West Indian planters lived as "absentees" in England, spending their profits on elegant townhouses or vast landed estates. Moreover the Navigation Acts, by requiring that American sugar be sold to British consumers or exported to continental markets through Britain, raised the level of trade and merchants' profits; by 1750 reexports of sugar and tobacco accounted for half of all British exports. Substantial profits also came from the slave trade, for the English merchants sold slaves in the West Indies for three to five times their cost in Africa. Finally, the trade in American sugar and tobacco stimulated manufacturing. Thousands of English and Scottish men and women worked in trade-related industries: building port facilities and warehouses, refining sugar and tobacco, distilling rum from molasses (a by-product of sugar), and manufacturing textiles and iron products for the growing markets in Africa and America. Shipyards built hundred of vessels to transport slaves (and machinery and settlers) to America, and the expansion of commerce provided a supply of experienced sailors, helping to make the Royal Navy the most powerful fleet in Europe. Thanks to the South Atlantic system, England was no longer dependent for its prosperity on trade in raw wool and textiles.

Despite the benefits for England, the South Atlantic system was an economic and human tragedy for West Africa and the areas of East Africa, such as Madagascar, where slavers also preyed. Between 1550 and 1870 the Atlantic slave trade uprooted about 15 million Africans, diminishing the wealth and population of the continent and provoking unspeakable human misery. On an economic balance-sheet the value of the iron, tinware, rum, and cloth that entered the African economy in exchange for slaves was worth from one-tenth (in the 1680s) to one-third (by the 1780s) as much as the goods those slaves produced in America for sale in Europe. Thus Atlantic slavery enhanced the prosperity of Europe at the expense of Africa.

Equally important, the slave trade changed the nature of West African society by promoting centralized states and military conquest. In 1739 an English observer noted that "whenever the King of Barsally wants Goods or Brandy . . . the King goes and ransacks some of his enemies' towns, seizing the people and selling them." War and slaving became a way of life in Dahomey, where the royal house made the sale of slaves a state monopoly and used the resulting access to European guns to create a regime of military despotism. Dahomey's army, which included a contingent of 5,000

TABLE 3.4	
Slave Destinations, 1520–1810	
Destination	*Number of Africans Exported*
South America	
Brazil	3,650,000
Dutch America	500,000
West Indies	
British	1,660,000
French	1,660,000
Central America	
Spanish	1,500,000
North America	
British colonies	500,000
Europe	175,000
Total	9,645,000

women, systematically raided the African interior for captives, disrupting families and exporting thousands of slaves each year. The Asante kings also used firearms and wealth acquired through the Atlantic trade to create a bureaucratic empire of 3 million to 5 million people. Yet slaving remained a choice for Africans, not a necessity. The old and still powerful Kingdom of Benin, famous for its cast bronzes and carved ivory, resolutely opposed the slave trade, prohibiting the export of men (and most women) for over a century.

The trade in human beings changed many aspects of African life and took a huge spiritual toll. Class divisions hardened as people of noble birth sold into slavery those of lesser status. Gender relations shifted as well. Men constituted two-thirds of the slaves sent across the Atlantic, both because European planters paid more for men than for women and because African traders directed women captives into local slave markets. The resulting imbalance between the sexes encouraged some African men to take several wives, changing the nature of marriage. Most important, the Atlantic trade prompted the rise of hereditary forms of slavery in Africa, eroding the dignity of human life there as well as on the plantations of the Western Hemisphere.

Slavery and Society in the Chesapeake

In 1619 the first Africans arrived on the North American mainland (in Virginia), but for the next forty years their numbers remained small and they were not legally enslaved. English common law acknowledged varying degrees of bondage, such as indentured servitude, but not *chattel slavery*—the ownership of one human being by another. If planters wanted legalized slavery, they would have to create it. In the West Indies and South

Sugar, Tea, and Gentility
In *The Honeymoon* (c. 1765), John Collet, an English artist, depicts the trappings of
upper-class life, which now include the products of empire: tea and coffee from the
East Indies and sugar from the West Indies. By the mid-1700s many ordinary families,
both in England and the American colonies, had acquired a taste for these exotic
beverages and for sugar, the universal sweetener.
Colonial Williamsburg Foundation.

Carolina they did exactly that, following the example of
Portuguese and Dutch sugar planters and quickly
enacting statutes permitting chattel slavery.

Virginia's Decision for Slavery. A legal system of
slavery developed more slowly in the tobacco colonies
of Maryland and Virginia than in the sugar colonies.

About 400 Africans were living in the Chesapeake
colonies in 1649, making up about 2 percent of the population; by 1670 their numbers had risen to 2,500,
about 5 percent of the population. These Africans were
forced to work hard and were ill fed and ill clothed, but
so were English indentured servants who worked next
to them in the fields.

Moreover, a significant number of these first African workers received their freedom by completing a term of service or converting to Christianity. Some African Christian freemen even purchased slaves or bought the labor contracts of English servants, which suggests that religion and personal initiative were as important as race in determining social status at this time. The English in the Chesapeake had always seen Africans as "different," sometimes referring in personal letters and official documents to skin color or language but focusing primarily on religion. To the colonists, Africans were first and foremost pagans or Muslims. By becoming a Christian and a planter, an enterprising African could aspire to achieving near equality with the English settlers.

Beginning in the 1660s, for reasons that are not completely clear, legislatures in the Chesapeake colonies enacted laws that lowered the status of Africans. Perhaps the English-born elite grew insecure as the tobacco boom ended and the number of Africans increased. Whatever the cause, by 1671 the Virginia House of Burgesses had forbidden Africans to own guns or join the militia. It had also barred them—"tho baptized and enjoying their own Freedom"—from buying the labor contracts of white servants and specified that conversion to Christianity did not qualify Africans for eventual freedom. Being black was becoming a mark of inferior legal status—of permanent and hereditary slavery.

The growth of the transatlantic trade in Africans hastened this transition. Following Bacon's rebellion of 1675–1676, planters imported thousands of Africans, primarily because they were now less expensive than white indentured servants (who were in short supply) but also because slaves had few legal rights and could be disciplined more strictly. To separate the two laboring groups, a Virginia law of 1692 prohibited sexual intercourse between English and Africans. Then, in 1705, a Virginia statute formally created a racially divided society by defining virtually all resident Africans as slaves: "All servants imported or brought into this country by sea or land who were not Christians in their native country shall be accounted and be slaves."

African slavery expanded not because it was *necessary*—indeed, white families and English indentured servants could have continued to grow tobacco and could have cultivated rice and sugar as well—but because it was *profitable*. To enhance its wealth, the Chesapeake elite chose to exploit the labor of African workers and create a racially divided society. By 1700 the number of enslaved blacks in the Chesapeake had risen to 9,600, or 10 percent of the population, and by 1720 to 32,000, a full 20 percent of the inhabitants.

The New Chesapeake Social Order. The years between 1675 and 1720 witnessed significant changes among whites as well. As settlement moved inland after 1675, away from the disease-ridden and swampy lowlands, English migrants lived much longer than before and formed stable families and communities. As their longevity increased, men reassumed their customary control of family property. When death rates had been high, many husbands had named their wives as executors of their estates and legal guardians of their children, and had given their widows large inheritances. After 1700 most Chesapeake property owners named male kin as executors and guardians, and once again gave priority to male children with respect to inheritance, limiting a widow's portion to the traditional one-third share during her lifetime.

The reappearance of strict patriarchy within the family mirrored broader social developments. The planter elite now stood at the top of a social hierarchy very much like that of Europe, exercising authority over a small yeoman class, a much larger group of white tenant farmers, and a growing host of enslaved black laborers—the American equivalent of oppressed peasants and serfs. Wealthy planters used Africans to grow food as well as tobacco; build houses, wagons, and tobacco casks; and make shoes and clothes. By increasing the self-sufficiency of their plantations, the planter elite survived the depressed tobacco market between 1660 and 1720. Small-scale planters who used family labor to grow tobacco fared less well, falling deeper into debt to their creditors among the elite.

However, to prevent another rebellion like Bacon's uprising (see Chapter 2), the Virginia gentry paid attention to the concerns of middling and poor whites. They gradually reduced the annual poll tax paid by every free man from 45 pounds of tobacco in 1675 to 5 pounds in 1750. And they allowed poor yeomen and some tenants to vote. The strategy of the leading families—the Carters, Lees, Randolphs, Robinsons—was to curry favor with these voters at election time, bribing them with rum, money, and the promise of favorable legislation. In return, they expected yeomen and tenants to elect them to political office and defer to their authority. As the planter elite solidified their social authority through this "horse-trading," they used their control of the House of Burgesses to cut the political power of the royal governor—bargaining with him over patronage and land grants.

The greater solidarity among whites fostered by the elite also served to protect slavery—which had rapidly become an important institution in the Chesapeake and throughout the South—by deterring black uprisings. By 1770 in the Chesapeake, 60 percent of English families owned at least one slave; thus they had a personal stake in this exploitative labor system. By now 500,000 slaves—roughly one-third of the population—toiled in the southern mainland colonies. The South had become a "slave society" rather than, as before 1700, a society with slaves.

Even as the expansion of voting and slaveholding created new ties between rich and poor whites, wealthy Chesapeake planters set themselves apart from their less affluent neighbors in other ways. Until the 1720s the ranks of the gentry were filled with boisterous, aggressive men who enjoyed many of the amusements of common folk—from hunting, hard drinking, and gambling on horse races to sharing tales of their manly prowess in seducing female servants and slaves. As time passed, however, affluent Chesapeake planters took on the trappings of wealth, modeling themselves after the English aristocracy (see American Lives, "William Byrd II and the Maturation of the Virginia Gentry," pp. 88–89). Between 1720 and 1750 they replaced their modest wooden houses with mansions of brick and mortar, and they sent their sons to London to be educated as lawyers and gentlemen. Most of the southern men who were educated in England returned to America, married, and followed in their fathers' footsteps, managing plantations, socializing with other members of the gentry, and participating in politics.

The lives of the women in well-to-do planter families changed as well. Wealthy Chesapeake and South Carolina women sought elegance and refinement by reading English newspapers and pamphlets, importing English clothes, and dining in the English fashion with an elaborate afternoon tea. To improve their daughters' chances of finding a desirable marriage partner, they hired English tutors to teach them etiquette. Once married, affluent gentry women deferred to their husbands' authority, reared pious children, and maintained elaborate social networks—gradually creating the southern ideal of the genteel woman.

Unlike the sugar magnates of the West Indies, who lived as absentee owners in Britain, the planter-merchants of the Chesapeake were committed to life in America. Using the profits of the South Atlantic system, they and their wives formed an increasingly well-educated, refined, and stable ruling class.

The Expansion of Slavery

For the enslaved Africans at the bottom of the social scale, the South Atlantic system was an unrelieved disaster. Torn from their village homes in Africa, captives were marched in chains to coastal ports where many of them died from disease. From there they made the perilous "middle passage" to the New World in hideously overcrowded ships. There was little to eat and drink, and the stench of excrement was nearly unbearable. Some Africans jumped overboard, choosing to drown rather than endure more suffering (see Voices from Abroad, "Olaudah Equiano: The Brutal 'Middle Passage,'" p. 87). About a million (15 percent of the estimated 9.6 million who crossed the Atlantic between 1700 and 1810) died on the journey, mostly from dysentery, smallpox, or scurvy.

Olaudah Equiano
This 1780 portrait by an unknown artist shows the freed slave Olaudah Equiano. Equiano was among the first Africans to develop a consciousness of an African identity that transcended traditional ethnic and national boundaries.
Royal Albert Memorial Museum, Exeter, England.

Like Olaudah Equiano, most survivors of the middle passage ended up on sugar plantations in Brazil and the West Indies, where they faced a short and degrading life of backbreaking labor and rampant disease. Tens of thousands of Africans died in epidemics of yellow fever, smallpox, and measles; thousands more perished from inadequate food, oppressive work, and inhuman living conditions. The planting and harvesting of sugarcane required intense labor under a tropical sun, with a pace set by the overseer's whip. With sugar prices high and the cost of slaves low, many planters worked slaves to death and then imported more. Between 1708 and 1735 about 85,000 Africans were brought into Barbados, but the black population increased only from 42,000 to 46,000.

Initially, because West Indian planters purchased four men for every woman, most slaves could not marry. But women survived at a much higher rate, possibly because they were whipped less often, and gradually female slaves formed half the work force. These women bore few children, because planters forced pregnant women to work in the fields up to the time of birth, and miscarriages were frequent. In the

OLAUDAH EQUIANO
The Brutal "Middle Passage"

⸻ ★ ⸻

Olaudah Equiano, known during his life in London as Gustavus Vassa, was born in the ancient kingdom of Benin (in present-day southern Nigeria) and was kidnapped and enslaved at the age of eleven. After experiencing short periods of domestic slavery in Africa and plantation slavery in Barbados and Virginia, he was purchased by an English sea captain. After buying his freedom in 1766, Equiano lived in London, where he became an anti-slavery activist and, twenty years later, published a memoir of his life.

My father, besides many slaves, had a numerous family of which seven lived to grow up, including myself and a sister who was the only daughter. . . . I was trained up from my earliest years in the art of war, my daily exercise was shooting and throwing javelins, and my mother adorned me with emblems after the manner of our greatest warriors. One day, when all our people were gone out to their works as usual and only I and my dear sister were left to mind the house, two men and a woman got over our walls, and in a moment seized us both, and without giving us time to cry out or make resistance they stopped our mouths and ran off with us into the nearest wood. . . . At length, after many days' travelling, during which I had often changed masters, I got into the hands of a chieftain in a very pleasant country. This man had two wives and some children, and they all used me extremely well and did all they could to comfort me, particularly the first wife, who was something like my mother. Although I was a great many days' journey from my father's house, yet these people spoke exactly the same language with us. This first master of mine, as I may call him, was a smith, and my principal employment was working his bellows.

I was again sold and carried through a number of places till . . . at the end of six or seven months after I had been kidnapped I arrived at the sea coast.

The first object which saluted my eyes when I arrived on the coast was the sea, and a slave ship which was then riding at anchor and waiting for its cargo. I now saw myself deprived of all chance of returning to my native country . . . ; and I even wished for my former slavery in preference to my present situation, which was filled with horrors of every kind. . . . I was soon put down under the decks, and there I received such a salutation in my nostrils as I had never experienced in my life; so that with the loathsomeness of the stench and crying together, I became so sick and low that I was not able to eat, nor had I the least desire to taste any thing. I now wished for the last friend, death, to relieve me; but soon, to my grief, two of the white men offered me eatables, and on my refusing to eat, one of them held me fast by the hands and laid me across I think the windlass, and tied my feet while the other flogged me severely. I had never experienced anything of this kind before, and although, not being used to the water, I naturally feared that element the first time I saw it, yet nevertheless could I have got over the nettings, I would have jumped over the side, but I could not. . . . One day, when we had a smooth sea and moderate wind, two of my wearied countrymen who were chained together (I was near them at the time), preferring death to such a life of misery, somehow made it through the nettings and jumped into the sea.

At last we came in sight of the island of Barbados; the white people got some old slaves from the land to pacify us. They told us we were not to be eaten but to work, and were soon to go on land where we should see many of our country people. This report eased us much; and sure enough soon after we were landed there came to us Africans of all languages.

⸻

Source: *The Interesting Narrative of the Life of Olaudah Equiano, or Gustavus Vassa, the African, Written by Himself* (London: 1789), 15, 22–23, 28–29.

sugar colonies, the African population did not increase through reproduction until after slavery was abolished.

Conditions were less severe in Maryland and Virginia, where many slaves lived relatively long lives. In terms of labor to produce a harvest, tobacco was not as physically demanding a crop as sugar. Slaves planted the young seedlings in the spring, hoed and weeded the crop throughout the summer, and in the fall picked and hung up the leaves to cure over the

William Byrd II and the Maturation of the Virginia Gentry

———————— ★ ————————

WILLIAM BYRD II (1674–1744) aimed high. In 1692, a mere youth of eighteen, he sought a post with the Lords of Trade, the body charged with administering England's colonial empire. Nearly two decades later, when he was a member of the Virginia Council, Byrd tried again, this time seeking to become the royal governor of Virginia. In 1714 and 1722 he renewed his quest for the governorship, without success.

His father's ambition explained much of the son's activity. Himself the son of a goldsmith and a London tradesman who became a planter-merchant in Virginia, the older William Byrd had high hopes for his son. He sent him across the Atlantic at the mere age of seven to be educated as an English gentleman at the Felsted School, in the county of Essex, hoping to smooth his entry into polite society. The goal was elusive. Ostracized as a "colonial" by his status-conscious classmates, the young Byrd had his first bitter taste of the gradations of rank that suffused English society.

Nonetheless, Byrd embraced his father's vision. Living in England until he was thirty-one years old, Byrd absorbed the precepts of self-control and courtesy laid down in a well-known manual of etiquette, Richard Brathwait's *The Perfect Gentleman* (1630). He became a learned man who read Hebrew, Greek, Latin, French, and Italian, and he wrote witty poetry and prose.

All to little avail. As a young man-about-town in London, Byrd practiced the arts of a gentleman but never mastered them. As he confessed in a revealing self-portrait, "Inamorato L'Oiseaux" (the Enamored Bird, a word play on his family name), "He wou'd look like a fool, and talk like a Philosopher, when both his eyes and his Tongue shou'd have sparked with wit and waggery." The failure was partly personal: despite Byrd's attempt at gallantry, he was essentially a shy man. And it was partly cultural: the stigma of birth to a colonial family with few aristocratic connections was difficult to overcome. What-

ever the cause, Byrd failed utterly in his almost desperate efforts to obtain a rich post or a rich wife.

In 1705 the death of his father brought him back to reality—his responsibility to manage the family's estate in Virginia, a "lonely . . . silent country" where life sometimes seemed like "being buried alive." In fact, Virginia was as medically dangerous as it was culturally barren, an untamed society still beset by epidemic disease and early death. But Byrd survived his stay in the provinces, succeeding his father as the proprietor of Westover, a tobacco estate on the James River. As a merchant, slaveowning planter, and minor royal official, he commanded a handsome annual income of some 1,500 English pounds sterling. He took as a wife Lucy Parke, the daughter of the colonial-born governor of the Leeward Islands, and became a man of importance. The parish vestry awarded him "the best pew in the church"; the royal governor appointed him commander in chief of the county militia; and, the biggest prize of all, the king's ministers named him a member of the Council, the advisory body to the governor and the highest court in the colony. By 1710, at age thirty-six, Byrd had risen about as high as a Virginia-born gentleman could go.

It was not enough. Driven by his father's ambition or his own inner compulsions and dazzled by English high society, Byrd embarked on a decade-long quest for power and wealth. The result was nearly calamitous for Byrd, even as it reveals the inner dynamics of the politics and culture of his time.

Byrd's first goal was political power: the governorship of Virginia, the most prestigious post on the mainland. From his long stay in England he had aristocratic friends, including the earl of Egmont and the duke of Argyll, who had influence at the Board of Trade. But these patronage connections were frail. The duke of Marlborough, the chief minister and a great general, curtly dismissed Byrd's petition, stating that "no one but soldiers should have the government of a plantation." Marlborough needed lucrative posts for his officers, and he wanted governors with military expertise in the event of an attack from New France or New Spain. He named Sir Alexander Spotswood to govern Virginia.

Rebuffed politically, the ambitious Byrd sought wealth. In an effort to inherit the Virginia estate of his wife's deceased father, Byrd agreed in 1712 to "pay all Colonel Parke's debts," a financial miscalculation that cost him dearly. Unknown to his son-in-law, Parke had incurred debts in England of £3,000, which Byrd now had to pay. Like other eighteenth-century Virginia planters who fell into debt, Byrd found himself

William Byrd II (1674–1744)
Virginia Historical Society.

[January 26, 1719] I rose about 8 o'clock, having taken my asses' milk, and read a chapter in Hebrew and some Greek in Lucian. I said my prayers and had milk porridge for breakfast. About 10 o'clock came Annie Wilkinson and I rogered her. . . .

Once again Byrd's colonial origins defeated him: his Virginia estate of 43,000 acres and 200 African slaves failed to impress Sabina's father: "an Estate out of this Island appears to him little better than an Estate in the moon." Rejected as a suitor, Byrd vented his hostility toward Sabina in verse:

> *Let Age with double speed oretake her;*
> *Let Love the room of Pride supply;*
> *And when the Fellows all forsake her*
> *Let her gnaw the sheets & dy.*

Nursing his wounded feelings, Byrd returned to Virginia in 1719 but stayed for only eighteen months before returning to London, where he lived for another five years.

Only in 1726, at age fifty-two and driven by financial necessity, did Byrd finally renounce his quest to be an English gentleman or imperial governor. He returned to Virginia with a young wife (who brought only a small dowry and bore him four children), at last prepared emotionally to accept a lesser destiny as a member of the Virginia gentry. He built an elegant two-story brick mansion on the family's estate at Westover and led an unsuccessful effort to prevent Parliamentary approval of the Colonial Debts Act (1732), which allowed English creditors to seize American lands and slaves to pay off debts. During the 1730s Byrd exercised his literary talents, writing an unpublished "History of the Dividing Line" between Virginia and North Carolina, an ironic yet celebratory portrait of America and its people.

The personal odyssey of William Byrd II mirrored that of the Virginia gentry. They had come to America to get rich and return to England in triumph, only to discover that they were bound to Virginia by the curse of their inferior colonial status. It was a hard and bitter lesson but far from a tragic one, for they became members of a privileged slaveowning provincial elite. As Byrd reflected after his return to America, "Like one of the patriarchs, I have my flocks and my herds, my bond-men and bond-women, and every soart of trade amongst my servants, so that I live in a kind of independance on every one, but Providence."

in a position of humiliating dependence on the credit of London merchant houses.

In 1714 Byrd returned to England to deal with Parke's debts and to undermine Governor Spotswood, whose policies threatened the power of the Council and Byrd's business in the Indian trade. Two years later Lucy Parke Byrd joined him, only to succumb to smallpox: "Gracious God what pains did she take to make a voyage hither to seek a grave," Byrd lamented. In premodern England as in early Virginia, death struck arbitrarily, without regard for age or social status.

The next years were unhappy ones for Byrd, who was unable to dislodge Spotswood, pay off Parke's debts, or marry a rich woman. As he avidly (and awkwardly) pursued an heiress twenty years younger than himself with flowery letters addressed to "Sabina" from "Veramour" (True Lover), Byrd satisfied his sexual desires with a string of prostitutes, recording the encounters in "Secret Diaries" that he wrote in code during most of his adult life:

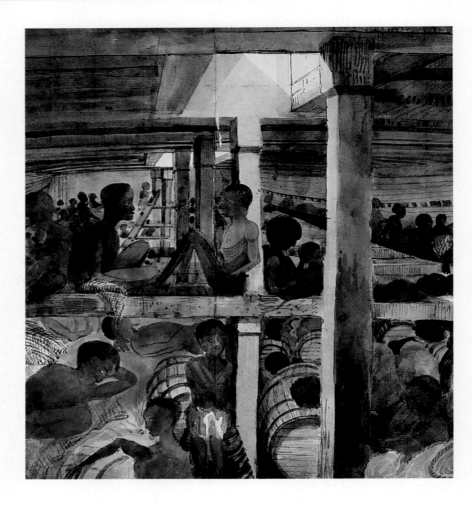

Two Views of the Middle Passage
As the slave trade boomed during the eighteenth century, ship designers packed in
more and more human cargo, treating enslaved Africans with no more respect than
hogsheads of sugar or tobacco. By contrast, a watercolor of 1846, painted by a ship's
officer on a voyage to Brazil, captures the humanity and dignity of the enslaved
Africans.
Peabody and Essex Museum; Royal Albert Memorial Museum, Exeter, England.

winter. Epidemic diseases did not spread easily
because the plantations were small and dispersed.
Also, because tobacco profits were low, planters could
not constantly buy new slaves and therefore treated
the slaves they had less harshly. Some tobacco
planters attempted to increase their work force
through reproduction, purchasing higher numbers of
female slaves and encouraging large families. In 1720
women made up about one-third of the African population of Maryland, and the black population had
begun to increase naturally. One absentee owner
instructed his plantation agent "to be kind and indul-
gent to the breeding wenches, and not to force them
when with child upon any service or hardship that will
be injurious to them." And, he added, "the children are

to be well looked after." Planters imported Africans
again when tobacco prices rose after 1720, but by mid-
century American-born slaves formed a majority
among Chesapeake blacks.

The most oppressive conditions for mainland slaves
existed in South Carolina, which was settled by land-
hungry whites from Barbados in the 1680s. The colony
grew slowly until Africans from rice-growing cultures,
who knew how to plant, harvest, and process that nutritious grain, turned rice into a profitable export crop (see
New Technology, "Rice: Riches and Wretchedness," p.
91). By 1730 merchants in Charleston were shipping
about 17 million pounds of rice a year to southern
Europe, where it was in demand; by 1775 annual rice
exports had reached 75 million pounds.

Rice: Riches and Wretchedness

★

TECHNOLOGY ALWAYS HAS cultural significance, for its use reveals the systems of value and power in a society. Occasionally, as in the case of the introduction of rice to America, the relation between culture and technology is particularly dramatic. Rice was not grown in England, but in the 1670s and 1680s the first English settlers in South Carolina tried, without success, to cultivate the exotic grain, to feed their slaves and sell as an export crop. As one planter later recalled, "The people being unacquainted with the manner of cultivating rice, many difficulties attended to the first planting and preparing it, as a vendable commodity."

Unlike northern Europeans, many West Africans had a thorough knowledge of rice. Along the semi-tropical western coast of Africa, an English traveler noted, rice "forms the chief part of the African's sustenance." As he explained, "The rice fields or *lugars* are prepared during the dry season, and the seed sown in the tornado season, requiring about four or five months to bring it to perfection." Enslaved blacks brought these skills to South Carolina. As early as 1690 an Englishman named John Steward was promoting rice production both as a potential export and as a cheap food for slaves. Africans welcomed the cultivation of a familiar food, and their knowledge was crucial to the crop's success.

English settlers were unfamiliar not only with the planting and harvesting of rice but also with its hulling. At first they tried to design a machine—a "rice mill"—that would separate the tough husk of the rice seed from the nutritious grain inside. In 1691 the government awarded Peter Jacob Guerard a two-year patent on a "Pendulum Engine, which doeth much better, and in lesser time and labour, huske rice." Machines did not prove equal to the task, so English planters turned to African technology. In 1700 a report informed the English Board of Trade that the settlers had "found out the true way of raising and husking rice" by having African women process it with a traditional mortar and pestle. The women placed the grain in large wooden mortars hollowed from the trunks of pine or cypress trees and then pounded it with long wooden pestles, eas-

Rice Hulling in Georgia
In this early twentieth-century photograph, the descendants of enslaved women use African technology to hull rice in Georgia.
Georgia Department of Archives and History, Atlanta.

ily removing the husks and whitening the grains. Their labor was prodigious. By the 1770s slaves were annually processing 75 million tons of rice for export and millions more for their own consumption.

African labor and technology brought both wealth and wretchedness to South Carolina. The planter-merchant aristocracy that controlled the rice industry became immensely wealthy; nine of the ten richest Americans who died around 1770 had grown rich as rice planters in South Carolina. The tens of thousands of enslaved Africans who actually labored on the plantations lived hard and short lives; many died of disease, and until the late eighteenth century, those slaves who survived had little to show—in material comforts or a stable family life—for their years of labor.

The technology for producing rice was simple and cheap, and it was used in many parts of the world to support egalitarian communities of independent farm families. But in America it became part of a slave-based plantation society with immense racial and economic divisions.

FIGURE 3.1
The Growth of Slavery in South Carolina
To grow more rice, white planters imported thousands of African slaves, giving South Carolina a black majority and prompting the development of an African-influenced language and culture.

To expand production of their lucrative crop, white planters and merchants imported tens of thousands of Africans (Figure 3.1). As early as the 1710s Africans made up a majority of the population of South Carolina and about 80 percent of those living in the rice-growing lowlands, but most met an early death. Mosquito-borne epidemic diseases flourished in the hot and swampy lowlands of coastal Carolina and took the lives of thousands of slaves. Overwork caused many other Africans to perish, for moving tons of dirt to construct irrigation works was brutally hard labor. As in the West Indies, there were many deaths and few births.

African American Community and Resistance

Slaves came from many regions of West Africa. South Carolina slaveowners preferred laborers from the Gold Coast and Gambia, but because the slave trade shifted to the south after 1730, they got more than 30 percent of their work force from Angola. As a result of such changes in the slave trade, there were no American colonies in which any African people or language group become dominant (Table 3.5). Moreover, many white planters consciously enhanced this cultural diversity to prevent slave revolts. "The safety of the Plantations," declared a widely read English pamphlet, "depends upon having Negroes from all parts of Guiny, who do not understand each other's languages and Customs and cannot agree to Rebel."

The Emergence of an African American Culture. In fact, slaves initially did not regard each other as "Africans" or "blacks" but as members of a specific people: for example, Mende, Hausa, Ibo, Yoruba. Gradually, however, enslaved peoples found it in their interest to transcend these cultural barriers. In the West Indies and also in the lowlands of South Carolina, the largely African-born population created new languages that combined English and African words in an African grammatical structure. Thus, South Carolina blacks created the Gullah dialect. In the Chesapeake, where there were more American-born blacks and a

TABLE 3.5

African Slaves Imported into North America, by Ethnicity, 1700–1775

African Region of Departure	Ethnicity	Number	Percent
Senegambia	Mandinka, Fulbe, Serer, Jola, Wolof, and Bambara	47,300	17
Sierra Leone	Vai, Mende, Kpelle, and Kru	33,400	12
Gold Coast	Ashanti and Fanit	19,500	7
Bight of Benin, Bight of Biafra	Ibo and Ibibio	47,300	17
West-Central	Kongo, Tio, and Matamba	44,600	16
Southeast Africa	Unknown	2,800	1
Other or Unknown		83,500	30
Total		278,400	100

The numbers are estimated from known voyages involving 195,000 Africans. Ethnic origins should be considered as very tentative because slaves from many regions left from the same port and because the ethnic and regional origins of 83,500 slaves (30 percent) are not known.
Source: Aaron S. Fogleman, "From Slaves, Convicts, and Servants to Free Passengers: The Transformation of Immigration in the Era of the American Revolution," *Journal of American History* 85 (June 1998), Table A4.

African Culture in South Carolina
The dance and the musical instruments are of Yoruba origin, the contribution of
Africans from the Niger River–Gold Coast region—a Yoruba-dominated area that
accounted for one-sixth of the slaves imported into South Carolina.
Colonial Williamsburg Foundation.

less concentrated slave population, many Africans gradually gave up their native tongues for English. A European visitor in the mid-eighteenth century reported with surprise that "all the blacks spoke very good English."

The acquisition of a common language, whether Gullah or English, was a prerequisite for the creation of an African American community. A more equal sex ratio, which would encourage stable families, was another. In South Carolina a high death rate undermined ties of family and kinship, but after 1725, blacks in the Chesapeake colonies created strong nuclear families and extended kin relationships. These "African Americans" gradually developed a culture of their own, passing on family names, traditions, and knowledge to the next generation.

As enslaved blacks forged an identity in an alien land, their lives continued to be shaped by their African past. This heritage took tangible form in wood carvings inspired by African motifs, the giant wooden mortars and pestles that slaves used to hull rice, and the design of shacks, which often had rooms arranged from front to back in a distinctive "I" pattern (not side by side, as was common in English houses). Traditional African values also persisted, as

some slaves retained Muslim religious beliefs and many more relied on the spiritual powers of conjurers, who knew the ways of African gods. Other slaves adopted Protestant Christianity but reshaped its doctrines, ethics, and rituals to fit their own needs and create a spiritually rich and long-lasting religious culture of their own.

Yet there were drastic limits on African American creativity because slaves were denied education and accumulated few material goods. A well-traveled European who visited a slave hut in Virginia in the late eighteenth century found it to be "more miserable than the most miserable of the cottages of our peasants. The husband and wife sleep on a mean pallet, the children on the ground; a very bad fireplace, some utensils for cooking. . . . They work all week, not having a single day for themselves except for holidays."

The comparison between slaves and peasants was apt. Both African American slaves and European peasants were peoples who, because of their poverty and dependence, had only limited ways in which to express their identity. Consequently, their primary legacies were not great works of art or literature but distinctive cultures based on language, family, community, and religion.

Slave Dwellings at Mulberry Plantation
Most pictures of plantations depict the imposing mansions of the slaveowners. However, this view of Mulberry plantation in South Carolina steals a look behind the big house to the meager dwellings of the slaves, whose labor produced the wealth of the plantation.
The Gibbes Museum of Art, Carolina Art Association.

Oppression and Resistance. Slaves resisted the rigorous work routine at their peril. To punish slaves who disobeyed, refused to work, or ran away, planters resorted to the lash and the amputation of fingers, toes, and ears (see American Voices, "Philip Fithian: Sadism under Slavery," p. 95). For example, declaring the chronic runaway Ballazore an "incorrigeble rogue," Robert "King" Carter of Virginia ordered all his toes cut off: "nothing less than dismembering will reclaim him." Thomas Jefferson, who witnessed such cruelty on his father's plantation in mid-eighteenth-century Virginia, noted that each generation of whites was "nursed, educated, and daily exercised in tyranny," for the relationship "between master and slave is a perpetual exercise of the most unremitting despotism on the one part, and degrading submission on the other." Nonetheless, Jefferson owned slaves throughout his life (and probably was the biological father of several of them).

The extent of violence by whites was related to the size and density of the slave population. English planters in the predominantly African West Indies routinely branded troublesome slaves with hot irons. In South Carolina, where whites in the lowlands were outnumbered 8 to 1, they maintained authority by imposing strict rules. Black workers were forbidden to leave the plantation without special passes, and rural patrols enforced those regulations.

Slaves dealt with their plight in a variety of ways. Some newly arrived Africans fled to the frontier, where they tried to establish African villages or, more often, married into Indian tribes. Blacks familiar with white ways, especially those fluent in English, fled to towns, where they tried to pass as free blacks. But the great majority of African Americans worked out their destinies as enslaved laborers on rural plantations. Some bargained with their owners, agreeing to do extra work in return for better food and clothes. Others resisted by working slowly or stealing. Still others attacked their owners or overseers even though this was punishable by mutilation or death. A successful rebellion was essentially impossible because whites were armed and, outside of coastal South Carolina, more numerous than Africans.

PHILIP FITHIAN
Sadism under Slavery

———————★———————

Planters relied on various incentives to get work from their African slaves. A few used rewards, providing cooperative laborers with food, leisure, and relatively good treatment. But many more planters wanted to maximize their profits and relied on force, extracting work by whipping recalcitrant laborers. Some brutal owners and overseers were so determined to demonstrate their power that they went much further, as described by Philip Fithian, a young Princeton college graduate who was employed as a tutor by Robert Carter III, one of the wealthiest Virginia planters.

[1773] This Evening, after I had dismissed the Children, & was sitting in the School-Room cracking Nuts, [I asked] . . . Mr. Carters Clerk, a civil, inoffensive agreeable young Man . . . what their [the slaves' food] allowance is? He told me that, excepting some favourites around the table their weekly allowance is a peck of Corn, & a pound of Meat a Head!—And Mr. Carter is allowed by all . . . [to be] by far the most humane to his Slaves of any in these parts! Good God! are these Christians?

While I am on the Subject, I will relate further, what I heard George Lee's Overseer, one Morgan, say the other day that he himself had often done to Negroes, and found it useful. He said that whipping of any kind does them no good, for they will laugh at your greatest Severity; But he told us he had invented two things, and by several experiments had proved their success.

For Sullenness, Obstinacy, or Idleness, says he, Take a Negro, strip him, tie him fast to a post; take then a sharp Curry-Comb, and curry him severely till he is well scrap'd; and call a Boy with some dry Hay, and make the Boy rub him down for several Minutes, then salt him, & unlose him. He will attend to his Business (said the inhuman Infidel) afterwards!

But savage Cruelty does not exceed His next diabolical Invention—To get a Secret from a Negro, says he, take the following Method—Lay upon your Floor a large thick plank, having a peg about eighteen inches long, of hard wood, & very Sharp, on the upper end, fixed fast in the plank—then strip the Negro, tie the Cord to a staple in the Ceiling, [and suspend the Negro from that cord] so that his foot may just rest on the sharpened Peg then turn him briskly around, and you would laugh (said our informer) at the Dexterity of the Negro, while he was relieving his Feet on the sharpen'd Peg!

I need say nothing of these seeing there is a righteous God, who will take vengeance on such Inventions.

———

Source: Philip Vickers Fithian, *Journals and Letters, 1773–1774*, Hunter Dulsingon Farish, ed. (Williamsburg, VA: Colonial Williamsburg Press, 1943), 50–51.

Predictably, South Carolina became the setting for the largest slave uprising of the eighteenth century—the Stono rebellion. The governor of Spanish Florida instigated the revolt in the late 1730s by promising freedom and land to slaves who would run away from their English owners. By February 1739 at least sixty-nine slaves had reportedly escaped to St. Augustine, and rumors circulated among whites in neighboring Georgia "that a Conspiracy was formed by Negroes in Carolina to rise and make their way out of the province." When war between England and Spain broke out later that year, seventy-five Africans—some of them Portuguese-speaking Christians from the African Kingdom of Kongo—killed a number of whites near the Stono River, stole guns and ammunition, and marched south toward Florida, a white observer reported, "with Colours displayed and two Drums beating." Unrest swept through the countryside, but the white militia killed many of the Stono rebels and dispersed the rest, preventing a general uprising. Thereafter, frightened whites imported fewer new slaves and tightened plantation discipline. For Africans the price of active resistance was high.

The Northern Maritime Economy

The South Atlantic system extended far beyond the staple-producing colonies in the South and the West Indies to include farmers and merchants in the northern mainland colonies. As early as the 1640s, New England farmers provided bread, lumber, fish, and meat to the sugar islands. As a West Indian explained, planters in the islands "had rather buy food at very dear rates than produce it by labour, so infinite is the profit of sugar works." By 1700 the economies of the West Indies and New England were closely interwoven. After 1720 farmers and merchants in New York, New Jersey, and Pennsylvania entered the West Indian trade, shipping wheat, corn, and bread to the islands.

The South Atlantic system tied the British Empire together economically. In return for sugar exports to England, West Indian planters received *bills of exchange* (credit slips) from merchant houses in London. The planters used those bills to buy slaves from Africa and also to reimburse American farmers and merchants for their provisions and shipping services. Farmers and merchants then exchanged the bills for British manufactures, primarily textiles and iron goods, thereby completing the cycle.

Urban Development.   The West Indian trade created the first American merchant fortunes and the first urban industries. Traders in Boston, Philadelphia, and New York built fine townhouses and invested the rest of their profits in new ships and factories. In Boston, Newport, and Providence, they set up factories that refined raw sugar into large (3 pound) loaves of granulated sugar (which previously had been imported from England) and distilled West Indian molasses into rum. By the 1740s Boston distillers were exporting more than half a million gallons of rum annually. In addition, merchants in smaller ports, such as Salem and Marblehead, established a major fishing industry, providing mackerel and cod to feed the slaves of the sugar islands and to export to southern Europe. Merchants farther to the south transformed Baltimore into an important port by developing a bustling trade in wheat, while Charleston traders exported deerskins, indigo, and rice to European markets (Map 3.4).

The expansion of commerce in the eighteenth century fueled rapid growth in American port cities and coastal towns. By 1750 Newport, Rhode Island, and Charleston, South Carolina, had nearly 10,000 resi-

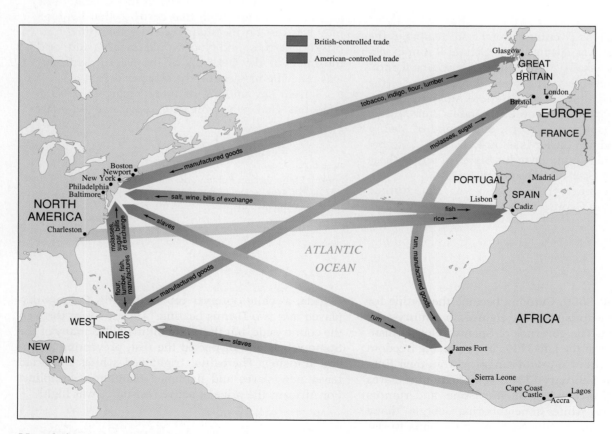

MAP 3.4
The Rise of the American Merchant, c. 1750
In accordance with mercantilist doctrine, British merchants controlled most of the transatlantic trade in manufactures, sugar, tobacco, and slaves. However, merchants in Boston, New York, and Philadelphia seized control of the West Indian trade, while traders in Newport imported slaves from Africa, and merchants in Boston and Charleston shipped fish and rice to southern Europe.

A View of Philadelphia in 1720
By 1720 Philadelphia was well on its way toward becoming the largest and wealthiest
seaport in North America, the home of scores of prosperous Anglican and Quaker mer-
chants; a multitude of English, German, and Scots-Irish artisans; and thousands of
English seamen, German indentured servants, and African American slaves.
Library Company of Philadelphia.

dents apiece, Boston had 15,000, and New York had
almost 18,000. The largest port was Philadelphia,
whose population reached 30,000 by 1776, the size of a
large European provincial city, such as Bristol or Bor-
deaux. Smaller coastal towns were centers of the shipbuilding and lumber industries. By the 1740s seventy
sawmills dotted the Piscataqua River in New Hampshire, providing low-cost wood for homes, warehouses,
and especially shipbuilding. Taking advantage of the
Navigation Acts, which allowed colonists to build and
own trading vessels, scores of shipwrights turned out
oceangoing ships, while hundreds of other artisans
made ropes, sails, and metal fittings for the new fleet.
Shipyards in Boston and Philadelphia launched about
15,000 tons of oceangoing vessels annually; eventually
colonial-built ships made up about one-third of the
entire British merchant fleet.

The impact of the South Atlantic system extended
into the interior of North America. A small fleet of trading vessels sailed back and forth between Philadelphia
and the villages along the Delaware Bay, exchanging
cargoes of European goods for barrels of flour and
wheat. Land-based trading networks also expanded. In
the 1750s hundreds of professional wagon-drivers in
Maryland carried to market some 370,000 bushels of
wheat and corn and 16,000 barrels of flour annually—
over 10,000 wagon trips. To service this traffic, entrepreneurs and artisans set up taverns, horse stables, and
barrel-making shops in small towns along the wagon
roads, thereby providing additional jobs. In the prosperous interior town of Lancaster, Pennsylvania, there
were more than 200 artisans, both German and English. The South Atlantic system thus provided not only

markets for farmers (by far the largest group of northern residents) but also opportunities for merchants,
artisans, and workers in country towns and seaport
cities.

Seaport Society.　　Seaport society was dominated by
the prosperous merchants who maintained the South
Atlantic system (Figure 3.2). By 1750 about forty merchants controlled over 50 percent of Philadelphia's
trade and had taxable assets averaging £10,000, a
huge sum at the time. Like the Chesapeake gentry,
urban merchants imitated the British upper classes,
using architectural designs from England to build
large brick mansions to showcase their wealth. Their
wives created a genteel culture, decorating their
houses with fine furniture and entertaining guests at
elegant dinners.

Artisan and shopkeeper families formed the middle
ranks of seaport society and numbered nearly half the
population. Some artisans aspired to wealth and status,
an entrepreneurial ethic that prompted them to hire
apprentices and expand production. But most craft
workers—innkeepers, butchers, seamstresses, shoemakers, weavers, bakers, carpenters, masons, and
dozens of other specialists—had more modest goals.
They worked to gain a *competency*—an income sufficient to maintain their families in modest comfort and
dignity. Wives and husbands often worked as a team,
teaching what artisans called the "mysteries of the
craft" to their children. To alleviate the distress caused
by unemployment, sickness, and death, they formed
mutual self-help societies with other members of their
craft. These efforts enabled some artisans to buy

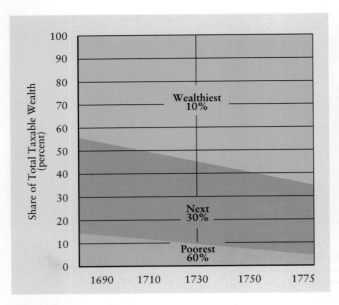

FIGURE 3.2
Wealth Inequality in the Northern Cities
As commerce expanded, the wealth of merchants grew much more rapidly than did that of artisans and laborers. By the 1770s the poorest 60 percent of the taxable inhabitants of Boston, New York, and Philadelphia owned less than 5 percent of the taxable wealth, whereas the top 10 percent—the merchant elite and its allies—controlled 65 percent.

houses and shops (sometimes run by widows continuing a family business), but most craft workers were not well-to-do. These middling people had taxable assets averaging about £300, a fraction of that owned by merchants. Many artisans were quite poor; a tailor was lucky to accumulate £30 worth of property in his lifetime—some tools and clothes, a few pots and pans, assorted pieces of bedding, and not much more.

Laboring men and women formed the lower ranks of urban society. The merchants of Boston, Philadelphia, and New York needed hundreds of dockworkers to unload manufactured goods and molasses from inbound ships, and reload the ships with barrels of wheat, fish, and rice for export. They often filled these demanding jobs with black slaves and white indentured servants, or they hired unskilled men who worked for daily wages. Merchants also gave work to hundreds of seamen, who manned the vessels that carried trade to and from the West Indies.

Indispensable to the economy yet without homes of their own, these bound laborers, wage earners, and merchant seamen lived in crowded tenements in back alleys. In good times, hard work brought enough money to drink cheap New England rum in waterfront taverns and to support their families. Poor women eked out a

living for themselves or helped provide for their families by washing clothes, spinning wool, or working as servants or prostitutes. To make ends meet, most laboring families sent their children out to work at an early age.

Periods of stagnant commerce affected all members of seaport society, threatening merchants with bankruptcy and artisans with irregular work. For laborers and seamen, whose household budgets left no margin for sickness or unemployment, depressed trade meant hunger, dependence on charity handed out by town-appointed overseers of the poor, and—for the most desperate—a life of petty thievery. Involvement in the South Atlantic system between 1660 and 1750 brought economic uncertainty as well as jobs and opportunities to northern workers and farmers.

The New Politics of Empire, 1714–1750

The triumph of trade changed the politics of empire. British ministers, pleased with the prosperous commerce in staple crops, were content to rule the colonies with a gentle hand. Two generations later the British political philosopher Edmund Burke would praise this strategy as "salutary [healthy] neglect." But by allowing the colonists a significant degree of self-government and economic autonomy, British authorities put them in a position to challenge the rules of the mercantilist system.

The Rise of the Assembly

Before 1689 political affairs in most colonies were dominated by royal governors or authoritarian elites. The duke of York ran New York without a representative assembly, Puritan magistrates suppressed dissent in New England, and Governor Berkeley and his Green Spring faction ruled Virginia with an iron hand. The strict control of society by leading men reflected the traditional view that "Authority should Descend from *Kings* and *Fathers* to *Sons* and *Servants*," as a royalist political philosopher put it. Governors and powerful political leaders denounced critics of their policies as traitors, and condemned opposition groups as illegitimate "factions."

In the Glorious Revolution of 1688 in England, the political faction known as the Whigs challenged this authoritarian outlook. They advocated a constitutional monarchy, a "mixed government" that divided power among the three traditional social orders, or ranks: the monarchy, the aristocracy, and the commoners. The Whigs did not advocate democracy, which they condemned as a dangerous "levelling" doctrine, but they championed the interests of non-noble property owners, especially with respect to the levying of taxes. When Whig politicians forced William and Mary to accept a Declaration of Rights in 1689, they strengthened the powers of the House of Commons, the elected branch of Parliament, at the expense of the Crown.

Having survived James II's attempt to abolish them, the American representative assemblies also wished to limit the powers of the Crown and the royal governors. They copied the Whigs by establishing the same committees as existed in the House of Commons and insisting on their authority over taxes—refusing to fund military projects and other programs advocated by royal governors. Gradually the legislatures won partial control of patronage and the budget, angering imperial bureaucrats and English proprietors. In Massachusetts during the 1720s the assembly refused repeatedly to obey the king's instructions to provide a permanent salary for the royal governor; subsequently legislatures in North Carolina, New Jersey, and Pennsylvania declined to pay their governors any salary for several years. "The people in power in America," complained the proprietor William Penn during a struggle with the Pennsylvania assembly, "think nothing taller than themselves but the Trees."

The rising power of the colonial assemblies created an elitist rather than a democratic political system. Although most property-owning whites had the right to vote after 1700, only men of considerable wealth and status stood for election (Figure 3.3). For example, in the 1750s in Virginia seven members of the influential Lee family sat in the House of Burgesses and, along with members of other powerful families, dominated its main committees. In New England descendants of the original Puritans intermarried and formed dynasties of political leaders in dozens of communities. "Go into every village in New England," the future Patriot leader John Adams declared in 1765, "and you will find that the office of justice of the peace, and even the place of representative, have generally descended from generation to generation, in three or four families at most."

Neither elitist assemblies nor wealthy property owners could impose unpopular edicts on the people. The crowd actions that had sparked the Glorious Revolution in England in 1688 and overthrown the colonial Dominion of New England in 1689 were a regular part of political life and were particularly powerful in America, where there were few sheriffs or other police officials. Indeed, the colonists often used disciplined crowd actions rather than legal means to enforce community values: in New York, mobs closed houses of prostitution; in Salem, Massachusetts, crowds ran people with

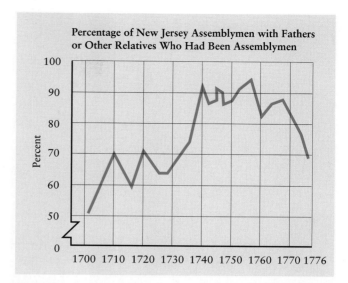

FIGURE 3.3
Family Connections and Political Power
By the 1750s nearly every member of the New Jersey assembly came from a family with a history of political leadership. This is clear testimony to the emergence of an experienced governing elite in the colonies.

infectious diseases out of town; in Boston, crowds prevented merchants from exporting grain during a time of shortage; and in New Jersey during the 1730s and 1740s, angry mobs obstructed proprietors who were trying to oust tenants from disputed lands.

Astute officials generally outmaneuvered angry crowds by waiting for their passion to subside. Likewise, entrepreneurs and land speculators often imposed their will on protestors because they had money and, usually, the law on their side. But mobs were always forces to be reckoned with. When officials in Boston tried to restrict the sale of farm produce to a designated public marketplace, a crowd destroyed the building and defied the authorities to arrest them. "If you touch One you shall touch All," an anonymous letter warned the sheriff, "and we will show you a Hundred Men where you can show one."

Such expressions of popular opinion—in the give-and-take of New England town meetings, in the rum-warmed conviviality of Virginia electioneering, in the political contests between ambitious men in Pennsylvania and New Jersey—gradually undermined the dominant position of the ruling hierarchy. As a royal governor remarked, "the ordinary sort of planters, [who] have land of their own, though not much, look upon themselves to be as good as the best of them." By 1750 most of the colonies had developed political institutions—town and county governments and colony-

Sir Robert Walpole, the King's Minister
All eyes are on Walpole (left) as he offers advice to the
Speaker of the House of Commons. A brilliant tactical politi-
cian, Walpole used patronage to command a majority in the
Commons and to win the support of George I and George II—
the German-speaking monarchs from the duchy of Hanover.
Walpole's personal motto, "Let sleeping dogs lie," helps to
explain his colonial policy of salutary neglect.
© National Trust Photographic Library/John Hammond.

wide assemblies—that were broadly responsive to
popular pressure and increasingly immune to British
control.

Salutary Neglect

British colonial policy during the reigns of George I
(r. 1714–1727) and George II (r. 1727–1760) contributed
significantly to the rise of American self-government.
Royal bureaucrats focused their attention on trade and
defense, relaxing their supervision of internal colonial
affairs.

This policy of "salutary," or healthy, neglect was a
by-product of the political system developed by Sir
Robert Walpole, leader of the Whigs in the House of
Commons between 1720 and 1742 and also the king's
chief minister. By strategically dispensing appointments, pensions, and gifts, Walpole won parliamentary

support for his policies and transformed the antagonistic relationship between king and Parliament into one
of cooperation. But Walpole's tactics offended some
members of Parliament. His chief opponents, who
called themselves Real (or Radical) Whigs, argued that
by using patronage and bribery to create a strong *Court*
(or *Crown*) *party*, Walpole had betrayed the constitutional monarchy established by the Glorious Revolution. Other critics, organized in a loose *Country party* of
landed gentlemen, warned that high taxes, a bloated
royal bureaucracy, and a peacetime army threatened
the liberties of the people.

The arguments of the Radical Whigs and the Country party appealed to Americans who wanted to
enhance the power of the provincial assemblies. In
their eyes the royal governors in America still had too
much arbitrary power; they could veto legislation and
use land grants and political appointment to influence
voting in the assemblies. "By increasing the number of
officers dependent on the Crown," a writer in the
Boston *Weekly Newsletter* charged, the royal governor
sought to destroy "the liberties of the people." Such
rhetoric was excessive. Few governors could actually
wield despotic power, but the accusation nevertheless
stirred public anxiety.

Even as Walpole's political tactics were alarming the
colonists, his patronage policies were undermining the
royal bureaucracy in America. His ministers filled colonial posts with mediocre officials who had good political connections and whose main goal was not to
advance imperial policies but to enrich themselves. In
New York, for example, William Cosby became governor during the 1730s primarily because his wife was
related to Lord Halifax, an influential English aristocrat.
Cosby was hungry for money, and his salary demands
and selling of offices threw the province into political
chaos for a decade. His successor, George Clinton,
appointed through a family connection with the duke of
Newcastle, Walpole's chief political manager, lacked the
will or political insight to uphold imperial interests (see
American Voices, "Governor George Clinton: The Waning of British Authority," p. 101). In 1744, for example,
Clinton cautioned his superiors against imposing a
stamp tax, warning that "the people in North America
are quite strangers to any Duty but such as they raise
themselves."

Walpole's patronage policies also weakened the
imperial system by filling the Board of Trade with men
of little talent. These "placemen" did little and undermined the morale of more capable imperial officials.
When Governor Gabriel Johnson went to North Carolina in the 1730s, determined to "make a mighty
change in the face of affairs" by curbing the assembly,
he was soon discouraged by the lack of support from
other British officials. Forsaking reform, he decided "to

GOVERNOR GEORGE CLINTON
The Waning of British Authority

———★———

Authority has to be exercised firmly if it is to command respect. During the era of "salutary neglect," lax administration in London and weak officials in America opened the way for colonial assemblies to defy imperial policy. In a letter to the Lords of Trade written in 1742, Governor Clinton describes how the New York assembly has seized power over the appointment of military officers. But the governor, who had received his appointment because of family ties in England, was unwilling to do battle with the New York assembly—which might refuse to approve his own salary. So he meekly—and unsuccessfully—requests the assistance of the home government.

My Lords,

I have in my former letters inform'd Your Lordships what Incroachments the Assemblys of this province have from time to time made on His Majesty's Prerogative & Authority in this Province in drawing an absolute dependence of all the Officers upon them for their Saleries & Reward of their services, & by their taking in effect the Nomination to all Officers. . . .

1stly, That the Assembly refuse to admit of any amendment to any money bill, in any part of the Bill; so that the Bill must pass as it comes from the Assembly, or all the Supplies granted for the support of Government, & the most urgent services must be lost.

2ndly, It appears that they take the Payment of the [military] Forces, passing of Muster Rolls into their own hands by naming the Commissaries for those purposes in the Act.

3rdly, They by granting the Saleries to the Officers personally by name & not to the Officer for the time being, intimate that if any person be appointed to any Office his Salery must depend upon their approbation of the Appointment. . . .

I must now refer it to Your Lordships' consideration whether it be not high time to put a stop to these usurpations of the Assembly on His Majesty's Authority in this Province and for that purpose may it not be proper that His Majesty signify his Disallowance of the Act at least for the payment of Saleries.

———

Source: E. B. O'Callaghan, ed., *Documents Relative to the Colonial History of the State of New York* (Albany: Weed, Parsons and Company, printers, 1853–1887), IX, 84.

---

do nothing which can be reasonably blamed, and leave the rest to time, and a new set of inhabitants."

Salutary neglect did not "cause" Americans to seek independence; in fact, in the short run, mild rule under Walpole strengthened the colonists' allegiance to Britain (as did the increasing popularity of British goods and culture). But over the long run the chief minister's policies weakened imperial rule in America. In the first place, his support for a merchant-run empire based on trade inhibited strong rule over the American colonies and allowed the "rise of the assembly." Second, Walpole's corrupt domestic policies persuaded American Radical Whigs that British rule posed a threat to their political liberties, thereby reducing their respect for royal governors. Finally—and most directly—his patronage system undermined the royal bureaucracy in America. Ultimately, the legislative and administrative autonomy allowed by salutary neglect encouraged Americans to expect a position of political equality within the empire and eventually to rise up to claim it.

Consolidating the Mercantilist System

During the years of salutary neglect the main preoccupation of Walpole and other ministers was the protection of Britain's commercial interests. To safeguard the profits of British planters and merchants, they subsidized the colony of Georgia, went to war against Spain, and supported new mercantilist controls on the mainland colonies.

Georgia and War with Spain. In the early 1730s General James Oglethorpe and a group of social reformers influenced by the Enlightenment (see Chapter 4) successfully petitioned King George II for land south of the Carolinas. They named the new colony Georgia in honor of the king and planned it as a refuge for Britain's poor. Envisioning a society of small farms worked by independent landowners and white indentured servants, the trustees of Georgia limited most land grants to 500 acres and outlawed slavery. Walpole arranged for Parliament to subsidize Georgia because he wanted it as a buffer between the valuable rice colony of South Carolina and Spanish Florida.

Spain had long resented the British presence in Carolina, which it had claimed since the 1540s, and was outraged by the expansion into Georgia, where Spanish Franciscans operated Indian missions. Moreover, Spanish officials were alarmed by the activities of English merchants, who had illegally expanded their trade in slaves and manufactured goods to New Spain. To deter further British imperialism and expansion into Georgia, in 1739 the Spanish governor of Florida incited a slave uprising in South Carolina, and Spanish naval forces stepped up their patrols against smugglers in the Caribbean, prompting sporadic naval combat.

Bristol Docks and Quay

The triangular trade with Africa, the West Indies, and the mainland colonies made Bristol, in southwest England, a bustling and prosperous seaport. In this detail from an eighteenth-century painting, horses draw large hogsheads of West Indian sugar to local factories, and workers prepare smaller barrels of rum for export to Africa.

City of Bristol Museum and Art Gallery/Bridgeman Art Library.

Under pressure in Parliament for an aggressive anti-Spanish policy, Walpole reacted strongly when Spanish naval forces mutilated an English smuggler. In 1740 he instructed General Oglethorpe, now the governor of Georgia, to attack Spanish Florida. Assembling an army of British regulars, provincial troops from South Carolina and Georgia, and some Indian allies, Oglethorpe launched an unsuccessful expedition against St. Augustine, which was defended by Spanish soldiers and escaped African slaves. Later that year another expedition against the Spanish seaport of Cartagena (in present-day Colombia) also failed. For the next eight years the British Navy clashed repeatedly in the West Indies with the navies of Spain and its ally France, but neither side scored a decisive victory on sea or land. By the end of the war in 1748, Britain had guaranteed the security of Georgia and access of its merchants to the markets of New Spain.

The Politics of Mercantilism. An unexpected threat to Britain's economic ascendancy in the Western Hemisphere was competition from its American colonies. According to the mercantilist Navigation Acts, the colonies were expected to produce agricultural goods and other raw materials that British merchants would carry to England and Scotland, where they would be consumed or turned into manufactured goods. To enforce the monopoly enjoyed by British manufacturers, Parliament passed a series of acts that prohibited Americans from selling colonial-made textiles (1699), hats (1732), and iron products such as plows, axes, and skillets (1750).

However, the Navigation Acts had a loophole because they allowed Americans to own ships and transport goods. Colonial merchants exploited those provisions, securing 95 percent of the commerce between the mainland and the West Indies and 75 percent of the trade in manufactures shipped from London and Bristol to the mainland colonies. Quite unintentionally, British mercantilism had created a dynamic and wealthy community of colonial merchants.

The flour, fish, and meat produced by the rapidly growing mainland colonies raised another set of problems for the British authorities. By the 1720s the British sugar islands could not absorb all the goods available for export, so enterprising colonial merchants sold them in the French West Indies. These inexpensive supplies of food helped French planters produce low-cost sugar and seize control of the competitive European sugar market. When American rum distillers began to buy cheap molasses from the French West Indies rather than molasses from the British islands in the Caribbean, planters petitioned Parliament for help.

Parliament responded by enacting the Molasses Act of 1733, which permitted the mainland colonies to export fish and farm products to the French islands but—to enhance the competitiveness of British molasses—placed a high tariff on imports of French molasses. American merchants and public officials protested that the act would cut farm exports and cripple their distilling industry, making it more difficult for colonists to purchase British goods. When Parliament ignored their petitions, American merchants turned to smuggling, importing French molasses and bribing customs officials to ignore the new tax. Luckily for the Americans, in the mid-1730s the demand for sugar surged, raising sugar prices and restoring prosperity to the British West Indies. In these circumstances, British customs officials chose not to enforce the Molasses Act.

The lack of adequate currency in the colonies led to another confrontation between the home government and the settlers. American merchants sent most of the gold and silver coins and the bills of exchange they earned in the West Indian trade to Britain to pay for manufactured goods, draining the domestic money supply. To provide currency and thereby encourage domestic trade, the assemblies of ten mainland colonies established banks that lent paper money to farmers, taking their land as collateral (hence the term *land banks*). Farmers used the paper money to buy tools or livestock or to pay their creditors, thereby stimulating trade. But some assemblies, such as that of Rhode Island, issued large amounts of currency, causing it to fall in value. Eventually a Rhode Island bill with a face value of £10 would buy only £5 worth of goods. Moreover, the legislature required merchants to accept this depreciated money at its face value. Creditors, especially English merchants, complained that they were being forced to accept worthless currency.

Because Rhode Island was a small colony and did not have a royal governor, British officials tolerated this fiscal abuse. But when Massachusetts tried to issue paper currency in 1740, the British government intervened, strongly supporting Governor Belcher's veto of the proposed legislation. Then, in 1751, Parliament passed a broad Currency Act that prevented all the New England colonies from establishing new land banks and, with Rhode Island in mind, prohibited the use of public bills of credit as legal tender for the payment of private debts. Many British merchants thought such decisive action was long overdue.

These economic conflicts and the growing power of the colonial assemblies angered a new generation of British political leaders, who believed that the Americans had too much autonomy. In 1749 Charles Townshend of the Board of Trade charged that the American assemblies had assumed many of the "ancient and established prerogatives wisely preserved in the Crown." Townshend and other officials were determined to replace salutary neglect with a more rigorous system of imperial control.

Summary

★

When Charles II ascended to the English throne in 1660, he paid his political and personal debts by giving away millions of acres of land in America. He granted the Carolina colony to a group of aristocratic proprietors; gave New York, which England had conquered from the Dutch in 1664, to his brother James, duke of York; and bestowed Pennsylvania on William Penn. However, Charles also pursued mercantilist goals, securing the enactment of Navigation Acts that regulated colonial exports and imports. In 1685 his successor, James II, tried to impose tighter political controls as well, abolishing the existing charters of the northern mainland colonies and creating the Dominion of New England. The Glorious Revolution of 1688 cost James his throne, and revolts in Maryland, Massachusetts, and New York helped to secure the restoration of the colonists' traditional rights and institutions.

The Navigation Acts ensured that the profits of the South Atlantic system, which depended primarily on the sugar trade, would flow into Britain. To work the sugar plantations of the West Indies and Brazil, planters from Britain and other European countries imported millions of African slaves and brutally exploited their labor. In the Chesapeake colonies, where Africans mainly raised tobacco and the conditions of servitude were less severe, the number of black laborers grew dramatically through importation and natural increase. Both in the Chesapeake and the Carolinas, the production of tobacco and rice brought great profits to white planters and fostered the creation of African American communities. By providing markets in the West Indies, the South Atlantic system also brought prosperity to northern seaports, merchants, and farmers.

Between 1713 and 1739 the European powers were at peace, and both the American population and economy grew at a rapid pace. Aided by the unofficial British policy of salutary neglect, American political leaders strengthened the power of the provincial assemblies, which were controlled by the elite but were responsive to the views of ordinary people. However, because of the influx of non-English migrants and the increasing complexity of economic life, American politics was becoming more complex and conflict-ridden.

Moreover, after 1730 pressure from British interests prompted greater imperial control of American affairs. In 1733, alarmed by the decline of the British sugar industry because of colonial trade with the French West Indies, the British Parliament passed the Molasses Act, which tightened mercantilist controls on colonial trade. By 1750, the enactment of other legislation restricting manufacturing in the American colonies and regulating their financial policies signaled that the era of salutary neglect was rapidly coming to an end.

T I M E L I N E

1651	First Navigation Act
1660s	Virginia moves toward slave system
1663	Carolina proprietorship granted
1664	New Netherland captured; becomes New York
1681	William Penn founds Pennsylvania
1686–1689	Dominion of New England
1688–1689	Glorious Revolution in England; William and Mary rule
	Revolts in Massachusetts, Maryland, and New York
1689–1713	England, France, and Spain at war
1696	Board of Trade created
1705	Full legal slavery enacted in Virginia
1714–1750	British policy of "salutary neglect"
	Rise of American assemblies
1718	Spanish establish missions and garrisons in Texas
1720–1742	Sir Robert Walpole chief minister
1720–1750	African American community forms
	Rice exports from Carolina soar
	Rise of planter aristocracy
	Expansion of seaport cities
1732	Georgia chartered
	Hat Act
1733	Molasses Act
1739	Stono rebellion
	War with Spain in the Caribbean
1740	Veto of Massachusetts land bank
1750	Iron Act
1751	Currency Act

Suggested Readings

———————★———————

The best overview of England's empire is Michael Kammen, *Empire and Interest: The American Colonies and the Politics of Mercantilism* (1970); for a more recent and detailed account, see Alison Olson, *Making the Empire Work: London and American Interest Groups, 1690–1790* (1992). On Africa, consult Paul Bohannan and Philip Curtin, *Africa and the Africans* (3rd ed., 1988). Two fine syntheses of the African American experience are Philip D. Morgan, *Slave Counterpoint: Black Culture in the Eighteenth-Century Chesapeake and Low Country* (1998), and Ira Berlin, *Many Thousands Gone: The First Two Centuries of Slavery in North America* (1999).

The Politics of Empire, 1660–1713

Robert Bliss, *Revolution and Empire: English Politics and the American Colonies in the Seventeenth Century* (1990), explores the impact on the colonies of the Puritan Revolution, while Jack M. Sosin, *English America and the Restoration Monarchy of Charles II: Transatlantic Politics, Commerce, and Kinship* (1980), examines the colonial policy of the restored king. See also Stephen S. Webb, *1676: The End of American Independence* (1984). For the events of 1688–1689, consult the comprehensive discussion by David S. Lovejoy, *The Glorious Revolution in America* (1972). A good case study is Lois Green Carr and David W. Jordan, *Maryland's Revolution of Government, 1689–1692* (1974). Ethnic tension in New York can be traced in Robert C. Ritchie, *The Duke's Province: Politics and Society in New York, 1660–1691* (1977); Thomas J. Archdeacon, *New York City, 1664–1710: Conquest and Change* (1976); Donna Merwick, *Possessing Albany, 1630–1710: The Dutch and English Experiences* (1990); and Joyce Goodfriend, *Before the Melting Pot: Society and Culture in Colonial New York City, 1664–1730* (1992). Jack M. Sosin, *English America and Imperial Inconstancy: The Rise of Provincial Autonomy, 1696–1715* (1985), outlines the new imperial system.

The Imperial Slave Economy

For the African background, see John Thornton, *Africa and Africans in the Making of the Atlantic World, 1400–1680* (1992), and Richard Olaniyan, *African History and Culture* (1982). Specialized studies of forced African migration include Philip Curtin, *The Atlantic Slave Trade: A Census* (1969); Paul Lovejoy, ed., *Africans in Bondage: Studies in Slavery and the Slave Trade* (1986); Hugh Thomas, *The Slave Trade* (1991); Joseph E. Inikori and Stanley L. Engerman, eds., *The Atlantic Slave Trade* (1992); and Barbara L. Solow, ed., *Slavery and the Rise of the Atlantic System* (1991).

Richard S. Dunn, *Sugar and Slaves: The Rise of the Planter Class in the English West Indies, 1624–1713* (1972), provides a graphic portrait of the brutal slave-based economy, while Sidney W. Mintz, *Sweetness and Power: The Place of Sugar in Modern History* (1985), explores the impact of the major crop of the slave economy. Winthrop D. Jordan, *White over Black, 1550–1812* (1968), remains the best account of Virginia's deci-sion for slavery, but see also Thomas D. Morris, *Southern Slavery and the Law, 1619–1860* (1996).

Lorena Walsh, *From Calabar to Carter's Grove* (1998), closely examines the lives of Africans in Virginia. For the development of African American society, see Allan Kulikoff, *Tobacco and Slaves: Southern Cultures in the Chesapeake, 1680–1800* (1986); Daniel C. Littlefield, *Rice and Slaves: Ethnicity and the Slave Trade in Colonial South Carolina* (1981); Peter H. Wood, *Black Majority: Negroes in Colonial South Carolina through the Stono Rebellion* (1974); and Marvin L. Michael Kay and Lorin Lee Cary, *Slavery in North Carolina, 1748-1775* (1995). See also Richard Price, ed., *Maroon Societies: Rebel Slave Communities in the Americas* (1973); Ira Berlin and Philip D. Morgan, eds., *Cultivation and Culture: Labor and the Shaping of Slave Life in the Americas* (1992); and Mechel Sobel, *The World They Made Together* (1987), which discusses the mingling of cultures in Virginia.

On white society in the South, read Richard Bushman, *The Refinement of America* (1992); Daniel Blake Smith, *Inside the Great House: Planter Family Life in Eighteenth-Century Chesapeake Society* (1980); Rhys Isaac, *The Transformation of Virginia, 1740–1790* (1982); Timothy H. Breen, *Tobacco Culture* (1985); and a fine older study of political practices, Charles Sydnor, *American Revolutionaries in the Making* (1952). Urban society and trade are explored in Gary B. Nash, *The Urban Crucible* (1979); Gary M. Walton and James F. Shephard, *The Economic Rise of Early America* (1979); and Christine L. Heyrman, *Commerce and Culture: The Maritime Communities of Colonial Massachusetts, 1690–1750* (1984). See also Marcus Rediker, *Between the Devil and the Deep Blue Sea: Merchant Seamen, Pirates, and the Anglo-American Maritime World, 1700–1750* (1987).

The New Politics of Empire, 1714–1750

The appearance of a distinctive American system of politics is traced in Bernard Bailyn, *The Origins of American Politics* (1968). Studies of various colonies include Jack P. Greene, *The Quest for Power: The Lower Houses of Assembly in the Southern Royal Colonies, 1689–1776* (1963); Patricia U. Bonomi, *A Factious People: Politics and Society in Colonial New York* (1971); A. Roger Ekirch, *"Poor Carolina": Politics and Society in Colonial North Carolina, 1729–1776* (1981); and Richard Bushman, *King and People in Provincial Massachusetts* (1985). John Schutz, *William Shirley* (1961), shows how a competent colonial governor wielded power, while Thomas C. Barrow, *Trade and Empire: The British Customs Service in Colonial America, 1660–1775* (1967), and Alison G. Olson, *Anglo-American Politics, 1660–1775* (1973), explore various aspects of British mercantilism.

Douglas E. Leach, *Roots of Conflict: British Armed Forces and Colonial Americans, 1677–1763* (1986), covers the diplomatic and military conflicts of the period, but this Anglo-American perspective is balanced by Patricia Wood, *French-Indian Relations on the Southern Frontier* (1992); David J. Weber, *The Spanish Frontier in North America* (1992); and Ian K. Steele, *Warpaths: Invasions of North America* (1993).

Susanna Truax
Gebooren den 8 g⁹ʳ 1726,
Geschildert Maart 1730.

Chapter 4

Growth, Diversity, and Crisis: Colonial Society,

1720–1765

B Y 1720 BRITAIN's North American settlements were well established. The early dangers were past. The Indians in coastal areas had been expelled or pacified, and the colonists were growing enough foodstuffs and other goods to feed themselves and to export their staples to markets in Europe and the West Indies. Steady immigration, the slave trade, and natural increase had brought the European and African population of the settlements to 400,000.

During the next forty-five years, natural increase more than tripled the population of New England, which increased from 150,000 to 500,000, while the mid-Atlantic colonies, with their promise of freehold land, political liberties, and religious tolerance, drew hundreds of thousands of new migrants from many regions of Europe. In addition, planters in the southern colonies imported tens of thousands of enslaved Africans, causing a society *with some slaves* to become an actual *slave society*. By 1765 the mainland population had grown fivefold, to almost 2 million people.

Accompanying the increase in population and ethnic diversity were greater complexity and conflict in intellectual and religious life. Many educated Americans embraced the ideas of the European Enlightenment, or Age of Reason, and assumed an increasingly optimistic view of the world. Beginning in the 1740s even more colonists—some of African ancestry, but mostly those of European descent—were swept up in a new wave of religious enthusiasm known to historians as the First Great Awakening, which also had its origin in Europe. Moreover, rapid economic change, the product of population growth and increased domestic and

A Young Dutch American Girl, 1730
This painting of four-year-old Susanna Truax of Albany, New York, was the work of the "Gansevoort Limner," an unknown Dutch portrait painter with an informal but realistic style. The upper left-hand corner shows her birth date. Susanna never married and lived to the ripe old age of seventy-nine.
National Gallery of Art, Washington, DC; gift of Edgar William and Bernice Chrysler Garbisch.

transatlantic commerce, divided many communities along the lines of wealth, thereby increasing social divisions and strife.

These developments were not restricted to well-established coastal areas. As new arrivals and the landless younger children of long-settled families headed toward the frontier looking for cheap land and new opportunities, they fought with speculators and landlords and demanded that colonial governments accord them greater political rights and representation in the assemblies. Equally important, this movement of farmers into the interior reignited conflict with native peoples and with France and Spain, the other European powers contesting for dominance of North America. By 1750 the residents of Britain's North American colonies lived in a complicated world filled with challenges and crises.

Freehold Society in New England

——————★——————

In the 1630s the Puritans had migrated from a country where a handful of nobles and gentry owned 75 percent of the farming and pasture land and worked it by using servants, leaseholding tenants, and wage laborers. In their new home in New England, the Puritans created a much more egalitarian society composed primarily of yeomen farm families who owned their land as *freeholders*—without feudal dues or leases. By 1750, however, the rapidly growing population threatened to outstrip the supply of easily farmed land. This posed a severe challenge to the freehold ideal.

Farm Families: Women's Place

The Puritans' vision of relative social equality did not extend to the family, which by English common law and social custom remained a patriarchy dominated by the husband. Just as men occupied all positions of public power, they also claimed authority within the private realm of the family. As the Reverend Benjamin Wadsworth of Boston advised women in his pamphlet *The Well-Ordered Family* (1712), it made no difference if they were richer, more intelligent, or of higher social status than their husbands: "Since he is thy Husband, God has made him the head and set him above thee." Therefore, Wadsworth concluded, it is "thy duty to love and reverence him."

Throughout their lives, New England women saw firsthand that their role was a subordinate one. Small girls watched their mothers defer to their fathers. As young adults they learned that their inheritances would be much smaller than those of their brothers,

and inferior in kind: daughters usually received livestock and household goods rather than land, the most prized economic resource. In a typical will, Ebenezer Chittendon of Guilford, Connecticut, left all his land to his sons, decreeing that "Each Daughter have half so much as Each Son, one half in money and the other half in Cattle."

In rural New England—indeed, throughout the colonies—women were raised to be dutiful helpmeets (helpmates) to their husbands and providers for their families. Farmwives spun thread and yarn from flax or wool and wove it into cloth for shirts and gowns. They knitted sweaters and stockings, made candles and soap, churned milk into butter and pressed curds into cheese, brewed malt and fermented it for beer, preserved meats, and mastered dozens of other household tasks. The most exemplary or "notable" practitioners of these domestic arts won praise from the community, for their labor was crucial to the rural household economy. "I have a great longing desire to be very notable," one woman wrote upon her marriage.

Reproduction—becoming a mother—was no less central a responsibility for the great majority of women. In New England between 1700 and 1750, most women married in their early twenties; by their early forties many of these women had given birth to six or seven children, usually delivered with the assistance of midwives. Bearing and rearing children was not an easy task. Managing a large family sapped a woman's physical and emotional strength, and it required her to expend her energies on domestic activities for about twenty of her most active years. Sarah Ripley Stearns, a Massachusetts farmwife, explained that she had no time for religious activities because "the care of my Babes takes up so large a portion of my time and attention."

In long-settled communities, the shrinking size of farms prompted many couples to have fewer children. After 1750 women in the eastern farming town of Andover, Massachusetts, bore an average of only four children, thus giving them the time and energy to pursue other tasks. Farm women now made extra yarn, cloth, or cheese to exchange with neighbors or sell to shopkeepers, thereby enhancing their families' standard of living. Some women, like Susan Huntington of Boston (who, as the wife of a prosperous merchant, had the good fortune to be rich), spent more time in "the care & culture of children, and the perusal of necessary books, including the scriptures."

But women's participation in the daily affairs of life was limited by cultural rules. For example, Puritan men were reluctant to have their wives work in the fields. "Women in New England," Timothy Dwight reported approvingly, "are employed only in and about the house and in the proper business of the sex." Yet strong-minded wives often defied their husbands and assumed authority in the household or over their own lives.

The Character of Family Life: The Cheneys
Life in a large colonial-era family was very different from that in a small modern one.
Mrs. Cheney's face shows the rigors of having borne ten children, a task that occupied
her entire adult life. Her children grew up with many older (or younger) siblings,
which blurred differences between the generations.
National Gallery of Art, Washington, DC; gift of Edgar William and Bernice Chrysler Garbisch.

One such woman was Hannah Heaton of North Haven, Connecticut, a devout Puritan wife who rebuked her husband's family for "wicked practices" and left his church. Like other Puritan women, Heaton had taken advantage of the Protestant emphasis on reading the Bible and had learned to read and write. She chafed under the restrictions in most Congregational churches that denied women the opportunity of voting or even speaking on church matters. Like Anne Hutchinson (see Chapter 2), Heaton questioned the authority of her minister, thinking him a "blind guide" who had not been reborn as a Saint. Eventually she joined an evangelical Congregational church that, like those in radical Protestant sects, gave women an active role in religious matters. For example, Quakers believed "that women can be called to the ministry as well as men," as a French visitor noted, and Baptists in Rhode Island permitted women to vote on church affairs.

Yet these differences among churches were only variations on the general theme of women's subordination. Despite their increasing freedom from child raising, most women—not only in New England but also in other regions of British America—remained in an infe-rior position, their lives tightly bound by a web of laws, cultural expectations, and religious restrictions.

Farm Property: Inheritance

By contrast, European men who migrated to the colonies escaped many traditional constraints, including the curse of landlessness. Indeed, land was the base of economic life for most inhabitants of the preindustrial world, and it was much in demand. "The hope of having land of their own & becoming independent of Landlords is what chiefly induces people into America," a British official reported in the 1730s. Acquiring a farmstead was relatively easy for the first settlers in New England, where the Puritan governments gave free land to most household heads. But the many European migrants who came as indentured servants, as well as the native-born children of propertyless parents, found it much more difficult to become landowners. In the colonies and in England, poor parents often indentured their sons and daughters to more prosperous households, where they would have enough to eat and could learn the ways of the world. When the indentures ended once the youths reached age eighteen or twenty-one,

Tavern Culture
By the eighteenth century, many taverns were run by women, such as this "Charming Patroness," who needed all her charm to deal with her raucous clientele. It was in taverns, declared puritanical John Adams, that "diseases, vicious habits, bastards, and legislators are frequently begotten."
Connecticut Historical Society.

the more ambitious of the young men would begin the long ten- to twenty-year climb up the agricultural ladder, from servant to laborer to tenant and finally to free-holding farm owner.

Having learned the importance of owning property from bitter experience in Europe, most yeomen farmers in New England—and in other regions as well—tried to provide for their children. As their sons and daughters reached marriageable age—usually twenty-three to twenty-five—fathers provided them with a *marriage portion:* land, livestock, farm equipment, or money. This marriage gift repaid children for their labor on the parents' farm and ensured their future loyalty. Parents knew they would need help from their offspring in their old age, for there were no pension or social security systems. To guarantee that they would not be left helpless, some farmers retained legal title to their land until they died.

Because the economic security of the parents—and of the newlyweds themselves—depended on a wise choice of marriage partners, most property-owning parents decided whom their children would marry. Although these youth did not have the luxury of "falling in love" with whomever they pleased, they could usually withdraw from an unacceptable match. Thus, Jane Hent, a young Quaker woman in Pennsylvania, refused to marry Thomas Martin, explaining that she "could not love him well enough to be her husband."

Marriage under English common law was hardly a contract between equals. A bride relinquished to her husband the legal ownership of her land and personal property, receiving in compensation a *dower right:* if her husband died, the widow received the right to use (but not to sell) one-third of the family's estate. Death or remarriage canceled this dower right, and her portion was then divided among the children. In this way the wife's property rights in New England and the other English colonies were subordinated to those of the family "line" that stretched, through the children, across the generations. By contrast, wives in New Netherland before 1664 and in New York's Dutch families until 1700 fared much better, for under Dutch law they retained inheritance rights over the property they brought into marriage.

As each generation passed property to the next, families divided their lands to provide farms for their sons. Eventually most properties were too small to split, so yeomen devised other strategies to maintain a society of freehold farm families. Some fathers willed the ancestral property to one son, specifying that it remain undivided and in the family forever. Thus Ebenezer Perry of Barnstable, Massachusetts, willed his land to his son, Ebenezer Jr., stipulating that it devolve in turn on the younger Ebenezer's "eldest son surviving and so on to the male heirs of his body lawfully begotten forever." If they were prosperous, farmers provided their other children with money, apprenticeship contracts, or frontier tracts with which to become freeholders in other communities. Other parents bequeathed their land to the oldest son and required him to pay money or goods to the younger children. Finally, some yeomen moved to frontier regions, first in New England and then in eastern New York and northeastern Pennsylvania, where life was hard but land for the children was cheap and abundant. "The Squire's House stands on the Bank of the Susquehannah," the traveler Philip Fithian reported from the Pennsylvania backcountry in the early 1760s. "He tells me that he will be able to settle all his sons and his fair Daughter Betsy on the Fat of the Earth."

The historic accomplishment of New England farmers was the creation of whole communities composed of independent property owners. A French visitor remarked on the sense of personal worth and dignity in

Lady Undressing for a Bath, c. 1730–1740
This delightful painting attributed to Gerardus Duyckinck captures a moment of intimacy between an unknown but obviously well-to-do American couple. Many marriages were "arranged" but grew into love matches. Others began with strong emotional bonds that withered over time. One affluent Philadelphia woman celebrated her match, writing to her husband: "Our Hearts have been united from the first, in so firm, so strong, so sweet an affection, that words are incapable of setting it forth." National Gallery of Art, Washington, DC; gift of Edgar William and Bernice Chrysler Garbisch.

this rural world, which contrasted sharply with that of European peasant life. Throughout the northern colonies, he wrote, he had found "men and women whose features are not marked by poverty, by lifelong deprivation of the necessities of life, or by a feeling that they are insignificant subjects and subservient members of society."

The Crisis of Freehold Society

By 1750, however, the threat of landlessness and poverty had increased as a result of the relentless growth of the New England population. The Puritan colonies had about 100,000 people in 1700, nearly 200,000 in 1725, and approximately 350,000 by 1750. In long-settled areas, farms that had once been ample in size had been divided and subdivided, leaving parents in a quandary. In the 1740s the Reverend Samuel Chandler of Andover, Massachusetts, confided to his diary that he was "much distressed for land for my children," seven of whom were boys. Dispersing the land among so many heirs usually meant a decline in the family's living standards (Table 4.1). In Concord, Massachusetts, by the 1750s, about 60 percent of farmers would never own as much land as their fathers had.

Because parents had less to give their children, they had less control over their children's lives, and the system of arranged marriages soon broke down. Young people either migrated from their town or engaged in premarital sex and used the urgency of pregnancy to win their fathers' permission to marry. Throughout New England the number of firstborn children con-

ceived before marriage rose spectacularly, from about 10 percent in the 1710s to 30 percent or more in the 1740s. Given another chance, young people "would do the same again," an Anglican minister observed, "because otherwise they could not obtain their parents' consent to marry."

After 1750 farm communities in New England responded to the threat to their freehold ideal in three ways. First, many towns petitioned the provincial government for assistance. In 1740 Massachusetts farmers demanded a land bank that would issue paper currency and thereby provide them with loans and stimulate trade, but this initiative was vetoed by the royal governor (see Chapter 3). With greater success, they created new communities of freehold farmers by obtaining land grants from the Massachusetts government or buying land from speculators in New Hampshire and the area of present-day Vermont.

Second, settlers who remained on the original farmsteads planted different crops. Even before 1750 they had replaced the traditional English crops of wheat and barley (used in making bread and beer) with crops that supported a grazing economy based on corn, cattle, and hogs. Corn offered a hardy food for the settlers, and its cobs and abundant leaves furnished feed for cows and pigs, which provided milk and meat. After 1750 New England farmers raised the output of this mixed-crop grazing economy by planting potatoes, whose high yield offset the disadvantage of smaller farms. Farmers also introduced nutritious nitrogen-bearing English grasses, such as red clover and timothy, to provide forage for their livestock and restore the fertility of depleted fields. New England boosted its

TABLE 4.1

Diminishing Property in the Fuller Family, Kent, Connecticut

	Date of Birth	Highest Assessment on Tax List
First Generation		
Joseph Fuller	1699	203 pounds
Second Generation		
Joseph Jr.	1723	42
Zachariah	1725	103
Jeremiah	1728	147
Nathaniel	?	67
Adijah	?	46
Simeon	?	49
Abraham	1737	136
Jacob	1738	59
Isaac	1741	7
	Average:	72 pounds
Third Generation		
Abel	?	40
Abraham Jr.	?	50
Oliver	1747	50
Daniel	1749	65
Howard	1750	28
Benejah	1757	32
Ephraim	1760	100
John	1760	?
Asahel	1770	48
James	1770	40
Revilo	1770	35
Samuel	?	14
	Average:	42 pounds

Charles S. Grant, *Democracy in the Connecticut Frontier Town of Kent* (New York: Columbia University Press, 1961), 30–40.

economy, becoming the major supplier of salted and pickled meat to the West Indies; in 1770 preserved meat accounted for about 5 percent of the value of all exports from the mainland colonies.

Finally, farmers compensated for their smaller plots by exchanging goods and labor among themselves, developing the full potential of what one historian has called the "household mode of production." Men loaned each other tools, draft animals, and grazing land. Women and children joined other families in spinning yarn, sewing quilts, and shucking corn. Farmers plowed the fields of artisans, who in turn fixed the pots, plows, and furniture brought to them for repair. Typically, no money changed hands between relatives or neighbors. Instead, farmers, artisans, and shopkeepers recorded debts and credits in personal account books, and every few years they "balanced" the accounts by transferring small amounts of cash. This system of exchange allowed households—and the entire economy—to achieve maximum output, thereby preserving the freehold ideal.

The Mid-Atlantic: Toward a New Society, 1720–1765

————————★————————

The middle colonies—New York, New Jersey, and Pennsylvania—lacked the cultural uniformity of New England, being populated instead by a mixture of settlers from many European countries with diverse traditions and religions (Map 4.1). Yet these settlements had more order and purpose than one might think. Strong ethnic ties bound German settlers to one another, as did deep religious loyalties among the members of various churches: Scots-Irish Presbyterians, English and Welsh

Quakers, German Lutherans, and Dutch Reformed Protestants. Nevertheless these religious and ethnic ties generated conflicts between cultural groups, as did increasing economic inequality.

Opportunity and Equality

Ample fertile land and a long growing season attracted migrants to the mid-Atlantic, and profits from the sale of wheat financed its settlement. Between 1720 and 1770 wheat prices doubled in Western Europe because of an explosion of population, and American farmers increased their exports to meet the demand (Figure 4.1, box insert). By 1770 the value of the wheat, corn, and flour shipped from the mid-Atlantic colonies to Europe and the West Indies amounted to over 15 percent of all mainland exports. Agricultural prosperity helped the combined population of New York, New Jersey, and Pennsylvania surge from 50,000 in 1700 to 120,000 in 1720 and 350,000 in 1765.

Tenancy in New York. As the colonial population rose, so did the demand for land. Nonetheless many migrants refused to settle in New York's fertile Hudson River Valley. There, long-established Dutch families—such as the Rensselaers, the Van Cortlandts, the Beekmans—presided over patroonships created by the Dutch West India Company, and wealthy English families—such as the Morris and Heathcote clans—owned vast estates granted by English governors between 1700 and 1714 (Map 4.2). Like the planter elite in the Chesapeake colonies, these propertied New York families sought to live like European gentry by dominating a dependent peasantry, but few migrants were interested in becoming their tenants.

As freehold land became scarce in eastern New York, more families were forced to accept tenancy leases. To attract and retain good tenants, many manorial lords offered longer leases that gave farmers the right to sell any improvements they made to the property to the next tenant. This policy worked. In 1714 only 82 families lived on the vast manor of Rensselaerswyck, but it had 345 tenants by 1752 and nearly 700 by 1765.

Most tenant families hoped that with hard work and good luck they could save enough to buy freehold farmsteads. However, they had to contend with the severe limits that preindustrial technology placed on their output. Before 1750, most farmers harvested grain by using a hand sickle or scythe, and they could reap only half an acre per day. Farm productivity improved following the introduction of the *cradle scythe*, a hand-held agricultural tool with wooden fingers that arranged the wheat for easy collection and binding; use of this tool doubled or tripled the amount of grain a worker could cut.

MAP 4.1
Ethnic and Racial Diversity, 1775
In 1700 most colonists were English, but by 1775 those of English descent constituted a minority. African Americans accounted for one-third of the population of the South, while the presence of Germans and Scots-Irish created ethnic and religious diversity in the middle colonies and southern backcountry.

Even so, few tenant families produced enough to grow rich—or even to buy a farmstead. Two adult workers could only harvest about 15 acres of wheat in a growing season, because ripe grain often sprouted and became useless before it could be cut. Consequently most families planted 10–15 acres, which yielded about 150–180 bushels of wheat. After reserving enough for family consumption and the next year's seeds, a tenant could sell the "surplus" wheat for about £15—enough to buy salt and sugar, tools, and cloth. Whereas farmers who owned their land could spend any remaining money to purchase a few acres of land to pass on to their children, most tenants had to use the remainder to pay the rent. It was not easy to rise into the ranks of the yeomanry.

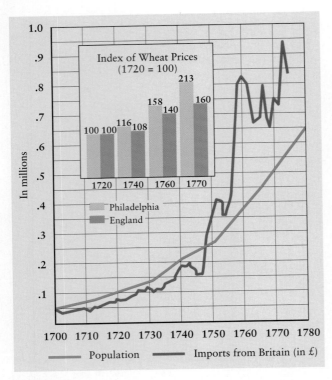

FIGURE 4.1
Population Growth, Wheat Prices, and Imports from Britain in the Middle Colonies
Wheat prices soared in Philadelphia because of demand in the West Indies and Europe. Exports of grain and flour paid for British manufactures, which were imported in large quantities after 1750.

MAP 4.2
The Hudson River Manors, c. 1765
Dutch and English manorial lords dominated the fertile eastern shores of the Hudson River Valley, leasing small farms to German tenant families and refusing to sell land to freehold-seeking migrants from overcrowded New England.

Prosperity and Inequality. Unlike New York, many communities in rural Pennsylvania and New Jersey were initially marked by relative economic equality. For example, the original migrants to Chester County, just outside Philadelphia, arrived with approximately equal resources. Around 1700, the poorest 30 percent of the taxpayers owned a substantial 17 percent of the assessed wealth and the top 10 percent controlled only 24 percent (Figure 4.2). Most settlers lived in small houses with one or two rooms and a sleeping loft and had few possessions: a couple of benches or stools, some wooden trenchers (platters), and a few wooden noggins (cups). Only the wealthiest families ate off pewter or ceramic plates imported from England or Holland.

Over the next two generations the rise of the wheat trade and an influx of poor settlers introduced marked social divisions. Some Chester County farmers grew wealthy by hiring propertyless laborers to raise large quantities of wheat for market sale. Others became successful entrepreneurs, providing newly arrived settlers with land, equipment, goods, and services. Gradually a new class of wealthy agricultural capitalists—large-

scale farmers, rural landlords, speculators, storekeepers, and gristmill operators—accumulated substantial estates. They built large houses and furnished them with mahogany tables, four-poster beds, couches, table linen, and imported Dutch dinnerware. Wealth and status now ordered the life of the community. By the 1760s the richest 10 percent of Chester County's property-owning families controlled 30 percent of their communities' assets, whereas the poorest 30 percent held a mere 6 percent.

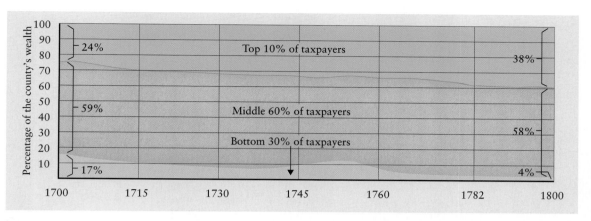

FIGURE 4.2
Increasing Social Inequality in Chester County, Pennsylvania
By renting land and selling goods to a growing population, the county's landed and commercial elite grew rich. Eventually the top 10 percent of taxpayers commanded nearly 40 percent of the wealth, far above the paltry 4 percent owned by the poorest 30 percent.

Moreover, a new landless class, one with *no* taxable property, had appeared at the bottom of the social order. By the 1760s half the young men in five New Jersey farming communities were without land and many of them would never become property owners. In Chester County, Pennsylvania, nearly half of *all* men were propertyless. Some of these men were the sons of property owners and would eventually inherit at least part of the family estate. But just as many were Scots-Irish *inmates*—single men or families "such as live in small cottages and have no taxable property, except a cow," according to one tax assessor. In the predominantly German settlement of Lancaster, Pennsylvania, a merchant likewise noted an "abundance of Poor people" who "maintain their Families with great difficulty by day Labour." Although these Scots-Irish and German migrants hoped to become tenants and eventually landowners, a sharp rise in land prices prevented many from realizing their dreams.

Merchants and artisans took advantage of the ample supply of labor by organizing a "putting-out" system such as that used in England. They bought wool or flax from large-scale producers and paid propertyless workers and the wives and daughters of subsistence farm families to spin it into yarn and weave it into cloth. In the 1760s an English traveler reported that hundreds of colonists in the region had turned "to manufacture, and live upon a small farm, as in many parts of England." In parts of New Jersey and eastern Pennsylvania, as in New England, the land had become as crowded and socially divided as that in rural England. Many farm families feared—with good reason—a return to the lowly status of the European peasant.

Cultural Diversity

The middle colonies were never a melting pot in which European cultures blended into a homogeneous "American" society. Rather, they evolved as a patchwork of ethnically and religiously diverse communities. When Swedish traveler Peter Kalm visited Philadelphia in 1748, he found no fewer than twelve religious denominations, including Anglicans, Quakers, Swedish and German Lutherans, Scots-Irish Presbyterians, and even Roman Catholics. Adding to this diversity were large communities of German sectarians—radical Protestants who had separated from established denominations—such as the Moravians in Bethlehem and Nazareth, Pennsylvania.

Most migrants tried to preserve their cultural identities, often by marrying within their own ethnic groups or maintaining the customs of their native lands. For example, 70 percent of the children of the original Welsh Quakers who migrated to Chester County, Pennsylvania, married other Welsh Quakers, as did 60 percent of the third generation. The main exception to this clannish pattern were the Huguenots, French Calvinists who were expelled from France and settled in New York and various seacoast cities. In part because of their small numbers, Huguenots intermarried with other Protestants and gradually lost their ethnic and religious identity.

The Quaker Experiment. Members of the Society of Friends (Quakers) became the dominant social group in Pennsylvania, at first because of their numbers and later because of their wealth and influence. Until the 1750s Friends controlled Pennsylvania's representative assembly, and members of the Society exercised considerable political power in New Jersey as well.

A German Farm in Western Maryland, 1738
Beginning in the 1730s, wheat became a major export crop in Maryland and Virginia.
This engraving probably depicts a German farm, because the harvesters are using
oxen, not horses, and women are working in the field alongside men. Using "A new
method of Reaping," possibly of German origin, the harvesters cut only the grain-
bearing tip and leave the wheat stalks in the fields, to be eaten by livestock.
Library of Congress.

Quakers had a distinct culture and set of moral ethics. Believing that all individuals were equal before God and that there should be no social distinction on earth, they wore plain clothes without elaborate decoration and refused to defer to their "superiors" by removing their hats. In talking among themselves and with strangers, they used old-English pronouns that emphasized intimacy—"How are thee today?" rather than "How are you?" Most members of the Society refused to use law courts to settle disputes among themselves, relying instead on Quaker arbitrators to judge what was "right" rather than what was "legal."

Around 1750 some Quakers extended these egalitarian values to their relations with African Americans, freeing their slaves. Indeed, some Quaker meetings not only condemned the institution of slavery but also expelled any members who continued to keep slaves, thereby making Quakers the first major religious group to advocate the abolition of slavery. The Quakers were also pacifists and did all they could to avoid conflict with native Americans. When William Penn first received a royal charter for his colony in 1681 (see Chapter 3), he had come to Pennsylvania and had personally negotiated a treaty with the Delaware Indians. Subsequently, the Quaker-dominated Pennsylvania government purchased land from the Indians rather than seizing it by force. This conciliatory policy enabled Pennsylvania to avoid a major Indian war until the 1750s, when aggressive Scots-Irish settlers sparked conflicts with the native peoples.

The Scots-Irish. A group of migrants known as the Scots-Irish formed the largest group of eighteenth-century European settlers, some 150,000 in number, and many of them settled initially in the mid-Atlantic colonies. Some of the migrants were Irish Catholics, but a substantial majority—about 70 percent—were the descendants of Presbyterian Scots who had been sent to Ireland between 1608 and 1650 to bolster English control of its Catholic population. In Ireland, both the Scots and the native Irish Catholics faced religious discrimination and economic regulation by the English. The Irish Test Act of 1704 had excluded Scottish Presbyterians as well as Irish Catholics from holding public office. English mercantilist regulations placed heavy import duties on the woolen goods Scots-Irish weavers produced, and farmers—both Scots-Irish and Irish— were heavily taxed. "Read this letter, Rev. Baptist Boyd," a settler in New York wrote to his former Presbyterian minister in Ireland, "and tell all the poor folk of ye place that God has opened a door for their deliverance . . . all that a man works for is his own; there are no revenue hounds [tax collectors] to take it from us here." Lured by such reports from America, after 1720 thousands of Scots-Irish families sailed for Pennsylvania, where there was more freehold land available than

A Quaker Meeting for Worship
Quakers dressed plainly and met in unadorned buildings, sitting in silence until
inspired by the "inner light." Women spoke with near equality to men, a tradition that
prepared Quaker women to take a leading part in the nineteenth-century women's
rights movement. In this British work, entitled *Quaker Meeting,* an elder (his hat on a
peg above his head) addresses the congregation.
Courtesy Museum of Fine Arts, Boston. Bequest of Maxim Karolik.

in New York and less danger from Indians. Debarking
in Philadelphia, they migrated to central Pennsylvania
and southward down the Shenandoah Valley into the
backcountry of Maryland, Virginia, and the Carolinas.

Like the Quakers, the Scots-Irish had a distinct linguistic culture, speaking English (an observer noted)
with "an Irish brogue." The Presbyterian migrants also
had a religious tradition that combined an active
revivalist-prone laity with a well-educated and well-
trained clergy. Like the Puritan ministers of the 1630s,
Presbyterian ministers pictured the exodus to America
as the communal migration of an oppressed people,

thus providing the Scots-Irish with a sustaining historical tradition. To maintain this identity, they encouraged young people to marry those of their own
ethnicity and religion.

The Pennsylvania Germans.   The Quaker vision of a
"peaceable kingdom" likewise attracted many German
settlers who were fleeing from war, religious persecution, and poverty in their homeland. First to arrive, in
1683, was a group of Mennonites, members of an evangelical Protestant sect founded around 1550 in Germany
by Menno Simons; as a persecuted group they were

German Artisanry
German artisans in Pennsylvania, carrying on the traditions of the old country, frequently decorated their furniture with abstract designs and simple folk motifs, such as the rectangular patterns and angels on this chest of drawers.
Philadelphia Museum of Art, Clarence W. Brazer Collection.

attracted by William Penn's promises of religious freedom. Other Germans soon followed, and because their language closely resembled that of the Dutch in New York, they were often called the "Pennsylvania Dutch." In the 1720s religious upheaval and population growth in southwestern Germany and Switzerland stimulated another wave of migrants. "Wages were far better" in Pennsylvania, Heinrich Schneebeli reported to his friends in Zurich after an exploratory visit to the Quaker colony, and "one also enjoyed there a free unhindered exercise of religion." Beginning in 1749, thousands of Germans and Swiss joined a huge exodus from their overcrowded and war-torn countries. By 1756, as many as 37,000 new migrants had landed in Philadelphia. Some came as *redemptioners*—a type of indentured servant—and struggled for years to pay off their debts (see Voices from Abroad, "Gottlieb Mittelberger: The Perils of Migration," p. 119). Many more Germans came with some economic resources; they had emigrated to raise their living standards and enhance the prospects for their children. Most migrants managed to improve their lives. As the German minister Gottlieb Mittelberger reported from Pennsylvania in the 1750s, "Even in the humblest or poorest houses, no one eats bread without butter or cheese."

German settlements soon dominated certain areas of Pennsylvania, such as the fertile plains near Lancaster. Other migrants moved down the Shenandoah Valley, establishing communities in the western parts of Maryland, Virginia, and the Carolinas. German settlers carefully guarded their heritage. Most migrants were members of Lutheran or Reformed congregations; to staff their churches, they often recruited ministers from Germany, thereby maintaining their ties to the homeland and its language. Well into the nineteenth century, their descendants conducted church services in German, published German-language newspapers, and used their native tongue in daily life. The settlers also preserved German agricultural practices, with women taking an active part in plowing and harvesting—activities that were frowned upon by New England Puritans and other English colonists. German women were "always in the fields, meadows, stables, etc.," an English observer noted with surprise, "and do not dislike any work whatsoever." Reflecting this participation, married German women had greater property rights than did English women, for they retained control of their personal property and could make wills.

Like other migrants, German parents encouraged their American-born children to take marriage partners of their own ancestry. A minister in North Carolina admonished his congregation "not to contract any marriages with the English or Irish," explaining that "we owe it to our native country to do our part that German blood and the German language be preserved in America." Despite this ethnic clannishness, the migrants did not seek to create an all-German colony. They slid easily into the status of loyal subjects of the English Crown, especially after 1714 when German (and German-speaking) princes from the duchy of Hanover ascended to the throne as George I (r. 1714–1727) and George II (r. 1727–1760). Most German migrants engaged in politics only to protect their religious liberty and property rights (such as those relating to married women) and were content to live in a British-defined political community.

By maintaining their ethnic and cultural identities, the German, Scots-Irish and English- and Welsh-Quaker European migrants created a pluralistic society in the mid-Atlantic colonies (Map 4.3). Only after the passage of several generations did a common "American" outlook begin to emerge.

Religious Identity and Political Conflict

In Western Europe religious diversity and freedom were condemned, and even in America most ministers remained committed to an established church and government enforcement of religious rules. Throughout the mid-Atlantic colonies "the preachers do not have

GOTTLIEB MITTELBERGER
The Perils of Migration

———————★———————

Gottlieb Mittelberger was a Lutheran minister who migrated to Pennsylvania with thousands of other Germans in the 1740s. Dismayed by the lax religious behavior of the colonial population and the lack of state support for religious authority, he returned to his homeland after a few years. In a book published in Germany in 1750, Mittelberger viewed America with a critical eye, warning his readers of the difficulties of migration and of life in a harsh, competitive society.

[The journey from Germany to Pennsylvania via Holland and England] lasts from the beginning of May to the end of October, fully half a year, amid such hardships as no one is able to describe adequately with their misery. Both in Rotterdam and in Amsterdam the people are packed densely, like herrings so to say, in the large sea-vessels. One person receives a place of scarcely 2 feet width and 6 feet length in the bedstead, while many a ship carries four to six hundred souls. . . .

During the journey the ship is full of pitiful signs of distress—smells, fumes, horrors, vomiting, various kinds of sea sickness, fever, dysentery, headaches, heat, constipation, boils, scurvy, cancer, mouth-rot, and similar afflictions, all of them caused by the age and the highly-salted state of the food, especially of the meat, as well as by the very bad and filthy water, which brings about the miserable destruction and death of many. . . .

Children between the ages of one and seven seldom survive the sea voyage; and parents must often watch their offspring suffer miserably, die, and be thrown into the ocean, from want, hunger, thirst, and the like. I myself, alas, saw such a pitiful fate overtake thirty-two children on board our vessel, all of whom were finally thrown into the sea. Their parents grieve all the more, since their children do not find repose in the earth, but are devoured by the predatory fish of the ocean. . . .

When the ships finally arrive in Philadelphia after the long voyage only those are let off who can pay their sea freight or can give good security. The others, who lack the money to pay, have to remain on board until they are purchased and until their purchasers can thus pry them loose from the ship. In this whole process the sick are the worst off, for the healthy are preferred and are more readily paid for. . . . Every day Englishmen, Dutchmen and High-German people select among the healthy persons; . . . adult persons bind themselves in writing to serve 3, 4, 5, or six years for the amount due to them. . . . Many parents must sell and trade away their children like so many head of cattle; for if their children take the debt upon themselves, the parents can leave the ship free and unrestrained. It often happens that whole families, husband, wife, and children, are separated by being sold to different purchasers, especially when they have not paid any part of their passage money. . . .

Thus let him who wants to earn his piece of bread honestly and in a Christian manner and who can only do this by manual labor in his native country stay *there* rather than come to America.

Source: Gottlieb Mittelberger, *Journey to Pennsylvania* (1756), ed. and trans. Oscar Handlin and John Clive (Cambridge, MA: Harvard University Press, 1960), 11–21.

---

the power to punish anyone, or to force anyone to go to church," complained the German-born minister Gottlieb Mittelberger. As a result, "Sunday is very badly kept. Many people plough, reap, thresh, hew or split wood and the like." Thus, Mittelberger concluded, religious liberty "does more harm than good to many people, both in soul and body."

However, religious congregations in the mid-Atlantic colonies and the southern backcountry enforced moral behavior among their members through communal self-discipline. "To preserve their people from falling off to the Church [of England]," the Anglican minister Charles Woodmason reported from the Carolina frontier, "the Synods of Pennsylvania and New England send out a sett of Rambling fellows yearly" (see American Voices, "Charles Woodmason: Social Chaos on the Carolina Frontier," p. 121). And German Lutherans established no fewer than forty schools from Virginia to Georgia to transmit their religious principles to the next generation.

The Quakers in Pennsylvania developed a particularly successful set of communal institutions. Each

MAP 4.3
Religious Diversity, 1750
By 1750 religious diversity was on the rise. Baptists had grown in numbers in New England—long the stronghold of Congregationalism—and would later dominate Virginia. Already there were pockets of Presbyterians and Lutherans in the South, where Anglicanism was the established religion.

portions and usually married within the sect. Those who lacked the resources remained unmarried or left the Society. In this way the Quakers maintained a community that was both prosperous and well defined, thereby perpetuating their political power even as thousands of Scots-Irish and Germans poured into Pennsylvania.

In the 1750s Quaker dominance in Pennsylvania finally came under attack. Scots-Irish Presbyterians who migrated to frontier settlements west of the Susquehanna River (which runs through present-day Harrisburg) challenged the pacifism of the Quaker-dominated assembly and demanded a more aggressive Indian policy. Many of the newer German migrants also opposed the Quakers; they wanted laws that respected their inheritance customs, and they sought representation in the provincial assembly in proportion to their numbers. Soon Scots-Irish Presbyterians, German Baptists, and German Lutherans began to cooperate against the Quakers. But as each of these churches had a distinct political agenda, the alliance was fragile. Moreover, as a European visitor reported, the anti-Quaker groups were divided by ethnicity and "a mutual jealousy, for religious zeal is secretly burning."

A similar religious and ethnic dispute broke out in New York, where members of the Church of England struggled with Scots-Irish Presbyterians for control of King's College, founded in 1754. These animosities carried over into the War of Independence, arraying ethnic groups and churches against one another (see Chapter 6). Yet the mid-Atlantic experiment in freedom and diversity managed to survive the passions of the American Revolution and became a model for the future. In the centuries to come cultural pluralism, an open political order, and passionate ethnic and social conflicts would characterize much of American society.

The Enlightenment and the Great Awakening, 1740–1765

Two great European cultural movements reached America between the 1720s and the 1760s: the Enlightenment and Pietism. The *Enlightenment*, which emphasized the power of human reason to shape the world, appealed especially to urban artisans and well-educated men and women from merchant or planter families. *Pietism*, a religious movement that stressed pious conduct (rather than theological beliefs) and a Christian's personal relation to God, attracted many adherents, especially among farmers and urban laborers. The two movements promoted independent behavior in differ-

Quaker family attended a weekly worship meeting and a monthly discipline meeting. Four times a year a committee met with each family to make certain the children were receiving proper religious instruction. The committee also reported on the moral behavior of adults; a Chester County meeting disciplined one of its members "to reclaim him from drinking to excess and keeping vain company." To sustain a self-contained and prosperous community, Quaker meetings granted permission to marry only to couples with sufficient land, livestock, and equipment to support themselves and their future children. And they usually prohibited marriage to non-Quakers. Over the generations this strict system shaped the character of the Quaker community. The children of well-to-do Friends had ample marriage

CHARLES WOODMASON
Social Chaos on the Carolina Frontier

———————★———————

To Church of England minister Charles Woodmason, the Carolina backcountry was the opposite of the ordered, civilized society for which he yearned. In his journal, he described poor communities filled with immoral people—a chaotic mixture of ethnic and religious groups who had little respect for established authority. But a careful reading of his entries reveals more order and prosperity than his tone indicates. There were nonchurched ruffians in the backcountry but also a multitude of church-going people who were members of dissenting Protestant congregations led by affluent planters and politically astute lawyers.

[February 1767] I had appointed a Congregation to meet me at the Head of Hanging Rock Creek— Where I arriv'd on Tuesday Evening—Found the Houses filled with debauch'd licentious fellows, and Scot Presbyterians who had hir'd these lawless Ruffians to insult me, which they did with Impunity—Telling me, they wanted no D_____d Black Gown Sons of Bitches among them—and threatening to lay me behind the Fire, which they assuredly would have done had not some travellers alighted very opportunely, and taken me under Protection—These Men sat up with, and guarded me all the Night. . . .

[June 1768] You must understand that all (or greatest Part) of this Part of the Province where I am, has been settled within these 5 years by Irish Presbyterians from Belfast, or Pennsylvania and they imagin'd that they could secure this large Tract of fine country to themselves and their Sect. Hereon, they built Meeting Houses, and got Pastors from Ireland, and Scotland. But with these there has also a Great Number of New Lights and Independants come here from New England, and many Baptists. . . .

To preserve their People from falling off to the Church established [Woodmason's Church of England], . . . the Synods of Pennsylvania and New England send out a Sett of Rambling fellows Yearly—who do no Good to the People, no Service to Religion—but turning of their Brains and picking up their Pockets of ev'ry Pistreen the Poor Wretches have, return back again, with double the profits I can make. . . . Of near 100 Couple that I've married, I have not been paid for ⅓. Their Poverty is so Great, that were they to offer me a fee, my Heart would not let me take it. . . .

These Sects are eternally jarring among themselves—The Presbyterians hate the Baptists far more than they do the Episcopalians, and so of the Rest—but (as in England) they will unite altogether in a body to distress or injure the Church established.

Hence it is, that when any Bills have been presented to the Legislature to promote the Interests of Religion, these Sectaries have found Means to have them overruled, for the leading men of the House being all Lawyers, those People know how to grease Wheels as make them turn.

If Numbers were to be counted here, the Church People would have the Majority—but in Point of Interest, I judge that the Dissenters possess most Money—and thereby they can give a Bias to things at Pleasure.

———————

Source: Charles Woodmason, *The Carolina Backcountry on the Eve of the Revolution*, ed. Richard Hooker (Chapel Hill: University of North Carolina Press, 1953), 16–18, 41–46.

ent ways; together they transformed American intellectual and cultural life.

The Enlightenment in America

Like most Europeans of the eighteenth century, the American colonists relied on religious teachings or folk wisdom to explain the workings of the natural world. Thus Swedish settlers in Pennsylvania attributed magical powers to the great white mullein, a common wildflower. When they had a fever, a traveler reported, they would "tie the leaves around their feet and arms." Even educated people believed that events occurred for reasons that today would be considered magical. When a measles epidemic struck Boston in the 1710s, the Puritan minister Cotton Mather tried to contain it by asking

God to sprinkle "our Houses [with] the Blood of the Great Passover"—referring to the ritual dabbing that had saved the Jews of the Old Testament from a terrible plague. Like most Christians, Mather believed that the earth stood at the center of the universe and that God intervened directly in human affairs.

The New Learning. Most Americans held to these beliefs despite the Scientific Revolution of the sixteenth and seventeenth centuries, which had challenged both traditional Christian and folk world views. As early as the 1530s the astronomer Copernicus had observed that the earth traveled around the sun, rather than vice versa, implying a more modest place for human beings in the universe. Other scholars conducted experiments using empirical methods—actual observed experience—to learn about natural phenomena such as earthquakes and lightning. Eventually the English scientist Isaac Newton, in his *Principia Mathematica* (1687), used mathematics to explain the movement of the planets around the sun. Newton's laws of motion and understanding of gravity described how the universe could operate without God's constant intervention, undermining traditional Christian explanations of the actions of the cosmos.

In the century between the publication of Newton's book and the outbreak of the French Revolution in 1789, the philosophers of the European Enlightenment applied scientific reasoning to all aspects of life, including social institutions and human behavior. Enlightenment thinkers believed that human beings could observe, analyze, understand, and improve their world. They advanced four fundamental principles: the lawlike order of the natural world, the power of human reason, the natural rights of individuals (including the right to self-government), and the progressive improvement of society.

The English philosopher John Locke was a significant contributor to the "new learning." In his *Essay Concerning Human Understanding* (1690), Locke emphasized the impact of environment, experience, and reason on human behavior. He proposed that the character of individuals and societies was not fixed by God's will but could be changed through education and purposeful action. Locke's *Two Treatises on Government* (1690) advanced the revolutionary theory that political authority was not divinely ordained, as kings such as James II insisted, but sprang from *"social compacts"* that people made to preserve their "natural rights" to life, liberty, and property. In Locke's view, not princes but people conferred political legitimacy, so that governments might change through the decision of a majority—as they did during the uprisings of the Glorious Revolution (see Chapter 3).

The Enlightenment ideas of Locke and other thinkers came to America with books and travelers and soon affected the beliefs of well-educated colonists about religion, science, and politics. As early as the 1710s the Reverend John Wise of Ipswich, Massachusetts, combined Locke's political principles with Calvinist theology to defend the decision of Congregational churches to vest power in the ordinary members—the laity. Wise argued that just as the social compact formed the basis of political society, the religious covenant made the congregation—not bishops or monarchs, as in the Church of England—the interpreter of spiritual authority.

Enlightenment science also made inroads against traditional religious beliefs and remedies. When a smallpox epidemic threatened Boston in the 1720s, Cotton Mather prayed for God's mercy but also sought a scientific remedy, joining with Zabdiel Boylston, a prominent Boston physician, to support the new technique of inoculation. Few of the inoculated people had died, another Boston physician reported, but "an exact scrutiny" revealed that 6,000 others "have now had the small Pox and of these 844 died."

Benjamin Franklin and the Enlightenment. Benjamin Franklin (1706–1790) was the epitome of the American Enlightenment. Born in Boston to a devout Calvinist family and apprenticed to a printer as a youth, Franklin was a self-made, self-taught man. As a tradesman, printer, and journalist in Philadelphia, he mastered a wide variety of political and scientific works and formed "a club of mutual improvement" that met weekly to discuss "Morals, Politics, or Natural Philosophy."

Franklin's imagination was shaped by Enlightenment literature rather than the Bible—which many Christians believed was God's direct revelation to humanity. As Franklin explained in his *Autobiography* (published first in 1771 and later expanded), "from the different books I read, I began to doubt of Revelation itself." Like many urban artisans, wealthy Virginia planters, and affluent seaport merchants, he became a *deist*. Influenced by Enlightenment science, deists believed that God had created the world but allowed it to operate in accordance with the laws of nature. The deists' God was a rational being, a divine "watchmaker" who did not intervene directly in history or in people's lives. Rejecting the authority of the Bible, deists relied on people's "natural reason" to define a moral code. Adherence to the code, they believed, would be rewarded by God after death.

Franklin popularized the practical outlook of the Enlightenment in *Poor Richard's Almanac* (1732–1757), which was published annually and read by thousands. Equally significant, his innovations and inventions supported the Enlightenment's progress, both in America and Europe. In 1743 he helped found the American Philosophical Society, an institution devoted to "the

Franklin's Influence
Benjamin Franklin's work as a scientist and inventor captivated subsequent generations of Americans. This painted panel (c. 1830) from a fire engine of the Franklin Volunteer Fire Company of Philadelphia depicts Franklin's experiment of 1752 that demonstrated the presence of electricity in lightning.
Cigna Museum and Art Collection. Photo by Joseph Painter.

promotion of useful knowledge," and he proceeded to invent bifocal lenses for eyeglasses, an improved stove (the Franklin stove), and the lightning rod. Franklin's book on electricity, first published in England in 1751, was praised by the English scientist Joseph Priestley as the greatest contribution to science since Newton's discovery of the laws of gravity and motion.

Thanks in part to Franklin's efforts, Philadelphia became the showplace of the American Enlightenment, the home of the first American medical school (1765) and a circulating library filled with the latest scientific treatises from Europe. Quaker and Anglican merchants built a Hospital for the Sick Poor and in 1767 added a Bettering House to shelter the aged and disabled and offer employment to the poor. These philanthropists acted from both moral conviction and economic self-interest, for they hoped these institutions would reduce the taxes they paid for "relief" of the poor. Nonetheless the hospital and the bettering house were tangible expressions of the Enlightenment belief that purposeful human action could improve society.

The life of the mind came of age in Philadelphia and other American cities—primarily among educated men and women but also among skilled artisans, who debated radical political principles in their clubs and workshops. By the 1760s nearly every colony had a reg-

ularly published newspaper, ambitious printers produced magazines for educated gentlemen, and booksellers had increased their stock of European books and papers. The European Enlightenment had added a secular dimension to colonial intellectual life, preparing the way for the great American contributions to republican political theory by Thomas Jefferson, John Adams, James Madison, Alexander Hamilton, and other patriots during the Revolutionary era.

Pietism in America

As a few Americans—mostly urban artisans and merchants and wealthy Virginia planters—turned to deism, many other colonists embraced the European devotional movement known as Pietism. Forsaking theological arguments, Pietists emphasized devout, or "pious," behavior, emotional church services, and striving for mystical union with God. Their preachers appealed to the hearts, not the minds, of their congregations.

The First Revivals. Pietist teachings came to America with German migrants in the 1720s and sparked religious revivals among farmers, artisans, and laborers. In Pennsylvania and New Jersey the Dutch minister Theodore Jacob Frelinghuysen moved from church

A Perspective View of the Pennsylvania Hospital, with the Buildings as intended to be erected

**Enlightenment Philanthropy:
The Philadelphia Hospital**
This imposing structure, built in 1753 with public funds and private donations, embodied two Enlightenment principles— that purposeful action could improve society and that the world should express reason and order (exhibited here by the symmetrical facade). Etchings such as this one drawn c. 1761 circulated widely, bolstering Philadelphia's reputation as the center of the American Enlightenment.
Historical Society of Pennsylvania.

to church, preaching rousing, emotional sermons to German settlers. In private prayer meetings he harnessed their enthusiasm and encouraged lay members to convey a message of spiritual urgency to their growing congregations. A decade later William Tennent and his son Gilbert—Presbyterian clergymen who copied Frelinghuysen's approach—drew upon the Scots-Irish revivalist tradition and raised great religious "enthusiasm" among the migrants from Ireland.

Simultaneously, a native-born pietistic movement developed in Puritan New England. Although Puritanism had its origins in a pietistic upsurge in England, many American Puritan congregations had lost their religious zeal over the decades. In the 1730s the minister Jonathan Edwards sought to restore spiritual commitment to the Congregational churches in the Connecticut River Valley. A philosopher as well as an effective preacher, Edwards urged his hearers—especially young men and women—to commit themselves to a life of piety and prayer. His sermons prompted hundreds of listeners to undergo conversion; being widely printed and distributed, his words also provided a strong theological justification for the revival movement (see American Lives, "Jonathan Edwards: Preacher, Philosopher, Pastor," pp. 126–127).

George Whitefield and the Great Awakening. In the 1740s religious revival was carried to new heights by George Whitefield, a young English evangelist who traversed the mainland settlements and sparked a "Great Awakening." Whitefield had experienced conversion in England after reading German pietistic tracts. He became a disciple of John Wesley, the founder of English Methodism, who combined enthusiastic preaching with prescribed rules of behavior and disciplined "methods" of worship, such as specific prayers and regularly scheduled meetings. Whitefield carried Wesley's preaching style to America and enjoyed equally great success.

As Whitefield traveled from Georgia to Massachusetts between 1739 and 1741, huge crowds of "enthusiasts" greeted him all along his route. "Religion is become the Subject of most Conversations," the *Pennsylvania Gazette* reported. "No books are in Request but those of Piety and Devotion." The usually skeptical and restrained Benjamin Franklin was so impressed by Whitefield's oratory that when the preacher asked for contributions, Franklin emptied his pockets "wholly into the collector's dish, gold and all." By the time the evangelist reached Boston, the Reverend Benjamin Colman reported, the people were "ready to receive him as an angel of God."

Whitefield's appeal was partly owing to his compelling personal presence. "He looked almost angelical; a young, slim, slender youth . . . cloathed with authority from the Great God," wrote a Connecticut farmer (see American Voices, "Nathan Cole: The Power of a Preacher," p. 125). Like most evangelical preachers, Whitefield did not read his sermons but spoke from memory, as if inspired, raising his voice for dramatic effect, gesturing eloquently, and making striking use of biblical metaphors. The young preacher evoked a deep emotional response when he impressed on his listeners the assertion that they had all sinned and must seek salvation. Hundreds of men and women suddenly felt the "new light" of God's

NATHAN COLE

The Power of a Preacher

———————★———————

The evangelist George Whitefield transformed the lives of thousands of Americans, such as the Connecticut farmer Nathan Cole, by convincing them of their sinfulness. In his reflections on his life (a short unpublished manuscript now in the archives of the Connecticut Historical Society), Cole described the impact that Whitefield's preaching made on his life in 1741 and his months of agony as he prayed for a sign that he was worthy enough to merit God's grace.

Now it please God to Send Mr. Whitefield into this land; and my hearing of his preaching at Philadelphia, like one of the old apostles, . . . I felt the Spirit of God drawing me by conviction; I longed to see and hear him and wished he would come this way. . . . Then of a sudden, in the morning about 8 or 9 of the clock there came a messenger and said Mr. Whitefield . . . is to preach at Middletown this morning at ten of the clock. I was in my field at work. I dropped my tool that I had in my hand and ran home to my wife, telling her to make ready quickly. . . .

When I saw Mr. Whitefield come upon the scaffold, he looked almost angelical; a young, slim, slender youth before some thousands of people with a bold undaunted countenance. And my hearing how

God was with him everywhere as he came, it solemnized my mind and put me into a trembling fear before he began to preach; for he looked as if he was clothed with authority from the Great God, and a sweet solemnity sat upon his brow, and my hearing him preach gave me a heart wound. By God's blessing my old foundation was broken up, and I saw that my righteousness would not save me.

Then I was convinced of the doctrine of Election: and went right to quarrelling with God about it; because that all I could do would not save me, and he had decreed from Eternity who should be saved and who not: I began to think I was not Elected, and that God had made some for heaven and me for hell. And I thought God was not Just in so doing. . . . Now this distress lasted Almost two years—Poor—Me—Miserable me. . . .

Hell fire was most always in my mind; and I have hundreds of times put my fingers into my pipe when I have been smoking to feel how fire felt: And to see how my Body could bear to lye in Hell fire for ever and ever. . . .

And while these thoughts were in my mind God appeared unto me and made me Skringe [cringe]. . . . I seemed to hang in open Air before God, and he seemed to Speak to me in an angry and Sovereign way: What won't you trust your Soul with God? My heart answered Oh yes, yes, yes. I was set free, my distress was gone. . . . Then I began to pray and praise God.

———————

Source: Richard Bushman, *The Great Awakening: Documents on the Revival of Religion, 1740–1745* (Chapel Hill: University of North Carolina Press, 1989), 67–71.

grace within them. Afterward, strengthened and self-confident, these so-called New Lights were prepared to follow in Whitefield's footsteps.

The Awakening in the North

Like all cultural explosions, the Great Awakening was controversial. Conservative ministers such as Charles Chauncy of Boston condemned (and feared) the "cryings out, faintings and convulsions" produced by emotional preaching. These so-called Old Lights persuaded the Connecticut legislative assembly to prohibit traveling preachers from speaking to established

congregations without the ministers' permission. When Whitefield returned to Connecticut in 1744, he found many pulpits closed to him. But the New Lights won repeal of the law in 1750, resisting attempts by civil authorities to silence them. "I shall bring glory to God in my bonds," a dissident New Light preacher wrote from jail. Dozens of farmers, women, and artisans roamed the countryside in New England, condemning the Old Lights as "unconverted" sinners. In New York and New Jersey the Dutch Reformed Church split in two, as New Lights in those colonies rejected the conservative-minded preachers assigned to them by church authorities in the Netherlands.

Jonathan Edwards: Preacher, Philosopher, Pastor

————————★————————

JONATHAN EDWARDS DID not mince words. Echoing the harsh theology of John Calvin, Edwards preached that men and women were helpless creatures completely dependent on God: "There is Hell's wide gaping mouth open; and you have nothing to stand upon, nor any thing to take hold of: there is nothing between you and Hell but the air; 'tis only the power and mere pleasure of God that holds you up."

Edwards spoke "without much noise of external emotion," a listener noted, and without a single gesture. But his intense "inner fervor" underlined the torments that awaited those who fell into the eternal flames:

> How dismal will it be . . . to know assuredly that you never, never shall be delivered from them; . . . after you shall have endured these torments millions of ages . . . your bodies, which shall have been burning and roasting all this while in these glowing flames, yet shall not have been consumed, but will remain to roast through an eternity yet.

Such was the terrible—and inevitable—fate that Edwards the preacher promised to complacent Christians in his most famous sermon, *Sinners in the Hands of an Angry God* (1742). But Edwards the pastor preached a more hopeful message of personal repentance and spiritual rebirth, telling congregations that this fate awaited only those who "never passed under a great change of heart, by the mighty power of the spirit of God upon your souls; all that were never born again, and made new creatures."

Blending passionate warnings with compassionate forgiveness, Edwards inspired a religious revival in the Connecticut River Valley in the mid-1730s and helped George Whitefield stir up an even greater one in the 1740s. But this minister, one of the leading revivalists of his age, was also a profound and original philosopher, perhaps the most intellectually brilliant colonial American.

Jonathan Edwards was born in 1703 in East Windsor, Connecticut, the fifth child and only son among the eleven children of Timothy and Esther Stoddard Edwards. His father came from a wealthy family but ended up a poorly paid rural minister who fought constantly with his congregation over his salary and authority, battles that Jonathan would later fight with his own church. His mother was the daughter of Solomon Stoddard, a famous Connecticut preacher and revivalist—a family legacy that would both help and haunt Jonathan Edwards throughout his life.

As a youth Jonathan embraced his grandfather Stoddard's theology, rejecting the Calvinist belief in God's omnipotence over people's lives and labeling it "a horrible doctrine." But at the age of seventeen he became a committed Calvinist, explaining in a *Personal Narrative* written later in life that he had then experienced "a *delightful* conviction" of the Almighty's absolute sovereignty, of "sweetly conversing with Christ, and wrapt and swallowed up in God." In fact, Edwards distorted the truth in his autobiography, for he found his Calvinist God only after many years of personal torment and a series of physical and emotional collapses.

The Enlightenment came more easily to Edwards. While studying for the ministry at Yale College, he read the works of Isaac Newton, John Locke, and other Enlightenment thinkers, thereby beginning a lifetime of philosophical inquiry into the meaning of words and things. He accepted Locke's argument in the *Essay Concerning Human Understanding* (1690) that ideas are not innate at birth but are the product of experience as conveyed through the senses—our ability to see, hear, feel, and taste the world around us. A person who has never *tasted* a pineapple, said Locke, will never have "the true idea of the relish of that celebrated and delicious fruit."

But Locke's theory of knowledge was less successful in explaining *abstract* ideas—such as God, love, salvation—and here Edwards made his contribution. Locke had suggested that abstract ideas resulted when the mind rationally analyzed various sense experiences. Edwards knew better. He had worked out his theological doctrines through intense personal torment; thus he knew they had an emotional component—that "love" (whether of God or a fellow human being) was "felt" and not merely understood. It followed that abstract ideas were emotional as well as rational entities, the product of the passions as well as the senses.

Jonathan Edwards, 1720
This portrait of Edwards, painted by Joseph Badger when Edwards was seventeen, shows that even as a young man Edwards was grave and dignified.
Yale University Art Gallery; bequest of Eugene Philips Edwards.

Edwards used his theory of knowledge to justify his style of preaching, arguing that vivid words promoted conversions. As he put it in *A Treatise Concerning Religious Affections* (1746), "true religion, in great part, consists in holy affection." He would save his congregation through powerful sermons: "to fright persons away from Hell." In the end the philosopher was at one with the preacher.

In 1729 Edwards put these ideas into practice as pastor of the Congregational church in Northampton, Massachusetts, taking over that ministry from his grandfather, Solomon Stoddard, and matching his success as a revivalist, especially among young people. Beginning in 1734, Edwards reported, "the number of true saints multiplied . . . the town seemed to be full of the presence of God." News of the Northampton revival stimulated religious fervor up and down the Connecticut River Valley "till there was a general awakening."

Edwards interpreted his success as "a remarkable Testimony of God's Approbation of the Doctrine . . . that we are justified only by faith in Christ, and not by any manner of virtue or goodness of our own."

He maintained that uncompromising Calvinist position during the widespread revivals of the 1740s. Also seeking to restore an older communal order, he took issue with those New Lights who asserted "the absolute Necessity for every Person to act singly . . . as if there was not another human Creature upon earth." Repudiating that spirit of individualism, Edwards insisted that aspiring Saints should heed their pastors, who were "skilful guides," and then make a "credible Relation of their inward Experience" to the congregation, thereby strengthening the covenant bonds that knit members together in a visible church. Edwards extended his critique of individualism to economic affairs, speaking out against "a narrow, private spirit" of greedy merchants and landlords, men who "are not ashamed to hit and bite others [and] grind the faces of the poor."

Edwards's rigorous standards and assault on individualism deeply offended the wealthiest and most influential members of his congregation. Continuing struggles over his salary and disciplinary authority culminated in a final battle in 1750, when Edwards repudiated Stoddard's practice of admitting almost all churchgoers to the sacrament of Communion; he would offer full church membership only to those whom God had chosen as Saints. By a vote of 200 to 20, the Northampton congregation dismissed the great preacher and philosopher from his pastorate. Impoverished and with a family of ten children to support, Edwards moved to Stockbridge, Massachusetts, a small frontier outpost. There he ministered, without great success, to the Housatonic Indians and wrote an impressive philosophical work, *Freedom of the Will* (1752).

In 1757, as Edwards was about to take up the presidency of the College of New Jersey (Princeton), he was inoculated against smallpox, had a severe reaction, and died. He left a pair of spectacles, two wigs, three black coats, and some 300 books, including 22 written by himself—but not much else in the way of earthly goods.

As he lay dying, this turn of fate puzzled America's first great philosopher. Why had God called him to Princeton only to give him no time to undertake his duties? As a preacher and pastor Edwards had always responded to such questions by stressing God's arbitrary power and the "insufficiency of reason" to understand God's purpose. Now he himself had to accept that grim and unsatisfying answer, showing through his personal experience why Calvinism was such a hard faith by which to live . . . and die.

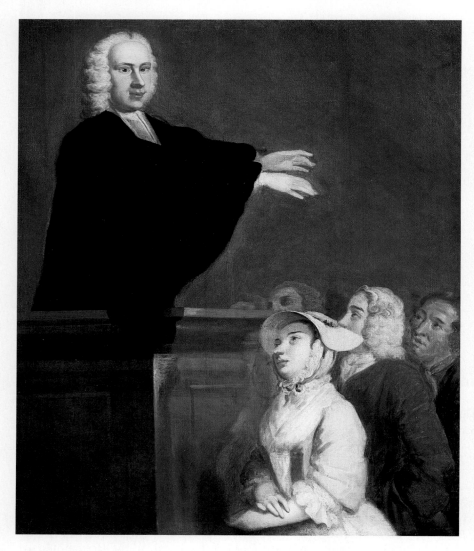

George Whitefield, 1742
One can only infer from this painting the magical appeal of George Whitefield as an orator. When he spoke to a crowd near Philadelphia, an observer noted, his words were "sharper than a two-edged sword. . . . Some of the people were pale as death; others were wringing their hands . . . and most lifting their eyes to heaven and crying to God for mercy." National Portrait Gallery, London.

The upheavals and debates that were a part of the Great Awakening altered American perceptions of the proper religious order. Except in Rhode Island and Pennsylvania, most colonists paid taxes that supported established churches. Like Roger Williams in the 1630s, New Lights and Baptists—another "enthusiastic" radical Protestant movement—challenged the authority of governments to impose such taxes or regulate spiritual affairs. In New England many New Lights left the established Congregational Church; by 1754 they had founded 125 "separatist" churches, supporting their ministers through "voluntary" contributions. Other religious dissidents joined Baptist congregations, which also favored a greater separation of church and state (Figure 4.3). According to the Baptist preacher Isaac Backus, "God never allowed any civil state upon earth to impose religious taxes."

The Awakening also challenged the authority of ministers, who had once commanded respect on the basis of their education and biblical knowledge.

Gilbert Tennent questioned those criteria in an influential pamphlet, *The Dangers of an Unconverted Ministry* (1740), in which he maintained that ministers became qualified to hold office not through theological training but through conversion. Reasserting Martin Luther's commitment to the priesthood of all believers, Tennent suggested that anyone who had experienced the saving grace of God could speak with ministerial authority. Not long afterward, Isaac Backus celebrated this spiritual democracy, noting that "the common people now claim as good a right to judge and act in matters of religion as civil rulers or the learned clergy."

By joining in religious revivals, farm families reaffirmed the cooperative work ethic that tied together their rural communities. Many preachers questioned the growing competition and pursuit of wealth that accompanied the expansion of the American economy and threatened to divide the colonists into distinct social classes. "In any truly Christian society," Gilbert

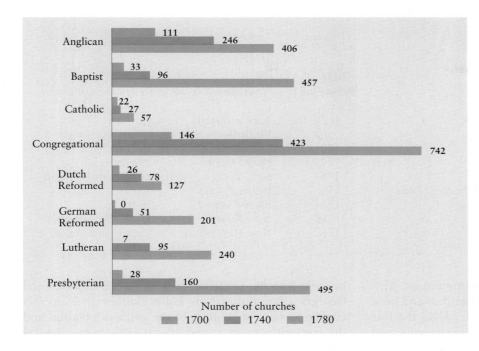

FIGURE 4.3
Church Growth by Denomination, 1700–1780
Some churches, such as the Dutch Reformed, grew only from the natural increase of their members. After 1740, the fastest-growing denominations were immigrant churches—the German Reformed, Lutheran, and Presbyterian—and those with an evangelical message, such as the Baptists.

Tennent declared, "mutual *Love* is the *Band and Cement*"—not the mercenary values of the marketplace. Suspicious of merchants and land speculators and dismayed by the erosion of traditional morality, Jonathan Edwards spoke for many rural Americans when he charged that a "private niggardly [miserly] spirit" was more suitable "for wolves and other beasts of prey, than for human beings."

As religious enthusiasm spread, churches founded new colleges to educate their youth and train ministers. New Light Presbyterians established the College of New Jersey (Princeton) in 1746, and New York Anglicans founded King's College (Columbia) in 1754. Baptists set up the College of Rhode Island (Brown); the Dutch Reformed Church subsidized Queen's College (Rutgers) in New Jersey (Table 4.2). The true intellectual legacy of the Awakening, however, was not a college education for the few but a new sense of religious authority among the many.

Social and Religious Conflict in the South

The Great Awakening also sparked religious conflict in the South, especially in Virginia. Although the established Church of England was supported by public taxes, it had never ministered to most Virginians. African Americans (about 40 percent of the population) were generally ignored by the church, and landless whites (another 20 percent) attended irregularly. Middling white freeholders, who accounted for about 35 percent of the population, formed the core of most Anglican (Church of England) congregations. But

prominent planters and their families (5 percent of the population) held real power in the church; as the vestrymen of the parish, they hired ministers and used their control over finances to discipline them. One Anglican clergyman complained that dismissal awaited any minister who "had the courage to preach against any Vices taken into favor by the leading Men of his Parish."

New Light Presbyterians. The Great Awakening challenged both Anglicanism and the power of the southern planter elite. In 1743 the bricklayer Samuel Morris, who had been inspired by his reading of George Whitefield's sermons, led a group of Virginia Anglicans out of the established church. Seeking a more vital religious experience, Morris and his followers invited New Light Presbyterian ministers from Scots-Irish settlements along the Virginia frontier to lead their prayer meetings. Soon these local revivals spread across the backcountry and into the long-settled Tidewater region (so called because ocean tides carried salt water far up coastal rivers), threatening the social authority of the Virginia gentry. Planters and their well-dressed families were used to arriving at Church of England services in elaborate carriages drawn by well-bred horses. Some routinely flaunted their power by marching in a body to their seats in the front pews. The gentry feared that these potent reminders of their social superiority would vanish if freeholders attended New Light Presbyterian rather than Church of England services. Moreover, they worried that religious pluralism would undermine their ability to tax the population to support the established church.

To prevent the spread of New Light doctrines, Virginia's governor denounced the "false teachings" of the Presbyterian ministers, and Anglican justices of the

TABLE 4.2

Colonial Colleges

	Date of Founding	Colony	Religious Affiliation
Harvard	1636	Massachusetts	Puritan
William and Mary	1693	Virginia	Church of England
Yale	1701	Connecticut	Puritan
College of New Jersey (Princeton)	1746	New Jersey	Presbyterian
King's (Columbia)	1754	New York	Church of England
College of Philadelphia (University of Pennsylvania)	1755	Pennsylvania	None
College of Rhode Island (Brown)	1764	Rhode Island	Baptist
Queen's (Rutgers)	1766	New Jersey	Dutch Reformed
Dartmouth	1769	New Hampshire	Congregationalist

peace closed down Presbyterian meetinghouses. This harassment kept most white yeoman families and poor tenants within the Church of England, as did the fact that most Presbyterian ministers were highly educated and sought converts mainly among skilled workers and propertied farmers.

Baptist Revivals and Black Protestantism. Baptists succeeded where Presbyterians failed. Like the Quakers, Baptists were a radical offshoot of the Protestant Reformation, direct descendants of the Anabaptists (see Chapter 1). Condemned or outlawed by the authorities throughout Europe, Baptists drew their congregations from among the poor, developing emotionally charged rituals that offered solace and hope in a world of trouble. Their central ritual was adult baptism, often involving complete immersion in water. Once men and women had experienced the infusion of grace—had been "born again"—they were baptized in an emotional public ceremony that celebrated the Baptists' shared fellowship. One Sunday "about 2,000 people came together," a Virginia Baptist minister recounted in his journal:

> We went to a field and making a circle in the center, there laid hands on the persons baptized. The multitude stood around weeping, but when we sang come we that love the lord *they lifted up their hands and faces toward heaven and discovered such cheerful countenances in the midst of flowing tears as I have never seen before.*

During the 1760s thousands of yeomen and tenant farm families in Virginia flocked to revivalist meetings, drawn by the enthusiasm and democratic ways of Baptist preachers.

Even slaves were welcome at Baptist revivals. As early as 1740 George Whitefield had openly condemned the brutality of slaveowners and urged that Africans be brought into the Christian fold. In South Carolina and Georgia a handful of New Light planters took up this challenge, but the hostility of the white population and the commitment of many Africans to their ancestral religions kept the number of converts low. The first sizable conversion of slaves took place in the 1760s among second- and third-generation African Americans in Virginia. Hundreds of those slaves, who knew English and English ways, joined Baptist churches run by ministers who taught that all people were equal in God's eyes.

The ruling gentry reacted violently to the Baptists, who posed a threat to their cultural dominance and political power. The Baptists courted blacks and poor whites and emphasized equality by calling one another "brother" and "sister." Baptist preachers urged their followers to work hard and lead virtuous lives, and condemned the customary pleasures of Chesapeake men such as gambling, drinking, whoring, and cockfighting. In response, Anglican sheriffs and justices of the peace organized armed bands of planters who broke up Baptist services by force. In Caroline County, Virginia, an Anglican posse attacked one Brother Waller. He had begun to pray when, a fellow Baptist reported, "he was violently jerked off the stage; they caught him by the back part of his neck, beat his head against the ground, and a gentleman gave him twenty lashes with his horsewhip." Despite such attacks, about 20 percent of Virginia's whites and hundreds of enslaved blacks had joined Baptist churches by 1775. In the South as in the North, Protestant revivalism was on the way to becoming a dominant American religious tradition.

Although Anglican slaveowners retained their economic and political power in Virginia, the revival began to alter the character of Chesapeake society. Belief in a living God gave meaning to the lives of poor families and better prepared yeomen and tenant farmers to assert their social values and economic interests. Moreover, as Baptist ministers spread Christianity among slaves, the cultural gulf between blacks and whites

The Founding of Dartmouth College
In 1769, to bring Protestant Christianity to European settlers and native Americans in the wilderness, Eleazar Wheelock moved his "Indian School" from Lebanon, Connecticut, to Hanover, New Hampshire. There it became Dartmouth College and, as this engraving shows, was dedicated to the education of both Indians and whites. Dartmouth College Archives.

shrank, undermining one justification for slavery and giving blacks a new sense of spiritual identity. Within a generation, African Americans would develop their own versions of Protestant Christianity.

The Midcentury Challenge: War, Trade, and Social Conflict, 1750–1765

─────── ★ ───────

Between 1740 and 1765 colonial life was transformed not only by Pietism and the Enlightenment but also by war, economic change, and violence on the frontier.

First, Britain embarked on a major war in America, the so-called French and Indian War, which became a worldwide conflict—the Great War for Empire—that redefined the British imperial system. Second, the expansion of transatlantic trade increased colonial prosperity but put Americans into debt to British creditors. Third, Britain's ouster of the French from North America in 1763 stimulated a great westward migration that led to new battles with the Indians, armed conflicts between settlers and landowners, and frontier rebellions against eastern governments.

The Great War for Empire

In 1745 Governor Shirley of Massachusetts predicted that within a century the population of Britain's mainland colonies in North America would equal that of

The Siege of Louisbourg, 1745
Assisted by British redcoats, blue-coated New England militiamen swarmed ashore on
Cape Breton island in May 1745 and laid siege to the formidable French citadel at
Louisbourg. By late June, the colonists' artillery had silenced a strategic French bat-
tery, allowing British warships to enter the harbor. Faced with a combined assault
from land and sea, the French surrendered.
Yale University Art Gallery, Mable Brady Garvan Collection.

France—which was then about 20 million people—and
"lay a foundation for a Superiority of British power
upon the continent of Europe." In fact, in North America the growth of the British colonies had already
begun to shift the balance of military and diplomatic
power. During the War of the Austrian Succession
(1740–1748), which pitted Britain and Austria against
Spain, France, and Prussia, a force of 3,000 New England militiamen captured the powerful French naval
fortress of Louisbourg near the mouth of the St.
Lawrence River, only to see it returned to France in the
Treaty of Aix-la-Chapelle (1748), which ended the war.
But in less than a decade the American colonists would
again join with Britain in a war against France and
Spain that ultimately solidified British control over all
of eastern North America.

Western Expansion and the Road to War. In 1750
the interior of North America was still inhabited primarily by Indians, who intended to remain in control of

these lands. Most French settlers lived along the St.
Lawrence River near the fur-trading centers of Mon-
treal and Quebec (Map 4.4). The more numerous
British inhabitants had not ventured across the
Appalachian Mountains because there were few natural
transportation routes and because of Indian resistance.

For more than a generation the Iroquois and other
native Americans had devised policies that protected
their lands, forming alliances among themselves and
using their control of the fur trade to bargain for guns
and subsidies from British and French officials. However, this strategy of playing off one European power
against another was breaking down as European governments refused to pay the rising cost of "gifts" of
arms and money, and as the Indian alliances crumbled;
along the Ohio River the Delaware and Shawnee
declared that they would no longer abide by Iroquois
policies.

Moreover, the rising Anglo-American demand for
Indian lands, the result of population growth in New

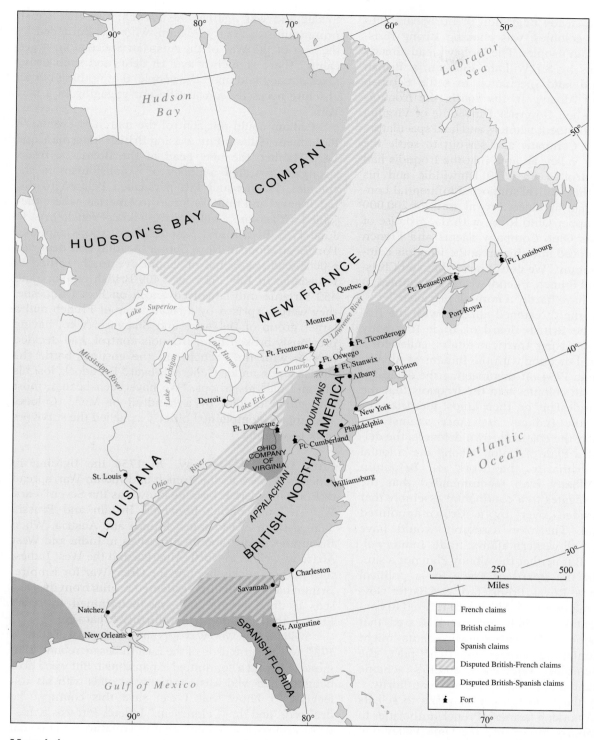

MAP 4.4

European Spheres of Influence, 1754

France laid claim to vast areas of North America and sought to use Indian allies to combat the numerical advantage of British settlers. For their part, native Americans played off one European power against another. As a British official observed, "To preserve the Ballance between us and the French is the great ruling Principle of Modern Indian Politics." By expelling the French from North America, the Great War for Empire disrupted this balance, leaving Indian peoples on their own to resist encroaching Anglo-American settlers.

England and the steady migration of Europeans into the mid-Atlantic colonies, was eliciting strong resistance among Indian peoples. The Mohawk had already rebuffed attempts by Sir William Johnson, a British Indian agent and land speculator, to settle Scottish migrants west of Albany. To the south, the Iroquois were infuriated when Governor Dinwiddie of Virginia and a group of prominent planters and land speculators created the Ohio Company and set out to settle the upper Ohio River Valley, an area that the Iroquois had traditionally controlled. In 1749 Dinwiddie and his associates, with the political support of influential London merchants, had obtained a royal grant of 200,000 acres along the upper Ohio River, with the promise of 300,000 more. As Ohio Company agents and French military forces moved into this area, the Iroquois complained in frustration: "We don't know what you Christians, English and French, intend; we are so hemmed in by both, that we have hardly a hunting place left."

To shore up the threatened alliance with the Iroquois Nations, the British Board of Trade (the body charged with supervising American affairs) called for a great intercolonial meeting with the Indians at Albany, New York, in June 1754. At this meeting the delegates from the American colonies told the Iroquois that the colonists had no designs on their lands; the delegates also asked for the Indians' assistance against the French. To bolster the colonists' own defenses, the delegates proposed a Plan of Union among the colonial governments. Primarily the work of Benjamin Franklin, the Albany Plan recommended that the colonies send delegates to a continental assembly that would be presided over by a Crown-appointed governor-general. The new assembly would have responsibility for all western affairs: trade, Indian policy, and defense. But neither the Albany Plan nor a similar proposal by the Board of Trade for a political "union between ye Royal, Proprietary, & Charter Governments" ever materialized. The board refused to consider a continental assembly because it feared that collaboration among American governments might encourage colonial autonomy; for their part, the provincial assemblies rejected Franklin's scheme because they wanted to preserve their own authority.

Alarmed by the Ohio Company's plans to sell its lands to Anglo-American farmers, French authorities in Quebec sent military forces into the Ohio Valley and ordered the construction of Fort Duquesne at the point where the Monongahela and Allegheny Rivers join to form the Ohio (present-day Pittsburgh). In response, Governor Dinwiddie dispatched an expedition to warn off the French and uphold the land claims of the Ohio Company. It was led by Colonel George Washington, a young planter eager to speculate in western lands. In July 1754 French troops seized Washington and his men, prompting expansionists in Virginia and Britain

to demand war against the French. But the British prime minister, Henry Pelham, who was burdened by the cost of the War of the Austrian Succession, urged calm: "There is such a load of debt, and such heavy taxes already laid upon the people, that nothing but an absolute necessity can justifie our engaging in a new War."

Pelham could not control the march of events. In Parliament William Pitt, a rising British statesman, and Lord Halifax, the new head of the Board of Trade, strongly advocated a policy of expansionism in the colonies. Halifax and Pitt persuaded Pelham to dispatch naval and military forces to America, where they joined with colonial militia in attacking French forts. In June 1755 British and New England troops captured Fort Beauséjour in Nova Scotia (Acadia) and deported 6,000 Acadians, some of whom eventually settled in Louisiana. In July 1755, as 1,400 British regulars and 450 Virginia militiamen advanced on Fort Duquesne, they were surprised by a small force of French and a larger group of Delaware and Shawnee (who, having previously broken from Iroquois control, had decided to side with the French). In the ensuing battle the British commander, General Edward Braddock, lost his life and half his troops. "We have been beaten, most shamefully beaten, by a handfull of Men," Colonel Washington complained bitterly as he led the survivors back to Virginia.

Pitt's Imperial Strategy. In 1756 the fighting in America, known as the French and Indian War, spread to Europe, where it became known as the Seven Years' War—a long conflict in which Britain and Prussia aligned themselves against France and Austria. When Britain decided to mount offensives in India and West Africa as well as in North America and the West Indies, the conflict quickly became the Great War for Empire. Britain had reaped unprecedented profits from its overseas trading empire and was determined to crush France, the main obstacle to further expansion.

William Pitt, who was appointed secretary of state in 1757, was the grandson of the East Indies merchant "Diamond" Pitt and a committed expansionist. Pitt was also a haughty man who was constantly at odds with his colleagues. "I know that I can save this country," he declared, "and that I alone can." Indeed, Pitt was a master of strategy, both commercial and military, and his goal was to cripple France by attacking its overseas empire.

In planning the critical American campaign against New France, Pitt exploited a demographic advantage: on the North American mainland, Britain's nearly 2 million subjects outnumbered the French by 14 to 1. To mobilize the colonists, Pitt agreed to pay half the cost of their troops and supply them with arms and equipment. He then committed a British fleet and thousands of British regulars to the American conflict, appointing

MAP 4.5

The Anglo-American Conquest of New France, 1754–1760
After years of preparation, British and American forces attacked the heartland of New France, capturing Quebec in 1759. The conquest both united and divided the allies. Colonists celebrated the great victory—"The Illuminations and Fireworks exceeded any that had been exhibited before," reported the South Carolina *Gazette*—but British officers viewed provincial soldiers with disdain: "the dirtiest, most contemptible, cowardly dogs you can conceive."

three young officers—James Wolfe, Jeffrey Amherst, and William Howe—as the top commanders. In 1758 British armies forced the French to abandon Fort Duquesne (which they renamed Fort Pitt) and then captured Louisbourg at the mouth of the St. Lawrence River.

The following year the British attacked Quebec, the heart of France's American empire. A British force—50 warships, 200 transports, and 8,500 troops—sailed up the St. Lawrence under the command of General Wolfe in June 1759 (Map 4.5). After several failed attacks, 4,000 British troops scaled the high cliffs protecting the city and overwhelmed the French, who were led by General Montcalm. Quebec's fall was the turning point of the war. The Royal Navy prevented French reinforcements from crossing the Atlantic, and when British forces captured Montreal in 1760, the conquest of Canada was complete.

Pontiac's Uprising. The war in America had one more scene to play. Early in 1763 the Ottawa chief Pontiac led a group of tribes in a major uprising that disrupted the frontier from New York to Michigan. During the war the tribes had been defrauded by rum-peddling British

traders, and they resented the British military occupation of the old French forts as well as General Amherst's decision to curtail "gifts" and supplies of gunpowder. Fearing the influx of Anglo-American settlers, Pontiac hoped to overwhelm British forces in the west and encourage continued French resistance. "I am French," Pontiac declared, "and I want to die French." Other Indians were inspired by Neolin, a Delaware prophet who, blending Christian doctrine with native American beliefs, urged the repudiation of all Europeans—along with their tools and clothes—and a return to traditional customs.

The warriors of Pontiac's confederation initially met with great success, capturing nearly every British garrison west of Fort Niagara and besieging the fort at Detroit. But the Indian alliance gradually weakened, and British military expeditions defeated the Delaware near Fort Pitt and broke the siege of Detroit. In the peace settlement that followed, Pontiac and his allies accepted the British as their new political "fathers." In return, the British addressed some of the Indians' concerns, temporarily barring Anglo-Americans from settling west of the Appalachians by establishing the Proclamation Line of 1763.

A Pipe of Peace
In 1760 the Ottawa chief Pontiac wel-
comed British troops to his territory, offer-
ing a pipe of peace to their commander,
Major Robert Rogers. Three years later,
Pontiac led a coordinated uprising against
British troops, traders, and settlers, accus-
ing them of cheating native American peo-
ples of their furs and lands.
Library of Congress.

The Treaty of Paris.   On other battlefields around the world, the British went from one success to another. Fulfilling Pitt's dream, the East India Company captured French commercial outposts and took control of trade in large sections of India. British forces seized French Senegal in West Africa, the French sugar islands of Martinique and Guadeloupe, and the Spanish colonies of Cuba and the Philippine Islands. When the war ended, Pitt was no longer in office, but his maritime strategy had extended British power around the world.

The Treaty of Paris of 1763 confirmed the triumph, granting Britain sovereignty over half the continent of North America, including French Canada, all French territory east of the Mississippi River, and Spanish Florida. To compensate Spain for the loss of Florida, Britain returned its colonies of Cuba and the Philippines, and France gave Spain title to Louisiana west of the Mississippi. The French empire in North America was reduced to a handful of sugar islands in the West Indies and two rocky islands off the coast of Newfoundland. The transatlantic British empire was at the height of its power.

British Economic Growth

Britain owed its triumph in large part to its unprecedented economic resources. Ever since it had wrested control of many oceanic trade routes from the Dutch at the end of the seventeenth century, Britain had been the dominant commercial power. Now, in the middle of the eighteenth century, it was becoming the first country to undergo industrialization. Its new technology and work discipline made Britain the first—and for over a century, the most powerful—industrial nation in the world.

Britain's Industrial Revolution.   New machines and new business practices enabled Britain to produce more wool and linens, iron tools, paper, chinaware, and glass than ever before—and to sell those goods at low prices. British artisans had designed and built water- and steam-driven machines that powered lathes for shaping wood, jennies and looms for spinning and weaving textiles, and hammers for forging iron. The new machines produced goods far more rapidly than human hands could. Furthermore, the entrepreneurs who ran the new factories drove their employees hard, forcing them to keep pace with the machines and work long hours.

To market their products, English and Scottish merchants launched aggressive campaigns in the rapidly growing mainland colonies. They extended a full year's credit, instead of the traditional six months' credit, to American traders. Colonial merchants and storekeepers took advantage of this longer repayment period to stock larger inventories and to offer better credit terms to their customers, enabling settlers to buy equipment and household goods for their farms. Soon Americans were purchasing 20 percent of all British exports, creating what some historians have called a "consumer revolution" that raised the living standard of many Americans (Figure 4.4).

American Exports.   To pay for these imported goods from Britain, Americans increased their agricultural exports. Tobacco from the Chesapeake remained the most important export, accounting for 25 percent of the total. Planters sent 52 million pounds of tobacco abroad in 1740 and more than 75 million pounds in 1765. Entre-

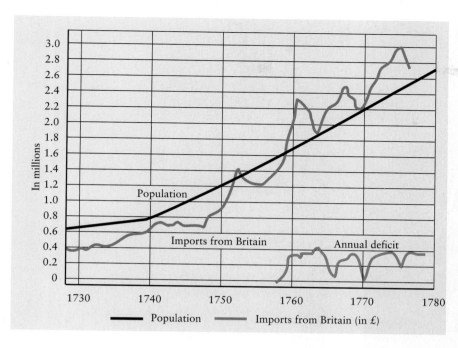

FIGURE 4.4
Colonial Population, Imports from Britain, and the American Trade Deficit
Around 1750 the rate of growth of imports from Britain into the American colonies outpaced the settlers' rate of population growth, indicating that consumption per capita was increasing. The colonists then went into debt to pay for these goods, running an annual deficit with their British suppliers.

preneurs in Scotland financed this export growth by subsidizing Virginia planters and Scots-Irish migrants who moved into the Piedmont, a region of plains and rolling hills inland from the Tidewater counties. Scottish-run stores granted ample credit to the planters—which they used to purchase land, slaves, and equipment—and took part of their tobacco crop in payment. By the 1760s merchants were buying nearly half the annual Chesapeake tobacco crop and reexporting most of it to expanding markets in France and central Europe.

Agricultural exports also supported the luxurious life-style of the white slaveowners of South Carolina and the planters and farmers of the mid-Atlantic region. The British government subsidized the cultivation of indigo, and by the 1760s planters were annually sending indigo valued at £117,000 to English textile factories and exporting about 65 million pounds of rice a year to Holland and southern Europe. Simultaneously New York, Pennsylvania, Maryland, and Virginia became the breadbasket of the Atlantic world, supplying Europe's exploding population with wheat at ever-increasing profits. In Philadelphia, wheat prices jumped almost 50 percent between 1740 and 1765.

This first American spending binge, like most subsequent splurges, landed many consumers in debt. Even during the boom times of the 1750s, exports paid for only 80 percent of imported British goods. The remaining 20 percent—worth millions of pounds—was financed by the British merchants who extended credit. The boom ended around 1762, as the war in America wound down and Britain slashed its troop levels and military expenditures. The loss of military markets, contracts, and cash subsidies made it more difficult for Americans to purchase British goods. Colonial merchants looked anx-

iously at their overstocked warehouses and feared bankruptcy. "I think we have a gloomy prospect before us," a Philadelphian noted in 1765, "as there are of late some Persons failed, who were in no way suspected." The increase in transatlantic trade had raised living standards but also had made Americans more dependent on overseas creditors and the fluctuating demand for American products in transatlantic markets.

Land Conflicts and Western Uprisings

In times of prosperity and in times of stagnating trade, the colonial population continued to grow. By 1750 the shortage of farmland in long-settled areas had become so acute that political conflicts broke out over disputed land rights granted by seventeenth-century charters.

Land Conflicts in the East. In 1738 Puritan families who traced their American ancestry back four generations had founded the town of Kent, Connecticut, which stood at the generally accepted western boundary of the colony. The next generation would have to find somewhere else to go. In the 1750s Connecticut farmers formed the Susquehanna Company and petitioned the Connecticut legislature to help them claim land in the Wyoming Valley in northeastern Pennsylvania. According to the colony's original charter (1662), its boundaries stretched all the way to the Pacific Ocean. But the Penn family also claimed this territory, invoking *its* charter rights, and issued its own land grants. Soon rival groups of settlers from Connecticut and Pennsylvania were burning down one another's houses. To avert further violence the two colonial

An American Merchant
James Tulley stands well-dressed and proud in his Philadelphia countinghouse, his ships in the background being
prepared for the next voyage. Merchants like Tulley were the
first great American entrepreneurs, exporting American products to the West Indies and Europe, and, as the advertisement
of a New York merchant shows, importing a vast array of
manufactured goods.
New York Social History Project; New-York Historical Society.

governments referred the dispute to the authorities in
London, where it remained undecided at the time of
American independence (Map 4.6).

Land disputes also broke out along the imprecise
border between New York and Massachusetts. Hundreds of yeomen families from New England moved
into disputed territory in the Hudson River Valley and
refused to accept the tenancy leaseholds that were customary on the great manorial estates in New York.
Instead, the migrants purchased freehold titles from
land speculators in Massachusetts and encouraged

long-settled Dutch and German tenants to dispute the
legitimacy of landlords' titles to their vast estates.

The manorial lords enforced their longstanding
claims to ownership in the New York courts, setting off
a rebellion. In 1766 New England migrants and tenant
farmers in Westchester, Dutchess, and Albany counties
refused to pay rent and used mob violence to close the
courts. On orders from the royal governor, General
Thomas Gage led two British regiments to assist local
sheriffs and manorial bailiffs in suppressing the tenant
uprising and evicting the New England squatters.

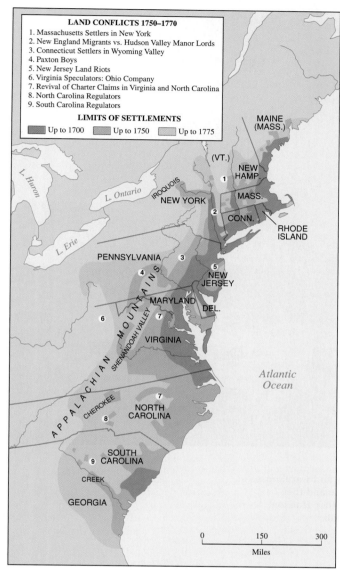

MAP 4.6
Westward Expansion and Armed Conflict, 1750–1775
Between 1750 and 1775 the mainland population doubled—from 1.2 million to 2.5 million—sparking legal battles over land, which became increasingly valuable. Violence broke out in newly settled regions, as backcountry settlers fought with Indians, rival claimants, and eastern-dominated governments.

decision awarded ownership of the entire northern neck of Virginia (along the Potomac River) to Lord Fairfax.

This revival of proprietary power underscored the growing extent of landed wealth—by the 1760s Lord Baltimore, the Maryland proprietor, and the Penn family were among the richest people in England, largely because of their holdings in the colonies—and the increasing resemblance between rural societies in Europe and America. Desirable land east of the Appalachians was getting more expensive, and much of it was controlled by manorial landlords and wealthy speculators. Tenants and yeomen farmers feared they might soon be reduced to the status of European peasants.

The Paxton Boys. As farmers moved west in search of cheap freehold land, they found themselves in the middle of disputes over Indian policy, political representation, and debts. In Pennsylvania, Scots-Irish migrants who lived along the western frontier had tried for decades to push the Indians out of the colony, but pacifistic Quakers had prevented such military action. In 1763 a band of Scots-Irish farmers known as the Paxton Boys took matters into their own hands and massacred twenty members of the Conestoga tribe.

When Governor John Penn tried to bring the murderers to justice, about 250 armed Scots-Irish advanced on Philadelphia. Benjamin Franklin intercepted the angry mob at Lancaster and arranged a compromise, narrowly averting a battle. Prosecution of the accused men failed for lack of witnesses. Although the Scots-Irish dropped their demand for the expulsion of the Indians, the episode left a legacy of racial hatred and political resentment. A decade later during the War of Independence, the Scots-Irish would take their revenge against the Indians in the west and the Quaker and Anglican elite in the east.

Uprisings in the Southern Backcountry. Violence also broke out in the backcountry of the Carolinas. During the war with France frontier settlers in South Carolina had clashed repeatedly with the Cherokee, who had allied themselves with the French in an attempt to protect their lands, creating social chaos in much of the backcountry. After the war ended in 1763 a group of vigilantes, known as the Regulators, tried to impose order on outlaw bands of whites who were roaming the countryside. The Regulators also disciplined the "low people," squatters and landless workers who eked out a meager living and were suspected of poaching or stealing property.

Many Regulators wanted greater political rights for their region, demanding that the eastern-controlled government provide them with more local courts, fairer taxes, and greater representation in the provincial

Simultaneously, in New Jersey and the southern colonies, resident landowners and English aristocrats also used long-dormant seventeenth-century land charters to reassert their control over lands settled by yeomen farmers. The British government and American judges supported most of these legal claims. For example, British authorities upheld the right of Lord Granville, an heir of one of the original Carolina proprietors of 1663, to collect quitrents—an annual tax on land—in a large area of North Carolina; and another

A New York Manor
The Philipse Manor stretched over 90,000 acres and included mills and warehouses as
well as a grand manor house. To preserve their aristocratic life-style and the
quasi-feudal leasehold system of agriculture, the Philipses joined other Hudson
River manorial lords in suppressing the tenant uprisings of the 1760s.
Historic Hudson Valley, Tarrytown, NY.

assembly. The assembly not only rejected these demands but, branding the Regulators' seizure of power as illegal, also threatened to suppress their movement with force. In the end the assembly decided to compromise because it feared slave revolts on lowland rice plantations if the militia were away in the backcountry. In 1767 the assembly met many of the rebels' demands, creating locally controlled courts in the west and reducing the fees for legal documents. However, lowland planter-merchants kept a firm grip on political power in South Carolina, refusing to reapportion the legislature to give western settlers representation proportionate to their growing numbers. And the assembly continued to tax the thin soil of the upland region at the same rate as the fertile lands of the low country.

Eventually a rival western group—the Moderators, who were led by affluent planters and justices of the

peace who resented Regulator rule—sided with the eastern government and raised an armed force of its own. In March 1769, 600 supporters of each back-country faction met near the Saluda River and exchanged angry words, then gunshots. To avert wholesale violence, Regulator and Moderator leaders agreed to disband their organizations and allow officials named by the provincial government to govern the western counties. Like the Paxton Boys in Pennsylvania, the South Carolina Regulators attracted attention to western needs but ultimately failed to wrest power from the eastern elite.

In 1766 another Regulator movement arose in the newly settled backcountry of North Carolina. After the Great War for Empire, tobacco prices plummeted, carrying many farmers into debt and into court. Judges directed sheriffs to seize the property of bankrupt farmers and auction it off to pay creditors and court costs.

A Backcountry Road
The first settlers in interior valleys lived in small, crude log cabins that were strung out along the road. Loneliness and desolation, suggested here by a solitary rider, were overcome by concerted efforts to build social communities, often through church-centered activities.
Library of Congress.

Backcountry farmers resented merchants' lawsuits, not just because they generated high fees for lawyers and court officials but also because they violated local custom. As in rural New England, farmers were used to extending credit to neighbors on the basis of mutual trust, and often allowed loans to remain unpaid for years.

To save their farms, North Carolina debtors joined together in a Regulator movement that intimidated judges, closed down courts, and broke into jails to free their comrades. Their leader, Herman Husband, told his followers not to vote for "any Clerk, Lawyer, or Scotch merchant. We must make these men subject to the laws or they will enslave the whole community." But ultimately the North Carolina Regulators—like their counterparts in South Carolina—were property owners, not political or social revolutionaries: they wanted orderly and fair government in the backcountry, greater political rights for the west, and more time to pay their debts. The North Carolina Regulators demanded passage of a law allowing them to pay their taxes in the "produce of the country" rather than in cash. And, echoing the demands of backcountry settlers from Pennsylvania to Georgia, they insisted on lower legal fees and greater legislative representation. In addition, the democratic-minded North Carolina Regulators demanded fairer taxes so that each person would be taxed "in proportion to the profits arising from his estate."

In 1771 the royal governor, William Tryon, mobilized the eastern militia and defeated a large Regulator force at the Alamance River; seven insurgent leaders were summarily executed. Not since Leisler's revolt in New York in 1689 (see Chapter 3) had a domestic political conflict caused so much bloodshed in America.

In 1771 as in 1689, colonial conflicts became intertwined with imperial politics. In Connecticut the Reverend Ezra Stiles defended the Regulators. "What shall an injured & oppressed people do," he asked, when faced with "Oppression and tyranny (under the name of Government)?" Stiles's remarks reflected growing resistance to British imperial control, a result of the profound changes that had occurred in the mainland colonies between 1720 and 1765. America was still a dependent society closely tied to Britain by trade, culture, and politics, but it was also an increasingly complex society with the potential for an independent existence. British policies would determine the direction the maturing colonies would take.

Summary

★

By 1720 a freeholding yeoman society was well established in New England. Its families were controlled by men, who assumed ownership of their wives' property and provided inheritances for their children. When rapid population growth began to threaten the freehold ideal, New England farmers planted higher-yielding crops and moved to new frontier settlements.

In the mid-Atlantic colonies the rising European demand for wheat brought prosperity to many farmers. An influx of German and Scots-Irish migrants created an ethnically diverse society in which religious groups held to their own beliefs. Ethnic conflict broke out, especially over the Quakers' pacifist Indian policy, and the emergence of stark economic inequality created new social divisions. Gentlemen farmers and entrepreneurs grew wealthy, and a landless class appeared at the bottom of the social order.

The American colonies became more integrated into the world economy and participated more fully in the intellectual life of Europe. Enlightenment rationalism influenced educated Americans such as Benjamin Franklin, and pietistic religion reinvigorated colonial churches. In the 1740s the preaching of George Whitefield prompted a Great Awakening that brought spiritual renewal to thousands of Americans and sparked conflicts. In the northern colonies enthusiastic New Lights condemned traditional Old Lights, and in Virginia evangelical Baptists converted white tenant farmers and black slaves, challenging the power of the Anglican elite.

In the 1750s rival claims to lands west of the Appalachians sparked a major war between Britain and France. With colonial aid, the British conquered Canada and wrote a peace treaty that excluded the French from North America. The war, along with the expansion of transatlantic trade, testified to the growing involvement of the colonies in the diplomatic and commercial life of Europe.

By this time the mainland colonies had become complex conflict-ridden societies. Manorial lords in New York suppressed dissident tenants and New England squatters, while landed proprietors from Pennsylvania to the Carolinas successfully asserted their legal rights to disputed lands. Yeomen families in the backcountry of Pennsylvania and the Carolinas fought with native Americans and formed Regulator movements that challenged the authority of eastern governments.

By the 1760s Britain's North American settlements had become mature provinces with substantial populations, increasingly complex economies, and great cultural diversity. As the years to come would show, they also had remarkably effective political institutions and considerable military resources.

TIMELINE

1700–1714	New Hudson River Valley manors created
1720s	German and Scots-Irish migration
	Theodore Jacob Frelinghuysen holds revivals
	Enlightenment ideas spread from Europe to America
1730s	William and Gilbert Tennent lead Presbyterian revivals among Scots-Irish migrants
	Jonathan Edwards preaches in New England
1739	George Whitefield and the Great Awakening
1740–1748	War of the Austrian Succession
1740–1760s	Great Awakening creates conflict between Old Lights and New Lights
	New colleges founded by religious denominations
	Population pressure on land in New England
	Rising grain and tobacco prices assist farmers
	Increasing inequality in rural communities
	Falling birthrate increases women's options
1743	Benjamin Franklin founds American Philosophical Society
1750s	Industrialization in Britain increases exports to colonies
	Americans export more to pay for British imports
	Ohio Company threatens French land claims in Ohio River Valley
	Connecticut's Susquehanna Company seeks land in Pennsylvania
	Proprietors assert charter rights to land
1754	French and Indian War begins
	Albany meeting and Plan
1756	Great War for Empire (Seven Years' War) begins
1759	Fall of Quebec
1760s	New York/New England border conflicts
	Regulator movements in the Carolinas
	Baptist revivals in Virginia
1763	Pontiac leads Indian uprising
	Treaty of Paris ends Great War for Empire
	Paxton Boys in Pennsylvania

Suggested Readings

———————★———————

Two collections of important articles are in Stanley Katz, John Murrin, and Douglas Greenberg, eds., *Colonial America: Essays in Politics and Social Development* (4th ed., 1993), and Bernard Bailyn and Philip D. Morgan, eds., *Strangers within the Realm: Cultural Margins of the First British Empire* (1991). John J. McCusker and Russell R. Menard, *The Economy of British America, 1607–1783* (1985), survey economic change, and Jon Butler, *Awash in a Sea of Faith: Christianizing the American People* (1990), covers religious developments. Jack P. Greene, *Pursuits of Happiness* (1988), offers a provocative comparative analysis of regional social evolution.

Freehold Society in New England

A good local study is Daniel Vickers, *Farmers & Fishermen: Two Centuries of Work in Essex County, Massachusetts, 1630–1830* (1994), whereas Bruce C. Daniels, *The Fragmentation of New England: Comparative Perspectives on Economic, Political, and Social Divisions in the Eighteenth Century* (1988), offers a wider view. See also Robert Gross, *The Minutemen and Their World* (1976). On women's lives, see Laurel Thatcher Ulrich, *Good Wives: Image and Reality in the Lives of Women of Northern New England, 1650–1750* (1982); Marylynn Salmon, *Women and the Law of Property in Early America* (1986); and Cornelia H. Dayton, *Women before the Bar: Gender, Law, and Society in Connecticut, 1639–1789* (1995). For studies of material culture, see Robert B. St. George, ed., *Material Life in America, 1600–1860* (1988), and Cary Carson et al., eds., *Of Consuming Interest* (1994).

The Mid-Atlantic: Toward a New Society, 1720–1765

On Pennsylvania, consult Michael Zuckerman, ed., *Friends and Neighbors: Group Life in America's First Plural Society* (1982), and Barry J. Levy, *Quakers and the American Family* (1988). James T. Lemon, *The Best Poor Man's Country* (1972), discusses ethnicity, as does Marilyn J. Westerkamp, *Triumph of the Laity: Scots-Irish Piety and the Great Awakening, 1625–1760* (1988). On white indentured servants and ethnic migration, see the classic study by Abbot E. Smith, *Colonists in Bondage* (1947); and A. G. Roeber, *Palatines, Liberty, and Property: German Lutherans in Colonial British America* (1993); Jon Butler, *The Huguenots in America* (1983); Ned Landsman, *Scotland and Its First American Colony, 1683–1775* (1985); and A. Roger Ekirch, *Bound for America: The Transportation of British Convicts to the Colonies, 1718–1775* (1987). Important studies on mid-Atlantic politics include Patricia U. Bonomi, *A Factious People: Politics and Society in Colonial New York* (1971); Thomas L. Purvis, *Proprietors, Patronage, and Money: New Jersey, 1703–1776* (1986); Alan Tully, *Forming American Politics* (1994); and Benjamin H. Newcomb, *Political Partisanship in the American Middle Colonies, 1700–1776* (1995).

The Enlightenment and the Great Awakening, 1740–1765

Henry F. May, *The Enlightenment in America* (1976), is still the standard treatment, but see also Douglas Anderson, *The Radical Enlightenment of Benjamin Franklin* (1997), and Paul Merrill Spurlin, *The French Enlightenment in America* (1984). For medical knowledge, consult Richard Shryock, *Medicine and Society in America, 1660–1860* (1960). Brooke Hindle, *The Pursuit of Science in Revolutionary America, 1735–1789* (1956), and John C. Greene, *American Science in the Age of Jefferson* (1984), are also relevant.

Good studies of the Great Awakening include David S. Lovejoy, *Religious Enthusiasm in the New World: Heresy to Revolution* (1985); Patricia U. Bonomi, *Under the Cope of Heaven: Religion, Society, and Politics in Colonial America* (1986); and Harry S. Stout, *The New England Soul: Preaching and Religious Culture in Colonial New England* (1986). Three good biographies of New England revivalists are Patricia Tracy, *Jonathan Edwards, Pastor* (1979); W. G. McLoughlin, *Isaac Backus and American Pietistic Tradition* (1957); and Christopher Jedrey, *The World of John Cleaveland* (1979). Harry S. Stout, *The Divine Dramatist* (1991), is a fine biography of George Whitefield. Richard Bushman, ed., *The Great Awakening* (1970), and Rhys Isaac, *The Transformation of Virginia, 1740–1790* (1982), capture the emotions of ordinary participants in the Awakening.

The Midcentury Challenge: War, Trade, and Social Conflict, 1750–1765

Douglas E. Leach, *Roots of Conflict: British Armed Forces and Colonial Americans, 1677–1763* (1986), sets the Great War for Empire in a broad context. See also Edward P. Hamilton, *The French and Indian Wars* (1962); Guy Fregault, *Canada: The War of the Conquest* (1969); George F. G. Stanley, *New France: The Last Phase, 1744–1760* (1968); and Fred Anderson, *A People's Army: Massachusetts Soldiers and Society in the Seven Years' War* (1984). Richard White, *The Middle Ground* (1991), and Francis Jennings, *Empire of Fortune: Crown, Colonies, and Tribes in the Seven Years' War* (1988), describe the crucial role played by Indians in the conflict. See also Richard Aquila, *The Iroquois Restoration: Iroquois Diplomacy on the Colonial Frontier, 1701–1754* (1983), and David H. Corkran, *The Cherokee Frontier: Conflict and Survival, 1740–1762* (1966).

Gary M. Walton and James F. Shepherd, *The Economic Rise of Early America* (1979), trace the growing importance of commerce. See also Paul G. E. Clemens, *The Atlantic Economy and Colonial Maryland's Eastern Shore: From Tobacco to Grain* (1980).

On backcountry political agitation see Richard D. Brown, *The South Carolina Regulators* (1963), and Alfred Young, ed., *The American Revolution: Essays in the History of American Radicalism* (1976). See also W. Stitt Robinson, *The Southern Colonial Frontier, 1607–1763* (1979), and Rachel N. Klein, *Unification of a Slave State: The Rise of the Planter Class in the South Carolina Backcountry, 1660–1808* (1994).

Chapter 5

─────────────★─────────────

Toward Independence: Years of Decision, 1763–1775

A S THE SEVEN Years' War—the Great War for Empire—drew to a close in 1763, the American colonists rejoiced over the triumph of the British nation, under whose banners their soldiers had fought. A mere twelve years later many of the same colonists were so angry at the British ministry that they took up arms to resist imperial authority. This rapid shift in attitude puzzled contemporary observers as well as later historians. How had it happened, asked the president of King's College in New York, that such a "happily situated" people had decided to "hazard their Fortunes, their Lives, and their Souls, in such a Rebellion"?

This swift and unexpected change had two broad sets of causes. First, the growing power of the American assemblies during the eighteenth century had fostered dreams of greater political autonomy than the settlers currently had. Unlike other colonial peoples of the time, Americans lived in a prosperous, stable society with a strong tradition of representative government. This unique historical circumstance created experienced leaders and a self-confident populace capable of supporting an independence movement. Still, despite recent disputes over the molasses trade and land banks, most Americans had been content for generations under British rule.

What sparked them to rebel—the second, and immediate, cause of the independence movement—was Britain's attempt to rule the colonies in a more rigorous fashion. A British effort to impose tighter administrative controls over the colonies began during the Great War for Empire and culminated in new tax legislation—the Stamp Act of 1765. The act provoked widespread

British Troops Occupy Concord
In April 1775 hundreds of British troops marched to Lexington and Concord, Massachusetts, searching houses for arms and munitions and prompting a violent confrontation with the Patriot militia. This painting by an unknown artist was done in 1775 as the events unfolded.
Courtesy, Concord Museum.

outrage among Americans, who were accustomed to governing and taxing themselves through their own assemblies, and prompted violent resistance. As successive British ministries ignored colonial protests and imposed additional taxes and controls, they set in motion a downward spiral of political conflict and ideological debate that ended in civil war. By 1775 armed Patriot rebels were prepared to do battle with British troops and Loyalist Americans.

This course of events was hardly predictable in 1765, when the Americans were indeed a "happily situated" people. And it was far from inevitable, for Britain and its colonies had lived for decades in a peaceful and prosperous union. Purposeful British statecraft could have saved the empire. Instead, passionate Patriot agitation brought about its demise.

The Reform Movement, 1763–1765

★

Since the late 1740s leading members of the British Board of Trade had favored tighter controls over the colonies, and by focusing attention on America, the Great War for Empire presented them with a golden opportunity. As soon as victory over the French was ensured, British officials launched a concerted effort to reform the colonial administrative system.

The Legacy of the War

The legacy of the Great War for Empire was a mixed one. By driving the French out of Canada, Britain had achieved dominance over eastern North America (Map 5.1). But the cost of the triumph was high: a mountain of debt and the need to spend even more money to station troops in the newly conquered provinces of Canada and Florida. This financial crisis prompted the British ministry not only to impose new taxes on its American possessions but also to redefine the character of the empire. Since 1689 Britain had exercised authority over the colonies indirectly, through mercantilist regulations on trade; now it proposed to govern them more directly, through Parliamentary legislation and taxation.

Disputes over Troops and Trade. The war made visible the differences between British and colonial society. Before 1754 only royal governors and a few merchants and naval officers had experienced life in the American provinces, but the fighting brought thousands of British troops to the mainland colonies. Few people liked what they saw. Many Americans were shocked by the arrogance of upper-crust British officers and the extent of their power over rank-and-file soldiers. British soldiers, a Massachusetts militiaman wrote in his diary, "are but little better than slaves to their officers." The hostility was mutual. The British general James Wolfe complained that colonial troops were drawn from the dregs of society and that "there was no depending on them in action."

Britain Triumphant
Celebrating the Great War for Empire, this painting honors George III, "The Best of Kings," and praises two wartime heroes, Prime Minister William Pitt and General James Wolfe, who was killed in the battle of Quebec. The artist also offers a political message with real Whig overtones, warning the king against "Evil and Corrupt Ministers."
Courtesy, American Antiquarian Society.

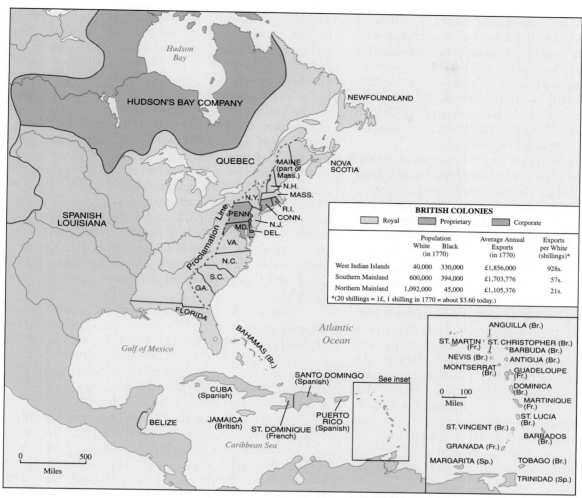

MAP 5.1
Britain's American Empire in 1763
In 1763 Britain was dominant in the West Indies and controlled all of eastern North America. British ministers dispatched troops to the conquered provinces of Florida and Quebec and, with the Proclamation Line of 1763, sought to prevent Anglo-American settlement west of the Appalachian Mountains.

In addition, the war once again exposed the weakness of British administrative control, especially the lack of authority exercised by the royal governors. For decades royal officials had struggled with the colonial assemblies over salaries, patronage, and taxes (losing more battles than they won), and the war only heightened these conflicts. In Virginia the House of Burgesses refused to levy additional taxes to pay for the war and resorted instead to deficit financing, printing huge amounts of paper currency to pay the province's bills. As the colony's currency declined in value, the Burgesses passed another act that required creditors to accept it at face value, prompting British merchants to apply to Parliament for relief.

Other conflicts arose over military policy. In theory the governors had command of the provincial militia, including the authority to appoint officers and set mil-

itary strategy. In reality they had to share power with the colonial assemblies, which refused to support the war effort with taxes and troops unless they also controlled military appointments and operations. In Massachusetts, complained Britain's Board of Trade, "almost every act of executive and legislative power is ordered and directed by votes and resolves of the General Court." This situation, British officials agreed, had to change.

Imperial authorities began by strictly enforcing the existing Navigation Acts. Before the war American merchants had routinely bribed customs officials to circumvent the Molasses Act of 1733. To curb such corruption, in 1762 Parliament passed a Revenue Act that prohibited English customs appointees from leasing their positions to deputies, who had often accepted bribes in order to pay their leases and augment their personal incomes. In addition, the ministry instructed the Royal Navy to stop the American merchants who were conducting a flourishing trade between the mainland colonies and the French islands. The fact that French armies attempting "to Destroy one English province, are actually supported by Bread raised in another" was absurd, declared an outraged British politician, because it enabled the French "to sustain and protract this long and expensive war."

Britain's wartime efforts to curb American autonomy culminated in 1763 with the deployment of a large peacetime army of about 10,000 men in North America. The decision stemmed from a variety of motives. First, the ministry wanted to discourage rebellion by the 60,000 French residents of the newly captured province of Quebec and also needed to safeguard its new province of Florida, which Spain wanted back and could potentially invade from neighboring Cuba. Second, the recent rebellion of the Ottawa chief Pontiac (see Chapter 4) had underscored the need for a substantial military garrison along the frontier. The troops would intimidate the Indians and, more important, deter white farmers from migrating west of the Proclamation Line of 1763—a boundary line along the crest of the Appalachian Mountains—and thus prevent new Indian wars. As one official warned, along the frontier there were thousands of land-hungry farmers, "too Lawless and Licentious ever to be restrained" by civil authorities; if not restrained by British soldiers, they would surely provoke new conflicts with the resident tribes.

Finally, some British politicians feared that with the French gone from Canada, Americans would seek greater freedom from imperial control, a fear that had been growing since the late 1740s. "I have been publickly told," the Swedish traveler Peter Kalm reported from America in 1748, "that within thirty or fifty years, the English colonies may constitute a separate state, wholly independent of England." To prevent this outcome, British ministers decided on a show of force. As Henry Knox, a Treasury official who had once served the Crown in Georgia, put it: "The main purpose of Stationing a large Body of Troops in America is to secure the Dependence of the Colonys on Great Britain." By stationing an army in America, the British ministry was indicating its willingness to use force to preserve its authority.

The National Debt. A more immediate problem was Britain's national debt, which had nearly doubled as a result of the war—from £75 million in 1754 to £133 million in 1763. To pay the rising interest charges, Lord Bute, the prime minister, would have to raise taxes. Treasury officials advised against increasing the English land tax, which was already at an all-time high and was paid by the propertied classes, whose support the government needed. Bute therefore imposed higher import duties on American-grown tobacco and sugar,

which manufacturers passed on to British consumers in the form of higher prices. The ministry also increased *excise levies*—essentially sales taxes—on domestic goods such as salt, beer, and distilled spirits, another measure that passed along the costs of the war to the king's ordinary subjects in Britain.

To collect these taxes and duties in Britain, the government doubled the size of the financial bureaucracy—from 5,000 to 11,000—and increased its legal powers. Customs agents and informers patrolled the coasts of southern Britain, arresting smugglers and seizing tons of European-produced goods, such as French wines and Flemish textiles, on which import duties had not been paid. Convicted smugglers faced heavy penalties, including death or "transportation" to America as indentured servants. The price of empire abroad had turned out to be debt, higher taxes, and a more powerful government at home (Figure 5.1).

These developments confirmed the worst fears of Country party aristocrats in Britain and Radical Whigs on both sides of the Atlantic. Since the ministry of Sir Robert Walpole (1721–1742), these political factions had emphasized the dangers of a big and expensive government and political corruption. Now opposition politicians in Britain went on the offensive against the ministry, charging that the British Treasury department was at the mercy of the "monied interest," the banks and financiers who were reaping millions of pounds in interest from government bonds. The bureaucracy, they protested, had become even more bloated, filled with thousands of "worthless *pensioners* and *placemen*"—appointees who collected salaries and occupied places but did little work.

Distressed by higher taxes and administrative corruption, the most outspoken British reformers insisted that Parliament be made more representative of the peoples' interests. The Radical Whig John Wilkes demanded an end to "rotten boroughs"—tiny districts whose few voters were controlled by wealthy aristocrats and merchants. In British domestic affairs as in American colonial policy, the Great War for Empire had transformed British political life, creating a more active and arguably a more oppressive government.

British Reform Strategy

This political transformation in Britain had a significant impact on American affairs because it brought to power a new generation of royal officials with a more expansive view of British authority. In 1760, George III (r. 1760–1820), a young, vigorous monarch, had become king and indicated his support for activist policies, both domestic and foreign. In a pamphlet published that same year, Thomas Pownall, a former governor of Massachusetts, had argued that the expanding trade

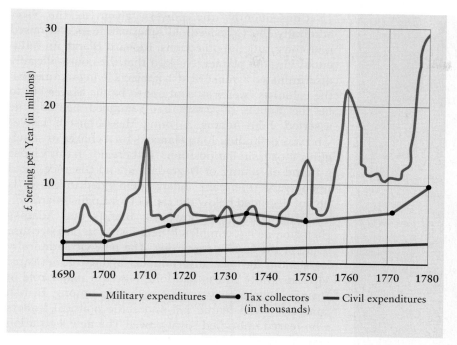

FIGURE 5.1
The Growing Power of the British State
As Britain built a great navy and subsidized the armies of its European allies, the government's military expenditures soared, as did the number of tax collectors. The tax bureaucracy more than doubled in size between 1700 and 1735 and increased sharply again between 1750 and 1780.

with the American colonies was crucial to Britain's future, because "the spirit of *commerce* will become the predominant power, which will rule the powers of Europe." Adopting Pownall's view, Charles Townshend and officials at the Board of Trade had vowed to enhance British prosperity by closely regulating colonial trade; further, during the war they had begun to reform the imperial administrative system.

George Grenville, who succeeded Bute as prime minister in 1763, continued the reform effort. In 1764, Grenville won Parliamentary approval of a Currency Act that protected the financial interests of British merchants in America. In 1751 Parliament had banned the use of paper money as legal tender in New England; spurred on by Virginia's abuse of paper currency during the war, the home legislature now extended the ban throughout the colonies. All Americans would have to pay their debts to merchants with British currency, foreign coins, or bills of exchange. Equally important, Parliament had seized control of the colonial monetary system from the American assemblies.

The Sugar Act. Grenville then introduced a new Navigation Act, the Sugar Act of 1764, to replace the widely evaded Molasses Act of 1733. The act reflected a shrewd effort by the ministry to balance American and British interests. Two Treasury officials, Thomas Whatley and Charles Jenkinson, had looked closely at the pattern of colonial trade and managed to convince Grenville that the mainland settlers had to sell some of their wheat, fish, and lumber in the French West Indies. Without the molasses, sugar, and bills of exchange those sales brought, Whatley and Jenkinson argued, the colonists would lack the funds to buy

British manufactured goods. The Treasury officials therefore advised Grenville to allow this trade and resist demands from British sugar planters to enforce the high duty of 6 pence per gallon tax on French molasses mandated by the act of 1733. Instead, they recommended a smaller duty of 3 pence per gallon, arguing that this tariff would allow British molasses to compete with the cheaper French product without destroying the mainland's export trade or distilling industry.

American merchants and manufacturers refused to support this carefully crafted compromise. Some New England traders, such as John Hancock of Boston, had made their fortunes by smuggling French molasses and thus had never paid the 6 pence duty; the new levy would severely cut their profits. These merchants—joined by New England distillers, who feared a rise in the price of molasses—orchestrated a political campaign against the Sugar Act. Publicly they protested that the new tax would wipe out trade with the French islands. Privately they vowed to evade the duty by smuggling or by bribing officials.

Merchants and their allies also raised constitutional objections to the new legislation. The British "constitution" was not a written document but rather the totality of the nation's legal tradition: Parliamentary statutes, case law decided by judges, and political understandings relating to such fundamental issues as royal power and taxation. Invoking one of these understandings, the speaker of the Massachusetts House of Representatives argued that the duties on sugar constituted a tax, so that the Sugar Act was "contrary to a fundamental Principall of our Constitution: That all Taxes ought to originate with the people."

George Grenville, Architect of the Stamp Act
As prime minister from 1763 to 1766, Grenville assumed leadership of the movement for imperial reform and taxation. This portrait of 1763 suggests Grenville's energy and ambition. As events were to show, the new minister was determined to reform the imperial system and ensure that the colonists shared the cost of the empire.
The Earl of Halifax, Garrowby, Yorkshire.

Vice-Admiralty Courts and the "Rights of Englishmen." The Sugar Act of 1764 raised other constitutional issues as well. To enforce the new duty, the act extended the jurisdiction of *vice-admiralty courts*— maritime tribunals that operated without the procedures and protections of English common law. There was no trial by jury in those courts. Rather, a judge (usually one with British sympathies) heard arguments and decided cases solely on the basis of Parliamentary legislation. For half a century colonial legislatures had vigorously opposed vice-admiralty courts, limiting their power by extending the jurisdiction of colonial courts to cover customs offenses occurring in the seaports or coastal waters. As a result, merchants charged with violating the Navigation Acts were often tried in common-law courts—and almost just as often acquitted by sympathetic local juries. By extending the jurisdiction of vice-admiralty courts to all customs offenses wherever they occurred, the Sugar Act closed this loophole.

Consequently, the powers given to the vice-admiralty courts revived old American fears and raised new constitutional objections. Richard Bland, an influential Virginia planter, charged that the courts illegally discriminated against British subjects living in America: the colonists "were not sent out to be the Slaves but to be the Equals of those that remained behind," he asserted. John Adams, a young Massachusetts lawyer who was defending John Hancock on a charge of smuggling, took a similar position. "Is there not in this Clause a Brand of Infamy, or Degradation, and Disgrace, fixed upon every American?" Adams demanded to know. "Is he not degraded below the rank of an Englishman?"

Although it was powerful, Bland's and Adams's rhetoric was not completely persuasive, in part because some of the facts were wrong. The new vice-admiralty legislation did *not* discriminate against Americans. Vice-admiralty courts had long played a major role in Britain, where they were unpopular among British smugglers who feared jail and some political leaders who feared unbridled royal power. The new legislation simply extended tough British legal practices and bureaucratic controls to the American colonies. What was really at issue in the conflict over the vice-admiralty courts was the British government's increased exercise of its authority over the colonists. Having lived for decades under a policy of salutary neglect, Americans soon realized that the new British reforms challenged the existing system of imperial politics and many of the freedoms they had traditionally enjoyed. As a committee of the Massachusetts House put it, the Sugar Act and other British edicts "have a tendency to deprive the colonists of some of their most essential Rights as British subjects."

For their part, British officials insisted on Parliament's power to enact such legislation and denied that the colonists could claim the traditional rights of Englishmen. When Royal Governor Francis Bernard of Massachusetts heard that the Massachusetts assembly had objected to the Sugar Act by asserting the doctrine of no taxation without representation, he denied that Americans should have that constitutional right. "The rule that a *British* subject shall not be bound by laws or liable to taxes, but what he has consented to by his representatives," Bernard argued, "must be confined to the inhabitants of Great Britain only." In the eyes of Bernard and most British officials and politicians, Americans were second-class subjects of the king, their rights limited by the Navigation Acts and the national interests of the British state, as determined by Parliament.

The Stamp Act

The issue of taxation brought about the first great imperial crisis. When Grenville introduced the Sugar Act in Parliament in 1764, he also announced his intention to seek a colonial stamp tax to cover part of the cost of keeping 10,000 British troops in America—some £200,000 per year, or about $15 million today. The new tax would raise revenue by requiring stamps (similar to modern postage stamps) on court documents, land titles, contracts, playing cards, newspapers, and other printed items. A similar English tax that had been levied since 1694 was yielding an annual revenue of £290,000, and Grenville hoped the American levy would raise at least £60,000 a year.

The prime minister knew that some Americans would object to the tax on constitutional grounds, so he asked explicitly whether any member of the House of Commons doubted "the power and sovereignty of Parliament over every part of the British dominions, for the purpose of raising or collecting any tax." No one rose to object.

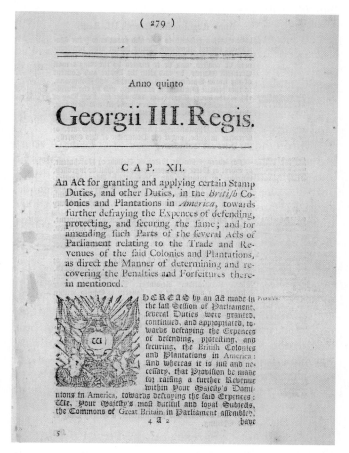

The Stamp Act
The official document that would fan the flames of patriotism in America begins in Latin, the ancient language of law and authority: "In the fifth year of the reign of George III. . . ." By imposing a direct tax on the colonists, the new legislation ignited a storm of opposition, much of it violent, and began a decade-long political confrontation between British ministers and American patriots.
Library of Congress.

Confident of Parliament's support, Grenville vowed to impose a stamp tax in 1765 unless the colonial legislatures would raise among themselves "a sum adequate to their defense." This challenge threw the London agents of the American assemblies into confusion. The agents—English merchants and Americans residing in London who presented petitions to British officials on behalf of their colonial clients—all agreed that the assemblies lacked the organizational means to create a continent-wide military force and to fund it. The agents knew that the colonies' representatives had met together only once, at the Albany Congress of 1754, and that not a single assembly had accepted that body's proposals. Lacking an alternative plan to raise the money and not convinced that the colonies had a constitutional immunity from Parliamentary taxation, some agents advised their assemblies to accept the new levy.

Benjamin Franklin, representing the Pennsylvania assembly, took an innovative approach to the constitutional issue by proposing American representation in Parliament. "If you chuse to tax us," he suggested to a British friend, "give us Members in your Legislature, and let us be one People." With the exception of William Pitt, who favored American representation in Parliament, British politicians rejected Franklin's radical idea. They argued that the colonists were "virtually" represented in the home legislature by the merchants who sat in Parliament and by other members with interests in America. Colonial leaders were equally skeptical of Franklin's plan; Americans were "situate at a great Distance from their Mother Country," the Connecticut assembly declared in a printed pamphlet that was quickly sent to London, and therefore "cannot participate in the general Legislature of the Nation." Influential merchants in Philadelphia, worried that a handful of colonial delegates would be powerless in Parliament, warned Franklin "to beware of any measure that might extend to us seats in the Commons."

The way was clear for Grenville to introduce the Stamp Act—both to raise revenue and, as his chief assistants observed, to assert a constitutional principle, "the Right of Parliament to lay an internal Tax upon the Colonies." The ministry's plan worked smoothly. The House of Commons refused to accept American petitions opposing the act and passed the new legislation by an overwhelming vote of 205 to 49. Parliament also approved Grenville's proposal that violations of the Stamp Act be tried in vice-admiralty courts.

Finally, at the request of General Thomas Gage, commander of British military forces in America, Parliament passed a Quartering Act. This measure directed colonial governments to contribute to the cost of defending the empire by providing barracks and food for the British troops stationed in America. During the recent war the assemblies of Massachusetts and New York had refused to accept this financial burden, and the ministry was determined to force the colonists to pay for their own defense.

Grenville's design was now complete. Using the doctrine of Parliamentary supremacy, the prime minister had begun to replace the mercantilist system of indirect regulation with a genuinely "imperial" administrative regime that directly controlled the king's subjects in the colonies. By placing British officials in control of taxation, legal proceedings, and military finances, Grenville deprived the American assemblies of many of their traditional powers and challenged their authority. He thus provoked a constitutional confrontation not only on specific issues of policy but on the fundamental question of representative self-government. It was that larger threat which spurred colonial resistance.

The Dynamics of Rebellion, 1765–1766

★

With the Sugar and Stamp Acts, Grenville had thrown down the gauntlet to the American colonists. Would they resist this curtailment of the political autonomy achieved during the decades of salutary neglect? If they did, what were their chances of success? Although the colonists had often opposed unpopular laws and arbitrary governors, they had never before faced a reform-minded ministry and Parliament. But many Americans were alarmed by the new British policies and were questioning their wisdom. And some Patriots—as the defenders of colonial rights came to be called—were prepared to take up Grenville's challenge by delivering speeches that bordered on treason, by rioting in the streets, and by organizing an intercolonial protest against the new legislation.

The Crowd Rebels

The American response to the Stamp Act was more drastic than Grenville had predicted. In May 1765 an eloquent young Virginian, Patrick Henry, addressed the House of Burgesses and heaped blame not only on Grenville but also on the new king, George III, who had appointed Grenville to office and apparently supported his policies. Comparing George III to the tyrannical Charles I, Henry seemed to call for a new Oliver Cromwell—the Puritan general and leader of the republican revolution of the 1640s—to lead a similar uprising. Although dismayed by Henry's nearly treasonous remarks, the Burgesses nonetheless endorsed his attack on the Stamp Act, declaring that any attempt to tax the colonists without their consent "has a manifest Tendency to Destroy American freedom." In Massachusetts, James Otis, another republican-minded firebrand, persuaded the House of Representatives to call for a general meeting of the colonies in New York in October to consider a "loyal and humble representation" to the king and Parliament "to implore Relief" from the act.

The Sons of Liberty. Events moved more quickly than words. Before the meeting in New York could be convened, disciplined mobs led by men who called themselves the Sons of Liberty demanded the resignation of newly appointed stamp-tax collectors. One of the first incidents took place in Boston in August 1765, when the Sons of Liberty made an effigy of the collector Andrew Oliver, which they beheaded and burned before destroying a new brick building that he owned. Boston merchants who opposed the Stamp Act advised Oliver to resign; otherwise "his House would be immediately destroyed and his Life in Continual Danger." Two weeks later Bostonians attacked the house of Lieutenant Governor Thomas Hutchinson. As a defender of social privilege and imperial authority, Hutchinson had many enemies. Now, in the heat of crisis, the common people took their revenge by destroying his house, looting his wine cellar, and burning his library and clothes (see American Voices, "Josiah Quincy Jr.: The Threat of Mob Rule," p. 154).

Throughout New England similar crowds of angry but purposeful people—the "rabble," as their American and British detractors called them—intimidated royal officials. Near Wethersfield, Connecticut, 500 farmers and artisans confronted the tax collector Jared Ingersoll. He came from a prominent Connecticut family and, as the assembly's agent in London, had tried to prevent passage of the Stamp Act. But once the act passed, he looked to his pocketbook and signed on as a tax collector. Now the crowd voiced its anger, refusing to be swayed by Ingersoll's previous service to the colony or his high social status. One rioter shouted that he "lookt upon this as the Cause of the People" and would not "take Directions about it from any Body." Ingersoll finally capitulated. At the direction of the mob, he gave three half-hearted cheers for "Liberty and Property," tossed his hat into the air, and, duly humbled, resigned from his office.

The Stamp Act Congress and the First Boycott. In the midst of this turmoil, nine colonial assemblies sent delegates to the Stamp Act Congress, which met in New York City in October 1765. Most of the twenty-eight delegates were cautious men and politicians trained in the art of compromise. Seeking to persuade Parliament to repeal the Stamp Act, the delegates issued a set of well-argued Resolves that carefully avoided any reference to the ongoing anti-imperial riots. In the Resolves the delegates contested the constitutionality of the Stamp and

The BOSTONIAN'S Paying the EXCISE-MAN, or TARRING & FEATHERING

A British View of American Mobs
This satiric attack on the Sons of Liberty questions their brutal treatment of John Malcolm, the Commissioner of the Customs in Boston, who was tarred and feathered and forced to drink huge quantities of tea. Note the men in the background pouring tea into Boston harbor. The Liberty Tree in the background raises the question, does liberty mean anarchy?
Courtesy of the John Carter Brown Library at Brown University.

ports pledged their support. Soon the import of manufactures from Britain slowed to a trickle.

Meanwhile, the Sons of Liberty increased their agitation against British policy. On November 1, Isaac Sears and other minor New York merchants mobilized shopkeepers, tradesmen, artisans, laborers, and seamen in a mass protest meeting. The protesters marched through the streets, breaking street lamps and windows and crying "Liberty!" The next night nearly 3,000 New Yorkers joined a mob that plundered the house of an unpopular British officer. And on November 5 a large crowd surrounded Fort George, where the tax stamps were stored, and demanded their destruction. Fearing an open assault on the fort, Lieutenant Governor Cadwallader Colden called on General Gage to use his small military force against the crowd. But the British commander refused. "Fire from the Fort might disperse the Mob, but it would not quell them," he told Colden, "and the consequence would in all appearances be an Insurrection, the Commencement of Civil War." Colden had to surrender the tax stamps.

Throughout the colonies popular resistance nullified the Stamp Act. Frightened collectors distributed few stamps, and royal officials and judges accepted legal documents without the stamps while they awaited instructions from Britain. Slow communication across the Atlantic meant that the ministry's response to the riots would not be known until the following spring. But already royal officials in America knew that they could no longer count on the deferential political behavior that had ensured stability for three generations. "What can a Governor do without the assistance of the Governed?" the Philadelphia customs collector lamented.

Motives of the Crowds. The strength of the Liberty mobs was surprising, but their existence was not. Crowd actions against houses of prostitution and other nuisances were a regular feature of British and colonial life. So were parades on Guy Fawkes Day, November 5, during which Protestants celebrated the failure of an English Catholic plot led by Fawkes against Parliament by ritually beheading the pope and burning an effigy of "Guy." Colonial mobs had attacked royal officials in the past, harassing the Surveyors of the Woods who protected huge trees for the use of the Royal Navy and intimidating overly zealous customs officials. In 1747 Boston crowds had rioted for three days to protest the impressment (forcible seizure) of merchant seamen for service on British warships.

The Stamp Act rioters came primarily from the middle and lower ranks of colonial society. The leaders of the Sons of Liberty were mostly minor merchants and property-owning artisans who knew each other through their jobs, churches, or neighborhoods. The mobs they led contained a diverse assortment of artisans and

Sugar Acts, declaring that only the colonists' elected representatives could impose taxes on them. They also rejected direct representation in the House of Commons, citing their distance from Britain and their distinct local interests, and they protested strongly against the loss of traditional colonial "rights and liberties," especially trial by jury. Then, assuring Parliament that Americans "glory in being subjects of the best of Kings having been born under the most perfect form of government," the delegates humbly petitioned for repeal of the Stamp Act.

Many Americans favored a more assertive stance. On November 1, 1765, when the Stamp Act went into effect, 200 important merchants in New York City announced a boycott against British merchandise. Traders in Boston and Philadelphia also vowed not to import British goods, and most merchants in smaller

JOSIAH QUINCY JR.
The Threat of Mob Rule

———— ★ ————

Although crowd actions were a familiar aspect of English and colonial life, they were rarely treated as completely legitimate and were often condemned. To Josiah Quincy Jr., a Boston gentleman who opposed the Stamp Act, the destruction of the house of Chief Justice Thomas Hutchinson by the Sons of Liberty in August 1765 was an unjust attack against a loyal American. As Quincy suggested in this passage in his private diary, the mob's violence raised the prospect of popular tyranny and "lawless despotism." Although Quincy later became a leading Boston Patriot, he concludes this entry by praising the ordered liberty provided by the British Constitution.

There cannot, perhaps, be found in the records of time a more flagrant instance to what a pitch of infatuation an incensed populace may arise than the last night afforded. . . . And that peculiar inflammation, which fired the breasts of the people of New England in particular, will always distinguish them as the warmest lovers of liberty; though undoubtedly, in the fury of revenge against those who they thought [were the] . . . enslavers and oppressive tax-masters of their native country, they committed acts totally unjustifiable.

The populace of Boston . . . assembled in King's Street; where, after having kindled a fire, they proceeded, in two separate bodies, to attack the houses of two gentlemen of distinction, who, it had been suggested, were accessories to the present burthens; and did great damage in destroying their houses, furniture, &c., and irreparable damage in destroying their papers. Both parties . . . then unitedly pro-

ceeded to the Chief-Justice's house, who, not expecting them, was unattended by his friends who might have assisted, or proved his innocence. . . .

This rage-intoxicated rabble . . . beset the house on all sides, and soon destroyed every thing of value. . . . The destruction was really amazing. . . .

The distress a man must feel on such an occasion can only be conceived by those who the next day saw his Honor the Chief-Justice come into court . . . with tears starting from his eyes, and a countenance which strongly told the inward anguish of his soul.

GENTLEMEN [he said]: There not being a quorum of the court without me, I am obliged to appear. Some apology is necessary for my dress: indeed, I had no other. Destitute of every thing,—no other shirt; no other garment but what I have on, and not one of my family in a better situation than myself. . . .

I call my Maker to witness, that I never, in New England or Old, in Great Britain or America, neither directly nor indirectly, was aiding, assisting, or supporting—in the least promoting or encouraging—what is commonly called the Stamp Act; but, on the contrary, did all in my power, and strove as much as in me lay, to prevent it. . . .

Who, that marks the riotous tumult, confusion, and uproar of a democratic . . . state [would not fly] . . . to that best asylum, that glorious medium, the British Constitution? Happy people who enjoy this blessed constitution! Happy, thrice happy people, if ye preserve it inviolate! May ye never lose it through a licentious abuse of your invaluable rights. . . .

Source: Jack P. Greene, ed., *Colonies to Nation: 1763–1789* (Baltimore: Johns Hopkins University Press, 1967), 61–63.

struggling journeymen, many of them drawn into the streets by frustration over economic issues. Imports of low-priced British shoes and other manufactured goods threatened the livelihood of some artisans, so they opposed any taxes that would further reduce their declining standard of living. Unlike "the Common people of England," a well-traveled colonist observed, "the people of America . . . never would submit to be taxed

that a few may be loaded with palaces and Pensions and riot in Luxury and Excess, while they themselves cannot support themselves and their needy offspring with Bread."

Other crowd members were moved by the religious passions aroused by the Great Awakening. These evangelical and hard-working Protestants led disciplined lives and resented the arrogance and immorality of

British military officers and the corruption of royal bureaucrats. Still other crowd members had absorbed from their parents and grandparents the antimonarchical sentiments of the seventeenth-century Puritan revolution. A letter sent to a Boston newspaper promising to save "all the Freeborn Sons of America" from "tyrannical ministers" was signed "Oliver Cromwell" (in yet another reference to that zealous revolutionary). Finally, a significant portion of many mobs was made up of apprentices, day laborers, and unemployed sailors—young men seeking adventure and excitement who, when fortified by drink, were more than ready to resort to violence against the well-to-do officials who represented imperial authority.

Traditional fears of tyrannical power thus merged with economic self-interest, religious passion, and class resentments to create a potent anti-imperial outlook among ordinary Americans. The resulting crowd actions imparted a democratic cast to the emerging American Patriot movement. "Nothing is wanting but your own Resolution," a New York Son of Liberty declared during the upheaval, "for great is the Authority and Power of the People."

Ideological Sources of Resistance

Regardless of the motives of the crowd, most Patriot leaders were moved by intellectual principles. These educated men drew on their reading of history and political philosophy to construct an ideology of resistance.

The Actors: Merchants and Lawyers. The colonial opposition movement began in the seaport cities because urban residents were directly affected by the new British policies. The Stamp Act taxed city-based products and services, such as the newspapers merchants relied on for news and the legal documents that were at the heart of the lawyers' business; the Sugar Act raised the cost of molasses to seaport merchants and distillers; and the Currency Act complicated urban trade and financial transactions. Moreover, British firms had begun selling low-cost manufactured goods directly to colonial shopkeepers, thereby threatening the livelihood of American artisans and merchants. All in all, an official in Rhode Island reported, the interests of Britain and the colonies were increasingly "deemed by the People almost altogether incompatible in a Commercial View."

American lawyers took an especially prominent role in the protest movement. In part, this involvement stemmed from their work: merchants hired lawyers to defend them from accusations by customs officials and to prevent seizure of their ships by vice-admiralty judges. But the lawyers' own professional values and training provided another motive for opposing various imperial measures. For example, most American lawyers were against the extension of vice-admiralty courts; as men trained in English common law, they strongly favored trial by jury. Lawyers protested again when the terms of appointment for colonial judges were altered from "during good behavior" to "at the pleasure" of the royal governor, arguing that the change in wording compromised the independence of the judiciary. Although a deep respect for established institutions led many older lawyers to remain loyal to the Crown, younger lawyers tended to embrace the Patriot movement; of the fifty-six men who signed the Declaration of Independence in 1776, twenty-five were lawyers.

As merchants and lawyers debated political and constitutional issues in taverns and coffeehouses, on streetcorners, and in public meetings, they broadened the terms of debate. Initially the American Patriots emphasized economic hardship and traditional privileges. One pamphleteer complained that colonists were being compelled to give the British "our money, as oft and in what quantity they please to demand it." Other writers alleged that the British had violated particular "liberties and privileges" embodied in colonial charters. However, the Patriots gradually came to define "liberty" as an abstract ideal—a "natural right" of all people— rather than as a set of historical privileges. Pamphlets of remarkable political sophistication circulated throughout the colonies, swaying the outlook of the political representatives from rural communities—who dominated the assemblies in terms of numbers—and providing the resistance movement with both an intellectual rationale and a political agenda.

The Intellectual Traditions. As Patriot merchants and lawyers formulated their arguments, they drew on three intellectual traditions. The first was English *common law*, the centuries-old body of legal rules and procedures that protected the king's subjects against arbitrary acts by the government. In 1761 the Boston lawyer James Otis had cited English legal precedents in the famous Writs of Assistance case; he used common-law precedents to dispute the constitutionality of a general search warrant that permitted customs officials to inspect the property and possessions of any and all persons. Similarly, in demanding a jury trial for John Hancock, who was about to be tried for smuggling in a vice-admiralty court, John Adams invoked the common-law tradition. "This 29th Chap. of Magna Charta," Adams argued, referring to an ancient English document that had established the right to trial by jury, "has for many Centuries been esteemed by Englishmen, as one of the noblest Monuments, one of the firmest Bulwarks of their Liberties." Such customary legal practices and common-law rights, Adams and other Patriot lawyers maintained, could not be abridged by bureaucratic edict or even Parliamentary statute.

Sam Adams, Boston Agitator
This portrait by John Singleton Copley (c. 1772) shows the radical Patriot pointing to the Massachusetts Charter of 1692, suggesting that "charter rights" accounted for Samuel Adams's opposition to British policies. But Adams was also influenced by the "natural rights" tradition.
Deposited by the City of Boston. Courtesy, Museum of Fine Arts, Boston.

A second important intellectual resource for educated Americans was the rationalist thought of the Enlightenment. Unlike common-law attorneys, who valued precedent and venerated the ways of the past, Enlightenment philosophers questioned the past and appealed to reason to discover and correct the ills of society. Most Enlightenment thinkers followed John Locke in believing that all individuals possessed certain "natural rights"—such as life, liberty, and property—and that it was the responsibility of government to protect those rights. For many educated colonists this belief provided a strong philosophical justification for resistance to British authority. Samuel Adams, John's cousin and a radical Patriot, asked rhetorically if it was "lawful to resist the Supreme Magistrate, if the Commonwealth cannot be otherwise preserved," and used arguments based on the individual's natural rights to justify the Stamp Act uprising.

The republican and Whig strands of the English political tradition provided the third ideological basis for the American Patriot movement. In some places, particularly Puritan New England, Americans had long venerated the Commonwealth era—the brief period between 1649 and 1660 when England was a republic

dominated by Puritans. After the Glorious Revolution of 1688 even more colonists had applauded the constitutional restrictions placed on the monarchy by English Whigs, such as the ban on royally imposed taxes. Later, many educated Americans absorbed the arguments of Radical Whig spokesmen who denounced political corruption. "Bribery is so common," John Dickinson of Pennsylvania had complained during a visit to London in the 1750s, "that there is not a borough in England where it is not practiced." These republican and Radical Whig sentiments predisposed many Americans to distrust imperial reform. Indeed, Joseph Warren, a Boston physician and Patriot, reported that many townspeople thought the Stamp Act was intended "to force the colonies into rebellion," after which the ministry would use "military power to reduce them to servitude."

Thus, as the ideology of Enlightenment thinkers altered American views of fundamental political rights, Patriot lawyers drew on common-law precedents to defend their clients, and Radical Whig politicians questioned the motives of British ministers and royal governors. By stating colonial grievances in terms of the broad principles of these intellectual traditions, Patriot leaders endowed colonial opposition to British control with high moral significance, turning a series of tax protests into a broad and deeply charged resistance movement.

The Informal Compromise of 1766

As the colonists' resistance intensified, the British Parliament was in turmoil, with various political factions advocating radically different responses to the American challenge. George III had lost confidence in Grenville because of issues unrelated to the Stamp Act and had replaced him as prime minister with Lord Rockingham (Table 5.1). For Americans, Rockingham was an ideal prime minister. Young, inexperienced, and open to persuasion, he led a party of Old Whigs hostile to Grenville's American policies. His followers favored a return to the policy of salutary neglect, believing that America was more important for its "flourishing and increasing trade" than as a source of tax revenue. Indeed, some Old Whigs declared the Stamp Act to be unconstitutional: "I can never give my assent to any bill for taxing the American colonies while they remain unrepresented," declared Lord Camden, a leading English jurist.

British merchants also favored repeal of the Stamp Act, because the colonial boycott of British goods had caused a drastic decrease in their sales. In January 1766 the leading commercial centers of London, Liverpool, Bristol, and Glasgow deluged Parliament with petitions, pointing out the threat to British prosperity. "The Avenues of Trade are all shut up," complained a Bristol merchant with large inventories on hand. "We have no Remittances and are at our Witts End for want of Money to fulfill our Engagements with our Tradesmen."

TABLE 5.1

Ministerial Instability in Britain

Leading Minister	Dates of Ministry	American Policy
Lord Bute	1760–1763	Mildly reformist
George Grenville	1763–1765	Ardently reformist
Lord Rockingham	1765–1766	Accommodationist
William Pitt/ Charles Townshend	1766–1770	Ardently reformist
Lord North	1770–1782	Coercive

But hard-liners in Parliament, outraged by the popular rebellion in America, demanded that substantial numbers of British soldiers be sent to the seaport cities to suppress the riots and force the Americans to submit to the constitutional supremacy of Parliament. "The British legislature," declared Chief Justice Sir James Mansfield, "has authority to bind every part and every subject, whether such subjects have a right to vote or not."

Former prime minister William Pitt devised a third, more ambiguous response to the American resistance movement, demanding that "the Stamp Act be repealed absolutely, totally, and immediately," primarily because it had failed to achieve its goals. Pitt—pro-American in sentiment yet firmly committed to British national power—argued both that Parliament could not tax the colonies and that British authority over America was "sovereign and supreme, in every circumstance of government and legislation whatsoever."

Rockingham successfully reconciled these conflicting views and factions by enacting a series of related measures. To assist British merchants and mollify colonial opinion with respect to taxation, he repealed the Stamp Act and ruled out the use of troops against colonial crowds. He also modified the Sugar Act, reducing the import duty on French molasses from 3 pence to 1 penny a gallon and, to raise revenue, extending the tax to include British molasses as well. Finally, Rockingham pacified imperial reformers and hard-liners with the Declaratory Act of 1766, which explicitly reaffirmed the British Parliament's "full power and authority to make laws and statutes . . . to bind the colonies and people of America . . . in all cases whatsoever."

The Stamp Act crisis ended in compromise. The Americans won important points: their riots, boycott, and petitions had secured repeal of the hated stamp tax and revision of the Sugar Act. Yet Grenville and other advocates of imperial reform had also triumphed by obtaining a statement of Parliamentary supremacy. Both sides could claim victory. And because the confrontation had ended quickly, it seemed possible that it might be forgotten even more quickly. The constitu-

tional status of the American provinces remained uncertain, but political positions had not hardened. Leaders of good will could still hope to work out an imperial relationship acceptable to both sides.

Patrick Henry, a Great Orator
This portrait of Henry, painted in 1795 when he was in his sixties, captures his lifelong seriousness and intensity. As an orator, Henry drew on evangelical Protestantism to create a new mode of political oratory. "His figures of speech . . . were often borrowed from the Scriptures," a contemporary noted, and the content of his speeches mirrored "the earnestness depicted in his own features."
Mead Art Museum, Amherst College.

Celebrating the Repeal of the Stamp Act
When news of the repeal of the Stamp Act reached Boston in May 1766, the colonists
erected an illuminated obelisk, depicted here in an engraving made by Paul Revere.
Made of oiled paper stretched on a wooden frame and lit from within by candles, the
obelisk was decorated with American symbols, such as Indians, and portraits of sympathetic British political leaders, including John Wilkes and Lord Camden (at far right,
lower portraits). Alas, such celebratory structures were temporary, and this one
burned down five hours after it was illuminated.
Library of Congress.

The Growing Confrontation, 1767–1770

★

The compromise of 1766 was short-lived. Within a year
political rivalries in Britain sparked a new and more
prolonged struggle with the American provinces over
taxes. On both sides of the Atlantic, economic self-
interest and ideological rigidity aggravated the conflict,
resurrecting the passions and violence of 1765 and
dashing prospects for a timely resolution of the crisis.

The Townshend Initiatives

Often the course of history is changed by a small
event—a leader's illness, a personal grudge, a chance
remark. So it was in 1766, when Rockingham's Old
Whig ministry collapsed and George III named William
Pitt to head the new ministry. Pitt, the master strategist
of the Great War for Empire, was chronically ill with
gout and often missed cabinet meetings and Parliamentary debates, leaving Chancellor of the Exchequer
Charles Townshend in command. Pitt was sympathetic
toward America; Townshend was not. Since his service
on the Board of Trade in the 1750s, Townshend had

favored imperial reform; with Pitt partially incapacitated, the chancellor had the power to push it through.

The Townshend Act. Even so, Townshend had other pressing concerns and no specific plans for the colonies. But in 1767 when he presented the military budget to Parliament, his longtime rival, Lord Grenville, rose to demand that the colonists pay for the British troops in America. On the defensive, Townshend made an unplanned, fateful policy decision. Convinced of the necessity of imperial reform and eager to reduce the English land tax, he promised that he would find a new source of revenue in America.

The new tax legislation, known as the Townshend Act of 1767, was intended to provide royal officials with a guaranteed income, freeing their salaries from the control of colonial assemblies and enabling them to enforce Parliamentary laws and royal directives. The tax imposed duties on paper, paint, glass, and tea imported into the colonies and was expected to raise about £40,000 a year. To pacify Grenville, part of the revenue would be used to defray military expenses, but the major part would be used to pay the salaries of governors, judges, and other imperial officials. To enhance further the power of the royal bureaucracy, Townshend devised the Revenue Act of 1767. This new act created a Board of American Customs Commissioners in Boston and vice-admiralty courts in Halifax, Boston, Philadelphia, and Charleston. These administrative innovations were far-reaching and posed a greater threat to American autonomy than did the small sums raised by the import duties.

The Restraining Act. The New York assembly gave Townshend another chance to challenge the colonial assemblies when it refused to comply with the Quartering Act of 1765, which required Americans to house and feed British troops. Fearing an unlimited drain on its treasury, the New York assembly first denied General Gage's requests for barracks and supplies and then limited the extent of its assistance. Dissatisfied, the British ministry instructed New York to assume complete financial responsibility for its defense against Indian attacks. If the assembly refused, some members of Parliament threatened that an extra port duty would be imposed on New York imports and exports to raise the needed funds.

The new secretary of state—William Petty, earl of Shelburne—took an even more aggressive stance. He recommended the appointment of a military governor with authority to seize funds from New York's treasury to pay for quartering the troops and "to act with Force or Gentleness as circumstances might make necessary." Townshend decided on a less provocative measure, the so-called Restraining Act of 1767, which suspended the New York assembly until it submitted to the Quartering

Act. Faced with the loss of self-government, New Yorkers appropriated the required funds.

The Restraining Act was of great significance because it threatened the very existence of representative government in the colonies. The British Privy Council had always supervised the assemblies, invalidating about 5 percent of all colonial laws, such as those establishing land banks or vesting new powers in the assemblies. Townshend's Restraining Act went much further by defining American governmental institutions as completely dependent on Parliamentary favor.

America Again Resists

The Townshend Duties revived the constitutional debate over taxation. During the Stamp Act crisis of 1765 some Americans had suggested that "external" duties on trade (which Britain had always regulated) were acceptable but that direct or "internal" taxes (which had never before been levied) were not. Townshend thought this distinction between internal and external taxes was "perfect nonsense," but he told Parliament that "since Americans were pleased to make that distinction, he was willing to indulge them [and] . . . to confine himself to regulations of Trade."

A Second Boycott. In reality, only a few colonial leaders argued that there was a significant difference between internal and external taxes. The majority agreed with John Dickinson, author of *Letters from a Farmer in Pennsylvania* (1768), that the real issue was not whether the tax was internal or external but the *intention* of the legislation. They refused to accept the legitimacy of Townshend's taxes on colonial imports because the measures were not designed to regulate trade but to bring revenue to the imperial government, and thus amounted to taxation without consent. As Dickinson sarcastically declared, "I think it evident that we *must* use paper and glass; that what we use *must* be *British*; and that we *must* pay the duties imposed, unless those who sell these articles are so generous as to make us presents of the duties they pay."

Many Americans joined Dickinson in opposing the new legislation. In February 1768 the Massachusetts House of Representatives sent a letter to the other assemblies condemning the Townshend Act for taxing the colonists and thereby infringing on their "natural & constitutional Rights." Meanwhile, Patriot merchants in Boston launched a new boycott of British goods, and New York traders followed in August. But public opinion was divided. Philadelphia merchants, sailors, and dockworkers, who were more heavily involved in direct trade with Britain, refused to join the nonimportation movement, believing they had too much to lose.

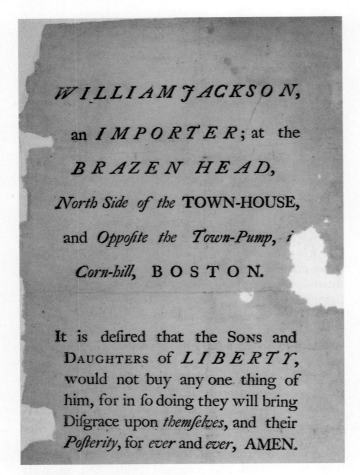

WILLIAM JACKSON,

an *IMPORTER*; at the

BRAZEN HEAD,

North Side of the TOWN-HOUSE,

and *Oppofite the Town-Pump, i*

Corn-hill, BOSTON.

It is defired that the Sons and
DAUGHTERS of *LIBERTY,*
would not buy any one thing of
him, for in fo doing they will bring
Difgrace upon *themfelves,* and their
Pofterity, for *ever* and *ever,* AMEN.

A Nonimportation Broadside
To punish merchants who defied the boycott against the
Townshend Duties, Patriots in Boston and other seaports
posted broadsides urging residents not to patronize their businesses. Some Sons and Daughters of Liberty resorted to more
violent tactics, harassing the merchants' customers and van-
dalizing their buildings.
Massachusetts Historical Society.

Nonetheless, public support for the boycott gradually spread to smaller port cities, such as Salem, Newport, and Baltimore, and into the countryside. In
Puritan New England, ministers and public officials
supported nonimportation by condemning "luxury and
dissipation" and the use of "foreign superfluities," and
promoted the domestic manufacture of necessities
such as paper and cloth.

The boycott prompted new crowd actions that
united thousands of Americans in a common political
movement. The Sons of Liberty published the names of
merchants who imported British goods, broke their
store windows, and harassed their employees. In
Charleston, South Carolina, the merchant Christopher
Gadsden joined the Sons of Liberty and helped persuade his fellow traders to support the boycott. But in
many seaports, merchants deeply resented the crowd's

attacks on their reputations and property. Fearing mob
rule, they condemned nonimportation and stood by the
royal governors.

Despite this split between radical Patriots and
future Loyalists, the boycott gathered momentum. In
March 1769 most Philadelphia merchants responded to
growing public pressure and joined the nonimportation
movement. Two months later the members of the Virginia House of Burgesses agreed not to buy dutied articles, British luxuries, or slaves. "The whole continent
from New England to Georgia seems firmly fixed," the
Massachusetts Gazette proudly announced; "like a
strong, well-constructed arch, the more weight there is
laid upon it, the firmer it stands; and thus with America, the more we are loaded, the more we are united."

The Daughters of Liberty. American women, especially religious women, added their support to the nonimportation movement through the production of
"homespun" textiles. Ordinarily women were excluded
from prominent roles in public affairs; in times of religious and social upheaval, such as the Great Awakening
or a severe shortage of food, a few women would
emerge as prophets or preachers or would lead a mob,
demanding that shopkeepers provide reasonably priced
grain. But the boycotts against Britain prompted a
more sustained involvement by women in the public
world. During the Stamp Act crisis, groups of young
women with ties to Patriot leaders had supported the
boycott of British goods and textiles by increasing their
production of yarn and cloth. For example, in March
1766, a newspaper reported that in Providence, Rhode
Island, "eighteen daughters of liberty, young ladies of
good reputation," met to spin yarn for cloth, and
declared that they would not purchase British manufactures.

The contest over the Townshend Duties elicited support from a much broader group of women, including
religious women in New England, who organized dozens
of spinning matches, bees, and demonstrations at the
homes of their ministers. Some of these gatherings were
openly patriotic, such as that at Berwick, Maine, where
the spinners—"as true Daughters of Liberty"—celebrated American goods, "drinking rye coffee and dining
on bear venison." But many more pious women combined support for nonimportation with the fulfillment of
social obligations and charitable work by gathering to
spin flax and wool, which they donated to their ministers
and needy members of the community. Just as the
tradition of crowd actions influenced men's response to
the imperial crisis, so women's concerns with the well-
being of their communities guided their efforts.

Ultimately, the efforts of patriotic young ladies and
religious women prompted thousands of other women
to redouble their efforts at the spinning wheel and the
loom. Newspapers celebrated these patriotic heroines,

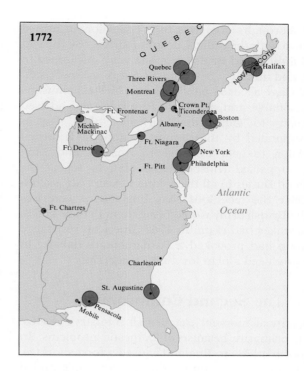

whose production of "homespun" cloth made America less dependent on British textile imports than in previous years. It was a newsworthy event when the women of the Freeman, Smith, and Heard families of Woodbridge, New Jersey, announced that they had attained an annual household output of 500 yards. One Massachusetts town claimed an annual output of 30,000 yards of cloth, while East Hartford, Connecticut, reported 17,000 yards. Although this surge in domestic production did not compensate for the loss of British imports, which had averaged about 10 million yards a year, it inspired support for nonimportation in hundreds of communities. Reflecting colonial confidence that the boycott was succeeding, Benjamin Franklin called for a return to the pre-1763 mercantilist system. "It is easy to propose a plan of conciliation," Franklin declared, "*repeal* the laws, *renounce* the right, *recall* the troops, *refund* the money, and *return* to the old method of requisition."

Britain Responds. British patience was exhausted. When a copy of the Massachusetts House's letter opposing the Townshend Duties reached London in late spring of 1768, Lord Hillsborough, the secretary of state for American affairs, branded it as "unjustifiable opposition to the constitutional authority of Parliament." He instructed Governor Francis Bernard to dissolve the House if it refused to rescind its action. To strengthen the "Hand of Government" in Massachusetts and assist the Commissioners of the Customs, who had been forced by a mob to take refuge on the *Liberty*, a British naval vessel, Hillsborough dispatched four regiments of troops to Boston (Map 5.2).

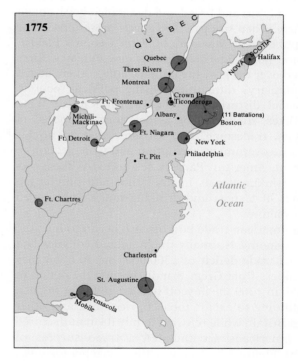

MAP 5.2
British Troop Deployments, 1763–1775
As the imperial crisis deepened, British military priorities changed. In 1763 most British battalions (the large circles represent 350 men) were stationed in Canada to deter Indian attacks and French-Canadian revolts. After the Stamp Act riots of 1765, the British established larger garrisons in New York and Philadelphia. By 1775 eleven battalions of British regulars occupied Boston, the center of the American Patriot movement.

Hillsborough's goal was to prepare for an armed showdown with the radical Boston Patriots. By the end of 1768 a thousand British regulars were encamped in Boston, and military coercion was a very real prospect. General Gage accused public leaders in Massachusetts of "Treasonable and desperate Resolves" and advised the ministry to "Quash this Spirit at a Blow." Parliament responded by threatening to appoint a special commission to hear evidence of treason, and King George supported Hillsborough's plan to repeal the Townshend Duties in all the colonies except Massachusetts. Once the rebellious New Englanders were isolated, the British army would bring them to their knees.

The stakes had risen. In 1765 American resistance to taxation had provoked a Parliamentary debate. In 1768 it produced a plan for military coercion.

The Second Compromise

At this critical moment the British ministry's resolve faltered, primarily because of domestic problems. In 1768 poor harvests in England caused a food shortage, and riots swept the countryside. English mobs raided supplies of grain and bread and demanded government assistance. When troops killed seven protesters in the highly publicized "Massacre of Saint George's Fields," opposition politicians called for a new ministry. Riots in Ireland over the growing military budget there added to the ministry's difficulties. Giving political focus to these social disturbances, the British Radical Whig John Wilkes, supported by associations composed of merchants, tradesmen, and artisans, stepped up his attacks on government corruption and won election to Parliament. American Patriots celebrated Wilkes's victory by drinking toasts in his honor and purchasing thousands of teapots and drinking mugs emblazoned with his picture.

The American trade boycott also began to hurt the British economy. Normally the mainland colonies had an annual trade deficit of £500,000, but in 1768 they imported less from Great Britain, cutting the deficit to £230,000. In 1769 the boycott had a significant impact. By continuing to export tobacco, rice, fish, and other goods to Britain while refusing to buy its manufactured goods, Americans accumulated a trade surplus of £816,000 (Figure 5.2). To revive their flagging fortunes, British merchants and manufacturers petitioned Parliament for repeal of the Townshend Duties. By late 1769 merchants' petitions had persuaded some ministers that the Townshend Duties were a mistake, and the king had withdrawn his support for Hillsborough's plan of military coercion.

The Crisis Resolved. Early in 1770 Lord North became prime minister and decided to arrange a new compromise with the colonists. Arguing that it was

John Wilkes, British Radical
Wilkes won fame as the author of *North Briton, Number 45*, a pamphlet that called for major reforms in the British political system. At a dinner in Boston, Radical Whigs raised their wineglasses to Wilkes—toasting him 45 times!
Miriam and Ira D. Wallach Division of Art, Prints and Photographs, The New York Public Library. Astor, Lenox and Tilden Foundations.

foolish for Britain to tax its own exports to America (thereby raising their price and decreasing consumption), North persuaded Parliament to repeal the duties on glass, paper, paint, and other manufactured items. But the prime minister retained the tax on tea as a symbol of Parliament's supremacy. This strategy worked. In a spirit of good will (and to restore their own flagging businesses), merchants in New York and Philadelphia renewed the importation of British manufactures, rejecting pleas from zealous Patriots in Boston to continue the boycott until North acknowledged their constitutional rights by repealing the tax on tea. Most ordinary Americans accepted the symbolic levy and simply avoided paying the tax by drinking smuggled Dutch tea, which was cheaper than British tea.

Even new outbreaks of violence in New York City and Boston did not rupture the compromise. During

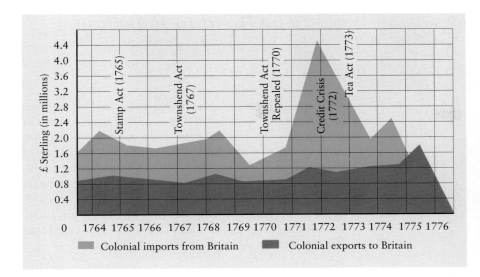

FIGURE 5.2
Trade as a Political Weapon, 1763–1776
Political upheaval did not affect the mainland colonies' exports to Britain, which remained steady (and rose slightly) over the period, but imports fluctuated greatly. The American boycott of 1768–1769 brought a sharp decline in the importation of British manufactures, which then soared after the repeal of the Townshend Duties.

the boycott New York artisans and workers had taunted British troops, mostly with words but occasionally with stones and fists. In retaliation the soldiers tore down a Liberty pole (a Patriot flagpole) in front of a tavern, setting off a week of street fighting—known as the Golden Hill riots.

In Boston friction arose between the townspeople and British soldiers on a much broader range of issues. Leading Patriots contested the constitutional legitimacy of the occupation of the town by what they called a "standing army." For decades Radical Whigs in England had emphasized the dangers to liberty posed by a peacetime army, and educated Americans had absorbed their arguments without fully understanding them. Now, with 4,000 British soldiers encamped in a town of 15,000 people, Bostonians knew firsthand the dangers of a standing army: its intimidation of political leaders, the daily challenges to residents by sentries, fights between soldiers and young men over women and jobs. In March 1770 tensions came to a head when a patrol of soldiers, taunted by a throng of laborers and seamen, fired into the crowd and killed five men, one of whom was Crispus Attucks, an escaped mulatto slave who was working as a seaman.

Seeking to uphold the honor of Boston while condemning British policy, Patriot leaders played a double game. No less a Patriot than John Adams defended the soldiers in a Boston court, blaming the incident on "a motley rabble of saucy boys, negroes and mulattoes, Irish teagues and outlandish jack tarrs," and won their acquittal. Simultaneously another Patriot, James Bowdoin, wrote *A Short Narrative of the Horrid Massacre in Boston*, accusing the British of deliberately planning the killing by imposing a standing army on the town. Bowdoin's inflammatory pamphlet circulated widely in the colonies and, by depicting the event not as an accident but as

the "Boston Massacre," inflamed public opinion against the imperial authorities.

Sovereignty Debated. Although most Americans still remained loyal to the empire, five years of conflict over taxes and constitutional principles had significantly altered their sentiments. In 1765 American public leaders had accepted Parliament's authority; the Stamp Act Resolves had opposed only certain "unconstitutional" legislation. By 1770 the most outspoken Patriots—Benjamin Franklin in Pennsylvania, Patrick Henry in Virginia, and Samuel Adams in Massachusetts—had repudiated Parliamentary supremacy, emphasizing instead the authority of the American assemblies. Beginning from this premise, Franklin looked for a way to redefine the imperial relationship so that the colonies would have political equality within the empire. Perhaps thinking of various European "composite monarchies" (in which kings ruled far-distant and semiautonomous provinces acquired by inheritance or conquest), Franklin suggested that the colonies were now "distinct and separate states" but ones that had "the same Head, or Sovereign, the King."

This proposal horrified Thomas Hutchinson, the American-born royal governor of Massachusetts, who rejected the idea of "two independent legislatures in one and the same state." For Hutchinson, the British Empire was a single entity, its sovereignty indivisible—it was all or nothing. "I know of no line," he told the Massachusetts House of Representatives, "that can be drawn between the supreme authority of Parliament and the total independence of the colonies." But a House committee disagreed, adopting Franklin's position: if Britain and its American colonies were united by the king as their "one head and common sovereign," they could "live happily in

Clerical Resistance in New England
Puritan ministers had long opposed the Church of England, and by the 1760s they feared that the British ministry would soon dispatch Anglican bishops to America. Jonathan Mayhew (1720–1766) vigorously opposed such schemes (note the bishop's miter hanging empty at the bottom of the engraving) and was an articulate advocate of religious self-government as practiced in the Congregational churches of New England.
Courtesy, American Antiquarian Society.

The Road to Rebellion, 1771–1775

The repeal of the Townshend Duties (with the exception of the tax on tea) in 1770 restored harmony to the British Empire. For the next three years most disputes were resolved peacefully. The continued existence of the empire seemed assured. Yet history moves in unpredictable ways, and below the surface lay strong fears and passions and mutual distrust. Suddenly, in 1773, those undercurrents erupted, overwhelming any hope for compromise. In less than two years the Americans and the British stood on the brink of war.

The Compromise Overturned

The repeal of the Townshend Duties did not satisfy radical Patriots, who now wanted American independence. From Boston, Patriots kept the Boston Massacre vivid in public memory and continued to warn Americans of the dangers of imperial domination. In November 1772 Samuel Adams persuaded the Boston town meeting to establish a Committee of Correspondence "to state the Rights of the Colonists of this Province." Within a few months eighty Massachusetts towns had similar committees. Other colonies copied the practice when the British government set up a royal commission to investigate the burning of the *Gaspée*, a British customs vessel, in Rhode Island. The commission's powers, particularly its authority to send Americans to Britain for trial, first aroused the Virginia House of Burgesses, which created a Committee of Correspondence "to communicate with the other colonies" about the situation in Rhode Island. By July 1773 committees had sprung up in Connecticut, New Hampshire, and South Carolina.

The Tea Act.   Parliament's passage of a Tea Act in May 1773 initiated the chain of events that led directly to civil war. Lord North had designed the act to provide financial relief for the British East India Company, a royally chartered firm that was deeply in debt because of mismanagement and military expeditions undertaken to extend British trade in India. The Tea Act provided the company with a government loan and, more important, eliminated the customs duties on the company's tea as it passed through Britain to be reexported to the American colonies. This provision allowed the East India Company to sell tea at a lower price than other British merchants, giving it a virtual monopoly of the American market.

   Lord North failed to understand how unpopular the Tea Act would be in America. Since 1768, when the

that connection." (More than a century and a half later, this idea would come to fruition in the British Commonwealth of Nations.)

   There the matter rested. The British had twice tried to impose taxes on the colonies, and American Patriots had twice forced them to retreat. If Parliament or the king insisted on exercising Britain's claim to sovereign power, at least some Americans were prepared to resist by force. Nor did they flinch when reminded that George III condemned their agitation. As the Massachusetts House told Hutchinson, "There is more reason to dread the consequences of absolute uncontrolled supreme power, whether of a nation or a monarch, than those of total independence." Fearful of civil war, the ministry hesitated to take the final fateful step.

Townshend Act had placed a duty of 3 pence a pound on tea, American traders had greatly increased their illegal imports of Dutch tea. By the 1770s about 90 percent of the tea consumed in the colonies was contraband. However, the Tea Act of 1773 was designed to make the British East India Company's tea cheaper than Dutch tea—even with 3 pence tax. Radical Patriots accused the ministry of using low prices to bribe Americans to give up their principled opposition to Parliamentary taxation; as an anonymous woman wrote in the *Massachusetts Spy,* "the use of tea is considered not as a *private* but as a *public* evil . . . a handle to introduce a variety of . . . oppressions amongst us." For his part, North saw the tax on tea as an initial wedge that would eventually allow the imposition of other levies. Like Grenville and Townshend before him, the prime minister was not content to declare Parliament's authority to tax the colonies—he wanted to demonstrate it.

North's insensitivity to the fragile state of the colonial relationship cost the empire dearly, for it revived American resistance. The East India Company decided to distribute the tea directly to shopkeepers in major American cities, a tactic that would eliminate most colonial merchants from the trade. American merchants immediately protested. "The fear of an Introduction of a Monopoly in this Country," General Haldimand reported from New York, "has induced the mercantile part of the Inhabitants to be very industrious in opposing this Step and added Strength to a Spirit of Independence already too prevalent."

The Committees of Correspondence took the lead in organizing resistance to the Tea Act. They held public bonfires at which they persuaded their fellow citizens—sometimes gently, sometimes not—to consign British tea to the flames. The Sons of Liberty prevented East India Company ships from landing new supplies, forcing the company's captains to return the tea to Britain or store it in public warehouses, and thus effectively nullified the legislation.

The Boston Tea Party. In Boston events took a more ominous turn. For decades Massachusetts had steadfastly resisted British authority, and in the 1760s it had assumed leadership of the anti-imperial movement. Boston lawyers James Otis and John Adams had raised the first constitutional objections to legislation enforcing imperial reform, Boston mobs were the first to oppose the Stamp Act, and Boston merchants such as John Hancock had led colonial opposition to the Townshend Duties. As early as 1768 Bostonians had condemned the tax on tea as a devious plot by "the politicians who planned our ruin," and it was they who provoked the Boston Massacre two years later. Now it was Boston's destiny to spark the final conflagration with Great Britain.

Chance also figured in this outcome. The governor of Massachusetts, Thomas Hutchinson, bitterly opposed the Patriots, and with good reason. Stamp Act rioters had looted his house, Benjamin Franklin and Boston Patriots had smeared his reputation by stealing and publishing his private correspondence, and the Massachusetts House had condemned his defense of Parliamentary power.

Motivated by both personal grudges and constitutional principles, Hutchinson came up with a scheme to land the tea and collect the tax. When a shipment of tea arrived on the *Dartmouth* on November 28, 1773, it was consigned to his sons, who were Boston merchants. The governor had his sons pass the ship through customs immediately but not pay the tax, which meant that the ship could not depart. He intended to wait twenty days, at which time customs officials could seize the cargo for non-payment of the tax, land it with the help of the British army, and sell the tea at auction to collect the tax. But Patriots foiled the governor's plan by raiding the *Dartmouth*: on December 16, a group of artisans and laborers disguised as Indians boarded the ship, broke open 342 chests and threw 45 tons of tea (valued at about £10,000, or roughly $800,000 today) into the harbor (see *American Lives,* "George R. T. Hewes and the Meaning of the Revolution," pp. 166–167). "This destruction of the Tea is so bold and it must have so important Consequences," John Adams wrote in his diary, "that I cannot but consider it as an Epoch in History."

The Coercive Acts. The British Privy Council was outraged by the Tea Party, as was the king. "Concessions have made matters worse," George III declared. "The time has come for compulsion." Early in 1774 Parliament decisively rejected a proposal to repeal the duty on American tea and instead enacted four Coercive Acts to force Massachusetts into submission. The Port Bill closed Boston Harbor until the East India Company received payment for the destroyed tea. The Government Act annulled the Massachusetts charter and prohibited most local town meetings. The new Quartering Act required the colony to build barracks or accommodate British soldiers in private houses. To protect royal officials from Massachusetts juries, the Justice Act allowed the transfer of trials for capital crimes to other colonies or to Britain.

In response, Patriot leaders throughout the mainland condemned these laws—which they called the Intolerable Acts—and rallied support for Massachusetts. In far-off Georgia a Patriot warned the "Freemen of the Province" that "every privilege you at present claim as a birthright, may be wrested from you by the same authority that blockades the town of Boston." To assist Bostonians to "stand more firm in the glorious cause," Patriots in Brooklyn, New York, sent 125 sheep to feed the town's poor. "The cause of Boston," George Washington declared from Virginia, "now is and ever will be considered as the cause

George R. T. Hewes and the Meaning of the Revolution

———————★———————

GEORGE ROBERT TWELVES Hewes was born in Boston in 1742. He was named George for his father, Robert for a paternal uncle, and Twelves for his maternal grandmother, whose maiden name was Twelves. Apart from his long name, Hewes received little from his parents—not size, for he was unusually short, at five feet, one inch; not wealth, for his father, a failed leather tanner, died a poor soap boiler when Hewes was seven years old; not even love, for Hewes spoke of his mother only as someone who whipped him for disobedience. When he was fourteen she apprenticed him to a shoemaker, one of the lower trades.

This harsh upbringing shaped Hewes's outlook on life. As an adult he spoke out against all brutality, even the tarring and feathering of a Loyalist who had almost killed him. And throughout his life he was extremely sensitive about his class status. He was "neither a rascal nor a vagabond," Hewes retorted to a Boston gentleman who pulled rank on him, "and though a poor man was in as good credit in town as he [the gentleman] was."

The occupation of Boston by 4,000 British soldiers in 1768 drew the twenty-six-year-old Hewes into the resistance movement. At first his concerns were personal: he took offense when British sentries challenged him and when a soldier refused to pay for a pair of shoes. Then they became political: Hewes grew angry when some of the poorly paid British soldiers moonlighted, taking jobs away from Bostonians, and even angrier when a Loyalist merchant fired into a crowd of apprentices who were picketing his shop, killing one of them. And so on March 5, 1770, when British soldiers came out in force to clear the streets of rowdy civilians, Hewes joined his fellow townspeople: "They were in the king's highway, and had as good a right to be there" as the British troops, he said.

Fate—and his growing political consciousness—placed Hewes in the middle of the Boston Massacre. He knew four of the five workingmen shot down that night by British troops, and one of them, James Caldwell, was standing by his side. Hewes caught him as he fell. Outraged, Hewes armed himself with a cane, only to be confronted by Sergeant Chambers of the

George Hewes
In this portrait Joseph Cole presents the elderly Hewes as a dignified gentleman, not the impoverished shoemaker and farmer that he actually was.
Bostonian Society/Old State House.

29th British Regiment and eight or nine soldiers, "all with very large clubs or cutlasses." Chambers seized his cane, but as Hewes stated in a legal deposition, "I told him I had as good a right to carry a cane as they had to carry clubs." This deposition, which told of the soldiers' threats to kill more civilians, was included in *A Short Narrative of the Horrid Massacre in Boston* (1770), published by a group of Boston Patriots.

Hewes had chosen sides, and his political radicalism did not go unpunished. His deposition roused the ire of one of his creditors, a Loyalist merchant tailor. Hewes had never really made a go of it as a shoemaker and lived on the brink of poverty. Unable to make good on a two-year-old debt of £6. 8s. 3p. (about $300 today) for "a sappled coat & breeches of fine cloth," in September 1770 he landed in debtor's prison for over a month. Hewes's extravagance was not in character; his purchase of the suit had been the desperate ploy of a propertyless artisan to win the hand of Sally Summer, the daughter of the sexton of the First Baptist Church, whom Hewes married in 1768.

Prison did not blunt Hewes's enthusiasm for the Patriot cause. On the night of December 16, 1773, he volunteered at the Tea Party organized by the radical Patriots of Boston. He "daubed his face and hands with coal dust in the shop of a blacksmith" and then found, to his surprise, that "the commander of the division to which I belonged, as soon as we were on board the ship, appointed me boatswain, and ordered me to go to the captain and demand of him the keys to the hatches."

Hewes had been singled out and made a minor leader, and he must have played the part well. Thompson

Maxwell, a volunteer sent to the Tea Party by John Hancock, recalled that "I went accordingly, joined the band under one Captain Hewes; we mounted the ships and made tea in a trice." In the heat of conflict the small man with the large name had been elevated from a poor shoemaker to "Captain Hewes."

A man of greater ability or ambition might have seized the moment, using his reputation as a Patriot to win fame or fortune, but that was not Hewes's destiny. During the War of Independence he fought as an ordinary sailor and soldier, shipping out twice on privateering voyages and enlisting at least four times in the militia, about twenty months of military service in all. He did not win riches as a privateer (although, with four children to support, that was his hope). Nor did he find glory or even adequate pay in battle: "we received nothing of the government but paper money, of very little value, and continually depreciating." Indeed, the war cost Hewes his small stake in society: "The shop which I had built in Boston, I lost"; it was pulled down and burned by British troops.

In material terms, the American Revolution did about as much for Hewes as his parents had. When a journalist found the shoemaker in New York State in the 1830s, he was still "pressed down by the iron hand of poverty." The spiritual reward was greater. As his biographer, Alfred Young, aptly put it: "He was a nobody who briefly became a somebody in the Revolution and, for a moment near the end of his life, a hero." Because Americans had begun to celebrate the memory of the Revolution, Hewes was brought back to Boston in triumph in 1835 as one of the last surviving participants in the Tea Party—the guest of honor on Independence Day.

But an even more fundamental spiritual reward had come to Hewes when he became a revolutionary, casting off the deferential status of a "subject" in a monarchy and becoming a proud and equal "citizen" in a republic. What this meant to Hewes, and to thousands of other poor and obscure Patriots, appeared in his relationship—both real and fictitious—with John Hancock. As a young man Hewes had sat rapt and tongue-tied in the rich merchant's presence. But when he related his story of the Tea Party, Hewes elevated himself to the same level as Hancock, placing the merchant at the scene (which was almost certainly not the case) and claiming that he "was himself at one time engaged with him in the demolition of the same chest of tea." In this lessening of social distance—this declaration of *equality*—lay one of the profound meanings of the American Revolution.

The Boston Tea Party
Led by radical Patriots disguised as Mohawk Indians, Bostonians dumped taxed British tea into the harbor. The rioters underlined their "pure" political motives by punishing those who sought personal gain; a man who stole some of the tea was "stripped of his booty and his clothes together, and sent home naked."
Library of Congress.

MAP 5.3
British Western Policy, 1763–1774
The Proclamation Line of 1763 restricted white settlement west of the Appalachian Mountains, but colonial land speculators planned the new colonies of Vandalia and Transylvania. However, the Quebec Act of 1774 designated these western lands as Indian reserves and, by vastly increasing the boundaries of Quebec, eliminated the sea-to-sea land claims of many eastern colonies. The act, which also allowed the French residents to practice Catholicism, angered many Americans: settlers and land speculators who wanted easy access to the west, New England Protestants who had long feared Catholicism, and colonial political leaders who condemned its failure to provide a representative assembly in Quebec.

of America." Clearly, the Committees of Correspondence had created a firm sense of unity.

In 1774 Parliament passed the Quebec Act, which heightened the Americans' sense of common danger. The law extended the boundaries of Quebec into the Ohio River Valley, threatening to restrict the western boundaries of Virginia and other seaboard colonies (Map 5.3). It also gave legal recognition to Roman Catholicism—a humane concession to French Canadians but one that aroused old religious hatreds, especially in New England, where Puritans detested Catholicism and associated it with arbitrary royal government. Although the ministry had not intended the Quebec Act as a coercive measure, many colonial leaders saw it as another demonstration of Parliament's power to intervene in American domestic affairs.

The Response of the First Continental Congress

To respond to the new British measures, American leaders called for a new all-colony assembly, the Continental Congress. The newer colonies—Florida and Quebec, which had just been acquired from Spain and France, and Nova Scotia and Newfoundland, recently settled provinces with few people and weak assemblies—did not attend. But delegates chosen by all the other mainland assemblies (except Georgia, whose legislature was effectively controlled by a royal governor) met in Philadelphia in September 1774.

The stakes at the First Continental Congress were high, and understandably the delegates were divided. Southern leaders, fearing a British plot "to overturn the constitution and introduce a system of arbitrary government," favored a new economic boycott. Representatives of the New England colonies wanted to go further, advocating political union and defensive military preparations. But many delegates from the middle colonies wanted to seek a political compromise with the British ministry.

Led by Joseph Galloway of Pennsylvania, these men of "loyal principles" outlined a scheme for a new imperial system that resembled the Albany Plan of Union of 1754. Under Galloway's proposal, America would have a legislative council selected by the colonial assemblies and a president-general appointed by the king. Moreover, the new council would have veto power over Parliamentary legislation that affected America. Despite this feature, the delegates refused to endorse Galloway's plan. With British troops occupying Boston and enforcing the Coercive Acts, they thought it was too conciliatory.

Instead, the First Continental Congress passed a Declaration of Rights and Grievances that condemned the Coercive Acts and demanded their repeal. The Congress also repudiated the Declaratory Act of 1766, which had proclaimed Parliament's supremacy over the colonies, and demanded that Britain restrict its supervision of American affairs to matters of external trade. Finally, the Congress began a program of economic retaliation, beginning with nonimportation and nonconsumption agreements that would take effect in December 1774. If Parliament did not repeal the Coercive Acts by September 1775, all colonial exports to Britain, Ireland, and the West Indies would be cut off. Ten years of constitutional conflict had culminated in all-out commercial warfare.

Even at this late date a few British leaders continued to hope for compromise. In January 1775 the earl of Chatham (William Pitt) asked Parliament to give up its claim to tax the colonies and to recognize the Continental Congress as a lawful body. In return for these and other concessions, he proposed that the Congress acknowledge Parliamentary supremacy and grant a continuing revenue to help defray the British national debt.

Chatham's dramatic intervention, like Galloway's in the colonies, was doomed to failure. The British ministry was unyielding. In 1766 and again in 1770, it had backed down when faced with American resistance; now a third retreat was impossible. The honor of the nation was at stake. The ministry rejected Chatham's plan, branding the Continental Congress an illegal assembly. It also rejected a proposal by Lord Dartmouth, the colonial secretary, to send commissioners to America to negotiate a settlement.

Instead, Lord North set stringent terms: Americans must pay for their own defense and administration and acknowledge Parliament's authority to tax them. To give teeth to these demands, North imposed a naval blockade on American trade with foreign nations and ordered General Gage to suppress dissent in Massachusetts. "Now the case seemed desperate," the prime minister told former governor Thomas Hutchinson, who was living in exile in London. "Parliament would not—could not—concede. For aught [I can] see it must come to violence."

The Rising of the Countryside

Although the Patriot movement began in the seaport cities, its success would ultimately depend on the support of the predominantly rural population. Before

William Pitt
Hobbled by gout and age, William Pitt (Lord Chatham) addresses the House of Lords on the American question. By 1775 Pitt's eloquence could not soothe the mutual suspicion and anger created by a decade of conflict.
Metropolitan Museum of Art, Bequest of Charles Allen Munn, 1924.

1750 most farmers had little interest in imperial issues. Their lives were deeply rooted in the soil, and their primary allegiance was to their families and communities. Then the Great War for Empire took their sons away from home and reduced their income. For example, in the community of Newtown on Long Island, farmers had paid an average of 10 shillings in taxes before 1754 (less than 5 percent of their cash income); by 1756 taxes had jumped to 30 shillings to cover New York's military expenses. Peace brought only slight relief; the Quartering Act cost each Newtown resident 20 shillings in taxes in 1771. Although in fact they paid much less in taxes than did most Britons, many rural Americans found these exactions onerous.

The Expansion of the Patriot Movement. The political doctrines of urban Patriots gradually infiltrated the countryside. The merchant-led boycott of 1765 attracted some rural supporters, and by 1768 Daughters munities merchants were seizing farmsteads for delinquent debts. Patriots warned that the new demands of the British government would further drain "this People of the Fruits of their Toil," as the town meeting of Petersham, Massachusetts, put it. "The duty on tea," a Patriot pamphlet added, "was only a prelude to a window-tax, hearth-tax, land-tax, and poll-tax, and these were only paving the way for reducing the country to lordships." By the 1770s many northern yeomen felt personally threatened by British imperial policy (Table 5.2).

Despite their higher standard of living, southern slaveowners had similar fears. Many Chesapeake planters had fallen deeply into debt to British merchants. A Virginia planter observed in 1766 that a debt of £1,000 had once been considered excessive, but "ten times that sum is now spoke of with indifference and thought no great burthen on Some Estates." High living had led to economic anxiety. Accustomed to being masters on their plantations, planters resented their financial dependence on British merchants and feared the prospect of political dependence raised by the Coercive Acts. Once Parliament had subdued Massachusetts, it might seize control of Virginia's county courts and House of Burgesses, depriving the gentry of the political power it had so long enjoyed. This threat moved Patriot planters to action. "The spark of liberty is not yet extinct among our people," one planter declared, "and if properly fanned by the Gentlemen of influence will, I make no doubt, burst out again into a flame."

The Loyalists. While many wealthy planters and affluent merchants supported the Patriot cause, other prominent Americans had worried for years that resistance to Britain would destroy respect for all political institutions and would end in mob rule (see American Voices, "Anonymous Broadside, May 18, 1775: 'To the Associators of the City of Philadelphia,'" p. 172). When the Sons of Liberty turned to violence to enforce nonimportation, these prominent men's fears increased. "No man can be in a more abject state of bondage than he whose Reputation, Property and Life are exposed to the discretionary violence . . . of the community," complained one well-to-do New Yorker. In 1774, these Americans of "loyal principles"—mostly royal officials, merchants with military contracts, clergy who were members of the Church of England, and well-established lawyers—began to denounce the Patriot goal of independence. Ministers such as Jonathan Boucher of Virginia denounced Patriot agitators from their pulpits, while landlords and merchants used the threat of economic retaliation to persuade indebted tenants and workers to oppose Patriot policies. These leaders and their followers gradually coalesced in a small but articulate pro-British faction known as the Loyalists.

Plate V.
A SOCIETY of PATRIOTIC LADIES,
AT
EDENTON in NORTH CAROLINA.

Political Propaganda: The Empire Strikes Back
A British cartoon attacks the women of Edenton, North Carolina, for supporting the boycott of British trade, hinting at their sexual lasciviousness and—by showing an enslaved black woman among these supposed advocates of liberty—their moral hypocrisy.
Library of Congress.

of Liberty in hundreds of small towns and villages were weaving homespun cloth to aid the second boycott of British goods. When the Continental Congress declared a new nonimportation movement in 1774, it had little difficulty in setting up a network of local Committees of Safety and Inspection to support it. In Concord, Massachusetts, 80 percent of male heads of families and a number of single women signed a Solemn League and Covenant vowing support for nonimportation. Appealing to rural thriftiness, the Congress condemned the wearing of expensive imported clothes to funerals, approving only "a black crape or ribbon on the arm or hat for gentlemen, and a black ribbon and necklace for ladies."

Patriots also appealed to the yeoman tradition of agricultural independence, which was everywhere under attack. Arable land had become scarce and expensive in long-settled regions; in many new com-

TABLE 5.2

Patriot Resistance, 1762–1775

British Action	Date	Patriot Response
Revenue Act	1762	Merchants complain privately
Proclamation Line	1763	Land speculators voice discontent
Sugar Act	1764	Protests by merchants and Massachusetts House
Stamp Act	1765	Riots by Sons of Liberty Stamp Act Congress First nonimportation movement
Quartering Act	1765	New York Assembly refuses to implement until 1767
Townshend Duties	1767	Second nonimportation movement Harassment of pro-British merchants
Troops occupy Boston	1768	Boston Massacre of 1770
Gaspée affair	1772	Committees of Correspondence created
Tea Act	1773	Widespread resistance Boston Tea Party
Coercive Acts and Quebec Act	1774	First Continental Congress Third nonimportation movement
British raids on Lexington and Concord	1775	Armed resistance by Minutemen Second Continental Congress

Thousands of ordinary colonists also refused to support the Patriot resistance movement, for a variety of reasons. Class antagonism was one factor. In regions where many wealthy landlords became Patriots, such as the Hudson Valley of New York, tenant farmers often favored the maintenance of imperial authority. Similar social divisions prompted about half of the backcountry regulators in North Carolina and many smallholding farmers on the eastern shore of Chesapeake Bay in Maryland to oppose the policies advocated by the local Patriot gentry. Ethnic and religious conflicts in the mid-Atlantic colonies also prompted colonists to support the king. In New Jersey, many members of Old Light Dutch Reformed congregations became Loyalists whereas many Dutch New Lights joined the Patriots. In Pennsylvania, Quakers and sectarian Germans tried to remain neutral because of their pacifist principles but were nonetheless labeled as Loyalists.

In most areas the Loyalists failed to organize potential supporters and were therefore unable to affect the course of events. A Tory Association started by Governor Wentworth of New Hampshire drew only fifty-nine members, fourteen of whom were the governor's relatives. At this crucial juncture Americans who favored resistance to British rule commanded the allegiance—or at least the acquiescence—of the majority of white Americans. Exploiting their advantage in public opinion, the Patriots prepared for full-scale rebellion.

The Failure of Compromise

When the First Continental Congress met in September 1774, New England was already openly defying British authority. A month earlier, 150 delegates from neighboring towns had gathered in Concord, Massachusetts, for a Middlesex County Congress. This illegal convention had advised Patriots to close the royal courts of justice and transfer their political allegiance to the popularly elected House of Representatives. Armed crowds had prevented judges appointed by the royal governor from holding court and had harassed supporters of the imperial regime.

General Thomas Gage, who was now the military governor of Massachusetts, tried desperately to maintain imperial power. In September 1774 he ordered British troops to march out of Boston and seize Patriot armories and storehouses at Charlestown and Cambridge. Far from subduing the Patriots, Gage's expedition only created more support for their cause. In response, 20,000 colonial militiamen mobilized to safeguard military supply depots in Concord and Worcester. The Concord town meeting voted to raise a

Anonymous Broadside, May 18, 1775

"To the Associators of the City of Philadelphia"

———★———

*L*oyalist fears that the "lower sort" would seize power had a basis in fact. When the republican Patriots of Philadelphia mobilized laborers, sailors, and other workers into a military "Association" to take control of the city, they unleashed democratic aspirations for respect and equality. At first this quest took the form of protests against concrete grievances, as in the following broadside by a well-educated Philadelphian who supported the demands of ordinary Associators for an inexpensive uniform that they could afford. These aspirations soon turned into appeals for political rights, and they partly account for the radically democratic character of the Pennsylvania Constitution of 1776 (see Chapter 7).

A Considerable number of the Associators of this city, on considering the plan of an uniform recommended by a Committee of the Officers, at a late meeting are of opinion that it will be found too expensive for the generality, as well as inconvenient to them; that the aforesaid Officers could not, with propriety, take upon them to adopt of themselves an uniform for the whole city, without the approbation of the people, who are entitled to an equal consultation.

That by adopting the cheapest uniform, such as that of a **HUNTING SHIRT,** as it will level all distinctions, answers the end of coat and jacket, and is within the compass of almost *every* person's ability, not costing at the utmost above ten shillings. The officers say that they did not mean to impose any particular uniform upon the people, but then they should have given the privates an opportunity of making known *their* sentiments. An uniform is granted by *all* to be absolutely necessary, but let it be something cheap, which the generality can afford.

A very material advantage which the **HUNTING SHIRTS** have above [over] the present uniform recommended, is that they will answer all seasons of the year, as a person may wear neither coat nor jacket in warm weather, and in winter he may cloath under them as warm as he pleases.

Had the hunting shirts been recommended by the Officers, it would have met the approbation of ninety-nine out of an hundred. A meeting of the Associators ought to be called immediately, that each man may have a voice in what so nearly concerns himself. The author is informed that some of the Captains of the different companies have proposed, that any of the men, who think they are not able to buy uniforms, may be supplied by *them*; now there are *hundreds* who could not afford it, yet would never submit to *ask* any man for a coat, neither would they appear in the ranks to be pointed at by those who *had* uniforms.

The author [hopes] . . . those gentlemen, who have partly fixed upon an expensive uniform, to concur in sentiment with him.

———

Source: Pennsylvania History, 52 (October 1985): 255–256.

defensive force—the famous Minutemen—to "Stand at a minutes warning in Case of alarm," and neighboring towns likewise prepared their militia for rapid action.

This stalemate lasted for six months. Unwilling to undertake new raids that might precipitate an armed conflict, Gage waited for orders from Britain. In the meantime, the Massachusetts House met on its own authority. It issued regulations for the collection of taxes, strengthened the militia, and—in concert with Patriot-dominated town meetings—assumed the responsibilities of government. Governor Gage's

authority was limited to Boston, where it rested primarily on the bayonets of his 4,000 troops.

Even before the news of the House's extralegal seizure of power reached London, the colonial secretary, Lord Dartmouth, had proclaimed Massachusetts to be in a state of "open rebellion." Declaring that "force should be repelled by force," he ordered Gage to march quickly against the "rude rabble." On the night of April 18, 1775, Gage dispatched 700 soldiers to capture colonial leaders and supplies at Concord. But Paul Revere and two other Bostonians warned the Patriots, and at dawn on April 19 local militiamen met the British at Lexington.

LIEUTENANT COLONEL FRANKLIN SMITH

A British View of Lexington and Concord

---★---

The past is made up of concrete events, but it is the written or oral accounts of those events that provide historians with the materials to interpret them. On April 26, 1775, a week after British troops marched on Lexington and Concord, the Patriot-controlled Massachusetts assembly (now called the Provincial Congress) issued what it called a "true, and authentic account" of the resulting hostilities. The Congress alleged that at Lexington "the regulars rushed on with great violence and first began the hostilities" and that in the subsequent retreat of the British troops from Concord "houses on the road were plundered, . . . women in child-bed were driven by soldiery naked in the streets, old men peaceably in their houses were shot dead, and such scenes exhibited as would disgrace the annals of the most uncivilized nation." Four days earlier, in his official report to General Gage, British lieutenant colonel Franklin Smith offered a very different account of those events. Which version should the historian find more "true, and authentic"?

Sir,—In obedience to your Excellency's commands, I marched on the evening of the 18th inst. with the corps of grenadiers and light infantry for Concord, . . . to destroy all ammunition, artillery, tents &c. . . . Notwithstanding we marched with the utmost expedition and secrecy, we found the country had intelligence or strong suspicion of our coming, and fired many signal guns. . . .

At Lexington . . . [we] found on a green close to the road a body of the country people drawn up in military order, with arms and accoutrements, and, as appeared afterward, loaded. . . . Our troops advanced towards them, without any intention of injuring them . . . ; but they in confusion went off, principally to the left, only one of them fired before he went off, and three or four more jumped over a wall and fired from behind it among the soldiers; on which the troops returned it, and killed several of them. They likewise fired on the soldiers from the Meeting and dwelling-houses. . . .

While at Concord we saw vast numbers assembling in many parts; at one of the bridges they marched down, with a very considerable body, on the light infantry posted there. On their coming pretty near, one of our men fired on them, which they returned; on which an action ensued and some few were killed and wounded. In this affair, it appears that, after the bridge was quitted, they scalped and otherwise ill treated one or two of [our] men who were either killed or severely wounded. . . .

On our leaving Concord to return to Boston they began to fire on us from behind walls, ditches, trees, &c., which, as we marched, increased to a very great degree, and continued . . . for, I believe, upwards of eighteen miles; so that I can't think but it must have been a preconcerted scheme in them, to attack the King's troops the first favorable opportunity that offered; otherwise, I think they could not, in such a short a time from our marching out, have raised such a numerous body. . . .

Source: Massachusetts Historical Society, *Proceedings, 1876* (Boston: 1876), 350ff.

Shots rang out, and a British volley killed 8 Americans and wounded several others. Pressing on to Concord, the 700 British soldiers confronted 400 Patriots. At Concord the British took the heavier losses: 3 dead and 12 wounded. The worst was yet to come. As the British retreated along the narrow, winding roads to Boston, they were repeatedly ambushed by 1,000 militiamen from neighboring towns. By the end of the day, 73 British soldiers lay dead, 174 were wounded, and 26 were missing. British fire had killed 49 American militiamen and wounded 39 (see Voices from Abroad, "Lieutenant Colonel Franklin Smith: A British View of Lexington and Concord," above).

Too much blood had now been spilled to allow a peaceful compromise. Twelve years of economic conflict and constitutional debate had ended in civil war.

Summary

★

The Great War for Empire brought a decisive end to the era of salutary neglect and began an era of imperial reform. The war had exposed the weakness of Britain's control over its American colonies and had left that nation with a crushing load of debt. When George Grenville became prime minister in 1763, he embraced the cause of reform. To raise money—and reassert British authority—he enacted the Sugar Act, which extended the jurisdiction of vice-admiralty courts, and the Stamp Act, which for the first time imposed a direct tax on the colonists.

Because they had long taxed and governed themselves, the colonists resisted reform, protesting against the stamp duty through mob violence, a trade boycott, and an extralegal Stamp Act Congress. Well-read colonists based their arguments for American rights on English common law, Enlightenment thought, and the writings of Radical Whigs, while the thousands of less-educated people who served as Sons and Daughters of Liberty opposed the new British legislation out of economic self-interest or a commitment (because of evangelical Protestant beliefs or residence in Puritan New England) to a republican form of government. To assist British merchants and manufacturers, Parliament repealed the Stamp Act in 1766, but it explicitly reaffirmed its complete authority over the colonies.

In 1767 Charles Townshend undermined this first political compromise by imposing a new tax on trade goods. Americans responded with a second boycott and new constitutional arguments proclaiming the authority of their assemblies over provincial affairs. When the British ministry devised a plan to crush American resistance by force, domestic problems forced its abandonment; by 1770 Lord North had implemented a second compromise, repealing most of the Townshend Duties but retaining a tax on tea.

North personally disrupted this second informal agreement by passing the Tea Act in 1773. When Bostonians resisted the new law, the British imposed coercive measures on Massachusetts in order to destroy the Patriot movement there. But in 1774 American political leaders met in the First Continental Congress, which supported Massachusetts and mandated a new program of economic warfare. The Congress had the backing of a majority of American farmers and planters, who were now prepared to resist British rule. The failure to find a new compromise resulted in bloodshed at Lexington and Concord in April 1775 and then in war between Patriot forces and British troops attempting to put down the American rebellion.

TIMELINE

1754– 1763	British national debt doubles
1760	George III becomes king
1762	Revenue Act reforms customs service
	Royal Navy arrests smugglers
1763	Treaty of Paris ends Great War for Empire
	Proclamation Line restricts settlement west of Appalachians
	George Grenville becomes British prime minister
	John Wilkes demands reform in England
1764	Currency Act protects British merchants
	Sugar Act places duty on French molasses
	Colonists oppose vice-admiralty courts
1765	Stamp Act imposes direct tax on colonists
	Quartering Act provides for British troops
	Riots by Sons of Liberty
	Stamp Act Congress
	First nonimportation movement
1766	First compromise: Stamp Act repealed and Declaratory Act passed
1767	Townshend Duties on certain colonial imports
	Restraining Act in New York temporarily suspends colonial assembly there
	Daughters of Liberty make "homespun" cloth
1768	Second nonimportation movement
	British army occupies Boston
1770	Second compromise: Townshend Duties repealed
	Boston Massacre
1772	Committees of Correspondence formed
1773	Tea Act assists British East India Company
	Boston Tea Party
1774	Coercive Acts punish Massachusetts
	Quebec Act offends Patriots
	First Continental Congress
	Third nonimportation movement
	Loyalists organize
1775	General Thomas Gage marches to Lexington and Concord

Suggested Readings

★

Jack P. Greene and J. R. Pole, eds., *The Blackwell Encyclopedia of the American Revolution* (1991), illuminates both obscure and well-known aspects of the Revolutionary era. A good interpretive synthesis is Edward Countryman, *The American Revolution* (1985); for a more recent overview, see Theodore Draper, *A Struggle for Power: The American Revolution* (1996).

The Reform Movement, 1763–1765

For the state of the empire in 1763, see Alison Gilbert Olson, *Making the Empire Work: London and the American Interest Groups, 1690–1790* (1992); and Jack P. Greene, *Peripheries and Center: Constitutional Development in the Extended Polities of the British Empire and the United States, 1607–1788* (1986). The impact of the Seven Years' War is traced in the classic study by Lawrence H. Gipson, *The Coming of the Revolution, 1763–1775* (1954), and in the following works: Richard Middleton, *The Bells of Victory: The Pitt-Newcastle Ministry and the Conduct of the Seven Years' War, 1757–1762* (1985); Howard H. Peckham, *Pontiac and the Indian Uprising* (1947); and Joseph A. Ernst, *Money and Politics in America, 1755–1775* (1973). Marc Egnal, *A Mighty Empire: The Origins of the Revolution* (1988), provides synthesis.

British politics and imperial reform can be traced in John Brewer, *Party Ideology and Popular Politics at the Accession of George III* (1976); P. D. G. Thomas, *British Politics and the Stamp Act Crisis: The First Phase of the American Revolution, 1763–1767* (1975); Thomas C. Barrow, *Trade and Empire: The British Customs Service in Colonial America, 1660–1775* (1967); John L. Bullion, *A Great and Necessary Measure: George Grenville and the Genesis of the Stamp Act, 1763–1765* (1982); Carl Ubbelohde, The *Vice-Admiralty Courts and the American Revolution* (1960); and Philip Lawson, *George Grenville* (1984).

The Dynamics of Rebellion, 1765–1766

For the American response to the British reform laws, see Edmund S. Morgan and Helen M. Morgan, *The Stamp Act Crisis* (1963); Pauline Maier, *From Resistance to Revolution: Colonial Radicals and the Development of Colonial Opposition to Britain, 1765–1776* (1972); and Gary B. Nash, *The Urban Crucible: Social Change, Political Consciousness, and the Origins of the American Revolution* (1979). Merrill Jensen, *The Founding of a Nation: A History of the American Revolution, 1763–1776* (1968), and Robert Middlekauff, *The Glorious Cause: The American Revolution, 1763–1789* (1982), provide detailed narratives of the Revolutionary era.

Studies of individual colonies capture the spirit of the resistance movement. See Paul A. Gilje, *The Road to Mobocracy: Popular Disorder in New York City, 1763–1834* (1986), and Ronald Hoffman, *A Spirit of Dissension: Economics, Politics, and the Revolution in Maryland* (1973). The motives of Patriots are best addressed through biographies. See Francis Jennings, *Benjamin Franklin, Politician* (1996); Pauline Maier, *The Old Revolutionaries: Political Lives in the Age of Samuel Adams* (1980); Milton E. Flower, *John Dickinson, Conservative Revolutionary* (1983); Richard R. Beeman, *Patrick Henry: A Biography* (1974); John R. Alden, *George Washington: A Biography* (1984); Helen Hill Miller, *George Mason: Gentleman Revolutionary* (1975); and Page Smith, *John Adams* (1962).

The most important single study of Patriot ideology is Bernard Bailyn, *The Ideological Origins of the American Revolution* (1967), but see also Robert M. Calhoon, *Dominion and Liberty: Ideology in Anglo-American Political Thought, 1660–1801* (1994). Other works include Caroline Robbins, *The Eighteenth-Century Commonwealthman* (1959); Morton White, *The Philosophy of the American Revolution* (1978); Garry Wills, *Inventing America: Jefferson's Declaration of Independence* (1978); and H. T. Dickinson, *Liberty and Property: Political Ideology in Eighteenth-Century Britain* (1978). For a discussion of the legal tradition, see Charles H. McIlwain, *The American Revolution: A Constitutional Interpretation* (1923), and John Phillip Reid's *Constitutional History of the American Revolution* (1986–1996).

The Growing Confrontation, 1767–1770

Peter D. G. Thomas, *The Townshend Duties Crisis: The Second Phase of the American Revolution, 1767–1773* (1987), is the most comprehensive treatment, but see also Colin Bonwick, *English Radicals and the American Revolution* (1977). On American resistance, consult Richard Alan Ryerson, *The Revolution Is Now Begun: The Radical Committees of Philadelphia, 1765–1776* (1978); Peter Shaw, *American Patriots and the Rituals of Revolution* (1981); and Stanley Godbold Jr. and Robert W. Woody, *Christopher Gadsden* (1982). The military confrontation is covered in John Shy, *Toward Lexington: The Role of the British Army in the Coming of the American Revolution* (1965), and Hiller B. Zobel, *The Boston Massacre* (1970).

The Road to Rebellion, 1771–1775

Benjamin Labaree, *The Boston Tea Party* (1964), is a stimulating account. See also Peter D. G. Thomas, *Tea Party to Independence* (1991); Bernard Donoughue, *British Politics and the American Revolution: The Path to War, 1773–75* (1972); and David Ammerman, *In the Common Cause: American Response to the Coercive Acts of 1774* (1968). A fine study of the resistance movement is Edward F. Countryman, *A People in Revolution: The American Revolution and Political Society in New York* (1983). On prewar Loyalism, see Bernard Bailyn, *The Ordeal of Thomas Hutchinson* (1974); and Janice Potter, *The Liberty We Seek: Loyalist Ideology in Colonial New York and Massachusetts* (1983). For the rising of the countryside, see David Hackett Fischer, *Paul Revere's Ride* (1994); Gregory H. Nobles, *Divisions throughout the Whole: Politics and Society in Hampshire County, Massachusetts, 1740–1775* (1983); and Richard Bushman, *King and People in Provincial Massachusetts* (1985). The transfer of authority is described in Jerrilyn Greene Marston, *King and Congress: The Transfer of Political Legitimacy, 1774–1776* (1987).

Part Two

★

The New Republic, 1775–1820

THEMATIC TIMELINE

	Government	Diplomacy	Economy	Society	Culture
	Creating Republican Institutions	**European Entanglements**	**Expansion of Commerce and Manufacturing**	**Defining Liberty and Equality**	**Pluralism and National Identity**
1775	State constitutions written	Independence declared (1776) French alliance (1778)	Wartime expansion of manufacturing	Emancipation of slaves in the North Judith Sargent Murray, "On the Equality of the Sexes" (1779)	Paine's *Common Sense* calls for a republic
1780	Articles of Confederation ratified (1781) Legislative supremacy in states Philadelphia convention drafts U.S. Constitution (1787)	Treaty of Paris (1783) British trade restrictions in West Indies	Bank of North America (1781) Commercial recession (1783–1789) Western land speculation	Virginia Statute of Religious Freedom (1786) Idea of republican motherhood	Land ordinances create a national domain in the West German settlers preserve own language Noah Webster defines American English
1790	Bill of Rights (1791) First national parties: Federalists and Republicans	Wars of the French Revolution Jay's and Pinckney's treaties (1795) Undeclared war with France (1798)	First Bank of the United States (1792–1812) States charter business corporations Outwork system expands	Sedition Act limits freedom of the press (1798)	Indians form Western Confederacy Sectional divisions emerge between South and North
1800	Revolution of 1800 Activist state legislatures Chief Justice Marshall asserts judicial power	Napoleonic wars (1802–1815) Louisiana Purchase (1803) Embargo of 1807	Cotton expands into Old Southwest Farm productivity improves Embargo encourages domestic manufacturing	Youth-run marriage system New Jersey ends woman suffrage (1807) Atlantic slave trade legally ended (1808)	African Americans absorb Protestant Christianity Tenskwatawa develops Indian identity
1810	Triumph of Republican Party State constitutions democratized	War of 1812 Treaty of Ghent (1816) Monroe Doctrine (1823)	Second Bank of the United States (1816–1836) Supreme Court protects contracts and corporations Emergence of a national economy	Expansion of suffrage for white men New England abolishes established church (1820s)	War of 1812 tests national unity Second Great Awakening shapes American identity

THE AMERICAN WAR is over, the Philadelphia Patriot Benjamin Rush declared in 1787, "but this is far from being the case with the *American revolution*. On the contrary, nothing but the first act of the great drama is closed. It remains yet to establish and perfect our new forms of government." The job was even greater than Rush imagined, for the republican revolution of 1776 challenged nearly all the values and institutions of the colonial social order, forcing changes not only in politics but also in economic, religious, and cultural life.

Government. The first and most fundamental task was to devise a republican system of government. In 1775 no one in America knew how the new state governments should be organized and if there should be a permanent central authority along the lines of the Continental Congress. It would take time and experience to find out. It would take even longer to assimilate a new institution—the political party—into the workings of government. Yet by 1820 these years of constitutional experiment and party strife had produced a successful republican system on both the state and national levels. This system of political authority had three striking characteristics: popular sovereignty—government of the people; activist legislatures that pursued the public good—government for the people; and democratic decision making by most white adult men—government by the people.

Diplomacy. Second, to create and preserve their new republic, Americans of European descent had to fight two wars against Great Britain, an undeclared war against France, and many battles with Indian peoples and confederations. The wars against Britain divided the country into bitter factions—Patriots against Loyalists in 1776, and prowar Republicans against antiwar Federalists in 1812—and expended much blood and treasure. Tragically, the extension of American sovereignty over the trans-Appalachian West brought cultural disaster to many Indian peoples, as their lives were destroyed by European diseases and alcohol and their lands were seized by gun-toting white settlers. Despite the costs, by 1820 the United States had emerged as a strong independent state, free from a half-century of entanglement in the wars and diplomacy of Europe and prepared to exploit the riches of the continent.

Economy. Third, by this time the expansion of commerce and the market system had established the foundations for a strong national economy. Beginning in the 1780s merchants financed a banking system and organized a rural-based system of manufacturing, while state governments used charters and legal incentives to assist their efforts and provide improved transportation. During these years southern planters carried slavery westward to Alabama and Mississippi and grew rich by exporting a new crop—cotton—to markets in Europe and the North. Simultaneously northern farm families settled lands in the West, produced raw materials such as leather and wool for the burgeoning manufacturing enterprises, and undertook additional labor as handicraft workers. As a result of these efforts, by 1820 the young American republic had begun to achieve economic as well as political independence.

Society. Fourth, as Americans defined the character of their new republican society, they divided along lines of gender, race, religion, and class, disagreeing on fundamental issues—legal equality for women, the status of slavery, the meaning of free speech and religious liberty, and the extent of public responsibility for social inequality. They resolved some of these disputes, extinguishing slavery in the North and broadening religious liberty by allowing freedom of conscience and (except in New England) ending the system of established churches. However, they continued to argue over social equality, in part because their republican creed placed authority in the family and society in the hands of men of property and thus denied equality not only to slaves but also to free blacks, women, and poor white men.

Culture. The fifth and final task Americans set themselves—creating a distinct culture and identity—was complicated by the diversity of peoples and regions. Native Americans still lived in their own clans and nations, while black Americans, one-fifth of the enumerated population, were developing a new, African American culture. The white inhabitants created vigorous regional cultures and preserved parts of their ancestral heritage—English, Scottish, Scots-Irish, German, and Dutch. Nevertheless, political institutions began to unite Americans, as did their increasing participation in the market economy and in evangelical Protestant churches. By 1820 to be an American meant, for the dominant white population, being a republican, a Protestant, and an enterprising individual in a capitalist-run market system.

War and Revolution,
1775–1783

THE BATTLES AT Lexington and Concord transformed the decade-long debate over the character of the empire into an armed rebellion. American Patriots had become rebels resisting British authority with military force. Although only a minority of Patriots demanded independence at this point in time, the outbreak of fighting gave them the advantage. By the end of 1775 radical-minded rebels dominated local meetings and most provincial assemblies, and their followers demanded a complete break from Britain. "To know whether it be the interest of the continent to be independent," declared Thomas Paine, an English republican who had migrated to the colonies in 1774 and become a Patriot, "we need only ask this easy, simple question: Is it the interest of a man to be a boy all his life?"

On July 4, 1776, the Patriots in the Continental Congress answered Paine's question by agreeing to a Declaration of Independence that severed their ties to Great Britain. More momentous, the rebels became revolutionaries by rejecting the authority of kings and princes and creating republican state governments. "From subjects to citizens the difference is immense," remarked the South Carolina physician and Patriot David Ramsay. "Each citizen of a free state contains, within himself, by nature and the constitution, as much of the common sovereignty as another." Rejecting aristocratic and monarchical rule, the Patriots had placed sovereignty in the people, thereby launching the age of democratic revolutions.

Washington at Verplanck's Point
Arrayed in the ceremonial uniform of the Continental army (in the traditional Whig colors of buff and blue), General Washington watches the reunion of the American and French armies in New York in 1782, following their victory the previous September over Cornwallis at Yorktown, Virginia. The artist, John Trumbull (1756–1843), served as an aide-de-camp to Washington during the war. After the war, Trumbull studied painting in London with the American-born artist Benjamin West. He completed this picture in 1790.
Courtesy, Winterthur Museum.

To preserve their independence, Patriot men and women fought a long and costly war against an invading British army. As the battles of the War of Independence ground on, Patriots began to define the meaning of their new republican ideology and to extend its bounds. By the time the war formally ended in 1783, some Americans had repudiated the legitimacy of slavery and of an established church, expanding the principle of political liberty to challenge long-existing social institutions.

Toward Independence, 1775–1776

★

The ties that bound American colonists to the British Empire were strong. The Battle of Concord was fought on April 19, 1775, but fourteen months would elapse before the rebel leaders could muster sufficient support among themselves—and the populace—to issue a formal declaration of independence. During these months Patriot legislators seized political power from the royal governors and resisted armed Loyalists who tried to restore imperial rule. These violent conflicts forced ordinary Americans to choose sides and pushed Patriots toward a complete break with Britain.

From Confrontation to Civil War

Armed struggle in Lexington and Concord in Massachusetts lent urgency to the Second Continental Congress, which met in Philadelphia in May 1775. Soon after the Congress opened, more than 3,000 British troops attacked new American fortifications on Breed's Hill and Bunker Hill, overlooking Boston. It took three British assaults, at the cost of 1,000 casualties, to dislodge the Patriot militia, which also suffered heavy losses.

Congress versus the King.   Inspired by the Patriots' valor at the Battle of Bunker Hill, John Adams exhorted the Congress to rise to the "defense of American liberty." Along with other radical members of Congress, Adams pressed for the creation of a Continental army, headed by George Washington of Virginia, and a call for military volunteers. More cautious delegates and those with Loyalist sympathies opposed these measures, warning that they would surely lead to more violence and commit the colonists irretrievably to rebellion. After bitter debate, Congress approved the proposals—but as Adams lamented, only "by bare majorities."

Despite the blood that had been shed, a majority of the members of the provincial assemblies and the Congress still hoped for reconciliation with Britain. The Pennsylvania assembly "strictly" enjoined its delegation to Congress to "dissent from and utterly reject" any propositions that might lead to independence. Led by Pennsylvanian John Dickinson, moderates in Congress passed the "Olive Branch" petition, expressing loyalty to George III and asking the king to seek the repeal of oppressive Parliamentary legislation, which they blamed on the influence of hard-line ministers such as Chief Justice Sir James Mansfield. But zealous Patriots such as Samuel Adams of Massachusetts and Richard Henry Lee of Virginia countered this initiative by convincing Congress to approve a Declaration of the Causes and Necessities of Taking Up Arms. Americans dreaded the "calamities of civil war," the Declaration asserted, but were "resolved to die Freemen rather than to live [as] slaves."

King George chose not to exploit these divisions among the Patriots, refusing even to receive the Olive Branch petition. Instead, in August 1775 the king issued a Proclamation for Suppressing Rebellion and Sedition. Now personally committed to a repressive policy, George III condemned the Americans as "traitors" and vowed to crush the revolt. The king's hard-line stance may have been justified. Following the battle at Bunker Hill in June, radicals in the Continental Congress won support for an invasion of Canada, hoping to unleash a popular uprising in the former French colony and thereby deny the British a strategically located military base. In November a small Patriot expeditionary army easily captured Montreal, but another American force suffered heavy losses in an unsuccessful attack on Quebec City. When the French inhabitants expressed little interest in joining the rebellion, the Americans were forced to withdraw.

Meanwhile Patriot merchants waged financial warfare, implementing the Congress's resolution to cut off all exports to Britain and its West Indian possessions. By squelching the trade in tobacco and disrupting the production of sugar, they hoped to undermine the British economy. Parliament retaliated at the end of 1775 with a Prohibitory Act that outlawed all trade with the rebellious colonies.

Rebellion in the South.   By this time armed rebellion had spread from Massachusetts to the southern colonies, where Patriots and Loyalists vied for power. In June 1775 the Patriot-dominated House of Burgesses forced Lord Dunmore, the royal governor of Virginia, to take refuge on a British warship in Chesapeake Bay. Citing the king's proclamation, Dunmore branded the Patriots as "traitors" and organized two military forces—one white, the Queen's Own Loyal Virginians, and one black, the Ethiopian Regiment—to uphold

George III, 1771
This portrait of George III was painted by Johann Zoffany in 1771, four years before the American rebellion broke out in 1775. Like George Washington (b. 1732), King George III (b. 1738) was a young man when the War of Independence began. A headstrong monarch, he tried to impose his will on Parliament, sparking a constitutional crisis in Britain. But George III strongly supported Parliament's attempts to tax the colonies and continued the war long after most of his ministers agreed that it had been lost.
The Royal Collection. © Her Majesty Queen Elizabeth II.

royal authority. Then, in November, Dunmore issued a controversial proclamation of his own, offering freedom to any slaves and indentured servants who would join the Loyalist cause. Faced with the possibility of black uprisings as well as military attack, Patriot planters threatened runaway slaves with death and called for a final break with Britain.

In the Carolinas, demands for independence also grew more insistent in response to British military threats. Early in 1776 North Carolina's royal governor, Josiah Martin, tried to reestablish imperial authority with a force of 1,500 Scottish Highlanders from the Carolina backcountry. But the Patriot militia in the lowcountry quickly mobilized and in February defeated Martin's army at the Battle of Moore's Creek Bridge, capturing more than 800 troops. As the violence escalated, radical Patriots transformed the North Carolina assembly into an independent Provincial Congress. In April 1776 that body instructed its representatives in

Philadelphia "to concur with the Delegates of other Colonies in declaring Independency, and forming foreign alliances."

"'Tis Time to Part"

The fact that the colonies moved very slowly toward independence was not surprising, for many ordinary Americans retained a deep loyalty to the Crown. Colonists celebrated the marriage of George III in 1762 and toasted the health of the king after the repeal of the Stamp Act in 1766. Even as the imperial crisis worsened and Patriots repudiated the legitimacy of Parliament's power over the colonies, Benjamin Franklin proposed that George III remain as their head or "Sovereign." Americans had condemned the tax legislation enacted by Parliament, not the king or the institution of monarchy.

The roots of this loyalty ran deep in the structure of American society. Like most men and women in early modern Europe, Americans used metaphors of age and family to describe both social authority and imperial rule. Colonists often pictured their settlements as the dependent offspring—the children—of Britain, the "mother country." Similarly, they accorded great respect to male "elders" in town meetings, churches, and families, and they honored the king as the "father" of the British people. Denial of George III's legitimacy might threaten all paternal authority and weaken the hierarchical social order.

Yet events had prepared many Americans to reject their traditional political father. In many communities the shortage of land and conflict among religious congregations had caused the power and authority of biological fathers and customary leaders to diminish. And by 1775 zealous Patriots were accusing George III of supporting ministers who passed oppressive legislation and—most serious of all—of ordering the use of military force against his "children."

Surprisingly, agitation against the king became especially intense in Philadelphia, the largest but hardly the most tumultuous seaport city. Because of their pacifist beliefs, the Quaker inhabitants of Philadelphia had refused to support violent opposition to British measures. Moreover, the city had been slow to join the boycott against the Townshend Duties because many of its merchants were members of the Church of England and harbored Loyalist sympathies. However, Philadelphia's artisans, who accounted for about half the city's population, had gradually become a powerful force in the Patriot movement. Worried that British imports threatened their small-scale manufacturing enterprises and that Parliament was attempting to abolish their "just Rights and Privileges," they organized a Mechanics Association and demanded resistance. By February 1776 forty resistance-minded artisans sat with forty-seven merchants on the Philadelphia Committee of Resistance, the extralegal body that enforced the trade boycott ordered by the Second Continental Congress.

The artisans' opposition to British measures stemmed from both economic self-interest and religious ideology. Some artisans, and even more of the city's laborers, were Scots-Irish Presbyterians who had left northern Ireland to escape the hard times brought on by British mercantilist policies. Many of these migrants had joined congregations led by Gilbert Tennent and other New Light ministers. As pastor of Philadelphia's Second Presbyterian Church, Tennent had told his congregation that all men and women were equal before God. Translating that assertion into political terms, New Light Presbyterians shouted in street demonstrations during the 1760s that they had "no king but King Jesus." In addition, republican ideas derived from the European Enlightenment circulated freely among all ranks of society in Philadelphia. Scientists and statesmen such as Benjamin Franklin, David Rittenhouse, and Benjamin Rush questioned not only the wisdom of George III but the idea of monarchy itself. And many artisans in the highly skilled trades shared their republican outlook.

At this pivotal moment, with artisans mostly supporting independence and merchants generally opposing it, a single pamphlet tipped the balance. In January 1776 an anonymous author—who turned out to be Thomas Paine—published *Common Sense*, a strident call for independence and republicanism. Paine, formerly a corset maker and minor bureaucrat in England, had been fired from the Customs Service there for protesting the low wage schedule. In 1774, armed with a letter of introduction from Benjamin Franklin, whom he had met in London, Paine migrated to Philadelphia, where he mingled with Benjamin Rush and others who shared his republican sentiments. In *Common Sense* Paine launched a direct assault on the traditional political order in language that the general public could understand. "Monarchy and hereditary succession have laid the world in blood and ashes," Paine proclaimed, leveling a personal attack against George III, "the hard hearted sullen Pharaoh of England." Mixing insults with biblical quotations, Paine blasted the British system of "mixed government" among the three estates of king, lords, and commoners. "That it was noble for the dark and slavish times in which it was created," Paine granted, but now this system of governance yielded only "monarchical tyranny in the person of the King and aristocratical tyranny in the persons of the peers" (see American Voices, "Thomas Paine: *Common Sense*," p. 184).

Paine also made a compelling case for independence by suggesting the absurdity of an island ruling or conquering a continent. Within six months *Common Sense* went through twenty-five editions and reached hundreds of thousands of people throughout the colonies. "There is great talk of independence," a worried New York Loyalist wrote in March 1776, "and the unthinking multitude are mad for it. . . . A pamphlet called Common Sense has carried off . . . thousands." Paine's message was not only popular but clear: reject the arbitrary powers of king and Parliament and create independent republican states. "A government of our own is our natural right, TIS TIME TO PART."

Independence Declared

Throughout the colonies Patriot conventions, inspired by Paine's arguments and escalating military conflict with Loyalists, called urgently for a break from Britain. In March 1776, the Congress dispatched a mission to France to seek military aid. Two months later Virginia Patriots—led by George Mason, James Madison, and Patrick Henry—called a special convention in Virginia at which they resolved unanimously to support independence. In June, Richard Henry Lee presented the Virginia convention's resolution to the Continental Congress: "That these United Colonies are, and of right ought to be, free and independent states . . . absolved from all allegiance to the British Crown." Faced with certain defeat when this measure came to a vote, staunch Loyalists and anti-independence moderates withdrew from the Congress, leaving committed Patriots to take the fateful step. On July 4, 1776, the Congress formally approved a Declaration of Independence.

The Declaration was the work of a committee led by Thomas Jefferson, a young Virginia planter and legislative leader who in 1775 had mobilized resistance to the Coercive Acts with the pamphlet *A Summary View of the Rights of British America*. Now Jefferson attempted to legitimize the colonies' demand for independence, using two sets of arguments. First, Jefferson appealed to the rights of man as defined by the laws of nature. Drawing upon the ideas and rhetoric of the European Enlightenment, he proclaimed a set of "self-evident" truths: "that all men are created equal" and possess the "unalienable rights" of "Life, Liberty, and the pursuit of Happiness." When a government "becomes destructive of these ends," Jefferson argued, it can rightly be overthrown and replaced by a new political system that derives its "just powers from the consent of the governed."

Second, to persuade domestic critics and foreign observers that British rule had been destructive of American rights, Jefferson listed a long series of the imperial laws and actions that had oppressed the colonists. Unlike previous Patriots, he heaped most of the blame not on Parliament but on George III himself: "He has plundered our seas, ravaged our coasts, burned our towns, and destroyed the lives of our people. . . . A prince, whose character is thus marked by every act which may define a tyrant, is unfit to be the ruler of a free people." Jefferson's indictment of the king, together with his celebration of individual liberty and popular

Independence Declared
In this painting by John Trumbull, Thomas Jefferson and the other drafters (John
Adams of Massachusetts, Roger Sherman of Connecticut, Robert Livingston of New
York, and Benjamin Franklin of Pennsylvania) present the Declaration of Indepen-
dence to John Hancock, the president of the Continental Congress. When the Declara-
tion was read at a public meeting in New York City on July 10, 1776, Patriot
Lieutenant Isaac Bangs reported that a massive statue of George III was "pulled down
by the Populace" and its four thousand pounds of lead melted down to make "Musquet
balls" for use against the British troops massed on Staten Island.
Yale University Art Gallery, Mabel Brady Garven Collection.

sovereignty, justified republicanism as well as independence. Indeed, the Declaration established revolutionary republicanism as a defining value of the new nation.

For Jefferson as for Paine, the pen proved mightier
than the sword. Almost overnight many once
monarchical-minded Americans became republican
revolutionaries. In rural hamlets and seaport cities,
crowds celebrated the Declaration by burning George III
in effigy; in New York City, they toppled a huge statue
of the king. With these acts of destruction the Patriots
broke their psychological ties to the mother country
and the father-monarch. Americans were ready to create *republics*, state governments that would derive their
authority from the people.

The Perils of War and Finance, 1776–1778

The Declaration of Independence prompted Britain to
launch a full-scale military assault against the Patriots.
For the next two years British forces outfought the Continental army commanded by George Washington, winning nearly every battle. A few inspiring American
victories kept the rebellion alive, but in late 1776 and
during the winter of 1777–1778 at Valley Forge, the
Patriot cause hung in the balance.

THOMAS PAINE

Common Sense

———★———

Thomas Paine was a sharp critic and an acute observer. Before arriving in Philadelphia from his native England in mid-1774, he had already rejected the validity of monarchical rule. And he quickly came to understand that the existing system of American politics was republican in spirit and localist in character. In the widely read political pamphlet Common Sense (1776), he showed the colonists that their customary practices of self-rule had intellectual legitimacy and could easily be adapted to create independent republican governments.

I draw my idea of the form of government from a principle in nature, which no art can overturn, viz. [that is] that the more simple any thing is, the less liable it is to be disordered, and the easier repaired when disordered; and with this maxim in view, I offer a few remarks on the much boasted constitution of England. . . .

If we will suffer ourselves to examine the component parts of the English constitution, we shall find them to be the base remains of two ancient tyrannies, compounded with some new republican materials.

First. The remains of monarchical tyranny in the person of the king.

Secondly. The remains of aristocratic tyranny in the person of the peers.

Thirdly. The new republican materials in the persons of the commons, on whose virtue depends the freedom of England. . . .

The plain truth is, that *it is wholly owing to the constitution of the people, and not to the constitution of the government,* that the crown is not as oppressive in England as in Turkey. . . . For it is the republican and not the monarchical part of the constitution of England which Englishmen glory in, viz. the liberty of choosing a house of commons from out of their own body—and it is easy to see that when republican virtue fails, slavery ensues. . . .

If there is any true cause of fear respecting independence, it is because no plan is yet laid down. Men do not see their way out—Wherefore, . . . I offer the following hints. . . .

Let the assemblies [in all of the former colonies] be annual, with a President only . . . their business wholly domestic, and subject to the authority of a Continental Congress.

Let each colony be divided into six, eight, or ten convenient districts, each district to send a proper number of delegates to Congress, so that each colony sent at least thirty. The whole number in Congress will be at least 390. . . .

But where, say some, is the King of America? I'll tell you. Friend, he reigns above, and doth not make havoc of mankind like the Royal Brute of Britain. Yet that we may not appear to be defective even in earthly honors, let a day be solemnly set apart for proclaiming the charter [of the new Continental republic]; let it be brought forth placed on the divine law, the word of God; let a crown be placed thereon, by which the world may know . . . that in America THE LAW IS KING. For as in absolute governments the King is law, so in free countries the law ought to be King; and there ought to be no other. . . . Let the crown at the conclusion of the ceremony, be demolished, and scattered among the people whose right it is.

———

Source: Thomas Paine, *Common Sense* (Philadelphia: 1776).

War in the North

When the British decided to use military force to crush the American revolt, few European observers gave the rebels a chance. Great Britain had 11 million people, compared with the mainland colonies' population of 2.5 million, nearly 20 percent of whom were slaves. The British also had a profound economic advantage because of the immense profits from the South Atlantic system and the emerging Industrial Revolution. These financial resources paid for the most powerful navy in the world, a standing army of 48,000 men, and thousands of German mercenaries—soldiers hired to fight for the British cause. Moreover, British military officers had been tested in combat, and their soldiers were well armed. The imperial government also had the potential support of tens of thousands of Loyalists in America and could count on the assistance of many Indian peoples (Map 6.1). The Cherokee in the Carolinas had long opposed the expansion of white settlement and were

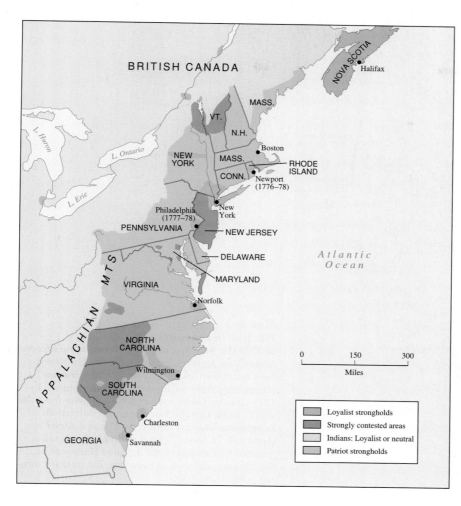

MAP 6.1
Loyalist Strength and Rebel Support
Patriot supporters formed the dominant faction in most areas of the thirteen colonies and used the local governments to back the rebel cause. Loyalists were powerful only in Nova Scotia, eastern New York and New Jersey, and in certain localities in the South. However, most native Americans favored the British cause and joined with Loyalist militia to fight Patriot forces in the backcountry of the Carolinas and in western New York.

firmly committed to the British side. So also were four of the six Iroquois Nations of New York—the Mohawk, Seneca, Cayuga, and Onondaga—who were led by the pro-British Mohawk chief Joseph Brand; only the Oneida and Tuscarora peoples supported the rebel side.

By contrast, the rebellious Americans looked militarily weak. They had no navy, and General Washington's newly formed and poorly trained army consisted of about 18,000 troops, mostly men who had hastily been recruited by state governments in Virginia and New England and who had agreed to serve for only three to six months. True, the Patriots could field thousands more militiamen, but only for short periods and only near their own farms and towns. Although some American officers were capable veterans of the French and Indian War, even the most experienced had never commanded a large force or faced a disciplined army capable of the intricate maneuvers of European warfare.

To exploit this military advantage, Britain's prime minister, Lord North, decided to act swiftly. Surprised by the American invasion of Canada in 1775, North ordered an ambitious military mobilization and replaced the ineffective General Thomas Gage with a new commander, General William Howe. Howe had

served in the colonies during the Great War for Empire and had distinguished himself in the siege of Quebec in 1759. North ordered him to capture New York City and seize control of the Hudson River, a strategic move that would isolate the radical Patriots of New England from the other colonies.

Howe proceeded with dispatch. In March 1776 he moved the besieged British forces in Boston to a new military headquarters in Halifax, Nova Scotia, where they were joined by dozens of new regiments from Europe. By the summer he was ready to attack. While the Continental Congress was declaring independence in Philadelphia, Howe was landing 10,000 troops—British regulars and German mercenaries—outside New York City. By August the British army had swollen to 32,000 soldiers, supported by a fleet of 30 warships and 10,000 sailors. This formidable force faced, on the American side, General Washington's new and untested Continental army.

British superiority was immediately apparent. On August 27, 1776, Howe attacked the Americans in the Battle of Long Island and forced their retreat to Manhattan Island. There Howe demonstrated the tactical superiority of his units and exposed the inexperience of

MAP 6.2
The War in the North, 1776–1777
In 1776 the British army drove Washington's forces across New Jersey into Pennsylvania. The Americans counterattacked at Trenton and Princeton, setting up winter headquarters at Morristown. In 1777 General Howe captured Philadelphia from the south, while General Burgoyne and Colonel St. Leger launched invasions from Canada. Aided by thousands of New England militia, troops commanded by General Gates defeated Burgoyne at Bennington and then at Saratoga, the military turning point of the war.

Washington and his subordinates. His troops continually outflanked the American forces, nearly trapping them on several occasions. Outgunned and outmaneuvered, the Continental army again retreated, first to Harlem Heights, then to White Plains, and finally across the Hudson River to New Jersey—an unbroken series of British victories. By December the invading army had pushed the rebels out of New Jersey and across the Delaware River into Pennsylvania, forcing Congress to flee from Philadelphia to Baltimore (Map 6.2).

From the Patriots' perspective, winter came just in time. Rather than pursue their advantage, the British chose to follow eighteenth-century custom and halt their military campaign during the cold and snowy months of winter. Moreover, the overconfident imperial forces let down their guard, allowing the Americans to score a triumph. On Christmas night in 1776, Washington crossed the Delaware River and staged a surprise attack on Trenton, New Jersey, forcing the surrender of a thousand German troops. Then, early in January 1777, the Continental army continued its winter offensive and won a small engagement at nearby Princeton. The two victories raised sagging Patriot

morale and allowed the Continental Congress to return to Philadelphia. Bright stars in a dark night, these momentary triumphs could not mask the British military superiority. These are the times, wrote Tom Paine, that "try men's souls."

Armies and Strategies

British superiority did not break the will of the Continental army, and partly because of Howe's tactical decisions and mistakes, the rebellion continued. While in Britain Howe had opposed the Coercive Acts of 1774, and as British military commander he still hoped for a political compromise—indeed, he had authority from Lord North to negotiate with the rebels and allow them to surrender on honorable terms. Consequently, instead of following up his early victories with a ruthless pursuit of the retreating American army, Howe was content to show his superior power and tactics, hoping to convince the Continental Congress that resistance was futile.

Howe's caution also reflected another convention of eighteenth-century warfare, which prescribed outmaneuvering the opposing forces and winning their

A British Camp, c. 1778
While American troops at Valley Forge huddled from the cold in thin tents, British troops stationed just outside New York City (on upper Manhattan Island) lived in simple but well-constructed and warm log cabins. Each hut housed either a few officers or as many as ten soldiers of the 17th Regiment of Foot. This painting, based on careful archaeological fieldwork, was executed in 1915 by John Ward Dunsmore.
New-York Historical Society.

surrender rather than destroying them. Moreover, the British general knew that his troops were 3,000 miles from supplies and reinforcements. In case of a major defeat, replenishing his force would take six months, especially since neither the British ministry nor the royal governors had encouraged Loyalists to join or supply the army. Although Howe's prudent tactics were understandable, they cost the British the opportunity to nip the rebellion in the bud.

Howe's failure to win a decisive victory was paralleled by Washington's success in avoiding a major defeat. Given the inexperience of his troops he too was cautious, challenging Howe on occasion but retreating in the face of superior strength. As Washington advised Congress, "On our Side the War should be defensive." His strategy was to draw the British away from the seacoast to extend their lines of supply, and to keep the Continental army intact as a symbol and instrument of American resistance.

To achieve this goal, Washington had to contend with Congress as well as with Howe. Patriot leaders had promised Washington a Continental army of 75,000 men, but the number of troops under Washington's command never reached even half that number. Most yeomen farmers preferred to serve in the local militia, in which they could defend their families and farms; few wanted to enlist for many months of service, subject themselves to strict military discipline, and fight in a far-off state. Consequently, the Continental army drew recruits from the lower ranks of society. For example, the soldiers in the Continental units commanded by General William Smallwood of Maryland were either poor American-born youths or older foreign-born men—British ex-convicts and former indentured ser-

vants. Some of these men enlisted for patriotic reasons, but most were motivated by economic factors; upon signing up, they received a cash bonus of $20 (equal to about $300 today) and the promise of 100 acres of land at the end of their three-year term of service.

Molding these men into a fighting force took time and skilled officers, both of which were in short supply. Thrown immediately into battle, many raw recruits panicked in the face of a British artillery bombardment or flank attack; hundreds of others deserted, unwilling to submit to the discipline and danger of military life. The soldiers who stayed resented the contemptuous way Washington and other American officers treated the women who came along with the recruits. Often referred to by the officers as "prostitutes," these women not only kept up the morale of the men but also contributed to the war effort by feeding the troops and repairing their clothes.

Such support from the friends and families of the soldiers was crucial because the Continental army received faint praise from Congress or the public. Radical Whig Patriots had long viewed a peacetime standing army as a threat to liberty; even in wartime they preferred the militia to a professional force. Consequently, the Continental army went begging, without ready volunteers from the populace and adequate supplies and pay from Congress. In 1776 General Philip Schuyler of New York complained that his troops were "weak in numbers, dispirited, naked, destitute of provisions, without camp equipage, with little ammunition, and not a single piece of cannon." Given these political and military handicaps, Washington was fortunate to escape overwhelming defeat in the first year of the war.

Wahrhafte Abbildung der Soldaten des Congreßes in Nordamericka, nach der Zeich=
nung eines Deutschen Officiers. Die Mütze ist von Leder, mit der Aufschrift Congreß. Die
gantze Kleidung von Zwillich überall mit weißen Franzen besetzt, die Beinkleider gehen bis
auf die Knochel herunter. Die Meisten laufen barfuß. Ihre Feuer-gewehre sind mit sehr langen
Bayonets versehen, welche Sie auch Statt eines Seiten gewehrs gebrauchen.

American Militiamen
Because of the shortage of cloth, the Patriot army dressed in a
variety of fashions that used many different kinds of fabrics.
This German engraving, based on a drawing by a German
officer, shows two barefoot American militiamen arrayed in
hunting shirts and trousers made of ticking, a strong woven
linen fabric that was often used as coverings for mattresses
and pillows.
Anne S. K. Brown Military Collection, Brown University.

Victory at Saratoga

Howe's failure to achieve a decisive victory surprised
and dismayed Lord North and his colonial secretary,
Lord George Germain, who now realized that restoration of the empire would require a long-term military
commitment similar to that of the Great War for
Empire. Accepting the challenge, the government
increased the British land tax to finance war and prepared to mount a major campaign in 1777.

The isolation of New England remained the primary British goal. To accomplish this, Lord George
Germain devised a three-pronged attack converging on
Albany, New York. General John Burgoyne was to lead
the main force, a large contingent of British regulars;
from Montreal it would advance up the Richelieu River,
across Lake Champlain, and then down the upper Hudson River to Albany. A second, smaller force under
Lieutenant Colonel Barry St. Leger would attack

Albany from the west, moving through the Mohawk
River Valley. Most of Leger's troops were Iroquois warriors from central New York; Germain expected them to
cut down rebel supporters all along the New York frontier. Finally, to link up with Burgoyne from the south,
Germain ordered Howe to dispatch a contingent from
his army northward from New York City.

Howe had a plan of his own. He proposed to attack
Philadelphia, the home of the Continental Congress,
hoping to force Washington into a fixed battle and end
the rebellion with a single stinging victory. With Germain's apparent approval, Howe set his forces in
motion—but very slowly. Rather than march overland
through New Jersey, the troops sailed south from New
York and then up Chesapeake Bay to approach
Philadelphia from the southwest. Once on the ground,
the British army showed its tactical skill. Howe's troops
easily outflanked the American positions along Brandy-
wine Creek, forcing Washington's troops to withdraw.
The British marched triumphantly into Philadelphia on
September 26, half assuming that the capture of the
rebels' capital would end the uprising. However, the
Continental Congress fled into the interior, first to Lancaster and then to York, and would hear no words of
surrender.

The British paid a high price for Howe's decision to
attack Philadelphia, for it contributed directly to
Burgoyne's defeat. Initially Burgoyne's troops had sped
across Lake Champlain, overwhelming the American
defenses at Fort Ticonderoga and driving toward the
upper reaches of the Hudson River. Then they stalled,
for Burgoyne—"Gentleman Johnny," as he was called—
fought with style, not speed. His heavy baggage train
moved slowly, weighed down by large tents and ample
stocks of food and wine. Burgoyne's progress was further impeded by General Horatio Gates, whose troops
felled trees across the crude wagon trail Burgoyne was
following and raided his long supply lines to Canada.
By the end of the summer Burgoyne's army—6,000 regulars (half of them German mercenaries) and 600 Loyalists and Indians—was in trouble, bogged down in the
wilderness near Saratoga, New York (see Map 6.2).

The Patriot militia delivered the final blows. On
August 15, fully 2,000 militiamen left their farms to
defend a military depot at Bennington, Vermont, winning a bitter pitched battle and depriving British
raiders of much-needed supplies of food, horses, and
oxen. Burgoyne then received more bad news: Patriot
militiamen in the Mohawk Valley had forced St. Leger
and his Iroquois allies to retreat. Moreover, to meet
Howe's request for additional troops to occupy
Philadelphia, the British commander in New York City
had recalled the relief force he had sent toward Albany.
While Burgoyne waited in vain for help, thousands of
Patriot militiamen from Massachusetts, New Hampshire, and New York joined Gates's forces. They

Joseph Brant

The Mohawk chief Thayendanegea, known to the whites as Joseph Brant, was a devout member of the Church of England who helped translate the Bible into the Iroquois language. An influential leader, Brant secured the support of four of the Six Iroquois Nations for the British. In 1778 and 1779, he led Iroquois warriors and Tory rangers in devastating attacks on American settlements in the Wyoming Valley of Pennsylvania and Cherry Valley of New York. This portrait by Charles Willson Peale was painted in 1797.

Independence National Historic Park.

"swarmed around the army like birds of prey," an English sergeant wrote in his journal, and on October 17, 1777, they forced Burgoyne to surrender (see Voices from Abroad, "Baroness Von Riedesel: The Surrender of Burgoyne, 1777," p. 190).

The battle at Saratoga proved to be the turning point of the war. The Americans captured five thousand British troops and their equipment—a reward in men, materiel, and morale that far outweighed Howe's capture of Philadelphia. More important, their victory virtually ensured the success of American diplomats in Paris, who were seeking a military alliance with France. Patriots on the home front were delighted, despite the wartime difficulties they faced.

Wartime Trials

In the twentieth century two world wars and many lesser conflicts have disrupted the lives of millions of ordinary women and men, conscripting them into war industries, destroying their property, turning them into refugees, taking their lives. On a much smaller scale, the War of Independence exposed tens of thousands of

American civilians to deprivation, displacement, and death. "An army, even a friendly one, are a dreadful scourge to any people," a Connecticut soldier wrote home from Pennsylvania. "You cannot imagine what devastation and distress mark their steps." New Jersey was particularly hard hit by the fighting as British and American armies marched back and forth across the state. Those with reputations as Patriots or Loyalists fled from their homes to escape arrest—or worse. Soldiers and partisans looted farms, seeking food or political revenge. Drunk and disorderly troops harassed or raped women and girls. Wherever the armies went, families lived in fear.

People learned to fear their neighbors as well, for the War of Independence was in many respects a civil war. Mobs of Patriot farmers in New England beat suspected Loyalists or destroyed their property. "Every Body submitted to our Sovereign Lord the Mob," a Loyalist preacher lamented. "Now we are reduced to a State of Anarchy." To restore order, Patriot leaders in many communities quickly organized a new institution of local government called a Committee of Safety. Those committees collected taxes, sent food and clothing to the Continental army, and imposed fines or jail sentences on those who failed to support the Patriot cause. "There is no such thing as remaining neutral," declared the Committee of Safety of Farmington, Connecticut.

Financial Crisis. Wars are not won by guns alone. Armies have to be fed, clothed, and paid, and victory often goes to the side that has the most money or is prepared to make the greatest financial sacrifices. When the War of Independence began, the new American governments were neither wealthy nor politically secure. Opposition to taxes had fueled the independence movement, so the Patriot-dominated assemblies hesitated to raise taxes for fear of undermining their fragile authority.

To finance the war, the state governments adopted a variety of strategies. First, they borrowed money—gold, silver, and British currency—from wealthy individuals, but those funds soon ran out. So, second, the states adopted a new monetary system based on the dollar (rather than the English pound) and issued $260 million in paper money and transferable bonds, using the paper currency to pay soldiers and purchase supplies. Theoretically the new notes could be redeemed at a stated time in gold or silver, but because they were printed in huge quantities and were not backed by tax revenues or mortgages on land, many Americans refused to accept them at their face value. Indeed, North Carolina's paper money came to be worth so little that even the state government refused to accept it. Many state governments teetered on the brink of bankruptcy.

The Continental Congress was equally hard-pressed for financial resources. Until 1781, when all the states finally ratified the Articles of Confederation, the

BARONESS VON RIEDESEL

The Surrender of Burgoyne, 1777

★

Friederike Charlotte Louise, Baroness Von Riedesel, was the wife of General Von Riedesel, commander of the Hessian soldiers in General John Burgoyne's army. An intrepid woman, the baroness was an eyewitness of the Saratoga campaign and a forthright critic of "Gentleman Johnny" Burgoyne. After Burgoyne's surrender, she and her children, as well as her husband, were held as prisoners of war in Massachusetts and Virginia.

We were halted at six o'clock in the morning [October 9, 1777], to our general amazement. General Burgoyne ordered the artillery to be drawn up in a line, and to have it counted. This gave much dissatisfaction, as a few marches more would have ensured our safety. . . . At length we recommenced our march; but scarcely an hour had elapsed, before the army was again halted, because the enemy was in sight. They were but two hundred in number, who came to reconnoitre, and who might easily have been taken, had not general Burgoyne lost all his presence of mind.

We reached Saratoga about dark, which was but half an hour's march from the place where we had spent the day. I was quite wet, and was obliged to remain in that condition, for want of a place to change my apparel. I seated myself near the fire, and undressed the children, and we then laid ourselves upon some straw.—I asked general Phillips, who came to see how I was, why we did not continue our retreat, my husband having pledged himself to cover the movement, and to bring off the army in safety. "My poor lady," said he, "you astonish me.

Though quite wet, you have so much courage as to wish to go farther in this weather. What a pity it is that you are not our commanding general! He complains of fatigue, and has determined upon spending the night here, and giving us a supper."

About 2 o'clock [the next afternoon] we heard again a report of muskets and cannon, and there was much alarm and bustle among our troops. My husband sent me word, that I should immediately retire into a house which was not far off. Soon after our arrival, a terrible cannonade began, and the fire was principally directed against the house, where we had hoped to find a refuge, probably because the enemy inferred, from the great number of people who went towards it, that this was the headquarters of the generals, while, in reality, none were there except women and crippled soldiers. We were at last obliged to descend into the cellar, where I laid myself in a corner near the door. My children put their heads upon my knees. An abominable smell, the cries of the children, and my own anguish of mind, did not permit me to close my eyes, during the whole night.

On the next morning, the cannonade begun anew, but in a different direction. . . . Eleven cannon-balls passed through the house, and made a tremendous noise. A poor soldier, who was about to have a leg amputated, lost the other by one of these balls. All his comrades ran away at that moment, and when they returned, they found him in one corner of the room, in the agonies of death. . . .

On the 17th of October, the capitulation was carried into effect. The generals waited upon the American general Gates, and the troops surrendered themselves prisoners of war and laid down their arms.

Source: Friederike Von Riedesel, *Letters and Memoirs Relating to the War of American Independence, and the Capture of the German Troops at Saratoga* (New York: G. & C. Carvill, 1827), 173–183.

Congress lacked legal authority over the states. After ratification, the Confederation government was still dependent on the funds requisitioned from the states, which frequently paid late or not at all. To raise money, Congress depended on loans from France and from wealthy Americans, but without the power to tax, it could not assure creditors they would be repaid. When those loans and credits from the French and Dutch were exhausted, Congress followed the lead of the states and financed the war by printing bills of credit. Between 1775 and 1779 it issued $191 million in bills, which were used as currency. By 1780 tax revenues from the states had retired only $3 million of these notes, and the value of the bills fell dramatically.

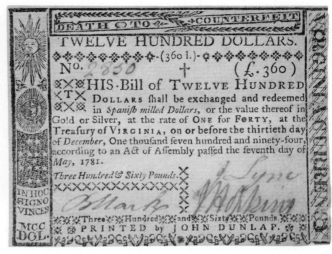

Paper Currency
To symbolize their independent status, the new state governments printed their own currency. Initially Pennsylvania retained the British system of pounds and shillings; Virginia chose the Spanish dollar as the basic unit of currency but included the equivalent in pounds ($1,200 was equal to £360). By 1781 Virginia had printed so much currency in order to pay its soldiers and wartime expenses that its value had depreciated. It now took forty Virginia paper dollars to buy the same amount of goods as one Spanish gold dollar.
The American Numismatic Society.

In fact, the enormous increase in the volume of paper money created the worst inflation in American history. The amount of goods available for purchase—both domestic foodstuffs and foreign manufactures—had shrunk significantly because of the fighting and the British naval blockade, whereas the amount of money in circulation had multiplied. Because consumers had lots of currency, they "bid up" the price of goods. By 1778 a family needed $7 in Continental bills to buy goods worth $1 in gold or silver. And things only got worse, with the ratio increasing to 42 to 1 in 1779 and 100 to 1 in 1780. In Maryland a bag of salt that in 1776 had cost $1 sold four years later for $3,900.

Unwilling to accept the virtually worthless currency, hard-pressed farmers refused to sell their crops, even to the Continental army. To supply their own needs, farmers used barter—trading grain for tools or clothes—or sold goods only to those who could pay in gold or silver. In towns, women who were distressed by the high prices of bread, tea, and sugar formed mobs and seized the goods they needed from storekeepers. Civilian morale and social cohesion crumbled, causing some Patriot leaders to doubt that the rebellion could succeed.

Valley Forge. Fears of defeat reached their peak during the winter of 1777–1778. Howe camped in Philadelphia and with his officers partook of the finest wines, foods, and entertainment the city could offer. Washington's army retreated to Valley Forge, some 20 miles to the west, where about twelve thousand soldiers and hun-

dreds of accompanying women suffered horribly. "The army . . . now begins to grow sickly," a surgeon confided to his diary. "Poor food—hard lodging—cold weather—fatigue. . . . Why are we sent here to starve and freeze?"

Nearby farmers refused to help. Some were pacifists—Quakers and German Mennonites—unwilling to support either side. Others were self-interested, hoarding their grain in hopes of higher prices in the spring or willing to accept only the gold and silver offered by British quartermasters. "Such a dearth of public spirit, and want of public virtue," Washington complained—but to no effect. By spring, a thousand of his hungry soldiers had vanished into the countryside and another three thousand had died from malnutrition and disease, along with scores of camp followers. A single winter at Valley Forge took as many American lives as had two years of fighting against General Howe.

In this dark hour Baron von Steuben raised the self-respect and readiness of the American army at Valley Forge. A former Prussian military officer, von Steuben was one of a handful of foreigners who had volunteered their services to the American cause. To counter falling morale, he instituted a standardized system of drill and maneuver. His efforts encouraged officers to become more professional in their demeanor and behavior and instilled greater order and discipline in the ranks. Thanks to von Steuben, the smaller Continental army that emerged from Valley Forge in the spring was a much tougher and better-disciplined force with a renewed sense of purpose.

The Path to Victory, 1778–1783

★

The Patriots' prospects improved dramatically in 1778 when the United States formed a military alliance with France, the most powerful nation on the European continent. The alliance brought the Americans money, troops, and supplies, and changed the conflict from a colonial rebellion to an international war.

The French Alliance

France and America were unlikely partners. France was a Catholic state and a monarchy; the United States, a mostly Protestant society and a federation of republics. The two peoples had been on opposite sides in wars from 1689 to 1763. But France was intent on avenging its defeat in the Great War for Empire and its loss of Canada. In 1776 the Comte de Vergennes, the French foreign minister and an early supporter of American independence, persuaded King Louis XVI to extend a secret loan to the rebellious colonies and supply them with gunpowder. Then in 1777 Vergennes opened wide-ranging commercial and military negotiations with Benjamin Franklin and two other American diplomats, Arthur Lee and Silas Deane. When news of the American victory at Saratoga reached Paris in December 1777, Vergennes urged the king to approve a formal alliance with the Continental Congress.

Negotiating the Treaty.   Franklin and his associates craftily exploited the rivalry between France and Britain, using the threat of a negotiated settlement with Britain to win an explicit French commitment to American independence. The Treaty of Alliance of February 6, 1778, specified that once France had entered the war against Great Britain, neither partner would sign a separate peace before the "liberty, sovereignty, and independence" of the United States were assured. In return, the American diplomats pledged that their government would recognize any French conquests in the West Indies, where France hoped to capture a rich sugar island from the British.

Although the French did not enter the war until June 1778, news of the alliance immediately gave new life to the Patriots' cause. Now certain of access to European military supplies and loans, the American army soon strengthened and hopes soared. "There has been a great change in this state since the news from France," a Patriot soldier reported from Pennsylvania; farmers—"mercenary wretches," he called them—"were as eager for Continental Money now as they were a few weeks ago for British gold."

With renewed energy and purpose, the Congress addressed the pressing demands for pensions by the offi-cers in the Continental army. Most officers came from the upper ranks of society and had used their own funds to equip themselves and sometimes their men as well; as compensation the officers wanted lifetime pensions at half-pay. At first Congress rejected this demand out of hand. John Adams likened the petitioners to "Mastiffs, scrambling for rank and pay like apes for nuts," while Henry Laurens, a leading Patriot merchant from South Carolina, condemned their request as a "total loss of virtue." Raised as gentlemen, officers were supposed to be exemplars of public service and give freely to preserve the republic. But General Washington urged Congress to grant the pensions, warning the lawmakers that "the salvation of the cause depends upon it." Buoyed by the French alliance, Congress reluctantly agreed to grant the officers half-pay after the war, but only for seven years.

The British Response.   The conflict with America had never been popular in Britain. During the late 1760s British political radicals and republican-minded artisans had supported American demands for greater rights as part of their own campaign for electoral reform at home; they wanted broader voting rights and more equitable representation for cities in Parliament. Now, as the cost of the war mounted, the landed gentry and urban merchants voiced discontent, denouncing increases in the land tax and the stamp duty as well as new levies on carriages, wine, and imported goods. "It seemed we were to be taxed and stamped ourselves instead of inflicting taxes and stamps on others," a British politician complained. But George III remained determined to crush the rebellion. If America won independence, he warned Lord North in 1777, "the West Indies must follow them. Ireland would soon follow the same plan and be a separate state, then this island would be reduced to itself, and soon would be a poor island indeed."

Following the British defeat at Saratoga, the king assumed a more pragmatic attitude. Worried about a Franco-American alliance, he allowed North to seek a negotiated settlement that would meet various Patriot demands. In February 1778 North had Parliament repeal the Tea and Prohibitory Acts and, in an amazing concession, renounce its right to tax the colonies. Then he appointed Lord Carlisle to negotiate with the Continental Congress and offer a return to the constitutional "condition of 1763," before the Sugar and Stamp Acts. But the gesture was too little too late. Many ordinary Americans had embraced independence and republicanism, and the Patriot leadership, emboldened by the alliance with France, rejected the overture.

War in the South

The French alliance expanded the war into a global conflict but did not rapidly conclude it. When France entered the conflict in June 1778, it concentrated some of its naval forces in the West Indies, where it hoped to acquire a rich sugar island, and dispatched other naval units to attack British merchant vessels trading to Europe and Africa. Spain, which joined the war as an ally of France in 1779, also had its own agenda: it wanted to regain from Britain its former colony of Florida and the fortress of Gibraltar at the entrance to the Mediterranean Sea. Indeed, the destiny of the new American republic had become enmeshed in a web of European territorial quarrels and the conflict between France and Britain for global maritime superiority.

The British ministry, now beset by war on many fronts, placed the highest priority on retaining control of its islands in the West Indies and adopted a modest strategy in North America. Rather than seeking to crush the Patriots, it tried to confine the rebellion to the relatively poor northern colonies and to recapture the rich tobacco- and rice-growing colonies of Virginia, the Carolinas, and Georgia. Once these staple-producing colonies had been conquered by the British army, they would be held and administered by local Loyalists. The British knew that Scottish Highlanders in North Carolina retained an especially strong alle-

giance to the Crown and hoped to recruit other Loyalists from the ranks of the backcountry Regulators, who had long opposed Patriot planters along the seacoast.

The ministry also hoped to take advantage of southern racial divisions. In 1776 over one thousand slaves had fled from their owners to fight for Lord Dunmore under the banner "Liberty to Slaves!" Now, thousands more African Americans might support a new British offensive. At the least, racial conflicts would undermine the Patriots' military efforts. Because blacks formed 30 to 50 percent of the population, owners were afraid to arm them. For the same reason many planters refused to allow their sons or white overseers to join the Continental forces, fearing that their absence would promote slave revolts.

Implementing this southern strategy became the responsibility of Sir Henry Clinton, who replaced the discredited Howe early in 1778. In June Clinton ordered the main British army to evacuate Philadelphia and to move to more secure quarters in New York. In December he launched his southern campaign, capturing Savannah, Georgia, and mobilizing hundreds of blacks to build barricades and unload supplies. Then

Marion Crossing the Pedee, *William T. Ranney, 1850*
In 1780, the war in the south went badly for the Patriots. General Lincoln surrendered one American army at Charleston, North Carolina, in May, and General Gates lost another at Camden, South Carolina, in August. But the tide soon turned, thanks in part to Patriot guerrilla forces led by Francis Marion, known as the "Swamp Fox," whose raids on enemy forts and supply lines forced the British to withdraw from the interior of South Carolina. Here Marion (on the chestnut horse) and his men cross the Pee Dee River on their way to a raid.
Amon Carter Museum of Western Art.

MAP 6.3
The Campaign in the South, 1778–1781
The British ministry's southern strategy started
well. British forces captured Savannah in December 1778 and Charleston in May 1780. Brutal
warfare raged in the interior over the next eighteen
months, fought more by small bands of irregulars
than by disciplined armies. When Lord Cornwallis
carried the battle into Virginia in late 1781, a
Franco-American army led by Washington and
Lafayette surrounded his forces at Yorktown, aided
by the French fleet under Admiral de Grasse.

Clinton moved inland, capturing Augusta early in
1779. By the end of the year, aided by local Loyalists,
the British had reconquered Georgia and had 10,000
troops poised for an assault on South Carolina. To
counter this threat, the Continental Congress suggested that South Carolina raise 3,000 African American troops, but the state assembly overwhelmingly
rejected the proposal.

During most of 1780 British forces marched from
victory to victory (Map 6.3). In April Clinton laid siege to
Charleston, South Carolina, which fell six weeks later. In
the most impressive British victory of the war, Clinton
won the surrender of General Benjamin Lincoln and his
5,000 troops. Shortly after this triumph, Lord Cornwallis
assumed control of the British forces in the South and
set out to secure the countryside. In August at Camden,
South Carolina, Cornwallis's army routed an American
force commanded by General Horatio Gates, the hero of
Saratoga. Only about 1,200 Patriot militiamen joined
Gates at Camden—one-fifth the number that had rallied
behind the American general at Saratoga. And many of
these militiamen panicked and fled without firing a shot,

handing the British control of South Carolina. Hundreds
of enslaved African Americans took the opportunity to
flee to freedom in Florida, while hundreds more sought
protection behind British lines, providing much-needed
labor for the invading army.

Then the tide of battle turned, thanks in part to
events in Europe. Hoping to restore its supremacy in
world commerce, the Dutch declared war against
Britain, creating yet another threat to British shipping
and the Royal Navy. Equally important, France dispatched troops to the American mainland. The French
decision was partly the work of the Marquis de
Lafayette, a republican-minded aristocrat who had
offered his services to the American cause long before
the alliance of 1778 and now served as one of
Washington's generals. In 1780 Lafayette returned to
France and personally persuaded Louis XVI to change
French military priorities and directly support the
Patriot rebellion. In July the king sent General Comte
de Rochambeau and a French army of 5,500 men to
Newport, Rhode Island, where it posed a threat to the
British forces in New York City.

American prospects likewise improved in the South. Unhappy with General Gates's leadership, Washington replaced him with Nathaniel Greene, who soon devised a military strategy to recapture the Carolinas and Georgia. To make the best use of Patriot militiamen, many of whom were "without discipline and addicted to plundering," Greene divided them into small groups commanded by strong leaders. Then he directed them to avoid pitched battles but instead to harass the larger but less mobile British forces.

The new approach evened up the conflict. In October 1780, a militia force of Patriot farmers defeated a regiment of Loyalists at Kings Mountain, North Carolina, taking about a thousand prisoners. In South Carolina, American guerrillas led by the "Swamp Fox," General Francis Marion, won a series of small but fierce battles, while General Daniel Morgan led another band of Patriot militia to a bloody victory at Cowpens, South Carolina, in January 1781. But Loyalist garrisons and militia remained powerful, assisted by Cherokee warriors led by the determined chief Dragging Canoe. "We fight, get beaten, and fight again," General Greene declared doggedly. In March 1781 Greene's soldiers fought Cornwallis's seasoned army to a draw at North Carolina's Guilford Court House (see Map 6.3).

The fighting in the South had become a war of attrition, one in which each side suffered hundreds of casualties. As his forces slowly weakened, Cornwallis made a crucial decision: he would concede Georgia and the Carolinas to Greene and seek a decisive victory in Virginia, the largest and most important southern state. Bolstered by military reinforcements from New York, the British general invaded Virginia's Tidewater region. There Benedict Arnold, the renegade Patriot general (see American Lives, "The Enigma of Benedict Arnold," pp. 196–197), led Cornwallis's troops in raids against plantations and towns along the James River, where they met with only slight resistance from a small American force commanded by Lafayette.

Then, in May 1781, as the two armies sparred near the York Peninsula in Virginia, the Franco-American leaders made a crucial decision of their own. Responding to American pleas, Louis XVI ordered Admiral François de Grasse to sail his large fleet from the West Indies to North America. Emboldened by the addition of this naval power, Washington decided to undertake a major offensive against Cornwallis's army. The American general arranged for Admiral de Grasse to position his fleet off the coast of Virginia, where, in combination with a smaller French naval force from Rhode Island, it outnumbered and outgunned Britain's American squadron. Simultaneously he ordered General Rochambeau's army to march in secrecy from Rhode Island to Virginia, where it joined Washington's force and prepared to attack Cornwallis's army. By the time the British discovered Washington's audacious

Lafayette at Yorktown, *J. B. Le Paon*
This painting, executed by the French artist J. B. Le Paon in 1780, depicts the Marquis de Lafayette and James Armistead, an enslaved African American who served as a spy for the Patriot army commanded by the French general. Receiving his freedom as a reward for his exploits, James took Lafayette's surname, becoming James Lafayette. The two Lafayettes met again in 1824, when the Frenchman visited the United States.
Lafayette College Art Collection, Easton, PA. Gift of Mrs. John Hubbard.

plan, it was impossible for the British troops in New York City to come to the rescue. Cornwallis found himself surrounded, his army of 9,500 men outnumbered two to one on land and cut off from reinforcement or retreat by sea. Abandoned by the outmatched Royal Navy, the British general surrendered at Yorktown on October 19, 1781.

The Franco-American victory at Yorktown broke the resolve of the British government. "Oh God! It is all over!" Lord North exclaimed when he heard the news. His ministry lacked the will or resources to raise a new army to continue the long war in America, and British prospects elsewhere were equally dim. The combined French and Spanish fleet menaced Britain's sugar islands, Dutch merchants were capturing European and Asian markets from British traders, and a newly formed group of European states—the League of

The Enigma of Benedict Arnold

———★———

BENEDICT ARNOLD WAS an exceptional man, and so too was his military career. During the American War of Independence, Arnold became a hero for *both* sides.

Arnold began his military exploits as an American Patriot. In May 1775 he devised a plan to capture Fort Ticonderoga on Lake Champlain and then joined with Ethan Allen, an avid Patriot from Vermont, and the Green Mountain Boys to do it. Arnold's heroics continued in September when he led an expedition of 1,150 riflemen against Quebec City, the capital of British Canada. The American commander drove his men hard through the Maine wilderness, overcoming leaky boats, spoiled provisions, treacherous rivers, and near starvation to arrive at Quebec in November, his force reduced to 650 men. These losses did not deter Arnold. Joined by General Richard Montgomery, who had arrived with 300 troops after capturing Montreal, Arnold's forces attacked the strongly fortified city, only to have the assault end in disaster. One hundred Americans were killed, including Montgomery; 400 were captured; and many were wounded—among them Arnold, who fell as he stormed over a barricade, a musket ball through his leg.

Ticonderoga and Quebec were only the beginning. For the next five years Arnold served the Patriot side with distinction in one battle after another, including a dangerous assault against the center of the British line at Saratoga, where he was again wounded in the leg. No general was more imaginative than Arnold, no field officer more daring, no soldier more courageous.

Yet Arnold has become immortalized not as a Patriot hero but as a villain, a military traitor who, as commander of the American fort at West Point, New York, in 1780, schemed to hand it over to the British. Of his role in this conspiracy there is no doubt. His British contact, Major John André, was caught with incriminating documents in Arnold's handwriting, including routes of access to the fort. Arnold, fleeing down the Hudson River on a British ship, defended his conduct in a letter to George Washington stating that "love to my country actuates my present conduct, however it may appear inconsistent to the world, who very seldom judge right of any man's actions."

But judge we must. Why did Arnold desert the cause for which he had fought so gallantly and twice been wounded? Was there any justification for his conduct?

Arnold was descended from respectable Puritan ancestors and grew up in modest circumstances. As a young man he served in a Connecticut regiment in the Great War for Empire. When the fighting began at Lexington and Concord in April 1775, Arnold was thirty-four years old, a minor merchant in New Haven, Connecticut, and also a militia captain and an ardent Patriot. Eager to support the rebellion, Arnold marched his men off to join in the siege of British forces in Boston. Along the way Arnold realized that the cannon at Fort Ticonderoga could be used to bombard General Thomas Gage's army and force it out of Boston. Once the victory was achieved, the former merchant submitted an inflated claim for expenses (£1,060 in Massachusetts currency, or about $60,000 today), then protested vehemently when suspicious legislators closely examined each item.

This adventure revealed Arnold's great strengths and equally great flaws. Bold and creative, he sized up a situation and acted quickly. Ambitious and extravagant, he craved power and the financial rewards that came with it. Intrepid and ruthless, he risked his life—and the lives of others—to get what he wanted.

Such larger-than-life figures are often resented as much as they are admired, and so it was with Benedict Arnold. At Quebec some New England officers accused him of arrogance , but Congress rewarded the colonel's bravery by making him a brigadier general. When Arnold again distinguished himself in battle in early 1777—having his horse shot out from under him— Congress promoted him to major general "as a token of their admiration of his gallant conduct." Then, in the middle of the struggle at Saratoga, General Horatio Gates relieved Arnold of his command, partly for insubordination and partly because the American commander considered him a "pompous little fellow." Nonetheless George Washington rewarded Arnold, appointing him commandant at Philadelphia in July 1778 following the British evacuation of the city.

But by then Arnold was an embittered man, disdainful of his fellow officers and resentful toward Congress for not promoting him more quickly and to even higher rank. A widower, he threw himself into the social life of Philadelphia, courting and marrying Margaret Shippen—a talented young woman from a wealthy merchant family—and falling deeply into debt. Arnold's extravagance drew him into shady financial schemes and into disrepute with Congress, which investigated his accounts and recommended a

Benedict Arnold, 1776
This engraving credits Arnold for the liberation of Boston (pictured in the background). By mounting the cannon he had seized at Fort Ticonderoga on the hills surrounding the seaport, Arnold forced the British to depart.
Anne S. K. Brown Military Collection, Brown University.

Major John André Executed as a British Spy
Unable to catch Benedict Arnold, the American army executed his British accomplice, whose intelligence and dignity won the hearts of his captors. "He died universally esteemed and universally regretted," noted Alexander Hamilton.
Library of Congress.

court-martial—which Arnold managed to avoid. "Having . . . become a cripple in the service of my country, I little expected to meet [such] ungrateful returns," he complained to Washington.

Faced with financial ruin, uncertain of future promotion, and disgusted with congressional politics, Arnold made a fateful decision: he would seek fortune and fame in the service of Great Britain. With cool calculation Arnold initiated correspondence with Sir Henry Clinton, the British commander, promising to deliver West Point and its 3,000 defenders for £20,000 sterling (about $1 million today), a momentous act that he hoped would spark the collapse of the American cause. Persuading Washington to place the fort under his command, in September 1780 Arnold began to execute his audacious plan, only to see it fail when André was captured and executed as a spy. The British ministry nonetheless rewarded Arnold, who received £6,000 and appointment as a brigadier general.

Arnold served George III with the same skill and daring he had shown in the Patriot cause. In 1781 in Virginia he looted Richmond and destroyed munitions and grain intended for the American army opposing Lord Cornwallis; in Connecticut he burned ships, warehouses, and much of the town of New London, a major port for Patriot privateers.

In the end, Benedict Arnold's moral failure resided not in his disenchantment with the Patriot cause—for many other American officers left the army in disgust. Nor did his infamy stem from his transfer of allegiance to the British side—for other Patriots chose to become Loyalists, sometimes out of principle but just as often for personal gain. Arnold's treason lay in the abuse of his position of authority: he would betray West Point and its garrison to secure his own success. His treachery was not that of a principled man but that of a selfish one, and he never lived that down. Hated in America as a consort of "Beelzebub . . . the Devil," after the war Arnold was treated with coldness and even contempt in Britain. He died as he lived—a man without a country.

Armed Neutrality—was demanding an end to Britain's commercial blockade of France. Isolated diplomatically in Europe, stymied militarily in America, and lacking public support at home, the British ministry gave up active prosecution of the war. For the next eighteen months only small and inconsequential attacks by British garrisons, Loyalists, and Indians reminded Patriots that they were still at war.

The Patriot Advantage

Angry members of Parliament demanded an explanation for this stinging military defeat. How could mighty Britain, victorious in the Great War for Empire, be defeated by a motley group of colonists? The ministry blamed the military leadership, pointing with some justification to a series of blunders. Why had Howe not been more ruthless in pursuing Washington's army in 1776? How could Germain, Howe, and Burgoyne have failed to coordinate the movement of British armies in 1777? Why were not the 60,000 Loyalists and thousands of native Americans who fought for the British used to greater military advantage? Why had Cornwallis marched deep into the powerful rebel state of Virginia in 1781?

Although historians have been equally critical of the British military command, they also have noted the high odds against British success, given broad-based American support for the rebel cause. Unlike most revolutionaries, the Patriots were led by experienced politicians who commanded public support. Although only a third of the white population zealously backed the rebellion, another third acknowledged the legitimacy of the Patriot-dominated local and state governments, paid taxes, and supported the war effort. And even though the Continental army had to be built from scratch and was never very large, it was fighting on familiar terrain with the assistance of thousands of militiamen. Once the rebels had the financial and military support of France, they could reasonably hope for victory. A charismatic leader such as William Pitt or an inspired general might have been able to suppress the rebellion, but ordinary politicians and mediocre military men were destined to fail.

The Americans, by contrast, were extremely lucky to have an impressive leader such as George Washington as commander of the Continental army. Politically astute, Washington deferred to the civil authorities, thereby winning support from the Congress and the state governments alike. Personally confident, he held the respect not only of his fellow American generals but also of European aristocrats such as von Steuben and Lafayette. And being militarily flexible, Washington came to understand that warfare in a lightly governed agricultural society required the deft use of rural militia units.

Finally, the American general had a greater margin for error than did the British generals because Patriots controlled local governments and could mobilize the militia to intervene at crucial moments. Thousands of militiamen had besieged General Gage in Boston in 1775, surrounded Burgoyne at Saratoga in 1778, and forced Cornwallis from the Carolinas in 1781. In the end the American people decided the outcome of the conflict. Preferring Patriot rule, a majority of white Americans refused to support local Loyalists or welcome invading British armies. Consequently, while the British won many military triumphs, they achieved few political victories, and their defeats at Saratoga and Yorktown proved catastrophic.

Diplomatic Triumph

After Yorktown it took nearly two years to conclude the war with a diplomatic settlement. Peace talks began in Paris in April 1782, but the French and Spanish negotiators stalled for time, hoping for a major naval victory or territorial conquest. Their delaying tactics infuriated the American diplomats—Benjamin Franklin, John Adams, and John Jay—who feared that drawn-out negotiations would tempt France to sacrifice American interests. For this reason the Americans negotiated secretly with the British; if necessary they were prepared to repudiate the treaty with France (which called for a jointly negotiated peace) and to sign a separate agreement with Britain. The British ministry was also eager to obtain a settlement. Many members of Parliament no longer supported the war, and ministers feared the loss to France of a rich West Indian sugar island. Franklin and his colleagues craftily exploited this rivalry between Britain and France, winning a diplomatic settlement that was extremely favorable to the United States.

In the Treaty of Paris, signed on September 3, 1783, Great Britain formally recognized American independence. Britain retained Canada, which now had a southern boundary at the Great Lakes. However, all land south of the lakes between the Appalachian Mountains and the Mississippi River, which Britain had wrested from France just twenty years before, was ceded to the new American republic. Although this territory was still the domain of undefeated native Americans, Britain did not secure its allies' rights to the land by insisting on a separate Indian territory. Leaving the Indians to their fate, negotiators promised to withdraw British garrisons from the region "with all convenient speed." As an Indian of the Wea people complained to a British official, "In endeavouring to assist you it seems we have wrought our own ruin."

Other treaty provisions granted Americans fishing rights off Newfoundland and Nova Scotia, forbade the British from "carrying away any negroes or other prop-

Drawing Boundary Lines for the Treaty of Paris
This map, drawn by John Mitchell in 1755, was used by British and American diplomats to help establish the boundaries of the United States as they negotiated the peace treaty of 1783. The map shows the "sea-to-sea" boundaries prescribed by the royal charters of the Carolinas and Virginia, and extends the limits of Pennsylvania north into present-day New York. In the treaty the British relinquished all claims to lands south of the Great Lakes and east of the Mississippi River.
Library of Congress Map Division.

erty," and guaranteed freedom of navigation on the Mississippi to British subjects and American citizens "forever." In its only major concessions, the American government promised not to hinder British merchants from recovering prewar debts and to recommend to the state legislatures that they treat Loyalists as equal citizens and return the property that had been confiscated from them during the war.

In the Treaty of Versailles, signed at the same time as the Treaty of Paris, Britain made a separate peace with France and Spain. Neither American ally gained very much. Spain failed in its main objective of retaking Gibraltar, though it retained Louisiana and reclaimed Florida from Britain (Map 6.4). France had the pleasure of reducing British power in North America, but its only territorial gain was the small Caribbean island of Tobago. Moreover, the war had quadrupled France's national debt; only six years later cries for tax relief and political liberty at home would spark the French Revolution. Only the Americans profited handsomely from the treaties, which gave them independence and, by opening up the lands east of the Mississippi River to American settlers, laid the foundation for the creation of a large and powerful nation.

Republicanism Defined and Challenged

————★————

From the moment they became revolutionary republicans, Americans began to define the character of their new social order. In the Declaration of Independence, Thomas Jefferson proclaimed that all individuals have the right to "Life, Liberty, and the pursuit of Happiness." Jefferson drew his list from the writings of the Enlightenment philosopher John Locke, but he substituted the word *happiness* for Locke's *property*. Jefferson's choice suggested that many Americans considered the private ownership of property a prerequisite for happiness. But it also reflected the idealism of many Patriots and their commitment to *republican virtue*, an enlightened quest for the public interest. As the New Hampshire constitution phrased it, "Government [was] instituted for the common benefits, protection, and security of the whole community."

The tension between self-interest and public interest shaped the history of the new nation from the very

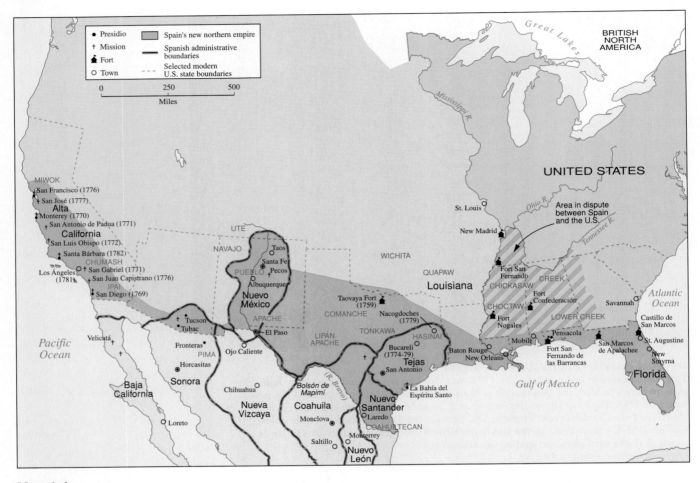

MAP 6.4
New Spain's Northern Empire in 1800
Following its acquisition of Louisiana in 1763, Spain tried to create a great northern empire. It established missions and forts in California, expanded Spanish settlements in New Mexico, and, by joining in the American War of Independence, reclaimed Florida from Britain. By the early nineteenth century, this dream of a great empire had been shattered by Indian uprisings in California and Texas, Napoleon's seizure of Louisiana, and American threats to Florida.

moment of its inception. Even as the War of Independence was being fought, Patriots argued over a series of important issues—who should bear the cost of the war, whether the property rights of Loyalists should be respected, whether slavery was compatible with republicanism, whether the government should support religion—in which the rights of the individual stood in tension with the welfare of the community.

Republican Ideals and Wartime Pressures

Simply put, a republic is a state without a monarch and with institutions of representative government. Yet for many Americans republicanism meant more than a political system; it was a social philosophy. In Latin, Thomas Paine noted, "The word republic means the

public good," which citizens have a duty to secure. "Every man in a republic is public property," asserted the Philadelphia Patriot Benjamin Rush (who eventually extended the notion to include women as well). "His time and talents—his youth—his manhood—his old age—nay more, life, all belong to his country."

The Ideal Tested. Because republicanism lauded public virtue and community service, the Continental Congress praised the self-sacrifice of the militiamen who fought and fell at Lexington and Concord. But as the war continued, the willingness of soldiers to endure military hardships diminished. During the hard winters of 1779 and 1780, Continental troops stationed at Morristown, New Jersey, mutinied because of low pay and sparse rations. To restore authority, Washington ordered the execution of several leaders of the revolt and urged Congress to use monetary incentives—back pay and new clothing—to pacify the recruits. In 1783 unrest among officers erupted at Newburgh, New York, and Washington had to use his personal authority to thwart a potentially dangerous challenge to the Congress's policies.

Economic distress also tested the republican virtue of ordinary citizens. The British naval blockade nearly destroyed the New England fishing industry and cut off the supply of European manufactured goods. The British occupation of Boston, New York, and Philadelphia caused domestic trade and manufacturing to decline, as did the recruitment of men for military service and the depredations of the warring armies. Unemployed shipwrights, dock laborers, masons, coopers, and bakers left cities and towns and drifted into the countryside; in New York City the population declined from 21,000 residents in 1774 to less than half that number by the war's end. In the Chesapeake the British blockade deprived tobacco planters of European markets, forcing them to turn to the cultivation of grain, which could be sold at home. All across the land the character of commercial activity changed as farmers and artisans adapted to a war economy.

In most areas the scarcity of goods brought a sharp rise in prices, and hard-pressed consumers decried merchants and traders as "enemies, extortioners, and monopolizers." Responding to widespread appeals for government regulation, in 1777 a convention of New England states restricted increases in the price of domestic commodities and imported goods to 75 percent above their prewar level. To enforce this directive, the Massachusetts legislature passed an "Act to prevent Monopoly and Oppression," only to find that many farmers and artisans refused to sell goods at the established prices. Some producers wanted to pass along their own rising costs, but others were determined to profit from wartime shortages. In the end consumers had to pay the market price, a government official admitted, "or submit to starving."

The struggle over regulation came to a head in Philadelphia. Following the British withdrawal from the city in 1778, severe food shortages and soaring prices prompted a sharp conflict over regulated versus free trade. In May 1779 the city's artisans and laborers, angered by a merchant who was illegally exporting flour, used their political influence to persuade a town meeting to establish a Committee on Prices. The Committee promptly set wholesale and retail prices for thirty-two commodities, justifying this regulation by invoking the traditional concept of the "just price" and urging citizens to act with "republican virtue."

Led by the influential Patriot financier Robert Morris, the merchant community condemned the price controls and espoused the "classical liberal" ideas of free trade and enlightened self-interest. Morris argued that regulation would only encourage farmers to hoard their crops, whereas allowing prices to rise would bring more goods to market and relieve scarcity. Most farmers agreed with Morris, as did members of the Continental Congress, including Benjamin Franklin, who condemned price controls as "contrary to the nature of commerce."

Nonetheless, most Philadelphians favored "fair" trade rather than "free" trade—at least in principle. At a second town meeting in August 1779, over 2,000 Philadelphians voted for regulation, and fewer than 300 opposed it. In practice, however, many artisan-republicans—shoemakers, tanners, and bakers—found that they could not support their families on fixed prices and so refused to abide by them. In civilian life as in the military, self-interest tended to triumph over republican virtue.

Women and Household Production. Faced with a shortage of goods and with constantly rising prices, government officials found it almost impossible to purchase supplies for the troops. They met this challenge by requisitioning goods directly from the people. For example, in 1776 Connecticut officials called on the citizens of Hartford to provide 1,000 coats and 1,600 shirts, and assessed smaller towns on a proportionate basis. In 1777 Connecticut officials again pressed the citizenry to provide shirts, stockings, and shoes for the men from their communities serving in the Continental army. Soldiers added personal pleas to these official exhortations. During the Battle of Long Island in 1776, Captain Edward Rogers lost "all the shirts except the one on my back." "The making of cloath," he wrote to his wife, " . . . must go on. . . . I must have shirts and stockings & a jacket sent me as soon as possible & a blankit."

In those difficult times Patriot women contributed to the war effort by increasing their production of "homespun" textiles, spinning wool and flax fibers into threads and weaving them into a coarse but serviceable cloth. One Massachusetts town produced 30,000 yards of homespun, and women in Elizabeth, New Jersey, promised "upwards of 100,000 yards of [homespun] linnen and woolen cloth." Other women assumed the burdens of farm production while their men were away at war. Some went into the fields, plowing, harvesting, and loading grain, while others supervised hired laborers or slaves, in the process acquiring a taste for decision making. "We have sow'd our oats as you desired," Sarah Cobb Paine wrote to her absent husband; "had I been master I should have planted it to Corn." Women's contribution to the war effort boosted their self-esteem and prompted some to claim greater rights in the new republican society. It also sparked an increase in farm household productivity that would soon create a dynamic rural economy.

Mobilizing for War
A few Patriot women disguised themselves as men and fought in the war, and thousands more traveled with the Continental army, providing the troops with food and support. This 1779 woodcut (which accompanied a poem by Molly Guttridge, a "Daughter of Liberty") symbolized the contributions of the Patriot women of the war-torn seaport of Marblehead, Massachusetts.
New-York Historical Society.

Taught from childhood to act selflessly—to value the welfare of their fathers, brothers, and husbands above their own—most Patriot women did not experience a sharp conflict between republican virtue and self-interest. But women often found that their *family's* interest differed from that of the Patriot cause. So, like many American men, they carefully calculated every financial transaction, refusing to sell their grain, meat, and cloth to Patriot commissaries who offered low prices or payment in rapidly depreciating Continental currency.

Fiscal Crisis.   Indeed, the spiraling inflation posed the most severe challenge to American families and the notion of public virtue. When the rate of exchange between Continental currency and specie reached 146 to 1 in 1781, not even the most virtuous

Patriots would accept paper money. To restore the value of its currency, the Continental Congress asked the states to assess taxes that citizens could pay by using forty paper dollars as the equivalent of a silver dollar. This plan brought in $120 million in Continental bills as tax payments, but it also provided a financial windfall for speculators. Many of them had bought Continental bills by paying one silver dollar (or goods worth that amount) for 100 paper dollars; now that paper currency was worth more than twice as much, giving them a handsome profit. At the end of the war these speculators still held $71 million in Continental notes, hoping eventually to redeem the currency at an even greater profit. "Private Interest seemed to predominate over the public weal," a leading Patriot complained.

In this financial game there were many more losers than winners. The losers were the tens of thousands of farmers, artisans, and soldiers who had received Continental bills for supplies or as military pay. As soon as they had received the currency, it lost purchasing power, literally depreciating in their pockets. Individually these losses were small, amounting to a tiny "tax" every time an ordinary citizen received a paper dollar, kept it for a week, and then spent it. But collectively such "currency taxes" paid the huge cost of the war. Indeed, it was these personal sacrifices made by hundreds of thousands of American citizens that financed the struggle for independence.

The experience was a sobering one. "Avaricious and ambitious men" seemed to be everywhere, protested one zealous Patriot. Was this the society for which Americans had fought and died? "Let us have patience," Benjamin Rush replied to such questions. He admitted that self-interest might be in the ascendancy, but he had faith that "our republican forms of government will in time beget republican opinions and manners. All will end well." Events would not completely bear out this optimism, but for Rush and many other Patriots, public virtue remained one of the preeminent ideals of the new American republics.

The Loyalist Exodus

As the war turned in favor of the Patriots, Loyalists faced disaster. Fearing for their lives, more than 100,000 Americans who had supported the Crown immigrated to the West Indies, Britain, and Canada. The exodus disrupted the established social order, for some of the Loyalists were wealthy and politically powerful merchants, lawyers, and landowners. Those who migrated to Canada became known as the United Empire Loyalists, and influential emigrés assumed the leadership of the English-speaking colonies of Nova Scotia, New Brunswick, and Ontario.

The land, buildings, and goods left behind by the Loyalists raised the touchy issue of the sanctity of property rights. Some Patriots denounced them as "traitors" whose property should be confiscated, and the passions of war lent urgency to their demands. In North Carolina the state government assumed temporary control of Loyalists' estates and rented them out to defray military expenses. But when the British army invaded the South, the Patriot-dominated assembly confiscated the estates and sold them at auction. Officials in New York also seized Loyalists' lands and goods, claiming the "sovereignty of the people of this state in respect to all property."

However, many public officials opposed the seizure of Loyalist property as contrary to Patriot principles. Following the classical liberal thought of John Locke as well as the dictates of common law, the Massachusetts Constitution of 1780 declared that every citizen should be protected "in the enjoyment of his life, liberty, and property, according to the standing laws," and state officials extended these rights to Loyalists. Most Tory property in Massachusetts was handled by the court system under the Act to Provide for the Payment of Debts. The courts mandated the seizure of land and goods needed to reimburse creditors, but the remaining property reverted to the families or agents of departed Loyalists.

Thus during the independence struggle there was no government-led social revolution. Most states seized only a limited amount of Loyalist property—that owned by notorious Loyalists—and sold it to the highest bidder, usually a wealthy Patriot rather than a yeoman or foot soldier. For example, Georgia seized 128,000 acres of land from 166 Tories but sold it to only 188 Patriots. Only in a few cases did these confiscations produce a democratic result. In North Carolina, about half the new owners of Loyalist lands were small-scale farmers. And on the former Philipsburg manor in New York, Patriot tenants successfully converted their leases into fee-simple ownership. But in general the revolutionary upheaval did not drastically alter the structure of rural society.

Social turmoil was greater in the cites, as Patriot merchants replaced Tories at the top of the economic ladder. In Massachusetts, the Lowell, Jackson, and Cabot families moved their trading enterprises to Boston to fill the vacuum created by the departure of the Loyalist Hutchinsons and Apthorps. In Philadelphia, small-scale traders stepped into the vacancies created by the collapse of Anglican and Quaker mercantile firms. These changes heralded the appearance of a more dynamic economic order. Many Loyalist merchants had imbibed the English values and consequently invested their profits from trade in real estate, becoming country gentlemen and landlords who lived off their rents. The

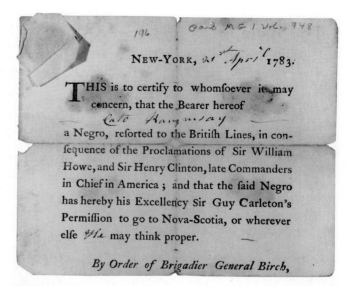

A Black Loyalist Pass, 1783
White Patriots claimed their freedom by fighting *against* the British, while thousands of black slaves won liberty by fighting *for* them. This pass certifies that Cato Rammsay, "a Negro," supported the Loyalist cause in New York and is now a free man, able to migrate to British Nova Scotia "or wherever else He may think proper."
Nova Scotia Archives and Records Management.

Patriot merchants who replaced them tended to be more entrepreneurial-minded. Some became speculators in western lands, but others promoted new trading ventures and domestic manufacturing. In economics as in politics, the War of Independence changed the character and the direction of American life.

The Problem of Slavery

The American Revolution generated intense debate over the institution of slavery, in part because of the active role played by African Americans on both sides of the struggle. Thousands of slaves in the South took refuge by fleeing behind British lines; in Virginia, Patriot Richard Henry Lee reported that two of his neighbors lost "every slave they had in the world." Many of these slaves won their freedom by working or fighting for the king. When British forces evacuated Charleston, more than 6,000 former slaves went with them; another 4,000 African Americans left Savannah with the British. Hundreds of black Loyalists settled permanently in Canada, but over 1,000 others, poorly treated and having been settled on inferior land in Nova Scotia, sought a better life in the abolitionist settlement in Sierra Leone in West Africa (see Chapter 9, American Lives, "Richard Allen and African American Identity," pp. 300–301).

Symbols of Slavery—and Freedom
The scar on the forehead of this black woman, who was
widely known as "Mumbet," underlined the cruelty of slavery.
Winning emancipation through a legal suit in Massachusetts,
she chose a name befitting her new status: Elizabeth
Freeman. This watercolor, by Susan Sedgwick, was painted
in 1811.
Massachusetts Historical Society.

Thousands of African Americans also served the
Patriot cause. Free blacks from New England enrolled
in Patriot units such as the First Rhode Island Company and the Massachusetts "Bucks." In Maryland,
Patriots recruited a large number of slaves for military
service and later freed them, a policy that was rejected
by other southern states. But many slaves struck informal bargains with their Patriot masters, trading loyalty
in wartime for a promise of eventual liberty. In 1782 the
Virginia assembly passed an act allowing manumission
(legal release); within a decade planters had freed ten
thousand slaves.

Slavery revealed a contradiction in the Patriots'
republican ideology. "How is it that we hear the loudest
yelps for liberty among the drivers of Negroes?" the
British author Samuel Johnson chided. Some white
Patriots took his point to heart. "I wish most sincerely
there was not a Slave in the province," Abigail Adams
wrote to her husband, John, as Massachusetts went to
war in 1776. "It always appeared a most iniquitous
Scheme to me—to fight ourselves for what we are daily
robbing and plundering from those who have as good a
right to freedom as we have."

Gradual Emancipation in the North. The intense
questioning of slavery was new. Before the American

and French Revolutions, Europeans did not believe in
political or social equality. Inequality of condition and
status was the norm in European society, regarded as
part of God's design for the world. Slavery in Europe's
American possessions pushed this doctrine of natural
inequality to the extreme.

The Quakers, whose belief in religious equality had
made them sharp critics of many social inequities in
Europe, took the lead in condemning slavery in America. Beginning in the 1750s, the evangelist John
Woolman and a few other Quakers urged their coreligionists to free their slaves. The outbreak of the independence struggle led many North Carolina Quakers to
"clear their hands" of the institution by manumitting
their slaves. Other rapidly growing pietistic religious
denominations, notably the Methodists and the Baptists, advocated emancipation and admitted both
enslaved and free blacks into their congregations. In
1784 a conference of Virginia Methodists declared that
slavery was "contrary to the Golden Law of God on
which hang all the Law and Prophets."

Enlightenment philosophy also played a role in the
debate. Many slaveowners justified slavery by depicting
Africans as "savage" or "inferior"—suited to bondage by
their nature. Such beliefs ran counter to the thought of
John Locke, who argued that ideas and habits were not
innate but stemmed from a person's impressions and
experiences in the world. Accordingly, Enlightenment
thinkers suggested that the oppressive conditions of slavery, not inherent inferiority, accounted for the debased
situation of Africans in the Western Hemisphere. As one
American writer put it, "A state of slavery has a mighty
tendency to shrink and contract the minds of men."
Anthony Benezet, a Quaker philanthropist who founded
and financed a school for blacks in Philadelphia, defied
popular opinion in declaring that African Americans
were "as capable of improvement as White People" (see
American Voices, "Benjamin Banneker: On Jefferson
and Natural Rights," p. 205).

These religious and secular arguments placed slavery on the defensive, especially in the North, where
there were relatively few African Americans. By 1784,
Massachusetts had abolished slavery outright and
three other states—Pennsylvania, Connecticut, and
Rhode Island—had provided for its gradual termination. Within another twenty years every state north of
Delaware had implemented a policy of *gradual emancipation*. This policy gave priority to white property
rights, for it required blacks to endure more years of
unpaid labor. For example, the New York Emancipation Edict of 1799 granted freedom only to enslaved
children—not their parents—and then only when they
reached the age of twenty-five. As late as 1810, fully
thirty thousand blacks in the northern states—nearly
one-fourth of their African American population—
were still enslaved.

BENJAMIN BANNEKER

On Jefferson and Natural Rights

★

In his Notes on Virginia *(1785), Thomas Jefferson suggested the inherent inferiority of the black race. In 1791 Benjamin Banneker, a free African American farmer and mathematician who helped to survey the District of Columbia, sent Jefferson a manuscript copy of his forthcoming "Almanac," an annotated and illustrated guide to the coming agricultural year. In the accompanying letter Banneker asks Jefferson, now the secretary of state, to reconsider his view of Africans, pointing out the contradiction between Jefferson's position and the doctrine of natural rights that he had articulated in the Declaration of Independence.*

I suppose it is a truth too well attested to you, to need a proof here, that we are a race of Beings who have long laboured under the abuse and censure of the world . . . considered rather as brutish than human, and Scarcely capable of mental endowments. . . .

Sir, I hope . . . that you are a man far less inflexible in Sentiments of this nature, than many others. . . . Now, Sir, if this is founded in truth, I apprehend you will readily embrace every opportunity to eradicate that train of absurd and false ideas and opinions which so prevail with respect to us, and that your Sentiments are concurrent with mine, which are that the one universal Father has given to us all, and that he hath not only made us all of one flesh, but that he hath also without partiality afforded us all the Same Sensations, and imbued us all with the same faculties, and that however diversified in Situation or colour, we are all of the Same Family, and Stand in the Same relation to him. . . .

Sir, Suffer me to recall to your mind that time in which the Arms and tyranny of the British Crown were exerted with very powerful effort in order to reduce you to a State of Servitude. . . . This, Sir, was a time in which you clearly saw into the injustice of a State of Slavery [and] . . . that you publickly held forth this true and invaluable doctrine . . . : "We hold these truths to be Self evident, that all men are created equal . . ."; but Sir, how pitiable it is to reflect, that . . . in detaining by fraud and violence so numerous a part of my brethren under groaning captivity and cruel oppression that you should at the Same time be found guilty of that most criminal act, which you professedly detested in others, with respect to yourselves.

Source: John J. Patrick, ed., *Founding the Republic: A Documentary History* (Westport, CT: Greenwood Press, 1995), 102–105.

Emancipation in the North came slowly for several reasons. Many whites feared that freed blacks would compete with them for jobs and housing. And they were horrified by the thought of race melding, so they opposed marriages between blacks and whites with much greater intensity than they resisted marriages between those from different Christian churches. In 1786 Massachusetts reenacted a colonial-era law that prohibited whites from marrying blacks, Indians, or mulattoes. Most important, whites' right to property had priority over blacks' rights to liberty.

Emancipation in the Chesapeake Region. The tension between the republican values of liberty and property was greatest in the South. By the last quarter of the eighteenth century slaves made up about 30 percent of the population of the Chesapeake region and represented a significant financial investment. However,

some Chesapeake planters were moving away from slavery, either because they had joined Methodist or Baptist churches or because their plantations were oversupplied with workers. Consequently, they allowed blacks to buy their freedom through paid work as artisans or laborers. By 1810 manumission and self-purchase had brought the number of freed blacks in Maryland to about one-third of the African American population, leading some observers to predict that slavery in the Chesapeake would gradually "wither away."

But these developments were not strong enough to dislodge such a deeply rooted institution as slavery. Even more than in the North, most southern whites did not want a society filled with free African Americans. In 1776 the North Carolina legislature condemned Quaker manumissions as "highly criminal and reprehensible" and passed laws ordering the enslavement of freed blacks or their expulsion from the state. In 1792 the Virginia legislature rejected a proposal for gradual emancipation and made it more difficult for individual masters to free their slaves. Following the lead of Thomas Jefferson, who continued to own more than a hundred slaves, many Chesapeake planters argued that slavery was a "necessary evil" required to maintain white supremacy and their luxurious life-styles. In South Carolina and Georgia, where blacks constituted 50 to 60 percent of the population and rice-growing was immensely profitable, there was virtually no discussion of ending slavery.

The southern debate over emancipation ended in 1800 when whites thwarted an uprising planned by the slave-artisan Gabriel Prosser. For months Prosser and his fellow conspirators had traveled the countryside laying the basis for a revolt, which was to begin when two hundred slaves in Richmond set fires, captured arms, and killed whites who opposed them. Alerted at the last moment by African American informers, Virginia authorities captured and hanged Prosser and about thirty of his followers. "Liberty and equality have brought the evil upon us," a letter to the *Virginia Herald* proclaimed in the aftermath, for such doctrines are "dangerous and extremely wicked in this country, where every white man is a master, and every black man is a slave." Throughout the South, most whites reaffirmed their commitment to slavery and white property rights, regardless of the cost to republican principles.

A Republican Religious Order

Before 1776 most colonies had a legally established church, supported by public taxes and often by laws that mandated attendance at Sunday services. Only the Quaker- and Baptist-controlled colonies of Pennsylvania and Rhode Island allowed individuals to support and worship at churches of their own choosing. Political revolution, however, broadened the appeal of religious liberty, forcing Patriot lawmakers to devise a new relationship between church and state.

Separation of Church and State. The most dramatic change in the religious situation came in those states where the Church of England had been legally estab-

A Lutheran Church Service, 1799
This detail of a sketch, by the German American folk artist Lewis Miller, shows a Lutheran congregation in York County, Pennsylvania. Like other migrants, Germans carried their faith and social practices to America. The minister preaches in German from the pulpit (far right), and the worshippers are segregated by sex, the men on the minister's right and the women on his left (and front, not included in this detail). Note the image of Martin Luther and scenes from the Old Testament along the balcony railing.
Historical Society of York County.

lished. For example, in Virginia most Anglicans immediately renounced allegiance to the king and the Church of which he was the head. By 1778 they had reorganized themselves as the Protestant Episcopal Church of America.

To win support for the war, the Virginia Episcopalians accepted the legitimacy of Presbyterian and Baptist churches, thereby undermining the idea of a single, state-supported church. Leading Virginia Patriots who embraced the Enlightenment also questioned the wisdom of an established church. In 1776 James Madison and George Mason persuaded the Virginia convention to issue a Declaration of Rights that would guarantee the "free exercise of religion" to all Christians. Later that year the Virginia legislature passed an act exempting dissenters from paying taxes to support the Anglican Church.

The debate over state support for religion continued after the war. Baptists in particular opposed the use of taxes to support religion. In Virginia their political influence prompted lawmakers to reject a bill supported by George Washington and Patrick Henry that would have imposed a general tax to fund all Christian churches. Instead, in 1786 the Virginia legislature enacted Thomas Jefferson's Bill for Establishing Religious Freedom, which made all churches equal before the law and granted direct financial support to none. In New York and New Jersey the sheer number of churches—Episcopalian, Presbyterian, Dutch Reformed, Lutheran, and Quaker, among others—prevented legislative agreement on an established church or compulsory religious taxes.

Yet many Americans clung to traditional European principles, arguing that a firm union of church and state would promote morality and respect for authority. "Pure religion and civil liberty are inseparable companions," a group of North Carolinians advised their minister. "It is your particular duty to enlighten mankind with the unerring principles of truth and justice, the main props of all civil government." Accepting this premise, most state governments provided churches with indirect aid by exempting their property and ministers from taxation.

Thus the separation of church and state came slowly, especially in New England, where congregationalist ministers who had strongly supported the independence movement were able to preserve a legally established church until the 1830s. But even there Baptists and Methodists could now have their religious taxes paid to their own churches rather than to the Congregational Church. After the Revolution an established church and compulsory religious taxes were no longer the norm.

Freedom of Conscience. Nonetheless, the meaning and extent of religious freedom remained controversial.

In Virginia, Jefferson's Bill for Establishing Religious Freedom instituted the principle of liberty of conscience by outlawing religious affiliation as a requirement for holding political and civil offices. However, other states enforced religious criteria for voting and officeholding, penalizing individuals who dissented from the doctrines of Protestant Christianity. The North Carolina constitution of 1776 disqualified from public office any citizen "who shall deny the being of God, or the Truth of the Protestant Religion, or the Divine Authority of the Old or New Testament." New Hampshire's constitution contained a similar provision until 1868.

Such restrictive doctrines commanded widespread support, both among the public at large and in courts of law. In one celebrated case decided shortly after 1800, Chancellor James Kent of the New York Supreme Court defined religious liberty in very narrow terms by upholding the conviction of Timothy Ruggles for blasphemy (publicly and disrespectfully shouting the name of Christ). Kent rejected Ruggles's contention that the charge infringed on his liberty of conscience under the New York Constitution of 1777, which guaranteed "the free, equal and undisturbed enjoyment of religious opinion." Kent declared that "the people of this State profess the general doctrines of Christianity" and that for Ruggles to slander Christ was "to strike at the root of moral obligation and weaken the security of social ties." For Kent and many others, the preservation of social cohesion had a higher priority than the individual's right of free speech.

Americans who were influenced by Enlightenment values condemned such restrictions on freedom of conscience. Leading American Patriots, including Thomas Jefferson and Benjamin Franklin, extended republican principles to religion, arguing that God had given human beings the power of reason so they could determine moral truths for themselves. Ethan Allen of Vermont wrote a widely circulated pamphlet called *Reason: The Only Oracle of Man* (1784). These rationalists demanded complete freedom of expression to protect society from what Allen and Jefferson called "ecclesiastical tyranny."

Many evangelical Protestants also favored freedom of conscience, but their main goal was to protect their churches from state control. The Massachusetts Baptist minister Isaac Backus warned his coreligionists not to incorporate their churches or accept state funding because that might lead to state interference in their affairs. Backus and other evangelicals welcomed "voluntarism" (the voluntary funding of churches by their members) because it allowed the laity to control the clergy, furthering "the principles of republicanism." In religion as in politics, Americans had begun to create a new republican order.

Summary

———————★———————

The War of Independence changed the course of American history by creating the United States as a separate nation with a republican system of government. This dramatic change began in earnest in April 1775, when the American colonists challenged British authority with military force. Thomas Paine's *Common Sense* attacked the monarchical system and persuaded many Americans to support republicanism and independence, which was formally declared by the Continental Congress on July 4, 1776.

The British ministry dispatched a large British army under General Howe to put down the rebellion. Howe's force defeated Washington's Continental army in a series of battles during 1776, but Patriot triumphs at Trenton and Princeton revived American morale. Howe captured Philadelphia, the Patriots' capital, in the summer of 1777, but the rebels won a major victory at Saratoga in New York in October. The Patriots nearly lost their main army to cold and hunger at Valley Forge, Pennsylvania, during the winter of 1777–1778. Simultaneously, a severe inflation caused by an excess of paper money undermined public support for the new republican governments.

The tide turned in February 1778, when an alliance with France aided the Patriot cause. Congress rejected British overtures for a negotiated settlement, and Lord North embarked on a southern military strategy. British troops won important victories in Georgia and the Carolinas during 1779 and 1780, but Patriot troops finally forced General Cornwallis and his army into Virginia, where they suffered a stinging defeat at Yorktown in October 1781. The Treaty of Paris in 1783 acknowledged the independence of the United States and defined its western boundary at the Mississippi River. Thousands of Loyalists immigrated to various parts of the British Empire, and thousands of slaves escaped to freedom by departing with the British army.

During the war some Patriots defined republicanism as pursuit of the common good. Other Americans embraced the liberal outlook inspired by John Locke and celebrated the pursuit of individual self-interest. Wartime hardships—such as currency inflation, the hidden tax that paid for the Patriots' military effort—increased the tension between these republican and liberal ideals.

Long after the war ended, Americans continued to debate the social and cultural implications of republicanism. State governments in the North began the gradual abolition of slavery, but those in the South refused to extend freedom to most African Americans. However, throughout the new nation there was growing commitment to freedom of religious worship and the separation of church and state.

T I M E L I N E

1775	Second Continental Congress meets
	Battle of Bunker Hill
	Congress submits Olive Branch petition
	Lord Dunmore's proclamation offers freedom to slaves
	American invasion of Canada
1776	Patriots and Loyalists skirmish in South
	Thomas Paine's *Common Sense*
	Declaration of Independence (July 4)
	British general William Howe defeats General George Washington in New York
	Virginia Declaration of Rights
1777	Patriot women become important in war economy
	Howe occupies Philadelphia
	General Horatio Gates defeats British general John Burgoyne at Saratoga
	Continental army suffers at Valley Forge
	Severe inflation of paper currency
1778	Franco-American alliance (February 6)
	Lord North seeks negotiated settlement
	British begin southern strategy; capture Savannah
1780	Sir Henry Clinton seizes Charleston (May 12)
	French army lands in Rhode Island
1781	Lord Cornwallis invades Virginia; surrenders at Yorktown
	Loyalist immigration
	Partial redemption of Continental currency at 40 to 1
1782	Slave manumission in Virginia (reversed, 1792)
1783	Treaty of Paris (September 3) officially ends war
1786	Virginia Bill for Establishing Religious Freedom
1800	Gabriel Prosser's conspiracy in Virginia

Suggested Readings

Gordon Wood, *The Radicalism of the American Revolution* (1992), offers a fine overview. For contrasting interpretations, see the essays in Alfred F. Young, ed., *Beyond the American Revolution: Explorations in the History of American Radicalism* (1993). Jack P. Greene and J. R. Pole, eds., *The Blackwell Encyclopedia of the American Revolution* (1991), provides illuminating essays on important topics.

Toward Independence, 1775–1776

Jerrilyn Green Marston, *King and Congress: The Transfer of Political Legitimacy, 1774–1776* (1987), and Jack N. Rakove, *The Beginnings of National Politics* (1979), discuss the movement toward independence. See also Eric Foner, *Tom Paine and Revolutionary America* (1976); Jack Fruchtman Jr., *Thomas Paine: Apostle of Freedom* (1994); and Pauline Maier, *American Scripture: Making the Declaration of Independence* (1997). On Loyalism, read William N. Nelson, *The American Tory* (1961), and the essays collected in Robert M. Calhoon, Timothy M. Barnes, and George A. Rawlyk, eds., *Loyalists and Community in North America* (1994).

The Perils of War and Finance, 1776–1778

The military history of the war is covered in James L. Stokesbury, *A Short History of the American Revolution* (1991), and Piers Mackesy, *The War for America, 1775–1783* (1964). Don Higginbotham, *George Washington and the American Military Tradition* (1985), and Ronald Hoffman and Peter Albert, eds., *Arms and Independence: The Military Character of the American Revolution* (1984), offer a more analytical perspective. The war in the North can be followed in Ira D. Gruber, *The Howe Brothers and the American Revolution* (1972), and Richard J. Hargrove Jr., *General John Burgoyne* (1983).

Studies of ordinary soldiers include Rodney Attwood, *The Hessians* (1980); Sylvia R. Frey, *The British Soldier in America* (1981); Robert K. Wright Jr., *The Continental Army* (1983); Charles P. Neimeyer, *America Goes to War: A Social History of the Continental Army* (1996); and John C. Dann, ed., *The Revolution Remembered: Eyewitness Accounts of the War for Independence* (1980). For the military bureaucracy, see R. Arthur Bowler, *Logistics and the Failure of the British Army in America, 1775–1783* (1975), and E. Wayne Carp, *To Starve the Army at Pleasure: Continental Army Administration and American Political Culture, 1775–1783* (1984).

Local studies include Jean Butenhoff Lee, *The Price of Nationhood: The American Revolution in Charles County* (1994); David Hackett Fischer, *Paul Revere's Ride* (1994); Richard Buel Jr., *Dear Liberty: Connecticut's Mobilization for the Revolutionary War* (1980); and Donald Wallace White, *A Village at War: Chatham, New Jersey, and the American Revolution* (1979).

African American participation in the war is discussed in Sidney Kaplan, *The Black Presence in the Era of the American Revolution* (rev. ed., 1989), and Gary B. Nash, *Race and Revolution* (1990). The native American response is described in Barbara Graymont, *The Iroquois in the American Revolution* (1972); Isabel T. Kelsey, *Joseph Brant, 1743–1807* (1984); and James H. O'Donnell III, *Southern Indians in the American Revolution* (1973).

A classic discussion of the fiscal problems created by the war is E. James Ferguson, *The Power of the Purse: A History of American Public Finance: 1776–1790* (1961); a more recent study is William G. Anderson, *The Price of Liberty: The Public Debt of the American Revolution* (1983).

The Path to Victory, 1778–1783

Bradford Perkins, *The Creation of a Republican Empire, 1776–1865* (1993), and Jonathan R. Dull, *A Diplomatic History of the American Revolution* (1985), provide good overviews. More specialized studies include James H. Hutson, *John Adams and the Diplomacy of the American Revolution* (1980); Richard B. Morris, *The Peacemakers: The Great Powers and American Independence* (1965); and Ronald Hoffman and Peter Albert, eds., *Peace and the Peacemakers: The Treaty of 1783* (1986).

For the southern campaign, consult W. Robert Higgins, ed., *The Revolutionary War in the South* (1979); Ronald Hoffman, Thad W. Tate, and Peter J. Albert, eds., *An Uncivil War: The Southern Backcountry during the American Revolution* (1985); and Jeffrey J. Crow and Larry E. Tise, eds., *The Southern Experience in the American Revolution* (1978). Studies of military action include Hugh F. Rankin, *Francis Marion: The Swamp Fox* (1973), and John S. Pancake, *The Destructive War, 1780–1782* (1985).

Republicanism Defined and Challenged

Milton M. Klein et al., *The Republican Synthesis Revisited* (1992), explores the debate over the importance of republican thought. See also Charles Royster, *A Revolutionary People at War: The Continental Army and American Character, 1775–1783* (1979). On women's lives, see Ronald Hoffman and Peter J. Albert, eds., *Women in the Age of the American Revolution* (1989); Mary Beth Norton, *Liberty's Daughters: The Revolutionary Experience of American Women, 1750–1800* (1980); Lynn Withey, *Dearest Friend: A Life of Abigail Adams* (1980); and Joy Day Buel and Richard Buel Jr., *The Way of Duty: A Woman and Her Family in Revolutionary America* (1984).

On the black experience, consult Sylvia R. Frey, *Water from the Rock: Black Resistance in a Revolutionary Age* (1991); Ira Berlin and Ronald Hoffman, eds., *Slavery and Freedom in the Age of the American Revolution* (1983); and Gary B. Nash, *Forging Freedom: The Formation of Philadelphia's Black Community, 1720–1840* (1988). See also James W. St. G. Walker, *The Black Loyalists: The Search for a Promised Land in Nova Scotia and Sierra Leone, 1783–1870* (1976), and Shane White, *Somewhat More Independent: The End of Slavery in New York City, 1770–1810* (1991).

On changes in American religion, see Ronald Hoffman and Peter J. Albert, eds., *Religion in a Revolutionary Age* (1994); Rhys Isaac, *The Transformation of Virginia, 1740–1790* (1982); Fred Hood, *Reformed America, 1783–1837* (1980); and Nathan O. Hatch, *The Democratization of American Christianity* (1989). The spiritual roots of a new secular religion are traced by Catharine Albanese, *Sons of the Fathers: The Civil Religion of the American Revolution* (1976), and Ruth Bloch, *Visionary Republic: Millennial Themes in American Thought* (1985).

The New Political Order,

1776–1800

MANY REVOLUTIONS END in political chaos or military rule, but the new American republic escaped those unhappy fates. The departure of zealous Loyalists ended support for the restoration of monarchy, and most Continental army officers strongly supported civilian rule. Still, General George Washington stunned the world in 1783 when he voluntarily left public life to return to his plantation. "Tis a Conduct so novel," the American painter John Trumbull reported from London, "so inconceivable to People [here], who, far from giving up powers they possess, are willing to convulse the empire to acquire more." Washington's retirement bolstered the authority of civilian Patriot leaders, who were firmly committed to representative government.

Fashioning republican institutions absorbed the energy and intellect of an entire generation. Between 1776 and 1800 Americans not only wrote new state and federal constitutions but also devised a representative system of politics that was broadly responsive to the popular will. Indeed, some Patriots thought it was *too* responsive. When a bill was introduced into a state legislature, grumbled Ezra Stiles, the conservative president of Yale College, the elected official "instantly thinks how it will affect his constituents," not how it would affect the good of the public as a whole. But what Stiles disparaged as an excess of democracy, most ordinary Americans welcomed. For the first time their interests were directly represented in the halls of government. One crowd of citizens in New York, a British visitor noted in 1792, watched a procession of newly

Frederick Muhlenberg, First Speaker of the U.S. House of Representatives
The son of German Lutherans who migrated to Pennsylvania in the 1740s, Muhlenberg was destined for the ministry but ended up in politics, serving as Speaker of the Pennsylvania Assembly. A man of "portly person and handsome rotundity," a journalist noted, Muhlenberg nearly filled the oversized chair intended to bestow dignity on those who led the House of Representatives. This portrait was painted by Joseph Wright (1756–1793) in 1790.
National Portrait Gallery, Smithsonian Institution/Art Resource, NY.

elected officials "with Transports and Tears of Joy. The People gazed at them, with a Kind of Rapture."

However, the sheer number of interests complicated the task of governing, and political life became increasingly conflict-ridden. During the 1790s Alexander Hamilton's system of public finance and the ideological passions of the French Revolution divided Americans into warring camps and led to the rise of organized political parties. Before the election of President Thomas Jefferson in 1800 brought an end to this political crisis, the national government had curtailed the rights of citizens and had almost gone to war with France.

Despite these conflicts—and in part *because* of them—the period between 1776 and 1800 was the most creative era in American political and constitutional development. Everywhere people with democratic views saw the United States as the exemplar of political liberty and, as Tom Paine had put it, "the last best hope of mankind."

Creating New Institutions, 1776–1786

───────★───────

The Revolution of 1776 was both a struggle for home rule (independence) and, in the words of the historian Carl Becker, a conflict over "who should rule at home." Who would control the new representative institutions of government—traditional elites or ordinary citizens? Patriots first answered this question at the state level, as they wrote state constitutions establishing the structure of government. Simultaneously, in the Articles of Confederation of 1781 and the Constitution of 1787, they addressed a related question—the division of authority between the states and the central government. These two issues relating to power—that held by ordinary citizens and that exercised by the different levels of government—stood at the core of a generation-long constitutional debate that divided Americans into rival camps.

The State Constitutions: How Much Democracy?

In May 1776 the Continental Congress passed a resolution calling for the authority of the Crown to be "totally suppressed" and "all the powers of government exerted under the authority of the people." Patriots in the states quickly complied, electing delegates to legislatures or conventions charged with the task of forming new institutions of government. Within six months Virginia, Maryland, North Carolina, New Jersey, Delaware, and Pennsylvania had written new constitutions, and Connecticut and Rhode Island had transformed their colonial charters into republican constitutions by deleting references to the king.

The Dilemma of Popular Sovereignty. In devising these constitutions, delegates heeded the principle of popular sovereignty stated in the Declaration of Independence: that governments derive "their just powers from the consent of the governed." The Delaware constitution provided concrete meaning to that high-minded phrase by linking sovereignty with power, declaring that "the Right of the People to participate in the Legislature, is the Foundation of Liberty and of all free government."

But who were the people? During the colonial period, propertyless white men, blacks, women, and native Americans had been excluded from public life, and although men who owned small amounts of property could vote, those of wealth held most political offices. In the heat of revolution, many Patriots moved toward a less elitist definition of politics—one based on citizenship, not property. Every man who supported the rebellion—property owner or not—had "an equal claim to all privileges, liberties and immunities," declared an article in the Maryland *Gazette*. In North Carolina the backcountry farmers of Mecklenburg County instructed their delegates to the state's constitutional convention to "oppose everything that leans to aristocracy or power in the hands of the rich and chief men exercised to the oppression of the poor." And in Virginia voters elected a new assembly that "was composed of men not quite so well dressed, nor so politely educated, nor so highly born," an observer remarked. "They are the People's men."

This populist impulse received its fullest expression in Pennsylvania, where a coalition of Scots-Irish farmers, Philadelphia artisans, and Enlightenment-influenced intellectuals created the most democratic government in America or Europe. Pennsylvania's constitution of 1776 abolished property owning as a requirement for political participation, granting all men who paid taxes the right to vote and hold office, and reapportioned the legislature to give more power to poorer backcountry regions. It also created a *unicameral* (one-house) assembly with complete legislative power. No council or upper house was reserved for the wealthy, and no governor exercised veto power. Other constitutional provisions mandated an extensive system of public elementary education, protected citizens from imprisonment for debt, and called for a society of economically independent freemen.

Pennsylvania's non-elitist constitution alarmed many leading Patriots, who continued to believe that voting and officeholding should be restricted to "men of learning, leisure and easy circumstances." Jeremy Belknap of New Hampshire insisted that "the people be

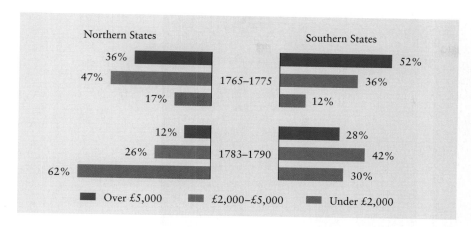

Northern States   Southern States

36%
47%   1765–1775   52%
17%   36%
                                       12%

12%   28%
26%   1783–1790   42%
62%   30%

■ Over £5,000   ■ £2,000–£5,000   ■ Under £2,000

FIGURE 7.1
Change in the Wealth of Elected Officials, 1765–1790
Before the Revolution men of wealth and property predominated in the colonial assemblies. In the new republic the proportion of less prosperous men in state legislatures increased dramatically, especially in the North.
Source: Adapted from Jackson T. Main, "Government by the People: The American Revolution and the Democratization of the Legislatures." *William and Mary Quarterly,* 3d ser., vol. 23 (1966).

taught . . . that they are not able to govern themselves." He and other conservative Patriots feared that popular rule would lead to the tyranny of legislative majorities, allowing ordinary citizens to use their numerical advantage to tax the rich. By 1778 prosperous Anglican merchants in Philadelphia had founded a Republican Society to lobby for repeal of their state's constitution.

For these merchants and many other Americans in the late eighteenth century, republicanism meant representative government run by men of wealth and "civic virtue." It did not mean "democracy," which they feared would lead to "mob rule"—with the entire people of a city or town meeting together in great undisciplined assemblies and crushing anyone who opposed their will. Consequently they denounced the broad suffrage prescribed by the Pennsylvania constitution of 1776 and assailed its unicameral legislature as little better than direct popular rule; as John Adams remarked, it was "so democratical that it must produce confusion and every evil work." To dissuade Patriots in other states from following Pennsylvania's example, Adams composed his *Thoughts on Government* (1776). In this treatise he celebrated the British Whig theory of mixed government (in which power was divided among the king, lords, and commons) and adapted this Whig system to a republican society. Rather than concentrating authority in a single-house assembly, as in Pennsylvania, Adams wanted to disperse power by creating a *bicameral* (two-house) legislature in which men of property in the upper house would check the excesses of popularly elected majorities in the lower house. As a further curb on popular rule, he proposed an elected governor with the power to veto laws and an appointed—not elected—judiciary to review them. By assigning the different functions—lawmaking, administering, and judging—to separate branches of the government, Adams argued, his plan would preserve liberty.

Leading Patriots endorsed Adams's plan both because they feared a democratic system in which ordinary men would determine public policy and because his proposal called for governments that resembled those of the colonial period while remedying their deficiencies. Consequently most states adopted constitutions that provided for bicameral legislatures in which membership in both houses was elective. Recalling the arbitrary conduct of royal governors, most state constitutions also reduced the powers of the executive; only three—New York, Massachusetts, and New Hampshire—gave veto power to the governor. In addition, New York's constitution of 1777, written chiefly by John Jay (with a copy of Adams's *Thoughts on Government* by his side), limited suffrage by property qualifications so that only 40 percent of white men were eligible to vote for the governor and members of the upper house.

But the most flagrant use of property qualifications to maintain elite power occurred in South Carolina. That state's constitution of 1778 required candidates for governor to have a debt-free estate of £10,000 (about $450,000 today), senators to be worth £2,000 (about $90,000), and assemblymen to have property valued at £1,000 (about $45,000). These provisions ruled out officeholding for about 90 percent of the white adult population; high property qualifications similarly restricted voting to a minority of South Carolina's white men.

Toward a Democratic Political System. Nonetheless, post-Revolutionary politics revealed a democratic tinge (Figure 7.1). As in Pennsylvania, most state constitutions apportioned seats in the lower houses of the legislatures on the basis of population, giving small-holding farmers in western areas the representation they had long demanded. Indeed, backcountry delegates showed their power by transferring the capitals of various states from merchant-dominated seaports such as New York City and Philadelphia to inland cities such as Albany and Harrisburg. Even conservative South Carolina moved its seat of government inland, from Charleston to Columbia.

Moreover, most of the state legislatures were filled by new sorts of political leaders. During the war Patriot militiamen in Philadelphia had asserted a right to elect

John and Abigail Adams
Both Adamses had strong personalities. In 1794, John fondly accused his wife of being
a "Disciple of Wollstonecraft," but Abigail's commitment to legal equality for women
long predated Wollstonecraft's *A Vindication of the Rights of Woman* (1792).
Boston Athenaeum; New-York State Historical Association.

their officers on a regular basis, "for annual election is so essentially necessary to the Liberty of Freemen." Subsequently many veterans, whether or not they had property, demanded the right to vote in regular elections and no longer automatically elected their social betters; rather, one New York observer noted, they often chose men of "middling circumstances" who knew "the wants of the poor." By the mid-1780s, smallholding farmers and urban artisans controlled the lower houses in most northern states and formed a sizable minority in southern assemblies. Flexing their new political muscles, these "middling men" took the lead in opposing the collection of back taxes and other measures that, they said, tended "toward the oppression of the people."

The political legacy of the Revolution was complex. Conservative Patriots such as John Adams blunted the edge of the democratic movement in that the structure of most political institutions remained conservative. Only in Pennsylvania—and Vermont, which copied Pennsylvania's constitution—were radical Patriots able to take power and create democratic governmental institutions. Yet everywhere, the day-to-day politics of electioneering and interest-group bargaining became much more responsive to the demands of ordinary property-holding white men.

The Political Status of Women.   Equally important, the extraordinary excitement of the years between 1776 and 1800 tested the dictum that only men could engage in politics. While men continued to control all public institutions—legislatures, juries, government offices—upper-class women entered into political debate, filling their letters and diaries (and undoubtedly their conversations) with opinions on public issues. "The men say we have no business [with politics]," Eliza Wilkinson of South Carolina complained in 1783, "but I won't have it thought that because we are the weaker sex as to bodily strength we are capable of nothing more than domestic concerns. They won't even allow us liberty of thought, and that is all I want."

American women did not demand complete political or social equality with men, but many did want to end discriminatory customs and legal rules. Abigail Adams insisted on equal legal rights for married women, pointing out that under existing common law they could not own most forms of property and could not enter into contracts or initiate lawsuits without their husbands' action. "Men would be tyrants" if they continued to hold such power over women, Adams declared to her husband, John, criticizing him and other Patriots for "emancipating all nations" from monarchical despotism while "retaining absolute power over Wives" (see American Voices, "Abigail and John Adams: The Status of Women," p. 215).

The most famous call for equality of the sexes—in public life as well as in legal rights—came not from America but from Britain. In 1792 Mary Wollstonecraft,

ABIGAIL AND JOHN ADAMS
The Status of Women

★

Most American women of European descent accepted the subordinate status of their sex; it was the way life had always been and, many believed, the way God intended it to be. Yet the rhetoric of liberty and equality prompted a few women, including Abigail Adams, the wife of the prominent Massachusetts Patriot John Adams, to challenge men's dominant position. However, as this exchange between the Adamses suggests, most of these challenges were very tentative and very brief.

March 31, 1776   Abigail Adams to John Adams
I long to hear that you have declared an independancy—and by the way in the new Code of Law . . . be more generous and favorable to [the Ladies] than your ancestors. Do not put such unlimited power into the hands of Husbands. Remember all Men would be tyrants if they could. If perticuliar care and attention is not paid to the Ladies we are determined to foment a Rebellion, and will not hold ourselves bound by any Laws in which we have no voice, or Representation. . . . Men of Sense in all Ages abhor those customs which treat us only as the vassals of your Sex. Regard us then as Beings placed by providence under your protection. . . .

April 14, 1776   John Adams to Abigail Adams
As to your extraordinary Code of Laws, I cannot but laugh. We have been told that our Struggle [for independence] has loosened the bonds of Government every where. That Children and Apprentices were disobedient—that schools and Colledges were grown turbulent—that Indians slighted their Guardians and Negroes grew insolent to their Masters. But your letter was the first Intimation that another Tribe more numerous and powerful than all the rest were grown discontented. . . .

Depend on it, We know better than to repeal our Masculine System. Altho they are in full Force, you know they are little more than Theory. We dare not exert our Power in its full Latitude. We are obliged to go fair, and softly, and in Practice you know We are the subjects. We have only the Name of Masters, and rather than give up this, which would compleatly subject Us to the Despotism of the Peticoat, I hope General Washington, and all our brave Heroes would fight. . . .

May 7 and August 14, 1776   Abigail Adams to John Adams
Notwithstanding all your wise Laws and Maxims we have it in our power not only to free ourselves but to subdue our Masters, and without violence to throw both your natural and legal authority at our feet—

"Charm by accepting, by submitting sway
Ye have our Humour most when we obey."

I most sincerely wish that some more liberal plan might be laid or executed for the Benefit of the rising Generation, and that our new constitution may be distinguished for Learning and Virtue. If we mean to have Heroes, Statesmen and Philosophers, we should have learned women. The world would laugh at me, and accuse me of vanity, But you I know have a mind too enlarged and liberal. . . . If much depends as is allowed upon the early Education of youth and the first principles which are instilld take the deepest root, great benifit must arise from litirary accomplishments in women.

Source: Lyman H. Butterfield, ed., *Adams Family Correspondence,* 4 vols. (Cambridge, MA: Harvard University Press, 1963), vol 1: 370, 382–383, 402–403; vol. 2: 94.

a British republican influenced by the French Revolution, published the pathbreaking manifesto *A Vindication of the Rights of Woman.* Reasoning from liberal ideals of natural rights and republican principles of civic equality, she demanded equal status for women in all public and political activities. Those American women who knew of Wollstonecraft generally condemned her sexually adventurous personal life but respected her political arguments.

American men generally treated the *Rights of Woman* with a disdain born of a lack of understanding, for they were unwilling to reassess their own dominant social position. Most husbands remained patriarchs; even men who embraced the republican ideal of

Judith Sargent (Murray), Age Nineteen
The well-educated daughter of a wealthy Massachusetts merchant, Judith Sargent enjoyed a privileged childhood. She endured a difficult seventeen-year marriage to John Stevens, a bankrupt who fled from his creditors and died in the West Indies. In 1788 she wed the Reverend John Murray, who became a leading American Universalist. Her portrait, painted around 1771 by the renowned artist John Singleton Copley, captures Murray's skeptical view of the world, an outlook that enabled her to question customary gender roles.
Private Collection. Photo courtesy Frick Art Reference Library.

"companionate" marriage—in which wives shared in decision making—did not support a public role for women. A partial exception was New Jersey. Its constitution of 1776 granted suffrage to *all* free adult inhabitants worth £50. This ambiguous phrasing was apparently intentional—chosen perhaps by men who felt the vote should be extended to propertied widows, who, as heads of households, were almost as independent as propertied men. But when a significant number of widows (and never-married propertied women) began to exercise this option, the New Jersey legislature redefined the franchise, bestowing voting rights in 1807 on all white men who paid taxes and excluding property-owning women.

Ultimately, the republican belief in the need for an educated citizenry provided an avenue for the most important advances made by American women during the Revolutionary era. In her 1779 essay "On the Equality of the Sexes" (published in 1790), Judith Sargent Murray, the well-educated daughter of a Massachusetts merchant, advocated the expansion of women's education. Systematically comparing the intellectual facul-

ties of men and women, Murray argued that women had an equal capacity for memory and a superior imagination. She conceded that most women were inferior to men in judgment and reasoning, but only because of a lack of training. "We can only reason from what we know," Murray pointed out, and most women had been denied "the opportunity of acquiring knowledge." Her goal was no less than "the female right to that *equality with their brethren which . . . is assigned them in the Order of Nature.*"

Such arguments yielded both short-term and long-term effects. In the 1790s the attorney general of Massachusetts persuaded a jury that girls had an equal right to schooling under the state constitution. With greater access to public elementary schools and new private female academies, many young women became literate, knowledgeable, and intellectually prepared for a role in public life. By 1850 as many women as men in the northeastern states would be able to read and write, and literate women would again challenge their subordinate legal and political status.

The Articles of Confederation

As the Patriots moved toward independence in 1776, they envisioned a central government with limited powers. Carter Braxton of Virginia thought the Continental Congress should have the authority over foreign affairs, regulating matters of "trade, war, peace, alliances, &c.," but "should by no means have authority to interfere with the internal police [governance] or domestic concerns of any Colony."

This outlook informed the Articles of Confederation, America's first national constitution, which was passed by Congress in November 1777 and essentially made permanent the ad hoc authority exercised by the various Continental Congresses. The Articles provided for a loose association in which "each state retains its sovereignty, freedom, and independence" as well as all powers and rights not "expressly delegated" to the central government. Most delegated powers pertained to diplomacy and defense: the Articles gave the Confederation the authority to declare war and peace, make treaties with foreign nations, adjudicate disputes between the states, borrow and print money, and requisition funds from the states "for the common defense or general welfare." These powers were to be exercised by a central legislature, the Congress, in which each state had one vote regardless of its wealth or population. There was no separate executive branch or judiciary. Important laws needed approval by at least nine of the thirteen states, and changes in the Articles required unanimous consent.

Because of disputes over western lands, the Articles were not ratified by all the states until 1781. States with no claims to land in the West, such as Maryland and

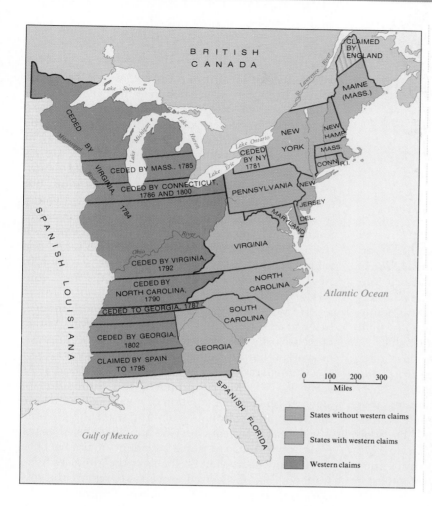

MAP 7.1

The Confederation and Western Land Claims
The Confederation Congress resolved the conflicting land claims of the states by creating a "national domain" to the west of the Appalachian Mountains. From 1781 to 1802 all the seaboard states with western land claims ceded them to the national government. The Confederation Congress established territories with democratic political institutions in this domain and declared that all of those territories were to be open to settlement by citizens from every state.

Pennsylvania, refused to approve the Articles until Virginia and other states that did have such claims (usually based on royal charters that defined their boundaries as stretching to the Pacific Ocean) agreed to relinquish them to Congress to create a common national domain in the West. Threatened by Lord Cornwallis's army in 1781 (see Chapter 6), Virginia finally agreed to give up its land claims, and Maryland, the last holdout, then ratified the Articles (Map 7.1 shows dates of the actual cessions).

The Ongoing Fiscal Crisis. Indeed, formal ratification of the Articles was anticlimactic, because the Congress had been exercising de facto constitutional authority for four years, and with considerable success. It raised the Continental army, negotiated the Franco-American alliance of 1778, and directed the successful war effort. The Confederation's weakness stemmed primarily from its limited fiscal powers. Lacking the authority to impose taxes, the Congress had to requisition funds from the state legislatures and hope they would pay. Most states failed to do so because they had their own wartime debts to pay and were unwilling to

impose heavier taxes on their citizens. Worried in 1780 that the Confederation would go bankrupt, General Washington called urgently for a national system of taxation, warning Patriot leaders that otherwise "our cause is lost."

In response, nationalist-minded members of Congress campaigned to expand the Confederation's authority. Robert Morris, who became superintendent of finance in 1781, persuaded Congress to charter the Bank of North America, a private institution in Philadelphia, hoping to use its notes to stabilize the inflated Continental currency. In concert with Gouverneur Morris of New York (see American Lives, "Gouverneur Morris: An Elitist Liberal in a Republican Age," pp. 218–219), he also developed a comprehensive financial plan that apportioned some war expenses among the states while centralizing control of army expenditures and foreign debt. Morris hoped that the existence of a national debt would draw attention to the Confederation's need for the authority to impose an import duty.

But Morris and other nationalists faced resistance to their plans to increase the Confederation's powers,

Gouverneur Morris: An Elitist Liberal in a Republican Age

———★———

THE AMERICAN REVOLUTION was significant on many levels, and the life of Gouverneur Morris (1752–1814) reveals its complexity. Born into the New York aristocracy, Morris had an acute understanding of the dangers to his class posed by a "democratic" revolution supported by social nobodies such as George Robert Twelves Hewes (see Chapter 5, American Lives, pp. 166–167). In 1774, at the tender age of twenty-two, Morris advised the New York elite "to seek for reunion with the parent state." Otherwise, "I see, and I see it with fear and trembling, that . . . we shall be under the worst of all possible dominions . . . the domination of a riotous mob." "The mob begin to think and reason," he warned again in 1775 after watching a debate between radical tradesmen and conservative Patriot merchants. "Poor reptiles! it is with them a vernal [spring] morning, . . . they bask in the sunshine, and ere noon they will bite, depend on it."

Family background had a lot to do with Morris's disdain of ordinary men and women. His grandfather, Lewis Morris, was the first lord of "Morrisania," a large estate in Westchester County, New York, and the king's governor of New Jersey from 1738 to 1746. His father, Lewis Jr., was also a royal official, serving as a judge of the vice-admiralty court of New York. On his deathbed Lewis Jr. gave instructions that Gouverneur, a younger son, should have "the best Education that is to be had in Europe or America." So the young man studied at the Academy of Philadelphia and King's College in New York, and then took up an apprenticeship with William Smith Jr., an eminent New York lawyer. Highly privileged but lacking inherited wealth, the young lawyer would need to use his social connections and personal talents—a fine mind, sophisticated manners, and great personal charm—to make his own way in the world.

The dispute with Britain forced Gouverneur Morris to make a fateful decision. Breaking with his mother, many relatives, and Smith, his legal mentor, who remained loyal to the Crown, Morris became a Patriot. In 1775 he won election to the Patriot Provincial Congress of New York and did his best to shape the course of the revolutionary struggle. At the Provincial Convention that drafted New York's relatively conservative state constitution of 1777, Morris argued strenuously for maintaining the old aristocratic method of voting by public declaration, but more republican-minded members mandated voting by ballot. Still, the convention heeded Morris's call to impose high property qualifications for voting: a freehold worth £20 to vote for the assembly, and one valued at £100 to vote for the senate or governor. In New York Morris was a republican of the most conservative stripe.

He was equally active—but much more innovative—in Patriot politics at the national level. As one of New York's delegates to the Continental Congress, he worked hard to remedy the financial weakness of the Confederation and to enhance its authority. As early as 1778 Morris proposed the elimination of state currencies, the creation of a national domain in the West, and national tariffs to pay off the growing war debt. Three years later he happily enlisted as the assistant to the new superintendent of finance, the merchant Robert Morris. Together the Morrises (who were not related) devised measures to restore the government's credit. In 1781 they won approval for the Bank of North America; in the following year they issued a "Report on Public Credit" that called for the Confederation government to assume the entire national debt, issue new interest-bearing debt certificates, and impose tariffs and internal taxes to pay the interest costs. Here in outline was the fiscal program implemented a decade later by Alexander Hamilton.

Like Hamilton, Gouverneur Morris was a man of "spirit and nerve" (according to George Washington) who never doubted his own judgment and rarely respected that of others. Washington chastised Morris for displaying his "brilliant imagination" too quickly and recklessly, and a French aristocrat predicted that "his [air of] superiority, which he has taken no pains to conceal, will prevent his ever occupying an important place" in republican America. Never humbled, not even by an accident in 1780 that left him with a wooden leg, Morris used charm and brilliance to compensate for these flaws in his character. He played a prominent role at the Philadelphia convention in 1787, insisting that "property was the sole or primary object of Government & Society." To protect property rights, Morris argued for an elitist Senate whose

Gouverneur Morris, Federalist Statesman
Morris almost became a Loyalist because he was a snob who liked privilege and feared the people ("The mob begins to think and reason," he once noted with disdain), and for similar reasons he became a Federalist, helping to write the Philadelphia Constitution and strongly supporting the Federalist Party.
National Portrait Gallery, Smithsonian Institution/Art Resource, NY.

members would serve without pay and for life, a national freehold property qualification for voting, and a strong president with the power of the veto.

But Morris rejected the legitimacy of two traditional types of property rights—the feudal dues paid by tenants to landowners, and the ownership of slaves. In debates in 1777 over the New York constitution Morris had argued for "abolishing all quit rents within this State." He also called for the end of "domestic slavery . . . so that in future ages, every human being who breathes the air of the State, shall enjoy the privileges of a freeman," a proposition he reiterated with great force at the Philadelphia convention.

Morris's defense of freedom for individuals—in their personal lives, their rights over property, their ability to form legal contracts—aligned him with those Patriots who gave a "classical liberal" definition to the American Revolution, and it placed him at odds with Patriots who gave greater weight to "classical republican" values of public virtue and the public good. Valuing individual liberty more highly than the public good as determined by majority rule, liberal Patriots such as Morris hoped the new Constitution would protect property rights from popularly elected state legislatures and encourage economic growth.

Indeed, Morris's outlook—and increasingly his life—reflected the emergent principles of a free-market capitalism that claimed immunity from governmental regulation. After serving as Robert Morris's assistant, Gouverneur became his business partner. The two men invested jointly in land in New York and Pennsylvania, a maritime venture in Massachusetts, and the sale of tobacco to the French tobacco monopoly. Such speculations landed Robert Morris in debtor's prison but made Gouverneur Morris a rich man, able at last to live in the elegant style to which he had been bred.

Beginning in 1788, Morris resided in Europe for ten years, first as a speculating merchant, then as the American minister to France (1792–1794), and finally as a cultured man of independent wealth. Fluent in French, polished in manners, confident of his talents, Morris fit easily into Parisian high society. He took as his mistress the young wife of an aging aristocrat, formed a lifelong friendship with the formidable Madame de Staël (a leading figure in Paris society), and came to share the hopes and fears of the endangered French monarch and his aristocratic supporters. While disparaging the French nobility for "Hugging the Privileges of Centuries long elapsed," Morris refused to support the constitutional monarchy proposed by the Marquis de Lafayette and other republican-minded French reformers, declaring that he was "opposed to the Democracy from Regard to Liberty." Indeed, as republicans seized control of France in 1792, Morris joined an unsuccessful aristocratic plot to smuggle King Louis XVI out of Paris.

In the end Gouverneur Morris stands forth as an elitist liberal, an American precursor of Alexis de Tocqueville (see Chapters 8 and 11, Voices from Abroad). Patrician in manners and fearful of mob rule, Morris was a political conservative, arguing that men of property and status should govern the new American republic. More democratic in his economic views, he celebrated the classical liberal principles of personal freedom, entrepreneurial enterprise, and equal opportunity.

which required the unanimous consent of the states. In 1781 the Rhode Island legislature rejected Morris's proposal for a national *tariff*, an import duty of 5 percent on foreign goods. Two years later the New York legislature refused to accept a similar plan, pointing out that in the 1760s it had opposed British import duties and would not now accept them from Congress. In another setback to Morris's plan, each state began to assume its share of the national debt by paying interest on it directly to its own citizens rather than by sending funds to Congress. By 1786 Pennsylvania, Maryland, New York, and New Jersey had assumed nearly one-third of the national debt, showing that the Confederation was essentially a league of states, not a powerful government in its own right.

Western Lands and the Northwest Ordinance. Despite its limited powers, Congress successfully planned the settlement of the trans-Appalachian West, which it had acquired as a result of the Treaty of Paris and the cessions of states. Congress wanted to assert the Confederation's clear title to this great treasure in order to sell it and raise revenue for the government. Consequently in 1783 Congress began to negotiate with resident Indian tribes, hoping to persuade them that the Treaty of Paris had extinguished their land rights. The Congress also bargained with white squatters who had set up farms, allowing them to stay only if they paid for their lands.

Congress was also determined to bind these western settlements firmly to the United States by providing for their eventual admission to the Union. Given the natural barrier of the Appalachian Mountains, many members of Congress feared that westerners might establish separate republics or even link up with Spanish Louisiana. The danger was real: in 1784 thousands of settlers—"white savages," John Jay called them—set up a new state, Franklin, in what is now eastern Tennessee. To preserve its authority over the West, Congress refused to recognize the state of Franklin or consider its application to join the Confederation. Instead, the delegates directed the states of Virginia, North Carolina, and Georgia to supervise the sale of lands and the creation of new states south of the Ohio River—a process that resulted in the transmission of slavery and other institutions of those southern states into the newly settled region.

To the north of the Ohio River, Congress established a national domain, the Northwest Territory, and issued three ordinances for its settlement and administration. The Ordinance of 1784, written by Thomas Jefferson, called for the admission of states carved out of the territory as soon as their populations equaled that of the smallest existing state. To deter squatters, the Land Ordinance of 1785 established a grid survey-

ing system and specified that the lands be surveyed before settlement (see Map 8.2). Land was to be sold in fee simple (a form of tenure giving the purchaser all ownership rights) and mostly in large blocs, a provision that favored large-scale investors and speculators. The ordinance also earmarked funds from the sale of some land for the support of public schools.

Finally, the Northwest Ordinance, which Congress devised in 1787, provided for the creation of three to five territories, which would eventually become the states of Ohio, Indiana, Illinois, Michigan, and Wisconsin. Reflecting the Enlightenment social philosophy of Thomas Jefferson and many other Patriots, the new ordinance prohibited slavery in those territories. It specified that each new territory be ruled by a governor and judges appointed by Congress. Once the number of free adult men reached 5,000, settlers could elect their own legislature. When the population grew to 60,000, residents could write a republican constitution and apply to join the Confederation. Once admitted, a new state would enjoy all the rights and privileges of the existing states, a provision that explicitly rejected the "colonial" model for new settlements used by Britain and other European governments.

In many respects the land ordinances of the 1780s were a great achievement, because they provided for the orderly settlement of the area to the north of the Ohio River and reduced the prospect of secessionist movements throughout the West. The Northwest Ordinance also acknowledged for the first time the validity of native American property rights in this region, stating that Indian "lands and property shall never be taken from them without their consent" (a provision whose spirit would be consistently violated in subsequent decades; see Chapter 8). By turning the attention of white Americans to the West, the ordinances added a new dimension to the national identity. The United States was no longer confined to thirteen governments on the eastern seaboard; it had space to expand.

The Postwar Crisis

Success was far from guaranteed, however, and the 1780s was the first of two critical decades for the new nation. Peace had brought recession rather than prosperity. The war had destroyed many American merchant ships and cut the export of tobacco and other farm goods. Deprived of a subsidy from the British government, South Carolina's lucrative indigo industry nearly vanished. The British Navigation Acts, which once had nurtured colonial commerce, now barred Americans from trading with the British West Indies. And low-priced British manufactures flooded American markets, driving many artisans and wartime textile firms out of business. Responding to protests by artisans, the legislatures of New York, Rhode Island, Pennsylvania, and Massachusetts imposed tariffs on imported manufactures.

Economic Conflict. As the postwar recession lowered the American standard of living, the financial legacy of the war threatened to undermine the new state governments. Most states emerged from the conflict with worthless currencies and big debts. North Carolina owed its creditors $1.7 million, and Virginia was liable for $2.7 million in war bonds. Wealthy speculators had purchased many state debt certificates for far less than their face value. Now these shrewd and influential merchants and landowners advocated high taxes so that the states could redeem the bonds quickly and at full value.

As economic recession and high taxes pressed hard on debtors, they sought political relief. In South Carolina farmers won the passage of a law that prevented sheriffs from selling seized farms to repay debts; instead, creditors had to accept installment payments over a three-year period. Such prodebtor measures were controversial. David Ramsay, a physician and the future author of the well-known *History of the American Revolution* (1789), assailed the South Carolina legislature for undermining "the just rights of creditors." To avert similar prodebtor legislation and preserve elite rule in Maryland, Charles Carroll of Carrollton persuaded the landlord-dominated Maryland legislature to replace the customary poll tax, which bore hard on the yeomen farmers and poor tenants, with a graduated property tax. But when the Maryland House of Delegates enacted additional profarmer and prodebtor measures in 1785 and 1786, they were rejected by the more conservative state senate.

As James Madison of Virginia pointed out, these political struggles were not primarily between "the Class with, and Class without, property." The real battle was between wealthy merchants and landowners on the one hand and a larger coalition of middling farm owners, small-scale traders, and artisans on the other. Creditors might be angered by legislation favoring farmers and artisans, but prodebtor laws eased the financial strain and probably prevented a major social upheaval.

Shays's Rebellion. In Massachusetts, the lack of debtor-relief legislation provoked the first armed uprising in the new nation. When the war ended, merchants and creditors in eastern Massachusetts lobbied successfully for high taxes and against paper money. These procreditor policies facilitated rapid repayment of the state's war debt but undermined the fragile finances of farmers in newly settled areas. Creditors and sheriffs hauled delinquent farmers into court, saddled them

Daniel Shays and Job Shattuck
This woodcut was published in *Bickerstaff's Boston Almanack for 1787* by "Friends of Government," who attacked the rebel leaders as upstarts and demagogues. "Liberty is still the object I have in view," a Shaysite declared in reply, but the former Radical Sam Adams would have none of it: "The man who dares to rebel against the laws of a republic ought to suffer death." Shattuck was sentenced to death for treason but then pardoned. Shays fled to New York State, where he died in 1821, still a poor farmer.
National Portrait Gallery, Smithsonian Institution/Art Resource, NY.

with high legal fees, and threatened to imprison them for debt or repossess their property. In 1786 residents of western counties called public meetings to protest against high taxes and aggressive eastern creditors. Meanwhile, bands of angry farmers closed the courts by force and freed debtors and fellow protesters from jail. Resistance gradually grew into open defiance of the state government and then became armed revolt. When their protests were ignored by the state legislature, hundreds of farmers in western and central Massachusetts organized an army under the leadership of Daniel Shays, a former Continental army captain, and prepared to resist state authority.

As a struggle against taxes imposed by a nonlocal government, Shays's Rebellion resembled colonial resistance to the Stamp Act. "The people have turned against their teachers the doctrines which were inculcated to effect the late revolution," complained the conservative Massachusetts political leader Fisher Ames. But even the Radical Patriots of 1776 condemned the Shaysites' actions as anti-republican. "Those Men, who . . . would lessen the Weight of Government lawfully exercised must be Enemies to our happy Revolution and Common Liberty," charged Samuel Adams.

To preserve its authority, the Massachusetts legislature passed a Riot Act outlawing illegal assemblies. Governor James Bowdoin, supported by eastern merchants, equipped a strong fighting force to put down the rebellion and called for additional troops from the Continental Congress. A national army was not needed. Shays's army dwindled during the winter of 1786–1787, falling victim to freezing weather and inadequate supplies, and Bowdoin's military force easily dispersed the rebels.

The collapsed rebellion provided graphic proof that the costs of war and the fruits of victory were not being shared evenly. Many of those who had fought for independence from Britain felt they had exchanged one tyranny for another. Massachusetts voters turned Governor Bowdoin out of office, and farmers in New York, northern Pennsylvania, Connecticut, New Hampshire, and Vermont (admitted as a state in 1791) closed courthouses, demanding economic relief.

These events shocked many leading Patriots. State economies were in disarray, the Confederation government was nearly bankrupt, and political conflicts over taxes and debts had erupted in almost every state. British officials in Canada predicted the imminent demise of the United States, and many Americans feared that they might be right. "I am really more distressed by the posture of our public affairs, than I ever was by the most gloomy appearances during the war," confessed William Livingston of New Jersey. In these dire times politicians with a nationalist outlook redoubled their efforts to create a stronger central government.

The Constitution of 1787

★

From the moment of its creation, the Constitution was a controversial document. Written in a time of crisis, it embodied the values and interests of men with a personal stake in its outcome. But, reflecting the intellectual talents of the framers and intense arguments over political principles, the Constitution was also a well-reasoned and innovative contribution to the centuries-long debate over republican political theory. And it addressed in a creative fashion the specifically American issue of federalism: the distribution of power between the states and the central government.

The Rise of a Nationalist Faction

The prime loyalty of the Patriots who led the fight against Great Britain was to particular states, so in forming the Confederation they tried to maximize the status of the states as independent republics. Like pre-1763 British imperial rule, the Confederation govern-

ment had minimal authority over the states and their internal affairs. Having restored power to the local legislatures, Patriots such as Patrick Henry and Sam Adams were content. New state-based leaders, such as Governor George Clinton of New York, shared their localist perspective and opposed a stronger central authority.

But other American Patriots favored a stronger national government. Prominent among these leaders were the military officers, diplomats, and officials who had served in the Continental Congress and acquired a "national" outlook. They included those of mature years, such as General Washington, the financier Robert Morris, and the diplomats Benjamin Franklin, John Jay, and John Adams. And they drew energy from younger men, such as Alexander Hamilton and James Madison, who had a vision of American grandeur. The nationalists thought "continentally," as Hamilton put it, and they advocated a government that would safeguard the nation's credit by imposing tariffs. They worried that Shays's Rebellion would undermine the promise of republicanism. "What a triumph for the advocates of despotism," lamented Washington, "to find that we are incapable of governing ourselves."

During the 1780s the nationalists had struggled hard to enhance the authority and the scope of the Confederation government but had been stymied at almost every turn. First the Rhode Island and then the New York legislature vetoed proposed national tariffs on imports. Then Congress's attempt to negotiate commercial treaties ran afoul of regional interests: southern planters insisted on free trade agreements while northern merchants, artisans, and manufacturers insisted that the agreements protect their economic interests. Rebuffed at the national level, they persuaded state governments in New York, Massachusetts, and Pennsylvania to provide shipping subsidies and impose tariffs on imported goods. The "stubborn Dignity" of the states, a nationalist complained, "will never permit a federal Government to exist."

By 1786 the nationalists were increasingly worried about the creditworthiness of the state governments and the private debts owed by their citizens. Legislatures in Virginia and other southern states had granted tax relief to various groups, diminishing public revenue and delaying the redemption of state debts. Public creditors feared that their government-issued bonds would become worthless; as Charles Lee of Virginia lamented, taxpayers were being led to believe "they will never be compelled to pay." State governments had also jeopardized the repayment of private debts by providing relief to hard-pressed debtors—delaying the collection of private debts or exempting personal property from legal seizure. Four states had gone much further, forcing merchants and creditors to accept depreciated paper currency in payment for debts. "The debtor interest . . . operates in all the forms of injustice & oppression," a South Carolina creditor complained. "While men are madly accumulating enormous debts, their legislators are making provisions for their nonpayment."

To address trade issues, James Madison and other nationalists persuaded the Virginia legislature to issue a call for a special convention to discuss tariff and taxation policies. Although nine state legislatures responded positively, only five—New York, New Jersey, Pennsylvania, Delaware, and Virginia—sent commissioners to the meeting in Annapolis, Maryland, in September 1786. Undaunted, the commissioners called for another meeting in Philadelphia to undertake a broad review of the problems facing the Confederation. Frightened by Shays's Rebellion, which was then in full swing, nationalist-minded politicians in Congress secured a resolution approving the Philadelphia convention and calling for a revision of the Articles of Confederation "adequate to the exigencies of government and the preservation of the Union." "Nothing but the adoption of some efficient plan from the Convention," a fellow nationalist wrote to James Madison, "can prevent anarchy first & civil convulsions afterwards."

Drafting a New National Constitution

By May 1787, fifty-five delegates had arrived in Philadelphia; they represented every state except Rhode Island, whose legislature opposed any increase in central authority. Some delegates, such as Benjamin Franklin and George Washington, had been leaders of the independence movement, but several other famous Patriots missed the convention. John Adams and Thomas Jefferson were in Europe, serving as the American ministers to Britain and France. Thomas Paine was also in Europe, and his fellow Radical Samuel Adams was not chosen as a delegate by the Massachusetts legislature. The Virginia firebrand Patrick Henry was selected but refused to attend because he favored a limited national government and "smelt a rat." The places of these "old Patriots" were taken by younger nationalists such as James Madison and Alexander Hamilton.

Most delegates to the Philadelphia convention came from the highest social ranks; they were merchants, slaveowners, and "monied men." There were no artisans, backcountry settlers, or tenants in attendance, and only a single yeoman farmer. Consequently most delegates supported creditors' property rights and favored a central government that would protect the republic from "the imprudence of democracy," as Hamilton put it.

The delegates began by electing Washington as the presiding officer. To forestall popular opposition, they

Portrait of James Madison, 1805–1807, Gilbert Stuart
A learned and thoughtful man, Madison was also a successful politician—especially in the decade beginning in 1785, when he helped to enact the Virginia Statute of Religious Liberty, became a prime architect and advocate of the Constitution of 1787, won passage of the Bill of Rights in the House of Representatives, and founded the Democratic-Republican Party.
Bowdoin College Museum of Art, Brunswick, ME. Bequest of James Bowdoin III.

decided to deliberate behind closed doors. (In fact, Americans learned of the proceedings only in the 1840s, when Madison's notebooks were published.) The delegates agreed that each state would have one vote, as in the Confederation, and that a majority of states would decide any given issue. Then the delegates took the first step toward creating a new constitution by agreeing to consider the Virginia Plan, a scheme for a truly national government devised by James Madison.

The Virginia and New Jersey Plans. Madison had arrived in Philadelphia determined to fashion a new political order that would ensure government by men of high character. A graduate of Princeton, he had read classical and modern political theory and served in both the Confederation Congress and the Virginia assembly. His experience in Virginia had convinced him of the "narrow ambition" and lack of public virtue of many state political leaders. He wanted to design a national government that would inhibit petty factional disputes, what he called the "Vices of the Political System."

Madison's Virginia Plan differed from the Articles of Confederation in three crucial respects. First, it rejected state sovereignty in favor of the "supremacy of national authority": the central government would have the power to overturn state laws and "legislate in all cases to which the separate States are incompetent." Second, the plan called for a *national* republic that drew its authority directly from all the people and had direct power over them. As Madison explained, the new government would bypass the states, operating directly "on the individuals composing them." Third, the plan created a three-tier national government with a lower house elected by voters in the states, an upper house elected by members of the lower house, and an executive and judiciary chosen by the entire legislature.

From a political perspective, Madison's plan contained a fatal flaw. By assigning great power to the lower house, whose composition was based on population, it would have dramatically increased the influence of the larger states. Consequently delegates from the less populous states rejected the plan, for their states had enjoyed equal representation in the Confederation Congress. They feared, as a Delaware delegate put it, that the states with many inhabitants would "crush the small ones whenever they stand in the way of their ambitious or interested views."

To protect their interests, delegates from the small states rallied behind the New Jersey Plan devised by William Paterson. This plan had many nationalist aspects, for it gave the Confederation government the power to raise revenue, control commerce, and make binding requisitions on the states. But the New Jersey Plan preserved the equality of the states by limiting each state to one vote in a unicameral legislature, as in the Confederation. Delegates from the larger states refused to accept this provision, and after a month of debate a bare majority of the states voted to accept the Virginia Plan as the basis for further discussion.

This decision raised the prospect of a dramatically new constitutional system, prompting two New York representatives—Robert Yates and John Lansing—to accuse the delegates of exceeding their mandate and to leave the convention (see American Voices, "Robert Yates and John Lansing: A Protest against the Philadelphia Convention," p. 225). During the hot, humid summer of 1787 the remaining delegates met six days a week, debating lofty principles and considering a multitude of technical details. Experienced and realistic politicians, they knew that their plan had to be acceptable to existing political factions and social groups.

Pierce Butler of South Carolina invoked a classical Greek precedent: "We must follow the example of Solon, who gave the Athenians not the best government he could devise but the best they would receive."

The Great Compromise. Representation remained the central problem. To satisfy both large and small states, the Connecticut delegates suggested amending the Virginia Plan so that the upper house, the Senate, would always seat two members from each state, whereas seats in the lower chamber, the House of Representatives, would be apportioned on the basis of population. The size of each state's delegation would be determined every ten years on the basis of a national census. This "Great Compromise" over representation was accepted, but only after bitter debate; to some it seemed less a compromise than a victory for the smaller states.

Other state-related matters were soon settled by restricting (or leaving ambiguous) the extent of central authority. Some delegates opposed establishing national courts within the states, warning that "the states will revolt at such encroachments." The convention therefore defined the judicial power of the United States in broad terms, vesting it "in one supreme Court" and leaving the new national legislature to decide whether or not to establish lower courts within the states. The convention also decided against imposing a uniform freehold property qualification for voting, as Gouverneur Morris and other political conservatives proposed. "Eight or nine states have extended the right of suffrage beyond the freeholders," George Mason of Virginia pointed out in response. "What will people there say if they should be disfranchised?"

Ultimately the delegates devised ingenious ways to give the states a prominent role in the new constitutional structure. For example, they placed the selection of the relatively powerful chief executive of the national government in the hands of an *electoral college* that would be chosen on a state-by-state basis. And they specified that state legislatures, not the voters at large, would elect members of the Senate. By giving state governments an important role in the new constitutional system, the delegates hoped to encourage them to accept a reduction in their sovereignty.

Compromise over Slavery. Although slavery was not a prominent issue in the convention, it intruded into various debates and revealed important regional divisions. Although no one proposed the abolition of slavery, Gouverneur Morris of New York spoke for many northern delegates in condemning it as "a nefarious institution." George Mason, reflecting the outlook of many Chesapeake planters, who already had ample numbers of slaves, argued eloquently for prohibition of the Atlantic slave trade. But delegates from the rice-

ROBERT YATES AND JOHN LANSING

A Protest against the Philadelphia Convention

─────★─────

Robert Yates and John Lansing attended the Philadelphia Convention as delegates from New York but left in protest when the Virginia Plan became the basis for a new constitutional order. In a letter to the governor of New York, Yates and Lansing explained their reasons: the Convention lacked the authority to create the "consolidated" government implicit in the Virginia Plan, and a centralized system of rule would undermine civil liberties and republican principles of representative government. These Antifederalist arguments failed to prevent ratification of the Constitution, but they remained powerful and were restated by hundreds of American politicians—from the North as well as the South—for the next seventy years.

We beg leave, briefly, to state some cogent reasons, which, among others, influenced us to decide against a consolidation of the states. . . .

Our powers were explicit, and confined to the sole and express purpose of revising the Articles of Confederation. . . . [We believed] that a system of consolidated government could not, in the remotest degree, have been in contemplation of the legislature of this state; for that so important a trust, as adopting measures which tended to deprive the state government of its most essential rights of sovereignty, could not have been confided by implication. . . .

Reasoning in this manner, we were of opinion that the leading feature of every amendment ought to be the preservation of the individual states in their uncontrolled constitutional rights, and that, in reserving these, a mode might have been devised of granting to the Confederacy, the moneys arising from a general system of revenue, the power of regulating commerce and enforcing the observance of foreign treaties, and other necessary matters of less moment.

. . . we [also] entertained an opinion that a general government, however guarded by declarations of rights, or cautionary provisions, must unavoidably, in a short time, be productive of the destruction of the civil liberty of such citizens who could be coerced by it, by reason of the extensive territory of the United States, the dispersed situation of its inhabitants, and the insuperable difficulty of controlling or counteracting the views of a set of men (however unconstitutional and oppressive their acts might be) possessed of all the power of government, and who [were remote] . . . from their constituents. . . . [Moreover, we believed] that however wise and energetic the principles of the general government might be, the extremities of the United States could not be kept in due submission and obedience to its laws, at the distance of so many hundred miles from the seat of government;

[And finally] that, if the general legislature was composed of so numerous a body of men as to represent the interests of all the inhabitants of the United States, in the usual and true ideas of representation, the expense of supporting it would become intolerably burdensome; and that, if a few only were vested with a power of legislation, the interests of a great majority of the inhabitants of the United States must necessarily be unknown. . . . These reasons were, in our opinion, conclusive against any system of consolidated government.

─────

Source: J. Elliot, ed., *Debates in the Several State Conventions on the Adoption of the Constitution* (New York: 1861), vol. 1: 480–483.

growing states of South Carolina and Georgia insisted that slave imports continue, warning that otherwise their states "shall not be parties to the Union." At their insistence, the new constitution denied Congress the power to regulate slave imports for twenty years; thereafter the slave trade could be abolished by legislative action (which Congress proceeded to do in 1808).

For the sake of national unity, the delegates had decided to treat slavery as a political rather than a moral issue. To protect the property of southern slaveowners, they agreed to a "fugitive" clause that would enable masters to reclaim enslaved blacks (or white indentured servants) who had taken refuge in other states. To mollify northern antislavery sentiment, they declined to mention slavery explicitly in the Constitution (referring instead to citizens and "all other Persons"), thus denying the institution national legal status.

Another compromise resolved the slavery-related issues of taxation and representation. Southern delegates wanted to count slaves when determining a state's representation in Congress, for this would increase southern power in the national legislature. In defense of this demand, they pointed out that slaves were property and would be taxed as wealth if Congress enacted a direct tax, as the Constitution permitted. But northerners objected to calculating representation on the basis of total population. They argued that propertyless slaves, lacking the vote, were not full or active members of the republic and should not be counted at all. To resolve the issue, the delegates reached a compromise; they agreed that for the purposes of both representation *and* taxation, a slave would be counted as three-fifths of a free person. White southerners would thereby have more political power, but they would be subject to higher taxes.

National Power. Having resolved the three issues of representation in the upper and lower houses, the states' role in national elections, and the status of slavery, the delegates proceeded to create a powerful, pro-creditor central government. The final document declared that the Constitution and all national legislation and treaties made under its authority would be the "supreme" law of the land. It gave the central government broad powers over taxation, military defense, and external commerce as well as the authority to make all laws "necessary and proper" to implement those and other provisions. To establish the fiscal reputation of the central government and protect creditors, the Constitution mandated that the United States honor the existing national debt.

While enhancing national authority, the Constitution restricted the range of state powers, particularly in economic matters. The new charter prohibited state governments from issuing money, preventing them from using currency inflation to assist debtors. It also barred states from enacting any "Law impairing the Obligation of Contracts," thus prohibiting other types of debtor-relief legislation.

The proposed Constitution was not a "perfect production," Benjamin Franklin admitted on September 17, 1787, as he urged the forty-two delegates still present to sign it. Yet the great diplomat confessed his astonishment at finding "this system approaching so near to perfection as it does." His colleagues apparently agreed; all but three—George Mason and Edmund Randolph of Virginia, and Elbridge Gerry of Massachusetts—signed the document. Their handiwork would now be judged by their fellow Americans.

The Debate over Ratification

The procedures for ratifying the new Constitution were as controversial as the political issues raised by the document itself. The delegates hesitated to submit the Constitution to the state legislatures for their unanimous consent, as required by the Articles of Confederation, because they knew that Rhode Island and possibly a few other states would reject it. Instead, they specified that the Constitution would go into effect upon ratification by special conventions in at least nine of the thirteen states. The Confederation Congress, because of its nationalist sympathies, winked at this extralegal procedure. Surprisingly, so too did most state legislatures, which promptly arranged for the election of delegates to ratification conventions.

As the debate over the Constitution began, the nationalists seized the initiative with two bold moves. First, they called themselves "Federalists," a term that suggested a loose, decentralized system of government and partially obscured their quest for a strong central authority. Second, they launched a coordinated campaign to ratify the proposed Constitution, publishing dozens of pamphlets and newspaper articles.

The Antifederalists. The opponents of the Constitution, who became known as Antifederalists, came from diverse backgrounds and were less organized than the Federalists. Some, like Governor George Clinton of New York, enjoyed power in a state and did not want to lose it. Others were rural democrats who feared that the proposed national government would be powerful and, what was worse, be controlled by merchants and creditors. "These lawyers and men of learning and monied men expect to be managers of this Constitution," worried a Massachusetts farmer, "and get all the power and all the money into their own hands and then they will swallow up all of us little folks . . . just as the whale swallowed up Jonah."

Well-educated Americans with a traditional republican outlook also opposed the new system. To keep government "close to the people," they wanted the nation to remain a collection of small sovereign republics tied together only for trade and defense—not the "United States" but the "States United." Citing the French political philosopher Montesquieu, these Antifederalists argued that republican institutions were best suited to cities or small states. "No extensive empire can be governed on republican principles," James Winthrop of Massachusetts declared.

Winthrop and other Antifederalists worried that a strong national administration and a powerful president would restore the worst features of British rule—high taxes, an oppressive bureaucracy, and a standing army controlled by a tyrannical chief executive—thereby ending the state-based republican experiment of 1776. As George Mason of Virginia put it, the new charter was "totally subversive of every principle which has hitherto governed us. This power is calculated to annihilate totally the state governments."

To bolster their claim that the Constitution was antirepublican, Antifederalists focused on specific deficiencies. Melancton Smith of New York warned that the large electoral districts prescribed by the Constitution would give power to a few wealthy upper-class men, whereas "a representative body, composed principally of respectable yeomanry, is the best possible security to liberty." Patrick Henry called attention to the immense taxing authority of the central government and the powers enjoyed by the chief executive—who would appoint members of the national judiciary, veto legislation passed by Congress, and command the military forces, and who could be reelected to office indefinitely. "A great and mighty President" would "be supported in extravagant munificence," he predicted;

"the whole of our property may be taken by this American government, by laying what taxes they please, and suspending our laws at their pleasure." Most compelling of all, Antifederalists pointed out that the Constitution, unlike most state constitutions, lacked a bill of rights that protected liberty of conscience in religious matters, the right to a jury trial, and other basic liberties.

The Federalist. In New York, where ratification was hotly contested, James Madison, John Jay, and Alexander Hamilton countered these arguments in a series of newspaper articles collectively called *The Federalist*. Writing under the pen name of "Publius" ("the public voice"), they stressed the need for a strong government to conduct foreign affairs and insisted that central authority would not foster domestic tyranny. Citing Montesquieu's praise for "mixed government" (and drawing on John Adams's *Thoughts on Government)*, the

The First "White House"
In 1790, New York City became the home of the new national government. To keep the capital at New York, the city began to build an imposing mansion for the president. To symbolize the nation's commitment to republicanism, the architects gave the residence a classical columned facade like those of the Roman republic, creating a sharp contrast with nearby Dutch-influenced buildings. Shortly before the completion of the mansion, the national government moved to the District of Columbia, a federal territory created by cessions from Maryland and Virginia.
New-York Historical Society.

authors of *The Federalist* pointed out that the power of the national government would be divided among a president, a bicameral legislature, and a judiciary. Each branch of government would "check and balance" the others, thereby preserving liberty.

James Madison went further, making a significant contribution to the theory of representative government by denying that republicanism was suited only to small states. Indeed, in *The Federalist*, No. 10, Madison maintained that the sheer size of the American national republic would be its greatest protection against tyranny. It was "sown in the nature of man," Madison wrote, that individuals would seek power and form factions to advance their interests. Indeed, "a landed interest, a manufacturing interest, a mercantile interest, a moneyed interest, with many lesser interests, grow up of necessity in civilized nations." The task of government in a free society should not be to suppress those groups, the young Virginian argued, but to prevent any one of them from becoming dominant. And this end could best be achieved not in a small republic, as Montesquieu and James Winthrop had claimed, but in a large one. "Extend the sphere," Madison concluded with true brilliance, "and you take in a greater variety of parties and interests; you make it less probable that a majority of the whole will have a common motive to invade the rights of other citizens."

Madison's hardheaded realism—his classical liberal emphasis on self-interest as the source of human conduct—was tempered by a traditional republican belief in public virtue. "I go by this great republican principle," Madison told the Virginia ratifying convention, "that the people have virtue and intelligence to select men of virtue and wisdom."

The Ratification Conventions. Madison's hopes were tested in the ratifying conventions, which met in eleven states between December 1787 and July 1788 (Map 7.2). (North Carolina and Rhode Island were the exceptions; they ratified only in 1789 and 1790.) Unlike the men at the Philadelphia convention, the delegates elected to the state caucuses came from many social groups: untutored farmers, middling artisans, and well-educated gentlemen. Generally, delegates from the backcountry were Antifederalists, whereas those from the seacoast were Federalists. Thus in Pennsylvania a coalition of merchants, artisans, and commercial farmers from Philadelphia and its vicinity spearheaded an easy Federalist victory. Other early Federalist successes came in the less populous states of Delaware, New Jersey, Georgia, and Connecticut, where delegates counted on a strong national government to offset the power of their larger neighbors.

The Constitution's first real test came in January 1788 in Massachusetts, one of the most populous states and a hotbed of Antifederalist sentiment. Influential local-minded Patriots, including Samuel Adams and Governor John Hancock, opposed the new constitution, as did Shaysite sympathizers in the west. But Boston artisans, who wanted tariff protection from British imports, supported ratification, and astute Federalist politicians won over wavering delegates by promising a national bill of rights. By a close vote of 187 to 168, the Federalists carried the day.

Spring brought new Federalist victories in Maryland and South Carolina. When New Hampshire ratified in June (by 57 votes to 47), the required nine states had approved the Constitution. But the outcome was still in doubt, for the large and powerful states of Virginia and New York had not yet acted. Leading Federalists reiterated their promise to amend the Constitution with a bill of rights, addressing a powerful Antifederalist argument. In the end the Federalists won narrowly in Virginia, 89 to 79, and that success, along with the influence of *The Federalist*, carried them to victory in New York by the even smaller margin of 30 to 27.

Given their defeats during the 1780s, few Federalists had expected a more resounding victory. Working against great odds, they had created a national republic, a triumph that had profound political and social implications. The United States Constitution of 1787 re-created a strong central authority, partially reversing the autonomy won by the states during the war of independence. It also restored creditors and merchants to positions of power, undermining the political gains made by yeomen, artisans, and other ordinary citizens. The Revolutionary era had come to an end.

The Constitution Implemented

The Constitution expanded the dimensions of American political life, allowing voters to fill national as well as local and state offices. Within a decade a single political system tied together the interests and concerns of Georgia planters, Pennsylvania artisans, Massachusetts merchants, and scores of other social groups.

Devising the New Government. The Federalists swept the election of 1788. No fewer than forty-four of the ninety-one members of the first United States Congress had helped to write or ratify the Constitution; only eight Antifederalists won election. Most of those selected (by voters in the states) as members of the electoral college were also Federalists. As expected, they chose George Washington as president and gave John Adams the second highest number of votes, making him the vice-president. The two men took up their posts in New York City, the temporary home of the national government.

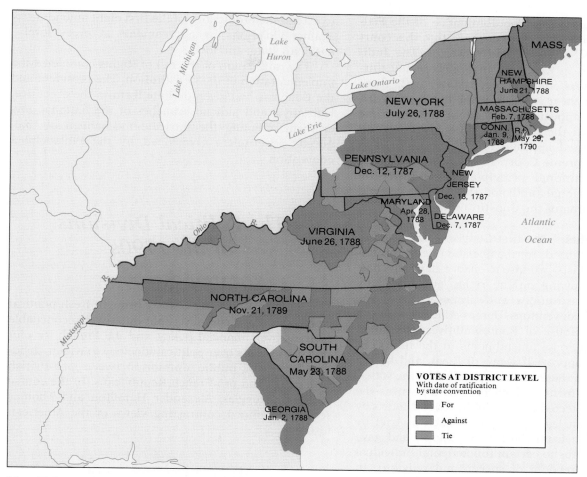

MAP 7.2
Ratifying the Constitution of 1787
In 1907 the geographer Owen Libby plotted the votes of the state ratification conventions on a map. He noted that most delegates from seaboard or commercial farming districts favored the Constitution, whereas those from backcountry areas opposed it. Subsequent research has confirmed Libby's socioeconomic interpretation in North and South Carolina and Massachusetts; however, other factors influenced delegates in some states with frontier districts, such as Georgia, where the Constitution was ratified unanimously.

Washington, the military savior of his country, became its political father as well, establishing many enduring institutions and practices. At age fifty-seven, he was a man of great personal dignity and influence. Instinctively cautious, he generally followed the administrative practices of the Confederation, asking Congress to reestablish the existing executive departments: Foreign Affairs (State), Finance (Treasury), and War. The president had the power, with the consent of the Senate, to appoint major officials. To head the Department of State, Washington chose Thomas Jefferson, a fellow Virginian and an experienced diplomat. For secretary of the Treasury he turned to Alexander Hamilton, a lawyer and wartime military aide. Although the Con-

stitution was silent on the issue, Washington also insisted that he had the sole authority to remove those officials, thus ensuring that he and future presidents would have exclusive control over the bureaucracy. The new president also designated Jefferson, Hamilton, and Secretary of War Henry Knox as his official *cabinet*, or advisory body (although the Constitution was silent on this matter as well).

The first Congress also played a crucially important role in determining the character of the national government, especially with respect to legal questions. Because the issue was so controversial, the Philadelphia convention had left it to Congress to establish the number, structure, and jurisdiction of the lower federal courts. The dominance of the Federalists in the first legislature ensured that this court system would be extensive and powerful. The Judiciary Act, passed by Congress in 1789, created thirteen *district courts*, one for each state, with three *circuit courts* to hear appeals from the district tribunals; further appeals would go to the Supreme Court, which had the final say. Moreover, the Judiciary Act permitted appeals from the various state courts to the Supreme Court, provided that the case involved constitutional principles. This provision ensured that national (and not state) judges would decide the meaning of the Constitution.

The Bill of Rights.   The first Congress also acted to provide legal safeguards for the liberties of citizens, fulfilling the Federalists' promise to enact a national charter of rights. Drawing on the rights guaranteed by various state constitutions and proposals from the states' ratifying conventions, James Madison, now a member of the House of Representatives, submitted nineteen constitutional amendments to the first Congress. Congress approved twelve of them, and by the end of 1791 ten of these had been ratified by the states. These ten amendments, which became known as the Bill of Rights, protected citizens in the federal courts by mandating certain legal procedures (such as trial by jury and freedom from self-incrimination), and gave constitutional status to certain fundamental individual rights (such as freedom of speech and religion). In addition, the Tenth Amendment prohibited the national government from claiming powers that were not delegated by the Constitution by explicitly reserving those powers to the states or the people.

As a political maneuver, the Bill of Rights yielded immediate results by quieting the fears of the Antifederalists and thus enhancing the legitimacy of the Constitution. As a safeguard against improper governmental authority, the amendments have had a complex history. Like all constitutional clauses and ordinary laws, they are subject to judicial interpretation, which has changed with time and circumstance. For example, the Second Amendment, which gives the people the right "to keep and bear Arms," has been interpreted by most twentieth-century courts to allow the states and Congress to forbid citizens from owning certain types of guns (such as automatic weapons) and to require the registration of others (such as handguns in cities). Moreover, in 1833 the Supreme Court (in the case of *Barron v. Baltimore*) declared that the amendments safeguarded rights only from infringement by the national government; for protection from state authorities, citizens would have to rely on the state constitutions. But nearly a century later, in the 1920s, federal courts began to use the Fourteenth Amendment (1868)

to extend the protections of the first eight amendments against violations by governments at every level—national, state, and local.

The ratification of the Bill of Rights completed the implementation of the Constitution. The president and the Congress had given definite form to the executive, legislative, and judicial branches of the national government, creating the intricate mechanism of "balanced" government envisioned by the Philadelphia convention.

The Political Divisions of the 1790s

The final decade of the century brought fresh political challenges. The Federalists split into two irreconcilable factions over financial policy, and the French Revolution caused rifts over political ideology to widen, dividing American public opinion between pro-British Federalists and pro-French Republicans. In the course of these struggles, Alexander Hamilton and Thomas Jefferson defined contrasting views of the American future.

Hamilton's Program

One of George Washington's most important decisions was his choice of Alexander Hamilton as secretary of the Treasury. An ambitious self-made man, Hamilton was the son of a Scottish merchant in the West Indies who soon abandoned the family. The precocious child learned the ways of trade from his shopkeeper mother, Rachel Faucett, and was apprenticed to a merchant firm. He moved to the mainland in 1772 and enrolled at King's College in New York. During the war Hamilton's military abilities and personal charm impressed Washington, who chose him as his personal aide. In the 1780s, Hamilton married the daughter of a wealthy Hudson River landowner and became a leading lawyer in New York City. At the Philadelphia convention Hamilton condemned the "amazing violence and turbulence of the democratic spirit," calling for an authoritarian government headed by a president with nearly monarchical powers.

As Treasury secretary, Hamilton devised bold policies that addressed the fiscal problems that had bedeviled the Confederation (Figure 7.2). Not surprisingly, his ambitious program favored his immediate acquaintances, many of them financiers and seaport merchants. He outlined his plan in three pathbreaking and

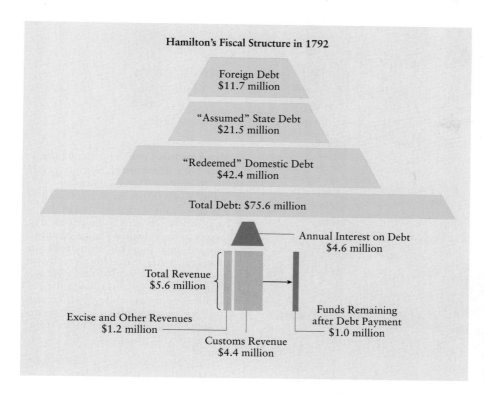

Hamilton's Fiscal Structure in 1792

Foreign Debt
$11.7 million

"Assumed" State Debt
$21.5 million

"Redeemed" Domestic Debt
$42.4 million

Total Debt: $75.6 million

Annual Interest on Debt
$4.6 million

Total Revenue
$5.6 million

Excise and Other Revenues
$1.2 million

Customs Revenue
$4.4 million

Funds Remaining
after Debt Payment
$1.0 million

FIGURE 7.2
Hamilton's Fiscal Structure, 1792
Alexander Hamilton used the revenue from excise taxes and customs duties to defray the annual interest on the national debt. He did not pay off the debt because he wanted to tie wealthy American bondholders to the new national government.

interrelated reports to Congress: on public credit (January 1790), a national bank (December 1790), and tariffs and manufactures (December 1791).

Public Credit. The financial and social implications of Hamilton's "Report on the Public Credit" made it instantly controversial. The report asked Congress to redeem at face value the millions of dollars in securities issued by the Confederation, a *redemption* plan that would bolster the government's credit but also provide windfall profits to speculators. For example, the merchant firm of Burrell & Burrell had paid about $600 for Confederation notes with a face value of $2,500; their redemption at face value would bring an enormous profit of $1,900. Moreover, Hamilton's plan involved a controversial *funding* system, for he proposed to pay off the Burrells and other noteholders with newly issued government securities, which would become a *permanent* national debt. Hamilton hoped that investors, attracted by the relatively high interest rate of about 6 percent per year, would hold (and not speculate with) the new securities, keeping their value high and enhancing the government's credit. The Treasury chief expected that these bonds would tie the financial interests of the wealthy Americans who invested in them to the new national government, thereby enhancing its authority.

Hamilton's plan for a permanent national debt funded by monied men reawakened Radical Whig and republican fears of scheming British financiers and governmental favoritism. "Money in a state of civilization is power," argued John Taylor of Virginia, who was wary of the rising wealth and power of the northern commercial elite. Speaking for the Virginia House of Burgesses, Patrick Henry declared that "to erect, and concentrate, and perpetuate a large monied interest, must prove fatal to the existence of American liberty."

James Madison opposed Hamilton's proposal on moral grounds. Madison wanted to do justice to the thousands of shopkeepers, farmers, and soldiers who had accepted government securities during the dark days of the war and then sold them to speculators. He proposed giving the present bondholders only "the highest price which has prevailed in the market," then distributing the remaining funds to the original owners. But identifying the original owners would have been difficult; furthermore, nearly half the members of the House of Representatives were owners of Continental or Confederation securities and stood to profit from Hamilton's plan. Melding practicality with self-interest, the House defeated Madison's proposal by a solid margin of 36 to 13. By way of protest, an angry citizen composed an ode, "On the Rejection of Mr. Madison's Motion":

A soldier's pay are rags and fame,
A wooden leg—a deathless name.
To specs, both in and out of Cong.
The four and six per cents belong.

***Membership Certificate from the
New York Mechanick Society, 1791***
"By Hammer & Hand, all Arts do
Stand" reads the motto at the top of
this certificate of membership in the
New York Mechanick Society. The first
members were divided almost equally
between the owners of substantial manufacturing enterprises (who hired wage
laborers to do the work) and independent artisans, who worked with their
families or employed a few journeymen
and apprentices. Both groups demanded
tariffs to protect their livelihoods from
lower-priced British goods.
Courtesy, Winterthur Museum.

Hamilton then advanced a second proposal that
favored wealthy creditors, an *assumption* plan by
which the national government would take over the
war debts of the states. This proposal unleashed the
flurry of speculation and governmental corruption that
critics of redemption had feared. Before Hamilton
announced it, Assistant Secretary of the Treasury
William Duer and other speculators used insider
knowledge to buy up over half of the depreciated war
bonds in various southern states; they sold these notes
after the announcement of Hamilton's assumption plan
caused bond values to rise.

Concerned members of Congress protested that
some state legislatures had already levied high taxes to
pay off their states' war debts. Responding to that argument, Hamilton modified his plan to reimburse those
states. Other representatives, particularly those from
Virginia and Maryland, argued that assumption would
further enhance the already excessive powers of the
national government. To quiet the fears of those representatives about a runaway central government, the
Treasury chief backed their bid to locate the national
capital (which the Constitution specified would consist
of a special "district") along the banks of the Potomac—
where they could easily watch its operations. Such
astute political bargaining gave Hamilton the votes he
needed in the House of Representatives to enact his
assumption plan.

The Bank of the United States. His confidence
bolstered by this success, in December 1790 Hamilton
asked Congress to charter a national financial institu-

tion, the Bank of the United States. The bank, to be
jointly owned by private stockholders and the
national government, would make loans to merchants, handle government funds, and issue financial
notes. Persuaded by Hamilton's arguments that the
bank would provide a sound currency for the specie-
starved American economy and make the new
national debt easier to fund, a majority in Congress
approved Hamilton's bill and sent it to the president
for approval.

At this critical juncture, Secretary of State Thomas
Jefferson joined ranks with Madison against Hamilton.
Jefferson had condemned the shady dealings in southern war bonds and the "corrupt squadron of paper deal-
ers" who had arranged them. Now he charged that
Hamilton's scheme for a national bank was unconstitu-
tional. "The incorporation of a Bank," Jefferson told
President Washington, was not "delegated to the United
States by the Constitution." Giving a *strict interpretation* to the national charter, Jefferson maintained that
the central government had only the limited powers
explicitly assigned to it in that document. In response,
Hamilton articulated a *loose interpretation*, noting that
Article 1, section 8, empowered Congress to make "all
Laws which shall be necessary and proper" to carry out
the Constitution's provisions. In the Treasury chief's
view, the Bank would assist the government to collect
taxes and pay its debts and therefore clearly fell "within
the compass of national authority." Washington agreed
with Hamilton and signed the legislation creating the
bank, a decision that prompted Jefferson to resign his
position as secretary of state.

Two Visions of America
Thomas Jefferson and Alexander Hamilton confront each other in these portraits, as they did during the political battles of the 1790s. Jefferson was pro-French; Hamilton, pro-British. Jefferson favored farmers and artisans; Hamilton supported merchants and financiers. Jefferson believed in democracy and rule by legislative majorities; Hamilton argued for a strong executive branch and for judicial review. But Hamilton's timely intervention in 1800 secured the presidency for his longtime political foe.
"Jefferson" by Rembrandt Peale © White House Historical Association/Photo by National Geographic Society; Yale University Art Gallery, Mabel Brady Garven Collection.

Tariffs and Manufactures. Hamilton now turned to the final element of his financial system: a national revenue that would be used to pay the interest on the permanent national debt. At his insistence, in 1792 Congress imposed a variety of internal taxes, including a duty on whiskey distilled in the United States. But the revenue from those internal levies was too small, a mere $1 million a year. To raise another $4–5 million, Hamilton asked Congress for modest increases in the schedule of tariffs on foreign goods enacted in 1789. At that time Congress had imposed a tax of 50 cents a ton on foreign ships entering American ports and a customs duty of 5 to 15 percent on the value of imported goods. By continuing to tax imports at a relatively low rate, Hamilton wanted to encourage the expansion of foreign trade. This would not only please his merchant allies but also increase the government's income from customs duties, which he desperately needed to pay interest on the national debt.

However, by using tariffs to raise revenue rather than to protect American industries, Hamilton undercut the arguments made in 1791 in his "Report on Manufactures." In that document, written jointly with Tench Coxe, a former secretary of the Pennsylvania Manufacturing Society, Hamilton had equated national power with self-sufficiency in manufactures and had advocated government assistance to enable American producers to compete with European firms. But because of his need for customs revenue, the Treasury chief now refused to assist manufacturers by imposing high tariffs that would cut foreign imports. As these European manufactures poured into the United States, customs revenue steadily increased (providing about 90 percent of the national government's income between 1792 and 1820), allowing him to fund his redemption and assumption programs.

Hamilton's carefully devised plan worked brilliantly. In less than two years he had restored public credit by creating a strikingly modern fiscal system in which a national bank and customs revenue provided the new government with financial stability.

Jefferson's Vision

Hamilton paid a high price for this success. By 1793, when Washington began his second four-year term as president, Hamilton's financial measures had split the Federalists into two irreconcilable factions. Most northern Federalists, in Congress and the states, adhered to the political alliance led by the Treasury chief, and most southerners joined a rival group headed by Madison and Jefferson. By the elections of 1794 the two factions had acquired names. Hamilton's supporters retained their original name: Federalists; Madison and Jefferson's supporters called themselves Democratic-Republicans, or simply Republicans.

Thomas Jefferson, a man of great learning as well as an able politician and diplomat, spoke for the southern planters and western farmers who became Republicans. As well read in architecture and scientific farming as in natural history and political theory, Jefferson embraced the optimistic spirit of the Enlightenment, declaring his

Machine Technology and Republican Values

★

Household Industry
This woodcut by Alexander Anderson shows the home as factory.
Miriam and Ira D. Wallach Division of Art, Prints and Photographs, The New York Public Library. Astor, Lenox and Tilden Foundations.

In 1805 the young American scientist Benjamin Silliman visited the industrial city of Manchester, England. He was impressed by the great factories, "the wonder of the world and the pride of England," but troubled by the degraded character of the workers—"at best an imbecile people," he wrote—and the unhealthy conditions in which they lived and worked. "Heaps of dung, rubble from buildings, putrid, stagnant pools are found here and there among the houses, and a sort of black smoke covers the city," another visitor reported. "Under this half daylight 300,000 human beings are ceaselessly at work. . . . The crunching wheels of machinery, the shriek of steam from boilers, the regular beat of the looms, the heavy rumble of the carts, these are the noises from which you can never escape."

Silliman contrasted this dismal scene of early industrialization with a peaceful image of rural America: "fields and forests, in which pure air . . . and simple manners, give vigour to the limbs, and a healthful aspect to the face." Were the wonders of British technology, he asked, worth "the physical and . . . moral evils which they produce?"

No American struggled harder with this question than Thomas Jefferson. "Those who labour in the earth are the chosen people of God," Jefferson wrote in his *Notes on the State of Virginia* (1785), and he remained committed to the moral superiority of a society of yeomen farm families. Yet Jefferson knew that "a people who are *entirely* dependent upon foreigners for food or clothes, must always be subject to

them." Even before the Embargo of 1807 and the War of 1812 convinced him of the necessity of American manufacturing, Jefferson advocated the use of advanced technology. He introduced cast-iron plows and improved threshing machines on his plantation near Monticello, Virginia, and rotated crops in accordance with the latest scientific theory.

Jefferson championed manufacturing on the plantation as well. As early as 1796 he bought an iron-cutting machine to make nails and, by employing a dozen slave men, made 10,000 nails a day. By 1812 Jefferson had built two water-powered mills at another plantation and had equipped his Monticello slaves to manufacture textiles. He and other Americans, the former president boasted to a European friend, "have reduced the large and expensive machinery for most things to the compass of a private family. . . . I need 2,000 yards of linen, cotton

firm conviction in the "improvability of the human race." But he knew that progress was not inevitable, and he deplored both the speculative practices of merchants and financiers and the emerging social divisions of an urban industrial economy. Having visited the manufacturing regions in Britain and seen the masses of propertyless laborers there, Jefferson had concluded that

workers who depended on wages lacked the economic independence required to sustain a republic (see New Technology, "Machine Technology and Republican Values," above).

Jefferson's vision of the American future was agrarian and democratic. Although himself a privileged slaveowner, Jefferson understood the needs and

Coalbrookdale by Night, *Philip James de Loutherbourg*
This painting depicts an ironworks, which poet William Blake called one of the "dark Satanic mills" of industrial England.
The Science Museum, London.

and woolen yearly, to cloth my family [of slaves], which this machinery, costing $150 only, and worked by two women and two girls, will more than furnish."

Here, then, was Jefferson's way of avoiding the "dark Satanic mills" of Manchester. Each American household would become a small factory, using the labor of "women, children, and invalids" to enhance the prosperity and independence of American freehold farmers. For Jefferson, the key was democratic ownership of the means of agricultural and industrial production.

This dream was noble and not at all unrealistic. The United States did become a nation of household producers between 1790 and 1820 (see Chapter 8). Hundreds of rural men made nails as a wintertime employment, thousands of farm women made butter and cheese for market sale, and tens of thousands of families worked in their homes manufacturing shoes, textiles, and other goods for merchant entrepreneurs. Particularly in the Northeast, the American countryside became a vast workshop.

Yet Jefferson's vision concealed important aspects of American rural life and was flawed by internal contradictions. Many families in the Northeast were driven to home manufacture by the threat of poverty; their subdivided farms yielded only a bare subsistence. The situation in the southern states was even more problematic. Was the enslaved labor that produced Jefferson's nails and textiles more compatible with republican moral and economic principles than was the waged labor in Manchester factories? And, over the long run, could household producers compete successfully with the water- and steam-driven factories owned by wealthy capitalists?

A candid observer must answer "No" to these questions. With his customary skill, Jefferson had identified the crucial issues: how the means of production should be owned and organized, and who should benefit financially from the new technology. He was unable, however, to show how the technological advances and social conditions of his age could be made compatible with the republican value of liberty and the democratic ideal of equality. That question remains unresolved to this day.

aspirations of yeomen farmers and other ordinary white Americans. His vision took form in the *Notes on the State of Virginia* (1785): "Those who labor in the earth are the chosen people of God," the very soul of the republic. Jefferson hoped that westward expansion and foreign commerce would remedy two of the worst features of eighteenth-century agriculture—widespread tenancy in the South and subdivided farms in New England. When drafting the Ordinance of 1784, he pictured a national domain settled by productive yeomen farm families. Their bountiful harvests of grain and meat would feed European nations, which "would manufacture and send us in exchange our clothes and other comforts,"

Urban Affluence
Beginning in the 1790s, New York merchants built large townhouses and furnished them with fine pieces of furniture. This detail of John Rubens Smith's watercolor, *The Shop and Warehouse of Duncan Phyfe* (c. 1816), illustrates the success of America's most skilled furniture designer and manufacturer, who employed more than a hundred skilled joiners and carvers in his New York factory. Metropolitan Museum of Art, Rogers Fund, 1922.

an international division of labor similar to that proposed by the Scottish economist Adam Smith in *The Wealth of Nations* (1776).

During the 1790s, Jefferson's vision moved closer to reality as turmoil in Europe created new opportunities for American farmers. The French Revolution began in 1789, and four years later France's new republican government went to war against a British-led coalition of monarchical states. As warfare disrupted European farming, wheat prices leapt from 5 to 8 shillings a bushel and remained high for twenty years thereafter. Chesapeake and Middle Atlantic farmers increased their grain exports, reaping substantial profits. Simultaneously a boom in cotton exports, fueled by the mechanization of cloth production in Britain and the invention of the cotton gin in the United States, boosted the economy of the Lower South. As Jefferson had hoped, European markets brought prosperity to American farmers and planters.

War and Party Politics

American merchants profited even more handsomely from the European war. President Washington issued a Proclamation of Neutrality, the first important decision on foreign policy by an American president. The Proclamation allowed U.S. citizens to trade with both sides, angering those Americans who favored France (and the smaller number who supported Britain), but American merchants were delighted. As neutral carriers, American ships could pass through the British naval blockade along the French coastline, so American merchants soon took over the lucrative trade between France and its West Indian sugar islands. The American merchant fleet became one of the largest in the world, increasing from 355,000 tons in 1790 to more than 1.1 million tons in 1808. Commercial earnings rose spectacularly, averaging $20 million annually in the 1790s—twice the value of cotton and tobacco exports.

This commerce brought prosperity to American port cities, which had languished for two decades. Shipowners invested part of their rising profits in new vessels, providing work for thousands of shipwrights, sailmakers, laborers, and seamen. Hundreds of carpenters, masons, and cabinetmakers found work building warehouses and elegant Federal-style townhouses for newly affluent merchants. In Philadelphia, a European visitor reported, scores of new buildings went up, "chiefly of red brick, and in general three stories high. A great number of private houses have marble steps to the street door, and in other respects are finished in a style of elegance." Real-estate values soared, reflecting the growth in population and wealth. In New York City,

Federalist Gentry

A prominent New England Federalist, Oliver Ellsworth served as Chief Justice of the United States (1796–1800). His wife, Abigail Wolcott Ellsworth, was the daughter of a Connecticut governor. In 1792 the portraitist Ralph Earl captured the aspirations of the Ellsworths by giving them an aristocratic demeanor and prominently displaying their mansion (in the window). Like other Federalists who tried to reconcile their wealth and social authority with republican values, Ellsworth dressed with restraint, and his manners, remarked Timothy Dwight, were "wholly destitute of haughtiness and arrogance."

Wadsworth Athenaeum, Hartford.

for example, the assessed value of property jumped from $5.8 million to $20.7 million during the 1790s.

The French Revolution and America. Simultaneously, the passions of the European struggle convulsed the new republic. Many Americans had welcomed the French Revolution of 1789 because it attacked aristocratic privileges and established a constitutional monarchy. But the creation of the more democratic French republic in 1792 and the execution of King Louis XVI the following year divided public opinion in America and widened the existing split between the parties led by Hamilton and Jefferson.

Many Americans praised the egalitarian principles of the French republicans: in Boston, they had Royal Alley renamed Equality Lane. More important, urban artisans founded Democratic-Republican clubs modeled on the radical democratic societies in Paris—the controversial Jacobin clubs. The Democratic-Republicans of Philadelphia celebrated the beheading of Louis XVI at a dinner where, an observer reported, "the head of a roasted pig was severed from its body, and being recognized as an emblem of the murdered King of France, was carried round to the guests. Each one placing the cap of liberty on its head, pronounced the word 'tyrant.'" Adopting French republican practice, some Americans began addressing each other as "citizen," a symbol of equality, and condemned Hamilton's economic policies as "aristocratic."

On the other side of the ideological controversy were men and women of wealth, conservative Christian

VOICES FROM ABROAD

WILLIAM COBBETT

Peter Porcupine Attacks Pro-French Americans

★

American Democratic-Republicans declared that "he who is an enemy to the French Revolution, cannot be a firm republican." William Cobbett, a British journalist who settled in Philadelphia and wrote under the pen name "Peter Porcupine," contested this definition of republicanism. A strong supporter of the Federalist Party, Cobbett was eager to attack its opponents and did so frequently in caustic and widely read pamphlets and articles. Here he evokes the horrors of the Terror in France, during which thousands of aristocrats and ordinary citizens were executed, and warns that the triumph of Radical Republicanism would bring the same fate to the United States.

France is a *republic,* and the decrees of the Legislators were necessary to maintain it a republic. This *word* outweighs, in the estimation of some persons (I wish I could say they were few in number), all the horrors that have been and that can be committed in that country. One of these modern republicans will tell you that he does not deny that hundreds of thousands of innocent persons have been murdered in France; that the people have neither religion nor morals; that all the ties of nature are rent asunder; . . . that its riches, along with millions of the best of the people, are gone to enrich and aggrandize its enemies; that its commerce, its manufactures, its sciences, its arts, and its honour, are no more; but at the end of all this, he will tell you that it must be happy, because it is a *republic.* I have heard more than one of these republican zealots declare, that he would sooner see the last of

the French exterminated, than see them adopt any other form of government. Such a sentiment is characteristic of a mind locked up in a savage ignorance.

Shall we say that these things never can take place among us? . . . We are not what we were before the French revolution. Political projectors from every corner of Europe, troublers of society of every description, from the whining philosophical hypocrite to the daring rebel, and more daring blasphemer, have taken shelter in these States.

We have seen the *guillotine* toasted to three times three cheers. . . . And what would the reader say, were I to tell him of a Member of Congress, who wished to see one of these murderous machines employed for lopping off the heads of the French, permanent in the State-house yard of the city of Philadelphia?

If these men of blood had succeeded in plunging us into a war; if they had once got the sword into their hands, they would have mowed us down like stubble. The word *Aristocrat* would have been employed to as good account here, as ever it had been in France. We might, ere this, have seen our places of worship turned into stables; we might have seen the banks of the Delaware, like those of the Loire, covered with human carcasses, and its waters tinged with blood: ere this we might have seen our parents butchered, and even the head of our admired and beloved President rolling on a scaffold.

I know the reader will start back with horror. His heart will tell him that it is impossible. But, once more, let him look at the example before us. The attacks on the character and conduct of the aged *Washington,* have been as bold, if not bolder, than those which led to the downfall of the unfortunate French Monarch [Louis XVI, executed in 1793]. Can it then be imagined, that, had they possessed the power, they wanted the will to dip their hands in his blood?

Source: William Cobbett, *Peter Porcupine in America,* ed. David A. Wilson (Ithaca: Cornell University Press, 1994), 150–154.

beliefs, and Federalist sympathies. They denounced the Terror—a reign of state-sponsored violence in France that resulted in hundreds of aristocrats having their heads cut off by the newly invented guillotine—and condemned the new French regime for abandoning Christianity in favor of atheism. Election of Jefferson and his supporters, they warned, would bring the same fate to America (see Voices from Abroad, "William Cobbett: Peter Porcupine Attacks Pro-French Americans," above).

238

These conflicts sharpened the debate over Hamilton's economic policies and helped to foment a domestic insurrection. In 1794 farmers in western Pennsylvania mounted the Whiskey Rebellion to protest Hamilton's excise tax on distilled spirits, which had raised the price—and thus cut the demand—for the corn whiskey they sold locally and bartered for eastern manufactures. Like the Sons of Liberty of 1765 and the Shaysites of 1786, the Whiskey rebels attacked local tax collectors and challenged the authority of a distant government. But these protesters also waved banners proclaiming the French revolutionary slogan "Liberty, Equality, and Fraternity!" To uphold national authority (and deter secessionist movements along the western frontier), President Washington raised an army of twelve thousand troops that soon suppressed the rebels.

Jay's Treaty. Britain's maritime strategy also widened the growing political divisions in the United States. In November 1793 the Royal Navy began to seize American ships bound for France from the West Indies, capturing 250 vessels and confiscating their cargoes of sugar. To avoid war, President Washington sent John Jay as a special envoy to Britain to seek compensation for these seizures and to settle financial and territorial disputes dating back to the War of Independence.

Jay returned with a treaty that was both comprehensive and controversial. The treaty required the U.S. government to make "full and complete compensation" to British merchants for all pre–Revolutionary War debts owed by American citizens. The treaty also acknowledged Britain's right to remove French property from American-owned ships, overturning the American merchants' claim that "free ships make free goods." In return, the agreement allowed American merchants to submit claims to the British government for compensation for illegal seizures. It also required the British to end their aid to the western Indians and remove all their military garrisons from American territory in the trans-Appalachian West.

Although Jefferson and his Republican followers denounced Jay's Treaty as too conciliatory, the Senate ratified it by a vote of 20 to 10, the bare two-thirds majority required by the Constitution. As long as Hamilton and his Federalist allies were in power, the United States would have a pro-British foreign policy.

Parties and the Election of 1796. The appearance of rival political parties marked a new stage in American politics. Although colonial legislatures had often divided into temporary factions based on family alliances, ethnicity, or regional concerns, they had lacked well-organized parties. And the new state and national constitutions made no provision for such political bodies. Indeed, most of the framers of the various constitutions considered parties unnecessary and dangerous; following classical republican principles, they wanted voters and legislators to act independently and in the public interest.

But the revolutionary ideology of popular sovereignty had drawn ordinary citizens into politics, and the emergence of economic and ideological interest groups sparked the appearance of a competitive party system. Northern merchants, commercial-minded farmers, and wheat-growing Chesapeake slaveowners generally favored Federalist policies. The emerging Republican Party was more diverse in its social makeup; by the mid-1790s it included not only southern tobacco and rice planters and debt-conscious western farmers but also artisans in the seaport cities, German and Scots-Irish in the southern backcountry, and subsistence-oriented eastern farmers.

Party identity crystallized during the election campaign of 1796. As president, Washington had tried to stand above the emerging parties, but his continuing support for Hamilton's policies exposed him to partisan attack and influenced his decision not to seek a third term. To prepare for the election, Federalist and Republican leaders called legislative caucuses in Congress and conventions in the states to discuss policies, nominate candidates, and mobilize supporters. For virtually the first time, American voters chose between candidates who represented political parties standing for distinct principles.

Many Federalist candidates triumphed in the 1796 election, giving their party a majority in Congress and the electoral college, which chose John Adams as president. But when some Federalist electors refused to vote for Adams's choice for vice-president, Thomas Pinckney of South Carolina (because they were offended by a treaty he had negotiated with Spain), Thomas Jefferson, the Republican presidential candidate, won the second highest number of electoral votes and became vice-president. Thus the nation had a divided administration.

President Adams continued Hamilton's pro-British foreign policy, angering the French, who began to seize American merchant ships. When agents of Prince Talleyrand, the French foreign minister, solicited a loan and a bribe from American diplomats, Adams urged Congress to prepare for war. To overcome Republican objections, he charged that Talleyrand's agents, whom he dubbed X, Y, and Z, had insulted the honor of the United States. Outraged by the XYZ affair (as it came to be called), the Federalist-controlled Congress cut off trade with France and authorized American privateers to seize French ships. Party conflict, which had begun

An Anti-French Cartoon
A five-headed monster, representing the leaders of France under the Directory, demands a bribe ("Money, Money, Money") from American diplomats. Federalists used the bribery incident—named the XYZ affair for the three anonymous French agents who asked for the bribe—to whip up anti-French sentiment in the United States and launch an undeclared naval war.
Huntington Library.

over Hamilton's domestic policies, now extended to foreign affairs as well.

The Crisis of 1798–1800

For the first (but not the last) time in the history of the republic, a controversial foreign policy prompted domestic protest and governmental repression. With the United States fighting an undeclared war against France, pro-Republican emigrants from France and Ireland viciously attacked Adams's foreign policy in newspapers and pamphlets. Some Federalists responded in kind: "Were I president, I would hang them for otherwise they would murder me," declared a Philadelphia pamphleteer.

The Alien and Sedition Acts. To silence its critics, in 1798 the administration pushed a series of coercive measures through Congress. The Naturalization Act increased the residency requirement for citizenship from five to fourteen years; the Alien Act authorized the president to deport any foreigner or immigrant he judged "dangerous to the peace and safety of the United States"; and the Sedition Act prohibited the publication of ungrounded or malicious attacks on the president or Congress. "He that is not for us is against us," thundered the Federalist *Gazette of the United States.* Using

the legal powers granted by the new act, Federalist prosecutors arrested more than twenty Republican newspaper editors and politicians, accused them of sedition, and imprisoned some of them.

Republicans assailed these repressive prosecutions, charging that the Sedition Act contradicted the First Amendment's prohibition against "abridging the freedom of speech, or of the press." Although the Sedition Act was probably unconstitutional, Republicans did not turn to the federal courts for redress. The authority of federal courts to review congressional legislation had not been established, and the entire judiciary—including the Supreme Court—was packed with Federalists.

Instead, Madison and Jefferson took the fight to the state legislature of Virginia, and also that of Kentucky, which had joined the union in 1792. In November 1798 the Kentucky legislature passed a resolution drafted by Jefferson declaring the Alien and Sedition Acts to be "unauthoritative, void, and of no force." The resolution asserted that the national government owed its existence to a compact among the states, which meant that *"each party has an equal right to judge for itself."* In December the Virginia legislature passed a similar resolution, drafted by Madison, claiming that states had the right to refuse to enforce federal laws that exceeded the powers granted by the Constitution. The Kentucky and Virginia Resolutions thus laid the theoretical basis for subsequent "states' rights" interpretation of the Constitution.

The Election of 1800. The debate over the Sedition Act set the stage for the election of 1800. Jefferson, once opposed in principle to political parties, now saw them as a valuable way "to watch and relate to the people" the activities of the government. Republicans strongly supported Jefferson's bid for the presidency, pointing to the wrongful imprisonment of newspaper editors and championing states' rights.

President Adams responded to the Republican attacks by reevaluating his foreign policy. Adams was a complicated man, easily offended, dogmatic, but possessed of great personal strength and determination. Rejecting the advice of Hamilton and others to intensify the undeclared war with France (so that Federalists would benefit from an upsurge in patriotism), Adams put country ahead of party and entered into diplomatic negotiations that brought an end to the war.

Federalists attempted to win the election by branding Jefferson as an irresponsible pro-French Radical, "the archapostle of irreligion and free thought," but their strategy failed. Republicans won a resounding victory as voters protested against the undeclared foreign war with France—and the special national tax on land and houses that Congress had imposed to pay for it. They gave the Republicans a majority in both houses of

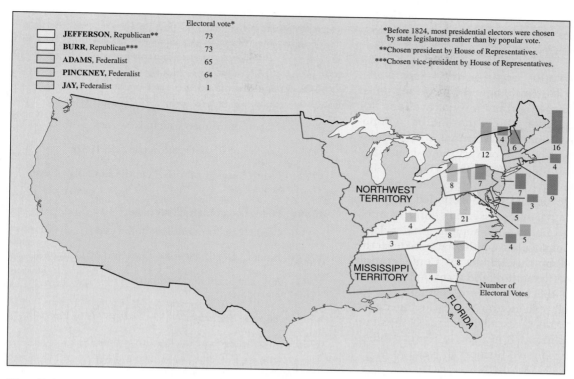

	Electoral vote*
JEFFERSON, Republican**	73
BURR, Republican***	73
ADAMS, Federalist	65
PINCKNEY, Federalist	64
JAY, Federalist	1

*Before 1824, most presidential electors were chosen by state legislatures rather than by popular vote.

**Chosen president by House of Representatives.

***Chosen vice-president by House of Representatives.

MAP 7.3

The Election of 1800

The voting in the election of 1800 followed regional lines. John Adams of Massachusetts carried every New England state and, reflecting Federalist strength in maritime and commercial areas, the eastern districts of various Mid-Atlantic states. But the Republicans led by Thomas Jefferson of Virginia eked out a narrow victory by winning most of the electoral votes of the South and, thanks to the efforts of vice-presidential candidate Aaron Burr, the twelve votes of the pivotal state of New York.

Congress and a narrow edge in the electoral college. But the electors gave Aaron Burr, Jefferson's choice for vice-president, the same number of votes as they gave to Jefferson; this tie threw the presidential election into the House of Representatives (Map 7.3). (The Twelfth Amendment, ratified in 1804, would remedy the constitutional defect that caused the tie by requiring electors to vote separately for president and vice-president.)

Ironically, as the era of Federalism and its aristocratic outlook came to an end, Alexander Hamilton ushered in a more democratic era. For thirty-five ballots Federalists in the House of Representatives blocked Jefferson's election. Then the former Treasury secretary intervened. Calling Burr an "embryo Caesar" and the "most unfit man in the United States for the office of president," Hamilton persuaded key Federalists to permit the selection of Jefferson, his longtime rival. The

Federalists' concern for political stability also played a role. As Senator James Bayard of Delaware explained, "it was admitted on all hands that we must risk the Constitution and a Civil War or take Mr. Jefferson."

Jefferson called the election the "Revolution of 1800," and so it was. For nearly a decade Federalists had attacked Republicans as social radicals and atheists, yet they peacefully relinquished power to their adversaries. The transfer of power demonstrated that governments elected by the people could be changed in an orderly way, even in times of bitter partisan conflict. In his inaugural address in 1801 Jefferson praised this achievement, declaring: "We are all Republicans, we are all Federalists." The new republican constitutional order—as defined in 1776 and reinterpreted in 1787— had survived a quarter-century of domestic conflict and foreign crisis.

Summary

———★———

The republican revolution began in the states, which between 1776 and 1780 wrote new constitutions. Most constitutions established property qualifications for voting and a separation of powers that inhibited popular rule. The Pennsylvania and Vermont constitutions were more democratic, with a powerful one-house legislature and broad voting rights for men. The New Jersey constitution allowed a few women to vote, but most American women continued to be excluded from the political sphere. A few women asserted claims of intellectual and social equality and sought greater legal rights, mostly without success. On the national level the government created by the Articles of Confederation began the orderly settlement of the trans-Appalachian West, but it lacked the authority to regulate foreign trade or raise enough revenue to pay off wartime debts. Clashes over debts and taxes also disrupted the state governments and culminated in 1786 in Shays's Rebellion, an uprising of indebted farmers in western Massachusetts.

The perceived weaknesses of the Confederation led nationalists and creditors to convene a constitutional convention in Philadelphia in 1787. The delegates devised a new constitution that derived its authority not from the states but from the people, who were directly represented in the lower house of the legislature. The delegates also created a strong national government with the power to levy taxes, issue money, and control trade. Its legislation was to be the supreme law of the land. In several important states the Constitution was ratified by narrow margins because it diminished the sovereignty of the states and seemed to create a potentially oppressive central government immune from popular control.

George Washington was elected as the first president under the new government and, along with the first Congress, established the executive and judicial departments. The economic policies of Washington's secretary of the Treasury, Alexander Hamilton, favored northern merchants and financiers and led to the creation of the Federalist Party. Thomas Jefferson and James Madison organized farmers, planters, and artisans into a rival Republican Party. The French Revolution prompted bitter ideological struggles in the United States and, during an undeclared war with France, political repression in the form of the Alien and Sedition Acts of 1798. The peaceful transfer of power to Jefferson and the Republicans in 1800 ended a decade of political strife.

TIMELINE

1776	Pennsylvania's democratic constitution
	John Adams, *Thoughts on Government*
	Propertied women vote in New Jersey (until 1807)
1777	Articles of Confederation (ratified 1781)
1779	Judith Sargent Murray, "On the Equality of the Sexes"
1780s	Postwar commercial recession
	Creditor-debtor conflicts in the states
1781	Bank of North America chartered by Congress
1784– 1785	Political and Land Ordinances outline policy for new states
1785	Thomas Jefferson, *Notes on the State of Virginia*
1786	Annapolis commercial convention
	Shays's Rebellion in Massachusetts
1787	Northwest Ordinance
	Philadelphia constitutional convention
1787– 1788	Ratification conventions
	The Federalist (John Jay, James Madison, Alexander Hamilton)
1789	George Washington inaugurated as first president
	Judiciary Act establishes federal court system
	Outbreak of French Revolution
1790	Alexander Hamilton's program: redemption and assumption
1791	Bill of Rights ratified
1792	Mary Wollstonecraft, *A Vindication of the Rights of Woman*
1793	First French Republic; Louis XVI executed
	Democratic-Republican Party founded
	War between Britain and France; Washington's Proclamation of Neutrality
1794	Whiskey Rebellion
1795	Jay's Treaty
1798	XYZ affair (1797) prompts war with France
	Alien, Sedition, and Naturalization Acts
	Kentucky and Virginia Resolutions
1800	Jefferson elected in "Revolution of 1800"

Suggested Readings

★

Jack N. Rakove, *Original Meaning: Politics and Ideas in the Making of the Constitution* (1996), and Richard B. Bernstein and Kym S. Rice, *Are We to Be a Nation? The Making of the Constitution* (1987), are the best recent overviews of the creation of a national republic. Stanley Elkins and Eric McKitrick, *The Age of Federalism: The Early Republic, 1788–1800* (1993), offer a comprehensive assessment of the 1790s.

Creating New Institutions, 1776–1786

Elisha P. Douglass, *Rebels and Democrats* (1965), documents the struggle for equal political rights. See also Merrill Jackson, *The New Nation* (1950); Jackson T. Main, *The Sovereign States, 1775–1783* (1973); and Ronald L. Hoffman and Peter Albert, eds., *Sovereign States in an Age of Uncertainty* (1981). Important studies of state constitutions include Willi Paul Adams, *The First American Constitutions* (1980); Edward Countryman, *A People in Revolution: The American Revolution and Political Society in New York, 1760–1790* (1981); and Donald Lutz, *Popular Consent and Popular Control: Whig Political Theory in the Early State Constitutions* (1980).

On women and republicanism, see Linda K. Kerber, *Women of the Republic* (1980), and Ronald Hoffman and Peter Albert, eds., *Women in the Age of the American Revolution* (1989). Fine in-depth studies include Rosemarie Zagarri, *A Woman's Dilemma: Mercy Otis Warren and the American Revolution* (1995); Judith Sargent Murray, *The Gleaner*, ed. Nina Baym (1992); and Lynn Withey, *Dearest Friend: A Life of Abigail Adams* (1982).

Gordon Wood, *The Creation of the American Republic, 1776–1790* (1965), links state and national constitutional development. Other important works on the 1780s include Peter S. Onuf, *The Origins of the Federal Republic: Jurisdictional Controversies in the United States, 1775–1787* (1983); Roger H. Brown, *Redeeming the Republic: Federalists, Taxation, and the Origins of the Constitution* (1993); Richard B. Morris, *The Forging of the Union, 1781–1789* (1987); and Robert A. Gross, ed., *In Debt to Shays* (1993).

The Constitution of 1787

In 1913 two studies initiated the modern analysis of the Constitution: Charles A. Beard offered *An Economic Interpretation of the Constitution of the United States*, and Max Farrand, *The Framing of the Constitution*, presented a detailed analysis of the Philadelphia convention. For critiques of Beard's work, see Leonard Levy, ed., *Essays on the Making of the Constitution* (rev. ed., 1987); for an update of Farrand, read Christopher Collier and James L. Collier, *Decision in Philadelphia* (1987).

Other significant works include Forrest McDonald, *Novus Ordo Seculorum: The Intellectual Origins of the Constitution* (1985); Edmund S. Morgan, *Inventing the People: The Rise of Popular Sovereignty in England and America* (1988); and Michael Kammen, *A Machine That Would Go by Itself: The Constitution*

in American Culture (1986). Three fine collections of essays are Richard R. Beeman et al., eds., *Beyond Confederation: Origins of the Constitution and American National Identity* (1987); Ellen Frankel Paul and Howard Dickman, eds., *Liberty, Property and the Foundations of the American Constitution* (1989); and Herman Belz et al., eds., *To Form a More Perfect Union: The Critical Ideas of the Constitution* (1992).

On the Antifederalists and ratification, see Patrick T. Conley and John P. Kaminiski, eds., *The Constitution and the States* (1988); Stephen L. Schechter, *The Reluctant Pillar: New York and the Adoption of the Federal Constitution* (1985); and Herbert Storing, *The Antifederalists* (1985). Two insightful studies of the Federalist papers are David F. Epstein, *The Political Theory of "The Federalist"* (1984), and Charles R. Kesler, ed., *Saving the Revolution* (1987).

R. A. Rutland, *The Birth of the Bill of Rights, 1776–1791* (rev. ed., 1983), offers the basic narrative; more analytic treatments include Michael J. Lacey and Knud Haakonssen, *A Culture of Rights* (1991), and Joyce Lee Malcolm, *To Keep and Bear Arms: The Origins of an Anglo-American Right* (1993). Akhil Reed Amar, *The Bill of Rights: Creation and Reconstruction* (1998), offers a persuasive "republican" interpretation.

The Political Divisions of the 1790s

Two good syntheses are John C. Miller, *The Federalist Age* (1957), and James Rogers Sharp, *American Politics in the Early Republic* (1993). Studies of important statesmen include Forrest McDonald, *Alexander Hamilton: A Biography* (1979), and James T. Flexner, *George Washington and the New Nation, 1783–1793* (1970), and *George Washington: Anguish and Farewell, 1793–1799* (1972). For Jeffersonian ideology, see Joyce Appleby, *Capitalism and a New Social Order: The Republican Vision of the 1790s* (1984); Drew McCoy, *The Elusive Republic: Political Economy in Jeffersonian America* (1982); Lance Banning, *The Jeffersonian Persuasion: The Evolution of a Party Ideology* (1978); and John R. Nelson Jr., *Liberty and Property: Political Economy and Policymaking in the New Nation, 1789–1812* (1987).

Richard Hofstadter, *The Idea of a Party System: The Rise of Legitimate Opposition in the United States, 1790–1840* (1969), offers an overview of the subject; see also John F. Hoadley, *Origins of American Political Parties, 1789–1803* (1993), and Thomas P. Slaughter, *The Whiskey Rebellion* (1986). On diplomatic and military history, consult Henry Ammon, *The Genêt Mission* (1973); Jerald A. Combs, *The Jay Treaty* (1970); Richard H. Kohn, *Eagle and Sword* (1975); and Lawrence D. Cress, *Citizens in Arms: The Army and the Military to the War of 1812* (1982).

On Adams's administration, see Ralph Brown Adams, *The Presidency of John Adams* (1975). More specialized studies are William Sinchcombe, *The XYZ Affair* (1980); Leonard Levy, *The Emergence of a Free Press* (1985); and James M. Smith, *Freedom's Fetters: The Alien and Sedition Laws and American Civil Liberties* (rev. ed., 1966).

Good state histories include Patricia Watlington, *The Partisan Spirit: Kentucky Politics, 1779–1792* (1972); Richard R. Beeman, *The Old Dominion and the New Nation, 1788–1801* (1972); and Mary K. Bonsteel Tachau, *Federal Courts in the Early Republic: Kentucky, 1789–1816* (1978).

Chapter 8

Westward Expansion and a New Political Economy, 1790–1820

Westward Expansion
Native American Resistance
Settlers, Speculators, and Slaves
The Transportation Bottleneck

The Republicans' Political Revolution
The Jeffersonian Presidency
Jefferson and the West
Conflict with Britain and France
The War of 1812

The Capitalist Commonwealth
A Merchant-Based Economy: Banks, Manufacturing, and Markets
Public Policy: The Commonwealth System
Law and the Commonwealth: Republicans versus Federalists
Federalist Law: John Marshall and the Supreme Court

MANY GENERATIONS IN the past, a Shawnee delegation told American officials in 1803, their Shawnee ancestors had stood on the shores of the Atlantic Ocean and seen a strange object: "At first they took it for a great bird, but they soon found it to be a monstrous canoe filled with . . . people who had got the knowledge which belonged to the Shawnees." "After these white people had landed," the delegation continued, they were "not content" with having robbed the Shawnee of their wisdom. These people also "usurped their land," purchasing it with goods that "were more the property of the Indians than the white people, because the knowledge which enabled them to manufacture these goods actually belonged to the Shawnees."

Whatever the truth of this legend, the Shawnee had great cause for alarm. The young American republic was growing at an astounding pace, thanks in part to purposeful political leadership and innovative public policies. In the Treaty of Paris of 1783, American diplomats had won British agreement to an extension of the boundary of the United States to the Mississippi River, which had doubled the young nation's size and added millions of acres of fertile, well-watered land—all of them belonging to the Shawnee and other native peoples. Even as the Shawnee were protesting against this usurpation in 1803, President Thomas Jefferson was again doubling the American claim to western lands with the Louisiana Purchase. With extraordinary self-confidence and a nearly complete disregard for Indian property rights, tens of thousands of American settlers

The Fairview Inn, Thomas Coke Ruckle (detail)
Scores of inns dotted the roads of the new republic, providing food, accommodations, and livery services for settlers moving west and for cattle drovers and teamsters carrying western produce to eastern markets. Although executed in 1889, this painting accurately depicts the architecture of an early-nineteenth-century Maryland inn and captures the character of its work force, showing free and enslaved African Americans driving cattle and tending to horses.
Maryland Historical Society.

trekked into the interior, imposing a new system of political power and economic production—a new political economy—on the land. "[No] territory can be too large," declared Dr. David Ramsay of South Carolina, "for a people, who multiply with such unequalled rapidity."

As American national policy promoted farming in the West, state legislatures devised legal innovations and financial incentives to stimulate economic growth in the East. The results of these twin initiatives were soon apparent. Beginning around 1800, per capita income in the United States increased by more than 1 percent per year—over 30 percent in a single generation. By the 1820s the extraordinary increase in productivity had laid the foundation for a new economic order. After half a century of political independence, the nation was well on its way to becoming a republic that was continental in scope and capitalist in character.

Westward Expansion

—————★—————

In 1790 the combined white and black population of the United States encompassed 3.9 million people, but only 200,000 Americans lived west of the Appalachian Mountains. During the next thirty years the West grew at a much more rapid rate than the rest of the nation. By 1820 there were 9.6 million white and black Americans, and 2 million of them inhabited nine new states and three new territories west of the Appalachians.

Native American Resistance

In the Treaty of Paris of 1783, Great Britain had relinquished its claims to the trans-Appalachian region and its peoples. As one British statesman put it, the Indian nations were "remitted to the care of their neighbours," a care that was far from benevolent. A few influential Americans advocated extermination of the native peoples: "Cut up every Indian Cornfield and burn every Indian town," proclaimed William Henry Drayton of South Carolina, so that their "nation be extirpated and the lands become the property of the public."

Many other political leaders, including Henry Knox, President Washington's first secretary of war, favored assimilation of the Indians into American society. As the first step in this process, Knox advocated the redistribution of commonly owned tribal land to individual Indian families as their private property. Most Indians firmly rejected that idea, for they were not accustomed to possessing wealth as individuals; instead, their custom was to circulate goods to fulfill social obligations.

Conflict over Land Rights. In fact, the first major struggle between Indians and whites arose not over assimilation but over land rights. Invoking the terms of the Paris treaty and claiming that pro-British Indians were conquered peoples, the new American republic asserted its ownership over all Indian lands in the trans-Appalachian West. Native Americans rejected this claim, pointing out that they had not signed the treaty and had never been conquered.

The Confederation Congress and the state governments brushed aside those arguments. In 1784, U.S. commissioners used military threats to force pro-British Iroquois peoples—the Mohawk, Onondaga, Cayuga, and Seneca—to sign the Treaty of Fort Stanwix, relinquishing much of their land in New York and Pennsylvania. Freely dispensing liquor, manufactured goods, and bribes, New York officials and land speculators secured other treaties that gave them title to millions of acres of Iroquois lands in central and western New York. By 1800 the once-powerful Iroquois peoples were confined to relatively small reservations.

American negotiators used similar tactics to extract agreements from Indian peoples farther to the west. In 1785 they induced the Chipewyan, Delaware, Ottawa, and Wyandot to sign away most of the future state of Ohio, but the tribes quickly repudiated the agreements, claiming—justifiably—that the treaties had been signed under duress. Soon those peoples, along with the Shawnee, Miami, and Potawatomi, formed a Western Confederacy to defend their lands and lives from aggressive settlers from Kentucky. Led by Little Turtle, a Miami chief, they defeated an American expeditionary force commanded by General Josiah Hamar in 1790 and crushed an army led by General Arthur St. Clair in 1791.

Fearing an alliance between the Western Confederacy and the British in Canada, President Washington doubled the size of the U.S. Army to five thousand men and ordered General "Mad Anthony" Wayne to lead a new expedition. In August 1794 Wayne defeated the Indian allies in the Battle of Fallen Timbers (near present-day Toledo, Ohio). Despite Wayne's victory, the Western Confederacy remained strong and forced the American negotiators to accept a compromise peace. In the Treaty of Greenville (Ohio) in 1795, the United States acknowledged Indian ownership of the trans-Appalachian West, renouncing a claim to the land that had been based on conquest. However, the treaty also required native Americans to cede the entire southeastern corner of the Northwest Territory as well as certain strategic areas along the Great Lakes, including Detroit and the future site of Chicago. Acknowledging American sovereignty over the entire region, the Indians agreed to place themselves "under the protection of the United States, and no other Power whatever." This agreement had great diplomatic significance, for it diminished the prospect of an Indian alliance with Britain and thus increased the likelihood that Britain would finally withdraw its military garrisons from American territory in the West. Recognizing the changed balance of power, Britain reaffirmed its obligation (under the Paris treaty) to remove its garrisons in Jay's Treaty of 1795.

As the fighting ended, the pace of American westward migration picked up. In 1805, two years after Ohio entered the Union, the new state had more than 100,000 residents, many of them clamoring for fertile Indian lands. Thousands more migrants moved into the future states of Indiana and Illinois, sparking new conflicts with the native peoples over land and hunting rights. As the Delaware put it, "The Elks are our horses, the buffaloes are our cows, the deer are our sheep, & the whites shan't have them."

Attempts at Assimilation.   Until the 1820s the U.S. government continued to pursue a twofold policy toward native Americans: the acquisition of their lands and their assimilation into white society. To provide new land for American farmers, Governor William Henry Harrison of the Indiana Territory and other federal officials used threats, bribes, and deceit to purchase millions of acres (Map 8.1). State officials and land speculators in Georgia, Tennessee, and the Mississippi Territory made similar deals with other Indian nations. At the same time government agents allowed—and often encouraged—the Indians to settle in farming communities on adjacent lands, hoping that Christian missionaries could persuade them to adopt white culture. The goal, as one Kentucky minister put it, was to make the Indian "a farmer, a citizen of the United States, and a Christian."

Most native Americans resisted attempts to confine them to farming and reshape their identity. "Born free and independent," an observer noted, Indians were "struck with horror at whatever has the shadow of despotic power." Many Indian peoples drove out the white missionaries and forced converts to Christianity to participate in traditional tribal rites. To explain their continuing respect for ancestral values, native American leaders devised dualistic cultural and religious theories. As a Munsee prophet put it, "there are two ways to God, one for the whites and one for the Indians."

Nevertheless, many tribes broke up into hostile religious factions. Among the Seneca of New York,

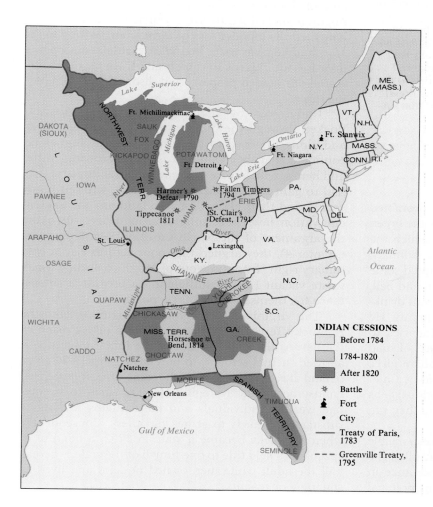

INDIAN CESSIONS
- ☐ Before 1784
- ☐ 1784–1820
- ☐ After 1820
- ✳ Battle
- ♣ Fort
- • City
- —— Treaty of Paris, 1783
- – – – Greenville Treaty, 1795

MAP 8.1
Military and Diplomatic Expansion, to 1840
The United States claimed sovereignty over the entire trans-Appalachian West by virtue of the Treaty of 1783 with Britain. When the tribes of the Western Confederacy contested this claim, the American government upheld it by force, sending armies into the West during the 1790s and the War of 1812. During the 1820s and 1830s this armed diplomacy forced native American peoples to cede by treaty most of their lands east of the Mississippi River.

An Iroquois Husk Mask
Each February the Iroquois peoples welcomed in the new year with a nine-day midwinter ceremony. On the sixth day members of the Husk Face Society, donning masks like this one made from braided corn leaves, invaded the council house and began a dialogue with those dancing inside. Eventually the Husk Faces identified themselves as a race of supernatural cultivators, who long ago had introduced corn growing to the Iroquois; then their women (actually men in women's dress) did the Woman's Dance to honor the "Three Sisters" that sustained the Iroquois: corn, squash, and beans.
Musée de l'Homme.

power; for example, the Shawnee chose women "war" and "civil" chiefs, who could decide whether to dispatch a war party or torture captives. Consequently, most women insisted on retaining their role as cultivators, and even those Indians who embraced Christian teachings retained many traditional values. To view themselves as individuals, as the Europeans demanded, would have been to repudiate the clan, the essence of Indian life. Most Indians therefore resisted assimilation into white culture, and most tribes resisted white attempts to acquire their lands.

Settlers, Speculators, and Slaves

Native American resistance did not deter the advance of American settlement, as migrants poured across the Appalachians into the Ohio River Valley and moved along the coastal plain of the Gulf of Mexico into the future states of Alabama and Mississippi.

The Rush to Kentucky and Tennessee. The migrants who settled Kentucky and Tennessee between 1790 and 1820 were mostly tenant farmers and struggling yeomen families fleeing the depleted soils and planter elite of the Chesapeake region. As more than 225,000 migrants moved westward, a worried eastern landlord lamented the massive loss of farm labor, writing to the *Maryland Gazette* that "boundless settlements open a door for our citizens to run off and leave us, depreciating all our landed property and disabling us from paying taxes."

Undeterred by such sentiments, the migrants flocked through the Cumberland Gap into Kentucky and along the road to the future state of Tennessee, confident that they would prosper by growing cotton and hemp, which were in great demand. But first they had to gain title to the land. Migrants without ready cash based their claims for free land on "the ancient cultivation law" governing frontier tracts. Invoking the argument of the North Carolina Regulators (see Chapter 4), they argued that poor settlers had a customary right "from time out of Mind" to occupy "back waste vacant Lands" sufficient "to provide a subsistence for themselves and their posterity."

The Virginia government, which administered the Kentucky Territory, had a much more elitist vision of the new settlements. To satisfy the initial migrants, it allowed "actual settlers" to purchase up to 1,400 acres of land at reduced prices. At the same time, it dispensed handsome grants averaging 100,000 acres to twenty-one wealthy individuals and partnerships and made substantial awards to scores of others. Consequently, when Kentucky became a state in 1792, a handful of speculators held title to one-fourth of the state, whereas half the adult white men owned no land and lived as squatters or tenants.

for example, the prophet Handsome Lake promoted traditional agricultural ceremonies—such as the green corn dance and the strawberry festival—in which the celebrants gave thanks to the earth, plants, animals, water, and sun. But Handsome Lake also adopted some Christian precepts, such as a belief in heaven and hell, and used them to discourage his followers from drinking alcohol, gambling, and practicing witchcraft. He also endorsed the efforts of Quaker missionaries to teach farming skills to Indian boys and the arts of soap making, spinning, and weaving to young Indian girls. The more conservative among the Seneca, led by Chief Red Jacket, opposed some of these innovations, such as expecting men to work in the fields, because they ran counter to longstanding Indian practice.

Traditionally, Indian women had been responsible for growing staple foods and had often controlled the inheritance of cultivation rights. Their importance in the economic sphere gave Indian women some political *nigger selling*   Charleston S.C. 4th March 1833 " The Land of the free & the home of the brave"

A Slave Auction in Charleston, South Carolina, 1833

As one slave departs with his new master (far right), the auctioneer tries to interest the
assembled planters in his next sale item, a black family. The artist, a British Canadian
named Henry Byam Martin, showed his disdain for these proceedings in the sketch
itself (compare the family's dignified bearing with the planters' slouching postures)
and in its sarcastic title: *The Land of the Free and the Home of the Brave.*
National Archives of Canada.

The Spread of Slavery into the Southwest.   As poor
whites fled from the Chesapeake states to Kentucky and
Tennessee, wealthy planters and up-and-coming young
men from the Chesapeake and the Lower South set up
new slave plantations in the Old Southwest—the future
states of Alabama, Mississippi, and Louisiana. Consequently, the southwestern frontier became a stronghold
not of yeoman agriculture but of slavery.

As planters established new plantations, first in the
interior of Georgia and South Carolina and then in the
Old Southwest, they imported thousands of new slaves
from Africa. Between 1776 and 1809, when Congress
banned American participation in the transatlantic
slave trade, about 115,000 Africans were brought to the
United States (see Table 9.2). The black population also
grew through reproduction, increasing from half a million in 1775 to 1.8 million in 1820. Many of these
Africans and African Americans still toiled in tobacco
fields in the Chesapeake, but as soil depletion caused a
drop in output, white planters took the crop and the
slaves who grew it into the Virginia Piedmont, North
Carolina, Kentucky, and Tennessee. Rice planters in

South Carolina and Georgia also expanded their plantations until the 1820s, when the overseas markets were
lost to less costly rice from Asia. By that time thousands
of blacks in Louisiana worked in a small and booming
sugar economy.

But it was a new crop—cotton—that provided the
impetus for the expansion of slavery into the Old Southwest. For centuries most Europeans had worn clothing
made from wool or flax; cotton textiles imported from
India were only for the rich. Then, after 1750, the European population explosion caused an increased demand
for clothing. Simultaneously, the technological breakthroughs of the Industrial Revolution, such as the newly
invented water-powered spinning jennies and weaving
mules, boosted the production of textiles and lowered
their prices. The result was a seemingly insatiable
demand for raw wool and cotton. In the 1790s, American inventors—including Connecticut-born Eli Whitney—helped to meet this demand by developing
machines that extracted the seeds from short-staple cotton (a variety with relatively short fibers), which grew
well in many regions of the South.

Before long, thousands of white planters in South Carolina and Georgia were growing cotton; beginning in 1815, a vast migration of planters—and their slaves—carried the production of cotton into Alabama and Mississippi, which entered the Union in 1817 and 1819, respectively. In a single year a government land office in Huntsville, Alabama, sold $7 million of uncleared land. The expression "doing a land-office business"—a metaphor for rapid commercial expansion—dates from this time (see American Voices, "Reuben Davis: Settling the Southwestern Frontier," p. 251).

Exodus from New England. As cotton planters moved southwest, a northern wave of migrants flowed out of New England into New York State and beyond, seeking to plant new yeomen farm communities. The quest for land had already propelled New England farmers north into New Hampshire and Vermont and east along the coast of Maine. But, after two centuries of population growth, many New England communities were crowded and subdivided into small farms, their rocky soils on the verge of depletion. Unable to provide farmsteads for the four or five children who survived to adulthood, thousands of New England parents hitched their oxen and horses to wagons and carried tools, plows, and household goods to the fertile plains and rolling hills of upstate New York. By 1820, as many as 800,000 migrants were living in a string of settlements stretching from Albany to Buffalo. Thousands more had pressed on to Ohio.

This vast migration was organized not by governments or joint-stock companies but by the people themselves. To lighten the burdens of migration, many settlers moved in large groups linked by family and religion. As a traveler reported from central New York, "The town of Herkimer is entirely populated by families come from Connecticut. We stayed at Mr. Snow's who came from New London with about ten male and female cousins." When 176 residents of Granville, Massachusetts, moved to Ohio, they transplanted their Congregational church whole, complete with ministers and elders, along with their system of freehold agriculture. Throughout the trans-Appalachian West, many "new" communities were not actually new; they were old communities that had moved inland.

As in Kentucky, much land in New York was snapped up by politically well-connected speculators. In the 1780s the financier Robert Morris acquired 1.3 million acres in the Genesee region of central New York for $75,000—about 6 cents an acre. Speculation drove up the price of farms, making it difficult for yeomen families to realize their dream of landed independence. Moreover, wealthy eastern landlords established new estates in the West. In the Genesee region the Wadsworth family bought thousands of acres of prime land and created leasehold farms similar to those on the manors of the Hudson River Valley. To attract tenants, the Wadsworths leased farms rent-free for the first seven years, after which they charged rents.

Seeking freehold ownership, many New England yeomen shunned these terms and signed lease-purchase agreements with the Dutch-owned Holland Land Company, which allowed them to buy the land as they worked it. But thousands of these aspiring yeomen became mired in debt because of high interest rates and the difficulty of transporting goods to market. Soon the number of tenants far surpassed the number of freeholders in the counties west of the Genesee River. Having fled declining prospects in the East, these farmers found themselves at the bottom of the economic ladder in the West.

Changes in Eastern Agriculture. The massive exodus drained eastern towns of money and workers, forcing established farmers to plant different crops and upgrade their equipment. In New England farmers turned to potatoes, a nutritious, high-yielding crop. In the wheat-growing Middle Atlantic states enterprising farmers replaced metal-tipped wooden plows with cast-iron models that dug a deeper furrow and required a single yoke of oxen instead of two or three. By using cast-iron plows farmers could get by with fewer draft animals and workers, thereby maintaining production levels even if their sons and daughters had gone west.

Eastern farmers also took advantage of the progressive farming methods advocated by British agricultural reformers. Wealthy "improvers" rotated their crops to maintain the soil's fertility, ordering workers or tenants to plant nitrogen-rich clover and follow it with wheat, corn, wheat, and then clover. In Pennsylvania, crop rotation enabled farmers to increase the average wheat yield from 12 to 25 bushels per acre. Yeomen were equally innovative, diversifying their output by raising sheep and selling the wool to textile manufacturers. Many farmers adopted a year-round planting cycle, sowing wheat in the winter for eventual market sale and planting corn in the spring to provide fodder for their milk cows. Women and girls milked the cows and developed a major new industry, making butter and cheese to sell in the growing towns and cities.

In the new agricultural economy families worked harder and longer, laboring even during the cold months of the year. But whether they were hacking fields out of western forests or carting manure to replenish eastern soils, their labor was rewarded by higher output and a better standard of living. Westward migration boosted the entire American economy, bringing new resources into production in the West and increasing farm productivity in the East.

Reuben Davis

Settling the Southwestern Frontier

———————★———————

Born around 1810, Reuben Davis grew up on the southwestern frontier, where his slaveowning father had migrated to find land and opportunities for his many children. Davis eventually became a successful lawyer in Mississippi and in 1890 published a memoir that describes—in a partly realistic, partly romantic fashion—the interaction among whites, Indians, and African Americans in early Alabama.

My father was one of the earliest settlers in this country. He was a man of limited means, and though of strong and vigorous intellect, had only the imperfect education of the pioneers of that day. His chief study was the Bible and a few volumes of history, which formed his only library. Although a Baptist minister of high standing, he occupied himself, during the week, with ordinary farm labor, and could never be induced to accept any compensation for his services in the church. . . .

Both my parents were born in Virginia, and remained there after marriage until ten children were added to their family. They then removed to Tennessee, and settled near Winchester, where I, their twelfth and last child, was born. . . . When I was about five years of age, my father removed from Tennessee to North Alabama. The land had been recently purchased from the Indians, and many of them yet roamed the dense forests of that section. I well remember how I hunted with these wild companions, and was taught by them to use the bow and arrow. Even now I can recall something of the emotion excited in my youthful breast by the wild yells of a party of drunken savages passing near my father's house. Occasional deeds of frightful atrocity were committed in the immediate neighborhood. Long before I was competent to reason on it, the problem of race-hatred was forced upon my observation. The fierce antagonism of one race for another and the frequent rising of the conquered against the conqueror were met then as practical questions,—as the fashion of the day was,—without much speculation or moralizing. . . .

At that time the country was as wild and unsettled as possible; there were no laws, no schools, and no libraries. Every man did what was right in his own eyes, but in spite of general recklessness and lawlessness, there was a rough code of honor and honesty which was rarely broken. The settlers lived a life of great toil and many privations, but they were eminently social, kindly, and friendly. . . .

Clearing land and opening a farm required constant and severe labor, and I, with my five brothers, performed our full share. Upon this farm I remained until I was sixteen years old. . . . My brothers and myself, assisted by six colored hands, cultivated the land, and attended school only about three months in the year. In this way we learned to read and write, as well as the rudiments of arithmetic and a little Latin. . . .

There was this great advantage that, while none were very wealthy, few were poor enough to suffer actual want. . . . The simple habits of the laboring man were not shamed by the ostentation of his more prosperous neighbor; and there was none of that silent, perpetual contrast of luxury and penury, which now adds bitterness to class hatreds.

———————

Source: Reuben Davis, *Recollections of Mississippi and Mississippians* (Boston: Houghton Mifflin, 1890), 2–4.

The Transportation Bottleneck

But the geography of the American continent threatened to cut short this economic advance. In America as in Europe, the pattern of settlement and trade had long been determined by water routes, the quickest and cheapest way to get goods to market—costing only 5 or 6 cents a ton-mile. Farmers and planters without access to rivers had to haul their crops by oxcart over narrow dirt trails that became mudholes during the wet season. Even in dry weather, ox-drawn carts moved slowly, carried small loads, and were expensive—costing 30 cents a ton-mile, or roughly five times as much as water transport. Incredibly, Pennsylvania farmers paid as much to send wheat and corn 30 miles overland to Philadelphia as merchants did to ship it from Philadelphia to London. Without access to waterways, settlers—especially those west of the Appalachian Mountains—could

Hop Picking, *Lucy Sheldon, 1801*
Hard work was nothing new for rural women and children, who had always labored on the farm. What was different in the early nineteenth century was the number of farm families, some of them propertyless, who now worked for employers such as shopkeepers and manufacturers. In this watercolor by Lucy Sheldon, then a schoolgirl at the Litchfield Female Academy in Connecticut, a young couple and their children pick hops, which they will sell to a storekeeper or local brewer to be made into beer.
Litchfield Historical Society.

not afford to send goods to eastern markets or export them to Europe or the West Indies.

The enhancement of inland trade became a high priority for the new state governments, which actively encouraged transportation ventures. Between 1793 and 1812, the Pennsylvania legislature granted corporate charters to fifty-five private turnpike companies, and Massachusetts chartered over a hundred. The turnpike companies charged tolls for the use of the level gravel roads they built, but the roads reduced travel time significantly. State governments and private entrepreneurs also undertook the construction of inland waterways, which were even more cost-efficient. They dredged rivers to make them navigable and constructed short canals, mostly to bypass waterfalls or rapids. By 1816 the United States had about 100 miles of canals, but only three were more than 2 miles long and none breached the great Appalachian barrier.

The great rivers of the interior represented the hope of the West. Western settlers paid premium prices for land along navigable streams, and speculators bought up property in growing towns—such as Cincinnati, Louisville, Chattanooga, and St. Louis—along the Ohio, Tennessee, and Mississippi Rivers. To take cotton and surplus grain and meat to market, western farmers and merchants built shallow barges and floated them down this interconnected river system to the port of New Orleans. By 1815 the southern port was processing about $5 million in agricultural products yearly.

The tens of thousands of migrants in the interior of New York faced a more serious transportation problem, for no rivers connected their settlements to the East. As one pioneer recalled, "In the early years, there was none but a home market and that was mostly barter— it was so many bushels of wheat for a cow; so many bushels for a yoke of oxen." Only in 1819, when the first section of the Erie Canal connected the central counties of New York with the Hudson River, could these inland farmers ship their crops to eastern markets.

Even then, many settlers in the West remained isolated and made their own clothes, repaired old tools, and bartered goods and labor with their neighbors. "A noble field of Indian corn stretched away into the forest on one side," an English visitor to an Ohio farm in the 1820s noted, waxing romantic,

and immediately before the house was a small potato garden, with a few peach and apple trees. The woman told me that they spun and wove all the cotton and woollen garments of the family, and knit all the stockings; her husband, though not a shoemaker by trade, made all the shoes. She manufactured all the soap and candles they use.

Self-sufficiency meant a low standard of living. As late as 1840, per capita income in states formed out of the Northwest Territory was only 70 percent of the national average.

Despite these hardships and the transportation bottlenecks, white Americans continued to migrate westward. They knew it would take a generation to clear land; build houses, barns, and roads; and plant orchards. Even if markets proved elusive, the settlers were confident that their sacrifices would yield future security—a farmstead and an independent livelihood for themselves and their children. The humble achieve-

View of Cincinnati, *John Caspar Wild, c. 1835*
Thanks to its location on the Ohio River, Cincinnati quickly became one of the major commercial cities of the trans-Appalachian West. By the 1820s, passenger steamboats as well as freight barges connected the city with Pittsburgh to the north and the ocean port of New Orleans to the far south.
Museum of Fine Arts, Boston.

ments of thousands of yeomen and tenant families slowly transformed the landscape of the trans-Appalachian West, turning forests into farms and beginning the conquest of the interior of the continent.

The Republicans' Political Revolution

★

Supported by voters in the new western states and by strong majorities in Congress, between 1801 and 1825 three Republicans from Virginia—Thomas Jefferson, James Madison, and James Monroe—each served two terms as president. This "Virginia Dynasty" of Republican presidents reversed many Federalist policies, completing what Jefferson called the Revolution of 1800. The West played a prominent role in Republican policy and, together with maritime disputes with Great Britain, precipitated the War of 1812.

The Jeffersonian Presidency

Thomas Jefferson was a brilliant man, perhaps the most accomplished and versatile statesman in American history. A seasoned diplomat and an insightful political philosopher, he was also a superb politician. On becoming president in 1801, Jefferson won over some of his Federalist opponents by appointing them to important government posts; he used other patronage positions to bolster the Republican Party in New England.

Courts and Politics. Jefferson was the first chief executive to be inaugurated in the District of Columbia, the new national capital, but he did not begin with a clean slate. After a dozen years of Federalist presidents, the government was filled with his political opponents, especially in the judiciary. The most important Federalist judge was the formidable John Marshall of Virginia, who sat at the head of the Supreme Court of the United States. Moreover, in 1801 the outgoing Federalist-controlled Congress passed a Judiciary Act creating sixteen new judgeships, six additional circuit courts, and a variety of patronage posts, which President Adams had filled in a series of "midnight appointments" just before he left office. The Federalists "have retired into the judiciary as a stronghold," Jefferson complained, "and from that battery all the works of Republicanism are to be beaten down and destroyed."

Republicans in Congress fought back by repealing the Judiciary Act of 1801 and impeaching two Federalist judges for their partisan political activities, winning the removal of one. For his part, James Madison, the new secretary of state, refused to commission one of the midnight appointees, William Marbury, as a justice of the peace in the District of Columbia. When Marbury asked the Supreme Court to issue a legal writ on his behalf, Marshall ruled in *Marbury v. Madison* (1803) that while Marbury had a right to his commission, the right was not enforceable by the Court. This was so, Marshall declared, because the Judiciary Act of 1789 had violated the Constitution by expanding the powers given to the Supreme Court in that document. Marshall's decision was politically astute, condemning Madison's action while avoiding a direct confrontation with the Republican administration. For his part, Jefferson pursued a conciliatory appointment policy, judging each Federalist bureaucrat on the basis of his ability. During eight years as chief executive, he removed only 109 of 433 Federalist officeholders. Forty of those removed had been midnight appointees of Adams.

The "Revolution of 1800." Nonetheless Jefferson was determined to change the character of the national government. The Federalists, he charged, had grossly expanded its size and power; Republicans would shrink it back to its correct constitutional size and shape. When the Alien and Sedition Acts expired in 1801, Congress did not reenact them, charging that they were politically motivated and unconstitutional. It also amended the Naturalization Act to permit resident aliens to become citizens after five years.

Jefferson likewise modified many Federalist policies. During the 1790s Federalist administrations had paid tribute to the Barbary States of North Africa—bribing them not to attack American merchant ships in the Mediterranean Sea. In 1801 Jefferson stopped the payments, and when the Barbary "pirates" renewed their assaults, he ordered the U.S. Navy to retaliate. But Jefferson wanted to avoid an expensive war, which would increase taxes and the national debt, and therefore he accepted a diplomatic solution in which the United States paid a small tribute.

In domestic affairs, too, Jefferson set his own course—moderate but clearly Republican. He abolished all internal taxes, including the excise tax that had sparked the Whiskey Rebellion of 1794. Addressing

his party's fears of a military takeover of the government, Jefferson reduced the size of the permanent army. He came to accept the Bank of the United States, which he had condemned as unconstitutional in 1791, because of its importance to the nation's economy, but he continued to oppose a large public debt. To remedy that he chose as secretary of the Treasury Swiss-born Republican Albert Gallatin, a fiscal conservative who believed that the national debt was "an evil of the first magnitude." By carefully controlling government expenditures and using customs revenues to redeem government bonds, Gallatin reduced the debt from $83 million in 1801 to $45 million in 1808. With Jefferson and Gallatin at the helm, the nation was no longer run in the interests of northeastern creditors and merchants.

Jefferson and the West

Long before he became president, Jefferson had championed the settlement of the West. He had celebrated the yeoman farmer in *Notes on the State of Virginia* (1785), helped compose the Confederation's western land ordinances, and strongly supported Pinckney's Treaty of 1795, which allowed settlers to ship crops down the Mississippi River for export through the Spanish-held port of New Orleans.

The Northwest Territory. As president, Jefferson had a new opportunity to encourage western settlement. The ordinances of 1785 and 1787, which had created the Northwest Territory, had divided it into uniform sections or townships. These townships were about the same size as New England communities, 6 miles square, and were divided into 36 sections of 1 square mile, or 640 acres, surveyed in a grid pattern (Map 8.2).

Despite Jefferson's efforts, the ordinance of 1785 had a class bias, favoring speculators over yeomen. It specified a minimum price of $1 per acre and required that 50 percent of the townships be sold in single blocks of 23,040 acres each, making direct purchase impossible for all but the wealthy. The other 50 percent of the townships were divided into 36 parcels of 640 acres each, but even those were prohibitively expensive for many migrants, who lacked ready cash. High-quality or well-located parcels were even more expensive. The poorer settlers demanded better terms, but the Federalist-dominated Congresses of the 1790s turned a deaf ear. Many Federalist politicians were eastern landlords and had no desire to lose their tenants to cheap land in the West. In fact, the Federalist Land Act of 1796 doubled the minimum price to $2 per acre. Much of the best land fell into the hands of speculators, such as those in the Ohio and Scioto Land Companies, as the authors of the ordinances had intended.

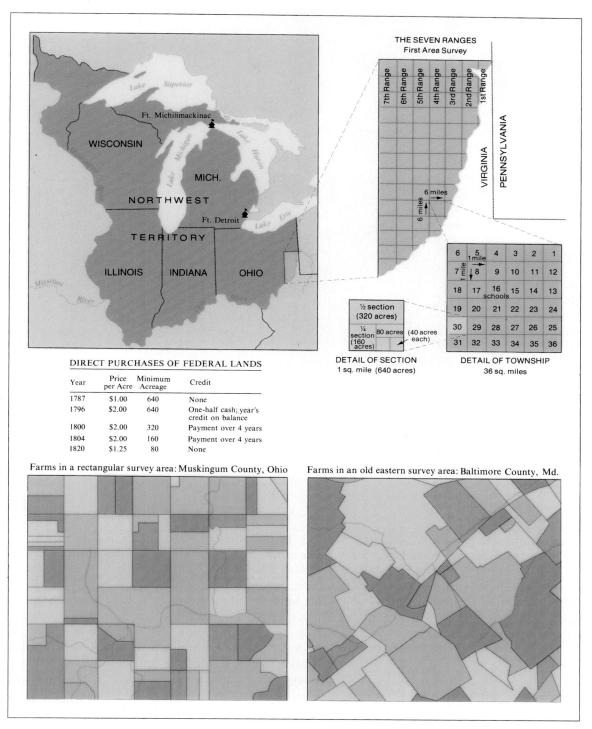

THE SEVEN RANGES
First Area Survey

7th Range | 6th Range | 5th Range | 4th Range | 3rd Range | 2nd Range | 1st Range

VIRGINIA | PENNSYLVANIA

6 miles

6 miles

DETAIL OF SECTION
1 sq. mile (640 acres)

½ section (320 acres)
¼ section (160 acres) | 80 acres | (40 acres each)

DETAIL OF TOWNSHIP
36 sq. miles

6	5	4	3	2	1
7	8	9	10	11	12
18	17	16 schools	15	14	13
19	20	21	22	23	24
30	29	28	27	26	25
31	32	33	34	35	36

1 mile / 1 mile

WISCONSIN

Ft. Michilimackinac

MICH.

NORTHWEST

Ft. Detroit

TERRITORY

ILLINOIS | INDIANA | OHIO

Lake Superior / Lake Michigan / Lake Huron / Lake Erie

Missouri River

DIRECT PURCHASES OF FEDERAL LANDS

Year	Price per Acre	Minimum Acreage	Credit
1787	$1.00	640	None
1796	$2.00	640	One-half cash; year's credit on balance
1800	$2.00	320	Payment over 4 years
1804	$2.00	160	Payment over 4 years
1820	$1.25	80	None

Farms in a rectangular survey area: Muskingum County, Ohio

Farms in an old eastern survey area: Baltimore County, Md.

MAP 8.2
Land Divisions in the Northwest Territory
Throughout the Northwest Territory, surveyors imposed a rectangular grid on the landscape in advance of settlement, so that farmers bought neatly defined properties. Thus
the right-angled property lines in Muskingum County, Ohio (lower left), contrasted
sharply with those in Baltimore County, Maryland (lower right), where—as in most
eastern states—boundaries followed the contours of the land.

The American Eagle over New Orleans
Jefferson's purchase of Louisiana made New Orleans part of the United States, but many districts in the city retained their French look (note the steeply pitched roofs on the right) and culture for decades. A traveler noted that "the great enmity existing between the Creoles [the French settlers] . . . and the Americans results in fights and Challenges—there are some of both sides in jail." This *View of New Orleans Taken from the Plantation of Marigny* was painted by John L. Boqueto de Woiserie in 1803.
Chicago Historical Society.

Because Jefferson wanted to see the West populated with yeomen farm families, the Republicans in Congress won the passage of laws in 1800 and 1804 that reduced the minimum allotment to 320 and then 160 acres and allowed payment in installments over four years. Eventually the Land Act of 1820 cut the minimum purchase to 80 acres and the price to $1.25 per acre, enabling a farmer with only $100 in cash to buy a western farm.

The Louisiana Purchase. But international events challenged Jefferson's vision for the West. In 1799 the daring general Napoleon Bonaparte seized power in revolution-torn France and began an ambitious campaign to establish a French empire in both Europe and America. In 1801 Napoleon coerced Spain into signing a secret treaty that returned to France its former colony of Louisiana; a year later he directed Spanish officials to restrict American access to New Orleans. Meanwhile, Napoleon had mobilized an expeditionary force to restore French rule in Haiti (then called Saint-Domingue), a rich sugar island that had been seized in

1793 by rebellious black slaves led by Toussaint L'Ouverture.

Napoleon's intention to reestablish a vast American empire prompted Jefferson to question his party's traditionally pro-French foreign policy. Trade down the Mississippi River, which was guaranteed by Pinckney's Treaty of 1795 with Spain, was crucial to the West; any nation that denied Americans access to New Orleans, Jefferson declared, must be "our natural and habitual enemy." To avoid crossing swords with Napoleon, Jefferson instructed Robert R. Livingston, the American minister in Paris, to purchase New Orleans. Simultaneously Jefferson sent James Monroe to Britain to seek its assistance in case of war. "The day that France takes possession of New Orleans," the president warned, "we must marry ourselves to the British fleet and nation."

Jefferson's diplomacy yielded a magnificent prize: the entire territory of Louisiana. By 1802 the French invasion of Haiti was faltering, a victim of yellow fever and spirited black resistance. Moreover, a new war was threatening to break out in Europe, and Napoleon

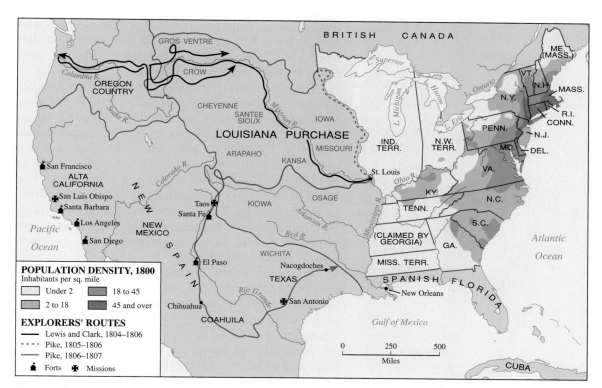

MAP 8.3
The Louisiana Purchase, 1803
The Louisiana Purchase ended France's quest for a North American empire. It doubled the size of the United States, prompting Thomas Jefferson to predict that the vast Mississippi Valley "from its fertility . . . will ere long yield half of our whole produce, and contain half of our whole population." Now only New Spain stood in the way of an American continental empire.

feared an American invasion of Louisiana. Acting with characteristic decisiveness, the French ruler gave up his dream of an empire in America and in April 1803 offered to sell not just New Orleans but the entire territory of Louisiana. For about $15 million ($180 million today), Livingston and Monroe concluded what became known as the Louisiana Purchase (Map 8.3). "We have lived long," Livingston remarked to Monroe, "but this is the noblest work of our lives."

The importance of the Louisiana Purchase forced the president to reconsider his interpretation of the Constitution. Jefferson had always been a strict constructionist, arguing that the national government possessed only the powers "expressly" delegated to it in the Constitution. However, there was no provision in the Constitution for adding new territory, so to fulfill his dreams for the West, Jefferson adopted a pragmatic stance: accepting a loose interpretation of the national charter, he used the treaty-making powers granted by the Constitution to complete the deal with France.

Spain reacted strongly to the American acquisition of Louisiana, for it feared that the expansion of the United States would endanger the northern territories of New Spain. Spanish diplomats argued that

Louisiana was limited to lands along the Mississippi River (the present-day states of Louisiana, Arkansas, and Missouri). But Jefferson claimed that the territory extended to the Rio Grande and the Rocky Mountains, which would place all of present-day Texas, half of New Mexico, and all the lands to the north under American control. This boundary dispute remained unresolved for two decades.

Being a scientist as well as a statesman, Jefferson wanted detailed information about the physical features of the new territory and its plant and animal life. In 1804 he sent his personal secretary, Meriwether Lewis, to explore the region along with William Clark, an army officer. Aided by Indian guides, Lewis and Clark traveled up the Missouri River, across the Rocky Mountains, and (venturing beyond the Purchase) down the Columbia River to the Pacific Ocean. After two years the explorers returned with the first maps of the immense wilderness and vivid accounts of its natural resources and native American inhabitants.

Threats to the Union. The Louisiana Purchase was a stunning accomplishment, doubling the size of the nation at a single stroke, but it brought a new threat.

The handwritten diary text beside the drawing reads (partially legible):

Monday March 17th 1806.

The Continent Described

Meriwether Lewis and William Clark fulfilled Jefferson's injunction to explore the trans-Mississippi West by filling their journals with drawings and descriptions of its topography, plants, and animals. Clark drew this picture of the white salmon trout along the Columbia River (in present-day Washington State) in his diary in March 1806.

Missouri Historical Society, Voorhis Number 2, William Clark Papers.

New England Federalists had long feared that western expansion would diminish their region's power, and some of them now talked openly of leaving the Union. When Alexander Hamilton refused to support their plan for a separate Northern Confederacy, the secessionists enlisted the support of Aaron Burr, the ambitious vice-president, who was seeking election as governor of New York. When Hamilton accused Burr of plotting to dismember the nation, Burr challenged him to a duel—the preferred aristocratic method for set-

tling personal disputes. The illegal duel took place in New Jersey in July 1804. Hamilton died from a gunshot wound, and Burr was indicted for murder by state courts in New York and New Jersey.

This tragic event propelled Burr into yet another secessionist scheme. After completing his term as vice-president early in 1805, he moved west to avoid prosecution. There he conspired with General James Wilkinson, the military governor of the Louisiana Territory. Their plan remains a mystery, but it is thought to have involved either the capture of territory in New Spain or a rebellion to establish Louisiana as a separate nation headed by Burr. Regardless of their intentions, Wilkinson betrayed his ally, arresting Burr on a charge of treason as the former vice-president led an armed force down the Ohio River.

In a highly publicized and politicized trial presided over by Chief Justice John Marshall, Burr was acquitted. But the verdict was less important than the dangers to national unity that it revealed. The Republicans' expansionist policies had increased sectional tension and party conflict, giving new life to states' rights sentiment and secessionist schemes.

Conflict with Britain and France

Simultaneously, the outbreak of the Napoleonic Wars in Europe (1802–1815) threatened the interests of the American republic because Great Britain and France, the major belligerents, refused to respect the neutrality of its merchant vessels. Napoleon established the Continental System, which authorized customs officials in the many European ports under French control to seize neutral ships that stopped in Britain. For its part, Britain seized American ships carrying sugar and molasses from the French West Indies and required merchants to obtain special licenses—and carry British goods—to pass through its naval blockade of Europe. The Royal Navy also searched American ships for deserters and *impressed* (or forced) them back into military service. Between 1802 and 1811 British officers seized nearly eight thousand sailors, many of whom were actually not British deserters but American citizens.

Long-simmering American resentment erupted in 1807, when a British warship attacked the U.S. Navy vessel *Chesapeake*, killing or wounding twenty-one men and seizing four alleged deserters. "Never since the battle of Lexington have I seen this country in such a state of exasperation as at present," Jefferson declared, demanding that Britain pay monetary reparations and put an end to impressment. To demonstrate his resolve, he barred British warships from American ports, preventing their resupply. The British government apologized and promised compensation but continued to seize French goods from American ships and impress suspected deserters.

The Embargo of 1807. To protect American interests while avoiding war, Jefferson pursued a policy of peaceful coercion. Working closely with Secretary of State James Madison, the president devised the Embargo Act of 1807. As passed by Congress, this legislation prohibited American ships from leaving their home ports until Britain and France repealed their restrictions on U.S. trade. Though the embargo was imaginative—an economic weapon similar to the nonimportation movements between 1765 and 1775—it was also naive. Jefferson and Madison overestimated the belligerents' dependence on American shipping and underestimated resistance from New England merchants, who feared the embargo would ruin them.

In fact, the embargo crippled American exports, which plunged from $108 million in 1806 to $22 million in 1808, hurting farmers as well as merchants and prompting Federalists to demand its repeal. Federalists grew more alarmed when the Republican Congress passed a Force Act to prevent smuggling across the border between New England and Canada. The act gave customs officials extraordinary legal powers, reviving fears of government tyranny. "Would to God," exclaimed one Federalist, "that the Embargo had done as little evil to ourselves as it has done to foreign nations."

Despite public discontent with the embargo, voters elected James Madison, one of its authors, to the presidency in 1808. As the main architect of the Constitution, an advocate of the Bill of Rights, and a prominent congressman and party leader, Madison had served the nation well. But as John Beckley, a loyal Republican, complained in 1806, he had performed poorly as secretary of state: "Madison is deemed by many too timid and indecisive as a statesman." Thus, at a crucial juncture in foreign affairs, a man with little understanding of the devious, cutthroat world of international politics became president.

Madison promptly acknowledged the embargo's failure. In 1809 he replaced it with the Nonintercourse Act, which permitted trade with all nations except France and Britain, and offered the promise of normal commerce if the belligerents respected America's neutral rights. When Britain and France ignored this overture, in 1810 Madison bowed to pressure from Congress and accepted an act (called Macon's Bill No. 2) that reopened legal trade but threatened to cut off trade with any nation interfering with American commerce. The British ministry refused to alter its policies, and Napoleon astutely exploited the ill-conceived legislation by publicly exempting American commerce from seizure while privately instructing his customs officials to seize ships. "The Devil himself could not tell which government, England or France, is the most wicked," an exasperated congressman declared.

Tecumseh's Challenge and Republican Policy. Other Republicans were pretty sure it was Britain. Republican congressmen from the West—the future "war hawks" of 1812—accused Britain of arming the Indian tribes in the Ohio River Valley. Since 1808 Governor General James Craig of Canada had quietly renewed military assistance to native Americans, hoping that the Indians could defend their territory and continue to trade with the British. Then, in 1809, the Shawnee chief Tecumseh, assisted by his brother, the Prophet Tenskwatawa, revived the Western Confederacy of the 1790s and tried to extend it to the southern tribes, vowing to exclude whites from all lands west of the Appalachian Mountains (see American Lives, "Tenskwatawa: Shawnee Prophet," pp. 260–261).

But thousands of white settlers already lived in the West, and their concerns had a decisive impact on American policy. Expansionists in Congress condemned British support of Tecumseh and threatened to retaliate by invading Canada and seizing Florida from Spain, Britain's ally. Urged on by such talk, southern planters campaigned for the conquest of eastern Florida to prevent fugitive slaves from taking refuge among the Seminole Indians. Americans living near and in the western (panhandle) region of Florida did not wait; they took up arms and occupied this region, hoping to annex it to the United States. Violence also broke out in the Ohio Valley. In 1811, responding to Indian raids against new settlements in the Indiana Territory, Governor William Henry Harrison marched on Prophetstown, Tenskwatawa's sacred village, fended off the confederation's warriors at the Battle of Tippecanoe, and burned the town to the ground (see American Voices, "Chief Shabonne: The Battle of Tippecanoe, 1811," p. 262).

Prompted by these events, Henry Clay of Kentucky, the new Speaker of the House of Representatives, and John C. Calhoun, a rising young congressman from South Carolina, pushed Madison toward war with Great Britain. Along with other southern and western war hawks in Congress, they eyed new territory in Florida and Canada and hoped war would discredit the Federalists. With national elections approaching, Madison demanded that the British respect American sovereignty in the West and neutral rights on the Atlantic. When the British failed to respond quickly, Madison abandoned the policy of economic coercion and asked Congress for a declaration of war. In June 1812 a sharply divided Senate voted 19 to 13 for war; the House of Representatives concurred, 79 to 49.

The causes of the War of 1812 have been much debated. Officially, the United States went to war because of violations of its neutral rights: the seizure of its ships and the impressment of its sailors. However, the resort to arms was opposed by the Federalist congressmen who represented merchants' interests

Tenskwatawa: Shawnee Prophet

★

BY 1800 INDIAN peoples in the interior of North America were in a state of crisis—their warriors dying at the hands of aggressive frontiersmen, their families and communities disintegrating from the violence and sexual promiscuity that flowed from the white man's whiskey, their very existence threatened by the spread of the European diseases of influenza, measles, and smallpox. War, alcoholism, disease—the trilogy of social disasters that had virtually wiped out the Indian peoples to the east of the Appalachians—now ravaged the tribes of the American heartland.

Everywhere along the frontier new Indian leaders appeared to explain these disastrous happenings and to prescribe solutions. The religious prophet Handsome Lake urged the Seneca of New York to abstain from alcohol and revive traditional Indian spiritual beliefs and practices. Eight hundred miles to the west, the eloquent Potawatomi shaman Main Poc denounced American soldiers and settlers for disrupting Indian life and spread his message of Indian renewal not only among the Potawatomi of Illinois and Wisconsin but also among the neighboring Sac, Winnebago, and Chippewa peoples.

But the most important Indian prophet was Tenskwatawa. He was born in 1775 at Old Piqua, a Shawnee village on the Mad River in western Ohio. His father, a prominent Shawnee warrior, had died four months before his birth, killed in battle against the Virginia militia; four years later his Creek mother abandoned the village, leaving her young Shawnee children to be raised by kinfolk. As a young man the future prophet was known as Lalawethika ("Rattle" or "Noisemaker") because of his boastful ways, blatant alcoholism, and flagrant disrespect for sacred Shawnee laws. Then in 1805, at age thirty, he had a profound emotional experience, lapsing for hours into an unconscious state resembling death.

Upon awakening Lalawethika claimed to have died and to have visited the Master of Life, the Good Spirit and main Shawnee god, who allowed him a glimpse of heaven: "a rich fertile country, abounding in game, fish, pleasant hunting grounds and fine corn fields," where virtuous Shawnee would go after death. He also observed the spirits of sinful Indians suffering fiery tortures (similar to those described by Jonathan Edwards, the great eighteenth-century Puritan preacher). Transformed by this experience, Lalawethika renounced his wicked ways and old identity, taking the name Tenskwatawa ("The One That Opens the Door") and founding a new settlement at Greenville in western Ohio. There he lived as a holy man, vowing to deliver the Shawnee from their present woes.

Like other Indian prophets, Tenskwatawa (pronounced Tens-qua-ta-wa) preached a nativist message, urging his followers to shun Americans, "the children of the Evil Spirit . . . who have taken away your lands." He denounced the consumption of the Long Knives' alcohol, a "poison and accursed" drink, and called for a return to traditional food and clothes: "You must not dress like the White Man . . . you must go naked Excepting the Breach cloth, and when you are clothed, it must be in skins or leather of your own Dressing." To spread these teachings, Tenskwatawa founded a new religion, its rituals derived in part from Catholicism, which French Jesuits had carried to the Indian peoples of the region. Converts were to confess their sins and then to worship an effigy of Tenskwatawa, fingering a string of beads (similar to a rosary) and thereby "shaking hands with the Prophet."

The new religion spread like wildfire among the Delaware of Indiana, who in 1806 showed their zeal by burning alive six suspected Indian witches. Shocked by these deaths, William Henry Harrison, the American governor of the Indiana Territory, denounced Tenskwatawa as a "pretended prophet" who was leading the Shawnee down "a dark, crooked, and thorny road." "If he is really a prophet," Harrison told the Indians, "ask of him to cause the sun to stand still . . . or the dead to rise from their graves. If he does these things, you may then believe that he has been sent from God." Harrison soon regretted these words. Learning from visiting American astronomers of an imminent eclipse of the sun in Indiana and Illinois, Tenskwatawa announced that on June 16 he would darken the sun at midday. "Did I not speak the truth?" he asked those—Delaware and Wyandot as well as Shawnee—who gathered at Greenville at the appointed time. "See, the sun is dark." As reports of this "miracle" circulated, warriors and wise men from many western tribes—Kickapoo, Potawatomi,

Tenskwatawa, "The Prophet," 1836
Tenskwatawa added a spiritual dimension to native American resistance, urging a holy war against the invading whites. His religious message transcended differences among Indian peoples, helping to create a formidable political and military alliance.
Library Company of Philadelphia.

Winnebago, Ottawa, Chippewas—journeyed to Greenville to learn the Prophet's teachings.

In 1808 the new religion took on a political cast. Fearing attacks by Americans and seeking closer proximity to his western followers, Tenskwatawa founded a new holy village, Prophetstown, near the juncture of the Tippecanoe and Wabash Rivers. There, he said, "they would be able to watch the Boundary Line between the Indians and white people—and if a white man put his foot over it [the Wabash River] that the warriors could easily put him back." To secure this newly defined boundary line, the Prophet dispatched his older brother Tecumseh to Canada, where he secured food, manufactures, and guns from British officials. The deter-

mination of the Shawnee brothers stiffened in September 1809 when "government chiefs" (Miami, Delaware, and Potawatomi leaders who received annuities from U.S. officials) ceded more than 3 million acres of land in Indiana and Illinois to the United States. Arguing that the land belonged to all Indians, Tenskwatawa declared that "no sale was good unless made by all the Tribes." Meeting with Harrison in August 1810, Tecumseh demanded that the governor "restore the land"; otherwise he would "kill all the chiefs that sold you this land" and form a great confederation of Indian peoples who would unite with the British to expel American invaders. What had begun as a movement of religious revitalization had become a crusade for Indian political unity and land rights.

As the movement changed its focus, Tecumseh seized the reins of leadership. After meeting Tecumseh in August 1811, Harrison reported to the secretary of war that he was "really the efficient man—the Moses of the family . . . a bold, active, sensible man, daring in the extreme and capable of any undertaking." When Tecumseh left for the South (to persuade the Chickasaw, Choctaw, and Creeks to join the Indian Confederation), Harrison mobilized an army of 1,000 men and marched on Prophetstown. Ignoring his brother's instructions to avoid conflict, Tenskwatawa defended his village. Assuring his force of 600 warriors that the Master of Life would make them invulnerable to the Long Knives, the Prophet attacked Harrison's camp near the Tippecanoe River. In a bitter but inconclusive battle, the Americans suffered 62 dead and 124 wounded while the Indians lost 50 dead and 80 wounded. But the victory ultimately went to Harrison. Shocked by their losses, Tenskwatawa's followers now scoffed at his claims of religious power, threatened him with death, and melted away, allowing Harrison's troops to burn Prophetstown.

Mortally wounded on the battlefield at Tippecanoe, the Prophet's religion died during the War of 1812, as American bullets took the life of Tecumseh and killed many of Tenskwatawa's remaining followers. After a decade of exile in British Canada, Tenskwatawa returned to the United States in 1824 as one of the "government chiefs" he had long despised, working for U.S. officials and persuading hundreds of Shawnee to leave Indiana and move with him to a reservation on the plains of eastern Kansas. There he died in 1836, without power, influence, or followers.

Chief Shabonne

The Battle of Tippecanoe, 1811

★

In this interview with a newspaper reporter some years after the Battle of Tippecanoe, the Potawatomi chief Shabonne recalls the events surrounding the confrontation and offers a penetrating view of reality: the unfaithfulness of allies, the confidence and impulsiveness of youth, and the false promises of war leaders.

It was fully believed among the Indians that we should defeat General Harrison, and that we should hold the line of the Wabash and dictate terms to the whites. The great cause of our failure was the Miamies, whose principal country was south of the river, and they wanted to treat with the whites so as to retain their land, and they played false to their red brethren and yet lost all. They are now surrounded and will be crushed. The whites will shortly have all their lands and they will be driven away. . . .

Our young men said: We are ten to their one. If they stay upon the other side, we will let them alone. If they cross the Wabash, we will take their scalps or drive them into the river. They cannot swim. Their powder will be wet. The fish will eat their bodies. The bones of the white men will lie upon every sand bar. Their flesh will fatten buzzards. These white soldiers are not warriors. Their hands are soft. Their faces are white. One half of them are calico ped-

dlers. The other half can only shoot squirrels. They cannot stand before men. They will all run when we make a noise in the night like wild cats fighting for their young. . . .

Such were the opinions and arguments of our warriors. They did not appreciate the great strength of the white men. I knew their great war chief [General William Harrison], and some of his young men. He was a good man, very soft in his words to his red children, as he called us; and that made some of our men with hot heads mad. I listened to his soft words, but I looked into his eyes. They were full of fire. I knew that they would be among his men like coals of fire in the dry grass. The first wind would raise a great flame. I feared for the red men that might be sleeping in its way. . . .

Our women and children were in the town only a mile from the battle-field waiting for victory and its spoils. They wanted white prisoners. The Prophet [Tenskwatawa, the Shawnee religious leader] had promised that every squaw of any note should have one of the white warriors to use as her slave, or to treat as she pleased. Oh how these women were disappointed! Instead of slaves and spoils of the white men coming into town with the rising sun, their town was in flames and women and children were hunted like wolves and killed by hundreds or driven into the river and swamps to hide. With the smoke of that town and the loss of that battle I lost all hope of the red men being able to stop the whites.

Source: Wesley Whickar, ed., "Shabonne's Account of Tippecanoe," *Indiana Magazine of History* 18 (December 1921): 355–359.

and also by a majority of voters in New England and the Middle Atlantic states; those seaboard regions gave 89 electoral votes to the Federalist candidate for president, De Witt Clinton of New York. Conversely, Madison amassed most of his 128 electoral votes in the South and West—regions whose congressmen had heeded the demands of their constituents and voted for war. Western farmers feared Indian raids and were angry because the British blockade had caused the price of their crops to fall.

In addition, many Americans in all regions were enraged by British arrogance during the decade-long conflict over neutral rights and Indian aid. Demanding

respect for America's status as an independent nation, Republicans mobilized patriotic support for war. As President Madison put it, "National honor is national property of the highest value."

The War of 1812

The War of 1812 was a near disaster for the United States, both militarily and politically. Republican congressmen had predicted an easy victory over British forces in Canada, but when General William Hull invaded western Canada in the summer of 1812, he was immediately forced to retreat. Nonetheless, American

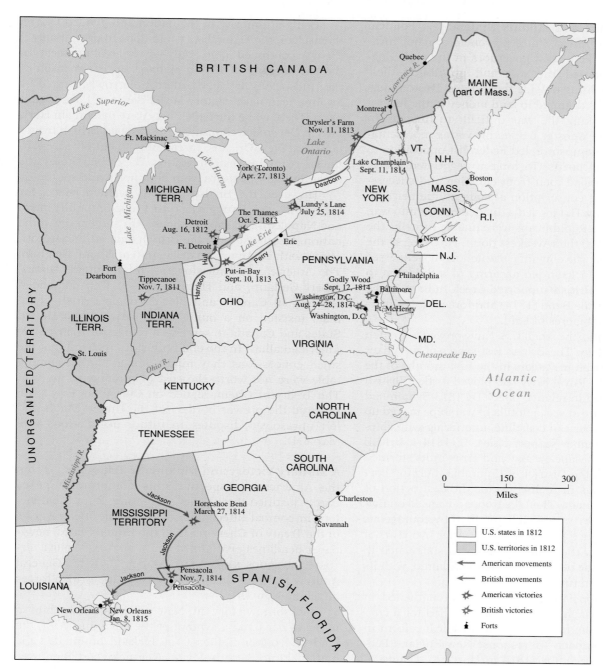

MAP 8.4
The War of 1812
The war had two main phases. In 1812 and 1813, American armies led by Generals Hull, Harrison, and Dearborn and a naval force commanded by Commodore Perry attacked British targets along the Canadian border with mixed success. The British took the offensive in 1814, successfully attacking Washington and Baltimore in the Chesapeake region, but suffering heavy losses when they invaded the United States along Lake Champlain in the northeast and at New Orleans in the southwest.

forces stayed on the offensive. Commodore Oliver Hazard Perry defeated a small British flotilla on Lake Erie, and in October 1813 General William Henry Harrison invaded Canada and defeated a combined British and Indian force at the Battle of the Thames, killing Tecumseh, who had become a general in the British army. Another American force captured and burned the Upper Canada capital of York (now Toronto) but, lacking men and supplies, quickly withdrew (Map 8.4).

Political Conflict and Military Stalemate. Political divisions in the United States prevented a major invasion of Canada. Federalist governors in the New England states opposed the war and prohibited their militias from fighting outside their states. Boston merchants and banks declined to lend money to the federal government, making the war difficult to finance. In Congress, Daniel Webster, a dynamic young representative from New Hampshire, led Federalist opposition to higher taxes and tariffs. To force a negotiated peace, Webster discouraged men from enlisting and successfully opposed the conscription of state militiamen into the national army. Having led a divided nation into war, Madison and the Republicans were unable to strike the British in Canada, their weakest point. However, in the South, a rugged slaveowning planter from Tennessee named Andrew Jackson led an army of militiamen to victory over the British-supported Creek Indians in the Battle of Horseshoe Bend (1814) and forced the Indians to cede 23 million acres of land.

In the Atlantic, the small U.S. Navy proved no match for the Royal Navy. The British lost scores of merchant vessels to American privateers in the first months of the war, but after the Royal Navy redeployed its fleet British commerce moved in relative safety. By 1813 Britain had taken the initiative at sea: a flotilla of warships moved up and down the American coastline, interfering with shipping and threatening seaport cities. In 1814 a British fleet sailed up Chesapeake Bay and army units stormed ashore to attack the District of Columbia, burning government buildings in retaliation for the destruction of York in Upper Canada. Then the troops advanced on Baltimore, where they were finally repulsed by courageous American resistance at Fort McHenry. After two years of sporadic warfare, the United States was stalemated in Canada and on the defensive along the Atlantic, with its new capital city in ruins.

Sectional opposition to the war strengthened in 1814 as the Massachusetts legislature called for a convention "to lay the foundation for a radical reform in the National Compact." In response New England Federalists met in December 1814 in Hartford, Connecticut. Some delegates to the Hartford Convention proposed outright secession by their states, but the majority favored a revision of the Constitution in order to reverse the declining role of the Federalist Party—and New England—in the expanding nation. To end the Virginia Dynasty, the delegates proposed a constitutional amendment that would limit the presidency to a single four-year term and require the office to rotate among citizens from different states. Other delegates suggested amendments restricting commercial embargoes to sixty days and requiring a two-thirds' majority in Congress to declare war, prohibit trade, or admit a new state to the Union.

Being a minority in the nation and divided among themselves, the Federalists could hope to prevail only if the war continued to go badly—a very real prospect. In the late summer of 1814 a planned British invasion of the Hudson River Valley had been narrowly averted by an American naval victory at the Battle of Lake Champlain. Then, while the Federalists were meeting in Hartford in December, thousands of seasoned British troops landed at New Orleans, threatening to cut off access to the sea from the western regions. The United States was under military pressure from both north and south.

However, the British ministry wanted peace, for the twenty-year struggle against French republicanism and Napoleon had sapped the wealth and energy of the nation. In August 1814 the British entered into negotiations with an American delegation at Ghent, Belgium. The American commissioners—John Quincy Adams, Albert Gallatin, and Henry Clay—at first demanded territory in Canada and Florida while British diplomats insisted on a buffer state between the United States and Canada to serve as a refuge for their native American allies. In the end both sides realized that the small concessions they might win at the bargaining table were not worth the cost of prolonging the war. The Treaty of Ghent, signed on Christmas Eve 1814, restored the prewar borders of the United States and left unresolved disputes to future negotiations (see Map 8.4).

A Military Victory and Diplomatic Triumphs. From the American perspective, this compromise peace hardly justified three years of fighting. But a final victory in combat lifted Americans' morale. Before news of the Treaty of Ghent reached the United States, newspaper headlines proclaimed an "ALMOST INCREDIBLE VICTORY!! GLORIOUS NEWS." On January 8, 1815, General Andrew Jackson's troops had crushed the British forces attacking New Orleans.

Jackson's victory at New Orleans made him a national hero and a symbol of the emerging West, the land of frontier fighters. Yet Jackson dominated the battlefield not because of his Kentucky and Tennessee sharpshooters in their coonskin caps but through a traditional deployment of regular troops, including a contingent of French-speaking black Americans, the Corps d'Afrique. The Americans fought from carefully constructed breastworks and were amply supplied with cannon, which rained "grapeshot and cannister bombs" on the massed British formations. The British lost thousands of their finest troops, with 700 dead and 2,000 wounded or taken prisoner. American casualties totaled only 13 dead and 58 wounded. This victory redeemed the nation's battered pride and, together with the coming of peace, undercut the Hartford Convention's demands for a revised Constitution.

Battle of New Orleans, *Jean Hyacinthe de Laclotte (detail)*
As their artillery (right center) bombarded the American lines, British troops attacked
the center of General Andrew Jackson's troops while a column of redcoats (foreground) tried to turn the right flank of the American fortifications. Secure behind their
battlements, Jackson's forces repelled the assaults, leaving the ground littered with
British casualties and taking thousands of prisoners.
New Orleans Museum of Art, gift of Edgar William and Bernice Chrysler Garbisch.

Just as Jackson emerged as a hero of the war, John
Quincy Adams rose to national prominence for his
diplomatic efforts at Ghent and his subsequent success
in resolving the boundary disputes intensified by the
conflict. The son of Federalist president John Adams,
John Quincy joined the Republican Party before the
war, and in 1817 became secretary of state under President James Monroe (1817–1825). Shortly after entering office, Adams turned a diplomatic crisis caused by
General Andrew Jackson to the advantage of the United
States. Jackson had led an unauthorized military expedition into the Spanish colony of East Florida, seized
two forts, and executed two British subjects, accusing
them of encouraging Seminole raids into the United
States. While condemning Jackson's aggressive behavior in private conversations, Adams defended him in
public and used the threat of new attacks to persuade
Spain to cede all of Florida to the United States. American settlers had already occupied parts of western

Florida in 1810 and 1813, and the Adams-Onís Treaty of
1819 extended U.S. control over the entire peninsula. In
return, the American government accepted responsibility for the financial claims of its citizens against Spain,
renounced Jefferson's dubious claim to Spanish Texas,
and agreed on a compromise boundary between New
Spain and the Louisiana Purchase (Map 8.5).

Adams also negotiated important agreements with
Great Britain. The Rush-Bagot Treaty of 1817 limited
British and U.S. naval forces on the Great Lakes. More
important, in 1818 the two countries agreed to establish
the border between the Louisiana Purchase and British
Canada at the 49th parallel. As a result of Adams's
efforts, the United States gained undisputed possession
of nearly all the land south of the 49th parallel and
between the Great Lakes and the Rocky Mountains.
Americans could now look purposefully westward, envisioning a nation that would span the continent, stretching from the Atlantic to the Pacific.

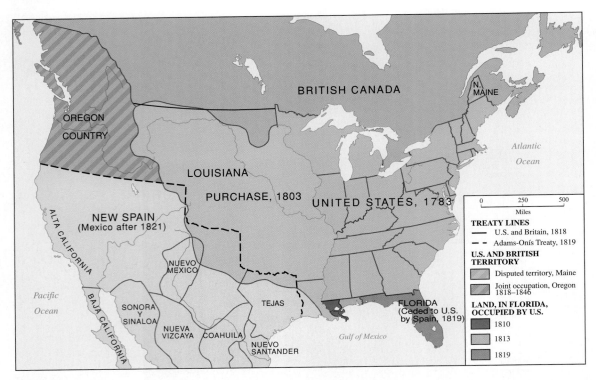

MAP 8.5
Defining the National Boundaries, to 1840
After the War of 1812, American diplomats negotiated treaties with Great Britain and
Spain that defined the national boundaries with Canada to the north and New Spain
(which in 1821 became the independent nation of Mexico) to the west. These treaties
eliminated the threat of war until the 1840s, providing the United States with a much-
needed period of peace and security.

The Capitalist Commonwealth

★

The increase in the geographic size of the United States
was paralleled by the growth of its economic institutions
and wealth. Before 1790 the American republic was an
agricultural society, dependent on Great Britain for markets, credit, and manufactured goods. Over the next generation the United States gradually achieved a measure
of economic independence, as rural Americans became
manufacturers, bankers supplied credit to expand industry and trade, merchants developed regional markets,
and state governments actively encouraged economic
development.

The emerging American economic order had a
capitalist character both because it was based on private property and market exchanges and because
those who had capital (money to invest), such as
financiers, bankers, and wealthy entrepreneurs,
shaped its political and economic policies. Yet the new
system of political economy was also influenced by
the ideology of the republican commonwealth, which

meant that some policies sought the public good
rather than private gain.

A Merchant-Based Economy: Banks, Manufacturing, and Markets

Merchants had dominated the economic life of port
cities in colonial times; with the departure of the
British, they began to set the social and cultural tone as
well. America was "a Nation of Merchants," a British
visitor reported from Philadelphia in 1798, "always
alive to their interests; and keen in the pursuit of wealth
in all the various modes of acquiring it." And acquire it
they did, especially during the European wars that
dragged on from 1792 to 1815.

Daring entrepreneurs, such as the fur trader John
Jacob Astor and the merchant Robert Oliver, became
the nation's first millionaires. Astor migrated from Germany to New York in 1784 and became wealthy by carrying furs from the Pacific Northwest to markets in
China. Investing his profits in real estate, he became the
largest landowner in New York City. Oliver made his fortune in Baltimore, beginning as an agent for Irish linen

merchants and then starting his own mercantile firm. Exploiting the wartime shipping boom, he reaped enormous profits in the West Indian coffee and sugar trade.

Banking and Credit. To finance the expansion of such mercantile enterprises, Americans had to devise an entirely new banking system. Before 1776 economically ambitious colonists had found it difficult to secure loans. Farmers had relied on government-sponsored land banks, pledging their land as security, while merchants such as Oliver had arranged partnerships, borrowed funds from other merchants, or obtained credit from British suppliers. Then, in 1781, several Philadelphia merchants, the enterprising Robert Morris among them, persuaded the Confederation Congress to charter the Bank of North America to provide short-term commercial loans; traders in Boston and New York founded similar banks in 1784. Those institutions provided merchants with the credit they needed to finance their transactions. "Our monied capital has so much increased from the Introduction of Banks, & the Circulation of the Funds," the Philadelphia merchant William Bingham noted as early as 1791, "that the Necessity of Soliciting Credits from England will no longer exist, & the Means will be provided for putting in Motion every Specie of Industry."

In 1791, on Alexander Hamilton's initiative, Congress chartered the Bank of the United States. The bank had the power to issue notes and make commercial loans, and although the bank's managers used their lending powers cautiously, profits still averaged a handsome 8 percent annually. By 1805, in response to the continuing demand for commercial credit, the bank had set up branches in eight major cities.

Nonetheless, for political reasons, the First Bank of the United States did not survive. Jeffersonians had long condemned the idea of a national bank, warning that it would produce "a consolidated, energetic government supported by public creditors, speculators, and other insidious men lacking in public spirit of any kind." When the bank's twenty-year charter expired in 1811, President Madison did not seek its renewal, a decision that forced merchants, artisans, and farmers to ask their state legislatures to create new banks. New York chartered the Mechanics' and Farmers' Bank of Albany in 1811, and other states followed suit. By the time Madison changed his mind with respect to a national bank and chartered the Second Bank of the United States in 1816, there were no fewer than 246 state-chartered banks.

However, many state banks issued notes without adequate reserves of specie, a shortsighted policy that inhibited commercial growth by undermining the notes' value. Poorly managed state banks were one cause of the Panic of 1819, a credit crisis sparked by a sharp drop in world agricultural prices. With farm

A Cloth Merchant
Elijah Boardman (1760–1823) was a prosperous storekeeper in New Milford, Connecticut, who eventually became a U.S. senator. Along with other American traders, he imported huge quantities of cloth from Britain. When war cut off trade, some merchants financed the domestic production of textiles, first in rural households and then in factories. Others, including Boardman, turned to land speculation. In 1795 he joined the Connecticut Land Company and bought huge tracts in Connecticut's "Western Reserve," including the present towns of Medina, Palmyra, and Boardman, Ohio. Ralph Earl painted this portrait of Boardman in 1789.
Metropolitan Museum of Art, bequest of Susan W. Tyler, 1979.

income suddenly cut by one-third, many American farmers were unable to pay their creditors, setting in motion successive bankruptcies among local storekeepers, wholesale merchants, and overextended state banks. The economic recession continued for two years, giving many Americans their first taste of the business cycle—the periodic expansion and contraction of profits and employment that is an inherent part of a market economy.

The Yankee Peddler, c. 1830
Even in 1830 most Americans
lived too far from market towns
to go there regularly to buy
needed goods. Instead, farm families, such as this affluent one represented by an unknown artist,
purchased most of their tinware,
clocks, textiles, and other manufactures from peddlers, often
from New England, who traveled
far and wide in small horse-
drawn vans such as that pictured
in the doorway.
Collection IBM Corporation,
Armonk, NY.

Rural Manufacturing. The Panic of 1819 revealed
that more and more Americans—artisans and yeomen
as well as merchants—depended on regional or
national markets. Before 1790, thousands of artisans in
New England and the Middle Atlantic states had hand-
crafted furniture, tools, wagons, shoes, saddles, clothing, and dozens of other items, but most of those goods
had remained within the local community. For example, John Hoff of Lancaster, Pennsylvania, sold his fine
wooden-cased clocks locally and bartered them with
his neighbors for such things as a dining table, a bedstead, shoes, pine boards, and labor on his small farm.

Other artisans—especially those who worked in
large, specialized groups—had an eye on more distant
markets. Even before independence, shipbuilders in
seacoast towns, iron smelters in Pennsylvania and
Maryland, and shoemakers in Lynn, Massachusetts,
had sold their products in far-flung markets. During the
Revolutionary War, merchants financed the expansion
of other enterprises, encouraging rural men and
women to make cheese, textiles, paper, and gunpowder.
Later, national pride prompted calls for the expansion
of *all* domestic handicrafts. "Until we manufacture
more, it is absurd to celebrate the Fourth of July as the
birthday of our independence," declared a contributor
to the Boston *Gazette*.

With peace restored, many merchants stopped
investing in domestic manufacturing for they could
amass greater profits by selling low-priced British
goods. But a small group of dynamic merchant-

entrepreneurs continued to develop a rural-based manufacturing system in a manner similar to the European
outwork, or *putting-out*, system (see Chapter 1). The
merchants stood at the center of this system, buying the
raw materials, organizing the workers, and selling the
finished products. At the periphery were hundreds of
thousands of farm families that supplied the labor.
When a French traveler visited central Massachusetts
in 1795, he found "almost all these houses . . . inhabited
by men who are both cultivators and artisans; one is a
tanner, another a shoemaker, another sells goods, but
all are farmers."

The outwork system achieved its greatest success in
the shoe and boot trade. In the 1780s merchants and
master craftsmen in Lynn, Massachusetts, began buying
large quantities of leather, thread, and awls and put thousands of farm families to work. Women and their older
sons and daughters stitched together the thin leather and
canvas uppers; then the half-finished shoes were taken by
wagon to Lynn for assembly by journeymen shoemakers.
When the Embargo of 1807 cut off competition from
British-made shoes, merchants in Lynn and over thirty
other Massachusetts towns expanded their output,
making millions of shoes.

By the 1820s entrepreneurs had mobilized an enormous work force in the New England countryside.
Farm families produced shoes, brooms, palm-leaf hats,
and tinware—baking pans, cups, utensils, lanterns.
Merchants shipped these products to cities and slave
plantations while New England peddlers, equipped

"with a horse and a cart covered with a box or with a wagon," blanketed the South, where they acquired the dubious reputation of crafty, hard-bargaining "Yankees." The commercial success of these peddlers and merchants extended the size of the capitalist sector of the American domestic economy. This economic advance stemmed primarily from innovations in organization and marketing rather than in technology, however. Even as their markets expanded, tinworkers, shoemakers, and other artisans continued to use traditional *preindustrial* manufacturing methods.

Power-driven machines—the product of the Industrial Revolution in Britain—were adopted slowly in America, beginning in the textile industry. In the 1780s merchants built scores of small mills along the creeks and rivers of New England and the Middle Atlantic states. They installed water-powered machines and hired workers to card and comb wool—and later cotton—into long strands. For several decades, the next steps in the manufacturing process were accomplished under the outwork system rather than in factories. Farm women and children spun the strands into yarn, receiving wages for their work, while men in other households used foot-powered looms to weave the yarn into cloth. In his *Letter on Manufactures* (1810), Secretary of the Treasury Albert Gallatin estimated that there were 2,500 outwork weavers in New England. A decade later more than 12,000 household workers in that region were weaving woolen cloth, which was then taken to water-powered fulling mills to be pounded flat and finished smooth. Thus, even before textile production was centralized in factories, the nation had a profitable and expanding preindustrial outwork system of manufacturing.

Toward a Market Economy. The rise of rural manufacturing transformed agriculture by motivating farmers to produce more goods for market sale. As a Polish traveler in central Massachusetts reported in 1798, "Along the whole road from Boston, we saw women engaged in making cheese." To provide the milk for cheese production, ambitious farm families switched from mixed-crop agriculture to keeping large herds of dairy cows. Other families expanded their holdings of cattle—selling their hides to the booming shoe industry—and their flocks of sheep—providing wool to textile manufacturers. Rising prices for these raw materials brought prosperity and new businesses to many farming towns. In 1792 Concord, Massachusetts, had one slaughterhouse and five small tanneries; a decade later the town had eleven slaughterhouses and six large tanneries. Foul odors from the stockyards and tanning pits drifted over Concord, but its residents were able to acquire more goods and live more comfortably.

At first, barter transactions were a central feature of the emergent market system, as the records of the book-manufacturing firm of Ebenezer and Daniel Merriam of Brookfield, Massachusetts, demonstrate. When the Merriams began selling books to publishing houses in New York City, Philadelphia, and Boston in the 1810s, they received neither cash nor credit in return but other books, which they had to exchange with local storekeepers to get supplies for their business. The Merriams also paid their employees on a barter basis; a journeyman printer received the use of a small house, credit at local stores, and a third of his "wages" in books, which he had to peddle for himself to gain more than a literary profit from his labors.

Gradually a cash economy replaced this complex barter system. As farm families joined the outwork system, they stopped producing all their own food, clothing, and bedding. Instead they supplied merchants with specialized goods in return for cash or store credit. "Straw hats and Bonnets are manufactured by many families," a Maine official commented in the Census of Manufacturing of 1820, while another observer noted that "probably 8,000 females" in the vicinity of Foxborough, Massachusetts, braided rye straw into hats for market sale. The women used the income from the sale of their labor to shop for clothes, household necessities, and other manufactures in local stores.

The new capitalist-run market economy had some drawbacks. Rural parents—and their children—now worked longer and harder, making shoes, hats, and cloth during the winter, and planting, weeding, and harvesting crops during the warmer seasons. Perhaps more important, they lost some of their economic independence. Instead of working solely for themselves as yeomen farm families, they toiled as part-time wage earners for merchants and manufacturers. The new market system decreased the self-sufficiency of families and communities even as it made them more productive. But the tide of change was unstoppable.

Public Policy: The Commonwealth System

Throughout the nineteenth century, state governments were the most important political institutions in the United States. Beginning in the late 1810s, many states rewrote their constitutions to make them more democratic, decreasing the property requirements for voting, reapportioning legislatures, and increasing the number of elected (rather than appointed) officials. State legislatures also took the lead in regulating social life. They abolished slavery in the North but retained it in the South, enacted laws governing criminal and civil affairs, established taxation systems, and oversaw county, city, and town officials. Consequently, state governments had a much greater impact on the day-to-day lives of Americans than did the national government.

Ballot Box
Elections in Pennsylvania were often contentious affairs, marred by riots and fistfights as rival political groups tried to keep their opponents from the polls. Once safely inside the voting place, citizens deposited their ballots in containers such as this nicely crafted late-eighteenth-century walnut box from the Delaware Valley.
Independence National Historic Park.

As early as the 1790s, many state legislatures attempted to enhance their states' prosperity by devising an American plan of mercantilism, known to historians as the "commonwealth" system (because its goal was to increase the common-wealth of the society). Just as the British Parliament had promoted the imperial economy through the Navigation Acts (1651–1696), state legislatures enacted measures to stimulate commerce and economic development. In particular, they granted hundreds of *corporate charters* to private businesses that were intended, as the act establishing the Massachusetts Bank put it, to be "of great public utility." Chartered companies were not new, of course; English investors had used them to establish the first American colonies. Under English law, however, colonial governments had been discouraged from creating corporations. As a result, American merchants had financed their mills, shipyards, and trading ventures through private partnerships, which lacked some of the economic advantages of government-chartered corporations, such as tax exemptions and monopoly privileges.

Private partnerships also lacked the funds required to build the large-scale transportation projects—the economic infrastructure—that had become a high priority. State legislatures therefore issued numerous charters of incorporation to promote investment in roads, bridges, and canals. In 1794 the Lancaster Turnpike Company received a monopoly charter from the Pennsylvania assembly to lay a graded gravel road between Lancaster and Philadelphia—a distance of 65 miles. The venture was expensive—nearly $500,000 ($6 million today)—but the road made a modest profit for the investors, and the reward to the regional economy from the greatly enhanced flow of people and goods was much greater. "The turnpike is finished," noted a farm woman, "and we can now go to town at all times and in all weather." The success of the Lancaster Turnpike set off a boom in turnpike construction, and improved roads soon connected dozens of inland market centers to seaport cities.

By 1800 state governments had granted more than 300 corporate charters. Incorporation enhanced the status of private companies in two ways. First, some charters protected investors by granting them *limited liability;* in the event of a business failure, shareholders' personal assets could not be seized to pay the corporation's debts. Second, most transportation charters included the power of *eminent domain,* which enabled turnpike, bridge, and canal corporations to use the judicial system to force the sale of land along their routes. This power—previously available only to the government—permitted private corporations to take land from property owners for a reasonable price, even if the owners did not want to sell. In granting corporations the power of eminent domain, state legislatures promoted the good of the commonwealth at the expense of the property rights of private citizens.

Such uses of state power by private companies were controversial, and in the eyes of some critics, they were contrary to republicanism, "which does not admit of granting peculiar privileges to any body of men." Charters not only violated the "equal rights" of all citizens, opponents argued, but restricted the sovereignty of the people. As a Pennsylvanian put it, "whatever power is given to a corporation, is just so much power taken from the State, in derogation of the original power of the mass of the community." Nonetheless, state courts consistently upheld the validity of corporate charters. Judges routinely approved grants of eminent domain to private corporations. "The opening of good and easy internal communications is one of the highest duties of government," a New Jersey court declared.

State mercantilism soon encompassed much more than transportation. In the years immediately following the Embargo of 1807, which cut off goods and credit from Europe, New England state governments awarded charters to 200 iron-mining, textile-manufacturing, and banking firms. Over the next few decades the Pennsylvania legislature was even more active, chartering more than 1,100 corporations and authorizing them to hold

Conestoga Wagon on the Pennsylvania Turnpike, *Thomas Birch, 1816*
To speed the settlement of western regions, state governments chartered private turnpike companies, which built broad roads and sturdy bridges, and collected tolls to pay for them. American inventors met the demand for better transportation by designing lightweight but durable rigs—such as the Conestoga Wagon—that could carry substantial loads.
Shelburne Museum, Shelburne, VT.

over $150 million in capital. Corporations—whether in the form of incorporated towns and cities, incorporated charitable institutions, or chartered private businesses—were becoming a central institution in American society. As one contemporary put it, "the whole political system" was "made up of concatenations of various corporations, political, civil, religious, social and economical."

Thus, by 1820 the innovative policies of state governments had created a new political economy: the commonwealth system. This system elevated the good of the public above that of private individuals. But because state legislatures relied on private corporations, this system also enhanced the economic and political power of capitalist entrepreneurs. The instru-

mental use of state incentives to encourage business enterprise and improve the general welfare would continue for another generation. In 1820 Missouri lawmakers incorporated this outlook into that state's first constitution, specifying that "internal improvements shall forever be encouraged by the government of this state."

Law and the Commonwealth: Republicans versus Federalists

Both Federalists and Republicans endorsed the idea of the commonwealth, but in different ways. Federalists looked to the national government for economic leadership and supported Hamilton's program of *national* mercantilism: a funded debt, tariffs, and a central bank. Jeffersonian Republicans generally opposed such policies, relying instead on *state* legislatures to promote economic development.

After the War of 1812, some Republicans, led by Henry Clay of Kentucky, began to support national economic initiatives. As Speaker of the House of Representatives, Clay supported the creation of the Second Bank of the United States in 1816. In the following year he won passage of the Bonus Bill, sponsored by Representative John C. Calhoun of South Carolina, which would have established a national fund for roads and other internal improvements. But most Republicans still opposed national mercantilist policies; they agreed with President Madison, who vetoed the Bonus Bill because he felt it exceeded the powers delegated to the national government by the Constitution. This fundamental disagreement over the role of the national government would become a key issue of political debate for the next thirty years (see Chapter 11).

Common Law versus Statute Law. Differing conceptions of law also separated Federalists and Republicans. From the earliest colonial times, American jurisprudence had followed English common law. In deciding cases, judges relied on *precedents*—previous decisions in similar cases—and assumed, as a Maryland lawyer put it, that "the Common Law takes in the Law of Nature, the Law of Reason and the Revealed Law of God." In this view, which was held by many Federalists, law was venerable and unchanging.

Beginning in 1776, the revolutionary republican doctrine of popular sovereignty undermined the intellectual foundations of the old legal order. In the debate over constitutional principles, many Americans recognized that law was a human invention, the product of politics rather than a sacred body of timeless truths. During the 1790s Thomas Jefferson and other Republican Party leaders attacked the common-law system, maintaining that law made by judges following common-law precedent was inferior to the statute ("positive") law enacted by representatives of the people. As a Republican jurist put it, a magistrate "should be governed himself by *positive* law" while executing and enforcing "the will of the supreme power, which is the will of THE PEOPLE."

In response, Federalist judges and politicians warned that popular sovereignty had to be curbed. Without safeguards, representative government would result in the "tyranny of the majority"—the passage of statutes that would infringe on the property rights of individual citizens. To prevent state legislatures from overriding property rights, Federalist lawyers asserted that judges had the power to void laws that violated traditional common-law principles or were contrary to "natural law" or "natural rights" (see Chapter 4).

Common Law versus Economic Development. Because common-law precedents had evolved in a relatively static agricultural economy, they often discouraged new modes of enterprise. For example, capitalist entrepreneurs who erected dams to power flour or textile mills often flooded adjacent farmlands; outraged farmers sued, charging that the dams infringed on their property rights, constituted a public "nuisance," and should be pulled down. At first the farmers won most of these cases as judges used common-law precedents to rule that interfering with the natural flow of a river for nonfarming purposes was illegal.

But when it became clear that such decisions would stifle economic development, state legislatures enacted statutes that overrode common law. In Massachusetts, the Mill Dam Act of 1795 allowed mill proprietors to flood adjacent farmland and required farmers to accept "fair compensation" for their lost acreage. Prodevelopment legislators justified the taking of private property by asserting the superior rights of those who made dynamic, rather than static, use of their property.

State judges with Republican leanings accepted the doctrines of popular sovereignty and legislative power and tended to uphold mill acts, just as they supported legislative statutes that granted eminent domain to private turnpike and canal corporations. To these judges, *social utility*—the greatest good for the greatest number of people—justified the government's intrusion into individual citizens' property rights. Such rulings shocked the Federalist lawyer and politician Daniel Webster, who considered them no less than a "revolution against the foundations on which property rests." Although both political parties favored economic development, Federalists gave a higher priority to national mercantilism, common law, and a static theory of property rights; Republicans emphasized state activism, statute law, and a dynamic concept of property (see Voices from Abroad, "Alexis de Tocqueville: Law and Lawyers in the United States," p. 273).

Federalist Law: John Marshall and the Supreme Court

When Thomas Jefferson became president in 1801, he warned that his Federalist opponents still controlled the judiciary and would use its power to thwart Republican policies. The legal career of John Marshall confirmed Jefferson's prediction. Appointed Chief Justice of the Supreme Court by President Adams in January 1801,

ALEXIS DE TOCQUEVILLE
Law and Lawyers in the United States

★

A French aristocrat and lawyer, Alexis de Tocqueville came to the United States to study its innovative prison system but ended up writing Democracy in America (1835), a comprehensive and astute analysis of its dynamic society. Here Tocqueville argues that the raw vigor of American democracy was restrained by the ingrained conservatism of men of the law, who dominated the political system.

The political activity that pervades the United States must be seen in order to be understood. No sooner do you set foot upon American ground than you are stunned by a kind of tumult . . . everything is in motion around you; here the people of one quarter of a town are met to decide upon the building of a church; there the election of a representative is going on; . . . in another place, the laborers of a village quit their plows to deliberate upon the project of a road or a public school. . . .

The political agitation of American legislative bodies, which is the only one that attracts the attention of foreigners, is a mere episode, or a sort of continuation, of that universal movement which originates in the lowest classes of the people and extends successively to all the ranks of society. . . .

In visiting the Americans and studying their laws, we perceive that the authority they have entrusted to the members of the legal profession, and the influence that these individuals exercise in the government, are the most powerful existing security against the excesses of democracy. This effect seems to me to result from a general cause, which it is useful to investigate. . . . Men who have made a special study of the laws derive from [that] occupation certain habits of order, a taste for formalities, and a kind of instinctive regard for the regular connection of ideas, which naturally render them very hostile to the revolutionary spirit and the unreflecting passions of the multitude. . . .

[Moreover,] the government of democracy is favorable to the political power of lawyers; for when the wealthy, the noble, and the prince are excluded from the government, the lawyers take possession of it, in their own right, as it were, since they are the only men of information and sagacity, beyond the sphere of the people, who can be the object of popular choice. . . .

The people in democratic states do not mistrust the members of the legal profession, because it is known that they are interested to serve the popular cause. . . . Lawyers belong to the people by birth and interest, and to the aristocracy by habit and taste; they may be looked upon as the connecting link between the two great classes of society. . . . When the American people are intoxicated by passion or carried away by the impetuosity of their ideas, they are checked and stopped by the almost invisible influence of their legal counselors.

As most public men are legal practitioners, they introduce the customs and technicalities of their profession into the management of public affairs. The jury extends this habit to all classes. The language of the law thus becomes, in some measure, a vulgar tongue . . . so that at last the whole people contract the habits and the tastes of the judicial magistrate.

Source: Alexis de Tocqueville, *Democracy in America*, ed. Philip Bradley (New York: Vintage, 1945), 1:283–290.

Marshall upheld Federalist principles until his death in 1835. His success stemmed not from a mastery of legal principles and doctrines but from the power of his logic and the force of his personality. Especially in the years before 1822, Marshall dominated the Supreme Court and shaped the meaning given to the Constitution. Three principles shaped his jurisprudence: a commitment to judicial authority, the supremacy of national over state legislation, and a traditional, static view of property rights.

Judicial Authority: *Marbury v. Madison.* In 1798, during the dispute over the Alien and Sedition Acts, Republican-dominated legislatures in Kentucky and Virginia had asserted the authority of the state legislatures to determine the constitutionality of national deciding that the Judiciary Act of 1789 violated the Constitution, the Chief Justice did both. "It is emphatically the province and duty of the judicial department to say what the law is," Marshall declared.

Thereafter, the doctrine of judicial review evolved slowly. During the first half of the nineteenth century, the Supreme Court and the state courts used it only to overturn *state* laws that conflicted with constitutional principles. Not until the *Dred Scott* decision of 1857 would the Supreme Court void another national law (see Chapter 13).

Nationalism: *McCulloch v. Maryland.*

Marshall's second principle—the supremacy of national over state legislation—was most eloquently expressed in the controversial case *McCulloch v. Maryland* (1819). When Congress created the Second Bank of the United States in 1816, it gave that bank the authority to handle the notes of state-chartered banks and thus to monitor their financial reserves. To preserve the independence and competitive position of its state banks, the Maryland legislature passed a statute imposing an annual tax of $15,000 on notes issued by the Second Bank's Baltimore branch.

The Second Bank contested the constitutionality of that action, claiming that it infringed on the powers of the national government. In response, lawyers for the state of Maryland adopted Jefferson's argument against the First Bank of the United States, maintaining that Congress lacked the constitutional authority to charter a national bank. Even if such a bank could be created, the lawyers argued, Maryland had a right to tax its activities within the state.

Marshall firmly rejected both arguments. The Second Bank was constitutional, he declared, because its existence was "necessary and proper," given the national government's responsibility to control currency and credit. Like Alexander Hamilton and other Federalists, Marshall preferred a loose construction of the Constitution. If the goal of a law is "legitimate [and] . . . within the scope of the Constitution," he wrote, then "all means which are appropriate" to secure that goal are also constitutional even if they are not explicitly mentioned in the Constitution.

As for Maryland's right to tax all institutions within its borders, the Chief Justice embraced the nationalist position advanced by Daniel Webster, a fellow Federalist and the legal counsel to the Second Bank. "The power to tax involves the power to destroy," Marshall observed, suggesting that Maryland's bank tax would render the national government "dependent on the states"—an outcome that "was not intended by the American people" who ratified the Constitution.

John Marshall, *Chester Harding, c. 1830*
Even at age seventy-five, John Marshall (1755–1835) had a commanding personal presence. Upon becoming Chief Justice of the U.S. Supreme Court in 1801, Marshall elevated the court from a minor department of the national government to a major institution in American legal and political life. His constitutional decisions dealing with judicial review, contract rights, regulation of commerce, and national banking permanently shaped the character of American law.
Boston Athenaeum.

laws. However, the Constitution stated that "the judicial Power shall extend to all Cases . . . arising under this Constitution [and] the Laws of the United States," implying that the Supreme Court held the final power of *judicial review* over such legislation.

Before 1803, when Marshall rendered the decision in the celebrated case of *Marbury v. Madison,* the Supreme Court had never overturned a national law or explicitly claimed the power of judicial review. In

Marshall asserted the dominance of national statutes over state legislation again in *Gibbons v. Ogden* (1824), which struck down a monopoly the New York legislature had granted to Aaron Ogden for steamboat passenger service across the Hudson River to New Jersey. Asserting that the Constitution gave the federal government the authority to regulate interstate commerce, the Chief Justice upheld the claim of Thomas Gibbons, who held a federal license to transport people and goods.

Property Rights: *Fletcher v. Peck*. Marshall also turned to the Constitution to uphold his third principle: property rights. To protect individuals against government interference with their property, Marshall seized on the *contract clause* of the Constitution (Article 1, section 10), which prohibits the states from passing any law "impairing the obligation of contracts." Delegates at the Philadelphia convention in 1787 had included this clause primarily to void state laws that protected debtors from merchants and other creditors, but Marshall expanded the scope of the contract clause by using it to defend other property rights against legislative challenge.

To do this, Marshall gave a broad definition to the term *contract,* extending it to embrace state grants and charters. For example, the important case of *Fletcher v. Peck* (1810) involved a large grant of land made by the Georgia legislature to the Yazoo Land Company. When a newly elected state legislature canceled the grant, alleging that it had been obtained through fraud and bribery, speculators who had already purchased Yazoo lands appealed to the Supreme Court to uphold their titles. Speaking for the Court, Marshall ruled that the purchasers held valid contracts that could not be voided by the state of Georgia. This decision was far-reaching. It not only gave constitutional protection against subsequent legislation to those who purchased state-owned lands but, by upholding the rights of out-of-state speculators, also promoted the development of a national capitalist economy.

The court extended its defense of property rights even further in *Dartmouth College v. Woodward* (1819). Dartmouth College was a private institution established by a charter granted by King George III. In 1816 the Republican-dominated legislature of New Hampshire tried to convert the college into a public university so that it could educate more of the state's citizens, thereby enhancing the commonwealth. The Dartmouth trustees resisted the plan and engaged Daniel Webster to plead their case before the Supreme Court. Webster invoked the Court's decision in *Fletcher v. Peck*, arguing that the royal charter constituted a contract and there-fore could not be tampered with by the New Hampshire legislature.

Marshall had difficulty persuading his colleagues to accept this position. Although he was still the dominant member of the Supreme Court, by 1819 five of the seven justices had been appointed by the Republican presidents Jefferson and Madison. Some of those justices embraced the commonwealth ideal, arguing that a public university would better serve the common good. Other Republican judges hesitated to restrict the powers of state legislatures or expand the broad protection for property rights already set forth in *Fletcher v. Peck*. Only after months of deliberation did the other justices on the Court follow Marshall and rule in favor of the college. Marshall's triumph seemed complete: he had incorporated Federalist principles into the law of the land. Indeed, many of these legal doctrines, such as judicial review and corporate rights, have become central fixtures of American law.

The Decline of Federalism. Even as Marshall announced the decisions in *Dartmouth* and *McCulloch* in 1819, the Federalist cause for which he labored was in severe decline, in part because of the expansion of the nation to the west. In a growing and increasingly democratic nation, the Federalists' eastern-oriented and elitist policies received little popular support. "No Federal character can run with success," Gouverneur Morris of New York lamented, and the election results of 1818 bore out his pessimism. Following the election, Republicans outnumbered Federalists 37 to 7 in the Senate and 156 to 27 in the House of Representatives.

The attack on Federalism and its principles gradually extended into the judiciary as Republican presidents and state legislatures appointed new judges. Jurists who valued the rights of states began to limit Marshall's nationalist vision, and state legislators evaded the restrictions of the *Dartmouth* decision by granting charters that included clauses allowing the state to alter their terms. In law as in politics, the transformation in American government begun by Jefferson's Revolution of 1800 finally moved toward completion, bringing the tumultuous era of Federalist-Republican conflict to an end.

The decline of the political controversy prompted contemporary observers to dub James Monroe's two terms as president (1817–1825) as the Era of Good Feeling. Actually, national political harmony was more apparent than real, for the Republican Party—by then home to many former Federalists—soon split into factions that struggled over power, patronage, and, after 1820, economic policy. One cycle of American politics and economic debate had ended, but another was soon to begin.

Summary

★

Between 1790 and 1820 the United States acquired immense new lands in the West and developed a capitalist economy in the East. The pace of westward expansion was slowed by native Americans fighting to defend their lands, the difficulties of transport and trade across the mountains, and the high price of land sold by both the U.S. government and speculators. Nonetheless, by 1820, fully 2 million Americans, white and black, were living west of the Appalachians.

Led by Thomas Jefferson, who favored westward expansion, the Republicans wrested political power from the Federalists. While retaining the Bank of the United States and many Federalist bureaucrats, Jefferson eliminated excise taxes, reduced the national debt, cut the size of the army, and lowered the price of national lands in the West. Faced with British and French seizures of American ships and sailors, he devised the Embargo of 1807, but it failed to change the policies of the warring nations. Eventually, Indian uprisings and expansionist demands by western Republicans led President James Madison into the War of 1812 against Britain. The war split the nation, prompting a secessionist movement in New England, but a negotiated peace ended the military stalemate and Andrew Jackson's victory at New Orleans preserved American honor. The diplomacy of John Quincy Adams led to the annexation of Florida and the settlement of boundaries with British Canada and Spanish Texas.

As Americans imposed a new political economy on the lands of the West, they developed a capitalist economy in the East. Beginning in the 1790s merchant capitalists created a flourishing outwork system of rural manufacturing, and state governments devised the commonwealth system—awarding corporate charters and subsidies to assist transportation companies, manufacturers, and banks. Republican-minded state legislatures enacted statutes that promoted economic development by redefining common-law property rights. Led by the Federalist John Marshall, the Supreme Court protected the traditional rights of property owners and the charter privileges of business corporations. Entrepreneurs took advantage of state legislation and judicial protection to create new business enterprises, strong regional economies, and the beginnings of a national market system.

TIMELINE

1787	Northwest Ordinance
1790s	Turnpikes and short canals are built
	Rural outwork system begins in shoes and textiles
	State mercantilism emerges: corporate charters
1790–1791	Little Turtle defeats American armies
1791	First Bank of the United States (1791–1811)
1792	Kentucky joins Union; Tennessee follows (1796)
1794	Battle of Fallen Timbers; Treaty of Greenville (1795)
	Lancaster Turnpike Company chartered
1795	Massachusetts Mill Dam Act promotes industry development
	Pinckney's Treaty with Spain allows U.S. use of Mississippi River
1801	Spain restores Louisiana to France
	John Marshall becomes Chief Justice
1801–1807	Treasury secretary Albert Gallatin reduces national debt
	Seizures of American ships by France and Britain
	Handsome Lake revives traditional beliefs
1803	Louisiana Purchase; Lewis and Clark expedition
	Marbury v. Madison asserts judicial review
1807	Embargo Act cripples American shipping
1809	Tecumseh and Tenskwatawa mobilize Indians
	Congress bans importation of slaves
1810s	Expansion of slavery into Old Southwest
	Fletcher v. Peck extends contract clause
1811	Battle of Tippecanoe
1812–1815	War of 1812
1817–1818	British-American agreements establish U.S.-Canadian boundary
1817–1825	Era of Good Feeling during James Monroe's presidency
1819	Adams-Onís Treaty: Florida annexed, Texas boundary defined
	McCulloch v. Maryland enhances power of national government
	Dartmouth College v. Woodward protects property rights

Suggested Readings

Gregory Evans Dowd, *A Spirited Resistance: The North American Indian Struggle for Unity, 1745–1815* (1992), presents a fine survey of the Indian peoples. Donald R. Hickey, *The War of 1812: A Forgotten Conflict* (1989), puts the war in an economic and diplomatic context. R. Kent Newmyer, *The Supreme Court under Marshall and Taney* (1968), and Gregory Nobles, *American Frontiers: Cultural Encounters and Continental Conquest* (1997), offer excellent overviews.

Westward Expansion

For studies of white policy toward native Americans, see Bernard Sheehan, *Seeds of Extinction: Jeffersonian Philanthropy and the American Indian* (1973); Reginald Horsman, *Expansion and American Indian Policy, 1783–1812* (1967); and Richard Slotkin, *Regeneration through Violence: The Mythology of the American Frontier* (1973). Works dealing with the impact of Christian missions include William W. Fitzhugh, ed., *Cultures in Contact* (1985); William G. McLoughlin, *Cherokees and Missionaries, 1789–1839* (1984); and Earl P. Olmstead, *Blackcoats among the Delaware* (1991). Other analyses of cultural interaction are William G. McLoughlin, *Cherokee Renascence in the New Republic* (1986); J. Leitch Wright Jr., *Creeks and Seminoles: The Destruction and Regeneration of the Muscogulge People* (1986); and John Mack Faragher, *Daniel Boone* (1992).

Two fine accounts of settlers and speculators are Alan Taylor, *Liberty Men and Great Proprietors* (1990) and *William Cooper's Town* (1995). For developments west of the Appalachian Mountains, see Malcolm J. Rohrbough, *The Transappalachian Frontier: Peoples, Societies, and Institutions, 1775–1850* (1978), and John Mack Faragher, *Sugar Creek: Life on the Illinois Prairie* (1986). For detailed analyses of the Old Northwest, see Andrew R. L. Cayton, *The Frontier Republic: Ideology and Politics in the Ohio Country, 1789–1812* (1986), and Andrew R. L. Cayton and Peter S. Onuf, *The Midwest and the Nation* (1990).

The Republicans' Political Revolution

Two good general accounts are Marshall Smelser, *The Democratic Republic, 1801–1815* (1968), and Ralph Ketcham, *Presidents above Party: The First American Presidency, 1789–1829* (1984). Detailed studies of Jefferson's presidency include Daniel Sisson, *The Revolution of 1800* (1974); Dumas Malone, *Jefferson the President* (2 vols., 1970 and 1974); and Richard E. Ellis, *The Jeffersonian Crisis: Courts and Politics in the New Republic* (1971). On the Louisiana Purchase, see Stephen E. Ambrose, *Undaunted Courage: Meriwether Lewis, Thomas Jefferson, and the Opening of the American West* (1996), and James P. Ronda, *Lewis and Clark among the Indians* (1984).

The activities of Aaron Burr are covered in Milton Lomask, *Aaron Burr* (1979). For the Federalists see David Hackett Fischer, *The Revolution of American Conservatism: The Federalist Party in the Age of Jeffersonian Democracy* (1965), and James Banner, *To the Hartford Convention: The Federalists and the Origins of Party Politics in the Early Republic, 1789–1815* (1970).

American attempts to avoid involvement in the Napoleonic Wars are traced in Lawrence Kaplan, *"Entangling Alliances with None": American Foreign Policy in the Age of Jefferson* (1987), and Bradford Perkins, *Prologue to War: England and the United States, 1805–1812* (1961). See also Clifford L. Egan, *Neither Peace nor War: Franco-American Relations, 1803–1812* (1983), and Doron S. Ben-Atar, *The Origins of Jeffersonian Commercial Policy and Diplomacy* (1993). On James Madison, see Robert A. Rutland, *The Presidency of James Madison* (1990); J. C. A. Stagg, *Mr. Madison's War: Politics, Diplomacy, and Warfare in the Early Republic, 1783–1830* (1983); and Drew McCoy, *The Last of the Fathers: James Madison and the Republican Legacy* (1989). For native Americans and the War of 1812 consult R. David Edmunds, *Tecumseh and the Quest for Indian Leadership* (1984), and H. S. Halbert and T. H. Ball, *The Creek War of 1813 and 1814* (1970).

Spain's activities are covered in David Weber, *The Spanish Frontier in North America* (1992), and American initiatives are the subject of Walter LaFeber, ed., *John Quincy Adams and American Continental Empire* (1965).

The Capitalist Commonwealth

Thomas Doerflinger, *A Vigorous Spirit of Enterprise: Merchants and Economic Development in Revolutionary Philadelphia* (1986); John Denis Haeger, *John Jacob Astor* (1991); and Stuart Bruchey, *Robert Oliver: Merchant of Baltimore* (1956), are fine studies of merchant enterprise. The standard history is Curtis R. Nettels, *The Emergence of a National Economy, 1775–1815* (1965). See also Ronald Hoffman, John J. McCusker, and Peter Albert, eds., *The Economy of Revolutionary America* (1987), and Daniel P. Jones, *The Economic and Social Transformation of Rhode Island, 1780–1850* (1992).

On banking, consult the classic study by Bray Hammond, *Banks and Politics in America* (1957), and Richard H. Timberlake, *Monetary Policy in the United States* (1992). Studies of manufacturing include Thomas C. Cochran, *Frontiers of Change: Early Industrialism in America* (1981), and Judith A. McGaw, *Early American Technology* (1994).

The classic studies of state mercantilism are Oscar Handlin and Mary Handlin, *Commonwealth: A Study of the Role of Government in the American Economy: Massachusetts, 1774–1861* (1947), and Louis Hartz, *Economic Policy and Democratic Thought: Pennsylvania, 1776–1860* (1948). State support for transportation can be traced in Carter Goodrich, *Government Promotion of American Canals and Railroads* (1960); Erik F. Hiates et al., *Western River Transportation: The Era of Early Internal Development, 1810–1860* (1975); and Harry N. Scheiber, *Ohio Canal Era: A Case Study of Government and the Economy* (1969).

The legal implications of commonwealth ideology are analyzed in Leonard Levy, *The Law of the Commonwealth and Chief Justice Shaw* (1955), and Morton Horwitz, *The Transformation of American Law, 1790–1860* (1976). On the Supreme Court, see Robert K. Faulkner, *The Jurisprudence of John Marshall* (1968); Francis N. Stites, *John Marshall: Defender of the Constitution* (1981); Thomas C. Shevory, ed., *John Marshall's Achievement* (1989); and C. Peter McGrath, *Yazoo: Law and Politics in the New Republic* (1966).

The Quest for a Republican Society, 1790–1820

FOR MOST WHITE Americans, July 4, 1826, was a day of celebration. For fifty years they had lived in a self-governing society, free of an arbitrary government that imposed high taxes and of an established church that enforced rigid dogma. Not even a tragic occurrence—the nearly simultaneous deaths on that Independence Day of former presidents John Adams and Thomas Jefferson—shook their optimism. Rather, many citizens interpreted this astounding coincidence in timing as divinely inspired, a sign that God looked with favor on their experiment in self-government. Two of the greatest founders had died, but the republic lived on.

During that first half-century, the nation had matured into a full-fledged "republican" society. After independence, Americans tried to become "republicans" not just in their constitutional and legal systems but also in their political outlook, social behavior, and cultural values. By the 1820s they had made considerable progress toward that goal, for their state and society now reflected many of the values of ordinary citizens. Attesting to the self-confident spirit of the new republic, leading citizens hailed their society as a model for all peoples. "The temperate zone of North America," a Kentucky judge declared in a Fourth of July speech, "already exhibits many signs that it is the promised land of civil liberty, and of institutions designed to liberate and exalt the human race."

Yet this pursuit of republican ideals was conflict-ridden and complex, for three partially competing, partially complementary visions of republican society

The Fourth of July in Philadelphia, c. 1811
By the early nineteenth century, July Fourth had become a popular holiday, a time for political speeches, leisurely conversations, and youthful revelry. This detail from a painting by J. Krimmel shows a crowd celebrating the holiday. The young man buying an alcoholic drink from a street vendor (left side) may well engage in some rowdy behavior before Independence Day is over.
Pennsylvania Academy of the Fine Arts, Philadelphia. Pennsylvania Academy Purchase (from the estate of Paul Beck Jr.).

emerged during this formative era. Many white Americans, especially in the northern states, subscribed to an ideology of democratic republicanism. Seeking to implement their ideals, they tried to instill greater equality into political and family life. Sometimes these initiatives succeeded, but just as often they failed because of the strength of entrenched cultural values and economic interests. In the South many whites shared these democratic aspirations, but because their society was even more sharply divided along the lines of class and race than that of the North, they found such ideals much more difficult to attain. Consequently, southern leaders gradually devised an aristocratic-republican ideology that better represented the dominant cultural values and hierarchical character of their society. Yet a third vision of American republican society took shape in the wake of the massive religious revival that swept through American society during the first half of the nineteenth century. For the many Americans—white and black, southern and northern—who embraced this vision, the United States was both a great experiment in republican government and the seedbed of a new Christian civilization.

Democratic Republicanism

-------------★-------------

After independence, leading Americans developed a political system based on the republican principle of "ordered liberty," which in practice meant continued rule by the traditional elite. Gradually ordinary citizens—white men of modest means—condemned the aristocratic pretensions of old-style political leaders and used the republican doctrines of legal equality and social mobility to gain the right to vote and improve their social status. These citizens also used republican ideals to reorganize traditional social institutions such as families and schools; they sought more egalitarian marriages and more affectionate ways of rearing and educating their children. As a result, many individuals—women as well as men—gained more freedom to choose their marriage partners and social values.

Social and Political Equality for White Men

Between 1780 and 1820 hundreds of well-educated Europeans visited the United States to observe life in a republican society. These visitors came from countries with monarchical governments, established churches, male-dominated families, and profound divisions between social classes. They wondered—as have successive generations of historians—whether America represented a different and a more just social order than their own. Comparing the Old World with the New in his famous *Letters from an American Farmer* (1782), the French-born essayist St. Jean de Crèvecoeur wrote that European society was composed "of great lords who possess everything, and of a herd of people who have nothing." America, by contrast, had "no aristocratical families, no courts, no kings, no bishops." Foreign visitors were well aware of the class and racial divisions that existed in the United States, but they saw them as different from those in Europe.

Social Mobility. The absence of a hereditary aristocracy encouraged enterprising white Americans to condemn inherited social privilege. Republican ideology further undermined hierarchical authority by proclaiming that all free men were equal before the law. "The law is the same for everyone both as it protects and as it punishes," noted one European traveler. As a result, many citizens came to value personal achievement and upward social mobility. As one letter to a newspaper put it, individuals should be valued not for their "wealth, titles, or connections" but for their "talents, integrity, and virtue." Divisions among social classes were acceptable only if they were based on achievement and not inheritance.

As a result of the expansion of the American economy after 1790 and the ability of ordinary citizens to purchase land in the West, many individuals attained substantial wealth. And, unlike in Europe, this success was rewarded by a higher social standing. "In Europe to say of someone that he rose from nothing is a disgrace and a reproach," remarked an aristocratic Polish visitor. "It is the opposite here. To be the architect of your own fortune is honorable. It is the highest recommendation."

Popular belief in the superiority of a competitive, achievement-oriented society was apparent in the legal profession. During the Revolutionary era, American attorneys established associations and won legislation that prevented untrained lawyers from practicing law. By 1800 most of the sixteen states required lawyers to have three to seven years of formal schooling or apprenticeship training, requirements that benefited young men from well-established families. As legal rules became a more central part of American life, the legal profession grew in importance (Table 9.1). As early as 1820, 15 percent of the members of the Massachusetts assembly and 35 percent of those in the Senate were lawyers, though men of the law constituted only 1 percent of the state's adult male population.

The enhanced status of the legal profession inspired calls for its reform. Republican-minded critics attacked what they called the "professional aristocracy" of lawyers, demanding the regulation of attorneys' fees and the creation of small-claims courts in which ordi-

TABLE 9.1

Number of Lawyers in Three Selected States, to 1820

	Number of Lawyers	Lawyers per 10,000 Population
Massachusetts (including Maine)		
1740	15	10
1775	71	24
1780	34	11
1785	92	24
1790	112	24
1800	200	35
1810	492	70
1820	710	87
Connecticut		
1790	129	54
1800	169	67
1820	248	90
South Carolina		
1771	24	19
1820	200	40

Source: George Dargo, *Law in the New Republic: Private Law and the Public Estate* (New York: Knopf, 1983), 49. Reprinted by permission of McGraw-Hill, Inc.

nary citizens could represent themselves. Democratic-minded reformers also succeeded in obtaining more relaxed standards for admission to the bar. By the 1820s only eleven of the twenty-six states required a fixed period of legal instruction, a change that lowered the intellectual quality of the legal profession but made it more democratic in composition and spirit.

Some Americans from long-distinguished families questioned the moral legitimacy of a social order based primarily on individual achievement and financial success. "The aristocracy of Kingston [New York] is more one of money than any village I have ever seen," complained Nathaniel Booth in 1825. Booth's ancestors had once ruled Kingston, but his family had lost its prominence in the rapidly growing Hudson River town. "Man is estimated by dollars," he lamented; "what he is worth determines his character and his position at once." But Booth spoke for a minority of Americans. For most white men, republicanism meant the opportunity to advance their interests and those of their families. For them, America was the "best poor man's country."

A Wider Franchise for Men. By the 1810s republicanism was also coming to mean voting rights for free white men. With the advent of popular sovereignty and provisions in state constitutions in Pennsylvania, Vermont, and elsewhere that allowed all taxpayers to vote, property ownership no longer constituted the foundation of citizenship. Increasingly, Americans repudiated the hierarchical ideal of Federalists such as Samuel Stone, who had called for "a *speaking* aristocracy in the face of a *silent* democracy." Rejecting the deferential politics of the eighteenth century, ordinary citizens refused to vote for Federalist politicians who flaunted their high social status, with their "top boots, breeches, and shoe buckles," their hair in "powder and queues." Instead, they elected Republican politicians who dressed simply and advocated extending the franchise, even if many of these Republicans favored policies that benefited the economic elite.

Moreover, as Jeffersonian Republicans became the majority political party, state legislatures expanded political democracy. Maryland extended the vote to all adult men in 1810, and the new states of Indiana (1816), Illinois (1818), and Alabama (1819) provided for a broad male franchise in their constitutions. If such "democratic doctrines" had been advanced ten years earlier, the Federalist chancellor James Kent of New York protested, they "should have struck the public mind with astonishment and terror." Within another decade fifteen states allowed all male taxpayers to vote and another seven had instituted universal white manhood suffrage, leaving only three states with property qualifications (Map 9.1).

Concurrently, state legislators redefined political citizenship on the basis of gender and race, thereby raising the status of middling and poor white men and lowering that of white women and free blacks. This redefinition was apparent in Ohio, which disfranchised blacks in 1802, and in New York, which in 1821 retained substantial property-holding requirements for black voters while eliminating such conditions for whites. The most striking case was New Jersey, where the state constitution of 1776 had granted suffrage to all property holders, raising the prospect that propertied black men, unmarried women, and widows might vote. (This provision did not apply to married women, for husbands owned all the family's property.) When some blacks and unmarried women began to exercise the franchise during the electoral battles between Federalists and Republicans, in 1807 New Jersey abolished property-holding requirements for voting and consciously defined full citizenship as an attribute of white men only. To justify the exclusion of women, legislators invoked traditional biological and social arguments. As one letter to a newspaper put it, "Women, generally, are neither by nature, nor habit, nor education, nor by their necessary condition in society fitted to perform this duty with credit to themselves or advantage to the public."

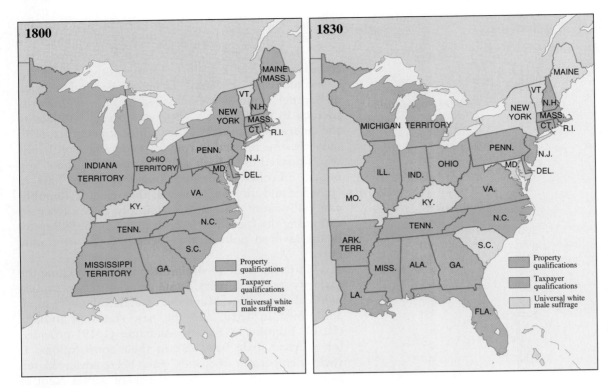

MAP 9.1
The Expansion of Voting Rights for White Men, 1800–1830
Between 1800 and 1830 the United States moved steadily toward political democracy for
white men. Many existing states revised their constitutions, replacing property ownership
with taxpaying or militia service as a qualification for voting. Some states extended the
franchise to all adult white men. As parties sought votes from a broader electorate, the
tone of politics became more open and competitive—swayed by the interests and values
of ordinary people.

Republican Women: Marriage and Motherhood

The debate over gender in New Jersey pointed to the
fact that republicanism was a revolutionary ideology.
As tradition-minded John Adams had lamented in
1776, the doctrine of political equality "spread where it
was not intended," threatening the husband's control of
the family. Both in Europe and America, husbands had
long dominated wives and controlled the family's property. But in the eyes of some Revolutionary-era white
women who wanted to control their inheritances or
speak out on public matters, the subordination of
women to men seemed arbitrary, at odds with a belief
in equal natural rights. In their view patriarchy was not
"natural" and could be justified only on practical
grounds, "for the sake of order in families," as the
Patriot writer Mercy Otis Warren put it.

Economic and cultural changes also eroded customary family relations. Landowning parents had traditionally arranged their children's marriages in an attempt to
ensure their own economic well-being during old age.
But as land holdings shrank in long-settled rural com-

munities, parents could no longer bequeath substantial
farms—the economic incentive they had used to control
their children's lives. Young men and women began to
choose their own marriage partners, influenced by the
new cultural attitude of sentimentalism.

The Effects of Sentimentalism. Originating in
Europe during the Romantic movement of the late
eighteenth century, *sentimentalism* celebrated the
importance of "feeling"—that is, a physical, sensuous
appreciation of God, nature, and other human beings.
By 1820 sentimentalism had touched all classes of
American society. It dripped from the pages of the German and English literary works that were read in educated circles. It fell from the lips of actors in tear-jerking
melodramas, which soon became the most popular theatrical entertainments in the United States. And it
infused the rhetoric of revivalist preachers, who
appealed to the passions of the heart rather than the
cool logic of the mind.

Individuals who were touched by the new cultural
outlook of sentimentalism often wanted to marry "for
love." Parents had always taken physical attraction and

The Wedding, *1805*
The unknown artist who painted this watercolor depicts the bride and groom staring intently into each other's eyes as they exchange marriage vows, suggesting that their union stems more from love than from economic calculation. Given the plain costumes of the assembled guests and the sparse furnishings of the room, this may be a rural Quaker wedding.
Philadelphia Museum of Art.

emotional compatibility into account in arranging marriages for their children, but romance in and of itself did not have a high cultural value. Most parents were more concerned with the personal habits and financial resources of a prospective son- or daughter-in-law. A skeptical mother in Virginia remarked that young women should remain single "till they were old enough to form a proper *judgement* of mankind." However, the new marriage system gave greater importance to personal feelings and less to rational calculation. Magazines promoted marriages "contracted from motives of affection, rather than of interest"; this outlook encouraged a young person to seek a spouse who was, as Eliza Southgate of Maine put it, "calculated to promote my happiness" (see American Voices, "Eliza Southgate: The Dilemmas of Womanhood," p. 284).

As young people began to arrange their own marriages on the basis of emotional attraction, parents adopted new strategies to protect their children's well-being. To prevent family resources from being squandered by a free-spending son-in-law, wealthy fathers placed funds for their daughters in legal trusts—effectively out of the control of their husbands. As a Virginia planter wrote to his lawyer, "I rely on you to see the property settlement properly drawn *before the marriage*,

for I by no means consent that Polly shall be left to the Vicissitudes of Life." By such means fathers gave up the hope of patriarchal dominance and became paternalists, protecting the interests of children who married for love.

For some of these young adults, freedom had a high cost. Those who lacked the maturity and experience to choose wisely were severely disappointed when their spouses failed as providers or faithful companions; a few sought divorces. Before 1800 most petitioners for divorce had charged their spouses with neglect, abandonment, or adultery—serious offenses against the moral order of society—but after that date emotional grounds dominated divorce petitions. One woman complained that her husband had "ceased to cherish her," and one man lamented that his wife had "almost broke his heart." Reflecting these changed cultural values, some states expanded the legal grounds for divorce to include personal cruelty and drunkenness and made divorce available through judicial decree rather than only (as in the past) through a special act of the legislature.

Still, most unions, happy or not, lasted until death and, especially among urban Americans of middling status, were influenced by the republican ideal of a

ELIZA SOUTHGATE

The Dilemmas of Womanhood

————— ★ —————

Eliza Southgate was born into a wealthy Maine family in 1783. While at school in Boston, she discovered radical doctrines of sexual equality as well as the reality of female subordination. In this excerpt from a letter to a male cousin, written in 1801, she tries to resolve these contradictory messages and define her own stance toward the world of men.

But every being who has contemplated human nature on a large scale will certainly justify me when I declare that the inequality of privilege between the sexes is sensibly felt by us females, and in no instance is it greater than in the liberty of choosing a partner in marriage; true, we have the liberty of refusing those we don't like, but not of selecting those we do. This is undoubtedly as it should be. . . .

I never was of opinion that the pursuits of the sexes ought to be the same; on the contrary, I believe it would be destructive to happiness, there would be a degree of rivalry incompatible with the harmony we wish to establish. I have ever thought it necessary that each should have a separate sphere of action—in such a case there could be no clashing unless one or the other should leap their respective bounds. Yet to cultivate the qualities with which we are endowed can never be called infringing the prerogatives of man. . . .

The cultivation of the power we possess, I have ever thought a privilege (or I may say duty) that belonged to the human species, and not man's exclusive prerogative. Far from destroying the harmony that ought to subsist, it would fix it on a foundation that would not totter at every jar. Women would be under the same degree of subordination that they now are; enlighten and expand their minds, and they would perceive the necessity of such a regulation to preserve the order and happiness of society. . . .

It does not follow (O what pen!) that every female who vindicates the capacity of the sex is a disciple of Mary Wolstoncraft [sic]. Though I allow her to have said many things which I cannot approve, I confess I admire many of her sentiments.

Source: David J. Rothman and Sheila Rothman, eds., Sources of the American Social Tradition (New York: Basic Books, 1975), vol. 1: 285.

"companionate" marriage. But this noble ideal, which (one Boston man claimed) gave wives "true equality, both of rank and fortune" with their husbands, often fell short in the face of deeply ingrained cultural habits that favored men, and laws that placed all property in men's hands. Moreover, because the new marriage system discouraged parents from playing an active role in their children's lives, young wives could no longer rely on their parents for emotional or financial support; they became even more dependent on their husbands than their mothers had been. The marriage contract "is so much more important in its consequences to females than to males," a young man at the Litchfield Law School in Connecticut noted astutely in 1820, "for besides leaving everything else to unite themselves to one man, they subject themselves to his authority. He is their all—their only relative—their only hope."

Fewer Children. In all societies, marriage has many purposes: it channels sexuality, facilitates the inheritance of property, and, by creating strong family and kinship ties, eases the rearing of children. Traditionally, most American women had focused their lives on family duties: the bearing and nurture of children, and work in the home or farm. However, in long-settled regions of the United States the early nineteenth century witnessed a dramatic drop in the birth rate. For example, in the farm village of Sturbridge, Massachusetts, women who had married around 1750 bore an average of 8 or 9 children, whereas women who married around 1810 had only about 6 children. The decline was even greater in the urban areas of Massachusetts, where by the 1820s native-born white women bore an average of 4 children.

The United States was one of the first countries in the world to experience this sharp decline in the birth rate, which is known as the *demographic transition*. The causes were several. The migration of thousands of young men to the trans-Appalachian West left many women without marriage partners and delayed the marriages of many more. Women who married later had fewer children because they were married for

Republican Motherhood
Art often reveals much of the
cultural values of the time. In this
1795 painting, the artist James
Peale, brother of the famous
portraitist Charles Willson Peale,
depicts himself with his wife and
children. The mother stands in
the foreground, offering advice to
her eldest daughter, while her
husband stands in the rear,
pointing to the other children.
The father, previously the center
of attention in family portraits
during the colonial era (see pp. 32
and 109), now gives pride of place
to his wife and offspring.
Pennsylvania Academy of the Fine Arts.

fewer of their most fertile years. More important, thousands of white American couples deliberately began to limit the size of their families. After having four or five children, they used birth control or abstained from sexual intercourse to avoid conception (see New Technology, "Women's Health and Fertility: From Folk Remedies to Pharmacies," pp. 286–287). The motives for limiting family size were various. Many fathers wanted to provide each of their children with an adequate inheritance and so favored smaller families; many mothers, affected by new ideas of individualism and self-achievement, were no longer willing to spend all of their active years bearing and rearing children.

Women as Moral Educators.   Despite this decline in fertility, American women did not immediately pursue new social roles. During the Revolution a few upper-class women sought a public voice, but most women—and certainly most men—did not assume that the egalitarian logic of republican ideology would dramatically change customary gender roles. However, some change did occur because clergymen and political leaders redefined the traditional notion of a separate women's sphere. By exercising their special domestic

skills and responsibilities, these men argued, women could make an important contribution to the republican state and society.

This enhanced domestic role for white women stemmed in part from changes in Christian thought. Traditionally, most religious writers had viewed women as morally inferior to men—as sexual temptresses or witches. By 1800 the Protestant clergy had revised this negative image and placed responsibility for sexual misconduct primarily on men. Indeed, Christian moralists now claimed that modesty and purity were inherent in woman's nature, making women uniquely qualified to educate the spirit. Thus, the cultivation of virtue became part of women's sphere.

Political leaders called on women to develop these talents in order to ensure the republican integrity of American men. In *Thoughts on Female Education* (1787), the Philadelphia physician Benjamin Rush argued that a young woman should receive intellectual training so that she would be "an agreeable companion for a sensible man"; her responsibility, as another moralist put it, was to ensure "his perseverance in the paths of rectitude." Rush and other political leaders also welcomed the emergence of loyal "republican mothers"

Women's Health and Fertility: From Folk Remedies to Pharmacies

★

Technology Comes to the Nursery
By the 1830s a woman who lost a child through stillbirth or early death could use a new technical advance—the breast pump—to ease her recuperation.
Miriam and Ira D. Wallach Division of Art, Prints and Photographs, The New York Public Library. Astor, Lenox and Tilden Foundations.

"I ONCE WAS VERRY Bad with a violent pain in my Back and Bowells and three months Gone with Child," Philadelphia shopkeeper Elizabeth Coates Pascall noted in her Receipt Book around 1760. As her condition steadily worsened from this "violent Chollick Pain," Pascall consulted medical professionals, who advised an abortion. "It was Judged Both By the Doctor and midwife that if I was not Speedily Delivered I should Dye." The midwife "tryed to Deliver me butt found it impossible," so Pascall turned to a folk healer, "an Elderly woman [who] proposed Giving me a Glister [an herbal potion]." "I took it and Lay Still Near an hour after it: Being presently Eased and the Child came from me [and] the after Birth all together and with very Little pain."

Like most American women in the eighteenth century, Elizabeth Pascall was not trying to control her fertility or restrict the number of her offspring. She would bear and rear the number of children that her husband and her God gave to her. But to do so she needed to protect her health, and like countless other Americans of her time, she turned to folk medicine.

The general state of medical knowledge was low. Most women knew the link between menstruation and pregnancy: that, as Dr. Samuel Jennings's *The Married Lady's Companion* (1808) put it, "An entire suppression of the menses attends almost every case of pregnancy." But they also believed that the absence of menstruation could be a sign of illness, either "mental

who would instruct "their sons in the principles of liberty and government." As the author of a list of "Maxims for Republics" commented, "Some of the first patriots of ancient times were formed by their mothers."

Ministers readily embraced the idea of republican motherhood, devising new roles for women in moral and religious education. "Preserving virtue and instructing the young are not the fancied, but the real 'Rights of Women,'" the Reverend Thomas Bernard told the Female Charitable Society of Salem, Massachusetts. He urged his audience to dismiss the public roles advocated by Mary Wollstonecraft and other campaigners for women's equality. Instead, he advised, women should be content to care for their children, a responsibility that gave them "an extensive power over the fortunes of man in every generation." Although Bernard wanted women to remain in their traditional domestic sphere, he campaigned to enhance its value.

Many American women from the middling classes accepted this limited revision of their role. As young Eliza Southgate of Maine put it, "She is still *woman*, with duties prescribed her by the God of Nature essendespondency" that took the form of "Grief and Distress," or "hysteria," characterized by "lowness of spirits, oppression and anxiety" as well as by stomach pains that caused "inflation, sickness and sometimes vomiting." In 1805 Lydia Tallender "had not had the female customs for 2 mos [months], and had been unwell," so she took medicines to cure her "illness."

In popular discourse, Lydia Tallender had "taken a cold"; the absence of "hot" menstrual blood indicated that a cold "humor" had taken control of her body. To restore her flow, an afflicted woman normally drank a medicine made of water suffused with herbs and minerals such as savin (a variety of juniper), red cedar, rue, aloes, or seneca snakeroot. When Elizabeth Drinker found her daughter Molly Rhoads "disorder'd and in pain . . . oweing to takeing colds," she administered "mint water," probably peppermint and magnesia.

Health manuals and diaries written in English did not mention the abortive qualities of such potions, but German publications were more forthright. The *Small Herbal of Little Cost*, printed in Germantown, Pennsylvania, between 1762 and 1778 by Christopher Sauer, provided women with recipes "to expel the dead fruit," and German midwifery manuals explained that such tonics would expel the fetus, "be it dead or alive." However, English women clearly understood the potions' effect; nursing mothers commonly drank savin tea to delay a new pregnancy—both to preserve their own health and to ensure a supply of milk for their nursing babies. But the cost of taking such tonics was high, for they caused physical pain and might label a woman as weak, dependent, and "hysterical."

By the late eighteenth century, American women no longer had to turn to folk healers for such medicines. Pharmacists in England and America had learned how to make pills and tonics to promote menstruation (or induce abortions), and they were quickly marketed by energetic entrepreneurs. One of the most popular was *Hooper's Female Pills*, which were composed of Barbados aloes, iron sulfate, hellebore, and myrrh. These patent medicines—including rosemary-laced *Hungary Water; Dr. Ryans's Sugar Plums;* and *Fraunce's Female Elixir*—were advertised in newspapers as "highly serviceable to the Female Sex" and, by the beginning of the nineteenth century, were widely available in rural shops as well as urban pharmacies.

This advance in technology (as well as the importation in the 1790s of French syringes that could be used to prevent conception or induce abortion) may have played a role in the decision of some American women to limit their fertility. Previously, women had used folk remedies to preserve their health or lengthen the interval between births. Now some upper-class women and Quaker women in Pennsylvania used patent medicines and other means in a conscious program of family planning. "It gives me great pleasure to hear of your prudent resolution of not increasing your family," Margaret Shippen Arnold of Philadelphia wrote to her sister around 1790. "I have determined upon the same plan; and when our Sisters have had five or six [children], we will likewise recommend it to them."

tially different from those of *man.*" However, some educated and strong-willed women insisted on the equality of the separate male and female worlds. "I will never consent to have our sex considered in an inferior point of light," Abigail Adams, the wife of President John Adams, proclaimed in 1799. And some ministers envisioned a public role for women based on their domestic virtues. As Thomas Grimké, a South Carolina minister, asserted, "Give me a host of educated pious mothers and sisters and I will revolutionize a country, in moral and religious taste."

Rearing and Educating Republican Children

The triumph of republican values in the United States altered assumptions not only about women's social roles but also about inheritance and child rearing. Under English common law the property owned by fathers who died without a will passed to the eldest son, a practice known as *primogeniture* (first-born). In most American states, republican-minded legislators repudiated primogeniture by enacting statutes that provided

The Battle over Education
The artist pokes fun at a tyrannical school-master and, indirectly, at the evangelicals' strict approach to child rearing. The students' faces reflect the rationalist outlook of the artist. As one Enlightenment-influenced minister put it, we see in their eyes "the first dawn of reason, beaming forth its immortal rays."
Copyright The Frick Collection.

for the equal distribution of an estate among all the children (while continuing to respect the traditional common-law *dower right* of the widow to the use of one-third of the estate during her lifetime). Most American parents supported this legal stress on equality because they had already begun to treat their children in this fashion and to teach all of them—including the eldest son—how to make their own way in the world.

Encouraging Independence.   Child-rearing practices are difficult to document, not being matters of public record, but reports from foreign visitors suggest that some white American parents indulged their children and failed to discipline them. "Mr. Schuyler's second son is a spoiled little child, as are all American children, very willful, mischievous, and likeable," the Marquis de Chastellux observed during the 1780s.

Visitors attributed this behavior, at least in part, to republican ideology. Because of the "general ideas of Liberty and Equality engraved on their hearts," suggested a Polish aristocrat who traveled through the United States around 1800, American children had "scant respect" for their parents. A few decades later a

British traveler was dumbfounded when an American father excused his son's "resolute disobedience" with a smile and the remark, "a sturdy republican, sir." The traveler guessed that parents encouraged such independence to enable young people to "go their own way" in the world.

The child-rearing literature of the period gives some support to this interpretation of lenient parental treatment. Ministers, who wrote most of the pamphlets and books giving advice on raising children, were divided into two camps. Religious writers influenced by John Locke and the Enlightenment argued that children were "rational creatures" who should be encouraged to act correctly by means of praise, advice, and reasoned restraint. However, another group of writers held to Calvinist principles and taught that infants were "full of the stains and pollution of sin" and needed strict discipline.

These two approaches—the affectionate rationalist and the authoritarian Calvinist—appealed to different social and religious groups in the United States. Educated or wealthy Americans, who were often members of Episcopal or Presbyterian churches, usually treated their children kindly. Since foreign commentators mixed primarily with these well-to-do Americans, they reported this set of customs as the social norm. Actually, most yeomen and tenant farmers were much stricter and more authoritarian in their dealings with children, especially in families that belonged to Calvinist-oriented Baptist and Congregational churches.

However, republican ideas gradually softened the harsh treatment of children even in these Calvinist-influenced churches. In the 1820s evangelical Baptists and Methodists still insisted on the need to instill humility in children and teach them to subordinate their desires to God's will. Fear was a "useful and necessary principle in family government," the minister John Abbott advised parents; a child "should submit to your authority, not to your arguments or persuasions." However, Abbott and other writers cautioned that it was wrong "exclusively to control him by this motive."

By this time rationalist writers were placing even more emphasis on children's capacity for education. They suggested that training should be focused on developing children's consciences so that young people would learn to control their own behavior. To that end, affectionate parents read their children stories that stressed self-discipline. They encouraged children to accept the burdens of independence: they must think and act for themselves. Foreigners observed that American children had greater freedom than did their counterparts in Europe, being allowed to participate in conversations among adults and venture into public without a chaperon. What passed unnoticed was the responsibility these young Americans had to assume for their own lives. In private life as in public affairs, republicanism balanced rights with duties.

Expanding Education. Worried about the fragility of their republican experiment, many Americans tried to buttress its principles through education. Before independence, formal education had played a minor role in the lives of most American youth. In New England locally funded public schools provided most boys and some girls with basic instruction in reading and writing, and other girls received instruction from parents or in private "dames' schools." In other regions fewer white children (and virtually no African American children) were given an education: among whites, about a quarter of the boys and perhaps 10 percent of the girls attended privately funded schools or had personal tutors. Even in New England, only a small fraction of the men—and almost no women—went on to grammar (high) school, and only 1 percent of men graduated from college.

After independence, Caleb Bingham, an influential textbook author from Boston, called for "an equal distribution of knowledge to make us emphatically a 'republic of letters.'" Thomas Jefferson and Benjamin Rush separately proposed ambitious schemes for educational reform. Both mapped out plans for a comprehensive system of primary and secondary schooling, followed by college attendance to educate young men (but not women) in the liberal arts—classical literature, history, and philosophy. They also proposed the establishment of a university where distinguished scholars would lecture on law, medicine, theology, and political economy.

These ideas fell on deaf ears. To ordinary citizens such elaborate schemes smacked of elitism. Farmers, artisans, and laborers looked to schools for basic instruction in the "three R's": reading, 'riting, and 'rithmetic. They supported public funding for primary schools but not for secondary schools or colleges, which were of no use to their teenage children, who had to go to work as apprentices, domestic servants, or farm laborers. "Let anybody show what advantage the poor man receives from colleges," an anonymous "Old Soldier" wrote to the Maryland *Gazette*. "Why should they support them, unless it is to serve those who are in affluent circumstances, whose children can be spared from labor, and receive the benefits?"

Reflecting the broad popular support for elementary education, the constitutions of many states encouraged or required the legislatures to use public resources to fund primary schools. However, these ambitious plans made little headway before 1820, when a new generation of reformers campaigned successfully for the improvement of public elementary schools. Led by merchants and manufacturers, they secured more funding for schools and raised standards by certifying qualified teachers and appointing state superintendents of education. They wanted schools to instill the virtues of self-discipline and individual enterprise. Consequently, textbooks praised honesty and hard work while condemning gambling, drinking, and laziness.

Promoting Patriotism. Reformers also demanded that students be required to study American history, for they thought patriotic instruction would foster shared cultural ideals. The experience of Thomas Low, a New Hampshire schoolboy of the 1820s, would have satisfied their fondest hopes:

> We were taught every day and in every way that ours was the freest, the happiest, and soon to be the greatest and most powerful country of the world. This is the religious faith of every American. He learns it in his infancy and can never forget it.

As early as the 1780s the author Noah Webster took up this patriotic crusade, asserting that "America must be as independent in *literature* as she is in politics." Before the Revolution most American writers were ministers who published sermons and moral tracts, and most of the books read by the colonists—whether they were religious publications, political treatises, or literary

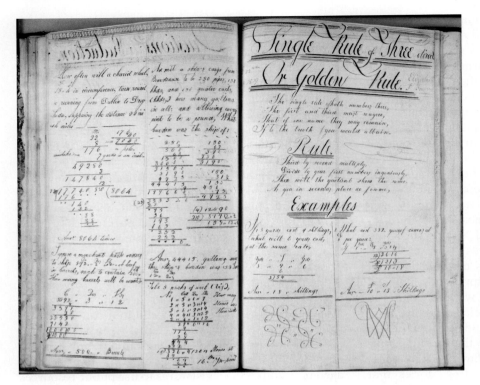

An Arithmetic Notebook
By 1819, when Elizabeth Braswell inscribed the "Single Rule of Three" into this notebook, female academies were providing instruction for young women in mathematics as well as in reading, spelling, penmanship, and geography. Education remained solidly traditional in its emphasis on "rote learning"; Braswell was told to follow a "rule" ("Third [number] by second [number] multiply, divide by your first numbers . . .") rather than being taught to understand how the calculations actually worked.
Chicago Historical Society.

works—were composed by European authors. To promote American literary independence, Webster published a *Dissertation on the English Language* (1789), which introduced an American spelling of various words (such as *labor* for the British *labour*) and defined their meaning in terms of American usage. Webster's "blue-backed speller," first published in 1783, carried this message to the general public; it sold 60 million copies over the next half-century and helped give Americans of all backgrounds a common vocabulary and grammar. "None of us was 'lowed to see a book," an enslaved African American recalled, "but we gits hold of that Webster's old blue-back speller and we . . . studies that spelling book." In other publications Webster called on his fellow republican citizens to detach themselves "from the dependence on foreign opinions and manners, which is fatal to the efforts of genius in this country."

Echoing Webster's plea, Joel Barlow, a Yale graduate and an ardent Jeffersonian Republican, called for an epic literature that would celebrate America. To that end he offered his own epic poem, *The Columbiad* (1807), an ambitious but undistinguished work in which Christopher Columbus predicted the future glory of North America. Mercy Otis Warren's *History of the American Revolution* (1805) contained stirring portraits of leading American patriots, as did the best-selling *Life of George Washington* written around 1800 by "Parson" Mason Weems, an Episcopal minister. Neither work had

much literary or historical merit; still, they won acclaim as contributions to popular culture and patriotism.

The most accomplished and successful writer in the new republic was Washington Irving, a Federalist in politics and outlook. His essays and histories, including *Salmagundi* (1807) and *Diedrich Knickerbocker's History of New York* (1809), had substantial American sales and won fame abroad because Europeans were fascinated by his tales of Dutch-American life. Irving himself grew impatient with the slow pace of American literary development; he lived in Europe for seventeen years, drawn by its aristocratic manners and intense intellectual life.

Apart from Irving, no American author was well known in Europe, partly because most American writers had their primary careers as planters, merchants, or lawyers. "Literature is not yet a distinct profession with us," Thomas Jefferson told an English friend, explaining the lack of intellectual life in the United States. "Now and then a strong mind arises, and at its intervals from business emits a flash of light. But the first object of young societies is bread and covering." Not until Ralph Waldo Emerson and the Transcendentalists would American-born authors make a real contribution to the great literature of the Western world (see Chapter 12). Regardless of the aspirations of Americans to create a society that reflected their democratic-republican ideals, cultural change came slowly.

Slavery and Aristocratic Republicanism in the South

———————★———————

Both in the North and the South, by the 1820s republicanism had come to mean voting rights for most free white men. But especially in the South, an extended franchise did not mean equality of influence, opportunity, or condition. The South was a complex society based on race and class, and it was much more stratified than the northern states. White planters grew rich by exploiting the labor of enslaved African Americans, who numbered one-third of the South's population, and they used their wealth to rule over dependent white tenants and independent yeomen families. In economics, politics, and many other spheres of life, the structure and character of southern society imparted an elitist and aristocratic flavor to the republican experiment.

Sectional Contrasts and Conflicts

Generations of observers had contrasted the societies of the Chesapeake and the Carolinas with the freehold farming regions of the North, particularly New England. In defining these differences, colonial-era writers paid little attention to human bondage (because there were slaves and indentured servants in all regions) and instead focused on behavior and popular speech of the white inhabitants. "Yankee," a foreign traveler learned, was originally "a name given derisively, or merely jestingly," by the Dutch in New Amsterdam to the residents of New England and, by the late eighteenth century, referred to the shrewd bargaining habits of people from that region. "The name of 'Buckskin' is given to the inhabitants of Virginia," he went on to observe, "because their ancestors were hunters and sold buck, or rather deer skins."

Cultural Differences. European visitors saw genuine cultural differences in the popular stereotypes. In 1800 a British observer detected religious "fanaticism" in New England as well as "a great strain of industry among all ranks of people." He thought that "the lower orders of citizens have a better education, are more intelligent, and better informed" than those he met in the southern states. "The state of poverty in which a great number of white people live in Virginia" surprised the Marquis de Chastellux during the 1780s. Other visitors to the Chesapeake commented on the rude manners, heavy drinking, and lack of a strong work ethic among white tenant farmers and small freeholders. As an observer remarked, they seemed only to have a "passion for gaming at the billiard table, a cockfight or cards." Some southerners felt that slavery was

one cause of the widespread poverty among whites; "where there are Negroes," a South Carolina merchant remarked, "a White Man despises to work, saying *what, will you have me a Slave and work like a Negroe?*" (Map 9.2).

New Englanders did indeed set a higher store by education than did white residents of the Chesapeake. The Puritan legacy included strong traditions of primary schooling and Bible reading. As a result, most of the men and more than half the women in New England in 1790 could read and write. In Virginia, most white women and a third of adult white men could not even write their names; they signed legal documents such as wills and marriage licenses with an "X" or another mark. This disparity in the literacy rate reflected different social and fiscal priorities. The slaveholding elite that ruled southern society refused to provide services or schooling for ordinary white families. In 1800 the 4,000 free inhabitants of Essex County in Virginia spent about $1,000 for local government, including schooling. In the same year the 900 residents of Acton, Massachusetts, spent $950 for public purposes—four times as much per capita as in Essex County—$550 on education alone.

Regional differences were also apparent in the observance of holidays. In Virginia, South Carolina, and other states where the Church of England had been dominant during the colonial period, Christmas was an occasion for feasting and celebration. Not so in New England, where Puritans condemned such celebrations as profane. Most New England churches did not celebrate Christmas until the 1850s; for them, Thanksgiving Day, commemorating the trials and triumphs of the first Pilgrim and Puritan settlers, was the focus of celebration.

Political Conflicts and the Missouri Compromise. Following independence and the creation of a national government, these regional differences found political expression. "When I was in Congress," Timothy Bloodworth of North Carolina recalled in 1789, there were distinct "Southern and Northern Interests" over slavery and other regional issues. After 1800 the expansion of the South's agricultural economy caused these tensions to increase. The invention of the cotton gin and the buoyant demand of British textile mills drove up the price of cotton—and also of slaves to grow it. British mercantile houses furnished ample capital for new plantations, and planters moved to new land because cotton depleted the fertility of the soil more quickly than did most other crops. In addition, poor farming practices ruined much land. Less than a generation after they had been settled, the farms of Georgia's eastern plantation belt were described as "red old hills stripped of their native growth and virgin soil, and washed with deep gullies."

MAP 9.2
Regional Cultures Move West, 1720–1820
By 1720 four distinct "core" cultures had developed along the Atlantic seaboard. By 1775 settlers from the Middle Atlantic and Chesapeake regions had carried their customs and institutions into the southern backcountry. Then, between 1780 and 1820, the descendants of these migrants moved into the trans-Appalachian West, while Carolinians transplanted their slave society to the Old Southwest and New Englanders transmitted their customs to upstate New York and the Old Northwest.

As slavery marched westward, millions of acres of newly cleared fertile soil were brought into cultivation. Entire black communities were uprooted from the Chesapeake region and the Carolinas and forced to move west with their masters (Map 9.3). Some migrating slaves—perhaps as many as one-half—moved with relatives and friends, as their owners sold their old plantations and began new ones on the fertile plains of the Mississippi Valley. Many other African Americans were "sold South" through a new domestic slave trade that provided tobacco and cotton planters in Maryland, Virginia, and other long-settled regions with a major source of income. Between 1790 and 1820 whites relocated more than 250,000 African Americans.

The expansion of slavery into the Southwest dashed the hopes of many northerners, who had hoped that slavery would "die a natural death" after the decline of the tobacco economy and the legal end of the Atlantic slave trade in 1809. To hasten the end of forced bondage, antislavery advocates worked to prevent the illegal importation of enslaved Africans and persuaded the legislatures of northern states to pass personal liberty laws to protect free blacks from being kidnapped and from slave catchers who abused the provisions of the Fugitive Slave Act of 1793.

More important, reformers opposed the expansion of slavery into the western territories. Despite their efforts, during the 1810s Louisiana, Mississippi, and Alabama joined the Union with state constitutions permitting slavery. When Missouri applied for admission on a similar basis in 1819, the antislavery forces rallied. Congressman James Tallmadge of New York proposed a ban on the importation of slaves into Missouri and the gradual emancipation of its black inhabitants. When Missouri whites rejected those conditions, the northern majority in the House of Representatives blocked the territory's admission to the Union. In response, southerners used their power in the Senate, which was equally divided between eleven free and eleven slave states, to withhold statehood from Maine, which was seeking to separate itself from Massachusetts. Tempers flared in the heat of debate. Senator Thomas W. Cobb of Georgia accused Tallmadge of kindling "a fire which all the waters of the ocean cannot put out and which seas of blood can only extinguish."

Controversy raged for two years before Congress resolved the stalemate. Henry Clay of Kentucky and other skilled politicians put together a series of agreements known collectively as the Missouri Compromise,

*Arise! Arise! and weep no more
dry up your tears, we shall part
no more. Come rose we go to
Tennessee.
that happy Shore To old virginia
never — never — return.*

The Internal Slave Trade
Mounted whites escort a convoy of slaves from Virginia to Tennessee in Louis Miller's *Slave Trader, Sold to Tennessee*. For white planters, the trade was a lucrative one, pumping money into the declining Chesapeake economy and providing workers for the expanding plantations of the cotton belt. For blacks, it was a traumatic journey, a new Middle Passage that broke up families and communities.
Abby Aldrich Rockefeller Folk Art Center.

by which Maine entered the Union as a free state in 1820 and Missouri was admitted as a slave state in the following year (Map 9.4). This bargain preserved the existing sectional balance in the Senate and set a precedent for the future admission of states in pairs—one free and one slave. To mollify antislavery sentiment in the House of Representatives, southern congressmen accepted the prohibition of slavery in the rest of the Louisiana Purchase north of latitude 36°30′, the southern boundary of Missouri.

The tradition of political compromise on the issue of slavery thus continued. In 1821 as in 1787, the white leaders of the North and the South gave prior-

ity to the Union, finding complex but workable ways by which to reconcile the interests of their regions. But the task had become more difficult. The Philadelphia delegates had resolved their sectional differences in two months; Congress took two years to work out the Missouri Compromise, and there was no guarantee that it would work. The fates of western lands, the Union, and the black race had become inextricably intertwined, raising the prospect of civil war. As the aging Thomas Jefferson exclaimed at the time of the Missouri controversy, "This momentous question, like a fire-bell in the night, awakened and filled me with terror."

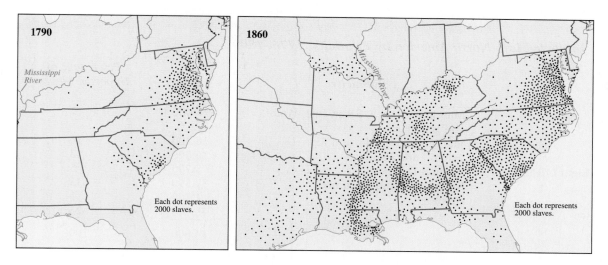

MAP 9.3
Distribution of the Slave Population, 1790–1860
The cotton boom brought the forced migration of enslaved African Americans to the Old Southwest. In 1790 most slaves lived and worked on the tobacco plantations of the Chesapeake and in the rice and indigo areas of South Carolina. By 1860 hundreds of thousands were laboring on the cotton and sugar lands of the lower Mississippi Valley and along an arc of fertile cotton land—the "black belt"—sweeping from Mississippi through Georgia.

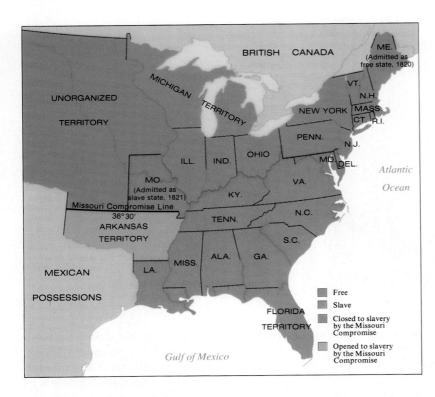

MAP 9.4
The Missouri Compromise, 1820
The Missouri Compromise resolved for a generation the issue of slavery in the lands of the Louisiana Purchase. Slavery was forbidden north of the Missouri Compromise line (36°30′ north latitude), with the exception of the state of Missouri. To maintain an equal number of free and slave states in the U.S. Senate, the compromise provided for the nearly simultaneous admission of Maine and Missouri.

African American Society and Culture

As whites debated the future of slavery, three developments helped to create a more unified African American culture in the United States. First, the end of the transatlantic slave trade in 1809 gradually created an entirely American-born black population. Even in South Carolina—the destination of most of the slaves imported since independence—only about 20 percent of the black inhabitants in 1820 had been born in Africa. Second, the movement of slavery into the Old Southwest slowly reduced cultural differences among slaves. For example, the Gullah dialect spoken by slaves from the Carolina low country gradually died out on the cotton plantations of Alabama and Mississippi, replaced by the black English spoken by slaves from the

TABLE 9.2

African Slaves Imported into North America by Ethnicity, 1776–1809

African Region of Departure	Ethnicity	Number	Percentage of Imported Slaves
Senegambia	Mandinka, Fulbe, Serer, Jola, Wolof, and Bambara	8,000	7
Sierra Leone	Via, Mende, Kpelle, and Kru	18,300	16
Gold Coast	Ashanti and Fanit	15,000	13
Bight of Benin; Bight of Biafra	Ibo and Ibibio	5,700	5
West-Central Africa	Kongo, Tio, and Matamba	37,800	33
Southeast Africa	Unknown	1,100	1
Other or Unknown		28,700	25
TOTAL		114,600	100

Note: The numbers are estimated from known voyages involving 65,000 Africans. Ethnic origins should be considered as very tentative because slaves from many regions left from the same port and because the ethnic and regional origins of 28,700 slaves (25 percent) are not known.

Source: Aaron S. Fogleman, "From Slaves, Convicts, and Servants to Free Passengers: The Transformation of Immigration in the Era of the American Revolution," *Journal of American History* (June 1998): table A.6.

Chesapeake. Third, in both southern and northern cities, free blacks consciously created a distinct African American community.

Even as the black population became more homogeneous, African cultural elements remained important in the lives of slaves. At least one-third of the slaves who entered the United States between 1776 and 1809 came from west-central Africa, the home of the Kongo, Tio, and Matamba peoples (Table 9.2). Consequently, the cultures of these African peoples had a considerable impact on nineteenth-century slave society. As the traveler Isaac Holmes reported in 1821, "In Louisiana, and the state of Mississippi, the slaves . . . dance for several hours during Sunday afternoon. The general movement is in what they call the Congo dance." Similar descriptions of blacks who "danced the Congo and sang a purely African song to the accompaniment of . . . a drum" appeared as late as 1890.

Enslaved blacks in South Carolina and elsewhere also retained the incest taboos of their African homeland. Unlike the white elite families in South Carolina and Georgia, who allowed cousins to marry one another in order to keep inherited property in the family, enslaved blacks shunned such marriages. For example, on the Good Hope plantation in South Carolina, where 40 percent of the 175 slave children born between 1800 and 1857 were related by blood to just three slaves from Africa, only one marriage took place between cousins.

Slave Families and Communities. Southern state legislatures and law courts prohibited legal marriages between blacks, so that slaves could be sold without breaking a marriage bond. "Our law requires no solemnity or form in regard to the marriage of slaves," declared the North Carolina Supreme Court. African Americans therefore devised their own rituals. Young men and women first asked their parents' consent to marry and then sought their owner's permission to live together in their own cabin. Following African custom, many couples symbolized their married state by jumping over a broomstick together in a public ceremony. Christian slaves often had a religious service performed by a white or black preacher, but these rites never ended with the customary phrase "until death do you part." Everyone knew that black marriages could end with the sale of one or both of the spouses.

Indeed, the geographical expansion of the cotton economy and the creation of a domestic slave trade caused the division of tens of thousands of African American families. For example, in 1790 many of the African Americans who lived on the Tayloe family's Mount Airy plantation in Virginia came from families who had lived there since the 1720s. Over the years these families had intermarried and increased their numbers, so that there were more workers than the plantation could employ. So in 1792 John Tayloe III

African American Banjos
Elements of African culture persisted in many aspects of African American life. In 1794, an English visitor to Virginia watched slaves dancing to the music of an African-style banjo "made of a gourd something in the imitation of a Guitar, with only four strings and played with the fingers in the same manner."
Collection of the Blue Ridge Institute & Museums/Ferrum College.

advertised a sale of fifty Mount Airy slaves, selling husbands away from their wives and children away from their parents. Over the next two generations, Tayloe and his sons continued to disrupt black family life at Mount Airy, moving 180 other slaves to new plantations in Alabama, where they worked "from day clean to first dark" clearing the land and planting it with cotton.

Other planters remained on their ancestral estates and sold their "surplus" blacks to slave traders. "I am

TABLE 9.3

African American Naming Patterns

Good Hope Plantation Slaves, Orangebury, South Carolina

Date of Birth	Baby's Name	Parents' Names	Source of Baby's Name
1793	Hector	Bess, Hector	Father
1806	Clarinda	Patty, Primus	Mother's mother
1811	Sambo	Affy, Jacob	Mother's father
1813	Primus	Patty, Primus	Father
1824	Sarah	Phoebe, Jack	Mother's mother
1828	Major	Clarinda, Abram	Father's father

Sold to a man by the name of Peterson a trader," lamented a Georgia slave. "My Dear wife for you and my Children my pen cannot Express the griffe I feel to be parted from you all." Some of these slaves forever lost touch with their families. "Dey sole [sold] my sister Kate," Anna Harris remembered decades later, ". . . and I ain't seed or heard of her since."

Although forced separations split many black families, the majority of slave marriages were stable. Among the slaves on the Good Hope plantation in South Carolina, about 70 percent of the women had all their children by the same man. Most other Good Hope women had their first child (by a slave father) before marriage in what the community called an "outside" birth and then bore the rest of their children within a stable union. On plantations in Louisiana black family ties were much more fragile because the hot climate and the demanding work of planting and cutting sugarcane took the lives of many men. Thirty percent of the slave women on one Louisiana plantation lived alone with their children, who were fathered by a succession of men. Northern opponents of slavery who were influenced by the sentimentalist ideal of the family increasingly condemned slavery because of the damage it inflicted on black family life.

To maintain their cultural identity, many recently imported slaves in the Lower South bestowed African names on their children. Males born on Friday were often called Cuffee—the name of that day in several West African languages. Most Chesapeake slaves chose names of British origin and bound one generation to another by naming sons after fathers, uncles, or grandfathers. Daughters were often named after grandmothers (Table 9.3). Like incest rules and marriage rituals, these naming patterns solidified kinship ties, thereby creating order in a harsh and arbitrary world.

As African American cultural communities developed, the quality of slave life gradually improved. During the eighteenth century the diverse origins of African-born slaves had enabled white men to take easy advantage of blacks—to rape women and punish defiant men by branding them or cutting off their fingers or ears. Although these abuses did not stop after 1800, they were questioned more often. Politicians and community leaders condemned rape as an aristocratic vice ill suited to a republican society, while the spread of evangelical Christianity prompted many masters to treat slaves more humanely.

Meanwhile, by forming stable families and strong communities, African Americans were better able to resist the worst forms of oppression. Because of their numerical dominance, blacks in the rice-growing lowlands of South Carolina were particularly successful in gaining some control over their lives. In particular, they won the right to labor by the *task* rather than work under constant supervision. Under the task system, each day a worker would have to complete a precisely defined task—for example, turn over a quarter acre of land, hoe half an acre, or pound seven mortars of rice. By working hard, many lowland slaves finished their tasks "by one or two o'clock in the afternoon," a Methodist preacher reported, and had "the rest of the day for themselves, which they spend in working their own private fields . . . planting rice, corn, potatoes, tobacco &c. for their own use and profit." "Should any owner increase the work beyond what is customary," a rice planter in South Carolina warned around 1800, "he subjects himself . . . to such discontent amongst his slaves as to make them of little use to him."

In fact, because of the prosperity of the nineteenth-century plantation system, slaves in most regions of the South were increasingly better clothed and housed. The slaves' food was also fairly nutritious, particularly when supplemented by greens from their own garden plots and by game and fish. And, on some large plantations, children, the sick, and the elderly received decent care. But few enslaved African Americans enjoyed a comfortable standard of living, and slaves clearly under-

Jacob Stroyer

A Child Learns the Meaning of Slavery

————————★————————

Jacob Stroyer, born into slavery in South Carolina, was emancipated and became a minister in Salem, Massachusetts. In My Life in the South *(1855), he relates a dramatic incident that revealed his family's subordinate and powerless status as slaves.*

Father had a surname, Stroyer, which he could not use in public, as the surname Stroyer would be against the law; he was known only by the name of William Singleton, because that was his master's name. . . . Mother's name was Chloe. She belonged to Colonel M.R. Singleton too; she was a field hand, and was never sold, but her parents once were. . . .

Father . . . used to take care of horses and mules. I was around with him in the barnyard when but a small boy; of course that gave me an early relish for the occupation of hostler, and soon I made known my preference to Colonel Singleton, who was a sportsman and had fine horses. . . . Hence I was allowed to be numbered among those who took care of the fine horses, and learned to ride. . . .

It was not long after I had entered my new work before they put me upon the back of a horse which threw me to the ground almost as soon as I reached his back. . . . When I got up there was a man standing near with a switch in hand, and he immediately began to beat me. . . . This was the first time I had been whipped by anyone except Mother and Father, so I cried out in a tone of voice as if I would say, this is the first and last whipping you will give me when Father gets hold of you.

When I got away from him I ran to Father with all my might, but soon my expectation was blasted, as Father very coolly said to me, "Go back to your work and be a good boy, for I cannot do anything for you." But that did not satisfy me, so I went on to Mother with my complaint and she came out to the man who whipped me. He was a groom, a white man whom master hired to train his horses . . . [and] he took a whip and started for her, and she ran from him, talking all the time. . . .

Then the idea first came to me that I, with my dear father and mother and the rest of my fellow Negroes, was doomed to cruel treatment through life and was defenseless. . . .

One day, about two weeks after Boney Young and Mother had the conflict, he . . . gave me a first-class flogging. That evening when I went home to Father and Mother, I said to them, "Mr. Young is whipping me too much now; I shall not stand it. I shall fight him." Father said to me, "You must not do that, because if you do he will say that your mother and I advised you to do it, and it will make it hard for your mother and me, as well as yourself. You must do as I told you my son. . . . I can do nothing more than pray to the Lord to hasten the time when these things shall be done away."

———————

Source: Linda R. Monk, ed., *Ordinary Americans: U.S. History through the Eyes of Everyday People* (Alexandria, VA: Close Up Publications, 1994), 71–72.

---

stood that planters gave them material favors not out of benevolence but to protect their investment.

Increased Labor Discipline. In theory, white masters had virtually unlimited power, both legal and physical, over their slaves. By law enslaved individuals were *chattel*—personal property. They could be disciplined at the will of their owners and bought and sold as if they were horses. As Thomas Ruffin, a justice of the North Carolina Supreme Court, declared in a court decision in 1829, "The power of the master must be absolute to render the submission of the slave perfect" (see American Voices, "Jacob Stroyer: A Child Learns the Meaning of Slavery," above).

But planters had never been able to turn slaves into willing workers. So in the upland cotton-growing regions of South Carolina and Georgia and in Alabama and Mississippi, owners devised a new gang-labor system to increase the output of their workers. Planters with twenty or more slaves organized the hands into disciplined teams, or "gangs," that were supervised by black "drivers" or white overseers and assigned specific tasks. To clear and plant newly settled lands, profit-conscious masters instructed drivers and overseers to use the lash to extract labor from exhausted field workers. Gangs worked at a feverish pace, clearing and plowing the land or hoeing and picking cotton.

Black Labor, White Leisure
In this watercolor, sarcastically entitled *An Overseer Doing His Duty* (1798), Benjamin Henry Latrobe underlines the exploitation inherent in slavery in his depiction of female slaves hard at work while their white master stands idly by. Only a small percentage of female slaves were domestic servants. The majority of female slaves in the South worked long, hard hours as unskilled field hands. Later in his life, Latrobe became the architect of the U.S. Capitol.
Maryland Historical Society.

Even on well-established plantations, gang labor became the norm. A traveler glimpsed two gangs returning from work in Mississippi:

> First came, led by an old driver carrying a whip, forty of the largest and strongest women I ever saw together; they were all in a simple uniform dress of a bluish check stuff, the skirts reaching little below the knee; their legs and feet were bare; they carried themselves loftily, each having a hoe over the shoulder, and walking with a free, powerful swing.

Next marched the plow hands with their mules, "the cavalry, thirty strong, mostly men, but a few of them women." Finally, "a lean and vigilant white overseer, on a brisk pony, brought up the rear." By forcing their slaves to work in gangs, owners extracted more labor, increasing output and profits.

Resistance and Flight. To resist the innovations of gang labor and forced separations, African Americans used the same tactics as previous generations of slaves. To slow the pace of work they feigned illness and were deliberately careless with the master's property, losing or breaking tools and setting fire to houses and barns. To maintain kin ties they insisted that work gangs be sold "in families" and defied their masters when they were not. One Maryland slave, faced with transport to Mississippi and separation from his wife (who was owned by another master), "neither yields consent to accompany my people, or to be exchanged or sold," his owner reported. Masters ignored such resistance at their peril, because a slave's relatives might retaliate with arson, poison, or destruction of crops or equipment.

A few blacks, such as Gabriel and Martin Prosser in Virginia (1800) and Denmark Vesey in South Carolina (1822), plotted mass uprisings and murders. But blacks realized that a revolt was unlikely to be successful. In most areas they accounted for less than half the population, and everywhere they lacked the strong institutions—such as the communes of free peasants or serfs in Europe—needed to organize a rebellion. Moreover, their white adversaries were well armed, unified, and militant, and there were only a few places to which the blacks could flee and set up their own communities. One such refuge was Spanish Florida, but that option was cut off in 1819 when the United States annexed that territory. Even so, hundreds of blacks continued to flee into the interior of Florida, where they intermarried with the Seminole people and joined with the Indians to expel white settlers. Elsewhere in the South small groups of escaped slaves eked out a bare subsistence in deserted marshy areas, such as Dismal Swamp in Virginia, or in mountain valleys, hoping that they would be tolerated—and not killed, enslaved, or returned—by Indian warriors.

Given these limited options, most slaves had no choice but to build the best possible lives for themselves on the plantations where they were born. As the black abolitionist Frederick Douglass observed, most slave communities were "pegged down to a single spot" and "must take root there or nowhere." Like the oppressed peasantry of Europe, enslaved African Americans worked as dependent agricultural laborers and built close-knit communities based on family, kinship, and religion.

Free Blacks. Meanwhile, free African Americans explored the opportunities, and encountered the racial

CLASS No. 1.
Comprises those prisoners who were found guilty and executed.

Prisoners Names.	Owners' Names.	Time of Commit.	How Disposed of.
Peter	James Poyas	June 18	Hanged on Tuesday the 2d July, 1822, on Blake's lands, near Charleston.
Ned	Gov. T. Bennett,	do.	
Rolla	do.	do	
Batteau	do.	do.	
Denmark Vesey	A free black man	22	
Jessy	Thos. Blackwood	23	
John	Elias Horry	July 5	Do. on the Lines near Ch.; Friday July 12.
Gullah Jack	Paul Pritchard	do.	
Mingo	Wm. Harth	June 21	
Lot	Forrester	27	
Joe	P. L. Jore	July 6	
Julius	Thos. Forrest	8	
Tom	Mrs. Russell	10	
Smart	Robt. Anderson	do.	
John	John Robertson	11	
Robert	do.	do.	
Adam	do.	do.	
Polydore	Mrs. Faber	do.	Hanged on the Lines near Charleston, on Friday, 26th July.
Bacchus	Benj. Hammet	do.	
Dick	Wm. Sims	13	
Pharaoh	— Thompson	do.	
Jemmy	Mrs. Clement	18	
Mauidore	Mordecai Cohen	19	
Dean	— Mitchell	do.	
Jack	Mrs. Purcell	12	
Bellisle	Est. of Jos. Yates	18	
Naphur	do.	do.	
Adam	do.	do.	
Jacob	John S. Glen	16	
Charles	John Billings	18	
Jack	N. McNeill	22	
Cæsar	Miss Smith	do.	
Jacob Stagg	Jacob Lankester	23	Do. Tues. July 30.
Tom	Wm. M. Scott	24	
William	Mrs. Garner	Aug. 2	Do. Friday, Aug. 9.

"An Account of the Late Intended Insurrection, Charleston, South Carolina"
In 1822, Charleston had a free black population of 1,500 that boasted an array of its own institutions, including a Brown Fellowship Society (for those of mixed racial ancestry) and an African Methodist Episcopal (AME) church. Denmark Vesey, one of these free African Americans, organized a conspiracy to free the city's slaves. When his plan was discovered, South Carolina authorities hanged Vesey and thirty-four co-conspirators and, as punishment to the black community, tore down the AME church where the insurrection had been plotted.
Rare Book, Manuscript & Special Collections, Duke University Library.

limits, of republican liberty. In the post-Revolutionary era a few free blacks were able for the first time to make full use of their talents, and some achieved great distinction. The mathematician and surveyor Benjamin Banneker published an almanac and helped lay out the new national capital in the District of Columbia. Joshua Johnston, a skilled painter, won praise for his portraiture, and merchant Robert Sheridan acquired a small fortune from his business enterprises.

More impressive and enduring than these individual achievements were the community institutions created by this first generation of free African Americans. In the major cities of the North and in Charleston, South Carolina, hundreds of free blacks pooled their resources and talents to found schools, mutual-benefit organizations, and fellowship societies. Reacting to discriminatory treatment in white Protestant churches, free blacks formed their own congregations and an independent religious denomination—the AME (African Methodist Episcopal) Church (see American Lives, "Richard Allen and African American Identity," pp. 300–301). Over the years these institutions gave free African Americans a sense of cultural, if not political, autonomy.

Between 1790 and 1820 the number of free blacks steadily rose, from 8 percent of the total African American population to about 13 percent. About half of all free blacks lived in the North, where they were treated as second-class citizens and consigned by custom to the most menial and low-paying work. In rural areas, free blacks worked as farm laborers or tenant farmers; in towns and cities, as domestic servants, laundresses, or day laborers. Prejudice further circumscribed the lives of these African Americans: even in the North they were usually forbidden to vote, attend public schools, or sit next to whites in churches. Of the states admitted to the Union between 1790 and 1821, only Vermont and Maine extended the vote to free blacks, and they could testify against whites in court only in Massachusetts. Virtually all public facilities in the North were segregated. The federal government did not allow free African Americans to work for the postal service, claim public lands, or hold a U.S. passport.

Most free African Americans in the slave states lived in the Upper South. In Maryland a quarter of the black population was free by 1820, and in Delaware free blacks outnumbered slaves by three to one. However, these free blacks faced substantial legal restrictions; those accused of crimes were often denied a jury trial, and those who lacked work were threatened by vagrancy and apprenticeship laws intended to force them back into slavery. To prove their free status, free blacks had to carry manumission documents; in some states they needed official permission just to travel across county lines. Even if they had valid papers, free African Americans had to be careful; kidnapping and sale into slavery was a constant threat. However, the shortage of skilled workers in southern cities did create opportunities for a few blacks to become carpenters, blacksmiths, barbers, butchers, and shopkeepers. Skilled African American workers in Baltimore, Richmond, Charleston, and New Orleans formed their own benevolent societies and churches, which became the core of their urban communities, providing education, recreation, and social welfare programs.

As a privileged group among African Americans, free blacks felt pulled in two directions: loyalty to the welfare of their families, which often meant assimilating white culture, and loyalty to their race, which meant identification with the great mass of enslaved African Americans. In some places wealthier free blacks, particularly the mulatto children of white masters and black women, drew apart from common laborers and field hands and adopted the outlook of the

Richard Allen and African American Identity

---★---

RICHARD ALLEN LIVED a full life. Born into slavery in Philadelphia in 1760 and sold with his family as a child to a farmer in Delaware, he died in 1831 not only free but influential, a founder of the African Methodist Episcopal Church and its first bishop. Allen's rise to fame reflects much of the classic American success story, but it bears a larger significance: as one of the first African Americans to be emancipated during the Revolutionary era, Allen worked to forge an identity for his people as well as for himself.

Allen began his ascent in 1777, when he was converted to Methodism by Freeborn Garretson, an itinerant preacher. A powerful foe of slavery, Garretson also converted Allen's master and convinced him that on Judgment Day slaveholders would be "weighted in the balance, and . . . found wanting." Allowed by his repentant owner to buy his freedom, Allen earned a living sawing cordwood and driving a wagon during the Revolutionary War. After the war he enlisted in the Methodist cause, becoming a "licensed exhorter" and preaching to blacks and whites from New York to South Carolina.

Allen's skill and success as a preacher soon attracted the attention of white Methodist leaders, including Francis Asbury, the first American bishop of the Methodist Church. In 1786 Allen won appointment as an assistant minister in Philadelphia, serving the racially mixed congregation of St. George's Methodist Church. The following year he and Absalom Jones, another black preacher, joined other former slaves and Quaker philanthropists to establish the Free African Society, a quasi-religious benevolent organization that offered fellowship and mutual aid to "free Africans and their descendants."

Allen remained a staunch Methodist throughout his life. In 1789, when the Free African Society adopted the Quaker custom of having fifteen minutes of silence at its meetings, Allen led a withdrawal of those who preferred more enthusiastic Methodist practices. Five years later he rejected an offer to become the pastor of the St. Thomas's African Church, the Episcopal-affiliated church that the Free African Society had built and that a majority of its members had joined. "I informed them that I could not be anything else but a Methodist, as I was born and awakened under them," Allen recalled.

Now Allen confronted a more difficult challenge: reconciling his Methodist faith and his African American identity. Gathering a group of ten black Methodists, Allen decided to form his own congregation. He took over a blacksmith's shop in the increasingly black southern section of the city, converting it to the Bethel African Methodist Episcopal Church. Although the Bethel Church opened in a ceremony led by Bishop Francis Asbury in July 1794, its tiny congregation worshipped "separate from our white brethren."

Allen's decision to found a black congregation was partly a response to white racism. Although most white Methodists in the 1790s favored emancipation, they did not treat free blacks as social equals. They refused to allow African Americans to be buried in the congregation's cemetery and, in a famous incident in 1792, segregated black worshippers in a newly built gallery of St. George's Methodist Church. But Allen's initiative also reflected a desire among African Americans to control their religious lives. For example, his congregation wanted the power "to call any brother that appears to us adequate to the task to preach or exhort as a local preacher." By 1795 the congregation of Allen's Bethel Church numbered 121; a decade later it had grown to 457, and by 1813 it had reached 1,272.

Bethel's rapid expansion reflected the growth of Philadelphia's black population, which numbered nearly ten thousand by 1810, as well as the appeal of Methodist practices. Newly freed blacks welcomed Methodist "love feasts," which allowed the full expression of emotions repressed under slavery. They were also attracted by the church's strict system of discipline—its communal sanctions against drinking, gambling, and marital infidelity—which helped them bring order to their lives. Allen's preaching also played a role; in 1799 the Methodist Church recognized his excellence by ordaining him as its first black deacon.

But over the years Allen and his congregation grew dissatisfied with Methodism. White ministers gradually retreated from their antislavery principles and the church hierarchy attempted to curb the autonomy of African American congregations. In 1807 the Bethel Church added an "African Supplement" to its articles of incorporation, and in 1816 it won legal recognition as an independent church. In the same year Allen and representatives from four

The Mount Bethel African Methodist Episcopal Church, Philadelphia
In 1816, the Mount Bethel Church was the site of a meeting between Richard Allen and representatives of other black Methodist congregations. Out of this meeting was born the first independent black denomination in America: the African Methodist Episcopal Church.
Mount Bethel A.M.E. Church, Philadelphia.

other black Methodist congregations (in Baltimore, Maryland; Wilmington, Delaware; Salem, New Jersey; and Attleboro, Pennsylvania) met at the Bethel Church to organize a new denomination—the African Methodist Episcopal Church. The delegates chose Allen as the first bishop of the church, the first fully independent black denomination in America. After a forty-year journey as a Methodist, he had embarked upon the new adventure of charting a distinct religious identity for African Americans.

Allen had long recognized the importance of education to the future of his community. In 1795 he opened a day school for sixty children and in 1804 founded the "Society of Free People of Colour for Promoting the Instruction and School Education of Children of African Descent." By 1811 there were no fewer than eleven black schools in the city.

But where did Allen think "free people of colour" should look for their future? This question had arisen in Philadelphia as early as 1787, when William Thornton promoted a plan devised by English antislavery organizations to settle free American and West Indian blacks in Sierra Leone, a new state they had created on the west coast of Africa. Many blacks in Boston and Newport had endorsed this scheme, but the members of Philadelphia's Free African Society had rejected it, declaring their intention to seek advancement in America.

Philadelphia's blacks adopted a dual strategy to deal with their subordinate position in American society. As a social group, they embraced their ancestral heritage by forming "African" churches and benevolent societies. But as individuals, they asserted their American identity by taking English names (although virtually never those of their former owners). Although their initial efforts did not yield significant gains in wealth and status, Philadelphia's African Americans once again rejected colonization when the issue was revived around 1800. Only four people signed up for immigration to Sierra Leone.

Instead, the city's black community took political action to enhance the situation of their race. Hundreds of African Americans signed petitions to the state and national governments to end slavery and the slave trade, and to repeal the Fugitive Slave Act of 1793, which allowed slaveowners to seize blacks without a warrant. As if to underline the importance of these political initiatives, in 1806 Allen himself was seized and held temporarily as a fugitive slave, showing that even the most prominent northern blacks could not be sure of their freedom.

Allen's new brush with slavery may account for his initial support for the American Colonization Society, a predominantly white organization founded in 1817 to promote the settlement of free blacks in Africa. But nearly three thousand Philadelphia blacks condemned colonization in a mass meeting and set forth a different vision of the African American future: "Whereas our ancestors (not of choice) were the first successful cultivators of the wilds of America, we their descendants feel ourselves entitled to participate in the blessings of her luxuriant soil."

Philadelphia's black community, including Allen, was more favorably inclined toward the Haitian Emigration Society, founded in 1824 to help African Americans settle in the black-run republic of Haiti. When the venture failed, Allen forcefully urged blacks to remain in the United States. In November 1827 he made a compelling argument in *Freedom's Journal*, the nation's first black newspaper: "This land which we have watered with *our tears* and *our blood* is now our *mother country*."

Born a slave of African ancestry, Allen had learned to live as a free man in white America. Rejecting emigration, he had undertaken to create a new African American cultural identity for his people. This decision meant that he cast his lot, and that of his descendants, with a society pervaded by racism. It was a brave decision, characteristic of the man who made it but also indicative of the limited choices available to those freed from the bonds of slavery.

Captain Absalom Boston
Absalom Boston was born in 1785 on the island of Nantucket, the heart of the American whaling industry. Part of a community of free blacks whose ancestors had been liberated from slavery by their Quaker owners, Boston went to sea at age fifteen. By the age of thirty he had used his whaling earnings to become the proprietor of a public inn. In 1822, Boston became the first black master with an all-black crew to undertake a whaling voyage from Nantucket. He later added to his notable accomplishments by serving as a trustee of the island's African School. Nantucket Historical Association.

chical in its structure and values. At the time of independence, nearly 60 percent of white families in the South owned at least one slave. The percentage of white owners dropped steadily over time; within a few generations only about 25 percent of white families held slaves, and the top 2 percent of southern whites owned about half of the slaves and much of the most fertile land. Wealthy, socially influential, politically powerful, this planter elite dominated the society and gave an aristocratic republican definition to politics and culture.

A "Natural" Aristocracy. Adopting the outlook of a landed gentry, the members of the wealthy slaveholding elite described themselves as natural aristocrats. They married their children to one another, and their sons and daughters became commercial and cultural leaders—the men working as planters, merchants, lawyers, newspaper editors, and ministers, and the women hosting plantation balls and church fetes.

Planters marked their success by building splendid mansions and indulging in displays of conspicuous consumption. The Greek Revival mansion on the rural estate of John Henry Hammond, a leading South Carolina planter and politician, boasted a center hall, 53 feet by 20 feet, its floor embellished with stylish Belgian tiles and expensive Brussels carpets. "Once a year, like a great feudal landlord," a guest recounted, Hammond "gave a fete or grand dinner to all the country people." To retain the allegiance of ambitious men from modest backgrounds, Hammond and other planters encouraged them to buy slaves and grow rich as they had.

Like all ruling classes, the planters sought to justify their power by endowing it with moral purpose. This task became more difficult following the Revolution as Quakers and other antislavery advocates in the North called for an end to human bondage. Initially many planters responded by defending slavery as a "necessary evil" to maintain white living standards and prevent racial warfare. Other southern apologists employed religious justifications, noting that the Hebrews, God's chosen people, had owned slaves and that Christ had never condemned slavery. Many of these writers also invoked St. Paul's injunction: "Servants, obey your masters," interpreting it to justify slavery.

Finally, some defenders of slavery constructed a social defense of the institution. They depicted planters as exemplars of aristocratic *noblesse oblige*, models of "disinterested benevolence" who ensured that their workers were adequately fed and housed, and provided for the sick and elderly who could no longer work. As part of the social defense of slavery, southern writers praised planters' wives as the managers of large households and their work as nurses, caring for sick African American children. As these views became widespread,

planter class. In New Orleans free African Americans sponsored an opera company and established literary journals. A few owned land and slaves themselves.

Generally, however, free blacks and enslaved African Americans saw themselves as one people. "We's different [from whites] in color, in talk and in 'ligion and beliefs," as one put it. Knowing their own freedom was not secure as long as slavery existed, free blacks sought to win freedom for their "brothers" and "sisters." Free blacks in the South aided fugitive slaves while those in the North supported the antislavery movement. In the rigid caste system of American race relations, free blacks stood as symbols of hope to enslaved African Americans and as omens of danger to the majority of whites.

The Southern Social Order

As blacks developed a more homogeneous culture, white society in the South became increasingly hierarthe planter elite came to view itself as a republican aristocracy, privileged by birth and by its role in maintaining a stable, orderly society.

Southern Yeomen and Tenant Farmers. In fact, southern society remained divided by property and regional outlook. As the slave system expanded into the cotton South, many white families became the tenants of aristocratic landlords, and others retreated into the backcountry near the Appalachians, where they hoped to maintain autonomy as yeomen farmers and control local county governments. Owning hilly farms of 50 to 100 acres, these yeomen families grew some cotton but primarily raised corn and livestock, especially hogs. Their goal was modest: to preserve their holdings and secure enough new land or goods to set up all of their children as farmers.

However, wealthy slaveowners continued to force yeomen into less fertile regions by buying up the best land and using their power in the state legislatures to serve their own interests. By the 1830s in Alabama, slaveowners numbered only 30 percent of the electorate but constituted 75 percent of the legislators; a fourth of the legislators were large planters who owned fifty or more slaves. These men kept taxes low on slaves and other personal property and taxed land by acreage rather than by value—so that backcountry farmers paid relatively high taxes on their marginal land. In addition, planters enacted laws that forced yeomen to "fence in" their livestock (sparing themselves the cost of building fences around their large properties) and prohibited them from hunting on unused private lands. Finally, legislatures forced all white men—whether they owned slaves or not—to serve in patrols and militias that deterred slaves from running away or rising in rebellion.

Slaveowners relied on racial prejudice to prevent non-slaveholding southerners from resenting their dominance. They warned tenants and yeomen that they had to support slavery or face economic competition and race warfare with freed African Americans. As John Henry Hammond told his poor white neighbors, "In a slave country every *freeman* is an aristocrat."

In reality, despite the continued expansion of the South's economy, few yeomen or tenants prospered as farmers, and they had few other economic opportunities. Because planters concentrated their resources in cotton and slaves, the percentage of southerners who lived in towns and worked in manufacturing remained small. The only major cities in the South were the old seaports of Baltimore, Charleston, and New Orleans, which remained predominantly commercial centers.

Moreover, the level of education in the South never improved. The wealthy planters who controlled southern society wanted a compliant labor force, content with the drudgery of agricultural work. Consequently, they trained most of their slaves as field hands (allowing only a few to learn the arts of the blacksmith, carpenter, or bricklayer), and they made little or no effort to provide ordinary whites with elementary instruction in reading or arithmetic. No state had a comprehensive system of public schools for whites. As a result, even as the cotton boom of the 1820s and 1830s increased the prosperity of the slave regime, about 20 percent of white southerners could not read or write (as compared to less than 1 percent in New England).

Lacking cities, factories, and educated workers, the South could not provide a majority of its people with a rising standard of living. Enslaved African Americans and white tenant farmers had little or no property, and landholding yeomen in the backcountry lacked access to profitable markets. Prosperity was limited primarily to those families—25 percent of the white population—who owned plantations and slaves. The prospect of political and social equality raised during the Revolutionary era had been dashed by the reality of the South's aristocratic social order.

Protestant Christianity as a Social Force

★

Religion had always been a significant part of American life. But in the decades between 1790 and 1820, a series of revivals planted the values of Protestant Christianity deep in the American national character and created new public roles for women. Religion played the most important role after the family in the lives of enslaved African Americans. Some blacks maintained African practices, invoking traditional spirits in time of need, but many became Christians, absorbing the religious views of white Baptists and Methodists and creating a distinctive and powerful institution—the black church. This upsurge of religious fervor changed the character of American life and gave a new definition to American republicanism.

The Second Great Awakening

The revivals that began around 1790 were much more complex than those of the Great Awakening of the 1740s. Then, most revivals had occurred in existing congregations; fifty years later they took place in frontier camp meetings as well, and often involved the creation of new churches and denominations. Even more striking, the Second Great Awakening spawned a wide variety of organizations dedicated to the cause of social and political reform.

Republican Churches and Revivalism. The churches that prospered in the new nation were typically republican in their outlook or organization. Because it was dominated by bishops and priests, the Roman Catholic

A Wealthy Planter Family at Play
In this painting, *The Fourth of July Picnic*, Lilly Martin Spencer depicts a wealthy
southern family, served by their domestic slaves, celebrating the holiday with a picnic
by the river. The artist focuses the viewer's attention on the patriarch, whose antics
delight his deferential children and grandchildren, and on the tense interaction
between the wife and the African American butler—a reminder of white fears of the
prospect of a slave revolt.
Courtesy Michael N. Altman & Company.

Church attracted few converts either among Protestants, who embraced Luther's doctrine of the priesthood of all believers, or among the unchurched, who feared clerical power. Likewise, few ordinary Americans joined the Episcopal Church (created by former members of the Church of England), which had a similar hierarchical structure and was dominated by its wealthiest members. The Presbyterian Church was more popular, in part because it was more "republican": ordinary members elected laymen to the synods (congresses) where doctrine and practice were formulated.

Methodism attracted even more adherents. It retained the traditional religious hierarchy, as bishops took the lead on theological issues and enforced order in the church. But most Methodist preachers were fervent evangelists and won converts by creating an egalitarian religious culture—encouraging lay preaching, emotional worship services, and communal singing. The most democratic forms of church government belonged to Quakers, Baptists, and congregationalists. No bishops or governing bodies stood above the local congregations, and most church decisions—on matters of theology as well as administration—rested with church members.

A continuous wave of revivalism fueled the expansion of many Protestant churches. Beginning in the 1780s, Baptists and Methodists evangelized the older cities and the backcountry of New England. A new sect of Universalists, who repudiated the Calvinist doctrine of predestination and preached universal salvation, attracted thousands of converts, especially in northern New England.

After 1800, enthusiastic camp meeting revivals swept the frontier regions of South Carolina, Kentucky, Tennessee, and Ohio. James McGready, a Scots-Irish Presbyterian preacher, "could so array hell before the wicked," an eyewitness reported, "that they would tremble and Quake, imagining a lake of fire and brimstone yawning to overwhelm them." When frontier preachers got together at a revival meeting, they were electrifying. One young man, James Finley, was so moved by the Cane Ridge, Kentucky, revival of 1802 that he became a Methodist minister:

> *The noise was like the roar of Niagara. The vast sea of human beings seemed to be agitated as if by a storm. I counted seven ministers, all preaching at one time, some on stumps, others on wagons. . . . Some of the people were singing, others praying, some crying for mercy. A peculiarly strange sensation came over me. My heart beat tumultuously, my knees trembled, my lips quivered, and I felt as though I must fall to the ground.*

Through such revivals, Baptist and Methodist preachers reshaped the spiritual landscape of the South and the Old Southwest. They won over most of the white population, and with the assistance of black ministers, they began to implant evangelical Protestant Christianity among African Americans as well (see Voices from Abroad, "Frances Trollope: A Camp-Meeting in Indiana," p. 306).

Unlike the Great Awakening of the 1740s, which had split many churches into hostile New Light and Old Light factions, the Second Awakening brought friendly competition among Protestant churches, which used new methods of spreading the faith to reach the unconverted. In New England and the Middle Atlantic states, pious women supplemented the work of preachers and lay elders, doubling the amount of organized spiritual energy. In the South and West, Baptist and Methodist preachers traveled constantly. Instead of settling in a congregation, a Methodist cleric followed a circuit, "riding a hardy pony or horse . . . with his Bible, hymnbook, and Discipline." Wherever they went, these "circuit riders" established new churches by searching out devout families, bringing them together for worship, then appointing lay elders to lead the congregation and enforce moral discipline until the circuit rider returned.

Evangelical ministers copied the techniques of George Whitefield and other eighteenth-century revivalists, codifying their intuitive genius in manuals on "practical preaching." To attract converts, preachers were cautioned to emphasize piety over theology; extemporaneous speech was deemed more powerful than a written sermon. "Preach without papers," advised one minister, "seem earnest & serious; & you will be listened to with Patience, & Wonder; both of your hands will be seized, & almost shook off as soon as you are out of the Church."

These missionary innovations shifted the denominational base of American religion away from the leading churches of the colonial period—the Congregationalists, Episcopalians, and Quakers—which declined in relative membership. Their leaders and members were content for the most part to maintain existing congregations or to grow slowly through natural increase. Because of their evangelism and democratic outlook, Methodist and Baptist churches grew spectacularly; by the early nineteenth century they had become the largest religious denominations in the United States.

Black Protestantism. After the family, the religious community played the most important role in the lives of enslaved African Americans. Initially, most blacks maintained the practices of their African homeland. "At the time I first went to Carolina," remembered Charles Ball, an escaped slave, "there were a great many African slaves in the country. . . . Many of them believed their [sic] were several gods [and] I knew several . . . Mohamedans [Muslims]."

Over time, many slaves became Christians, absorbing the religious views of white Baptists and Methodists and adapting them to their needs. Black Christians generally preferred to envision God as a warrior who had liberated the Jews, his chosen people. "Their cause was similar to the Israelites'," Martin Prosser told his fellow slave conspirators during a thwarted rebellion in Virginia in 1800. "I have read in my Bible where God says, if we worship him, we should have peace in all our land and five of you shall conquer a hundred and a hundred of you a hundred thousand of our enemies."

After 1800 tens of thousands of blacks embraced Protestant revivalism, seeing a message of freedom and ultimate justice in its doctrines and tone. Black Christians generally ignored the doctrines of original sin and predestination as well as biblical passages that portrayed the church as a lawgiver and symbol of authority. The Christianity of the slaves repudiated the virtue of unthinking obedience: when a white minister urged slaves in Liberty County, Georgia, to obey their masters, he noted that "one half of my audience deliberately rose up and walked off." Slaves also identified with the persecuted Christ, who had suffered and died so that his followers might gain salvation. Amid the manifest injustice of their lives, African Americans used Christian principles to affirm their equality with whites in the eyes of God.

Black Christianity thus developed as a religion both of emotional fervor and of stoical endurance. By offering hope of eventual liberation from life's sorrows, the Christian message helped many slaves endure their bondage. African American Protestants took heart from stories of the Israelites' exile in Egypt and Christ's compassion for the oppressed. Confident of their special

FRANCES TROLLOPE

A Camp-Meeting in Indiana

──────★──────

Frances Trollope, a successful English author and the mother of novelist Anthony Trollope, resided in the United States during the late 1820s. She lived for a time in Cincinnati, where she established an unprofitable bazaar for the sale of European goods. Her critical and at times acerbic Domestic Manners of the Americans *(1832) achieved wide popularity in both Europe and the United States. Here she provides her readers with a vivid description of a revivalist meeting in Indiana around 1830.*

We reached the ground about an hour before midnight, and the approach to it was highly picturesque. The spot chosen was the verge of an unbroken forest, where a space of about twenty acres appeared to have been partially cleared for the purpose. Tents of different sizes were pitched very near together in a circle round the cleared space. . . .

Four high frames, constructed in the form of altars, were placed at the four corners of the inclosure; on these were supported layers of earth and sod, on which burned immense fires of blazing pinewood. On one side a rude platform was erected to accommodate the preachers, fifteen of whom attended this meeting, and with very short intervals for necessary refreshment and private devotion, preached in rotation, day and night, from Tuesday to Saturday.

When we arrived, the preachers were silent; but we heard issuing from nearly every tent mingled sounds of praying, preaching, singing, and lamentation. . . . The floor [of one of the tents] was covered with straw, which round the sides was heaped in masses, that might serve as seats, but which at that moment were used to support the heads and arms of the close-packed circle of men and women who kneeled on the floor.

Out of about thirty persons thus placed, perhaps half a dozen were men. One of these [was] a handsome-looking youth of eighteen or twenty. . . . His arm was encircling the neck of a young girl who knelt beside him, with her hair hanging dishevelled upon her shoulders, and her features working with the most violent agitation; soon after they both fell forward on the straw, as if unable to endure in any other attitude the burning eloquence of a tall grim figure in black, who, standing erect in the center, was uttering with incredible vehemence an oration that seemed to hover between praying and preaching. . . .

One tent was occupied exclusively by Negroes. They were all full-dressed, and looked exactly as if they were performing a scene on a stage. . . . The men were in snow white pantaloons, with gay colored linen jackets. One of these, a youth of coal-black comeliness, was preaching with the most violent gesticulations. . . .

At midnight, a horn sounded through the camp, which, we were told, was to call the people from private to public worship; and we presently saw them flocking from all sides to the front of the preacher's stand. . . . There were about two thousand persons assembled.

One of the preachers began in a low nasal tone, and, like all other Methodist preachers, assured us of the enormous depravity of man. . . . Above a hundred persons, nearly all females, came forward, uttering howlings and groans so terrible that I shall never cease to shudder when I recall them. They appeared to drag each other forward, and on the word being given, "let us pray," they fell on their knees . . . and they were soon all lying on the ground in an indescribable confusion of heads and legs.

───────────

Source: Frances Trollope, *Domestic Manners of the Americans* (London: Whittaker, Treacher and Co., 1832), 139–142.

relationship with God, the slaves prepared themselves spiritually for emancipation, which they saw as deliverance to the Promised Land.

New Religious Thought and Institutions. The Second Great Awakening changed the character of American thought—and social action—in dramatic ways. Before the Awakening, the Calvinist preoccupation with human depravity and weakness had shaped the thinking of many writers, teachers, and statesmen. But by the early nineteenth century, ministers—whether or not they were revivalists—had begun to place greater stress on human ability and individual free will. Such views imparted a new optimism to the religious culture of the United States and made it more compatible with republican doctrines of liberty and equality.

In New England, the primary source of the new rationalist theology, many educated and economically well-off Congregationalists became Unitarians. Rejecting the concept of the Trinity—God the Father, Son, and Holy Spirit—Unitarians worshipped an indivisible and "united" God (hence the name Unitarian). Reacting against the emotionalism of Methodist and Baptist services, they stressed the power of human reason. "The ultimate reliance of a human being is, and must be, on his own mind," argued the famous Unitarian minister William Ellery Channing, "for the idea of God is the idea of our own spiritual nature, purified and enlarged to infinity." This emphasis on a believer's reason, a legacy of the Enlightenment, gave Unitarianism a humanistic and individualistic aspect.

Optimistic ideas affected mainstream Congregational churches as well. Lyman Beecher, the preeminent New England clergyman, accepted the Universalists' doctrine of universal salvation. Although Beecher continued to believe that humans had a natural tendency to sin, he retreated from the Calvinist doctrine of predestination, declaring that men and women had the capacity to choose God. In emphasizing choice—the free will of the believer—Beecher testified to the growing confidence in the power of human action.

Reflecting this optimistic outlook, the minister Samuel Hopkins linked individual salvation with social reform through the concept of religious *benevolence*. Benevolence was the practice of disinterested virtue, to be undertaken by those who had received God's sanctifying grace. According to the New York Presbyterian minister John Rodgers, such fortunate individuals had a duty "to dole out charity to their poorer brothers and sisters." Inspired by such arguments, pious merchants founded the New York Humane Society and other charitable organizations. By the 1820s some conservative church leaders were complaining that through their benevolence, lay men and women were devoting themselves to secular reforms—such as the prevention of pauperism—to the neglect of spiritual goals. Their criticism underlined a key element of the new religious outlook: its emphasis on improving society. It was her belief, the social reformer Lydia Maria Child later recalled, that "the *only* true church organization [is] when heads and hearts unite in working for the welfare of the human-race."

These new ideas spread quickly through the founding of new theological seminaries such as Andover in Massachusetts and Lane in Ohio, two Congregationalist institutions that fostered cooperation among the denominations. As individual clergymen of different denominations cooperated with one another, American Protestant churches became less dogmatic. Many congregations abandoned orthodox books and pamphlets such as the Watts Hymnal, which took controversial stances on old theological debates over predestination

MAP 9.5

Ethnicity and Religion in Eastern Pennsylvania and New Jersey, c. 1780

Long-established churches, founded by English Quakers and Dutch Reformed Protestants, stood side by side with those established by new ethnic groups, such as German Lutherans and Scots-Irish Presbyterians. Many communities had churches for two or three different denominations, a situation that fostered religious toleration and undermined the idea of a legally established church.

and replaced them, a layman explained, with publications that would not give "offense to the serious Christians of any denomination" (Map 9.5).

Indeed, five interdenominational societies were founded between 1815 and 1826: the American Education Society (1815), the American Bible Society (1816), the American Sunday School Union (1824), the American Tract Society (1824), and the American Home Missionary Society (1826). The new organizations were based in New York, Boston, and Philadelphia, but they ministered to a national congregation. Each year the societies dispatched hundreds of missionaries to small towns and rural villages and distributed tens of thousands of religious pamphlets.

Organization on this scale united the individual energies of thousands of church members in a great col-

lective undertaking, providing the Second Great Awakening with momentum and power. "I want to see our state evangelized," declared one pious New York layman: "Suppose the great State of New York in all its physical, political, moral, commercial, and pecuniary resources should come over to the Lord's side. Why it would turn the scale and could convert the world. I shall have no rest until it is done." For the first time in America, men and women in small villages scattered across the nation saw themselves as part of a large religious movement, one that could change the course of history.

As a result of the Second Awakening, religion became a central force in American life. Thus, on July 4, 1827, the Reverend Ezra Stiles Ely called on the members of the Seventh Presbyterian Church in Philadelphia to begin a "Christian party in politics." In his sermon entitled "The Duty of Christian Freemen to Elect Christian Rulers," Ely set out for the American republic a new religious goal—one that Thomas Jefferson and John Adams would have found strange if not troubling. The two recently deceased presidents had believed that America's mission was to spread political republicanism. In contrast, Ely urged the United States to become an evangelical Christian nation, dedicated to religious conversion at home and abroad. As Ely put it, "All our rulers ought in their official capacity to serve the Lord Jesus Christ." The Second Great Awakening had added moral issues and social reform to the agenda of American politics and, in the process, gave a religious definition to American republicanism.

Women's New Religious Roles

Revivalism created new opportunities for women in the public sphere. Taking advantage of their enhanced moral status, pious women assumed a leading role in many Protestant churches and even founded new sects. Mother Ann Lee organized the Shaker sect in Britain and migrated in 1774 to America, where she and a handful of followers attracted numerous recruits; by the 1820s Shaker communities dotted the American countryside from New Hampshire to Kentucky and Indiana (see Chapter 12). In 1776 in Rhode Island Jemima Wilkinson, a young Quaker woman stirred by the sermons of George Whitefield, had a vision in which she died and her body was infused by the "Spirit of Light." Repudiating her birth name, Wilkinson declared herself to be the Publick Universal Friend and won scores of converts to her new religion, which blended the Calvinist warning of "a lost and guilty, gossiping, dying World" with a Quaker-inspired social gospel that advocated plain dress, pacifism, and the emancipation of slaves.

Increasing Public Activity. Far more important were the activities undertaken by women in mainstream churches. To give but a few examples, in New Hampshire women managed more than fifty local "cent" societies that raised funds for the Society for Promoting Christian Knowledge. Evangelical women in New York City founded a charitable institution, the Society for the Relief of Poor Widows. And young Quaker women in Philadelphia ran the Society for the Free Instruction of African Females.

Women became active in religion and charitable work partly because they were excluded from other spheres of public life and partly because they formed a substantial majority in many denominations. After 1800 no less than 70 percent of the members of New England Congregational churches were women because many men were pursuing economic rather than spiritual goals. Some ministers acknowledged the predominance of women by changing longstanding practices. In many Protestant faiths, men and women had traditionally sat on opposite sides of the church during regular Sunday services, and ministers had conducted separate prayer meetings for each sex. Now evangelical Methodist and Baptist preachers began to encourage mixed seating and praying. Although critics condemned the practice as "promiscuous," Presbyterian and Congregational churches in frontier areas achieved impressive results with it. "Our prayer meetings have been one of the greatest means of the conversion of souls," a minister in central New York reported in the 1820s, "especially those in which brothers and sisters have prayed together."

As women began to transcend traditional gender roles, their religious activities and organizations became controversial. Many laymen resented the clergy's emphasis on women's moral superiority, and the religious and social activism that sprang from it. "Women have a different *calling*," one man argued. "They are neither required nor permitted to be exhorters or leaders in public assemblies. . . . That they *be chaste, keepers at home* is the Apostle's direction." But many ministers continued to encourage the creation of women's organizations, and women became increasingly conscious of their new social power. By the 1820s, mothers throughout the United States had founded local maternal associations to encourage Christian child rearing. Newsletters such as *Mother's Magazine* were widely read in hundreds of small towns and villages, giving women a sense of shared purpose and identity.

In their capacity as moral paragons, women had an immediate and direct impact on social behavior. Absorbing the principle of female virtue, many young women, and the men who courted them, postponed sexual intercourse until after marriage—a form of self-restraint that had not been common in the eighteenth century. In Hingham, Massachusetts, and many other New England towns, about 30 percent of the women who married between 1750 and 1800 had borne a child within eight months of their wedding day. By the 1820s, the proportion had dropped to 15 percent.

Women in the Awakening
In this detail from the painting *Religious Camp Meeting* by J. Maze Burbank (1839), all
the preachers are men, but women fill the audience and form the majority of those
visibly "awakened." In fact, the Second Great Awakening was one of the pivotal times
in the history of American women. It transformed millions of women into devout
Christians, providing Protestant churches with dedicated workers, teachers, and
morally minded mothers. And by encouraging tens of thousands of women to join
movements for temperance, abolition, and women's rights, the Awakening spurred a
great wave of social reform.
Old Dartmouth Historical Society/New Bedford Whaling Museum.

Women's Education.   Religious activism also advanced
the education of women. Churches established scores
of seminaries and academies where girls—mostly from
the middling classes—received sound intellectual training as well as moral instruction. Emma Willard, the
first American to advocate higher education for
women, opened the Middlebury Female Seminary in
Vermont in 1814 and later founded girls' schools in
Waterford and Troy, New York.

The women who were educated in these seminaries
and academies gradually displaced men from their customary roles as public school teachers. By the 1820s
women were teaching the summer session in many
schools; in the following decade they would work the
more demanding winter term as well. Women took over
teaching in primary schools because they had few other
opportunities and because they would accept lower pay
than would men. As schoolteachers women earned from
$12 to $14 per month with room and board—less than
a farm laborer did. But they benefited from the higher
moral status accorded to women and from the impera-
tives of republican motherhood: they would instruct the
young not only at home but also in school. As schoolteachers, women had an acknowledged place in public
life, one that had been beyond their reach in colonial
and Revolutionary times. Thus, the Second Great Awakening had transformed both the character of American
republicanism and the scope of women's lives.

Summary

★

Three variants of republican society developed in the United States in the early nineteenth century: democratic republicanism in the North, aristocratic republicanism in the South, and an evangelical Protestant vision of republicanism that was embraced by many people in both regions. In the North the ideal of a democratic republican society based on liberty and equality encouraged the emergence of a white male citizenry that demanded voting rights, pursued social mobility, and looked with suspicion on those with aristocratic pretensions. Political and religious leaders promoted a different path for women, developing the notion of a separate sphere consisting primarily of domestic responsibilities. Republicanism and sentimentalism influenced the private lives of many Americans, encouraging young people to marry for love as well as for economic security, and prompting parents to rear their children using reason as well as authority.

Responding to the demand for cotton, southern planters extended the slave regime into the Old Southwest. This expansion led to a sectional confrontation over slavery that the Missouri Compromise temporarily resolved by allowing some free and some slave states to be carved out of the Lousiana Purchase. Enslaved blacks adopted English and some white religious practices but, along with free blacks in northern cities, forged a distinct African American culture. Slaves developed increasingly strong family, community, and religious values, which helped them survive the forced migration to the cotton South and the relentless demands of gang labor.

The planter elite solidified its control of the southern social order, constructing an elaborate intellectual defense of slavery and depicting itself as a natural aristocracy. Using the ideology of white supremacy, it retained the loyalty of white tenants and yeomen, most of whom did not own slaves and resided on small farms in backcountry districts. The hierarchical character of southern society encouraged the formation of an aristocratic republican system of values.

Simultaneously, the Second Great Awakening made Americans a fervently Protestant people and dramatically increased the influence of evangelical Baptist and Methodist churches. Religious revivalism also enhanced the status of women, whose moral activism broadened the dimensions of their sphere to encompass teaching in public schools and managing charitable groups and religious societies. Religious institutions thus gave women a new and growing presence in public life and added a new dimension to the American republican experiment. The shared religious experience of hundreds of thousands of Americans between the 1770s and the 1820s formed the core of an emerging national identity, even as the citizens of the North and the South defined republicanism in distinctly different ways.

TIMELINE

1782	St. Jean de Crèvecoeur, *Letters from an American Farmer*
1787	Benjamin Rush, *Thoughts on Female Education*
1790s	Parents limit family size
	Second Great Awakening
	"Republican motherhood" defined
1800	Gabriel Prosser's rebellion in Virginia
1800s	Rise of sentimentalism and republican marriage system
	Women's religious activism and female academies
	Spread of evangelical Baptists and Methodists
	Beginnings of benevolent reform
	Chesapeake blacks adopt Protestant beliefs
1807	New Jersey excludes propertied women from suffrage
1810s	Expansion of suffrage for men
	Slavery defended as a "necessary evil"
	Expansion of cotton South and domestic slave trade
1819–1821	Conflict over admission of Missouri
1820s	Reform of public education
	Women become schoolteachers

Suggested Readings

———————★———————

Two fine local studies—Alan Taylor, *William Cooper's Town: Power and Persuasion on the Frontier of the Early American Republic* (1995), and Laurel Thatcher Ulrich, *A Midwife's Tale: The Life of Martha Ballard* (1990)—capture the texture of northern life in the early republic. James Oakes, *The Ruling Race: A History of American Slaveholders* (1982), offers an important perspective on the expansion of slavery, while Nathan O. Hatch, *The Democratization of American Christianity* (1987), presents an interpretation of religious change.

Democratic Republicanism

Warren S. Tryon, *A Mirror for Americans: Life and Manners in the United States, 1790–1870, as Recorded by European Travelers* (3 vols., 1952), suggests the distinctive features of republican society. Clement Eaton, *Henry Clay and the Art of American Politics* (1957), perceptively describes the coming of political democracy. More detailed studies are Ronald Formisano, *The Transformation of Political Culture: Massachusetts Parties, 1790s–1840s* (1983), and Chilton Williamson, *American Suffrage from Property to Democracy* (1960).

Michael Grossberg, *Governing the Hearth* (1985), discusses changing marriage rules. Catherine M. Scholten, *Childrearing in American Society, 1650–1850* (1985), should be supplemented by Philip Greven's pathbreaking analysis, *The Protestant Temperament: Patterns of Childrearing, Religious Experience, and the Self in Early America* (1977). On sentimentalism, see Shirley Samuels, *The Culture of Sentiment: Race, Gender and Sentimentality in Nineteenth Century America* (1992). Other important works include Daniel Blake Smith, *Inside the Great House: Planter Family Life in Eighteenth-Century Chesapeake Society* (1980); Bernard Wishy, *The Child and the Republic* (1970); and Jan Lewis, *The Pursuit of Happiness: Family and Values in Jefferson's Virginia* (1983).

Slavery and Aristocratic Republicanism in the South

Peter Kolchin, *American Slavery, 1619–1877* (1993), provides a fine overview. See also Lawrence W. Levine, *Black Culture and Black Consciousness* (1977). On the expansion of slavery, see Ira Berlin and Ronald Hoffman, eds., *Slavery and Freedom in the Age of the American Revolution* (1983); Donald L. Robinson, *Slavery in the Structure of American Politics, 1765–1820* (1971); and Albert Raboteau, *Slave Religion* (1968). Also see Ira Berlin and Philip D. Morgan, eds., *Cultivation and Culture: Labor and the Shaping of Slave Life* (1993); Peter W. Bardaglio, *Reconstructing the Household: Families, Sex, and the Law in the Nineteenth-Century South* (1996); and Dena J. Epstein, *Sinful Tunes and Spirituals: Black Folk Music to the Civil War* (1977). Two good studies of the Carolina region are Joyce E. Chaplin, *Agricultural Innovation and Modernity in the Lower South, 1730–1815* (1993), and Peter A. Coclanis, *The Shadow of a Dream: Economic Life and Death in the South Carolina Low Country, 1670–1920* (1988).

For blacks in the northern states, see Gary B. Nash, *Forging Freedom: Philadelphia's Black Community, 1720–1840* (1988). Glover Moore, *The Missouri Compromise* (1953), provides a detailed analysis of that crisis.

The culture of the planter class and non-slaveholding whites can be explored in O. Vernon Burton, *In My Father's House Are Many Mansions: Family and Community in Edgefield, South Carolina* (1985); Drew Gilpin Faust, *Southern Stories: Slaveholders in Peace and War* (1992); and Eugene Genovese, *Roll, Jordan, Roll* (1974). The best studies of women in southern slave society are Catherine Clinton, *The Plantation Mistress* (1983), and Elizabeth Fox-Genovese, *Within the Plantation Household: Black and White Women of the Old South* (1988). Catherine Clinton, ed., *Half Sisters of History: Southern Women and the American Past* (1994), is a collection of important articles. Other important studies include Jacqueline Jones, *Labor of Love, Labor of Sorrow: Black Women, Work, and the Family from Slavery to the Present* (1986), and Deborah G. White, *Ar'n't I a Woman? Female Slaves in the Plantation South* (1985).

J. Mills Thornton III, *Politics and Power in a Slave Society: Alabama, 1800–1860* (1978), connects southern culture with southern politics. On the nature of violence in southern society, see John Hope Franklin, *The Militant South, 1800–1861* (1956), and Bertram Wyatt-Brown, *Southern Honor: Ethics and Behavior in the Old South* (1982). On slave revolts, see Stephen B. Oates, *The Fires of Jubilee: Nat Turner's Fierce Rebellion* (1975); Eugene D. Genovese, *From Rebellion to Revolution: Afro-American Slave Revolts in the Making of the Modern World* (1979); and Douglas R. Egerton, *Gabriel's Rebellion* (1995). On the ambiguous position of free blacks in a slave society, consult Ira Berlin, *Slaves without Masters: The Free Negro in the Antebellum South* (1974).

Protestant Christianity as a Social Force

Perry Miller, *The Life of the Mind in America* (1966), offers a good overview of the Second Great Awakening. For revivalism, see Stephen A. Marini, *Radical Sects of Revolutionary New England* (1982); Bernard A. Weisberger, *They Gathered at the River* (1958); and Ian H. Murray, *Revival and Revivalism: The Making and Marring of American Evangelicalism, 1750–1858* (1994). The course of religious thought in New England is traced in Daniel Walker Howe, *The Unitarian Conscience* (1970).

Recent studies touching on evangelical religion include Christine L. Heyrman, *Southern Cross: The Beginnings of the Bible Belt* (1997); Diana Hockstedt Butler, *Standing against the Whirlwind: Evangelical Episcopalians in Nineteenth-Century America* (1995); Randy J. Sparks, *On Jordan's Stormy Banks: Evangelicalism in Mississippi, 1773–1876* (1994); and John G. West Jr., *The Politics of Revelation and Reason: Religion and Civic Life in the New Nation* (1996).

For women's lives, see Susan Juster, *Disorderly Women: Sexual Politics and Evangelicalism in Revolutionary New England* (1994), and Harriet B. Applewhite and Darline G. Levy, eds., *Women and Politics in the Age of Democratic Revolution* (1990). Specialized studies include Joan M. Jensen, *Loosening the Bonds: Mid-Atlantic Farm Women, 1750–1850* (1986), and Jeanne Boydston, *Home and Work* (1990).

Women's religious initiatives are discussed in Mary P. Ryan, *Cradle of the Middle Class* (1981); Barbara Epstein, *The Politics of Domesticity: Women, Evangelism, and Temperance* (1978); and Keith Melder, *Beginnings of Sisterhood: The American Women's Rights Movement, 1800–1850* (1977), which also traces the growth of female academies.

Part Three

★

Economic Revolution and Sectional Strife,

1820–1877

THEMATIC TIMELINE

	Economy	Society	Government	Culture	Sectionalism
	The Economic Revolution Begins	The Emergence of a New Class Structure	Creating a Democratic Polity	Reforming People and Institutions	From Compromise to Civil War and Reconstruction
1820	Waltham textile factory (1814) Erie Canal completed (1825); market economy expands	Business class emerges Rural women and girls recruited as factory workers	Universal white male suffrage Rise of Jackson and Democratic Party	American Colonization Society (1817) "Benevolent" Reform Revivalist Charles Finney	Missouri Compromise (1820) Walker's Appeal to the Colored Race (1829)
1830	Protective tariffs aid owners and workers Panic of 1837	Mechanics form craft unions Depression shatters labor movement	Anti-Masonic movement Whig Party formed (1834); Second Party System emerges	Joseph Smith founds Mormonism Female Moral Reform Society (1834) Temperance Crusade	Nullification crisis (1832) Garrison forms American Anti-Slavery Society (1833)
1840	Irish join labor force Commonwealth v. Hunt (1842) legalizes unions Manufacturing increases	Working-class districts emerge in cities Irish immigration accelerates	Log Cabin campaign mobilizes voters Antislavery parties: Liberty and Free Soil	Fourierist and other communal settlements founded Seneca Falls convention (1848)	Mexican War and Wilmot Proviso (1846) increase sectional conflict
1850	Panic of 1857	Expansion of farm society into Midwest and Far West Free labor ideology justifies inequality	Whig Party disintegrates; Republican Party founded (1854): Third Party System	Stowe's Uncle Tom's Cabin (1852)	Compromise of 1850 Kansas-Nebraska Act (1854) and "Bleeding Kansas" Dred Scott decision (1857)
1860	Republicans enact agenda: Homestead Act, aid to railroads, high tariffs	Emancipation Proclamation (1863) Free blacks struggle for control of land	Thirteenth Amendment (1865) ends slavery; Fourteenth Amendment (1868) extends legal and political rights	U.S. Sanitary Commission and American Red Cross founded	South Carolina secedes (1860) Confederate States of America (1861–1865)
1870	Panic of 1873	Rise of sharecropping in the South	Fifteenth Amendment extends vote to black men (1870)	Freed African Americans create schools and institutions	Compromise of 1877 ends Reconstruction

BETWEEN 1820 AND 1877 the United States changed from a predominantly agricultural society into one of the world's most powerful industrial economies. This profound transformation began slowly in the Northeast and then accelerated after 1830, affecting every aspect of life in the northern and midwestern states and bringing important changes to the South as well.

Economy. First, two revolutions—in industrial production and the market system—transformed the nation's economy. Factory owners used high-speed machines and a new system of labor discipline to boost production, and enterprising merchants employed a newly built network of canals and railroads to create a vast national market. The industrial sector produced an ever-increasing share of the country's wealth—from less than 5 percent in 1820 to more than 30 percent in 1877.

Society. Second, this new economic system spurred the creation of a class-based society. A wealthy elite of merchants, manufacturers, bankers, and other entrepreneurs emerged at the top of the social order and tried to maintain social stability through a paternalistic program of religious reform. However, an urban middle class with a distinct material and religious culture grew in size and political importance. Equally striking was the increasing number of propertyless workers, many of them immigrants from Germany and Ireland, who labored for wages in the new factories and built the new canals and railroads. By 1860, half the nation's free workers labored for wages, and wealth had become concentrated in the hands of relatively few families.

Government. Third, these economic and social changes facilitated the development of political parties and a more open, democratic polity. Farmers, workers, and entrepreneurs turned to politics, seeking improved transportation, shorter work days, and special corporate charters, and Catholic immigrants from Ireland and Germany entered the political arena to protect their religion and culture from attacks by nativists and reformers. Led by Andrew Jackson, the Democratic Party took a primary role in advancing the interests of southern planters, farmers, and urban workers, and it carried through a democratic political and constitutional revolution that reduced the scope of governmental authority. To compete with the Democrats, the Whig Party (and, beginning in the 1850s, the Republican Party) campaigned widely for votes, promoting reform

and a vision of a society with few class barriers and a high rate of individual social mobility. The result was a two-party system that engaged the energies of the vast majority of the electorate and unified the fragmented social order.

Culture. Fourth, a series of reform movements, many with religious roots and goals, swept across America. Dedicated men and women preached the gospel of temperance, observance of Sunday, prison reform, and dozens of other causes. A few reformers pursued their visions in utopian communities in the midwestern states, but many radical activists sought dramatic changes in American society by campaigning for equal rights for women and the end of slavery. Abolitionists condemned slavery as a sin, prompting southern leaders to defend the institution as beneficial to both planters and slaves. During the 1840s and 1850s antislavery advocates turned to political action, campaigning for "free soil" in the western territories and alleging that the southern "Slave Power" threatened free labor and republican values.

Sectionalism. Fifth, these economic, political, and cultural changes combined to sharpen sectional divisions: the North developed into an urbanizing and industrializing society based on free labor, whereas the South remained a rural, slaveholding society dependent on the production and export of cotton. Following the conquest of vast areas of the West during the Mexican War (1846–1848), northern and southern politicians vigorously debated the future of these lands. Conflicts over the issue of slavery in the new territories could not be resolved by political compromise, leading in 1861 to the secession of the South from the Union and, thereafter, civil war. The conflict became a "total war," a struggle between two societies as well as two armies. Because of new technology and the mass mobilization of armies, the two sides endured unprecedented casualties and costs before the North emerged victorious.

The fruits of victory were substantial. During Reconstruction, the Republican Party ended slavery, imposed its economic policies and constitutional doctrines on the nation, and began to extend full democratic rights to the former slaves. But in the face of massive resistance from white southerners, northern leaders lacked the will to undertake the fundamental transformation of the economic and political order of the South that was required to provide African Americans with the full benefits of freedom.

Chapter 10

★

The Economic Revolution,
1820–1860

The Rise of Manufacturing
Division of Labor and the Factory
The Textile Industry and British Competition
American Mechanics and Technological
    Innovation
Wage Workers and the Labor Movement

The Expansion of Markets
Migration to the West
The Transportation Revolution
The Growth of Cities and Towns

Changes in the Social Structure
The Business Elite
The Middle Class
The New Urban Poor
The Benevolent Empire
Revivalism and Reform
Immigration and Cultural Conflict

THE UNITED STATES WAS founded as an agrarian republic and over the next half-century matured into a commercially advanced agricultural society. Then enterprising Americans initiated a century-long process of change that transformed the nation into the world's most powerful industrial economy. The years from 1820 to 1836 were crucial to this transition, for they saw a dramatic acceleration in the growth of its two central components: the factory system of manufacturing and the market economy. A second leap forward occurred between 1843 and 1857, as the business leaders of the Northeast drove mechanization forward and incorporated the trans-Appalachian West into the industrial economy.

Together, the "industrial revolution" and the "market revolution" created a new American economy. A significant change in manufacturing methods enabled Americans to increase their economic *productivity* (making more goods per worker), while the building of new transportation networks—turnpikes, canals, and railroads—allowed those products to be sold throughout the land. The economic results were phenomenal. By 1860 the United States was not only the world's leading exporter of cotton and wheat but also the third-ranking manufacturing nation, behind only Great Britain and France.

The French aristocrat Alexis de Tocqueville captured a key feature of this economic revolution in his treatise entitled *Democracy in America* (1835). "What most astonishes me," he remarked after a two-year stay in the United States, "is not so much the marvelous grandeur of some undertakings, as the innumerable magnitude of small ones." It was the individual efforts

A New England Textile Village, 1822
Because of the need for water power, the American industrial revolution began in small rural settlements like that shown in Francis Alexander's Globe Village *on the Blackstone River near Southbridge, Massachusetts. The mill in the center of the picture was begun in 1814. By 1822, the date of the painting, New England textile mills were giving British manufacturers a run for their money.*
Jacob Edwards Library, Southbridge, MA.

of tens of thousands of artisan-inventors, entrepreneurial storekeepers and manufacturers, and commercially minded planters and farmers that propelled the country into a new economic era. As the editor of *Niles Weekly Register* in Baltimore put it, there was an "almost *universal ambition to get forward.*"

Not all Americans embraced the new ethic of enterprise, and many who did failed to share in the new prosperity. Industrial and commercial expansion created new social classes, challenging the founders' vision of an agricultural republic with few distinctions of wealth or power. "The invasion of Nature by Trade with its Money, its Credit, its Steam, its Railroad," the philosopher Ralph Waldo Emerson wrote in 1839, "threatens to . . . establish a new, universal Monarchy."

The Rise of Manufacturing

———★———

Industrialization came to the United States after 1790 as American merchants increased productivity by reorganizing work and building factories. These innovations in manufacturing boosted output and living standards to an unprecedented extent; the average per capita wealth of Americans increased by nearly 1 percent per year—30 percent over the course of a generation. Goods that had once been luxury items became part of everyday life.

Division of Labor and the Factory

The impressive gain in output stemmed primarily from the way in which workers made goods. Since the 1790s American merchants had broadened the scope of the outwork system, which made domestic manufacturing more efficient than before—even without technological improvements. For example, during the 1820s and 1830s the shoe industry greatly expanded the scale and extent of the outwork system developed after the Revolution (see Chapter 8). Tens of thousands of rural women, laboring on a piecework basis, fabricated the "uppers" of shoes, which were bound to the soles by wage-earning journeymen shoemakers in Lynn and dozens of other Massachusetts towns. This system of production made the master a powerful employer, the "shoe boss," and eroded workers' control over the pace and conditions of labor. However, it also dramatically increased the output of shoes while cutting their price.

For tasks that were not suited to the outwork system, entrepreneurs created an even more important new organization, the modern *factory*, which used power-driven machines and assembly-line techniques to turn out large quantities of well-made goods. As early as 1782 the prolific Delaware inventor Oliver Evans had built a highly automated labor-saving flour mill driven by water power. His machinery lifted the grain to the top of the mill, cleaned it as it fell into hoppers, ground it into flour, and then conveyed the flour back to the top of the mill to allow it to cool as it descended into barrels. Evans's factory, remarked one observer, "was as full of machinery as the case of a watch." It needed only six men to mill 100,000 bushels of grain a year.

Subsequently, manufacturers made use of newly improved stationary steam engines to power their mills. This new technology enabled them to build factories in the nation's largest cities, taking advantage of urban concentrations of cheap labor, good transportation networks, and eager customers. By 1838 there were about 2,000 steam engines in the United States, including 133 in Pittsburgh alone, where they were used in the glass industry, sawmills, machine shops, and iron-rolling mills.

Manufacturers also concentrated as many of the elements of production as possible under one roof and divided the work into specialized tasks. For example, in the 1830s Cincinnati merchants built slaughterhouses that included "disassembly" lines for butchering hogs. A simple system of overhead rails moved the carcasses past workers, each of whom had a specific task: cutting the animals in half, removing various organs, and trimming the carcasses before packers stuffed them in barrels and pickled them. The system was highly efficient; every hour more than sixty hogs were butchered and packed. In the 1840s Cincinnati was disassembling so many hogs that the city became known as "Porkopolis."

Gradually factory owners extended the use of power-driven machines and assembly lines from the processing of agricultural goods—pork, leather, wool, cotton—to the manufacturing of other machines made of metal: guns, sewing machines, clocks and watches, and agricultural machinery. Cyrus McCormick of Chicago developed power-driven conveyor belts to assemble reapers, and Samuel Colt built an assembly-line factory in Hartford, Connecticut, to produce his invention—the "six-shooter," as it became known. By the late 1850s Colt's factory was turning out 60,000 weapons annually, and five Connecticut clockmakers were using machine tools to make intricate works for half a million clocks a year. As a team of British observers noted with admiration, those products were made "in large factories, with machinery applied to almost every process, the extreme subdivision of labor, and all reduced to an almost perfect system of manufacture."

The Textile Industry and British Competition

The most dramatic gains in productivity occurred in the textile industry, where manufacturers *combined* the new technology with the new organization of labor. In

the 1760s textile manufacturers in northern England had begun to use water-driven machines to produce huge quantities of inexpensive cloth, and in the 1790s American entrepreneurs tried to duplicate their success. This task was difficult because British law prohibited the export of textile machinery and the emigration of *mechanics* (as skilled workers were then called) who knew how to build it. Lured by high wages or offers of partnerships, thousands of British mechanics disguised themselves as ordinary laborers and set sail for the United States. By 1812 there were more than 300 British mechanics at work in the Philadelphia area alone.

The most important was Samuel Slater, who came to America in 1789. He had worked as an apprentice for the partner of Richard Arkwright, the inventor and operator of the most advanced machinery for spinning cotton. Having memorized the design of Arkwright's machinery, the young Slater contacted Moses Brown, a wealthy American merchant who had been trying to duplicate British spinning technology. Slater took over the management of Brown's cotton mill in Providence, Rhode Island, and replicated Arkwright's machines. The opening of Slater's Mill in 1790 marks the advent of the American Industrial Revolution (see New Technology, "Cotton Spinning: From Spinsters to Machines," p. 318).

American and British Advantages. In competing with British mills, American manufacturers had one clear advantage: an abundance of natural resources. Southern plantations produced a wealth of cotton, northern farmers developed a booming wool industry, and rivers from Maine to Delaware provided a cheap source of energy. As rivers cascaded from the Appalachian foothills to the Atlantic coastal plain, they were easily harnessed to run power machinery. All along these waterways, industrial villages and towns

Pork Packing in Cincinnati
The only form of modern technology in this Cincinnati pork packing plant was the overhead pulley system that carried hog carcasses past the workers. The plant's efficiency came from its organization: labor was divided so that each worker performed a specific task. Such plants pioneered the moving assembly line, which reached a high level of sophistication in the early twentieth-century automobile factories of Henry Ford.
Cincinnati Historical Society.

Cotton Spinning: From Spinsters to Machines

★

Samuel Slater's Spinning Frame
Samuel Slater's spinning frame was powered by water and could spin thread onto 96 bobbins simultaneously (48 on each side of the lower part of the machine). The introduction of the spinning frame revolutionized textile manufacturing by dramatically increasing the output of a single worker.
Museum of History and Technology, Smithsonian Institution, Washington, DC.

SINCE THE DAWN of civilization the making of cloth had been slow and laborious work, mostly done by women. Taking raw wool or cotton, women pulled out burrs and seeds and separated the fibers into strands by running them through a comb or "card," a flat paddle studded with twigs or nails. They next began the even more time-consuming task of spinning the fibers into cotton or woolen thread (or more bulky woolen yarn) by using hand- or foot-powered spinning machines. Only then could the fibers be fitted into hand-powered looms and woven into cloth, sometimes by women but more often by men.

Despite its importance, spinning had a low social value, in part because it was drudge work—slow, repetitive, and uninteresting. It became the work of women without power, those dependent on the good will of others: young girls, grandmothers, and especially unmarried women. Living in the households of their fathers or brothers, unmarried women stood at the bottom of the family hierarchy, condemned to the menial tasks of cleaning, mending, and especially spinning. Indeed, the connection between spinning and never-married older women was so close that such women became (and remain) known as "spinsters."

The name should not have survived the Industrial Revolution, which transformed the processing of cotton and wool and made spinsters obsolete. Carding was no longer hand-work. By 1800 water- or hand-powered carding machines were turning raw cotton into clean fibers. Consisting of two or more cylinders covered with wire pins, the machines combed the fibers into parallel strands and fed them into other machines that wound the carded cotton into a loose roll (or "roving").

Mechanization also revolutionized the technology of spinning. The key tool in spinning had always been the spindle, which first elongated the strands of fiber and then twisted them together to make threads or yarn. In 1765 the British inventor James Hargreaves devised a "spinning jenny" that imitated the function of spinning wheels. The jenny's operator manually turned a wheel that spun a series of spindles—from 24 to 100—each of which simultaneously drew out the roving and twisted it into thread. Using a jenny, one person could now do the work of dozens, and in less time.

However, American textile manufacturers preferred another British invention—the spinning frame, patented by Richard Arkwright in 1769 and brought to the United States by Samuel Slater. The spinning frame separated the functions of drawing and twisting. After two pairs of rollers had elongated the thread, it was passed down the arm of a flier, a device attached to a spindle. The flier twisted the thread and wound it onto a bobbin attached to the spindle.

The spinning frame lowered production costs dramatically. The machine ran hundreds of spindles continuously on inexpensive water power and produced yarn that was both coarse enough for the rugged cloth used for most American clothing and strong enough to be processed on the water-powered looms that came into use during the 1820s. Most important from the manufacturers' perspective, the spinning frame required only low-skilled and low-priced labor. The operative had only to affix the roving to the frame and tie any threads that broke. In many American factories, tending spinning frames became the ill-paid work of young women and, increasingly, of young boys and girls.

By a cruel twist of fate, spinning had once again become drudge work—repetitive, uninteresting, and low-paid. But now it was the work not of family-dependent "spinsters" but of wage-dependent industrial "proletarians" (workers who had nothing to sell but their labor). In a myriad of such small transformations, the Industrial Revolution changed the character of American economic—and social—life.

sprang up—especially in New England, where the relative lack of good farmland promoted the growth of manufacturing (Map 10.1).

However, the British producers easily undersold their American competitors. Thanks to cheap shipping and low interest rates in Britain, it was profitable to import raw cotton from the United States, manufacture it into cloth, and then ship the textiles back across the Atlantic. Moreover, because British companies were better established, they could engage in ruthless competition, cutting prices briefly but sharply to drive the newer American firms out of business. But the most important British advantage was low-cost labor. Britain

had a larger population than the United States—about 12.6 million in 1810 compared with 7.3 million—and thousands of landless laborers who were willing to take low-paying factory jobs. Since unskilled American workers could obtain good pay for farm or construction work, American manufacturers had to pay higher wages to attract them to factory jobs.

To offset these British advantages, American entrepreneurs sought assistance from the federal government. In 1816 Congress imposed a small tax on imported cloth, giving American manufacturers of cotton and wool goods modest protection from low-cost imports. More stringent protective legislation in 1824 levied a tariff of 35 percent on imported iron products, woolen and cotton textiles, and various agricultural products, and the rate rose to 50 percent in 1828. But in 1833, under pressure from southern planters, western farmers, and urban consumers—all of whom wanted to keep down the price of manufactured goods—Congress began to reduce tariffs (see Chapter 11). Without governmental assistance many American textile manufacturers failed, unable to compete with the British producers.

Improved Technology and Cheap Labor. American producers adopted two strategies to challenge their British rivals. First, they improved on British technology. In 1811 Francis Cabot Lowell, a wealthy Boston merchant, spent a holiday touring British textile mills. A well-educated and charming young man, he flattered his hosts by asking a great many questions, but his easy manner hid a serious purpose. Lowell listened closely to the answers and, each night in his hotel room, secretly made detailed drawings of the power machinery he had seen. Paul Moody, an experienced American mechanic, then copied the machines and made improvements on their design.

In 1814, armed with this technology, Lowell joined two other merchants, Nathan Appleton and Patrick Tracy Jackson, to form the Boston Manufacturing Company. Raising the staggering sum of $400,000, they built a textile plant in Waltham, Massachusetts, on the Charles River. The Waltham factory was the first in America to perform under one roof all the operations of cloth making—cleaning, carding, spinning, and weaving (see New Technology, "Cotton Spinning: From Spinsters to Machines," p. 318). More important, thanks to Moody's improvements, Waltham's power looms operated at higher speeds than British looms and required fewer workers.

The second American strategy was to lower the cost of labor. The Boston Manufacturing Company again took the lead, pioneering a manufacturing system that became known as the Waltham plan. The company recruited thousands of farm girls and women as textile operatives. Although the wages of operatives were low, they were

MAP 10.1

Industrial Enterprise in New England, 1790–1840

As entrepreneurs built new factories, they installed the most efficient equipment used in existing plants, thus diffusing technological innovations across New England. Because of the availability of water power, textile plants became concentrated in towns such as Waltham and Lowell in eastern Massachusetts; the size of each circle indicates the relative number of spindles or employees in that town.

higher than those paid to maids or cooks or outwork laborers. To attract female workers to the new mills, the owners also provided boardinghouses and cultural activities such as evening lectures. They reassured anxious parents about their daughters' moral lives by enforcing strict curfews, prohibiting alcoholic beverages, and requiring regular church attendance. At Lowell (1822), Chicopee (1823), and other sites in Massachusetts and New Hampshire, the Boston Manufacturing Company built new cotton factories on the Waltham plan; other Boston-owned firms quickly followed suit.

By the early 1830s more than 40,000 young women were working in textile mills in New England. Eleven-year-old Lucy Larcom of Lowell, Massachusetts, went to work in a mill, she later recalled, so that she could support herself and not be "a trouble or burden or expense" to her widowed mother. Many operatives sent their savings home to help their fathers pay off farm mortgages, defray the cost of schooling for their broth-ers, or accumulate a dowry for themselves. Although the women often found the work oppressive (and therefore moved from mill to mill, taking vacations in between jobs), many gained a new sense of freedom and autonomy. "Don't I feel independent!" mill worker Lucy Larcom wrote to her sister in the 1840s. "The thought that I am living on no one is a happy one indeed to me" (see American Voices, "Lucy Larcom: Early Days at Lowell," p. 321).

The owners of the Boston Manufacturing Company were even happier. By using improved technology and cheap female labor, they finally achieved competitive superiority over their British rivals in American markets. They also had an advantage over textile manufacturers in New York and Pennsylvania, where agricultural workers were better paid than in New England and textile workers thus earned higher wages. Producers in those states used a different strategy, modifying traditional technology to produce higher-quality cloth, also with good results. In 1825 Thomas Jefferson, formerly a critic of industrialization, expressed his pride in the American achievement: "Our manufacturers are now very nearly on a footing with those of England."

American Mechanics and Technological Innovation

By the 1820s American-born craftsmen had replaced British immigrants at the cutting edge of technological innovation. Although few of these men had a formal education and all had once been viewed as "mean" or even "servile" workers, they now claimed respect as "men professing an ingenious art." One such inventor, Richard Garsed, began working in a textile mill when he was eight years old. Ten years later, in 1837, Garsed began experimenting with improvements on power looms in his father's factory and in three years nearly doubled their speed. By 1846 he had patented a cam and harness device that allowed elaborately figured fabrics such as damask to be woven by machine.

In the Philadelphia region, the most important inventors came from the remarkable Sellars family. Samuel Sellars Jr. invented a machine for twisting long-stapled woolen yarn. His son John devised more efficient ways of using water power to run the family's sawmills and gristmills, and built a machine to weave wire sieves. John's sons and grandsons built machine shops that turned out a variety of new products: riveted leather fire hoses, papermaking equipment, and—eventually—locomotives. In 1824 members of the Sellars family and other mechanics founded the Franklin Institute in Philadelphia. Named after Benjamin Franklin, whom the mechanics admired for his scientific accomplishments and idealization of hard work, the institute fostered a sense of professional identity. The Franklin Institute published a journal; provided high school–level

Mill Girl, c. 1850
This fine daguerreotype (an early form of photography) shows a neatly dressed textile worker who is about twelve years old. The harsh working conditions in the mill have taken a toll on her spirit and body: the young girl's face shows little joy or life and her hands are rough and swollen. She probably worked either as a knotter, tying broken threads on spinning jennies, or as a warper, straightening out strands of cotton or wool as they entered the loom.
Jack Naylor Collection.

LUCY LARCOM

Early Days at Lowell

★

Lucy Larcom (1824–1893) went to work in a Lowell, Massachusetts, textile mill when she was eleven years old and remained there for a decade. She then migrated to Illinois with her sisters and a great tide of other New Englanders. In later life Larcom became a teacher and a writer, and in her autobiography she suggested the impact of the Industrial Revolution on the lives of working women.

I never cared much for machinery. The buzzing and hissing and whizzing of pulleys and rollers and spindles and flyers around me often grew tiresome. I could not see into their complications, or feel interested in them. But in a room below us we were sometimes allowed to peer in through a sort of blind door at the great waterwheel that carried the works of the whole mill. It was so huge we could only watch a few of its spokes at a time, and part of its dripping rim, moving with a slow, measured strength through the darkness that shut it in. It impressed me with something of the awe which comes to us in thinking of the great Power which keeps the mechanism of the universe in motion.

. . . We did not call ourselves ladies. We did not forget that we were working girls, wearing coarse aprons suitable to our work, and that there was some danger of our becoming drudges. I know that sometimes the confinement of the mill became very wearisome to me. In the sweet June weather I would lean far out of the window, and try not to hear the unceasing clash of sound inside. Looking away to the hills, my whole stifled being would cry out

Oh, that I had wings!

Still I was there from choice, and

The prison unto which we doom
ourselves,
No prison is.

I regard it as one of the privileges of my youth that I was permitted to grow up among these active, interesting girls, whose lives were not mere echoes of other lives, but had principle and purpose distinctly their own. Their vigor of character was a natural development. The New Hampshire girls who came to Lowell were descendants of the sturdy backwoodsmen who settled that State scarcely a hundred years before. Their grandmothers had suffered the hardships of frontier life. . . . Those young women did justice to their inheritance. They were earnest and capable; ready to undertake anything that was worth doing. My dreamy, indolent nature was shamed into activity among them. They gave me a larger, firmer ideal of womanhood. . . .

Country girls were naturally independent, and the feeling that at this new work the few hours they had of every-day leisure were entirely their own was a satisfaction to them. They preferred it to going out as "hired help." It was like a young man's pleasure in entering upon business for himself. Girls had never tried that experiment before, and they liked it. It brought out in them a dormant strength of character which the world did not previously see.

Source: Lucy Larcom, *A New England Girlhood* (Boston: Houghton Mifflin, 1889), 153–155, 181–183, 196–200.

---

instruction in mechanics, chemistry, mathematics, and mechanical drawing; and organized annual fairs to exhibit the most advanced products. Craftsmen in Ohio and other states soon established their own mechanics institutes, which played a crucial role in spreading technical knowledge and encouraging innovation. Around 1820 the United States Patent Office issued about 200 patents on new inventions each year; by 1850 it was awarding 1,000 annually, and ten years later over 4,000.

During these years American mechanics pioneered the development of *machine tools*—that is, machines for making other machines. This technical advance was crucial because it facilitated the rapid spread of the Industrial Revolution. For example, mechanics serving the textile industry invented lathes, planers, and boring machines that made standardized parts. These machine-tooled parts, which required a minimum of filing and fitting, made it possible to manufacture new spinning jennies and weaving looms at a low cost and to repair broken machines easily. Moreover, the American machinery was precise enough in design and construction to operate at higher speeds than British equipment.

Technological innovation swept through the rest of American manufacturing. For example, in 1832 the mechanics employed by Samuel W. Collins in his Connecticut ax-making company built a vastly improved die-forging machine—a device that pressed and hammered hot metal into dies, or cutting forms. Using the improved machine, a skilled worker could increase the production of ax heads from 12 to 300 a day. A few years later mechanics in Massachusetts perfected a power-driven shoe-stitching machine, boosting the output of well-made boots while cutting the cost. In the South, Welsh- and American-born mechanics at the Tredegar Iron Works helped to make Richmond, Virginia, a regional manufacturing center.

The most important advances in machine building came in the firearms industry. To fill large-scale contracts from the federal government, Eli Whitney and his co-workers in Connecticut developed machine tools that produced parts that were not only interchangeable but also precision-crafted (see American Lives, "Eli Whitney: Machine Builder and Promoter," pp. 324–325). After Whitney's death this innovative work in machine design was continued by his partner, John H. Hall, an engineer at the federal armory in Harpers Ferry, Virginia. By the 1840s Hall had developed an array of machine tools to work metal: turret lathes, milling machines, and precision grinders. Thereafter, manufacturers could use those machine tools to produce complicated machinery with great speed, at low cost, and in large quantities.

Through this expansion in the availability of machines, the Industrial Revolution in the United States came of age. American manufacturers now produced goods that were comparable in quality and in price with British imports, enabling them to compete in the rapidly expanding domestic market. Between 1840 and 1860 the American population grew from 17 million to more than 31 million, as the result of a high birth rate (45 births per thousand people per year, compared with 30 per thousand in Europe) and a massive surge in immigration from western Europe. As the destination of most immigrants, the northeastern and Great Lakes states dominated this demographic surge, providing a ready market for American industrial goods.

Northern manufacturers easily met the growing demand for goods. They not only expanded production in the fall-line towns but also used the coal-powered stationary steam engine to set up factories in the older seaports and, with stunning swiftness, the new cities of the interior—Buffalo, Detroit, Chicago, St. Louis. The sheer volume of output caused some products—Remington rifles, Singer sewing machines, Waltham watches, and Yale locks as well as Colt handguns and McCormick reapers—to become household words in the United States and abroad. After showing their machine-tooled goods at the Crystal Palace Exhibition in London in 1851 (the first major international display of industrial goods), McCormick and Colt built factories in Great Britain that used American machinery and production techniques. Soon their products dominated many European markets.

Wage Workers and the Labor Movement

As the Industrial Revolution gathered momentum, it changed the character of the American social order. Each decade, more and more white Americans gave up their economic independence and took work as wage-earning employees, hired for a specific job or by the day, week, or season. Seeking security of employment and a good measure of control over their working conditions, they often banded together in labor unions.

Some wage workers labored in traditional crafts, such as the building trades, and found it relatively easy to form unions and bargain with the master artisans who employed them. Stonecutters, masons, and cabinetmakers had specialized skills that were much in demand, and other wage-earning journeymen—carpenters, housepainters, roofers—often followed the same occupations as their fathers and had a strong sense of craft identity. A main concern of their unions was the increasing length of the workday, which deprived workers of time to spend with their families or improve their education. Rapid urbanization during the 1820s and the building of homes, stores, and factories had triggered a strong demand for construction, leading many bosses to demand more work and longer hours. The traditional workday for artisans was "sun-up to sun-down," which had averaged out over the winter and summer seasons at about twelve hours. By the 1820s masters were abusing the old work rules—requiring workers to begin at the first sign of light, cutting the length of their breaks for lunch and dinner, and ending only when darkness descended. Despite this increase in the length of the workday, employers paid journeymen the old daily rate.

In response, building-trade workers formed unions and went on strike. In 1825 in Boston, 600 carpenters laid down their tools and demanded a ten-hour day, from 6 A.M. to 6 P.M., with an hour each for breakfast and a midday meal. Although the Boston protest failed, two years later several hundred journeymen carpenters in Philadelphia won a similar strike for a ten-hour day and then helped found the Mechanics' Union of Trade Associations. This citywide organization of 50 unions and 10,000 Philadelphia wage earners articulated a broad reform program, demanding "a just balance of power . . . between all the various classes and individuals which constitute society at large."

To secure this goal, in 1828 the Philadelphia artisans founded the Working Men's Party, which campaigned for the abolition of banks, equal taxation, and universal education. For many workers, the advancement of public education was the most important goal. They wanted publicly funded schools that would provide their children with the skills needed to move quickly into the ranks of the propertied classes. Training in "one or more mechanical arts" combined with "literary and scientific instruction," they insisted, would "place the citizens of this extensive republic on an equality [and] bring the children of the poor and rich to mix together as a band of republican brethren." The Working Men's Party won the expansion of public schooling in Philadelphia and, in 1834, persuaded the Pennsylvania legislature to authorize a system of universal, tuition-free, tax-supported schools.

Indeed, by the mid-1830s skilled building-trade workers in many cities had forced employers to accept ten hours as the standard workday. In 1835 the Philadelphia city council set a ten-hour day for local public works, and in the following year President Andrew Jackson established a ten-hour day at the Philadelphia navy yard. These victories were significant, giving skilled American workers the same hours that British building-trade workers had enjoyed since the 1750s and enabling many artisan families to live comfortably.

Artisans whose occupations were threatened by industrialization were less prosperous. As machines and factory discipline changed the nature of their work, shoemakers, hatters, printers, furniture makers, and weavers faced declining incomes, unemployment, and loss of status. To avoid the regimentation of factory work, some artisans moved to small towns or opened small, specialized shops that catered to a limited market. For example, in New York City about 800 highly skilled cabinetmakers continued to ply their craft in the traditional way, fashioning custom-made products in shops with only a few employees. However, a much larger group of 3,200 semitrained workers—derogatively called "botches"—now worked for low pay in small factories, turning out cheap, mass-produced furniture. The coming of the new industrial system had divided the traditional artisan class into two groups: self-employed craftsmen and wage-earning workers.

In many industries these wage-earning workers banded together to form craft unions. As early as 1794 Philadelphia shoemakers formed the Federated Society of Journeymen Cordwainers (taking the name *cordwainers* from the high-quality cordovan leather they worked). To prevent wage cuts, the journeymen went out on strike repeatedly until 1806, when their leaders were convicted of criminal conspiracy in the case of *Commonwealth v. Pullis.* According to English and American common law, workers' organizations for raising wages were illegal—"a government unto themselves," in the words of the Philadelphia court—because they prevented other workers from hiring out for whatever wages they wished.

Despite such legal setbacks, unions sprang up whenever wages fell and working conditions became intolerably onerous. In 1830 in Lynn, Massachusetts,

Woodworker, c. 1850
Skilled cabinetmakers took great pride in their work, which was often intricately designed and beautifully executed. To underline the dignity of his occupation, this woodworker poses in formal dress and proudly displays his hammer and chisel, the tools of his craft. A belief in the value of labor was an important ingredient of the artisan-republican ideology held by many workers. Library of Congress.

journeymen shoemakers responded to the proliferation of factories and the wealthy employers who ran them by founding a Mutual Benefit Society. "The division of society into the producing and nonproducing classes," they explained, had made workers like themselves into a mere "commodity" whose labor could be bought and sold without regard for their welfare, whereby "the natural order of things is entirely reversed." Because of its appeal to workers, the society spread quickly to other shoemaking centers and joined with other craft unions in labor federations. In 1834 local federations from Boston to Philadelphia combined their resources in the National Trades' Union, the first regional union of different trades. Two years later, thirty-seven unions in various northern cities demonstrated the potential of labor solidarity, providing financial support that enabled striking journeymen bookbinders in Philadelphia to hold out for over two months and win a compromise settlement over wages with their employers.

Leaders of the new union movement mounted a critique of the industrial order. Warning that workers were becoming "slaves to a monied aristocracy" (their term for commercial middlemen and capitalist employers),

Eli Whitney: Machine Builder and Promoter

★

E LI WHITNEY (1765–1825) thought life was "a Lottery in which many draw blanks," but thanks to the opportunities offered by the Industrial Revolution, that was not to be his fate. Whitney's luck, combined with intense social ambition and exceptional talents for self-advertisement and mechanical innovation, allowed him to rise in the world and to exert a significant influence on the development of industry in America.

Eli Whitney was born in Westborough, Massachusetts, the son of a well-respected middling farmer. As a child, Eli found routine farm chores boring and even depressing. As often as he could, the young lad fled to the farm's workshop to repair household furniture and farm tools. A sociable youth, he took great pleasure in talking with his family's neighbors and friends. As his sister recalled, Eli "possessed a great measure of affability." Those conversations sharpened Whitney's awareness of the limits of New England's mature farm economy—how its poor soil and overcrowded towns condemned most young people to lives of unrelenting labor and few economic rewards.

The outbreak of the American Revolution in 1776 opened new doors for the restless youth. In 1779, when he was fourteen years old, Eli persuaded his father to install a forge in the workshop so that he could produce nails and knife blades as substitutes for the British imports that were no longer available. His enterprise flourished, as did many like it in New England, and he soon hired a worker to help him meet the demand. Following the end of the war, an avalanche of cheap nails from Britain ruined Eli's market. So the young entrepreneur shifted his production to women's hatpins and men's walking sticks.

Despite this early success in household manufacturing, Whitney realized that his workshop and his father's small farm would not provide a living for himself, two younger brothers, and four sisters. Beyond that, the ambitious young man aspired to wealth and status and looked to a college education—then the privileged preserve of a mere 1 percent of American men—to assist him to rise in the world. But

Eli Whitney
Eli Whitney posed for this portrait in the 1820s, when he had achieved both prosperity and social standing. Whitney's success as an inventor inspired the artist, his young New Haven neighbor Samuel F. B. Morse, to turn his energies from painting to industrial technology. By the 1840s Morse had devised the first successful commercial telegraph.
Yale University Art Gallery. Gift of George Hoadley, B.A. 1801.

Eli lacked the required preparation in English grammar, classics, and mathematics. So he enrolled at Leicester Academy, a private secondary school, financing his studies by teaching primary school for six years. By 1789, at age twenty-four, Whitney had the skills and, more important, the social connections necessary to win admission to Yale College.

At Yale, Whitney might have studied engineering or science if the college had offered those subjects. But like the other colleges of the day Yale followed a traditional curriculum, placing heavy emphasis on ancient languages, history, rhetoric, and religion. In any event, Whitney was more interested in exploiting the social advantages of his Yale education. At graduation in 1792 the president of Yale found him a job as a tutor on a Georgia plantation.

In traveling south Whitney met Catherine Greene, the young widow of the Revolutionary War general Nathanael Greene, who was charmed by his "affability" and Yale-bred manners. When Whitney's tutoring position fell through, she invited him for an extended visit to her Georgia plantation, Mulberry Grove, which was managed by Phineas Miller, another Yale alumnus. For his part, the young New Englander grew fascinated by the exclusive world of the southern planters and paid close attention to their efforts to expand cotton production. Encouraged by Catherine Greene and Phineas Miller, he set up a workshop and built a simple machine to separate the cotton seeds from the delicate fibers. Applying the technique he had used to produce women's hatpins, Whitney fashioned thin tines of metal and arrayed them in ranks, creating a rudimentary cotton gin, the machine that would ultimately revolutionize the processing of cotton.

In 1793 Whitney returned to New Haven and began manufacturing gins in quantity, using special machine tools he had built. "One of the most Respectable Gentlemen in N. Haven," the young manufacturer proudly reported to his father, said "he would rather be the author of the [my] Invention than the prime minister of England." If the cotton gin brought prestige, it did not yield wealth. Although Whitney had patented his invention in 1794, he was unable to control the market. Using some of Whitney's ideas, numerous planters made their own gins, and other manufacturers marketed gins, with slight improvements on his design, but no one paid him royalties. In a futile bid to protect his patent rights, Whitney filed scores of lawsuits, using up the profits from the sales of his own gins and then falling into debt.

To restore his finances, Whitney decided to manufacture a product that would have a guaranteed market: military weapons. His Yale network again served him well. In his effort to patent his gin, he had formed a friendship with another Yale alumnus, Oliver Wolcott, who had become secretary of the Treasury in 1795. In 1798 Whitney convinced Wolcott that he could mechanize the production of firearms and thus turn them out at an unprecedented scale and pace. Whitney's timing was superb. The new national government had established two armories—in Springfield, Massachusetts, and Harpers Ferry, Virginia—but their production was dismal. To prepare for a possible war with France, Congress had just authorized the Treasury to contract for arms with private parties. Almost immediately Wolcott engaged Whitney to manufacture 10,000 muskets within twenty-eight months.

Whitney knew little about the details of musket manufacture, but he had a clear understanding of machine tools. He was confident that he could design tools that would produce interchangeable musket parts. As Whitney stated in a letter to Wolcott, "[I will] form the tools so that the tools themselves shall fashion the work and give to every part its just proportion—which when once accomplished will give expeditious uniformity, and exactness to the whole." The young inventor quickly devised improved forms and jigs to guide the hands of mechanics; crafted the first milling machine, which used sharp teeth on a gearlike wheel to cut metal; and achieved a greater degree of interchangeability of parts than anyone before him had managed to do.

Despite these technical advances, Whitney was unable to fulfill his original contract on time. Indeed, it took ten years to produce the 10,000 muskets, and even then Whitney had to make some components with traditional handicraft skills. But Wolcott remained loyal, as did the government inspector in New Haven, yet another Yale alumnus. Also helpful was a group of ten prominent citizens of New Haven, including Pierpont Edwards, the wealthy son of the preacher and philosopher Jonathan Edwards (see Chapter 4).

Whitney also had the support of Thomas Jefferson, who had been interested in interchangeability since the 1780s. Because of his curiosity about science and manufacturing, Jefferson had followed Whitney's career from the time he patented the cotton gin, and as president-elect he had witnessed the dramatic public demonstration of interchangeability that Whitney staged in Washington. Jefferson understood that the perfection of Whitney's techniques would vastly increase the productivity of American manufacturers.

With Jefferson's encouragement, Whitney continued to develop his innovations. During the War of 1812 and thereafter, he won new contracts for military weapons. The new work, along with shrewd investment advice from Oliver Wolcott, provided Whitney with the wealth and social position of which he had long dreamed. He dined regularly with New Haven's elite, and Yale awarded him an honorary master's degree. In 1817 Whitney joined one of New England's most respected families by marrying Henrietta Edwards, the daughter of Pierpont Edwards.

When Whitney died in 1825, he had still not achieved his goal of mass production. But his technical advances, as well as his promotion of interchangeability and mechanization, provided a great stimulus to American industry. By mid-century American manufacturers led the world in the production of goods that used standardized, interchangeable parts. As a team of British observers noted with admiration, many American products were made "with machinery applied to almost every process . . . all reduced to an almost perfect system of manufacture."

they condemned the new organization of production in which "capital and labor stand opposed." To restore a just society, they advocated a *labor theory of value*, arguing that the price of a product should reflect the labor required to make it and should be paid primarily to the producer, to "enable him to live as comfortably as others." Appealing to the spirit of the American Revolution, which had destroyed the aristocracy of birth, they called for a new revolt to destroy the aristocracy of capital. Armed with this artisan-republican ideology and pressured by rapidly increasing prices, in 1836 union men organized nearly fifty strikes for higher wages, many of which were temporarily successful.

This agitation for workers' rights drew support from women operatives in cotton and woolen textile mills. As competition among cloth producers cut profit margins and threatened bankruptcy, employers reduced the pay of their workers and imposed increasingly stringent work rules. In 1828 women mill workers in Dover, New Hampshire, struck against new rules, winning some relief; six years later more than 800 Dover women walked out to protest wage cuts. That same year 2,000 women in Lowell, Massachusetts, backed up a strike by withdrawing their savings from an employer-owned bank. The *Boston Transcript* reported that "one of the leaders mounted a pump, and made a flaming . . . speech on the rights of women and the iniquities of the 'monied aristocracy.'"

However powerful the rhetoric, most strikes by factory operatives failed. Employers often fired the leaders, and the rest of the workers either returned to work or moved to another factory. Even the more successful strikes by building-trade workers and shoemakers did not alter the inferior position of wage laborers in the new industrial order. They lacked access to financial capital, business know-how, and a broad education—three key ingredients of success in the new society. In these circumstances, a group of Philadelphia workers declared, "liberty is but an unmeaning word, and equality an equal shadow."

Exploiting their advantage over workers, manufacturers continued to upgrade their factories to increase productivity and output. To pay for the new machinery, they cut wages; and to use the equipment most efficiently, they increased the pace of work, which employees resisted. For example, in 1845 the weaver Sarah G. Bagley and other operatives formed the Female Labor Reform Association in an unsuccessful attempt to protest wage cuts and speedups in Massachusetts textile mills. When conditions did not improve, young New England women refused to enter the mills, and most older female employees left to marry and raise families. First Irish and later French-Canadian immigrants took their places, forced by poverty to work for extremely low wages. A majority of the new workers were men, foreshadowing the emergence of a predominately male system of factory labor (see Chapter 17).

By the 1850s workers faced yet another threat to their jobs. As mechanization caused the output of manufactures to increase, the supply of goods often exceeded the demand, prompting the laying off or dismissal of workers. One episode of overproduction preceded the Panic of 1857—a financial crisis sparked by excess railroad investments—and resulted in a full-scale depression. Unemployment remained at about 10 percent until the outbreak of the Civil War in 1861, reminding Americans of the social costs of the new—and otherwise very successful—system of industrial production.

The Expansion of Markets

As American factories turned out more manufactures, merchants and legislators sought faster and cheaper ways to obtain raw materials and get their finished products to consumers. As early as the 1820s, they promoted the construction of a massive system of canals and roads to link eastern manufacturers and markets to the trans-Appalachian West, where hundreds of thousands of farm families had settled. By 1860 nearly one-third of the nation's people lived in the midwestern states—Ohio, Indiana, Illinois, Michigan, and Wisconsin, (the five states carved out of the Northwest Territory), along with Missouri, Iowa, and Minnesota—where they created a complex society and economy that increasingly resembled that of the Northeast.

Migration to the West

In the generation after independence vast numbers of men and women left the seaboard states, taking with them their savings, personal property, and skills. By the 1820s the Carolinas and New England were losing as many people through migration as they gained through natural increase. Abandoned farms and homes dotted the countryside, their owners gone in search of better lands. Some families wanted to acquire enough land to settle their children on nearby farms, re-creating traditional rural communities. Others were more entrepreneurial and hoped for greater profits from the fertile soil of the West. "It is useless to seek to excite patriotic emotions" and loyalty to one's state of birth, complained an easterner, "when self-interest speaks so loudly." By 1840 about 5 million people lived west of the Appalachians (Map 10.2).

These pioneers migrated in three great streams. In the South, plantation owners moved their slaves into the Old Southwest, where they hoped to prosper by meeting the voracious demand of British and New England factories for raw cotton. Deserting depleted fields in Georgia and the Carolinas, they established what became known as the Cotton Kingdom in the new states of Louisiana (admitted to the Union in 1812), Mississippi (1817), Alabama (1819), Missouri (1821), and Arkansas (1836). *"The Alabama Feaver* rages here with great violence," a North Carolina planter complained, "and has *carried off* vast numbers of our Citizens."

Small-scale farmers from the Upper South, especially Virginia and Kentucky, created a second stream as they crossed over the Appalachian Mountains and settled in the Ohio River Valley. Many of these migrants owned small hilly farms and were seeking better lands; others were simply fleeing the planter-dominated slave states. In a free community, thought Peter Cartwright, a Methodist lay preacher from southwestern Kentucky, "I would be entirely clear of the evil of slavery . . . [and] could raise my children to work where work was not thought a degradation." These migrants introduced corn and hog farming to the southern portions of Ohio (admitted in 1803), Indiana (1816), and Illinois (1818).

The third stream of migrants came from the overcrowded farms of New England. Thousands of New Englanders had poured into upstate New York during the 1790s, and now thousands more abandoned the rocky soils of Vermont and New Hampshire for the rich lands of the Old Northwest. They wanted to maintain their traditional life as yeomen farmers and keep their children on the land, sparing them from industrial work. These settlers established wheat farms and small towns throughout the Great Lakes Basin: northern Ohio, northern Illinois, Michigan (admitted in 1837), Iowa (1846), and Wisconsin (1848).

To meet the demand for cheap land, in 1820 Congress reduced the price of federal land from $2.00 an acre to $1.25—just enough to cover the cost of surveying and sale through government land offices. For $100 a farmer could buy eighty acres, the minimum required under federal law. With huge quantities of public land available at that price, the market price for all undeveloped land remained low. Many American families saved enough in a few years to make the minimum purchase and used money from the sale of their old farm to finance the move. After 1830 wealthy southerners eagerly snapped up low-priced federal land, carrying their slaves and the "Cotton Kingdom" across the Mississippi River. Taken together, these migrations of farmers, planters, and enslaved African Americans brought a dramatic westward shift in the population center of the United States (see Maps 9.3 and 10.2).

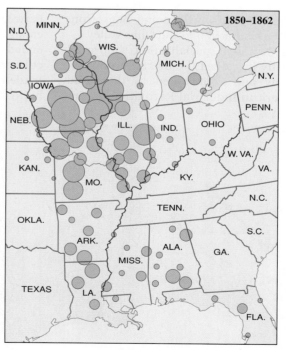

MAP 10.2

Western Land Sales

The federal government opened land offices along the frontier to sell farmland to settlers. During the 1830s, the offices sold huge amounts of land in the Old Northwest (especially Indiana, Michigan, and Illinois) and in the Old Southwest (Alabama and Mississippi). By the 1850s, the boom in land sales had moved to the upper Mississippi River Valley (particularly Iowa and Wisconsin). Each circle centers on a land office, and the size of the circle depends on the relative amount of land sold at that office.

The Transportation Revolution

Extending the market economy into the interior required a revolution in transportation. Previously most overland trade had been local, consisting of an exchange of goods between towns and nearby rural areas. For example, merchants and artisans in Philadelphia traded their textiles and ironware for farm products grown close by: flour and corn, dairy products, fruits and vegetables, and wood for heating and cooking. More distant trade was virtually impossible because there was no system of well-maintained roads.

To enhance the "common-wealth" of their citizens, the federal and state governments tried to create a larger market. Beginning in the 1790s, they chartered private companies to build turnpikes (toll roads) in well-populated areas and subsidized road construction in the West. The most significant feat was the National Road, which started in Cumberland, Maryland; passed Wheeling (then in Virginia) in 1818; crossed the Ohio River in 1833; and reached Vandalia, Illinois, in 1850 (Map 10.3). At first these interregional highways mostly carried migrants and their heavily loaded wagons to the West and herds of livestock to the East, but gradually they became conduits for manufactured goods and farm products. Merchants in the Northeast exchanged textiles, clothing, boots and shoes, muskets, and farm equipment for wheat, corn, whiskey, and hogs from farms in the Great Lakes Basin and the Ohio Valley.

By facilitating regional specialization, improved transportation greatly increased the overall productivity of the economy and contributed to the rapid progress of the American Industrial Revolution. Farmers in the West supplied wool and leather to eastern manufacturers and inexpensive grain, meat, vegetables, and fruit to factory workers and cities in the Northeast, spurring urban growth. Northern textile mills consumed ever greater quantities of southern cotton; by the 1840s the South was producing more than two-thirds of the world's cotton and accounted for almost two-thirds of the total value of American exports.

Canals and Steamboats.   To get these heavy and bulky goods to market, Americans replaced slow and expensive overland trade with a water-borne transportation system of unprecedented size, complexity, and cost. As early as 1790 entrepreneurs had begun to build canals to connect inland areas with coastal cities and towns, but progress was slow. When the New York legislature approved construction of the Erie Canal in 1817, no canal in the United States was longer than 28 miles—a reflection of the huge capital investment canals required and the lack of American engineering expertise. But the New York project had three things in its favor: the vigorous support of New York City merchants, who wanted access to western markets; the backing of New York's governor, DeWitt Clinton, who persuaded the legislature to finance the waterway from tax revenues, tolls, and bond sales to foreign investors; and the relative gentleness of the terrain between Albany, the Hudson River city where the canal began, and Buffalo, on Lake Erie, where it ended. Even so, the task was enormous. Millions of cubic yards of dirt had to be dug out by hand and hauled away, thousands of tons of rock quarried to build huge locks in which boats could be raised and

Building the Erie Canal
The success of the Erie Canal prompted the nationwide canal system of 1820–1860, which was equal in scope to the later construction of the national railroad network and the interstate highway system. Tens of thousands of workers—many of them Irish immigrants—dug thousands of miles of canals by hand and, with the aid of the simple hoists shown here, built hundreds of stone locks. The unknown artist who sketched this scene was, like the canal planners, more interested in the scale of the project than in the personalities of the faceless workers. The work was hard and dangerous; in 1819, in the marshes near Syracuse, New York, a thousand workers fell ill with fever and many died.
Miriam and Ira D. Wallach Division of Art, Prints and Photographs, The New York Public Library. Astor, Lenox and Tilden Foundations.

MAP 10.3

The Transportation Revolution: Roads and Canals, 1820–1850

By 1850 the United States had an efficient transportation system based on roads, natural waterways, and canals. Short canals and navigable rivers carried cotton, tobacco, and other products from the upcountry of the seaboard states into the Atlantic commercial system. Major canals—the Erie, Chesapeake and Ohio, and Pennsylvania Mainline—linked major seaport cities to the vast trans-Appalachian region, and a set of regional canals connected most of the Great Lakes region to the Ohio and Mississippi Rivers and New Orleans.

lowered, and vast reservoirs constructed to ensure a steady supply of water.

The first great engineering project in American history, the Erie Canal altered the ecology as well as the economy of an entire region. Hundreds of streams and rivers soon flowed into the canal, depriving some areas of the water needed to sustain wildlife and settlers. As towns and farming communities sprang up along the waterway, millions of trees were cut down to provide wood for building and land for farms. Cows and pigs now foraged in forests where deer and bear had once held sway.

The Erie Canal was an instant success. The first section, a stretch of 75 miles opened in 1819, quickly generated enough revenue to repay its cost. When the canal was completed in 1825, a 40-foot-wide ribbon of water stretched 364 miles from Albany to Buffalo. The canal carried lightweight mail and passenger boats from New York City to Buffalo in only six days, and 100-ton freight barges pulled by two horses moved along at a steady 24 miles a day, greatly accelerating the flow of goods and dramatically cutting transportation costs. (In comparison, on New York roads four horses could pull a 1-ton wagon only 12 miles a day.)

The Erie Canal brought prosperity to central and western New York, carrying wheat and meat from farming communities in the interior to eastern cities and foreign markets. In 1818 the mills in Rochester, New York, had processed only 26,000 barrels of flour from the wheat of local farmers; ten years later production soared to 200,000 barrels, and in 1840 to 500,000 barrels. After a trip on the canal, the novelist Nathaniel Hawthorne suggested that its water "must be the most fertilizing of all fluids, for it causes towns with their masses of brick and stone, their churches and theaters, their business and hubbub, their luxury and refinement, their gay dames and polished citizens, to spring up."

The spectacular benefits of the Erie Canal prompted a national canal boom. Civic and business leaders in Philadelphia and Baltimore proposed their own waterways to compete for the trade of the West. Copying New York's fiscal innovations, they persuaded their state governments to allocate tax money to canal projects, making it easier to raise the needed capital. Some state governments invested directly in canal companies or forced state-chartered banks to do so; other states guaranteed repayment of the bonds issued by canal companies and thus encouraged British and Dutch banks and wealthy financiers to provide almost three-quarters of the $200 million invested in canals by 1840. Canals soon became the most important part of the inland American transportation system, connecting the Great Lakes region with the port cities of New York (via the Erie and Pennsylvania Canals) and New Orleans (via the Ohio and Mississippi Rivers) (see Map 10.3).

The steamboat, another product of the industrial age, ensured the success of this vast water transportation system. The engineer-inventor Robert Fulton built the first American steamboat, the *Clermont*, which he navigated up the Hudson in 1807. However, the first steamboats were expensive to run because their engines consumed large amounts of wood or coal; moreover, they could not navigate shallow western rivers. During the 1820s engineers broadened the hulls of these boats, which increased their cargo capacity, facilitated loading and unloading, and gave them a shallower draft. The improved design cut the cost of upstream river transport in half, dramatically increasing the flow of goods into the interior—especially in the South, where there were many navigable rivers. Steam-powered shipping also speeded the transit of people and news, both on inland waterways and along the coasts (Map 10.4). In 1800 a traveler or a letter leaving New York had taken three days to get to Boston, ten days to arrive in Charleston, and an entire month to reach New Orleans or Detroit. Thirty years later these times had been cut in half, and by 1857 the entire region east of the Mississippi River could be reached in less than a week.

Railroads and Regional Ties.   The rapid emergence of this national system of transportation was encouraged by the Supreme Court under Chief Justice John Marshall. In the crucial case of *Gibbons v. Ogden* (1824) the Court declared that the federal government had paramount authority over interstate commerce (see Chapter 8). This decision meant that no local or state monopolies—or tariffs—would impede the flow of goods and services across the nation.

The free movement of goods over a growing transportation system created a national economy, linking the manufacturing Northeast not only to the cotton-producing South but also to the wheat-growing Midwest. Midwestern farmers shipped their grain to northeastern markets on the Great Lakes and the Erie Canal. To cultivate their fields, many midwestern farmers bought the cast-iron plow invented in 1819 by Jethro Wood, a farmer in upstate New York. Wood's plow cut cultivating time in half, allowing farmers to till much larger fields, and it could easily be repaired with replaceable cast-iron parts. Northeastern factories likewise supplied low-cost, high-quality shovels and

MAP 10.4
The Speed of Business News in 1817 and 1841
The transportation revolution increased the speed of trade and communication between the Atlantic seaports and the towns of the interior. Aggressive entrepreneurs provided for the national circulation of daily newspapers from New York, and by 1841 many parts of the country received economic news from New York in less than ten days.

spades fabricated from rolled iron at the Delaware Iron Works, axes forged in Connecticut factories, and steel horseshoes manufactured in Troy, New York. Indeed, the production of farm implements consumed fully half the nation's output of iron.

Soon midwestern inventors and entrepreneurs copied the technology and mass-production techniques of northeastern manufacturers and began to produce farm machinery. The story of John Deere was typical. As a blacksmith in Grand Detour, Illinois, Deere made his first steel plow out of old saws in 1837; ten years later he opened a factory in Moline that used mass-production techniques. His steel plows, superior in strength to cast-iron models, soon dominated the midwestern market. Other companies—McCormick, Hussey, Atkins, and Manny—mass-produced reapers that revolutionized the harvesting of grain. Previously, one worker with a cradle scythe had cut two to three acres a day. With a self-raking reaper, a farmer could cut twelve acres daily. Because their farms were large and laborers were in short supply, midwesterners led the way in using modern agricultural technology, increasing their productivity more than 20 percent during the 1850s.

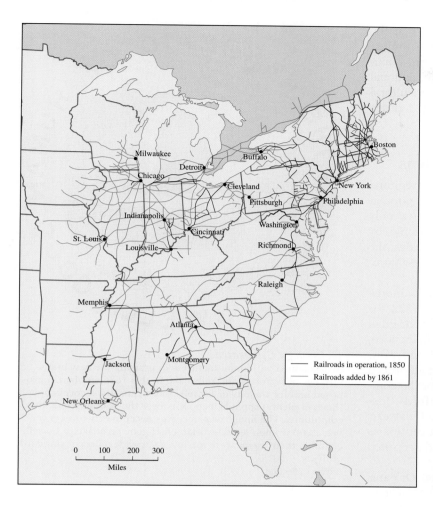

MAP 10.5
Railroads of the North and South, 1850–1860
In the decade before the Civil War, the rapid construction of railroads provided the Northeast and the Midwest with extensive and dense transportation systems that stimulated economic development. The South built a much simpler system. In all regions, railroad lines used different track gauges, hindering the efficient flow of traffic.

Another product of industrial technology—the railroad—cemented the union between the Northeast and the Midwest. As late as 1852 canals were carrying twice the tonnage of railroads, but over the next six years track mileage increased dramatically. The new railroads included trunk lines that stretched across New York and Pennsylvania to provide through traffic from New York City and Philadelphia to Cleveland and Chicago. More convenient and faster than canals, railroads became the main carriers of freight by 1859 (Map 10.5). They hastened the settlement of areas that canal and river transport could not serve and made western farming more profitable by lowering the cost of transporting farm goods to market. This *national* market in wheat forced some eastern farmers out of business and prompted others to turn to market gardening.

Railroad construction facilitated the modernization of the iron industry, a critical component of northeastern manufacturing. Railroad building required high-quality iron and steel, so Philadelphia rail mills raised their technical standards. The engineering requirements for train engines had a similar effect on steam engine production in the Northeast and the Mid-

west, where railroad companies also built a large network of machine shops to service their locomotives. Although separated by geography, the Midwest and the Northeast increasingly resembled each other in ethnic composition, cultural values, and technical skills.

However, the commercial links between the Northeast and the South did not produce similar types of economies. Southern investors concentrated their resources in cotton and slaves, so that the percentage of southerners who lived in towns and worked in manufacturing remained small; only Richmond developed as an important industrial center. Moreover, the South did not develop a well-educated work force. Wealthy planters wanted compliant workers who would be content with the drudgery of agricultural work, so they trained most of their slaves as field hands (allowing only a few to learn the arts of the blacksmith, carpenter, or bricklayer). And they made few efforts to provide blacks, or ordinary whites, with elementary instruction in reading or arithmetic. At the height of the prosperity of the slave regime, most African Americans and about 20 percent of white southerners could not read or write (as compared to less than 1 percent in New England). Lacking cities, factories, and educated workers, the South could not provide a majority of its people with a rising standard of living. In 1860 the per capita income was $141 in the North but only $103 in the South. Prosperity was limited primarily to those families—25 percent of the white population—who owned plantations and slaves. The national system of commerce had accentuated the agricultural character of the South even as it helped to create a diversified economy in the Midwest.

The Growth of Cities and Towns

Industrialization and the expansion of interregional trade caused a dramatic increase in the urban population of the United States. In 1820 there were only 58 towns in the nation with 2,500 to 50,000 people; by 1840 there were 126. During those two decades the total urban population grew fourfold, from 443,000 to 1,844,000.

The most rapid growth occurred in the new industrial towns that sprang up along the fall line. In 1822, for example, the Boston Manufacturing Company decided to build a new complex of mills in East Chelmsford, Massachusetts, on the Merrimack River. Within a few years the sleepy river village was transformed into a bustling town, now named Lowell in honor of the company's founder, Francis Cabot Lowell. Hartford, Connecticut; Trenton, New Jersey; Wilmington, Delaware; and Richmond, Virginia, also became urban centers as mill owners exploited local water power and recruited workers from the surrounding countryside.

Western commercial cities such as New Orleans, Pittsburgh, Cincinnati, and Louisville grew almost as rapidly. Initially these cities expanded because of their location at points where goods were transferred from one mode of transport, such as canal boats or farmers' wagons, to another, such as steamboats or sailing vessels. As the western population grew during the 1830s, St. Louis, Rochester, Buffalo, and Detroit emerged as dynamic centers of commerce. Merchants, bankers, shopkeepers, and insurance brokers settled in those cities, developing the marketing, provisioning, and financial services that were essential to farmers and small-town merchants in the hinterland (Map 10.6).

Within a few decades these western commercial hubs—joined by Cleveland and Chicago—became manufacturing centers as well. As key junctions for railroad lines and steamboats, these cities' manufacturers and entrepreneurs established flour mills, packing plants, and docks, and provided work for hundreds of artisans and laborers. In 1846 Cyrus McCormick moved his reaper factory from western Virginia to Chicago to be closer to his midwestern customers. St. Louis and Chicago were the biggest boom towns, and they grew rapidly—thanks in part to the balloon-frame house (see p. 335), which was first developed in Chicago. By 1860 St. Louis and Chicago had surpassed Boston and Baltimore in size, and had become the nation's third and fourth largest cities, respectively, after New York and Philadelphia.

Technology Celebrated
Artists joined with manufacturers in praising the new industrial age of factories and railroads. In this 1836 emblem, a proposed seal for the city of Lowell, Massachusetts, a cornucopia (horn of plenty) spreads its bounty over the booming industrial community. The image of plenty was deceptive; two years earlier, 2,000 women textile workers had gone on strike in Lowell, claiming their wages were too low to provide a decent standard of living.
Private Collection.

Yet the old Atlantic seaports—Boston, Philadelphia, Baltimore, Charleston, and especially New York—remained important both for their foreign commerce and increasingly as centers of finance and manufacturing. In 1817 New York merchants founded the New York Stock Exchange, which soon became the nation's chief market for securities. The New York metropolis grew at a phenomenal rate, diversifying into small-scale manufacturing and becoming the center of the ready-made clothing industry, which relied on the labor of thousands of low-paid seamstresses, both native- and foreign-born. "The wholesale clothing establishments are . . . absorbing the business of the country," a "Country Tailor" complained to the New York *Tribune*, "casting many an honest and hardworking man out of employment [and allowing] . . . the large cities to swallow up the small towns."

New York's growth stemmed primarily from its control of foreign trade and immigration. It had the best harbor in the United States, and oceangoing vessels could sail or steam 150 miles up the Hudson River to Albany. The city's merchants benefited from these natural advantages. In 1818 four Quaker merchants founded the Black Ball Line as the first regularly scheduled transatlantic service. Black Ball ships carried cargo, people, and mail between New York and Euro-

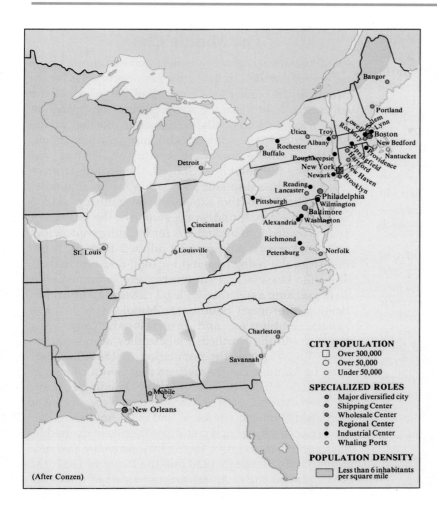

MAP 10.6
The Nation's Major Cities in 1840
By 1840 most American cities in the interior had developed specialized economic roles—Cincinnati and Pittsburgh became industrial centers, Hartford and Lancaster grew as regional centers for farm communities, and Brooklyn and Buffalo developed as wholesaling centers. The oldest ports on the Atlantic had more diversified economies, serving as centers for import merchants, banks, insurance companies, ready-made clothing manufacturers, and many other activities.

pean ports such as Liverpool, London, and Le Havre. New York merchants also gained an unassailable lead in commerce with the newly independent Latin American nations of Brazil, Peru, and Venezuela. Finally, they moved into the cotton trade. Their agents in southern ports offered finance, insurance, and shipping to cotton exporters and won for New York a dominant share of the cotton that passed through northern harbors. In their most aggressive stroke, New York merchants persuaded the state government to build the Erie Canal, which solidified New York's position as the nation's premier port. By the 1840s and 1850s New York's merchants controlled almost two-thirds of foreign imports and almost half of all foreign trade.

Changes in the Social Structure

★

The industrial and market revolutions transformed the material lives of many Americans, allowing them to live in larger houses, cook more easily, and wear better-made clothes. But the new economic order also

widened social distinctions among a wealthy industrial and commercial elite, a substantial urban middle class, and a mass of propertyless wage earners who included many immigrant laborers. In helping to create a society divided by class and ethnicity, industrialization posed a momentous challenge to American republican ideals.

The Business Elite

Before industrialization, white Americans had been divided into various *ranks*, with a group of "notables" at the top ruling over the "lower orders." But in rural areas the different ranks shared a common culture: gentlemen farmers talked easily with yeomen about crop yields and livestock, while their wives conversed with humble farm women about the arts of quilting and preserving food. In the South needy tenants and aristocratic slaveowners shared the same amusements: gambling, cockfighting, and betting on horse races. In northern towns rich and poor attended the same Quaker meetinghouse or the same Presbyterian or Congregational church. "Almost everyone eats, drinks, and dresses in the same way," a European visitor to Hartford, Connecticut, reported in 1798, "and one can see the most obvious inequality only in the dwellings."

The Industrial Revolution shattered this traditional order and created a society of *classes*, each with its own culture. The new economic system pulled many farm youth into small towns and larger cities and made some merchants, manufacturers, bankers, and landlords very rich. In 1800 the top 10 percent of the nation's families owned about 40 percent of the wealth; by 1860 the wealthiest 10 percent owned nearly 70 percent, a proportion similar to that in western Europe. Inequality was greatest in the American cities, where the richest 1 percent of the population held more than 40 percent of all *tangible* property—such as land and buildings—and an even higher share of *intangible* property—such as stocks and bonds.

Government policies encouraged the inequality of wealth by placing heavier taxes on the middling and poorer classes than on the rich. Like most national governments, the U.S. Treasury raised most of its revenue from tariffs—hidden taxes that raised the cost of imported goods (such as textiles) purchased mostly by ordinary citizens. The tax policies of state and local governments also favored the wealthier classes. They usually taxed real estate and tangible personal property (such as furniture, tools, and machinery) but almost never stocks and bonds owned by the rich or the inheritances they passed on to their children.

Still, the uncertainties of the new capitalist world doomed some wealthy men to financial disaster. Unprofitable investments, fraud, and shifting markets took their toll even in times of prosperity, and increasingly frequent financial panics drove some of even the most cautious and calculating merchants, manufacturers, and investors into bankruptcy. In 1827 Jeremiah Thompson, New York's largest cotton trader and an organizer of the Black Ball Line, went bankrupt; in addition, the Panic of 1837 destroyed the fortunes of thousands, including Philip Hone, a wealthy merchant and one-time mayor of New York (Chapter 11).

Over time families of wealth consciously set themselves apart from the rest of society. Such people dressed well, rode around town in fancy carriages pulled by fine horses, and lived in well-furnished houses tended by butlers, cooks, coachmen, and other servants. The women of the family no longer socialized with those of lesser wealth, and the men no longer labored side by side with their journeymen but became managers and directors, issuing orders through trusted subordinates to hundreds of factory operatives. Similarly, merchants, manufacturers, and bankers chose to live in separate residential areas, turning away from traditional practices such as boarding unmarried workers in their own homes. By the 1830s most employers had moved their families to distinct upper-class enclaves, often at the edge of the city. The desire for greater privacy by privileged families divided many American cities into class-segregated communities for the first time.

The Middle Class

Standing between wealthy owners and entrepreneurs at one end of the social spectrum and nonpropertied wage earners at the other was a growing middle class. In the words of a Boston printer and publisher, the "middling class" was made up of "the farmers, the mechanics, the manufacturers, the traders, who carry on professionally the ordinary operations of buying, selling, and exchanging merchandize." Indeed, the economic revolution brought a dramatic increase in its size and prosperity. Thanks to the expansion of industry, skilled mechanics easily found work; similarly, the growth of cities provided jobs and profits for building contractors and shopkeepers. Commercial-minded farmers benefited from the rising demand for food and raw materials, while lawyers and surveyors were swamped with clients seeking assistance on legal matters and the clarification of property boundaries. Middle-class business owners, employees, and professionals were most numerous in the Northeast, where they accounted for about 30 percent of the population in 1840, but they could be found in every American town, even villages in the rural South. In the boom town of Oglethorpe, Georgia (population 2,500) in 1854, there were no fewer than eighty "business houses" and eight hotels.

The size, wealth, and cultural influence of the middle class continued to grow, fueled by a dramatic increase in prosperity. Between 1830 and the Panic of 1857, the per capita income of Americans increased by about 2.5 percent a year, a remarkable rate that the United States has never since matched. This surge in income, along with the availability of inexpensive mass-produced goods, facilitated the creation of a distinct middle-class culture, especially in urban areas of the North.

The Character of Middle-Class Life. One of the defining features of the urban middle class was the character of family life. Unlike the situation in yeoman and artisan households, where both husbands and wives worked to support the family, middle-class husbands had sufficient earnings to free their wives (and their children) from such labor. Many middle-class men saved about 15 percent of their income, depositing it in banks and using it to buy well-built houses in a "respectable part of town." With ample leisure time at their disposal, middle-class wives were literate and accomplished; they bought books and pianos as well as commodious furniture for their front parlors. The more affluent hired a servant or two to work in the kitchen and the stables. Middle-class parents had the means to provide their children with a full high school education (at a time when most white children received only four or five years of elementary schooling), thereby enhancing their chances for success in the new economic world.

Middle-Class Family Life, 1836
The family of Azariah Caverly boasted many of the amenities of middle-class life—handsome clothes, finely decorated furniture, and a striking floor covering. Underlining the social conventions of the time, an unknown artist depicts the father and his son holding a newspaper and a square, symbolizing commerce and industry, while the mother and her daughter are pictured next to a Bible, indicating their domestic and moral vocations.
New York State Historical Association.

Improvements in housing reflected this prosperity and gave middle-class life a distinctive character. During the 1830s American carpenters devised an efficient method to build wooden houses: the balloon frame. Traditional wood construction depended on the careful fitting together of heavy timbers; in the East experienced housewrights fashioned a strong frame with mortise-and-tenon joints, and in the West farmers fitted trimmed logs together. The *balloon frame,* much lighter in weight (as its name implied) but almost as strong, formed a house with a vertical grid of thin wooden studs joined by nails to crosspieces at the top and bottom. Once the carpenter had constructed the frame, he simply nailed wood sheathing to the studs to make the walls, then added a layer of clapboard siding. The new technology reduced the cost of housing by 40 percent, and the four-room balloon-frame house soon became the standard residence, replacing the typical two-room-with-a-loft house of preindustrial society.

The new house design helped change the character of family life. Urban middle-class parents had already begun to have fewer children by using various means of birth control: abstinence, coitus interruptus, animal-skin condoms, and abortions induced by patent medicines. Larger houses allowed members of these smaller families to have "individual" spaces; to enhance privacy, architects published manuals featuring house plans with many bedrooms. Andrew Jackson Downing, the leading architectural philosopher of the era, praised the new houses in his famous book *The Architecture of Country Houses* (1850). Downing argued they would promote a "refinement of manners" and strengthen the life of the family, which was "the best social form."

Prosperous urban families lived not only in more space but also in greater luxury. Beds with springs of woven rope or iron wire replaced beds with wooden slats, and as mass-produced ticking (fabric for pillow or mattress coverings) and sheeting became available in stores, homemade featherbeds, mattresses, and down pillows became standard items. Middle-class residences now boasted furnaces that heated water for bathing and for radiators that warmed entire rooms, eliciting complaints from visiting Europeans that it was impossible to escape the hot air: "It meets you the moment the street-door is opened to let you in, rushes after you when you emerge again, half-stewed and parboiled into the wholesome air."

Most affluent urban house owners acquired goods that eased the burden of domestic chores. Stoves with ovens, including broilers and movable grates, replaced inefficient open hearths, and women had access to a variety of pots, pans, and kettles; mechanical equipment such as grinders and presses; and washboards. Many middle-class householders owned treadle-operated sewing machines and iceboxes, which ice-company wagons filled daily. They also bought packaged goods: as early as 1825 the Underwood Company of Boston was marketing well-preserved Atlantic salmon in jars. Following the introduction of the air-tight Mason jar in 1858, housewives bought perishable farm produce when it was cheap and preserved it, thereby providing their families with a varied diet even in winter.

Middle-Class Culture and Values. The technology of the Industrial Revolution allowed the creation of a middle-class "book culture." The Napier steam-driven press (1825) and the Hoe rotary press (1847) led to the mass production of inexpensive books; soon publishing houses in New York, Philadelphia, and Boston competed with each other, offering discounts to booksellers, sending sales agents into the field, and recruiting popular authors. Between 1820 and 1850 American book publishers such as Harper Brothers and G. P. Putnam's Sons increased their annual sales from about $2.5 million to $12.5 million. The religious press contributed to the explosion in print. The American Bible Society and dozens of other organizations published more than 1 million Bibles and 6 million books, pamphlets, and magazines each year.

The middle class provided a virtually insatiable market for these books. By 1850 nine of ten American-born white adults could read—double the proportion in the nations of western Europe—and millions of them bought books or borrowed the nearly 13 million volumes available in over 50,000 public libraries. Fiction constituted a large proportion of literary consumption. One of the first successful American writers of fiction was James Fenimore Cooper. Beginning with *The Pioneers* (1823) and *The Last of the Mohicans* (1826) and ending with *The Deerslayer* (1841), Cooper built an enormous readership for the adventures of his hero, the frontier scout Leatherstocking, a model of American self-reliance and nonconformity. Corresponding in popularity was the poetry of Henry Wadsworth Longfellow, who romanticized the American past in *Hiawatha* (1855) and *The Courtship of Miles Standish* (1858).

Many novels and even more works of nonfiction engaged in moral instruction, placing particular emphasis on discipline, hard work, and social mobility. Ambitious parents reinforced these values, for they wanted to pass on their hard-earned status to their children. Puritans and other American Protestants had long believed that work in an earthly "calling" was a duty people owed to God. In the 1820s and 1830s the business elite and the middle class gave this idea a secular twist: they celebrated work as the key to a higher standard of living for the nation and social mobility for the individual.

Benjamin Franklin gave classical expression to the secular work ethic in his *Autobiography*, which was published in full in 1818 and immediately found a huge audience. Heeding Franklin's suggestion that an industrious man would become a rich one, tens of thousands of young American men worked hard, saved their money, shunned alcoholic beverages, and practiced honesty in their business dealings. Countless magazines, children's books, self-help manuals, and novels taught the same lessons. The ideal of the "self-made man" became a central theme of American popular culture.

Just as a rural-producer ethic had united the social ranks in pre-1800 America, this new goal of personal achievement and social mobility tied together the upper and middle classes of the new industrializing society. There might have been an enormous economic gulf between a wealthy factory owner and his middle-class clerks, foremen, and skilled mechanics, but the two groups increasingly shared the same values. Knowing that many affluent families had risen from modest beginnings, middle-class men and women took them as models and shunned the rapidly increasing numbers of working families who owned nothing and had to struggle just to survive.

The New Urban Poor

Indeed, as thoughtful members of the business elite and the middle class surveyed the emerging social landscape, they worried that the poor might never improve their status. In large cities and small towns there were more and more factory districts and working-class neighborhoods, where laborers lived in cheap rooming houses and drank in dark saloons. As horse-drawn buses (which were too costly for most workers) moved slowly through the city streets, their affluent riders could not avoid the sight of disorderly, sometimes drunken crowds.

In this new urban and industrial world, a yeoman-like society made up of independent families no longer seemed possible or even desirable. "Entire independence ought not to be wished for," Ithamar A. Beard, the paymaster of the Hamilton Manufacturing Company, told a mechanics association in 1827. "In large manufacturing towns, many more must fill subordinate stations and must be under the immediate direction and control of a master or superintendent, than in the farming towns."

Beard had a point. By 1840 as many as half the nation's free workers were laboring for others rather than for themselves. The bottom 10 percent of this wage-earning labor force consisted of casual workers—those hired on a short-term basis, often by the day, for the most arduous jobs. Poor women washed clothes, while their husbands and sons carried lumber and bricks for construction projects, loaded ships and wagons, and dug out dirt and stones to help build canals. Most casual laborers owned no property except the clothes they wore. During business slumps they bore the brunt of unemployment, and even in the best of times their jobs were unpredictable, seasonal, and dangerous.

Other laborers had greater security of employment, but few were prospering. In Massachusetts in 1825 the daily wage of an unskilled worker was about two-thirds that of a mechanic; two decades later it was less than half as much. The 18,000 needlewomen in New York City in the 1850s were no better off, averaging less than $80 a year, meager wages that did not buy much. While middle-class families spent about one-third of their income on food, poorer urban workers had to spend nearly $2 of every $3 they earned just for sustenance. After paying rent for housing, they were broke—unable to take advantage of the rapidly falling prices of manufactured goods. Only the most fortunate working families could afford to educate their children, pay the fees required for apprenticeship in a trade, or accumulate small dowries so that their daughters could marry men with better prospects. Most had to send their children out to work to help support the family. An economic

The Hot Corn Seller, c. 1840
Free African Americans faced discrimination and harsh economic conditions, eking out a living with long hours of work that yielded meager returns. This woman, painted by Nicolino Calyo, may have been lucky enough to have a garden plot that grew more food than her family needed, offering her the opportunity to sell the extra produce in order to make some much-needed cash.
Museum of the City of New York. Gift of Mrs. Francis P. Garvan in memory of Francis P. Garvan.

recession or the death of a spouse often threw them into dire poverty. As one charity worker noted, "What can a bereaved widow do, with 5 or 6 little children, destitute of every means of support but what her own hands can furnish (which in a general way does not amount to more than 25 cents a day)."

By the 1830s most urban factory workers, journeymen, and unskilled casual laborers resided in well-defined neighborhoods. Certain blocks were dominated by large boardinghouses where single men and women lived, often in unhealthy conditions caused by crowding and inadequate sanitary facilities. Elsewhere landlords converted houses, including the basements and attics, into tiny apartments and then used the profits from rentals to build more workers' housing. Often the developers squeezed a number of buildings, interspersed with outhouses and connected by foul-smelling courtyards and dark alleys, onto a single lot.

Living in such distressing conditions, many wage earners turned to the dubious solace of alcohol. Liquor had long been an integral part of American life; beer, wine, and rum had "lubricated" ceremonies, work breaks, barn raisings, and games. But during the 1820s urban wage earners led Americans to new heights of alcohol consumption. Aiding them were western farmers, who distilled corn and rye into gin and whiskey as a low-cost way to get their grain to market. By 1830 the per capita consumption of liquor had risen to more than 5 gallons a year, three times present-day levels (see Voices from Abroad, "Frances Trollope: American Workers and Their Wives," p. 338).

Drinking patterns changed as well. Workers in many craft unions "swore off" liquor, convinced that it would undermine their skilled work as well as their health and finances. But other workers began to drink on the job—and not just during the traditional 11 A.M. and 4 P.M. "refreshers." Journeymen used apprentices to smuggle whiskey into shops, and then, as one baker recalled, "One man was stationed at the window to watch, while the rest drank." Grogshops and tippling houses appeared on almost every block in working-class districts. The saloons became focal points for urban disorder and crime, including assault, burglary, and vandalism. Fueled by unrestrained drinking, a fist-fight among young men could turn into a brawl or a full-scale riot. The urban police forces, consisting of low-paid watchmen and untrained constables, were unable to contain the lawlessness.

The Benevolent Empire

The disorder among urban wage earners sparked concern among many well-to-do Americans. Inspired by the religious ideal of "benevolence," they created a number of reform organizations that were linked by overlapping membership and shared ideals. Because of these groups' aggressive quest for moral purity and firm belief in charity, historians have labeled them the "Benevolent Empire."

During the 1820s Congregational and Presbyterian ministers united with like-minded merchants and their wives to launch a program whose purpose, according to Presbyterian minister Lyman Beecher of Boston, was to restore "the moral government of God." The reformers introduced new forms of moral discipline into their own lives and the lives of working people. They would regulate behavior—by persuasion if possible, by law if necessary.

Although the Benevolent Empire targeted age-old evils such as drunkenness, prostitution, and crime, its methods were new. Instead of relying on church sermons and moral persuasion by community leaders, the reformers set out to institutionalize charity and combat evil systematically. They established large-scale organizations—the Prison Discipline Society and the American Society for the Promotion of Temperance, among many others. Each had a managing staff, a network of volunteers and chapters, and a newspaper.

FRANCES TROLLOPE
American Workers and Their Wives

——★——

During her four-year stay in the United States, Mrs. Trollope traveled widely and proved to be an acute social commentator. Her book, Domestic Manners of the Americans (1832), was a best seller on both sides of the Atlantic. She frequently compared life in America with that in Britain, as in this discussion of the living conditions and habits of working people.

Mohawk [in southern Ohio], as our little village was called, gave us an excellent opportunity of comparing the peasants of the United States with those of England, and of judging the average degree of comfort enjoyed by each. . . .

Mechanics, if good workmen, are certain of employment, and good wages, rather higher than with us; the average wages of a labourer throughout the Union is ten dollars a month, with lodging, boarding, washing, and mending; if he lives at his own expense he has a dollar a day. It appears to me that the necessaries of life, that is to say, meat, bread, butter, tea, and coffee (not to mention whiskey), are within the reach of every sober, industrious, and healthy man who chooses to have them; and yet I think that an English peasant, with the same qualifications, would, in coming to the United States, change for the worse. . . .

[This result, says Trollope, is because American men indulge in various money-consuming vices.] Tobacco grows at their doors, and is not taxed: yet this too costs something, and the air of heaven is not in more general use among the men of America than chewing tobacco. . . . Ardent spirits, though lamentably cheap, still cost something, and the use of them among the men . . . is universal. . . . I am not now pointing out the evils of dram-drinking, but it is evident, that where this practice prevails universally, and often to the most frightful excess, the consequence must be, that the money spent to obtain the dram [a small glass of whiskey] is less than the money lost by the time consumed in drinking it.

Long, disabling, and expensive fits of sickness are incontestably more frequent in every part of America than in England, and the sufferers have no aid to look to, but what they have saved, or what they may be enabled to sell. I have never seen misery exceeded what I have witnessed in an American cottage where disease has entered.

But if the condition of the labourer be not superior to that of the English peasant, that of his wife and daughters is incomparably worse. It is they who are indeed the slaves of the soil. One has but to look at the wife of an American cottager, and ask her age, to be convinced that the life she leads is one of hardship, privation, and labour. It is rare to see a woman in this station who has reached the age of thirty, without losing every trace of youth and beauty.

Even the young girls, though often with lovely features, look pale, thin, and haggard. . . . The horror of domestic service, which the reality of slavery, and the fable of equality, have generated, excludes the young women from that sure and most comfortable resource of decent English girls; and the consequence is . . . the daughters are, to the full extent of the word, domestic slaves.

Source: Frances Trollope, *Domestic Manners of the Americans* (New York: Whittaker, Treacher & Co., 1832), n.p.

Together these groups set out to "improve" society. First, by campaigning for temperance in drinking habits and the end of female prostitution, they encouraged individuals to lead well-disciplined and moral lives. As part of this effort they persuaded local governments to ban carnivals of drink and dancing, such as Negro Election Day in New England (mock elections in which African Americans symbolically took over the government), which had been enjoyed by whites as well as blacks. Second, they created new institutions for people who were considered to be threats to society or who were unable to handle their own affairs. Reformers provided homes of refuge for the abandoned children of the poor, removed the insane from isolation in attics and cellars and placed them in newly built asylums, and campaigned for an end to corporal punishment for criminals and their rehabilitation through moral training in penitentiaries.

Women played an increasingly active role in the Benevolent Empire. Since the 1790s upper-class women had sponsored a number of charitable organizations, such as the Society for the Relief of Poor Widows with Small Children, founded in New York in 1797 by

Benevolent Reform
Epidemics of virulent diseases—
smallpox, yellow fever, and
cholera—killed thousands of residents in seaport cities between
1800 and 1860 and left hundreds
of children orphans. Reformers
addressed this serious social problem by establishing asylums for
poor orphan boys and girls, such
as the handsome Louisiana-style
cottage in New Orleans depicted
in this hand-colored engraving by
W. P. Knox and L. Hill, c. 1840.
Historic New Orleans Collection.

Isabella Graham, a devout Presbyterian widow. By the 1820s Graham's society was assisting hundreds of widows and their children in New York City. Her daughter, Joanna Bethune, set up other charitable institutions, including the Orphan Asylum Society and the Society for the Promotion of Industry, which gave hundreds of poor women employment as spinners and seamstresses.

Some reformers believed that one of the gravest threats to the "moral government of God" was the decline of the traditional Sabbath. As the pace of commercial activity accelerated, merchants and shippers began to conduct business on Sunday, since they did not want their goods and equipment to be idle one day in every seven. In response, in 1828 Lyman Beecher and other ministers formed the General Union for Promoting the Observance of the Christian Sabbath, and hundreds of local union chapters sprang up—usually with women's auxiliaries—from Maine to the Ohio Valley. Seeking a symbolic issue around which to rally Christians, the union focused on a law Congress had enacted in 1810 allowing mail to be transported—though not delivered—on Sunday. In an unsuccessful attempt to repeal this law, the union adopted the tactics of a political party, organizing rallies and circulating petitions. Its members boycotted shipping companies that did business on the Sabbath and campaigned for municipal laws forbidding games and festivals to be held on that day.

Not everyone agreed with the program of the Benevolent Empire. Men who labored twelve hours daily for six days in a row refused to spend their one day of leisure in meditation and prayer. Shipping company managers demanded that the Erie Canal provide lock keepers on Sundays and joined antitemperance advocates in arguing that laws enforcing morality were "contrary to the free spirit of our institutions." And when the reform-minded evangelical Baptists in the South proposed to teach Christianity to slaves and extend church membership to African Americans, many white planters were outraged. Such popular resistance or indifference limited the success of the Benevolent Empire. A different kind of message was required if religious reformers were to do more than preach to the already converted and discipline the already disciplined.

Revivalism and Reform

The seeds of this message had already been sown in England, where ambitious, self-disciplined men from dissenting Protestant backgrounds—mostly Methodist but also Congregational and Presbyterian—had become manufacturers and members of a rising middle class. The Presbyterian minister Charles Grandison Finney brought this program of personal uplift and middle-class ambition to Americans. Finney was not part of the traditional religious elite. Born to poor farmers in Connecticut in 1792, he initially pursued a career in the law but in 1823, following an intense conversion experience, decided to become a minister. Beginning in towns along the Erie Canal, Finney conducted emotional revival meetings that ignored deep instruction in church doctrine; what counted was the individual's will to be saved. God would welcome *any* sinner who submitted to the Holy Spirit, he told his listeners, and only an infusion of God's grace, poured into the heart of the believer, made

Charles Finney, Evangelist
Finney (1792–1875) had a long and influential career after his New York revivals. In 1835 he established a theology department at the newly founded Oberlin College in Ohio, where he helped train a generation of ministers. Finney served as president of the college from 1851 to 1866. This daguerreotype, taken in 1850 while Finney and his second wife, Elizabeth Atkinson, were on an evangelistic tour of Great Britain, suggests the determination and moral intensity of the great preacher.
Oberlin College Archives.

a moral life possible. Finney's ministry drew upon—and greatly accelerated—the Second Great Awakening, the wave of Protestant revivalism that had begun after the Revolution (see Chapter 9).

Finney's message that "God has made man a moral free agent" was particularly appealing to propertied farmers and members of the urban middle class, who had already chosen to improve their material lives. But he became famous for converting those at the ends of the social spectrum: the haughty rich, who had placed themselves above God; and the abject poor, who seemed lost to drink, sloth, and misbehavior. His goal was to humble the pride of the rich and relieve the shame of the poor by celebrating their common fellowship in Christ. Conversion changed not only people's eternal fate but also their moral standing, identifying them spiritually with pious middle-class respectability.

Finney's most spectacular triumph came in 1830, when he moved his revivals from farming villages and small towns to Rochester, New York—a major city on the Erie Canal. For six months he preached every day

and added a new tactic: group prayer meetings in family homes, in which women played an active role. Finney's wife, Lydia, and other pious middle-class wives carried the message to the homes of the unconverted. Soon, one convert reported, "You could not go upon the street and hear any conversation, except upon religion."

This effort won over the influential merchants and manufacturers of Rochester, who pledged to reform their lives and those of their workers. In one Presbyterian church, members pledged to "renounce all the ways of sin, and to make it the business of our life to do good and promote the glory of God." They would attend church, take the "cold water cure" by giving up alcohol, and work steady hours. To encourage their employees and poor workers to follow suit, wealthy businessmen founded a new Free Presbyterian Church—"free" because members did not have to pay for pew space—and other evangelical Protestants formed two similar churches. To encourage morality, Rochester's business elite established a savings bank to promote thrift, Sunday schools for poor children, and the Female Charitable Society to provide relief for the families of the unemployed.

The attempt to create a harmonious community of morally disciplined Christians was somewhat effective. During the 1830s many workers, often led by their wives, followed their employers' example and became converts and church members, receiving raises and promotions as a reward. But skilled workers who belonged to strong craft organizations—bootmakers, carpenters, stonemasons, and boat builders—resisted the message, arguing that workers needed higher wages and schools more urgently than sermons and prayers. And Finney's revival seldom moved poor people, especially the Irish Catholic immigrants who had recently begun arriving in American cities, including Rochester, and who thought of Protestants as religious heretics and as their political oppressors in Ireland.

This resistance only heightened the converts' zeal for rebuilding society into an evangelical Christian order. In farming villages and towns from New England to the Ohio Valley, younger ministers—Baptist and Methodist as well as Congregationalist and Presbyterian—adopted Finney's techniques and pushed the revival forward. In New York City, where Finney established himself after leaving Rochester, the wealthy silk merchants Arthur and Lewis Tappan founded a magazine, *The Christian Evangelist*, to promote his ideas. The success of the revival "has been so general and thorough," concluded a General Assembly of Presbyterians, "that the whole customs of society have changed."

The temperance movement proved to be the most effective arena for evangelical reform on a national scale. In 1832 evangelicals gained control of the American Temperance Society, which grew quickly to 2,000 local chapters with more than 200,000 members. The society adapted the methods that had worked so well in the revivals—group confession and prayer, a focus on

The Temperance Crusade
Reformers urged those addicted to alcohol to take the "cold water cure," swearing off liquor and drinking water instead. To promote temperance, Reverend Thomas Hunt founded the Cold Water Army, an organization that grew to embrace several hundred thousand children, all of whom pledged "perpetual hate to all that can intoxicate." This Cold Water Army fan shows a young supporter of the movement pumping water as the army of boys and girls marches by.
Museum of American Political Life.

the family and the spiritual role of women, and sudden, emotional conversion—and took them into every town and city. On one day in New York City in 1841, as many as 4,000 people took the temperance "pledge" to avoid alcohol completely. As Americans reduced their intake of alcohol, the average annual consumption of spirits fell from about 5 gallons per person in 1830 to about 2 gallons in 1845 (see American Voices, "John Gough: The Vice of Intemperance," p. 342).

Evangelical reformers reinforced the traditional moral foundations of the American work ethic. Laziness and drinking could not be cured by Benjamin Franklin's patient methods of self-discipline, they argued; rather, individuals had to experience the profound change of heart achieved only through God's grace and religious conversion. In this perspective, even the poorest family could look forward to a prosperous new life. Through such means, evangelical Protestantism reinforced the sense of common identity between the business elite and the middle class and

spread the values of individual enterprise and moral discipline among wage earners. Religion and the ideology of social mobility served as a powerful cement, holding society together amid the massive changes brought by the spread of markets and industry.

Immigration and Cultural Conflict

During the 1840s and 1850s the influx of hundreds of thousands of immigrants from Ireland, the German states, and Great Britain created new strains in the American social order. There was no federal legislation regulating immigration, and state laws, which attempted to set minimum health standards and exclude paupers, were generally ineffective. Consequently, there were no legal barriers to immigrants fleeing poverty and famine or seeking a better life. Between 1840 and 1860 about 2 million Irish men and women poured into the United States, along with 1.5 million Germans and 750,000 Britons. Most immigrants avoided the South because they opposed slavery, shunned blacks, or feared competition from enslaved workers. Many German migrants moved to states in the Midwest such as Wisconsin, Iowa, and Missouri, where they made up a majority of the settlers in many areas (see Map 10.2). Other Germans, and most of the other immigrants, settled in the northeastern states, where they accounted for nearly one-third of white adults by 1860.

Irish Poverty. The economic situation of immigrants varied greatly. The wealthiest were the British, many of whom were professionals, landowning farmers, and skilled workers. The majority of German immigrants came from farming and artisan families and could afford to buy land in America. The poorest migrants were peasants and laborers from Ireland, who fled from a famine in the 1840s caused by severe overpopulation, a devastating blight on the potato crop, and inadequate policies on the part of the English-run government. Arriving in dire poverty and unable to buy farms, the Irish found new homes in the cities of New England and New York, where they took low-skilled jobs in factories, construction projects, docks, warehouses, and private residences. Because they were willing to work for long hours, at low wages, and with great intensity, Irish workers gave a competitive edge to industrialists in New York City and Boston, where they numbered nearly one-third of the population by 1850. In Boston, the large clothing factories employed hundreds of young Irishwomen.

Many Irish immigrants, like the majority of unskilled native-born day laborers, lived in poverty, unable to afford the food they needed to keep up with the intense pace of factory work. Crowded living conditions threatened their health, for sanitation systems in large cities were primitive. Poorly sealed privies drained into wells used for drinking water, and open

John Gough
The Vice of Intemperance

———★———

John Gough (1817–1886) was twelve years old when his impoverished English parents shipped him to America, where he found work as a book-binder in New York City—and eventually turned to drink. In 1842, at age twenty-five, Gough converted to temperance. For the next four decades he used his elo-quence as a lecturer—and his considerable talents as an actor—to command high fees and persuade thou-sands to join the temperance movement. The following selection is taken from his Autobiography *(1869).*

Will it be believed that I again sought refuge in rum? Yet so it was. Scarcely had I recovered from the fright, than I sent out, procured a pint of rum, and drank it all in less than an hour. And now came upon me many terrible sensations. Cramps attacked me in my limbs, which racked me with agony; and my temples throbbed as if they would burst. . . . Then came on the drunkard's remorse-less torturer—delirium tremens, in all its terrors, attacked me. For three days I endured more agony than pen could describe, even were it guided by the mind of Dante. . . . I was at one time surrounded by millions of monstrous spiders, that crawled slowly over every limb, whilst the beaded drops of perspi-ration would start to my brow, and my limbs would shiver until the bed rattled. . . . All at once, whilst gazing at a frightful creation of my distempered mind, I seemed struck with sudden blindness. I knew a candle was burning in the room, but I could not see it—all was so pitchy dark. . . . And then the scene would change: I was falling—falling swiftly as an arrow—far down into some terrible abyss. . . .

By the mercy of God, I survived this awful seizure; and when I rose, a weak, broken-down man, and surveyed my ghastly features in the glass, I thought of my mother, and asked myself how I had obeyed the instructions received from her lips, and to what advantage I had turned the lessons she taught me. I remembered her countless prayers and tears. . . . Oh! how keen were my rebukes; and, in the excitement of the moment, I resolved to lead a better life, and abstain from the accursed cup.

For about a month, terrified by what I had suf-fered, I adhered to my resolution; then my wife came home, and, in my joy at her return, I flung my good resolutions to the wind, and, foolishly fancy-ing that I could now restrain my appetite, which had a whole month remained in subjugation, I took a glass of brandy. That glass aroused the slumbering demon, who would not be satisfied by so tiny a liba-tion. Another and another succeeded, until I was again far advanced in the career of intemperance. The night of my wife's return, I went to bed intoxi-cated.

———

Source: David Brion Davis, ed., *Antebellum American Culture: An Interpretive Anthology* (Lexington, MA: Heath, 1979), 402–403.

---

sewers ran through the streets. Epidemics of cholera, yellow fever, typhoid, smallpox, diphtheria, and tuber-culosis struck with increasing frequency. In the sum-mer of 1849 cholera epidemics hit New York, St. Louis, and Cincinnati. More than 5,000 people, mostly poor immigrants, died in New York City alone.

Catholicism and Nativism. In times of hardship and sorrow, immigrants turned to their churches. Many Germans and virtually all the Irish were devout Catholics, and they fueled the growth of the Catholic Church. In the 1840s there were 16 Catholic dioceses and 700 churches in the United States, and the number increased to 45 dioceses and 3,000 churches by 1860. With the guidance of their priests and bishops, the Irish built a network of institutions: charitable societies, orphanages, militia companies, parochial schools, newspapers, social clubs, and political organizations. These community organizations had few equivalents in Ireland, for they had sprung up in America to help immigrants in their search for housing, jobs, and edu-cation. Through these Catholic institutions and urban political organizations, the Irish and Germans—and, subsequently, later immigrant groups—would maintain their cultural identity and attain considerable political power.

When the first Irish immigrants—about 50,000—arrived in the 1830s, they were greeted by a rash of anti-Catholic publications. One of the most militant critics of Catholicism was Samuel F. B. Morse (who would later make the first commercial adaptation of the telegraph). In 1834 Morse published *Foreign Conspiracy against the Liberties of the United States,* which warned of a Catholic threat to American republican institutions. The "past history" of Roman Catholics, Morse suggested, clearly showed that "they everywhere act together, as if guided by one mind"—the pope. Morse believed that Catholic immigrants would obey the dictates of Pope Pius IX, who strongly opposed republican reformers in Italy and condemned republicanism as a false political ideology based on the sovereignty of the people rather than the sovereignty of God. To resist this perceived threat, he advocated the formation of an "Anti-Popery Union." Republican-minded Protestants of many denominations shared Morse's fears, and *Foreign Conspiracy* became their textbook. Millions of young Americans read it in Protestant Sunday schools.

The social tensions stemming from industrialization intensified anti-Catholic sentiment. Unemployed Protestant mechanics and poorly paid factory workers joined mobs that attacked Catholics, blaming immigrant labor for their economic woes. They organized Native American Clubs, which called for increasing the waiting period for citizenship from five to twenty-one years, restricting public office to native-born Americans, and using only the Protestant version of the Bible in public schools. Other native-born citizens supported the anti-Catholic movement for reasons of public policy. They wanted a strong system of public schools and therefore opposed proposals from Catholic clergymen and Democratic legislators in many northeastern states that the local taxes paid by Catholics be reserved for parochial (religious) schools. Evangelical ministers and temperance advocates were alarmed by the abuse of alcohol on the part of some Irish men and called for an end to immigration. As in certain parts of England, where Irish Catholics also migrated, cultural conflicts among ethnic and religious groups inhibited the development of a strong labor movement. Many Protestant laborers felt they had more in common with their Protestant employers than with their Catholic co-workers.

In almost every city with a large immigrant population, religious and cultural conflicts resulted in violence. In 1834 in Charlestown, Massachusetts, a quarrel between Catholic laborers repairing a convent owned by the Ursuline order of nuns and Protestant workers in a neighboring brickyard turned into a full-scale riot. An anti-Catholic mob drove the nuns out of the convent and burned it to the ground. Rioting escalated in the 1840s as the Irish began to acquire political influence in northeastern cities. In Philadelphia the violence peaked in 1844 when the Catholic bishop persuaded public school officials to use both Protestant and Catholic versions of the Bible. Anti-Irish rioting incited by the city's Native American Clubs lasted for two months and escalated into open warfare between Protestants and the Pennsylvania militia.

An Anti-Catholic Riot
When riots against Irish Catholics broke out in Philadelphia in 1844, the governor of Pennsylvania called out the militia to protect Catholic churches and residential neighborhoods. In the foreground of this engraving, two Protestant rioters, depicted by the artist as well-dressed gentlemen, attack an Irish family with sticks, while in the background the state militia exchanges musket fire with other members of the mob.
Library Company of Philadelphia.

Thus, even as economic revolution brought prosperity and a higher standard of living to many Americans, it divided the society along the lines of class and, by encouraging the influx of immigrants, created new ethnic and religious tensions. Differences of class and culture now split the North in much the same way that race and class had long divided the South. But the majority of white Americans remained closely tied to their fellow citizens, bound together not only by a quest for advancement in an economic system based on private property and capitalist enterprise but also by participation in a vibrant political culture of democratic republicanism.

Summary

───────★───────

Between 1820 and 1860 the United States experienced an "industrial" and a "market" revolution that created a new economic structure. Merchants and manufacturers organized increasingly efficient systems of production and, aided by skilled mechanics, introduced water- and steam-powered machines to turn out huge quantities of goods. Simultaneously merchants, traders, and shop-keepers created a vast market system in which they exchanged these manufactures for grain, meat, cotton, leather, and wool produced by a rapidly growing—and westward-moving—farm population.

Three streams of migrants moved into the West, transplanting the cultures of the plantation South and yeoman New England into the Old Southwest, the Ohio River Valley, and the Old Northwest. State governments promoted this westward movement—and the creation of regional and national markets—by subsidizing the building of roads, canals, and railroads and creating a transportation system that was unprecedented in size and complexity. As domestic markets and production grew, urbanization accelerated in the Northeast, where industrial towns dotted the landscape, and New York City became the nation's largest city and leading trading center.

Economic growth fostered the creation of new social classes: a wealthy urban business elite of merchants and manufacturers; a prosperous, educated, and well-housed middle class; and a mass of wage-earning laborers with little or no property. Some artisans and workers formed trade unions in generally unsuccessful efforts to improve their economic welfare; other working people lived in poverty and sought solace in drink.

To improve the living conditions and the morals of the poor, upper-class Americans formed "benevolent" reform societies that promoted temperance, dispensed charity, and encouraged respect for the Christian Sabbath. Simultaneously, Charles Grandison Finney and other evangelical clergymen gave new life to the Second Great Awakening, enlisting millions of propertied farmers and middle-class Americans in a massive religious revival. Preaching the doctrine of "free moral agency," Finney urged Americans both to assist in their own salvation and to reform the world in which they lived.

Protestant evangelicalism heightened the cultural conflict between native-born Americans and millions of Catholic immigrants from Ireland and Germany. Nativist writers attacked Irish Catholics as anti-republican, and American workers blamed immigrant labor for their economic woes—attitudes that led to ethnic riots in many northern cities. By 1860 the United States was a more prosperous society than ever before, and also a more socially divided one.

TIMELINE

1782	Oliver Evans develops automated flour mill
1790	Samuel Slater opens spinning mill in Providence, R.I.
1793	Eli Whitney manufactures cotton gins
1807	Robert Fulton launches the *Clermont*, the first steamboat
1810s	Cotton Kingdom begins in Old Southwest
1814	Boston Manufacturing Co. opens cotton mill in Waltham, Mass.
1817	Erie Canal begun; completed in 1825
1820	Minimum federal land price reduced to $1.25 per acre
1820s	Women become textile operatives
	Building-trade workers seek ten-hour day
	Rise of Benevolent Empire
1821	End of Panic of 1819; fifteen-year boom begins
1824	Congress raises tariffs; raised again in 1828
	Gibbons v. Ogden promotes interstate trade
1830s	Expansion of western commercial cities
	Union movement; class-segregated cities
	Growth of temperance movement
	Creation of middle-class culture
1830	Charles Grandison Finney begins Rochester revival
1837	Panic of 1837; seven-year recession begins
1840s–1850s	Irish and German immigration; ethnic riots
	Expansion of railroads
	Rise of machine tool industry
1857	Financial panic after fourteen-year boom

Suggested Readings

Three important studies of the economic revolution and its consequences are Stuart Bruchey, *Enterprise: The Dynamic Economy of a Free People* (1990); Charles G. Sellers Jr., *The Market Revolution: Jacksonian America, 1815–1840* (1991); and Stuart M. Blumin, *The Emergence of the Middle Class: Social Experience in the American City, 1760–1900* (1989).

The Rise of Manufacturing

Surveys of the Industrial Revolution in America include W. Elliot Brownlee, *Dynamics of Ascent: A History of the American Economy* (1979), and Thomas C. Cochran, *Frontiers of Change: Early Industrialism in America* (1981). See also the pioneering work in economic geography by Donald W. Meinig, *The Shaping of America: A Geographical Perspective*, Vol. 2: *Continental America, 1800–1867* (1993). Good regional studies are Peter J. Coleman, *The Transformation of Rhode Island* (1963), and Anthony F. C. Wallace, *Rockdale: The Growth of an American Village in the Early Industrial Revolution* (1978).

Books on technological change include Judith A. McGaw, ed., *Early American Technology* (1994); Gary Cross and Rick Szostak, *Technology and American Society: A History* (1995); David Freeman Hawke, *Nuts and Bolts of the Past: A History of American Technology, 1776–1860* (1988); Brooke Hindle and Steven Lubar, *Engines of Change: The American Industrial Revolution, 1790–1860* (1986); and Barbara M. Tucker, *Samuel Slater and the Origins of the American Textile Industry* (1984).

On American workers during this period, see Alan Dawley, *Class and Community: The Industrial Revolution in Lynn* (1976); Jonathan Prude, *The Coming of Industrial Order: Town and Factory Life in Rural Massachusetts* (1983); Jeanne Boydston, *Home and Work: Housework, Wages, and the Ideology of Labor in the Early Republic* (1990); and Thomas Dublin, *Transforming Women's Work: New England Lives in the Industrial Revolution* (1994). Other useful analyses are Paul A. Gilje and Howard B. Rock, eds., *Keepers of the Revolution: New Yorkers at Work in the Early Republic* (1992); Susan E. Hirsch, *Roots of the American Working Class* (1978); and Paul Faler, *Mechanics and Manufacturers in the Early Industrial Revolution* (1983).

The Expansion of Markets

For the development of the Midwest, see Stephen Aron, *How the West Was Lost: The Transformation of Kentucky from Daniel Boone to Henry Clay* (1996), and Andrew R. L. Cayton and Peter S. Onuf, *The Midwest and the Nation* (1990). On agricultural expansion, consult Paul W. Gates, *The Farmer's Age: Agriculture, 1815–1860* (1960).

For urban development, see the classic study by R. G. Albion, *The Rise of New York Port, 1815–1860* (1939), and the fine analysis of Chicago by William Cronon, *Nature's Metropolis* (1992). Also consult Richard C. Wade, *The Urban Frontier: Pioneer Life in Early Pittsburgh, Cincinnati, Lexington, Louisville, and St. Louis* (1964).

A comprehensive study of the role of transportation is presented in George R. Taylor, *The Transportation Revolution, 1815–1860* (1951). On canals, consult Carol Sherrif, *The Artificial River: The Erie Canal and the Paradox of Progress, 1817–1862* (1996); Peter Way, *Common Labour: Workers and the Digging of North American Canals* (1993); Carter Goodrich et al., *Canals and American Economic Development* (1961); and Ronald E. Shaw, *Canals for a Nation: The Canal Era in the United States, 1790–1860* (1990). On the growth of railroads, consult Albert Fishlow, *American Railroads and the Transformation of the Ante-Bellum Economy* (1965). For the contribution of the law to the economic revolution, see Oscar Handlin and Mary Flug Handlin, *Commonwealth: A Study in the Role of Government in the American Economy, Massachusetts, 1774–1861* (1947), and Christopher L. Tomlins, *Law, Labor and Ideology in the Early American Republic* (1993).

Changes in the Social Structure

For the distribution of wealth and income in the early nineteenth century, see Frederic C. Jaher, *The Urban Establishment: Upper Strata in Boston, New York, Charleston, Chicago, and Los Angeles* (1982), and Edward Pessen, *Riches, Class, and Power before the Civil War* (1973). Social mobility is analyzed in Robert Doherty, *Society and Power: Five New England Towns, 1800–1860* (1977), and Don H. Doyle, *The Social Order of a Frontier Community: Jacksonville, Illinois, 1825–1870* (1978).

Some of the disruptive effects of economic change are addressed in Karen Haltunen, *Confidence Men and Painted Women: A Study of Middle-Class Culture in America, 1830–1870* (1982); W. J. Rorabaugh, *The Alcoholic Republic: An American Tradition* (1979); and Christine Stansell, *City of Women: Sex and Class in New York, 1789–1860* (1986). For a stimulating discussion of the effects of markets and manufacturing on the countryside, see Christopher Clark, *The Roots of Rural Capitalism: Western Massachusetts, 1789–1860* (1990). See also Suzanne Lebsock, *The Free Women of Petersburg* (1987).

The concept of the business class is developed in Michael Katz et al., *The Social Organization of Early Industrial Capitalism* (1982). Surveys of reform movements closely linked to the Second Great Awakening include Alice F. Tyler, *Freedom's Ferment* (1944), and Ronald G. Walters, *American Reformers, 1815–1860* (1978). Studies of religious evangelism and social reform are particularly abundant for New York State. See Paul E. Johnson, *A Shopkeeper's Millennium: Society and Revivals in Rochester, New York, 1815–1837* (1978), and Mary Ryan, *Cradle of the Middle Class: The Family in Oneida County, New York, 1790–1865* (1981). On the relationship between religion and labor protest, see Jama Lazerow, *Religion and the Working Class in Antebellum America* (1996). For more general studies of religious ferment in the early republic, see John Butler, *Awash in a Sea of Faith: Christianizing the American People* (1990), and R. Lawrence Moore, *Selling God: American Religion in the Marketplace of Culture* (1994).

On European immigration, consult Philip Taylor, *The Distant Magnet: European Immigration to the U.S.A.* (1971), and Oscar Handlin, *Boston's Immigrants: A Study in Acculturation* (1979). See also Kathleen Neils Conzen, *Immigrant Milwaukee, 1836–1860* (1976), and Bruce Laurie, *Working People in Philadelphia, 1800–1850* (1980).

Chapter 11

A Democratic Revolution,

1820–1844

The Rise of Popular Politics, 1820–1829

The Decline of the Notables and the Ascent of Parties

The Election of 1824

The Presidency of John Quincy Adams, 1825–1829

Adams and the Jacksonians in the Election of 1828

The Presidency of Andrew Jackson, 1829–1837

Jackson's Agenda: Patronage and Policy

The Tariff and Nullification

The Bank War

Indian Removal

The Jacksonian Legacy

Class, Culture, and the Second Party System

The Whigs and Their Outlook

Labor Politics and the Depression of 1837–1843

"Tippecanoe and Tyler Too!"

"I FEEL THAT I belong to a later age," President Martin Van Buren declared in 1837 in his inaugural address, depicting himself as a mere "public servant" who was about to tread "in the footsteps of the illustrious men" who had founded the republic and served as its first presidents. As Van Buren knew all too well, the nation had changed dramatically in many ways over the previous half-century. The economic revolution had transformed the lives of millions of Americans, disrupting the traditional society in which most white people had lived and worked together on family farms and in close-knit communities. But geographical expansion and economic change pushed many people out of those intimate settings and divided society along class lines. The new world was very different from that of the founding generation: less predictable, less personal, and far more complicated.

To address the problems of the new society, Americans turned not only to evangelical religion but also to democratic politics. In the early years of the nation the slogan had been *republicanism*, that is, rule by property-owning "men of TALENTS and VIRTUE," as one Patriot put it. By the 1820s the watchword had become *democracy*, that is, power exercised by party politicians elected by the people as a whole. "That the majority should govern was a fundamental maxim in all free governments," Van Buren had declared in 1821, and he and other middle-class professional politicians gradually came to dominate American political life. By uniting Americans from different classes and regions, the new democratic political parties that they created held together an increasingly fragmented social order.

Presidential Inauguration of William Henry Harrison, March 4, 1841 (detail)
After being sworn into office, President Harrison stands on the steps of the U.S. Capitol building reviewing a parade of military units. Many women attended the ceremony, despite the fact that they could not vote, because the Whig Party encouraged them to support its policies.
Anne S. K. Brown Military Collection, Brown University.

As the stakes of national politics increased, so also did the scale of conflict. Between 1820 and 1844 the nation was rocked by a series of bitter disputes over government policy—internal improvements, tariffs, banks, and Indian removal. Informing all these controversies were far-reaching debates over the proper powers of the national government and, following the election of Andrew Jackson, over those of the president as well. During these years the American people tested—and redefined—the character of their nation's republican constitutional order.

The Rise of Popular Politics, 1820–1829

★

Expansion of the franchise was the most dramatic expression of the democratic revolution. Beginning in the late 1810s, one state after another revised its constitution to remove property qualifications for voting, giving ordinary farmers and wage earners the franchise and laying the foundation for the rise of mass politics. Regardless of its flaws—for women, most African Americans, and Indians were largely excluded from the political arena—the emerging American political system was the most democratic in the world; nowhere else did ordinary men have so much political power.

The Decline of the Notables and the Ascent of Parties

In the former agricultural society, local notables—northern landlords, slaveowning planters, and seaport merchants—controlled the political system. As former Supreme Court Chief Justice John Jay noted approvingly in 1810, "Those who own the country are the most fit persons to participate in the government of it." The notables dominated local elections by building up an "interest": lending money to small farmers, buying supplies from storekeepers and artisans, and treating their workers or tenants to rum at election time. An outlay of £5 for refreshments, an experienced poll watcher told an office seeker, "may produce about 100 votes." As Martin Van Buren, whose father was an ordinary tavern keeper, knew from personal experience, this gentry-dominated system excluded men of modest means, who lacked land, wealth, and "the aid of powerful family connections."

The main assault on the old deferential order came in the newly settled states of the Midwest. As smallholding farmers and ambitious laborers settled the trans-Appalachian region, they broke free of control by the gentry; "no white man or woman will bear being called a servant," reported a traveler in Ohio. The constitutions of the new states of Indiana (admitted to the Union in 1816), Illinois (1818), and Alabama (1819) reflected this egalitarian ethic by allowing all white men who paid taxes to vote. Armed with the vote, ordinary citizens usually elected middling men to local and state offices. A well-to-do migrant in Illinois was surprised to find that his plowman "was a colonel of militia, and a member of the legislature." Once in public office, men from modest backgrounds responded to the demands of their constituents by restricting imprisonment for debt, keeping taxes low, and making it easier for farmers to claim "squatters' rights" to unoccupied land.

To deter migration to the Midwest and unrest at home, the elites in most eastern states grudgingly accepted a broader franchise. Responding to reformers who condemned property qualifications as a "tyranny" that endowed "one class of men with privileges which are denied to another," Maryland legislators extended the vote to all adult men in 1810; by the 1830s five other states—New York, Kentucky, South Carolina, Maine, and Missouri—had followed suit (see Map 9.1, p. 282). By then only a few states—North Carolina, Virginia, and Rhode Island—required the ownership of freehold property for voting. In all the others, most white men could vote because they either paid taxes or served in the militia.

Although every state denied women the franchise and the right to hold office, and many states limited the political rights of free African American men, the dramatic loosening of suffrage restrictions ushered in the era of democratic politics. The United States now boasted a system of representative government that was very different from that in all European states, where voting was still restricted to a small minority of the adult population; even after the British Reform Bill of 1832, only 900,000 out of 6 million men—a mere 15 percent—had the right to vote.

Popular pressure also brought major revisions in the state constitutions of Connecticut, Massachusetts, and New York. Between 1818 and 1821 popularly elected conventions in those states wrote new charters that reapportioned legislatures on the basis of population—giving more votes to growing cities and towns—and instituted more democratic forms of local government, such as the *election* rather than the *appointment* of judges and justices of the peace.

The politics of democracy was more complex and contentious than the politics of deference. Newly powerful entrepreneurs and speculators demanded governmental assistance and protection for their business enterprises, and used their wealth to elect friendly candidates and lobby for favorable legislation. Financiers sought state charters for their banking enterprises and opposed limits on interest rates; land speculators petitioned for roads and canals to enhance the value of their holdings and demanded the eviction of squatters. Other Americans entered the political arena for religious and cultural reasons. In 1828 evangelical Presbyterians in Utica, New York, campaigned for town ordinances to restrict secular activities on Sunday; in response, a member of the local Universalist church (a free-thinking Protestant denomination) attacked this effort at coercive reform, calling for "Religious Liberty."

The rise of the political party allowed the voices of such ordinary voters to be heard. Political "factions" and "parties" had been condemned as antirepublican by the nation's founders and were not mentioned in state constitutions or the federal constitution of 1787. But as the power of notables declined, the political party emerged as the central element in the American system of government. The new parties were disciplined organizations run by professional politicians from middle-class backgrounds, especially lawyers and journalists. To some observers, they resembled the mechanical innovations of the Industrial Revolution, political "machines" that, like a well-designed textile loom, wove the diverse threads of social groups and economic interests into an elaborate tapestry—a coherent legislative program.

Martin Van Buren of New York was the chief architect—and advocate—of the emerging system of party government. Between 1817 and 1821 Van Buren created the first statewide political machine, the Albany Regency; then, as a senator in Congress during the mid-1820s, the "Little Magician" organized the first nationwide political party, the Jacksonian Democrats. In each case Van Buren repudiated republican principles that disparaged political parties as dangerous to the commonwealth. Indeed, he maintained that the opposite was true. "All men of sense know that political parties are inseparable from free government," Van Buren argued, because they checked the government's "disposition to abuse power . . . [and] the passions, the ambition, and the usurpations of individuals." To staff his party Van Buren recruited ambitious lawyers and journalists from middling backgrounds, men who were part of a new breed of bourgeois Americans pursuing careers "open to talent" (rather than those dependent on aristocratic patronage).

One key to Van Buren's success as a politician was his systematic use of the *Albany Argus* and other newspapers to promote a *platform*—a statement of party principles—and drum up the vote to support it. *Patronage* was even more important, for the awarding of state jobs gave Van Buren a greater "interest" than any landed aristocrat could claim—some 6,000 appointments to the legal bureaucracy of New York (judges, justices of the peace, sheriffs, deed commissioners, and coroners), carrying salaries and fees worth $1 million. Finally, Van Buren insisted on party *discipline*, requiring state legislators to follow the majority decisions of a party meet-

ing, or *caucus*. On one crucial occasion, Van Buren pleaded with seventeen Republicans to "magnanimously sacrifice individual preferences for the general good," and rewarded their loyalty with patronage and a formal banquet at which, one observer wrote, they were treated with "something approaching divine honors."

The Election of 1824

The advance of political democracy disrupted the traditional system of national politics that had been managed by leading notables. By the 1820s the aristocratic Federalist Party had virtually disappeared, and the Republican Party had broken up into competing factions. As the election of 1824 approached, no fewer than five candidates, all calling themselves Republicans, campaigned for the presidency. Three were veterans of President James Monroe's cabinet: Secretary of State John Quincy Adams, the son of John Adams; Secretary of War John C. Calhoun; and Secretary of the Treasury William H. Crawford. The fourth candidate was Henry Clay from Kentucky, the influential Speaker of the House of Representatives, and the fifth was General Andrew Jackson, now a senator from Tennessee.

Although Crawford had been selected as the "official" nominee by a poorly attended caucus of the Republicans in Congress, the other candidates refused to accept that result. Instead, they introduced competition to national politics by seeking support among ordinary voters in the various states. Thanks to democratic reforms, eighteen of the twenty-four states now held popular elections (rather than relying on a vote of the state legislature) to choose members of the electoral college, the body charged with selecting the president. As a result, in three-quarters of the states the struggle for the presidency became literally a "popularity" contest that would be won by the candidate who commanded the most support among the voters and thus among the electors.

The battle was closely fought. Secretary of State John Quincy Adams enjoyed national recognition, having negotiated the acquisition of Florida, resolved boundary disputes with Spanish Mexico and British Canada, and outlined a new foreign policy (which, thirty years later, became known as the Monroe Doctrine). In an address to Congress in 1823, Monroe, at Adams's behest, had warned Spain and other European powers not to interfere in the affairs of the former Spanish colonies in Latin America that had revolted and established independent republics. Indeed, Monroe declared that the American continents were not "subject for further colonization" by the nations of Europe. In return, Adams and Monroe reiterated the policy of the United States "not to interfere in the internal concerns" of European nations. Such diplomatic successes—and his lineage—made Adams a formidable candidate.

For his part, Henry Clay framed his candidacy around domestic issues. During his many years in Congress, Clay had gradually articulated a program known as the American System, a plan for economic development in which the national government would use the Second Bank of the United States—the nationally chartered bank that held the government's funds—to regulate state banks and guide the nation's financial affairs, and spend tariff revenues to subsidize internal improvements such as roads and canals. Because it called for an activist central government, Clay's program had evoked political controversy in Congress and various states, especially in Virginia and the South. A strong contingent of "Old Republicans," claiming to be heirs of the political principles of Thomas Jefferson, attacked the American System as a danger to the authority and powers of the state governments. William Crawford of Georgia, one of the most influential of the Old Republicans, promised strong support for the rights of the states, a position that enhanced his popularity in his native South. Recognizing Crawford's strength in his home region, John C. Calhoun of South Carolina switched to the vice-presidential race and endorsed Andrew Jackson for the presidency.

As the hero of the Battle of New Orleans, nicknamed "Old Hickory" by the press (after the toughest American hardwood tree), Jackson embodied the nationalistic pride that had swelled in the wake of the War of 1812. Born in the Carolina backcountry, Jackson had settled in Nashville, Tennessee, where he had formed ties to influential families through his marriage and his career as an attorney, cotton planter, and slaveowner. Jackson's reputation as a man of civic virtue and, as one newspaper editor put it, "plain solid *republican utility*" appealed to many voters, and his rise from common origins fit the tenor of the new democratic age. Nominated for the presidency by the Tennessee legislature, Jackson did not campaign actively but soon commanded nationwide attention. His supporters vigorously promoted him as a man of integrity who would root out corruption and preserve American freedom.

The results of the election surprised many political leaders, who had predicted a close contest among Adams, Clay, and Crawford. When the electoral college met, Jackson received 99 votes; Adams, 84; Crawford, who had suffered a stroke during the campaign, 41; and Clay, 37 (Map 11.1). In such cases, with no candidate

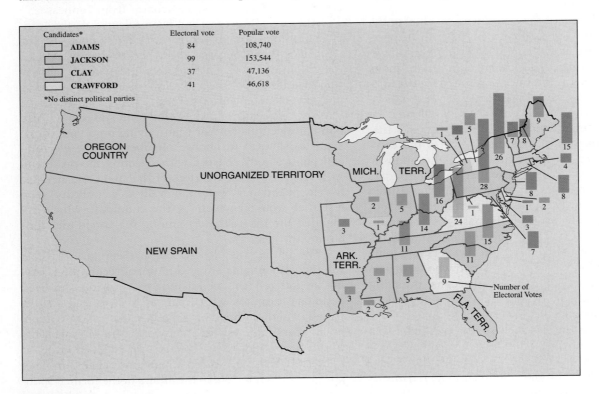

MAP 11.1
The Election of 1824
This map clearly shows the importance of regional ties in the election of 1824. John Quincy Adams captured every electoral vote in New England and most of those in New York. Henry Clay carried Ohio and Kentucky, the two most populous western states, and William Crawford garnered most of his votes in the South. Only Andrew Jackson claimed a national constituency, winning Pennsylvania and New Jersey in the East, Indiana and Illinois in the Midwest, and most of the southern states. In this last national election of the predemocratic era, only 356,000 Americans voted, about 27 percent of the eligible electorate.

having received an absolute majority of electoral votes, the Constitution specifies that the House of Representatives choose the president from among the three leading contenders. The congressional allies of Jackson, Adams, and the incapacitated Crawford would decide the issue.

This constitutionally mandated process hurt Jackson's chances because many congressmen were horrified at the thought of a rough-hewn westerner and blunt general in the White House. Clay in particular feared Jackson, considering him a "military chieftain" and—because of Old Hickory's iron will and determination—a potential tyrant. Personally out of the race, Clay resolved to use his powers as Speaker to thwart Jackson's election. By the time the House met in February 1825, Clay had put together a coalition of representatives from New England and the Ohio Valley that voted Adams into the presidency. Adams immediately showed his gratitude by appointing Clay secretary of state, the traditional stepping-stone to the highest office.

Clay's appointment was a fatal mistake for both men. Calhoun accused Adams of thwarting the will of the people by using "the power and patronage of the Executive" to select his successor. It was, he wrote, "the most dangerous stab, which the liberty of this country has yet received." Jackson's supporters in Congress, their numbers increased by the election results, condemned Clay, claiming that Adams appointed him secretary not out of gratitude but as part of a "corrupt bargain" that gave Adams the presidency. They vowed that Clay would never become president. Soon Senator Martin Van Buren joined the Jacksonians and used his formidable political skills to oppose the policies advanced by Adams and Clay.

The Presidency of John Quincy Adams, 1825–1829

As president, Adams called for bold leadership. "The moral purpose of the Creator," he told Congress, was to use the president and every other public official to "improve the conditions of himself and his fellow men." To that end, Adams advocated legislation to promote "the cultivation of the mechanic and the elegant arts, the advancement of literature and the progress of science." He called for the establishment of a national university in Washington, extensive scientific explorations in the Far West, and the adoption of a uniform standard of weights and measures. Most important, the president embraced key elements of Clay's American System: (1) a protective tariff to stimulate manufacturing, (2) federally subsidized internal improvements (roads and canals) to aid commerce, and (3) continued support for the Second Bank of the United States.

Adams's policies favored his most loyal supporters—the business elite of the Northeast—and assisted entrepreneurs and commercial farmers in the Midwest. However, they won little support among the planters of the South, who opposed tariffs, and among smallholding farmers, who feared powerful banks. Writing from his deathbed in 1826, Thomas Jefferson spoke for these agriculturalists, condemning Adams for promoting "a single and splendid government of [a monied] aristocracy . . . riding and ruling over the plundered ploughman and beggared yeomanry."

Other politicians objected to the American System on constitutional grounds. In 1817 President Madison had vetoed the Bonus Bill sponsored by Calhoun and Clay. Madison declared that the bill, which would have used federal funds to build roads, harbors, lighthouses, and other projects in various states, exceeded the national government's constitutional powers. Adams's

John Quincy Adams (1767–1848)
This famous daguerreotype of John Quincy Adams, taken about 1843 by Philip Haas, conveys his rigid personality and high moral standards, attributes that hindered his effectiveness as president but contributed to his success as an antislavery congressman from Massachusetts in the 1830s and 40s. Metropolitan Museum of Art. Gift of I. N. Phelps Stokes, Edward S. Hawes, Alice Mary Hawes, Marion Augusta Hawes.

program was even more ambitious and raised similar constitutional issues. Moreover, there was little public support for an active national government; most politically aware Americans believed that the state governments should assume the primary responsibility for economic development. Declaring his allegiance on "Constitutional questions . . . with the doctrines of the Jefferson School," Martin Van Buren joined with the Old Republicans in voting against federal subsidies for roads and canals, and proposed constitutional amendments to limit them. A hostile Congress defeated most of Adams's proposals, approving only a few navigation improvements and a short extension of the National Road from Wheeling, Virginia, into Ohio.

The most far-reaching battle of the Adams administration, however, was fought over tariffs. In 1824, Congress had raised the tariffs imposed on various imported manufactures, such as iron goods and woolen and cotton cloth, nearly doubling the tax from 20 to 35 percent of the goods' value. And Adams and Clay wanted even higher protective duties to safeguard the profits of eastern factory owners and the jobs of the workers.

When Van Buren and his Jacksonian allies took control of Congress after the 1826 elections, they also supported higher tariffs, but on different imports and for different reasons. By raising tariffs on raw materials and agricultural imports, they hoped to help their supporters, many of whom were smallholding farmers. Indeed, Van Buren's main objective was to bolster Jackson's prospects among the iron producers and farmers of the Middle Atlantic states, which he needed to carry in the 1828 election. The tariff had become a prisoner of politics. "I fear this tariff thing," warned Thomas Cooper of South Carolina, who strongly opposed higher import duties; "by some strange mechanical contrivance . . . it will be changed into a machine for manufacturing Presidents, instead of broadcloths, and bed blankets."

Disregarding southern opposition, northern Jacksonians joined forces with New England textile manufacturers to enact the Tariff of 1828, which raised duties on raw materials *and* manufactures. To win support for Jackson in New York, Pennsylvania, Ohio, and Kentucky, Van Buren and his allies proposed tariffs on iron, flax, hemp, lead, molasses, and raw wool. But to muster a majority in Congress to vote for those duties—which helped farmers, miners, and iron workers—they had to seek the support of New England representatives, who wanted to protect the domestic textile industry. These New Englanders demanded—and secured—a duty that added about 50 percent to the cost of imported cloth.

The new tariff enraged politicians and planters from the South, which gained nothing from the new

A CARTOON COMPARING CONDITIONS UNDER FREE TRADE AND PROTECTIVE TARIFF
From "The United States Weekly Telegram," November 5, 1832.

The "Tariff of Abominations"
Political cartoons were widely used in eighteenth-century England and became popular in the United States during the political battles of the First Party System (1794–1815). By the 1820s cartoons were an important part of American political life, published on a daily basis in party-subsidized newspapers. This cartoon of 1828 attacks the new tariff as hostile to the interests and prosperity of the South. The gaunt figure on the left represents a southern planter, oppressed by the weight of the tariff, while the northern textile manufacturer on the right has grown stout by feasting on the bounty of protection.
Corbis-Bettmann.

legislation. As the world's cheapest producer of raw cotton, the South did not need a tariff to protect its main industry, and by raising the price of British manufactures, the new legislation cost southern planters about $100 million a year. To obtain cloth, plows, and other manufactured goods, they would now have to buy either high-cost American products, thereby enriching northeastern businesses and workers, or highly taxed British goods, thereby increasing tariff revenues and, in effect, placing the cost of the national government on the South. In either event, they were the losers and vented their anger in righteous indignation. The new legislation was "little less than legalized pillage," declared an Alabama legislator; with equal fervor other southern politicians denounced the new legislation as the "Tariff of Abominations."

Adams and the Jacksonians in the Election of 1828

Despite the role played by Van Buren and other Jacksonians in enacting the tariff, most southerners did not blame their woes on Jackson. Rather, they attacked

Adams both because of his support for higher tariffs and because of his position on another important issue: the land rights of native Americans in Georgia and other southern states. In 1825 U.S. commissioners and a faction of the Creek people had concluded a treaty that relinquished Creek control over their remaining lands in Georgia. When the Creek National Council repudiated the treaty as fraudulent, Adams supported the Indians' position and ordered new negotiations. In response, Governor George M. Troup vowed to take the lands by force. Defying Adams's assertion of federal jurisdiction over Indian lands and affairs, Troup attacked the president as a "public enemy . . . the unblushing ally of the savages." Confronted by Georgia's resistance and widespread sentiment in Congress to extinguish Creek land titles, Adams backed down. By 1828 most Creeks had left the state. Adams had alienated white planters without protecting native American land rights.

Adams's failure in this and other political battles stemmed in part from his deficiencies as a practical politician. As the son of a Federalist president and as a notable himself, John Quincy had not been prepared by history or personal experience for the competitive democratic politics of the 1820s. As president, he acted the part of an aristocrat: aloof, haughty, paternalistic. When Congress rejected his activist economic policies, Adams lashed out at his opponents, questioning the wisdom of the people and advising elected officials not to be "palsied by the will of our constituents." Ignoring his waning popularity, the president failed to use patronage to reward his supporters; indeed, he allowed hostile politicians to keep their appointed positions as long as they were competent. As the election of 1828 approached, Adams did not mount a full-scale campaign. Rather than "run" for reelection, he "stood" for it, expecting voters to acknowledge his merit and accomplishments. As he told supporters, "If my country wants my services, she must ask for them."

Martin Van Buren and the professional politicians handling Jackson's campaign had no reservations about running for office. Beginning in 1827, Van Buren devised the first national campaign organization. By allying with leading Virginia politicians, he re-created the old Jeffersonian coalition, uniting farmers and artisans (the "plain Republicans of the North") with the southern slaveowners who had voted Jefferson, Madison, and Monroe into the presidency. When Calhoun, Jackson's semiofficial running mate, brought his South Carolina allies into Van Buren's party, it dominated the South. And Jackson's close friends in Tennessee rallied voters there and in Kentucky to the cause.

With strong direction from above, state leaders orchestrated a newspaper campaign (in New York, fifty

Van Burenite newspapers declared for Jackson on the same day) and mobilized local groups to run mass meetings, torchlight parades, and barbecues to excite public interest. Jackson's supporters attacked Adams for the "corrupt bargain" with Clay and, in an early example of "negative" campaigning, made the sensational (but untrue) charge that as minister to Russia, Adams had tried to persuade an American girl to become the mistress of the tsar. In contrast, they exalted Jackson's virtue, celebrating his frontier origins and rise to wealth and fame without the advantages of influential parents, extensive education, or political intrigue: to his supporters Old Hickory was a "natural" aristocrat, a self-made man.

Initially the Jacksonians called themselves Democratic-Republicans, but as the campaign wore on, they became Democrats. The name conveyed their message. The republic, Jacksonians charged, had been corrupted by "special privilege," which they would root out and replace by rule of the majority—the democracy. "Equality among the people in the rights conferred by government," Jackson would declare, was the "great radical principle of freedom."

Jackson's message appealed to a variety of social groups. His hostility to special privileges for business corporations and to Clay's American System won support among farmers and small property holders who resented state subsidies to those who were rich or had political clout. Jackson's mistrust of banks and "monied aristocrats" drew votes from urban workers and artisans who felt threatened by industrialization and the spread of the market system. In the Southeast and Midwest, Old Hickory's well-known hostility toward native Americans reassured white farmers who wanted to force Indians to leave their ancestral lands and move to the West. On the controversial Tariff of 1828, Jackson benefited from the financial boost it gave to Pennsylvania iron workers and western farmers; at the same time, he declared his support for a "judicious" tariff, appealing for votes in the South by suggesting that the existing rates were too high.

The Democratic strategy of seeking votes from a wide variety of social and economic groups worked to perfection. In 1824, only about one-fourth of the eligible electorate had voted; in 1828, more than half went to the polls, and they voted overwhelmingly for Jackson (Map 11.2 and Figure 11.1). The senator from Tennessee received 178 of 261 electoral votes, becoming the first president to be elected from the trans-Appalachian West, indeed from any state other than Virginia and Massachusetts. The massive outpouring of popular support for Jackson frightened the northern business elite. When the new president came to Washington, warned former Federalist Daniel Webster, he would "bring a breeze with him. Which way it will

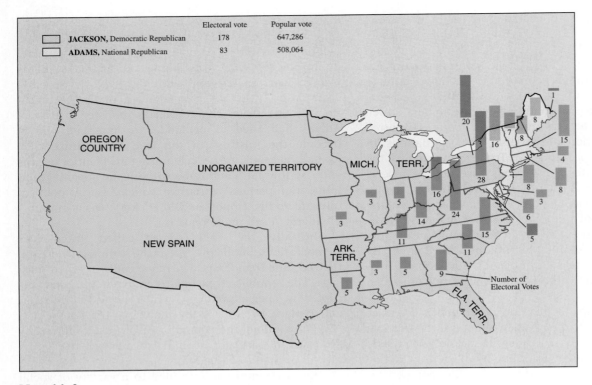

MAP 11.2
The Election of 1828
As in the election of 1824, John Quincy Adams captured the electoral votes of New England and won some support in the mid-Atlantic states. However, Andrew Jackson dominated the voting in every other state and won a resounding victory in the electoral college. Nearly 1.2 million American men cast ballots in 1828, three times the number who went to the polls just four years before.

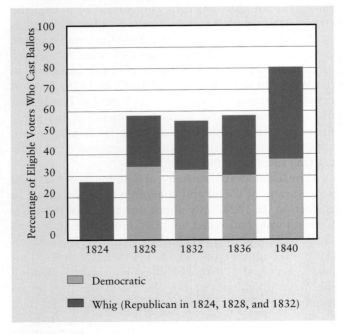

FIGURE 11.1
Changes in Voting Patterns, 1824–1840
With the return of two-party competition, voter participation soared in the critical presidential elections of 1828 and 1840.

blow, I cannot tell. . . . My *fear* is stronger than my *hope.*" Watching an unruly crowd clamber over the elegant furniture in the White House to shake the hand of the newly inaugurated president, Supreme Court Justice Joseph Story lamented that "the reign of King 'Mob' seemed triumphant" (see American Voices, "Margaret Bayard Smith: Republican Majesty and Mobs," p. 355).

The Presidency of Andrew Jackson, 1829–1837

Political democracy—a broad franchise, a disciplined political party, and policies tailored to specific social groups—had carried Andrew Jackson to the presidency. Jackson used that popular mandate to enhance his personal authority and the power of the chief executive. Invoking the sovereignty of the people, he attacked Clay's American System and proposed a different—and much more limited—role for national government.

MARGARET BAYARD SMITH
Republican Majesty and Mobs

──────★──────

As Andrew Jackson ascended to the presidency in 1829, he and his followers were seen by many observers as threats to the established political and social system because they adopted democratic rhetoric and questioned the legitimacy of a powerful central government. Writing to her son, the Washington socialite Margaret Bayard Smith revealed a mixture of pride and anxiety about the coming of popular democracy.

The inauguration . . . was one grand whole—an imposing and majestic spectacle. . . . Thousands and thousands of people, without distinction of rank, collected in an immense mass around the Capitol, silent, orderly, and tranquil, with their eyes fixed on the front of the Capitol, waiting the appearance of the president. . . . The door from the Rotunda opens, preceded by the marshall surrounded by the judges of the Supreme Court, the old man [President Jackson] with his grey hair, that crown of glory, advances, bows to the people, who greet him with a shout that rends the air. The cannon, from the heights around from Alexandria and Fort Washington, proclaim the [oath of office] he has taken and all the hills around reverberate the sound. It was grand; it was sublime! An almost breathless silence succeeded and the multitude was still—listening to catch the sound of his voice, though it was so low as to be heard only by those nearest to him.

After reading his speech, the oath was administered to him by the chief justice. The marshall presented the Bible. The president took it from his hand, pressed his lips to it, laid it reverently down, then bowed again to the people. Yes, to the people in all their majesty—and had the spectacle closed here, even Europeans must have acknowledged that a free people, collected in their might, silent and tranquil, restrained solely by a moral power, without a shadow around of military force, was majesty, rising to sublimity, and far surpassing the majesty of kings and princes, surrounded with armies and glittering in gold. . . .

[But at the White House reception that followed,] what a scene did we witness!! The *majesty of the people* had disappeared, and [instead] a rabble, a mob . . . scrambling, fighting, romping . . . [crowded around] the president, [who,] after having literally been nearly pressed to death . . . escaped to his lodgings at Gadsby's. Cut glass and bone china to the amount of several thousand dollars had been broken in the struggle to get refreshments. . . . Ladies fainted, men were seen with bloody noses. . . . Ladies and gentlemen only had been expected at this [reception], not the people *en masse*. . . . But it was the people's day, and the people's president. . . .

God grant the people do not put down all rule and rulers. I fear . . . as they have been found in all ages and countries where they get power in their hands, that of all tyrants, they are the most ferocious, cruel, and despotic. The . . . rabble in the president's house brought to my mind descriptions I had read of the mobs in the Tuileries and at Versailles [during the French Revolution].

──────────

Source: M. B. Smith to J. B. H. Smith, March 1829, Smith Family Correspondence, Library of Congress, in Linda R. Monk, ed., *Ordinary Americans: U.S. History through the Eyes of Ordinary People* (Alexandria, VA: Close-Up Foundation, 1993), 49–50.

Jackson's Agenda: Patronage and Policy

To decide policy, Jackson relied primarily on an informal group of advisors, his so-called Kitchen Cabinet. Its most influential members were Francis Preston Blair of Kentucky, who edited the *Washington Globe*, the main newspaper of the Democratic Party; Amos Kendall, also from Kentucky, a Treasury department official who helped Jackson write many of his state papers; Roger B. Taney of Maryland, who became attorney general and then Chief Justice of the Supreme Court; and, most influential of all, Secretary of State Martin Van Buren.

Following Van Buren's practice in New York, Jackson used patronage to create a loyal and disciplined party. He insisted on rotation in office: when a new administration came to power, Jackson demanded that bureaucrats appointed by its predecessor leave government service and return "to making a living as other people do." Dismissing the argument that forced rotation would cause government service to suffer from lack of administrative expertise, Jackson maintained that most public duties were "so plain and simple that men of intelligence may readily qualify themselves for their performance." William L. Marcy, a New York Jacksonian, explained the rationale of rotation more bluntly, telling a Senate committee that government jobs were like the spoils of war and that there was "nothing wrong in the rule that to the VICTOR belong the spoils of the ENEMY." Using the policy of rotation as a *spoils system*, Jackson dispensed government jobs to loyal Democrats and to friends of influential members of Congress, thereby enhancing support for his legislative program. But to ensure the smooth operation of government offices, he also protected some talented administrators who had no political connections.

Jackson's main priority was policy, not patronage. He wanted to block any legislation that would further Clay's American System and to overthrow those laws that had already expanded the powers of the national government. Responding to western supporters who argued that the "voice of the people" called for "economy in the expenditures of the Government," Jackson rejected federal support for most internal improvements. In 1830 he vetoed a bill that would have extended the National Road from Maysville, Kentucky (on its border with Ohio), to Lexington, Kentucky, arguing that it was "an infringement of the reserved powers of states." Then Jackson turned his attention to two other parts of the American System: protective tariffs and the national bank. Those issues were so complex and politically charged that it took years of effort—and great political skill—for Jackson to emerge triumphant, but by the end of his two terms in office, the American System lay in disarray.

The Tariff and Nullification

The Tariff of 1828 had helped Jackson win the presidency, but it saddled him with a serious political crisis. The fiercest opposition to the tariff was in South Carolina, where slaveowners suffered from chronic insecurity. South Carolina was the only state with an African American majority—in 1830 blacks constituted 56 percent of the total population and 90 percent of the residents of many lowland counties—which made it more like the West Indian islands of Jamaica or Barbados than the rest of the South.

Like their counterparts in the West Indies, South Carolina planters had long lived in fear of slave rebellions. By the late 1820s, they were also worried about the forced abolition of slavery. The British Parliament was about to end slavery in the West Indies (and it did so in August 1833, paying compensation to

President Andrew Jackson, 1830
The new president came to Washington with a well-deserved reputation as an aggressive Indian fighter and dangerous military chieftain. Some of Jackson's intensity shows through in this lithograph by Albert Newsam, after an original painting by William James Hubard, but in this "official" portrait Jackson appears "presidential"—his dress and posture creating an image of a calm and deliberate statesman. Subsequent events would show that Jackson had not lost his hard-edged personality.
Library of Congress.

the slaveowners), and southern planters worried that the U.S. government might do the same. To prevent that, South Carolina's leaders wanted to limit the power of the federal government and chose the (already controversial) tariff as their target.

The Crisis of 1832. The conflict over tariffs escalated in July 1832, when Congress ignored southern demands to repeal the Tariff of Abominations and enacted new tariff legislation that retained high duties on cloth and iron. Arguing that this policy unfairly aided the North at the expense of the South, leading planters and politicians in South Carolina called a state convention, which on November 24 boldly adopted an Ordinance of Nullification. The ordinance declared the

Fashion and Fear in South Carolina, c. 1831
This painting, executed by South Carolina artist S. Barnard around the time of the nullification crisis, shows fashionably dressed whites strolling along the East Battery of Charleston. To the left, two African Americans resort to fisticuffs, while other blacks sit and watch. To the right stand a pack of dogs, perhaps indicating the artist's fear of an uprising by enslaved blacks, who formed a majority of the state's population.
Yale University Art Gallery.

tariffs of 1828 and 1832 null and void; forbade the collection of those duties in the state after February 1, 1833; and threatened secession from the Union if the federal government tried to collect them.

South Carolina's act of nullification rested on the constitutional arguments developed in a tract published in 1828, *The South Carolina Exposition and Protest.* Written anonymously by Vice-President Calhoun, a native of that state, the *Exposition* challenged the proposition that majority rule lay at the heart of republican government. "Constitutional government and the government of a majority are utterly incompatible," Calhoun wrote. "An unchecked majority is a despotism," he continued, declaring that a government "will be permanent in proportion to the number, complexity, and efficiency of the checks, by which its powers are controlled."

The Philadelphia Convention of 1787 had addressed these very issues. To limit the power of the

new national government, it required the passage of legislation by both houses of Congress, gave a veto power to the president, and provided a broad scope to the judicial power of the Supreme Court. Calhoun rejected the founders' "checks and balances" as inadequate, in part because the appearance of party discipline and pronounced sectional differences over policy had increased the possibility of controversial—and potentially oppressive—legislation.

To devise a mechanism by which to check congressional majorities, Calhoun turned to the arguments advanced by the Antifederalists of the 1780s and by Jefferson and Madison in the Kentucky and Virginia resolutions of 1798. Developing a constitutional theory that advocates of states' rights would use well into the twentieth century, Calhoun maintained that sovereignty resided not in the American people *as a whole* but in citizens acting *through their state governments.* Consequently, he argued that a state convention could determine that a congressional law was unconstitutional and declare it null and void within the state's borders. According to Calhoun, the law would remain nullified unless three-fourths of the other states ratified an amendment assigning Congress the power in question; even then the dissident state could secede from the republic.

Jackson's Defense of the Union. In 1830 Calhoun's arguments on the issue of states' rights sparked a long Senate debate over the nature of the Union between Robert Y. Hayne of South Carolina and Daniel Webster of Massachusetts. The debate arose when Hayne, protesting a resolution by Senator Samuel A. Foot of Connecticut to restrict western land sales, suggested that the South and the West join forces to oppose the land and tariff policies that had been enacted because of the political and economic power of the Northeast. Defending the Northeast and the primacy of national laws, Webster challenged Hayne to debate the issue of states' rights. Hayne responded with the arguments of the *Exposition,* and Calhoun—widely rumored to be its author—watched approvingly. Often looking directly at Calhoun, Webster replied with a stirring defense of national power, ending with the resounding appeal: "Liberty *and* Union, now and forever, one and inseparable." Webster's powerful address, known as his "Second Reply to Hayne," immediately became famous and circulated widely among those who favored a strong national government.

Although Jackson had come into office determined to limit the reach of national legislation, he was also a staunch supporter of the Union. When the *Exposition* first appeared, Jackson had dismissed its arguments out of hand. Now, in April 1830, he sided with Webster and confronted Calhoun at a banquet celebrating Jefferson's birthday. While opening the formal toasts, Jackson looked squarely at his vice-president and declared: "Our Federal Union—*it must be preserved.*" Not to be outdone, Calhoun rose to deliver the second toast, the glass trembling in his hand: "The Union—next to our liberty the most dear! May we remember that it can only be preserved by respecting the rights of the states and distributing equally the benefits and burdens of the Union."

In May 1832, after Calhoun had admitted his authorship of the *Exposition,* Jackson dropped him as the Democrats' candidate for vice-president. The newly reelected president responded to South Carolina's Nullification Ordinance of November 1832 in an equally forthright manner. "Disunion by armed force is *treason,*" Jackson declared in December. Appealing to patriotism, the president asserted that nullification violated the Constitution and was *"unauthorized by its spirit, inconsistent with every principle on which it is founded, and destructive of the great object for which it was formed."* Given Jackson's vigorous rejection of his doctrines, Calhoun resigned as vice-president three months before his term expired and took up the defense of his state from the floor of the Senate, to which he was immediately appointed by the South Carolina legislature.

In defending the Union, Jackson had not only the authority of his office and the power of the Democratic Party behind him but also the weight of public opinion. Regardless of their complaints about the tariff or other policies, most Americans supported the governmental institutions created by the constitution of 1787 and basked in the growing size and prosperity of their national republic. Even in the South no other state supported nullification, in part because most planters did not perceive an imminent threat to slavery and were strong supporters of President Jackson. At Jackson's request, Congress enacted a Force Bill in March 1833 that authorized the president to use the army and navy to compel obedience to national laws.

Both to reward his southern supporters and to meet their long-expressed requests for tariff relief, the president also proposed new legislation providing for a reduction in duties. Under the terms of the Tariff Act of 1833, import taxes would gradually be cut; by 1842 they would revert to the modest levels set in 1816, an outcome that would not only please the South but also advance Jackson's efforts to destroy Clay's American System.

The compromise worked. Having saved face on the tariff issue, the South Carolina convention rescinded its nullification of the tariff (while defiantly nullifying the now-meaningless Force Bill). Jackson was satisfied. He had established the principle that no state could nullify a law of the United States.

The Bank War

In the middle of the tariff crisis Jackson faced a serious challenge from the supporters of the Second Bank of the United States. The Second Bank stood at the center of the American financial system. A privately managed entity, the Bank had operated since 1816 under a twenty-year charter from the federal government, which owned 20 percent of its stock. Its most important role was to stabilize the nation's money supply. Most American money consisted of notes—in effect, paper money—issued by state-chartered commercial banks. The banks promised to redeem the notes with "hard" money—gold or silver coins, also known as *specie*—on demand. By collecting those notes and regularly demanding specie, the Second Bank kept the state banks from issuing too many notes (which would produce monetary inflation and cause prices to rise).

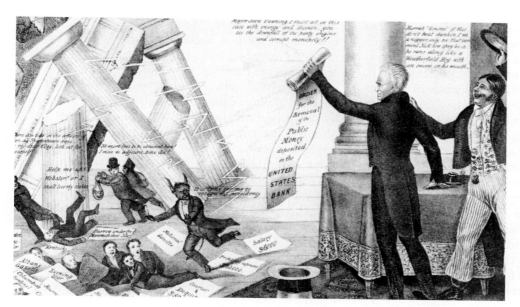

Jackson Destroys the Bank
In this political cartoon Jackson proudly orders the withdrawal of "public money" from the privately run Second Bank of the United States. Crushed by the subsequent collapse of the Bank are its director Nicholas Biddle, depicted here as the Devil; wealthy British and American investors; and the newspapers that supported Biddle during the bank war. Standing behind the president is "Major Jack Downing," the pseudonym for Seba Smith, a pro-Jackson humorist.
Library of Congress.

During the prosperous 1820s, under the leadership of Nicholas Biddle, the Second Bank maintained monetary stability and restrained expansion-minded banks in the West, forcing some to close. Biddle's policy was welcomed by bankers and entrepreneurs in Boston, New York, and Philadelphia, whose capital was underwriting economic development, but it aroused hostility among some state bankers and in the public at large. Most Americans did not understand the regulatory role of the Second Bank and feared its ability to force bank closures, which often left ordinary citizens holding worthless paper notes. Some wealthy Americans also resented the financial power wielded by Biddle and his bank, especially its monopoly of government funds and its regulation of the nation's credit. Thus some New York bankers, including supporters of Martin Van Buren, wanted federal monies deposited in their institutions; and expansion-minded bankers in western cities, including friends of Jackson in Nashville, wanted to escape supervision by a central bank.

However, neither Jackson nor Van Buren was a strong advocate of state-chartered banks. The president blamed banks for financial instability in general and for the substantial sums he had lost in speculative investments during the 1790s in particular. For his part, Van Buren had long opposed the expansion of the New York banking industry and, as governor, had enacted a Safety Fund system imposing strict controls on bank investments and note issuance, and setting up a fund to reimburse the noteholders of failed banks. Despite their reservations about the Second Bank, the two leaders would not destroy it in order to assist state bankers.

Jackson's Veto and the Election of 1832. Rather, it was a political miscalculation by the supporters of the Second Bank that brought about its downfall. In 1832 Jackson's opponents in Congress, led by Clay and Webster, persuaded Biddle to request an early recharter of the Bank. They knew that many Democrats favored the Bank and calculated that they had the votes to get a rechartering bill through Congress. Their strategy was to lure Jackson into an unpopular veto that would split the Democratic Party just before the 1832 elections.

Jackson turned the tables on Clay and Webster. He not only vetoed the bank bill but, by justifying his action in a masterful public statement that blended constitutional arguments with class rhetoric and patriotic fervor, became a public hero. Taking Jefferson's position, the president declared that Congress had no constitutional authority to charter a national bank, in part because it was "subversive of the rights of the States." Jackson also employed the egalitarian republican rhetoric of the American Revolution, attacking the Second Bank as "dangerous to the liberties of the people." He assailed the Bank as a nest of special privilege and monopoly power that promoted "the advancement of the few at the expense of the many" and damaged the "humbler members of society—the farmers, mechanics, and laborers—who have neither the time or the means to secure like favors for themselves." Finally, the president evoked popular support by pointing to the heavy investments in the Bank's stock made by British aristocrats; such a powerful institution should be *"purely American,"* he declared.

Jackson's attack on the Bank carried him to victory in the presidential election of 1832. Prior to the campaign he had rejected Calhoun as his running mate, partly because of the South Carolinian's continuing support of nullification and partly because of a dispute over etiquette. Peggy O'Neale was the attractive married daughter of the owner of the tavern where Jackson and John H. Eaton had lived while representing Tennessee in the Senate. Rumors linked O'Neale and Eaton in a sexual affair, and following the death of her husband in 1828, O'Neale and Eaton married. However, when Jackson appointed his longtime friend as secretary of war, Mrs. Calhoun encouraged other cabinet wives to shun Mrs. Eaton, angering Jackson, whose deceased wife had also been subject to sexual rumors. In place of Calhoun, Jackson chose Martin Van Buren, the architect of his victory in 1828 and now his personal friend and closest advisor.

Together, Old Hickory and the Little Magician confronted Clay, who headed the National Republican ticket. Clay attacked Jackson for abusing patronage and the veto power and promised a revitalization of the American System, including the rechartering of the Second Bank. Clay was a popular campaigner, but Jackson and Van Buren benefited from a decade-long surge in prosperity. They won nearly 55 percent of the popular vote and overwhelmed Clay in the electoral college, 219 to 49. Jackson's most fervent supporters were farmers and workers whose lives had been disrupted by price fluctuations or falling wages. But many promoters of economic growth were also Jacksonians. Thousands of middle-class Americans—lawyers, clerks, shopkeepers, artisans—cheered his attacks on privileged corporations. They wanted equal opportunity to rise in the world (see Voices from Abroad, "Alexis de Tocqueville: Parties in the United States," p. 361).

Destruction of the Second Bank. Immediately after his reelection Jackson launched an outright attack on the Second Bank. The Bank still had four years left on its charter, but Jackson decided to destroy it immediately by withdrawing the funds of the national government. After removing from office two Treasury secretaries who opposed this scheme because they feared it would damage the American economy, the president appointed Roger B. Taney to the post. Taney was a strong opponent of corporate privilege and a loyal supporter of the president. On Jackson's instructions, Taney withdrew the government's gold and silver from the Bank and deposited it in state institutions, which critics called the administration's "pet banks." To justify this abrupt (and probably illegal) act, Jackson claimed that the recent election had given him a mandate to destroy the Second Bank. It was the first time a president claimed that victory at the polls allowed him to act independently of Congress.

The bank war continued to escalate. Democrats in the House of Representatives defended Jackson, but in March 1834 his opponents in the Senate passed a resolution, written by Clay, that censured the president and warned of despotism: "We are in the midst of a revolution," the resolution declared, "hitherto bloodless, but rapidly descending towards a total change of the pure republican character of the Government, and the concentration of all power in the hands of one man." For his part, Nicholas Biddle tried to bring down Jackson by sharply reducing loans by the Second Bank. Although this contraction in the supply of credit caused a brief economic recession, Jackson and Taney refused to recharter the Bank. When its original charter expired in 1836, it became a state institution in Pennsylvania— still wealthy but without national public responsibilities. There would be no more national banking until the Civil War.

Indian Removal

The status of the native American peoples was as problematic as the tariff and the Second Bank, and it also raised issues of federal versus state power. As John Quincy Adams had learned to his dismay, by the 1820s white voices throughout the trans-Appalachian West were calling for the removal of Indians and their resettlement west of the Mississippi River. Removal was also favored by many eastern whites, including those who were sympathetic to native Americans; in their view it was a humane way to protect Indians from direct competition with a superior race.

Political and Legal Maneuvers. Jackson endorsed Indian removal in his first inaugural address in 1829 and soon began to implement it, especially in the Old Southwest. This region was the home of the so-called Five Civilized Tribes: the Cherokee and Creeks in Georgia, Tennessee, and Alabama; the Chickasaw and Choctaw in Mississippi and Alabama; and the Seminole in Florida. During the War of 1812, Jackson's military expeditions against the Creeks had forced them to relinquish millions of acres. But Indian peoples still controlled vast tracts of land in the region, and some of them had adopted European practices and values.

This assimilation to white culture was especially apparent among the Cherokee, who lived in Georgia and the Carolinas. Beginning in the late eighteenth century, the Cherokee had organized an unusually centralized political system to resist the advancing white settlers, who wanted the Indian lands for growing cotton. A national council headed by two respected chiefs oversaw all 18,000 members of the tribe with respect to certain activities—maintaining a mounted police force and replacing clan revenge for murder with a formal legal process. Reflecting European ideas, the council declared that inheritances should pass from father to son (rather than mother to daughter, as was the Cherokee custom).

These innovations were primarily the work of a small faction of Christian Cherokee mixed-bloods,

ALEXIS DE TOCQUEVILLE
Parties in the United States

─────★─────

In Democracy in America *(1835) Tocqueville presented both a philosophical analysis of the society of the United States and an astute description of its republican institutions. Here the republican-minded French aristocrat explains the motivating principles of American political parties during the early 1830s.*

The political parties that I style great are those which cling to principles rather than to their consequences; to general and not to special cases; to ideas and not to men. . . . In them private interest, which always plays the chief part in political passions, is more studiously veiled under the pretext of the public good. . . .

Great political parties . . . are not to be met with in the United States at the present time. Parties, indeed, may be found which threaten the future of the Union; but there is none which seems to contest the present form of government or the present course of society. The parties by which the Union is menaced do not rest upon principles, but upon material interests. These interests constitute, in the different provinces of so vast an empire, rival nations rather than parties. Thus, upon a recent occasion [the Tariff of 1832 and the nullification crisis] the North contended for the system of commercial prohibition, and the South took up arms in favor of free trade, simply because the North is manufacturing and the South an agricultural community; and the restrictive system that was profitable to the one was prejudicial to the other.

In the absence of great parties the United States swarms with lesser controversies. . . . The pains that are taken to create parties are inconceivable, and at the present day it is no easy task. In the United States there is no religious animosity, . . . no jealousy of rank, . . . no public misery. . . . Nevertheless, ambitious men will succeed in creating parties. . . . A political aspirant in the United States begins by discerning his own interest . . . [and] then contrives to find out some doctrine or principle that may suit the purposes of this new organization, which he adopts in order to bring forward his party and secure its popularity. . . .

The deeper we penetrate into the inmost thought of these parties, the more we perceive that the object of the one is to limit and that of the other to extend the authority of the people. I do not assert that the ostensible purpose or even that the secret aim of American parties is to promote the rule of aristocracy or democracy in the country; but I affirm that aristocratic or democratic passions may easily be detected at the bottom of all parties. . . .

To quote a recent example, when President Jackson attacked the Bank of the United States, the country was excited, and parties were formed; the well-informed classes rallied round the bank, the common people round the President. But it must not be imagined that the people had formed a rational opinion upon a question which offers so many difficulties to the most experienced statesmen. By no means. The bank is a great establishment, which has an independent existence; and the people . . . are startled to meet with this obstacle to their authority [and are] led to attack it, in order to see whether it can be shaken, like everything else.

Source: Alexis de Tocqueville, *Democracy in America* [1835] (New York: Random House, 1981), vol. 1: 94–99.

mostly the offspring of white fur traders and Indian women. Growing up in a bicultural world, they learned the language and political ways of whites, and some emulated the life-style of southern planters. James Vann, a Georgia Cherokee, eventually owned more than twenty black slaves, two trading posts, and a gristmill. Forty other Cherokee mixed-blood families owned a total of more than 1,000 slaves. To protect their land and that of their tribe, the mixed-bloods attempted to

forge a strong national identity. Sequoyah, a mixed-blood, developed a system of writing for the Cherokee language, and the tribe published a newspaper. In 1827 they introduced a new charter of government modeled directly on the U.S. Constitution. Full-blooded Cherokee, who made up 90 percent of the tribe, resisted many of the mixed-bloods' cultural and political innovations but were equally determined to retain their ancestral lands. "We would not receive money for land in which our fathers and friends are buried," one chief declared. "We love our land; it is our mother."

Cherokee preferences carried no weight with Jackson, who was a committed Indian fighter (and alleged Indian hater), or with the political leaders of Georgia. When the Cherokee adopted their new constitution and proclaimed themselves a separate nation within the United States, the Georgia legislature rejected their claim. It declared that the Cherokee were merely a collection of individuals who were tenants on state-owned land. Upon becoming president, Jackson threw his support to Georgia, repudiating Adams's pro-Indian policies and withdrawing the federal troops that had protected Indian enclaves there and in Alabama and Mississippi. The states, Jackson argued, were sovereign within their borders and were free to do as they wished with respect to the native peoples.

Jackson then pushed through Congress the Indian Removal Act of 1830, which offered native Americans land west of the Mississippi in exchange for their ancestral holdings in the East. To encourage native Americans to accept these terms, Jackson instructed his agents to promise that in the trans-Mississippi West "their white brothers . . . will have no claim to the land" so that they "can live upon it, they and all their children, as long as grass grows and water runs." Unwilling to fight against well-armed federal troops and land-hungry American settlers, some seventy Indian peoples negotiated treaties with the U.S. government; taken together, those agreements exchanged 100 million acres of land in the East for $68 million and 32 million acres in the area of present-day Oklahoma and Kansas.

As Jackson determinedly pursued Indian removal, mixed-blood Cherokee carried their case to the Supreme Court, claiming that the Cherokee were a "foreign nation" whose affairs fell under the Court's jurisdiction. However, in *Cherokee Nation v. Georgia* (1831), Chief Justice John Marshall denied the Indians' claim of national independence. Speaking for a majority of the justices, Marshall declared that Indian peoples enjoyed only partial autonomy and defined them as "domestic dependent nations." Then, in the case of *Worcester v. Georgia* (1832), Marshall sided with the Cherokee, voiding Georgia's extension of state law over the tribe and holding that Indian nations were "distinct political communities, having territorial boundaries, within which their authority is exclusive . . . [and] guaranteed by the United States." But Jackson had no interest in protecting the Cherokee and reputedly responded, "John Marshall has made his decision; now let him enforce it."

Indian Wars and the Trail of Tears. Ignoring the Court, Jackson pressed ahead with his removal policy. In 1832 he dispatched U.S. troops to dislodge Chief Black Hawk and his Sauk and Fox followers from their ancestral villages in rich farmland along the Mississippi River

Black Hawk (1767–1838)
George Catlin (1796–1872) was a prolific artist and chronicler of Indian tribes, who depicted Indians in realistic and dignified poses. His portrait of Black Hawk, rendered when the Indian leader was about sixty years old, shows a man who has endured the vicissitudes of life and become stronger as a result of these experiences. To protect ancestral lands in Illinois, Black Hawk mobilized Sauk and Fox warriors to resist the Indian Removal Act. "It was here that I was born—and here lie the bones of many friends and relatives," the aging chief declared in 1830. "I . . . could never consent to leave it." Thomas Gilcrease Institute of American History and Art.

in western Illinois (see American Voices, "Black Hawk: A Sacred Reverence for Our Lands," p. 363). After a series of clashes, the American forces rejected Black Hawk's offer to surrender and pursued him into the Wisconsin Territory. There, on August 3, the pursuit ended in the brutal eight-hour-long Bad Axe Massacre, which took the lives of 850 of Black Hawk's 1,000 warriors. During the next five years a combination of diplomatic pressure and military power forced virtually all the remaining Indian peoples to move west of the Mississippi.

The greatest Indian resistance continued to occur in the Old Southwest. Beginning in the mid-1830s, 4,000 Seminole Indians and their 1,500 African American allies (including many fugitive slaves who had married into the tribe) held the American army troops at bay. Unable to secure a military victory, in October 1837 the U.S. Army resorted to deceit, flagrantly violating a flag of truce to capture Osceola, the leading Seminole warrior. Soon the army had removed half the Indians, but the war dragged on. Despite mounting

BLACK HAWK

A Sacred Reverence for Our Lands

———————★———————

Black Hawk (1767–1838), or Makataimesheki-akiak in the language of his people, was a chief of the Sauk and Fox. In 1833 he dictated his life story to a government interpreter, and a young newspaper editor published it. Here Black Hawk describes the coming of white settlers to his village, near present-day Rock Island, Illinois, and his decision to resist removal to lands west of the Mississippi River.

We had about eight hundred acres in cultivation. The land around our village . . . was covered with bluegrass, which made excellent pasture for our horses. . . . The rapids of Rock river furnished us with an abundance of excellent fish, and the land, being good, never failed to produce good crops of corn, beans, pumpkins, and squashes. We always had plenty—our children never cried with hunger, nor our people were never in want. Here our village had stood for more than a hundred years.

[In 1828] Nothing was now talked of but leaving our village. Ke-o-kuck [the principal chief] had been persuaded to consent to . . . remove to the west side of the Mississippi. . . . [I] raised the standard of opposition to Ke-o-kuck, with full determination not to leave my village. . . . I was of the opinion that the white people had plenty of land and would never take our village from us. . . .

During the [following] winter, I received information that three families of whites had arrived at our village and destroyed some of our lodges, and were making fences and dividing our corn-fields for their own use. . . . I requested them [to remove, but some weeks later] we came up to our village, and found that the whites had not left it—but that others had come, and that the greater part of our corn-fields had been enclosed. . . . Some of the whites permitted us to plant small patches in the fields they had fenced, keeping all the best ground for themselves. . . . The white people brought whiskey into our village, made people drunk, and cheated them out of their homes, guns, and [beaver] traps!

That fall [1829] I paid a visit to the agent, before we started to our hunting grounds. . . . He said that the land on which our village stood was now ordered to be sold to individuals; and that, when sold, *our right* to remain, by treaty, would be at an end, and that if we returned next spring, we would be forced to remove! I refused . . . to quit my village. It was here, that I was born—and here lie the bones of many friends and relatives. For this spot I felt a sacred reverence, and never could consent to leave it, without being forced therefrom.

[In the spring of 1831] I directed my village crier to proclaim, that my orders were, in the event of the [Indian] war chief coming to our village to remove us [to honor the treaty], that not a gun should be fired, nor any resistance offered. That if he determined to fight, for them to remain quietly in their lodges, and let them *kill them if he chose.*

———————————

Source: David Jackson, ed., *Black Hawk: An Autobiography* (Urbana: University of Illinois Press, 1964), 88–90, 95–97, 111–113.

opposition to forced removal in Congress, Martin Van Buren, who had succeeded Jackson as president, refused to compromise. The Seminole had to be "totally expelled," he declared, so as not to set an "evil example" for other tribes facing resettlement.

When the Cherokee repudiated a treaty that had been signed by a minority faction and had not left their lands by the May 1838 deadline, the president ordered General Winfield Scott and an army of 7,000 troops to remove them. Scott's army rounded up about 14,000 Cherokee and forcibly marched them 1,200 miles to the new Indian Territory (present-day Oklahoma), an arduous journey they remembered as the Trail of Tears (Map 11.3). Along the way 3,000 Indians died of starvation and exposure. Using military power, the national government had asserted its control over the Indian peoples and forced their removal to the West.

The Jacksonian Legacy

During his presidency Jackson had destroyed both national banking—the achievement of Alexander Hamilton—and the American System of protective tariffs and internal improvements advocated by John Quincy Adams and Henry Clay. The result was a significant constriction in the economic policies and powers of

MAP 11.3
***The Removal of Native Americans,
1820–1840***
Between 1820 and 1840 the U.S. government con-
cluded treaties with native Americans in the East,
giving them designated tracts of land west of the
Mississippi River. During the 1830s the Five Civilized
Tribes of the Old Southwest—the Cherokee,
Chickasaw, Choctaw, Creeks, and Seminole—were
forced to move to these reservations in the Indian
Territory, the present-day state of Oklahoma; other
eastern tribes were settled in Kansas.

the national government. "All is gone," observed a Washington newspaper correspondent as Jackson completed
his dismantling work; "All is gone, which the General
Government was instituted to create and preserve."

Although generally correct, this assessment overlooked the ways in which Jackson enhanced the powers
of the national government and the presidency. During
the nullification crisis, Old Hickory stood firmly for the
Union, denying the right of secession and threatening
the use of military force, thus providing the basis for
Abraham Lincoln's defense of the Union during the secession crisis of 1861 (Chapter 14). Moreover, Jackson's policy of Indian removal enhanced the scope of federal
power over native Americans. Finally, Jackson greatly
expanded the authority of the nation's chief executive,
using the rhetoric of popular sovereignty to declare that
"the President is the direct representative of the American people." Jackson's legacy as chief executive, like that
of other great presidents, was complex and rich.

As Jackson and his followers came to dominate
American politics, they used their new power to infuse
many American institutions—the federal judiciary,
state legislatures and constitutions, and local governments—with their principles. Following the death of
John Marshall, Jackson made a crucially important
decision by appointing Treasury secretary Roger B.
Taney as Chief Justice of the Supreme Court. During
his long tenure (1836–1864), Taney used his legal skills
and powerful personality to persuade the Court to

reverse or modify many of his predecessor's decisions.
Whereas Marshall's jurisprudence had emphasized
vested property rights and national power, Taney's
Court bestowed constitutional legitimacy on Jackson's
policies of antimonopoly and states' rights.

Thus, in the landmark case of *Charles River Bridge
Co. v. Warren Bridge Co.* (1837), Taney undermined the
legal position of chartered monopolies by ruling that
the charter issued to the Charles River Bridge Company
did not convey an exclusive, monopolistic right to carry
goods and people over the river because no such right
was explicitly stated by the Massachusetts legislature.
Consequently, Taney ruled, the legislature retained the
power to charter a competing bridge company to serve
the public. As the Chief Justice put it, "While the rights
of private property are sacredly guarded, we must not
forget that the community also has rights, and the happiness and well-being of every citizen depends on their
faithful preservation."

Taney's decision in the Charles River Bridge case
qualified John Marshall's interpretation of the contract
clause in cases such as *Dartmouth College v. Woodward*
(1819). There Marshall had emphasized the binding
nature of public charters and had limited the power of
states to alter or repeal them (see Chapter 8). It also
encouraged competitive enterprise, opening the way
for legislatures to charter railroads that could compete
with existing canal and turnpike companies without
fear of crippling lawsuits.

The Trail of Tears
This depiction of the forced march of the Cherokee to Oklahoma, rendered in 1957 by native American artist Brummett Echohawk, portrays the hardship and anguish of the long journey. A grieving family lays a relative in a shallow grave as one of the military escorts watches. The other Indians march on, shielding their faces from the harsh winds of late autumn and pushing heavily loaded supply wagons over rocky trails. At the end of the 1,200-mile march, as many as 3,000 Cherokee lay dead along the trail that became known as the Trail of Tears.
Thomas Gilcrease Institute of American History and Art.

Other decisions by the Taney Court retreated from Marshall's nationalist interpretation of the commerce clause and enhanced the regulatory role of state governments. For example, in *Mayor of New York v. Miln* (1837) the Taney Court ruled that in the absence of federal regulations, New York State could use its "police power" to inspect the health of arriving immigrants. The Taney Court also restored to the states some of the economic powers they had exercised before 1787. In *Briscoe v. Bank of Kentucky* (1837) the Court approved the issuance of currency by a bank owned and controlled by the state of Kentucky, ruling that it did not violate the provision (in Article 1, section 10, of the U.S. Constitution) that forbade states from coining money or issuing bills of credit.

Jacksonian Democrats in the various states mounted their own constitutional revolutions. Between 1830 and 1860 no fewer than twenty states called conventions that fundamentally revised their constitutions and greatly enhanced their democratic aspects. Most states extended the vote to all white men and reapportioned their legislatures on the basis of population. They also brought government "near to the people" by cutting the number of appointed posts and mandating the election of most officials, including sheriffs, justices of the peace, and judges. For the first time in the his-

tory of the republic, popular sovereignty achieved full implementation in everyday political life.

Most constitutions likewise implemented Jacksonian economic ideals by prohibiting states from granting special charters to corporations or extending loans or credit guarantees to private businesses. "If there is any danger to be feared in a republican government," declared a New Jersey Democrat, "it is the danger of associated wealth, with special privileges." Finally, the Jacksonian constitutions protected taxpayers by setting strict limits on state indebtedness and encouraging judges to enforce them. As a New York reformer put it, "We will not trust the legislature with the power of creating indefinite mortgages on the people's property." Just as Jackson had undermined the American System of government subsidies on the national level, his disciples in the states subverted the "commonwealth" philosophy of economic development that depended on chartered monopolies and state subsidies. Declaring that "the world is governed too much," Jacksonian Democrats embraced a small-government outlook, rejecting regulation of the economy and society in favor of a laissez-faire (or "let alone") policy that allowed more decisions to be made by ordinary people acting in the marketplace and the voting booth.

Class, Culture, and the Second Party System

The rise of the Democrats and Jackson's tumultuous presidency sparked the creation in the mid-1830s of a second national party—the Whigs. For the next two decades Whigs and Democrats dominated American politics, forming what historians call the Second Party System. Many evangelical Protestants became Whigs, whereas most Catholics and non-evangelical Protestants joined the Democrats. The two parties competed fiercely for votes, debating issues of economic policy, class power, and moral reform and offering Americans a clear choice between political programs.

The Whigs and Their Outlook

The Whig Party began in Congress in 1834, when opponents of Jackson banded together to protest his policies and high-handed actions. They took the name *Whigs* to identify themselves with the pre-Revolutionary American and British parties—also called Whigs—that had opposed the arbitrary actions of King George III and previous monarchs. The congressional Whigs labeled Jackson as "King Andrew I," accusing him of acting like an American monarch and violating the Constitution through "executive usurpation." By creating a "spoils system" and increasing presidential authority, they charged, Jackson had undermined government by elected legislators, the true representatives of the sovereign people.

Initially, the congressional Whigs were led by Senators Webster of Massachusetts, Clay of Kentucky, and Calhoun of South Carolina, who were united primarily by their opposition to Jackson. Webster and Clay also held a similar economic outlook, for Webster spoke on behalf of New England's business elite while Clay represented merchants and traders in the Ohio and Mississippi Valleys. Both men advocated a national program of economic development; this placed them at odds with Calhoun, now the most prominent defender of the interests of the white planters of the South. Having broken with Jackson over nullification, however, Calhoun had little choice but to join the Whigs regardless of his reservations about their economic policies.

Whig Ideology. During the election of 1836 the Whigs elaborated their plan for the nation's future, formulating a party platform and seeking votes among evangelical Protestants and upwardly mobile middle- and working-class citizens in the North. Their philosophy took issue with the assumption of many Jacksonians and radical reformers, such as Frances Wright, who believed that all men were born equal and therefore condemned most

BORN TO COMMAND.

OF VETO MEMORY.

HAD I BEEN CONSULTED.

KING ANDREW THE FIRST.

A Whig Cartoon
Lampooning the president as "KING ANDREW THE FIRST," this political cartoon accuses Andrew Jackson of acting arbitrarily, like a monarch, and trampling on the principles of the Constitution. It emphasizes Jackson's contempt for judges and criticizes many of his political appointments. Seeking to turn democratic fervor to the advantage of the Whig Party, the caption asks: "Shall he reign over us, or shall the PEOPLE RULE?"
New-York Historical Society.

distinctions of wealth and status (see American Lives, "Frances Wright: Radical Reformer," pp. 368–369). Beginning from different premises, Whigs reasoned to different conclusions. Like the Federalists, they believed that it was natural for individuals to have different abilities and acquire different amounts of wealth. To reconcile the resulting economic hierarchy with republican ideals, they exalted the *equality of opportunity;* unlike the Federalists, Whigs wanted an elite selected on the basis of talent, not birth. "This is a country of *self-made men,*" they boasted, pointing to the relative absence of permanent distinctions of class and status among white citizens of the United States.

The Whigs also justified elite rule by celebrating the role played by enterprising entrepreneurs and activist governments in increasing the nation's wealth. Suggesting that industrialization had increased social harmony, Whig leaders such as congressman Edward Everett welcomed the investments of "moneyed capitalists" as increasing the "chances of improvement for those who had little" and providing "bread, clothing and homes to the poor." As Everett told a Fourth of July crowd in Lowell, Massachusetts, national prosperity depended on a "holy alliance" among laborers, owners, and governments. Many workers agreed, especially those holding jobs in the New England textile factories and Pennsylvania iron mills that benefited from state subsidies and protective tariffs. To continue economic progress, Everett and northern Whigs called for a return to the American System of Henry Clay and John Quincy Adams.

Southern Whigs like Calhoun had a different perspective. While they condemned Jackson's "executive usurpation" and advocated rapid economic development, they opposed high tariffs and social fluidity advocated by the northern Whigs. Indeed, Calhoun argued that the northern Whig ideal of equal opportunity was contradicted not only by slavery, which he considered a fundamental American institution, but also by the wage-labor system of industrial capitalism. "There is and always has been in an advanced state of wealth and civilization a conflict between labor and capital," he argued in 1837, urging southern slaveowners and northern factory owners to unite in a defensive alliance against their common foe: the working class composed of enslaved blacks and propertyless whites.

Most northern Whigs rejected Calhoun's class-conscious vision. "A clear and well-defined line between capital and labor" might fit the slave South or class-ridden Europe, Daniel Webster admitted, but in the North "this distinction grows less and less definite as commerce advances." Pointing to Massachusetts with its strong tradition of yeoman farming and its growing urban middle class, Webster declared: "I do not believe there is on earth, in a highly civilized society, a greater equality in the condition of men than exists here."

Webster and other Whigs counted on the growing size and prosperity of the northern middle class, which had become the backbone of their party. In the election of 1834 the Whigs won a majority in the House of Representatives by appealing to prosperous farmers, small-town merchants, and skilled industrial workers in New England, New York, and the new communities along the Great Lakes. Those voters were particularly attracted to the Whigs' ideology of individual social mobility.

The Influence of Anti-Masonry. Many Whig voters had previously been Anti-Masons, members of a powerful but short-lived political movement directed against the secret Order of Freemasonry. Masonry originated among free-thinking intellectuals in eighteenth-century Europe, where the order was condemned by princes and priests because of its republican and deist beliefs. Spreading rapidly to America, it attracted leading political leaders—including George Washington, Henry Clay, and Andrew Jackson—and ambitious businessmen. By the mid-1820s there were 20,000 Masons in New York State alone, organized into 450 local lodges. But because Masonry developed as a secret order (to protect its early members from prosecution), and had mysterious rituals and handshakes, it evoked widespread concern. Many Americans feared that Masons formed an aristocratic fraternity whose members unfairly used their influence to assist one another.

In 1826 this resentment turned into anger following the kidnapping and murder of William Morgan, a New York Mason who had threatened to reveal the Order's secrets. Accusing the Masons of conspiring to protect the murderers and repudiating republican principles, Thurlow Weed, a Rochester newspaper editor, spearheaded an Anti-Masonic political party. By 1830 Anti-Masonic agitation had spread to other states in the North and Midwest, and the party held a national convention. Many Anti-Masons were strongly religious migrants from New England or those who shared their Yankee faith in moral discipline and self-improvement.

Once the Anti-Masons had driven their Masonic enemies from local and state offices, their movement collapsed. Many former Anti-Masons—including Thurlow Weed—gravitated to the new Whig Party. Picking up on Anti-Masonic themes—temperance, equality of opportunity, evangelical religious values—Whigs developed a political program that was far broader than congressional opposition to King Andrew's "usurpations" had been. On the state and local levels Whigs revived the program of moral reform of the Benevolent Empire, advocating legal restrictions on the sale of alcohol and bylaws that preserved Sunday as a day of worship. Thanks to the influx of Anti-Masons, the Whigs became the party of evangelical religion and social reform as well as of nationalistic economic policies. Nearly everywhere New Englanders had migrated, the Whigs were strong.

Whigs and the Election of 1836. Henry Clay carried the Whig message into the Ohio and Mississippi Valleys, where it appealed to farmers, bankers, and shopkeepers who favored public investment in roads, canals, and bridges. In the South, support for the Whigs was much more fragmentary and rested more on the appeal of specific policies than on agreement with the Whigs' social vision. Thus many nonslaveholding whites in the backcountry voted Whig to break the grip over state politics held by rich planters, most of whom were Democrats. Yet a significant minority of wealthy planters became Whigs, especially those who had invested heavily in railroads, banks, and factories and had close ties to northern markets and New York capitalists. Finally, some states' rights Democrats in

Frances Wright: Radical Reformer

————————★————————

FRANCES WRIGHT (1795–1852) arrived in New York City on January 1, 1829, intent upon beginning the new year with a new life and a new message. Born into a wealthy, republican-minded merchant family in Glasgow, Scotland, Wright had first discovered America at age sixteen. "From that moment on," she recalled, "my attention became rivetted on this country as upon the theatre where man might first awake to the full knowledge and exercise of his powers." Of the many Europeans drawn to America by the egalitarian doctrines of the Declaration of Independence, Wright was among the most radical and controversial. She was an advocate of black emancipation, a socialist society without private property, deism, and women's rights.

In 1818 Wright first crossed the Atlantic to her promised land. Returning to Britain three years later, she published an enthusiastic account of life in the United States, *Views of Society and Manners in America* (1821), which was translated into three languages. Among her readers was the French hero of the American Revolution, the Marquis de Lafayette, who became Wright's friend and patron. She and her sister subsequently moved to France and resided at the country estate of the sixty-four-year-old widower. Ignoring the objections of his family, Wright stayed with Lafayette for almost two years, at one point begging him to either marry her or adopt her as a daughter.

Wright's tie to Lafayette provided a new link to the United States. In 1824 she accompanied the republican-minded aristocrat on his triumphal tour of the United States, using his social contacts to good advantage. During a six-week stay with Thomas Jefferson at Monticello, the young Scot outlined a bold plan to set up a community of whites and freed slaves who would live together in full equality. Like other utopian visionaries (those who believe in the possibility of human perfection), Wright had great ambitions.

Encouraged by Jefferson, in 1825 Wright founded the community, called Nashoba, on 320 acres in the wilderness of western Tennessee. Joined by young American idealists, Wright enlarged Nashoba to 2,000 acres and purchased about thirty enslaved African Americans. Believing in the dignity of labor and self-reliance, she wanted the slaves to earn emancipation by working the land. While they labored, the Nashoba community would provide their children with an education. Displaying her egalitarianism, Wright joined the slaves in the arduous task of clearing and ditching the marshy land. But she soon lost the willing support of the black workers, who saw little improvement in their lives.

Wright remained undaunted. She embraced the ideals of Robert Owen, a Scottish manufacturer and philanthropist who in 1824 had founded his own utopian community in New Harmony, Indiana. Taking up Owen's quest for alternatives to marriage, organized religion, and private property, Wright called on those at Nashoba to form a society "where affection shall form the only marriage, kind feelings and kind action the only religion, respect for the feelings and liberties of others the only restraint, and reunion of interest the bond of peace and security." But potential recruits were repelled by the rude conditions of life at Nashoba, and its numbers dwindled.

By 1828 Wright had concluded that an "individual experiment" such as Nashoba could not succeed. What was required was a more general effort, a campaign to reform the "collective body politic." Leaving her faltering utopian community, she joined forces with Owen's son, Robert Dale Owen, who had become infatuated with her. Together they launched a lecture campaign that brought her to New York, the high temple of the emerging American capitalist economic system and a center of trade unionism.

Wright took New York by storm, unveiling a radical plan to persuade the city's workers to reject the authority of the business elite and the religious organizations that it supported. As a lecturer Wright attracted large audiences, in part because rumors of free love and racial mixing at Nashoba had preceded her, and she lived up to her advance billing. Sweeping onto the stage with a group of women apostles, Wright would throw off her cloak to reveal her unorthodox attire—a tunic of white muslin. She would then wave a copy of the Declaration of Independence and elaborate on its ideals in a resonant, musical voice. The poet Walt Whitman, who heard Wright lecture when he was a young lad, remembered that "we all loved her; fell down before her: her very appearance seemed to enthrall us."

Echoing Robert Dale Owen's socialist message, Wright told her listeners that the "laboring class of the community" faced oppression from the united

Frances Wright

Frances Wright not only preached radical doctrine but also lived by its precepts. In this portrait, painted at Nashoba in 1826, the thirty-two-year-old Wright wears the simple and practical (but also culturally subversive) women's costume adopted by Robert Owen's socialist community at New Harmony, Indiana—pantaloons covered by a tunic that reached the knees.

Miriam and Ira D. Wallach Division of Art, Prints and Photographs, The New York Public Library. Astor, Lenox and Tilden Foundations.

To nurture a radical culture among New York's workers, Wright and Owen took over an abandoned church near the Bowery, in the heart of a working-class neighborhood, and transformed it into a "Hall of Science." There they established a newspaper, *The Free Enquirer*, a printing press for other radical publications, a reading room and lecture auditorium, a free medical dispensary, and a deist Sunday school. They hoped that rationalist science, the religion of the Enlightenment, would displace church dogma and evangelical Protestantism as the guiding principles of workers' lives. In fact, Wright won a substantial following among artisans and journeymen, some of whom turned to politics and energized the Working Men's Party. In 1829 twenty devotees wrote her name on their ballots for the New York Assembly.

But most New York workers rejected Wright's message. They believed that a maldistribution of wealth and opportunity—not traditional religion—was the primary cause of their poverty and powerlessness. Disheartened, in 1831 Wright and Owen sold the Hall of Science to a Methodist congregation and went their separate ways. Owen returned to New Harmony and pursued a political career as a Jacksonian reformer. Wright transported her freed slaves to the black-run nation of Haiti and then sailed for Paris, where she married a French reformer.

Wright never abandoned her dreams. Inspired by Andrew Jackson's war against the Second Bank, she returned to America in 1835. But her time had passed; audiences greeted her lectures, including speeches for presidential candidate Martin Van Buren, with indifference or hostility. Newspaper editors labeled her the "Red Harlot of Infidelity" (a phrase that simultaneously condemned her socialism, feminism, and deism), and Christian parents compared her to Satan, invoking her name to frighten their children.

Wright settled in Cincinnati, where she lived out her life in obscurity, writing her memoirs, occasionally promoting her old causes, and winning a pioneering suit for divorce. In her later years she became increasingly pessimistic about the American republic. Thomas Paine's great hope of mankind seemed to have squandered its egalitarian ideals as its citizens engaged in a mad quest for wealth and mobility. Wright no longer felt at home in her chosen land. At times, she mused, it seemed as if she had "fallen from a strange planet among a race whose sense and perceptions are all different from my own."

forces of a "monied aristocracy" of bankers and financiers and a "professional aristocracy" of ministers, lawyers, and politicians. She lashed out at evangelical ministers, challenging their claims of divine inspiration and describing the Benevolent Empire as the "would-be Christian Party in politics."

Wright preached peaceful reform, not violent revolution. To attack the fundamental flaws in society, she called for the compulsory training in boarding schools of all children between the ages of two and sixteen. She argued that such an educational system would encourage social equality, insulate children from organized religion, and benefit young women, who would learn to break their "mental chains" and seek equality under the law.

Virginia and South Carolina shared Calhoun's anger at Andrew Jackson's forceful suppression of nullification and joined the Whigs in protest.

In the election of 1836 the Whigs faced Martin Van Buren, the architect of the Democratic Party and Jackson's hand-picked successor. Following in Jackson's footsteps, Van Buren emphasized his opposition to the American System and support for "equal rights." The Little Magician also promised to preserve American "liberty." He warned that Whigs would use national laws and subsidies to encourage economic development, undermining the rights of the states and creating an oppressive system of "consolidated government." Positioning himself as a defender of individual rights, Van Buren likewise opposed the plans of Whigs and moral reformers to use legal means—the power of government—to impose temperance, evangelical religious values, or abolition of slavery. Underlining the Democratic Party's ties to the South, Van Buren declared himself an "inflexible and uncompromising opponent" of the use of governmental power to restrict slavery, as many abolitionists and some Whigs were demanding. "The government is best which governs least" became his motto.

Celebrating a Political Triumph, 1836
To commemorate Martin Van Buren's election to the presidency and to reward friends for their support, the Democratic Party distributed thousands of snuff boxes inscribed with his portrait. By using such innovative measures to enlist the loyalty of voters, Van Buren and his allies transformed American politics from an upper-class avocation to a democratic contest for votes and power.
Collection of Janice L. and David J. Frent.

To oppose Van Buren, the Whigs put forward four candidates, each of whom had a strong regional base. Party leaders counted on their candidates garnering enough electoral votes to throw the contest into the House of Representatives, which they controlled. The plan failed. The Whig tally—73 electoral votes collected by William Henry Harrison of Ohio, 26 by Hugh L. White of Tennessee, 14 by Daniel Webster, and 11 by W. P. Magnum of Georgia—fell far short of Van Buren's 170 votes. Still, the size of the popular vote for the Whig candidates—49 percent of the total—showed that the party's message of economic improvement and moral uplift had appealed not only to middle-class Americans but also to farmers and workers with little or no property. Most important, the election of 1836 witnessed the creation of the Second Party System, a closely fought struggle between Whigs and Democrats that defined American political life for the next two decades.

Labor Politics and the Depression of 1837–1843

The prolonged and steady expansion of the economy from 1821 to 1836 had led many Americans to consider prosperity a permanent feature of life. Benefiting from a shortage of labor, skilled workers organized labor unions and, beginning in 1827, supported the Working Men's parties that sprang up in Pennsylvania and fourteen other states.

Working Men's Parties and the Employers' Response. This new political movement was partly a response to the inequities of early capitalist industrialization. As employers increased the length of the workday during the 1820s, workers demanded a ten-hour day and organized politically. "Past experience teaches us that we have nothing to hope from the aristocratic orders of society," declared the New York Working Men's Party; "our only course . . . is . . . to send men of our own description, if we can, to the Legislature at Albany." In Philadelphia workers demanded higher taxes on the wealthy to finance a system of universal public education that would assist their children to advance into the ranks of the propertied. By 1834 the Philadelphia Working Men's Party had persuaded the Pennsylvania legislature to authorize universal, free, tax-supported schools.

By this time a rapid rise in prices was bringing new recruits into the Working Men's movement. By the early 1830s huge amounts of British capital were flowing into the United States—to build canals in the North and finance the expansion of cotton plantations in the South—and American state banks were increasing the money supply even further by lending more money and issuing more notes. By 1836 the nation was awash with money, and many basic commodities had tripled in price.

Further, rising prices and stagnant wages had lowered the standard of living of many urban artisans and wage earners, who condemned "the glaring inequality of society."

The ideology underlying the Working Men's parties was artisan republicanism. Party publicists called for a society in which (as the radical Massachusetts Democrat Orestes Brownson put it) "instead of one man's working for another and receiving wages thereof, all men will be independent proprietors, working on their own capitals, on their own farms, or in their own shops." In New York City, the Working Men's Party demanded "equal rights" for all Americans and called for the abolition of private banks and chartered monopolies that promoted "the benefit of the rich and the oppression of the poor." "The only safeguard against oppression," argued William Leggett, a leading member of the New York Loco-Foco (Equal Rights) Party, "is a system of legislation which leaves to all the free exercise of their talents and industry."

At first these parties did well in urban areas, but divisions over policy and voter apathy soon took a toll. By the mid-1830s most politically active workers had joined the Democratic Party, where they continued to agitate against monopolies, banks, and the system of imprisonment for debt. They also condemned protective tariffs, which gave "bounties to particular interests," and they supported legislation placing taxes on the personal property of the wealthy: stocks, bonds, machinery, and furniture.

Many labor activists continued to focus on the workplace, encouraging artisans to take advantage of the shortage of skilled labor and bargain hard with their employers. They organized new unions in small cities and General Trade Union federations in New York City and Philadelphia. Employers responded by attacking the union movement. In 1836 clothing manufacturers in New York City agreed not to hire workers belonging to the Union Trade Society of Journeymen Tailors and circulated a list—a so-called blacklist—of its members.

More important, the employers brought a series of lawsuits to overturn *closed shop* agreements that required them to hire only union members. They argued that such contracts violated the common law and, in New York State, legislative statutes that prohibited "conspiracies" in restraint of trade. Judges usually agreed with the manufacturers' arguments. In 1835, New York's supreme court found that a shoemaker's union in Geneva had illegally caused "an industrious man" to be "driven out of employment." "It is important to the best interests of society," the court declared, "that the price of labor be left to regulate itself." When another court upheld a conspiracy verdict against the New York City tailors' union, a crowd of 27,000 people demonstrated outside City Hall and tailors circulated handbills proclaiming that the "Freemen of the North are now on a level with the slaves of the South." In 1836 popular demonstrations encouraged local juries to acquit shoemakers in Hudson, New York; carpet makers in Thompsonville, Connecticut; and plasterers in Philadelphia of similar conspiracy charges. Although this resistance by workers kept some union members out of jail, the threat of legal attack remained.

The Panic of 1837 and Labor's Decline. At this juncture the Panic of 1837 threw the American economy into disarray. The panic began early in 1837 when the Bank of England, needing to increase the domestic supply of specie to bolster the British economy, sharply curtailed the flow of money and credit to America. For the previous decade and a half, British manufacturers and investors had stimulated the American economy, providing southern planters with credit to expand cotton production and purchasing millions of dollars worth of canal bonds in northern states. As the British economy faltered, textile mills cut their purchases of raw cotton from the South, causing its price to collapse from 20 cents a pound to 10 cents or less.

Deprived of British funds, American planters, merchants, and canal corporations had to withdraw specie from domestic banks to pay their foreign loans and commercial debts. This drain of funds set off a general financial crisis. On May 10 the Dry Dock Bank of New York City closed its doors, and panicked depositors withdrew more than $2 million in coin from other city banks, forcing them to suspend all payments in specie. Within two weeks every bank in the United States had followed suit, shocking high-flying entrepreneurs and ordinary citizens (Map 11.4).

Lacking access to new bank loans, many businesses had to cut production, and trade, manufacturing, and farming quickly slid into decline. "It would be difficult . . . to render intelligible in Europe, the stunning effect which this sudden overthrow of the commercial credit and honor of the nation has caused," British diplomat Henry Fox wrote to the prime minister, Lord Palmerston. "The conquest of this land by a foreign power could hardly have produced a more general sense of humiliation and grief." Soon the crisis engulfed state governments as tax revenues and canal tolls fell. Nine states defaulted on the bonds they had issued to finance canal building; others declared a moratorium on debt payments, undermining British confidence in the American economy and cutting the flow of new investment. Bumper crops during the late 1830s drove down cotton prices even further, causing more bankruptcies.

The American economy fell into a deep depression. By 1843 canal construction had dropped by 90 percent and the general price level by nearly 50 percent. Simultaneously the rate of unemployment rose, reaching almost 20 percent of the work force in seaports and industrial centers. From his pulpit in New York City, minister Henry Ward Beecher described a land "filled with lamentation . . . its inhabitants wandering like bereaved citizens among the ruins of an earthquake,

MAP 11.4
Anatomy of a Panic: Bank Suspensions in May 1837
The first failures occurred in the South (Natchez, Tallahassee, and Montgomery) as planters withdrew specie to pay their British creditors. But it was the collapse of New York City banks on May 10 that precipitated a chain reaction; within twelve days most banks along the Atlantic coast, the Erie Canal, and the Ohio River had shut their doors. This pattern of bank failures clearly reveals the central importance of New York in the economic nervous system of the nation.

mourning for children, for houses crushed, and property buried forever."

By creating a surplus of skilled workers, the depression devastated the labor movement. In 1837, over 6,000 masons, carpenters, and other building-trade workers lost their jobs in New York City, depleting the membership of unions and destroying their bargaining power. By 1843 most local unions and all the national labor organizations had disappeared, along with their newspapers and other publications. It would be thirty years before labor organizations again played an important role in national life.

During the depression years two events improved the long-term prospects of the labor movement. One was a major legal decision that gave legitimacy to the labor movement. In *Commonwealth v. Hunt* (1842), Chief Justice Lemuel Shaw of Massachusetts upheld the rights of workers to form unions and enforce a closed shop. Shaw, one of the great jurists of the nineteenth century, overturned common-law precedents by making two critical rulings: (1) a union was not an inherently illegal organization, and (2) union members could legally attempt to enforce a closed shop, even by striking. Shaw's opinion was generally accepted by courts in other states, so that unions were free to organize. However, judges (who were mostly Whigs) found other methods, such as court injunctions, to restrict strikes and boycotts, thereby depriving unions of bargaining power.

Labor's second success was political. Continuing Jackson's effort to attract workers to the Democratic Party, in 1840 President Van Buren signed an executive order establishing a ten-hour workday for federal employees. Significantly, this achievement came after the unions had lost their power in the marketplace, underlining the fact that the struggle between labor and capital—like conflicts over tariffs, banks, and internal improvements—had moved into the political arena.

"Tippecanoe and Tyler Too!"

The depression had a significant impact on American politics. Because few people understood the workings of the international economy, many Americans blamed the Democrats for their financial woes. In particular, they derided Jackson for destroying the Second Bank and for issuing the Specie Circular of 1836, which required western settlers to use bullion instead of the notes issued by private banks to pay for land purchases. Not

The Panic of 1837
Thousands of workers, like the carpenter depicted in this cartoon, lost their jobs during the Panic of 1837 and the subsequent depression, threatening their families with disaster. "I'm so hungry," laments one of the children in the cartoon, while the landlord stands at the door, eviction notice in hand. Another child asks whether his father can get some "specie claws," a pun on Jackson's Specie Circular. By placing portraits of Jackson and Van Buren on the wall, the artist implicitly blames them for the suffering of the family and encourages workers to renounce their support for the Democratic Party.
Library of Congress.

realizing that shipment of gold and silver to Britain (to pay off past debts) was the main cause of the financial panic, Whigs heaped blame on Jackson's specie policy.

The public then turned its anger on Van Buren, who entered office just as the panic began. Ignoring the pleas of influential bankers, the new president refused to revoke the Specie Circular or take other actions to reverse the economic downturn. Holding to his philosophy of limited government, Van Buren advised Congress that "the less government interferes with private pursuits the better for the general prosperity" and explicitly ruled out any financial intervention involving "the aid of legislative grant or regulations by law."

As the depression continued, this laissez-faire outlook commanded less and less political support. Speaking for the Whigs, Daniel Webster condemned the president for his "refusal to prescribe for the sickness and distress of society." Worse, Van Buren's major piece of economic legislation, the Independent Treasury Act of 1840, actually delayed recovery. The act pulled federal specie out of Jackson's "pet banks" (which had used it to back loans) and placed it in government vaults (where it did no economic good at all). Regard-

less of its value in placing the nation's financial reserves above politics, the Independent Treasury Act did little to enhance Van Buren's popularity.

The Election of 1840. Determined to exploit Van Buren's weakness, the Whigs organized their first national convention in 1840 and nominated William Henry Harrison of Ohio for the presidency and John Tyler of Virginia for the vice-presidency. A military hero of the Battle of Tippecanoe and the War of 1812, Harrison at age sixty-eight was well advanced in years and had little political experience. But the Whig leaders in Congress, Clay and Webster, did not want a strong president; they planned to have Harrison rubber-stamp their program for protective tariffs and a national bank. Party strategists such as Thurlow Weed of New York had chosen Harrison primarily because of his military record and western background, promoting him as the Whig version of Andrew Jackson. An unpretentious, amiable man, Harrison warmed to that task, telling voters that Whig policies were "the only means, under Heaven, by which a poor industrious man may become a rich man without bowing to colossal wealth."

The Log-Cabin Campaign, 1840
During the Second Party System, politics became more responsive to the popular will, as ordinary people voted for candidates who shared their values and life-styles. The barrels of hard cider surrounding this campaign banner evoke the drink of the common man, while the central image falsely portrays William Henry Harrison as a poor and simple frontier farmer—a man of the people.
New-York Historical Society.

Panic and depression stacked the political cards against Van Buren, but the contest itself turned as much on style as on substance. It became the great "log-cabin" campaign and the first occasion on which two well-organized parties competed for the loyalties of a mass electorate. One result was a new political style of festive celebrations. Whig pamphleteering, songfests, parades, and well-orchestrated mass meetings dominated the contest, drawing new voters and new social groups into the political arena. Recognizing the importance of women in evangelical churches and reform organizations, Whigs hailed Harrison as "a good Sunday school . . . church going man," invited "the ladies" to political meetings, and called on women to infuse government and society with "pure morality." Whig speakers assailed "Martin Van Ruin" as a manipulative politician with aristocratic tastes—a devotee of fancy wines and elegant clothes, as indeed he was. With less candor they praised Harrison (actually the son of a wealthy planter who had signed the Declaration of Independence) as a self-made soldier and statesman who lived in a simple log cabin and enjoyed hard cider, a drink of the common man.

Each party relied on newspapers to convey its message. From the nation's capital the Democrat *Washington Globe* and the Whig *National Intelligencer* carried the parties' message to local Jacksonian and Whig newspapers, which relayed it to voters in thousands of crossroads towns. The Democrats relied on party discipline to bring out their supporters, and the Whigs drew on the wealth of the business elite to orchestrate their carnival-like campaign. More than 80 percent of the eligible electorate went to the polls in 1840 (up from less than 60 percent in 1832 and 1836; see Figure 11.1). Heeding the Whig slogan "Tippecanoe and Tyler Too," they voted Harrison into the White House and gave the Whigs a majority in Congress (Map 11.5).

The Tyler Administration. The Whig triumph was short-lived. One month after his inauguration, Harrison died of pneumonia and the nation got "Tyler Too." Vice-President Tyler, who became president, was not a typical Whig. Like Calhoun, he was a former Democrat who had joined the Whig Party primarily in opposition to Jackson's stance against nullification. On economic issues Tyler shared many of Jackson's views. Favoring rapid settlement of the West, Tyler signed the Preemption Act passed by the Whig-controlled Con-

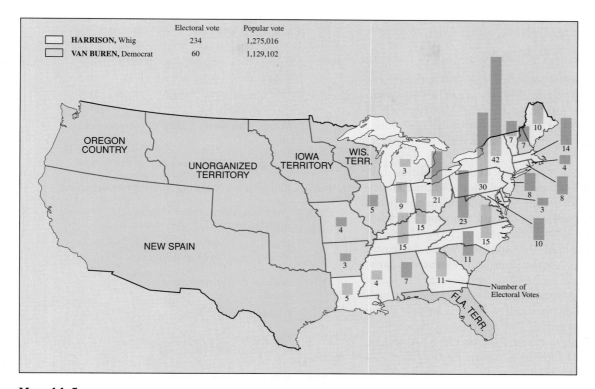

	Electoral vote	Popular vote
HARRISON, Whig	234	1,275,016
VAN BUREN, Democrat	60	1,129,102

MAP 11.5
The Election of 1840
William Henry Harrison carried the Whigs to victory, winning the presidency by amassing support in every section of the country. As a result of Harrison's popularity, the Whigs also won majorities in the House and the Senate, giving them the opportunity to reverse the policies of Andrew Jackson and Martin Van Buren.

gress in 1841. The act allowed American citizens and immigrants to claim up to 160 acres of federal land and, if they built a house on the property and improved the land, to purchase it later at the low price of $1.25 an acre. However, Tyler opposed other aspects of Clay's American System and betrayed the Whig voters who had elected him to office. Acting more like a Democrat than a Whig, he vetoed bills that would have created a new national bank and significantly raised tariffs. Consequently, Whig successes during the Tyler administration were few and limited: repeal of the independent Treasury in 1841 and a modest tariff increase in 1842 that was too small either to protect eastern industries or to finance western canals and railroads.

The split between Tyler and the Whigs gave the Democrats time to regroup. By opposing Whig measures on the state level that favored bankers and manufacturers, the Democrats won support among subsistence farmers in the North. They also recruited planters by continuing to support low tariffs. The Democrats were particularly successful in winning the votes of the Irish-Catholic and German immigrants, who now formed a substantial minority in many cities in the North and Midwest. Supporting the immigrants' demands for religious and cultural freedom, they opposed Whig proposals to use the Protestant Bible in public schools and to regulate saloons and the consumption of beer and spirits. In New York City during the 1840s about 95 percent of Irish-Catholic voters supported Democratic candidates. Thanks to these recruits, the Democrats remained the majority party: in most parts of the nation, their program of "equal rights" (no special privileges for business corporations), states' rights, and cultural liberty was more attractive than the Whig platform of economic nationalism, moral reform, and individual mobility.

The continuing struggle between Whigs and Democrats, each claiming to speak for "the people," completed the democratic revolution among white American men. The United States now boasted not only white male universal suffrage but also a highly organized system of party government that was responsive to ordinary citizens. In their scope and significance for American life, these political innovations matched the advances of the economic revolution. But the new political system would soon be tested by the growing sectional conflict over slavery.

Summary

─────★─────

With the rise of popular politics in the states, the power of the notables declined, and political parties assumed control of American public life. Martin Van Buren and other party leaders used patronage to build disciplined organizations and enact legislation favorable to powerful social groups.

Political democracy came to national politics during the election of 1824, as John Quincy Adams, Henry Clay, William Crawford, and Andrew Jackson competed for the presidency. Jackson received the most electoral votes, but because he lacked a majority the House of Representatives decided the contest. What Jackson's supporters labeled a "corrupt bargain" elevated Adams to the presidency and made Clay his secretary of state. Adams failed to win congressional approval for Clay's American System because many citizens opposed the expansion of federal power. The high rates imposed by the Tariff of 1828 caused many southerners to oppose Adams's reelection. Partly as a result, Andrew Jackson won an overwhelming victory in the election of 1828.

During his eight years as president, Jackson carried through a political revolution, introducing the spoils system of patronage and dramatically reducing the economic agenda of the national government. He ended federal subsidies for internal improvements, vetoing a bill to extend the National Road, and won a gradual reduction in tariff rates. Jackson likewise eliminated national banking by vetoing a bill to recharter the Second Bank of the United States and withdrawing all government funds from its vaults.

In other respects Jackson enhanced the power of the national government, using its military power to carry through his policy of Indian removal and to coerce South Carolina to renounce nullification. He was the first "modern" president in claiming that his victory at the polls gave him a political mandate.

Charging that "King Andrew" had abused his powers, Henry Clay, Daniel Webster, and John C. Calhoun formed the Whig Party. It drew support from members of the growing middle class and from former Anti-Masons, who were attracted by the Whigs' ideology of equality of opportunity, social mobility, and moral reform. For the next two decades Whigs and Democrats struggled for dominance in the Second Party System.

The Panic of 1837 destroyed Working Men's parties and most labor unions. The panic also brought victory to the Whigs in the famous log-cabin campaign of 1840, but President Tyler's vetoes prevented them from instituting Clay's American System. By the early 1840s the American democratic revolution was complete, and the new political system was about to be tested by the growing conflict over slavery.

TIMELINE

1810s	Revision of state constitutions and expansion of voting rights
	Martin Van Buren's political innovations
1825	John Quincy Adams elected president by House; advocates Henry Clay's American System
1827	Philadelphia Working Men's Party organized
1828	"Tariff of Abominations" raises duties on imported materials and manufactures
	The South Carolina Exposition and Protest challenges idea of majority rule
1830	Andrew Jackson vetoes extension of National Road
	Indian Removal Act
1831	*Cherokee Nation v. Georgia* denies Indians' claim of national independence
1832	Bad Axe Massacre of Sauk and Fox by American troops
	Jackson vetoes Second Bank bill
	South Carolina nullifies Tariff of 1832
1833	Force Bill and Tariff Act
1834	Whig Party formed by Henry Clay, John C. Calhoun, and Daniel Webster
1835	Roger Taney named Supreme Court Chief Justice
1837	*Charles River Bridge Co. v. Warren Bridge Co.* undermines legal position of chartered monopolies
	Panic of 1837 begins depression of 1837–1843
1838	Trail of Tears: thousands of Cherokee die on forced march to new Indian Territory
1840	Independent Treasury Act
	Whig victory in "log-cabin" campaign
1841	John Tyler succeeds William Henry Harrison as president
	Preemption Act promotes purchase of federal land
1842	*Commonwealth v. Hunt* legitimates trade unions

Suggested Readings

──────────★──────────

Two fine surveys of the Jacksonian era are Charles Sellers, *The Market Revolution: Jacksonian America, 1814–1846* (1992), and Harry L. Watson, *Liberty and Power: The Politics of Jacksonian America* (1990). See also Daniel Feller, *The Jacksonian Promise: America, 1815–1840* (1995).

The Rise of Popular Politics, 1820–1829

The classic study of American politics between 1815 and 1828 is George Dangerfield, *The Era of Good Feelings* (1952). More recent studies include James Sterling Young, *The Washington Community, 1800–1828* (1966); Harry Ammon, *James Monroe: The Quest for National Identity* (1971); and Merrill Peterson, *The Great Triumvirate: Webster, Clay, and Calhoun* (1987). The political innovations of Martin Van Buren are traced in John Niven, *Martin Van Buren: The Romantic Age of American Politics* (1983), and Robert V. Remini, *Martin Van Buren and the Making of the Democratic Party* (1959). See also Norman Risjord, *The Old Republicans* (1965), and Chilton Williamson, *American Suffrage from Property to Democracy, 1760–1860* (1960).

For John Quincy Adams and his administration, see Samuel Flagg Bemis, *John Quincy Adams and the Union* (1956); Leonard L. Richards, *The Life and Times of Congressman John Quincy Adams* (1986); and Mary Hargreaves, *The Presidency of John Quincy Adams* (1985). For foreign policy, see Ernest R. May, *The Making of the Monroe Doctrine* (1975).

The Presidency of Andrew Jackson, 1829–1837

Arthur M. Schlesinger Jr., *The Age of Jackson* (1945), initiated the modern reexamination of Andrew Jackson and his significance. Among the most provocative subsequent studies are Lee Benson, *The Concept of Jacksonian Democracy: New York as a Test Case* (1961); Marvin Meyers, *The Jacksonian Persuasion: Politics and Belief* (1957); and John William Ward, *Andrew Jackson: Symbol for an Age* (1962). For a comprehensive view of Jackson's life, see Robert V. Remini, *The Election of Andrew Jackson:* (1963), *Andrew Jackson and the Course of American Freedom, 1822–1833* (1977), *Andrew Jackson and the Course of American Democracy, 1833–1845* (1984), and *The Life of Andrew Jackson* (1988). Other studies include Donald Cole, *The Presidency of Andrew Jackson* (1992), and Leonard D. White, *The Jacksonians: A Study in Administrative History, 1828–1861* (1954).

On the politics of the bank war, see Robert V. Remini, *Andrew Jackson and the Bank War* (1967); Thomas P. Govan, *Nicholas Biddle: Nationalist and Public Banker, 1786–1844* (1959); and John M. McFaul, *The Politics of Jacksonian Finance.* On the nullification crisis, see Richard E. Ellis, *The Union at Risk* (1987), and two studies by William W. Freehling: *Prelude to Civil War* (1966), and *The Road to Disunion*, vol.1: *Secessionists at Bay, 1776–1854* (1990).

Works treating Jackson's Indian policy include Ralph S. Cotterill, *The Southern Indians* (1954); Grant Forman, *Indian Removal* (1953); Michael D. Green, *The Politics of Indian Removal* (1982); William G. McLoughlin, *Cherokee Renascence in the New Republic* (1986); Gary E. Moulton, *John Ross: Cherokee Chief* (1978); Francis P. Prucha, *American Indian Policy in the Formative Years* (1962), and *American Indian Treaties: The History of a Political Anomaly* (1994); and Ronald N. Satz, *American Indian Policy in the Jacksonian Era* (1975).

For a fine study of Jackson's successor, consult Major J. Wilson, *The Presidency of Martin Van Buren* (1984); see also James C. Curtis, *The Fox at Bay* (1970). Biographies of the leading Whig opponents of Jackson include Richard N. Current, *John C. Calhoun* (3 vols., 1944–1951); Irving H. Bartlett, *Daniel Webster* (1978); and Robert V. Remini, *Henry Clay: Statesman for the Union* (1991).

Class, Culture, and the Second Party System

A rich literature describes the emergence of the Whigs in the context of a changing political culture and the creation of the Second Party System. Books that deal broadly with these topics include John Ashworth, *"Agrarians" & "Aristocrats": Party Political Ideology in the United States, 1837–1846* (1983); Richard Hofstadter, *The Idea of a Party System* (1972); Daniel W. Howe, *The Political Culture of the American Whigs* (1979); and Robert Kelley, *The Cultural Pattern in American Politics: The First Century* (1979). Also see Stephen C. Bullock, *Revolutionary Brotherhood: Freemasonry and the Transformation of the American Social Order, 1730–1840* (1994); Lawrence F. Kohl, *The Politics of Individualism: Parties and the American Character in the Jacksonian Era* (1989); Richard P. McCormick, *The Second American Party System: Party Formation in the Jacksonian Era* (1966); and Joel H. Silbey, *The Partisan Imperative: The Dynamics of American Politics before the Civil War* (1985).

More specialized studies include Thomas Brown, *Politics and Statesmanship: Essays on the American Whig Party* (1985); Ronald P. Formisano, *The Birth of Mass Political Parties: Michigan, 1827–1861* (1972), and *The Transformation of Political Culture: Massachusetts Parties, 1790's–1840's* (1983); William G. Shade, *Banks or No Banks: The Money Issue in Western Politics, 1832–1865* (1972); and Harry L. Watson, *Jacksonian Politics and Community Conflict: The Emergence of the Second Party System in Cumberland County, North Carolina* (1981). For the presidency of John Tyler, see Robert J. Morgan, *A Whig Embattled* (1954).

For the impact of the Panic of 1837 on workers, see Norman Ware, *The Industrial Worker, 1840–1860* (1924); Mary H. Blewett, *Men, Women, and Work: Class, Gender, and Protest in the New England Shoe Industry, 1780–1910* (1988); Paul G. Faler, *Mechanics and Manufacturers in the Early Industrial Revolution* (1981); Ronald Schultz, *The Republic of Labor: Philadelphia Artisans and the Politics of Class* (1993); and Sean Wilentz, *Chants Democratic: New York City and the Rise of the American Working Class, 1788–1850* (1984). See also Christopher L. Tomlins, *Law, Labor and Ideology in the Early American Republic* (1993).

Little acts of kindness
Little words of love

Make our earthly eden
like our Heaven above

Is our
Home a
Heaven

Heaven
is our
Home

Peace Be still

Kind
words
Never
Die

Forgive
as you
hope to be
forgiven

Earth has
no sorrow
Heaven
cannot
heal

Be still
and know
that I am
God

No Cross No Crown

Thy will be done

Oh sacred
Patience
with my
soul abide

There is a
magic in
kindness
that springs
from above

Maria
Cadman
Hubbard
aged 79

If you can
not be a
Golden Pipp
indon't turn
crab epple

abide with us

Love one
another

1848

Chapter 12

The Ferment of Reform,
1820–1860

Individualism
Emerson and Transcendentalism
Emerson's Literary Influence
The Brook Farm Experiment

Communalism
The Shakers
The Fourierist Movement
Noyes and the Oneida Community
The Mormons

The Women's Movement
New Social Roles for Women
The Influence of Abolitionism
The Program of Seneca Falls

Abolitionism
African Colonization
Slave Rebellion
Evangelical Abolitionism
Opposition and Disunity

THE WHIRLWIND PACE of economic and political change in the 1820s and 1830s transformed the way Americans thought about themselves as individuals and as a society. Increasing opportunities encouraged many men and women to believe that they could improve not just their personal lives but society as a whole. Some dedicated themselves to the cause of reform. At first an antislavery advocate, William Lloyd Garrison went on to embrace women's rights, pacifism, and the abolition of all prisons. Such individuals—the Unitarian minister Henry W. Bellows cautioned—had committed themselves to the pursuit of "an object, which in its very nature is unattainable—the perpetual improvement of the outward condition."

Many obstacles stood in their way. America's social order was still rigidly divided by race and gender as well as by wealth and religious belief. As much as it liberated some individuals, the developing industrial and market economy meant new forms of social control for others, such as gang labor for enslaved African Americans, the strict work routine imposed on factory operatives, and the commitment to self-discipline and self-improvement among members of the middle class. Even the rise of democratic politics brought new norms of required conduct. Democratic Party officials would keep their positions "if they face the enemy" and resolutely followed the commands of the party's leaders, remarked one of Martin Van Buren's political lieutenants, "but the first man we see *step to the rear*, we *cut down*." Moreover, the

"Pieties Quilt," Maria Cadman Hubbard, 1848
Maria Cadman Hubbard may have been a Quaker, for "No Cross, No Crown" (the inscription on the far right) was the title of William Penn's pamphlet of the 1670s attacking the Church of England. Whatever her affiliation, she used her considerable skills as a quiltmaker to express her deeply held religious beliefs. Prior to the 1850s, women's names were not routinely kept in town records. Apart from the family bible, quilts such as this one might be the only record of a woman's life. By including her name (lower left-hand corner) and date (lower right-hand corner) in this unique quilt of pious sayings, Hubbard immortalized herself for future generations.
Museum of American Folk Art. Gift of Cyril Irwin Nelson in loving memory of his parents, Cyril Arthur and Elise Mary Nelson.

first wave of American "improvers," the Benevolent Empire of the 1820s, had seized on social discipline as the answer to the nation's ills, championing regular church attendance, temperance, and the strict moral codes of the evangelical churches.

Then, in the 1830s and 1840s, a more powerful reform wave spilled out of these conservative channels and washed over American society, threatening to submerge traditional values. Mostly middle-class northerners in origin, the new reformers propounded a bewildering assortment of radical ideals—extreme individualism, common ownership of property, sexual equality, the immediate emancipation of slaves—and demanded action to satisfy their visions. The result was a far-reaching intellectual and cultural debate that challenged the premises of the American social order. As a fearful southerner saw it, the goal of the reformers was a world in which there would be "No-Marriage, No-Religion, No-Private Property, No-Law and No Government."

Individualism

"Individualism" as we know it today was a product of the nineteenth century. Indeed, the term itself was coined in 1835 by Alexis de Tocqueville following his visit to the United States. He used it to describe those Americans who were "no longer attached to each other by any tie of caste, class, association, or family." The French aristocrat worried that as the numbers of such rootless individuals grew, organized society would disintegrate, first in America and then in Europe. Unlike Tocqueville, the New England author and lecturer Ralph Waldo Emerson celebrated this liberation of the individual from the constraints of traditional social ties and institutions. Emerson's vision of individual freedom influenced thousands of ordinary Americans and a generation of important artists and writers.

Emerson and Transcendentalism

Ralph Waldo Emerson (1803–1882) was the leading spokesman for transcendentalism, an intellectual movement rooted in the religious soil of New England. Its first advocates were spiritually inclined young men, often Unitarian ministers from well-to-do New England families, who questioned the constraints imposed by their Puritan heritage. For inspiration they turned to Europe, drawing on a new conception of self and society known as Romanticism. Romantic thinkers, such as the English poet Samuel Taylor Coleridge, rejected the ordered, rational world of the eighteenth-century Enlightenment. Instead they tried to capture the pas-

Success through Hard Work
During the nineteenth century many artists turned away from portraits, doing them only to earn a living, and began rendering scenes from life. In this painting, *A Farmer Whetting His Scythe*, William Sidney Mount (1807–1868), an accomplished artist who lived in rural New York, depicts a farmer who enjoys his work and, as is apparent from his dress, has prospered from his labor.
The Museums at Stony Brook, NY. Gift of Mr. and Mrs. Ward Melville, 1955.

sionate character of the human spirit and sought deeper insights into the mysteries of existence. Drawing on ideas borrowed from the German philosopher Immanuel Kant, English Romantics and their American followers believed that behind the concrete world of the senses was an *ideal* world. To reach this deeper reality, people had to "transcend," or go beyond, the ways in which they normally comprehended the world around them. By tapping mysterious intuitive powers, people could soar beyond the limits of ordinary experience and gain mystical knowledge of the ultimate and eternal.

Emerson had followed in the footsteps of his father and become a Unitarian minister, thus placing himself outside the religious mainstream. Unlike most Christians, Unitarians held that God was a single, unified being and not a trinity of Father, Son, and Holy Spirit (see Chapter 9). In 1832 Emerson moved still further from orthodox Christianity. After a crisis of conscience the twenty-nine-year-old minister resigned his Boston pulpit, rejecting organized religion in favor of individual moral insight.

Emerson moved to Concord, Massachusetts, and turned to writing essays and lecturing on his transcendentalist philosophy, supported in part by a legacy from his first wife. His subject was what he called "the infinitude of the private man," the idea of the radically free individual.

The young New England philosopher saw people as being trapped in inherited customs and institutions. "Our age is retrospective," he complained. People looked back, wearing the ideas fabricated in earlier times—the tenets of New England Calvinism, for example—as a kind of "faded masquerade," and needed to shed those values and practices. "What is a man born for but to be a Reformer, a Remaker of what man has made?" he asked. For Emerson, an individual's remaking depended on the discovery of his or her own "original relation with Nature," an insight that would lead to a mystical private union with the "currents of Universal Being." The ideal setting for such a discovery was solitude under an open sky, among nature's rocks and trees.

Emerson's genius lay in his capacity to translate abstract ideas into examples that made sense to ordinary middle-class Americans. He also succeeded in tempering the radical implications of these concepts, thus extending their appeal to a much wider audience. Strictly speaking, pantheism is the doctrine that the universe, conceived of as a whole, *is* God, an idea that underlay Emerson's attack on organized religion and that most Christians would have rejected. But Emerson described his pantheism as the idea that all of nature was saturated with the presence of God, leaving open the possibility that God existed separately from the universe, a concept that many Christians could accept.

Emerson's attitude toward the new industrial society was equally ambiguous. On the one hand, he condemned the deadening routine of the factory work that stifled people's creativity. Emerson also worried that a preoccupation with work, profits, and the consumption of factory-made goods would drain the nation's spiritual energy. "Things are in the saddle," he wrote, "and ride mankind." On the other hand, Emerson took the edge off his hostility to materialism by applauding human innovations in technology that philosophers had traditionally ignored or scorned, such as canals and railroads. At times he even celebrated money itself. Rather than being a source of corruption, it "represents the prose of life. [It] is in its effects and laws, as beautiful as roses."

The transcendentalist message of inner change and self-realization reached hundreds of thousands of people, primarily through Emerson's writings and lectures. Public lectures had become a spectacularly successful new way of spreading information and fostering discussion among the middle classes. Beginning in 1826, a Massachusetts organization known as the American Lyceum attempted to "promote the general diffusion of knowledge" by organizing lecture tours by all sorts of speakers—poets, preachers, scientists, and reformers. The

The Founder of Transcendentalism
As this painting of Ralph Waldo Emerson by an unknown artist indicates, the young New England philosopher was an attractive man, his face brimming with confidence and optimism. Because of his radiant personality, Emerson deeply influenced dozens of influential writers, artists, and scholars, and enjoyed great success as a lecturer among the emerging middle class. The Metropolitan Museum of Art. Bequest of Chester Dale, 1962 [64.97.4].

Lyceum movement—named in honor of the place where the ancient Greek philosopher Aristotle taught—soon took firm hold, especially in the North. In 1839, for example, 137 local Lyceum groups in Massachusetts invited lecturers to their towns during the fall and winter "season" to speak to more than 33,000 subscribers. Among the hundreds of lecturers on the Lyceum circuit, Emerson was the most popular. Between 1833 and 1860 he gave 1,500 lectures in more than 300 towns in twenty states.

Emerson's celebration of the liberated individual tapped currents that already ran deep in his middle-class audiences. The publication of Benjamin Franklin's *Autobiography* in 1818 had given Americans a down-to-earth model of an individual seeking "moral perfection" through self-discipline. Charles Grandison Finney's account of his conversion experience in 1823 also pointed in Emersonian directions. Finney, the foremost business-class evangelist, pictured his conversion as a mystical union of an individual, alone in the woods, with God. And the great revivalist's message, like that of Emerson, affirmed the importance of individual action. As Finney put it, "God has made man a moral free agent," endowing individuals with the ability to determine their spiritual as well as their worldly fate.

Emerson's Literary Influence

Emerson took as one of his tasks the remaking of American literature. In an address entitled "The American Scholar" (1837) the philosopher issued a literary declaration of independence from the "courtly muse" of old Europe. He urged American writers to celebrate democracy and individual freedom and find inspiration not in the doings and sayings of aristocratic courts but in the "familiar, the low . . . the milk in the pan; the ballad in the street; the news of the boat; the glance of the eye; the form and gait of the body."

Thoreau and Fuller. A young New England intellectual, Henry David Thoreau (1817–1862), heeded Emerson's call by looking to the American environment for inspiration. Shortly after his graduation from college, Thoreau turned away from society and embraced self-reliance and the natural world, building a cabin at the edge of Walden Pond near Concord, Massachusetts, and living alone there for two years—mostly on his own produce. In 1854 he published *Walden, or Life in the Woods,* an account of his spiritual search for meaning that went beyond the artificiality of life in a "civilized" society:

> I went to the woods because I wished to live deliberately, confront only the essential facts of life, and see if I could not learn what it had to teach, and not, when I came to die, discover that I had not lived.

In writing *Walden,* Thoreau did not wish to promote a life of hermit-like subsistence farming but rather to urge his readers to probe the deeper, spiritual meanings of their lives. Although Thoreau's book had little impact outside transcendentalist circles during his lifetime, *Walden* has become an essential text of American literature and an inspiration to those who reject the dictates of society. Its most famous metaphor provides an enduring justification for independent thinking: "If a man does not keep pace with his companions, perhaps it is because he hears a different drummer." Beginning from this premise, Thoreau became an advocate for social nonconformity and a philosopher of civil disobedience—arguing that it was morally acceptable to refuse to obey unjust laws.

As Thoreau sought independence and self-realization for men, Margaret Fuller (1810–1850) explored the possibilities of freedom for women. Born into a wealthy Boston family, Fuller learned to read the classic works of literature in six languages and educated her four siblings.

Margaret Fuller, 1848
At the age of 38, Fuller moved to Italy, where she worked as a correspondent during Italy's revolution of 1848. While there, Fuller became enamored of Thomas Hicks (1823–1890), a much younger American artist. Hicks rebuffed Fuller's advances but painted this rather flattering portrait, softening her features and giving her a pensive look. After this portrait was painted, Fuller married a Roman nobleman, Giovanni Angelo, Marchese d'Ossoli, and gave birth to a son in September 1848.
Constance Fuller Threinen.

After teaching in a girls' school, she became interested in Emerson's ideas and in 1839 began a transcendental "conversation," or discussion group, for elite Boston women. Soon Fuller was editing the leading transcendentalist journal, the *Dial,* and in 1844 she published *Woman in the Nineteenth Century,* which proclaimed that a "new era" was coming for men and women.

Although Fuller had been influenced by the feminist ideas of Mary Wollstonecraft (see Chapter 7), her philosophy began with the transcendental belief that women, like men, had a mystical relationship with God that gave them identity and dignity. It followed that every woman deserved psychological and social independence—the ability "to grow, as an intellect to discern, as a soul to live freely and unimpeded." Thus, she declared, "We would have every arbitrary barrier thrown down" and "every path laid open to Woman as freely as to Man." Embracing that vision, Fuller became the literary critic of the *New York Tribune* and went to

Italy to report on the revolution of 1848. Her adventurous life brought an early death; while returning to the United States at the age of forty, she drowned in a shipwreck. But Fuller's example and writings inspired the rising generation of women reformers.

Whitman. Another writer who responded to Emerson's call was the poet Walt Whitman (1819–1892). Whitman said that when he first encountered Emerson, he had been "simmering, simmering." Then Emerson "brought me to a boil." Whitman had been a journalist, an editor of the *Brooklyn Eagle* and other newspapers, and an active publicist for the Democratic Party. But it was poetry that was the "direction of his dreams." In *Leaves of Grass*, first published in 1855 and constantly revised and expanded for almost four decades afterward, he recorded his attempt to pass a number of "invisible boundaries": between solitude and community, between prose and poetry, and even between the living and the dead. It was a wild, exuberant poem in both form and content, self-consciously violating every poetic rule and every canon of respectable taste. Unlike the cautious Emerson, Whitman dared readers to shut the book in revulsion or accept his idiosyncratic vision.

At the center of *Leaves of Grass* is the individual—the figure of the poet, "I, Walt." He begins alone: "I celebrate myself, and sing myself," loafing in nature, "observing a spear of summer grass." But because he has what Emerson called an "original relation" with nature, Whitman claims not solitude but perfect communion with others: "For every atom belonging to me as good belongs to you." Whitman was celebrating democracy as well as himself, arguing that a poet could claim a profoundly intimate, mystical relationship with a mass audience. For Emerson, Thoreau, and Fuller the individual had a divine spark. For Whitman the individual had expanded to *become* divine, and democracy assumed a sacred character.

Despite their hopes for Americans, the transcendentalists were not naive optimists. Whitman wrote of human suffering with as much passion as he wrote of everything else. Emerson's accounts of the exhilaration that could come in communion with nature were tinged with anxiety. "I am glad," he said, "to the brink of fear." Thoreau's gloomy judgment of everyday life is well known: "The mass of men lead lives of quiet desperation." Still, such dark murmurings were muted in their work, woven into triumphant and expansive assertions that nothing was impossible for an individual who could break free from tradition, law, and other social restraints.

Darker Visions. Emerson's influence also reached two great novelists, Nathaniel Hawthorne and Herman Melville, and two other important writers, Edgar Allan Poe and Emily Dickinson, all of whom had more pessimistic visions. In their novels Hawthorne and Melville

addressed the opposition between individual transcendence and the legitimate requirements of social order, discipline, and responsibility. Like Tocqueville, they sounded powerful warnings that unfettered egoism could destroy individuals and the fragile bonds of social life. They embraced the ideal of individual freedom but at the same time urged the acceptance of an inner discipline.

Hawthorne's most brilliant exploration of the theme of excessive individualism appeared in his novel *The Scarlet Letter* (1850). The two main characters, Hester Prynne and Arthur Dimmesdale, challenge their seventeenth-century New England community in the most blatant way—by committing adultery, producing a child, and refusing to bend to the community's condemnation. The result of their assertion of individual freedom from social discipline is not exaltation but tragedy. Racked by guilt and unable to confess, Dimmesdale dies in anguish. Prynne learns from her experience that the way to a truly virtuous life can be found only by a person who is willing to do good within the social order.

Melville explored the limits of individualism in even more extreme and tragic terms, and emerged as a scathing critic of transcendentalism. He made his most powerful statement in *Moby Dick* (1851), the story of Captain Ahab's obsessive hunt for a mysterious white whale that had severed his leg during an earlier expedition. Ahab is a version of Emerson's liberated individual with an intuitive grasp of hidden meanings in nature. Believing that the whale is pure, demonic evil, Ahab is determined to hunt it down, no matter what the cost. In the end this quest for spiritual meaning in nature brings death, not transcendence, to Ahab and his crew. Only one member of the crew, the social outcast Ishmael, is left to tell the sorry tale.

Moby Dick was a commercial failure. The middle-class audience that was the primary target of American publishers was unwilling to follow Melville into the dark, dangerous realm of individualism gone mad. It also did not relish the visions of terror and evil that Edgar Allan Poe, a southern-born admirer of Hawthorne, created in "The Raven" (1845) and other poems and short stories. Poe won respect in New York literary circles but could not find a broader audience. Emily Dickinson, another poet whose work expressed doubts about individualism, did not even try to find readers. During the 1850s she kept private the poetry she had begun to write in isolation in Amherst, Massachusetts.

Even more optimistic works such as *Walden* and *Leaves of Grass* failed to find a large readership. American readers had little enthusiasm for Thoreau's advocacy of civil disobedience and Whitman's boundless claims for a mystical union between the individual of genius and the democratic mass. What they emphatically preferred were the more modest examples of individualism offered by Emerson and Hawthorne—self-improvement through hard work and personal discipline.

The Brook Farm Experiment

To escape the constraints of life in industrializing America, transcendentalists and other radical reformers created ideal communities, or *utopias.* They hoped that these planned societies, which organized community life in new ways, would allow members to realize their full spiritual and moral potential. The most important communal experiment of the transcendentalists was Brook Farm, founded in West Roxbury, Massachusetts, in 1841. Freed from the tension and degradation of an urban competitive society, its members hoped to develop their minds and souls and uplift society through their example. The Brook Farmers supported themselves by selling milk, vegetables, and hay for cash but organized their farming so that they could remain relatively independent from the market. Residents who did not work on the farm made cash payments—in effect, tuition for what was virtually a transcendentalist boarding school.

The intellectual life at Brook Farm was electric. Hawthorne lived there for a time and later used the setting for *The Blithedale Romance* (1852). All the important transcendentalists, including Emerson, Thoreau, and Fuller, were residents or frequent visitors. A former member recalled that they "inspired the young with a passion for study, and the middle-aged with deference and admiration, while we all breathed the intellectual grace that pervaded the atmosphere." Music, dancing, games, plays, parties, picnics, and dramatic readings filled the leisure hours. For many Brook Farmers, this cultural education transformed their lives—"a French Revolution in small," as Emerson put it.

Although Brook Farm provided intellectual fulfillment, it faltered in achieving economic self-sufficiency. At first most of its members were ministers, teachers, writers, and students who had few productive skills; to succeed it needed practical men and women. In 1844 a reorganization attracted more farmers and artisans but yielded only marginal economic gains. And these changes resulted in a more disciplined routine that, as one resident put it, suppressed "the joyous spirit of youth." After a devastating fire in 1846, the organizers disbanded and sold the farm.

After the failure of Brook Farm, the transcendentalists abandoned their attempts to fashion a new system of social organization. Most accepted the brutal reality of industrial society but continued to try to reform it, especially through the education of workers. However, the passion of the transcendentalists for individual freedom lived on in the movement to abolish slavery, which many of them joined.

Communalism

——————★——————

Even as Brook Farm faded, thousands of Americans joined other communal settlements during the 1840s, primarily in the Northeast and Midwest. Most were

Brook Farm, *Josiah Walcott, 1844*
Unlike most other nineteenth-century communal settlements, the Brook Farm transcendentalist enclave did not begin as a rude wilderness camp. Thanks to the generosity of social reformer George Ripley and his wife, Sophia, Brook Farm took shape in 1841 on a well-established farm in West Roxbury, Massachusetts, near Boston. Consequently, its residents could restrict their farmwork to half of the day and spend the other half engaged in literary and intellectual pursuits.
Courtesy of Mrs. Robert Blake Watson.

ordinary people seeking refuge and security from the seven-year economic depression that had begun with the Panic of 1837. But these rural utopias were also symbols of social protest, explicitly challenging the values of the larger society by organizing themselves along socialist lines with common ownership of property, or by experimenting with unconventional forms of marriage and family life. In questioning acquisitive capitalist values and traditional gender roles, the communalists pointed to major cultural strains in American society.

The Shakers

The Shakers, the first successful American communal movement, dated back to the era of the Revolution. In 1770 Ann Lee Stanley (Mother Ann), an illiterate cook and factory worker in Manchester, England, had a vision in which God revealed to her that Adam and Eve had been banished from the Garden of Eden because of their sexual lust. Consequently, Ann Lee embraced the practice of celibacy, because it restored the purity of Paradise. In 1774 she led a band of eight followers to America, where they established a church near Albany, New York. Because of the ecstatic dances that became part of their worship, the sect became known as "Shaking Quakers" or, more simply, "Shakers" (see Voices from Abroad, "The Mystical World of the Shakers," p. 386). After Mother Ann's death the Shakers venerated her as the Second Coming of Christ, and they decided to withdraw from the evils of the world into strictly run communities of believers. Members had to declare themselves "sick of sin" and follow a program of confession. To the Shakers, sin was wholly the product of a society that put obstacles in the way of a chaste and self-denying life.

Shaker communities embraced the common ownership of property and vowed to abstain from politics and war. Over time Shaker doctrine also included a ban on tobacco and alcoholic drink. Most striking, Shakers eliminated marriage and made a commitment to celibacy, in accordance with Mother Ann's testimony against "the lustful gratifications of the flesh as the source and foundation of human corruption." Men and women lived apart in gender-segregated dormitories.

The Shakers believed that God was "a dual person, male and female," and that Mother Ann represented God's female element. These doctrines provided the underpinning for their attempt to banish distinctions between the sexes. In practice, Shakers maintained the traditional division of labor between men and women, but they vested the authority for governing each community—in both its religious and its economic spheres—in women and men alike, the Eldresses and Elders. And they welcomed blacks as well as whites; to Rebecca Cox Jackson, an African American seamstress from Philadelphia who joined their community, the Shakers seemed to be "loving to live forever."

The Shaker Community at Poland Hill, Maine (detail)
Like all Shaker communities, the settlement at Poland Hill, Maine, painted by Joshua H. Bussell around 1850, was built on a regular gridlike plan. There was a large dwelling for communal living, surrounded by various workshops and farm buildings. The design of the architecture, like that of Shaker furniture, was plain and sparse.
Collection of the United Society of Shakers, Sabbathday Lake, Maine.

Between the 1780s and the 1840s Shakers founded twenty communities, mostly in New England, New York, and Ohio (Map 12.1). Their agriculture and crafts, especially furniture making, acquired a reputation for quality that enabled most of these communities to become self-sustaining and even comfortable. Thanks to this economic success and their ideology of sexual equality, Shaker communities attracted more than 3,000 converts during the 1830s, with women outnumbering men more than two to one. Because Shakers had no children of their own, they had to rely on converts and the adoption of young orphans to replenish their numbers. As these sources dried up in the 1840s and 1850s, the communities stopped growing and eventually began to decline.

Because of their celibacy, Shaker communities could never provide a model for society as a whole; at best, they could serve as a place of refuge for those fleeing life in an individualistic, industrial world. By the end of the nineteenth century most Shaker communities had disappeared, leaving as their material legacy a distinctive and much-imitated furniture style.

The Mystical World of the Shakers

★

Foreigners were both attracted to and distressed by the strange religious practices they found in the United States. In either case, they made certain to include reports of revivals and communal settlements in their letters and journals. In a book recounting his travels in America in the 1830s, an anonymous British visitor describes a Shaker dance and the sect's intimate contact with spiritual worlds inaccessible to those without faith.

At half past seven p.m. on the dancing days, all the members retired to their separate rooms, where they sat in solemn silence, just gazing at the stove, until the silver tones of the small tea-bell gave the signal for them to assemble in the large hall. Thither they proceeded in perfect order and solemn silence. Each had on dancing shoes; and on entering the door of the hall they walked on tip-toe, and took up their positions as follows: the brothers formed a rank on the right, and the sisters on the left, facing each other, about five feet apart. After all were in their proper places the chief Elder . . . gave an exhortation for about five minutes, concluding . . . "go forth, old men, young men and maidens, and worship God with all [your] might in the dance.". . .

They commenced dancing, and continued it until they were pretty well tired. During the dance the sisters kept on one side, and the brothers on the other, and not a word was spoken by any one of them. . . . [Then] each one took his or her place in an oblong circle formed around the room, and all waited to see if anyone had received a "gift," that is, an inspiration to do something odd. Then two of the sisters would commence whirling round like a top, with their eyes shut; and continued this motion for about fifteen minutes. . . .

On some occasions when a sister had stopped whirling, she would say, "I have a communication to make"; . . . The first message I heard was as follows. "Mother Ann has sent two angels to inform us that a tribe of Indians has been round here two days, and want the brothers and sisters to take them in." . . . The first Elder exhorted the brothers "to take in the poor spirits and assist them to get salvation." He afterward repeated more of what the angels had said, viz., "that Indians were a savage tribe who had all died before Columbus discovered America, and had been wandering about ever since.". . . Whereupon eight or nine sisters became possessed of the spirits of Indian squaws, and about six of the brethren became Indians. Then ensued a regular pow-wow, with whooping and yelling and strange antics, such as would require a Dickens to describe. . . .

At one of the meetings . . . two or three sisters commenced whirling . . . and revealed to us that Mother Ann was present at the meeting, and that she had brought a dozen baskets of spiritual fruit for her children. . . . Accordingly they all stepped forth and went through the various motions of taking fruit and eating it. You will wonder if I helped myself to the fruit, like the rest. No; I had not faith enough to see the baskets or the fruit. . . .

Source: Noel Rae, ed., _Witnessing America_ (New York: Penguin Press, 1966), 372–373.

The Fourierist Movement

The rise of the American Fourierist movement in the 1840s was one cause of the Shakers' decline. Charles Fourier (1777–1837) was a French utopian reformer who devised an eight-stage theory of social evolution and predicted the imminent decline of the present stage of individualism and capitalism. Arthur Brisbane, Fourier's idealistic American disciple, gave a republican twist to his theories. For Brisbane, Fourierism meant "completion of our great political movement of 1776" through the creation of new social institutions that would end the "menial and slavish system of Hired Labor or Labor for Wages."

In the place of capitalist wage-labor, Fourierists would work and live cooperatively in groups called _phalanxes_. The members of a phalanx would be its shareholders; they would own all its property in common, including stores and a bank as well as a school and a library. Fourier and Brisbane saw the phalanx as a practical, more humane alternative to the emerging capitalist society and one that would liberate women as well as men. "In society as it is now constituted," Brisbane wrote, "Woman is subjected to unremitting and slavish

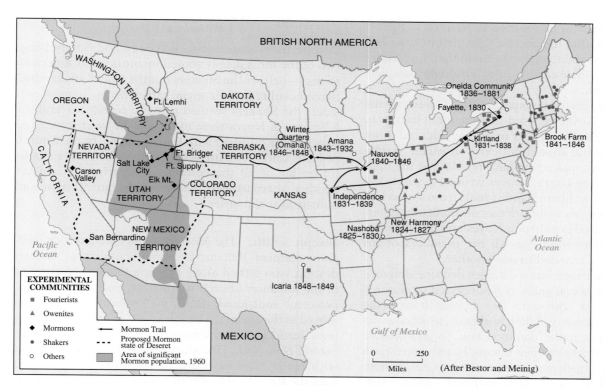

MAP 12.1
Communal Experiments before 1860
Some experimental communities settled in frontier regions, but the vast majority chose relatively secluded regions in well-settled areas. Because of their opposition to slavery, most communalists avoided the South. Those Mormons who in the late 1840s followed Brigham Young into what was then Mexican territory (becoming part of the United States in 1848) formed the largest and most enduring communal society.

domestic duties"; in the "new Social Order . . . based upon Associated households," women's domestic drudge-work would be eliminated or shared with men.

Brisbane skillfully promoted Fourier's ideas in his influential book *The Social Destiny of Man* (1840), in a regular column in Horace Greeley's *New York Tribune,* and in hundreds of lectures, many of them in towns along the Erie Canal. These ideas found a receptive audience among educated farmers and craftsmen, some of whom had joined the socialist community of Robert Owen in New Harmony, Indiana (1824–1827), and who now yearned for economic stability and communal solidarity in the wake of the Panic of 1837. In the 1840s Brisbane and his followers started nearly 100 cooperative communities from Massachusetts to Michigan, but almost all were unable to support themselves and soon collapsed. Despite its failure to establish viable communities, the Fourierist movement underscored the extent of the social discontent caused by the economic depression. It also revealed the difficulty of establishing a utopian community in the absence of a charismatic leader or a compelling religious vision.

Noyes and the Oneida Community

The radical minister John Humphrey Noyes was both charismatic and deeply religious. He believed that the Fourierists had failed because their communities lacked the strong religious ethic required for sustained altruism and cooperation. Instead, he pointed to the success of the Shakers, praising them as the true "pioneers of modern Socialism" because they questioned men's control of property and of women. Noyes was attracted by the Shakers' marriageless society and set about creating a community that defined sexuality and gender roles as well as property rights in dramatically new and radical ways.

Noyes was a well-to-do graduate of Dartmouth College, who was inspired to join the ministry by the preaching of Charles Finney. When Noyes developed radical religious doctrines and was expelled from his Congregational church, he became a leading advocate of "perfectionism." Perfectionism was a Christian evangelical movement that gathered thousands of followers during the 1830s, primarily among religiously minded

New Englanders who had settled in New York. Perfectionists believed that the Second Coming of Christ had already occurred and that people could therefore aspire to perfection in their earthly lives, attaining complete freedom from sin.

Unlike most perfectionists (who lived conventional personal lives), Noyes believed that the main barrier to achieving this ideal state was marriage, which did not exist in heaven and should not exist on earth. "Exclusiveness, jealousy, quarreling have no place at the marriage supper of the Lamb," Noyes wrote. He wanted to reform marriage to liberate individuals from sin, as had the Shakers, but his solution was dramatically different: instead of Shaker celibacy, Noyes and his followers embraced *complex marriage*—all the members of his community were married to one another.

Complex marriage was a complex doctrine designed to attain various social goals. Noyes rejected monogamy partly because he wished to free women from being regarded as the property of their husbands, which was virtually their status under common law. To give women more freedom to develop their talents, he advocated birth control. Noyes urged men to have intercourse without orgasm, which also demonstrated their self-discipline. For those children that were born, Noyes established community nurseries. By freeing women from endless childbearing and child raising, Noyes hoped to make them full members of the community. To symbolize their equality with men, the women cut their hair short and wore pantaloons under their calf-length skirts.

In the late 1830s Noyes gathered an initial group of followers in his hometown of Putney, Vermont, but local opposition to the practice of complex marriage prompted him in 1848 to move the community to the more isolated setting of Oneida, New York. By the mid-1850s more than 200 people were living at Oneida, and it became financially self-sufficient when the inventor of a highly successful steel animal trap joined the community. With the profits from the production of traps and various household goods, Oneida diversified into making silverware with the brand name Community Plate. After Noyes fled to Canada in 1879 to avoid prosecution for adultery, the community abandoned complex marriage and founded a joint-stock silverware manufacturing company, the Oneida Community, Ltd., which survived well into the twentieth century.

As with the Shakers and Fourierists, the primary historical significance of Noyes and his followers does not lie in their numbers, which were small. Nor does it reside in their crafts, despite their lasting impact on the design of American silverware. The importance of all these experiments lies rather in their determined effort to create alternative communities that repudiated the class divisions and sexual norms of American society. They stood as countercultural blueprints for a more egalitarian social order.

The Mormons

Despite their challenge to marriage and family life—two of the most deeply rooted institutions in American society—neither the Shakers nor the Oneidians aroused fierce hostility to their social experiments. To most outsiders the Shakers seemed pathetic eccentrics, and the followers of Noyes were too few to be worrisome. The case was far different with the Mormons, or the Church of Jesus Christ of Latter-Day Saints—the most successful by far of all the communal experiments and yet another alternative to the emerging individualist and industrial social order.

Joseph Smith. The Mormons emerged from the religious ferment that arose among families of Puritan descent who settled along the Erie Canal. The founder of the Mormon Church was Joseph Smith, a vigorous, powerful individual. Born in Vermont in 1805, he moved at the age of ten with his very religious but rather poor farming and shopkeeping family to Palmyra in central New York. His education was rudimentary, but with his mother he heard innumerable sermons and read the Bible constantly. In a series of religious experiences that began in 1820, Smith came to believe that God had singled him out to receive a special revelation of divine truth. Like the prophets of the Old Testament, he would carry a message that would redeem a society fatally flawed by excessive individualism.

In 1830 Smith published *The Book of Mormon*, claiming he had translated it from ancient hieroglyphics on gold plates shown to him by an angel named Moroni. *The Book of Mormon* told the story of ancient civilizations from the Middle East that had migrated to the Western Hemisphere, and of the visit of Jesus Christ, soon after the Resurrection, to one of them. On a metaphorical level, the book describes the success of societies that follow the Ten Commandments and biblical revelations.

Smith proceeded to organize the Church of Jesus Christ of Latter-Day Saints, which claimed control over many aspects of members' lives and reaffirmed the primacy of the husband within the family. Like Charles Finney and other Protestant ministers of the time, Smith and other church leaders encouraged followers to adopt practices central to success in the age of capitalist markets and factories: hard work, saving, and risk taking. Unlike those ministers, they placed equal emphasis on a communal framework that would protect the Mormon "New Jerusalem" from outside threats and create a structure for the achievement of human perfection.

Smith struggled for years to establish a sanctuary for his new religion. In the face of persecution in various neighboring settlements, Smith and his growing congregation trekked from western New York to Kirtland, Ohio, then to Independence, Missouri, finally settling in

Mob Violence against Mormons
In this lithograph of the *Martyrdom of Joseph and Hiram Smith in Carthage Jail, June 27, 1844*, the artist, G. N. Fasel after C. G. Crehen, evokes sympathy for the fallen Mormon leader by depicting one of the assailants as a masked ruffian, prevented from mutilating the corpse only by the intervention of a gentleman. In fact, many leading politicians and businessmen feared Smith and welcomed the mob's action. The murders of the Smith brothers prompted the decision of Brigham Young, the new head of the Mormon Church, to lead his followers out of the United States into the wilderness. The migrating people, more than 10,000 strong, settled in what is now Salt Lake City, Utah.
Library of Congress.

Nauvoo, Illinois, a town they founded on the Mississippi River. By the early 1840s Nauvoo had become the largest utopian community in the United States, with 30,000 inhabitants. But the rigid discipline and secrecy of the Mormons, along with their prosperity, hostility to other sects, and bloc voting in Illinois elections, fueled resentment among their neighbors (see American Voices, "An Illinois 'Jeffersonian' Attacks the Mormons," p. 390). This resentment became overt hostility when Smith refused to abide by any Illinois law that he did not approve of personally, asked Congress to turn Nauvoo into a federal territory, and (in 1844) declared himself a candidate for president of the United States.

Moreover, Smith had a new revelation that justified *polygamy*—the practice of a man having multiple wives at the same time. A few Mormon leaders began to practice polygamy, dividing the community from within, while economic and political issues encouraged assaults from without. In 1844 Smith was arrested and charged with treason for allegedly conspiring with foreign powers to create a Mormon colony in Mexico. An anti-Mormon mob stormed the jail in Carthage, Illinois, where Smith and his brother were being held, and murdered them.

Brigham Young and Utah. Now led by Brigham Young, an early convert to the church, the Mormon elders sought religious independence by leaving the United States to create a new settlement in the western wilderness. In 1846 Young began a phased migration of more than 10,000 people across the Great Plains. (Many of the migrants accepted the practice of polygamy;

those who remained in the United States did not. Led by Smith's son, Joseph Smith III, they formed the Reorganized Church of Jesus Christ of Latter-Day Saints, headquartered in Independence, Missouri.) Young's party eventually reached the Great Salt Lake in what was still Mexican territory. Using communal labor and an elaborate irrigation system based on communal water rights, the Mormon pioneers transformed the desert. They quickly spread planned agricultural communities along the base of the Wasatch Range in present-day Utah.

When the United States acquired Utah from Mexico in 1848 (see Chapter 13), Congress rejected a Mormon petition to create a new state, Deseret, stretching all the way to Los Angeles and San Diego. Instead, in 1850 it set up the much smaller Utah Territory, with Young as territorial governor. Eight years later, Democratic president James Buchanan removed Young from the governorship. Responding to pressure from Christian churches and the rival Republican Party, whose members denounced polygamy as one of the "relics of barbarism," Buchanan dispatched a small army to Salt Lake City. However, the "Mormon War" proved bloodless because Buchanan withdrew the troops when the Mormons refused to change their marriage practices. Buchanan feared that the forced abolition of the "domestic institution" of polygamy would serve as a precedent for the ending of slavery as well. Subsequently, preoccupation with the Civil War and Reconstruction prevented Republican administrations from paying much attention to Utah. Consequently, the national government did not succeed in pressuring the

An Illinois "Jeffersonian" Attacks the Mormons

———★———

The corporate solidarity of the Mormon community enraged many Illinois residents, who feared both the political power wielded by the Mormons' large and nearly independent city-state at Nauvoo and the military might of the 2,000-strong "Legion" commanded by Joseph Smith. In 1844 a mob led by "respectable citizens" assassinated Smith and his brother, and some Illinois residents—such as the author of this letter to the Warsaw Signal, a newspaper in a town near Nauvoo—called for the forcible expulsion of the Mormons from the state.

Mr. Editor,

. . . It is a low pitiable contemptable kind of electioneering, that old Tom Jefferson would have been ashamed of—when a body of men acting under the garb of religion (as the Mormons themselves say they are) shall decide our elections and act together as a body politically, we might as well bid a final farewell to our liberties and the common rights of man.

Now Sir, under all these circumstances, it is high time that every individual should come out and clearly define the position that he occupies. I too am an Anti-Mormon both in principle and in practice. . . . Mr. Editor when I speak harshly of the Mormons, I wish it to be perfectly understood I do not mean every individual that advocates the Mormon cause. By no means; that there are some good, law-abiding peaceable citizens belonging to the Mormon profession I verily believe . . . but I am opposed to them because of the unprincipled manner in which the leaders of that fanatical sect, set at defiance the laws of the land . . . (as was the case in Missouri) claiming to be the chosen people of God; not subject to the laws of the state in any respect whatever, and receiving revelations direct from Heaven almost daily commanding them to take the property of the older citizens of the county and confiscate it to the use of the Mormon church. . . .

It was for the commission of such deeds together with deeds ten fold more dark and damning in their nature that finally led to their expulsion from that state, and one of the brightest pages in the history of Missouri is that, on which is written "Governor Boggs's exterminating order" directing that the lawless rabble should be driven beyond the limits of the state, or exterminated at their own option. They chose the former, [which was] a most unfortunate thing for the state of Illinois.

Strange to tell, yet such is the fact, they have commenced nearly the same operation here that they did in Missouri . . . they have attempted to subsidize the press, thereby attempting to corrupt the very fountains of public virtue,—they have went [sic] into the legislative halls and attempted to bribe the representatives of the people in their seats and made them their tools.

They have in short, by a long series of high handed outrages . . . forfeited all claims (if any they ever had) to confidence and respect, and ought justly to receive the condemnation of every individual, not only in this community, but in this nation.

Source: David Brion Davis, Antebellum America: An Interpretive Anthology (University Park: Pennsylvania State University Press, 1997), 226–227.

Utah Mormons to abolish polygamy until 1890, six years before Utah became a state.

The Mormon Church in Utah and the Reorganized Church in Missouri had succeeded where other social experiments and utopian communities had failed. They endorsed the private ownership of property and encouraged individualistic economic enterprise, accepting the entrepreneurial spirit of market society. But Mormon leaders resolutely used strict religious controls to create disciplined communities and patriarchal families, reaffirming values inherited from the eighteenth century. This blend of economic innovation, social conservativism, and hierarchical leadership continued into the twentieth century, creating prosperous churches with a strong missionary impulse and millions of members.

The Women's Movement

———★———

The prominence of gender issues—sexual behavior, marriage, family authority—among Mormons, Shakers, and Noyesites was the product of a broad shift in American culture, particularly in the North. After the American Revolution northern women played an increasingly prominent role in public life, joining religious revivals and reform movements. Slavery was among the targets of women reformers, and their abolitionist activities created great controversy and caused some of them to become advocates of women's rights. These activists argued that women had social and political rights as individuals—rights that equaled those of men.

New Social Roles for Women

During the American Revolution, upper-class women had demanded increased legal rights for married women and more educational opportunities for their daughters, but they had been given only a slightly enhanced status as "republican mothers." Subsequently the economic revolution presented young farm women with new opportunities for outwork and factory labor; at the same time, it helped to relegate middle-class married women to a "separate" domestic sphere (see Chapter 9). Rather than working as household producers (the traditional roles of the wives of farmers and artisans), middle-class women became full-time providers of household services, such as child care. However, many of these women achieved greater authority within their families by joining religious revivals and becoming guardians of morality. Such activities bolstered their self-esteem and encouraged them to expand their influence over decisions in all areas of family life, including the timing of pregnancies.

Women Authors. The advent of a popular press directed at middle-class readers, the majority of whom were women, also influenced women's social roles. Publications such as *Godey's Lady's Book* (1821–1858) and Catharine Beecher's *Treatise on Domestic Economy* (1841) taught women how to make their homes more efficient and moral, and justified a life of child rearing and middle-class domesticity. But the most popular women writers wrote fiction. The author Catharine Maria Sedgwick won wide popularity in the 1820s, as did Caroline Howard Gilman and Caroline Lee Hentz in the next decade. Writers whose names are virtually unknown today—Sara Parton, Augusta Evans Wilson, and Susan Warner—reached even larger audiences in the 1850s. The sentimental melodramas composed by these women authors were often punctuated by tearful domestic scenes and suggested that women could achieve their potential only within the sphere of marriage and the family. In her last novel, *Married or Single* (1857), Sedgwick concluded that marriage was "the great circumstance" of a woman's life whereby she could form the character of her husband and children.

The most successful woman author of the period was Harriet Beecher Stowe, one of the daughters of the influential congregationalist minister Lyman Beecher. Stowe's novel *Uncle Tom's Cabin* (1852), which sold 350,000 copies in its first year, was first and foremost an antislavery tract, but it was also an argument for the superior morality of women and the importance of family life. Stowe gave the home a deeply religious meaning, writing in *The Minister's Wooing* (1859) that it was the "appointed sphere for woman, more holy than cloister, more saintly and pure than church and altar."

There was an ironic twist to this celebration of the private sphere of home, marriage, and family. These writers were actually engaged in a very public—and commercial—enterprise. Bargaining with their publishers, often making their own living, and supporting their families, they were among the first successful professional women in the United States. These talented and energetic women were erasing the contradiction between "domestic" and "public" life and justifying the concept of the independent woman. But they did so in a subtle and nonthreatening fashion by promoting morality and thereby assuming one of the roles of the minister. Indeed, Caroline Lee Hentz described her writing career as the "vocation . . . for which God has endowed me."

Reformers and Teachers. For most middle-class women, a greater influence over family life was enough, but some women used their new religious authority to expand their involvement outside the home. Moral reform was among the first of their efforts in the public arena. In 1834 a group of middle-class women in New York City launched an aggressive campaign to end prostitution, redeem their "fallen" sisters from a life of sin, and protect single women from sexually predatory men. Founding the New York Female Moral Reform Society, they elected Lydia Finney, the wife of Charles Finney, as its president. By 1837 the Society had 250 chapters in towns and villages throughout New York State, and 15,000 members. Three years later it had grown into a national association—the American Female Moral Reform Society—with 555 chapters throughout the North.

Employing only women as its agents, bookkeepers, and staff, the society attempted to provide moral "government" for factory girls, seamstresses, clerks, and servants who lived away from their families. Women reformers even invaded brothels, where they sang hymns, offered prayers, searched for runaway girls, and noted the names of clients. They also founded homes of refuge for prostitutes and homeless women, and won the passage of laws regulating sexual behavior—including making seduction a crime—in Massachusetts in 1846 and New York in 1848.

Women also turned their energies to the reform of social institutions. They worked to improve conditions in traditional settings, such as hospitals and community-run shelters for the poor, and in new asylums and prisons, which grew in number in the 1830s and 1840s. The

Massachusetts reformer Dorothea Dix was a leader in these efforts, persuading legislatures in many states to expand state hospitals to accommodate the poor and mentally ill women rather than jail them with criminals (see American Lives, "Dorothea Dix: Public Woman," pp. 394–395).

Both as reformers and as teachers, northern women played a significant role in education. From Maine to Wisconsin, women vigorously supported the movement led by Horace Mann to expand public elementary schools. As secretary of the newly created Massachusetts Board of Education from 1837 to 1848, Mann lengthened the school year; established teaching standards in reading, writing, and arithmetic; and improved instruction by recruiting well-educated women as teachers.

The intellectual leader of the new corps of women educators was Catharine Beecher, another daughter of Lyman Beecher, who founded academies for young women in Hartford and Cincinnati and whose writings inspired a multitude of women teachers. In a series of publications Beecher argued that "moral and religious education must be the foundation of national instruction" and that "energetic and benevolent women" were the best qualified to impart moral and intellectual instruction to the young. By the 1850s most teachers were women, both because school boards heeded Beecher's arguments and because women could be paid less than men.

The Influence of Abolitionism

The public accomplishments of moral reformers such as Dix and Beecher inspired other women to assume public roles, and many of them found a cause in the movement to end slavery. During the Revolutionary era, Quaker women in Philadelphia had established schools for freed slaves, and subsequently many Baptist and Methodist women endorsed religious arguments against slavery. When William Lloyd Garrison, a Massachusetts-born printer, began his radical campaign for *abolition*— the immediate, uncompensated end to slavery—in 1831, a few women rallied to his cause. One of the first Garrisonian abolitionists was Maria W. Stewart, an African American in Boston who carried his message to free blacks and whites in the early 1830s. As the abolitionist movement grew, scores of white women delivered lectures condemning slavery and hundreds more conducted home "visitations" to win converts among women and their husbands.

Influenced by abolitionist ideas and their own experience of discrimination, a few women challenged the subordinate status of their sex. The most famous were Angelina and Sarah Grimké, sisters of reform minister Thomas Grimké. The Grimkés had left their father's South Carolina slave plantation, converted to Quakerism and abolitionism in Philadelphia, and become antislavery lecturers. In 1837 some Congregationalist clergymen demanded that the sisters cease speaking to mixed audiences of men and women, claiming that the true duty of women was to obey men and not to lecture them on their moral responsibilities. In response, Sarah Grimké turned to the Christian Bible for justification: "The Lord Jesus defines the duties of his followers in his Sermon on the Mount . . . without any reference to sex or condition," she wrote. "Men and women are CREATED EQUAL! They are both moral and accountable beings and whatever is right for man to do is right for woman."

To defend this position, Angelina Grimké composed a series of *Letters to Catharine E. Beecher* and published them in 1838. In reply to Beecher's argument that women should exercise power primarily as wives, mothers, and schoolteachers, Angelina Grimké pushed the argument beyond religion, using Enlightenment principles to claim equal civic rights for women:

> *It is a woman's right to have a voice in all the laws and regulations by which she is governed, whether in Church or State. . . . The present arrangements of society, on these points are a* violation of human rights, a rank usurpation of power, *a violent seizure and confiscation of what is sacredly and inalienably hers.*

By 1840 the Grimkés were asserting that traditional gender roles amounted to the "domestic slavery" of women. Not all abolitionist women shared this view, but many demanded equality with men within the antislavery movement.

These demands, along with the controversial lecturing of the Grimké sisters, alarmed many abolitionist men. They feared that allowing women to exercise power would offend many Americans and damage the political fortunes of the antislavery movement. In 1840 William Lloyd Garrison leaped to the defense of women activists. Arguing that "our object is *universal* emancipation, to redeem women as well as men from a servile to an equal condition," he demanded that the abolitionist movement support a broad reform platform that included women's rights. When Garrison's stance split the abolitionist movement, women activists such as Abby Kelley, Lucretia Mott, and Elizabeth Cady Stanton remained with Garrison. They recruited new women agents, including the future women's rights leader Lucy Stone, to proclaim the common interests of enslaved blacks and free women.

In the 1840s and 1850s, women increasingly used abolitionist ideas and organizations to underline the special horrors of slavery for women. Apologists for slavery had exalted the sexual purity of white plantation women, contrasting them with stereotypical descriptions of passionately sexual black men and women and defending the brutal punishments of male slaves accused of rape or sexual intimacy with white women. Abolitionist women now pointed out that the reality of plantation life was much more complex and contradictory, underlining the fact that many masters had sex with their female slaves and fathered children by them. "I cannot tell how much I suffered in the presence of these wrongs," the black abolitionist Harriet Jacobs confessed in anguish in her autobiography, *Incidents in the Life of a Slave Girl* (1861). As Jacobs and other former slaves testified, sexual assault by their masters was compounded by cruel treatment at the hands of mistresses enraged by their husbands' promiscuity. In *Uncle Tom's Cabin*, Harriet Beecher Stowe charged that among the greatest moral failings of slavery was its degradation of slave women. Sojourner Truth, a former slave who lectured to both antislavery and women's rights conventions, hammered home the point that women slaves were denied both basic human rights and the protected separate sphere enjoyed by free women. "I have ploughed and planted and gathered into barns, and no man could head me—and ain't I a woman?" she asked. Drawn into public life by abolitionism, thousands of northern women had become firm advocates of greater rights both for themselves and for enslaved African American women.

The Program of Seneca Falls

The commitment to full civil equality for women emerged during the 1840s as activists devised a pragmatic program of reform. While championing the rights of women, they did not challenge the institution of marriage or even the conventional division of labor within the family. Instead, harking back to the efforts of Abigail Adams and other Revolutionary era women, they tried to strengthen the legal rights of married women, especially with respect to property. This initiative won crucial support from affluent men, who wanted to protect their wives' assets in case their own businesses went into bankruptcy, a constant threat in the volatile economy of mid-nineteenth-century America. By giving property rights to married women, they also hoped to guard against irresponsible sons-in-law who might waste their daughters' inheritances. Such considerations influenced legislatures in three states—Mississippi, Maine, and Massachusetts—which enacted Married Women's Property Acts between 1839 and 1845. In New York, women activists entered the campaign and won a more comprehensive statute (1848) that gave a woman full legal control over the property she brought to a marriage, and became the model for similar laws in fourteen other states.

To push forward the nascent women's movement, Elizabeth Cady Stanton and Lucretia Mott, who had become friends at the World's Anti-Slavery Convention in London in 1840, called a convention in Seneca Falls in upstate New York in 1848. The convention was attended by seventy women activists and thirty men sympathetic to their cause. It outlined for the first time a coherent program for women's equality. Taking the republican ideology of the Declaration of Independence as a starting point, the convention issued a "Declaration of Sentiments" affirming that "all men and women are created

Sojourner Truth
Few women had as interesting a life as Sojourner Truth. Born Isabella in Dutch-speaking rural New York in about 1797, she labored as a slave until 1827. Following a religious vision, Isabella moved to New York City, learned English, and worked for deeply religious—and ultimately fanatical—Christian merchants. In 1843, seeking spiritual enlightenment, she took the name Sojourner Truth and left New York. After briefly joining the Millerites, who believed the world would end in 1844, Truth became famous as a forceful speaker on behalf of abolitionism and women's rights. This photograph, taken when she was in her seventies, suggests Truth's powerful personal presence.
Massachusetts Historical Society.

Dorothea Dix: Public Woman

---★---

AT HER BIRTH women were second-class citizens, excluded by law and custom from voting and from nearly all public institutions and civic activities. They could not sit on juries, attend secondary school or college, or speak in public about the issues of the day. At her death the world had begun to change; some women were demanding complete civic equality with men, and many more were already playing active roles in society. Few women had more to do with this social revolution than Dorothea Dix (1802–1887)—teacher, author, moral reformer, and political activist.

"I never knew childhood," Dix once remarked, for she had been forced to fend for herself from her earliest days. Her paternal grandparents, Elijah and Dorothy Dix, were prominent Bostonians, but her father, Joseph Dix, had dropped out of Harvard and married an older woman of whom his family disapproved. After moving to Maine to manage his father's land developments, he suffered one business failure after another, ending up as an itinerant (and alcoholic) Methodist minister. For Dorothea and her two brothers, family life was marked by poverty, frequent moves, and emotional abuse. When Dorothea was twelve years old her grandmother rescued her from this squalid existence by bringing her to Boston. But grandmother Dix, a rigid and remote person, proved a poor mentor for a precocious and willful child.

These emotionally scarring early experiences made Dix into a compassionate young woman. At age fourteen she began her own school for young children. Realizing her lack of education, she embarked upon a rigorous regime of reading under the direction of private tutors. By 1821 she was ready to impart this knowledge to others, setting up a school at her grandmother's Boston mansion. Like other "dame" or "marm" schools, it offered private instruction to young children, preparing young boys for further education in public secondary (or grammar) schools, and providing young girls with the only intellectual training most of them would ever get. Dorothea also persuaded her grandmother to allow her to open a "charity school" to "rescue some of

America's miserable children from vice and guilt." She ran such schools for the next seventeen years except during periods when bouts of physical illness and mental stress compelled her to rest.

When she was too weak to teach, Dix would write. In 1824 she published a short book of knowledge, *Conversations on Common Things,* that focused on natural science and moral improvement. The book was a great success, going through sixty editions over the next four decades. By 1832 Dix had published six more books, establishing herself as a public personality. Substantial royalties, along with an inheritance from her grandmother, gave her financial independence.

Dix's literary achievements—and her family background—gave her access to the highest reaches of society. William Ellery Channing, a prominent Boston Unitarian minister, invited her to teach his children. Forming a close friendship with Channing, Dix incorporated Unitarian ideas into her work. When her health and spirits broke again in 1836, she spent eighteen months on the English estate of William Rathbone, a wealthy Unitarian merchant and philanthropist. There she met British reformers who were interested in pragmatic programs to correct the maladies of industrial society, and they inspired her to look for similar possibilities in America.

In March 1841 Dix found her cause. Teaching a Sunday School class for incarcerated women, she was outraged to find that insane women were jailed along with criminals. She petitioned the court to provide separate facilities for the women and mobilized Boston philanthropists on their behalf. Expanding her goals, Dix undertook a systematic two-year investigation of the institutions that treated the insane and mentally retarded. She praised reformers for founding new asylums that lavished love and not punishment on mentally ill patients, but she complained that those programs served only the families of New England's elite. Poorer patients continued to endure neglect and cruelty.

In 1843 Dix presented her findings in an extensive *Memorial to the Legislature of Massachusetts* that detailed "the condition of the miserable, the desolate, the outcast," and she mobilized powerful reformers to aid their plight. The legislature responded by enlarging the state hospital in Worcester to accommodate the indigent.

Exhilarated by this success, Dix began a national crusade to establish separate, well-funded state hospitals for the mentally ill. Between 1843 and 1854 she traveled more than 30,000 miles and visited 18 state penitentiaries, 300 county jails and houses of correc-

Dorothea Dix (1802–1887)
This daguerreotype captures Dix's firm character, which helped her endure emotional abuse as a child and accounted for her great success as a social reformer. Dorothea Dix pointed to the need for institutions that would strengthen individuals in the face of the pressures of industrialization. Her call for government intervention into social relations put her on the frontier of reform.
Boston Athenaeum.

tion, and more than 500 almshouses in addition to innumerable hospitals and houses of refuge. She prepared dozens of reports and memorials to state legislatures and became an exceptional student of the legislative process. Her success in arousing public opinion led many states to create or significantly expand their state hospitals.

Because Dix worried that state governments would not be willing to provide sufficient tax revenues to support mental hospitals, she sought assistance from the national legislature. "The insane poor," she wrote, "through the Providence of God, are wards of the nation." In 1848 she asked Congress to place 5 million acres into a national trust that would fund asylums for the mentally ill. If canal and railroad developers could lobby for public lands to sub-

sidize their ventures, "Why can I not too, go in with this selfish, struggling throng, and plead for God's poor . . . that they shall not be forgotten?"

Spurred by Dix's relentless lobbying, the House of Representatives passed her funding proposal in 1850, but the Senate failed to act. In 1851 her legislation got through the Senate but not the House and so could not be presented for final approval to President Millard Fillmore. A Whig sympathetic to moral reform, Fillmore was also Dix's personal friend and was ready to sign her bill. Finally, in 1854, Dix persuaded both houses of Congress to pass legislation setting aside 12.5 million acres of land to fund asylums. But President Franklin Pierce, a Democrat, vetoed the bill, charging that it was an unconstitutional expansion of the powers of the national government and encroached on responsibilities vested in the states. Given the growing national crisis over slavery, Pierce and other supporters of the South feared any measure that might create precedents enhancing national authority, especially with respect to social matters.

This defeat threw Dix into a temporary depression but did not destroy her energy and optimism. She continued her reform work at the state level and founded an international movement to improve the treatment of the mentally ill. Following the outbreak of the Civil War, she accepted an appointment by Abraham Lincoln as superintendent of nurses. This important position placed her in charge of hospital nursing for the entire Union army and made her the highest-ranking woman in the federal government. Exhausted from her wartime labors, in 1866 Dix returned to private life but remained active in reform for the next fifteen years. As her health deteriorated, Dix retired to the New Jersey state hospital in Trenton, an institution she had helped establish in 1845, where she lived out the rest of her life.

In some respects Dix's career embodied the temper of her age. During her lifetime women became active participants in the religious and social reform of their society. And Dix was in the forefront of that movement, one of the first "public women." But in many other ways this formidable Boston woman was far in advance of her time. More politically aware than most women reformers, Dix became a successful legislative lobbyist. Her systematic investigations of social problems were also pathbreaking, making Dix a precursor of the scientific-minded social reformers of the late nineteenth century. Finally, in her campaign for national social welfare programs, Dorothea Dix went far beyond accepted political norms. It was only in the 1920s that the national government became involved in the kinds of social programs advocated by Dix in the 1850s.

equal." "The history of mankind is a history of repeated injuries and usurpations on the part of man toward woman," it continued, "having in direct object the establishment of an absolute tyranny over her." To persuade Americans to right this longstanding wrong, those attending the convention resolved to "use *every instrumentality within our power . . .* [to] employ agents, circulate tracts, petition the State and National legislatures, and endeavor to enlist the pulpit and the press on our behalf." By staking out claims for equality for women in public life, the Seneca Falls convention repudiated the idea that the assignment of separate spheres for men and women was the natural order of society.

Although most men dismissed the Seneca Falls Declaration as nonsense, it drew women—and a few radical men—into the movement. During the 1850s conventions of women—at the local, regional, and national levels—hammered out a diverse reform program. They called on churches to revise concepts of women's inferiority in their theology. They also worked for legal changes that would give married women control over their property and earnings, guarantee a mother's custody of her children in the event of divorce or the father's death, and ensure women's right to sue and testify in court. Finally, and above all else, they began a concerted campaign to win the vote for women. In 1851 a national convention of women declared that suffrage was "the corner-stone of this enterprise, since we do not seek to protect woman, but rather to place her in a position to protect herself" (see American Voices, "Lucy Stone: The Question of Women's Rights," p. 398).

The struggle for legislation required new tactics and new leaders who had talents as organizers rather than lecturers. The most prominent was Susan B. Anthony. She came from a Quaker family and as a young woman had participated in moral reform and a women's antislavery society. She had resigned from a teaching position in bitter protest over discrimination against women, and joined the temperance movement as a paid fundraiser. Her experience in the temperance movement, Anthony explained, had taught her "the great evil of woman's utter dependence on man for the necessary means to aid reform movements."

In 1851, at age thirty-one, Anthony joined the movement for women's rights. Forging an enduring friendship with Elizabeth Cady Stanton, Anthony created a network of political "captains," all women, in every county in New York State. Using their local ties, Anthony and Stanton collected thousands of signatures on petitions and relentlessly lobbied the state legislature. In 1860 their efforts resulted in the passage of a New York law granting women the right to collect and spend their own wages (which fathers or husbands previously could insist on controlling), bring suit in court, and, if widowed, acquire full control of the property

they had brought to the marriage. Such successes would provide the basis for more aggressive attempts after the Civil War to secure equal rights for women.

Abolitionism

For women as well as men, for blacks as well as whites, the drive to end slavery gradually became the dominant American reform movement. In part the increasing focus on slavery stemmed from the success of other initiatives: by the 1840s the Second Great Awakening had drawn millions of Americans into churches, temperance was on the rise, hospitals for the sick and mentally ill had been created, and prisons had been reformed. But more important was the new attitude of many northern whites toward the South's "peculiar institution." Early-nineteenth-century antislavery activists had criticized human bondage as contrary to the tenets of republicanism and liberty but had accepted it as a "necessary evil." Beginning in the 1830s abolitionists condemned slavery as a *sin* and saw it as their moral duty to end this violation of God's law.

African Colonization

The new antislavery crusade had a strong sectional character. By 1820 republican-minded reformers had persuaded northern legislatures to abolish slavery and provide for gradual emancipation in those states. They had also induced Congress to outlaw the importation of enslaved Africans and, in the Missouri Compromise, to prohibit slavery in most of the Louisiana Purchase. But the most difficult problem remained untouched: ending the institution in the "slave societies" of the South, where it was most deeply entrenched, and in neighboring states of Kentucky, Tennessee, and Missouri, which also had significant numbers of slaves.

The founders of the American Colonization Society, which was created in 1817, thought they had the answer. Slaveowners would gradually emancipate their slaves— some 1.5 million people in 1820—and the society would arrange for their resettlement in Africa. This plan was the brainchild of prominent leaders from the Upper South, including President James Monroe, who wanted to eradicate slavery in order to foster economic and social development along northern lines. As Speaker of the House Henry Clay put it, racial bondage had placed his state of Kentucky and the other slaveholding states "in the rear of our neighbors . . . in the state of agriculture, the progress of manufactures, the advance of improvement, and the general prosperity of society."

Susan B. Anthony, c. 1850
As a child, Susan B. Anthony (1820–1906) worked on the
Rochester, New York, farm of her father, a failed textile manufacturer. During the Civil War she showed her organizational
skills as the founder—with Elizabeth Cady Stanton—of the
National Women's Loyal League, which promoted the cause of
woman suffrage and gathered 400,000 signatures in favor of a
constitutional amendment prohibiting slavery.
Meserve-Kunhardt Collection.

Elizabeth Cady Stanton and Daughter, 1856
Elizabeth Cady Stanton (1815–1902) was the daughter of a
judge in Johnstown, New York. As a child she learned from
her father's lawbooks that married women could not own
property and, perhaps with her own daughter's future in mind,
devoted her adult life to remedying that crucially important
disability. As Stanton put it: "The right to property will of
necessity [lead] . . . to the elective franchise, and then . . . [to]
the right to hold office."
Seneca Falls Historical Society.

Slavery had to go, as did the freed slaves. The first
advocates of African colonization, in the 1770s, had
been British antislavery reformers concerned primarily
with the welfare of those in bondage; they believed that
enslaved Africans would welcome the chance to return
to the continent and culture of their birth, and were
surprised when they did not (see Chapter 9). The new
colonizers had a different outlook and goal. Unable to
envision a society in which free blacks and whites could
live peaceably together, they wanted to make the United
States a "white-man's country." Emancipation without
colonization, Clay predicted, "would be followed by
instantaneous collisions between the two races, which
would break out into a civil war that would end in the
extermination or subjugation of the one race or the
other." Northerners who joined the Colonization Society had much the same outlook. They regarded the
250,000 free blacks in the northern states as "notoriously ignorant, degraded and miserable, mentally diseased, brokenspirited," as one society report put it, and

hoped they would leave the United States. What they
wanted was "African removal."

However, the American Colonization Society was a
dismal failure. Despite appeals to wealthy individuals,
churches, and state governments, it raised enough money
to purchase freedom for only a few hundred slaves. Most
free blacks continued to reject colonization, agreeing
with Bishop Richard Allen of the African Methodist Episcopal Church that "this land which we have watered with
our *tears* and our *blood* is now our *mother country*." In
1817 three thousand African Americans met in Philadelphia's Bethel Church to condemn colonization, declaring
that their goal was to advance in American society using
"those opportunities . . . which the Constitution and the
laws allow to all." In the end, the society transported only
6,000 African Americans to Liberia, a colony it established on the west coast of Africa.

Life in Liberia was never easy for the migrants and
often difficult for the resident African peoples. In 1847
the African American colonists declared Liberia an

LUCY STONE

The Question of Women's Rights

──────★──────

*L*ucy Stone (1818–1893) graduated in 1847 from Oberlin College in Ohio and, like many other early advocates of women's rights, came to the movement for sexual equality as a result of her activities as an abolitionist. In 1855 Stone reflected upon women's burdens in an extemporaneous speech at a national women's rights convention in Cincinnati.

The last speaker alluded to this movement as being that of a few disappointed women. From the first years to which my memory stretches, I have been a disappointed woman. When, with my brothers, I reached forth after sources of knowledge, I was reproved with "It isn't fit for you; it doesn't belong to women." Then there was but one college in the world where women were admitted, and that was in Brazil. I would have found my way there, but by the time I was prepared to go, one was opened in the young state of Ohio—the first in the United States where women and negroes could enjoy opportunities with white men. I was disappointed when I came to seek a profession worthy of an immortal being—every employment was closed to me, except that of the teacher, the seamstress, and the housekeeper.

In education, in marriage, in religion, in everything, disappointment is the lot of woman. It shall be the business of my life to deepen this disappoint-ment in every woman's heart until she bows down to it no longer. I wish that women, instead of begging of their fathers and brothers the latest and gayest new bonnet, would ask of them their rights.

The question of Women's Rights is a practical one. . . . The flour merchant, the house-builder, and the postman charge us no less on account of our sex; but when we endeavor to earn money to pay all these, then, indeed we find the difference. Man, if he have energy, may hew out for himself a path where no mortal has ever trod, held back by nothing but what is in himself; the world is all before him, where to choose; and we are glad for you, brothers, men, that it is so. But the same society that drives forth the young man, keeps woman at home—a dependent . . . ; but if she goes heartily and bravely to give herself some worthy purpose, she is out of her sphere and she loses caste. . . .

I know not what you believe of God, but I believe He gave yearnings and longings to be filled, and that He did not mean all our time should be devoted to feeding and clothing the body. The present condition of woman causes a horrible perversion of the marriage relation. It is asked of a lady, "Has she married well?" "Oh yes, her husband is rich." Woman must marry for a home, and you men are the sufferers by this; for a woman who loathes you may marry you because you have the means to get money which she cannot have. But when woman can enter the lists with you and make money for herself, she will marry you only for deep and earnest affection.

───────────

Source: Elizabeth Cady Stanton, Susan B. Anthony, and Matilda Joslyn Gage, *History of Woman Suffrage* (Rochester, NY: Susan B. Anthony, 1881), vol. 1: 165–166.

---

independent republic and adopted a constitution modeled after that of the United States. But the American government did not extend diplomatic recognition to the new nation until 1862, after the Confederate states had left the Union. The African American colonists and their descendants, who remained Protestant and continued to speak English, formed a small ruling class—little more than 10 percent of the population by the mid-twentieth century—that dominated the native tribes. Liberia's economic life remained closely tied to that of the United States, and in the twentieth century American rubber companies, working with the local elite, largely controlled the economy. In recent decades, splits within the ruling group and rebel-lions by the native peoples have produced bloody civil wars that have devastated Liberian society.

Slave Rebellion

Having rejected colonization, free blacks demanded an end to slavery. To build support for emancipation in the South, in 1827 John Russwurm and Samuel D. Cornish began the first African American newspaper, *Freedom's Journal*, in New York. The Boston agent for the newspaper was David Walker, a free black from North Carolina who made a living selling secondhand clothes. A self-educated man, Walker studied the speeches of

A Call for Revolution
David Walker (1785–1830), who ran a used clothing shop in Boston, Massachusetts, used his own savings to publish the *Appeal . . . to the Colored Citizens of the World*, a learned and passionate attack against racial slavery. In the *Appeal*, published in 1829, Walker depicts Christ as an avenging "God of justice and of armies," and raises the banner of slave rebellion. A year later he was found in his shop, dead from unknown causes.
Library of Congress.

Thomas Jefferson and other slaveowners and devoured volumes of history, seeking to place racial slavery within a coherent historical context. In 1829 Walker published a stirring pamphlet entitled *Appeal . . . to the Colored Citizens of the World* that ridiculed the religious pretensions of slaveholders, justified slave rebellion, and in biblical language warned white Americans that the slaves would revolt if justice was delayed. "We must and shall be free," he told white Americans, "And woe, woe, will be it to you if we have to obtain our freedom by fighting. . . . your DESTRUCTION *is at hand*, and will be speedily consummated unless you REPENT." Within a year Walker's *Appeal* had gone through three printings and, carried by black merchant seamen, had begun to reach free African Americans in the South.

In 1830 Walker and other African American activists called a national convention in Philadelphia. The delegates did not adopt Walker's radical position but, invoking the ideals of freedom and equality in the Declaration of Independence, urged free blacks to use every legal means to improve the condition of their race and asked for divine assistance in breaking "the shackles of slavery." To assist free African Americans, who were threatened by expulsion from some states and cities, they pushed forward plans for a refuge for blacks in British Canada.

As Walker was calling for violent black rebellion from Boston, Nat Turner, a slave in Southampton County, Virginia, staged a bloody revolt—a coincidence that had far-reaching consequences. As a child Turner

had taught himself to read and had hoped to be emancipated, but a new master forced him into fieldwork and another master separated him from his wife. Turner became deeply spiritual and had considerable success as a preacher. Then, in a religious vision, "the Spirit" told him that "Christ had laid down the yoke he had borne for the sins of men, and that I should take it on and fight against the Serpent, for the time was fast approaching when the first should be last and the last should be first."

Interpreting an eclipse of the sun as an omen, Turner plotted with a handful of relatives and close friends to overturn the evil regime of slavery. They would meet the masters' terror with violence of their own. In August 1831 his men killed almost sixty men, women, and children, in many cases dismembering and decapitating them. Turner had hoped that a vast army of slaves would rally to his cause, but he had mustered only sixty men by the time a white militia dispersed his poorly armed and exhausted followers. In retaliation, vengeful whites took slaves' lives at random. One company of cavalry killed forty in two days, putting the heads of fifteen on poles to warn "all those who should undertake a similar plot." Fifty slaves were formally prosecuted, and twenty were hanged. After hiding for nearly two months, Turner was captured and hanged, still identifying his mission with that of the Savior: "Was not Christ crucified?" he asked.

Deeply shaken by Turner's rebellion, the Virginia legislature debated a bill providing for gradual emancipation and colonization. When the bill was rejected in 1832 by a vote of 73 to 58, the possibility that southern planters would legislate an end to slavery faded forever. Instead, the southern states marched down another path, toughening their slave codes, limiting the movement of slaves, and prohibiting anyone from teaching them to read. They would meet Walker's radical *Appeal* and Turner's rebellion with radical measures of their own.

Evangelical Abolitionism

Frightened by the prospect of a bloody racial revolution and inspired by the antislavery efforts of free blacks, evangelical northern whites launched a moral crusade to abolish slavery. Previously, Quakers, along with some Methodists and Baptists, had freed their own slaves and campaigned for gradual emancipation in the North. Now radical Christian abolitionists demanded that southerners free their slaves immediately and without compensation. The issue was absolute: slaveowners and their supporters were sinning by depriving slaves of their God-given status as free moral agents. If the slaveowners did not repent, the evangelical abolitionists believed, they faced the prospect of revolution in this world and damnation in the next.

Garrison, Weld, and the Grimkés. The most uncompromising leader of the abolitionist movement during the 1830s was William Lloyd Garrison. He had collaborated in Baltimore during the 1820s with a Quaker, Benjamin Lundy, who published the *Genius of Universal Emancipation*, the leading antislavery newspaper of the decade. In 1830 Garrison went to jail, convicted of writing and publishing an article that libeled a New England merchant engaged in the domestic slave trade; after seven weeks he was released when Arthur Tappan, a wealthy New York merchant and moral reformer, paid his fine. In 1831 Garrison moved to Boston and founded his own antislavery weekly, *The Liberator*, which attracted many free black subscribers. The next year he spearheaded the formation of the New England Anti-Slavery Society.

From the outset *The Liberator* took a radical stance, demanding the immediate abolition of slavery without reimbursement for slaveholders. In pursuing this goal, Garrison declared, "I will be harsh as truth and as uncompromising as justice. . . . I am in earnest—I will not equivocate—I will not excuse—I will not retreat a single inch—AND I WILL BE HEARD." He lived up to his word, condemning the American Colonization Society and charging that its real aim was to strengthen slavery by removing troublesome African Americans who were already free. He then assailed the U.S. Constitution for its implicit acceptance of racial bondage, labeling it "a covenant with death, an agreement with Hell." As time went on, Garrison concluded that slavery was a sign of deep corruption infesting *all* American institutions and called for comprehensive reform of society. He

demanded not only the equality of women but also the repudiation of all governments because their rule, like that of slaveowners, rested ultimately on force. In his view the true Christian should not vote, hold office, or obey the laws of men—only those of God.

Theodore Dwight Weld, who joined Garrison as a leading abolitionist, came to the movement from the religious revivals of the 1830s. The son of a congregationalist minister and inspired by Charles Finney, Weld first became an advocate of temperance and educational reform. Turning to abolitionism, he worked in Presbyterian and Congregational churches in the North, preaching the moral responsibility of all Americans for the denial of liberty to slaves. In 1834 Weld inspired a group of students at Lane Theological Seminary in Cincinnati to form an antislavery society and, when it was repressed, to enroll at Oberlin College, a hotbed of abolitionist activity. Weld's crusade gathered force, buttressed by the theological arguments he advanced in *The Bible against Slavery* (1837). Collaborating closely with Weld were Angelina Grimké, whom he married in 1838, and her sister, Sarah.

Weld and the Grimkés provided the abolitionist movement with a mass of evidence in *American Slavery as It Is: Testimony of a Thousand Witnesses* (1839). The book set out a simple question: "What is the actual condition of the slaves in the United States?" To answer it, the authors presented documentary evidence from southern newspapers and firsthand testimonies. In one account, Angelina Grimké told of a treadmill that slaveowners used for punishment: "One poor girl, [who was] sent there to be flogged, and who was accordingly stripped naked and whipped, showed me the deep gashes on her back—I might have laid my whole finger in them—*large pieces of flesh had actually been cut out by the torturing lash*." The book sold over 100,000 copies in its first year alone.

The American Anti-Slavery Society. In 1833 Weld, Garrison, Arthur Tappan and his brother Lewis Tappan, along with sixty other delegates, black and white, met in Philadelphia to establish the American Anti-Slavery Society. The Society received financial support from the Tappans, using it to promote their cause to the northern middle class. Women abolitionists soon established their own organizations, such as the Philadelphia Female Anti-Slavery Society, founded by Lucretia Mott in 1833, and the Anti-Slavery Conventions of American Women, formed by a network of local societies in the late 1830s. The women's societies raised money for *The Liberator* and were a major force in the movement, distributing abolitionist literature, collecting tens of thousands of signatures on antislavery petitions, and running schools for free blacks.

Abolitionist leaders developed a three-pronged plan of attack, beginning with an appeal to public opinion. To

William Lloyd Garrison
As this portrait, c. 1835, of Garrison at age thirty suggests, William Lloyd Garrison was an intense and righteous man. In 1854 he publicly burned the U.S. Constitution, declaring: "So perish all compromises with tyranny." His attack on slavery began a passionate quest to destroy all institutions that prevented individuals—whites as well as blacks, women as well as men—from discovering their full potential.

foster intense condemnation of slavery in the North, the American Anti-Slavery Society adopted the tactics of the religious revivalists: large rallies led by stirring speakers, the distribution of antislavery manifestos by the members of local chapters, and home visits by agents of the movement. The abolitionists also used the latest techniques of mass communication. Assisted by steam-powered printing presses, the Society distributed more than 100,000 pieces of literature in 1834. In 1835 the organization launched its "great postal campaign," which flooded the nation, including the South, with a million abolitionist pamphlets. In July 1835 alone, abolitionists mailed more than 175,000 items at the New York City post office.

The abolitionists' second strategy was to encourage slaves to flee from slavery and to assist those who did. By the late 1830s thousands of slaves were fleeing each year from their masters, defying white patrols with bloodhounds. Those blacks who lived near a free state had the greatest chance of success. In those areas

enslaved women, whose concern for their children often deterred flight, joined the exodus along with their families. Fugitives from plantations deeper in the South counted on receiving aid from the "underground railroad," an informal network of whites and African Americans that included free blacks in Baltimore, Richmond, Charleston, New Orleans, and other southern cities. In Baltimore, a free African American sailor lent his identification papers to the future abolitionist Frederick Douglass, who used them to escape to New York and then returned them by mail. Many escaped slaves, such as Harriet Tubman, returned repeatedly to the South, risking reenslavement or death. As Tubman wrote, "I should fight for . . . liberty as long as my strength lasted, and when the time came for me to go, the Lord would let them take me." Thanks to the "railroad," by the 1840s about 1,000 African Americans reached freedom in the North each year.

There they faced an uncertain future. Not only were the northern and western states hotbeds of racial prejudice, but the Fugitive Slave Law (1793) allowed masters and hired slave-catchers to capture suspected fugitives and carry them back to bondage. To thwart these efforts, abolitionists financed the settlement of some escapees in Canada and forcibly prevented the reenslavement of others. Throughout the 1830s and 1840s white abolitionists in northern cities joined with crowds of free blacks to defy the Fugitive Slave Law by seizing recaptured slaves and driving slave-catchers out of town.

The third element of the abolitionists' program was to seek support among state and national legislators. In 1835 the American Anti-Slavery Society encouraged local chapters and members to bombard Congress with petitions demanding the abolition of slavery in the District of Columbia, an end to the domestic slave trade, and denial of the admission of new slave states to the Union. By 1838, petitions with nearly 500,000 signatures had arrived in Washington.

This agitation drew thousands of middle-class men and women to abolitionism. During the late 1830s the number of local abolitionist societies grew swiftly, from about 200 in 1835 to more than 500 in 1836 and nearly 2,000 by 1840—when they had nearly 200,000 members, including many leading transcendentalists. Emerson condemned the moral failure of a free society that tolerated slavery, and Thoreau was even more assertive. In 1846 he protested against the Mexican War (see Chapter 13), which he saw as an attempt to extend slavery, by refusing to pay his taxes and submitting to arrest. Two years later he published an anonymous essay entitled "Civil Disobedience" that outlined how a few individuals, by resisting unjust legislation—such as the Fugitive Slave Law—and through loyalty to a higher moral law, could redeem themselves and the state. "A minority is powerless while it conforms to the majority," Thoreau declared, but it becomes "irresistible when it clogs by its whole weight."

Opposition and Disunity

As Thoreau discerned, the abolitionist crusade had won the wholehearted allegiance of only a small minority of white Americans. By 1850 perhaps 10 percent of the northern population embraced its cause, while another 20 percent were sympathetic. Many other northerners were openly hostile. Most men of wealth feared that the abolitionist attack on slave property could turn into a general assault on all property rights. Tradition-minded clergymen warned that the abolitionists threatened the stability of the family by encouraging public roles for women. New York merchants and New England textile manufacturers rallied to the support of the slaveowners who provided them with cotton and purchased their products. Native-born white wage earners and recent Irish and German immigrants feared that freed slaves willing to work for subsistence wages would pour into northern cities and take their jobs.

Indeed, a substantial majority of northern whites wanted to deny political rights and civil equality to the free blacks who lived and worked among them. Only five states, all in New England, allowed African American men to vote. During the 1830s and 1840s other states—Connecticut in New England, New Jersey and Pennsylvania in the mid-Atlantic region, and Ohio, Indiana, and Illinois in the Midwest—changed their laws so as to deprive free blacks of the franchise, and New York restricted voting to those blacks who owned $250 in property. Even fewer whites welcomed the prospect of racial mixing and intermarriage, which the abolitionists seemed to advocate indirectly through their attacks on racism and colonization. Such fears were particularly intense in the communities in the Ohio River Valley, which had been founded and peopled by migrants from the South.

Attacks on Abolitionism.   Moved by such sentiments, staunch northern opponents of abolitionism turned to violence. Mobs, often led by "gentlemen of property and standing," intimidated free blacks and abolitionists. In 1833 an anti-abolitionist mob of 1,500 in New York City stormed a church in search of Garrison and Arthur Tappan. In the next year prominent New Yorkers cheered as a mob of laborers vandalized and set fire to Lewis Tappan's house. Other white mobs swept through Philadelphia's African American neighborhoods, clubbing and stoning residents, destroying homes and churches, and forcing crowds of black women and children to flee the city. In 1835 in Utica, New York, a group of lawyers, local politicians, merchants, and bankers broke up an abolitionist convention and beat several delegates. In the same year a Boston mob dragged Garrison through the streets, threatening to hang him. And two years later in the southern Illinois town of Alton, a mob shot and killed an abolitionist editor, Elijah P. Lovejoy.

THE PARTING "Buy us too."

Antislavery Card
"Buy us too," cries the enslaved mother with her child, as a trader leads her husband away in chains. This card was part of a series of twelve produced in 1863 by H. T. Helmbold, a drug and chemical warehouse in New York City. The cards were used to promote Helmbold's line of products (such as "Helmbold's Fluid Extract of Sarsaparilla" and "Helmbold's Rose Wash") while at the same time mobilizing support for abolition among consumers that bought its wares. Scenes such as this one showing the breakup of African American families were highly effective because the spread of sentimentalism enhanced the importance of family ties for many middle-class northerners.
William Gladstone.

White southerners reacted to abolitionism with equal fervor. Stung by the attacks of northern antislavery groups, some slaveowners encouraged politicians, newspaper editors, and clergymen to defend slavery not as a "necessary evil" (as they had done in the past) but as a "positive good" required to raise Africans from their savage condition. "That the African negro is an inferior variety of the human race, is, I think now generally admitted," William Harper, the chancellor of

South Carolina, declared in 1837; does not it improve their condition, the former U.S. senator continued, "to make them the slaves of civilized masters?"

To preserve slavery, masters whipped those caught with antislavery pamphlets and threatened to enslave any free black sailor who smuggled in these tracts. Southern legislatures enacted laws that prohibited their citizens from belonging to an abolitionist organization or advocating its doctrines, and they passed resolutions demanding that northern legislatures do the same. The Georgia legislature offered a $5,000 reward to anyone who would kidnap Garrison and bring him to the South to be tried for inciting rebellion. In Nashville vigilantes whipped a northern college student for distributing abolitionist pamphlets, and a mob in Charleston attacked the post office and destroyed sacks of abolitionist mail. After 1835, southern postmasters simply refused to deliver mail of suspected abolitionist origin.

National politicians joined the fray. President Andrew Jackson, though a radical on many issues, was a slaveowner and a firm supporter of the southern social order. Jackson privately applauded the South Carolina mob that removed abolitionist pamphlets from the U.S. post office, and in 1835 he asked Congress to restrict the use of the mails by abolitionist groups. Congress did not comply, but in 1836 the House of Representatives adopted the so-called *gag rule*. Under this informal rule, which remained in force until 1844, the House automatically placed antislavery petitions "on the table" as soon as they were received, a parliamentary maneuver that rendered them inactive and kept them from becoming the subject of public debate.

Internal Divisions. Assailed from outside, abolitionists were also divided among themselves. Many antislavery clergymen denounced the Grimké sisters for lecturing to mixed audiences. Influential reformers such as Theodore Weld, who wanted to concentrate all of their energies on abolitionism, left the American Anti-Slavery Society as Garrison broadened his attacks to include other American values and institutions. In response Garrison grew more radical, supporting pacifism abroad and the abolition of prisons, asylums, and other places of confinement at home. At the 1840 convention of the American Anti-Slavery Society he precipitated a split with more conservative abolitionists by demanding a broad platform that supported women's rights and helping to elect the activist Abby Kelley to the organization's business committee.

Garrison's opponents founded a new organization, the American and Foreign Anti-Slavery Society, which received financial backing from Lewis Tappan. Its members worked primarily through their churches to win public support for practical measures against slavery. Other abolitionists turned to electoral politics,

Retribution, Southern Style
Jonathan Walker, a Massachusetts shipwright, paid for his abolitionist activities, as this daguerreotype shows, by being branded. Captured off the coast of Florida in 1844 while trying to smuggle seven slaves to freedom in the Bahama Islands, where slavery had been abolished by the British, Walker had the initials "SS" (for "slave stealer") burnt onto his hand. Massachusetts Historical Society.

establishing the Liberty Party and nominating James G. Birney for president in 1840. Birney was a former Alabama slaveowner who had been converted to abolitionism by Theodore Weld and who had founded an antislavery newspaper in Cincinnati. Birney and the Liberty Party argued that the Constitution did not recognize slavery; that the Fifth Amendment, by barring any congressional deprivation of "life, liberty, or property," prevented the federal government from supporting slavery; and that slaves became automatically free when they entered areas of federal authority, such as the District of Columbia and national territories. But Birney won few votes in the election of 1840, and the future of the party and political abolitionism appeared dim.

Coming hard on the heels of popular violence and political suppression, these schisms and electoral failures stunned the leaders of the abolitionist movement. In less than a decade they had mobilized the energies and ideas of thousands of evangelical Protestants, moral reformers, and transcendentalists. Now they realized the extent to which their activities had aroused the hostility of a substantial majority of the white population. Many Americans had come to fear that abolitionism—and the feminist movement that accompanied it—might not perfect their society but destroy it. The movement for reform, begun with such confidence in the North in the 1820s, now divided the people of that region and threatened the unity of the nation.

Summary

★

After 1820 rapid economic and political change prompted many Americans to question traditional values and to support social reform movements. Ralph Waldo Emerson and other transcendentalists urged men—and women—to reject the outworn ideas of the past and realize their complete potential as individuals. To promote full spiritual growth, transcendentalists founded utopian communities such as Brook Farm. Transcendental thought influenced a generation of American writers, many of whom probed the tensions between individual freedom and social responsibility.

Thousands of other Americans joined utopian communities that questioned traditional gender roles and the acquisitive capitalist values of the market-oriented, industrializing society. Shakers, Fourierists, and members of the Oneida community endorsed the communal ownership of property, and devised various schemes—celibacy, phalanxes, multiple marriage—to promote greater equality between men and women. Although most of these communities did not prosper, their existence suggested the extent of the social dislocation caused by rapid growth and especially the Panic of 1837.

Joseph Smith and his Mormon followers created the most successful communitarian enterprise. They encouraged their members to pursue capitalist enterprise but subjected them to strict religious controls. Mormons celebrated the traditional patriarchal family, and some practiced polygamy. The Mormons' unorthodox marriage practices, along with their bloc voting, resulted in mob attacks on their communities and the migration of many Mormons to Utah.

During the 1830s thousands of middle-class white women also questioned traditional social practices. Many women became active in moral reform, which attacked the sexual double standard and tried to eliminate prostitution. Other women enlisted in the abolitionist movement and, when denied an equal role, demanded complete political and civil equality for women. In 1848 they issued a "Declaration of Sentiments," beginning the modern women's rights movement.

The most dramatic expression of reform was a new attack on slavery by William Lloyd Garrison, who demanded the immediate, uncompensated emancipation of slaves. His crusade soon attracted the support of thousands of reformers. In 1835 the great postal campaign of the American Anti-Slavery Society prompted widespread mob violence against abolitionists. In 1840 some abolitionists turned to politics, forming the Liberty Party. Over the next two decades, political struggles over slavery would gradually come to dominate the nation's history.

TIMELINE

1817 American Colonization Society founded

1829 David Walker's *Appeal* encourages slave revolts

1830 Joseph Smith publishes *The Book of Mormon*

1831 William Lloyd Garrison begins *The Liberator,* an antislavery weekly

Nat Turner's rebellion

1832 Ralph Waldo Emerson resigns his pulpit

New England Anti-Slavery Society founded

1834 New York Female Moral Reform Society established

1836 House of Representatives adopts gag rule

1840 Liberty Party runs James G. Birney for president

1841 Transcendentalists found Brook Farm, a utopian community

Dorothea Dix promotes investigations for the insane

1844 Margaret Fuller's *Woman in the Nineteenth Century*

1845 Henry David Thoreau withdraws to Walden Pond

1846 Mormons trek to Salt Lake under Brigham Young

1848 John Humphrey Noyes founds Oneida community

Seneca Falls convention proposes women's equality

1851 Herman Melville's *Moby Dick*

Susan B. Anthony joins movement for women's rights

1852 Harriet Beecher Stowe's *Uncle Tom's Cabin*

1855 Walt Whitman's *Leaves of Grass*

1858 The "Mormon War" over polygamy

Suggested Readings

─────★─────

General surveys of antebellum reform movements include Robert H. Abzug, *Cosmos Crumbling: American Reform and the Religious Imagination* (1994); C. S. Griffen, *The Ferment of Reform, 1830–1860* (1967); and Ronald G. Walters, *American Reformers, 1815–1860* (1978).

Individualism

The leading study linking transcendentalism and reform is Ann C. Rose, *Transcendentalism as a Social Movement, 1830–1850* (1981). See also Catherine L. Albanese, *Corresponding Motion: Transcendental Religion and the New America* (1977). Studies that relate literary developments to reform themes and cultural history include Harold Kaplan, *Democratic Humanism and American Literature* (1972); David S. Reynolds, *Beneath the American Renaissance: The Subversive Imagination in the Age of Emerson and Melville* (1988), and *Walt Whitman's America: A Cultural Biography* (1995); and Larzer Ziff, *Literary Democracy: The Declaration of Cultural Independence in America* (1981). On Margaret Fuller, see Paula Blanchard, *Margaret Fuller: From Transcendentalism to Revolution* (1978); Charles Capper, *Margaret Fuller: An American Romantic Life* (1992); and Joan von Mehren, *Minerva and the Muse: A Life of Margaret Fuller* (1995).

Communalism

On communitarian experiments, see Arthur Bestor Jr., *Backwoods Utopias: The Sectarian and Owenite Phases of Communitarian Life in America* (1970); Lawrence Foster, *Religion and Sexuality: Three American Communal Experiments of the Nineteenth Century* (1981); Jean McMahon Humez, ed., *Gifts of Power: The Writings of Rebecca Jackson, Black Visionary, Shaker Eldress* (1981); Louis J. Kern, *An Ordered Love: Sex Roles and Sexuality in Victorian Utopias—The Shakers, the Mormons, and the Oneida Community* (1981); Spencer Klaw, *Without Sin: The Life and Death of the Oneida Community* (1995); and Stephen J. Stein, *The Shaker Experience in America* (1992).

On the Mormon experience, see James B. Allen and Glen M. Leonard, *The Story of the Latter-Day Saints* (1992); Leonard J. Arrington, *The Mormon Experience: A History of the Latter-Day Saints* (1992); John L. Brooke, *The Refiner's Fire: The Making of Mormon Cosmology, 1644–1844* (1994); Grant Underwood, *The Millennarian World of Early Mormonism* (1993); and Kenneth H. Winn, *Exiles in a Land of Liberty: Mormons in America, 1830–1846* (1989). On the linkages between religion and the utopians, see Paul E. Johnson and Sean Wilentz, *The Kingdom of Matthias: A Story of Sex and Salvation in 19th-Century America* (1995); and Timothy L. Smith, *Revivalism and Social Reform: American Protestantism on the Eve of the Civil War* (1980).

The Women's Movement

The most comprehensive history of women in the United States is Nancy Woloch, *Women and the American Experience* (1992). On the social history of women, see Nancy F. Cott, *The Bonds of Womanhood: "Women's Sphere" in New England, 1780–1835* (1977); Carl N. Degler, *At Odds: Women and the Family in America from the Revolution to the Present* (1980); and Mary P. Ryan, *Cradle of the Middle Class: The Family in Oneida County, New York, 1790–1865* (1981). The most complete discussion of women in education and benevolent reform is Keith Melder, *Beginnings of Sisterhood: The American Women's Rights Movement, 1800–1850* (1977). For studies of specific aspects of women's involvement in reform, see Barbara J. Berg, *The Remembered Gate: Origins of American Feminism: The Woman and the City, 1800–1860* (1978); Estelle B. Freedman, *Their Sisters' Keepers: Women's Prison Reform in America, 1830–1860* (1981); Lori D. Ginzberg, *Women and the Work of Benevolence: Morality, Politics, and Class in the Nineteenth-Century United States* (1990); Nancy A. Hewitt, *Women's Activism and Social Change: Rochester, New York, 1822–1872* (1984); and Jean F. Yellin, *Women and Sisters: The Antislavery Feminists in American Culture* (1989). See also Elizabeth R. Varon, *We Mean to Be Counted: White Women and Politics in Antebellum Virginia* (1996).

On Dorothea Dix, see David Gollaher, *Voice for the Mad: The Life of Dorothea Dix* (1995); and Charles M. Snyder, *The Lady and the President: The Letters of Dorothea Dix and Millard Fillmore* (1975). The leading studies of the early women's rights movement include Kathleen Barry, *Susan B. Anthony—A Biography: A Singular Feminist* (1988); Ellen Du Bois, *Feminism and Suffrage: The Emergence of an Independent Women's Movement, 1848–1869* (1978); and Eleanor Flexner, *Century of Struggle: The Woman's Rights Movement in the United States* (1959). But see also Jeanne Boydston et al., *The Limits of Sisterhood: The Beecher Sisters on Women's Rights and Woman's Sphere* (1990).

Abolitionism

Surveys of antislavery reform include Robert H. Abzug, *Passionate Liberator: Theodore Dwight Weld and the Dilemma of Reform* (1980); David Brion Davis, *The Problems of Slavery in the Age of Revolution, 1770–1823* (1975); Louis Filler, *The Crusade against Slavery, 1830–1860* (1960); Stanley Harrold, *The Abolitionists and the South, 1831–1861* (1995); Leon F. Litwack, *North of Slavery: The Negro in the Free States, 1790–1860* (1961); Stephen B. Oates, *To Purge This Land with Blood: A Biography of John Brown* (1970); Lewis Perry, *Childhood, Marriage, and Reform: Henry Clarke Wright, 1797–1870* (1980); Benjamin Quarles, *Black Abolitionists* (1969); James B. Stewart, *Holy Warriors: The Abolitionists and American Slavery* (1976); John L. Thomas, *The Liberator: William Lloyd Garrison* (1963); and Bertram Wyatt-Brown, *Lewis Tappan and the Evangelical War against Slavery* (1959). For the role of women in the antislavery movement, consult Blanche Hersh, *The Slavery of Sex: Female Abolitionists in Nineteenth-Century America* (1978); Gerda Lerner, *The Grimké Sisters from South Carolina: Pioneers for Women's Rights and Abolition* (1967); and Alma Lutz, *Crusade for Freedom: Women of the Antislavery Movement* (1968). On northern hostility to abolition, see Leonard L. Richards, *"Gentlemen of Property and Standing": Anti-Abolition Mobs in Jacksonian America* (1970).

The Crisis of the Union,
1844–1860

I N THE EARLY summer of 1856, as antislavery settlers from the northern states fought a guerrilla war in Kansas with proslavery migrants from the South, Senator Charles Sumner of Massachusetts delivered an inflammatory speech in the Senate. Denouncing the South, he singled out for attack Senator Andrew P. Butler of South Carolina, accusing him of having taken "the harlot slavery" as his mistress. Outraged by Sumner's speech, Butler's nephew and protégé, Congressman Preston Brooks, accosted the Massachusetts senator at his desk and beat him over the head with a walking cane to near unconsciousness. Passion had replaced compromise as the hallmark of American politics.

The political conflict that sparked this violence stemmed from events in the 1840s. By that decade a generation of rapid economic growth and intense reform activity had expanded the wealth of both the North and the South and had accentuated longstanding differences between those regions. The North was increasingly industrial and urban, a busy land of movement and markets and social mobility, whereas the South remained overwhelmingly agricultural and rural, a vast expanse of white cotton and black slaves. More important, those sectional differences were increasingly *felt*, especially in the South. As John C. Calhoun warned in 1850, white southerners had come to fear the North's wealth and political power and resent its "long-continued agitation of the slavery question."

The awareness of sectionalism was much more intense and widespread than it had been in the 1790s, when Thomas Jefferson had contested Alexander Hamilton's economic program, or even in the 1830s, when

Reading the News, **Christian Friedrich Mayr, 1844 (detail)**
Born in Germany in 1803, Mayr earned his living as a portraitist in New York, Charleston, and New Orleans. Mayr also painted scenes of American life. Here Mayr shows how Americans who lived in small towns were consumed by events in the larger world.
National Academy Museum, NYC.

the sections had nearly come to blows over the high tariffs on imported manufactures. Those were battles over issues. Now the conflict was between different ways of life. Northerners and southerners were living in different social systems, with different ways of thinking about the individual and society. Middle-class northerners hailed the principles of "free labor," individualism, and social mobility; southern slaveowners celebrated the traditions of slavery, hierarchy, and authority.

Simultaneously, the massive westward migration of Americans shifted attention to the vast lands of the trans-Mississippi West. Many Americans came to believe that the nation's "Manifest Destiny" was to extend republican institutions to the Pacific Ocean. But whose institutions—those of the North or those of the South? As the bloodshed in Kansas demonstrated, the issue of westward expansion was becoming inextricably entangled with those of slavery and sectional identity.

Manifest Destiny

──────★──────

For nearly a generation after the Missouri Compromise of 1820, American politicians had prevented a new sectional conflict over slavery by devising party platforms that were national in appeal. This strategy worked only as long as territorial issues remained unimportant. When Texas won independence from Mexico in 1836 and petitioned for annexation to the United States, it set in motion a long and fateful political struggle.

The Independence of Texas

During the 1830s, as northeastern farmers and European immigrants were settling the Midwest, settlers from the Ohio Valley and the South were claiming the best lands in Arkansas and southern Missouri, pushing just beyond the western boundaries of those states to the 95th meridian of longitude. Beyond this imaginary north-south line stretched lands with little rainfall, the semiarid Great Plains. In 1820 an army explorer, Major Stephen H. Long, had described the entire area between the Missouri River and the Rocky Mountains as a Great American Desert "almost wholly unfit for cultivation." Sharing this assumption, land-hungry American planters looked southward toward Mexican territory, especially the province of Texas.

Texas had long been a zone of conflict between European nations. During the eighteenth century the Spanish rulers of Mexico had employed Tejas, or Texas (so called after the local native American word for "friends"), as a buffer against the French in Louisiana. After the United States purchased Louisiana from

France in 1803, Texas became Spain's buffer against the expanding American republic. Although adventurers from the United States did arrive there, the Adams-Onís treaty of 1819 guaranteed Spanish sovereignty over the region, and after winning independence from Spain in 1821, the Mexican government encouraged its own citizens to settle in Texas. Realizing that it could not deter illegal immigrants from the United States, the new Mexican government also welcomed American settlers and tried to make them loyal Mexican citizens by granting them some of the best land in Texas. One early grantee was Moses Austin, whose son Stephen F. Austin established a thriving American settlement by offering large plots at a low cost (Map 13.1). The Americans did not assimilate Mexican culture and defied various Mexican laws, including an edict of 1829 ending slavery. By 1835, fully 27,000 Americans and their 3,000 slaves were living in Texas, raising cotton and cattle, and far outnumbered the 4,000 Mexicans in the southwestern towns of Goliad and San Antonio.

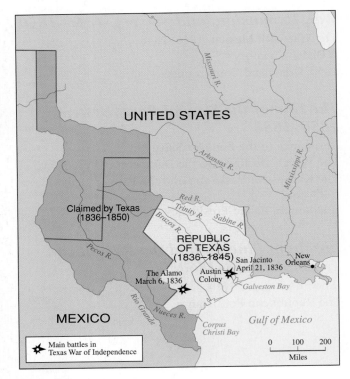

MAP 13.1
American Settlement in Texas, 1821–1850
In 1821 Stephen F. Austin established the first organized Anglo-American settlement in Texas on land granted to his father by the Mexican authorities. By 1835 he had issued land titles to more than 1,000 families, who grew cotton and exported it from Corpus Christi Bay and Galveston Bay. At the time of rebellion in 1836, there were nearly 30,000 Americans in Texas; anticipating a flood of settlers, the new Texas republic claimed all Mexican lands east of the Rio Grande.

SIEGE OF THE ALAMO.

Assault on the Alamo
After a thirteen-day siege, a Mexican army of 4,000 stormed the small mission in San Antonio, Texas, on March 6, 1836. "The first to climb were thrown down by bayonets . . . or by pistol fire," reported a Mexican officer. Only a half-hour of continuous assaults gave the attackers control of the wall. This contemporary woodcut shows fierce battles, which took the lives of all 250 American defenders; the Mexicans suffered 1,500 dead or wounded.
Archives Division, Texas State Library.

In the early 1830s, as the Mexican government tried to enforce the ban on slavery, the Americans in Texas split into two groups. The "peace party," under the leadership of Stephen Austin, worked to win more self-government for the province within the Mexican republic, whereas the "war party" demanded independence. Austin won significant concessions from Mexican authorities, but before these were fully implemented General Antonio López de Santa Anna became president. A strong nationalist, Santa Anna appointed a military commandant for Texas and centralized power in Mexico City.

In October 1835 the American war party reacted to Santa Anna's action by spearheading a rebellion that most of the American settlers ultimately supported. By the beginning of 1836 the rebels had ousted all Mexican troops from the province, prompting Santa Anna to lead a large army across the Rio Grande and march on San Antonio. To rally support for their cause, on March 2 the rebellious Americans declared Texas an independent nation and adopted a constitution legalizing slavery. Four days later, Santa Anna responded with vengeance as his army wiped out the garrison defending the Alamo, an old mission in San Antonio that had been turned into a fortress. After capturing the settlement of Goliad, 80 miles to the southeast, the Mexican chief ordered the execution of 371 rebel prisoners, whom he regarded as mercenaries rather than as Texans because many of them had just arrived from the United States (see Voices from Abroad, "Colonel José Enrique de la Peña: A Mexican View of the Battle of the Alamo," p. 411).

Santa Anna thought he had crushed the rebellion, but the battle of the Alamo had captured the attention of newspapers in New Orleans and New York. Their correspondents romanticized the heroism of the Texans at the Alamo and the deaths of the folk heroes Davy Crockett and Jim Bowie, who were famous because of their widely published exploits as frontiersmen. Using some of the strongest anti-Catholic rhetoric of the day, the newspapers described the Mexicans as tyrannical butchers in the service of the pope. Thousands of American adventurers, lured by Texan offers of land bounties, set sail from New York, the Gulf states, and the Mississippi Valley. Reinforced by the new arrivals and led by General Sam Houston, the rebels routed the Mexicans in the Battle of San Jacinto, just east of present-day Houston, on April 21, 1836, establishing de facto independence. The Mexican government refused to recognize the new republic but abandoned efforts to reconquer it.

The Texans immediately voted by plebiscite for annexation by the United States. Just before leaving office President Andrew Jackson extended diplomatic recognition to the rebellious province, but his successor, Martin Van Buren, firmly rebuffed Texas's request for annexation because of its potential effect on domestic politics. Long an advocate of "mutual forbearance and reciprocal concession" between the sections (as he put it during the Nullification Crisis), Van Buren gave a higher priority to political harmony than to territorial expansion. As a Texas diplomat reported to his government, the new president and many other American politicians

Sam Houston, *Martin Johnson Heade, 1846*
Military hero, president of the Lone Star Republic, and senator from the state of Texas, Sam Houston cut an impressive figure and had many admirers both inside and outside politics. According to a Nashville belle who knew the Texan as a young man, "two classes of people pursued Sam Houston all his life—artists and women." Heade's portrait, painted when Houston was the senator from Texas, conveys the Texan's flamboyant character and personal charm.
Texas State Library & Archives Commission.

feared that annexation would spark both a war with Mexico and a "desperate death-struggle . . . between the North and the South; a struggle involving the probability of a dissolution of the Union."

The Push to the Pacific

The annexation of Texas became a more pressing issue in the 1840s, when American expansionists developed continental ambitions. Those dreams were captured by the term *Manifest Destiny,* coined in 1845 by John L. O'Sullivan, editor of the New York–based *Democratic Review.* As O'Sullivan put it, "Our manifest destiny is to overspread the continent allotted by Providence for the free development of our yearly multiplying millions." O'Sullivan left the geographic scope of Manifest Destiny vague but clearly implied that the United States had a divinely inspired mission to bring parts of Mexico and British Canada into the American republic. Behind his

rhetoric was a sense of cultural and even racial superiority; "inferior" peoples who were resident in the West—such as native Americans and Mexicans—were to be brought under American dominion, taught about republican forms of government, and converted to Protestantism.

Oregon. In fact, many residents of the Ohio River Valley were casting their eyes far to the west—to the fertile valleys of the Oregon Country, which was claimed by Great Britain as well as the United States. In 1818 a British-American convention had established the 49th parallel as the Canadian-American boundary up to the Rocky Mountains but no farther, allowing both Britons and Americans to settle anywhere in the disputed region to the west. At that time Oregon stretched from the 42nd parallel in the south, which formed the border with the Mexican province of California, to 54°40′ in the north, which formed the border with Russian Alaska (Map 13.2). Subsequently, the British-run Hudson's Bay Company carried on a lucrative fur trade north of the Columbia River, while several hundred Americans settled to the south, mostly in the Willamette Valley. On the basis of this settlement, the United States established a claim to the zone between the 42nd parallel and the Columbia River.

In 1842 American interest in Oregon increased dramatically. Navy lieutenant Charles Wilkes published glowing reports of the potential harbors he had found in the Strait of Juan de Fuca, Admiralty Inlet, and Puget Sound, which were of great interest to New England

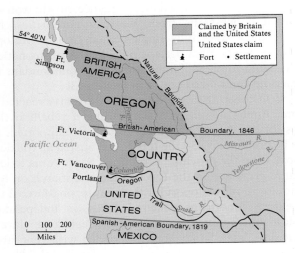

MAP 13.2
Territorial Conflict in Oregon, 1819–1846
As thousands of American settlers poured into the so-called "Oregon Country" in the early 1840s, British authorities tried to confine them south of the Columbia River. But the migrants—and fervent Midwestern expansionists—asserted that American (and British) citizens could settle anywhere in the territory. In 1846 British and American diplomats resolved the dispute by drawing the boundary at the 49th parallel.

Colonel José Enrique de la Peña

A Mexican View of the Battle of the Alamo

———— ★ ————

In February 1836 a Mexican army led by General Antonio López de Santa Anna laid siege to the Alamo, an old San Antonio mission building held by about 250 Americans commanded by William B. Travis. In his personal narrative of the war in Texas, Colonel José Enrique de la Peña offers a dramatic and critical account of the ensuing events, in which he played a prominent role.

. . . Our commander [president-general Santa Anna] became more furious when he saw that the enemy resisted the idea of surrender. He believed as others did that the fame and honor of the army were compromised the longer the enemy lived. . . . But prudent men . . . were of the opinion that victory over a handful of men concentrated in the Alamo did not call for a great sacrifice. In fact, it was necessary only to await the artillery's arrival at Béjar for these to surrender. . . .

Travis's resistance was on the verge of being overcome, for several days his followers had been urging him to surrender, giving the lack of food and the scarcity of munitions as reasons. . . . on the 5th he promised them if no help arrived on that day they would surrender the next day or would try to escape under the cover of darkness. . . . it was said as a fact . . . that the president-general knew of Travis's decision, and it was for this reason that he precipitated the assault, because he wanted to create a sensation and would have regretted taking the Alamo without clamor and without bloodshed, for some believed that without these there is no glory. . . .

The columns, bravely storming the fort in the midst of a terrible shower of bullets and cannon-fire, had reached the base of the walls. . . . A lively rifle fire coming from the roof . . . caused painful havoc. . . . [Finally] our soldiers, some stimulated by courage and others by fury, burst into the quarters . . . our losses were grievous. . . . [But our men] turned the enemy's own cannon to bring down the [inner] doors . . . a horrible carnage took place, and some [Americans] were trampled to death. . . . This scene of extermination went on for an hour before the curtain of death covered and ended it. . . .

Some seven men had survived the general carnage and, under the protection of General Castrillon, they were brought before Santa Anna. Among them was one of great stature, well proportioned, with regular features, in whose face there was the imprint of adversity, but in whom one noticed a degree of resignation and nobility that did him honor. He was the naturalist David Crockett, well known in North America for his unusual adventures, who had undertaken to explore the country and who, finding himself at Béjar at the very moment of surprise, had taken refuge in the Alamo, fearing his status as a foreigner might not be respected. Santa Anna answered Castrillon's intervention in Crockett's behalf with a gesture of indignation and . . . ordered his execution. The commanders and officers were outraged at this action and did not support the order. . . . [But several officers] thrust themselves forward, in order to flatter their commander, and with swords in hand, fell upon these unfortunate, defenseless men just as a tiger leaps upon his prey. . . .

To whom was this sacrifice useful and what advantage was derived by increasing the number of victims? . . . the taking of the Alamo was not considered a happy event, but rather a defeat that saddened us all.

Source: José Enrique de la Peña, *With Santa Anna in Texas: A Personal Narrative of the Revolution*, trans. Carmen Perry (College Station: Texas A&M University Press, 1975), 40–57.

merchants plying the China trade. Also in 1842 the first large party, over a hundred people, crossed the Oregon Trail, which fur traders and explorers had blazed through the Great Plains and the Rocky Mountains (Map 13.3). Their reports told of a mild climate and fertile soil.

"Oregon fever" suddenly raged. In May 1843 over a thousand men, women, and children gathered in Independence, Missouri, for the trek to Oregon. The migrants were mostly farming and trading families from Missouri and the Ohio Valley: Kentucky, Tennessee, and the southern

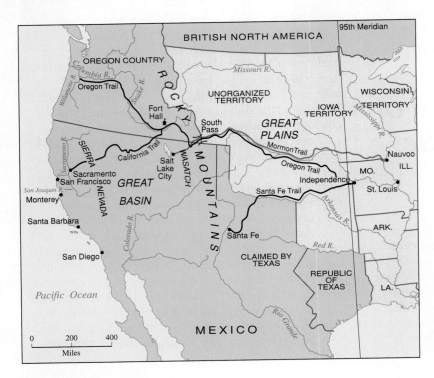

MAP 13.3
Settlement of the Trans-Missouri West, 1840s
In the 1840s tens of thousands of Americans crossed the Great Plains in huge wagon trains. The Mormons settled in the Salt Lake Basin; other pioneers pressed on to Mexican California and the Oregon Country. There was remarkably little crime on these treks because most migrants were deeply religious or were committed to the rule of Anglo-American law, which they enforced through political compacts and self-created institutions.

parts of Indiana and Ohio. With military-style organization and formations, the pioneers started westward with more than 100 wagons and 5,000 oxen and cattle. They overcame flooding streams, dust storms, dying livestock, attacks by Indians, and illness and death. After a journey of six months, they reached the Willamette Valley more than 2,000 miles across the continent. During the next two years another 5,000 people reached Oregon.

By 1860, approximately 350,000 Americans, including many from the Midwest, had braved the Oregon Trail. Over 34,000 people died in the effort, mostly from disease and exposure; only 400 deaths resulted from Indian attacks. The walking migrants wore 3-foot-deep paths, and their wagons carved 5-foot-deep ruts, across sandstone formations in southern Wyoming—tracks that are visible today. More men than women died on the trail, but many women found the long journey to be emotionally draining because it pulled them away from friends, heightened the authority of their husbands, and added to their traditional chores the strenuous work of driving wagons and animals.

California.   Some pioneers ended up in the Mexican province of California. They left the Oregon Trail just past Fort Hall on the Snake River and struggled southward down the California Trail, settling in the interior valley of the Sacramento River. California had been the remotest corner of Spain's empire in North America and was settled only during the reign of Carlos III (1759–1788), a dynamic monarch who had taken a personal interest in Spain's provinces in the Western Hemisphere. Under his orders, Spanish troops established

military *presidios* (garrisons) at San Diego, Santa Barbara, Monterey, and San Francisco, while the Franciscan friar Junípero Serra set up missions in those settlements and elsewhere along the California coast. As the friars converted the resident Indian peoples to Christianity and drafted many of them to work and live at the missions, European diseases cut the native population along the coast nearly in half, from 60,000 in 1769 to 35,000 in 1800.

New England merchants soon struck up trade with the new Mexican settlements in California, exchanging manufactured goods for sea otter pelts that they carried to China. Commerce increased after Mexico won independence from Spain in 1821. To promote the economic development of California, the new Mexican government secularized the California missions, liberating more than 20,000 Indians who had been forced to work for the friars and granting mission lands to entrepreneurs who imported large herds of cattle.

The rise of cattle ranching created a new society and economy. While some of the mission Indians joined the 200,000 native American peoples who lived in the interior of California, many remained in the coastal region. They intermarried with the local *mestizos* (Mexicans of mixed Spanish and Indian ancestry) and worked as laborers and cowboys on the large *ranchos*. New England merchants carried the leather and tallow produced by these workers to customers in the booming Massachusetts boot and shoe industry. To handle the increased business, New England firms dispatched dozens of resident agents to California. Unlike the Americans in Texas, many of these New Englanders assimilated Mexican

**The Promised Land—
The Grayson Family,
*William S. Jewett, 1850***
For adventurous nineteenth-century Americans, the West symbolized a brighter future. Here Andrew Jackson Grayson (1819–1869) and his family catch their first glimpse of the fertile lands of California's Sacramento Valley. The Graysons had traveled west with a group of ill-fated migrants who perished when trapped by a blizzard at the Donner Pass; fortunately, they left the main group and made their way over the Sierra Nevada by themselves. Mr. Grayson's journey west held great meaning for him. To celebrate his family's safe arrival, he commissioned William S. Jewett to paint a portrait of his family, actually bringing him to the precise spot where they first saw their new home.
Terra Museum of American Art, Chicago, Illinois. Daniel J. Terra Collection.

culture. They married into the families of the elite Mexican residents—the *Californios*—and adopted their dress, manners, outlook, and Catholic religion. An important exception was Thomas Oliver Larkin, the most successful merchant in Monterey. Larkin established a close working relationship with Mexican authorities and often lent them money, but he remained an American citizen and plotted for the peaceful annexation of California to the United States. In 1843 he became the U.S. consul in California.

Like Larkin, the American migrants who braved the Oregon Trail and settled in the Sacramento Valley had no desire to assimilate into Mexican society. Their legal standing was uncertain because they received dubious land grants or squatted without any title. Some of them hoped to emulate the Americans who had colonized Texas and then sought annexation into the United States. However, there were too few settlers in the Sacramento Valley to turn those dreams into reality; in the mid-1840s they numbered only about 700, compared to the coastal population of 7,000 Mexicans and 300 American traders.

The Fateful Election of 1844

The course of the American government's policy toward California, Oregon, and Texas was determined by the election of 1844. Since 1836, when Texas first requested annexation to the United States, some southern leaders had favored territorial expansion to protect and extend the slave system. They had been opposed not only by

cautious party politicians and northern abolitionists but also (southerners came to think) by British diplomacy. In 1839 Britain and France had intervened in Mexico to force it to pay its foreign debts, and there were rumors that Britain wanted the province of California as payment. Southern leaders also saw evidence that Britain was encouraging Texas to remain independent and had designs on Spanish Cuba, which some southerners wanted to annex as a slave state. In the minds of certain southern leaders, these British actions seemed to be part of a grand scheme concocted by British abolitionists to block American expansion—and the spread of slavery—to the south and west. To thwart this design, southern expansionists demanded the annexation of Texas.

Simultaneously, "Oregon fever" and a rage for expansion altered the political and diplomatic landscape in the North. By 1843 Americans throughout the Ohio Valley and the Great Lakes states were calling on the federal government to renounce the joint occupation of Oregon and oust the British. Democrats and Whigs worked together to organize "Oregon conventions," and in July a bipartisan national convention demanded that the United States seize Oregon all the way to 54°40′ north latitude, the southern limit of Russian Alaska.

Now that northerners were demanding expansion, southern Democrats thought they could champion the annexation of Texas without threatening the unity of their party. President John Tyler, disowned by the

A Californio *Patriarch*
The descendant of a Spanish family that had lived—and prospered—in Mexico since the Spanish conquest, Mariano Guadalupe Vallejo served in California as a military officer. In the 1820s he acquired more than 270,000 acres of land in the Sonoma Valley, north of San Francisco. Vallejo, the father of nine children, presents himself in this photograph as a proud patriarch, surrounded by two daughters and three grand-daughters. During the American takeover in 1846 he was imprisoned for a short period. The new government was to have a profound effect on Vallejo. Although he lived out his life in California, Vallejo gradually lost most of his vast hold-ings due to property disputes and squatters.
University of California at Berkeley, Bancroft Library.

Whigs because of his opposition to Henry Clay's nation-alist economic program, hoped to win reelection in 1844 as a Democrat or as the head of a new political party. To curry favor among expansionists, Tyler pro-posed the annexation of Texas and the seizure of Ore-gon to the 54°40′ line. In April 1844 Tyler and John C. Calhoun, his new secretary of state, began to execute this plan, submitting a treaty for the annexation of Texas to the Senate. As debate began, two other leaders with presidential ambitions, Democrat Martin Van Buren and Whig Henry Clay, declared their opposition. Being experienced politicians, they knew that support-ing the annexation of Texas would alienate many north-ern voters and threaten the existing political system. At their urging, Whigs and northern Democrats united to defeat the treaty.

The annexation of Texas became the central issue in the presidential election of 1844. The Democrats passed over Tyler, whom they did not trust, and Van Buren, whom southern Democrats despised for his stance on Texas. Instead, they selected former Tennessee governor James K. Polk, a slaveowner who was Andrew Jackson's personal favorite and who carried the nickname "Young Hickory." Unimpressive in appearance, Polk was a man of iron will and boundless ambition for the nation. Like Tyler, he called for annexing Texas and taking all of Oregon. "Fifty-four forty or fight!" became the patriotic cry of his campaign.

The Whigs nominated Clay, who once again cham-pioned his American System of internal improvements, high tariffs, and national banking. Throughout the cam-paign Clay dodged the issue of Texas, finally suggesting that under certain circumstances he might support annexation. His wavering position disappointed thou-sands of northern Whigs and Democrats who opposed any expansion of slavery. Rather than vote for Clay, some of these antislavery advocates supported the Liberty Party's candidate, James G. Birney of Kentucky. Birney won less than 3 percent of the popular vote in the nation as a whole, but he probably took enough votes from Clay in New York to cause Clay to lose that state by 5,000 votes. By winning New York's 36 electoral votes, Polk won by a margin of 170 to 105 in the electoral college. (Without a victory in New York, Polk would have lost the election, with 134 votes as compared to Clay's 141.)

After Polk's victory, congressional Democrats closed ranks and moved immediately to bring Texas into the Union. Because of northern Whig opposition to the addition of another slave state, they could not secure a two-thirds majority in the Senate for a treaty with the Texas Republic. So the Democrats approved annexation by a joint resolution of Congress, which required only a majority vote in each house. The long-standing effort of cautious party politicians to avoid sectional conflict over slavery had collapsed in the midst of reckless political ambition and popular enthu-siasm for westward expansion.

War, Expansion, and Slavery, 1846–1850

James K. Polk and the Democrats swept to victory in 1844 by promising the immediate annexation of Texas and laying claim to all of Oregon. But Polk had even greater territorial ambitions: he wanted all of Mexico west of Texas to the Pacific Ocean and was prepared to go to war to get it. What he was not prepared for was the major crisis over slavery unleashed by the success of his expansionist dreams.

Polk for President, 1844
By the 1840s political campaigns were major events, marked by rousing speeches, torchlight parades, and party propaganda. This banner evokes patriotism as it calls for both the election of Polk, who is pictured in the upper left corner, and the annexation of Texas, represented by the "lone star" outside the group of twenty-six stars.
Collection of Janice L. and David J. Frent.

The War with Mexico, 1846–1848

Mexico had not prospered in the twenty-five years since it won independence from Spain in 1821. Its population remained small at seven million people, and its stagnant economy yielded only modest tax revenue, much of which was eaten up by interest payments on foreign debt and a bloated and often corrupt government bureaucracy. Consequently, the Mexican republic lacked the money and people to settle its distant northern provinces. The Spanish-speaking population of California and New Mexico remained small—about 75,000 in 1840—and contributed little to the national economy. Still, the fledgling Mexican government was determined to retain all its historical territories, and when the breakaway Texas Republic accepted American statehood on July 4, 1845, Mexico broke off diplomatic relations with the United States.

Polk's Expansionist Program. President James Polk viewed Mexico's action as a great opportunity. Since taking office in March 1845, Polk had moved quickly to implement Congress's resolution annexing Texas and had devised a secret plan to acquire all of Mexico's far northern provinces. To intimidate the Mexican government, Polk ordered General Zachary Taylor and an American army force of two thousand soldiers to occupy the disputed lands between the Nueces River (the historical boundary of the Mexican province of Texas) and the Rio Grande, which the expansionist-minded Texas Republic claimed as its southern and western border (see Map 13.4). Taylor camped near the town of Corpus Christi, just south of the mouth of the Nueces.

Simultaneously Polk launched a diplomatic initiative, dispatching John Slidell on a secret mission to Mexico City. The president instructed Slidell to secure Mexico's acceptance of the Rio Grande boundary and buy the Mexican provinces of New Mexico and California, paying as much as $30 million. When Slidell arrived in December 1845, Mexican officials refused to see him, declaring that the American annexation of Texas was illegal.

Anticipating that the Mexicans would refuse to sell California and New Mexico, Polk had already embarked on an alternative plan to take California. The president's strategy was to foment a revolution there that, as in Texas, would lead to the creation of an independent republic and a request for annexation. In October 1845 he had Secretary of State James Buchanan advise Thomas O. Larkin, the U.S. consul in the major port of Monterey, that the United States would protect Californians if they sought independence from Mexico. Larkin immediately encouraged leading Mexican residents of California to support a peaceful shift of sovereignty. To add military muscle to any uprising, Polk sent orders to John Sloat, the commander of the U.S. naval squadron in the Pacific, to seize San Francisco Bay and California's coastal towns in the event of war. The president also had the War department dispatch Captain John C. Frémont and an "exploring" party of heavily armed soldiers deep into Mexican territory. As Frémont later noted, "in arranging his expedition, the eventualities of war were taken into consideration." By December 1845 Frémont had reached California's Sacramento Valley, and in March 1846 he engaged in a show of force, confronting Mexican authorities in the port of Monterey before moving on to the Oregon Country.

Events now moved quickly toward war. When Polk learned of the complete failure of Slidell's mission, he ordered General Taylor to build a fort near the Rio Grande, hoping to incite an armed response by Mexico. As Ulysses S. Grant, a young officer serving with Taylor, said much later, "We were sent to provoke a fight, but it was essential that Mexico should commence it." When Mexican and American forces clashed near the Rio Grande in May 1846, Polk delivered the war message he had drafted much earlier, saying that Mexico "has passed the boundary of the United States, has invaded our territory, and shed American blood upon the American soil."

Ignoring Whig pleas for a peaceful resolution to the dispute, the Democratic majority in Congress voted for war with Mexico, unleashing large and almost hysterical demonstrations of popular support. To avoid a simultaneous war with Britain over the occupation of Oregon, the president retreated from his campaign pledge of "Fifty-four forty or fight!" He accepted a British proposal to divide the Oregon Country at the 49th parallel, and in June 1846 the Senate ratified a treaty establishing that boundary. (In 1848 Congress organized the Oregon Territory, and in 1859 it admitted the state of Oregon into the Union.)

American Military Success. As the Senate acted, American settlers in California's Sacramento Valley rose in revolt. Supported by Frémont's forces, which had returned from Oregon, the rebels captured the town of Sonoma and, fashioning a crude flag that displayed the strongest animal in California, proclaimed the Bear Flag Republic on July 4, 1846. Meanwhile, U.S. naval commander John Sloat, knowing that hostilities with Mexico had broken out south of the Nueces, landed 250 marines and seamen in Monterey. He declared that California "henceforward will be a portion of the United States" and raised the American flag.

To ensure American control of territory along the Rio Grande, Polk ordered army units under General Stephen Kearney into the northern Mexican province of Nuevo Mexico, where they captured Santa Fe without opposition in August. Then Kearney's army marched on to southern California, where the Mexicans mounted stiff resistance. They drove the Americans from Los Angeles and then won a victory over Kearney's forces at the Battle of San Pascual outside San Diego. Only the arrival of reinforcements under Commodore Robert F. Stockton turned the tide, allowing the American army to retake Los Angeles in a decisive battle at the San Gabriel River. By mid-January 1847 the American forces had also captured San Francisco, Santa Barbara, and San Diego (Map 13.4). In his diary, Polk wrote that he would accept no treaty that failed to cede New Mexico and California to the United States.

The American president had reason for optimism because Zachary Taylor's army in Texas had been equally successful. In May 1846 the American forces had crossed the Rio Grande, occupied Matamoros, and moved southward, using their advantage in artillery to win a series of victories against a larger Mexican army.

An American Volunteer Goes to War, 1846
"People here are all in a state of delirium," the novelist Herman Melville reported from New York as the Mexican War began, with thousands of young men volunteering for military service. Knowing that they faced death on the battlefield, many soldiers used the new technology of the daguerreotype to leave their families with visual mementos. This man was a major in the infantry.
Courtesy of Michael Bremer.

After a fierce six-day battle in September, Taylor took the interior town of Monterrey. Two months later a U.S. naval squadron in the Gulf of Mexico seized Tampico, Mexico's second most important port. By the end of 1846 the United States controlled much of northeastern Mexico.

Polk expected that these American victories would prompt the Mexicans to sue for peace, but he had underrated their national pride and strength. Under the leadership of General Antonio López de Santa Anna, who had just been reelected as president, the Mexican government refused to agree to a peace, let alone a cession of territory. Instead Santa Anna went on the offensive, attacking the depleted units of Zachary Taylor at Buena Vista in February 1847. Only superiority in artillery enabled Taylor to eke out a victory and hold the American line in northeastern Mexico.

Street Fighting in the Calle de Iturbide, 1846
The American conquest of Monterrey, which Spain's troops had been unable to capture during the Mexican War, came after bloody house-to-house fighting. Protected by thick walls and shuttered windows, Mexican defenders pour a withering fire on dark-uniformed American troops and buckskin-clad frontier fighters. A spacious Catholic cathedral looms in the background, its foundations obscured by the smoke from Mexican cannons.
West Point Museum, United States Military Academy, West Point, NY. From *The Old West: The Mexican War*, photographed by Paulus Lesser. © 1978 Time-Life Books.

To bring the Mexican government to terms, Polk accepted a military strategy devised by General Winfield Scott, a veteran army officer, which called for a strike deep into the heart of Mexico. In March 1847 Scott captured the Gulf Coast port of Veracruz and began the 260-mile march to Mexico City, which the Spanish conquistador Hernando Cortés had taken three centuries earlier. Leading Scott's 14,000 troops was a cadre of talented West Point officers who would later become famous during the Civil War: Robert E. Lee, George Meade, and P. G. T. Beauregard. Taking heavy casualties, Scott's troops crushed Santa Anna's attempt to block their march at Cerro Gordo and inflicted heavy losses on the Mexican army at the battle of Churubusco, just outside Mexico City. Finally, in September 1847, Scott's much-depleted army seized the Mexican capital, and the Mexican government had little choice but to make peace.

A Divisive Victory

Initially many Americans had viewed the war with Mexico as a noble struggle to extend their republican institutions across the continent and to free Mexico from a corrupt, weak regime that might fall under the influence of ambitious European monarchies. And at the end of the bloody conflict, many citizens agreed with Polk's judgment that the war had demonstrated that a

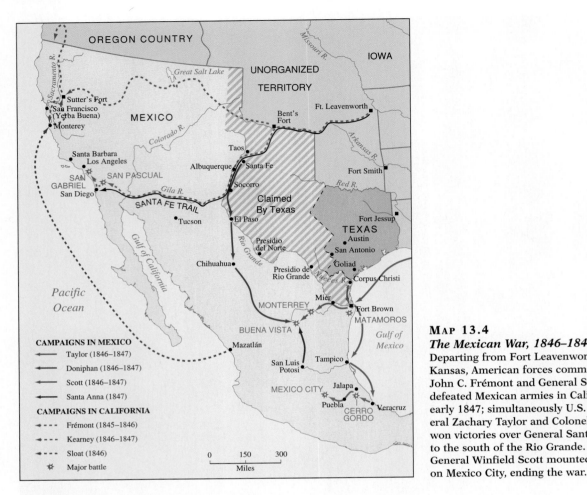

MAP 13.4
The Mexican War, 1846–1848
Departing from Fort Leavenworth in present-day Kansas, American forces commanded by Captain John C. Frémont and General Stephen Kearney defeated Mexican armies in California in 1846 and early 1847; simultaneously U.S. armies under General Zachary Taylor and Colonel Alfred A. Doniphan won victories over General Santa Anna's forces far to the south of the Rio Grande. Then, in mid-1847, General Winfield Scott mounted a successful attack on Mexico City, ending the war.

democratic republic could fight a foreign war "with the vigor" characteristic of "more arbitrary forms of government." Even so, the conflict had divided the nation.

Antislavery Whigs. As Clay and Van Buren had feared, the annexation of Texas and the resulting war with Mexico altered the character of American politics. From the very beginning of the war a few Whigs, such as Charles Francis Adams of Massachusetts, strongly opposed the war on moral grounds and became known as "conscience Whigs." They maintained that the war was part of a southern conspiracy to add new slave states in the West and thereby ensure control of the federal government by slaveholding Democrats. These antislavery Whigs grew bolder after the elections of 1846, which gave their party control of Congress. After Taylor's victory at Buena Vista in February 1847, Whigs in the House passed a resolution that congratulated the army but condemned the war, declaring that it had been "unconstitutionally and unnecessarily begun by the President." Whigs grew more vocal as American casualties mounted, particularly during the bloody march to Mexico City.

Whig leaders moved toward an antislavery stance partly because their economic program—especially

their support for high tariffs—had lost popular appeal. In 1846 Polk and the congressional Democrats had passed the Walker Tariff, which dramatically reduced duties on imported goods. The Walker Tariff came hard on the heels of Britain's repeal of the Corn Laws (which had placed high duties on imported wheat and corn) and seemed to herald the adoption of free trade throughout the Anglo-American world. American consumers welcomed cheaper prices on imported goods, and their increased purchases pushed up tariff revenues, allowing Polk to finance the war without raising taxes. Given the popularity of free trade, the Whigs could no longer count on winning elections by championing higher tariffs and the American System.

The Wilmot Proviso and Free Soil. But the Democrats had even worse political problems because Polk's expansionist policy had split the party. In August 1846, David Wilmot, a Democratic representative from Pennsylvania, proposed a simple amendment to a military appropriations bill: slavery would be prohibited in any new territories acquired from Mexico. This provision, known as the Wilmot Proviso, soon became a rallying point for northerners who feared the expansion of slav-

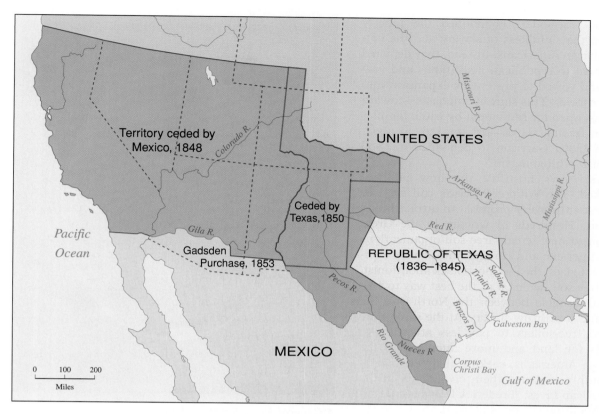

MAP 13.5
The Mexican Cession, 1848–1853
In the Treaty of Guadalupe Hidalgo (1848) and the Gadsden Purchase (1853), Mexico
ceded to the United States its vast northern territories—the present-day states of California, Nevada, Utah, Arizona, New Mexico, and half of Colorado and Texas. These new
territories, President Polk boasted to Congress, "constitute of themselves a country large
enough for a great empire, and the acquisition is second in importance only to that of
Louisiana in 1803."

ery. In the House the Democratic Party was divided as
supporters of Martin Van Buren joined forces with antislavery Whigs to pass the Proviso on several occasions.
The Senate, dominated by southerners and proslavery
northern Democrats, killed the measure each time.

In this heated atmosphere, the most fervent Democratic expansionists became even more aggressive.
Polk, along with Secretary of State Buchanan and Senators Stephen A. Douglas of Illinois and Jefferson Davis
of Mississippi, wanted the United States to take at least
part of Mexico south of the Rio Grande. But many
southerners, including John C. Calhoun, worried that
the United States could not absorb the resident Mexicans, whom they regarded as an "inferior" people, and
feared that a longer war would augment the power of
the federal government. Calhoun supported taking only
California and New Mexico, the most sparsely populated areas of Mexico. Midwestern Democrats also
opposed a major expansion to the south, in part
because of their anger at Polk's compromise with
Britain over Oregon.

To reunify the Democratic Party before the next
election, Polk and Buchanan abandoned their expansionist dreams of "All Mexico" and accepted Calhoun's
policy. In February 1848 Polk signed the Treaty of
Guadalupe Hidalgo, in which the United States agreed
to pay Mexico $15 million in return for its northern-
most provinces: Texas north of the Rio Grande, New
Mexico, and California (Map 13.5). The United States
also agreed to assume all the claims of American citizens, totaling $3.2 million, against the Mexican govern-
ment. The Senate ratified the treaty in March 1848.

This settlement did not restore political tranquility.
The Wilmot Proviso energized abolitionists who had
been seeking a legislative solution to the problem of
slavery, and the Senate's refusal to pass it alarmed
them. Echoing the arguments of the conscience Whigs,
antislavery advocates claimed that southern planters
and their northern business allies had entered into a
massive "Slave Power" conspiracy to expand the
bounds of slavery. To defeat this alleged plan, a significant number of northerners joined a new "free-soil"

movement. The free-soilers abandoned the Liberty Party's focus on the sinfulness of slavery and the natural rights of African Americans. Instead, they depicted slavery as a threat to republican institutions and yeoman farming and vowed to prevent its expansion into the western territories. This shift in emphasis—toward keeping the West open for settlement by white families and away from freeing slaves—led the radical abolitionist William Lloyd Garrison to denounce free-soil doctrine as racist "whitemanism."

Despite Garrison's hostility, the new political approach worked. The Wilmot Proviso's call for free soil was the first antislavery proposal to attract broad popular support. Hundreds of women in the Great Lakes states joined new female free-soil organizations formed by the American and Foreign Anti-Slavery Society. Frederick Douglass, the foremost black abolitionist, also endorsed free soil, seeing it as the best way to provoke a political struggle between the North and the South that would overthrow slavery. At the same time Douglass urged free-soilers to pay less attention to white demands for land and more attention to the needs of African Americans, seeking their emancipation in the South and giving them civil rights in the North (see American Lives, "Frederick Douglass: Development of an Abolitionist," pp. 422–423).

The Election of 1848. The conflict over slavery played a critical role in the election of 1848. Opposed by free-soilers and reduced to exhaustion by his rigorous dawn-to-midnight work regime, Polk declined to run for a second term and died three months after leaving office. In an attempt to maintain party unity, the Democrats nominated another expansionist, Senator Lewis Cass of Michigan. Cass had previously advocated buying Cuba, annexing Mexico's Yucatan Peninsula, and taking all of Oregon. But now he campaigned on a platform that was deliberately vague regarding the question of slavery in the West. He promoted a new idea—which he called "squatter sovereignty"—that would give the settlers in each territory the power to determine its status as free or slave.

Cass's political ingenuity failed to hold the party together. Demanding unambiguous opposition to the expansion of slavery, some northern Democrats joined the newly formed Free Soil Party, which nominated Martin Van Buren for president. Van Buren's conversion to free soil was genuine, but he also wanted to punish southern Democrats for having denied him the presidential nomination in 1844. To attract Whig votes, the Free Soil Party chose a conscience Whig, Charles Francis Adams, as its candidate for vice-president.

To keep their ranks intact, the Whigs nominated General Zachary Taylor. Although he was a southerner and a Louisiana slaveowner, Taylor had not taken a position on the politically charged issue of slavery in

A General Runs for President
Of the first nine presidents, three—Washington, Jackson, and Harrison—owed their political success to their exploits as military commanders. Fresh from the battlefields of the Mexican War, General Zachary Taylor tried to follow in their footsteps, posing for this daguerreotype campaign portrait in his uniform. In part because of his popular appeal as a military hero, Taylor—running on the Whig ticket—won a narrow victory over Democrat Lewis Cass.
Collection of Janice L. and David J. Frent.

the territories. Equally important, the general's exploits during the Mexican War had made him a popular hero in the North as well as the South. Known as "Old Rough and Ready," Taylor possessed a common touch that had won him the affection of his troops. "Our Commander on the Rio Grande," wrote Walt Whitman, "emulates the Great Commander of our revolution"—George Washington.

In 1848, as in the election of 1840, running a military hero worked for the Whigs, but only barely. Taylor took 47 percent of the popular vote against 42 percent for Cass, but the margin in the electoral college was thin: 163 to 127. The Free Soil ticket of Van Buren and Adams made the difference in the election, winning 10 percent of the total popular vote and depriving the Democrats of enough votes in New York to cost Cass that state and the presidency. The popularity of the Wilmot Proviso and the rapid growth of the Free Soil Party had changed the dynamics of American politics, causing southern planters to fear for the future of slavery.

California Gold Prospectors
Beginning in 1849, thousands of fortune seekers from all parts of the world converged
on the California goldfields. By 1852 the state had 200,000 residents, including 25,000
Chinese, many of whom worked as wage laborers in the goldfields. Working at the
head of the Auburn Ravine in 1852, these prospectors are using a primitive technique—panning—to separate gold from sand and gravel.
California State Library.

1850: Crisis and Compromise

Even before President Taylor took office, events in California sparked a serious political crisis that threatened
the Union. In January 1848, just a few months before
the Treaty of Guadalupe Hidalgo made California part
of the United States, workmen building a mill for John
A. Sutter discovered flakes of gold in the Sierra Nevada
foothills in northern California. Sutter was a Swiss
immigrant who arrived in California in 1839, became a
Mexican citizen, and established a kind of feudal estate
in the Sacramento Valley. He tried to keep the discovery
a secret, but by May scores of Americans were pouring
into the foothills from San Francisco in search of the
precious metal. When President Polk confirmed the
discovery in December, the gold rush was on. By Janu-

ary 1849 sixty-one crowded ships had departed from
northeastern ports to sail around Cape Horn for San
Francisco, and by May 12,000 wagons had crossed the
Missouri River, also bound for the goldfields. In 1849
alone more than 80,000 migrants—the "forty-niners"—
arrived in California (Map 13.6).

Statehood for California. The rapid influx of settlers
revived the national debate over free soil. The forty-
niners, who lived in crowded, chaotic towns and mining camps, demanded the formation of a territorial
government to protect their lives and property. To avoid
an extended debate over slavery, President Taylor
advised the Californians to apply for statehood immediately, and in November 1849 they ratified a state constitution that prohibited slavery. Few of the many

Frederick Douglass: Development of an Abolitionist

————— ★ —————

FREDERICK DOUGLASS WAS born a slave in 1818. Thirty years later he was a famous man, author of the acclaimed *Narrative of the Life of Frederick Douglass* (1845) and a leading moral abolitionist. Within another five years Douglass had become active in politics, convinced that only the power of the government would bring an end to the institution of slavery.

There was much luck in Douglass's rapid ascent to fame and influence, but even more determination and sheer ability: he was a man of remarkable talents. Douglass began his life on a plantation on the eastern shore of Maryland as Frederick Bailey, having been given his mother's family name. He never knew who his father was, although talk in the slave quarters pointed toward a man Douglass later described as "his master." This intimate tie to the white community may explain Frederick Bailey's rather fortunate early life. In 1827 he became the property of Thomas Auld, as part of a family property settlement. Auld immediately dispatched the nine-year-old boy to live with his brother, Hugh Auld, in Baltimore.

There were no other slaves in Hugh Auld's household, and quite remarkably, for the next five years Frederick was treated much like the other children. He listened to Sophia Auld read the Bible, learned to read from a spelling book borrowed from the Auld children, figured out the meaning of *abolition* from newspapers, and heard about slaves running away to the North. At age twelve he purchased a copy of *The Columbian Orator,* a collection of speeches for young boys learning to declaim the virtues of the republic—including its devotion to "the rights of man." Enthralled, Douglass memorized and recited the speeches to his friends, including the free blacks he sought out at Methodist and Baptist churches. Despite his legal status, the young Frederick Bailey had begun to think and act like a free man.

In 1833 Thomas Auld returned Frederick to the sleepy eastern shore town of St. Michaels, perhaps to prevent him from running away or becoming mixed up in antislavery agitation. Frederick became rebel-

lious, organizing a Sabbath school and refusing to work. So in 1834 Auld hired Douglass out to Edward Covey, a farmer with a reputation for "breaking" unruly slaves. After enduring six months of disciplined labor and regular beatings, Frederick reached his own breaking point and had it out with Covey. Their brutal fight "was the turning point in my *'life as a slave,'*" Douglass recalled, the point at which his future became clear. "I was nothing before; I WAS A MAN NOW," and determined "to be a FREEMAN."

In 1835 the seventeen-year-old Frederick hatched a plan. Betrayed by a fellow conspirator, he found himself in jail, facing sale into the Deep South. Once again Thomas Auld intervened, returning Frederick to his brother's charge in Baltimore and promising him freedom in eight years, at the age of twenty-five. Becoming a journeyman caulker in the shipyards, the young slave soon worked independently, giving Hugh Auld a weekly payment.

Douglass plunged into the life of Baltimore's free African American community, almost 30,000 in number. He courted a free black woman, Anna Murray, and became a member of the East Baltimore Mental Improvement Society, a self-improvement society of free black caulkers. But this life came to an abrupt end when he fell behind in his payments to Hugh Auld, who ordered him to give up his independence. Frederick decided to run away. In the fall of 1838 he borrowed the identification papers of a free African American sailor and sailed to New York City, where he and Anna married.

Frederick Bailey began his life of freedom by taking a new name—Douglass—and settling in the seaport town of New Bedford, Massachusetts. Inspired by the lectures of William Lloyd Garrison, a leading abolitionist, he began to deliver antislavery speeches to white audiences. In 1841 Douglass delivered a powerful address at a meeting of the Massachusetts Anti-Slavery Society, winning the admiration of Garrison, who hired him as an agent of the American Anti-Slavery Society.

Soon Douglass's commanding personal presence, dramatic rhetoric, and forceful intellect made him a celebrity. He lectured in hundreds of communities in the Northeast, where his speeches held audiences spellbound. In 1842 Elizabeth Cady Stanton, a proponent of women's rights, heard Douglass address a meeting in Boston's Faneuil Hall and was deeply impressed:

Around him sat the great antislavery orators of the day watching the effect of his eloquence on that immense audience, that laughed and wept by turns, completely carried away by the won-

Frederick Douglass, c. 1848
This daguerreotype of Douglass was taken when he was about thirty years of age. Describing Douglass, an admirer wrote: "He was more than six feet in height, and his majestic form . . . straight as an arrow, muscular, yet lithe and graceful, his flashing eye, and more than all, his voice, that rivaled Webster's in its richness, and in the depth and sonorousness of its cadences, made up such an ideal of an orator as the listeners never forgot."
Chester County Historical Society.

drous gifts of his pathos and humor. On this occasion, all the other speakers seemed tame after Frederick Douglass.

In his speeches Douglass denounced both slavery in the South and racial discrimination in the North. But he grew uncomfortable with Garrison's willingness to expel the southern states from the Union, which Douglass believed would leave the slaves completely at the mercy of their owners. Gradually the young African American orator moved toward an independent position, especially in the wake of the great success of his *Narrative* and a triumphal lecturing tour of the British Isles between 1845 and 1847.

Upon his return to the United States, Douglass moved to Rochester, New York, where he founded an antislavery newspaper, *The North Star,* which was financed primarily by Gerrit Smith, one of the leaders of the Liberty Party. Departing from Garrison's moral

radicalism, Douglass gravitated toward political abolitionism. In 1848 he attended the Buffalo convention that established the Free Soil Party, ignoring Garrison's charge that the party was a species of "whitemanism," a racist effort to keep the territories white. In that year Douglass also attended the women's rights convention at Seneca Falls, where he was the only man to play a prominent role. Subsequently, he endorsed a wider public role for women, writing in *The North Star* "that in respect to political rights, we hold woman to be justly entitled to all we claim for men."

In 1851 Douglass publicly separated himself from Garrison and the American Anti-Slavery Society by defending the Constitution, which Garrison had previously condemned as "a covenant with death." A year later he delivered his "Fifth of July" speech, probably the most moving and influential of his career. Now he specifically denied that the Constitution was proslavery. "In that instrument, I hold there is no warrant, license, nor sanction of the hateful thing; but, interpreted as it ought to be interpreted, the Constitution is a GLORIOUS LIBERTY DOCUMENT."

Douglass's involvement in practical politics deepened during the 1850s. Although he believed that violence would be necessary to abolish slavery, he was cautious in encouraging slave insurrections, declining to join John Brown's raid on Harpers Ferry. Nonetheless, popular suspicion that he was a key conspirator led Douglass to flee to Canada and then to Britain. When he resumed speechmaking in America in 1860, the victory of the Republican Party and its program of free soil seemed imminent.

Douglass remained a leader of the African American community. During the Civil War he pressed the Republicans to embrace the abolition of slavery as a war aim and was delighted when President Lincoln adopted his view of the Constitution. He also helped the War department recruit black soldiers. Throughout Reconstruction he spoke and lobbied effectively for equal treatment—including the right to vote—for African Americans. But his service to the Republican Party went virtually unrewarded until he reached the age of seventy, when he was appointed as American minister to the black nation of Haiti.

By the time of his death in 1895 Douglass's optimism about race relations had waned, as Jim Crow laws in the southern states fastened new bonds of discrimination on African Americans. In his last major speech he warned that the "presence of eight millions of people . . . constituting an aggrieved class, smarting under terrible wrongs, denied the exercise of the commonest rights of humanity . . . [is] a disgrace and scandal to . . . the whole country."

MAP 13.6
The California Gold Rush, 1849–1857
Traveling from all parts of the world—Europe, China, and Australia, as well as the eastern United States—hundreds of thousands of bonanza seekers converged on the California goldfields. Miners traveling by sea landed at San Francisco, which became an instant metropolis, and then stocked up on food and supplies at Stockton and Sacramento. By the mid-1850s the seaborne boom was over; almost as many people departed from San Francisco each year as had arrived to seek their fortune.

southerners who flocked to the goldfields or to San Francisco owned slaves or wanted to; only ranchers in sparsely populated southern California had strongly promoted slavery. For his part, Taylor wanted to attract Free-Soilers and northern Democrats into the Whig Party and urged Congress to admit California as a free state. At the same time he assured southern Whigs that he would protect slavery in the South.

Nonetheless, most southern politicians were alarmed by the swift victory of the antislavery forces in California. Not only had a valuable area been lost to free soil, but the admission of California would threaten the carefully maintained balance in the Senate. In 1845 the entry of Texas and Florida to the Union had raised the total of slave states to fifteen, as opposed to thirteen free states. However, the entry of Iowa in 1846 and Wisconsin in 1848 had reestablished the balance. Now southern leaders feared that the admission of California would give the North a majority in the Senate as well as the House, placing their section at a political disadvantage from which it would never recover. They were prepared to block the entry of California as a free state unless the federal government guaranteed the future of slavery.

Constitutional Conflict. The resulting impasse produced passionate debates in Congress and a variety of political and constitutional solutions. As usual, John C. Calhoun took the most extreme southern position, warning of possible secession by the slave states and even civil war. To avoid that outcome, Calhoun proposed that slavery be guaranteed in all the territories and that the Constitution be amended to ensure a permanent balance of power between the sections. He wanted the presidency to become a dual office, with authority divided between executives from the South and the North, each with full veto power.

In making those proposals, Calhoun advanced a radically new constitutional doctrine: that Congress had no authority to regulate slavery in the territories and thus citizens of any state were free to take their property—including human chattel—into these areas, which were the common property of all the states. Regardless of its constitutional merits, Calhoun's argument gathered little backing from leading politicians because it ran counter to a half-century of practice. In 1787 the Continental Congress had banned slavery in the Northwest Territory, and in the Missouri Compromise of 1820 the U.S. Congress had prohibited bondage in most of the area encompassed by the Louisiana Purchase.

While Calhoun's new doctrine did attract some support in the Deep South, most southern planters were prepared to accept a second, more moderate, solution: an extension of the Missouri Compromise line to the Pacific Ocean. This policy would guarantee slaveowners access to some western territory (in a separate state in southern California, for example) and add more slave states to the Union. Some northern Democrats, including former secretary of state James Buchanan, also favored this plan as a way to resolve the crisis.

A third alternative was squatter sovereignty, the idea advanced by Lewis Cass during the election of 1848 and now championed by Democratic senator Stephen Douglas of Illinois. Douglas called his plan *popular sovereignty* to emphasize its roots in republican ideology, and it had considerable appeal to many politicians. Popular sovereignty would place decisions about slavery in the hands of local settlers and their territorial governments rather than in the hands of Congress, thereby removing the explosive issue from national politics. However, the concept was vague and slippery, in part because its proponents did not clearly specify at what point the people of a territory could legalize or ban slavery—when it was first organized or when it applied for statehood.

However, antislavery politicians were unwilling to accept *any* expansion of slavery, lending credence to Calhoun's warning of the possible breakup of the Union. In 1850 Senator Salmon P. Chase of Ohio, elected by a Democratic–Free Soil coalition, and Senator William H. Seward, an abolitionist-minded New York Whig, urged federal authorities to contain slavery and then extinguish it completely. Condemning human bondage as "morally unjust, politically unwise, and socially pernicious," Seward invoked "a higher law than the Constitution" and demanded bold action to protect freedom, "the common heritage of mankind."

A Complex Compromise. Standing on the brink of disaster, senior Whigs and Democrats desperately sought a compromise. Through a long, complex legislative process, the Whig leaders Henry Clay and Daniel Webster and the Democrat Stephen A. Douglas fashioned a complex package of six laws known collectively as the Compromise of 1850. To mollify the South, the Compromise included a new Fugitive Slave Act, strengthening a law enacted in 1793 by requiring federal magistrates to assist slaveowners seeking runaway slaves. To satisfy the North, the Compromise admitted California as a free state, abolished the slave trade (but not slavery itself) in the District of Columbia, and restricted the spread of slavery by denying claims of Texas to the land east of the Rio Grande (see Map 13.5). Finally, the Compromise organized the rest of the lands acquired from Mexico into the territories of New Mexico and Utah on the basis of popular sovereignty.

The Compromise averted a secession crisis in 1850—but only barely. Some of the new laws squeaked through Congress by only a few votes, and there was little popular enthusiasm for the settlement. In the midst of the struggle the governor of South Carolina declared that there was not "the slightest doubt" that his state would secede. He and other "fire-eaters" (the name given to rabid secessionists) in Georgia, Mississippi, and Alabama organized special conventions to protect "Southern Rights" and demand secession. Moderate southern politicians persuaded the convention delegates to support the Compromise but had to promise that they would back secession in the future if Congress abolished slavery anywhere, failed to recognize slavery in a new territory, or refused to admit a territory with a proslavery constitution into the Union. Lacking the support of other slave states, the South Carolina radicals drew back from secession, averting a constitutional crisis. The fact that the Compromise of 1850 elicited such a passionately negative response throughout the Deep South—and among many northern Whigs and Free-soilers as well—did not bode well for its success.

The End of the Second Party System, 1850–1858

───────★───────

The architects of the Compromise of 1850 hoped that their agreement, like the Missouri Compromise of 1820, would resolve the issue of slavery for another generation. But their hopes were quickly dashed as one conflict after another divided Americans along sectional lines. Demanding freedom for fugitive slaves and free soil in the West, antislavery northerners blocked implementation of parts of the Compromise, while southern expansionists insisted that slavery be extended not only into the West but also into the Caribbean and even the North. "That Union should so long have been preserved in a confederacy which contains an element of discord of such magnitude and of so disturbing a nature as that of Slavery is a wonder," Martin Van Buren reflected in 1856. Even as the former president spoke, the trust and good will that had preserved the Union for nearly three generations were being shattered.

Resistance to the Fugitive Slave Act

The most controversial element of the Compromise proved to be the Fugitive Slave Act. Under its terms, federal judges or special commissioners in the northern states determined the status of blacks who were accused of being runaway slaves. A commissioner would receive

Uncle Tom's Cabin, 1852
The cover of this "Young Folks Edition" of *Uncle Tom's Cabin* shows Tom as a well-dressed and kindly older man, reading the Bible to Little Eva, whom he has saved from drowning. Like the book's text, this image offered whites a sympathetic view of African Americans, challenging generations of negative stereotypes.
The Charles L. Blockson Afro-American Collection, Temple University.

catcher out of town. Abandoning pacifism, Frederick Douglass declared that "the only way to make a Fugitive Slave Law a dead letter is to make half a dozen or more dead kidnappers."

As if in response, in September 1851 a deadly confrontation took place in the Quaker village of Christiana, Pennsylvania. About twenty African Americans, including several escaped slaves, exchanged gunfire with a group of slave catchers from Maryland; the slaves' owner was killed and his son was severely wounded. Millard Fillmore, who had become president in 1850 following the sudden death of Zachary Taylor, sent in troops and federal marshals, who arrested thirty-six blacks and four whites. To underline their resolve, federal prosecutors indicted the suspects for treason (waging war against the United States), but a local jury acquitted one defendant, and northern public opinion forced the government to drop its charges against the rest. Nonetheless, the law was effectively enforced in many northern regions, and a significant number of fugitives (as well as some free blacks) were sent to the South and enslaved.

It was in reaction to the Fugitive Slave Act that Harriet Beecher Stowe composed her abolitionist novel, *Uncle Tom's Cabin* (1852). The novel tells of a compassionate but weak slaveholder in Kentucky who sells two slaves, an older man named Tom and a five-year-old boy, to a slave trader to pay off debts. The beautiful Eliza Harris, the boy's mother, refuses to be separated from her son. With the child in her arms, she crosses the Ohio River on cakes of ice just ahead of the vicious slave trader. Eliza reaches the house of an Ohio politician who, to preserve the Union, has set aside his "private feeling" and voted for a fugitive slave law. His wife persuades him to follow his heart and help Eliza and her child escape to Canada. Meanwhile, Tom has fallen under the control of Simon Legree, a brutal overseer on a southern plantation, who beats Tom to death but never conquers his Christian soul. By translating the moral principles of abolitionism into heart-rending personal tragedies, Beecher's novel evoked a mixture of empathy and outrage throughout the North. More than 300,000 Americans bought copies of *Uncle Tom's Cabin*, and countless families flocked to an emotionally charged stage version produced by local theater companies (see American Voices, "Mary Boykin Chesnut: A Slaveholder's Diary," p. 427).

In the mid-1850s northern legislatures responded to the growing popular opposition to slave catching by enacting *personal liberty* laws that extended legal rights to accused fugitives. In 1857 the Wisconsin Supreme Court went even further. In *Ableman v. Booth* the Wisconsin judges claimed the authority to void federal statutes, ruling that the Fugitive Slave Law could not be enforced in their state because it violated the Constitution. Then they contested the power of the federal courts to review their decision, directly challenging a

a $10 fee (about $150 today) if an alleged fugitive was found to be a runaway, but only $5 (or $75 today) if the accused was declared a free person—a significant incentive for a guilty verdict. The accused African Americans were also denied jury trials and even the right to testify. Moreover, federal marshals were legally required to support the slave catchers, and federal magistrates could impose heavy penalties on anyone who helped a slave escape or used force to protect a fugitive.

The act aroused great hostility among free blacks and abolitionists. Declaring "that it is the cruel mockery of all justice, inhuman, anti-Christian, [and] diabolical," the Antislavery Society of Rochester, New York, organized a vigilante force to block its enforcement. In October 1850 in Boston, Theodore Parker and other abolitionists openly defied the law by helping two slaves escape to freedom and driving a Georgia slave

MARY BOYKIN CHESNUT

A Slaveholder's Diary

★

During the 1850s, in response to Harriet Beecher Stowe's Uncle Tom's Cabin *and Republican celebrations of free labor, proslavery advocates such as George Fitzhugh (in* Sociology for the South; or, the Failure of Free Society *and other works) contrasted the slaveowners' benevolent concern for their enslaved workers with the factory owners' indifference toward the welfare of their wage laborers. Mary Boykin Chesnut (1823–1886), wife of the South Carolina senator James Chesnut, held a more complex view. Although believing that blacks were innately inferior and celebrating the benevolence of white women, she hated slavery, in part because she thought that it oppressed the women of both races. Chesnut revealed her views in the extensive diary she kept during the Civil War.*

March 18, 1861 . . . I wonder if it be a sin to think slavery a curse to any land. [Massachusetts senator Charles] Sumner said not one word of this hated institution which is not true. Men and women are punished when their masters and mistresses are brutes and not when they do wrong—and then we live surrounded by prostitutes. An abandoned woman is sent out of any decent house elsewhere. Who thinks any worse of a negro or mulatto woman for being a thing we can't name? God forgive us, but ours is a *monstrous* system and wrong. . . . Like the patriarchs of old our men live all in one house with their wives and their concubines, and the mulattoes one sees in every family exactly resemble the white children—and every lady tells you who is the father of all the mulatto children in everybody's household, but those in her own she seems to think drop from the clouds, or pretends so to think. Good women we have . . . the purest women God ever made. Thank God for my countrywomen—alas for the men! No worse than men everywhere, but the lower their mistresses, the more degraded they must be.

November 27, 1861 . . . Now what I have seen of my mother's life, my grandmother's, my mother-in-law's: These people were educated at Northern schools mostly—read the same books as their Northern condemners, the same daily newspapers, the same Bible—have the same ideas of right and wrong—are highbred, lovely, good, pious—doing their duty as they conceive it. They live in negro villages. They do not preach and teach hate as a gospel and the sacred duty of murder and insurrection, but they strive to ameliorate the condition of these Africans in every particular. . . . These women are more troubled by their duty to negroes, have less chance to live their own lives in peace than if they were African missionaries. They have a swarm of blacks about them as children under their care—not as Mrs. Stowe's fancy paints them, but the hard, unpleasant, unromantic, undeveloped savage Africans. And they hate slavery worse than Mrs. Stowe. . . .

We are human beings of the nineteenth century—and slavery has to go, of course. All that has been gained by it goes to the North and to negroes. The slave-owners, when they are good men and women, are the martyrs. And as far as I have seen, the people here are quite as good as anywhere else. I hate slavery.

Source: C. Vann Woodward, *Mary Chesnut's Civil War* (New Haven: Yale University Press, 1981), 29–30, 245–246.

jurisdictional doctrine that had been accepted for more than a generation. When the case was finally considered by the U.S. Supreme Court in 1859, Chief Justice Taney led a unanimous Court in affirming the supremacy of federal over state courts—a position that has stood the test of time—and upheld the constitutionality of the Fugitive Slave Act. But by that time popular sentiment in many northern states had made it impossible to catch fugitive blacks or secure their conviction. As Douglass had hoped, the act had become a "dead letter."

The Whigs' Decline and the Democrats' Diplomacy

The conflict over fugitive slaves split the Whig Party, which entered the election of 1852 weakened by the deaths of Henry Clay and Daniel Webster, two of its greatest leaders. Passing over Fillmore because of his reputation as an aristocratic snob and his vigorous enforcement of the Fugitive Slave Act, the Whigs nominated General Winfield Scott, another hero of the Mexican War. But

The Election of 1852
In this cartoon, Franklin Pierce races toward the White House on a swift Democratic horse while General Winfield Scott futilely beats his stubborn Whig mule, which is pulled by members of the Know-Nothing Party (represented by the "Native American") and prodded by a group of African Americans. By identifying Scott and the Whigs with the anti-immigrant platform of the Know-Nothing Party and as pro-black (because many Whigs opposed the Fugitive Slave Act of 1850), the cartoonist seeks to garner votes for Pierce and the Democrats from New York's large population of Irish and German immigrants.
Collection of Janice L. and David J. Frent.

about a third of southern Whigs refused to support Scott because they were angry over the party's longstanding support of pro-northern economic policies and its refusal to uphold the Fugitive Slave Act.

As the Democrats met in their national convention, they too were divided. Southerners wanted a candidate who would support Calhoun's position that all territories should be open to slavery. Northern delegates rejected that idea but were sharply divided among the three candidates who supported the alternative policy of popular sovereignty: Lewis Cass, Stephen Douglas, and James Buchanan. For forty-eight ballots none of the three men could secure the necessary two-thirds majority. Exhausted, the convention settled on a compromise candidate—Franklin Pierce of New Hampshire, a congenial man reputed to be sympathetic to the South.

The Democrats' cautious strategy paid off, and they swept the election. Pleased by the admission of California as a free state, Martin Van Buren and many other Free-Soilers voted for Pierce, reuniting the Democratic

Party. Conversely, the election destroyed the Whig Party as a national organization, as massive numbers of southerners deserted its ranks. The Whigs would never again wage a national campaign (see Map 13.8).

As president, Pierce pursued an expansionist foreign policy. To assist northern merchants who wanted to expand trade with Asia, he gave his support to Commodore Matthew C. Perry, who had been dispatched to Japan with a naval squadron. When Perry's show of force persuaded Japanese leaders to sign a treaty of friendship with the United States, Pierce used the opportunity to establish full diplomatic and trading relations with the island nation. In 1854 he sent Townsend Harris, an experienced China trader, to negotiate with Japan; four years later Harris returned with a commercial treaty, the first such agreement the rigidly traditionalist Japan had made with any industrial power.

Pierce was even more solicitous of southern interests. To resolve a dispute over the southern boundary of New Mexico, the president revived Polk's plan to annex

Mexican territory south of the Rio Grande. Pierce and his secretary of war, Jefferson Davis, sent James Gadsden to negotiate the purchase of a major portion of northern Mexico and Baja (Lower) California. Mexican officials refused to part with those large territories but in 1853 agreed to the sale of 30,000 square miles of land south of the Gila River. Gadsden, a South Carolina politician and railroad promoter, wanted this territory to expedite the construction of a southern transcontinental railroad to the Pacific. The Gadsden Purchase, as it became known, rubbed salt into Mexico's war wounds, reminding it of the power of its northern neighbor (see Map 13.5).

Pierce's most dramatic foreign policy initiatives came in the Caribbean. During the 1840s southern expansionists had funded three clandestine military expeditions to Spanish Cuba, where they hoped to prod the slaveowning elite into declaring independence. Once Cuba was independent, it would be invited to join the Union as a slave state. In 1853 Pierce covertly supported a new Cuban expedition led by John A. Quitman, a former governor of Mississippi. While Quitman was building up his forces, the Pierce administration threatened war with Spain over the seizure of the American ship *Black Warrior*, demanding an apology and a large indemnity. But when northern Democrats in Congress refused to support this aggressive attempt to create an incident and take Cuba by force, Pierce and Secretary of State William L. Marcy had to back down.

Determined to seize Cuba to enhance his presidential ambitions, Secretary Marcy instructed the American minister in Spain to offer to buy Cuba; if rebuffed, he should "detach that island from the Spanish dominion" by other means. When that initiative also failed, Marcy encouraged the minister and the American ambassadors in France and Great Britain to pressure Pierce to seize the island. The result was an inflammatory message to Pierce that became known as the Ostend Manifesto (1854). Invoking the rhetoric of Manifest Destiny, the three American diplomats (who met in Ostend, Belgium) declared that the United States would be justified in seizing Cuba "by every law, human and Divine." Quickly leaked to the press by antiexpansionists, the Ostend Manifesto triggered a new wave of northern resentment against the South and forced Pierce to halt his efforts to acquire Cuba. The Democrats' policy of expansionism in the Caribbean had not unified the nation in a patriotic cause; instead, it had accentuated sectional tensions by reviving northern fears of a Slave Power conspiracy.

The Kansas-Nebraska Act and the Rise of New Parties

Almost immediately a new struggle over westward expansion deepened sectional divisions. Because the Missouri Compromise prohibited slavery in the Louisiana Purchase north of 36°30′, southern senators

had delayed the political organization of that area, allowing only the admission of Iowa to the Union in 1846 and the formation of the Minnesota Territory. Even though much of the remaining area was in the "Great American Desert," westward-looking residents of the Ohio River Valley and the Upper South demanded that it be organized for settlement. Senator Stephen A. Douglas of Illinois became their foremost spokesman, championing western development and the building of a northern transcontinental railroad from Chicago to California. In 1854 Douglas introduced a bill to extinguish native American rights on the central Plains and to organize a large territory to be called Nebraska.

Douglas's bill conflicted with the plans of southern senators, who were determined to extend slavery throughout the Louisiana Purchase and, like James Gadsden, hoped that a city in a slaveholding state—New Orleans, Memphis, or St. Louis—would become the eastern terminus of a transcontinental railroad. To win southern support for creating the Nebraska Territory, Douglas proposed that it be organized on the basis of popular sovereignty. In a further concession Douglas amended his bill so that it explicitly repealed the Missouri Compromise, which had prohibited slavery in the northern part of the Louisiana Purchase. He also agreed to the formation of two new territories—Nebraska and Kansas—rather than one, giving slaveholders a chance to dominate the settlement of Kansas, the more southern territory (Map 13.7). To encourage northerners to support this policy, Douglas argued that Kansas would be settled primarily by non-slaveholders because its climate and terrain were not suited to plantation agriculture. Supported primarily by southern members of Congress (and a few northern Democrats), the Kansas-Nebraska Act passed in May 1854.

Republicans and Know-Nothings. The Kansas-Nebraska Act proved to be the last nail in the coffin of the Second Party System of Whigs and Democrats. Abolitionists and free-soilers denounced the act for opening new territories to slavery, calling it "part of a great scheme for extending and perpetuating supremacy of the slave power." Antislavery northern Whigs and "anti-Nebraska" Democrats abandoned their respective parties to create a new party, taking the Jeffersonian name *Republican*. Emphasizing uncompromising opposition to the expansion of slavery, the Republicans ran a slate of candidates, primarily in the Midwest, in the congressional election of 1854.

Like most American parties, the Republican Party was a coalition of diverse groups—Free-Soilers, antislavery Democrats, conscience Whigs—but its founders shared many values. In the Republican view, slavery produced only two classes of people: haughty masters and submissive dependents. The masters were corrupted by wielding unlimited power, a system of rule that produced ignorance and sloth among slaves and poor whites. In

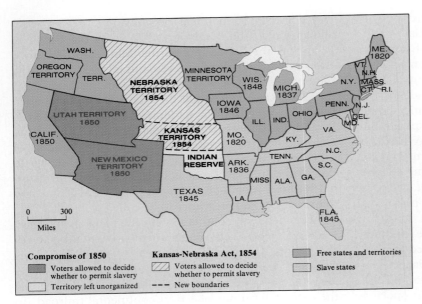

MAP 13.7

The Compromise of 1850 and the Kansas-Nebraska Act of 1854

Vast territories were at stake in the contest over the extension of slavery. The Compromise of 1850 resolved the status of lands in the Far West: California would be a free state, and the settlers of the Utah and New Mexico territories would decide their own fate. But in 1854 the implementation of popular sovereignty in Kansas and Nebraska sparked a bitter local war between the advocates of free soil and of slavery, revealing a fatal flaw in the concept.

contrast, Republicans such as Congressman Thaddeus Stevens of Pennsylvania celebrated the virtues of a society based on "the middling classes who own the soil and work it with their own hands." They envisioned communities in which no person would have unlimited power over another and social mobility would prevent the division of society into fixed classes. Abraham Lincoln, an Illinois Whig who became a Republican, articulated the party's vision. "There is no permanent class of hired laborers among us," he argued. "The man who labored for another last year, this year labors for himself, and next year he will hire others to labor for him." To combat the effects of slavery in the South and growing class divisions in the industrializing North and Midwest, Lincoln and his fellow Republicans asserted the values of republican freedom, individual enterprise, and social mobility.

Competing for Whig and Democratic votes was another new party, the "Know-Nothing," or American, Party. The American Party had its origins in the anti-immigrant, anti-Catholic passions of the 1830s and 1840s (see Chapter 10). In 1850 various secret anti-Catholic societies banded together in the Order of the Star-Spangled Banner; a year later they formed the American Party. The secrecy-conscious members of the party sometimes answered outsiders' questions by saying "I know nothing," which gave the party its nickname, but its program was far from secret. Know-Nothings attempted to unite northern and southern voters behind a program of nativist opposition to the "alien menace": Irish and German Catholics. Many Know-Nothings supported a ban on immigration and advocated literacy tests for voters, which they thought would disfranchise most recent immigrants. In 1854 the American Party gained control of the state governments of Massachusetts and Pennsylvania and, allied with the Whigs, commanded a majority in the U.S. House of

Representatives. The emergence of a strong new party led by nativists suddenly became a real possibility.

"Bleeding Kansas" and the Election of 1856. Just at that moment the settlement of Kansas prompted a new political crisis. In 1854 thousands of ideologically motivated settlers rushed into the new territory, putting Douglas's theory of popular sovereignty to the test. On the side of slavery, Senator David R. Atchison of Missouri organized residents of his state to move to Kansas or to vote there in crucial elections. Opposing him were abolitionists in the New England Emigrant Aid Society, who were colonizing Kansas with free-soilers. When the struggle moved to Washington in March 1855, the Pierce administration recognized the territorial legislature in Lecompton, Kansas, as the legitimate government. This legislature, which had been elected largely by proslavery Missourians who had crossed the border to cast ballots, promptly enacted laws that outlawed the questioning of slavery and made aiding a fugitive slave into a capital offense. To assist the Lecompton legislature, Pierce dispatched federal troops and proslavery judicial appointees. In response, free-soilers rejected its legitimacy.

In May 1856 both sides turned to violence (see American Voices, "Axalla John Hoole: 'Bleeding Kansas': A Southern View," p. 432). A proslavery gang, 700 strong, sacked the free-soil town of Lawrence, destroying two newspaper offices, looting stores, and burning down buildings. The attack on Lawrence enraged John Brown, an abolitionist from New York and Ohio, whose free-state militia force arrived too late to save the town. Brown was a complex man with a checkered past. Born in 1800, he had started more than twenty businesses in six states, had fallen into bankruptcy, and had often been sued by his creditors. Nonetheless, he had an intelligence and a

"Bleeding Kansas"
The confrontation between the North and South in Kansas took many forms. In the spring of 1859, Dr. John Doy (seated) slipped across the border into Missouri and tried to lead thirteen escaped slaves to freedom in Kansas, only to be captured and jailed in St. Joseph, Missouri. This serious-minded band of antislavery men, well-armed with guns and Bowie knives, attacked the jail, freeing Dr. Doy and bringing him back to Kansas.
Kansas State Historical Society.

moral intensity that won the trust of influential people, including leading abolitionists. According to a free-soil minister who knew him, Brown believed "that God had raised him up on purpose to break the jaws of the wicked." Seeking revenge for the sack of Lawrence, he and a few followers murdered and mutilated five proslavery settlers. We must "fight fire with fire" and "strike terror in the hearts of the proslavery people," Brown declared. The "Pottawatomie massacre," as the killings became known, initiated a guerrilla war in Kansas that cost about 200 lives.

The violence in Kansas dominated the presidential election of 1856. The two-year-old Republican Party counted on anger over "Bleeding Kansas" to boost its electoral fortunes. The party's platform denounced the Kansas-Nebraska Act and, alleging a "Slave Power" conspiracy to expand slavery, insisted that the federal government prohibit slavery in all the territories. As one Republican put it, "If we do not exclude slavery from the Territories, it will exclude us." The Republican platform also called for federal subsidies to transcontinental railroads, reviving the element of the Whig economic program that was most popular among midwestern Democrats. For president, the Republicans nominated John C. Frémont, a free-soiler famous for his role in the conquest of California.

The American Party entered the election with high hopes, but it quickly split into warring factions—North and South—over the struggle in Kansas. The Republicans cleverly maneuvered the northern faction into endorsing Frémont and won the support of many Know-Nothing workingmen by adding anti-Catholic nativism to their program of high tariffs on imported manufactures. As a Republican congressman declared, "Let our motto be, protection to *everything American, against everything foreign.*" The southern faction of the American Party nominated Millard Fillmore, who ran an effective campaign and found supporters in all regions.

The Democrats reaffirmed their support for popular sovereignty and the Kansas-Nebraska Act and nominated James Buchanan of Pennsylvania, who emerged victorious in the three-way race. Some southern Democrats openly threatened secession if Frémont won, and fearful of such a cataclysm, enough northern Democrats remained loyal to the party to provide Buchanan with a solid margin in the popular vote. Buchanan drew 1.8 million votes (45 percent), against 1.3 million (33 percent) for Frémont and 0.9 million (22 percent) for Fillmore, who garnered just 8 electoral votes. Frémont showed the strength of the new Republican Party in the North by carrying eleven free states with 114 electoral votes. Buchanan captured 174 electoral votes but took

AXALLA JOHN HOOLE

"Bleeding Kansas": A Southern View

——————★——————

Early in 1856 Axalla John Hoole and his bride left South Carolina to build a new life in the Kansas Territory (K.T.). These letters from Hoole to his family show that things did not go well from the start and only got worse; after eighteen months the Hooles returned to South Carolina. A Confederate militia captain during the Civil War, Axalla Hoole died in the Battle of Chickamauga in September 1863.

Kansas City, Missouri, Apl. 3d., 1856. The Missourians . . . are very sanguine about Kansas being a slave state & I have heard some of them say it *shall* be . . . but generally speaking, I have not met with the reception which I expected. Everyone seems bent on the Almighty Dollar, and as a general thing that seems to be their only thought. . . . the supper bell has rung and I must close. Give my love to [the family] and all the Negroes. . . .

Lecompton, K.T., Sept. 12, 1856. I have been unwell ever since the 9th of July. . . . I thought of going to work in a few days, when the Abolitionists broke out and I have had to stand guard of nights when I ought to have been in bed, took cold which . . . caused diarrhea. . . . Betsie is well—

You perceive from the heading of this that I am now in Lecompton, almost all of the Proslavery party between this place and Lawrence are here. We brought our families here, as we thought that we would be better able to defend ourselves. . . .

Lane [and a free-state army] came against us last Friday (a week ago to-day). As it happened we had about 400 men with two cannon—we marched out to meet him, though we were under the impression at the time that we had 1,000 men. We came in gunshot of each other, but the regular [U.S. Army] soldiers came and interfered, but not before our party had shot some dozen guns, by which it is reported that five of the Abolitionists had been killed or wounded. We had strict orders . . . not to fire until they made the attack, but some of our boys would not be restrained. I was a rifleman and one of the skirmishers, but did all that I could to restrain our men though I itched all over to shoot myself. . . . but we were acting on the defensive, and did not think it prudent to commence the engagement. I firmly believe we would have whipped them, though we would have lost a good many men. . . .

July the 5th., 1857. I fear, Sister, that [our] coming here will do no good at last, as I begin to think that this will be made a Free State at last. 'Tis true we have elected Proslavery men to draft a state constitution, but I feel pretty certain, if it is put to a vote of the people, it will be rejected, as I feel pretty confident that they have a majority here at this time. The South has ceased all efforts, while the North is redoubling her exertions. We nominated a candidate for Congress last Friday—Ex-Gov. Ransom of Michigan. I must confess I have not much faith in him, tho he professes to hate the abolitionists bitterly . . . . If we had nominated a Southern man, he would have been sure to have been beaten. . . .

———————

Source: William Stanley Hoole, ed., "A Southerner's Viewpoint of the Kansas Situation, 1856–1857," *Kansas Historical Quarterly* 3 (1934): 43–65, 149–171, passim.

only five free states, and a small shift of the popular vote to Frémont in Illinois and Pennsylvania would have given the election to the Republicans.

The dramatic restructuring of parties was now apparent (Map 13.8). The Know-Nothings had lost their bid to become a major party, and the Republicans had replaced the Whigs in the contest with the Democrats for national supremacy. Because the Republicans had no support in the South, the implications for the sectional crisis were ominous; a victory for the new party might mean the end of the Union. The fate of the republic hinged on the ability of President Buchanan to achieve a new compromise that would protect free soil in the West and slavery in the South.

Buchanan's Failed Presidency

Events—and his own values and weaknesses—conspired against James Buchanan. A tall, dignified, white-haired figure sixty-four years of age, Buchanan was an experienced party politician but an uninspiring statesman of limited vision. In this time of crisis he stuck doggedly to the traditional Democratic policy of support for southern interests.

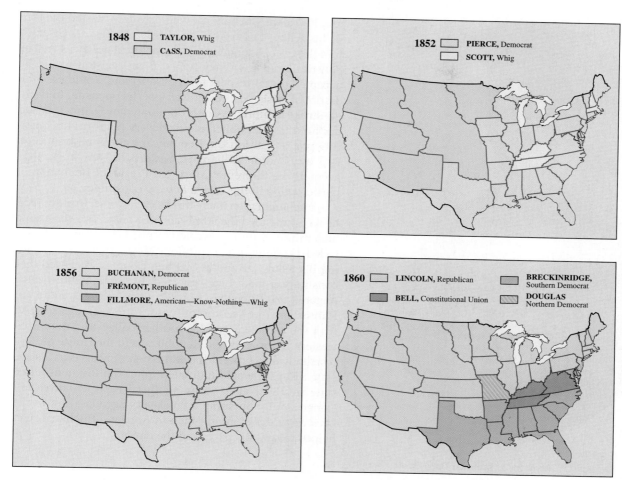

MAP 13.8
Political Realignment, 1848–1860

In 1848 both the Whigs and the Democrats boasted *national* parties, with strong support in most parts of the country. Then political conflict over slavery and the Compromise of 1850 destroyed the Whig Party in the South, making the Democrats the only nationwide party and giving them an easy victory in 1852. The Democratic supremacy was short-lived: by 1856 the passions aroused by "Bleeding Kansas" resulted in the creation of the Republican Party, which carried most of the states of the Northeast and Midwest. By 1860 this *regional* realignment of the party system was complete and would persist for the next seventy years, with Democrats dominant in the South and Republicans dominant in the Northeast and Midwest.

Although Congress had long regulated slavery in the territories, its authority to do so had never been subjected to a clear test of constitutionality. But now in 1856 the case of Dred Scott reached the Supreme Court. Scott was an enslaved African American who had lived for a time with his master, an army surgeon, in the free state of Illinois and at Fort Snelling, then in the Wisconsin Territory, where the Northwest Ordinance (1787) and the Missouri Compromise (1820) prohibited slavery. In his suit, which he filed in Missouri in 1846, Scott claimed that his residency in a free state and a free territory had made him a free man. In March 1857, only days after Buchanan's inauguration, the Court announced its decision in *Dred Scott v. Sandford*.

Seven members of the Court concurred on one critical point: Scott remained a slave. But the judges in the majority could not agree on the legal issues raised by the case, and each justice wrote a separate opinion. In the most influential opinion, Chief Justice Roger B. Taney of Maryland declared that blacks, slave *or* free, could not be citizens of the United States and that Scott therefore had no right to sue in federal court. That argument was controversial enough because free African Americans could be citizens of a state (which would give them the right to enter federal courts), but Taney went on to make two even more controversial points. First, he repeated John C. Calhoun's argument that because the Fifth Amendment prohibited the taking of property without due process of law, Congress could not prevent

Dred Scott (1857)
The case of *Dred Scott v. Sandford* is famous; Dred Scott himself is not. Scott was born into slavery in Virginia around 1800, taken to St. Louis in 1830, and sold to Dr. John Emerson, whose travels formed the legal basis of Scott's suit. Voluntarily freed in June 1857, Scott worked as a hotel porter in St. Louis and was described by a local reporter as "a small, pleasant-looking negro" who looked "somewhat the worse for wear and tear." He died in September 1858, survived by his wife Harriet, a laundress, and by two daughters, who were parties to his original lawsuit of 1846. The suit did not begin as an abolitionist effort to test constitutional principles but as an individual act: Scott and his children wanted to be free.
Library of Congress.

southern citizens from taking their slaves into the territories or owning them there. Therefore, the Chief Justice concluded, the Northwest Ordinance and the Missouri Compromise—which prohibited slavery in the territories—had *never* been constitutional, so Scott's residency at Fort Snelling could not have freed him. Second, Taney declared that Congress could not give to territorial governments any powers that Congress itself did not possess. Since Congress had no authority to prohibit slavery in a territory, neither did a territorial government. Thus Taney endorsed Calhoun's position that slavery could not be banned from any territory.

Five of the seven justices in the majority, including the Chief Justice, were Democrats from slave states. They

and President Buchanan—who privately twisted the arm of his fellow Pennsylvanian, Justice Robert C. Grier, to join the five—intended to make political policy as well as constitutional law. They hoped their decision would be accepted out of respect for the Court and would ease the sectional crisis. The result was just the opposite. In a single stroke a Supreme Court dominated by Democrats had declared the Republicans' antislavery platform unconstitutional, a decision the Republicans could never accept. Led by Senator William H. Seward of New York, they accused the Supreme Court and President Buchanan of participating in the "Slave Power" conspiracy.

Buchanan then made things even worse. In early 1858 he recommended the admission of Kansas as a slave state under the constitution written by proslavery forces, the so-called Lecompton constitution. Most observers—including his fellow Democrat Stephen Douglas—believed that constitution had been enacted by fraudulent means. Angered that Buchanan would not permit a referendum in Kansas on the Lecompton constitution, Douglas broke with the president and his southern allies and mobilized western Democrats and Republicans in the House of Representatives to prevent the admission of Kansas as a slave state. (Kansas would ultimately enter the Union as a free state in 1861, after many southern representatives left Congress.) By pursuing a proslavery agenda—first in the *Dred Scott* decision and then in Kansas—Buchanan had helped to split his party and the nation.

Abraham Lincoln and the Republican Triumph, 1858–1860

⭐

The crisis of the Union intensified as the national Democratic Party fragmented into sectional factions and the Republicans gained the support of a majority of northern voters. During this transition Abraham Lincoln emerged as the pivotal figure in American politics. Lincoln was the only Republican leader whose policies and temperament might have saved the Union, but few southerners trusted him, and his election to the White House in 1860 threatened to reinvigorate the secessionist movement that had smoldered for over a decade.

Lincoln's Early Career

Lincoln's rise from poverty to power through determination and hard work is legendary. The future president came from a hardscrabble farming family that, searching for prosperity, had moved from Kentucky, where he was born in 1809, to Indiana and then Illinois. In 1831, at the age of twenty-two, Lincoln rejected the life of a farmer and began working as a store clerk in New Salem, a small town on the Sangamon River in central Illinois. There he won the admiration of the young workingmen who hung out in local saloons; they elected him captain of a company of militia. A socially ambitious young man, Lincoln also sought entry into the cultured world of the middle class, becoming a member of the New Salem Debating Society. With the help of the local schoolmaster he studied English grammar and elementary mathematics, and another villager introduced him to the works of Shakespeare.

Indeed, Lincoln's ambition was "a little engine that knew no rest," as a close associate later remarked, an ambition that ran not to business but to politics. In 1832 Lincoln ran unsuccessfully for the state legislature, advocating increased state aid for internal improvements and a broad system of public education; in 1834 he ran again and won. After studying law with a prominent Whig attorney, Lincoln moved to Springfield, Illinois, the small country town that had become the new state capital. There he met Mary Todd, the daughter of a successful Kentucky businessman and politician; they married in 1842. The couple were a picture in contrasts. She was short, slender, and elegantly dressed; he was tall, gaunt, and frequently disheveled. Her tastes were aristocratic; his were plain. She was volatile; he was easygoing and deliberate. Bouts of depression, which plagued Lincoln throughout his life, tried her patience and tested his character.

Avidly pursuing a political career, Lincoln served four terms in the lower house of the Illinois legislature. As Whig floor leader and chairman of the finance committee, he promoted education, state banking, and internal improvements such as turnpikes, canals, and railroads. An effective speaker, the rising politician campaigned actively in 1840 for William Henry Harrison and in 1844 for his political hero, Henry Clay. In 1846 he drew on his network of Whig friends to win election to Congress.

As a member of the House of Representatives during the Mexican War, Lincoln had to take a stand on the contentious issue of slavery. He had long felt that human bondage was unjust but did not believe that the federal government had the constitutional authority to tamper with slavery in the southern states. Consequently, he had little sympathy for abolitionism and condemned those New York Whigs who voted for the Liberty Party in 1844, thereby denying the presidency to Henry Clay. Yet Lincoln knew that some Whigs supported abolition and that, like himself, many more were strongly opposed to the expansion of slavery.

A political realist by instinct, Lincoln sought a middle ground. He supported the appropriations bill that sustained President Polk's war in Mexico but, to express his opposition to the spread of slavery, voted for the Wilmot Proviso. Lincoln also proposed the gradual abolition of bondage in the District of Columbia, advancing a plan that would provide compensation to slaveowners and require approval in a referendum of the "free white citizens" of the District. Lincoln argued that such measures—firm opposition to the expansion of slavery, gradual emancipation, and the colonization of freed slaves in Africa and elsewhere—represented the only practical way to address the issues of bondage and race relations. His ideas were derided by those who were driven by emotions and by doctrines. Because of Lincoln's support for gradual emancipation, the abolitionist Wendell Phillips assailed him as "the slave hound of Illinois," and proslavery voters in southern Illinois condemned his support for the Wilmot Proviso.

Dismayed, in 1849 Lincoln withdrew from politics and devoted his energies to an increasingly lucrative legal practice representing railroads and manufacturers in Illinois. But he spoke out against those who fomented the growing sectional crisis. In a speech in 1852 eulogizing Henry Clay for his contributions to national unity, Lincoln condemned both the proslavery fanatics, who denied the tenet of the Declaration of Independence that "all men are created equal," and the abolitionists, who would "shiver into fragments the Union of these States; tear to tatters its now venerated constitution; and even burn the last copy of the Bible, rather than slavery should continue a single hour."

Lincoln returned to the political fray after the passage of Stephen Douglas's Kansas-Nebraska Act, which "aroused" him, his longtime friend and law partner William Herndon observed, "as he had never been before." As a Whig candidate for a seat in the Illinois legislature, Lincoln protested that the opening of Kansas to slaveowning planters placed freedom and human bondage on the same ethical level. Attacking Douglas's position on popular sovereignty in what became known as his Peoria address, Lincoln articulated a clear position on slavery. He would not threaten the institution in the states where it existed, but he hoped that white southerners themselves would adopt "some system of gradual emancipation." Lincoln was outraged that Douglas was willing to permit the expansion of slavery, an institution founded "in the selfishness of man's nature." For his part, he would use the authority of the national government to exclude slavery from the territories and would urge Americans eventually to cut out slavery like a "cancer."

The Republican Politician

Despite his personal victory in the election of 1854, Lincoln abandoned the Whigs because he was unwilling to tie his political career to a dying party. Committing himself to the Republican cause, Lincoln soon emerged as the party's leader in Illinois, working to unite all the anti-Nebraska forces—reformist Whigs, Free-Soilers, abolitionists, Know-Nothings, and radical Democrats.

Following the *Dred Scott* decision and Buchanan's endorsement of the Lecompton constitution, Lincoln won new Republican converts by alleging that there was a "Slave Power" conspiracy to extend slavery into the territories. Moreover, as a lawyer, Lincoln was well aware that a certain case, *Lemmon v. New York*, involving the constitutionality of New York laws prohibiting slavery in that state, might soon come before the proslavery Supreme Court. So he warned Illinois voters that the Court might soon declare that the Constitution "does not permit a *state* to exclude slavery from its limits," just as it had decided (in *Dred Scott*) that "neither Congress nor the territorial legislature can do it." In that event, Lincoln pointed out, "we shall *awake* to the *reality* . . . that the *Supreme Court* has made *Illinois* a *slave* state."

Lincoln versus Douglas.   The fear that slavery would be extended throughout the nation was widely felt in the North. In accepting his party's nomination to challenge Douglas for the U.S. Senate in 1858, Lincoln played on this theme in the most radical speech of his career. Quoting from the Bible, "A house divided against itself cannot stand," the Republican politician predicted a constitutional crisis that would bring either the triumph or the demise of slavery:

> *I believe this government cannot endure permanently half* slave *and half* free. *I do not expect the Union to be dissolved—I do not expect the house to* fall*—but I do expect it will cease to be divided. It will become* all *one thing, or* all *the other.*

Lincoln's duel with Douglas for election to the U.S. Senate attracted national interest because of Douglas's prominence and Lincoln's reputation as a formidable attorney and stump speaker. To increase his national exposure, Lincoln challenged Douglas to a series of seven debates. During those debates Lincoln attacked slavery as an institution that subverted equality of opportunity. While expressing doubts about the innate abilities of those of African descent and rejecting proposals that would give blacks social and political equality, he declared that they were entitled to "all the natural rights enumerated in the Declaration of Independence." This meant, Lincoln explained, that "in the right to eat the bread, without leave of anybody else, which his own hand earns," the black was "the equal of every living man." Taking the offensive, Lincoln pressed Douglas to explain how he could accept the *Dred Scott* decision (which allowed slaveowners to bring their property into the territories) and at the same time advocate popular sovereignty.

In a debate in Freeport, Illinois, Douglas responded by reformulating popular sovereignty. In what became known as the Freeport doctrine, he asserted that settlers could exclude slavery from a territory simply by not adopting local legislation to protect it. Even if territorial

governments lacked the power to prohibit slavery, as Taney had argued in his *Dred Scott* opinion, municipalities could still do so by refusing to support the "peculiar institution." Douglas's Freeport statement upset both proslavery advocates, who feared they would be denied the victory won in *Dred Scott,* and abolitionists, who were not convinced that local regulations would halt the expansion of slavery. Nonetheless the Democratic majority in the Illinois legislature reelected the "Little Giant," as the 5 feet 4 inch Douglas was called, to the Senate. Yet Lincoln's performance had made him into a national figure, and the Republican Party, by winning control of the House of Representatives in the election of 1858, had moved a step closer to national power.

In the wake of Republican gains, southern Democrats divided into two groups. Moderates such as Senator Jefferson Davis of Mississippi, who were known as Southern Rights Democrats, pursued the traditional policy of seeking ironclad commitments to protect slavery in the territories. More radical southern politicians, such as Robert Barnwell Rhett of South Carolina and William Lowndes Yancey of Alabama, abandoned cooperation and actively promoted secession. They proposed extreme measures, such as the reopening of the Atlantic slave trade, in the hope of driving a wedge between the North and the South.

John Brown's Raid.   Radical northerners played into their hands. During the election of 1858 Senator William Seward of New York had declared that freedom and slavery were locked in "an irrepressible conflict," and in October 1859 the militant abolitionist John Brown gave violent expression to those words. Brown led eighteen heavily armed black and white men in a raid to seize the federal arsenal at Harpers Ferry, Virginia; he hoped to use the guns in a slave rebellion that would establish an African American state in the South. The local militia and U.S. Marines under the command of Colonel Robert E. Lee quickly reclaimed the arsenal, capturing Brown and killing ten of his party.

Republican leaders disavowed Brown's raid, but Democrats called his plot, in the words of Stephen Douglas, "a natural, logical, inevitable result of the doctrines and teachings of the Republican party." Fueling the Democratic charges were letters that linked six leading abolitionists to the financing of Brown's raid. The group included two Unitarian ministers—Theodore Parker, who was active in the underground railroad, and Thomas Wentworth Higginson, a Free-Soiler who would command a regiment of African American soldiers during the Civil War. Higginson admitted his involvement and declared that Brown's "acquittal or rescue would do half as much good as [his] being executed; so strong is the personal sympathy with him."

Virginia gave the abolitionists the Christian martyr they wanted. Brown was charged with treason, sentenced to death, and hanged. At a church meeting in Concord, Massachusetts, Henry David Thoreau described Brown as "an angel of light," "the bravest and humanest man in all the country," while Ralph Waldo Emerson proclaimed that Brown would "make the gallows as glorious as the cross." Slaveholders were horrified that some northerners admired Brown, and they looked toward the future with fear. "The aim of the present black republican organization is the destruction of the social system of the Southern States, without regard to consequences," warned one proslavery newspaper.

The Election of 1860. Nor could the South count on the Democratic Party to protect its interests. At the April 1860 party convention in Charleston, South Carolina, northern Democrats rejected Jefferson Davis's program to protect slavery in the territories, prompting the delegates from eight southern states to leave the hall. When neither Douglas nor anyone else could win the required two-thirds majority for the presidential nomination, the convention adjourned. At a second Democratic convention in Baltimore, northern and western delegates nominated Douglas; southern Democrats met separately and nominated Buchanan's vice-president, John C. Breckinridge of Kentucky, as their candidate for president. The Democratic Party had broken into two sectional pieces.

The Republicans sensed victory. They courted white voters by opposing both slavery and racial equality: "Missouri for white men and white men for Missouri," declared that state's Republican platform. On the national level, the Republican convention chose Lincoln as its presidential candidate. Lincoln's position on slavery was more moderate than that of the best-known Republicans, Senators William H. Seward of New York and Salmon P. Chase of Ohio, who demanded that the federal government actively promote abolition. Lincoln also conveyed a compelling egalitarian image that appealed to smallholding farmers and wage earners. And Lincoln's home territory—the rapidly growing Midwest—was crucial in the competition between Democrats and Republicans. The Republican platform followed Lincoln's views and struck a moderate tone, upholding free soil in the West and ruling out direct interference with slavery in the South. It also denied the right of states to secede and endorsed the old Whig program of economic development, which had gained increasing support in the Midwest.

The Republican strategy was successful. Lincoln received only 40 percent of the popular vote but garnered a clear majority of 180 electoral votes by winning every northern and western state except New Jersey. As the candidate of moderate Democrats who wanted compromise, Douglas drew support from all regions except the South; but, while the Little Giant took 30 percent of the total vote, he won only in Missouri and New Jersey—giving him a mere 12 electoral votes. As the secessionists' candidate, Breckinridge captured every state in the Deep South as well as Delaware, Maryland, and North Car-

Abraham Lincoln and Stephen Douglas, 1860
When Douglas and Lincoln squared off in the presidential election of 1860, they distributed thousands of silk campaign ribbons bearing their portraits and signatures. The well-known photographer Matthew Brady took these pictures and retouched the images to make them more flattering—smoothing out Lincoln's gaunt and well-lined face and slimming down Douglas's ample cheeks.
Collection of Janice L. and David J. Frent.

olina, taking 18 percent of the popular ballot and 79 electoral votes. John Bell, a former Tennessee Whig who became the nominee of the compromise-oriented Constitutional Union Party, carried the Upper South states where moderate Whigs had been strongest: Kentucky, Tennessee, and Virginia, giving him 12 percent of the tally and 39 electoral votes (see Map 13.8).

As the vote indicated, the nation was confused and divided. Many white Americans favored continued sectional compromise, but many others were profoundly discouraged by a decade and a half of bitter constitutional debates and failed political bargains. The logic of events now favored those who demanded confrontation and clean solutions. "No man knows what will happen next," the poet Walt Whitman reflected, "but all know some such things are to happen as mark the greatest moral convulsions of the earth." The Republican Party had united majorities in the states of the Northeast, Midwest, and Pacific coast behind the doctrine of free soil and had seized the presidency. Although the Republicans did not control the Congress, to many southerners it now seemed time to think carefully about the meaning of Lincoln's words of 1858: the Union must "become *all* one thing, or *all* the other."

Summary

★

Westward expansion carried American settlers into the Mexican province of Texas, where they mounted a successful rebellion and petitioned for annexation to the United States, and into the Oregon Country and Mexican California. The popular appeal of Manifest Destiny prompted southern leaders such as John Tyler and John C. Calhoun to advocate the immediate annexation of Texas and to support northern politicians who laid claim to all of Oregon. This expansionist program carried James B. Polk to the presidency in the election of 1844.

Polk's expansionist dreams led the United States into a successful war of conquest against Mexico, but the acquisition of new territory in the West undermined the longstanding political compromise over the spread of slavery and threatened to split the Union. Democratic and Whig leaders joined in framing a political settlement known as the Compromise of 1850; its most important aspects were laws admitting California as a free state and providing federal assistance to planters seeking the return of fugitive slaves.

The Compromise and the Second Party System died in the political conflicts and armed violence of the 1850s. Antislavery northerners defied the Fugitive Slave Act by battling southern slave catchers in the courts and on the streets. When northern Whigs refused to support the act, southerners deserted the party, killing it as a national organization. The Democratic Party also lost its national appeal because of southern attempts to annex land in Mexico and the Caribbean and the failure of Stephen Douglas's doctrine of popular sovereignty to allow the peaceful settlement of Kansas and Nebraska. As northern opponents and southern supporters of slavery fought a guerrilla war in "Bleeding Kansas," northern Whigs and Free-Soilers established the Republican Party, which also attracted anti-Nebraska Democrats and former Know-Nothings. By 1856 the Second Party System of Democrats and Whigs had given way to a new alignment in which Democrats confronted Republicans.

The national Democratic Party disintegrated following the Supreme Court's proslavery decision in the *Dred Scott* case and President James Buchanan's support for a proslavery constitution in Kansas. Following John Brown's attempt to raise a black rebellion to end slavery, southern Democrats unsuccessfully demanded ironclad protection for the institution. In the 1860 election the Democrats were divided along sectional lines, which facilitated the election of Abraham Lincoln and the Republican Party with its platform of "free soil, free speech, free labor, and free men." The nation stood poised on the brink of secession and civil war.

TIMELINE

1836	Texas proclaims independence from Mexico
1842	Overland migration to Oregon begins
1844	Fate of Texas and Oregon dominate presidential election
1845	John O'Sullivan coins term *Manifest Destiny*
	Texas admitted to Union as a slave state
	John Slidell's diplomatic mission to Mexico fails
1846	United States declares war on Mexico
	Oregon treaty ratified; 49th parallel becomes boundary
	Walker Tariff lowers duties on imported goods
	Wilmot Proviso proposes prohibiting slavery in territories acquired from Mexico
1847	Winfield Scott captures Mexico City
1848	Gold discovered in California
	Treaty of Guadalupe Hidalgo gives northernmost provinces of Mexico to the United States
	Free Soil Party organized
1850	Compromise of 1850
1851	American (Know-Nothing) Party formed
1854	Kansas-Nebraska Act
	Republican Party formed
1856	"Bleeding Kansas" undermines popular sovereignty
1857	*Dred Scott v. Sandford* allows slavery in territories
1858	James Buchanan backs Lecompton constitution
	Lincoln-Douglas debates
1859	John Brown's raid on Harpers Ferry
1860	Abraham Lincoln elected president

Suggested Readings

———————★———————

Histories that offer a comprehensive analysis of the disruption of the Union between the time of the Mexican War and the election of Lincoln are rare. The best is David M. Potter, *The Impending Crisis, 1848–1861* (1976). A recent treatment of the 1850s is Michael A. Morrison, *Slavery and the American West: The Eclipse of Manifest Destiny and the Coming of the Civil War* (1995).

Manifest Destiny

Historians have recently begun to reexamine the development of the trans-Appalachian West in the antebellum period. See Gregory N. Nobles, *American Frontiers* (1996); Stephen Aron, *How the West Was Lost: The Transformation of Kentucky from Daniel Boone to Henry Clay* (1996); Andrew R. L. Cayton and Peter S. Onuf, *The Midwest and the Nation* (1990); and Nicole Etcheson, *The Emerging Midwest: Upland Southerners and the Political Culture of the Old Northwest, 1787–1861* (1996). See also William Cronon, *Nature's Metropolis* (1992).

The ideology of Manifest Destiny is discussed in Norman Graebner, *Empire on the Pacific: A Study of American Continental Expansion* (1955), and Reginald Horsman, *Race and Manifest Destiny: The Origins of American Racial Anglo-Saxonism* (1981).

New approaches to the history of the trans-Mississippi West include Patricia Nelson Limerick, *The Legacy of Conquest: The Unbroken Past of the Unbroken West* (1987); Clyde A. Milner II, *The Oxford History of the American West* (1994); David J. Weber, *The Mexican Frontier, 1821–1846* (1982); and Richard White, *"It's Your Misfortune and None of My Own": A History of the American West* (1991). This newer scholarship presents a more complete view of women in the West. See, for example, Susan Armitage and Elizabeth Jameson, eds., *The Women's West* (1987); John Mack Faragher, *Women and Men on the Overland Trail* (1979); Julie R. Jeffrey, *Frontier Women: The Trans-Mississippi West, 1840–1860* (1979); and Joanna L. Stratton, *Pioneer Women: Voices from the Kansas Frontier* (1981).

War, Expansion, and Slavery, 1846–1850

Study of expansionism in the 1840s should begin with Frederick Merk, *The Monroe Doctrine and American Expansion, 1843–1849* (1972), and William J. Cooper, *The South and the Politics of Slavery, 1828–1856* (1978). On the coming of the Mexican War, consult Paul H. Bergeron, *The Presidency of James K. Polk* (1987); David Pletcher, *The Diplomacy of Annexation: Texas, Oregon, and the Mexican War* (1973); and Charles G. Sellers, *James K. Polk: Continentalist, 1843–1846* (1966). On the fighting of the war, see K. Jack Bauer, *The Mexican War, 1846–1848* (1974), and Otis A. Singletary, *The Mexican War* (1960). For an analysis of the relationship between the war experience and American culture, see Robert W. Johannsen, *To the Halls of the Montezumas: The Mexican War in the American Imagination* (1985). For the Mexican viewpoint, see Gene M. Brack, *Mexico Views Manifest Destiny, 1821–1846: An Essay on the Origins of the Mexican War* (1975).

On congressional politics during the 1840s, see Chaplain Morrison, *Democratic Politics and Sectionalism: The Wilmot Proviso Controversy* (1967); Merrill Peterson, *The Great Triumvirate: Webster, Clay, and Calhoun* (1987); and Joel H. Silbey, *The Shrine of Party: Congressional Voting Behavior, 1841–1852* (1967). The Compromise of 1850 is covered in Holman Hamilton, *Prologue to Conflict: The Crisis and Compromise of 1850* (1964). For an interpretation stressing the contingency of the South's commitment to the Union, consult William W. Freehling, *The Road to Disunion: Secessionists at Bay, 1776–1854* (1991).

The End of the Second Party System, 1850–1858

An older but still valuable study of sectional conflict is Avery O. Craven, *The Growth of Southern Nationalism* (1953). On the Fugitive Slave Act, consult Stanley W. Campbell, *The Slave Catchers* (1970). The best study of the politics of southern expansionism is Robert E. May, *The Southern Dream of a Caribbean Empire, 1854–1861* (1973). Important studies of Frederick Douglass include Nathan I. Huggins, *Slave and Citizen: The Life of Frederick Douglass* (1980), and William S. McFeely, *Frederick Douglass* (1991); for Douglass's own accounts, read *The Narrative of the Life of Frederick Douglass, an American Slave* (1845) and *Life and Times of Frederick Douglass, Written by Himself* (1881).

On the development of the Republican Party, see Eric Foner, *Free Soil, Free Labor, Free Men: The Ideology of the Republican Party before the Civil War* (1970), and William E. Gienapp, *The Origins of the Republican Party, 1852–1856* (1987). The crisis over Kansas is discussed in James A. Rawley, *Race and Politics: Bleeding Kansas and the Coming of the Civil War* (1969), and Gerald W. Wolff, *The Kansas-Nebraska Bill: Party, Section, and the Coming of the Civil War* (1977). On the Buchanan administration, see Kenneth M. Stampp, *America in 1857: A Nation on the Brink* (1990). On *Dred Scott*, see Don E. Fehrenbacher, *The Dred Scott Case: Its Significance in American Law and Politics* (1978). For a biography of Stephen A. Douglas, see Robert W. Johannsen, *Stephen A. Douglas* (1973). The best biography of John Brown is Stephen Oates, *To Purge This Land with Blood: A Biography of John Brown* (1970).

Abraham Lincoln and the Republican Triumph, 1858–1860

The fate of the Democratic Party is discussed in Michael Holt, *The Political Crisis of the 1850s* (1978). Abraham Lincoln has inspired a host of biographies. Classic studies include James G. Randall, *Mr. Lincoln* (1957); Carl Sandburg, *Abraham Lincoln: The Prairie Years* (1929); and Benjamin Thomas, *Abraham Lincoln: A Biography* (1952). The most recent important biography of Lincoln is David Herbert Donald, *Lincoln* (1995). On Lincoln's formative political years see Don E. Fehrenbacher, *Prelude to Greatness: Lincoln in the 1850s* (1962). Other treatments include George B. Forgie, *Patricide and the House Divided* (1979); Stephen Oates, *With Malice toward None: A Life of Abraham Lincoln* (1977); and Garry Wills, *Lincoln at Gettysburg* (1992).

Chapter 14

Two Societies at War,
1861–1865

"WHAT A SCENE it was," the Union soldier Elisha Hunt Rhodes wrote in his diary as the battle of Gettysburg ended in July 1863; "Oh the dead and the dying on this bloody field." Two years after the secession of the southern states from the Union, the passions of sectionalism and war still inspired thousands of ordinary men to give up their lives in battle, and the slaughter would continue for two more years. "What is this all about?" asked Confederate lieutenant R. M. Collins at the end of another gruesome battle. "Why is it that 200,000 men of one blood and tongue . . . [should be] seeking one another's lives? We could settle our differences by compromising and all be at home in ten days." But there was no compromise— not in 1861 nor even in 1865.

To explain why the war was fought—and fought to the bitter end—is not a simple task, but slavery is an important part of the answer. For political leaders in the South, the victory of Abraham Lincoln and the Republicans in the election of 1860 presented a clear and immediate danger to their way of life. They knew that Lincoln regarded slavery as morally wrong and that the Republicans would seek to unite northern society against the "Slave Power." At the very least the Republicans would try to prevent the extension of slavery into the territories, and they might well launch an all-out attack against the institution itself. Unlike any preceding president, Lincoln owed the South not a single electoral vote, and soon, a southern senator warned, "cohorts of Federal office-holders, Abolitionists, may be sent into [our] midst" to mobilize the African American population. The result, he and other leaders predicted, would be waves of bloody slave revolts.

Victory March, 1865, Victor Nehlig (detail)
When the long and bloody war finally ended, railroads carried the victorious Union troops back to army camps, from which they walked the final miles to their towns and villages. Here top-hatted men and barefooted boys join the troops in a spontaneous celebration as they march through the New York countryside.
Courtesy of Edenhurst Gallery, Los Angeles, Daniel Nicodemo, Thomas Gianetto, and Donald Merrill.

To save slavery—the bedrock of the planters' wealth and of white supremacy—radical southern leaders embarked on the dangerous journey of secession. Adopting John C. Calhoun's constitutional theory that sovereignty lay not with the American people as a whole but with collections of people acting through their state governments, the rebels led their states out of the American Union and established their own nation, the Confederate States of America. If Lincoln and the Republicans would not allow them to leave peacefully, they would fight.

And so came the Civil War. Called the "War between the States" by southerners and the "War of the Rebellion" by northerners, the struggle went on until the great issue of slavery had been resolved once and for all. The cost was incredibly high: more lives lost than in all the nation's subsequent wars put together, and a century-long legacy of bitterness between the triumphant North and the vanquished South.

Secession and Military Stalemate, 1861–1862

——————★——————

After Lincoln's election in November 1860, secessionist fervor quickly swept through the Deep South. In Washington, political leaders spent the next four months in a desperate race against time. Before Lincoln was inaugurated in March 1861, they hoped to forge a new compromise over slavery that (like the agreements of 1789, 1820, and 1850) would preserve the Union.

Choosing Sides

The movement toward secession was most rapid in South Carolina—the home of Calhoun, the nullification controversy over tariffs in 1831, and the Southern Rights movement. Since 1850 Robert Barnwell Rhett and other South Carolina "fire-eaters" had been planning for secession, and upon Lincoln's election they immediately called a convention to achieve their long-delayed goal. On December 20, delegates to the convention voted unanimously to dissolve "the union now subsisting between South Carolina and other States."

Over the next six weeks, secessionists in the six cotton states of the Deep South called similar conventions. They also organized vigilante groups to suppress local Unionists and mobilized the state militia to prepare for war. In early January, in an atmosphere of public celebration, Mississippi enacted a secession ordinance. Within a month Florida, Alabama, Georgia, Louisiana, and Texas had also left the Union (Map 14.1). In early February the jubilant secessionists met

in Montgomery, Alabama, to proclaim a new nation—the Confederate States of America. They adopted a provisional constitution and named Jefferson Davis of Mississippi, a former U.S. senator and secretary of war, as provisional president.

Secessionist fervor was less widespread in the eight Upper South states (Virginia, Delaware, Maryland, North Carolina, Kentucky, Tennessee, Missouri, and Arkansas), where there were fewer slaves and yeomen farmers had greater political power. For decades many yeomen had resented the authority claimed by the slaveowning gentry, and some actively opposed it. In the 1850s Hinton Helper of North Carolina sought to rouse the "Non-slaveowners of the South! farmers, mechanics and workingmen," warning that "the slaveholders, the arrogant demagogues whom you have elected to offices of honor and profit, have hoodwinked you, . . . used you as mere tools for the consummation of their wicked designs." Influenced by such sentiments, the legislatures of Virginia and Tennessee did not join the secessionist movement in January 1861 but, to uphold the cause of states' rights, voted to resist any federal invasion of the seceded states. Seeking a compromise that would restore the Union, Upper South leaders proposed that the federal government guarantee that slavery would be protected in the states where it already existed.

Meanwhile, the Democratic-controlled Union government floundered. In his last message to Congress in December 1860, President Buchanan declared secession illegal but said that the federal government lacked the authority to restore a state to the Union by force. South Carolina immediately claimed that Buchanan's message implied recognition of its independence and demanded the surrender of Fort Sumter, a federal garrison in Charleston harbor. Reluctant to turn over federal property, Buchanan decided to test the secessionists' resolve by ordering an unarmed merchant ship to resupply the fort. When the South Carolinians fired on the ship, Buchanan backed down, refusing to order the navy to escort the ship into the harbor.

The Crittenden Plan. As the crisis continued, Buchanan urged Congress to find a compromise. The proposal that received the most support was submitted by Senator John J. Crittenden of Kentucky, an aging follower of Henry Clay, who had been a prime architect of the Compromise of 1850. Crittenden's proposal had two parts. The first, which won congressional approval, called for a constitutional amendment that would permanently protect slavery from federal interference in any state where it already existed. To deal with the territories, Crittenden offered a second provision that called for the westward extension of the Missouri Compromise line (36°30′ north latitude) to the California border. Slavery would be barred north of the line and

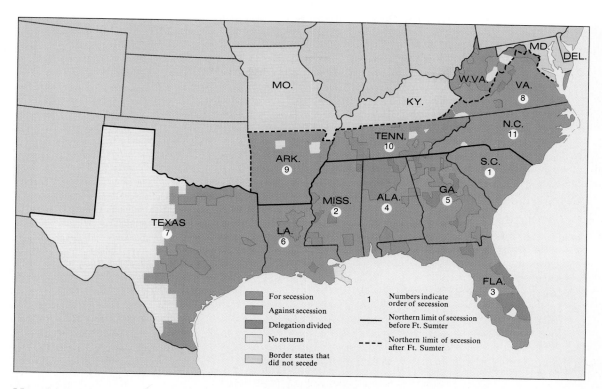

MAP 14.1

The Process of Secession, 1860–1861

The states with the highest concentration of slaves (see Map 9.3) led the secessionist movement and, after the attack on Fort Sumter, were joined by the states of the Upper South. Yeomen farmers in Tennessee and the backcountry of Alabama, Georgia, and Virginia opposed secession but, with the exception of the future state of West Virginia, generally rallied to the Confederate cause and, until 1864, supported the war effort.

protected to the south, including any territories "hereafter acquired."

After consulting with President-elect Lincoln, congressional Republicans rejected Crittenden's plan for the territories. Lincoln was determined to uphold the doctrine of free soil and feared that extending the Missouri Compromise line would encourage the South to embark on an imperialist expansion of slavery into Mexico, the Caribbean, and Latin America. If adopted, Lincoln charged, Crittenden's plan would be "a perpetual covenant of war against every people, tribe, and State owning a foot of land between here and Tierra del Fuego [the southern tip of South America]."

The Seizure of Fort Sumter. In his inaugural address on March 4, 1861, Lincoln carefully balanced a call for reconciliation with a firm commitment to the Union. Lincoln repeated his oft-stated position not "to interfere with the institution of slavery in the States where it exists," but stood firm for free soil in the territories. Most important, he stated that the Union was "perpetual" and consequently that secession was illegal and that acts of violence in its support constituted insurrec-

tion. He announced equally clearly that he intended to enforce federal law throughout the Union and—of particular relevance to Fort Sumter—continue to "hold, occupy, and possess" federal property in the seceded states and "to collect duties and imposts." If force was necessary to preserve the Union, Lincoln—like Andrew Jackson during the Nullification crisis—promised to use it. The choice was the South's: return to the Union or face war.

The decision came quickly. Within a month of Lincoln's inauguration the garrison at Fort Sumter urgently needed supplies. To maintain his credibility, the new president dispatched a relief expedition; but, to avoid giving the Confederacy an excuse to go to war, he informed South Carolina authorities that his naval force would not land troops or arms unless the delivery of food and medicine was disrupted.

Jefferson Davis and his Confederate government decided to use this opportunity to take Fort Sumter by force. They hoped that an armed confrontation would turn the wavering Upper South against the North and win British and French support for their cause. Resolving to take the fort before the arrival of the Union ships,

The Bombardment of Fort Sumter, 1861
Currier and Ives, a New York publishing house, brought colorful art into thousands of middle-class homes by printing inexpensive lithographs of pastoral scenes and dramatic historical events. This fairly realistic depiction of the Confederate bombardment of Fort Sumter in Charleston harbor in April 1861 was especially popular in the South.
Library of Congress.

Davis instructed General P. G. T. Beauregard, the Confederate commander in Charleston, to demand its surrender. When Major Robert Anderson refused to comply, the Confederate forces opened fire. On April 14, after two days of bombardment that destroyed large portions of the fort but took no lives, Anderson surrendered. The next day Lincoln called 75,000 state militiamen into federal service for ninety days to put down an insurrection "too powerful to be suppressed by the ordinary course of judicial proceedings." All talk of compromise was past.

Northern states responded to Lincoln's call to arms with enthusiasm. Asked to provide thirteen regiments of volunteers, Republican governor William Dennison of Ohio sent twenty. "The lion in us is thoroughly roused," he explained. Many northern Democrats were equally committed to the Union cause. Asserting that the Constitution was "a perpetual and irrevocable compact," elder statesman Martin Van Buren called on Democrats in New York to support the call to arms.

Stephen Douglas was equally forthright. "Every man must be for the United States or against it," he declared. "There can be no neutrals in this war, *only patriots—or traitors.*"

The Contest for the Upper South. The white residents of the Upper South now had to choose between the Union and the Confederacy, and their decision was crucial. Those eight states accounted for two-thirds of the South's white population, more than three-fourths of its industrial output, and well over half its supplies of food and fuel. They were home to many of the nation's best military leaders, including Colonel Robert E. Lee of Virginia, whom General in Chief Winfield Scott recommended to Lincoln as field commander of the new Union army. And they were geographically strategic. Kentucky, with its 500-mile border on the Ohio River, was essential to the movement of troops and supplies. Maryland was also vital because it contained the major port of Baltimore and surrounded the nation's capital on the north.

The weight of history decided the outcome in Virginia, the original home of North American slavery and a longtime advocate of the rights of the states. Three days after the fall of Fort Sumter, a Virginia convention passed an ordinance of secession by a vote of 88 to 55, with nearly all the dissenting votes coming from the yeoman-dominated northwestern counties (see Map 14.1). Elsewhere in Virginia whites rallied to the Confederate cause. As William Poague, a former Unionist lawyer, explained his decision to enlist in a Virginia artillery unit: "The North was the aggressor. The South resisted her invaders." Refusing Scott's offer to command the Union troops, Robert E. Lee resigned from the army and assumed command of the Confederate army. "Save in defense of my native state," Lee told Scott, "I never desire again to draw my sword." North Carolina, Tennessee, and Arkansas soon joined Virginia in the Confederacy and sent their militias to that state's defense.

Lincoln moved aggressively to hold the rest of the Upper South. In May he ordered General George B. McClellan to take control of northwestern Virginia, thus securing the railway line between the District of Columbia and the Ohio Valley. Five months later, the region's yeomen voters overwhelmingly approved the creation of a new state, West Virginia, which was ultimately admitted to the Union in 1863. In Maryland, where support for slavery was still strong, there was much less enthusiasm for the Union cause. In Baltimore in April 1861 a pro-Confederate mob attacked Massachusetts troops marching between railroad stations, causing the war's first combat deaths: four soldiers and twelve civilians. When other Maryland secessionists destroyed railroad bridges and telegraph lines, Lincoln ordered a military occupation of the state and imprisoned suspected secessionists, including members of the state legislature. He released them only in November 1861, after Unionists had gained control of the state legislature.

Lincoln also mobilized support for the Union among German Americans in Missouri, a key state with respect to trade and military operations on the Missouri and upper Mississippi Rivers. In July a force of German American militia defeated Confederate sympathizers commanded by Governor Claiborne Jackson. Despite continuing raids by Confederate guerrilla bands led by William Quantrill and Jesse and Frank James, the Union retained control of Missouri throughout the war (see Voices from Abroad, "Ernest Duveyier de Hauranne: German Immigrants and the Civil War within Missouri," p. 446).

In Kentucky secessionist and Unionist sentiment was evenly balanced, and Lincoln moved cautiously. Not until August, after Unionists had taken control of the state government, did he order federal troops to cut Kentucky's thriving export trade in horses, mules, whiskey, and foodstuffs to the Lower South. When the Confederacy responded by moving troops into Kentucky, the Unionist legislature asked for federal protection. In September, Illinois volunteers under the command of the relatively unknown brigadier general Ulysses S. Grant crossed the Ohio River and drove out the Confederates. Of the eight states of the Upper South, Lincoln had kept four (Delaware, Maryland, Kentucky, and Missouri) and a portion of a fifth (western Virginia) in the Union.

Setting War Aims and Devising Military Strategies

Upon secession, Confederate leaders called on their people to defend the independence of the new nation. At his inauguration in February 1861, Jefferson Davis identified the Confederate cause with that of the American Revolution; like their grandfathers, white southerners were fighting against tyranny and for the "sacred right of self-government." As Davis put it, the Confederacy sought "no conquest, no aggrandizement, no concession of any kind from the states with which we were lately confederated; all we ask is to be let alone." This decision to focus on the defense of the Confederacy (and not to conquer western territories) gave southern leaders a strong advantage: they needed only a military stalemate to guarantee Confederate independence.

However, the Confederacy's firm commitment to slavery undermined its support in Europe, where opposition to forced labor was strong. Shortly after his election as vice-president of the Confederacy, Alexander Stephens of Georgia refused to consider any plan for gradual emancipation, declaring that his nation's "cornerstone rests upon the great truth that the Negro is not equal to the white man, that slavery—subordination to the superior race—is his natural or normal condition." Slavery made democracy for whites possible, Stephens argued, for otherwise ordinary whites would be reduced to the position of menial wage workers and oppressed serfs.

To muster support in the North, Lincoln made an important statement on Union goals and war policy in a speech to Congress on July 4, 1861. He portrayed secession as an attack on republican government and the rule of law. As such it was important not only to the United States but "to the whole family of man" because it raised the question of "whether a constitutional republic, or a democracy—a government of the people, by the same people—can or cannot maintain its territorial integrity against its domestic foes." Only by crushing the rebellion could the nation preserve its democratic-republican principles.

This politically driven need for a decisive victory determined Lincoln's military strategy. He considered,

ERNEST DUVEYIER DE HAURANNE

German Immigrants and the Civil War within Missouri

————— ★ —————

Tens of thousands of German immigrants settled in Missouri and other midwestern states in the two decades before the Civil War, and as the following letter by the Frenchman Ernest Duveyier de Hauranne indicates, most of them supported the Union cause. De Hauranne traveled widely, and his letters home offer an intelligent commentary on American politics and society during the Civil War.

St. Louis, September 12, 1864
Missouri is to all intents and purposes a rebel state, an occupied territory where the Federal forces are really nothing but a garrison under siege; even today it is not certain what would happen if the troops were withdrawn. Party quarrels here are poisoned by class hatreds. . . . The old Anglo-French families, attached to Southern institutions, harbor a primitive, superstitious prejudice in favor of slavery. Conquered now, but full of repressed rage, they exhibit the implacable anger peculiar to the defenders of lost causes. . . .

The more recent German population is strongly abolitionist. They have brought to the New World the instincts of European democracy, together with its radical attitudes and all-or-nothing doctrines. Ancient precedents and worn-out laws matter little to them. They have not studied history and have no respect for hallowed injustices; but they do have, to

the highest degree, that sense of moral principle which is more or less lacking in American democracy. They aren't afraid of revolution: to destroy a barbarous institution they would, if necessary, take an axe to the foundations of society. Furthermore, their interests coincide with their principles. . . .

The immigrant arrives poor and lives by his work. A newcomer, having nothing to lose and caring little for the interests of established property owners, sees that the subjection of free labor to the ruinous competition of slave labor must be ended. At the same time, his pride rebels against the prejudice attached to work in a land of slavery; he wants to reestablish its value. . . .

There is no mistaking the hatred the two parties, not to say the two peoples, have for each other. . . . As passions were coming to a boil, the Federal government sent General [John C.] Frémont here as army commander and dictator. . . . An abolitionist and a self-made man, he put himself firmly at the head of the German party, determined to crush the friends of slavery. He formed an army of Germans who are completely devoted to their chief. . . .

[However,] bands of guerrillas hold the countryside, where they raid as much as they please; politics serves as a fine pretext for looting. Their leaders are officers from the army of the South who receive their orders from the Confederate government. . . . These "bushwackers," who ordinarily rob indiscriminately, maintain their standing as political raiders by occasionally killing some poor, inoffensive person. Finally, people bent on personal vengeance take advantage of the state of civil war: sometimes one hears of villages divided against themselves so bitterly that massacres are carried on from door to door with incredible ferocity. . . . You can see what emotions are still boiling in this region that is supposed to be pacified.

Source: Ernest Duveyier de Hauranne, *A Frenchman in Lincoln's America* (Chicago: 1974), Lakende Press, 305–309.

and rejected, the policy of attrition proposed by Winfield Scott, which called for blockading the Confederacy on all sides and squeezing it into submission through economic sanctions. Instead, Lincoln called for an aggressive military strategy, hoping that an early Union triumph would quickly bring an end to the rebellion.

The Union Thrust toward Richmond. Because of Virginia's size and its historic importance as the home of presidents and the defender of states' rights, the Confederacy located its capital at Richmond—a mere 125 miles from the District of Columbia. Aware that the northern public would welcome a strike toward the

Confederate capital, Lincoln launched a significant attack. He ordered General Irwin McDowell and a Union army of 30,000 men to attack P. G. T. Beauregard's force of 20,000 troops at Manassas, a major rail junction in Virginia 30 miles southwest of Washington. On July 21, McDowell began a strong offensive near Manassas Creek (also called Bull Run), but panic swept through his troops during a Confederate counterattack. For the first time Union soldiers heard the hair-raising rebel yell. "The peculiar corkscrew sensation that it sends down your backbone under these circumstances can never be told," a Union veteran wrote. "You have to feel it." McDowell's troops retreated in disarray to Washington, along with the many civilians who had come down from the capital with their Sunday picnic baskets and binoculars to observe the battle. The victorious Confederate troops also dispersed, confused and without the wagons and supplies they needed to pursue McDowell's army.

Quickly realizing that the rebellion would not be easily crushed, the president called on Congress to raise an additional 100,000 men, who would serve for three years. To bolster northern morale, which had been shattered by the rout at Bull Run, he replaced McDowell with General George B. McClellan, and in November he made McClellan his general in chief. A cautious military engineer, McClellan took advantage of the cold winter months (a period when armies traditionally did not fight) to train raw recruits and organize the newly created Army of the Potomac.

In April 1862, McClellan launched the first sustained offensive of the war, a thrust toward Richmond. In a maneuver that required skillful logistics, the Union general transported about 100,000 troops by boat down the Potomac River and Chesapeake Bay, landing them near Yorktown, Virginia (Map 14.2). Slowly but surely, the Union forces fought their way up the peninsula between the York and James Rivers toward the South's capital. But McClellan failed to anticipate a Confederate counterstroke. In May, the Confederate commander Robert E. Lee dispatched an army under Thomas J. ("Stonewall") Jackson on a quick march up the Shenandoah Valley, threatening the army of Nathaniel P. Banks that was protecting the District of Columbia. To head off the danger to the Union's capital, Lincoln diverted 30,000 troops from McClellan's army, but Jackson, a brilliant general, defeated three Union armies in the valley. Then Jackson rejoined Lee's army, which had

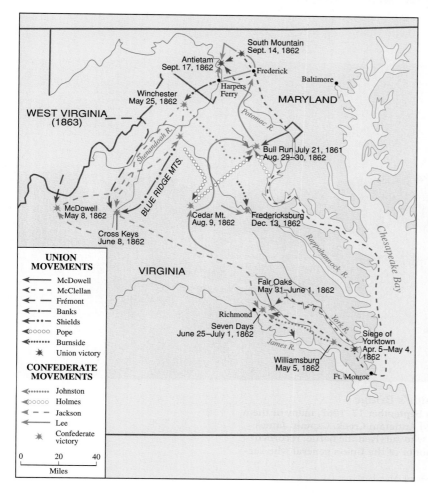

MAP 14.2
The Eastern Campaigns, 1861–1862
Many of the great battles of the Civil War took place in the area (of about 125 miles) between Washington and Richmond and in the adjacent Shenandoah Valley. During the eastern campaigns of 1861 and 1862, the audacity and imagination of Confederate generals Thomas J. "Stonewall" Jackson and Robert E. Lee helped secure victories here that were almost decisive. But, as was often the case in the Civil War, the victors were too exhausted and had suffered too many casualties to exploit their advantage.

448   Part Three: *Economic Revolution and Sectional Strife, 1820–1877*

confronted McClellan outside Richmond. Lee launched a ferocious attack that lasted for seven days (June 25–July 1), suffering heavy casualties (20,000 to the Union's 10,000). But McClellan failed to exploit the resulting weakness of the Confederate forces, refusing to renew the offensive unless he received fresh troops. Lincoln ordered the withdrawal of the Army of the Potomac, and Richmond remained secure.

Lee's First Invasion of the North. Lee promptly went on the offensive, hoping for victories that would humiliate Lincoln's government. Joining with Jackson in northern Virginia before McClellan could send reinforcements, Lee routed a small Union army in the Second Battle of Bull Run (August 1862). Then the Confederate commander advanced toward the northern states through western Maryland, where he met with near disaster. When Lee divided his army—dispatching a force under Stonewall Jackson to capture Harpers Ferry in northwestern Virginia—a copy of his orders fell into McClellan's hands. Once again the Union general failed to take advantage of a Confederate weakness, delaying his attack until Lee's depleted army had occupied a strong defensive position behind Antietam Creek, near Sharpsburg, Maryland (see Map

14.2). Outnumbered 87,000 to 50,000, Lee desperately fought off McClellan's assaults. Just as Union regiments were about to overwhelm his right flank, Jackson's troops arrived, saving the Confederates from a serious defeat. Appalled by his casualties, McClellan let Lee retreat to Virginia while he buried the dead and set up field hospitals for the wounded.

The fighting at Antietam on September 17, 1862, was the bloodiest single day in U.S. history. A Wisconsin officer described his men as "loading and firing with demoniacal fury and shouting and laughing hysterically." At a critical point in the battle a sunken road nicknamed Bloody Lane was filled with Confederate bodies two and three deep, and the attacking Union troops knelt on "this ghastly flooring" to shoot at the retreating Confederates. Together, the Confederate and Union dead numbered 4,800 and the wounded 18,500, of whom 3,000 soon died. (In comparison, 6,000 Americans were wounded or killed on D-Day, which began the Allied invasion of Nazi-occupied France during World War II.)

In public Lincoln declared Antietam a victory, but privately he believed that McClellan should have fought Lee to the finish. A masterful organizer of men and supplies, McClellan lacked the stomach for a major com-

The Battle of Antietam: The Fight for Burnside's Bridge
Nearly 8,000 soldiers lost their lives at Antietam on September 17, 1862, many of them in the struggle for the Rohrbach Bridge that crossed Antietam Creek. Captain James Hope of the 2nd Vermont Volunteers, one of those who survived the battle, recorded the event in this painting, renaming the bridge in honor of the Union general who sacrificed many of his troops trying to capture it.
Antietam National Battlefield, National Park Service, Sharpsburg, Maryland.

mitment of his forces. Dismissing McClellan as his general in chief, Lincoln began what turned out to be a long search for an effective replacement. His first choice was Ambrose E. Burnside, who proved to be more daring but less competent than McClellan. In December, after heavy losses in futile attacks against well-entrenched Confederate forces at Fredericksburg, Virginia, Burnside resigned his command, and Lincoln replaced him with Joseph ("Fighting Joe") Hooker. As 1862 ended, the Confederates had reason to be content: the war in the East was a stalemate.

The War in the West. In the West, Union forces were more successful. Their goal was to control the Ohio, Mississippi, and Missouri Rivers, thereby dividing the Confederacy and reducing the mobility of its armies. The decision of Kentucky not to join the rebellion gave the Union dominance in the Ohio River Valley. Early in 1862 the Union army launched a series of highly innovative land and water operations to gain control of the Tennessee and Mississippi Rivers as well. As the architect of the northern part of the Union offensive in the West, General Ulysses S. Grant used riverboats clad with iron plates to take Fort Henry on the Tennessee River and Fort Donelson

on the Cumberland. Grant then moved south along the Tennessee River to take control of critical railroad lines.

A Confederate army under Albert Sidney Johnston and P. G. T. Beauregard caught Grant by surprise early in April near a small log church named Shiloh. Grant relentlessly threw troops into the battle, forcing a Confederate withdrawal but suffering extensive casualties. Grant described a large field "so covered with dead that it would have been possible to walk over the clearing in any direction, stepping on dead bodies, without a foot touching the ground." At the cost of many lives Grant had maintained the Union's military momentum in the West (Map 14.3).

Three weeks after the battle at Shiloh, Union naval forces commanded by David G. Farragut struck from the south, moving through the Mississippi Delta from the Gulf of Mexico to capture New Orleans. This victory gave the Union the South's financial center and largest city as well as a major base for future naval operations. As 1862 ended, Union armies pushed Confederate troops out of Kentucky and most of Tennessee. Stalemated in the East, Union armies in the West had scored some significant victories that undermined Confederate strength in the Mississippi Valley.

Lincoln Visits the Army of the Potomac, 1862
Following the battle of Antietam, President Lincoln journeyed to the headquarters of General McClellan. Supported by his military advisors (standing to his rear), the towering commander in chief vigorously urged his principal general to exploit the opportunity offered by Lee's heavy casualties and launch an all-out attack against Richmond. McClellan (pictured here facing the president) did not undertake this offensive, and Lincoln removed him from command of the Army of the Potomac a month later.
Library of Congress.

MAP 14.3
The Western Campaigns, 1861–1862
As the Civil War intensified during the course of 1861, Union and Confederate military and naval forces fought to control the great valleys of the Ohio, Tennessee, and Mississippi Rivers. By the end of 1862 Union forces had achieved dominance over most of these crucial transportation routes, allowing them to keep Missouri in the Union, drive Confederate armies out of Kentucky and half of Tennessee, and capture New Orleans. With their victory at Shiloh (along the Tennessee River), northern forces carried the war to the borders of the states of the Deep South.

Toward Total War

The carnage at Antietam and Shiloh made it clear that the war would be long and costly. After Shiloh, Grant later noted, he "gave up all idea of saving the Union except by complete conquest." The conflict now became a *total war*—a struggle that arrayed the entire resources of the two societies against each other and would eventually result in warfare against enemy civilians on both sides. Aided by a strong party and a talented cabinet, Lincoln skillfully mobilized the North for all-out war, organizing an effective central government. Jefferson Davis, who remained at the head of the Confederacy, was less successful because he led eleven states that were deeply suspicious of centralized rule.

Mobilizing Armies and Civilians

At first, patriotic fervor prompted partisans on both sides to support the war. When nineteen-year-old Elisha Hunt Rhodes of Pawtuxet, Rhode Island, wanted to join the Union army following the attack on Fort Sumter, his widowed mother gave her consent, saying, "My son, other mothers must make sacrifices and why should not I?" Writing home from the Confederate army in February 1862, James B. Griffin of Edgefield, South Carolina, was certain that his wife, Leila, felt the same way: "Would you, My Darling, . . . be willing to leave

your Children under such a [despotic Union] government? No—I know you would sacrifice every comfort on earth, rather than submit to it."

The Military Draft. Given such sentiments the initial calls for soldiers were greeted with enthusiasm, especially in the South, which had a strong military tradition and an ample supply of trained officers. But the surge of enlistments fell off as the people saw the realities of war: heavy losses to outbreaks of smallpox and dysentery, and dreadful carnage on the battlefields. Soon both governments faced the necessity of forced enlistment—a military draft.

The Confederacy was the first to act. In April 1862, after its huge loss of soldiers at Shiloh, the Confederate Congress imposed the first legally binding draft in American history. One law extended all existing enlistments for the duration of the war; another required three years of military service from all able-bodied men between the ages of eighteen and thirty-five. In September, after the even heavier casualties at Antietam, the Congress raised the age limit for enlistees to forty-five.

This Confederate legislation had two controversial provisions. First, it exempted one white man on any plantation—either the planter or an overseer—for each twenty slaves, allowing the owners and supervisors of large plantations to avoid military service. Second, the law permitted drafted men to hire substitutes. By the time this provision was repealed in 1864, the price for

Draft Riots in New York City
The Enrollment Act of 1863 enraged many workers and recent Irish and German immigrants who opposed the war. In July in New York City, they took out their anger on free blacks in a week-long riot. This engraving depicts the violence that accompanied the worst riots in all of U.S. history: as the club-waving mob hangs an African American, three other blacks escape by climbing over a fence. The violence against African Americans received wide publicity (this engraving appeared in the *Illustrated London News* on August 8, 1863) and generally strengthened support for the war effort in the North.
Culver Pictures.

a substitute had risen to $300 in gold, about three times the annual wages of a skilled worker. Laborers and yeomen farmers angrily complained that it was "a rich man's war and a poor man's fight."

Consequently, some southerners refused to serve, and the Confederate government lacked the power to compel them. Because the Confederate constitution vested sovereignty in the individual states, determined governors such as Joseph Brown of Georgia and Zebulon Vance of North Carolina simply ignored Davis's first draft call. Elsewhere, state judges issued writs of *habeas corpus* (a legal process designed to protect people from arbitrary arrest and detention) and ordered the Confederate army to release protesting draftees. The Confederate Congress was reluctant to override the judges' authority to free conscripted men, but as the war progressed the army's need for new recruits prompted the Congress to suspend habeas corpus for two periods totaling sixteen months. This coercive measure, along with long enlistments, enabled the Confederate government to keep substantial armies in the field well into 1864.

Because of its better-established institutions, the Union government took a more authoritarian stance toward potential foes and ordinary citizens. To prevent opposition to the war, Lincoln suspended habeas corpus and imprisoned thousands of Confederate sympathizers without trial. The president also extended martial law to those civilians who discouraged enlistment or resisted the draft, making them subject to military courts rather than local juries. This firm policy had the desired effect. The Militia Act of 1862 set a quota of volunteers for each state, and enough recruits came forward to satisfy Union needs for a year. As the scale of hostilities increased, Congress passed the Enrollment Act of 1863,

which raised the age limit for military service to forty-five and instituted high quotas for each congressional district, which could be met with either conscripts or volunteers. Knowing that conscription would be unpopular, northern officials used cash bounties to entice volunteers, prompting the enlistment or reenlistment of almost a million men. As in the South, wealthy men could avoid the draft by providing a substitute or paying a $300 commutation, or exemption, fee.

The Enrollment Act sparked the first significant opposition to the northern war effort. Ordinary artisans and laborers protested against the high commutation fee—which equaled a worker's annual income—and thousands of recent immigrants from Ireland and Germany refused to serve, saying it was not their fight. Northern Democrats exploited these resentments against the Enrollment Act by charging that Lincoln was drafting poor whites in order to free the slaves and flood the cities with black laborers who would work for lower wages. Some of these Democrats opposed the war, arguing that the South should be allowed to secede; others simply wanted to protect the interests of immigrants, most of whom were Democrats.

In July 1863 hostility to the draft and to African Americans spilled onto the streets of New York City. For five days immigrant Irish and German workers ran rampant, burning the draft office, sacking the homes of important Republicans, and attacking the police. Venting their anger against blacks, the rioters lynched and mutilated at least a dozen African Americans, drove hundreds of black families from their homes, and burned down the Colored Orphan Asylum. Lincoln rushed in Union troops, who killed more than a hundred rioters and suppressed the insurrection, but many immigrants continued to oppose conscription.

Hospital Nursing
Working as nurses in battlefront hospitals, thousands of Union and Confederate women gained firsthand experience of the horrors of war. A sense of calm prevails in this behind-the-lines Union hospital in Nashville, Tennessee, as nurse Anne Belle tends to the needs of those recovering from their wounds. Most Civil War nurses served as unpaid volunteers and spent time cooking and cleaning for their patients as well as tending to their injuries. In contrast, conditions at field hospitals were chaotic under the pressure of heavy casualties and shifting battle sites.
U.S. Army Military History Institute.

The Civilian War Effort. The Union government's determination to wage total war won greater support among native-born citizens. In 1861 prominent New Yorkers established the United States Sanitary Commission. Its task was to provide medical services and prevent a repeat of the debacle of the recently concluded Crimean War between Britain and Russia (1854–1856), in which disease accounted for over three-fourths of British casualties. Through its network of seven thousand local auxiliaries, the Sanitary Commission gathered supplies; distributed clothing, food, and medicine to the army; improved the sanitary standards of camp life; and recruited battlefield nurses and doctors for the Union Army Medical Bureau.

The efforts of the Sanitary Commission were not consistently successful. Diseases—dysentery, typhoid, and malaria as well as childhood viruses such as mumps and measles, to which many rural men had not developed an immunity—killed twice as many Union soldiers (about 250,000) as died in combat. Surgeons inadvertently took more lives by spreading infection than they saved by performing operations. Still,

because of better sanitation and high-quality food, the mortality rate among Union troops from disease and wounds was substantially lower than that in other major nineteenth-century wars (see American Voices, "Jane Swisshelm: The Common Lemon: The Difference between Life and Death," p. 453). Confederate soldiers were less fortunate. Although thousands of white women volunteered as nurses, the Confederate health system was poorly organized. Thousands of southern soldiers contracted scurvy because of the lack of vitamin C in their diets, and they died from camp diseases at higher rates than did Union soldiers.

Women took a leading role in the Sanitary Commission and other wartime governmental agencies. As superintendent of women nurses, Dorothea Dix became the first woman to receive an important federal appointment. Dix used her influence to combat the prejudice against women treating men, opening a new occupation to women (see Chapter 12, American Lives, pp. 394–395). Thousands of educated Union women joined the war effort as clerks in the expanding governmental bureaucracy. In the South women staffed the efficient Confederate postal service. Indeed, in both sections millions of women assumed new economic responsibilities and worked with far greater intensity than before the war. They took over many farm tasks previously done by men, and went to work in schools as well as textile, clothing, and shoe factories. A number of women took on military duties as spies, scouts, and (disguised as men) soldiers. As the nurse Clara Barton, who later founded the American Red Cross, recalled, "At the war's end, woman was at least fifty years in advance of the normal position which continued peace would have assigned her."

Mobilizing Resources and Money

Wars usually are won by the side with superior resources and economic organization, and in this regard the Union entered the war with a distinct advantage. With nearly two-thirds of the American people, about two-thirds of the nation's railroad mileage, and nearly 90 percent of American industrial output, the North's economy was far superior to the South's (Figure 14.1). The North had an especially great advantage in the manufacture of cannon and rifles because many of its arms factories were equipped for mass production.

But the Confederate position was far from weak. Virginia, North Carolina, and Tennessee had substantial industrial capacity. Richmond, with its Tredegar Iron Works, was an important industrial center, and in 1861 the Confederacy transported to Richmond the gun-making machinery captured at the U.S. armory at Harpers Ferry. The production of the Richmond armory, the purchase of Enfield rifle-muskets from Britain, and

JANE SWISSHELM

The Common Lemon: The Difference between Life and Death

———— ★ ————

During the Civil War diseases took more lives than bullets did, and the northern toll would have been even higher without the work of the doctors and nurses of the United States Sanitary Commission. In 1861 Dr. Elizabeth Blackwell organized the Woman's Central Association for Relief in New York, which trained women as army nurses. This narrative by Jane Swisshelm, a social reformer who worked on her own as a volunteer nurse, shows the crucial role played by public support for military hospitals—in this case by providing lemons that were rich in vitamin C and inhibited a common hospital disease.

About nine o'clock I returned to the man I had come to help. I had sat by him but a few moments when I noticed a green shade on his face. It darkened, and his breathing grew labored—then ceased. I think it was not more than twenty minutes from the time I observed the green tinge until he was gone. I called the nurse, who brought the large man I had seen at the door of the bed ward, and now I knew he was a surgeon, knew also, by the sudden shadow on his face when he saw the corpse, that he was alarmed; and when he had given minute directions for the removal of the bed and its contents, the washing of the floor and sprinkling with chloride of lime, I went close to his side, and said in a low voice:

"Doctor, is not this hospital gangrene?"

He looked down on me, seemed to take my measure, and answered:

"I am very sorry to say, madam, that it is."

"Then you want lemons!"

"We would be glad to have them!"

"Glad to have them?" I repeated, in profound astonishment, "why, you *must* have them!"

He seemed surprised at my earnestness, and set about explaining:

"We sent to the Sanitary Commission last week, and got half a box."

"Seven hundred and fifty wounded men! Hospital gangrene, and half a box of lemons!". . .

I went to the head nurse . . . who . . . gave me writing materials, and I wrote a short note to the *New York Tribune:*

"Hospital gangrene has broken out in Washington, and we want lemons! *lemons!* LEMONS! LEMONS! No man or woman in health, has a right to a glass of lemonade until these men have all they need; send us lemons!"

I signed my name and mailed it immediately, and it appeared next morning. . . . That day lemons began to pour into Washington, and soon, I think, into every hospital in the land. Gov. Andrews sent two hundred boxes to the Surgeon General. I received so many, that at one time there were twenty ladies, several of them with ambulances, distributing those which came to my address, and if there was any more hospital gangrene that season I neither saw nor heard of it.

———————

Source: Jane Swisshelm, *Half a Century* (Chicago: Jansen, McClurg & Co., 1880), 251–253.

the capture of 100,000 Union-made Springfield rifle-muskets enabled the Confederacy to provide every infantryman with a modern weapon by 1863 (see New Technology, "The Rifle-Musket," p. 455).

Moreover, with 9 million people, the Confederacy could mobilize enormous armies. Although one-third of that number were slaves, their masters kept them in the fields, producing food for the armies and cotton for export. The Confederacy counted on "King Cotton" to provide revenue to purchase clothes, boots, blankets, and weapons from abroad. It also counted on cotton as a diplomatic weapon, hoping that the British, who depended on southern cotton to supply their textile factories, would grant diplomatic recognition and provide military and economic aid. And indeed the British government did regard the conflict as a war, giving the rebels the status of a belligerent power with the right under international law to borrow money and purchase weapons. Thus the odds did not necessarily favor the Union, despite its superior resources.

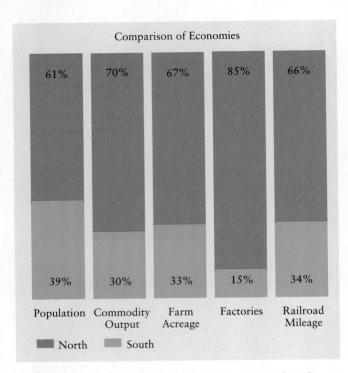

Comparison of Economies

	Population	Commodity Output	Farm Acreage	Factories	Railroad Mileage
North	61%	70%	67%	85%	66%
South	39%	30%	33%	15%	34%

■ North   ■ South

Source: Stanley Engerman, "The Economic Impact of the Civil War," in Robert W. Fogel and Stanley L. Engerman, *The Reinterpretation of American Economic History* (New York: Harper & Row, 1971), U.S. Census data.

FIGURE 14.1
Economies, North and South, 1860
The military advantages of the North were even greater than this chart suggests because the population figures included slaves whom the South feared to arm and because its commodity output was dominated by farm goods rather than manufactures. Moreover, southern factories were, on average, much smaller than those in the North.

Forging New Economic Policies. The outcome of the conflict hinged on the ability of the two governments to mobilize the resources of their respective societies. Lincoln and the Republicans had a clear economic agenda. To build political support for their party and boost industrial output, they enacted virtually the entire economic program—the American System—previously advocated by Henry Clay and the Whig Party. First, the Republicans raised tariffs to double their prewar levels, winning praise from northeastern manufacturers and laborers and farmers who feared competition from cheap foreign goods and labor. Second, Secretary of the Treasury Salmon P. Chase created a new national banking system—an important element in a modern centralized government—by linking thousands of existing local banks. This integrated system was far more extensive in scope and far more effective in raising capital and controlling inflation than earlier efforts by the First and Second Banks of the United States had been.

Finally, the Lincoln administration fulfilled Clay's program for a nationally financed system of internal improvements. In 1862 Congress devised an extensive network of transcontinental railroads, chartering the Union Pacific and Central Pacific railways and subsidizing them lavishly. It awarded those railroads 20 square miles of federal land for every mile of track they put down and in 1864 provided a similar subsidy to the Northern Pacific. In addition, the Republicans moved aggressively to provide northern farmers with "free land" in the West. The Homestead Act of 1862 gave heads of families or individuals aged twenty-one or older the right to own 160 acres of public land after five years of residence and improvement. This economic program not only sustained the allegiance of a majority of northerners to the Republican Party but, by helping northern industries and raising money for military expenses, also bolstered the Union's ability to fight the war.

In contrast, the Confederate government had a much less coherent and far-reaching economic policy. True to its states' rights philosophy, the Confederacy left most economic matters in the hands of the state governments. But as the realities of total war became clear, Jefferson Davis's administration took extraordinary measures: it built and operated shipyards, armories, foundries, and textile mills; commandeered food and scarce raw materials such as coal, iron, copper, and lead; requisitioned slaves to work on fortifications; and exercised direct control over foreign trade. As the war wore on, ordinary citizens increasingly resented these coercive measures, in part because the Confederate leaders failed to explain their wartime needs or deal with civilians' misery on the home front. To sustain the war effort they increasingly counted on racial solidarity: President Davis warned whites that a Union victory would destroy slavery "and reduce the whites to the degraded position of the African race."

Raising Money in the North. For both the North and the South, the cost of fighting a total war was enormous. In the Union, spending by the federal government shot up from less than 2 percent of the gross national product to about 15 percent. To pay for those expenditures, the Republicans established a powerful modern state that raised money in three ways: by imposing broad-based taxes, borrowing from the middle class as well as wealthy Americans and foreign investors, and creating a national monetary system.

The Union government increased taxes by raising tariff rates, placing excise duties on consumer goods such as alcoholic beverages, and for the first time imposing direct taxes on business corporations, large inheritances, and the incomes of affluent citizens. Those levies paid for about 20 percent of the cost of the war.

The sale of Treasury bonds financed an even greater part of the northern war effort: no less than

The Rifle-Musket

★

"WAR IS THE continuation of politics by other means," the Prussian military strategist Karl Von Clauswitz declared in the 1820s, and the American Civil War showed just how bloody that politics would be. The war was the first conflict fought with the new technology: railroad transport, ironclad ships, and highly efficient deadly weapons.

Among the most deadly was the rifle-musket. By 1855 U.S. secretary of war Jefferson Davis had ended production of the traditional smooth-bore musket and begun equipping American soldiers with the new weapon. Consequently, during the Civil War most Union infantrymen used Springfields, rifle-muskets first manufactured by the U.S. armory at Springfield, Massachusetts. Many Confederate soldiers carried Enfields, a similar weapon manufactured in Britain.

In many respects, the rifle-musket was a traditional weapon. Like a musket, it had a long barrel (usually 40 inches), fired a single shot, and was loaded through the muzzle, a cumbersome process. Before aiming and firing, a soldier had to rip open a paper-wrapped cartridge of gunpowder with his teeth, pour the powder and a bullet down the barrel, jam them tight with a ramrod, half-cock the hammer to insert a percussion cap, and then—finally—cock the hammer. Some soldiers could do all this lying on their backs, but to fire two or three times a minute, most men had to load from a kneeling or standing position, exposing themselves to enemy fire.

That fire was now much more accurate because the new rifle-muskets used the technology of eighteenth-century hunting weapons: tapered barrels that were rifled—lined with spiral grooves—to give the bullet greater speed and accuracy. But these hunting rifles (which had given Daniel Boone his reputation as a "Kentucky sharpshooter") had not been issued to combat soldiers because the grooved barrel quickly accumulated gunpowder and required frequent cleaning.

A technological innovation solved that problem. In the early 1850s James S. Burton, an American mechanic working at the Harpers Ferry armory, developed a new bullet based on an earlier French model. Burton's cylindro-conoidal bullet had a radically different shape from the round bullets of the day and was cast with a cavity at its base. When powder exploded, hot gas expanded the soft-metal cavity and forced the bullet to engage the grooves of the rifling, cleaning them as it sped through the barrel.

The rifle-musket revolutionized warfare and military strategy by enormously strengthening defensive forces. Infantrymen could now kill reliably at 300 yards—triple the previous range—and thus keep attackers from getting close enough for hand-to-hand combat. As a result, bayonets accounted for less than 1 percent of all wounds in the Civil War.

Elaborate entrenchments strengthened defensive positions even more. Firing from deep trenches, infantrymen with rifle-muskets could easily turn back assaults by forces three to four times their size, as the great success of the depleted Confederate forces defending Atlanta and Richmond in 1864 and 1865 clearly showed. Indeed, the grinding trench warfare around Petersburg, Virginia, provided a chilling preview of World War I, by which time defensive positions had been strengthened even more by quick-firing breech-loaded rifles and machine guns.

The new technology baffled most Civil War commanders, who continued to use the tactics perfected during the heyday of the musket and bayonet. They ordered thousands of infantrymen into dense close-order formations and sent them against enemy positions in successive waves. The result was brutally tragic. In battle after battle charging infantrymen went down like harvested wheat. Finally, the terrible losses at Gettysburg forced officers to search for ways to cope with the rifle-musket—the new and deadly weapon of war.

1861 Springfield Rifle-Musket
From *The Civil War: The Killing Ground.* Photograph by Larry Sherer. © 1986 Time–Life Books, Inc.

Industrial Richmond
Exploiting their city's location at the falls of the James River, Richmond entrepreneurs developed a wide range of industries: flour mills, tobacco factories, railroad and port facilities, and, most important, a profitable and substantial iron industry. In 1861 the Tredegar Iron Works employed nearly 1,000 workers and, as the only facility in the South that could manufacture large machinery and heavy weapons, made a major contribution to the Confederate war effort.
Virginia State Library.

65 percent of the Union's expenditures came with borrowed money. Following the advice of Jay Cooke, a Philadelphia banker, the Treasury paid interest on the bonds in gold, which made them financially attractive to foreign investors, and marketed them widely throughout the Union. Using newspaper advertisements and 2,500 subagents, Cooke persuaded nearly a million northern families—one-fourth of all households—to buy war bonds. In addition, the National Banking Acts of 1863 and 1864 induced many state banks to purchase bonds. If state banks invested one-third of their capital in these bonds, the U.S. government granted them a national charter, allowing them to issue national banknotes and freeing them from various taxes. By the end of 1865, the number of national banks had tripled and their purchases of U.S. bonds had increased nearly fourfold.

The Union financed most of the remaining cost of the war by printing paper money. The Legal Tender Act of 1862 authorized the issue of $150 million in Treasury notes—which soon became known as "greenbacks"—and required the public to accept them as legal tender.

As with the "Continentals" issued during the War of Independence, these Treasury notes were backed by faith in the government rather than by specie. Unlike the Continentals, however, this paper money did not depreciate significantly in value. Although $500 million in greenbacks had been issued by the end of the war, this paper money funded only 15 percent of wartime expenses (as opposed to 80 percent during the Revolutionary War) and consequently did not spark an inflationary rise in prices.

Resorting to Inflation in the South. The financial demands on the South were just as great, but it lacked a powerful central government that could tax and borrow. The Confederate Congress fiercely opposed taxes on cotton exports and slaves, the most valuable property of wealthy planters. Thus, an 1861 Confederate revenue measure exempted slave property from taxation and left the collection of the taxes of other property to the states. Only South Carolina imposed these centrally legislated taxes directly on its citizens; the other states either borrowed the money or paid the Confed-

The War's Toll on Civilians
Fighting along the Mississippi River in the spring of 1862 and the Union blockade along the Gulf of Mexico disrupted the supply of foodstuffs that usually came down the river into New Orleans. By the time Union troops captured the city in May, food stocks were severely depleted. In June, hungry citizens—men in top hats and fashionably dressed women, as well as barefoot children and white and black working people—stormed the stores and emptied them of their last supplies of food. This engraving of the *Starving People of New Orleans* appeared in *Harper's Weekly*, a prominent New York journal.
Library of Congress.

eracy with state-issued IOUs. Even the more comprehensive tax legislation enacted in 1863 by the Confederate Congress excluded slave property. Consequently, taxes fell primarily on urban middle-class and nonslaveholding yeomen farm families, who often refused to pay. In 1864 a new measure that included a 5 percent tax on the value of slaves came too late to raise much revenue, so that the Confederate government covered less than 5 percent of its expenditures through taxation.

The Confederacy had an equally difficult time in borrowing money. Although wealthy planters had enough capital to fund a relatively large part of the war, most of them refused to buy Confederate bonds by pledging their cotton revenues. At first they were unwilling to accept low interest rates; later they began to doubt that the Confederacy would prevail. Europeans came to share those doubts, and the only major loan to the Confederacy came from a French banking house in 1863. In the end the Confederate government paid only 35 percent of its war costs through borrowing.

And so the Confederacy was forced to finance about 60 percent of its expenses with unbacked paper money. This flood of currency created soaring inflation, which was compounded by counterfeit copies of the poorly printed Confederate notes. The great battles and sieges brought a reduction in the food supply, thereby causing food prices to rise even higher. As the huge supply of money (and shortages of goods) brought rising food prices, riots broke out in more than a dozen southern cities and towns. In early 1863 several hundred women in Richmond broke into bakeries, crying, "Our children are starving while the rich roll in wealth."

The situation got worse as the paper money depreciated. By the spring of 1865 prices had risen to ninety-two times their 1861 levels. Inflation not only undermined civilian morale but also caused farmers to refuse to accept Confederate money for the produce needed to feed the armies. Supply officers had to seize what they needed, offering payment in virtually worthless IOUs; some military units simply took what they needed without even intending to pay. The fear among white southerners of a strong government and high taxes had an ironic result. Unable legally to raise money, the Confederacy had to resort to outright seizures—a gross violation of its citizens' property rights—to sustain the war effort.

The Turning Point: 1863

——————★——————

By 1863 the Lincoln administration had mobilized northern society, creating a complex war machine and a coherent economic and financial system. "Little by little," the young diplomat Henry Adams noted from his post at the American embassy in London, "one began to feel that, behind the chaos in Washington power was taking shape; that it was massed and guided as it had not been before." Slowly but surely the tide of battle shifted toward the Union side.

Emancipation

From the beginning of the conflict, antislavery Republicans had tried to persuade their party and their president to make abolition—as well as the restoration of

"Contrabands" Go to School
Forbidden as slaves to learn how to read and write, the African Americans who fled behind Union lines were eager students. Arrayed in front of the barracks erected to house them, black women and children are shown learning to read at a school for contrabands. Adult men are notably absent because during the war most men were employed as military workers or soldiers.
Brady Collection, National Archives.

the Union—a central war aim. They based their argument not just on morality but on "military necessity," pointing out that slave-grown crops sustained the Confederate war effort. As Frederick Douglass put it, "The very stomach of this rebellion is the Negro in the form of a slave. Arrest that hoe in the hands of the Negro, and you smite the rebellion in the very seat of its life." As war casualties mounted in 1862, Lincoln and some Republican leaders accepted Douglass's argument and began to redefine the war as a struggle against slavery—the cornerstone of southern society.

"Contrabands." But it was enslaved African Americans who forced the issue of emancipation by seizing freedom for themselves. Exploiting the disorder of wartime, slaves escaped from their plantations and sought refuge behind Union lines. The first Union official who had to decide what to do with escapees was General Benjamin Butler. When three slaves reached his camp on the Virginia coast in May 1861, Butler labeled them "contraband of war" and refused to return them to their owner. His term stuck, and for the rest of the war escaped slaves who lived behind Union lines were known as *contrabands*. Within a few months a thousand contrabands were camping with Butler's army.

As the number of runaway slaves who fled to freedom grew into tens of thousands, the Union government undertook to define their status. In August 1861 Lincoln signed a Confiscation Act, which authorized the seizure of all property—including slaves—used to support the rebellion. However, this law applied only to slaves within the reach of Union armies and only protected them from seizure by their owners; it did not make them free.

The debate over the Confiscation Act revealed a threefold division among Republicans over emancipation. Conservative members of the party wanted to prevent the spread of slavery into the territories but leave the responsibility for emancipation in the South and in existing pro-Union states, such as Kentucky and Maryland, to the state governments—even if this would preserve the institution for decades. Moderate Republicans, the most numerous faction and the one led by Lincoln, wanted to end slavery quickly but feared that immediate abolition would cause a dramatic loss of Union support in the border states and stimulate a racist backlash in northern cities.

Radical Republicans discounted such fears. They had long condemned slavery and saw that the war provided the ideal opportunity to destroy it. As battlefield casualties among Union forces mounted, they mobi-

First Reading of the Emancipation Proclamation, *Francis Bicknell Carpenter*
Treasury Secretary Salmon P. Chase (far left) and Secretary of State William H.
Seward (center foreground) were longtime foes of slavery. As thousands of black contrabands sought freedom behind Union lines, they pressed Lincoln to make abolition
one of his war aims. In July 1862, the president drew up a draft proclamation but
Seward, himself a successful politician who knew the importance of timing, persuaded
him to "postpone its issue until you can give it to the country supported by military
success." On September 21, four days after the battle of Antietam, Lincoln read the
Emancipation Proclamation to his cabinet and the next day issued it to the public.
United States Capitol Historical Society.

lized popular support for a policy of punishing rebel
planters by taking away their slaves. By the spring of
1862 leading Radicals—Treasury Secretary Chase;
Charles Sumner, chair of the Senate Committee on
Foreign Relations; and Thaddeus Stevens, chair of the
House Ways and Means Committee—had convinced
moderate Republicans to move toward abolition. A
long-time congressman from Pennsylvania, Stevens
was particularly effective. An uncompromising foe of
slavery, he was also a masterful politician, adept at
fashioning legislation that commanded majority support. In April 1862 Stevens and his Radical allies persuaded Congress to end slavery in the District of
Columbia, with compensation for owners. In June the
legislature outlawed slavery in the federal territories,
finally enacting the Wilmot Proviso and the Republicans' free-soil policy. And in July Congress passed a
second Confiscation Act, which, overriding the property rights of Confederate slaveowners, declared "forever free" all fugitive slaves and all slaves captured by
the Union army. Emancipation had become an instrument of war.

The Emancipation Proclamation.   Sensing a shift in
public opinion in the Union, Lincoln seized the initiative from the Radical Republicans. In July 1862 he pre-

pared a general proclamation of emancipation and,
viewing the battle of Antietam as "an indication of
the Divine Will," issued it on September 22, 1862. The
proclamation declared Lincoln's intention to free the
slaves in all states that were still in rebellion on January 1, 1863. This decree had its constitutional basis in
the president's war powers. To fulfill his responsibilities
as commander in chief, Lincoln believed he could deny
resources—in this case, enslaved workers—to the
enemy. The proclamation gave the seceding states one
hundred days to preserve slavery by returning to the
Union. None chose to do so.

The proclamation was politically astute. Since Lincoln needed to keep the loyalty of whites in the border
states that had remained loyal to the Union, he left slavery intact there. The president also wanted to win the
allegiance of the areas occupied by Union armies—
western and central Tennessee, western Virginia, and
southern Louisiana, including New Orleans—so he left
slavery untouched there. Consequently, because
Lincoln's order had no immediate, practical effect
within the Confederacy, the Emancipation Proclamation did not free a single slave.

Nonetheless, Lincoln's initiative dramatically
changed the nature of the conflict by making emancipation a central goal of Union policy. As antislavery

activist Wendell Phillips put it, Lincoln had advanced abolition to "the edge of Niagara," where it would soon be swept over the brink, bringing freedom to all enslaved African Americans. For his part, the president predicted that the conflict would now become a war of "subjugation" in which "the old South is to be destroyed and replaced by new propositions and ideas."

As a war aim, emancipation was controversial both in the Confederacy, where Jefferson Davis labeled it the "most execrable measure recorded in the history of guilty man," and in the North, where it produced the backlash among whites that the moderate Republicans had feared. Some Union officers did not want to fight for emancipation, and many more, including General in Chief George McClellan, worried that the proclamation would incite slave rebellions. As McClellan said privately, he "could not make my mind to fight for such an accursed doctrine as that of a servile insurrection." But McClellan, who had political aspirations as a Democrat, nonetheless remained loyal to civilian authorities in the Lincoln administration. The "remedy for political errors," he reminded his officers, " . . . is to be found only in the action of people at the polls."

The verdict of the American people on emancipation was mixed. In the congressional elections of 1862 Democrats denounced emancipation as unconstitutional, warned of slave uprisings and massive bloodshed in the South, and claimed that a "black flood" would wash away the jobs of northern workers. In New York, this message worked: Democrat Horatio Seymour won the governorship by declaring that if abolition was the purpose of the war, the South should not be conquered. Other Democrats also swept to victory in New York—and in Pennsylvania, Ohio, and Illinois as well—giving the party a gain of 34 seats in Congress. However, Republicans retained a 25-seat majority in the House and gained 5 seats in the Senate.

Blaming their losses on the inability of soldiers at the front to vote, the Republicans continued their assault against slavery. In December the House endorsed the preliminary proclamation and passed an act requiring West Virginia to abolish slavery as a condition of statehood. Lincoln also pressed ahead. After the election he removed McClellan from command of the Army of the Potomac, both because of his cautious generalship at Richmond and Antietam and because of his opposition to emancipation, which was well known. Then, on New Year's Day 1863, the president signed the Emancipation Proclamation. As a gesture to northerners who sympathized with the South and feared racial warfare, Lincoln urged slaves to "abstain from all violence." But he now justified emancipation as an "act of justice." "If my name ever goes into history," he said, "it was for this act."

Vicksburg and Gettysburg

The fate of the proclamation and of African Americans would depend on the success of Union armies. The outlook was not particularly encouraging. Not only had Democrats registered gains in the elections of 1862, but there was also increased popular support for those Democrats who favored a negotiated peace. Two brilliant victories by Lee, whose Confederate army defeated Hooker's forces at Fredericksburg (December 1862) and Chancellorsville, Virginia (May 1863), further eroded northern support for the war, as did rumors of the new military draft.

Vicksburg. At this crucial juncture, General Grant mounted a major offensive in the West designed to split the Confederacy in two. In the spring of 1863 Grant drove southward along the western bank of the Mississippi and then moved his troops across the river near Vicksburg, Mississippi, where he defeated two Confederate armies and laid siege to the city. After repelling Union assaults for six weeks, the exhausted and starving Vicksburg garrison surrendered on July 4, 1863. Five days later Union forces took Port Hudson, Louisiana, establishing Union control of the entire Mississippi River. Grant had taken 31,000 prisoners; cut off Louisiana, Arkansas, and Texas from the other Confederate states; and prompted hundreds of slaves along the river to desert their plantations (see American Voices, "Elizabeth Mary Meade Ingraham: A Vicksburg Diary," p. 461).

When Grant began his advance down the Mississippi in early 1863, he caused a division over strategy within the Confederate leadership. Davis and other civilian leaders wanted to counter Union pressure in the West by throwing in reinforcements to defend Vicksburg and sending troops into Tennessee to draw Grant out of Mississippi. But Robert E. Lee, buoyed by his recent victories over Hooker, favored a new invasion of the North. He argued that a military thrust into the free states would relieve the pressure on Vicksburg by drawing the Union armies eastward. Beyond that, Lee hoped for a significant victory that would undermine northern support for the war.

Gettysburg. Lee's strategy won out. In June 1863 he maneuvered his army northward through Maryland into Pennsylvania. The Army of the Potomac moved along with him, positioning itself between Lee and Washington, until the two great armies met in an unplanned but decisive confrontation at Gettysburg, Pennsylvania (Map 14.4). On the first day of the battle, July 1, Lee drove the Union's advance guard to the south of town. There General George G. Meade, who had just taken over command of the Union forces from Hooker, placed his troops in well-defended hilltop posi-

ELIZABETH MARY MEADE INGRAHAM

A Vicksburg Diary

———★———

Elizabeth Mary Meade Ingraham (1806–?) was the sister of Union general George Meade but sided with the Confederacy. In 1831 she and her husband, who had been an agent of the Second Bank of the United States, moved from Philadelphia to Mississippi, where they lived on Ashwood Plantation, 30 miles from Vicksburg. Her diary, which covers the six weeks between May 2 and June 13, 1863, describes how Ulysses S. Grant's Vicksburg campaign dramatically changed the relationship between masters and slaves.

May 4. [Union general] Osterhaus' Division, scum of St. Louis, camped in the big field. All the corn ruined in the field, and nearly all consumed in the granaries. . . . Nancy [a slave] sent me a little. Elsy, faithful and true, and Jack and Emma [all slaves] very attentive.

May 8. The last thing Eddens [a slave] did was to save some meat for me. He slept in the spare room Sunday night, and Monday at noon he had quit our service. . . . Parker, Sol, Mordt, Jim Crow, Isaiah, and Wadloo, have quit us, but the rest are here, and very attentive and willing. . . .

May 13. Elsy still faithful, feeds us, and does what she can; Rita Jane too; Bowlegs very attentive. Emma beginning to tire of waiting on me, did not come up at noon; Nancy not true.

May 15. Edward's [Ingraham's son] sash and six pairs of gloves taken out of my wardrobe. I am afraid Emma has done this; don't feel as if I could trust any one but Elsy; she feeds and takes care of me.

May 18. [We] have reason to think the hands will all leave; only a question of time, they are not quite ready; Elsy still true; but Jack doubtful. . . .

May 27. Negro meetings are being held, and the few whites left begin to be very anxious. . . . Powers was burnt out by his own negroes. I fear the blacks more than I do the Yankees. Jack trying to persuade Elsy to leave. . . . She tells him to get her a home and a way of earning a living, and she is ready to go, but [I] told her, if he left here, to move up into the washhouse with her children. I would give her $12 a month and free her four children.

June 3. Our darkeys in great commotion, yesterday, on account of Secesh [secessionists], who, about twenty-five in number, have been going the rounds, and setting the negroes to work; they whipped one fellow . . . and hung another; and we thought last evening all ours but a few meant to go. . . . I wish the Secesh would come [here]. . . .

June 6. Martha with her three children and Emma, left at midnight Friday . . . and the rest are packing to-day. Hays resolved to go, and I dread lest he take his wife with him, for I can hardly get along as it is, and shall die if I have the cooking to do.

June 10. Fanny, John Smith, and the children, Buck and his family, Dave and his, Kate and hers, making in all thirteen who have gone—Dave intending to come back, but the Yankees would not let him. . . . those who have stayed are utterly demoralized; if they work for you, the job is only half done.

Source: W. Maury Darst, "The Vicksburg Diary of Mrs. Alfred Ingraham," Journal of Mississippi History 44 (May 1982): 148–179.

tions and called up reinforcements. By the morning of the second day Meade had 90,000 troops under his command, whereas Lee had 75,000. Aware that he was outnumbered but bent on victory, Lee decided to advance, attacking both of Meade's flanks but failing to turn them. General Richard B. Ewell, assigned to attack the Union right, was unwilling to risk his men in an all-out assault, and General Longstreet on the Union left was unable to dislodge Meade's forces from a hill known as Little Round Top.

On July 3 Lee decided to attempt a frontal assault on the center of the Union lines. He had enormous confidence in his troops and realized that this might be his last chance to inflict a crushing psychological defeat on the North. After the heaviest artillery barrage of the war, Lee ordered 14,000 men under General George E. Pickett to take Cemetery Ridge. But Meade had reinforced the center of his line with artillery and his best troops. Pickett's men charged across a mile of open terrain and, despite massive, withering fire, nearly

MAP 14.4
The Battle of Gettysburg, 1863
After Lee's victory at Chancellorsville in May 1863, the two armies jockeyed for position
as the Confederate forces moved northward. At Gettysburg, the Union army commanded
by General George Meade emerged victorious, primarily because it was much larger than
the Confederate army and held well-fortified positions along Cemetery Ridge, which gave
its units a major tactical advantage.

reached the Union lines, but once again artillery and the new rifle-musket demonstrated their potency against a traditional infantry assault. Thousands of Pickett's troops were killed, wounded, or captured. When ordered to rally his troops to repel a possible counterattack, Pickett answered, "General Lee, I *have* no division, now."

Gettysburg was a great Union victory. By the end of the battle, Lee had suffered 28,000 casualties, one-third of the Army of Northern Virginia. Never again would a southern army threaten a major invasion of the North. But Meade, like McClellan at Antietam, was so shocked by the bloodletting and his own losses—some 23,000 killed or wounded—that he allowed the remaining Confederate soldiers to escape, thereby losing an opportunity to end the war. "As it is," Lincoln brooded, "the war will be prolonged indefinitely."

Political and Diplomatic Effects. Nonetheless, the outcome at Gettysburg and the simultaneous Union victory at Vicksburg decisively changed the political climate in the North. In the state and local elections in the fall of 1863, Democrats once again challenged Republi-

cans on the issue of emancipation, accusing them of favoring social equality for blacks. For the position of governor of Ohio, the Democrats nominated Clement L. Vallandigham, a politician whom Lincoln had banished from the Union for giving aid and comfort to the enemy by denouncing the war as one fought "for the freedom of the blacks and the enslavement of the whites." Lincoln intervened in the election, declaring that to oppose emancipation was to oppose northern victory, and Republicans swept to decisive victories in the three key states of New York, Pennsylvania, and Ohio, where Vallandigham's opponent won a record share of the vote.

In the South, the military setbacks accentuated war weariness. The Confederate elections of 1863 went sharply against the politicians who supported Jefferson Davis, and a large minority in the new Confederate Congress was outspokenly hostile to his policies. A few representatives advocated peace negotiations, and many more criticized the ineffectiveness of the war effort, with the Confederate vice-president, Alexander Stephens, comparing Davis to "my poor old blind and deaf dog."

Vicksburg and Gettysburg also represented a great diplomatic victory for the North, ending the Confederacy's chances to gain foreign recognition and acquire advanced naval weapons. Since the war began, Britain had recognized the Confederacy as a belligerent power and allowed it to buy arms and other military goods from British manufacturers. But Britain had not recognized the Confederacy as a sovereign state or interfered with the ever-tightening Union naval blockade of southern ports. Nonetheless, because British textile mills imported four-fifths of their raw cotton from the South, the Confederacy continued to hope that Britain would actively intervene on its side.

Two disputes between the British ministry and Lincoln's government heightened the prospect of intervention. In November 1861, a Union sloop seized a British steamer, the *Trent*, on the high seas and arrested two Confederate commissioners, James Mason and John Slidell, who were on their way to Britain and France. To secure the release of the diplomats, the British ordered troops to Canada and threatened war. Then, in the spring of 1862, British shipbuilders began to supply armed cruisers to the Confederacy, and one of them, the *Alabama*, soon sank or captured more than a hundred Union merchant ships. Charles Francis Adams, the son of John Quincy Adams and the American minister in London, despaired of preventing the scheduled delivery of two other ironclad cruisers in mid-1863. But news of the great Union victories changed everything, and Adams persuaded the British government to impound the ships.

Other factors also influenced the British decision to deny active assistance to the Confederacy. Cotton had not proved to be "King," as the South had hoped. British manufacturers had stockpiled raw cotton before the war, and when those stocks were depleted they found new sources of raw cotton in Egypt and India. Equally important, the dependence of British consumers on cheap wheat from the North deterred the government from supporting the Confederacy. Finally, British workers and reformers were enthusiastic champions of abolition, which the Emancipation Proclamation established as a Union war aim. The results at Vicksburg and Gettysburg then guaranteed British neutrality by demonstrating the military might of the Union. The British ministry did not want to risk Canada or the merchant marine by provoking a strong, well-armed United States.

France's emperor, Napoleon III (r. 1852–1870), was less cautious. He dreamed of an empire in Mexico and, taking advantage of American preoccupation with the Civil War, imposed a new colonial regime there. Beginning in the summer of 1862 Napoleon dispatched thousands of troops to Mexico, using as a pretext its failure to pay debts to French bankers. Overthrowing the established republican government, in 1864 Napoleon installed Archduke Ferdinand Maximilian, the brother of the emperor of Austria, as the emperor of Mexico. Union diplomats protested in vain against France's contempt for republican institutions and, citing President James Monroe's address to Congress in 1823 opposing new European colonies, its intrusion into what they claimed was the sphere of influence of the United States. But Confederate hopes that France might assist their struggle were dashed by the Union's great victories in 1863 and by Lincoln's armed diplomacy. Late in the year the president ordered an American expeditionary force to seize Brownsville, Texas (just north of the Mexican border), a warning heeded by the French-sponsored regime. Like the British ministry, Napoleon III had no stomach for a confrontation with an ever more powerful Union war machine.

The Union Victorious, 1864–1865

★

With the Union victories of 1863, it became clear that the South could not win the war on the battlefield. Now the Confederacy could only hope for a military stalemate that would persuade a war-weary North to give up the fight. Lincoln and his generals faced the daunting task of quickly winning a decisive victory; otherwise a majority of northern voters might desert the Republican Party and its policies.

Soldiers and Strategy

Two key developments strengthened the ability of the Union to prosecute the war with continued vigor and eventually to prevail: the enlistment of African American soldiers, and the discovery of generals capable of fighting a modern war.

The Impact of Black Troops. Free African Americans and fugitive slaves had tried to enlist in the Union army as early as 1861, and the black abolitionist Frederick Douglass had embraced their cause: "Once let the black man get upon his person the brass letters, 'U.S.,' . . . a musket on his shoulder and bullets in his pockets, and there is no power on earth which can deny that he has earned the right to citizenship in the United States." Such a prospect frightened many northern whites, who were determined to keep blacks in an inferior political and economic position. Moreover, most Union generals doubted that former slaves would make good soldiers, so the Lincoln administration initially refused to encourage black aspirations for military

Black Soldiers in the Union Army
Tens of thousands of African Americans volunteered for military service and the
chance to fight for their freedom. These proud soldiers were members of the 107th
Colored Infantry, stationed at Fort Corcoran near Washington, DC. In January 1865,
their regiment participated in the daring capture of Fort Fisher, which protected
Wilmington, North Carolina, the last Confederate port open to blockade runners.
Their chaplain declared that in nine battles the regiment "never faltered, gave way, or
retreated, unless ordered by the General commanding."
Library of Congress.

service. Nonetheless, by 1862 free and contraband
blacks had formed regiments in South Carolina,
Louisiana, and Kansas.

The Emancipation Proclamation changed popular
thinking and military policy. If blacks were to benefit
from a Union victory, some northern whites now
argued, they should share in the fighting and dying.
The valor exhibited by the first African American regiments also influenced northern opinion. In January
1863 Thomas Wentworth Higginson, the white abolitionist commander of the First South Carolina (Black)
Volunteers, wrote a glowing newspaper account of their
military prowess: "No officer in this regiment now
doubts that the key to the successful prosecution of the
war lies in the unlimited employment of black troops."
In July the heroic but costly attack on Fort Wagner,
South Carolina, by another black regiment, the 54th
Massachusetts Infantry, seemed to confirm Higginson's
prediction and convinced many white northerners,
including Union officers, of the value of black soldiers.

The War department authorized the enlistment of
free blacks and contraband slaves, and as white resistance to conscription increased, the Lincoln administration recruited as many African Americans as it
could. Without black soldiers, the president suggested

in the autumn of 1864, "we would be compelled to
abandon the war in three weeks." By the following
spring there were nearly 200,000 African American soldiers and sailors.

Military service did not end racial discrimination,
however. Black soldiers served under white officers in
segregated regiments and were used primarily to build
fortifications, garrison forts, and guard supply lines.
Army authorities routinely denied officers' commissions to African Americans and, until black soldiers
protested to Congress in June 1864, paid them less than
white soldiers ($7 versus $13 per month). Moreover, the
Lincoln administration did not consistently protect
captured African American soldiers from Confederate
violations of their rights as prisoners of war. When the
Confederacy threatened in 1863 to execute or enslave
captured blacks, the Union's War department retaliated
by refusing to exchange captured Confederate officers
and troops. But when the Confederates did execute or
enslave captured African Americans, Lincoln did not
carry through on his threat to take the lives of captured
rebels or put them to work at hard labor.

Despite such treatment, African Americans volunteered for military service in disproportionate numbers—forming about 10 percent of those who served in

Union armies during the entire war—and diligently served the northern cause. They knew they were fighting for freedom and the possibility of a new social order. "Hello, Massa," said one black soldier to his former master, who had been taken prisoner. "Bottom rail on top dis time." The worst fears of the secessionists had come true; through the agency of the Union army, slaves had risen in a great rebellion.

The Influence of New Generals. As African Americans enlisted in the ranks, Lincoln finally found a commanding general in whom he had confidence. In March 1864 he put General Ulysses S. Grant in charge of all the Union armies and created a command structure appropriate to the large, complex organization that the Union army had become. From then on, the president would determine general strategy and Grant would decide how best to implement it. Aiding the process was General Henry W. Halleck, the consummate office-soldier. He served as chief of staff, channeling communications and lifting administrative burdens from both Lincoln and Grant. Along with the general staff of the Prussian army in Europe, the Union's military command structure now was the most efficient in the world.

Grant Planning an Attack
On June 2, 1864, the day this photograph was taken, Grant moved his headquarters to the Bethesda Church, carried the pews out under the shade of the surrounding trees, and planned the costly attack he would make at Cold Harbor the next day. While Grant (to the left) leaned over a pew, gesturing at a map, his officers smoked their pipes and read reports of the war in newspapers that had just arrived from New York City.
Library of Congress.

Moreover, Lincoln's new commander understood how to fight a modern war. During his cadet days at West Point, Grant had been bored with studying conventional strategies—ones that stressed, for example, the advantages of interior lines of supply. As the war proceeded, he recognized how the new technology—especially ironclad ships, the telegraph, and railroads—created new strategic possibilities. During his successful western campaigns of 1862 and 1863, Grant employed ironclads to advance along the South's rivers; then, in November 1863, he used railroad transport to charge to the rescue of a Union army near Chattanooga, Tennessee, and drive an invading Confederate army back into Georgia.

Grant also came to believe that it was necessary to accept heavy casualties to overpower strongly defended positions. Abandoning the caution of earlier Union commanders, he threw reinforcements into the battle until he forced the Confederates to surrender or retreat. These aggressive tactics earned Grant a reputation as a butcher both of his own men and of enemy armies. Grant himself had few qualms about his tactics: "To conserve life, in war, is to fight unceasingly," he declared. Finally, the Union commander understood that a modern war was directed not just at the army of the enemy but at its entire society. At Vicksburg he had besieged an entire city and forced its surrender; to crush the Confederacy's will to resist, he was willing to terrorize the civilian population.

In May 1864 Lincoln approved Grant's plan to advance simultaneously against all the main Confederate forces, hoping for a decisive victory before the election of 1864. Personally taking charge of General George Meade's 115,000-strong Army of the Potomac, Grant set out to destroy Lee's force of 75,000 troops in Virginia. At the same time he instructed General William Tecumseh Sherman, who shared his views on modern warfare, to invade Georgia and take Atlanta. As Sherman prepared for battle, he wrote that "all that has gone before is mere skirmish. The war now begins."

Grant's Virginia Campaign

In Virginia, Grant advanced toward Richmond, hoping to force Lee to fight in open fields, where the Union's superior manpower and artillery could prevail. Lee, remembering Gettysburg, maintained strong defensive positions, attacking only when he held a tactical advantage. He twice seized such opportunities, winning narrow victories in the battles of the Wilderness on May 5–7 and Spotsylvania Court House on May 8–9. Nevertheless Grant drove on toward the Confederate capital (Map 14.5). In early June the Union general attacked Lee at Cold Harbor but withdrew after losing 7,000 men in a frontal assault that lasted less than sixty minutes. Grant had severely eroded Lee's forces, which had suffered 31,000 casualties, but Union losses were even higher at 55,000 men.

MAP 14.5
The Closing Virginia Campaigns, 1864–1865
During the last eight months of 1864 the armies of Grant and Lee were locked in a deadly dance across the Virginia countryside. By threatening Lee's lines of communication, Grant attempted to lure him into open battle. But Lee avoided a major test of strength, falling back and taking defensive positions that forced the Union army to undertake protracted sieges. As the number of casualties mounted, northern support for the war declined dramatically.

The fighting took a heavy psychological toll. "Many a man has gone crazy since this campaign began from the terrible pressure on mind and body," observed a Union captain, Oliver Wendell Holmes Jr. (a future eminent justice of the Supreme Court). Previous battles had lasted only a few days and had been separated by long intervals. But in this campaign Grant's relentless offensive advance toward Richmond and Lee's defensive tactics produced sustained fighting and grueling attrition.

In June, Grant altered his strategy, pulling some of his troops away from Richmond and laying siege to Petersburg, an important railroad center. The two armies now faced each other in well-designed and fortified trenches, foreshadowing the deadly trench warfare of World War I. Soldiers built complex networks of ditches, tunnels, and artillery emplacements for almost 50 miles around Richmond and Petersburg, and dared the other side to attack. As a Union soldier wrote home in December 1864,

> *In front of our works are deep ditches now filled with water and in front of this an abatis [barrier] made of limbs and trees driven slanting into the ground and with the points sharpened. Then we have wires stretched about in every direction about six inches or a foot above the ground. . . . I wish the Rebels would try to take our lines.*

The ensuing stalemate brought as much psychological as physical hardship. One Union officer reported that his men felt "a great dread and horror of attacking earthworks again," and another officer invoked biblical imagery, describing the continuous artillery firing and sniping as "living night and day within the 'valley of the shadow of death.'" The stress was especially great for the outnumbered Confederate troops, who spent months in the muddy, sickening trenches without being rotated to the rear for rest. As time passed, Lincoln and Grant felt pressures of their own; indeed, the enormous casualties and military standoff threatened Lincoln with defeat in the November election.

The outlook for the Republicans worsened in July 1864 when Confederate general Jubal Early's cavalry moved from its bases in the Shenandoah Valley and mounted attacks near Washington. To neutralize Early, Grant had to pull some of his best troops out of the Petersburg campaign and dispatch them to the north. Even so, two of Early's brigades managed to invade southern Pennsylvania and, when the city council of Chambersburg refused to pay a ransom of $500,000, burned the town to the ground. To exact revenge for this arson and punish the Confederate sympathizers in the Shenandoah Valley who had supported Early, Grant ordered General Philip H. Sheridan to turn the region

into "a barren waste." During the fall Sheridan's troops conducted a scorched-earth campaign, destroying grain supplies, barns, farming implements, and gristmills.

This terrorism went beyond the military norms of the day, for most officers regarded civilians as noncombatants and feared that a punitive policy against them would erode military discipline. But Grant's decision to carry the war to Confederate civilians had changed the definition of conventional warfare.

The Election of 1864 and Sherman's March

As the siege at Petersburg dragged on, Lincoln's reelection hopes came to rest on General William Tecumseh Sherman in Georgia (see American Lives, "William Tecumseh Sherman: An Architect of Modern War," pp. 468–469). Following Grant's orders Sherman had gradually penetrated to within about 30 miles of Atlanta, a great railway hub that controlled the heart of the Confederacy. Although his army outnumbered that of General Joseph E. Johnston 90,000 to 60,000, he avoided a direct attack and slowly pried the Confederates out of one defensive position after another (see Map 14.6). Finally, on June 27, at Kennesaw Mountain, Sherman engaged Johnston in a set battle but took 3,000 casualties while inflicting only about 600. Nonetheless, the Union general pressed on and by late July had laid siege to Atlanta, which was defended by Confederate troops under General John B. Hood. The next month brought little gain; like Grant, Sherman seemed to be bogged down in a hopeless campaign.

The Rise of the Peace Democrats. Meanwhile, the presidential campaign of 1864 was well under way. In June the national convention of the Republican Party endorsed Lincoln's war measures, demanded the unconditional surrender of the Confederacy, and called for a constitutional amendment to abolish slavery. To attract Democratic support, the Republicans temporarily renamed themselves the National Unionists and, as their candidate for vice-president, chose Andrew Johnson of Tennessee, a Democrat who had remained loyal to the Union. Despite these political maneuvers, public support for the Republicans continued to decline over the summer. By August, some party leaders wanted to call a new convention and drop Lincoln from the ticket. To end dissent within the party and rally support among northern voters, the Republican National Committee urged Lincoln to renounce emancipation as a war aim and offer peace to the Confederacy, requiring only an acknowledgment of "the supremacy of the constitution." While admitting that he would probably be beaten, "and unless some great change takes place badly beaten," Lincoln refused to abandon emancipation.

William Tecumseh Sherman: An Architect of Modern War

──────★──────

THE CIVIL WAR rescued William Tecumseh Sherman (1820–1891) from a life of disappointment and failure, and it gave him the opportunity to use his talents as a ruthless soldier and strategist. By the end of the war Sherman emerged as a major force in the Union victory and an important architect of modern warfare.

Disappointment had come early in Sherman's life. He was born into a socially prominent clan in Connecticut, but his immediate family fell on hard times when his parents moved to Lancaster, Ohio. His father's law practice did not prosper there, and his early death in 1829 shattered the family. Able to support only two of her eleven children, Sherman's mother put out the rest to friends and relatives. The sixth child, Tecumseh (named after the great Indian chief), was one of the more fortunate. At the age of nine he went to live with Thomas Ewing, a close family friend and a wealthy Lancaster lawyer.

Life with the Ewings brought many privileges but not much pleasure. His foster mother insisted that Tecumseh be baptized into her Catholic faith and take a Christian name (William). Sherman never adjusted to his new life, always carrying with him a sense of embarrassment over his father's financial failure and his family's inability to provide him with a home. In 1836 he gladly left Ohio to enter the United States Military Academy at West Point, where Ewing, who had been elected to the U.S. Senate in 1831, had found a place for him.

Sherman adopted the army as his real family, finding in the corps of professional officers the sense of identity, order, and belonging that he had missed as a child. After his graduation in 1840, the young officer used assignments in Florida, Alabama, South Carolina, and Georgia to travel widely and satisfy his curiosity about American life and geography. However, the Ewings had grandiose plans for their foster son, approving his marriage to their daughter Ellen and encouraging the young officer to enter the world of business. Sherman refused to leave the army, hoping that service in the Mexican War would allow him to rise in the ranks. But by the time he took up his assignment in California in 1847 there was little to do except paperwork. Six years later, depressed by his failure to advance, Sherman finally resigned his commission.

He was no more successful as a businessman than as a soldier. Unstable financial times ruined Sherman's budding career as head of the San Francisco and New York branches of a St. Louis bank, and he was forced to accept a junior partnership in a business run by two of his foster brothers. Unwilling to remain a dependent of the Ewings, in 1860 Sherman rejoined the army as superintendent of the brand-new Louisiana Military Seminary.

Sherman's earlier assignments in the South had made him sympathetic to the planter class and its institutions. In particular, he believed that slavery was necessary to maintain the stability of southern social order. However, Sherman remained a staunch Unionist. As a Whig in politics and a soldier by profession, he was convinced that a strong and purposeful national government was the key to American prosperity and greatness. In 1861 there was no question on which side William Tecumseh Sherman would stand. When Louisiana troops seized the U.S. arsenal at Baton Rouge in January 1861 and deposited captured weapons at his academy, Sherman resigned his position. Secession meant "anarchy," he told his southern friends, and had to be crushed. "There can be no peaceable secession," he continued. "If war comes, as I fear it surely will, I must fight your people whom I best love."

Sherman understood how costly and bloody the war would be, and he doubted that Abraham Lincoln and his administration would pay the price. But his family was firmly committed to the war effort, and they carried him along. Urged on by Senator Ewing and his younger brother John Sherman, who had just been elected as a Republican senator from Ohio, William Tecumseh became a colonel in a newly formed Union brigade.

Bull Run was Sherman's first taste of combat, and the rout of the Union army confirmed his longstanding doubts about democratic individualism. "The want of organization and subordination of our people

William Tecumseh Sherman
Sherman was a nervous man who smoked cigars and talked continuously. When he was seated, he crossed and uncrossed his legs incessantly, and a journalist described his fingers as constantly "twitching his red whiskers—his coat buttons—playing a tattoo on the table—or running through his hair." But he was a decisive general who commanded the loyalty of his troops. This photograph was taken at the end of the war in 1865.
Library of Congress.

is a more dangerous enemy than the armies of the South," he wrote. By October 1861 Sherman had risen to the rank of brigadier general and had command of all the Union forces in Kentucky, but he remained so darkly pessimistic about Union prospects that Lincoln and his military staff relieved him of his command.

But Sherman had important allies in the military and the strong support of his politically influential family. In February 1862 Sherman was back in Kentucky, serving under Ulysses S. Grant, who provided just the sense of direction and confidence that Sherman needed. Grant agreed with Sherman's

emphasis on strict military discipline and on the swift and decisive deployment of forces. Under Grant's leadership, Sherman enjoyed a string of successes. He distinguished himself at Shiloh, winning a promotion to major general. As military governor of Memphis he pacified a strategic sector along the Mississippi River and then served under Grant in the successful campaign against the Confederate stronghold at Vicksburg.

Now experienced and increasingly self-confident, Sherman began to develop his innovative military ideas. Assuming command of a Union army in Tennessee, he began to wage war against pro-southern civilians, especially those who assisted anti-Union guerrillas. "When one nation is at war with another, all the people of one are enemies of the other," he declared. When guerrillas fired on a boat with Unionist passengers and goods near Randolph, Tennessee, Sherman sent a regiment to level the town. "We are justified in treating all inhabitants as combatants," he asserted.

In March 1864 Sherman became commander of all military operations in the West and worked closely with Grant on a coordinated plan to destroy the Confederacy. Over the next year, Sherman's army dealt the secessionist cause a series of blows, taking and burning Atlanta, and devastating the countryside as he marched through Georgia to the sea and then swept across the Carolinas. These campaigns demonstrated both his tactical military genius and understanding of psychological warfare: he would destroy the Confederate army by laying waste to southern society.

After the Union victory Sherman received international acclaim. His former troops revered him, grateful American businessmen made him wealthy, and world leaders honored him. Unlike Grant and other Union generals who pursued political careers, Sherman maintained his identity as a military man, leading a war against the Great Plains Indians and serving as commanding general of the army from 1869 until his retirement in 1883. His longstanding contempt for democratic politics prompted Sherman to rebuff all overtures from Democratic and Republican leaders who wanted to exploit his prestige. Asked to run for the presidency in 1883, Sherman replied with the oft-quoted words: "If nominated, I will not accept; if elected, I will not serve." He prized order and discipline too much to join the anarchic and increasingly corrupt world of American politics.

Atlanta in Ruins
Not all of the destruction in Atlanta came at the hands of Sherman's forces; as the Confederate army retreated from Atlanta, it blew up manufacturing facilities and munitions factories to keep them out of Union hands. The wreckage seen in this photograph is of a factory that Hood's retreating troops blew up. Union troops destroyed the remaining industries, including the roundhouse and car repair sheds of the Georgia Central Railroad (on the right). The devastation of Atlanta and southern Georgia during Sherman's "march to the sea" dealt a severe blow to Confederate morale.
National Archives.

Increasingly hopeful of victory, the Democrats' national convention met in late August and nominated General George B. McClellan for president. Agreeing with McClellan, who had long opposed emancipation, the delegates rejected freedom for blacks and condemned Lincoln's uncompromising repression of domestic dissent. But the Democrats split into two camps over the issue of continuing the war. By threatening to bolt from the convention, the "Peace Democrats" forced through a platform calling for "a cessation of hostilities" and a "convention of the states" to restore peace "on the basis of the Federal Union." Although personally a "War Democrat" who wanted to suppress the rebellion by force, McClellan promised that as president he would seek an immediate armistice and a peace convention.

Confederate leaders cheered the decline of Radical Republicanism and the rise of the Peace Democrats. Rejoicing in "the first ray of real light I have seen since the war began," Confederate vice-president Alexander Stephens declared that if Atlanta and Richmond held out, Lincoln would go down to defeat. Once the Peace Democrats ended hostilities, Stephens believed, eventual independence of the Confederacy would be assured.

The Fall of Atlanta and Lincoln's Victory. Then, on September 2, Atlanta fell to Sherman. In a stunning move, the Union general pulled his troops from the trenches to the north of the city and swept around to the south, cutting its road and rail links to the rest of the Confederacy. Fearing that Sherman would be able to trap and destroy his army, Hood abandoned the city. "Atlanta is ours, and fairly won," Sherman telegraphed Lincoln, sparking 100-gun salutes and wild Republican celebrations in northern cities.

A deep pessimism settled over the Confederacy. In her diary Mary Chesnut, a slaveowning plantation mistress (see Chapter 13, American Voices, p. 427), confessed that she "felt as if all were dead within me, forever" and for the first time despaired of the possibility of a Confederate victory: "We are going to be wiped off the earth." Acknowledging the dramatic change in the military situation, McClellan repudiated the Democratic peace platform and dissident Republicans abandoned all efforts to dump Lincoln. Instead, the Republican Party went on the offensive, charging that McClellan was still a peace candidate and that his Peace Democrat supporters, whom they

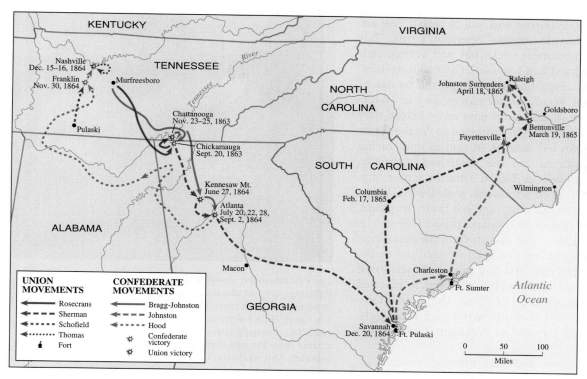

MAP 14.6
Sherman's March through the Confederacy, 1864–1865
The Union victory in November 1863 at Chattanooga, Tennessee (on that state's border with Georgia), was almost as critical as those in July at Gettysburg and Vicksburg. Having already split the Confederacy along the Mississippi, the Union was now in position to divide it again by driving through Georgia to the sea. After capturing Atlanta in September 1864, Sherman relied on other Union armies to repulse General John B. Hood's invasion of Tennessee, and swept to the Atlantic.

called *Copperheads* (after a poisonous snake), were hatching treasonous plots in the border states.

Sherman's success in Georgia gave Lincoln a clear-cut victory in the November elections. The president captured 212 of 233 electoral votes, winning 55 percent of the popular vote in the free and border states and carrying every state except Delaware, Kentucky, and New Jersey. Republicans now dominated Congress, winning 145 of the 185 seats in the House of Representatives and increasing their Senate majority to 42 of 52 seats. Many Republican victories resulted from the support of Union troops, three-quarters of whom voted for Lincoln. Many soldiers—and many Republican politicians—wanted the war to continue until the Confederacy met every Union demand, including emancipation.

Already the pace of legal emancipation had accelerated. In 1864 Maryland and Missouri amended their constitutions to free their slaves, and the three Union-occupied states of Tennessee, Arkansas, and Louisiana followed suit. But abolitionists worried that the Emancipation Proclamation, which was based on the president's wartime powers, would lose its force at the end

of the war and that the southern states would reestablish slavery. Urged on by Lincoln, the Republican-dominated Congress took the final step toward full legal emancipation. On January 31, 1865, it approved the Thirteenth Amendment, which prohibited slavery throughout the United States. Now slavery was nearly dead.

Sherman's Total War. And so was the Confederacy. After capturing Atlanta, Sherman did not follow the retreating Confederate army into Alabama and Tennessee and decided instead on a bold strategy. Rather than spread his troops dangerously thin by protecting supply lines to the rear, he would simply "cut a swath through to the sea," living off the land. To persuade Lincoln and Grant to approve this unconventional plan, Sherman pointed out that such a march would devastate Georgia and score a major psychological victory. It would be "a demonstration to the world, foreign and domestic, that we have a power [Jefferson] Davis cannot resist" (Map 14.6).

Sherman carried out the concept of total war that he and Sheridan had pioneered: destruction of the enemy's economic resources and will to resist. "We are not only fighting hostile armies," Sherman wrote, "but a hostile people, and must make old and young, rich and poor, feel the hard hand of war." The Union general admitted that his army "cannot change the hearts of those people of the South but we can make war so terrible . . . that generations would pass away before they would again appeal to it." He promised to "make Georgia howl!" Sherman left Atlanta in flames and during his 300-mile march to the sea destroyed railroads, property, and supplies. A Union veteran wrote that "[we] destroyed all we could not eat, stole their niggers, burned their cotton & gins, spilled their sorghum, burned & twisted their R.Roads and raised Hell generally." Letters from their families in Georgia describing the havoc so demoralized Confederate soldiers at the front that many deserted and fled home to their loved ones. Others refused to fight. When Sherman reached Savannah, Georgia, in mid-December, the 10,000 Confederate defenders left without putting up a struggle. Sherman presented the city to President Lincoln as a Christmas gift.

In February 1865 Sherman invaded South Carolina. He planned to link up with Grant at Petersburg in Virginia and along the way punish the state where secession had begun. "The truth is," Sherman wrote, "the whole army is burning with an insatiable desire to wreak vengeance upon South Carolina." His troops cut a comparatively narrow swath across the state but ravaged the countryside even more thoroughly than they had in Georgia. On February 17 his troops captured South Carolina's capital, Columbia, and burned the business district, most churches, and the wealthiest residential neighborhoods. "This disappointment," lamented Jefferson Davis, "to me is extremely bitter." By March Sherman had reached North Carolina and was on the verge of linking up with Grant and crushing Lee's army.

The Confederate Collapse. Sherman's march exposed an internal Confederate weakness: rising class resentment on the part of poor whites. For decades wealthy slaveowners had forced yeomen into less fertile regions by buying up the best land, and had used their power in the state legislatures to tax their slaves at low rates while imposing substantial levies on the marginal lands of backcountry farmers. During the war, the planter elite had imposed new burdens on white yeomen, conscripting them for military service while using the "twenty-Negro" exemption to keep some of their sons and overseers on the plantation. In late 1864 these undercurrents of discontent rose to the surface. Resentful of the planter elite and fearing that the Confederacy was doomed, many ordinary southern men actively resisted conscription. Equally important, more than 100,000

Lee's Surrender, April 9, 1865
Paintings are not always accurate, as this rather fanciful depiction of Lee's surrender to Grant in the town of Appomattox Court House demonstrates. The surrender actually took place in a farmer's parlor that was much more modestly furnished than the one depicted here (note the fine vases on the mantle). And while the Confederate general was in fact splendidly attired in his best uniform, Grant wore his unpressed combat jacket and muddy trousers and boots.
Appomattox Court House National Historic Park.

Confederate soldiers deserted their units. Some deserters linked up with draft evaders to form guerrilla forces that ruled backcountry areas. To add to the South's troubles, societies of Unionists formed militias in the Appalachian Mountains, the hill country of Alabama, the Ozarks of Arkansas, parts of Texas, and other areas where there were few slaves. These Unionists aided northern troops and sometimes joined the Union army when it marched nearby.

By early 1865 the Confederacy was experiencing such a severe manpower crisis that its leaders debated an extreme measure: arming its own slaves. "If slaves will make good soldiers," Howell Cobb of Georgia pointed out, "our whole theory of slavery is wrong." Urged on by Lee, the Confederate Congress disregarded such theoretical arguments. It voted to enlist black soldiers, and President Davis issued an executive order granting freedom to all blacks who would serve in the Confederate army. But the military struggle ended too soon to reveal whether any slaves would have fought for the Confederacy.

The final act of the war took place in Virginia. In April 1865 Grant finally forced Lee into a showdown by gaining control of the crucial railroad junction at Petersburg, thus cutting off supplies to his army in Richmond. Lee abandoned the defense of the city and

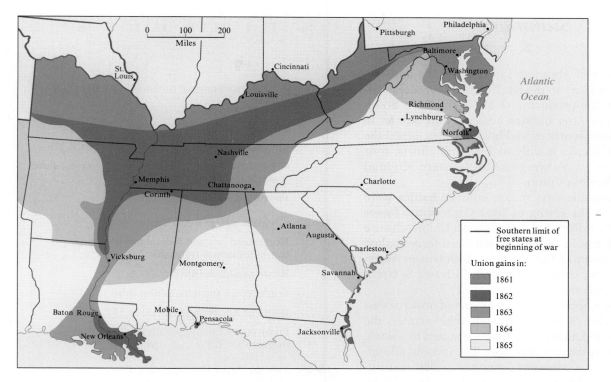

MAP 14.7
The Conquest of the South, 1861–1865
It took four years for the Union army to occupy the territory of the Confederacy, much of
which remained under southern control until the last year of the war. Most of the Union's
victories came on the western front, where control of strategic lines of communication
allowed the Union army to mount large-scale attacks against Confederate armies.

moved westward, hoping to join up with Confederate
forces in North Carolina (see Map 14.5). While Lincoln
visited the ruins of the Confederate capital, mobbed
by joyful former slaves, Grant cut off Lee's escape
route. On April 9, almost precisely four years after the
attack on Fort Sumter, Lee surrendered to Grant at the
town of Appomattox Court House, Virginia. In accepting the surrender of the impeccably dressed Confederate general, Grant set a tone of egalitarianism and
generosity, wearing an unpressed jacket and muddy
trousers and allowing Lee's men to take their horses
home for spring planting. Afterward, Grant's soldiers—grateful that the long conflict was nearly
over—willingly shared their ample rations with the
hungry Confederates.

Apart from this ceremony, there was no formal conclusion to the hostilities: the Confederate army and
government simply dissolved (Map 14.7). Nine days
after the agreement at Appomattox, General Johnston
signed an armistice with Sherman near Durham, North
Carolina, and soon surrendered his forces. By May 26
all the other Confederate generals had also ordered
their men to lay down their arms. After fleeing from
Richmond, hoping that the South would continue to
resist, Jefferson Davis was captured by Union cavalry in
Georgia.

The armies of the Union had destroyed the Confederacy and much of the South's economy. Its factories,
warehouses, and railroads were in ruins, as were many
of its farms and some of its most important cities.
Almost 260,000 Confederate soldiers—nearly one in
three of those who served—had paid for secession with
their lives. Most significant, the Union had been preserved and slavery destroyed. The cost of this victory
was enormous in terms of money, wasted resources,
and lives; over 360,000 Union soldiers were dead, and
hundreds of thousands were maimed and crippled.

The hard and bitter war was over, and a reunited
nation turned to the tasks of peace. Freed slaves faced
the question of what freedom would bring, while their
former masters tried to salvage what they could from
defeat. People in all parts of the North pondered the
meaning of their victory, at once so complete and so
costly. Would the "terrible, swift sword" of abolitionist
John Brown and his God, celebrated by Unionist Julia
Ward Howe in the "Battle Hymn of the Republic," be
sheathed in reconciliation or loosed again in a hard and
bitter peace?

Summary

★

With the victory of Abraham Lincoln and the antislavery Republican Party in the election of 1860, secessionists led the cotton-producing states of the Deep South out of the Union. After fighting began at Fort Sumter in April 1861, other southern and border states joined the rebellion, but thanks mainly to Lincoln's efforts, four border states and a portion of a fifth (western Virginia) remained within the Union.

In the East, the first major military battles were inconclusive. In the spring of 1862 Confederate forces commanded by Robert E. Lee repulsed a Union advance on Richmond, and in September northern forces halted Lee's first invasion of the North at Antietam in Maryland. In the West, Union forces under Ulysses S. Grant scored significant victories.

The conflict became a total war, one of unsurpassed cost in lives and resources. To staff their armies, the Union and Confederate governments resorted to a draft, which sparked resistance and riots. The Lincoln administration pursued a coherent economic policy, instituting Henry Clay's American System. It also created an efficient system of taxation and borrowing to finance the war, whereas Jefferson Davis's Confederate government had to pay its troops and suppliers by printing paper money, which produced a runaway inflation.

The turning point of the war came in 1863, which began with Lincoln's call for emancipation as a war aim. Tens of thousands of African American slaves fled behind Union lines, and many of those eventually enlisted in the northern army. In July 1863 Grant's capture of Vicksburg gave the Union control of the Mississippi and split the Confederacy. Simultaneously, George Meade's victory over Lee at Gettysburg ended the Confederate hope for a military victory.

The war turned into a stalemate, threatening Lincoln's bid for reelection and raising the prospect of a negotiated peace that would give independence to the Confederacy. Then, in September 1864, Union forces under William Tecumseh Sherman captured the key city of Atlanta, Georgia, giving military momentum to the North and ensuring Lincoln's reelection. Sherman's devastating "march to the sea" undermined Confederate morale, and Grant's capture of Petersburg in early 1865 led to the surrender of Lee's army in April and the rest of the Confederate forces in May.

The Union victory ended the secessionist rebellion and ensured the triumph of nationalist constitutional principles. The Republicans enacted and ratified the Thirteenth Amendment, which ended slavery and ensured that the South would have a new social order. However, the extent of African American freedom remained to be determined.

T I M E L I N E

1861   Confederate States of America formed (February 4)

Abraham Lincoln inaugurated (March 4)

Confederates fire on Fort Sumter (April 12)

Virginia convention votes to secede (April 17)

General Benjamin Butler declares runaway slaves "contraband of war" (May)

First Battle of Bull Run (July 21)

1862   Congress passes Legal Tender Act

Homestead Act and federal aid to transcontinental railroads

Battle of Shiloh (April 6–7)

Confederacy introduces first draft

Battle of Antietam (September 17)

Preliminary Emancipation Proclamation (September 22)

1863   Lincoln issues Emancipation Proclamation (January 1)

Enrollment Act begins draft in North; riots in New York City (July)

Battles of Gettysburg and Vicksburg (July)

1864   Ulysses S. Grant advances on Richmond; seige of Petersburg

Atlanta falls to William T. Sherman (September 2)

Lincoln reelected; Sherman marches through Georgia

1865   Robert E. Lee surrenders (April 9)

Passage and ratification of Thirteenth Amendment

Suggested Readings

──────★──────

The best up-to-date, comprehensive one-volume surveys of the Civil War are James M. McPherson, *Battle Cry of Freedom: The Civil War Era* (1988) and *Ordeal by Fire: The Civil War and Reconstruction* (1993). An excellent brief survey is Charles P. Roland, *An American Iliad: The Story of the Civil War* (1991). For a compelling older survey, see Shelby Foote, *The Civil War: A Narrative*, 3 vols. (1958–1974).

Secession and Military Stalemate, 1861–1862

Classic studies of the secession crisis include Richard N. Current, *Lincoln and the First Shot* (1963); David M. Potter, *Lincoln and His Party in the Secession Crisis, 1860–61* (1950); and Kenneth M. Stampp, *And the War Came: The North and the Secession Crisis, 1860–61* (1950). Histories of the secession of the Deep South include William L. Barney, *The Secessionist Impulse: Alabama and Mississippi in 1860* (1974), and Michael P. Johnson, *Toward a Patriarchal Republic: The Secession of Georgia* (1977). On the Upper South, see Daniel Crofts, *Reluctant Confederates: Upper South Unionists in the Secession Crisis* (1989).

Toward Total War

To study northern society and politics during the war, consult Iver Bernstein, *The New York City Draft Riots* (1990); Gabor S. Boritt, ed., *Lincoln the War President: The Gettysburg Lectures* (1992); George M. Fredrickson, *The Inner Civil War: Northern Intellectuals and the Crisis of Union* (2nd ed., 1993); J. Matthew Gallman, *The North Fights the Civil War: The Home Front* (1994); Mary E. Massey, *Bonnet Brigades: American Women and the Civil War* (1966); Mark E. Neely Jr., *The Fate of Liberty: Abraham Lincoln and Civil Liberties* (1991); Phillip S. Paludan, *The Presidency of Abraham Lincoln* (1994); Susan M. Reverby, *Ordered to Care: The Dilemma of American Nursing, 1850–1945* (1987); Joel Silbey, *A Respectable Minority: The Democratic Party in the Civil War Era* (1977); Hans Trefousse, *The Radical Republicans* (1969); and Garry Wills, *Lincoln at Gettysburg* (1992). Important biographies of Union leaders include Michael Fellman, *Citizen Sherman: A Life of William Tecumseh Sherman* (1995); William McFeely, *Grant: A Biography* (1981); Stephen B. Oates, *With Malice toward None: A Life of Abraham Lincoln* (1977); Stephen W. Sears, *George B. McClellan: The Young Napoleon* (1988); and the Abraham Lincoln studies cited in Chapter 13.

Among the best histories of the Confederacy are George C. Rable, *The Confederate Republic: A Revolution against Politics* (1994), and Emory M. Thomas, *The Confederate Nation: 1861–1865* (1979). Important biographies of leading Confederates include William C. Davis, *Jefferson Davis, the Man and His Hour: A Biography* (1991), and Thomas E. Schott, *Alexander H. Stephens of Georgia: A Biography* (1988). Studies of the Confederacy include Paul Escott, *After Secession: Jefferson Davis and the Failure of Southern Nationalism* (1978); Drew Gilpin Faust, *The Creation of Confederate Nationalism: Ideology and Identity in the Civil War* (1988); and Philip S. Paludan, *Victims: A True History of the Civil War* (1981).

The Turning Point: 1863

Studies of wartime emancipation include Herman Belz, *A New Birth of Freedom: The Republican Party and Freedmen's Rights, 1861–1866* (1976); John Hope Franklin, *The Emancipation Proclamation* (1963); Louis S. Gerteis, *From Contraband to Freedom: Federal Policy toward Southern Blacks, 1861–1865* (1973); and James M. McPherson, *The Struggle for Equality: Abolitionists and the Negro in the Civil War and Reconstruction* (1964). The best scholarship on the lives of slaves during the war is found in Ira Berlin et al., eds., *Freedom: A Documentary History of Emancipation, 1861–1867*, series 1, vol. 1: *The Destruction of Slavery* (1985), and series 1, vol. 3: *The Wartime Genesis of Free Labor: The Lower South* (1990).

The Union Victorious, 1864–1865

The most useful introduction to the military aspects of the war is T. Harry Williams, *The History of American Wars* (1981). On the experiences of Civil War soldiers, consult Albert Castel, *Decision in the West: The Atlanta Campaign* (1992); Gerald F. Linderman, *Embattled Courage: The Experience of Combat in the American Civil War* (1987); James M. McPherson, *What They Fought For, 1861–1865* (1994); and Reid Mitchell, *Civil War Soldiers* (1988) and *The Vacant Chair: The Northern Soldier Leaves Home* (1993). On the participation of African Americans in the war, read Ira Berlin et al., *Freedom: A Documentary History of Emancipation, 1861–1867*, series 2: *The Black Military Experience* (1982), and Joseph T. Glatthaar, *Forged in Battle: The Civil War Alliance of Black Soldiers and White Officers* (1990). For Confederate military tactics, refer to Grady McWhiney and Perry D. Jamieson, *Attack and Die: Civil War Military Tactics and the Southern Heritage* (1982), and Steven E. Woodworth, *Jefferson Davis and His Generals: The Failure of Confederate Command in the West* (1990). An innovative exploration of the dynamics of violence is found in Charles Royster, *The Destructive War: William Tecumseh Sherman, Stonewall Jackson, and the Americans* (1991). The most graphic account of a single battle is Stephen W. Sears, *Landscape Turned Red: The Battle of Antietam* (1983). On the Civil War in the Far West, consult Alvin M. Josephy Jr., *The Civil War in the American West* (1991). For insightful analyses of the war's outcome, see Richard E. Beringer et al., *Why the South Lost the Civil War* (1986); Herman Hattaway and Archer Jones, *How the North Won: A Military History of the Civil War* (1983); and Archer Jones, *Civil War Command and Strategy: The Process of Victory and Defeat* (1992).

Absorbing personal accounts of the war years include C. Vann Woodward, ed., *Mary Chesnut's Civil War* (1981); David Donald, ed., *Inside Lincoln's Cabinet: The Civil War Diaries of Salmon P. Chase* (1959); T. W. Higginson, *Army Life in a Black Regiment* (1867); and W. T. Sherman, *Memoirs* (1990).

Reconstruction,
1865–1877

I<small>N HIS SECOND</small> inaugural address, President Lincoln spoke of the need to "bind up the nation's wounds." No one knew better than Lincoln how daunting a task reconstruction of the Union would be. Foremost were the terms for restoring to the Union the states that had rebelled. But America's civil war had opened more fundamental questions. Slavery was finished. That much was certain. But what system of agricultural labor should replace plantation slavery? What rights should the freedmen be accorded beyond emancipation itself? How far should the federal government go to settle these questions? And who should decide? The president? Or Congress?

While the war was still on, the North began to grope for answers. Relying on his wartime powers, President Lincoln in December 1863 offered the secessionist states a chance to return to the Union on easy terms: the organization of loyal governments by 10 percent of the number of voters in 1860 who accepted Lincoln's general amnesty offer and took an oath of allegiance to the Union. Although it reflected Lincoln's conciliatory bent, his Ten Percent Plan, which only states under military occupation (Louisiana, Arkansas, and Tennessee) accepted, was really aimed at subverting the southern war effort. What it also did, however, was reveal the rocky road that lay ahead for Reconstruction. Thus, in Louisiana, sugar planters used the restored government to regain control over the freed slaves, employing curfew laws to restrict their movements and vagrancy regulations to force them back to work. But

Chloe and Sam, 1882 (detail)
After the Civil War the country went through the wrenching peacemaking process known as Reconstruction. The struggle between the victorious North and the vanquished South was fought out on a political landscape, but Thomas Hovenden's warmhearted painting reminds us of the deeper meaning of Reconstruction: that Chloe and Sam, after lives spent in slavery, might end their days in the dignity of freedom.
Thomas Colville Fine Art.

the Louisiana freedmen fought right back. Led by the free-black community of New Orleans, they began to agitate for political rights. No less than their former masters, the former slaves intended to be actors in the savage drama of Reconstruction.

With Louisiana very much in mind, Republicans in Congress put forth a stricter substitute for Lincoln's Ten Percent Plan. The initiative came from the Radical wing of the party—those seeking a stern peace and full rights for the freedmen—but had broad support among more moderate Republicans. The Wade-Davis bill, passed on July 2, 1864, laid down, as conditions for the restoration of the rebellious states to the Union, the following: (1) an oath of allegiance by a majority of each state's adult white men, (2) new state governments formed and operated only by those who had never carried arms against the Union, and (3) permanent loss of voting rights by Confederate civil and military leaders. The Wade-Davis bill served notice that the congressional Republicans were not about to hand reconstruction policy over to the president.

Lincoln was not perturbed. Rather than openly challenging Congress, he executed a "pocket" veto of the Wade-Davis bill by not signing it before Congress adjourned. At the same time he initiated informal talks with congressional leaders aimed at finding common ground. Lincoln sensed that he had the upper hand. He could exploit the divisions among his fellow Republicans. And after four years of war, Americans were accustomed to strong executive leadership. The last speech Lincoln ever delivered, on April 11, 1865—two days after General Robert E. Lee's surrender at Appomattox—demonstrated his cautious realism. Reconstruction, Lincoln pleaded, had to be regarded as a practical, not a theoretical, problem. It could be solved only if Republicans remained united (even if that meant compromise) and only if the defeated South gave its consent (even if that meant forgiveness). What the speech showed, above all, was Lincoln's sense of the fluidity of events, of policy toward the South as an evolving, not a fixed, position.

What course Reconstruction might have taken had Lincoln lived is one of the unanswerable questions of American history. Three days after his speech, Lincoln was shot in the head at Ford's Theater in Washington by an unstable actor named John Wilkes Booth. (Ironically, Lincoln might have been spared if the war had dragged on longer, for Booth and his Confederate associates had originally plotted to kidnap the president to force a negotiated settlement.) Without regaining consciousness, Lincoln died on April 15. In one stroke John Wilkes Booth had sent Lincoln to martyrdom, hardened many northerners against the South, and handed the presidency to a man utterly lacking in Lincoln's moral sense and political judgment, Vice-President Andrew Johnson.

Presidential Reconstruction

At the end of the Civil War, a crucial constitutional question remained in dispute—whether, by seceding, the Confederate states had legally left the Union. If so, they were now conquered territories, and the terms of their readmission demanded the gravest consideration by Congress. If not, if even in defeat they retained their constitutional status, the initiative for restoring them to the Union might appropriately be taken by the president. This was Andrew Johnson's view, and by an accident of timing he was free to act on it: the Thirty-ninth Congress elected in November 1864 was not scheduled to convene until December 1865.

Johnson's Initiative

Andrew Johnson was a self-made man from the hills of eastern Tennessee. A Jacksonian Democrat, he saw himself as the champion of the common man. He hated what he called the "bloated, corrupt aristocracy" of the Northeast, and he was just as disdainful of the wealthy southern planters, whom he blamed for the poverty of the South's small farmers. But it was the poor *whites* that he championed; Johnson, himself a former slaveowner, had little sympathy for the slaves and was, in fact, implacably racist. His political career had taken him to the U.S. Senate, where he remained when the war broke out, loyal to the Union. After federal forces captured Nashville, Johnson became Tennessee's military governor. The Republicans nominated him for vice-president in 1864 in an effort to promote wartime political unity and to court the support of southern Unionists.

In May 1865, just a month after Lincoln's death, Johnson launched his own reconstruction plan. He offered amnesty to all southerners who took an oath of allegiance to the Union except for high-ranking Confederate officials and wealthy planters, whom Johnson held responsible for secession. Such persons could be pardoned only by presidential order. He appointed provisional governors for the southern states and laid down as conditions for their restoration only that they revoke their ordinances of secession, repudiate their Confederate debts, and ratify the Thirteenth Amendment, which abolished slavery. Within months all the former Confederate states had met Johnson's requirements and had functioning, elected governments.

At first Republicans responded favorably. The moderates among them were sympathetic to Johnson's argument that it was up to the states, not the federal government, to settle questions of the ballot and civil rights for the freedmen. Even the Radicals were optimistic. They liked the stern treatment of Confederate

Andrew Johnson
The president was not an easy man. This photograph of Andrew Johnson (1808–1875) conveys some of the prickly qualities that contributed so centrally to his failure to reach an agreement with Republicans on a moderate reconstruction program.
Library of Congress.

crats, and disgruntled conservative Republicans. To retain the appearance of nonpartisanship, Johnson called his movement "National Union." The Civil War had left in disgrace the Democratic Party because it represented secession in the South and disloyalty in the North. Now Democrats realized that Johnson's gambit offered an avenue by which their discredited party could be restored to respectability. As the president warmed to Democratic applause, he granted more and more pardons to influential southerners—an average of a hundred a day in September 1865.

His perceived indulgence of their efforts to restore white supremacy emboldened the ex-Confederates. They packed the delegations to the new Congress with old comrades—nine members of the Confederate Congress, seven former officials of Confederate state governments, four generals and four colonels, and even the vice-president of the Confederacy, Alexander Stephens. For Republicans, this was the last straw.

Republican Response. Under the Constitution, Congress is "the judge of the elections, returns and qualifications of its own members" (Article 1, section 5). On this basis, the Republican majorities in both houses refused to admit the southern delegations when Congress convened in early December 1865, blocking Johnson's reconstruction program. Although relations with the president had frayed, the Republicans still assumed he would cooperate with them in formulating the new terms on which the South would be readmitted to Congress. To that end, a House-Senate committee—the Joint Committee on Reconstruction—was formed and began public hearings on conditions in the South.

In the meantime, the southern states backed away from the most flagrant of the Black Codes—those targeting one race—but in their place brought forth nonracial ordinances that were administered in the same way; they were applied to blacks, not to whites. Moreover, a wave of violence erupted across the South, intended to terrorize the freedmen into submission. In Tennessee, a Nashville paper reported that white gangs "are riding about whipping, maiming and killing all negroes who do not obey the orders of their former masters, just as if slavery existed." Listening to the vivid testimony of officials, observers, and victims, Republicans concluded that the South was trying to circumvent the Thirteenth Amendment. The only possible response was for the federal government to intervene.

Back in March 1865, the previous Congress had established the Bureau of Refugees, Freedmen and Abandoned Lands (known as the Freedmen's Bureau) to provide emergency aid to ex-slaves during the chaotic transition from war to peace. Now in early 1866, under the leadership of the moderate Republican senator Lyman Trumbull, Congress voted to extend the Freedmen's Bureau's life, gave it direct funding for the

leaders, and they hoped that the new southern governments would respond positively to Johnson's conciliatory approach and offer the vote at least to African Americans who were literate and owned property.

Nothing of the sort happened. The South lay in ruins (see Voices from Abroad, "David Macrae: The Devastated South," p. 480). But southerners had not lost their fierce attachment to the old order. The newly seated legislatures moved to restore slavery in all but name. They enacted laws—known as Black Codes—designed to drive the freed slaves back to the plantations and to deny them elementary civil rights. The new governments had mostly been formed by southern Unionists, but when it came to racist attitudes, not a lot distinguished these loyalists from the Confederates. The latter, moreover, soon filtered back into the corridors of power. It turned out that Johnson, despite his hard words against them, forgave the former Confederate leaders easily, as long as he got the satisfaction of making them submit to his personal authority.

Stung by Republican criticism, Johnson began to rethink his political options. If the Republican establishment turned against him, then he would build a new coalition of white southerners, northern Demo-

David Macrae
The Devastated South

——★——

In this excerpt from The Americans at Home *(1870), an account of his tour of the United States, the Scottish clergyman David Macrae describes the war-stricken South as he found it in 1867–1868.*

I was struck with a remark made by a Southern gentleman in answer to the assertion that Jefferson Davis [the president of the Confederacy] had culpably continued the war for six months after all hope had been abandoned.

"Sir," he said, "Mr. Davis knew the temper of the South as well as any man in it. He knew if there was to be anything worth calling peace, the South must win; or, if she couldn't win, she wanted to be whipped—well whipped—thoroughly whipped." . . .

The further south I went, the oftener these remarks came back upon me. Evidence was everywhere that the South had maintained the desperate conflict until she was utterly exhausted. . . . Almost every man I met at the South, especially in North Carolina, Georgia, and Virginia, seemed to have been in the army; and it was painful to find many who had returned were mutilated, maimed, or broken in health by exposure. When I remarked this to a young Confederate officer in North Carolina, and said I was glad to see that *he* had escaped unhurt, he said, "Wait till we get to the office, sir, and I will tell you more about that." When we got there, he pulled up one leg of his trousers, and showed me that he had an iron rod there to strengthen his limb, and enable him to walk without limping, half of his foot being off. He showed me on the other leg a deep scar made by a fragment of a shell; and these were two of but seven wounds which had left their marks upon his body. When he heard me speak of relics, he said, "Try to find a North Carolina gentleman without a Yankee mark on him." . . .

Nearly three years had passed when I travelled through the country, and yet we have seen what traces the war had left in such cities as Richmond, Petersburg, and Columbia. The same spectacle met me at Charleston. Churches and houses had been battered down by heavy shot and shell hurled into the city from Federal batteries at a distance of five miles. Even the valley of desolation made by a great fire in 1861, through the very heart of the city, remained unbuilt. There, after the lapse of seven years, stood the blackened ruins of streets and houses waiting for the coming of a better day. . . . Over the country districts the prostration was equally marked. Along the track of Sherman's army especially, the devastation was fearful—farms laid waste, fences burned, bridges destroyed, houses left in ruins, plantations in many cases turned into wilderness again.

The people had shared in the general wreck, and looked poverty-stricken, careworn, and dejected. Ladies who before the war had lived in affluence, with black servants round them to attend to their every wish, were boarding together in half-furnished houses, cooking their own food and washing their own linen, some of them, I was told, so utterly destitute that they did not know when they finished one meal where they were to find the next. . . . Men who had held commanding positions during the war had fallen out of sight and were filling humble situations—struggling, many of them, to earn a bare subsistence. . . . I remember dining with three cultured Southern gentlemen, one a general, the other, I think, a captain, and the third a lieutenant. They were all living together in a plain little wooden house, such as they would formerly have provided for their servants. Two of them were engaged in a railway office, the third was seeking a situation, frequently, in his vain search, passing the large blinded house where he had lived in luxurious ease before the war.

Source: Allan Nevins, ed., *America through British Eyes* (Gloucester, MA: Peter Smith, 1968), 345–347.

first time, and authorized its agents to investigate cases in which blacks were being denied the "civil rights belonging to white persons."

More extraordinary was Trumbull's proposal for a civil rights bill, declaring all persons born in the United States to be citizens and granting them—without regard to race—equal rights of contract, access to the courts, and protection of person and property. Trumbull's bill nullified all state laws depriving citizens of these rights, authorized U.S. attorneys to bring enforcement suits in the federal courts, and provided for fines and imprisonment for anyone, including public officials, found guilty of depriving a citizen of civil rights. In response to an unrepentant South, Republicans of the most moderate persuasion concluded that the federal government had to assume responsibility for securing the basic civil rights of the freedmen.

Acting on Freedom

While Congress debated, African Americans acted on their own idea of freedom. News of emancipation left them exultant and hopeful. Freedom meant many things—the reunion of separated families; the end of punishment by the lash; the ability to move around; and the opportunity to begin schools, form churches and social clubs, and, not least, engage in politics. Across the South blacks held mass meetings, paraded, and formed organizations. In the cities, where free blacks took the lead, Union Leagues and Equal Rights Leagues were formed to give the freedmen a political voice. With the encouragement of Freedmen's Bureau agents, state conventions also began to meet, passing resolutions demanding equality before the law and the right to vote—"an essential and inseparable element of self-government."

Struggling for the Land. First of all, however, came economic independence, which emancipated blacks believed was the basis for true freedom. During the Civil War they had acted on this assumption whenever Union armies drew near. During the final months of the war, when the Union directed its military operations against civilians, freedmen found greater opportunities to take control of land. Most visibly, General William T. Sherman

reserved vast tracts of coastal lands in Georgia and South Carolina—the Sea Islands and abandoned plantations within 30 miles of the coast—for liberated slaves, and settled them on 40-acre tracts. Sherman only wanted to relieve the burdens the refugees were placing on his army as it drove across the South. But freedmen took seriously the assurances of one of Sherman's generals "that they were to be put in possession of lands, upon which they might locate their families and work out for themselves a living and respectability."

As the war ended, resettlement became the responsibility of the Freedmen's Bureau, which was charged with feeding and clothing war refugees, distributing confiscated land to "loyal refugees and freedmen," and regulating labor contracts between freedmen and planters. The bureau also assisted the northern voluntary associations that were sending missionaries and teachers to work with former slaves.

Encouraged by the Freedmen's Bureau, blacks across the South occupied confiscated or abandoned land. Many families stayed on their old plantations, awaiting redistribution of the land to them after the war. One Georgia freedman offered to sell his expected share back to his former master. When the South Carolina planter Thomas Pinckney returned home, his freed slaves told him, "We ain't going nowhere. We are going to work right here on the land where we were born and what belongs to us."

Johnson's amnesty plan, entitling pardoned Confederates to recover property seized during the war, squelched these hopes. In October 1865, Johnson ordered General Oliver O. Howard, head of the Freedmen's Bureau, to tell Sea Island blacks that the land

Schoolhouse, Port Hudson, Louisiana
This was probably the first schoolhouse built for freedmen by Union forces. In front, African American soldiers from the Port Hudson "Corps d' Afrique" pose with their textbooks. It stood to reason that former slaves who had taken up arms should be first to receive the education so coveted by all freedmen.
Chicago Historical Society.

they occupied would have to be restored to the white owners. When Howard reluctantly obeyed, the dispossessed farmers protested: "Why do you take away our lands? You take them from us who have always been true, always true to the Government! You give them to our all-time enemies! That is not right!" (see American Voices, "A Plea for Land," p. 483).

In the Sea Islands and elsewhere, former slaves resisted these efforts. Often led by black veterans of the Union army, they fought pitched battles with plantation owners and bands of ex-Confederate soldiers. Landowners responded by attempting to disarm and intimidate the black veterans. One soldier wrote from Maryland: "The returned colard Solgers are in Many cases beten, and their guns taken from them, we darcent walk out of an evening. . . . They beat us badly and Sumtime Shoot us." In this warfare federal troops often backed the local whites, who generally prevailed in recapturing their former holdings.

Resisting Wage Labor. As returning planters prepared for a new growing season, a battle began to take shape over the labor system that would replace slavery. Convinced that blacks could not work without supervision, planters insisted on retaining the gang system of plantation labor, only now paying low wages instead of the food, clothing, and shelter their slaves had once received. In this endeavor, the planters generally had the backing of the Freedmen's Bureau. The main thing, its planners had said from the outset, was that the Union not encourage dependency "in the guise of guardianship." The ex-slave had to be "self-supporting," with no special privileges or burdens, but treated "as any other freeman." This was the message that the Bureau's agents carried into the devastated southern countryside. Rely upon your "own efforts and exertions," an agent told a crowd of freedmen in North Carolina, "make contracts with the planters," and "respect the rights of property."

This was advice given with little regard for the world in which those North Carolina freedmen lived. It was not only the unequal bargaining power between them and their former masters that they feared, or even that their former masters' real desire was to reenslave them through the coercive regulations of the Black Codes. In their eyes, the condition of wage labor was itself debasing. The rural South was not like the Yankee North, where working for wages had become the norm and qualified a man as independent. Selling one's labor to another—and in particular, selling one's labor to work another's land—implied not freedom but dependency. In the South, to be a "freeman"—a fully empowered citizen—meant heading a household, owning some property, carrying on one's own affairs.

So the issue of wage labor cut to the very core of the former slaves' struggle for freedom. Nothing had been more horrifying than the fact that as slaves, their

Wage Labor of Former Slaves
This photograph, taken in South Carolina shortly after the Civil War, shows former slaves leaving the cotton fields. Ex-slaves were organized into work crews probably not that different from earlier slave gangs, although they now worked for wages and their plug-hatted boss bears little resemblance to the slavedrivers of the past.
New-York Historical Society.

A Plea for Land

———————★———————

Following is a painfully written letter by the freed-men of Edisto Island off the coast of South Car-olina to President Andrew Johnson. In it they plead for a reversal of his order that the lands they now worked be returned to their former masters.

Edisto Island S.C. Oct. 28th, 1865.
To the President of these United States. We the freedmen Of Edisto Island South Carolina have learned From you through Major General O O Howard commissioner of the Freedman's Bureau, with deep sorrow and Painful hearts of the possibil-ity of government restoring These lands to the for-mer owners. We are well aware of the many perplexing and trying questions that burden Your mind. and do therefore pray to god (the preserver of all. and who has through our Late and beloved President [Lincoln] proclamation and the war made Us A free people) that he may guide you in making Your decision. . . . Here is where secession was born and Nurtured Here is where we have toiled nearly all Our lives as slaves and were treated like dumb Driven cattle. This is our home, we have made These lands what they are. . . . Shall not we who Are freedmen and have always been true to this Union have the same rights as enjoyed by Others? Have we broken any Law of these United States? have we for-feited our rights of property In Land?—If not then!

are not our rights as A free people and good citizens of these United States To be considered before the rights of those who were Found in rebellion against this good and just Government . . . And we who have been abused and oppressed For many long years But be subject To the will of these large Land own-ers. God forbid. Land monopoly is injurious to the advancement of the course of freedom, and if Government Does not make some provision by which we Freedmen can obtain A Homestead, we have Not bettered our condition.

. . . We the freedmen of this Island and the State of South Carolina—Do hereby petition to you as the President of these United States, that some provi-sions be made by which Every colored man can pur-chase land. and Hold as his own. We wish to have A home if It be but A few acres. without some provi-sion is Made our future is sad to look upon. . . .

We pray that God will direct your heart in Making such provision for us as freedmen which Will tend to unite these states together stronger Than ever before—May God bless you in the Administration of your duties as the President of these United States is the humble prayer Of us all.—

In behalf of the Freedmen

Henry Bram

Committee   Ishmael. Moultrie

yates. Sampson

———————————

Source: Eileen Boris and Nelson Lichtenstein, eds., *Major Problems in the History of American Workers: Documents and Essays* (Lexington, MA: D.C. Heath, 1990), 137–139.

---

persons had been the property of others. In a famous oration celebrating the anniversary of emancipation, the Rev. Henry M. Turner spoke bitterly of the time when his people had "no security for domestic happi-ness," when "our wives were sold and husbands bought, children were begotten and enslaved by their fathers," and "we therefore were polygamists by virtue of our condition." That was why formalizing marriage was so urgent a matter after emancipation and why, when hard-pressed planters demanded that freedwomen go back into the fields, they resisted so resolutely. If the ex-slaves were to be free as white folk, then their wives could not, any more than white wives, labor for others. "I seen on some plantations," one freedman recounted, "where the white men would . . . tell colored men that their wives and children could not live on their places unless they work in the fields. The colored men

[answered that] whenever they wanted their wives to work they would tell them themselves; and if he could not rule his own domestic affairs on that place he would leave it and go someplace else."

The reader will see the irony in this definition of freedom: it assumed the wife's subordinate role and designated her labor the husband's property. But if that was the price of freedom, freedwomen were prepared to pay it. Far better to take a chance with their own men than with their former masters.

Many freedpeople voted with their feet, abandon-ing their old plantations and seeking better lives and more freedom in the towns and cities of the South. Those who remained in the countryside refused to work the cotton fields under the hated gang labor sys-tem or negotiated tenaciously over the terms of their labor contracts. When they could, families developed their own garden plots, guaranteeing at least a minimum level of subsistence. What was freedom all about if not to have a bit more leisure time, to labor less intensely than they had as slaves, and to work for themselves and their families?

The efforts of former slaves to control their own lives challenged deeply entrenched white attitudes. "The destiny of the black race," asserted one Texan, could be summarized "in one sentence—subordination to the white race." Southern whites, a Freedmen's Bureau official observed, could not "conceive of the negro having any rights at all." And when freedmen resisted, white retribution was swift and often terrible. The toll of murdered and beaten blacks mounted into untold thousands. The governments established under Johnson's plan only put the stamp of legality on the pervasive efforts to enforce white supremacy. Blacks "would be *just as well* off with no law at all or no Government," concluded a Freedmen's Bureau agent, as with the justice they got under the restored white rule.

In this unequal struggle, blacks turned to Washington. "We stood by the government when it wanted help," a black Mississippian wrote to President Johnson. "Now . . . will it stand by us?"

Congress versus President

Andrew Johnson was not the man to ask. In February 1866 he vetoed the Freedmen's Bureau bill, declaring it unconstitutional because Congress lacked authority to provide a "system for the support of indigent people" and because the states most directly affected by its provisions were not yet represented in Congress. The bureau, said Johnson, was an "immense patronage," showering benefits on blacks never granted to "our own people." A month later, rebuffing angry critics of his Freedmen's Bureau veto and overruling his own cabinet, Johnson vetoed Trumbull's civil rights bill, again arguing that federal protection of black civil rights constituted "a stride toward centralization." Johnson's racism, hitherto muted, now blazed forth. In his view, granting blacks the privileges of citizenship was discriminatory, operating "in favor of the colored and against the white race" and threatening all manner of evil consequences, including racial mixing.

Surprised by Johnson's attack on the civil rights bill, the Republicans were galvanized into action. They failed to override Johnson's veto of the Freedmen's Bureau bill, but in early April they got the necessary two-thirds majorities in both Houses and enacted the Civil Rights Act of 1866. This was a truly historic event, the first time Congress had prevailed over a presidential veto on a major piece of legislation. The Republican resolve was reinforced by news of mounting violence in the South, culminating in three days of rioting in Memphis. Forty-six blacks and two whites were left dead, and hundreds of black homes, churches, and schools were looted and burned. In July an angry Congress renewed the Freedmen's Bureau over a second veto by Johnson.

The Fourteenth Amendment. Anxious to consolidate their gains against Johnson, Republicans moved to enshrine black civil rights in an amendment to the Constitution. The heart of the Fourteenth Amendment was Section 1, which declared that "all persons born or naturalized in the United States" were citizens. No state could abridge "the privileges or immunities of citizens of the United States," deprive "any person of life, liberty, or property, without due process of law," or deny anyone "the equal protection of the laws." These phrases were intentionally vague, but they established the constitutionality of the Civil Rights Act and, more important, the basis on which the courts and Congress could establish an enforceable standard of equality before the law in the states.

For the moment, however, the Fourteenth Amendment was most important for its impact on national politics. With the 1866 congressional elections approaching, Johnson somehow figured he had a winning issue in the Fourteenth Amendment. He urged the states not to ratify it. Months earlier Johnson had begun to maneuver politically against the Republicans, aiming to build a coalition of white southerners, northern Democrats, and conservative Republicans under the banner of National Union. Any hope of creating a new national party, however, was shattered by Johnson's intemperate behavior and by escalating violence in the South. In New Orleans, a white mob attacked the delegates to a black convention and, aided by the local police, murdered thirty-seven blacks. A dissension-ridden National Union convention in July ended inconclusively, and Johnson's campaign against the Fourteenth Amendment became, effectively, a campaign for the Democratic Party.

Republicans responded with a scurrilous attack on the Democrats, unveiling a practice that would become known as "waving the bloody shirt." The Democrats were traitors, charged Indiana governor Oliver Morton, and their party was "a common sewer and loathesome recepticle, into which is emptied every element of treason North and South, every element of inhumanity and barbarism which has dishonored this age." In late August, Johnson embarked on a disastrous "swing around the circle"—a railroad tour from Washington to Chicago and St. Louis and back. It was unprecedented for a president to campaign personally, and Johnson made matters worse by engaging in shouting matches with hecklers and insulting members of the hostile crowds.

The 1866 congressional elections inflicted a humiliating defeat on Johnson. The Republicans won a three-to-one majority in Congress, so that, to begin with, the Republicans considered themselves "masters of the situation," free to proceed "entirely regardless of [Johnson's] opinions or wishes." As a referendum on the Fourteenth Amendment, moreover, the election registered strong popular support for the civil rights of the freedmen. The Republican Party emerged with a new sense of unity—a unity coalescing not at the center but on the left, around the program of the Radical minority.

Radical Republicans. The Radicals represented the abolitionist strain within the Republican Party. Most of them hailed from New England or from the area of the upper Midwest settled by New Englanders. In the Senate they were led by Charles Sumner of Massachusetts; in the House, by Thaddeus Stevens from Pennsylvania. For them, Reconstruction was never primarily about restoring the Union but about remaking southern society. "The foundations of their institutions . . . must be broken up and relaid," declared Stevens, "or all our blood and treasure will have been spent in vain."

Only a handful went as far as Stevens in demanding that the plantations be treated as "forfeited estates of the enemy" and broken up into small farms for the former slaves. But there was agreement about the need to guarantee the freedmen's civil rights and to grant them the suffrage. In this endeavor Radicals had no qualms about expanding the powers of the national government. "The power of the great landed aristocracy in those regions, if unrestrained by power from without, would inevitably reassert itself," warned Congressman George Julian. Radicals were aggressively partisan. They regarded the Republican Party as the instrument of the Lord, and black votes as the means by which the party could dominate the South and bring about its regeneration.

At first, in the months after the Confederacy's surrender at Appomattox, few but the Radicals themselves imagined they had any chance of putting across so extreme a program. Black suffrage especially seemed beyond reach, since the northern states themselves (except in New England) denied blacks the vote at this time. And yet, as fury mounted against the intransigent South, Republicans became ever more radicalized until, in the wake of the smashing victory of 1866, they embraced the Radicals' vision of a reconstructed South.

Resistance in the South
This engraving, entitled *If He Is a Union Man or Freedman: Verdict, Hang the D--- Yankee and Nigger*, appeared in *Harper's Weekly* on March 23, 1857, just as the Reconstruction Act was being adopted. Thomas Nast's cartoon encapsulated the outrage at the South's murderous intransigence that led even moderate Republicans to support radical Reconstruction. Library of Congress.

under the protection of the laws." Remarkably, the South remained defiant even after the 1866 elections. Every state legislature (except, back in July, Tennessee) rejected the Fourteenth Amendment, mostly by virtual acclamation. It was as if they could not imagine that governments installed under presidential approval and fully functioning might be swept away. But that, in fact, is just what the Republicans intended to do.

Radical Reconstruction

————————★————————

Afterward, thoughtful southerners admitted that the South had brought radical Reconstruction on itself. "We had, in 1865, a white man's government in Alabama," remarked the man who had been Johnson's provisional governor, "but we lost it." The state's "great blunder" was not to "have at once taken the negro right

Congress Takes Command

The Reconstruction Act of 1867, enacted in March by the Republican Congress, organized the South as a conquered land, dividing it (with the exception of Tennessee) into five military districts (Map 15.1), each under the command of a Union general. The price for reentering the Union involved granting the vote to the freedmen and disfranchising the South's prewar leadership class. Each military commander was ordered to register all eligible adult men (black as well as white), supervise the

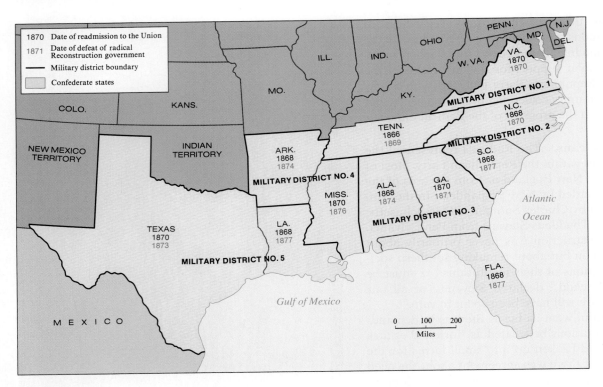

MAP 15.1

Reconstruction

The federal government organized the Confederate states into five military districts during radical Reconstruction. For each state the first date indicates when that state was readmitted to the Union; the second date shows when radical Republicans lost control of the state government. All the ex-Confederate states rejoined the Union from 1868 to 1870, but the periods of radical rule varied widely. Radicals lasted only a few months in Virginia; they held on until the end of Reconstruction in Louisiana, Florida, and South Carolina.

election of state conventions, and make certain that the new constitutions contained guarantees of black suffrage. Congress would readmit a state to the Union if its voters ratified the state constitution, if that document proved acceptable to Congress, and if the new state legislature approved the Fourteenth Amendment (thereby ensuring the needed ratification by three-fourths of the states). Johnson vetoed the Reconstruction Act, but Congress overrode the veto (Table 15.1).

The Tenure of Office Act. Republicans also attacked President Johnson's room for maneuver. The Tenure of Office Act, a companion to the Reconstruction Act, required Senate consent for the removal of any official whose appointment had required Senate confirmation. Congress chiefly wanted to protect Secretary of War Edwin M. Stanton, a Lincoln holdover and the only member of Johnson's cabinet who favored radical Reconstruction. In his position Stanton could do much to frustrate Johnson's anticipated efforts to undermine Reconstruction. Congress also required the president to issue all orders to the army through its commanding general, Ulysses S. Grant. In effect, Congress was attempting to reconstruct the presidency as well as the South.

Seemingly defeated, Johnson appointed generals recommended by Stanton and Grant to command the five military districts in the South. But he was just biding his time. In August 1867, after Congress had adjourned, he "suspended" Stanton and replaced him with Grant, believing that the general would act like a good soldier and follow orders. Next Johnson replaced four of the commanding generals, including Philip H. Sheridan, Grant's favorite cavalry general. Johnson, however, had misjudged Grant, who publicly registered his opposition to the president's machinations. When the Senate reconvened in the fall, it overruled Stanton's suspension. Grant, now an open enemy of Johnson, resigned so that Stanton could resume his office.

Impeachment. On February 21, 1868, Johnson formally dismissed Stanton. The feisty secretary of war, however, barricaded the door of his office and refused to admit the replacement Johnson had appointed. Three days later, House Republicans introduced articles of impeachment against the president, employing the power granted to the House of Representatives by the Constitution to charge high federal officials with "Treason, Bribery, or other high Crimes and Misde-

TABLE 15.1

Primary Reconstruction Laws and Constitutional Amendments

Law (Date of Congressional Passage)	Key Provisions
Thirteenth Amendment (January 1865*)	Prohibited slavery
Civil Rights Act of 1866 (April 1866)	Defined citizenship rights of freedmen
	Authorized federal authorities to bring suit against those who violated those rights
Fourteenth Amendment (June 1866†)	Established national citizenship for persons born or naturalized in the United States
	Prohibited the states from depriving citizens of their civil rights or equal protection under the law
	Reduced state representation in House of Representatives by the percentage of adult male citizens denied the vote
Reconstruction Act of 1867 (March 1867‡)	Divided the South into five military districts, each under the command of a Union general
	Established requirements for readmission of ex-Confederate states to the Union
Tenure of Office Act (March 1867)	Required Senate consent for removal of any federal official whose appointment had required Senate confirmation
Fifteenth Amendment (February 1869)	Forbade states to deny citizens the right to vote on the grounds of race, color, or "previous condition of servitude"
Ku Klux Klan Act (April 1871)	Authorized the president to use federal prosecutions and military force to suppress conspiracies to deprive citizens of the right to vote and enjoy the equal protection of the law

*Ratified by three-fourths of all states in December 1868.
†Ratified by three-fourths of all states in July 1868.
‡Ratified by three-fourths of all states in March 1870.

meanors." The House overwhelmingly approved eleven counts of presidential misconduct, nine of which dealt with violations of the Tenure of Office Act.

The case went to the Senate, which acts as the court in impeachment cases, with Supreme Court Chief Justice Salmon P. Chase presiding. After an eleven-week trial, thirty-five senators on May 15 voted for conviction, one vote short of the two-thirds majority required. Seven moderate Republicans had broken ranks, voting for acquittal along with twelve Democrats. The reluctant Republicans were overwhelmed by the drastic nature of the attack on Johnson; Congress had removed federal judges from office, but never a president. Even if Johnson had broken the law, they felt, the real issue was a political disagreement between Congress and the president. (In fact, the Supreme Court subsequently declared the Tenure of Office Act unconstitutional.) The vote for acquittal reflected fears that a conviction based on a policy dispute would establish a dangerous precedent and undermine the presidency—too high a price just to punish Johnson.

In any case, even without being convicted, Johnson had been defanged. For the remainder of his term he was helpless to alter the course of Reconstruction.

The Election of 1868. The impeachment controversy made Grant, already the North's most popular war hero, a Republican hero as well, and he easily won the party's presidential nomination in 1868. In the fall campaign he supported radical Reconstruction, but he also urged reconciliation between the sections. His Democratic opponent was Horatio Seymour, a former governor of New York who almost declined the nomination, certain that the Democrats could not overcome their identification with the disloyal South.

As Seymour feared, the Republicans "waved the bloody shirt," stirring up old wartime emotions against the Democrats to great effect. Seymour could only appeal lamely for a more moderate program that would permit the southern states to reorganize themselves. Grant won about the same share of the northern vote (55 percent) that Lincoln had won in 1864, and received 214 of 294 electoral votes. The Republicans also retained two-thirds majorities in both houses of Congress.

The Fifteenth Amendment. In the wake of their smashing victory, the Republicans produced the last major piece of Reconstruction legislation—the Fifteenth

THE POLITICAL DEATH OF THE BOGUS CÆSAR.

Johnson's Impeachment
By including provisions for the impeachment and removal of a president, the Constitution gives Congress an orderly proceeding by which to serve the cause of justice. Perhaps inadvertently, Thomas Nast's cartoon in *Harper's Weekly,* entitled *The Political Death of the Bogus Caesar,* reveals the true nature of Johnson's impeachment. Nast's Roman senators have not concluded a judicial proceeding. They have assassinated Caesar, and that is how we must regard the Republican impeachment of Johnson, although, thanks to the Senate's acquittal, Johnson's political end was not as final as Caesar's. He served out his term, and six years later, in 1874, was elected U.S. senator from Tennessee.
Harper's Weekly, March 13, 1869.

Amendment, which forbade either the federal government or the states from denying citizens the right to vote on the basis of race, color, or "previous condition of servitude." Proponents of the amendment were aware that it left open the use of poll taxes and property or literacy tests to discourage blacks from voting. But northern states also valued such qualifications, employing them against immigrants and the "unworthy" poor. A California senator warned that in his state, with its rabidly anti-Chinese sentiment, any restriction on that power would "kill our party as dead as a stone."

Despite grumbling by Radical Republicans, the amendment passed without modification in February 1869. Congress required the unreconstructed states of Virginia, Mississippi, Texas, and Georgia to ratify it before they were readmitted to the Union. A year later the Fifteenth Amendment became part of the Constitution.

Woman Suffrage Denied. If the Fifteenth Amendment troubled some proponents of black suffrage, this was nothing as compared to the outrage felt by women's rights advocates. They had fought the good fight for so many years for the abolition of slavery, only to be abandoned when the chance finally came to get the vote for women. Leading suffragists such as Susan B. Anthony and Elizabeth Cady Stanton did not want to hear from Radical Republicans that this was "the Negro's hour" and that women would have to wait for another day. How could suffrage be granted to former slaves, Stanton demanded to know, but not to them? In her despair, Stanton lashed out in ugly racist terms against "Patrick and Sambo and Hans and Ung Tung," clueless about the Declaration of Independence yet entitled to vote, while the best and most accomplished

of American women remained voteless. In 1869 the annual meeting of the Equal Rights Association, the champion of both black and woman suffrage, broke up in acrimony, and Stanton and Anthony came out against the Fifteenth Amendment.

At this searing moment, a schism opened in the ranks of the women's movement. The majority, led by Lucy Stone and Julia Ward Howe, reconciled themselves to disappointment and accepted the priority of black suffrage. The Stanton-Anthony group, however, struck out in a new direction. Stanton declared that woman "must not put her trust in man" in fighting for her rights. The new organization that she headed, the New York–based National Woman Suffrage Association, accepted only women, focused exclusively on women's rights, and resolutely took up the battle for a federal woman suffrage amendment. It was more realistic, moderates felt, to seek piecemeal advances at the state level. Organized into the American Woman Suffrage Association, they remained allied to the Republicans in the forlorn hope that once Reconstruction had been settled, it would be time for woman suffrage.

The fracturing of the women's movement concealed the common ground the two sides shared. Both now realized that a popular constituency had to be built broader than the elite of evangelical reformers who had founded the movement. Both elevated suffrage into the preeminent women's issue. And both were energized by a shared anger not evident in earlier times. "If I were to give vent to all my pent-up wrath concerning the subordination of woman," Lydia Maria Child wrote to the Republican warhorse Charles Sumner in 1872, "I might frighten *you*. . . . Suffice it, therefore, to say, either the theory of our government is *false,* or women have a right

A Woman Suffrage Quilt
Homemade quilts provided funds and a means of persuasion for the temperance and antislavery movements. Suffragists, however, regarded quilts and needlework as symbols of the domestic subjugation of women, so woman suffrage quilts, such as this one (c. 1860–1880) depicting a women's rights lecture, were rare.
Collections of Mrs. Nancy W. Livingston and Mrs. Elizabeth Livingston Jaeger. Photo courtesy of the Los Angeles County Museum of Art.

to vote." If radical Reconstruction seemed a barren time for women's rights, in fact it had planted the seeds of the modern feminist movement.

Republican Rule in the South

Between 1868 and 1871 all the southern states met the congressional stipulations and rejoined the Union. Protected by federal troops and encouraged by northern party leaders, state Republican organizations took hold across the South and won control of the newly established Reconstruction governments. These Republican administrations remained in power for periods ranging from a few months in Virginia to nine years in South Carolina, Louisiana, and Florida (see Map 15.1). African Americans participated prominently in the Reconstruction governments. In Alabama, Florida, South Carolina, Mississippi, and Louisiana they constituted a majority of registered voters. They provided the votes for Republican victories there and in Georgia, Virginia, and North Carolina as well, where they accounted for nearly half the registered voters.

Carpetbaggers and Scalawags. Democratic ex-Confederates mocked and scorned southern whites who became Republicans as *scalawags*—an ancient

Scots-Irish term for runty, worthless animals. Whites who had come from the North they denounced as *carpetbaggers*—self-seeking interlopers who carried all their property in cheap suitcases called carpetbags. Carpetbaggers held more than half the governorships in the new Republican administrations and almost half the southern seats in Congress.

Actually, few southern Republicans conformed to the hostile stereotypes. Some carpetbaggers did come south for personal profit, but they also brought capital and skills. Union army veterans taken with the South— its climate, people, and economic opportunities—also figured heavily among the carpetbaggers. And interspersed with the self-seekers were many idealists anxious to advance the cause of emancipation.

The scalawags were even more diverse. Some had once been slaveowners, Whigs, or even Democrats, now drawn to Republicanism as the best way to attract northern capital to southern railroads, mines, and factories. In southwestern Texas the large German population was strongly Republican. They sent to Congress Edward Degener, an immigrant San Antonio grocer whom Confederate authorities had imprisoned and whose sons had been executed for treason. But most numerous among the scalawags were backcountry farmers who wanted to rid the South of its slaveholding aristocracy. Scalawags had generally fought against (or at least refused to support) the Confederacy; they believed that slavery had victimized whites as well as blacks. "Now is the time," a Georgia scalawag wrote, "for every man to come out and speak his principles publickly [*sic*] and vote for liberty as we have been in bondage long enough."

African American Leadership. The Democrats' stereotype of black political leaders as ignorant field hands who could only play at politics was just as false as the stereotypes about white Republicans. Until 1867 most African American leaders in the South came from the elite that had been free before the Civil War. With the formation of the reconstructed Republican governments in 1867, this diverse group of ministers, artisans, shopkeepers, and former soldiers reached out to the freedmen. African American speakers, some financed by the Republican Party, fanned out into the old plantation districts and recruited former slaves for political roles. Still, few of the new leaders were field hands; most had been preachers or artisans. The literacy of one former slave, Thomas Allen, who was a Baptist minister and shoemaker, helped him win election to the Georgia legislature. "In my county," he recalled, "the colored people came to me for instructions, and I gave them the best instructions I could. I took the *New York Tribune* and other papers, and in that way I found out a great deal, and I told them whatever I thought was right."

Many African American leaders who emerged in 1867 had been born in the North or had spent many

THE FIRST COLORED SENATOR AND REPRESENTATIVES.
In the 41st and 42nd Congress of the United States.

African American Congressional Delegation, 1872
This Currier and Ives lithograph celebrates one of the notable achievements of radical Reconstruction—the representation that ex-slaves won, however briefly, in the U.S. Congress. Hiram Revels of Mississippi, the Senate's first African American member, is seated at the extreme left.
Granger Collection.

years there. They moved south when radical Reconstruction offered the prospect of meaningful freedom. Like white migrants, many were veterans of the Union army. Some had fought in the antislavery crusade, some were employed by the Freedmen's Bureau or northern missionary societies, and a few came from free families and had gone north for an education. Others had escaped from slavery and were returning home. One of these was Blanche K. Bruce, who had received tutoring on the Virginia plantation of his white father. During the war Bruce escaped to Kansas from Missouri (where his father had moved) and then returned to Missouri, establishing a school for former slaves in Hannibal. He arrived in Mississippi in 1869 and entered politics; in 1874 he became the second African American elected to the Senate and the first elected to a full term.

Although never proportionate to their numbers in the population, African American officeholders held positions of importance throughout the South. Sixteen African Americans served in the U.S. House of Representatives. In 1870 Mississippi sent Hiram R. Revels, a minister born in North Carolina, to the Senate as its first African American member. In 1868 blacks constituted a majority in the lower house of the South Carolina legislature. They were heavily represented in the state's executive offices, elected to three seats in Congress, and won a seat on the state supreme court. Over the entire course of Reconstruction twenty African Americans served as governor, lieutenant governor, secretary of state, treasurer, or superintendent of education; more than six hundred served as state legislators. Almost all who became state executives had been free

before the Civil War, but in the legislatures most black members were former slaves.

The Radical Program.   The Republicans who took office had ambitious plans for a reconstructed South. They wanted to end its dependence on cotton agriculture and create an advanced economy based on manufacturing, capital investment, and skilled labor. Southern Republicans fell far short of achieving this vision, but they accomplished more of it than their critics gave them credit for.

The Republicans modernized state constitutions, eliminated property qualifications for the vote, and made more offices elective. They attended especially to the personal freedoms of the former slaves, sweeping out the shadow Black Codes enforcing labor discipline on the freedmen and controlling their movements. Women also benefited from the Republican defense of personal liberty. Nearly all the new constitutions expanded the property rights of married women, enabling them to hold property and personal earnings independent of their husbands. This was, a Georgia woman wrote, "a wonderful reform" for "the cause of Women's Rights." The Republicans' social program called for hospitals, more humane penitentiaries, and asylums for orphans and the insane. South Carolina provided medical care for the poor, and Alabama offered free legal counsel. Republican governments built roads in areas where roads had never existed. They poured money into rebuilding the region's railroad network, and they provided subsidies to attract factories. They undertook major public works programs. And they did all this without federal financing.

To pay for their ambitious programs the Republican governments copied the taxes that northern states had introduced during the Jacksonian reforms of the 1830s. These were general property taxes applying not only to real estate but to personal wealth. The Republican goal was to make planters pay their fair share of taxes and to broaden the tax base by forcing them to sell off uncultivated land. In many plantation counties, especially in South Carolina, Louisiana, and Mississippi, former slaves served as tax assessors and collectors, administering the taxation of their onetime owners.

Increasing tax revenues never managed to overtake the burgeoning obligations assumed by the Reconstruction governments. State debts mounted rapidly, and as interest payments on bonds fell into arrears, public credit collapsed. On top of that, much of the spending was wasted or ended up in the pockets of state officials. Corruption was endemic to American politics, present in the southern states before the Republicans came on the scene and rampant everywhere in this era, not least in the Grant administration itself. But there was no question that in the free-spending atmosphere of the early Republican regimes, corruption was especially widespread and damaging to the cause of radical Reconstruction.

Nothing, however, could dim the achievement in public education. Here the South had lagged woefully; only Tennessee had a system of public schooling before the Civil War. Republican state governments vowed to make up for lost time, viewing education as the foundation for a democratic order. African Americans of all ages rushed to attend the newly established schools, even when they had to pay tuition. An elderly man in Mississippi explained his desire to go to school: "Ole missus used to read the good book [the Bible] to us . . . on Sunday evenin's, but she mostly read dem places where it says, 'Servants obey your masters.' . . . Now we is free, there's heaps of tings in that old book we is just suffering to learn." By 1875 about half of all the children in Florida, Mississippi, and South Carolina were enrolled in school.

Except in New Orleans, the new schools were segregated. Most African Americans did not complain. They agreed with Frederick Douglass, the black abolitionist, that separate schools were "infinitely superior" to no schools at all. Integration was an issue for another day.

The Role of Black Churches. The building of schools was part of a larger effort by African Americans to fortify the institutions that had sustained their spirit during the days before emancipation. Religious belief had struck deep roots in nineteenth-century slave society. Now, in freedom, the African Americans buttressed their new communities by founding their own churches. They left their old white-dominated congregations, where they had been relegated to segregated balconies and denied any voice in church governance, and built churches of their own. These churches joined together to form African American versions of the Southern Methodist and Southern Baptist denominations, including, most prominently, the National Baptist Convention and the African Methodist Episcopal Church. Everywhere the robust black churches served not only as places of worship but as schools, social centers, and political meeting halls.

Black ministers were community leaders and often political officeholders. As Charles H. Pearce, a Methodist minister in Florida, declared, "A man in this State cannot do his whole duty as a minister except he looks out for the political interests of his people." Calling for the brotherhood of man and the special destiny

Freedmen's School, c. 1870
This rare photograph shows the interior of one of the 3,000 freedmen's schools established across the South after the Civil War. Although many of these schools were staffed by white missionaries, a main objective of northern educators was to prepare black women to take over the classroom. The black teacher shown here is surely one of the first.
Library of Congress.

of the former slaves as the new "Children of Israel," black ministers provided a powerful religious underpinning for the Republican politics of their congregations.

Sharecropping

In the meantime, the freedmen were locked in a great economic struggle with their former owners. In 1869 the Republican government of South Carolina had established a land commission to buy acreage and resell it on easy terms to the landless. In this way about 14,000 black families acquired farms. South Carolina's land distribution plan showed what was possible, but it was the exception, not the rule. Despite a lot of rhetoric, Republican regimes elsewhere did little to help the freedmen fulfill their dreams of becoming independent farmers. Federal efforts proved equally feeble. The Southern Homestead Act of 1866 offered 80-acre grants to settlers, limited for the first year to freedmen and southern Unionists. The advantage was strictly symbolic, however, since the public land made available to homesteaders was off the beaten track in swampy, infertile parts of the Lower South, and in any case, the freed slaves lacked the resources to get started. Only about a thousand families finally succeeded.

There was no reversing President Johnson's order restoring confiscated lands to former Confederates, even after the radical Republicans had the power to do so. Property rights, it seemed, trumped everything else, even for most champions of black rights. The Freedmen's Bureau, which had earlier championed the land claims of the ex-slaves, now devoted itself to teaching them how to be good agricultural laborers.

So, while they yearned for farms, most freedmen started out landless, and with no option but to work for their former owners. But not, they vowed, under the conditions of slavery—no gang work, no overseers, no fines or punishments, no regulation of their private lives or personal freedom. In certain parts of the agricultural South wage work became the norm—for example, on the great sugar plantations of Louisiana taken over after the war by northern investors. The problem was that cotton planters lacked the money to pay wages, at least not until the crop came in, and sometimes, in lieu of a straight wage, they offered a share of the crop. As a *wage*, this was a bad deal for the freedmen, but it opened up interesting possibilities. They soon realized that if they could be paid in shares for their work, they could pay in those same shares to rent the land they worked.

This form of land tenantry was already familiar in parts of the South among white farmers, and the freedmen now seized on it for the independence it offered them. Planters resisted, believing, as one wrote, that "wages are the only successful system of controlling hands." But in a battle of wills that broke out all across the cotton South, the planters yielded to "the inveterate

MAP 15.2
The Barrow Plantation, 1860 and 1881
Comparing the 1860 map of this central Georgia plantation with the 1881 map reveals the changing patterns of black residence and farming. In 1860 the slave quarters were clustered near the planter's house, which sat on a small hilltop. The sharecroppers of 1881 built cabins along the spurs or ridges of land between the streams, scattering their community over the plantation. A black church and school were built by this date. A typical sharecropper on the plantation earned most of his income from growing cotton.

prejudices of the freedmen, who desire to be masters of their own time."

Thus there sprang up a distinctively southern system of agricultural labor—*sharecropping*, in which the freedmen worked as renters, exchanging their labor for the use of land, house, implements, and sometimes seed and fertilizer, typically turning over half to two-thirds of their crops to the landlord (Map 15.2). The sharecropping system joined laborers and the owners of land and capital in a common sharing of risks and returns. But it was a very unequal relationship, given the force of southern law and custom on the white landowner's side, and given the dire economic circum-

Sharecroppers
This sharecropping family stands proudly in front of their new cabin and young cotton crop, which is planted nearly up to the cabin door. But the presence of the white landlord in the background casts a shadow on them, suggesting their hard struggle for economic freedom.
Brown Brothers.

stances of the sharecroppers. Starting out in poverty, they had no way of making it through the first growing season without borrowing for food and supplies.

Country storekeepers stepped in. Bankrolled by their northern suppliers, they "furnished" the sharecropper and took as collateral a *lien* on the crop, effectively assuming ownership of the cropper's share. Once indebted at one store, the sharecropper was no longer free to shop around and thus became an easy target for inflated prices, unfair interest rates, and crooked bookkeeping. As cotton prices declined during the 1870s, more and more sharecroppers fell into permanent debt. And if the merchant was also the landowner, or conspired with the landowner, the debt became a pretext for compulsory labor, or *peonage*, although evidence now suggests that sharecroppers generally managed to pull up stakes and move on once things became hopeless. Sharecroppers always thought twice about moving, however, because part of their "capital" was being known and well-reputed in their home communities. Freedmen who lacked that local standing generally found sharecropping hard going and likely ended up in the ranks of agricultural laborers.

In the face of so much adversity, black families struggled to better themselves. The fact that it enabled *family* struggle was, in truth, the saving advantage of sharecropping, because it mobilized husbands and wives in common enterprise while shielding both from personal subordination to whites. The trouble with sharecropping, one planter grumbled, was that "it makes the laborer too independent; he becomes a partner, and has to be consulted." By the end of Reconstruction, about one-quarter of sharecropping families had managed to save enough to rent with cash payments, and eventually black farmers owned about one-third of the land they cultivated—but rarely the best land and usually at a cost greater than its fertility warranted.

A Comparative Perspective. The battle between planters and freedmen over the land was by no means unique to the American South. Wherever slavery ended—in Haiti after the slave revolt of 1791, in the British Caribbean by abolition in 1833, in Cuba and Brazil by gradual emancipation during the 1880s—a fierce struggle ensued between planters seeking to restore a gang labor system and former slaves seeking to gain economic autonomy. The outcome of this universal conflict depended crucially on the ex-slaves' access to land. Where vacant land existed, as in British Guiana on the South American mainland, or where plantations could be seized, as in Haiti, the ex-slaves became subsistence farmers; and insofar as the Caribbean plantation economy survived without the ex-slaves, it did so by the importation of laborers from India and China. Where land could not be had, as in the British islands of Barbados and Antigua, the ex-slaves returned to plantation labor as wage workers, although often in some combination with customary rights to housing and garden plots. The cotton South fit neither of these broad patterns. The freedmen did not get the land, but neither did the planters get field hands. What both got was sharecropping.

The source of this exceptional outcome was ultimately political. Elsewhere, emancipation almost never meant civil or political equality for the freed slaves. Even in the British islands, where substantial self-government existed, high property qualifications effectively disfranchised the former slaves. In the United States, however, hard on the heels of emancipation came civil rights, manhood suffrage, and, for a brief era, a real measure of political power for the freedmen. Sharecropping took shape during Reconstruction, and there was no going back afterward.

For the freedmen, sharecropping was not the worst choice; it certainly beat laboring for their former owners. But for southern agriculture, the costs were devastating.

Sharecropping committed the South inflexibly to cotton, the one cash crop capable of satisfying the financial demands of landowners and furnishing merchants. Crop diversification declined, costing the South its self-sufficiency in grains and livestock. And with farms leased year-to-year, neither tenant nor owner had any incentive to improve the property. The crop-lien system lined merchants' pockets with unearned profits that might otherwise have gone into agricultural improvement. The result was a stagnant farm economy, blighting the South's future and condemning it to economic backwardness—a kind of retribution, one could say, for the fresh injustices visited on the people it had once enslaved.

The Undoing of Reconstruction

————★————

Ex-Confederates were blind to the benefits of radical Reconstruction. Indeed, no amount of achievement could have persuaded them that it was anything but an abomination, undertaken without their consent and intended to deny them their rightful place in southern society. Led by the planters, ex-Confederates staged a massive counterrevolution—one designed to "redeem" the South and restore them to political power under the banner of the Democratic Party. But the Redeemers could not have succeeded on their own. They needed the complicity of the North. The undoing of Reconstruction is as much about northern acquiescence as it is about southern resistance.

Klan Portrait
Two armed Klansmen pose in their disguises, which they donned not only to hide their identity but also to intimidate their black neighbors. Northern audiences saw a lithograph based on this photograph in *Harper's Weekly* on December 28, 1868.
Rutherford B. Hayes Presidential Center.

Counterrevolution

Insofar as they could win at the ballot box, southern Democrats took that route. They worked hard to get former Confederates restored to the rolls of registered voters, they appealed to racial solidarity and southern patriotism, and they attacked black suffrage as a threat to white supremacy. By 1869 the Democrats had enough votes to regain office in Tennessee, and a year later, in Virginia. But force was equally acceptable. Throughout the Deep South, especially where black voters were heavily concentrated, ex-Confederate planters and their supporters organized secret societies and waged campaigns of terrorism against blacks and their white allies.

The Ku Klux Klan. The most widespread of these groups, the Ku Klux Klan, first appeared in 1866 as a Tennessee social club but soon became a paramilitary force under Nathan Bedford Forrest, the Confederacy's most decorated cavalry general. (See American Lives, "Nathan Bedford Forrest: Defender of Southern Honor," pp. 496–497.)

By 1870 the Klan was operating almost everywhere in the South as a terrorist force serving the Democratic Party. The Klan murdered and whipped Republican politicians, burned black schools and churches, and attacked Republican Party gatherings (see American Voices, "Harriet Hernandes: The Intimidation of Black Voters," p. 498). In October 1870 a group of Klansmen assaulted a Republican rally in Eutaw, Alabama, killing four African Americans and wounding fifty-four. For three weeks in 1873 Klansmen laid siege to the small town of Colfax, Louisiana, which was defended by black Union veterans holding the county seat after a contested election. On Easter Sunday, armed with a small cannon, the whites overpowered the defenders and slaughtered fifty-two of them after they had surrendered under a white flag. Such terrorist tactics enabled the Democrats to seize power in Georgia and North Carolina in 1870 and make substantial gains elsewhere. An African American politician in North Carolina wrote, "Our former masters are fast taking the reins of government."

Congress responded by passing enforcement legislation, including the Ku Klux Klan Act of 1871, authorizing President Grant to use federal prosecutions, military force, and martial law to suppress conspiracies to deprive citizens of the right to vote, hold office, serve on juries, and enjoy equal protection under the law. For the first time, crimes by private citizens became violations of federal law. Government agents penetrated the Klan and gathered evidence that provided the basis for widespread arrests; federal grand juries indicted more than 3,000 Klansmen. In South Carolina, where the Klan was most deeply entrenched, federal troops occupied nine counties, made hundreds of arrests, and drove as many as 2,000 Klansmen from the state.

The Failure of Federal Enforcement. The Grant administration's assault on the Klan raised the spirits of southern Republicans, but it also emphasized how dependent they were on the federal government. The potency of the Ku Klux Klan Act, a Mississippi Republican wrote, "derived alone from its source" in the federal government; "no such law could be enforced by state authority, the local power being too weak." If Republicans were to prevail over ex-Confederate terrorism, they needed what one carpetbagger described as "steady, unswerving power from without."

Northern Republicans, however, grew weary of the financial costs of Reconstruction and the endless guerrilla war it seemed to produce. Prosecuting Klansmen under the enforcement laws was an uphill battle. Indeed, U.S. attorneys usually faced all-white juries, and the Justice department lacked the resources to handle the cases. After 1872, prosecutions began to drop off, and many Klansmen received hasty pardons; few served significant prison terms. Moreover, the Supreme Court undercut the enforcement legislation by ruling that the Fourteenth Amendment protected citizens from actions by the *states*, not by other citizens, so that federal prosecution of private bodies like the Klan became legally questionable.

In a kind of self-fulfilling prophesy, the unwillingness of the Grant administration to shore up Reconstruction guaranteed that it would fail. Republican governments that were denied federal help found themselves overwhelmed by ex-Confederate politicians during the day and by terrorists at night. Democrats overthrew Republican governments in Texas in 1873, in Alabama and Arkansas in 1874, and in Mississippi in 1875.

The Mississippi campaign showed all too clearly what the Republicans were up against. As elections neared in 1875, paramilitary groups such as the Rifle Clubs and Red Shirts operated openly. Often local Democrats paraded armed, as if they were militia companies. They identified black leaders in assassination lists called "dead-books," broke up Republican meetings, provoked rioting that left hundreds of African Americans dead, and threatened voters. Mississippi's Republican governor, Adelbert Ames, appealed to President Grant for federal troops, but Grant refused. Ames then contemplated organizing a state militia but ultimately decided against it, believing that only blacks would join. Rather than escalate the fighting and turn it into a racial war, he conceded victory to the terrorists.

By 1877 Republican governments, backed by token U.S. military units, remained in only three states: Louisiana, South Carolina, and Florida. Elsewhere, the former Confederates were back in the saddle.

The Acquiescent North

At the outset, there was strong reason to believe that the North would stand fast on radical Reconstruction. The underlying ideal of equal rights inspired significant northern reform, especially in the treatment of northern blacks. This was partly because the Reconstruction amendments voided northern (as well as southern) laws denying blacks freedom to move between states and testify in court or vote. But northern states themselves moved against segregated public facilities and improved black access to education. In a typical rhetorical gesture, Michigan Republicans scorned "that political blasphemy which says, 'This is a white man's Government.' It is God's Government made for man!"

The spirit of equal rights extended to other causes—to women's rights, as already noted, and also to the labor movement. Trade unionism surged after the war. A new umbrella organization, the National Labor Union, formed in 1866 to fight "wage slavery" and advocate reforms that would bring about "the independence of the working class" and ensure "the success of our republican institutions."

The Civil War, moreover, brought into being an activist state. At the federal level, wartime Republicans legislated a national banking system, massive subsidies for interregional railroads, free homesteads for settlers, an expanded postal system, and improvements in rivers and harbors. The Republican Party sought "large and noble schemes of national advancement." The noblest of these was the U.S. Sanitary Commission, a privately funded body that started in 1861 by tending sick and wounded soldiers but ended by advancing an ambitious agenda for national betterment.

In Republican-controlled states, there was an equally dramatic increase in public programs after the war. The New York legislature established teacher-training colleges, the first state Board of Charities, a powerful Board of Health, and free public schools (in place of schools financed by parents according to the number of days their children attended). Everywhere in the North, education took pride of place, with public expenditures increasing from $19.9 million in 1860 to $61.7 million in 1870. "With free soil, free schools, a free press, and free men," a Republican journalist

Nathan Bedford Forrest: Defender of Southern Honor

Nathan Bedford Forrest, c. 1866
Tennessee State Museum.

NATHAN BEDFORD FORREST, the South's fiercest champion, as a boy had little stake in the old plantation order. His father was a blacksmith who followed the frontier to Tennessee, where Forrest, the oldest of eleven children, was born on July 13, 1821. When Forrest was only sixteen years old, his father died, leaving him as the primary breadwinner. With hardly any schooling the boy took charge of the family's rented farm; he also became an adept horsetrader. At age twenty-one, when his mother remarried, he left for Hernando, Mississippi, where his uncle ran a livery business.

Tall and physically impressive, Forrest normally spoke with great courtesy, but he had a violent temper. When four men attacked his uncle, Forrest leapt to his defense. The uncle died from a bullet meant for his nephew, but the young Forrest had shown his mettle. Admiring his raw courage, Hernando citizens rewarded Forrest by electing him town constable. Equally implacable in love, in 1845 Forrest so insistently wooed a young lady from a well-connected local family that at their third meeting she agreed to marry him.

For a hard-driving young man like Forrest, the booming cotton economy offered much opportunity. He took over his uncle's business, ran a stagecoach service, and traded livestock and—in due course—slaves as well. In 1851 ambition took him and his family to nearby Memphis, Tennessee, where he became a well-known slave trader. With his profits he purchased a large plantation in Mississippi. By now he had become a man of substance, a leading Memphis citizen. In the sectional crisis that was brewing at the time, Forrest was not a firebrand secessionist but fiercely championed southern rights and, of course, slavery.

When war broke out in 1861 he immediately organized a Tennessee cavalry regiment. In April 1862 he distinguished himself at the bloody Battle of Shiloh, although he was badly wounded during the retreat. Promoted to brigadier general, he began a brilliant career as a cavalry raider, mostly fighting behind Union lines. His aggressive spirit often carried him into the thick of battle, oblivious to the fact that he was a general and not a trooper.

That same explosiveness ignited one of the war's worst atrocities, the slaughter of black troops at Fort Pillow, Tennessee, on April 12, 1864, evidently because of rumors that the Fort Pillow garrison had been harassing local whites who were loyal to the Confederacy.

The Fort Pillow massacre foreshadowed the civil strife that would consume Tennessee for the next half-decade, especially after the Republican William G. Brownlow was elected governor in March 1865. A former Confederate prisoner, Brownlow was not shy about calling his enemies to account. Under his governorship the disfranchisement of former Confederates, hitherto partial, became general, leaving political power in the hands of a minority of Unionist whites and freed slaves. When racial tensions exploded into a bloody riot against blacks in Memphis in May 1866, Brownlow at once intervened, transferring the responsibility for maintaining order from local police to a commission appointed by him. Former Confederates around the state concluded that they could regain power only by waging a secret campaign of terror against Brownlow's base of support in the black community. This was the genesis, among other things, of the first "den" of the Ku Klux Klan in Pulaski, Tennessee, sometime in late 1865 or early 1866.

Home safe from the war, Forrest was absorbed by his own damaged fortunes. The wealth represented by his slaves had been wiped out by emancipation, and his Mississippi plantation was left heavily encumbered by his wartime debts. With the aid of the Freedmen's Bureau he managed to put his former slaves back to work. But flooding (probably caused by war-damaged levies) destroyed his cotton crop; in August 1866 he gave up, surrendering the plantation to his creditors. He then turned to other enterprises: a commission merchant firm, a fire and life insurance company, partnership in a Memphis street-paving firm, labor contracting for the Memphis & Little Rock Railroad. Forrest finally declared personal bankruptcy, having been swept down, like so many others, by the war-devastated economy. In desperation, he considered leading an expedition of former Confederate comrades to seize the riches of Mexico.

A more promising avenue for Forrest's energies, however, had by now opened up. From its obscure beginnings after the war, the Ku Klux Klan proliferated wildly across Tennessee and into neighboring states. What the Klan needed was a tough, respected figure able to impose order on the Invisible Empire and prevent it from spinning out of control—none other than Nathan Bedford Forrest. At a clandestine meeting in Nashville sometime in late 1866, he accepted the job and donned the robes of Grand Wizard, the Klan's highest office. Forrest's activities are mostly unknown because he worked in secrecy, but there is no mystery about why he gravitated to the Klan. For him, the Klan was politics by other means, the vehicle by which disfranchised former Confederates like himself might strike a blow against the despised Republicans who ran Tennessee.

In many towns, including Memphis, the Klan became virtually identical to the Democratic clubs; in fact, Klan members—including Forrest—dominated the state's delegation to the Democratic national convention of 1868. On the ground the Klan unleashed a murderous campaign of terror against Republican sympathizers. Governor Brownlow responded resolutely, threatening to mobilize the state militia and root out the Klan. If Brownlow tried, answered Forrest (for once emerging from secrecy), "there will be war, and a bloodier one than we have ever witnessed. . . . If the militia attack us, we will resist to the last; and, if necessary, I think I could raise 40,000 men in five days, ready for the field."

For many months, Tennessee endured a high state of tension. In September 1868 a new law identified membership in the Klan as a felony, and in the following February martial law was declared in nine Klan-ridden counties. But it was the Republicans, not the Klan, that cracked. In March 1869 the redoubtable Brownlow retreated to the U.S. Senate. The Democrats were on their way back to power, and the Klan, having served its purpose, was officially disbanded in Tennessee.

Like many other Confederate heroes, Forrest might now have anticipated a comfortable life in politics. But he had too much blood on his hands. He was among the very last to be pardoned by President Johnson. His appearance at the Democratic convention in 1868 brought forth bitter Republican denunciations against "the Fort Pillow Butcher." Physical violence, moreover, still dogged his life, including the killing (he claimed self-defense) of a sharecropper on his plantation. What sealed Forrest's political fate, however, was the Ku Klux Klan. This was, to some degree, undeserved. Forrest had regarded the Klan's mission in strictly political terms, its violence calibrated to the task of driving the Republicans from power. In this Forrest only reflected what conservative southerners generally favored. But he could not personally curb the senseless brutality against blacks done in the Klan's name. Any ruffian, he complained, could put on a white sheet and go after his neighbors. But Forrest was the Grand Wizard, and even after he resigned (probably late in 1869) his name could not be dissociated from Klan savagery. Celebrated though he might have been, when it came to supporting him for political office responsible Democrats kept their distance.

So Forrest had to cash in his chips elsewhere, which he did as president and chief promoter of the Memphis & Selma Railroad. Beginning in 1869 he worked tirelessly hawking bonds to communities along the proposed right of way, lobbying for state and county subsidies, and expending his considerable reputation to carry forward an ambitious project linking Memphis by rail to northern Alabama and eastern Mississippi. All in vain. The unfinished Memphis & Selma finally collapsed after the panic of 1873, and Forrest was left with nothing. Resilient to the end, he contracted with Selby County for convicts to work 1,700 acres of land he had rented on President's Island, four miles from Memphis. Leasing convicts was a practice that was notorious for horrendous abuses, but none were reported on President's Island. As a master Forrest had always been well reputed, even in the slave days. The swamp-ridden island, however, proved hard on him; he contracted a debilitating intestinal illness that ultimately proved fatal. After so many setbacks, his luck turned at least in this regard: against all odds, Nathan Bedford Forrest died peacefully in his bed on October 29, 1877.

HARRIET HERNANDES

The Intimidation of Black Voters

———— ★ ————

The following testimony was given in 1871 by Harriet Hernandes, a black resident of Spartanburg, South Carolina, to the Joint Congressional Select Committee investigating conditions in the South. The terrorizing of black women through rape and other forms of physical violence was among the means of oppression used by the Ku Klux Klan.

Question: How old are you?
Answer: Going on thirty-four years. . . .
Q: Are you married or single?
A: Married.
Q: Did the Ku-Klux come to your house at any time?
A: Yes, sir; twice. . . .
Q: Go on to the second time. . . .
A: They came in; I was lying in bed. Says he, "Come out here, sir; come out here, sir!" They took me out of bed; they would not let me get out, but they took me up in their arms and toted me out—me and my daughter Lucy. He struck me on the forehead with a pistol, and here is the scar above my eye now. Says he, "Damn you, fall." I fell. Says he, "Damn you, get up." I got up. Says he, "Damn you, get over this fence!" and he kicked me over when I went to get over; and then he went on to a brush pile, and they laid us right down there, both together. They laid us down twenty yards apart, I reckon. They had dragged and beat us along. They struck me right on top of my head, and I thought they had killed me;

and I said, "Lord o'mercy, don't, don't kill my child!" He gave me a lick on the head, and it liked to have killed me; I saw stars. He threw my arm over my head so I could not do anything with it for three weeks, and there are great knots on my wrist now.
Q: What did they say this was for?
A: They said, "You can tell your husband that when we see him we are going to kill him. . . ."
Q: Did they say why they wanted to kill him?
A: They said, "He voted the radical ticket [slate of candidates], didn't he?" I said, "Yes," that very way.

. . .

Q: When did [your husband] get back home after this whipping? He was not at home, was he?
A: He was lying out; he couldn't stay at home, bless your soul! . . .
Q: Has he been afraid for any length of time?
A: He has been afraid ever since last October. He has been lying out. He has not laid in the house ten nights since October.
Q: Is that the situation of the colored people down there to any extent?
A: That is the way they all have to do—men and women both.
Q: What are they afraid of?
A: Of being killed or whipped to death.
Q: What has made them afraid?
A: Because men that voted radical tickets they took the spite out on the women when they could get at them.
Q: How many colored people have been whipped in that neighborhood?
A: It is all of them, mighty near.

———————

Source: Report of the Joint Congressional Select Committee to Inquire into the Condition of Affairs in the Late Insurrectionary States, House Reports, 42d Cong., 2d sess. (Washington, DC: U.S. Government Printing Office, 1972), vol. 5, South Carolina, December 19, 1871.

---

boasted, "the future is full of hope and promise." It was in this spirit of reform that the North approved the use of federal power to defend radical Reconstruction.

The Civil War, finally, fueled an economic boom in the North. Industrial production increased 75 percent between 1865 and 1873, and 3 million immigrants entered the country. Investment shifted toward iron and steel production, machine tools, and coal mining, laying the basis for an advanced industrial economy. Corporate enterprise was beginning to emerge, especially the railroads, where building went forward at a frantic pace.

The North had entered the industrial age. It was an economic giant compared to the South, and amply able to bear the costs of seeing Reconstruction through.

The North's Loss of Faith. Yet the business sector was where enthusiasm flagged most quickly. Northern entrepreneurs complained that the turmoil of Reconstruction retarded the South's economic recovery and harmed their investment opportunities. A similar calculation led to trouble between Republicans and their allies in the National Labor Union. The break came over the eight-hour workday, which labor theorists saw as the key reform that would end wage slavery and complete the equal-rights revolution inaugurated by the Civil War. This grand theory did not much trouble Republicans, but the economic cost of the eight-hour workday did, and inevitably they sided with their business allies, driving the National Labor Union out of the party and into independent politics.

Sympathy for the freedmen also began to wane. The North was flooded with one-sided, often racist reports, such as James S. Pike's *The Prostrate State* (1873), describing extravagant, corrupt Republican rule and a South in the grip of "a mass of black barbarism." The impact of this propaganda could be seen in the fate of the Civil Rights bill, which Charles Sumner introduced in 1870 at the height of radical Reconstruction. Sumner's bill was a remarkable application of federal power against discrimination in the country, guaranteeing citizens equal access to public accommodation, schools, churches, and jury service. By the time the bill passed in 1875, it had been stripped of its key provisions and was of little account as a weapon against discriminatory treatment of African Americans. The Supreme Court finished the demolition job when it declared the remnant Civil Rights Act unconstitutional in 1883.

The political cynicism that overtook the Civil Rights Act signaled the Republican Party's reversion to the practical politics of earlier days. In many states a second generation took over the party—men like Senator Roscoe Conkling of New York, who treated the Manhattan Customs House, with its regiment of political appointees, as an auxiliary of his machine; or Simon Cameron, senator from Pennsylvania, who was in the pocket of the Pennsylvania Railroad. Politicos such as Conkling or Cameron had little enthusiasm for Reconstruction, except as it benefited the Republican Party, and as the party lost headway in the South, they abandoned any interest in the battle for black rights. In Washington, President Grant presided benignly over this transformation of his party, turning a blind eye on corruption even as it began to lap against the White House.

The Liberal Republicans. As Grant's administration lapsed into cronyism, a revolt took shape inside the Republican Party. Anti-Grant factions of many stripes accepted the leadership of an influential collection of intellectuals, journalists, and reform-minded businessmen who resented the dominance of professional politicians in the party's affairs. The first order of business for them was civil-service reform that would replace corrupt patronage with a merit-based system of appointments. The reformers also, however, disliked the thrust of government activism spawned by the Civil War crisis. They regarded themselves as classical liberals—believers in free trade, market competition, and limited government. Government activity was "by nature wasteful, cor-

rupt, and dangerous." And, with unabashed elitism, they spoke out against universal suffrage, which "can only mean in plain English the government of ignorance and vice." So it followed that liberal reformers would have little patience with the former slaves. Although mostly veterans of the anti-slavery movement, they now became strident critics of radical Reconstruction.

The Election of 1872. Unable to deny Grant renomination for a second term, the dissidents broke away and formed a new party under the name Liberal Republican. Their candidate was Horace Greeley, longtime editor and publisher of the New York *Tribune* and a warhorse of American reform in all its variety, including antislavery. The Democratic Party, still in disarray, also nominated Greeley, despite the fierce animus he had always shown for Democrats: "murderers, adulterers, drunkards, cowards, liars, thieves." An ineffective campaigner, Greeley was assailed so bitterly during the campaign that, as he said, "I hardly knew whether I was running for President or the penitentiary."

Grant won overwhelmingly, capturing 56 percent of the popular vote and every electoral vote. Yet the Liberal Republicans had managed to shift the terms of political debate in the country. The new agenda they had established—civil-service reform, limited government, reconciliation with the South—was now adopted by the Democrats as they shed their treasonous reputation and reclaimed their place as a legitimate American party. In the 1874 elections, the Democrats dealt the Republicans a crushing blow, gaining control of the House of Representatives for the first time since secession and triumphing in seven normally Republican northern states.

Scandal and Depression. Charges of Republican corruption, mounting ever since Grant's reelection, came to a head in 1875. The scandal involved the Whiskey Ring, a network of liquor distillers and Treasury agents who defrauded the Treasury of millions of dollars of excise taxes on whiskey. The ring was organized by a former Union general, John A. McDonald, whom Grant had appointed supervisor of internal revenue in St. Louis. Grant's private secretary, Orville Babcock, kept a protective eye on McDonald's activities and funneled some of the spoils into the campaign coffers of the Republican Party. In 1875, however, Grant's secretary of the Treasury, Benjamin Bristow, exposed the ring and prosecuted more than 350 distillers and government officials. Many of them, including McDonald, went to prison, but Grant stood by Babcock, possibly perjuring himself to save his secretary from jail. The stench of scandal, however, had engulfed the White House.

On top of this, the economy had fallen into a severe depression after 1873. The precipitating event was the bankruptcy of the Northern Pacific Railroad and its main investor, Jay Cooke. Both Cooke's privileged role as

"Grantism"
Grant was lampooned on both sides of the Atlantic for the behavior of his scandal-ridden administration. The British magazine *Puck* shows Grant only barely defying gravity to keep his corrupt subordinates aloft and out of jail. Despite the scandals, the British public welcomed Grant with admiration on his triumphant foreign tour in 1877.
Stock Montage.

a financier of the Civil War and the generous federal subsidies to the Northern Pacific (and other railroads) suggested to many suffering Americans that Republican financial manipulations had caused the depression. Grant's administration responded ineffectually, rebuffing the pleas of debtors for relief by increasing the money supply (see Chapter 18). In 1874 Democrats gained enough support from Republicans to push through Congress a bill that would have increased the volume of currency in circulation and eased the money pinch. But President Grant vetoed it, fueling Democratic charges that Republicans served only the interests of capitalists.

Among the casualties of the depression was the Freedman's Savings and Trust Company, which held the small deposits of thousands of former slaves. When the bank failed in 1874, Congress refused to compensate the depositors, and many lost their life savings. In denying their pleas for compensation, Congress was also signaling that Reconstruction had lost its moral claim on the country. National politics had moved on, and other concerns absorbed the voter as another presidential election approached in 1876.

The Political Crisis of 1877

Abandoning Grant, the Republicans nominated Rutherford B. Hayes, governor of Ohio. He was a colorless figure but untainted by corruption or by strong convictions—in a word, a safe man. His Democratic opponent was Samuel J. Tilden, governor of New York—a wealthy lawyer with ties to Wall Street and a reform reputation for helping to break the grip of the thieving Tweed Ring on New York City politics. The Democrat Tilden favored "home rule" for the South, but so did the Republican Hayes, though more discreetly. Reconstruction did not actually figure prominently in the campaign and was mostly subsumed under broader Democratic charges of "corrupt centralism" and "incapacity, waste, and fraud." By now, Republicans had written off the South and scarcely campaigned there. Not a lot was said about the states still ruled by Reconstruction governments—Florida, South Carolina, and Louisiana.

Once the returns started coming in on election night, however, those three states began to loom very large indeed. Tilden led in the popular vote, and being victorious in key northern states, he seemed headed for the White House. But sleepless politicians at Republican headquarters realized that if they kept Florida, South Carolina, and Louisiana, Hayes would win by a single electoral vote. The campaigns in those states had been bitterly fought, replicating the Democratic assaults on blacks that had overturned Republican regimes everywhere else in the South. But Republicans still controlled the election machinery in those states, and citing Democratic fraud and intimidation, they could certify Republican victories. Late on election night the audacious announcement came forth from Republican headquarters: Hayes had carried the three southern states and won the election. But newly elected Democratic officials in the three states also sent in electoral votes for Tilden, and when Congress met in early 1877, it faced two sets of electoral votes from those states.

The Constitution does not provide for this contingency. All it says is that the president of the Senate (in 1877, a Republican) opens the electoral certificates before the House (Democratic) and the Senate (Republican) and that "The votes shall then be counted." Ever since the November 1876 election, an air of crisis had gripped the country. There was talk of inside deals, of a new election, even of a violent coup and civil war. Just in case, the commander of the army, General William T. Sherman, deployed four artillery companies in Washington. Finally, Congress decided to appoint an electoral commission to settle the question. The commission included seven Republicans, seven Democrats, and, as the deciding member, David Davis, a Supreme Court justice not known to have fixed party loyalties. But Davis disqualified himself by accepting an Illinois seat in the Senate. He was replaced by Republican Justice Joseph P. Bradley, and by a vote of 8 to 7 the commission awarded the disputed votes to Hayes (Map 15.3).

Outraged Democrats had one more trick up their sleeves. They controlled the House, and they set about stalling a final count of the electoral votes so as to prevent Hayes's inauguration on March 4. But a week earlier, secret talks had begun in Washington between southern Democrats and Ohio Republicans representing Hayes. Other issues may have been on the table, but the main thing was the situation in South Carolina and Louisiana, where Republican governors physically occupied the statehouses, protected by Union troops. If not for the disputed federal election, ironically, the military would not have intervened, and the Redeemers

would already have seized power. Exactly what deal was struck, or how involved Hayes himself was, will probably never be known, but on March 1 the House Democrats suddenly ended their filibuster, the ceremonial counting of votes went forward, and Hayes was inaugurated on schedule. He soon ordered the Union troops back to their barracks, and the Republican regimes in South Carolina and Louisiana fell. Reconstruction had ended.

In 1877 political leaders on all sides seemed ready to say that what Lincoln had called "the work" was complete. But for the freedmen, the work had only begun. Reconstruction turned out to have been a magnificent aberration, a leap beyond what most white Americans actually felt was due their black fellow citizens. Redemption represented a sad falling back to the norm. Still, something real had been achieved—three rights-defining amendments to the Constitution, some elbow room to advance economically, and, not least, a stubborn confidence among blacks that by their own efforts they could lift themselves up. Things would, in fact, get worse before they got better, but the work of Reconstruction was imperishable and could never be erased.

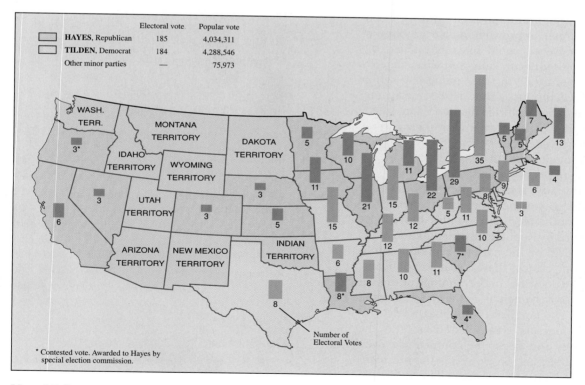

MAP 15.3
The Election of 1876
In this presidential election, the closest and most contested in U.S. history, the Republican Rutherford B. Hayes won only with the disputed votes of three states in the Deep South. (Hayes also needed to defeat the efforts of the governor of Oregon to replace a Republican elector from that state with a Democrat.)

Summary

★

When the Civil War ended in 1865, no one could have foreseen the course of Reconstruction. The slaves had been emancipated, but there was no consensus about their future status as citizens. The South had been defeated, but there was no consensus about its restoration to the Union. Had Abraham Lincoln lived, these questions might have been settled peaceably and with justice for all. But with his assassination, they were left to the mercy of unfolding events.

Without consulting Congress, Lincoln's successor, Andrew Johnson, offered the South easy terms for reentering the Union. This might have succeeded had the South responded with restraint, but instead former Confederates were welcomed back into leadership and a concerted effort was made to reenslave the freedmen through the Black Codes. Infuriated by southern intransigence, congressional Republicans closed ranks behind the Radicals, embraced the freedmen's demand for full equality, placed the South under military rule in 1867, and inaugurated radical Reconstruction.

Politically empowered freedmen participated on nearly equal terms with their white allies in the new Republican state governments that undertook to reconstruct the South through ambitious programs of economic and educational improvement. No amount of accomplishment, however, could have reconciled the ex-Confederates to Republican rule, and they staged a violent counterrevolution in the name of white supremacy and "redemption." But in the meantime, before the political balance shifted against them, freedmen prevailed in the battle of wills with their former masters over a postslavery labor system. Sharecropping had many disadvantages, but it was better than the gang labor that the planters wanted.

Despite an initially stern response, the Grant administration had no stomach for a protracted guerrilla war in the South. Northern politics moved on, increasingly absorbed by Republican scandals and, after depression hit in 1873, by the nation's economic problems. Grant's reform critics, the Liberal Republicans, fatally weakened the doctrinal underpinnings of radical Reconstruction in governmental activism and equal rights. By allying with the Liberal Republicans in 1872, the discredited Democrats scrambled back into the political mainstream and began to compete on even terms with the Republicans. So close was the presidential election of 1876 that both parties claimed victory. The constitutional crisis was resolved only by the Democrats' agreement to accept the Republican Hayes as president in exchange for an end to Republican rule in South Carolina and Louisiana, thereby signaling the conclusion of Reconstruction.

TIMELINE

1863	Lincoln announces his Ten Percent Plan
1864	Wade-Davis bill passed by Congress
	Lincoln gives Wade-Davis bill a "pocket" veto
1865	Freedmen's Bureau established
	Lincoln assassinated; Andrew Johnson succeeds as president
	Johnson implements his restoration plan
	Joint Committee on Reconstruction formed
1866	Civil Rights Act passes over Johnson's veto
	Memphis riots
	Johnson makes disastrous "swing around the circle"
	Johnson defeated in Congressional elections
1867	Reconstruction Acts
	Tenure of Office Act
1868	Impeachment crisis
	Fourteenth Amendment ratified
	Ulysses S. Grant elected president
1870	Ku Klux Klan at peak of power
	Fifteenth Amendment ratified
1871	Ku Klux Klan Act passed by Congress
1872	Grant's reelection as president
1873	Panic of 1873 ushers in depression of 1873–1877
1874	Democrats win majority in House of Representatives
1875	Whiskey Ring scandal undermines Grant administration
1877	Compromise of 1877
	Rutherford B. Hayes becomes president
	Reconstruction ends

Suggested Readings

The starting point for the study of Reconstruction is Eric Foner's synthesis, *Reconstruction: America's Unfinished Revolution, 1863–1877* (1988), which is also available in a shorter version. Two older surveys that provide useful introductions are John Hope Franklin, *Reconstruction: After the Civil War* (1961), and Kenneth M. Stampp, *The Era of Reconstruction* (1965). *Black Reconstruction in America* (1935), by the black activist and scholar W. E. B. Du Bois, deserves attention as the first book to challenge traditional interpretations that discounted the struggle of the emancipated slaves for full freedom.

Presidential Reconstruction

For important studies of presidential efforts to rebuild the Union, see the books on Abraham Lincoln listed in Chapter 14 and the following works on Andrew Johnson: Albert Castel, *The Presidency of Andrew Johnson* (1979); Eric L. McKitrick, *Andrew Johnson and Reconstruction* (1960); and James Sefton, *Andrew Johnson and the Uses of Constitutional Power* (1979). On the Radical resistance to presidential Reconstruction, see James M. McPherson, *The Struggle for Equality: Abolitionists and the Negro in the Civil War and Reconstruction* (1965).

Books that focus on Congress include LaWanda Cox and John H. Cox, *Politics, Principle, and Prejudice, 1865–1867* (1963); David Donald, *The Politics of Reconstruction, 1863–1867* (1965); and William R. Brock, *An American Crisis: Congress and Reconstruction, 1865–1867* (1963). For insight into developments in the South, see Dan T. Carter, *When the War Was Over: The Failure of Self-Reconstruction in the South, 1865–1867* (1985). Michael Perman, *Reunion without Compromise: The South and Reconstruction, 1865–1868* (1973), stresses the South's relations with President Andrew Johnson.

On the freedmen, see Willie Lee Rose, *Rehearsal for Reconstruction: The Port Royal Experiment* (1964); Peter Kolchin, *First Freedom: The Responses of Alabama's Blacks to Emancipation and Reconstruction* (1972); and Leon F. Litwack, *Been in the Storm So Long: The Aftermath of Slavery* (1979). More recent emancipation studies emphasize slavery as a labor system: Barbara Fields, *Slavery and Freedom on the Middle Ground: Maryland during the Nineteenth Century* (1985); Julie Saville, *The Work of Reconstruction: From Slave to Wage Laborer in South Carolina, 1860–1870* (1994); and Ira Berlin et al., *Slaves No More: Three Essays on Emancipation and the Civil War* (1992), incorporating the introductory essays in the initial volumes of a monumental edition of the emancipation records in the National Archives by Ira Berlin et al., *Freedom: A Documentary History of Emancipation, 1861–1867* (1985–). Eric Foner, *Nothing But Freedom: Emancipation and Its Legacy* (1983), places emancipation in a comparative context. Jacqueline Jones, *Labor of Love, Labor of Sorrow: Black Women, Work, and the Family from Slavery to the Present* (1985), is a pioneering work on the impact of emancipation on black women. An important new case study is Leslie A. Schwalm, *A Hard Fight for We: Women's Transition from Slavery to Freedom in South Carolina* (1997).

Radical Reconstruction

For Congress's role in radical Reconstruction, see Michael Les Benedict, *A Compromise of Principle: Congressional Republicans and Reconstruction* (1974), and Hans L. Trefousse, *Impeachment of a President: Andrew Johnson, the Blacks, and Reconstruction* (1975). William S. McFeely, *Grant: A Biography* (1981), explains the politics of Reconstruction. Also helpful is Brooks D. Simpson, *Let Us Have Peace: Ulysses S. Grant and the Politics of War and Reconstruction, 1861–1868* (1991). State studies of Reconstruction include Richard Lowe, *Republicans and Reconstruction in Virginia, 1856–1870* (1991), and Otto Olsen, ed., *Reconstruction and Redemption in the South* (1980). The best account of carpetbaggers is Richard N. Current, *Those Terrible Carpetbaggers: A Reinterpretation* (1988).

On blacks during radical Reconstruction, see Joel Williamson, *After Slavery: The Negro in South Carolina during Reconstruction, 1861–1877* (1965); Robert Cruden, *The Negro in Reconstruction* (1969); John Blassingame, *Black New Orleans, 1860–1880* (1973); Thomas Holt, *Black over White: Negro Political Leadership in South Carolina during Reconstruction* (1977); and Barry A. Crouch, *The Freedmen's Bureau and Black Texans* (1992). The emergence of the sharecropping system is explored in Roger L. Ransom and Richard Sutch, *One Kind of Freedom: The Economic Consequences of Emancipation* (1977); Jay Mandle, *The Roots of Black Poverty: The Southern Plantation Economy after the Civil War* (1978); Gavin Wright, *Old South, New South: Revolutions in the Southern Economy since the Civil War* (1986); Edward Royce, *The Origins of Southern Sharecropping* (1993); and Harold Woodman, *New South, New Law: The Legal Foundations of Credit and Labor Relations in the Postbellum Agricultural South* (1995).

The Undoing of Reconstruction

The most thorough study of the Ku Klux Klan is Allen W. Trelease, *White Terror: The Ku Klux Klan Conspiracy and Southern Reconstruction* (1972); on its leader, see Brian S. Wills, *A Battle from the Start: The Life of Nathan Bedford Forrest* (1992). To survey Reconstruction politics in the South, consult Michael Perman, *The Road to Redemption: Southern Politics, 1869–1879* (1984). On politics in the North, see James Mohr, ed., *The Radical Republicans in the North: State Politics during Reconstruction* (1976), and William Gillette, *Retreat from Reconstruction, 1863–1879* (1979). Laura F. Edwards, *Gendered Strife and Confusion: The Political Culture of Reconstruction* (1997), is an innovative study that explores the gendered dimension of reconstruction politics in a North Carolina county. Equally illuminating as a more traditional political narrative is Jonathan M. Bryant, *How Curious a Land: Conflict and Change in Greene County, Georgia, 1850–1885* (1996).

For the impact of Reconstruction on the national state, see Morton Keller, *Affairs of State: Public Life in Late Nineteenth-Century America* (1977), and Richard F. Bensel, *Yankee Leviathan: The Origins of Central State Authority in America, 1859–1877* (1990). On political corruption, see Mark W. Summers, *The Era of Good Stealings* (1993). On the contested election of 1876, see C. Vann Woodward's classic *Reunion and Reaction* (1956), and K. I. Polakoff, *The Politics of Inertia: The Election of 1876 and the End of Reconstruction* (1973).

Part Four

★

A Maturing Industrial Society, 1877–1914

THEMATIC TIMELINE

	Economy	Society	Culture	Government	Diplomacy
	The Triumph of Industrialization	Racial, Ethnic, and Gender Divisions	The Rise of the City	From Inaction to Progressive Reform	An Emerging World Power
1877	Carnegie launches modern steel industry Knights of Labor becomes national movement (1878)	Defeat of the struggle for black equality End of nomadic Indian life	National League founded (1876) Dwight L. Moody pioneers urban revivalism	Election of Rutherford B. Hayes ends Reconstruction	United States becomes a net exporter
1880	Gustavus Swift pioneers vertically integrated firm American Federation of Labor founded (1886)	Chinese Exclusion Act (1882) Dawes Severalty Act divides tribal lands (1887)	Electrification transforms city life First *Social Register* defines high society (1888)	Ethnocultural issues dominate state and local politics Civil service reform (1883)	Diplomacy of inaction Naval buildup begins
1890	United States surpasses Britain in iron and steel output Economic depression (1893–1897) Era of farm prosperity begins	Black disfranchisement and racial segregation in the South Immigration from southeastern Europe rises sharply	Settlement houses spread progressive ideas to cities Hearst's *New York Journal* pioneers yellow journalism	Populist Party founded (1892) William McKinley wins presidency; defeats Bryan's free silver crusade (1896)	Social Darwinism and Anglo-Saxonism promote expansionism Spanish-American War (1898–1899); conquest of the Philippines
1900	Great merger movement Immigrants dominate factory work Industrial Workers of the World founded (1905)	Women take leading roles in social reform Revival of the struggle for civil rights Immigration restriction movement launched	Muckraking journalism Movies begin to overtake vaudeville	Progressivism in national politics Theodore Roosevelt attacks the trusts Hepburn Act enforces government's regulation of railroads (1906)	Panama cedes Canal Zone to United States (1903) Roosevelt Corollary to Monroe Doctrine (1904) Root-Takahira agreement (1908)
1910	Ford builds first automobile assembly line	NAACP founded (1910) Women win the right to vote in western states World War I ends the great European migration	Urban liberalism	Election of Woodrow Wilson (1912) New Freedom legislation creates Federal Reserve, FTC	Taft's dollar diplomacy promotes American business Woodrow Wilson proclaims U.S. neutrality in World War I

WHILE THE NATION'S attention was focused on the political drama of Reconstruction, few people noticed an equally momentous watershed in American economic life. For the first time, as the decade of the 1870s passed, farmers no longer constituted a majority of working Americans. Henceforth, America's future would be linked irrevocably to its development as an industrial society.

Economy. The effects of accelerating industrialization were felt, first of all, on the manufacturing sector itself. As heavy industry emerged and the railroad system was completed, the modern techniques of industrial management took shape, and big nationwide firms began to dominate American enterprise. The modern labor movement became firmly established, and as immigration surged, the foreign-born and their children became America's workers. What had been partial and limited changes became general and widespread as America became a land of factories, great corporate enterprise, and restless workers.

The West. Second, the demands of industrialism largely drove the final surge of settlement across the Great Plains and the Rockies. Cities called for new sources of food, and industry needed the Far West's mineral resources. In the struggle for their way of life, western Indians were ultimately defeated not so much by the rifles of army troopers as by events taking place far away in the nation's industries and cities. These same economic forces set in motion the Asian, Mexican, and European migrations that made for a multiethnic western society. Rural America was likewise locked into the advancing Industrial Revolution. The distress American farmers experienced during this period resulted from their imperfect integration into the modern industrial order. They remained small-scale operators in an economic world increasingly dominated by far-flung railroads and giant corporations.

Culture. Third, industrialization transformed the physical and human makeup of the nation's cities. By 1900 one in five Americans lived in cities. That was where the jobs were—as workers in factories; as clerks and salespeople in offices and department stores; as members of a new salaried middle class of managers,

engineers, and professionals; and, at the apex, as a wealthy elite of property owners and entrepreneurs. But the city was more than just a place to make a living. It provided a setting for an urban way of life unlike anything seen before in the United States.

Government. Fourth, politics marched in step with the industrial order. In the years of unprecedented economic expansion between 1877 and 1893 there seemed little need for government intervention. The major parties were robust and active, but their vitality stemmed from a political culture of popular participation, from ethnocultural conflicts linked to party loyalties, and from the informal functions political parties performed as highly organized machines. Economic crisis during the 1890s triggered a serious challenge to the political status quo, first by distressed farmers active in the Populist Party and then, as economic troubles spread, by the divisive campaign for free silver. The election of 1896 turned back that challenge. Still unresolved, however, was another economic concern: the enormous concentration of business power that had accompanied the nation's corporate development. This issue dominated national politics during the Progressive Era. In those years, too, the nation belatedly began to address its social ills. Women progressives took the lead in the struggle to make life better for America's urban masses. African Americans, victimized by disfranchisement and segregation, found allies among white progressives and launched a new drive for racial equality.

Diplomacy. Fifth, the dynamism of America's economic development forced a decisive shift in the country's foreign relations. In the decades after the Civil War, America had been inward-looking, its indifference to global affairs reflected in an inactive diplomacy and a neglected navy. The economic crisis of the 1890s, however, brought home to American leaders the need for secure access to overseas markets for the nation's surplus products. In short order the United States fought a brief war with Spain, acquired an overseas empire, and asserted its national interests in Latin America and Asia. There was no mistaking America's standing as a Great Power and, as World War I approached, no evading the responsibilities and entanglements that came with that elevated status.

The American West

D URING THE LAST decades of the nineteenth century, America seemed like two nations. One was an advanced industrial society, the America of great factories and sprawling cities. The other still seemed to be frontier country, with pioneers streaming onto the Great Plains, repeating the dramas of "settlement" they had been performing ever since Europeans had first set foot on the continent. Not until 1890 did the U.S. Census declare that a "frontier of settlement" no longer existed: the country's "unsettled area has been so broken into . . . that there can hardly be said to be a frontier line."

In that same year the country surpassed Great Britain in the production of iron and steel. Newspapers reported Indian wars and labor strikes in the same edition. The last tragic episode in the war against the Sioux, the massacre at Wounded Knee, South Dakota, occurred only eighteen months before the great Homestead steel strike of 1892. This conjunction of events from the distant worlds of factory and frontier was not accidental. The final surge of settlement across the Great Plains and the Far West was powered primarily by American industrialism.

The Industrial Revolution likewise shaped the history of agricultural America in these years. Farmers had one foot in the agrarian past and the other in the industrial age. They remained small-scale operators in an economic world dominated by far-flung railroads and giant corporations. They were thinking as family farmers but producing for international markets. Rural America could no longer be understood on its own terms. Its history had become linked ever more tightly to the larger industrial society.

The Yo-Hamite Falls (1855)
This detail of one of the earliest artistic renderings of Yosemite Valley and its great waterfall was drawn, in fact, before the place came to be called Yosemite. The scale of the waterfall, which falls 2,300 feet to the valley below, is dramatized by the inclusion of the artist's (Thomas A. Ayres) companions in the foreground. In this romantic lithograph, one can already see the grandeur of the West that Yosemite came to represent for Americans.
University of California at Berkeley, Bancroft Library, Honeyman Collection.

The Great Plains

───────★───────

During the 1860s agricultural settlement reached the western margins of the tall-grass prairie. Beyond, roughly from the 98th meridian, stretched vast dry country uninviting to farmers accustomed to woodlands and ample rainfall (Map 16.1). They saw it much as did the New York publisher Horace Greeley on his way to California in 1859: "a land of starvation," "a treeless desert" with a "terrible" climate of baking heat in the daytime and "chill and piercing" cold at night.

Greeley was describing the Great Plains. The geologic event creating this wide, dry expanse occurred 60 million years ago when the Rocky Mountains arose

out of the ocean covering western North America. With no outlet, the shallow inland sea to the east dried up, forming a hard pan on which sediment washing down from the mountains built up a loose, featureless surface layer. The mountain barrier also made for a dry climate because moisture-laden winds from the Pacific spent themselves on the western slopes. Only vegetation capable of withstanding the bitter winters and periodic cycles of severe drought could take hold on the plains. The short gramma (buffalo) grass, the linchpin of this fragile ecosystem, matted the easily blown soil into place and sustained a rich wildlife dominated by grazing pronghorn antelope and buffalo. What the dry, short-grass country had not sustained, until the past few centuries, was human settlement.

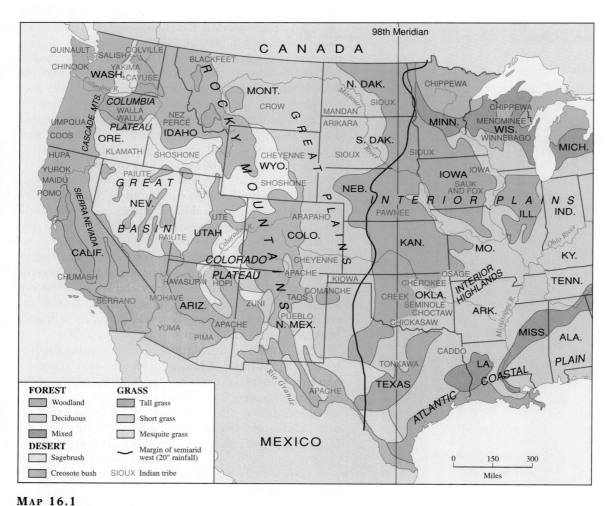

MAP 16.1

The Natural Environment of the West

As settlers pushed into the Great Plains beyond the line of semiaridity, they sensed the overwhelming power of the natural environment. In a landscape without trees for fences and barns, and without adequate rainfall, ranchers and farmers had to relearn their business. The native Americans peopling the plains and mountains had in time learned to live in this environment, but this knowledge counted for little against the ruthless pressure of the settlers to domesticate the West.

Indians of the Great Plains

Probably a hundred thousand native Americans lived on the Great Plains at mid-nineteenth century. They were a diverse people, divided into six linguistic families and at least thirty tribal groupings. The Mandan, Arikara, and Pawnee were mostly agriculturalists, planting maize and beans and living in permanent villages. Relatively concentrated and sedentary, these tribes were ravaged during the nineteenth century by smallpox and measles brought by Europeans. Less vulnerable to epidemics were the hunting tribes that had migrated onto the Great Plains since the seventeenth century: Kiowa and Comanche in the southwest; Arapaho and Cheyenne on the central plains; and, to the north, Blackfeet, Crow, Cheyenne, and the great Sioux nation (see Map 16.1).

The Teton Sioux.   Originally the Sioux had occupied semipermanent settlements in the lake country of northern Minnesota. With fish and game dwindling, some Sioux tribes drifted westward during the early eighteenth century. Around 1760 they began to cross the Missouri River into the vast short-grass country. These Sioux became nomadic, living in portable skin tepees and relying on the hunt for survival. From tribes to the south and west, they acquired horses. Now mounted, the Sioux became splendid hunters and formidable fighters, claiming the entire Great Plains north of the Arkansas River as their hunting grounds and driving out or subjugating longer-settled tribes.

The westernmost Sioux—they called themselves the Teton people, or Lakotas (meaning "allies")—made up a loose confederation of seven tribes. In the winter months the tribes broke up into small bands, but each spring the bands assembled and prepared for the summer hunt. Summer was also the season for making war. Mostly, raiding parties of thirty or forty warriors rode forth, intent on capturing horses and taking scalps, but occasionally larger, well-organized territorial campaigns were mounted against rival tribes.

A society that celebrates the heroic virtues of hunting and war is likely to define gender roles sharply. But before the Sioux got horses, chasing down the buffalo had involved the entire community: women and men worked collectively to construct a "pound" and to channel the herds in the right direction. With the arrival of horses, however, the men rode off to the hunt while the women stayed behind to prepare the mounting piles of buffalo skins. This was laborious, painstaking work. Fanny Kelly, who had been a Sioux captive, considered the women's lives "a servitude"; but she noticed also that they were "very rebellious, often displaying ungovernable and violent temper." Subordination to the men was not how Sioux women understood their unrelenting labor; this was their allotted share in a partnership on which the proud, nomadic life of the Teton depended.

Teton Culture.   Living so close to wild nature, depending on its bounty for survival, the Sioux saw sacred meaning in every manifestation of the natural world.

Tepee Liner
For the Plains Indians, tribal life revolved around the buffalo hunt and the battleground. These were the themes with which an unknown Indian artist decorated this dewcloth, which was hung inside a tepee to shield the occupants and provide some insulation from the cold.
American Hurrah, New York City.

Unlike Europeans, they conceived of God not as a supreme being but, in the words of ethnologist Clark Wissler, as a "series of powers pervading the universe"— Wi, the sun; Skan, the sky; Maka, the earth; Inyan, the rock. Below these came the moon, wind, buffalo—down through a hierarchy embodying the entire natural order.

By prayer and fasting in some isolated place, young Sioux prepared themselves for a vision of those mysterious powers. Medicine men provided instruction, but the religious experience was essentially personal and open to both sexes. The vision, when a supplicant achieved it, attached itself to some object—a feather, an animal skin, or a shell—that was tied into a sacred bundle and became that person's lifelong talisman, or charm. For the tribe as a whole, Sacred Pipe bundles served as the symbolic and ceremonial core of Sioux religion. In the annual Sun Dance, the entire tribe engaged in the rites of coming of age, fertility, the hunt, and combat, followed by four days of fasting and dancing in supplication to Wi, the sun.

The world of the Teton Sioux was not self-contained. All along they had been traders, exchanging pelts and buffalo robes for the agricultural products of other Plains Indians. These exchanges expanded to the white traders who had appeared on the upper Missouri River during the eighteenth century, and a substantial commerce in furs developed. Although the buffalo provided most of the essentials of life—not only food but clothing, shelter, fuel, carrying bags, and a variety of bone implements—the Sioux came to rely as well on the traders' pots, kettles, blankets, knives, and firearms. The trade system they had entered was linked to the Euro-American economy, yet it was also integrated into the traditional Sioux way of life. Everything depended on the survival of the Great Plains as the Sioux had found it—wild grassland on which the antelope and buffalo ranged free.

Intruders

On first encounter, settlers themselves saw no better use for the Great Plains. After exploring a drought-stricken stretch in 1820, Major Stephen H. Long declared it "almost wholly unfit for cultivation, and of course uninhabitable by a people depending upon agriculture for their subsistence."

For years thereafter, maps marked the plains region as the Great American Desert. And with that notion in mind, Congress formally designated the Great Plains in 1834 as permanent Indian country. The army general in charge, Edmund Gaines, wanted the border forts, stretching from Lake Superior to Fort Worth, Texas, to be constructed of stone because they would be there forever. Trade with the Indians—now closely supervised and licensed by the federal government—would continue with the Indian country otherwise off-limits to white intrusion.

Events swiftly overtook the nation's solemn commitment to the native Americans. During the 1840s settlers began a massive movement westward to Oregon and California. Indian country became a bridge to the Pacific. The first wagon train headed west for Oregon from Missouri in 1842. Over the next three decades, thousands of emigrants traveled the Oregon Trail to the Willamette Valley or, cutting south beyond Fort Hall, down into California. Approaching Fort Hall in 1859, it seemed to Horace Greeley as if "the white coverings of the many emigrant and transport wagons dott[ing] the landscape" gave "the trail the appearance of a river running through great meadows, with many ships sailing on its bosom." Only these "ships" left behind not a trailing wake of foam but a rutted landscape devoid of grass and game, and littered with abandoned wagons and rotting garbage.

The Railroads.   Talk about the need for a railroad to the Pacific soon began to be heard in Washington. How else could the distant territories stretching to the Pacific Ocean be firmly linked to the Union? Settlers bound for California and Oregon clamored for relief from the ordeal of the overland journey by wagon train. For nearly twenty years, however, the project languished while North and South argued over the eastern terminus for the route. Meanwhile, Indian country was crisscrossed by overland freight lines and Pony Express riders and, in 1861, by the telegraph lines that brought San Francisco into instant communication with the East. In the next year, with the South in rebellion, the federal government finally moved forward with the transcontinental rail project.

No private company could be expected to foot the bill by itself. The construction costs were staggering and, in the short run, not much demand for rail service existed in the thinly populated interior of the West. So the federal government offered generous land grants along the right-of-way, plus millions of dollars in public loans, to the two companies that undertook the transcontinental project.

The Union Pacific, building westward from Omaha, made little headway until the Civil War ended but then advanced rapidly across Indian country, reaching Cheyenne, Wyoming, in November 1867. It took the Central Pacific nearly that long moving eastward from Sacramento, California, to cross the crest of the Sierra Nevada. Both then worked furiously—since the government subsidy was based on miles of track built—until, to great fanfare, the tracks met at Promontory, Utah, in 1869. The transcontinental link was actually a pretty rickety affair, capable of moving people but not a lot of freight. It would eventually have to be wholly rebuilt. None of the other railroads following other westward routes made it as far as the Rockies before the Panic of 1873 hit, throwing them into bankruptcy and bringing work to an abrupt halt.

By then, however, railroad tycoons had changed their minds about the Great Plains. No longer did they see it through the eyes of the Oregon-bound settlers—as a place to be gotten through en route to the Pacific. Rail transportation, they realized, was laying the basis for the economic exploitation of the Great Plains. This calculation spurred the railroad boom that followed economic recovery in 1878. Construction soared. During the 1880s, 40,000 miles of track were laid west of the Mississippi, including links from southern California via the Southern Pacific to New Orleans and via the Santa Fe to Kansas City, and from the Northwest via the Northern Pacific to St. Paul, Minnesota.

The Cattle Kingdom. Of all the opportunities beckoning on the Great Plains, most obvious was cattle raising. The grazing buffalo made it easy to imagine the plains as cow country. But first, the buffalo had to go. A small market for buffalo robes had existed for years. And buffalo hunters like the famous William F. Cody (see American Lives, "Buffalo Bill and the Wild West," pp. 512–513) made a good living providing meat for labor gangs and army posts, and leading parties of sportsmen. Then, in the early 1870s, eastern tanneries discovered how to cure the hides, and a huge demand developed among shoe and harness manufacturers. Parties of professional hunters with high-powered rifles swept across the plains and began a systematic slaughter of the buffalo. The great herds, already diminished by disease and shrinking pasturage, almost vanished within ten years. Many people spoke out against this mass killing, but no way existed to stop people bent on making a quick dollar. Besides, as General Philip H. Sheridan pointed out, exterminating the buffalo would starve the Indians into submission and open up the feeding grounds for cattle.

About 5 million head of longhorn cattle roamed the ranches of south Texas in 1865, hardly worth bothering about because they could not be profitably marketed. In that year, however, the Missouri Pacific Railroad reached Sedalia, Missouri, far enough west to be accessible across open land to Texas cattle. At the Sedalia terminus, which connected to hungry eastern markets, a $3 longhorn might command $40. With this incentive, Texas ranchers inaugurated the famous Long Drive. Cowboys began to herd the longhorn cattle hundreds of miles north to the railroads that were pushing west across Kansas.

At Abilene, Ellsworth, and Dodge City, ranchers sold their cattle, and trail-weary cowboys went on a binge. These wide-open cattle towns captured the nation's imagination as symbols of the Wild West. The reality was much more ordinary. The cowboys, many of them blacks and Hispanics, were in fact farmhands on horseback, working long hours under harsh conditions for small pay. Colorful though it seemed, the Long Drive was actually a makeshift method of bridging a gap in the developing

Killing the Buffalo
This woodcut shows passengers shooting buffalo from a Kansas Pacific Railroad train—a small thrill added to the modern convenience of traveling west by rail.
North Wind Picture Archives.

transportation system. As soon as railroads reached the Texas range country during the 1870s, ranchers abandoned the hazardous and wasteful Long Drive.

In Texas, ranchers owned or leased the grazing land they used, sometimes in huge tracts. North of Texas, where the land was in the public domain, cattlemen simply helped themselves. Hopeful ranchers would spot a likely area along a creek and claim as much land as they could qualify for as settlers under federal homesteading laws, plus what might be added by the fraudulent claims taken out by one or two ranch hands. By a common usage that quickly became established, ranchers had a "range right" to all the adjacent land rising up to the divide—the point where the land sloped down to the next creek.

News of easy money traveled fast. Calves cost $5, and steers sold for maybe $60 on the Chicago market. Rail connections were in place or coming in. And the grass was free. Profits of 40 percent per year were a sure thing. The rush was on, drawing from as far away as Europe both hardheaded investors and romantics (like the recent Harvard graduate Teddy Roosevelt) eager for a taste of the Wild West. By the early 1880s the plains overflowed with cattle—as many as 7.5 million head, decimating the grass and trampling the water holes.

A cycle of good weather only postponed the inevitable disaster. When it came—a hard winter in 1885, a severe drought the following summer, then record blizzards and bitter cold—cattle died by the hundreds of thousands. An awful scene of rotting carcasses greeted the cowhands riding out onto the range the following spring. The recent slaughter of buffalo had produced equally ghastly sights, only no one owned the buffalo (and horror at their fate was therefore

Buffalo Bill and the Wild West

★

SCOTT COUNTY, IOWA, was still frontier country when William F. Cody was born there on February 26, 1846. Kansas, where his family moved in 1854, was even wilder, for it was not only frontier country but racked by bloody conflict between proslavery and free-soil settlers. Bill's father, Isaac Cody, was active on the free-soil side, serving in the Topeka legislature and frequently in harm's way from neighboring southern sympathizers and marauding Border Ruffians. One of Bill's first exploits was a wild gallop, with proslavery men in hot pursuit, to warn his father of a trap set for him near the family farm. Isaac Cody, however, was less an idealist than a typical enterprising westerner on the lookout for the main chance. He had been an Indian trader, a farm manager, a stagecoach operator, and, in Kansas, a land speculator around Grasshopper Falls. When he died suddenly in 1857, Cody left the family with a pile of land titles but little money.

Bill, never much for schooling anyway, had to find work. Only eleven, he was taken on by Majors and Waddell, the firm that transported goods from Fort Leavenworth to army posts west of the Missouri River. Bill worked as a messenger boy, livestock herder, and teamster helper on the freight wagons. When his employers organized the short-lived Pony Express in 1860, Cody became a stocktender and occasional rider in the Colorado- Nebraska division. Most of this was hard and tedious labor, but there were flashes of excitement—scrapes with Indians and with bandits (at fifteen, Bill killed one), buffalo stampedes, and brief encounters with Wild Bill Hickok and other tough western characters on whom Bill could model himself. In the early part of the Civil War Cody was at loose ends. Among other things, he engaged in horse thieving disguised as guerrilla activity in Missouri, and he became a heavy drinker. After a stint in the Seventh Kansas Cavalry and a halfhearted effort to settle down after the war

(in what turned out to be an unhappy marriage), Cody got his lucky break in 1867.

The Kansas Pacific Railroad was building a line through Indian country to Sheridan, Kansas. To provision the work crews, the contractors hired Cody at $500 a month—excellent pay—to supply the cooks with buffalo meat. Cody was a crack shot and an excellent horseman, and he knew buffalo hunting. This assignment was duck soup for him, and the aplomb with which he carried it off soon gave him the name "Buffalo Bill."

The next summer, 1868, Indian war broke out in Kansas, and Cody got his second claim to fame. He was hired as chief scout for the U.S. Fifth Cavalry. Cody knew the Kansas landscape intimately, seemed to have a remarkable instinct for following a trail, and was intrepid in the face of danger. At the height of the fighting in 1868–1869 Cody saw repeated action. In the climactic Battle of Summit Springs, his scouting played a decisive role, and he himself shot the Cheyenne chief Tall Bull. Although the legends later built up around Buffalo Bill (and the claims of others) have inclined scholars to be skeptical, Buffalo Bill was in fact an authentic hero. Perhaps the best testimony was the extra $100 awarded him by the normally tight-fisted army "for extraordinarily good services as a trailer and fighter in the pursuit of hostile Indians."

Out of these promising materials there began to emerge a mythic figure. In July 1869 the dime novelist Ned Buntline (Edward Zane Carroll Judson) came through Kansas, met Cody, and, after returning to New York, wrote *Buffalo Bill, the King of the Border Men*—the first of some seventeen hundred potboilers to feature Cody's name and exploits. Then there were the buffalo-hunting parties of the rich and famous that Cody periodically led, including a royal hunt in 1872 with Grand Duke Alexis of Russia that had the entire country agog. With his white horse, buckskin suit, crimson shirt, and broad sombrero, Buffalo Bill began to play his part to the hilt. "He realized to perfection the bold hunter and gallant sportsman of the plains," wrote one appreciative participant. In 1872 Cody was persuaded to appear as himself in a play Ned Buntline proposed to put on in New York. Buntline was said to have dashed off *The Scouts of the Prairie* in four hours, and critics pronounced it "execrable." But Buffalo Bill, who mostly ad-libbed, was a

Buffalo Bill's Wild West Show
The Wild West Show had worldwide appeal. This poster celebrates one of Buffalo Bill's
European tours.
Buffalo Bill Historical Center, Cody, Wyoming. Gift of The Coe Foundation.

great hit, and so was the production. Cody was launched on his career as a showman.

From then on, the lines between reality and make-believe began to blur. Not only did Buffalo Bill draw on his past exploits when he went on stage, but he had the stage in mind when he returned to the real world. During the Sioux wars of 1875–1876 Cody was again out in the field as an army scout. (Fortunately, the fighting took place during the theatrical off-seasons in the East.) Shortly after the annihilation of Custer's troops at Little Big Horn, Cody gained a measure of vengeance in a famous skirmish in which he killed and scalped a Sioux chief named Yellow Hand. Cody rode into that engagement wearing his stage vaquero outfit—black velvet and scarlet with lace—so that when he reenacted the mayhem on stage, he could say he was wearing the very clothes in which he had seen action. Over time, with some help from Cody, the fight with Yellow Hand assumed legendary proportions, becoming a formal duel, with a challenge laid down by the Indian chief and troopers and

Indian warriors lined up on opposing sides watching Buffalo Bill and Yellow Hand fight it out.

The mythic West that Cody was creating became full blown in his Wild West Show, first staged in 1883. Taking the circus and rodeo as his model, Cody put on an open-air extravaganza with displays of horsemanship, sharpshooting by Little Annie Oakley, real Indians (in one season Chief Sitting Bull toured with the company), and reenactments of stagecoach robberies and great events such as Custer's Last Stand. The Wild West Show toured the country every year and was a smashing success in Europe as well.

Buffalo Bill had been keen enough to see the hunger of city people for a legendary West. He traded on his talents as a showman, but he relied as well on his grasp of the authentic world behind the make-believe. When Cody died in 1917, that world was long gone, but his Wild West Show kept it alive in legend, where it still remains in the mythic figures of cowboys and Indians that populate our movies and television screens.

The Cowboy at Work
The cowboy, celebrated in dime novels, was really a farmhand on horseback, with the skills to work on the range, including the ability to stay glued to his saddle while lassoing a steer. He earned twenty-five dollars a month, plus meals and a bed in the bunkhouse, in return for long hours of lonesome, grueling work. But one can see in Charles Russell's vivid painting, *Jerked Down* (1907), why the cowhand could so readily be converted into a western hero.
Thomas Gilcrease Institute of American History and Art.

regarded as "sentimental"). Every dead steer, however, represented some rancher's investment. On top of these losses, beef prices collapsed when hard-pressed ranchers dumped the surviving cattle on the market. The boom had turned into a spectacular bust, and investors fled, leaving behind a more enduring ecological catastrophe: the native grasses never recovered from the relentless overgrazing in the drought cycle.

The ranchers who remained fenced their land and planted hay for the winter. No longer would cattle be left to fend for themselves on the open range. Elsewhere, Hispanic grazers from New Mexico brought in sheep to feed on the weeds and woody plants that had replaced the native grasses. Sheep raising, previously scorned by ranchers as unmanly and resisted as a threat to cattle, became a major enterprise in the sparser high country. Some ranchers even sold out to the despised "nesters"— those who wanted to try farming the Great Plains.

Homesteaders. Potential settlers, of course, needed first of all to be persuaded that crops would grow in that dry country. Powerful interests devoted themselves to overcoming the popular notion that the plains was a Great American Desert. Foremost were the railroads, eager to sell off the public land they had been granted— 180 million acres of it—and develop traffic for their routes. They aggressively advertised, offered cut-rate tickets, and sold off their landholdings at bargain prices. Land speculators, transatlantic steamship lines, and the western states and territories did all they could to encourage settlement of the Great Plains. And so did the federal government, with its offer under the Homestead Act (1862) of 160 acres of public land to settlers.

"Why emigrate to Kansas?" asked a testimonial in *Western Trail*, the Rock Island Railroad's gazette. "Because it is the garden spot of the world. Because it will grow anything that any other country will grow, and with less work. Because it rains here more than any other place, and at just the right time." Too boastful, a prospective settler might think, but surely holding a grain of truth. Besides, the climate might improve. "Why may we not suppose that the genial influences of civilization—that extensive cultivation of the earth— might contribute to the multiplication of showers?" asked Josiah Gregg, an early traveler on the plains. Might not "these sterile regions . . . be thus revived and fertilized, and their surface covered one day by flourishing settlements to the Rocky Mountains?"

Over time Gregg's vision became an article of faith among boosters of the plains. As if to confirm the optimists, an exceptionally wet cycle occurred between 1878 and 1886. "As the plains are settled up we hear less and less of drouth, hot winds, alkali and other bugbears that used to hold back the adventurous," remarked one Nebraska man. Some settlers attributed the increased rainfall to soil cultivation and tree planting. Others credited God. As a settler on the southern plains remarked, "The Lord just knowed we needed more land an' He's gone and changed the climate."

No amount of optimism, however, could dispel the emptiness of the treeless land. "Such an air of desolation," wrote a Nebraska-bound woman; and from another woman in Texas, "such a lonely country." One old hand likened these despairing feelings to an illness. "A stranger travelling on the prairie would get his hopes up, expecting to see something different on making the next rise." But all he found was "grass and then more grass—the monotonous, endless prairie! . . . To him the disappointment and monotony were terrible. 'He's got loneliness,' we would say of such a man." For a Swedish emigrant like Ida Lindgren (see American Voices, "Ida Lindgren: Swedish Emigrant in Frontier Kansas,"

IDA LINDGREN
Swedish Emigrant in Frontier Kansas

———————★———————

Like many emigrants, Ida Lindgren did not find it easy to adjust to the harsh new life on the frontier. Her diary entries and letters home show that the adjustment for the first generation was never complete.

May 15, 1870 [Lake Sibley, Nebraska]
What shall I say? Why has the lord brought us here? Oh, I feel so oppressed, so unhappy! Two whole days it took us to get here and they were not the least trying part of our travels. We sat on boards in the work-wagon packed in so tightly that we could not move a foot, and we drove across endless, endless prairies, on narrow roads; no, no, not roads, tracks like those in the fields at home when they harvested grain. No forest but only a few trees which grow along the rivers and creeks. And then here and there you see a homestead and pass a little settlement. The Indians are not so far away from here, I can understand, and all the men you see coming by, riding or driving wagons, are armed with revolvers and long carbines, and look like highway robbers.

No date [probably written July 1870]
Claus and his wife lost their youngest child at Lake Sibley and it was very sad in many ways. There was no real cemetery but out on the prairie stood a large, solitary tree, and around it they bury their dead, without tolling of bells, without a pastor, and some-times without any coffin. A coffin was made here for their child, it was not painted black, but we lined it with flowers and one of the men read the funeral service, and then there was a hymn, and that was all.

August 25, 1874 [Manhattan, Kansas]
It has been a long time since I have written, hasn't it? . . . When one never has anything fun to write about, it is no fun to write. . . . We have not had rain since the beginning of June, and then with this heat and often strong winds as well, you can imagine how everything has dried out. There has also been a general lamentation and fear for the coming year. We are glad we have the oats (for many don't have any and must feed wheat to the stock) and had hoped to have the corn leaves to add to the fodder. But then one fine day there came millions, trillions of grasshoppers in great clouds, hiding the sun, and coming down into the fields, eating up everything that was still there, the leaves on the trees, peaches, grapes, cucumbers, onions, cabbage, everything, everything. Only the peach stones still hung on the trees, showing what had once been there.

July 1, 1877 [Manhattan, Kansas]
. . . It seems so strange to me when I think that more than seven years have passed since I have seen you all. . . . I can see so clearly that last glimpse I had of Mamma, standing alone amid all the tracks of Eslov station. Oliva I last saw sitting on her sofa in her red and black dress, holding little Brita, one month old, on her lap. And Wilhelm I last saw in Lund at the station, as he rolled away with the train, waving his last farewell to me. . . .

———

Source: H. Arnold Barton, ed., *Letters from the Promised Land* (Minneapolis: University of Minnesota Press, 1975), 143–145, 150–156.

above), no place could have seemed so far from home and loved ones, and offered so little hope of seeing home and family again. Emigrants, indeed, had always taken parting as a kind of death, with reunion unlikely "on this side of the dark river."

For many women, this hard experience had a liberating side. Prescribed gender roles broke down as women shouldered men's work on new farms and gained a heightened sense of self-reliance. When husbands died or gave up, wives operated farms on their own. Other women started out alone. Under the Homestead Act, which accorded widows and single women the same rights as men, women filed 10 percent of the claims. "People afraid of coyotes and work and loneliness had better leave ranching alone," advised one woman homesteader. "At the same time, any woman who can stand her own company . . . and is willing to put in as much time at careful labor as she does at the washtub, will certainly succeed; will have independence, plenty to eat all the time, and a home of her own in the end."

Buffalo Chips
With no trees around for firewood, settlers on the plains had to make do with dried cow and buffalo droppings. Gathering the "buffalo chips" must have been a regular chore for Ada McColl and her daughter on her homestead near Lakin, Kansas (1893).
Kansas State Historical Society.

The vision of new land to be farmed drove people onto the plains. By the 1870s, Illinois, Wisconsin, and other midwestern states had filled up, and farmers looked hungrily westward. "Hardly anything else was talked about," recalled short-story writer Hamlin Garland about his Iowa neighbors. "Every man who could sell out had gone west or was going. . . . Farmer after farmer joined the march to Kansas, Nebraska, and Dakota. . . . The movement . . . had . . . become an exodus, a stampede."

The same excitement took hold in northern Europe, as Norwegians, Swedes, and Russians for the first time joined the older German migration. At the peak of the "American fever" in 1882, over 105,000 Scandinavians immigrated to the United States. Swedish and Norwegian became the primary languages in parts of Minnesota and the Dakotas. Roughly a third of the farmers on the northern plains were foreign-born (Map 16.2).

The motivation for most settlers, American or European, was to better themselves economically. But for some southern blacks, Kansas briefly represented something more precious—the modern Promised Land of racial freedom. In the spring of 1879, with Reconstruction over and federal protection withdrawn, black communities fearful of white vengeance were swept by religious enthusiasm for Kansas. Within a month or so, some 6,000 blacks left Mississippi and Louisiana, most of them with nothing more than the clothes on their backs and faith in the Lord. They called themselves Exodusters, members of the exodus to the dry prairie. The 1880 census reported

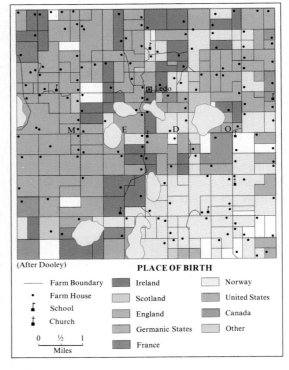

(After Dooley)

PLACE OF BIRTH

— Farm Boundary
• Farm House
School
Church

Ireland
Scotland
England
Germanic States
France

Norway
United States
Canada
Other

0   ½   1
Miles

MAP 16.2
The Rural Ethnic Mosaic: Blue Earth County, Minnesota, 1880
What could have been more natural for emigrants such as Ida Lindgren (see American Voices, p. 515) than to settle next to others sharing common ties to a homeland? This map of Medo Township reveals that in rural America, no less than in the cities, ethnicity strongly influenced where people lived.

Exodusters
Driven from their homes by terror raids, these southern blacks camped out on a Mississippi levee on the way to Kansas.
Library of Congress.

40,000 blacks in Kansas, by far the largest African American concentration in the West aside from Texas, whose expanding cotton frontier attracted hundreds of thousands of black migrants during the 1870s and 1880s.

Farming the Plains. No matter where they came from, homesteaders found the plains a harsh place. A cloud of grasshoppers might destroy a crop in a day; a brush fire or hailstorm could do the job in an hour. What forested land had always provided—springs for water, lumber for cabins and fencing, ample firewood—was absent. For shelter, settlers often cut dugouts into hillsides and, after a season or two, erected houses made of turf cut from the ground.

The absence of trees, however, meant far less labor clearing the land. New technology and better seed overcame obstacles once thought insurmountable: steel plows enabled homesteaders to break the tightly matted ground; barbed wire, invented in 1874 by Joseph F. Glidden, an Illinois farmer, provided cheap, effective fencing against roaming cattle; and strains of hard-kernel wheat tolerant of the extreme temperatures of the plains came in from northern Europe and Russia's Crimea. The open, level land was ideal for raising grain. Homesteaders had good crops while the wet cycle held, and they began to anticipate the wood-frame house, deep well, and full coal bin that might make life on the plains tolerable.

Then, in the later 1880s, the dry years came and wrecked those hopeful calculations. "From day to day," reported the budding novelist Stephen Crane from Nebraska, "a wind hot as an oven's fury . . . raged like a pestilence," destroying the crops and leaving farmers "helpless, with no weapon against this terrible and inscrutable wrath of nature." Land only recently settled emptied out as homesteaders fled. The Dakotas lost 50,000 settlers between 1885 and 1890, and comparable departures occurred up and down the drought-stricken plains.

Other settlers held on grimly. Stripped of the illusion that "rain follows the plow," the survivors came to terms with the semiarid climate prevailing west of the 98th meridian. The answer lay in dry-farming methods, which involved deep planting to bring subsoil moisture to the roots, and quick harrowing after rainfalls to turn over a dry mulch that slowed evaporation. Producing a low yield per acre, dry farming developed most fully on the corporate farms that covered up to 100,000 acres in the Red River Valley in North Dakota. But family farms, which remained the norm elsewhere, could not operate with less than 300 acres of grain crops. Congress came to the rescue in 1873 by amending the Homestead legislation to enable settlers to qualify for an additional 160 acres if they planted trees on a quarter of the land. No one, however, could hope to survive without machinery for plowing, planting, and harvesting. Dry farming was not for the unequipped homesteader.

By the turn of the century the Great Plains had fully submitted to agricultural development. About half of the nation's cattle and sheep, a third of its cereal crops—and nearly three-fifths of its wheat—came from the newly settled lands. This process displayed little of the "pioneering" that Americans associated with the westward movement. The railroads preceded the settlers, eastern capital financed the ranching bonanza, and agriculture depended on sophisticated dry-farming techniques and modern machinery.

And where was the economic capital of the Great Plains? Far off in Chicago. There, at the hub of the nation's rail system, the wheat pit traded western grain and consigned it to world markets, and great packing houses slaughtered western livestock and supplied the nation with sausage, bacon, and sides of beef. In return, western ranchers and farmers got lumber, barbed wire, McCormick reapers, and Sears Roebuck catalogues. Chicago was truly, as historian William Cronon has called it, "nature's metropolis."

The Fate of the Indians

What of the native Americans who had inhabited the Great Plains? Basically, their future has been told in the foregoing account of western settlement. "The white children have surrounded me and have left me nothing but an island," lamented the great Sioux chief Red Cloud in 1870, the year after the completion of the transcontinental railroad. "When we first had all this land we were strong; now we are all melting like snow on a hillside, while you are grown like spring grass."

No matter that provision for a permanent Indian country had been written into federal law and ratified by treaties with various tribes. As incursions into their lands increased from the late 1850s onward, the Indians struck back all along the frontier: the Apache in the Southwest, the Cheyenne and Arapaho in Colorado, the Sioux in the Wyoming and Dakota territories. Fighting ferociously between 1865 and 1867, the Sioux prevented a wagon road from being built through their prized Powder River hunting grounds to the booming mining town of Bozeman, Montana. The Indians hoped that if they resisted stubbornly enough, the whites would tire of the struggle and leave them in peace. This seemed not altogether fanciful, given the country's exhaustion after the Civil War. But the federal government did not give up; instead, it formulated a new policy for dealing with the western Indians.

The Reservation Solution. Few whites questioned the necessity of moving the native Americans out of the path of settlement. That, indeed, had been the fate of the eastern Indians. Now, however, Indian removal was linked to something new: a planned approach for weaning the Indians from their tribal way of life. In early 1867, Congress adopted a law "for establishing peace with certain Indian tribes now at war with the United States." To this end, a peace commission was appointed, charged especially with negotiating a settlement based on the removal of the western tribes to reservations, where, under the guidance of the Office of Indian Affairs, they would be wards of the government until they learned "to walk on the white man's road."

The government set aside two extensive areas for the Indians. It allocated the southwestern quarter of the Dakota Territory—present-day South Dakota west of the Missouri River—to the northern Plains tribes. The Indians on the southern plains were assigned to Oklahoma, where the Five Civilized Tribes—the Choctaw, Cherokee, Chickasaw, Creek, and Seminole—and other

eastern Indians had already been resettled. Scattered reservations went to the Apache, Navajo, and Ute in the Southwest and to the mountain Indians in the Rockies and beyond (Map 16.3).

As in the past, the transfer of land went through the legal process of treaty making. And, as in the past, the whites bribed and tricked the Indian chiefs and in the end forced them to accept what they could not prevent. In 1868 the western Sioux tribes signed a treaty ceding all their land outside the Dakota reservation but explicitly retaining their hunting grounds in the Powder River country. "We have now selected and provided reservations for all, off the great road," concluded the western commanding general that year. "All who cling to their old hunting-grounds are hostile and will remain so till killed off." That they would resist was inevitable. "You might as well expect the rivers to run backward as that any man who was born a free man should be contented when penned up and denied liberty to go where he pleases," said Chief Joseph of the Nez Percé. With that conviction, Joseph in 1877 led his tribe, including women and children, on an epic 1,500-mile march from eastern Oregon to escape confinement in a small reservation. In a series of heroic engagements, the Nez Percé fought off the pursuing U.S. Army until, after four months of extraordinary hardship, the remnants of the tribe were finally cornered and forced to surrender in Montana near the Canadian border.

The U.S. Army was thinly spread, having been cut back after the Civil War to a total force of 27,000. But these were veteran troops, including 2,000 black cavalrymen of the Ninth and Tenth regiments, whom Indians called, with grim respect, "buffalo soldiers." Technology also favored the army. Telegraph communications and railroads enabled the troopers to be quickly concentrated; repeating rifles and Gatling guns increased their firepower. As fighting intensified in the mid-1870s, a reluctant Congress made appropriations to augment the western troopers. Tribal rivalries meant that the army always had Indian allies. Worst of all for the Indians, however, beyond the formidable U.S. Army or their own disunity, was the overwhelming impact of white settlement.

Resisting the reservation solution, the Indians fought on for years—in Kansas in 1868–1869, in the Red River Valley of Texas in 1874, sporadically in Arizona among the Apache, who refused to be contained in the small reservation to which they had been removed in the mid-1870s. For more than a decade, bands of these fierce desert warriors made life miserable for white settlers in the Southwest until Geronimo—their wily chief—was finally captured in 1886 and began a lifetime of captivity. On the northern plains the crisis came in 1875, when the Indian Office—despite the treaty of

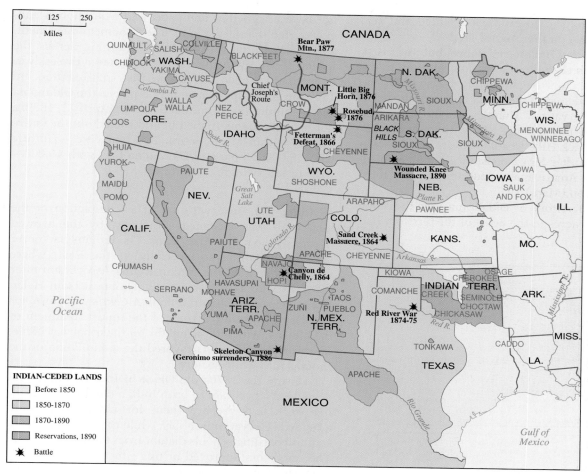

MAP 16.3
The Indian Frontier, to 1890
As settlement pushed onto the Great Plains after the Civil War, the Indians put up bitter
resistance, but ultimately to no avail. Over a period of decades they ceded most of their
lands to the federal government, and by 1890 they were confined to scattered reservations
where the most they could expect was an impoverished and alien way of life.

1868—ordered the Sioux to vacate their Powder River
hunting grounds and withdraw to the reservation.

Led by Sitting Bull, Sioux and Cheyenne warriors
gathered on the Little Big Horn River to the west of the
Powder River country. In a typical concentrating
maneuver, army columns from widely separated forts
converged on the Little Big Horn. The Seventh Cavalry,
commanded by Colonel George A. Custer, famous as a
Civil War cavalryman, came upon the Sioux encampment on June 25, 1876. Disregarding orders, the reckless Custer sought out battle on his own. He attacked
from three sides, hoping to capitalize on the element of
surprise. But his forces were spread too thin. The other
two army contingents fell back with heavy losses to
defensive positions, but Custer's own force of 256 men
was surrounded and annihilated by Crazy Horse's
Sioux warriors.

The victory was great but not decisive; it merely
postponed the day of reckoning. Weakened by unrelenting military pressure and increasing physical privation, the Sioux bands one by one gave up and moved
onto the reservation. Last to come in were Sitting Bull's
followers. They had retreated to Canada, but in 1881,
after five hard years, they recrossed the border and surrendered at Fort Buford, Montana.

By then the open plains were no more. Homesick
bands of southern Cheyenne learned this bitter truth in
1878 when they escaped from their reservation in the
Indian Territory of Oklahoma. Along the route to their
native grounds in the Wyoming Territory lay three railroads, numerous telegraph lines, and ranchers and
homesteaders eager to report the Cheyenne's movements. When the army eventually captured them, the
survivors declared that they preferred death to returning

to the reservation. The government relented and permitted them to stay on their native land.

In the end, not Indian resistance but relentless white pressure wrecked the reservation solution. In the mid-1870s prospectors began to dig for gold in the Black Hills, sacred land to the Sioux and entirely inside their Dakota reservation. Unable to hold back the prospectors or to buy out the Sioux, the government opened up the Black Hills to gold seekers at their own risk and in 1877, after Sioux resistance had crumbled, forced the native Americans to cede the western third of their reservation (Map 16.4).

The Indian Territory of Oklahoma met the same fate. Two million acres in the heart of the territory had not been assigned to any tribe, and white homesteaders coveted that fertile land. The "Boomer" movement, stirred up initially by railroads running across the Indian Territory during the 1880s, agitated tirelessly to open this so-called Oklahoma District to settlers. In 1889 the government gave in and placed the Oklahoma District under the Homestead Act. On April 22, 1889, a horde of claimants rushed in and staked out the entire district within a few hours. Two tent cities—Guthrie with 15,000 people and Oklahoma City with 10,000— were in full swing by nightfall.

Dividing the Reservations. The completion of the land grab was hastened, ironically, by the avowed friends of the native Americans. The Indians had never lacked sympathizers—especially in the East, where reformers created the Indian Rights Association after the Civil War. The movement got a boost from Helen Hunt Jackson's influential book *A Century of Dishonor* (1881), which told the story of the unjust treatment of the Indians. With little sympathy for the tribal way of life, however, the reformers favored the assimilation of the Indians into white society.

During the 1870s the Office of Indian Affairs had developed a program to train Indian children for farming work and prepare them for citizenship. Some attended reservation schools, while the less lucky were sent to boarding schools distant from family and home. The reformers approved of this educational program. They also favored efforts by the Indian Office to undercut tribal authority. In particular, they highly esteemed private property as a "civilizing" force. They felt, moreover, that defense of Indian lands against white encroachment was hopeless until the Indians became, individually, property owners.

The resulting policy was called *severalty*—the division of reservation lands into individually owned parcels. With the blessing of the reformers, the Dawes Severalty Act of 1887 authorized the president to divide tribal lands, giving 160 acres to each family head and smaller parcels to other individuals. The land would be held in trust by the government for twenty-five years, and the recipients would become U.S. citizens. Remaining reservation lands would be sold off and the proceeds placed in an Indian education fund.

MAP 16.4
The Sioux Reservations in South Dakota, 1868–1889
In 1868, when they bent to the demand that they move onto the reservation, the Sioux thought they had gained secure rights to a substantial part of their ancestral hunting grounds. But as they learned to their sorrow, fixed boundary lines only increased their vulnerability to the land hunger of the whites and sped up the process of expropriation.

The Last Battle: Wounded Knee. The Sioux were among the first to bear the brunt of the Dawes Act. The federal government, announcing it had gained the Sioux's approval, opened their "surplus" land to white settlement on February 10, 1890. But no surveys had been made of the reservation boundaries, nor had any provision been made for land allotments for the Indians living in the ceded areas. On top of these signs of bad faith by the whites, drought wiped out the Sioux's crops that summer.

Indian School
In this photograph at the Riverside Indian School in Anadarko, Oklahoma Territory, the pupils have been shorn of their braids and dressed in laced shoes, Mother Hubbard dresses, and shirts and trousers—one step on the journey into the mainstream of white American society. Children as young as five were separated from their families and sent to Indian schools like this one that taught them new skills while encouraging them to abandon traditional Indian ways.
University of Oklahoma, Western History Collections.

It seemed beyond endurance. They had lost their ancestral lands. They faced a future as sedentary farmers that was alien to all their traditions. And immediately confronting them was a winter of starvation.

But news of salvation had also come. An Indian messiah, a holy man who called himself Wovoka, was preaching a new religion on a Paiute reservation in Nevada. In a vision, Wovoka had gone to heaven and received God's word that the world would be regenerated: the whites would disappear, all the Indians of past generations would return to earth, and life on the Great Plains would go back to the time of the roaming buffalo. All this would come to pass in the spring of 1891. Awaiting that great day, the Indians should follow Wovoka's commandments and practice the Ghost Dance. Wovoka's teachings were nonviolent, but among his Sioux adherents the new religion took a belligerent and increasingly threatening tone against white settlers. As the frenzy of the Ghost Dance swept through some Sioux encampments in the fall of 1890, resident whites became alarmed and called for army intervention.

When Indian police backed by federal troops tried to arrest Sitting Bull on December 14, a gun battle broke out, killing the old chief and at least twelve others. Worse was to come. Among the Minneconjou, the medicine man Yellow Bird had stirred up a fervent Ghost Dance following. But their chief, Big Foot, had fallen desperately ill with pneumonia, and the Minneconjou had agreed to come in under military escort to an encampment at Wounded Knee Creek on December 28. The next morning, when the soldiers attempted to disarm the Indians, a battle exploded in the encampment. In American Voices ("Black Elk: Wounded Knee: Something Terrible Happened . . . ," p. 522), Black Elk describes what happened. Among the U.S. troopers, 25 died; among the Indians, 146 men, women, and children perished, many of them shot down as they fled.

The Aftermath. Wounded Knee was the final episode in the war against the Plains Indians, but not the end of their story. The process of severalty now proceeded without hindrance. On the Dakota lands the Teton Sioux fared relatively well, and many of the younger generation settled down as small farmers and stock grazers. Ironically, the more fortunate tribes were probably those occupying reservation lands that did not attract white settlement and thus were bypassed by the severalty process. The flood of whites into South Dakota and Oklahoma, in contrast, left the Indians as small minorities in lands once wholly theirs—20,000 Sioux in a South Dakotan population of 400,000 in 1900, 70,000 members of various tribes in a population of a million when Oklahoma became a state in 1907.

Even so, tribal life survived until, with the restoration of the reservation policy in 1934, it once again rested on a communal territorial basis. All along, native American cultures had been adaptive, changing in the face of adversity and even absorbing features of white society including, in some cases, developing written languages. This cultural resilience persisted—in religion, in tribal structure, in crafts—but the fostering native American world was gone: swept away, as an Oklahoma editor put it in the year of statehood, by "the onward march of empire."

The Far West

On the western edge of the Great Plains, the Rocky Mountains rise up to form a great barrier between the mostly flat eastern two-thirds of the country and the rugged Far West (see Map 16.1). Beyond the Rockies lie two vast plateaus: in the north the Columbia plateau,

BLACK ELK

Wounded Knee: Something Terrible Happened . . .

———————★———————

Black Elk, an Oglala Sioux holy man, was at Wounded Knee when the killing occurred on December 29, 1890. This is his account, as he recollected the event forty years later.

It was in the evening when we heard that the Big Foots were camped over there with the soldiers. . . . The [next] morning I went out after my horses, and while I was out I heard shooting off toward the east, and I knew from the sound that it must be wagon-guns [cannons] going off. The sounds went right through my body, and I felt that something terrible would happen. . . .

A little way ahead of us, just below the head of the dry gulch, there were some women and children who were huddled under a clay bank, and some cavalrymen were there pointing guns at them. . . .

I had no gun, and when we were charging, I just held the sacred bow out in front of me with my right hand. The bullets did not hit us at all. . . .

After the soldiers marched away, I heard from my friend, Dog Chief, how the trouble started, and he was right there by Yellow Bird when it happened. This is the way it was:

In the morning the soldiers began to take all the guns away from the Big Foots. Soldiers were on the little hill and all around, and there were soldiers across the dry gulch to the south and over east along Wounded Knee Creek too. The people were nearly surrounded, and the wagon-guns were pointing at them.

Some had not yet given up their guns, and so the soldiers were searching all the tepees, throwing things around and poking into everything. There was a man called Yellow Bird, and he and another man were standing in front of the tepee where Big Foot was lying sick. They had white sheets around and over them, with eyeholes to look through, and they had guns under these. An officer came to search them. He took the other man's gun, and then started to take Yellow Bird's. But Yellow Bird would not let go. He wrestled with the officer, and while they were wrestling, the gun went off and killed the officer. As soon as the gun went off, Dog Chief told me, an officer shot and killed Big Foot who was lying sick inside the tepee.

Then suddenly nobody knew what was happening, except that the soldiers were all shooting and the wagon-guns began going off right in among the people.

Many were shot down right there. The women and children ran into the gulch and up west, dropping all the time, for the soldiers shot them as they ran. There were only a hundred warriors and there were nearly five hundred soldiers. The warriors rushed to where they had piled their guns and knives. They fought soldiers with only their hands until they got their guns. . . .

It was a good winter day when all this happened. The sun was shining. But after the soldiers marched away from their dirty work, a heavy snow began to fall. The wind came up in the night. There was a big blizzard, and it grew very cold. The snow drifted deep in the crooked gulch, and it was one long grave of butchered women and children and babies, who had never done any harm and were only trying to run away.

———————

Source: John G. Neihardt, ed., *Black Elk Speaks: The Legendary "Book of Visions" of an American Indian* (1932; rpt. New York: Washington Square Press, 1971), 216–223.

---

extending into eastern Oregon and Washington, and, flanking the southern Rockies, the Colorado plateau. Where they break off, the plateaus open to the desert-like Great Basin, which covers western Utah and all of Nevada. To the southeast the Great Basin gives way to plains and mountain ridges that are equally dry but are drained by the rivers of lower Arizona and New Mexico.

Separating this arid interior from the Pacific are two great mountain ranges—the Sierra Nevada and, to the north, the Cascades. Beyond these mountains lies a coastal region, the Pacific slope, cool and rainy in the north but increasingly dry as one proceeds southward, until in southern California rainfall becomes almost as sparse as in the interior.

The Dead at Wounded Knee
In December 1890 U.S. soldiers massacred 146 Sioux men, women, and children in the
Battle of Wounded Knee in South Dakota. It was the last big fight on the northern
plains between the Indians and the whites. Black Elk, a Sioux holy man, related that
"after the soldiers marched away from their dirty work, a heavy snow began to fall. . . .
and it grew very cold." The body of Yellow Bird lay frozen where it had fallen.
National Anthropological Archives, Smithsonian Institution, Washington, DC.

What most impressed white Americans about the
far western country was its inhospitability. "Who are to
go there?" asked Senator George McDuffie in 1843
when the nation was preparing to seize this land from
Mexico. "The territory consists of mountains almost
inaccessible, and low lands . . . where rain never falls,
except during spring. . . . Why, sir, sir, of what use will
this be for agricultural purposes? I would not, for that
purpose, give a pinch of snuff for the whole territory."

The senator's assessment was too grim, perhaps,
but contained enough truth to explain why the Far
West could not be occupied in the familiar way—that
is, by a multitude of settlers moving westward along a
broad front, blanketing the land, and bringing it under
cultivation homestead by homestead. The wagon trains
moving to Oregon's Willamette Valley revealed an
entirely different strategy of occupation—the planting
of distant oases in a vast, mostly barren landscape. This
had been the strategy of Spanish colonizers ever since
they had sent the first wagon trains 700 miles northward from Mexico into the upper Rio Grande Valley
in 1598.

When the Southwest was taken from Mexico by the
United States 250 years later, in 1848, major Hispanic
settlements existed in New Mexico and California, and
smaller ones were scattered along the borderlands into
south Texas. At that time, aside from Oregon, the only
significant settlement of non-Hispanic whites was
around the Great Salt Lake in Utah, where Mormons
had moved to escape persecution and plant a New Zion.

Fewer than 100,000 people of European ancestry—
roughly 75,000 of them Hispanic—lived in the entire
Far West in 1848.

The Mining Frontier

More emigrants would be coming in, certainly, but Senator McDuffie's slight valuation of the nation's newly
acquired western territory seemed about right. California was "hilly and mountainous," commented a U.S.
naval officer in 1849, too dry for farming, and surely
not "susceptible of supporting a very large population."
He had not taken account of the recent discovery of
gold in the Sierra foothills, however. California would
indeed support a very large population, drawn not by
the lure of arable land but by dreams of gold.

Extraction of mineral wealth became the basis for
the Far West's development (Map 16.5). This meant,
first of all, explosive growth. By 1860, when the Great
Plains was still Indian country, California was a booming state with 300,000 residents. Overnight San Francisco became a bustling metropolis—it had 57,000
residents by 1860—and was the hub of a mining empire
that stretched to the Rockies. Similarly, Denver mushroomed into the metropolis for the mining camps on
the eastern slope.

In its swift urbanization, the Far West resembled
Australia, whose gold rush began in 1851, much more
than it resembled the American Midwest; like San
Francisco, Melbourne was a city incongruously grand

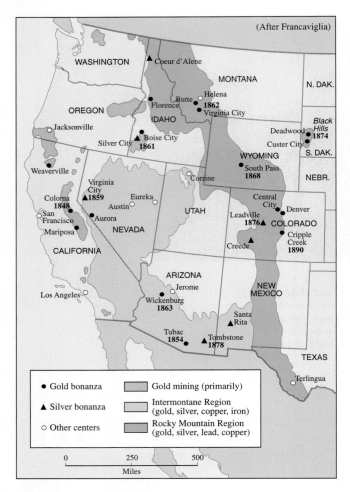

MAP 16.5
The Mining Frontier, 1848–1890
The Far West was America's gold country because of its geological history. Veins of gold and silver form when molten material from the earth's core is forced up into fissures caused by the tectonic movements that create mountain ranges, such as the ones that dominate the far western landscape. It was these veins, the product of mountain-forming activity many thousands of years earlier, that prospectors began to discover after 1848 and furiously exploit. Although widely dispersed across the Far West, the lodes that they found followed the mountain ranges, bisecting the region and bypassing the great plateaus not shaped by the ancient tectonic activity.

amid the empty spaces and rough mining camps of the Australian "outback." Finally, the distinctive pattern of isolated settlement persisted, driven now, however, by a proliferation of mining sites and by people moving not east to west but coming mainly from California and moving west to east.

By the mid-1850s, as easy pickings in the California gold country diminished, disappointed prospectors began to pull out and spread across the West in hopes of striking it rich elsewhere. Gold was discovered on the Nevada side of the Sierra, in the Colorado Rockies,

and along the Fraser River in British Columbia. New strikes of gold and silver occurred in Montana and Wyoming during the 1860s, in the Black Hills of South Dakota a decade later, and in the Coeur d'Alene region of Idaho during the 1880s.

As the news of each discovery spread, a wild, remote area turned almost overnight into a mob scene of prospectors, traders, gamblers, prostitutes, and saloon keepers. At least a hundred thousand fortune seekers flocked to the Pike's Peak area of Colorado in the spring of 1859. Trespassers on government or Indian land, the prospectors made their own law. The mining codes devised at community meetings limited the size of a mining claim to what a person could reasonably work. This kind of informal lawmaking also became an instrument for excluding or discriminating against Mexicans, Chinese, and African Americans in the gold fields. And it turned into hangman's justice for the many outlaws who infested the mining camps. Supplying these camps, especially in advance of the railroads, was a small industry in itself, dotting the far western interior with rough trading depots like Corinne, Utah (see Voices from Abroad, "Baron Joseph Alexander von Hübner: A Western Boom Town," p. 525).

The heyday of the prospectors was always brief. They were equipped only to skim gold from the surface of the earth and from stream beds. Extracting the metal locked in underground lodes required mine shafts and crushing mills, which called for capital, technology, and business organization. The original claim holders quickly sold out after exhausting the surface gold or when a generous bidder came along. At every gold-rush site the prospector soon gave way to entrepreneurial development and large-scale mining. Rough mining camps turned into big towns.

Virginia City. Nevada's Virginia City started out as a ramshackle mining camp. But once the Comstock silver lode came into production in 1859, Virginia City was rapidly transformed into a real urban center, boasting a stock exchange, five newspapers, and, in short order, ostentatious mansions for the mining kings, fancy hotels, opera, even Shakespearean theater. Virginia City was a magnet for job seekers of both sexes: the men laboring as miners below ground for $4 a day, many of the women becoming dance-hall entertainers and prostitutes because that was the best chance offered them by Virginia City's bonanza economy. In 1870 the ratio of men to women was two to one; children made up only 10 percent of the population. There were a hundred saloons, and brothels lined D Street.

Even so, when James Galloway arrived looking for work on February 4, 1875, he brought his family with him, and so did many other miners. By 1880 there were as many women and children as men in Virginia City.

BARON JOSEPH ALEXANDER VON HÜBNER

A Western Boom Town

─────── ★ ───────

During a leisurely trip around the world, Baron von Hübner, a distinguished Austrian diplomat, traveled across the United States, taking advantage of the newly completed transcontinental railroad to see the Wild West. After observing Mormon life in Salt Lake City, he went northward to Corinne, Utah, near the juncture where the Central and Union Pacific railroads met. He was struck not only by the crudeness of Corinne (see Map 16.5) but also by the tough "rowdies" inhabiting the place.

Corinne has only existed for four years. Sprung out of the earth as if by enchantment, this town now contains upwards of 2,000 inhabitants, and every day increases in importance. It is a victualing center for the advanced posts of the [miners] in Idaho and Montana. A coach runs twice a week to Virginia City and to Helena, 350 and 500 miles to the north. Despite the serious dangers and the terrible fatigue of the journeys, these diligences are always full of passengers. Various articles of consumption and dry goods of all sorts are sent in wagons. The "high road" is but a rough track in the soil left by the wheels of the previous vehicles.

The streets of Corinne are full of white men armed to the teeth, miserable looking Indians dressed in the ragged shirts and trousers furnished by the federal government, and yellow Chinese with a business-like air and hard, intelligent faces. No town in the Far West gave me so good an idea as this little place of what is meant by *border life*, the struggle between civilization and savage men and things. . . .

All commercial business centers in Main Street. The houses on both sides are nothing but boarded huts. I have seen some with only canvas partitions. . . . The lanes alongside of the huts, which are generally the resort of Chinese women of bad character, lead into the desert, which begins at the doors of the last houses. . . .

To have on your conscience a number of manslaughters committed in full day, under the eyes of your fellow citizens; to have escaped the reach of justice by craft, audacity, or bribery; to have earned a reputation for being "sharp," that is, for knowing how to cheat all the world without being caught—those are the attributes of the true rowdy in the Far West. . . . Endowed as they often are with really fine qualities—courage, energy, and intellectual and physical strength—they might in another sphere and with the moral sense which they now lack, have become valuable members of society. But such as they are, these adventurers have a reason for being, a providential mission to fulfill. The qualities needed to struggle with and conquer savage nature have naturally their corresponding defects. Look back, and you will see the cradles of all civilization surrounded with giants of Herculean strength ready to run every risk and to shrink from neither danger nor crime to attain their ends. It is only by the peculiar temper of the time and place that we can distinguish them from the backwoodsman and rowdy of the United States.

Source: Oscar Handlin, ed., *This Was America* (Cambridge, MA: Harvard University Press, 1949), 313–315.

───────────────

Galloway's diary describes a family life that was entirely ordinary—church going, picnics, the purchase of a lot for a small house. But Galloway was infected by Virginia City's pervasive gambling fever: he speculated regularly in mining stock and always lost money. In the end, he fell victim to the extraordinary hazards of hardrock mining. He was killed when his sleeve got caught in the gears of a mine machine. He might have survived had he permitted rescuers to hack off his arm, but he took a long chance on being cut loose and coming out whole, and lost.

Industrialization of Western Mining. In its final stage the mining frontier passed into the industrial world. At some sites gold and silver proved less important than the more common metals—copper, lead, zinc—for which there was a huge demand in eastern manufacturing. Beginning in the 1870s, copper mining thrived in the Butte district of Montana, especially after the opening of the fabulous Anaconda mine, and also flourished in the Globe and Copper Queen fields of New Mexico and Arizona. In the 1890s, Idaho's Coeur d'Alene silver district became the nation's main source of lead and zinc.

Hydraulic Mining
When surface veins of gold were played out, miners turned to hydraulic mining, which was invented in California in 1853. The technology was simple; it used high-pressure streams of water to wash away hillsides of gold-bearing soil. Although building the reservoirs, piping systems, and sluices cost money, the profits from hydraulic mining helped transform western mining into big business. But, as this daguerreotype suggests, hydraulic mining wreaked havoc on the environment.
Collection of Matthew Isenburg.

Entrepreneurs raised capital, built rail connections, devised the technology for treating the lower-grade copper deposits, constructed smelting facilities, and recruited a labor force. As elsewhere in American industry, trade-union organization appeared among the miners (see Chapter 17). And as elsewhere in corporate America, the western metal industries went through a process of consolidation. The Anaconda Copper Mining Company and other Montana mining firms came under the control of the Amalgamated Copper Company in 1899. Also in that year, the American Smelting and Refining Company brought together the bulk of the nation's lead-mining and copper-refining properties.

Blackfeet and Crow country in the 1860s, the Butte copper district was a center of industrial capitalism barely thirty years later.

The Pacific Slope. If the Far West had lacked mineral wealth, the history of California, Oregon, and Washington State would certainly have been very different. Before the discovery of gold in 1848, Oregon's Willamette Valley—not dry California—attracted most westward-bound settlers. And, but for the gold rush, California would likely have remained like the Willamette Valley—an agricultural backwater lacking markets for its products and slow to build population.

In 1860, Oregon, already a state, had scarcely 25,000 inhabitants, and its principal city, Portland, was little more than a village. Over the next few decades, however, booming California pulled Oregon from the doldrums by creating a market for the state's produce and timber. North of Oregon—territory very thinly settled during the 1870s—the arrival of rail transportation in the early 1880s had an equally tonic effect. On the coastal side, Washington's development was much like Oregon's, but east of the Cascades, on the fertile, semi-arid Columbia plateau, a rich grain-producing region also sprang up.

Oregon and Washington (which became a state in 1889) grew prodigiously. Where scarcely a hundred thousand settlers had lived twenty years earlier, there were by 1890 nearly three-quarters of a million (Map 16.6). Portland and, even more dramatically, Seattle blossomed into important commercial centers, both prospering from a mixed economy of farming, ranching, logging, and fishing.

California's fertile Central Valley and forested north coast experienced a comparable development, and so did the irrigated valleys of Utah, which by 1890 had over 200,000 inhabitants. At a certain point, especially as railroads opened up eastern markets, this diversified growth became self-sustaining. But what had triggered it, what had provided the first markets and underwritten the service infrastructure, was the bonanza mining economy, at the hub of which stood San Francisco, metropolis for the entire Far West.

Hispanics, Chinese, Anglos

California was the anchor of two distinct far western regions. First, with Oregon and Washington it formed the Pacific slope. Second, by climate and Hispanic heritage, California was linked to the Southwest, which today includes Arizona, New Mexico, and Texas.

The Hispanic Southwest. Along a 1,500-mile borderland, settlements planted over two centuries earlier by the Spanish viceroys formed, after the 1821 revolution, the northernmost provinces of independent Mexico. Most populous were the settlements along the upper Rio Grande Valley in New Mexico; Santa Fe, the main town and over 200 years old, contained 4,635 residents in 1860. Farther down the Rio Grande were El Paso, nearly as old but much smaller, and, as the Rio Grande emptied into the Gulf of Mexico, newer towns such as Laredo. To the north lay San Antonio, founded to establish Spain's claim to central Texas. At the other end of this Hispanic crescent, in California, a Hispanic population was spread thinly in the old *presidio*, or garrison, towns along the coast, and on a patchwork of great ranches.

The economy of the Hispanic Southwest was pastoral, consisting primarily of cattle and sheep ranching. In south Texas there were family-run ranches. Everywhere else the social order was highly stratified. At the top stood an elite, the ranching dons, who were beneficiaries of royal land grants, proudly Spanish, and devoted to the traditional life of a landed aristocracy. Below them, with little in between, was a laboring class of servants, artisans, *vaqueros* (cowboys), and farmworkers. In New Mexico there was also a large *mestizo* population, a peasantry of mixed Hispanic and Pueblo Indian blood, who were Spanish-speaking and Catholic but who, in their village life and farming methods, were faithful to their Pueblo heritage.

Pueblo Indians, though long past the golden age of their civilization, still occupied much of the Rio Grande Valley, living in the old ways in adobe villages and

POPULATION DENSITY
Per square mile

- Under 2
- 2 to 6
- 6 to 18
- 18 to 45
- 45 to 90
- Over 90

MAP 16.6
The Settlement of the Pacific Slope, 1860–1890
In 1860 the settlement of the Pacific slope was remarkably uneven—fully under way in northern California, scarcely begun anywhere else. By 1890 a new pattern had begun to emerge, with the swift growth of southern California foreshadowed and the settlement of the Pacific Northwest well launched.

Vaqueros *in a Corral*
On California cattle ranches owners relied on Mexican cowhands—*vaqueros*—whose
skills as riders and rope handlers were unexcelled. This striking painting was done in
1877 by James Walker, who came from New York City but had a special enthusiasm
for southwestern scenes.
Thomas Gilcrease Institute of American History and Art.

making the New Mexico countryside a patchwork of
Hispanic and Pueblo settlements. To the north a vibrant
new people, the Navajo, had appeared, warriors like the
Apache from whom they descended but also skilled
craft workers and sheep raisers.

New Mexico was one place where European and
native American cultures managed a successful, if
uneasy, coexistence and where the Indian inhabitants
were equipped to hold their own against the Anglo
challenge. In California, by contrast, the Hispanic
occupation had been harder on the native American
peoples, undermining their tribal structure, forcing
them to abandon hunting and gathering for compulsory labor, and making them easy prey for the aggressive Anglo miners and settlers, who, in short order,
nearly wiped out California's once numerous Indian
population.

Anglo-Hispanic Conflict. The fate of the Hispanic
Southwest after its incorporation into the United
States in 1848 depended on the rate of Anglo immigration. In New Mexico, which remained off the beaten
track even after the arrival of railroads in the 1880s,
the Santa Fe elite more than held its own, incorporat-

ing the Anglo newcomers into Hispanic society
through intermarriage and business partnerships. In
California, by contrast, aggressive Anglos grabbed
most of the great ranches even though the peace treaty
with Mexico had recognized the property rights of the
Californios and had made them U.S. citizens. The fact
that the ranch proprietors actually won most of the
lawsuits challenging their Mexican land titles did not
matter very much. Burdened by huge legal expenses,
rising taxes, and the costs of removing squatters, the
dons saw their lands auctioned off or lost in swindles
by Yankees swarming in with business deals. Around
San Francisco the great ranches disappeared almost in
a puff of smoke. Farther south, where Anglos were
slow to arrive, the dons held on longer, but by the
1880s just a handful of the original families still
retained their Mexican land holdings.

The New Mexico peasants found themselves similarly embattled. Crucial to their livelihood were their
grazing rights on communal lands. But these were customary rights that could not withstand legal challenge
when Anglo ranchers established title and began
putting up fences. The peasants responded as best they
could. Traditionally, women had raised much of the

family food in small gardens, bartered in the village markets, made the clothes, and plastered the adobe houses. With the loss of the communal lands, the men began to leave the villages seasonally to work on the railroads or in the Colorado mines and sugar-beet fields, earning crucial dollars while leaving the village economy in their wives' hands.

Elsewhere, hard-pressed Hispanics struck back for what they considered rightfully theirs. In El Paso, the inhabitants rose in unsuccessful revolt when title to their communal salt beds passed into private hands in 1879. After Anglo ranchers began to fence in communal lands in San Miguel County, the New Mexicans long settled there, *los pobres* (the poor ones), organized themselves into masked night-riding raiders and in 1889 and 1890 mounted an effective campaign of harassment against the interlopers. After 1900, when Anglo farmers swarmed into south Texas bent on exploiting new irrigation methods, the displaced *Tejano* ranchers responded with sporadic but persistent night-riding attacks. Much of the raiding by Mexican "bandits" from across the border in the years before World War I was really more in the nature of a civil war by embittered *Tejanos* who had lived north of the Rio Grande for generations.

In the long run, however, these *Tejanos*, like the New Mexico villagers who became seasonal wage laborers, could not avoid being driven into the ranks of a Mexican American working class as the Anglo economy developed. This same development also began to attract increasing numbers of immigrants from Old Mexico.

Mexican Migrants. All along the Southwest borderlands economic activity was picking up in the late nineteenth century. Railroads were being built, copper mines were opening in Arizona, and commercial agriculture was developing in south Texas (cotton and vegetable crops) and in southern California (fruit). There is no way of knowing how many people migrated to the work thus created, since the borders were open until 1917 and few bothered to register when they entered the United States. In Texas the Hispanic population increased from about 20,000 in 1850 to 165,000 in 1900. Some came as contract workers for railway track gangs and as harvest labor; virtually all were relegated to the lowest-paying and most backbreaking work; and everywhere they were discriminated against and reviled by Anglo workers.

Mostly the Mexicans came as short-term and casual workers—not as permanent settlers—but some remained and swelled the numbers and resources of established Mexican American communities. In Tucson, originally an isolated *presidio* planted in Apache country, a Mexican elite dominated the expanding local economy. But most Mexican urban dwellers were poor laboring people segregated in what was already identifiably the *barrio*—the Mexican ghetto—of the Southwest borderland cities.

What stimulated the Mexican migration was the enormous demand for workers by the region's explosive economic development—hence the exceptionally high numbers of immigrants to California. Between 1860 and 1890 roughly one-third of the state's residents were

Mexican Miners
When large-scale mining began to develop in Arizona and New Mexico in the late nineteenth century, Mexicans crossed the border to earn Yankee dollars. In this unidentified photograph from the 1890s, the men are wearing traditional clothing, indicating perhaps that they are recent arrivals at the mine.
Division of Cultural Resource, Wyoming Department of Commerce.

foreign-born, more than twice the level for the country as a whole. Many came from Europe. Most numerous were the Irish, followed by the Germans and British. But there was also another group that was unique to the West—the Chinese.

The Chinese Migration. Attracted first by the California gold rush of 1849, 200,000 Chinese came to the United States over the next three decades. In those years they constituted a considerable minority of California's population, nearly 10 percent. Because virtually all were actively employed, they represented a much larger proportion of the state's labor force, probably a quarter. Elsewhere in the West, at the crest of mining activity, their presence could surge remarkably, to over 25 percent of Idaho's population in 1870, for example.

The coming of the Chinese to North America was part of a worldwide Asian migration that began in the mid-nineteenth century. Driven by poverty from their overpopulated lands, the Chinese went to Australia, Hawaii, and Latin America; Indians to Fiji and South Africa; and Javanese to Dutch colonies in the Caribbean. Most of these Asians migrated under the system of indentured servitude, which in effect made them the property of others. In America indentured servitude was no longer lawful, so the Chinese came as free workers. Their passage was financed by a *credit-ticket system*, by which they were able to borrow passage money from a broker while retaining their personal freedom and their right to choose their employers.

Once in America, Chinese immigrants normally entered the orbit of the Six Companies, a powerful confederation of Chinese merchants in San Francisco's Chinatown. Most of the arrivals were young unmarried men eager to earn a stake and return to their native villages. The Six Companies not only acted as an employment agency but provided them with the social and commercial services they needed to survive in an alien world. The few Chinese women—the male/female ratio was thirteen to one—worked mostly as servants and prostitutes, sad victims of the desperate poverty that drove the Chinese to America. Some were sold by impoverished parents; others had been enticed into fraudulent marriages or kidnapped by procurers and transported to America.

Until the early 1860s, when surface mining played out, Chinese men labored mainly in the California goldfields—as prospectors where white miners permitted it, as laborers and cooks where they did not. Then, when construction began on the transcontinental railroad, the Central Pacific hired Chinese workers. Eventually they constituted four-fifths of the railroad's labor force, doing most of the pick-and-shovel work of laying the track across the Sierra. Many were recruited from around Canton by labor agents and worked in labor gangs under the control of "China bosses," who not only supervised but fed, housed, paid, and often cheated them.

When the transcontinental railroad was completed in 1869, the Chinese scattered. Some continued to work in railroad construction gangs, while others labored on swamp-drainage and irrigation projects in California's Central Valley and then became agricultural workers and, if they were lucky, small farmers and orchardists. The mining districts of Idaho, Montana, and Colorado also attracted large numbers of Chinese, but according to the 1880 census, nearly three-quarters remained in California. In San Francisco many of them became factory workers. The Chinese were excluded from higher-wage trades, but they soon dominated certain industries—such as cigar making—that competed with eastern products and could survive only with cheap labor. "Wherever we put them, we found them good," remarked Charles Crocker, one of the promoters of the Central Pacific. From the standpoint of employers, "their orderly and industrious habits make them a very desirable class of immigrants."

Anti-Chinese Agitation. White workers, however, did not share this enthusiasm for Chinese labor. Why they should have taken so venomous a view of the Chinese has never been easy to explain. It involved, most certainly, a sense of unfair competition that pitted them against "Chinamen's wages." But the hatred clearly went deeper. In other parts of the country, racism was directed against African Americans; in California, where there were few blacks, it found a target in the Chinese. They were "an infusible element" who could not be assimilated into American society, wrote the young journalist Henry George in a 1869 letter that made his reputation as a spokesman for California labor. "They practice all the unnameable vices of the East. [They are] utter heathens, treacherous, sensual, cowardly and cruel." Sadly, this vicious racism was intertwined with labor's republican ideals. The Chinese, argued George, would "make nabobs and princes of our capitalists, and crush our working classes into the dust . . . substitut[ing] . . . a population of serfs and their masters for that population of intelligent freemen who are our glory and our strength."

The anti-Chinese frenzy climaxed in San Francisco in the late 1870s when mobs ruled the streets, at one point threatening to burn the docks of the Pacific Mail Steamship Company at which the Chinese immigrants landed. The fiercest agitator, an Irish teamster named Denis Kearney, quickly became a dominant figure in the California labor movement. Under the slogan "The Chinese Must Go!" Kearney led a workingmen's party that strongly challenged the state's major parties. Democrats and Republicans, however, jumped on the bandwagon, joining together in 1879 to write a new state constitution replete with anti-Chinese provisions and pressuring Washington to take up the issue. Finally, after renegotiating the Burlingame Treaty (1868) with China, Congress in 1882 passed the Chinese Exclusion Act, which barred the further entry of Chinese laborers into the country. The injustice of this law—the United States remained totally open to every other nationality—rankled the Chinese. Why us, protested one woman to a federal agent, and not the Irish, "who were always drunk and fighting"? Merchants and American-born Chinese, who were free to come and go, routinely registered a newly born son after each trip, enabling many an unrelated "paper son" to enter the country. In this and other ways the Chinese were resourceful in evading the exclusion law, but the flow of immigrants nevertheless slowed to a trickle.

But the job opportunities that had attracted the Chinese to America did not subside. If anything, the West's agricultural development intensified the demand for cheap labor, especially in California, which was shifting from wheat, the state's first great cash crop, to fruits and vegetables. This intensive agriculture required lots of workers: stoop labor, meagerly paid, and mostly seasonal. This was not, as one San Francisco journalist put it, "white men's work." That ugly phrase serves as a touchstone for California agricultural labor as it would thereafter develop—a kind of caste labor system, always including some downtrodden, footloose whites, yet basically defined along color lines.

But if not the Chinese, then who? First, Japanese immigrants came in increasing numbers, and by the early twentieth century constituted half of the state's agricultural labor force. Then, when anti-Japanese agitation closed off that population flow in 1908, Mexico became the next, essentially permanent, provider of migratory workers for California's booming commercial agriculture.

The irony of the state's social evolution is painful to behold. Here was California, a land of limitless opportunity, boastful of its democratic egalitarianism. Yet simultaneously, and from its very birth, it was a racially torn society, at once exploiting and despising the Hispanic and Asian minorities whose hard labor helped make California the enviable land it was.

Golden California

Life in California contained all that the modern world of 1890 had to offer—a great cosmopolitan city, comfortable travel, a high living standard, colleges and universities, even accomplished painters and writers. By 1890 California counted over a million residents, a quarter of them in San Francisco. Yet California was still remote from the rest of America, still a long journey

Building the Central Pacific
Chinese laborers in 1867 at work on the great trestle spanning the canyon at Secrettown in the Sierra Nevada.
Huntington Library/Superstock.

away, and, of course, differently and spectacularly endowed by nature. Location, environment, and history all conspired to set California somewhat apart from the American nation. And so, in certain ways, did the Californians.

Creating a California Culture. What Californians yearned for was a cultural tradition of their own. Closest to hand was the bonanza era of the gold rush. California had the great good fortune of attracting to its parts one Samuel Clemens. He arrived in the Nevada Territory in 1861, did a bit of prospecting, worked as a reporter, and adopted the pen name Mark Twain. In 1864 he left for San Francisco and became a newspaper columnist, writing about what he pronounced "the livest, heartiest community on our continent."

Listening to the old miners in Angel's Camp in 1865, Twain jotted one tale down in his notebook, as follows:

Coleman with his jumping frog—bet stranger $50—stranger had no frog, and C. got him one:—in the meantime stranger filled C's frog full of shot and he couldn't jump. The stranger's frog won.

Market Scene, Sansome Street
This exuberant painting by William Hahn captures downtown San Francisco as he
saw it in 1872—a veritable boiling pot of races (note the black woman at left and the
Chinese group at right) and classes (note, in the middle of the market bustle, the
proper lady at far left with her Lord Fauntleroy son). It was its role as metropolis
for the entire Far West that gave San Francisco the great vitality conveyed in this
painting.
Crocker Art Museum.

In Twain's hands, this fragment was transformed into
a tall tale that caught the imagination of the country
and made his reputation as a humorist. What "The
Celebrated Jumping Frog of Calaveras County" had
somehow encapsulated was the entire world of make-
or-break optimism in the mining camps.

In such short stories as "The Luck of Roaring
Camp" and "The Outcasts of Poker Flat," Twain's fellow
San Franciscan Bret Harte developed this theme in a
more literary fashion and firmly implanted it in California's memory. But this past was too raw, too suggestive of the tattered beginnings of so many of the state's
leading citizens—in short, too disreputable for an up-
and-coming society.

Then, in 1884, Helen Hunt Jackson published her
novel *Ramona*. In this story of a half-Indian girl caught
between two cultures, Jackson intended to advance the
cause of the native Americans, but she placed her tale in
the evocative setting of Old California, and that rang a
bell. By then, the chain of Spanish missions planted by
the Catholic Church had been long abandoned. The
padres were wholly forgotten, their Indian converts scattered and in dire poverty. Now that lost world of "sun,
silence and adobe" became all the rage. Sentimental
novels and histories appeared in abundance. There was

a movement to restore the missions. The Spanish Mexican dons of the great *ranchos* became larger in death
than they had ever been in life. Many communities
began to stage Spanish *fiestas*, and the mission style of
architecture enjoyed a great vogue among developers.

In its Spanish past California found the cultural
traditions it needed. Elsewhere in the Southwest the
same kind of discovery was taking place, although in
Santa Fe and Taos there really were live Hispanic roots
to celebrate.

Land of Sunshine.   All this enthusiasm was strongly
tinged with commercialism. And so was a second distinctive feature of California's development. The southern part of the state was neglected, thinly populated,
and too dry for anything but grazing and some chancy
wheat growing. What it did have, however, was an
abundance of sunshine. At the beginning of the 1880s
there burst upon the country amazing news of the
charms of southern California: "There is not any
malaria, hay fever, loss of appetite, or languor in the air;
nor any thunder, lightning, mad dogs . . . or cold snaps."
This publicity was mostly the work of the Southern
Pacific Railroad, which had reached Los Angeles in
1876 and was eager for business.

When the Santa Fe arrived in 1885, a furious fare war broke out, and it became possible to travel by train from Chicago or St. Louis to Los Angeles for $25 or less. Thousands of people, mostly midwesterners, poured in; a dizzying real estate boom developed, along with the frantic building of such resort hotels as San Diego's opulent Hotel del Coronado. Los Angeles County, which had less than 3 percent of the state's population in 1870, had 12 percent by 1900 (see Map 16.6). By then southern California had firmly established itself as the land of sunshine and orange groves. It had found a way to translate climate into riches.

The Great Outdoors. That California was specially favored by nature some Californians knew even as the great stands of redwoods and sugar pine were being hacked down, the soil depleted by the relentless cycle of wheat crops, the streams polluted, and the hills torn apart by reckless mining techniques. Back in 1864 influential Americans who had seen it prevailed on Congress to grant to the state of California "the Cleft, or Gorge in the granite peak of the Sierra Nevada Mountain, known as Yosemite Valley," which would be reserved "for public pleasuring, resort, and recreation." When the young naturalist John Muir arrived in California four years later, he headed straight for Yosemite. Its "grandeur . . . comes as an endless revelation," he wrote. Muir, and others like him, became devoted to studying the High Sierra and protecting the mountains from "despoiling gain-seekers . . . eagerly trying to make everything immediately and selfishly commercial." One result was the creation of California's national parks in 1890—Yosemite, Sequoia, and King's Canyon. Another was the formation in 1892 of the Sierra Club, which became a powerful voice for the defenders of California's wilderness.

Champions of California's wild lands won some battles and lost some. Advocates of water-resource development insisted that California's irrigated agriculture and thirsty cities could not grow without tapping the abundant snowpack of the Sierra. By the turn of the century, Los Angeles faced a water crisis that threatened its growth. The answer was a 238-mile aqueduct to the southern Sierra, tapping the waters of the Owens River. Local residents and preservationists protested but could not prevent the damming up of the beautiful Owens Valley. More painful was the defeat suffered by John Muir and his allies in their battle to save the Hetch Hetchy gorge north of Yosemite National Park. In 1913, after years of controversy, the federal government approved the damming of Hetch Hetchy to serve the water needs of San Francisco.

When the development stakes became high enough, nature lovers like John Muir generally came out on the short end. Even so, something original and distinctive had been added to California's heritage—the linking of a society's well-being with the preservation of its natural environment.

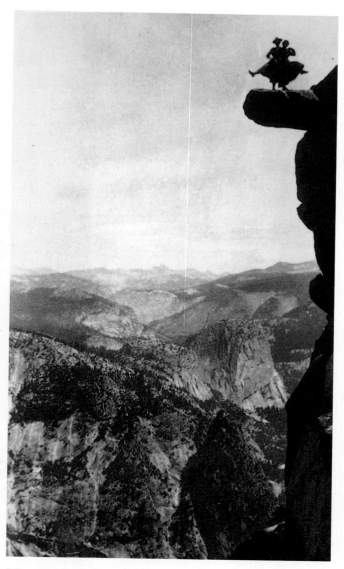

Kitty Tatch and Friend on Glacier Point, Yosemite
From the time the Yosemite Valley was set aside in 1864 as a place "for public pleasuring, resort, and recreation," it attracted a stream of tourists eager to experience the grandeur of the American West. As is suggested by this photograph taken sometime in the 1890s, the magic of Yosemite was enough to set even staid young ladies dancing.
The Yosemite Museum.

The Farmers' World

With the settlement of the Great Plains and the Pacific slope, the regional patterns of American agriculture became well defined (Map 16.7). Wheat growing, which had shifted steadily westward with the frontier, finally settled on the Great Plains, where hardy European strains produced a better bread flour than the soft-kernel

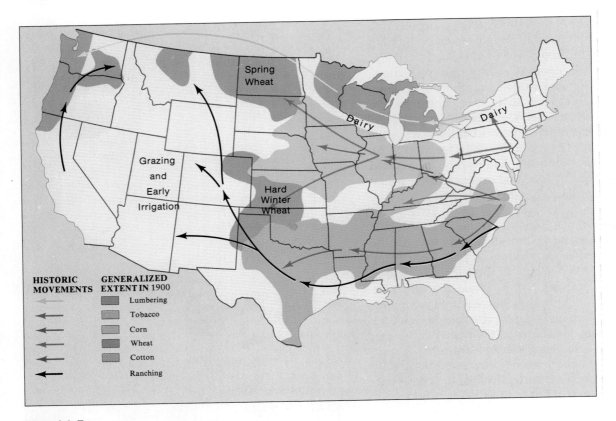

MAP 16.7
Agricultural Regions, 1900
The development of agricultural regions reflected the commercial bent of American agriculture—that is, farmers raised crops for market rather than for home consumption. Regional specialization matched climate and soil to the most suitable crops. The westward movement carried crops westward, of course. Wheat, generally a first crop choice in frontier areas, was finally concentrated in the northern and central plains and in the Northwest. By 1900 the basic pattern of crop specialization was well established in the United States.

wheat of milder regions. On the wheat-producing Columbia plateau in the Northwest, Spanish and Australian varieties did best. In the Midwest the main crop was corn—feed for the nation's livestock. North of the corn belt, dairy farming stretched from Minnesota eastward to New York and New England. In California wheat growing had given way by 1900 to orange groves, vineyards, and vegetable crops. Cotton dominated southern agriculture, spreading westward during the last third of the nineteenth century from the old Cotton Kingdom into Texas, Oklahoma, and Arkansas.

The Business of Agriculture

In certain grain-growing areas, such as California's Central Valley until the 1890s, farmers might be large-scale and even corporate operators. In the South after Reconstruction, the typical farmer was a tenant or sharecropper. Elsewhere, and most commonly, farmers owned their land. Deeply rooted in American tradition, Thomas Jefferson's ideal of a country of independent, family

farmers was enshrined in the national policy of providing land from the public domain for homesteaders. In an age of corporations and other large-scale enterprises, farmers succeeded as did no other group in retaining the *forms* of economic independence. But their *functions* took them far from the self-sufficiency of Jeffersonian America. They were not yeoman farmers but commodity producers in the modern economic order.

General farming, in which no crop represented as much as 40 percent of a farm's total production, was still common; and so was subsistence farming in the hilly and infertile areas of New England and the southern Appalachians. But a cash crop was what farmers wanted, and that preference led to the remarkable regional specialization of American agriculture. "The old rule that a farmer should produce all he required is part of the past," remarked one farm journal. "Agriculture, like all other business, is better for its subdivisions, each one growing that which is best suited for his soil, skill, climate and market, and with its proceeds purchasing his other needs."

Specialization in cash crops was one sign of the commercial leanings of American farmers. Another was their attitude toward land. Americans had little of the passionate identification with the soil that tied European peasants to their inherited plots. In 1910 more than half of all American farmers had moved within the previous five years. Farmers saw their acreage as a commodity. In frontier areas, where the value of newly developed land increased rapidly, they anticipated as much profit, if not more, from the land's value as from the crops it produced. Nor were farmers averse to borrowing money. In boom times they rushed into debt to buy more land and better farm equipment. They relished the innovations of the industrial age, especially the railroad, and supported whatever incentives might be necessary, such as the public purchase of railway bonds, to lure a line to their towns. All these enthusiasms—for cash crops, for land speculation, for borrowed money, for new technology—bore witness to the conviction that farming was a business "like all other business."

The bedrock of farmers' commercial identity was the knowledge that they stood at the center of a vast and complex network of trade and industry. A sophisticated array of commodity exchanges determined prices and found buyers throughout the country and beyond. Vast processing industries turned wheat into flour, livestock into dressed meat, and fruits and vegetables into canned goods. Entire rail systems, port facilities, and fleets of ships were devoted to moving the products of American farmers. All this activity gave farmers access to the expanding urban markets in the United States and overseas; about 20 percent of American agricultural production went abroad during the late nineteenth century. American farmers were likewise abundantly supplied with modern goods and services. The capital they needed came, via mortgage companies and banks, from distant eastern and European lenders.

No one could deny that the result was an agricultural system of amazing abundance; farm output more than tripled between 1860 and 1900. To an Austrian observer reflecting on the scarcity that had always been humankind's lot, the surplus produced by American agriculture seemed "the greatest event of modern times."

Farmers in Distress

Somehow, this triumph of American agriculture as a productive system did not translate into good times for farmers. On the contrary, the late nineteenth century was a time of deep agrarian discontent.

Farm Life. The grievances of farmers stemmed partly from the harshness of rural life. No one labored longer or harder. Farmers worked an average of sixty-eight hours a week in 1900, twelve hours longer than industrial workers. Mechanization did not reduce the workload on farms, as it generally did in factories. Crop acreage tended to increase in step with more efficient planting and harvesting machinery. Most other chores remained on the farmer's shoulders.

For women, too, farming demanded unrelenting labor. Like other work in America, farmwork was sex-typed. Except under dire necessity, northern farm women did not labor in the fields after the pioneering days. Substantial numbers of widows and single women did run farms on their own—300,000 were recorded in the 1900 census—but the evidence suggests that these women mostly relied on hired hands for the heavy fieldwork. In the South, especially among poor tenant farmers, it was different; wives, both black and white, commonly went into the fields, doing "whatever the occasion demands—plowing, hoeing, chopping, putting down fertilizer, picking cotton."

Even without working in the fields, however, farm women contributed crucially to the family enterprise. Farming could be thought of as a "dual economy," in which men's labor brought in the big payment at season's end and women's labor in the garden and barn provisioned the family day by day and produced a steady bit of money for groceries. And if the crop failed, it was women's income that carried the family through. No wonder rural society placed a high premium on marriage: a mere 2.4 percent of Nebraska women in 1900 had never married. The western farmer was well advised to take a wife for the "pecuniary advantage in the domestic economy of his household."

Throughout rural America children, too, pitched in with the farm chores and fieldwork. "Many a time a shudder has passed through the mother heart of me," said a Missouri woman, "at the sight of some little fellow struggling with the handles of a plow, jerking and stumbling over cloddy ground from daylight till dark. Boys 'making a full hand,' 'helping Pa.'" Farm children in 1900 attended school only two-thirds as many days as did city children, and they left school at an earlier age. In an era of rapidly advancing urban education, farm children still attended gloomy, ungraded one-room schools—hardly the little red schoolhouses of popular mythology.

Farm families may have accepted how hard they labored, how wives and husbands were worn out, how childhoods were sacrificed, for the living they wrested from the soil. Harder to swallow was the widening gap between life in the country and city. At the close of the nineteenth century, electricity, indoor plumbing, and paved roads were still rarities in rural areas. Work in the kitchen remained almost unaffected by appliances already commonplace in many urban homes. Laundry was "the most trying" of all household chores, long hours spent lugging and boiling water, bent over washtubs

Rural Schooling
In one-room schoolhouses such
as this one, probably in Colorado,
farm children got the rudiments
of an education. Teaching offered
one of the few opportunities for
rural women to support themselves and obtain a paying job,
albeit for very skimpy wages.
Note the pictures cut from a fashion magazine decorating the plain
log walls.
Denver Public Library, Western History
Division.

and rubbing boards. Even on well-equipped farms, one Michigan woman observed, "the women must still do the work much as their mothers did before."

Hardest to bear was the sense of isolation. On the Great Plains, with its cruel winters and long, empty distances, loneliness was hard on everyone but especially on Scandinavian immigrants accustomed to neighborly living in rural communities. "Think for a moment how great the change must be from the white-walled, red roofed village on a Norway fiord . . . to an isolated cabin on a Dakota prairie," wrote one critic of dispersed American farming practices in 1893, "and say if it is not any wonder that so many Scandinavians lose their mental balance." Farm life everywhere, however, tended to be narrow and circumscribed. Rural neighborhoods, even in long-settled areas, totaled 3 or 4 square miles, where perhaps a dozen families lived. As one writer remarked, "the end of the neighborhood was almost the end of the world." Hamlin Garland and other authors of the late nineteenth century wrote powerfully about the dullness of the countryside and the lure of the city. "I hate farm life," grumbled one of Garland's heroines. "It's nothing but fret, fret and work the whole time, never going any place, never seeing anybody but a lot of neighbors just as big fools as you are. I spend my time fighting flies and washing dishes and churning. I'm sick of it all."

Understandably, when farmers formed organizations, they provided for social activity first of all. The National Grange of the Patrons of Husbandry, whose local granges spread by the thousands across rural America in the early 1870s, became the social center for farm families through its fraternal ceremonies and its dances, picnics, and lectures. Oliver H. Kelley, the government clerk who founded the Grange in 1867, hoped that participation by "the young folks of both sexes . . . will have a tendency to instill in their minds a fondness of rural life, and prevent in great measure so many of them flocking to the cities."

Economic Problems. The hunger for social activity cemented organizational ties, but what drove agrarian movements was the farmers' economic grievances. The basic problem was that farmers remained individual operators in a economic world that was becoming highly organized. And they were, in certain ways, acutely aware of their predicament. They understood, for example, the disadvantages they faced in dealing with the big businesses that supplied them with machinery, arranged their credit, and marketed their products.

One answer was cooperation. Cooperatives had first appeared before the Civil War, mostly as stores and creameries. The Grange took up the cooperative idea in a big way by purchasing in bulk from suppliers and by setting up cooperative banks, insurance companies, grain elevators, and processing plants. The Iowa Grange even started to manufacture farm implements in 1873. But private business fought back hard and generally got the better of the poorly managed and underfinanced Grange cooperatives. Most of them eventually failed. The cooperative idea, however, was highly resilient and would be revived by every successive farmers' movement. The farmers' hostility to middlemen also left as a legacy the great mail-order house of Montgomery Ward, which had been founded in 1872 to serve Grange members. As a solution to the organizational weakness of the farmer in the marketplace, however, the cooperative had to be accounted a failure.

The power of government might also be enlisted to do for farmers what they could not do for themselves. The Grange in the early 1870s encouraged independent political parties that ran on antimonopoly platforms. In a number of prairie states these agrarian parties pushed through so-called Granger laws regulating grain elevators, fixing maximum railroad rates, and prohibiting discriminatory practices against small and short-haul shippers. Constitutional difficulties arose, however, over the question of whether the states were exceeding their police powers when they tried to regulate interstate commerce. In *Wabash v. Illinois* (1886), the Supreme Court decided that they were, voiding an Illinois railroad law and putting the Granger agenda in jeopardy. By then, however, a movement had started for federal regulation of the railroads. The Interstate Commerce Act (1887) created the Interstate Commerce Commission—the first federal regulatory agency—and made railroad regulation a permanent part of national public policy, although, for the next twenty years, without much practical effect.

Farmers turned to cooperatives and government regulation out of a deep sense of organizational disadvantage. But that disadvantage, tangible as it was, did not really account for the unprofitability of farming in this period. Manufacturers and banks lacked the degree of market control ascribed to them by angry farmers. The much-maligned mortgage companies actually could not rig credit markets in the western states; their interest rates matched those in the rest of the country. Nor, for the period 1865–1890, could manufacturers establish a relative price advantage over agriculture. In fact, the wholesale prices of all commodities fell at a slightly faster rate than did farm prices during those years. And on the railroads, freight rates fell steadily and East-West differentials narrowed as improved technology reduced operating costs and the volume of western traffic increased (Table 16.1).

The impact of the general fall in prices, or *deflation*, did have dire consequences for certain kinds of farmers, however. The crops of cotton and wheat farmers were subject to the wider, more unpredictable price swings of the international commodities markets. Also at risk in deflationary periods were farmers in debt, for falling prices forced them to pay back more in real terms than they had borrowed. Who was most deeply in debt? The same two groups: cotton and wheat farmers.

In the 1870s the major wheat-growing states had been Illinois, Wisconsin, and Minnesota. These states had been at the center of the Granger agitation of that decade. By the 1880s wheat had moved onto the Great Plains. Among the indebted wheat farmers of Kansas, Nebraska, and the Dakotas, along with the cotton farmers of the South, the deflationary economy of the 1880s made for stubbornly hard times. All that was needed to bring on a real crisis was a sharp drop in world prices for wheat and cotton.

TABLE 16.1

Freight Rates for Transporting Nebraska Crops

Grand Island to Omaha (150 miles)				Grand Island to Chicago (650 miles)			
Date Effective	Corn	Wheat	Oats	Date Effective	Corn	Wheat	Oats
	(in cents per hundredweight)				*(in cents per hundredweight)*		
January 1, 1883	18	19½	18	January 7, 1880	32	45	32
April 16, 1883	15	16½	15	September 15, 1882	38	43	38
January 10, 1884	18	19½	18	April 5, 1887	34	39	34
March 1, 1884	17	19½	17	November 1, 1887	25	30	25
August 25, 1884	20	20	20	March 21, 1890	22½	30	25
April 5, 1887	10	16	10	October 22, 1890	22	26	22
November 1, 1887	10	12	10	January 15, 1891	23	28	25

Source: Sigmund Diamond, ed., *The Nation Transformed* (New York: George Braziller, 1963), 352.

Summary

★

In 1860 the Great Plains was still ancestral home to nomadic Indian tribes with a vibrant society based on the horse and buffalo. By 1890 the Indians were crowded onto reservations and forced to abandon their tribal way of life. With railroads leading the way, cattle ranchers and homesteaders in short order displaced the Indians and domesticated the Great Plains. Beyond the Rockies, the pattern of settlement was different. Because so much of this region was arid and uninhabitable, occupation occurred in oases of settlement rather than as the progressive force moving along the broad frontier that had prevailed east of the Rockies. And while arable land had been the lure for settlers up to that point, what drove settlement beyond the Rockies was the discovery of mineral wealth. The pace of occupation of the entire trans-Mississippi West was accelerated by the nation's economic development. Industry needed the West's mineral resources; the cities demanded agricultural products; and, from railroads to barbed wire, the industrial economy provided the means for a swift and decisive conquest of the West.

By population, economy, and strategic position, California was the regional power dominating the Far West in the late nineteenth century. It was the anchor both of a crescent of Hispanic settlement to the Southwest and of the Pacific slope region stretching up to the Canadian border. The discovery of gold had set off a huge migration that overwhelmed the thinly spread Hispanic inhabitants and swiftly transformed California into a populous state with a large urban sector. California developed a distinctive culture that capitalized on its rediscovered Hispanic heritage and its climate and natural environment. The treatment of the Chinese, Japanese, and Mexicans who provided the state's cheap labor, however, infused a dark streak of racism into California society.

The settlement of the West completed a national agricultural development characterized by regional crop specialization. American farming became integrated into the modern industrial order. However, that integration was imperfect—in particular because farming remained a family operation in an economy dominated by large-scale enterprise. Most aggrieved, and most prepared to protest, were the cotton farmers of the South and the wheat farmers of the Great Plains.

TIMELINE

1849	California gold rush
	Chinese migration begins
1862	Homestead Act
1864	Yosemite Valley reserved as public park
1865	Long Drive of Texas longhorns begins
1867	Patrons of Husbandry (the Grange) founded
	U.S. government adopts reservation policy for Plains Indians
1868	Indian treaty confirms Sioux rights to Powder River hunting grounds
1869	Union Pacific–Central Pacific transcontinental railroad completed
1874	Barbed wire invented
1875	Sioux ordered to vacate Powder River hunting grounds; war breaks out
1876	Battle of Little Big Horn
1877	San Francisco anti-Chinese riots
1879	Exoduster migration to Kansas
1882	Chinese Exclusion Act
1884	Helen Hunt Jackson's novel *Ramona*
1886	Dry cycle begins on the Great Plains
	Wabash v. Illinois
1887	Dawes Severalty Act
	Interstate Commerce Act
1889	Oklahoma opened to white settlement
1890	Indian massacre at Wounded Knee, South Dakota
	U.S. Census declares end of the frontier

Suggested Readings

★

Western history has become a bitterly contested ground in recent years. The fountainhead of the voluminous traditional scholarship is Frederick Jackson Turner's famous essay "The Significance of the Frontier in American History" (1893), reprinted in Ray A. Billington, ed., *Frontier and Section: Selected Essays of Frederick Jackson Turner* (1961). The "new" western history is critical of Turnerian scholarship for being "Eurocentric"—for seeing western history only through the eyes of frontiersmen and settlers—and for masking the rapacious and environmentally destructive underside of western settlement. Patricia N. Limerick's skillfully argued *The Legacy of Conquest: The Unbroken Past of the American West* (1987) opened the debate. Richard White, *"It's Your Misfortune and None of My Own": A New History of the American West* (1991), provides the fullest synthesis of the new scholarship. For an authoritative, balanced treatment of the main themes of western history, see the essays in Clyde A. Milner II *et al.*, *The Oxford History of the American West* (1994). On women's experience—another primary concern of the new western history—the starting point is Susan Armitage and Elizabeth Jameson, eds., *The Women's West* (1987). There are incisive environmental essays in Donald Worster, *Under Western Skies: Nature and History in the American West* (1992).

The Great Plains

The classic book, stressing the settlers' adaptation to climate and environment, is Walter P. Webb, *The Great Plains* (1931). There is an excellent chapter on the ecological history of the southern plains in Donald Worster, *The Great Plains* (1979). Robert M. Utley, *The Indian Frontier of the American West, 1846–1890* (1984), is a good introduction; Robert H. Lowie, *Indians of the Great Plains* (1954), is a classic anthropological study. On the religious life of the Plains Indians, see Howard L. Harrod, *Renewing the World: Plains Indian Religion and Morality* (1987). The assault on Indian culture is recounted in Fredrick E. Hoxie, *A Final Promise: The Campaign to Assimilate the Indians, 1880–1920* (1984). On phases of plains settlement, see Oscar Winther, *The Transportation Frontier: The Trans-Mississippi West, 1865–1890* (1964); Lewis Atherton, *The Cattle Kings* (1964); Gilbert Fite, *The Farmer's Frontier, 1865–1900* (1966); and Mary W. M. Hargreaves, *Dry-Farming in the Northern Great Plains* (1954). The ecological impact is subtly probed in Frieda Knobloch, *The Culture of Wilderness: Agriculture as Colonization in the American West* (1996). The peopling of the plains can be explored in Craig Miner, *West of Wichita: Settling the High Plains of Kansas, 1865–1890* (1986); Frederick C. Luebke, ed., *Ethnicity and the Great Plains* (1980); Nell Irvin Painter, *Exodusters: Black Migration to Kansas after Reconstruction* (1976); Julie Roy Jeffrey, *Frontier Women: The Trans-Mississippi West, 1840–1880* (1979); Deborah Fink, *Agrarian Women: Wives and Mothers in Rural Nebraska, 1880–1940* (1992); and Elaine Lindgren, *Land in Her Own Name: Women as Homesteaders in North Dakota* (1991). On the integration of the plains economy with the wider world, an especially rich book is William Cronon,

Nature's Metropolis: Chicago and the Great West (1991). Richard Slotkin, *The Fatal Environment: The Myth of the Frontier in the Age of Industrialization, 1800–1890* (1985), deals with the process by which Americans translated the hard realities of conquering the West into a national mythology.

The Far West

The best book on western mining is Rodman Paul, *Mining Frontiers of the Far West: 1848–1880* (1963). A valuable case study of women in a mining town is Paula Petrik, *Women and Family on the Rocky Mountain Frontier: Helena, Montana, 1865–1900* (1987). On western miners, the standard book is Mark Wyman, *Hard Rock Epic: Western Miners and the Industrial Revolution, 1860–1910* (1979). Two valuable regional histories are Carlos A. Schwantes, *The Pacific Northwest: An Interpretive History* (1989), and David Alan Johnson, *Founding the Far West: California, Oregon, and Nevada* (1992). A very imaginative recent treatment of the New Mexico peasantry is Sarah Deutsch, *No Separate Refuge* (1987). On Hispanic Texas, an important book is David Montejano, *Anglos and Mexicans in the Making of Texas* (1987). Important local studies of laboring Hispanics and their communities are Mario T. Garcia, *Desert Immigrants: The Mexicans of El Paso, 1880–1920* (1981), and Richard Griswold del Castillo, *The Los Angeles Barrio, 1850–1890* (1979). On the Asian migration to America, the best introduction is Ronald Takaki, *Strangers from a Different Shore: A History of Asian Americans* (1989), which can be supplemented with Gunther Barth, *Bitter Strength: A History of the Chinese in the United States, 1850–1870* (1964); Sucheng Chan, *This Bittersweet Soil: The Chinese in California Agriculture, 1860–1910* (1986); and, on the impact of the exclusion laws, Lucy E. Salyer, *Laws Harsh as Tigers: Chinese Immigrants and the Shaping of Modern Immigration Law* (1995). Labor's opposition to the Chinese is skillfully treated in Alexander Saxton, *The Indispensable Enemy: Labor and the Anti-Chinese Movement in California* (1971). Kevin Starr, *California and the American Dream, 1850–1915* (1973), provides a comprehensive account of the emergence of a distinctive California culture. On John Muir and the California wilderness, see Michael L. Smith, *Pacific Visions: California Scientists and the Environment, 1850–1915* (1987), and on water, with special emphasis on California, Donald J. Pisani, *Water, Land, and Law in the West: The Limits of Public Policy, 1850–1920* (1996).

The Farmers' World

The standard works are Fred A. Shannon, *The Farmer's Last Frontier, 1860–1887* (1945), and Allan G. Bogue, *From Prairie to Corn Belt: Farming on the Illinois and Iowa Prairies* (1963). On farm women, see Deborah Fink, *Agrarian Women: Wives and Mothers in Rural Nebraska, 1880–1940* (1992), and on immigration and ethnic settlement, Jon Gjerde, *The Minds of the West: Ethnocultural Evolution in the Rural Middle West, 1830–1917* (1997). The flavor of farm life can best be captured in fiction: Hamlin Garland, *Main-Travelled Roads* (1891); Willa Cather, *My Antonia* (1918); and Ole E. Rolvaag, *Giants in the Earth* (1927).

Chapter 17

Capital and Labor in the Age of Enterprise, *1877–1900*

THE YEAR THAT Reconstruction ended, 1877, also marked the end of the first great crisis of America's emerging system of industrial capitalism. In 1873, four years earlier, a severe depression had set in, bankrupting forty-seven thousand firms and driving wholesale prices down about 30 percent. Railroad building ground to a halt. Orders for industrial products disappeared. Hundreds of thousands of workers lost their jobs, and suffering was widespread. Across the country workers demanded "bread for the needy, clothing for the naked, and houses for the homeless." Before long the foundations of the social order began to shake.

On July 16, 1877, railroad workers went on strike against the Baltimore and Ohio system to protest wage cuts. In towns along the B&O tracks crowds cheered as the strikers attacked company property and prevented trains from running. The strike spread across the country. In Pittsburgh the Pennsylvania Railroad roundhouse and Union Depot went up in flames, and at many rail centers rioters and looters roamed freely. President Rutherford B. Hayes called up the National Guard, which gradually restored order. On August 15, the president wrote in his diary: "The strikers have been put down *by force*." The Great Strike of 1877 had been crushed. But never had the nation edged so close to social revolution.

And then recovery came. Within months the economy was booming again. In the next fifteen years, the output of manufactured goods increased over 150 percent. America's confidence in its industrial future

The H. C. Frick Coke Company
Coke, a processed form of coal, is an essential ingredient in iron and steel making. The richest coking coal deposits in the country happened to be in Connellsville, Pennsylvania, not far south of Pittsburgh. The Connellsville coke industry contributed mightily to Pittsburgh's industrial preeminence as well as to H. C. Frick's millions. The men depicted in the center of this print are baking coke in beehive ovens. Once processed, the coke will be dispersed across America by train. As this picture (c. 1880) suggests, the coal industry forever altered Pennsylvania's pastoral landscape.
Library of Congress.

rebounded. "Upon [material progress] is founded all other progress," asserted a railroad president in 1888. "Can there be any doubt that cheapening the cost of necessaries and conveniences of life is the most powerful agent of civilization and progress?"

Industrial Capitalism Triumphant

★

Economic historians speak of the late nineteenth century as the age of the Great Deflation. Prices fell steadily, not only in the United States but worldwide. Normally, falling prices signal economic stagnation: there is not enough demand for the available goods and services. For England, a mature industrial power, the Great Deflation did indeed signal economic decline. But in the United States industrial expansion went into high gear during the Great Deflation (Figure 17.1). Because of increasing manufacturing efficiencies, American firms could cut prices and yet earn profits for financing still better equipment. And this achievement in turn meant a sustained upward trend in average real income, which rose for nonagricultural employees (in constant 1914 dollars) from $388 in 1877 to $573 in 1900—an increase of nearly 50 percent in scarcely a quarter of a century.

Growth of the Industrial Base

By the 1870s manufacturing was long established in America. But the early factories had really been appendages of the agricultural economy. What they produced—textiles, boots and shoes, paper and furniture—were *consumer* goods, which used familiar materials and mostly replaced things made at home or by individual artisans. Gradually, however, a different kind of demand developed. Railroads needed locomotives; new factories needed machinery; and the expanding cities needed trolley lines, sanitation systems, and commercial buildings. Locomotives, machinery, and construction materials were *capital* goods—that is, goods that themselves added to the productive capacity of the economy. Although consumer goods remained very important, it was the manufacture of capital goods that became the core of America's industrial economy.

From Iron to Steel. Central to the development of the capital-goods sector was a new technology for manufacturing steel. The country already produced large quantities of wrought iron, whose malleability made it ideally suited for use by country blacksmiths and farmers. But wrought iron was expensive—it was produced in small batches by skilled puddlers and rollers—and did not stand up under heavy use as railway track. In 1856 the British inventor Henry Bessemer designed a furnace— the Bessemer converter—that required little labor and refined raw pig iron into an essentially new product, steel, that was harder and more durable than wrought iron (see New Technology, "Iron and Steel," pp. 544–545). Others adopted Bessemer's invention, but it was Andrew Carnegie who demonstrated its revolutionary importance.

Carnegie arrived from Scotland in 1848 at the age of twelve with his poverty-stricken family. He became a telegraph operator, then went to work for the Pennsylvania Railroad and rapidly climbed the managerial ladder. In 1865, having amassed a fortune in wartime speculation, Carnegie struck out on his own as an iron manufacturer. His main customers were his former associates in the railroad business.

In 1872 Carnegie erected a massive steel mill outside Pittsburgh, designed to take maximum advantage of Bessemer's process. Named the Edgar Thomson

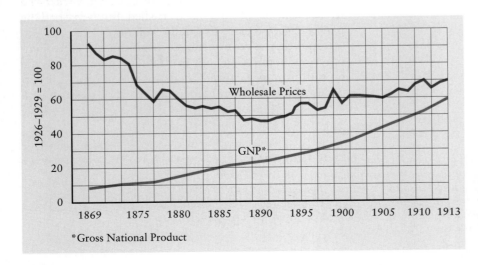

FIGURE 17.1
Business Activity and Wholesale Prices, 1869–1913
This graph shows the key feature of the performance of the late nineteenth-century economy: while output was booming, the price of goods was falling.

MAP 17.1

The Westward Movement of Iron and Steel Production, to 1900

Before the Civil War, the iron industry was concentrated in eastern Pennsylvania and northern New Jersey. With the shift to steel and the westward movement of population and industry, production moved first to western Pennsylvania and then to Ohio, Indiana, and Illinois, and southward into Alabama. The specific locations—Pittsburgh, Youngstown, Chicago, Birmingham—were dictated by the rail network, new sources of coal and iron ore, and markets for steel.

Works after Carnegie's admired boss at the Pennsylvania Railroad, the mill brought together all the stages of production—smelting, refining, and rolling—into a single coordinated operation. Iron ore entered the blast furnaces at one end and, with no break in operations, came out the other end as finished steel rails. Hugely profitable, the Edgar Thomson Works became a model for the modern steel industry. Large, integrated steel plants swiftly replaced the small iron mills that had once dotted western Pennsylvania.

Steel rails made up nearly three-quarters of the industry's output in 1885. But thereafter, as railroad building slowed, the demand became more diversified. More and more steel went into bridges, skyscrapers, machinery, and a host of other industrial uses, such as pipes and tubing, sheet steel and wire, and armor for the nation's new navy.

Minerals and Energy. The technological breakthrough in steel spurred the intensive exploitation of the country's mineral resources. Major discoveries of iron ore deposits occurred from the 1850s onward, first in upper Michigan and then in the huge Mesabi Range of northern Minnesota. The Mesabi ore, shipped down the Great Lakes, gave the lakeshore sites, such as South Chicago and Gary, Indiana, a competitive advantage over Pittsburgh and contributed to the westward shift of the industry (Map 17.1).

Coal mining, a minor enterprise before 1850, grew rapidly, first in the anthracite (hard coal) region of eastern Pennsylvania and then in the bituminous (soft coal) fields of western Pennsylvania and Ohio. The production of bituminous coal, the primary industrial fuel, doubled every decade between 1870 and 1910 (Table 17.1).

The Corliss Engine

The symbol of the Philadelphia Centennial in 1876 was the great Corliss engine, which towered over Machinery Hall and powered all the equipment on exhibit there. Yet the Corliss engine also signified the incomplete nature of American industrialism at that time; it soon became obsolete. Westinghouse turbines generating electricity would be the power source for the nation's next great World's Fair in Chicago in 1893.
Culver Pictures.

Iron and Steel

★

IRON WAS NOT a product new to the nineteenth century in the way that plastic was new to the twentieth century. Early Europeans had made iron tools and weapons at least a thousand years before Christ, and in the years since those remote times the underlying processes did not change, for they are dictated by the nature of iron metallurgy. What did change were the techniques for carrying out those processes.

The first break from ancient methods came when blast furnaces appeared in Belgium around 1340. Ore was melted in a charcoal-burning furnace to which limestone had been added. A blast of air then set off a combustion process that combined carbon from the charcoal with the molten iron while the impurities combined with the limestone to form a slag. The slag was drawn off from the top while the molten iron was tapped from the bottom into sand forms resembling piglets feeding from a sow—hence the term "pig iron."

Bessemer Converter, Bethlehem Works, Steelton, Pennsylvania, 1885
Workers for Bethlehem Steel in Steelton, Pennsylvania, pose for this 1885 photograph with a Bessemer converter. The late nineteenth century in America came to be known as "America's Age of Steel," thanks to the increased steel production that the Bessemer converter helped generate.
Hagley Museum and Library.

As steam engines became the nation's primary energy source, railroads and factories began to consume enormous amounts of coal. Industries previously dependent on water power converted rapidly to steam-driven machinery. By 1900, water wheels were disappearing, providing less than a sixth of the nation's industrial energy. The steam turbine, a further innovation introduced in the 1880s, provided still more power and efficiency by utilizing continuous rotation rather than the back-and-forth motion of conventional steam engines. With the coupling of the steam turbine to the electric generator, the nation's energy revolution was completed, and after 1900 factories began a massive conversion to electric power.

Thus, in the decades after the Civil War, the modern steel industry was established, the nation's mineral resources came under intensive exploitation, and energy was harnessed to the manufacturing system. All these basic elements of modern industrialism—steel, coal, and energy output—grew after 1870 at rates far exceeding that of manufacturing production itself.

The Railroads

Before the Civil War, most goods moved quite efficiently by water. But from the first appearance of primitive locomotives on iron tracks in the 1830s, Americans fell

By the late eighteenth century Great Britain was running out of wood for charcoal. The substitution of coke, made by superheating coal, saved the industry and gave Britain the competitive edge it needed to launch the Industrial Revolution. Endowed with ample forests, the United States was slow to adopt coke-using furnaces, but by 1860 it had caught up with Britain's technologically.

The search for a metal harder and more durable than wrought iron resulted in the invention in 1856 of an entirely different refining process by the Englishman Henry Bessemer. The Bessemer converter was a pear-shaped vessel that was open at the top and had a bottom perforated with many holes. Molten pig iron flowed into the top while the converter was tilted on its side. Air was blasted through the perforated bottom with great force, and the converter then swung back to its upright position. The resulting combustion set off a spectacular display of flame and smoke. Within fifteen minutes, the impurities in the molten iron burned off and the flames died down. The converter was again tilted on its side, and after manganese and other chemicals had been added, the purified iron was emptied into ingot molds. The refined metal, called steel, was ideally suited for use as railroad track.

Bessemer's device, though invented primarily with the aim of gaining a more durable metal, also proved vastly more efficient than the hand-operated puddling furnaces that produced wrought iron. The Bessemer converter turned out great quantities of steel with virtually no labor, and this forced changes up and down the line. To feed the converters' appetite for pig iron, blast furnaces were built larger and, with the introduction of the hot blast, became much faster. To handle the flow of steel from the converters, rolling mills became increasingly mechanized and automatic. Finally, blast furnaces, convertors, and rolling mills were brought together and linked into a single processing operation. The integrated steel plant of 1900—capable of producing 2,500 tons or more a day—became a voracious consumer of ore and coal.

The commanding lead the United States had built up by 1900 rested on the world's best reserves of coking coal in western Pennsylvania and the vast ore deposits in Minnesota's Mesabi Range, northern Michigan's older fields, and Alabama. The geographical face of American industrialism changed as the places best located in relation to raw materials, transportation, and markets—Pittsburgh, the steel towns along the Great Lakes, and Birmingham, Alabama—became the great centers of steel production. American cities relied on steel for the construction of skyscrapers, trolley lines, subways, and the vast underground complexes of pipe that supplied the urban millions with water and gas, and carried away their sewage. Without steel, the emerging automobile industry would not have grown, nor would a host of other industries.

It is no wonder that historians have called the last decades of the nineteenth century America's Age of Steel. What was overlooked at the time and for long afterward was the fact that the nation's natural resources were not inexhaustible. It is the exhaustion of the great Mesabi Range that has leveled the playing field among global competitors and helped trigger the recent decline of the American steel industry.

in love with railroads. They were impatient for the year-round, on-time service that canal barges and riverboats could not provide. By 1860, with a network of tracks already covering the states east of the Mississippi, the railroad clearly was on the way to being industrial America's mode of transportation (Map 17.2).

Constructing the Railroads. The question was, Who would pay for it? Railroads could be state enterprises, as most of the canals built before the Civil War had been. Or, alternatively, they could be financed by investors trying to make money. Unlike most European countries, which regarded railroads as a state responsibility, the United States left railroad building to private enterprise. Even so, government played a big role. Many states provided financial aid, mostly by buying railroad bonds but also, as in Texas and Maine, by offering state-owned land to railroad companies. Land grants were the principal means by which the federal government encouraged interregional railroads; huge tracts went to the transcontinental railroads because of the national interest in tying the Far West to the rest of the country.

The most important boost that government gave the railroads, however, was not money or land but a legal form of organization—the *corporation*—that enabled them to raise private capital in prodigious

TABLE 17.1

Increasing Output of Heavy Industry, 1870–1910

	Bituminous Coal (thousands of tons)	Rolled Iron and Steel (thousands of tons)	Copper (tons)	Industrial Machinery (millions of dollars)
1870	20,471	850*	14,112	110.4[†]
1880	50,757	3,301	30,240	98.6[‡]
1890	111,302	6,746	129,882	185.6
1900	212,318	10,626	303,059	347.6
1910	417,111	24,216	544,119	512.4

*Approximate total.
[†]Data for 1869.
[‡]Data for 1874.

amounts. Investors who bought stock in the railroads and thus became their legal owners enjoyed *limited liability:* they risked only the money they had invested and were not personally liable for the corporation's debts. A corporation also could borrow money by issuing interest-bearing bonds, which was how the railroads raised most of the money they needed.

The actual responsibility for railroad building was handed over to a construction company, which, despite the name, was really another part of the elaborate financing system. Hiring the contractors and suppliers often involved persuading them to accept the railroad's bonds as payment and, when that failed, wheeling and dealing to raise cash by selling or borrowing on the bonds. Since the promoters of the railroad and the owners of the construction company were one and the same, the opportunities for plunder were enormous. The most notorious of the construction companies, the Union Pacific's Crédit Mobilier, siphoned into the pockets of the promoters probably half of the money it paid out.

Railroad promotion was not for the faint of heart. Most successful were promoters with the best access to capital—their own or others'. John Murray Forbes, a great Boston merchant in the China trade, recruited New England money to develop the Chicago, Burlington and Quincy Railroad into the preeminent midwestern system. Cornelius Vanderbilt started with the fortune he had made in the steamboat business. He consolidated previously independent lines up the Hudson River and across New York State, and ultimately he developed the New York Central into an interregional trunk line connecting New York City to Chicago. James J. Hill, who without federal subsidy made the Great Northern into the best constructed of all the transcontinental railroads, was certainly the nation's champion railroad builder. In contrast, Jay Gould, who at one time or another controlled the Erie, Wabash, Union

Pacific, and Missouri Pacific systems, always remained a stock-market speculator at heart. Whether he was a *robber baron*—someone who loots commerce and gives nothing in return—can only be answered by closer inspection of his career (see American Lives, "Jay Gould: Robber Baron?" pp. 548–549).

Railroad development in the United States was often sordid, fiercely competitive, and subject to boom and bust. But vast sums of capital were raised—well over $10 billion, probably a quarter of it attracted from Europe—and a network was built whose track mileage exceeded that of the rest of the world combined. By 1900 virtually no corner of the country lacked rail service.

The Railway System. The railroads became increasingly efficient. Built by competing local companies, the early system was a jumble of discontinuous segments. Gauges of track—the width between the rails—varied widely, so at many points railroads were not physically connected. Moreover, each railroad company reserved its track exclusively for its own equipment. As late as 1880 goods could not be shipped through from Massachusetts to South Carolina. Eight times along the way, freight cars had to be emptied, and their contents loaded onto other cars across a river or at the other side of a city.

During the Civil War years, however, pressure increased for the physical integration of the railroads. Track was hastily laid through Philadelphia, Richmond, and other cities to speed the shipment of troops and equipment. The postwar economy, as it grew more complex and interdependent, demanded a better-organized rail system. Much railroad integration resulted from the expansion of great trunk lines, such as the New York Central, the Pennsylvania, and the Illinois Central, connecting different regions of the country. By the end of the 1880s a standard track gauge (4 feet, 8½ inches) had been adopted across the country. In 1883 the railroads rebelled

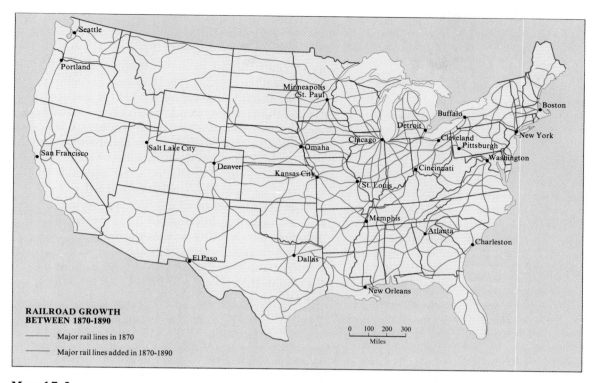

MAP 17.2

The Expansion of the Railroad System, 1870–1890

In 1870, the nation had 53,000 miles of rail track; in 1890, 167,000 miles. That burst of construction essentially completed the nation's rail network, although there would be additional expansion for the next two decades. The main areas of growth were in the South and west of the Mississippi. The Great Plains and the Far West accounted for over 40 percent of all railroad construction in this period.

against the confusion of local times that made scheduling a nightmare and, acting on their own, divided the country into the four standard time zones that we still use. Fast-freight firms and standard accounting procedures enabled shippers to use the railroad network as if it were a single unit, moving goods without the breaks in transit, transfers between cars, or other delays that had once bedeviled them.

At the same time, railroad technology was advancing. Durable steel rails permitted heavier traffic. The redesign of steam engines culminated in the Consolidation-type locomotive, with four sets of driving wheels and nearly triple the pulling power of its predecessors. To control the great mass and length of the new freight trains, the inventor George Westinghouse perfected the automatic coupler, the air brake, and the friction gear for starting and stopping a long line of cars. Costs per ton-mile fell by 50 percent between 1870 and 1890, resulting in a steady drop in freight rates for shippers.

The railroads brilliantly met the transportation needs of the maturing industrial economy. For investors, however, the costs of freewheeling competition and unrestrained growth were painfully high. On many routes there were too many railroads, and competitors fought for the available traffic by cutting rates to the bone. Many railroads were saddled with huge debt from bonds issued during the extravagant construction years; a fifth of these bonds failed to pay interest even in a pretty good year like 1889. So it was no wonder that when the economy turned bad, there were wholesale bankruptcies. A third of the industry went into receivership after the Panic of 1893.

Out of the rubble, however, came a major railroad reorganization. This was primarily the handiwork of Wall Street investment banks such as J. P. Morgan & Co. and Kuhn, Loeb & Co., whose main role had been to market railroad stocks and bonds. When railroads fell into bankruptcy, the investment bankers stepped in to pick up the pieces. They persuaded investors to help out by accepting lower interest rates or by putting up more money. And they eased the competitive pressures on the railroads by consolidating rivals. By the early twentieth century, half a dozen great regional systems had emerged, and the nerve center of American railroading had shifted to Wall Street.

Jay Gould: Robber Baron?

———★———

JAY GOULD WAS an operator pure and simple, although, in a general way of speaking, he was as far as possible from pure and as far as possible from simple. . . . It would be at least very difficult to show that the Nation as a whole is a dollar richer by the existence of JAY GOULD, while he himself has become the richer . . . from the expansion of the city and the Nation. He has simply absorbed what would have been made in spite of him.

Thus did the *New York Times* bid farewell to Jay Gould at his death on December 3, 1892. There was a name for the kind of businessman the *Times* thought Gould was: robber baron. In the Middle Ages the term described renegade knights who exacted tribute from all who passed by; by extension to Gould's time the term referred to capitalists who extracted riches from the economic system while adding nothing to it. By that definition, was Gould a robber baron? Yes, said historians for many years, following the thesis first advanced by Matthew Josephson in his book *The Robber Barons* (1934). Today historians are no longer so sure.

Jay Gould was born on May 27, 1836, in Roxbury, New York, in the mountainous Catskill region. John Gould wanted Jay, his only son, to take over the family farm, but the boy was small and sickly and detested farmwork. At sixteen he became a surveyor, at nineteen he wrote a flowery history of Delaware County, New York, for the money, and then at twenty he got a big break. An eccentric but wealthy tanner, Zadock Pratt, befriended Gould, taking him as a partner to set up a tannery in Pennsylvania, where Gould had located a rich new source of tanning bark. The venture succeeded thanks to Pratt's money and Gould's hard work, but after two years there was a falling-out and Pratt proposed terminating the partnership. He would buy Gould's share for $10,000 or sell out to the young man for $60,000. Gould found backers among the leather merchants who marketed the tannery's output and bought out the surprised Pratt. This was a typical Gould maneuver—bold, unexpected, and decisive. The new partnership

quickly turned sour, primarily because of the collapse of the leather market. The damage to well-reputed merchants left Gould discredited in the leather trade. He had made money amid the wreckage of other people's businesses, another Gould trademark. In 1860 he settled in New York, bent on satisfying what had become his obsession: he wanted to be rich.

Enlisting in the Union army probably never occurred to him. The Civil War offered too good a chance for turning quick profits; and besides, Gould had no taste for fighting. In 1863 he married the daughter of a wealthy New York merchant, sired six children in rapid succession, and became a devoted family man. These were, above all, schooling years for Gould. He learned about the railroads from a controlling interest he gained in a small Vermont railroad. And—no one knows exactly how—he developed a consummate mastery of the intricacies of Wall Street finance. Few could have been aware of this in 1867 when Gould was elected to the executive board of the Erie Railroad just as a titanic battle was taking shape for control of the Erie.

The aggressor was Cornelius Vanderbilt, who wanted to ally the Erie with his emerging New York Central system. Vanderbilt began secretly buying up Erie stock, a maneuver that had gained him control of other key railroad properties. This time, however, Erie stock mysteriously kept entering the market even though no more could legally be issued by the railroad. Gould was exploiting a dubious loophole: freshly minted convertible bonds that could immediately be converted to stock. Vanderbilt countered with court injunctions, forcing Gould and his confederates to decamp to New Jersey, while in Albany Vanderbilt lobbied to prevent legalization of the convertible-bond gambit. A bidding war began for legislators' votes, which, with the Erie dollars overflowing his satchel, Gould finally won. To settle things, however, Vanderbilt and his allies had to be compensated for their losses, which Gould ingeniously arranged by spending $9 million from the Erie Railroad treasury to buy back their stock at inflated prices. The railroad was effectively bankrupted, but it was now firmly in Gould's hands.

Gould proceeded to show how money—lots of it—could be made from control of a large enterprise that was itself unprofitable and badly managed. The trick was to manipulate stock prices, buying and selling with an insider's advance knowledge. For example, Gould announced that he was replacing the United States Express Company, which operated on the Erie line, with a new company that he intended to form.

Jay Gould
Culver Pictures.

United's stock dropped from 60 to 16, at which point Gould bought, renewed the contract, and sold on the stock's rebound. He walked away with a cool $3 million. Under Gould's rule, the Erie never earned enough even to service its debt. Long-suffering European stockholders finally rebelled, forcing him out in March 1872.

Gould was never able to shed the unsavory reputation he acquired during the Erie years. But even in that buccaneering period there was another side to him as a railroad man. Indifferent to day-to-day operations, Gould had a brilliant strategic sense for how railroads should grow. The key, he knew, was integrated development, with trunk-line service between major centers. Right off Gould moved to take over the local roads west of Pittsburgh and Buffalo, in hopes of making the Erie the dominant system linking the Atlantic seaboard and the Midwest. But he lacked the resources, and the Pennsylvania and the New York Central, spurred by his challenge, beat him out, capturing the key western lines and leaving the Erie a weak secondary system.

Yet the vision had been Gould's, and ten years later he found, in the area west of St. Louis and southward into Texas, greener fields for his strategic talents. The railroads in this region were a tangle of incomplete, disconnected lines when Gould came on the scene in 1879. He began buying control, finishing the lines, and linking them into a regional system operating more than 5,000 miles of track under his parent company, the Missouri Pacific. He also moved aggressively in other parts of the country, challenging established railroads and cutting rates ruthlessly to take traffic from them. By 1882 he controlled 15 percent of the nation's entire trackage, and Western Union and the New York Elevated besides.

The economic boom that fostered this empire building did not last, however, and after 1881 Gould found himself on the wrong side of the stock market, overextended in holdings that were falling in value. On the verge of ruin in early 1884, he managed to get a "corner" on the stock of the Missouri Pacific, forcing up its price and thus saving himself. But Gould was not the same man after that. He lost his iron nerve, and his health began to fail. He swore off speculation. His business dealings, while still far-flung, became more cautious and defensive. But to the end he remained a tough customer, never justifying himself, never cloaking himself in religious piety, not even seeking to make amends by a show of philanthropy. In death he thumbed his nose at the world: his entire fortune—$75 million—went in trust to his family.

A century later historians can perhaps appreciate better than Gould's obituarists the positive side of his amazing business career. The nation's railroad network bore in some considerable degree Gould's mark by virtue of his own system building and the spur he gave to others. Moreover, his forays into the territory of other railroads broke open monopoly markets and drove shipping prices down. Railroads might have made less money, but shippers and consumers benefited from cheaper transportation costs. Even Gould's purely speculative ventures may have contributed to the nation's economic growth. Economists say that money made in speculation is an especially efficient source of fresh capital, which is what Gould's winnings were to America's capital-hungry railroads.

Let us suppose that Gould never understood this. Let us suppose further that he was motivated by greed, that his methods were as unscrupulous as they needed to be, and that, had he lived at a later time, he probably would have ended up in prison. Are we justified in calling him a robber baron?

Union Pacific's Engine No. 149
The railroads invoked a new notion of time. How fast could a person cross the continent? In 1876, a troupe of actors, scheduled to present Shakespeare's *Henry V* in San Francisco, made the trip from New York City in eighty-four hours—a record. The Union Pacific's crack engine No. 149 carried them at open throttle on the last leg from Ogden, Utah. Union Pacific Museum Collection.

The Managerial Revolution

At one time, recalled a railroad expert in 1896, it had been thought "practically impossible to manage a great railway effectively." On the early railroads "management had been personal and autocratic; the superintendent, a man gifted with energy and clearness of perception, moulded the property to his own will. But as the properties grew, he found himself unable to give his personal attention to everything. Undaunted, he sought to do everything and do it well. He ended by doing nothing."

It is not hard to understand the mistake of that early railroad superintendent. In a world of small businesses, where could he find a model for running an enterprise that was too big for personal and direct control?

In 1856 Daniel C. McCallum, an Erie Railroad official, had come to grips with the problem. On a 50-mile railroad, McCallum noted, the superintendent could personally attend to every detail, "and any system, however imperfect, may prove comparatively successful." But not on 500-mile railroads: "I am fully convinced that in the want of a system lies the true secret of their failure." Thus McCallum identified the need for a *system*—a formal administrative structure—for the successful operation of large-scale, complex enterprises. He knew he was working in the dark: "We have no precedent or experience upon which we can fully rely."

Railroads were the most complex form of nineteenth-century enterprise. They had to raise huge amounts of capital, and their properties stretched over ever-greater distances. They employed armies of workers—nearly fifty thousand on the Pennsylvania system by 1890. And, unlike the leisurely traffic on canals, trains had to be precisely scheduled and closely coordinated. Even with the use of telegraphic communication, train accidents took a heavy toll.

Step by step, always under the prod of necessity, the early trunk lines pioneered the main elements of modern business administration. They separated overall management from day-to-day operations and created departments along functional lines—maintenance of way, rolling stock, and traffic. Then they carefully defined the lines of communication from the operating divisions upward to the central office. When Albert Fink perfected his cost-accounting system for the Louisville and Nashville Railroad after the Civil War, managers at last had precise data with which to assess performance. By the end of the 1870s the managerial crisis on the railroads had been resolved.

As industrial enterprises became comparably complex, they confronted the same kind of managerial problems. However, manufacturers benefited from the experience of the railroads. Andrew Carnegie, for example, drew on his early career with the Pennsylvania Railroad. Whether by learning from the railroads or through trial and error, large companies moved toward a modern management structure and solved the problems of administering far-flung business empires.

Mass Markets and Large-Scale Enterprise

The railroads sparked a revolution in marketing as well as management. Until well into the industrial age, all but a few manufacturers operated on a small scale, producing goods mainly for nearby markets. They left the marketing to wholesale merchants and commission agents. Products normally passed through numerous hands on their way from the factory to the consumer.

Then, after the Civil War, the scale of economic activity began to grow dramatically. "Combinations of capital on a scale hitherto wholly unprecedented constitute one of the remarkable features of modern business methods," the economist David A. Wells wrote in 1889. He could see "no other way in which the work of production and distribution can be prosecuted." What was there about the nation's economy that led to Wells's sense of inevitability?

The key to large-scale enterprise lay in the American market. Immigration and a very high birth rate swelled the population from 40 million to over 60 million between 1870 and 1890. People flocked to the cities. The railroads brought these dense consuming markets within the reach of distant producers. The telegraph, fully operational by the Civil War, created instant communication across the country. Unlike Europe, with its many nation-states, the American market was unified; no political frontiers impeded the flow of goods across the continent. Meanwhile, high tariffs protected American industry from foreign competition. Nowhere else did manufacturers have so vast and accessible an internal market for their products.

Gustavus Swift and Vertical Integration. The meatpacking industry was a case in point. Before the Civil War, Cincinnati and Chicago had become great processors of preserved products such as salt pork and

smoked beef. But fresh meat remained the province of local butchers, whose practices had scarcely changed since the preindustrial era. Fresh meat was a luxury item, and the diet of city dwellers, especially the poor, depended heavily on salt pork.

The coming of the railroads brought big changes to the fresh-meat business (Map 17.3). Cattle raising shifted to the grazing ranges of the Great Plains. With the opening of Union Stock Yards in 1865, Chicago became the main cattle market for the country. Livestock coming in by rail from the Great Plains was auctioned off at the Chicago stockyards and then shipped to eastern cities, where, as before, the animals were slaughtered in local "butchertowns." Such an arrangement—with distribution nationalized but processing still local—adequately met the demand of an exploding urban population indefinitely. In Europe no further development ever did occur.

But Gustavus F. Swift, a shrewd Massachusetts cattle dealer who settled in Chicago in 1875, saw the future differently. He recognized that livestock in cattle cars deteriorated en route to the East, and that small, local slaughterhouses could not utilize waste by-products and cut labor costs. If dressed beef could be kept fresh in transit, he could concentrate processing in

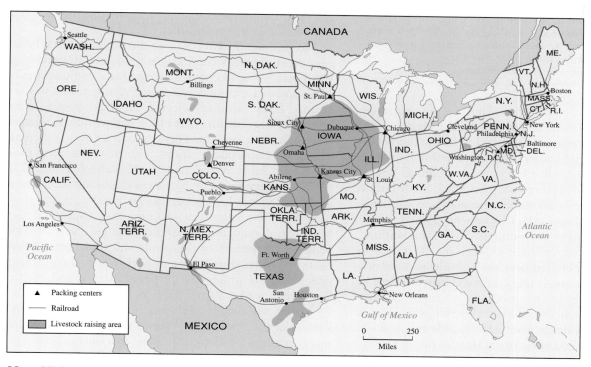

MAP 17.3

The Dressed Meat Industry, 1900

The meatpacking industry clearly shows how transportation, supply, and demand combined to foster the growth of the American industrial economy. The main centers of beef production in 1900—Chicago, St. Paul, Kansas City, Fort Worth—were rail hubs with connections westward to the cattle regions and eastward to cities hungry for cheap supplies of meat. Vertically integrated enterprises sprang from these elements, linked together by an efficient and comprehensive railroad network.

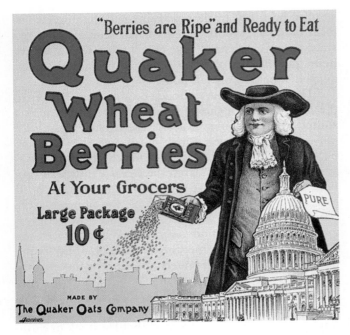

Quaker Oats

Like crackers, sugar, and other nonperishable foods, oatmeal had traditionally been marketed to consumers in bulk from barrels. In 1882 the grain merchant Henry P. Cowell completed the first continuous-process mill for oatmeal, cutting production costs and greatly increasing output. He also hit on the idea of selling oatmeal in boxes of standard size and weight to a national market. Broadsides showing the Quaker Oats man soon appeared in every American town, advertising a product of reliable quality and uniform price.
Division of Political History, Smithsonian Institution.

Chicago and reap the benefits of large-scale operation. Primitive refrigeration already enabled Chicago pork-packing plants to operate year-round during the 1860s. The problem was how to apply this technology to a railroad freight car. After his engineers figured out an effective system of air circulation in 1877, Swift built a fleet of refrigerator cars and constructed an immense beef-processing plant at the Chicago stockyards.

This was only the beginning of Swift's innovations. No refrigerated warehouses existed in the cities to which he shipped chilled beef, so he built his own network of branch houses. Next, he established a fleet of wagons to distribute his products to retail butcher shops. Swift constructed additional facilities to process the fertilizer, chemicals, and other usable by-products from his slaughtering operations. He also began to handle other perishable commodities, including dairy products, so that he could fully utilize his refrigerator cars and branch houses. As the demand grew, Swift built more packing houses in other stockyard centers, including Kansas City, Fort Worth, and Omaha.

Step by step, Swift created a new kind of enterprise, the *vertically integrated* firm—that is, a national company capable of handling within its own structure all the func-

tions of an industry. In effect, Swift & Co. replaced a large number of small specialized firms with one multifunctional national firm. Swift's lead was followed by several big Chicago pork packers, of which Armour & Co. was the most prominent. By the end of the 1890s five firms, all of them nationally organized and vertically integrated, produced nearly 90 percent of the meat shipped in interstate commerce. The entire geography of the meat industry had changed (see Map 17.3).

The Birth of Mass Marketing. The refrigerator car had made all this possible in the fresh-meat trade. In most other fields no single invention was so decisive. But other manufacturers did share Swift's insight that the essential step was to identify a mass market and then develop a national enterprise capable of serving it. In the petroleum industry John D. Rockefeller during the 1870s built the Standard Oil Company partly by taking over rival firms, but he also developed a national distribution system to reach the enormous market for kerosene as a fuel for lighting and heating homes. The Singer Sewing Machine Company formed its own sales organization, using both retail stores and door-to-door salesmen. Through such distribution systems, manufacturers provided technical information, credit, and repair facilities for their products. Like the meat packers, these companies became vertically integrated firms that served a national market.

To gain the benefits of mass distribution, retail business went through comparable changes. Montgomery Ward and Sears, Roebuck developed into national mail-order houses for rural consumers. From Vermont to California, farm families selected identical goods from catalogues and became part of the nationwide consumer market. In the cities, mass distribution followed different strategies. Department stores, a form of retailing pioneered by John Wanamaker in Philadelphia in 1875, spread to every large city. The most important innovators in this field were Jewish families such as the Strauses of New York, the Lazaruses of Columbus, Ohio, and the Mays of Colorado, most of whose founders had started as peddlers or owners of dry-goods shops. An alternative route to urban distribution was through chain stores, which was the strategy of the Great Atlantic and Pacific Tea Company (A & P) and the F. W. Woolworth Company.

American society prepared its citizens to be consumers of the standardized goods produced by national manufacturers and sold by mass marketers. The high rate of geographic mobility broke down local loyalties, so strong in Europe. Social class in America, though by no means absent, was blurred at the edges and did not, for example, call for distinguishing ways of dressing. Foreign visitors often noted that ready-made clothing made it difficult to tell salesgirls from debutantes on city streets.

The American consumer's receptivity to standardized goods should not be exaggerated. Gustavus Swift, for

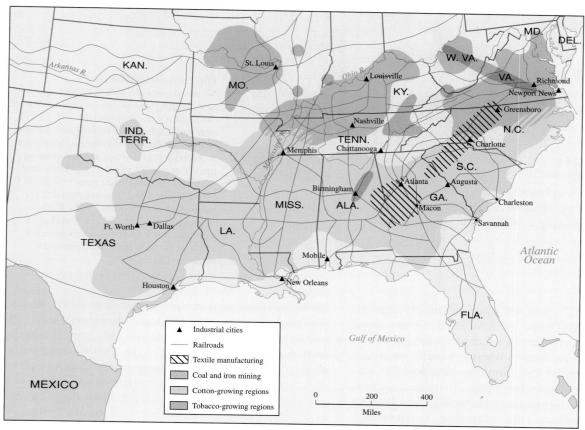

MAP 17.4
The New South, 1900
The economy of the Old South focused on raising staple crops, especially cotton and tobacco. In the New South staple agriculture continued to dominate, but there was marked industrial development as well. Industrial regions developed, producing textiles, coal and iron, and wood products. By 1900 the South's industrial pattern was well defined.

example, encountered great resistance to his Chicago beef: how could it be wholesome weeks later in Boston or Philadelphia? Cheap prices helped, but advertising mattered more. Modern advertising was born in the late nineteenth century, cluttering the urban landscape with billboards and signs. By 1900 advertisers were spending upwards of $90 million a year for space in newspapers and magazines. Advertisements urged readers to bathe with Pears' soap, eat Uneeda biscuits, sew on a Singer machine, and snap pictures with a Kodak camera. The active molding of demand for brand-name products became a major function of American business.

The New South

"Shall we dethrone our idols?" This was a question southerners had to ask themselves as they enviously observed the burst of economic activity in the North. For many, the answer was a resounding yes. Nostalgia

for the Old South, with its leisurely plantation ways, became the chief target of the advocates of southern economic development. The South, they argued, had always given "the places of trust and honor" to "warriors and orators," forgetting that "what it would most need was the practical wisdom of businessmen." Led by Henry W. Grady, editor of the Atlanta *Constitution*, an influential group of publicists made the "practical wisdom of businessmen" the credo of a "New South."

Catching up with the North was no easy task. The plantation economy of the Old South had strongly impeded industrial development. The slave states had few cities, a primitive distribution system, and not much manufacturing. This modest infrastructure was quickly restored after the Civil War. In 1877, with both Reconstruction and economic depression ended, a railroad boom developed. Track mileage doubled in the next decade and, at least by that measure, the South became nearly competitive with the rest of the country (Map 17.4).

But the South remained overwhelmingly agricultural; two of every three persons lived on the land. Farming and poverty are not necessarily linked, but in the South they were. Sharecropping, which required a cash crop (see Chapter 15), committed the South to cotton despite soil depletion, low productivity, and unprofitable prices. At a time of rapid technological advances in northern agriculture, cotton growing remained tied to the mule, the plow, and the hoe. Wages for southern farm labor fell steadily, dropping to scarcely half of the national average by the 1890s—roughly 75 cents a day without board.

Southern Industry.   From this low agricultural wage, surprisingly, sprang the South's hopes for industrialization. Consider, for example, how southern textile mills got started in the Piedmont upcountry of North Carolina, South Carolina, and Georgia in the mid-1870s. Capital was raised locally, subscribed in large amounts and small under a drumbeat of boosterism. The mills recruited workers mostly from the surrounding hill farms, where people struggled to make ends meet. To attract them, mill wages had to be higher than farm earnings, but not much higher. Paying rock-bottom wages, the new mills had a great competitive advantage over the long-established New England industry—as much as 40 percent in labor costs in 1897.

The labor system that evolved likewise reflected southern agrarian society. To begin with, it involved hiring whole families. "Papa decided he would come because he didn't have nothing much but girls and they had to get out and work like men," recalled one woman. It was not Papa, in fact, but his girls whom the mills wanted, for work as spinners and loom tenders. But they could not be recruited individually: no right-thinking parent would have permitted that. There was, however, no objection to hiring by families; after all, on

the farm everyone had been expected to work. And so the family system of textile labor developed, in which half or more of the mill operatives were female and the work force was very young. In the 1880s, a quarter of all southern textile workers were under fifteen years of age; three-quarters were twenty-four or younger.

The hours were long—twelve hours a day—but life in the mill villages was, in the words of one historian, "like a family." Employers tended to be highly paternalistic, providing company housing and a variety of services. The mill workers themselves built close-knit, supportive communities—but for whites only. Although blacks sometimes worked as day laborers and janitors, they hardly ever got jobs as operatives in the mills.

Cheap, abundant labor might have been termed the South's most valuable natural resource. But the South was also well endowed with other natural resources. From its rich soil came tobacco—after cotton, the region's largest cash crop. When cigarettes became fashionable in the 1880s, the young North Carolina entrepreneur James B. Duke seized the new market by taking advantage of a southern invention—James A. Bonsack's machine for producing cigarettes automatically. Blacks stemmed and stripped the tobacco leaf, as they always had, but Duke followed the textile example and restricted machine tending to white women.

Lumbering, by contrast, was largely racially integrated, with a labor force evenly divided between black and white men. The extensive pine forests of the South were rapidly exploited in the post-Reconstruction years. Alabama's rich coal and iron ore deposits also attracted investors; by 1890 the Birmingham district was producing nearly a million tons of pig iron a year.

Economic Retardation.   Despite the South's high hopes, this burst of industrial development did not lift the region out of poverty. Industrial output increased

TABLE 17.2

Comparison of Value Added per Worker, South and Non-South, 1910 (in dollars)

Type of Industry	South	Non-South
Lumber and timber products	820	1020
Cotton goods	544	764
Cars and general shop construction by steam railroad companies	657	746
Turpentine and resin	516	—
Tobacco manufactures	1615	1394
Foundry and machine-shop products	1075	1307
Printing and publishing	1760	2100
Cottonseed oil	1715	—
Hosiery and knit goods	461	724
Furniture and refrigerators	732	1052
Iron and steel	1182*	1433
Fertilizer	1833	1947

This table reveals the consistency with which northern industries (except tobacco manufactures) controlled the more skilled—and hence more value-creating—processes of production.
*Partially estimated.
Source: Gavin Wright, *Old South, New South: Revolutions in the Southern Economy since the Civil War* (New York: Basic Books, 1986), 163.

more rapidly than in the North but not rapidly enough to make much headway against the dominant agricultural sector. In 1900 two-thirds of all southerners made their living from the soil, just as they had in 1870. Moreover, most of the industries that did develop produced raw materials (forestry and mining) or engaged in the low-tech processing of coarse products. Industry by industry, the key economic statistic—the value added by manufacturing—showed the South consistently lagging behind the North (Table 17.2).

Southerners tended to blame the North: the South was a "colonial" economy controlled by New York and Chicago. There was some truth to this charge. Much of the capital—by no means all—did come from the North. And the integrating processes of the economy did subordinate regional to national interests. When the railway network moved to a uniform gauge in 1886, the southern railroads had to convert to the northern standard. Nor did northern interests hesitate to use their muscle to maintain the interregional status quo. Railroads, for example, varied freight rates so that it was cheap for southern cotton and timber to flow out and for northern manufactured goods to flow in.

Yet in the end the South's economic backwardness was mostly of its own making. The great advantage of the South—its cheap labor—actually kept it from becoming a more technologically advanced economy. First, low wages discouraged employers from replacing workers with machinery. Second, low wages attracted labor-intensive industry, such as textiles. Third, a cheap labor market inhibited investment in education because of the likelihood that better-educated workers would flee to higher-wage markets and the investment in them would be lost.

What distinguished the southern labor market was that it was *insulated* from the rest of the country. Why northern workers and arriving immigrants steered clear of the South is not hard to explain: wages were too low, attractive jobs were too scarce. Harder to understand is why so few southerners, black or white, left for the higher-wage North prior to World War I. At its core, the explanation has to do with the fact that the South was a place apart, with social and racial mores that discouraged all but its most resourceful inhabitants from seeking economic opportunity elsewhere. The result was that a normal flow of workers back and forth did not occur, and wage differentials did not narrow. So long as this condition persisted, the South would remain a tributary economy, a supplier on unequal terms to the advanced industrial heartland of the North.

The World of Work

———————★———————

In a free-enterprise system, profit drives the entrepreneur. But the industrial order is not populated only by profit makers. It includes—in vastly larger numbers—wage earners. What is done for profit always affects those who work for wages, but never so profoundly as in the late nineteenth century.

Labor Recruits

Wherever industrialism took hold, it set people in motion. Farm folk migrated to cities. Artisans moved into factories. An industrial labor force emerged. This happened in the United States just as it did in European countries, but with a difference: the United States could not rely primarily on its own population for a supply of workers.

The demand for labor was enormous. American industry required nearly three times more workers in 1900 than it had needed in 1870 (Figure 17.2). Rural Americans were highly mobile in the late nineteenth century, and half of those who moved ended up in cities. But the desirable factory jobs—puddlers, rollers, molders, and machinists—required industrial skills not held by rural Americans. Except in the South, moreover, native-born whites no longer wanted factory work. They had a basic education; they could read and calculate, and they understood American institutions and ways of doing things. City-bound white Americans found their opportunities in the multiplying white-collar jobs in offices and retail stores.

Modest numbers of blacks began to migrate northward and westward—roughly 80,000 between 1870 and 1890 and another 200,000 from 1890 to 1910. Most of them settled in cities, where the men were restricted to casual labor and janitorial work, the women to domestic service. Only 7 percent of all African American men held factory jobs in 1890. Employers turned black applicants away from the factory gates because immigrant workers were already supplying them with as much cheap labor as they needed.

Immigrant Workers. The great migration from the Old World started in the 1840s, when over a million Irish peasants fled the potato famine. In the following years, as European agriculture became increasingly commercialized, expanding peasant populations outstripped the available land. The peasant economy failed first in Germany and Scandinavia and then, later in the nineteenth century, across Austria-Hungary, Russia, Italy, and the Balkans. In the industrial districts of Europe, the forces of economic change also cut loose many workers in the declining artisan trades and in obsolete occupations such as hand-loom weaving.

Ethnic origin largely determined the kind of work that the immigrants found in their new country. Skilled artisans generally sought the types of jobs they had held in the Old World. The Welsh labored as tin-plate workers, the English as miners, the Germans as machinists and traditional artisans (for example, bakers and carpenters), the Belgians as glass workers, and the Scandinavians as seamen on the Great Lakes. For common labor, employers counted on the brawn of Irish rural immigrants.

As technology advanced, American employers had less need for European craft skills, while the demand for unskilled workers skyrocketed. The sources of

Ironworkers—Noontime
The qualities of the nineteenth-century craft worker—dignity, "unselfish brotherhood,"
a "manly" bearing—shine through in this painting by Thomas P. Anschutz.
Ironworkers—Noontime became a popular painting when it was reproduced as an
engraving in *Harper's Weekly* in 1884.
Fine Arts Museum of San Francisco.

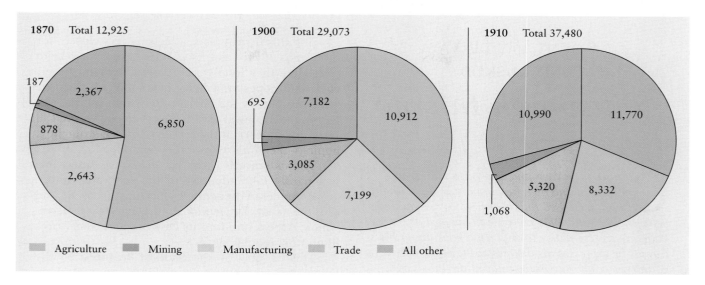

| 1870 | Total 12,925 | | 1900 | Total 29,073 | | 1910 | Total 37,480 |

Agriculture ■ Mining ■ Manufacturing ■ Trade ■ All other

FIGURE 17.2
Changes in the Labor Force, 1870–1910
The numbers represent thousands of people (for example, 12,925 = 12,925,000 workers). They reveal both the enormous increase in the labor force between 1870 and 1910 and the dramatic shift from agriculture to industry and other nonagricultural jobs.

immigration began to shift during the 1880s, and by the early twentieth century arrivals from eastern and southern Europe far outstripped immigration from northern Europe (Figure 17.3). Slavic immigrants without job skills flooded into the lowest rungs of American industry. Heavy, low-paid factory labor became the domain of the recent immigrants (see Voices from Abroad, "Count Vay de Vaya und Luskod: Pittsburgh Inferno," p. 558). Blast-furnace jobs, one job seeker heard, were "Hunky work," not suitable for him or any other native-born whites. The derogatory term refers to Hungarian workers, but it was applied indiscriminately to Poles, Slovaks, and all the other Slavic groups arriving in America's industrial districts.

Not only skill determined where immigrants ended up in American industry. The newcomers, though generally traveling on their own, moved within well-defined networks, following relatives or fellow villagers already in America, joining their households as family members or boarders, and relying on them to land a job. A high degree of ethnic clustering resulted, even within a single factory. At the Jones and Laughlin steelworks in Pittsburgh, for example, the carpentry shop was German, the hammer shop Polish, and the blooming (ingot-reducing) mill Serbian. Immigrants also had different job preferences. Men from Italy, for example, preferred outdoor work to factory labor, often laboring in gangs under a *padrone* (boss), much as they had in Italy.

Immigrants entered a modern industrial order, but they saw their surroundings through peasant eyes. With the disruption of the traditional rural economies of eastern and southern Europe, many had lost their lands and fallen into the class of dependent, propertyless servants.

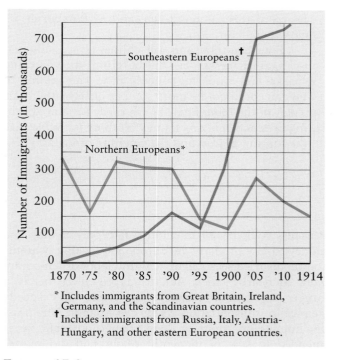

* Includes immigrants from Great Britain, Ireland, Germany, and the Scandinavian countries.
† Includes immigrants from Russia, Italy, Austria-Hungary, and other eastern European countries.

FIGURE 17.3
American Immigration, 1870–1914
This graph shows the surge of European immigration in the late nineteenth century. While northern Europe continued to send substantial numbers, it was overshadowed after 1895 by southern Europeans pouring into America to work in mines and factories.

COUNT VAY DE VAYA UND LUSKOD

Pittsburgh Inferno

★

*C*ount Vay de Vaya und Luskod, a Hungarian nobleman and high functionary in the Catholic Church, crossed the United States several times between 1903 and 1906 en route to his post as the Vatican's representative to Asia. In a book about his travels, he expresses his distress at the plight of his countrymen laboring in the mills of the Pittsburgh steel district.

The bells are tolling for a funeral. The modest train of mourners is just setting out for the little church-yard on the hill. Everything is shrouded in gloom, even the coffin lying upon the bier and the people who stand on each side in threadbare clothes and with heads bent. Such is my sad reception at the Hungarian workingmen's colony at McKeesport. Everyone who has been in the United States has heard of this famous town, and of Pittsburgh, its close neighbor. . . .

Fourteen-thousand tall chimneys are silhouetted against the sky . . . discharg[ing] their burning sparks and smok[ing] incessantly. The realms of Vulcan could not be more somber or filthy than this valley of the Monongahela. On every hand are burning fires and spurting flames. Nothing is visible save the forging of iron and the smelting of metal. . . .

And this fearful place affects us very closely, for thousands of immigrants wander here from year to year. Here they fondly seek the realization of their cherished hopes, and here they suffer till they are swallowed up by the inferno. He whom we are now burying is the latest victim. Yesterday he was in full vigor and at work at the foundry, toiling, struggling, hoping—a chain broke, and he was killed. . . .

This is scarcely work for *mankind.* Americans will hardly take anything of the sort; only immigrants rendered desperate by circumstances . . . and thus he is at the mercy of the tyrannous Trust, which gathers him into its clutches and transforms him into a regular slave.

This is one of the saddest features of the Hungarian emigration. In making a tour of these prisons, wherever the heat is most insupportable, the flames most scorching, the smoke and soot most choking, there we are certain to find compatriots bent and wasted with toil. Their thin, wrinkled, wan faces seem to show that in America the newcomers are of no use except to help fill the moneybags of the insatiable millionaires. . . . In this realm of Mammon and Moloch everything has a value—except human life. . . . Why? Because human life is a commodity the supply of which exceeds the demand. There are always fresh recruits to supply the place of those who have fallen in battle; and the steamships are constantly arriving at the neighboring ports, discharging their living human cargo still further to swell the phalanx of the instruments of cupidity.

Source: Oscar Handlin, ed., *This Was America* (Cambridge, MA: Harvard University Press, 1949), 407–410.

Peasants could avoid that bitter fate only if they had money to buy property. In Europe job-seeking peasants commonly tried seasonal agricultural labor or temporary work in nearby cities. America represented merely a larger leap, made possible by cheap and speedy steamship transportation across the Atlantic. The peasant immigrants, most of them young and male, never intended to stay permanently. About half did return, departing from America in great numbers during depression years. No one knows how many left because they had saved enough money and how many left for lack of work. For American employers, it scarcely mattered. What mattered was that the immigrants took the worst jobs and melted away when the jobs dried up. For the new industrial order, they made an ideal labor supply.

Railroading and a few other fields employed mostly native-born workers. Overall, however, immigrants manned American industry, constituting well over half of the labor force of the nation's principal manufacturing and mining industries after the turn of the century.

Working Women. Between 1870 and 1900 the number of wage-earning women grew by almost two-thirds. Women made up a quarter of the labor force in 1900 and were essential to America's economy. Their gender shaped their role as workers. Contemporary beliefs about womanhood determined which women entered the work force and how they were treated once they became wage earners.

Immigrant Workers

Many native-born Americans resented the influx of peasant immigrants from eastern and southern Europe that began in the 1880s. In fact, the newcomers provided most of the heavy labor on which the nation's industrial economy depended. They were Europe's gift—its most vigorous and hardworking people. In this photograph new arrivals are boarding a ferry at Ellis Island, the fabled immigration station in New York harbor, to be taken to the Battery, at the southern tip of Manhattan, from where they will scatter to factories and mines across America.

State Historical Society of Wisconsin.

Wives were not supposed to work outside the home, and in fact less than 5 percent did so in 1890. Only among African Americans did many married women, above 30 percent, work for wages. Among whites, the typical working woman at that time was

under twenty-four and unmarried. In most working-class households, daughters had no choice but to work, because their families needed their earnings. When older women worked, remarked one observer, it "was usually a sign that something had gone wrong"—their husbands had died, deserted, or stopped working.

Since women were held to be inherently different from men, it followed that they should not be permitted to do "men's work." Nor, regardless of the value of their labor, could they be paid a man's wage. The dominant view was that a woman did not require a "living wage" because, as one investigator reported, "it is expected that she has men to support her." Moreover, the occupation that served as the baseline for all women's jobs was domestic service, which was always very poorly paid or, in a woman's own home, not paid at all.

At the turn of the century women workers fell into three categories. One third worked as maids or other types of domestic servants. Another third held "female" white-collar jobs in teaching, nursing, sales, and office work. The remaining third worked in industry, heavily concentrated in the garment trades and textile mills but present also in many other industries as inspectors, packers, and assemblers, and in other "light" occupations. Few worked as supervisors, fewer in the crafts, and nearly none as day laborers.

Just how jobs came to be defined as male or female—in sociological lingo, the *sex-typing* of occupations—is not easy to explain. Jobs as telephone operators and store clerks, originally held by men, had by the 1890s been taken over by women. Once women dominated an occupation, people came to think of it as having feminine attributes, even though very similar or even identical work elsewhere was done by men. Jobs identified as women's work became unsuitable for men. There were no male telephone operators by 1900.

The sex-typing of work was legitimized by the sentimental view of women as the weaker sex, but powerful interests also played a role. Craft workers protected their male domain, and employers profited from cut-rate work. Wherever they worked, women earned less than the lowest-paid males. At the turn of the century the weekly wage of women factory workers came to roughly $7, $3 less than that of unskilled men and $5 below the average for all industrial employees.

As with male workers, ethnicity and race played a big part in the distribution of women's jobs among particular groups. Exclusion from all but the most menial jobs applied as rigidly to black women as it did to black men. White-collar jobs were reserved for the native-born, which in the cities increasingly included the second-generation daughters of immigrants. And as with men, ethnicity created clustering patterns in the jobs held by wage-earning women or, in the case of Italian families, restricted them to sewing and other subcontracting tasks that could be done at home.

Switchboard Operators
Telephone work offers a prime historical example of sex-typing in American employment. When the first telephone exchange was set up in Boston in 1878, it was operated by teenage boys, which followed the practice set in the telegraph industry. During the 1880s, however, young women increasingly replaced the boys, and by 1900 switchboard operation was defined as women's work. In this photograph of a telephone exchange in Columbus, Ohio, in 1907, the older woman at left has risen to the position of supervisor, but it is the two men in the picture who are clearly in charge. The other major occupations in this new industry—telephone installation and line maintenance—were just as strictly male as switchboard operation was female, but of course on a much higher pay scale. Corbis-Bettmann.

The Family Economy. Disapproval of wives working outside the home, though expressed in sentimental and moral terms, was based on solid necessity for working-class families. From the standpoint of the labor market, the basic economic unit consisted of the individual employee. For workers, however, the family was the economic unit, and the wife's contribution to it was crucial. Cooking, cleaning, and tending the children were not income-producing activities or reckoned in terms of money. But everyone knew that the family household could not function without the wife's contribution. Therefore, her place was in the home.

Working-class families, however, found the going hard on a single income. Only among highly skilled workers, wrote an investigator of the family budgets of miners and iron workers, "was it possible for the husband unaided to support his family." The rockiest period came during the child-bearing years, when there were many mouths to feed and only the earnings of the father to provide the food. Thereafter, as the children grew old enough to work, the family income began to increase. Not only older unmarried sons and daughters but the younger children as well contributed their share. In 1900 one of every five children under sixteen worked for wages, including probably a quarter of a million younger than ten. "When the people own houses," remarked a printer from Fall River, Massachusetts, "you will generally find that it is a large family all working together."

By the 1890s all the northern industrial states had passed laws prohibiting child labor and regulating work hours for teenagers. Most of those states also required children under fourteen to attend school for a certain number of weeks each year. Working-class families continued to need more than one income, but this money came increasingly from the wives. After 1890 the proportion of married women who worked crept steadily upward; about a fifth of the wives of unskilled and semiskilled men in Chicago held jobs in 1920. Wage-earning wives and mothers were on their way to becoming a primary part of America's labor force.

Autonomous Labor

No one supervised the nineteenth-century coal miner (see American Voices, "John Brophy: A Miner's Son," p. 561). He was a tonnage worker, paid for the amount of coal he produced. He provided his own tools, worked at his own pace, and knocked off early when he chose. Such autonomous craft workers—almost all of them men—flourished in many branches of nineteenth-century industry. They were mule spinners in cotton mills, puddlers and rollers in ironworks, molders in stove making, and machinists, glassblowers, and skilled workers of many other types.

In the shop they abided by the *stint*, a limit placed by themselves on the amount they would produce each day. This informal system of limiting output infuriated efficiency-minded engineers. But to the worker it signified personal dignity and "unselfish brotherhood" with fellow employees. The male craft worker took pride in a "manly" bearing toward both his fellows and the boss. One day a shop in Lowell, Massachusetts, posted regulations requiring all employees to be at their posts in work

JOHN BROPHY
A Miner's Son

★

John Brophy (1883–1963), an important mine union official, recalls in an oral history what mining was like in his boyhood, a time when mining was strictly pick-and-shovel work and machinery had not yet eroded the prized skills of the miner.

I got a thrill at the thought of having an opportunity to go and work in the mine, to go and work along side my father. After . . . I got experience and some strength, and the ability to work with a little skill, I was conscious of the fact that my father was a good workman; that he had pride in his calling. . . . It was a great satisfaction to me that my father was a skilled, clean workman with everything kept in shape, and the timbering done well—all of these things: the rib side, the roadway, the timbering, the fact that you kept the loose coal clean rather than cluttered all over the workplace, the skill with which you undercut the vein, the judgment in drilling the coal after it had been undercut and placing the exact amount of explosive so that it would do an effective job of breaking the coal from the solid— indicated the quality of his work. . . .

It was skill in handling the pick and the shovel, the placing of timbers, and understanding the vagaries of the workplace—which is subject to certain pressures from the overhanging strata as you advance into the seam. It's an awareness of roof conditions. And it's something else too. Under the older conditions of mining under which I went to work with my father, the miner exercised considerable freedom in his working place in determining his pace of work and the selection of the order of time in the different work operations. Judgment was everywhere along the line, and there was also necessary skill. It was the feel of all this. You know that another workman in another place was a good miner, a passable miner, or an indifferent one. . . . I think that was one of the great satisfactions that a

miner had—that he was his own boss within his workplace. . . .

The miner is always aware of danger, that he lives under dangerous conditions in the workplace, because he's constantly uncovering new conditions as he advances in the workingplace, exposing new areas of roof, discovering some weakened condition or break which may bring some special danger. There is also the danger that comes from a piece of coal slipping off the fast and falling on the worker as he lays prone on the bottom doing his cutting. The worker has got to be aware of all these conditions that may be in the coal, that may be in the roof. . . .

Then there is the further fact that the miners by and large lived in purely mining communities which were often isolated. They developed a group loyalty under all these circumstances. They were both individualists and they were group conscious. . . . It made them an extraordinary body of workers, these miners, because of these very special conditions, because involved in it was not only earning a living, but a matter of health and safety, life and death were involved in every way. You find time and again miners, in an effort to rescue their fellow workers, taking chances which quite often meant death for themselves. . . .

Along with that is a sense of justice. There was the very fact the miner was a tonnage worker and that he could be short weighed and cheated in various ways, and that the only safeguard against it was [union] organization. In that case it was important to have a representative of the miners to see that the weight was properly done and properly credited to the individual miner. There was the whole complex of circumstances that had been in the mining industry for generations which had been their experience. The miner in my day in the United States was aware that all knowledge didn't start with his generation. . . . At least on one side of my family there are at least four generations of [British] miners, and I say this with a sense of pride; very much so. I'm very proud of the fact that there is this long tradition of miners who have struggled with the elements.

Source: Jerold S. Auerbach, ed., *American Labor: The Twentieth Century* (Indianapolis: Bobbs-Merrill, 1969), 44–48.

Breaker Boys

In the anthracite districts of eastern Pennsylvania, giant machines called breakers processed the coal as it came out of the mines, crushing it and sorting it by size for sale as domestic fuel. The boys shown in this photograph had the job of picking out the slate and refuse as the processed coal came down the chutes, working long hours in a constant cloud of coal dust for less than a dollar a day. Breaker boy was the first job, often begun before the age of ten, in a lifetime in the mines. The photograph does not show any old men, but sick and disabled miners often ended their careers as breaker boys—hence the saying among coal diggers, "Twice a boy and once a man is the poor miner's life."

Library of Congress.

Women workers found much the same kind of social meaning in their jobs. Department store clerks, for example, developed a work culture and language just as robust as that of any male craft group. The most important fact about wage-earning women, however, was their youth. The first job freed many of them from family discipline. It was an opportunity to be independent; to form friendships with other young women; and to experience, however briefly, a fun-loving time of nice clothes, dancing, and other "cheap amusements." Young male workers, by contrast, underwent a process of job socialization presided over by seasoned, older co-workers. Being young mattered to male workers, certainly, but did not define work experience for them as it did for women.

To some degree, youthful preoccupations made it easier for working women to overlook or accept the miserable terms under which many of them labored. But this did not mean that they lacked a sense of group solidarity and self-respect. Pretty clothes might appear frivolous to the casual observer, but they also conveyed the message that the working girl considered herself as good as anyone. Rebellious youth culture sometimes united with job grievances to produce astonishing strike movements in the early twentieth century, as, for example, by the Jewish garment workers of New York and the Irish American telephone operators of Boston.

Rarely, however, did women workers wield the kind of authority that the male craft worker commonly enjoyed. In many factories, he hired his own helpers, supervised their work, and paid them from his earnings. In the late nineteenth century, when the scale of production was expanding, craft workers relieved their employers of the mounting burden of shop-floor management. Many factory managers deliberately shifted this responsibility to their employees. In metal-fabricating firms that did precise machining and complex assembling, for example, a system of inside contracting developed, in which skilled employees bid for a production run, hiring and paying their own workers, taking full responsibility for the operation, and pocketing the profits.

Foremen enjoyed a similar degree of authority over the labor of unskilled workers. A multitude of laborers had been needed to dig canals, lay railroad tracks, and build cities. They were equally important in heavy industry, where until the last years of the century virtually all hauling of materials was done by hand. In the steel mills, a third or more of the workers shoveled coal and iron ore from freight cars, loaded the furnaces, and handled the tons of hot metal that passed through the mill daily. They worked in gangs, completely under the charge of the foreman or gang boss. He hired them, told them what to do, and disciplined and fired them.

Dispersal of authority was thus characteristic of nineteenth-century industry. The aristocracy of the workers—the craftsmen, inside contractors, and foremen—had a high degree of autonomy. However,

clothes at the opening bell and remain, with the shop door locked, until the dismissal bell. A machinist promptly packed his tools and quit, declaring that he had not "been brought up under such a system of slavery."

Underlying this ethical code was a keen sense of the craft group, each with its own history and customs. Hatters—masters of the art of applying fur felting to top hats and bowlers—had a language of their own. When a hatter was hired, he was "shopped"; if fired, he was "bagged"; when he quit work, he "cried off"; and when he took an apprentice, the boy was "under teach." The hatters, most of whom worked in Danbury, Connecticut, or Orange, New Jersey, formed a distinctive, self-contained community.

their subordinates often paid dearly for that independence. Opportunities for abuse were endless. Any worker who paid his helpers from his own pocket might be tempted to exploit them. In the Pittsburgh area, foremen known as "pushers" were notorious for driving their gangs mercilessly. At the same time, industrial labor in the nineteenth century was still on a human scale. People dealt with each other face to face and often developed cohesive ties within the shop. Striking craft workers commonly received the support of helpers and laborers, and labor gangs sometimes walked out on behalf of a popular foreman.

Systems of Control

As technology advanced and modern management emerged, controls over the work process intensified. Despite fierce resistance, workers increasingly lost the proud independence that had characterized nineteenth-century craft work.

When mine owners introduced undercutting machines in the 1880s, they deprived coal miners of the pick work that was their most prized skill. "Anyone with a weak head and a strong back can load machine coal," grumbled one Kentucky miner. "But a man has to think and study every day like you was studying a book if he is going to get the best of the coal when he uses only a pick." Similar complaints came from many other craft workers as their skills fell victim to machinery—from hand-loom weavers early in the nineteenth century to glassblowers a hundred years later.

One main source of this de-skilling process was a new system of production—Henry Ford called it *mass production*—that turned out standardized, high-volume products. Agricultural implements, sewing machines, typewriters, bicycles, and, after 1900, automobiles were assembled from standardized, interchangeable parts. The machine tools that cut, drilled, and ground these metal parts were first operated by skilled machinists. But because they produced long runs of a single item, these machine tools became more specialized; they became *dedicated* machines—machines set up to do the same job over and over—and the need for skilled operatives disappeared. "A man never learns the machinist's trade now," John Morison, a machinist, complained in 1883 to a Senate investigating committee. In the manufacture of sewing machines "the trade is so subdivided that a man is not considered a machinist at all. One man may make just a particular part of a machine and may not know anything whatever about another part of the same machine." Such a worker, noted an observer, "cannot be master of a craft, but only master of a fragment."

Meatpacking did not become a mechanized industry, yet it also experienced the mass-production revolution. The key innovation in the Chicago packing houses was a shift from the traditional reliance on skilled

butchers to a highly specialized division of labor. At the Armour plant, workers performed seventy-eight distinct jobs, working efficiently and at high speed as the carcasses moved along, hooked to overhead conveyors. In a ten-hour day a gang of 157 workers could handle 1,050 head of cattle, many more per employee than if one skilled butcher did everything. "If you need to turn out a little more," boasted a superintendent at Swift & Co., "you speed up the conveyor a little and the men speed up to keep pace." Complaints about speedups were a sure sign of workers' loss of control over their jobs.

Frederick W. Taylor and Scientific Management. Employers were attracted to dedicated machinery and conveyor belts because these innovations increased output; the impact on workers was not uppermost in their minds. Employers recognized that mechanization made it easier to discipline workers, but that was only an incidental benefit of the efficiencies coming from the machinery itself. Gradually, however, the idea took hold that managing workers might itself be a way to reduce the cost of production.

The pioneer in this field was Frederick W. Taylor. An expert on metal-cutting methods, Taylor believed that the same engineer's approach might be applied to managing workers, hence the name for his method: *scientific management*. To get the maximum work from the individual worker, Taylor suggested two basic reforms. The first would eliminate the brain work from manual labor. Managers would assume "the burden of gathering together all of the traditional knowledge which in the past has been possessed by the workmen and then of classifying, tabulating, and reducing this knowledge to rules, laws, and formulae." The second reform, a logical consequence of the first, would deprive workers of the authority they had been exercising on the shop floor. Workers would "do what they are told promptly and without asking questions or making suggestions. . . . The duty of enforcing . . . rests with the management alone."

Once managers had the knowledge and the power, they would put labor on a "scientific" basis. This meant subjecting each task to a *time-and-motion study* by an engineer who would analyze and time each job with a stopwatch. A personnel office would hire and train the right person for each job. Workers would be paid at a differential rate—that is, a certain amount if they met the stopwatch standard and a higher rate for additional output. Taylor claimed that his techniques would guarantee the optimum level of worker efficiency. His assumption was that only money mattered to workers and that they would automatically respond to the lure of higher earnings.

Scientific management, in practice, was not a roaring success. Implementing it called for a total restruc-

The Killing Floor
To the modern eye, the labor process depicted in this 1882 engraving of a Chicago meatpacking plant seems primitive and inefficient, but it contains the seeds of America's mass-production revolution. At the far left the steer has already been stunned by one specialist, killed by a second, and attached to a chain that will lift it onto the overhead conveyor. The division of labor is already in place (each of the workers on the line does a single repetitive task), and the process is continuous. It would be only a small step from the killing floors of the Chicago packing plants to Henry Ford's assembly line.
Library of Congress.

turing of factory administration. No company ever adopted Taylor's entire system, and the few that tried paid dearly for the effort. His method of job analysis, which was widely used, met stubborn resistance from workers. "It looks to me like slavery to have a man stand over you with a stopwatch," complained one iron molder. A union leader insisted that "this system is wrong, because we want our heads left on us." Far from solving the labor problem, as Taylor claimed it would, scientific management embittered relations on the shop floor.

Yet Taylor achieved something of fundamental importance. He was a brilliant publicist, and his teachings spread throughout American industry. Taylor's disciples moved beyond his simplistic economic psychology, creating the new professions of personnel administration and industrial psychology, which purported to know how to extract more and better labor from workers. A threshold had been crossed into the modern era of labor management.

So the circle closed on American workers. With each advance, the quest for efficiency cut deeper into their cherished autonomy. Mechanization, scientific management, and the growing scale of industrial activity diminished workers and cut them down to fit the production system. The process occurred unevenly. For textile workers the loss had come early. Miners and iron workers felt it much more slowly. Others, such as craft workers in the building trades, escaped the process almost entirely. But increasing numbers of workers found themselves in an environment that crushed any sense of mastery or even understanding.

The Labor Movement

Wherever industrialization has taken hold, workers have organized and responded collectively. However, the movements they built have varied from one industrial society to another. In the United States, workers were especially uncertain about the path they wanted to take. Only in the 1880s did the American labor movement settle into a fixed course.

Reformers and Unionists

Thomas B. McGuire, a New York wagon driver, was ambitious. He had saved $300 from his wages "so that I might become something of a capitalist eventually." But his venture as a cab driver in the early 1880s soon failed:

> *Corporations usually take that business themselves. They can manage to get men, at starvation wages, and put them on a hack [hired carriage], and put a livery on them with a gold band and brass buttons, to show that they are slaves—I beg pardon; I did not intend to use the word slaves; there are no slaves in this country now—to show that they are merely servants.*

Slave or liveried servant, the symbolic meaning was the same to McGuire. He was speaking of the crushed aspirations of the independent American worker.

Labor Reform and the Knights of Labor. What would satisfy the Thomas McGuires of the nineteenth century? Only the restoration of an egalitarian society, one in which all citizens were equals and everyone might hope to become independent. This republican goal did not require returning to the agrarian past, but rather moving beyond the existing industrial order to a juster system that did not distinguish between capitalists and workers. All would be "producers" laboring together in what was commonly called the "cooperative commonwealth." This ideal inspired the Noble and Holy Order of the Knights of Labor.

Founded in 1869 as a secret society of Philadelphia garment cutters, the Knights of Labor gradually spread to other cities and in 1878 became a national movement. Led by Grand Master Workman Terence V. Powderly, the Knights boasted an elaborate ritual and ceremony calculated to appeal to the fraternal spirit of nineteenth-century workers. From the Knights of Labor they got a sense of belonging very much like that offered by the Masons or Odd Fellows. The Knights, however, harnessed fraternalism to labor-reform advocacy. Their goal was to "give voice to that grand undercurrent of mighty thought, which is today [1880] crystallizing in the hearts of men, and urging them on to perfect organization through which to gain the power to make labor emancipation possible."

But how was "emancipation" to be achieved? Through cooperation, the Knights argued. Funds would be raised to set up cooperative factories and shops owned and run by the employees. As these cooperatives flourished and spread, American society would be transformed into a cooperative commonwealth. But little was actually done. Instead, the Knights concentrated mainly on "education." Terence V. Powderly regarded the organization as a vast labor lyceum open to almost anyone (except lawyers and saloonkeepers). The cooperative commonwealth would arrive in some mysterious way as more and more "producers" became members and learned the group's message from lectures, discussions, and publications. Social evil would not end in a day but "must await the gradual development of educational enlightenment."

Trade Unionism. The labor reformers expressed the higher aspirations of American workers. Another kind of organization—the trade union—tended to their day-to-day needs. Unions had long been central in the lives of craft workers. Apprenticeship rules regulated entry into a trade, and the *closed shop*—by reserving all jobs for union members—kept out lower-wage and incompetent workers. Union rules specified the terms of work, sometimes in minute detail. Above all, trade unionism defended the craft worker's traditional skills and rights.

The trade union also expressed the social identity of a craft. Hatters took pride in their drinking prowess, an on-the-job privilege that was jealously guarded, and their unions sometimes resembled drinking clubs. More often, however, craft unions had an uplifting character. A Birmingham iron puddler claimed that his union's "main object was to educate mechanics up to a standard of morality and temperance, and good workmanship." Because operating trains was a high-risk occupation, the railroad brotherhoods stressed mutual aid, providing accident and death benefits and encouraging members to assist one another. On the job and off, the unions played a big part in the lives of craft workers.

The earliest unions organized local workers in the same craft, which, especially among German workers, was sometimes limited to a single ethnic group. As expanding markets broke down the insularity of these unions, they began to form national organizations. The first of them was the International Typographical

Terence V. Powderly, Labor Peacemaker
The Knights of Labor, unlike their trade-union rivals, in principle opposed strikes. In this cartoon from *Puck*, dated April 7, 1886, the little man depicted in the middle is Master Workman Powderly, leader of the Knights of Labor. The cartoon shows Powderly offering Capital and Labor the Knights' proposal for the peaceful settlement of labor disputes by means of "arbitration," which in those days meant mediation and negotiation rather than resolution by a third party. Powderly's judicious stance, however, could not keep the two sides from each other's throats, and in the national strikes soon to break out, Powderly's own members joined the picket lines.
Puck, April 17, 1886.

A Railroad Brotherhood

Locomotive firemen, who fed the boilers on nineteenth-century steam engines, ranked below locomotive engineers but still considered theirs a privileged occupation. This union certificate conveys the respectable values to which locomotive firemen adhered and, as depicted in the scenes on the right-hand side, the need they felt to protect their families (through the affordable insurance provided by their union) in the event of accidents that were so much a part of the dangerous trade they followed.

Library of Congress.

Union, in 1852. By the 1870s molders, iron workers, bricklayers, and about thirty other trades had formed national unions.

The practical job interests that trade unions espoused might have seemed a far cry from the reform idealism of the Knights of Labor. But both kinds of motives arose from a single workers' culture. Seeing no conflict, many workers carried membership cards in both the Knights of Labor and a trade union. The careers of many labor leaders, including Powderly, likewise embraced both kinds of activity. For many years even the functional lines were indistinct. At the local level, little separated a trade assembly of the Knights from a local trade union; both engaged in fraternal and job-oriented activities.

Trade unions generally barred women, and so did the Knights until, in 1881, women shoe workers in Philadelphia struck in support of their male co-workers and won the right to form their own local assembly. By 1886 probably fifty thousand women belonged to the Knights of Labor. Their courage on the picket line prompted Powderly's rueful remark that women "are the best men in the Order." For a handful of women, such as hosiery worker Leonora M. Barry, the Knights provided a rare chance to take up leadership roles as organizers and officials. For many others the liberation was more modest but very real: "timid young girls—girls who have been overworked from their cradle—stand[ing] up bravely . . . swayed . . . by the wrongs heaped upon their comrades, talk[ing] nobly and beautifully of the hope of redress to be found in organization."

Similarly, the Knights of Labor grudgingly expanded the opportunity for black workers to join, because of the need for solidarity and, just as important, in deference to the Order's egalitarian principles. The Knights could rightly boast that their "great work has been to organize labor which was previously unorganized."

The Triumph of "Pure and Simple" Unionism

In the early 1880s the Knights began to rival the trade unions. Boycott campaigns against the products of "unfair" employers achieved impressive results. With the economy booming and workers in short supply, the Knights began to win strikes, including a major victory against Jay Gould's Southwestern railway system in 1885. Workers flocked into the organization, and its membership jumped from 100,000 to perhaps 700,000 in less than a year. For a brief time the Knights stood poised as a potential industrial-union movement capable of bringing all workers into its fold.

The rapid growth of the Knights of Labor frightened the national trade unions. They tried to keep their local branches away from the Knights, but without success. The unions then began to insist on a clear separation of roles, with the Knights confined to the field of labor reform. This was partly a battle over turf, but it also reflected a deepening divergence of labor philosophies.

Samuel Gompers, a cigar maker from New York City, led the ideological assault on the Knights. Gompers hammered out the philosophical position that would become known as "pure and simple" unionism. His starting point was that grand theories and schemes such as those that excited the Knights should be avoided like the plague. Unions, Gompers believed, should focus instead strictly on concrete, achievable gains, and they should organize workers not as an undifferentiated mass of "producers" but by craft and occupation. The battleground should be where workers could mobilize their power, which was where they worked—not in the quicksands of politics. Gompers developed these views as general propositions, but they were grounded in the hard experience of unionists such as Abraham Bisno, who tried to organize his fellow workers and bargain collectively with employers (see American Voices, "Abraham Bisno: Trade Unionist," p. 568). Bisno would have nodded in agreement with Gompers's assertion that "no matter how just . . . unless the cause is backed up with power to enforce it, it is going to be crushed and annihilated."

The struggle for the eight-hour workday crystallized the tensions between the rival movements. Both of them favored a shorter workday, but for different reasons. To the Knights, more leisure was desirable because workers had duties "to perform as American citizens and members of society": a shorter workday was a precondition for a healthy republican society. Trade unionists took a more hard-boiled view of the eight-hour day: it would spread the available jobs among more workers, protect them against overwork, and (like higher wages) give them a better life. When the trade unions set May 1, 1886, as the deadline for achieving the eight-hour day, the Knights objected. But workers everywhere responded enthusiastically, and as the deadline approached, a wave of strikes and demonstrations broke out across the country.

The Haymarket Square Riot. At one such eight-hour strike, at the McCormick agricultural-implement works in Chicago, a battle erupted on May 3, leaving four strikers dead. Chicago was a hotbed of American *anarchism*—the revolutionary advocacy of a stateless society—and local anarchists, most of them German immigrants, called a protest meeting the next evening at Haymarket Square. The meeting went off peacefully, but when police moved in at the end to break it up, someone threw a bomb at the police, who responded with wild gunfire. Most of the casualties, including some police, came from police bullets.

The anarchist sponsors of the rally, some of them not even present, were arrested and charged wih criminal conspiracy, a legal doctrine so broad that no direct involvement in the bombing was required to justify a verdict of guilt. There was in fact no evidence linking them to the bombing. Four men were executed, one committed suicide, and the others received long prison sentences. They were victims of one of the great miscarriages of American justice.

Seizing on the anti-union hysteria set off by the Haymarket affair, employers took the offensive against the campaign for an eight-hour workday. They broke strikes violently, compiled blacklists of strikers, and forced others to sign *yellow-dog contracts* guaranteeing that, as a condition of employment, they would not join a union. If trade unionists needed any further confir-

mation of the tough world in which they lived, they found it in Haymarket and its aftermath.

In December 1886, having failed to persuade the Knights of Labor to desist from union activity, the national trade unions formed the American Federation of Labor (AFL), with Samuel Gompers as president. The AFL embodied the belief of the national unions that they constituted a distinctive movement. The federation in effect locked into place the trade-union structure as it had evolved by the 1880s. Underlying this structure was the conviction that workers had to take the world as it was, not as they dreamed it might be. At this point, the American movement's development definitely diverged from that of its European counterparts, for fundamental to Gompers's AFL was rejection of a separate political party for workers.

Samuel Gompers
This is a photograph of the labor leader in his forties taken when he was visiting striking miners in West Virginia, an area where mine operators resisted unions with special fierceness. The photograph was taken by a company detective.
George Meany Memorial Archives.

ABRAHAM BISNO
Trade Unionist
———★———

Repeated strikes in Chicago caused a government commission to come to that city in 1900 to investigate the reasons for the labor troubles. Bisno, a garment worker and "walking delegate"—a local union agent—gives the trade-union side of the story.

Q. Present occupation.
A. Collecting fares on the loop here for the Union Elevated Railway Company.
Q. Former occupation.
A. I am a cloak maker by trade—made cloaks for some years—and I have had several occupations within the last few years. I have been walking delegate for our union.
Q. What union is that?
A. The Chicago Cloak Makers' Union. . . .

Q. Is the union to which you belong still in existence?
A. It is lately organized again; it was broken up after the defeat of the strike 2 years ago. . . .
Q. Are you a believer in the union of labor?
A. Yes. . . . Unless a firm recognizes the union and agrees to employ nobody except members of the union, the union cannot exist. In my own trade, when our union was weak, our best men were victimized, and were out of a job most of the time; I mean our most intelligent men—men who do not want to put up with abuse easily. . . . So when these men demand that the union be recognized to the extent of not employing other people except members of their union, this is essential to the very existence of the organization. It is a life-and-death question with them. . . .

Q. You recognize that the strike is a coercive measure—an act of war and an interference with the civil rights of a concern?
A. . . . Yes; but then the reduction in wages, or failing to raise the wages when conditions warrant, are acts of war and interference with my civil rights in a time of peace. It is the same thing. . . .
Q. What are the steps of persuasion brought into use to influence a man who has failed to yield to argument and has gone to work?
A. Well several. For instance, in one case we have alienated a man from the affections of his co-church members.
Q. That you call persuasion?
A. Yes; we went into the church and denounced the fellow as a traitor to our interests, cutting our throats, sort of sinning against the religious laws, inflicting damage on so many families.
Q. That is one step?
A. That was one of the means; called him scab.
Q. Called him scab?
A. Yes; on the streets.
Q. To his face?
A. Yes. As I told you, it depends upon the temperament of the man. We would go after him in a hundred and one ways, if we can, to drive him out of the community.
Q. That you call persuasion?
A. Within the law; and I think under certain conditions it is right for a person to violate the law and take the consequences. Supposing I am fined for calling a man a scab. I am put into a fine, say, of $10 and have to go to jail for 20 days. The abuse I am suffering may be so great that I would take my medicine. I would tell a man he was a scab, and take my medicine for it and go to jail. . . .

———

Source: Report of the U.S. Industrial Commission, VIII (Washington, DC: U.S. Government Printing Office, 1901), 53–58, 79–82.

The Knights of Labor never recovered from the employer counteroffensive after the Haymarket affair. Powderly retreated to the rhetoric of labor reform, but wage earners had lost interest, and he was unable to formulate a workable new strategy. By the mid-1890s, the Knights of Labor had faded away. In the meantime, the trade unions experienced steady growth, justifying Gompers's confidence that he had found the correct formula for the American labor movement.

Industrial War

The trade unions were conservative: they accepted the economic order, and all they wanted was a larger share for working people. But it was precisely that claim against business profits that made American employers so opposed to collective bargaining. In the 1890s they unleashed a fierce counterattack on the trade-union movement.

The Homestead Strike. Skilled workers in Homestead, Pennsylvania, site of one of Andrew Carnegie's great steel mills, thought themselves safe from that threat. They earned good wages, lived comfortably, and generally owned their own homes. The town was very much their community, with a municipal government elected from their ranks. And they had faith in Carnegie. For had not Good Old Andy said in a famous magazine article that workers had as sacred a right to combine as did capitalists, and that workers had a moral claim on their jobs that forbade the use of strikebreakers by employers?

Espousing high-toned principles made Carnegie feel good, but a strong bottom line made him feel even better. He decided that collective bargaining had become too expensive, and he was confident that his skilled workers could be replaced by the advanced machinery he was installing. Lacking the stomach for the hard battle ahead, Carnegie hid himself in a remote estate in Scotland, leaving behind a second-in-command well qualified for the job at hand. This was Henry Clay Frick, a former coal baron and a veteran of labor wars in the coal fields.

After a brief pretense of bargaining, Frick announced that as of July 1, 1892, the company would no longer deal with the Amalgamated Association of Iron and Steel Workers. If the employees wanted to work, they would have to return on an individual basis. The plant had already been fortified so that strikebreakers could be brought in to resume operations and defeat the union. At stake now was not just wage cuts but the defense of a way of life. Town authorities—members of the union—turned away the county sheriff when he tried to take possession of the plant. The entire community—women no less than men—mobilized in defense of the union.

At dawn on July 6 two barges were seen approaching Homestead up the Monongahela River. On the barges were armed guards hired by the Pinkerton Detective Agency to take control of the steelworks on behalf of the company. Behind hastily erected barricades, the strikers opened fire, and a bloody battle ensued. When the Pinkertons finally surrendered, the enraged women of Homestead mercilessly pummeled them as they retreated to the railway station. Frick appealed to the governor of Pennsylvania, who called out state National Guard units and placed Homestead under martial law. The great steelworks was taken over and opened to strikebreakers, while strike leaders and town officials were arrested on charges of riot, murder, and treason.

The defeat at Homestead marked the beginning of the end for trade unionism in the iron and steel industry. Ended too were any lingering illusions about the sanctity of workers' communities such as Homestead. "Men talk like anarchists or lunatics when they insist that the workmen of Homestead have done right," asserted one conservative journal. Nothing could be permitted to interfere with private property or threaten law and order.

The Homestead strike ushered in an era of strife in which working people faced not only the formidable power of corporate industry but the even more formidable power of their own government.

The Great Pullman Boycott. The fullest demonstration of that hard reality came at a place that seemed an even less likely site for class warfare than Homestead. Pullman, Illinois, was a model factory town, famous for the amenities it offered to workers and the beauty of its landscaping and city plan. The town was named for its creator, George M. Pullman—inventor of the Pullman sleeping car, which brought comfort and luxury to railway travel. When the Panic of 1893 struck, business fell off and the Pullman Company cut wages but did not cut the rents for company housing. For many workers take-home pay shrank to pitiful levels. When a workers' committee finally complained to Pullman in May 1894, he responded that he saw no connection between his roles as employer and landlord. As for the committee members who had approached him, they were fired.

The strike that ensued would have been no more than a footnote in American labor history but for the fact that the Pullman workers belonged to the American Railway Union (ARU), a rapidly growing industrial union of railroad workers. Its leader, Eugene V. Debs, directed ARU members not to handle Pullman sleeping cars, which, though operated by the railroads, were owned and serviced by the Pullman Company. This action was a *secondary labor boycott*: force was applied at a secondary point (the railroads) to bring pressure on the primary target (Pullman).

Railroad officials, already fearful of the growing power of the ARU, saw the Pullman boycott as their chance to break the union. The General Managers' Association, which represented the railroads serving Chicago, insisted on running the Pullman cars. Since ARU members refused to operate trains with Pullman cars, a strike soon spread across the country and threatened to disrupt the entire economy.

Quite deliberately, the railroad managers maneuvered to bring the federal government into the dispute. Their hook was U.S. mail cars, which they attached to every train hauling Pullman cars. When strikers stopped these trains, the General Managers' Association appealed to President Grover Cleveland to send in troops to protect the U.S. mail and halt the growing violence. Richard Olney, Cleveland's attorney general, was a former railroad lawyer who unabashedly sided with his former employers. Disregarding the protests of Illinois governor John P. Altgeld, President Cleveland dispatched the U.S. Army. When federal troops failed to get the trains running again, Olney obtained court injunctions

The Pullman Strike
Chicago was the hub of the railway network and the strategic center of the battle
between the Pullman boycotters and the trunk line railroads. For the strikers, the crucial thing was to prevent those trains with Pullman cars attached from running; for
the railroads, it was to get the trains through at any cost. The arrival of federal troops
meant that the trains would move and that the strikers would be defeated.
Harper's Weekly, July 21, 1894.

prohibiting ARU leaders from conducting the strike.
Debs and his subordinates refused to obey, were held in
contempt of court, and were jailed. Now leaderless and
uncoordinated, the strike quickly disintegrated.

No one could doubt why the great Pullman boycott
had failed: it had been crushed by the naked use of government power on behalf of the railroad companies.

American Radicalism in the Making

Oppression does not radicalize all its victims, but it
does radicalize some of them. And when social injustice
is most painfully felt, when the underlying power realities stand openly revealed, the process of radicalization
speeds up. Such was the case during the depression of
the 1890s. Out of the industrial strife of that decade
emerged the main forces of twentieth-century American radicalism.

Eugene Debs and American Socialism. Very little in
Eugene Debs's background suggested that he would one
day become the nation's leading socialist. Born in 1855 to

middle-class French Alsatian parents, Debs grew up
believing in the essential goodness of American society,
as he found it in his hometown of Terre Haute, Indiana—
a prosperous midwestern railroad center. A popular
young man-about-town, Debs considered a career in
politics or business. Instead, he returned to the railway
yards where he had worked as a boy, got involved in the
local labor movement, and in 1880, at the age of
twenty-five, was elected national secretary-treasurer of
the Brotherhood of Locomotive Firemen, one of the
craft unions that represented the skilled operating
trades on the railroads.

These unions were conservative, opposed to strikes,
and indifferent to the well-being of low-paid track and
yard laborers. Troubled by this, Debs left his comfortable union post in 1892 to devote himself to a new organization, the American Railway Union, that would
organize all railroad workers irrespective of skill—that
is, an *industrial union*.

The Pullman boycott visibly changed Debs. He
declared it "a contest between the producing classes and
the money power of the country." And he went to jail for
his convictions. Debs was sentenced to six months in the

federal penitentiary not for violating any law but for refusing to obey a court order he knew to be trumped-up and prejudicial. He came out of jail an avowed radical committed to a lifelong struggle against a system that enabled employers to enlist the powers of government to enforce their arbitrary rule over working people. At first Debs identified himself as a Populist (see Chapter 18), but he quickly gravitated toward the socialist camp.

German refugees had brought the ideas of Karl Marx, the German radical philosopher, to America after the failed 1848 revolutions in Europe. Marx's prescription for revolution through class struggle inspired the most durable radical movements in the industrial world. Though little noticed in most parts of American society, Marxist socialism struck deep roots in the growing German American communities of Chicago and New York. In 1877 the Socialist Labor Party was formed, and from that time on Marxist socialism maintained a continuing, if narrowly based, presence in American politics.

When Eugene Debs appeared in their midst in 1897, the socialists were in a state of crisis. Although the economic hardship of the depression had just ended, they had failed to make much headway. Many blamed the party head, Daniel De Leon—an ideological purist not greatly interested in attracting voters. Debs joined the revolt against the dogmatic De Leon and helped found the rival Socialist Party of America in 1901, with the aim of building a broad-based political movement.

A spellbinding campaigner, Debs attracted a devoted national following. He talked socialism in an American idiom, making Marxism understandable and persuasive to many ordinary Americans. Under him the new party began to break down ethnic barriers and attract American-born voters. Many trade unionists, disillusioned as Debs himself had been by the events of the 1890s, went through the same kind of radical evolution and joined in large numbers. In Texas, Oklahoma, and Minnesota socialism exerted a powerful appeal among cotton and wheat farmers. The party was also highly successful at attracting women activists. Inside of a decade, with a national network of branches and state organizations, the Socialist Party had become a force to be reckoned with in American politics.

Western Radicalism. In the meantime, a different brand of American radicalism was taking shape in the West. After many years of mostly friendly labor relations, the situation in the western mining camps turned ugly during the 1890s. Powerful new corporations were taking over, and they wanted to be rid of the miners' union, the Western Federation of Miners (WFM). Moreover, silver and copper prices began to drop in the early 1890s, bringing pressure to cut miners' wages. When strikes resulted, they took a particularly violent turn.

In 1892 at Coeur d'Alene, a silver-mining district in northern Idaho, striking miners engaged in gun battles with company guards, sent a car of explosive powder careering into the Frisco mine, and threatened to blow up processing plants. Martial law was declared, federal troops came in, the strikers were crowded into "bullpens" (enclosed stockades), and the strike was broken. Equally violent strikes took place at Cripple Creek, Colorado, in 1894; at Leadville, Colorado, in 1896; and again in Coeur d'Alene in 1899.

In these western strikes, government intervention was particularly naked and unrestrained. This was partly in response to the level of violence, but it stemmed also from the character of politics in the lightly settled western states: either the miners would dominate state politics—as they did in coalition with the Populists during their successful strike at Cripple Creek—or, as was increasingly true, the mine owners would dominate, with disastrous consequences for the miners.

In 1897 WFM president Ed Boyce called on all union members to arm themselves with rifles, and his rhetoric—he called the wage system "slavery in its worst form"—had a hard edge. Any lingering faith in the political process died in the Colorado state elections of 1904, after bitterly fought strikes across the state in the previous two years. The miners thought they had defeated their archenemy, Republican governor James H. Peabody, only to have the Colorado Supreme Court overturn the election results and reinstall Peabody (who, by prearrangement, resigned in favor of his lieutenant governor).

In 1905 the Western Federation of Miners led the way in creating a new radical labor movement, the Industrial Workers of the World (IWW). Although the IWW initially had links to the Socialist Party, it soon repudiated political action and settled on its own radical course. The Wobblies, as IWW members were called, fervently supported the Marxist class struggle—but strictly in the industrial field. By action at the point of production and by an unending struggle against employers—ultimately by means of a general strike—they believed that the workers themselves would bring about a revolution. A workers' society would emerge, run directly by the workers through their industrial unions. The term *syndicalism* describes this brand of workers' radicalism.

In both of its major forms—the politically oriented Socialist Party and the syndicalist IWW—American radicalism flourished after the crisis of the 1890s, but only within certain limits. Socialists and Wobblies lived, in a sense, on the tolerance of society. They would later be crushed without ceremony. Nevertheless, they served a larger purpose. American radicalism, by its sheer vitality, bore witness to what was exploitative and unjust in the new industrial order.

Summary

★

American industrialism took its modern shape during the last decades of the nineteenth century. Central to this development were the shift from iron making to the manufacture of steel, the great expansion of coal mining, and the technology for generating steam and electrical power. These advances made possible the production of the capital goods and energy required by an expanding manufacturing economy. An efficient railway system provided access to national markets. A managerial revolution enabled entrepreneurs to master the complex business organizations they were building. The scale of enterprise grew very large, and the vertically integrated firm became the predominant form of business organization. Only in the South did prevailing conditions—in particular, the insulated, low-wage labor market—retard the growth of an advanced industrial economy.

In the North the enormous demand for labor led to a great influx of immigrants, making ethnic diversity a distinctive feature of the American working class. Gender likewise defined occupational opportunity. Women joined the labor force in growing numbers, but almost universally they were subjected to a sex-typing process that relegated them to "women's work," always at wage rates below those of men. Mass production—the high-volume output of standardized products—vastly improved the productivity of American manufacturing but also de-skilled workers and mechanized their jobs. Scientific management, the brainchild of Frederick W. Taylor, cut further into the traditional autonomy of American workers by systematizing the labor process and shifting control into the hands of supervisors.

The late nineteenth century gave rise to the American labor movement in its modern form. In the Knights of Labor, anticapitalist labor reform enjoyed one final surge during the mid-1880s and then succumbed to the "pure and simple" unionism of the American Federation of Labor. The AFL was conservative, in that it accepted the economic order, but its insistence on a larger share of the benefits for working people guaranteed that employers would fiercely resist the trade-union movement. The result was a series of bitter strikes: Homestead in 1892, the Pullman boycott of 1894, and, the most violent, the cycle of metal miners' strikes in the Far West. The industrial warfare of the 1890s stirred new radical impulses, leading on the one hand to the political socialism of Eugene Debs and on the other to the industrial radicalism of the IWW.

TIMELINE

1869 Knights of Labor founded in Philadelphia

1872 Montgomery Ward, first U.S. mail-order house, founded

Andrew Carnegie starts construction of Edgar Thomson steelworks near Pittsburgh

1873 Panic of 1873 ushers in economic depression

1875 John Wanamaker establishes first department store, in Philadelphia

1876 Philadelphia Centennial Exhibition showcases Corliss steam engine

1877 Baltimore and Ohio workers initiate nationwide railroad strike

1878 Gustavus Swift introduces refrigerator car

1879 Jay Gould begins to build Missouri Pacific railway system

1883 Railroads establish national time zones

1886 Haymarket Square bombing in Chicago

American Federation of Labor (AFL) founded

1892 Homestead steel strike crushed

1893 Panic of 1893 leads to national depression

Wave of railroad bankruptcies; reorganization by investment bankers begins

1894 President Cleveland sends troops to break Pullman boycott

1895 Southeastern European immigration exceeds northern European immigration for the first time

1901 Eugene V. Debs helps found Socialist Party of America

1905 Industrial Workers of the World (IWW) launched

Suggested Readings

⭑

The most useful introduction to the economic history of this period is Edward C. Kirkland, *Industry Comes of Age, 1860–1897* (1961). A more sophisticated analysis can be found in W. Elliot Brownlee, *Dynamics of Ascent* (rev. ed., 1979). For essays on many of the topics covered in this chapter, consult Glenn Porter, ed., *Encyclopedia of American Economic History* (3 vols., 1980).

Industrial Capitalism Triumphant

On railroads a convenient introduction is John F. Stover, *American Railroads* (1970). The growth of the railroads as an integrated system has been treated in George R. Taylor and Irene D. Neu, *The American Railway Network, 1861–1890* (1956). Julius Grodinsky, *Jay Gould: His Business Career, 1867–1892* (1957), is a complex study demonstrating the contributions this railroad buccaneer made to the transportation system. Books such as Grodinsky's have gone a long way to resurrect Gilded Age businessmen from the debunking tradition first set forth with great power in Matthew Josephson, *Robber Barons: Great American Fortunes* (1934). Peter Temin, *Iron and Steel in the Nineteenth Century* (1964), is the best treatment of that industry. Joseph F. Wall, *Andrew Carnegie* (1970), is the definitive biography of the great steel maker. On the development of mass production the key book is David A. Hounsell, *From the American System to Mass Production, 1800–1932* (1984). Alfred D. Chandler, *The Visible Hand: The Managerial Revolution in American Business* (1977), is not an easy book but will amply repay the labors of interested students.

On the New South the standard work has long been C. Vann Woodward, *Origins of the New South, 1877–1913* (1951). Equally essential as a modern reconsideration is Edward L. Ayers, *The Promise of the New South: Life after Reconstruction* (1992). A brilliant reinterpretation of the causes of the South's economic retardation is Gavin Wright, *Old South, New South* (1986). Jacqueline Jones, *The Dispossessed: America's Underclasses from the Civil War to the Present (1992),* contains an excellent treatment of southern labor.

The World of Work

For an understanding of the impact of industrialism on American workers, three collections of essays make the best starting points: Herbert G. Gutman, *Work, Culture and Society in Industrializing America* (1976); Michael S. Frisch and Daniel J. Walkowitz, eds., *Working-Class America: Essays on Labor, Community and American Society* (1983); and Leon Fink, *In Search of the Working Class* (1994). On the introduction of Taylorism, the most useful book is Daniel Nelson, *Managers and Workers: Origins of the New Factory System* (2nd ed., 1995). The impact of Taylorism on American workers is treated with insight in David Montgomery, *The Fall of the House of Labor: The Workplace, the State, and American Labor Activism, 1865–1925* (1987).

Two valuable collections of essays on immigrant workers are Richard Ehrlich, ed., *Immigrants in Industrial America* (1977), and Dirk Hoerder, ed., *American Labor and Immigration History, 1877–1920: Recent European Research* (1983). John Bodnar, *Immigration and Industrialization: Ethnicity in an American Mill Town* (1977), is an important case study of a single community. On women workers the best introduction is Alice Kessler-Harris, *Out to Work* (1982). Ava Baron, ed., *Work Engendered: Toward a New History of American Labor* (1991), is a rich collection of essays that apply gender analysis to the history of working people. Two excellent case studies in this vein are Mary Blewett, *Men, Women, and Work: Class, Gender, and Protest in the New England Shoe Industry, 1780–1910* (1988), and Stephen H. Norwood, *Labor's Flaming Youth: Telephone Operators and Worker Militancy, 1878–1923* (1990). On black workers, useful introductions are William H. Harris, *The Harder We Run: Black Workers since the Civil War* (1982), and Philip S. Foner, *Organized Labor and the Black Worker* (1974). Walter Licht, *Getting Work: Philadelphia, 1840–1950* (1992), is a pioneering history of a labor market in operation.

The Labor Movement

The standard book on the struggle between labor reform and trade unionism is Gerald N. Grob, *Workers and Utopia, 1865–1900* (1961). For the Knights of Labor, it should be supplemented by Leon Fink, *Workingmen's Democracy: The Knights of Labor and American Politics* (1983), which captures the cultural dimensions of labor reform not seen by earlier historians. Labor's place in the political environment is the subject of David Montgomery, *Citizen Worker* (1993). On the emergence of a political strategy, see Julie Greene, *Pure and Simple Politics: The American Federation of Labor, 1881–1915* (1997). Paul Krause, *The Battle for Homestead, 1880–1892* (1992), puts the great strike in a larger social context. The most recent survey, incorporating much of the latest scholarship, is Bruce Laurie, *Artisans into Workers: Labor in Nineteenth Century America* (1989).

The founder of the AFL is the subject of a lively brief biography by Harold Livesay, *Samuel Gompers and Organized Labor in America* (1978). Among the many books on individual unions, Robert Christie, *Empire in Wood* (1956), best reveals the way pure and simple unionism worked out in practice. On industrial conflict, the most vivid book is Robert V. Bruce, *1877: Year of Violence* (1959). On western miners, the standard work is Mark Wyman, *Hard-Rock Epic: Western Miners and the Industrial Revolution, 1860–1910* (1979). On the western labor movement, important new interpretations are David Brundage, *The Making of Western Working-Class Radicalism: Denver's Organized Workers, 1878–1905* (1994), and Elizabeth Jameson, *All That Glitters: Class, Conflict, and Community in Cripple Creek* (1998). The best book on the IWW is Melvyn Dubofsky, *We Shall Be All* (1969). On socialism, David Shannon, *The Socialist Party of America* (1955), remains the standard account. There is, however, a fine biography of that party's leader that supersedes previous studies: Nick Salvatore, *Eugene V. Debs: Citizen and Socialist* (1982). A dimension of American radicalism long neglected receives sensitive attention in Mari Jo Buhle, *Women and American Socialism, 1870–1920* (1982).

Chapter 18

The Politics of Late Nineteenth-Century America

EVER SINCE THE founding of the republic, foreign visitors had been coming to America to study its political system. Most famous of the early observers was the French aristocrat Alexis de Tocqueville, who had written *Democracy in America* in 1832. When an equally brilliant visitor, the Englishman James Bryce, sat down to write his own account fifty years later, he decided that Tocqueville's great book could not serve as his model. For Tocqueville, Bryce noted, "America was primarily a democracy, the ideal democracy, fraught with lessons for Europe." In his own book, *The American Commonwealth* (1888), Bryce was much less rhapsodic. The robust democracy celebrated by Tocqueville had devolved half a century later into the dreary machine politics of the industrial age.

Bryce was anxious, however, that European readers not misunderstand him. Europeans would find in his book "much that is sordid, much that will provoke unfavourable comment." But they needed to be aware of "the existence in the American people of a reserve of force and patriotism more than sufficient to sweep away all the evils now tolerated, and to make a politics of the country worthy of its material grandeur and of the private virtues of its inhabitants." Bryce was ultimately an optimist: "A hundred times in writing this book have I been disheartened by the facts I was stating: a hundred times has the recollection of the abounding strength and vitality of the nation chased away these tremours."

Just what it was that Bryce found so disheartening in the practice of American politics is this chapter's first subject; the second is the underlying vitality that Bryce

Bandanna, 1888 Election
During the late nineteenth century, politics became a vibrant part of America's culture. Party paraphernalia, such as this colorful bandanna depicting the Democratic presidential nominee Grover Cleveland and his running mate, A. G. Thurman, flooded the country.
Collection of Janice L. and David J. Frent.

sensed, and how it reemerged and began to reinvigorate the nation's politics by the century's end.

The Politics of the Status Quo, 1877–1893

★

In times of national ferment, as a rule, public life becomes magnified. Leaders emerge. Electoral campaigns debate great issues. The powers of government expand. All this was true of the Civil War era, when, in the crises of Union and Reconstruction, the nation's political structure was most severely tested. The final crisis, the contested election of 1876, rocked the constitutional foundations of presidential succession. In 1877, with the Republican Rutherford B. Hayes safely settled in the White House, the era of sectional strife finally ended.

Political life went on, but drained of its earlier drama. In the 1880s there were no Lincolns, no great national debates. Where defenders of the Union had once envisioned a social order and an economic system reshaped by an activist state, now, in the 1880s, the nation's political leaders retreated to a more modest conception of state power. There remained an irreducible core of public functions, and even, as on the question of railroad regulation, a grudging acceptance of new governmental responsibilities. But the dominant rhetoric celebrated the government that governed least, and as compared to the Civil War era, American government did govern less.

The Passive Presidency

There were five presidents from 1877 to 1893: Rutherford B. Hayes (Republican, 1877–1881), James A. Garfield (Republican, 1881), Chester A. Arthur (Republican, 1881–1885), Grover Cleveland (Democrat, 1885–1889), and Benjamin Harrison (Republican, 1889–1893). All were estimable men. Hayes, Garfield, and Harrison boasted distinguished war records. Hayes had served effectively as governor of Ohio for three terms, and Garfield had done well as a congressional leader. Arthur, despite his reputation as a hack politician, had shown fine administrative skills as head of the New York City customs house. Cleveland had an enviable reputation as a reform mayor of Buffalo and governor of New York. None was a charismatic leader, but circumstances, more than personal qualities, explain why these presidents did not make a larger mark on history.

The president's biggest job was to dispense political patronage. Under the spoils system, government

PUCK.

"WHERE IS HE?"

Where Is He?

This *Puck* cartoon, which appeared two weeks after Benjamin Harrison's defeat for reelection at Grover Cleveland's hands in 1892, is a commentary on Harrison's insignificance as president. The hat in Uncle Sam's hands belonged to Benjamin Harrison's grandfather, President William Henry Harrison. *Puck* started using the hat as a trademark for Benjamin Harrison after he had been elected in 1888. As his term progressed, the hat grew progressively larger, and the president progressively smaller. By the time of his defeat, just the hat is left and Harrison has disappeared altogether.
Bancroft Library, University of California at Berkeley. *Puck*, November 16, 1892.

appointments were treated as rewards for those who had served the victorious party. Reform of this system became an urgent issue after President Garfield was killed in 1881. His assassin, Charles Guiteau, was a deranged religious fanatic, but advocates of civil-service reform managed to blame Garfield's death on the poisonous atmosphere of the spoils system that left many disappointed in the scramble for government jobs. The resulting Pendleton Civil Service Act of 1883 created a list of civil-service jobs to be filled on the basis of examinations administered by the new Civil Service Commission. The list originally included only 10 percent of all federal jobs, however, and patronage remained a preoccupation in the White House. When the Democrats won the presidency in 1884 for the first time in nearly thirty years, the pent-up hunger for jobs among the party faithful nearly overwhelmed Grover Cleveland. He was known to complain bitterly about the "damned, everlasting clatter for office." The standards of public administration did rise measurably, but there was no American counterpart to the elite professional civil services taking shape in Britain and Germany in these years.

The executive branch, in any event, had very modest functions. As late as 1897 the White House staff consisted of half a dozen assistants plus a few clerks, doorkeepers, and messengers. Budgetary matters were not the president's province but Congress's; federal agencies accordingly paid more heed to Capitol Hill and the key money-dispensing committees than to the White House. Of the 100,000 federal employees in 1880, 56 percent worked for the U.S. Post Office. During the 1880s even the important government departments—Treasury, State, War, Navy, Interior—were sleepy places carrying on largely routine duties. Virtually all federal income came from customs duties and the excise tax on liquor and tobacco. These sources produced more money than the government spent. The question of how to reduce the federal surplus ranked as one of the most troublesome issues of the 1880s.

As for setting a national agenda, this was—unlike in Lincoln's day—not to be looked for from the White House. "The office of President is essentially executive in nature," Cleveland insisted, not policy making. In fact, as a Democratic president facing a hostile Republican Senate, Cleveland did begin to assert himself on policy matters, but in a mostly negative way: in his first term he vetoed a record number of bills.

Party Politics

On matters of national policy the president took a back seat to Congress. But Congress functioned badly. Procedural rules frequently stymied legislative business. Neither party ever stayed in power long enough to push through a coherent legislative program, and in any case congressional leaders lacked the power to keep party members in line.

Historically, Democrats and Republicans represented somewhat different traditions. The Democrats favored states' rights and limited government; the Republicans were heirs to the Whig enthusiasm for federally assisted economic development. After Reconstruction, however, the Republicans backed away from that activist position and, in truth, party differences became muddy. On most leading issues of the day—civil-service reform, the currency, and regulation of the railroads—the divisions occurred within the parties, not between them.

The Tariff Question. Only free trade remained a real fighting issue. From Lincoln's day onward, high duties had protected American industry against imported goods. It was an article of Republican faith, as President Harrison said in 1892, that "the protective system . . . has been a mighty instrument for the development of the national wealth." The Democrats, free-traders by tradition, regularly attacked Republican protectionism. In practice, however, the tariff was a negotiable issue like any other. Congressmen voted their constituents' interests, regardless of party rhetoric. As a result, every tariff bill was a patchwork of bargains among special interests.

In 1887 President Cleveland cast off his reluctance to lead the nation and took up the tariff issue. Ardently opposed to protectionism, Cleveland devoted his entire annual message to Congress to tariff reform and campaigned on that basis for reelection in 1888. His narrow defeat seemed to confirm the political wisdom of evading big issues. "They told me it would hurt the party," he later wrote. "Perhaps I made a mistake from the party standpoint; but damn it, it was right. I had at least that satisfaction."

Campaign Politics. Issues were treated gingerly partly because the parties were so equally balanced. The Democrats, in retreat immediately after the Civil War, quickly regrouped and by the end of Reconstruction stood on virtually equal terms with the Republicans. Every presidential election from 1876 to 1892 was decided by a thin margin, and neither party gained command of Congress. Political caution seemed wise; any false move on national issues might tip the scales to the other side.

James Bryce, accustomed to the ideological divisions between Tories and Liberals in Britain, grumbled about the pragmatism of American politics. "Neither party has any principles, any distinctive tenets," he wrote. Perhaps Bryce exaggerated when he added, "All has been lost, except office or the hope of it."

The weakening of principled politics was evident in the Republicans' retreat from their Civil War legacy. The major unfinished business after 1877 involved the plight of the former slaves. The Republican agenda called for federal funding to combat illiteracy and, even more threatening to the South, federal protection for black voters in southern congressional elections. Neither measure ever managed to make it through Congress. With little mileage left in Reconstruction politics, the Republicans backpedaled on the race issue and gradually abandoned the blacks to their fate.

That did not stop the Republicans from "waving the bloody shirt" against the "treasonous" Democrats. Service in the Union army gave candidates a strong claim to public office, and veterans' benefits always stood high on the Republican agenda. The Democrats played the same game in the South as the defenders of the Lost Cause. Bryce rightly criticized American politicians for "clinging too long to outworn issues and neglecting the problems . . . which now perplex the country."

Alternatively, campaigns could descend into comedy. In the hard-fought election of 1884, for example, the Democrat Cleveland burst on the scene as a reformer, fresh from his victories over corrupt machine politics in New York State. The Kansas editor William Allen White saw Cleveland as the champion of a people "sick with politics" and "nauseated at all politicians." But years earlier Cleveland, a bachelor, had fathered an illegitimate child, and throughout the campaign he was dogged by the chant "Maw, Maw, where's my Paw?" (after election day, Cleveland's supporters gleefully responded, "He's in the White House, haw-haw-haw"). Cleveland's opponent, James G. Blaine, already on the defensive for taking favors from the railroads, got tangled up in the scandalous charge by a too ardent Republican supporter that the Democrats were the party of "Rum, Romanism and Rebellion." In a twinkling, he had insulted Catholic voters who might have cast their votes for Blaine. In the midst of all the mudslinging, the issues got lost.

The characteristics of public life in the 1880s—the inactivity of the federal government, the evasiveness of the political parties, and the absorption in politics for its own sake—derived ultimately from the conviction that little was at stake in public affairs. In 1887 Cleveland vetoed a small appropriation for drought-stricken Texas farmers with the remark that "though the people support the Government, the Government should not support the people." Governmental activity was itself considered a bad thing. All that the state can do, said Republican senator Roscoe Conkling of New York, "is to clear the way of impediments and dangers, and leave every class and every individual free and safe in the exertions and pursuits of life." Conkling was expressing the political corollary to the doctrine of *laissez faire*—the belief that the government was best which governed least.

The Ideology of Individualism

At the peak of the labor strife of the 1880s, the cotton manufacturer Edward Atkinson gave a talk to the textile workers of Providence, Rhode Island. They had, he told them, no cause for discontent. "There is always plenty of room on the front seats in every profession, every trade, every art, every industry. . . . There are men in this audience who will fill some of those seats, but they won't be boosted into them from behind." (There were certainly women as well in the audience—at least half of the Rhode Island labor force was female—but, as was characteristic of the times, Atkinson assumed that economic opportunity was of interest only to men.) Every man, Atkinson continued, got what he deserved. For example, Cornelius Vanderbilt had amassed a fortune of $200 million by building the New York Central Railroad. Atkinson made some rapid calculations. Every person in the audience consumed about a barrel of flour a year. In 1865 it had cost $3.45 to ship that barrel from Chicago to Providence. In 1885, the New York Central carried it for 68 cents, taking 14 cents as profit while the workingman saved nearly $3.00. "Wasn't Vanderbilt a cheap man for you to employ as a teamster?" Atkinson asked. "Do you grudge him the fourteen cents?"

Atkinson's homely talk went to the roots of conservative American thought: any man, however humble, could rise as far as his talents would carry him; every person received his just reward, great or small; and the success of the individual, so encouraged, contributed to the progress of the whole. How persuasive the workers listening to Atkinson found his message we have no way of knowing. But the confidence with which Atkinson presented his case is evidence of the continuing appeal of the ideology of individualism in the age of industrial expansion.

A wide variety of popular writings trumpeted the individualist creed, from the rags-to-riches tales of Horatio Alger to the stream of success manuals with such titles as *Thoughts for the Young Men of America, or a Few Practical Words of Advice to Those Born in Poverty and Destined to Be Reared in Orphanages* (1871). It was a lesson celebrated in the lives of such self-made men as Andrew Carnegie, whose book *Triumphant Democracy* (1886) paid homage to a nation that had enabled a penniless Scottish child to rise from bobbin boy to steel magnate.

The Gospel of Wealth. From the pulpit came the assurances of the Episcopal bishop William Lawrence of Massachusetts that "Godliness is in league with riches." Bishop Lawrence was voicing a tradition in American Protestantism that went back to the Puritans: success in one's earthly calling signified the promise of eternal salvation. It was all too easy for a conservative ministry to make morally reassuring the furious acquisitiveness of industrial America. "To secure wealth is an honorable ambition," intoned the Baptist minister Russell H. Conwell in his lecture "Acres of Diamonds." "Money is power. Every good man and woman ought to strive for power, to do good with it when obtained." Conwell's lecture—its notion of wealth as stewardship—served as a text for what became known as the Gospel of Wealth. Its leading exemplar, Andrew Carnegie, argued that the rich had a duty to put their money to social use. They should not coddle the less

Facing the World
The cover of this Horatio Alger novel (1893) captures the myth of opportunity that Edward Atkinson extolled to his audience of textile workers. Our hero, Harry Vane, is a poor but earnest lad, ready to make his way in the world and, despite the many obstacles thrown in his path, sure to succeed. In some 135 books Horatio Alger repeated this story, with minor variations, for an eager reading public that numbered in the millions.
Frank and Marie-Therese Wood Print Collections, Alexandria, Virginia.

privileged, Carnegie said, but provide the libraries, education, and cultural and scientific institutions by which the worthy poor might prepare themselves for life's challenges.

Social Darwinism. American individualism drew strong intellectual support from science. In *The Origin of Species* (1859) the British naturalist Charles Darwin had developed a bold hypothesis to explain the evolution of plants and animals. In nature, Darwin wrote, all living things struggle and compete. Individual members of a species are born with characteristics that help them survive in their particular environment: camouflage coloring for a bird, for example, or resistance to

thirst in a desert animal. Because these survival characteristics are genetic, they are transmitted to future generations and become dominant in the species. This view of evolution, which Darwin called *natural selection*, created a revolution in biological science.

Drawing on Darwin, the British philosopher Herbert Spencer developed an elaborate analysis of how human society evolved through constant competition and "survival of the fittest." Social Darwinism, as Spencer's ideas became known, was championed in America by William Graham Sumner, a sociology professor at Yale. Competition, said Sumner, is a law of nature that "can no more be done away with than gravitation." And who are the fittest? "The millionaires. . . . They may fairly be regarded as the naturally selected agents of society. They get high wages and live in luxury, but the bargain is a good one for society."

Social Darwinists regarded with horror any government interference with social processes. "The great stream of time and earthly things will sweep on just the same in spite of us," Sumner wrote in a famous essay, "The Absurd Attempt to Make the World Over" (1894). "That is why it is the greatest folly of which a man can be capable to sit down with a slate and pencil to plan out a new social world." As for the government, it had "at bottom . . . two chief things . . . with which to deal. They are the property of men and the honor of women. These it has to defend against crime."

The Supremacy of the Courts

Suspicion of activist government not only paralyzed political initiative; it also shifted power away from the executive and legislative branches. "The task of constitutional government," declared Sumner, "is to devise institutions which shall come into play at critical periods to prevent the abusive control of the powers of a state by the controlling classes in it." Sumner meant the judiciary. From the 1870s onward the courts increasingly accepted the role that he assigned to them, becoming the guardians of the rights of private property.

Under the federal system as it was understood in the late nineteenth century, the states retained primary responsibility for social welfare and economic regulation. They were responsible for exercising their *police powers* to ensure the health, safety, and morals of their citizens. The leading contemporary question in American law was where to strike the balance between state responsibility for the general welfare and the liberty of individuals to pursue their private interests. Most states, caught up in the conservative ethos of the day, were themselves cutting back on expenditures and public services. Even so, there were more than enough state initiatives to alarm vigilant judges. Thus, in the landmark case *In Re Jacobs* (1885), the New York Supreme Court struck down a state law prohibiting cigar making in sweatshop tenements on the grounds that such regulation exceeded the police powers of the state. The high courts of the states declared unconstitutional a record number of laws during the 1880s.

Increasingly, however, it was federal judges who took up the battle against state activism. The Supreme Court's crucial weapon in this campaign was the Fourteenth Amendment (1868), which prohibited the states from depriving "any person of life, liberty, or property, without due process of law." The due-process clause had been adopted during Reconstruction to protect the civil rights of the former slaves. But due process protected the property rights and contractual liberty of any "person," and legally, corporations counted as persons. So interpreted, the Fourteenth Amendment became by the turn of the century a powerful means of restraining the states in the use of their police powers to regulate private business.

The Supreme Court similarly hamstrung the federal government by a narrow reading of its constitutional powers. In 1895 the Court ruled that the federal power to regulate interstate commerce did not cover manufacturing and struck down a federal income tax law. And in areas where federal power was undeniable—such as the regulation of railroads—the Supreme Court watched like a hawk for undue interferences with the rights of property.

The preeminent conservative jurist of the day, Stephen J. Field, made no bones about the dangers he saw in the nation's headlong industrial development. "As population and wealth increase—as the inequalities in the conditions of men become more and more marked and disturbing—as . . . angry menaces against order find vent in loud denunciations—it becomes more and more the imperative duty of the court to enforce with a firm hand every guarantee of the Constitution."

Power conferred status. The law, not politics, attracted the ablest people and held the public's esteem. A Wisconsin judge boasted: "The bench symbolizes on earth the throne of divine justice. . . . Law in its highest sense is the will of God." Judicial supremacy reflected how dominant the ideology of individualism had become in industrial America, and also how low American politicians had fallen in the esteem of their countrymen.

Sources of Popular Participation

———————★———————

For all the criticism leveled against it, politics figured centrally in the nation's life. Proportionately more voters turned out in presidential elections from 1876 to 1892 than at any other time in American history. People voted Democratic or Republican for a lifetime. Many actively participated. In New York City, a fourth of all Republican voters were dues-paying party members. National conventions attracted huge crowds. "The excitement, the mental and physical strains," remarked an Indiana Republican after the 1888 convention, "are surpassed only by prolonged battle in actual warfare, as I have been told by officers of the Civil War who later engaged in convention struggles." The convention he described had nominated the colorless Benjamin Harrison on a routine platform. What was all the excitement about?

Cultural Politics: Party, Religion, and Ethnicity

In the late nineteenth century, politics was a vibrant part of the nation's culture. The journalist George M. Towle told a British audience that America "is a land of conventions and assemblies, where it is the most natural thing in the world for people to get together in meetings, where almost every event is the occasion for speechmaking." Spellbinding orators such as Herbert G. Ingersoll held forth at Republican rallies. During the election season, the party faithful marched in impressive torchlight parades. Party paraphernalia flooded the country—handkerchiefs, mugs, posters, and buttons emblazoned with the Democratic donkey or the Republican elephant, symbols that had been adopted in the 1870s. In 1888 the presidential hopefuls were pictured on cards—like baseball players—packed into Honest Long Cut tobacco. Campaigns had the suspense of baseball pennant races plus the excitement of the circus coming to town. In an age before movies and radio, politics ranked as one of the great American forms of entertainment.

Party loyalty was a deadly serious matter, however. Long after the Civil War, emotions ran high. Among family friends in Cleveland, recalled urban reformer Brand Whitlock, the Republican Party was "a synonym for patriotism, another name for the nation. It was inconceivable that any self-respecting person should be a Democrat." Or, among southerners, that any self-respecting person could be a Republican.

Beyond these sectional differences, the most important determinants of party loyalty were religion and ethnicity. Statistically, northern Democrats tended to be foreign-born and Catholic, while Republicans tended to be native-born and Protestant. (The South, which received few immigrants, had a cultural politics driven by race rather than by ethnicity.) Among Protestants, the more *pietistic* a person's faith was—that is, the more personal and direct the believer's relationship to God—the more likely he or she was to be a Republican, and to favor using the powers of the state to legislate public morality and regulate individual behavior. Northern Democrats, in contrast, favored "the largest individual liberty consistent with public order."

During the 1880s ethnic tensions began to build up in many cities. Education became an arena of bitter conflict. One issue was whether instruction would be in English in the schools. Immigrant groups often wanted their children taught in their native languages. In response, native-born Americans passed laws making English the language of instruction. In St. Louis, a heavily German city, the longstanding policy of teaching German to the entire student body was overturned after a bitter campaign.

Religion was an even more explosive educational issue. Catholics fought a losing battle over public funding of parochial schools. By 1900 such aid had been prohibited by twenty-three states. In Boston a furious controversy broke out in 1888 over the use of an anti-Catholic history textbook. When the school board withdrew the offending book, angry Protestants mounted a campaign, threw the moderates off the board, and returned the text to the curriculum.

Then there was the regulation of public morals. In many states, so-called blue laws restricted activity on Sundays. When Nebraska banned Sunday baseball, the state supreme court approved the law as a blow struck in "the contest between Christianity and wrong." But German and Irish Catholics, who saw nothing evil in a bit of fun on Sunday, considered blue laws a violation of their personal freedom.

Ethnocultural conflict also flared over the liquor question. In a speech introducing the first attempt at national prohibition in 1876, Senator Henry W. Blair of New Hampshire laid down a challenge to his immigrant critics: "Upon discussion of this issue Irishman and German will in due time demonstrate that they are Americans." Although the Blair constitutional amendment languished, many states adopted strict licensing and local-option laws governing the sale and consumption of alcoholic beverages. Indiana permitted drinking, but only joylessly in rooms containing "no devices for amusement or music . . . of any kind."

Because the hottest social issues of the day—education, the liquor question, and observance of the Sabbath—were also party issues, they lent deep significance to party affiliation (Figure 18.1). And because these issues were fought out mostly at the state and local levels, they hit very close to home. Crusading Methodists thought of the Republican Party as the party of morality. Embattled Irish and German Catholics saw the Democratic Party as the defender of their freedoms.

Organizational Politics

Political life was also important because of the remarkable organizational activity it generated. By the 1870s both major parties had evolved formal, well-organized

The Presidential B.B. Club (1888)
On the left, Grover Cleveland is the baseman; at center Benjamin Harrison is at bat; and on the right, Cleveland tags Harrison out—not, alas, the right prediction, since Harrison won the 1888 election.

Collection of Janice L. and David J. Frent.

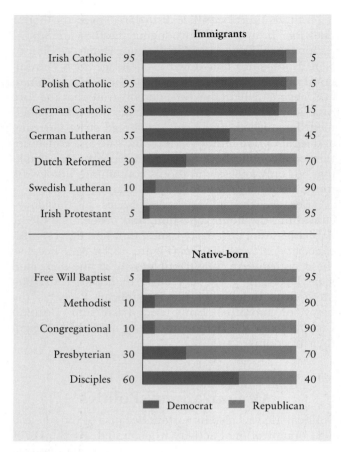

FIGURE 18.1
Ethnocultural Voting Patterns in the Midwest, 1870–1892
These figures demonstrate how voting patterns among midwesterners reflected ethnicity and religion in the late nineteenth century. Especially striking is the overwhelming
preference by immigrant Catholics for the Democratic Party.
Among Protestants there was an equally strong preference
for the Republican Party by certain groups of immigrants
(Swedish Lutherans and Irish Protestants) and native-born
(Free Will Baptists, Methodists, and Congregationalists), but
other Protestant groups were more evenly divided in their
party preferences.

structures. At the base lay the precinct or ward, whose
meetings could be attended by all party members.
County, state, and national committees ran the ongoing
business of the parties. Conventions determined party
rules, adopted platforms, and selected each party's candidates for public office.

At election time the party's main job was to get out
the vote. Wherever elections were close and hard
fought, the parties mounted intensive efforts organized
down to the individual voter. In Indiana, for example,
the Republicans appointed 10,000 "district men" in
1884, each responsible for turning out a designated
group of voters. The Pennsylvania Republican Party
maintained a list of 800,000 voters classified by degree
of voting reliability.

Only professionals could manage such a highly
organized political system. The German sociologist
Max Weber remarked that Americans regarded politics
as a "vocation." This factor, above all else, gave American politics its special character. The distinguishing
trait of American politicians, James Bryce observed,
was "that their whole time is more frequently given to
political work, that most of them draw an income from
politics . . . that they . . . are proficient in the arts of
popular oratory, of electioneering, and of party management." The party system required professionals, and
professionalism created careers. Politics, like professional sports and trade unionism, served as an avenue
of upward mobility for the many whose ethnic or class
background barred them from the opportunities open
to other Americans.

Machine Politics.   Party administration seemed, on
its face, highly democratic, since in theory all power
derived from the party members in the precincts and
wards. In practice, however, the parties were run by
unofficial internal organizations—*machines*—that consisted of insiders willing to accept discipline and do
party work in exchange for getting on the public payroll
or pocketing bribes and other forms of "graft." The
machines tended toward one-man rule, although the
"boss" ruled more by the consent of the secondary leaders than by his own absolute power.

Absorbed in the tasks of power brokerage,
machine bosses treated public issues as somewhat
irrelevant. The high stakes of money, jobs, and influence made for intense factionalism. In New York,
Manhattan's Tammany Hall was always at odds with
the upstate Democratic machine run by Senator
David B. Hill. At the national level, Republicans
fought bitterly among themselves after Ulysses S.
Grant left the White House in 1877. For the next six
years the party was divided into two warring factions—the Stalwarts, who followed Senator Roscoe
Conkling of New York, and the Halfbreeds, led by
James G. Blaine of Maine. The split was sparked by a
personal feud between Conkling and Blaine, but it
persisted because of a furious struggle over patronage. The Halfbreeds represented a newer Republican
generation that was more inclined to pay lip service
to political reform and was less committed to the old
Civil War issues. But issues were secondary in the war
between Stalwarts and Halfbreeds. They were really
fighting over the spoils of party politics.

And yet the record was not wholly negative.
Machine politics raised the standards of government in
certain ways. Disciplined professionals, veterans of
machine politics, improved the performance of state
legislatures and the Congress because they were more
experienced in the give-and-take of politics. More
important, party machines filled a void in the nation's

The Levi P. Morton Association
The top-hatted gentlemen in this photograph constituted the local Republican Party organization of Newport, Rhode Island, named in honor of Levi P. Morton, Republican leader and vice-president during the Benjamin Harrison administration (1889–1893). The maleness of party politics leaps from the photograph and asserts more clearly than a thousand words why the suffragist demand for the right to vote was met with ridicule and disbelief.
Newport Historical Society.

public life. They did informally much of what the government left undone in this era, especially in the cities (see Chapter 19).

The Mugwumps. But machine politics never managed to win the respect of the general public. Many of the nation's social elite—intellectuals, well-to-do businessmen, and old-line families—resented a politics that excluded people like themselves, the "best men." There was, too, a genuine clash of values. Political reformers called for "disinterestedness" and "independence"—the opposite of the self-serving careerism and party regularity fostered by the machine system. Many of them had earned their spurs as Liberal Republicans who had broken from the party and fought President Grant's reelection in 1872.

In 1884 Carl Schurz, Edwin L. Godkin, and Charles Francis Adams Jr. again left the Republican Party because they associated its presidential candidate, James G. Blaine, with corrupt politics. Mainly from New York and Massachusetts, these Republicans became known as Mugwumps—a derisive bit of contemporary slang, supposedly of Indian origin, referring to pompous or self-important persons. The Mugwumps threw their support to the Democrat Grover Cleveland and may have ensured his victory by giving him the margin for carrying New York State.

After the 1884 election, the enthusiasm for reform spilled over into local politics, spawning good-government campaigns across the country. Although they won some municipal victories, the Mugwumps were more effective at molding public opinion. Controlling the influential newspapers and journals read by the educated middle class, the Mugwumps defined the terms of debate and denied the machine system public legitimacy.

The Mugwumps registered their biggest success in the campaign for the secret ballot, which had been pioneered in Australia. Under this reform, citizens, in the privacy of a voting booth, would mark an official ballot listing the candidates of all the parties instead of submitting a party-supplied ticket in public view at the polling place. Adopted throughout the United States in the early 1890s, the Australian ballot freed voters from party surveillance as they exercised the right to vote.

The Mugwumps were reformers, but not on behalf of social justice. The problems of working people did not evoke their sympathy, nor did they favor using the powers of the state to ease the suffering of the poor. As far as the Mugwumps were concerned, that government was best which governed least. Theirs was the brand of "reform" perfectly in keeping with a politics of the status quo.

Women's Political Culture

The young Theodore Roosevelt, an up-and-coming Republican state politician in 1884, referred to the Mugwumps contemptuously as "man-milliners." The sexual slur was not accidental. In attacking organizational politics, the Mugwumps were challenging one of the bastions of male society. At party meetings and conventions, men carried on not only the business of politics but also the satisfying rituals of male sociability amid cigar smoke and whiskey. Politics was identified with manliness. It was competitive. It dealt in the commerce of power. It was frankly self-aggrandizing. Party politics, in short, was no place for a woman.

So, naturally, the woman suffrage movement met with fierce opposition. Blocked in their efforts to get a constitutional amendment introduced in Congress, suffragists concentrated on state campaigns. But except in Wyoming, Idaho, Colorado, and Utah, the most they could win in the late nineteenth century was the right to vote for school boards or on tax issues. "Men are ordained to govern in all forceful and material things, because they are men," asserted an anti-suffrage resolution, "while women, by the same decree of God and nature, are equally fitted to bear rule in a higher and more spiritual realm, where the strong frame and the weighty brain count for less"—that is to say, not in politics.

Yet this invocation of the doctrine of "separate spheres"—that men and women had different natures, and that women's nature fitted them for "a higher and more spiritual realm"—did open a channel for women to enter public life. "Women's place is Home," acknowledged the journalist Retha Childe Dorr. "But Home is not contained within the four walls of an individual house. Home is the community. The city full of people is the Family. . . . And badly do the Home and Family need their mother." Indeed, women since the early nineteenth century had engaged in charitable and reform activities. Women's organizations fought prostitution, assisted the poor, agitated for the reform of women's prisons, and tried to improve educational and job opportunities for women. Since many of these goals required state intervention, women's organizations of necessity became politically active, but not, they stressed, out of any desire to participate in partisan politics or to gain the ballot. Quite the contrary: women were bent on creating their own political sphere.

Thus in 1869, Sorosis, a women's professional club in New York City, convened a Women's Parliament in the hope of launching a parallel government responsible for public matters of concern to women. Nothing came of the Women's Parliament, but it did indicate the degree to which women's sphere could take a political form. If not a parallel government, the social activism of women certainly gave rise to a female political cul-

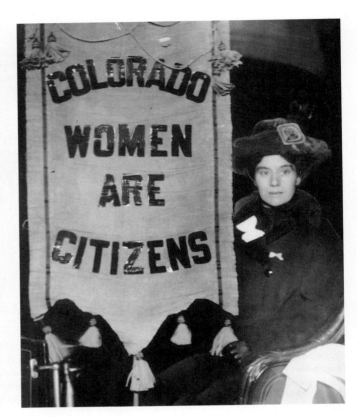

Colorado Women Are Citizens
Colorado was one of four western states to grant women full voting rights before 1900—and the first to do so by referendum. The next day, November 9, 1893, the *Denver Republican* congratulated "the men of Colorado who showed the world yesterday that they were neither afraid nor ashamed to give their women equal rights with themselves." It would be twenty-seven more years before other men of the country showed similar gumption by ratifying the Nineteenth Amendment (1920), granting women the right to vote.
Denver Public Library, Western History Division.

ture that made itself felt in the public life of late nineteenth-century America.

No issue joined home and politics more poignantly than did the liquor question. Just before Christmas in 1873 the women of Hillsboro, Ohio, began to hold vigils and prayer meetings in front of the town's saloons, pleading with the owners to close down and end the suffering of families of hard-drinking fathers. Thus began a spontaneous uprising of women that spread across the country and closed an estimated 3,000 saloons. From this agitation came the Woman's Christian Temperance Union (WCTU), which after its formation in 1874 rapidly blossomed into the largest organization of women in the country.

Because it excluded men, the WCTU was the spawning ground for a new generation of women leaders. Under the guidance of Frances Willard, who

OUT OF WORK—
And the reason why.

Wanted, Sober Men
This drawing appeared in a magazine in 1899, twenty-five years after the women of Hillsboro, Ohio, rose in revolt against the town's saloonkeepers and launched the Woman's Christian Temperance Union (WCTU). But the emotion it expresses had not changed—that the saloon was the enemy of the family.
Culver Pictures.

became president in 1879, the WCTU moved beyond temperance and adopted a "Do-Everything" policy. Alcoholism, women recognized, was not simply a personal failing; it stemmed from larger social evils afflicting men. Willard also wanted to attract women who had no particular interest in the liquor question. Local bodies were encouraged to undertake causes that were important in their own communities. By 1889 the WCTU had thirty-nine departments concerned with such issues as labor, prostitution, health, and international peace.

Most important, the WCTU was drawn to woman suffrage. This was necessary, Willard argued, "because the liquor traffic is entrenched in law, and law grows out of the will of majorities, and majorities of women are against the liquor traffic." The WCTU began by stressing moral persuasion and personal discipline—hence the word "temperance" in its name—but

expanded its attack on liquor to include prohibition by law. Women needed the vote, said Willard, to fulfill their social responsibilities *as women* (see American Voices, "Helen Potter: The Case for Women's Political Rights," p. 586). This was very different from the claim made by the suffragists—that voting was an inherent right of all citizens as individuals—and was less threatening to masculine pride.

Not much changed in the short run. The WCTU was internally divided on the suffrage issue and did not become a major participant in the later struggles for women's right to vote. But by linking women's social concerns and women's political participation, the WCTU helped lay the groundwork for a fresh, broader-based attack on male electoral politics in the early twentieth century. And in the meantime, even without the vote, the WCTU demonstrated how potent a voice women could find in the public realm, and how vibrant a political culture they could build.

The Crisis of American Politics: The 1890s

Benjamin Harrison's election to the presidency in 1888 was the last of the cliff-hanger victories: the Democrat Grover Cleveland actually got a larger popular vote. Over the next few years, the tide went heavily against the Republicans. In 1890 Democrats took the House of Representatives decisively, capturing 235 seats to the Republicans' 88, and won a number of governorships in normally Republican states. These losses can partly be explained by the lackluster performance of the Harrison administration and by the success of the Democrats at tarring the protectionist McKinley Tariff of 1890 as a giveaway for the vested interests. Less visible but more ominous for the Republicans was an erosion of grass-roots support. The Prohibition Party, which had first appeared in national elections in 1876, made inroads among evangelical Protestants, while the Democrats gained among moderates in local battles over education and public morality. In 1892 Cleveland regained the presidency by the largest margin in twenty years.

Had everything else remained equal, the events of 1890 and 1892 might have inaugurated a long period of Democratic supremacy. But everything else did not remain equal. By the time of Cleveland's inauguration, rising farm foreclosures and railroad bankruptcies signaled economic trouble. On May 3, 1893, the stock market crashed. By year's end, 16,000 firms and hundreds of banks had failed. In Chicago 100,000 jobless

HELEN POTTER
The Case for Women's Political Rights

———★———

In 1883 Helen Potter, a New York educator, testified before the Senate Committee on Education and Labor. She meant to speak about the sanitary conditions of the poor in New York City, but in the course of her testimony she delivered a powerful indictment of the unequal treatment of women that spoke volumes about the evolving women's political culture of the late nineteenth century.

The Witness. It is really an important question—this of the condition of women in our community. When I was a young girl I had some ambition, and when I heard a good speaker, or when I read something written by a good writer, I had an ambition to do something of that kind myself. I was exceedingly anxious to preach, but the churches would not have me; why, they said that a woman must not be heard. . . .

Q. I suppose you have an idea that women might abolish some of the tricks of the politician's trade?

A. Well, sir, it would take them a long time to learn to dare to do those things that men do in the way of politics—to sell and buy votes. . . .

Q. What would be the effect of conferring suffrage upon women? Would not the effect be injurious to the moral character and high influence of woman, if she should devote herself to the tricks of the politician's trade, which you very properly criticize so severely?

A. . . . I certainly think it would clean our streets, and I think it would purify politics, at least for the next two hundred years. It would take about that time to get women to understand the tricks of politi-cians as at present practiced. I do not think that women would be injured by it. . . . This Government is based upon the will of the people—women are "people," yet we have not a word to say about the laws. You will hear women in the course of your acquaintance say they wish they were men; I never heard a man say he wished he was a woman. . . .

Q. Why do you think that the suffrage is not extended to women by men—what is the true reason, the radical reason, why men do not give up one half their political power to women?

A. Well, it may arise from a false notion of gallantry. I think most men feel like taking care of, and protecting the ladies. . . . It would be all very well, perhaps, if all women had representatives, and if all had a generous, straightforward honorable man to represent them. But take the case of a good woman who has a drunken husband; how can he represent her? He votes for liquor and for everything he may happen to want, even though it may ruin her and turn her out of doors, and even though it may ruin her children. If the husband is a bad man would it not be better for that woman to represent herself?

Q. What effect do you think the extension of the suffrage to women would have upon their material condition, their wage-earning power and the like?

A. They would get equal pay for equal work of equal value. I do not think a woman ought to be paid the price of an expert, when she is not herself an expert, but I believe there would be a stimulus for a woman to fit herself for the very best work. What stimulus is there for woman to fit herself properly, if she never can attain the highest pay, no matter what sort of work she does? If women had a vote I think larger avenues of livelihood would be opened for them and they would be more respected by the governmental powers.

———

Source: U.S. Senate, Committee on Education and Labor, *Report upon Relations between Labor and Capital,* II (1885), 627, 629–632.

workers walked the streets; nationwide, the unemployment rate soared to over 20 percent. As always in hard times, suffering and unrest mounted alarmingly.

As the economic crisis of the 1890s set in, which party would prevail—and on what platform—became an open question. The first challenge to the political status quo arrived from the West and South, where the grievances of farmers had begun to crystallize into the radical program of the Populist Party.

The Populist Revolt

Farmers were of necessity joiners. They needed organization to overcome their social isolation and to obtain crucial economic services—hence the enormous appeal of the Patrons of Husbandry (see Chapter 16), which had spread across the Midwest after 1867, and, after the Grange's decline, of the farmers' alliances that began to spring up among southern and western farmers. From diffuse organizational beginnings, two dominant organizations emerged. One was the Farmers' Alliance of the Northwest, which was confined mainly to the midwestern states. More dynamic was the National (or Southern) Farmers' Alliance, which in the mid-1880s spread rapidly from Texas onto the Great Plains and eastward into the cotton South, as "travelling lecturers" extolled the virtues of cooperative activity and reminded farmers of "their obligation to stand as a great conservative body against the encroachments of monopolies and . . . the growing corruption of wealth and power." While thus recapitulating Granger resentment against railroads and merchants that had fueled earlier third-party movements, the alliances conceived of themselves as agents of social and economic reform rather than as new political parties.

The Texas alliance established a massive cooperative, the Texas Exchange, that marketed the crops of cotton farmers and provided them with cheap credit. When cotton prices fell sharply in 1891, the Texas Exchange failed. The Texas alliance then proposed a new scheme: a subtreasury system that would enable farmers to store their crops in public warehouses. Farmers would be able to borrow against those crops from a federally supplied fund at low interest rates until prices rose enough so that their cotton could be profitably marketed. The subtreasury plan would provide the same credit and marketing functions as had the defunct Texas Exchange, but with a crucial difference: the federal government would play the key role. When the Democratic Party declared the subtreasury plan too radical, the Texas alliance decided to strike out in politics independently.

These events in Texas revealed, with special clarity, a process of politicization that went on throughout the alliance movement. Rebuffed by the established parties, alliancemen more or less reluctantly abandoned their Democratic and Republican allegiances. Across the South and West, as state alliances grew stronger

and more impatient, they began to field independent slates. In 1890 third parties won control of the Nebraska and Kansas legislatures and in the South captured several governorships and eight state legislatures. These successes led to the formation of the national People's (Populist) Party. In the 1892 election, with the veteran antimonopoly campaigner James B. Weaver as their presidential candidate, the Populists captured a million votes and carried four western states (Map 18.1). For the first time agrarian protest truly challenged the national two-party system.

Populism was distinguished also by the many women in the movement. In the established parties, the grass-roots organizations—the local political clubs—were for men only. Populism, in contrast, arose from a network of suballiances that had formed for largely social purposes and that welcomed women. "The Alliance has come to redeem woman from her enslaved condition," proclaimed a female member from Texas. "She is admitted into the organization as an equal to her brother" and is free of "the ostracism which has impeded her intellectual progress in the past."

Although women participated actively and served prominently as speakers and lecturers, only a handful achieved high office in the alliances, and their role diminished once the Populist Party entered politics. In

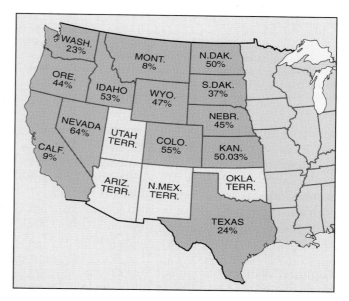

MAP 18.1

The Heyday of Western Populism, 1892

This map shows the percentage of the popular vote won by James B. Weaver, the People's Party candidate, in the presidential election of 1892. Except in California and Montana, the Populists won broad support across the West and genuinely threatened the established parties in that region.

Mary Elizabeth Lease
As a political movement, the Populists were short on cash and organization, but long on rank-and-file zeal and tub-thumping oratory. No one was more rousing on the stump than Mary Elizabeth Lease, who came from a Kansas homestead and pulled no punches. "What you farmers need to do," she proclaimed in her speeches, "is to raise less corn and more *Hell!*" Kansas State Historical Society.

the farmers, laborers, merchants and all the people who produce wealth. . . . Between these two there is no middle ground."

By this reasoning, farmers and workers formed a single producer class. Thus the Southern Farmers' Alliance renamed itself in 1889 the National Farmers' Alliance and Industrial Union. The title was not merely rhetorical. Organized in Knights of Labor assemblies, Texas railroad workers and Colorado miners cooperated with the farmers' alliances, got their support in strikes, and actively participated in forming state Populist parties. The platform of the national party contained strong labor planks, and party leaders earnestly sought the support of the labor movement. In its explicit class appeal—in recognizing that "the irrepressible conflict between capital and labor is upon us"—Populism parted company from the two mainstream parties.

In an age dominated by laissez-faire doctrine, what most distinguished Populism from the major parties was its positive attitude toward the state (see American Voices, "Datus E. Meyer: Angry Farmers," p. 590). The Populist platform declared: "We believe that the powers of government—in other words, of the people—should be expanded as rapidly and as far as the good sense of an intelligent people and the teachings of experience shall justify, to the end that oppression, injustice and poverty should eventually cease in the land." Populists such as Lorenzo Dow Lewelling, governor of Kansas, considered it to be "the business of the Government to make it possible for me to live and sustain the life of my family."

The Omaha platform, adopted at the founding convention of 1892, called for nationalization of the railroads and communications; protection of the land, including natural resources, from monopoly and foreign ownership; a graduated income tax; the creation of postal savings banks; the Texas alliance's subtreasury plan; and "the free and unlimited coinage of silver." From this array of issues, free silver emerged as the overriding demand of the Populist Party.

Free Silver. Cotton and grain farmers were especially vulnerable to falling commodity prices (see Chapter 16). In the early 1890s rock-bottom prices wreaked havoc among cotton, wheat, and corn growers. Under this pressure, farmers turned to free silver, which they hoped, by increasing the money supply, would raise farm prices and enable them to pay back their debts with cheaper dollars. In addition, free silver would bring in hefty contributions to the Populist Party from silver-mining interests. These mine operators, scornful though they might be of Populist radicalism, yearned for the day when the government would buy at a premium price all the silver they could produce, and to that end they were prepared to support the Populists.

deference to the southern wing, the Populist platform was silent on woman suffrage. Still, neither Democrats nor Republicans would have countenanced a spokeswoman such as the fiery Mary Elizabeth Lease, who became famous for calling on farmers "to raise less corn and more hell." Lease insisted just as strenuously on Populism's "grand and holy mission . . . to place the mothers of this nation on an equality with the fathers."

Populist Ideology. Populism was driven as much by ideology as by the quest for political power. The problems afflicting farmers, Populists felt, could stem only from some basic evil. They identified this evil as the control of the "money power" over the levers of the economic system. "There are but two sides," proclaimed a Populist manifesto. "On the one side are the allied hosts of monopolies, the money power, great trusts and railroad corporations. . . . On the other are

En Route to a Populist Rally, Dickinson County, Kansas
Farm people traveled miles to rallies and meetings for the chance to voice their grievances and socialize with like-minded folks. This tradition infused Populism with a special fervor. Gatherings such as the one these Kansans were heading to were a visible sign of what Populism meant—a movement of the "people."
Kansas State Historical Society.

Free silver was opposed by urban social reformers such as Henry Demarest Lloyd of Chicago and by agrarian radicals such as Georgia's Tom Watson. They argued that free silver would undercut the broader Populist program and drive away wage earners, who had no enthusiasm for inflationary measures. Any chance of a farmer-labor alliance that might transform Populism into an American version of the social democratic parties of Europe would be doomed. As Lloyd complained, free silver was "the cowbird of reform," stealing in and taking over the nest that others had built.

Despite the fierce debate within the party, the outcome was never in doubt. The political appeal of free silver was simply too great. But once Populists made that choice, they fatally compromised their party's capacity to maintain an independent existence. For free silver was not an issue over which the Populists held a monopoly. Free silver was, on the contrary, a question at the very center of mainstream politics in the 1890s.

Money and Politics

In a rapidly developing economy such as nineteenth-century America's, the money supply is bound to be a big political issue. Money has to increase rapidly enough to meet the economy's needs or growth will be stifled. How fast the money supply should grow, however, is a question that creates sharp divisions. Inflationists—debtors and producers of goods—want a larger money supply: more money in circulation raises prices and reduces the real cost of borrowing. The "sound-money" people—creditors, individuals on fixed incomes, those in the slower-growing sectors of the economy—have an opposite interest.

Before the Civil War the main source of the nation's money supply had been the banknotes circulated by several thousand state banks. Although more or less subject to state regulation, these banks issued notes in their private role as providers of credit to their customers. The banknotes they gave to borrowers circulated as money until presented to the banks for redemption. The burgeoning economy's need for money was amply met by the state banks, although the goodness of the banknotes—the ability of the issuing banks to stand behind their notes and redeem them at face value—was always uncertain. During the Civil War this freewheeling system came to an end. The Banking Act of 1863 sharply curtailed the freedom of the state banks to create money. They could still issue banknotes, but only insofar as these notes were backed by U.S. government bonds.

The economic impact of this nationalizing action was not immediately felt because the Lincoln administration itself was printing large amounts of paper money—greenbacks, so called—to finance the Civil War. After the war, however, the sound money interests lobbied powerfully for a return to the bimetallic policy prevailing ever since the founding of the republic, which was to base the federal currency on the *specie*—gold and silver—held by the U.S. Treasury. The issue was hotly debated for a decade, but in 1875 the inflationists were defeated, and the circulation of greenbacks as legal tender—that is, backed by nothing more than the good faith of the federal government—came to an end. With the state banknotes also in short supply, the country entered an era of chronic deflation and tight credit.

This was the context out of which the silver question emerged. The country had always operated on a

DATUS E. MEYER
Angry Farmers

————————★————————

In his testimony before a Senate committee, Datus Meyer, a Minnesota farmer, details farmers' grievances against the railroads. Underlying his remarks is his sense of farmers as victims of powers beyond their control—hence the demand for government intervention, one of the hallmarks of Populism.

St. Paul, Minnesota, June 25, 1885

Mr. Meyer. There is very great discontent among the smaller farmers of the State in regard to [the railroads], arising both from discrimination and what they consider extortion. To illustrate what I mean by that, I can produce for you freight receipts that will show where car-loads of stuff have been brought from Springfield, Ohio, to Saint Paul at a charge of $65, a distance of about 800 miles, and carried to Saint Vincent, a distance of about 400 miles, and charged $155. . . . The plan of discriminating, and charging more for a short than for a long haul near competing points, is almost universal. . . . Then there were discriminations [that] proved they absolutely refused to allow a small farmer to have a car at all, in which to load his corn and ship it away, unless he put it through that elevator system . . . on account of having given the exclusive privilege to those elevator lines. . . . Another thing that was practiced . . . was this: They have what they call a transit-rate system in the southern part of the State. If I wanted to ship grain to Milwaukee I would have to pay the rate clear through to Chicago before they would allow me to ship at all. Then they would give me a ticket for the difference between Milwaukee and Chicago, and I would have to sell that ticket for whatever I could get for it. These abuses have caused the farmers to think that they are very much abused in the matter.

You know how hard farmers are to organize; and yet there are over three hundred secret organizations in this State, organized for the purpose of obtaining redress. . . . They think they ought to have protection; and they look to Congress to give them some relief in these matters. . . . I tell you that the feeling through the country among the small farmers and dealers, who suffer, is much greater than you think. . . . If you could get a rule laid down by which the small farmer believed he was getting justice he would be contented; but as soon as he feels that he is not getting justice there is great discontent, and that discontent will grow. . . .

The Chairman. They have a right now to go into court and sue if they are charged an unreasonable rate?

Mr. Meyer. That is true. But suppose a farmer sues under the common law. The railroads have their attorneys hired and paid for all the time, and they can carry that suit on until an ordinary farmer is ruined. He cannot contend with the railroads.

The Chairman. What would you have done?

Mr. Meyer. I would put a commission between the farmer and the railroads that would see that he obtains justice. That is what I would have done, and what the farmers desire shall be done. You can depend on that.

Source: U.S. Senate, Select Committee on Interstate Commerce, *Report*, 49th Cong., 1st sess. (1886), Part 2, 1335–1337; reprinted in Stanley I. Kutler, ed., *Looking for America*, vol. 2, 2nd ed. (New York: Norton, 1975), 171–174.

bimetallic standard, but the supply of silver had gradually tightened, and as silver became more valuable as metal than as money, silver coins disappeared from circulation. In 1873 silver was officially dropped as a medium of exchange. Soon afterward, great silver discoveries occurred in the West, and silver prices fell. Inflationists began to agitate for a resumption of the traditional bimetallic policy: if the government resumed buying silver at the fixed ratio prevailing before 1873—16 ounces of silver equaling 1 ounce of gold—silver would flow into the Treasury and greatly expand the volume of currency.

With so much at stake for so many people, the currency question became one of the staple issues of post-Reconstruction politics. Twice the prosilver coalition in Congress won modest victories. First, the Bland-Allison Act of 1878 required the U.S. Treasury to purchase and coin between $2 million and $4 million worth of silver each month. Then, the more sweeping Sherman Silver Purchase Act of 1890 required 4.5 million ounces of silver bullion to be purchased monthly to serve as the basis for new issues of U.S. Treasury notes.

These legislative battles, though hard fought, cut across party lines in the characteristic fashion of post-Reconstruction politics. But in the early 1890s, silver suddenly became a defining issue between the parties; in particular, it had a radicalizing effect on the Democratic Party.

The Cleveland Administration and the Silver Question.

When the crash of 1893 hit, the Democrats held power in Washington. The party in office usually gets blamed if the economy falters, but President Cleveland made things worse for the Democrats. When jobless marchers—known as Coxey's Army—arrived in Washington in 1894 to appeal for federal relief, Cleveland's response was to disperse them forcibly and arrest their leader, Jacob S. Coxey. Cleveland's brutal handling of the Pullman strike (see Chapter 17) further alienated the labor vote. Nor was he able to deliver on his campaign promise of tariff reform. Cleveland lost control of the battle when the unpopular McKinley Tariff of 1890 came up for revision in Congress. The resulting Wilson-Gorman Tariff of 1894, which Cleveland allowed to pass into law without his signature, caved in to special interests and left the most important rates mostly unchanged.

Most disastrous, however, was Cleveland's rigidity on the silver question. A committed sound-money man, Cleveland had repeatedly denounced "the dangerous and reckless experiment of free, unlimited, and independent silver coinage." Nothing that happened after the depression set in—not collapsing prices, not the suffering of farmers, not the groundswell for free silver within his own party—budged Cleveland from his opposition to free silver.

Economic pressures, in fact, soon pushed him to abandon altogether a silver-based currency. The problem was a persistent drain on U.S. gold reserves held by the Treasury, caused partly by transfers of gold overseas to cover an unfavorable balance of international payments, and partly by redemptions of gold by holders of U.S. Treasury notes. To help preserve the government's gold reserves, Cleveland persuaded Congress in 1893 to repeal the Sherman Silver Purchase Act, effectively sacrificing the country's painfully crafted effort at maintaining a partial bimetallic standard.

As his administration's difficulties deepened, Cleveland turned in 1895 to a syndicate of private bankers led by J. P. Morgan to finance the gold purchases needed to replenish the Treasury's depleted reserves. The administration's secret negotiations with Wall Street, once discovered, enraged Democrats and completed Cleveland's isolation from his party.

William Jennings Bryan and the Election of 1896.

At their national convention in Chicago in 1896, the Democrats repudiated Cleveland and turned left. The leader of the triumphant silver Democrats was William Jennings Bryan of Nebraska. Only thirty-six years old, Bryan had already served two terms in Congress and become a passionate advocate of free silver. He was a consummate politician and, no less important, an inspiring public speaker. Bryan, remarked the journalist Frederic Howe, was "pre-eminently an evangelist," whose zeal sprang from "the Western self-righteous missionary mind." With biblical fervor, Bryan swept up his audiences when he joined the debate on free silver at the Democratic convention. He had been quietly building up delegate support while distancing himself from convention politicking. Bryan locked up the presidential nomination with a stirring attack on the gold

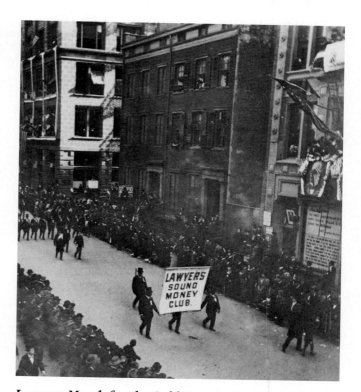

Lawyers March for the Gold Standard
Presidential campaigns of the late nineteenth century were always hard fought, none more so than the 1896 election. Big issues were at stake: would the country stay on the gold standard or drastically expand the money supply through the free coinage of silver? Lawyers paraded in the streets of New York City to demonstrate their conviction that the nation's fate hung on sound money and the election of the Republican William McKinley.
New-York Historical Society.

The Candidates, 1896
The 1896 presidential campaign marked one small step in the technology of election-eering—the introduction of the celluloid campaign button, which a party supporter could pin on his lapel. It is doubtful, however, that this innovation made any differ-ence in the outcome of the election.
Collection of Janice L. and David J. Frent.

standard: "You shall not press down upon the brow of labor this crown of thorns, you shall not crucify mankind on a cross of gold."

Bryan's nomination meant that the Democrats had become the party of free silver; his "cross of gold" speech meant that the money question would turn into a national crusade. No one could be neutral on this defining issue. Silver Republicans bolted their party; gold Democrats went for a splinter Democratic ticket or supported the Republican Party; even the Prohibition Party split into gold and silver wings. The Populists, meeting after the Democratic convention, accepted Bryan as their candidate. The free-silver issue had become so vital that they could not do otherwise. Although they nominated their own vice-presidential candidate, Tom Watson of Georgia, the Populists found themselves for all practical purposes absorbed into the Democratic silver crusade.

The Republicans took up the challenge. Their key party leader was Mark Hanna, a wealthy Cleveland iron maker, a brilliant political manager, and an exponent of the new industrial capitalism. He orchestrated an unprecedented money-raising campaign among Amer-ica's corporate interests. Hanna's candidate, William McKinley of Ohio, personified the virtues of Republi-

canism, standing solidly for prosperity, high tariffs, and sound money. While Bryan broke with tradition and crisscrossed the country in a furious whistle-stop cam-paign, the dignified McKinley received delegations at his home in Canton, Ohio. As Bryan orated with pas-sionate moral fervor, McKinley talked of industrial progress and a full dinner pail.

Not since 1860 had the United States witnessed such a hard-fought election over such high stakes. For the middle class, sound money stood symbolically for the soundness of the social order. With jobless workers tramping the streets and bankrupt farmers up in arms, Bryan's fervent assault on the gold standard struck fear in many hearts. Republicans denounced the Demo-cratic platform as "revolutionary and anarchistic." They called Bryan's supporters "social misfits who have almost nothing in common but opposition to the exist-ing order and institutions."

Though little noticed at the time, ethnocultural issues also figured strongly in the campaign. The Republicans, the party of morality, beat a strategic retreat from temperance and Sunday laws. McKinley himself had represented an ethnically mixed district of northeastern Ohio in Congress. In appealing to his immigrant and working-class constituents, he had

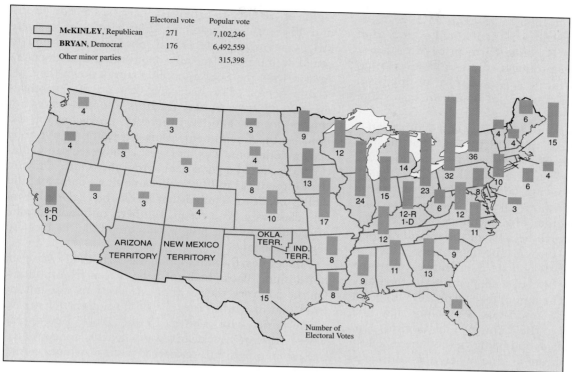

	Electoral vote	Popular vote
McKINLEY, Republican	271	7,102,246
BRYAN, Democrat	176	6,492,559
Other minor parties	—	315,398

MAP 18.2
The Election of 1896
The 1896 election was one of the truly decisive elections in American history. The Republican Party won by its largest margin since 1872. More important, the Republicans established a firm grip on the key midwestern and Middle Atlantic states—especially New York, Indiana, Ohio, and Illinois—that had been the decisive states in every national election since Reconstruction. The 1896 election broke a party stalemate of twenty years' duration and began a period of Republican domination that would last until 1932.

learned the art of easy tolerance, as expressed in his phrase "live and let live." Of the two candidates, the prairie orator Bryan, with his biblical rhetoric and moral righteousness, presented the more alien image to traditional Democratic voters in the big cities.

McKinley won handily, with 271 electoral votes to Bryan's 176 (Map 18.2). He kept the Republican ground that had been regained in the 1894 midterm elections and pushed into Democratic strongholds, especially in the cities. Boston, New York, Chicago, and Minneapolis, all taken by Cleveland in 1892, went for McKinley in 1896. Bryan ran strongly only in the South, in silver-mining states, and in the Populist West. The gains his evangelical style brought him in some Republican rural areas did not compensate for his losses in traditionally Democratic urban districts.

The paralyzing equilibrium of American politics ended in 1896. The Republicans had skillfully handled both the economic and the cultural challenges. They persuaded the nation that they were the party of pros-

perity and shifted some of the burdens of morality politics onto the Democrats. In 1896, too, electoral politics regained its place as an arena for national debate, setting the stage for the reform politics of the Progressive Era.

The Decline of Agrarian Radicalism

As for Populism, it simply faded away. Fusion with the Democrats in 1896 deprived the People's Party of its identity and undermined its organizational structure. After the election, the issue on which Populism had staked its fate—free silver—vanished. During the 1890s gold was discovered in South Africa, Colorado, and the Yukon, and the new cyanide refining method greatly increased ore yields. The newly abundant gold supply took the sting out of the lost battle for free silver. In 1897, moreover, the world market for agricultural commodities turned favorable. Wheat went from

72 cents a bushel in 1896 to 98 cents in 1909, corn from 27 cents a bushel to 57 cents, and cotton from 6 cents a pound to 14 cents. Farm prices rose faster than prices of other products, and as a result, so did the real income of farmers. A new spirit of optimism took hold in the "golden age" of American agriculture before World War I.

The farmers' sense of inferiority and deprivation—that they were "rubes" and "hicks" and that life was inherently better in the city—began to subside after 1900. The new prosperity meant that more farmers could afford labor-saving home appliances and farm machinery. Other inventions eased the isolation and monotony of rural life. The telephone became commonplace, not so much because of the spread of commercial service but through the determined efforts of farmers themselves. Telephone cooperatives were the most common type of farm cooperative in the early twentieth century. The automobile, especially the Ford Model T, gave rural Americans a mobility they had never before known. The Country Life Commission, formed in 1908, took an optimistic view of farm society: "There has never been a time when the American farmer was as well off as he is today, when we consider not only his earning powers but the comforts and advantages he may secure."

In an agrarian nation, the distress of farmers could readily be regarded as a disorder of the entire country. Pushed far enough, farmers might mobilize to seize political power. In short, they could become Populists. But by the opening of the twentieth century farmers no longer constituted a majority of the population. In 1900 scarcely a third of the labor force earned a living from the soil; the proportion doing so would shrink in each succeeding census until, in our own time, less than 3 percent of the labor force is engaged in agriculture (see the Appendix, p. A-10).

There would be times in the twentieth century when distressed farmers would turn again to insurgent politics, but never with the potency generated by the Populist Party. It would be as an organized interest group, not as a political movement, that farmers in the future would advance their cause.

Agriculture had long been at the heart of American life. In the twentieth century agriculture became just one more economic interest—important but subordinate in the larger scheme of the modern industrial order.

Race and Politics in the South

When Reconstruction ended in 1877, so did the hopes of African Americans that they would enjoy the equal rights of citizenship promised them by the Fourteenth and Fifteenth amendments. Southern schools were strictly segregated. Access to jobs, to justice, and to social welfare was racially determined and unequal. And in 1883 the Supreme Court struck down the Civil Rights Act of 1875, declaring that private citizens—owners of restaurants, theaters, hotels—were not subject to the antidiscriminatory provisions of the Fourteenth Amendment. But segregation in public accommodations was not yet legally required, and practices varied a good deal across the South. Only on the railroads, as rail travel became more common, did whites begin to demand that blacks be excluded from first-class cars. As a result, southern railroads became after 1887 the first public accommodation subject to segregation laws.

In politics, the situation in the early 1880s was even more fluid. Blacks had not been driven from politics. On the contrary, their turnout at elections was not far from that of whites. But blacks did not participate on equal terms with whites. In the Black Belt—areas where African Americans were heavily concentrated and sometimes outnumbered whites—whites gerrymandered the districts to ensure that while blacks got some electoral representation, political control remained in white hands. Blacks, moreover, were routinely intimidated during political campaigns—hence the large numbers whose votes were recorded as Democratic in those years. Even so, an impressive majority remained staunchly Republican, refusing, as the last black congressman from Mississippi told his House colleagues in 1882, "to surrender their honest convictions, even upon the altar of their personal necessities."

Whatever hope blacks entertained for better days, however, faded during the 1880s and then, in the next decade, expired in a terrible burst of racist terrorism. What made this outcome so tragic was that it coincided with a positive effort to overcome racial divisions. Black disfranchisement and rigid segregation stemmed directly from the crisis of the 1890s and, in particular, from a political upheaval that briefly challenged Democratic Party rule in the South.

The Triumph of White Conservatism

No democratic society can survive if it does not enable competing economic and social interests to be heard. In the United States the two-party system performs that role. The Civil War crisis severely tested the two-party system because, in both the North and the South, political opposition came to be seen as treasonous. In the victorious North, despite the best efforts of the Republicans, the Democrats shed their disgrace and reclaimed their status as a major party. In the defeated South, however, the scars of war cut deep, and Recon-

Disfranchisement

This political drawing that appeared in *Judge* magazine on July 30, 1892, shows members of the Ku Klux Klan barring black voters from the polls. By 1892, in fact, this drawing was behind the times. Literacy tests and poll taxes were beginning to disfranchise blacks with less menace and more likelihood of evading the constitutional requirement (note the sign behind the Ku Kluxers) under the Fifteenth Amendment that the right to vote not be denied "on account of race, color, or previous condition of servitude."

Museum of American Political Life.

struction cut even deeper. The struggle for "home rule" empowered the Democrats. They had "redeemed" the South from black Republican domination—hence the name that southern Democrats adopted: Redeemers. Cloaked in the mantle of the Lost Cause, the Redeemers claimed a monopoly on political legitimacy.

The Republican Party did not fold up, however. On the contrary, it soldiered on, sustained by stubborn black loyalty, by a hard core of white supporters, by patronage from Republican national administrations, and by a key Democratic vulnerability. This was the gap between the universality the Democrats claimed as the party of Redemption and the reality that the Democratic Party was controlled by an economic elite indifferent to the plight of poor whites.

Class antagonism, though often muted by sectional patriotism, was never absent from southern society. The Civil War had brought out long-smoldering differences between planters and hill-country farmers, who had little to gain from the slaveholding system they were called on to defend. Fresh sources of conflict now arose from the sharecropping system—which increasingly included whites as well as blacks—and from an emerging industrial working class. Unable to loosen the grip of the conservative elite, economically distressed white southerners broke with the Democratic Party in the early 1880s and mounted independent movements across the South. Most successful were the Readjusters, who briefly gained power in Virginia by opposing full repayment of Reconstruction debts, which would enrich bond-holding speculators while leaving the state destitute. Elsewhere, conservative Democrats also faced substantial challenges from disaffected farmers organized in Granges and acting through Independent or Greenback parties or, as in Tennessee, Louisiana, and Arkansas, by utilizing the Republican Party. After subsiding briefly, this agrarian discontent revived in the mid-1880s with a vengeance, welling out of the farmers' alliances that sprang up across the South, and spawning the formidable Populist challenge to Democratic rule. Refusing to accept any opposition as legitimate, the ruling Democrats stuffed ballot boxes, intimidated black voters, murdered opponents, and stirred up racial animosity by shouting "Negro domination!"

If opposition was illegitimate, moreover, did it not follow that the incurably disloyal should be excluded from politics altogether? Exclusion had been the purpose behind the cumulative poll tax—a tax for the privilege of voting—adopted by Georgia in 1877 and South Carolina's "eight-box" law (1882), which made voting a nightmare for uneducated voters. It was clear, too, which voters these disfranchising measures mainly targeted: the blacks, whose political participation everywhere insulted southern white sensibilities and, in black-belt districts, made rule by white Democrats perpetually uneasy (see Voices from Abroad, "Charles Boissevain: Touring the South, 1880," p. 597).

But Populists themselves were uneasy about black participation. Racism cut through southern white society and, so some thought, most infected the lowest rungs. "The white laboring classes here," wrote an Alabaman in 1886, "are separated from the Negroes, working all day side by side with them, by an innate consciousness of race superiority," which "excites a sentiment of sympathy and equality with the classes above them, and in this way becomes a healthy social leaven." Yet when times got bad enough, hard-pressed whites could also see blacks as fellow victims. "They are in the ditch just like we are," asserted one white Texan. Southern Populists never fully reconciled these contradictory impulses. They never questioned the conventions of social inequality: blacks had not been admitted to the suballiances. Nor were the economic interests of white landowning farmers and black tenants and laborers always in concert. But once agrarian protest turned political, the logic of racial solidarity became hard to deny.

Kept out of the Southern Farmers' Alliance, black farmers had organized separately into the Colored Farmers' Alliance, thereby gaining a certain amount of leverage with the emerging Populist movement. The Knights of Labor, which accepted blacks, also argued for interracial unity. The realities of partisan politics, once the alliances had taken that step, clinched the argument. Where the Populists fused with the Republican Party, such as in North Carolina and Tennessee, they automatically became allies of black leaders and gained a black constituency. Where fusion did not happen and the Populists fielded independent tickets, they needed to appeal to black voters. "The accident of color can make no difference in the interest of farmers, croppers, and laborers," argued the Populist leader Tom Watson. "You are kept apart that you may be separately fleeced of your earnings." By making this interracial appeal, even if not always wholeheartedly, the Populists put at risk the foundations of conservative southern politics.

In the face of this challenge, conservative Democrats played the race card to the hilt, parading as the "white man's party" while denouncing the Populists for courting "Negro rule." Yet at the same time they shamelessly competed for the black vote. In this, they had many advantages: money; control of the local power structures; a paternalistic relationship to the black community. When all else failed, mischief at the polls enabled the Democrats to beat back the Populists. Thus the Mississippian Frank Burkitt's bitter attack on the conservatives: they were "a class of corrupt office-seekers" who had "hypocritically raised the howl of white supremacy while they debauched the ballot boxes . . . disregarded the rights of the blacks . . . and actually dominated the will of the white people through the instrumentality of the stolen negro vote."

Black Disfranchisement.   In the midst of these deadly struggles the Democrats decided to settle matters once and for all. Disfranchising the blacks, hitherto pursued hesitantly, now turned into a potent movement throughout the South (Map 18.3). In 1890, Mississippi adopted a literacy test that effectively drove the blacks out of politics. The motives behind it were cynical, but the literacy test could be dressed up as a reform for Mississippians tired of electoral fraud and violence. Their children and grandchildren, argued one influential figure, should not be left "with shotguns in their hands, a lie in their mouths and perjury on their lips in order to defeat the negroes." Better, a Mississippi journalist wrote, to devise "some legal defensible substitute for the abhorrent and evil methods on which white supremacy lies." This argument even persuaded some weary Populists: Frank Burkitt, for example, was arguing *for* the Mississippi literacy test in the words quoted in the previous paragraph. Other disfranchising methods—registration laws, property qualifications, the secret ballot (which demanded some basic literacy), the already familiar poll tax—were also widely enacted during the 1890s, but none matched the literacy test as a flexible and efficient instrument for driving blacks from the polls.

The race issue had helped to bring down the Populists; now it helped reconcile them to defeat. Embittered poor whites, deeply ambivalent all along about interracial cooperation, turned their fury on the blacks. Insofar as disfranchising measures asserted militant white supremacy, poor whites approved. It was important, of course, that their own vulnerability be partially protected by lenient enforcement and by exemptions. The literacy test, for instance, was softened by Mississippi's understanding clause, which permitted illiterate voters to explain a constitutional passage that was read to them, and by Louisiana's grandfather clause, which exempted from the test

CHARLES BOISSEVAIN

Touring the South, 1880

———★———

In 1880, as the South was emerging from Reconstruction, the Dutch journalist Charles Boissevain toured the region. Like many visitors, Boissevain was captivated by the romance of the antebellum South, but he was not blind to the evils of slavery or the plantation system. Echoing his southern hosts in his disdain for the freedmen as voters, he also reflected a home-grown racism: if there was any contemporary equal in the world to American slavery, it was the relentless Dutch oppression of the blacks of South Africa. A decade ahead of his hosts, Boissevain came up with the solution they would eventually embrace—constitutional disfranchisement of southern blacks.

I visited an old-fashioned plantation and spoke with some intelligent whites, and with free Negroes who had once been slaves. Walking through the cotton fields in the thick red clay mud, a great deal out of the past and present became clearer than before. . . . The aristocracy of Virginia, which once gave America a Washington, was more and more degraded through the accursed system of slavery. The gentlemen became no more than overseers and slave drivers. It was a masterful, luxurious, merry life that they lived; and walking about here I wished, despite myself, that I might once have been the guest of one of the old masters of the land on his plantation. . . .

I have spoken with several old slaveholders who acknowledge that slavery was properly abolished and that free labor is more profitable than they had ever thought. But they complain bitterly because the government went too far in giving the right to vote to the emancipated Negroes, and thereby ruined both the land and the people. . . . The worst disservice that could have been done for the freedmen was to throw them, unprepared, into the American political battle, an enticing prey for the hungry adventurers from the North who received the picturesque name of carpetbaggers from the suitcase which was their only luggage when they came down the Mississippi. . . .

Now the carpetbagger instead of the slave owner is the master of the Negro, for the idea that the blacks in the South or elsewhere are able to govern whites is laughable. The white must remain the older brother, the leader; this can no more be resisted than can a law of nature. . . .

The Ku-Klux Klan is at present as good as suppressed, but the Negroes are in no better position to make free use of the right to vote. In addition to the fact that many employers make renunciation of the privilege a condition of employment, the colored people are directly prevented from voting for whomever they wish through trickery and through open frauds at the ballot box. . . . In other parts of the country not even that much attention is paid to the forms; the votes of the Negroes are simply not counted.

. . . All honest and thoughtful people, all those who recognize the sovereignty of the law and approve no low deception, must together protest against the frauds at the ballot box. . . . The Negro's lack of fitness for the exercise of the ballot can be the basis for a movement for amending the Constitution, but the defenders of a regime who know no better means that deceit at the polls will earn the confidence of no one. To rule by falsified rolls and by ballot boxes with double bottoms is worse than a military dictatorship.

Source: Oscar Handlin, ed., *This Was America* (Cambridge, MA: Harvard University Press, 1949), 337–342.

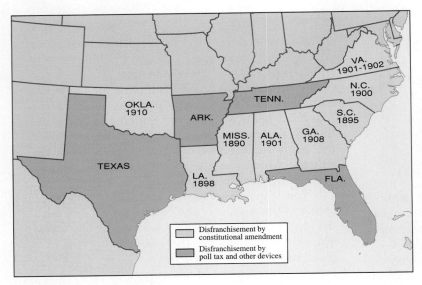

MAP 18.3
Disfranchisement in the South
In the midst of the Populist challenge to Democratic one-party rule in the South, a movement to deprive blacks of the right to vote spread from Mississippi across the South. By 1910 every state in the region except Tennessee, Arkansas, Texas, and Florida had made constitutional changes designed to prevent blacks from voting, and these four states accomplished much the same result through poll taxes and other exclusionary methods. For the next half-century the political process in the South would be for whites only.

those entitled to vote on January 1, 1867, together with their sons and grandsons. But poor whites were not protected from property and poll-tax requirements, and many stopped voting.

Poor whites might have objected more had their spokesmen not been given a voice within the Democratic Party. A new brand of southern politician came forward to speak for them, appealing not to their class interests but to their racial prejudices. Tom Watson, the fiery Georgia Populist, rebuilt his political career as a brilliant practitioner of race baiting. Starting in the early 1900s, he and other racial demagogues thrived throughout the South.

The Ascendancy of Jim Crow. With the collapse of Populism, a brand of white supremacy emerged that was more virulent than anything blacks had faced since Emancipation. The color line, hitherto incomplete, became rigid and comprehensive. Segregated seating in trains, already in force generally since first being enacted by Florida in 1887, provided a precedent for the legal separation of the races. The enforcing legislation, known as Jim Crow laws, soon applied to every type of public facility—restaurants, hotels, streetcars, even cemeteries. In the 1890s the South became for the first time a society fully segregated by law.

The Supreme Court of the United States soon ratified the South's decision. In the case of *Plessy v. Ferguson* (1896) the Court ruled that segregation was not discriminatory—that is, it did not violate black civil rights under the Fourteenth Amendment—provided that blacks had accommodations equal to those of whites. The "separate but equal" doctrine of course had little regard for the realities of southern life: segregated

facilities were rarely if ever "equal" in any material sense, and segregation itself was intended to underscore the inferiority of blacks. With a similar disregard for reality, the Supreme Court in *Williams v. Mississippi* (1898) validated the disfranchising devices of the southern states: so long as race was not a specified criterion for disfranchisement, the Fifteenth Amendment was not being violated, even though the practical effect was the virtual exclusion of blacks from politics in the South.

Race hatred became an accepted part of southern life, manifested in a wave of lynchings and race riots and in the public abuse of blacks. For example, Benjamin R. Tillman, governor of South Carolina and after 1895 a senator, excoriated blacks as "an ignorant and debased and debauched race." This ugly racism came from several sources, including intensified competition between whites and blacks for jobs during the depression of the 1890s and white anger against a less submissive black generation born after slavery. Recent scholarship also suggests more deep-seated psychological causes: the rage against blacks served as a way of reasserting a traditional sense of southern "manhood" that was under assault by rapid social and economic change. Lynching, moreover, occurred most frequently in developing areas such as the Gulf plain and in new cotton country where the population was thinly spread, community ties were weak, and blacks and whites were strangers to one another.

But what had triggered the antiblack offensive was the crisis in the South over Populism. From then on, white supremacy propped up the one-party system that the Redeemers had been fighting for ever since Reconstruction. If the southern elite had to share political

Frank J. Farrell, Black Delegate
In this illustration from a popular weekly, Farrell is introducing Master Workman Powderly to the Knights of Labor convention in Richmond, Virginia. It would be hard to exaggerate the fortitude it took for a black man to appear on such a podium in the South in 1886. By this display of interracial unity, the Knights intended to convey the message that class unity trumped racial prejudice. The Southern Farmers' Alliance, allies of the Knights, took this message to heart, at least for a while.
Library of Congress.

power with demagogic poor white leaders such as Tom Watson and James K. Vardaman, this sharing would be on terms agreeable to them—the exclusion from the political arena of any serious challenge to the economic status quo.

The Case of Grimes County. In 1890 African Americans composed more than half of the population of Grimes County, a cotton-growing area of east Texas. They had kept the local Republican Party going after Reconstruction and regularly sent black representatives to the Texas legislature during the 1870s and 1880s. More remarkably, the local Populist Party that appeared in 1892 among white farmers proved immune to the Democrats' taunts of "black rule." A Populist-

Republican coalition swept the county elections in 1896 and 1898, surviving well after the collapse of the national Populist movement.

In 1899 defeated Democratic office seekers and prominent citizens of Grimes County organized the secret White Man's Union. Armed men prevented blacks from voting in town elections that year. The two most important black leaders were shot down in cold blood. Night riders terrorized both white Populists and black Republicans.

When the Populist sheriff proved incapable of enforcing the law, the game was up. The White Man's Union, now out in the open, became the county Democratic Party in a new guise. The Democrats won Grimes County by an overwhelming vote in 1900. The day after the election, members of the Union laid siege to the Populist sheriff's office. They killed his brother and a friend and drove the sheriff, badly wounded, out of the county forever.

The White Man's Union ruled Grimes County for the next fifty years. The whole episode was the handiwork of the county's "best citizens," suggesting how respectable the use of terror had become in the service of white supremacy. The Union intended, as one of its leaders said, to "force the African to keep his place." After 1900 blacks could survive in Grimes County only if they tended to their own business and stayed out of trouble with whites.

Forms of Black Resistance

Like the blacks of Grimes County, southern blacks in many places resisted white oppression as best they could. When Georgia adopted the first Jim Crow law applying to streetcars in 1891, Atlanta blacks declared a boycott, and over the next fifteen years there were boycotts against segregated streetcars in at least twenty-five cities. "Do not trample on our pride by being 'jim crowed,'" the Savannah *Tribune* urged its readers: "Walk!" Ida Wells-Barnett emerged as the most outspoken black crusader against lynching, so enraging Memphis whites by the editorials in her newspaper *Free Speech* that she was forced in 1892 to leave the city. And individual blacks, such as Robert Charles, struck back, some of them sacrificing their own lives (see American Lives, "Robert Charles: Black Militant," pp. 600–601).

Like Charles, some were drawn to the back-to-Africa movement. It was a sign of their despair that Africa was again seen as the place of black salvation. But emigration was not a real choice, and like the blacks of Grimes County, African Americans everywhere had to bend to the raging forces of racism and find a way to survive.

Robert Charles: Black Militant

————————★————————

THE TROUBLE BEGAN in an ordinary way. The two black men were sitting quietly on the steps of a house on Dryades Street in New Orleans, between Washington and 6th streets. It was Monday evening, July 24, 1900. One was nineteen-year-old Leonard Pierce; the other was an older man named Robert Charles. They were waiting for a friend of Charles's, Virginia Banks, and her roommate to return from a day at Baton Rouge. Around 11 P.M. three policemen approached Pierce and Charles and began to question them roughly. When Charles stood up, Officer Mora grabbed him. A scuffle followed, and Mora began to beat Charles about the head with his billy club. Charles, a big man, broke away. There was an exchange of gunfire, wounding both in the thigh, Officer Mora more seriously. In a hail of bullets, Charles ran off.

"In any law-abiding community Charles would have been justified in delivering himself up immediately to the properly constituted authorities and asking for a trial by a jury of his peers," wrote the antilynching crusader Ida Wells-Barnett in her pamphlet on what followed. "Charles knew that his arrest in New Orleans, even for defending his life, meant nothing short of a long term in the penitentiary, and still more probable death by lynching at the hands of a cowardly mob." Those must have been Charles's thoughts. He made his way back to the room he shared with Pierce on 4th Street, took down his Winchester rifle, and got ready to fight.

In the meantime Pierce had been brought to the police station, where Charles's name and address were soon "sweated" out of him. Captain John T. Day, a local hero who had rescued fourteen people from a hotel fire, led a squad to bring Charles in. The entrance to Charles's room was along an alley. When the police arrived, Charles swung open the door, shot Day through the heart, then turned and fatally wounded a second officer. The other two policemen cowered along the wall and slipped into another house, where they hid in the dark. The officers on the street refused to enter the unlit alley. When reinforcements arrived at 5 A.M., Charles had slipped away, and the manhunt commenced.

The New Orleans newspapers labeled Charles a "fiend incarnate." No one who had known him would have said so. Robert Charles was one of thousands of rural blacks who had sought to escape from grinding poverty by migrating to southern cities. Robert Charles was born just after the end of slavery, in 1865 or 1866, in Copiah County, Mississippi. His parents were sharecroppers, and he was one of ten children. He worked as a day laborer on the railroads and, after arriving in New Orleans around 1894, at a variety of odd jobs. In July 1900 he was unemployed. Charles was unmarried and rather stylish in his dress, favoring a brown derby hat. Acquaintances remembered him as quiet and intelligent. He had received little education, but his room contained the well-thumbed books and papers of a studious man. One other thing about Charles: he ardently believed that blacks should return to Africa.

The back-to-Africa movement, which enjoyed a revival in these hard years, reflected the despair that poor blacks like Robert Charles felt about life in America. Africa was their only salvation, preached Bishop Henry M. Turner, the combative leader of the movement. "I see no other shelter from the stormy blast, from the red tide of persecution, from the horrors of American prejudice." Charles was a reader of Bishop Turner's fiery paper *Voice of Missions*, and in 1899 he began to sell subscriptions. He also became a local agent for the International Migration Society, working on commission to sign up members who would secure transportation to Liberia by contributing a dollar a month for forty months.

Recent events had fortified Charles's conviction that blacks had no hope in America. He was said to have been infuriated by the most infamous lynching of the era, the burning and dismemberment of Sam Hose in Georgia in 1899. In Louisiana, moreover, blacks had been disfranchised in 1898, and a crisis was brewing in state politics. As the elections of 1900 approached, the Democrats vowed that on no account would they allow the Republicans and Populists to emerge as winners. In Charles's pocket was a newspaper clipping about an opposition leader who had called on his supporters to "oil up their Winchesters and prepare to fight" if Democrats tried to steal the election. In *Voice of Missions* there was a similarly desperate message: in one editorial Bishop Turner had urged that "Negroes Get Guns" in self-defense.

Charles, in fact, habitually carried a Colt .38 revolver; it was in his belt when Officer Mora accosted

MOB RULE
IN
NEW ORLEANS.

ROBERT CHARLES
AND
His Fight to the Death.

THE STORY OF HIS LIFE.
BURNING HUMAN BEINGS ALIVE.
OTHER LYNCHING STATISTICS.

IDA B. WELLS-BARNETT,
CHICAGO.

PRICE 25 CENTS.

Robert Charles
This is the only known picture of Charles, an engraving done for the cover of Ida Wells-Barnett's pamphlet on Charles's slaying.
Miriam and Ira D. Wallach Division of Art, Prints and Photographs, The New York Public Library. Astor, Lenox and Tilden Foundations.

him. There is no knowing what went through his mind when he chose not to submit to the policeman's abuse. But by drawing his gun, Charles had stepped across the line. From then until his inevitable death, he was making a political statement.

That was how the whites of New Orleans saw Charles, too: he was challenging the white power structure. As a leader of the mob that gathered in the streets on Wednesday put it:

> The only way you can teach these niggers a lesson and put them in their place is to go out and lynch a few of them as an object lesson. String up a few of them, and the others will trouble you no more. . . . On to the Parish Prison and lynch Pierce!

The mob couldn't get at Pierce, but they took their fury out on any other unfortunate black they encountered as they surged through the city. In the next two days at least six people were killed and dozens of others brutally beaten. Only late on Thursday did the police and militia restore a semblance of law and order to New Orleans. But Charles remained at large. Then, on Friday afternoon, July 27, the police got a tip that he was hiding in a small house on Saratoga Street.

Springing from a back closet, Charles shot down the two police officers who came to investigate and then made his way up to the second story. A great crowd soon surrounded the house, peppering it with bullets. Dodging from window to window, Charles returned the fire for nearly two hours. In grudging admiration, one reporter wrote of his "diabolical coolness" and "wonderful marksmanship [that] never failed him for a moment." More than twenty of his attackers were hit, three fatally. As dusk began to fall, the building was set ablaze, and Charles was forced out. Still defiant, he almost made it across the courtyard when he was stopped by a bullet and went down. The crowd was at him in an instant, firing dozens of shots into him, stomping on his head. His body was carried off in a police wagon, his battered head hanging grotesquely from the back. Later that night the mob broke loose again, burning buildings and murderously attacking six more blacks.

No New Orleans black would have dared say out loud that Robert Charles had done right. But Ida Wells-Barnett, writing from the safety of Chicago, insisted that he had. "The white people of this country may charge that he was a desperado, but to the people of his own race Robert Charles will always be regarded as the hero of New Orleans." Five weeks after Charles's burial, a neighbor of Fred Clark's on South Rampart Street came up behind Clark, put a gun to his head, and shot him dead. Fred Clark was the black man who had given away Charles's hiding place to the police.

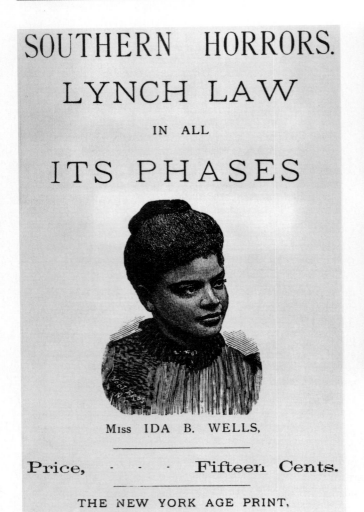

MISS IDA B. WELLS,

Price, - - - Fifteen Cents.

THE NEW YORK AGE PRINT,
1892.

Miss Ida B. Wells
In 1887 Ida Wells (Wells-Barnett after she married in 1895) was thrown bodily from a train in Tennessee for refusing to vacate her seat in a section reserved for whites, launching her into a lifetime crusade for racial justice. Her mission was to expose the evil of lynching in the South. This portrait is from the title page of a pamphlet she published in 1892 entitled, "Southern Horrors. Lynch Law in All Its Phases."
Miriam and Ira D. Wallach Division of Art, Prints and Photographs, The New York Public Library. Astor, Lenox and Tilden Foundations.

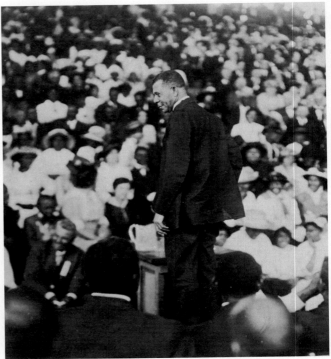

Booker T. Washington
In an age of severe racial oppression, Washington emerged as the acknowledged leader of black people in the United States. He was remarkable for both his ability as spokesman to white Americans and his deep understanding of the aspirations of black Americans. Born a slave, Washington suffered the indignities experienced by all blacks after Emancipation. But having been befriended by several whites as he grew to manhood, he also understood what it took to gain white support—and maneuver around white hostility—in the black struggle for equality.
Library of Congress.

The Atlanta Compromise. Booker T. Washington, the foremost black leader of his day, marked the path in a speech in Atlanta in 1895. Washington retreated from the defiant stand of an older generation of black abolitionists exemplified by Frederick Douglass, who died the same year that the Atlanta speech launched Washington into national prominence. Washington was conciliatory toward the South; it was a society that blacks understood and loved. He considered "the agi-

tation of the question of social equality the extremest folly." Washington accepted segregation, provided that blacks had equal facilities. He accepted educational and property qualifications for the vote, provided that they applied equally to blacks and whites.

Washington's doctrine came to be known as the Atlanta Compromise. His approach was "accommodationist," in the sense that it avoided a direct assault on white supremacy. Despite the humble face he put on before white audiences, however, Washington did not concede the struggle. Behind the scenes he did his best to resist Jim Crow laws and disfranchisement. More important, his Atlanta Compromise, while abandoning the field of political protest, opened up a second front of economic struggle.

Booker T. Washington sought to capitalize on a southern dilemma about the economic role of the black population. Racist dogma dictated that blacks be kept down and conform to their image as lazy, shiftless workers. But to prosper, the South needed an efficient labor force. Washington made this need the target of his efforts. As founder of the Tuskegee Institute in Alabama in 1881, Washington advocated *industrial education*—manual and agricultural training. He preached the virtues of thrift, hard work, and property ownership. Washington's industrial education program won generous support from northern philanthropists and businessmen and, following his Atlanta speech, applause from progressive supporters of the New South.

Washington assumed that black economic progress would be the key to winning political and civil rights. He regarded members of the white southern elite as crucial allies, because ultimately only they had the power to change the South. More important, they could see "the close connection between labor, industry, education, and political institutions." When it was in their economic interest, when they had grown dependent on black labor and black enterprise, white men of business and property would recognize the justice of black rights. As Washington put it, "There is little race prejudice in the American dollar."

The Limits of Self-Help. Do the facts suggest that Washington was right? Or, to put the question as an economist might: was it the impersonal market or race prejudice that most determined the economic treatment of blacks? For southern industry the answer seems mixed. Employers did not discriminate very much over wage rates—that is, they did not pay whites higher wages than they paid blacks for the same work. But racial barriers certainly prevented blacks from moving into better-paid and more highly skilled jobs. This hard truth is made graphically clear in the comparative wage distributions of whites and blacks shown in Figure 18.2. In agriculture, too, the picture was mixed. The opportunity for black farmers to advance themselves clearly did exist. The proportion who became landowners inched slowly upward to roughly 25 percent by 1900. But the racial gap remained very wide, with whites almost three times as likely as blacks to be landowners.

To what extent black self-help—hard work, industrial education, the husbanding of small resources—might counterbalance race prejudice was the nub of Booker T. Washington's problem. Where the almighty dollar reigned, there was some hope of progress. Elsewhere, as Washington saw it, there was none.

For twenty years after his Atlanta address, Washington dominated the organized African American community. In an age of severe racial oppression, no black dealt more skillfully with the leaders of white

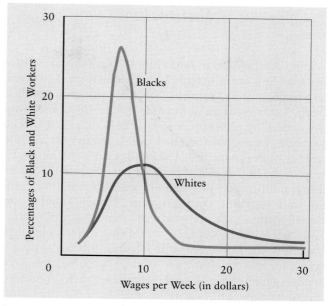

Source: Gavin Wright, *Old South, New South: Revolutions in the Southern Economy since the Civil War* (New York: Basic Books, 1986), 184.

FIGURE 18.2
Distributions of Weekly Wages for Black and White Workers in Virginia, 1907
This graph reveals that wages for common labor in the South were nondiscriminatory (otherwise no or few whites would have been bunched at the low end of the wage scale) but that discrimination denied blacks entry into higher-paying jobs.

America or wielded greater political influence than did Washington. Black leaders knew him as a hard taskmaster. Intensely jealous of his authority, he did not take opposition kindly. Black politicians, educators, and editors stood up to him at their peril.

Even so, opposition surfaced after 1900, especially among younger educated blacks. They thought Washington was conceding too much. He instilled black pride, but of a narrowly middle-class and utilitarian kind. What about the special genius of blacks that W. E. B. Du Bois, a Harvard-trained African American sociologist, celebrated in his collection of essays, *The Souls of Black Folk* (1903)? And what of the "talented tenth" of the black population, whose promise could only be stifled by manual education? Blacks also became increasingly impatient with Washington's silence on segregation and lynching. By the time of his death in 1915, Washington's approach had been superseded by a strategy that relied on the courts and political leverage, not on black self-help and accommodation.

Summary

★

When Reconstruction ended in 1877, national politics became less issue oriented and, as a formal process, less important in American life. This situation resulted from weaknesses in governmental institutions, from the prevailing philosophy of laissez faire, and from the paralysis of evenly matched political parties. Yet the politics of the years after 1877 had great vigor, as can be seen in the high levels of popular participation. For one thing, politics was the arena in which the nation's ethnic and religious conflicts were largely fought out. Equally important, the party machines were powerful and performed crucial functions that properly belonged to, but were still beyond the capacity of, governmental institutions. Finally, despite the slow headway made toward woman suffrage, women's organizations carved out for themselves a broadening public sphere of social reform activity.

During the 1890s national politics again became an important arena. Threatened by the rise of Populism, the Democratic Party committed itself to free silver and made the election of 1896 a contest over issues of real significance. The Republicans won decisively, ending a paralyzing party stalemate that had lasted for twenty years and assuring themselves of political dominance for the next thirty years. At the same time, the 1890s saw, in the failure of Populism, the last great challenge to the mainstream two-party system. And in the South the Populist failure turned into a grim reaction that disfranchised African Americans, completed a rigid segregation system, and let loose a terrible cycle of racial hatred and violence. Blacks resisted but had to bend to overwhelming white power. The accommodationist philosophy of Booker T. Washington seemed to be the best strategy for black survival in an age of extreme racism.

TIMELINE

1874   Woman's Christian Temperance Union founded

1877   Rutherford B. Hayes inaugurated as president, marking the end of Reconstruction

1881   President James A. Garfield assassinated

1883   Pendleton Civil Service Act

Supreme Court strikes down Civil Rights Act of 1875

1884   Mugwump reformers leave the Republican Party to support Grover Cleveland, first Democrat elected president since 1856

1887   Florida adopts first law segregating railroad travel

1888   James Bryce's *The American Commonwealth*

1890   McKinley Tariff

Democrats sweep congressional elections, inaugurating brief era of Democratic Party dominance

Mississippi becomes first state to adopt literacy test to disfranchise blacks

1892   People's (Populist) Party founded

1893   Panic of 1893 leads to national depression

Repeal of Sherman Silver Purchase Act (1890)

1894   "Coxey's Army" of unemployed fails to win federal relief

1895   Booker T. Washington sets out Atlanta Compromise

1896   Election of Republican president William McKinley; free-silver campaign crushed

Plessy v. Ferguson upholds constitutionality of "separate but equal" facilities

1897   Economic depression ends; era of agricultural prosperity begins

Suggested Readings

The best introductions to American politics in the late nineteenth century are John A. Garraty, *The New Commonwealth, 1877–1890* (1968), and R. Hal Williams, *Years of Decision: American Politics in the 1890s* (1978). More detailed and comprehensive is Morton Keller, *Affairs of State: Public Life in Late Nineteenth-Century America* (1977). Joel L. Silbey, *The American Political Nation, 1838–1893* (1991), focuses on the party system and political behavior.

The Politics of the Status Quo, 1877–1893

Various aspects of national politics are discussed in Robert D. Marcus, *Grand Old Party: Political Structure in the Gilded Age* (1971); J. Rogers Hollingsworth, *The Whirligig of Politics: The Democracy of Cleveland and Bryan* (1963); H. Wayne Morgan, *From Hayes to McKinley: National Party Politics, 1877–1896* (1969); and David J. Rothman, *Politics and Power: The Senate, 1869–1901* (1966). On the development of public administration, see Leonard D. White, *The Republican Era, 1869–1901* (1958), and Stephen Skowronek, *Building a New American State: The Expansion of National Administrative Capacities* (1982). The ideological basis for conservative national politics is fully treated in Sidney Fine, *Laissez Faire and the General Welfare State, 1865–1901* (1956), and Robert G. McCloskey, *American Conservatism in the Age of Enterprise* (1951). A useful introduction to the legal history of this era is Morton J. Horwitz, *The Transformation of American Law, 1870–1960* (1992).

Sources of Popular Participation

On popular participation in politics see especially Michael E. McGerr, *The Decline of Popular Politics: The American North, 1865–1928* (1986), and Paul Kleppner, *The Third Electoral Party System, 1853–1892: Parties, Voters, and Political Cultures* (1979). On the Mugwump reformers see John G. Sproat, *The "Best Men": Liberal Reformers in the Gilded Age* (1965), and Ari Hoogenboom, *Outlawing the Spoils: The Civil Service Reform Movement, 1865–1883* (1961). The existence of a women's political culture in the late nineteenth century can be traced in Carl N. Degler, *At Odds: Women and the Family from the Revolution to the Present* (1979). A valuable book setting the stage is Ellen Carol DuBois, *Feminism and Suffrage: The Emergence of an Independent Women's Movement in America, 1848–1869* (1978). The political role of the WCTU is one of the themes of Suzanne M. Marilley, *Woman Suffrage and the Origins of Liberal Feminism in the United States* (1997).

The Crisis of American Politics: The 1890s

The most recent synthesis on Populism is Robert C. McMath, *American Populism* (1993). Richard D. Hofstadter, *The Age of Reform* (1955), stresses the darker side of Populism, in which intolerance and paranoia figure heavily. Hofstadter's thesis once dominated debate among historians but has given way to a much more positive assessment. The key book here is Lawrence Goodwyn, *Democratic Promise: The Populist Moment in America* (1976), which argues that Populism was a broadly based radical response to industrial capitalism. Peter H. Argesinger, *The Limits of Agrarian Radicalism: Western Politics and American Politics* (1995), stresses the capacity of the political status quo to frustrate western Populism. Two stimulating books that follow the history of Populism into the twentieth century are Grant McConnell, *The Decline of Agrarian Democracy* (1953), which focuses on farm organizations, and Michael Kazin, *The Populist Persuasion* (1995), which describes how the language of Populism entered the discourse of mainstream American politics.

The money question is elucidated in Allan Weinstein, *Prelude to Populism: Origins of the Silver Issue* (1970), and, in the most recent and sophisticated account, Gretchen Ritter, *Goldbugs and Greenbacks: The Anti-Monopoly Tradition and the Politics of Finance in America, 1865–1896* (1997). On the politics of the 1890s see especially Robert F. Durden, *Climax of Populism: The Election of 1896* (1965), and Paul W. Glad, *McKinley, Bryan, and the People* (1964).

Race and Politics in the South

On southern politics the seminal book for the post-Reconstruction period is C. Vann Woodward, *Origins of the New South, 1877–1913* (1951), which still defines the terms of discussion among historians. The most far-reaching revision is Edward L. Ayers, *The Promise of the New South* (1992). Complementary books on the social basis of southern politics are Dwight B. Billings, *Planters and the Making of the "New South": North Carolina, 1865–1900* (1979), and Paul Escott, *Many Excellent People: Power and Privilege in North Carolina, 1850–1900* (1985).

The classic book on segregation is C. Vann Woodward, *The Strange Career of Jim Crow* (2nd ed., 1968), but it should be supplemented by Howard N. Rabinowitz, *Race Relations in the Urban South, 1865–1890* (1978). A powerful analysis of southern racism, stressing its psychosocial roots, is Joel Williamson, *A Rage for Order: Black/White Relations in the American South since Emancipation* (1986). Disfranchisement is treated with great analytic sophistication in J. Morgan Kousser, *The Shaping of Southern Politics: Suffrage Restriction and the Establishment of the One-Party South, 1880–1910* (1974). August Meier, *Negro Thought in America, 1880–1915* (1963), is a key analysis of black accommodation and protest. The preeminent exponent of accommodation is the subject of a superb two-volume biography by Louis B. Harlan, *Booker T. Washington: The Making of a Black Leader* (1973) and *Wizard of Tuskegee* (1983); and equally fine on Washington's main critic is David Levering Lewis, *W. E. B. Du Bois: Biography of a Race, 1868–1919* (1993).

The Rise of the City

Visiting his fiancée's Missouri farm home in 1894, Theodore Dreiser was struck by "the spirit of rural America, its idealism, its dreams." But this was an "American tradition in which I, alas!, could not share." Said Dreiser, "I had seen Pittsburgh. I had seen Lithuanians and Hungarians in their 'courts' and hovels. I had seen the girls of the city—walking the streets at night." Only twenty-three at the time, Dreiser would go on six years later to publish one of the great American urban novels—*Sister Carrie*—about one young woman in the army of small-town Americans flocking to the Big City in the late nineteenth century. But Dreiser, a member of that army, already knew that between rural America and Pittsburgh an unbridgeable chasm had opened up.

In 1820, after 200 years of settlement, fewer than one American in twenty had lived in a city with a population of 10,000. After that, decade by decade, the urban population swelled until, by 1900, one of every five Americans lived in cities of over 100,000 residents. The same process was happening in Europe, but at a slower pace. During the nineteenth century, the percentage of Europeans living in cities tripled while in the United States the increase was sevenfold, with the greatest growth taking place in the metropolitan centers. In 1900 nearly a tenth of the nation—6.5 million persons—lived in just three cities: New York, Chicago, and Philadelphia. The late nineteenth century, an economist remarked in 1899, was "not only the age of cities, but the age of great cities."

The city was the arena of America's vibrant economic life. Here the factories went up, and here the

Mulberry Street, New York City, c. 1900
The influx of southern and eastern Europeans created teeming ghettos in the heart of New York City and other major American cities. The view is of Mulberry Street, with its pushcarts, street peddlers, and bustling traffic. The inhabitants are mostly Italians, and some of them, noticing the photographer preparing his camera, have gathered to be in the picture.
Library of Congress.

multitudes of working people settled. New immigrants swelled the ranks of the working class: at the turn of the century upwards of 30 percent of the residents of major American cities were foreign-born. Here, too, lived the millionaires and a growing white-collar middle class. For all these people the city was more than a place to make a living; it provided the setting for an urban culture unlike anything seen before in the United States. City people, though differing vastly among themselves, became distinctively and recognizably urban.

Urbanization

★

The march to the cities seemed inevitable to nineteenth-century Americans (Map 19.1). "The greater part of our population must live in cities—cities much greater than the world has yet known," declared Congregational minister Josiah Strong in 1898. "In due time we shall be a nation of cities." There was "no

resisting the trend," said another writer. Urbanization became inevitable because of its link to another inevitability of American life—industrialization.

Industrial Sources of City Growth

Until the Civil War, cities were centers of commerce, not industry. They were the places where merchants bought and sold goods for distribution into the interior of the country or shipment out to the world market. Early industrialism sprang up in the countryside. Mills and factories needed water power from streams and rivers, access to sources of fuel and raw materials, and workers drawn from the surplus farm population. Of the nation's fifteen largest cities in 1860, only five reported as much as 10 percent of the labor force engaged in manufacturing activity.

After midcentury, industry began to abandon the countryside. Once steam engines came along, mill operators no longer needed to locate along streams. In the iron industry, coal replaced charcoal as the primary fuel, so iron makers did not have to be near forests. Improved transportation, especially the railroads, gave

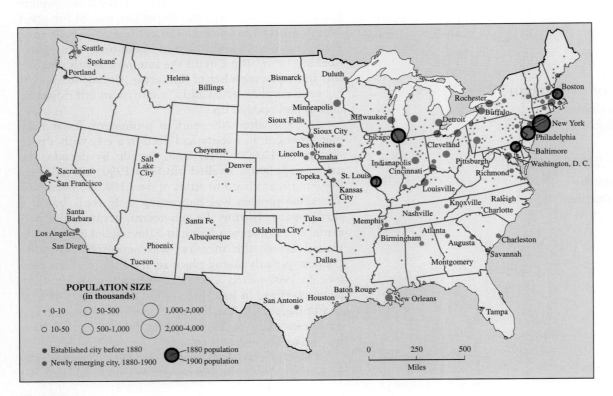

MAP 19.1

The Growth of America's Cities, 1880–1900

The number of Americans living in urban places more than doubled between 1880 and 1900. The most dramatic increases occurred in the largest metropolitan centers. New York grew from 1.2 million to 3.4 million, Chicago from 500,000 to 1.7 million. Notable among newly emerging cities—places that had been small towns or minor cities in 1880—were Los Angeles, Seattle, Birmingham, Omaha, and Atlanta.

TABLE 19.1

Ten Largest Cities by Population, 1870 and 1910

1870		1910	
City	Population	City	Population
1. New York	942,292	New York	4,766,883
2. Philadelphia	674,022	Chicago	2,185,283
3. Brooklyn*	419,921	Philadelphia	1,549,008
4. St. Louis	310,864	St. Louis	687,029
5. Chicago	298,977	Boston	670,585
6. Baltimore	267,354	Cleveland	560,663
7. Boston	250,526	Baltimore	558,485
8. Cincinnati	216,239	Pittsburgh	533,905
9. New Orleans	191,418	Detroit	465,766
10. San Francisco	149,473	Buffalo	423,715

*Brooklyn was consolidated with New York in 1898.
Source: U.S. Census data.

entrepreneurs greater latitude in selecting the best sites in relation to supplies and markets. The result was a geographic concentration of industry. Iron makers gravitated to Pittsburgh because of its access not only to coal and iron ore but also to markets for iron and steel products. Chicago, ideally located between western livestock suppliers and eastern consuming markets, became a great meatpacking center in the 1870s (see Map 17.3).

Many smaller cities became one-industry towns. Youngstown, Ohio, and Johnstown, Pennsylvania, specialized in iron and steel; Brockton and Haverhill, Massachusetts, in boots and shoes; Troy, New York, in collars and cuffs; East Liverpool, Ohio, in pottery. Other cities processed the raw materials of their regions. Sacramento canned fruits and vegetables, Richmond made cigarettes, Minneapolis milled grain, and Memphis handled lumber and produced cottonseed oil.

As factories became bigger, their size contributed to urban growth. A plant that employed thousands of workers instantly created a small city in its vicinity, sometimes a company town like Aliquippa, Pennsylvania, which became body and soul the property of the Jones and Laughlin Steel Company. Many firms set up their plants near a large city so they could draw on its labor supply and transportation facilities, as George Pullman did in 1880 when he located his sleeping-car works and model town southwest of Chicago.

Sometimes the nearby metropolis spread and absorbed the smaller city, which was the fate of Pullman's town. Elsewhere, as in northern New Jersey or along Lake Michigan south of Chicago, the lines

between industrial towns blurred and an extended urban-industrial area emerged. The same process could be seen in Europe, where industrial regions were emerging in northeastern France around Lille and in Germany's Ruhr Valley.

The established commercial cities also became more industrial. Warehouse districts could readily be converted to small-scale manufacturing; a distribution network and transportation facilities were right at hand. In addition, as gateways for immigrants, port cities offered abundant cheap labor. Boston, Philadelphia, Baltimore, and San Francisco became hives of small-scale, labor-intensive industrial activity. An enormous pool of immigrant workers made New York a magnet for the garment trades, cigar making, and diversified light industry. Preeminent as a city of trade and finance, New York also ranked in the late nineteenth century as the nation's largest manufacturing center.

By 1870, a core industrial region had formed from New England down through the Middle Atlantic states to Maryland. In this region the percentage of people living in urban areas was twice the national average. Forty years later, in 1910, the original industrial core was nearly three-quarters urbanized. It had also thrust westward to include the Great Lakes states, which became America's industrial heartland. Important new centers for steel making, manufacturing, and food processing sprang up in this region. Pittsburgh, Cleveland, Detroit, Milwaukee, Minneapolis—all of them small cities or modest commercial centers in 1870—had by 1910 grown into major industrial cities with from 300,000 to well over half a million inhabitants (Table 19.1).

City Building

The commercial cities of the early nineteenth century had been compact places, densely settled around a harbor or along a river. As late as 1850, when it had 565,000 people, greater Philadelphia covered only 10 square miles. From the foot of Chestnut Street on the Delaware River a person could walk almost anywhere in the city within forty-five minutes. Thereafter, however, Philadelphia—and indeed all American cities—tended to spread out as they developed.

A downtown area emerged, usually in what had been the original commercial city. Downtown in turn broke up into shopping, financial, warehousing, manufacturing, hotel and entertainment, and red-light districts. Somewhat fluid at their edges, all these districts were well-defined areas of specialized activity. Moving out from the center, industrial development tended to follow the arteries of transportation—railroads, canals, and rivers—and, at the city's outskirts, to spread out into complexes of heavy industry. At the same time the middle class in large numbers moved out to new suburban areas.

Urban development was markedly different in continental Europe, where even cities growing rapidly in population remained physically compact, with built-up areas ending abruptly at the surrounding countryside. In America cities constantly expanded, spilling beyond their formal boundaries and forming what the federal census began to designate in 1910 as metropolitan areas. While American cities were highly congested at the center, their population density was actually much below that of European cities: 22 persons per acre for fifteen American cities in the 1890s, for example, versus 157.6 for a comparable group of German cities. Given this difference, the development of efficient urban transportation had a much higher priority in the United States than in Europe.

"The only trouble about this town," wrote Mark Twain on arriving in New York in 1867, "is that it is too large. You cannot accomplish anything in the way of business, you cannot even pay a friendly call, without devoting a whole day to it. . . . The distances are too great." Finding ways of moving nearly a million New Yorkers around was not as hopeless as Twain thought, but it did pose a challenge to city builders. The city demanded innovation no less than industry itself did and, in the end, compiled an equally impressive record of technological achievement.

Mass Transit. The first innovation, dating back to the 1820s, had been the omnibus, an elongated version of the horse-drawn coach. The omnibus was a convenience but did not do much to relieve congestion; downtown, people could walk just as fast. Much more efficient was the horsecar, which ran on iron tracks, enabling the cars to carry more passengers, move them at a faster clip through congested city streets, and reach out into the residential areas. All this happened because of a modest but crucial refinement in railroad track design in 1852—a grooved rail that was flush with the pavement. From the 1850s onward, horsecars were the mainstay of urban transit across America, accounting for 70 percent of the traffic.

Then came the electric trolley car. Its development was primarily the work of Frank J. Sprague, an electrical engineer once employed by the great inventor Thomas A. Edison. In 1887 Sprague designed an electricity-driven system for Richmond, Virginia: a "trolley" carriage running along an overhead power line was attached by cable to streetcars equipped with an electric motor—hence the name trolley car. After Sprague's success, the electric trolley swiftly displaced the horsecar and by 1900 became the primary means of public transportation in most American cities.

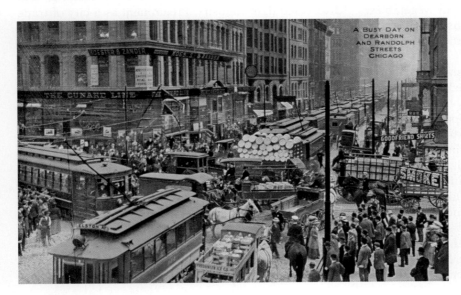

Traffic Jam in Downtown Chicago, 1905
The purpose of urban transit systems was to move masses of people rapidly and efficiently through the city. However, better transportation brought more congestion as well, as this scene of gridlock at Dearborn and Randolph streets in Chicago shows.
Curt Teich Postcard Archives.

In the great metropolitan centers, however, mounting congestion led to demands that public transit be moved off the streets. Affluent suburbanites had long used the railroad to commute to the city. The problem was how to harness railway technology to the needs of ordinary city dwellers. In 1879 the first elevated lines went into operation on Sixth and Ninth avenues in New York City. Powered at first by steam engine, the "els" converted to electricity following Sprague's success with the trolley. Chicago developed elevated transit most fully (Map 19.2). New York, meanwhile, turned to the subway. Boston opened a short underground line in 1897, but it was the completion in 1904 of a subway running the length of Manhattan that demonstrated the full potential of underground mass transit. Thinly settled areas of northern Manhattan and the Bronx, predicted the *New York Times*, would soon boast "a population of ten millions . . . housed comfortably, healthfully and relatively cheaply." The subway would especially delight "all who travel with the sole purpose of 'getting there' in the least time possible." Mass transit had become *rapid* transit.

In 1890 the number of passengers carried on American street railways was more than 2 billion per year, over twice that of the rest of the world combined. Berlin, which boasted the best system in Europe, had a per capita usage that was exceeded by twenty-one American cities. In Great Britain the horsecar remained dominant long after it had disappeared from American streets. In Tokyo, the biggest Asian city, the horsecar was not even introduced until 1882, and electric streetcars first appeared there in 1903.

City Structures: Bridges, Skyscrapers, Terminals. Rivers, in earlier times the city's lifeline of trade, now became barriers that interrupted rail traffic and hindered urban expansion. Hundreds of iron and steel bridges went up in the second half of the nineteenth century. Some from this great age of bridge construction—among them the Eads Bridge (1873), spanning the Mississippi River at St. Louis, and the Brooklyn Bridge (1883), over New York's East River—are still in use. Linking Brooklyn and Manhattan, the Brooklyn Bridge took fifteen years to build. A giant suspension structure, it was not only an engineering marvel but the symbol of the new industrial era—"the first product of the age of coal and iron to achieve completeness of expression," wrote the twentieth-century architectural critic Lewis Mumford.

If urban transit evolved in response to the geographic expansion of the American city, the need for more space in the downtown business districts drove advances in building construction. New materials made it possible to construct commercial buildings of greater height, interior space, and fire resistance. With the availability by the 1880s of steel girders, mass-produced durable plate glass, and the passenger elevator, a wholly new way of construction opened up. A steel skeleton would support the building, and the walls, previously weight bearing, would serve as curtains enclosing the structure. The sky, so to speak, became the limit.

The first "skyscraper" to be built on this principle was William Jenney's ten-story Home Insurance Building (1885) in Chicago. Although this pioneering effort was itself conventional in appearance—it looked just like the other commercial buildings in the downtown

The Chicago Elevated, 1900
This is Wabash Avenue, looking north from Adams Street. For Americans from farms and small towns, this photograph by William Henry Jackson captured something of the peculiarity of the urban scene. What could be stranger than a railroad suspended above the streets in the midst of people's lives?
KEA Publishing Services Ltd.

MAP 19.2

The Expansion of Chicago, 1865–1902

In 1865 Chicagoans depended on horsecar lines to get around town. By 1900 the city limits had expanded enormously, accompanied by an equally dramatic extension of streetcar service, by then electrified. Elevated trains also helped ease congestion in the urban core. New streetcar lines, some extending beyond the city limits, were important to suburban development in the coming years.

of the fifty-five story Woolworth Building. Aptly called the Cathedral of Commerce, the Woolworth Building towered over its neighbors and marked the beginning of the modern Manhattan skyline.

By contrast, the magnificent rail terminals that graced the great cities tried to mask their function. Reflecting the architectural forms of ages past, the terminals were marvels of structural design in their soaring interiors and use of steel, glass, and stone. New York's Grand Central Station (1913), built in the French baroque style, was completely electrified. It made superb use of underground space and had a loop system that enabled trains to turn around without reversing course.

The Electric City. For ordinary citizens the electric lights that dispelled the gloom of the city at night probably offered the most dramatic evidence that times had changed. The mainstay of city lighting since the early nineteenth century had been gaslight—illuminating gas produced from coal—but, at 12 candlepower, gaslight was too dim to brighten the downtown streets and public spaces of the modern city. The first use of electricity, when generating technology made it commercially feasible, was for better city lighting. Charles F. Brush's electric arc lamps, installed in the windows of the Wanamaker department store in Philadelphia in 1878, threw a brilliant light and soon replaced gas lamps in stores and hotel lobbies and on city streets across the country. The following year Thomas Edison created the first practical incandescent light bulb, which brought electric lighting into American homes. Edison's motto—"Let there be light!"—truly described the experience of the modern city. Before electricity had any significant effect on industry, it gave the city its modern tempo, lifting and lowering elevators, powering streetcars and subway trains, turning night into day.

Meanwhile the telephone, patented by Alexander Graham Bell in 1876, speeded up communication beyond anything imagined previously. Twain's complaint of 1867 that it was impossible to carry on business in New York had been answered: all he needed to do was pick up the phone.

The City as Private Enterprise

City building was very much an exercise in private enterprise. The lure of profit spurred the great innovations—the trolley car, electric lighting, the skyscraper, the elevator, the telephone—and drove urban real-estate development. The investment opportunities looked so tempting that new cities sprang up almost overnight from the ruins of the Chicago fire of 1871 and the San Francisco earthquake of 1906. Real-estate interests, eager to develop subdivisions, were often instrumental in pushing streetcar lines outward from the central districts of cities.

district—the steel-girdered structure swiftly liberated the aesthetic perceptions of American architects. A Chicago school sprang up, dedicated to the design of buildings whose form expressed, rather than masked, their structure and function. The masterpiece of the Chicago school was Louis Sullivan's Carson, Pirie, Scott and Company department store (1904).

Chicago pioneered skyscraper construction, but the island of Manhattan, with its unrelenting need for prime downtown space, took the lead after the mid-1890s. The climax of New York's turn-of-the-century construction surge came with the completion in 1913

Thomas Edison's Laboratories in Menlo Park, New Jersey, c. 1880
Thomas Edison's dream of illuminating the world is illustrated by this fanciful drawing
of his laboratories in Menlo Park, New Jersey. For the time being, however, it was the
American home that was the primary beneficiary of Edison's wonderful lightbulb, since
electricity was slow to arrive in many parts of the world.
U.S. Department of the Interior, National Park Service, Edison National Historic Site.

Urban transit became big business. In the early 1880s Peter A. B. Widener and William L. Elkins teamed up to unite much of Philadelphia's streetcar system in the Philadelphia Traction Company. They did the same in alliance with Charles T. Yerkes in Chicago and with William C. Whitney and Thomas Fortune Ryan in New York. By 1900 their syndicate controlled streetcar systems in more than a hundred cities, as well as utilities supplying gas and electricity to urban customers. The city, like industry, became an arena for enterprise and profit.

Providing services privately, however, was a political choice. Under state laws cities had extensive powers of self-development. In authorizing a municipally owned subway in New York City in 1897, for example, the state courts reaffirmed the right of cities to carry out their responsibilities as they saw fit. Even the use of privately owned land was subject to whatever regulations the city might impose. Thus the skylines of Chicago and Boston did not resemble Manhattan's partly because of the limits those cities imposed on the heights of buildings.

But, as compared to Europe, American cities used their broad powers sparingly. America produced what the urban historian Sam Bass Warner has called the "private city"—one shaped primarily by the actions of many private individuals. All these persons pursued their own goals and tried to maximize their own profit. The prevailing belief was that the sum of such private activity would far exceed what the community could accomplish through public effort. This meant that the city itself handled only functions that could not be undertaken efficiently or profitably by private enterprise.

Despite that limitation, American cities actually compiled an impressive record in the late nineteenth century. Though by no means free of the corruption and wastefulness of earlier days, city governments in these years became more centralized, better administered, and, above all, more expansive in the functions they undertook. Nowhere in the world were there more massive public projects: aqueducts, sewage systems, street paving, bridge building, extensive park systems.

The Urban Environment. Yet streets, mainly a matter of convenience for the people, were often filthy. "Three or four days of warm spring weather," remarked a New York journalist, would turn Manhattan's garbage-strewn, snow-clogged streets into "veritable mud rivers." The environment likewise suffered. A visitor to Pittsburgh noted "the heavy pall of smoke which constantly overhangs her . . . until the very sun looks coppery through the sooty haze." As for the lovely hills rising from the rivers, "they have been leveled down, cut into, sliced off, and ruthlessly marred and mutilated, until not a trace of their original outlines remains." Pittsburgh presented "all that is unsightly and forbidding in appearance, the original beauties of nature having been ruthlessly sacrificed to utility."

It was not that America lacked an urban vision. On the contrary, an abiding rural ideal had exerted a powerful influence on American cities for many years. Frederick Law Olmsted, who designed New York's Central Park, wanted cities that exposed people to the beauties of nature. One of Olmsted's projects, the Chicago World's Fair of 1893, gave rise to the influential "City Beautiful" movement. The results included larger park systems, broad boulevards and parkways, and, after the turn of the century, zoning laws and planned suburbs.

But cities usually heeded urban planners too little and far too late. "Fifteen or twenty years ago a plan might have been adopted that would have made this one of the most beautiful cities in the world," Kansas City's park commissioners reported in 1893. At that time, however, "such a policy could not be fully appreciated." Nor, the commissioners concluded, even if Kansas City had foreseen its future, would it have shouldered the "heavy burden" of trying to shape its development. The American city had placed its faith in the operations of the marketplace, not the restraints of a planned future.

Even with planning, the city's dynamism often confounded efforts to meet the needs of the people. When completed in 1842, New York's Croton aqueduct was hailed as "more akin in magnificence to the ancient and Roman aqueducts [than anything] achieved in our times." Yet less than a decade later water consumption was exceeding the capacity of the aqueduct. In 1885 New York started to build a second and larger aqueduct. That one also failed to meet the city's needs, so New York built still another aqueduct a hundred miles away in the Catskill Mountains. Each new facility and innovation seemed to fall short, not merely outstripped by the rising demand but also contributing to that demand. This occurred with urban transportation, high-rise buildings, and modern sanitation systems. They attracted more users, created new needs, and caused additional crowding and shortages.

Congested Housing. Hardest hit by urban growth were the poor. In earlier times low-income city residents had lived in makeshift wooden structures in alleys and back streets or in the subdivided homes of more prosperous families who had fled to better neighborhoods. When rising land values after the Civil War made this practice unprofitable, speculators began to build housing specifically designed for the urban masses. In New York City, the dreadful result was the "dumbbell" tenement, shaped to utilize nearly all the standard lot of 25 by 100 feet. A five-story building of this type could house twenty families in cramped, airless apartments (Figure 19.1). In New York's Eleventh Ward an average of 986 persons occupied each acre, a density matched only by Bombay, India. In other cities crowding was not as severe. Chicago, Boston, and St. Louis relied on two- and three-story buildings for low-income housing, while Philadelphia and Baltimore made do with dingy row houses.

FIGURE 19.1
Floor Plan of a Dumbbell Tenement
In a contest for a design that met an 1879 requirement that every room have a window, the dumbbell tenement won. The interior indentation, which created an airshaft between adjoining buildings, gave the tenement its "dumbbell" shape. What was touted as a "model" tenement demonstrated instead the futility of trying to reconcile maximum land usage with decent housing. Each floor contained four apartments of three or four rooms, the largest only 10 by 11 feet. The two toilets in the hall became filthy or broke down under the daily use by forty or more people. The narrow airshaft provided almost no light for the interior rooms and served mainly as a dumping ground for garbage. So deplorable were these tenements that they became the stimulus for the next wave of New York housing reform.

Civic-minded people everywhere considered these districts to be blights on the city. Here is how one investigator described Chicago's Halsted Street in 1896:

> *The filthy and rotten tenements, the dingy courts and tumble-down sheds, the foul stables and dilapidated outhouses, the broken sewer pipes, the piles of garbage fairly alive with diseased odors, and . . . children filling every nook, working and playing in every room, eating and sleeping in every windowsill, pouring in and out of every door, and seeming literally to pave every scrap of "yard."*

Reformers recognized the problem but seemed unable to solve it. Some favored model tenements financed by public-spirited citizens willing to accept a limited return on their investment. When private philanthropy failed to make much of a dent in the problem, cities turned to housing codes. The most advanced of these was New York's Tenement House Law of 1901, which required interior courts, indoor toilets, and fire safeguards for new housing, but did little about existing housing stock. Commercial development pushed up land values in downtown areas. Only high-density, cheaply built housing could earn a sufficient profit for the landlords of the poor. This economic fact defied nineteenth-century solutions.

A Balance Sheet: Chicago and Berlin. Chicago and Berlin had virtually equal populations in 1900. Their histories, however, were profoundly different. Seventy years earlier, when Chicago was just a muddy frontier outpost, Berlin was a city of 250,000 and the capital of the kingdom of Prussia.

With Prussia's unification of the German Empire in 1871, the Hohenzollern rulers rebuilt Berlin on a grander scale. "A capital city is essential for the state, to act as a pivot for its culture," proclaimed Prussian historian Heinrich von Treitschke. Berlin served that national purpose—"a center where Germany's political, intellectual, and material life is concentrated, and its people can feel united." Chicago had no such pretensions. It was strictly a place of business, made great by virtue of its strategic grip on the commerce of America's industrial heartland. Nothing in Chicago evoked the grandeur of Berlin's boulevards or its monumental palaces and public buildings, nor were Chicagoans ever witness to the pomp and ceremony of the imperial parades through the Brandenburg Gate and up broad, tree-lined Unter den Linden to the national cathedral.

Yet as a functioning city Chicago was in many ways superior to Berlin. Chicago's waterworks pumped 500 million gallons of water a day, providing 139 gallons of water per person, while Berliners had to make do with 18 gallons. Flush toilets, a rarity in Berlin in 1900, could be found in 60 percent of Chicago's homes. Its streets were lit by electricity while Berlin still relied mostly on gaslight. Chicago had a much more extensive streetcar system, twice as much acreage devoted to parks, and a public library containing many more volumes than Berlin's. And Chicago had just completed an amazing sanitation project, reversing the course of the Chicago River so that its waters—and the city's sewage—would flow away from Lake Michigan and southward down into the Illinois and Mississippi rivers.

Giant sanitation projects were one thing; an inspiring urban environment was something else. For well-traveled Americans admiring of things European, the sense of inferiority was palpable. "We are enormously rich," admitted the journalist Edwin L. Godkin, "but . . . what have we got to show? Almost nothing. Ugliness from an artistic point of view is the mark of all our cities." Thus the urban balance sheet: a utilitarian infrastructure that was superb by nineteenth-century standards but "no municipal splendors of any description, nothing but population and hotels."

City People

————————★————————

With its soaring skyscrapers, jostling traffic, and hum of business activity, the city symbolized energy and enterprise. When the budding writer Hamlin Garland and his brother arrived in Chicago from rural Iowa in 1881, they knew immediately that they had entered a new world: "Everything interested us. . . . Nothing was commonplace, nothing was ugly to us." In one way or another every city-bound migrant, whether from the American countryside or from a foreign land, experienced something of this exhilaration and wonder.

Newcomers

With the opportunity and boundless variety came disorder and uncertainty. The urban world was utterly unlike the rural communities the newcomers had left. In the countryside every person had been known to his or her neighbors. Mark Twain found New York "a splendid desert, where a stranger is lonely in the midst of a million of his race. A man walks his tedious miles through the same interminable streets every day, yet never seeing a familiar face, and never seeing a strange one the second time. . . . Every man rushes, rushes, rushes, and never has time to be companionable—never has any time at his disposal to fool away on matters which do not involve dollars and duty and business." If rural roles and obligations had been well understood, in the city the only predictable relationships were those dictated by the marketplace.

Italian Bread Peddlers, New York City
Because of crowded conditions in East Side tenements, immigrant life spilled out onto the streets, which offered a bit of fresh air, a chance to socialize with neighbors, and a place to shop for food, including bread.
KEA Publishing Services Ltd.

The newcomers could never re-create in the city the worlds they had left behind. But they found ways to gain a sense of belonging, they built a multitude of new institutions, and they learned how to function in an impersonal, heterogeneous environment. An urban culture emerged, and through it there developed a new breed of American who was entirely at home in the modern city.

Immigrants. At the turn of the century, upwards of 30 percent of the residents of New York, Chicago, Boston, Cleveland, Minneapolis, and San Francisco were foreign-born. The dominant groups still represented mainly the older migration from northern Europe. The biggest ethnic group in Boston was Irish; in Minneapolis, Swedish; in most other northern cities, German. But by 1910 the influx from southern and eastern Europe had changed the ethnic complexion of many of these cities. The experience of Philadelphia is shown in Table 19.2. In Chicago, Poles took the lead; in New York, eastern European Jews; in San Francisco, Italians.

All these immigrants—old and new—brought with them homeland experiences and customs that shaped their lives in the New World. But for the later arrivals from southern and eastern Europe there was less intermingling with the resident populations than in the earlier "walking cities." Beginning in the 1880s, observers invariably reported that only foreign-born people lived in the poorer downtown areas. "One may find for the asking an Italian, a German, a French, African, Spanish, Bohemian, Russian, Scandinavian, Jewish, and Chinese colony," remarked the Danish American journalist Jacob Riis in his study of New York in 1890. "The one thing you shall vainly ask for in the chief city of America is a distinctively American community."

The later arrivals from southern and eastern Europe had little choice about where they lived; they needed to be near their jobs and to find cheap housing. Some gravitated to the outlying factory districts; others settled in the congested downtown ghettos. The immigrants did not settle randomly in these districts, however. Even where this seemed to happen, as in Philadelphia, closer study revealed that ethnic groups clustered in certain houses and portions of blocks. More commonly, as Riis discovered, an ethnic group took over an entire neighborhood. In New York City, Italians crowded into the formerly Irish neighborhoods west of Broadway, and Russian and Polish Jews pushed the Germans out of the Lower East Side (Map 19.3). A colony of Hungarians lived around Houston Street, and Bohemians occupied stretches of the Upper East Side between Fiftieth and Seventy-sixth streets.

Within ethnic groups, one could also spot clusters of people from the same province or even village. Among New York Italians, for example, Neapolitans and Calabrians populated the Mulberry Bend district, while Genoese lived on Baxter Street. Other northern

TABLE 19.2		
Foreign-Born Population of Philadelphia, 1870 and 1910		
	1870	*1910*
Irish	96,698	83,196
German	50,746	61,480
Austrian	519	19,860
Italian	516	45,308
Russian	94	90,697
Hungarian	52	12,495
Foreign-born population	183,624	384,707
Total population	674,022	1,549,008

Source: Allen F. Davis and Mark Haller, *The Peoples of Philadelphia* (Philadelphia: Temple University Press, 1973), 205.

Italians occupied the Eighth and Fifteenth wards west of Broadway, while southern Italians moved into "Little Italy" far uptown in Harlem. In 1903, along a short stretch of Elizabeth Street there lived several hundred families from a single Sicilian fishing town, Sciacca, and Sciacca's patron saint was celebrated on Elizabeth Street, as in Sicily.

Capitalizing on the fellow-feeling that drew ethnic groups together, a variety of institutions sprang up to meet the immigrants' needs. Wherever substantial numbers lived, newspapers appeared. In 1911 the twenty thousand Poles in Buffalo, New York, supported two Polish-language daily papers. Immigrants throughout the country avidly read *Il Progresso Italo-Americano* and the Yiddish-language *Jewish Daily Forward*, both published in New York City (see American Voices, "Anonymous: Bintel Brief," p. 619). Companionship could always be found on streetcorners, in barbershops and club rooms, and in saloons. Italians marched in saint's-day parades, Bohemians gathered in singing societies, and New York Jews patronized a lively Yiddish theater. To provide help in times of sickness and death, the immigrants organized mutual-aid societies. The Italians of Chicago had sixty-six of these organizations in 1903, composed mainly of people from particular provinces and towns. Immigrants built a rich and functional institutional life in urban America, to an extent unimagined in their native villages.

Urban Blacks. The vast majority of African Americans—85 percent in 1880—lived in the rural South. In the ensuing years some of them migrated to the modestly growing southern cities. By 1900 blacks constituted roughly a third of the South's urban population, ranging from 20 percent in Louisville and Dallas to majorities in Memphis and Charleston.

The great African American migration to northern cities was just beginning. The black population of New York increased by 30,000 to 91,000 between 1900 and 1910, making New York second only to Washington, D.C. Blacks in New York in 1910 still represented less than 2 percent of that population, which was roughly their percentage in Chicago and Cleveland as well.

Despite their relatively small numbers, urban blacks could not escape discrimination. They retreated from the scattered black neighborhoods of older times into concentrated ghettos—Chicago's black belt on the South Side, for example, or the early outlines of New York's Harlem. Race prejudice likewise cut down job opportunities. Twenty-six percent of Cleveland's blacks had been skilled workers in 1870, but only 12 percent were by 1890, and entire occupations such as barbering (except for a black clientele) disappeared. Two-thirds of Cleveland's blacks in 1910 worked as domestics and day laborers, with little hope of moving up the job ladder.

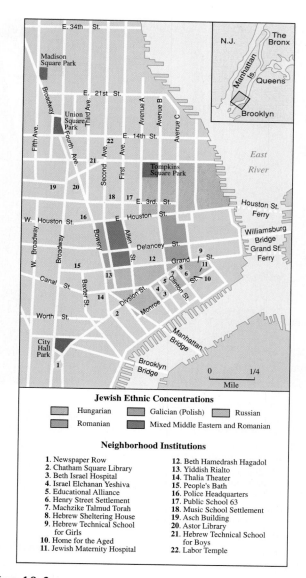

Map 19.3

The Lower East Side, New York City, in 1900

As this map shows, the Jewish immigrants dominating Manhattan's Lower East Side preferred living in neighborhoods populated by those from their home regions of eastern Europe. Their sense of a common identity made for a remarkable flowering of educational, cultural, and social institutions on the Jewish East Side.

In the face of pervasive discrimination, urban blacks built their own communities. They created a flourishing press, fraternal orders, a vast array of women's organizations, and a middle class of doctors, lawyers, and small entrepreneurs who catered to their needs. Above all, there were the black churches—twenty-five in Chicago in 1905, mainly Methodist and Baptist. More than any other institution, remarked one scholar in 1913, it was the church "which the Negro may call his own. . . . A new church may be built . . . and . . . all the machinery set in motion without ever con-

The Economy of the Ghetto
Downtown immigrant neighborhoods would not have struck
the casual observer as industrial districts, but tucked away in
the tenements were commercial lofts and small workshops.
An entire ready-made clothing industry flourished within the
ghettos of large cities, drawing especially on the young women
of the neighborhood to perform the low-paid sewing tasks in
often dangerous conditions.
Brown Brothers.

The Cherry Family, 1906
Wiley and Fannie Cherry migrated in 1893 from North Carolina to Chicago, settling in the small African American community on the West Side. The Cherrys apparently prospered,
and by 1906, when this family portrait was taken, had entered
the black middle class. When migration intensified after 1900,
longer-settled urban blacks like the Cherrys became uncomfortable, and relations with the needy, rural newcomers were
often tense.
Courtesy Lorraine Heflin/Chicago Historical Society.

sulting any white person. . . . [It] more than anything
else represents the real life of the race." As in the southern countryside, the church was the central institution
for city blacks, and the preacher the most important
local citizen. Manhattan's Union Baptist Church,
housed like many others in a storefront, attracted the
"very recent residents of this new, disturbing city" and,
ringing with spirituals and fervent prayer, made Christianity come "alive Sunday mornings."

Ward Politics

Race and ethnicity tended to divide newcomers to the
city and turn them in on themselves. Politics, in contrast,
acted as a powerful instrument for integrating them into
the larger urban society. Every migrant to an American
city automatically became a ward resident and, by living
on a particular street, immediately acquired a spokesman
at city hall in the form of an alderman.

In earlier days aldermen had been the dominant figures in urban politics, but that was no longer the case in
the late nineteenth century. Power had largely passed to

the mayor's office and various city administrative agencies. But the city council still represented the parochial
interests of the wards, and immigrants learned very
quickly that if they needed anything from city hall, the
alderman was the person to see. That was how streets got
paved, or water mains extended, or a variance granted—
so that, for example, in 1888 Vito Fortounescere could
"place and keep a stand for the sale of fruit, inside the
stoop-line, in front of the northeast corner of Twenty-
eighth Street and Fourth Avenue" in Manhattan, and the
parishioners of Saint Maria of Mount Carmel could set
off fireworks at their Fourth of July picnic.

Machine control of political parties, present at
every level, flourished most luxuriantly in the big cities.
Urban machines depended on a loyal grass-roots con-

ANONYMOUS
Bintel Brief

———————★———————

In Yiddish bintel brief *means "bundle of letters." That was the name of the famous section of the* Jewish Daily Forward *devoted to letters from immigrant readers about their trials and tribulations in America.*

I am a girl sixteen years old. I live together with my parents and my two old sisters. Last year I met a young man. We love one another. He is a very respectable man, and makes a fine living. My sisters have no fiances. I know that should I marry they will never talk to me. My parents are also strongly against it since I am the youngest child. I do not want to lose my parents' love, and neither do I want to lose my lover because that would break my heart. Give me some advice, dear Editor!

I was born in a small town in Russia, and until I was sixteen I studied in *Talmud Torahs* and *yeshivas,* but when I came to America I developed spiritually and became a freethinker. Yet every year when the time of *Rosh Hashana* and *Yom Kippur* comes around I become very gloomy. . . . So strong are my feelings that I enter the synagogue, not in order to pray to God but to heal and refresh my aching soul by sitting among *landsleit* [countrymen] and listening to the cantor's sweet melodies. The members of my Progressive Society don't understand. They say I am a hypocrite. . . . What do you think? *Answer.* No one can tell another what to do with himself on *Yom Kippur.*

I am a Russian revolutionist and a freethinker. Here in America I became acquainted with a girl who is also a freethinker. We decided to marry, but the problem is that she has Orthodox parents, and if we refuse a religious ceremony we will be cut off from them forever. I don't know what to do. Therefore, I ask you to advise me how to act. *Answer.* There are times when it is better to be kind in order not to grieve old parents.

To a man everything is permissible, to a woman nothing. A man is king over us and may do his will. When I argue that morality is more demanding on women, my husband gets angry and denies it with all his might. There is no such thing as a man with a bad name, but just let one spot fall upon a woman. . . . Why?!

I am in favor of giving women full rights, but most of my friends are against it. They argue that the woman would then no longer be the housewife, the mother to her children, the wife to her husband—in a word, everything would be destroyed. I do not agree because a woman is a human being just like a man, and if women are recognized as human beings, they must be granted all the rights of human beings. *Answer.* Justice can reign among people only when they all have equal rights.

Why do the police favor the clothing stores on Canal Street which remain open seven days a week? . . . Where else in the world do people sell their lives to make a living with no holidays and no rest? I am one of the corpses who works seven days a week in one of those electric-lit graves on Canal Street.

I am a young man of twenty-five, and I recently met a fine girl. She has a flaw, however—a dimple in her chin. It is said that people who have this lose their first husband or wife. I love her very much. But I'm afraid to marry her lest I die because of the dimple. *Answer.* The tragedy is not that the girl has a dimple in her chin but that some people have a screw loose in their heads.

———————————

Source: Irving Howe and Kenneth Libo, eds., *How We Lived* (New York: New American Library, 1979), 88–90.

stituency, so each ward was divided into election districts of a few blocks. The district captain reported to the ward boss, who was likely also to be the alderman. The main job of these functionaries was to be accessible and, as best they could, to serve the needs of the party faithful.

The machine similarly served the business community. Contractors sought city business; gas companies and streetcar lines wanted licenses and privileges; manufacturers needed services and not-too-nosy inspectors; and the liquor trade and numbers racket relied on a tolerant police force. All of them turned to the machine boss and his lieutenants. In addition to these everyday functions, the machine continuously mediated among conflicting interests and oiled the wheels of city government.

The machines filled a void in the public life of the nineteenth-century city. They did informally much of what the municipal system left undone. "Nowhere else in the world," remarked journalist Henry Jones Ford, "has party organization had to cope with such enormous tasks . . . and its efficiency in dealing with them is the true glory of our political system."

Of course, the machine exacted a price for these services. The tenement dweller gave his vote. The businessman wrote a check. Corruption permeated this informal system. Some of the money that changed hands inevitably ended up in the pockets of machine politicians. This "boodle" could take the form of outright corruption—kickbacks by contractors; protection money from gamblers, saloonkeepers, and prostitutes; payoffs from gas and trolley companies. The Tammany Ward boss George Washington Plunkitt, however, insisted that he had no need for kickbacks and bribes. He favored what he called "honest graft," the easy profits that came to savvy insiders. Plunkitt made most of his money building wharves on Manhattan's waterfront. Tim Sullivan used his contacts to build a vaudeville empire. One way or another, legally or otherwise, machine politics rewarded its supporters (see American Lives, "Big Tim Sullivan: Tammany Politician," pp. 622–623).

For ambitious young immigrants and blacks, this was reason enough to favor the machine system. In the mid-1870s, over half of Chicago's forty aldermen were foreign-born, sixteen of them Irish immigrants. The first Italian was elected to the board in 1885 and the first Pole in 1888. Blacks did not manage to get on Chicago's board of aldermen until after 1900; but in Baltimore an African American represented the Eleventh Ward from 1890 onward, and Philadelphia had three black aldermen by 1899. As a ladder for social mobility, machine politics (like professional sports, entertainment, and organized crime) was the most democratic of American institutions.

For the ordinary tenement dweller, however, the machine had a more modest value. It acted as a rough-and-ready social service agency, providing jobs for the jobless, a helping hand for a bereaved family, and intercession with an unfeeling city bureaucracy. As a Boston ward boss remarked, "There's got to be in every ward somebody that any bloke can come to—no matter what he's done—and get help. *Help, you understand; none of your law and justice, but help.*" The Tammany Ward boss Plunkitt had a "regular system" when fires broke out in his district. He arranged for clothing and shelter, to "fix them up till they get things runnin' again. It's philanthropy, but it's politics, too—mighty good politics."

Plunkitt was an Irishman, and so were most of the ward politicians controlling Tammany Hall. But by the

1890s Plunkitt's Fifteenth District was filling up with Italians and eastern European Jews. In general the New York Irish had no love for these newer immigrants, but Plunkitt played no favorites. On any given day (as he recorded in his diary) he might attend an Italian funeral in the afternoon and a Jewish wedding in the evening, and he probably paid his respects with a few Italian words and a bit of Yiddish. In an era when so many forces acted to isolate ghetto communities, politics served an *integrating* function, cutting across ethnic lines and giving immigrants and blacks a stake in the larger urban order.

Religion in the City

For African Americans, as we have seen, the church was a central institution of urban life. This was true for many other city dwellers as well. But the city was also difficult ground for religious practice, with much that had once seemed settled now contested. All the great faiths present in late nineteenth-century America—Judaism, Catholicism, Protestantism—had to scramble to reconcile how they practiced their beliefs with the secular demands of the new urban world.

Judaism: The Challenge to Orthodoxy. About 250,000 Jews, mostly of German origin, were living in America when the eastern European Jews began to arrive in the 1880s. Well established and prosperous, the German Jews had embraced Reform Judaism, abandoning religious practices—from keeping a kosher kitchen to conducting services in Hebrew—"not adapted to the views and habits of modern civilization." Anxious to preserve their traditional piety, Yiddish-speaking immigrants from eastern Europe founded their own Orthodox synagogues, often in vacant stores and ramshackle buildings, and practiced Judaism in the old way.

In the villages of eastern Europe, however, Judaism had stood not only for worship and belief but for an entire way of life. Insular though it might be, ghetto life in America could not re-create the communal environment on which strict religious observance depended. "The very clothes I wore and the very food I ate had a fatal effect on my religious habits," confessed the hero of Abraham Cahan's novel *The Rise of David Levinsky* (1917). "If you . . . attempt to bend your religion to the spirit of your surroundings, it breaks. It falls to pieces." Levinsky shaved off his beard and plunged into the Manhattan clothing business. Orthodox Judaism survived this shattering of faith, but only by sharply reducing its claims on the lives of the faithful.

"Americanism" and the Catholic Church. Catholics faced much the same problem. The issue, explicitly defined within the Roman Catholic Church as "Americanism," turned on the degree to which Catholicism

Immaculate Heart of Mary Church, 1908
In crowded immigrant neighborhoods the church rose from undistinguished surroundings to assert the centrality of religious belief in the life of the community. This photograph is a view of Immaculate Heart of Mary Church, taken from Polish Hill in Pittsburgh in 1908.
Archives of Industrial Society, University Library System, University of Pittsburgh.

should adapt to American society, with its Protestant majority and sharp separation of church and state. Should Catholic children attend parochial or public schools? Should they intermarry with non-Catholics? Should the traditional education for the clergy be changed? Bishop John Ireland of St. Paul, Minnesota, felt that "the principles of the Church are in harmony with the interests of the Republic." But traditionalists, led by Archbishop Michael A. Corrigan of New York, denied the possibility of such harmony and argued in effect for insulating the Church from the threatening American environment.

In 1895 Pope Leo XIII announced his support of the traditionalists, pronouncing America a country that did not afford "the most desirable status of the Church." The pope regretted the absence of state support for Catholicism and urged communicants "to prefer to associate with Catholics, a course which will be very conducive to the safeguarding of their faith." Immigrant Catholics generally supported the Church's conservatism because they wanted to preserve their religion as they had known it in Europe. But their concerns were not purely religious; church life also had to express their ethnic identities. Newly arrived Catholics wanted their own parishes where they could celebrate their own customs and holidays, speak their own languages, and educate their children in their own parochial schools. When they became numerous enough, they also demanded their own bishops.

The Church had difficulty responding. The demands of immigrant congregations seemed to challenge the Catholic hierarchy, which was dominated by Irish Catholics, and even the integrity of the Church

itself. The desire for ethnic parishes led to demands for local control of Church property. Moreover, if the Church appointed bishops with jurisdiction over specific ethnic groups, that would mean disrupting the diocesan structure that unified the Church.

The severity of the challenge depended partly on the religious convictions of each ethnic group. Italian men, for example, were known for religious apathy, and many Italians harbored strong anticlerical feelings, much strengthened by the papacy's stand against the unification of Italy. But the Church played such an important part in the lives of Polish immigrants that they resented any interference by the Catholic hierarchy. In 1907 fifty parishes formed the Polish National Catholic Church of America, which adhered to Catholic ritual without recognizing the pope's authority.

On the whole, the Church managed to satisfy the immigrant faithful. It met their demand for representation in the hierarchy by appointing immigrant priests as auxiliary bishops within existing dioceses. Ethnic parishes also flourished. Before World War I American Catholics worshiped in more than two thousand foreign-language churches and in many others that were bilingual. Not without strain, the Catholic Church made itself a central institution for the expression of ethnic identity in urban America.

Protestantism: Regaining Lost Ground. Protestantism was the dominant faith of the nation, but by 1890 the total church membership was only about 14 million, compared to 8 million practicing Catholics. The city posed the greatest challenge to Protestant

Big Tim Sullivan: Tammany Politician

★

TIMOTHY D. SULLIVAN was born on July 23, 1863, near the Hudson River docks in lower Manhattan. His parents were Irish immigrants, part of the mass migration of potato famine victims who flooded into New York in the 1840s. Four years later Tim's father died, leaving his young widow, Catherine Connelly Sullivan, with four small children. Soon after, Catherine married Lawrence Mulligan, an Irish laborer, and the family moved to the notorious Five Points district on the Lower East Side. There the 1870 census found them, a household of ten (including three boarders) living in an overcrowded tenement at 25 Baxter Street (see Map 19.3 for the urban geography of Sullivan's career).

Tim had a harsh childhood. His stepfather drank heavily and beat his wife and children regularly. To make ends meet, Catherine took in washing and Tim went to work at age seven bundling papers for $1.50 a week on Newspaper Row across from City Hall. Tim got through grammar school, but his family needed his earnings too much for him to go on to high school. "Free as it was," he later remarked, "it was not free enough for me to go there." Instead—Horatio Alger style—he made his way up in the newspaper business and by age eighteen was well established as a wholesale newspaper dealer. He soon became the proprietor of two saloons and in his early twenties was ready for politics. A handsome fellow, over six feet tall, Sullivan was quick with his fists. He gained a local reputation by thrashing a tough he had encountered on the street beating up a woman. True or not, the story helped him win the Democratic nomination at age twenty-three for the New York State Assembly from the Second District.

In 1889 Sullivan opposed a bill granting Manhattan's police virtually unlimited powers to detain people with jail records. The champion of the bill was Thomas F. Byrnes, chief inspector of the New York Police Department and the most celebrated detective in the country. Byrnes did not take kindly to opposition from small-time politicians. He raided Sullivan's saloons, arrested two barkeepers for excise tax violations, and denounced Sullivan as a consorter with

Big Tim Sullivan
Culver Pictures.

criminals. Against the advice of friends, Sullivan took the assembly floor to answer the charge.

In tearful tones Sullivan cast himself as an "honest Bowery boy," describing his impoverished childhood, his saintly mother, his struggle to rise in the world. "When, at the conclusion [so a reporter recorded], he asked if he had any time or money to spend with thieves, there was a 'No' on nearly every member's lips." The performance was the making of the obscure assemblyman. Although he gained notoriety with uptown New Yorkers that would dog him throughout his career, he won the hearts of his own constituents, who reveled in the success story of one of their own. They thought "Big Tim" a fine fellow, and so did the Tammany leaders.

When the Tammany machine swept into power in the 1892 elections, Boss Richard Croker tapped Sullivan to run the new Third Assembly District centering on the Bowery. Sullivan swiftly consolidated his power. His inner circle was all Irish, but for election district captains he appointed Jews, Italians, and Germans who were well connected in the immigrant communities that populated his fiefdom. Sullivan became famous for his summer "chowders," when he transported his constituents by riverboat to the country for a rowdy day of picnicking. At Christmas there was a fine dinner for all who were in need. And in February Sullivan handed out wool socks and shoes—always with the sentimental tale of how a teacher had given him free shoes one cold winter.

Big Tim also attended assiduously to the nitty-gritty business of running a political machine. He got jobs for his supporters, visited the jails regularly to offer bail and other aid to the inmates, and on election day made sure his strong-arm crews patrolled the polling places. Sullivan's district became the best organized in the city, and Tammany hailed him as "the most popular man on the East Side."

In the meantime, Sullivan was making his fortune. His particular form of "honest graft" was commercial entertainment. Big Tim knew instinctively how important a good time was to city people. Besides, the main street of his district, the Bowery, was the gaudy center of low-life entertainment for the entire city, lined with burlesque houses, concert saloons, restaurants, and cheap hotels. In the mid-1890s Sullivan formed a partnership with two theatrical producers and began to invest in vaudeville houses. He contributed not only money and a shrewd head but the political contacts that ensured lax enforcement of building codes and easy access to liquor licenses. Sullivan also became involved in pro-fessional boxing, horse racing, and, more illicitly, the gambling dens that dotted his district.

Sullivan was accused of trafficking in East Side prostitution, but this he indignantly denied: "Nobody who knows me well will believe I would take a penny from any woman, much less from the poor creatures who are more to be pitied than any other human beings on earth. I'd be afraid to take a cent from a poor woman of the streets for fear my old mother would see me. I'd a good deal rather break into a bank and rob the safe. That would be a more manly and decent way of getting money."

When Boss Croker resigned in 1902, Sullivan might have succeeded him, but Big Tim preferred his own district and threw his support to Charles F. Murphy, who ruled Tammany for the next twenty-two years. Sullivan served briefly in Congress, made a lot more money investing in the early movie industry and in vaudeville syndicates across the country, and in the final phase of his career became a champion of progressive social legislation in the New York Senate. In 1912 Sullivan suffered a severe mental breakdown, possibly caused by tertiary syphilis. A year later he died under the wheels of a freight train after running off from his brother's house outside New York. His funeral procession down the Bowery was one of the largest in memory and brought out an immense crowd from every stratum of New York society, from statesmen to prizefighters to scrubwomen.

churches. They had to find ways of attracting, or reaffiliating, the great numbers of native-born Americans flocking into the cities in the late nineteenth century from the nation's farms and small towns. At the same time, they had to keep up with congregations scattering into the suburbs as European immigrants occupied the older residential neighborhoods. Many formerly prosperous churches found themselves stranded in the squalid new ghettos. Seventeen Protestant churches moved out of lower Manhattan during the twenty years after 1868 as the area below Fourteenth Street filled up with immigrants.

Every major city retained great downtown churches where wealthy Protestants worshiped. Some of these churches, richly endowed, took pride in nationally prominent pastors, including Henry Ward Beecher of Plymouth Congregational Church in Brooklyn and Phillips Brooks of Trinity Episcopal Church in Boston. But the eminence of these churches, with their fashionable congregations and imposing edifices, could not disguise the growing remoteness of Protestantism from much of its urban constituency. "Where is the city in which the Sabbath day is not losing ground?" lamented a minister in 1887. The families of businessmen, lawyers, and doctors could be seen in any church on Sunday morning, he noted, "but the workingmen and their families are not there."

To counter this decline, the Protestant churches responded in two ways. They evangelized among the unchurched and indifferent, for example, through the Sunday-school movement. Protestants also made their churches instruments of social uplift. Starting in the 1880s, many city churches provided reading rooms, day nurseries, clubhouses, and vocational classes. Some churches linked evangelism and social uplift. The Salvation Army, which arrived from Great Britain in 1879, spread the gospel of repentance among the urban poor and built an assistance program that ranged from soup kitchens to homes for former prostitutes. When all else failed, the down-and-outers of American cities knew they could count on the Salvation Army.

For young single people new to the cities, there were the Young Men's and Women's Christian Associations, which had been transplanted from Britain before the Civil War. By the mid-1880s virtually all large cities had YMCAs equipped with gymnasiums, auditoriums, and dormitories. Housing for single women was an especially important mission of the YWCAs. No other organizations so effectively combined activities for young adults with an evangelizing appeal in the form of Bible classes, nondenominational worship, and a religious atmosphere.

The social meaning that urban Protestants sought in religion explained the enormous popularity of a book called *In His Steps* (1896). The author, the Congregational minister Charles M. Sheldon, told the story of a congregation that resolved to live by Christ's precepts for one year. "If the church members were all doing as Jesus would do," Sheldon asked, "could it remain true that armies of men would walk the streets for jobs, and hundreds of them curse the church, and thousands of them find in the saloon their best friend?"

The most potent form of urban evangelism—revivalism—said little about social uplift. From its beginnings in the eighteenth century, revivalism had steadfastly focused on individual redemption. The resolution of earthly problems, revivalists believed, would follow the conversion of the people to Christ. Beginning in the mid-1870s, revival meetings swept through the cities.

The pioneering figure was Dwight L. Moody, a former Chicago shoe salesman and YMCA official. After preaching in Britain for two years, Moody returned to America in 1875. With his talented chorister and hymn writer, Ira D. Sankey, Moody staged revival meetings that drew thousands. He preached an optimistic, uncomplicated, nondenominational message. Eternal life could be had for the asking, Moody shouted as he held up his Bible. His listeners needed only "to come forward and take, TAKE!"

Many other preachers followed in Moody's path. The most notable was Billy (William Ashley) Sunday, a hard-drinking former outfielder for the Chicago White Stockings who mended his ways and found religion. Like Moody and other city revivalists, Sunday was a farm boy. His rip-snorting attacks on fashionable ministers and the "booze traffic" carried the ring of rustic America. By realizing that many people remained villagers at heart, revivalists found a key for bringing city dwellers back into the church.

In a larger sense, however, revivalism was expressive of a more general fundamentalist movement that sought to preserve old-time religion against the increasing complacency and doctrinal liberalism of mainstream Protestantism. Just as Methodism had arisen against the Church of England in the eighteenth century, so now in the late nineteenth century new churches arose against Methodism. The Holiness evangelical movement was at first nondenominational but then began to spawn such new denominations as the Church of the Nazarene (1908). Out of the Holiness Revival came the more radical Pentecostal movement, which by 1914 had brought together many local bodies into the Assemblies of God.

Leisure in the City

City people compartmentalized life's activities, setting workplace apart from home and working time apart from free time. "Going out" became a necessity, demanded not only as relief from a day of hard work but as proof that life was better in the New World than

JOSÉ MARTÍ
Coney Island, 1881

———★———

*José Martí, a Cuban patriot and revolutionary
(p. 680), was by profession a journalist. In exile
from 1880 to 1895, he spent most of his time in
New York City, reporting to his Latin American readers on the customs of the Yankees. Martí took special
pleasure in observing Americans at play.*

From all parts of the United States, legions of intrepid ladies and Sunday-best farmers arrive to admire
the splendid sights, the unexampled wealth, the
dizzying variety, the herculean surge, the striking
appearance of Coney Island, the now famous island,
four years ago an abandoned sand bank, that today
is a spacious amusement area providing relaxation
and recreation for hundreds of thousands of New
Yorkers who throng to its pleasant beaches every
day. . . .

Other nations—ourselves among them—live
devoured by a sublime demon within that drives us
to the tireless pursuit of an ideal of love or glory. . . .
Not so with these tranquil souls, stimulated only by
a desire for gain. One scans those shimmering
beaches . . . one views the throngs seated in comfortable chairs along the seashore, filling their lungs
with the fresh, invigorating air. But it is said that

those from our lands who remain here long are
overcome with melancholy . . . because this great
nation is void of spirit.

But what coming and going! What torrents of
money! What facilities for every pleasure! What
absolute absence of any outward sadness or poverty! Everything in the open air: the animated groups,
the immense dining rooms, the peculiar courtship
of North Americans, which is virtually devoid of the
elements that compose the shy, tender, elevated love
in our lands, the theatre, the photographers' booth,
the bathhouses! Some weigh themselves, for North
Americans are greatly elated, or really concerned, if
they find they have gained or lost a pound. . . .

This spending, this uproar, these crowds, the
activity of this amazing ant hill never slackens from
June to October, from morning 'til night. . . . Then,
like a monster that vomits its contents into the hungry maw of another monster, that colossal crowd,
that straining, crushing mass, forces its way onto
the trains, which speed across wastes, groaning
under their burden, until they surrender it to the
tremendous steamers, enlivened by the sound of
harps and violins, convey it to the piers, and
debouch the weary merrymakers into the thousand
trolleys that pursue the thousand tracks that spread
through slumbering New York like veins of steel.

———

Source: Juan de Onís, trans., *The America of José Martí:
Selected Writings* (New York: Noonday Press, 1954), 103–110.

in the Old. "He who can enjoy and does not enjoy com-
mits a sin," a Yiddish-language paper told its readers.
And enjoyment now meant buying a ticket and being
entertained.

Public Entertainment. Amusement parks went up at
the ends of trolley lines in cities across the country.
Most glittering was Luna Park at New York's Coney
Island—"an enchanted, storybook land of trellises,
columns, domes, minarets, lagoons, and lofty aerial
flights. . . . It was a world removed—shut away from
the sordid clatter and turmoil of the streets." In fact,
that escape from everyday urban life explains the
appeal of amusement parks (see Voices from Abroad,
"José Martí: Coney Island, 1881," above). The creators
of Luna Park intended it to be "a different world—a
dream world . . . where all is bizarre and fantastic . . .
gayer and more different from the everyday world."

The theater likewise attracted huge audiences.
Chicago had six vaudeville houses in 1896 and twenty-
two in 1910. Evolving from cheap variety and minstrel
shows, vaudeville moved from boisterous beer halls into
grand theaters. Vaudeville cleaned up its routines, making them suitable for the entire family, and turned into
thoroughly professional entertainment handled by
national booking agencies. With its standard program of
nine acts of singing, dancing, and comedy, vaudeville
attained enormous popularity just as the movies arrived.
The first primitive films, a minute or so of humor or
glimpses of famous people, appeared in 1896 in penny
arcades and as filler in vaudeville shows. Within a decade
millions of city people were watching story films of
increasing length and artistry at nickelodeons (named
after the five-cent admission charge) across the country.

For young unmarried workers the leisure activities
of the city created a new social space. "I want a good

Amusement Park, Long Beach, California
The origins of the roller coaster go back to LaMarcus Thompson's Switchback Railway, installed at Coney Island in 1884 and featuring gentle dips and curves. By 1900,
when Long Beach's Jack Rabbit Race was constructed, the goal was to create the
biggest possible thrill. Angelenos journeyed out by trolley to Long Beach not only to
take a dip in the ocean but to ride the new roller coaster. The Airplane Ride in the
foreground is a further wrinkle on the peculiarly modern notion that the way to have
fun is to be scared to death.
Curt Teich Postcard Archives.

time," a New York clothing operator remarked. "And
there is no . . . way a girl can get it on $8 a week. I guess
if anyone wants to take me to a dance he won't have to
ask me twice." Hence the widespread ritual among the
urban working class of "treating." The girls spent what
money they had on dressing up; their beaus were
expected to pay for the fun. Parental control over
courtship broke down, and amid the bright lights and
lively music of the dance hall and amusement park
working-class youth forged a more easygoing culture of
sexual interaction and pleasure seeking.

The geography of the big city carved out ample
space for commercialized sex. Prostitution was not new
to urban life, but in the late nineteenth century it
became less closeted and more intermingled with other
forms of public entertainment. In New York the most
famous sex district in this period was the Tenderloin,
running northward from Twenty-third Street between
Fifth and Eighth avenues and eventually up to Times
Square and beyond. This was also the locale of the city's
fanciest restaurants, the best hotels, and the theater
district. On the side streets many of the brownstone

row houses, abandoned by their well-to-do owners for
the quieter parts of town, were taken over by brothels.
The nearby concert saloons—the forerunners of the
nightclub—featured not only stage shows and bar-
tenders but also well-dressed prostitutes working the
premises.

The Tenderloin and the Bowery district farther
downtown were also the sites of a robust gay subculture. The long-held notion that homosexual life was
covert, in the closet, in Victorian America appears not to
be true, at least not in the country's premier city. Homosexual activity was illegal, but as with prostitution, the
law was mostly a dead letter. In certain corners of the
city a gay world flourished, with a full array of saloons,
meeting places, and drag balls, which were widely
known and often patronized by uptown "slummers."

Baseball. Of all forms of (mostly) male diversion
none was more specific to the city, or so spectacularly
successful, as professional baseball. The game's promoters decreed that baseball had been created in 1839
by Abner Doubleday in the village of Cooperstown, New

York. Actually, baseball was neither of American origin—it developed from the British game of rounders—nor a product of rural life.

Organized play began in the early 1840s in New York City, where a group of gentlemen enthusiasts competed on an empty lot. During the next twenty years the aristocratic tone of baseball disappeared. Clubs sprang up across the country, and intercity competition developed on a scheduled basis. In 1868 baseball became openly professional, as other teams followed the example of the Cincinnati Red Stockings in signing players to contracts at a negotiated salary for the season.

Big-time commercial baseball came into its own with the launching of the National League in 1876. The team owners were profit-minded businessmen who carefully shaped the sport to please the fans. Wooden grandstands gave way to the concrete and steel stadiums of the early twentieth century, such as Fenway Park in Boston, Forbes Field in Pittsburgh, and Shibe Park in Philadelphia.

For the urban multitudes baseball grew into something more than an occasional afternoon at the ballpark. By rooting for the home team, fans found a way of identifying with the city they lived in. Amid the diversity and anonymity of urban life, baseball acted as a bridge among strangers.

Students of the game have suggested that baseball was peculiarly attuned to city life. It followed strict, precise rules, which suggested an underlying order to the chaotic city. Far from respecting the rules, however, the players tried to get away with whatever they could in order to win. Did this not match the competitive scramble of urban life? The blue-coated umpire, the symbol of authority, was scorned by players and derided by fans. What better substitute for the resentment against the powers-that-be who ruled the lives of city people? Baseball, like many other emerging urban institutions, served as a mechanism for inducting people into the life of the modern city.

Newspapers. Most efficient at this task, however, was the newspaper. James Gordon Bennett, founder of the *New York Herald* in 1835, wanted "to record the facts . . . for the great masses of the community." The news was everything that interested city readers, starting with crime, scandal, and sensational events. After the Civil War Charles A. Dana of the *New York Sun* added the human-interest story, which made news of ordinary, insignificant happenings. Newspapers also targeted specific audiences. A women's page offered recipes and fashion news, separate sections covered sports and high society, and the Sunday supplement helped fill the weekend hours.

When Joseph Pulitzer, the owner of the *St. Louis Post-Dispatch*, invaded New York in 1883 by buying the *New York World*, a furious circulation war broke out. In 1895 William Randolph Hearst, who owned the *San Francisco Examiner*, bought the *New York Journal* and challenged the *World* (see Chapter 21, American Lives, "William Randolph Hearst: Jingo," pp. 682–683). Hearst developed a sensational style of newspaper reporting and writing that became known as *yellow journalism*. The term, linked to the first comic strip to appear in color, "The Yellow Kid" (1895), referred to a type of reporting that treated accuracy as secondary to a good story.

"He who is without a newspaper," said the great circus showman P. T. Barnum, "is cut off from his species." Barnum was speaking of city people and their hunger for information. By meeting this need, newspapers revealed their sensitivity to the public they served.

The World of the Urban Elite

———— ★ ————

In the midst of this popular ferment, other institutions of culture were taking shape under the sponsorship of a new social and economic elite. A hunger for the cultivated life was not, of course, specifically urban or upper class. Before the Civil War the lyceum movement had sent lecturers to the remotest towns, bearing messages of culture and learning. The Chautauqua movement, founded in upstate New York in 1874, carried on this work of cultural dissemination in the last decades of the nineteenth century. However, great institutions such as museums, public libraries, opera companies, and symphony orchestras could flourish only in metropolitan centers and with the financial support of wealthy patrons.

Creating High Culture

The nation's first major art museum, the Corcoran Gallery of Art, opened in Washington, D.C., in 1869. New York's Metropolitan Museum of Art started in rented quarters two years later. In 1880 the museum moved to its permanent site in Central Park and launched an ambitious program of art acquisition. J. P. Morgan became chairman of the board in 1905, assuring the Metropolitan's preeminence. The Boston Museum of Fine Arts was founded in 1876, Chicago's Art Institute in 1879. By 1914 virtually every major city and about three-fifths of all cities above the size of 100,000 people had an art museum.

Top-flight orchestras also appeared, first in New York under the conductors Theodore Thomas and Leopold Damrosch in the 1870s, then in Boston and Chicago during the next decade. National tours by these leading orchestras planted the seeds for orchestral societies in many other cities. Public libraries grew from modest collections (in 1870 only seven had as

BOSTON BASE-BALL CLUB.

The National Pastime
This lithograph celebrates the opening game of the 1889 season, with the Boston Base-Ball Club taking on the New York Base-Ball Club. The National League was then scarcely twelve years old. The fielders played barehanded, but otherwise the game today is much as the artist pictured it a century ago, down to the umpire's characteristic stance.
Stock Montage.

many as 50,000 books) into major urban institutions. The greatest library benefactor was Andrew Carnegie, who announced in 1881 that he would build a library in any city that was prepared to maintain it. By 1907 Carnegie had spent more than $32.7 million to establish about a thousand libraries throughout the country.

The late nineteenth century was the great age not only of moneymaking but also of money *giving*. Surplus private wealth flowed in many directions, including to universities. These schools included Vanderbilt, Tulane, and Johns Hopkins universities, all named for their chief benefactors, and the University of Chicago, founded by John D. Rockefeller in 1892. The new millionaires also richly patronized the arts, partly out of a sense of civic duty, partly as a means to establish themselves in society, as in the founding of the Metropolitan Opera in New York (see p. 629). But museums and opera houses also received generous support as an expression of national pride.

"In America there is no culture," pronounced the English critic G. Lowes Dickinson in 1909. Science and the practical arts, yes, "every possible application of life to purposes and ends," but "no life for life's sake." Such condescending remarks received a respectful hearing in the United States because of a deep sense of cultural inferiority to the Old World. In 1873 Mark Twain and Charles Dudley Warner published a novel, *The Gilded Age*, satirizing America as a land of money-grubbers and speculators. This enormously popular book touched a nerve in the American psyche. Its title has in fact been appropriated by historians to characterize the late nineteenth century—America's "Gilded Age"—as an age of materialism and cultural shallowness.

Some members of the upper class, like the novelist Henry James, despaired of the country and moved to Europe. Others spent their lives in the kind of perpetual alienation that Henry Adams, descendant of U.S. presidents John and John Quincy Adams, described in his ironic memoir *The Education of Henry Adams* (1907).

The more common response was to try to raise the nation's cultural level. The newly rich had a hard time of it. With few exceptions, they did not have much opportunity to cultivate a taste for art, and a great deal of what they collected was mediocre and garish. One exception was George W. Vanderbilt, grandson of the rough-hewn Cornelius Vanderbilt, who became a patron of the Art Students League in New York and an early champion of French Impressionism. Another was the coal and steel baron Henry Clay Frick, who built a brilliant art collection that remains housed as a public museum in his mansion in New York City. The enthusiasm of moneyed Americans—not always well directed—largely fueled the great cultural institutions that arose in many cities during the Gilded Age.

A deeply conservative idea of culture sustained this generous patronage. The aim was to embellish urban life, not to probe or reveal its meaning. "Art," says the hero of Reverend Henry Ward Beecher's sentimental novel *Norwood* (1867), "attempts to work out its end solely by the use of the beautiful, and the artist is to select out only such things as are beautiful." The idea of culture also took on an elitist cast: Shakespeare, once a staple of popular stage entertainment (in various bowdlerized versions), was appropriated into the domain of "serious" theater.

Culture also became firmly linked to femininity. In America, remarked one observer, culture was "left entirely to women. . . . It is they, as a general rule, who have opinions about music, or drama, or literature, or philosophy. . . . Husbands or sons rarely share in those interests." Men represented the "force principle," said the clergyman Horace Bushnell, and women symbolized the "beauty principle."

The treatment of life, the eminent editor and novelist William Dean Howells wrote, "must be tinged with sufficient idealism to make it all of a truly uplifting character. We cannot admit stories which deal with false or immoral relations. . . . The finer side of things—the idealistic—is the answer for us." The *genteel tradition*, as this literary school came to be called, dominated such American cultural agencies as universities and publishers from the 1860s onward.

The New Millionaires

In the compact city of the early nineteenth century, class distinctions had been expressed by the way men and women dressed, how they behaved, and the deference they demanded from or granted to others. As the industrial city grew, these interpersonal marks of class began to lose their force. In the anonymity of a large city, recognition and deference no longer served as mechanisms for conferring status. Instead, the rich began to rely on external signs: conspicuous display of wealth, exclusive association in clubs and similar social organizations, and, above all, choice of neighborhood.

For the poor, place of residence depended, as it always had, on the location of their work. For higher-income urbanites, where to live became a matter of personal means and social preference.

Life-Styles of the Rich. As early as the 1840s Boston merchants took advantage of the new railway service to move out of the congested central city. Fine rural estates appeared in Milton, Newton, and other outlying towns. By 1848 roughly 20 percent of Boston's businessmen were making the long trip from the countryside to their downtown offices. Ferries that plied the harbor between Manhattan and Brooklyn or New Jersey served the same purpose for New Yorkers.

As commercial development engulfed downtown residential areas and as transportation services improved, the exodus from cities by the well-to-do spread across America. In Cincinnati wealthy families settled on the scenic hills rimming the crowded, humid tableland that ran down to the Ohio River. On those hillsides, a traveler noted in 1883, "the homes of Cincinnati's merchant princes and millionaires are found . . . elegant cottages, tasteful villas, and substantial mansions, surrounded by a paradise of grass, gardens, lawns, and tree-shaded roads." Residents of the area, called Hilltop, founded several country clubs, the Cincinnati Riding Club, the New England Society, five downtown gentlemen's clubs, and many other institutions that ensured an exclusive social life for Cincinnati's elite.

Despite the temptations of country life, many of the very richest people preferred the heart of the city. Chicago boasted its Gold Coast; San Francisco, Nob Hill; Denver, Quality Hill; and Manhattan, Fifth Avenue. The New York novelist Edith Wharton recalled how the comfortable midcentury brownstones gave way to the "'new' millionaire houses," which spread northward beyond Fifty-ninth Street and up Fifth Avenue along Central Park. Great mansions, emulating the homes of the European aristocracy, lined Fifth Avenue at the turn of the century.

But great fortunes did not automatically confer high social standing. An established elite stood astride the social heights even in such relatively raw cities as San Francisco and Denver. It had taken only a generation—and sometimes less—for money made in commerce or real estate to shed its tarnish and become "old" and genteel. In older cities such as Boston, wealth passed intact through several generations, creating a closely knit tribe of old-line families that kept moneyed newcomers at bay. Elsewhere urban elites tended to be more open, but only to the socially ambitious who were prepared to make visible and energetic use of their money.

New York's Metropolitan Opera was one of the products of this ongoing struggle among the wealthy. The Academy of Music, home to the city's opera since 1854, was controlled by the Livingstons, the Bayards, the Beekmans, and other old New York families. Frustrated in their efforts to purchase boxes at the Academy, the Vanderbilts and their allies decided to sponsor a rival opera house. In 1883, with its glittering opening to the strains of Gounod's *Faust*, the Metropolitan proclaimed its ascendancy in the opera world and in due course won the patronage of even the Beekmans and Bayards. During this battle of the opera houses the Vanderbilt circle achieved social recognition.

"High Society." New York became the home of a national elite as the most ambitious people gravitated to this preeminent center of American economic and cultural life. Manhattan's extraordinary vitality in turn kept the city's high society fluid and relatively open. In Theodore Dreiser's novel *The Titan* (1914), tycoon Frank Cowperwood reassures his unhappy wife that if Chicago society will not accept them, "there are other cities. Money will arrange matters in New York—that I know. We can build a real place there, and go in on equal terms, if we have money enough." New York thus came to be a magnet for millionaires. The city attracted them not only because of its importance as a financial center, but also because of the opportunities it offered for display and social recognition.

From Manhattan an extravagant life of leisure radiated outward to resorts such as Saratoga Springs, New York; Palm Beach, Florida; and Newport, Rhode Island, with its grand array of summer "cottages." To these

Going to the Opera, 1873
In this painting by Seymour J. Guy, William H. Vanderbilt, eldest son and successor of
the railroad tycoon Cornelius Vanderbilt, has gathered with his family and friends
preparatory to attending the opera. It was the sponsorship of New York's Metropolitan Opera that helped the Vanderbilts achieve social recognition among the older,
more established moneyed families of New York City.
Courtesy of Biltmore Estate, Asheville, North Carolina.

resorts, the affluent traveled in great comfort by private
railway car. Entertaining was on a grand scale; luxurious restaurants like Delmonico's and Sherry's sprang
up, catering to the rich. "Our forefathers would have
been staggered at the cost of hospitality these days,"
remarked one New Yorker.

This infusion of wealth shattered the older elite
society of New York. Seeking to be assimilated into the
upper class, the flood of moneyed newcomers simply
overwhelmed it. There followed a curious process of
reconstruction, a deliberate effort to define the rules of
conduct and identify those who properly "belonged" in
New York society.

The key figure in this process was Ward McAllister, a
southern-born lawyer who made a quick fortune in gold-
rush San Francisco and then devoted himself to a second
career as the arbiter of New York society. In 1888 McAllister compiled the first *Social Register*, which announced
that it would serve as a "record of society, comprising an
accurate and careful list" of all those deemed acceptable
to participate in New York society. McAllister instructed
the socially ambitious on how to select guests, set a
proper table, arrange a ball, and launch a young lady into

society. He presided over an ordered round of assemblies,
balls, and dinners that defined the boundaries of an elite
society. At the apex stood "the Four Hundred"—the true
cream of New York society. McAllister's list corresponded
to the list of guests invited to Mrs. William Astor's great
ball of February 1, 1892.

Social registers, coming-out balls for debutantes,
and lesser versions of Ward McAllister soon popped up
in cities throughout the country. In this fashion, the
socially ambitious struggled to master the fluidity at
the height of the social order.

Americans were adept at making money, noted the
journalist Edwin L. Godkin in 1896, but they lacked the
European traditions for spending it. "Great wealth has
not yet entered our manners," Godkin remarked. "No
rules have yet been drawn to guide wealthy Americans in
their manner of life." In their struggle to find the rules
and establish the manners, the moneyed elite made an
indelible mark on urban life. If there was magnificence in
the American city, it was mainly their handiwork. And if
there was conspicuous waste and vulgarity, it was also
their doing. In a democratic society wealth finds no easier outlet than through public display.

The Urban Middle Class

—————— ★ ——————

From colonial times onward, the American economy spawned a robust middle class of lawyers, merchants, doctors, and ship captains. What most distinguished this group was the independence that came with self-employment. This older middle class remained important, but in the late nineteenth century it was joined by a new salaried middle class brought forth by the emerging corporate economy.

Bureaucratic organizations required managers, accountants, and clerks. Advancing technologies called for engineers, chemists, and designers. The distribution system sought salesmen, advertising executives, and buyers. These salaried ranks increased sevenfold between 1870 and 1910—at a much faster rate than any other occupational group. Nearly 9 million people held white-collar jobs in 1910—more than a fourth of all nonagricultural employees.

The middle class left a smaller imprint than the rich on the public and cultural faces of urban society. Its members, unlike the wealthy, preferred privacy and retreated into the domesticity of suburban comfort and family life.

Expanding Suburbs

The American middle class, particularly its salaried ranks, was an urban population. Some of its members lived within the city, in the row houses of Baltimore or Boston or the comfortable apartment houses of New York and other metropolitan centers. But far more preferred to escape from the clamor and congestion of the city. They were attracted by a persisting "rural ideal." They agreed with landscape architect Andrew Jackson Downing, who thought that "nature and domestic life are better than the society and manners of town." With the extension of trolley service from the city center, middle-class Americans followed the wealthy into the countryside. All sought what a Chicago developer promised for his North Shore subdivision in 1875—"qualities of which the city is in a large degree bereft, namely, its pure air, peacefulness, quietude, and natural scenery."

No major American city escaped rapid suburbanization during the last third of the nineteenth century. City limits everywhere expanded rapidly, but even so, much of the suburban growth took place beyond city limits. By 1900 more than half of Boston's people lived in "streetcar suburbs" outside Boston proper; and nationwide, according to the 1910 census, about 25 percent of the urban population lived in such independent suburbs.

Cincinnati Suburb
The lives of the people inhabiting these neat homes along this tree-lined street were woven into the dynamic capitalism of a major industrial metropolis, including the children lounging on the corner, who were most certainly being educated for service in the new economic order. Looking at the bucolic setting of this Cincinnati street, no one would have thought so, and that was just the illusion that the suburb was intended to create: that Americans still partook of a rural ideal and could hold at bay the modern industrial order of which they were now a part.
Cincinnati Historical Society.

On the European continent, by contrast, cities remained highly concentrated; and when expansion did occur, it was the poor, not the well-to-do, who inhabited the margins. Unlike its American counterpart, the European middle class was not attracted (except in Britain) to the rural ideal and valued urban life for its own sake. The preconditions for suburbanization were likewise much weaker in Europe: mass transit developed more slowly; traditional beam-and-post house construction did not give way to the cheaper balloon-frame techniques; and there was little of the freewheeling real-estate development that spurred American suburbanization. Finally, because European cities were ethnically more homogeneous, the middle class was not driven, as was its American counterpart, to flee the diverse masses populating the city centers.

The geography of the American suburbs was truly a map of class structure, because where a family lived told where it ranked. The farther the distance from the center of the city, the finer were the houses and the larger the lots. Affluent businessmen and professionals had the leisure and flexible schedules to travel a long distance into town. People closer in wanted transit lines that went straight into the city center and carried them quickly between home and office. Lower-income suburbanites were more likely to have more than one wage earner in the family, less secure employment, and jobs requiring movement around the city. It was better for them to live closer to the city center, because they then had easy access to the cross-town lines that gave them the mobility they needed for their work.

Location on the suburban map, though always a precise measure of economic ranking, never became rigid. Working-class residents of the city center who wanted to better their lives moved to the cheapest suburbs. Those already settled there fled from these newcomers, in turn pushing the next higher group farther out in search of space and greenery.

Suburbanization was the sum of countless individual decisions. Each move represented an advance in living standards—not only more light, air, and quiet but also better housing than the city afforded. Suburban houses had more space and better design. They came equipped with indoor toilets, hot water, central heating, and, by the turn of the century, electricity. Even people in the inner suburbs soon regarded these amenities as necessities.

The suburbs also restored a basic opportunity that rural Americans thought they had sacrificed when they moved to the city. In the suburbs home ownership again became the norm. "A man is not really a true man until he owns his home," propounded Reverend Russell H. Conwell in "Acres of Diamonds," his famous sermon on the virtues of making money,

The small town of the rural past had fostered community life. Not so the suburbs. The grid street pattern, efficient for laying out lots and providing utilities, offered no natural focus for group life. Nor did the stores and services that lay scattered along the trolley-car streets. Not even schools and churches were located where they could become centers of community life. Suburban development conformed to the economics of real estate and transportation, and so did the thinking of middle-class home seekers entering the suburbs. They wanted a house that gave them good value and convenience to the trolley line.

The need for community had lost some of its force for middle-class Americans. Two other attachments assumed greater importance: work and family.

Middle-Class Families

In the preindustrial economy farmers, merchants, and artisans had carried on their work within family units, which counted as members not only blood relatives but all others living and working in the household. As industrialism progressed, production gradually moved out of the household. For the middle class in particular, the family became dissociated from economic activity. The father left the home to earn a living, and children

spent more years in school. Clothing was bought ready-made; food came increasingly in cans and packages. Middle-class families became smaller, excluding all but nuclear members and consisting typically by 1900 of husband, wife, and three children.

Within this family circle relationships became intense and affectionate. "Home was the most expressive experience in life," recalled literary critic Henry Seidel Canby of his growing up in the 1890s. "Though the family might quarrel and nag, the home held them all, protecting them against the outside world." In a sense, the family served as a refuge from the competitive, impersonal business world. The suburbs provided a fit setting for such middle-class families. The quiet, tree-lined streets created a domestic world insulated from the hurly-burly of commerce and enterprise.

The Wife's Role. The burdens of this domesticity fell heavily on the wife. It was nearly unheard of for her to seek an outside career; that was her husband's role. Her job was to manage the household. "The woman who could not make a home, like the man who could not support one, was condemned," Canby remembered. But with better household technology, greater reliance on purchased goods, and fewer children, the wife's workload declined. Moreover, servants still played an important part in middle-class households. In 1910 there were about 2 million domestic servants, the largest job category for women.

As the physical burdens of household work eased, higher-quality homemaking became the new ideal. This was the message of Catharine Beecher's best-selling book *The American Woman's Home* (1869) and of such magazines as *Ladies' Home Journal* and *Good Housekeeping*, which first appeared during the 1880s. This advice literature told women that in their domestic duties, they had the higher calling of bringing sensibility, beauty, and love to the household. "We owe to women the charm and beauty of life," wrote one educator. "For the love that rests, strengthens and inspires, we look to women." In this idealized view, the wife made the home a refuge for her husband and a place of nurture for their children.

Womanly virtue, even if a happy marriage depended on it, by no means put wives on equal terms with their husbands. Although the legal status of married women—the right to own property, control separate earnings, make contracts and bring suit, and get a divorce—improved markedly during the nineteenth century, sufficient legal discrimination remained to establish their subordinate role within the family. More important, custom dictated a wife's submission to her husband. She relied on his ability as the family breadwinner and, despite her superior virtues and graces, ranked as his inferior in vigor and intellect. Her mind could be employed "but little and in trivial matters," wrote one prominent physician, and her proper place was as "the companion or ornamental appendage to

Middle-Class Domesticity
For middle-class Americans the home was a place of nurture, a refuge from the world of competitive commerce. Perhaps that explains why their residences were so heavily draped and cluttered with bric-a-brac. All of it emphasized privacy and pride of possession.
Culver Pictures.

man" (see American Voices, "M. Carey Thomas: 'We Did Not Know . . . Whether Women's Health Could Stand the Strain of College Education,'" p. 634).

No wonder that bright, independent-minded women rebelled against marriage. The marriage rate in the United States fell to its lowest point during the last forty years of the nineteenth century. More than 10 percent of women of marriageable age remained single, and the rate was much higher among college graduates and professionals. Only half of the Mount Holyoke College class of 1902 married. "I know that something perhaps, humanly speaking, supremely precious has passed me by," remarked the writer Vida Scudder. "But . . . how much it would have excluded!" Married life "looks to me often as I watch it terribly impoverished, for women."

The strains of marriage were manifest in the number of middle-class families that broke up. The national divorce rate increased from 1.2 per 1,000 marriages in 1860 to 7.7 in 1900. Most domestic failures, however, went unrecorded because of the stigma attached to divorce. In a Chicago suburb in the 1880s, at a time when divorce was virtually unknown there, about 10 percent of households had an absent spouse.

Even harder to document were the other ways women responded to marriages that denied their autonomy and downplayed their sexuality. Middle-class women became the principal victims of neurasthenia, a disorder whose symptoms included depression and general disability. Some unhappy housewives found "silent friends" in opium and alcohol, which often were dispensed in well-laced patent medicines.

A healthier release came through the companionship of other women. In an age that defined separate spheres for men and women, close ties commonly formed between schoolmates, cousins, and mothers and daughters. The intimacy and intensity of such attachments can be sensed in the letters of separated friends. Such enduring female ties yielded an emotional gratification not often found in marriage. Husbands, absorbed in business, frequently played a secondary and remote role in the lives of their wives. Women's own sphere often filled that emotional vacuum.

Changing Views of Sexuality. In earlier times sexuality and reproduction had been more or less in harmony. A large family was considered a good thing, and the heavy toll of repeated pregnancies on the wife was accepted as God's will. In lower-class families this fatalism persisted, but not among middle-class couples, who increasingly wanted to limit their families. Birth control, however, was

M. CAREY THOMAS

"We Did Not Know . . . Whether Women's Health Could Stand the Strain of College Education"

———————— ★ ————————

President of Bryn Mawr College for many years, M. Carey Thomas (1857–1935) recalls in a retrospective essay her dreams of college as a girl growing up in Baltimore in the 1870s.

The passionate desire of women of my generation for higher education was accompanied thruout its course by the awful doubt, felt by women themselves as well as by men, as to whether women as a sex were physically and mentally fit for it. . . . I was always wondering whether it could be really true, as everyone always said, that boys were cleverer than girls. . . . I often remember praying about it, and begging God that if it were true that because I was a girl I could not successfully master Greek and go to college and understand things to kill me at once, as I could not bear to live in such an unjust world. When I was a little older I read the Bible entirely thru with passionate eagerness because I had heard it said that it proved that women were inferior to men. . . . To this day I can never read many parts of the Pauline epistles without feeling again the sinking of the heart with which I used to hurry over the verses referring to women's keeping silence in the churches and asking their husbands at home. . . .

It was not to be wondered at that we were uncertain in those old days as to the ultimate result of women's education. We did not know when we began whether women's health could stand the strain of college education. We were haunted in those early days by the clanging chains of that gloomy little specter, Dr. Edward H. Clarke's *Sex in Education*. With trepidation of spirit I made my mother read it, and was much cheered by her remark that, as neither she, nor any of the women she knew, had ever seen girls or women of the kind described in Dr. Clarke's book, we might as well act as if they did not exist. Still, we did not *know* whether college might not produce a crop of just such invalids. . . .

Before I myself went to college I had never seen but one college woman. I had heard that such a woman was staying at the house of an acquaintance. I went to see her with fear. Even if she had appeared in hoofs and horns I was determined to go to college all the same. But it was a relief to find this Vassar graduate tall and handsome and dressed like other women. When, five years later, I went to Leipzig to study after graduating from Cornell, my mother used to write me that my name was never mentioned to her by the women of her acquaintance. I was thought by them to be as much a disgrace to my family as if I had eloped with the coachman. . . .

We are now [1908] living in the midst of great and, I believe on the whole beneficent, social changes which are preparing the way for the coming economic independence of women. . . . The passionate desire of the women of my generation for a college education seems, as we study it now in the light of coming events, to have been part of this greater movement.

Source: Linda K. Kerber and Jane De Hart-Mathews, eds., *Women's America: Refocusing the Past,* 2nd ed. (New York: Oxford University Press, 1987), 263–265.

---

not an easy matter. From the 1830s onward information about contraception became widely available, as did an array of commercial devices—condoms, diaphragms, sponges, douches. But the knowledge purveyed was imperfect or, like advice about the rhythm method, absolutely wrong (doctors thought women were most fertile around the menstrual period). And the devices for the most part were not very effective or, as in the case of the condom, were stigmatized by association with the brothel.

Before these barriers could be surmounted, birth control was swept up in the social-purity campaign championed by Anthony Comstock. From the 1870s onward contraceptive devices and birth-control information were legally classified as obscene, barred from the mails, and criminalized in many states. Abortion, long protected by common law, became illegal except to save the mother's life. Although the practice of abortion probably remained widespread, it was expensive and dangerous—and considered shameful besides.

Around 1890 a change set in. Although the birth rate continued to decline, more young people married, and at an earlier age. These developments reflected the beginnings of a sexual revolution in the American middle-class family. Despite the Comstock laws, contraception became more acceptable and more reliable. Experts began to abandon the notion, put forth by one popular medical text, that "the majority of women (happily for society) are not very much troubled by sexual feeling of any kind." In succeeding editions of his book *Plain Home Talk on Love, Marriage, and Parentage,* physician Edward Bliss Foote began to favor a healthy sexuality that gave pleasure to both women and men.

During the 1890s the artist Charles Dana Gibson created the image of the "new woman" in his drawings for *Life* magazine. The Gibson girl was tall, spirited, athletic, and chastely sexual. Constrictive clothing such as bustles, hoop skirts, and hourglass corsets gave way to shirtwaists and other natural styles that did not hide or disguise the female form. In the city, women's sphere began to take on a more public character. Among the new urban institutions catering to women, the most important was the department store, which became a temple for their emerging role as consumers.

Attitudes toward Children.   The children of the middle class went through their own revolution. In the past, American children had been regarded as an economic asset—added hands for the family farm, shop, or countinghouse. That no longer held true for the urban middle class. Parents stopped treating their children as working members of the family. In the old days, Ralph Waldo Emerson remarked in 1880, "children had been repressed and kept in the background; now they were considered, cosseted, and pampered." There was such a thing as "the juvenile mind," lectured Jacob Abbott in his book *Gentle Measures in the Management and Training of the Young* (1871). The family was responsible for providing a nurturing environment in which the young personality could grow and mature.

Preparation for adulthood became increasingly linked to formal education. School enrollment went up 150 percent between 1870 and 1900. High school attendance, while still encompassing only a small percentage of teenagers, increased at the fastest rate. As the years between childhood and adulthood began to stretch out, a new stage of life—adolescence—emerged. While rooted in an extended period of dependency on the family, adolescence shifted much of the socializing role from parents to peer group. A youth culture—one of the hallmarks of American life in the twentieth century—was starting to take shape.

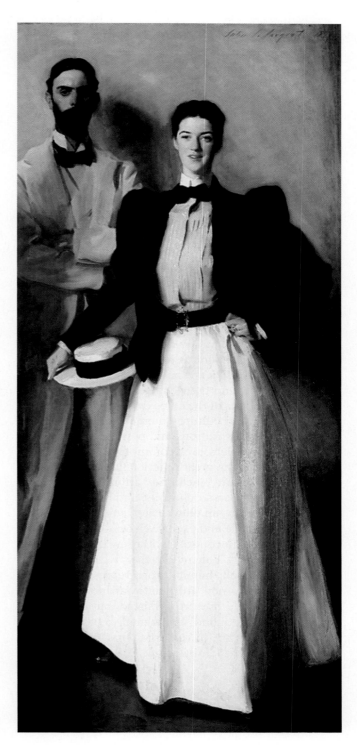

The New Woman
John Singer Sargent's painting *Mr. and Mrs. Isaac Newton Phelps Stokes* (1897) captures on canvas the essence of the "new woman" of the 1890s. Nothing about Mrs. Stokes, neither how she is dressed nor how she presents herself, suggests physical weakness or demure passivity. She confidently occupies center stage, a fit partner for her husband, who is relegated to the shadows of the picture.
The Metropolitan Museum of Art, New York. Bequest of Edith Minturn Phelps Stokes (Mrs. I. N.), 1938 (38.104).

Summary

★

America, an agrarian society since its birth, became increasingly urbanized after the Civil War. By 1900 about 20 percent of the population was living in cities with 100,000 or more people. City growth stemmed primarily from industrialization—the concentration of industry at key points, the increasingly large scale of production, and the need for commercial and administrative services that were best located in urban centers. A burst of innovation, including mass transit systems, steel-frame buildings, the telephone, and electric lighting, solved the problems arising from the concentration of large populations in a confined area. Although amply endowed with regulatory powers, American cities left decision making as much as possible in the hands of private interests. The result was dramatic growth but not much attention to the impact of growth on the urban environment.

In the cities geography defined the social order of the population. The poor were found in the city centers and the factory districts, the middle class spread out into the suburbs, and the rich lived insulated in exclusive central sections of the cities or beyond the suburbs. A distinctive urban culture emerged, drawing heavily on ethnic social institutions and new leisure activities, enabling city dwellers to accommodate themselves to the urban world. The great American cities became the sites of high culture, including art museums, opera companies, symphony orchestras, and libraries.

For the wealthy, an elite society emerged, stressing an opulent life-style and exclusive social organizations. The middle class, in contrast, withdrew into the private world of the family. For middle-class wives, the cult of domesticity reigned, but its more repressive features began to relax as a new attitude toward female sexuality took hold. Child nurture persisted, but as the years of dependent childhood lengthened, a new phase—adolescence—began to emerge that would draw teenagers out of the family orbit.

TIMELINE

1869	Corcoran Gallery of Art, the nation's first major art museum, opens in Washington, D.C.
1871	Chicago fire
1873	Mark Twain and Charles Dudley Warner publish *The Gilded Age*
1875	Dwight L. Moody launches urban revivalist movement
1876	Alexander Graham Bell patents the telephone
	National Baseball League founded
1878	Electric arc-light system installed in Philadelphia
1879	Thomas Edison creates a practical incandescent lightbulb
	Salvation Army arrives from Britain
1881	Andrew Carnegie offers to build a library for every American city that will maintain it
1883	New York City's Metropolitan Opera founded
	Brooklyn Bridge opens
	Joseph Pulitzer purchases the *New York World*
1885	William Jenney builds first steel-frame structure, Chicago's Home Insurance Building
1887	First electric trolley line constructed in Richmond, Virginia
1892	John D. Rockefeller founds University of Chicago
1893	Chicago World's Fair
	"City Beautiful" movement
1895	William Randolph Hearst enters New York journalism
	The comic strip "The Yellow Kid" appears
1897	Boston builds first American subway
1900	Theodore Dreiser publishes *Sister Carrie*
1901	New York Tenement House Law
1904	New York subway system opens
1906	San Francisco earthquake
1913	Fifty-five-floor Woolworth Building opens in New York City

Suggested Readings

★

Useful introductions to urban history are Charles N. Glaab and A. Theodore Brown, *A History of Urban America* (1967), and Raymond A. Mohl, ed., *The Making of Urban America* (1997). Arthur M. Schlesinger, *The Rise of the City* (1936), is a pioneering study. A sampling of the innovative scholarship that opened new historical paths can be found in Stephan Thernstrom and Richard Sennett, eds., *Nineteenth-Century Cities: Essays in the New Urban History* (1969).

Urbanization

Allan Pred, *Spatial Dynamics of U.S. Urban Growth, 1800–1914* (1971), traces the patterns in which cities grew. On the revolution in urban transit, see the pioneering book by Sam B. Warner, *Streetcar Suburbs: The Process of Growth in Boston, 1870–1900* (1962). In a subsequent work, *The Private City: Philadelphia in Three Periods* (1968), Warner broadened his analysis to show how private decision making shaped the character of the American city. Innovations in urban construction are treated in Carl Condit, *American Building Art: Nineteenth Century* (1969) and *Rise of the New York Skyscraper, 1865–1913* (1996); Robert C. Twombly, *Louis Sullivan* (1986); Alan Trachtenberg, *The Brooklyn Bridge* (1965); Harold L. Platt, *The Electric City: Energy and the Growth of the Chicago Area, 1880–1930* (1991); and Mark H. Rose, *Cities of Light and Heat: Domesticating Gas and Electricity in Urban America* (1995). The problems of meeting basic human needs are treated in Jon C. Teaford, *The Unheralded Triumph: City Government in America, 1870–1900* (1984); and David B. Tyack, *The One Best System: A History of American Urban Education* (1974). The struggle to reshape the chaotic nineteenth-century city can be explored in John D. Fairchild, *The Mysteries of the Great City: The Politics of Urban Design, 1877–1937* (1993); James Machor, *Pastoral Cities: Urban Ideals and the Symbolic Landscape of America* (1987); and David Schuyler, *The New Urban Landscape: The Redefinition of City Form in Nineteenth-Century America* (1986).

City People

A useful introduction to American immigration history is John Bodnar, *The Transplanted* (1986). Among the leading monographs are Moses Rischin, *The Promised City: New York's Jews, 1870–1914* (1962); Joseph Barton, *Peasants and Strangers: Italians, Rumanians, and Slovaks in an American City, 1890–1950* (1975); and Robert A. Orsi, *The Madonna of 115th Street: Faith and Community in Italian Harlem, 1880–1950* (1985). On blacks in the city see Gilbert Osofsky, *Harlem: The Making of a Ghetto, 1890–1930* (1966); Allan H. Spear, *Black Chicago, 1860–1920* (1966); and Kenneth L. Kusmer, *A Ghetto Takes Shape: Black Cleveland, 1870–1930* (1976). David C. Hammack, *Power and Society: Greater New York at the Turn of the Century* (1982), is a sophisticated treatment that places the party machine in the larger context of municipal power politics. The encounter of Protestantism with the city is treated in Henry F. May, *Protestant Churches and Urban America* (1949);

William G. McLoughlin, *Modern Revivalism* (1959); and Paul Boyer, *Urban Masses and Moral Order in America, 1820–1920* (1978). On the Catholic Church, see Robert D. Cross, *Liberal Catholicism in America* (1958). Aspects of an emerging city culture are studied in Gunther Barth, *City People: The Rise of Modern City Culture in Nineteenth-Century America* (1982); Susan Porter Benson, *Counter Cultures: Saleswomen, Managers, and Customers in American Department Stores, 1890–1940* (1986); Timothy J. Gilfoyle, *City of Eros: New York City, Prostitution and the Commercialization of Sex, 1790–1920* (1991); Kathy Peiss, *Cheap Amusements: Working Women and Leisure in Turn-of-the-Century New York* (1986); Robert W. Snyder, *The Voice of the City, Vaudeville and Popular Culture in New York City, 1880–1930* (1990); and David Nasaw, *Going Out: The Rise and Fall of Public Amusements* (1993). George Chauncey, *Gay New York: Gender, Urban Culture, and the Making of the Gay New York World, 1890–1940* (1994), reveals terrain hitherto invisible to the historian.

The World of the Urban Elite

On the fostering of high culture in the American city, see Daniel M. Fox, *Engines of Culture: Philanthropy and Art Museums* (1963). The best introduction to intellectual currents in the emerging urban society is Alan Trachtenberg, *The Incorporation of America: Culture and Society, 1865–1893* (1983). On the social elite see Frederic C. Jaher, *The Urban Establishment: Upper Strata in Boston, New York, Charleston, Chicago, and Los Angeles* (1982).

The Urban Middle Class

Urban social mobility is the focus of Stephan Thernstrom, *The Other Bostonians: Poverty and Progress in an American City, 1880–1970* (1973), which also contains a useful summary of mobility research on other cities. Two recent books greatly advance our understanding of the urban middle class: Stuart S. Blumin, *The Emergence of the Middle Class: Social Experience in the American City, 1760–1900* (1989), and Olivier Zunz, *Making Corporate America, 1870–1920* (1990). Aspects of middle-class life are revealed in Margaret Marsh, *Suburban Lives* (1990); Michael A. Ebner, *Creating Chicago's North Shore: A Suburban History* (1988); Gwendolyn Wright, *Moralism and the Model Home: Domestic Architecture and Cultural Conflict in Chicago, 1873–1913* (1980); Susan Strasser, *Never Done: A History of American Housework* (1983); and John F. Kasson, *Rudeness and Civility: Manners in Nineteenth-Century America* (1990). Contemporary notions of sexuality are skillfully captured in John S. Haller and Robin M. Haller, *The Physician and Sexuality in Victorian America* (1980). Whether those views actually applied to the private world of the middle class is strongly questioned in Karen Lystra, *The Searching Heart: Women, Men, and Romantic Love in Nineteenth-Century America* (1989). Control over reproduction is fully explored in Janet Farrell Brodie, *Contraception and Abortion in Nineteenth-Century America* (1994). A good introduction to family development, including childhood, is Steven Mintz and Susan Kellog, *Domestic Revolutions: A Social History of the American Family* (1988).

Collier's

THE NATIONAL WEEKLY

AGAIN!!!

VOL XLIX NO 8   MAY 11 1912

Chapter 20

★

The Progressive Era

O**N THE FACE** of it, the political ferment of the 1890s ended after the election of 1896. The bitter struggle over free silver left the victorious Republicans with no stomach for political crusades. William McKinley's administration devoted itself to maintaining business confidence: sound money and high tariffs were the order of the day. The main thing, as party chief Mark Hanna said, was to "stand pat and continue Republican prosperity."

Yet beneath the surface a deep uneasiness had set in. The depression of the 1890s had unveiled harsh truths not acknowledged in better days. The fury of the decade's labor strikes, for example, revealed a frightening chasm opening between America's social classes. The outbreak of the great Pullman strike of 1894, declared Richard Olney, brought the country "to the ragged edge of anarchy." As Cleveland's attorney-general at the time, it was Olney's job to crush the strike, and he had done so with ruthless efficiency (see Chapter 17). But Olney took little satisfaction from his success. He asked himself what might be done in the future to avoid such one-sided state intervention. Olney advocated federal legislation, first expressed in the Erdman Mediation Act of 1898, that would regulate labor relations on the railroads and prevent "the evils and perils" of crippling rail strikes. In such ways did the crisis of the 1890s turn the nation's thinking to reform.

The problems themselves, however, were of much older origin. For half a century, Americans had been absorbed in developing their nation. At the beginning of the twentieth century they paused, looked around, and began to add up the costs. With industrialization

Again!
The Pure Food and Drug Act of 1906 was a monument to the muckraking journalism of the Progressive Era. Collier's, which had done the heavy work on this reform, revisited the patent-medicine scene in 1912 and found the villains alive and kicking. Vigilance seemed to be the price of permanent reform.
Boston Athenaeum.

had come a frightening concentration of corporate economic power and, equally troubling, a rebellious working class. The cities had spawned widespread misery and corrupt machine politics. The heritage of an earlier America seemed to be succumbing to the demands of the new industrial order.

Now, with the crisis of the 1890s over, reform became an absorbing concern of many Americans. It was as if social awareness had reached a critical mass around 1900 and set reform activity in motion as a major, self-sustaining phenomenon. For this reason the years from 1900 to World War I have come to be known as the Progressive Era.

The Intellectual Roots of Progressivism

————————★————————

Intellectual climates change. Why they change is usually hard to explain, but it is not so difficult to tell when new ideas are taking hold. That new ideas were taking hold was altogether evident as the twentieth century began. An intellectual style emerged that can be called "progressive."

A Sense of Mastery

The Progressive Era was an age of scientific investigation. The federal government conducted massive statistical studies of immigration, women's and children's labor, and working conditions in many industries. Vice commissions studied prostitution, gambling, and other moral ills of American cities. Among private investigations the most notable was the Pittsburgh Survey (1911–1914). Financed by New York City philanthropists, a team of investigators recorded in great detail living and working conditions in Pittsburgh's steel district.

The facts were important because they formed the basis for corrective action. When the young journalist Walter Lippmann wrote *Drift and Mastery* (1914), he asserted the progressives' confidence in people's ability to act purposefully and constructively. This sense of mastery expressed itself in many ways—for example, in the faith people had in academic experts. In Wisconsin the state university became a key resource for Governor Robert M. La Follette's progressive administration. "The close intimacy of the university with public affairs explains the democracy, the thoroughness, and the scientific accuracy of the state in its legislation," boasted one La Follette supporter. Similarly, progressives were strongly attracted to scientific management, which had

originally been intended to rationalize work in factories (see Chapter 17). But its founder, Frederick W. Taylor, argued that his basic approach—the "scientific" analysis of human activity—offered solutions to waste and inefficiency in municipal government, schools and hospitals, and even homes and churches. Scientific management, Taylor insisted, could solve all the social ills that arise "through such of our acts as are blundering, ill-directed, or inefficient."

Attacking Nineteenth-Century Formalism. The essential thing, in the progressive view, was to resist intellectual formulations that denied people this sense of mastery, as did the Social Darwinian writings of the British philosopher Herbert Spencer and his many American disciples (see Chapter 18). Spencer argued that society develops according to fixed laws that cannot be changed. Spencer's intellectual approach was *formalistic*—that is, it proceeded from unproven general principles rather than from factual investigation.

Critics of Spencer denied that the evolution of society is guided by absolute and unvarying rules. "It is folly," protested the Harvard philosopher William James, "to speak of the 'laws of history,' as of something inevitable, which science only has to discover, and which any one can then foretell and observe, but do nothing to alter or avert." Man could "shape environmental forces to his own advantage," the sociologist Lester F. Ward argued. Society could advance through "rational planning" and "social engineering."

In the law, too, formalism had dominated. The courts treated legal rights as if these were eternal principles not rooted in—or to be tested by—social reality. Thus in the *Lochner v. New York* decision (1905) the Supreme Court invalidated a law limiting the long working hours of bakers in New York State on the grounds that such regulation violated the contractual liberty of both employers and workers. Justice Oliver Wendell Holmes, the leading critic of legal formalism, dissented; in his view, the *Lochner* decision was based on a fictional equality. If the choice was between working and starving, could it really be said that bakers freely accepted jobs requiring that they labor fourteen hours a day or that limiting their working hours violated their liberty of contract?

Holmes had earlier asserted the essence of progressive legal reasoning: "The life of the law has not been logic; it has been experience. The felt necessities of the time, even the prejudices which judges share with their fellow-men, have had a good deal more to do than logic in determining the rules by which men shall be governed." "Sociological jurisprudence," as Dean Roscoe Pound of the Harvard Law School termed it, called for "the adjustment of principles and doctrines to the human conditions they are to govern rather than assumed first principles." The law, moreover, should not claim a false neutrality; on the contrary, as Pound's student Felix Frankfurter argued, law should be "a vital agency for human betterment."

The Academic Critique. The assault against formalism took place in many scholarly disciplines. In classical economics, for example, scholars assumed that markets were perfectly competitive and thus perfectly responsive to the laws of supply and demand. Such a system left no room for reform, which would only disrupt what could not be improved. Critics of classical economics—they called themselves "institutional economists"—denied that the market ever operated so perfectly. They conducted field research to determine how institutions and power relationships influenced the marketplace. In his *Theory of the Leisure Class* (1899) and *The Instinct of Workmanship* (1914) the economist Thorstein Veblen lampooned the classical economists' abstract image of "economic man." In the real world, Veblen contended, people acted not out of pure economic calculation but from complex motives ranging from vanity to pride in their work.

In philosophy, it was William James who led the assault on formalism as an intellectual system. James denied the existence of absolute truths. In his philosophy of *pragmatism*, ideas were judged by their consequences; ideas served as guides to action that produced desired results. Philosophy should be concerned with solving problems, argued James, not with contemplating ultimate ends.

James's most important disciple was John Dewey. Like James, Dewey had a great interest in psychology, whose insights he applied to education. In his Laboratory School at the University of Chicago Dewey broke from the rigid curriculum of traditional education and instead stressed problem solving and practical activity as the keys to children's personal growth. His pupils were encouraged to explore and discover for themselves rather than learning lessons by rote. Nowhere could the intellectual bent of progressivism in action be better seen than in Dewey's experiments, which, fittingly, came to be known as progressive education.

Sources of Progressive Idealism

The reformers prided themselves on being tough-minded, on being expert at making things happen. But they were not indifferent to the purposes of effective action. On the contrary, progressives were unabashed idealists. The progressive cause, pronounced Theodore Roosevelt, "is based on the eternal principles of righteousness."

Much of this idealism came from the American past. No American hero loomed larger for progressives

than Abraham Lincoln. Lincoln's example, in particular, inspired the battle for political reform. "Go back to the first principles of democracy; go back to the people," Robert La Follette told his audience when he launched his attack on the Republican machine in Wisconsin. Political reformers typically described their work as political restoration, frequently confessing that they had converted to reform after discovering how far party politics had drifted from the ideals of representative government.

Progressive idealism also derived from American radical traditions. Many progressives traced their conversion to Henry George's *Progress and Poverty* (1879), which asked why, in the midst of fabulous wealth, so many Americans lived in poverty. George's answer—that private control of land siphoned the community's wealth into the hands of nonproductive landlords—led to a Single Tax movement that served as a school for many budding progressives. Others traced their awakening to Edward Bellamy's novel *Looking Backward* (1888), with its utopian vision of an ordered, affluent American socialism, or to the Chicago social democrat Henry Demarest Lloyd's *Wealth against Commonwealth* (1894), with its powerful indictment of the Standard Oil trust. In later years this radical tradition was transmitted mainly through the Socialist Party, which flourished after 1900 under the leadership of Eugene V. Debs (see Chapter 17). Walter Lippmann and many other young reformers passed through socialism on their way to progressivism, while others, such as Charlotte Perkins Gilman, never left the socialist camp.

The most important source of progressive idealism, especially among social reformers, was religion. Protestant churches had long been concerned with the plight of the urban poor (see Chapter 19). Now this concern blossomed into a major school of religious thought—the Social Gospel. The Baptist cleric Walter Rauschenbusch, its most influential exponent, had been deeply affected by his ministry near the squalid Hell's Kitchen section of New York City. Rauschenbusch fought for more playgrounds and better housing in slum neighborhoods. The churches had to reassert the "social aims of Jesus," he argued. The "Kingdom of God on Earth" would be achieved not by striving for personal salvation but by struggling for social justice. To coordinate that effort, reform-minded clerical leaders formed the Federal Council of Churches in 1908. The council aimed at "promoting the application of the law of Christ in every relation to human life."

The Social Gospel was an explicitly religious movement, but secular progressivism was also infused with a strong element of faith. Progressive leaders characteristically grew up in families imbued with evangelical piety. Many went through a religious crisis and, having failed to experience a conversion, settled on careers in social work, education, journalism, or politics, where they could translate inherited religious belief into modern secular action. Jane Addams, for example, had taken up settlement-house work with this intention. She believed that by uplifting the poor in tenement districts, settlement workers themselves would be uplifted: they would experience "the joy of finding Christ" by acting "in fellowship" with the needy. Similarly, the philosopher John Dewey called democracy "a spiritual fact" and the "means by which the revelation of truth is carried on." At the Progressive Party national convention in 1912, Theodore Roosevelt's supporters marched around the hall singing "Onward Christian Soldiers."

The Muckrakers

The progressive mode of thought—idealistic in intent and tough-minded in approach—nurtured a new style of reform journalism. During the 1890s magazines such as *McClure's* and *Collier's* had found a wide audience of urban readers. Unlike the highbrow *Atlantic Monthly* or *Harper's*, these bright new journals, which sold for only 10 cents, specialized in lively and informative reporting. Almost by accident—Lincoln Steffens's article "Tweed Days in St. Louis" in the October 1902 issue of *McClure's* is credited with getting things started—

editors discovered that what most interested readers, and most lifted circulation, was the exposure of corruption in American life. Investigative reporters such as Charles Edward Russell fanned out on the trail of evildoers (see American Voices, "Charles Edward Russell: Muckraking," p. 643).

In a series of powerful articles, Steffens wrote about "the shame of the cities"—the corrupt ties between business and political machines. Ida M. Tarbell attacked Standard Oil, and David Graham Phillips told how money controlled the Senate. William Hard exposed industrial accidents in "Making Steel and Killing Men" (1907) and child labor in "De Kid Wot Works at Night" (1908). Hardly a sordid corner of American life escaped the scrutiny of these tireless reporters. They were moralists as well, infusing their factual accounts with a powerful spirit of personal indignation. "The sights I saw," wrote the slum investigator Jacob Riis, "gripped my heart until I felt I must tell of them, or burst, or turn anarchist."

President Roosevelt, among many others, thought these journalists went too far. In a 1906 speech he compared them to the man with the muckrake in *Pilgrim's Progress*, by the seventeenth-century English preacher John Bunyan. The man was too absorbed with raking the filth on the floor to look up and accept a celestial

Ida Tarbell Takes on Rockefeller
A popular biographer of Napoleon and Lincoln in the 1890s, Ida Tarbell turned her journalistic talents to muckraking. Her first installment of "The History of the Standard Oil Company" appeared in *McClure's* in November 1902. John D. Rockefeller, she wrote, "was willing to strain every nerve to obtain for himself special and illegal privileges from the railroads which were bound to ruin every man in the oil business not sharing them with him." As Tarbell built her case, criticism rained down on Rockefeller. A more sympathetic cartoon in the magazine *Judge* pleads with Rockefeller's critics: "Boys, don't you think you have bothered the old man just about enough?"
Ida M. Tarbell Collection, Reis Library, Allegheny College, Meadville, Pennsylvania; Culver Pictures.

Charles Edward Russell
Muckraking

———★———

*I*n this autobiographical account newspaperman *Charles Russell describes how he got into muck-raking journalism and what he thought it was all about. He never did, by the way, get back to writing music.*

All America had been accustomed to laud and bepraise the makers of great fortunes. . . . Money had become the touchstone and perfect measure of worth. . . . Now, of a sudden, men began to discover that these great and adored fortunes had been gathered in ways that not only grazed the prison gate but imposed burdens and disadvantages upon the rest of the community; that vast hoards for one man meant much less for others. In the shock of this discovery, a literature of exposition arose and daily the magazine editors looked for new dark, malodorous corners of money-grabbing upon which the spotlight could be turned.

Pure accident cast me, without the least desire, into the pursuit of this fashion. I had finally withdrawn from the newspaper business, and having enough money to live modestly I was bent upon carrying out a purpose long cherished in quite a different line. [I had concluded] that what we call the separate arts of music and poetry are really but one, and I now conceived that with a piano, my Swinburne, and some sheets of music paper I could

demonstrate this priceless fact to a palpitating world. Upon this task I was intent when the whole business was upset with a single telegram.

One day, Mr. J. W. Midgley, who was a famous expert on railroad rates and conditions . . . let loose a flood of startling facts about the impositions practised by the owners and operators of refrigerator cars. My friend, Mr. Erman J. Ridgway . . . of *Everybody's Magazine* wired asking me to see Mr. Midgley and get him to write for *Everybody's* an article along the lines of his testimony. I conferred accordingly and Mr. Midgley positively refused all offers to become an exposé writer. [So] Ridgway wire[d] asking me to furnish the article *Everybody's* wanted. I had not the least disposition to do so, except only that Ridgway was my friend. . . . The next thing I knew a muck-rake was put into my hand and I was plunged into the midst of the game. . . .

I wrote two or three articles on the refrigerator car scandal and then went on to write a series on the methods of the Beef Trust and was not in the least astonished to find that I was become an unmitigated scoundrel, a hired assassin of character, a libeller of good men, an enemy of society and of the government, and probably an Anarchist in disguise. . . . We were all up and away, full of the pleasures of the chase . . . and all that business about poetry and music sheets forgotten. It was exhilarating sport, hunting the money octopus.

———

Source: Charles Edward Russell, *Bare Hands and Stone Walls* (New York: Charles Scribner's Sons, 1933), 135–139.

---

crown. Thus the term *muckraker* became attached to journalists who exposed the underside of American life. Their efforts were in fact health giving. More than any other group, the muckrakers called the people to arms.

The Many Faces of Reform

———★———

Historians have sometimes spoken of a progressive "movement." But progressivism was not a movement in any meaningful sense. There was no single progressive

constituency, no agreed-upon agenda, and no unifying organization or leadership. At different times and places, different social groups became active. People who were reformers on one issue might be conservative on another. The term *progressivism* embraces a widespread, many-sided effort after 1900 to build a better society.

Political Reformers

One realm that cried out for reform was American politics. Like the Mugwumps of the Gilded Age, twentieth-century reformers denounced the boss rule of the party system, but the progressives' attack was much more skilled and aggressive. Indeed, because politics was about power, in this realm the motives of the progressives were always mixed, with the ideals of civic betterment elbowing uneasily with the drive for self-aggrandizement.

City Government. In many cities the demand for good government came from local businessmen. Taxes went up, they complained, but needed services always lagged. There had to be an end, as one manufacturer said, to "the inefficiency, the sloth, the carelessness, the injustice and the graft of city administrations." The solution, argued John Patterson of National Cash Register Company, lay in putting "municipal affairs on a strict business basis." Cities should be run "not by partisans, either Republican or Democratic, but by men who are skilled in business management and social service."

In 1900 a hurricane devastated Galveston, Texas, drowning five thousand people and destroying the municipal port. Local businessmen took over and, in the course of rebuilding the city, replaced the mayor and board of aldermen with a five-member commission. The Galveston plan, though widely copied, had a serious flaw: it concentrated too much power in the city commission. Dayton, Ohio, resolved this problem by assigning policy matters to a nonpartisan body and administrative functions to an appointed city manager. The commission-manager system, which aimed at running the American city "in exactly the same way as a private business corporation," was chiefly the work of the business community.

It was also a way of grabbing power. By making elections city-wide and professionalizing city administration, municipal reformers attacked the ward politics that had favored ethnic and working-class groups, shifting political power to the urban middle class. In fact, municipal reform contained a decidedly antidemocratic bias. "Ignorance should be excluded from control," said former Mayor Abram Hewitt of New York in 1901. "City business should be carried on by trained experts selected upon some other principle than popular suffrage."

Other urban progressives, however, opposed such elitism. Mayor Brand Whitlock of Toledo, Ohio, believed "that the cure for the ills of democracy was not less democracy . . . but more democracy." Whitlock's administration not only attacked municipal corruption and inefficiency but also concerned itself with providing better schools, cleaner streets, and more social services for Toledo's working people. An increasing number of cities came under the leadership of such progressive mayors, including Tom Johnson in Cleveland and Mark Fagan in Jersey City. By combining popular programs and campaign magic, they won over the urban masses and challenged the rule of the machines.

Robert M. La Follette
La Follette was transformed into a political reformer when a Wisconsin Republican boss attempted to bribe him in 1891 to influence a judge in a railway case. As he described it in his *Autobiography*, "Out of this awful ordeal came understanding; and out of understanding came resolution. I determined that the power of this corrupt influence . . . should be broken." This photograph captures La Follette at the top of his form, taking his case in 1897 to the people of Cumberland, Wisconsin.
State Historical Society of Wisconsin.

State Politics. The major battleground for democratic reform, however, was not the cities but the states. Robert M. La Follette of Wisconsin led the way. Born in 1855, La Follette had followed a conventional party career as a lawyer, district attorney, and then congressman for three terms before breaking with the Wisconsin Republican machine in 1891, allegedly because of an attempt by the top party boss to bribe him. La Follette became a tireless exponent of political reform, battling the Republican old guard for a decade before finally winning the governorship in 1900 on a platform of higher taxes for corporations, stricter utility and railroad regulation, and political reform.

La Follette's key proposal was a direct primary law requiring political parties to choose candidates by means of popular election rather than in machine-run conventions. Enacted in 1903, this democratic reform not only expressed La Follette's ideals but suited his particular political talents. Republican Party regulars opposing him were insiders, more comfortable in the caucus room than out on the hustings. But on the hustings was where La Follette, a superb campaigner, excelled. The direct primary gave him an iron grip on the Republican Party in Wisconsin that he did not relinquish until his death twenty-five years later.

What was true of La Follette was more or less true of all successful progressive politicians. Albert B. Cummins of Iowa, Harold U'Ren of Oregon, and Hiram Johnson of California all espoused democratic ideals, and all skillfully used the direct primary as the stepping-stone to political power and reform. If they were newcomers—as Woodrow Wilson was when he left academic life to enter New Jersey politics in 1910—they showed a quick aptitude for politics and gained a solid mastery of the trade. They practiced a new kind of popular politics, which in a reform age could be a more effective route to power than the back-room techniques of the old-fashioned machine politicians.

Even the most democratizing of progressive reforms—the initiative, the referendum, and the recall—were really exercises in power politics. The *initiative* let ordinary citizens place issues of interest to them on the ballot. The *referendum* enabled voters to decide big legislative issues (including propositions arising from the initiative) by popular vote. The *recall* empowered citizens to remove from office politicians who had lost the public's confidence. It soon became clear, however, that direct democracy did not supplant organized politics. Initiative, referendum, and recall campaigns put a premium on organization, money, and expertise, and these were attributes not of the people at large but of well-organized special interests. Like the direct primary, the initiative, referendum, and recall had as much to do with power relations as with democratic idealism.

The Woman Progressive

Reform movements arise through a process of recruitment. Why do people enlist in a great cause? Each mobilized group—the progressive politicians just described, for example—is linked in some personal way to the evil crying out for correction. For middle-class women of the Progressive Era, the link was through their long-established identity as "social housekeepers": it was women's duty to tend to the social well-being of their communities (see Chapter 18).

Middle-class women had long borne the burden of humanitarian work in American cities. They did most of the legwork for the charity-organization societies coordinating citywide private relief after the 1870s. As voluntary investigators, women visited needy families, assessed their problems, and referred them to relief agencies.

After many years of such dedicated charity work, Josephine Shaw Lowell of New York City concluded that it was not enough to give assistance to the poor. "If the working people had all they ought to have, we should not have the paupers and criminals," she declared. "It is better to save them before they go under, than to spend your life fishing them out afterward." Lowell founded the New York Consumers' League in 1890. Her goal was to improve the wages and working conditions of female clerks in the city's stores by issuing a "White List"—a very short one at first—of cooperating shops.

From these modest beginnings the league spread to other cities and blossomed into the National Consumers' League in 1899. By then the women who ran the league had lost faith in voluntary action; only the state could rescue poor urban families. Under the crusading leadership of Florence Kelley, formerly a chief factory inspector in Illinois, the Consumers' League became a powerful lobby for protective legislation for women and children.

Among its achievements, none was more important than the *Muller v. Oregon* decision (1908), which upheld an Oregon law limiting to ten hours the workday of women workers. The Consumers' League recruited the brilliant Boston lawyer Louis D. Brandeis to defend the Oregon law before the U.S. Supreme Court. In his brief, Brandeis devoted only two pages to the narrow constitutional issue—whether, under its police powers, Oregon had the right to regulate women's working hours. Instead Brandeis rested his case on data gathered by the Consumers' League showing how long hours damaged women's health and family roles. The *Muller* decision, which accepted Brandeis's reasoning, was a victory for the new "sociological jurisprudence" and cleared the way for a wave of protective laws across the country (Table 20.1).

Women's organizations became a mighty lobbying voice on behalf of women and children (see American Lives, "Frances Kellor: Woman Progressive," pp. 646–647). Their victories included the first law providing public assistance for mothers with dependent children, in Illinois in 1911; the first minimum wage law for women, in Massachusetts in 1912; more effective child labor laws, in many states; and, at the federal level, the Children's and Women's bureaus in the Labor department, in 1912 and 1920, respectively. The welfare state, insofar as it arrived in America in these years, was what women progressives made it; they erected a "maternalist" welfare system.

Settlement Houses.   Meanwhile, other women were launching the settlement-house movement. In 1889, inspired by Toynbee Hall in the slums of London, two young American women, Jane Addams and Ellen Gates Starr, established Hull House on Chicago's West Side. During the next fifteen years, scores of settlement houses sprang up in the slum neighborhoods of the nation's cities. The settlement houses served as community centers run by middle-class residents, who acted as amateur social workers for the surrounding immigrant communities. Hull House had meeting rooms, an art gallery, clubs for children and adults, and a kindergarten. Addams herself led battles for garbage

Frances Kellor: Woman Progressive

——————★——————

FROM THE DAY its doors opened in 1892, the University of Chicago was a major center of American learning. Financed by John D. Rockefeller, the university modeled itself on the great German research universities and, unlike Yale and Harvard, concentrated on graduate education. At Chicago and other American universities, modern social science was taking shape, breaking from its nineteenth-century moral foundations and seeking a scientific basis for the study of society. Economics, political science, and sociology demanded a rigorous course of study certified by the granting of the Ph.D. But if the social sciences were becoming professional, their guiding purpose was not yet disinterested research but the improvement of society. The University of Chicago saw the city surrounding it as a great laboratory for social betterment. Its students were being prepared, whether they knew it or not, to be in service to the American progressivism of the next decade. The University of Chicago, moreover, was receptive to the admission of women, and for them in particular, graduate education was a breeding ground for careers as social reformers.

Among the women entering in 1898 was Frances Alice Kellor, a recent graduate of Cornell University. Kellor was born in Columbus, Ohio, in 1873. Her father abandoned the family before she was two, and her mother made a hard living as a domestic and laundress. This was not the kind of privileged background from which most woman progressives sprang, but Kellor's experience came closer to the norm than her threadbare circumstances might have suggested. In 1875 her family moved to Coldwater, Michigan, a former abolitionist center (and station on the underground railroad) and a stronghold of Yankee culture. From the Coldwater community, with its high moral standards and strong educational institutions, Kellor received the reformist values that other budding progressives learned from their families. Kellor, moreover, had a remarkable talent for finding patrons, gaining by her wits the financial means her fellow progressives were born to. Her first patrons were the well-to-do librarians of Coldwater, Mary and Frances Eddy, who befriended her and took her into their home. Born Alice, Kellor began to call herself "Frances" as a sign that she considered herself adopted by the Eddy sisters. She graduated from high school, became a reporter for the *Coldwater Republican,* and then, with the backing of the Eddys, enrolled at Cornell in 1895. Highly athletic, Kellor made her first mark as a fighter for equal rights on a sports issue: she led the campaign for a women's crew. She got a solid education in the social sciences at Cornell and decided to become a criminologist.

When Frances Kellor arrived in Chicago in 1898, sociology was an infant discipline, with little in the way of systematic theory and an emphasis on high-minded investigations of social problems. Kellor's interest in crime was encouraged by the Chicago faculty. The prevailing theory of the time, advanced by the Italian Cesare Lombroso, was that criminality was an inherited trait—that criminals were born criminal and that this tendency was manifest in their physical features. Skeptical, Kellor conducted a study of the female inmates of five midwestern prisons. Comparing them with a control group of college women, she could find no physical differences. Kellor concluded that not heredity but social environment, economic disadvantage, and poverty produced criminality. Kellor also rejected "the prevailing opinion that when women are criminal they are more degraded and more abandoned than men." People thought so, she asserted, only because of "the difference in the standards which we set for the two sexes."

A second project on criminality among southern blacks likewise rejected heredity and stressed environmental factors, but Kellor's conclusions were pessimistic and racially conservative: centuries of slavery and indolent southern life had left blacks so morally weakened that "the Negro at present has neither the perceptions nor the solidity of character that would enable him to lead his race." She considered the southern restrictions on blacks' legal and political rights unfortunate but necessary, and she believed that "the free intermingling of the two races is impossible, at least for many generations." In drawing these illiberal conclusions, Kellor was echoing the views of her teachers and indeed of most white progressives of her generation.

Frances Kellor
This photograph of Kellor was taken in her early twenties, when she was a student at Cornell University.

Despite her precocious record, Kellor left the university in 1902 without a degree. The reasons are not altogether clear but doubtless had something to do with a painful truth of which Kellor must have been aware: the University of Chicago almost never placed its female graduate students in university teaching jobs. To be a professor, it seemed, was still a male prerogative. There was, however, a positive side to Kellor's decision. Like many of her fellow students, she had fallen under the spell of Jane Addams. Kellor lived periodically at Hull House, joined the circle of social reformers that congregated there, and began to see her future out among the disadvantaged rather than in the university. When she left Chicago, it was to do social research for New York's College Settlement Association.

Her first project was a study of unemployment. Kellor rejected the prevailing notion that being jobless was a sign of personal weakness. She was among the first investigators to see that unemployment was an economic problem, the result not primarily of individual shiftlessness or incompetence but of the impersonal operations of the labor market. Her book *Out of Work* (1904) was a pioneering investigation, paving the way for the modern study of unemployment. Kellor was especially concerned with the plight of jobless women and their exploitation by commercial employment agencies. Representing the Women's Municipal League of New York, Kellor lobbied successfully for state regulation of these agencies. Kellor thus employed her research to bring about social change. The combination of professional investigation and robust political advocacy became the hallmark of Kellor's progressivism. Her next study, on the problems of immigrants in New York, led to the establishment of the New York State Bureau of Industries and Immigration in 1910. Kellor was chosen to be its head, the first woman to hold so high a post in New York's state government.

The high point of Kellor's career came two years later, when Theodore Roosevelt launched the Progressive Party. Convinced that social reform required strong government, Kellor was drawn to the New Nationalism. She linked it with her own fervent advocacy of women's political rights. Always a fighter, she was entirely at ease in the rough-and-tumble of partisan politics. After Roosevelt's defeat in 1912, the Progressive Party set up the National Progressive Service, a kind of think tank to study social problems and formulate legislative proposals. The idea was mainly Kellor's, and she was tapped to chair the Service. This was truly a pinnacle for a woman in American politics at a time when women in most states could not vote in national elections. Unfortunately, Kellor's emphasis on scientific investigation put her at odds with the practical politicians, and she was forced out in early 1914. Hers was a brief run in national politics, exhilarating while it lasted and unique for a woman of her generation.

Kellor never married. Like many other woman progressives, including Jane Addams, she found personal fulfillment in an enduring relationship with another woman. This was Mary Dreier, one of two wealthy sisters who played leading roles in New York progressivism. From the time Kellor moved into the Dreier home in Brooklyn Heights in 1904 until her death almost fifty years later, she and Mary were constant companions. Kellor's later professional life was devoted to a distinguished career with the American Arbitration Association.

TABLE 20.1

Progressive Legislation and Supreme Court Decisions

State Laws	Federal Laws	Supreme Court Decisions
1903 Wisconsin primary law Oregon ten-hour law for women	1898 Erdman Railway Mediation Act	1895 *U.S. v. E.C. Knight* shelters manufacturing from antitrust law
1910 New York Bureau of Industries and Immigration Washington State adopts woman suffrage	1902 Newlands Reclamation Act 1903 U.S. Bureau of Corporations Elkins Act	1897 *U.S. v. Trans-Missouri* quashes "rule of reason" in antitrust suits
1911 Illinois law providing aid for mothers with dependent children New York State Factory Commission	1906 Hepburn Railway Act Pure Food and Drug Act Meat Inspection Act 1909 Payne-Aldrich Tariff Act	1904 *U.S. v. Northern Securities* orders dissolution of a company ruled a monopoly under the Sherman Act
1912 Massachusetts minimum-wage law for women and children	1913 Underwood Tariff Act Federal Reserve Act 1914 Federal Trade Commission Act Clayton Antitrust Act 1916 Seamen's Act Federal Farm Loan Act	1905 *Lochner v. New York* invalidates a state law limiting hours of bakers
		1908 *Muller v. Oregon* approves a state law limiting working hours of women *Loewe v. Lawlor* (Danbury Hatters case) finds a labor boycott to be a conspiracy in restraint of trade
		1911 *U.S. v. Standard Oil* restores rule of reason as guiding principle in antitrust cases

removal, better street lighting, and police protection. At the Henry Street Settlement in New York City, Lillian D. Wald made visiting nursing a major service. Mary McDowell, head of the University of Chicago Settlement, installed a bathhouse, a playground, and a citizenship school for immigrants.

Besides the modest good they did in slum neighborhoods, settlement houses also satisfied the hunger of their middle-class residents for meaningful lives. In a famous essay, Jane Addams spoke of the "subjective necessity" of the settlement house. She meant that it was as much a response to the desire of educated young men and women to serve as it was a response to the needs of slum dwellers. Addams herself was a case in point. Born in 1860 in Cedarville, Illinois, she grew up in a comfortable middle-class family and graduated from Rockford College. Then Addams faced an empty future—as an ornamental wife if she married, as a sheltered spinster if she did not. Hull House became her salvation, enabling her to "begin with however small a group to accomplish and to live." At least half of the women residents went on to careers in social service. Settlement houses thus contributed significantly to the emerging profession of social work. To a remarkable degree, the leaders of social reform—both men and women—served apprenticeships in settlement houses.

Revival of the Suffrage Movement. Almost imperceptibly, women activists such as Jane Addams and Florence Kelley breathed new life into the suffrage movement. Why, they asked, should a woman who was capable of running a settlement house or lobbying a bill be denied the right to vote? If women had the right to vote, moreover, they would demand more enlightened legislation and better government. Finally, by encouraging working-class women to help themselves, women progressives got a whole new class interested in fighting for suffrage.

In 1903 social reformers founded the National Women's Trade Union League. Financed and led by wealthy supporters, the league organized women workers, played a considerable role in their strikes, and, perhaps most important, helped to develop working-class leaders. Rose Schneiderman became a union organizer among garment workers in New York City, and Agnes Nestor led women glove workers in Illinois; both were also lobbyists for protective legislation. Athough they often resented the patronizing ways of their well-to-do sponsors, such trade-union women identified their cause with the broader struggle for women's rights. When New York State held referenda on woman suffrage in 1915 and 1917, strong support came from the Jewish and Italian precincts inhabited by unionized garment workers.

Saving the Children
In the early years at Hull House, Jane Addams recalled, toddlers sometimes arrived for kindergarten tipsy from a breakfast of bread soaked in wine. To settlement-house workers, the answer to such ignorance was in child-care education, and so began the program to send visiting nurses into immigrant homes. They taught mothers the proper methods of caring for children—including, as this photograph shows, the daily infant bath, given in a dishpan if necessary.
Chicago Historical Society.

Suffrage activity began to revive nationwide. Women won the right to vote in the state of Washington in 1910, in California in 1911, and in four more western states during the next three years (Map 20.1). Women also altered their tactics. In Britain suffragists had begun to picket Parliament, assault politicians, and go on hunger strikes in jail. Following their lead, Alice Paul, a young Quaker who had lived in Britain, applied these confrontational tactics to the American battle for woman suffrage. Rejecting the slower route of enfranchisement by the states, Paul advocated a constitutional amendment that in one stroke would give women across the country the right to vote. In 1916 she organized the militant National Woman's Party.

The National American Woman Suffrage Association (NAWSA), from which Paul had split off, was also rejuvenated. Carrie Chapman Catt, a skilled political organizer from the New York movement, took over as national leader in 1915. Under her guidance, NAWSA brought a broad-based organization to the campaign for a federal amendment.

Birth of Feminism. In the midst of this suffrage struggle something new and more fundamental began to happen. A new generation of college-educated women, out in the world and self-supporting, refused to be hemmed in by the social constraints of women's "separate sphere." "Breaking into the Human Race"

Rose Schneiderman, 1913
In their battles for better conditions, women garment workers produced their own leaders, and none was more devoted to their cause or more fiery on the platform than Rose Schneiderman. The daughter of a widowed immigrant woman, Schneiderman went to work at thirteen, quickly got caught up in union activities, and fashioned for herself a lifetime career as a trade unionist, including becoming president of the National Women's Trade Union League.
Brown Brothers.

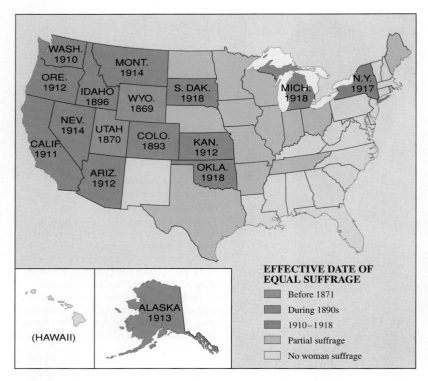

MAP 20.1
Woman Suffrage, 1869–1918
By 1909, after more than sixty years of agitation, only four lightly populated western states had granted women full voting rights. A number of other states offered partial suffrage, limited mostly to voting for school boards and such issues as taxes. Between 1910 and 1918, as the effort shifted to the struggle for a constitutional amendment, eleven states (and Alaska) joined the list granting full suffrage. The most stubborn resistance was in the South.

was the intention they proclaimed at a mass meeting in New York in 1914. "We intend simply to be ourselves," declared the chair Marie Jenny Howe, "not just our little female selves, but our whole big human selves."

The women at this meeting called themselves *feminists*, a term that was just coming into use. In this, its first incarnation, *feminism* meant freedom for full personal development, which in its specifics covered many things—freedom to follow a career, freedom from the double standard in sexual morality, freedom from social convention—but in a larger sense it meant freedom from the stifling stereotypes of women's separate sphere. Thus did Charlotte Perkins Gilman, famous for her advocacy of communal kitchens as a means of liberating women from homemaking, imagine the new woman: "Here she comes, running, out of prison and off pedestal; chains off, crown off, halo off, just a live woman."

Feminists were militantly prosuffrage, but unlike their more traditional suffragist sisters, they did not stake their claim on any presumed uplifting effect of the women's vote on American politics. Rather, they demanded the right to vote because they considered themselves fully equal to men. At the point that the suffrage movement was about to triumph, it was overtaken by a larger revolution that redefined the struggle for women's rights as a battle against all the constraints that prevented women from achieving their potential as human beings.

Feminism brought forth a new and more radical type of woman progressive: Margaret Sanger. As a public health nurse in New York, Sanger had been repeatedly asked by immigrant women the "secret" of how to avoid having more babies. When one of her patients died of a botched abortion, Sanger decided to devote herself to teaching poor immigrant women about birth control. This brought her up against the Comstock laws, which outlawed contraceptive literature and devices as obscene materials (see Chapter 19). While it was easy enough for the educated middle class to evade these laws, birth control could reach the poor only by an open campaign of education. Undeterred by police raids or public disapproval, Sanger gave speeches, published the pamphlet *Family Limitation*, and in 1916 opened the first birth-control clinic in the United States. If her ends were not different from Jane Addams's—both wanted to uplift the downtrodden—the means that Sanger used posed a more provocative challenge to the status quo.

Urban Liberalism

When Hiram Johnson first ran for governor of California on the Republican ticket in 1910, he was the reform candidate of the urban middle class and the farming community. Famous as prosecutor of the corrupt San Francisco boss Abe Ruef, Johnson pledged to purify California politics and curb the Southern Pacific Rail-

Suffragists on Parade, 1912
After 1910 the suffrage movement went into high gear. Suffragist leaders decided to demand a constitutional amendment rather than rely on gaining the vote state by state. In 1912 they served notice on both parties that they meant business and, as shown in this suffragist parade in New York, made their demands a visible part of the presidential campaign.
Corbis-Bettmann.

road—the dominating power in the state's economic and political life. By his second term Johnson was championing social and labor legislation. His original base in the middle class had eroded and been replaced by an immigrant working-class vote that made him an invincible power in California for years.

Johnson's career illustrated an enduring achievement of progressivism: the activation of America's working people as a force in reform politics. The elements in this achievement were, first, the emergence of committed leaders, like Hiram Johnson; second, the crafting of a reform program keyed to the needs of the urban masses; and, perhaps most important, a rising level of popular engagement by these immigrant working people. This last development crucially altered the composition of progressivism, which had begun as a movement of the middle class but then took on board America's working people. The effect was a brand of reform politics that historians have labeled *urban liberalism*. To understand this phenomenon, we need to begin with city boss politics.

Machine Politicians as Reformers. Thirty minutes before quitting time on Saturday afternoon, March 25, 1911, fire broke out at the Triangle Shirtwaist Company in downtown New York City. The flames trapped the workers, mostly young immigrant women. Forty-seven leapt to their deaths; another ninety-nine never made it to the windows (see American Voices, "Pauline Newman: Working for the Triangle Shirtwaist Company," p. 652). The tragedy caused a national furor and led to the creation of the New York State Factory Commission.

Over the next four years the commission developed a remarkable program of labor reform: fifty-six laws dealing with fire hazards, unsafe machines, homework, and wages and hours for women and children. The chairman of the commission was Robert F. Wagner; the vice-chairman, Alfred E. Smith. Both were Tammany Hall politicians, Democratic Party leaders in the state legislature. They established the commission, participated fully in its work, and marshaled the party regulars to pass the proposals into law. All this Wagner and Smith did with the approval of the Tammany machine.

Tammany's reform role reflected something new in urban politics. Party machines increasingly recognized their limitations as social agencies in the modern industrial age. Only the state could prevent future Triangle fires or cope with the evils of factory work and city life. A new generation had entered machine politics. Al Smith and Robert Wagner, men of social vision, absorbed the lessons of the Triangle investigation. They formed durable ties with such middle-class progressives as the social worker Frances Perkins, who sat on the commission as the representative of the New York Consumers' League.

For all their organizational muscle, the urban machines could not ignore the will of the people. In the successes of such progressive politicians as Jersey City's Mark Fagan and Cleveland's Tom Johnson, the machines saw the appeal of reform programs in working-class wards. They faced a threat from the left as well. The Socialist Party was making headway in the cities, electing Milwaukee's Victor Berger as the nation's first socialist congressman in 1910 and winning municipal elections in towns and cities across the country. The political universe of the urban machines had changed, and they had to pay more attention to opinion in the precincts.

PAULINE NEWMAN

Working for the Triangle Shirtwaist Company

———— ★ ————

*P*auline Newman was an organizer and educational director for the International Ladies Garment Workers Union until her death in 1986. As a child she had worked at the notorious Triangle Shirtwaist factory in New York.

A cousin of mine worked for the Triangle Shirtwaist Company and she got me on there in October of 1901. It was probably the largest shirtwaist factory in the city of New York then. They had more than two hundred operators, cutters, examiners, finishers. Altogether more than four hundred people on two floors. . . . We started work at seven-thirty in the morning, and during the busy season we worked until nine in the evening. They didn't pay you any overtime and they didn't give you anything for supper money. . . . What I had to do was not really very difficult. It was just monotonous. When the shirtwaists were finished at the machine there were some threads that were left, and all the youngsters— we had a corner on the floor that resembled a kindergarten—we were given little scissors to cut the threads off. It wasn't heavy work, but it was monotonous, because you did the same thing from seven-thirty in the morning until nine at night.

Well, of course, there were [child labor] laws on the books, but no one bothered to enforce them. The employers were always tipped off if there was going to be an inspection. "Quick," they'd say, "into the boxes!" And we children would climb into the big boxes the finished shirts were stored in. Then some shirts were piled on top of us, and when the inspector came—no children. The factory always got an okay from the inspector, and I suppose someone at City Hall got a little something, too.

The employers didn't recognize anyone working for them as a human being. . . . If you went to the toilet and you were there longer than the floor lady thought you should be, you would be laid off for half a day and sent home. And, of course, that meant no pay. You were not allowed to have your lunch on the fire escape in the summertime. The door was locked to keep us in. That's why so many people were trapped when the fire broke out. . . .

I stopped working at the Triangle Factory during the strike in 1909 and I didn't go back. The union sent me out to raise money for the strikers. I apparently was able to articulate my feelings and opinions about the criminal conditions, and they didn't have anyone else who could do better so they assigned me. . . .

After the 1909 strike I worked with the union, organizing in Philadelphia and Cleveland and other places, so I wasn't at the Triangle Shirtwaist Factory when the fire broke out, but a lot of my friends were. . . . It's very difficult to describe the feeling because I knew the place and I knew so many of the girls. The thing that bothered me was the employers got a lawyer. . . . One hundred and forty-six people were sacrificed, and the judge fined Blank and Harris seventy-five dollars!

Conditions were dreadful in those days. But . . . even when things were terrible, I always had that faith. . . . Only now, I'm a little discouraged sometimes when I see the workers spending their free hours watching television—trash. We fought so hard for those hours and they waste them. We used to read Tolstoy, Dickens, Shelley, by candlelight, and they watch the "Hollywood Squares." Well, they're free to do what they want. That's what we fought for.

———

Source: Joan Morrison and Charlotte Fox Zabusky, eds., *American Mosaic: The Immigrant Experience in the Words of Those Who Lived It* (New York: E. P. Dutton, 1980), 9–14. Copyright © 1980 by Joan Morrison and Charlotte Fox Zabusky. Reprinted by permission.

The Labor Movement. City machines, always pragmatic, adopted urban liberalism without much of an ideological struggle. The same could not be said of trade unions, the other institution that spoke for American working people. During its early years the American Federation of Labor (AFL) had strongly opposed state interference in labor's affairs. Samuel Gompers preached that workers should not seek from government what they could accomplish through their own economic power and self-help. Voluntarism, as trade unionists called this doctrine, did not die out, but it weakened substantially during the progressive years.

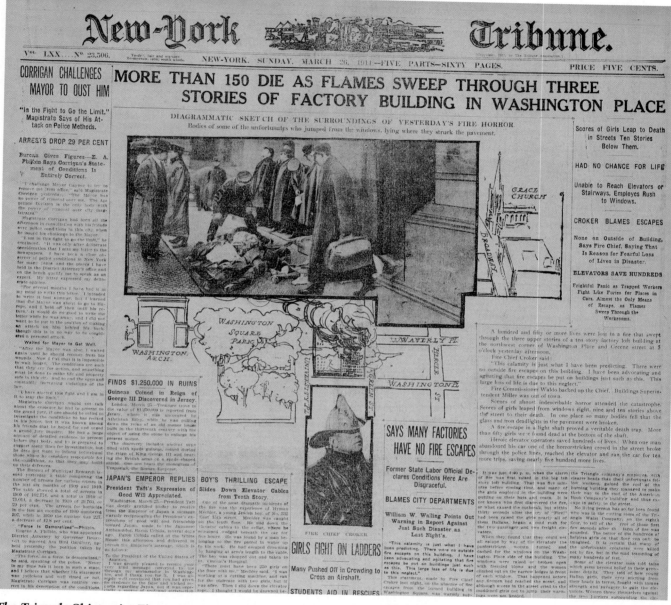

The Triangle Shirtwaist Fire

The doors were the problem. Most were locked (to keep the working girls from leaving early); the few that were open became jammed by bodies as the flames spread. When the fire trucks finally came, the ladders were too short. Compared with those caught inside, the girls who leapt to their deaths were the lucky ones. "As I looked up I saw a love affair in the midst of all the horror," a reporter wrote. A young man was helping girls leap from a window. The fourth "put her arms about him and kiss[ed] him. Then he held her out into space and dropped her." He immediately followed. "Thud—dead, Thud—dead . . . I saw his face before they covered it. . . . He was a real man. He had done his best."

The New York Tribune, March 26, 1911.

In the early twentieth century the labor movement came under severe attack by the courts. In the Danbury Hatters case (1908), the U.S. Supreme Court found a labor boycott—a call by the Hatters' Union for people not to patronize the anti-union D. E. Loewe & Company—to be a conspiracy in restraint of trade under the Sherman Antitrust Act and awarded triple damages to the company. Hundreds of union members stood to lose their homes and life savings until the labor movement raised the money to pay the fines. Even worse was the willingness of many judges to grant employers labor injunctions—court orders—prohibiting a union from carrying on a strike or boycott. The justification was to prevent "irreparable damage" to an employer while the legality of a union's acts was being adjudicated. But the effect of this "temporary" measure was to immobilize and defeat the union, as had happened, for example, to the American Railway Union in the great Pullman strike of 1894 (see Chapter 17).

Only a political response could blunt these assaults on labor's economic weapons. In its "Bill of Grievances" of 1906 the AFL demanded that Congress grant unions immunity from court attack. Rebuffed by Congress, the unions became more politically active, entering campaigns and giving nonpartisan support to candidates who favored their program. The AFL intended to "reward our friends and punish our enemies." In principle, this was "nonpartisan" politics, but in practice, labor became allied to the Democratic Party, which was more responsive than the Republican Party to labor's pleas for a curb on the courts.

Once into politics, the labor movement had difficulty denying the case for social legislation. The AFL, after all, claimed to speak for the entire working class. When muckrakers exposed exploitation of workers and middle-class progressives came forward with solutions, how could the labor movement fail to respond? Gompers served on the Triangle factory commission, and if—according to Frances Perkins—he was a less eager student than the Tammanyite members, learn he did. In state after state, organized labor joined the battle for progressive legislation and increasingly became its strongest advocate.

Conservative labor leaders offered the excuse that protective laws were for women and children, who could not defend themselves. In practice, however, trade unions became more flexible about legislative protection for men as well, and on the issue of workers' compensation they took the lead.

Social Insurance Deferred. Accidents took an awful toll in American factories and mines. Two thousand coal miners were killed every year, dying from cave-ins and explosions at a rate 50 percent higher than in German mines. Liability laws, which were still governed by common-law principles, so heavily favored the employer that victims of industrial accidents rarely got compensation. Nothing cried out more for reform than the plight of maimed workers and penniless widows. Citing state-funded accident insurance in Germany and Britain, the unions demanded comparable protections for American workers, although they were willing to compromise with the insurance industry and employers on a funding system based on accident rates. Between 1910 and 1917 workers' compensation on this basis went into effect in all the industrial states.

Compared to Europe, however, the United States was slow to protect workers against the hazards of

Maimed Factory Worker
Lewis Hine, a great photographer of immigrant life, took this undated picture of a disabled factory worker. Two of his four children are in the background. How was he to support them? If his accident occurred before the passage of workers' compensation laws in 1910, they were probably out of luck.
George Eastman House.

modern industrial life. Health insurance and unemployment compensation, familiar in Europe, scarcely made it onto the American political agenda. Old-age pensions, which Britain adopted in 1908, got a serious hearing, only to come up against the fact that the United States already had a pension system of a kind, for Civil War veterans: as many as half of all native-born white men over sixty-four or their survivors were receiving veterans' pensions in the early twentieth century. It did not help, moreover, that the Republican Party had shamelessly exploited veterans' pensions as a campaign issue, or that administration of the program was notoriously corrupt and laced with patronage, or, finally, that easy access to veterans' benefits often reinforced fears of state-induced dependency. Clarence J. Hicks, an industrial-relations expert, recalled Civil War pensioners idling away the hours around the wood stove in the grocery store in his Wisconsin town. They had decided "that the country owed them a living," lost their initiative, and "retreated from the battle of life."

Not until a later generation experienced the Great Depression of the 1930s would the country be ready for social insurance. A secure old age, unemployment compensation, health insurance—these human needs of a modern industrial order were beyond the reach of urban liberals in the Progressive Era.

Cultural Pluralism Embattled. Urban liberalism was driven not only by the plight of the economically downtrodden but also by a sharpening attack on immigrants. Old-stock evangelical Protestants had long agitated for laws that would impose their moral and cultural norms on American society. After 1900 this impulse again beat strongly, expressing, in fact, one strand of progressive reform. The Anti-Saloon League, which called itself "the Protestant church in action," became a formidable force for prohibition in many states. Outlawing the sale of liquor was related to other reform targets: the saloon made for dirty politics, poverty, and bad labor conditions. Like progressives on other fronts, prohibitionists pronounced their movement the "Revolt of Decent Citizens."

The moral-reform agenda expanded to include a new goal: restricting the immigration of southern and eastern Europeans into the United States. "No intelligent patriot," pronounced M.I.T. president Francis A. Walker, can observe "the entrance . . . of such vast masses of peasantry, degraded below our utmost concepts . . . without the gravest apprehension and alarm." La Follette's close advisor, Edward A. Ross of the University of Wisconsin, denounced the "pigsty mode of life" of immigrants. The danger, respected social scientists argued, was that the nation's Anglo-Saxon population would be "mongrelized" and its civilization swamped by "inferior" Mediterranean and Slavic cultures. Feeding on this fear, the Immigration Restriction League spearheaded a movement to end America's historic open-door policy. Like prohibition, immigration restriction was considered by its proponents to be a progressive reform.

Urban liberals thought otherwise. They denounced prohibition and immigration restriction as attacks on the personal liberty and worthiness of urban immigrants. Prohibition, protested one Catholic academic, was "despotic and hypocritical domination." The Tammany politician Martin McCue accused the Protestant ministry of "seeking to substitute the policeman's nightstick for the Bible."

Urban liberal leaders championed both the economic needs of city dwellers and their religious and cultural freedom. In many ways, certainly until the Great Depression, the second issue provided the stronger basis for urban liberal politics. And because their party cultivated the immigrant vote, the Democrats became the beneficiaries of the rise of urban liberalism. The rapid growth of this city vote destined the

Democrats to become the majority party. The shift from Republican domination, though not completed until the 1930s, began during the Progressive Era.

Racism in an Age of Reform

The direct primary was the flagship of progressive politics—the crucial reform, as La Follette said, for defeating the party bosses and returning politics to "the people." The primary originated not in Wisconsin, however, but in the South, and by the time La Follette got his primary law in 1903, it was already operating in seven southern states. As in the North, the direct primary in the South was celebrated as a democratizing reform and frequently set the stage for bringing reform state administrations into power.

The southern primary, however, sprang from the furious political battles of the 1890s (see Chapter 18). In the course of those battles, as the challenge to Democratic rule failed, one of the devices that emerged for driving blacks out of politics was the primary. In the South the Democratic primary was a *white* primary. Since the Democratic nomination was tantamount to election, excluding African Americans from the nominating process effectively disfranchised them. The southern primary was dressed up as an attack on backroom party rule, but it served also to drive blacks out of politics.

White Supremacy in the Progressive Vein. How could democratic reform and white supremacy be united in this fashion? Because of the racism of the age. In a 1902 book on Reconstruction, Professor John W. Burgess of Columbia University denounced the Fifteenth Amendment. Granting the vote to the freedmen after the Civil War was a "monstrous thing," wrote Burgess. "A black skin means membership in a race of men which has never of itself succeeded to reason." Burgess was southern-born, but he was confident that his northern audience saw the "vast differences in political capacity" between blacks and whites and approved of black disfranchisement. Not even the Republican Party offered a rebuttal. Indeed, as president-elect in 1908, William Howard Taft applauded the southern laws as necessary to "prevent entirely the possibility of domination by . . . an ignorant electorate" and reassured southerners that "the federal government has nothing to do with social equality."

In the North, racial tensions were on the rise. Over 200,000 blacks migrated from the South between 1900 and 1910. Their arrival in northern cities invariably sparked white resentment. Attacks on blacks became widespread, capped by a bloody race riot in Springfield, Illinois, in 1908. Equally reflective of racist sentiment was the huge success of D. W. Griffith's epic film *Birth of a Nation* (1915), which depicted Reconstruction as a moral struggle between rampaging blacks and a chivalrous Ku Klux Klan. Woodrow Wilson found the film's history "all so terribly true." His Democratic administration marked a low point for the federal government as the ultimate guarantor of equal rights: during Wilson's tenure, segregation of the U.S. civil service would have gone into effect had there not been an outcry among black leaders and a handful of influential white allies.

Revival of the Civil Rights Struggle.   In these bleak years a core of young black professionals, mostly northern-born, began to fight back. The key figure was William Monroe Trotter, the pugnacious editor of the *Boston Guardian* and an outspoken critic of Booker T. Washington (see Chapter 18). "The policy of compromise has failed," Trotter argued. "The policy of resistance and aggression deserves a trial." In this endeavor, Trotter was joined by W. E. B. Du Bois, whose *The Souls of Black Folk* (1903) had challenged Washington's accommodationism for "practically accept[ing] the alleged inferiority of the Negro." In 1906 the two of them, having broken with Washington, called a meeting of twenty-nine supporters at Niagara Falls—in Canada, because no hotel on the U.S. side would admit blacks. The Niagara Movement, which resulted from that meeting, had an impact far beyond the scattering of members and local bodies it organized. The principles it affirmed would define the struggle for the rights of African Americans: first, encouragement of black pride

by all possible means; second, an uncompromising demand for full political and civil equality; and above all, a resolute denial "that the Negro-American assents to inferiority, is submissive under oppression and apologetic before insults."

Going against the grain, a handful of white reformers rallied to the African American cause. Among the most devoted was Mary White Ovington, who grew up in an abolitionist family. Like Jane Addams, Ovington became a settlement-house worker, but among blacks in New York City rather than in an immigrant Chicago neighborhood. News of the Springfield race riot of 1908 changed her life. Convinced that her duty was to fight racism, Ovington called a meeting of sympathetic white progressives, which led to the formation of the National Association for the Advancement of Colored People (NAACP) in 1909.

Torn by internal disagreements, the Niagara Movement was breaking up, and most of the black activists joined the NAACP. Whites dominated the organization's leadership, with one crucial exception: Du Bois became editor of the NAACP's journal, *The Crisis*. With a passion that only an African American voice could provide, Du Bois used that platform to proclaim the demand for black equality.

In social welfare, the National Urban League became the lead organization, uniting in 1911 the many groups serving black migrants arriving in northern cities. Like the NAACP, the Urban League was interracial, including white reformers such as Ovington and

W. E. B. Du Bois
No activity undertaken by the NAACP in the early years was more important than the publication of its journal, *The Crisis*, which under the brilliant editorship of W. E. B. Du Bois became the strongest voice for equal rights and black pride in the country. In this photograph, Du Bois is pictured at his desk at the magazine's editorial office.
Schomburg Center for Research in Black Culture, New York Public Library.

black welfare activists such as William Lewis Bulkley, a New York school principal who was the main architect of the Urban League. In the South, social welfare was very much the province of black women, whose civic activities to some extent filled the vacuum left by the disfranchisement of black men. African American women's progressivism sprang organizationally from the churches and schools, but also from the southern affiliates of the National Association of Colored Women's Clubs, which had started in 1896. And because their activities seemed unthreatening to white supremacy, black women were able to reach across the color line and find allies and supporters among white women in the South.

Progressivism was a house of many chambers. Most were infected by the respectable racism of the age, but not all. A saving remnant of white progressives rallied to the cause of African Americans. In the interracial NAACP and Urban League, and in such black organizations as the National Association of Colored Women's Clubs, national institutions were formed that would lead the black struggle for a better life over the next half-century.

Colored Women's League of Washington, D.C.
At a time when black men were being driven from politics in the South, their wives and sisters organized themselves and became an alternative voice of black conscience. Sara Iredell Fleetwood, superintendent of the Freedman's Hospital Training School for Nurses, founded the Colored Women's League of Washington, D.C., in 1892 for purposes of "racial uplift." This picture of the League was taken on the steps of Frederick Douglass's home in Anacostia, Washington. Mrs. Fleetwood is seated at the far right, third row from the bottom. The notations are by someone seeking to identify the other members, a modest effort to save for posterity these women, mostly teachers, who did their best for the good of the race.
Library of Congress.

Progressivism and National Politics

---★---

The gathering forces of progressivism reached the national scene slowly. Reformers had been spurred by immediate and visible problems. Washington seemed distant from the battles they were waging in their cities and states. But in 1906 Robert La Follette left the governor's office in Wisconsin for the U.S. Senate. Other seasoned progressives, also ambitious for a wider stage, made the same move. By 1910 a highly vocal progressive Republican bloc was making itself heard in both houses of Congress.

Progressivism came to national politics not from Congress, however, but by way of the presidency. This was partly because the White House provided a "bully pulpit"—to use Theodore Roosevelt's phrase—for mobilizing national opinion. But just as important was the twist of fate that brought Roosevelt to the White House on September 14, 1901.

T. R.: The Making of a Progressive President

Except for his aristocratic background, Theodore Roosevelt was cut from much the same cloth as other progressive politicians. Born in 1858, he came from a wealthy old-line New York family, attended Harvard, and might have chosen the life of a leisured man of letters. Instead, scarcely out of college, he plunged into Republican politics and in 1882 entered the New York State legislature. Like many other budding progressives, he was motivated by a moralistic, Christian upbringing. Roosevelt always identified himself—loudly—with the cause of righteousness. But he did not scorn power and its uses. He showed contempt for the amateurism of the Mugwumps, and much preferred the company of party professionals. Roosevelt rose in the New York party because he skillfully translated his moral fervor into broad popular support and thus forced himself on reluctant state Republican bosses.

After returning from the Spanish-American War as the hero of San Juan Hill (see Chapter 21), Roosevelt won the New York governorship in 1898. During his single term he clearly signaled his reformist inclinations by pushing through civil-service reform and a tax on corporate franchises. He discharged the corrupt superintendent of insurance over the Republican Party's objections and asserted his confidence in the government's capacity to improve the life of the people.

Hoping to neutralize him, the party bosses promoted Roosevelt in 1900 to what seemed a dead-end job, as William McKinley's vice-president. Roosevelt

Theodore Roosevelt at Yellowstone National Park, 1903
President Roosevelt, a devoted conservationist, is pictured here about to enter Yellowstone, the first of America's national parks and a favorite of his. The photograph of him on horseback must have delighted Roosevelt. It showed him as he liked to be seen—as a great outdoorsman.
Picture Research Consultants & Archives.

accepted reluctantly. But on September 6, 1901, an anarchist named Leon F. Czolgosz shot the president. When McKinley died eight days later, Roosevelt became president. It was a sure bet, groaned Republican boss Mark Hanna, that "that damn cowboy" would make trouble in the White House.

Roosevelt in fact moved cautiously, attending first of all to politics. He understood the power of the conservative Republican bloc in Congress and treated the Senate leader, Nelson W. Aldrich of Rhode Island, with kid gloves while consolidating his position. He adroitly used the patronage powers of the presidency to gain control of the Republican Party. But Roosevelt was also restrained by uncertainty about what reform role the federal government ought to play. At first the new president might have been described as a progressive without a cause.

First Steps: Conservation and the Coal Strike. Even so, Roosevelt displayed his activist bent. An ardent outdoorsman, he devoted part of his first annual message to Congress to conservation. Unlike John Muir (see Chapter 16), Roosevelt was not a preservationist broadly opposed to exploitation of the nation's wilderness. Rather, he wanted to conserve the country's resources.

He was not against commercial development as long as it was regulated and mindful of the public interest. The Forest Reserve Act of 1891 had begun the process of withdrawing timberland from unregulated private use. Roosevelt added more than 125 million acres to the national forests and brought mineral lands and water power sites into the reserve system. In 1902 he backed the Newlands Reclamation Act, which designated the proceeds from public land sales for irrigation in arid regions. His administration upgraded the management of public lands and, to the chagrin of some Republicans, energetically prosecuted violators of federal land laws. In the cause of conservation Roosevelt showed his enthusiasm for exercising executive authority and his disdain for those who sought profit "by betraying the public."

The same inclinations influenced Roosevelt's handling of the anthracite miners' strike of 1902. Hard coal (anthracite) was the main fuel for home heating in those days. As cold weather approached with no settlement in sight, the government faced a national emergency. The United Mine Workers, led by John Mitchell, were willing to submit to arbitration, but the coal operators adamantly opposed recognizing the union. Roosevelt's advisors told him there was no legal basis for federal intervention. Nevertheless, the president called both sides to the White House on October 1, 1902. When the conference failed, Roosevelt threatened the operators with a government takeover of the mines. He also persuaded the financier John Pierpont Morgan to use his considerable influence with them. At that point the coal operators caved in. The strike ended with the appointment by Roosevelt of an arbitration commission to rule on the issues, another unprecedented step. While not especially supportive of organized labor, Roosevelt became positively livid at the "arrogant stupidity" of the mine owners.

"Of all the forms of tyranny the least attractive and the most vulgar is the tyranny of mere wealth," Roosevelt wrote in his autobiography. He was prepared to deploy all his presidential authority against the "tyranny" of irresponsible business.

The Problem of the Trusts. The economic issue that most concerned Roosevelt was the assault on the competitive market by big business. The drift toward large-scale enterprise had been under way for many years, as entrepreneurs sought the efficiencies of nationwide, vertically integrated firms (see Chapter 17). But they knew that creating bigger businesses also meant gaining power to control markets. This was the motive behind the scramble to merge rival firms in the aftermath of the depression of the 1890s. These mergers—*trusts*, as they were called—greatly increased the degree of business concentration in the economy. Of the 73 largest industrial companies in 1900, 53 had not existed three years earlier. By 1910, 1 percent of the nation's manufacturers accounted for 44 percent of the nation's industrial output (see Voices from Abroad, "James Bryce: America in 1905: 'Business Is King,'" p. 660).

Most of these new combines were heavily watered—that is, the stocks and bonds they issued greatly exceeded the real value of the properties they controlled. For their underwriting services in launching the new trusts, moreover, investment bankers such as J. P. Morgan charged huge fees. Worse yet, financiers did not relinquish control over the combines they had fathered, for they sat on the boards of directors of the new firms and exerted a back-room influence on the

Jack and the Wall Street Giants
In this vivid cartoon from the humor magazine *Puck*, Jack (Theodore Roosevelt) has come to slay the giants of Wall Street. To the country, trust-busting took on the mythic qualities of the fairy tale—with about the same amount of awe for the fearsome Wall Street giants and hope in the prowess of the intrepid Roosevelt. J. P. Morgan is the giant leering at front right.
Library of Congress.

JAMES BRYCE

America in 1905: "Business Is King"

———————★———————

James Bryce, British author of The American Commonwealth *(1888), a great treatise on American politics, visited the United States regularly over many years. In an essay published in 1905, Lord Bryce took stock of the changes he had seen during the previous quarter century. What most struck him, beyond the sheer growth of material wealth, was the loss of individualism and the intensifying concentration of corporate power. In this, he was at one with his old friend Theodore Roosevelt, who at that very time was gearing up to do battle with the trusts.*

That which most strikes the visitor to America today is its prodigious material development. Industrial growth, swift thirty or forty years ago, advances more swiftly now. The rural districts are being studded with villages, the villages are growing into cities, the cities are stretching out long arms of suburbs, which follow the lines of road and railway in every direction. The increase of wealth, even more remarkable than the increase of population, impresses the European more than ever before because the contrast with Europe is greater. The huge fortunes, the fortunes of those whose income reaches or exceeds a million dollars a year, are of course far more numerous than in any other country. . . . With this extraordinary material development it is natural that in the United States, business, that is to say, industry, commerce, and finance, should have more and more come to overshadow and dwarf all other interests, all other occupations. . . . Business is king.

Commerce and industry themselves have developed new features. Twenty-two years ago there were no trusts. . . . Even then, however, corporations had covered a larger proportion of the whole field of industry and commerce in America than in Europe, and their structure was more flexible and efficient. Today this is still more the case; while as for trusts, they have become one of the most salient phenomena of the country. They fix the attention, they excite the alarm of economists and politicians as well as of traders in the Old World, while they exercise and baffle the ingenuity of American legislators. Workingmen follow, though hitherto with unequal steps, the efforts at combination which the lords of production and distribution have been making. The consumer stands, if not with folded hands, yet so far with no clear view of the steps he may make for his own protection. Perhaps his prosperity—for he is prosperous—helps him to be quiescent.

The example of the United States, the land in which individualism has been most conspicuously vigorous, may seem to suggest that the world is passing out of the stage of individualism and returning to that earlier stage in which groups of men formed the units of society. The bond of association was, in those early days, kinship, real or supposed, and a servile or quasi-servile dependence of the weak upon the strong. Now it is the power of wealth which enables the few to combine so as to gain command of the sources of wealth. . . . Is it a paradox to observe that it is because the Americans have been the most individualistic of peoples that they are now the people among whom the art of combination has reached its maximum? The amazing keenness and energy, which were stimulated by the commercial conditions of the country, have evoked and ripened a brilliant talent for organization. This talent has applied new methods to production and distribution and has enabled wealth, gathered into a small number of hands, to dominate even the enormous market of America.

Source: Allan Nevins, ed., *America through British Eyes* (Gloucester, MA: Peter Smith, 1968), 384–387.

operating executives. Almost overnight a "money power"—a cabal of Wall Street bankers—seemed to have gained a stranglehold on the American economy.

Roosevelt's sense of the nation's uneasiness became evident as early as his first annual message, in which he referred to the "real and grave evils" of economic concentration. But what weapons could the president use in response?

The basic legal principles upholding free competition were already firmly established. Under common law—the body of judge-made legal precedents that America had inherited from Britain—it was illegal for anyone to restrain or monopolize trade. Persons who were economically injured by such actions could sue for damages. These common-law rights had been enacted into statute law in many states during the

1880s and then, because the problem went beyond state jurisdictions, had been incorporated into the Sherman Antitrust Act of 1890 and become part of federal law.

Neither the Cleveland administration nor the McKinley administration had been much inclined to enforce the Sherman Act. But the law was there to be used. Its potential rested above all on the fact that it incorporated common-law principles of unimpeachable validity. In the right hands, the Sherman Act could be a strong weapon against the abuse of economic power.

Trust-Busting. Roosevelt made his opening move in 1903 by establishing the Bureau of Corporations, empowered to investigate business practices. On the basis of facts gathered by the bureau, the Department of Justice was enabled to mount antitrust suits. The department had already filed such a suit in 1902 against the Northern Securities Company, a combination of the railroad systems of the Northwest. In a landmark decision, the Supreme Court ordered Northern Securities dissolved in 1904.

In the presidential election that year, Roosevelt handily defeated a weak conservative Democratic candidate, Judge Alton B. Parker. Now president in his own right, Roosevelt stepped up the attack on the trusts. He took on forty-five of the nation's giant firms, including Standard Oil, American Tobacco, and Du Pont. His rhetoric rising, Roosevelt became the nation's trust-buster, a crusader against "predatory wealth."

But Roosevelt was not antibusiness. He regarded large-scale enterprise as a natural result of modern industrialism. Only firms that abused their power deserved punishment. But how would those companies be identified? Under the Sherman Act, following common-law doctrine, the courts decided whether an act in restraint of trade was "unreasonable"—that is, actually harmed the public interest—and the courts thus had the discretion to evaluate the actions of corporations on a case-by-case basis. In the *Trans-Missouri* decision of 1897, however, the Supreme Court repudiated this "rule of reason." As a result, after 1897, actions that restrained or monopolized trade automatically put a firm in violation of the Sherman Act, regardless of their impact on the public interest.

Little-noticed when it was first decided, *Trans-Missouri* placed Roosevelt in an awkward position. He had no desire to hamstring legitimate business activity, but he could not rely on the courts to distinguish between "good" and "bad" trusts. The only solution was for Roosevelt to assume that responsibility. This the president could do because it was up to him—or to his attorney general—to decide whether to initiate antitrust prosecutions in the first place.

In November 1904, with an antitrust suit looming, the United States Steel Corporation's chairman, Elbert

J. Pierpont Morgan
J. P. Morgan was a giant among American financiers. He had served an apprenticeship in investment banking under his father, a leading Anglo-American banker in London. A gruff man of few words, Morgan had a genius for instilling trust and the strength of will to persuade others to follow his lead and do his bidding—qualities the great photographer Edward Steichen captured in this portrait.
George Eastman House.

H. Gary, approached Roosevelt and proposed a deal: cooperation in exchange for preferential treatment. The company would open its books to the Bureau of Corporations; if the bureau found evidence of wrongdoing, the company would be warned privately and given a chance to set matters right. Roosevelt accepted this "gentlemen's agreement," as well as a similar one with International Harvester the next year. J. P. Morgan controlled both firms, and from Morgan's standpoint the arrangement seemed entirely sensible. Two great powers, one political and the other economic, would meet as equals and settle matters between them. For Roosevelt, the gentlemen's agreements solved a serious dilemma: he could accommodate the realities of the modern industrial order while maintaining his public image as champion against the trusts.

Railroad Regulation. The railroads posed a different kind of problem for Roosevelt. As quasi-public enterprises, the railroads had always been subject to public regulation. Initially, this had been the responsibility of the states, but with the passage of the Interstate Commerce Act of 1887, the federal government had entered the field, establishing in the Interstate Commerce

Commission (ICC) the nation's first federal regulatory agency. Nevertheless, like the Sherman Act, railroad regulation remained pretty much a dead letter in its early years. Convinced, however, that the railroads needed firm regulation, Roosevelt pushed through the Elkins Act of 1903, which prohibited discriminatory rebates—that is, reductions on published rates for preferred or powerful customers. Then, with the 1904 election behind him, Roosevelt launched the drive for real railroad regulation.

The central issue was government rate-setting, which the conservative Republican bloc in Congress firmly opposed. In 1906, after nearly two years of wrangling, Congress passed the Hepburn Railway Act, which empowered the ICC to set maximum rates upon complaint of a shipper and to prescribe uniform methods of bookkeeping. But as a concession to conservatives, the courts retained broad powers to review the ICC's rate decisions.

The Hepburn Act was a triumph of Roosevelt's skills as a political operator. He had maneuvered brilliantly against determined opposition and come away with the essentials of what he wanted. Despite grumbling by Senate progressives critical of any compromise, Roosevelt was satisfied. He had achieved a landmark expansion of the government's regulatory powers over business.

Consumer Protection.   The regulation of consumer products, another hallmark of progressive reform, was very much the handiwork of muckraking journalists. In 1905 Samuel Hopkins Adams published a series of articles on the patent-medicine business in *Collier's*. The first paragraph opened with these riveting words:

> *Gullible America will spend this year some seventy-five millions of dollars in the purchase of patent medicines. In consideration of this sum it will swallow huge quantities of alcohol, an appalling amount of opiates and narcotics, a wide assortment of varied drugs ranging from powerful and dangerous heart depressants to insidious liver stimulants; and, far in excess of all other ingredients, undiluted fraud. For fraud, exploited by the skillfullest of advertising bunco men, is the basis of the trade.*

For a time, industry lobbies stymied food and drug regulation. Then, in 1906, Upton Sinclair's novel *The Jungle* appeared. Sinclair had meant to expose labor exploitation in Chicago meatpacking plants, but his graphic descriptions of rotten meat and filthy conditions excited—and sickened—the nation. President Roosevelt, previously not greatly concerned about consumer issues, weighed into the legislative battle, initiating a federal investigation of the stockyards. The Pure Food and Drug Act and the Meat Inspection Act passed within months, and another administrative agency was added to the federal bureaucratic structure Roosevelt was building: the Food and Drug Administration.

The Square Deal.   During the 1904 presidential campaign Roosevelt had taken to calling his program the Square Deal. This kind of labeling was new to American politics, introducing a political style that dramatized issues, mobilized public opinion, and asserted leadership. But the label identified something of substance as well. After many years of passivity, the federal government was reclaiming the activist role it had abandoned after the Civil War. Now, however, the target was the new economic order. When companies misused corporate power, the government had the responsibility to intercede and assure ordinary Americans a "square deal."

During his two terms as president Theodore Roosevelt struggled to bring a modern corporate economy under regulatory control. He was well aware, however, that his Square Deal was built on nineteenth-century foundations; in particular, antitrust doctrine, which aimed at enforcing competition, seemed inadequate in the face of a large-scale industrial order. Better, Roosevelt felt, to give the federal government administrative powers to regulate big business than to try to

Campaigning for the Square Deal
When William McKinley ran for president in 1896, he sat on his front porch in Canton, Ohio, and received delegations of voters. That was not Theodore Roosevelt's way. He considered the presidency a "bully pulpit," and he used the office brilliantly to mobilize public opinion and to assert his leadership. The preeminence of the presidency in American public life begins with Roosevelt's administration. Here, at the height of his crusading power, he stumps for the Square Deal in the 1904 election.
Library of Congress.

break it up. Roosevelt's final presidential speeches dwelt on the need for a reform agenda for the twentieth century. This was the task he bequeathed to his chosen successor, William Howard Taft.

The Fracturing of Republican Progressivism

William Howard Taft was an estimable man in many ways. An able jurist and a superb administrator, he had served Roosevelt loyally and well as governor general of the Philippines and as secretary of war. He was an avowed Square Dealer. But he was not by nature a progressive politician. Taft was incapable of dramatizing issues or stirring the people. He disliked the give-and-take of politics, he distrusted power, and he generally deferred to Congress. In fundamental ways, moreover, Taft was deeply conservative. After years as a federal judge, Taft sanctified property rights, revered the processes of the law, and, unlike Roosevelt, found it hard to trim his means to fit his ends.

Taft's Democratic opponent in the 1908 campaign was William Jennings Bryan. This was Bryan's last hurrah, his third attempt at the presidency, and he made the most of it. Eloquent as ever, Bryan showed again why he was known as the Commoner, the voice of the people. He attacked the Republicans as the party of the "plutocrats," and he outdid them in urging tougher antitrust legislation, lower tariffs, stricter railway regulation, and advanced labor legislation. So favorable was Bryan to the unions that despite its formal nonpartisanship, the AFL endorsed him. Bryan's campaign moved the Democratic Party into the mainstream of national progressive politics, but that was not enough to offset Taft's advantages as Roosevelt's candidate.

Taft won comfortably, if by a smaller margin than Roosevelt's smashing 1904 victory, and he entered the White House with a mandate to pick up where Roosevelt had left off. That, alas, was not to be.

Taft's Troubles. By 1909 the ferment of reform had unsettled the Republican Party. On the right, the conservatives were bracing themselves against further losses. Led by the formidable Senator Nelson W. Aldrich, they were still a force to be reckoned with. On the left, progressive Republicans were rebellious. They had broad popular support—especially in the Midwest—and, in Robert La Follette, a fiery leader. They felt that Roosevelt had been too easy on business, and with him gone from the White House, the congressional progressives were determined to make up for lost time. Reconciling these conflicting forces within the Republican Party would have been a daunting task for the most accomplished politician. For Taft, it spelled disaster.

First there was the tariff. Progressives considered protective tariffs a major reason why competition had declined and the trusts had sprung up. Although Taft had campaigned for tariff reform, he was won over by the conservative Republican bloc during the prolonged drafting process and gave his approval for the protectionist Payne-Aldrich Tariff Act of 1909, which sheltered eastern industry from foreign competition.

Next came the Pinchot-Ballinger affair. U.S. Chief Forester Gifford Pinchot, an ardent conservationist and a chum of Roosevelt, accused Secretary of the Interior Richard A. Ballinger of conspiring to transfer Alaskan public land—rich in natural resources—to a private syndicate. When Pinchot made the charges public in January 1910, Taft fired him for insubordination. Despite Taft's strong conservationist credentials, in the eyes of the progressives the Pinchot-Ballinger affair marked him for life as a friend of the "interests" bent on plundering the nation's resources.

Solemnly pledged to carry on in Roosevelt's tradition, Taft found himself propelled into the conservative Republican camp, an ally of "Uncle Joe" Cannon, the dictatorial Speaker of the House of Representatives. When a House revolt finally broke Cannon's power in 1910, it was regarded as a defeat for the president as well. Largely in reaction to Taft, the reformers in the Republican Party turned into a distinct, organized faction. By 1910 they were calling themselves "Progressives" or, in more belligerent moments, "Insurgents." Taft answered by backing their conservative foes in the Republican primaries that year. This vendetta climaxed Taft's record of clumsy leadership.

The agents of historical change sometimes take strange forms. A person out of tune with the times can, by the sheer friction he or she generates, serve as the catalyst for great events. Such was the fate of President Taft.

The Taft-Roosevelt Split. The progressives emerged from the 1910 elections stronger and angrier. In January 1911 they formed the National Progressive Republican League and began a drive to take over the Republican Party. La Follette was the progressives' leader and designated presidential candidate, but they knew that their best chance to win lay with Theodore Roosevelt.

Home from a year-long safari in Africa, Roosevelt yearned to reenter the political fray. He would have been troublesome for Taft under any circumstances. As it was, the president's handling of the progressives fed Roosevelt's mounting sense of outrage. But Roosevelt was too loyal a party member to defy the Republican establishment and too astute a politician not to recognize that a party split would benefit the Democrats. He could be spurred into rebellion only by the discovery of a true clash of principles. On the question of the trusts, just such a clash materialized.

By distinguishing between good and bad trusts, Roosevelt had managed to reconcile public policy (the Sherman Act) and economic reality (the inevitable tendency toward corporate concentration). But this was a makeshift solution that depended on a president who was willing to stretch his powers to the limit. Taft had no such inclination. His legalistic mind rebelled at the notion that he as president should decide which trusts should be prosecuted. The Sherman Act was on the books. "We are going to enforce that law or die in the attempt," Taft promised grimly.

In its *Standard Oil* decision (1911) the Supreme Court eased Taft's problem by reasserting the common-law principle of the "rule of reason," which meant that, once again, the courts themselves would distinguish between good and bad trusts. With that burden lifted from the executive branch, Attorney General George W. Wickersham picked up the pace of antitrust actions.

United States Steel Corporation became an immediate target. Among the charges against the steel trust was that it had violated the antimonopoly provision of the Sherman Act by acquiring the Tennessee Coal and Iron Company in 1907. The purchase had been made from a banking house that had fallen into trouble and urgently needed to sell its Tennessee Coal and Iron stock to raise capital. As president, Roosevelt had personally approved the acquisition as a necessary step—as United States Steel representatives had explained it to him—to prevent a financial collapse on Wall Street. Taft's suit against United States Steel thus amounted to an attack on Roosevelt. Nothing was better calculated to propel Roosevelt into action than an issue that was both an affair of personal honor and a question of broad principle.

The New Nationalism. Ever since leaving the White House, Roosevelt had been pondering the trust problem. There was, he concluded, a third way between breaking up big business and submitting to corporate rule. The federal government could be empowered to oversee the nation's industrial corporations to make sure they acted in the public interest. They could be regulated by a federal trade commission, with powers comparable to those exerted by the Interstate Commerce Commission over the railroads or by state commissions over public utilities. In the modern age, Roosevelt was suggesting, industrial corporations were becoming, like railroads and utilities, "natural" monopolies and therefore were subject to the same degree of public oversight.

In a speech at Osawatomie, Kansas, in August 1910 Roosevelt made the case for what he now called the New Nationalism. The central issue, Roosevelt argued, was human welfare versus property rights. In modern society, property had to be controlled "to whatever degree the public welfare may require it." The government would become "the steward of the public welfare."

This formulation removed the restraints from Roosevelt's thinking. Ultimately, after breaking with Taft, he went so far as to embrace government price-fixing for corporate industry. He took up the cause of social justice, adding to his program a federal child labor law, regulation of labor relations, and a national minimum wage for women. Most radical, perhaps, was Roosevelt's attack on the legal system. Insisting that the courts should not be making social policy, Roosevelt proposed sharp curbs on their powers, even raising the possibility of popular recall of court decisions.

Beyond these specifics, the New Nationalism advanced a distinctive political philosophy. The key source was a book by the journalist Herbert Croly, *The Promise of American Life* (1909), which called for a uniting of rival strains in the American political tradition. From Alexander Hamilton's federalism Croly drew his emphasis on strong national government; from Thomas Jefferson's republicanism came Croly's enthusiasm for democracy and the primacy of the interests of the common citizen. The result, however, was a genuine break from America's political past. To the problem of corporate power the New Nationalism offered a statist solution—an enormous expansion of the role of the federal government.

Early in 1912 Roosevelt announced his candidacy for the presidency and immediately swept the progressive Republicans into his camp. A bitter party battle ensued. Taft proved to be a tenacious opponent. Roosevelt won the states that held primary elections, but Taft controlled the party organizations elsewhere. Dominated by the party regulars, the Republican convention chose Taft.

Considering himself cheated out of the nomination, Roosevelt led his followers into a new Progressive Party, soon nicknamed the "Bull Moose" Party. In a crusading campaign Roosevelt offered the New Nationalism to the people.

Woodrow Wilson and the New Freedom

While the Republicans battled among themselves, the Democrats were on the move. The scars caused by the free-silver campaign of 1896 had faded (see Chapter 18), and in the 1908 campaign William Jennings Bryan had established the rejuvenated party's progressive credentials. The Democrats made dramatic gains in 1910, taking over the House of Representatives for the first time since 1892, winning ten Senate seats, and capturing a number of traditionally Republican governorships. After fourteen years as the party's standard-bearer, Bryan reluctantly made way for a new generation of leaders.

HARPER'S WEEKLY

EDITED BY GEORGE HARVEY

July 13 1912   THE NEW RIDER   Price 10 Cents

On to the White House

At the Democratic convention of 1912 Woodrow Wilson only narrowly defeated the front-runner, Champ Clark of Missouri. *Harper's Weekly* triumphantly depicted Wilson immediately after his nomination—the scholar turned politician riding off on the Democratic donkey, with his running mate, Thomas R. Marshall, hanging on behind. The magazine's editor, George Harvey, had identified Wilson as presidential timber back in 1906, long before the Princeton president had thought of politics, and had worked on his behalf from then on. Newberry Library.

The ablest was Woodrow Wilson of New Jersey, a noted political scientist who, as university president, had brought Princeton into the front rank of American universities. In 1910, with no political experience, he accepted the Democratic nomination for governor of New Jersey and won. Wilson compiled a brilliant record: he cleaned up the boss system and passed a direct-primary law, workers' compensation, and stronger regulation of railroads and utilities. With these credentials as a reformer, Wilson went on to win the Democratic presidential nomination in 1912 in a bruising battle.

Forging the New Freedom. Wilson possessed, to a fault, the moral certainty that characterized the progressive politician. A brilliant speaker, he instinctively assumed the mantle of righteousness and showed little tolerance for the views of his critics. Only gradually, however, did Wilson hammer out, in reaction to Roosevelt's New Nationalism, a coherent reform program, which he called the New Freedom.

Wilson actually had much in common with Roosevelt. "The old time of individual competition is probably gone by," Wilson stressed. "We will do business henceforth, when we do it on a great and successful scale, by means of corporations." Like Roosevelt, Wilson opposed not bigness but the abuse of economic power. Nor did Wilson think that the abuse of power could be prevented without a strong federal government. He parted company from Roosevelt over *how* government should restrain private power.

As he warmed to the debate, Wilson cast the issue in the fundamental terms of slavery and freedom. "This is a struggle for emancipation," he proclaimed in October 1912. "If America is not to have free enterprise, then she can have freedom of no sort whatever." Wilson also scorned Roosevelt's social program. Welfare might be benevolent, he declared, but it also would be paternalistic and contrary to the traditions of a free people. The New Nationalism meant collectivism, Wilson warned, whereas the New Freedom would preserve political and economic liberty.

How, then, did Wilson propose to deal with the problem of corporate power? Court enforcement of the Sherman Act was Wilson's basic answer. His task was to figure out how to make that long-established antitrust approach work better. In this effort Wilson relied heavily on a new advisor—Louis D. Brandeis, famous as the "people's lawyer" for his public service in many progressive causes (including the landmark *Muller* case).

An expert on regulatory matters, Brandeis understood that an all-powerful trade commission was likely to end up not as defender of the public interest but in a cozy relationship with the industries it was supposed to regulate. Nor did Brandeis believe that bigness meant efficiency. On the contrary, he argued that trusts were wasteful compared with firms that vigorously competed in a free market. The main thing was to prevent the trusts from unfairly using their power to curb free competition. It should be the aim of public policy "so [to] restrict the wrong use of competition that the right use of competition will destroy monopoly."

The Election of 1912. Despite the rhetoric of the campaign, the election itself fell short of being a referendum on the New Nationalism versus the New Freedom. The outcome turned on a more humdrum reality: Wilson was elected because he kept the traditional Democratic vote while the Republicans split between Roosevelt and Taft (Map 20.2). Although he won by a landslide in the electoral college, Wilson received only 42 percent of the popular vote, 115,000 fewer votes than Bryan had amassed

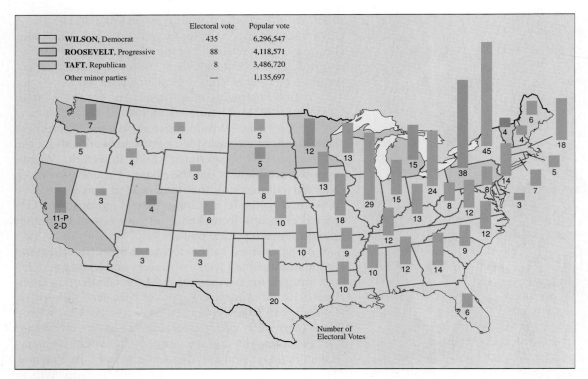

	Electoral vote	Popular vote
WILSON, Democrat	435	6,296,547
ROOSEVELT, Progressive	88	4,118,571
TAFT, Republican	8	3,486,720
Other minor parties	—	1,135,697

MAP 20.2
The Election of 1912

The 1912 election reveals why the two-party system is so strongly rooted in American politics. The Democrats, though a minority party, won an electoral landslide because the Republicans divided their vote between Roosevelt and Taft. This result indicates what is at stake when major parties splinter. The Socialists, despite a record vote of 900,000, got no electoral votes. To vote Socialist in 1912 meant in effect to throw away one's vote.

against Taft in 1908. If there was a beneficiary of the reform ferment sparked by the presidential campaign, it was not Wilson but the Socialist candidate, Eugene V. Debs, who captured 900,000 votes, 6 percent of the total. At best it could be said that the 1912 election signified that the American public was in the mood for reform: only 23 percent, after all, had voted for the one candidate who stood for the status quo, President Taft. Woodrow Wilson's own reform program, however, had not received a mandate from the people.

Yet the 1912 election proved to be decisive in the history of national reform. The debate between Roosevelt and Wilson had brought forth, in the New Freedom, a program capable of finally resolving the crisis over corporate power that had gripped the nation for a decade. Just as important, the election created a rare legislative opportunity in Washington. Wilson became president with the Democrats in firm control of both houses of Congress and united in their eagerness to get on with the New Freedom.

The First Phase: Tariff Reform and the Federal Reserve. Upon entering the White House, Wilson chose a flanking attack on the problem of economic power. So long out of office, the Democrats were hun-

gry for tariff reform. From the prevailing average of 40 percent, the Underwood Tariff Act of 1913 pared rates down to an average of 25 percent. Targeting especially the trust-dominated industries, Democrats confidently expected the Underwood Tariff Act to spur competition and reduce prices for consumers by opening protected American markets to foreign products.

Wilson's administration then turned to the nation's banking system, whose key weakness was the absence of a central bank. The main function of a central bank at that time was to regulate commercial banks and back them up in case they could not meet their obligations to depositors. In practice, in the United States this role had been assumed by the great New York banks, which handled the accounts of outlying banks and assisted them when they came under pressure. However, if the New York banks weakened, the entire system could collapse. This had nearly happened in 1907, when the Knickerbocker Trust Company failed and panic swept through the nation's financial markets.

The need for a reserve system became widely accepted, but the form it should take was hotly debated. Wall Street wanted a centralized system controlled by the bankers. Rural Democrats and their spokesman, Senator Carter Glass of Virginia, preferred a decentralized network of reserve banks. Progressives in both parties agreed that the essential feature should be public control over the reserve system. The bankers, whose practices were already under scrutiny by Congress, were on the defensive in this contest.

President Wilson, no expert to begin with, learned quickly and reconciled the reformers and bankers. The monumental Federal Reserve Act of 1913 gave the nation a banking system that was resistant to financial panic. The act delegated reserve functions to twelve district reserve banks, which would be controlled by their member banks. The Federal Reserve Board imposed public regulation on this regional structure. In one stroke the act strengthened the banking system and placed a measure of restraint on the "money trust."

Settling the Trust Question. Having dealt with tariff and banking reform, Wilson turned to the big question of how to curb the trusts. During the presidential campaign, Wilson had championed a strengthened Sherman Act, but the strategy he proposed—defining with precision what constituted illegal practices that shut out competition—proved unexpectedly hard to implement. Was it feasible to state precisely when interlocking directorates, discriminatory pricing, or exclusive contracts became illegal? Wilson's advisor Louis D. Brandeis finally decided that it was not, and the president assented. In the Clayton Antitrust Act of 1914, amending the Sherman Act, the definition of unlawful practices was left flexible, subject to the test of whether the effect "substantially lessen[ed] competition or tend[ed] to create a monopoly in any line of commerce."

Brandeis realized that this retreat from a definitive antitrust prescription meant that a federal trade commission would be needed to aid the executive branch in enforcing the Sherman and Clayton acts. Wilson was understandably hesitant, given his principled opposition to Roosevelt's conception of a powerful trade commission overseeing American business. At first Wilson wanted only an advisory, information-gathering agency. But ultimately, under the 1914 law establishing it, the Federal Trade Commission (FTC) received broader powers to investigate companies and issue "cease and desist" orders against unfair trade practices that violated antitrust law. FTC decisions, however, were subject to court review, so that Wilson's entire program was situated within the original conception of antitrust enforcement. As before, the courts would ultimately decide which business practices were illegal.

Despite a good deal of commotion, this arduous legislative process was actually an exercise in consensus building. Wilson himself had opened the debate in a conciliatory way. "The antagonism between business and government is over," he said, and the time was ripe for a program representing the "best business judgment in America." Afterward, Wilson felt he had brought the long controversy over corporate power to a successful conclusion, and in fact he had. Steering a course between Taft's conservatism and Roosevelt's radicalism, Wilson carved out a middle way that brought to bear the powers of government without threatening the constitutional order, and that curbed abuse of corporate power without threatening the capitalist system.

What few Americans recognized, in the midst of this protracted struggle, was how very odd it seemed from a European standpoint. Neither of America's industrial rivals—Britain nor Germany—made such a fuss over competitive markets. It was true that the fundamental concept—restraint of trade—originated in English common law, but the British, free-traders and export oriented, lacked the opportunity to engage in market-controlling behavior and hence found no need for antitrust legislation. Germany, by contrast, was a veritable hotbed of conspiracies in restraint of trade, only they were called "cartels"—trade associations that divided the market and rigged prices, and operated with the approval of the imperial government.

Wilson's Social Program. On social policy, as with antitrust policy, President Wilson carved out a middle way. Having denounced the New Nationalism as paternalistic, he at first was unreceptive to what he saw as special-interest demands of labor and farm organizations. On the leading issue—that they be exempted from antitrust prosecution—the most Wilson was willing to accept was cosmetic language in the Clayton Act that did not give them the immunity they sought.

The labor vote had grown increasingly important to the Democratic Party, however. As his second presidential campaign drew near, Wilson lost some of his scruples about prolabor legislation. In 1915 and 1916 he championed a host of bills beneficial to American workers: a model federal workers' compensation law, a child labor law, the Adamson eight-hour law for railroad workers, and the landmark Seamen's Act, which eliminated age-old abuses of sailors aboard ship and granted them the individual rights held by other workers. Likewise, after earlier resistance, in 1916 Wilson approved the Federal Farm Loan Act, which provided the low-interest rural credit system long demanded by farmers.

Wilson encountered the same dilemma that confronted all successful progressives: the claims of moral principle versus the unyielding realities of political and economic life. Progressives were high-minded but not radical. They saw evils in the system, but they did not consider the system itself evil. They also prided themselves on being realists as well as moralists. So it stood to reason that Wilson, like other progressives who achieved power, would find his place at the center.

Summary

★

A new chapter in American reform began at the start of the twentieth century. For decades the problems resulting from industrialization and urban growth had been mounting. Now, after 1900, reform began to dominate the nation's public life. The unifying element in progressivism was a common intellectual outlook, highly principled and idealistic as to goals, and confident of the human capacity to find the means.

Beyond this shared outlook, progressives broke up into diverse and often conflicting groups. Political reformers included business groups concerned chiefly with improving the efficiency of city government. Other progressives, such as Robert La Follette, opposed privilege and wanted to democratize the political process. Both groups worked to enhance their power at the expense of entrenched party machines.

Social welfare became the province of American women, and that effort reinvigorated the struggle for women's rights. In the cities, working people and immigrants also became reform minded and set in motion a new political force—urban liberalism. While progressivism was infected by the endemic racism in American life, there was a reform wing that joined with black activists to forge the major institutions of black protest and uplift of the twentieth century: the National Association for the Advancement of Colored People, and the Urban League.

At the national level, progressives focused primarily on controlling the economic power of corporate business. This overriding problem led to Theodore Roosevelt's Square Deal, then to his New Nationalism, and finally to Woodrow Wilson's New Freedom. The role of the federal government expanded dramatically, but in service to a cautious and pragmatic approach to the problems of the country.

T I M E L I N E

1889	Jane Addams and Ellen Gates Starr found Hull House
1893	Panic of 1893 starts depression of the 1890s
1899	National Consumers' League founded
1900	Robert M. La Follette elected Wisconsin governor
	Commission form of city government first appears, in Galveston, Texas
1901	President McKinley assassinated; Theodore Roosevelt succeeds him
1902	President Roosevelt settles national anthracite strike
1903	National Women's Trade Union League founded
1904	Supreme Court dissolves the Northern Securities Company
1905	*Lochner v. New York* overturns law restricting length of the workday
1906	Upton Sinclair's *The Jungle*
	Hepburn Railway Act
	AFL adopts "Bill of Grievances"
1908	*Muller v. Oregon* upholds regulation of working hours for women
	Federal Council of Churches founded
	William Howard Taft elected president
1909	NAACP formed
	Herbert Croly's *Promise of American Life*
1910	Roosevelt announces the New Nationalism
	Woman suffrage movement revives; suffrage victory in Washington State
1911	*Standard Oil* decision restores "rule of reason"
	Triangle Shirtwaist fire
1912	Progressive Party formed
	Woodrow Wilson elected president
1913	Federal Reserve Act
	Underwood Tariff Act
1914	Clayton Antitrust Act

Suggested Readings

The most recent survey of the Progressive Era is John Milton Cooper, *Pivotal Decades: The United States, 1900–1920* (1990). A highly influential interpretation of progressive reform that is worth reading despite its disputed central arguments is Richard Hofstadter, *Age of Reform* (1955). Robert H. Wiebe, *The Search for Order, 1877–1920* (1967), places progressive reform in a broader context of organizational development. On the debate over progressivism as a movement see Daniel Rodgers, "In Search of Progressivism," *Reviews in American History* 10 (1982).

The Intellectual Roots of Progressivism

The progressive mind has been studied from many different angles. The religious underpinnings are stressed in Robert M. Crunden, *Ministers of Reform: The Progressives' Achievement in American Civilization, 1889–1920* (1982). In *The New Radicalism in America, 1889–1963* (1965), Christopher Lasch sees progressivism as a form of cultural revolt. Most useful on political thinkers is Charles Forcey, *The Crossroads of Liberalism: Croly, Weyl, Lippmann, and the Progressive Era* (1961). A provocative study set in an international context is James T. Kloppenberg, *Uncertain Victory: Social Democracy and Progressivism in European and American Thought, 1870–1920* (1986). On the journalists see David M. Chalmers, *The Social and Political Ideas of the Muckrakers* (1964), and Harold S. Wilson, *"McClure's" Magazine and the Muckrakers* (1970).

The Many Faces of Reform

Political reform has been the subject of a voluminous literature. Wisconsin progressivism can be studied in David P. Thelen, *The New Citizenship: Origins of Progressivism in Wisconsin, 1885–1900* (1972). Important progressives are discussed in Spencer C. Olin, *California's Prodigal Son: Hiram Johnson and the Progressive Movement* (1968), and Richard Lowitt, *George W. Norris: The Making of a Progressive* (1963). On city reform see Bradley R. Rice, *Progressive Cities: The Commission Government Movement* (1972); Jack Tager, *The Intellectual as Urban Reformer: Brand Whitlock and the Progressive Movement* (1968); and Melvin G. Holli, *Reform in Detroit: Hazen S. Pingree and Urban Politics* (1969).

The best treatment of the settlement-house movement is Allen F. Davis, *Spearheads of Reform* (1967). Allen F. Davis, *American Heroine: Jane Addams* (1973); George Martin, *Madame Secretary: Frances Perkins* (1976); and Kathryn Kish Sklar, *Florence Kelley and the Nation's Work: The Rise of Women's Political Culture* (1995), deal with leading woman progressives. The connection to working women is effectively treated in Nancy S. Dye, *As Equals and Sisters: Feminism, the Labor Movement, and the Women's Trade Union League of New York* (1980). Women garment workers, the key labor constituency for women progressives, are studied with great skill and insight in Susan A. Glenn, *Daughters of the Shtetl: Life and Labor in the Immigrant Generation* (1990). Two path-breaking books on the origins of American feminism are Rosalind Rosenberg, *Beyond Separate Spheres: The Intellectual Origins of Modern Feminism* (1982), and Nancy F. Cott, *The Grounding of Modern Feminism* (1987). The most recent study of the battle for the vote, Sara Hunter Graham, *Woman Suffrage and the New Democracy* (1996), treats it as a precocious exercise of the single-issue pressure politics of our own times. The leading social reformer to spring from feminism is treated in Ellen Chesler, *Woman of Valor: Margaret Sanger and the Birth Control Movement* (1992).

On urban liberalism the standard book is John D. Buenker, *Urban Liberalism and Progressive Reform* (1973). Two important recent books by historical sociologists treat the halting progress toward the welfare state: Theda Skocpol, *Protecting Soldiers and Mothers* (1992), and, in a comparison of the United States with Canada and Britain, Ann Shola Orloff, *The Politics of Pensions* (1993). Linda Gordon, *Pitied but Not Entitled: Single Mothers and the History of Welfare, 1890–1935* (1994), brilliantly uses the current crisis over welfare reform as a lens for probing the tangled history of this central concern of social progressives. The most comprehensive survey is Morton Keller, *Regulating a New Society: Public Policy and Social Change in America, 1900–1933* (1994). On the South see Jack Temple Kirby, *Darkness at the Dawning: Race and Reform in the Progressive South* (1972), and Dewey Grantham, *Southern Progressivism* (1983); on southern black women as social reformers, Glenda Elizabeth Gilmore, *Gender and Jim Crow: Women and the Politics of White Supremacy in North Carolina, 1869–1920* (1996); and on the racial conservatism of social progressives, Elizabeth Lasch-Quinn, *Black Neighbors: Race and the Limits of Reform in the American Settlement-House Movement* (1993). The revival of black protest is vigorously described in Stephen R. Fox, *The Guardian of Boston: William Monroe Trotter* (1971), and David Levering Lewis, *W. E. B. Du Bois: Biography of a Race, 1868–1919* (1993).

Progressivism and National Politics

National progressivism is best approached through its leading figures. John Milton Cooper, *The Warrior and the Priest* (1983), is a provocative joint biography of Roosevelt and Wilson that emphasizes their shared world view. Lewis S. Gould, *The Presidency of Theodore Roosevelt* (1991), provides a useful synthesis. Aspects of national progressive politics can be followed in James Penick, *Progressive Politics and Conservation: The Ballinger-Pinchot Affair* (1968); James Holt, *Congressional Insurgents and the Party System* (1969); and David Sarasohn, *The Party of Reform: The Democrats in the Progressive Era* (1989). Naomi Lamoreaux, *The Great Merger Movement in American Business, 1895–1904* (1985), offers a sophisticated modern analysis of trust activity; Thomas K. McCraw, ed., *Regulation in Perspective* (1981), contains valuable interpretative essays on the problems of trust regulation; and James Livingston, *Origins of the Federal Reserve System: Money, Class, and Corporate Capitalism, 1890–1913* (1986), treats banking reform. A comprehensive rethinking of the progressive struggle to fashion a regulatory policy for big business is offered in Martin J. Sklar, *The Corporate Reconstruction of American Capitalism, 1890–1916: The Market, the Law, and Politics* (1988).

An Emerging World Power,

1877–1914

IN 1881 GREAT BRITAIN sent a new envoy to Washington. He was Sir Lionel Sackville-West, son of an earl, brother-in-law of Tory Party leader Lord Denby, but otherwise distinguished only as the lover of a celebrated Spanish dancer. His well-connected friends wanted to park Sir Lionel somewhere comfortable but out of harm's way. So they made him minister to the United States.

Twenty years later such an appointment would have been unthinkable. All the major European powers had by then elevated their missions in Washington to embassies and staffed them with top-of-the-line ambassadors. And they treated the United States, without question, as a fellow Great Power.

In Sir Lionel's day, the United States scarcely cast a shadow on the world stage. As a military power the United States was puny, even comical. Its army was smaller than Bulgaria's; its navy ranked thirteenth in the world and was a threat mainly to the crews of its unseaworthy ships. By 1900, however, the United States was flexing its muscles. It had just made short work of Spain in a brief but decisive war, and acquired for itself an empire stretching from Puerto Rico to the Philippines. America's standing as a rising naval power was manifest, and so was its aggressive assertion of national interest in the Caribbean and the Pacific.

In practice, the United States still acted as a regional power, but Europeans were keenly aware of its capacity to cut a wider swath when it chose to do so. "Are we to be confronted by an American peril . . . before which the Old World is to go down to irretrievable defeat?" wondered a former French foreign minister. The notion of an "American peril" became a lively topic after 1900 among

Battle of Santiago de Cuba, 1898
James G. Tyler's dramatic painting of the final sea battle of the Spanish-American War (detail) showcased America's newest weapon of war, the battleship.
Franklin D. Roosevelt Library.

Europeans surveying the industrial and military potential of the United States. No one could be sure what America's role would be, since the United States retained its traditional policy of nonintervention in European affairs. But by 1914, when a great world war engulfed Europe, one could be sure that the United States would have a big role to play. How the United States emerged onto the world stage in the decades before World War I is the subject of this chapter.

The Roots of Expansionism

——————★——————

In 1880 the United States had a population of 50 million, and by that measure ranked with the great European powers. It was the world's leading producer of wheat and cotton. In industrial production the United States was second only to Britain and was rapidly closing the gap. Anyone who doubted the military prowess of the Americans needed only to recall the ferocity with which they had fought one another in the Civil War. The great campaigns of Lee, Sherman, and Grant had entered the military textbooks and were closely studied by army strategists everywhere.

And when its vital interests were at stake, the United States had not shown itself to be lacking in diplomatic vigor. The Civil War had put the United States at odds with both France and Britain. The issue with France involved the establishment in Mexico of a French-sponsored regime under Archduke Maximilian, a move regarded by the United States as a threat to its security in the Southwest. When American troops under General Philip Sheridan began to mass on the Mexican border in 1867, the French military withdrew, abandoning Maximilian to a Mexican firing squad.

With Britain, the issue involved damages done to Union shipping by the *Alabama* and other Confederate sea raiders operating from English ports. American hopes of achieving the annexation of Canada out of this dispute were dashed by Britain's grant of dominion status to Canada in 1867. But four years later, after lengthy negotiations, Britain expressed regret for its unneutral acts against the Union and agreed to the arbitration of the *Alabama* claims, settling to America's satisfaction the last outstanding diplomatic issue of the Civil War.

Diplomacy in the Gilded Age

In the years that followed, the United States lapsed into diplomatic isolation, not out of weakness but for lack of any clear national purpose in world affairs. George Washington's warning against entangling alliances with foreign countries seemed as pertinent as it had when

America was a thinly populated land of farmers. The business of building the nation's industrial economy absorbed Americans and turned their attention inward. And while the new international telegraphic cables provided the country with swift overseas communication after the 1860s, wide oceans still kept the world at a distance and gave Americans a sense of isolation and security.

Nor did European power politics, which centered on Franco-German rivalry and on nationalistic conflict in the Balkans, seem to matter very much. As far as President Grover Cleveland's secretary of state, Thomas F. Bayard, was concerned, "we have not the slightest share or interest [in] the small politics and backstage intrigues of Europe . . . upon which we look with impatience and contempt."

As for the empires that the European powers were avidly building by the 1880s in Africa and Asia, this expression of national prowess did not tempt the United States. Even so ardent an American nationalist as the young Theodore Roosevelt saw the folly of overseas expansion. "We want no unwilling citizens to enter our Union," he wrote in 1886. "European nations war for the possession of thickly settled districts which, if conquered, will for centuries remain alien and hostile to the conquerors; we, wiser in our generation, have seized the waste solitudes that lay near us."

In these circumstances, with no external threat to be seen, what was the point of maintaining a big navy? After the Civil War, the fleet gradually deteriorated. Of the 125 ships on the navy's active list in the 1870s, only about 25 were seaworthy at any one time. No effort was made to keep up with European advances in weaponry or battleship design; the American fleet consisted mainly of sailing ships and obsolete ironclad ships like the *Monitor* and *Merrimack* of Civil War fame.

During the administration of Chester A. Arthur (1881–1885), the navy began a modest upgrading program, commissioning new ships, raising standards for the officer corps, and founding the Naval War College. But the fleet remained small, lacked a unified naval command, and had little more to do than maintain coastal defenses and a modest cruising fleet whose task in wartime would be to harass enemy commerce. An expenditure of 1 percent of the gross domestic product for the entire military establishment seemed entirely adequate in the 1880s.

The conduct of diplomacy was likewise of little account. Appointment to the foreign service was mostly made through the spoils system. American envoys and consular officers were a mixed lot, with many idlers and drunkards among the hardworking and competent. Domestic politics, moreover, made it difficult to develop a coherent foreign policy. Although diplomacy was a presidential responsibility, the U.S. Senate jealously guarded its constitutional right to give "advice and consent" on treaties and diplomatic appointments. Partisan

Sugarcane Plantation, Hawaii
Over 300,000 Asians from China, Japan, Korea, and
the Philippines came to work in the Hawaiian cane
fields between 1850 and 1920. The hardships they
endured are reflected in plantation work songs,
such as this one by Japanese laborers:
  Hawaii, Hawaii
  But when I came what I saw was Hell
  The boss was Satan
  The lunas [overseers] his helpers.
George Bacon Collection, Hawaii State Archives.

squabbling between Democrats and Republicans left the
White House even less room for maneuver. For its part
the State department tended to be inactive, exerting
little control either over policy or over its missions
abroad. Remarkably often, ministers and naval officers
set policy in the field, only to see their actions repudiated or ignored by the State department. In remote
areas, the American presence was likely to be religious:
intrepid missionaries eager to Christianize the native
populations of Asia, Africa, and the Pacific islands.

Latin American Diplomacy. In the Caribbean the
United States remained the dominant power, but the
expansionist enthusiasms of the Civil War era subsided.
Nothing came of the grandiose plans of William H.
Seward, Andrew Johnson's secretary of state, for an
American empire reaching into Latin America and
across the Pacific, or of President Grant's efforts to purchase Santo Domingo (the future Dominican Republic)
in 1870; and the Senate regularly blocked later moves
to acquire bases in Haiti, Cuba, and Venezuela (see
Map 21.3). The long-cherished interest in an interoceanic canal across Central America also faded.
Despite its claims of exclusive building rights, the
United States stood by when a French company headed
by the builder of the Suez Canal, Ferdinand de Lesseps,
started to dig across the Panama isthmus in 1880. That
project failed after a decade, but the reason was bankruptcy, not American opposition.

Diplomatic activity quickened when James G. Blaine
became secretary of state in 1881. He got involved in a

border dispute between Mexico and Guatemala, tried to
settle a war Chile was waging against Peru and Bolivia,
and called the first Pan-American conference of the
Western Hemisphere countries. Blaine's interventions in
Latin American disputes went badly, however, and his
successor canceled the Pan-American conference after
Blaine left office in late 1881. This was a characteristic
instance of Gilded Age diplomacy, driven partly by partisan politics and carried out without any clear sense of
national purpose.

Pan-Americanism—the notion of a community of
American states—took root, however, and Blaine, on
returning in 1889 for a second stint at the State department, took up the plans of the outgoing Cleveland
administration for a new Pan-American conference.
But little came of it, except for an agency in Washington that was later named the Pan-American Union. Any
Latin American goodwill won by Blaine's efforts was
soon blasted by the humiliation the United States visited upon Chile because of a riot against American
sailors in the port of Valparaiso in 1891. Threatened
with war, Chile was forced to apologize to the United
States and pay an indemnity of $75,000.

Pacific Episodes. American interest in the Pacific
centered on Hawaii, where American missionaries had
long been proselytizing among the islanders. With a climate ideal for raising sugarcane, Hawaii had also
attracted American planters and investors. Nominally
an independent monarchy, Hawaii fell increasingly
under American control. In an 1875 treaty, Hawaiian

sugar gained duty-free entry to the American market, and the islands were declared off-limits to other powers. A second treaty in 1887 granted the United States the right to establish a naval base at Pearl Harbor.

When Hawaii's favored access to the American market was abruptly canceled by the McKinley Tariff of 1890, sugar planters began to plot an American takeover of Hawaii. Aided by the U.S. minister to Hawaii and with American sailors conspicuously present, the planters revolted in January 1893 against Queen Liliuokalani and quickly negotiated a treaty of annexation with the administration of President Benjamin Harrison. Before the Senate could approve annexation, however, Grover Cleveland returned to the presidency and, after an investigation of the Hawaiian episode, withdrew the treaty. To annex Hawaii, he declared, would violate both America's "honor and morality" and its "unbroken tradition" against acquiring territory far from the nation's shores.

Meanwhile, the American presence elsewhere in the Pacific was growing. The 1867 purchase of Alaska from imperial Russia gave the United States not only a huge territory with vast natural resources but an unlooked-for presence stretching across the northern Pacific. And far to the south, with even less forethought, the United States had become involved in the remote Samoan Islands (see Map 21.2).

In 1878 the United States secured the right to a coaling station in Pago Pago harbor—a key link on the route to Australia—and in exchange promised local Polynesian leaders to assist in Samoa's relations with other foreign powers. An informal protectorate resulted. In the mid-1880s Germany began to press its claims to the islands, and the United States, stung by German arrogance, responded with equal fervor. In 1889 naval warfare might have broken out but for a hurricane that wrecked the German and American fleets. At that point, agreement on a three-power protectorate (the third country was Britain) averted further strife and preserved American rights in Pago Pago.

American diplomacy in these years has been characterized as a series of incidents, not the pursuit of a foreign policy. Many things happened but intermittently and without a plan, driven by individuals and pressure groups—not by any well-founded and coherent conception of national objectives. This was possible because, as Englishman James Bryce remarked in 1888, America still sailed "upon a summer sea." In the stormier waters that lay ahead, a different kind of American diplomacy would be required.

Economic Sources of Expansionism

"A policy of isolation did well enough when we were an embryo nation," remarked Senator Orville Platt of Connecticut in 1893. "But today things are different. . . . We are 65 million people, the most advanced and powerful on earth, and regard to our future welfare demands an abandonment of the doctrines of isolation." What especially demanded that Americans look outward was their enormously productive economy.

The Search for Foreign Markets. America's gross domestic product—the total value of all goods and services produced annually—quadrupled between 1870 and 1900, and industrial output quintupled. But were there markets big enough to absorb the staggering volume of goods flowing from America's farms and factories? Over 90 percent of American output in the late nineteenth century was consumed at home. Even so, foreign markets were important. Roughly a fifth of the nation's agricultural output was exported, and the proportion of major staple crops—cotton, wheat, tobacco—was much higher, up to 80 percent, for example, in the case of cotton.

As the industrial economy expanded, so did factory exports. Between 1880 and 1900, the industrial share of total exports jumped from 15 percent to over 30 percent. Although only 9 percent of manufactured output went overseas in 1900, the export share in key industries was much larger: 57 percent for petroleum products, 50 percent for copper, 25 percent for sewing machines, 15 percent for iron and steel.

Major American firms began to establish themselves overseas. As early as 1868, the Singer Sewing Machine Company established its first foreign plant in Glasgow, Scotland. The giant among American firms doing business abroad was Standard Oil. Starting with the Anglo-American Oil Company in 1888, Rockefeller's firm created European affiliates to operate its oil tankers and market its kerosene across the continent. In Asia, Standard Oil kerosene cans, converted into utensils and roofing tin, became a visible sign of American market penetration. Brand names such as Kodak (cameras), McCormick (agricultural equipment), and later Ford (the Model T) became household words around the world.

Foreign trade was important partly for reasons of international finance. As a developing economy, the United States attracted a lot of foreign investment capital but sent relatively little abroad—scarcely 1 percent of all the money Americans invested in the late nineteenth century. The result was a heavy outflow of dollars from the United States in the form of interest and dividend payments to foreign investors. To balance this account, the United States needed to export more goods than it imported. In fact, a favorable import-export balance was achieved in 1876 (Figure 21.1). But because of its dependence on foreign capital, America would have to be constantly vigilant about its foreign trade.

Even more important, however, was the relationship that many Americans perceived between foreign

The Singer Sewing Machine
The sewing machine was an American invention that swiftly found markets abroad. The Singer Company, the dominant firm, not only exported large quantities but produced 200,000 machines annually at a Scottish plant that employed 6,000 workers. Singer's advertising rightly boasted of its prowess as an international company and of a product that was "The Universal Machine." New-York Historical Society.

markets and the nation's social stability. In hard times, farmers took up radical politics, and workers became militant strikers. The problem, many thought, was that the nation's capacity to produce was outrunning its capacity to consume. And when the economy slowed and domestic demand fell, the impact on farmers and workers was devastating, driving down farm prices and wages and causing layoffs and farm foreclosures across the country. The answer was to make sure that there would always be enough buyers for America's surplus products, and this meant, more than anything else, ensuring access to foreign markets.

Overseas Trade and Foreign Policy. How did these concerns about foreign markets link up to America's foreign policy? The bulk of American exports in the late nineteenth century—over 80 percent—went to Canada and Europe (Table 21.1). In those countries the normal instruments of diplomacy sufficed. In Europe, for example, a major issue during the 1880s was restrictions placed on imports of American pork, allegedly for health reasons. The United States protested vigorously, threatened to embargo the imports of countries that discriminated against American meat products, and in 1891 negotiated a satisfactory settlement.

But in Asia, Latin America, and other regions that Americans considered "backward," a tougher brand of American intervention seemed necessary because there the United States was competing with other industrial powers. Asia and Latin America represented only a modest part of America's export trade—roughly an eighth of the total in the late nineteenth century. Still, this trade was growing—it was worth $200 million in 1900—and parts of it mattered a great deal to specific industries, for example, the China market for American textiles manufacturers. The real importance of these non-Western markets, however, was not so much their current value as their future promise. China, with its enormous population of potential customers, exerted a powerful hold on the American mercantile imagination. Many felt that the China trade, though quite small, would one day be the key to American prosperity. Therefore, China and other beckoning markets must not be closed to the United States.

In the mid-1880s, the pace of imperialist activity picked up. After the Berlin Conference of 1884, the European powers rapidly colonized Africa. In a burst of modernizing energy, Japan transformed itself into a major power and began to challenge China's claims to Korea. In the Sino-Japanese War of 1894–1895, Japan won an easy victory and started a scramble among the Great Powers, including Russia, to carve China into spheres of influence. In Latin America, Britain, France, and Germany began to challenge U.S. interests more aggressively. On the European continent, moreover, the free-trade liberalism of earlier years gave way after the 1870s to protectionism, threatening established European markets for American goods just as empire building was closing off new markets elsewhere.

On top of all this came the Panic of 1893, setting in motion industrial strikes and agrarian protests that many Americans, such as Cleveland's secretary of state, Walter Q. Gresham, took to be "symptoms of revolution." With the nation's social stability seemingly at stake, securing the markets of Latin America and Asia took on new urgency, inspiring the expansionist diplomacy of the 1890s.

Creating an Expansionist Foreign Policy

"Whether they will or no, Americans must now begin to look outward. The growing production of the country requires it." So wrote Captain Alfred T. Mahan, America's leading naval strategist, in his book *The Influence of Seapower upon History* (1890). While serving aboard

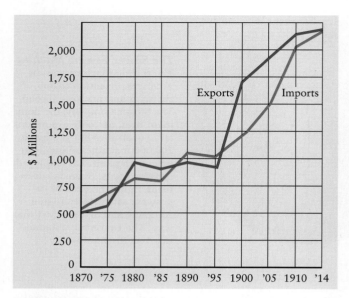

FIGURE 21.1
Balance of U.S. Imports, 1870–1914
By 1876 the United States had become a net exporting nation. The brief reversal after 1888 aroused fears that the United States was losing its foreign markets and helped fuel the expansionist drive of the 1890s.

a warship cruising the coast of Latin America, Mahan had spent his spare time reading history. In a library in Lima, Peru, he hit upon the idea that the key to imperial power was control of the seas. From this insight Mahan developed a naval analysis that became the cornerstone of American strategic thinking.

A Global Strategy. "When a question arises of control over distant regions . . . it must ultimately be decided by naval power," Mahan advised. The United States should regard the oceans not as barriers but as "a great high-

way . . . over which men pass in all directions." Traversing that highway required a robust merchant marine (America's had fallen on hard times since its heyday in the 1850s), a powerful navy to protect American commerce, and strategic overseas bases. Here technology played a role because, having converted from sails to steam, navies required coaling stations far from home. Without such stations, Mahan warned, warships were "like land birds, unable to fly far from their own shores."

Mahan called for a canal across Central America to connect the Atlantic and Pacific oceans. Such a canal would enable the eastern United States to "compete with Europe, on equal terms as to distance, for the markets of East Asia." The canal's approaches would need to be guarded by bases in the Caribbean Sea. And Hawaii would have to be annexed to extend American power into the Pacific, a step Mahan considered "natural, necessary, irrepressible." What Mahan envisioned was a form of colonialism different from Europe's. Mahan aspired not to U.S. rule over large territories and native populations but to U.S. control over strategic bases for the defense of America's trading interests.

Mahan was offering the United States a *coherent* foreign policy: first, foreign markets secured for the nation's surplus products; second, the nation's development as a naval power; and third, to sustain both of those goals, an expansionist strategy anchored on an interoceanic canal and bases in the Caribbean and the Pacific.

Other advocates of a powerful America flocked to Captain Mahan, including such up-and-coming politicians as Theodore Roosevelt and Henry Cabot Lodge. The influence of these men, few in number but strategically placed, increased during the 1890s. They pushed steadily for what Lodge called a "large policy." But mainstream politicians also accepted Mahan's underlying logic, and from the inauguration of Benjamin Harrison in 1889 onward, a surprising consistency began to emerge in the conduct of American foreign policy.

TABLE 21.1

Exports to Canada and Europe Compared with Exports to Asia and Latin America, 1875–1900

Year	Exports to Canada and Europe ($)	Percentage of Total	Exports to Asia and Latin America ($)	Percentage of Total
1875	494,000,000	86.1	72,000,000	12.5
1885	637,000,000	85.8	87,000,000	11.7
1895	681,000,000	84.3	108,000,000	13.4
1900	1,135,000,000	81.4	200,000,000	14.3

Source: Compiled from information in *Historical Statistics of the United States,* 1960; U.S. Department of Commerce, *Long Term Growth, 1860–1965,* 1966; National Bureau of Economic Research, *Trends in the American Economy in the Nineteenth Century,* 1960.

Alfred T. Mahan
Mahan's theory about the influence of sea power on history came to him while he was killing time on a tour of naval duty reading Roman history in a library in Lima, Peru, in 1885. His insight was personal as well as intellectual: embarrassed by the decrepit ships on which he served, Mahan thought the United States should have a modern fleet in which officers like himself could serve with pride (and with some hope of professional advancement).
U.S. Naval Historical Foundation.

Rebuilding the Navy. Mahan argued strongly for a battleship fleet capable of roaming the high seas and striking a decisive first blow against an enemy. In 1890 Congress appropriated funds for the first three battleships in the two-ocean fleet envisioned by Benjamin F. Tracy, Harrison's ambitious secretary of the navy. Battleships might be expensive, said Tracy, but they were "the premium paid by the United States for the insurance of its acquired wealth and its growing industries." The battleship took on a special aura for those—like the young Roosevelt—who had grand dreams for the United States: "Oh, Lord! if only the people who are ignorant about our Navy could see those great warships in all their majesty and beauty, and could realize how [well fitted they are] to uphold the honor of America!" (see New Technology, "The Battleship," pp. 678–679.)

The incoming Cleveland administration was less spread-eagled and established its antiexpansionist credentials by canceling Harrison's scheme for annexing Hawaii. But after hesitating briefly, Cleveland picked up the naval program of his Republican predecessor, pressing Congress just as forcefully for additional battleships (five were authorized) and making the same basic argument. The nation's commercial vitality—"free access to all markets," in the words of Cleveland's second secretary of state, Richard Olney—depended on its naval power.

While rejecting the colonialist aspects of Mahan's thinking, Cleveland absorbed the underlying strategic arguments about where America's vital interests lay. This explains the remarkable crisis that suddenly blew up in 1895 with Great Britain over Venezuela.

The Venezuela Crisis. For years a border dispute had simmered between Venezuela and British Guiana. Now the United States demanded that it be resolved. The Europeans were carving up Africa and Asia in this period. How could the United States be sure that Europe did not have similar designs on Latin America? Indeed, prompted by President Cleveland, Secretary of State Olney made that point in a bristling note to London on July 25, 1895, demanding that Britain accept arbitration or face the consequences.

Invoking the Monroe Doctrine, Olney warned that the United States could not tolerate any European attempt to intimidate or overthrow nations in the Western Hemisphere. "Today the United States is practically sovereign upon this continent, and its fiat is law upon the subjects to which it confines its interposition." Olney intended to convey a clear message that the United States would brook no challenge to its vital interests in the Caribbean. These vital interests were strictly America's, not Venezuela's; Venezuela was not consulted during the entire dispute.

Despite its suddenness, the tough stand of the Cleveland administration was not an aberration but a logical step in the new American foreign policy. Once the British realized that Cleveland meant business, they backed off and agreed to arbitration of the boundary dispute. Afterward, Olney remarked with satisfaction that as a great industrial nation, the United States needed "to accept [its] commanding position" and take its place "among the Powers of the earth." Other countries would have to accommodate the American need for access to "more markets and larger markets for the consumption and products of the industry and inventive genius of the American people."

The Ideology of Expansionism. As policy makers hammered out the new foreign policy, it was receiving strong ideological support from a variety of sources. One was the social Darwinist theory that dominated the political thought of this era (see Chapter 18). If, as Charles Darwin had shown, animals and plants evolved through the survival of the fittest, so did nations. "Nothing under the sun is stationary," warned the

The Battleship

————— ★ —————

IN THE ANNALS of naval warfare, ancient gave way to modern when sea battles ceased to be combat between shipborne soldiers. We can date that fault line quite precisely. It occurred at the defeat of the Spanish Armada in 1588, when the lumbering Spanish vessels of Philip II were pounded by the guns of the English ships without ever managing to board their troops on Elizabeth's nimble galleons. Ever since, the objective of naval combat has been to sink enemy ships. The tactical division of labor, as it evolved, called for sailing ships of many types—frigates, sloops-of-war, and smaller boats. But for a nation aspiring to command the seas, the essential weapon was the *capital* ship, carrying the biggest guns and heaviest armament. A superb example was the *Victory*, Lord Horatio Nelson's flagship at the battle against the Napoleonic fleet at Trafalgar in 1805. The *Victory* carried one hundred guns on three decks, and was among the most formidable fighting ships of her time. Because these capital ships entered battle in a line, guns blazing against the enemy fleet, they were called ships of the line or line-of-battle ships—hence the name for the next generation of capital ships: *battleships*.

In this drama of capital ships the United States figured not at all. Indeed, Trafalgar confirmed the nation's early policy against challenging Britain's command of the seas. In the War of 1812, the American fleet contained no ships of the line. At the time, this strategy was recommended by the country's few naval resources, but even after the United States developed the means for challenging Britain, geography and aspirations argued against doing so. As long as the United States defined itself as a continental nation, the mission of the U.S. Navy could be limited to coastal defense and harassing enemy commerce. The ship of the line, glorious though it was, had no place in American naval doctrine.

Even so, given America's industrial prowess, the United States contributed to the battleship's emergence as the capital ship of the age of steam and iron. The first steam-powered vessel in any navy was the U.S.S. *Fulton* (1815), and another American warship, the *Princeton* (1844), first demonstrated the superiority of the screw propeller over paddle wheels. The Civil War taught the world that wooden warships were finished. In a celebrated battle on March 8, 1862, the Confederacy's ironclad *Merrimack* rammed a sloop-of-war, sank a frigate with its

U.S.S. Atlanta
Pictured at its launching in 1884, the cruiser *Atlanta* was the first step in the navy's modernization program. The ship's transitional nature is suggested by the sailors manning the yardarms, which were there to support the sails assisting the *Atlanta*'s engines.
United States Naval Institute.

U.S.S. Oregon
Launched twelve years after the *Atlanta*, the *Oregon* was in an altogether different league, not only because of heavier tonnage and weaponry but because this vessel had left the age of sail behind and was recognizably a modern battleship.
U.S. Naval History Center.

guns, and might have destroyed the entire Union fleet blockading the Chesapeake but for the arrival of the ironclad U.S.S. *Monitor*. Unlike its European predecessors or the *Merrimack*, the *Monitor* was not a converted man-of-war. Here was an entirely new design, a ship with a low, flat deck, a dominating turret mounting two cannons, and no auxiliary sails—a prototype of the modern battleship, in fact, but in miniature, since the *Monitor* was only a shallow-draft gunboat (soon fated to founder in high seas).

Though it had helped create these technological advances, the United States had little to do with incorporating them into the battleship. The first example, completed in late 1861, was Britain's 9,210-ton *Warrior*, with a speed of 14 knots, a crew of 707, and eight 7-inch guns. Over the next twenty-five years, all the essential features of battleship design fell into place: in weaponry, rifled guns mounted on revolving turrets (the H.M.S. *Monarch*, 1869); in motive power, steam engines exclusively (H.M.S. *Devastation*, 1873); in construction, all-steel hulls and superstructures (H.M.S. *Colossus*, 1886).

Only after the battleship was an accomplished fact did the United States, heeding Captain Alfred T. Mahan's advice, shed its small-navy doctrine and build capital ships. The *Indiana*, *Massachusetts*, and *Oregon*, authorized in 1890, were, at 11,700 tons, world-class battleships, but they had some flaws.

They listed when the big guns pointed abeam; and the 8-inch turrets suffered blast effects from the 13-inch guns. Even so, these first American battleships proved more than adequate against the Spanish fleet in 1898, and the shipbuilding program then went into high gear, producing by 1914 the world's third most formidable battleship fleet, after Britain's and Germany's.

This achievement brought the United States into the front rank of twentieth-century sea powers; the battleship was Theodore Roosevelt's "big stick," and he took much pride in the Great White Fleet that circumnavigated the globe at the close of his administration. Yet after 1898 the American battleship's war record proved to be scant. By 1917, when the United States entered World War I, the German fleet had already been defeated, leaving for the U.S. Navy only convoy and blockading duties. By World War II, battleships verged on obsolescence. Like the ships of the Spanish Armada, they were vessels of great power but incapable of closing with an elusive opponent—in this instance, the aircraft carrier, which launched its planes from one hundred miles off and hoped never to see the enemy's ships. Thus, the Japanese attack on Pearl Harbor on December 7, 1941, meant little strategically because only the U.S. battleship fleet was at anchor on that Sunday morning; the U.S. aircraft carriers, safely at sea, were unscathed.

American social theorist Brooks Adams in *The Law of Civilization and Decay* (1895). "Not to advance is to recede." By this criterion, the United States had no choice; if it wanted to survive, it had to expand.

Linked to social Darwinism was a spreading belief in the inherent superiority of the Anglo-Saxon "race." In the late nineteenth century, Great Britain basked in the glory of its representative institutions, industrial prosperity, and far-flung empire—all ascribed to the supposed racial superiority of its people and, by extension, of their American cousins as well. On both sides of the Atlantic, Anglo-Saxonism was in vogue. John Fiske, an American philosopher and historian, lectured the nation on its future responsibilities: "The work which the English race began when it colonized North America is destined to go on until every land on the earth's surface that is not already the seat of an old civilization shall become English in its language, in its religion, in its political habits, and to a predominant extent in the blood of its people."

Fiske titled his lecture "Manifest Destiny." A half-century earlier this term had been used to express Americans' sense of their national mission to sweep aside the native American peoples and occupy the continent. In his widely read book *The Winning of the West* (1896), Theodore Roosevelt drew a parallel between the expansionism of his own time and the suppression of the Indians. To Roosevelt, what happened to "backward peoples" mattered little because their conquest was "for the benefit of civilization and in the interests of mankind. It is indeed a warped, perverse and silly morality which would forbid a course of conquest that has turned whole continents into the seats of mighty and flourishing civilized nations." More than historical parallels, however, linked the Manifest Destiny of the past and present.

In 1890 the U.S. Census reported the end of the westward movement on the North American continent: there was no longer a frontier line beyond which land remained to be conquered. The psychological impact of that news on Americans was profound, spawning among other things a new historical interpretation that stressed the importance of the frontier in shaping the nation's character. In a landmark essay setting out this thesis—"The Significance of the Frontier in American History" (1893)—the young historian Frederick Jackson Turner suggested a link between the closing of the frontier and overseas expansion. "He would be a rash prophet who should assert that the expansive character of American life has now entirely ceased," Turner wrote. "Movement has been its dominant fact, and, unless this training has no effect upon a people, the American energy will continually demand a wider field for its exercise." As Turner predicted, Manifest Destiny did turn outward.

Thus a strong current of ideas, deeply rooted in American experience and ideology, justified the new diplomacy of expansionism. The United States was eager to step onto the world stage. All it needed was the right occasion.

An American Empire

After Spain lost its South American empire in the early nineteenth century, Cubans yearned to join their mainland brothers and sisters in freedom. Independence movements sprang up repeatedly, most recently in a rebellion that had lasted from 1868 to 1878. In February 1895, inspired by the poet José Martí, Cuban patriots again rebelled against Spanish rule. Although Martí died in an early skirmish and no mass uprising occurred, the rebels built up substantial fighting forces and mounted a guerrilla war against the Spaniards. A standoff developed; the Spaniards controlled the towns, the insurgents held much of the countryside. Then, in early 1896, the newly appointed Spanish captain general, Valeriano Weyler, adopted the harsh policy of *reconcentration*. The Spaniards forced entire populations into armed camps and treated any Cubans on the outside as rebels. Because reconcentration was not followed by aggressive pursuit, it only inconvenienced the guerrilla fighters. The toll on civilians, however, was brutal. Out of a population of 1,600,000, as many as 200,000 may have died of starvation, exposure, or dysentery.

The Cuban Crisis

Rebel leaders shrewdly saw that their best hope was not military but political: they had to draw the United States into their struggle. Some Cubans lived there, mostly in Florida, where Cuban cigar makers taxed themselves heavily for the cause of independence. But the nerve center of the United States was New York City, and it was there that a key group of exiles—the *junta*—set up shop to make the case for *Cuba Libre*.

By itself, their cause would not have stirred much interest. The Spaniards were behaving no more dishonorably than any other colonial power in similar circumstances; nor were atrocities in short supply elsewhere in the world. The Cuban exiles, however, came on the scene at a critical juncture in American sensationalist journalism. William Randolph Hearst had just purchased the nearly moribund *New York Journal* and was in a hurry to build circulation (see American Lives, "William Randolph Hearst: Jingo," pp. 682–683). Cuba was ideal for his purposes. Locked in a furious circulation war, Hearst's *Journal* and Joseph Pulitzer's *New York World* elevated Cuba's agony into flaming front-page headlines.

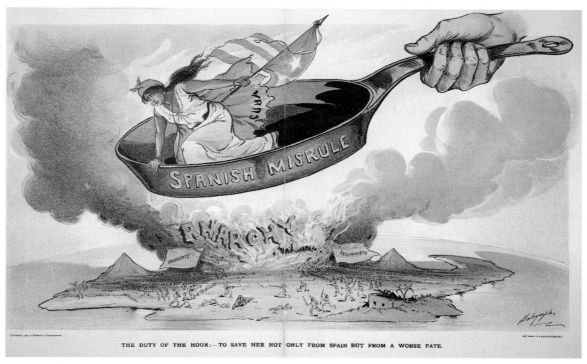

THE DUTY OF THE HOUR:—TO SAVE HER NOT ONLY FROM SPAIN BUT FROM A WORSE FATE.

Free Cuba?
Independence for Cuba was not an unalloyed good for many Americans, including this
cartoonist. Here he depicts Cuba as a woman about to jump from the frying pan
(Spanish misrule) into the fire (anarchy). Hence the revealing caption: "The Duty of
the Hour—To Save Her Not Only from Spain but from a Worse Fate."
Granger Collection.

Across the country powerful sentiments stirred:
humanitarian concern for the Cubans, sympathy with
their aspirations for freedom, and a superpatriotism
that became known as *jingoism*. Congress began calling
for Cuban independence.

Presidential Politics. Grover Cleveland, still in
office when the rebellion broke out, took a cooler view
of the situation. His concern was America's vital interests, which, he told Congress, were "by no means of a
wholly sentimental or philanthropic character." The
Cuban civil war was disrupting the sizable trade
between the two countries and destroying profitable
American investments, especially in Cuban sugar plantations. Of course, it was the rebels who were burning
the crops, but Spain was accountable for not maintaining security. The president was also worried that
Spain's troubles might draw other European powers
into the situation. A chronically unstable Cuba was not
compatible with America's increasing strategic interests in the region, especially its plans for an interoceanic canal whose approaches would have to be
safeguarded. If Spain could put down the rebellion,
that was fine with Cleveland. But as Spain's impotence
became clear, he urged the Spanish government to
make reforms and resolve the crisis.

Taking over in March 1897, the McKinley administration adopted much the same line. Like Cleveland,
William McKinley considered the United States to be
the dominant Caribbean power, with vital interests that
had to be defended. But McKinley was inclined to be
tougher on the Spaniards. He was appalled by Spain's
"uncivilized and inhumane conduct" in Cuba and more
sympathetic than his predecessor to the aspirations of
the rebels. In addition, McKinley had to contend with
the jingoism in the Republican Party, manifest at the
1896 national convention in a bristling platform calling
for Cuban independence and proclaiming a new American imperialism. But the notion, long held by historians, that McKinley was swept along against his better
judgment by popular opinion and by a Republican war
faction led by Theodore Roosevelt, Henry Cabot Lodge,
and other aggressive advocates of a "large policy" was
not true. McKinley was very much his own man. A
skilled politician and a canny if undramatic president,
he would not proceed until he sensed a broad national
consensus for war. In particular, McKinley was sensitive to business interests fearful of disruption to an
economy just recovering from depression.

The Road to War. On September 18, 1897, the American minister in Madrid asked the Spanish government

William Randolph Hearst: Jingo

★

WILLIAM RANDOLPH HEARST, born in San Francisco on April 29, 1863, was no Horatio
Alger hero. His father, George Hearst, had
struck it rich in Nevada's Comstock lode, and Willie
grew up in the lap of luxury: grand houses, trips to
Europe, private tutors, Harvard. His mother, Phoebe,
doted on him, at once indulging and smothering her
only child. From these unpromising beginnings
sprang a strappingly handsome young man of
remarkable contradictions, beginning with his voice,
which was incongruously thin and high pitched.
Hearst was painfully shy but simultaneously hell-
bent on mischief; his pranks at Harvard (which
finally got him expelled) were legendary. He was out-
wardly diffident but had to dominate everyone
around him. He was sentimental and generous but
also without scruples. When he wanted something,
he really wanted it, and he was known late into his
life to throw tantrums when he was denied. All this
would be of no historical moment—doubtless there
were others like him among the progeny of the new
millionaires—except for one thing: Hearst did not
end up a dissipated alcoholic or, as was known to
happen, even a quietly exemplary citizen. Hearst
became a great newspaperman and, driven by his
inner demons, cut a swath through American history.

His father happened to own the *San Francisco
Examiner*, a money-loser that served as the elder
Hearst's political organ. At Harvard the son took to
reading the *Examiner* and decided that he wanted to
run it. His inspiration was Joseph Pulitzer, who a few
years earlier had taken over the moribund *New York
World* and transformed it into a hugely successful
daily. While still a college junior, Hearst wrote a
remarkable letter to his father outlining his plans for
the paper, which, like the *World*, would be "of that
class which appeals to the people and which depends
for its success upon enterprise, energy and a certain
startling originality and not upon the wisdom of its
political opinions or the lofty style of its editorials."
The elder Hearst was unimpressed. He was thinking
about unloading the paper, not pouring more money
into it. Supposing it became a great success, he asked
the business manager, how much might it make?

Maybe $100,000 a year, came the answer. "Hell!"
snorted Hearst. "That ain't no money." But the son
wasn't interested in the money; he was interested in
the *circulation* and the delight he would take from
orchestrating the emotions—and maybe even the
actions—of thousands upon thousands of readers.

In early 1887 the young Hearst, not yet twenty-
four, finally got his wish and, on taking command,
immediately pronounced the sleepy *Examiner*
"Monarch of the Dailies." It would be "THE LARGEST,
BRIGHTEST AND BEST NEWSPAPER ON THE PACIFIC COAST,"
providing readers with the best news and "THE LATEST
AND MOST ORIGINAL SENSATIONS." Sensation was what
Hearst was after—copy that would arouse, in his editor's words, "the gee-whiz emotion." For example,
were any grizzly bears left in California? Hearst dispatched an intrepid newsman to the Tehachapi
Mountains, where after three months of arduous
trapping he caught a grizzly. The beast was chained
in a beer wagon, paraded with great fanfare around
San Francisco, and given a home in Golden Gate
Park. Naturally, it was named Monarch. All this the
Examiner reported in exhaustive detail, building
suspense as the search progressed and ending triumphantly with the carnival display of the unfortunate bear. There was much more of the same:
rescues, murders, scandal, sob stories, anything that
might give readers the "gee-whiz emotion." The other
string in Hearst's bow was that he became a champion of "the people." The *Examiner* embarked on a
series of noisy crusades—against the water trust, and
got rates cut by 15 percent; against a city charter
crafted by venal politicos and their business cronies,
and got it defeated; and, on many fronts, against the
rapacious Southern Pacific Railroad.

By the early 1890s the *Examiner*'s circulation was
soaring and Hearst was making money. Looking
around for greener fields, his eye fixed on New York
City. The *Journal* was for sale, and Hearst got it
cheaply. It was an anemic paper, close to folding, but
Hearst didn't care. He intended to transform it, pouring money in as he had with the *Examiner* and applying everything he had learned in San Francisco. He
was going to war against Pulitzer's *New York World*.

When Hearst took over the *Journal* in October
1895, the Cuban insurrection had already begun.
Until then Hearst had shown no interest in foreign
affairs, but he genuinely felt for the underdog
Cubans and, more to the point, saw in their cause
just what he needed to drive his circulation war
against Pulitzer. Not much actual news could be gotten out of Cuba, for the sporadic fighting took place
in the remote interior, beyond the reach of Hearst's

William Randolph Hearst
Archive Photos.

correspondents in Havana. It did not matter. Rebel claims were good enough for Hearst, and a drumbeat of superheated articles began to appear about mostly nonexistent battles and about Spanish atrocities. When General Valeriano Weyler took command, the *Journal* immediately dubbed him the "Butcher":

> Weyler the brute, the devastator of haciendas, the destroyer of families and the outrager of women. . . . Pitiless, cold, an exterminator of men . . . inventing tortures and infamies of bloody debauchery. . . .

Weyler's reconcentration program soon put meat into the *Journal*'s wild charges, and American public opinion began to harden against the Spanish.

The *Journal* was stridently for war. Hearst's jingoism sounded very much like his old crusade against the San Francisco water trust: it was the people versus the interests all over again, the freedom-loving masses against the peace-at-any-price plutocrats. President McKinley was Wall Street's puppet, with the nefarious Senator Hanna pulling the strings. When the *Maine* went down, the *Journal* was ablaze with fiery headlines charging Spanish treachery. That week circulation passed a million. Impatient for action, Hearst found ammunition even in the suicide of poor Mrs. Mary Wayt:

GRIEVED OVER OUR DELAY

"The Government May Live
in Dishonor," Said She,
"I Cannot."

The next day, April 19, the Senate passed the war resolution, and hostilities commenced. The news from Manila Bay got this screaming headline: "VICTORY . . . Complete! . . . Glorious! . . . THE MAINE IS AVENGED." A few days later, the front page asked readers: "HOW DO YOU LIKE THE JOURNAL'S WAR?"

Was it true? Had Hearst caused the war? For many years historians thought so. Now, with a better understanding of McKinley's administration, they are more inclined to stress the country's endangered strategic interests. Yet there is no denying Hearst's contribution. The war hysteria he nurtured was like a ticking bomb, forcing the president's hand because, as New York's Senator Platt noted, McKinley knew "that the people of the United States will not tolerate much longer the war in Cuba." There were also longer-term consequences. For one, public opinion became a weightier factor in the conduct of American foreign policy; whether democracy and diplomacy are compatible has been debated ever since Hearst's time. Second, Hearst introduced and never let go of a superpatriotism—"Americanism," he called it—that became a permanent, if volatile, element of the nation's political debate.

As for the war with Spain, Hearst had a grand time of it. He hired a boat, took a crew of newsmen down to Cuba, came under fire at El Caney, wrote some creditable dispatches when his star reporter was wounded, rounded up Spanish survivors of the Santiago naval battle, and returned to New York feeling that the world was his oyster.

At that time Hearst was thirty-five, with another fifty-three years to live. The news business, ultimately a huge empire, remained the core of his being. But he also entered New York politics in a quixotic quest for the presidency. He plunged into Hollywood moviemaking and formed a permanent liaison with one of his creations, the movie star Marion Davies. He built a castle at San Simeon, California, and extravagantly entertained the rich and famous. All the while he became more enigmatic, more dictatorial, more alone.

In the end Hearst gained immortality in an utterly modern way: he became the inspiration for Orson Welles's great movie *Citizen Kane* (1941). Ordinarily, we do not look to the movies for historical insight, but Welles captured something about Hearst. The plot turns on Kane's dying word, *rosebud*, which proves to be only the name of a sled remembered from his childhood.

"whether the time has not arrived when Spain . . . will put a stop to this destructive war." If Spain could not ensure an "early and certain peace," the United States would take whatever steps it "should deem necessary to procure this result." The American pressure on Spain at first seemed to pay off. The conservative regime fell, and a liberal government, upon taking office in October 1897, moderated its Cuban policy. Spain recalled Weyler, limited reconcentration, and adopted an autonomy plan granting Cuba a degree of self-rule but not independence. Madrid's incapacity soon became clear, however. In January 1898, Spanish loyalists in Havana rioted against the offer of autonomy. Cuban rebels, encouraged by the prospect of American intervention, demanded full independence.

On February 9, 1898, the *New York Journal* published a private letter written by Dupuy de Lôme, Spanish minister to the United States. In it de Lôme called President McKinley "weak" and "a bidder for the admiration of the crowd." Worse, the letter suggested that the Spanish government was not taking the American demands for reform seriously. De Lôme immediately resigned, but the damage had been done.

A week later the U.S. battleship *Maine* blew up and sank in Havana harbor, with the loss of 260 seamen. "Whole Country Thrills with the War Fever," proclaimed Hearst's *New York Journal*. From that moment on, popular passions against Spain became a major factor in the march toward war.

President McKinley kept his head. He assumed that the sinking was accidental: what motive could the Spanish have had for attacking the *Maine*? An American naval board of inquiry, however, submitted a damaging report. Disagreeing with a separate Spanish inquiry, the American board concluded that the sinking was caused by a mine, not—as the latest studies find just as likely—by an accidental explosion aboard the *Maine*. (A 1976 naval inquiry faulted the ship's design, which located the ship's explosives too close to coal bunkers prone to spontaneous fires.) No evidence linked the Spanish to the purported mine. But if a mine did in fact sink the ship, then the Spanish were at least at fault for not protecting an American vessel within their jurisdiction.

The impression that Spanish control over Cuba had broken down was reinforced by a memorable speech by Senator Redfield Proctor of Vermont after a visit to Cuba. The account by this anti-imperialist senior Republican of the devastation in the Cuban countryside convinced even the skeptical that Spain had lost its claim to Cuba.

President McKinley had no enthusiasm for the martial spirit engulfing the country. He was not swept along by calls to avenge the sinking of the *Maine*. But he did have to pay attention to an aroused public opinion. Business leaders now also became impatient for the dispute with Spain to end. War was preferable to

the unresolved Cuban crisis. On March 27 McKinley cabled Madrid what was in effect an ultimatum: an immediate armistice for six months, abandonment of reconcentration, and, with the United States as mediator, peace negotiations with the rebels. A telegram the next day added that only Cuban independence would be regarded as a satisfactory outcome to the negotiations. Spain categorically rejected these humiliating demands, although, as a final concession, it unilaterally declared on April 9 an armistice whose duration would be at the discretion of the Spanish military.

On April 11 McKinley sent a message to Congress asking for authority to intervene to end the fighting in Cuba. His motives were as he described them: "In the name of humanity, in the name of civilization, in behalf of endangered American interests which give us the right and the duty to speak and to act, the war in Cuba must stop." The War Hawks in Congress—a mixture of Republicans and western Democrats—were impatient with McKinley's cautious progress. But the president did not lose control, and he defeated the War Hawks on the crucial issue of recognizing the rebel republican government, which would have greatly reduced the administration's freedom of action in dealing with Spain.

The resolutions authorizing intervention in Cuba contained an amendment by Senator Henry M. Teller of Colorado disclaiming any intention by the United States of taking possession of Cuba. No European government should say that "when we go out to make battle for the liberty and freedom of Cuban patriots, that we are doing it for the purpose of aggrandizement for ourselves or the increasing of our territorial holdings." This policy had to be made clear with regard to Cuba, "whatever," Senator Teller added, "we may do as to some other islands."

Did McKinley have in mind "some other islands"? Was this really a war of aggression, secretly motivated by a desire to seize strategic territory from Spain? In a strict sense, almost certainly no. It was not *because* of expansionist ambitions that McKinley forced Spain into a corner. But once war came, McKinley saw it as an opportunity. As he wrote privately after hostilities began: "While we are conducting war and until its conclusion, we must keep all we get; when the war is over we must keep what we want." Precisely what would be forthcoming, of course, would depend on the fortunes of battle.

The Spoils of War

Hostilities formally began when Spain declared war on April 24, 1898. Across the United States volunteer regiments began to form up. Theodore Roosevelt immediately resigned as assistant secretary of the navy, ordered a fancy uniform, and was commissioned lieutenant colonel in a volunteer cavalry regiment that became known as the Rough Riders. Raw recruits poured into makeshift bases around Tampa, Florida. Confusion

"Remember the Maine!"
In late January 1898 the *Maine* entered Havana harbor on a courtesy call. On the evening of February 15 a mysterious blast sent the U.S. battleship to the bottom. This dramatic lithograph conveys something of the impact of that event on American public opinion. Although no evidence ever linked the Spanish authorities to the explosion, the sinking of the *Maine* fed the emotional fires that prepared the nation for war with Spain.
Granger Collection.

reigned. Tropical uniforms did not arrive; the food was bad, the sanitation worse; and rifles were in short supply. No provision had been made for getting the troops to Cuba; the government hastily began to collect a fleet of yachts, lake steamers, and commercial boats. Fortunately, the small regular army was a disciplined, highly professional force, and its seasoned 28,000 troops provided a nucleus for the 200,000 civilians who had to be turned into soldiers inside of a few weeks.

The navy was in much better shape. Spain had nothing to match America's seven battleships and armored cruisers, and the ships Spain did have were undermanned and ill prepared for battle. The Spanish admiral Pascual Cervera gloomily expected that his navy would "like Don Quixote go out to fight windmills and come back with a broken head."

On April 23, acting on plans already drawn up, Commodore George Dewey's small Pacific fleet set sail from Hong Kong for the Philippines. There, at this Spanish possession in the far Pacific, not in Cuba, the decisive engagement of the war took place. On May 1 American ships cornered the Spanish fleet in Manila Bay and destroyed it (Map 21.1). The victory produced euphoria in the United States. Immediately, part of the army being trained for the Cuban campaign was diverted to the Philippines. Manila, the Philippine capital, fell on August 13, 1898.

With Dewey's naval victory, American strategic thinking clicked into place. "We hold the other side of the Pacific and the value to this country is almost beyond imagination," declared Senator Lodge. "We must on no account let the [Philippine] Islands go." President McKinley agreed, and so did his key advisors. An anchorage in the western Pacific had long been coveted by naval strategists. At this time, too, the Great Powers were carving China into spheres of influence. If American commerce wanted a place in that glittering market, the power of the United States would have to be projected into Asia. "With a strong foothold in the Philippine Islands, we can and will take a large slice of the commerce of Asia," Senator Mark Hanna asserted. "That is what we want . . . and it is better to strike while the iron is hot."

Once the decision for a Philippine base had been made, other decisions followed almost automatically. The question of Hawaii was quickly resolved. After stalling the previous year, in July 1898 Hawaiian annexation went through Congress by joint resolution. Hawaii had acquired a crucial strategic value: it was a halfway station on the way to the Philippines. The navy pressed for a coaling base in the central Pacific; that meant Guam, a Spanish island in the Marianas. There was need also for a strategically located base in the Caribbean; that meant Puerto Rico. By July, before the assault on Cuba, the full scope of McKinley's war aims

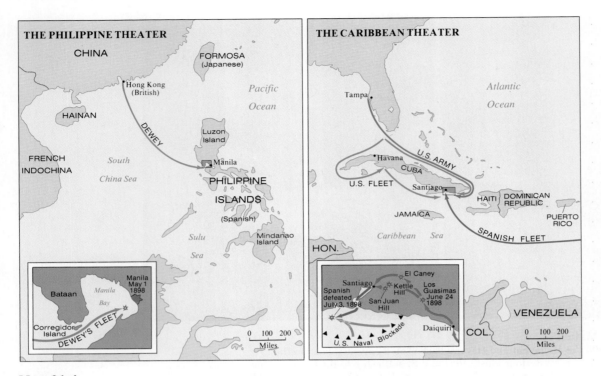

MAP 21.1
The Spanish-American War of 1898
The swift American victory in the Spanish-American War resulted from overwhelming naval
superiority. Dewey's destruction of the Spanish fleet in Manila harbor doomed the Spaniards
in the Philippines. In Cuba, American ground forces won a hard victory on San Juan Hill,
for they were ill equipped and poorly supplied. With the United States in control of the seas,
the Spaniards saw no choice but to give up the battle for Cuba.

had taken shape. The American people were vocifer-
ously behind him. In the wake of Dewey's victory,
enthusiasm for colonial annexations swept the country
and, as one close reader of the nation's press reported,
was "getting so strong it will mean the political death of
any man to oppose it pretty soon."

The campaign in Cuba was something of an anti-
climax. The Spanish fleet was bottled up in Santiago
harbor, and the city itself became the strategic key to
the military campaign. Half trained and ill equipped,
the American forces moving on Santiago might have
been checked by a determined opponent. The Spaniards
fought to maintain their honor but had no stomach for
a real war against the Americans.

The main battle, on July 1, occurred near Santiago
on the heights of San Juan Hill. On foot because there
had been no room for horses on the transports,
Roosevelt's Rough Riders seized Kettle Hill. Then a
frontal assault against the San Juan heights began.
Four black regiments took the brunt of the fighting.
White observers grudgingly credited much of the victory to the "superb gallantry" of the black soldiers (see
American Voices, "George W. Prioleau: Black Soldiers
in a White Man's War," p. 688). In fact, it was not quite
a victory. The Spaniards, driven from their forward

positions, retreated to a well-fortified second line. The
Americans had suffered heavy casualties and were
exhausted by the heat; whether they could mount a
second assault was questionable. They were spared
this test, however, by the Spanish. On July 3 Cervera's
fleet in Santiago harbor made a suicidal daylight
attempt to run the American blockade and was
destroyed. A few days later, convinced that Santiago
could not be saved, Spanish forces surrendered.

The two nations signed an armistice in which
Spain agreed to give up Cuba and cede Puerto Rico and
Guam to the United States. American forces occupied
Manila pending a peace treaty.

The Imperial Experiment

The big question was the Philippines, an archipelago of
over 7,000 islands populated—as William R. Day,
McKinley's secretary of state, put it in the racist language
of that era—by "eight or nine millions of absolutely ignorant and many degraded people." Not even the most avid
American expansionists had advocated colonial rule over
such a population—that was European-style imperialism, not the acquisition of strategic bases that Mahan
and his followers had in mind. Both Mahan and Lodge

The Battle of San Juan Hill
On July 1, 1898, the key battle for Cuba took place on heights overlooking Santiago. African American troops bore the brunt of the fighting. Although generally overlooked, the black role in the San Juan battle is done justice in this contemporary lithograph, without the demeaning stereotypes by which blacks were normally depicted in an age of intensifying racism. Even so, the racial hierarchy is maintained. The blacks are the foot soldiers; their officers are white.
Library of Congress.

initially advocated keeping only Manila. It gradually became clear, however, that Manila was not defensible without U.S. control of the whole of Luzon, the large island on which the city is located.

Taking the Philippines. McKinley and his advisors surveyed the options. One possibility was to return most of the islands to Spain, but the reputed evils of Spanish rule made that a "cowardly and dishonorable" solution. Another possibility was to partition the Philippines with one or more of the other Great Powers. But as McKinley observed, to turn over valuable territory to "our commercial rivals in the Orient—that would have been bad business and discreditable."

Most plausible was the option of granting the Philippines independence. As in Cuba, Spanish rule had already stirred up a rebellion, led by the fiery patriot Emilio Aguinaldo. An arrangement might have been possible like the one being negotiated with the Cubans: the lease of a naval base to the Americans as the price for freedom. But after some hesitation McKinley was persuaded that "we could not leave [the

Filipinos] to themselves—they were unfit for self-rule—and they would soon have anarchy and misrule over there worse than Spain's was."

In October 1898, while the peace negotiations were in progress, McKinley made a two-week speaking tour of the Midwest to get a reading on public opinion. What he heard from the crowds confirmed his own belief that the United States would have to take the entire archipelago. On October 26 he cabled instructions to that effect to the American delegation in Paris. He had concluded that the United States "cannot let go."

As for the Spaniards, they had little choice against what they considered "the immoderate demands of a conqueror." In the Treaty of Paris they ceded the Philippines to the United States for a payment of $20 million. The treaty encountered harder going at home and was ratified by the Senate (requiring a two-thirds majority) on February 6, 1899, with only a single vote to spare.

The Anti-Imperialists. The narrowness of the administration's victory signaled the revival of an anti-expansionist tradition that had been briefly silenced by

GEORGE W. PRIOLEAU

Black Soldiers in a White Man's War

———— ★ ————

The chaplain of the Ninth Cavalry regiment expresses his bitterness toward the racism experienced by black troopers in the South on their way to battle in Cuba.

Hon. H. C. Smith
Editor, Gazette

Dear Sir:
The Ninth Cavalry left Chickamauga on the 30th of April for Tampa, Fla. We arrived here (nine miles from Tampa) on May 3. From this port the army will sail for Cuba. We have in this camp here and at Tampa between 7,000 and 8,000 soldiers, artillery, one regiment of cavalry (the famous fighting Ninth) and the Twenty-fourth and Twenty-fifth infantries. The Ninth Cavalry's bravery and their skillfulness with weapons of war . . . is well known by all who have read the history of the last Indian war. . . .

Yesterday, May 12, the Ninth was ordered to be ready to embark at a moment's notice for Cuba. . . . These men are anxious to go. The country will then hear and know of the bravery of these sable sons of Ham.

The American Negro is always ready and willing to take up arms, to fight and to lay down his life in defense of his country's flag and honor. All the way from northwest Nebraska this regiment was greeted with cheers and hurrahs. At places where we stopped the people assembled by the thousands. While the Ninth Cavalry band would play some national air the people would raise their hats, men, women and children would wave their handkerchiefs, and the heavens would resound with their hearty cheers. The white hand shaking the black hand. The hearty "goodbyes," "God bless you," and other expressions aroused the patriotism of our boys. . . . These demonstrations, so enthusiastically given, greeted us all the way until we reached Nashville. At this point we arrived about 12:30 A.M. There were about 6,000 colored people there to greet us (very few white people) but not a man was allowed by the railroad officials to approach the cars. From there until we reached Chattanooga there was not a cheer given us, the people living in gross ignorance, rags and dirt. Both white and colored seemed amazed; they looked at us in wonder. Don't think they have intelligence enough to know that Andrew Jackson is dead. . . .

The prejudice against the Negro soldier and the Negro was great, but it was of heavenly origin to what it is in this part of Florida, and I suppose that what is true here is true in other parts of the state. Here, the Negro is not allowed to purchase over the same counter in some stores that the white man purchases over. The southerners have made their laws and the Negroes know and obey them. They never stop to ask a white man a question. He (Negro) never thinks of disobeying. You talk about freedom, liberty, etc. Why sir, the Negro of this country is a freeman and yet a slave. Talk about fighting and freeing poor Cuba and of Spain's brutality; of Cuba's murdered thousands, and starving reconcentradoes. Is America any better than Spain? Has she not subjects in her very midst who are murdered daily without a trial of judge or jury? Has she not subjects in her own borders whose children are half-fed and half-clothed, because their father's skin is black. . . . Yet the Negro is loyal to his country's flag. . . .

The four Negro regiments are going to help free Cuba, and they will return to their homes, some then mustered out and begin again to fight the battle of American prejudice. . . .

Yours truly,
Geo. W. Prioleau
Chaplain, Ninth Cavalry

Source: Cleveland *Gazette* (May 13, 1898), reprinted in Willard B. Gatewood, *"Smoked Yankees" and the Struggle for Empire, 1898–1902* (Urbana: University of Illinois Press, 1971), 27–29.

---

the patriotic passions of a nation at war. In the Senate, opponents of the treaty invoked the country's republican principles. Under the Constitution, argued conservative Republican George F. Hoar, "no power is given to the Federal Government to acquire territory to be held and governed permanently as colonies" or "to conquer alien people and hold them in subjugation." Hoar rejected "the fundamental idea [of the European imperial powers] that the people of immense areas of territory can be held as subjects, never to become citizens."

But making 8 million Filipinos eligible for citizenship was equally objectionable to the anti-imperialists, who were no more champions of "these savage people" than were the expansionists who denigrated the self-governing capacity of the Filipinos.

Leading citizens enlisted in the anti-imperialist cause, including Andrew Carnegie, who offered a check for $20 million to purchase the independence of the Philippines; Samuel Gompers, who feared the competition of cheap Filipino labor; and Jane Addams, who believed that women should stand for peace. The key group, however, was a social elite of old-line Mugwump reformers including Carl Schurz, Charles Eliot Norton, and Charles Francis Adams. In November 1898 a Boston group formed the first Anti-Imperialist League, from which blossomed a national movement over the next year.

Although skillful at publicizing their cause, the anti-imperialists never managed to build a truly popular

Emilio Aguinaldo
At the start of the war with Spain, U.S. military leaders brought the Filipino patriot Aguinaldo back from Singapore because they thought he would stir up a popular uprising that would help defeat the Spaniards. Aguinaldo came because he thought the Americans favored an independent Philippines. These differing intentions—it has remained a matter of dispute what assurances Aguinaldo received—were the root cause of the Filipino insurrection that proved far costlier in American and Filipino lives than the war with Spain that preceded it.
Corbis-Bettmann.

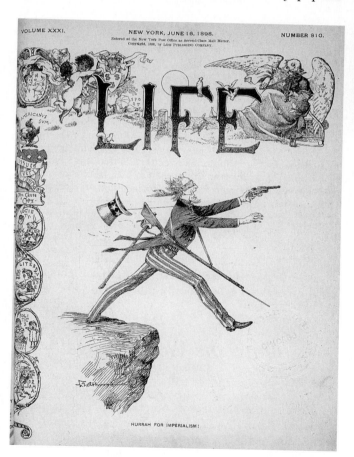

Hurrah for Imperialism!
Amid the patriotic frenzy over Dewey's naval victory, cooler heads wondered whether the United States knew what it was getting into with all the talk about creating an American empire. Here, *Life* magazine, often a skeptical commentator on American public life, pictures a blindfolded Uncle Sam stepping off a cliff.
LIFE, 1898, Newbury Library.

movement. They shared little but their anti-imperialism and, within the Mugwump core, lacked the common touch. Nor was anti-imperialism easily translated into a viable political cause, because the Democrats, once the treaty was adopted, waffled on the issue. Although an outspoken anti-imperialist, William Jennings Bryan, the Democratic standard-bearer, provided confused leadership. He confounded his friends by favoring ratification of the treaty and afterward hesitated to stake his party's future on a crusade against a national policy that he privately believed to be irreversible. Still, if it was an accomplished fact, Philippine annexation lost the moral high ground because of grim events that began to unfold in the Philippines.

War in the Philippines. On February 4, 1899, two days before the Senate ratified the treaty, fighting broke out between American and Filipino patrols on the edge of Manila. Confronted by American annexation, Aguinaldo asserted his nation's independence and turned his guns on the occupying American forces. The ensuing conflict far exceeded in ferocity the war just concluded with Spain.

Fighting tenacious guerrillas, the U.S. Army resorted to the reconcentration tactics the Spaniards had used in Cuba, moving people into towns, carrying out indiscriminate attacks beyond the perimeters, and burning crops and villages (see American Voices, "Robert P. Hughes and Richard T. O'Brien: Subduing the Filipinos—The Realities," p. 691). Atrocities became commonplace on both sides. In three years of warfare 4,200 Americans and thousands more Filipinos died. The fighting ended in 1902, and Judge William Howard Taft, who had been appointed governor general, set up a civilian administration. He intended to make the Philippines a model of American road building and sanitary engineering.

McKinley's convincing victory over Bryan in the 1900 election, though by no means a referendum on American expansionism, suggested popular satisfaction with the country's overseas adventure. Yet a strong undercurrent of misgivings was evident. Americans had not anticipated the brutal methods needed to subdue the Filipino guerrillas. "We are destroying these islanders by the thousands, their villages and cities," protested the philosopher William James. "No life shall you have, we say, except as a gift from our philanthropy after your unconditional surrender to our will. . . . Could there be any more damning indictment of that whole bloated ideal termed 'modern civilization'?" And when the fighting ended, it was not apparent just what the United States had achieved.

There were, moreover, disturbing constitutional issues to be resolved. Did the U.S. Constitution extend to the acquired territories? Did their inhabitants automatically become U.S. citizens? In 1901 the Supreme Court ruled negatively on both questions; these were matters for Congress to decide. A special commission appointed by McKinley recommended independence for the Philippines after an indefinite period of U.S. rule, during which the Filipinos would be prepared for self-government. In 1916 the Jones Act formally committed the United States to granting Philippine independence but set no date.

The ugly business in the Philippines rubbed off some of the moralizing gloss but left undimmed America's global aspirations. In a few years the United States had acquired the makings of a strategic overseas empire: Hawaii, Puerto Rico, Guam, the Philippines, and finally, in 1900, several of the Samoan islands that had been jointly administered with Germany and Britain. The United States, remarked the legal scholar John Bassett Moore in 1899, had moved "from a posi-

Fighting the Filipinos, 1899
The United States went to war against Spain in 1898 partly out of sympathy with the Cuban struggle for independence. Yet the United States found it necessary to use the same brutal tactics against the Filipino insurrectionists that the Spaniards had employed against the Cubans. Here U.S. troops man a defensive perimeter near Pasay in 1899 against an elusive foe. California Museum of Photography.

tion of comparative freedom from entanglements into a position of what is commonly called a world power."

Onto the World Stage

In Europe the flexing of America's muscles caused some consternation. The assault on Spain seemed, in the words of the French envoy to Washington, "ignorant, brutal, and quite capable of destroying the complicated European structure." At the instigation of Kaiser Wilhelm II of Germany, the major powers had tried before war broke out to intercede on Spain's behalf—but tentatively, because no one was looking for trouble with the Americans. President McKinley had listened politely to the presentations of their envoys on April 6, 1898, then proceeded with his war.

ROBERT P. HUGHES AND RICHARD T. O'BRIEN

Subduing the Filipinos—The Realities

———————★———————

When Arthur MacArthur, the commanding general of U.S. forces in the Philippines, appeared in 1902 before a Senate committee investigating conditions there he boasted of "planting the best traditions, the best characteristics of Americanism . . . down deep in that fertile soil."

Brigadier General Hughes offered the Senate committee a different picture of the implanting of American ideals in Filipino soil.

Sen. Rawlins: . . . [In] burning towns, what would you do? Would the entire town be destroyed by fire or would only offending portions of the town be burned?

Gen. Hughes: I do not know that we have ever had a case of burning what you would call a town in this country, but probably a barrio or a sitio; probably half a dozen houses, native shacks, where the insurrectos would go in and be concealed, and if they caught a detachment passing they would kill some of them.

Sen. Rawlins: What did I understand you to say would be the consequences of that?

Gen. Hughes: They usually burned the village.

Sen. Rawlins: All the houses in the village?

Gen. Hughes: Yes, every one of them.

Sen. Rawlins: What would become of the inhabitants?

Gen. Hughes: That was their lookout. . . .

Sen. Rawlins: If these shacks were of no consequence what was the utility of their destruction?

Gen. Hughes: The destruction was as a punishment. They permitted these people to come in there and conceal themselves and they gave no sign. It is always—

Sen. Rawlins: The punishment in that case would fall, not upon the men, who could go elsewhere, but mainly upon the women and little children.

Gen. Hughes: The women and children are part of the family, and where you wish to inflict punishment you can punish the man probably worse in that way than in any other.

Sen. Rawlins: But is that within the ordinary rules of civilized warfare? . . .

Gen. Hughes: These people are not civilized.

Richard T. O'Brien, of M Company, 26th Infantry Volunteers, U.S. Army, gave this account to the Senate committee.

[How] the order started and who gave it I don't know, but the town was fired on. I saw an old fellow come to the door, and he looked out: he got a shot in the abdomen and fell to his knees and turned around and died. . . .

After that two old men came out, hand in hand. I should think they were over 50 years old, probably between 50 and 70 years old. They had a white flag. They were shot down. At the other end of the town we heard screams, and there was a woman there; she was burned up, and in her arms was a baby, and on the floor was another child. The baby was at her breast, the one in her arms, and this child on the floor was, I should judge, about 3 years of age. They were burned. Whether she was demoralized or driven insane I don't know. She stayed in the house.

Source: U.S. Senate, Committee on the Philippines, *Hearings,* 57th Congress, 1st Session (1902).

The decisive outcome confirmed what the Europeans already suspected. After Dewey's naval victory the semi-official French paper *Le Temps* observed that "what passes before our eyes is the appearance of a new power of the first order." And in a long editorial the London *Times* concluded: "This war must . . . effect a profound change in the whole attitude and policy of the United States. In the future America will play a part in the general affairs of the world such as she has never played before" (see Voices from Abroad, "James Bryce, Jean Hess, and Émile Zola: On American Expansionism," p. 692).

A Power among Powers

The politician most ardently agreeing with the London *Times*'s vision of America's future was the man who,

JAMES BRYCE, JEAN HESS, ÉMILE ZOLA

On American Expansionism

————————★————————

America's emergence as an imperial power provoked much anxious comment abroad. Not surprisingly, this commentary tended to mirror the concerns of the commentators. What was unexpected, as the following excerpts suggest, was how seriously Europeans had taken America's high estimate of itself. If U.S. actions violated professed ideals and traditions, Europeans were not averse to calling the United States to account.

As the debate over Hawaiian annexation raged in late 1897, James Bryce, the renowned British observer, reminded America of the wisdom of the Founding Fathers.

What have the United States to gain by territorial extension? . . . The United States has already a great and splendid mission in building up between the oceans a free, happy, and prosperous nation of two hundred millions of people. And one of the noblest parts of her mission in the world has been to show the older peoples and states an example of abstention from the quarrels and wars and conquests that make up so large and so lamentable a part of the annals of Europe. Her remote position and her immense power have, as I have said, delivered her from that burden of military and naval armaments which presses with crushing weight upon the peoples of Europe. It would be, for her, a descent from what may be called the pedestal of wise and pacific detachment on which she now stands, were she to yield to that earth hunger which has been raging among the European states, and to imitate the aggressive methods which some of them have pursued. The policy of creating great armaments and of annexing territories beyond the sea would be, if a stranger may venture to say so, an un-American policy, and a complete departure from the maxims—approved by long experience—of the illustrious founders of the republic.

Jean Hess, a Frenchman well traveled in East Asia, questioned in 1899 American motives for intervening in the Philippines.

Nowhere, in my opinion, better than in the Philippines, has it been shown that modern wars are simply "deals." The American intervention in the struggle engaged in by the revolutionary Tagals [Filipinos] against the Spanish government has turned out to be nothing but a speculation of "business men," and not the generous effort of a people paying a debt in procuring for others the liberty that it concedes belongs to all. . . . Back of all these battles, this devastation and mourning, in spite of the newly-born Yankee imperialism, there was only, there is only, what the people of the Bourse [stock market] call a deal.

Writing in 1900, Émile Zola, the great French novelist, feared that America's military adventurism was dealing a blow to the cause of world peace.

I know that, for belief in peace and future disarmament, the time is scarcely auspicious, as we are now beholding an alarming recrudescence of militarism. Nations which till now seem to have held aloof from the contagion, to have escaped this madness so prevalent in Europe, now appear to be attacked. Thus, since the Spanish war, the United States seems to have become a victim of the war fever. . . . I can see in that great nation a dangerous inclination toward war. I can detect the generation of vague ideas of future conquest. Until the present time that country wisely occupied itself with its domestic affairs and let Europe severely alone, but now it is donning plumes and epaulets, and will be dreaming of possible campaigns and be carried away with the idea of military glory—notions so perilous as to have been responsible for the downfall of nations.

Source: Philip S. Foner and Robert C. Winchester, eds., *The Anti-Imperialist Reader: A Documentary History of Anti-Imperialism in the United States* (New York: Holmes and Meier Publishers, 1984), vol. 1: 98–99, 417–418.

with the assassination of William McKinley, became president on September 14, 1901: Theodore Roosevelt. An avid student of foreign affairs, Roosevelt had widely traveled abroad and was acquainted with many of the European leaders. He had no doubt about America's role in the world.

It was important, first of all, to uphold the country's honor in the community of nations. "I am not hostile to any European power in the abstract," Roosevelt once wrote. "I am simply American first and last, and therefore hostile to any power which wrongs us." Nor should the country ever shrink from righteous battle. "All the great masterful races have been fighting races," Roosevelt declared. But when he spoke of war, Roosevelt had in mind actions by the "civilized" nations against "backward peoples" (such as the Filipinos, whose struggle for freedom was being subdued when he entered the White House). Roosevelt felt "it incumbent on all civilized and orderly powers to insist on the proper policing of the world." That was why he sympathized with European imperialism and how he justified American dominance over the Caribbean states.

As for the "civilized and orderly" policemen of the world, the worst thing that could happen was for them to fall to fighting among themselves. Roosevelt had an acute sense of the fragility of world peace, and he was farsighted about the likelihood—in this he was truly exceptional among Americans—of a catastrophic world war. He believed in American responsibility for helping to maintain the balance of power.

Anglo-American Amity. After the Spanish-American War, the European powers had been uncertain about how to deal with the victor. Germany toyed briefly with the notion of an American alliance, but only Great Britain had a clear view of what it wanted from the United States. In the late nineteenth century Britain's position in Europe was steadily worsening in the face of industrial and military challenges by a unified Germany. Clashing expansionist ambitions in North Africa and across Asia soured Britain's relations with France and Russia. And there was general European hostility toward British imperial policy in South Africa, a policy that resulted in the Boer War against the independent-minded Dutch settlers at the end of the 1890s. In its growing isolation Britain turned to the United States. This explains why Britain bowed to American demands in the Venezuela dispute of 1895. From that time onward, after a century of cool relations (or worse) with its former colonies in North America, Britain strove for *rapprochement* (literally, a "coming together") with the United States.

In the Hay-Pauncefote Agreement of 1901 Britain gave up its treaty rights to joint participation in any Central American canal project, clearing the way for a canal exclusively under U.S. control. And two years later the last of the vexing U.S.–Canadian border disputes—this one involving British Columbia and Alaska—was settled, again to American satisfaction. The lone British member of the U.S.–Canadian tribunal cast the deciding vote, awarding to the United States the Pacific inlets and ports that provided the only convenient access to the Klondike goldfields of the Canadian Yukon.

No formal alliance was forthcoming, but Anglo-American friendship was so firm that British planners after 1901 based their war plans on the assumption that America was "a kindred state with whom we shall never have a parricidal war." Roosevelt heartily agreed: "Eng-land and the United States, beyond any other two powers, should be friendly." In his unflagging efforts to maintain a global balance of power, the cornerstone of Roosevelt's policy was the British relationship.

The Big Stick. Among nations, however, what counted was strength, not merely goodwill. Roosevelt wanted "to make all foreign powers understand that when we have adopted a line of policy we have adopted it definitely, and with the intention of backing it up with deeds as well as words." As Roosevelt famously said: "Speak softly and carry a big stick." By a "big stick," he meant above all naval power.

Under Roosevelt, the battleship program (see New Technology, pp. 678–679) went on apace. By 1904 the U.S. Navy stood fifth in the world, and by 1907 it was third. At the top of Roosevelt's agenda, however, was a canal across Central America. Indeed, the Spanish-American War had demonstrated that strategic need in the most graphic way: the entire country had waited breathlessly while the battleship *Oregon* steamed at full speed from the Pacific around the tip of South America to join the final action against the Spanish fleet in Cuba.

The Panama Canal. After Britain's surrender of its joint rights in 1901, Roosevelt proceeded to the more troublesome task of leasing from Colombia the needed strip of land across Panama, which was a Colombian province. To this end, the United States had purchased from the New Panama Canal Company the assets of de Lesseps's earlier project. The Colombian legislature, however, voted down the proposed treaty, partly because the company's rights were about to expire and the lease to the United States could then be renegotiated on terms more favorable to Colombia. Furious over what seemed to him a breach of faith, Roosevelt contemplated outright seizure of Panama but settled on a more devious solution.

The key intermediary in the sale of the de Lesseps assets, an engineer named Philippe Bunau-Varilla, let Roosevelt know that an independence movement was brewing in Panama. The United States in turn informed Bunau-Varilla that American ships were steaming toward Panama. The idea was that the Americans would covertly assist the expected uprising. But when the cruiser *Nashville* arrived at Colón, on Panama's northern coast, there was a mix-up and the American commander failed to prevent the landing of 400 troops sent by the Colombian government to hold the province. Using their wits, the conspirators managed to keep these troops from proceeding to Panama City, where the bloodless revolution against Colombian rule went off on schedule. On November 7, 1903, the United States recognized Panama. Less than two weeks later, with Bunau-Varilla serving as the representative of the new republic, Panama signed a treaty that granted the

The Panama Canal

The Canal Zone was acquired through devious means from which Americans could take little pride (and which led in 1978 to the Senate's decision to restore the property to Panama). But the building of the Panama Canal itself was a triumph of American ingenuity and drive. Dr. William C. Gorgas cleaned out the malarial mosquitoes that had earlier stymied the French. Under Colonel George W. Goethals, the U.S. Army overcame formidable obstacles in a mighty feat of engineering. This photograph shows the massive effort underway in December 1904 to excavate the Culebra Cut so that oceangoing ships would be able to pass through.

Corbis-Bettmann.

United States a perpetually renewable lease on a canal zone. Roosevelt never regretted the victimization of Colombia, although the United States, as a kind of conscience money, paid Colombia $25 million in 1922.

Building the canal was one of the heroic engineering feats of the twentieth century, involving a swamp-clearing project to rid the area of malaria and yellow fever, the construction of a series of great locks, and the excavation of 240 million cubic yards of earth. It took the U.S. Army Corps of Engineers eight years to finish the huge project. When the Panama Canal opened in 1914, it gave the United States a commanding commercial and strategic position in the Western Hemisphere (Map 21.2).

Policeman of the Caribbean. Next came the task of making the Caribbean basin secure. The countries there, said Secretary of State Elihu Root, had been placed "in the front yard of the United States" by the Panama Canal. Therefore, as Roosevelt put it, they had to "behave themselves."

In the case of Cuba, good behavior was readily managed in the settlement that followed the Spanish-American War. Before the United States withdrew from Cuba in 1902, it reorganized Cuban finances and concluded a swamp-clearing program that eliminated yellow fever, a disease that had ravaged Cuba for many years (and had killed probably 4,000 of the occupying U.S. troops). As a condition for gaining independence, Cuba was required to include in its constitution a proviso called the Platt amendment, which gave the United States the right to intervene if Cuban independence was threatened or if Cuba failed to maintain internal order. Cuba also granted the United States a lease on Guantánamo Bay, where the U.S. Navy built a large base.

Roosevelt believed that instability in the Caribbean invited the intervention of European powers. For example, Britain and Germany blockaded Venezuela in 1902–1903 for failing to meet its debt payments. In 1904 Roosevelt announced that the United States would act as "policeman" of the region, stepping in

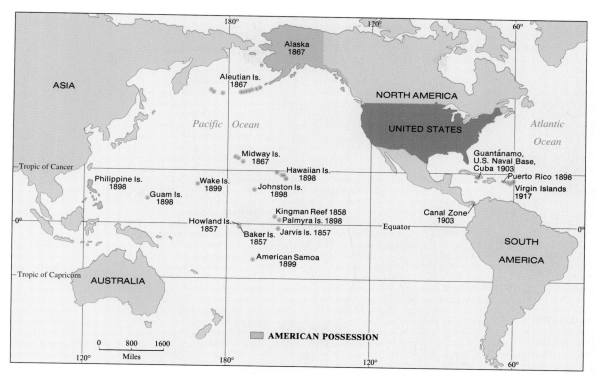

MAP 21.2
The American Empire
In 1890 Alfred T. Mahan wrote that the United States should regard the oceans as "a great highway" across which America would carry on world trade. That was precisely what resulted from the empire the United States acquired after the Spanish-American War. The Caribbean possessions, the strategically located Pacific islands, and, in 1903, the Panama Canal Zone gave the United States commercial and naval access to a wider world.

"however reluctantly, in flagrant cases . . . of wrong doing or impotence." This policy became known as the Roosevelt Corollary to the Monroe Doctrine, transforming that doctrine's broad principle of opposition to European interference in Latin America into the unrestricted right of the United States to regulate Caribbean affairs. The Roosevelt Corollary was not a treaty with other states; it was a unilateral declaration sanctioned only by American power and national interest.

Citing the Roosevelt Corollary, the United States intervened regularly in the internal affairs of Caribbean states. In 1905 American authorities took over the customs and debt management of the Dominican Republic, and similar financial supervision was imposed on Nicaragua in 1911 and on Haiti in 1916. When internal order broke down, the United States did not hesitate to send in the marines. Cuba was occupied in 1906, Nicaragua in 1909, Haiti and the Dominican Republic in later years (Map 21.3).

Roosevelt's thinking was primarily strategic; his successor, William Howard Taft, took a more commercial view. American investments in the Caribbean region grew dramatically after 1900. United Fruit Company owned about 160,000 acres in Central America by 1913, and U.S.

investments in Cuban sugar plantations quadrupled in fifteen years. Taft quickly intervened when disorder threatened American property. But he also regarded business investment as a force for stability in underdeveloped areas. Taft spoke for *dollar diplomacy*—the aggressive coupling of American diplomatic and economic interests abroad.

The Open Door in Asia

Commercial interests dominated American policy in East Asia, especially the prospect of the huge China market. But by the late 1890s Japan, Russia, Germany, France, and Britain had all carved out spheres of influence in China and instituted discriminatory trade practices in their zones. Fearful that the United States was being frozen out, Secretary of State John Hay in 1899 sent them an "open-door" note advancing the right of equal trade access—an open door—for all nations that wanted to do business in China. Despite U.S. control of the Philippines, the United States lacked real leverage and received no better than ambiguous and noncommittal responses from the occupying powers. But Hay chose to interpret them as accepting the American open-door position.

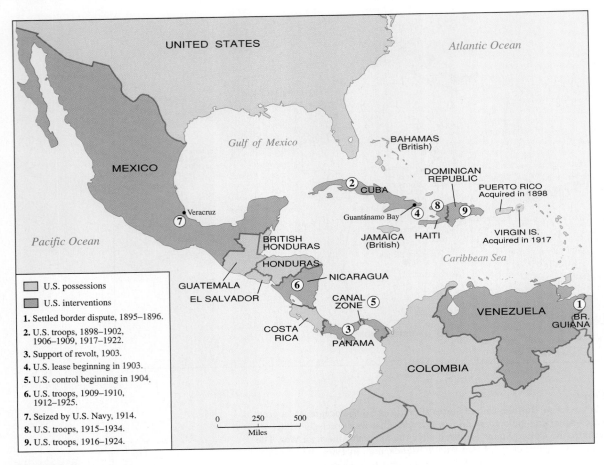

MAP 21.3
Policeman of the Caribbean
After the Spanish-American War the United States vigorously asserted its interest in the
affairs of its neighbors to the south. As the record of interventions shows, the United States
truly became the "policeman" of the Caribbean.

When a secret society of Chinese nationalists, the
Boxers, rebelled against the foreigners in 1900, the
United States sent 5,000 troops from the Philippines
and joined the multinational campaign to raise the siege
of the diplomatic missions in Peking (Beijing). America
took this opportunity to assert a second principle of the
open door: that China would be preserved as a "territorial and administrative entity." As long as the legal fiction of an independent China survived, so would
American claims to equal access to the China market.

The European powers had acceded to American
claims to preeminence in the Caribbean. But Britain,
Germany, France, and Russia were strongly entrenched
in East Asia and not inclined to defer to American interests. The United States also confronted a powerful
Asian nation—Japan—that had its own vital interests.
Although the open-door policy was important to him,
Roosevelt quickly saw in the Pacific a deadlier game
that called for American involvement.

Japan had unveiled its military strength in the
Sino-Japanese War of 1894–1895, which began the dis-

membership of China. With the formation of the
Anglo-Japanese Alliance in 1902, the strategic advantage in East Asia shifted to Japan, emboldening Japan
to confront Russia over their rival claims in Manchuria
and Korea. In 1904, provoked by Russian demands for
a military withdrawal from northern Korea, Japan suddenly attacked the Russian fleet at Port Arthur, Russia's
leased port in China. In a series of brilliant victories the
Japanese smashed the Russian military forces in Asia.
Eager to restore some semblance of a balance of power,
Roosevelt mediated a settlement of the Russo-Japanese
War at Portsmouth, New Hampshire, in 1905. Japan
emerged as the predominant power in East Asia.

Contemptuous of other Asian nations, Roosevelt
admired the Japanese—"a wonderful and civilized
people . . . entitled to stand in absolute equality with all
the other peoples of the civilized world." He conceded
that Japan had "a paramount interest in what surrounds
the Yellow Sea, just as the United States has a paramount interest in what surrounds the Caribbean." But
American strategic and commercial interests in the

The Japanese in California
The Japanese who flocked into California from 1890 onward made a mighty contribution to the state's agriculture, and through tireless labor many of them became independent and highly productive farmers. But the prejudice against them was unrelenting, and when San Francisco's school board sought to segregate Japanese children in 1906, an international incident occurred. President Roosevelt got the segregation order rescinded, and Japan voluntarily agreed to limit immigration to the United States. Despite this so-called Gentlemen's Agreement, a festering wound had been opened in the relations between the two countries.
Pat Hathaway Collection of California Views.

Pacific had to be accommodated. In exchange for Japanese acceptance of American sovereignty over the Philippines, the United States approved of Japan's protectorate over Korea in 1905 and then of its claim of full sovereignty six years later. However, a surge of anti-Asian feeling in California complicated Roosevelt's efforts. In 1906 San Francisco's school board placed all Asian students in a segregated school, infuriating Japan. In 1907 a "Gentlemen's Agreement" in which Japan agreed to restrict immigration to the United States smoothed matters over, but periodic resurgences of racism in California led to continuing tensions with the Japanese.

Roosevelt meanwhile moved to balance Japan's military power by increasing American naval strength in the Pacific. American battleships visited Japan in 1908 and then made a global tour in an impressive display of sea power. Late that year, near the end of his administration, Roosevelt achieved a formal accommodation with Japan. The Root-Takahira Agreement confirmed the status quo in the Pacific as well as the principles of free oceanic commerce and equal trade opportunity in China.

William Howard Taft, however, entered the White House in 1909 convinced that the United States had been shortchanged. He pressed for a larger role for American bankers and investors in East Asia, especially in the railroad construction going on in China. An exponent of dollar diplomacy, Taft hoped that American capital would counterbalance Japanese power and pave the way for increased commercial opportunities. When the Chinese Revolution of 1911 toppled the ruling Manchu dynasty, Taft supported the Chinese Nationalists as a counterforce to the Japanese. The United States thus entered a long-term rivalry with Japan that would end in war thirty years later.

The United States had become embroiled in a distant struggle that promised many future liabilities but few of the fabulous profits that had lured Americans to Asia.

Woodrow Wilson and Mexico

When Woodrow Wilson became president in 1913, he was bent on reform in American foreign policy no less than in domestic politics. Wilson did not really differ with his predecessors on the importance of economic development overseas. He applauded the "tides of commerce" that would arise from the Panama Canal. But he opposed dollar diplomacy, which bullied weaker countries into inequitable financial relationships and gave undue advantage to American business. It seemed to Wilson "a very perilous thing to determine the foreign policy of a nation in terms of material interest."

Within two weeks of taking office, Wilson demonstrated what he had in mind. American banks had joined an international consortium to provide a loan to China. When the investment banker J. P. Morgan sought Wilson's approval, the president refused on the grounds that the terms of the loan threatened the independence of the Chinese government. The plan "was obnoxious to the principles upon which the government of our people rests."

The United States, Wilson insisted, should conduct its foreign policy in conformity with its democratic principles. He intended to foster the "development of constitutional liberty in the world" and, above all, to extend it to the nation's neighbors in Latin America. In a major policy speech in October 1913 Wilson promised those nations that the United States would "never again seek one additional foot of territory by conquest." The president committed himself to advancing "human rights, national integrity, and opportunity" in Latin America. To do otherwise would make "ourselves untrue to our own traditions." Guided by such a moral policy, future generations would arrive at "those great heights where there shines unobstructed the light of the justice of God."

Mexico became the primary object of Wilson's ministrations. A cycle of revolutions had begun there in 1911. The dictator Porfirio Díaz was overthrown by Francisco Madero, who spoke much as Wilson did about liberty and constitutionalism. But before Madero got very far with his reforms, he was deposed and murdered in February 1913 by one of his generals, Victoriano Huerta. Other powers quickly recognized Huerta's provisional government, but the United States did not, despite America's longstanding tradition of granting quick recognition to new governments. Wilson abhorred Huerta, called him a murderer, and pledged "to force him out."

Wilson also subjected Mexico to other pressures, including the threatened use of force. By intervening in this way, Wilson insisted, "we act in the interest of Mexico alone. . . . We are seeking to counsel Mexico for its own good." Wilson meant that he intended to put the Mexican Revolution back on the constitutional path started by Madero. Wilson was not deterred by the fact that American business interests, with enormous investments in Mexico, favored Huerta. On the contrary, that seemed to spur Wilson on.

The emergence of armed opposition to Huerta in northern Mexico under Venustiano Carranza strengthened Wilson's hand. Carranza's Constitutionalist movement gave Wilson some grounds for denying recognition to Huerta, whose government did not fully control the country. More important, Carranza signified to Wilson the vitality of the reformist politics he wanted to foster in Mexico.

But the Constitutionalists, ardent nationalists, had no desire for American intervention in Mexican affairs. Carranza angrily rebuffed Wilson's efforts to bring about elections through a compromise between the rebels and the Huerta government. He also promised to resist by force any intrusion of U.S. troops into his country. All he wanted from Wilson, Carranza asserted, was recognition of the Constitutionalists' belligerent status, so that they could purchase arms in the United States. In exchange for vague promises to respect property rights and "fair" foreign concessions, Carranza finally got his way in 1914. American weapons began to flow to his troops.

When it became clear that Huerta was not about to fall, the United States threw its own forces into the conflict. On the pretext of a minor insult to the U.S. Navy at Tampico, Wilson ordered the occupation of the major port of Veracruz on April 21, 1914, at the cost of 19 American and 126 Mexican lives. At that point the Huerta regime began to crumble. Carranza nevertheless condemned the United States, and his forces came close to engaging the Americans. When he entered Mexico City in triumph in August 1914, Carranza had some cause to thank the Yankees. But if any sense of gratitude existed, it was overshadowed by the anti-Americanism inspired by Wilson's insensitivity to Mexican pride and revolutionary zeal.

The later phases of the Mexican Revolution dragged the United States ever more deeply into the morass of interventionism. No sooner had the Constitutionalists triumphed than Carranza was challenged by his northern general, Pancho Villa, who was encouraged by some American interests in Mexico. Defeated and driven northward, Villa began to stir up trouble along the border, in January 1916 killing sixteen American civilians taken from a train and two months later attacking the town of Columbus, New Mexico. Wilson sent troops led by General John J. Pershing into Mexico after the elusive Villa. Soon Pershing's force resembled an army of occupation rather than a punitive expedition. Mexican public opinion demanded that Pershing withdraw, and armed clashes with Mexican troops began. At the brink of war, the two governments backed off, and U.S. forces began to leave in early 1917. Soon after, with a new constitution ratified and elections completed, the Carranza government finally received official recognition from Washington.

The Gathering Storm in Europe

In the meantime, Europe had begun to drift toward world war. There were two main sources of tension. One was the deadly rivalry between Germany, the new military and economic superpower of Europe, and the European states threatened by its might—above all France, which had been humiliated in the Franco-Prussian War of 1870 and forced to cede the Alsace-Lorraine provinces to Germany. The second danger zone was the Balkans, where the Ottoman Empire was disintegrating and where, in the midst of explosive ethnic rivalries, Austria-Hungary and Russia were maneuvering for dominance. Out of these conflicts an alliance system had emerged: Germany, Austria-Hungary, and Italy (the Triple Alliance) were on one side, France and Russia (the Dual Alliance) on the other.

The tensions in Europe were partially released by European imperial adventures, especially by France in Africa and by Russia in Asia. These activities placed France and Russia in opposition to imperial Britain, effectively excluding Britain from the European alliance system. Fearful of Germany, however, Britain in 1904 resolved its differences with France, and the two countries reached a friendly understanding, or *entente*. In 1907 Britain came to a similar understanding with Russia, and the basis was laid for the Triple Entente. A deadly confrontation between two great European power blocs became possible.

In these European quarrels Americans had no obvious stake nor any inclination, in the words of a cau-

In Pursuit of Pancho Villa
Pancho Villa's attacks on American citizens prompted General Pershing's punitive expedition into Mexico in 1916. U.S. troops captured some of Villa's followers, but he and his main force escaped. It was an early lesson about the difficulties Great Powers have against a guerrilla foe able to melt away into a larger civilian society.
Corbis-Bettmann.

tionary Senate resolution, "to depart from the traditional American foreign policy which forbids participation . . . [in] political questions which are entirely European in scope." But on becoming president, Theodore Roosevelt took a lively interest in European affairs and was eager, as the head of a Great Power, to make a contribution to the cause of peace in Europe. In 1905 he got his chance.

The Moroccan Crisis. The Anglo-French entente of the previous year was based partly on an agreement over spheres of influence in North Africa: the Sudan was conceded to Britain, Morocco to France. Then Germany suddenly challenged France over Morocco—a disastrous move, conflicting with Germany's self-interest in keeping France's attention diverted from Europe. The German ruler, Kaiser Wilhelm, turned to Roosevelt for help. Finding in an obscure commercial treaty with Morocco the basis for American involvement, Roosevelt persuaded France to attend an international conference, which was held in January 1906 at Algeciras, Spain. With U.S. diplomats playing a key role, the crisis was defused. Germany got a few token concessions, but France's dominance over Morocco was sustained.

Algeciras marked an ominous turning point—the first time the power blocs that would become locked in battle in 1914 squared off against one another. But in 1906 the outcome of the conference seemed a diplomatic triumph, and Roosevelt's secretary of state, Elihu Root, boasted of America's success in "preserv[ing] world peace because of the power of our detachment."

Root's words prefigured how the United States would define its role among the Great Powers: it would be the apostle of peace, distinguished by its "detachment," by its lack of selfish interests in European affairs. Opposing this internationalist impulse, however, was America's strongly held isolationism.

The Peace Movement. Americans had applauded the international peace movement launched by the Hague Peace Conference of 1899. The Permanent Court of Arbitration created by the Hague conference offered new hope for the peaceful settlement of international disputes. Both the Roosevelt and the Taft administrations negotiated arbitration treaties with other countries, pledging to submit disputes to the Hague Court, only to see the treaties emasculated by a Senate unwilling to compromise the nation's sovereignty. Nor was there any sequel to Roosevelt's initiative at Algeciras. It was coolly received in the Senate and by the nation's press. Roosevelt's successor, William Howard Taft, was not inclined to challenge the doctrine of nonentanglement.

When Wilson became president, he chose William Jennings Bryan to be secretary of state. A great apostle of world peace, Bryan devoted himself to negotiating a series of "cooling off" treaties with other countries—so called because the parties agreed to wait for one year before taking other measures while disputed issues were submitted to a conciliation process. Though admirable, these bilateral agreements had no bearing on the explosive power politics of Europe. As tensions there reached the breaking point in 1914, the United States remained effectively on the sidelines.

Yet at Algeciras Roosevelt had correctly anticipated what the future would demand of America. So did the French writer Andre Tardieu, who remarked in 1908:

> The United States is . . . a world power. . . . Its power creates for it . . . a duty—to pronounce upon all those questions that hitherto have been arranged by agreement only among European powers. These powers themselves, at critical times, turn toward the United States, anxious to know its opinion. . . . The United States . . . is seated at the table where the great game is played, and it cannot leave it.

Summary

★

In 1877 the United States was, by any economic or population measure, already a great power. But America was inward-looking. The lax conduct of its foreign policy and the neglect of its naval power reflected the absence of significant overseas concerns. America's rapid economic development, however, began to force the country to look outward, in particular because of the felt need for outlets for its surplus products. By the early 1890s a new strategic outlook had taken hold, best expressed in the writings of Alfred Thayer Mahan. Mahan called for a battleship navy, an interoceanic canal, and overseas bases from which American naval power could be projected to ensure access to markets in Latin America and Asia. Supporting this new expansionism were arguments drawn from social Darwinism, Anglo-Saxon racism, and America's earlier tradition of Manifest Destiny.

The Spanish-American War created an opportunity for acting on these imperialist impulses. Swift victory enabled the United States to seize from Spain the key possessions it wanted, while wartime patriotism briefly silenced America's traditional antiexpansionism. In taking the Philippines, however, the United States overstepped the bounds of the limited kind of colonialism palatable to the country—overseas bases, not dominance over alien populations. The result was a resurgence of anti-imperialist sentiment that was deepened by Filipino resistance to American rule. Even so, the McKinley administration achieved the strategic goals it had set, and the United States entered the twentieth century poised to fulfill its destiny as a Great Power.

In Europe the immediate consequences were few. Only in its *rapprochement* with Britain and in Roosevelt's involvement in the Moroccan crisis did the United States begin to depart from its traditional policy of avoiding European entanglements. But in the Caribbean and Asia, where it had strong regional interests, the United States moved more decisively, building the Panama Canal, asserting its dominance over the nearby states, and pressing for the open door in China. In Japan, however, the United States encountered a formidable opponent whose interests were not easily reconciled with America's. When Woodrow Wilson became president, he tried to bring the conduct of America's foreign policy into closer conformity with the nation's political ideals, only to have the limitations of that approach driven home by his intervention in the Mexican Revolution. As world war engulfed Europe in 1914, Wilson's idealism was about to receive a much harder test.

TIMELINE

1875	Treaty brings Hawaii within U.S. orbit
1876	United States achieves favorable balance of trade
1881	Secretary of State James G. Blaine inaugurates Pan-Americanism
1889	Conflict with Germany in Samoa
1890	Alfred Thayer Mahan's *The Influence of Seapower upon History*
1893	Annexation of Hawaii fails
	Frederick Jackson Turner's "The Significance of the Frontier in American History"
	Panic of 1893 ushers in economic depression (until 1897)
1894	Sino-Japanese War begins breakup of China into spheres of influence
1895	Venezuela crisis
	Cuban civil war
1898	Outbreak of Spanish-American War
	Hawaii annexed
	Anti-imperialist movement launched
1899	Treaty of Paris
	Guerrilla war in the Philippines
	Open-door policy in China
1901	Theodore Roosevelt becomes president; diplomacy of the "big stick"
	Hay-Pauncefote Agreement
1902	U.S. withdraws from Cuba; Platt amendment gives United States right of intervention
1903	U.S. recognizes Panama and receives grant of Canal Zone
1904	Roosevelt Corollary
1906	U.S. mediates Franco-German crisis over Morocco at Algeciras
1907	Gentlemen's Agreement with Japan
1908	Root-Takahira Agreement
1909	Taft becomes president; dollar diplomacy
1913	Wilson asserts new principles for American diplomacy
	Intervention in the Mexican Revolution
1914	Panama Canal opens
	World War I begins

Suggested Readings

Two useful surveys of late nineteenth-century diplomatic history are Charles S. Campbell, *The Transformation of American Foreign Relations, 1865–1900* (1976), and Walter LaFeber, *The American Search for Opportunity, 1865–1913* (vol. 2, *The Cambridge History of American Foreign Relations*, 1993). Invaluable as a historiographical guide is Robert L. Beisner, *From the Old Diplomacy to the New, 1865–1900* (2nd ed., 1986).

The Roots of Expansionism

Standard works on the preexpansionist era are David M. Pletcher, *The Awkward Years: American Foreign Relations under Garfield and Arthur* (1963), and Milton Plesur, *America's Outward Thrust: Approaches to American Foreign Affairs, 1865–1890* (1971). Walter LaFeber's highly influential *The New Empire, 1860–1898* (1963) places economic interest—especially the need for overseas markets—at the center of scholarly debate over the sources of American expansionism. On American business overseas the definitive work is Myra Wilkins, *The Emergence of the Multinational Enterprise: American Business Abroad from the Colonial Era to 1914* (1970). Other important books dealing with aspects of American expansionism are David Healy, *U.S. Expansionism: The Imperialist Urge in the 1890s* (1970); Robert Seager, *Alfred Thayer Mahan* (1977); Emily S. Rosenberg, *Spreading the American Dream: American Economic and Cultural Expansionism* (1982); Michael Hunt, *Ideology and U.S. Foreign Policy* (1987); Mark R. Shulman, *Navalism and the Emergence of American Sea Power, 1882–1893* (1995); and Kenneth J. Hagan, *This People's Navy: The Making of American Seapower* (1991).

An American Empire

On the war with Spain the liveliest narrative is still Frank Freidel, *A Splendid little War* (1958). For fuller treatments see John Offner, *An Unwanted War: The Diplomacy of the United States and Spain over Cuba, 1895–1898* (1988); David S. Trask, *The War with Spain in 1898* (1981); Ivan Musicant, *Empire by Default* (1998); and Lewis Gould, *The Spanish-American War and President McKinley* (1982), which emphasizes McKinley's strong leadership. Ernest R. May, *Imperial Democracy: The Emergence of America as a Great Power* (1961), exemplifies the earlier view that McKinley was a weak figure driven to war by jingoistic pressures. On the Philippines see Richard E. Welch, *Response to Imperialism: The United States and the Philippine-American War, 1898–1903* (1979), and, for the subsequent history, Peter Stanley, *A Nation in the Making: The Philippines and the United States, 1899–1921* (1974). Robert L. Beisner, *Twelve against Empire: The Anti-Imperialists, 1898–1900* (1968), remains the best book on that subject.

Onto the World Stage

On the European context a useful introduction can be found in the early chapters of Felix Gilbert, *The End of the European Era, 1890 to the Present* (4th ed., 1991). For a stimulating interpretation see L. C. B. Seaman, *From Vienna to Versailles* (1955). On American relations with Britain the standard work is Bradford Perkins, *The Great Rapprochement: England and the United States, 1895–1914* (1968). On Roosevelt's diplomacy the starting point remains Howard K. Beale, *Theodore Roosevelt and the Rise of America to World Power* (1956). There are keen insights into the diplomatic views of both Roosevelt and Wilson in John Milton Cooper, *The Warrior and the Priest* (1983). On the thrust into the Caribbean see Walter LaFeber, *The Panama Canal* (1979); Richard Lael, *Arrogant Diplomacy: U.S. Policy toward Colombia, 1903–1922* (1987); David Healy, *Drive to Hegemony: the United States in the Caribbean, 1898–1917* (1988); and Thomas D. Schoonover, *The United States in Central America, 1860–1911* (1991). America's Asian involvements are treated in Thomas J. McCormick, *China Market: America's Quest for Informal Empire, 1893–1901* (1967); Michael H. Hunt, *The Making of a Special Relationship: The United States and China to 1914* (1983); and Akira Iriye, *Pacific Estrangement: Japanese and American Expansion, 1897–1911* (1972). On the Mexican involvement see John S. D. Eisenhower, *Intervention! The United States and the Mexican Revolution* (1993). There is a lively and critical analysis of Wilson's misguided policies in Robert E. Quirk, *An Affair of Honor: Woodrow Wilson and the Occupation of Veracruz* (1962). The revolution as experienced by the Mexicans is brilliantly depicted in John Womack, *Zapata and the Mexican Revolution* (1968). The standard work on the American peace movement is Roland Marchand, *The American Peace Movement and Social Reform, 1898–1918* (1973).

Part Five

The Modern State and Society, 1914–1945

THEMATIC TIMELINE

	Government	Diplomacy	Economy	Society	Culture
	The Rise of the State	**From Isolation to World Leadership**	**Prosperity, Depression, and War**	**Nativism, Migration, and Social Change**	**The Emergence of a Mass National Culture**
1914	Wartime agencies expand power of the federal government	United States enters World War I (1917) Wilson's Fourteen Points (1918)	Shift from debtor to creditor nation Agricultural glut	Southern blacks begin migration to northern cities	Silent screen; Hollywood becomes movie capital of the world
1920	Republican ascendancy Prohibition (1920–1933) Business-government partnership	Treaty of Versailles rejected by U.S. Senate (1920) Washington Conference sets naval limits (1922)	Economic recession (1920–1921) Booming prosperity (1922–1929) Rise of welfare capitalism	Rise of nativism National Origins Act (1924) Mexican American immigration increases	Jazz Age (1920s) Advertising promotes consumer culture, supports radio and new magazines
1930	Franklin D. Roosevelt becomes president (1933) The New Deal: unprecedented government intervention in economy, social welfare, arts	Roosevelt's Good Neighbor Policy toward Latin America (1933) Abraham Lincoln Brigade fights in Spanish Civil War U.S. neutrality proclaimed (1939)	Great Depression (1929–1941) Rise of labor movement	Farming families migrate from Dust Bowl states to California and the West Indian New Deal	Documentary impulse Federal patronage of the arts
1940	Government mobilizes industry for war production and rationing	United States enters World War II (1941) Allies defeat Axis powers; bombing of Hiroshima (1945)	War mobilization ends depression	Rural whites and blacks migrate to war jobs in cities Civil rights movement revitalized	Film industry enlisted to aid war effort

By 1914 INDUSTRIALIZATION, economic expansion abroad, massive immigration, and the growth of a vibrant urban culture had set the foundations for a distinctly *modern* American society. In all facets of politics, the economy, and daily life, American society was becoming more organized, more bureaucratic, and more complex. By 1945, after having fought in two world wars and weathering a dozen years of economic depression, the edifice of the new society was largely complete.

Government. First, an essential building block of modern American society was a strong national state. This state came late and haltingly to America compared with that of the industrialized countries of Western Europe. American participation in World War I called forth an unprecedented mobilization of the domestic economy, but policy makers quickly dismantled the centralized wartime bureaucracies in 1919. During the 1920s the Harding and Coolidge administrations embraced a philosophy of business-government partnership, believing that unrestricted corporate capitalism would provide for the welfare of the American people. Ultimately the Great Depression, with its uncounted business failures and unprecedented levels of unemployment, overthrew that long-cherished idea. Franklin D. Roosevelt's New Deal dramatically expanded federal responsibility for the economy and the welfare of ordinary citizens. An even greater expansion of the national state resulted from the massive mobilization necessitated by America's entry into World War II. Unlike the experience after World War I, the new state apparatus remained in place when the war ended.

Diplomacy. Second, America was slowly and somewhat reluctantly drawn into a position of world leadership, which it continues to hold today. World War I provided the major impetus: before 1914 the world had been dominated by Europe, but from that point on the United States increasingly dominated the world. In 1918 American troops provided the margin of victory for the Allies, and President Wilson helped shape the treaties that ended the war. The United States, however, refused to join the League of Nations. America's dominant economic position guaranteed an active role in world affairs in the 1920s and 1930s nonetheless. The globalization of America accelerated in 1941, when the nation threw all its energies into a second world war that had its roots in the imperfect settlement of the first one. Of all the powers that participated in this most devastating of global conflagrations, only America emerged physically unscathed from World War II. The country was also the only one to possess a dangerous new weapon—the atomic bomb. Within wartime decisions and strategies lay the roots of the Cold War that followed.

Economy. Third, modern America developed a strong domestic economy. In fact, between 1914 and 1945 the nation's industrial economy was the most productive in the world. Even the Great Depression, which hit the United States harder than any other industrialized nation, did not permanently affect America's global economic standing. Indeed, American businesses successfully competed in world markets, and American financial institutions played the leading role in international economic affairs. Large-scale corporate organizations replaced smaller family-run businesses. The automobile industry symbolized the ascendancy of mass-production techniques. Many workers shared in the general prosperity but also bore the brunt of economic downturns. These uncertainties fueled the dramatic growth of the labor movement in the 1930s.

Society. Fourth, American society was transformed by the great wave of European immigration and the movement from farms to cities. The growth of metropolitan areas gave the nation an increasingly urban tone, and geographical mobility broke down regional differences. Many old-stock white Americans viewed these processes with alarm; in 1924 nativists succeeded in all but eliminating immigration except from within the Western Hemisphere, where migration across the border from Mexico continued to shape the West and Southwest. In other ways internal migration changed the face of America as African Americans moved north and west to take factory jobs, and Dust Bowl farmers in the 1930s moved to the Far West to find better livelihoods. World War II accelerated these migration patterns even more.

Culture. Fifth, modern America saw the emergence of a mass national culture. By the 1920s Americans were increasingly drawn into a web of interlocking cultural experiences. Advertising and the new entertainment media—movies, radio, and magazines—disseminated the new values of consumerism; the movies exported this vision of the American experience worldwide. Not even the Great Depression could divert Americans from their desire for leisure, self-fulfillment, and consumer goods. The emphasis on consumption and a quest for a rising standard of living would define the American experience for the rest of the twentieth century.

SEPT 29th 1917

Price 10 Cents
In Canada, 15 Cents

Leslie's

Illustrated Weekly Newspaper

Paul Stahr

Be Patriotic

sign your country's pledge to save the food

★

War and the American State, *1914–1920*

"IT WOULD BE the irony of fate if my administration had to deal chiefly with foreign affairs," Woodrow Wilson told a friend early in his first term as president. But the United States was no longer just a regional power—it was seated at the table of what the president called the "great game" of international politics. Wilson responded to World War I with the same idealism he had brought to domestic concerns during the Progressive Era (see Chapter 20). In the first major U.S. intervention in Great Power politics, Wilson aimed for a new international order based on democratic ideals.

The American decision to enter the conflict in 1917 confirmed one of the most important shifts of power in the twentieth century. The pre–World War I world had been dominated by Europe; the postwar world was increasingly dominated by the United States. The historian Akira Iriye calls this broad transformation the "globalization" of America: the United States increasingly became "involved in security, economic, and cultural affairs in all parts of the world." This process, which is usually thought to begin with World War II and its aftermath, actually started in 1917.

Victory in a modern, global war involved more than armies. New federal bureaucracies had to be created to coordinate the efforts of business, labor, and agriculture, a process that hastened the emergence of a national administrative state. The federal government became an increased presence in the lives of Americans in everything from conscription to taxation to food conservation. War meant new opportunities, albeit temporary, for women and for blacks and other racial and ethnic minorities. The wartime experience united the nation behind a common goal of military victory, but in the

America and the War Effort
Popular magazines like Leslie's Illustrated Weekly Newspaper *teamed up with the federal government to promote food conservation. If a patriotic reader affixed a 1 cent stamp to the cover's top right corner, the magazine would be sent to soldiers or sailors at the front.*
Leslie's, September 29, 1917/Picture Research Consultants & Archives.

process it spawned new divisions among Americans and new hatreds—first of Germans and Austrians, and then of "Bolshevik" Reds. When the war ended, the United States was forced to confront the deep class, racial, and ethnic divisions that had surfaced during wartime mobilization in the Red Scare of 1919.

The Great War, 1914–1918

★

When war erupted in August 1914, most Americans saw no reason to get involved in a struggle among Europe's imperialistic powers. No vital American interests were at stake; indeed, the United States had good relationships with both sides. But a combination of factors—economic interests, violations of neutral rights, cultural ties with Great Britain and France, and German miscalculations—drew the United States into the war on the Allied side in 1917.

War in Europe

Almost from the moment France, Russia, and Britain formed the Triple Entente in 1907 to counter the Triple Alliance of Germany, Austria-Hungary, and Italy (see Chapter 21), European leaders began to prepare for what they saw as an inevitable conflict. The spark that

ignited war came in Europe's perpetual tinderbox—the Balkans—where Austria-Hungary and Russia competed for power and influence. Austria's seizure of the provinces of Bosnia and Herzegovina in 1908 had enraged Russia and its client, the independent state of Serbia. Serbian terrorists responded by recruiting Bosnians to agitate against Austrian rule. On June 28, 1914, a nineteen-year-old Bosnian student assassinated Franz Ferdinand, the heir to the Austro-Hungarian throne, and his wife in Sarajevo.

After the assassination the complex European system of alliances that had for years maintained a fragile peace pulled all the major powers into war. Austria-Hungary, blaming Serbia for the assassination, declared war on that country on July 28. Russia, which had a secret treaty with Serbia, mobilized its armies; Germany responded by declaring war on Russia and its ally, France, and by invading neutral Belgium. The brutality of the invasion, as well as Britain's commitment to Belgian neutrality, prompted Great Britain to declare war on Germany on August 4. Within a few days all the major European powers had formally entered the conflict.

The combatants were divided into two rival blocs. The Allied Powers—Great Britain, France, Japan, Russia, and, in 1915, Italy—were pitted against the Central Powers: Germany, Austria-Hungary, and Turkey, joined by Bulgaria in 1915 (Map 22.1). Because of the alliance system, the conflict spread to parts of the world far beyond Europe, making this a truly global war. The Austrians and Germans faced the Russians on the Eastern

MAP 22.1
Europe at the Start of World War I
In early August 1914 a complex set of interlocking alliances drew the major European powers into war. At first the United States avoided the conflict. Not until April 1917 did America enter the war on the Allied side.

The Landscape of War
World War I devastated the countryside: this was the battleground at Ypres in western Belgium in 1915. The carnage of trench warfare also scarred the soldiers who served in these surreal settings, causing "gas neurosis," "burial-alive neurosis," and "soldiers' heart"—all symptoms of shell shock.
Imperial War Museum, London.

Front; Turkey squared off against Russian and British troops in the Middle East and Mesopotamia; and the British, French, and Japanese seized German territories in Africa, China, and the South Pacific. The worldwide scope of the conflict and the staggering number of resulting casualties caused it to be known as the Great War or, later, World War I. It was also the first modern war in which extensive harm was done to civilian populations.

Modern wars drew on increasingly destructive military technology. Since the American Civil War and the Franco-Prussian War in 1870, massive industrialization and an escalating arms race among the Great Powers had transformed the technology of war. Every soldier in World War I carried a long-range, high-velocity rifle that could hit a target at 1,000 yards, a vast improvement over the 300-yard range of the rifle-musket used in the American Civil War. Significantly, the mass production of rifles in Europe relied on the adoption of technology developed in the United States. Another innovation, the machine gun, also had American roots. Its American inventor,

Hiram Maxim, had heeded a friend's advice when he moved to Great Britain in the 1880s: "If you want to make your fortune, invent something which will allow those fool Europeans to kill each other more quickly."

The concentrated fire of rifles and machine guns gave a tremendous advantage to troops in defensive positions. For four bloody years, between 1914 and 1918, the Allies and the Central Powers faced each other on the Western Front, a narrow swath of territory in Belgium and northern France crisscrossed by 25,000 miles of heavily fortified trenches, enough to circle the globe. (Barbed wire, invented to fence the western range in America, became a devastating weapon of war when coiled above the trenches: if soldiers tried to climb over the barrier or cut the barbed wire, they suffered cuts and lacerations, as well as exposed themselves to enemy sharpshooters, an often deadly situation.) Trench warfare produced unprecedented numbers of casualties. If one side tried to break the stalemate by venturing into the "no-man's land" between the trenches, its soldiers were mowed down by artillery fire or poison gas, first used by the Germans at the Belgian border town of Ypres in April 1915. Between February and December 1916 the French suffered 550,000 casualties and the Germans 450,000 as Germany tried to break through the French lines at Verdun. The front did not move.

The Perils of Neutrality

As the bloody stalemate continued, the United States grappled with its role in the international conflagration. Two weeks after the outbreak of war in Europe, President Wilson had made the American position clear. In a message widely printed in the newspapers, the president called on Americans to be "neutral in fact as well as in name, impartial in thought as well as in action."

Wilson wanted to keep out of war in order to play a larger, not a smaller, role in world affairs. The child of a Presbyterian minister, Wilson approached foreign affairs with missionary zeal. He never doubted the superiority of the Christian values he had learned as a boy or questioned the widely held belief that the United States was better than the rest of the world. Only if he kept America aloof from the European quarrel, Wilson reasoned, could he impartially arbitrate—and influence—its ultimate settlement.

The nation's divided loyalties also influenced Wilson's policy. Many Americans, including Wilson, felt deep cultural ties to the Allies, especially Britain and France. Yet most Irish Americans resented the centuries-long British occupation of their home country and the deferral of Irish home rule, authorized by Parliament in 1914, for the duration of the war. Also, the 10 million immigrants from Germany and Austria-Hungary made up one of the largest and best-established ethnic groups in the United States. Many aspects of German culture, including classical music and Germany's university system, were widely admired. It would not have been easy for Wilson to rally Americans to the Allied side in 1914.

Many isolationist Americans had no sympathy for either side. Pacifist sentiment was diffuse but broad. Progressive Republicans such as Senators Robert La Follette of Wisconsin and George Norris of Nebraska vehemently opposed American participation in the European conflict. Progressive Democrats, including Secretary of State William Jennings Bryan, and many western and southern progressives felt the same. Newly formed pacifist groups, among them the American Union against Militarism and the Women's Peace Party, both founded in 1915, also mobilized popular opposition. Practically the entire political left, led principally by Eugene Debs and the Socialist Party, condemned the war as imperialism, whereas African American leaders such as A. Philip Randolph identified it as a conflict of the white race only. Prominent industrialists, notably Andrew Carnegie and Henry Ford,

bankrolled antiwar activities. In December 1915 Ford spent almost half a million dollars to send more than a hundred men and women to Europe on a "peace ship" to negotiate an end to the war.

Conflict on the High Seas.   With no stake in the territorial struggles among the European powers, the United States might well have remained neutral if the conflict had not spread to a new theater—the high seas. Here the United States initially had as many arguments with Britain as with Germany. The most troublesome issue concerned freedom of the seas and neutrality rights— the freedom to trade with nations on both sides of a conflict. By the end of August 1914 the British had imposed a naval blockade on the Central Powers, hoping to cut off military supplies and starve the German people into submission. But their actions also prevented neutral nations such as the United States from trading with Germany and its allies. The United States chafed at this infringement of its neutrality rights but chose to do little besides complain, largely because the spectacular increase in trade with the Allies more than made up for the lost trade with the Central Powers. American trade with Britain and France grew from $824 million in 1914 to $3.2 billion in 1916, and by 1917 U.S. bankers had lent the Allies $2.5 billion. In contrast, American trade with and loans to Germany in 1917 totaled only $29 million and $27 million, respectively.

To challenge British control of the seas, the German navy launched a devastating new weapon—the U-boat, short for *Unterseeboot* (undersea boat, or submarine). In February 1915, Germany announced a naval blockade of Great Britain: German submarines would attack any ship transporting military supplies to the British Isles. Traditional rules of naval warfare required submarine commanders to warn and search a ship before sinking it. If a submarine surfaced to do this, however, it would lose its greatest advantage—surprise—and leave itself vulnerable to attack. The Germans began sinking enemy ships without warning.

What if a U-boat attacked a neutral trading vessel or unarmed passenger ship by mistake? This situation occurred when the Germans sank a British luxury liner, the *Lusitania*, off the Irish coast on May 7, 1915, killing 1,198 people, including 128 Americans. The attack on the unarmed passenger ship incensed Americans— newspapers branded it a "mass murder"—and prompted President Wilson to send a series of strongly worded protests to Germany.

The *Lusitania* crisis divided Wilson's government into pro- and anti-British factions. Secretary of State William Jennings Bryan resigned in protest, unable to support Wilson's harsh criticism of Germany's violation of neutrality rights while the president remained silent about Britain's violation of American rights with its blockade. The crisis continued until September 1915, when Germany announced that submarine commanders would not attack passenger ships without warning. A temporary lull set into the naval war.

Throughout 1915 and 1916, Wilson tried at several points to mediate an end to the European conflict through his aide, Colonel Edward House. But House concluded that neither side was seriously interested in peace negotiations. Worsening tensions with Germany in turn caused Wilson to rethink his earlier opposition to preparedness. In the fall of 1915 he endorsed a $1 billion buildup of the army and navy, and by 1916 rearmament was well under way.

The 1916 Election. The presidential election of 1916 did not serve as a referendum on the American stance toward the war. The Republican Party passed over the belligerently prowar Theodore Roosevelt in favor of Supreme Court Justice Charles Evans Hughes, a former governor of New York. The Democrats renominated

Woodrow Wilson, whose campaign emphasized the progressive reform record he had accomplished during his first term (see Chapter 20). The Democrats also gained votes with their widely circulated campaign slogan, "He kept us out of war." They won a narrow victory over a Republican Party reunited after its 1912 split. Despite getting 3 million more votes than he had in 1912, Wilson defeated Hughes by only about 600,000 votes and by 277 to 254 in the electoral college. That slender margin limited Wilson's options in mobilizing the nation for war and planning the postwar peace.

Toward War. The events of early 1917 further diminished Wilson's hopes of staying out of the conflict. On January 31 Germany, frustrated by the impasse in the land war, announced the resumption of unrestricted submarine attacks. In response, Wilson broke off diplomatic relations with Germany on February 3. A few weeks later the release of the "Zimmermann telegram"

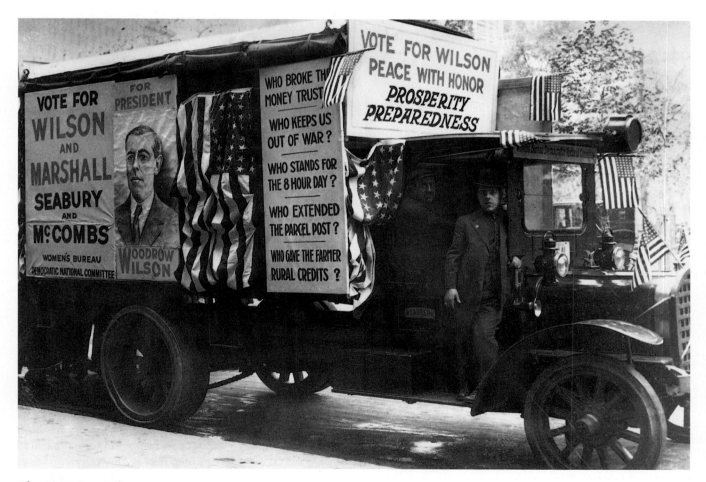

The 1916 Campaign
This campaign van sponsored by the Women's Bureau of the Democratic National Committee linked Woodrow Wilson to the themes of progressivism, prosperity, and preparedness. Note the variation on the popular slogan, "He kept us out of war."
Corbis-Bettmann.

moved the country closer to war. Newspapers published an intercepted communication from Germany's foreign secretary, Arthur Zimmermann, to the German minister in Mexico City, in which Zimmermann urged Mexico to join the Central Powers in the war. In return, Germany promised to help Mexico recover "the lost territory of Texas, New Mexico, and Arizona." When the telegram was made public on February 27, this threat to the territorial integrity of the United States jolted both congressional and public opinion—especially in the West, where support for the war had lagged. Combined with the resumption of unrestricted submarine warfare, the telegram inflamed anti-German sentiment.

Throughout March, U-boats attacked American shipping vessels without warning, sinking three ships on March 18 alone. On April 2, 1917, after consulting his cabinet, Wilson appeared before a special session of Congress to ask for a declaration of war. "It is a fearful thing to lead this great peaceful people into war," Wilson declared. It was a conflict that had already proved extremely costly—

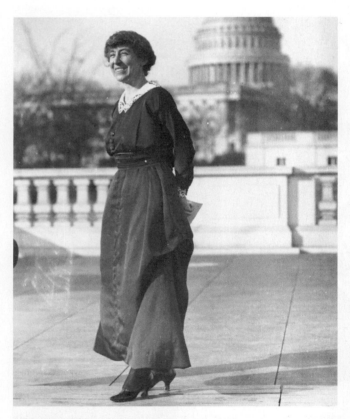

The First Woman in Congress
In 1916, Jeannette Rankin, a former suffrage organizer, became the first woman elected to Congress. Her vote against U.S. entry into World War I cost her a chance for election to the Senate in 1918. In 1940 Rankin again won election to Congress from Montana. True to her lifelong pacifism, she cast the only vote against American entry into World War II.
Corbis-Bettmann.

millions of Europeans killed, their landscapes and social structures destroyed. America had no selfish aims, he told the country: "We desire no conquest, no dominion. We seek no indemnities for ourselves, no material compensation for the sacrifices we shall freely make. We are but one of the champions of the rights of mankind." In a memorable phrase intended to ennoble America's role, Wilson proposed that U.S. participation in the war would make the world "safe for democracy."

Four days later, on April 6, 1917, the United States declared war on Germany. Reflecting the divided feelings of the country as a whole, the congressional vote was far from unanimous. Six senators and fifty members of the House voted against the action, including Representative Jeannette Rankin of Montana, the first woman elected to Congress. "I want to stand by my country," she declared, "but I cannot vote for war."

Over There

To native-born Americans, Europe seemed a great distance away—literally "over there," as the lyrics of George M. Cohan's popular song described it. After the declaration of war many citizens were surprised to learn that the United States planned to send troops to Europe, optimistically having assumed that the nation's participation could be limited to military and economic aid.

In May 1917 General John J. Pershing, recently returned from the unsuccessful pursuit of Pancho Villa in Mexico (see Chapter 21), traveled to London and Paris to determine how America could best support the war effort. The answer, as Marshal Joseph Joffre of France put it, was clear: "Men, men, and more men." The problem was that the United States had never maintained a large standing army in peacetime. Only about 200,000 soldiers, mostly lifetime volunteers, were on active duty in early 1917. To field a fighting force large enough to enter a global war, the government turned to conscription.

Conscription. The passage of the Selective Service Act in May 1917 demonstrated the increasing impact of the state on ordinary citizens. Unlike the resistance to the draft during the Civil War, no major riots occurred. The selective service system worked in part because it combined central direction from Washington with local administration and civilian control, and thus did not tread too heavily on the tradition of individual freedom and local autonomy. Draft registration also demonstrated the potential bureaucratic capacity of the American state. On a single day, June 5, 1917, more than 9.5 million men between the ages of twenty-one and thirty registered for military service in their local voting precincts.

Although compliance was not universal, most male citizens went along with the draft's premise of *service—*

WWI Pillow Cover
The three stars on this pillow
cover indicated that three family
members were fighting in the war.
The images in the frames are of
President Woodrow Wilson and
General John J. Pershing.
Picture Research Consultants &
Archives.

a key progressive word—as a responsibility of modern
citizenship. By the end of the war almost 4 million
men, plus several thousand female navy clerks and
army nurses, were in uniform. Another 300,000 men—
known as slackers—evaded the draft, and 4,000 were
classified as conscientious objectors.

Wilson chose General Pershing to head the American Expeditionary Force (AEF), but the newly raised
army did not have an immediate impact on the fighting.
The new recruits had to be trained and outfitted, and
then they had to wait for one of the few available transport ships to take them across the submarine-infested
Atlantic. By June 1917 only 15,000 AEF troops had
arrived in France.

At first the main American contribution was to
secure the safety of the seas. When the United States
entered the war, German submarines were sinking
Allied ships at a rate of about 900,000 tons a month and
threatening the transport of American troops to the
European front. Adopting a plan that aimed for safety

in numbers, the government began sending armed convoys across the Atlantic. The plan worked: no American
soldiers were killed on the way to Europe, and Allied
shipping losses were cut dramatically.

Meanwhile, trench warfare continued its deadly
grind on the Western Front. Allied commanders pleaded
for American reinforcements for their units, but Pershing was reluctant to put his independent fighting unit
under foreign commanders. Because the AEF was not
ready as a fighting force until May 1918, the brunt of the
fighting continued to fall on the French and British.

**The Russian Revolution and the Collapse of the
Eastern Front.** On the Eastern Front the strain of
fighting the Germans had exposed the weaknesses of
the Russian government of Tsar Nicholas II, and a general mutiny of the troops led to the overthrow of the
monarchy in March 1917. The new provisional government, which Woodrow Wilson supported, promised
democratic reforms but insisted on continuing the war.

Russian workers and peasants saw no end in sight to the seemingly endless food shortages at home and the horrendous casualties at the front. Conditions were ripe for a second, more sweeping, revolution.

The communist theorist and political activist Vladimir Ilych Lenin, who had been living in exile in Switzerland when the March revolution took place, saw his chance. Lenin was a follower of German political philosopher Karl Marx and anticipated that a period of "dictatorship of the proletariat" (workers) would be necessary to root out capitalism before an ideal, classless society could emerge. The Germans, hoping to promote internal strife in Russia, cannily arranged Lenin's safe passage home in a sealed railroad car. Lenin and members of the Russian Social Democratic Workers' Party, or Bolsheviks, arrived in Petrograd (later renamed Leningrad and now St. Petersburg) in April 1917 and began to agitate against the provisional government. On November 6 Lenin directed a Bolshevik-led coup and quickly consolidated his control by promising "peace, land, and bread" to the long-suffering masses.

The new Bolshevik government kept the first part of its promise: Russia agreed to a cease-fire with Germany and Austria-Hungary on December 15, 1917, and signed the Treaty of Brest-Litovsk on March 3, 1918. In return for an end to hostilities, the Bolsheviks surrendered about one-third of Russia's territories, including Russian Poland, Ukraine, the Baltic provinces, and Finland. Yet instead of peace the Russian people got three more years of a devastating civil war.

Allied Victory in the West. The civil war in the new Soviet state would command the Allies' attention only after the end of World War I. No longer facing a hostile Russia, Germany launched a major offensive on March 21, 1918, designed to break the stalemate on the Western Front. By May the German army had advanced to the Marne River, within 50 miles of Paris. Allied leaders intensified their calls for American troops, and Pershing, who was under orders to keep the AEF a separate fighting unit, relented a bit to help the Allies bolster their defenses. About 60,000 American soldiers helped the French repel the Germans in the battles of Château-Thierry and Belleau Wood in May and June. During the fighting, the AEF encountered firsthand the terrible effects of poison gas (see American Voices, "Frederick Pottle: Mustard Gas," p. 713).

American reinforcements soon began to arrive in large numbers. Fresh troops flooded the ports of Liverpool in Britain and Brest and Saint Nazaire in France—245,000 in May 1918, 278,000 in June, an additional 306,000 in July. From there they slowly worked their way to the front along the clogged French transportation system. Augmented by 85,000 American troops, the Allied force brought the German offensive to a halt in mid-July. The counteroffensive began with a successful campaign to drive the Germans back from the Marne (Map 22.2). In mid-September 1918 American and French troops led by General Pershing forced the Germans to retreat from Saint-Mihiel. On September 26 Pershing launched the last major assault of the war, which pitted over a million American soldiers

MAP 22.2
U.S. Participation on the Western Front, 1918
When American troops reached the European front in significant numbers in 1918, the Allied and Central Powers had been grinding each other down in a war of attrition for almost four years. The influx of American troops and supplies broke the stalemate. Successful offensive maneuvers by the American Expeditionary Force included those at Belleau Wood and Château-Thierry, and the Meuse-Argonne campaign.

FREDERICK POTTLE
Mustard Gas

———— ★ ————

Frederick Pottle volunteered for service as an enlisted man in the Medical Corps. He describes here the effects of mustard gas during the battles of Belleau Wood and Château-Thierry in June 1918.

Indeed, those dreadful mustard-gas cases were probably the most painful we had to witness in all our service. As a matter of fact, the majority were in much less serious plight than the wounded men. Mustard gas (it has nothing to do with mustard) is a heavy liquid, which, though fairly volatile, will remain for some time clinging to grass and undergrowth, and will burn any flesh with which it comes in contact. It is especially adapted for use by a retreating army. By soaking down with mustard gas the area through which the pursuing American troops had to advance, the Germans made sure that a large number of the advancing force would be incapacitated. The soldier's clothing soon becomes impregnated with the stuff as he brushes through the undergrowth, and the burns develop through the help of moisture. Those parts of the body subject to excessive perspiration are especially affected. The burns are extremely painful, but in general not fatal unless the gas has been inhaled, or (as with other surface burns) a third or more of the total skin area has been affected. A bad feature of mustard gas, however, is that it almost invariably produces temporary, but complete, blindness. Nothing demoralizes a man so much as the fear of losing his sight, and telling him that he will see again in a day or two generally fails to reassure him. The gas cases began to arrive at Juilly as early as June 12. Since most of them were immediately evacuable, we made temporary wards for them in the great cloisters which ran around two sides of the court in front of Wards F and G—the children's dormitories. By the sixteenth there were nearly seven hundred gassed men there, just out of the glare of the sunny court, lying fully dressed on blanket-covered cots, some of them badly gassed in the lungs and fighting horribly for breath, which could be a little prolonged by giving them oxygen; nearly all blinded, many delirious, all crying, moaning, tossing about. For most of the patients there was nothing to do but renew frequently the wet dressings which relieved somewhat the smart of the burns, and to try to restore their lost morale. For those who had been gassed worst, nothing effectual could be done. They were spared much by being in general delirious, but it required the constant attention of several orderlies to keep some of them in bed. Later on, the hospital service was so organized that the gas cases were handled by special gas hospitals. After we left Juilly we almost never received gas victims unless they were also wounded.

———

Source: Frederick A. Pottle, *Stretchers: The Story of a Hospital Unit on the Western Front* (New Haven: Yale University Press, 1929), 117–118.

against vastly outnumbered and exhausted German troops. The Meuse-Argonne campaign, the main American military contribution to the fighting, pushed the enemy back across the Selle River near Verdun and broke the German defenses at a cost of over 26,000 American lives.

World War I ended on November 11, 1918, when German and Allied representatives signed an armistice in the railway car of Marshal Ferdinand Foch of France. The flood of American troops and supplies during the last six months of the war helped provide the Allied margin of victory. In many ways this contribution was emblematic of the shift in international power as European diplomatic and economic dominance declined and the United States emerged as a world leader.

The American Fighting Force

About 2 million American soldiers were in France when the war ended. Two-thirds of them had seen at least brief action on the Western Front, but most American "doughboys" had escaped the horrors of sustained trench warfare that had sapped the morale of Allied and German troops. (The origin of the nickname *doughboy* is unclear, but it may involve the buttons on the uniforms of American infantrymen, which resembled dumplings made of dough.) During the eighteen months in which the United States fought, 48,000 American servicemen were killed in action or died from wounds. Another 27,000 died from other causes, mainly the influenza epidemic that swept the world in 1918–1919.

Fighting the Flu
The influenza epidemic of 1918–1919 strained the resources of a public health system
already fully mobilized for the war effort. Here doctors, army officers, and reporters
don surgical masks and gowns before touring hospitals that treat influenza patients.
Note the patriotic poster entreating citizens to buy bonds on the wall behind them.
Corbis-Bettmann.

But these casualties were minimal compared with the 8 million soldiers lost by the Allies and the Central Powers. The French lost far more soldiers in the siege of Verdun than the United States did during the entire war.

Although individual bravery was increasingly anachronistic in modern warfare, the war generated its share of American heroes. Sergeant Alvin York single-handedly killed 25 Germans and took 132 prisoners at the battle of Châtel-Chéhéry in the Meuse-Argonne campaign. Although air power played only a minor role in the conduct of the war, it captivated the popular imagination. One of America's best-known aces (the word coined for pilots who destroyed five or more enemy aircraft) was the former professional race car driver Eddie Rickenbacker, known as the "American Ace of Aces" for shooting down more enemy aircraft than any other pilot. The aerial exploits of daredevil pilots, often fighting in single combat like medieval knights, provided a thrill that contrasted with the monotony of trench warfare. The popular fascination with York and Rickenbacker suggests a deep-seated need on the part of the American public to anoint heroes in what had become an increasingly depersonalized and mechanized pursuit of war.

Military Morality. Another characteristic of World War I was the growing influence of the state—in this case, army officials—over the private lives of American soldiers. The high ideals of progressivism set the tone for military service. Reformers urged the adoption of

Flying Aces
One of America's best-known aces was former professional race car driver Eddie
Rickenbacker (middle) of the 94th Aero Pursuit Squadron. Note the insignia on the
plane. The 94th was known as the hat-in-the-ring squadron for the American custom
of throwing a hat into the ring as an invitation to fight.
Corbis-Bettmann.

progressive solutions to the "vices" of alcohol and sex, and government and military officials agreed. Reflecting the antiliquor fever taking hold in America, Secretary of the Navy Josephus Daniels declared navy ships dry. The army banned drinking by soldiers in uniform and prohibited the sale or consumption of liquor on army bases and in the surrounding localities.

The army also mounted an ambitious program of sex education. In an era when people rarely discussed sex in public, the army brought the subject into the open. Concerned that venereal disease (VD) might sap the strength of the fighting men (antibiotics had not yet been developed), the army launched an anti-VD campaign. Posters proclaimed "A German bullet is cleaner than a whore" and "How could you look the flag in the face if you were dirty with gonorrhea?" In France the army continued its campaign for moral purity, although it could not entirely stop American soldiers from patronizing French prostitutes. Army-issue condoms and safety razors, a novelty that changed the

shaving habits of future generations of men, were two of the souvenirs that American soldiers brought home from France.

World War I also marked the first time that homosexuality emerged as a major social issue. Urban reformers were concerned that military recruits would fall prey to the "urban degeneracy" of "male perversion" while passing through embarkation points such as New York City. As they cracked down on prostitution, they also attempted to curb the city's thriving gay subculture. The military also targeted male homosexuality as part of its campaign against vice. At the Newport (Rhode Island) Naval Training Station in 1919, the navy undertook an extensive undercover operation against suspected "sexual perverts" that led to more than twenty arrests.

Racism in the Armed Forces. Reformers expressed high hopes for democratization and education in the military services, yet the army reflected the divisions in American society. About one-fifth of the American soldiers had been born in another country, leading some people to call the AEF the American Foreign Legion. Army censors had to be able to read forty-nine languages to check letters written home by American doughboys.

To sort its conscripts, the army used the newly developed Stanford-Binet intelligence test, putting the progressive belief in social science at the service of wartime needs. Army psychologists, who administered the test to all recruits, expressed shock at the level of illiteracy among draftees—as high as 25 percent. Racial and ethnic variations in the test scores reinforced stereotypes about the supposed intellectual inferiority of blacks and immigrants, although in fact their lower

Portrait of a Corporal
Black soldiers such as this corporal in the 15th New York Infantry received segregated and unequal treatment at every level of military service. Yet their pride in serving their country remained strong, as this 1918 painting by Raymond Desvarraus suggests.
West Point Museum, United States Military Academy, West Point, NY.

scores stemmed from the cultural and environmental biases of the tests. (How many recent immigrants or rural blacks knew the importance of the French painter Rosa Bonheur?) The army dropped the test in 1919, but revised versions of intelligence tests soon became a standard part of assessment measures in the American educational system.

The "Americanization" of the army remained imperfect at best, with African American soldiers receiving the worst treatment. Blacks were organized into rigidly segregated units, almost always under the control of white officers. In addition, blacks were assigned to the most menial tasks, working as stevedores (workers who loaded and unloaded the ships) and messboys (workers who cleaned up kitchen and dining facilities). Although the policy of segregation minimized contact between black and white recruits, racial violence erupted at several camps. The worst incident occurred in Houston in August 1917, when black members of the Twenty-fourth Infantry's Third Battalion killed fifteen white soldiers and police officers in retaliation for a string of racial incidents, including the beating of a black woman by a white police officer. Sixty-four soldiers were tried in military courts, and nineteen were hanged. The army quickly disbanded the battalion, but the legacy of racial mistrust lingered throughout the rest of the war.

Racial equality had never been a central concern on the progressive agenda, and the black experience in World War I reflected the persistent gap between democratic rhetoric and reality. Over 400,000 black men served in the military, accounting for 13 percent of the armed forces; 92 percent were draftees, a far higher rate than that of whites. Black soldiers often found the French more willing to socialize with them on an equal basis than white American soldiers. Despite documented cases of extreme heroism, no black received the Congressional Medal of Honor, the nation's highest military award, even though they had been so honored in the Civil War and the Spanish-American War. The French, however, had no qualms about awarding the Croix de Guerre (Legion of Honor) to several hundred African American soldiers (see Voices from Abroad, "A German Propaganda Appeal to Black Soldiers," p. 717).

Demobilization.   Just as it had taken months to get American troops to Europe to join the fighting, similar delays slowed demobilization at the war's end. June 1919 was the peak month for returns, with 368,000 men—plus the women who had served ·in France as telephone operators, canteen workers, and nurses—coming home to begin the process of readjusting to civilian life. When their ships sailed into New York harbor, many mouthed the old vaudeville saying: "If the Statue of Liberty wants to see my face again, she'll have to turn around."

A German Propaganda Appeal to Black Soldiers

★

In an effort to undermine enemy morale, each side distributed propaganda tracts behind the lines. This piece of German propaganda was specifically directed toward black soldiers in France. According to Charles Williams—who, with the cooperation of the secretary of war, the Federal Council of Churches, and the Phelps-Stokes Fund, investigated conditions for black soldiers—the reaction of soldiers who read the propaganda was clear: "We know what they say is true, but don't worry; we're not going over."

"To the Colored Soldiers of the U.S. Army,
September, 1918, Vosges Mountains.

"Hello, boys, what are you doing over there? Fighting the Germans? Why? Have they ever done you any harm? Of course, some white folks and the lying English-American papers told you that the Germans ought to be wiped out for the sake of humanity and democracy. What is democracy? Personal freedom, all citizens enjoying the same rights socially and before the law. Do you enjoy the same rights as the white people do in America, the land of freedom and democracy? Or aren't you rather rated over there as second class citizens? Can you go to a restaurant where white people dine, can you get a seat in a theatre where white people sit, can you get a pullman seat or berth in a railroad car, or can you ride in the South in the same street car with white people? And how about the law? Is lynching and the most horrible cruelties connected therewith a lawful proceeding in a democratic country?

"Now all of this is entirely different in Germany, where they do like colored people, where they do treat them as gentlemen and not as second class citizens. They enjoy exactly the same social privileges as every white man, and quite a number of colored people have mighty fine positions in Berlin and other big German cities.

"Why, then, fight the Germans only for the benefit of the Wall Street robbers to protect the millions they have lent to the English, French, and Italians? You have been made the tool of the egotistic and rapacious rich in England and America, and there is nothing in the whole game for you but broken bones, horrible wounds, broken health or—death. No satisfaction whatever will you get out of this unjust war. You have never seen Germany; so you are fools if you allow people to teach you to hate it. Come over and see for yourself. Let those do the fighting who make profit out of this war; don't allow them to use you as cannon food. To carry the gun in their defense is not an honor but a shame. Throw it away and come over to the German lines. You will find friends who will help you along."

Source: Charles H. Williams, *Sidelights on Negro Soldiers* (Boston: B. J. Brimmer Co., 1923), 70–71.

After the armistice the war lived on in the minds of the men and women who had gone "over there." Spared the horror of sustained battle, many members of the AEF had experienced the war more as tourists than as soldiers. Before joining the army, most recruits had barely traveled beyond their hometowns, and for them the journey across the ocean to Europe was a monumental, once-in-a-lifetime event. In 1919 a group of former AEF officers formed the American Legion "to preserve the memories and incidents of our association in the great war." The word *legion* perfectly captured the romantic, almost chivalric memories that many veterans held of their wartime service. Only later did disillusionment set in over the contested legacy of World War I.

War on the Home Front

★

The fighting of World War I required extraordinary economic mobilization on the home front: business, the work force, and the public all cooperated. At the height of mobilization fully one-fourth of the gross national product went for war production. Business and government proved especially congenial partners, a collaboration that typified the pattern of state building in America. Similarly, the rapid dismantling of that apparatus when the war ended reflected the unease that Americans felt about a strong bureaucratic state.

Mobilizing Industry and the Economy

Even before the formal declaration of war the United States had geared up as the arsenal for the Allied Powers. As hundreds of tons of American grain and military supplies crossed the Atlantic and the Allies paid for their purchases in gold, the United States reversed its historical position as a debtor and became a leading creditor. In addition, U.S. financial institutions increasingly provided capital for investment in the world market once British financial reserves started to be diverted to the war effort. This shift from debtor to creditor status, which would last until the 1980s, guaranteed the nation a major role in international financial affairs after the war and confirmed the new role of the United States as a world power.

Paying for the War.   The monetary cost to the United States of World War I reached $33 billion, a huge sum for a government unaccustomed to large expenditures. The disruption in international trade after the outbreak of war in 1914 had reduced the money raised by tariffs, ordinarily a major source of federal revenues. Wilson's Treasury secretary, William McAdoo, had two options: to impose a national sales tax, or to increase income taxes. (The Sixteenth Amendment to the Constitution, which instituted a federal income tax, had been approved in 1913.) Wilson and McAdoo, in conjunction with progressive Democratic leaders in Congress, chose the second option.

The resulting War Revenue bills of 1917 and 1918 transformed the previously limited income tax into the foremost instrument of federal taxation, one of the lasting legacies of World War I. And the Wilson administration did this along lines influenced by progressivism: following the lead of the steeply graduated Revenue Act of 1916, it rejected a tax on all wages and salaries in favor of placing the burden on corporations and wealthy individuals. The corporate excess-profits tax contained in the 1917 law signaled a direct and unprecedented intrusion of the state into the workings of corporate capitalism. By 1918 U.S. corporations were paying over $2.5 billion in excess-profits taxes per year, more than half of all federal taxes.

In all, the United States raised about one-third of the cost of the war through taxes; the rest came from loans, especially the popular Liberty bonds, which encouraged public support for the war effort. The government also paid for the war by using the Federal Reserve System to expand the money supply, making it easier to borrow money. Even so, the federal debt increased from $1 billion in 1915 to $20 billion in 1920. Federal expenditures never again dropped to their pre-war levels, but by 1920 the federal budget was posting a surplus.

Wartime Economic Regulation.   In addition to financing the war, mobilization required the coordination of economic production. The government never seriously considered exercising total control over the economy, but the war sped up the creation of a centralized national administrative structure that ultimately would match the consolidated power of the business and banking communities. The government also created an added incentive for business cooperation by suspending antitrust laws, which ordinarily outlawed business practices that restrained or monopolized trade. For economic expertise the government turned primarily to those who knew the capacities of the economy best—the nation's business leaders. Executives flocked to Washington, regarding war work as both a duty and an opportunity for professional advancement.

A series of boards and agencies tried to rationalize and coordinate the economy. The Overman Act of 1918 granted the president control over these agencies, a significant milestone in the growth of presidential power. A network of industrial committees linked war agencies to organizations in private industry, and government leaders used a combination of public and private power to enforce their decisions. This semivoluntarist approach represented an attempt to find a middle ground between total state control of the economy and letting business operate without direction. Like most compromises, it had mixed results.

The Fuel Administration, directed by Harry Garfield, the president of Williams College, allocated the coal needed for operation of the nation's railroads and factories. Its task became more difficult during the severe winter of 1917–1918, when there were coal shortages in major cities and industries of the Northeast. At one point Garfield ordered all factories east of the Mississippi River to shut down for four days. By raising the price of coal to artificially high levels, the Fuel Administration stimulated the production of coal from previously unprofitable mines to meet the nation's energy needs.

The Railroad War Board, under Secretary of the Treasury McAdoo, coordinated the nation's sprawling transportation system. Because the army needed trains to move its troops, the board took over the railroads in December 1917. In return it guaranteed railroad owners a "standard return" equal to their average earnings between 1915 and 1917, and promised that the carriers would be returned to private control no later than twenty-one months after the war.

Perhaps the most successful government agency was the Food Administration, created in August 1917 and led by Stanford University–trained engineer Herbert Hoover. Using the slogan "Food will win the war," Hoover encouraged the expansion of domestic production of wheat and other grains from 45 million acres in

1917 to 75 million in 1919. The increased output not only fed the large domestic market but also allowed a threefold rise in food exports to war-torn Europe. At no time did the government contemplate domestic food rationing. "Wheatless" Mondays, "meatless" Tuesdays, and "porkless" Thursdays and Saturdays resulted in substantial voluntary conservation of food resources, as consumers patriotically responded to snappy jingles like "If U fast U beat U boats—if U feast U boats beat U." Hoover emerged from the war as one of the nation's most admired public figures.

The War Industries Board. The central agency for mobilizing wartime industry was the War Industries Board (WIB), which was established in July 1917. After a fumbling start that showed the limits of voluntarism in a national emergency, in March 1918 the Wilson administration reorganized the board under the centralized control of Bernard Baruch, a Wall Street financier. The WIB reflected the ambivalent attitude of Americans toward government intervention in the economy. Although Wilson recognized the need for central authority in wartime, he always saw the WIB as a temporary expedient. Baruch organized the WIB around specific commodities and industries, whose administrators then negotiated issues such as market allocation with their equivalents in private industry. This frequent consultation blurred the lines between the needs of business and those of government and often left patterns of private power undisturbed.

The WIB produced an unparalleled expansion of the economic powers of the federal government: it allocated scarce resources, gathered economic data and statistics, controlled the flow of raw materials, ordered the conversion of factories to war production, set prices, imposed efficiency and standardization procedures, and coordinated purchasing. The board had the authority to compel compliance, but Baruch preferred to win voluntary acceptance from industry, often through personal intervention. Business generally supported this governmental expansion because federal growth coincided with its own interests. Despite higher taxes, corporate profits soared, aided by the suspension of antitrust laws and guaranteed prices for war work. War profits produced an economic boom that continued without interruption until 1920.

With the signing of the armistice in November 1918, the United States scrambled to dismantle wartime controls. Wilson, determined to "take the harness off," disbanded the WIB effective January 1, 1919, resisting suggestions from economists and reformers that keeping the board in place would help stabilize the economy during demobilization. Like most Americans, he could tolerate putting planning power in the hands of the government during an emergency but not as a permanent feature of the economy.

Although U.S. participation in the war lasted only eighteen months, it left an important legacy for the modern bureaucratic state. Entire industries had been organized as never before, linked to a maze of government agencies and executive departments. A modern system of income taxation had been established, with the potential for vastly increasing federal reserves. Finally, the collaboration between business and government had been

ON THE JOB FOR VICTORY
UNITED STATES SHIPPING BOARD ——— EMERGENCY FLEET CORPORATION

On the Job for Victory
Shipping was a critical area of war mobilization because troops and supplies had to be transported back and forth to Europe. This poster by the United States Shipping Board highlights the bustling activity at a shipyard of the Emergency Fleet Corporation.
Library of Congress.

mutually beneficial, a lesson that both partners would put to use in the state building that occurred in the 1920s and thereafter.

Mobilizing American Workers

Modern wars are never won solely by armies and business and government leaders. Farmers, factory workers, and other civilians play crucial roles. However, World War I produced fewer rewards for workers than it did for owners and managers.

Organized Labor.   Labor's position improved during the war, although it remained a junior partner to business and government. Samuel Gompers, leader of the American Federation of Labor (AFL), traded labor's support of the war for a voice in government policy, specifically a spot on the National Defense Advisory Commission. That bargain proved acceptable to government and business leaders concerned with averting crippling strikes. The War Labor Policies Board headed by Felix Frankfurter, a Harvard law professor, coordinated labor and welfare programs in government and industry, while the United States Employment Service placed 4 million workers in war jobs.

Far more important to workers, however, was the April 1918 establishment of the National War Labor Board (NWLB), which arbitrated labor disputes. Composed of representatives of labor, management, and the public, the NWLB was chaired by former president William Howard Taft, spokesperson for management, and Frank P. Walsh, a labor lawyer. The board's decisions favored labor more often than management, giving important federal support to the goals of the labor movement. During the eighteen months of the NWLB's existence it arbitrated approximately 1,250 cases. The board established an eight-hour day for war workers, with time and a half for overtime, and endorsed equal pay for women workers. Workers were not allowed to disrupt war production through strikes or other disturbances; in return, the NWLB supported their right to organize unions and required employers to deal with shop committees representing workers in the workplace. The NWLB had ample power to enforce its decisions and intervene in disputes. For example, when the Smith and Wesson arms plant in Springfield, Massachusetts, flouted NWLB rules by discriminating against union employees, the federal government took over the firm.

After years of federal hostility toward labor, the actions of the NWLB improved labor's status and power and demonstrated the wisdom of labor's decision to support the war effort to advance its own interests. From 1916 to 1919 AFL membership grew by almost a million workers, reaching over 3 million at the end of the war. Few of the wartime gains lasted, however. Wartime inflation ate up most of the wage hikes, and a virulent postwar anti-union movement caused a rapid decline in union membership that lasted into the 1930s. The labor movement did not yet have enough power to bargain on an equal basis with business and government.

Black and Mexican American Workers.   When soldiers go to war, jobs open up for workers who normally are excluded from them. Black men, for example, found jobs in northern defense industries that would not have hired them in peacetime. The magnet of industrial jobs and escape from the southern agricultural system lured between 400,000 and 450,000 African Americans to northern and midwestern cities such as St. Louis, Chicago, Cleveland, and Detroit during the war. This "Great Migration," which began around 1910 and continued until the 1970s, was one of the largest population shifts of the twentieth century (see American Voices, "Southern Migrants," p. 721).

Mexican Americans in California, Texas, New Mexico, and Arizona also found new opportunities during the war. When urban growth in the Southwest made the wartime labor shortage more severe, many Mexican Americans left farm labor for new industrial opportunities. Continuing political instability in Mexico following the revolution there caused many Mexicans to relocate, temporarily or permanently, across the border, a process facilitated by newly opened railroad lines. At least 100,000 Mexican Americans entered the United States between 1917 and 1920, often settling in segregated neighborhoods (*barrios*) in urban areas, where they met discrimination similar to that experienced by African Americans.

Women and the War Effort.   Women were the largest group that took advantage of new wartime opportunities. White women and, to a lesser degree, black and Mexican American women found that factory jobs formerly reserved for men were now open to them. About 1 million women joined the labor force for the first time. In addition, many of the nation's 8 million women who already held jobs switched from low-paying work such as domestic service to higher-paying industrial work. Americans soon got used to the sight of female streetcar conductors, train engineers, and defense workers. But everyone—including the working women—expected that those jobs would return to men after the war ended.

Professional women also found opportunities in government service. Mary Van Kleeck, an industrial sociologist and an expert on the problems of woman workers, joined the Department of Labor to lobby for equal pay and better working conditions for woman workers. Pauline Goldmark, a social reformer from the National Consumers' League, acted as a women's rights advocate at the Railroad Administration. Mary Anderson, a trade unionist who had been Van Kleeck's assistant, became

Southern Migrants

───────★───────

*T*he Great Migration of southern African Americans to the cities of the North disrupted communities and families, but the migrants kept in touch with friends and kin through letters and visits. Cities like Chicago offered new opportunities and experiences, as these letters suggest, and migrants eagerly promoted their promise to the folks back home.

CHICAGO, ILLINOIS.

My dear Sister: I was agreeably surprised to hear from you and to hear from home. I am well and thankful to say I am doing well. The weather and everything else was a surprise to me when I came. I got here in time to attend one of the greatest revivals in the history of my life—over 500 people joined the church. We had a Holy Ghost shower. You know I like to have run wild. It was snowing some nights and if you didnt hurry you could not get standing room. Please remember me kindly to any who ask of me. The people are rushing here by the thousands and I know if you come and rent a big house you can get all the roomers you want. You write me exactly when you are coming. I am not keeping house yet I am living with my brother and his wife. My sone is in California but will be home soon. He spends his winter in California. I can get a nice place for you to stop until you can look around and see what you want. I am quite busy. I work in Swifts packing Co. in the sausage department. My daughter and I work for the same company—We get $1.50 a day and we pack so many sausages we dont have much time to play but it is a matter of a dollar with

me and I feel that God made the path and I am walking therein.

Tell your husband work is plentiful here and he wont have to loaf if he want to work. . . . Well goodbye from your sister in Christ.

CHICAGO, ILLINOIS, 11/13/17.

Mr. H⸺
Hattiesburg, Miss.

Dear M⸺: Yours received sometime ago and found all well and doing well. hope you and family are well.

I got my things alright the other day and they were in good condition. I am all fixed now and living well. I certainly appreciate what you done for us and I will remember you in the near future.

M⸺, old boy, I was promoted on the first of the month I was made first assistant to the head carpenter when he is out of the place I take everything in charge and was raised to $95. a month. You know I know my stuff.

Whats the news generally around H'burg? I should have been here 20 years ago. I just begin to feel like a man. It's a great deal of pleasure in knowing that you have got some privilege My children are going to the same school with the whites and I dont have to umble to no one. I have registered—Will vote the next election and there isnt any "yes sir" and "no sir"—its all yes and no and Sam and Bill.

Florine says hello and would like very much to see you.

All joins me in sending love to you and family. How is times there now? Answer soon, from your friend and bro.

───────────

Source: Journal of Negro History 4, no. 4 (1919): 457, 458–459.

the first director of the Women's Bureau established by the Labor department in 1920.

World War I proved especially liberating for middle-class women outside the work force. Women's clubs and groups turned much of their organizational energy to the war effort. Suffragist leaders such as Anna Howard Shaw mobilized women's support for the war through the Women's Committee of the Council of National Defense. Housewives played a crucial role in the success of Herbert Hoover's Food Administration. Other groups, including the American Red Cross and

the Young Women's Christian Association (YWCA), sent volunteers to France to organize relief work and recreational activities in conjunction with the AEF.

Suffrage Victory. The war especially affected the battle for woman suffrage. The main suffrage organization, the National American Woman Suffrage Association (NAWSA), threw the support of its 2 million members behind the Wilson administration. Carrie Chapman Catt, president of the organization, argued that women had to prove their patriotism to avoid jeopardizing the suffrage

Wartime Opportunities
Women took on new jobs during the war, working as mail carriers, police officers, drill-press operators, and farm laborers attached to the Women's Land Army. These Newark, New Jersey, women, decked out in snazzy uniforms, clearly enjoyed their work as dispatch riders for local munitions plants and shipyards. When the war ended, women usually lost such employment.
National Archives.

movement. At the same time, NAWSA continued to lobby for the proposed woman suffrage amendment to the Constitution. The suffragists posed a simple but effective moral challenge: How could the United States fight to make the world safe for democracy while denying half its citizens the right to vote?

Alice Paul and the National Woman's Party (NWP) took a more militant and confrontational tack, widening the split in the suffrage movement that had occurred after 1914 (see Chapter 20). To the dismay of NAWSA leaders, suffrage militants led by the NWP began picketing in front of the White House in July 1917 to protest their lack of the vote. Arrested and sentenced to seven months in jail, an unusually harsh sentence, Paul and other women prisoners went on a hunger strike. Prison authorities responded by force-feeding the suffragists, which involved inserting a 20-inch-long tube through the nostril to the stomach, a

process that was excruciatingly painful as well as demeaning. Public shock at their treatment caused them to be regarded as martyrs. Suffragist Rose Winslow stated forcefully, "God knows we don't want other women ever to have to do this over again."

In the end it took both suffrage militancy and the NAWSA's policy of patient persuasion to break the logjam. In January 1918 Woodrow Wilson withdrew his opposition to a federal woman suffrage amendment. The constitutional amendment quickly passed the House but took eighteen months to get through the Senate. Then came another year of hard work for ratification by the states. Finally, on August 26, 1920, Tennessee gave the Nineteenth Amendment the last vote it needed. The goal that had first been declared at the Seneca Falls convention in 1848 was finally reached seventy-two years later, its enactment spurred by women's contributions to the war effort.

Promoting National Unity

The course of American participation in World War I was fundamentally shaped by the progressive period that preceded the war. Reformers eagerly embraced American involvement as an opportunity to put progressive ideals into practice. The educator and philosopher John Dewey, a staunch supporter of the war, argued that wars represented a "plastic juncture" in which societies became more open to reason and new ideas. Dewey's optimistic view matched the spirit of the times. But the dissenting observation voiced by Randolph Bourne, an outspoken pacifist and intellectual who had once been a pupil of Dewey's, came closer to reality. "If the war is too strong for you to prevent," Bourne asked, "how is it going to be weak enough for you to control and mould to your liberal purposes?"

Although the enactment of woman suffrage confirmed Dewey's prediction that social progress could occur in a war context, the excesses committed in the name of building national unity supported Bourne's warning. Woodrow Wilson shared that foreboding: "Once lead this people into war, and they'll forget there ever was such a thing as tolerance." But the president also realized the need to manufacture support for the war: "It is not an army we must shape and train for war, it is a nation."

Wartime Propaganda. In April 1917 Wilson formed the Committee on Public Information (CPI) to promote public backing for the war, a critical task given the lack of a strong national consensus on American participation. This government propaganda agency, headed by the journalist George Creel (see American Lives, "George Creel: Holding Fast the Inner Lines," pp. 724–725), acted as a magnet for progressive reformers and muckraking journalists such as Ida Tarbell (see Chapter 20). Professing lofty goals such as educating citizens about democracy, promoting national unity, Americanizing immigrants, and breaking down the isolation of rural life, the committee also indirectly acted as a nationalizing force by promoting the development of a common ideology.

The CPI touched the life of practically every American during World War I. It distributed 75 million pieces of patriotic literature. At local movie theaters before the feature presentation (which sometimes was a CPI-supported film such as *The Hun Within* or *Pershing's Crusaders*), a volunteer called a "four-minute man" made a short speech supporting the war. (The name, a reference to Revolutionary War heroes, also reassured audiences and theater owners that the featured entertainment would be delayed only briefly.) Those speeches reached an audience estimated at more than 300 million—three times the population of the United States at the time. But the CPI sometimes went too far. In early 1918, for example, it encouraged speakers to use inflammatory stories of alleged German atrocities, such as rapes and murders of innocent citizens, to build support for the war effort.

A Climate of Suspicion. As is often true during wartime, a spirit of conformity pervaded the home front and many Americans found themselves targets of suspicion. Posters such as "Spies and Lies" warned that "German agents are everywhere." Local businesses paid for newspaper and magazine ads that asked citizens to report to the Justice department "the man who spreads pessimistic stories, cries for peace, or belittles our efforts to win the war." And quasi-vigilante groups such as the American Protective League mobilized approximately 250,000 self-appointed "agents," furnished with badges issued by the Justice department, to spy on neighbors and co-workers.

The CPI also urged ethnic groups to give up their Old World customs in the spirit of "One Hundred Percent Americanism." All new immigrants were the target of this Americanization campaign, but German Americans bore the brunt of it because of questions about their loyalty and the anti-German sentiments stirred up by the CPI propaganda. Suddenly everything German became suspect. German music and opera were banished from concert halls, publishers removed pro-German references from textbooks, and many communities banned the teaching of the German language. Sauerkraut was renamed "liberty cabbage," and hamburgers were transformed into "liberty sandwiches." Even the German measles became "liberty measles." Although anti-German hysteria dissipated when the war ended, uncertainty and hostility toward "hyphenated" Americans survived, spurring a rise of nativism in the 1920s.

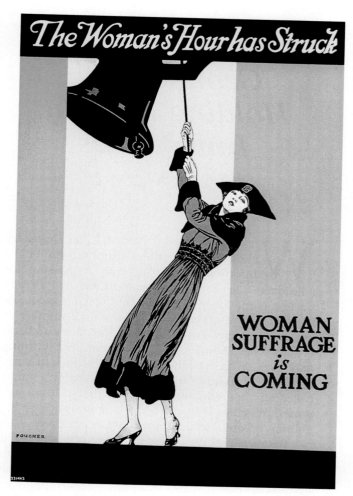

Woman Suffrage Triumphant
This 1919 poster celebrating the passage of the Nineteenth Amendment by Congress promised that woman suffrage was coming, but it took still another year of intense lobbying to win the necessary ratification by the states. Then, finally, the woman's hour struck.
Poster Collection, US5084, Hoover Institution Archives, Stanford University, CA.

Curbing Dissent. Law enforcement officials tolerated little criticism of established values and institutions in wartime, as the militant suffragists picketing the White House had discovered. The main legal tools for curbing dissent were the Espionage Act of 1917 and the Sedition Act of 1918. The espionage law imposed stiff penalties for antiwar activities and allowed the federal government to ban treasonous material from being sent through the mails. The definition of treason was left to the postmaster general. The sedition law went further, punishing anyone who might "utter, print, write, or publish any disloyal, profane, scurrilous, or abusive language about the form of government of the United States, . . . or the uniform of the Army or the Navy."

George Creel: Holding Fast the Inner Lines

— ★ —

George Creel
George Creel in 1917, at the time of his appointment as head of the Committee on Public Information.
Corbis-Bettmann.

WOODROW WILSON CALLED George Creel, his choice to lead the Committee on Public Information, a man with a "passion for adjectives." The forty-one-year-old Creel had already made a name for himself as a muckraking journalist and unabashed progressive, picking up a number of detractors along the way for his impetuous and flamboyant style. "A little shrimp of a man with burning dark eyes set in an ugly face under a shock of curly black hair" was how one critic described him; another called him "a fascinating talker who looked like a gargoyle." Whether it concerned his appearance or his politics, no one was neutral about George Creel.

George Creel was born on December 1, 1876, in Lafayette County, Missouri, the son of a Confederate officer who had moved west from Virginia after the Civil War. His mother, who ran a boardinghouse while his father brooded and drank, made sure that her son heard the Southern version of the War Between the States. "The battle of Antietam, indeed!" she exclaimed after he recounted one history lesson from school. "Why, honey, it was the battle of Sharpsburg, and we *whipped* them." The young boy concluded about his upbringing, "The open mind was no part of my inheritance. I took in prejudice with mother's milk, and was weaned on partisanship."

Quitting high school after one year, Creel worked briefly on a Kansas City newspaper before hopping on a cattle train to New York City to try his luck as a writer and freelance journalist. By 1900 he was back in the Midwest to found the Kansas City *Independent*, a weekly paper whose slogan was "A Clean, Clever Paper for Intelligent People." With zeal shared by early twentieth-century urban progressives all around the country, he lead battles to clean up municipal government, pass laws to protect workers, and stop prostitution.

In 1909 Creel moved to Denver, a hotbed of progressive activity. When reformers won a majority in the 1912 city elections, he became police commissioner but was fired from the job a year later when his campaigns to dismiss political holdovers and rehabilitate criminals went too far even for his fellow progressives. Freed from the straitjacket of public office, he intensified his muckraking activities, exposing, for example, the glowing personal endorsements that often accompanied advertisements for quack medical remedies by printing the death dates of these supposedly cured patients. He was an ardent woman suffragist, and he coauthored a book on child labor with Edwin Markham and Denver's crusading judge, Ben Lindsey. Along the way he married Hollywood actress Blanche Bates, star of *The Darling of the Gods* and other films, and starred in a cowboy movie himself. He also boxed professionally. Who says progressive reformers have to be dull?

Creel had been impressed by Woodrow Wilson's idealism as far back as 1905, and he became an enthusiastic backer of Wilson's presidential ambitions in 1912. In the 1916 campaign Creel wrote an influential pamphlet called *Wilson and the Issues*, which stressed Wilson's reform record and endorsed his stand of neutrality toward the European war. In return the reelected president offered him a position in Washington, but Creel declined. When America was on the verge of entering the war in the spring of 1917, Creel had a change of heart. If there was going to be someone in charge of public opinion, he told a Wilson aide, he wanted "to be *it*."

Reaction to Creel's appointment was decidedly mixed. Many newspapers, including the *New York Times*, saw him as "a radical writer" and questioned whether such an outspoken and thin-skinned figure would be able to work effectively with the press. Creel brushed these criticisms aside and promptly got down to work.

The jurisdiction of the Committee on Public Information was "everything related to public opinion, both at home and abroad," and Creel enlisted the cooperation of journalists, movie makers, advertising executives, and others in the common battle of "holding fast the inner lines" of American public opinion during wartime. His goal was affirmative propaganda, not rank appeals to emotion—to "inspire, not inflame." So confident was he of "the absolute justice of America's cause, the absolute selflessness of America's aims," that he believed "no other argument was needed than the simple, straightforward presentation of the facts." "Words evaporate," he said repeatedly, but "facts remain."

Creel later called the CPI "the world's greatest adventure in advertising." In the days before radio, printed publicity played a crucial role in reaching, and then binding together, a diverse nation. By the end of 1917 the CPI was sending each newspaper in California an average of six pounds of publicity copy a day. One unintended by-product of this government-sponsored media campaign was the stimulation of the advertising industry, which became a major force in shaping patterns of consumption in the 1920s. The war also stimulated the nascent film industry, which cooperated wholeheartedly with CPI efforts.

George Creel quickly demonstrated that he aimed not just to shape the minds of American citizens but to "fight for the mind of mankind" worldwide. The foreign section of the CPI exported ideas about American life and values to three target audiences: neutral nations, America's allies, and the civilian populations of the Central Powers. German and Austrian citizens were bombarded with propaganda leaflets dropped from balloons and airplanes or smuggled behind enemy lines. And in the newly formed Soviet Union, the CPI distributed a million pamphlets, "sounding alarms against typhus as well as against Lenin and Trotsky." Propaganda became part of a global network.

At war's end, the CPI was quickly dismantled and Creel returned to journalism. Always the publicist, he wrote a book about his CPI experiences entitled *How We Advertised America* (1920) in which he took great delight in settling old scores with his opponents, especially Republican members of Congress. He also ardently defended, to no avail, the Treaty of Versailles out of loyalty to his friend Woodrow Wilson. In 1926 he and his family moved to San Francisco, where he continued to write for national publications such as *Collier's* magazine, as well as publish books of popular history and biography.

The upheavals of the 1930s and 1940s drew Creel back into public life. He warmly supported Franklin Roosevelt's efforts to end the Great Depression and served on a variety of New Deal advisory boards. He was far more critical, however, of the administration's conduct of World War II, especially the "blundering" (in his words) propaganda efforts undertaken by the Office of War Information. With his usual inflated pride and self-justification, he commented, "A full twenty organizations now spend more than $130,000,000 a year to do the work that I did with $2,500,000 a year." By the 1940s he was moving away from his former progressive belief in reform, fearing that the federal government had gotten so big that it was stifling individual initiative. Creel died in 1951, having spent the last years of his life battling what he saw as a huge international conspiracy of communists and their sympathizers.

George Creel always thought of himself as a "rebel at large," the title he chose for his 1947 autobiography. Reflecting on the changes that had occurred in America during his lifetime, he concluded, "At twenty, when I enlisted in the progressive movement, I was appalled at the magnitude of the task of reform. Today, at seventy, I am amazed at the swiftness of our approach to equal justice." Despite his ideological journey away from progressivism toward the end of his life, Creel never deviated from his wartime creed: "Democracy is a religion with me, and throughout my adult life I have preached America as the hope of the world."

More than a thousand people were convicted under these broad restrictions on freedom of speech.

The Justice department also targeted the radical Industrial Workers of the World (IWW), or Wobblies (see Chapter 17), who passionately argued that war benefited the capitalist class at the expense of workers. When Wobblies threatened to disrupt war production in the western lumber and copper industries, the Justice department arrested 113 IWW leaders in September 1917. Vigilante groups contributed their own reprisals: a mob in Butte, Montana, dragged IWW organizer Frank Little through the streets and hanged him from a railroad trestle. By the end of the war the Wobblies had been decimated.

Socialists encountered similar reprisals for criticizing the war and the draft. In 1919 party leader Eugene Debs was sentenced to ten years in federal prison for a speech in which he stated that the master classes declared wars while the subject classes fought the battles. (He was pardoned by President Warren G. Harding in 1921.) Victor Berger, a Milwaukee socialist, was twice prevented from taking his seat in the U.S. House of Representatives because he had been jailed under the Espionage Act for his antiwar views. The Supreme Court reversed Berger's conviction in 1921, and he served in the House again from 1923 to 1929.

The reversal in the Berger case was an exception, however. The Supreme Court rarely overturned these cases of wartime excesses. In *Schenck v. United States* (1919), the justices upheld the conviction of the general secretary of the Socialist Party, Charles T. Schenck, who had mailed pamphlets urging draftees to resist induction. In a unanimous decision Justice Oliver Wendell Holmes wrote, "When a nation is at war many things that might be said in time of peace are such a hindrance to its effort that their utterances will not be endured." Therefore, an act of speech uttered under circumstances that would "create a clear and present danger to the safety of the country" could be constitutionally restricted. In *Abrams v. United States* (1919), the Court upheld the conviction for sedition of Jacob Abrams, a Russian anarchist and recent immigrant who had dumped from tenement windows in New York many Yiddish and English pamphlets denouncing American military intervention in Russia. Holmes dissented in this case, seeing no clear threat to the conduct of the war. He and Justice Louis Brandeis made up the minority in the 7-to-2 decision. Because of the national war emergency, the Court upheld limits on freedom of speech that would not have been acceptable in peacetime.

The Eighteenth Amendment. The century-old campaign for Prohibition was also affected by the wartime climate. In early twentieth-century America, Prohibition was viewed as a progressive reform, not a denial of individual freedom. Urban reformers, concerned about good government, urban poverty, and public morality, supported a nationwide ban on drinking. Among the Progressive Era leaders who supported Prohibition were William Jennings Bryan, Supreme Court Justice Louis Brandeis, former presidents William Howard Taft and Theodore Roosevelt, and settlement-house leader Jane Addams. On the eve of World War I, nineteen states had passed Prohibition laws and many more allowed communities to regulate liquor sales and consumption (Map 22.3).

The drive for Prohibition also had substantial backing in rural communities. Many people equated liquor with the sins of the city: prostitution, crime, machine politics, and public disorder. In addition, the churches with the greatest strength in rural areas, such as the Methodists, Baptists, and Mormons, strongly condemned drinking. Protestants from rural areas dominated the membership of the Anti-Saloon League, which in the 1910s supplanted the Woman's Christian Temperance Union as the leading proponent of Prohibition.

Support for the right to drink existed primarily in heavily urbanized states with large immigrant populations, such as New York, Massachusetts, Rhode Island, Illinois, and California. Alcoholic beverages, especially beer and whiskey, played an important role in certain ethnic cultures, especially those of German Americans and Irish Americans. Many saloons were in working-class neighborhoods and served as gathering places for workers; machine politicians conducted much of their business in bars. Many immigrant and working-class people rightly interpreted Prohibition as an imposition of middle-class cultural values on them.

During World War I those who supported a constitutional amendment to prohibit drinking gained political momentum. One spur was the intense anti-German hysteria of the war years. Because several major breweries (Pabst and Busch, for example) had German names, beer drinking became unpatriotic in many people's minds. To conserve food, Congress prohibited the use of foodstuffs such as hops and barley to make distilled beverages. Finally, in December 1917, Congress passed the proposed Eighteenth Amendment, which prohibited the "manufacture, transport, and sale of intoxicating liquors." Among its few exceptions were alcohol prescribed for medicinal reasons and wine consumed for sacramental purposes.

Ratified in 1919 and made effective on January 16, 1920, the Eighteenth Amendment was another example of how "progressive" solutions to issues of purity, poverty, and public safety were adopted in wartime. It also demonstrated the widening influence of the state on matters of personal behavior. Yet the ethnic and urban-rural clashes over Prohibition also foreshadowed the political and cultural debates of the 1920s.

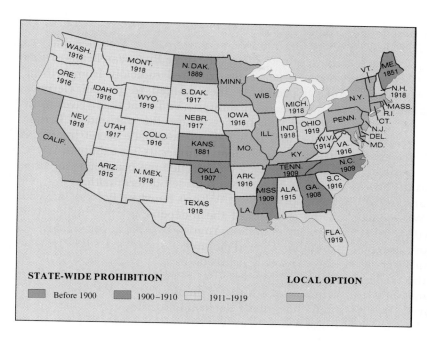

MAP 22.3
Prohibition on the Eve of the Eighteenth Amendment
Prohibition had already made headway in the states before the adoption of the Eighteenth Amendment in 1919. States such as Maine, North Dakota, and Kansas had been dry since the nineteenth century; by 1919 two-thirds of the states had passed laws banning liquor. Most states that resisted the trend were industrial centers or had large immigrant populations.

Unlike woman suffrage, the other constitutional amendment that won passage at this time, Prohibition would never gain general acceptance.

An Unsettled Peace, 1919–1920

— ★ —

In January 1917 Woodrow Wilson had proposed a "peace without victory," since only a "peace among equals" could last. His goal was "not a balance of power, but a community of power; not organized rivalries, but an organized common peace." With victory achieved, Wilson confronted the task of constructing this new moral international order, whose keystone was a permanent league of nations. But he would first have to win over a Senate that was controlled by Republicans and deeply divided over the peace treaty. At the same time, ethnic and racial tensions that had smoldered during the war erupted in controversy and strife, and fears of domestic radicalism boiled over in the Red Scare.

The Treaty of Versailles

Wilson scored an early victory when the Allies accepted his Fourteen Points as the basis for the peace negotiations that began in January 1919. First put forward in a speech to Congress in early 1918, the Fourteen Points represented Wilson's clearest articulation of his blueprint for the postwar world. The president called for

open diplomacy, "absolute freedom of navigation upon the seas," arms reduction, the removal of trade barriers, and an international commitment to territorial integrity and national self-determination. Essential to Wilson's vision was the creation of a multinational organization "for the purpose of affording mutual guarantees of political independence and territorial integrity to great and small States alike." This League of Nations became Wilson's obsession.

The Fourteen Points matched the spirit of progressivism. Widely distributed as propaganda during the final months of the war, Wilson's declaration proposed to extend the benefits of the American way of life—democracy, freedom, and peaceful economic expansion—to the rest of the world. The League of Nations, acting as a kind of Federal Trade Commission for the world, would supervise disarmament and, according to the crucial Article X of its covenant, curb unilateralism (the tendency to conduct foreign affairs with minimal consultation with other countries or even allies) in favor of collective military action. More grandiosely, Wilson anticipated that the league would mediate disputes between nations, prevent future wars, and thereby ensure that the Great War would be "the war to end all wars." By emphasizing such lofty goals, Wilson courted disappointment: his ideals for world reformation proved too far-reaching to be practical or attainable.

The U.S. peace delegation sailed for Europe in December 1918. Wilson toured the major European capitals and received a tumultuous welcome: in Paris 2 million people lined the Champs-Élysées to pay tribute to "Wilson the Just." This reception encouraged Wilson to press ahead with his plan to dominate the peace conference. Twenty-seven countries sent representatives to the peace conference in Versailles, near Paris, although the Big Four—Wilson, Prime Minister David Lloyd George of Great Britain, Premier Georges Clemenceau of France, and Prime Minister Vittorio Orlando of Italy—did most of the negotiating. Neither Germany nor the Soviet Union were invited.

The exclusion of the Soviet Union from the Versailles negotiations was the result of the Allies' profound unease about the ideological direction of the new Soviet state. Lenin's calls for a proletarian revolution to liberate the world from capitalism and imperialism posed a direct challenge to the Wilsonian concept of international order represented by the League of Nations. Not only did Wilson refuse to recognize Lenin's legitimacy, but the Allies also took steps to topple the Bolshevik regime. Using the excuse of helping 60,000 trapped Czechoslovakians return west to fight the Germans, Wilson deployed 2,000 American troops to Vladivostok in eastern Russia in June 1918 and sent an additional 3,000 troops to northwestern Russia in July. Britain and Japan also sent troops. The unstated purpose of this military maneuver was to support anti-Bolshevik forces within Russia. American troops remained on Soviet soil until the spring of 1920, leaving a bitter legacy for American-Soviet relations.

Negotiating the Treaties. The Big Four concurred about excluding Lenin from the peace negotiations, but in other respects the three European heads of state sought a peace that differed radically from Wilson's plan. Specifically they wanted to punish Germany through heavy reparations and treat themselves to the spoils of war. In fact, before the war ended, Britain, France, and Italy had already made secret treaties to divide up the German colonies. It is a tribute to Wilson that he managed to influence the peace agreement as much as he did. National self-determination, a fundamental principle of Wilson's Fourteen Points, bore fruit in the creation of the independent states of Austria, Hungary, Poland, Yugoslavia, and Czechoslovakia from the defeated empires of the Central Powers (Map 22.4). The establishment of the new nations of Finland, Estonia, Lithuania, and Latvia not only upheld the principle of self-determination but also served Wilson's (and the Allies') determination to isolate the Soviet Union from the rest of Europe. Wilson was also able to soften some of the harshest demands for reprisals against Germany.

He had less success in achieving other goals. Certain topics, such as freedom of the seas and free trade, never made the agenda because of Allied resistance. The old central and eastern European empires were dismantled, but instead of becoming independent

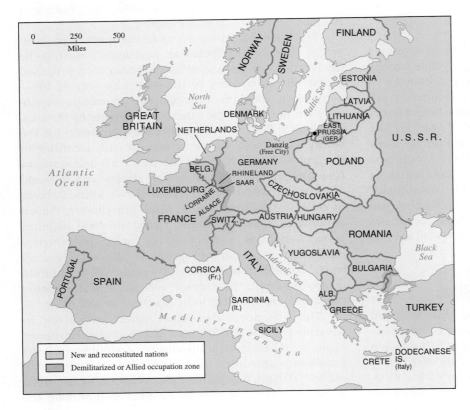

MAP 22.4
Europe after World War I
World War I and its aftermath dramatically altered the landscape of Europe, most notable with the creation of new countries such as Poland, Yugoslavia, and Czechoslovakia from territory of the defeated powers of Germany and Russia. Twenty years later, these new countries were the battlegrounds of the next world war.

The Peace at Versailles
This painting by Sir William Orpen of the signing of the peace treaty in the Hall of Mirrors at Versailles in June 1919 captures the solemnity of the occasion and the grandeur of the surroundings. Wilson was justifiably proud of his role in the peace negotiations, but he faced strong opposition in the Senate.
Imperial War Museum, London.

countries, the colonies were assigned to victorious Allied nations to administer as trustees. The transfer of Germany's colonies to imperialist powers such as Britain and Japan hardly constituted national self-determination. More troubling, economic issues were not faced as squarely as were territorial ones. Wilson yielded to French and British demands for a "war guilt" clause, which provided justification for the restitution demanded from Germany. The final figure, set in 1921, was a staggering $33 billion.

In the face of his many disappointments, Wilson consoled himself with the negotiators' commitment to his proposed League of Nations. He acknowledged that the treaty had defects but expressed confidence that they could be resolved by a permanent international organization dedicated to the peaceful resolution of disputes. The American public seemed enthusiastic about a league of nations, at least in principle. Major newspapers and the Federal Council of Churches in Christ of America supported the treaty; even a declared opponent, Senator Henry Cabot Lodge, acknowledged that "the people of the country are very naturally fascinated by the idea of eternal preservation of the world's peace."

On June 28, 1919, representatives gathered in the Hall of Mirrors in the Palace of Versailles to sign the peace treaty. Wilson sailed for home immediately after the ceremony and presented it to the Senate on July 10. The treaty was already in trouble, however, with support in the Senate being far short of the two-thirds vote necessary for ratification. Wilson had failed to pay attention to political realities, neglecting, for example, to include a prominent Republican in the American commission that represented the United States at Versailles. When the Senate balked at ratification, Wilson adamantly refused to compromise. "I shall consent to nothing," he told the French ambassador. "The Senate must take its medicine."

The Battle for Ratification. Opposition to the treaty came from several sources. One group, called the "irreconcilables," consisted of western progressive senators such as William E. Borah of Idaho, Hiram W. Johnson of California, and Robert M. La Follette of Wisconsin, who disagreed fundamentally with the premise of permanent U.S. participation in European affairs. Moreover, they were horrified at the harshness of the treaty toward Germany. Less dogmatic but more influential was a group of Republicans led by Senator Lodge of Massachusetts. Lodge's Republicans proposed a list of amendments centered around Article X, the section of the covenant that called for collective security measures if a member nation should be attacked. Lodge argued that this provision restricted Congress's constitutional authority to declare war. More important, Lodge and many other senators felt that the treaty imposed unacceptable restrictions on the freedom of the United States to pursue a unilateral foreign policy.

Wilson refused to budge—especially to placate Lodge, his hated political rival. Hoping to mobilize support for the treaty, in September 1919 the president launched an extensive speaking tour in a last great effort to take his case directly to the American people. In three weeks he traveled 10,000 miles by train and gave forty speeches, sometimes to tens of thousands of people, without the aid of public address systems. He brought large audiences to tears with his impassioned defense of the treaty, but the strain proved too much for the ailing sixty-two-year-old president, who collapsed in Pueblo, Colorado, in late September. The tour had to be cut short. One week later in Washington, Wilson suffered a severe stroke.

Defeat. We will never know whether a healthy Wilson could have mobilized public support for the League of Nations and gained Senate ratification. If he had allowed the Democrats to compromise, the treaty might have been saved. From his sickbed, however, Wilson ordered Democratic senators to vote against all Republican amendments. The treaty came up for a vote in November 1919 and was not ratified. When another attempt in March 1920 fell seven votes short of approval, the issue was dead.

While the president's wife—Edith Bolling Galt Wilson—his physician, and the various cabinet heads oversaw the routine business of government, Wilson slowly recovered but was never the same. He had delusions of making the 1920 election campaign "a great and solemn referendum" on the League of Nations and even briefly hoped to run for a third term. Neither dream was a serious possibility. Wilson died in 1924, "as much a victim of the war," David Lloyd George noted, "as any soldier who died in the trenches."

United States never ratified the Versailles treaty or joined the League of Nations. Many wartime issues remained only partially resolved, notably Germany's future, the fate of colonial empires, and rising nationalist demands for self-determination. These unsolved problems would play a major role in the coming of World War II, and some, like competing nationalisms in the Balkans, would remain unresolved for the rest of the century.

Racial Strife and Labor Unrest

Wilson spent only ten days in the United States between December 1918 and June 1919. Totally preoccupied with the peacemaking process at Versailles, for more than six months he was practically an absentee president. Unfortunately, many urgent domestic problems demanded his attention.

The war years and the immediate postwar period brought a severe decline in race relations throughout the country. The volatile mix of black migration and raised black expectations as a result of service in World War I combined to worsen white racism. In the South the number of lynchings rose from forty-eight in 1917 to seventy-eight in 1919, and several African American men were lynched in their military uniforms. In the North race riots broke out in more than twenty-five cities, with one of the first and most deadly occurring in 1917 in East St. Louis, Illinois, where nine whites and more than forty blacks died in a conflict sparked by competition over jobs at a defense plant.

Chicago Race Riot
Racial violence exploded in Chicago during the summer of 1919, and photographer Jun Fujita was on the scene to capture it. As one of the few Japanese immigrants in Chicago at the time, Fujita was probably no stranger to racism, but it took personal courage to put himself in the midst of the escalating violence. When the riot finally ended, thirty-eight people were dead and more than five hundred injured.
Chicago Historical Society, photo by Jun Fujita.

Riots in Chicago. By the summer of 1919, the death toll from racial violence had reached 120. One of the worst race riots in American history took place in Chicago that July. It began at a Lake Michigan beach when a black teenager named Eugene Williams swam into an area customarily reserved for whites. Someone threw a rock that hit him on the head, and he drowned. The incident touched off five days of rioting in which twenty-three blacks and fifteen whites died.

Chicago on the eve of the riot was ready to ignite. The arrival of 50,000 black newcomers during the war years had strained the city's social fabric. In politics black voters often determined the winners of close elections. (Unlike in the South, northern blacks generally were not prevented from voting.) Blacks and whites competed for jobs, and the more heavily unionized white population deeply resented blacks who became strikebreakers; white stockyard workers considered the words *Negro* and *scab* to be synonymous. Blacks and whites competed for scarce housing as well, and blacks soon overflowed the racially segregated South Side and moved into Chicago's intensely ethnic neighborhoods. Even before that sultry July afternoon at the beach, tensions had led to bombing of black homes and other forms of harassment.

Chicago blacks did not sit meekly by as whites destroyed their neighborhoods. They fought back both in self-defense and for their rights as citizens. World War I had an indirect effect on their actions, since many blacks had served in the armed forces. The rhetoric about democracy and self-determination raised their expectations, too.

1919—A Year of Strikes. Workers harbored similar hopes for a better life after the war. The war years had brought many industrial employees higher pay, shorter hours, and better working conditions. Yet many native-born Americans continued to identify unions with radicals and foreigners, and after the armistice many employers resumed their attacks on union activity. In addition, rapidly rising inflation—in 1919 the cost of living was 77 percent higher than its prewar level—threatened to wipe out workers' wage increases. Nevertheless workers hoped to keep, perhaps even expand, their wartime gains.

The result of workers' determination and employers' resistance was a dramatic wave of strikes. More than 4 million workers—one in every five—went on strike in 1919, a proportion never before or since equaled. The year began with a walkout by shipyard workers in Seattle, a strong union town. Their action spread into a general strike that crippled the city. In the fall the Boston police force went on strike. The idea of public employees trying to unionize shocked many Americans. Declaring "there is no right to strike against the public safety by anybody, anywhere, any time," Governor Calvin Coolidge of Massachusetts fired the entire police force, and the strike failed. The public supported this harsh reprisal, and Coolidge was rewarded with the Republican vice-presidential nomination in 1920.

The most extensive labor disruption in 1919 was the hard-fought steel strike in which more than 350,000 steelworkers across the country walked off the job in late September. The main issue was union recognition,

General Strike in Seattle
Seattle was a strong union town and 110 local unions took part in the 1919 general strike that paralyzed the city. Although the strike was peaceful, city officials deputized local citizens for police duty, such as this ragtag group of volunteers being issued guns.
Museum of History and Industry, Seattle, Washington.

but the strikers were also protesting twelve-hour shifts and seven-day workweeks. Elbert H. Gary, chair of the United States Steel Corporation, refused even to meet with representatives of the steelworkers' union to discuss their demands. The company hired Mexicans and blacks to break the strike and maintained steel production at about 60 percent of the normal level. This high production rate doomed the strike. Striker solidarity began to slacken as winter approached, and in January the strike collapsed. The union charged that U.S. Steel's "arbitrary and ruthless misuse of power" had crushed the strike, but just as important was the lack of public support for the goals of organized labor. Unions had made important gains during the war, but they were unable to hold on to them.

The Red Scare

Underlying many of the social and political tensions in the aftermath of World War I was the fear of radicalism. Wartime hatred of the German Hun was quickly replaced by postwar hostility toward the Bolshevik Red. The Bolshevik Revolution of 1917 and the founding of the Third International (or Comintern) in 1919 to export revolution throughout the world set those fears in motion. Ironically, as public concern about domestic Bolshevism mounted, American radicalism rapidly lost supporters and political influence. No more than 70,000 Americans belonged to the fledgling U.S. Communist Party or the Communist Labor Party in 1919, and the IWW and the Socialist Party had been gravely weakened by wartime repression and internal dissension. Yet the public and the press continued to blame almost every disturbance, especially labor conflicts, on radicals. "REDS DIRECTING SEATTLE STRIKE—TO TEST CHANCE FOR REVOLUTION," warned a typical newspaper headline.

Then a series of bombings shocked the nation in the early spring. "The word 'radical' in 1919," the historian Robert Murray observed, "automatically carried with it the implication of dynamite." Thirty-four mail bombs addressed to prominent government officials were discovered by postal workers before they exploded. Many people suspected that the intended bombings had been timed to coincide with the communist celebration of International Labor Day on May 1. In June a bomb exploded outside the Washington townhouse of the recently appointed attorney general, A. Mitchell Palmer. His family escaped unharmed, but the bomber was blown to bits. President Wilson's debilitating stroke prevented him from providing decisive leadership as hysteria mounted in the fall of 1919, but Attorney General Palmer seized the moment. Angling for the presidential nomination, Palmer rode the crest of public fears about domestic radicalism into 1920.

The Palmer Raids. One aspect of the wartime expansion of state power was increased surveillance of citizens and repression of dissent. Palmer set up an antiradicalism division in the Justice department, appointing as its director a young government attorney named J. Edgar Hoover. In November 1919, on the second anniversary of the Bolshevik Revolution, the attorney general staged the first of what became known as "Palmer raids." Federal agents stormed the headquarters of radical organizations and captured such supposedly revolutionary booty as a set of drawings that turned out to be blueprints for a phonograph, at first thought to be sketches for a bomb. The dragnet pulled in thousands of alien residents who had committed no crime but were suspect because of their anarchist or revolutionary beliefs or their immigrant background. Lacking the protection of U.S. citizenship, these aliens faced deportation without formal trial or indictment. In December 1919 the U.S.S. *Buford*, nicknamed the "Soviet Ark," embarked for Finland and the Soviet state with a cargo of 294 deported radicals. Its passengers included two famous anarchists, Emma Goldman and Alexander Berkman.

The peak of Palmer's power came with his New Year's raids in January 1920. In one night, with the greatest possible newspaper publicity, Palmer rounded up 6,000 radicals. Agents invaded private homes, union headquarters, and meeting halls, holding citizens and aliens without specific charges and denying them legal counsel, a violation of their civil liberties. But then Palmer overstepped himself, predicting that on May Day 1920 an unnamed conspiracy would attempt to overthrow the U.S. government. State militia units and police went on twenty-four-hour alert to guard the nation against the threat of revolutionary violence, but not a single incident occurred. The hysteria of the Red Scare began to abate as the summer of 1920 passed without major labor strikes or renewed bombings.

The Sacco-Vanzetti Case. One dramatic episode kept the wartime legacy of antiradicalism alive well into the next decade. In May 1920, at the height of the Red Scare, Nicola Sacco, a shoemaker, and Bartolomeo Vanzetti, a fish peddler, were arrested for the robbery and murder of a shoe company's paymaster in South Braintree, Massachusetts. Sacco and Vanzetti were self-proclaimed anarchists and Italian aliens who had evaded the draft; both were armed at the time of their arrest.

Convicted in 1921, Sacco and Vanzetti sat on death row for six years while supporters appealed their verdicts. Although new evidence suggesting their innocence surfaced, Judge Webster Thayer denied a motion for a new trial. Scholars still debate the question of their guilt, but most agree that they did not receive a

Awaiting Their Fate
As the executions of Nicola Sacco and Bartolomeo Vanzetti approached in 1927, they
sparked protests from around the world. This painting by Ben Shahn shows the two
handcuffed together as they wait to hear whether their verdicts will be overturned. The
judicial system declined to reopen the case.
Ben Shahn, *Bartolomeo Vanzetti and Nicola Sacco*, 1931–1932. Estate of Ben Shahn/Licensed by VAGA,
New York, NY.

fair trial. Shortly before his execution in the electric
chair on August 23, 1927, Vanzetti claimed triumph:

> *If it had not been for these thing, I might have live
> out my life among scorning men. I might have die,
> unmarked, unknown, a failure. Now we are not a
> failure. This is our career and our triumph. Never in
> our full life can we hope to do such work for toler-
> ance, for justice, for man's understanding of man, as
> now we do by an accident.*

This often-quoted elegy captures the eloquence and tolerance of a person caught in the last spasm of antiradicalism and fear that capped America's participation in
World War I.

That participation left other legacies as well. World
War I did not have the catastrophic effect on the United
States that it did on European countries. With relatively
few casualties and no physical destruction at home,
America emerged from the conflict stronger than ever
before. Consolidating developments that had begun
with the Spanish-American War, the United States
became a major international power, both economically and politically. Increased efficiency and technological advancements fostered exceptional industrial
productivity that made the United States the envy of the
rest of the world in the postwar decade. And though
mobilization was accompanied by an insistence on as
much voluntarism as possible, the war emergency did
leave a legacy of a stronger federal government and an
enlarged bureaucracy. Finally, the war—especially the
nationalism that accompanied it—contributed to a climate that was inhospitable to liberal social reforms, a
climate that would persist until the crisis of the Great
Depression.

Summary

★

American participation in World War I set in motion one of the most important shifts in international power in the twentieth century, as the United States emerged from the war as a dominant world power. The outbreak of the Great War in 1914 initially posed a great challenge to American diplomacy. For more than two years President Wilson attempted to use American power and prestige to mediate between the two sides. The United States finally entered the war in 1917 because of violations of its neutral rights at sea but, more broadly, because the country's foreign policy reflected the same moral concerns that animated the domestic reform movement. On April 6, 1917, Congress declared war on Germany.

American participation in the war was brief but decisive. Two million freshly recruited "doughboys" helped to turn the tide for the Allies on the Western Front in 1918. Flush with victory, Wilson sought to bring about a peace that would reflect his vision of a new world order. Yet the Versailles treaty only partially reflected the president's hopes for freedom of the seas, peaceful economic expansion, and national self-determination. His postwar plans suffered a worse blow when the U.S. Senate refused to ratify the treaty, which included American participation in the League of Nations.

As the Wilson administration put the nation on a war footing, progressive reform energies were largely diverted to the war effort. An army had to be created almost from scratch, American agriculture and manufacturing had to be federally coordinated to produce for the Allies as well as for the home market, and American workers had to be recruited for war work and kept on the job. All this absorbed the energies of a new group of professional-experts-turned-government-bureaucrats. World War I thus helped create the tools of the modern bureaucratic state, which (though laid aside temporarily at the war's end) would be taken up again during the nation's worst peacetime crisis, the Great Depression.

The government tried to mobilize the minds of the American people as well but succeeded mainly in inflaming passions. Certain groups, such as woman suffragists, found success during the war. But others became targets of repression, including blacks who migrated to northern cities, labor activists, and socialists and other radicals who criticized the government. Domestic tensions erupted in race riots in many northern cities, widespread labor strikes in 1919, and the Red Scare of 1919–1920. The story of U.S. involvement in World War I, then, is a story of battles and diplomacy abroad, and mobilization and strife at home—all of which ultimately had a lasting impact on the nation's future.

T I M E L I N E

1914	Outbreak of war in Europe
	United States declares neutrality
1915	German submarine sinks British ship *Lusitania*
1916	Wilson reelected president
	Revenue Act of 1916
1917	United States enters World War I
	War Revenue bill passed
	Selective Service Act passed
	War Industries Board established
	Suffrage militancy
	East St. Louis race riot
	Espionage Act
	Bolshevik Revolution
	Committee on Public Information established
1918	Wilson proposes Fourteen Points peace plan
	Meuse-Argonne campaign
	Socialist Eugene Debs imprisoned under Sedition Act
	Armistice ends war
	U.S. troops intervene in Russia
1919	Treaty of Versailles signed, ending World War I
	Chicago race riot
	Steel strike
	Red Scare and Palmer raids
	Schenck v. United States
	American Legion founded
	League of Nations defeated in U.S. Senate
	Eighteenth Amendment (Prohibition) ratified
	War Industries Board disbanded
1920	Nineteenth Amendment (woman suffrage) ratified
1924	Woodrow Wilson dies

Suggested Readings

————————★————————

Ronald Schaffer, *America in the Great War: The Rise of the War Welfare State* (1991), and David M. Kennedy, *Over Here: The First World War and American Society* (1980), provide comprehensive overviews of the period. See also Meirion Harries and Susie Harries, *The Last Days of Innocence: America at War, 1917–1918* (1997). On the links between the Progressive Era and the war, see Neil A. Wynn, *From Progressivism to Prosperity: World War I and American Society* (1986); John A. Thompson, *Reformers and War* (1987); and Robert M. Crunden, *Ministers of Reform* (1982). Ellis W. Hawley, *The Great War and the Search for a Modern Order, 1917–1933* (1979), stresses the continuities between the war years and the 1920s.

The Great War, 1914–1918

On America's entry into World War I, see John Coogan, *The End to Neutrality* (1981); Ross Gregory, *The Origins of American Intervention in the First World War* (1971); and Thomas A. Bailey and Paul Ryan, *The Lusitania Disaster* (1975). Studies of Wilson include August Heckscher, *Woodrow Wilson* (1991); Kendrick Clements, *The Presidency of Woodrow Wilson* (1992); Robert Ferrell, *Woodrow Wilson and World War I* (1985); and John Milton Cooper Jr., *The Warrior and the Priest: Woodrow Wilson and Theodore Roosevelt* (1983). See also David Steigerwald, *Wilsonian Idealism in America* (1994).

For American participation in the war, Russell Weigley, *The American Way of War* (1973), and Edward M. Coffman, *The War to End All Wars* (1968), provide useful introductions. They can be supplemented by David F. Trask, *The AEF and Coalition War-Making, 1917–1918* (1993); and A. E. Barbeau and Florette Henri, *The Unknown Soldiers: Black Troops in World War I* (1974). John Whiteclay Chambers II, *To Raise an Army* (1987), covers the draft. Allan Brandt, *No Magic Bullet* (1985), discusses anti–venereal disease campaigns, and Mary E. Odem, *Delinquent Daughters* (1995), looks at attempts to control sexuality during the war years. Paul Chapman, *Schools as Sorters* (1988), describes the intelligence-testing movement.

War on the Home Front

Robert D. Cuff, *The War Industries Board: Business-Government Relations during World War I* (1973), provides an excellent case study of mobilization for war. See also Stephen Skowronek, *Building a New American State: The Expansion of National Administrative Capacities, 1877–1920* (1982). Valerie Jean Conner, *The National War Labor Board* (1983), and Melvyn Dubofsky, *The State and Labor in Modern America* (1994), cover federal policies toward labor. Jordan Schwarz, *The Speculator* (1981), is an insightful biography of Bernard Baruch.

Maurine Greenwald, *Women, War, and Work* (1980), and Barbara Steinson, *American Women's Activism in World War I* (1982), provide good overviews of women's wartime experiences. Ellen Carol DuBois, *Harriet Stanton Blatch and the Winning of Woman's Suffrage* (1997); and Christine A. Lunardini, *From Equal Suffrage to Equal Rights: Alice Paul and the National Woman's Party, 1910–1928* (1986), cover the final stages of the woman suffrage campaign. On the peace movement, see C. Roland Marchand, *The American Peace Movement and Social Reform, 1898–1918* (1973); Charles Chatfield, *For Peace and Justice: Pacifism in America, 1914–1941* (1971); and Charles DeBenedetti, *Origins of the Modern Peace Movement* (1978).

Efforts to promote national unity are covered in Stephen Vaughan, *Holding Fast the Inner Lines: Democracy, Nationalism, and the CPI* (1980). For George Creel's story, see his *How We Advertised America* (1920) and *Rebel at Large* (1947). On free speech, see Richard Polenberg, *Fighting Faiths: The Abrams Case, the Supreme Court, and Free Speech* (1987). For the experiences of Mexican Americans, see David C. Gutierrez, *Walls and Mirrors: Mexican Americans, Mexican Immigrants and the Politics of Ethnicity* (1995); and George Sanchez, *Becoming Mexican American* (1993).

An Unsettled Peace, 1919–1920

On Wilson's diplomacy, see Thomas Knock, *To End All Wars: Woodrow Wilson and the Quest for a New World Order* (1992); Lloyd Ambrosius, *Woodrow Wilson and the American Diplomatic Tradition* (1987); Arthur Walworth, *Wilson and the Peacemakers* (1986); and N. Gordon Levin Jr., *Woodrow Wilson and World Politics* (1968). For more on Versailles and the League of Nations, see Ralph A. Stone, *The Irreconcilables: The Fight against the League of Nations* (1970), and Arno J. Mayer, *Politics and Diplomacy of Peacemaking: Containment and Counter Revolution at Versailles* (1967). See also William Widenor, *Henry Cabot Lodge and the Search for an American Foreign Policy* (1980), and Ronald Steel, *Walter Lippmann and the American Century* (1980). On American intervention in Russia, see David Foglesong, *America's Secret War against Bolshevism: U.S. Intervention in the Russian Civil War, 1917–1920* (1995); John L. Gaddis, *Russia, the Soviet Union, and the United States* (1978); and Peter Filene, *Americans and the Soviet Experiment, 1917–1933* (1967).

Robert K. Murray, *The Red Scare* (1955), summarizes the antiradicalism of the postwar period. See also John Higham, *Strangers in the Land* (1955); Burl Noggle, *Into the Twenties* (1974); and William D. Miller, *Pretty Bubbles in the Air: America in 1919* (1991). David Brody, *Labor in Crisis* (1965), describes the steel strike of 1919. On race relations, see Joe William Trotter Jr., ed., *The Great Migration in Historical Perspective* (1991); James R. Grossman, *Land of Hope: Chicago, Black Southerners, and the Great Migration* (1989); William M. Tuttle Jr., *Race Riot: Chicago in the Red Summer of 1919* (1970); Robert V. Haynes, *A Night of Violence: The Houston Riot of 1917* (1976); and Elliot M. Rudwick, *Race Riot at East St. Louis, July 2, 1917* (1964). For an introduction to the Sacco and Vanzetti case, see Louis Joughin and Edmund Morgan, *The Legacy of Sacco and Vanzetti* (1948), and Roberta Strauss Feuerlicht, *Justice Crucified* (1977).

LOOK WHO'S HERE!

WORDS BY
HAROLD ADAMSON
MUSIC BY
BURTON LANE

25¢

Famous Music
CORPORATION
719 SEVENTH AVENUE · · · NEW YORK

MADE IN U.S.A.

Modern Times: The 1920s

I N 1924 THE sociologists Robert Lynd and Helen Merrell Lynd arrived in Muncie, Indiana, to study the life of a small American city. They observed how the citizens of Middletown (the fictional name they gave the city, which they chose for its middle-of-the-road quality) made their living, maintained their homes, educated their children, practiced religion, organized community activities, and spent their leisure time. As the Lynds' fieldwork proceeded, they were struck by how much had changed over the past thirty-five years—the actual lifetime of many Middletown residents. When *Middletown* was published in 1929, this "study in modern American culture" became an unexpected best seller. Americans wanted to better understand the forces that were transforming their society.

The transformation to a modern society had begun with World War I. Participation in the war had made the United States a major player in the world economy, and the foundations of large-scale corporate enterprise and a modern state had been firmly established. The 1920s, rather than World War I, however, were the watershed in the development of a mass national culture. Only then did the Protestant work ethic and the traditional values of self-denial and frugality begin to give way to a fascination with consumption, leisure, and self-realization that is the essence of modern American culture. Despite ambivalence toward these changes, the patterns that appeared during the "new era" of the 1920s quickly became part of American life. In economic organization, political outlook, and cultural values, the 1920s have more in common with the United States today than with the industrializing America of the late nineteenth century.

"Look Who's Here!"
This sheet music from the 1920s depicts the flapper, prosperity, and big-time athletics—all central images of the decade called the Roaring Twenties.
Picture Research Consultants & Archives.

As movies, radio, advertising, and mass production industries helped to transform the country into a modern, cosmopolitan nation, many Americans welcomed these changes as exciting evidence of progress. But others were uneasy. Flappers dancing to jazz, youthful sexual experimentation in the backseat of a Ford, hints of a decline in religious values—these harbingers of a new era worried more tradition-minded folk. In the nation's cities, the powerful presence of immigrants and African Americans suggested the waning of white Protestant cultural dominance. Beneath the clichéd images of the "Roaring Twenties" were deeply felt tensions that surfaced in conflicts over immigration, religion, Prohibition, and race relations.

The Business-Government Partnership of the 1920s

——————★——————

The business-government partnership accelerated by World War I continued to expand on an informal basis throughout the 1920s. As the *Wall Street Journal* enthusiastically proclaimed, "Never before, here or anywhere else, has a government been so completely fused with business." From 1922 to 1929 the nation's prosperity seemed to confirm the economy's ability to regulate itself with minimal government intervention. Gone, or at least submerged, was the reform impulse of the Progressive Era. Business leaders were no longer seen as villains but as respected public figures. President Warren Harding captured the prevailing political mood when he offered the American public "not heroics but healing, not nostrums but normalcy."

The Economy

America's transition from a wartime to a peacetime economy was not smooth. The worst problem was runaway inflation: prices jumped by one-third in 1919, accompanied by feverish economic activity. Federal efforts to halt inflation through spending cuts and a contraction of the supply of credit produced the recession of 1920–1921, the sharpest short-term downturn the United States had ever faced. Unemployment reached 10 percent, and foreign trade dropped by almost half as European nations resumed production after the disruptions of war. Prices fell so dramatically—by more than 20 percent—that much of the inflation of World War I was wiped out.

The recession lasted only a short time. By 1922 the economy began a recovery that continued with only brief interruptions until 1929. Unemployment hovered around 3 or 4 percent, and inflation stayed low. Between

1922 and 1929 the gross national product grew from $74.1 billion to $103.1 billion, approximately 40 percent. Per capita income rose from $641 in 1921 to $847 in 1929, giving the United States the highest standard of living in the world. Soon the federal government was recording a budget surplus. This economic expansion provided the backdrop for the partnership between business and government that flourished in the 1920s.

An abundance of new consumer products, particularly the automobile, stimulated recovery and prosperity. Manufacturing output expanded by 64 percent, as industries churned out cars, appliances, chemicals,

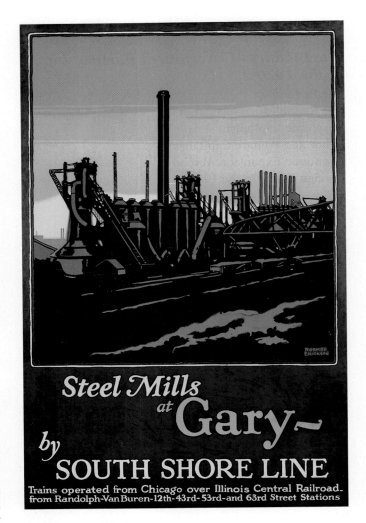

Modern Industry
This highly stylized 1928 poster promotes the steel mills of Gary, Indiana, as a tourist attraction on par with Yellowstone or Yosemite. The Gary that steelworkers experienced was more likely to be full of soot, grime, and hard work than recreation or beauty. The sky in Gary was often similar in color to that eerie shade of orange shown in the poster due to the high levels of pollution generated by the steel mills.
Chicago Historical Society.

electricity, radios, aircraft, and movies. The value of new construction increased from $6 billion in 1921 to $12 billion in 1927. Behind the growth lay new management and mass-production techniques, many of which had been developed during the war years, which resulted in a 40 percent increase in workers' productivity. High employment rates combined with low inflation enhanced the spending power of many American consumers, especially skilled workers and members of the middle class.

The booming economy, however, had some weaknesses. Income distribution reflected significant disparity: 5 percent of the nation's families received one-third of all income. In addition, not all industries were healthy. Agriculture never fully recovered from the recession of 1920–1921. During the inflationary period of 1914–1920, farmers had borrowed heavily to finance mortgages and equipment in response to government incentives, increased demand, and rising prices. When the war ended, European countries resumed agricultural production, glutting the world market. The price of wheat dropped 40 percent as the government withdrew wartime price supports. Corn prices fell 32 percent and hog prices 50 percent. Farmers' share of national income plummeted from 16 percent in 1919 to 8.8 percent at the end of the 1920s.

Farmers were not the only ones whose income plunged: certain "sick industries," such as coal and textiles, missed out on the prosperity of the 1920s. These industries, which had expanded in response to wartime demands, now faced overcapacity or unprofitability and grew sluggishly, if at all, during the 1920s. This underside of economic life would play a role in the coming of the Great Depression of the 1930s.

The Republican Ascendancy

Except for Woodrow Wilson's two terms, the presidency had been controlled by the Republican Party since 1896. When Wilson's progressive coalition floundered in 1918, the Republicans had a chance to regain the White House. With the ailing Wilson out of the picture, in 1920 the Democrats nominated Governor James M. Cox of Ohio, with Assistant Secretary of the Navy Franklin D. Roosevelt as the candidate for vice-president. The Democratic platform called for ratification of U.S. participation in the League of Nations and a continuation of Wilsonian progressivism. The Republicans, led by Warren G. Harding and Calvin Coolidge, promised a return to "normalcy," which meant a strong probusiness stance and conservative cultural values. Hardly a towering national figure, Harding had built an uninspiring record in Ohio politics before winning election to the U.S. Senate in 1914. With a Republican victory almost a certainty in 1920, party leaders wanted a candidate they could dominate. Genial, loyal, and

mediocre, "Uncle Warren" filled the bill. Harding and Coolidge won in a landslide, marking the beginning of a Republican dominance that would last until 1932.

Central to what Republicans termed the *New Era* was business-government cooperation. Although Republican administrations generally opposed expanding state power to promote progressive reforms, they did use federal policy and power to assist corporations. Thus, Harding's secretary of the Treasury, financier Andrew W. Mellon, engineered a tax cut that undercut the wartime Revenue Acts, benefiting wealthy individuals and corporations. The Republican-dominated Federal Trade Commission (FTC) for the most part ignored antitrust laws rather than using federal power to police industry. In this the FTC followed the lead of the Supreme Court, which in 1920 had dismissed the long-pending antitrust case against U.S. Steel, ruling that bigness in business was not against the law as long as some competition remained.

Perhaps the best example of government-business cooperation emerged in the Department of Commerce, headed by Herbert Hoover, a firm believer in what historian Ellis Hawley has called the "associative state." Hoover thought that with government assistance, businessmen would work in behalf of the public interest, thereby benefiting the entire country. Under Hoover the Commerce department expanded dramatically, offering new services like the compilation and distribution of trade and production statistics to American business. It also assisted private trade associations, which brought together leading business executives from a single industry such as mining or railroads, in their efforts to make business and commerce more efficient, such as through product standardization and wage and price controls.

Unfortunately, not all government-business cooperation was as high-minded as Hoover had anticipated. Harding was an honest man, but some of his political associates had low ethical standards. When Harding died suddenly in San Francisco in August 1923 of a heart attack, evidence of widespread fraud and corruption in his administration had just started to come to light. A particularly damaging scandal concerned the government's secret leasing of oil reserves in Teapot Dome, Wyoming, and Elk Hills, California, to private companies without prior competitive bidding. Secretary of the Interior Albert Fall was eventually convicted of taking $300,000 in bribes, and became the first cabinet officer in American history to serve a prison sentence.

After Harding's death the taciturn vice-president, Calvin Coolidge, moved into the White House. In contrast to his predecessor's political cronyism and outgoing style, Coolidge personified moral rectitude. As vice-president, "Silent Cal" often sat through official functions without uttering a word. A dinner partner once challenged him by saying, "Mr. Coolidge, I've made a rather sizable bet with my friends that I can get you to speak three words this evening." Responded Coolidge icily, "You lose." Like Harding, Coolidge backed business and believed in limited government; he was said to perform all his presidential duties in four hours a day. Coolidge's image of unimpeachable morality reassured voters in the wake of the Harding scandals, and he soon announced that he would run for president in 1924.

The 1924 Election. When the Democrats gathered that July in the sweltering heat of New York City, they faced a divided party. The party drew its support mainly from the South and from northern urban political machines like Tammany Hall in New York, and the two constituencies' interests often collided. In 1924 the main disagreements were over Prohibition, immigration restriction, and, most serious, the mounting power of the Ku Klux Klan. The resolutions committee deadlocked over whether the party should condemn the racist and anti-immigrant Klan, eventually reaching a weak compromise that affirmed its general opposition to "any effort to arouse religious or racial dissension."

The convention was the first to be broadcast live on national radio, and it lasted seventeen days, prompting the humorist Will Rogers to say, "This thing has got to come to an end. New York invited you people here as

The Election of 1924
President Coolidge had a reputation for being a man of few words, but evidently he found enough to fill this 78-rpm phonograph record, which was distributed during his campaign.
Collection of Janice L. and David J. Frent.

guests, not to live." The convention became hopelessly deadlocked between Alfred E. Smith of New York, who had the support of northern urban politicians, and William G. McAdoo of California, Wilson's secretary of the Treasury (and son-in-law), the western and southern choice. McAdoo also had the backing of a large faction of Klan members, causing opponents to jeer "Ku, Ku, McAdoo." After 103 ballots the delegates compromised on John W. Davis, a Wall Street lawyer who had served as a West Virginia congressman and an ambassador to Great Britain. To attract rural voters the Democrats chose as their vice-presidential candidate Governor Charles W. Bryan of Nebraska, the brother of three-time presidential candidate William Jennings Bryan.

The 1924 campaign also featured a third-party challenge by Senator Robert M. La Follette of Wisconsin, who ran on the Progressive Party ticket. La Follette's candidacy mobilized reformers and labor leaders as well as disgruntled farmers in an effort to reinvigorate the reform movement both parties had abandoned. The Progressive Party platform called for nationalization of railroads, public ownership of utilities, and the right of Congress to overrule Supreme Court decisions. It also favored the election of the president directly by the voters rather than by means of the electoral college.

The Republicans won an impressive victory, with Coolidge receiving 15.7 million popular votes to 8.4 million for Davis and winning decisively in the electoral college. La Follette got almost 5 million popular votes but carried only Wisconsin in the electoral college. In the end the Democrats were unable to mount an effective challenge to their more popular and better-financed Republican rivals, whose strength came chiefly from the native-born Protestant middle class, augmented by small business people, skilled workers, farmers, northern blacks, and wealthy industrialists. Until the Democrats could overcome their sectional and cultural divisions and build an effective national organization to rival that of the Republicans, they would remain a minority party.

Perhaps an even more significant aspect of the 1924 election than its outcome was the low voter turnout. Only 52 percent of the electorate voted, compared with the more than 70 percent who had regularly voted in presidential elections in the late nineteenth century. The nation's newly enfranchised women were not to blame, however: the long-term drop in voting by men, not apathy among women, was responsible for the decline.

Women in Politics. Instead of resting after their suffrage victory, women increased their political activism in the 1920s. African American women struggled for voting rights in the Jim Crow South and pushed unsuccessfully for a federal anti-lynching law. Many women tried to break into party politics, but Republicans and Democrats granted them only token positions on party committees. Political officeholding remained a "widow's game": about two-thirds of the women in Congress had been appointed to finish their late husbands' terms.

Women were more influential as lobbyists. The Women's Joint Congressional Committee, a Washington-based coalition of ten major women's organizations including the newly formed League of Women Voters, lobbied for reform legislation. Its major accomplishment was the passage in 1921 of the Sheppard-Towner Federal Maternity and Infancy Act, the nation's first federally funded health care program. In an attempt to reduce the high rate of death associated with childbirth, Congress appropriated $1.25 million for well-baby clinics, educational programs, and visiting-nurse projects. Rural women were especially grateful for this government aid and eagerly sought information from government agencies such as the Children's Bureau, which administered the program (see American Voices, "Women Write the Children's Bureau," p. 742).

The Sheppard-Towner bill had passed in part because politicians feared that if it didn't, women would vote them out of office. As one supporter noted, "If the members could have voted in the cloak room, it would have been killed." Once politicians realized that women did not vote as a bloc, they stopped listening so intently to the women's lobby. Instead they listened to other powerful lobbying groups, such as the American Medical Association, which had strenuously objected to the state being involved in health care at all. In 1929 Congress cut off Sheppard-Towner's funding.

The roadblocks that women activists faced were part of a broader public antipathy to ambitious reform. Although some states—such as New York, where an urban liberalism was coalescing under leaders like Al Smith—did enact legislation that promoted workmen's compensation, public health, and conservation, on the national level reforms that would have strengthened federal power made little headway. After years of progressive reforms and an expanded presence in World War I, many Americans were unenthusiastic about increased taxation or more governmental bureaucracy. The Red Scare had given ammunition to opponents of reform by making it easy to claim that legislation calling for governmental activism was the first step toward Bolshevism. Finally, the general prosperity of the 1920s hampered the reform spirit. With a strong economy, the Republican policy of an informal partnership between business and government seemed to work and made reforms regulating corporations and the economy seem unnecessary and even potentially harmful.

Corporate Capitalism

The 1920s saw the triumph of the management revolution that had been reshaping American business since the late nineteenth century (see Chapter 17). Large-scale corporate organizations with bureaucratic structures of authority replaced family-run businesses. There were more mergers in the 1920s than at any time since the heyday of combinations in the 1880s and 1890s; the largest number occurred in rapidly growing industries such as chemicals, electrical appliances and machinery, and automobiles. By 1930 the 200 largest corporations controlled almost half the nonbanking corporate wealth in the United States. It was rare for one corporation to monopolize an entire industry; instead, *oligopolies* (in which a few large producers controlled an industry) became the norm, such as in auto manufacturing, oil refining, and steelmaking. The nation's financial institutions expanded and consolidated along with its corporations. Total bank assets rose dramatically as mergers between Wall Street banks enhanced New York's role as the financial center of the world. In 1929 almost half the nation's banking resources were controlled by 1 percent, or 250, of American banks.

By 1920 many American industries, especially in manufacturing, had modern organizational structures. The multi-unit enterprise coordinated production and distribution through divisions organized by functions, such as sales, operations, and investment. Alfred P. Sloan Jr., an engineer and midlevel manager at General Motors in the 1920s, refined this structure by relieving top management of the day-to-day control of production. This shift in responsibility freed management to concentrate on long-range planning while autonomous, integrated divisions met short-range production goals. General Motors' innovative structure set the pattern for large American companies in the 1920s and 1930s and was later adopted by companies worldwide. In addition, corporations greatly increased their commitment to research and development, using current earnings to create future profits. By 1927 more than a thousand corporations had set up independent research programs, among them Bell Laboratories, the research arm of the American Telephone and Telegraph Company, which was formally incorporated in 1925.

These huge modern corporate structures called for a new breed of employee, the professional manager (nearly always a man, as women found few opportunities in the corporate hierarchy until the 1970s). Increasingly, corporations relied on elite graduate schools of business, such as Wharton and Harvard, to produce managers, consultants, and executives, many of whom had engineering training. The chief executives at General Motors, General Electric, Singer, Du Pont, and Goodyear had all been engineering classmates at the Massachusetts Institute of Technology.

Business leaders enjoyed enormous popularity and respect in the 1920s, their reputations often surpassing those of the era's lackluster politicians. Many politicians and commentators drew parallels between

AMERICAN VOICES

Women Write the Children's Bureau

───────★───────

The Children's Bureau in the Department of Labor was in charge of administering the Sheppard-Towner Act from 1921 to 1929. In addition to setting up clinics and offering correspondence courses, the staff answered letters from anxious mothers, such as the two excerpted here—yet another example of how the state was becoming part of everyday life.

Dear Doctor Sherbon:
You can not imagine how much I have enjoyed the Course. As soon as I received it I lay down and never stopped until I read it through. It is splendid, and if every woman could follow each lesson to the letter there would be less suffering. But how are we going to convince our families that such care is necessary? Of course the children can be taught these things, but the husbands and our mothers think it is foolishness to take such care of ourselves.

Do you think it proper to explain to children where they come from and the science of life? I have told my stepson, age 18, all of these things and how he should take care of himself, and also how he should treat girls and how much suffering there was to childbirth, and I was very much criticized by some of the family.

I must close. I am taking up your valuable time and am losing much time of my own. Thank you for all the help and the good you are doing, not only for myself but others.

Dear Madam:
I took your correspondence course last winter and enjoyed it very much although I have been a mother three times and expect to be again as [I] am pregnant three months now. Maybe you have something for me or that might help me in some way, so [I] thot that I would drop you a line.

We are a poor family and live in western Kansas and [are] heavily in debt, so this ordeal is hard for me at present. But what I would like to ask you is if a poor mother can get any county or state aid. My teeth are badly in need of dental work, and [I have] no money to pay the bill and the doctor bill worries me too. The doctor we have gone to is so high I don't see how we can afford it. We owe $125 in doctor bills in another county . . . and I dread any more until back ones are paid.

Isn't there a law in Kansas that unless a confinement case is obstetrical the limit charge is $15 and if obstetrical the limit is $25? He says he charges $25 for a confinement case and $1.00 mileage which would make a total of $37 for us for doctor bill, besides a nurse or lady to nurse and do the work too. But if you know anything about such things you know that mother and babe are sadly neglected if the nurse has all the house work to do too. . . .

Does the county doctor tend to such cases and look to the community for his money? It looks like we ought to be able to do and care for such things without asking for help, but you know there are just lots and lots of mothers in my fix that just drag along and worry because they have no way of buying the most needy things at such a time and are too proud to find out if there is any way to get help. My husband thinks it's awful to get help in any way besides paying for it, but when I know he is not financially able to help, I don't see why I should suffer if there is any way to help me, as any mother or doctor knows at that time a mother needs the best of care in every way. And it's because I have always had to work too soon after childbirth that I am broken down now.

I will see what I hear from you before going into details any more. Hoping you will not think it too trifling a matter to interest you and will answer me as soon as possible. Yours truly.

───────────

Source: Molly Ladd-Taylor, *Raising a Baby the Government Way: Mothers' Letters to the Children's Bureau, 1915–1932* (New Brunswick, NJ: Rutgers University Press, 1986), 131–132, 136–138.

religious activity and business leadership. President Coolidge solemnly declared, "The man who builds a factory builds a temple. The man who works there worships there." The glorification of business reached a new height in a book called *The Man Nobody Knows* (1924), by the advertising executive Bruce Barton.

The man of the title is Jesus Christ, whom Barton portrays as the founder of modern business: Christ "picked up twelve men from the bottom ranks of business and forged them into an organization that conquered the world." Barton's parable was an instant best seller.

The most respected businessman of the decade was Henry Ford, whose rise from poor farm boy to corporate giant symbolized the values of rural society and American individualism in a rapidly changing world. Ford's automobile factories, especially the gigantic River Rouge plant in suburban Detroit, represented the triumph of mass production. Ironically, this American capitalist hero achieved great popularity in the Soviet Union. At a time when the United States and the Soviet Union had no formal diplomatic relations, Ford sold the Russians 25,000 tractors between 1920 and 1926.

Labor and Welfare Capitalism

Workers shared in the good times of the 1920s, although unskilled African Americans, Mexican Americans, and immigrants participated less fully in the prosperity of the decade. Most members of the working class enjoyed higher wages and a better standard of living. With a shorter workweek (five full days and a half day on Saturday), many workers had more leisure time; large firms such as International Harvester offered employees two weeks of paid vacation a year. But scientific management techniques, such as time-and-motion studies to increase worker efficiency, reduced workers' control over their labor and the work environment. First put forth in 1895 by Frederick W. Taylor, these techniques were not widely implemented until the 1920s.

The 1920s was the heyday of "welfare capitalism," a system of labor relations that stressed management's responsibility for the well-being of its employees. Though tinged with paternalism, this system provided benefits to workers at a time when unemployment compensation and retirement pensions did not exist. Employee security was not, however, the primary concern of those corporate programs, which were established mainly to deter the formation of unions.

Welfare capitalism appeared primarily in the largest, most prosperous firms, such as General Electric, Bethlehem Steel, Goodyear, and International Harvester, which meant that its benefits reached only a minority of American workers. Industrial workers could increase their stake in the company by buying stock below the market price, though only a small minority could actually afford to do so. Some firms subsidized mortgages or contributed to employees' savings funds; others set up insurance and pension plans. Many adopted programs for consultation between management and elected representatives of the workers. These employee representation schemes, another device to avert unionization, were called the *American Plan* in order to establish the idea that unions were un-American. Management's long-term goals included control over the workplace, an open shop (where only nonunion members were employed), and worker loyalty.

Welfare capitalism represented a form of labor relations that was squarely in keeping with the conservative values of the 1920s. It placed the responsibility for economic welfare in the private sector rather than the public sector, avoiding the possibility of government interference. It also satisfied management's desire to reverse the tide of unionization: union membership dropped from 5.1 million in 1920 to 3.6 million in 1929, about 10 percent of the nonagricultural work force. The number of strikes also fell dramatically from the level in 1919. Welfare capitalism seemed to represent the wave of the future in industrial relations.

Economic Expansion Abroad

The power of American corporations also emerged in the international arena. During the 1920s the United States was the most productive country in the world, with an enormous capacity to compete in foreign markets that eagerly desired American consumer products such as radios, telephones, automobiles, and sewing machines. The demand for U.S. capital was just as great. American investment abroad more than doubled between 1919 and 1930; by the end of the 1920s American corporations had invested $15.2 billion in foreign companies. Soon the United States became the world's largest creditor nation, reversing its pre–World War I status and causing a dramatic shift of power in world capital markets away from Europe and toward North America. This American capital sustained the international economic system in the 1920s.

Manufacturers led the way in foreign investment. Electric companies, including General Electric, built new plants in Latin America, China, Japan, and Australia. Ford had major facilities throughout the British Empire, and General Motors took over established automakers such as Vauxhall in England and Opel in Germany. The International Telephone and Telegraph Corporation, founded in 1920, employed 95,000 workers outside the country, more than did any other U.S. company.

Other American companies invested internationally during the 1920s to take advantage of lower production costs or to procure raw materials and supplies, concentrating mainly on Latin America. The three major American meat packers—Swift, Armour, and Wilson—built plants in Argentina to capitalize on low livestock prices there. Fruit growers such as the United Fruit Company established plantations in Costa Rica, Honduras, and Guatemala. American capital ran sugar plantations in Cuba and rubber plantations in the Philippines, Sumatra, and Malaya. The Anaconda Copper Corporation owned Chile's largest copper mine, and Standard Oil of New Jersey led American oil companies in acquiring oil reserves in

Bananas
... a good mixer
with every fruit that grows

Oranges, apples, grapefruit, pineapples, pears, melons, grapes—all these and many others—blend perfectly with bananas. The distinctive flavor of the banana, when added to a fruit cup, a fruit salad, or any fruit combination, brings out the flavor of the other fruits and makes them taste better.

"EAT plenty of fresh fruits" is now an accepted principle of diet—and the mere sight of mellow, luscious bananas is an invitation to serve many delicious and nourishing fruit combinations.

All year round from the tropics... Easter, Fourth of July, Thanksgiving, Christmas—every season, every day—bananas are available. Thanks to the nearness and all-year-round productiveness of the tropics, they always can be had at your grocery or fruit store.

Children crave the temptingly flavored banana instinctively. And it is well that they do, for bananas are one of the most important energy-producing foods. Doctors and dietitians consider the banana not only one of the most *valuable* foods, but also one of the most *easily digested* . . . as beneficial for grown-ups as for children.

Serve bananas with other fruits, with cereals, with milk or cream . . . or serve them plain. But always be sure they are fully ripe (generously flecked with brown spots). If they are not at the proper stage of ripeness when you buy them, let them ripen at room temperature. Never place them in the ice-box.

"*Ripe bananas are good for little children.*"

UNIFRUIT BANANAS
Reg. U. S. Pat. Off.
A United Fruit Company Product
Imported and Distributed by Fruit Dispatch Company
17 Battery Place, New York, N. Y.

American Companies Abroad
United Fruit was one of the many American companies that found opportunities for investment in South America in the 1920s. Bananas were such a new and exotic fruit that advertisements had to tell consumers such facts as how to tell when bananas are ripe and never to put them in the icebox.
Duke University Library, Special Collections.

Mexico and Venezuela. (American involvement in the oil-rich Persian Gulf became significant only after World War II.)

American banks supported U.S. enterprises abroad, especially in Europe. European countries, particularly Germany, needed private American capital to finance economic recovery after World War I. Germany had to rebuild its economy and pay reparations to the Allies; Britain and France had to repay wartime loans. As late as 1930 the Allies still owed the United States $4.3 billion. American political leaders, responding to voters' disenchantment with the cost of the nation's participation in the war, rigidly demanded payment. Referring to the European nations, President Coolidge scoffed, "They hired the money, didn't they?"

European countries had trouble repaying their debts in part because the United States maintained high protective tariffs against foreign-made goods. The Fordney-McCumber Tariff of 1922 and the Hawley-Smoot Tariff of 1930 advanced the long-standing Republican policy of protectionism and economic nationalism. Most American manufacturers favored those high tariffs because they believed that foreign competition would reduce their profits. But the difficulty of selling goods in the United States made it harder for European nations to pay off their debts in dollars.

In 1924, at the prodding of the United States, the nations of France, Great Britain, and Germany joined with the United States in a plan to improve and promote European financial stability. The Dawes Plan (named for Charles G. Dawes, a Chicago banker who negotiated the agreement) offered substantial loans to Germany and a reduction in the amount of reparations owed to the Allies. But the Dawes Plan did not provide a permanent solution. The international economic system was inherently unstable. It depended on the flow of American capital to Germany, reparations payments from Germany to the Allies, and the repayment of debts to the United States. If the flow of capital from the United States were to slow or stop, the world financial structure might collapse.

Foreign Policy in the 1920s

American efforts to stabilize the international economy belie the common view of U.S. foreign affairs in the interwar period as isolationist—as representing a time when the United States, disillusioned after World War I, willfully retreated from involvement in the rest of the world. In fact, the United States played an active role in global affairs during this period. Economic expansion into new markets was a major component of the prosperity of the 1920s, and the United States ardently sought a peaceful and stable world order to facilitate American investments in Latin American, European, and Pacific Rim markets. This expansion abroad, which was a continuation of Taft's policy of Dollar Diplomacy (see Chapter 21), was warmly supported by the appropriate agencies of the federal government, such as the State and Commerce departments. There was little popular or political support, however, for entangling diplomatic commitments to allies, European or otherwise.

In the 1920s the United States continued its quest for peaceful ways to dominate the Western Hemisphere economically and diplomatically, but it retreated slightly from military intervention in Latin America. The United States withdrew troops from the Dominican Republic in 1924 but maintained military forces in Nicaragua almost continuously from 1912 to 1933. American troops also occupied Haiti from 1915 to 1934. Relations with Mexico remained tense as a legacy of U.S. intervention during the Mexican Revolution.

Since the United States never joined the League of Nations or the Court of International Justice (the World Court), international cooperation had to come through other forums. The Washington Conference of 1921 represented a milestone in the history of disarmament and the fulfillment of one of Woodrow Wilson's goals. By placing limits on naval expansion, policy makers hoped to encourage stability in areas such as East Asia and to protect the fragile postwar world economy from excessive spending on arms. A hidden agenda was to contain Japan, whose expansionist tendencies were already regarded as threatening two decades before the outbreak of World War II.

Led by Secretary of State Charles Evans Hughes, the three leading naval powers—Britain, the United States, and Japan—joined other countries in agreeing to halt construction of large battleships for ten years and maintain current tonnage among Britain, the United States, Japan, Italy, and France. The conferees even agreed to scrap some existing warships, leading one commentator to exclaim that in a thirty-five-minute speech the secretary of state had sunk "more ships than all the admirals of the world have sunk in a cycle of centuries." Not until the 1980s would the world see another such concerted effort to disarm.

In a similar spirit of international cooperation, the United States joined other nations in condemning militarism through the Kellogg-Briand Pact, named for its main drafters: the French foreign minister, Aristide Briand, and Coolidge's secretary of state, Frank Kellogg. Fifteen nations signed the pact in Paris in 1928, with forty-eight more approving it later. Peace groups in the United States such as the Women's International League for Peace and Freedom and the Conference on the Cause and Cure of War enthusiastically supported the pact, and the U.S. Senate ratified it 85 to 1. Yet critics claimed that it lacked enforcement machinery, calling it little more than an "international kiss." For many who abhorred war, however, the pact's broad moral statement was an important contribution to the maintenance of peace.

In the end, fervent hopes and pious declarations were no cure for the massive economic, political, and territorial problems that World War I had left in its wake. The United States vacillated, as it would in the 1930s, between wanting to play a larger role in world affairs and fearing that treaties and responsibilities would limit its ability to act unilaterally or draw the country into another world war. Diplomatic efforts ultimately proved inadequate to resolve the mounting crises of the interwar years; but rather than criticize such initiatives as naive or misguided, it is better to see them as honest but ultimately inadequate efforts to find a will to peace.

A New National Culture

The 1920s represented an important watershed in the development of a mass national culture. A new emphasis on leisure, consumption, and amusement characterized the modern era, although its benefits remained most accessible to the white middle class. Automobiles, paved roads, the parcel post service, movies, radios, telephones, mass-circulation magazines, brand names, and chain stores—all these linked mill towns in the southern Piedmont, rural outposts on the Oklahoma plains, and ethnic enclaves on the coasts in an expanding web of national experience. In fact, with the exportation of automobiles, radios, and movies to consumers throughout the world, the American experience became a global model.

Consumption and Advertising

In homes across the country in the 1920s, Americans sat down to a breakfast of Kellogg's corn flakes and toast from a General Electric toaster. They got into a Ford Model T to go about their business, perhaps shopping

The Amazing Talking Machine
The Victrola, or phonograph, brought music and entertainment into the homes of many Americans in the 1920s. Italian tenor Enrico Caruso was one of the first opera singers to master this new medium, broadening his appeal beyond opera houses and concert halls through his extensive recordings.
Leslie's, December 18, 1920/Picture Research Consultants & Archives.

at one of the chain stores, such as Safeway and A & P, that had sprung up across the country. In the evening the family gathered to listen to radio programs such as "Great Moments in History" and "True Story" or to read the latest issue of the *Saturday Evening Post, Reader's Digest,* or *Collier's.* On weekends they might hop in the car to see the latest Charlie Chaplin film at the local movie theater. Millions of Americans, in other words, now shared the same daily experiences.

The 1920s was a critical decade in the development of the American consumer society. Although not every family participated in the new life-style, consumption became a cultural ideal for most of the middle class, often providing the criterion for judging self-worth that had once been supplied by character, religion, and social standing. Spending money on more and better possessions became a form of self-fulfillment, a gratification of personal needs. Yet participation in commercial mass culture did not necessarily mean a total conversion to

American middle-class values. For example, buying a Victrola or a radio on credit could have been a way for Italian immigrants to keep their culture alive by listening to the opera singer Enrico Caruso. The historian Lizabeth Cohen concluded that "Chicago's ethnic workers were not transformed into more Americanized, middle-class people by the objects they consumed. Buying an electric vacuum cleaner did not turn Josef Dobrowolski into *True Story*'s Jim Smith."

The unequal distribution of income limited many consumers' ability to buy the enticing new products, however. At the height of prosperity in the 1920s, about 65 percent of America's families had an income of less than $2,000 a year, which barely supported a decent living standard. The average family income in the bottom 40 percent of the population was $725. Of that amount, a family spent about $290 a year for food, $190 for housing, and $110 for clothing, leaving only $135 for everything else, including medical expenses and emergencies.

Retailers and automobile manufacturers addressed this situation by selling on the installment plan. In those days, "buy now, pay later" was a revolutionary concept. Before World War I most urban families paid cash for everything except a house, but in the 1920s the automobile became such an object of desire that consumers put aside their fears of buying "on time." In 1927 two-thirds of the cars in the United States were being paid for on the installment plan. Once people saw how easy it was to finance a car, they bought radios, refrigerators, and sewing machines on credit. "A dollar down and a dollar forever," a cynic remarked. By 1929 banks, finance companies, credit unions, and other institutions were lending consumers over $7 billion a year, and consumer lending had become the tenth largest business in the United States.

Many of the new products were household appliances, made feasible by the rapid electrification that had reached 85 percent of American nonfarm households by 1930. Irons and vacuum cleaners were the most popular appliances, followed by phonographs, sewing machines, and washing machines. Radios, whose production increased twenty-five-fold in the 1920s, sold for around $75. One of the most expensive items was a refrigerator, which cost $900 at the beginning of the decade. Technological improvements soon brought the price down to $180, but many families still had to make do with an old-fashioned icebox, which supplied cooling through blocks of ice delivered to the house.

Because much of the new technology was concentrated in the home, it had a dramatic impact on women's lives. Despite enfranchisement and participation in the work force, the primary role for most women remained that of housewife. Electric appliances made housewives' chores less arduous: plugging in an electric iron was far easier than heating an iron on the stove; using a vacuum cleaner was quicker and easier than wielding a broom and a rug beater. Paradoxically, however, the time women spent on housework did not decline. More middle-class women began to do their own housework and laundry as electric servants replaced human ones. Technology also raised standards of cleanliness so that a man could wear a clean shirt every day instead of just on Sunday, and a house could be vacuumed daily rather than swept weekly.

Few of the new consumer products could be considered necessities, so the advertising industry spent billions of dollars (in 1929 an average of $15 annually on every man, woman, and child in the United States) to entice consumers to buy automobiles, cigarettes, radios, and refrigerators. Advertisements appealed to people's social aspirations by projecting images of successful and elegant sophisticates who smoked a certain brand of cigarettes or drove a recognizable make of car. Ad writers also sold products by preying on people's insecurities, coming up with a variety of socially unacceptable "diseases," including "office hips," "ashtray breath," and the dreaded "BO" (body odor). After the term *halitosis* was discovered in a British medical journal, many consumers rushed out to buy Listerine mouthwash. Advertising became a big business in the 1920s, accounting for 3 percent of the gross national product, comparable to its share after World War II. Yet American consumers were not passive victims of advertisers who manipulated their every whim: America gloried in its role as the world's first mass-consumption economy.

Many of these cultural images were embodied in the flapper, the media version of the emancipated woman of the 1920s. (The term originated with

The Flapper
The flapper phenomenon was not limited to Anglos. This 1921 photograph of a young Mexican American woman named Luisa Ronstadt Espinel shows how American fads and fashions reached into Latino communities across the country.
Arizona Historical Society.

women's fad of leaving galoshes unbuckled, which made them flap.) With her slim, boyish figure, bobbed hair, short skirt, and rolled-down silk stockings, the flapper symbolized the personal freedom trumpeted by movies, advertisements, and other elements of the emerging mass culture. Neither maternal nor wifely, the flapper wore makeup (previously assumed to be a sign of sexual availability in lower-class women) and lit up cigarettes in public, a shocking affront to ladylike decency. Like so many cultural icons, the flapper represented only a tiny minority of women. Yet the image mass-marketed the belief in women's postsuffrage emancipation.

The Automobile Culture

No possession typified the new consumer culture of the 1920s better than the automobile. "Why on earth do you need to study what's changing this country?" a resident of Muncie, Indiana, asked the sociologists Robert and Helen Lynd. "I can tell you what's happening in just four letters: A-U-T-O!" Another Middletowner volunteered, "We'd rather do without clothes than give up the car."

The showpiece of modern capitalism and the ultimate consumer toy, the automobile revolutionized the way Americans spent their money and leisure time. The isolation of rural life broke down in the wake of the automobile. New phrases such as "filling station" (or, as they were known west of the Rockies, "service stations") entered the nation's vocabulary. The automobile even affected crime, providing gangsters with a "getaway car" and the possibility of "taking someone for a ride." Cars touched so many aspects of American life that the word *automobility* was coined to describe their impact on production methods, the landscape, and American values.

The mass production of cars helped to stimulate the prosperity of the 1920s. Before the introduction of the moving assembly line in 1913, it took Ford workers twelve and a half hours to assemble one auto; it took only ninety-three minutes on an assembly line. In 1927 Ford produced a car every twenty-four seconds. Car sales climbed from 1.5 million in 1921 to 5 million in 1929, when Americans spent $2.58 billion on new and used cars. By the end of the decade Americans owned about 80 percent of all the automobiles in the entire world, an average of one car for every five people.

The success of the auto industry had a ripple effect on the American economy. In 1929, 3.7 million workers directly or indirectly owed their jobs to the automobile. Auto production stimulated the steel, petroleum, chemical, rubber, and glass industries. Total U.S. demand for oil, mainly in the form of gaso-

All in a Day's Work
Parked in the testing ground at Ford's huge River Rouge plant in Dearborn, Michigan, sit 1,000 assembled chassis, a single day's production.
Henry Ford Museum and Greenfield Village.

line, multiplied two and a half times between 1919 and 1929, and domestic oil production expanded to meet the need. (The United States was the world's chief supplier of oil in the 1920s.) The advertising industry grew along with the automobile; cars and cigarettes were two of the most heavily marketed products of the decade. Highway construction became a billion-dollar-a-year enterprise financed by federal subsidies and state gasoline taxes. Car ownership also spurred the growth of suburbs, contributed to real estate speculation, and spawned the first shopping center, Country Club Plaza, in Kansas City in 1924. Not even the deaths of 25,000 people a year in traffic accidents, 70 percent of them pedestrians, could dampen America's passion for the automobile.

Nowhere was this more obvious than in the way Americans spent their leisure time. They took to the roads, becoming a nation of tourists. The American Automobile Association, founded in 1902, reported that

Fourth of July at the Beach
Nantasket Beach became a favorite outing for Bostonians during the 1920s, and one of
the most popular ways to get there was by car. After a day lounging at the beach and
sampling the nearby amusements, families must have had trouble remembering where
they parked their cars when they first arrived.
Archive Photos/Hirz.

in 1929 about 45 million people—almost one-third of
the population—took vacations by automobile. People
preferred the freedom of automobiles to the rigid
timetables and predetermined routes of trains. With
improved roads, motorists could average more than
45 miles an hour on their way to the "autocamps" and
tourist cabins that were the forerunners of motels.

Like movies and other products of the new mass
culture, cars changed the dating patterns of young
Americans. Contrary to many parents' views, premarital sex was not invented in the backseat of a Ford, but
the Model T did indeed offer more privacy and comfort
than did the family living room or the front porch. City
elders in Muncie overreacted by calling automobiles
"prostitution on wheels."

The Model T was the most popular car of the
decade. The Ford Motor Company manufactured over
15 million Model T's between 1908 and 1927. A "Tin
Lizzie," as these dependable cars were called, required a
mechanically inclined driver. The motorist had to hand
crank the car to start it, and keep one hand on the accelerator and the other on the wheel while driving. There
was no gas gauge, and as late as 1919 only about 10 percent of cars had roofs. As for color, Henry Ford intoned,
"The customer can have a Ford any color he wants—so
long as it's black." By the late 1920s a new Model T,
which had cost $1,000 in 1908, sold for only $295.

Consumers eventually became discontented with
the plain Model T, and Ford faced stiff competition from
General Motors (GM). GM's five automobile divisions

turned out cars for specialized markets and introduced the concept of "trading up." The luxury Cadillac cost the most and had the lowest volume of sales; the Chevrolet cost the least and had the highest volume of sales; Oldsmobile, Pontiac, and Buick were geared to incomes in between. GM cars also featured self-starters and foot accelerators. Henry Ford finally bowed to consumer demands when he introduced the Model A in 1927. More than a million New Yorkers visited the Ford showroom during the five days after the new model was unveiled. At prices ranging from $495 to $570, the Model A fulfilled consumers' demands for different styles, more colors, and greater comfort, and helped make the automobile a permanent part of American culture.

The Movies and Mass Culture

The movie industry, whose growth coincided with America's transformation into a predominantly urban, industrial society, probably did more than anything else to disseminate common values and attitudes throughout the United States. In contrast to Europe, where cinema developed as an avant-garde, highbrow art form, American movies were part of popular culture almost from the start, a mass-entertainment industry that was both democratic and highly lucrative.

The Silent Era. Movies began around the turn of the century in nickelodeons, or theaters where for a nickel the mostly working-class audience could see a one-reel silent film such as *What Demoralized the Barbershop* (1901) and the spectacularly successful *The Great Train Robbery* (1903). Because the films, mostly comedies and melodramas, were silent, they could be understood by immigrants who did not speak English. The new medium grew in popularity and profitability.

During the first years of the twentieth century most films were made in New York City or nearby Fort Lee, New Jersey. After 1910 moviemakers such as D. W. Griffith and Cecil B. De Mille flocked to southern California, which had cheap land, plenty of sunshine, and varied scenery—mountains, deserts, cities, and the Pacific Ocean—within easy reach. Another attraction was Los Angeles's reputation as an anti-union town. Actors flocked to California as well, especially to Hollywood, a rapidly growing suburb of Los Angeles. The early movie stars—the comedians Buster Keaton, Charlie Chaplin, and Harold Lloyd; Mary Pickford (though born in Canada, "America's Sweetheart"); and dashing leading men Douglas Fairbanks, Wallace Reid, and John Gilbert—became national idols. So did Clara Bow, one of the biggest stars, male or female, of the decade (see American Lives, "Clara Bow: The 'It' Girl," pp. 752–753).

The Tramp
Charlie Chaplin did not invent the tragicomic figure of the tramp, but it soon became his screen persona. Chaplin grew up poor in the London slums, but the movies brought him wealth and fame. In 1919 he joined Douglas Fairbanks, Mary Pickford, and D. W. Griffith to form United Artists.
Archive Photos.

Movies quickly outgrew their working-class origins and reached middle-class audiences. D. W. Griffith's epic *Birth of a Nation* (1915), which glorified the Reconstruction-era Ku Klux Klan, helped establish the feature film as popular entertainment. The outbreak of World War I in Europe eliminated competition from Italian and French moviemakers, in part because the chemicals used to produce celluloid for film were needed for the manufacture of gunpowder. By the war's end the United States was making 90 percent of the world's films. For the next several decades Hollywood reigned as the world movie capital, with foreign distribution of Hollywood films stimulating the market for the American material culture so lavishly displayed on the screen.

Movies fed the desires of a mass-consumption economy and set national trends in clothing and hairstyles. They also served as a form of sex education. Rudolph Valentino, best known as the romantic hero of *The Sheik* (1921), epitomized sexual passion on the screen, and the message was not wasted on the nation's youth. "It was directly through the movies that I learned to kiss a girl on her ears, neck, and cheeks, as well as on the mouth," confessed one boy. The sociologist Edward Alsworth Ross concluded that movies made young people more "sex-wise, sex-excited, and sex-absorbed" than they'd been in any previous generation. The impact of the movies on sexual attitudes and morality has remained strong ever since.

The Coming of Sound. Movies were a big business. Power was concentrated in large studios such as United Artists, Paramount, and Metro-Goldwyn-Mayer, which were controlled mainly by Eastern European Jewish immigrants such as Adolph Zukor and Samuel Goldfish (later Goldwyn) who believed deeply in the American dream and used their studios to reinforce core American values. Though most movies were made in Hollywood, the studios were financed by eastern banks, which were more interested (as were the studio heads) in maximum profitability than in artistic expression or creativity. In 1926 the movie industry grossed $1.5 billion a year. The studios controlled distribution as tightly as they did production by establishing chains of theaters, thereby achieving complete vertical integration of the movie industry.

In the late 1920s the major studios borrowed close to $300 million to convert from silent production to "talkies," but the overwhelming success of the new films quickly paid back the investment. Warner Brothers' *The Jazz Singer* (1927), starring Al Jolson, was the first feature-length film to offer sound, and by 1929 all the major studios had completed the changeover to talkies. Although no one had thought of movies as silent until talkies took their place, silent films soon became obsolete.

By the end of the 1920s the nation had almost 23,000 movie theaters, including elaborate palaces built by the studios in major cities. Movie attendance rose from 60 million in 1927 to 90 million in 1930. In two short decades movies had become thoroughly entrenched as the most popular—and probably the most influential—form of the new urban-based mass media.

Jazz. It is perhaps no coincidence that the first talkie was *The Jazz Singer*. Jazz was such a popular part of the new mass culture that the 1920s are often called the Jazz Age. An improvisational style whose notes were (and are still) rarely written down, jazz originated in the dance halls and bordellos of New Orleans's Sto-

ryville quarter around the turn of the century. A synthesis of earlier African American music, such as ragtime and the blues, it also drew on African and European styles. With roots in urban culture, jazz gave black people an outlet for expressing dissent and opposition to mainstream white values, but it also appealed to whites. Phonograph records capturing the spontaneity of jazz were so popular that they boosted the infant recording industry. The interracial appeal of jazz suggested the close, symbiotic relationship between African American and American culture in the 1920s and beyond, and jazz remains one of the most distinctly American art forms.

Most of the early jazz musicians were black. As they left the South, they took jazz to Chicago, New York, Kansas City, Los Angeles, and other cities. Some of the best known were the composer-pianist Ferdinand "Jelly Roll" Morton, the trumpeter Louis Armstrong, the singer Bessie Smith (the "Empress of the Blues"), and composer-bandleader Edward "Duke" Ellington. Soon this uniquely American art form had caught on in Europe, especially in France.

Journalism and Radio. Besides movies and sound recordings, other forms of mass media helped establish national standards of taste and behavior. In 1922 ten magazines claimed a circulation of at least 2.5 million, including the *Saturday Evening Post*, the *Ladies' Home Journal*, and *Good Housekeeping*. Moreover, *Reader's Digest*, *Time*, and the *New Yorker*—still found today in homes across the country—all started publication in the 1920s. Thanks to syndicated columns and features in newspapers, people could read the same articles anywhere in the United States. They could also read the same books, preselected by a board of expert judges for the Book of the Month Club, which was founded in 1926.

Tabloid newspapers—sometimes called jazz journalism—also became part of the national scene. In 1919, just two days before the signing of the Versailles treaty, publisher Joseph Medill Patterson introduced the *New York Illustrated Daily News*. Half the size of a regular newspaper, with bold headlines, large photographs, and short, sensational stories, tabloids were meant to be read quickly—for instance, while riding the subway to work. All the major cities had at least one tabloid by 1932.

The newest instrument of mass culture was truly a child of the 1920s. On November 2, 1920, professional radio broadcasting began when station KDKA in Pittsburgh carried the presidential election returns. By 1929 about 40 percent of the nation's households had a radio. More than 800 stations—most affiliated with the Columbia Broadcasting Service (CBS), formed in 1928, or the National Broadcasting Company (NBC), started in 1926—were on the air. (These corporations would

Clara Bow:
The "It" Girl

———★———

WHEN CLARA BOW, the "It" Girl of the 1920s, was asked to define what "it" meant, she replied, "I ain't real sure." To most fans, "it" was synonymous with sex appeal, but Elinor Glyn, the British writer who coined the phrase, had a more nuanced definition: "To have 'It' the fortunate possessor must have that strange magnetism which attracts both sexes. 'It' is a purely virile quality belonging to a strong character. . . . There must be physical attraction, but beauty is unnecessary. Conceit or selfconsciousness destroys 'It' immediately." Whatever "it" was, when Paramount released a movie in 1927 based on the Elinor Glyn novella of the same name and starring Clara Bow, the film grossed $1 million. Soon Bow was receiving almost 35,000 fan letters a month, many addressed simply to "The 'It' Girl, Hollywood U.S.A." In 1927 she was all of twenty-two years old.

The thin plot of the film hardly seems capable of launching a national obsession. Bow played a department store clerk named Betty Lou Spense who is out to catch her rich, handsome boss. He too is smitten, and when he calls on her in her modest home, he

Twenties Sex Symbol
Clara Bow was not the girl next door, as this seductive film still from *Her Wedding Night* (1930) confirms.
Culver Pictures.

finds her minding a friend's baby. However, he jumps to the mistaken conclusion that she is an unmarried mother and propositions her. She is indignant at the insult, but after several plot twists they resolve their differences. In the final scene they kiss on the store owner's yacht, *Itola,* with the embrace obscuring all but the first two letters of the yacht's name. That's right—IT!

"It" was typical of Hollywood's fascination with flapper themes in the 1920s. On screen and off, the flapper was emancipated, urban, and young, befitting the worship of youth that was characteristic of the 1920s. The flapper was a working girl with money to spend, time on her hands, and a wardrobe of mass-produced fashions, especially short skirts suitable for dancing and dating. On screen she was sensual but not promiscuous, often marrying the male lead at the film's end. The Hollywood stars Colleen Moore and Louise Brooks also played flapper roles.

Before Bow became indelibly known as the "It" Girl, her studio had tried to promote her as the "Brooklyn Bonfire." The name never stuck, but it revealed her background. Clara Bow was born on July 29, 1905, into an extremely poor family in Brooklyn, New York; her mother was mentally unstable, and her father was often unemployed. She dropped out of school during the eighth grade. The only place she found refuge from her grim family life was at the movies. Like many other young girls, Bow decided that she wanted to be an actress.

Her break came when she won a 1921 "Fame and Fortune" beauty contest sponsored by three movie magazines, which helped her land a bit part in *Beyond the Rainbow* (1922). Her scenes ended up on the cutting room floor, but they were restored after she became a star. In 1923 Bow won a Hollywood contract, and by 1924 she had made thirteen films, none memorable. Her roles improved when she signed with Paramount in 1925; her performances in *Dancing Mothers* (1926) and *Mantrap* (1926), two movies with Jazz Age themes, led Elinor Glyn to pronounce that Bow had "it" on the screen.

Clara Bow had an amazing screen presence. On screen she never seemed to stay still. Studio executive B. P. Schulberg called her "the hottest jazz baby in films." A young man who first saw her at age seventeen observed, "I've never taken dope, but it was like a shot of dope when you looked at this girl." The *New York Times* wrote of her performance in *Mantrap,* "She could flirt with a grizzly bear." She had a boyish figure and what one reviewer called "flirts' eyes." She was especially known for her shock of red hair. In the 1920s redheads were thought to be highly sexed. Just as the vamp of the 1910s had dark hair and the typical star of the 1930s was a platinum blonde, the 1920s was the decade of the redhead.

Yet Bow's career lasted less than five years after the success of *It.* Somewhat unstable emotionally, she had several nervous breakdowns. As she once said, "A sex symbol is a heavy load to carry when one is tired, hurt, and bewildered." She was also hurt by scandals in her personal life, including widely publicized affairs with actor Gary Cooper and director Victor Fleming and a legal dispute with a former secretary. Furthermore, like many silent stars, she found the transition to talkies difficult. It was not just her Brooklyn accent—voice lessons could have smoothed that out. But her whole style of acting, which was very emotional and involved constant movement around the set, was not suited to the early days of sound recording, when an actor had to stay close to a stationary microphone to speak dialogue.

In 1931 Bow announced that she was leaving Hollywood to live with Rex Bell, a Nevada rancher whom she married later that year. She returned briefly to make two films before declaring "I've had enough" in 1933. She devoted her time to marriage and the two sons she and Bell had in 1934 and 1938, but her emotional instability made it hard for her to find happiness, and she and Bell eventually separated. She died in Los Angeles in 1965, long before her films had become cult classics. On seeing *It* for the first time in 1987, sixty years after its release, her son said, "If I ever saw Mother, I saw her in that movie. The tremendous facial expression. . . . It brought back so vividly what she was like." But it also reinforced the deep gulf between the on-screen charisma of the "It" Girl and Bow's fragile off-screen persona.

Toward the end of her life Bow reflected on the differences between Hollywood in the 1920s and the 1960s in a way that makes clear where her sympathies lay: "We had individuality. We did as we pleased. We stayed up late. We dressed the way we wanted. Today, stars are sensible and end up with better health. But we had more fun."

CRAZY BLUES

By PERRY BRADFORD

Get this number for your phonograph on Okeh Record No. 4169

PUBLISHED BY
PERRY BRADFORD
MUSIC PUB. CO.
1547 BROADWAY, N. Y. C.

All That Jazz
The phonograph dramatically expanded the popularity and market for jazz recordings like this one by Mamie Smith and her Jazz Hounds. The success of "Crazy Blues" convinced record companies that there was a market to be tapped in black communities for what were called "race records," and Mamie Smith skyrocketed to fame with this 1920 recording.
Division of Political History, Smithsonian Institution, Washington, DC.

dominate the next leap forward in mass communication: television.) Unlike European networks, which were government monopolies, American radio stations operated for profit. Though the federal government licensed the stations, their revenue came primarily from advertisers and corporate sponsors.

Americans fell in love with radio. They listened avidly to the World Series and other sports events and to variety entertainment shows featuring performers such as the Lucky Strike Orchestra and the A & P Gypsies, sponsored (not surprisingly) by advertisers of those brand-name products or companies. One of the most popular radio shows of all time, "Amos 'n' Andy," premiered on NBC in 1928, featuring two white actors playing stereotypical black characters. Soon fractured phrases from "Amos 'n' Andy," such as "check and double check," became part of everyday speech. So many people "tuned in" (another new phrase of the 1920s) that the country seemed to come to a halt during popular programs—a striking example of the pervasiveness of mass media.

New Patterns of Leisure

One of the most significant developments in modern life has been the growing freedom of workers from constant physical toil. As the workweek shrank and some workers won the right to paid vacations, Americans had more time—and energy—to spend on leisure. Like so much else in the 1920s, leisure became increasingly tied to consumption and mass culture.

Public recreation flourished in the 1920s as cities and suburbs built baseball diamonds, tennis courts, swimming pools, and golf courses. In the New York met-

MAMIE SMITH AND HER JAZZ HOUNDS

Boxing Heroes
George Bellows (1882–1925) often painted boxing scenes. *Dempsey and Firpo* (1924) depicts a heavyweight fight between Jack Dempsey, the "Manassa Mauler," and challenger Luis Firpo, the "Wild Bull of the Pampas." Dempsey is the one being unceremoniously knocked out of the ring. Boxing was one of the most popular sports in the sports-crazy 1920s.
Whitney Museum of American Art, NY.

ropolitan area the city planner Robert Moses masterminded a vast system of parks, playgrounds, and picnic areas. His greatest achievement was Jones Beach on Long Island. Moses not only created the state park but built limited-access highways to it. Any New Yorker with a car—an important limit on freedom of consumption—could escape to a public beach in less than forty minutes.

People not only played sports but had the time and money to watch them. Newspapers, especially the tabloids, capitalized on popular interest; fans could also listen to contests on the radio or see highlights in a newsreel at a movie theater. Baseball continued to be the national pastime, drawing as many as 10 million fans a year to the ballpark. Tarnished in 1919 by the "Black Sox" scandal, in which gamblers bribed Chicago White Sox players to throw the World Series, baseball bounced back with the rise of heroes such as Babe Ruth of the New York Yankees, nicknamed the "Sultan of Swat." African Americans, however, had different heroes. Excluded from white teams, black athletes like Satchel Paige played in Negro leagues formed during the 1920s.

Thanks to media coverage, the popularity of sports figures rivaled that of movie stars. In football Red Grange of the University of Illinois was a major star, and Jack Dempsey and Gene Tunney attracted loyal followings in boxing. Bobby Jones helped to popularize golf. Bill Tilden dominated men's tennis, and Helen Wills and Suzanne Lenglen reigned in the women's game. The decade's best-known swimmer, male or female, was Gertrude Ederle, who swam the English Channel in 1926 in just over fourteen hours.

The decade's most popular hero was neither an athlete nor a movie star. On May 20, 1927, Charles Lindbergh made the first successful solo nonstop flight between New York and Paris in his plane, the *Spirit of St. Louis* (see New Technology, "Aviation," pp. 756–757). For the 3,610-mile flight that lasted 33½ hours, the pilot took only five sandwiches and one day's worth of tinned rations, saying, "If I get to Paris, I won't need any more, and if I don't get to Paris, I won't need any more either." Returning home to ticker-tape parades and effusive celebrations, Lindbergh captivated the nation because he combined the mastery of new technology (the airplane) with the traditional American virtues of individualism, self-reliance, and hard work. His charm and boyish good looks contributed further to his appeal. He was twenty-five years old at the time of his flight, and in 1928 *Time* magazine chose him as its first Man of the Year.

Dissenting Values and Cultural Conflict

———————★———————

Despite the attractions of modern times, many Americans were deeply disturbed by the new secular values of the 1920s. Cultural and political conflict broke out over issues such as immigration restriction, Prohibition, and race relations. Tension between city and country played

Aviation

★

CHARLES LINDBERGH CAPTIVATED an American public that was already captivated by aviation. In the 1910s and 1920s many Americans embraced this new technology, investing in the airplane almost utopian hopes for a new world order. There was something about seeing an airplane for the first time that called forth these feelings—it was so different from anything that anyone had ever seen before that they could only describe it in miraculous, almost mystical, terms. As a Chicago minister said of his first experience at an airshow, "Never have I seen such a look of wonder in the faces of a multitude. From the gray-haired man to the child, everyone seemed to feel that it was a new day in their lives."

World War I acted as a great accelerator to the aviation industry in both its commercial and its military applications. When the war ended, a glut of

Lucky Lindy
Charles Lindbergh stands beside the *Spirit of St. Louis*, the plane he flew solo nonstop across the Atlantic in 1927 on his way to becoming the most popular hero of the 1920s. His plane—named in honor of St. Louis, Missouri, investors and aviation enthusiasts who backed his venture—is permanently on display at the National Air and Space Museum in Washington, D.C.
Hulton Getty/Liaison.

a part in all those conflicts, but fear of and resistance to change, and ambivalence about modernity—feelings that transcended the urban-rural polarity—probably had a greater influence.

The Rise of Nativism

The cultural conflicts of the 1920s occurred in part because both rural and urban dwellers realized how far they had already strayed from previous values—especially devotion to a traditional way of life rooted in small towns and farming communities. As farmers struggled with severe economic problems, rural communities lost residents to the cities at an alarming rate. When the 1920 census revealed for the first time that city dwellers outnumbered rural people, Americans realized that a dramatic change had taken place, rivaling the closing of the frontier in 1890. In 1920 a full inexpensive training planes became available, and these craft became the vehicles of choice for the barnstorming pilots of the 1920s. With their open cockpits, canvas wings, and rudimentary controls, these planes were tricky and often dangerous to fly, but that didn't stop the pilots from spreading the "winged gospel" through stunts, shows, and air races. These "birdmen"—and a fair number of "bird-women"—brought aviation to towns and hamlets all across America. Said Amelia Earhart, who learned to fly in 1921, "Not to have had a ride in an airplane today is like not having heard the radio."

Hollywood discovered aviation in the 1920s, cranking out dozens of aviation-related films whose plots, often on World War I themes, featured production thrillers like dogfights and fiery crashes. Flying became a popular hobby for Hollywood celebrities like Cecil De Mille and Colleen Moore, which further added to its allure. In newspapers and tabloids across the country, aviation was front-page news precisely because aviation stories, especially crashes (of which there were many, given the technologically unsophisticated equipment of the time), sold papers. So did coverage of long-distance record-setting flights. When Admiral Richard Byrd became the first person to fly over the North Pole in 1926, he became a national hero.

It took railroads half a century to complete a cycle of pioneering, merger, regulation, and stabilization; the airlines did it in just over a decade, culminating in the 1938 Civil Aeronautics Act. An important milestone was the 1925 Contract Air Mail Act, whereby the federal government awarded contracts for airmail delivery on a competitive basis. These contracts were essential to the emergence of modern airlines, because they offered a guaranteed profit at a time when neither the technology nor the demand existed for commercial transport of passengers. Charles Lindbergh had been both a stunt pilot and an airmail pilot in Minnesota before his record-breaking flight.

Lindbergh's transatlantic solo set off a boom—often called the Lindbergh boom—that saw the number of airlines expand from sixteen in 1927 to forty-seven in 1930. But commercial air travel was still very much in its infancy. In 1929 Lindbergh joined other investors to found TAT (Transcontinental Air Transport), which promised passengers coast-to-coast passage in forty-eight hours by flying during the day and taking the train at night. (Night flying, especially over mountainous regions, was considered too dangerous a risk to paying customers.) TAT was not that much more efficient than the fastest train, however, and was much more expensive, so it never turned much of a profit despite its nickname of "the Lindbergh line." The airline was soon absorbed into TWA. In fact, by the early 1930s the outlines of the other major airline dynasties, including United, Eastern, and Northwest, were firmly in place. These companies would dominate the domestic and, in the case of Pan American, the international markets until airline deregulation in the 1970s.

Aviation technology took a quantum leap forward with the introduction in 1936 of the DC-3. With its seating capacity of twenty-one passengers, the DC-3 offered airlines the possibility of generating profits through passenger travel rather than being dependent on airmail contracts. The DC-3, manufactured by the Douglas Aircraft Company, proved to be the most influential piece of aircraft in history, as well as one of the most dependable. Hundreds of its models are still flying today.

52 percent of the population lived in urban areas, compared with 28 percent in 1870.

Though the 1920 census exaggerated the extent of urbanization—its guidelines classified towns with as few as 2,500 people as cities—there was no mistaking the trend (Map 23.1). By 1929, ninety-three cities had a population of over 100,000. During the 1920s New York City exceeded 7 million inhabitants, Chicago had close to 3 million, and the population of Los Angeles doubled to more than 1.2 million. Outside the major cities, growth was even more impressive. As a result of the availability of cheap land and better transportation—notably the automobile—expanded metropolitan areas and suburbs sprang up. This trend started long before the post–World War II suburban boom.

The mass media generally reflected the cosmopolitan values of these urban centers, and many old-stock Americans worried that the cities, and the immigrants

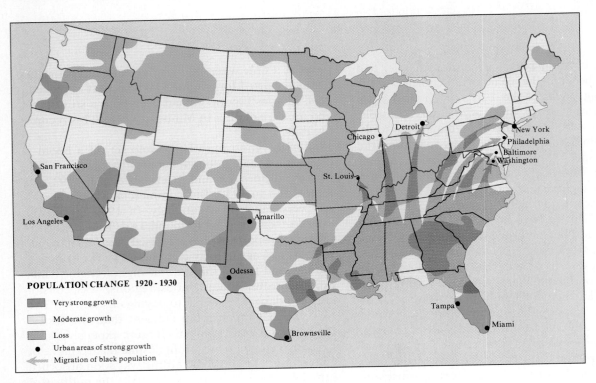

MAP 23.1
The Shift from Rural to Urban Population, 1920–1930
Despite the increasingly urban tone of modern America after 1920, regional patterns of
population growth and decline were far from uniform. Cities in the South and West grew
most dramatically as southern farmers moved to more promising areas with familiar climates. An important factor in the growth of northern cities, such as New York and
Chicago, was the migration of southern blacks set in motion by World War I.

who clustered there, would soon dominate the culture.
Yet polarities between city and country should not be
overstated. The lives of rural people had been affected by
the same forces that influenced urban life. Much of the
new technology—especially electricity and automobiles—enhanced rural life. Indeed, rural people, like
their urban counterparts, were tempted by the new
materialistic values proclaimed by radio programs, magazines, and movies. Moreover, urban Americans were far
from monolithic: many urban residents—immigrant
Catholics, for example—were just as alarmed about
declining moral standards as rural Protestants were. A
simplified urban-rural duality misrepresents the complexity of the decade's cultural conflicts.

Immigration Restriction.   These conflicts often centered on the question of growing racial and ethnic
pluralism. When native-born white Protestant Americans—both rural and city dwellers—looked at their
communities in 1920, they saw a nation that had
changed vastly in only forty years. During that time
more than 23 million immigrants had come to America,

many of them Catholics or Jews, most from peasant
stock. Senator William Bruce of Maryland called them
"indigestible lumps" in the "national stomach," implying that the nation would be unable to absorb their
large numbers and different customs. Such sentiments,
which were widely shared, came to be known as
nativism.

Nativist animosity fueled a new drive against immigration. The Chinese had been totally excluded in 1882,
and Theodore Roosevelt had negotiated a "gentlemen's
agreement" to limit Japanese immigration in 1908. Yet
efforts to restrict European immigration did not meet
with much success until after World War I, which had
heightened suspicion of "hyphenated" Americans. During the Red Scare, nativists had played up the supposed
association of immigrants with radicalism and labor
unrest, charging that southern and eastern European
Catholics and Jews were incapable of becoming true
Americans.

In response Congress passed an emergency bill in
1921, limiting the number of immigrants to 3 percent
of each national group as counted in the 1910 census.

Kazuo Kawai
A Foreigner in America

★

Before the 1920s, the laws regulating immigration from Asia contained more loopholes for the Japanese than the Chinese. As a result, there were approximately 110,000 Japanese living in the United States in 1920. Asian immigrants' experience of prejudice was much sharper than that of Europeans; in California, for example, the Alien Land Law of 1913 barred foreign-born Japanese from purchasing land or leasing it for more than three years. At the same time, the experiences of Japanese immigrants such as Kazuo Kawai echoed the problems that many young ethnic Americans faced in the 1920s as they recognized that they did not belong in the old country but were not accepted as "One Hundred Percent Americans."

But it hurt because I couldn't say: "This is my own, my native land." What was my native land? Japan?

True, I was born there. But it had seemed a queer, foreign land to me when I visited it. America? I had, until now, thought so. I had even told my father once that even in case of war between Japan and America, I would consider America as my country. In language, in thought, in ideals, in custom, in everything, I was American. But America wouldn't have me. She wouldn't recognize me in high school. She put the pictures of those of my race at the tail end of the year book. (I was a commencement speaker, so they had to put my picture near the front.) She won't let me play tennis on the courts in the city parks of Los Angeles, by city ordinance. She won't give me service when I go to a barber's shop. She won't let me own a house to live in. She won't give me a job, unless it is a menial one that no American wants. I thought I was American, but America wouldn't have me. Once I was American, but America made a foreigner out of me—Not a Japanese, but a foreigner—a foreigner to any country, for I am just as much a foreigner to Japan as to America.

Source: Stanford Survey of Race Relations (Stanford, CA: Stanford University, 1924), Hoover Institute Archives.

President Wilson refused to sign it, but the bill was reintroduced and passed during Warren Harding's administration. The new law produced immediate results. In the twelve-month period ending in June 1921, 805,228 immigrants had entered the United States; over the next twelve months, the number dropped to 309,556. In 1924 a more restrictive measure, the National Origins Act, reduced immigration through 1927 to 2 percent of each nationality as reflected in the 1890 census—which included relatively small numbers of people from southeastern Europe and Russia. After 1927 the law set a cap of 150,000 immigrants per year and continued to tie admission to a quota system that intentionally limited immigration from those regions. Japanese and Chinese immigrants were excluded entirely (see American Voices, "Kazuo Kawai: A Foreigner in America," above).

Puerto Rico provided a different source of immigration. After the Jones Act of 1917 conferred U.S. citizenship on Puerto Ricans, they could go to and from the mainland without restriction. Most of the movement was to New York, which was only a four-day sea voyage away. Thriving Puerto Rican communities, or *colonias*, sprang up in East Harlem and the Greenpoint section of Brooklyn. As it was for other migrants, the lure of New York City was primarily economic, and Puerto Ricans took jobs that had previously gone to European immigrants. But when hard times hit in the 1930s, the flow of Puerto Ricans stopped temporarily.

One remaining loophole permitted unrestricted immigration from countries in the Western Hemisphere. This source became increasingly significant over the years as Mexicans and Central and Latin Americans crossed the border to fill jobs made available by the cutoff of immigrants from Europe and Asia (Figure 23.1). Over 1 million Mexicans entered the United States between 1900 and 1930, including a wave who crossed the border after the Mexican Revolution of 1910 and another who entered during the labor shortages of World War I. Nativists and representatives of organized labor, who viewed Mexican immigrants as unwanted competition, lobbied Congress to close the loophole but met with strong

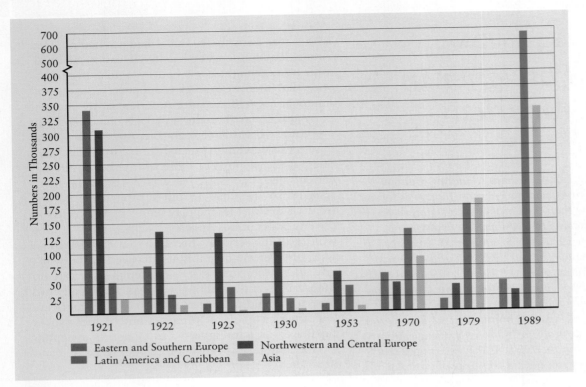

FIGURE 23.1
American Immigration after World War I
Legislation reflecting nativism slowed the influx of immigrants after 1920, as did the dislocations brought on by depression and war in the 1930s and 1940s. Note the higher rate of non-European immigration since the 1970s.

resistance until the 1930s and the economic devastation of the Great Depression.

Nativism took other forms during the 1920s. Many elite colleges instituted quotas to limit the enrollment of Jewish students, and many law firms refused to hire Jewish lawyers. Henry Ford spoke for many Americans when he warned of the menace of the "International Jew," referring to the supposed Jewish domination of international finance. Ford became so closely identified with anti-Semitism that decades passed before some Jewish families could bring themselves to buy his company's cars.

The New Klan. The most striking example of nativism in the 1920s was the revival of the Ku Klux Klan (KKK). Shortly after the 1915 premiere of *Birth of a Nation*, a group of southerners gathered on Stone Mountain outside Atlanta to revive the racist organization. Taking as its motto "Native, white, Protestant supremacy," the modern Klan appealed to both urban and rural folk, though its largest "klaverns" were found in urban areas. Spreading out from its southern base and encouraged by the superpatriotism of the war years, it found significant support in the Far West, the

Southwest, and the Midwest—especially Indiana, Oklahoma, and Oregon. Unlike its earlier incarnation after the Civil War, the Klan of the 1920s did not limit its harassment to blacks; Catholics and Jewish immigrants were just as likely to be its targets. Its tactics, however, remained the same: arson, physical intimidation, and economic boycotts directed at Klan targets. The new Klan also turned to politics, succeeding in electing hundreds of Klansmen to public office and emerging as a significant force in the Democratic Party.

At the height of its power in 1925 the Klan had over 3 million members, including a strong contingent of women who pursued their own distinctive political agenda combining racism, nativism, and a commitment to equal rights for white Protestant women. But after mid-decade the Klan declined rapidly. Battles between rival factions and disclosures of rampant corruption hurt its image. Especially damaging was the revelation that Grand Dragon David Stephenson, the Klan's national leader, had kidnapped and sexually assaulted his former secretary, driving her to commit suicide. And the passage of the 1924 immigration act reduced the nativist fervor that was a legacy of World War I, robbing the Klan of its most potent issue.

Patrolling the Texas Border
These Border Patrol officers in Laredo, Texas, in 1926 were deputized to stop illegal immigration from Mexico. Their guns, military uniforms, and stern expressions did not present a warm welcome to immigrants arriving from south of the border.
University of Texas at Austin.

Religious Fundamentalism

Other cultural tensions erupted over religion. The debate between modernist and fundamentalist Protestants, which had been simmering since the 1890s (see Chapter 20), came to a boil in the 1920s. Modernists tried to reconcile religion with scientific discoveries such as Darwin's theory of evolution and the avalanche of recent technological and scientific discoveries. Fundamentalists favored a literal interpretation of the Bible that could not be reconciled with science. Most major Protestant denominations, especially the Baptists and the Presbyterians, had heated internal conflicts in the 1920s, with the losers frequently splitting off to form their own churches. The most conspicuous evangelical figures, however, were outside the established denominations. Popular preachers like Billy Sunday and Aimee Semple McPherson used revivals, storefront churches, and open-air preaching to popularize their own brands of charismatic fundamentalism and traditional values.

Women of the Klan
The Ku Klux Klan was so well integrated into the daily life of white Protestants that one woman from rural Indiana remembered her time in the KKK in the 1920s as "just a celebration . . . a way of growing up." Perhaps as many as 500,000 women joined the Women of the Ku Klux Klan (WKKK) in the 1920s, including these Indiana Klanswomen in August 1924.
W. A. Swift Collection, A. M. Bracken Library, Ball State University, Muncie, IN.

Religious controversy soon entered the political arena when fundamentalists, worried about declining morality and increasing secularism, turned to the law to shore up their vision of a righteous Protestant nation. Some states enacted legislation to prevent the teaching of evolution in schools. In 1925, for example, Tennessee passed a law declaring that "it shall be unlawful . . . to teach any theory that denies the story of the Divine creation of man as taught in the Bible, and to teach instead that man has descended from a lower order of animals." In a test case involving John T. Scopes, a high school biology teacher in Dayton, Tennessee, the recently formed American Civil Liberties Union (ACLU) challenged the constitutionality of that law. Clarence Darrow, a famous criminal lawyer, defended Scopes. William Jennings Bryan, a spellbinding orator and ardent fundamentalist, was the most prominent member of the prosecution team.

The Scopes trial came to be known as the "monkey trial," referring both to Darwin's theory that human beings and other primate species share a common ancestor and to the circus atmosphere that prevailed in the courtroom. In July 1925 more than a hundred journalists crowded the sweltering courthouse, and the Chicago radio station WGN broadcast the proceedings live. The trial quickly turned to volatile questions of faith and scientific theory. The judge rebuffed defense efforts to call expert scientific witnesses on evolution, dismissing such testimony as hearsay because the scientists had not been present when lower forms of life had evolved. Darrow countered by calling Bryan to the stand as an expert on the Bible. Under oath, Bryan asserted his belief that a "big fish" had swallowed Jonah, that Eve had been created from Adam's rib, and that God had created the world in six days. He hedged, however, about whether the "days" were literally twenty-four hours long, an inconsistency that Darrow ruthlessly exploited.

Even so, the jury took only eight minutes to find Scopes guilty. Though the Tennessee Supreme Court overturned the conviction on a technicality, the reversal prevented further appeal of the case and the controversial law remained on the books for more than thirty years. Historically the trial symbolizes the conflict between the two competing value systems, scientific and religious, that clashed in the 1920s. It suggests that despite the period's image as frivolous and decadent, religion continued to matter deeply to many Americans.

Prohibition

The most notorious cultural debate of the 1920s was the battle over the Eighteenth Amendment, which took effect on January 20, 1920 (see Chapter 22). More than any other issue, Prohibition gave the decade its reputation as the Roaring Twenties. In major cities, whose ethnic populations had always opposed Prohibition, noncompliance was widespread. Illegal saloons called speakeasies sprang up—more than 30,000 in New York City alone. People who preferred to drink at home imitated rural moonshiners by learning to distill "bathtub gin." Liquor smugglers operated with ease along borders and coastlines. Organized crime, already a factor in major cities, supplied a ready-made distribution network for bootleg liquor, and gangsters used the "noble experiment" of Prohibition to entrench themselves more deeply in city politics. Said the decade's most notorious gangster, Chicago's Al Capone, "Everybody calls me a racketeer. I call myself a businessman. When I sell liquor, it's bootlegging. When my patrons serve it on a silver tray on Lake Shore Drive, it's hospitality."

By the middle of the decade Prohibition was clearly failing. Government appropriations for its enforcement were woefully inadequate, and the few highly publicized raids hardly made a dent in the liquor trade. In 1929 Attorney General William D. Mitchell conceded that liquor could be bought "at almost any hour of the day or night, either in rural districts, the smaller towns, or the cities." A committee appointed by President Hoover in 1931 to study Prohibition only weakly recommended that it be retained.

But Prohibition was not just the law—it was part of the Constitution. So the forces for repeal—the "wets," as opposed to the "drys," who continued to support the Eighteenth Amendment—began the long process of gaining the necessary majorities in Congress and state legislatures to amend the Constitution again. The Women's Organization for National Prohibition Repeal, headed by Pauline Sabin, a wealthy New York Republican, lobbied Congress and mobilized support from other national organizations. The onset of the Great Depression hastened the repeal process. People argued that liquor production would create jobs and prop up the faltering economy. On December 5, 1933, the Eighteenth Amendment was repealed. Ironically, drinking became more socially acceptable, although not necessarily more widespread, than it had been before the Prohibition experiment began its rocky course.

Intellectual Crosscurrents

The most articulate and embittered dissenters in the 1920s were writers and intellectuals who were disillusioned by the horrors of World War I and the crass materialism of the new American consumer culture. Some artists felt so at odds with what they saw as the complacent, anti-intellectual, moralistic tone of American life that they settled in Europe—some temporarily, such as the novelists Ernest Hemingway and F. Scott Fitzgerald, and others permanently, such as the writer Gertrude Stein. (The strong dollar, another legacy of

Ignoring Prohibition
Despite their popularity, speakeasies were rarely drawn or photographed; after all, they were supposed to be private clubs tucked away beyond the reach of the law. Fancy hotels were unable to compete with speakeasies once their bars were shut down, and many went out of business in the 1920s. But John Sloan's 1928 painting shows the rich enjoying themselves at New York's posh Lafayette Hotel. It is likely that these gentlemen and ladies had flasks concealed somewhere in their evening finery.
John Sloan, *The Lafayette*, 1928, Metropolitan Museum of Art, New York. Gift of Friends of John Sloan, 1929 (28.18).

World War I, made this a cheap and attractive way to leave American materialism behind.) African Americans such as the dancer Josephine Baker, the writer Langston Hughes, and the painter Henry O. Tanner also sought a temporary escape from racism by moving to France. The poet T. S. Eliot, who left the United States before the war, became a British citizen. His despairing poem *The Waste Land* (1922), with its images of a fragmented civilization in ruins after the war, influenced a generation of writers.

Other writers also made powerful statements against war and contemporary culture, including John Dos Passos, whose first novel, *The Three Soldiers* (1921), was inspired by the war, and whose *1919* (1932), the second volume in his *USA* trilogy, railed against the obscenity of "Mr. Wilson's war." Ernest Hemingway described the dehumanizing consequences and futility of the war in *In Our Time* (1924), *The Sun Also Rises* (1926), and *A Farewell to Arms* (1929), which drew on his experience as an ambulance driver in Italy. In 1925 F. Scott Fitzgerald published *The Great Gatsby*, which showed the corrosive consequences of the mindless pursuit of wealth.

But the artists and writers who migrated to Europe, particularly to Paris, were not just a "Lost Generation" fleeing America; they were also drawn to Paris as the cultural and artistic capital of the world. Paris, as Gertrude Stein put it, was "where the twentieth century was happening." Indeed, the *modernist movement*, the term for the deliberate departure from tradition and the use of experimental forms in many styles of twentieth-century literature, art, and music, invigorated American writing abroad and at home.

In the 1920s the business culture and corruption of the Harding years caused intellectuals to cast a more critical eye on American society. One of the sharpest critics, the Baltimore journalist H. L. Mencken, directed his mordant wit against mass culture, small-town America, and the "booboisie," his contemptuous term for the middle class. In the *American Mercury*, the journal he founded in 1922, Mencken championed writers such as Sherwood Anderson, Sinclair Lewis, and Theodore Dreiser, who satirized the provincialism of American society.

The literature of the 1920s was varied and rich. Poetry enjoyed a renaissance in the works of Robert Frost, Wallace Stevens, Marianne Moore, and William Carlos Williams. Edith Wharton won a Pulitzer Prize for *The Age of Innocence* (1920), the first woman to be so honored. Influenced by Freudian psychology, the novelist William Faulkner achieved his first critical success with *The Sound and the Fury* (1929), set in the fictional Mississippi county of Yoknapatawpha, where inhabitants cling to the old values of the agrarian South as they try to adjust to modern industrial capitalism. The dramatist Eugene O'Neill also showed the influence of Freudian psychology in his experimental plays, including *The Hairy Ape* (1922) and *Desire under the Elms* (1924). Although Faulkner and O'Neill went on to produce major works in the 1930s, on the whole the creative energy of the literary renaissance of the 1920s did not survive into the next decade. The Great Depression, social and ideological unrest, and the rise of totalitarianism would reshape the intellectual landscape.

Harlem Renaissance. A different kind of cultural affirmation took place in the black community of Harlem in the 1920s. In the words of the Reverend Adam Clayton Powell Sr., pastor of the influential Abyssinian Baptist Church, Harlem loomed as "the symbol of liberty and the Promised Land to Negroes everywhere." One aspect of this hope was the Harlem Renaissance, an artistic movement of young writers and artists who broke with the older, genteel traditions of black literature to reclaim a cultural identity with African roots. Alain Locke, editor of the influential anthology *The New Negro* (1926), summed up the movement when he stated that, through art, "Negro life is seizing its first chances for group expression and self-determination."

The Harlem Renaissance championed racial pride and cultural identity in the midst of white society. The poet Langston Hughes, who became a leading exponent of the Harlem Renaissance, captured its affirmative spirit when he asserted, "I am a Negro—and beautiful." Authors such as Claude McKay, Jean Toomer, Jessie Fauset, and Zora Neale Hurston explored the black experience and represented the "New Negro" in fiction. Countee Cullen and Langston Hughes turned to poetry, and Augusta Savage used sculpture to draw attention to black accomplishments. Their outpouring of literary work showed the ongoing African American struggle to find a way, as W. E. B. Du Bois put it, "to be both a Negro and an American."

The artistic outpouring encouraged a wide range of creative expression. Jean Toomer, a writer passionately committed to black self-expression, wrote the influen-

The Harlem Renaissance
The Crisis, edited by W. E. B. Du Bois, was the magazine of the National Association for the Advancement of Colored People (NAACP). This 1929 cover suggests the cultural and political awakenings associated with the Harlem Renaissance.
Henry Lee Moon Library and Civil Rights Archive, NAACP, Washington, DC.

tial novel *Cane* in 1923. With its poems, sketches, and stories about a northern black's discovery of the rural black South, it inspired other African American artists and writers. Langston Hughes drew on the black artistic forms of blues and jazz in *The Weary Blues* (1926), a groundbreaking collection of poems. Considered the most original black poet and the most representative African American writer of the time, Hughes also wrote novels, plays, and essays. Zora Neale Hurston, born in Florida to a family of poor tenant farmers, attended Howard University in Washington, D.C., and won a scholarship to study anthropology at Barnard College in New York City. She spent a decade collecting folklore in the South and the Caribbean and incorporated that material into her short stories and novels. Her genius for storytelling won her acclaim.

The vitality of the Harlem Renaissance was short-lived. Although the NAACP's magazine *The Crisis* was a forum for the Harlem writers, the black middle class and the intellectual elite in Harlem were relatively small and could not support the group's efforts. Its main audience consisted of white intellectuals and philanthropists, and many writers were ambivalent about depending on white patronage as they struggled to attain an authentic voice in their fiction. Langston Hughes became disillusioned with his white patron when she withdrew support as he began to write about common black people in Kansas and New York rather than keeping with African themes.

During the Jazz Age, when Harlem was in vogue, the publishing industry courted its writers, but the stock market crash of 1929 brought that interest to a sudden end. The movement waned in the 1930s as the depression deepened. Nonetheless, the writers of the Harlem Renaissance would influence a future generation of black writers when their works were rediscovered by black intellectuals during the civil rights movement of the 1960s.

Marcus Garvey and the UNIA. Although the Harlem Renaissance was mainly an artistic movement, other African American movements sought to challenge white political and cultural hegemony. The most successful was the Universal Negro Improvement Association (UNIA), which championed black separatism under the leadership of the Jamaican-born Marcus Garvey. Based in Harlem, the UNIA was the black working class's first mass movement. At its height it claimed 4 million followers, many of whom were recent migrants to northern cities. Garvey's wife, Amy Jacques Garvey, appealed to black women by combining black nationalism with an emphasis on women's contributions to culture and politics. Like several nineteenth-century reformers, Marcus Garvey urged blacks to return to Africa because, he said, blacks would never be treated justly in countries ruled by whites. Although he did not anticipate a mass migration, he did envision that a strong black Africa could use its power to protect blacks everywhere.

The UNIA grew rapidly in the early 1920s. It published a newspaper called *Negro World*, and it opened "liberty halls" in New York, Chicago, Detroit, New Orleans, Mobile, Jacksonville, and other cities. The UNIA also undertook business ventures to support black capitalism. Its most ambitious project was the Black Star Line steamship company, which was supposed to ferry cargo between the West Indies and the United States and take African Americans back to Africa. The Black Star Line caused the downfall of the UNIA. Irregularities in fundraising led to Garvey's conviction for mail fraud in 1925, and he was sentenced to five years in prison. President Coolidge paroled him in 1927, and Garvey was deported to Jamaica. Without his charismatic leadership the organization collapsed, but his ideas remained influential even after his death in 1940.

The 1928 Election

The works of the Lost Generation and the Harlem Renaissance touched only a small minority of Americans in the 1920s, but emotionally charged issues such as Prohibition, religious fundamentalism, and nativism spilled over into national politics. The Democratic Party, which drew on Protestant rural supporters in the South and West as well as ethnic voters in northern cities, was especially vulnerable to the urban-rural conflicts of the time (see Voices from Abroad, "Li Gongpu: The Presidential Election of 1928," p. 766).

Alfred E. Smith. In 1924 the Democratic National Convention had revealed an intensely polarized party, split between the urban machines and its rural wing. In 1928 the urban wing held sway and succeeded in nominating New York's governor, Alfred E. Smith, on the first ballot. Al Smith, the grandson of Irish immigrants and a Catholic, was the first presidential candidate to reflect the aspirations of the urban working classes. Proud of his urban background, he adopted "The Sidewalks of New York" as his campaign song. Democrats hoped Smith would attract recent immigrants and workers who traditionally voted Republican. Belle Moskowitz, a New York social worker who served as Smith's political advisor, helped him appeal to women and liberal urban Jews.

But Smith had liabilities. He spoke in a heavy New York accent, sprinkling his speeches with "ain't" and "he don't," which did not play well on the radio. His early career in Tammany Hall troubled many voters, suggesting—incorrectly—that he was little more than a cog in a political machine. Smith's stand on Prohibition alienated even more voters. Although he promised to enforce Prohibition, he made no secret of his support for repeal. Smith chose John J. Raskob, a wealthy entrepreneur and one of the nation's most ardent "wets," as head of the Democratic National Committee.

By far the most damaging handicap to Smith's campaign was his Catholicism. In the midst of the heightened nativism of the decade, most Protestant Americans were not ready for a Roman Catholic president in 1928. Although Smith insisted that his religion would not interfere with his duties as president, being Catholic cost him support from Democrats and Republicans alike. Protestant clergymen, who already opposed Smith because he supported the repeal of Prohibition, led the drive against him. "No Governor can kiss the papal ring and get within gunshot of the White House," declared a Methodist bishop from Buffalo.

Herbert Hoover. Just as Smith marked a new kind of presidential candidate for the Democrats, so did Herbert Hoover for the Republicans. Coolidge's unexpected decision not to run for reelection in 1928 opened the

Li Gongpu

The Presidential Election of 1928

★

In 1927 Li Gongpu (1902–1946) came to America as an exchange student at Reed College in Oregon. As a Chinese intellectual and political activist, he was especially interested in the workings of the American electoral system. His description of going to a polling place on November 6, 1928, with a Reed classmate drew comparisons between the American system and China's ongoing struggle to live up to the promise of the 1911 revolution.

A week before the election I made preparations to go to a polling place on election day to watch the excitement and to observe the attitude of the people of this country at the time of the election. Who would have imagined that when I went with my schoolmate Cane on the afternoon of the sixth, the so-called polling place turned out to be nothing more than a little house! A small sign outside the door stated that this was Municipal Electoral Polling Place No. 137. In one half of the ground floor sat a ballot issuer, a checker, a ballot receiver, and four overseers; in the other half was room for ten people to fill out ballots. While Cane did his, I asked in detail about the procedures for filling out a ballot, and I also received an explanation of the ballot from the lady who was issuing them.

Lastly, after getting permission from the chairman of the polling place, I went upstairs and observed how the ballots were counted. Four people were counting the votes, one calling them out and three recording them. Each ballot had on it not only the presidential candidates of the various parties but also important state officials whose terms had expired, the city's mayor, and a number of important state referendum questions, such as whether to increase firemen's disability benefits and old-age pensions, whether to increase the automobile gasoline tax, and so on, with detailed rationales included, to be decided by the opinion of the majority of the people. The poll workers were deputed by a state administrative organ; each precinct has no more than three or four hundred voters registered in it, and there was not the slightest crowding or clamor.

Election regulations require that the parties stop all propaganda activities on election day, so that day was unusually peaceful everywhere. I watched two workers and an old lady fill out their ballots with extraordinary care. Such an atmosphere is truly worthy of our respect! It is extremely discouraging to compare this with our own former elections for provincial assemblymen and national assemblymen, which were confused and disorganized, without the slightest order, even to the point of knives and guns, beheadings, and bloodletting!

But if we carry our examination of the American electoral system and its true nature a bit further, the conclusion will be that the democratic form of government in the United States has so far only taken the first step and not yet reached perfection. In political matters the people are still completely manipulated by the two parties. Before an election, promises are made: if elected, this will be done or that will be carried out. Once the election period is past, the party that has gained power exercises its authority in any way it wishes. The policies and matters they had promised are for the most part treated only perfunctorily, and there is nothing that the people can do. In this respect, the external expression and inner strength of America's so-called democratic spirit are not as great as those of the English people.

As for the election of state government officials and city mayors, most are controlled by political parties, and the majority of the people do not know about the record of experience or character of nine out of ten people on the ballot and just mark any name when voting. This is a fact admitted by many of my schoolmates and professors of government. Of the personnel employed in various organs of state government and so on, more than half are mediocrities interested only in making a living, as was declared by a Democratic senator in a public speech in the city.

If people at the level of Americans still have politics that are so imperfect, then it is clear that the realization of "democracy" is not an easy matter. At the same time we should also be aware that if from now on the Nationalist government actively devotes itself to constructive work, strengthening the five-branch organization of the government, and at the same time education and the economy suddenly develop and spread, then after twenty years the progress of our politics, industry, and commerce could easily be equal to that of England and the United States. It all depends on the wisdom and hard work of us Chinese.

Source: R. David Arkush and Leo O. Lee, eds. and trans., *Land without Ghosts: Chinese Impressions of America from the Mid-Nineteenth Century to the Present* (Berkeley: University of California Press, 1989), 140–141.

field, and Hoover led from the start. As a professional administrator and engineer, Hoover embodied the new managerial and technological elite that was restructuring the economic order. He had never been elected to political office. During his campaign, in which he gave only seven speeches, Hoover promised that his vision of individualism and cooperative endeavor would banish poverty from the United States. That rhetoric, as well as his reputation for organizing humanitarian relief during the war, caused many voters to consider him more progressive than Smith.

Hoover won a stunning victory, receiving 58 percent of the popular vote to Smith's 41 percent, and 444 electoral votes to 87 for Smith (Map 23.2). For the first time since Reconstruction a Republican candidate carried Virginia, Texas, and North Carolina, largely because many Democrats refused to vote for a Catholic. The strong economy also aided the Republicans. The voter turnout rose from 52 percent in 1924 to 56.9 percent in 1928, partly as a result of extensive education campaigns undertaken by the League of Women Voters. Also, the transfer of polling places to schools and churches from their former locations in saloons made women feel more comfortable with

their new role as voters. Many Catholic and immigrant women voted for Smith, but even more native-born Republican women supported Herbert Hoover.

The 1928 election reflected important underlying political changes. Despite the party's overwhelming loss, the Democratic turnout increased substantially in urban areas. Smith won the industrialized states of Massachusetts and Rhode Island and carried the nation's twelve largest cities. The Democrats were on their way to forging a new identity as the party of the urban masses, including ethnic voters—a reorientation that the New Deal completed in the 1930s.

It is unlikely that any Democratic candidate, let alone a Catholic, could have won the presidency in 1928. With a seemingly prosperous economy, a national consensus on foreign policy, and strong support from the business community, the Republicans were unbeatable. Ironically, Herbert Hoover's victory put him in the unenviable position of leading the United States when the Great Depression struck in 1929. Having claimed credit for the prosperity of the 1920s, the Republicans found it difficult to escape blame for the depression. Twenty-four years would pass before a Republican won the presidency again.

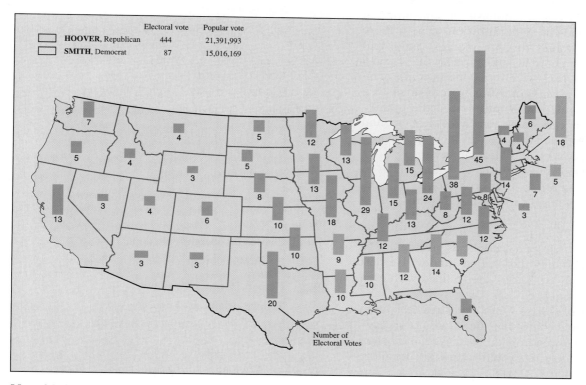

	Electoral vote	Popular vote
HOOVER, Republican	444	21,391,993
SMITH, Democrat	87	15,016,169

Number of Electoral Votes

MAP 23.2

The Election of 1928

Historians still debate the extent to which 1928 was a critical election—that is, one that produced a significant realignment in voting behavior. Although the Republican Herbert Hoover swept the electoral college, Democrats were heartened by the fact that Alfred E. Smith won the heavily industrialized states of Rhode Island and Massachusetts. For the first time, the Democratic ticket carried the nation's twelve largest cities, garnering strong support from immigrants and urban dwellers.

Summary

★

By the 1920s modern America had arrived, a transformation that had begun with World War I. The Republican Party controlled the national government and cemented the partnership between business and government that had been accelerated by the war and that characterized the pattern of state building during the era. In foreign policy the United States promoted disarmament and the reduction of German war reparations but otherwise generally steered clear of European political affairs. The chief U.S. interest was to ensure a stable environment for economic expansion abroad, especially in the Western Hemisphere. With the exception of the 1920–1921 recession the economy performed well, although agriculture never recovered from the postwar slump, and some industries remained overextended after their wartime expansion. The automobile industry typified the new mass-production techniques that dominated economic life in the United States and revolutionized American society.

During the 1920s a national culture began to develop. It was characterized by new ways of spending leisure time, a heightened emphasis on consumption and advertising, and the wide diffusion of new, more secular ideas and values through movies, radio, and other mass media. The new life-styles of the decade, often called the Roaring Twenties or the Jazz Age, captured the popular imagination but were limited to a minority of the population. Families needed a middle-class income to buy cars, radios, vacuum cleaners, and toasters. Those left outside the circle of prosperity included farmers, blacks, and Mexican Americans.

Not everyone welcomed the new secular values of the 1920s. Conflicts arose over Prohibition, religion, race, and immigration. Those cultural disputes spilled over into politics, disrupting the already fractured Democratic Party. The 1928 election showed that the nation could not yet accept a Catholic as president. The Republican ascendancy continued under Herbert Hoover, who looked forward to a term filled with even greater prosperity and progress.

The advances of the New Era, and the expectation that the nation would continue to be vigorous and powerful at home and abroad, made the harsh realities of the Great Depression that would follow all the more shocking.

TIMELINE

1920	First commercial radio broadcast
	Warren G. Harding elected president
	Census reveals shift in population from farms to cities
	Sinclair Lewis, *Main Street*
	Edith Wharton, *The Age of Innocence*
1920–1921	National economic recession
1921	Sheppard-Towner Act
	Congress limits immigration
	Washington Conference supports naval disarmament
1922	Fordney-McCumber Tariff
	T. S. Eliot, *The Waste Land*
1923	Calvin Coolidge succeeds Harding as president
	Time magazine founded
	Jean Toomer, *Cane*
1924	Dawes Plan reduces German reparation payments
	Bruce Barton, *The Man Nobody Knows*
	Teapot Dome scandal
	U.S. troops withdraw from Dominican Republic
	National Origins Act
1925	F. Scott Fitzgerald, *The Great Gatsby*
	Height of Ku Klux Klan
	Scopes ("monkey") trial
1926	Alain Locke, *The New Negro* anthology
1927	First "talkies"
	Charles Lindbergh's solo flight
	Ford's Model A car
1928	Herbert Hoover elected president
	Kellogg-Briand Pact signed
1929	*Middletown* published
	Ernest Hemingway, *A Farewell to Arms*
	William Faulkner, *The Sound and the Fury*

Suggested Readings

General overviews of the 1920s are provided by Lynn Dumenil, *Modern Temper* (1995); Ellis Hawley, *The Great War and the Search for a Modern Order, 1917–1933* (1979); William Leuchtenburg, *The Perils of Prosperity*, 2nd ed. (1995); and Ann Douglas, *Terrible Honesty: Mongrel Manhattan in the 1920s* (1995). Robert S. Lynd and Helen Merrell Lynd, *Middletown: A Study in Modern American Culture* (1929), remains a superb study of American life in the 1920s.

The Business-Government Partnership of the 1920s

Discussion of corporate developments can be found in Alfred Chandler, *The Visible Hand* (1977), and Robert Himmelberg, *The Origins of the National Recovery Administration: Business, Government, and the Trade Association Ideal, 1921–1933* (1976). On labor developments, see Irving Bernstein, *The Lean Years* (1960); David Brody, *Workers in Industrial America* (1980); and David Montgomery, *The Fall of the House of Labor* (1987).

The domestic and international aspects of the economy are treated in Jim Potter, *The American Economy between the Wars* (1974), and Emily Rosenberg, *Spreading the American Dream* (1982). Interpretations of foreign policy include Akira Iriye, *The Globalizing of America, 1913–1945* (1993); Warren Cohen, *Empire without Tears* (1987); William Appleman Williams, *The Tragedy of American Diplomacy* (1962); and Walter LaFeber, *Inevitable Revolutions* (1983).

General introductions to politics in the 1920s can be found in David Burner, *The Politics of Provincialism* (1967); Robert Murray, *The Politics of Normalcy* (1973); and Alan Dawley, *Struggles for Justice* (1991). Biographies of the decade's major political figures include Donald McCoy, *Calvin Coolidge* (1967); David Burner, *Herbert Hoover* (1979); and Paula Elder, *Governor Alfred E. Smith: The Politician as Reformer* (1983). On women in politics, see Nancy Cott, *The Grounding of Modern Feminism* (1987); Elisabeth Israels Perry, *Belle Moskowitz* (1987); and Molly Ladd-Taylor, *Mother-Work: Women, Child Welfare and the State, 1890–1930* (1994).

A New National Culture

Daniel Boorstin, *The Americans: The Democratic Experience* (1973), and David Nasaw, *Going Out: The Rise and Fall of Public Amusements* (1993), introduce the emerging mass culture. On movies, see Steven J. Ross, *Working-Class Hollywood: Silent Film and the Shaping of Class in America* (1998); Robert Sklar, *Movie-Made America*, 2nd ed. (1987); Larry May, *Screening Out the Past* (1980). Material on Clara Bow can be found in David Stenn, *Clara Bow, Runnin' Wild* (1988). Erik Barnouw, *A Tower in Babel* (1966), and Susan Douglas, *Inventing American Broadcasting* (1987), discuss radio. See also Melvin Patrick Ely, *The Adventures of Amos 'n' Andy: A Social History of an American Phenomenon* (1991). On adver-

tising, see Roland Marchand, *Advertising the American Dream* (1985), and T. J. Jackson Lears, *Fables of Abundance* (1994). Paula Fass, *The Damned and the Beautiful* (1977), and Beth L. Bailey, *From Front Porch to Back Seat* (1988), cover youth, and Susan Strasser, *Never Done* (1982), and Ruth Schwartz Cowan, *More Work for Mother* (1983), discuss the lives of white middle-class women. Lizabeth Cohen, *Making a New Deal: Industrial Workers in Chicago, 1919–1939* (1990), suggests how working-class communities adapted mass culture for their purposes. Joan Shelley Rubin describes the middle class in *The Making of Middlebrow Culture* (1992).

The impact of the automobile on modern American life is amply documented by James Flink, *The Car Culture* (1975) and *The Automobile Age* (1988); on women and the automobile, see Virginia Scharff, *Taking the Wheel* (1991). For sports, see Allen Guttmann, *A Whole New Ball Game* (1988); Harvey Green, *Fit for America* (1986); and Susan Cahn, *Coming on Strong: Gender and Sexuality in 20th Century Women's Sport* (1994). The Negro Leagues are covered in Robert W. Peterson, *Only the Ball Was White* (1970), and Donn Rogosin, *Invisible Men* (1985).

Dissenting Values and Cultural Conflict

Paul Carter, *Another Part of the Twenties* (1977), outlines the decade's deeply felt cultural controversies. Background on rural and urban life is provided by Don Kirschner, *City and Country: Rural Responses to Urbanization in the 1920s* (1970); Zane Miller, *The Urbanization of America* (1973); and Jon Teaford, *The Twentieth-Century American City* (1986). John Higham, *Strangers in the Land* (1955), describes immigration restriction and nativism. Richard K. Tucker, *The Dragon and the Cross* (1991), and Leonard Moore, *Citizen Klansmen* (1991), cover the Klan's rise and fall, and Kathleen M. Blee, *Women of the Klan* (1991), and Nancy MacLean, *Behind the Mask of Chivalry* (1994), offer a provocative discussion of racism and gender in the 1920s. George M. Marsden, *Fundamentalism and American Culture* (1980), and William G. McLoughlin, *Fundamentalism in American Culture* (1983), cover religion; Edward J. Larson, *Summer of the Gods* (1997), treats the Scopes trial. On intellectual development, see Robert Crunden, *From Self to Society, 1919–1941* (1972); Roderick Nash, *The Nervous Generation: American Thought, 1917–1930* (1969); and Daniel Singal, ed., *Modernist Culture in America* (1991). Virginia Sanchez Korrol, *From Colonia to Community* (1983), covers the history of Puerto Ricans in New York City. On the Harlem Renaissance, see George Hutchinson, *The Harlem Renaissance in Black and White* (1995); David Levering Lewis, *When Harlem Was in Vogue* (1981); Nathan Huggins, *Harlem Renaissance* (1971); and Cheryl A. Wall, *Women of the Harlem Renaissance* (1995). For jazz and blues, see Burton Peretti, *The Creation of Jazz* (1992), and Angela Y. Davis, *Blues Legacies and Black Feminism* (1998). Judith Stein, *The World of Marcus Garvey* (1985), describes the reformer. On Prohibition, see Andrew Sinclair, *Prohibition: The Era of Excess* (1962), and Norman Clark, *Deliver Us from Evil* (1976). The 1928 election is covered in Oscar Handlin, *Al Smith and His America* (1958); Kristi Andersen, *The Creation of a Democratic Majority, 1928–1936* (1979); and Allan J. Lichtman's quantitative study, *Prejudice and the Old Politics* (1979).

The Great Depression

FOR MOST AMERICANS, the year 1929 means only one thing—the stock market crash that touched off the Great Depression. By 1932, more than one-fourth of the nation's workers were unemployed and industrial production had fallen to barely half the 1929 level. President Herbert Hoover, formerly the symbol of business prosperity, had become the scapegoat for the depression. Images from the 1920s of flappers and movie stars, admen and stockbrokers, were replaced by depression-era images of hoboes standing in breadlines, unemployed men selling apples on city street corners, and displaced farm families piling into dilapidated jalopies to head west to California.

Did the country really go from unprecedented prosperity to the poorhouse overnight? Of course not. The extreme contrast between the flush times of the 1920s and the hard times of the 1930s is too stark. The vaunted prosperity of the 1920s was never as widespread or as deeply rooted as many believed at the time. Although America's mass-consumption economy was the envy of the world, many people lived on its margins. This unequal distribution of wealth was one of the main causes of the depression. Nor was every American devastated by the depression. Those with a secure job or a fixed income survived the economic downturn in relatively good shape, and some people even managed to get rich. Yet few could escape the depression's wide-ranging social, political, and cultural effects. Although not every event of the 1930s should be viewed through the lens of the depression, the great economic contraction unifies the history of the decade more than any other factor.

Looking for Work
This detail of Moses Soyer's painting Employment Agency (1940) *captures the despair and bleak resignation of a victim of the Great Depression—a white male, down on his luck but still trying to keep up appearances and hope.*
Collection of Philip J. and Suzanne Schiller.

Almost all our impressions of the 1930s are black and white, in part because widely distributed photographs taken by Farm Security Administration photographers etched this stark visual image of depression America on the popular consciousness. Yet conditions were not uniformly grim. The depression was not on everyone's mind twenty-four hours a day. People continued their daily routine of work, family, and leisure. Literature and the arts flourished, and Hollywood movies and radio provided a welcome relief from hard times. Novelist Josephine Herbst recalled "an almost universal liveliness that countervailed universal suffering."

The Coming of the Great Depression

———————★———————

Since the beginning of the Industrial Revolution early in the nineteenth century the United States had experienced recessions or panics at least every twenty years. But none was as severe or lasted as long as the Great Depression. Only as the economy shifted toward war mobilization in the late 1930s did the grip of the depression finally ease.

The Causes of the Depression

The downturn began slowly and almost imperceptibly. After 1927, consumer spending declined and housing construction slowed. Inventories piled up, and in 1928 and 1929 manufacturers began to cut back on production and lay off workers; reduced incomes and buying power in turn reinforced the downturn. By the summer of 1929 the economy was clearly in a recession.

Stock Market Speculation and the Great Crash. Among the causes of the Great Depression, a flawed stock market was an important but not the dominant influence. By 1929 the market had become the symbol of the nation's prosperity and an icon of American business culture. The financier John J. Raskob captured this attitude in a *Ladies' Home Journal* article, "Everyone Ought to Be Rich." Invest $15 a month in sound common stocks, Raskob advised, and in twenty years the investment will grow to $80,000. Not everyone was playing the stock market, however. Only about 4 million Americans, representing about 10 percent of the nation's households, owned stock in 1929, and less than one-third of them had portfolios large enough to require the services of a stockbroker.

Stock prices had been rising steadily since 1921, but in 1928 and 1929 they surged forward, with the average price of stocks rising over 40 percent. All this economic activity was essentially unregulated. Margin buying in particular proceeded at a feverish pace as customers borrowed up to 75 percent of the purchase price of stocks. That easy credit lured more speculators and less creditworthy investors into the market. The Federal Reserve Board warned member banks not to lend money for stock speculation—if prices dropped, many investors would not be able to repay their debts—but no one listened. As long as prices continued to soar, everyone felt like a winner. A noted economist proclaimed in mid-October 1929 that "stock prices have reached what looks like a permanently high plateau."

The stock market began sliding in early September, but people ignored the warning. Then on "Black Thursday" (October 24, 1929) and again on "Black Tuesday" (October 29, 1929) the bubble burst. More than 28 million shares changed hands in frantic trading. Overextended investors, suddenly finding themselves heavily in debt, began to sell their stocks. Waves of panic selling ensued, during which many stocks found no buyers. Practically overnight, stock values fell from a peak of $87 billion (at least on paper) to $55 billion.

The precipitous decline of stock prices became known as the Great Crash, and its impact was felt far beyond the trading floors of Wall Street. Speculators who had borrowed from banks to buy their stocks could not repay the loans because they could not sell the stocks. These defaults in turn caused bank failures. Since bank deposits were uninsured before the 1930s, a bank failure meant that all the depositors' money was lost. This sudden loss of their life savings was a tremendous shock to members of the middle class, many of whom had no other resources with which to cope with the crisis.

The stock market crash intensified the course of the Great Depression in several ways. Besides wiping out the savings of thousands of Americans, it hurt commercial banks that had invested heavily in corporate stocks. Less tangibly, it destroyed the optimism of people who had regarded the stock market as the crowning symbol of American prosperity, causing a crisis of confidence that prolonged the depression.

Structural Weaknesses. Although the stock market crash and its immediate consequences contributed to the Great Depression, longstanding weaknesses in the American economy accounted for its length and severity, especially the deep plunge between 1931 and 1933. Agriculture, in particular, had never recovered from the recession of 1920–1921. Farmers faced high fixed costs for equipment and mortgages incurred during the inflationary war years. At the same time prices fell because of overproduction, forcing farmers to default on mortgage payments and risk foreclosure. In 1929 the yearly income of a farmer averaged only $273, compared with $750 in other occupations. Because farmers accounted

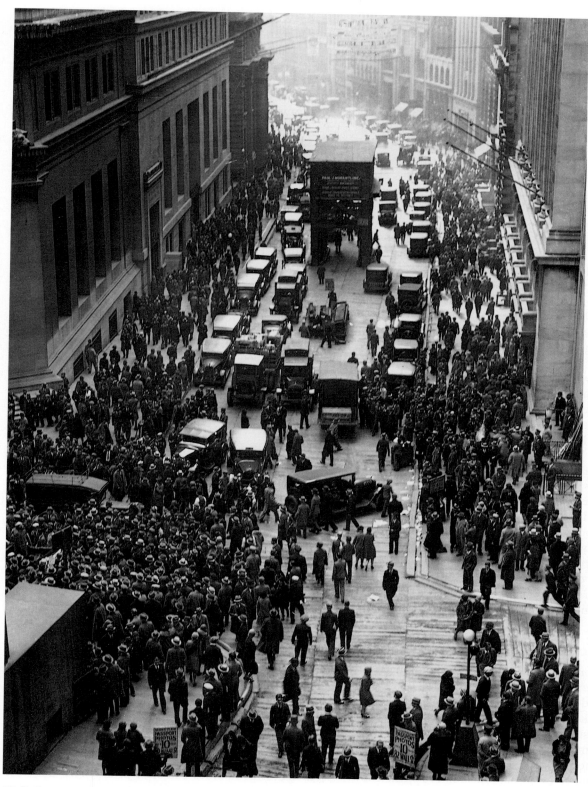

Wall Street, October 1929
Crowds gather in front of the New York Stock Exchange on October 25, 1929, the day
after "Black Thursday." The mood would be even darker after "Black Tuesday," October 29, the day the bubble burst.
Corbis-Bettmann.

for about one-fourth of the nation's gainfully employed workers in 1929, their difficulties weakened the general economic structure.

Certain basic industries also had experienced economic setbacks during the prosperous 1920s. Textile manufacturers, facing a steady market decline after the war, abandoned New England for cheaper labor markets in the South but continued to suffer from decreased demand and overproduction. Mining and lumbering, which had expanded in response to wartime demands, experienced the same problem. Coal mining was especially battered by overexpansion, outdated technology, and competition from new energy sources, including hydroelectric power, fuel oil, and natural gas, as well as a legacy of bitter labor struggles. And the railroad industry, damaged by stiff competition from truck transportation on publicly subsidized roads, faced shrinking passenger revenues and stagnant freight levels. While these older sectors of the economy faltered, newer and more successful consumer-based industries, such as chemicals, appliances, and food processing, proved not yet strong enough to lead the way to recovery.

Unequal Distribution of Wealth. The country's unequal distribution of wealth also contributed to the severity of the depression. During the 1920s the share of national income going to families in the upper- and middle-income brackets increased. The tax policies of Secretary of the Treasury Andrew Mellon contributed to that concentration of wealth by lowering personal income tax rates, eliminating the wartime excess-profits tax, and increasing deductions that favored affluent individuals and corporations. In 1929, the poorest 40 percent of the population received only 12.5 percent of aggregate family personal income, whereas the wealthiest 5 percent of the population received 30 percent. Once the depression began, this skewed income distribution prevented people from spending the amounts of money necessary to revive the economy.

The Deepening Economic Crisis

The Great Depression became self-perpetuating. The more the American economy contracted, the longer people expected the depression to last; and the longer they expected it to last, the more afraid they were to spend or invest their money, if they had any—and spending and investing was exactly what was needed to stimulate economic recovery. The economy showed some improvement in the summer of 1931 when low prices encouraged consumption, but it plunged again late in the fall.

At that point the chronically depressed agricultural sector put pressure on the commercial banking system, worsening the economic contraction. The nation's banks had already been weakened by the stock market crash. When agricultural prices and incomes fell more steeply than usual in 1930, many farmers went bankrupt, causing rural banks to fail in alarming numbers. By December 1930 so many rural banks had defaulted on their obligations that urban banks also began to fail. The wave of bank failures frightened depositors into withdrawing their savings, further deepening the crisis.

A change in the nation's monetary policy in 1931 added to the banking problems. During the first phase of the depression the Federal Reserve System had reacted cautiously. But in October 1931 the Federal Reserve Bank of New York significantly increased the discount rate—the interest rate it charged on loans to member banks—and cut back the amount of money placed in circulation through purchase of government securities. This miscalculation squeezed the money supply, forcing prices down and depriving businesses of funds for investment. By March 1933, when the economy reached its lowest point, the money supply had fallen by about one-third from its August 1929 level.

In the face of that money shortage, the country could have been pulled out of the depression only if the American people spent at a higher rate. But because of falling prices, rising unemployment, and a troubled banking system, Americans preferred to hold on to their dollars, stashing them under the mattress rather than depositing them in the bank. Economic stagnation set in.

The Worldwide Depression

President Hoover later blamed the severity of the depression on the international economic situation. Although domestic factors far outweighed international causes of America's protracted economic decline, Hoover was correct in surmising that economic problems in the rest of the world affected the United States, and vice versa. Indeed, the international economic system had been out of kilter since World War I. It functioned only as long as American banks exported enough capital to allow European countries to repay their debts and continue to buy American manufactured goods and agricultural products. By the late 1920s European economies were staggering under the weight of large debts and trade imbalances with the United States, which undercut the recovery that had seemed possible earlier in the decade. By 1931 most European economies had collapsed.

In an interdependent world, the downturn of the American economy had enormous repercussions. When U.S. companies cut back production, they also cut back their purchases of raw materials and supplies from abroad, and this devastated many foreign economies. When American financiers sharply reduced foreign investment and consumers bought fewer European goods, debt repayment became even more difficult. As European economic conditions worsened,

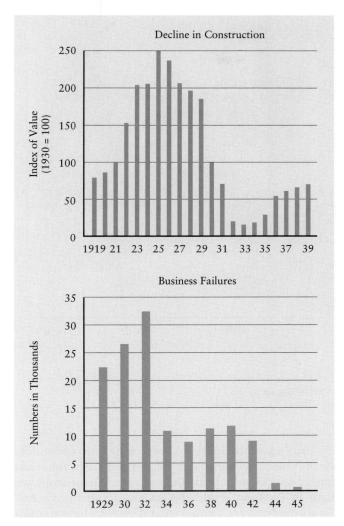

FIGURE 24.1
Statistics of the Depression
The top graph shows the decline in construction, as reflected in the value of new building permits; the bottom graph shows the numbers of business failures.
Source: Historical Statistics of the United States, Colonial Times to 1970 (Washington, DC: U.S. Government Printing Office, 1975), 626, 912.

the stock market crash in 1929 to the depths of the depression in 1932–1933, the U.S. gross national product was cut almost in half, declining from $103.1 billion to $58 billion in 1932. Consumption expenditures dropped by 18 percent, construction fell by 78 percent, private investment plummeted by 88 percent, and farm income, already low, was more than cut in half. During this period 9,000 banks went bankrupt or closed their doors, and 100,000 businesses failed. The consumer price index declined by 25 percent, and corporate profits fell from $10 billion to $1 billion.

Most telling, unemployment rose from 3.2 percent in 1929 to 24.9 percent in 1933, affecting approximately 12 million workers (Figure 24.2). Statistical measures at that time were fairly crude, and it is likely that unemployment was even higher. At least one in four workers was out of a job. Even those who had jobs faced wage cutbacks or the possibility of being laid off. Their stories put a human face on the almost incomprehensible dimensions of this economic downturn.

Hard Times

"We didn't go hungry, but we lived lean." That statement sums up the experiences of many American families during the Great Depression. The vast majority were neither very rich nor very poor. For most, the depression did not mean losing thousands of dollars in the stock market or pulling children out of a fancy boarding school, nor did it mean going on relief or living in a shantytown. In a typical family in the 1930s, the husband still had a job and the wife was still a homemaker. Life was not easy, but it usually consisted of "making do" rather than suffering stark deprivation.

Making Do

"You could feel the depression deepen," recalled the writer Caroline Bird, "but you could not look out the window and see it." Many people never saw a breadline or entered a soup kitchen. The depression caused a private kind of despair that often simmered behind closed doors. "I've lived in cities for many months broke, without help, too timid to get in breadlines," the writer Meridel LeSueur remembered. "I've known many women to live like this until they simply faint on the street from privations, without saying a word to anyone. A woman will shut herself up in a room until it is taken away from her, and eat a cracker a day and be as quiet as a mouse." (See Voices from Abroad, "Mary Agnes Hamilton: Breadlines and Beggars," p. 777.)

demand for American exports fell dramatically; this strained the gold standard, which provided a fixed standard against which the value of currencies could be pegged. Finally, when the Hawley-Smoot Tariff of 1930 (see Chapter 23) raised rates to all-time highs, foreign governments retaliated by imposing their own trade restrictions, further limiting the market for American goods—especially agricultural products. All these factors deepened the worldwide depression.

By 1933 the world economy was showing signs of recovery, although progress remained uneven. No other major trading nation was hit as hard as the United States, however. The statistics paint a stark picture (Figure 24.1). From the height of the prosperity before

FIGURE 24.2
Unemployment, 1915–1945
As this graph shows, the historically low unemployment levels of the 1920s began to rise in 1930. By 1933 one in four American workers was out of a job.

"Mass unemployment is both a statistic and an empty feeling in the stomach," observed the writer Cabell Phillips. "To fully comprehend it, you have to both see the figures and feel the emptiness." The victims of the depression were a varied group. The depression did not create poverty; it merely publicized the conditions of the poor. People who had always been poor were joined by the newly poor. Those formerly solid working-class and middle-class families strongly believed in the Horatio Alger ethic of upward mobility through hard work but suddenly found themselves floundering in a society that no longer had a place for them. They were proud people who felt humiliated by their plight, and many blamed themselves for their misfortune. "What is going to become of us?" asked a man in Arizona. "I've lost twelve and a half pounds this last month, just thinking. You can't sleep, you know. You wake up at 2 A.M. and you lie and think."

Hard times weighed heavily on senior citizens, many of whom faced utter destitution after losing their savings in bank failures. In a cartoon from the 1930s a squirrel asks a man on a park bench why he did not save for a rainy day. "I did," the man replies listlessly. Children, by contrast, often escaped the sense of bitterness and failure that gripped their elders; some youngsters thought it was fun to stand in a soup line. Yet hard times made children grow up fast.

Downward mobility was especially hard for middle-class Americans because it challenged basic American tenets of individualism and success. An unemployed man in Pittsburgh told the journalist Lorena Hickok, "Lady, you just can't know what it's like to have to move your family out of the nice house you had in the suburbs, part paid for, down into an apartment, down into another apartment, smaller and in a worse neighborhood, down, down, down, until finally you end up in the slums." Before a laid-off chauffeur started a relief construction job, he spent the day watching how the other men handled their picks and shovels so he could "get the hang of it and not feel so awkward." A woman broke into tears when her husband, formerly a white-collar worker, put on his first pair of overalls to go to work.

The key to surviving the depression was to maintain one's self-respect. One man spent two years painting his father's house (in fact, he painted it twice). Keeping up appearances, keeping life as close to normal as possible, was an essential strategy. Camaraderie and cooperation helped many families and communities survive as people found that they were all in the same boat. When a driver "accidentally" dumped a load of oranges or coal off the back of his truck, he was contributing to the welfare of the neighborhood. Hoboes developed an elaborate system of sidewalk chalk marks to tell one another at which back doors they could get a meal, an old coat, or some spare change.

Mary Agnes Hamilton
Breadlines and Beggars

————— ★ —————

British writer and Labor Party activist Mary Agnes Hamilton arrived in the United States on a gloomy morning in December 1931 for a lecture tour that eventually took her as far west as Nebraska and as far south as Virginia. Her observations of conditions in New York during that grim winter confirm the devastation and despair gripping urban America.

One does not need to be long in New York (or for that matter in Chicago, in Cleveland, in Detroit, in Kansas, or in Buffalo) to see that there are plenty of real tragedies, as well as plenty of not-so-real ones. If those who have turned in the second or third car talk the most, the others talk—when they get the chance. In New York, one has only to pass outside the central island bounded by Lexington and Sixth Avenues to see hardship, misery, and degradation, accentuated by the shoddy grimness of the shabby houses and broken pavements. Look down from the Elevated, and there are long queues of dreary-looking men and women standing in "breadlines" outside the relief offices and the various church and other charitable institutions. Times Square, at any hour of the day and late into the evening, offers an exhibit for the edification of the theater-goer, for it is packed with shabby, utterly dumb and apathetic-looking men, who stand there, waiting for the advent of the coffee wagon run by Mr. W. R. Hearst of the New York *American*. Nowhere, in New York or any other city, can one escape from the visible presence of those who with perhaps unconscious cruelty are called "the idle." At every street corner, and wherever taxi or car has to pause, men try to sell one apples, oranges, or picture papers. Not matches—matches, in book form, are given away with every fifteen-cent package of cigarettes, lie on every restaurant table, litter the street, half used, and exemplify how little, as yet, the depression has done to overcome the national habit of easy-going wastefulness. On a fine day, men will press on one gardenias at fifteen cents apiece; on any day, rows of them line every relatively open space, eager to shine one's shoes. It is perhaps because so many people are doing without this "shine," or attempting with unfamiliar hands and a sense of deep indignity to shine their own, that the streets look shabby and the persons on them so much less well-groomed than of yore. The well-shod feet of the States struck me forcibly on my first visit; the ill-cleaned feet of New York struck me as forcibly in January and April 1932. In 1930 an English friend, long domesticated in New England, told me that she hesitated to bring her children to London, since the sight of beggars would make so painful an impression on them; in 1932 there are more beggars to be met with in New York than in London. Yes, distress is there; the idle are there. How many, no one really knows. Ten million or more in the country; a million and a half in New York are reported. They are there; as is, admittedly a dark undergrowth of horrid suffering that is certainly more degraded and degrading than anything Britain or Germany knows. Their immense presence makes a grim background to the talk of depression: there is an obscure alarm as to what they may do "if this goes on," and the charitable relief funds (about which more later) dry up, as they are in many centers already doing; their existence, in numbers that grow instead of diminishing, constitutes the fact that largely justifies the feeling of gloom. . . .

The American people, unfamiliar with suffering, with none of that long history of catastrophe and calamity behind it which makes the experience of European nations, is outraged and baffled by misfortune. Depression blocks its view: it cannot see round it. Misled in the onset by leaders who assured it, in every soothing term and tone, that reverse was to last but for a little while; that it was the preliminary to recovery; that American institutions were immune to the ills that had laid the countries of the rest of the world upon their backs; that prosperity was native to the soil of the Union, and all that was needed was to wait till the clouds, blown up by the wickedness of other lands, rolled by, as they were bound to do, and that speedily; the nation now suffers from a despair of any and every kind of leadership. Every institution is assailed; even the sacred foundations of democracy are being undermined. The defeatism that has been so lamentably evidenced in Congress is not peculiar to Congressmen, any more than is the crude individualism of their reactions. It lies like a pall over the spirit of the nation. It is felt by most people to be, in fact, the greatest obstacle to recovery, to that restoration of confidence for which everybody pleads, which everybody sees as necessary. But how to break it nobody knows.

Source: Mary Agnes Hamilton, *In America Today* (1932), in Allan Nevins, ed., *America through British Eyes* (Gloucester, MA: Peter Smith, 1968), 443–444.

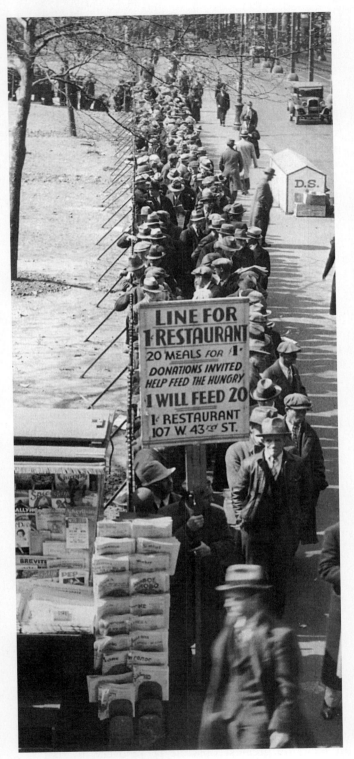

The Breadline

Some of the most vivid images from the depression were breadlines and men selling apples on street corners. Note that all the people in this breadline are men. Women rarely appeared in breadlines, often preferring to endure private deprivation rather than violate standards of respectable behavior by appearing in public to ask for help.

Franklin D. Roosevelt Library, Hyde Park, NY.

After their savings and credit had been exhausted, many families faced the humiliation of going on relief. Seeking aid from state or local governments hurt people's pride and disrupted the traditional pattern of turning to relatives, neighbors, churches, and mutual-aid societies in times of need. Even if families survived the demeaning process of being certified for state or local relief, the amount they received was a pittance. In New York State, for example, where benefits were among the highest in the nation, a family received only $2.39 a week.

Such hardships left deep wounds—Caroline Bird called it an "invisible scar." One elderly civil servant bought a plot of land outside Washington so that if the depression recurred, she would have the means to live. The labor organizer Larry Van Dusen described a common reaction: "The depression left a legacy of fear, but also a desire for acquisition—property, security. I now have twenty times more shirts than I need, because all during that time, shirts were something I never had" (see American Voices, "Larry Van Dusen: A Working-Class Family Encounters the Great Depression," p. 779). Virginia Durr, a white civil rights activist from Alabama, concurred: "The great majority reacted by thinking money is the most important thing in the world. Get yours. And get it for your children. Nothing else matters. Not having that stark terror come at you again." For many Americans, "that stark terror" of losing control over their lives summed up the Great Depression.

Families Face the Great Depression

Sociologists who studied family life during the 1930s found that the depression generally intensified existing behavior. If a family had been stable and cohesive before the depression, it pulled together to overcome the new obstacles. However, if a family had shown signs of disintegration, the depression made the situation worse. On the whole, researchers thought that far more families hung together than broke apart.

Men and women experienced the Great Depression differently, partly because of the traditional gender roles that governed behavior in the 1930s. Men had been trained from childhood to be breadwinners and considered themselves failures if they could no longer support their families. Women, however, felt their self-importance increase as they struggled to keep their families afloat. The sociologists Robert and Helen Lynd noticed this phenomenon in their follow-up study of Middletown (Muncie, Indiana), published in 1937: "The men, cut adrift from their usual routine, lost much of their sense of time and dawdled helplessly and dully about the streets; while in the homes the women's world remained largely intact and the round of cooking, housecleaning, and mending became if anything more absorbing." Even if a wife took a job when her husband lost his, she retained almost total responsibility for housework and child care.

Larry Van Dusen

A Working-Class Family Encounters the Great Depression

———————★———————

Although many families endured the privations of the Great Depression with equanimity, others, like Larry Van Dusen's family, experienced tremendous strains. In this passage from his oral history account to journalist Studs Terkel, he describes the pressures on male wage earners and their children.

One of the most common things—and it certainly happened to me—was this feeling of your father's failure. That somehow he hadn't beaten the rap. Sure things were tough, but why should I be the kid who had to put a piece of cardboard into the sole of my shoe to go to school? It was not a thing coupled with resentment against my father. It was simply this feeling of regret, that somehow he hadn't done better, that he hadn't gotten the breaks. Also a feeling of uneasiness about my father's rage against the way things are.

My father was very much of an individualist, as craftsmen usually are. He would get jobs he considered beneath his status during this period. Something would happen: he'd quarrel with the foreman, he'd have a fight with the boss. He was a carpenter. He couldn't be happy fixing a roadbed or driving a cab or something like that. He was a skilled tradesman and this whole thing had him beat. I think it bugged the family a lot.

Remember, too, the shock, the confusion, the hurt that many kids felt about their fathers not being able to provide for them. This reflected itself very often in bitter quarrels between father and son. I recall I had one. I was the oldest of six children. I think there was a special feeling between the father and the oldest son. . . .

My father led a rough life: he drank. During the Depression, he drank more. There was more conflict in the home. A lot of fathers—mine, among them—had a habit of taking off. They'd go to Chicago to look for work. To Topeka. This left the family at home, waiting and hoping that the old man would find something. And there was always the Saturday night ordeal as to whether or not the old man would get home with his paycheck. Everything was sharpened and hurt more by the Depression.

Heaven would break out once in a while, and the old man would get a week's work. I remember he'd come home at night, and he'd come down the path through the trees. He always rode a bicycle. He'd stop and sometimes say hello, or give me a hug. And that smell of fresh sawdust on those carpenter overalls, and the fact that Dad was home, and there was a week's wages—well, this is something you remember, too. That's the good you remember.

And then there was always the bad part. That's when you'd see your father coming home with the toolbox on his shoulder. Or carrying it. That meant the job was over. The tools were home now, and we were back on the treadmill again.

I remember coming back home, many years afterwards. Things were better. It was after the Depression, after the war. To me, it was hardly the same house. My father turned into an angel. They weren't wealthy, but they were making it. They didn't have the acid and the recriminations and the bitterness that I had felt as a child.

Source: Studs Terkel, *Hard Times* (New York: Pantheon Books, 1986), 107–108.

Despite the hard times, Americans maintained a fairly high level of consumption. As in the 1920s, households in the middle-income range—the 50.2 percent of American families with an income of $500 to $1,500 in 1935—did much of the buying. Several factors enabled those families more or less to maintain their former standard of living despite pay cuts or unemployment—especially the deflation that lowered the cost of living by almost 20 percent between 1929 and 1935. For example, milk sold for 10 cents a quart, bread for 7 cents a loaf, and butter for 23 cents a pound. Families also spent their reduced income differently. Telephone use and clothing sales dropped sharply, but cigarettes, movies, radio, and newspapers, once considered luxuries, now became necessities. The automobile proved to be one of the most depression-proof items in the family budget. Though sales of new cars dropped, gasoline sales were stable, suggesting that people bought used cars or kept their old models running longer.

Some families maintained their life-styles in the 1930s through "deficit living"—that is, using install-ment payments and credit to stretch their income. By 1936 consumer credit in the United States had increased by 20 percent over 1929 levels. A Middletown resident summed up the prevailing attitude toward installment buying: "Most of the families I know are after the same things today that they were after before the Depression, and they'll get them in the same way—on credit."

To maintain their families' life-styles, housewives substituted their own labor for goods and services they had formerly purchased. Women sewed their own clothes and canned fruits and vegetables. They prac-ticed small economies such as buying day-old bread and heating several dishes in the oven at once to save fuel; two friends who often bought hamburger together split 2 pounds for 25 cents and took turns keeping the extra penny. Women who had formerly employed ser-vants now did their own housework. Those economies helped pay for cars and trips to the movies. Women generally accepted their new work stoically. "We had no choice," remembered one housewife. "We just did what had to be done one day at a time."

Another way for families to make ends meet in the 1930s was to send an additional member of the house-hold to work. At the turn of the century that additional family worker was often a child or a young unmarried adult; in the 1930s it was increasingly a married woman. Instead of expelling women from the work force, the depression solidified their position in it. The 1940 census reported almost 11 million women in the work force, approximately one-fourth of the nation's workers and a small increase over 1930. The number of married women employed outside the home rose 50 percent.

Working women, especially married ones, encoun-tered sharp resentment and outright discrimination when they entered the depression workplace. After calculating that the number of employed women roughly equaled the 1939 unemployment total, the editor Norman Cousins suggested this tongue-in-cheek remedy: "Simply fire the women, who shouldn't be working anyway, and hire the men. Presto! No unemployment. No relief rolls. No depression." A 1936 Gallup poll asked whether wives should work when their husbands had jobs, and 82 percent of the people interviewed said no. From 1932 to 1937 the federal government would not allow a husband and wife to hold government jobs at the same time, and many states adopted laws that prohibited married women from working, especially in the field of education.

The attempt to make women scapegoats for the depression rested on shaky moral and economic grounds. Most women worked because they had to. A sizable minority were the sole support of their families

Women Face the Depression
Most information for the 1930 census, conducted just as the depression gripped the nation, was gathered in personal inter-views. This well-dressed census taker, Marie Cioffi, was proba-bly lucky to get the job. The woman she is interviewing on East 112th Street in New York City, Margaret Napolitana, was likely a homemaker and, from her attire and expression, a struggling one. Meanwhile her daughter is not quite sure what to make of the two women's conversation.
Corbis-Bettmann.

because their husbands had left home or lost their jobs. Single, divorced, deserted, or widowed women had no husbands to support them. Moreover, women rarely took jobs away from men. "Few of the people who oppose married women's employment," observed one feminist in 1940, "seem to realize that a coal miner or steel worker cannot very well fill the jobs of nurse-maids, cleaning women, or the factory and clerical jobs now filled by women." Custom, rather than law or eco-nomics, made crossovers rare.

The division of the work force by gender gave women a small edge during the depression. Many fields with large numbers of female employees, including clerical, sales, and service and trade occupations, suffered less from economic contraction than did the steel industry, mining, and manufacturing, which employed men almost exclusively. As a result, unemployment rates for women, although extremely high, were somewhat lower than those for men. This small bonus came at a high price, however. The jobs women held reinforced the traditional stereotypes of women's work. When the depression ended, women found themselves even more concentrated in low-paying, dead-end jobs than when it began.

The depression workplace also benefited white women at the expense of nonwhite women. To make ends meet, white women willingly took jobs usually held by blacks or minority workers—domestic service, for example. White men also took jobs previously held by minority group men. In both cases employers were quick to act on their preference for a white work force.

During the Great Depression there were few feminist demands for equal rights at home or on the job. On an individual basis, women's self-esteem probably rose because of their importance to family survival. Most men and women, however, continued to believe that the two sexes should have fundamentally different roles and responsibilities and that a woman's life cycle should be shaped by marriage, child rearing, and her husband's career. The substantial contributions made by women in the 1930s actually reinforced their overall identification with the home, laying the foundation for the so-called feminine mystique of the 1950s.

Demographic Trends

Another measure of the impact of the depression on family life was the change in demographic trends during the 1930s. The marriage rate fell from 10.14 per thousand persons in 1929 to 7.87 in 1932. The divorce rate dropped as well because people could not afford the legal expenses of dissolving failed marriages. Although marriage and divorce rates rebounded after 1933, postponement of marriage sometimes became permanent. Elsa Ponselle, a Chicago schoolteacher who later became the principal of one of that city's largest elementary schools, recalled her experience:

> *Do you realize how many people in my generation are not married? . . . It wasn't that we didn't have a chance. I was going with someone when the Depression hit. We probably would have gotten married. He was a commercial artist and had been doing very well. . . . Suddenly he was laid off. It hit him like a ton of bricks. And he just disappeared.*

The birth rate was the demographic factor most affected by the depression. The birth rate had fallen steadily since 1800, but from 1930 to 1933 it dropped from 21.3 live births per thousand population to 18.4, a

14 percent decrease. The 1933 level, if maintained, would have led to a population decline. The birth rate rose slightly after 1934, but by the end of the decade it had reached only 18.8. In contrast, at the height of the baby boom following World War II, the birth rate was 25 per thousand population.

The 1930s marked a significant stage in the long history of the birth control movement in America. In 1936, in *United States v. One Package of Japanese Pessaries*, a federal court struck down all federal restrictions on the dissemination of contraceptive information. Doctors now had wide discretion in prescribing birth control for married couples, which became legal in all states except Massachusetts and Connecticut. Public support for contraception increased: in a 1936 Gallup poll, 63 percent of those interviewed favored making birth control information more widely available. These changing attitudes meant thriving business for the makers of diaphragms and condoms, the most common forms of birth control at that time.

Margaret Sanger played a major role in encouraging the availability and popular acceptance of birth control. As a public health nurse in the slums of New York in the 1910s, she had fielded questions from anxious immigrant women eager to know the "secret" of how to avoid having more babies. When a patient who had been referred to her died after a botched abortion, Sanger dedicated her life to expanding access to birth control. At first she joined forces with socialist movements aimed at the working class. In the 1920s and 1930s, however, she appealed to the middle class for support, identifying this segment of the population as the key to the movement's success. Sanger also courted the medical profession, pioneering the establishment of birth control clinics staffed by doctors, and winning the American Medical Association's endorsement of contraception in 1937. Birth control became less a feminist demand and more a medical issue.

Contraception had long been a private matter between individuals. Its public acceptance increased greatly during the 1930s because of the widespread desire to limit family size for economic reasons. In 1942 the American Birth Control League, which Sanger had founded in 1921, became Planned Parenthood, an organization that remains active today.

Hard Times for Youth

The depression hit the nation's 21 million young people especially hard. Although children only dimly glimpsed the sacrifices made in the 1930s, adolescents knew that making do usually meant doing without. The writer Maxine Davis, who traveled 10,000 miles in 1936 interviewing the nation's youth, described them as "runners, delayed at the gun." She added, "The depression years have left us with a generation robbed of time and

American Youth in the 1930s
Farm Security Administration photographer Russell Lee took this photograph of a soda jerk in Corpus Christi, Texas, in 1939. A job at the local drugstore as a soda jerk (the name came from the machine handles used to make ice-cream sodas and shakes) was a great way for a teenage boy to make a little extra cash in the depression, plus show off for his peers.
Library of Congress.

opportunity just as the Great War left the world its heritage of a lost generation." Studies of social mobility confirm that the young men who entered adulthood during the depression era had less successful careers than did those before or since. About 250,000 young people became so demoralized that they took to the road as hoboes and "sisters of the road," as female tramps were called.

Because job prospects were so dim, some young people chose to stay in school longer. Public schools were free and were warm in the winter. In 1930 less than half the nation's youth attended high school, compared with three-fourths in 1940 at the end of the depression. This was partly due to increased attendance by boys, who had traditionally dropped out of school to work at an earlier age than did girls. College, however, remained the privilege of a distinct minority. With times so rough, the "college of hard knocks" was about all most depression-era youths could expect. About 1.2 million young people, or 7.5 percent of the population between the ages of eighteen and twenty-four, attended college in the 1930s, 40 percent of them women. After 1935 college became a little more affordable because of the National Youth Administration (NYA), which provided part-time employment to more than 2 million college and high school students. This government agency also provided work for 2.6 million out-of-school youths.

Financial sacrifices contributed to the seriousness of purpose among college students in the 1930s. The influence of fraternities and sororities declined during the depression, and many students became involved in political movements. Fueled by disillusionment with World War I, thousands took the "Oxford Pledge" never to support a war in which the United States might be involved. In 1936 the Student Strike against War drew support from several hundred thousand students across the country.

Despite the economic sacrifices demanded by the depression, adolescence became increasingly institutionalized in the 1930s. Through high school and college attendance, organized athletics, and extracurricular activities, young people developed their own values and patterns of behavior. Peers, rather than parents, influenced their values and tastes. Magazines and movies promoted a youth culture that was closely tied to an ethos of consumption. Teenagers throughout the country read the same comics, wore the same style of clothes, and saw the same movies. They also experimented with necking, petting, and dating rituals that shocked their elders. By now the youth culture first noticed in the 1920s had became a permanent feature of modern life.

Dancing Cheek to Cheek
During the Great Depression, Americans turned to inexpensive recreational activities such as listening to the radio and going to the movies. One of the most popular attractions in Hollywood movies was the dance team of Fred Astaire and Ginger Rogers, who starred together in ten movies.
Steve Schapiro.

The Grapes of Wrath
John Steinbeck's best-selling 1939 novel became one of the top movies of the 1940s. Ma Joad, played by Jane Darwell, expressed the central message of both the book and the film: "We're the people that live. They ain't gonna wipe us out. Why, we're the people—we go on."
Steve Schapiro.

Popular Culture

Americans turned to popular culture to alleviate some of the worst trauma of the depression. The mass culture that grew so dramatically in the 1920s flourished in the decade that followed, offering not just entertainment but commentary on the problems that beset the nation. Movies and radio served as a forum for criticizing the system—especially politicians and bankers—as well as vehicles for reaffirming traditional ideals.

Movies. Despite the closing of one-third of the country's theaters by 1933, the movie industry and its studio system prospered. More than 60 percent of Americans saw at least one movie a week, with weekly attendance ranging from 60 million to 75 million. One of the most popular (and highly paid) stars was Mae West, who titillated—or shocked—moviegoers with sexual innuendos like "I used to be Snow White, but I drifted" and "It's not the men in my life, but the life in my men that counts." In response to public outcry by the Catholic Legion of Decency and other religious groups that were against supposed immorality in the early talkies, the industry set up the Production Code Administration in 1934. Committing themselves to a form of self-censorship, studios agreed to banish explicit sex, immorality, and violence from the screen. The new standards were so strict that censors barely permitted Rhett Butler to utter the famous last line of *Gone with the Wind*: "Frankly, my dear, I don't give a damn."

Hollywood movies offered more than just escape from hard times. Many of the 5,000 movies produced during the depression decade contained complex messages that reflected a real sense of the societal crisis that engulfed the nation. The cultural historian Lawrence W. Levine has argued that depression-era films were "deeply grounded in the realities and intricacies of the Depression" and thus offer a wealth of information about the period. Even if they did not deal specifically with the economic or political crisis, many films reaffirmed traditional values such as democracy, individualism, and egalitarianism. They also contained criticisms—suggestions that the system was not working, or that law and order had broken down. Thus, popular gangster movies—such as *Public Enemy* (1931), with James Cagney, or *Little Caesar* (1930), starring Edward G. Robinson—can be seen as perverse Horatio Alger tales in which the main character struggles to succeed in a harsh environment. Often these movies suggested that incompetent or corrupt politicians, police, and business leaders were as much to blame for organized crime as the gangsters themselves.

Depression-era films repeatedly portrayed politicians as cynical and corrupt. In *Washington Merry-Go-Round* (1932), lobbyists manipulated weak congressmen to undermine democratic rule. The Marx Brothers' irreverent comedies criticized authority and most everything else. In *Duck Soup* (1933), Groucho Marx played Rufus T. Firefly, president of the mythical nation of Freedonia, who sings gleefully:

The last man nearly ruined this place,
He didn't know what to do with it.
If you think this country's bad off now,
Just wait till I get through with it.

Few filmmakers left more of a mark on the decade than Frank Capra. An Italian immigrant who personified the possibilities of success the United States offered, Capra made films that spoke to Americans' idealism. In movies like *Mr. Deeds Goes to Town* (1936) and *Mr. Smith Goes to Washington* (1939), he pitted the virtuous small-town hero against corrupt urban shysters—business leaders, lobbyists, and newspaper publishers—whose schemes subverted the nation's ideals. Though the hero usually prevailed, Capra was realistic enough to suggest that the victory was not necessarily permanent, that the problems the nation faced were very serious.

At the height of the depression, movies continued to influence consumers. One of the decade's top box-office stars was a curly-headed little girl named Shirley Temple, who made twenty-one films by 1941. Shirley Temple dolls, books, and clothes flooded the market. Similarly, because of the popularity of glamorous blondes such as Jean Harlow, Carole Lombard, and Mae West, sales of peroxide hair rinse skyrocketed. Sales of undershirts fell drastically after Clark Gable, a leading sex symbol of the 1930s, took off his shirt in *It Happened One Night* and revealed his bare chest.

Radio Days. Radio occupied an increasingly important place in popular culture during the 1930s (Map 24.1). At the beginning of the decade about 13 million households had a radio set; by the end of the decade, 27.5 million owned one. Listeners tuned in to daytime serials such as "Ma Perkins" or picked up useful household hints on "The Betty Crocker Hour." Variety shows featured Jack Benny, George Burns and Gracie Allen, and the ventriloquist Edgar Bergen and his impudent dummy, Charlie McCarthy. Millions of listeners followed the adventures of the Lone Ranger (with his trademark cry, "Hi-Ho Silver"), Superman, and detective Dick Tracy.

Radio also brought music to depression-era audiences. Classical music devotees could listen to live Saturday afternoon performances of New York's Metropolitan Opera (begun in 1931 and still being broadcast) or the NBC Symphony Orchestra under the baton of Arturo Toscanini. On the lighter side, people loved the new Big Band "swing" music of Benny Goodman, Duke Ellington, and Tommy Dorsey—an outgrowth of the jazz craze of the 1920s—and Cole Porter songs such as "Begin the Beguine" and "Night and Day" from Broadway shows. Radio increased the consumer market for 78-rpm. phonograph records of classical music, swing, and Broadway show tunes.

Like the movies, radio offered Americans more than escape. A running gag in comedian Jack Benny's show was his stinginess: audiences could certainly identify with an unwillingness, or inability, to spend money. Even more relevant was Benny's distrust of banks. He kept his money in an underground vault guarded by a polar bear named Carmichael—presumably a more reliable place than the nation's financial institutions.

The radio program "Amos 'n' Andy" is remembered primarily for its racial stereotyping (see Chapter 23), but the popular show also dealt with hard times, often referring explicitly to the depression. A central theme of the program was the contrast between Amos's hard work and Andy's more carefree approach to life. As the historian Arthur Frank Wertheim notes, "The way that the characters' hopes for monetary success were turned into business failures mirrored the lives of many Americans."

Not all leisure time was filled by commercial entertainment. In a resurgence of traditional values, attendance at religious services rose. The home once again became a center of leisure activity, with an evening by the radio providing an inexpensive form of family entertainment. Amateur photography and stamp collecting enjoyed tremendous vogue (President Franklin Roosevelt was an avid stamp collector), as did board games like Monopoly. Reading aloud from books borrowed from the public library was another affordable diversion. But Americans bought books too, taking advantage of new manufacturing techniques that made books less expensive. Readers made best sellers of Margaret Mitchell's *Gone with the Wind* (1936), Dale Carnegie's *How to Win Friends and Influence People* (1936), Pearl Buck's *The Good Earth* (1932), and James Hilton's *Lost Horizon* (1933). Columnist Russell Baker

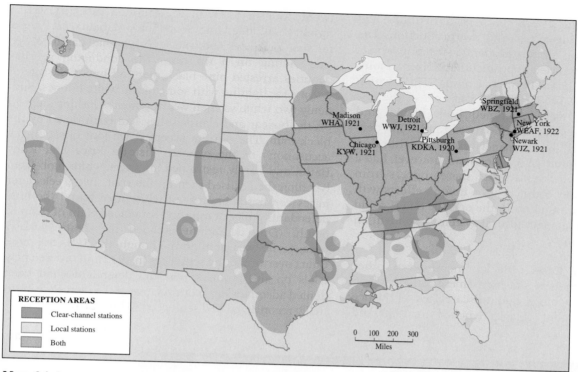

MAP 24.1

The Spread of Radio

In 1938 more than 26 million American households, or about three-quarters of the population, had a radio. Four national networks dominated the field, broadcasting news and entertainment across the country. Powerful clear-channel stations reached listeners hundreds of miles away. By 1939 only a few sparsely populated areas were beyond radio's reach.

recalled an activity everyone could afford: "Talking was the Great Depression pastime. Unlike the movies, talk was free."

Harder Times

★

Much writing about the 1930s has focused on white working-class or middle-class families that were caught in a spiral of downward social mobility. For such groups as African Americans, farmers, and Mexican Americans, times had always been hard, and during the 1930s they just got harder. As the poet Langston Hughes noted, "The depression brought everybody down a peg or two. And the Negroes had but few pegs to fall."

Blacks in the Depression

African Americans had always known discrimination and limited opportunity, so they viewed the depression differently than most whites did. "It didn't mean too much to him, the Great American Depression, as you call it," one man remarked. "There was no such thing. The best he could be is a janitor or a porter or shoeshine boy. It only became official when it hit the white man." The novelist and poet Maya Angelou, who grew up in Stamps, Arkansas, recalled, "The country had been in the throes of the Depression for two years before the Negroes in Stamps knew it. I think that everyone thought the Depression, like everything else, was for the white folks."

Despite the black migration to northern cities that had begun before World War I, as late as 1940 more than 75 percent of African Americans still lived in the South. Nearly all the farmers who were black lived in the South, their condition scarcely better than it had been at the end of Reconstruction. Only 20 percent of black farmers owned their own land; the rest toiled at the bottom of the exploitative southern agricultural system as tenant farmers, farmhands, and sharecroppers. During the 1930s African Americans rarely earned more than $200 a year, and in one Louisiana parish black women averaged only $41.67 a year picking cotton.

Throughout the 1920s southern agriculture had suffered from falling prices and overproduction. The depression made an already desperate situation worse. Some black farmers tried to protect themselves by joining the Southern Tenant Farmers Union (STFU), which was founded in 1934. The STFU was one of the few southern groups that welcomed both blacks and whites. "The same chain that holds you holds my people, too," an elderly black farmer reminded whites on the organizing committee. Landowners, however, had a stake in keeping black and white sharecroppers from organizing, and they countered the union's efforts with repression and harassment. In the end the STFU could do little to reform an agricultural system dependent on a single crop—cotton.

The Scottsboro Case. Blacks encountered other forms of discrimination and harassment, often violent, in the 1930s. Lynchings and miscarriages of justice increased, with twenty blacks lynched in 1930 and twenty-four in 1933. In a celebrated case in 1931, a freight train pulled into Scottsboro, Alabama, carrying a number of hoboes and transients who had caught a free ride. Acting on a tip from the conductor, sheriff's deputies arrested nine black men, all under the age of twenty, for fighting with some of the white hoboes. Suddenly two white women wearing men's clothing stepped off the boxcar and claimed they had been raped by the black men. The officers accepted without question the accusations of the women, Victoria Price and Ruby Bates, and barely restrained an angry white mob from lynching the accused men on the spot. Two weeks later juries composed entirely of white men found the nine defendants guilty of rape and sentenced eight of them to death. (One defendant escaped the death penalty because he was a minor.) Though the U.S. Supreme Court overturned the sentences in 1932 and ordered new trials on the grounds that the defendants had been denied adequate legal counsel, five of the men were eventually reconvicted and sentenced to long prison terms.

Lynching
The threat of lynching remained a terrifying part of life for African Americans in the 1930s, and not just in the South. Artist Joe Jones set this canvas in 1933, perhaps influenced by the fact that twenty-four blacks were lynched that year. He gave it the ironic title of *American Justice, 1933 (White Justice)*.
Collection of Philip J. and Suzanne Schiller.

The youth of the Scottsboro defendants, their hasty trials, and the harsh sentences stirred public protest, prompting the International Labor Defense (ILD), a labor organization closely tied to the American Communist Party, to take over their defense. The Communist Party had targeted the struggle against racism as a priority in the early 1930s but was making little headway in its recruitment of blacks. "It's bad enough being black, why be red?" was a common reaction. White southerners resented the interference of those radicals as well as the fact that almost all those involved in the Scottsboro defense were northerners and Jews. In the words of a local solicitor, "Alabama justice cannot be bought and sold with Jew money from New York."

The case was complicated by the southern myth of the inviolate honor and chastity of white womanhood. The stories of the two women contained many inconsistencies, and Ruby Bates later recanted. However, when a white southern woman claimed to have been raped by a black man, she was taken at her word. As a court observer remarked, Victoria Price "might be a fallen woman, but by God she is a white woman."

The Scottsboro case received wide coverage in black communities across the country. Along with the increase in lynching in the early 1930s, it provided black Americans with a strong incentive to head for northern and midwestern cities. However, the lure of the North was offset by the lack of economic opportunities caused by the depression. About 400,000 black men and women left the South during the 1930s, only about half the number that had departed in the 1920s. Nevertheless, by 1935 eleven northern cities were home to more than 100,000 African Americans. Two of the most popular destinations were the South Side of Chicago and Harlem in New York City.

Harlem in the 1930s. Harlem's housing facilities and community services had already been strained by the enormous influx of African Americans in the 1920s, and the depression aggravated the situation. Residential segregation kept blacks from moving elsewhere, so African Americans paid excessive rents to live in deteriorating buildings. Crowded living conditions caused disease and death rates to climb, and tuberculosis became a leading cause of death in Harlem. As whites clamored for jobs traditionally held by blacks—waiters, domestic servants, elevator operators, and garbage collectors—unemployment in Harlem rose to 50 percent, twice the national rate. At the height of the depression, shelters and soup kitchens staffed by the Divine Peace Mission, under the leadership of the charismatic black religious leader Father Divine, provided 3,000 meals a day for Harlem's destitute.

In March 1935 Harlem exploded in the nation's only major race riot of the decade. Anger about the lack of jobs, a slowdown in relief services, and the economic exploitation of the black community had been building for years. Although white store owners depended entirely on black trade, they would not employ blacks. The arrest of a teenage black shoplifter, followed by rumors that he had been severely beaten by white police officers, triggered the riot. False reports of his death fueled the panic, and the city mobilized 500 police officers in response. Four blacks were killed, and property damage totaled $2 million.

The picture was not totally bleak for African Americans in the 1930s, however. The New Deal under President Franklin Delano Roosevelt would channel significant amounts of relief money toward blacks outside the South, partly in response to the 1935 riot but mainly in return for growing black allegiance to the Democratic Party (see Chapter 25). The National Association for the Advancement of Colored People continued to publicly challenge the status quo of race relations. And although calls for racial justice went largely unheeded during the depression, World War II and its aftermath would further the struggle for black equality.

Dust Bowl Migrations

Distressed conditions in agriculture had been one of the causes of the Great Depression. In the 1930s things only got worse for farmers, especially those living on the Great Plains. The decade became known as the "Dirty Thirties" because of dust storms caused by a drought, the worst in the country's history, that began in 1930 and lasted until 1941. Throughout the decade the three words most often uttered by farmers were "if it rains."

Farmers who moved onto the semiarid Great Plains after the 1870s had always risked the ravages of drought (see Chapter 16). Even in wet years the average rainfall was 20 inches or less—barely enough to raise grain crops. But low rainfall alone did not create the Dust Bowl. National and international market forces, such as the demand for wheat during World War I, had caused farmers to push the farming frontier beyond its natural limits by working increasingly marginal land to capture a profit. After that land had been stripped of its natural vegetation, the delicate ecological balance of the plains was destroyed, leaving nothing to hold the soil when the rains dried up and the winds came.

Dust became a plague of everyday life throughout the Great Plains but especially in Oklahoma, Texas, New Mexico, Colorado, Arkansas, and Kansas (Map 24.2). When the clouds of dust rolled in, streetlights blinked on as if night had fallen. Dust seeped into houses and "blackened the pillow around one's head, the dinner plates on the table, the bread dough on the back of the stove." The dust storms were not confined to the plains.

Litigating Civil Rights
In 1935 the NAACP represented Donald Gaines Murray (middle), a black
Amherst College graduate who had
been refused admission to the University of Maryland law school. NAACP
attorneys Thurgood Marshall (left)
and Charles H. Houston (right) won
the case, setting an important legal
precedent for later challenges to racial
discrimination in education. In 1967
Thurgood Marshall became the first
black to be appointed to the Supreme
Court.
Library of Congress.

In May 1934 the wind took dust clouds to Chicago,
where filth fell like snow, dumping the equivalent of
4 pounds of debris per person on the city. Several days
later the same clouds blackened the skies and dirtied
the streets of Buffalo, Boston, New York, and Washington. That winter, red snow fell on New England.

This ecological disaster caused a mass exodus from
the land. Their crops ruined, their lands barren and dry,
their homes foreclosed for debts they could not pay,
thousands of farm families loaded their belongings into
beat-up Fords and headed west along Route 66 to the
promised land of California. The migrants were called
"Okies," whether or not they were from Oklahoma.
John Steinbeck's novel *The Grapes of Wrath* (1939)
immortalized them and their journey. In the novel the
Joads abandon their land not only because of drought
but also as a result of the economic forces changing
American agriculture. Large-scale commercialized
farming was spreading to the plains. After the bank
forecloses on the Joads' farm, a gasoline-engine tractor,
the symbol of mechanized farming, plows under their
crops and demolishes their house.

Although it is a powerful work of fiction, *The
Grapes of Wrath* did not convey the diversity of the
westward migration, which was both a response to
hard times and part of the larger migration out of the
nation's agricultural heartland that had begun around

World War I and continued through the 1970s. Not all
Okies were destitute dirt farmers; approximately one in
six was a professional, a business proprietor, or a white-
collar worker. Many were participating in chain migrations, that is, following family members or friends to a
specific place. For most the drive west was fairly easy,
not the life-and-death saga portrayed in Steinbeck's
book. Route 66 was a paved two-lane road, and in a
decent car it took just three to four days to make it from
Oklahoma or Texas to California.

Before the 1930s, California had already pioneered
a type of agriculture different from that practiced by
southwestern and midwestern farmers. Agriculture in
California was large-scale, intensive, and diversified.
The state's wealth came primarily from specialty crops
such as citruses, grapes, and potatoes, whose staggered
harvests required a great deal of transient labor for
short picking seasons. The steady supply of cheap
migrant labor provided by Chinese, Mexicans, Okies,
and, briefly, East Indians made such farming economically feasible. Journalist Carey McWilliams, whose nonfiction book *Factories in the Field* (1939) focused
national attention on migrant workers, noted that California agriculture was basically industrial in nature:

> *Ownership is represented not by physical possession
> of the land, but by ownership of corporate stock;*

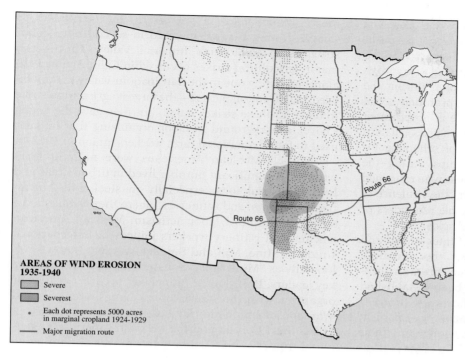

MAP 24.2
The Dust Bowl
A U.S. Weather Bureau scientist called the drought of the 1930s "the worst in the climatological history of the country." Conditions were especially severe in the southern plains, where the dramatic increases in farming on marginal land had strained production even before the drought struck. Many farm families saw no choice but to follow Route 66, the highway that went west through Missouri, Oklahoma, and north Texas, to California, the promised land.

AREAS OF WIND EROSION 1935-1940
Severe
Severest
Each dot represents 5000 acres in marginal cropland 1924-1929
Major migration route

Route 66

farm labor, no longer pastoral in character, punches a time clock, works at piece or hourly wage rates, and lives in a shack or company barracks, and lacks all contact with the real owners of the farm factory on which it is employed.

Encouraged by handbills promising good jobs in California, at least 350,000 southwesterners headed west in the 1930s. Some went to metropolitan areas, but about half settled in rural areas. White, native-born Americans had made up about 20 percent of the migratory farm labor force before the depression, but their proportion increased to more than 85 percent in the late 1930s. Since growers needed only 175,000 workers at the peak of the picking season, this surplus ensured them a cheap supply of labor, usually docile and willing to work at any price. That price was incredibly low in the 1930s. The average yearly family income of migrant farm workers in California ranged from $350 to $450, less than one-third of the subsistence level. Yet what they earned in California was more than what they had left behind.

Those migrants had a lasting impact on California culture. At first they met outright hostility from old-time Californians, a demoralizing experience for white, native-born Protestants who were ashamed of the negative Okie stereotype. But they stayed, filling important roles in the expanding California economy. Soon communities in the rich agricultural region of central California's San Joaquin Valley—Bakersfield, Fresno, Merced, Modesto, Stockton—took on a distinctly Okie cast, identifiable by southern-influenced evangelical religion and the growing popularity of country music.

Mexican American Communities

The Mexican American experience in the West differed from that of Dust Bowl refugees. In the depths of the depression, with American fears about competition from foreign workers at a peak, perhaps one-third of the Mexican American population, most of them immigrants, returned to Mexico. A formal deportation policy instituted by the U.S. government was partly responsible for the exodus, but many more Mexicans left "voluntarily" when work ran out and local relief agencies refused to extend assistance to them. Pervasive racism, coupled with the proximity of Mexico, made Mexicans the only immigrants targeted for deportation during the depression.

The deportation of Mexican Americans was not a response to the arrival of migrants from the Dust Bowl. The largest number of deportations occurred during the Hoover administration, well before the Dust Bowl exodus reached its peak. Most occurred in California and Texas, but Indiana, Illinois, Michigan, and Colorado also deported unwanted workers. In 1932, a one-way train ticket cost the equivalent of a week's relief allotment, and officials in many southwestern and western communities realized that it was cheaper to send migrant workers back to Mexico than to support them during the winter, when there were no crops to pick.

In 1930 Los Angeles was home to 150,000 Mexican Americans, giving it the largest concentration of Mexicans outside Mexico. Mexican Americans spilled out of the downtown area, known as "Sonoratown," into neighborhoods, or *colonias*, in Belvedere and East Los Angeles, where mutual-aid societies (*mutalistas*), Spanish-language newspapers, and the Catholic Church fostered a sense of community. But Los Angeles's loss of approximately one-third of its Mexican population during the repatriation drives of the 1930s caused profound social dislocations. Although the free trip home at government expense was the source of some *chistes* (jokes), it also caused family separations, disruptions of schooling for children, and extreme financial hardships during the worst years of the depression. And for those who remained in America, the threat of deportation and the virulence of anti-Mexican sentiment were unmistakable reminders of their inferior status in the eyes of most Anglos.

Mexican migration to the United States—legal and illegal—increased steadily throughout the twentieth century. The first *bracero* (day laborer) program promoting Mexican immigration had been established during World War I to meet labor shortages. (*Bracero* comes from *brazo*, which means "arm" in Spanish; *braceros* are hired hands, those who work with their arms.) The importation of cheap Mexican labor continued throughout the 1920s. After being deported during the depression, Mexican workers were coaxed back again when World War II caused another labor shortage. Ultimately the influx of Spanish-speaking migrants with their own culture helped shape the patterns of life and work in the Southwest and the West.

Discrimination and exploitation were omnipresent in Mexican communities. The harsh experiences of César Chávez's family as migrant workers during the 1930s influenced him to become one of the twentieth century's most influential labor organizers. In the mid-1930s Chávez's father became involved in several bitter labor struggles in California's Imperial Valley. Thirty-seven major agricultural strikes occurred in California in 1933 alone, including one in the San Joaquin Valley that mobilized 18,000 cotton pickers—the largest agricultural strike to date. All these strikes failed, but they gave the young Chávez a background in labor organizing that he later used to found a national farm workers' union in 1962.

Not all Mexican Americans were migrant farm workers. A significant number lived in urban areas and held industrial jobs, especially in steel mills, meat-packing plants, and refineries, where they established a strong tradition of labor activism. Mexican American smelter and refinery workers joined the International Union of Mine, Mill and Smelter Workers (known colloquially as "Mine-Mill") in large numbers and became key leaders. Bert Corona launched his career as a labor organizer with the International Longshoremen's and Warehousemen's Union in Los Angeles (see American Lives, "Bert Corona and the Mexican American Generation," pp. 792–793). Labor activism was not limited to men, however. Mexican American women made up 75 percent of the dressmakers who toiled in Los Angeles's sweatshops, many for less than $5 a week. In 1933 Rose Pesotta, a Polish immigrant labor organizer for the International Ladies' Garment Workers Union (ILGWU), used bilingual appeals to lead a four-week strike in which Mexican American women were the most active participants.

In California, Mexican Americans also found employment in fruit and vegetable processing plants,

A Bitter Harvest
In the early 1930s California was rocked by strikes, and one of the largest was the cotton-pickers' strike of 1933. Demanding higher wages and better working conditions, the predominantly Mexican American work force set up camps for the duration of the strike. As usual, it was the women who bore most of the responsibility for cooking, cleaning, and child care.
Bancroft Library, University of California, Berkeley.

especially young single women who preferred the higher wages of cannery work to domestic service, needlework, and farm labor. Corporate giants such as Del Monte dominated California's food-processing industry. In those plants Mexican American women earned around $2.50 a day, whereas their male counterparts earned $3.50 to $4.50. So pervasive was the "cannery culture" that workers could say, "We met in spinach, fell in love in peaches, and married in tomatoes," and their friends would know they were referring to the harvests of March, August, and October. In 1939 labor unions came to the canneries in the form of the United Cannery, Agricultural, Packing, and Allied Workers of America—an unusually democratic union in which women, who formed a majority of the rank-and-file workers, played a leading role.

This activism of the 1930s, both in the fields and in the factories, demonstrated how the second generation of Mexican immigrants, born in the United States, increasingly turned its orientation toward issues of political and economic justice in the United States, rather than retaining primary allegiance to Mexico. According to historian George Sanchez, they were creating "their own version of Americanism without abandoning Mexican culture." Joining American labor unions and becoming more involved in American politics were thus important steps in the creation of a distinct Mexican American ethnic identity.

Herbert Hoover and the Great Depression

During the presidential campaign of 1928 Herbert Hoover predicted that "the poorhouse is vanishing from among us" and stated that America was "nearer to the final triumph over poverty than ever before in the history of any land." Once elected, Hoover promised, he would preside over an era of Republican prosperity and governmental restraint. Even after the stock market crash in 1929, he stubbornly insisted that the downturn was only temporary. He greeted a business delegation in June 1930 with these words: "Gentlemen, you have come sixty days too late. The Depression is over." In 1931 and 1932, as the country hit rock bottom, Hoover finally acted, but by then it was too little, too late.

The Republican Response

In 1932 the journalist William Allen White wrote an article about the outgoing president entitled "Herbert Hoover—The Last of the Old Presidents, or the First of the New?" White concluded that Hoover had been a

little of both, as have historians ever since. Hoover's early efforts to fight the depression are now seen as predecessors of many New Deal programs, and his reputation among historians has risen steadily over the years. Hoover, who lived until 1964, offered a simple explanation for the improvement in his historical stature, telling Chief Justice Earl Warren of the Supreme Court that he had simply managed "to outlive the bastards."

Hoover's approach to the Great Depression was shaped by his priorities as secretary of commerce: he turned to the business community for leadership in overcoming the economic downturn. Hoover asked business to maintain wages voluntarily, keep up production, and work with the government to build confidence in the system.

Fiscal Policy. Hoover did not rely solely on public pronouncements but also used public funds and federal action to encourage recovery. Soon after the stock market crash he cut federal taxes and called on state and local governments to increase capital spending in the "energetic yet prudent pursuit" of public construction. The 1929 Agricultural Marketing Act gave the federal government its largest role to date in a program of agricultural stabilization and farm relief. In 1930 and the first half of 1931 Hoover raised the federal public-works budget to $423 million, a dramatic increase in an area not traditionally considered to be the federal government's responsibility. Hoover also eased the international crisis by declaring a moratorium on the payment of Allied debts and reparations early in the summer of 1931. The federal government's efforts to stimulate business activity were moderately effective, but the depression continued.

By 1931 more drastic action was required, but Hoover faced a cruel dilemma that had been created by the Federal Reserve's contraction of the money supply. If he embraced deficit financing and encouraged recovery through increased government spending, interest rates would remain high, since the federal government would be competing for borrowed capital with corporations and private investors. Hoover decided that significantly higher interest rates posed the greater danger to recovery, so in December 1931 he asked Congress for a 33 percent tax increase to balance the budget. The Revenue Act of 1932 represented the largest peacetime tax increase in the nation's history. Like monetary restriction, higher taxes choked both consumption and investment and contributed significantly to the severity of the Great Depression.

Not all the steps taken by the Hoover administration were so ill conceived. The president pushed Congress to create a system of government home-loan banks in 1932 and supported the Glass-Steagall Banking Act of 1932, which made government securities available to guarantee

Bert Corona and the Mexican American Generation

★

BERT CORONA ALWAYS considered himself a child of the revolution—the Mexican Revolution. His father, Noe Corona, had crossed the border from Mexico to the United States around 1915 or 1916, seeking safety after being wounded while fighting in Pancho Villa's army. Settling temporarily in El Paso, he married Margarita Escápite Salayandia, and they had four children, including Humberto (his Anglo teachers later Americanized his name to Bert), who was born in 1918.

The border is an apt metaphor for Mexican American life, capturing the fluidity of crossing back and forth between two countries and two cultures. Bert's family returned to Mexico in 1922, where two years later Noe Corona was assassinated by unknown assailants, presumably political enemies. This loss had a profound effect on Noe's six-year-old son: "The Revolution, my father's role in it, and his martyrdom symbolized the struggle for social justice. This would be the same struggle I would later pursue."

Strong female role models influenced Bert as well. The Corona family resettled in El Paso, where Bert's mother secured a job at the Mexican customs house on the El Paso–Ciudad Juarez border, and his grandmother, a doctor, pursued her practice of medicine and midwifery. The El Paso school system provided a searing introduction to the discrimination and unequal treatment that Mexican immigrants in the Southwest faced. Corona's segregated "Mexican" school in the barrio, geared primarily toward vocational education, was far inferior to white schools. Although he attended an integrated high school with a good academic reputation, racism and discrimination remained very much a part of his education, both in daily encounters with his Anglo teachers and classmates and in the general lack of respect for Mexican history and culture in the curriculum. His grandmother said tartly, "Well, you have to understand that the United States writes its history to its own convenience. It always has, and these people always will."

Bert Corona
Bert Corona addresses a press conference at the National Chicano Political Caucus in 1972.
Bert Corona.

When Bert graduated from high school in 1934 at age sixteen, it was the height of the Great Depression, and El Paso was hard hit. Fortunately, his mother kept her job at the Juarez customs house, but hard times forced many Mexicans to leave. El Paso was a major border crossing for *los repatriados* (those returning to their old country), as they fled the depression and the threat of deportation, but Mexicans were not the only group on the move. The Corona backyard faced the train tracks, and Bert vividly remembered the thousands of Dust Bowl migrants traveling through El Paso on their way west. A hundred-car freight train could carry a thousand Dust Bowlers, and there were three trains in the morning and three in the evening. "It was like the population of a small town coming in every day," he later recalled.

After working for two years in El Paso, Bert headed to the University of Southern California, where he hoped to play basketball and continue his education on an athletic scholarship. But an injury cut short his sports career, and he soon found new interests that took him away from his studies, although he later regretted not getting a college degree. What took precedence over his family's strong belief in education? Participating in the revitalized labor movement and fostering Mexican American political consciousness—the two causes that shaped the rest of Corona's life.

The Congress of Industrial Organizations, or CIO (see Chapter 25), became his vehicle for labor activism: "I had a sense of the historical importance of the CIO, and I viewed the CIO as a movement whose time had come. Nothing could stop it, and—for a time—nothing did." In the 1930s many labor activists focused on organizing Mexican American migrant workers in the fields, but Corona concentrated on recruiting Los Angeles industrial workers into the newly constituted International Longshoremen's and Warehousemen's Union (ILWU). His organizing was not restricted to Mexican workers, however. Like the CIO, he wanted the entire working class to join unions to work for social change in the workplace and in society as a whole. While organizing at an aviation plant in 1941 he met his future wife, Blanche Taff. The daughter of Polish Jewish immigrants, she shared his commitment to progressive social change. Their marriage fit right in with the interracial and interethnic culture of the CIO. So great was their commitment to organized labor that they gave up their honeymoon to participate in a major CIO organizing drive.

In addition to labor organizing, Bert Corona felt a deep commitment to the political mobilization of Spanish-speaking peoples throughout the United States. In 1939 he joined El Congreso Nacional del Pueblo de Habla Español (the National Congress of Spanish-Speaking Peoples), a militant organization founded to fight for the rights of Mexican Americans and other Latinos as part of the larger struggle against racial and class oppression. There he worked with noted activists such as Luisa Moreno, a Guatemalan-born CIO organizer who had been active in the cannery industry, and Josefina Fierro, a radical young Mexican American married to the screenwriter John Bright, who was part of Hollywood's leftist community. Their activist agenda was far to the left of that of organizations such as the League of United Latin American Citizens (LULAC), founded in 1929, which focused on assimilation and citizenship from a distinctly middle-class perspective.

After serving in the armed forces during World War II, Corona continued to be a labor and community activist. In the 1960s he became involved in the Mexican-American Political Association, or MAPA, which mobilized Latino political power to force the Kennedy and Johnson administrations to do more for those constituencies. Since then he has been involved in community organizing, especially of undocumented Mexican workers, arguing that they have just as legitimate claims to live, work, and be protected by the basic guarantees of American law as any other workers.

Bert Corona exemplifies what the historian Mario Garcia has called the "Mexican-American Generation." These men and women, who were born and raised in the United States, came of political age between the 1930s and the 1950s. They filled the leadership vacuum created when *los repatriados*, mainly older and Mexican-born, returned permanently to that country in the 1930s. Even before terms such as *Mexican American*, *Hispanic*, and *Latino* were widely used, this generation had the "double consciousness" that W. E. B. Du Bois described in African Americans: a sense of being both *mexicanos* and American citizens. Many members of the Mexican-American Generation shared Corona's commitment to organizing for social change—in their communities, on the job, and in the wider political arena. Tracing their political activism over the years provides a window on the changing character of Mexican American communities in the United States.

Since the 1930s Bert Corona has seen a dramatic expansion of Latino empowerment, but he remains modest about his role in this story. "It's hard for me to think how I would like to be remembered by history," he told Mario Garcia as they collaborated on a book about his life. "I never planned my life. It just happened the way it did. . . . If my life has meant anything, I would say that it shows that you can organize workers and poor people if you work hard, are persistent, remain optimistic, and reach out to involve as many people as possible. . . . But my life is not over yet, and I continue *la lucha*, the struggle." For Bert Corona, that commitment to *la lucha* had its roots in his Mexican heritage, but it first began to flower during the turbulent 1930s.

Federal Reserve notes and thus temporarily propped up the ailing banking system. The federal government under Hoover also spent $700 million—an unprecedented sum for the time—on public works.

The Reconstruction Finance Corporation.   The centerpiece of Hoover's new initiative to combat the depression was the Reconstruction Finance Corporation (RFC), which Congress approved in January 1932. Modeled on the War Finance Corporation of World War I and developed in collaboration with the business and banking communities, the RFC was the first federal institution created to intervene directly in the economy during peacetime. To alleviate the credit crunch for business, the RFC would provide federal loans to railroads, financial institutions, banks, and insurance companies in a strategy that has been called *pump priming*. In theory, money lent at the top of the economic structure would stimulate production, which in turn would create new jobs and increase consumer spending. Benefits would thus "trickle down" to the rest of the economy.

Congress allocated $500 million for the RFC, but the agency's cautiousness in lending money limited its influence. In July 1932 Congress doubled that amount and authorized loans to the states for relief and public works. Once again the RFC acted far too cautiously, lending only $30 million by the end of 1932 and spending only 20 percent of the $1.5 billion appropriated for public works projects.

The RFC was a watershed in American political history and the rise of the state. When voluntary cooperation failed, the president turned to federal action to stimulate the economy. Yet Hoover's break with the past had clear limits. In many ways his support of the RFC was just another attempt to encourage business confidence. Compared with previous presidents, and in contrast to his image as a "do-nothing" president, Hoover responded to the national emergency on an unprecedented scale. But the nation's needs during the Great Depression were also unprecedented, and Hoover's initiatives failed to meet them.

In particular, federal programs fell far short of helping the growing ranks of the unemployed. Hoover

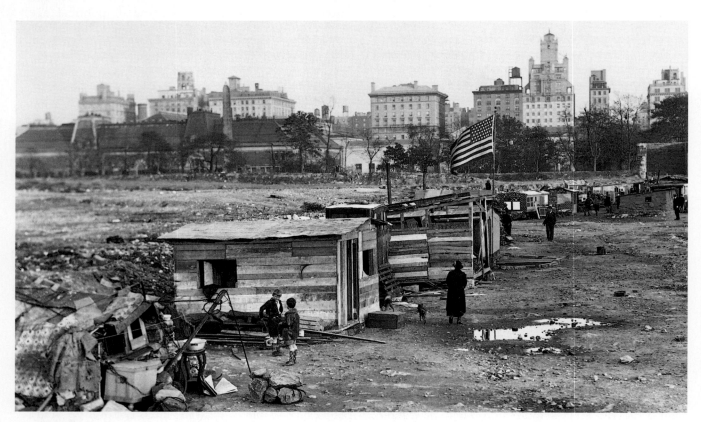

Hoovervilles
By 1930 shantytowns had sprung up in most of the nation's cities. In New York City squatters camped out along the Hudson River railroad tracks, built makeshift homes in Central Park, or lived in the city dump. This scene from the old reservoir in Central Park looks east toward the fancy apartment buildings of Fifth Avenue and the Metropolitan Museum of Art, at left.
Grant Smith/Corbis.

The Despair of the Unemployed

★

In 1931 an unemployed tool and dye designer wrote to the director of the President's Organization for Unemployment Relief (POUR), but his letter drew only this penciled response: "no use answering."

Detroit, Mich.
September 29, 1931

Mr. Walter Gifford
Dear Sir:

You and Pres. Hoover shows at times about the same degree of intelligence as Andy [of the "Amos 'n' Andy" radio show] does. The other night Andy was going to send a fellow a letter to find out his address.

You have told us to spend to end the slump, but you did not tell us what to use for money, after being out of work for two years you tell us this, Pres. Hoover on the other hand tells the working man to build homes, and in face of the fact nearly every working man has had his home taken off him, "some more intelligence." This is a radical letter but the time is here to be radical. when an average of two a day has to take their own life right in the City of Detroit because they can not see their way out. right in the city where one of the worlds riches men lives who made last year 259 000 000 dollars. where hundreds of peoples are starving to death. . . . Mr. Gifford why not come clean . . . remember you have the all seeing eye of God over you. Tell us the reason of the depression is the greed of Bankers and Industrialist who are taking too great of amount of profits. . . . The other day our Pres. Hoover came to Detroit and kidded the soldier boys out of their bonus. Pres Hoover a millionaire worth about 12 000 000 dollars drawing a salary of 75 000 per year from the government asking some boys to forgo their bonus some of them have not 12 dollars of their own "Some more nerve."

Am I right when I say you and he shows the same degree of intelligence as Andy.

J.B.

Source: Quoted in Robert S. McElvaine, *Down and Out in the Great Depression* (Chapel Hill: University of North Carolina Press, 1983), 46–47.

---

remained adamant in his refusal to consider any plan for direct federal relief for unemployed Americans. Throughout his career he had believed that private organized charities were sufficient to meet social welfare needs. During World War I Hoover had headed the Commission for Relief of Belgium, a private group that distributed 5 million tons of food to relieve the suffering of Europe's civilian population. In 1927 he coordinated a rescue and cleanup operation after a devastating Mississippi River flood left 16.5 million acres of land under water in seven states. This effort involved private charities, including the Red Cross and the Rockefeller Foundation, as well as government agencies such as the U.S. Public Health Service and the National Guard. The success of these and other predominantly voluntary responses to public emergencies confirmed Hoover's belief that private charity, not federal aid, was the "American way" of solving social problems. Unfortunately, evidence from across the country supported a different conclusion: charities and state and local relief agencies could not meet the growing needs of the unemployed.

Rising Discontent

As the depression deepened, many citizens came to hate Herbert Hoover. Formerly the symbol of business prosperity, he became the scapegoat for the depression. "In Hoover we trusted, now we are busted" read hand-lettered signs carried by the down and out. New terms entered the vocabulary: *Hoovervilles* (shantytowns where people lived in packing crates and other makeshift shelters), *Hoover flags* (empty pockets turned inside out), and *Hoover blankets* (newspapers). The president's declarations that no one was starving and that hoboes were better fed than ever before seemed cruel and insensitive, and his apparent willingness to bail out business and banks while leaving individuals to fend for themselves added to his reputation for cold-heartedness (see American Voices, "The Despair of the Unemployed," above).

In 1932, as the country entered its fourth year of the depression, signs of rising discontent and rebellion began to emerge. Farmers were among the most vocal groups, banding together to harass the bank agents and government officers who enforced evictions and farm foreclosures and to protest the low prices they received for their crops. Midwestern farmers had watched the price of wheat fall from $3 a bushel in 1920 to barely 30 cents in 1932. Now they formed the Farm Holiday Association under the charismatic leadership of Milo Reno, the sixty-four-year-old former president of the Iowa Farmers' Union. Farmers barricaded local roads and dumped milk, vegetables, and other farm produce because the prices they would fetch on the market would not cover the farmers' costs. Nothing better captured the cruel irony of underconsumption and maldistribution than farmers dumping food at a time when so many people were hungry.

Protest was not confined to rural America. Bitter labor strikes occurred during the depths of the depression, despite the threat that strikers would lose their jobs. In Harlan County, Kentucky, miners struck in 1931 over a 10 percent wage cut, only to see their union crushed by the mine owners and the National Guard. In 1932, at Ford's River Rouge factory outside Detroit, a demonstration provoked violence from police and Ford security forces; three demonstrators were killed, and fifty were seriously injured. Some 40,000 people viewed the coffins under a banner charging that "Ford Gave Bullets for Bread."

In 1931 and 1932 violence broke out in the nation's cities. Groups of unemployed citizens battled local authorities over inadequate relief; people staged rent riots and hunger marches. Some of these urban actions were organized by the Communist Party, such as "unemployment councils" that agitated for jobs and food and coordinated a hunger march on Washington, D.C., in 1931. The marches were well attended and often got results from local and federal authorities, but they did not necessarily win converts to communism. In the early 1930s the American Communist Party was still a tiny organization with only 12,000 members, although it would grow dramatically later in the decade.

It was not radicals but veterans who staged the most publicized—and tragic—protest. In the summer of 1932 the "Bonus Army," a ragtag group of about 15,000 unemployed World War I veterans, hitchhiked to Washington from throughout the nation to demand immediate payment of their bonuses, originally scheduled for distribution in 1945. While their leaders unsuccessfully lobbied Congress, members of the "Bonus Expeditionary Force" (parodying the wartime American Expeditionary Force) camped out in the capital, a visible reminder of the plight of the unemployed. "We were heroes in 1917, but we're bums now," one veteran remarked bitterly. When the marchers refused to leave their camp, Hoover called out riot troops to clear the area. Led by General Douglas MacArthur, assisted by Majors Dwight D. Eisenhower and George S. Patton, the troops burned the encampment to the ground. In the fight that followed, more than a hundred marchers were injured. Newsreel footage captured the deeply disturbing spectacle of the U.S. Army firing on its own veterans, and Hoover's popularity plunged even further.

The 1932 Election

Despite evidence of discontent, the nation was not in a revolutionary mood as it approached the 1932 election. Despair and apathy, not anger, characterized the feelings of most citizens. The Republicans, who could find no credible way to abandon an incumbent president, unenthusiastically renominated Hoover. The Democrats turned to Governor Franklin Delano Roosevelt of New York, who capitalized on that state's innovative relief and unemployment programs to win the nomination.

Roosevelt's route to the presidential nomination began on a Hudson River estate north of New York City. Born into a wealthy family in 1882, he attended the Groton School (in Connecticut), Harvard College, and Columbia Law School. He had served in the New York State legislature and as assistant secretary of the navy in the Wilson administration, a post that earned him the vice-presidential nomination on the losing Democratic ticket in 1920. Except for his allegiance to Democratic rather than Republican Party ideology, he consciously modeled his career on that of his distant cousin Theodore Roosevelt, whose niece Eleanor he married in 1905.

Franklin Roosevelt was sidetracked from his path to the White House in 1921 by an attack of polio that left both his legs paralyzed for the rest of his life. Roosevelt fought back from his infirmity, emerging from the ordeal a stronger, more resilient man. "If you had spent two years in bed trying to wiggle your toe,

1932 Campaign Memorabilia
Mechanical buttons of the 1932 campaign gave voters a choice between a Republican elephant rearing its trunk to bring back prosperity and a Democratic donkey that kicked out the depression by kicking an elephant. All you had to do was pull the string.
Collection of David J. and Janice L. Frent.

after that anything would seem easy," he said. Eleanor Roosevelt strongly supported her husband's return to public life and helped to mastermind his successful campaign for the New York governorship in 1928.

The 1932 campaign foreshadowed little of the governmental activism that would characterize the New Deal. Roosevelt hinted at new approaches to the depression but stated his goals in vague terms: "The country needs and, unless I mistake its temper, the country demands bold, persistent experimentation." Roosevelt won easily, receiving 22.8 million votes to Hoover's 15.7 million. Despite the economic collapse, Americans remained firmly committed to the two-party system. The Socialist Party candidate, Norman Thomas, got fewer than a million votes. The Communist Party drew only 100,000 votes for its candidate, party leader William Z. Foster (Map 24.3).

The 1932 election marked a turning point in American politics—the emergence of a Democratic coalition that would dominate political life for the next four decades. In 1932 Roosevelt won with the support of the Solid South, which returned to the Democratic fold after defecting in 1928 because of Al Smith's religion and views on Prohibition. Roosevelt also drew substantial support in the West and in the cities, continuing a trend first noticed in the 1928 election when the Democrats successfully appealed to recent immigrants and urban ethnic groups. Roosevelt's election was

hardly a mandate to reshape American political and economic institutions, however. Many people voted as much against Hoover as for Roosevelt.

Having spoken, the voters had to wait until March 1933 before Roosevelt could put his ideas into action. (Inauguration Day was moved up to January 20 by the Twentieth Amendment in 1933.) In the worst winter of the depression, Americans could do little but hope that things would get better. According to the most conservative estimates, unemployment stood at 20 to 25 percent. The rate was as high as 50 percent in Cleveland, 60 percent in Akron, and 80 percent in Toledo—cities dependent on manufacturing jobs in industries that had essentially shut down. The nation's banking system was so close to collapse that many state governors temporarily closed banks to avoid further panic.

By the winter of 1932–1933 the depression had totally overwhelmed public welfare institutions. Private charity and local public relief, whose expenditures had risen dramatically, still reached only a fraction of the needy. Hunger haunted cities and rural areas alike. When a teacher tried to send a coal miner's daughter home from school because she was weak from hunger, the girl replied, "It won't do any good . . . because this is sister's day to eat." In New York City, hospitals reported ninety-five deaths from starvation. This was the America that Roosevelt inherited when he took the oath of office on March 4, 1933.

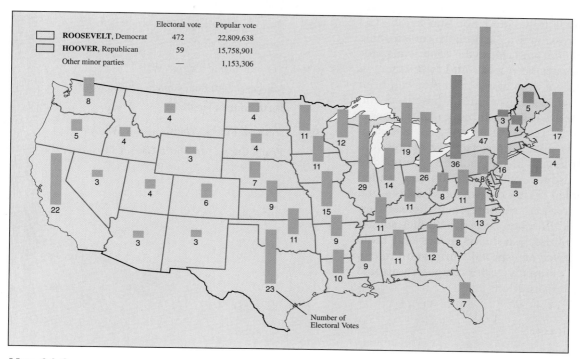

	Electoral vote	Popular vote
ROOSEVELT, Democrat	472	22,809,638
HOOVER, Republican	59	15,758,901
Other minor parties	—	1,153,306

Number of Electoral Votes

MAP 24.3

The Election of 1932

Franklin Roosevelt's convincing electoral victory over Herbert Hoover in 1932 resulted from a political realignment and dissatisfaction with the incumbent president. Even in the midst of the gravest crisis capitalism had ever faced, candidates of the Communist and Socialist Parties received fewer than 1 million votes out of almost 40 million cast.

Summary

★

The Great Depression of the 1930s was the longest and most severe economic downturn the United States had ever faced, and it had wide-ranging social, political, and cultural effects. The economic prosperity of the 1920s had rested on shaky ground. After the stock market crash of 1929 the economy entered a downward spiral that did not bottom out until 1932–1933. In addition to the collapse of the stock market, the main causes of the depression were underconsumption, an unequal distribution of wealth, an unstable international financial situation, a legacy of "sick industries" and agricultural distress from the 1920s, and the flawed monetary policies of the Federal Reserve System. At first President Hoover did not want to intervene in the economy because of his reliance on private charities and his adamant stance on maintaining a balanced budget. Then in 1932 the Hoover administration authorized the first direct federal intervention in the economy during peacetime, the Reconstruction Finance Corporation, to win business and public confidence. Though unprecedented, such measures did not end the Great Depression. In 1932 the nation turned to Franklin D. Roosevelt and the Democrats.

The Great Depression left an invisible scar on many people who lived through the 1930s, especially white middle-class Americans. Those who wanted to work blamed themselves if they could not find a job. The impact of the depression was especially catastrophic for African Americans and Mexican Americans, for whom times had always been hard. And for farmers in the Midwest, things got even worse than they had been in the 1920s. Misguided agricultural practices and drought created the Dust Bowl, forcing many farmers off their land.

Despite the devastating impact of the depression, many aspects of American life and culture continued to conform to traditional patterns. Families pulled together, with women taking on expanded roles—and often new jobs—to help support their households. Young people stayed in school longer. Families sought relief in popular culture, especially movies and radio programs, which played an especially important role in reaffirming—and obliquely criticizing—traditional American ideals and institutions.

T I M E L I N E

1929	Stock market crash
	Agricultural Marketing Act
1930	Midwestern drought begins
	Hawley-Smoot Tariff
1931	Scottsboro case
	Hoover declares moratorium on Allied war debts
	Miners strike in Harlan County, Kentucky
1932	Reconstruction Finance Corporation created
	Bonus Army rebuffed by Congress
	Height of deportation of Mexican migrant workers
	Strike at Ford's River Rouge plant in Michigan
	Communist-led hunger marches
1933	Unemployment rises to highest level
	Franklin Delano Roosevelt becomes president
	Birth rate drops to lowest level due to depression
	The Marx Brothers in *Duck Soup*
1934	Southern Tenant Farmers Union founded
	It Happened One Night sweeps Oscars
1935	National Youth Administration created
	Harlem race riot
1936	Student Strike against War
	Margaret Mitchell, *Gone with the Wind*
	Birth control legalized
1939	John Steinbeck, *The Grapes of Wrath*
	Frank Capra, *Mr. Smith Goes to Washington*

Suggested Readings

─────────────★─────────────

Useful overviews of the Great Depression are T. H. Watkins, *The Great Depression: America in the 1930s* (1993); John A. Garraty, *The Great Depression* (1987); and Robert S. McElvaine, *The Great Depression, 1929–1941* (1984).

The Coming of the Great Depression

Historians and economists continue to debate the causes of the Great Depression. See John Kenneth Galbraith, *The Great Crash* (1954); Milton Friedman and Anna Schwartz, *The Great Contraction, 1929–1933* (1965); Charles Kindleberger, *The World in Depression* (1974); Peter Temin, *Did Monetary Forces Cause the Great Depression?* (1976); and Michael Bernstein, *The Great Depression: Delayed Recovery and Economic Change in America, 1929–1939* (1988). Irving Bernstein, *The Lean Years* (1960), offers a compelling portrait of hard times during the Hoover years.

Hard Times

A wealth of material brings the voices of the 1930s to life. The Federal Writers' Project, *These Are Our Lives* (1939); Tom Terrill and Jerrold Hirsch, eds., *Such as Us: Southern Voices of the Thirties* (1978); and Ann Banks, ed., *First-Person America* (1980), all draw on oral histories collected by the Works Progress Administration during the 1930s. See also Robert S. McElvaine, ed., *Down and Out in the Great Depression* (1983). Evocative secondary sources include Studs Terkel, *Hard Times: An Oral History of the Great Depression* (1970), and Caroline Bird, *The Invisible Scar* (1966).

Descriptions of family life in the 1930s include Robert and Helen Lynd, *Middletown in Transition* (1937); Mirra Komarovsky, *The Unemployed Man and His Family* (1940); and Roger Angell, *The Family Encounters the Depression* (1936). Russell Baker's autobiography, *Growing Up* (1982), provides an often humorous description of family life in the 1930s. Glen H. Elder Jr., *Children of the Great Depression* (1974), and John A. Clausen, *American Lives: Looking Back at the Children of the Great Depression* (1993), consider the long-term effects. For more on youth, see Maxine Davis, *The Lost Generation* (1936); Eileen Eagan, *Class, Culture, and the Classroom* (1981); and John Modell, *Into One's Own: From Youth to Adulthood, 1920–1975* (1989).

Frederick Lewis Allen, *Since Yesterday* (1939), provides an impressionistic overview of popular culture in the 1930s. See also the essays in Lawrence W. Levine, *The Unpredictable Past* (1993), and Michael Denning, *Cultural Front: The Laboring of American Culture in the Twentieth Century* (1996). Specific studies of movies and Hollywood include Andrew Bergman, *We're in the Money* (1971); Molly Haskell, *From Reverence to Rape: The Treatment of Women in the Movies* (2d ed., 1987); and Thomas Schatz, *The Genius of the System: Hollywood Film Making in the Studio Era* (1988). On radio, see Arthur Frank Wertheim, *Radio Comedy* (1979).

Material on women in the 1930s can be found in Susan Ware, *Holding Their Own* (1982); Winifred Wandersee, *Women's Work and Family Values, 1920–1940* (1981); and Lois Scharf, *To Work and to Wed* (1981). For the special dimensions of white rural women's lives, see Margaret Hagood, *Mothers of the South* (1939). Jeane Westin, *Making Do: How Women Survived the '30s* (1976), is a lively account drawn from interviews. The birth control movement is surveyed in Linda Gordon, *Woman's Body, Woman's Right* (2d ed., 1990); Estelle Freedman and John D'Emilio, *Intimate Matters: A History of Sexuality in America* (1988); and Ellen Chesler, *Woman of Valor: Margaret Sanger and the Birth Control Movement in America* (1992).

Harder Times

Developments in the black community during the 1930s are covered in Cheryl Lyn Greenberg, *"Or Does It Explode?" Harlem in the Great Depression* (1991); Jervis Anderson, *This Was Harlem, 1900–1950* (1982); and Robert Weisbrot, *Father Divine and the Struggle for Racial Equality* (1983). James Goodman, *Stories of Scottsboro* (1994), and Dan T. Carter, *Scottsboro* (1969), discuss that case. Donald Grubbs, *Cry from Cotton* (1971), tells the story of the Southern Tenant Farmers Union. Robin D. G. Kelley, *Hammer and Hoe* (1990), is an excellent account of Alabama communists during the Great Depression. Donald Worster, *Dust Bowl* (1979), evokes the plains during the "Dirty Thirties." James N. Gregory, *American Exodus: The Dust Bowl Migration and Okie Culture in California* (1989), treats the experiences of migrants and their impact on California culture and the economy. See also Kevin Starr, *Endangered Dreams: The Great Depression in California* (1996).

On the experiences of Mexican Americans during the 1930s, see Mario T. Garcia, *Mexican Americans: Leadership, Ideology, and Identity, 1930–1960* (1989), and *Memories of Chicano History: The Life and Narrative of Bert Corona* (1994). George J. Sanchez, *Becoming Mexican American* (1993), examines Chicano Los Angeles from 1900 to 1945; and David Gutierrez, *Walls and Mirrors* (1995), looks at Mexican immigration and the politics of ethnicity. See also Richard A. Garcia, *The Rise of the Mexican-American Middle Class* (1990). For Mexican American women's lives in the twentieth century, see Vicki Ruiz's overview, *From Out of the Shadows* (1998), as well as her *Cannery Women, Cannery Lives* (1987), and Patricia Zavella, *Women's Work and Chicano Families* (1987).

Herbert Hoover and the Great Depression

Hoover's response to the depression is chronicled in Alfred Romasco, *The Poverty of Abundance* (1965), and Jordan Schwartz, *The Interregnum of Despair* (1970). Eliot Rosen, *Hoover, Roosevelt, and the Brain Trust* (1977), treats the transition between the two administrations, as does Frank Freidel, *Launching the New Deal* (1973). On the 1932 election and the beginnings of the New Deal coalition, see David Burner, *The Politics of Provincialism* (1967); Samuel Lubell, *The Future of American Politics* (1952); and John Allswang, *The New Deal in American Politics* (1978).

The New Deal,
1933–1939

IN HIS BOLD inaugural address on March 4, 1933, President Franklin Delano Roosevelt declared, "The only thing we have to fear is fear itself." That memorable phrase rallied a nation that had already endured almost four years of the worst economic contraction in its history, with no end in sight.

With his demeanor grim and purposeful, Roosevelt preached his first inaugural address like a sermon. Only in the most general terms did he speak of the economic and social problems that the nation faced, and their possible solutions. Promising "a leadership of frankness and vigor," Roosevelt issued ringing declarations of his vision of governmental activism: "This Nation asks for action, and action now." Roosevelt repeatedly compared combating the depression to fighting a war. The most explicit parallel was his willingness to ask Congress for "broad Executive power to wage a war against the emergency, as great as the power that would be given to me if we were in fact invaded by a foreign foe." This conception of presidential leadership was well suited to Roosevelt's self-confident personality and pragmatic political style.

In the end, however, Roosevelt intended not to scare the American people but to reassure them. The democratic system was basically sound, he told them, and hard times could be overcome, but only if a dispirited nation chose not to wallow in lethargy. On that cold March day in 1933 Roosevelt urged his fellow citizens to return to the values of hard work, cooperation, and sacrifice that had made the country great. Roosevelt's restoration of hope and confidence was likely his greatest contribution to American life during the Great Depression.

The CCC
The Civilian Conservation Corps (CCC) was one of the most popular New Deal programs. Over ten years, it enrolled 2.75 million young Americans who worked for $1 a day on projects such as soil conservation, disaster relief, reforestation, and flood control. The CCC was limited to men, although a few camps employed out-of-work young women.
Library of Congress.

The federal government dominated political and economic life so thoroughly during the 1930s that the term *New Deal* is often used as a synonym for that decade. In a time of deep crisis, the New Deal was meant to relieve suffering and conserve the nation's political and economic institutions through unprecedented activity on the part of the national government. Its legacy would be an expanded federal presence in the economy and the lives of ordinary citizens. By the late 1930s, however, Roosevelt became increasingly preoccupied with international relations, as Europe moved toward war and Japan flexed its muscles in East Asia. As war mobilization finally began to pull the country out of its decade-long depression, calls for further social reform stalemated.

The New Deal Takes Over, 1933–1935

———— ★ ————

Franklin Roosevelt first used the term *New Deal* in his acceptance speech at the Democratic National Convention in 1932. Plucked from deep within the speech by the newspaper cartoonist Rollin Kirby, the term came to stand for the Roosevelt administration's complex set of responses to the depression. The New Deal was not a carefully formulated plan. Its ideology contained many contradictions, but it provided a measure of economic security against the worst depression in U.S. history.

The Roosevelt Style of Leadership

Although the New Deal represented many things to many people, one unifying factor was the personality of its master architect, Franklin Delano Roosevelt. Every president since the 1930s has lived in the shadow of FDR, although few of his successors have matched his raw political talent and none have had to face and surmount the twin crises of depression and war. "I have no expectation of making a hit every time I come to bat," Roosevelt disarmingly told his critics. "What I seek is the highest possible batting average." Roosevelt parlayed that experimental tone into a highly effective political and governmental style.

The New Deal was "a very personal enterprise," and President Roosevelt established an unusually close rapport with the American people. "Mr. Roosevelt is the only man we ever had in the White House who would understand that my boss is a son of a bitch," remarked one worker. Many ordinary citizens credited him with the positive changes in their lives, saying, "He gave me a job" or "He saved my home." Roosevelt's masterful use of the new medium of radio, typified by the sixteen "fireside chats" he broadcast during his first two terms, fostered this personal identification. More than 450,000 letters poured into the White House in the week after

FDR
President Franklin Delano Roosevelt was a consummate politician who loved the adulation of a crowd, such as this one greeting him in Warm Springs, Georgia, in 1933. He consciously adopted a cheerful mien to keep people from feeling sorry for him because of his infirmity, knowing that he could not be a successful politician if the public pitied him.
Corbis-Bettmann.

the inauguration, and an average of 5,000 to 8,000 arrived weekly for the rest of the decade. One person had handled public correspondence during the Hoover administration, but it took a staff of fifty under Roosevelt. He also became the first president to hire a press secretary.

Franklin Roosevelt's personal charisma and political talent allowed him to continue the expansion of presidential power begun during the administrations of Theodore Roosevelt and Woodrow Wilson. From the beginning Roosevelt centralized decision making in the White House; in doing so, he dramatically expanded the role of the executive branch in initiating policy and helped to create the modern presidency. During the interregnum (the period between election and inauguration) he relied so heavily on the advice of Columbia University professors Raymond Moley, Rexford Tugwell, and Adolph A. Berle Jr. that the press dubbed them the "Brains Trust." Once in the White House, for policy formulation he turned to his talented cabinet, which included Interior Secretary Harold Ickes, Frances Perkins at Labor, Henry A. Wallace at Agriculture, and an old friend, Henry Morgenthau Jr., at the Treasury.

When searching for new ideas and fresh faces, Roosevelt was just as likely to turn to advisors and administrators scattered throughout the New Deal bureaucracy. Eager young people flocked to Washington to join the New Deal—"men with long hair and women with short hair," wags quipped (see American Voices, "Joe Marcus: A New Deal Activist," p. 804). Lawyers in their mid-twenties fresh out of Harvard found themselves drafting legislation or being called to the White House for strategy sessions with the president. Paul Freund, a Harvard Law School professor who worked in the Department of Justice, remembered, "It was a glorious time for obscure people." Many young New Dealers who went on to distinguished careers in government or pub-

lic service later recalled that nothing could match the excitement of the early New Deal.

The Hundred Days

The first problem that the new president confronted was the collapse of the banking system, which, far more than the stock market crash, had brought the depression home to the middle class. On the eve of Roosevelt's inauguration thirty-eight states had closed their banks, and banks operated on a restricted basis in the rest. On March 5, 1933, the day after his inauguration, the president declared a national "bank holiday" (a euphemism for closing all the banks) and called Congress into special session. Four days later Congress passed Roosevelt's proposed emergency banking bill, which permitted banks to reopen beginning on March 13, but only if a Treasury department inspection showed that they had sufficient cash reserves. The House approved the plan after only thirty-eight minutes of debate.

The Emergency Banking Act.   The Emergency Banking Act, which Roosevelt developed in consultation with banking leaders, was such a conservative document that it could have been proposed by Herbert Hoover. The difference was the public's reaction. On the Sunday evening before the banks reopened Roosevelt gave his first "fireside chat" to a radio audience estimated at 60 million. In simple terms he reassured the people that the banks were now safe, and Americans believed him. When the banks reopened on Monday morning, deposits exceeded withdrawals. "Capitalism was saved in eight days," observed Raymond Moley, who had served as Roosevelt's speech writer during the 1932 campaign. The banking bill did its job: more than 4,000 banks failed in 1933 (the vast majority in the months before the law took effect), but only 61 closed their doors in 1934 (Table 25.1).

TABLE 25.1

American Banks and Bank Failures, 1920–1940

Year	Total Number of Banks	Total Assets ($ billion)	Bank Failures
1920	30,909	53.1	168
1929	25,568	72.3	659
1931	22,242	70.1	2,294
1933	14,771	51.4	4,004
1934	15,913	55.9	61
1940	15,076	79.7	48

Source: Historical Statistics of the United States: Colonial Times to 1970 (Washington, DC: U.S. Government Printing Office, 1975), 1019, 1038–1039.

JOE MARCUS
A New Deal Activist

★

As an economist working for Harry Hopkins, Joe Marcus was one of thousands who formed the growing New Deal bureaucracy. Marcus's account, as told to Studs Terkel, captures some of the excitement that the New Deal generated. Marcus also suggests the way in which Roosevelt's administration expanded opportunities for Jews and other "outsiders."

I graduated college in '35. I went down to Washington and started to work in the spring of '36. The New Deal was a young man's world. Young people, if they showed any ability, got an opportu-nity. I was a kid, twenty-two or twenty-three. In a few months I was made head of the department. We had a meeting with hot shots: What's to be done? I pointed out some problems: let's define what we're looking for. They immediately had me take over. I had to set up the organization and hire seventy-five people. Given a chance as a youngster to try out ideas, I learned a fantastic amount. The challenge itself was great.

It was the idea of being asked big questions. The technical problems were small. These you had to solve by yourself. But the context was broad: Where was society going? Your statistical questions became questions of full employment. You were not prepared for it in school. If you wanted new answers, you needed a new kind of people. This is what was exciting.

Ordinarily, I might have had a job at the university, marking papers or helping a professor. All of a sudden, I'm doing original research and asking basic questions about how our society works. What makes a Depression? What makes for pulling out of it? Once you start thinking in these terms, you're in a different ball game.

The climate was exciting. You were part of a society that was on the move. You were involved in something that could make a difference. Laws could be changed. So could the conditions of people.

The idea of bring involved close to the center of political life was unthinkable, just two or three years before all this happened. Unthinkable for someone like me, of lower middle-class, close to ghetto, Jewish life. Suddenly you were a significant member of society. It was not the kind of closed society you had lived in before.

. . . You were really part of something, changes could be made. Bringing *immediate* results to people who were starving. You could do something about it: that was the most important thing. This you felt.

A feeling that if you had something to say, it would get to the top. As I look back now, memoranda I had written reached the White House, one way or another. The biggest thrill of my life was hearing a speech of Roosevelt's, using a selection from a memorandum I had written.

Everybody was searching for ideas. A lot of guys were opportunists, some were crackpots. But there was a search, a sense of values . . . that would make a difference in the lives of people.

We weren't thinking of remaking society. That wasn't it. I didn't buy this dream stuff. What was happening was a complete change in social attitudes at the central government level. The question was: How can you do it within this system? People working in all the New Deal agencies were dominated by this spirit. . . .

It was an exciting community, where we lived in Washington. The basic feeling—and I don't think this is just nostalgia—was one of excitement, of achievement, of happiness. Life was important, life was significant.

Source: Studs Terkel, *Hard Times* (New York: Pantheon Books, 1986), 265–266.

The Banking Act was the first of fifteen pieces of major legislation enacted by Congress in the opening months of the Roosevelt administration. This legislative session, which came to be called the Hundred Days, remains one of the most productive ever. Congress created the Home Owners Loan Corporation to refinance home mortgages threatened by foreclosure; a full 20 percent of the nation's homeowners took advantage of it. A second banking law, the Glass-Steagall Act, curbed speculation by separating investment banking from commercial banking and also created the Federal Deposit Insurance Corporation (FDIC), which insured bank deposits up to $2,500. Another act created the Civilian Conservation Corps (CCC), through which 250,000 young men went to live in camps where they did reforestation and conservation work. The Tennessee

Valley Authority (TVA) received legislative approval for its innovative plan of government-sponsored regional development and public energy. And in a move that lifted public spirits immeasurably, Roosevelt legalized beer in April. Full repeal of Prohibition came eight months later, in December 1933.

The Agricultural Adjustment Act. The Roosevelt administration targeted three pressing problems for immediate attention: agricultural overproduction, business failures, and unemployment. Roosevelt considered a farm bill "the key to recovery." The Agricultural Adjustment Act (AAA) was developed by Secretary of Agriculture Henry A. Wallace, Assistant Secretary Rexford Tugwell, and the agricultural economist M. L. Wilson in close collaboration with the leaders of major farmers' organizations. The AAA established a domestic allotment system for seven commodities (wheat, cotton, corn, hogs, rice, tobacco, and dairy products), with cash subsidies to farmers who cut production—a pattern of federal subsidies that continues to the present. Those benefits were financed by a tax on processing (such as the milling of wheat), which was passed on to consumers. New Deal planners hoped prices would rise in response to the federally subsidized scarcity, halting the steep deflation and thus spurring a more general recovery.

The AAA stabilized the agricultural situation, but its benefits were distributed unevenly. Subsidies for reducing production went primarily to the owners of large and medium-size farms, who often cut production by reducing their renters' and sharecroppers' acreage rather than their own. In the South, where many sharecroppers were black and the landowners and government administrators were white, that strategy had racial overtones, displacing as many as 200,000 black tenant farmers from their land. New Deal agricultural policies thus fostered the migration of small farmers in the South and Midwest to northern cities and California, and consolidated the economic and political clout of larger landholders.

The National Recovery Administration. The New Deal attacked the problem of economic recovery with the National Industrial Recovery Act (NIRA), which created the National Recovery Administration (NRA). The NRA, which drew on the World War I experience of Bernard Baruch's War Industries Board, set up a system of industrial self-government to handle the problems of overproduction, cutthroat competition, and price instability. For each industry a code of prices and production quotas, similar to those for farm products, was established. In effect, those legally enforceable agreements suspended the antitrust laws. The codes also established minimum wages and maximum hours and outlawed child labor. One of the most far-reaching

provisions, Section 7(a), guaranteed workers the right to organize and bargain collectively "through representatives of their own choosing." These union rights dramatically spurred the growth of the labor movement in the 1930s.

General Hugh Johnson, a colorful though erratic administrator, headed the NRA. He supervised negotiations for more than 600 NRA codes, ranging from large industries such as coal, cotton, and steel to dog food, costume jewelry, and even burlesque theaters. The negotiating process theoretically took into account equal input from management, labor, and consumers; but trade associations, controlled by large companies, tended to dominate the code-drafting process, thereby solidifying the power of large businesses at the expense of smaller enterprises. Labor had little input, and consumer interests had almost none. To sell the program to skeptical consumers and businesspeople, the NRA launched an extensive public relations campaign, complete with plugs in Hollywood films and stickers with the NRA slogan, "We Do Our Part."

Unemployment Legislation. The early New Deal also addressed the critical problem of unemployment. In the fourth year of the depression, the total exhaustion of private and local sources of charity made it essential to provide some form of federal relief. Roosevelt was basically a fiscal conservative, fearful of large federal deficits, and he moved reluctantly toward federal responsibility for the unemployed. The Federal Emergency Relief Administration (FERA), set up in May 1933 under the direction of Harry Hopkins, a New York social worker, offered federal money to the states for relief programs. FERA was designed to keep people from starving until other recovery measures took hold. In his first two hours in office, Hopkins distributed $5 million. When told that some of the projects he had authorized might not be sound in the long run, Hopkins replied, "People don't eat in the long run—they eat every day." During its two-year existence FERA spent $1 billion.

Roosevelt always maintained a strong distaste for the dole. Wherever possible, New Deal administrators promoted work relief over cash subsidies; they also consistently favored relief jobs that did not compete directly with the private sector. When the Public Works Administration (PWA), under Secretary of the Interior Harold L. Ickes, received a $3.3 billion appropriation in 1933, Ickes's cautiousness in initiating projects limited the agency's effectiveness. In November 1933 Roosevelt assigned $400 million in PWA funds to a new agency, the Civil Works Administration (CWA), headed by Harry Hopkins. Within thirty days the CWA put 2.6 million men and women to work; at its peak in January 1934 it employed 4 million. CWA workers received $15 a week for jobs such as repairing bridges, building highways, constructing public buildings, and setting up community projects. The CWA, regarded as a stopgap measure to get the country through the winter of 1933–1934, lapsed the following spring after exhausting all its funds.

Many of these early emergency measures were deliberately inflationary; that is, they were designed to trigger price rises that were thought necessary to halt the steep deflation and thus stimulate recovery. Another element of this strategy was Roosevelt's executive order on April 18, 1933, to abandon the gold standard and let gold rise in value like any other commodity. As the price of gold rose, administrators hoped, so too would the price of manufactured and agricultural goods. Although abandoning the gold standard did not have much of an impact on the domestic economy, it did allow the Federal Reserve System to manipulate the value of the dollar in response to economic conditions, an important shift in economic power from the private to the public sector.

When an exhausted Congress recessed in June 1933, much had been accomplished. Rarely had a president so dominated a legislative session. A mass of "alphabet agencies," as the New Deal programs came to be known, flowed from Washington, and for the first time since 1929 Americans saw a ray of hope. In April 1933, at the height of the excitement over the Hundred Days, Walt Disney released a cartoon film called *The Three Little Pigs*. Echoing FDR's assertion that they had nothing to fear but fear itself, many people hummed the film's theme song, "Who's Afraid of the Big Bad Wolf?" as they started down the road toward renewed confidence.

If the measures taken during the Hundred Days had cured the Great Depression, the rest of the New Deal probably would not have occurred. But despite a slight upturn in the economy, the depression stubbornly persisted. FDR and the Seventy-third Congress now turned to more far-reaching structural changes to replace the emergency recovery measures of 1933. The reform of business practices, they argued, would be crucial to preventing future depressions.

One obvious target was Wall Street, where insider trading, fraud, and other abuses had contributed to the 1929 crash. In 1934 Congress established the Securities and Exchange Commission (SEC) to regulate the stock market. The commission had the power to regulate the purchase of stocks on credit, or margin buying, and to restrict speculation by those with inside information on corporate plans. The banking system also came under scrutiny. The Banking Act of 1935 enhanced the federal government's role in controlling the economy and business. The act authorized the president to appoint a new Board of Governors of the Federal Reserve System, placing control of interest rates and other money market policies at the federal level rather than with regional banks. By requiring all large state banks to join the Federal Reserve System by 1942 in order to take advantage of the federal deposit insurance system, the law further encouraged centralization of the nation's banking system.

"Gulliver's Travels"
So many new agencies flooded out of Washington in the 1930s that one almost needed a scorecard to keep them straight. Here a July 1935 *Vanity Fair* cartoon by William Gropper substitutes Uncle Sam for Captain Lemuel Gulliver, tied to the ground by Lilliputians, in a parody of Jonathan Swift's *Gulliver's Travels*.
Courtesy Vanity Fair. © 1935 (renewed 1963) by The Conde Nast Publications, Inc.

The New Deal under Attack

As Congress and the president consolidated the early New Deal, their work came under attack from several quarters. Although Roosevelt billed himself as the savior of capitalism, noting that "to preserve we had to reform," his actions provoked strong hostility from many Americans. To the wealthy, Roosevelt became simply "That Man," a traitor to his class. Business leaders and conservative Democrats formed the Liberty League in 1934 to lobby against the New Deal and its "reckless spending" and "socialist" reforms.

The conservative majority on the Supreme Court also disagreed with the direction of the New Deal. On "Black Monday," May 27, 1935, the Supreme Court struck down the NRA, Roosevelt's business recovery plan. In the case of *Schecter v. United States*, the Court unanimously ruled that the National Industrial Recovery Act represented an unconstitutional delegation of legislative power to the executive branch. The so-called sick-chicken case concerned a Brooklyn, New York, firm convicted of violating NRA codes by selling diseased poultry. In its decision the Court ruled that the NRA regulated commerce *within* states, whereas the Constitution limited federal regulation to *interstate* commerce. Roosevelt protested that the Court's narrow interpretation would return the Constitution "to the horse-and-buggy definition of interstate commerce" and worried privately that the Court might invalidate the entire New Deal.

Other citizens thought the New Deal had not gone far enough. Francis Townsend, a physician from Long Beach, California, spoke for the nation's elderly. Many Americans feared poverty in old age because few had pension plans and many had lost their life savings in bank failures. In 1933 Townsend proposed an Old Age Revolving Pension Plan that would give $200 a month (a considerable sum at the time) to citizens over the age of sixty. To receive payments, people would have to retire from their jobs, thereby opening their positions to others, and agree to spend the money within a month, thereby pumping cash into the economy. The plan was never enacted, but Townsend Clubs soon sprang up across the country, particularly in the West.

Father Charles Coughlin also challenged Roosevelt's leadership and attracted a large following, especially in the Midwest. Coughlin, a parish priest in the Detroit suburb of Royal Oak, had turned to the radio in the mid-1920s to increase membership in his pastorate. In 1933 about 40 million Americans listened regularly to the "Radio Priest." At first Coughlin supported the New Deal, but he soon broke with Roosevelt over the president's refusal to support nationalization of the banking system and expansion of the money supply. In 1935 Coughlin organized the National Union for Social Justice to promote his views as an alternative to

The Kingfish
Huey Long, the Louisiana governor and senator, was one of the most controversial figures in American political history. He took his nickname "Kingfish" from a character in the popular radio show "Amos 'n' Andy." Long inspired one of the most powerful political novels of all time, Robert Penn Warren's *All the King's Men*, which won a Pulitzer Prize in 1946.
Corbis-Bettmann.

"Franklin Double-Crossing Roosevelt." Because he was Canadian-born and a Catholic priest, Coughlin could not run for president, but his rapidly growing constituency threatened to become a factor in the 1936 election.

The most direct threat to Roosevelt came from Democratic senator Huey Long. In a single term as governor of Louisiana, the flamboyant Long had achieved stunning popularity. He had increased the share of taxes paid by corporations and embarked on an ambitious program of public works, which included the construction of new highways, bridges, hospitals, and schools. But Long's accomplishments came at a price: to push through his reforms he seized almost dictatorial control of the state government, and he maintained that control even after his election to the U.S. Senate in 1930. Although he supported Roosevelt in 1932, Long made no secret of his own presidential ambitions.

In 1934 Senator Long broke with the New Deal, arguing that its programs did not go far enough. Like Coughlin, he established his own national movement, the Share Our Wealth Society, which had over 4 million followers in 1935. Arguing that the unequal distribution of wealth in the United States was the fundamental cause of the depression, Long advocated taxing 100 percent of all incomes over $1 million, and all inheritances over $5 million, and distributing the money to the rest of the population. Every family would be guaranteed about $2,000 annually, he promised, even though he secretly knew his plan was unworkable. "When they figure that out," he confided privately, "I'll have something new for them." Long's rapid rise in popularity suggested the potential depth of public dissatisfaction with the Roosevelt administration. The president's strategists feared that Long might join forces with Coughlin and Townsend to form a third party, enabling the Republicans to win the 1936 election.

The Second New Deal, 1935–1938

─────────★─────────

By 1935 Roosevelt had abandoned his hope of building a classless coalition of rich and poor, workers and farmers, and rural and urban dwellers. Pushed from the left to do more, and bitterly criticized by the right for what he had already done, the president had no choice but to abandon the middle ground. For both political and ideological reasons, and with an eye fixed firmly on the 1936 election, Roosevelt moved dramatically to the left. Historians use the term *Second New Deal* to describe the outpouring of legislation that followed.

Legislative Accomplishments

The first beneficiary of Roosevelt's change of direction was the labor movement. The rising number of strikes in 1934, about 1,800 involving a total of 1.5 million workers, reflected the dramatic growth of rank-and-file militancy. After the Supreme Court declared the NIRA unconstitutional in 1935, invalidating Section 7(a), labor representatives demanded legislation that would protect the right to organize and bargain collectively.

The Wagner Act. Democratic senator Robert F. Wagner of New York, one of labor's staunchest supporters in Congress, had introduced similar legislation even before the Supreme Court decision of 1935. Roosevelt

was at best a lukewarm supporter of the labor movement, but he realized the importance of organized labor to the Democratic Party and his own political future. Only when Congress was on the verge of passing Wagner's bill did Roosevelt reluctantly support the legislation, signing the National Labor Relations Act, also known as the Wagner Act, on July 5, 1935.

The Wagner Act placed the weight of the federal government on labor's side in the struggle to organize. Most important, it upheld the right of industrial workers to join a union (farm workers were not covered) and outlawed many unfair labor practices used by employers to squelch unions, such as firing or blacklisting workers because of their union activities. The act also established the nonpartisan National Labor Relations

General Strike, San Francisco, 1934
A general strike in San Francisco began with the longshoremen and soon spread to almost every union member (and some middle-class supporters as well) in the city. This striker has been shot in the head during an altercation with police. On July 19, union leaders voted to accept government arbitration, and the strike ended.
Corbis-Bettmann.

Board (NLRB) to protect workers from employer coercion, supervise representation elections, and enforce the guarantee of collective bargaining. If a union won a majority of the votes in a secret election, usually conducted by the NLRB, it was entitled to recognition as the sole bargaining agent for all the employees in a factory or other appropriate bargaining unit. The NLRB had the authority to force employers to comply.

Social Security. The Social Security Act signed by Roosevelt on August 14, 1935, was the second major piece of legislation in this phase of the New Deal. The law was partly a response to the political mobilization of the nation's elderly through the Townsend and Long movements, but it also reflected the prodding of social reformers such as Grace Abbott, head of the Children's Bureau, and Secretary of Labor Frances Perkins. The Social Security Act provided pensions for most workers in the private sector, although originally agricultural workers and domestics were not covered. The pensions were paid out of a federal-state pension fund to which both employers and employees contributed. The act also established a joint federal-state system of unemployment compensation, funded by an unemployment tax on employers and employees.

The Social Security Act was a milestone in the creation of the modern welfare state. With this law, the United States joined industrialized countries such as Great Britain and Germany in providing old-age pensions and unemployment compensation to its citizens. (The Roosevelt administration chose not to push for national health insurance, even though most other industrialized nations offered such protection.) The law also mandated categorical assistance, such as aid to the blind, deaf, and disabled and to dependent children. Those recipients were the so-called deserving poor, people who could not support themselves through no fault of their own. The categorical assistance programs, which formed a small part of the New Deal, gradually expanded over the years until they became the mainstay of the American welfare system.

The Works Progress Administration. Roosevelt was never enthusiastic about large expenditures for social welfare programs. As he said in January 1935, the government "must and shall quit this business of relief." But in the sixth year of the depression 10 million Americans were still out of work, a pressing political and moral issue for FDR and the Democrats. Under the direction of Harry Hopkins, the Works Progress Administration (WPA) became the main federal relief agency for the rest of the depression. Whereas the FERA had supplied grants to the states for relief programs, the WPA put relief workers on the federal payroll. Between 1935 and 1943 the WPA employed 8.5 million Americans and spent $10.5 billion. The agency constructed

Posters of the WPA
During its eight-year existence the WPA produced 2 million posters from 35,000 designs. WPA posters—such as this one designed to promote the Indian Court at the Golden Gate International Exposition in San Francisco in 1939—spotlight the vitality of American graphic design in the 1930s.
Library of Congress.

651,087 miles of roads, 125,110 public buildings, 8,192 parks, and 853 airports, and built or repaired 124,087 bridges.

The WPA, although an extravagant operation by the standards of the 1930s (it inspired nicknames such as "We Putter Around" and "We Poke Along"), never reached more than one-third of the nation's unemployed. Its average wage of $55 a month, well below the government-defined subsistence level of $100 a month, enabled workers to eke out only a bare living. The government cut back the program severely in 1941 and ended it in 1943, when the WPA was no longer deemed necessary in the full-employment economy that resulted from World War II.

The Revenue Act of 1935 showed Roosevelt's willingness to push for reforms that were considered too controversial earlier in his presidency. Much of the business community had already turned violently against Roosevelt in reaction to the NRA, the Wagner Act, and the Social Security Act. Wealthy conservatives quickly labeled this tax reform bill—which included federal inheritance and gift taxes, higher personal income tax rates in the top brackets, and increased corporate taxes—an attempt to "soak the rich." Roosevelt, seeking to defuse the popularity of Huey Long's Share Our Wealth plan, was just as interested in the political mileage of the tax bill as in its actual results, which increased federal revenues by only $250 million a year.

The 1936 Election

As the 1936 election approached, the broad range of New Deal programs (Table 25.2) brought new voters into the Democratic coalition. Many had been personally helped by federal programs; others benefited because their interests had found new support in the expanded functions of the government. Roosevelt could count on an impressive urban-based coalition of workers, organized labor, northern blacks, white ethnic groups, Catholics, Jews, liberals, intellectuals, progressive Republicans, and middle-class families concerned about old-age dependence and unemployment. The Democrats also held on, though with some difficulty, to their traditional strength among white southerners.

The Republicans realized that they could not compete directly with Roosevelt's popularity and the potent New Deal coalition. To run against Roosevelt, they chose the progressive governor of Kansas, Alfred M. Landon, who accepted the general precepts of the New Deal. But Landon and the Republicans stridently criticized the inefficiency and expense of many New Deal programs and accused FDR of harboring dictatorial ambitions.

Roosevelt's victory in 1936 was one of the biggest landslides in American history. The assassination of Huey Long in September 1935 by a Baton Rouge doctor whose motives were never explained had deflated the threat of a serious third-party challenge; the candidate of the combined Long-Townsend-Coughlin camp, Congressman William Lemke of North Dakota, garnered fewer than 900,000 votes (1.9 percent) for the Union Party ticket. Roosevelt received 60.8 percent of the popular vote and carried every state except Maine and Vermont; Landon received 36.5 percent. Landon fought such an uphill battle that the columnist Dorothy Thompson quipped, "If Landon had given one more speech, Roosevelt would have carried Canada."

Stalemate

"I see one-third of a nation ill-housed, ill-clad, ill-nourished," the president declared in his second inaugural address in January 1937. Roosevelt's appraisal suggested that he was considering further expansion of

TABLE 25.2

Major New Deal Legislation

Agriculture

1933	Agricultural Adjustment Act (AAA)
1935	Resettlement Administration (RA)
	Rural Electrification Administration
1937	Farm Security Administration (FSA)
1938	Agricultural Adjustment Act of 1938

Business and Industry

1933	Emergency Banking Act
	Glass-Steagall Act (FDIC)
	National Industrial Recovery Act (NIRA)
1934	Securities and Exchange Commission (SEC)
1935	Banking Act of 1935
	Revenue Act (wealth tax)

Conservation and the Environment

1933	Tennessee Valley Authority (TVA)
	Civilian Conservation Corps (CCC)
1936	Soil Conservation and Domestic Allotment Act

Labor and Social Welfare

1933	Section 7(a) of NIRA
1935	National Labor Relations Act (Wagner Act)
	National Labor Relations Board (NLRB)
	Social Security Act
1937	National Housing Act
1938	Fair Labor Standards Act (FLSA)

Relief

1933	Federal Emergency Relief Administration (FERA)
	Civil Works Administration (CWA)
	Public Works Administration (PWA)
1935	Works Progress Administration (WPA)
	National Youth Administration (NYA)

the welfare state that had begun to form late in his first term. However, retrenchment, controversy, and stalemate—not further reform—marked the second term.

The Supreme Court Fight. Only two weeks after his inauguration Roosevelt stunned Congress and the nation by asking for fundamental changes in the structure of the Supreme Court. Shortly after finding the NIRA unconstitutional in *Schecter v. United States* (1935), the Court had struck down the Agricultural Adjustment Act, a coal conservation act, and New York State's minimum wage law. With the Wagner Act, the TVA, and Social Security coming up on appeal, the future of New Deal reform legislation appeared in doubt.

In response, Roosevelt proposed adding one new justice to the Court for each currently sitting justice over the age of seventy. That scheme, which Roosevelt tried to promote as a way to reduce the workload of the elderly justices, would have increased the number of justices from nine to fifteen. Roosevelt's opponents quickly accused him of trying to "pack" the Court with justices favorable to the New Deal. The president's proposal was also regarded as an assault on the principle of separation of powers. The issue became moot when the Supreme Court, in what journalists tagged "a switch in time that saved nine," upheld several key pieces of New Deal legislation, including the Social Security Act, Washington State's minimum wage law, and the Wagner Act. A timely series of resignations allowed Roosevelt to reshape the Supreme Court with seven new appointments over the next four years, including Hugo Black, Felix Frankfurter, Stanley F. Reed, and William O. Douglas. Yet his handling of this issue was a costly blunder at a time when he was vulnerable to the lame-duck syndrome that often afflicts second-term administrations. No one yet suspected that FDR would break with tradition by seeking a third term.

Congressional Opposition. Congressional conservatives had long opposed the direction of the New Deal, but the Court-packing episode galvanized the conservatives by demonstrating that Roosevelt was no longer politically invincible. Throughout Roosevelt's second term a conservative coalition, composed mainly of southern Democrats and Republicans from rural areas, blocked or impeded social legislation. Two pieces of reform legislation that did win passage were the National Housing Act of 1937, which mandated the construction of low-cost public housing, and the Fair Labor Standards Act of 1938, which made permanent the minimum wage, maximum hours, and anti–child labor provisions in the NRA codes.

Roosevelt's attempts to reorganize the executive branch met a different fate. In both 1937 and 1938 Congress refused to consider a plan that would have consolidated all independent agencies into cabinet-rank departments, extended the civil service system, and created the new position of auditor general. Conservatives effectively played on lawmakers' fears that centralized executive management would dramatically reduce congressional power and linked the plan to popular fears of fascism and dictatorship abroad, fears fanned by Hitler's rise to power in Germany. Roosevelt settled for a weak bill in 1939 that allowed him to create the Executive Office of the President and name six administrative assistants to the White House staff. The White House also took control of the all-important budget process by moving the Bureau of the Budget to the Executive Office from its old home in the Treasury department.

The Roosevelt Recession. The "Roosevelt recession" of 1937–1938 dealt the most devastating blow to the president's political standing in the second term. Until that point the economy had made steady progress. From 1933 to 1937 the gross national product grew at a yearly rate of about 10 percent, and industrial output finally regained 1929 levels in 1937, as did real income. Unemployment declined from 25 percent to 14 percent, which meant that almost half the people without a job in 1933 had found one by 1937. Many Americans agreed with Senator James F. Byrnes of South Carolina that "the emergency has passed."

The steady improvement cheered Roosevelt, who had never overcome his dislike of large federal expenditures and the resulting deficits. Accordingly, Roosevelt slashed the federal budget in 1937. Between January and August, Congress cut the WPA's funding in half, causing layoffs of about 1.5 million workers. Moreover, the $2 billion withheld from workers' paychecks to initiate the new Social Security system further reduced purchasing power. The Federal Reserve, fearing inflation, tightened credit, causing a sharp drop in the stock market. Unemployment soared to 19 percent, which translated into more than 10 million workers without jobs. At this point Roosevelt found himself in the same situation that had confounded Hoover. Having taken credit for the recovery between 1933 and 1937, he now had to take the blame for the recession.

Shifting gears, Roosevelt spent his way out of the downturn. Large WPA appropriations and a resumption of public works projects poured enough money into the economy to lift it out of the recession by early 1938. Roosevelt and his economic advisors were groping toward the general theories advanced by John Maynard Keynes, a British economist. Keynes proposed that governments use deficit spending (the spending of public funds obtained by borrowing rather than through taxation) to stimulate the economy when private spending proved insufficient. But Keynes's theory would not be widely accepted until a dramatic increase in federal defense spending for World War II finally ended the Great Depression.

Still struggling with attacks on the New Deal, Roosevelt decided to "purge" some of his most conservative opponents from the Democratic Party as the 1938 election approached. In the spring primaries he campaigned against members of his own party who had been hostile or unsympathetic to New Deal initiatives. The effort failed abysmally and widened the liberal-conservative rift in the Democratic Party. In the general election of 1938, Republicans capitalized on the Roosevelt recession and the Court-packing backlash to pick up 8 seats in the Senate and 81 in the House. The Republicans also gained 13 governorships.

By 1938 the New Deal had basically run out of steam. For six years Roosevelt had inspired confidence that hard times could be overcome, skillfully balancing demands for more government programs with his own assessment of what was politically feasible. However, the president always set clear limits on how far he was willing to go. His instincts were basically conservative, not revolutionary—he wanted only to save the capitalist economic system by reforming it. This new activism was a major step beyond the informal and one-sided business-government partnership of the previous decade, but only because the emergency of the depression pushed Roosevelt in that direction. Under normal circumstances, he would have served out his second term and a new president would have been elected in 1940. Roosevelt won a third term (and eventually a fourth) primarily because the outbreak of World War II in Europe in 1939 made Americans reluctant to risk a change in leadership during such perilous times.

The New Deal's Impact on American Society

———★———

The New Deal was "somehow more than the sum of its parts." To understand its impact on society, one must look beyond the federal programs that poured out of Washington and consider broader changes in American political and social life. The New Deal set in motion dramatic growth in the federal bureaucracy and opened unprecedented opportunities for new constituencies to participate in public life. Its programs and priorities had an enormous impact on the public landscape and the arts, and it laid the groundwork for the welfare system that lasted until the 1990s. Its main legacy was an expanded federal presence in the economy and in the lives of ordinary citizens.

New Deal Constituencies and the Broker State

The New Deal accelerated the expansion of the federal bureaucracy that had been under way since the turn of the century. In one decade, the number of civilian government employees increased by 80 percent; the number of federal employees who worked in Washington grew at an even more rapid rate, doubling between 1929 and 1940. Power was increasingly centered in the nation's capital, not in the states. In 1939 a British observer summed up the new orientation: "Just as in 1929 the whole country was 'Wall Street conscious,' now it is 'Washington conscious.'"

The new bureaucrats administered federal budgets of unprecedented size. In 1930 the Hoover administration had spent $3.1 billion and had run a surplus of almost $1 billion. With the increase in federal programs to fight the depression, federal expenditures grew steadily to $4.8 billion in 1932, $6.5 billion in 1934, and $7.6 billion in 1936. In 1939, the last year before war mobilization affected the federal budget, expenditures reached $9.4 billion. Government spending outstripped receipts throughout this period, producing yearly deficits of about $3 billion. Roosevelt had come close to balancing the budget in 1938 but had triggered a major recession. The deficit climbed toward $3 billion again in the following year.

The beginnings of big government and bureaucracy are often associated with the Roosevelt years, but many of the problems commonly ascribed to the New Deal belong to later eras. The real step toward expanded government spending came during World War II, not during the depression. Federal outlays routinely surpassed $95 billion in the 1940s, and deficits grew to $50 billion. Although the deficit declined in the postwar era, government expenditures never returned to pre–World War II levels.

The growth of the federal government increased the potential impact of its decisions (and spending) on various constituencies. And the New Deal included a broader spectrum of the population in the political process, especially those people who organized themselves into pressure groups. During the 1930s the federal government operated as a *broker state*—that is, as a mediator between contending groups seeking power and influence. Democrats realized the importance of satisfying certain blocs of voters in order to cement their allegiance to the party. Even before the depression, they had begun to build a coalition based on urban political machines and white ethnic voters. In the 1930s, organized labor, women, African Americans, and other groups joined that coalition, receiving more attention from the Democrats and the federal government they controlled.

Organized Labor. During the 1930s, labor relations became a legitimate arena for federal action and intervention, and organized labor claimed a place in national political life. Labor's dramatic growth in the 1930s was one of the most important social and economic changes of the decade, an enormous contrast to its demoralized state at the end of the 1920s. Several factors encouraged the growth of the labor movement: the inadequacy of welfare capitalism in the face of the depression, New Deal legislation such as the Wagner Act, the rise of the Congress of Industrial Organizations (CIO), and the growing militancy of rank-and-file workers. By the end of the decade the number of unionized workers had tripled to almost 9 million, or 23 percent of the nonfarm work force. Organized labor won the battle not only for union recognition but also for higher wages, seniority systems, and grievance procedures.

The CIO served as the cutting edge of the union movement by promoting industrial unionism, that is, by organizing all the workers in an industry, both skilled and unskilled, into a single union. John L. Lewis, the leader of the United Mine Workers and a founder of the CIO, was the leading exponent of industrial unionism. His philosophy put him at odds with the American Federation of Labor (AFL), which favored organizing workers on a craft-by-craft basis. Lewis began to detach himself from the AFL in 1935, and the break was complete by 1938. Although the CIO generated much of the excitement on the labor front in the 1930s, the AFL gained more than a million new members between 1935 and 1940.

The CIO scored its first major victory in the automobile industry. On December 31, 1936, General Motors workers in Flint, Michigan, staged a sit-down strike, vowing to stay at their machines until management agreed to bargain collectively. The workers lived in the factories and machine shops for forty-four days before General Motors recognized the United Automobile Workers (UAW). The CIO soon won another major victory at the U.S. Steel Corporation. Despite a long history of bitter opposition to unionization (as demonstrated in the 1919 steel strike), "Big Steel" capitulated without a fight and recognized the Steel Workers Organizing Committee (SWOC) on March 2, 1937.

The victory in the steel industry was not complete, however. A group of companies known as "Little Steel" chose not to follow the lead of U.S. Steel in making peace with the CIO, causing steelworkers to strike the Republic Steel Corporation plant in South Chicago. On Memorial Day, May 31, 1937, strikers and their families gathered for a holiday picnic and rally outside the plant's gates. Tension mounted, rocks were thrown, and the police fired on the crowd, killing ten protesters. All were shot in the back. A newsreel photographer recorded the scene, but Paramount Pictures considered the film of the "Memorial Day Massacre" too inflammatory for distribution. Workers in Little Steel did not win union recognition until 1941. The road to recognition for labor, even with New Deal protections, was still long and violent.

The 1930s constituted one of the most active periods of labor solidarity in American history. The sit-down tactic spread rapidly. In March 1937, a total of 167,210 workers staged 170 sit-down strikes. Labor unions called for nearly 5,000 strikes that year and won favorable terms in 80 percent of them. Yet large numbers of middle-class Americans felt alienated by sit-down strikes, which they considered attacks on private property. The Supreme Court agreed and in 1939 upheld a law that banned the practice.

Meanwhile, the CIO attracted new groups to the union movement. Mexican Americans and blacks found the CIO's commitment to racial justice a strong

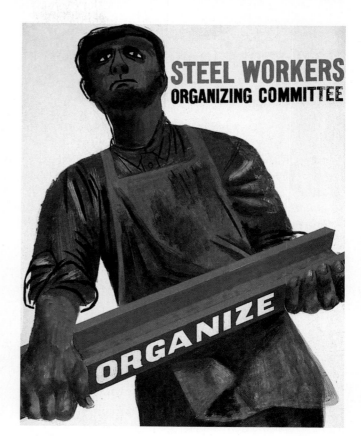

Organize
The Steel Workers Organizing Committee was one of the most vital labor organizations contributing to the rise of the CIO. Note that the artist Ben Shahn chose a male figure to represent the American labor movement in this poster from the late 1930s. Such iconography reinforced the notion that the typical worker was male, despite the large number of women who joined the CIO.
Library of Congress.

contrast to the AFL's long-established patterns of exclusion and segregation. About 800,000 women workers also found a limited welcome in the CIO. Women participated in major CIO strikes and served as union organizers, especially in textile organizing drives in the South. Few blacks, Mexican Americans, or women held leadership positions, however.

Women found other ways to participate in the labor movement. During the Flint sit-down strike in 1937 the Women's Emergency Brigade, a group of wives, sisters, and girlfriends of striking workers, supplied food and first aid. Wearing distinctive red berets and armbands, they picketed, demonstrated, and occasionally resorted to tactics such as breaking windows to disperse the tear gas used against the strikers (see American Voices, "Genora Johnson Dollinger: Labor Militancy," p. 814). After the strike, however, UAW leaders politely but firmly told the women to go back home where they supposedly belonged.

Genora Johnson Dollinger
Labor Militancy

——————★——————

During the Flint, Michigan, sit-down strike Genora Johnson Dollinger, the wife of a General Motors striker and the mother of two small children, organized the Women's Emergency Brigade. Women like Dollinger played a major role in the Flint victory.

I was twenty-three years old on December 30, 1936, when the strike started. It lasted forty-four days, a very dramatic forty-four days, until February 11, 1937.

It was New Year's Eve when I realized women had to organize and join in the fight. I was on the picket lines when the men's wives came down. They didn't know why their husbands were sitting inside the plant. Living in a company town, you see, they got only company propaganda through the press and radio. So when they came down on New Year's Eve, many were threatening to divorce their striking husbands if they didn't quit and get back to work to bring home a paycheck.

I knew then that union women must organize on their own in order to talk with these wives. . . .

This was an independent move. It was not under the direction of the union or its administrators—I just talked it over with a few women—the active ones—and told them this is what we had to do.

Women might, after all, be called upon to give their lives. That was exactly the appeal I made while we were forming the brigade—I told the women, "Don't sign up for this unless you are prepared. If you are prone to hysteria or anything like that you'd only be in our way." I told them they'd be linking arms and withstanding the onslaughts of the police and if one of our sisters went down shot in cold blood there'd be no time for hysteria.

Around 500 women answered that call. We bought red berets and made arm bands with the white letters "EB" for Emergency Brigade. It was a kind of military uniform, yes, but it was mainly identification. We wore them all the time so we'd know who to call on to give help in an emergency. I had five lieutenants—three were factory women. I chose them because they could be called out of bed at any hour, if necessary, or sleep on a cot at the union hall. Mothers with children couldn't answer calls like that—although they did sign up for the brigade. Even a few grandmothers became brigadiers and, I remember, one young girl only sixteen.

We had no communication system to speak of. Very few people had telephones so we had to call one woman who was responsible for getting the messages through to many others.

We organized a first aid station and child care center—the women who had small children to tend and couldn't join the EB took care of these jobs.

Listen, I met some of the finest women I have every come across in my life. When the occasion demands it of a woman and once she understands that she's standing in defense of her family—well, God, *don't fool around with that woman then. . . .*

It's a measure of the strength of those women of the Red Berets that they could perform so courageously in an atmosphere that was often hostile to them. We organized on our own without the benefit of professional leadership, and yet, we played a role, second to none, in the birth of a union and in changing working families' lives forever.

Source: Genora Johnson Dollinger, quoted in Jeane Westin, *Making Do* (Chicago: Follett Publishing, 1976), 223, 225–226, 229.

Labor's new vitality spilled over into political action. The AFL had always stood aloof from partisan politics, but the CIO quickly allied itself with the Democratic Party, giving $770,000 to Democratic campaigns in 1936 through Labor's Non-Partisan League. Labor also provided one of the few solid lobbies behind Roosevelt's plan to reorganize the Supreme Court. In the 1940s the CIO would become a major contributor to the Democratic war chest.

Yet despite the breakthroughs of the New Deal, the labor movement never developed into the dominant force in American life that had seemed possible in the heyday of the late 1930s. Roosevelt never made the growth of the labor movement a high priority, and many workers remained indifferent or hostile to unionization. Although the Wagner Act guaranteed unions a permanent place in American industrial relations, it did not revolutionize working conditions. The right to collective bargaining granted labor a measure of legitimacy, but it did not redistribute power in American industry. Management even found that unions could be a useful buffer against rank-and-file militancy. New Deal social welfare programs also diffused some of the pre-1937 radical spirit by channeling economic benefits to workers whether they belonged to unions or not. During the 1940s the labor movement entered a period of consolidation and then stagnation that continued for several decades.

Women and the New Deal. In the experimental climate of the New Deal unprecedented numbers of women were offered positions in the Roosevelt administration, both as policy makers and as middle-level bureaucrats. Frances Perkins served as secretary of labor throughout all four terms, the first woman named to a cabinet post. Molly Dewson, a social reformer turned politician, headed the Women's Division of the Democratic National Committee, where she promoted an issue-oriented program that supported New Deal reforms. Roosevelt's appointments of women included the first woman director of the mint, the head of a major WPA division, and a judge on the circuit court of appeals. Many of those women were close friends as well as professional colleagues and cooperated in an informal network to advance feminist and reform causes.

Eleanor Roosevelt exemplified the growing prominence of women in public life. In the 1920s she had worked closely with other reformers to increase women's clout in political parties, labor unions, and education—an invaluable apprenticeship for her White House years. Franklin and Eleanor's marriage represented one of the most successful political partnerships of all time. He was the pragmatic politician, always aware of what could be done; she was the idealist, always pushing him—and the New Deal—to do more. Indeed, Eleanor Roosevelt served as the conscience of the New Deal.

Although Franklin Roosevelt's expansion of the personalized presidency had roots in the administrations of Theodore Roosevelt and Woodrow Wilson, the nation had never seen a first lady like Eleanor Roosevelt. She held press conferences for women journalists, wrote a popular syndicated column called "My Day," and traveled extensively throughout the country. Some people wondered why the first lady did not stay home at the White House like a good wife, but in a Gallup poll in January 1939, 67 percent approved of her conduct, a higher approval rating than the president's at that time. In 1938 *Life* magazine hailed her as the greatest American woman alive.

Despite the vocal support of prominent women such as Eleanor Roosevelt, Molly Dewson, and the rest of the female political network, grave flaws still marred the treatment of women in New Deal programs. For

A First Lady without Precedent
Reflecting Eleanor Roosevelt's tendency to turn up in odd places, a famous 1933 *New Yorker* cartoon has one coal miner saying to another, "For gosh sakes, here comes Mrs. Roosevelt." Life soon imitated art. Here the first lady emerges from a coal mine in Dellaire, Ohio, still carrying her miner's cap in her left hand, while speaking with Joseph Bainbridge on May 22, 1935.
Wide World Photos, Inc.

example, one-fourth of the NRA codes set a lower minimum wage for women than for men performing the same jobs. New Deal agencies such as the Civil Works Administration and the Public Works Administration gave jobs almost exclusively to men, mainly because construction work was considered unsuitable for women. The Social Security and the Fair Labor Standards Acts did not cover major areas of traditional employment for women, such as domestic service. And the CCC excluded women entirely, leaving critics to ask, "Where is the 'she-she-she'?"

Women fared somewhat better under the Works Progress Administration. At the WPA's peak, 405,000 women were on its rolls. The Women's and Professional Projects Division of the WPA, headed by Ellen Sullivan Woodward, a Mississippi social worker, created hundreds of programs to put women to work, although these job assignments—most women were sent to work on sewing projects, which became a sort of dumping group for unemployed women—tended to reinforce gender and racial attitudes. African American and Mexican American women, if they had access to work relief at all, often found themselves shunted into training as domestics. For the most part, progress for women did not come from specific attempts to single them out as a group but occurred as part of a broader effort to improve the economic security of all Americans.

Blacks and the New Deal. Just as the New Deal did not seriously challenge gender inequities, it did little to battle racial discrimination. In the 1930s, the vast majority of the American people did not regard civil rights as a legitimate area for federal intervention. Indeed, many New Deal programs reflected prevailing racist attitudes. CCC camps segregated blacks, and many NRA codes did not protect black workers. Most telling, Franklin Roosevelt repeatedly refused to support legislation making lynching a federal crime, claiming that it would antagonize southern members of Congress whose support he needed to pass New Deal measures.

Nevertheless, blacks did receive enormous benefits from New Deal relief programs directed toward poor Americans, regardless of race or ethnicity. Blacks made up about 18 percent of the WPA's recipients although they constituted only 10 percent of the population. Public works projects channeled funds into black communities. The Resettlement Administration—established in 1935 to aid in the resettlement of sharecroppers and tenant farmers onto more productive land by helping small farmers buy property—fought for the rights of black tenant farmers in the South—that is, until angry southerners in Congress cut its appropriation. Nevertheless, many blacks reasoned that the tangible aid coming from Washington outweighed the discrimination that marred many federal programs.

African Americans were also pleased to see blacks appointed to federal office. Mary McLeod Bethune, an educator who ran the Office of Minority Affairs of the National Youth Administration, headed the "Black Cabinet" (see American Lives, "Mary McLeod Bethune: Black Braintruster," pp. 818–819). This informal network worked for fairer treatment of blacks by New Deal agencies in the same way that the women's network advocated feminist causes. Both groups benefited greatly from the support of Eleanor Roosevelt. The first lady's promotion of equal treatment for blacks ranks as one of her greatest legacies.

Help from the WPA and other New Deal programs and a belief that the White House—at least Eleanor Roosevelt—cared about their plight caused a dramatic change in blacks' voting behavior. Since the Civil War blacks had voted Republican, a loyalty resulting from Abraham Lincoln's freeing of the slaves and radical Reconstruction, as well as the Democratic Party's off-and-on associations with the Ku Klux Klan. As late as 1932 black voters in northern cities overwhelmingly supported Republican candidates. Then, in less than four years, blacks turned Lincoln's portrait to the wall and substituted that of Franklin Roosevelt. Because of the harshness of the depression, national politics assumed a new relevance for black Americans outside the South, who gave Roosevelt 71 percent of their votes in 1936. In Harlem, where relief dollars increased dramatically in the wake of the 1935 riot (see Chapter 24), the support was an extraordinary 81.3 percent. Black voters have remained overwhelmingly Democratic ever since.

Mexican Americans and the New Deal. The election of Franklin Roosevelt had an immediate effect on Mexican American communities demoralized by the depression and the deportations of the Hoover years. In cities such as Los Angeles and El Paso, Mexican Americans found it easier to qualify for relief under New Deal guidelines, and there was more relief to go around. Even though New Deal guidelines prohibited discrimination on the basis of an immigrant's legal status, the new climate encouraged a marked rise in requests for naturalization papers, the first step toward citizenship. Inspired by New Deal rhetoric about economic recovery and social progress through cooperation, Mexican Americans increasingly identified their future with the United States, not Mexico. This shift was especially evident among members of Bert Corona's "Mexican American generation"—the American-born children of Mexican immigrants who filled the leadership vacuum created by the deportations in the early 1930s (see Chapter 24). Mexican Americans supported and benefited from the New Deal's labor policies, such as Section 7(a) of the NIRA and the Wagner Act, which fostered an upsurge in labor organizing. For many Mexican Americans, joining the CIO was an important step in becoming an American.

Many Mexican Americans felt a personal connection to President Roosevelt, and participating in the political system increasingly became a part of Mexican American life. Los Angeles activist Beatrice Griffith noted, "Franklin D. Roosevelt's name was the spark that started thousands of Spanish-speaking persons to the polls." In 1939 El Congreso Nacional del Pueblo de Habla Español, the first national civil rights conference for Spanish-speaking peoples, called on its members to become American citizens and vote. The New Deal made it clear that it welcomed the votes of Mexican Americans and considered them to be an important part of the New Deal coalition. This politicalization was well under way before World War II, and it provided additional spurs to political activism.

Native Americans and the New Deal. But what about groups that were not politically mobilized or that were not recognized as key components of the New

Deal coalition? The New Deal's impact on those groups and communities often depended on whether sympathetic government administrators in Washington undertook to promote their interests. Native Americans were one of the nation's most disadvantaged and powerless minorities. The annual individual income of a native American in 1934 was only $48, and the unemployment rate of native Americans was three times the national average. Concerned New Deal administrators such as Secretary of the Interior Harold Ickes and Commissioner of the Bureau of Indian Affairs John Collier tried to correct some of those inequities. The Indian Section of the Civilian Conservation Corps brought needed money and projects to reservations throughout the West. Indians also received benefits from FERA and CWA work relief projects.

Of far greater significance was the Indian Reorganization Act of 1934, sometimes called the Indian New Deal. That law reversed the Dawes Severalty Act of 1887 (see Chapter 16) by promoting more extensive self-government through tribal councils and constitutions. The government also abandoned the attempt to force native Americans to assimilate into mainstream society in favor of promoting cultural pluralism. The New Deal pledged to help preserve Indian languages, arts, and traditions. The problems of native Americans were so severe, however, that these changes in federal policy did little to improve their lives or reinvigorate tribal communities.

The New Deal and the Land

Concern with the land was one of the dominant motifs of the New Deal, and the shaping of the public landscape is among its most visible legacies. Roosevelt brought to the presidency a love of forestry and a conservation ethic nurtured from childhood on his Hudson River estate. The expansion of federal responsibilities in the 1930s, especially the need to put the unemployed to work on public projects, created a climate conducive to action, as did public concern heightened by dramatic images of the drought and devastation of the Dust Bowl. The resulting national resources policy stressed scientific management of the land, conservation instead of commercial development, and the aggressive use of public authority to safeguard both private and public holdings.

The most extensive New Deal environmental undertaking was the Tennessee Valley Authority (TVA). The need for dams to control flooding and erosion in the Tennessee River Basin, a seven-state area with some of the country's heaviest rainfall, had been recognized since World War I. During the 1920s progressives led by Senator George Norris of Nebraska pushed for a public corporation to control flooding and to create a cheap source of electric power on the Tennessee River, but utility companies blocked the project. In 1933 the Tennessee Valley

A New Deal for Indians
John Collier, the New Deal's Commissioner for Indian Affairs, was a former social worker who had become interested in native American tribal cultures in the 1920s. Here Collier speaks with Chief Richard of the Blackfoot Nation, one of the Indian chiefs attending the Four Nation celebration at historic Old Fort Niagara, New York, in 1934.
Corbis-Bettmann.

Authority won approval to develop the region's resources under public control (Map 25.1). The TVA integrated flood control, reforestation, and agricultural and industrial development, including the production of chemical fertilizers. A hydroelectric grid provided inexpensive electric power for the valley's residents. Admired worldwide, the Tennessee Valley became one of the most popular destinations for visitors to the United States (see Voices from Abroad, "Odette Keun: A Foreigner Looks at the Tennessee Valley Authority," p. 821).

The Dust Bowl helped to focus attention on land management and ecological balance as well. Agents from the Soil Conservation Service in the Department of Agriculture taught farmers the proper technique for tilling hillsides. Government agronomists (experts in the science of agriculture) also tried to remove marginally productive land from cultivation and prevent soil erosion through better agricultural practices. One of their most widely publicized programs was the creation of the Shelterbelts, which involved planting a line of 220 million trees running northward roughly along the 99th meridian from Abilene, Texas, to the Canadian border. Planted as a windbreak, the trees also prevented soil erosion. The Shelterbelt program was a personal favorite of Franklin Roosevelt.

Sometimes political reality dictated specific legislation affecting the environment, such as the Soil Conservation and Domestic Allotment Act of 1936, which

Mary McLeod Bethune: Black Braintruster

★

THE NEW DEAL brought many remarkable people to Washington, but few had traveled as far as Mary McLeod Bethune. As the Reverend Adam Clayton Powell Sr. wrote to her in 1935 when she received the prestigious Spingarn Medal from the National Association for the Advancement of Colored People, "It is a long way from the rice and cotton fields of South Carolina to this distinguished recognition, but you have made it in such a short span of years that I am afraid you are going to be arrested for breaking the speed limit." In terms of her contributions to black history, Mary McLeod Bethune deserves to be remembered alongside such luminaries as Frederick Douglass, W. E. B. Du Bois, and Martin Luther King Jr.

Born on July 10, 1875, near Mayesville, South Carolina, Mary was the fifteenth of seventeen children born to Sam and Patsy McLeod, former slaves liberated after the Civil War. She was educated at the Scotia Seminary in Concord, North Carolina, and the Bible Institute for Home and Foreign Missions in Chicago (later the Moody Bible Institute) in preparation for her chosen career as a missionary. Turning from her original plan to go to Africa, she redirected her missionary zeal to the United States and the field of education and racial uplift. In 1898 she married Albertus Bethune, and their only child, Albert McLeod Bethune, was born in 1899. The family moved to Florida, but the marriage foundered and the couple separated in 1907. She never remarried, and Albertus Bethune died in 1918.

In 1904, "with $1.50 and a prayer," Mary McLeod Bethune opened the school in Daytona Beach, Florida, that eventually became the prestigious Bethune-Cookman College, the only historically black college founded by a black woman that continues to thrive today. The initial student body consisted of five girls and her son; by 1923 the school had more than 300 students and a faculty and staff of twenty-five. Bethune was intimately involved with this institution—and by extension with the issue of providing

Mary McLeod Bethune
This 1943 painting by Betsy Graves Reyneau captures the strength and dignity of one of the twentieth century's most important African Americans. Behind Bethune is a picture of the first building at the Daytona Literary and Industrial School for Training of Negro Girls, which later became Bethune-Cookman College.
National Portrait Gallery, Smithsonian Institution/Art Resource, NY.

expanded educational opportunities for African Americans—for the rest of her life. Through her extensive civic involvement in Daytona Beach and the constant fundraising needed to keep her school afloat, she was quickly drawn into wider national networks, especially through the National Association of Colored Women (NACW)—the leading black women's organization in the first quarter of the twentieth century. Bethune served as president of that organization from 1924 to 1928. In 1935 she organized the National Council of Negro Women (NCNW), a coalition of the major national black women's associations, serving as its president until 1949.

Mary McLeod Bethune was a forceful personality and a born leader. The New Deal offered her a national platform through which to promote her agendas on race, education, women, and youth when she was named—at Eleanor Roosevelt's suggestion—to the advisory committee of the National Youth Administration in 1935. In the next year she was named director of the division of Negro Affairs in the NYA, where she served until 1944. One of her greatest contributions was the leadership she provided to the other black administrators who found opportunities in the New Deal. The Federal Council of Negro Affairs, known informally as the Black Cabinet, met on Sunday nights at her home in Washington. As the Washington correspondent for the Associated Negro Press noted, "Mrs. Bethune has gathered everything and everybody under her very ample wing since her arrival last June." Along with NAACP general secretary Walter White, she was the only ranking black administrator who had access to the White House.

Bethune recognized the limits of the New Deal's commitment to civil rights, but she remained a loyal supporter of Franklin Roosevelt, with whom she enjoyed an easy friendship. But it was Eleanor Roosevelt who became her staunchest political ally. When funding for a black housing project in Daytona Beach was stalled by bureaucratic red tape, local activists contacted Bethune, who in turn reached Eleanor Roosevelt, who with one call to the head of the Federal Housing Authority had the project back on track. On several occasions the first lady opened the White House to Bethune for conferences, thereby ensuring that they would receive national attention. Along the way the two women became personal friends as well as allies, although Roosevelt admitted that it took her a while to feel comfortable giving Bethune the customary peck on the cheek she bestowed when greeting white friends. Not until she kissed Mrs. Bethune without thinking about it, she told her daughter, did she feel that she had overcome the racial prejudice that was so much a part of Roosevelt's—and many white Americans'—background.

Bethune's basic strategy was to win policy-making positions for African Americans and then use those bases to work for more equitable treatment for blacks throughout the New Deal. Sometimes her small gestures were just as telling as her larger public stances. She always insisted on being called "Mrs. Bethune" as a term of respect, refusing to go down in history as "Mary from Florida." When a White House guard addressed her as "Auntie," a term whites often used indiscriminately for older black women, she looked at him sweetly and asked, "Which one of my brother's children are you?" Her entire adult life was devoted to improving conditions and access for her race. "The drums of Africa beat in my heart," she often said. "I

cannot rest while there is a single Negro boy or girl lacking a chance to prove his worth."

There must have been many times when Bethune, a deeply religious woman, had to suppress personal feelings of disappointment or outright anger at the pace of change, but she always favored conciliation and compromise over confrontation. "I am diplomatic about certain things. I let people infer a great many things, but I am careful about what I say because I want to do certain things." But she also knew when to apply pressure, twist arms, appeal to publicity, and move a group toward concensus. As she once said forthrightly, "The White man has been thinking for us too long. We want him to think with us instead of for us."

When the National Youth Administration ceased operation in 1944, Bethune left government service but continued to be active in educational and charitable work. In 1952 she fulfilled a lifelong dream when she visited Liberia as an official U.S. representative at the inauguration of William Tubman as that country's president. She died of a heart attack in 1955 and was buried on the Bethune-Cookman campus. In 1974, on the ninety-ninth anniversary of her birth, the National Council of Negro Women dedicated the Mary McLeod Bethune Memorial Statue at Lincoln Park in Washington, D.C., just a short distance from the Capitol.

"Most people think I am a dreamer," Mary McLeod Bethune once said. "Through dreams many things come true." A dream come true was the 1938 gathering organized in conjunction with the National Council of Negro Women that brought sixty-seven black women leaders to the White House. Bethune recalled its significance soon thereafter:

> It certainly was history-making. . . . The pressure we have been making, the intercessions . . . they are finding their way. . . . The position I hold now—I give you that as an example. The first time in history that a Negro woman filled a national, federal position with the leeway, the opportunity . . . the contacts. Because one got in there, sixty-seven got in one day and many others are getting in here and there and there and there.

"A door has been sealed up for two hundred years," she concluded. "You can't open it overnight but little crevices are coming." Mary McLeod Bethune cracked open that door, and generations of African American activists, male and female, have been opening it wider and wider ever since.

filled the void created when the Supreme Court ruled the Agricultural Adjustment Act unconstitutional in January of that year. Under the new act, farmers received payments for cutting back the commercial production of crops such as wheat and cotton, which depleted the soil, and planting instead soil-building grasses and legumes such as clover and soybeans. Wheat and cotton were in fact major surplus commodities, and the law provided a way to cut production as well as encourage soil conservation. The Agricultural Adjustment Act of 1938 continued the policy of price supports and payments to farmers to limit production and established soil conservation as a permanent program.

Another priority of the Roosevelt administration was helping rural Americans stay on the land. The Rural Electrification Administration, established in 1935, brought power to farms in an attempt to improve the quality and productivity of rural life (see New Technology, "Rural Electrification," pp. 822–823). The New Deal also encouraged urban dwellers to return to rural areas. This "back to the land" motif animated many New Deal projects, especially those planned by the Resettlement Administration under the direction of Rexford Tugwell. Some of the best-known examples were planned cooperative communities in rural areas, such as Arthurdale in West Virginia, and the "Greenbelt" residential towns outside Washington, Cincinnati, and Milwaukee.

Although the TVA, Shelterbelts, and Greenbelt towns were primarily environmental programs, they also put large numbers of the unemployed to work. The Civilian Conservation Corps—the so-called Tree Army—planted some 2 billion trees by 1941, a dozen for every American citizen at the time. Not only was this sound conservation, but it gave the 2.5 million CCC workers a job to do. Similarly, many WPA projects helped achieve conservation and recreational goals.

Today, New Deal projects affecting the natural environment can be seen throughout the country, artifacts from the depression era. CCC and WPA workers built the Blue Ridge Highway—the consummate parkway of the 1930s—connecting the Shenandoah National Park in Virginia with the Great Smoky Mountain National Park in North Carolina. In the West, government workers built the San Francisco Zoo,

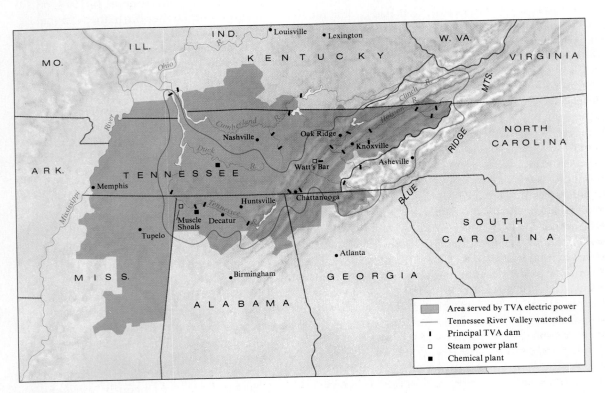

MAP 25.1
The Tennessee Valley Authority, 1933–1952
The Tennessee Valley Authority was one of the New Deal's most far-reaching environmental projects. Between 1933 and 1952 the TVA built twenty dams and improved five others. The cheap hydroelectric power generated by the dams brought electricity to hundreds of thousands of area residents.

ODETTE KEUN

A Foreigner Looks at the Tennessee Valley Authority

———★———

French writer Odette Keun visited the United States in 1936 and was so impressed by the TVA that she wrote a book about it. Among other observations, Keun felt that experiments like the TVA might help inhibit the development of an American variety of fascism.

The vital question before democracy is, therefore, not how to bring back an economic freedom which is irretrievably lost, but how to prevent the intellectual freedom, which is still our heritage, from being submerged. It is already threatened. It will be threatened more and more strongly in the years ahead—and the menace, of course, is dictatorship. But to fight dictatorship it is necessary first to understand in what circumstances it arises, and then to think out the counterattack which democracy can launch against its approaching force.

Dictatorship springs from two very clear causes. One is the total incapacity of parliamentary government: total, as in Germany in 1933 and in Spain in 1935. To such a breakdown neither the democratic nations of Europe nor America have yet been reduced, although everywhere there are very ominous creaks and cracks, and the authority and prestige of parliamentary institutions have greatly and perilously diminished. The other cause, infinitely closer to us and more dynamic, is the failure of the economic machine to function properly, and by functioning properly I mean ensuring a livelihood for the entire population. No system can survive if it cannot procure food and wages for the people who live under it. Man has to get subsistence from his rulers, for the most immediate and the most imperious law of our nature is that the belly must be filled. It is perfectly futile to orate on fine, high, and abstract principles to human beings who are permanently hungry, permanently harassed, permanently uncertain, who hear their wives begging for the rent and their children crying out for nourishment. . . .

One of the main tenets of liberalism—I reiterate this like a gramophone, but I must get it to sink in—is that all necessary overhauling and adjustment ought to be done in a manner which will minimize the shock to the greatest number, and soften as much as possible the unavoidable human suffering which these changes entail. This opposition to extremes, this practice of a graduated change, we can call "the middle of the road in time and space." But it is not nearly enough to conceive it and to bestow upon it a name. We must reach it. It is unutterably foolish to look at the middle of the road, to talk of the middle of the road, to hope for the middle of the road—and never get there.

Now I have tried to show that the middle of the road is already being laid down in America. The Tennessee Valley Authority is laying it down. Handicapped and restricted though it is in all sorts of ways, it is the noblest, the most intelligent, and the best attempt made in this country or in any other democratic country to economize, marshal, and integrate the actual assets of a region, plan its development and future, ameliorate its standards of living, establish it in a more enduring security, and render available to the people the benefits of the wealth of their district, and the results of science, discovery, invention, and disinterested forethought. In its inspiration and its goal there is goodness, for goodness is that which makes for unity of purpose with love, compassion, and respect for every life and every pattern of living. The economic machine, bad though it is, has not been smashed in the Tennessee Watershed; it is being very gradually, very carefully, very equitably reviewed and amended, and the citizens are being taught and directed, but not bullied, not coerced, not regimented, not frightened, within the constitutional frame the nation itself elected to build. It is not while the Tennessee Valley Authority has the valley in its keeping that despair or disintegration can prepare the ground for a dictatorship and the loss of freedom. The immortal contribution of the TVA to liberalism, not only in America but all over the world, is the blueprint it has drawn, and that it is now transforming into a living reality, of the road which liberals believe is the only road mankind should travel.

Source: Odette Keun, A Foreigner Looks at the TVA (1937), in Oscar Handlin, ed., This Was America (Cambridge, MA: Harvard University Press, 1949), 547–549.

Rural Electrification

──── ★ ────

IN 1935 FEWER than one-tenth of the nation's 6.8 million farms had electricity. For millions of farm families that stark fact meant a life of unremitting toil made even harsher by the lack of simple conveniences. Farm families used an average of 200 gallons of water a day. Any chore requiring water—and most did—meant pumping the water from a distant well and carrying it to the house or barn in a pair of buckets that weighed as much as 30 pounds each. Water had to be heated on a wood-stove that required constant tending. Meeting a family's yearly water needs took 63 eight-hour days and involved carrying water a distance of 1,750 miles.

Rural women suffered especially from the lack of electricity. Canning, a necessity before refrigeration, kept women standing over steaming vats of fruit or vegetables, often in the worst summer heat, before the freshly harvested produce spoiled. Wash day, traditionally Monday, called for three large zinc wash-tubs for washing, rinsing, and bleaching. A week's wash consisted of four to eight loads, each requiring three washtubs of clean water hauled from the well. Few rural households could afford commercial soap,

"Blue Monday"
Laundry was one of women's hardest household chores. Although this woman did not have to haul water from an outdoor well, she still had to pump it by hand in order to do the wash because her home lacked electricity. She also had to wring out the wet clothes manually, another arduous task.
Corbis-Bettmann.

Berkeley's Tilden Park, and the canals of San Antonio. The CCC helped complete the East Coast's Appalachian Trail and the West Coast's Pacific Crest Trail through the Sierras. In state parks across the country, cabins, shelters, picnic areas, lodges, and observation towers were built in a style that has been called "government rustic." All those projects shared the New Deal ethos of leisure and recreation coexisting with conservation.

Although the New Deal was ahead of its time in its attention to conservation, its legacy to later environmental movements is mixed. Many of the tactics used in New Deal projects—damming rivers, blasting fire roads, altering the natural landscape with buildings and shelters—are now considered too intrusive. In the 1970s the TVA came under attack for its longstanding practice of strip mining (removing topsoil to get at outcrops of coal near the surface rather than mining in shafts underground) and the pollution caused by its

power plants and chemical factories. Because of environmental concerns, a project as massive as the TVA probably could never be undertaken today—an ironic conclusion to what was hailed at the time as an enlightened use of government power for the public good.

The New Deal and the Arts

In the arts, the depression had dried up traditional sources of private patronage, and like most Americans, creative artists had nowhere to turn except to Washington. The WPA project known as "Federal One" put unemployed artists, actors, and writers to work, but its spirit and purpose extended far beyond relief. New Deal administrators wanted to redefine the relationship between artists and the community so that art would no longer be the province of the elite. "Art for the millions" became a popular New Deal slogan.

so women used lye, which barely removed ground-in dirt from soiled clothes and was very harsh on hands. But if farm women dreaded Monday, they hated Tuesday even more. Tuesday meant ironing, another all-day job. The iron, a 6- or 7-pound wedge of metal, had to be heated on the stove, and because it did not retain heat for more than a few minutes, it took several irons to do a shirt. The women in Texas's hill country called them "sad irons."

A day that began in darkness and was given over to twelve hours of backbreaking toil brought few comforts in the evening. Reading by kerosene lamps strained the eyes. Children's eyes might be strong enough to read in the semidarkness, but few older people could read without squinting. The absence of electricity also meant no radios, which meant no contact with the outside world.

Studies showed that farmers would find many uses for electricity and would make good customers, but power companies balked at the prospect of bringing electricity to the countryside, claiming that it was not economically feasible to run lines to individual farms. In 1935 the federal government made a commitment to bring power to rural America. The Rural Electrification Administration, an independent agency, promoted the formation of nonprofit farm cooperatives to bring electricity to their regions. For a $5 down payment, local farmers could join an association and become eligible for low-interest federal loans covering the cost of installing power lines. Each household was committed to a monthly minimum usage, usually about $3, but as usage increased, the rates came down. By 1940, 40 percent of the nation's farms had electricity; in 1950, the rate reached 90 percent.

Electricity brought relief from the drudgery and isolation of farm life. An electric milking machine saved hours of manual labor, most of it previously done before dawn by the faint glow of a kerosene lamp so farmers could devote the daylight hours to outdoor chores. An electric water pump lightened many chores, especially the hauling of water. Electric irons, vacuum cleaners, and washing machines eased women's burdens.

People's responses to rural electrification were poignant. A small child told his mother, "I didn't realize how dark our house was until we got electric lights." One farm woman remembered, "I just turned on the light and kept looking at Paw. It was the first time I'd ever really seen him after dark." Another family, caught unaware by the timing of the hookup, saw their house from a distance and thought it was on fire. Schoolteachers noticed that children did better at school when they had light to do homework by at night. Along with the automobile, electricity probably did more than any other technological innovation to break down the barriers between urban and rural life in twentieth-century America.

The Federal Art Project (FAP) gave work to many of the twentieth century's leading painters, muralists, and sculptors at a point in their careers when the lack of private patronage might have prevented them from continuing their artistic production. Under the direction of Holger Cahill, an expert on American folk art, the FAP commissioned murals for public buildings and post offices across the country. Jackson Pollack, Alice Neel, Willem de Kooning, and Louise Nevelson all received support from the FAP.

The Federal Music Project employed 15,000 musicians under the direction of Nicholas Sokoloff, the conductor of the Cleveland Symphony Orchestra. Under this project, government-sponsored orchestras toured the country, presenting free concerts of classical and popular music. Like many New Deal programs, the Music Project emphasized American themes. The composer Aaron Copland wrote his ballets *Billy the Kid* (1938) and *Rodeo* (1942) for the WPA, basing them on western folk motifs. The federal government also employed the musicologist Charles Seeger and his wife, the composer Ruth Crawford Seeger, to catalog hundreds of American folk songs.

The former journalist Henry Alsberg headed the Federal Writers' Project (FWP), which at its height employed about 5,000 writers. Young FWP writers who would later achieve fame included Saul Bellow, Ralph Ellison, Tillie Olsen, Richard Wright, and John Cheever. The FWP produced more than a thousand publications. It collected oral histories of Americans from many walks of life, including a set of 2,000 narratives of former slaves. Its most ambitious project was a set of state guidebooks. Fifty-one state and territorial guides and twenty regional guides, including *U.S. One: Maine to Florida*, were published, mostly by commercial presses. Combining tourism, folklore, and history, the guides

New Deal Murals
The social-realist painter William Gropper (who also created the *"Gulliver's Travels"*
cartoon on p. 806) portrayed the contributions of labor to modern industry in the
heroic, dynamic style that was typical of public art during the depression. This mural,
Construction of a Dam, was commissioned in 1937 for the Department of the Interior
building in Washington, D.C.
National Museum of American Art/Art Resource.

reflected the resurgence of interest in everything American.

Of all the New Deal arts programs, the Federal Theatre Project (FTP) was the most ambitious. American drama thrived in the 1930s, the only time that the United States has had a federally supported national theater. (In contrast, most European countries have state-supported theater and arts companies.) Under the gifted direction of Hallie Flanagan, former head of Vassar College's Experimental Theater, the Theatre Project reached an audience of 25 to 30 million in the four years of its existence. Talented directors, playwrights, and actors, including Orson Welles, John Huston, and Arthur Miller, offered their talents and services. But the leftist leanings of many actors and productions left the FTP vulnerable to conservative attack, and Congress terminated the program in 1939. Federal One limped along under federal-state sponsorship until 1943, when wartime priorities dealt it a final blow.

The WPA arts projects were influenced by a broad artistic trend known as the *documentary impulse*. Combining social relevance with uniquely American themes, this approach—which presented actual facts and events in a way that aroused the interest and emotions of the audience—characterized artistic expression in the 1930s. The documentary, probably the decade's most distinctive genre, influenced practically every aspect of American culture: literature, photography, art, music, film, dance, theater, and radio.

The documentary impulse is evident in John Steinbeck's fiction and John Dos Passos's *USA* trilogy, which used actual newspaper clippings, dispatches, and headlines in its fictional story. The commercially produced *March of Time* newsreels, which movie audiences saw before the feature film, presented the news of the world for the pretelevision age. The filmmaker Pare Lorentz commissioned the composer Virgil Thompson to create music that set the mood for documentary movies such as *The Plow That Broke the Plains* (1936), about Midwestern farming, and *The River* (1936), a lyrical tribute to the Mississippi. The new photojournalism magazines, including *Life* and *Look* (founded in 1936 and 1937, respectively), also reflected this documentary approach. The New Deal institutionalized the trend by sending investigators such as journalists Lorena Hickok and Martha Gellhorn into the field to report on the conditions of people on relief.

Finally, the federal government played a leading role in compiling the photographic record of the 1930s. The Historical Section of the Resettlement Administration had a mandate to document and photograph the American scene for the government. Through their haunting images of sharecroppers, Dust Bowl migrants, and the urban homeless, photographers like Dorothea Lange, Walker Evans, Ben Shahn, and Margaret Bourke-White permanently shaped the popular image of the Great Depression. The government hired photographers solely for their professional skills—not to provide relief, as in Federal One's projects. Their photographs, collected by the Historical Section and, after 1937, the Farm Security Administration (FSA), rank as the best visual representation of life in the United States during the depression decade.

The Legacies of the New Deal

The New Deal set in motion far-reaching changes, notably the growth of a modern state of significant size.

For the first time people experienced the federal government as a concrete part of everyday life. During the 1930s more than one-third of the population received direct government assistance from new federal programs such as Social Security, farm loans, relief, and mortgage guarantees. Furthermore, the government had made a commitment to intervene in the economy when the private sector could not guarantee economic stability. New legislation regulated the stock market, reformed the Federal Reserve System by placing more power in the hands of Washington policy makers, and brought many practices of modern corporate life under federal regulation. The New Deal thus continued and accelerated the pattern begun during the Progressive Era of using federal regulation to bring order and regularity to economic life.

The New Deal also laid the foundations of America's welfare state—that is, the federal government's accep-

tance of primary responsibility for the individual and collective welfare of the people. Although the New Deal offered more benefits to American citizens than they had ever received before, its safety net had many holes, especially in comparison with the far more extensive welfare systems in Western Europe. Another serious defect of the emerging welfare system was its failure to reach a significant minority of American workers. For example, the Social Security program excluded domestic workers and farm workers for many years. And since state governments administered the programs, benefits varied widely, with southern states consistently providing the lowest amounts. Not until the Great Society programs of President Lyndon Johnson in the 1960s would social welfare programs reach significant numbers of America's poor.

To its credit, the New Deal recognized that poverty was a structural economic problem, not a matter of

Relief Blues
Between 1934 and 1939 O. Louis Guglielmi, an Italian immigrant, found work on the Federal Art Project of the WPA, to which he submitted this painting in 1938. Entitled *Relief Blues*, it represents the social concern and urban realism prominent in American painting during the 1930s. The starkness of the room and its occupants is intensified by the bright red slippers, the pink rose on the floor, and the red lipstick and nail polish of the woman on the left.
National Museum of American Art/Art Resource.

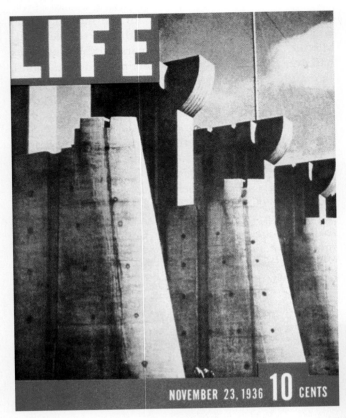

Life

Margaret Bourke-White's photograph of the Fort Peck Dam, with the two human figures in the foreground establishing its scale, graced the inaugural cover of *Life* magazine in 1936. Fort Peck was part of a series of dams the WPA was constructing in the Columbia River Basin for flood control. *Life's* first issue also contained a photo essay about the town nearest to the Fort Peck Dam, which was named, appropriately, New Deal, Montana.

Margaret Bourke-White, *Life* Magazine. © 1936 Time, Inc.

relation to the economic benefits that poured into their communities. The Women's Division of the Democratic National Committee mobilized 80,000 women at the grass-roots level who supported what the New Deal had done for their communities. The unemployed also looked kindly on the Roosevelt administration. According to one of the earliest Gallup polls, 84 percent of those on relief voted the Democratic ticket in 1936.

The Democratic Party attracted more than the down-and-out. Roosevelt's charismatic personality and the dispersal of New Deal benefits to families throughout the social structure brought middle-class voters, many of them first- or second-generation immigrants, into the Democratic fold. The New Deal thus completed the transformation of the Democratic Party that had begun in the 1920s toward a coalition that reflected the

The Human Face of the Great Depression

Migrant Mother by Dorothea Lange is perhaps the most famous documentary photograph of the 1930s. Lange spent only ten minutes in the pea-picker's camp in California where she captured this image, and did not even get the name of the woman whose despair and resignation she so powerfully recorded. She was later identified as Florence Thompson, a full-blooded Cherokee from Oklahoma.

Library of Congress.

personal failure. But New Deal reformers assumed that once the depression was over, full employment and an active economy would take care of welfare needs, and poverty would wither away. It did not. When later administrations confronted the persistence of inequality and unemployment, they grafted welfare programs onto the jerry-built system left over from the New Deal. Thus, the American welfare system would always be marked by its birth during the crisis of the Great Depression.

But even if the early welfare system had serious flaws, it was brilliant politics. The Democratic Party courted the allegiance of citizens who benefited from New Deal programs. Organized labor aligned itself with the administration that had made it a legitimate force in modern industrial life. Blacks voted Democratic in direct interests of ethnic groups, city dwellers, organized labor, blacks, and a broad cross-section of the middle class. Those voters provided the backbone of the Democratic coalition for decades to come.

Yet even in the 1930s the New Deal coalition contained potentially fatal contradictions, mainly involving the issue of race. Because Roosevelt depended on the support of southern white Democrats to pass New Deal legislation, he was unwilling to challenge the economic and political marginalization of blacks in the South. At the same time, New Deal programs were changing the face of southern agriculture by undermining the sharecropping tenant system and encouraging the migration of southern blacks to northern and western cities. Outside the South blacks were not prevented from voting, thus guaranteeing that civil rights would enter the national agenda. The resulting cracks would eventually weaken the coalition that had seemed so invincible at the height of Roosevelt's power.

America and an Insecure World Peace

Throughout the 1930s much of Franklin Roosevelt's, and the country's, attention was focused on the domestic crisis, but international events did not stand still. The rise of fascism in Europe and Asia in the 1930s threatened the fragile peace that had prevailed since the end of World War I. When the League of Nations proved too weak to deal with threats to world peace, President Roosevelt foresaw the possibility of America's participation in another war but bowed to the strong isolationist sentiment that predominated in the country. By 1939, however, the world—and the United States—was once again edging toward war.

Depression Diplomacy

During the early years of the New Deal, America's involvement in international affairs, especially in Europe, remained limited. Roosevelt put the national interest first, reasoning that only when the United States regained a stable economy could it act as an effective international leader. One of Roosevelt's few diplomatic initiatives in the early days of the New Deal was formal recognition of the Soviet Union in November 1933.

The Good Neighbor Policy. A significant development closer to home was the Good Neighbor Policy, under which the United States voluntarily renounced the use of military force and armed intervention in the Western Hemisphere. At the core of this policy, which was developed by Roosevelt and Secretary of State Cordell Hull, was the recognition that the friendship of Latin American countries was essential to the security of the United States and that to win that trust the United States had to develop more equal partnerships with its neighbors. At the Pan American Conference in Montevideo, Uruguay, in December 1933 Hull proclaimed that "no state has the right to intervene in the internal or external affairs of another." In 1934 Congress repealed the Platt Amendment, a relic of the Spanish-American War, which had asserted the right of the United States to intervene in Cuba's internal affairs. Indicating the limits to the Good Neighbor Policy, however, the U.S. Navy kept (and still keeps) a major base at Cuba's Guantanamo Bay and continued to meddle in Cuban politics. And in numerous Latin American countries, U.S. diplomats frequently resorted to economic pressure to solidify the influence of the United States and benefit its multinational corporations.

Debates over Isolationism. An internationalist at heart, Franklin Roosevelt—like his predecessor, Woodrow Wilson—wanted the United States to play a prominent role in the international economic and political system. But FDR was hampered by the isolationism that had been building in both Congress and the nation throughout the 1920s, a product of growing disillusionment with American participation in World War I. In 1934 Gerald P. Nye, a Republican senator from North Dakota, began a congressional investigation into the profits of munitions makers during World War I, which then expanded into a wide investigation of the influence of economic interests on America's decision to declare war. Nye's committee concluded that war profiteers, whom it called "merchants of death," had maneuvered the nation into the war for financial gain.

Most of the committee's charges were dubious or simplistic, but they gave momentum to the isolationist movement and contributed to the passage of the Neutrality Act of 1935. Explicitly designed to prevent a recurrence of the events that had pulled the United States into World War I, the act imposed an embargo on trading arms with countries at war and declared that American citizens traveling on the ships of belligerent nations did so at their own risk. In 1936 Congress expanded the Neutrality Act to ban loans to belligerents, and in 1937 it adopted a "cash and carry" provision: if a country at war wanted to purchase nonmilitary goods from the United States, it had to pay for them in cash and pick them up in its own ships.

In that same year Congress explicitly reinforced earlier bans on sales of arms to Spain, where a bloody civil war had erupted in 1936. In Spain, army forces led by Generalissimo Francisco Franco, with strong support from the fascist regimes in Germany and Italy, were leading a rebellion against the elected republican coalition government. Only the Soviet Union and Mexico backed the Spanish government forces, called the Loyalists; the governments of the United States, Great Britain, and France sympathized with the Loyalists but remained neutral. Because Franco was receiving substantial military aid from Germany and Italy, the neutrality policy doomed the Loyalists.

Many American activists and intellectuals expressed shock at the policy of nonintervention. The Spanish Civil War was the most vital issue of their generation. "People of my sort," observed the writer Malcolm Cowley, "were more deeply stirred by the Spanish Civil War than by any other international event since the World War and the Russian Revolution." Ernest Hemingway immortalized the conflict in his novel *For Whom the Bell Tolls* (1940). Approximately 3,200 American men and women volunteered to fight on the Loyalist side. Calling themselves the Abraham Lincoln Brigade, they formed part of an international force of soldiers, ambulance drivers, and support personnel. Years later survivors recalled the struggle as the "good fight." Despite assistance from the Soviet Union, the Loyalists were outnumbered and inadequately supplied; more than half the American volunteers died in the carnage, which claimed over 700,000 lives altogether.

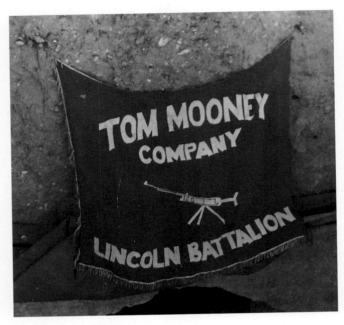

The Spanish Civil War
American volunteers who fought on the Loyalist side against Franco in the Spanish Civil War associated their fight against fascism with the figure of Abraham Lincoln, symbol of democracy and human rights. In a similar spirit, the American machine gun detachment of the Abraham Lincoln Brigade called itself the Tom Mooney Company in honor of the World War I labor activist imprisoned for his alleged role in planting a bomb during a preparedness parade in 1916.
Archive Photos.

Aggression and Appeasement

The Spanish Civil War was just one of several world crises that challenged the neutrality policy of the United States during the 1930s. Even more threatening were aggressive actions by Germany, Italy, and Japan, all determined to expand their borders and widen their influence. The first crisis was precipitated by Japan, a country with a militaristic regime intent on dominating the Pacific Basin. Japan needed raw materials and markets for its goods to become an imperial and industrial power. In 1931, desiring a buffer against its enemy, the Soviet Union, Japan occupied Manchuria, the northernmost province of China; in 1937 Japan launched a full-scale invasion of China. In both instances, the League of Nations condemned Japan's action but was helpless to stop the aggression.

Japan's defiance of the League gave encouragement to a fascist dictator half a world away. Italy's Benito Mussolini, who had come to power in 1922, had long been unhappy with the Versailles treaty, which had not awarded Italy any former German or Turkish colonies.

Nor had Italy ever forgotten its stinging defeat by Abyssinia (modern Ethiopia) in 1896, the first time Africans had successfully defended themselves against white imperialists. In 1935 Italy invaded Ethiopia, one of the few independent countries left in Africa. The Ethiopian emperor, Haile Selassie, appealed to the League of Nations, which condemned the invasion as aggression and this time imposed sanctions, but to little effect. By 1936 Italian subjugation of Ethiopia was complete.

The Rise of Hitler. Not Italy, but Germany presented the gravest threat to the world order in the 1930s. The German Weimar Republic of the 1920s was fundamentally unstable, saddled with huge reparations payments and national passions inflamed by the guilt clause imposed by the Treaty of Versailles, in which Germany was made to take sole blame for World War I. Runaway inflation, fear of communism, labor unrest, and rising unemployment fueled the rise of Adolf Hitler and his National Socialist (Nazi) Party. On January 20, 1933, during the interregnum between the Hoover and

Roosevelt administrations, Hitler became chancellor of Germany and assumed dictatorial powers. Aiming at nothing short of world domination, as he made clear in his book *Mein Kampf* (My Struggle), Hitler sought to overturn the territorial settlements of the Versailles treaty, "restore" all the Germans of Central and Eastern Europe to a single greater German fatherland, and annex large areas of Eastern Europe. In his warped vision, "inferior races" such as Jews, Gypsies, and Slavs, as well as "undesirables" such as homosexuals and the mentally impaired, would have to make way for the "master race." In 1933 Hitler established the first concentration camp at Dachau in southeast Germany and opened a campaign of persecution against the Jews.

Hitler's strategy for gaining territory was to provoke a series of crises that gave Britain and France little alternative but to let him have his way. British prime minister Neville Chamberlain was a particularly insistent proponent of the policy that became known as "appeasement." In 1933 Germany withdrew from the League of Nations, and two years later Hitler announced that he planned to rearm Germany in violation of the Versailles treaty. No one stopped him. In 1936 Germany reoccupied the Rhineland, a region that had been declared a demilitarized zone under the treaty. Once again France and Britain took no action. Later that year Hitler and Mussolini joined forces in the Rome-Berlin Axis, a political and military alliance, and when the Spanish Civil War broke out, they supplied arms to the Spanish fascists. On November 26, 1936, Germany and Japan signed the Anti-Comintern Pact, a precursor to the military alliance between Japan and the Axis powers that was formalized in 1940.

As early as 1936, President Roosevelt had foreseen the possibility of U.S. participation in another European war, but he was determined to stay in line with public opinion. During the 1936 campaign, Roosevelt made a stirring antiwar statement that drew on his experience as assistant secretary of the navy during World War I: "I have seen blood running from the wounded. I have seen men coughing out their gassed lungs. . . . I have seen children starving. I have seen the agony of mothers and wives. I hate war." But in October 1937 Roosevelt seemed to take a small step away from isolationism when he denounced "the present reign of terror and international lawlessness" and called on peace-loving nations to oppose such aggression through a "quarantine." Roosevelt's statement reflected rhetorical opposition to militarism more than a specific call for collective security. In any case, at a time when Gallup polls showed that two-thirds of the American people believed the United States had made a mistake in entering World War I, there was no broad-based support for changing the isolationist course.

The Popular Front. Fearful of a world war set in motion by fascist aggression, the Soviet Union attempted to mobilize liberals in democratic countries into what was called a "popular front." In Europe and the United States, communist parties welcomed the cooperation of any group concerned about the threat of fascism to civil rights, organized labor, and world peace. The popular front coincided with the period of the Communist Party's greatest appeal in America, from 1935 to 1939, when party membership peaked at about 100,000, including many intellectuals and writers but also union organizers, working-class activists, and even a few New Deal administrators. The participation of the Abraham Lincoln Brigade on the Loyalist side in the Spanish Civil War was part of the popular front strategy, although these collective efforts could not keep the Spanish republic from falling to Franco's forces in March 1939.

The Failure of Appeasement. As persecution of the Jews and other minorities escalated in Germany, Hitler's ambitions grew. In 1938 he sent troops to annex Austria, while at the same time he schemed to seize part of Czechoslovakia, the keystone of Central Europe. Because Czechoslovakia had an alliance with France, war seemed imminent. But at the Munich Conference in September 1938, Britain and France capitulated, agreeing to let Germany annex the Sudetenland, the German-speaking border areas of Czechoslovakia, in return for Hitler's pledge to seek no more territory.

Within six months, however, Hitler's forces had overrun the rest of Czechoslovakia and threatened to march into Poland, exposing the folly of Neville Chamberlain's pronouncement that the Munich agreement had guaranteed "peace with honor . . . peace for our time." Britain and France prepared to take a stand. Then in August 1939 Hitler shocked the world by signing the Nonaggression Pact with the Soviet Union, allowing Germany to avoid waging war on two fronts. Just as shocked were supporters of the popular front, who were devastated by Stalin's willingness to strike a deal with the hated Hitler to stay out of war. The heyday of American communism ended abruptly.

With the signing of the Nazi-Soviet pact, the world again stood on the brink of war. Although most Americans hoped the United States would remain aloof from the coming European conflict, many began to realize that the nation faced a greater enemy than the economic problems that had gripped it for the past decade. Barely twenty years after the "war to end all wars," the United States prepared once again to enter a worldwide struggle for the survival of democracy.

Summary

★

The New Deal was the response of Franklin Roosevelt and the Democratic Party to the crisis of the Great Depression. The New Deal offered a broad-based program of political and economic reform, but its programs were hardly revolutionary. President Hoover had taken the first steps toward involving the federal government more actively in economic life, a trend that Roosevelt continued and expanded. The New Deal never cured the depression, but it restored confidence that Americans could overcome hard times. It provided a measure of economic security against the worst depression in American history by relieving many of its tragic effects. And legislation such as the Social Security Act of 1935 laid the foundation of the modern welfare state, bringing the United States more in line with other industrialized countries in its acceptance of responsibility for the collective welfare of its citizens.

The New Deal dramatically expanded the size and power of the federal government, continuing a trend that had begun in the late nineteenth and early twentieth centuries. Decisions made in Washington touched millions of individual lives. The New Deal provided new opportunities and a larger role in public life for blacks, women, Mexican Americans, and the labor movement. The collapse of the economy encouraged a reassertion of American values in literature and the arts. This artistic flowering was partly supported by a unique experiment in government patronage of the arts through the WPA. In politics the Democratic coalition of white southerners and the urban working class that had begun to emerge in the 1920s reached a climax in the landslide presidential victory of 1936. By 1938, however, the New Deal had run out of steam and hard times were far from over.

Although the attention of the country was focused on the domestic crisis throughout the decade, the rise of fascism in Germany, Italy, and Japan threatened the fragile world peace established by the Treaty of Versailles. American public opinion remained strongly isolationist, even as Europe stood on the edge of war in 1939, but President Roosevelt was already leading the nation toward participation in its second global war in a generation.

TIMELINE

1933	Emergency Banking Act
	Glass-Steagall Act establishes FDIC
	Agricultural Adjustment Act (AAA)
	National Industrial Recovery Act (NIRA)
	Tennessee Valley Authority (TVA)
	United States abandons gold standard
	Repeal of Prohibition
1934	Securities and Exchange Commission
	Indian Reorganization Act
	Platt Amendment repealed
1935	Supreme Court finds NIRA unconstitutional
	National Union for Social Justice created, led by Father Coughlin
	Resettlement Administration
	National Labor Relations (Wagner) Act
	Social Security Act
	Works Progress Administration
	Huey Long assassinated
	Congress of Industrial Organizations (CIO) formed
	Italy invades Ethiopia
1935–1937	Neutrality Acts
1936	Supreme Court finds AAA unconstitutional
	Black Cabinet (Federal Council of Negro Affairs)
	Roosevelt reelected
	Life magazine founded
1936–1939	Spanish Civil War
1937	Sit-down strikes
	Memorial Day Massacre
	Supreme Court reorganization fails
	Japan invades China
1937–1938	"Roosevelt recession"
1938	Fair Labor Standards Act
1939	Munich Conference
	Federal Theatre Project terminated
	Nazi-Soviet pact
	World War II breaks out in Europe

Suggested Readings

——————★——————

Comprehensive introductions to the New Deal include Robert S. McElvaine, *The Great Depression* (1984); William E. Leuchtenburg, *Franklin D. Roosevelt and the New Deal* (1963); John A. Garraty, *The Great Depression* (1987); Roger Biles, *A New Deal for the American People* (1991); and Harvard Sitkoff, ed., *Fifty Years Later: The New Deal Evaluated* (1985).

The New Deal Takes Over, 1933–1935

The New Deal has inspired a voluminous bibliography. Frank Freidel, *Launching the New Deal* (1973), covers the first hundred days in detail. Monographs include Bernard Bellush, *The Failure of the NRA* (1975); Thomas K. McCraw, *TVA and the Power Fight* (1970); John Salmond, *The Civilian Conservation Corps* (1967); Roy Lubove, *The Struggle for Social Security* (1968); Mark Leff, *The Limits of Symbolic Reform: The New Deal and Taxation, 1933–1939* (1984); and Bonnie Fox Schwartz, *The Civilian Works Administration, 1933–1934* (1984). Ellis Hawley, *The New Deal and the Problem of Monopoly* (1966), provides a stimulating account of economic policy. Claire Bond Potter, *War on Crime* (1998), analyzes the Federal Bureau of Investigation and statebuilding in the 1930s. Agricultural developments are covered in Theodore Saloutos, *The American Farmer and the New Deal* (1982); and Sidney Baldwin, *Poverty and Politics: The Rise and Decline of the Farm Security Administration* (1968). Alan Brinkley, *Voices of Protest* (1982), covers the Coughlin and Long movements.

The Second New Deal, 1935–1938

Roosevelt's second term has drawn far less attention than has the 1933–1936 period. James MacGregor Burns, *Roosevelt: The Lion and the Fox* (1956), provides an overview, as does Barry Karl, *The Uneasy State* (1983). Alan Brinkley, *The End of Reform* (1995), discusses the New Deal and liberalism between 1937 and 1945. The growing opposition to the New Deal is treated in Clyde P. Weed, *The Nemesis of Reform: The Republican Party during the New Deal* (1994); and James T. Patterson, *Congressional Conservatism and the New Deal* (1967).

The New Deal's Impact on American Society

Katie Louchheim, ed., *The Making of the New Deal: The Insiders Speak* (1983), provides an engaging introduction to some of the men and women who shaped the New Deal. On women in the New Deal, see Susan Ware, *Beyond Suffrage* (1981). Blanche Cook, *Eleanor Roosevelt* (1991), takes the story to 1933; see also Lois Scharf, *Eleanor Roosevelt* (1987). Also of interest is Frances Perkins's memoir, *The Roosevelt I Knew* (1946).

On minorities and the New Deal, see Harvard Sitkoff, *A New Deal for Blacks* (1978); John B. Kirby, *Black Americans in the Roosevelt Era* (1980); Robert Zangrando, *The NAACP Crusade against Lynching, 1909–1950* (1980); and Nancy J. Weiss, *Farewell to the Party of Lincoln* (1983). For material on Mary McLeod Bethune, see Darlene Clark Hine, ed., *Black Women in America: An Historical Encyclopedia* (1993). George J. Sanchez, *Becoming Mexican American: Ethnicity, Culture and Identity in Chicano Los Angeles, 1900–1945* (1993), and David G. Gutierrez, *Walls and Mirrors: Mexican Americans, Mexican Immigrants, and the Politics of Ethnicity* (1995), describe the politicization of Mexican Americans in the 1930s.

Irving Bernstein, *The Turbulent Years* (1970) and *A Caring Society: The New Deal, the Worker, and the Great Depression* (1985), chronicle the story of the labor movement through 1941 in compelling detail. Additional studies include Ronald Schatz, *The Electrical Workers* (1983); Bruce Nelson, *Workers on the Waterfront* (1988); and Lizabeth Cohen, *Making a New Deal: Industrial Workers in Chicago, 1919–1939* (1990). Steven Fraser, *Labor Will Rule* (1991), is a fine biography of CIO leader Sidney Hillman. For women and the labor movement, see Annelise Orleck, *Common Sense and a Little Fire* (1995).

On Indian policy, see Donald Parman, *Navajos and the New Deal* (1976); Laurence Hauptman, *The Iroquois and the New Deal* (1981); and Laurence C. Kelly, *The Assault on Assimilation: John Collier and the Origins of Indian Policy Reform* (1983). For rural electrification, see D. Clayton Brown, *Electricity for Rural America* (1980).

The various New Deal programs have found historians in Jerry Mangione, *The Dream and the Deal: The Federal Writers' Project, 1935–1943* (1972); Richard McKinzie, *The New Deal for Artists* (1973); and Jane DeHart Mathews, *The Federal Theater, 1935–1939* (1967). Marlene Park and Gerald Markowitz, *Democratic Vistas* (1984), survey New Deal murals and art, and Barbara Melosh, *Engendering Culture* (1991), looks at New Deal public art and theater. General studies of cultural expression include William Stott, *Documentary Expression and Thirties America* (1973), and Richard Pells, *Radical Visions and American Dreams* (1973). The creation of the New Deal's welfare system is treated in James T. Patterson, *America's Struggle against Poverty* (1981), which carries the story through 1980. See also Michael Katz, *In the Shadow of the Poorhouse: A Social History of Welfare in America* (1986). For the enduring impact of Franklin Roosevelt on the political system, see William Leuchtenburg, *In the Shadow of FDR* (1983).

America and an Insecure World Peace

Robert Dallek, *Franklin Delano Roosevelt and American Foreign Policy, 1932–1945* (1979), and Wayne Cole, *Roosevelt and the Isolationists, 1932–1945* (1983), provide comprehensive overviews. See also Kenneth S. Davis, *FDR: Into the Storm, 1937–1940* (1993); Arnold Offner, *American Appeasement* (1976); and David Schmitz, *The United States and Fascist Italy, 1922–1940* (1988). On Latin America, see Walter LaFeber, *Inevitable Revolutions* (1983). Material on the relationship between American intellectuals and the Communist Party can be found in Harvey Klehr, *The Heyday of American Communism* (1984). Peter Carroll, *The Odyssey of the Abraham Lincoln Brigade* (1994), tells the story of Americans in the Spanish Civil War.

Back Him Up!

BUY WAR BONDS

The World at War,

1939–1945

O N A SUNDAY night in October 1938 the actor Orson Welles's "Mercury Theater of the Air" broadcast a modern version of *The War of the Worlds* (1898) by the British writer H. G. Wells. The fictional news bulletins, interspersed with simulated on-the-spot reports, convinced many people that Martians had landed near Princeton, New Jersey, and were invading the countryside. Even though the broadcast included four announcements that the radio program was a dramatization, some people fled their homes. No one doubted the power of radio anymore.

One reason that so many people believed in Orson Welles's fictional invasion may have been that in September 1938, radio programs had been interrupted repeatedly by ominous news bulletins about a possible European war. Even the September 30 reports of the Munich agreement among Britain, France, and Germany, which prevented war for another year, did not ease people's fears of imminent catastrophe. In the late 1930s popular culture reflected America's connection to international events, an involvement that the coming of World War II would intensify. When radios announced on December 7, 1941, that the Japanese had attacked Pearl Harbor, Americans realized that this news flash was not a hoax.

World War II ranks with the New Deal as a crucial period of political, social, and economic change in America. Mobilization for war pumped money and confidence into the economy, ending the Great Depression. The task of fighting a global war increased the government's influence on people's lives and caused dramatic social changes on the home front. But the most far-reaching

Mobilizing the Hearts and Minds of America
To offset the enormous cost of the war, the U.S. government sponsored a series of bond drives. This poster by Thomas Hart Benton, which the prominent artist donated in 1943 to the war effort, captured the spirit of unity and sacrifice needed to win World War II.
Library of Congress.

impact was international, as the United States accepted a leading—and continuing—role in world affairs. Within wartime strategies lay the seeds of the Cold War that would follow.

American Neutrality, 1939–1941

★

World War II officially began when German troops attacked Poland on September 1, 1939, and two days later Britain and France declared war on Germany. For more than two years the United States debated its course of action. Most Americans held two contradictory positions. The overwhelming majority supported the Allies. A 1939 poll showed that 84 percent wanted an Allied victory, 2 percent supported the Nazis, and 14 percent had no opinion. Even so, most Americans did not want to be drawn into another European war. This strong isolationist sentiment severely limited President Roosevelt's options.

The Road to War

Because the United States had become a major world power, whatever stand the country adopted after 1939 would affect the course of the European conflict. Two days after the outbreak of hostilities, the United States officially declared its neutrality. Roosevelt made no secret of his sympathies, however, pointedly rephrasing Woodrow Wilson's declaration of 1914: "This nation will remain a neutral nation, but I cannot ask that every American remain neutral in thought as well." So began what *Time* magazine would later call America's "thousand-step road to war."

At first the need for American intervention seemed remote. After the German conquest of Poland in September 1939, a false calm settled over Europe. This "phony war" lulled many Americans into believing that arming the Allies would be enough to defeat Germany. Hitler soon shattered that complacency. In a few hours on April 9, 1940, Nazi tanks overran Denmark. Norway fell to the Nazi *Blitzkrieg* ("lightning war") next, and the Netherlands, Belgium, and Luxembourg soon followed. Then the Germans stormed into France from the north, making short work of the combined British and French troops. On June 22, 1940, France fell. Only Britain stood between the United States and Hitler's plans for world domination.

Support for Intervention Grows.   During the summer and fall of 1940 German planes bombarded Britain mercilessly in the Battle of Britain, destroying the myth of its island invincibility. In America the debate over the nation's neutrality intensified. The journalist William Allen White and his Committee to Defend America by Aiding the Allies led the interventionists. Isolationists, including the aviator Charles Lindbergh, Senator Gerald Nye, and the former National Recovery Act administrator Hugh Johnson, formed the America First Committee in 1940 to keep the nation out of the war. They attracted the support of the *Chicago Tribune*, the Hearst chain of newspapers, and other conservative publications—especially those in the Midwest.

Despite the efforts of the America First Committee, in 1940 the United States moved closer to involvement in the war. In May, Roosevelt created the National Defense Advisory Commission and the Council of National Defense to advise on strategies for putting the economy and government on a defense footing. In June of that election year he brought two prominent Republicans, Henry Stimson and Frank Knox, into his cabinet as secretaries of war and the navy, respectively, to give a bipartisan character to the war preparations. During the summer the president traded fifty World War I destroyers to Great Britain in exchange for the right to build military bases on British possessions in the Atlantic, thereby circumventing the nation's neutrality laws by executive order. In October a bipartisan majority in Congress approved a large increase in defense spending and instituted the first peacetime draft registration and conscription in American history. Another draft law, which came up in August 1941, lengthening draftees' service from one year to two and a half years, passed by a single vote.

The 1940 Election.   While the war expanded in Europe, Asia, North Africa, and the Middle East, the United States prepared for the 1940 election. Would Roosevelt seek an unprecedented third term? He had not designated a successor, and the war in Europe convinced him that he should run. Roosevelt submitted to a "draft" at the Democratic National Convention in Chicago, but convention delegates balked at his choice for vice-president, liberal Secretary of Agriculture Henry A. Wallace, to replace John Nance Garner of Texas, a conservative who had long since broken with the New Deal. Wallace's nomination went through only after Eleanor Roosevelt, reminding delegates that this was "no ordinary time," asked them to put politics aside in a national crisis.

The Republicans nominated a political newcomer, Wendell Willkie of Indiana, a lawyer and the president of the Commonwealth and Southern Electric Utilities Company. Willkie, a former Democrat, supported many of the New Deal's domestic and international policies, including Roosevelt's trade of destroyers for military bases. The platforms of the two parties differed only slightly. Both pledged aid to the Allies but stopped short of calling for American participation in the war.

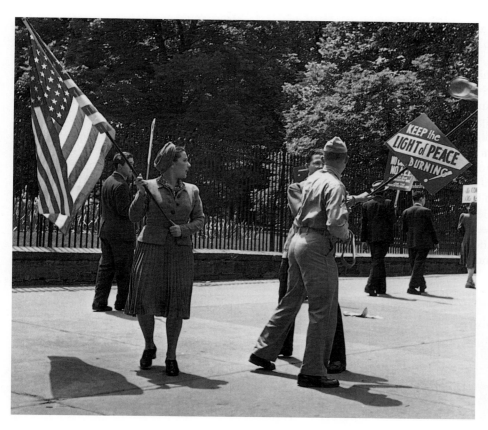

The Debate over Intervention Gets Personal
Playing out the nationwide debate between interventionists and isolationists, a soldier grabs a picket sign from a peace activist in front of the White House in 1941.
T. McAvoy, *Life* Magazine. © Time, Inc.

Initially Willkie conducted his campaign in a bipartisan spirit, but as the election approached, Republican leaders pressured him to go on the offensive. Charging that Roosevelt was leading the country into war, Willkie promised that he would not send "one American boy into the shambles of another war." Roosevelt's reply on October 28, 1940, probably clinched his victory: "I have said this before, but I shall say it again and again and again: Your boys are not going to be sent into foreign wars." (Of course, if the United States was attacked, it would no longer be a foreign war.) Willkie's spirited campaign resulted in a closer election than those of 1932 and 1936, but Roosevelt and the vital Democratic coalition won 55 percent of the popular vote and a more lopsided victory in the electoral college.

The Lend-Lease Act. With the election behind him, Roosevelt concentrated on persuading the American people to increase aid to Britain, whose survival he viewed as the key to American security. In November 1939 FDR had won a bitter battle in Congress to amend the Neutrality Act of 1935 to allow the Allies to buy weapons from the United States—but only on the cash-and-carry basis established for nonmilitary goods in 1937. In March 1941, with German submarines sinking British ships more rapidly than they could be replaced, and Britain no longer able to afford to pay cash for arms, Roosevelt convinced Congress to pass the Lend-

Lease Act. The legislation authorized the president to "lease, lend, or otherwise dispose of" arms and other equipment to any country whose defense was considered vital to the security of the United States. In a press conference designed to build popular support for the plan, Roosevelt had used the analogy of lending a neighbor a garden hose to put out a fire: "I don't say to him, . . . 'Neighbor, my garden hose cost me $15; you have to pay me $15 for it.' . . . I don't want $15—I want my garden hose back after the fire is over." To administer the program, Roosevelt turned to the former relief administrator Harry Hopkins, who became one of his most trusted advisors during the war years. After Germany invaded the Soviet Union in June 1941 (an abandonment of the Nazi-Soviet pact of two years earlier), the United States extended lend-lease to the Soviet Union, which became part of the Allied coalition.

In his State of the Union address to Congress in January 1941, Roosevelt had connected lend-lease to the defense of democracy at home as well as in Europe. He spoke about what he called "four essential human freedoms everywhere in the world"—freedom of speech and expression, freedom of worship, freedom from want, and freedom from fear. Although Roosevelt avoided stating explicitly that America had to enter the war to protect those freedoms, he intended to justify exactly that, for he now regarded U.S. participation as inevitable. And, indeed, the implementation of lend-lease marked the unofficial entrance of the United States into the European war.

The Atlantic Charter. The United States became even more involved in August 1941, when Roosevelt and the British prime minister, Winston Churchill, conferred secretly aboard a battleship off the Newfoundland coast to discuss goals and military strategy. It was the first time the two world leaders had met. Their joint press release, which became known as the Atlantic Charter, provided the ideological foundation of the Western cause and of the peace to follow. Like Wilson's Fourteen Points, the charter called for postwar economic collaboration and guarantees of political stability to ensure that "all men in all the lands may live out their lives in freedom from fear and want." The charter also supported free trade, national self-determination, and the principle of collective security.

As in World War I, when Americans started supplying the Allies, Germany attacked American and Allied ships. By September 1941 Nazi submarines and American vessels were fighting an undeclared naval war in the Atlantic, unknown to the American public. Without an actual enemy attack, however, Roosevelt still hesitated to ask Congress for a declaration of war.

The Attack on Pearl Harbor

The final provocation came not from Germany but from Japan. Tensions between Japan and the United States had been building throughout the 1930s. Japanese military advances in China had upset the balance of

Pearl Harbor
The U.S. battleship *West Virginia* exploded into flames after receiving a direct hit during the surprise Japanese attack on Pearl Harbor on December 7, 1941. It was early Sunday morning, and many of the servicemen were still asleep. More than 2,400 Americans were killed; the Japanese suffered only light losses.
U.S. Navy.

political and economic power in the Pacific, where the United States had long enjoyed the economic benefits of the open-door policy, especially access to China's raw materials and large markets (see Chapter 21). It was the Japanese invasion of China in 1937 that caused Roosevelt to suggest that such aggressors should be "quarantined" by peace-loving nations. Despite such rhetoric, the United States avoided taking a stand, mainly because isolationism was still strong in the country. During the brutal sack of Nanking in 1937 the Japanese had sunk an American gunboat, the *Panay*, in the Yangtze River. In exchange for more than $2 million in damages, the United States allowed Japan to apologize and the incident was quickly smoothed over.

With the attention of the major powers focused on the war in Europe, Japan's imperial intentions became more expansionist. In 1940 Japan signed the Tri-Partite Pact, a defensive alliance with Germany and Italy that extended the Axis into Asia, and in the fall of 1940 Japanese troops occupied the northern part of French Indochina. The United States retaliated by effectively cutting off trade with Japan, including vital oil shipments that accounted for almost 80 percent of Japanese consumption. (At that time the United States was producing two-thirds of the world's oil.) Before its supplies ran down, Japan faced a choice: accept American demands that it cease its expansionism in Asia, or try to find alternative sources for those resources, most likely by seizing British and Dutch possessions in the Pacific. In July 1941 Japanese troops occupied the rest of Indochina; Roosevelt froze Japanese assets in the United States and instituted an embargo on trade with Japan.

In September 1941 the government of Prime Minister Hideki Tojo began secret preparations for war against the United States. Talks between the two nations continued without progress. By November American military intelligence knew that Japan was planning an attack but did not know where it would occur. Early on Sunday morning, December 7, 1941, Japanese bombers attacked the naval base at Pearl Harbor in Hawaii, killing more than 2,400 Americans. Eight battleships, three cruisers, three destroyers, and almost two hundred airplanes were destroyed or heavily damaged. Luckily for the United States, there were no aircraft carriers in port at the time—those vessels would be far more important in the war to come. The Japanese also failed to destroy Pearl Harbor's oil reserves, which would have stranded the navy in Hawaii until oil shipments arrived from the West Coast, thousands of miles away.

Although the attack was devastating, it united the American people in anger and a determination to fight. Pearl Harbor Day is still etched in the memories of millions of Americans who remember precisely what they were doing when they heard about the attack. The next day Roosevelt went before Congress. Calling December 7 "a date which will live in infamy," he asked for a declaration of war against Japan. The Senate unanimously voted for war, and the House concurred by a vote of 388 to 1. The lone dissenter was Jeannette Rankin of Montana, who had also opposed American entry into World War I. Three days later Germany and Italy declared war on the United States, and the United States in turn declared war on those nations.

Organizing for Victory

——————★——————

The task of fighting a global war accelerated the growing influence of the state on American life. Coordinating the changeover from civilian to war production, raising an army, and assembling the necessary work force taxed government agencies to the limit. Mobilization on such a scale demanded cooperation between business executives and political leaders in Washington, solidifying a partnership that had been growing since World War I. But the most dramatic expansion of power occurred at the presidential level when Congress passed the War Powers Act of December 18, 1941, giving Roosevelt unprecedented authority over all aspects of the conduct of the war.

Mobilizing for Defense

Defense mobilization had a powerful impact on the federal government's role in the economy (Figure 26.1). The federal budget of $95.2 billion in 1945 was ten times that of 1939, and the national debt grew sixfold, topping out at $258.6 billion in 1945. Along with huge federal budgets came greater acceptance of Keynesian economics, that is, the use of government fiscal policy to stimulate economic growth. The war also brought significant changes in the federal bureaucracy. The number of civilians employed by the government increased almost fourfold, to 3.8 million—a far more dramatic growth than the New Deal period had witnessed. At the height of wartime hiring the government gave the civil service exam two or three times a day.

Financing the War. Taxes paid about half the cost of the war, compared with 30 percent of the cost of World War I. The Revenue Act of 1942 continued the income tax reform that had begun during World War I by taxing not just wealthy individuals and corporations but average citizens as well. The number of people paying income tax increased from 3.9 million in 1939 to 42.6 million in 1945; tax collections rose from $2.2 billion to $35.1 billion, facilitated by payroll deductions and tax

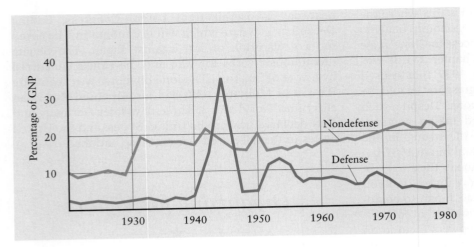

FIGURE 26.1
Government Spending as a Percentage of GNP
Government defense spending was a minuscule percentage of the gross national product in the 1930s, but it ballooned during World War II and rose again during the Korean War and, to a lesser degree, during the Vietnam War. Nondefense government spending did not display such wild fluctuations—just a steady, upward trend.

withholding, which were instituted in 1943. This mass-based tax system, a revolutionary change in the financing of the modern state, was sold to the taxpayers as a way to express their patriotism. War bond drives also gave people a patriotic opportunity to put their savings at the disposal of the government by buying long-term Treasury bonds, which financed the remaining cost of the war. War bonds had the additional benefit of withdrawing money from circulation, which helped hold down inflation.

Running the Economy.   Like Woodrow Wilson during World War I, Roosevelt turned to business leaders to run the war economy. (Many of these executives became known as "dollar-a-year men" because they volunteered for government service while remaining on the corporate payroll.) Defense preparations had been under way since 1940; before Pearl Harbor 25 percent of the economy was already devoted to war production. In January 1941 Roosevelt established the Office of Production Management under William Knudsen, the president of General Motors. After the Japanese attack Roosevelt disbanded that agency and replaced it with the War Production Board (WPB), headed by Donald Nelson, a former Sears, Roebuck executive. The WPB awarded defense contracts, evaluated military and civilian requests for scarce resources, and oversaw the conversion of industries to military production. The WPB used the carrot more often than the stick. To encourage businesses to convert to war production, the board granted generous tax write-offs for plant construction and approved contracts with cost-plus provisions that guaranteed a profit and promised that businesses could keep the new factories after the war. As Secretary of War Henry Stimson put it, "you had better let business make money out of the process or business won't work."

In the interest of efficiency and maximum production, the WPB preferred to deal with large corporations rather than with small businesses. The fifty-six largest corporations got three-fourths of the war contracts, with one-third going to the top ten. This system of allocating contracts, along with the suspension of antitrust prosecution during the war, hastened the trend toward large corporate structures. In 1940 the hundred largest companies manufactured 30 percent of the nation's industrial output; in 1945 their share was 70 percent. Those giant businesses would form the core of the military-industrial complex that came to link the federal government, corporations, and the military in an interdependent partnership in the postwar era (see Chapters 27 and 28).

The Office of Price Administration and Civilian Supply (OPA) supervised the domestic economy, allocating resources and trying to keep inflation down. By February 1942 retail prices were rising by 2 percent a month, as consumers had more income to spend than there were available goods and services. In April the OPA froze most prices and rents at their March 1942 levels. When loopholes, especially regarding food prices, undermined that effort, Congress passed the Anti-Inflation Act, which stabilized prices, wages, and salaries. The consumer price index rose by 28.3 percent between 1940 and 1945, but most of the inflation occurred before 1943.

Roosevelt remained unsatisfied with the mobilization effort; there were too many government agencies, and their actions often overlapped. In October 1942 he persuaded Justice James F. Byrnes to resign from the Supreme Court to head the Office of Economic Stabilization and, after 1943, the Office of War Mobilization. Byrnes soon became the second most powerful person in the administration and finally brought order to production goals for civilian and military needs. The results were remarkable.

The peak of mobilization occurred in late 1943, when two-thirds of the economy was directly involved

Why We Fight

This 1942 award-winning lithograph by Karl Koehler and Victor Ancona painted a sinister, menacing portrait of a Nazi officer, leaving little room for doubt as to why it was necessary to end Nazism.

National Museum of American Art, Smithsonian Institution, Washington, DC.

How We Fight

One way that America defeated the Axis powers was through war production. Government posters such as this 1942 lithograph by Jean Carlu supported the home front effort.

National Museum of American Art, Smithsonian Institution, Washington, DC.

in the war effort, as opposed to only one-quarter in World War I. Shipbuilding showed that American productive capacity was at full strength. By 1941 the German navy had crippled transatlantic transport, sinking about 12 million tons of mostly U.S.-built Allied shipping in the North Atlantic. Producing replacement vessels became a high priority. By turning out clunky but easy-to-build Liberty ships, the United States produced 19 million tons of merchant shipping by 1943, up from 1 million tons two years earlier.

Henry J. Kaiser, a West Coast shipbuilder, performed shipyard production miracles. Using the mass-production techniques of the automobile industry, Kaiser cut the time needed to build a transport ship from 300 days to 17. He motivated workers through high pay and fringe benefits, including one of the country's first prepaid medical programs (see American

Lives, "Henry J. Kaiser: World War II's 'Miracle Man,'" pp. 840–841). Kaiser's name became synonymous with getting things done in a hurry.

Although not all industries could boast of freedom from *snafus* (an acronym coined during the war from the expression "situation normal, all fouled up"), business and government compiled an impressive record. As in World War I, industry played a significant role in the military victory. By 1945 the United States had turned out 86,000 tanks, 296,000 airplanes, 15 million rifles and machine guns, 64,000 landing craft, and 6,500 ships. Mobilization on this gigantic scale gave a tremendous boost to the economy, causing the gross national product to more than double. It rose from $99.7 billion in 1940 to $211 billion by the end of the war. After years of depression, Americans' faith in the capitalist system was restored. But it was a transformed economy that relied heavily on the government's participation.

Mobilizing the American Fighting Force

An expanded state presence was also evident in the government's mobilization of a fighting force. Under the chief of staff, George C. Marshall, the army grew from 200,000 soldiers in 1939 to over 8 million in 1945. By the end of World War II the U.S. armed forces numbered more than 15 million men and women. The army, including those who served in the Army Air Force, enlisted the most, but almost 4 million served in the navy, 600,000 in the marines, and 240,000 in the coast guard.

Henry J. Kaiser: World War II's "Miracle Man"

★

Henry Kaiser was a workaholic. His motto was "Find a Need and Fill It." He hated being alone and hated taking vacations. He worked twenty-hour days and expected his top managers to do the same. If ordinary mortals were trying to sleep in California, he made long-distance calls to associates in other time zones. "Whenever he had a new idea—and he commonly had a score or so daily—he reached for the telephone," noted his biographer, Mark Foster. As early as 1942 his company was running up then-extravagant phone bills of $250,000 a year.

Kaiser was one of the most widely known figures of the 1940s, a genuine folk hero to many for his ability to get things done. After shipyard triumphs such as the construction of an entire Liberty ship in four days, fifteen hours, and twenty-six minutes in November 1942, the press dubbed him the "Miracle Man." He was a special darling of media mogul Henry Luce: 40 percent of the popular articles on Kaiser between 1941 and 1943 appeared in *Time*, *Life*,

and *Fortune*, Luce's three major publications. Even the staid *Wall Street Journal* called him "Fabulous Mr. Kaiser." Franklin Roosevelt seriously considered the industrialist for the vice-presidential slot on the 1944 Democratic ticket and, according to FDR's cousin Margaret Suckley, even thought Kaiser could be the best man to succeed him if he chose not to run for reelection. A Roper poll in spring 1945 found that the public believed Henry Kaiser had done more than any other civilian to help the president win the war.

Kaiser's career and the rise of the modern American West went hand in hand. Born in upstate New York in 1882 to German immigrant parents, he left school at age thirteen to make his way in the world. In 1906 he headed west to Spokane, Washington, to establish himself in business so that he could marry his fiancée; in 1921 he and his family settled permanently in Oakland, California. From 1914 to 1931 Kaiser's contracting business built roads, trying to keep up with the West's insatiable demand for highways for the new cars rolling off the assembly lines in Detroit. In the 1930s Kaiser was part of a six-company partnership that successfully bid for massive engineering projects such as building the Hoover and Grand Coulee Dams, federally funded public works projects that permanently changed the western landscape. In the 1930s he also lobbied extensively in Washington, developing contacts with New Deal bureaucrats that would prove invaluable during the war years.

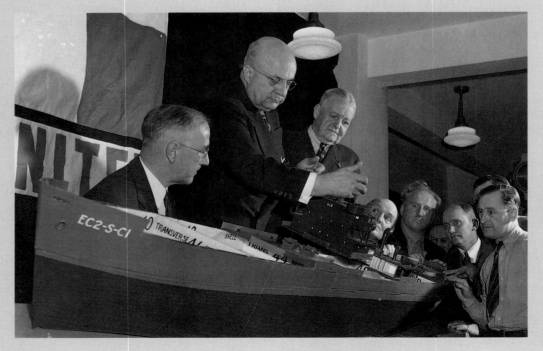

The Miracle Man
In November 1942, Henry Kaiser used an 81-piece, 14-foot-long model of the 10,400-ton Liberty freighter to show shipowners and navy representatives how it was built in the amazing time of 4 days, 15 hours, and 26 minutes.
Corbis-Bettmann.

Moved largely by wartime opportunities, Kaiser left construction to launch a career as an industrialist. He made his first big splash—literally—building Liberty ships faster and better than anyone else. Shipbuilding was an ideal choice for an inveterate self-promoter like Henry Kaiser. The World War II era boasted few photo opportunities better than a ship launching, and Kaiser invited Hollywood stars, members of the president's family, and a host of other celebrities to christen the ships, always with the newsreel cameras rolling and the photographers' flash bulbs popping. Thanks to his public relations machine, Kaiser's name was all over the news.

But before Kaiser could build ships he had to build shipyards. Drawing on the availability of vacant tracts of West Coast waterfront (something the older shipyards in the East did not have), he constructed work spaces large enough to accommodate the assembly of prefabricated ship components. Kaiser's shipyards in Richmond, California, were designed like a city grid, complete with numbered and lettered streets. "It was a city without houses," remembered one worker, "but the traffic was heavy. Cranes, trucks, trains noised by." Recalled a recent migrant from a small Iowa town, "It was such a huge place, something I had never been in. People from all walks of life, all coming and going and working, and the noise. The whole atmosphere was overwhelming to me."

Although Kaiser did not invent the subassembly technique, he was the most successful at applying mass production to shipbuilding. Previously, most jobs in shipbuilding had been skilled or semiskilled, requiring apprenticeship and training far too lengthy for the wartime emergency. To train new workers more quickly, the work process was broken down into small, specialized tasks, in effect de-skilling what had previously been a craft. As Kaiser put it, "production is not labor anymore, but a process."

The Kaiser shipyards were known as much for their corporate welfare programs as for their bureaucratized work climate. Kaiser offered his workers day care, financial and job counseling, subsidized housing, and especially health care, his most significant long-term contribution. The Kaiser Permanente Medical Care Program was founded in 1942, an outgrowth of prepaid health care plans first tried on remote federal construction projects in the 1930s. This health care system, the forerunner of today's health maintenance organizations (HMOs), was available to Kaiser workers for the nominal paycheck deduction of 50 cents a week. Almost 90 percent of his workers chose that option. Kaiser provided health care for both philanthropic and business reasons. The initial investment was quickly repaid in the form of healthier workers, lower absenteeism, and greater productivity. As a Permanente executive explained, "To the private physician, a sick person is an asset. To Permanente, a sick person is a liability. We'd go bankrupt if we didn't keep most of our members and their families well most of the time."

At the core of Kaiser's popularity was a dichotomy. The public saw him as a man who broke the rules for them, a self-made outsider who made things happen in wartime Washington despite the bureaucrats. Yet Kaiser could never have achieved his business miracles without a close working relationship with the federal government, which, for example, allowed him to borrow $300 million from the Reconstruction Finance Corporation during World War II to construct new plants. Noting the symbiotic relationship between business and government that increasingly characterized the twentieth century, historian Stephen B. Adams calls Henry Kaiser a *government entrepreneur*. But the public persisted in seeing him as an individualist, a symbol of a "can-do" age.

While many business executives faced the postwar period with caution, Kaiser looked forward to peacetime reconversion with the boundless optimism of a far-sighted entrepreneur. He was especially excited about opportunities for industrial expansion in the West. Between 1944 and 1946 he identified opportunities in areas such as steel, magnesium, and aluminum as well as foreseeing a demand for mass-produced suburban tract housing. In the 1950s he headed a multinational corporate empire that included many companies with assets close to $1 billion. In 1965 he became the first industrialist to win the AFL-CIO's highest honor, the Philip Murray–William Green Award.

To many Americans Henry Kaiser was a twentieth-century incarnation of Horatio Alger, even though he was a portly sixty years old in 1942 when he launched the Richmond shipyards. In terms of managerial style, he was more an old-style "seat-of-the-pants" entrepreneur than a modern corporate bureaucrat. He was a maverick, challenging traditional ways of doing business at every stage of his career at the same time that he seized the opportunities presented by the growth of the administrative state. He was a visionary in the role that he saw for an industrial West, a dream that was amply fulfilled during the postwar era. But he was also lucky, his success being the product of a highly favorable set of economic conditions both regionally in the West and globally during World War II and its aftermath. After his death in 1967 his industrial empire largely disappeared, but Kaiser Permanente lives on, one of the country's largest and most successful health maintenance organizations.

Draft boards registered about 31 million men between the ages of eighteen and forty-four and ordered physical examinations for about one-sixth of the male population. More than half the men failed to meet the physical standards, with defective teeth and poor vision causing the greatest number of rejections. The military also tried to screen out homosexuals, but its attempts were ineffectual. Once in military service, homosexuals found that the sex-segregated environment offered new possibilities for same-sex attraction. Wartime experiences also weakened patterns that traditionally channeled men and women toward heterosexuality: instead of going directly from parental homes into marriage, gay men and lesbians in the military lived away from kin in settings where they found opportunities to participate in a gay subculture that was more extensive than that found in civilian life.

Racial discrimination prevailed in the armed forces, mainly directed against the approximately 700,000 blacks in uniform. African Americans served in all branches of the armed forces but were assigned the most menial duties; a great number served as messboys on navy ships, for example. The army even segregated black and white blood banks, a policy that had no scientific merit. The National Association for the Advancement of Colored People (NAACP) and other civil rights groups chided the government with reminders such as "A Jim Crow army cannot fight for a free world," but the military refused to change its practices. In contrast, Mexican Americans were never officially segregated. Unlike blacks, they were welcomed into combat units, and seventeen Mexican Americans won the Congressional Medal of Honor.

Women found both opportunities and discrimination in the armed services. Approximately 350,000 American women enlisted in the armed services and achieved a permanent status in the military. There were about 140,000 WAC (Women's Army Corps) members, 100,000 naval WAVES (Women Accepted for Volunteer Emergency Service), 23,000 members of the Marine Corps Women's Reserve, and 13,000 SPARs (for Semper Paratus, or Always Ready, the coast guard's motto) in the coast guard. In addition, about 1,000 WASPs (Women's Airforce Service Pilots) ferried planes and supplies in noncombat areas. One-third of the nation's registered nurses, almost 75,000 overall, volunteered for military duty.

The armed forces limited the types of duty assigned to women, as it did with blacks. Women were barred from combat, although nurses and medical personnel sometimes served close to the front lines, risking capture or death. The social lives of women soldiers, most of whom were single, were more strictly regulated than those of their male counterparts, mainly out of fear of sexual impropriety. Most military jobs reflected stereotypes of women's roles in civilian life—clerical work,

The WACs Overseas
Not all military women were relegated to stateside duty. These eager WACs, members of the first Women's Army Corps unit to go overseas, have just arrived in North Africa in 1943 to begin their assignments.
Archive Photos.

communications, and health care. The widely distributed pinups of Betty Grable in a bathing suit, Rita Hayworth in a flimsy nightgown, and, for the black soldiers, the singer Lena Horne, were probably closer to the average GI's view of women than a WAC or a WAVE was.

Workers and the War Effort

When millions of citizens entered military service, a huge hole opened in the American work force. The backlog of depression-era unemployment quickly disappeared, and the United States faced a critical labor shortage. The nation's defense industries provided jobs for about 7 million new workers, including great numbers of women, blacks, and Mexican Americans who were given employment opportunities for the first time.

Rosie the Riveter. Government planners "discovered" women while looking for workers to fill the jobs vacated by departing servicemen. The recruiting campaign drew on patriotism. One poster urged, "Longing won't bring him back sooner . . . GET A WAR JOB!" Recruiters promised that women would take to riveting machines and drill presses "as easily as to electric cake-mixers and vacuum cleaners." The artist Norman Rockwell supported the campaign by creating his famous "Rosie the Riveter" cover for the *Saturday Evening Post*.

Although the government directed its propaganda at housewives, women who were already employed gladly abandoned low-paying "women's" jobs as domestic servants or file clerks for higher-paying jobs in defense factories. Suddenly the nation's factories were full of women working as riveters, welders, blast furnace cleaners, and drill press operators. Women made up 36 percent of the labor force in 1945, compared with 24 percent at the beginning of the war.

Government planners and employers regarded women as just "filling in" while the men were away. Employers rarely offered day care or flexible hours, and government child care programs established by the 1940 Lanham Act reached only 10 percent of those who needed them. Because women were responsible for home care as well as their jobs, they had a higher absentee rate than did men. Often, the only way to get shopping done or take a child to the doctor was to skip work. Women war workers also faced discrimination on the job. In shipyards women with the most seniority and responsibility earned $6.95 a day, whereas the top men made as much as $22.

When the men came home from war and the plants returned to peacetime operations, Rosie the Riveter was out of a job. But many women refused to put on an apron and stay home. Women's participation in the labor force dropped temporarily when the war ended but rebounded steadily for the rest of the 1940s, especially among married women.

Organized Labor. Wartime mobilization also opened up opportunities to advance the labor movement and solidify the industrial breakthroughs of the 1930s. By the end of the war almost 15 million workers—one-third of the nonagricultural labor force, up from 9 million at the end of the previous decade—belonged to unions.

Organized labor responded to the war with an initial burst of patriotic unity. On December 23, 1941, representatives of major unions made a "no strike" pledge—although nonbinding—for the duration of the war. In January 1942 Roosevelt created the National War Labor Board (NWLB) composed of representatives of labor, management, and the public. The board established wages, hours, and working conditions and had the authority to order government seizure of plants that did not comply. Forty plants were seized during the war.

During its tenure the NWLB handled 17,650 disputes affecting 12 million workers. It resolved the controversial issue of union membership through a compromise. Under the principle of maintenance of membership, new hires did not have to join a union, but those who already belonged to a union had to maintain their membership over the life of the contract. Agitation for wage increases caused a more serious disagreement. Because managers wanted to keep production running smoothly and profitably, they were willing to pay higher wages. However, pay raises would conflict with OPA's attempt to combat inflation by stabilizing prices and salaries. In 1942 the NWLB established the "Little Steel Formula," which granted a 15 percent wage increase to match the increase in the cost of living since January 1, 1941, and another 24 percent by 1945. Actually, incomes rose by as much as 70 percent because workers earned overtime pay, which was not covered by wage ceilings. The tremendous increase in output during World War II occurred largely because people worked overtime.

Although incomes were now higher than anyone could have dreamed of during the depression, many union members felt cheated as they watched corporate profits soar in relation to wages. The high point of dissatisfaction came in 1943, when a nationwide railroad strike was narrowly averted. Then John L. Lewis led more than half a million United Mine Workers out on strike, demanding wages higher than the Little Steel Formula allowed. Although Lewis won concessions, he alienated Congress; because he had defied the government during wartime, he became one of the most disliked public figures of the 1940s.

Congress countered Lewis's action by overriding Roosevelt's veto of the Smith-Connally Labor Act of 1943, which required a thirty-day cooling-off period before a strike and prohibited strikes in defense industries entirely. Nevertheless, about 15,000 strikes occurred during the war. Though less than one-tenth of a percent of working hours were lost to strikes, the public perceived the disruptions as far more extensive. Labor unions won acceptance during the war years but also provoked significant public and congressional hostility, which would hamper the labor movement in the postwar years.

Civil Rights during Wartime

A new mood of militancy appeared among the nation's minorities during wartime. World War II disrupted a number of traditional patterns, and many barriers to racial equality tottered or fell. "A wind is rising throughout the world of free men everywhere," Eleanor Roosevelt wrote during the war, "and they will not be kept in bondage." Civil rights leaders pointed out parallels between anti-Semitism in Germany and racial discrimination in America and pledged themselves to a "Double V" campaign: victory over Nazism abroad and victory over racism and inequality at home.

Even before Pearl Harbor, activism was on the rise. In 1940 only 240 of the nation's 100,000 aircraft workers were black, and most of them were janitors. Black leaders demanded that the government require defense contractors to integrate their work forces. When the government took no action, A. Philip Randolph, head of the Brotherhood of Sleeping Car Porters, a black union,

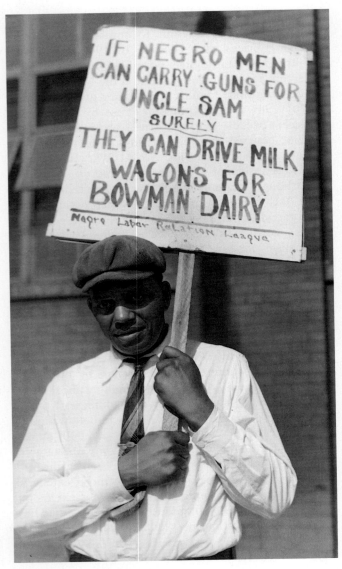

Fighting for Freedom at Home and Abroad
This protester from the Negro Labor Relations League pointedly drew the parallel between blacks serving in the armed
forces and a 1941 labor discrimination dispute at a Chicago
dairy.
Library of Congress.

announced plans for a "March on Washington" in the
summer of 1941. Roosevelt was not a strong supporter
of civil rights, but he feared the embarrassment of a
massive public protest. Even more, he worried about a
disruption of war preparations.

In June 1941, in exchange for Randolph's cancella-
tion of the march, Roosevelt issued Executive Order
8802, declaring "that there shall be no discrimination
in the employment of workers in defense industries or
government because of race, creed, color, or national
origin." To oversee the policy, he established the Fair
Employment Practices Committee (FEPC) in the Office
of Production Management. Although this federal com-

mitment to minority employment rights was unprecedented, it was limited in scope. For instance, it did not
affect segregation in the armed forces. Moreover, the
FEPC could not require compliance with its orders and
often found that the needs of defense production took
precedence over fair employment practices. The FEPC
resolved only about one-third of the more than 8,000
complaints it received. Blacks made up 8 percent of
defense workers in 1944, probably owing more to the
labor shortage than to FEPC prodding.

Encouraged by the ideological climate of the war
years, civil rights organizations increased in number and
membership. Although the NAACP generally favored
lobbying and legal strategies, the student chapter of the
NAACP at Howard University used direct tactics. In 1944
it forced several restaurants in Washington, D.C., to
serve blacks by picketing them with signs that read, "Are
You for Hitler's Way or the American Way? Make Up
Your Mind." In Chicago James Farmer helped found the
Congress of Racial Equality (CORE), a group that
became known nationwide for using direct action such
as demonstrations and sit-ins.

An awareness of civil rights was heightened in other
ways as well. The Swedish sociologist Gunnar Myrdal
wrote an extensive analysis of race relations, *An American Dilemma: The Negro Problem and Modern Democracy*
(1944), focusing many white Americans' attention on the
issue for the first time. In 1944 the Supreme Court ruled
in *Smith v. Allwright* that Texas's all-white primary election, commonly used to disfranchise blacks in southern
states, was unconstitutional. These wartime developments laid the groundwork for the civil rights revolution
of the 1950s and 1960s (see Voices from Abroad, "German POWs: American Race Relations," p. 845).

Mexican Americans also used the ideological climate of the war to press for change, building on their
community's patriotic contributions to national defense
and the armed services to challenge long-standing patterns of discrimination and exclusion. In Texas, where it
was still common to see signs reading "No Dogs or Mexicans Allowed," community leaders protested segregation in schools and public facilities. In California,
Mexican American labor activists argued that defense
contractors' refusal to hire resident Mexican aliens violated Executive Order 8802's prohibition of discrimination on the basis of race, creed, color, or national origin.

The Sleepy Lagoon case of 1942 explicitly linked
the experiences of Mexican Americans with the broader
ideological underpinnings of the war effort. In the summer of 1942 a Mexican American youth was found dead
near Sleepy Lagoon, a popular place to hang out in
south-central Los Angeles. On exceedingly flimsy evidence, the police charged twenty-two members of a
Mexican American gang called the 38th Street Club
with murder and conspiracy, and in January 1943 an
all-white jury convicted seventeen of the defendants.
The Sleepy Lagoon Defense Committee, which one

GERMAN POWs
American Race Relations

———★———

During World War II, Nazi prisoners of war were assigned to various army camps throughout the United States, where their labor was often contracted out to help with the acute shortage of workers caused by war mobilization. German prisoners thus had a unique opportunity to observe American life. Here are some of their observations, mainly centered on the issue of race.

We picked cotton the length of the Mississippi. I'm an agriculturalist, and I know how to handle hard work, but there it was truly very, very hard. It was terribly hot, and we had to bend over all day. We had nothing to drink. . . . There were a great number of Blacks on the plantation. They required us to gather 100 lbs. of cotton a day; but of the Blacks, they demanded two or three times more. . . . For them it was worse than for us. And you have to see how they lived. Their farms: very ugly, very primitive. These people were so exploited. . . .

Me, I was in peas; picking and the canning factory. The farmers liked me, and wanted me to stay after the war, but I wasn't sure. . . . I met some old people of German origin one day, and these poor old people told me: "We feel alone here. It's sad. It's too big. If we could, we would walk back to Germany on foot. . . ." And the Blacks! They were always saying: "We are just like you: Prisoners; Oppressed; Second-class men. . . ."

There was a plumber who came to work in the camp. His name was Gutierrez, and he was Mexican. . . . He was a very nice guy. When he went to the barbershop, he stood in the corner, he did not move, and, as he was "colored," he had to wait until all the Whites were done. You know, things like that upset us very much. . . .

I was in a camp near Miami in Florida. I was one of the scavenger commandos; every morning we went to gather the garbage in the city. . . . People of German origin were the least nice to us. . . . Those who helped us the most, on the contrary, were the Jews. . . . Ah, the Jews and the Blacks.

Source: Arnold Krammer, *Nazi Prisoners of War in America* (New York: Stein and Day, 1979), 92–93.

---

scholar has called "the best known and most influential Mexican American–oriented advocacy organ to emerge in California in this period," eventually succeeded in getting the convictions overturned on appeal. The Defense Committee's premise was that the defendants had been deprived of their basic civil rights solely because of their ethnic background. As America fought to preserve democracy abroad, they argued, it must live up to democratic ideals at home.

In Los Angeles white hostility toward Mexican Americans had been smoldering for some time. Male Latino teenagers had organized *pachuco* (youth) gangs, sometimes also called *cholos*. Speaking a hybrid English-Spanish slang called *calo*, they sported slicked-down hair, tattoos, and a distinctive style of dress called the zoot suit, which featured padded shoulders, pegged trousers, clunky shoes, and broad-brimmed felt hats. The young women they escorted favored long coats, huarache sandals, and pompadour hairdos. Although zoot suits were most popular among Latinos, that style was also taken up by blacks and by a few white working-class teenagers in Los Angeles, Detroit, New York, and Philadelphia as a symbol of alienation and self-assertion.

In July 1943 rumors that a *pachuco* gang had beaten a white sailor set off a four-day riot in Los Angeles, during which white servicemen entered Mexican American neighborhoods and attacked zoot suiters, taking special pleasure in slashing the pegged pants of their victims. The attacks occurred in full view of white police officers, who did nothing to stop the violence. Even as the war years opened new avenues for Mexican American participation in American life, they also brought ugly reminders of the persistence of racism and ethnic hostility.

Politics in Wartime

At a press conference late in 1943 Roosevelt playfully announced that "Dr. Win the War" had replaced "Dr. New Deal." In fact, business executives had already replaced many of the reformers and social activists who had staffed New Deal relief agencies in the 1930s. Although the federal government expanded dramatically during the war years, there was little attempt to use the state to promote social reform on the home front, as had occurred in World War I. An enlarged federal presence was justified only insofar as it assisted war aims.

During the early years of the war Roosevelt rarely pressed for social and economic change, in part because he was preoccupied with military matters but also because he faced certain political realities. The Republicans had picked up 10 seats in the Senate and 47 seats in the House in the 1940 elections, thus bolstering conservatives in Congress who sought to roll back New Deal measures. With little protest, Roosevelt agreed to drop several popular New Deal programs, including the Civilian Conservation Corps, the Works Progress Administration, and the National Youth Administration, which were deemed less necessary once war mobilization brought full employment. Severe budget cuts crippled the Farm Security Administration, which had represented the interests of poor farmers. The speed with which the government terminated those agencies suggested that they had been more a response to the crisis of the depression than a commitment to promoting the general welfare through federal programs. Programs with broad popular support such as Social Security were left untouched, however.

Later in the war Roosevelt began to promise new social welfare measures. In his State of the Union address in 1944 he called for a second bill of rights, which would serve as "a new basis of security and prosperity." This extension of the New Deal identified jobs, adequate food and clothing, decent homes, medical care, and education as basic rights. But the president's sweeping commitment remained largely rhetorical; congressional support for this vast extension of the welfare state did not exist in 1944. It was possible, however, to win some of those rights for a special group of American citizens: veterans. The Servicemen's Readjustment Act (1944), known as the GI Bill of Rights, provided education, job training, medical care, pensions, and mortgage loans for men and women who had served in the armed forces during the war.

Roosevelt's call for more social legislation was part of a plan to woo Democratic voters. In the 1942 election, Republicans picked up seats in both houses of Congress and increased their share of state governorships. The Democrats realized they would have to work hard to maintain the strength of their coalition in 1944. Once again Roosevelt headed the ticket, concluding that the continuation of the war made a fourth term necessary, but the years had taken their toll. Concern about Roosevelt's health and the need for a successor prompted the Democrats to drop Vice-President Henry Wallace, whose outspoken support for labor, civil rights, and domestic reform was too extreme for many party leaders. In Wallace's place they chose Senator Harry S Truman of Missouri. Truman, a World War I veteran and Kansas City haberdasher whose business had failed in the 1920–1921 recession, found more success in politics. Sponsored by Thomas Pendergast, the Democratic boss in Kansas City, he was elected to the Senate in 1934 and again in 1940. Truman became known for heading a Senate investigation of government waste and inefficiency in defense contracts during the war.

The Republicans nominated Governor Thomas E. Dewey of New York. Only forty-two years old, Dewey had won fame fighting organized crime as a U.S. attorney. He accepted the broad outlines of the welfare state and belonged to the internationalist wing of the Republican Party. The 1944 election was the closest since Woodrow Wilson had narrowly defeated Charles Evans Hughes in 1916: Roosevelt received 53.5 percent of the popular vote. The Democrats lost ground among farmers, but most ethnic groups remained solidly Democratic. Roosevelt got his customary support from the South, augmented by the overwhelming allegiance of members of the armed forces, who voted by absentee ballot. The party's margin of victory came from the cities. In urban areas with more than 100,000 people the president drew 60 percent of the vote.

Roosevelt also received strong support from organized labor. Under the prodding of CIO leaders Sidney Hillman and Philip Murray, labor contributed more than $1.5 million, or about 30 percent of the Democratic Party's election funds. The CIO's Political Action Committee canvassed door to door and conducted voter registration campaigns. Organized labor continued to play a significant role in the Democratic Party after the war.

Life on the Home Front

In contrast to World War I, once Congress declared war there was almost no domestic opposition to the nation's role in World War II. Americans fought for their way of life and to preserve democracy against Nazism and Japanese imperialism. Because the enemies seemed so evil and America's will to win was so strong, many remember it as the "good war." By the spring of 1945 soldiers who had completed their military duty, which averaged sixteen months, were beginning to return home. Fighting had been a dirty, bloody job—a far cry from their visions of saving democracy and stopping fascism. Dreams of marriage, a house in the suburbs, and a new car sustained many soldiers through the horror and tedium of the war. In 1947 veterans and their families made up one-fourth of the American population.

"For the Duration"

Although the United States did not suffer the physical devastation that ravaged much of Europe and the Pacific, the war affected the lives of those who stayed behind. Every time relatives of a loved one overseas saw the Western Union boy on his bicycle, they feared a telegram from the War department telling them that their son, husband, or father would not be coming home. Other Americans tolerated small deprivations daily. "Don't you know there's a war on?" became the standard reply to any request that could not be fulfilled. People accepted the fact that their lives would be different "for the duration."

Just like the soldiers in uniform, people on the home front had a job to do. They worked on civilian defense committees, donated blood, collected old newspapers and scrap material for recycling, and served on local rationing and draft boards. About 20 million home "Victory gardens" produced 40 percent of the vegetables grown in the United States. Advertising campaigns displaying the popular "V for Victory" slogan stressed patriotism, and all seven war bond drives were oversubscribed. These endeavors were encouraged by various federal agencies, especially the Office of War Information (OWI).

Perhaps the major source of American's high morale was wartime prosperity. Unemployment disappeared, and per capita income rose from $691 in 1939 to $1,515 in 1945. Despite geographical dislocations and shortages of many items, about 70 percent of Americans admitted midway through the war that they had personally experienced "no real sacrifices." A Red Cross worker put it bluntly: "The war was fun for America. I'm not talking about the poor souls who lost sons and daughters. But for the rest of us, the war was a hell of a good time."

During the war years demographic patterns rebounded from their depression-induced declines. Young people could afford to marry, and the imminent departure of men for military service induced many couples to take that step sooner rather than later. Not all those marriages survived the strain of separation or wartime relocation, and the divorce rate also rose. The birth rate went up, with many babies being conceived before their fathers went off to war. In effect, the wartime birth patterns marked the beginning of the "baby boom" that characterized American culture in the postwar period.

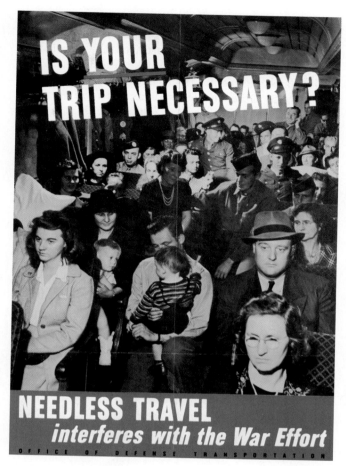

Please Stay Home
With the economy booming and most citizens reporting no great hardships or dislocations, Americans sometimes had to be reminded that there was a war on. A poster from the Office of Defense Transportation pointing out that needless travel interfered with the war effort jogged their memory.
Picture Research Consultants & Archives.

Popular Culture. Popular culture, especially the movies, reinforced the connection between the home front and the troops serving overseas. Average weekly movie attendance soared to over 100 million during the war. Demand was so high that many theaters operated around the clock to accommodate defense workers on the swing and night shifts. Hollywood escaped the restrictions and cutbacks that affected other industries, in part because studio heads argued that movies built morale. Popular actors like Jimmy Stewart and Clark Gable donned uniforms, and many Hollywood directors lent their services to the military. Director Frank Capra's "Why We Fight" films, a documentary series produced for the War department, explained war aims to new soldiers and sailors. John Huston provided an intense portrayal of men in combat in his documentary *The Battle of San Pietro* (1944).

Many movies, encouraged in part by the OWI, had patriotic themes. Stars such as John Wayne, Anthony Quinn, and Spencer Tracy portrayed the heroism of American fighting men in films like *Guadalcanal Diary* (1943), *Back to Bataan* (1945), and *Thirty Seconds over Tokyo* (1945). Other movies, such as *Watch on the Rhine* (1943) and Frank Capra's *Meet John Doe* (1943), warned of the danger of fascism at home and abroad, and the Academy Award–winning *Casablanca* (1943) demonstrated the heroism and patriotism of ordinary citizens. The box-office hit *Since You Went Away* (1943), starring Claudette Colbert as a housewife who took a war job after her husband left to fight, was one of many films that portrayed struggles on the home front. Newsreels accompanying feature films kept the public up to date on the war, as did on-the-spot radio broadcasts by commentators such as Edward R. Murrow. Thus, popular culture reflected America's new international responsibilities at the same time that it built up morale on the home front.

Entertaining the Troops

The original Stage Door Canteen opened in the basement of a Broadway theater in 1942. It provided servicemen with coffee, doughnuts, and big-time entertainment volunteered by Broadway and Hollywood stars. The canteen's popular weekly radio show was the inspiration for the 1943 movie *Stage Door Canteen*.

Lee Boltin Picture Library.

War correspondents such as John Hersey and Ernie Pyle (who was killed in a foxhole on Ie Shima by a Japanese bullet) reported on the GIs (short for "government issue") for readers back home. Reporters often portrayed the GIs as ordinary boys doing their patriotic duty. "When you looked into the eyes of those boys, you did not feel sorry for the Japs: you felt sorry for the boys," John Hersey wrote of the marines fighting in the Pacific battle of Guadalcanal in 1944. Another marine who fought there remembered it as simply a matter of survival: "The only way you could get it over with was to kill them off before they killed you. The war I knew was totally savage."

Throughout the war the Japanese were hated far more than the Germans, in part because Japan had attacked the United States but also because of the racism that was a constant undercurrent of World War II. Whereas Americans often differentiated between evil Nazi leaders and ordinary "good Germans" forced to go along with Nazi excesses, they lumped all Japanese together. Racial epithets such as "slant eyes" and "yellow monkeys" were widely used in conversation, and even respected magazines such as *Time*, *Life*, and *Newsweek* routinely referred to the enemy as "Japs."

Rationing. For many Americans, the main inconveniences of the war were the limitations placed on consumption. In contrast to the largely voluntaristic approach used during World War I, federal agencies such as the Office of Price Administration subjected almost everything that Americans ate, wore, or used during World War II to rationing or regulation.

Rubber became the first scarce item. The Japanese conquest of Malaya and the Netherlands East Indies cut off 97 percent of America's imports of natural rubber, an essential raw material for war production. An entire new industry in synthetic rubber was born, and by late 1944 the United States was producing 762,000 tons of it a year, mostly for the war effort. Meanwhile, to conserve rubber, the government restricted the sale of tires, a difficult sacrifice for the nation's 30 million car owners, many of whom put their autos up on blocks for the duration. The government also rationed gasoline and fuel oil. Shortages of fuel oil forced schools and restaurants to shorten their hours, and home thermostats were lowered to 65 degrees. Gasoline rationing, introduced in December 1942, represented both a response to depleted domestic gasoline supplies and an attempt to save wear on precious rubber tires. To further discourage gasoline consumption, Congress imposed a nationwide speed limit of 35 miles per hour; as a result, highway death rates dropped dramatically.

By 1943 the amount of meat, butter, and other foods Americans could buy was regulated by a complicated system of rationing points and coupons. Most people cooperated with the restrictions, but almost one-fourth of the population occasionally bought items on the black market, especially meat, gasoline, and cigarettes. People found it especially hard to cut back on sugar. When sugar disappeared from grocery shelves, the government rationed it at a rate of 1 to 1½ cups per person a week. However, the manufacturers of products such as Coca-Cola and Wrigley's chewing gum received unlimited quantities of sugar by convincing the government that their products helped the morale of the men and women in the armed forces.

Shortages of other consumer products also hit the home front. People finally had enough money to buy refrigerators, cars, and radios, but the components of those items—including rubber, copper, and steel—were earmarked for war production. The last Ford rolled off the assembly line in 1942 as automobile plants converted to bomber production. To placate consumers, many companies ran advertisements promising delayed gratification: after the war, they told the public, you can buy that new house and fill it with all the appliances you want.

But some purchases could not wait. Among the most sought-after items on the black market were women's stockings. During the 1930s women had worn silk stockings, but when the war with Japan cut off imports of silk, they switched to nylon. Yet nylon was essential to war production: thirty-six pairs of nylons equaled one parachute. In a dramatic fashion change (and one associated with the image of Rosie the Riveter), many women began wearing slacks in public. The strict rationing of food and other items eased in the summer of 1944, when victory appeared on the horizon.

Migration and Family Life. The war not only affected what people ate, drank, and wore but also affected where they lived. People moved from one part of the country to another in unprecedented numbers. When men volunteered for or were drafted into the armed services, their families often followed them to training bases or points of debarkation. The lure of high-paying defense jobs encouraged others to move. About 15 million Americans changed residence during the war years, half of them by moving to another state. The pace of urbanization increased, but this movement was not simply an exodus from rural to urban areas. About 5.4 million people left farms, but 2.5 million moved onto them. The greatest number of people went west. The western states not only served as staging areas for the war in the Pacific but also had room for the new ship- and airplane-building industries. Their remote regions (for instance, Hanford, Washington, and Los Alamos, New Mexico) were ideal places to conduct top-secret research.

As a center of defense production California was affected by wartime migration more than any other state. "The Second Gold Rush Hits the West," headlined the *San Francisco Chronicle* in 1943. During the war one-tenth of all federal dollars went to California, and the state turned out one-sixth of total war production. California welcomed nearly 3 million new residents during the war, a 53 percent growth in population. They went where the defense jobs were—to Los Angeles, San Diego, and the San Francisco Bay area. Some towns grew practically overnight: just two years after the

A Family Effort
After migrating from the Midwest to Portland, Oregon, fifteen members of the family of John R. Brauckmiller (sixth from left) found jobs at Portland's Swan Island shipyard. A local newspaper pronounced them "the shipbuildingest family in America."
Ralph Vincent, *The Journal*, Portland, OR.

Kaiser Corporation opened a shipyard in Richmond, the population had quadrupled.

Migration and relocation often caused strains. In many towns with defense industries, housing was scarce and public transportation inadequate. Conflicts over public space and recreation erupted between old-timers and newcomers. Of special concern were the young people the war had set adrift from traditional community restraints. Newspapers were filled with stories of "latchkey" children who stayed home alone while their mothers worked in defense plants. Adolescents were even more of a problem. Teenage girls who hung around army bases looking for a good time were known as "victory girls." In 1942 and 1943 juvenile delinquency seemed to be reaching epidemic proportions.

Another significant result of the growth of war industries was the migration of more than a million African Americans to defense centers in California, Illinois, Michigan, Ohio, and Pennsylvania. The migrants'

need for jobs and housing led to racial conflict in several cities, with some of the worst racial violence taking place in the Detroit area. Early in 1942 black families encountered resistance and intimidation when they tried to move into the Sojourner Truth housing project in the Polish community of Hamtramck. In June 1943 a major race riot in Detroit itself left 34 people dead, including 25 blacks. Racial conflicts broke out in 47 cities across the country during 1943.

Although racial confrontations and zoot suit riots recalled the widespread racial tensions of World War I, the mood on the home front was generally calm in the 1940s. Leftists and communists faced little domestic repression, mainly because the Soviet Union became an ally of the United States after Pearl Harbor. German culture and German Americans did not come under suspicion, nor did most Italian Americans (unless they were fascist sympathizers), largely because there was little threat of either a German or Italian invasion.

Japanese Relocation

The internment of Japanese Americans on the West Coast was a glaring exception to this record of tolerance. California had a long history of antagonism toward both Japanese and Chinese immigrants (see Chapters 16 and 21). The Japanese Americans, who clustered together in highly visible communities, were a small, politically impotent minority, numbering only about 112,000 in the three coastal states. Unlike German Americans and Italian Americans, the Japanese stood out. "A Jap's a Jap," General John DeWitt stated. "It makes no difference whether he is an American citizen or not." This sort of sentiment, coupled with fears of the West Coast's vulnerability to attack and the inflammatory rhetoric of newspapers and local politicians, fueled mounting demands that the region be rid of supposed Japanese spies.

In early 1942, in Executive Order 9022, Roosevelt approved a War department plan to intern Japanese Americans in relocation camps for the rest of the war. In March 1942 Milton Eisenhower, a career civil servant and the brother of General Dwight D. Eisenhower, took over the War Relocation Authority (WRA), a civilian agency created to carry out that policy. Despite the lack of evidence of disloyalty or sedition—no Japanese American was ever charged with espionage—few public leaders opposed the plan.

The relocation announcement shocked Japanese Americans, more than two-thirds of whom were native-born American citizens. (They were *Nisei*, the children of the foreign-born *Issei*.) The government gave families only a few days to dispose of their belongings and prepare for relocation. Businesses that had taken a lifetime to build were liquidated overnight, and speculators snapped up Japanese real estate for a fraction of its value.

Zoot Suits
Zoot suits gained wide popularity among American youth during the war. In 1943 this well-dressed teenager greased his hair in a ducktail and wore a loosely cut coat with padded shoulders ("fingertips") that reached midthigh, baggy pleated pants cut tight ("pegged") around the ankles, and a long gold watch chain.
Corbis-Bettmann.

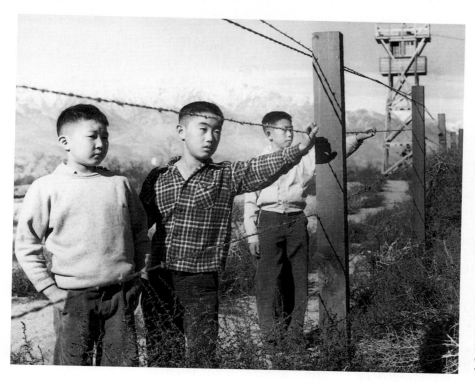

Behind Barbed Wire
As part of the forced relocation of 120,000 Japanese Americans, Los Angeles photographer Toyo Miyatake and his family were sent to Manzanar, a camp in the California desert east of the Sierra Nevada. Miyatake secretly began shooting photographs of the camp, although he eventually received permission from the authorities to document life in the camp. This photograph of three young boys behind barbed wire with a watchtower in the distance must have been shot with official sanction because the photographer is on the other side of the barbed wire. It gives new meaning to the phrase "prisoners of war."
Toyo Miyatake.

A Japanese American music teacher got only $30 for her treasured piano. Another woman broke every piece of her family's heirloom porcelain rather than accept $17.50 from a secondhand dealer for it. But most Japanese Americans accepted the policy stoically. "*Shikata gu nai,*" they said—it can't be helped, hardships must be borne.

Relocation took place in two stages. First the government sent Japanese Americans to temporary assembly centers such as the Santa Anita racetrack in Los Angeles, where they lived in stables that horses had occupied a few days earlier. Then they were moved to ten permanent camps away from the coast. Those internment camps in California, Arizona, Utah, Colorado, Wyoming, Idaho, and Arkansas "were in places where nobody had lived before and no one has lived since," a historian commented (Map 26.1). Milton Eisenhower had hoped the relocation camps would resemble the CCC youth camps of the New Deal, but the barbed wire and enforced communal living mocked his hopes. Although they were sometimes compared to Nazi concentration camps, the relocation centers more closely resembled Indian reservations (see American Voices, "Monica Sone: Japanese Relocation," p. 852).

All ten camps were in hot, dusty places, and their communal bathroom and dining facilities made family life nearly impossible. Eight people often lived in a space measuring 25 by 20 feet. No one had any privacy: when one baby cried, babies cried up and down the barracks. Boredom and generational differences between the *Issei*, with an average age of fifty-five, and the *Nisei*, with an average age of seventeen, added to the tensions.

Almost every Japanese American in California, Oregon, and Washington was involuntarily detained for some period during World War II. Ironically, the Japanese Americans who made up one-third of the population of Hawaii, and presumably posed a greater threat because of their numbers and proximity to Japan, were not affected. Less vulnerable to detention because of

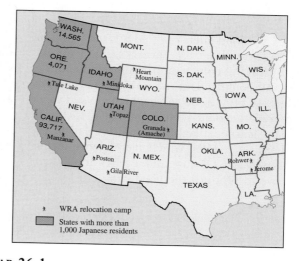

MAP 26.1
WRA Relocation Camps
In 1942 the government ordered 112,000 Japanese Americans living on the West Coast into internment camps in the nation's interior because of their supposed threat to public safety. Some of the camps were as far away as Arkansas.

MONICA SONE

Japanese Relocation

———— ★ ————

Monica (Itoi) Sone's autobiography, Nisei Daughter (1953), tells the story of Japanese relocation from the perspective of a young woman in Seattle, Washington. Here she describes the Itoi family's forced evacuation to a temporary encampment called Camp Harmony; later they were moved to a settlement in Idaho. Although her parents spent the entire war in the camp, Monica Sone was allowed to leave in 1943 to attend college in Indiana.

We felt fortunate to be assigned to a room at the end of the barracks because we had just one neighbor to worry about. The partition wall separating the rooms was only seven feet high with an opening of four feet at the top, so at night, Mrs. Funai next door could tell when Sumi was still sitting up in bed in the dark, putting her hair up. "*Mah*, Sumi-*chan*," Mrs. Funai would say through the plank wall, "are you curling your hair tonight again? Do you put it up every night?" Sumi would put her hands on her hips and glare defiantly at the wall.

The block monitor, an impressive Nisei who looked like a star tackle with his crouching walk, came around the first night to tell us that we must all be inside our room by nine o'clock every night. At ten o'clock, he rapped at the door again, yelling, "Lights out!" and Mother rushed to turn the light off not a second later.

Throughout the barracks, there were a medley of creaking cots, whimpering infants and explosive night coughs. Our attention was riveted on the intense little wood stove which glowed so violently I feared it would melt right down to the floor. We soon learned that this condition lasted for only a short time, after which it suddenly turned into a deep freeze. Henry and Father took turns at the stove to produce the harrowing blast which all but singed our army blankets, but did not penetrate through them. As it grew quieter in the barracks, I could hear the light patter of rain. Soon I felt the "splat! splat!" of raindrops digging holes into my face. The dampness on my pillow spread like a mortal bleeding, and I finally had to get out and haul my cot toward the center of the room. In a short while Henry was up. "I've got multiple leaks, too. Have to complain to the landlord first thing in the morning."

All through the night I heard people getting up, dragging cots around. I stared at our little window, unable to sleep. I was glad Mother had put up a makeshift curtain on the window for I noticed a powerful beam of light sweeping across it every few seconds. The lights came from high towers placed around the camp where guards with Tommy guns kept a twenty-four hour vigil. I remembered the wire fence encircling us, and a knot of anger tightened in my breast. What was I doing behind a fence like a criminal? If there were accusations to be made, why hadn't I been given a fair trial? Maybe I wasn't considered an American anymore. My citizenship wasn't real, after all. Then what was I? I was certainly not a citizen of Japan as my parents were. On second thought, even Father and Mother were more alien residents of the United States than Japanese nationals for they had little tie with their mother country. In their twenty-five years in America, they had worked and paid their taxes to their adopted government as any other citizen.

Of one thing I was sure. The wire fence was real. I no longer had the right to walk out of it. It was because I had Japanese ancestors. It was also because some people had little faith in the ideas and ideals of democracy. They said that after all these were but words and could not possibly insure loyalty. New laws and camps were surer devices. I finally buried my face in my pillow to wipe out burning thoughts and snatch what sleep I could.

———

Source: Monica Sone, *Nisei Daughter* (Boston: Little, Brown and Co., 1953), 176–178.

———

the islands' multiracial heritage, the Japanese also provided much of the unskilled labor on the islands. The Hawaiian economy could not function without them.

Cracks soon appeared in the relocation policy. Even with stepped-up recruitment of Mexican Americans through the *bracero* program, a labor shortage in farming led the government to furlough seasonal Japanese American agricultural workers from the camps as early as 1942. About 4,300 young people who had been in college when the relocation order came through were allowed to stay in school as long as they transferred out of the West Coast military zone. Another route out of the camps was enlistment in the armed services. The 442d Infantry Combat Team, a segregated unit serving in Europe and composed entirely of *Nisei* volunteers, was actually the most decorated unit in the armed forces.

The Supreme Court upheld the constitutionality of internment as a legitimate exercise of power during wartime in *Hirabayashi v. United States* (1943) and in *Korematsu v. United States* (1944). It was not until 1988, after years of lobbying by Japanese American groups, that Congress decided to issue a public apology and to give $20,000 in cash to each of the 60,000 surviving internees—small restitution indeed, but evidence that this shameful episode has been burned into the national conscience.

Fighting and Winning the War

------------★------------

World War II, noted the military historian John Keegan, was "the largest single event in human history." Fought on six continents at a cost of 50 million lives, it was far more global than World War I. At least 405,000 Americans were killed and 671,000 were wounded in the fighting, representing less than half of 1 percent of the U.S. population. In contrast, the Soviets counted as many as 21 million military and civilian dead during the war, about 8 percent of their people. Dropping atomic bombs on Hiroshima and Nagasaki in 1945 was the final stage in this most destructive of human conflicts.

Wartime Aims and Strategies

The Allied coalition was composed mainly of Great Britain, the United States, and the Soviet Union, with other nations, notably China and France, playing lesser roles. Franklin Roosevelt, Britain's Winston Churchill, and Joseph Stalin, the premier of the Soviet Union, took the lead in setting overall strategy. The Atlantic Charter, drafted aboard ship during the Churchill-Roosevelt rendezvous off the Newfoundland coast in August 1941, formed the basis of the Allied vision of the postwar international order. However, Stalin had not been part of the agreement, and that would cause later disagreement over its goals.

Roosevelt's unswerving commitment to Britain's survival provided the basis for a strong, if not always smooth, relationship with Churchill. (Roosevelt's aide Harry Hopkins described his own role as that of a "catalytic agent between two prima donnas.") Stalin, however, was something of a mystery. He and Roosevelt did not meet until late in 1943. Although the United States and Great Britain disagreed on issues such as the postwar fate of colonial empires, the potential for conflict with the Soviet Union was far greater.

As far back as the lend-lease negotiations of early 1941, Churchill and Roosevelt had agreed that defeating Germany would be the first military priority because of that country's huge armies, massive industrial capacity, and mastery of technology. One way to wear down the Germans was to open a second front on the European continent, preferably in France. The Russians strongly argued for this strategy because it would draw German troops away from the Eastern Front and Russian soil. The issue came up so many times that the Soviet foreign minister, Vyacheslav Molotov, was said to know only four English words: *yes, no,* and *second front.*

Though Roosevelt assured Stalin informally that such a front would be opened in 1942, Churchill opposed the idea because he feared British troops would be trapped in a destructive ground war in France just as they had been during World War I. More practically, a second front was moot until American war production was raised to full capacity, since such a huge undertaking would depend primarily on American troops and supplies. As a result, for most of the war the Soviet Union bore the brunt of the land battle against Germany. Roosevelt and Churchill's foot-dragging infuriated Stalin, who was already suspicious about American and British intentions. His mistrust and bitterness carried over into the postwar world in the Cold War that followed the Allied victory.

At various points during the war the three leaders of the Grand Alliance met to discuss military strategy and plan the postwar peace. In January 1943 Roosevelt and Churchill met in Casablanca, Morocco; Stalin did not attend because the Battle of Stalingrad had reached a crucial point. The main outcome of the conference was the Allied demand for unconditional surrender of the Axis powers as a condition for peace. In November 1943 Roosevelt, Churchill, and the Chinese leader, Jiang Jieshi (Chiang Kai-shek), met in Cairo to discuss military operations in the Pacific theater; this conference was designed to keep China in the war. To Roosevelt's dismay, Jiang seemed more interested in fighting the communist revolution in his own country (see Chapter 27) than in mobilizing the Chinese people to expel the Japanese invaders.

Traveling directly from Cairo to Teheran, Iran, Roosevelt finally met Stalin late in November 1943. At the Teheran Conference Roosevelt and Churchill agreed to Stalin's demand for a second front within six months. In return, Stalin promised to join the fight against Japan after the war in Europe ended, a promise he kept. The three leaders also issued the Teheran Declaration, in which they welcomed the cooperation of all nations in the war and invited them to join the Big Three in a "world family of democratic nations." Churchill and Roosevelt also agreed tacitly to Stalin's demand that Poland's borders be redrawn to give the Soviet Union more territory. But the three leaders disagreed sharply about who should control the rest of Poland and the other Eastern European states. Roosevelt expressed confidence that the personal rapport he had developed with Stalin would aid postwar relations among the superpowers, but Stalin's territorial ambitions in Eastern Europe foreshadowed later divisions.

The War in Europe

During the first six months of 1942 the military news was so bad that it threatened to swamp the Grand Alliance. The Allies suffered severe defeats on land and sea throughout Europe and Asia. German armies pushed deeper into Soviet territory, reaching the outskirts of Moscow and Leningrad; simultaneously they started an offensive in North Africa aimed at seizing the Suez Canal, the critical transportation link to Africa and the Asian subcontinent. At sea German submarines were crippling American convoys carrying supplies to Europe. Since the United States was the main supplier of oil to the Allies, those attacks struck at the heart of the war effort, which was increasingly dependent on petroleum-based military equipment such as tanks and airplanes.

The turning point of the war in Europe occurred in the winter of 1942–1943, when the Soviets halted the German advance in the Battle of Stalingrad. By 1944, Stalin's forces had driven the German army out of the Soviet Union. Meanwhile the Allies launched a major offensive in North Africa, Churchill's substitute for a second front in France. Between November 1942 and May 1943 Allied troops under the leadership of Generals Dwight D. Eisenhower and George S. Patton defeated Germany's crack Afrika Korps led by General Erwin Rommel.

From Africa the Allied command followed Churchill's strategy of attacking the Axis powers through what he called its "soft underbelly": Sicily and the Italian peninsula. In July 1943 the fascist regime of Benito Mussolini fell, and Italy's new government joined the Allies. The Allied forces invaded Italy in the following fall, but the mountainous terrain and heavy resistance from German troops kept them from entering Rome until June 1944 (Map 26.2). The last German forces in Italy did not surrender until May 1945.

D-Day.   The long-awaited invasion of France to open the second front came on D-Day, the code name for the date of the Allied landing—June 6, 1944. That morning, after an agonizing delay caused by bad weather, the largest fleet ever assembled moved across the English Channel.

Hitting the Beach at Normandy
These American soldiers, part of almost 150,000 Allied troops, stormed the beaches of Normandy, France, on D-Day, June 6, 1944. More than a million Allied troops came ashore during the next month. Filmmaker Stephen Spielberg re-created the carnage and confusion of the landing in the opening scene of *Saving Private Ryan* (1998).
Library of Congress.

MAP 26.2
World War II in Europe

a. 1941–1943 Hitler's Germany reached its greatest extent in 1942, when Nazi forces stalled at Leningrad and Stalingrad. The tide of battle turned in the fall, when the Soviet army launched a massive counterattack at Stalingrad and Allied forces began to drive the Germans from North Africa. In 1943 the Allies invaded Sicily and the Italian mainland. **b. 1944–1945** On June 6, 1944 (D-Day), the Allies finally invaded France. It took almost a year for the Allied forces to close in on Berlin—the Soviets from the east and the Americans, British, and French from the west. Germany surrendered on May 8, 1945.

While airplanes and battleships offshore bombarded the German defenses, more than 4,000 vessels ferried troops, trucks, tanks, and supplies ashore. The beaches of Normandy where the Allies landed—code-named Utah, Omaha, Juno, Gold, and Sword—soon became household words in the United States, sites of great and quiet bravery as well as terrible casualties and death. Under the command of General Dwight Eisenhower, more than 1.5 million American, British, and Canadian soldiers crossed the Channel over the next few days. In August the Allied troops helped liberate Paris, and by September they had driven the Germans out of most of France and Belgium.

In the autumn of 1944 the German military situation looked hopeless. All that year, long-range Allied bombers had made daring daylight raids, damaging Nazi military and industrial installations and pulverizing cities such as Cologne, Dresden, and Berlin, the German capital. In the air campaign 305,000 people were killed and 780,000 were wounded, both soldiers and civilians. In modern war no one was safe from attack.

Victory in Europe. The Germans were not ready to give up, however. In December 1944 their forces in Belgium mounted an attack that began the Battle of the Bulge, so called because it made a dent in the Allied defenses. After ten days of heavy fighting in what was to be the final German offensive of the war, the Allies regained their momentum and pushed the Germans back across the Rhine River. Their goal was to take Berlin. American and British troops led the drive from the west, while Soviet troops advanced from the east through Poland, reaching Berlin first. On April 30, with much of Berlin in rubble from Allied bombing, Hitler committed suicide in his bunker. Germany surrendered on May 8, 1945, the date that became known as V-E (Victory in Europe) Day.

The Holocaust. When Allied troops advanced into Germany in the spring of 1945, they came face to face with Hitler's "final solution of the Jewish question": the extermination camps where 6 million Jews had been put to death, along with another 6 million Poles, Slavs, Gypsies, homosexuals, and other "undesirables." Photographs from Nazi death camps at Buchenwald, Dachau, and Auschwitz, showing bodies stacked like firewood and survivors so emaciated that they were barely alive, horrified the American public and the rest of the world. But government officials could not claim that no one knew about the camps before the German surrender. The Roosevelt administration had had reliable information about the death camps as early as November 1942.

The lack of response by the U.S. government to the Holocaust—the Nazi regime's systematic near-annihilation of European Jewry—ranks as one of the gravest failures of the Roosevelt administration. So few Jews escaped the Holocaust because the United States—and the rest of the world—would not take them in. State department policies allowed only 21,000 refugees to enter this country during the war. The War Refugee Board, established in 1944 with little support from the Roosevelt administration, eventually helped save about 200,000 Jews. Several factors combined to inhibit U.S. action: anti-Semitism; fear of economic competition from a flood of refugees in a country just recovering from the depression; failure of the media to grasp the magnitude of the horror and publicize it accordingly; and failure of religious leaders, Jews and non-Jews alike, to speak out.

In justifying the American course of action, Roosevelt claimed that winning the war would be the strongest con-

The Living Dead
When Allied troops advanced into Germany in the spring of 1945, they came face to face with what had long been rumored—concentration camps, Adolf Hitler's "final solution of the Jewish question." Margaret Bourke-White was one of the first photographers on the scene. This haunting image from the Buchenwald death camp appeared in *Life* magazine.
Margaret Bourke-White, *Life* Magazine. © Time, Inc.

tribution America could make to liberating the camps. But it is hard to escape the conclusion that the United States could have done much more to lessen the Holocaust's terrible human toll.

The War in the Pacific

After the victory in Europe the Allies still had to defeat Japan. American forces bore the brunt of the fighting in the Pacific, just as the Russians had done in the land war in Europe. At the beginning of 1942 the news from the Pacific was uniformly grim. In the wake of Pearl Harbor, Japan had scored quickly with seaborne invasions of Hong Kong, Wake Island, and Guam. Japanese forces conquered much of Burma, Malaya, and the Philippines as well as the Solomon Islands and began to threaten Australia and India (see American Voices, "Anton Bilek: The War in the Pacific," p. 858). Japan achieved this huge territorial expansion in only three months. One of the few boosts for American morale came on April 18, 1942, when Colonel James H. Doolittle led sixteen American bombers on the first air raid on Tokyo, but the attack had little military value.

The more significant battles were far to the south. On May 7–8, 1942, in the Battle of the Coral Sea near southern New Guinea, American naval forces halted the Japanese offensive against Australia. In June, at the island of Midway, the Americans inflicted crucial damage on the Japanese fleet. For the first time, a major sea battle was waged—and decided—primarily by planes launched from aircraft carriers that never came within sight of each other. Submarines also played an important role in the naval battles, but the human cost was high: 22 percent of American submariners lost their lives during the war—the highest death rate in any branch of the armed services.

After the Battle of Midway the American military command, under General Douglas MacArthur and Admiral Chester W. Nimitz, took the offensive in the Pacific, adopting a plan of winning strategic positions essential for an eventual direct assault against Japan. For the next eighteen months American forces advanced arduously from one island to the next, winning major victories at Tulagi and Guadalcanal in the Solomon Islands and at Tarawa and Makin in the Gilberts. They reached the Marshall Islands in early 1944. In October 1944 the reconquest of the Philippines began with a victory in the Battle of Leyte Gulf, a massive naval encounter in which the Japanese lost practically their entire fleet whereas the Americans suffered only minimal losses (Map 26.3).

By early 1945 victory over Japan was in sight. The campaign in the Pacific moved slowly toward what military leaders anticipated would be a massive and costly invasion of Japan. To put U.S. planes within striking distance of Tokyo, Americans needed to capture Iwo Jima and Okinawa. In some of the fiercest fighting of the war, the marines sustained more than 20,000 casualties at Iwo Jima, including 6,000 dead; at Okinawa the toll reached 7,600 dead and 32,000 wounded. The closer U.S. forces got to the Japanese home islands, the more fiercely the Japanese fought. On Iwo Jima almost all of the 21,000 Japanese died.

By mid-1945 Japan's army, navy, and air force had suffered devastating losses. American bombing of the mainland had killed about 330,000 civilians and crippled the Japanese economy. In a last-ditch effort to stem the tide, Japanese pilots began suicidal kamikaze missions, crashing their planes and boats into American ships. This desperate action, combined with the Japanese military leadership's refusal to surrender, suggested that Japan would keep up the fight despite overwhelming losses. Based on the fighting at Okinawa and Iwo Jima, American military commanders grimly predicted millions of casualties in the upcoming invasion.

Planning the Postwar World

In February 1945 Roosevelt, Churchill, and Stalin held what would be their last conference at Yalta, a Black Sea resort. Victory in Europe and the Pacific was in sight, but no agreement had been reached on the peace to come. Roosevelt remained focused on maintaining Allied unity, which he saw as the key to postwar peace and stability. The fate of British colonies such as India, where an independence movement had already begun, caused friction between Roosevelt and Churchill. A more serious source of conflict was Stalin's desire for a band of Soviet-controlled satellite states to protect the Soviet Union's western border. With Soviet armies in control of much of Eastern Europe, Stalin had become increasingly inflexible on that issue, insisting that he needed friendly (that is, Soviet-dominated) governments there to provide a buffer zone to guarantee Soviet national security. Roosevelt acknowledged the legitimacy of that demand but, with the Atlantic Charter's principle of self-determination in mind, hoped for democratically elected governments in Poland and the neighboring countries. The two goals proved mutually exclusive.

At Yalta, Roosevelt and Churchill agreed in principle to the idea of a Soviet sphere of influence in Eastern Europe but deliberately left its dimensions vague. Stalin in return pledged to hold "free and unfettered elections" at an unspecified time. (Those elections never took place.) The compromise reached at Yalta was open to multiple interpretations. Admiral William D. Leahy, Roosevelt's chief military aide, described the agreement as "so elastic that the Russians can stretch it all the way from Yalta to Washington without technically breaking it."

ANTON BILEK

The War in the Pacific

———————★———————

Anton Bilek grew up in Southern Illinois and enlisted in the army in 1939 at nineteen because jobs were hard to get. Sent to the Philippines in 1940, he was taken prisoner when the Japanese overran the Bataan peninsula in April 1942. He describes the infamous "Bataan Death March" and its aftermath.

The next morning, we got orders to get rid of all our arms and wait for the Japanese to come. General King had surrendered Bataan. They came in. First thing they did, they lined us up and started searchin' us. Anybody that had a ring or a wristwatch or a pair of gold-rimmed spectacles, they took 'em. Glasses they'd throw on the floor and break 'em and put the gold rims in their pockets. If you had a ring, you handed it over. If you couldn't get it off, the guy'd put the bayonet right up against your neck. Fortunately I never wore a ring. I couldn't afford one.

They moved us about on the road. Here was a big stream of Americans and Filipinos marchin' by. They told us to get in the back of this column. This was the start of the Death March. (A long, deep sigh.) That was a sixty-mile walk. Here we were, three, four months on half-rations, less. The men were already thin, in shock. Undernourished, full of malaria. Dysentery is beginning to spread. This is even before the surrender. We had two hospitals chuck-full of men. Bataan peninsula was the worst malaria-infected province of the Philippines.

The Japanese emptied out the hospitals. Anybody that could walk, they forced 'em into line. You found all kinda bodies along the road. Some of 'em bloated, some had just been killed. If you fell out to the side, you were either shot by the guards or you were bayoneted and left there. We lost somewhere between six hundred and seven hundred Americans in the four days of the march. The Filipinos lost close to ten thousand. At San Fernando, we were stuffed into boxcars and taken about thirty-five miles further north. The cars were closed, you couldn't get air. In the hot sun, the temperature got up there. You couldn't fall down because you were held up by the guys stacked around you. You had a lot of guys blow their top, start screamin'. From there, they marched us another seven, eight miles to Camp O'Donnell, which was built hurriedly for the Philippine army. It was built like the huts were built, of native bamboo and *nipa* and grass. There must've been about nine thousand of us and about fifty thousand Filipinos. Americans in one camp, Filipinos in the other. We had to leave after a month and a half. The monsoon season was starting. A hurricane blew down two of the barracks. Eighty men were killed. Just crushed.

I went blind, momentarily. It scared the hell out of me. I was at the hospital for about two weeks, and the doctor, an American, said, "There's nothing I can do with you. Rest is the only thing. Eat all the rice you can get. That's your only medicine." That's the one thing that pulled me through. He said, "You won't have to go on details." The Japanese were comin' in and they'd take two, three hundred and start 'em repairing a bridge that was blown up. We were losin' a lot of men there. They couldn't work any more. They were dyin'. . . .

I'm back home. It's all over with. I'd like to forget it. I had nothin' against the Japanese. But I don't drive a Toyota or own a Sony. . . . A lotta friends I lost. We had 185 men in our squadron when the war started. Three and a half years later, when we were liberated from a prison camp in Japan, we were 39 left. It's them I think about. Men I played ball with, men I worked with, men I associated with. I miss 'em.

———————

Source: Studs Terkel, *"The Good War": An Oral History of World War Two* (New York: Pantheon Books, 1984), 85, 90–91, 95–96.

At Yalta the three leaders also proceeded with plans to divide Germany into four zones to be controlled by the United States, Great Britain, France, and the Soviet Union. Berlin, the capital city that lay in the middle of the Soviet zone, would also be partitioned among the four powers. The divisive issue of German reparations remained unsettled.

The Big Three made further progress toward the establishment of a postwar international organization in the form of the United Nations. Roosevelt, determined to

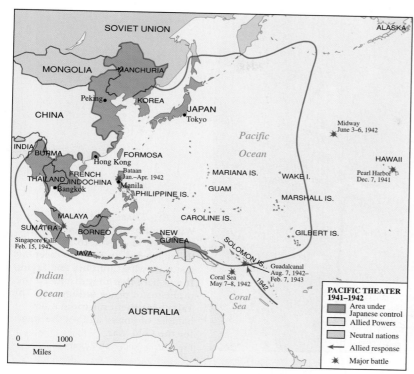

MAP 26.3
World War II in the Pacific
a. 1941–1942 After the attack on Pearl Harbor in December 1941 the Japanese rapidly extended their domination in the Pacific. The Japanese flag soon flew as far east as the Marshall and Gilbert Islands and as far south as the Solomon Islands and parts of New Guinea. Japan also controlled the Philippines, much of Southeast Asia, and parts of China, including Hong Kong. American naval victories at the Coral Sea and Midway stopped further Japanese expansion.

b. 1943–1945 Allied forces retook the islands in the Central Pacific in 1943 and 1944 and the Philippines early in 1945. The capture of Iwo Jima and Okinawa put U.S. bombers in position to attack Japan itself. The Japanese offered to surrender on August 10, after the United States dropped atomic bombs on Hiroshima and Nagasaki.

avoid Woodrow Wilson's mistakes in regard to the League of Nations, had already cultivated congressional backing; realizing that such an organization would be impotent without the Soviets' participation, he cultivated their support as well. British, American, and Soviet representatives had already met at Dumbarton Oaks, an estate in Washington, D.C., in September 1944 to begin

planning the structure of the organization. At Yalta the Big Three agreed that the Security Council of the United Nations would include the five major Allied powers—the United States, Britain, France, China, and the Soviet Union—plus six nations elected on a rotating basis. They also decided that the permanent members of the Security Council should have veto power over decisions of the

The Big Three at Yalta
With victory in Europe at hand, Roosevelt journeyed to Yalta, on the Black Sea, in 1945, to meet one last time with Churchill and Stalin. It was here that they discussed the problems of peace settlements. The Yalta agreement mirrored a new balance of power and set the stage for the Cold War.
Franklin D. Roosevelt Library.

General Assembly, in which all nations would be represented. Roosevelt, Churchill, and Stalin announced that the United Nations would convene in San Francisco on April 25, 1945.

Roosevelt returned to the United States in February, visibly exhausted by his 14,000-mile trip. He neglected to inform the American public of the concessions he had made to maintain the increasingly fragile wartime alliance. When he reported to Congress on the Yalta agreements, he made an unusual acknowledgment of his physical infirmity. Referring to the heavy steel braces he wore on his legs, he asked Congress to excuse him if he gave his speech sitting down. The sixty-three-year-old president was a very sick man, suffering from heart failure and high blood pressure. On April 12, 1945, during a short visit to his vacation home in Warm Springs, Georgia, Roosevelt suffered a cerebral hemorrhage and died.

Many Americans could not imagine any leader other than Franklin Roosevelt in the White House. Those who reached adulthood in the 1930s and 1940s had never known another president. In both depression and war he led the country through perilous times. As a global strategist he grasped America's predominant role and helped educate the country to accept its new international responsibilities. Roosevelt's model of leadership proved a difficult legacy for future presidents to match.

V-E Day came less than a month after Roosevelt died and Harry Truman succeeded to the presidency.

The war in the Pacific ended after Truman ordered the dropping of atomic bombs on two Japanese cities, Hiroshima on August 6 and Nagasaki on August 9, 1945. Many later questioned why the United States did not warn Japan about the attack or choose a noncivilian target; the rationale for dropping the second bomb was even less clear. Other critics suggested that the fact that the Japanese were a nonwhite race facilitated the momentous decision to drop the bombs. At the time, however, the belief that Japan's military leaders would never surrender unless their country was utterly devastated convinced policy makers that they had to deploy the devastating new weapon. The atomic bombs killed 100,000 people at Hiroshima and 60,000 at Nagasaki. Tens of thousands more died slowly of radiation poisoning. Japan offered to surrender on August 10 and signed a formal treaty of surrender on September 2, 1945. World War II had ended, but a new atomic age of insecurity had begun.

The Onset of the Atomic Age

The development of the atomic bomb was closely linked to wartime military strategy. In December 1938 German scientists had discovered that the nuclei of atoms could be split into smaller particles, a process called fission. With materials prepared from uranium, a chain reaction of nuclear fission would release tremendous amounts of energy. American scientists, including many refugees from fascist Italy and Nazi

Hiroshima
This was all that remained of Hiroshima after the dropping of an atomic bomb on August 6, 1945. The shell of Hiroshima's Museum of Science and Industry (visible in the photo), one of the few buildings left standing after the bomb, later became the center of a memorial to those who died in the blast.
National Archives.

Germany, produced the first controlled chain reaction on December 2, 1942, at the University of Chicago.

Scientists soon began working frantically to harness nuclear reactions for military purposes. Their goal was the development of an atomic bomb for use against Germany or, later, Japan. The secret research, called the Manhattan Project, cost $2 billion, employed 120,000 people, and involved the construction of thirty-seven installations in nineteen states under the direction of General Leslie R. Groves of the U.S. Army Corps of Engineers. In the final stages a team consisting of most of the country's top physicists assembled the bomb at an isolated desert site in Los Alamos, New Mexico. All this was hidden from Congress, the American people, and even Vice-President Truman. The secrecy and scope of this alliance between science and government constitute a dramatic example of how much the power of the state grew during wartime.

Roosevelt had followed the bomb's progress closely. He and his advisors had planned to deploy the bomb to end the war without the dreadful number of American casualties projected to result from an invasion of Japan. At the same time, policy makers hoped that the possession of such a powerful weapon—the "master card," in the words of Secretary of War Henry Stimson—might enhance American power in the postwar world. Instead, the new weapon became the first step in a deadly arms race between the United States and the Soviet Union.

Until the last moment the scientists did not know if the atomic bomb would work. On July 16, 1945, near Alamogordo, New Mexico, they watched in wonder as the test bomb exploded in a huge mushroom cloud. President Truman received news of the successful detonation in Potsdam, near Berlin, where he was about to meet with Churchill and Stalin in the final wartime conference about the shape of postwar Europe (see Chapter 27). Truman, who had not known about the bomb before he became president, was ecstatic about its potential, telling aides, "This is the greatest thing in history." Others were not so sure. J. Robert Oppenheimer, one of the leading scientists on the Manhattan Project, watched the test on that July morning in the New Mexico desert. Overwhelmed by its frightening power, he recalled the words from the Bhagavad Gita, a Hindu sacred text: "I am become Death, Destroyer of Worlds."

Franklin Roosevelt's death and the dropping of the atomic bomb came at a critical juncture in world affairs. Many questions had been left deliberately unresolved in the hopes of keeping the wartime alliance intact to guide the transition to peace. But as the war ended, issues such as the fate of Poland and Germany demanded action. The resulting compromises, not all of which were fully reported to the American people, tended to promote spheres of influence as the new basis of international power, rather than the ideals of national self-determination and economic cooperation laid out in the Atlantic Charter. Once the common enemies had been defeated, the wartime alliance became strained and then began to split apart in ways so fundamental that it is unlikely that Roosevelt could have kept it together if he had lived. Perhaps the greatest legacy of World War II was the Cold War that followed.

Summary

⸻ ★ ⸻

With the rise of fascism and imperialism in Germany, Italy, and Japan, the world was at war by 1939. Although most Americans clung to strong isolationist sentiment, President Roosevelt began mobilizing public opinion for intervention and converting the economy to war production. The Japanese attack on Pearl Harbor on December 7, 1941, brought the nation into World War II.

Defense mobilization ended the Great Depression and caused the economy to rebound. As with World War I, mobilization led to a dramatic expansion of the state. On the home front, the war resulted in rationing and shortages of many items but no serious hardships. Geographical mobility increased as labor shortages opened job opportunities for women, blacks, and Mexican Americans. The labor movement surged, and the ideological climate of fighting Nazism aided the cause of civil rights. However, Japanese Americans on the West Coast suffered a devastating denial of civil liberties when the government moved them into internment camps.

World War II was a global war, consisting of massive military campaigns in both Europe and the Pacific. The war news was bleak at first, but by 1943 the Allies had started to move toward victory, first in Europe and then in the Pacific. Soviet forces bore the brunt of the fighting in the European theater, while American forces primarily orchestrated the war effort in the Pacific. More than 15 million American men and women served in the armed forces, and at least 405,000 lost their lives.

While the Allied forces mobilized to defeat Germany and Japan, Roosevelt attempted to maintain harmony among the United States, Great Britain, and the Soviet Union. Many of the disagreements over wartime diplomacy would become serious problems in the postwar world, especially the fate of Eastern Europe and the intentions of the Soviet Union. Of all the major powers that fought in World War II, only the United States emerged physically unharmed. And at the end of the war, only the United States had a powerful new weapon, the atomic bomb. But the most enduring legacy of World War II was the onset of the Cold War, which would dominate American foreign policy for the next four decades.

TIMELINE

1938	Munich agreement
1939	Nazi-Soviet pact
	War breaks out in Europe
1940	Conscription reinstated
	America First Committee
	Roosevelt reelected to third term
1941	Roosevelt promulgates Four Freedoms
	Hitler invades Soviet Union
	Lend-Lease Act
	Fair Employment Practices Commission
	Atlantic Charter
	Japanese attack Pearl Harbor
1942	Battles of Coral Sea and Midway halt Japanese advance in the Pacific
	Women recruited for war industries
	Relocation of Japanese Americans
	Revenue Act of 1942
1942–1945	Rationing
1943	Race riots in Detroit and Los Angeles
	Fascism falls in Italy
	Teheran Conference
1944	Gunnar Myrdal, *An American Dilemma*
	D-Day invasion
	Reconquest of Philippines
	GI Bill of Rights
	Roosevelt reelected to fourth term
1945	Germany surrenders
	Battles of Iwo Jima and Okinawa
	Yalta Conference
	Harry Truman becomes president after Roosevelt's death
	United Nations convenes
	U.S. drops atomic bombs on Hiroshima and Nagasaki
	Japan surrenders

Suggested Readings

John Morton Blum, *V Was for Victory* (1976); William O'Neill, *A Democracy at War* (1993); Michael C. C. Adams, *The Best War Ever* (1994); and Geoffrey Perret, *Days of Sadness, Years of Triumph* (1973), offer good introductions to American politics and culture during the war years. A valuable collection of articles is found in Lewis A. Erenberg and Susan E. Hirsch, eds., *The War in American Culture* (1996). Studs Terkel, *"The Good War"* (1984), offers a powerful and provocative oral history of the war. John Keegan, *The Second World War* (1990), offers the best one-volume account of the battlefront aspects.

American Neutrality, 1939–1941

Depression and wartime diplomacy are covered in Robert Dallek, *Franklin D. Roosevelt and American Foreign Policy, 1932–1945* (1979), and Akira Iriye, *The Globalizing of America, 1913–1945* (1993). On American isolationism, see Wayne Cole, *Roosevelt and the Isolationists, 1932–1945* (1983). Warren T. Kimball, *The Most Unsordid Act* (1969), describes the lend-lease controversy of 1939–1941, whereas Kimball's *The Juggler: Franklin Roosevelt as Wartime Statesman* (1991), provides an overview of Roosevelt's leadership. Roberta Wohlstetter, *Pearl Harbor* (1962); Herbert Feis, *The Road to Pearl Harbor* (1950); and Gordon W. Prange, *At Dawn We Slept* (1981), describe the events that led to American entry into the war.

Organizing for Victory

George Flynn, *The Mess in Washington* (1979), and Harold G. Vatter, *The U.S. Economy in World War II* (1985), discuss America's economic mobilization. Mark S. Foster, *Henry J. Kaiser: Builder in the Modern American West* (1989), and Stephen B. Adams, *Mr. Kaiser Goes to Washington: The Rise of a Government Entrepreneur* (1997), are comprehensive accounts of Kaiser's career. Alan Winkler, *The Politics of Propaganda* (1978), covers the Office of War Information. On labor's role during war, see George Lipsitz, *Rainbow at Midnight: Labor and Culture in the 1940s* (1994); and Nelson Lichtenstein, *Labor's War at Home: The CIO in World War II* (1982). For more on politics in wartime, see James McGregor Burns, *Roosevelt: The Soldier of Freedom* (1970); Doris Kearns Goodwin, *No Ordinary Time* (1994); and Alan Brinkley, *The End of Reform* (1995).

Women's roles in wartime are covered by Susan Hartmann, *The Home Front and Beyond* (1982); Karen Anderson, *Wartime Women* (1980); D'Ann Campbell, *Women at War with America* (1984); Ruth Milkman, *Gender at Work* (1987); and Sherna B. Gluck, *Rosie the Riveter Revisited: Women, the War, and Social Change* (1987). Judy Barrett Litoff and David C. Smith, *We're in This War, Too* (1994), includes letters from American women in uniform, and Leisa D. Meyer, *Creating GI Jane* (1996), discusses the Women's Army Corps.

Life on the Home Front

William M. Tuttle Jr., *"Daddy's Gone to War"* (1993), describes World War II from the perspective of the nation's children. Alan Clive, *State of War* (1979), provides a case study of Michi-

gan during the war; Marilynn S. Johnson, *The Second Gold Rush* (1993), describes Oakland, California, and the East Bay. See also Gerald D. Nash, *The American West Transformed: The Impact of the Second World War* (1985). Clayton R. Koppes and Gregory D. Black, *Hollywood Goes to War* (1987), and Thomas Doherty, *Projections of War* (1993), cover the film industry. The experience of black Americans is treated in Albert Russell Buchanan, *Black Americans in World War II* (1977), and Neil Wynn, *The Afro-American and the Second World War* (1975). On racial tensions, see Dominic Capeci Jr., *Race Relations in Wartime Detroit* (1984), and Mauricio Mazan, *The Zoot Suit Riots* (1984). Richard Dalfiume, *Desegregation of the U.S. Armed Forces* (1969), covers black soldiers in the military, and Phillip McGuire, *Taps for a Jim Crow Army* (1993), offers a collection of letters from black soldiers. Alan Berube, *Coming Out under Fire* (1990), is an oral history of gay men and lesbians in the military; see also John D'Emilio, *Sexual Politics, Sexual Communities* (1983), for the impact of the war on gay Americans. Maurice Isserman, *Which Side Were You On?* (1982), analyzes the American Communist Party during the war. Two compelling accounts of Japanese relocation are Audre Girdner and Anne Loftus, *The Great Betrayal* (1969), and Roger Daniels, *Prisoners without Trial: Japanese-Americans in World War II* (1993). See also John Tateishi, ed., *And Justice For All: An Oral History of the Japanese-American Detention Camps* (1984); Peter Irons, *Justice at War: The Story of the Japanese-American Internment Cases* (1983); and Page Smith, *Democracy on Trial: The Japanese American Evacuation and Relocation in World War II* (1995).

Fighting and Winning the War

Extensive material chronicles the American military experience during World War II. Albert Russell Buchanan, *The United States and World War II* (1962), and Russell F. Weigley, *The American Way of War* (1973), provide overviews; Ronald Schaffer, *Wings of Judgement: American Bombing in World War II* (1985), and Bradley F. Smith, *The Shadow Warriors: OSS and the Origins of the CIA* (1983), are more specialized. Stephen Ambrose, *D-Day, June 6, 1944* (1994) and *Citizen Soldiers* (1997), describe the end of the fighting in Europe. David S. Wyman, *The Abandonment of the Jews* (1984), describes the lack of American response to the Holocaust from 1941 to 1945. On East Asia, see John W. Dower, *War without Mercy: Race and Power in the Pacific War* (1986); Ronald H. Spector, *Eagle against the Sun: The American War with Japan* (1984); and John Toland, *Rising Sun: The Decline and Fall of the Japanese Empire* (1970).

American diplomacy and the strategy of the Grand Alliance are surveyed in Lloyd Gardner, *Spheres of Influence* (1993). The relationship between the wartime conferences and the onset of the Cold War is treated in Walter LaFeber, *America, Russia, and the Cold War* (8th ed., 1996), and Stephen Ambrose and Douglas Brinkley, *Rise to Globalism* (8th ed., 1997). Richard Rhodes, *The Making of the Atomic Bomb* (1987), and Martin Sherwin, *A World Destroyed* (1975), provide compelling accounts of the development of the bomb. See also Gar Alperowitz, *The Decision to Use the Atomic Bomb* (1995); Ronald Takaki, *Hiroshima: Why America Dropped the Atomic Bomb* (1995); and Robert Jay Lifton and Greg Mitchell, *Hiroshima in America: Fifty Years of Denial* (1995).

Part Six

★

America and the World, 1945–1996

THEMATIC TIMELINE

	Diplomacy	Government	Economy	Society	Culture
	The Cold War Era— and After	**Redefining the Role of the State**	**Ups and Downs of U.S. Economic Dominance**	**Social Movements and Demographic Diversity**	**Consumer Culture and the Information Revolution**
1945	Truman Doctrine (1947) Marshall Plan (1948) NATO founded (1949)	Truman's Fair Deal liberalism Taft-Hartley Act (1947)	Bretton Woods system established: World Bank, IMF, GATT	Migration to cities accelerates Armed forces desegregated (1948)	End of wartime rationing Rise of television
1950	Permanent mobilization: NSC-68 (1950) Korean War (1950–1953)	Eisenhower's modern Republicanism Warren Court activism	Rise of military-industrial complex Service sector expands	*Brown v. Board of Education* (1954) Montgomery bus boycott (1955)	Growth of suburbia Baby boom
1960	Cuban missile crisis (1962) Nuclear test ban treaty (1963) Vietnam War escalates (1965)	High tide of liberalism: Great Society, War on Poverty Nixon ushers in conservative era	Kennedy-Johnson tax cut, military expenditures fuel economic growth	Student activism Civil Rights Act (1964); Voting Rights Act (1965) Revival of feminism	Shopping malls spread Baby boomers swell college enrollment Youth counterculture
1970	Nixon visits China (1972) SALT initiates détente (1972) Paris Peace Accords (1973)	Watergate scandal; Nixon resigns (1974) Deregulation begins under Ford and Carter	Arab oil embargo (1973–1974); inflation surges Deindustrialization brings unemployment to "Rustbelt" Income stagnation	*Roe v. Wade* (1973) Televangelists mobilize evangelical Protestants New Right urges conservative agenda	First Earth Day (1970) Gasoline shortages Apple introduces first personal computer (1977)
1980	Reagan arms buildup INF treaty (1988) Berlin Wall falls	Reagan Revolution Supreme Court conservatism	Reaganomics Budget and trade deficits soar Savings and loan bailout	New Hispanic and Asian immigration	MTV debuts AIDS epidemic
1990	War in the Persian Gulf USSR disintegrates; end of the Cold War U.S. peacekeeping forces in Bosnia	Democratic party adopts "moderate" policies Republican Congress shifts federal government tasks to states	Corporate downsizing NAFTA (1993) Asian economies decline	Third wave of feminism Affirmative action challenged Welfare reform	Health care crisis Information superhighway Biotech revolution

I N 1945 THE United States entered an era of unprecedented international power and influence. Unlike the period after World War I, American leaders did not avoid international commitments; instead, they aggressively pursued U.S. interests abroad, vowing to contain communism around the globe. The consequences of that struggle profoundly influenced the nation's domestic economy, political affairs, and social and cultural trends for the next half-century.

Diplomacy. First and most important, the United States took a leading, or hegemonic, role in global diplomatic and military affairs. When the Soviet Union challenged America's vision of postwar Europe, the Truman administration responded by crafting the policies and alliances that came to define the Cold War. That bipolar struggle lasted for more than forty years, spawned two "hot" wars in Korea and Vietnam, and fueled a terrifying and debilitating nuclear arms race. Although the moderate policy of détente pursued by Richard Nixon and later presidents helped ease tensions, the Cold War mentality prevailed until the collapse and disintegration of the Soviet Union in 1991.

Government. Second, America's global commitments had dramatic consequences for American government and politics. Until the national consensus fractured over the Vietnam War, liberals and conservatives agreed on keeping the country in a state of permanent mobilization and maintaining a large and well-equipped military establishment. The end of the Cold War brought modest cutbacks in defense spending, but an explosion of ethnic and religious conflicts in the former Yugoslavia, Africa, and other areas required U.S. military participation in several international peacekeeping missions in the 1990s. In the area of economic policy, all administrations, Republican and Democratic, were willing to intervene in the economy when private initiatives could not maintain steady growth. But liberals also pushed for a larger role for the federal government in the areas of social welfare and environmental protection. Under Harry S Truman, John F. Kennedy, and especially Lyndon B. Johnson, the government went beyond the New Deal by erecting an extensive federal and state apparatus to provide for the social well-being of the people. In subsequent years, particularly under the presidency of Ronald Reagan in the 1980s and the Republican control of Congress in the mid-1990s, conservatives cut back on many of the major programs and tried to delegate federal powers to the states.

Economy. Third, thanks to the growth of a military-industrial complex of enormous size and the expansion of consumer culture, the quarter-century after 1945 represented the heyday of American capitalism. Economic dominance abroad translated into unparalleled affluence at home. In the early 1970s, however, competition from other countries began to challenge America's economic supremacy, and for the next two decades many American workers experienced high unemployment, declining real wages, stagnant incomes, and a standard of living that could not match that of their parents. Following this period of global economic restructuring, the U.S. economy rebounded in the mid-1990s, reclaiming a position of undisputed dominance but sharing its leadership role with other industrial powers.

Society. Fourth, the victory over fascism in World War II led to renewed calls for America to make good on its promise of liberty and equality for all. In great waves of protests in the 1950s and 1960s, African Americans—and then women, Latinos, and other groups—challenged the political status quo. The resulting hard-won reforms brought concrete gains for many Americans, but since the late 1970s conservatives have challenged many of these initiatives. As the century drew to a close, the promise of true equality remained unfulfilled.

Culture. Fifth, American economic power in the postwar era accelerated the development of a consumer society based on suburbanization and technology. As millions of Americans migrated to new suburban developments after World War II, growing baby-boom families provided an expanded market for household products of all types. Among the most significant were new technological devices—television, video recorders, personal computers—that helped break down the isolation of suburban and rural living. Beginning in the 1960s, however, some people began to question the American obsession with material consumption and the environmental degradation it caused. In the 1990s the popularization of the Internet initiated an "information revolution," which both expanded and challenged the power of corporate-sponsored consumer culture.

Today, more than half a century after the end of World War II, Americans are living in an increasingly interwoven network of national and international forces. Outside events shape ordinary lives in ways that were inconceivable a century ago. As the Cold War era fades into history, the United States remains the sole military superpower, but it shares economic leadership in the new interdependent global system.

Cold War America,
1945–1960

WHEN HARRY TRUMAN arrived at the White House on April 12, 1945, after learning of Franklin D. Roosevelt's death, he asked the president's widow, "Is there anything I can do for you?" Eleanor Roosevelt responded, "Is there anything we can do for you? For you are the one in trouble now."

Truman inherited the presidency at a perilous time in modern American history. World War II had profoundly disrupted the global balance of power, leaving the United States and the Union of Soviet Socialist Republic (USSR) as the two most powerful nations. Each quickly moved to reshape the postwar world to serve its own national interests. Because the Soviet peoples had been victims of German aggression in both world wars, the USSR sought to create a buffer zone of friendly governments in Eastern Europe—a development that also advanced the Soviet agenda of promoting communist revolution. For its part, the Truman administration set out to contain communist influence in the region and to fortify noncommunist governments in Western Europe that shared America's commitment to a free-market system. Soon the two superpowers were locked in the confrontation known as the Cold War—a protracted economic, political, and military conflict that spread from Europe to Asia and around the world. The Cold War continued in the 1950s under the Republican presidency of Dwight Eisenhower, who modified some of Truman's initiatives but did little to ease tensions.

The Soviet-American conflict of the postwar years had important domestic repercussions for the United States. As World War II drew to a close, Americans

The Perils of the Cold War
In this detail of a 1948 Pulitzer Prize–winning cartoon, Rube Goldberg depicts the perilous nature of America's postwar peace—one that was based largely on atomic supremacy and the threat of nuclear annihilation.
University of California at Berkeley, Bancroft Library.

Postwar Devastation, 1945
Cologne, Germany, was one of many European cities reduced to rubble during World War II. Here one of the 120,000 remaining inhabitants of Cologne (from a prewar population of 780,000) sits homeless with all of her belongings amid the ruins of this once beautiful and prosperous city. United States policy makers worried that physical devastation and economic disorder would make many areas of Europe vulnerable to communist influence.
Johnny Florea, LIFE Magazine, © 1945 Time, Inc.

looked forward to reducing foreign and military spending, and many Republicans called for a return to prewar isolationism. But as U.S.-Soviet tensions escalated, Cold War policies boosted military expenditures and fueled an arms race. The Cold War also fostered a climate of fear and suspicion that led to a hunt for "subversives" in government, education, and the media. But the economic benefits of international involvement also gave rise to a period of unprecedented affluence and prosperity. That prosperity helped to underwrite a continuation and, in some cases, an expansion of federal power, perpetuating the New Deal in the postwar era.

The Early Cold War

---★---

When World War II ended, many parts of the world lay devastated. Fifty million people had perished in the conflict, and tens of millions were left homeless. Six years of war unsettled the international system by creating power vacuums in Germany, Japan, and other occupied countries, devastating Western Europe, and dissolving colonial empires. Even before the war ended, the United States and the Soviet Union were struggling for advantage in those unstable areas; after the war they engaged in a protracted global conflict. Hailed as

a battle between communism and capitalism, the Cold War was in reality a more complex struggle over a broad range of ideological, economic, and strategic issues. As each side tried to protect its own national security and way of life, its actions aroused fear in the other, fueling a cycle of distrust and animosity that would shape U.S.-Soviet relations for the next four decades.

Sources of Conflict

Despite 400,000 American casualties, the United States emerged from the war as the world's strongest, wealthiest nation. Unscathed by bombing, U.S. industry and agriculture had grown rapidly during the war, making America the world's leading manufacturer and exporter. The nation's gross national product soared, growing by 1945 to three times that of the Soviet Union, its nearest competitor. The United States also wielded enormous military power. American air and naval forces were the world's best, and the United States alone possessed the atomic bomb. In the postwar era U.S. policy makers tried to maintain that supremacy and rebuild the world in America's image.

The Soviet Union, in comparison, was relatively weak. Sustaining the greatest casualties of any nation, the USSR lost more than 20 million people—or one-ninth of its total population—as a result of the war. The Soviet economy was devastated; more than 30,000 industrial plants had been destroyed, and the nation's agricultural output fell to half of what it had been in 1940. The Soviet Union's greatest asset was its army, including a vast force of troops occupying Eastern Europe and parts of Germany at the end of the war. Although the USSR hoped to preserve its influence in these areas, its dominance did not extend beyond the region.

The Soviet regional presence in Eastern Europe, however, raised serious concerns among U.S. policy makers, who feared the spread of communism across the European continent. With the defeat and dismantling of the Nazi government, American leaders worried that Soviet influence would expand across postwar Germany. Elsewhere in Europe economic chaos threatened to disrupt the political status quo, as did the growing popularity of communist and labor-led parties in Britain, Czechoslovakia, France, Greece, Italy, and Sweden. Although those parties generally remained independent of Moscow, American policy makers viewed them as sympathetic to Soviet initiatives and therefore as potential tools of the Kremlin. American security, those policy makers argued, required a strong, noncommunist Europe that could serve as a military and economic partner of the United States.

Political instability also characterized the "Third World," where World War II hastened the disintegration of colonial empires. Rising nationalist movements in developing regions and financial pressures on war-torn European countries after 1945 led to a severing of colonial ties and client-state relationships. American-Soviet rivalry for these areas was keen, for they provided essential markets for finished goods and had vital resources such as oil, tin, zinc, and manganese. In an air-age world where national defense stretched far beyond domestic borders, Third World nations also offered strategic sites for U.S. and Soviet military bases. The struggle for these economic and strategic benefits sparked a series of conflicts in Asia, the Middle East, and other regions.

Finally, the end of World War II marked the beginning of the nuclear age and the rise of atomic diplomacy. In 1945 the United States had sole possession of the atomic bomb and held it, as Secretary of War Henry Stimson explained, "rather ostentatiously on our hip." Emboldened by that monopoly, President Harry Truman decided to "get tough" with the Russians, a stance matched with equally stubborn resistance by the Soviet leader, Joseph Stalin. Both sides were inflexible in their demands and remained suspicious of each other's motives and actions. Stalin and Truman came to dislike each other so much that they refused to meet after the war. From 1945 to 1955, some of the most

tense years of the Cold War, there were no summit meetings between Soviet and American heads of state. In this climate of mutual distrust, negotiation or compromise became virtually impossible.

Descent into Cold War, 1945–1946

During the war Franklin Roosevelt had worked effectively with Stalin, and he had intended to continue good relations with the Soviet Union in peacetime. In particular, he hoped that the United Nations would provide a forum for resolving postwar conflicts. Avoiding the disagreements that had doomed American membership in the League of Nations after World War I, the Senate approved America's participation in the United Nations in December 1945. A marked departure from earlier isolationist sentiment, the vote was a firm acknowledgment of the importance of American leadership in global affairs as well as a memorial to the late president's hopes for postwar peace.

Shortly before his death, however, Roosevelt had been disturbed by Soviet actions in Eastern Europe. As the Soviet army drove the Germans out of Russia and back through Eastern Europe, the USSR sponsored provisional governments in Poland, Romania, Hungary, and Bulgaria. At the Yalta Conference in February both America and Britain had agreed to recognize this Soviet "sphere of influence" with the condition that "free and unfettered elections" would be held as soon as possible. But in succeeding months the Soviets made no move to hold elections and rebuffed Western attempts to reorganize Soviet-installed governments.

When Truman assumed the presidency after Roosevelt's death, he quickly took a belligerent stance toward the Soviet Union. Recalling Britain's disastrous appeasement of Hitler in 1938, Truman decided that the United States had to stand up to the Soviet dictator. At a meeting a week after he took office, the new president berated the Soviet foreign minister, V. M. Molotov, for not honoring agreements on Poland. Truman used what he called "tough methods" again in July at the 1945 Potsdam Conference, which brought together the United States, Britain, and the Soviet Union. After learning of the successful test of America's atom bomb, Truman "told the Russians just where they got off and generally bossed the whole meeting," recalled British prime minister Winston Churchill. Negotiations on critical postwar issues deadlocked, revealing serious cracks in the Grand Alliance.

Policies governing the fate of occupied Germany were the only points of agreement between the United States and the Soviet Union at Potsdam. At Yalta the defeated German state had been divided into four occupation zones controlled by the United States, France, Britain, and the Soviet Union. At Potsdam the

Allies agreed to disarm the country, dismantle its military production facilities, and permit the occupying powers to extract reparations from the zones they controlled. Plans for future reunification stalled, however, as the United States and the Soviet Union each worried that a reunited German state would fall into the other's sphere. The economic base was thus laid for what would become the political division into East and West Germany four years later.

In March 1946 Winston Churchill issued an ominous warning to Americans about the deepening divide between Eastern and Western Europe. At the invitation of President Truman, Churchill delivered a major policy address in Fulton, Missouri. At Yalta, Churchill had gone along with plans for a Soviet sphere of influence in Eastern Europe, but now, out of office, he denounced the "expansive tendencies" of the Soviet Union: "From Stettin in the Baltic to Trieste in the Adriatic, an Iron Curtain has descended across the Continent." The former prime minister's widely publicized "Iron Curtain" speech helped convince many Americans that the Soviet Union posed a serious threat to national security.

As tensions over Europe divided the former allies, hopes of international cooperation in the control of atomic weapons also faded. In a plan that Truman's arms negotiator Bernard Baruch submitted to the United Nations in 1946, the United States proposed a system of international control that relied on manda-

The "Iron Curtain" Speech
At the invitation of President Truman, former British prime minister Winston Churchill delivered a historic address in Fulton, Missouri, on March 9, 1946, in which he warned Americans of the growing threat of Soviet expansion in Europe. It was during this speech that Churchill coined the expression "Iron Curtain," a metaphor that eerily foreshadowed the Soviet order in 1961 to build the Berlin Wall, dividing the Allied and Soviet sections of the city.
Winston Churchill Memorial and Library.

tory inspection and supervision but preserved the American nuclear monopoly. The Soviets rejected the plan and concentrated efforts to complete their own bomb. The Truman administration likewise pursued its plans to develop more advanced nuclear energy and weapons systems. The failure of the Baruch Plan signaled the beginning of a frenzied nuclear arms race between the two superpowers.

Containing Communism

As tensions mounted between the superpowers, a new American policy, called *containment*, began to take shape. The most articulate and influential expression of the policy in 1946 and 1947 came from George F. Kennan, a scholarly diplomat who had devoted his career to studying the Soviet Union (see American Lives, "George F. Kennan: Architect of Containment," pp. 872–873). According to Kennan, the Soviets were moving "inexorably along the prescribed path, like a persistent toy automobile wound up and headed in a given direction, stopping only when it meets unanswerable force." To stop Soviet expansionism, Kennan argued, the United States should pursue a policy of "firm containment . . . at every point where [the Soviets] show signs of encroaching upon the interests of a peaceful and stable world."

Kennan's initial formulation recommended economic and diplomatic means to enforce containment, but the policy soon took on a military cast. In one version or another containment defined the foreign policy of every subsequent administration, both Democratic and Republican, well into the 1980s. In addition to the effort to stop the spread of communism, the containment doctrine served at least three other purposes: it provided a rallying cry for Americans of both parties to unite in fighting the Soviet threat; it justified the creation of a vast peacetime military machine; and it obscured other objectives of American foreign policy in the economic arena and the Third World.

The Truman Doctrine and the National Security Act. The emerging containment policy crystallized in 1947 over a crisis in Greece. In the spring of 1946, several thousand local communist guerrillas, who American advisors mistakenly believed were controlled by Moscow, launched a full-scale civil war against the government and the British occupation authorities. In February 1947 the British informed Truman that they could no longer afford to assist the Greek anticommunists. U.S. policy makers worried that Soviet influence in Greece threatened American and European interests in the eastern Mediterranean and the Middle East, especially in strategically located Turkey and the oil-rich state of Iran.

In response, the president announced what became known as the Truman Doctrine. In a speech to

Congress on March 12 he requested large-scale military and economic assistance to Greece and Turkey and called for all Americans "to support free peoples who are resisting attempted subjugation by armed minorities or by outside pressures." To win popular support for the global fight against communism, and to squeeze money out of a Congress committed to reducing military spending, the president followed the advice of Republican senator Arthur Vandenberg. Chair of the Senate Foreign Relations Committee and a former isolationist, Vandenberg advised Truman to "scare hell" out of the American people—advice that the president apparently took to heart. If Greece fell to communism, Truman warned, the effects would be serious not only for Turkey but for the entire Middle East and even the world. Not just Greece but freedom itself was at issue, Truman declared: "If we falter in our leadership, we may endanger the peace of the world—and we shall surely endanger the welfare of our own nation." Despite the open-endedness of this military commitment, Congress quickly approved Truman's request for $300 million in aid to Greece and $100 million for Turkey. The appropriation reversed the postwar policy of sharp cuts in foreign spending and marked a new level of commitment to the emerging Cold War.

The Truman administration also worked with Congress to pass the National Security Act, which was designed to strengthen and streamline defense operations. Signed in July 1947, the act created three new bodies: a single Department of Defense to replace the previous Departments of War and the Navy; the National Security Council (NSC), an advisory body charged with helping the president set defense and military priorities; and the Central Intelligence Agency (CIA), a national intelligence-gathering operation that replaced the wartime Office of Strategic Services. The Atomic Energy Commission, established in 1946 under the executive branch, worked with the new agencies in the development of atomic energy and weapons. The establishment of these new bureaucratic structures marked the emergence of the national security state, a collection of powerful and highly secretive operations in the executive branch. Such structures accelerated the shift of policy-making initiative to the White House.

The Marshall Plan. As the president was promoting the Truman Doctrine, other members of his administration were busy devising the Marshall Plan, which Truman called "the other half of the walnut." A program of large-scale economic and military aid to Europe, the Marshall Plan—or European Recovery Program—was designed to complement the aggressive containment policy of the Truman Doctrine. Speaking at Harvard University's commencement in June 1947, Secretary of State George Marshall urged the nations

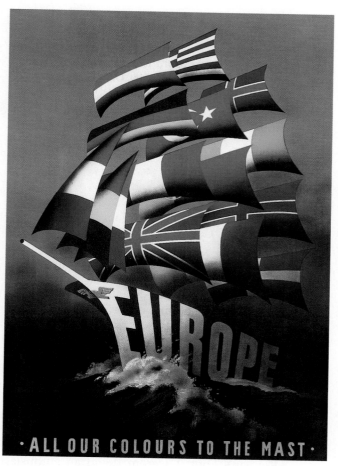

Charting a New Course for Europe with the Marshall Plan
Between 1948 and 1951 the European Recovery Program—popularly known as the Marshall Plan, after Secretary of State George C. Marshall—contributed over $12 billion toward its objective of "restoring the confidence of the European people in the economic future of their own countries and of Europe as a whole." This poster, targeted at Great Britain, stresses European cooperation in the rebuilding effort.
Courtesy Marshall Foundation.

of Europe to work out a comprehensive recovery program and then ask the United States for aid. By bolstering European economies devastated by the war, the United States could forestall the severe economic dislocation that might encourage the spread of communism. American economic self-interest was also a contributing factor—the legislation required that foreign aid dollars be spent on U.S. goods and services. A revitalized Europe centered on a strong West German economy would also provide a better market for American products.

Within Congress, however, there was significant opposition to Truman's pledge of economic aid to European economies. Isolationist Republicans attacked the Marshall Plan as a huge "international W.P.A." and a

George F. Kennan: Architect of Containment

———————★———————

O N FEBRUARY 22, 1946, A diplomatic advisor named George Kennan dictated an 8,000-word telegram from the U.S. embassy in Moscow. Responding to a Department of State request for an assessment of Soviet foreign policy, Kennan described the USSR as an insecure state intent on expansion, subversion, and the export of communist revolution. It was, he argued, "a political force committed fanatically to the belief that with the U.S. there can be no permanent modus vivendi." A preliminary blueprint of the containment theory, this "Long Telegram" was a confidential communiqué to President Harry Truman and Secretary of State James Byrnes. Within weeks, however, it became required reading for hundreds of U.S. military and diplomatic personnel around the world.

Kennan's Long Telegram found an enthusiastic audience among Washington policy makers who were eager to redefine U.S.-Soviet relations in the early postwar period. Its alarmist language helped convince the Truman administration to take a harder line against the Soviet Union and provided the ideological foundations for the emerging Cold War. Summoned back to Washington a few months later, Kennan became one of the most influential advisors in the Truman administration. Writing and lecturing continuously for the next forty years, he would also become one of the foremost foreign policy theorists of the twentieth century.

Kennan's containment theory was shaped by his many years of experience in the diplomatic corps. Born in Milwaukee in 1904, Kennan graduated from Princeton University in 1925 and entered the foreign service the following year. After holding minor positions in Switzerland and Germany, he was offered training as a Soviet specialist in 1929. Under the tutelage of anticommunist Russian émigrés in Berlin, Kennan studied Russian history, language, and literature and later served as a Soviet expert at the U.S. embassy in Latvia. In 1933, when Franklin Roosevelt initiated diplomatic relations with the Soviet Union, Kennan helped open the new U.S. embassy in Moscow and joined the embassy staff. During his four years in the USSR, he witnessed the horrors of the Stalinist purges, an experience that fueled his animosity toward the Russian leader Joseph Stalin and the Soviet Communist regime. Between 1937 and 1944, Kennan occupied a variety of diplomatic posts in the United States and Europe, none of which truly satisfied him. When the new ambassador to the Soviet Union, Averell Harriman, requested him as an advisor in 1944, he jumped at the opportunity to return to Moscow.

Still deeply antagonistic toward the Soviet Union, Kennan disagreed with Roosevelt's wartime alliance with Stalin and issued a steady stream of anti-Soviet memoranda. During the war, most of these pronouncements fell on deaf years. With the end of the war and the rise of Soviet-American conflict over Poland, however, Harriman and other members of the Truman administration became more receptive to Kennan's views. Widespread praise for his Long Telegram won Kennan an offer to lecture at the National War College in Washington in April 1946. A year later, Secretary of State George Marshall appointed him director of the department's new Policy Planning Staff (PPS), which helped devise the Marshall Plan and other long-range foreign policy initiatives.

While serving as PPS director from 1947 to 1950, Kennan refined his ideas about containment. His best-known articulation of the theory appeared in a July 1947 article in *Foreign Affairs*, which he wrote anonymously as "Mr. X." Kennan's identity, however, was soon revealed, and his views of an antagonistic and deceitful Soviet state won wide currency. Conceding Soviet influence in Eastern Europe, he urged the United States and its allies to contain the Soviet threat through "the adroit and vigilant application of counter-force at a series of constantly shifting geographical and political points." By pursuing such a policy, Kennan speculated, Soviet power could be diminished since it "bears within it the seeds of its own decay."

As Kennan himself would later admit, his formulation of containment was ambiguous and imprecise. His use of the term *force* was vague; he failed to specify whether the United States should use political, economic, or military force to contain the Soviets. Nor did he place any geographical limits on Ameri-

With the election of Republican Dwight D. Eisenhower in 1952, Kennan's influence in Washington was further diminished. Eisenhower's secretary of state, the staunchly conservative John Foster Dulles, condemned containment as immoral and denounced Kennan for his "appeasement" of the Soviets in Eastern Europe. Kennan briefly returned to the diplomatic corps in 1961 as ambassador to Yugoslavia under President John F. Kennedy. Two years later, however, Congress revoked that country's most-favored-nation trading status, undermining Kennan's work and prompting his permanent retirement from government service.

As Kennan's diplomatic career waned, he became a renowned historian and theorist of American foreign relations. Working from his office at the Institute for Advanced Studies, he produced dozens of books and articles, including two Pulitzer Prize–winning works, *Russia Leaves the War* (1950) and his often-quoted *Memoirs* (1967). His popular historical text *American Diplomacy, 1900–1950* (1951) introduced millions of Americans to the "realist" critique of foreign policy—an approach that stresses national interests and power politics over the idealistic motives of both conservatives and liberals.

On numerous occasions, Kennan aired his realist views of controversial Cold War developments. During the 1950s he condemned McCarthyism and advocated Soviet and U.S. disengagement from Europe. Later he became an outspoken opponent of the Vietnam War, testifying before the Senate Foreign Relations Committee in 1966 that the containment doctrine was poorly suited to Indochina. Opposing moralistic foreign policy, he criticized Jimmy Carter's preoccupation with human rights in the 1970s and Ronald Reagan's dramatic arms buildup and anti-Soviet pronouncements in the 1980s. As an outspoken critic of the nuclear arms race, he called for "no first use" of nuclear weapons in 1984 and pressed for comprehensive arms control agreements.

The demise of the Soviet Union in 1991 seemed to fulfill Kennan's prophecy in the 1947 article and brought him renewed public attention. But historians continue to debate the usefulness of containment in ending the Cold War. During his long career, Kennan himself served as both chief architect and key critic of containment. His evolving views highlight the complexities and perils of Cold War policy making in the late twentieth century.

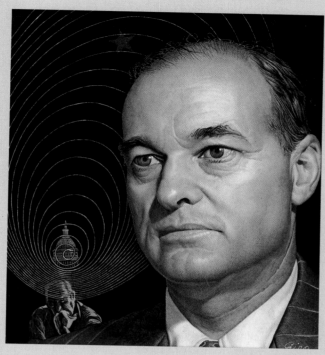

George F. Kennan

As a diplomat, foreign policy theorist, and historian, George F. Kennan has enjoyed a long and distinguished career spanning more than 70 years. This portrait by Guy Rowe dates from 1955.

National Portrait Gallery, Smithsonian Institution/Art Resource, NY.

can intervention. Although Kennan later claimed that containment was primarily a political/economic strategy intended to protect the world's key industrial areas, the ambiguity of the 1947 article invited American policy makers to interpret containment in the broadest possible fashion.

By 1950 Truman's increasingly hard-line approach toward the Soviet Union had alienated Kennan. He criticized the open-ended commitment of the Truman Doctrine, the militarization of containment under NSC-68, and the division of Europe under the NATO treaty. Increasingly marginalized by the new secretary of state, Dean Acheson, Kennan took a leave of absence to attend the Institute for Advanced Study at Princeton University. In 1952 he returned to the administration to serve as ambassador to the Soviet Union; within months, however, he was forced to resign after making disparaging remarks comparing Stalin's regime to Nazism.

JEAN MONNET

Truman's Generous Proposal

————— ★ —————

Jean Monnet was an eminent French statesman and a tireless promoter of postwar European union. As head of a French postwar planning commission, he helped oversee the dispersal of Marshall Plan funds, the importance of which he described in his memoirs.

So we had at last concerted our efforts to halt France's economic decline; but now, once more, everything seemed to be at risk. Two years earlier [1947], we thought that we had plumbed the depths of material poverty. Now we were threatened with the loss of even basic essentials. . . . Our dollar resources were melting away at an alarming rate, because we were having to buy American wheat to replace the crops we had lost during the winter. This alone cost us $200m. instead of the $30m. we had expected to pay. In addition, we had to increase our coal imports at a time when prices had risen in the United States. In June, we met the cost with gold bullion from the Bank of France; in August, we cut off inessential imports. A further American loan was soon exhausted.

Nor was this grim situation confined to France. Britain too had come to the end of her resources. In February 1947 she had abruptly cancelled her aid to Greece and Turkey, whose burdens she had seemed able to assume in 1945. Overnight, this abrupt abdication gave the United States direct responsibility for part of Europe. Truman did not hesitate for a moment: with the decisiveness that was to mark his actions as President, he at once asked for credits and arms for both Turkey and Greece. . . . [Soon after], he announced the Truman Doctrine of March 12, 1947. Its significance was general: it meant that the United States would prevent Europe from becoming a depressed area at the mercy of Communist advance. On the very same day, the Four-Power Conference began in Moscow. There, for a whole month, George Marshall, Ernest Bevin, and Georges Bidault argued with Vyacheslav Molotov about all the problems of the peace, and above all about Germany.

When Marshall returned to Washington, he knew that for a long time there would be no further genuine dialogue with Stalin's Russia. The 'cold war', as it was soon to be known, had begun. . . . Information from a number of sources convinced Marshall and his Under-Secretary Dean Acheson that once again, as in 1941, the United States had a great historic duty. And once again there took place what I had witnessed in Washington a few years earlier: a small group of men brought to rapid maturity an idea which, when the Executive gave the word, turned into vigorous action. This time, it was done by five or six people, in total secrecy and at lightning speed. Marshall, Acheson, Clayton, Averell Harriman, and George Kennan worked out a proposal of unprecedented scope and generosity. It took us all by surprise when we read the speech that George Marshall made at Harvard on June 5, 1947. Chance had led him to choose the University's Commencement Day to launch something new in international relations: helping others to help themselves.

Source: Jean Monnet, *Memoirs*, trans. Richard Mayne (New York: Doubleday, 1978), 264–266.

"bold Socialist blue-print." But in the midst of this congressional stalemate, the Soviets staged a brutal coup in Czechoslovakia, one of the few Eastern European countries to have held free elections after the war and elected a coalition government that was widely admired in the West. When the Communists seized control of the country on February 25, 1948, and installed a new government, Congress rallied in support of the Marshall Plan. In March both houses voted overwhelmingly to approve funds for the program.

Historian Thomas J. McCormick calls the Marshall Plan "arguably the most innovative piece of foreign policy in American history." Over the next four years the United States contributed over $12 billion to a highly successful recovery effort (see Voices from Abroad, "Jean Monnet: Truman's Generous Proposal," above).

The Berlin Airlift
For 321 days American planes like this one flew 272,000 missions to bring food and other supplies to Berlin after the Soviet Union had blocked all surface routes into the former German capital. The blockade was finally lifted on May 12, 1949, after the Soviets conceded that it had been a failure.
Wide World Photos, Inc.

Western European economies revived and industrial production increased 64 percent, opening new areas for international trade. The Marshall Plan did not specifically exclude Eastern Europe or the Soviet Union, but it required that all participating nations exchange economic information and work toward the elimination of tariffs and other trade barriers. Soviet leaders denounced those conditions as attempts to draw Eastern Europe into the American orbit and forbade their satellite states of Czechoslovakia, Poland, and Hungary to participate.

The Berlin Airlift and the Creation of NATO. The Marshall Plan accelerated American and European efforts to rebuild and reunify the West German economy. In June 1948, after agreeing to fuse their zones of occupation, the United States, France, and Britain began a currency reform program in West Berlin. The economic revitalization of West Berlin, located deep within the Soviet zone of occupation (see Map 27.1), alarmed Soviet policy makers, who feared a resurgent Germany aligned with the West. To forestall that development, the Soviet Union imposed a blockade on all highway, rail, and river traffic to West Berlin. Truman responded with an airlift. For nearly a year American and British pilots, who had been dropping bombs on Berlin only four years earlier, flew in 2.5 million tons of food and fuel, nearly a ton for each West Berlin resident. On May 12, 1949, Stalin lifted the blockade, which by then had made the city a symbol of resistance to communism.

The coup in Czechoslovakia and the crisis in Berlin convinced U.S. policy makers of the need for a collective security pact. In April 1949, for the first time since the American Revolution, the United States entered into a peacetime military alliance, the North Atlantic Treaty Organization (NATO). To back up America's new stance, Truman asked Congress for $1.3 billion in military assistance to NATO and authorized the basing of four U.S. Army divisions in Western Europe. Under the NATO pact, twelve nations—the United States, Canada, Britain, France, Italy, Portugal, Belgium, the Netherlands, Luxembourg, Denmark, Norway, and Iceland—agreed that "an armed attack against one or more of them in Europe or North America shall be considered an attack against them all." In May 1949 those nations also agreed to the creation of the Federal Republic of Germany (West Germany), which joined NATO in 1955.

In response to the creation of NATO, the Soviet Union tightened its grip on Eastern Europe in October 1949 by creating a separate government for East Germany, which became the German Democratic Republic. The Soviets also organized an economic association, the Council for Mutual Economic Assistance (COMECON), in 1949 and a military alliance for Eastern Europe, the Warsaw Pact, in 1955. The postwar division of Europe was nearly complete (Map 27.1).

The "Fall" of China. As mutual suspicion between the United States and the Soviet Union deepened, Cold War doctrines began to influence the American position toward Asia as well. American policy there was

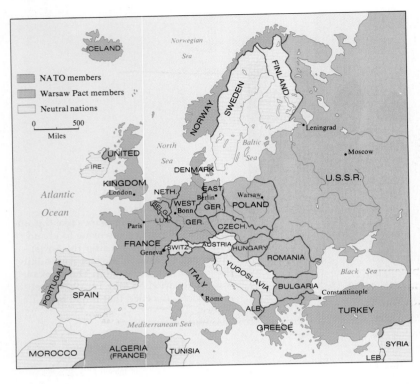

MAP 27.1
Cold War Europe, 1955
In 1949 the United States sponsored the creation of
the North Atlantic Treaty Organization—an alliance
of ten European nations, the United States, and
Canada. West Germany was formally admitted to
NATO in May 1955. A few days later the Soviet
Union and seven other communist nations estab-
lished a rival alliance, the Warsaw Pact.

based on Asia's importance in the world economy as
much as on the desire to contain communism. At first,
American plans for the region centered on a revitalized
China, but political instability there prompted the
Truman administration to focus instead on developing
the Japanese economy. After dismantling Japan's military forces and weaponry, American occupation forces
under General Douglas MacArthur began the job of
transforming Japan into a bulwark of Asian capitalism.
MacArthur drafted a democratic constitution and oversaw the rebuilding of the economy, paving the way for
the restoration of Japanese sovereignty in 1951.

In China the situation was more precarious. Since
the 1930s a civil war had been raging as Communist
forces led by Mao Zedong (Mao Tse-tung) and Zhou
Enlai (Chou En-lai) contended for power with conservative nationalist forces under Jiang Jieshi (Chiang
Kai-shek). Although dissatisfied with the corrupt and
inefficient Jiang regime, the Truman administration
saw it as the only alternative to Mao and resigned itself
to working with the nationalists. Between 1945 and
1949 the United States provided more than $2 billion to
Jiang's forces, but to no avail. In 1947, Truman's key
military advisor in China insisted that the nationalist
government undertake "drastic political and economic
reforms" in order to win the struggle against the Communists. When those reforms did not occur, the
Truman administration cut off aid to the Nationalists in

August 1949, sealing their fate. The People's Republic of
China was formally established on October 1, 1949, and
what was left of Jiang's government fled to the island of
Formosa (Taiwan).

Although nothing less than a massive U.S. military
commitment could have stopped the Chinese Communists, many Americans viewed Mao's success as a
defeat for the United States. Republican statesman
John Foster Dulles, who would become secretary of
state in the Eisenhower administration, assailed the
communist victory in China as "the worst defeat the
United States has suffered in its history." A pro-
nationalist "China lobby," led by the powerful publisher Henry R. Luce (born in China to missionary
parents) and Republican senators Karl Mundt of
South Dakota and William S. Knowland of California,
protested that the Department of State under the leadership of Truman's newly appointed secretary of state,
Dean Acheson, was responsible for the "fall of China."
As a result of pressure from the China lobby, most
Department of State experts on East Asia were forced
to resign. The loss of those experts created a critical
knowledge gap that would handicap the United States
for decades in dealing with Vietnam and other Asian
trouble spots.

Although the Chinese Communists remained independent of Moscow, the United States refused to recognize what it called "Red China," instead giving

diplomatic recognition to the exiled Nationalist government in Taiwan. The United States also used its influence to block China's admission to the United Nations. For almost twenty years, U.S. administrations treated the People's Republic of China, the world's most populous country, as a diplomatic nonentity.

Containment Militarized: NSC-68. New impetus for the policy of containment came in September 1949, when American military intelligence detected a rise in radioactivity in the atmosphere—proof that the Soviet Union had detonated an atomic bomb. The American atomic monopoly, which some military and political advisors had argued would last for decades, ended in only four years, forcing a major reassessment of the nation's foreign policy.

To devise a new diplomatic and military blueprint, Truman turned to the National Security Council. In April 1950 it delivered its report, known as NSC-68, to the president. Expressing alarm over the Soviet threat, the writers of the document made several specific recommendations, including the development of a hydrogen bomb, an advanced weapon that was a thousand times more destructive than the atomic bombs that had destroyed Hiroshima and Nagasaki. NSC-68 also supported increases in U.S. conventional forces and a strong system of alliances—reflections of the increasing militarization of the Cold War. Most important, it called for a tax hike to finance "a bold and massive program of rebuilding the West's defensive potential to surpass that of the Soviet world."

NSC-68 called for defense budgets totaling up to 20 percent of the gross national product, four times their level at that time. Now that the U.S. atomic monopoly had been broken, Truman's advisors also looked to build up conventional military forces to maintain American superiority. Truman, however, was reluctant to commit to a major defense buildup, fearing that it would overburden the budget. But the Korean War, which began just two months after NSC-68 was completed, helped transform the report's recommendations into reality.

The Cold War Heats Up: The Korean War

Although Truman acknowledged that communist success in China raised urgent questions for American foreign policy, he recognized the limits of American power in Asia. In December 1949 Secretary of State Dean Acheson clarified American policy. The United States, he said, would help Asian nations realize their aspirations but would consider itself bound to protect only a "defensive perimeter" extending from the Aleutian Islands in Alaska to Japan, the Ryukyus (a chain of

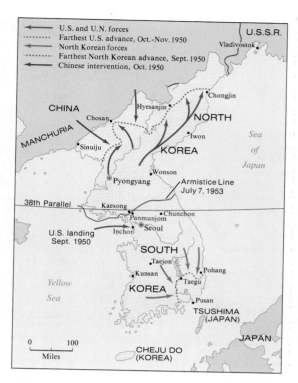

MAP 27.2
The Korean War, 1950–1953
The first months of the Korean War featured dramatic shifts in control up and down the 600-mile peninsula. From June to September 1950 North Korean troops overran most of the territory south of the 38th parallel. On September 15, U.N. forces under General Douglas MacArthur counterattacked behind enemy lines at Inchon and pushed north almost to the Chinese border. Massive Chinese intervention forced the U.N. troops to retreat to the 38th parallel in January 1951, and the war was a stalemate for the next two years.

small islands stretching from Japan to Taiwan), and the Philippines (a former American protectorate that had won its independence from the United States in 1946). If an attack occurred outside that perimeter—in Korea, Taiwan, or Southeast Asia, for example—"the initial reliance must be on the people attacked to resolve it and then upon . . . the United Nations."

A test of the new policy came quickly in Korea, a country whose artificial division after World War II contained the seeds for later conflict. Both the United States and the Soviet Union had troops in Korea at the end of the war, and neither side was willing to abandon its occupied territories. As a result, Korea was divided at the 38th parallel into competing spheres of influence (Map 27.2). The Soviets supported a communist government, led by Kim Il Sung, in North Korea; the United States backed Syngman Rhee, a longtime Korean nationalist, in South Korea. Soon sporadic fighting between North and South Koreans broke out along the 38th parallel, and a civil war began.

The Korean War
These men of the Second Infantry battalion, shown here in Korea in 1950, helped pave
the way for the formal integration of all U.S. Army units by 1954. The Korean War
marked the first time in the nation's history that all troops served in racially integrated
combat units.
National Archives.

On June 25, 1950, the North Koreans launched a surprise attack across the 38th parallel. The initiative for
Korean reunification came from Kim Il Sung, but Stalin
approved of the mission. Soviet and North Korean leaders may have expected Truman to ignore this armed challenge, but the president immediately asked the United
Nations Security Council to authorize a "police action"
against the invaders. Because the Soviet Union was temporarily boycotting the Security Council to protest the
exclusion of the People's Republic of China from the
United Nations, it could not veto Truman's request. Three
days after the Security Council voted to send a peacekeeping force, Truman ordered U.S. troops to Korea.

The American intervention in Korea revealed the
extent to which foreign policy formulation had been
transferred from Congress to the president. When isolationist Republican senator Robert A. Taft of Ohio argued
that the president should have obtained congressional
approval before committing American troops to Korea,
Truman boldly insisted that he already had the power he
needed as commander in chief of the armed forces and
executor of the treaty binding the United States to the
United Nations. The Truman administration enjoyed
widespread popular support for this action: in a July
1950 poll, 77 percent of the respondents approved of
U.S. intervention. The Korean conflict—the first Ameri-

can combat effort to implement containment—thus
became the first major American war undertaken without a formal declaration of war by Congress.

Fighting the War. Although fourteen other noncommunist members of the United Nations sent troops, the
rapidly assembled United Nations army in Korea was
overwhelmingly American. At the request of the Security Council, President Truman named General Douglas
MacArthur, hero of the American victory in the Pacific
and head of the postwar occupation of Japan, to lead
the U.N. forces. At first the North Koreans held an overwhelming advantage, controlling practically the entire
peninsula except the area around Pusan. But on September 15, 1950, MacArthur launched a surprise
amphibious attack at Inchon, far behind the North
Korean front line, while U.N. forces staged a breakout
from Pusan. Within two weeks the U.N. forces controlled Seoul, the South Korean capital, and almost all
the territory up to the 38th parallel (see Map 27.2).

Encouraged by this success, MacArthur sought the
authority to lead his forces across the 38th parallel into
North Korea. Truman's original plan had been to restore
the 1945 border, but he managed to win U.N. support for
the broader goal of creating "a unified, independent and
democratic Korea." Although the Chinese government in

Beijing warned repeatedly that such a move would provoke its retaliation, American officials dismissed the warnings as a bluff. MacArthur's troops crossed the 38th parallel on October 9, reaching the Chinese border at the Yalu River by the end of the month. Just after Thanksgiving, a massive Chinese counterattack of almost 300,000 troops forced a retreat to the 38th parallel. On January 4, 1951, Communist troops reoccupied Seoul.

Two months later the American forces and their allies counterattacked, regained Seoul, and pushed back to the 38th parallel. Then stalemate set in. Public support for U.S. involvement dropped after Chinese intervention increased the likelihood of a long war. According to one poll in early January 1951, 66 percent of Americans thought the United States should withdraw, and 49 percent believed it was a mistake to have intervened at all. Given those domestic and international constraints, Truman and his advisors decided to work for a negotiated peace. They did not want to tie down large numbers of U.S. troops in Asia, far from what they considered more strategically important trouble spots in Europe and the Middle East. If the Korean War had become a larger war with China, General Omar N. Bradley, chairman of the Joint Chiefs of Staff, reasoned, it would have been "the wrong war, at the wrong place, at the wrong time, with the wrong enemy."

The Fate of Douglas MacArthur. MacArthur disagreed. Headstrong, arrogant, and brilliant, the general fervently believed that the nation's future opportunities lay in Asia, not in Europe. Disregarding Truman's instructions, MacArthur traveled to Taiwan and urged the nationalists to join in an attack on mainland China. He pleaded for U.S. permission to use the atomic bomb against targets in China. In an inflammatory letter to the House minority leader, the Republican Joseph J. Martin of Massachusetts, he denounced the Korean stalemate. "We must win," MacArthur declared. "There is no substitute for victory."

Martin released MacArthur's letter on April 6, 1951, as part of a concerted Republican campaign to challenge Truman's conduct of the war. The strategy backfired. On April 11 Truman relieved MacArthur of his command in Korea and Japan, accusing him of insubordination—a decision the Joint Chiefs of Staff supported. Truman's decision was nonetheless highly unpopular. The allure of decisive victory under a charismatic military leader temporarily pushed aside doubts about the war. Returning to tumultuous receptions in San Francisco, Chicago, and New York, MacArthur delivered an impassioned televised address to a joint session of Congress watched by millions of Americans. Although he failed to win the 1952 Republican presidential nomination, which he coveted, MacArthur's determination to roll back (rather than just contain) communist influence remained popular with many Americans.

The Korean War dragged on for more than two years after MacArthur's dismissal. Truce talks began in Korea in July 1951, but a final armistice was not signed until July 1953. Approximately 45 percent of American casualties were sustained in this period. The final settlement left Korea divided very near the original border at the 38th parallel and established a demilitarized zone between the two countries (see Map 27.2). North Korea remained firmly allied with the Soviet Union; South Korea signed a mutual defense treaty with the United States in 1954.

The Impact of the Korean War. The three-year conflict was costly for the United States: 54,200 American soldiers died, 103,000 were wounded, and military expenditures totaled $54 billion. Defense mobilization helped stimulate the American economy but did not foster the patriotic fervor that had characterized World War II. Struggling against heavy snow and subzero cold, American troops in Korea grew to hate the endless fighting that characterized the stalemate. "I'll fight for my country," a corporal from Chicago complained, "but I'm damned if I see why I'm fighting for this hell-hole." When the armistice was signed, there were few public celebrations.

The Korean War had a lasting impact on the conduct of American foreign policy. Truman's decision to commit troops to Korea without congressional approval set a precedent for future undeclared wars. The war also expanded American involvement in Asia, transforming containment into a truly global policy. During and after the war the United States stationed large numbers of troops in South Korea and increased military aid to French forces fighting communist insurgents in Indochina (see Chapter 29). Such commitments were costly. Overall defense expenditures grew from $13 billion in 1950, roughly one-third of the federal budget, to $50 billion in 1953, nearly two-thirds of the budget. Although military expenditures dropped briefly after the Korean War, defense spending remained at over $35 billion annually throughout the 1950s. American foreign policy had become more global, more militarized, and more costly. Even in times of peace, the United States now functioned in a state of permanent mobilization.

Harry Truman and the Cold War at Home

Harry S Truman brought a complex personality to the presidency. Alternately humble and cocky, he had none of Franklin D. Roosevelt's patrician ease and was a distinctly unpopular president. Yet he handled affairs with an assurance and crisp dispatch that have endeared him to later generations. "If you can't stand the heat, stay out of the kitchen," he liked to say of presidential responsibility. The major domestic issues that he faced were reconversion to a peacetime economy and fears of communist infiltration and subversion—fears that his administration played a part in fanning. Truman kept the New Deal coalition alive by proposing new federal programs to advance the interests of its constituencies, and his Fair Deal would influence the Democratic Party's agenda for the next twenty years.

The Challenge of Reconversion

When Truman became president in 1945, Americans welcomed him with an approval rating of 87 percent, according to Gallup polls. Within a year his popularity had dropped to 32 percent, and new phrases such as "To err is Truman" entered the political language. What had happened? New to the presidency, Truman had to oversee the complex conversion of a wartime economy to a peacetime one. In part because government planners had not known about the atomic bomb, they had assumed that reconversion could be phased in while the country went through the process of winning a land war in Japan that was expected to last through 1946. Instead World War II ended before adequate reconversion plans were in place.

The public's main fear in 1945 was that the depression would return once war production ended. To the relief of those who had lived through the hardships of the 1930s, the economy did not collapse. Despite a drop in government spending after the war, consumer spending increased because workers had amassed substantial wartime savings that they were eager to spend once wartime restrictions were lifted. The Servicemen's Readjustment Act of 1944, popularly known as the GI Bill, also put money into the economy by providing educational and economic assistance to returning veterans. Despite some temporary dislocations as war production shifted back to civilian uses and veterans were reabsorbed into the work force, unemployment did not increase significantly. The most visible layoffs involved the "Rosie the Riveters" who had taken high-paying defense jobs during the war and were now forced to find jobs in traditional areas of women's employment at much lower pay.

Economic Policy. But the transition was hardly trouble-free. The main domestic problem was inflation. Consumers wanted an end to wartime restrictions and price rationing, but Truman feared economic chaos if he lifted all controls immediately. In the summer of 1945 he eased industrial controls but retained the wartime Office of Price Administration (OPA). When

the OPA was disbanded and almost all controls were lifted in November 1946, prices soared. That year saw an annual inflation rate of 18.2 percent. The persistent shortages of food and products prompted by unfettered consumer spending also irritated many shoppers.

With the Employment Act of 1946, the federal government began developing mechanisms to pursue a more coherent economic policy. The legislation introduced federal fiscal planning on a permanent basis—not just in times of economic crisis—to achieve full employment. Besides supporting the Keynesian notion of government spending to spur economic growth, the act promoted the use of tax policy as a tool for managing the economy, using tax cuts to spur economic growth and tax increases to slow inflation. Yet the legislation was weak. It merely advocated rather than mandated such planning measures and gave the new three-member Council of Economic Advisors only an advisory role. It also failed to establish clear economic priorities, such as the proper relationship between the commitment to full employment and the need for a balanced budget. Nevertheless, the Employment Act of 1946 was an important milestone in establishing federal responsibility for the performance of the economy.

Postwar Strikes. The rapidly rising cost of living prompted demands for higher wages by the nation's workers. By 1945 the number of union members had swelled to more than 14 million—representing over one-third of the nonagricultural work force and two-thirds of all workers in the mining, manufacturing, construction, and transportation industries. Under government-sanctioned agreements the labor movement had held the line on wages during the war, but unions expressed frustration as postwar corporate profits doubled while real wages declined in the face of increasing inflation and the loss of wartime overtime pay. Determined to make up for their war-induced sacrifices, workers mounted strikes in major sectors of the economy, crippling the automobile, steel, and coal industries. By the end of the year 5 million workers had idled factories and mines for a total of 107,476,000 lost workdays.

Truman never doubted his course of action, even if it meant alienating organized labor, an important component of the Democratic coalition. "If you think I'm going to sit here and let you tie up this whole country, you're crazy as hell," he told the leaders of a nationwide railroad strike in the spring of 1946. Truman used his executive authority to place the nation's railroad system under federal control and asked Congress for the power to draft striking workers into the army, a move that infuriated labor but pressured strikers to go back to work. A few days later, on April 1, 1946, he seized control of the nation's coal mines to end a strike led by John L. Lewis and the United Mine Workers. Such actions won Truman support from Americans fed up with labor disruptions but angered organized labor.

These domestic upheavals did not bode well for the Democrats at the polls. In the 1946 congressional elections Republicans capitalized on popular dissatisfaction with reconversion with the simple slogan "Had enough?" Many voters answered in the affirmative, and the Republicans gained control of both houses of Congress for the first time since 1928. Truman and the Democrats seemed to have been thoroughly repudiated.

The Taft-Hartley Act. The Republican Congress elected in 1946 was determined to trim back several New Deal social welfare measures, and it singled out labor legislation as a special target. In 1947 Congress passed the Taft-Hartley Act, a rollback of several provisions of the 1935 National Labor Relations Act. Unions especially disliked section 14b, which allowed states to pass "right to work" laws that outlawed the *closed shop* (a workplace employing only union labor). The act also restricted the political power of unions by prohibiting the use of their dues for political activity, and it allowed the president to declare an eighty-day cooling-off period in strikes with a national impact. Truman issued a ringing veto of the Taft-Hartley bill in June 1947, calling it "bad for labor, bad for management, and bad for the country." Congress easily overrode the veto, but Truman's action brought labor back into the Democratic fold.

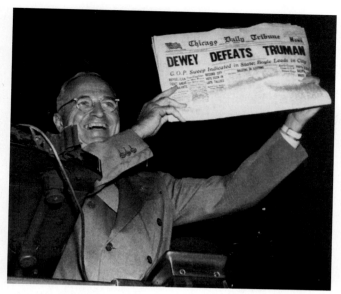

Truman Triumphant
In one of the most famous photographs in American political history, Harry S Truman gloats over an inaccurate headline in the Chicago *Tribune*. Pollsters had predicted an overwhelming victory for Thomas E. Dewey. Their primitive techniques, however, did not reflect the dramatic surge in support for Truman during the last days of the campaign.
Corbis-Bettmann.

The 1948 Election

Most observers believed that Truman faced an impossible task in the presidential campaign of 1948. The Republicans were united and well organized, maintaining the firm support of most white middle- and upper-income Protestant voters outside the South and that of many farmers and skilled workers. Eager to attract votes from traditional Democratic constituencies, the Republicans nominated Thomas E. Dewey, the politically moderate governor of New York who had demonstrated his attractiveness as a national candidate by garnering 46 percent of the popular vote in his 1944 campaign against Roosevelt. To increase their appeal in the West, the Republicans nominated Earl Warren, governor of California, for vice-president. Their brief platform promised to continue most New Deal reforms and supported a bipartisan foreign policy.

Truman, in contrast, led a party in disarray. Both the left and right wings of the Democratic Party split off and nominated their own candidates. Henry A. Wallace, a former New Deal liberal whom Truman had fired as secretary of commerce in 1946 because he was perceived as too "soft" on communism, ran as the candi-

date of the new Progressive Party. Wallace advocated increased government intervention in the economy, more power for labor unions, and cooperation with the Soviet Union.

Southern Democrats bolted the party over the issue of civil rights. At the Democratic national convention, northern liberals such as Mayor Hubert H. Humphrey of Minneapolis and gubernatorial candidate Adlai E. Stevenson of Illinois had pushed through a platform calling for the establishment of a permanent Fair Employment Practices Commission and federal antilynching and anti–poll tax legislation. Southern Democrats, unwilling to tolerate federal interference in race relations, walked out of the convention and created the States' Rights Party, popularly known as the Dixiecrats. They nominated Governor J. Strom Thurmond of South Carolina for president.

Truman responded to these challenges with one of the most effective presidential campaigns ever waged. He dramatically called Congress back into summer session to give the Republicans a chance to enact their platform into law. When they failed to do so, he launched a strenuous cross-country speaking tour, blasting the "do-nothing Republican Congress." He also hammered away at the Republicans' support for the antilabor Taft-Hartley Act and their opposition to legislation on housing, medical insurance, and civil

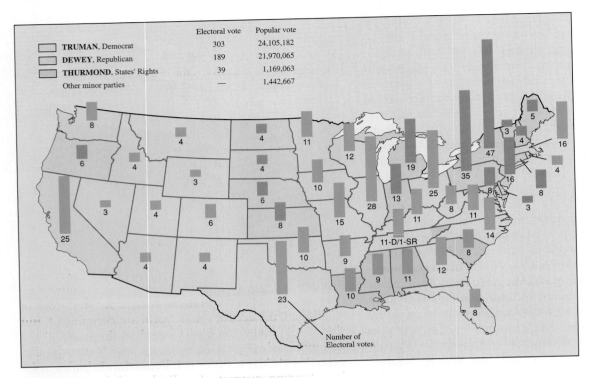

MAP 27.3
The Election of 1948
Political advisor Clark Clifford planned Truman's electoral strategy in 1948, arguing that the president should concentrate his campaign in urban areas where the Democrats had their greatest strength. In an election with a low turnout Truman held onto enough support from the Roosevelt coalition of blacks, union members, and farmers to defeat Dewey by more than 2 million votes.

rights. By combining these domestic themes with attacks on the Soviet menace abroad, Truman revived his troubled campaign. At his rallies enthusiastic listeners took up the cry "Give 'em hell, Harry!"

Truman won a remarkable victory, receiving 49.6 percent of the vote to Dewey's 45.1 percent (Map 27.3). Strom Thurmond carried only four southern states, and Henry Wallace failed to win any electoral votes. The Democrats also regained control of both houses of Congress. Truman retained the support of organized labor and Jewish and Catholic voters in the big cities; the loyalty of northern black voters to the Democratic Party offset southern losses to the Dixiecrats. Most important, Truman appealed effectively to people like himself who hailed from the farms, towns, and small cities in the nation's heartland. He had grasped something the pollsters had missed: "Everybody's against me but the people."

Fair Deal Liberalism

Shortly after becoming president, Truman had proposed to Congress a twenty-one-point plan for expanded federal responsibilities. Anticipating a period of afflu-

ence rather than the austerity that had shaped the New Deal, Truman phrased his proposals in terms of the rights of individual citizens—the right to a "useful and remunerative" job, protection from monopoly, good housing, "adequate medical care," "protection from the economic fears of old age," and a "good education." Later Truman added support for civil rights and called his program the Fair Deal.

Truman's Fair Deal represented the essential aspects of postwar liberalism. Liberals believed in an activist federal government that would use its powers to stimulate economic growth, redress imbalances, and encourage social progress. With a rhetorical commitment to civil rights and economic abundance for all, liberalism called for the modern state to extend the benefits of capitalism to ever greater numbers of citizens. By expanding the welfare state at home while fighting communism abroad, Truman sought to steer a middle course between socialism on the left and fascism on the right. Historian Arthur Schlesinger Jr. dubbed this brand of liberalism "the Vital Center."

Truman's agenda ran up against a generally hostile Congress, despite its Democratic majority. The same conservative coalition that had blocked Roosevelt in his second term and had dismantled or cut popular New Deal programs during wartime continued to fight against Truman's proposals. Only parts of the Fair Deal won adoption: the minimum wage increased from 40 cents to 75 cents an hour, the Social Security system was extended to cover 10 million new workers, and Social Security benefits were raised by 75 percent. The National Housing Act of 1949 called for the construction of 810,000 units of low-income housing, although only half of that number was actually built under the program.

Truman's record on civil rights illustrates the opportunities and obstacles facing proponents of the Fair Deal. Although the struggle for civil rights had preoccupied African Americans since Reconstruction, it took on a new urgency in the 1940s. The callous treatment of black soldiers during World War II and the lynching of more than forty black men after the war—many of them veterans—sparked widespread anger. At the same time, black expectations had been raised by wartime opportunities and by symbolic victories such as Jackie Robinson's joining the Brooklyn Dodgers in 1947, breaking the color line in major league baseball. Truman's sympathies for civil rights were reinforced by the realization that black voters were playing an increasingly large role in the Democratic Party as they migrated from the South, where they were effectively disfranchised, to northern and western cities. Finally, Truman was sensitive to the world's view of America's treatment of blacks, especially since the Soviet Union often compared segregation of southern blacks with the Nazis' treatment of Jews.

Lacking a popular mandate on the civil rights issue, Truman turned to executive action. In 1946 he appointed a National Civil Rights Commission, whose 1947 report called for an expanded federal role that foreshadowed much of the civil rights legislation of the 1960s. He ordered the Justice department to prepare an *amicus curiae* ("friend of the court") brief in the Supreme Court case of *Shelley v. Kraemer* (1948), which struck down as unconstitutional restrictive covenants that enforced residential segregation by barring home buyers on the basis of race or religion. In the same year, Truman signed an executive order desegregating the armed forces. The Truman administration also proposed a federal antilynching law, federal protection of voting rights (such as an end to poll taxes), and a permanent federal agency to guarantee equal employment opportunities. A filibuster by southern conservatives, however, blocked such legislation in Congress.

Interest groups successfully opposed other key items on the Fair Deal agenda. The American Medical Association quashed a labor-backed movement for national health insurance by denouncing it as the first step toward "socialized medicine." Catholic groups successfully opposed legislation for aid to education because it did not include subsidies for parochial schools. Farmers, many of whom relied on unorga-

nized seasonal workers, refused to join labor in supporting repeal of the Taft-Hartley Act.

Two factors further limited the Fair Deal's chances for legislative success. One was the outbreak of the Korean War in 1950, which diverted national attention to foreign affairs. The other was the nation's growing fear of internal subversion. The anticommunist crusade was only one manifestation of the way the Cold War was increasingly permeating all facets of American life. Truman's administration played a significant role in heightening those domestic tensions.

The Great Fear

As American relations with the Soviet Union deteriorated in the late 1940s and early 1950s, fear of communism fueled a widespread campaign of domestic repression. Americans often call this phenomenon "McCarthyism," after Senator Joseph R. McCarthy of Wisconsin, the decade's most vocal anticommunist. But this "Great Fear" involved more than the work of just one man and was shared by many Americans who disagreed with McCarthy's vitriolic tactics. It built on the longstanding distrust of radicals and foreigners that had exploded in the Red Scare after World War I. Worsening Cold War tensions and partisan politics intersected with those deep-seated anxieties to spawn an obsessive concern with internal subversion. Ultimately, few Communists were found in positions of power; far more Americans became innocent victims of false accusations and innuendo. Although anticommunism also flourished in England, France, and other Western European nations, it took a particularly virulent form in the United States, where the term *communist* became synonymous with "un-American."

HUAC. The roots of postwar anticommunism date back to the late 1930s, when Democratic congressman Martin Dies of Texas and other conservatives launched the House Committee on Un-American Activities (HUAC) to investigate alleged fascist and communist subversion in labor unions and New Deal agencies. During America's World War II alliance with the Soviet Union, HUAC's visibility declined, but the committee reemerged after the war as Americans grew concerned over Soviet expansion in Eastern Europe. Revelations in 1946 of a Soviet spy ring operating in Canada and the United States accentuated American fears of Soviet subversion. Republicans in Congress capitalized on these fears, using accusations of communist subversion to discredit the Truman administration.

In 1947 HUAC helped launch the postwar red scare by holding widely publicized hearings on communist infiltration of the film industry. A group of writers and directors, soon dubbed the "Hollywood Ten," went to jail for contempt of Congress when they

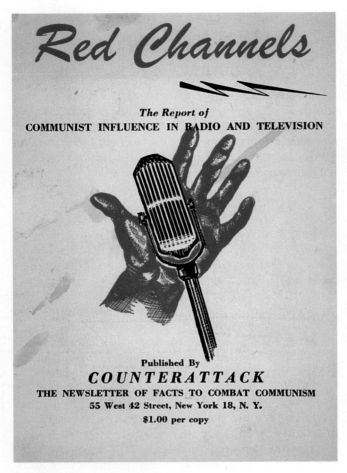

Red Channels

The Report of
COMMUNIST INFLUENCE IN RADIO AND TELEVISION

Published By
COUNTERATTACK
THE NEWSLETTER OF FACTS TO COMBAT COMMUNISM
55 West 42 Street, New York 18, N. Y.
$1.00 per copy

The Red Scare and the Media
After HUAC's 1947 investigation of the film industry, television and radio sponsors became wary of possible communist subversion on the airwaves. In 1950 three former FBI agents employed by a private consulting firm produced *Red Channels*, a booklet identifying 151 allegedly subversive entertainers. *Red Channels* was widely circulated among producers and was one of the key tools of the cultural Cold War.
The Michael Barson Collection/Past Perfect.

cited the First Amendment in refusing to testify about their past associations. Soon afterward former FBI agents in Hollywood circulated a list of actors, directors, and writers whose names had been mentioned in the HUAC investigation or whose associates and friends had been labeled as "reds." Industry executives denied the existence of a blacklist, but for ten years hundreds of people were shut out of work in the entertainment industry (see American Voices, "Mark Goodson Red Hunting on the Quiz Shows; or, What's My Party Line?" p. 885). The Weavers, a popular folk-singing group led by Pete Seeger, were blacklisted, and politically active actors such as Zero Mostel and John Garfield had difficulty finding work. One day the actress Jean Muir headlined the popular radio show

"The Aldrich Family"; the next she was out of a job— fired, according to the network, not because she was a Communist but because gossip about her alleged communist sympathies had made her too "controversial."

Anticommunism also emerged as a divisive force in the labor movement. In the 1930s and early 1940s Communists had been very active in labor organizing, and their contributions had been welcomed, if not openly acknowledged. But as conservatives charged that Soviet-led Communists were taking over American unions, the labor movement reversed itself in the late 1940s and purged Communists. The Taft-Hartley Act fueled this campaign by requiring labor leaders to take oaths swearing they were not Communists before their unions could participate in federally supervised elections. The president of the Congress of Industrial Organizations, Philip Murray, subsequently denounced communist sympathizers as "skulking cowards . . . apostles of hate." Eleven unions that refused to oust their communist or communist-sympathizing leaders were expelled from the CIO.

Truman's Loyalty Program. Attempting to protect himself against charges that he was "soft on communism" in the wake of the Soviet spy ring revelations, Truman fed the hysteria in March 1947 by issuing an executive order initiating a comprehensive investigation into the loyalty of all federal employees. More than 6 million individuals were subjected to security checks, 14,000 underwent intensive FBI investigation, and 2,000 were dismissed. The case of Dorothy Bailey reflects the experience of many of those who were dismissed. Bailey lost her job with the U.S. Employment Service, where she had worked for fourteen years, because an unidentified informer claimed that she was a Communist and associated with known Communists. Denying the charge, she was brought before the District of Columbia regional loyalty board, which introduced no evidence against her and called no witnesses to support its case. She was fired anyway.

Following Washington's lead, many state and local governments, universities, political organizations, churches, and businesses undertook their own antisubversion campaigns. Part of a broad-based "Popular Front" against fascism in the late 1930s and early 1940s, American Communists had worked in a wide variety of occupations and political organizations. In the chilling climate of the Cold War, however, many Americans began to fear these radicals, believing they would co-opt their political agendas or discredit their organizations. Loyalty programs and purges were seen as the solution. All 11,000 faculty members in the University of California system were required to take a loyalty oath; UCLA alone fired 157 who refused to do so. Many Catholic organizations became hotbeds of anticommunism, urging their members to combat "enemies" within the church. Because of the Communist

MARK GOODSON

Red Hunting on the Quiz Shows; or, What's My Party Line?

———★———

Active in the television industry from its earliest days, Mark Goodson was a highly successful producer whose game shows included "What's My Line?" "To Tell the Truth," "Password," and "Family Feud." In this interview, Goodson recalls his experience in the industry in the early 1950s when rampant anticommunism plagued the entertainment business.

I'm not sure when it began, but I believe it was early 1950. At that point I had no connection with the blacklisting that was going on, although I heard about it in the motion picture business and heard rumors about things that had happened on other shows, like *The Aldrich Family.* . . .

Soon afterwards, CBS installed a clearance division. There wasn't any discussion. We would just get the word—"drop that person"—and that was supposed to be it. Whenever I booked a guest or a panelist on *What's My Line?* or *I've Got a Secret*, one of our assistants would phone up and say, "We're going to use so-and-so." We'd either get the okay, or they'd call back and say. "Not clear," or "Sorry, we can't use them." Even advertising agencies—big ones, like Young & Rubicam and BBD&O—had their own clearance departments. They would never come out and say it. They would just write off somebody by saying, "He's a bad actor." You were never supposed to tell the person what it was about; you'd just

unbook them. They never admitted there was a blacklist. It just wasn't done. . . .

Anna Lee was an English actress on a later show of ours called *It's News to Me*. The sponsor was Sanka Coffee, a product of General Foods. The advertising agency was Young & Rubicam. One day, I received a call telling me we had to drop one of our panelists, Anna Lee, immediately. They said she was a radical, that she wrote a column for the *Daily Worker*. They couldn't allow that kind of stuff on the air. They claimed they were getting all kinds of mail. It seemed incongruous to me that this little English girl, someone who seemed very conservative, would be writing for a Communist newspaper. It just didn't sound right.

I took her out to lunch. After a little social conversation, I asked her about her politics. She told me that she wasn't political, except she voted Conservative in England. Her husband was a Republican from Texas.

I went to the agency and said, "You guys are really off your rocker. Anna Lee is nothing close to a liberal." They told me, "Oh, you're right. We checked on that. It's a different Anna Lee who writes for the *Daily Worker*." I remember being relieved and saying, "Well, that's good. You just made a mistake. Now we can forget this." But that wasn't the case. They told me, "We've still got to get rid of her, because the illusion is just as good as the reality. If our client continues to get the mail, no one is going to believe him when he says there's a second Anna Lee." At that point I lost it. I told them their demand was outrageous. They could cancel the show if they wanted to, but I would not drop somebody whose only crime was sharing a name. When I got back to my office, there was a phone call waiting for me. It was from a friend of mine at the agency. He said, "If I were you, I would not lose my temper like that. If you want to argue, do it quietly. After you left, somebody said, 'Is Goodson a pinko?'"

Source: Griffin Fariello, *Red Scare* (New York: Norton, 1995), 320–324.

Party's historic defense of racial equality, civil rights organizations such as the National Association for the Advancement of Colored People and the National Urban League were attacked as communist-influenced. To fend off such charges, civil rights groups subsequently purged themselves of Communists or sympathetic "fellow travelers." Some postwar liberals, such as Henry Wallace and his followers in the Progressive Party, continued to seek cooperation with the Soviet Union and defended the participation of Communists in their organizations. But many other liberals, most notably those in Americans for Democratic Action, founded in 1947, shunned potential left-wing allies and embraced a strident anticommunism.

The anticommunist crusade intensified in 1948 when HUAC began an investigation of Alger Hiss, a former New Dealer and State department official who had accompanied Franklin Roosevelt to Yalta. Republican congressman Richard M. Nixon of California orchestrated the HUAC investigation, an event that brought him national recognition and boosted his political career. The case against Hiss rested on the testimony of former Communist Whittaker Chambers, a senior editor at *Time* magazine. Chambers claimed that Hiss was a member of a secret communist cell in the government and had passed him classified documents in the 1930s. Hiss categorically denied the allegations and denied even knowing Chambers. Because the statute of limitations on espionage had expired by 1949, Hiss was charged with perjury for lying about his communist affiliations and acquaintance with Chambers. The first trial resulted in a hung jury; the second, in early 1950, found Hiss guilty and sentenced him to five years in federal prison. Even after Alger Hiss's death in 1996, the media continued to debate the question of his guilt or innocence. Recently released evidence from the Soviet archives suggests that he was in fact working with the Soviets at the time.

The Rise and Fall of McCarthy.   The conviction of Hiss increased paranoia about a communist conspiracy in the federal government and contributed to the meteoric rise of Senator Joseph McCarthy of Wisconsin. In February 1950, just a few weeks after the Hiss verdict, McCarthy delivered a bombshell during a speech in Wheeling, West Virginia: "I have here in my hand a list of the names of 205 men that were known to the Secretary of State as being members of the Communist Party and who nevertheless are still working and shaping the policy of the State Department." McCarthy never revealed the names on his list and later lowered the number to 81 and then to 57. Despite these inconsistencies, the public responded enthusiastically to his charges.

A Marine Air Corps veteran who had won a Senate seat in the 1946 Republican landslide, McCarthy discovered that anticommunist rhetoric could boost his political fortunes. Like other Republicans in the late 1940s, he leveled accusations of communist subversion

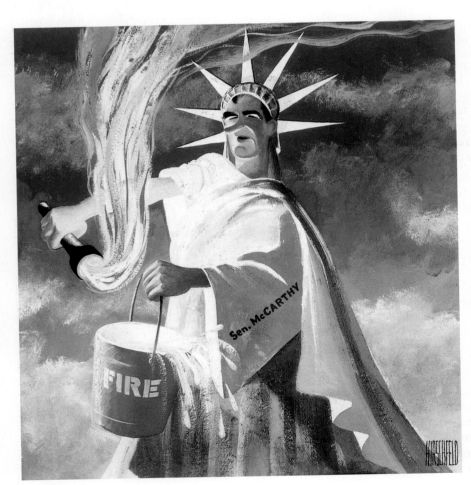

McCarthy's Assault on Civil Liberties
Senator Joseph McCarthy's reckless attacks on alleged Communists in the U.S. government stirred widespread public fears of Soviet subversion in the 1950s. His critics, such as cartoonist Al Hirschfeld, expressed alarm at what they saw as McCarthy's assault on American liberty.
© Al Hirschfeld. Drawing reproduced by special arrangement with The Margo Feiden Galleries, NY.

to embarrass Truman and the Democrats. Truman called McCarthy's charges "slander, lies, character assassination," but he could do nothing to curb them. McCarthy's political genius lay in his ability to make his name synonymous with the cause of uncovering subversives in government. Politicians who attacked him exposed themselves to charges of being "soft" on communism, the kiss of death in the postwar political climate. Because McCarthy charged that his critics themselves were part of "this conspiracy so immense," few political leaders challenged him. When Republican Dwight D. Eisenhower was elected president in 1952, he did not publicly challenge his party's most outspoken senator despite his personal dislike for McCarthy.

Although McCarthy never identified a single Communist in the federal government, a series of national and international events allowed him to retain credibility. Besides the Hiss case, the sensational 1951 espionage case of Julius and Ethel Rosenberg fueled McCarthy's allegations. Convicted of passing atomic secrets to the Soviet Union in a highly controversial trial, the Rosenbergs were executed in 1953. (As in the case of Alger Hiss, their convictions continue to be debated; the recent release of declassified documents from Project Venona, a top-secret intelligence mission during World War II, provided new evidence of Julius Rosenberg's guilt.) The Korean War, which embroiled the United States in a frustrating fight against communism in a faraway land, also made Americans susceptible to McCarthy's claims.

After four years of relentless red hunting, McCarthy overreached himself by launching an investigation into possible subversion in the U.S. Army in 1954. When lengthy televised hearings brought McCarthy's smear tactics and innuendos into the nation's living rooms, support for him declined. Joseph Welch, an attorney representing the army in the hearings, voiced the growing public disapproval of McCarthy when he burst out, "Senator, have you no decency?" Moreover, the end of the Korean War and the death of Stalin in 1953 also undercut public interest in McCarthy's anticommunist campaign. In December 1954 the Senate voted 67 to 22 to censure McCarthy for unbecoming conduct. He died from alcohol-related illness three years later at the age of forty-eight, his name forever attached to a period of political repression of which he was only the most flagrant manifestation.

"Modern Republicanism"

──────────★──────────

The 1952 election occurred in the middle of the Korean stalemate and at the height of the Great Fear. The newly elected president, Dwight D. Eisenhower, worked quickly to end the Korean War, but the grip of McCarthyism

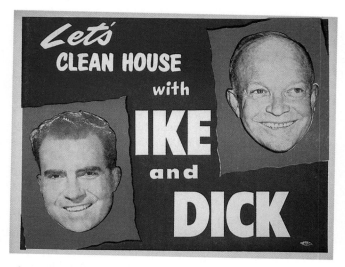

The 1952 Presidential Campaign
The 1952 Republican ticket of Dwight D. Eisenhower and Richard M. Nixon launched an effective attack on the Democratic leadership by stressing the Truman administration's involvement in bribery and influence-peddling scandals, and by capitalizing on Truman's failure to end the war in Korea. Collection of Janice L. and David J. Frent.

lasted longer. Eisenhower set the tone for what historians call "modern Republicanism"—an updated GOP approach that emphasized a slowdown, but not a dismantling, of federal responsibilities. Compared with their predecessors in the 1920s and their successors in the 1980s and 1990s, Eisenhower and other modern Republicans were more tolerant of the federal government's intervention in social and economic affairs, though they sought to limit its scope. More important to the average voter than Eisenhower's political philosophy, however, was his proven leadership in trying times; he seemed the right person to guide the nation through the perils of the continuing Cold War.

They Liked Ike

Eisenhower's status as a war hero was his greatest political asset. Born in 1890 and raised in Abilene, Kansas, he had graduated from the United States Military Academy at West Point in 1915. General Douglas MacArthur chose him as his aide in the early 1930s, and Eisenhower rose quickly through the ranks. After the Japanese attack on Pearl Harbor, he came to Washington under the sponsorship of a second mentor, General George C. Marshall. Eisenhower oversaw the Allied invasion of North Africa in 1942, and in 1944 became Supreme Commander of Allied Forces in Europe, where he had the mammoth task of coordinating the D-Day invasion of France. To hundreds of thousands of soldiers and to the millions who followed the war on newsreels, he was simply "Ike," the best known and most respected of the nation's military leaders.

A professional military man, Eisenhower claimed to stand "above politics." While in the army he had never voted, insisting that such political activity represented an intrusion of the military into civilian affairs. Many Democrats had hoped to make him their candidate for president in 1948 and again in 1952. Eisenhower wanted the office, but as a Republican. Resigning his position as commander of NATO forces in Europe, he quickly won several primaries and took delegates away from his rival, Senator Robert A. Taft of Ohio, in a tough fight at the Republican national convention. Eisenhower then asked Senator Richard M. Nixon of California to be his running mate. Young, tirelessly partisan, and sporting a strong anticommunist record from his crusade against Alger Hiss, Nixon brought regional balance and an aggressive campaign style to the ticket.

The Democrats never seriously considered renominating Harry Truman, who by 1952 was a thoroughly discredited leader. Lack of popular enthusiasm for the Korean War dealt the most severe blow to Truman's support, but a series of widely publicized scandals involving federal officials in bribery, kickbacks, and influence-peddling schemes caused voters to complain about the "mess in Washington." The Democrats turned instead to the popular governor of Illinois, Adlai E. Stevenson, who enjoyed the support of organized labor and respected liberals such as Eleanor Roosevelt. To appease southern voters who feared Stevenson's liberal agenda, the Democrats nominated Senator John A. Sparkman of Alabama for vice-president.

Throughout the 1952 campaign Stevenson advocated New Deal and Fair Deal policies with an almost literary eloquence, but Eisenhower's artfully unpretentious speeches were more effective with the voters. Eager to win the support of the broadest possible electorate, Eisenhower played down specific questions of policy. Instead, he attacked the Democrats with the "K1C2" formula—"Korea, Communism, and Corruption." In a campaign pledge that clinched the election he vowed, "I shall go to Korea," to end the stalemated war if elected.

The Republican campaign was temporarily set back by the revelation that wealthy Californians had set up a secret slush fund for Richard Nixon. Eisenhower contemplated dropping him from the ticket, but Nixon adroitly used a televised speech to convince voters that he had not misused campaign funds. Whereas Truman appointees had accepted mink coats from contractors— a reference to a widely reported case involving a loan examiner for the Reconstruction Finance Corporation— Nixon's wife wore a "respectable Republican cloth coat." Nixon did admit accepting one gift, a puppy his young daughters had named Checkers. That gift he would not give back, he declared earnestly. Nixon's televised pathos turned an embarrassing incident into an advantage, as sympathetic viewers flooded Republican headquarters with telegrams and phone calls. Outmaneuvered, Republican leaders had no choice but to keep Nixon on the ticket. The "Checkers speech" showed how politicians could use the powerful medium of television to their advantage.

That November Eisenhower won 55 percent of the popular vote, carrying all the northern and western states and four southern states as well. Republican candidates for Congress did not fare quite as well. They regained the Senate but won control of the House of Representatives by only a slender margin of four seats. In 1954 the Democrats would regain control of both houses, an advantage that they held even when the enormously popular Eisenhower won easy reelection in 1956.

The Hidden-Hand Presidency

Eisenhower offered modern Republicanism as an alternative to the Democrats' liberal agenda. He did his best to set a quieter national mood, hoping to decrease the need for federal intervention in social and economic issues. He refused to speak out publicly against Senator McCarthy and displayed little leadership in the emerging area of civil rights. As columnist Richard L. Strout observed in *The New Republic*, "The less he does the more they love him. Here is a man who doesn't rock the boat."

Yet Eisenhower was no stooge as president. Political scientist Fred Greenstein has characterized his style of leadership as the "hidden-hand presidency," pointing out that Eisenhower maneuvered deftly behind the scenes while not seeming to concern himself publicly with partisan questions. Others cite the president's skillful handling of the press. When his press secretary, James Hagerty, asked what he would say about a tricky foreign policy issue at a press conference, Eisenhower replied, "Don't worry, Jim. If that question comes up, I'll just confuse them."

Eisenhower presided cautiously over increases in federal activity. When the Soviet Union launched *Sputnik*, the first space satellite, in 1957, Eisenhower reluctantly approved a U.S. space program to catch up in this new Cold War competition. The National Aeronautics and Space Administration (NASA) was founded the following year. Arguing that the Cold War required more scientists and experts on foreign affairs, he persuaded Congress to appropriate additional money for college scholarships and to increase its support for research and development in universities and industry. Federal outlays for veterans' benefits, unemployment compensation, housing, and Social Security were increased, and the minimum wage was raised from

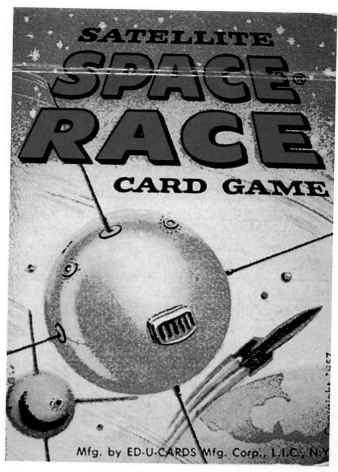

The Sputnik *Crisis*
The Soviet launching of the *Sputnik* space satellite in 1957 precipitated a crisis of confidence in American science and education. That sense of crisis was reflected in a 1950s "Space Race" card game, in which those dealt the *Sputnik* card would lose two turns.
The Michael Barson Collection/Past Perfect.

75 cents an hour to a dollar. The creation of the new Department of Health, Education and Welfare (HEW) in 1953 consolidated government control of social welfare programs.

The most extensive federal activity took place in the realm of transportation. In a move that drastically altered the American landscape and favored the trend toward privately owned automobiles, the Interstate Highway Act of 1956 authorized $26 billion over a ten-year period for the construction of a nationally integrated highway system. (This network of highways was also promoted to speed civilian evacuation in case of nuclear attack.) To link the Great Lakes with the Atlantic Ocean, the United States and Canada cosponsored in 1959 the construction of the St. Lawrence Sea-

way, a project that had been discussed since the 1930s. The interstate highway and the St. Lawrence Seaway projects were the largest public works programs to date, surpassing anything the New Deal had undertaken. They highlighted the vital role of federal spending in American life, even under a Republican administration.

Eisenhower realized that the vast federal budget, which reached almost 23 percent of the gross national product in the late 1950s, gave the government a major responsibility for the overall health of the nation's economy. The president made the fight against inflation, not full employment, his top economic priority. Eisenhower believed that a balanced budget and stable prices would encourage business confidence and lead to prosperity. His policies pleased investors: the economy grew 2.9 percent per year between 1953 and 1961, while inflation averaged only 1.5 percent annually. Periodic bouts of unemployment and recession continued (1953–1954, 1957–1958, and 1960–1961), but the unemployment rate stayed below 7 percent throughout the Eisenhower years.

Modern Republicanism, it turned out, resisted the unchecked expansion of the state but did not generally cut back federal power. Only in the area of natural resource development did the Eisenhower administration move to reduce federal activity—turning federal offshore oil contracting over to the states in 1953 and authorizing privately financed hydroelectric dams on the Snake River in 1955. In most other areas the responsibilities that the federal government had accepted—social welfare programs inherited from the New Deal, Keynesian intervention in the economy, and increased defense expenditures necessitated by the nation's growing role abroad—signaled an abandonment of the Republican style of limited government that had prevailed in the 1920s. When Eisenhower retired from public life in 1961, the federal government was an even greater presence in everyday life than it had been when he took office. Some of the most controversial federal initiatives occurred in the area of civil rights.

Emergence of Civil Rights as a National Issue

The civil rights movement was arguably the most important force for change in postwar America, and its accelerating momentum had profound implications for the federal government. Legal segregation of the races still governed the southern way of life in the early 1950s. In most states it was illegal for whites and blacks to eat in the same rooms in restaurants and luncheonettes, use the same waiting rooms and toilet facilities at bus and train stations, or ride in the same taxis.

All forms of public transportation were rigidly segregated by custom or by law. Even drinking fountains were labeled "White" and "Colored."

Brown v. Board of Education.

Unlike Harry Truman, Dwight Eisenhower showed little commitment to civil rights. In fact, he proved extremely reluctant to intervene in what was widely seen as a state issue. Inadvertently, though, he contributed to the advancement of the black cause by naming Governor Earl Warren of California as Chief Justice of the U.S. Supreme Court in September 1953. Warren's quiet persuasion convinced the Court to rule unanimously in *Brown v. Board of Education of Topeka* (1954) that racial segregation in the public schools was unconstitutional.

The 1954 decision was the culmination of a series of test cases challenging segregation in housing, transportation, and other areas that the NAACP had been litigating since the 1940s. The NAACP had filed the Topeka case on behalf of Linda Brown, a black student who attended a segregated school several miles from her home rather than the nearby white elementary school. The NAACP's chief counsel, Thurgood Marshall, argued that the legal segregation mandated by the Topeka, Kansas, Board of Education was inherently unconstitutional because it stigmatized an entire race and thereby denied it the "equal protection of the laws" guaranteed by the Fourteenth Amendment. In a unanimous decision announced on May 17, 1954, the Supreme Court agreed, overturning the "separate but equal" doctrine of *Plessy v. Ferguson* (see Chapter 18). Speaking for the Court, Chief Justice Earl Warren ruled:

> To separate Negro children . . . solely because of their race generates a feeling of inferiority as to their status in the community that may affect their hearts and minds in a way unlikely ever to be undone. . . . We conclude that in the field of public education the doctrine of "separate but equal" has no place. Separate educational facilities are inherently unequal. . . . Any language in Plessy v. Ferguson *contrary to these findings is rejected.*

Integration at Little Rock, Arkansas

With chants such as "Two-four-six-eight, we ain't gonna integrate," angry crowds taunted Elizabeth Eckford (shown here walking past white students and National Guardsmen) and eight other black students who tried to register at the previously allwhite Central High School in Little Rock, Arkansas, on September 4, 1957. The courtordered integration proceeded only after President Eisenhower reluctantly nationalized the Arkansas National Guard to protect the students.

Francis Miller, LIFE Magazine, © Time, Inc.

In response to NAACP suits over the next several years, the Supreme Court used the *Brown* precedent to overturn segregation in city parks, public beaches and golf courses, all forms of interstate and intrastate transportation, and public housing. Meanwhile, progress in desegregating schools was frustratingly slow. In a 1955 decision implementing the *Brown* decision, the Court declared that integration should proceed "with all deliberate speed." Many critics would later note that the deliberation was far more evident than the speed.

When it became clear that the Court was not going to back down on civil rights, white resistance solidified. In 1956, 101 members of Congress signed a "Southern Manifesto" denouncing the *Brown* decision as "a clear abuse of judicial power" and encouraging their constituents to defy it. In that year 500,000 southerners joined White Citizens' Councils dedicated to blocking school integration and other civil rights measures. Some whites revived the old tactics of violence and intimidation, swelling the ranks of the Ku Klux Klan to levels not seen since the 1920s.

Crisis in Little Rock. President Eisenhower was disturbed by the *Brown* decision, asserting, "I don't believe you can change the hearts of men with laws or decisions." (He later complained that his appointment of Earl Warren was "the biggest damn fool mistake I ever made.") While acknowledging *Brown* as the law of the land, he did not commit federal power to enforcing it. A crisis in Little Rock, Arkansas, finally forced him to intervene on the side of desegregation. In September 1957 nine black students attempted to enroll at the all-white Central High School after the local school board won a court order to implement a desegregation plan. Governor Orval Faubus called out the state National Guard to bar the children from entering the school, despite the court order. Then the mob took over. Every day a white crowd taunted the poised but obviously terrified black students with chants such as "Go back to the jungle." As the vicious scenes were replayed on television night after night, Eisenhower reluctantly decided to act. He sent 1,000 federal troops to Little Rock and nationalized 10,000 members of the Arkansas National Guard, ordering them to protect the students.

Eisenhower thus became the first president since Reconstruction to use federal troops to enforce the rights of blacks. He also signed the Civil Rights Act of 1957, a Democratic bill that created the U.S. Commission on Civil Rights to study federal laws and policies dealing with equal protection. Though admittedly weak, the act was the first national civil rights legislation passed since Reconstruction.

Montgomery Bus Boycott. White resistance to the *Brown* decision, as well as Eisenhower's hesitancy to act in Little Rock, showed that court victories were not enough to overthrow segregation. Black southerners had also grown alarmed with the rising level of white violence, particularly the brutal lynching of fourteen-year-old Emmett Till in Mississippi in 1955. Later that year, on December 1, a new strategy of nonviolent protest emerged when Rosa Parks, a seamstress and member of the NAACP in Montgomery, Alabama, refused to give up her seat on a city bus to a white man. She was promptly arrested and charged with violating a local segregation ordinance. "I felt it was just something I had to do," Parks stated. Although Parks was hardly the first black southerner to challenge Jim Crow laws, her upstanding social reputation and political connections with the civil rights movement soon made her case famous in the black community.

When local black residents met to discuss the proper response, they turned to the Reverend Martin Luther King Jr., who had become pastor of Dexter Street Baptist Church the year before. The son of a prominent black minister in Atlanta, King had received a B.A. from Morehouse College and a Ph.D. in theology from Boston University. King endorsed a plan by a local black women's organization to boycott Montgomery's bus system until it was integrated. For the next 381 days members of a united black community formed car pools or walked to work. The bus company neared bankruptcy, and downtown stores complained about the loss of business. But not until the Supreme Court ruled in November 1956 that bus segregation was unconstitutional did the city of Montgomery finally relent. "My feets is tired, but my soul is rested," said one woman boycotter.

The Montgomery bus boycott catapulted Martin Luther King to national prominence. In 1957, with the Reverend Ralph Abernathy and other southern black clergy, he founded the Southern Christian Leadership Conference (SCLC), based in Atlanta. The black church had long been the center of African American social and cultural life; now it lent its moral and organizational strength, as well as the voices of its most inspirational preachers, to the civil rights movement. Female black church members were one of the movement's strongest constituencies, transferring the skills that they had honed through years of church work to the fight for racial equality. The SCLC joined the NAACP as one of the main advocacy groups for racial justice. Even though these groups received little support from national political leaders in the 1950s, their limited victories laid the organizational groundwork for the dynamic civil rights movement that would emerge in the 1960s.

The Political Baptism of Martin Luther King Jr.
After the arrest of Rosa Parks in December 1955, the black community of Montgomery, Alabama, organized a citywide bus boycott with the help of Martin Luther King Jr., a local Baptist pastor. Many black women served as grass-roots organizers of the boycott, but it was King who rose to prominence as an eloquent and highly respected spokesperson for the emerging civil rights movement in the region. He is shown here in Montgomery, Alabama, in 1956 addressing a crowd during the bus boycott.
Dan Weiner, courtesy Sandra Weiner.

The "New Look" of Foreign Policy

Eisenhower felt far more comfortable exercising leadership in military and diplomatic affairs than in civil rights. One of his first acts as president was to negotiate an armistice in the Korean War. As he had pledged in the campaign, he visited Korea in December 1952. The final settlement was signed in July 1953 at Panmunjom (see Map 27.2) after the parties reached a compromise on the tricky issue of prisoner exchange. The war ended with both sides occupying the territory they had held at the start of the conflict in 1950.

Once the Korean War was settled, Eisenhower turned his attention to Europe and the Soviet Union. Stalin's death in March 1953 had precipitated an intraparty struggle that lasted until 1956, when Nikita S. Khrushchev emerged as Stalin's successor. Although Khrushchev surprised Westerners by calling for "peaceful coexistence" between communist and capitalist societies, he made certain that the Soviet Union's Eastern European satellites did not drift too far from the Soviet path. When nationalists revolted in Hun-

gary in 1956 and moved to take the country out of the Warsaw Pact, Soviet tanks rapidly moved into Budapest—an action the United States could condemn but not realistically resist. Soviet repression of the Hungarian revolt showed that American policy makers had few, if any, options for rolling back Soviet power in Eastern Europe short of going to war with the USSR.

Although Eisenhower strongly opposed communism, as a fiscal conservative he hoped to keep the cost of containment at a manageable level. Under his New Look defense policy, the president sought to enhance American nuclear capabilities and encourage U.S. allies to bear greater military responsibility through increased foreign aid and an extensive system of defense alliances.

Massive Retaliation. Eisenhower and Secretary of State John Foster Dulles believed that the nation's main foreign enemy was a worldwide communist movement led by Moscow. They reasoned that the United States could economize by developing a massive nuclear arsenal as an alternative to more expensive conventional forces. Because nuclear weapons delivered "more bang for the buck" (in the words of Defense Secretary Charles E. Wilson), the Eisenhower administration relied on the threat of nuclear weapons to check Soviet expansion—a policy known as *massive retaliation*. The administration thus expanded its commitment to the hydrogen bomb, approving extensive atmospheric testing in the South Pacific and in western states such as Nevada, Colorado, and Utah beginning in 1952. To improve the nation's defenses against possible air attack from the Soviet Union, the administration supported research to develop the long-range bombing capabilities of the Strategic Air Command, and installed the Distant Early Warning line of radar stations in Alaska and Canada in 1958.

Those efforts, however, did not give the United States the military superiority it hoped for because the Soviets matched the United States weapon for weapon in an escalating arms race. The Soviet Union carried out its own atmospheric tests of hydrogen bombs between 1953 and 1958 and developed a fleet of long-range bombers. By 1958 both nations had intercontinental ballistic missiles (ICBMs). When an American nuclear submarine launched an atomic-tipped Polaris missile in 1960, Soviet leaders raced to produce an equivalent weapon. While boosting the military-industrial sectors of the United States and the Soviet Union, the arms race funneled immense resources into soon-to-be obsolete weapon systems.

The New Look policy also extended collective security agreements between the United States and its allies, encouraging the latter to take greater responsibility for their own military defense. To complement the NATO alliance in Europe, Secretary of State Dulles negotiated bilateral defense treaties with South Korea and the nationalist Chinese regime in Taiwan in 1954. In the same year, he orchestrated the creation of the Southeast Asia Treaty Organization (SEATO), linking America and its major European allies with Australia, Pakistan, Thailand, New Zealand, and the Philippines. This "pactomania," as some called it, required that the United States come to the defense of more than forty other countries. U.S. policy makers tended to support stable governments, no matter how repressive, as long as they were overtly anticommunist. Some of America's staunchest allies—the Philippines, Iran, Cuba, South Vietnam, and Nicaragua—were governed by military dictatorships or repressive right-wing civilian governments that lacked broad-based popular support.

CIA Activities. Secretary of State Dulles did not shrink from covert intervention against governments that were, in his opinion, too closely aligned with com-

Testing an Atomic Bomb
Throughout the 1950s the Atomic Energy Commission (AEC) conducted above-ground tests of atomic and hydrogen bombs. Thousands of soldiers were exposed to fallout during the tests, such as this one at Yucca Flats, Nevada, in April 1952. The AEC, ignoring or suppressing medical evidence to the contrary, mounted an extensive public relations campaign to convince local residents that the tests did not endanger their health. FPG International.

munism. For such tasks he used the Central Intelligence Agency, which was headed by his brother, Allen Dulles. During the Eisenhower administration the CIA moved beyond its original mandate of intelligence gathering to active, albeit secret, involvement in the internal affairs of foreign countries.

In the 1950s the CIA successfully directed the overthrow of several foreign governments. When Iran's nationalist premier, Muhammad Mossadegh, seized British oil properties in 1953, CIA agents helped the young shah of Iran, Muhammad Reza Pahlavi, depose him. In 1954 the CIA supported a coup in Guatemala against the popularly elected Jacobo Arbenz Guzman, who had expropriated 250,000 uncultivated acres held by the American-owned United Fruit Company and accepted arms from the communist government of Czechoslovakia. The CIA also tried, unsuccessfully, to overthrow Achmed Sukarno of Indonesia in 1958 because of his tolerance for growing communist influence in that country's government. Eisenhower specifically approved those efforts. "Our traditional ideas of international sportsmanship," he wrote privately in 1955, "are scarcely applicable in the morass in which the world now flounders."

The Emerging Third World

American leaders had devised the containment policy in response to Soviet expansion in Eastern Europe, but they soon extended it to the new nations that were emerging in the Third World. Before World War II, nationalism, socialism, and religion had inspired powerful anticolonial movements; in the 1940s and 1950s those forces intensified and spread, especially in the Middle East, Africa, and Asia. Between 1947 and 1962 the British, French, Dutch, and Belgian empires all but disintegrated. Seeking to draw the newly created countries into an American-led world system, U.S. policy makers encouraged the development of stable market economies in those areas. They also sought to further the ideal of national self-determination. But under the growing East-West tensions of the Cold War, both the Truman and the Eisenhower administrations often failed to recognize that indigenous nationalist or socialist movements in emerging nations had their own goals and were not necessarily under the control of either local communists or the Soviet Union.

The Middle East. The Middle East, an oil-rich area that was playing an increasingly central role in the strategic planning of both the United States and the Soviet Union, presented one of the most complicated challenges. Zionism, the Jewish nationalist movement, had long encouraged Jews to return to their ancient homeland of Israel (Palestine). After World War II many Jewish survivors of the Nazi extermination camps had resettled in Palestine, which was still controlled by Britain under a World War I mandate. On November 29, 1947, the U.N. General Assembly voted to partition Palestine into two states, Jewish and Arab—a decision that Egypt, Jordan, and other Arab League states resisted. On May 14, 1948, the British mandate ended, and Zionist leaders proclaimed the state of Israel. President Truman quickly recognized the new state, alienating the Arabs but winning crucial support from Jewish voters in the 1948 election.

The Birth of Israel, 1948
Prime Minister David Ben-Gurion reads Israel's Declaration of Independence to the new country's assembled officials. The photograph on the wall is of Theodor Herzl, one of the founders of Zionism.
Corbis-Bettmann.

Egypt was another site of conflict with the Arab nations, one that reflected the way in which Third World countries became embroiled in the Cold War. When Gamal Abdel Nasser came to power in Egypt in 1954, two years after independence from Britain, he pledged to lead not just his country but the entire Middle East out of its dependent, colonial relationship through a form of pan-Arab socialism. Nasser obtained arms and promises of economic assistance from the Soviet Union, including help in building the Aswan Dam on the Nile, a major water and energy development project. Secretary of State Dulles countered with an offer of American assistance, but Nasser refused to distance himself from the Soviets, declaring Egypt's neutrality in the Cold War. Unwilling to accept this stance of nonalignment, Dulles abruptly withdrew his offer in July 1956.

A week later Nasser retaliated against the withdrawal of Western financial aid by nationalizing the Suez Canal, over which Britain had retained administrative authority and through which three-quarters of Western Europe's oil was transported. Nasser said he would use the tolls from the canal to build the dam himself. After several months of fruitless negotiation, Britain and France, in alliance with Israel, attacked Egypt and retook the canal. Their attack occurred at the same time as the Soviet repression of the Hungarian revolt, placing the United States in the potentially awkward position of denouncing Soviet aggression while tolerating a similar action by its own allies. Eisenhower and the United Nations forced France and Britain to pull back. Egypt retook the Suez Canal and built the Aswan Dam with Soviet support. In the end the Suez crisis increased Soviet influence in the Third World, intensified anti-Western sentiment in Arab countries, and produced dissension among leading members of the NATO alliance.

The Eisenhower Doctrine. In early 1957, in the aftermath of the Suez crisis, the president persuaded Congress to approve the Eisenhower Doctrine. Addressing concerns over declining British influence in the Middle East, the policy stated that American forces would assist any nation in the region "requiring such aid, against overt armed aggression from any nation controlled by International Communism." Later that year Eisenhower invoked the doctrine when he sent the U.S. Sixth Fleet to the Mediterranean Sea to aid King Hussein against a Nasser-backed revolt in Jordan. A year later he landed 14,000 troops to back up a pro-U.S. government in Lebanon.

The attention that the Eisenhower administration paid to developments in the Middle East in the 1950s demonstrated how the desire for access to steady supplies of oil increasingly affected foreign policy. More broadly, attention to the Middle East confirmed the global scope of American interests. Just as the Korean War had stretched the application of containment from Europe to Asia, the Eisenhower Doctrine revealed U.S. intentions to influence events in the Middle East as well.

The Impact of the Cold War

★

The Cold War extended to the most distant areas of the globe, but it also had powerful effects on the domestic economy, politics, and cultural values of the United States. The Soviet-American conflict also affected Americans in a personal way: for the first time in the nation's history there was a peacetime draft. In the past the armed forces had shrunk to a skeleton volunteer force at the end of each war or foreign engagement. But when World War II ended, the draft was kept in place to meet the military commitments associated with the Cold War: occupation forces in defeated Axis countries, missile deployment operations in Europe, and counterinsurgency forces in the Third World. Sud-

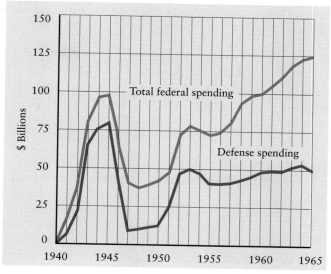

FIGURE 27.1
National Defense Spending, 1940–1965
In 1950 the defense budget was $13 billion, less than a third of total federal outlays. In 1961 defense spending reached $47 billion, fully half of the federal budget and almost 10 percent of the gross national product.

denly every neighborhood seemed to have a boy in the armed forces; many people made military service a career.

The postwar expansion of the military produced a dramatic shift in the country's economic priorities, as military spending took up a greater percentage of national income. Between 1900 and 1930, except for the two years that the United States fought in World War I, the country spent less than 1 percent of its GNP for military purposes. When Eisenhower left office in January 1961, the figure was closer to 10 percent, fully half of the federal budget (Figure 27.1). Even though the country was at peace during most of his administration, the economy and the government operated practically on a war footing.

The Military-Industrial Complex and Nuclear Proliferation

With its headquarters at the sprawling Pentagon in Arlington, Virginia, the Department of Defense had evolved into a massive bureaucracy that profoundly influenced the postwar economy. Aircraft companies such as Boeing and Lockheed did so much of their business with the government that they became dependent on Defense department orders. Federal money underwrote 90 percent of the cost of research on aviation and space, and also subsidized the scientific

The Computer Revolution

———————★———————

THE FIRST MODERN computers—information-processing machines capable of storing and manipulating data according to specified programs—appeared in the 1940s. During World War II engineers and mathematicians at the University of Pennsylvania developed a general-purpose, programmable electronic calculator called ENIAC (Electronic Numerical Integrator and Computer), which could add 5,000 ten-digit decimal numbers in one second. It stood 8 feet tall, measured 80 feet long, and weighed 30 tons; it used 18,000 vacuum tubes for computations. When it performed complex mathematical computations, one scientist noted, ENIAC sounded "like a roomful of ladies knitting." Although ENIAC lacked a central memory and could not store a program, it was the bridge to the modern computer revolution.

Six computers were under construction by 1947, including UNIVAC (Universal Automatic Computer), the first commercial computer system. To the general public in the 1950s, the word *UNIVAC* was synonymous with *computer*. UNIVAC was basically a data-processing system that could be tailored to an individual customer's needs. In 1951 the U.S. Census Bureau bought the first UNIVAC. Soon CBS-TV signed on, using a UNIVAC to predict the outcome of the 1952 presidential election. At 9 P.M., after only the East Coast polls had closed and with only 7 percent of the votes counted, UNIVAC predicted that Dwight D. Eisenhower would sweep the election with 438 electoral votes. CBS programmers and network executives, who had expected a closer election, got jittery and altered the program to give Eisenhower a far narrower margin. When the final tally gave him 442 electoral votes, only 4 votes off the original projection, commentator Edward R. Murrow observed, "The trouble with machines is people."

Computers are essentially collections of switches; the programs tell the machine which switches to turn on and off. The puzzle early computer scientists had to solve was how to increase the speed of this basic operation while lowering the cost. The first generation of computers needed vacuum tubes for computation power and used punched cards for writing programs and analyzing data. Computers such as ENIAC were room-size machines, and programming them could take several days because the programmers had to manually set thousands of switches in the on or off position. The vacuum tubes were the weakest part of early computers; the burnout of just a few of them could

---

instruments, automobile, and electronics industries. With the government paying part of the bill, corporations developed products with unprecedented speed. After the Pentagon backed IBM's investment in integrated circuits in the 1960s, these new devices—crucial to the computer revolution (see New Technology, "The Computer Revolution," above)—were in commercial production within three years. The impact of permanent mobilization was thus felt far beyond the defense industry.

The Cold War defense buildup brought mixed blessings. In positive terms, it created jobs: by the 1960s, perhaps as many as one in seven Americans owed his or her job to the military-industrial complex. In the South and West, where much of the new military activity was concentrated, dependence on federal defense spending was even greater (Map 27.4). That increased spending put money in the pockets of the millions of people working in defense-related industries, but it also limited the resources available for domestic needs. Moreover, the Cold War spurred a dangerous cycle of nuclear proliferation that would long outlive the Soviet-American conflict that spawned it.

The nuclear arms race affected all Americans by fostering a climate of fear and uncertainty. Bomb shelters and civil defense drills provided a daily reminder of the threat of nuclear war, and atomic research and testing had a devastating impact on human health. In the 1950s a small but growing number of citizens became concerned about the effects of radioactive fallout from above-ground bomb tests. In later years federal investigators documented a host of illnesses, deaths, and birth defects among families of veterans who had worked on weapons tests and among "downwinders"—residents near nuclear test sites and weapons facilities (see American Voices, "Isaac Nelson: Atomic Witness," p. 899).

An Early Computer Center
This computer–data-processing center featured an IBM 704 computer.

shut down the entire system. Furthermore, the tubes gave off enormous amounts of heat, necessitating noisy and cumbersome air-conditioning units wherever computers operated. After a critical signal relay stopped one early program, scientists finally located the problem—a dead moth trapped in the apparatus, the origin of the term *debugging*.

The 1948 invention of the transistor revolutionized computers and the whole field of electronics, making the second generation of computers possible. Like vacuum tubes, transistors served as on-off switches, but they did not generate heat, burn out, or consume a lot of energy. They also were inexpensive to manufacture.

The invention of integrated circuits in 1959 ushered in the third computer generation, characterized by greater sophistication in miniaturization: the number of transistors that could be installed on a silicon chip increased dramatically, with a corresponding increase in computational power. The fourth computer generation arrived in 1971 with the development of the microprocessor, which placed the entire central processing unit (CPU) of a computer on a single silicon chip (about the size of the letter "O" on this page).

Miniaturization progressed so rapidly that by the mid-1970s a $1 chip provided as much processing power as had the ENIAC of thirty years earlier. Since then, transistor size has continued to shrink, resulting in chips with twice as many transistors roughly every eighteen months. The increased speed and memory of these chips, together with the immense data storage capabilities of the Internet (an online network first established by the Department of Defense in 1969), have made today's compact personal computers incredibly powerful tools. At the same time, scientists have been developing large-scale "supercomputers"—an integrated series of smaller computers that can be used to simulate complex natural and human phenomena such as weather, transportation systems, and genetics. Computers and computer technology have become so much a part of modern life that it is hard to remember how recent the origins of this technological revolution are.

The most shocking revelations came to light in 1993 when the Department of Energy released millions of previously classified documents on human radiation experiments conducted under government auspices in the late 1940s and 1950s. The documents described over sixteen thousand cases involving the deliberate irradiation of human subjects, often without their consent or understanding. Some of the tests involved research for legitimate medical procedures, but others simply measured human tolerance of radioactive substances, some of which were known at the time to be extremely dangerous.

Arms Control

By the late 1950s, public concern over nuclear testing and fallout had become a high-profile issue, and new antinuclear groups such as SANE (the National Committee for a Sane Nuclear Policy) and Physicians for Social Responsibility called for an international test ban. Even Eisenhower, whose policies accelerated the arms race, had second thoughts about a nuclear policy—the aptly named MAD (Mutual Assured Destruction)—that was based on the premise of annihilating the enemy even if one's own country was destroyed. He also found spiraling arms expenditures a serious hindrance to balancing the federal budget, one of his chief fiscal goals. Consequently, Eisenhower tried to negotiate an arms limitation agreement with the Soviet Union. Laying the diplomatic groundwork for a possible arms treaty, Eisenhower and Khrushchev held a summit meeting in Geneva, Switzerland, in 1955—the first such meeting since the Potsdam Conference ten years before—and followed up with further disarmament talks over the next two years.

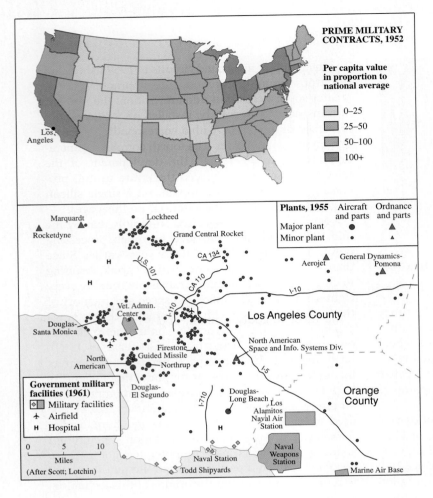

PRIME MILITARY CONTRACTS, 1952

Per capita value in proportion to national average

- 0–25
- 25–50
- 50–100
- 100+

Los Angeles

Plants, 1955

	Aircraft and parts	Ordnance and parts
Major plant	●	▲
Minor plant	•	▲

Marquardt
Rocketdyne
Lockheed
Grand Central Rocket
CA 134
U.S. 101
CA 110
Aerojet
General Dynamics-Pomona
I-10
Vet. Admin. Center
Los Angeles County
I-110
Douglas-Santa Monica
North American
Firestone
Guided Missile
Northrup
Douglas-El Segundo
North American Space and Info. Systems Div.
I-5
Orange County
I-710
Douglas-Long Beach
Los Alamitos Naval Air Station
Naval Weapons Station
Naval Station
Todd Shipyards
Marine Air Base

Government military facilities (1961)
- Military facilities
- ✈ Airfield
- H Hospital

0   5   10
Miles
(After Scott; Lotchin)

MAP 27.4
The Military-Industrial Complex in Los Angeles
The development and expansion of military facilities and defense contracting during the Cold War helped boost the populations and economies of Los Angeles and other Sun Belt cities and made the economies of California and other states highly dependent on defense expenditures.

Although those meetings did not yield the "open skies" mutual arms inspection treaty Eisenhower wanted, they did produce plans for another summit meeting in May 1960. Then, on May 5, the Soviets shot down an American U-2 spy plane over their territory and captured its pilot. Eisenhower at first denied that the plane was engaged in espionage but later admitted that he had authorized this and other secret flights over the USSR. In the midst of the dispute the summit meeting was canceled, and Eisenhower's last chance to negotiate an arms agreement evaporated.

Nuclear proliferation was not the only aspect of the Cold War that troubled Eisenhower. In his final address to the nation Eisenhower warned against the power of what he termed the "military-industrial complex," which by then was employing 3.5 million Americans. Its pervasive influence, he said, "is felt in every city, every statehouse, every office of the federal government." Even though his administration had fostered this growth in the defense establishment to contain the Soviet threat, Eisenhower was gravely concerned about its implications for a democratic people: "We must guard against the acquisition of unwarranted influence, whether sought or unsought, by the military-industrial complex," he warned. "We must never let the weight of this combination endanger our liberties or democratic processes." With those words Dwight Eisenhower showed how well he understood the major transformations that the Cold War had brought to American life.

ISAAC NELSON
Atomic Witness

———————★———————

Isaac Nelson, a naval veteran of World War II, returned to his hometown of Cedar City, Utah, in 1945 and went to work for a nearby hardware company. Like many other residents of southern Utah, he and his wife Oleta lived downwind from the Nevada Test Site, where the U.S. government detonated 126 atomic bombs into the atmosphere between 1951 and 1963.

After 1951 they were going to start the testing in Nevada, and everybody was really excited, and thought maybe we'd get a part to play in it and show our patriotism. We wanted to help out what little we could. My wife and I and a hundred or so residents of Cedar drove out to see the first one. We huddled up, our blankets around us because it was cold, so early in the morning before daylight, and we were chattering like chipmunks, so excited! Pretty soon, why, the whole sky just flared up in an orange-red flash, and it was so brilliant that you could easily see the trees ten miles across the valley, and if you had a newspaper you could have easily read it, it was so bright. . . .

Later on in the day, you'd see these fallout clouds drifting down in Kanarraville, and up through Cedar, and if you'd ever seen one you'd never mistake it because it was definitely different from any rain cloud, kind of a pinkish-tan color strung out all down through the valley there for several miles. They'd float over the city and everyone would go out and ooh and aah just like a bunch of hicks. We was never warned that there was any danger involved in going out and being under these fallout clouds all the time I lived here. . . .

Along about 1955 a cloud came over Cedar, and my wife and I, the kids and the neighbors stood outside looking at it and talking about it. Later on towards evening, my wife, her skin, her hands, arms, neck, face, legs, anything that was exposed just turned a beet red. . . . She got a severe headache, and nausea, diarrhea, really miserable. We drove out to the hospital, and the doctor said, "Well it looks like sunburn, but then it doesn't." Her headache persisted for several months, and the diarrhea and nausea for a few weeks.

Four weeks after that I was sittin' in the front room reading the paper and she'd gone into the bathroom to wash her hair. All at once she let out the most ungodly scream, and I run in there and there's about half her hair layin' in the washbasin! You can imagine a woman with beautiful, raven-black hair, so black it would glint green in the sunlight just like a raven's wing. . . . She was in a state of panic. . . . After that she kept getting weaker, and listless, and she didn't even have any desire to go out in the garden to work with her flowers. . . . Finally [the doctors] said it looked like a large tumor in her brain, and they operated and removed a tumor about the size of a large orange or softball, but they couldn't get it all out, it was too embedded in the brain tissue. Oleta lived two years or so after that operation. She started going downhill from 1955 and died in 1965 at 41.

—————————

Source: Carole Gallagher, *American Ground Zero* (Cambridge, MA: MIT Press, 1993), 133–135.

Summary

★

Emerging from World War II as the world's most powerful nation, the United States soon became embroiled in a conflict with the Soviet Union over Eastern Europe. Twice a victim of German aggression, the Soviet Union used its occupation forces to establish a buffer zone of friendly governments in the region. The Truman administration, alarmed at what it saw as naked Soviet expansionism, set out to contain communist influence and to support noncommunist governments that shared America's commitment to a free-market system. Originally intended to curb the communist threat in Europe through economic and political aid, containment soon became a policy of military aid against communist and left-wing movements around the world.

Tension over communism abroad fostered a period of domestic repression and fear at home. Government, unions, schools, and other organizations instituted loyalty oaths as a requirement for employment; media organizations blacklisted suspected Communists; and congressional committees conducted sensationalized public investigations of alleged communist subversion. Red-hunting activities peaked during the anticommunist crusade of Senator Joseph McCarthy in the early 1950s, shattering the lives and careers of many innocent victims through false accusations and innuendo.

The Cold War also enhanced the power of the presidency and the national security state. With bipartisan support for the Cold War, the president gained greater latitude in foreign policy making and increasingly relied on covert operations of the Central Intelligence Agency to maintain friendly governments in the Third World. But these changes came at a price. The national security state required increased defense expenditures, which consumed an ever larger part of the gross national product. Americans now lived in a world where small foreign wars were a constant possibility and fear of a nuclear attack and radioactive fallout was part of daily life.

Under both Democratic and Republican presidents, New Deal reforms were modestly expanded during the postwar era. Harry Truman's Fair Deal proposed a sweeping program of social and economic reform but won only limited legislative victories in the areas of economic policy, social welfare, and civil rights. The Republican administration of Dwight Eisenhower did not roll back the New Deal and in fact presided over cautious increases in federal power through new initiatives in aerospace, education, and transportation. A growing civil rights movement in the South spurred federal activism on behalf of racial equality and put civil rights back on the national political agenda. Ultimately, the civil rights movement would usher in a broader wave of social activism in the 1960s, a development that was rooted in the affluence of the Cold War era.

TIMELINE

1945	Yalta and Potsdam conferences
	Harry S Truman succeeds Roosevelt as president
	End of World War II
1946	Kennan sends "Long Telegram" outlining containment policy
	Churchill's "Iron Curtain" speech
	Baruch Plan for international control of atomic weapons fails
	Employment Act
1947	Taft-Hartley Act
	Truman Doctrine
	National Security Act
	Marshall Plan
	House Un-American Activities Committee (HUAC) begins to investigate Hollywood
1948	Desegregation of U.S. armed forces
	Berlin airlift
1949	North Atlantic Treaty Organization (NATO) founded
	People's Republic of China established
	National Housing Act
	USSR detonates atomic bomb; U.S. atomic monopoly ends
1950	Senator Joseph McCarthy presents list of alleged Communists in government
	NSC-68 calls for permanent mobilization
1950– 1953	Korean War
1952	Dwight D. Eisenhower elected president
	U.S. detonates hydrogen bomb
1953	Joseph Stalin dies
1954	U.S. Army–McCarthy hearings
	Brown v. Board of Education of Topeka
1956	Suez crisis
	Interstate Highway Act
1957	Eisenhower Doctrine
	USSR launches *Sputnik*
	Eisenhower sends U.S. troops to Little Rock to ensure school integration
1958	NASA established
1960	American U-2 spy plane shot down over USSR

Suggested Readings

———————★———————

General works on the politics and diplomacy of the Cold War era include William Chafe, *The Unfinished Journey* (4th ed., 1999), and Paul Boyer, *Promises to Keep* (1995).

The Early Cold War

The best overviews of the Cold War are Walter LaFeber, *America, Russia, and the Cold War, 1945–1990* (8th ed., 1997); Thomas G. Paterson, *On Every Front: The Making and Unmaking of the Cold War* (rev. ed., 1992); and Stephen Ambrose and Douglas Brinkley, *Rise to Globalism* (8th ed., 1997). Melvyn P. Leffler presents a masterful and exhaustive synthesis of Truman's foreign policy in *A Preponderance of Power* (1992). For critical views of American aims, see H. W. Brands, *The Devil We Knew* (1993), and Richard Ned Lebow and Janice Gross Stein, *We All Lost the Cold War* (1994). John Lewis Gaddis blames the Cold War on both the United States and the Soviet Union in *Strategies of Containment* (1982), although his more recent works, *The Long Peace* (1987) and *The United States and the End of the Cold War* (1992), are more sympathetic to American policy making. For international perspectives on the Cold War, see Melvyn P. Leffler and David S. Painter, eds., *Origins of the Cold War: An International History* (1994), and Thomas J. McCormick, *America's Half-Century* (1989). Specialized studies include Ernest R. May, ed., *American Cold War Strategy: Interpreting NSC-68* (1993); Laurence S. Kaplan, *The United States and NATO* (1984); Michael Hogan, *The Marshall Plan* (1987); and Richard Freeland, *The Truman Doctrine and the Origins of McCarthyism* (1972).

The descent into the Cold War can also be viewed through the works of individual policy makers. Indispensable are Dean Acheson's modestly titled *Present at the Creation* (1970) and George F. Kennan's *American Diplomacy, 1900–1950* (1952), and *Memoirs, 1925–1950* (1967). Walter L. Hixson, *George F. Kennan: Cold War Iconoclast* (1989), presents a complex portrait of the architect of containment. Walter Lippmann, *The Cold War* (1947), offers a thoughtful critique of American foreign policy by a contemporary.

McGeorge Bundy, *Danger and Survival* (1989); Martin J. Sherwin, *A World Destroyed* (1975); and Gar Alperovitz, *Atomic Diplomacy* (2d ed., 1994), cover the impact of atomic weapons on American policy. For general discussions of America and nuclear weapons, see Paul Boyer, *By the Bomb's Early Light* (1985).

For developments in Asia, Akira Iriye, *The Cold War in Asia* (1974), is a good starting point. See also William Borden, *The Pacific Alliance* (1984); Warren I. Cohen, *America's Response to China* (2d ed., 1980); and Michael Schaller, *The United States and China in the Twentieth Century* (1979) and *The American Occupation of Japan* (1985).

There is an abundance of scholarship on the Korean War, including William Stueck, *The Korean War: An International History* (1995); Clay Blair, *The Forgotten War* (1988); Max Hastings, *The Korean War* (1987); Callum McDonald, *Korea: The War before Vietnam* (1987); Burton Kaufman, *The Korean War* (1986); and Rosemary Foot, *The Wrong War* (1985). Especially influential are the two volumes of *The Origins of the Korean War* by Bruce Cumings: *Liberation and the Emergence of Separate Regions, 1945–1947* (1981) and *The Roaring of the Cataract, 1947–1950* (1990). William Manchester, *American Caesar* (1979), and Michael Schaller, *Douglas MacArthur* (1989), offer stimulating biographies of a leading figure of the war.

Harry Truman and the Cold War at Home

Harry Truman, *Memoirs* (1952–1962), tells Truman's story in characteristically pointed language; see also Merle Miller's oral history, *Plain Speaking* (1980); David McCullough, *Truman* (1992), offers a generally sympathetic biography; Alonzo Hamby presents a more mixed view in *Man of the People: A Life of Harry S. Truman* (1995). General accounts of the Truman presidency can be found in Robert J. Donovan, *Tumultuous Years: The Presidency of Harry S. Truman, 1949–1953* (1982); Donald R. McCoy, *The Presidency of Harry S. Truman* (1984); and William Pemberton, *Harry S. Truman* (1989). Critical perspectives are presented in Barton J. Bernstein, ed., *Politics and Policies of the Truman Administration* (1970).

The literature on McCarthyism is voluminous. Recent works include Richard Gid Powers, *Not without Honor* (1996); Richard Fried, *Nightmare in Red: The McCarthy Era in Perspective* (1990); and Stephen J. Whitfield, *The Culture of the Cold War* (1991). David Caute, *The Great Fear* (1978), provides a detailed account, which can be supplemented by Victor Navasky, *Naming Names* (1980), and Athan Theoharis, *Spying on Americans* (1978). Two useful biographies are Thomas C. Reeves, *The Life and Times of Joe McCarthy* (1982), and David Oshinsky, *A Conspiracy So Immense* (1983).

"Modern Republicanism"

Two standard overviews of the Eisenhower administration, Herbert S. Parmet, *Eisenhower and the American Crusades* (1972), and Charles C. Alexander, *Holding the Line* (1975), can be supplemented by Fred I. Greenstein, *The Hidden-Hand Presidency* (1982), and Stephen Ambrose, *Eisenhower the President* (1984).

Robert F. Burk, *The Eisenhower Administration and Black Civil Rights* (1984), looks at what the administration did and did not do. Richard Kluger, *Simple Justice* (1975), and Mark Tushnet, *The NAACP's Legal Strategy against Segregated Education* (1987), analyze the *Brown* decision and its context. Martin Luther King Jr. recounts his experience in the Montgomery bus boycott in *Stride toward Freedom* (1958); and Taylor Branch, *Parting the Waters: America in the King Years, 1954–1963* (1988), provides a good account of King's early years.

The Impact of the Cold War

For the complex foreign policy of the 1950s, consult LaFeber, *America, Russia, and the Cold War*; Ambrose and Brinkley, *Rise to Globalism*; and McCormick, *America's Half-Century*. Gabriel Kolko, *Confronting the Third World, 1945–1980* (1988), offers a highly critical view of U.S. policy. On American involvement in the Middle East, see Bruce Kuniholm, *The Origins of the Cold War in the Near East* (1980), and Michael Stoff, *Oil, War, and American Security* (1980). On Latin America, see Stephen Rabe, *Eisenhower and Latin America: The Foreign Policy of Anticommunism* (1988).

Chapter 28

The Affluent Society and the Liberal Consensus,

1945–1965

IN 1959, VICE-PRESIDENT Richard Nixon traveled to Moscow to open the American National Exhibit, one of several efforts to reduce Cold War tensions in the late 1950s. After sipping Pepsi-Cola, Nixon and Soviet Premier Nikita Khrushchev got into a heated debate about the relative merits of Soviet and American societies. Instead of discussing rockets, submarines, and missiles, however, they talked dishwashers, toasters, and televisions. Both the subject of the animated conversation and its site—the kitchen of a model American home—led to its popular designation as the "kitchen debate." What was so striking about the Moscow exhibition was how its American planners enlisted affluence and mass consumption in the service of Cold War politics. The suburban life-style portrayed in the exhibit was intended to symbolize the superiority of capitalism over communism and imply that the American way of life would win the Cold War.

During the postwar era, millions of Americans pursued the promise of consumer society in the burgeoning suburbs, enjoying the highest standard of living in the nation's history. But this affluence was never as widespread as the Moscow exhibit implied. The middle-class suburban life-style was beyond the reach of many poor and nonwhite Americans, particularly those in the decaying central cities. Hoping to spread the abundance of a consumer society to greater numbers of Americans, the Democratic administrations of the early 1960s pressed for the expansion of New Deal social welfare programs. The administrations of John F. Kennedy and—to a much greater extent—Lyndon B. Johnson

The Growing Middle Class
Postwar affluence resulted in an unprecedented standard of living for the rapidly expanding middle class of the 1950s and 1960s. This 1951 photograph shows Du Pont worker Steve Czekalinski and his family amid a year's supply of food. Prior to the 1950s, most families relied on a diet of starches and smoked meats. The newfound prosperity of the growing middle class enabled families like the Czekalinskis to enrich their diets with fresh meats and vegetables and frozen food. The cost to the Czekalinskis in 1951 for a year's supply of food: $1,300.
Alexander Henderson/Hagley Museum and Library.

tried to use federal power to ensure the public welfare in areas such as health care, education, and civil rights. In the Great Society program—a burst of social legislation in 1964–1965 that marked the high tide of postwar liberalism—the Johnson administration attempted to use the fiscal powers of the state to redress the imbalances of the economy without directly challenging capitalism.

Liberal politicians also pursued an activist stance abroad. Continuing and in some cases expanding the Cold War policies of Truman and Eisenhower, the Kennedy and Johnson administrations took aggressive action against communist influence in Europe, the Caribbean, Vietnam (see Chapter 29), and other areas. The growing financial and political costs of that ambitious agenda, however, hampered further progress on the domestic front and revealed ominous cracks in the postwar liberal coalition.

The Affluent Society

★

By the end of 1945 war-induced prosperity had made the United States the richest country in the world. Because the government had curtailed new housing construction and rationed many consumer goods during the war, Americans in 1945 had accumulated savings of $140 billion, which they were eager to spend. Over the next two decades the gross national product (GNP) more than tripled, benefiting a wider segment of society than anyone would have dreamed possible in the dark days of the Great Depression. Millions of Americans, particularly working-class and middle-class whites, moved their families to new homes in the suburbs in a search for security and stability.

The Economic Record

The twenty-year period following World War II was the heyday of modern American capitalism. U.S. corporations and banking institutions so dominated the world economy that the period has been called the *Pax Americana* (American peace). U.S. military policy and foreign aid, as well as the absence of major economic competitors, were vital factors in extending the global reach of American corporate capitalism, which enjoyed remarkable growth in productivity and profits. American economic leadership abroad translated into affluence at home.

Corporate Strategies. The predominant thrust of modern corporate life was the consolidation of economic and financial resources by oligopolies, a few large producers who controlled the national and, increasingly, the world market. In 1970 the top four U.S. firms produced 91 percent of the motor vehicles sold in the domestic market and 90 percent of all breakfast cereal foods; the top four in tires produced 72 percent, in cigarettes 84 percent, and in detergents 70 percent. Despite laws restricting branch banking to a single state, in 1970 the four largest banks held 16 percent of the nation's banking assets; the top fifty banks held 48 percent.

Diversification—undertaking new activities and investments and moving into new markets—was the most important corporate strategy in the postwar era. By combining companies in unrelated industries, larger firms called conglomerates offered protection from instability in any single market, making them more effective international competitors. International Telephone and Telegraph became a diversified conglomerate by acquiring Continental Baking, Sheraton Hotels, Avis Rent-a-Car, Levitt and Sons (home builders), and Hartford Fire Insurance. Ling-Temco-Vought, another conglomerate, simultaneously produced steel, built ships, developed real estate, and brought cattle to market. These and other corporate acquisitions resulted in the nation's third great merger wave (the first two had taken place in the 1890s and the 1920s), which reached its peak in the 1960s.

The development of giant corporations was also based on the penetration of foreign markets. Unlike the Soviet Union, Western Europe, and Japan, America emerged physically unscathed from the war, with its defense industries eager to convert to consumer production. Soon American companies provided products and services for war-torn European and Asian markets, giving the nation a trade surplus close to $5 billion in 1960. International strategies enabled American business to enter these regions when domestic markets became saturated or when American recessions cut into sales. American products were considered the best in the world and were widely sought after abroad.

The Bretton Woods System. American global supremacy rested in part on decisions made at a United Nations economic conference held in Bretton Woods, New Hampshire, in July 1944, which established the U.S. dollar as the capitalist world's principal reserve currency. Two global institutions—the International Bank for Reconstruction and Development (commonly known as the World Bank) and the International Monetary Fund (IMF)—resulted from this meeting. The World Bank provided private loans for the reconstruction of war-torn Europe as well as for the development of Third World countries. The IMF was set up to stabilize the value of currencies, providing a secure and predictable monetary environment for trade. It did this by encouraging fixed exchange rates, which facilitated the

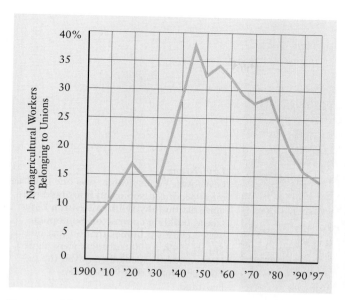

FIGURE 28.1
Labor Union Strength, 1900–1997
Labor unions reached their peak strength immediately after World War II. For the next thirty years they consistently represented more than a quarter of the nonfarm work force. After 1975, the influence of labor unions declined dramatically.
Source: AFL-CIO Information Bureau, Washington, DC.

free convertibility of currencies to gold or to the currencies of other trading nations; the strong U.S. dollar served as the benchmark. In 1947 multinational trade negotiations resulted in the first General Agreement on Tariffs and Trade (GATT), which led to the establishment of an international body to oversee trade rules and practices.

The World Bank, the IMF, and GATT were the cornerstones of the so-called Bretton Woods system, which guided the world economy after the war. The United States dominated the World Bank and the IMF because it contributed the most capital to them and because the U.S. dollar had a pivotal role in international currency exchange. Thus, these independent international organizations worked along lines that favored American-style internationalism over the economic nationalism that was traditional in most other countries. The World Bank, the IMF, and GATT encouraged stable prices, the liberalization of trade barriers and the reduction of tariffs, flexible domestic markets, and free trade based on fixed exchange rates. As long as the U.S. dollar remained the strongest currency, the Bretton Woods system would effectively serve America's global economic interests.

The Domestic Boom. U.S. economic supremacy abroad helped boost the domestic economy, creating millions of new jobs. One of the fastest-growing groups was salaried office workers, whose numbers increased

by 61 percent between 1947 and 1957. Growing corporate bureaucracies and increased access to a college education through the GI Bill helped expand the male white-collar ranks. These "organization men," as sociologist William Whyte called them, were joined by millions of women who moved into clerical work and other lower-paying service-sector occupations. Although the percentage of blue-collar manufacturing jobs declined slightly during this same period, the power of organized labor reached an all-time high (Figure 28.1). In 1955 the Congress of Industrial Organizations made a formal alliance with its old adversary, the American Federation of Labor. That merger created a single organization—the AFL-CIO—which represented more than 90 percent of the nation's 17.5 million union members. George Meany, a New York building-trades unionist, led this organization for the next twenty-four years with the goal of securing for labor its share of the record postwar profits. In exchange for labor peace and stability—that is, fewer strikes—corporate managers often cooperated with unions, agreeing to contracts that gave many workers secure, predictable, and steadily rising incomes.

As the income of many American workers grew, consumer spending soared. That spending, combined with federal outlays for defense and domestic programs, seemed to promise a continuously rising standard of living. The GNP grew from $213 billion in 1945 to more than $500 billion in 1960 (Figure 28.2). With the inflation rate under 3 percent in the 1950s, this steady economic growth meant a 25 percent rise in real income between 1946 and 1959. American homeownership rates reflected the rising standard of living: in 1940, 43 percent of American families owned their homes; by 1960, 62 percent did. The postwar boom was marred, however, by periodic bouts of recession and unemployment that particularly hurt low-income and nonwhite workers. Moreover, the rising standard of living was not accompanied by a redistribution of income: the top

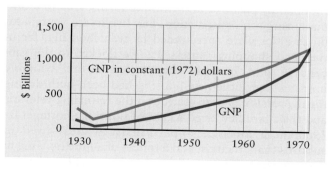

FIGURE 28.2
Gross National Product (GNP), 1929–1972
After a sharp dip during the Great Depression, the gross national product rose steadily in both real and constant dollars in the postwar period.

Levittown
Levittown, Pennsylvania, was one of three mass-produced suburban housing developments built by William Levitt, a Long Island building contractor. So popular were Levittown homes that on just one day in 1949, 1,400 contracts were signed. Homeowners especially enjoyed the privacy and space that such homes provided.
Van Bucher/Photo Researchers.

10 percent of Americans still earned more than the bottom half. Nevertheless, most Americans had more money to spend than ever before.

The Suburban Explosion

One of the most dynamic areas of the economy was the expanding suburban housing market. Although Americans had been gravitating toward urban areas throughout the twentieth century, the postwar period was characterized by two new patterns: one was a shift away from older cities in the Northeast and Midwest and toward newer urban centers in the South and West; the other, a mass defection from the cities to the suburbs. In the 1950s all but one of the nation's twelve most populous cities lost population. (The exception was Los Angeles, where vast tracts of undeveloped land allowed for suburban-style development.)

At the end of World War II many cities were surrounded by pastures and working farms. Due to a dramatic surge in construction, just five to ten years later those cities were surrounded by tract housing, factories, and shopping centers. People flocked to the suburbs in part because they followed the available housing. Very little new housing had been built during the depression or war years, and the returning veterans and their families faced a critical housing shortage. By 1960 more Americans—particularly whites—lived in suburbs than in cities, and a fourth of all the housing in the country had been built during the preceding decade, most of it single-family, owner-occupied homes.

The Housing Boom. William Levitt, an innovative Long Island building contractor, revolutionized the suburban housing market by applying mass-production techniques to home construction. Levitt's company could build 150 homes per week, a rate of one house every sixteen minutes. A basic four-room house, complete with kitchen appliances and an attic that a handy homeowner could convert into two additional bedrooms, was priced at less than $10,000 in 1947. Levitt built planned communities in New York, New Jersey, and Pennsylvania—all named Levittown. Soon other developers were snapping up the cheap farmland surrounding urban areas. On the West Coast, the former shipbuilding magnate Henry Kaiser (see Chapter 26, American Lives, "Henry J. Kaiser: World War II's 'Miracle Man,'" pp. 840–841) moved into housing construction in the postwar era, building subdivisions in and around Los Angeles and San Francisco. Dozens of other developers followed suit, hastening the exodus from the farm and the central city.

Many families financed their homes with mortgages from the Federal Housing Administration and the Veterans Administration at rates dramatically lower than those offered by private lenders. In 1955 those two agencies wrote 41 percent of all nonfarm mortgages. Such lending demonstrated the quiet yet revolutionary way in which the federal government was entering and influencing daily life.

The new suburban homes—and much of the savings and loan and Veterans Administration money—were reserved almost exclusively for whites. Levittown homeowners had to sign a covenant prohibiting occupation "by members of other than the Caucasian Race"; Levitt did not sell houses directly to blacks until 1960. Other communities adopted similar covenants to exclude Jews or Asians. Although the Supreme Court had ruled in *Shelley v. Kraemer* (1948) that restrictive covenants were illegal, the custom continued infor-

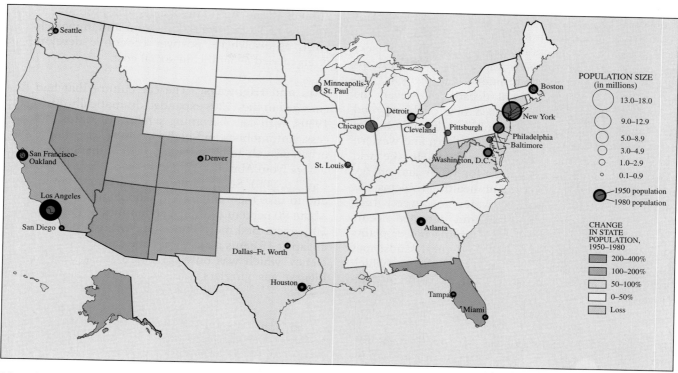

MAP 28.1

Metropolitan Growth, 1950–1980

A metropolitan area is generally defined as a central city that in combination with its surrounding territory forms an integrated economic and social unit. The U.S. Census Bureau introduced the Standard Metropolitan Statistical Area (SMSA) in 1950, but later changes in the definition of SMSA make it difficult to generalize from the 1950 figures. This map compares the population of central cities in 1950 with population figures for the more broadly defined metropolitan areas in 1980 to illustrate the extent and geographical distribution of metropolitan growth in the postwar period.

mally until the civil rights laws of the 1960s banned private discrimination.

Even though suburbia was often portrayed as a homogeneous, even bland, environment, there were strong cultural and class variations among suburbs. When less affluent firefighters, plasterers, machine-tool makers, and sales clerks moved to the suburbs, they were far more likely to settle in a modest Levittown than in an upper-middle-class suburb such as Winnetka, Illinois, or Shaker Heights, Ohio. Blacks shut out of white suburbs established their own communities, such as Lincoln Heights outside Cincinnati, Robbins on the edge of Chicago, and Kinloch near St. Louis. In well-equipped living quarters at bargain prices, working-class white and black families could share in the ultimate postwar suburban dream of giving "every kid an opportunity to grow up with grass stains on his pants."

The Sun Belt. The new patterns of growth and development were most striking in the South and West, where open space allowed for sprawling suburban-style expansion. Fueled by World War II defense spending,

the postwar development of the southern and western cities accelerated as industry took advantage of inexpensive land, unorganized labor, low taxes, and warm climates (now made livable through the new technology of air conditioning). Some of the most explosive growth occurred in Florida, Texas, and California—states that would become the industrial leaders of the emerging Sun Belt economy (Map 28.1). Between 1940 and 1970, Miami's metropolitan population increased by 79 percent with the addition of more than a million new residents, many of them older or retired. Texas cities, especially Houston and Dallas, grew as the petrochemical industry expanded rapidly after 1945. Spurred by massive defense spending, California grew the most rapidly, adding 2.6 million people in the 1940s and 3.1 million more in the 1950s. In 1970 California had about a tenth of the U.S. population, and in 1972 it replaced New York as the state with the largest number of electoral votes.

Business boosters in California and other Sun Belt states worked tirelessly to promote regional development. Local leaders lobbied for new defense installations and contracts, wooed scientific and artistic talent from the Northeast, and even purchased professional sports teams. In 1958 investors moved the Brooklyn Dodgers to Los Angeles and the New York Giants to San Francisco, allowing boosters to promote their towns as "big-league" cities. In subsequent decades, however, the success of Sun Belt cities raised new problems and challenges. Booming urban populations brought higher crime and poverty rates, making southern and western cities more like those in the Northeast. In the arid Southwest, increasing demands for water and energy resulted in environmental and health problems. As cities competed for scarce water resources, they depleted underground aquifers and dammed scenic rivers. The proliferation of coal-burning power plants increased air pollution and scarred rural landscapes through strip mining. The nuclear industry, which brought jobs and income to the West, also brought radi-

ation contamination to residents near atomic test sites, nuclear waste facilities, and uranium mines. In the West, as elsewhere, postwar economic development often carried a significant social cost.

Cars and Highways.   The car culture that had first emerged in the 1920s expanded dramatically during the 1950s, with cars becoming symbols of status and success. Automobiles and highways were essential to suburban growth and the development of the Sun Belt (see Voices from Abroad, "Hanoch Bartov: 'Everyone Has a Car,'" p. 909). Suburbanites needed cars to get to work and to take their children to school and piano lessons. About 90 percent of suburban families owned cars, and 20 percent had more than one. With gas plentiful and cheap at 15 cents a gallon, no one cared about fuel efficiency, which was only 8 miles to the gallon for the biggest gas guzzlers. American cars became heavier

Highway Building
Federal funding of interstate transportation resulted in a burgeoning network of highways that transformed both urban and rural landscapes. This photograph shows the construction of the Congress (later renamed Eisenhower) Expressway in Chicago in 1950. The new expressway cut a wide swath through many West Side neighborhoods, forever altering the urban landscape and introducing city residents to traffic jams and air pollution.
Chicago Tribune.

HANOCH BARTOV

"Everyone Has a Car"

★

One of Israel's foremost writers and journalists, Hanoch Bartov spent two years in the United States working as a correspondent for the newspaper Lamerchav. As a newcomer to Los Angeles in the early 1960s, he was both fascinated and appalled by Americans' love affair with the automobile.

Our immediate decision to buy a car sprang from healthy instincts. Only later did I learn from bitter experience that in California, death was preferable to living without one. Neither the views from the plane nor the weird excursion that first evening hinted at what I would go through that first week.

Very simple—the nearest supermarket was about half a kilometer south of our apartment, the regional primary school two kilometers east, and my son's kindergarten even farther away. A trip to the post office—an undertaking, to the bank—an ordeal, to work—an impossibility.

Truth be told: the Los Angeles municipality . . . does have public transportation.

Buses go once an hour along the city's boulevards and avenues, gathering all the wretched of the earth, the poor and the needy, the old ladies forbidden by their grandchildren to drive, and other eccentric types. But few people can depend on buses, even should they swear never to deviate from the fixed routes. . . . There are no tramways. No one thought of a subway. Railroads—not now and not in the future.

Why? Because everyone has a car. A man invited me to his house, saying, "We are neighbors, within ten minutes of each other." After walking for an hour and a half I realized what he meant—"ten minute drive within the speed limit." Simply put, he

never thought I might interpret his remark to refer to the walking distance. The moment a baby sees the light of day in Los Angeles, a car is registered in his name in Detroit. . . .

At first perhaps people relished the freedom and independence a car provided. You get in, sit down, and grab the steering wheel, your mobility exceeding that of any other generation. No wonder people refuse to live downtown, where they can hear their neighbors, smell their cooking, and suffer frayed nerves as trains pass by bedroom windows. Instead, they get a piece of the desert, far from town, at half price, drag a water hose, grow grass, flowers, and trees, and build their dream house. . . .

The result? A widely scattered city, its houses far apart, its streets stretched in all directions. Olympic Boulevard from west to east, forty kilometers. Sepulveda Boulevard, from Long Beach in the south to the edge of the desert, forty kilometers. Altogether covering 1200 square kilometers. As of now.

Why "as of now"? Because greater distances mean more commuting, and more commuting leads to more cars. More cars means problems that push people even farther away from the city, which chases after them.

The urban sprawl is only one side effect. Two, some say three, million cars require an array of services. . . .

. . . Why bother parking, getting out, getting in, getting up and sitting down, when you can simply "drive in"? Mailboxes have their slots facing the road, at the level of the driver's hand. That is how dirty laundry is deposited, electricity and water bills paid. That is how love is made, how children are taken to school. That is how the anniversary wreath is laid on the graves of loved ones. There are drive-in movies. And, yes, we saw it with our own eyes: drive-in churches. Only in death is a man separated from his car and buried alone. . . .

Source: Oscar and Lilian Handlin, eds., *From the Outer World* (Cambridge, MA: Harvard University Press, 1997), 293–296.

and bigger, creating a disparity in size with Japanese or European models that persists to this day, despite the downsizing of American vehicles since the 1970s.

More cars required more highways, which were funded largely by the federal government. In 1947 Congress authorized the construction of 37,000 miles of highways; the National Interstate and Defense Highway Act of 1956 increased this commitment by another 42,500 miles. One of the largest civil engineering projects in world history, the new interstate system would link the entire country with roads at least four lanes wide. The interstate system changed both the cities and the countryside. It rerouted traffic through rural areas and created new communities of gas stations, fast-food outlets, and motels around highway exits. In urban areas new highways cut wide swaths through old neighborhoods and caused air pollution and traffic jams; critics complained about "autosclerosis," a hardening of the urban arteries.

The federally constructed highways also siphoned funding away from mass transit. With the support of the interstate trucking industry, Congress established the Highway Trust Fund in 1956 to collect fees to finance road building and maintenance; it specifically prohibited the use of its funds to promote urban mass transit. As municipal governments committed increasing resources to matching funds for federal highway construction, mass-transit systems languished. By 1960 two-thirds of Americans were driving to work each day. The percentage was even higher—between 80 and 95 percent—in Sun Belt cities like Los Angeles and Phoenix.

Highway construction had far-reaching effects on patterns of consumption and shopping. Instead of taking a train into the city or walking to a corner grocery store, people drove to suburban shopping malls and supermarkets. The first mall had appeared in Kansas City in the 1920s, and there were still only 8 in 1945; by 1960 the number had mushroomed to almost 4,000. When a 110-store complex at Roosevelt Field on suburban Long Island opened in 1956, it was conveniently situated at an expressway exit and had parking for 11,000 cars. Downtown retail areas and department stores soon declined.

Highways and suburbs also lured corporate business and manufacturing away from the cities. In the early 1950s, Stanford University in Palo Alto, California, built one of the nation's first *industrial parks*, a suburban, campuslike facility for light manufacturing. Exploiting its ties with university researchers, Stanford Industrial Park attracted Cold War defense contractors such as General Electric, Lockheed, and Hewlett-Packard. Those firms soon formed the nucleus of an electronic and high-tech region known as Silicon Valley. On the East Coast, a similar high-tech boom occurred outside Boston along Route 128, led by firms such as Polaroid and computer manufacturers Digital Equipment and Wang. In the Midwest the number of factories in suburban Chicago doubled between 1947 and 1954, and suburban Detroit saw a 220 percent increase.

The U.S. government's financing of highways and home building after World War II helped fuel a suburban explosion that was unique to North America. In war-ravaged European cities postwar housing construction was centered in high-density city neighborhoods or along mass-transit lines. Not until the 1960s and 1970s would Europeans experiment with low-density suburban housing, and their central cities never declined as precipitously as American cities did.

American Life during the Baby Boom

Hula-Hoops and poodle skirts, sock hops and rock 'n' roll, shiny cars and gleaming appliances—all signify the "fifties," a period that really stretched from 1945 through the early 1960s. The postwar years are remembered as a time of affluence and stability, a time when Americans enjoyed an optimistic faith in progress and technology and a serene family-centered culture enshrined in television sitcoms such as "Father Knows Best." This powerful myth, like many myths, has some truth to it, but there were other sides to the story. Focusing solely on affluence, popular culture, and consumption does not do justice to this complex period of economic and social transformation, which included challenges to the status quo as well as conformity.

Consumer Culture. In some respects the consumer culture of the 1950s seemed like a return to the 1920s—a wealth of new gadgets and appliances, the expansion of consumer credit and advertising, more leisure time, the growing importance of the automobile, and the development of new types of mass media. Yet there was a significant difference: the postwar economy was far better balanced than that of the 1920s. By the 1950s consumption had become a hallmark of middle-class culture, but even blue-collar families had discretionary income to spend on consumer goods because of rising incomes.

As in the 1920s, though, prosperity was helped along by a dramatic increase in consumer credit, which enabled families to stretch their incomes. Between 1946 and 1958 short-term consumer credit rose from $8.4 billion to almost $45 billion. The Diners Club introduced the first credit card in 1950, followed by the American Express card and Bank Americard in 1959. By the 1970s the omnipresent plastic credit card had revolutionized personal and family finances.

Aggressive advertising contributed to the massive increase in consumer spending. In 1951 businesses spent more on advertising ($6.5 billion) than taxpayers did on primary and secondary education ($5 billion). The 1950s gave Americans the Marlboro man; M&Ms that "melt in your mouth, not in your hand"; Wonder Bread to "build strong bodies in twelve ways"; and the "Does she or doesn't she?" Clairol woman. Automobiles continued to be the most heavily advertised item in the 1950s, but advertising also promoted a variety of new consumer appliances to fill the suburban home. In 1946 automatic washing machines and electric dryers came on the market; commercial laundries across the country struggled to stay in business. The home freezer enabled families to eat seasonal foods, such as fruits and vegetables, all year long and encouraged the dramatic growth of the frozen-food industry. Partly because of the purchase of electrical appliances for the home, consumer use of electricity doubled during the 1950s.

Consumers had more free time in which to spend their money than ever before. In 1960 the average worker put in a five-day week, with eight paid holidays a year (double the 1946 standard) plus a paid two-week vacation. The travel industry grew rapidly during the 1950s, with Americans devoting a seventh of the GNP to spending on leisure and entertainment. Americans took to the interstate highway system by the millions, encouraging the dramatic growth of motel chains, roadside restaurants, and fast-food eateries. The first McDonald's restaurant opened in 1954 in San Bernardino, California; the Holiday Inn motel chain started in Memphis in 1952. Among the most popular destinations were national and state parks and Disneyland, which opened in Anaheim, California, in 1955. Aided by the strong U.S. dollar and the introduction of jet air travel in 1958, families flooded Europe each summer, earning the unflattering epithet of "ugly Americans" because many expected things to be just like home.

Television. Perhaps the most significant hallmark of postwar consumer culture was television. TV's leap to cultural prominence was swift and overpowering. There were only ten broadcasting stations in the country and a meager 7,000 sets in American homes in 1947. By 1960, 87 percent of American families had at least one television set. Viewers had only three or four channels to choose from, however; public television did not begin until 1967, and cable was a phenomenon of the 1980s.

Television developed as a government-controlled or subsidized service in other countries, but in the United States it emerged as private enterprise geared toward entertainment. Although stations were licensed by the Federal Communications Commission after 1941, television, like radio, depended entirely on advertising and corporate sponsorship for profits. Soon television supplanted radio as the chief diffuser of popular culture, its national programming promoting shared interests and tastes and reducing regional and ethnic differences. Movie attendance shrank throughout the postwar period, and studios increasingly relied on overseas distribution of American films to earn a profit.

Television encouraged the consumerism and advertising that have characterized mass culture since the 1920s. As in the golden era of radio in the 1920s and 1930s, corporations produced and sponsored major television shows such as "Texaco Star Theater" with Milton Berle and "General Electric Theater" hosted by Ronald Reagan. New products entered the home, such as frozen TV dinners, first introduced in 1954. *TV Guide,* founded in 1948, became the most successful new periodical of the 1950s. Television even affected city services. In 1954 the Toledo water commissioner wondered why water consumption rose dramatically during certain three-minute periods. The answer? All

Advertising in the TV Age
Aggressive advertising and the development of new products, such as color television, helped fuel the surge in consumer spending during the 1950s. Electricity usage more than doubled in the 1950s, as growing numbers of Americans purchased TVs and other appliances.
Courtesy Motorola Museum of Electronics. © 1999 Motorola Inc.

across Toledo, TV watchers flushed their toilets during commercials.

What Americans saw on television, besides the omnipresent commercials, was an overwhelmingly white, middle-class world of nuclear families living in suburban homes. "Leave It to Beaver," "Ozzie and Harriet," and similar sitcoms featured characters who adhered to clear-cut gender roles and plots based on small family crises that were always happily resolved by the end of the show. Programs such as "The Honeymooners," starring Jackie Gleason as a Brooklyn bus driver, and "Life of Reilly," a situation comedy featuring a California aircraft worker, were rare in their treatment of working-class lives. Nonwhite characters appeared mainly as servants, such as comedian Jack Benny's black "houseboy" Rochester or the Latino gardener with the anglicized name "Frank Smith" on "Father Knows Best."

The types of television programs developed in the 1950s built on older entertainment genres but also pioneered new ones. Taking over a popular radio and movie category, television offered some thirty westerns by 1959, including "Bonanza," the first color show.

National television coverage made professional sports big-time entertainment and big business—far exceeding the potential of radio. Programming geared to children, such as Walt Disney's "Mickey Mouse Club," "Howdy Doody," and "Captain Kangaroo," created the first generation of children to grow up glued to the tube. The appeal of popular quiz shows such as "Twenty-One" and "The $64,000 Question" was not diminished even when it was revealed in 1959 that contestants had received the questions in advance. Although the new medium did offer some serious programming, notably live theater and documentaries, Federal Communications Commissioner Newton Minow concluded in 1963 that television was "a vast wasteland." Its reassuring images of family life and postwar society, however, dovetailed with the social expectations of many Americans.

Religion and the Search for Security. The dislocations of the depression and war years made Americans yearn for security and a reaffirmation of traditional values. Some of this sentiment was expressed in a renewed emphasis on religion. Church membership rose from 49 percent of the population in 1940 to 69 percent in 1960. All the major denominations shared in the growth, which was accompanied by an ecumenical movement to bring Catholics, Protestants, and Jews together. The stress on religious harmony meshed with Cold War Americans' view of themselves as a righteous people opposed to "godless communism." In 1954 the phrase "under God" was inserted into the Pledge of Allegiance, and in 1956 Congress added "In God We Trust" to all U.S. coins.

Beyond patriotism, religion also served more deeply felt needs. In his popular television program Bishop Fulton Sheen asked, "Is life worth living?" He and countless others optimistically answered in the affirmative. None was more positive than Norman Vincent Peale, whose best-selling book *The Power of Positive Thinking* (1952) embodied the trend toward the therapeutic use of religion to assist men and women in coping with the stresses of modern life. Evangelical religion also experienced a resurgence, most evident in the dramatic rise to popularity of the Reverend Billy Graham, who used television, radio, advertising, and print media to spread the gospel. His nondenominational Evangelistic Association, founded in 1950, was a tremendous success. Although critics suggested that middle-class interest in religion stemmed less from spirituality than from the impulse toward conformity, the revival nonetheless spoke to Americans' search for spiritual meaning in uncertain times.

The Baby Boom. Even more dramatic testimony to the desire for stability in the postwar era was the emphasis Americans placed on the family and children.

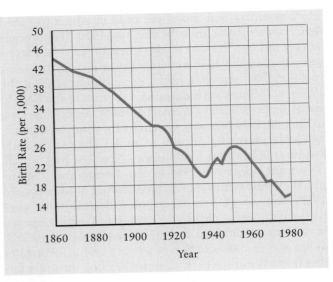

FIGURE 28.3
The Declining American Birth Rate, 1860–1980
When birth rates are viewed over more than a century, the postwar baby boom is clearly an aberration.

As one popular advice book put it, "The family is the center of your living. If it isn't, you've gone astray." Two things were noteworthy about the men and women who formed families between 1940 and 1960. First, their marriages were remarkably stable. Not until the mid-1960s did the divorce rate begin to rise sharply. Second, they were intent on having children.

After a century and a half of declining family size, the birth rate shot up: more babies were born between 1948 and 1953 than were born in the previous thirty years (Figure 28.3). Women who came of age in the 1930s had an average of 2.4 children; their counterparts in the 1950s averaged 3.2 children. As a result of this trend and a lengthened life expectancy due to improvements in diet, public health, and medicine, the American population rose dramatically from 140 million in 1945 to 179 million in 1960 and then to 203 million in 1970.

There are several reasons for this twenty-year upsurge that demographers call the *baby boom*, which peaked in 1957. Because a sustained rise in the birth rate did not occur in all the countries affected by World War II, it was not simply a response to the losses of war. More important was the drop in the average marriage age—to twenty-two for men and twenty for women—a trend that had begun during the war. The drop in the marriage age resulted in a surge of young married couples who produced a bumper crop of children.

To rear all those baby-boom children and keep them healthy, middle-class parents increasingly relied on the advice of experts. Accepting the advice of doctors and the federal government, they had their children inoculated with the Salk polio vaccine,

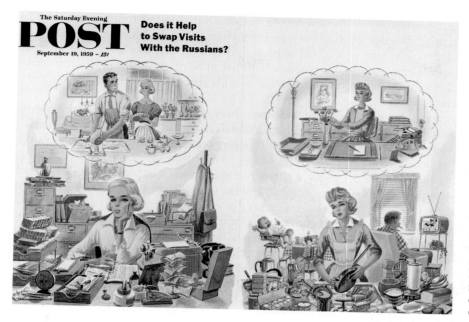

A Woman's Dilemma in Postwar America
This 1959 cover of the *Saturday Evening Post* depicts some of the difficult choices facing women in the postwar era. Women's consignment to low-paid, dead-end jobs in the service sector encouraged many to become full-time homemakers. Once back in their suburban homes, however, many middle-class women felt isolated and trapped amid endless rounds of cooking, cleaning, and diaper changing.
© The Curtis Publishing Company.

administered free in the nation's schools. The conquest of polio, which demonstrated the potential of government-sponsored public health programs, made the children of the 1950s one of the healthiest generations ever. Just as important was the widespread use of new "miracle drugs" such as penicillin (introduced in 1943), streptomycin (1945), and cortisone (1946).

Parents also embraced scientific child rearing, buying a million copies of Dr. Benjamin Spock's *Baby and Child Care* (1946) in the year it was published. New mothers found Spock's insistence that they abandon the rigid feeding and baby care schedules of an earlier generation liberating, though the book did not remove all their insecurities. Mothers who wanted to work outside the home felt guilty because Spock recommended that they be constantly available to respond to their children's needs. But if a mother was too protective of her children, Spock and others argued, she might hamper their adjustment to a normal adult life.

The baby boom had a broad and immediate impact on American society. It prompted a major expansion of the nation's educational system: by 1970 school expenditures were double those of the 1950 level. In addition, the consumer needs of all those babies fueled the economy as families bought food, diapers, toys, and clothing for their expanding broods. Together with federal expenditures on national security, family spending on consumer goods fueled the unparalleled prosperity and economic growth of the 1950s and 1960s.

The postwar baby boom would have a continuing impact on America for many decades. In the 1960s the baby-boom generation swelled college enrollments and, not coincidentally, the ranks of student protesters. By the 1970s, when the baby-boom generation entered the workplace, it had to compete for a limited number of jobs in what had become a stagnant economy. The delayed marriages and later childbearing of the career-oriented baby boomers temporarily caused the birth rate to rise again in the 1980s. The 1990s produced the first baby-boom president (Bill Clinton) and widespread concern about the future viability of old-age assistance programs such as Social Security and Medicare as the baby boomers aged. The decisions made by many couples in the immediate postwar period to have large families would continue to affect American life well into the twenty-first century.

Contradictions in Women's Lives. The 1950s were characterized by a strong allegiance to traditional gender roles: a masculine ideal that emphasized men's roles as responsible breadwinners and a feminine ideal that pronounced that woman's place was in the home. What feminist Betty Friedan called the "feminine mystique" of the 1950s—that "the highest value and the only commitment for women is the fulfillment of their own femininity"—bore remarkable similarities to the nineteenth-century cult of true womanhood (see Chapter 19). However, the 1950s version of the cult of domesticity drew on twentieth-century science and culture, particularly psychology. Pronouncing motherhood the only "normal" female sex role, psychologists berated mothers who worked outside the home, charging that they damaged their children's development. Television, popular music, films, and advertising reinforced that notion by depicting career women as social and sexual misfits.

In her book *The Feminine Mystique* (1963) Betty Friedan identified "the problem that has no name"—the frustration and depression of many women who chafed under these narrowly prescribed gender roles (see

American Voices, "Joy Wilner: A Fifties Housewife," p. 915). Speaking from her own experience, Friedan described how she gave up a psychology fellowship and career in journalism to marry, move to the suburbs, and raise three children—only to find herself isolated and dissatisfied. Thousands of middle-class women responded enthusiastically to Friedan's theory, making her book a best seller. But not all housewives of the baby-boom era were unhappy or neurotic. Many working-class women embraced their new roles as housewives, delighted not to have to toil at low-paying jobs outside the home. Middle-class wives found constructive outlets for their energy in groups such as the League of Women Voters, the PTA, and the Junior League. And as in earlier periods, some women used the rhetoric of domesticity and maternalism to justify political activism, organizing around issues of community improvement, racial integration, and nuclear disarmament.

Another contradictory aspect of postwar culture was that despite the feminine mystique, more than one-third of American women held jobs outside the home. Many women took jobs to supplement family income and keep pace with rising standards of living, causing a dramatic rise in the number of older, married middle-class women in the labor force. At the turn of the twentieth century the typical female worker was a young recent immigrant who worked only until she married. By mid-century the typical female worker was in her forties, was married, and had children in school.

Occupational segmentation remained characteristic of women's work in the postwar period. Until 1964 the classified sections of most newspapers separated employment ads into columns headed "Help Wanted Male" and "Help Wanted Female." Staffing the expanding postwar service sector, more than 80 percent of all working women did stereotypical "women's work" as salespeople, health-care technicians, waitresses, flight attendants, servants, receptionists, telephone operators, and secretaries. In 1960 women represented only 3.5 percent of all lawyers and 6.1 percent of all physicians, but 97 percent of all nurses, 85 percent of all librarians, and 57 percent of all social workers. Along with women's jobs went women's pay, which averaged 60 percent of men's pay in 1963.

How could postwar society so steadfastly uphold the domestic ideal while an increasing number of wives and mothers took jobs? In many ways the women themselves kept the dramatic increase invisible. Fearing public disapproval of their decisions, such women usually justified their work in individual or family-oriented terms: "Of course I believe a woman's place is at home, but I took this job to save for college for our children." Moreover, when women took jobs outside the home, they retained full responsibility for child care and household management, which allowed families and society to avoid facing the implications of women's new roles. As one overburdened woman noted, she now had "two full-time jobs instead of just one—underpaid clerical worker and unpaid housekeeper." The absence of an active feminist movement in the 1940s and 1950s meant most women had to cope on their own.

Youth Culture. Beneath the surface of family togetherness and traditional gender roles lay other tensions—those between parents and children. Dating back to the 1920s, the emergence of a mass youth culture had its roots in the democratization of education, the growth of peer culture, and the growing consumer independence of teenagers in an age of affluence. Youth, eager to escape the climate of suburban conformity of their parents, had become a distinct new market that advertisers eagerly exploited. In 1956 advertisers projected an adolescent market of $9 billion for items such as transistor radios (introduced in 1952), clothing, and fads such as Silly Putty (1950) and Hula-Hoops (1958). Increasingly, advertisers targeted the young, both to capture their spending money and to exploit their influence on family spending patterns. Notice the changing slogans for Pepsi-Cola: "Twice as much for a nickel" (1935), "Be sociable—have a Pepsi" (1948), "Now it's Pepsi for those who think young" (1960), and finally "the Pepsi Generation" (1965).

Hollywood movies played a large role in fostering and legitimizing a teen culture separate from the safe and insulated suburban world that teenagers' parents had worked so hard to create. At a time when general movie attendance was declining because of competition from television, young people made up the largest audience for motion pictures. Hollywood studios catered to this market with films such as *The Wild One* (1951), starring Marlon Brando, and *Rebel without a Cause* (1955), starring James Dean, Natalie Wood, and Sal Mineo. "What are you rebelling against?" a waitress asks Brando in *The Wild One*. "Whattaya got?" he replies.

What really defined this generation, however, was its music. Rejecting the rigid boundaries of traditional popular music, teenagers in the 1950s discovered rock 'n' roll, an amalgam of white country and western music and the black urban music known as rhythm and blues. The Cleveland disc jockey Alan Freed played a major role in introducing white America to the new African American sound by playing rhythm and blues records on white radio stations beginning in 1954. Young white performers such as Bill Haley, Buddy Holly, and especially Elvis Presley incorporated the new mixture into their own music and capitalized on the new market (see American Lives, "Elvis Presley: Teen Idol of the 1950s," pp. 916–917). Between 1953 and 1959 record sales increased from $213 million to $603 million, with 45-rpm rock-'n'-roll records as the driving force. The new teen music shocked many white adults, who saw rock 'n' roll as an invitation to race-mixing, sexual promiscuity, and juvenile delinquency.

JOY WILNER

A Fifties Housewife

★

Like millions of other middle-class women in the 1950s, Joy Wilner married an ambitious young professional and had children in quick succession. In this interview she recounts the joys and frustrations of her early years of marriage and motherhood and her struggle to accommodate herself to what Betty Friedan has termed the "feminine mystique."

I felt totally fulfilled, totally happy. We were the perfect couple—Ted was supportive of me and I was supportive of him and we never argued. Well, we didn't know how. We'd had no experience with conflict. Everything was fine. I had my next child sixteen months after the first. The second child was neither exactly planned nor unplanned. I didn't really intend to get pregnant again, but on the other hand, we weren't using birth control because, after all, we already had one. . . .

After the second baby, that was the first time I can remember conflict, feelings of being trapped, wondering what I was doing with my life. These weren't very distinct feelings, not like I wonder if this is the right man for me. Just uncomfortable feelings. At some point I expressed some of these feelings, in a very tentative way, to Ted and he said, "Well, if you feel that way, maybe we should get a divorce." I was terrified. The idea of divorce was inconceivable. I never mentioned the subject again.

At the same time, I got such pleasure, real physiological pleasure from my children—from playing with them, feeding them, watching them develop. Then we moved and Ted went into general practice, and at about the same time I had another child. I became his secretary, his nurse, and I was also handling the children, keeping them out of his hair. And of course, we were also establishing our identity as the doctor and his wife, so there was a lot of socializing. It was a busy time.

What amazes me now is that it never occurred to me not to do this. His career was just my life. There came a time when I felt I didn't have the strength for all this and I started breaking down. I can remember going into the shower and screaming—in the shower so that no one could hear me. Even then I didn't have conscious thoughts of "I hate this life"—I didn't think there was anything objectively wrong with the way I was living, just that I couldn't take it any more.

Source: Brett Harvey, ed., *The Fifties: An Oral History* (New York: HarperCollins, 1993), 103–104.

Cultural Dissenters. The youth rebellion was only one aspect of a broader undercurrent of discontent with the conformist culture of the 1950s. Postwar artists, jazz musicians, and writers also expressed their alienation from mainstream society through intensely personal, introspective art forms. In New York Jackson Pollock and other painters rejected the social realism of the 1930s for an unconventional style that became known as *abstract expressionism*. Swirling and splattering paint onto giant canvases, Pollock emphasized self-expression in the act of painting, capturing the chaotic atmosphere of the nuclear age. A similar trend developed in jazz, as black musicians originated a hard-driving improvisational style known as *bebop*. Whether the "hot" bebop of saxophonist Charlie Parker in the 1940s or the more subdued "cool" West Coast sound of the 1950s epitomized by Miles Davis, postwar jazz was cerebral, intimate, and individualistic.

Black jazz musicians found eager fans not only in the African American community but among young white Beats in New York and San Francisco. Disdaining the middle-class conformity, corporate capitalism, and suburban materialism of the 1950s, the Beats were a group of writers and poets who were both literary innovators and outspoken social critics. In his poem "Howl" (1956), which became a manifesto of the beat generation, Allen Ginsberg lamented: "I saw the best minds of my generation destroyed by madness, starving hysterical naked, dragging themselves through the angry streets at dawn looking for an angry fix." In works such as Jack Kerouac's novel *On the Road* (1957) the Beats glorified spontaneity, sexual adventurism, drug use, and spirituality. Although they were apolitical—their rebellion was strictly cultural—in the 1960s they inspired a new generation of rebels who would champion both political and cultural change.

915

Elvis Presley: Teen Idol of the 1950s

───── ★ ─────

WHEN ELVIS PRESLEY performed on "The Ed Sullivan Show" in 1956, the television cameras zoomed in on his head and shoulders. The close-ups were inspired not by the young singer's good looks but by a desire to conceal his lower body. After several scandalous TV appearances earlier that season, CBS decided that Presley's sexually suggestive bumping and grinding were unsuitable for family viewing. Despite the censorship, Presley's performance was an unprecedented success, claiming over 80 percent of the television audience. His records sold 10 million copies that year alone and would account for a quarter of RCA's record sales over the next decade. More than any other recording artist of the 1950s Presley popularized the new hybrid music known as rock 'n' roll.

Born in East Tupelo, Mississippi, in 1935, Elvis Aron Presley grew up in a white working-class family that keenly felt the hardships of the Great Depression. Like many poor southerners, the Presleys moved frequently, in search of work as laborers and mill hands. When Elvis was thirteen, his father found a job at a paint factory in Memphis, and the Presleys settled in one of that city's new public-housing projects.

Elvis's earliest exposure to music came through gospel singing at the Pentecostal First Assembly of God Church, where his uncle was pastor. Later, when his family lived in or adjacent to the black districts of Tupelo and Memphis (as the South's poorest whites often did), Elvis gravitated toward local churches, bars, and clubs, where he gained a lifelong love of blues, gospel, and other black music.

Local radio was an equally powerful force in his musical education. In the late 1940s, commercial radio offered a diverse selection of musical programming, catering to the growing audience of rural migrants who had been moving to southern cities since World War II. Although there had always been significant cross-fertilization between white and black musical styles, industry promoters maintained an artificial distinction between "hillbilly" and "race" music. After World War II those derogatory labels gave way to the more respectable terms "country and western" and "rhythm and blues," but the programming remained rigidly segregated.

Young white southerners like Presley listened to both types of programs. They admired the traditional vocal styles and guitar picking they heard on "The Grand Ole Opry" and other country shows, and they developed a keen appreciation for the blues progressions and driving rhythms of black music. White youngsters' growing fascination with rhythm and blues was not generally acknowledged and was considered somewhat scandalous. But a small group of disc jockeys and record promoters spotted the potential of the new market. As Memphis record producer Sam Phillips once said, "If I could find a white man who had the Negro sound and the Negro feel, I could make a billion dollars."

Phillips found that man in Elvis Presley. In 1953 nineteen-year-old Presley was working as a truck driver and occasionally stopped by Phillips's Sun Studios to make sample recordings for his friends and family. Phillips remembered his unusual vocal style and later asked him to cut a record with a local band. The result was an eclectic mix of musical styles: on one side a white version of a black blues song, "That's All Right," on the other side a black-influenced interpretation of a bluegrass number, "Blue Moon of Kentucky." The record was an overnight local sensation and launched Presley into a national recording career the following year. Over the next decade he produced dozens of hits for RCA, including "Hound Dog," "Heartbreak Hotel," "Jailhouse Rock," and "Blue Suede Shoes."

Presley's success was based not only on his music but also on his stage presence and his relationship with the audience. With his slicked-back hair, long sideburns, and tight pants, Presley cultivated a lower-class "greaser" look that proved immensely popular with teenage fans. His quivering legs, gyrating pelvis, and playful sneer drove young female fans wild; they frequently mobbed the stage, grabbing at his clothes

RCA VICTOR
LPM-1254
A "NEW ORTHOPHONIC" HIGH FIDELITY RECORDING

ELVIS PRESLEY

Elvis Presley
The young Elvis Presley, shown here on the cover of his first album in 1956, embodied cultural rebellion against the conservatism and triviality of adult life in the 1950s. © 1956 BGM Music.

for souvenirs. Many adults, however, condemned such antics, associating them with juvenile delinquency, sexual immorality, and race-mixing. After his first television appearance, one critic described Presley's performance as "suggestive and vulgar, tinged with the kind of animalism that should be confined to dives and bordellos," and another critic called it "a strip-tease with clothes on." To many adults rock 'n' roll seemed an invitation to rebellion by the younger generation.

African Americans found Presley's success and notoriety somewhat ironic. Chuck Berry and other black musicians had been performing such music for years—but with little commercial success among white audiences. Many of them viewed the appropriation of black rhythm and blues by white artists as out-and-out theft. In the long run, however, the pop-ularity of rock 'n' roll introduced black performers such as Little Richard, Fats Domino, and James Brown to white as well as black audiences.

Presley's musical popularity declined with his induction into the army in 1958 (the long arm of the state reached even the most popular stars). Afterward he headed for Hollywood, acting and singing in dozens of mostly mediocre teen-oriented movies. He enjoyed a comeback starting in 1968, but his career was hampered by personal problems. In 1977 he died of an accidental drug overdose. Since then he has become a cult figure, spawning hundreds of books and articles and a spate of Elvis impersonators. Graceland, his ornate home in Memphis, attracts more visitors per year than does George Washington's estate at Mount Vernon.

The Other America

As middle-class whites flocked to the suburbs, a diverse group of poor and working-class migrants, many of them nonwhite, moved into the central cities. With jobs and financial resources flowing to the suburbs, urban newcomers inherited a declining economy and a decaying environment. This "other America," as the social critic Michael Harrington called it, remained largely invisible to affluent white suburbanites.

Urban Migration

Newly arrived immigrants were one of several groups moving into the nation's cities in the postwar era. Although prior to 1965 U.S. immigration policy followed the restrictive national origins quota system set up in 1924 (see Chapter 23), Congress modified the law during and after World War II. The War Brides Act of 1945, permitting the entry and naturalization of the wives and children of Americans living abroad (mainly servicemen), brought thousands of new immigrants between 1950 and 1965, including some 17,000 Koreans. Three years later, the Displaced Persons Act admitted approximately 415,000 European refugees. The repeal of the Chinese Exclusion Act in 1943, made in deference to America's wartime alliance with China, and the passage of the McCarran-Walter Act in 1952 ended the exclusion of Chinese, Japanese, Korean, and Southeast Asian immigrants. Finally, in recognition of the freeing of the Philippines from American control in 1946, Filipinos received their own quota (Figure 28.4).

Latino Immigration. One of the largest groups of postwar migrants came from Mexico. Nearly 275,000 Mexicans came in the 1950s, and almost 444,000 in the 1960s. They moved primarily to western and southwestern cities such as Los Angeles, El Paso, and Phoenix, where they found jobs as migrant workers or in the expanding service sector. Large numbers of Mexican Americans also settled in Chicago, Detroit, Kansas City, and Denver. Before World War II, most Mexican Americans had lived in rural areas and engaged in agricultural work; by 1960, a majority were living in urban areas where they joined more settled communities of service and manufacturing workers.

Part of the stimulus for Mexican immigration came from the reinstitution of the *bracero* program from 1951 to 1964. Originally devised as a means of importing temporary labor during World War II, the *bracero* program brought 450,000 Mexican workers to the United States at its peak in 1959. But even as the federal government welcomed *braceros*, it deported those who stayed on illegally. In response to the recession of 1953–1954, which caused high unemployment throughout the nation, federal authorities deported nearly 4 million Mexicans in a program called "Operation Wetback." For a few years the level of illegal immigration was reduced, but it rose again after the *bracero* program ended.

Another group of Spanish-speaking migrants came from the American-controlled territory of Puerto Rico.

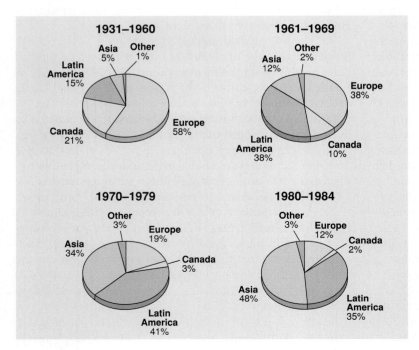

FIGURE 28.4
Legal Immigration to the United States by Region, 1931–1984
Source: Robert W. Gardner, Bryant Robie, and Peter C. Smith, "Asian Americans: Growth, Change, and Diversity," *Population Bulletin*, vol. 40, no. 4 (Washington, DC: Population Reference Bureau, 1985), 2.

Residents of that island had been American citizens since 1917, so their migration was not subject to immigration laws. The inflow from the island increased dramatically after World War II, when mechanization of the island's sugarcane industry pushed many rural Puerto Ricans off the land. When airlines began to offer cheap direct flights between San Juan and New York City (in the 1940s the fare was about $50, or two weeks' wages), Puerto Ricans became this country's first group to immigrate by air. Most Puerto Ricans went to New York, where they settled first in East ("Spanish") Harlem and then in other areas of the city. This massive migration, which grew from 70,000 in 1940 to 613,000 just twenty years later, transformed the ethnic composition of the city. More Puerto Ricans were living in New York City than in San Juan.

Cuban refugees constituted the third large group of Spanish-speaking immigrants. In the six years after Fidel Castro's seizure of power and institution of communist rule in 1959, an estimated 180,000 people fled Cuba for the United States. The Cuban refugee community grew so quickly that it turned Miami into a cosmopolitan, bilingual city almost overnight. Unlike most new immigrants, Miami's Cubans prospered, in large part because they had arrived with more resources. Cubans differed from most other Latino immigrants in that they were predominantly middle class and politically conservative.

Internal Migration. Internal migration also brought large numbers of people to the cities, especially African Americans, continuing a trend that had begun during World War I (see Chapter 22). Black migration was hastened by the transformation of southern agriculture. New Deal agricultural policies and the development of synthetic fibers such as rayon and Dacron after World War II caused cotton acreage in the South to decline from 43 million acres in 1929 to less than 15 million in 1959. In addition, the ongoing mechanization of agriculture reduced the demand for farm labor. The mechanical cotton picker, introduced in 1944, could pick 1,000 pounds an hour compared with the 20 pounds picked by an experienced farmhand. As a result of these changes, the southern farm population fell from 16.2 million in 1930 to 5.9 million in 1960. Although both whites and blacks left the land, the starkest decline was among black farmers.

Some of the migrants settled in southern cities, where they found industrial jobs. White southerners from Appalachia moved north to "hillbilly" ghettos such as Cincinnati's Over the Rhine neighborhood and Chicago's Uptown. In the most dramatic population shift, as many as 3 million blacks headed to Chicago, New York, Washington, Detroit, Los Angeles, and other cities between 1940 and 1960. So pervasive were the migrants that certain sections of Chicago seemed like

Harlem in the Fifties
During and after World War II, thousands of African Americans left the rural South for northern and western cities, expanding the population of Harlem and other black neighborhoods. Ironically, the migrants arrived just as declining employment, deteriorating housing, and shrinking tax revenues were making life more difficult for inner-city residents. Henry Hammond/Archive Photos.

the Mississippi Delta transplanted. By 1960 about half of the nation's black population was living outside the South, compared with only 23 percent before World War II.

In western cities, an influx of native Americans also contributed to the rise in the nonwhite urban population. Seeking to end federal involvement in Indian affairs, Congress in 1953 authorized a program to terminate the legal standing of native tribes and move their members off reservations. The program, which reflected a Cold War preoccupation with conformity and assimilation, enjoyed strong support from mining, timber, and agricultual interests that wanted to open reservation lands for private development. The Bureau of Indian Affairs encouraged voluntary migration to urban areas by subsidizing moving costs and establishing relocation centers in San Francisco, Denver, Chicago, and other cities. The relocation program proved problematic, however, as many Indians found it difficult to adjust to an urban environment and culture. Although the policy of forced termination was halted in 1958, by 1960 some 60,000 Indians had moved to the cities. Despite the program's stated goal of assimilation, most native American migrants settled together in poor urban neighborhoods alongside other nonwhite groups.

The Urban Crisis

American cities thus saw their nonwhite populations swell at the same time that whites were flocking to the suburbs. From 1950 to 1960 the nation's twelve largest cities lost 3.6 million whites and gained 4.5 million nonwhites. Tax revenues followed the more affluent whites out of the city and into the suburbs. A wealthy community such as Grosse Pointe, a suburb of Detroit, could far more easily fund first-rate schools and police and fire protection than could the city of Detroit, whose tax base shrank as businesses and middle-class residents relocated to the suburbs. The decay of urban services and infrastructure, coupled with growing racial fears, only accelerated white suburban flight in the 1960s.

By the time that blacks, Latinos, and native Americans moved into the inner cities, urban America was in poor shape. Housing continued to be a crucial problem. City planners, politicians, and real-estate developers responded with urban renewal programs, razing blighted city neighborhoods to make way for modern construction projects. Local residents were rarely consulted about whether they wanted their neighborhoods "renewed," and redevelopment programs often produced grim high-rise housing projects that destroyed community bonds and created anonymous open areas that were vulnerable to crime. Between 1949 and 1967 urban renewal demolished almost 400,000 buildings and displaced 1.4 million people. The 575,000 units of public housing built nationwide by 1964 came nowhere close to satisfying the need for affordable urban housing.

Urban renewal projects often benefited the wealthy at the expense of the poor. Many downtown "revitalization" projects replaced established racial-ethnic neighborhoods with expensive rental housing or office buildings where suburban commuters worked. Boston's West End, a poor but vibrant Italian American community, was razed by a private developer between 1958 and 1960 to build Charles River Park, an apartment complex whose rents were far too steep for the former residents. In San Francisco some 4,000 residents of the Western Addition, a predominantly black neighborhood, were displaced under an urban renewal program that built luxury housing, a shopping center, and an express boulevard. In both cities residents were forced into less desirable parts of the city, cut off from the vitality of their former neighborhoods.

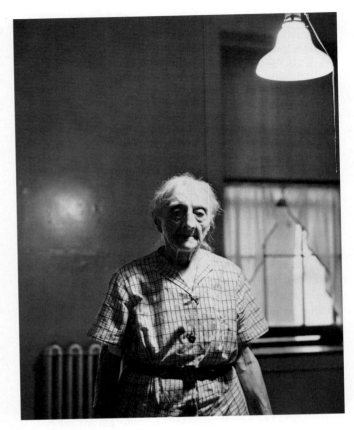

The Other America
While many celebrated the "affluent society" of the postwar era, critics like Michael Harrington noted that thousands of Americans remained in poverty. Among them were many elderly people who struggled to survive on fixed incomes and without medical insurance.
Cincinnati Historical Society.

Despite pockets of "urban gentrification," postwar cities were increasingly becoming places of last resort for the nation's poor. Unlike earlier immigrants, for whom cities were gateways to social and economic betterment, inner-city residents in the postwar period faced diminishing hopes for improvement. Lured by the promise of plentiful jobs, migrants found that many of those opportunities had relocated to the suburban fringe, making steady employment out of reach for those who needed it most. The poor were also trapped in the cities because of racism. Migrants to the city, especially blacks, faced racial hostility and institutional barriers to mobility—biased school funding, hiring and promotion decisions, and credit practices. Two separate Americas were emerging: a largely white society in suburbs and peripheral areas, and an inner city populated by blacks, Latinos, and other disadvantaged groups.

The Fifties—The Way We Were?

Despite the contradictory developments of the postwar era, many Americans continue to view the 1950s as the historical norm—a time when families were close-knit and intact, children were happy, and the economy was growing. Despite the fear of nuclear annihilation, Americans were confident that theirs was the strongest country, both economically and morally, in the world. Changes in American family, political, and social life since then are often seen as declines from this ideal.

But perhaps the fifties should be regarded more as unique than as ideal—the result of a special combination of circumstances that could not be sustained on a permanent basis. In a 200-year trend toward smaller families, the postwar baby boom was certainly atypical, as was the remarkable stability of marriages. Scarred by memories of depression and World War II–era dislocations and scared by the ambiguities of living in the atomic age, the postwar generation embraced family life with a vengeance—a phenomenon that historian Elaine Tyler May calls "cold war, warm hearth." When social conditions changed in the 1960s, the profamily orientation gave way to the more individualistic ethos that characterized the rest of the century.

Our tendency to view the 1950s as the historical norm also fails to recognize that America's postwar affluence was based on international economic conditions that could not continue indefinitely. The war-devastated economies of Japan and West Germany would rebuild, taking advantage of new technology to compete with and eventually challenge American economic supremacy. So too would emerging industrial centers in the Pacific Rim such as South Korea, Hong Kong, and Singapore. For Americans who regard the economic dominance of the 1950s as the norm, any decline appears to be a disturbing loss of American power and economic strength rather than a return to a more balanced state of economic affairs.

The stereotypes of boundless affluence in the 1950s are also misleading, for they hide those persons who did not share equally in the American dream—displaced factory workers, destitute old people, female heads of households, blacks and other racial minority groups. Not until the publication of Michael Harrington's *The Other America* in 1962 did Americans begin to realize that in the richest country in the world more than a quarter of the population was poor. In the turbulent decade that followed, three contrasts—between suburban affluence and the "other America"; between the lure of the city for the poor and minorities and its grim, segregated reality; and between a heightened emphasis on domesticity and the widening opportunities for women—would spawn growing demands for social change that the nation's leaders could not ignore.

John F. Kennedy and the Politics of Expectation

——— ★ ———

In his 1961 inaugural address President John Fitzgerald Kennedy challenged a "new generation of Americans" to take responsibility for the future: "Ask not what your country can do for you, ask what you can do for your country." Few presidents came to Washington more primed for action than John F. Kennedy. His New Frontier program promised to "get America moving again" through vigorous governmental activism at home and abroad. British journalist Henry Fairlie referred to this activist impulse as the "politics of expectation." But the legislative achievements of Kennedy's New Frontier, particularly in domestic affairs, were modest.

The New Politics

The Republicans would have been happy to renominate Dwight D. Eisenhower for president, but the Twenty-second Amendment prevented them from doing so. Passed in 1951 by a Republican-controlled Congress to prevent a repetition of Franklin Roosevelt's four-term presidency, the amendment limited future presidents to two full terms. So in 1960 the Republicans turned to Vice-President Richard M. Nixon, who, like a good

The Kennedy Magnetism
John Kennedy, the Democratic candidate for president in 1960, used his youth and personality to attract voters. Here the Massachusetts senator draws an enthusiastic crowd on a campaign stop in Elgin, Illinois.
Wide World Photos, Inc.

1950s junior executive, had patiently waited for his turn at the top. Nixon campaigned for an updated version of Eisenhower's policies but was hampered by lukewarm support from the popular president. Asked by reporters whether Nixon had helped make any major policy decisions in his administration, Eisenhower replied, "If you give me a week I might think of one."

The Democrats chose Senator John Kennedy of Massachusetts, with the Senate majority leader, Lyndon B. Johnson of Texas, as the vice-presidential nominee. Kennedy, an alumnus of Harvard and a World War II hero, had inherited his love of politics from his grandfathers, both of whom had been colorful Irish-Catholic politicians in Boston. His wealthy father, Joseph P. Kennedy, had headed the Securities and Exchange Commission and served as ambassador to Great Britain under Roosevelt. First elected to Congress in 1946, John Kennedy moved to the Senate in 1952. Ambitious and hard-driven, Kennedy launched his campaign in 1960 with a platform calling for civil rights legislation, health care for the elderly, aid to education, urban

renewal, expanded military and space programs, and containment of communism abroad. With the country in the middle of a recession that had pushed unemployment to a postwar high, Kennedy vowed to "get America moving again."

At forty-three, Kennedy was poised to become the youngest man ever elected to the presidency and the nation's first Catholic chief executive. Turning his age into a powerful campaign asset, Kennedy practiced what came to be called the "new politics," an approach that emphasized youthful charisma, style, and personality rather than issues and platforms. Using the power of the media—particularly television—to reach voters directly, practitioners of the new politics relied on professional media consultants, political pollsters, and mass fundraising. Kennedy's family wealth and the contributions he raised from sources outside traditional party networks paid for his expensive campaign.

A series of four televised debates between the two principal candidates, a major innovation of the 1960 campaign, showed how important television was becoming to political life. Nixon, far less photogenic

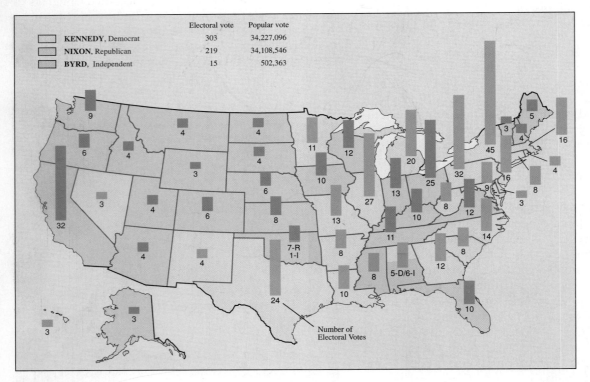

MAP 28.2
The Election of 1960
The Kennedy-Nixon contest was the closest since 1884. Kennedy won twelve states, including Illinois, by less than 2 percent of the two-party vote tally; he lost six others, including California, by a similarly small margin. Fifteen electors cast their votes for the Independent Democrat, Harry F. Byrd. Despite his razor-thin margin of victory, Kennedy won 303 electoral votes, the same number Truman had won in 1948, showing that the electoral college vote can be a misleading indicator of popular support.

than Kennedy, looked sallow and unshaven under the intense studio lights. Kennedy, in contrast, looked vigorous, cool, and self-confident on screen. Polls showed that television did sway political perceptions: voters who listened to the first debate on the radio concluded that Nixon had won, but those who viewed it on TV judged in Kennedy's favor.

Despite the edge Kennedy enjoyed in the debates, he won only the narrowest of electoral victories, receiving 49.7 percent of the popular vote to Nixon's 49.5 percent (Map 28.2). Kennedy successfully appealed to the diverse elements of the Democratic coalition, attracting large numbers of Catholic and black voters and a significant sector of the middle class; the vice-presidential nominee, Lyndon Johnson, brought in southern white Democrats. Yet only 120,000 votes separated the two candidates, and the shift of a few thousand votes in key states such as Illinois (where there were confirmed cases of voting fraud) would have reversed the outcome.

Activism Abroad

Although Kennedy's New Frontier platform included a long list of domestic social reforms, his greatest priority as president was foreign affairs. A resolute Cold Warrior, Kennedy took a hard line against communist expansionism. In contrast to Eisenhower, whose cost-saving New Look program had built up the American nuclear arsenal at the expense of conventional weapons, Kennedy proposed a new policy of *flexible response*, stating that the nation must be prepared "to deter all wars, general or limited, nuclear or conventional, large or small." Congress quickly granted Kennedy's military requests, and by 1963 the defense budget reached its highest level as a percentage of total federal expenditures in the Cold War era, greatly expanding the military-industrial complex (see Figure 27.1).

Flexible response measures were designed to deter direct attacks by the Soviet Union. To prepare for a new kind of warfare, evident in the wars of national liberation that had broken out in many Third World countries, Kennedy adopted a new military doctrine of *counterinsurgency*. Soon U.S. Army Special Forces, called Green Berets for their distinctive headgear, were receiving intensive training in repelling the random, small-scale attacks typical of guerrilla warfare. Vietnam would soon provide a testing ground for counterinsurgency techniques (see Chapter 29).

Peace Corps and Foreign Aid.   Another of Kennedy's projects, the Peace Corps (established in 1961 and headed by his brother-in-law, Sargent Shriver), embodied the commitment to public service that the president had called for in his inaugural address. Thousands of men and women, many of them recent college gradu-

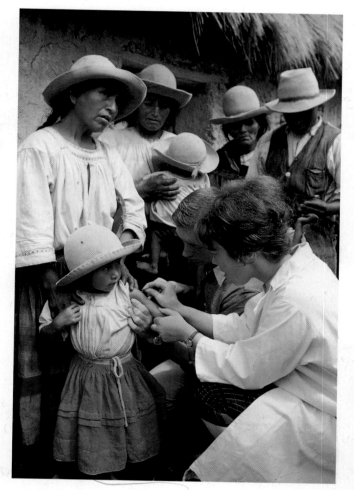

The Peace Corps
The Peace Corps, a New Frontier program initiated in 1961, attracted thousands of idealistic young Americans, including these volunteers who worked in a vaccination program in Bolivia.
David S. Boyer/National Geographic Society Image Collection.

ates, agreed to devote two or more years to programs that had them teaching English to Filipino schoolchildren or helping African villagers obtain adequate supplies of water. Embodying the idealism of the early 1960s, the Peace Corps was also a Cold War weapon designed to bring Third World countries into the American orbit and away from communist influence.

For the same reason, Kennedy pushed for economic aid to developing countries. The State department's Agency for International Development coordinated foreign aid for the Third World, including surplus agricultural products distributed to developing nations through its Food for Peace program. In Latin America, the Alliance for Progress provided funds for food, education, medicine, and other services, although it did little to enhance economic growth or improve social conditions there.

Bay of Pigs Invasion. In April 1961 Kennedy undertook his first major initiative—an effort to overthrow the new Soviet-supported regime in Cuba. The United States had long maintained a naval base at Guantánamo Bay and exercised nearly total economic and political dominance of the island. But on New Year's Day in 1959 Fidel Castro overthrew the corrupt and unpopular dictator Fulgencio Batista and called for a revolution to reshape Cuban society. When Castro began agrarian reforms at odds with American interests, and nationalized American-owned banks and industries, relations with Washington deteriorated. By early 1961 the United States had declared an embargo on all exports to Cuba, cut back on imports of Cuban sugar, and broken off diplomatic relations with Castro's regime.

Isolated by the United States, Cuba turned increasingly toward the Soviet Union for economic and military support. Concerned about Castro's growing friendliness with the Soviets, in early 1961 Kennedy used plans originally drawn up by the Eisenhower administration to dispatch Cuban exiles living in Nicaragua to foment an anti-Castro uprising. The invaders had been trained by the Central Intelligence Agency (CIA) but were ill prepared for their task and

had little popular support. After landing at Cuba's Bay of Pigs on April 17, the tiny force of 1,400 men was crushed by Castro's troops (Map 28.3). Symptomatic of inept CIA planning, pilots taking off from Nicaragua to provide air cover for the landing forces forgot to set their watches ahead to Cuban time and arrived at the beach an hour late. The anticipated rebellion never occurred. The embarrassing failure of the Bay of Pigs invasion cast doubts on Kennedy's activist approach to international affairs.

U.S.-Soviet relations deteriorated further in June 1961, when Soviet premier Khrushchev deployed soldiers to sever communist-controlled East Berlin from the western sector of the city controlled by West Germany. Khrushchev took this action after the United States flatly rejected his proposal to withdraw both Soviet and Western occupation forces from the city. Determined to confront the Soviets publicly, Kennedy declared in a televised speech on July 25 that Berlin was the "great testing place of Western courage and will." With congressional approval, Kennedy added 300,000 troops to the armed forces and promptly dispatched 40,000 of them to Europe. In mid-August, to stop the exodus of East Germans to the West, the Sovi-

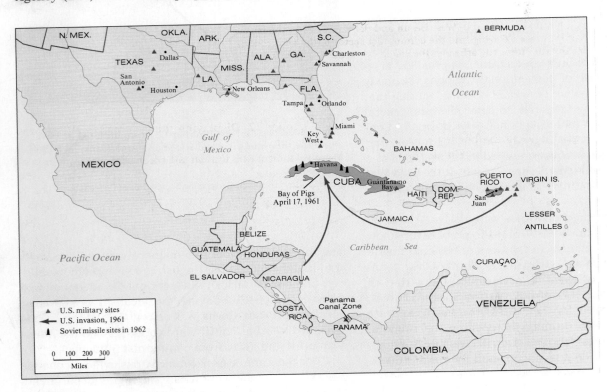

MAP 28.3
The United States and Cuba, 1961–1962
Fidel Castro's takeover in Cuba in 1959 brought Cold War tensions to the Caribbean. In 1961 the United States tried unsuccessfully to overthrow Castro's regime by supporting the Bay of Pigs invasion of Cuban exiles launched from Nicaragua and other points in the Caribbean. In 1962 a major confrontation with the Soviet Union occurred over Soviet missile sites in Cuba. The Soviets removed the missiles after President Kennedy ordered a naval blockade of the island, which lies just 90 miles south of Florida.

The Berlin Wall
In June 1962, President Kennedy traveled to West Berlin and delivered one of the most memorable speeches of his career. Gazing into the communist sector of the city from a podium beside the Berlin Wall, Kennedy affirmed the solidarity of the free world and declared, "Let them come to Berlin."
Corbis-Bettmann.

ets ordered construction of the Berlin Wall, and East German guards began policing the border. Visiting the city in June 1963, Kennedy—standing beside the wall—invoked the solidarity of the free world by declaring "Ich bin ein Berliner" ("I am a Berliner") and denounced the barrier as proof of the failure of communism. Until it was dismantled in 1989, the Berlin Wall remained the supreme symbol of the Cold War.

Cuban Missile Crisis. The climactic confrontation of the Cold War came in October 1962. After the failed Bay of Pigs invasion, the Kennedy administration increased economic pressure against Cuba and resumed covert efforts to overthrow the Castro regime. In response, the Soviets stepped up military aid to Cuba, including the installation of missiles (see Map 28.3). In early October, American reconnaissance planes photographed Soviet-built bases for intermediate-range ballistic missiles (IRBMs), which could reach U.S. targets as far as 2,200 miles away. At least some of those nuclear weapons had already been installed, and more were on the way.

Rather than work through Department of State or diplomatic channels, Kennedy confronted the Soviet Union publicly in a somber televised address on Mon-

day, October 22. Displaying the reconnaissance photos as evidence, he announced that the United States would impose a "quarantine on all offensive military equipment" intended for Cuba. As the two superpowers went on full military alert, people around the world believed that this long-dreaded direct confrontation between the two superpowers would end in nuclear war. Americans living in cities within range of the missiles restocked their bomb shelters and calculated the fastest routes out of town.

While the world held its breath, the Russian ships halted their voyage. Khrushchev wrote to Kennedy that if the United States agreed not to invade Cuba, the Soviets would remove the missiles. In a second letter Khrushchev demanded the removal of American missiles in Turkey as a condition for resolving the crisis. On his brother Robert's advice, the president publicly agreed to the terms of the first letter but ignored the second one. (He later secretly agreed to remove the missiles from Turkey, a move that the United States had already planned.) On the following Sunday, October 28, after the most harrowing week of the nuclear age, Kennedy and Khrushchev both announced concessions: Kennedy pledged not to invade Cuba, and Khrushchev promised to dismantle the missile bases. "We're eyeball to eyeball," Secretary of State Dean Rusk observed, "and I think the other fellow just blinked."

Although the risk of nuclear war was greater during the Cuban missile crisis than it was at any other time in the postwar period, it led to a slight thaw in U.S.-Soviet relations. In the words of national security advisor McGeorge Bundy, "having come so close to the edge, the leaders of the two governments have since taken care to keep away from the cliff." Kennedy softened his Cold War rhetoric and began to strive for peaceful coexistence. Soviet leaders, similarly chastened, were willing to talk. In August 1963 the three nuclear powers—the United States, the Soviet Union, and Great Britain—agreed to ban the testing of nuclear weapons in the atmosphere, in space, and underwater. Underground testing, however, was allowed to continue. The new emphasis on peaceful coexistence also led to the establishment of a Washington-Moscow telecommunications "hot line" in 1963 so that leaders could contact each other quickly during potential crises.

But no matter how often American leaders talked about opening channels of communication with the Soviets, the preoccupation with the Soviet military threat to American security remained a cornerstone of U.S. policy. Nor did Soviet leaders moderate their concern over the threat that they believed the United States posed to the survival of the USSR. The Cold War, and the escalating arms race that accompanied it, would continue for another twenty-five years.

The New Frontier at Home

The expansive vision of presidential leadership that Kennedy and his advisors brought to the White House worked less well at home than it did abroad. Hampered by the lack of a popular mandate in the 1960 election, Kennedy could not mobilize public support for the domestic agenda of the New Frontier. A conservative coalition of southern Democrats and western and midwestern Republicans effectively stalled most liberal initiatives. More important, Kennedy was not nearly as impassioned about domestic reform as he was about foreign policy.

NASA. One program that did win both popular and congressional support was increased funding for the National Aeronautics and Space Administration (NASA), whose Mercury space program had begun in 1958. On May 5, 1961, just three months after Kennedy took office, Alan Shepard became the first American in space. (The Soviet cosmonaut Yuri Gagarin earned the distinction of being the first person in space when he made a 108-hour flight in April 1961.) The following year, American astronaut John Glenn manned the first space mission to orbit the earth. At the height of American fascination with space flight, Kennedy proposed that the nation commit itself to landing a man on the moon within the decade. To support this mission (accomplished in 1969), Kennedy persuaded Congress to greatly increase NASA's budget.

Economic Policy. Kennedy's most striking domestic achievement was his use of modern economic theory to shape government fiscal policy. New Dealers had gradually moved away from the ideal of a balanced budget, turning instead to deliberate deficit spending to stimulate economic growth. In addition to relying on federal spending to create the desired deficit, Kennedy and his advisors proposed a reduction in income taxes. A tax cut, they argued, would put more money in the hands of taxpayers, who would spend it, thereby creating more jobs. For a time federal expenditures would exceed federal income, but after a year or two the expanding economy would raise American incomes and generate higher tax revenues.

Congress balked at this unorthodox proposal, and the measure failed to pass. But Lyndon Johnson pressed for it after Kennedy's assassination, signing it into law in February 1964. The Kennedy-Johnson tax cut—the Tax Reduction Act (1964)—marked a milestone in the use of fiscal policy to encourage economic growth, an approach that Republicans and other fiscal conservatives would later embrace. Although an economic expansion started before the effects of the tax cut could be felt, Kennedy and his economic advisors got credit for it anyway. The gross national product grew at a rate of 5 percent during the 1960s, nearly twice the rate of the Eisenhower years. Much of the growth, however, was fueled by massive defense expenditures, especially spending for the escalating Vietnam War.

Kennedy's interest in stimulating economic growth did not include a commitment to spending for domestic social needs, although he did not entirely ignore the liberal legislative agenda of Franklin Roosevelt and Harry Truman. Kennedy managed to push through legislation raising the minimum wage and expanding Social Security benefits. But on other issues—federal aid to education, wilderness preservation, federal investment in mass transportation, and medical insurance for the elderly—he ran into determined congressional opposition from both Republicans and dissenters in his own party.

The Warren Court. Some of the most significant policies of the early 1960s came not from the Kennedy administration but from the Supreme Court. Much of the Court's judicial activism in these years was linked to Earl Warren, Chief Justice from 1953 to 1969. Warren's leadership had already influenced the Court's most important decision, *Brown v. Board of Education* (1954), requiring the desegregation of public schools (see Chapter 27). In the 1960s the Court continued to make landmark decisions. It reinforced defendants' rights in cases like *Miranda v. Arizona* (1966), which required arresting officers to notify a suspect that "he has a right to remain silent, that any statement he does make may be used in evidence against him, and that he has a right to the presence of an attorney, either retained or appointed." Tackling the issue of the reapportionment of state legislatures in *Baker v. Carr* (1962) and *Reynolds v. Sims* (1964), the Court put forth the doctrine of "one person, one vote," meaning that all citizens' votes should have equal weight, no matter where they lived. The ruling substantially increased the representation of both suburban and urban areas, with their concentrations of black and Spanish-speaking residents, at the expense of rural regions. One of the most controversial decisions was *Engel v. Vitale* (1962), which banned organized prayer in public schools as a violation of the First Amendment's injunction that "Congress shall make no law respecting an establishment of religion."

JFK and Civil Rights

Perhaps the gravest failure of the Kennedy administration was its reluctance to act on civil rights—the most important domestic issue of the 1960s. Building on the strategy of nonviolent direct action pioneered by Martin Luther King Jr. and the Montgomery bus boycotters in the 1950s, a younger generation of activists in the 1960s initiated new, more assertive tactics such as sit-ins, freedom rides, and voter registration campaigns.

Sit-Ins and Freedom Rides. This new phase of the civil rights movement began in Greensboro, North Carolina, on February 1, 1960, when four black college students took seats at the "whites only" lunch counter of a local Woolworth's, determined to "sit in" until they were served. Although the protesters were arrested, the sit-in tactic worked and quickly spread to other southern cities. A few months later Ella Baker, an administrator with the Southern Christian Leadership Conference and a lifelong activist, helped to organize the Student Non-Violent Coordinating Committee (SNCC, known as "Snick") to facilitate student sit-ins. By the end of the year, about 50,000 people had participated in sit-ins or other demonstrations, and 3,600 of them had been jailed, usually for disturbing the peace. But lunch counters had been desegregated in 126 cities throughout the South (see American Voices, "Anne Moody: 'We Would Like to Be Served,'" p. 928).

The success of SNCC's unorthodox tactics encouraged the Congress of Racial Equality (CORE), an interracial group founded in 1942, to adopt a more confrontational strategy. In 1961 CORE's executive director, James Farmer, organized a series of *freedom rides* on interstate bus lines throughout the South to call attention to the continuing segregation of public trans-

portation despite the Supreme Court rulings. The bus-riding activists, mostly young, both black and white, were brutally attacked by white mobs. In Anniston, Alabama, club-wielding Ku Klux Klansmen attacked one of the buses with stones and set it on fire. Governor John Patterson refused to intervene, claiming, "I cannot guarantee protection for this bunch of rabble rousers."

Although the Kennedy administration generally opposed the freedom riders' activities, films of their beatings and the bus burning shown on the nightly news prompted Attorney General Robert Kennedy to send federal marshals to Alabama to restore order. Faced with Department of Justice intervention against those who defied the Interstate Commerce Commission's prohibition of segregation in interstate vehicles and facilities, most southern communities quietly acceded to the changes. And civil rights activists learned the lesson that nonviolent protest could succeed if it provoked vicious white resistance and generated publicity. Only when forced to, it appeared, would the federal authorities act.

Except for protecting the freedom riders, the Kennedy administration lent little support to the growing civil rights movement. Kennedy seemed to view civil rights protests as irritating political embarrassments that distracted him from more important domestic and international issues. Behind the scenes Kennedy even authorized clandestine FBI surveillance of Martin Luther King Jr. and a smear campaign against him.

Political realities, especially tensions within the Democratic coalition, also dampened Kennedy's enthusiasm for civil rights. Blacks had given Kennedy strong support in the 1960 election and he needed to keep them in the coalition, but Kennedy also needed the votes of southern Democrats to get his programs through Congress. Kennedy reached out to black constituencies by appointing former NAACP lawyer Thurgood Marshall to the U.S. Circuit Court of Appeals at the same time he appointed a number of white segregationist judges to southern benches. But as the civil rights movement became more confrontational, Kennedy could not maintain that delicate balancing act.

Birmingham. Events came to a head in 1963 in Birmingham, Alabama, when Martin Luther King Jr. and the Reverend Fred Shuttlesworth called for a protest against conditions in what King called "the most segregated city in the United States." In April thousands of black demonstrators marched downtown to picket Birmingham's department stores. They were met by Eugene "Bull" Connor, the city's commissioner of public safety, who used snarling dogs, electric cattle prods, and high-pressure fire hoses to break up the crowd. The hoses were so powerful that they ripped bark from trees and tore bricks from buildings, a scene captured for the evening news by television cameras. "The civil rights movement

Anne Moody

"We Would Like to Be Served"

———★———

Born in rural Mississippi in 1940, Anne Moody was one of thousands of black college students who joined the Student Non-Violent Coordinating Committee in the early 1960s. In her senior year, she participated in a sit-in at a Woolworth's lunch counter in Jackson, Mississippi, which she described in her autobiography.

At exactly 11 A.M., Pearlena, Memphis, and I entered Woolworth's from the rear entrance. We separated as soon as we stepped into the store, and made small purchases from various counters. . . .

Seconds before 11:15 we were occupying three seats at the previously segregated Woolworth's lunch counter. In the beginning the waitresses seemed to ignore us, as if they really didn't know what was going on. Our waitress walked past us a couple of times before she noticed we had started to write our own orders down and realized we wanted service. She asked us what we wanted. We began to read to her from our order slips. She told us that we would be served at the back counter, which was for Negroes.

"We would like to be served here," I said. . . .

At noon, students from a nearby white high school started pouring in to Woolworth's. When they first saw us they were sort of surprised. They didn't know how to react. A few started to heckle and the newsmen [who had arrived earlier] became interested again. Then the white students started chanting all kinds of anti-Negro slogans. We were called a little bit of everything. The rest of the seats except the three we were occupying had been roped off to prevent others from sitting down. A couple of the boys took one end of the rope and made it into a hangman's noose. Several attempts were made to put it around our necks. . . .

Memphis suggested that we pray. We bowed our heads, and all hell broke loose. A man rushed forward, threw Memphis from his seat, and slapped my face. Then another man who worked in the store threw me against an adjoining counter.

Down on my knees on the floor, I saw Memphis lying near the lunch counter with blood running out of the corners of his mouth. As he tried to protect his face, the man who'd thrown him down kept kicking him against the head. . . .

. . . The mob started smearing us with ketchup, mustard, sugar, pies, and everything on the counter. Soon Joan [Trumpauer, a white college student and NAACP member] and I were joined by John Salter, but the moment he sat down he was hit on the jaw with what appeared to be brass knuckles. Blood gushed from his face and someone threw salt into the open wound. . . .

. . . The mob took spray paint from the counter and sprayed it on the new demonstrators. The high school student had on a white shirt; the word "nigger" was written on his back with red spray paint.

We sat there for three hours taking a beating when the manager decided to close the store because the mob had begun to go wild with stuff from other counters. . . .

After the sit-in, all I could think of was how sick Mississippi whites were. They believed so much in the segregated Southern way of life, they would kill to preserve it. I sat there in the NAACP office and thought of how many times they had killed when this way of life was threatened. I knew that the killing had just begun. . . .

Source: Anne Moody, *Coming of Age in Mississippi* (New York: Dell Publishing, Laurel Editions, 1968), 264–267.

should thank God for Bull Connor," President Kennedy noted. "He's helped it as much as Abraham Lincoln."

Realizing that he could no longer straddle the issue, Kennedy decided to step up the federal role in civil rights. On June 11, 1963, he went on television to promise major civil rights legislation banning discrimination in public accommodations and empowering the Department of Justice to seek desegregation on its own authority. Black leaders hailed the speech as a "Second Emancipation Proclamation," but for one person Kennedy's speech came too late. That night, Medgar Evers, president of the Mississippi chapter of the NAACP, was shot in the back and killed in his driveway in Jackson. The martyrdom of Evers became a spur to further action.

The March on Washington. To rouse the conscience of the country and to marshal support for Kennedy's bill, civil rights leaders turned to a tactic that A. Phillip

Racial Violence in Birmingham
When thousands of blacks marched through downtown Birmingham, Alabama, to protest racial segregation in April 1963, they were met with fire hoses and attack dogs unleashed by Police Chief "Bull" Connor. The violence, which was televised on the national evening news, shocked many Americans and helped build sympathy for the civil rights movement among northern whites.
Bill Hudson/Wide World Photos, Inc.

Randolph had first suggested in 1941 (see Chapter 26): a massive march on Washington. Organized by Martin Luther King Jr. and other prominent black civil rights leaders, the march drew support from a broad coalition, including the National Council of Churches, the National Conference of Catholics for Interracial Justice, the American Jewish Congress, and the AFL-CIO's Industrial Union Department.

On August 28, 1963, about 250,000 black and white demonstrators—the largest demonstration up to that time—gathered at the Lincoln Memorial. The march culminated in a memorable speech delivered, indeed preached, by King in the evangelical style of the black church:

I have a dream that one day on the red hills of Georgia the sons of former slaves and the sons of former slaveowners will be able to sit down together at the table of brotherhood. I have a dream that one day even the state of Mississippi, a desert state sweltering with the heat of injustice and oppression, will be transformed into an oasis of freedom and justice. I have a dream that my four little children will one day live in a nation where they will not be judged by the color of their skin but by the content of their character.

King ended with an exclamation from an old Negro spiritual: "Free at last! Free at last! Thank God almighty, we are free at last!"

King's eloquence and the sight of blacks and whites marching solemnly together did more than any other event to make the civil rights movement acceptable to white Americans. The March on Washington marked the climax of the nonviolent phase of the civil rights movement and confirmed King's position, especially among white liberals, as the leading speaker for the black cause. In 1964 King won the Nobel Peace Prize for his leadership.

Despite the impact of the march on public opinion, few congressional votes were changed by the event. Southern senators continued to block Kennedy's legislation by threatening a filibuster. Even more troubling was a new outbreak of violence by white extremists determined to oppose equality for

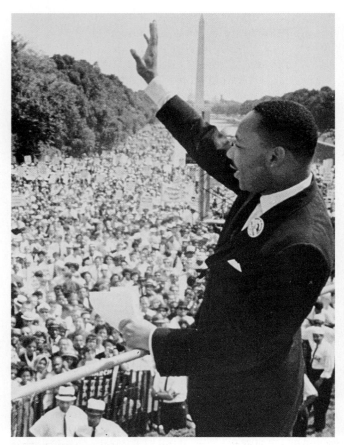

Martin Luther King Jr.
The Reverend Martin Luther King Jr. (1929–1968) was one of
the most eloquent advocates of the civil rights movement. For
many, his "I have a dream" speech at the 1963 March on
Washington was the high point of the event.
Wide World Photos, Inc.

blacks at all costs. In September a Baptist church in
Birmingham was bombed, and four black Sunday
school students were killed. Two months later, President Kennedy was assassinated.

The Kennedy Assassination

Although the first two years of Kennedy's presidency
had been plagued by foreign policy crises and domestic
inaction, many political observers believed that by 1963
Kennedy was maturing as a national leader. On November 22, 1963, Kennedy went to Texas, a state he needed
to win for reelection in 1964, to heal divisions in the
party organization there. As he and his wife,
Jacqueline, rode in an open car past the Texas School
Book Depository in Dallas, he was shot through the
head and neck by a sniper. Kennedy died a half hour
later. (Whether accused killer Lee Harvey Oswald, a

twenty-four-year-old loner who had spent three years in
the Soviet Union, was the sole gunman is still a matter
of considerable controversy.) Before *Air Force One* left
Dallas to take the president's body back to Washington,
a grim-faced Lyndon Johnson was sworn in as president. Kennedy's stunned widow, still wearing her blood-
stained pink suit, looked on.

By 1 P.M. Dallas time, just thirty minutes after the
shooting, 68 percent of adults in the United States
knew that Kennedy had been shot. By late afternoon,
the proportion had risen to 99.8 percent, showing
how the mass media could reach virtually every person in the nation within a few hours. As on Pearl
Harbor Day in 1941, people never forgot what they
were doing when they heard that Kennedy had been
shot.

Kennedy's youthful image, the trauma of his
assassination, and the collective sense that Americans had been robbed of a promising leader contributed to a powerful mystique. Only forty-six at the
time of his death, he was the first president born in
the twentieth century. The Kennedy myth had begun
even before his tragic death. In June 1963 about
59 percent of the people surveyed claimed to have
voted for Kennedy, a big jump over the 49.7 percent
who actually had; after the assassination, that figure
rose to 65 percent. A British journalist called it "a
posthumous landslide."

The Kennedy mystique has overshadowed what
most historians agree was at best a mixed record.
Kennedy exercised bold presidential leadership in foreign affairs, but his initiatives in Cuba and Berlin
marked the height of superpower confrontation during
the Cold War. Moreoever, his enthusiasm for fighting
communism abroad had no domestic equivalent.
Kennedy's proposals for educational aid, medical insurance, and other liberal reforms stalled, and his tax cut
bill languished in Congress until after his death.
Lyndon Johnson's decision to turn passage of civil
rights legislation into a memorial to his slain predecessor provided an ironic climax to Kennedy's lukewarm
support for the cause.

Lyndon B. Johnson and the Great Society

———★———

Lyndon Baines Johnson, a seasoned politician who was
best at negotiating in the backrooms of power, was no
match for the Kennedy style, and he knew it. But less
than a year after assuming office, Johnson won the
1964 presidential election in a landslide that far sur-

passed Kennedy's meager mandate in 1960. Johnson then used his astonishing energy and genius for compromise to bring to fruition many of Kennedy's stalled programs and more than a few of his own. Those legislative accomplishments are referred to as the "Great Society," Johnson's own phrase to describe his policies for ending poverty and racial injustice. It was the Great Society, not the much less ambitious New Frontier, that fulfilled and in many cases surpassed the New Deal liberal agenda of the 1930s (Table 28.1).

A Southern President and Civil Rights

Johnson brought to the presidency far more legislative experience than had any other modern president, and he used his talent to great effect. Born in the central Texas hill country in 1908, Johnson had served in government since 1932 as a congressional aide, New Deal administrator, congressman, senator, Senate majority leader, and finally vice-president. In his first year as president he used his powers of persuasion to push through the Kennedy-Johnson tax cut and a major piece of civil rights legislation.

Civil Rights Act of 1964. As a southerner, Johnson was eager to prove to the nation and to Kennedy's skeptical staff that he was a true liberal and a champion of racial equality. The Civil Rights Act, passed in June 1964 after a two-and-a-half-month filibuster by southern senators, was a landmark in the history of American race relations and one of the greatest achievements of the 1960s. Its keystone, Title VII, outlawed discrimination in employment on the basis of race, religion, sex, or national origin. Another section barred discrimination in public accommodations. The law gave integrationists two powerful new weapons: they could ask the U.S. attorney general to withhold federal funds from any government-run program that was not desegregated, and they could appeal discrimination in public accommodations and employment to the newly established Equal Employment Opportunity Commission. The Civil Rights Act resulted in the desegregation of public facilities throughout the South, including many public schools, but obstacles to black voting rights persisted.

Freedom Summer. In 1964, with the Civil Rights Act on the brink of passage, black organizations and churches mounted a major civil rights campaign in Mississippi known as Freedom Summer. Drawing on several thousand volunteers from across the country, including many idealistic white college students, Freedom Summer workers established freedom schools for black children, conducted a major voter registration drive, and organized the Mississippi Freedom Democratic Party, a political alternative to the all-white Mississippi Democratic organization.

White southerners reacted swiftly and violently to those efforts. In June, James Chaney, a CORE volunteer from Mississippi; Andrew Goodman, a student from New York; and Michael Schwerner, a New York social worker, disappeared from Philadelphia, Mississippi, and were presumed murdered. As public demand for an investigation grew, Rita Schwerner, Michael's wife, noted, "We all know that this search . . . is because Andrew Goodman and my husband are white. If only Chaney was involved, nothing would have been done." Six weeks later the FBI discovered the three bodies inside a newly constructed dam five miles away. Goodman and Schwerner had been killed by a single bullet each; Chaney had been brutally beaten with a chain and shot several times. An investigation later determined that members of the Ku Klux Klan had committed the crime. During Freedom Summer, fifteen civil rights workers were murdered, and only about twelve hundred black voters were registered.

The 1964 Election. If 1964 was a year of growing momentum in the civil rights movement and significant liberal legislative accomplishments in Congress, it was a year of conservative retrenchment in the Republican Party. The Republican nominee for president in 1964 was Senator Barry Goldwater of Arizona. Determined to offer "a choice, not an echo," Goldwater campaigned against the expansion of federal power in areas such as the economy and civil rights. Goldwater's crisp speeches rejected Republican efforts to build a moderate coalition. "Extremism in the defense of liberty is no vice," he stated in his acceptance speech at the Republican convention. "Moderation in the pursuit of justice is no virtue." On foreign affairs Goldwater was an aggressive anticommunist who once joked about "lobbing [a nuclear bomb] into the men's room of the Kremlin."

President Johnson easily won the Democratic nomination. Reaffirming his commitment to the party's liberal agenda but putting some distance between himself and the Kennedy clan, Johnson passed over Robert F. Kennedy for vice-president in favor of the Senator Hubert H. Humphrey of Minnesota, a well-known civil rights advocate. An attempt by the avowed segregationist George C. Wallace, governor of Alabama, to exploit a white backlash against civil rights showed early strength but then fizzled. Ironically, given his growing involvement in Vietnam, Johnson presented himself as the peace candidate. Using a frightening TV commercial showing a billowing mushroom cloud, Johnson campaigners exploited public fears about Goldwater's belligerent foreign policy. (The ad was pulled two days later in response to public outcries against fear mongering.) The Johnson-Humphrey ticket won by one of the largest margins in history, receiving 61.1 percent of the popular

TABLE 28.1

Major Great Society Legislation

Civil Rights

1964	Twenty-fourth Amendment	Outlawed poll tax in federal elections
	Civil Rights Act	Banned discrimination in employment and public accommodations on the basis of race, religion, sex, or national origin
1965	Voting Rights Act	Outlawed literacy tests for voting; provided federal supervision of registration in historically low-registration areas

Social Welfare

1964	Economic Opportunity Act	Created Office of Economic Opportunity (OEO) to administer War on Poverty programs such as Head Start, Job Corps, and Volunteers in Service to America (VISTA)
1965	Medical Care Act	Provided medical care for the poor (Medicaid) and the elderly (Medicare)
1966	Minimum Wage Act	Raised hourly minimum wage from $1.25 to $1.40 and expanded coverage to new groups

Education

1965	Elementary and Secondary Education Act	Granted federal aid for education of poor children
	National Endowment for the Arts and Humanities	Provided federal funding and support for artists and scholars
	Higher Education Act	Provided federal scholarships for postsecondary education

Housing and Urban Development

1964	Urban Mass Transportation Act	Provided federal aid to urban mass transit
	Omnibus Housing Act	Provided federal funds for public housing and rent subsidies for low-income families
1965	Housing and Urban Development Act	Created Department of Housing and Urban Development (HUD)
1966	Metropolitan Area Redevelopment and Demonstration Cities acts	Designated 150 "model cities" for combined programs of public housing, social services, and job training

Environment

| 1964 | Wilderness Preservation Act | Designated 9.1 million acres of federal lands as "wilderness areas," barring future roads, buildings, or commercial use |
| 1965 | Air and Water Quality acts | Set tougher air quality standards; required states to enforce water quality standards for interstate waters |

Miscellaneous

1964	Tax Reduction Act	Reduced personal and corporate income tax rates
1965	Immigration Act	Abandoned national quotas of 1924 law, allowing more non-European immigration
	Appalachian Regional Development Act	Provided federal funding for roads, health clinics, and other public works projects in economically depressed regions

vote and surpassing even the 1936 landslide of that great coalition builder Franklin D. Roosevelt, Johnson's political idol and mentor. And Johnson's coattails were long—his sweeping victory brought Democratic gains in both Congress and the state legislatures.

Enacting the Liberal Agenda

Like most New Deal liberals, Johnson took an expansive view of presidential leadership and the positive role of the federal government. The 1964 election gave him not only the popular mandate but, more important, the filibuster-proof Democratic Senate majority that he needed to push his programs forward. "Hurry boys, hurry," he urged his staff. "Get that legislation up to the Hill and out. Eighteen months from now ol' Landslide Lyndon will be Lame-Duck Lyndon." The Eighty-ninth Congress enacted more social reform measures than any session had since Franklin Roosevelt's first term, offering legislation for every important element of the Democratic coalition (see Table 28.1).

One of Johnson's first big successes was breaking the congressional deadlock on aid to education. Passed in April 1965, the Elementary and Secondary Education Act authorized $1 billion in federal funds to benefit impoverished children. By dispensing aid to schools on the basis of the number of needy children in attendance, the act sidestepped the religious issue by granting funds to public and parochial schools alike. That same year the Higher Education Act provided the first federal scholarships for college students and library grants to colleges and universities. The Eighty-ninth Congress also gave Johnson enough votes to enact the federal health insurance legislation first proposed by Truman. The result was two new programs: Medicare, a health plan for the elderly funded by a surcharge on Social Security payroll taxes, and Medicaid, a health plan for the poor paid for by general tax revenues. Because Congress did not impose a cap on medical expenses, which the medical industry opposed, federal expenditures for the two programs quickly escalated.

Although the Great Society is usually associated with programs for the disadvantaged, many of the Johnson administration's programs benefited more affluent Americans as well. Federal urban renewal and home mortgage assistance helped those who could afford to live in single-family homes or modern apartments. Medicare assistance went to every elderly person covered by Social Security, regardless of need. Federal aid for general public education programs benefited children of the middle class as well as the poor. Finally, the creation of the National Endowment for the Arts and the National Endowment for the Humanities in 1965 supported artists and scholars in their efforts to understand and interpret the nation's cultural heritage.

Another aspect of public welfare addressed by the Great Society was the environment. President Johnson pressed for the expansion of the national park system, improvement of air and water quality, and increased land-use planning. At the insistence of his wife, Lady Bird Johnson, he promoted the Highway Beautification Act of 1965. His approach marked a significant break with past conservation efforts, which had tended to concentrate on maintaining natural resources and national wealth. As Secretary of the Interior Stewart Udall explained, Great Society environmental programs emphasized quality of life, battling the problem "of vanishing beauty, of increasing ugliness, of shrinking open space, and of an overall environment that is diminished daily by pollution and noise and blight."

Taking advantage of the Great Society's reform climate, liberal Democrats also brought about significant changes in immigration policy. The Immigration Act of 1965 abandoned the quota system of the 1920s that had discriminated against Asians and southern and eastern Europeans, replacing it with more equitable numerical limits on immigration from Europe, Africa, Asia, and countries in the Western Hemisphere. Since close relatives of individuals who were already legal residents of the United States could be admitted over and above the numerical limits, the legislation led to an immigrant influx far greater than anticipated, with the heaviest volume coming from Asia and Latin America.

Voting Rights Act of 1965. The federal government also stepped up its commitment to voting rights, although once again it took violence to provoke congressional action. During a voter registration march in February 1965, sheriff's deputies in Marion, Alabama, killed Jimmy Lee Jackson, a black voting rights advocate. In protest, King and other black leaders called for a massive march on Sunday, March 7, from nearby Selma to the state capital, Montgomery, 54 miles away. A staunch opponent of integration, Governor George Wallace banned the march, citing concern for public safety. As soon as the marchers left Selma, mounted state troopers attacked them in broad daylight with tear gas and clubs. Scenes from "Bloody Sunday" were shown on national television later that night; ironically, ABC interrupted *Judgment at Nuremberg*, a film about the Nazi war crimes trials, to show police officers attacking American citizens on the Pettus Bridge.

Lyndon Johnson called Bloody Sunday "an American tragedy" and redoubled his efforts to get Congress to pass his pending voting rights legislation. In a televised speech to a joint session of Congress on March 15 Johnson asserted, "It is wrong—deadly wrong, to deny any of your fellow Americans the right to vote in this country." Then, dramatically and repeatedly, Johnson invoked the best-known slogan of the civil rights movement, "We shall overcome." Watching the speech on television, Martin Luther King was moved to tears.

On August 6 Congress passed the Voting Rights Act of 1965, the second legislative landmark of the civil rights movement. The act suspended the literacy tests and other measures that most southern states had used to prevent blacks from registering to vote. It also authorized the attorney general to send federal examiners to register voters in any county where less than 50 percent of the voting-age population was registered, placing the entire registration and voting process under federal to register in 1964, later declared, "It won't never go back where it was."

War on Poverty. In the midst of his campaign for civil rights legislation, Johnson was also pursuing his ambitious goal of putting "an end to poverty in our time." During his presidency, those who lived below the poverty line—three-fourths of whom were white—made up about a quarter of the American population. They included isolated farmers and miners in Appalachia, blacks and Puerto Ricans in urban ghettos, Mexican Americans in migrant labor camps and urban *barrios*, native Americans on reservations, women raising families on their own, and the destitute elderly. Because programs such as Old Age Assistance, Aid to

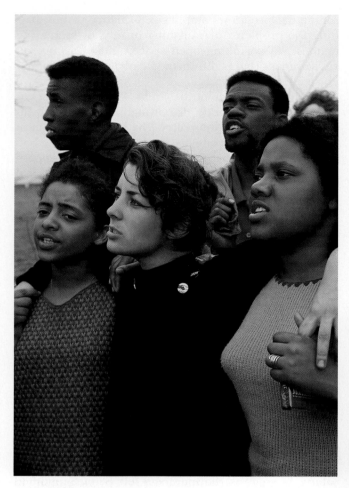

Civil Rights Protesters in Selma
Protesting the killing of a black voting rights advocate, thousands of civil rights activists staged a 54-mile march from Selma to Montgomery, Alabama, on March 7, 1965. The men and women in this photograph, shown here singing songs of freedom, were part of the historic march. The peaceful protest turned violent when state troopers clubbed and tear-gassed demonstrators on the Pettus Bridge outside Selma. Public outrage over the violence on "Bloody Sunday," as the incident became known, helped Johnson push the Voting Rights Act through Congress that summer.
Bob Adelman/Magnum Photos, Inc.

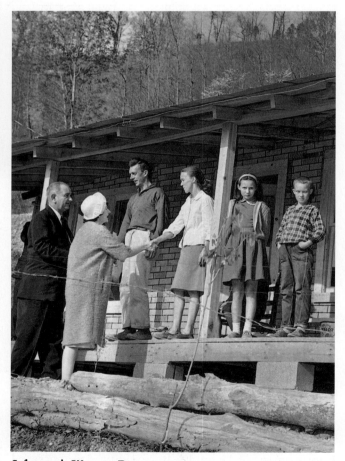

Johnson's War on Poverty
During his five years in office, President Lyndon Johnson launched a political crusade against poverty and racial inequality. Here LBJ and his wife, Lady Bird, visit with the Fletcher family in Inez, Kentucky, a town in rural Appalachia—one of the regions targeted by Johnson's War on Poverty.
Corbis-Bettmann.

control. Together with the adoption in 1964 of the Twenty-fourth Amendment to the Constitution, which outlawed the federal poll tax, the Voting Rights Act allowed millions of blacks to register and vote for the first time. Congress reauthorized the Voting Rights Act in 1970, 1975, and 1982. The results in the South were stunning. In 1960 only 20 percent of eligible blacks were registered; by 1964 the figure had risen to 39 percent and by 1971 to 62 percent (Map 28.4). Hartman Turnbow, a Mississippi farmer who had risked his life

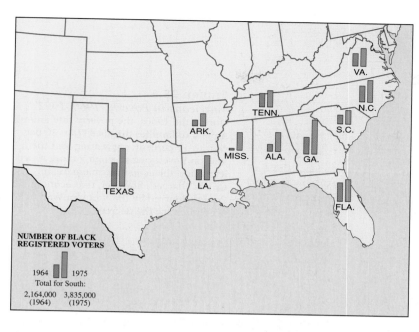

MAP 28.4
Black Voter Registration in the South, 1964 and 1975
After passage of the Voting Rights Act of 1965, black registration in the South increased dramatically. The bars show the number of blacks registered in 1964, before the act was passed, and in 1975, after it had been in effect for ten years. States in the Deep South, such as Mississippi, Alabama, and Georgia, had the biggest rises.

Dependent Children, and Aid to the Blind had strict eligibility restrictions, New Deal social welfare programs had failed to reach many of these people.

To reduce poverty, the Johnson administration expanded long-established social insurance, welfare, and public works programs. It broadened Social Security to include waiters and waitresses, domestic servants, farmworkers, and hospital employees. Social welfare expenditures increased rapidly, especially for Aid to Families with Dependent Children (AFDC), as did public housing and rent subsidy programs. Food Stamps, begun in 1964 largely to stabilize farm prices, grew into a major program of assistance to low-income families. The Appalachian Regional Development Act of 1965 provided federal funding for local roads, health clinics, and other public works projects in that poverty-stricken region. As during the New Deal, these social welfare programs developed in piecemeal fashion, without overall coordination.

The Office of Economic Opportunity (OEO), established by the Economic Opportunity Act of 1964, was the Great Society's showcase in the War on Poverty. Built around the twin strategies of equal opportunity and community action, OEO programs were so numerous and diverse that they recalled the alphabet agencies of the New Deal (see Table 28.1). Sargent Shriver, who moved from the Peace Corps to head the new agency, admitted, "It's like we went down to Cape Kennedy [the NASA space center in Florida] and launched a half dozen rockets at once."

OEO programs produced some of the most innovative measures of the Johnson administration. Head Start provided free nursery schools to prepare disad-vantaged preschoolers for kindergarten. The Job Corps and the Neighborhood Youth Corps provided jobs and vocational training for young people. Upward Bound gave low-income teenagers the skills and motivation to go to college. Volunteers in Service to America (VISTA), modeled on the Peace Corps, promoted community service among youths in impoverished rural and urban areas. The Community Action Program encouraged the poor to demand "maximum feasible participation" in decisions that affected them. Community Action organizers worked closely with 2,000 lawyers employed by the Legal Services Program to provide the poor with free legal aid.

Cracks in the New Deal Coalition

By the end of 1965, the Johnson administration had compiled the most impressive legislative record of liberal reforms since the New Deal. It had put issues of poverty, justice, and access at the center of national political life, and it had expanded the federal government's role in protecting citizens' welfare. Yet the Great Society never quite measured up to the extravagant promises made for it, and by the end of the decade many of its programs were under attack.

In part, the political necessity of bowing to pressure from various interest groups hampered Great Society programs. For example, the American Medical Association used its influence to shape Medicare and Medicaid in ways that contributed to skyrocketing medical costs. And entrenched Democratic mayors such as Richard J. Daley of Chicago and Sam Yorty of Los Angeles vigorously resisted VISTA and Community

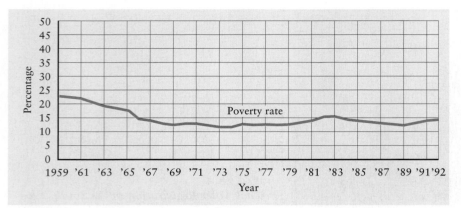

FIGURE 28.5
Americans in Poverty, 1960–1992
During the 1960s, the poverty rate among American families dropped from 20 percent to 13 percent, suggesting that the War on Poverty was bringing more Americans into the economic mainstream. Critics charged, however, that economic growth spurred by the Vietnam War accounted for the decrease.

Action Program agents who encouraged poor (and often nonwhite) people to demand the public services long withheld by unresponsive local governments. Many white working-class Democrats seconded these views, convinced that organized black and Latino groups were winning a disproportionate share of federal benefits. In response to such pressure, Johnson gradually phased out the Community Action Program and instead channeled spending for housing, social services, and other urban poverty programs through local municipal governments. That decision increased tensions between the Johnson administration and urban minority groups, while not fully mending the breach between the administration and its white working-class constituents—a rift that Republicans would later exploit.

Another inherent problem was the limited funding of Great Society programs. The annual budget for the War on Poverty, for example, was less than $2 billion. Still, the statistical decline in poverty during the 1960s suggests that the Great Society was successful on some levels. From 1963 to 1968, the proportion of Americans living below the poverty line dropped from 20 percent to 13 percent (Figure 28.5). Economic advancement of African Americans was even more marked: in the 1960s the black poverty rate was cut in half, and millions of blacks moved into the middle class, some through federal jobs in antipoverty programs. But critics charged that the reduction in the poverty rate was due to the decade's booming economy—fueled by defense spending for the Vietnam War—not to the War on Poverty. Moreover, although the overall standard of living increased, distribution of wealth was still uneven. The poor were better off in an absolute sense, but they remained far behind the middle class in a relative sense.

The implementation of the Great Society revealed deep contradictions in the New Deal coalition, which was torn among its diverse constituencies and their conflicting priorities. Those contradictions had been lurking in political life since Roosevelt and Truman had begun to expand the power of the federal government, but they surfaced forcefully in the climate fostered by the politics of expectation. Kennedy and Johnson had gathered an extraordinarily diverse set of groups into the New Deal coalition—middle-class and poor; white and nonwhite; Protestant, Jewish, and Catholic; urban and rural. For a brief period between 1964 and 1966 the coalition held together. But inevitably the claims of certain groups—such as the demand of blacks for civil rights and that of the urban poor for increased political power—conflicted with the interests of other Democratic supporters, such as white southerners and northern political bosses who wanted to maintain the status quo. In the end the New Deal coalition, which had fostered a vast expansion of federal power, could not sustain a consensus over the purposes that such a government ought to serve.

Democrats were also plagued by public disillusionment over the shortcomings of their reforms. In the early 1960s the lofty rhetoric of the New Frontier and the Great Society raised unprecedented expectations for social change. But competition for federal largesse was keen, and the shortage of funds for programs such as the War on Poverty left many promises unfulfilled, especially after 1965, when the escalation of the Vietnam War siphoned funding away from domestic programs. In 1966 the government spent $22 billion on the Vietnam War and only $1.2 billion on the War on Poverty. In the haunting phrase of Martin Luther King, the Great Society was "shot down on the battlefields of Vietnam."

Project Head Start
Project Head Start, which offered free early education programs for poor children, was one of the most acclaimed programs of LBJ's War on Poverty. In 1965, folk singer Tom Glazer staged a series of concerts for the more than 25,000 children enrolled in Head Start throughout New York City.
Wide World Photos.

Summary

★

In the postwar era, American dominance of the global economy ensured an unprecedented level of domestic prosperity. Increased levels of spending on defense and consumer goods led to new economic development concentrated in the southern and western states and in the suburbs. Federal intervention in the economy, especially Cold War defense spending, boosted the economies and populations of California, Texas, Florida, and other emerging Sun Belt states. Federal home loan programs and highway construction spurred rapid suburban development, siphoning jobs and middle-class residents out of the central cities. At the same time, many blacks, Latinos, native Americans, and other low-income groups were migrating into these declining urban areas, where they encountered growing unemployment, rising crime, and deteriorating housing and education.

After years of depression and war-induced insecurity, Americans turned inward toward religion, home, and family. Postwar couples married young, had several children, and—if they were white and middle class—raised their children in a climate of suburban affluence and consumerism. The profamily orientation of the 1950s celebrated social conformity and traditional gender roles, even though millions of women entered the work force in those years. Many of the smoldering contradictions of the postwar period—unequally shared affluence, institutionalized racism, tensions in women's lives—helped spur the civil rights movement and other social reform efforts of the 1960s.

As Americans looked to Washington for solutions to the nation's social and economic ills, the Democrats offered a diverse array of federal programs designed to appeal to a broad range of constituencies. John F. Kennedy first set the agenda for this politics of expectation in his 1960 presidential bid, but the domestic accomplishments of his New Frontier were limited. Kennedy's activism was more evident in foreign policy, where he proved a resolute Cold Warrior. Following Kennedy's assassination in 1963, Lyndon Johnson played a critical role in pushing civil rights legislation through Congress. Moreover, Johnson used his formidable political skills to usher in the most ambitious legislative reform program since the New Deal. Congress funded an array of Great Society programs in education, medical care, social welfare, housing, transportation, and environmental protection. But although the Great Society raised hopes, it could not always deliver on its promises. Increasing military expenditures for the Vietnam conflict limited federal funds for domestic programs. And as federal functions and responsibilities grew, accommodating the diverse and often competing constituencies in the Democratic coalition became increasingly difficult. By the mid-1960s the liberal consensus was breaking apart.

TIMELINE

1944	Bretton Woods economic conference
	World Bank and International Monetary Fund (IMF) founded
1947	Levittown, New York, built
1953–1958	Operation Wetback and Indian termination programs
1954	*Brown v. Board of Education of Topeka*
1955	AFL and CIO merge
	Montgomery bus boycott
1956	National Interstate and Defense Highway Act
1957	Peak of postwar baby boom
	School desegregation battle in Little Rock, Arkansas
	Southern Christian Leadership Conference (SCLC) founded
1960	Sit-ins in Greensboro, North Carolina
	John F. Kennedy elected president
1961	Peace Corps established
	Freedom rides
	Bay of Pigs invasion
	Berlin Wall erected
1962	Michael Harrington's *The Other America*
	Cuban missile crisis
1963	Betty Friedan, *The Feminine Mystique*
	Civil rights protest in Birmingham, Alabama
	March on Washington
	Nuclear test-ban treaty
	John F. Kennedy assassinated; Lyndon B. Johnson assumes presidency
1964	Freedom Summer
	Civil Rights Act
	Economic Opportunity Act inaugurates War on Poverty
	Johnson elected president
1965	Immigration Act abolishes national quota system
	Civil rights march from Selma to Montgomery
	Voting Rights Act
	Medicare and Medicaid programs established
	Elementary and Secondary Education Act

Suggested Readings

──────────★──────────

General introductions to postwar society include Paul Boyer, *Promises to Keep* (1995); John Diggins, *The Proud Decades* (1988); and David Halberstam, *The Fifties* (1993).

The Affluent Society

For overviews of the economic changes of the postwar period see David P. Calleo, *The Imperious Economy* (1982). Herman P. Miller, *Rich Man, Poor Man* (1971), and Gabriel Kolko, *Wealth and Power in America* (1962), discuss inequality in income distribution. Michael Harrington, *The Other America* (1962), documents the persistence of poverty in the postwar era.

Kenneth Jackson, *Crabgrass Frontier* (1985), provides an overview of suburban development. Herbert Gans, *The Levittowners* (1967), and Bennett M. Berger, *Working-Class Suburb* (1960), are sociological studies of suburbia written by contemporaries. On postwar development in the South and West see Carl Abbott, *The Metropolitan Frontier: Cities in the Modern American West* (1993); Numan V. Bartley, *The New South, 1945–1980* (1995); and Richard Bernard and Bradley Rice, eds., *Sunbelt Cities* (1983).

Books that highlight the social and cultural history of the 1950s include Larry May, ed., *Recasting America* (1989), and Douglas T. Miller and Marion Nowak, *The Fifties* (1977). For popular culture, George Lipsitz, *Time Passages* (1991), surveys postwar television, music, film, and popular culture, and his *Rainbow at Midnight* (2d ed., 1994) looks at working-class culture and rock 'n' roll. Other treatments of the mass media include James L. Baughman, *The Republic of Mass Culture* (1992); Peter Biskind, *Seeing Is Believing* (1983); and Nora Sayre, *Running Time* (1982). Vance Packard's influential unmasking of the advertising industry, *The Hidden Persuaders* (1957), can be supplemented by Stephen Fox, *The Mirror Makers* (1984).

Richard Easterlin, *American Baby Boom in Historical Perspective* (1962), analyzes the demographic changes, as does Landon Y. Jones, *Great Expectations* (1980). Elaine May's *Homeward Bound* (1988) is the classic introduction to postwar family life, providing a historical corollary to Betty Friedan's *Feminine Mystique* (1963). Recent revisionist work challenging this view can be found in Joanne Meyerowitz, ed., *Not June Cleaver* (1994).

Youth culture is the subject of William Graeber's *Coming of Age in Buffalo* (1990). James Gilbert, *A Cycle of Outrage* (1986), looks at juvenile delinquency in the 1950s. Peter Guralnick, *Last Train to Memphis* (1994), is the definitive biography of Elvis Presley's early years. Discussions of cultural dissent in the 1950s can be found in Bruce Cook, *The Beat Generation* (1971), and Dan Wakefield, *New York in the Fifties* (1992).

The Other America

Reed Ueda, *Postwar Immigrant America* (1994), examines new trends in immigration since 1945. Jacqueline Jones compares black and white urban migrants in *The Dispossessed* (1992). Thomas Sugrue, *Origins of the Urban Crisis* (1996), analyzes the economic decline and racial antagonism that plagued postwar Detroit. Donald Fixico, *Termination and Relocation* (1986), looks at federal Indian policy from 1945 to 1970.

Jon C. Teaford, *Rough Road to Renaissance* (1990); John Mollenkopf, *The Contested City* (1983); and Kenneth Fox, *Metropolitan America* (1985), offer the most complete accounts of postwar urban development.

John F. Kennedy and the Politics of Expectation

The literature on the Kennedy years is voluminous. Among the best general accounts are Richard Reeves, *President Kennedy: Profile of Power* (1993); James Giglio, *The Presidency of JFK* (1991); David Burner, *JFK and a New Generation* (1988); and Jim F. Heath, *Decade of Disillusionment: The Kennedy-Johnson Years* (1975). Critical views appear in Seymour Hersh, *The Dark Side of Camelot* (1997); David Halberstam, *The Best and the Brightest* (1972); and Henry Fairlie, *The Kennedy Promise: The Politics of Expectation* (1973).

On foreign policy in the Kennedy years see Michael Beschloss, *The Crisis Years: Kennedy and Khrushchev, 1960–1963* (1990), and Thomas Paterson, *Kennedy's Quest for Victory* (1989). Ernest R. May and Philip D. Zelikow, eds., *The Kennedy Tapes: Inside the White House during the Cuban Missile Crisis* (1997), provide verbatim accounts of the Cuban missile crisis. Secondary treatments include James Nathan, *The Cuban Missile Crisis Revisited* (1992), and Thomas Paterson, *Contesting Castro* (1994). Gerald Posner, *Case Closed* (1993), provides the most definitive treatment of the Kennedy assassination.

The best overviews of the postwar civil rights movement are Robert Weisbrot, *Freedom Bound* (1990); Harvard Sitkoff, *The Struggle for Black Equality* (2d ed., 1993); and Clayborne Carson et al., *The Eyes on the Prize Civil Rights Reader* (1991). Histories of the major civil rights organizations include Carson's study of SNCC, *In Struggle* (1981), and August Meier and Elliot Rudwick, *CORE* (1973). Doug McAdam, *Freedom Summer* (1988), describes the experiences of northern volunteers during Freedom Summer. Two fine oral histories of the civil rights movement are Howell Raines, *My Soul Is Rested* (1977), and Henry Hampton and Steve Fayer, *Voices of Freedom* (1990).

Local accounts of grass-roots organizing include William H. Chafe's superb study of Greensboro, North Carolina, *Civilities and Civil Rights* (1980), and two recent studies of Mississippi: John Dittmer, *Local People* (1994), and Charles M. Payne, *I've Got the Light of Freedom* (1995). The role of women in the civil rights movement is examined in Vicki L. Crawford et al., *Women in the Civil Rights Movement: Trailblazers and Torchbearers, 1941–1965* (1990). Martin Luther King Jr. told his own story in *Why We Can't Wait* (1964). His biographers include David Garrow, *Bearing the Cross* (1986), and Taylor Branch, *Parting the Waters* (1988) and *Pillar of Fire* (1998).

Lyndon B. Johnson and the Great Society

Lyndon Johnson's account of his presidency can be found in *The Vantage Point* (1971). Doris Kearns, *Lyndon Johnson and the American Dream* (1976), and Merle Miller, *Lyndon: An Oral Biography* (1980), are based on extensive conversations with LBJ. Robert A. Caro focuses on Johnson's early career in *The Path to Power* (1982) and *Means of Ascent* (1989); Robert Dallek offers his own exhaustive account in *Lone Star Rising* (1991) and *Flawed Giant* (1998).

Chapter 29

War Abroad and at Home: The Vietnam Era, 1961–1975

LYNDON JOHNSON, IN the crude language that characterized this tough-talking Texan, posed the trade-off starkly: "If I left the woman I really love—the Great Society—in order to get involved with that bitch of a war on the other side of the world, then I would lose everything at home. All my programs. All my hopes to feed the hungry and shelter the homeless. . . . But if I left that war and let the Communists take over South Vietnam, then I would be seen as a coward and my nation would be seen as an appeaser and we would both find it impossible to accomplish anything for anybody anywhere on the entire globe." In the end, his priorities were clear. "Losing the Great Society was a terrible thought, but not so terrible as the thought of being responsible for America's losing a war to the Communists. Nothing could possibly be worse than that."

Although most Americans first learned about Vietnam in the mid-1960s, the conflict occupied U.S. presidential administrations from Truman's to Ford's. U.S. troops fought in Vietnam for more than a decade—from the early 1960s to 1973—making it the nation's longest war. Moreover, as the country's first major military defeat, the war shook American confidence and damaged the international credibility it was supposed to uphold. The war took a toll at home, too. Defense spending temporarily boosted the economy but fueled inflation and diverted resources from domestic uses. As the war dragged on, antiwar sentiments spread across college campuses to the nation's streets, living rooms, and halls of state. Not since the Civil War was the nation so deeply and bitterly divided. Debates about the meaning and lessons of the war still resonate in American life.

The Longest War
American combat troops fought in Vietnam from 1965 to 1973, making it the longest war in the nation's history. Ambushed during a search-and-destroy mission, these soldiers await the arrival of a medical evacuation helicopter. More than 58,000 Americans lost their lives in the conflict, while another 300,000 were injured.
© Tim Page.

The "war at home" was part of a larger movement for social change in the 1960s. The postwar affluence of the middle class produced a self-assured generation of young whites who were optimistic about their ability to cure the nation's social ills. For young African Americans the affluence of the white middle class was a stark reminder of racial inequality. In the 1960s that same baby-boom generation swelled college enrollments, providing recruits for the civil rights campaign and other protest movements. Among women, increased access to education and greater participation in the work force in the postwar era sparked a revival of feminism. And the lofty Cold War rhetoric of international freedom and democracy prompted many to press for economic and racial justice at home.

Into the Quagmire, 1945–1968

★

Like many new nations that emerged from the dissolution of European empires after World War II, Vietnam was characterized by a volatile mix of nationalist sentiments, religious and cultural conflicts, economic need, and political turmoil. The rise of communism there was just one phase of that nation's larger struggle, which would eventually result in a bloody civil war. But American policy makers viewed these events singlemindedly through the lens of the Cold War, interpreting them as part of an internationally inspired communist movement toward global domination. Their failure to understand the complexity of Vietnam's internal conflicts led to a long and ultimately disastrous war.

The Roots of American Involvement

Vietnam, which had been part of the French colony of Indochina since the late nineteenth century, was occupied by Japan during World War II. Native resistance to the Japanese was led by Ho Chi Minh, a former schoolteacher and maritime worker, and the Vietnam Independence League, the Vietminh. First and foremost, the Vietminh were nationalists who wanted to end foreign rule in Vietnam. When the Japanese surrendered in 1945, Ho Chi Minh took advantage of the resulting power vacuum to proclaim—with words drawn from the American Declaration of Independence—the establishment of an independent republic of Vietnam. When France rejected his claim and reasserted control over the country the next year, an eight-year struggle that the Vietminh called the Anti-French War of Resistance ensued. Ho Chi Minh called on President Truman to support the struggle for Vietnamese independence, but Truman instead offered covert support to the French in

hopes of stabilizing a politically chaotic region and rebuilding the French economy.

By the end of the 1940s, American fears of communist expansion prompted the United States to step up its assistance to the French through the Marshall Plan and other Cold War measures. After the Chinese Revolution of 1949, the United States became concerned that China—along with the Soviet Union—might actively support anticolonial struggles in Asia and that newly independent countries would align themselves with the communists. At the same time, Republican charges that the Democrats had "lost" China influenced Truman to take a firmer stand against perceived communist aggression in both Korea and Vietnam. Truman also wanted to maintain good relations with France, whose support was crucial to the success of the new NATO alliance (see Chapter 27). Finally, Indochina played a strategic role in Secretary of State Dean Acheson's plans for an integrated Pacific Rim regional economy centered on a reindustrialized Japan.

When the Soviet Union and the new Chinese leaders recognized Ho Chi Minh's government early in 1950, the United States—along with Great Britain—recognized the noncommunist government of Bao Dai that the French had installed the previous year. Subsequently, the Truman and Eisenhower administrations provided substantial military support to the French—more than $2 billion by mid-1954. Eisenhower argued that such aid was essential to prevent the collapse of all the non-communist governments in the region in a chain reaction that he called the *domino effect*: "You have a row of dominoes set up, you knock over the first one, and what will happen to the last one is the certainty that it will go over very quickly."

Despite joint French-American efforts, Vietminh forces gained strength in northern Vietnam. In the spring of 1954, the French made a last stand at the isolated administrative fortress of Dienbienphu. France asked the United States to launch air strikes from nearby carriers to break the siege, but congressional opposition at home and Britain's refusal to join a pro-French coalition convinced Eisenhower to abstain from direct military intervention. Dienbienphu fell in May after a fifty-six-day siege.

The dramatic turn of events at Dienbienphu gave the Vietminh negotiating leverage at a conference in Geneva sponsored by Britain and the Soviet Union to discuss problems in Southeast Asia. The resulting 1954 Geneva Accords temporarily partitioned Vietnam at the 17th parallel and committed France to withdraw its forces from the area north of that line (Map 29.1). The accords also provided that within two years free elections would be held to choose a unified government for the entire nation. Eight of the nine national delegations in attendance signed the agreements, including China and the Vietminh, but the United States refused, instead issuing a separate protocol acknowledging the

MAP 29.1
The Vietnam War, 1954–1975
The Vietnam War was a guerrilla war, fought in skirmishes and inconclusive encounters rather than decisive battles. Supporters of the National Liberation Front filtered into South Vietnam along the Ho Chi Minh Trail, which wound through Laos and Cambodia. In January 1968 Vietcong forces launched the Tet offensive, a surprise attack on several South Vietnamese cities and provincial centers. American vulnerability to these attacks served to undermine U.S. credibility and fueled opposition to the war.

agreements and promising to "refrain from the threat or use of force to disturb them."

Eisenhower had no intention of allowing a communist victory in Vietnam's upcoming election. With the help of CIA military operatives, he made sure that a pro-American government took power in South Vietnam in June 1954, just before the accords were signed. Ngo Dinh Diem, an anticommunist Catholic who had spent the previous eight years in the United States, returned to Vietnam as premier of the French-backed South Vietnamese government. The next year Diem, in a rigged election in which he won an unlikely 98.2 percent of the vote, became president of an independent South Vietnam. With the support of the United States, he then called off the reunification elections scheduled for 1956, mainly because everyone realized that the popular Ho Chi Minh would win easily in both the north and south.

From the perspective of the Vietnamese, the Geneva Accords marked only a brief interlude between two wars, one to end French colonial control and another to reunify Vietnam. In March 1956 the last French soldiers left Saigon, the capital of South Vietnam, and the United States replaced France as the dominant foreign power in that country. Diem's was just one in a long line

of U.S.-backed governments that failed to win the allegiance of the Vietnamese population.

Between 1955 and 1961 the Eisenhower administration viewed South Vietnam as vital to the security interests of the United States, sending Diem an average of $200 million a year in aid and stationing approximately 675 American military advisors in Saigon. But in reality, Vietnam was too small a country to play a significant role in the international balance of power. Furthermore, its communism was regional and intensely nationalistic, not expansionist. Nevertheless, the United States continued to see Vietnam as a critical battleground in the Cold War struggle to contain communism. Having stepped up U.S. involvement considerably, Eisenhower passed the Vietnam situation to his successor, John F. Kennedy.

The Kennedy Years

President Kennedy saw Vietnam as an ideal laboratory to try out the counterinsurgency techniques that were the centerpiece of his military policy (see Chapter 28). But first he had to prop up the faltering regime of Ngo Dinh Diem, who was highly unpopular because of his

Buddhist Protesters, 1966
Beginning in 1963, militant Buddhist monks staged a series of protests against the war that helped bring down the American-backed regime of Ngo Dinh Diem. Here, robed monks, part of a group of 250 Buddhist protesters, stage an antigovernment demonstration in Saigon. They are surrounded by barbed wire put there by government troops. Strongly nationalistic, the monks appealed for peace talks with the Vietcong and for free elections that would allow the Vietnamese to decide their own fate. The South Vietnamese military government arrested Buddhist leaders in 1966 and effectively crushed their movement.
Wide World Photos, Inc.

administration's corruption and brutality, aloofness from the peasantry, and greedy land policy. The Diem regime also faced a growing military threat. In December 1960, the Communist Party in North Vietnam organized most of Diem's opponents in South Vietnam into a revolutionary movement known as the National Liberation Front (NLF). To counter the threat, Kennedy increased the number of American military "advisors" (an elastic term that included helicopter units and special forces assigned to train the South Vietnamese in counterinsurgency techniques) to more than 16,000 by November 1963. To win the "hearts and minds" of Vietnamese peasants, he also sent economic development specialists. Kennedy refused, however, to send American combat troops to assist the South Vietnamese.

The American aid did little good. Diem's political inexperience and corruption, combined with his Catholicism in a predominantly Buddhist country, prevented him from creating a stable government. He enjoyed much more support in faraway America than he did in his native land, and he consistently misled his American allies about South Vietnamese military and social progress. The NLF's guerrilla forces—called the Vietcong by their opponents—made considerable headway against the Diem regime, using the revolutionary tactics of the Chinese leader Mao Zedong to blend into the South Vietnamese civilian population "like fish in the water." They found a receptive audience among peasants who had been alienated by Diem's strategic hamlet program, which uprooted families and whole villages and moved them into barbed-wire-enclosed compounds in a vain attempt to separate them from Ho Chi Minh's sympathizers.

Anti-Diem sentiment was also strong among Buddhists, who charged the government with religious persecution. Starting in May 1963, militant Buddhists staged dramatic demonstrations against Diem. Several of the protesters set themselves on fire, and their suicides were recorded by American television crews. Diem's regime retaliated with raids on temples and mass arrests of Buddhist priests in August, prompting more antigovernment demonstrations. As opposition to Diem deepened, Kennedy decided that Diem would have to be removed. Ambassador Henry Cabot Lodge Jr. let it be known in Saigon that the United States would support a military coup that had "a good chance of succeeding." On November 1, 1963, Diem was driven from office and assassinated by officers of the South Vietnamese army.

Less than a month later, Kennedy himself was assassinated. Although historians continue to debate whether Kennedy would have withdrawn American forces from Vietnam had he lived, the actions of his administration clearly accelerated U.S. involvement. When Lyndon Johnson became president, he retained many of Kennedy's foreign policy advisors and quickly declared his intention to maintain support for South Vietnam. "I am not going to be the President who saw Southeast Asia go the way China went," Johnson asserted weeks after taking office. A new phase in the Americanization of the war was about to begin. When Johnson assumed the presidency in November 1963, 16,000 American troops were in Vietnam; when he left office in January 1969, there were more than 500,000.

Escalation under Johnson

The removal of Diem did not improve the efficiency or popularity of the Saigon government. Secretary of Defense Robert McNamara and other top advisors argued that only a rapid, full-scale deployment of U.S.

Aerial Bombing in Vietnam
The bombs dropped by U.S. forces in an attempt to root out Vietcong sympathizers inflicted heavy damage on the countryside and caused many civilian deaths. B-52 jets dropped most of the bombs.
Larry Burrows/LIFE Magazine © Time, Inc.

forces could prevent the imminent defeat of the South Vietnamese. But Johnson would need at least tacit congressional support, perhaps even a declaration of war, to commit U.S. forces to an offensive strategy. Originally Johnson wanted to wait until after the 1964 election to place this controversial request before Congress, but events gave him an opportunity to win authorization sooner.

The Gulf of Tonkin Resolution.   During the summer of 1964 American naval forces conducted surveillance missions off the North Vietnamese coast to aid amphibious attacks by the South Vietnamese. When the North Vietnamese resisted the attacks, President Johnson told the nation that on two separate occasions North Vietnamese torpedo boats had fired on American destroyers in international waters in the Gulf of Tonkin (see Map 29.1). At Johnson's request, Congress authorized him to "take all necessary measures to repel any armed attack against the forces of the United States and to prevent further aggression." On August 7 the Gulf of Tonkin Resolution passed by 88 to 2 votes in the Senate and 416 to 0 in the House. Only Senators Wayne Morse of Oregon and Ernest Gruening of Alaska opposed it as a "predated declaration of war" that further increased the president's ability to carry out foreign policy without consulting Congress.

Many questions were later raised about the resolution. A draft version had been ready for several months, awaiting just such an incident. The evidence of a North Vietnamese attack was sketchy at best. As the president admitted to his advisors soon afterward, "For all I know, our navy was shooting at whales out there." But this unverified attack got Johnson what he wanted—a sweeping mandate to conduct Vietnam operations as he

saw fit. It was the only formal approval of American intervention in Vietnam that Congress ever granted.

During the 1964 presidential campaign, Johnson declared, "We are not going to send American boys nine or ten thousand miles away from home to do what Asian boys ought to be doing for themselves." Yet plans were already being drawn up for a possible escalation of American efforts. With congressional support assured and the 1964 election safely over, the Johnson administration began the fateful move toward the total Americanization of the war. The escalation, which was accomplished during the first several months of 1965, took two forms: the initiation of direct bombing campaigns against North Vietnam and the deployment of ground troops.

Operation Rolling Thunder.   The first phase of escalation began on March 2, 1965, with Operation Rolling Thunder, a protracted campaign of bombing attacks against North Vietnam designed to cripple the economy and force the communists to the bargaining table. A special target was the Ho Chi Minh Trail, an elaborate network of paths, bridges, and shelters that stretched from North Vietnam through Cambodia and Laos into South Vietnam (see Map 29.1). By 1967 some 20,000 Vietnamese soldiers were moving southward along that route each month, along with the military equipment and other resources necessary to supply them.

Between 1965 and 1968 Operation Rolling Thunder (named for a Protestant hymn) dropped a million tons of bombs on North Vietnam, 800 tons a day for three and a half years. Each B-52 bombing sortie cost $30,000, and by early 1966, the direct costs of the air war had exceeded $1.7 billion. From 1965 to 1973 the United States dropped three times as many bombs on North Vietnam, a country roughly the size of Texas, as had fallen on Europe, Asia, and Africa during World War II. The several hundred captured American pilots downed in the raids then became pawns in negotiations with the North Vietnamese over the fate of prisoners of war.

To the amazement of American advisors, the bombing had little effect on the ability of the Vietnamese to wage war. Despite continuous sorties and the use of chemical defoliants to deny the Vietcong cover, the flow of troops and supplies to the south continued. The North Vietnamese quickly rebuilt roads and bridges, moved munitions plants underground, and constructed a network of tunnels and shelters. Instead of destroying enemy morale and bringing the North Vietnamese to the bargaining table, Operation Rolling Thunder intensified their will to fight. The bombing continued nevertheless.

The Arrival of U.S. Ground Troops.

A week after the launch of Operation Rolling Thunder, the United States sent its first official ground troops into combat duty when U.S. Marines waded ashore at Danang, South Vietnam's second largest city. Initially assigned to protect the nearby American air base, they were soon patrolling the countryside and skirmishing with the enemy. Beginning in the summer of 1965, combat operations shifted from a defensive stance to search-and-destroy missions designed to uncover and kill Vietcong forces. Fearing congressional opposition to this expanded military commitment, the Johnson administration did not reveal that a major change in policy had occurred.

Over the next three years the number of American troops in Vietnam grew dramatically. Although in 1965 U.S. troops were accompanied by military forces from Australia, New Zealand, and South Korea, the war increasingly became an American struggle, fought to achieve American aims. In 1966 more than 380,000 American soldiers were stationed in Vietnam; by 1968, there were 536,000 (Figure 29.1). The increasing demands of General William Westmoreland, commander of U.S. forces in Vietnam, confirmed a prediction made by presidential advisor George Ball in 1961 when

he warned an incredulous President Kennedy that if American ground troops were committed to Vietnam, 300,000 would be on the ground within five years. But as Kennedy observed before his death, requests for troops were like having a drink: "The effect wears off, and you have to take another."

The massive commitment of troops and air power threatened to destroy Vietnam's countryside and fragile resources. Taking to the extreme Johnson's call "to leave the footprints of America in Vietnam," the campaign of extensive defoliation and military bombardment made it difficult for peasants to practice the agriculture that provided the economic and cultural base of Vietnamese society. After one devastating but not unusual engagement the commanding U.S. officer remarked, "It became necessary to destroy the town in order to save it." Graffiti on a plane that dropped defoliants said, "Only you can prevent forests." (In later years chemicals such as Agent Orange were found to have highly toxic effects on humans and the environment.) The devastation was not limited to North Vietnam. South Vietnam, America's ally, absorbed more than twice the total bomb tonnage dropped on the north as U.S. forces tried to flush out Vietcong sympathizers. In Saigon and other South Vietnamese cities the influx of American soldiers and dollars distorted the local economy, spread corruption and prostitution, and triggered uncontrollable inflation and black-market activities.

Why did the dramatically increased American presence in Vietnam from 1965 on fail to turn the tide of the war? Certain advisors, such as former lieutenant colonel John Paul Vann, argued that military intervention would do little unless it was accompanied by reform of the Saigon government and increased popular support in the countryside. Other critics claimed that the United States never fully committed itself to total victory, although what total victory would have entailed remains in dispute. It is true, however, that military strategy was inextricably tied to political considerations. For domestic reasons, policy makers often searched for the elusive "middle ground" between an

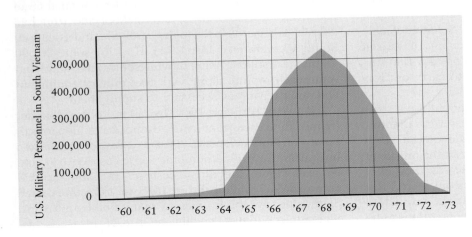

FIGURE 29.1
U.S. Troops in Vietnam, 1960–1973
When Lyndon Johnson escalated the Vietnam War, troop levels rose from 23,300 in December 1964 to 184,300 a year later. Troop levels eventually peaked at more than 543,000 personnel. Under Richard Nixon's Vietnamization program, beginning in the summer of 1969, levels drastically declined; the last U.S. military forces left South Vietnam on March 29, 1973.

all-out invasion (and the possibility of sparking a nuclear exchange between the superpowers) and the politically unacceptable alternative of disengagement. But this limited commitment was never enough to ensure victory, however defined.

The tremendous determination of the Vietnamese was a major factor. In the 1940s Ho Chi Minh had told his French imperialist foes, "You can kill ten of my men for every one I kill of yours, but even at those odds, you will lose and I will win." That same statement held true twenty years later against the Americans. The Vietcong were prepared to accept limitless casualties and to fight for as many years as necessary. North Vietnamese strategists astutely realized that the war did not have to be won on the battlefield, accurately predicting that American public opinion would not tolerate endless casualties and a long war of attrition. Time was on the Vietcong's side, although at an enormous cost to both sides.

The Combat Experience

Approximately 2.8 million Americans served in Vietnam. With an average age of only nineteen, this fighting force was one of the youngest in U.S. history. Most of those servicemen were too young to vote or drink (the voting age was twenty-one until the passage of the Twenty-sixth Amendment in 1971), but they were old enough to fight and die. They served for a variety of reasons. Some, including 7,000 women enlistees, were volunteers who joined out of a sense of patriotic duty or because they wanted to "see the world." But many more served because they were drafted. Until the country shifted to an all-volunteer force in 1973, the draft stood as a concrete reminder of the government's impact on the lives of ordinary Americans.

As troop needs increased, the draft reached deeper into the male population. In 1965 draftees accounted for 16 percent of total battle deaths; that figure rose to 34 percent in 1967 and 62 percent in 1969. Even more than in other recent wars, sons of the poor and the working class shouldered a disproportionate amount of the fighting, forming an estimated 80 percent of the enlisted ranks. Young men from more affluent backgrounds were more likely to avoid combat through student deferments, medical exemptions, and appointments to National Guard and reserve units—alternatives that made Johnson's Vietnam policy more palatable to the middle class.

At first many draftees and enlistees shared Cold War assumptions about the need to fight communism and the superiority of the American military. Service in Vietnam, however, quickly challenged simple notions of patriotism and the inevitability of victory (see American Voices, "Dave Cline: A Vietnam Vet Remembers," p. 948). The first thing new soldiers noticed when they got off the plane was the stench of napalm (a lethal incendiary substance), human waste, and death in this torrid jungle country. Sometimes they had to sprint from the plane to the safety of the base buildings because of mortar attacks, a sign of the boldness with which enemy forces operated throughout the country.

Unlike World War II soldiers who served "for the duration," Vietnam soldiers had a one-year tour of duty. For many it was simply a matter of getting through 365 days. For the first ninety days or so they were "cherries," slang for virgins, or inexperienced newcomers. Once they neared the end of the tour, soldiers might carry a "short-timer's stick," notched for the remaining days left; as each day passed, they would cut off a notch until only a small stub remained. Some soldiers longed for "million-dollar wounds"—serious but nonfatal injuries that would result in permanent removal from the battlefield. Some "grunts" (ordinary infantrymen) and "bloods" (a name that black draftees called themselves) deliberately avoided making close friends in case their buddies caught a grenade or triggered a booby trap on a routine patrol.

In "Nam" (soldiers' shorthand for Vietnam) days passed in boring menial work punctuated by flashes of intense fighting. "Most of the time, nothing happened," a soldier recalled, "but when something did, it happened instantaneously and without warning." The fighting had a surreal quality. Combat often intensified at night. Incoming and outgoing firepower lit up the sky while soldiers huddled sleeplessly on watch. There were rarely large-scale battles, only skirmishes; no front lines or conquering of territory, just operations during the day in areas that reverted to Vietcong control at night. Although some whole units were ambushed, casualties typically came in twos and threes.

A former marine captain recalled, "You never knew who was the enemy and who was the friend. They all looked alike. They all dressed alike. They were all Vietnamese. Some of them were Vietcong." He concluded graphically, "It wasn't like the San Francisco Forty-Niners on one side of the field and the Cincinnati Bengals on the other. The enemy was all around you." Because differentiating between friendly South Vietnamese and Vietcong sympathizers was difficult, many soldiers lumped them together as "gooks." A draftee noted of his indoctrination, "The only thing they told us about the Vietcong was they were gooks. They were to be killed."

Because territorial gains were often temporary and illusory, American success was measured in "body counts"—the number of enemy soldiers killed—and "kill ratios"—the ratio between enemy losses and U.S. casualties. "If it's dead and Vietnamese, it's VC [Vietcong]" was the rule of thumb in the bush. Casualty figures were often deliberately inflated. As a twenty-four-year-old army captain recalled, "I went out and killed one VC and liberated a prisoner. Next day the major called me in and told me that I'd killed fourteen VC and liberated six prisoners. You want to see the medal?"

AMERICAN VOICES

DAVE CLINE
A Vietnam Vet Remembers

⸻ ★ ⸻

Born in 1947, Dave Cline grew up in a working-class family outside Buffalo, New York. Drafted by the army in 1967, the twenty-year-old Cline was eager to help fight communist aggression in Vietnam. But after his arrival in Danang seven months later, his attitude toward the war quickly changed. Cline described this transformation in an interview conducted in 1992.

I went to basic training at Fort Dix. . . .

Down there, they used to give you basically two raps on why you were going to Vietnam. One was that rap about we're going to help the heroic South Vietnamese people. We're going to go fight for freedom [and repel] communist aggression. They'd show you the maps and stuff, the domino theory, the Red Chinese are trying to engulf all of southeast Asia. The other rap was: killing communists was your duty. . . .

The boat came into Danang, and then they flew us from Danang to Cu Chi. I remember it was humid and hot and smelled. First thing you do when you get in-country is, they give you these indoctrination classes and they say, "Forget all that shit they told; you can't trust any of these people. They're not really people anyway; they're gooks." . . . In other words: You see anyone with slant eyes, that's your potential enemy—don't trust them. That sort of blows away any "help the people" thing. . . .

I got wounded the last time out near the Cambodian border. This happened on December 20, 1967. Again, we were doing these sweeps and we were overrun about two in the morning. The North Vietnamese launched a massive human wave attack. We could hear them yelling orders maybe 25, 30 feet away, and these guys were charging. . . .

A guy came running up to my foxhole. We saw him coming from the next hole over and we didn't know if it was an American retreating over to us or a Vietnamese, because it was two in the morning. So we didn't shoot him.

I was sitting there with my rifle waiting to see, and all of a sudden he stuck his rifle in. I saw the front side of an AK-47 and a muzzle flash, and then I pulled my trigger. I shot him through his chest. I blacked out initially, but then I came to and found a round went right through my knee. They threw me in a foxhole and gave me a bottle of Darvons. I lay there until the battle ended. In the morning they medivaced me out.

They carried me over to this guy I had shot. He was sitting up against this tree stump. He was just sitting there with his rifle across his lap. He was dead. The sergeant started giving me this pep talk, "Here's the gook you killed!" In my unit they had a big thing about confirmed kills. If you had a confirmed kill and the person had an automatic weapon, then you were supposed to get a three-day in-country pass. . . .

This kid looked about the same age as me. The first thing I started thinking was, Why is he dead and I'm alive? . . .

Then after going into the hospital, I started thinking about that guy. I wonder if his mother knows he's dead? I wonder if he had a girlfriend? Looking back, I think I was retaining the sense that he was a human being.

⸻

Source: Richard Stacewicz, *Winter Soldiers: An Oral History of the Vietnam Veterans against the War* (New York: Twayne Publishers, 1997), 135–136, 140–141.

Fighting and surviving in such conditions took its toll. "Killing is the easiest part of the whole thing," one soldier recalled. "Sweating twenty-four hours a day, seeing guys drop all around you of heatstroke, not having food, not having water, sleeping only three hours a night for weeks at a time, that's what war is. Survival." Another veteran echoed that sentiment: "The hardest thing to come to grips with was the fact that making it through Vietnam—surviving—is probably the only worthwhile part of the experience. It wasn't going over there and saving the world from communism or defending the country." The pressure of waging war in those conditions drove many soldiers to seek escape in alcohol or cheap and readily available drugs.

The American women who served in Vietnam shared some of these experiences. As WACs, nurses, and civilian service workers with organizations such as the United Services Organization, women volunteers

948

witnessed massive doses of death and mutilation, mainly inflicted on soldiers barely out of their teens. They tried not to get caught up in it emotionally, but as a navy nurse recalled, "It's pretty damn hard not getting involved when you see a nineteen- or twenty-year-old blond kid from the Midwest or California or the East Coast screaming and dying. A piece of my heart would go with each."

After the intensity and the boredom of the tour of duty, there remained one last hurdle. Unlike veterans of World War II or the Korean War, who usually came back home in groups by a long boat ride, Vietnam veterans were in Saigon one day and back on the American mainland the next. Soldiers returned home alone and received no deprogramming or counseling. As support for the war evaporated at home, veterans felt increasingly out of place.

The Consensus Unravels

During the Kennedy and early Johnson years most Americans supported the administration's conduct of foreign affairs, as they had throughout the Cold War period. But in the late 1960s public opinion began to turn against the war. In July 1967 a Gallup poll revealed that for the first time, a majority of Americans disapproved of Johnson's Vietnam policy and believed that the war had reached a stalemate.

The Television War. Television had much to do with shaping these attitudes. Vietnam was the first war in which television brought the fighting directly into the nation's living rooms. The escalation in Vietnam came just two years after the expansion of the nightly network news broadcasts from fifteen minutes to half an hour. By 1967 CBS and NBC were spending $5 million a year to cover the war from their expanded Saigon bureaus, an investment that guaranteed reports from Vietnam would appear on the news every night. Reporters soon learned that combat footage—what they called "shooting bloody"—had a better chance of airing than did reports about social reform or political developments. Every night Americans watched U.S. soldiers advancing steadily in the countryside and heard reporters detail staggering Vietcong losses and minimal U.S. casualties.

Despite the glowing reports that were fed to the American public about the progress of the war, a number of congressmen and administration officials grew pessimistic. In 1966, the Senate Foreign Relations Committee (chaired by J. William Fulbright, an outspoken critic of the war) conducted televised hearings that raised questions about the administration's Vietnam policies. In November of the following year, Secretary of Defense McNamara, one of the architects of the war, sent a memo to the president arguing that con-

A Televised War
This harrowing scene from Saigon during the Tet offensive in 1968 was broadcast on U.S. network news. The NBC bureau chief described the film in a terse telex message: "A VC officer was captured. The troops beat him. They bring him to [Brigadier General Nguyen Ngoc] Loan who is head of South Vietnamese national police. Loan pulls out his pistol, fires at the head of the VC, the VC falls, zoom on his head, blood spraying out. If he has it all it's startling stuff."
Wide World Photos, Inc.

tinued escalation "would be dangerous, costly in lives, and unsatisfactory to the American people." A few weeks later McNamara left the Defense department for the World Bank. "I do not know," he later wrote, "whether I quit or was fired." Pentagon analysts confirmed McNamara's doubts, estimating that the Vietcong could marshal 200,000 guerrillas a year indefinitely. But President Johnson continued to insist that victory was within reach. Journalists, especially those who had spent time in Vietnam, soon commented that the Johnson administration suffered from a "credibility gap."

Economic events put Johnson and his advisors even more on the defensive. In 1966 the federal deficit was $9.8 billion; in 1967, it jumped to $23 billion, with the Vietnam War costing the taxpayers $27 billion. Although the war was consuming only 3 percent of the gross national product, compared with 42 percent at the height of World War II and 12 percent during the Korean War, its costs became more evident as the growing federal deficit nudged the inflation rate upward. But only in the summer of 1967 did Johnson ask for a 10 percent surcharge on individual and corporate income, which Congress delayed approving until 1968. By then the inflationary spiral that would plague the American economy throughout the 1970s was already well under way.

The Rise of the Antiwar Movement. Another major problem facing the Johnson administration was the growing strength and visibility of the antiwar movement. As in every American military conflict, a small group of dissenters opposed the war from the beginning, including pacifist organizations such as the War Resisters League and the Women's International League for Peace and Freedom, and religious groups such as the Quakers and the Fellowship for Reconciliation. Those groups were joined by a new generation of activists who had emerged in the 1950s in groups such as SANE (the National Committee for a Sane Nuclear Policy), Physicians for Social Responsibility, and Women Strike for Peace. These activists opposed the accelerating arms race in general and atmospheric testing in particular and lobbied successfully for the 1963 nuclear test-ban treaty between the United States and the Soviet Union (see Chapter 28).

Between 1963 and 1965, peace activists in both older and newer organizations staged protests, vigils, and letter-writing campaigns against U.S. involvement in the war. After the escalation in the spring of 1965, the antiwar movement was swelled by growing numbers of students, housewives, politicians, and artists, and a few elected officials. Critics of intervention argued that the war was morally wrong and antithetical to American ideals; that the goal of an independent, anticommunist South Vietnam was unattainable; and that American military involvement would not help the Vietnamese people. Though a diverse lot, all shared a common skepticism about the means and aims of U.S. policy.

Some Americans felt so strongly against the war that they adopted extreme methods of protest. In November 1965 Norman Morrison, a thirty-two-year-old Quaker activist—married and the father of an eighteen-month-old daughter—set himself on fire and burned to death near the gates of the Pentagon, 40 yards from Defense Secretary McNamara's office. Morrison undertook this protest after reading an account by a French priest who had despaired at seeing his Vietnamese parishioners burned by napalm during a bombing attack. Like the priest, Morrison was anguished about his inability to stop the carnage. To his wife he left this note: "Know that I love thee but must act for the children of the priest's village."

Morrison's suicide shocked the nation. Even McNamara later admitted that he was horrified by this "outcry against the killing that was destroying the lives of so many Vietnamese and American youth." Three weeks later an estimated 30,000 antiwar protesters converged on the White House, including a large contingent of college students. Over the next few years student protesters flocked to the antiwar movement, increasing its visibility and political clout. The fervor of this new generation drove not only the antiwar movement but a youthful rebellion that challenged authority on nearly every front.

The Challenge of Youth, 1962–1970

"There is everywhere protest, reevaluation, attack on the Establishment," social critic Paul Goodman asserted at the end of the 1960s. Novelist Norman Mailer agreed: "We're in a time that's divorced from the past. . . . There's utterly no tradition anymore." The civil rights movement had ignited the challenge to established institutions, teaching college students protest tactics such as marches, sit-ins, and mass confrontations. The idealism of Kennedy's New Frontier and Johnson's Great Society raised students' expectations of what they and their society could accomplish. Finally, the escalation of the Vietnam War in 1965 offered a compelling political cause to rally around, especially as the draft affected more and more college-age men. Vietnam would become the defining political issue of their generation.

Student Activism

The 1960s witnessed the first active student movement since the 1930s (see Chapter 24). Most of that depression-scarred generation had been unable to afford higher education, but its children—the baby boomers—flocked to colleges and universities in the postwar period. In addition, many soldiers who had served in World War II and the Korean War used the benefits of the GI Bill to finance higher education for themselves and later sent their children to college as well. In 1940 only 15 percent of all youth between the ages of eighteen and twenty-one attended college; in 1963 the proportion reached almost 50 percent.

The youthful rebelliousness so evident in 1950s popular culture infiltrated college campuses in the early 1960s, taking a distinctly political form. In June 1962 forty students from Big Ten and Ivy League universities met at a United Auto Workers conference center in Port Huron, Michigan, to found Students for a Democratic Society (SDS). Their manifesto, written by Tom Hayden, a University of Michigan student, drew heavily on the writings of the radical Columbia University sociologist C. Wright Mills. The Port Huron Statement expressed hostility toward bureaucracy, rejected Cold War ideology (including but not limited to the Vietnam conflict), emphasized participatory politics, and designated students as the major force for change in society. To distinguish themselves from the "Old Left"—communists, socialists, and other left-wing sectarians of the 1930s and 1940s—the founders of SDS referred to their movement as the "New Left." Consciously adopting the activist tactics pioneered by the civil rights movement, SDS devoted much of its early attention to grass-roots organizing in cities and on college campuses.

The Free Speech Movement. The first student protests broke out in the fall of 1964 at the University of California at Berkeley after the administration banned political activity near the Telegraph Avenue entrance to the campus, where student groups had traditionally distributed leaflets and recruited volunteers. In response, all the major student organizations, from SDS to the conservative Youth for Goldwater, formed a coalition called the Free Speech Movement and organized a sit-in at the main administration building. The university agreed to drop the ban.

The Free Speech Movement owed a strong debt to the civil rights movement. Berkeley had sent more volunteers to Freedom Summer in Mississippi in 1964 than had any other campus, and the students had been radicalized by the experience. Mario Savio spoke for many of them:

> *Last summer I went to Mississippi to join the struggle there for civil rights. This fall I am engaged in another phase of the same struggle, this time in Berkeley. The two battlefields may seem quite different to some observers, but this is not the case. The same rights are at stake in both places—the right to participate as citizens in a democratic society and to struggle against the same enemy. In Mississippi an autocratic and powerful minority rules, through organized violence, to suppress the vast, virtually powerless majority. In California, the privileged minority manipulates the university bureaucracy to suppress the students' political expression.*

On a deeper level Berkeley students were challenging a university that in their view had grown too big, too impersonal, and too insulated from the major social issues of the day. The largest universities, like the largest corporations, had grown the fastest in the postwar era. In 1940 only two campuses had as many as 20,000 students; in 1969 thirty-nine "multiversities" were at least that large. Emboldened by the Berkeley experience, college students across the country were soon protesting everything from dress codes to course requirements, tenure decisions, and academic grading systems.

Students also protested their universities' complicity in the problems of the ghettos that surrounded many urban campuses. Columbia, for example, was a major property owner in Harlem, which bordered its campus. When the university announced plans in 1968 to build a new gymnasium, displacing local stores and housing, students chanting "Gym Crow must go" tore down the fence at the construction site and took over several university buildings. At Berkeley, students and administrators

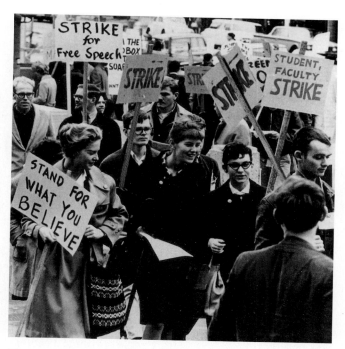

Free Speech at Berkeley, 1964
Students at the University of California's Berkeley campus protested the administration's decision to ban political activity in the school plaza. Free speech demonstrators, many of them active in the civil rights movement, relied on tactics and arguments that they learned during that struggle.
University of California at Berkeley, Bancroft Library.

clashed in 1969 over a parcel of vacant land near the campus that a coalition of students and residents had turned into a "People's Park." When the university asserted its right to the land, a violent confrontation broke out and an onlooker was killed. At both Columbia and Berkeley, administration decisions to use local police officers to break up the demonstrations radicalized many more students than had originally supported the protests. As campus disturbances spread, more and more university buildings were blocked, occupied, or picketed, and classes were frequently dismissed or canceled.

The Antiwar Movement. No issue provoked more impassioned and sustained protest than the Vietnam War. A strong spur to activism was a change in the Selective Service System. In the past, young men could use deferments for college, graduate school, teaching, and parenthood to avoid the draft until they reached the cut-off age of twenty-six; a disproportionate number of deferments went to affluent whites. In response to criticism of the class and racial bias inherent in the system, automatic student deferments were abolished in January 1966. To avoid the draft, some young men enlisted in the National Guard or the reserves; others declared themselves conscientious objectors. Several thousand ignored

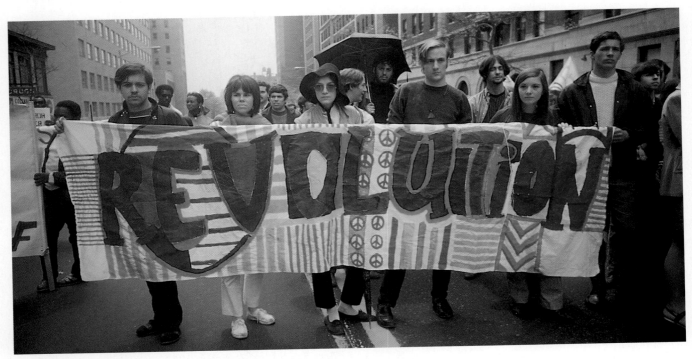

Columbia University Protests, 1968
At the height of the Vietnam War in 1968, Columbia University students launched a
series of protests against military research contracts, university governance, and the
construction of a gymnasium in a nearby Harlem neighborhood.
Steve Schapiro/Black Star.

their induction notices entirely, risking prosecution for
draft evasion. Others left the country, most often for
Canada or Sweden. Opponents of the war burned their
draft cards in public acts of civil disobedience, closed
down induction centers, and on a few occasions broke
into Selective Service offices to destroy or mutilate files.

As antiwar and draft protests multiplied, students
realized that their universities were deeply implicated in
the war effort. In some cases as much as 60 percent of a
university's research budget came from government contracts, especially from the Department of Defense. Protesters blocked campus recruitment by Dow Chemical
Company because it produced napalm and Agent
Orange. Arguing that universities should not train students for war, protesters demanded that the Reserve Officer Training Corps (ROTC) be removed from campus.

Mass demonstrations against the war consumed
much of the energy of the student movement in the late
1960s as students became part of the larger antiwar
movement. Rallies, "teach-ins," and student strikes
became commonplace, and in October 1967 more than
100,000 antiwar demonstrators, many of them students, marched on Washington as part of "Stop the
Draft Week." Criticism of American policy also came
from abroad. Cuban revolutionary leader Che Guevara
denounced the war as an imperialist struggle, a view
embraced by a growing number of young American
radicals (see Voices from Abroad, "Che Guevara: Viet-

nam and the World Freedom Struggle," p. 953). Lyndon
Johnson, who had earlier dismissed antiwar protesters
as "nervous Nellies" or communist dupes, now faced
large-scale public opposition to his policies. The
administration thus waged a two-front offensive: a military operation in Vietnam and a war for public opinion
at home.

The Rise of the Counterculture

The antiwar movement accelerated the erosion of confidence in established American institutions and values.
While the New Left took to the streets in protest, a
growing number of young Americans undertook their
own revolution against authority and middle-class
respectability. Building on the cultural rebellion articulated by the Beat generation in the 1950s, the *counterculture* (so-called because it challenged so many
established values) encouraged personal liberation
through new musical and clothing styles, spiritual
exploration, and experimentation with sex and drugs.

The impact of the counterculture was soon evident
even to the uninitiated. For one thing, young people's
clothing and hairstyles changed radically. At Berkeley's
free speech demonstrations in 1964, young men wore
coats and ties and women wore skirts and sweaters. At
antiwar protests just three or four years later, youths
defiantly dressed in unisex ragged blue jeans, tie-dyed

CHE GUEVARA

Vietnam and the World Freedom Struggle

———————★———————

*C*he Guevara, a leader of the Cuban Revolution, later worked with revolutionary nationalist movements in Africa and Latin America. Between his departure from Cuba in 1965 and his death in Bolivia in 1967, he made only one public statement. His message, "Vietnam and the World Freedom Struggle," helped convince some young American radicals of the necessity of armed struggle at home and abroad.

This is the painful reality: Vietnam, a nation representing the aspirations and the hopes for victory of the entire world of the disinherited, is tragically alone. . . .

And—what grandeur has been shown by this people! What stoicism and valor in this people! And what a lesson for the world their struggle holds!

It will be a long time before we know if President Johnson ever seriously thought of initiating some of the popular reforms necessary to soften the sharpness of the class contradictions that are appearing with explosive force and more and more frequently.

What is certain is that the improvements announced under the pompous label of the Great Society have gone down the drain in Vietnam.

The greatest of the imperialist powers feels in its own heart the drain caused by a poor, backward country; and its fabulous economy feels the effect of the war. . . .

And for us, the exploited of the world, what should our role be in this? . . .

Our part, the responsibility of the exploited and backward areas of the world, is to eliminate the bases sustaining imperialism—our oppressed peoples, from whom capital, raw materials, technicians and cheap labor are extracted, and to whom new capital, means of domination, arms and all kinds of goods are exported, submerging us in absolute dependence.

The fundamental element of this strategic goal will be, then, the real liberation of the peoples, a liberation that will be obtained through armed struggle in the majority of cases, and which, in the Americas, will have almost unfailingly the property of becoming converted into a socialist revolution.

In focusing on the destruction of imperialism, it is necessary to identify its head, which is none other than the United States of North America. . . .

The adversary must not be underestimated; the North American soldier has technical ability and is backed by means of such magnitude as to make him formidable. He lacks the essential ideological motivation which his most hated rivals of today have to the highest degree—the Vietnamese soldiers. . . .

Over there, the imperialist troops encounter the discomforts of those accustomed to the standard of living which the North American nation boasts. They have to confront a hostile land, the insecurity of those who cannot move without feeling that they are walking on enemy territory; death for those who go outside of fortified redoubts; the permanent hostility of the entire population.

All this continues to provoke repercussions inside the United States; it is going to arouse a factor that was attenuated in the days of the full vigor of imperialism—the class struggle inside its own territory.

Source: Ernesto C. Guevara, *Che Guevara Speaks* (New York: Pathfinder Press, 1967), 144–159.

T-shirts, beads, and army fatigues. Unorthodox clothes and long, unkempt hair identified a new phenomenon of American youth culture: the hippie. The uncomprehending older generation often had a simple response: "Get a haircut."

Popular music mirrored changing political moods. Folksinger Pete Seeger set the tone for the era with idealistic songs such as the antiwar ballad "Where Have All the Flowers Gone?" Joan Baez gained national prominence singing "We Shall Overcome" and other political anthems at protest rallies. In 1963, the year of the Birmingham demonstrations and President Kennedy's assassination, Bob Dylan's "Blowin' in the Wind" reflected the impatience of people whose faith in liberalism was wearing thin.

Other winds of change came from abroad. Early in 1964 the Beatles, four working-class youths from Liverpool, England, burst onto the American scene. As Elvis

Sgt. Pepper's Lonely Hearts Club Band
The colorful collage on the cover of this 1967 Beatles album allowed fans to debate (occasionally under the influence of marijuana or LSD) the symbolism of those depicted. Can you identify Mae West, Karl Marx, Bob Dylan, Albert Einstein, Lenny Bruce, and Marilyn Monroe, as well as the "Fab Four" in their various disguises?
© Apple Corps Ltd.

now celebrated the new drug-induced consciousness of "tangerine trees and marmalade skies" in hits such as "Lucy in the Sky with Diamonds" (1967).

For a brief time adherents of the counterculture believed that a new age was dawning. In 1967 the "world's first Human Be-In" drew 20,000 people to Golden Gate Park in San Francisco. The Beat poet Allen Ginsberg "purified" the site with a Buddhist ritual, political activists embraced "drug freaks," and the LSD advocate Timothy Leary, a former Harvard psychology instructor, urged the gathering to "turn on to the scene, tune in to what is happening, and drop out." That summer—dubbed the "Summer of Love"—San Francisco's Haight-Ashbury, New York's East Village, and Chicago's Uptown neighborhoods swelled with "flower children." Their faith in instant love and peace was soon tested, however, as dropouts, drifters, and teenage runaways coped with bad drug trips, venereal disease, and violence. In 1967 seventeen murders and more than a hundred rapes were reported in Haight-Ashbury alone.

Meanwhile, the appeal of rock music and drugs continued to spread. In August 1969 more than 400,000 people journeyed to Bethel, New York, to "get high" on music, drugs, and sex at the three-day Woodstock Music and Art Fair. Despite torrential rain and numerous drug overdoses, most enjoyed the festival, which was heralded as the birth of the "Woodstock nation." A few months later, however, an outdoor concert by the Rolling Stones at Altamont Speedway near San Francisco degenerated into a near riot, leaving four dead and hundreds injured.

Rejecting both the mainstream culture and the growing anarchy of the counterculture, some young people headed for rural communes located in areas such as the mountains between Santa Cruz and San Francisco, the wide-open spaces of New Mexico, and the pastoral solitude of Vermont. Following in the tradition of earlier American utopian communities, communes provided economic and sexual alternatives to nuclear families and were removed from the watchful eye of mainstream America (and local drug enforcement agents). Members grew their own food, baked their own bread, and rejected materialism and commercialism in favor of rural self-sufficiency. But the communes of the 1960s did not just look backward. Their advocacy of organic farming—growing food without chemicals or pesticides—anticipated and influenced the environmental concerns that would emerge in the 1970s (see Chapter 30).

The Widening Struggle for Civil Rights

The counterculture and the antiwar movement were not the only social movements to challenge the status quo in the 1960s. Black frustration and anger fueled a new racial militance as the civil rights struggle moved outside the South to take on the more stubborn problems of

Presley had done eight years earlier, they thrust their way into the national consciousness through a series of television appearances on "The Ed Sullivan Show." The Beatles' music, by turns lyrical and driving, was phenomenally successful, spawning a commercial and cultural phenomenon called Beatlemania that deepened the generational divide begun by rock 'n' roll in the 1950s. After the Beatles came the angrier, more rebellious music of other British groups, notably the Rolling Stones, whose raunchy 1965 hit "(I Can't Get No) Satisfaction" signaled a new openness about sexuality.

Drugs were almost as important as rock music in the youth culture of the 1960s. Drugs were hardly new to the American scene: the Beats had experimented with mind-altering drugs, and many jazz musicians had used heroin and cocaine for decades. But the recreational use of drugs—especially marijuana and the hallucinogen lysergic acid diethylamide, popularly known as LSD or "acid"—had never been so widespread, or so celebrated in popular music. San Francisco bands such as the Grateful Dead and the Jefferson Airplane and musicians like the Seattle-born guitarist Jimi Hendrix developed a style of music known as "acid rock," characterized by long, heavily amplified guitar solos and psychedelic lighting effects. The Beatles, whose early songs had simply stated "I want to hold your hand," entrenched poverty and racism. The rhetoric and tactics of the emerging black power movement shattered the existing civil rights coalition and galvanized white opposition. At the same time, the tactics that the civil rights movement had pioneered—legislative and judicial challenges, nonviolent direct action, and mobilization of public opinion—were adopted by women, Mexican Americans, native Americans, and other groups to press their demands. As a civil rights worker observed, "What started out as an identity crisis for Negroes turned out to be an identity crisis for the nation."

Rising Militance.

Once the system of legal, or *de jure*, segregation had fallen, the civil rights movement turned to the more difficult task of eliminating the *de facto* segregation, enforced by custom, that made blacks second-class citizens throughout the nation. Outside the South, racial discrimination was less flagrant, but it was pervasive, especially in education, housing, and employment. Although the *Brown* decision outlawed separate schools, it did nothing to change educational systems in areas where schools were all-black or all-white because of residential segregation. Not until 1973 did federal judges begin to extend the desegregation that had begun in the South two decades earlier to schools in the rest of the country.

As civil rights leaders took on the new target of northern racism, the movement fractured along generational lines. Students who had risked assault to sit in at lunch counters or to register to vote grew impatient with the gradualism of their elders. Some younger black activists, eager for confrontation and faster change, questioned the very goal of integration into white society. Black separatism, espoused by earlier black leaders such as Marcus Garvey in the 1920s (see Chapter 23), was revived in the 1960s by the Nation of Islam, which had more than 10,000 members and many more sympathizers. Popularly known as the Black Muslims, the Nation of Islam was extremely hostile to whites, whom its leader Elijah Muhammad called "blue-eyed devils." Forcefully promoting black nationalism, the group stressed black pride, unity, and self-help.

The Black Muslims' most charismatic figure was Malcolm X. Born Malcolm Little in Omaha in 1925, he converted to the Nation of Islam while serving time in prison for attempted burglary. Replacing his "slave name" with an X to signify his lost African name, Malcolm X was a brilliant debater and spellbinding speaker who preached a philosophy quite different from Martin Luther King's. Malcolm X advocated militant protest and separatism and condoned the use of violence for self-defense and self-assertion. He was hostile to the traditional civil rights organizations, caustically referring to the 1963 march as the "Farce on Washington."

In 1964, after a power struggle with Elijah Muhammad, Malcolm X broke with the Nation of Islam. He then made a pilgrimage to Mecca, the holiest site of traditional Islam, and toured Africa, where he embraced the liberation struggles of all colonized peoples. On his return to the United States, Malcolm X moved away from antiwhite rhetoric toward an internationalist vision of the black future. On February 21, 1965, he was assassinated while giving a speech at the Audubon Ballroom in Harlem. Three Black Muslims were later convicted for the murder. Malcolm X's autobiography, cowritten by Alex Haley and published soon after his death, became one of the decade's most influential books.

Black Power.

Although Malcolm X's call for black cultural and political independence appealed to young black activists in SNCC and CORE, many balked at the idea of converting to Islam, preferring a secular black nationalist movement. In 1966 SNCC leader Stokely Carmichael christened a new era in the black struggle when he called for black self-reliance and racial pride under the banner of "black power." Amid growing distrust of white domination, SNCC embraced black power and effectively ejected its white members. In the same year Huey Newton and Bobby Seale, two college students in Oakland, California, founded the Black Panthers as a militant self-defense organization to protect local blacks from police violence. The Panthers undertook a wide range of community-organizing projects in several cities, but their affinity for Third World revolutionary movements and armed struggle became their most publicized attribute.

Among the most significant legacies of black power was the assertion of racial pride. Many young blacks insisted on being called Afro-American rather than Negro, a term they found demeaning because of its historical association with slavery and racism. Rejecting white tastes and standards, blacks wore African clothing and Afro hairstyles and helped awaken interest in black history, art, and literature. Black students demanded courses in African American history and culture, the forerunners of the Afro-American or black studies departments established by many universities in the late 1960s and early 1970s. By acknowledging race as a key factor in American life, these new courses and programs had an enduring impact on the way American history was taught and written.

The new black assertiveness alarmed many white Americans. They had been willing to go along with the moderate reforms of the 1950s and early 1960s but became wary when blacks started demanding higher-paying jobs, housing in white neighborhoods, integrated schools, and increased political power. In 1966, 84 percent of all whites thought blacks were demanding too much change, up from 34 percent five years earlier. White backlash soon became a powerful force in both political parties.

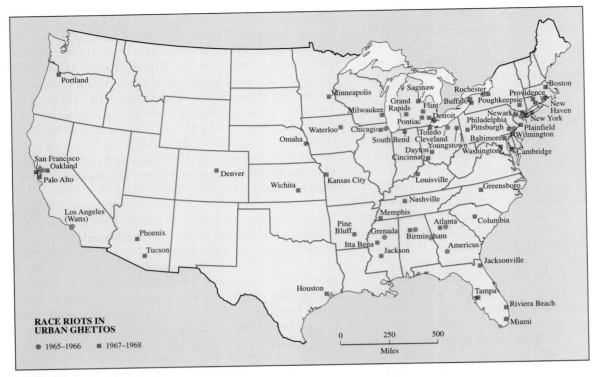

MAP 29.2
Racial Unrest in America's Cities, 1965–1968
American cities suffered through four "long hot summers" of rioting in the mid-1960s. In
1967, the worst year, riots broke out across the United States, including the South and
West. Major riots did not usually occur in the same city two years in a row.

Summer in the City. A major reason for the erosion
of white support was a wave of riots that struck the
nation's cities. Every summer from 1964 to 1968 images
of defiant black youths and burning buildings filled the
nightly TV news. Mired in declining urban neighborhoods with high unemployment, dilapidated housing,
and substandard education and services, black residents angrily denounced the racism of white employers, landlords, shopkeepers, and labor unions. Many
blacks especially resented the police, whose violent
presence in black neighborhoods made them seem like
"an occupying army." Stimulated by the successes of
southern blacks who had challenged whites and gotten
results, young urban blacks expressed their grievances
through their own brand of direct action.

The first "long hot summer" began in July 1964 in
New York City, when police shot a young black criminal
suspect in Harlem. Angry youths looted and rioted for a
week. The volatile issue of police brutality would set off
riots in a number of cities over the next four years
(Map 29.2). In August 1965 the arrest of a young black
motorist in the Watts section of Los Angeles sparked six
days of rioting that left thirty-four blacks dead. Ironically,
Watts erupted only five days after President Johnson
hailed the passage of the Voting Rights Act of 1965 as the

next great step toward racial equality. For many young
urban blacks the legal gains of the civil rights movement
were irrelevant to their daily experience of poverty and
economic exploitation. Instead of singing "We shall overcome," Watts rioters shouted "Burn, baby, burn."

The riots of 1967 were the most serious of all,
engulfing twenty-two cities in July and August. The
most devastating outbreaks occurred in Newark and
Detroit. Forty-three people were killed in Detroit alone,
nearly all of them black, and $50 million of property
was destroyed; federal paratroopers, some just back
from service in Vietnam, were sent in to restore order.
As in most of the riots, the arson and looting in Detroit
targeted white-owned stores and property, though there
was little physical violence against white people.

On July 29, 1967, President Johnson appointed a
special commission to investigate the riots. The final
report of the National Advisory Commission on Civil
Disorders (also known as the Kerner Commission),
released in March 1968, detailed the continuing inequality and racism of urban life. It also issued a warning:
"Our nation is moving toward two societies, one black,
one white—separate and unequal. . . . What white Americans have never fully understood—but what the Negro
can never forget—is that white society is deeply impli-

cated in the ghetto. White institutions created it, white institutions maintain it, and white society condones it."

The Assassination of Martin Luther King Jr. On April 4, 1968, barely a month after the Kerner Commission released its report, Martin Luther King was assassinated in Memphis, Tennessee, where he had gone to support a strike by predominantly black sanitation workers. King's death set off an explosion of urban rioting, with major violence breaking out in more than a hundred cities.

With King's assassination the civil rights movement lost the black leader best able to stir the conscience of white America. At the time of his death, King was only thirty-nine years old. During the last years of his life he had moved toward a broader view of the structural problems of poverty and racism faced by blacks in contemporary America. He spoke out eloquently against the Vietnam War, and in 1968 he was planning a poor people's campaign to raise issues of economic injustice and inequality. How successful King would have been in those endeavors will never be known, but his death marked the passing of an important national leader and symbolized the troubled course of the civil rights movement.

The Legacy of the Civil Rights Movement

The 1960s brought permanent, indeed revolutionary, changes in American race relations. Jim Crow segregation was overturned in less than a decade, and federal legislation was passed to ensure protection of black Americans' most basic civil rights. The enfranchisement of blacks in southern states ended political control there by a lily-white Democratic Party and allowed black candidates to enter the political arena. White candidates who had once been ardent segregationists now courted the black vote. In time Martin Luther King's

Mourning Martin Luther King Jr.
Thousands of African Americans mourned the death of the country's foremost civil rights leader, Martin Luther King, who had been assassinated in Memphis, Tennessee, on April 4, 1968. Among those who marched alongside King's casket, borne by a simple farm wagon pulled by mules, were future presidential candidate Jesse Jackson (in green) and future U.N. ambassador Andrew Young (at the left corner of the casket). During that week racial uprisings broke out in more than a hundred cities.
Wide World Photos, Inc.

greatness was recognized even among whites in the South; in 1986 his birthday became a national holiday.

Yet much remained undone. The more entrenched forms of segregation and discrimination persisted despite the legal reforms of the 1960s. African Americans, particularly those in the central cities, continued to make up a disproportionate number of the poor, unemployed, and undereducated. As the civil rights movement gradually disintegrated, its agenda remained unfinished.

The Chicano Movement.   Despite its limitations, the civil rights movement provided a fresh and innovative model for social change. Although Mexican Americans had been actively working for civil rights since the 1930s (see Chapter 24), poverty, an uncertain legal status, and language barriers made political mobilization difficult. That situation began to change when the Mexican-American Political Association (MAPA) mobilized support for Kennedy in 1960; in return Kennedy appointed several Mexican American leaders to posts in Washington. Over the next four years, MAPA and other political organizations successfully worked to elect Mexican American candidates to Congress, including Edward Roybal of California and Henry Gonzalez and Elizo de la Garza of Texas in the House, and Joseph Montoya of New Mexico in the Senate.

Younger Mexican Americans quickly grew impatient with MAPA, however. The *barrios* of Los Angeles and other western cities produced the militant Brown Berets, who modeled themselves on the Black Panthers (who wore black berets). Rejecting the assimilationist approach of their elders, 1,500 Mexican American students met in Denver in 1969 to hammer out a new nationalist political and cultural agenda. They proclaimed a new term, *Chicano*, to replace *Mexican American* and subsequently organized a political party, La Raza Unida (The United Race), to promote Mexican American interests and candidates. In California and other southwestern states, students staged demonstrations and boycotts to press for bilingual education, the hiring of more Chicano teachers, and the creation of programs in Chicano studies. By the 1970s dozens of universities in the region were offering such programs.

Chicano strategists also pursued economic objectives. Working in the fields around Delano, California, labor leader César Chávez organized the United Farm Workers (UFW), the first union to represent migrant workers successfully. A 1965 grape pickers' strike and a nationwide boycott of table grapes brought Chávez and his union national publicity and won support from the AFL-CIO and Senator Robert F. Kennedy of New York. Chávez was soon receiving almost as much media attention as Martin Luther King Jr. Victory came in 1970, when California grape growers signed contracts recognizing the UFW.

The Native American Movement.   North American Indians also found a model in the civil rights movement.

Native Americans, who numbered nearly 800,000 in the 1960s, were an exceedingly diverse group, divided by language, tribal history, region, and degree of integration into mainstream American life. Moreover, the termination policy that had begun in the 1950s had accelerated the breakdown of tribal life and the dispersal of native American populations. But native Americans also shared an unemployment rate ten times the national average, as well as the worst poverty, the most inadequate housing, the highest disease rates, and the least access to education of any group in the United States.

As early as World War II, the National Council of American Indians had lobbied for the improvement of those conditions, but now some Indian groups became more assertive. Like the young militants in other movements, they challenged the accommodationist approach of their elders. Proposing a new name for themselves—native Americans—they organized protests and demonstrations to build support for their cause. In 1968 several Chipewyan from Minnesota organized the militant American Indian Movement (AIM), which modeled itself on the black power movement and drew its strength from the third of the native American population that lived in "red ghettos" in cities throughout the West.

In November 1969 AIM seized the deserted federal penitentiary on Alcatraz Island in San Francisco Bay, offering the government $24 worth of trinkets to pay for it, supposedly the sum the Dutch had paid the native inhabitants for Manhattan Island in 1626. The occupation of Alcatraz lasted until the summer of 1971. A year later, a thousand protesters occupied the headquarters of the Federal Bureau of Indian Affairs in Washington, D.C., which was to many native Americans a hated symbol of the inconsistent federal policy on tribal welfare (see American Voices, "Mary Crow Dog: The Trail of Broken Treaties," p. 960).

In February 1973, a group of Sioux organized by AIM leaders began an occupation of the tiny village of Wounded Knee, South Dakota, the site of the army massacre of the Sioux in 1890 (see Chapter 16). They were protesting the light sentences given to a group of white men convicted of killing a Sioux in 1972. To dramatize their cause, the protesters took eleven hostages and occupied several buildings. But when a gun battle with the FBI left one protester dead and another wounded, the seventy-one-day siege collapsed. Although the new native American activism alienated many whites, it helped spur government action on tribal issues (see Chapter 31).

Identity Politics.   Civil rights, once seen as a movement exclusively for the rights of black people, also sparked a new awareness among some predominantly white groups. Americans of Polish, Italian, Greek, and Slavic descent, most of them working class and Catholic, proudly embraced their ethnic identity. Through groups like the Grey Panthers, elderly Americans organized to demand better health, social security, and other benefits.

Wounded Knee Revisited
In 1973 members of the American Indian Movement staged a seventy-one-day protest at Wounded Knee, South Dakota, the site of the 1890 massacre of two hundred Sioux by U.S. soldiers. The takeover was sparked by the murder of a local Sioux by a group of whites but quickly expanded to include demands for basic reforms in federal Indian policy and tribal governance.
Corbis-Bettmann.

Similarly, homosexual men and women banded together to protest legal and social oppression based on sexual orientation. Going beyond an older legalistic approach to homosexual rights, the gay liberation movement was born in 1969 in the Stonewall riot in New York City, in which patrons of a gay bar in Greenwich Village fought back against police harassment. Activists took the new name *gay* rather than *homosexual;* founded advocacy groups, newspapers, and political organizations to challenge discrimination and prejudice; and provided emotional support for those who "came out" by publicly affirming their homosexual identity.

For many gays and members of various ethnic and cultural groups, political activism based on heightened group identity represented one of the most significant legacies of the African American struggle. It also posed dilemmas for those who had multiple social identities (such as gay or elderly nonwhites) and were pressured to choose one primary identity over others.

The Revival of Feminism

The civil rights movement also helped reactivate feminism, a movement that had been languishing since the 1920s. Just as the abolition movement had been the training ground for an earlier generation of women's rights advocates in the nineteenth century, the black struggle inspired and influenced young feminists in the 1960s. But the revival of feminism also grew out of postwar social and demographic changes that affected younger and older women alike. More women were attending college and working outside the home than ever before, the birth rate was falling again after its baby-boom high, and divorce rates were skyrocketing— all developments that undercut traditional gender expectations. Those changing social realities created a major constituency for the emerging women's movement.

Throughout the 1960s, older, politically active professional women sought change by working through the political system. Many of them came together in the President's Commission on the Status of Women, a group appointed by John F. Kennedy to counter criticism about his administration's poor record on women's issues. In 1963 the commission issued a report that documented the employment and educational discrimination faced by women. More important than the report's conservative recommendations was the nationwide network of women in public life that formed during the course of the commission's work.

Another spark that ignited the revival of feminism was Betty Friedan's best-selling book, *The Feminine Mystique*, published in 1963. A pointed indictment of women's suburban domesticity that grew out of Friedan's experiences as a housewife in the 1950s, the book explored what she called "the problem that has no name": "As she made the beds, shopped for groceries, matched slipcover material, ate peanut butter sandwiches with her children, chauffeured Cub Scouts and Brownies, lay beside her husband at night—she was afraid to ask even of herself the silent question—'Is this all?'" Women responded enthusiastically to Friedan's story, especially white, college-educated women whose backgrounds resembled the author's. *The Feminine Mystique* gave women a vocabulary for their dissatisfaction and introduced many of them to the powerful ideas of modern feminism.

Like so many constituencies in postwar America, women's rights activists looked to the federal government for help. The first step occurred in 1963 when Congress passed the Equal Pay Act, which directed that men and women be paid the same wages for doing the same job. Even more important was the Civil Rights Act of 1964, which had as great an impact on women as it did on blacks and other minorities. Title VII, which barred discrimination in employment on the basis of race, color, religion, national origin, or sex, eventually became a powerful tool in the fight against sex discrimination. Initially, however, the Equal Employment Opportunity Commission avoided implementing it.

MARY CROW DOG

The Trail of Broken Treaties

———★———

In November 1972, 19-year old Mary Crow Dog traveled to Washington, D.C., with several hundred other Sioux from the Rosebud and Pine Ridge reservations in South Dakota. As she explains in her autobiography, their group was one of several caravans participating in a protest known as the Trail of Broken Treaties, which ended in a six-day occupation of the Bureau of Indian Affairs headquarters.

When we arrived in Washington we got lost. We had been promised food and accommodation, but due to government pressure many church groups which had offered to put us up and feed us got scared and backed off. . . .

Somebody suggested, "Let's all go to the BIA." It seemed the natural thing to do, to go to the Bureau of Indian Affairs building on Constitution Avenue. They would have to put us up. It was "our" building after all. Besides, that was what we had come for, to complain about the treatment the bureau was dishing out to us. . . . Next thing I knew we were in it. We spilled into the building like a great avalanche. Some people put up a tipi on the front lawn. . . . The building finally belonged to us and we lost no time turning it into a tribal village. . . .

We pushed the police and guards out of the building. Some did not wait to be pushed but jumped out of the ground-floor windows like so many frogs. We had formulated twenty Indian demands. These were all rejected by the few bureaucrats sent to negotiate with us. . . . Soon we listened to other voices as the occupation turned into a siege. I heard somebody yelling, "The pigs are here." I could see from the window that it was true. The whole building was surrounded by helmeted police armed with all kinds of guns. A fight broke out between the police and our security. Some of our young men got hit over the head with police clubs and we saw the blood streaming down their faces. . . .

We barricaded all doors and the lowest windows with document boxes, Xerox machines, tables, file cabinets, anything we could lay our hands on. . . .

From then on, every morning we were given a court order to get out by six P.M. Come six o'clock and we would be standing there ready to join battle. I think many brothers and sisters were prepared to die right on the steps of the BIA building. . . .

In the end a compromise was reached. The government said . . . they would appoint two high administration officials to seriously consider our twenty demands. Our expenses to get home would be paid. Nobody would be prosecuted. Of course, our twenty points were never gone into afterward. From the practical point of view, nothing had been achieved. . . . But morally it had been a great victory. We had faced White America collectively, not as individual tribes. We had stood up to the government and gone through our baptism of fire. We had not run.

Source: Mary Crow Dog, *Lakota Woman* (New York: Grove Weidenfeld, 1990), 84–85, 88–91.

Dissatisfied with the commission's reluctance to promote women's rights, Friedan and others founded the National Organization for Women (NOW) in 1966. Modeling itself on groups such as the NAACP, NOW aimed to be a civil rights organization for women. "The purpose of NOW," its statement of purpose declared, "is to take action to bring women into full participation in the mainstream of American society now, exercising all the privileges and responsibilities thereof in truly equal partnership with men." Under Friedan, who served as NOW's first president, its membership grew from 1,000 in 1967 to 15,000 in 1971. Men made up a fourth of NOW's early membership. It is still the largest feminist organization in the United States.

Under the banner "women's liberation," a younger generation of women came to feminism by a different path. White women had made up about half of the students who went south with SNCC in the 1964 Freedom Summer project. College women developed self-confidence and organizational skills working in the South and found role models in older women, both black and white, who were prominent in the movement. Yet women volunteers also found that they were expected to do all the cleaning and cooking at the Freedom Houses where SNCC volunteers lived. "We didn't come down here to work as maids this summer," one complained.

After 1965 black power militancy made white women as well as white men unwelcome in the civil

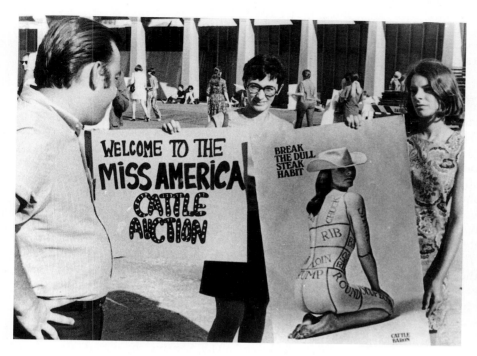

Women's Liberation
Arguing that beauty contests were degrading to women, members of the National Women's Liberation Party staged a protest against the Miss America pageant held in Atlantic City, New Jersey, in September 1968.
Wide World Photos, Inc.

rights movement. But when these women transferred their energies to the student and antiwar groups that were emerging, they found the New Left groups equally male dominated and unsupportive. When the antiwar movement adopted draft resistance as its central strategy, women found themselves relegated to roles as sex objects. "Girls say yes to guys who say no" was a popular slogan. Women who tried to raise feminist issues at conventions were shouted off the platform with jeers such as "Move on, little girl, we have more important issues to talk about here than women's liberation."

Around 1967 the contradiction between the New Left's lip service to egalitarianism and women's treatment by male leaders caused radical women to found their own movement. In contrast to women's rights groups such as NOW, which had traditional organizational structures and dues-paying members, radical women formed loose collectives whose shifting memberships often lacked any coordinating structure. The women's liberation movement (or "women's lib," as it was dubbed by the media) went public in 1968 when it staged a protest at the Miss America pageant. The demonstration included a "freedom trash can" into which women were encouraged to throw false eyelashes, hair curlers, brassieres, and girdles—all considered symbols of female oppression. The media quickly labeled the radical feminists "bra burners." The derisive name stuck, although no brassieres were actually burned.

An activity with a more lasting impact was *consciousness raising*, group sessions in which women shared their experiences of being female. Swapping stories about being passed over for promotion, needing a husband's signature on a credit card application, or enduring the humiliation of whistles and leers while walking down the street helped participants realize that their individual problems were part of a wider pattern of oppression. The slogan "The personal is political" became a rallying cry of the movement.

Feminism's potential as a mass movement was demonstrated on August 26, 1970, when thousands of women throughout the country marched to celebrate the fiftieth anniversary of the Nineteenth Amendment. A flood of new converts broke down the barriers between radical and more traditional activists, as did a growing convergence of interests. Radical women realized that key feminist goals—child care, equal pay, abortion rights—could best be achieved in the political arena. At the same time, more traditional feminists developed a broader view of women's oppression, including tentative support for divisive issues such as abortion and lesbian rights. Although the movement remained largely white and middle class, feminists were beginning to think of themselves as part of a broad and increasingly influential social movement that would continue to grow.

The Long Road Home, 1968–1975

———————★———————

The United States in 1968 was deeply polarized. Riots in the cities, black and Chicano power, campus unrest, and a host of protests and challenges were in the eyes of many citizens tearing the country in two. But Vietnam remained the central domestic and foreign policy issue. Although the Johnson administration insisted that there was "light at the end of the tunnel," the reality was otherwise. The war would continue, at home and in Vietnam, for another five years.

1968: A Year of Shocks

By 1968, as Lyndon Johnson planned his reelection campaign, antiwar protests and rising battlefield casualties had eroded public support for the war. Since the assassination of Diem in 1963, South Vietnam had undergone a series of military coups and counter-coups. In the spring of 1966, the Johnson administration pressured the South Vietnamese government to adopt democratic reforms, including a new constitution and popular elections. In September 1967, U.S. officials helped elect Nguyen Van Thieu president of South Vietnam. Thieu's regime, the administration hoped, would broaden its support at home, legitimize the South Vietnamese government in the eyes of the American public, and advance the military struggle against the communists.

The Tet Offensive. Those hopes were quickly shattered on January 30, 1968, when the Vietcong unleashed a massive, well-coordinated assault on major urban areas in the south. Known as the Tet offensive, the assault was timed to coincide with the Vietnamese holiday of Tet, celebrating the lunar New Year. Vietcong forces struck thirty-six of the forty-four provincial capitals and five of the six major cities, including Saigon, where they raided the supposedly impregnable U.S. embassy (see Map 29.1). Once again the United States and South Vietnamese forces had seriously underestimated the capabilities of their foes, who had been planning the attack since the previous fall. "Even had I known exactly what was to take place," an intelligence officer explained, "it was so preposterous that I probably would have been unable to sell it to anybody."

In strictly military terms the Tet offensive was a failure for the Vietcong, for it did not bring about the collapse of the South Vietnamese government. But its effect on American morale was devastating. With congressional support already slipping, the Tet offensive convinced many of Johnson's advisors that the war was unwinnable. When General Westmoreland asked for 206,000 additional troops, a deployment that would have required the politically explosive course of calling up the reserves, Johnson turned him down.

Covered extensively by the media, the Tet offensive made a mockery of official pronouncements that the United States was winning in Vietnam and helped swing American public opinion more clearly against the war. Just before Tet, a Gallup poll found that 56 percent of Americans considered themselves "hawks" (supporters of the war) and only 28 percent identified themselves as "doves" (opponents). Women and blacks consistently opposed the war more than white men did,

and younger people more than older. Three months after the Tet offensive, doves outnumbered hawks by 42 to 41 percent. This turnaround, however, did not mean that a majority supported the peace movement. Many who called themselves doves had concluded that the war was unwinnable and opposed it on pragmatic, rather than moral, grounds. As one housewife told a pollster, "I want to get out, but I don't want to give up."

Political Turmoil. The growing opposition to the war spilled over into the 1968 presidential campaign. Senator Eugene J. McCarthy of Minnesota had already entered the Democratic primaries as an antiwar alternative to Lyndon Johnson. A core of student activists went "clean for Gene" by cutting their hair and putting away their blue jeans to avoid alienating voters. In March President Johnson won the first state primary election in New Hampshire, but McCarthy received a stunning 42.2 percent of the vote. His strong showing against an incumbent president reflected profound dissatisfaction with the course of the war, even among those who were hawks. Sensing the president's vulnerability, Senator Robert Kennedy of New York, who had earlier decided against entering the race, announced his candidacy.

Johnson realized that his political support was evaporating. On March 31, at the end of an otherwise mundane televised address, he stunned the nation by announcing that he would not seek reelection. Johnson had already reversed his policy of incremental escalation of the war when he turned down Westmoreland's request for more troops. Now he called a partial bombing halt and vowed to devote his remaining months in office to the search for peace. On May 10, 1968, preliminary peace talks between the United States and North Vietnam began in Paris.

Just four days after Johnson's withdrawal from the presidential race, Martin Luther King Jr. was assassinated in Memphis. Soon afterward, a major student confrontation at Columbia University ended only when police forcibly removed protesters from the administration buildings they had occupied, beating and injuring dozens of demonstrators in the process. Student unrest seemed likely to become a worldwide phenomenon in May, when a massive strike by students and labor unions toppled the French government in protest over working conditions, university policies, and other issues.

Then came another tragedy. As Robert Kennedy celebrated his California primary victory over Eugene McCarthy on June 5, 1968, he was shot dead by Sirhan Sirhan, a young Palestinian who was thought to oppose Kennedy's pro-Israel stance. Once again the nation went through the ritual of burying a Kennedy. In two strokes—the assassinations of Martin Luther King and Robert Kennedy—liberalism, as the student leader Tom Hayden put it, was "decapitated."

Robert Kennedy's assassination shattered the dreams of many who hoped that social change could be achieved through the political system. In his brief but dramatic campaign Robert Kennedy had energized the traditional components of the New Deal coalition, including blue-collar workers and black voters, in a way that the more cerebral Eugene McCarthy never did. So widespread was Kennedy's appeal that election-day exit polls in Indiana found that many voters who had supported him in the primary voted for the conservative candidate George Wallace in November.

Kennedy's death also weakened the Democratic Party, which had not fully recovered from Johnson's withdrawal. McCarthy proceeded listlessly through the rest of his campaign, and Senator George S. McGovern of South Dakota entered the Democratic race in an effort to keep the Kennedy forces together. Meanwhile, Vice-President Hubert H. Humphrey lined up pledges from the traditional Democratic constituencies— unions, city machines, and state political organizations. The Democrats thus found themselves on the verge of nominating not an antiwar candidate but a public figure closely associated with Johnson's war policies. The stage was set for the Democratic National Convention in Chicago in August.

The Siege of Chicago. With Vietnam emerging as the central campaign issue in the 1968 elections, the political divisions generated by the war consumed the Democratic Party. Most of the drama at the national convention occurred not in the main hall but outside, on the streets of Chicago. Led by "Yippie" (Youth International Party) activists Jerry Rubin and Abbie Hoffman, approximately ten thousand protesters descended on Chicago. With theatrics geared toward maximum media exposure, they called for an end to the war, the legalization of marijuana, and the abolition of money. To mock the "pigs" who ruled America, they nominated a live pig for president, which was promptly confiscated by Chicago's humane society. Their stunts diverted attention from the more serious, and far more numerous, antiwar activists who had come to Chicago as convention delegates or volunteers.

Chicago's old-line Democratic mayor, Richard J. Daley, had little tolerance for antiwar protesters and called out the police to break up the demonstrations. Several nights of skirmishes between protesters and police culminated on the evening of the nominations in what an official report later described as a "police riot." Officers dispersed protesters with Mace, tear gas, and clubs. While protesters chanted "The whole world is watching," the television networks ran film of the riot during the nominating speeches. In one memorable moment, Senator Abraham Ribicoff of Connecticut interrupted his nominating speech for Senator McGovern to interject, "With George McGovern we wouldn't have Gestapo tactics on the streets of

RFK
Bobby Kennedy inspired strong passions during his 1968 campaign. Followers often tore off his cuff links as they tried to touch him or shake his hand.
Steve Schapiro/Black Star.

Chicago." The cameras panned to Mayor Daley, livid with rage and clearly mouthing obscenities.

Television coverage of the riots was hardly excessive—about 32 minutes on CBS and less than 14 minutes on NBC—but it cemented an impression of the Democrats as the party of disorder. The Democrats dispiritedly gave the nomination to Hubert H. Humphrey, who chose Senator Edmund S. Muskie of Maine as his running mate. The convention approved a middle-of-the-road platform that endorsed Johnson's policy of continuing the fighting in Vietnam while exploring diplomatic means to end the conflict.

Backlash. Among the general public, the turmoil at the Democratic convention unleashed a backlash against antiwar protesters and strengthened support for proponents of "law and order," which became the conservative catch phrase of the next several years. Many Americans, though opposed to the war, were fed up with protest and dissent. Governor George C. Wallace of Alabama, who left the Democrats to head a third-party ticket called the American Independent Party, skillfully exploited their growing hostility by making student protests and urban riots his chief campaign issues. But Wallace, who in 1963 had promised to enforce "segregation now . . . segregation tomorrow . . . and segregation forever," also exploited the mounting backlash against the civil rights movement. Articulating the resentments of many working-class whites, he delivered a populist message that combined attacks on liberal intellectuals and government elites with strident denunciations of school desegregation and forced busing.

Even more than George Wallace, Richard Nixon effectively tapped the growing conservative mood of the electorate. After his unsuccessful presidential campaign in 1960 and his loss in the California gubernatorial race in 1962, Nixon engineered an amazing political come-back. In 1968 the "new" Nixon easily beat back primary challenges by three governors—Ronald Reagan of California, George Romney of Michigan, and Nelson Rockefeller of New York—to win the Republican nomination. He chose Spiro Agnew, the conservative governor of Maryland, as his running mate to attract southern voters, especially Wallace supporters, who opposed Democratic civil rights initiatives. In what his campaign advisor Kevin Phillips called the "southern strategy," Nixon hoped to make impressive inroads in the once solidly Democratic South. He also used traditional populist appeals, pledging to represent the "quiet voice" of the "great majority of Americans, the forgotten Americans, the nonshouters, the nondemonstrators."

Despite the Democratic debacle in Chicago, the election was closely contested. Humphrey rallied in the last weeks of the campaign by gingerly disassociating himself from Johnson's war policies. Then, in a televised address on October 31, President Johnson announced a complete halt of the bombing of North Vietnam. Nixon countered by intimating that he had his own plan for ending the war, although in reality no such plan existed. On election day Nixon received 43.4 percent of the popular vote to Humphrey's 42.7 percent, defeating Humphrey by a scant 510,000 votes out of the 73 million cast (Map 29.3). Wallace finished with 13.5 percent of the popular vote, becoming the most successful third-party candidate since the Progressive Party's Robert M. La Follette in 1924. Nixon owed his election largely to the split in the Democratic coalition, but his southern strategy produced a decisive victory in the electoral college and hinted at the future emergence of a new Republican majority. In the meantime, however, the Democrats retained a majority in both houses of Congress.

The 1968 election revealed the growing polarization of American society over the Vietnam War and other events of the 1960s. Nixon appealed to a segment of society that came to be known as the "silent majority"—hardworking, nonprotesting, and generally white Amer-

icans. According to social scientists Ben J. Wattenberg and Richard Scammon in their influential book *The Real Majority* (1970), the typical American was a white forty-seven-year-old machinist's wife from Dayton, Ohio, and this was what she was concerned about:

> To know that the lady in Dayton is afraid to walk the streets alone at night, to know that she has a mixed view about blacks and civil rights because before moving to the suburbs she lived in a neighborhood that became all black, to know that her brother-in-law is a policeman, to know that she does not have the money to move if her new neighborhood deteriorates, to know that she is deeply distressed that her son is going to a community junior college where LSD was found on campus—to know all this is the beginning of contemporary political wisdom.

Although Nixon's victory suggested a growing national consensus around the law-and-order perspective of the silent majority, heated protest and controversy would persist until the war ended.

Nixon's War

Long Lyndon Johnson's war, Vietnam now became Richard Nixon's and would drag on for another four years. At first Nixon sought to end the war by expanding its scope as a means of pressuring the North Vietnamese to negotiate. But Nixon and his national security advisor, Henry Kissinger, soon realized that the public would not support such an approach. So shortly after taking office, Nixon sent a letter to North Vietnamese leaders proposing mutual troop withdrawals, an offer they flatly refused. In March 1969, to convince Hanoi that the United States meant business, Nixon ordered secret bombing raids on the neighboring country of Cambodia, through which the North Vietnamese transported supplies and reinforcements. To keep Congress and the public ignorant about those sorties, the air force officials in charge of the bombings fed accurate information about the raids into one Defense department computer while placing data omitting the Cambodian targets into another. The faulty projections from the second computer were the ones given to Congress.

Vietnamization and Its Critics.   When the intensified bombing failed to end the war, Nixon and Kissinger adopted a policy of *Vietnamization*. On June 8, 1969, Nixon announced that 25,000 American troops would be withdrawn by August and replaced by South Vietnamese forces. Antiwar protesters denounced the new policy, which protected American lives at the expense of the Vietnamese and would not end the war. Even the U.S. ambassador to Vietnam, Ellsworth Bunker, noted that it was just a matter of changing "the color of the bodies." On October 15, 1969, millions of people in cities across the country joined a one-day "moratorium" to protest

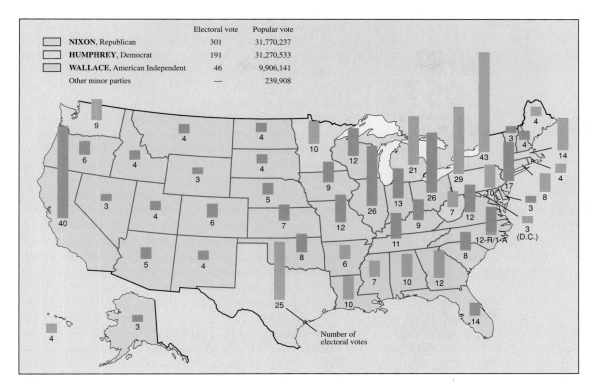

	Electoral vote	Popular vote
NIXON, Republican	301	31,770,237
HUMPHREY, Democrat	191	31,270,533
WALLACE, American Independent	46	9,906,141
Other minor parties	—	239,908

Number of electoral votes

MAP 29.3
The Election of 1968
As late as mid-September the third-party candidate George C. Wallace of Alabama had the support of 21 percent of the voters. But in November he received only 13.5 percent of the vote, winning five states and showing that the South was no longer solidly Democratic. The Republican Richard M. Nixon defeated Hubert H. Humphrey with only 43.4 percent of the popular vote.

the war. A month later, more than a quarter of a million people mobilized in Washington to call for an end to the fighting, the largest antiwar demonstration to date.

Nixon staunchly insisted that he would not be swayed by the mounting protests against the war, stating that "North Vietnam cannot defeat or humiliate the United States; only Americans can do that." Vice-President Spiro Agnew attacked dissenters as "ideological eunuchs" and "nattering nabobs of negativism." During the November 1969 march on Washington the president closeted himself in the White House and watched football on television.

On April 30, 1970, the previously secret bombing of Cambodia culminated in an "incursion" into that country by American ground forces to destroy enemy havens there. The invasion proved only a short-term setback for the North Vietnamese, who continued to boycott the Paris peace talks. More critically, the American action— along with the ongoing North Vietnamese intervention there—destabilized the country, exposing it to a takeover by the ruthless Khmer Rouge later in the 1970s.

Nixon's televised address announcing the invasion, followed by *New York Times* revelations of the earlier U.S. bombing campaign in Cambodia, prompted antiwar leaders to organize a national student strike. On May 4, at

Kent State University outside Cleveland, panicky National Guardsmen fired into a crowd of students at a noontime antiwar rally on May 4. Four people were killed, eleven wounded. Only two of those killed, Jeffrey Miller and Alison Krause, had participated in the demonstration; William Shroeder and Sandra Scheur were passing by on their way to class. Soon afterward, amid campus protests over Vietnam and other issues, National Guardsmen stormed a dormitory at Jackson State College in Mississippi, killing two black students. Over the next few months, more than 450 colleges closed because of strikes, and 80 percent of all American college campuses experienced some kind of protest. In June 1970, soon after the Kent State slayings, a Gallup poll reported that campus unrest—either student protests or the violent responses to them—was the main issue troubling Americans.

At the same time, dissatisfaction with the war continued to spread. Congressional opposition intensified with the invasion of Cambodia, and in June 1970 the Senate voted to repeal the Gulf of Tonkin Resolution and cut off funding for operations in Cambodia. Even American troops in Vietnam showed mounting opposition to their mission. From 1969 to 1971 the number of troops refusing combat orders steadily increased, and thousands of U.S. soldiers deserted. Many among the

WHO LOST VIET NAM?

"NOT I," SAID IKE. "I JUST SENT MONEY."

"NOT I," SAID JACK. "I JUST SENT ADVISORS."

"NOT I," SAID LYNDON. "I JUST FOLLOWED JACK."

"NOT I," SAID DICK. "I JUST HONORED JACK AND LYNDON'S COMMITMENTS."

"NOT I," SAID JERRY. "WHAT WAS THE QUESTION?"

"**YOU** LOST VIETNAM," SAID HENRY, "BECAUSE YOU DIDN'T TRUST YOUR LEADERS."

Passing the Buck
Highlighting the long and tortured history of the war, Jules Feiffer's 1975 cartoon offered a biting commentary on the lack of presidential accountability for U.S. policies in Vietnam.

majority who continued to fight sewed peace symbols onto their uniforms. At home a group called Vietnam Veterans against the War turned in their combat medals at mass demonstrations at the U.S. Capitol.

The My Lai Massacre. In 1971 Americans were confronted with the sheer brutality of the Vietnamese conflict when Lieutenant William L. Calley was court-martialed for atrocities committed in the Vietnamese village of My Lai (see Map 29.1). In March 1968 Calley had commanded a platoon on a routine search-and-destroy mission. Retaliating for casualties sustained by their fellow troops in an earlier engagement, the platoon apparently murdered 350 Vietnamese villagers on Calley's order. The incident came to light because one member of the platoon refused to go along with a military cover-up; investigative reporter Seymour Hersh of the *New York Times* broke the story in November 1969. In the court-martial proceedings, a jury of six soldiers who had served in Vietnam sentenced Calley to life imprisonment for his part in the massacre. Yet George Wallace and some congressional conservatives called Calley a hero, and after President Nixon's intervention, his sentence was reduced, and he was paroled in 1974.

The Decline of Antiwar Protest. After the outbreak of protest and violence following Kent State, antiwar activism began to ebb. Student strikes in the spring of 1971 and 1972, though large in number, never approached the emotional intensity of earlier demonstrations. SDS and other antiwar groups fell victim to police harassment, and FBI and CIA agents infiltrated and disrupted radical organizations. After 1968 the New Left splintered into factions, its energy spent. One radical faction formed the Weathermen, a tiny band of self-styled revolutionaries who embraced terrorist tactics—such as the destruction of the Army Math building at the University of Wisconsin at Madison in 1970—that alienated more moderate activists.

Nixon's Vietnamization policy also played a role in the decline of antiwar protest by dramatically reducing the number of U.S. soldiers in combat. When Nixon took office, more than 543,000 American soldiers were serving in Vietnam; by the end of 1970, 334,000; two years later, 24,200 (see Figure 29.1). Nixon's promise to continue troop withdrawals, end the draft, and institute an all-volunteer army by 1973 deprived the antiwar movement of important organizing issues, particularly on college campuses. Some students simply "burned

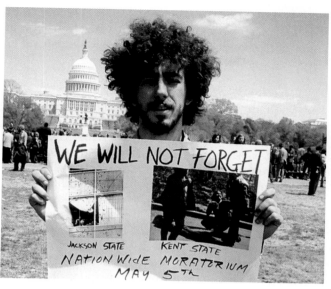

Kent State

The shootings by National Guardsmen of four students at Kent State University in Ohio on May 4, 1970, set off campus demonstrations and protests across the country. The protester shown here holds a placard memorializing the slain students as well as the two black students killed soon afterward at Jackson State College in Mississippi. The president of Columbia University called May 1970 "the most disastrous month . . . in the history of American higher education."

Michael Abramson/Black Star.

out," but commitment to social causes did not disappear altogether. In the early 1970s many student activists refocused their energies on causes such as feminism and environmentalism.

Détente.   While Nixon was prosecuting the war in Vietnam to halt the spread of communism, he and Henry Kissinger were formulating a new policy toward the Soviet Union and China. Known as *détente* (the French word for a relaxation of tensions), Nixon's policy was to seek peaceful coexistence with the two communist powers and to link those overtures with his plan to end the Vietnam War. Nixon encouraged the Soviet and Chinese leaders to reduce military aid to North Vietnam as a means of pressuring the North Vietnamese to the negotiating table.

As a lifelong anticommunist crusader, Nixon was better able than a Democratic president would have been to seek accommodation with the two communist superpowers. After all, no one could accuse Richard Nixon of being soft on communism. Since the Chinese Revolution of 1949 the United States had refused to recognize the government of the People's Republic of China, instead giving unconditional support to the Nationalist Chinese government in Taiwan. Nixon moved away from that policy, reasoning that the United States could exploit the growing rift between the People's Republic of

China and the Soviet Union. In February 1972, Nixon journeyed to China, walked along the Great Wall, and toasted Chinese leaders in Beijing. Nixon's visit set the stage for the formal establishment of diplomatic relations, which took place in 1979.

In a similar spirit of détente Nixon journeyed to Moscow in May 1972 to sign the Strategic Arms Limitations Treaty (SALT I) between the United States and the Soviet Union. Although SALT I fell far short of ending the arms race, it did limit the production and deployment of intercontinental ballistic missiles (ICBMs) and antiballistic missile systems (ABMs). Yet the treaty was also an acknowledgment that the United States was unwilling to shoulder the massive military spending that would have been necessary to regain the nuclear and military superiority it had enjoyed immediately after World War II. Most critically, Nixon hoped that rapprochement with the Soviets would help resolve the prolonged crisis in Vietnam.

American Withdrawal from Vietnam.   The Paris peace talks had been stalemated since 1968. The war had been "Vietnamized" and American casualties had decreased, but the South Vietnamese military was unable to hold its own. In late 1971, as American troops withdrew from the region, communist forces stepped up their attacks on Laos, Cambodia, and South Vietnam. The next spring North Vietnamese forces launched a major new offensive against South Vietnamese targets south of the demilitarized zone, in Binh Long province and in the Central Highlands (see American Lives, "John Paul Vann: Dissident Patriot," pp. 970–971). As the fighting intensified, Nixon ordered B-52 bombing raids against North Vietnam in April and the mining of all North Vietnamese ports a month later.

Increased combat activity in the spring of 1972 helped revive the Paris peace talks. Anxious to advance détente, Soviet and Chinese leaders pressured Hanoi back to the negotiating table. With the fall presidential election looming in the United States, Nixon hoped to undercut his antiwar critics by making concessions to the North Vietnamese. That October Henry Kissinger and North Vietnamese negotiator Le Duc Tho reached a cease-fire agreement calling for the withdrawal of the remaining U.S. troops, the return of all American prisoners of war, and the continued presence of North Vietnamese troops in South Vietnam (a major sticking point in earlier negotiations). Nixon and Kissinger also promised the North Vietnamese substantial aid for postwar reconstruction. On the eve of the 1972 presidential election Kissinger announced that "peace is at hand." With serious negotiations under way, Nixon returned to the White House with a resounding electoral victory (see Chapter 30).

The peace initiative, however, stalled once more when the South Vietnamese rejected the provision concerning

North Vietnamese troop positions, and the North declined to compromise further. With negotiations deadlocked, Nixon stepped up military action again. In a final destructive demonstration of American military strength—the "Christmas bombings" from December 17 to December 30, 1972—North Vietnamese civilian and military targets in Hanoi and Haiphong were subjected to the most devastating bombing of the war. Finally, on January 27, 1973, a cease-fire was signed in Paris by representatives of the United States, North and South Vietnam, and the Vietcong. The Paris Peace Accords differed little from the proposal of the previous October, and they failed to deliver on Nixon's often-repeated promise of "peace with honor." Basically, they mandated the unilateral withdrawal of American troops in exchange for the return of American prisoners of war held in North Vietnam. For most Americans, that amount of face-saving was enough.

The 1973 cease-fire did not resolve Vietnam's civil war. Without massive U.S. military and economic aid and with North Vietnamese guerrillas operating freely throughout the countryside, it was only a matter of time before the South Vietnamese government of General Nguyen Van Thieu fell to the more disciplined and popular communist forces. In March 1975 North Vietnamese forces launched a final offensive. Horrified American viewers watched on television as South Vietnamese officials and soldiers struggled with American embassy personnel for space on the last helicopters that flew out of Saigon before North Vietnamese troops entered the city. On April 29, 1975, Vietnam was reunited; Saigon was renamed Ho Chi Minh City in honor of the communist leader, who had died in 1969.

The Legacy of Vietnam

The Vietnam War exacted an enormous cost from America in human terms. Some 58,000 U.S. soldiers died, and another 300,000 were wounded. Even those who came back unharmed returned to an often hostile or indifferent reception. As one vet recalled, "Bringing up the Nam was like farting at the dinner table. Everybody looks away embarrassed and acts like nothing happened. Well, pardon me." The psychological tensions of serving in Vietnam and the abrupt transition back to America sowed the seeds of what is now recognized as post-traumatic stress disorder—recurring physical and psychological problems, often leading to higher than average rates of divorce, unemployment, and suicide. Only in the 1980s did America begin to make its peace with those who had served in the nation's most unpopular war.

In Southeast Asia the damage was even greater. The war claimed an estimated 1.5 million Vietnamese lives and devastated the country's physical and economic infrastructure. Neighboring Laos and Cambodia also suffered, particularly Cambodia, where the Khmer Rouge killed an estimated 2 million Cambodians (25 percent of the population) in a brutal "relocation" campaign between 1975 and 1979. All told, the war pro-

Hanoi Devastated
The North Vietnamese capital of Hanoi sustained heavy damage from bombing raids by American B-52 jets. The most devastating raids occurred during the "Christmas bombings" in December 1972, just weeks before the Paris Peace Accords were signed.
Marc Riboud/Magnum Photos, Inc.

duced nearly 10 million Southeast Asian refugees, many of whom immigrated to the United States. Among the refugees were thousands of Amerasians, the offspring of American soldiers and Vietnamese women. Spurned by their fathers and most Vietnamese, more than 30,000 Amerasians immigrated to the United States in the 1990s.

The defeat in Vietnam prompted Americans to think differently about foreign affairs and acknowledge the limits of U.S. power abroad. The United States became less willing to plunge into overseas military commitments, a controversial development that conservatives dubbed the "Vietnam syndrome." In 1973 Congress expressed its hostility to undeclared wars like those in Vietnam and Korea by passing the War Powers Act, which required the president to report any use of military force within forty-eight hours and directed hostilities to cease within sixty days unless Congress declared war. On those occasions when Congress did agree to foreign intervention, as in the Persian Gulf

War of 1990–1991, American leaders would insist on obtainable military objectives and careful handling of the media—elements often lacking in Vietnam. Perhaps most important, any future foreign entanglement would be evaluated in terms of its potential for becoming "another Vietnam."

The Vietnam War also distorted American economic and social life. At a total price of over $150 billion, the war siphoned economic resources from domestic needs, added to the deficit, and fueled inflation. The war critically shattered the liberal consensus that had supported the Democratic coalition. Even more serious, the conduct of the war—the lies about American successes on the battlefield, the questionable representation of events in the Gulf of Tonkin, the secret war on Cambodia—spawned deep distrust of government among American citizens. The discrediting of liberalism, the increased cynicism about government, and the growing social turmoil that accompanied the war paved the way for a new era of conservatism.

The Vietnam Veterans' Memorial
Conceived and funded by a small group of veterans, the Vietnam Veterans' Memorial was dedicated in Washington, D.C., in November 1982. The memorial, designed by Maya Ling Lin, a Yale architecture student, consists of two walls of black granite inscribed with the names of 58,183 men and women who died in the war. The wall of names has tremendous emotional impact on viewers and has become one of the most popular tourist destinations in the nation's capital.
Peter Marlow/Magnum Photos, Inc.

John Paul Vann: Dissident Patriot

★

T HE DIVISIONS CAUSED by the Vietnam War haunted Arlington National Cemetery on June 16, 1972, when three hundred mourners assembled for the funeral of John Paul Vann. "The soldier of the war in Vietnam," Vann had been killed in a helicopter crash in the Central Highlands the week before. Politicians and military leaders closely associated with the war effort were very much in evidence—General William Westmoreland, CIA Director William Colby, the conservative journalist Joseph Alsop, and Secretary of State William Rogers. But so were Daniel Ellsberg, a former Pentagon official who had publicly turned against the war, and Senator Edward Kennedy, another war opponent who had shared Vann's concern about the plight of Vietnamese refugees. In a time of intense polarization over a war that was still going on, this assemblage of hawks and doves was an exceptional sight.

Vann's family also showed the rifts over Vietnam that day. His wife of twenty-six years, Mary Jane, had requested two pieces of music: the upbeat "Colonel Bogie March" from the film *The Bridge on the River Kwai,* one of her husband's favorites, and the haunting antiwar ballad "Where Have All the Flowers Gone?" to express her opposition to the war. One of Vann's sons, twenty-one-year-old Jesse, hated the war so profoundly that he tore his draft card in two at the funeral, placing half of it on his father's casket. He planned to give the other half to President Richard Nixon at the White House ceremony after the funeral, where his father would be presented posthumously with the Presidential Medal of Freedom. Only at the last moment was Jesse talked out of his act of defiance, agreeing that this was, after all, his father's day.

Also at the funeral was *New York Times* reporter Neil Sheehan, who decided at that moment to write a biography of Vann, which he published sixteen years later, *A Bright and Shining Lie.* Sheehan, along with David Halberstam and other reporters, had fallen under Vann's spell during his first tour of duty in Vietnam in 1963, when Vann seemed to be the only American official who was willing to admit that the war

was not going well. Sheehan had continued to rely on Vann's outspoken assessments for the rest of the war. "In this war without heroes, this man had been the one compelling figure," Sheehan concluded. "By an obsession, by an unyielding dedication to the war, he had come to personify the American endeavor in Vietnam."

John Paul Vann was an enormously complicated person—a born leader, a visionary, a man who knew no physical fear, but most of all a true believer in America's mission to share democracy with countries "less fortunate" than the United States. His early years were shaped by poverty and lack of opportunity. Born in 1924 to a working-class family in Norfolk, Virginia, he grew up poor during the Great Depression. A colleague later remembered him as a "cocky little red-necked guy with a rural Virginia twang." World War II offered a ticket out; when Vann turned eighteen in 1943, he enlisted and made the army his career. He served with distinction in the Korean War and then took assignments in West Germany and the United States. But in 1959 his service record was stained by accusations of the statutory rape of a fifteen-year-old girl. Even though the army eventually dropped the charges, the scandal effectively prevented him from moving up in the military bureaucracy. Neil Sheehan later concluded that Vann's "moral heroism" in speaking out against the conduct of the war to the seeming detriment of his career was rooted in his awareness that he had nothing to lose, although reporters did not know the full story at the time.

In 1963 the thirty-nine-year-old Lieutenant Colonel Vann was sent to Vietnam, where he served as a senior advisor to a South Vietnamese infantry division in the Mekong Delta. At the battle of Ap Bac he watched his South Vietnamese counterpart purposely refuse to fight the battle the way it had been planned and let the enemy escape. In a moment of epiphany Vann realized that the rosy reports being fed to Saigon and Washington were false, that Saigon suffered from "an institutionalized unwillingness to fight." After unsuccessful attempts to enlighten his superiors, he leaked his meticulously documented assessments to reporters such as Halberstam and Sheehan. His candor won him few friends in the military, and at the end of his tour of duty he was reassigned to the Pentagon. He tried to alert the Joint Chiefs of Staff that the war was not being won, but at the last moment the scheduled briefing was canceled, in large part because the Joint Chiefs did not want to

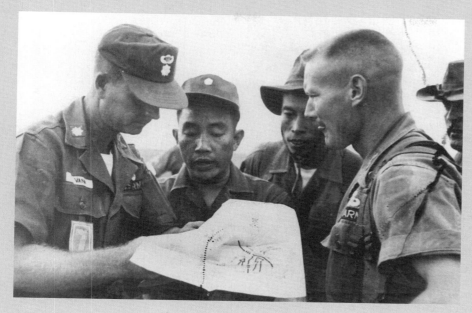

Planning Strategy
Lieutenant Colonel John P. Vann (left) shown during his tour of duty in Vietnam in 1963, discussing a tactical decision.
U.S. Army Photo/U.S. Department of Defense, Still Media Records Center, Washington, DC.

hear his version of the problem. Frustrated and disillusioned, Vann resigned from the army soon afterward and went to work for a civilian defense contractor.

Before long, however, Vann grew restless with stateside life and tried to rejoin the military. Wary of Vann's public criticism of the war, the army refused to accept him. In 1965 Vann found civilian employment with the Agency for International Development in a pacification program to win over the peasants to the South Vietnamese side rather than the National Liberation Front. Arriving just as the major escalation of the war was getting under way, Vann would stay in Vietnam (except for brief trips home) until his death. His honesty and unmatched familiarity with conditions in the countryside led him to conclude that the communists were doing a far better job at appealing to the local population than was the corrupt Saigon government. As he wrote to a friend in 1965, "If I were a lad of eighteen faced with the same choice—whether to support the GVN [Government of Vietnam] or the NLF—and a member of a rural community, I would surely choose the NLF." His concern for winning over the local peasantry made him an outspoken opponent of the heavy bombing inflicted on the Vietnamese countryside to roust Vietcong sympathizers. He also strongly criticized General Westmoreland's strategy of sending in more American troops to wear down the Vietcong in a war

of attrition, arguing that this would be useless without major reforms in the Saigon government.

Despite his role as a gadfly and even though he was now a civilian, Vann assumed more and more responsibility in the day-to-day conduct of the war. In 1971 he was given authority over all the U.S. military forces in the Central Highlands, the equivalent of the position of major general. But by then, according to Sheehan, Vann had "lost his compass." He was no longer able to assess realistically the ability or will of the South Vietnamese to fight without American aid. He continued to insist that the war could be won through pacification and reform in Saigon despite evidence of growing Vietcong strength. When his helicopter went down at Kontum in 1972, he had almost single-handedly saved the Central Highlands from a North Vietnamese offensive. Within six months the United States formally ended its involvement. Two years later Vietnam was reunited under communist rule.

John Paul Vann never wavered in his belief that in Vietnam America's cause was just and its intentions good. He had no quarrel with the war itself, just with the way it was fought. Vann thought he knew the answers, but Saigon and Washington chose not to listen. His life and death serve as a reminder of the complexities of the Vietnam experience: could it ever really have been "won," and what would "winning" have meant? Neil Sheehan is convinced that Vann "died believing he had won his war."

Summary

★

America's involvement in Vietnam lasted nearly thirty years, growing incrementally from one administration to the next. Under Truman, Eisenhower, and Kennedy, the United States threw its support behind the French and later the South Vietnamese government in an effort to contain the communist threat in Asia. Lyndon Johnson escalated the war in 1965 from an ostensibly defensive action to an offensive combat mission. Between 1965 and 1968 sustained bombing attacks on North Vietnam were accompanied by ever larger infusions of U.S. ground troops. But the Tet offensive of January 1968 highlighted the discrepancy between the administration's glowing accounts of the war and its tortuous reality, and marked the beginning of U.S. efforts to disengage from the conflict. Richard Nixon spent another five years trying to end the war, promising Americans "peace with honor." Under his program of Vietnamization Nixon gradually withdrew U.S. troops while secretly bombing and later invading Cambodia in a futile attempt to destroy enemy havens. The final withdrawal of American troops took place in 1973 under the terms of the Paris Peace Accords. The war marked a turning point in U.S. foreign relations, revealing the limitations of American military power in a complex postwar world.

The war also had serious consequences at home, as Americans turned against one another in bitter conflict. Galvanized by opposition to military escalation and the draft, the antiwar movement spread rapidly among college students and other young people who staged a series of mass protests between 1967 and 1971. The spirit of rebellion was not limited to the antiwar movement. The New Left challenged university policies and corporate dominance of society, while the more apolitical counterculture preached personal liberation through sex, drugs, music, and spirituality. As the civil rights struggle moved beyond the South, rising militancy and racial strife divided the movement and fueled white opposition to change. At the same time, however, the new black power movement encouraged racial pride and assertiveness, serving as a model for Mexican Americans, native Americans, and other ethnic groups. The civil rights movement also helped inspire a resurgence of feminism and the birth of the gay liberation movement.

The domestic struggle over the war and other issues divided the Democratic Party, resulting in a Democratic National Convention riven with protest and violence in the summer of 1968. The assassinations of Martin Luther King and Robert Kennedy and a series of urban riots that year further shocked the nation and fueled a growing public desire for law and order. Although antiwar protests continued into the early 1970s, a new mood of conservatism took hold in the country, contributing to the resurgence of the Republican Party under Richard Nixon.

T I M E L I N E

1946   War begins between French and Vietminh

1950   China and Soviet Union recognize Ho Chi Minh's government

United States recognizes French-backed government of Bao Dai and sends military aid

1954   French defeat at Dienbienphu

Geneva Accords partition Vietnam at 17th parallel

1962   Students for a Democratic Society (SDS) founded

1963   Coup ousts Ngo Dinh Diem in South Vietnam

1964   Free Speech Movement at Berkeley

Gulf of Tonkin Resolution authorizes military action in Vietnam

1965   Malcolm X assassinated

Operation Rolling Thunder escalates war through mass bombing campaigns

First U.S. combat troops arrive in Vietnam

Race riot in the Watts district of Los Angeles

1966   National Organization for Women (NOW) founded

Stokely Carmichael proclaims black power

1967   Hippie counterculture's "Summer of Love"

Race riots in Detroit and Newark

1968   Tet offensive dashes American hopes of victory

Martin Luther King Jr. assassinated

Robert F. Kennedy assassinated

Riot at Democratic National Convention in Chicago

Women's liberation movement emerges

1969   Stonewall riot leads to gay liberation movement

Vietnam moratorium

American Indian Movement seizes Alcatraz

1970   Nixon orders invasion of Cambodia; renewed antiwar protests

Killings at Kent State and Jackson State

1972   Nixon visits People's Republic of China

SALT I Treaty with Soviet Union

Christmas bombings of Hanoi and Haiphong

1973   Paris Peace Accords

War Powers Act

1975   Fall of Saigon

Suggested Readings

Among the best general accounts of the Vietnam War are George Herring, *America's Longest War* (3rd ed., 1996); Stanley Karnow, *Vietnam: A History* (rev. ed., 1991); and Marilyn Young, *The Vietnam Wars, 1945–1990* (1991). Guenter Lewy offers a controversial defense of American involvement in *America in Vietnam* (1978).

Into the Quagmire, 1945–1968

The origins of American involvement in Vietnam are covered in Loren Baritz, *Backfire: A History of How American Culture Led Us into Vietnam* (1985); Larry Berman, *Planning a Tragedy* (1982) and *Lyndon Johnson's War* (1989); Robert Buzzanco, *Masters of War* (1996); Lloyd Gardner, *Approaching Vietnam* (1988); David Halberstam, *The Making of a Quagmire* (rev. ed., 1988); and Brian VanDeMark, *Into the Quagmire* (1991). A fascinating insight into Vietnam policy making in the 1960s can be found in Neil Sheehan, *The Pentagon Papers* (1971). Secretary of Defense Robert McNamara offers an insider's view and belated apologia in *In Retrospect* (1995).

For a sense of what the war felt like to the soldiers who fought it, see Mark Baker, *Nam* (1982); Philip Caputo, *Rumor of War* (1977); Michael Herr, *Dispatches* (1977); Tim O'Brien, *If I Die in a Combat Zone* (1973); and Ron Kovic, *Born on the Fourth of July* (1976). Wallace Terry, *Bloods* (1984), surveys the experiences of black veterans, and Keith Walker, *A Piece of My Heart* (1985), introduces the often forgotten stories of the women who served in Vietnam. Christian G. Appy offers a class analysis of the Vietnam experience in *Working-Class War* (1993). Neil Sheehan surveys the entire Vietnam experience through the life of career soldier John Paul Vann in *A Bright and Shining Lie* (1988).

The Challenge of Youth, 1962–1970

There are a growing number of survey works on the 1960s, including David Steigerwald, *The Sixties and the End of Modern America* (1995); Terry Anderson, *The Movement and the Sixties* (1994); David Farber, *The Age of Great Dreams: America in the 1960s* (1994); Todd Gitlin, *The Sixties: Years of Hope, Days of Rage* (1987); and Allen J. Matusow, *The Unraveling of America* (1984).

The student activism of the 1960s is the subject of dozens of eyewitness accounts and scholarly works. See Kenneth Keniston, *The Uncommitted* (1965) and *Young Radicals* (1969); Nathan Glazer, *Remembering the Answers* (1970); and Philip Slater, *The Pursuit of Loneliness* (1970). On student revolt see W. J. Rorabaugh, *Berkeley at War* (1989); Kirkpatrick Sale, *SDS* (1973); Wini Breines, *Community and Organization in the New Left, 1962–1968* (1982); and James Miller, *Democracy Is in the Streets* (1987). The definitive book on the antiwar movement is Charles DeBenedetti, with Charles Chatfield, *An American Ordeal* (1990).

Morris Dickstein, *Gates of Eden* (1977), is an excellent account of cultural developments in the 1960s. Other sources include Theodore Roszak, *The Making of a Counter-Culture* (1969); and Charles Reich, *The Greening of America* (1970). Gerald Howard, ed., *The Sixties* (1982), is a good anthology of the decade's art, politics, and culture. Philip Norman, *Shout! The Beatles in Their Generation* (1981), and Jon Weiner, *Come Together: John Lennon in His Times* (1984), cover developments in popular music.

Major texts of the black power movement include Stokely Carmichael and Charles Hamilton, *Black Power* (1967); James Baldwin, *The Fire Next Time* (1963); and Eldridge Cleaver, *Soul on Ice* (1968). *The Autobiography of Malcolm X* (cowritten with Alex Haley, 1966) has become a black literary classic; it can be supplemented by Michael Eric Dyson, *Making Malcolm: The Myth and Meaning of Malcolm X* (1995). William L. Van Deburg, *New Day in Babylon* (1992), provides a general historical account of the black power movement.

Report of the National Advisory Commission on Civil Disorders (1968) analyzes the decade's major race riots. See also Joe R. Feagin and Harlan Hahn, *Ghetto Revolts* (1973), and Robert Fogelson, *Violence as Protest* (1971). Sidney Fine's book on the Detroit riot, *Violence in the Model City* (1989), provides the most thorough historical treatment of race rioting in this period.

Carlos Muñoz Jr., *Youth, Identity and Power: The Chicano Movement* (1989), and Juan Gomez-Quiñones, *Chicano Politics* (1990), examine the rise of the Chicano movement in the 1960s. Peter Matthiessen, *In the Spirit of Crazy Horse* (1983), chronicles the American Indian Movement's ongoing conflict with the FBI and the federal government. Martin Duberman, *Stonewall* (1993), looks at the birth of the gay movement in the late 1960s.

General histories of women's activism in the 1960s include Cynthia Harrison, *On Account of Sex: The Politics of Women's Issues, 1945–1968* (1988), and Susan M. Hartmann, *From Margin to Mainstream: American Women and Politics since 1960* (1989). The revival of feminism is examined in Jo Freeman, *The Politics of Women's Liberation* (1975), and Judith Hole and Ellen Levine, *The Rebirth of Feminism* (1971). Sara Evans, *Personal Politics* (1979), traces the roots of feminism in the civil rights movement and the New Left.

The Long Road Home, 1968–1975

The Tet offensive is the subject of Don Oberdoffer's *Tet! The Turning Point in the Vietnam War* (1971). The domestic events of 1968 are covered in David Caute, *The Year of the Barricades* (1968), and David Farber, *Chicago '68* (1988). Norman Mailer provides a contemporary view of the national political conventions in *Miami and the Siege of Chicago* (1968). William C. Berman, *America's Right Turn* (2nd ed., 1998), chronicles the rightward shift in politics. Kevin Phillips, *The Emerging Republican Majority* (1969), and Richard Scammon and Ben J. Wattenberg, *The Real Majority* (1970), describe the voters Richard Nixon tried to reach. Dan Carter, *The Politics of Rage* (1996), examines the political career of George Wallace.

William Bundy, *The Tangled Web* (1998), and Robert S. Litwak, *Détente and the Nixon Doctrine* (1984), are overviews of Nixon's foreign policy. On his Vietnam policy see the general works on Vietnam listed above as well as the highly critical study by William Shawcross, *Sideshow: Kissinger, Nixon, and the Destruction of Cambodia* (1979). An account of the My Lai massacre can be found in Seymour Hersh, *Cover-Up* (1972). Robert Jay Lifton, *Home from the War* (1973); Paul Starr, *The Discarded Army* (1973); and Lawrence Baskir and William A. Strauss, *Chance and Circumstance*, discuss the problems of returning Vietnam veterans.

The Lean Years,
1969–1980

A S THE VIETNAM War ended, Americans turned inward to attend to their own needs and interests, just as they had done in the years after World Wars I and II. But the 1970s, unlike the 1920s and 1950s, were not a time of postwar prosperity and optimism. To many Americans the withdrawal from Vietnam represented a humiliating defeat that underscored the diminished role of U.S. power in the international arena. Growing economic problems in the early 1970s—rising oil prices, runaway inflation, declining productivity, and stagnating incomes—compounded that sense of disillusionment. In the mid-1970s industrial competition abroad, together with the newly asserted independence of the oil-producing Arab nations, produced a severe economic crisis at home. As the dollar plummeted on the world market and the trade deficit soared, the overwhelming postwar economic superiority of the United States came to an end.

Americans also grew disenchanted with political leadership in the 1970s as one public official after another resigned for misconduct, including (for the first time in history) the president, Richard Nixon. The Watergate scandal, which forced Nixon's resignation, became the defining experience of the decade, a symbol of the growing cynicism and lack of confidence that pervaded the nation in the 1970s. In the wake of Watergate, the lackluster administrations of Gerald Ford and Jimmy Carter contributed to Americans' growing skepticism about government and its capacity to improve people's lives.

Earth Day
One of the most dynamic areas of social activism in the 1960s and 1970s was the environmental movement, which addressed issues such as wilderness preservation, energy policy, and toxic dumping. The growing significance of this movement was demonstrated on Earth Day, May 4, 1970, when thousands gathered in New York (shown here) and in other cities and towns across the country to register their concern for the endangered planet.
Ken Regan.

But the 1970s was a paradoxical decade: in the midst of growing disaffection with national politics was ongoing commitment to social change. Social movements such as feminism and environmentalism had their greatest impact in the 1970s. But like the civil rights and antiwar movements of the 1960s, social activism in the 1970s stirred fears and uncertainty among some blue-collar and middle-class Americans. Furthermore, the darkening economic climate undercut the sense of social generosity that had characterized the 1960s and fueled what political commentator Alan Crawford called a "politics of resentment." The 1970s was thus a complex and transitional decade in which expanding social activism helped spur a conservative reaction that would influence the nation for the next several decades.

The Nixon Years

With his election to the presidency in 1968, Richard Nixon set the stage for the new conservatism. His policies heralded a long-term Republican effort to trim back the Great Society, shifting a number of federal responsibilities back to the states. But unlike his Republican successors, Nixon actively embraced the use of federal power—within limits—to uphold government responsibility for social welfare, environmental protection, and economic stability. While maintaining a strong federal government, he hoped to reduce governmental inefficiency through better management. Ultimately, however, Nixon's suspicion of his political opponents and his ruthless efforts in the 1972 campaign led to his downfall in the Watergate scandal, a political drama that consumed the nation.

The Republican Domestic Agenda

In a 1968 campaign pledge to "the average American," Nixon vowed to "reverse the flow of power and resources from the states and communities to Washington and start power and resources flowing back . . . to the people." Nixon's New Federalism marked a retreat from the long-term consolidation of federal power that had characterized American political life since the New Deal. One of its hallmarks was the 1972 program of *revenue sharing*, which distributed a portion of federal tax revenues to the states as block grants to be spent as state officials saw fit. In subsequent years revenue sharing would become a key Republican strategy for reducing federal social programs and bureaucracy.

Nixon also worked to scale down certain government programs that had grown dramatically during the Johnson administration. Viewing many Democratic

social programs as bloated and inefficient, he reduced funding for most of the War on Poverty and dismantled the Office of Economic Opportunity altogether in 1971. Nixon also *impounded* (refused to spend) billions of dollars appropriated by Congress for urban renewal, pollution control, and other environmental initiatives. Although his administration claimed to support civil rights, Nixon adopted a cautious approach toward racial issues so as not to alienate southern white voters. In a leaked 1970 memo, presidential advisor Daniel Patrick Moynihan, a Democrat who had joined the Nixon White House, suggested that "the issue of race could benefit from a period of benign neglect"—a revelation that scandalized liberals and embarrassed the administration. Nixon also vetoed a 1971 bill to establish a comprehensive national child-care system, fearing that such "communal approaches to child rearing" would "Sovietize" American children.

As an alternative to Democratic social legislation, the administration put forward its own antipoverty program in an ambitious attempt to overhaul the jerry-built welfare system. In 1969, following the advice of Moynihan, Nixon proposed a Family Assistance Plan that would provide a family of four a small but guaranteed annual income. The appeal of this proposal lay in its simplicity: it would eliminate the multiple layers of bureaucrats (caseworkers, local and state officials, and federal employees) who administered Aid to Families with Dependent Children (AFDC), the nation's largest welfare program. But the bill floundered in the Senate: conservatives attacked it for putting the federal government too deeply into the welfare business, and liberals and social welfare activists opposed it for not going far enough. Welfare reform would remain a contentious political issue for the next twenty-five years.

Although Nixon sought to streamline or scale back certain antipoverty programs, he actively expanded federal entitlement programs and the regulatory apparatus. Facing Democratic majorities in both houses of Congress, Nixon agreed to the growth of major entitlement programs such as Medicare, Medicaid, and Social Security. In 1970, he signed a bill establishing the Environmental Protection Agency (EPA) to coordinate the growing federal responsibilities for environmental action. In 1972, to monitor the health and safety of workers and consumers, Nixon approved legislation creating the Occupational Safety and Health Administration (OSHA) and the Consumer Products Safety Commission. As inflation spiraled upward in 1971, he also made use of the federal powers granted under the Economic Stabilization Act of 1970 to institute wage and price controls, the first such measures since World War II. Although Nixon offered only lukewarm support for much of this legislation, his administration generally continued the expansion of federal power that had been under way since the New Deal.

Nixon demonstrated his commitment to conservative social values most clearly with his appointments to the Supreme Court. One of his first acts was to nominate the conservative Warren Burger to replace retired Chief Justice Earl Warren in the spring of 1969. Over the next five years, Nixon named three more Supreme Court justices—Harry Blackmun, Lewis F. Powell Jr., and William Rehnquist—the last becoming the leading conservative force on the Court through the 1990s.

Conservative judges did not always give Nixon the decisions he wanted. Despite attempts by the Justice Department to halt further desegregation in the face of determined white opposition, the Court ordered busing to achieve racial balance in the case of *Swann v. Charlotte-Mecklenburg Board of Education* (1971). In *Furman v. Georgia* (1972) the Supreme Court issued strict guidelines restricting the implementation of capital punishment, although it did not rule the death penalty unconstitutional. And in the controversial 1973 case of *Roe v. Wade*, Justice Harry Blackmun wrote the decision striking down Texas and Georgia laws prohibiting abortion.

The 1972 Election

Nixon's reelection in 1972 was never much in doubt. In May, the threat of a conservative third-party challenge from Alabama's governor, George Wallace, ended abruptly when an assailant in a suburban Maryland shopping mall shot Wallace, paralyzing him from the waist down. With Wallace out of the picture, Nixon's strategy of wooing southern white voters away from the Democrats got a boost. Nixon also benefited from the disarray in the Democratic Party, which was deeply divided over Vietnam and civil rights. After the 1968 Chicago convention the party had changed its way of selecting delegates and candidates, pledging to include "minority groups, young people and women in reasonable relationship to their presence in the population." The ratification of the Twenty-sixth Amendment in 1971, lowering the national voting age to eighteen, reinforced the power of the youth vote. Tensions soon arose between those groups and the old-line Democratic officeholders and labor union leaders who had formerly dominated the party.

Senator George McGovern of South Dakota, a noted liberal and an outspoken opponent of the Vietnam War, reaped the greatest benefit from the new Democratic guidelines. By 1972 he was supported by an army of antiwar activists who blitzed precinct caucuses and won delegate commitments far beyond his support among voters. In the past, an alliance of party bosses and union leaders almost certainly would have rejected an upstart candidate such as McGovern, but few old-line leaders qualified as delegates to the nominating convention under the changed rules. Typical of the new

Richard Nixon on the Campaign Trail
One of the most resilient political figures in American history, Richard Nixon won the presidential elections of 1968 and 1972 after losing campaigns for president in 1960 and for governor of California in 1962. Even after his resignation in 1974, Nixon reemerged as an elder statesman and was frequently consulted for his views on foreign affairs.
Charles Moore/Black Star.

Democratic look, the black minister and civil rights veteran Jesse Jackson replaced Mayor Richard Daley of Chicago as head of the Illinois delegation.

McGovern's campaign against Nixon was an unrelieved disaster. Surprised to learn that his running mate, Senator Thomas F. Eagleton of Missouri, had undergone electroshock therapy for depression some years earlier, McGovern first supported him "1,000 percent," then abruptly insisted that he quit the ticket. Sargent Shriver, the former head of the Peace Corps and the Office of Economic Opportunity, replaced Eagleton, but McGovern's waffling made him appear weak and indecisive. Moreover, he was far too liberal for many traditional Democrats, who rejected his ill-defined proposals for welfare reform, did not rally around his calls for unilateral withdrawal from Vietnam, and ignored his charges that the Nixon administration had corruptly abused its power.

Nixon's campaign took full advantage of McGovern's weaknesses. Although the war in Vietnam dragged on, Nixon's Vietnamization policy had reduced weekly American combat deaths from three hundred in 1968 to almost none in 1972. Henry Kissinger's premature declaration that "peace is at hand" raised hopes for a negotiated settlement (see Chapter 29). Not only did those initiatives rob the Democrats of their greatest appeal—their antiwar stance—but an improving economy further favored the Republicans.

Nixon won handily, receiving nearly 61 percent of the popular vote and carrying every state except Massachusetts and the District of Columbia. The Democrats maintained control of both houses of Congress, but McGovern's showing pointed to a significant erosion of the traditional Democratic coalition: he received only 18 percent of the southern white Protestant vote and 38 percent of the big-city Catholic vote. Only blacks, Jews, and low-income voters remained loyal.

Watergate

Watergate, the great constitutional crisis of the early 1970s, was a direct result of Nixon's ruthless political tactics, his secretive style of governing, and his obsession with the antiwar movement. Many Americans saw Watergate as consisting of only the evil deeds of one person (Richard Nixon) and one unlawful act (obstruction of justice). But Watergate was not an isolated incident; it was part of a broad pattern of illegality and misuse of power that flourished in the crisis atmosphere of the Vietnam War.

Before the Break-In. The new administration began to stretch the boundaries of the law under the guise of national security just four months into Nixon's first term. In the spring of 1969, after the *New York Times* reported the secret bombing of Cambodia, the White House asked the FBI to find out who had leaked the story. Without seeking a warrant, the FBI illegally tapped the phone conversations of several journalists and low-level staffers on the National Security Council. The source of the leak was never found, but the precedent for warrantless surveillance had been set.

Over the next several years the Nixon administration would repeatedly invoke supposed domestic threats to national security to justify its actions. In 1970 the White House asked Tom Huston, a former army intelligence officer, to draw up an extensive plan for secret domestic counterintelligence—opening mail, tapping phones, and arranging break-ins—to discredit the antiwar movement. President Nixon approved the scheme, which involved coordinated efforts by the FBI, CIA, and Justice Department. FBI director J. Edgar Hoover, however, refused to cooperate with other government agencies in activities that he interpreted as being exclusively within the domain of the FBI.

Nixon's obsession with the antiwar movement grew in June 1971, when Daniel Ellsberg, a former Defense department analyst who had become disillusioned with the war, leaked the so-called Pentagon Papers to the *New York Times*. Commissioned by Secretary of Defense Robert McNamara in 1967, the Pentagon Papers was a classified study of American involvement in Vietnam that included hundreds of government documents from the Kennedy and Johnson years. The report detailed so many American blunders and misjudgments that McNamara had commented on first reading it, "You know, they could hang people for what is in there." In a subsequent court challenge the Nixon administration attempted to block publication of the Pentagon Papers. In an effort to discredit Ellsberg, White House underlings broke into his psychiatrist's office to look for damaging information. The burglars failed to turn up anything embarrassing on Ellsberg, and the judge dismissed the pending case against him when the break-in was revealed.

In another abuse of presidential power committed prior to the 1972 campaign, the White House established a clandestine intelligence group led by former CIA agents G. Gordon Liddy and Howard Hunt. Known as the "plumbers" because they were supposed to plug leaks of government information, they relied on tactics such as using the Internal Revenue Service and other agencies to harass opponents of the administration named on an "enemies list" drawn up by the presidential counsel John Dean. A major target of the plumbers was the Democratic Party, whose front-running candidate, Senator Edmund Muskie of Maine, was the object of several "dirty tricks" during the primaries. For example, white New Hampshire voters were awakened in the middle of the night by callers from the "Harlem for Muskie" committee, and posters appeared in Florida saying "Help Muskie in Busing More Children Now." Most damaging was a letter to a New Hampshire newspaper forged by one of Nixon's campaign aides accusing Muskie of ethnic insensitivity to French Canadians. Together those dirty tricks derailed Muskie's primary campaign.

These secret and highly questionable activities were financed by massive illegal fundraising efforts by the Committee to Re-Elect the President (known as CREEP), which was headed by Attorney General John Mitchell. In soliciting funds from major corporations, Nixon's fundraisers used high-pressure tactics that included implied threats of federal tax audits and other punitive measures for companies that failed to contribute. CREEP subsequently raised over $20 million, a portion of which was used to finance various dirty tricks, including the break-in that led to the Watergate scandal.

The Break-In. Early on the morning of June 17, 1972, an alert security guard noticed something amiss at the headquarters of the Democratic National Committee at the Watergate apartment complex in Washington. Five men carrying cameras, wiretapping equipment, and a large amount of cash were arrested; two accomplices were apprehended soon afterward. Three of the accused men had ties either to the White House or to CREEP; the remaining four, all from Miami, had been involved in CIA-linked anti-Castro activities. Nixon's press secretary, Ronald Ziegler, promptly dismissed the break-in as a "third-rate burglary attempt." Nixon soon claimed that White House counsel John Dean had conducted a full investigation of the incident (no such investigation ever took place) and stated categorically that "no one on the White House staff, no one in this administration, presently employed, was involved in this very bizarre incident." The cover-up had begun.

Subsequent investigations revealed that six days after the break-in the president had ordered his chief of staff, H. R. Haldeman, to instruct the CIA to tell the FBI not to probe too deeply into connections between the White House and the burglars. That action constituted obstruction of justice. Nixon apparently feared that the Watergate burglary would lead to an investigation of the dubious fundraising methods and political sabotage practiced by his reelection committee.

The Watergate burglars were convicted in January 1973. With Nixon's approval, John Dean tried to buy their continued silence with $400,000 in hush money and hints of presidential pardons. However, prodded by the presiding judge, John Sirica, one of the convicted burglars began to talk. Two tenacious investigative reporters at the *Washington Post*, Carl Bernstein and Bob Woodward, exposed the attempted cover-up and traced it back to the White House. In February the Senate voted 77 to 0 to establish a select committee to investigate the scandal. Dean started to get nervous, and in March 1973 he warned Nixon, referring to the cover-up, that "there is a cancer within, close to the presidency, that is growing." In April Nixon accepted the resignations of Haldeman, Assistant Secretary of Commerce Jeb Stuart Magruder, and Chief Domestic Advisor John Ehrlichman, all of whom had been implicated in the cover-up. He also fired Dean, who had agreed to testify in the case in exchange for immunity from prosecution. As evidence mounted linking the scandal directly with the White House, press secretary Ziegler declared all previous statements on Watergate "inoperative."

In May the Senate Watergate Committee, chaired by Senator Sam Ervin of North Carolina, began nationally televised hearings that riveted the nation for the next six months. On June 14 Magruder testified before the committee, confessing his guilt and implicating Attorney General John Mitchell, Dean, and others in the Water-

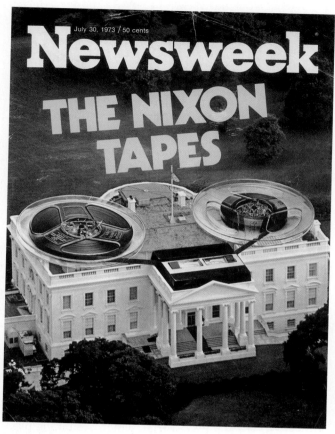

Watergate

In July 1973, White House aide Alexander Butterfield testified before the Senate Watergate Committee that all oval office telephone communications had been recorded on a secret taping system. Although Nixon tried in vain to suppress the tapes by claiming executive privilege, their eventual release—including statements directly implicating the president in the Watergate cover-up—led to Nixon's resignation in August of 1974.

gate affair. In five days of riveting testimony in late June, Dean implicated Nixon in the cover-up (see Voices from Abroad, "Watergate and Due Process," p. 980). Even more startling testimony came from an aide who revealed that Nixon had a secret taping system in the Oval Office. "I was hoping you fellows wouldn't ask me about that," Alexander Butterfield sheepishly told the committee. Until the existence of the tapes was disclosed, it had been Dean's word against Nixon's; now finding out what had actually been said seemed possible.

The president steadfastly "stonewalled" the committee's demand that he surrender the tapes, citing executive privilege and national security. Archibald Cox, a special prosecutor appointed by Nixon to investigate the Watergate events, successfully petitioned a lower federal court to order the president to hand over the tapes. Still Nixon refused to comply, ordering Attorney General Elliott Richardson to fire Cox. Richardson

Watergate and Due Process

———————————— ★ ————————————

Foreign reaction to the Watergate scandal included both praise and condemnation of America's handling of the crisis. One of the sharpest criticisms came from the venerable British daily newspaper the Times (London), which ran an editorial in 1973 attacking the American press for publishing highly prejudicial material, including damaging testimony before the Senate investigating committee by White House counsel John Dean.

The President of the United States is in the unenviable position of being tried by his fellow countrymen in three different forums, each of which has its own particular deficiencies. . . . What Mr. Nixon is now receiving is a Washington variant of lynch law, and that while he may or may not be innocent, he may never be proved guilty by a process so clearly lacking in justice.

The three forms of trial, which are taking place simultaneously, are the Ervin Committee in the Senate . . . the Grand Jury, and the media, including The New York Times and the Washington Post.

The Ervin Committee is investigating precisely because the Senate thought that the due process of law was working too slowly. The Senators are trying to ask fair and relevant questions. . . . Yet Senate committees are not courts: they do not have an adversary procedure; they do not have cross examination by Counsel for the accused; they can take and certainly do take hearsay evidence. . . . The enormous publicity given to hearsay evidence in televised hearings is so prejudicial that it alone would seem to preclude the possibility of fair trial for any accused, even including the President himself if there were impeachment proceedings.

The second tribunal is the Grand Jury. No student of British law will forget that we abandoned the Grand Jury procedure because of its notorious weaknesses as an instrument of justice. Grand Jury proceedings provide the prosecutor with opportunities to introduce prejudicial evidence, which would not be admissible in a trial. The Watergate Grand Jury proceedings have been held in camera but have been widely leaked. The public has therefore a partial and unreliable account of these proceedings; that must be more damaging to the administration of justice than if there were a full account or no account at all. . . .

The third tribunal is the press, with television. . . . The American press, and particularly the Washington Post, deserve their full credit for forcing the Watergate affair into the open. They are however now publishing vast quantities of prejudicial matter, that would be contempt under British law, which again must tend to prejudice the fair trial of any accused, or, if it came to that, of the President. . . .

What the President is accused of that really matters is to have interfered with the course of justice. That would be as grave an offence as a President could commit. Yet are not the Senate committee who are taking and publishing hearsay evidence to the whole country also interfering with the course of justice? . . .

And what about the press? . . . How can one justify the decision to publish the Dean leak? . . . Here is a piece of wholly suspect evidence—unsworn, unverified, not cross-examined, contradicting previous evidence, subject to none of the safeguards of due process, given by a man who may be bargaining for his freedom. How can the newspapers defend themselves from the very charge that they are bringing against the President, the charge of making a fair trial impossible, if they now publish evidence so damning and so doubtful with all the weight of authority that their publication gives?

———————————

Source: Times (London) editorial, June 5, 1973, 17.

refused and resigned in protest, as did Assistant Attorney General William Ruckelshaus. Solicitor General Robert Bork, third in command in the Justice department, finally carried out his order, but the action backfired. The "Saturday Night Massacre" sparked public outrage and renewed demands for release of the tapes.

After additional federal subpoenas the following spring, Nixon released heavily edited transcripts of the tapes, whose most frequent words seemed to be "expletive deleted," a phrase necessitated by the extensive profanity on the tapes. Senate Republican leader Hugh Scott called the edited transcripts "deplorable, disgusting, shabby, immoral." Most suspicious was an eighteen-minute gap in the tape of a crucial meeting of Nixon, Haldeman, and Ehrlichman on June 20, 1972, three days after the break-in.

The Final Days. The Watergate affair moved into its final phase in the summer of 1974, when a committee of the House of Representatives convened impeachment hearings. On July 30 seven Republicans joined the Democratic majority to vote three articles of impeachment against Richard Nixon: obstruction of justice, abuse of power, and subverting the Constitution. Two days later the Supreme Court ruled unanimously that Nixon had no right to claim executive privilege as a justification for refusing to turn over additional tapes. Under pressure, on August 5 Nixon released the unexpurgated tapes, which contained shocking evidence (the so-called smoking gun) that he had ordered the cover-up as early as six days after the break-in. In effect, the president had been lying to the American people since that time. A delegation of the most senior members of Congress, led by Senator Barry Goldwater, informed the president that no more than fifteen senators still supported him. Facing certain conviction in a Senate trial, on August 9, 1974, Nixon became the first U.S. president to resign.

The next day Vice-President Gerald Ford was sworn in as president. Ford, a former Michigan congressman and House minority leader, had replaced Spiro Agnew in 1973 after Agnew resigned under indictment for accepting kickbacks on construction contracts while serving as governor of Maryland and vice-president. The transfer of power from Nixon to Ford went remarkably smoothly. A month later, however, Ford stunned the nation by granting a "full, free, and absolute" pardon of Nixon "for all offenses he had committed or might have committed during his presidency." Ford took that action, he said, to spare the country the agony of reliving Watergate. While Nixon retired to his estate in San Clemente, California, twenty-five members of his administration went to prison, including Nixon's closest advisors, H. R. Haldeman, John Ehrlichman, and John Mitchell. Named only as an "unindicted co-conspirator" in their trials, Nixon refused to admit guilt for what had happened, conceding only that Watergate represented an error of judgment.

The Aftermath. In response to the abuses of the Nixon administration, Congress adopted several reforms to contain the power of what historian Arthur M. Schlesinger Jr. called "the imperial presidency." In 1974 a strengthened Freedom of Information Act gave citizens greater access to files that federal government agencies had amassed on them. The 1974 Congressional Budget and Impoundment Control Act restricted the president's authority to impound federal funds (that is, to refuse to spend money appropriated by Congress for programs opposed by the White House). The Fair Campaign Practices Act of 1974 limited campaign contributions and provided for stricter accountability and public financing of presidential campaigns. Finally, in cases of alleged criminal activity in the executive branch, the Independent Counsel Act of 1978 required the attorney general to call on a panel of three federal judges to appoint a special prosecutor—thus precluding future "Saturday Night Massacres."

Perhaps the most significant legacy of Watergate, however, was the wave of cynicism that swept the country in its wake. Beginning with Lyndon Johnson's "credibility gap" in the Vietnam War, public distrust of government had risen steadily with the disclosure of Nixon's secret bombing of Cambodia and the illegal surveillance and harassment of antiwar protesters and other political opponents. The saga of Watergate seemed to confirm the suspicions of many Americans that politicians were hopelessly corrupt and that the federal government was out of control. Ironically, some of the post-Watergate legislation intended to curb political abuses ended up further undermining public confidence. In the case of the Fair Campaign Practices Act, which allowed an unlimited number of political action committees (PACs) to donate up to $5,000 per candidate, corporations and lobbying groups found they could actually increase their political influence by making multiple donations. By the end of the decade close to 3,000 PACs were playing an increasingly pivotal—and some would argue unethical—role in national elections. The Independent Counsel Act, which would be invoked twenty-one times between 1978 and 1999, revealed a string of political scandals in both parties and raised doubts about the political "independence" of some of the appointed prosecutors. Such measures fueled public cynicism about politics for the foreseeable future.

The Economic Downturn

Economic difficulties compounded Americans' political disillusionment. After twenty-five years of world leadership, the economic dominance of the United States had begun to fade. Growing international demands for natural resources, particularly oil, and unstable access to foreign supplies wreaked havoc with the domestic economy. At the same time, foreign competitors were successfully expanding their share of the world market, edging out American-made products. The result was a sharp downturn in the economy that marked the end of America's overwhelming economic superiority in the postwar era.

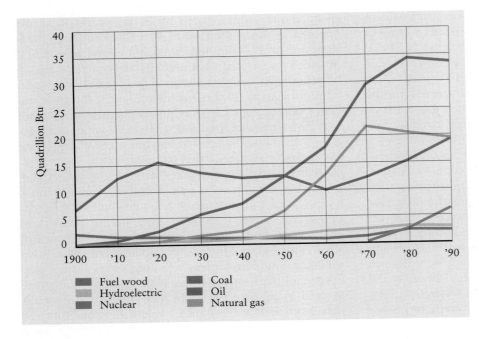

FIGURE 30.1
U.S. Energy Consumption, 1900–1990
Coal was the nation's primary source of energy until the 1950s, when oil and natural gas became the dominant fuels. The use of nuclear and hydroelectric power also rose substantially in the postwar era. Since the late 1970s fuel-efficient automobiles and conservation measures have reduced total energy use.

The Energy Crisis

"Without oil," Interior Secretary Harold Ickes had noted back in 1933, "American civilization as we know it could not exist." That continues to be true today, when not only the United States but the entire modern world lives in a hydrocarbon age, dependent on petroleum and its by-products. In the twentieth century, oil supplanted coal as the main energy source for the industrial world because it was cheaper, cleaner, and more abundant (Figure 30.1). Between 1949 and 1972, world energy consumption more than tripled, and the demand for oil increased more than five and a half times. Access to oil, especially at the low prices that prevailed in the 1950s and 1960s, fostered rapid economic growth and rising standards of living in most of the world, especially in the United States.

Until well into the twentieth century, the United States was the world's leading producer and consumer of oil. During World War II, America still produced two-thirds of the world's oil, but by 1972 its share had fallen to only 22 percent, even though domestic production continued to rise. By the late 1960s the United States was buying more and more oil on the world market to keep up with shrinking domestic reserves and growing demand.

The imported oil came primarily from the Middle East, where production increased a stupendous 1,500 percent in the twenty-five years after World War II. The rise of nationalism and the corresponding decline of colonialism in the postwar era had encouraged Persian Gulf nations to wrest control of the industry from the European and American oil companies that had previously dominated petroleum exploration and production

in that region, reaping enormous profits along the way. In 1960 oil-producing countries in the Third World formed the Organization of Petroleum Exporting Countries (OPEC) in an attempt to exercise more control over the world oil market. Five of the founding countries—the Middle Eastern states of Saudi Arabia, Kuwait, Iran, and Iraq, plus Venezuela—were the source of more than 80 percent of the world's crude oil exports. In 1960 the oil industry was in the middle of a twenty-year period of surplus capacity, and prices stayed low.

In the early 1970s, however, the balance shifted. Several trends—a sharp increase in worldwide demand, the end of excess capacity, political instability in the Middle East, the shift of the United States from a net exporter to a net importer of oil—came together to set the stage for what would soon be OPEC's "golden age." The year 1973 was the turning point. Between 1973 and 1975 OPEC deliberately raised the price of a barrel of oil from $3 to $12. By the end of the decade the price had peaked at $34 a barrel. Because the United States depended heavily on Middle Eastern oil, the price rise set off furious inflation.

OPEC members also found that oil could be used as a weapon in global politics. In 1973 OPEC instituted an oil embargo against the United States, Western Europe, and Japan, in retaliation for their aid to Israel during the Yom Kippur War. (The conflict had begun earlier that year on October 6, Yom Kippur—the holiest day in Judaism—when Egypt and Syria invaded Israel in an attempt to retake lands occupied by Israel in the Six Day War of 1967.) The embargo, which lasted until 1974, forced the United States to scramble to meet its domestic energy needs. Americans either had to curtail their driving or had to spend long hours in line at the pumps; gas prices climbed 40 percent in a matter of months. A national speed limit of 55 miles per hour was instituted to conserve fuel.

Drivers wanted to buy more fuel-efficient cars, but the U.S. automobile industry had little to offer except "gas-guzzlers" built to run on cheap gasoline. Soon the domestic auto industry was in a slump as Americans bought cheaper, more fuel-efficient foreign cars, primarily those manufactured in Japan and West Germany. Since the United States owed much of its twentieth-century prosperity to the automobile (one in six jobs was tied directly or indirectly to the auto industry in the 1970s), this downturn had profound implications for the American economy. Moreover, the energy crisis was an enormous shock to the American psyche. Suddenly Americans felt like hostages to economic forces beyond their control.

Economic Woes

While the energy crisis dealt a swift blow to the U.S. economy, a series of long-term economic developments had equally damaging results. The high cost of the Vietnam War and the Great Society had contributed to a steadily growing federal deficit and spiraling inflation. In the industrial sector growing competition from the reviving economies of West Germany and Japan reduced demand for American goods worldwide. In 1955 American-made goods had accounted for 32 percent of all imports by major capitalist countries; by 1970 U.S. products accounted for only 18 percent of the total, and the percentage continued to decline in the 1970s. As a result, in 1971 the dollar fell to its lowest level on the world market since 1949, and the United States posted its first trade deficit in almost a century.

Nixon's Remedies.   That year, with the 1972 election looming, Nixon took several bold steps to turn the economy around and avoid a recession. To stem the decline in currency and trade, he suspended the 1944 Bretton Woods system, one of the pillars of the postwar economic order (see Chapter 28). Once again, the dollar would fluctuate in relation to the price of an ounce of gold, which increased from its former set price of $35 to as much as $800 on the international market during the 1970s. The abandonment of Bretton Woods, which effectively devalued the dollar in hopes of encouraging foreign trade, represented a frank acknowledgment that America's currency was no longer the world's strongest. Nixon also instituted wage and price controls to curb inflation and offered a "full employment" budget for 1972, including $11 billion in deficit spending to boost the sluggish economy.

These measures brought a temporary improvement in the economy, but the general decline persisted. Overall economic growth as measured by the gross national

No Gas
During the energy crisis of 1973–1974, American motorists faced widespread gasoline shortages for the first time since World War II. Although gas was not rationed, gas stations were closed on Sundays, air travel was cut by 10 percent, and a national speed limit of 55 miles per hour was imposed.
Tony Korody/Sygma.

product (GNP) had averaged 4.1 percent per year in the 1960s; in the 1970s, this measure dropped to only 2.9 percent. Tellingly, all the real growth occurred before 1973, the year the OPEC oil embargo began. By 1980 nine Western European countries had surpassed the United States in per capita GNP. Between 1973 and the mid-1990s, most American workers saw their real incomes drop and maintained their family income levels only by working longer hours or by having additional family members join the paid work force.

Many of these new workers were women employed in the expanding service sector. Women in particular entered the clerical work force, where jobs dominated by narrow and repetitive tasks did not allow for control and autonomy. In most cases their salaries were lower than the hourly wages of unionized blue-collar workers. Millions of other women entered blue-collar service

FIGURE 30.2
The Consumer Price Index, 1960–1994
The annual inflation rate peaked in 1980, the last year of Carter's presidency.
Source: U.S. Statistical Abstract, 1995.

occupations, performing manual labor for hourly wages under factory-like conditions in laundries, restaurants, warehouses, and other businesses. For nonwhite and working-class women, a "pink-collar" ghetto offered minimum-wage jobs in hotels, hospitals, and beauty salons.

Stagnating wages and the growth of the low-paying service sector produced a noticeable decline in most Americans' standard of living. Discretionary income per worker dropped 18 percent between 1973 and the early 1980s. At the same time, galloping inflation forced consumer prices upward. The Consumer Price Index (CPI) reached double-digit peaks of around 10 percent in 1974 and over 13 percent in 1980 (Figure 30.2). Housing prices rose even more rapidly, with the average cost of a single-family home more than doubling in the 1970s. Homeownership thus became less accessible to many working-class and middle-class Americans, including many baby boomers who were entering adulthood.

Young adults also faced a constricted job market in the late 1970s as a record number of baby-boom job seekers competed for a limited number of positions. Unemployment peaked at around 9 percent in 1975, declined briefly, and then edged upward again to around 6 to 7 percent in the late 1970s. The devastating combination of inflation and unemployment—dubbed *stagflation*—was resistant to traditional government remedies such as deficit spending and tax reduction and bedeviled presidential administrations from Nixon to Reagan.

Deindustrialization. American economic woes were most acute in the industrial sector, which entered a prolonged period of decline. The economists Barry Bluestone and Bennett Harrison estimate that the United States lost between 32 million and 38 million jobs in the 1970s as a direct result of deindustrialization, "the widespread, systematic disinvestment in the nation's productive capacity." Investors who had for-

merly bought stock in basic U.S. industries began to speculate on risky new ventures in the stock market or put their money into foreign companies or mergers (that often resulted in job layoffs). Many U.S. firms relocated overseas, partly to take advantage of cheaper labor and production costs and partly because federal tax law permitted corporations to deduct foreign expenses from their domestic profits. By the end of the 1970s the hundred largest multinational corporations and banks were earning more than a third of their overall profits abroad.

The most dramatic consequences of deindustrialization occurred in the older northeastern and midwestern industrial regions, which came to be known as the Rust Belt. Nightly newscasts were full of stories of the closings of unprofitable plants. The dominant images of American industry in the mid-twentieth century—huge factories such as Ford's River Rouge plant outside Detroit; the General Electric plant in Lynn, Massachusetts; and the United States Steel Corporation compound in Gary, Indiana—were becoming relics of a past stage of industrial development.

When a community's major employer closed up shop and left town, the effect was devastating. In 1977 the Lykes Corporation shut the Campbell Works of the Youngstown Sheet and Tube Company, laying off 4,100 Ohio steelworkers. Two years later Youngstown was still reeling. A third of the displaced workers, considered too old to retrain for new positions, had been forced to take early retirement at half of their previous salaries. Ten percent had moved, many of them to nonunion jobs in the Sun Belt, where the economy continued its dramatic postwar growth. Another 15 percent were still looking for work, their unemployment compensation long since exhausted. Among the 40 percent who were the "success stories" (those who had found other jobs), many had taken huge wage cuts. A former rigger, for instance, was selling women's shoes for $2.37 an hour. The impact of such plant closings rippled through communities across America's heartland.

Deindustrialization
Scores of industrial plants closed in the 1970s, putting many American workers out of work. At the same time, more Americans were buying cheaper imported cars, fueling anger toward foreign competitors. David Helfferich of Greenburg, Pennsylvania, bashed this Japanese-made Honda Civic and urged others to "buy American" as a means of protecting U.S. jobs.
Wide World Photos, Inc.

The changing economic conditions that fostered foreign investment and plant closings posed critical problems for the labor movement. As foreign competition cut into American corporate profits in the 1970s, industry was less willing to treat labor as a partner in making economic decisions. Union leaders often learned about a plant closing from the TV news at the same time that ordinary workers and the general public learned about it. Under such conditions, the power of organized labor declined in the 1970s, with a drop in union membership from 28 percent to 23 percent of the work force. Labor's bargaining position was increasingly vulnerable in the face of multinational conglomerates with vast international resources and mobility. Some employers facing strikes or labor problems simply closed their domestic operations and turned to a cheaper, more compliant work force abroad. In a competitive global environment, labor's prospects for regaining its earlier strength were dim, and union leaders shifted their priorities to holding on to gains they had already won.

Reform and Reaction in the 1970s

The nation's economic problems and growing cynicism about government led to deep public anxiety and resentment, and caused many Americans to turn inward to private satisfactions. The journalist Tom Wolfe labeled the 1970s the "Me Decade" because of its widespread obsession with life-styles and personal well-being, and the historian Christopher Lasch referred derisively to the decade's "culture of narcissism." But those labels hardly do justice to a decade in which environmentalism, feminism, lesbian and gay rights, and other social movements blossomed. Furthermore, such characterizations neglect the growing social conservatism that was in part a response to such movements. In the transitional decade of the 1970s, all these trends coexisted in a complex pattern of shifting crosscurrents.

The New Activism: Environmental and Consumer Movements

After 1970, many baby boomers left the counterculture behind and settled down to pursue careers and material success. But these young adults sought personal fulfillment as well. In a quest for physical and spiritual well-being, millions of Americans began jogging, riding bicycles, or working out at the gym. The fitness craze coincided with heightened environmental awareness, which spurred demands for pesticide-free foods and vegetarian cookbooks. Some young people embraced the spiritual and self-help techniques of the human potential, or New Age, movement, while others turned to new religious movements such as the Hare Krishna, the Church of Scientology, and the Unification Church of the Reverend Sun Myung Moon.

A few baby boomers continued to pursue the unfinished social and political agendas of the 1960s. Moving into law, education, social work, medicine, and other

Rachel Carson
A pioneer of the modern environmental movement, biologist
Rachel Carson documented the adverse effects of DDT and
other pesticides in her 1962 best seller, *Silent Spring*. This pho-
tograph, taken in 1961, shows Carson conducting fieldwork.
Alfred Eisenstadt/LIFE Magazine © Time, Inc.

fields, former radicals practiced their activism at a
grass-roots level. Some moved into the left wing of the
Democratic Party, while others helped establish a host
of community-based organizations such as health clinics, food co-ops, and day-care centers. On the local
level, the progressive spirit of the 1960s lived on.

Environmental Awareness.   One of the most dynamic
sources of activism in the 1970s was the environmental
movement. The birth of America's modern environmental movement can be dated to the 1962 publication of
Rachel Carson's *Silent Spring*, a powerful analysis of the
impact of pesticides, especially DDT, on the food chain.
Other issues that galvanized public opinion included a
huge oil spill in January 1969 off the coast of Santa Barbara, California, which devastated beaches and sea life
along the Pacific coast, and the environmental impact of
projects such as the Alaska pipeline and a proposed air-
port in the Florida Everglades. New scientific research
also revealed the harmful effects of chlorofluorocarbons
and other fossil fuel by-products on the ozone layer of
the earth's atmosphere, potentially destroying its protective properties and causing global warming. Environmentalism became a mass movement on the first
Earth Day, April 22, 1970, when 20 million citizens gathered across the country to show their support for their
endangered planet.

The United States had long consumed vast quantities
of natural resources and had built a vigorous economy
based on resource exploitation. Even as Americans
became increasingly aware of the possible exhaustion of
the earth's resources, the idea that there were limits to
growth was revolutionary and difficult to accept, but so
too were unhealthy air and polluted water. Concern about
environmental quality and ecological values may be seen
as an offshoot of the advanced consumer economy that
defined the postwar period. Moving beyond basic necessities, many Americans demanded an even higher standard
of living that included a healthy environment and corresponding life-styles. That desire led to new demands on
the state, as citizens expected the federal government to
take responsibility for environmental issues.

Many of the new environmentalists had been
1960s-style activists, and they brought their radical
political sensibilities to environmental issues. For
example, environmental activists talked about the
"rights of nature" just as they talked about the rights of
women or blacks. They construed the search for alternative technologies (especially solar power) as a political statement against a corporate structure that seemed
increasingly hostile to human-scale technology—and to
humans as well. Activists used sit-ins and other protest
tactics developed in the civil rights and antiwar movements to mobilize mass support for specific issues or
pieces of legislation. Like those movements, environmentalism was characterized by its decentralized
nature and local orientation.

The environmental movement also raised public
awareness of the dangers resulting from the dumping
or release into the environment of toxic wastes. In
1978, outside Niagara Falls, New York, the Love Canal
housing development made headlines when local residents discovered that it had been built over an underground chemical waste-disposal site. Lois Gibbs and
other residents became aware of abnormally high rates
of illness, miscarriages, and birth defects among Love
Canal families. In 1980 a state of emergency was
declared, and the New York State government paid
homeowners to relocate (see American Lives, "Lois
Marie Gibbs: Environmental Activist," pp. 988–989).

One of the worst offenders was the federal government itself. In the Cold War rush to produce bombs and
weapons for national security, nuclear weapons plants
carelessly released billions of gallons of radioactive
waste into the environment. For example, the uranium-
processing plant built in 1954 at Fernald, Ohio, dumped
liquid wastes into open-air waste-storage pits, which
then leaked into regional waterways. At the Hanford
Nuclear Reservation near Richland, Washington, pluto-
nium waste and toxic chemicals contaminated the soil
and seeped into the Columbia River. Environmentalists
called on the federal government to clean up this chemical legacy of the Cold War, but with only limited success.

Nuclear Power. Nuclear energy also became a subject of citizen action in the 1970s, when rising oil prices and shortages pitted environmental concerns against the need for alternative energy sources. To reduce the nation's dependence on foreign oil, some politicians and utility companies promoted the expansion of nuclear power. By January 1974, forty-two nuclear power plants were in operation, and over a hundred more were planned. The construction of nuclear power plants and reactors had gone largely unchallenged in the 1950s and 1960s, but it suddenly became controversial in the 1970s. Community activists protested plans for new reactors, citing inadequate disaster evacuation plans and the unresolved problem of disposing of radioactive waste. The mass protests of the Clamshell Alliance and other antinuclear groups helped to prevent or delay the start-up of nuclear reactors in Seabrook, New Hampshire, and Shoreham, New York.

Public fears about nuclear safety seemed to be confirmed in March 1979 when the central core reactor of a nuclear plant at Three Mile Island near Harrisburg, Pennsylvania, came critically close to a meltdown. Nearly a hundred thousand residents were evacuated as a precaution. A prompt shutdown brought the problem under control before any radioactive material was released into the environment, but a member of the panel investigating the accident admitted, "We were damn lucky." Ultimately, Three Mile Island made Americans reassess whether nuclear power could be a viable solution to the nation's energy needs. Grass-roots activism, combined with public fears about the potential dangers of nuclear energy, convinced many utility companies to abandon nuclear power despite its short-term economic advantages.

Environmental Legislation. Citizens' concerns over nuclear power, chemical contamination, pesticide poisoning, and other environmental issues created bipartisan support for an array of new federal legislation. In 1969 Congress passed the National Environmental Policy Act, requiring the developers of public projects to file an environmental impact statement (EIS) to assess the consequences of changing use patterns on a particular ecosystem. The EIS soon became a useful tool for citizens' groups trying to block unwanted development by private industry or government. The next year Nixon established the EPA and signed the Clean Air Act, which toughened standards for auto emissions to reduce smog and air pollution. Two years later Congress banned the use of DDT. And in 1973 the Endangered Species Act expanded the Endangered Animals Act of 1964, granting species such as snail darters and spotted owls protected status. Environmental protection thus joined social welfare, defense, and national security as areas for federal intervention in the postwar era.

But the environmental movement did not go uncontested. EPA-mandated fuel economy standards for cars, for example, provoked criticism for threatening the health of the auto industry as it struggled to keep up with foreign competitors. Corporations resented environmental regulations, but so did many of their workers, who believed that tightened standards threatened their jobs and placed nature over human beings. "If you're hungry and out of work, eat an environmentalist" read one labor union's bumper sticker. In a time of rising unemployment and deindustrialization, activists clashed head-on with proponents of economic development, full employment, and global competitiveness.

The Consumer Movement. Paralleling the rise of environmentalism was a growing consumer protection movement to eliminate harmful consumer products and curb dangerous practices by American corporations. The consumer movement had originated in the Progressive Era with the founding of government agencies such as the Food and Drug Administration (see Chapter 20). After decades of inertia, the consumer movement reemerged in the 1960s under the leadership of Ralph Nader, a young Harvard-educated lawyer whose book *Unsafe at Any Speed* (1965) attacked General Motors for putting flashy style ahead of safe handling and fuel economy in its engineering of the Chevrolet Corvair.

In 1969 Nader launched a Washington-based consumer protection organization that gave rise to the Public Interest Research Group, a national network of consumer groups that focused on issues ranging from product safety to consumer fraud and environmental pollution. Staffed by a handful of lawyers and hundreds of student volunteers known as "Nader's Raiders," the organization pioneered legal tactics such as the class-action suit, which allowed people with common grievances to sue as a group. Nader's organization became a model for dozens of other groups that emerged in the 1970s and afterward to combat the health hazards of smoking, unethical insurance and credit practices, and other consumer problems. The establishment of the federal Consumer Products Safety Commission in 1972 reflected the growing importance of consumer protection in American life.

Challenges to Tradition: The Women's Movement and Gay Rights

Along with environmentalism, feminism proved to be the most enduring movement to emerge from the 1960s. In the next decade the women's movement grew more sophisticated, generating an array of women-oriented services and organizations, from rape crisis centers and battered women's shelters to feminist health collectives and women's bookstores. *Our Bodies, Ourselves,* a

Lois Marie Gibbs: Environmental Activist

———————★———————

IN 1978 LOIS GIBBS was a twenty-seven-year-old housewife living in Niagara Falls, New York. A chemical worker's wife and the mother of two children, Gibbs spent her days cooking, shopping, and cleaning the family's modest three-bedroom home. Two years later Gibbs was a nationally known figure. As leader of the fight against toxic waste at Love Canal, she organized hundreds of local families, squared off with the governor of New York State, testified before Congress, appeared on national television, and was recognized by President Jimmy Carter for her efforts. She was, as she liked to put it, "the housewife who went to Washington."

Born in Grand Island, New York, in 1951, Lois Conn was one of six children in a blue-collar family in the industrial region surrounding Buffalo. After graduating from high school in 1969, she worked as a nurse's aide at a convalescent home and married Harry Gibbs, a worker at a local chemical plant. After the birth of their first child, Michael, they purchased a home in a quiet, tree-lined neighborhood. Lois quit her job to stay at home and in 1975 gave birth to a daughter. With no inkling of what lay beneath them, the Gibbses finished their basement, tended their garden, and enjoyed a peaceful suburban existence.

The first sign of trouble came in 1977, when their son Michael entered kindergarten at the neighborhood school. Within three months, he developed epilepsy and soon contracted asthma and chronic urinary and ear infections. The following spring Gibbs read newspaper reports about toxic chemicals buried beneath the school and tried to have her son transferred. When school officials rejected her request, insisting that the school was safe, Gibbs launched a petition drive to have the school closed.

At first Gibbs was reticent about approaching her neighbors, afraid of having doors slammed in her face. But what she found surprised her. Not only were people interested in and concerned about the dangers of chemicals, but many of them had health problems of their own, including respiratory ailments, cancer,

miscarriages, and birth defects. "The more I heard, the more frightened I became," said Gibbs. "The entire community seemed to be sick."

Gibbs set out to educate herself about the area's history. Consulting local newspaper files, she learned about Love Canal, a six-mile-long canal project developed by William T. Love in the 1890s to connect the upper and lower branches of the Niagara River. Construction had been under way when the depression of 1893 doomed the project, leaving a partially dug trench. The land later became a dump site used mainly by the Hooker Chemical Corporation, which disposed of 22,000 tons of chemical wastes there between 1942 and 1953. (Health officials eventually identified over 200 different compounds at the site, including highly toxic substances such as dioxin—used in the herbicide Agent Orange—toluene, and benzene.) After filling and covering over the site in 1953, Hooker sold the land to the Board of Education for one dollar, stipulating that the company not be held responsible for any future injury or death. Housing subdivisions soon sprang up around the site, and a new elementary school near the corner of the canal opened in 1955.

By the time Gibbs began meeting with her neighbors in 1978, rusted metal drums were surfacing in backyards, chemical sludge was seeping into basements, and residents were complaining about dead trees, burned feet, and a recurring stench. In June of that year the New York State Health Department began collecting air, soil, and blood samples from households closest to the canal. After finding abnormally high rates of birth defects and miscarriages, the health department issued an order on August 2 for reconstruction of the canal site and recommended the evacuation of all pregnant women and children under age two. Soon afterward concerned residents established the Love Canal Homeowners Association (LCHA) to fight for permanent relocation of Love Canal families and elected Lois Gibbs as LCHA president. Under pressure from Gibbs and the LCHA, New York's governor, Hugh Carey, agreed a few days later to relocate the 239 families closest to the canal, purchasing their homes at the replacement value.

While Gibbs and the LCHA applauded Carey's action, they worried about the other 810 families remaining in the neighborhood, many of whose homes also showed dangerous levels of chemicals. Gibbs appealed to federal and local officials for further action but encountered repeated delays, denials, and rebuffs. The mayor of Niagara Falls denounced Gibbs's efforts, claiming that the adverse publicity would destroy the city's tourist industry. Meanwhile,

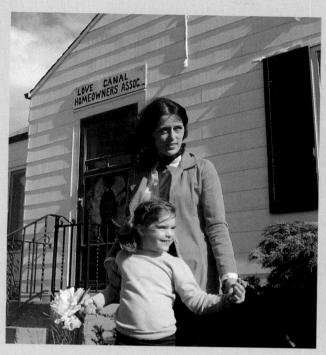

Lois Marie Gibbs
A twenty-seven-year-old housewife in Niagara Falls, New York, Lois Gibbs became the leader of a campaign against toxic waste in her neighborhood in 1978. As president of the Love Canal Homeowners Association, Gibbs fought successfully for the permanent relocation of more than a thousand Love Canal families.
Corbis-Bettmann.

Gibbs made frequent trips to Albany and Washington to negotiate with state officials, the governor's office, Senator Daniel Patrick Moynihan, and other federal representatives.

Like other housewives involved in the crisis, Gibbs gained a new independence through her activities outside the home. Those activities, however, also caused tension in her marriage. "My husband was getting upset with me," she recalled. "I was never home . . . dinner was never on time." She and her husband divorced in 1980.

In May of that year events at Love Canal came to a head when the U.S. Environmental Protection Agency released a study showing abnormally high levels of chromosome breakage in Love Canal residents (suggesting increased risks of cancer, miscarriage, and birth defects). In an act of desperation Gibbs and two other housewives took two EPA officials hostage in the LCHA office while hundreds of angry residents surrounded the building, demanding federal relocation of Love Canal families. Coming in the middle of the Iranian hostage crisis, the women's ploy brought national media coverage but also a threat of reprisal from the FBI. To avoid violence, Gibbs released the officials, but she also demanded a response from President Jimmy Carter within forty-eight hours. Two days later, on May 21, Carter declared a health emergency at Love Canal, authorizing the temporary relocation of the remaining 810 families. Later that year he signed a bill permitting the permanent relocation of those families and the purchase of their homes; he also signed a bill establishing a "Superfund" to clean up Love Canal and thousands of other toxic waste sites identified by the EPA.

Using part of the $30,000 the state paid for her home, Gibbs and her children moved to Washington, D.C., in 1981. There she founded the Citizens Clearinghouse for Hazardous Waste, a consulting group for grass-roots organizations working on problems related to pesticides, solid waste, asbestos, and other toxic substances. She married a toxicologist, gave birth to two more children, and continues to work as director of the Citizens Clearinghouse.

One of the communities the Citizens Clearinghouse has been watching is Love Canal. In 1990 the EPA declared Love Canal habitable again after a twelve-year, $250 million cleanup. The elementary school and the 239 houses closest to the canal had been demolished, but 236 other homes were rehabilitated and sold at discount prices to eager buyers. Public officials insist the new containment system has safely and permanently sealed off the dump. Lois Gibbs is not so sure.

the state health department refused to relocate more families until it could complete further studies. At one point in 1979 the department claimed to have lost the residents' health records and instructed them to start the lengthy documentation process all over again.

Faced with bureaucratic inertia, Gibbs sought out sympathetic scientists to help the residents conduct their own studies. Their most important finding came from a neighborhood survey showing health problems clustered around swales—underground drainage ditches that led away from the canal—and suggesting more widespread contamination. The LCHA promptly released the findings to the media. Gibbs got publicity in other ways as well: she appeared on talk shows, organized picketing at the canal construction site, and was arrested for blocking truck traffic. When state officials still failed to take action, Gibbs led a group of citizens to the state capitol in Albany, bearing cardboard coffins symbolizing Love Canal victims. Throughout the Love Canal crisis

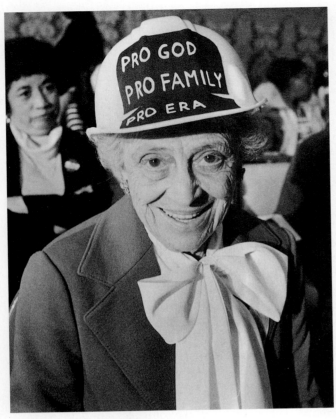

The Expanding Women's Movement
By the late 1970s the feminist movement had broadened its base, attracting women of all ages and backgrounds, such as this delegate to the 1977 National Women's Conference in Houston, Texas. As the slogan on her hat implies, though, the movement was already on the defensive against right-wing claims that it undermined traditional values.
Bettye Lane.

women's health manual published by a group of Boston women in 1973, quickly became a best seller. In 1972 Gloria Steinem and other journalists founded *Ms.* magazine, the first consumer magazine aimed at a feminist audience. Formerly all-male bastions, such as Yale, Princeton, and the U.S. Military Academy at West Point, admitted women undergraduates for the first time, and hundreds of colleges started women's studies programs. By 1977 the National Organization for Women (NOW) had sixty-five thousand members.

Women were also increasingly visible in politics and public life. The National Women's Political Caucus, founded in 1971, actively promoted the election of women to public office. Among the women to enter Congress were Bella Abzug and Geraldine Ferraro from New York and Patricia Schroeder from Colorado. Ella Grasso won election as Connecticut's governor in 1974, and Dixie Lee Ray as Washington's in 1976. In November 1977 twenty thousand women came to Houston for the first National Women's Conference, part of the

observance of the United Nations' International Women's Year. Their "National Plan of Action" represented a hard-won consensus on topics ranging from violence against women to homemakers' rights, the needs of older women, health, and, most controversial, abortion rights and other reproductive issues.

Women's political mobilization resulted in significant legislative and administrative gains. With the passage of Title IX of the Educational Amendments Act of 1972, which broadened the 1964 Civil Rights Act to include educational institutions, Congress prohibited colleges and universities that received federal funds from discriminating on the basis of sex, a change that particularly benefited women athletes. In 1972 Congress authorized child-care deductions for working parents; in 1974 it passed the Equal Credit Opportunity Act, which significantly improved women's access to credit, including charge cards and mortgages, in their own names and on the basis of their own (not their husbands') incomes.

Abortion Rights. The Supreme Court also significantly advanced the cause of women's rights. In several rulings the Court read a right of privacy into the Ninth and Fourteenth Amendments' concept of personal liberty to give women more control over their reproductive lives. In 1965 *Griswold v. Connecticut* had overturned state laws against the sale of contraceptive devices to married adults, a protection that was extended to single persons in 1972. In 1973 *Roe v. Wade* struck down Texas and Georgia statutes that allowed abortions only if the mother's life was in danger. According to this 7-to-2 decision, states could no longer outlaw abortions performed during the first trimester, or three months, of pregnancy. Rather than addressing the issue in feminist terms, such as women's right to control their own bodies, the justices interpreted abortion as a medical issue, basing their controversial decision on the confidentiality of the doctor-patient relationship as well as the individual's right to privacy.

Roe v. Wade nationalized the liberalization of state abortion laws that had begun in New York in 1970, but it also fueled the development of a powerful anti-abortion movement. Believing that the "right to life" of the unborn took precedence over a woman's right to choose whether to terminate a pregnancy, abortion opponents attempted to overturn *Roe v. Wade*. In 1976 they convinced Congress to deny Medicaid funds for abortions for poor women, one of the opening rounds in a protracted legislative and judicial campaign to chip away at the *Roe* decision.

The Equal Rights Amendment. In the 1970s the women's movement increasingly united around the proposed Equal Rights Amendment (ERA) to the Constitution. The ERA, first introduced in Congress in 1923

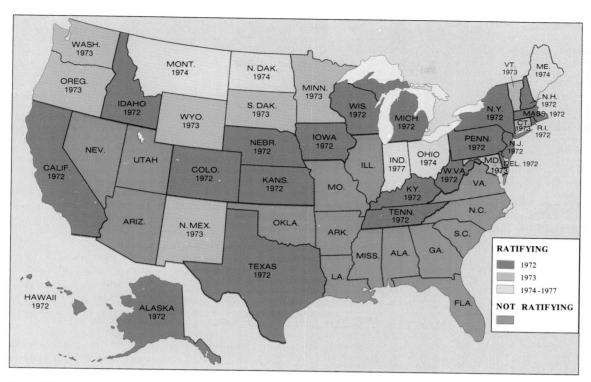

MAP 30.1
States Ratifying the Equal Rights Amendment
The Equal Rights Amendment quickly won support in 1972 and 1973 but then stalled. ERAmerica, a coalition of women's groups formed in 1976, lobbied extensively, particularly in Florida, North Carolina, and Illinois, but failed to sway the conservative legislatures in those states. Efforts to revive the ERA in the 1980s were unsuccessful.

by the National Woman's Party, stated in its entirety, "Equality of rights under the law shall not be denied or abridged by the United States or any State on the basis of sex." In 1970 feminists revived the amendment, which passed the House but died in the Senate. In the next session it passed in both houses of Congress and was submitted to the states for ratification.

Thirty-four states quickly passed the ERA between 1972 and the end of 1974, but then the momentum stopped (Map 30.1). Only Indiana ratified after that point, leaving the amendment three states short of the necessary three-fourths' majority. Most of the nonratifying states were in the South and the West; Illinois also held out despite spirited campaigns there by ERA supporters. Congress extended the deadline for ratification until June 30, 1982, but the Equal Rights Amendment still fell short.

Stalemate. The fate of the ERA and the battle over abortion rights show that by the mid-1970s the momentum of the women's movement was beginning to slow. The contradictions of identity politics created internal divisions within the feminist movement based on race, class, age, and sexual orientation. Most critically, for many nonwhite and working-class women, feminism

seemed to represent the interests only of self-seeking white career women. The ERA, for example, promised to open certain high-paying occupations to individual women but also to eliminate gender-specific protective legislation such as maximum hours laws considered essential to many women workers. The feminist movement also faced growing social conservatism among Americans generally. Although 63 percent of the women polled in 1975 said that they favored "efforts to strengthen and change women's status in society," a growing number of men and women expressed concern over what seemed to be revolutionary changes in women's traditional roles. Especially disturbing to many women were attitudes that seemed to denigrate those who chose to be full-time housewives.

Phyllis Schlafly, long active in conservative causes, led the antifeminist backlash. Notwithstanding her law degree and active career while raising five children, Schlafly advocated traditional roles for women. Schlafly's STOP ERA organization claimed that the amendment would create an unnatural "unisex society," permit women to be drafted, and prohibit separate toilets for men and women. (Feminists argued that those charges were groundless.) Grass-roots networks of conservative women showed up at statehouses with home-

MARLETTE ©1982 THE CHARLOTTE OBSERVER

FIRST DOLLAR

FIRST 59¢

The Income Gap
Although the feminist movement helped create greater opportunities for women, it could not redress the longstanding economic inequalities between men and women. Cartoonist Doug Marlette offered this satirical look at the income gap in 1982, when women earned only fifty-nine cents for every dollar men earned.
Doug Marlette. © The Charlotte Observer.

baked bread and apple pies, symbols of their traditional domestic roles. Their message, that women would lose more than they would gain if the ERA passed, found favor among many men and women, especially those troubled by the rapid pace of social change.

Although the feminist movement was on the defensive by the mid-1970s, women's lives showed no signs of returning to the patterns of the 1950s. Because of increasing economic pressures, the proportion of women in the paid work force continued to rise, from 44 percent in 1970 to 51 percent in 1980. Easier access to birth control permitted women to enjoy greater sexual freedom, although they also became more vulnerable to male sexual pressures. With a growing number of career options available to them, many women, particularly educated white women, stayed single or delayed marriage and child rearing. The birth rate continued its postwar decline, reaching an all-time low in the mid-1970s (see Figure 28.5). At the same time, the divorce rate rose 82 percent in the 1970s, as more men and women chose to leave unhappy marriages.

Such changes brought increased autonomy for many women, but they also caused new hardships, particularly in poor and working-class families. Divorce left many women with low-paying jobs and inadequate child care. More tolerant attitudes toward premarital sex, along with other social and economic factors, contributed to rising teenage pregnancy rates. Increasing rates of divorce and adolescent pregnancy produced a sharp rise in the number of female-headed families, which in turn resulted in a "feminization" of poverty. By 1980 women accounted for 66 percent of the nation's adults living below the poverty line. Such developments made many Americans uneasy and fueled a growing wave of social reaction.

Gays and Lesbians. Like the women's movement, the gay liberation movement achieved greater visibility in the 1970s. Thousands of gay men and lesbians "came out" in those years, publicly—and proudly—proclaiming their sexual orientation and often embracing alternative gender roles (see American Voices, "David Kopay: The Real Score: A Gay Athlete Comes Out," p. 993). Growing gay communities in New York's Greenwich Village, San Francisco's Castro, and other urban enclaves gave rise to hundreds of new gay and lesbian clubs, churches, businesses, and political organizations. In 1973 the National Gay Task Force launched a campaign to include gay men and lesbians as a protected group under civil rights laws covering employment and housing. Such efforts were most successful on the local level; during the 1970s Detroit, Boston, Los Angeles, Miami, San Francisco, and other cities passed laws barring discrimination on the basis of sexual orientation.

Like abortion and the ERA, gay rights came under attack from conservatives who defended traditional gender roles and believed that protecting gay people's rights would encourage immoral behavior. When the Miami city council passed a measure banning discrimination against gay men and lesbians in 1977, the singer Anita Bryant led a campaign to repeal the law by popular referendum. Later that year voters overturned the measure by a two-to-one majority, prompting similar anti–gay rights campaigns around the country.

Racial Minorities

Although the civil rights movement was in disarray by the late 1960s, minority group protests over the next decade continued to win social and economic gains. Native Americans saw some of the most significant changes. In

David Kopay

The Real Score: A Gay Athlete Comes Out

————————★————————

For ten years, David Kopay played professional football for the San Francisco Forty-Niners, the Detroit Lions, the Washington Redskins, the New Orleans Saints, and the Green Bay Packers. In 1975, at the end of his playing career, Kopay publicly acknowledged his homosexuality, creating a national furor in the sports world.

I always knew I was a bit different, but I kept it kind of quiet. I didn't think of myself as queer. In fact I couldn't even say that word for years and years. . . .

When I thought about the future, I assumed I'd be able to get a job in coaching because I was a player-coach my last few years playing. I was always working behind the scenes with the young ballplayers, coaching them. But I wasn't getting any interviews. There were all kinds of rumors about me being gay. . . .

By the time I spoke out, I really had nothing left to lose. It felt like I didn't have a choice—I just had to do it. Then one morning in 1975 I saw an article in the *Washington Star* about homosexual athletes and why they had everything to lose. There was an interview in the article with Jerry Smith [Washington Redskins tight end who died of AIDS in 1986]. . . .

. . . I was at a time and place in my own coming out where I felt that if I was going to survive, I had to speak out. It was do that or maybe go crazy.

So I called Lynn Rosellini, who was the reporter for the article that quoted Jerry Smith. Lynn was doing an entire series on gay athletes. . . .

Everybody said there was going to be a terrible backlash against me when Lynn's article was published. But there wasn't a backlash against me personally: There was a backlash against all the television shows and radio stations that I went on. And the newspapers. The *Washington Star* said they had never received more negative mail for anything they'd ever done—hundreds of horrible hate letters. Only two or three were addressed to me directly; the rest were addressed to the *Washington Star* editor and Lynn Rosellini for doing the series on gay athletes. The letters said things like, "It doesn't belong on the sports page as a model for our young boys and girls." "How could the *Washington Star* run an article like this?" I got letters that said, "I hope you never get a coaching job. Yours in Christ. Love. . . ." Just horrible things.

I never did get a coaching job. I was really quite frightened because I didn't know what I was going to do. No one would hire me to be a coach, I think, because of the image problem. They didn't think I could fill the role of the coach as guardian of the morals of the young students—the father figure. I also knew that I probably wouldn't get that really good sales-rep job that a lot of the other guys got. I had to make a spot for myself somehow, so I wound up working with Perry Young for a year on my book, *The Dave Kopay Story.*

I think we knew we were doing something good. . . .

A lot of kids still write. They say that the book meant so much to them. They remember that it changed them a lot or made a difference.

_____

Source: Eric Marcus, *Making History* (New York: Harper Collins, 1992), 275–277.

1971 the Alaska Native Land Claims Act restored 40 million acres to Eskimos, Aleuts, and other native peoples, along with $960 million in compensation. Smaller settlements were made with tribes in Maine, New Mexico, South Dakota, and Washington State. Most important, the federal government abandoned the tribal termination program that it had begun in the 1950s (see Chapter 28). Under the Indian Self-Determination Act of 1974, Congress restored the legal status of tribes to govern them-

selves and gave them authority over federal programs on their reservations (Map 30.2).

Busing. The court-mandated busing of children to achieve school desegregation proved to be the most disruptive social issue of the 1970s. Progress in achieving the desegregation mandated by *Brown v. Board of Education of Topeka* had been slow. In the 1970s both the courts and the Justice department pushed for more

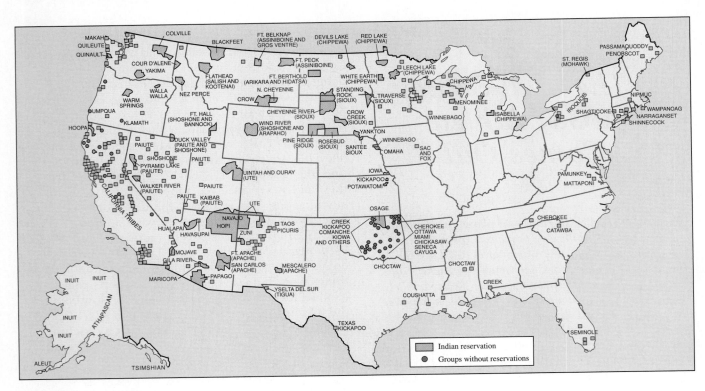

MAP 30.2
American Indian Reservations
Although native Americans have been able to preserve small enclaves in the northeastern
states, most Indian reservations are in the West. Beginning in the 1970s, various nations
filed land claims against federal and state governments.

action, first in the South, which grudgingly complied,
and then in the rest of the country. In *Millicent v.
Bradley* (1974), for example, the Court ordered cities
with deeply ingrained patterns of residential segregation to use busing within municipal boundaries to integrate their classrooms. The decision sparked both
race-based and class-based resentments; many white
working-class city dwellers objected to busing not only
because they opposed racial integration but because
such schemes had been devised by affluent suburbanites whose school districts were unaffected by the plans.

The most violent opposition occurred in Boston in
1974–1975. The strongly Irish-Catholic working-class
neighborhood of South Boston responded to the arrival of
black students from the Roxbury section with mob scenes
reminiscent of Little Rock in 1957 (see American Voices,
"Phyllis Ellison: Busing in Boston," p. 996). Armed riot
police were needed to keep South Boston High School
open. Threatened by court-ordered busing, many white
parents transferred their children to private schools; the
resulting "white flight" increased the racial imbalance
that busing was intended to redress. Some black parents
also opposed busing, calling instead for better schools in
predominantly black neighborhoods. By the late 1970s
federal courts were backing away from their earlier insistence on busing to achieve racial balance.

Affirmative Action. Almost as divisive as busing was
the implementation of *affirmative action*—procedures
designed to redress historical patterns of race and sex discrimination in employment and education. First put forward by Lyndon Johnson's administration in 1965,
affirmative action programs such as hiring and enrollment goals and recruitment and training programs
expanded opportunities for blacks and Latinos. The number of black students enrolled in colleges and universities
doubled between 1970 and 1977 to 1.1 million, or 9.3 percent of the total student enrollment. A small but growing
number of black graduates moved into white-collar professions in corporations, banks, universities, and law
firms. Others found new opportunities in civil service
occupations such as law enforcement and firefighting or
entered apprenticeships in the skilled construction
trades. Latinos experienced similar gains in education
and employment. On the whole, however, both groups
experienced only marginal economic improvement, since
poor and working-class nonwhites bore the brunt of job
loss and unemployment in the 1970s.

Nevertheless, many whites, who were also feeling
the economic pinch, came to resent affirmative action
programs as infringements on their rights. A growing
number of white men raised the cry of "reverse discrimination," claiming that they had been passed over

An Antibusing Confrontation in Boston
Tensions over court-ordered busing ran high in Boston in 1976. When a black lawyer tried to cross the city hall plaza during an antibusing demonstration, he became a victim of Boston's climate of racial hatred and violence. This Pulitzer Prize–winning photograph by Stanley Forman for the Boston *Herald American* shows a protester trying to impale the man with a flagstaff.
Stanley Forman.

in favor of less qualified minority group members or women. In 1978 a white man named Allan Bakke sued the University of California Medical School at Davis for rejecting him while admitting minority candidates with lesser qualifications. The Supreme Court ruling in *Bakke v. University of California* was inconclusive. Though it branded the medical school's strict quota illegal and ordered Bakke admitted, it stated that racial factors could be considered in making hiring and admission decisions, thus upholding the principle of affirmative action. But the *Bakke* decision was clearly a setback for the proponents of affirmative action, and it set the stage for subsequent efforts to eliminate those programs in the 1990s.

The Politics of Resentment

The often vociferous opposition to busing, affirmative action, gay-rights ordinances, and the Equal Rights Amendment, along with the rapidly growing anti-abortion movement, constituted a broad backlash against the social changes of the previous decade. The economic changes of the 1970s, which left many working-class and middle-class Americans with lower disposable incomes, rising prices, and higher taxes, further fueled what conservative writer Alan Crawford has termed the "politics of resentment"—a grass-roots revolt against "special-interest groups" (such as women, minorities, and gays) and growing expenditures on social welfare. Special groups and programs, conservatives believed, robbed other Americans of educational and employment opportunities and created a fiscal burden on the working and middle classes.

Although the politics of resentment most often centered on socioeconomic issues, it also took the form of local taxpayers' revolts. In 1978 California voters passed Proposition 13, a measure that reduced prop-

erty taxes and eventually undercut local governments' ability to maintain schools and other public services. Promising tax relief to middle-class homeowners and reduced funding for busing and other programs benefiting the urban poor (who were invariably viewed as nonwhite), Proposition 13 became the model for similar tax-cutting measures around the country in the late 1970s and 1980s.

Evangelical Religion. The rising popularity of evangelical religion also fueled the conservative resurgence of the 1970s. Evangelicalism, a conservative Protestant movement that emphasized strict moral codes based on the Bible and an emotional "born-again" experience, had been growing steadily since World War II under the leadership of charismatic preachers such as Billy Graham. Soon evangelical groups set up their own school systems, newspapers, and broadcasting networks. A new breed of televangelist, such as Jerry Falwell, built vast television ministries through religious programs aired on the new Christian Broadcasting Network founded by the Virginia preacher Pat Robertson.

In the 1970s, while membership in the liberal mainstream Protestant churches declined, evangelical denominations showed energetic growth. According to a Gallup poll conducted in 1976, some 50 million Americans, about a quarter of the population, were affiliated with evangelical churches. President Jimmy Carter, a member of the evangelical Southern Baptist Church, proudly proclaimed the influence of Jesus Christ in his life, as did the singers Pat Boone and Johnny Cash, the former Watergate convicts Jeb Magruder and Charles Colson, and the black-power activist Eldridge Cleaver.

The New Right. Addressing a broad range of social and cultural issues, a growing number of evangelicals

Phyllis Ellison
Busing in Boston

————————★————————

Nowhere in the North was busing more divisive than in Boston in 1974–1975. Phyllis Ellison was one of fifty-six black students from the predominantly black neighborhoods of Columbia Point and Roxbury who were assigned to South Boston High School. In this interview she describes incidents from her sophomore year, including the day a white student was stabbed by a black student during a melee at the school. The student's wound was not fatal, but the incident led to heightened resistance and recriminations.

I remember my first day going on the bus to South Boston High School. I wasn't afraid because I felt important. I didn't know what to expect, what was waiting for me up the hill. We had police escorts. I think there was three motorcycle cops and then two police cruisers in front of the bus, and so I felt really important at that time, not knowing what was on the other side of the hill.

Well, when we started up the hill you could hear people saying, "Niggers go home." There were signs, they had made a sign saying, "Black people stay out. We don't want any niggers in our school." And there were people on the corners holding bananas like we were apes, monkeys. "Monkeys get out, get them out of our neighborhood. We don't want you in our schools.". . .

You can't imagine how tense it was inside the classroom. A teacher was almost afraid to say the wrong thing, because they knew that that would excite the whole class, a disturbance in the classroom. The black students sat on one side of the classes. The white students sat on the other side of the classes. . . . In the lunchrooms . . . [it] was the same thing. . . . So really, it was separate, I mean, we attended the same school, but we really never did anything together. . . .

I remember the day Michael Faith got stabbed vividly, because I was in the principal's office and all of a sudden you heard a lot of commotion and you heard kids screaming and yelling and saying, "He's dead, he's dead. That black nigger killed him. He's dead, he's dead." And then the principal running out of the office. There was a lot of commotion and screaming, yelling, hollering, "Get the niggers at Southie." I was really afraid. And the principal came back into the office and said, Call the ambulance and tell all the black students that were in the office to stay there. A police officer was in there and they were trying to get the white students out of the building, because they had just gone on a rampage and they were just going to hurt the first black student that they saw. . . . The black students were locked in their rooms and all the white students were let go out of their classrooms. I remember us going into a room, and outside you just saw a crowd of people, I mean, just so many people, I can't even count. . . . I remember the police cars coming up the street, attempting to, and people turning over the police cars, and I was just amazed that they could do something like that. The police tried to get horses up. They wouldn't let the horses get up. They stoned the horses. They stoned the cars. And I thought that day that we would never get out of South Boston High School. . . .

Source: Henry Hampton and Steve Fayer, *Voices of Freedom: An Oral History of the Civil Rights Movement from the 1950s through the 1980s* (New York: Bantam, 1990), 600, 610, 612–613.

spoke out against abortion, busing, sex education, pornography, feminism, and gay rights. Hoping to bring these religious views to a wider public, Jerry Falwell founded the Moral Majority in 1979, a political pressure group that promoted staunch anticommunism and Christian "family values"—traditional gender roles, heterosexuality, family cohesion. Soon the extensive media and fundraising networks of the Christian right became the organizational base for a larger conservative movement known as the New Right. Using computerized mass mailing campaigns that targeted evangelical constituencies, New Right political groups such as the National Conservative Political Action Committee and the American Conservative Union mobilized thousands of followers and millions of dollars to support conservative candidates and causes.

During the 1970s conservatives were most active at the local level, building from the ground up a movement that would help elect Ronald Reagan in 1980. Lib-

Jerry Falwell

The resurgence of evangelical religion in the 1970s was accompanied by a conservative movement in politics known as the New Right. Founded in 1979 by televangelist Jerry Falwell, the Moral Majority was one of the earliest New Right groups, committed to promoting "family values" in American society and politics.

Dennis Brack/Black Star.

eral activists shared this grass-roots approach but were less effective in using modern technological tools to sustain a mass following. Among both liberals and conservatives, the dynamism of local organizing developed in the absence of effective political leadership on the national level.

From Ford to Reagan

— ★ —

In the wake of Watergate many citizens became cynical about the federal government and politicians in general. "Don't vote. It only encourages them" read one bumper sticker for the 1976 presidential campaign. Indeed, political leaders proved unable to deal with the rising inflation, stagnant growth, and declining productivity that plagued the U.S. economy in the 1970s. The fall of Saigon in 1975 reminded Americans of the failure of the nation's Vietnam policy. The world was changing, and Americans grappled with the unsettling idea that perhaps the United States would not continue to be the all-powerful country it had been for much of the postwar era. As Americans approached the 1980 election, this growing sense of impotence erupted in fury over the Iranian hostage crisis.

Ford's Caretaker Presidency

During the two years Gerald Ford held the nation's highest office, he failed to establish his legitimacy as president. His pardon of Nixon a month after taking office hurt his political credibility. Moreover, he was a less activist executive than Nixon, preferring voluntary action by the private sector over federal initiatives. Ford's hostility to government activism often put him at odds with the Democrats, who, in the wake of Watergate, increased their majorities in both houses of Congress in the 1974 elections.

Ford's biggest problem was the economy, which was reeling from inflation set in motion by the Vietnam War, rising OPEC prices, and the growing trade deficit. In an attempt to curtail prices, the Federal Reserve Board in 1974 tightened the money supply and drove up interest rates. The following year the economy entered its deepest downturn since the Great Depression. Production declined more than 10 percent, and nearly 9 percent of the work force was unemployed. Though many of the nation's economic problems were beyond the president's control, Ford's failure to take vigorous action made him appear timid and ineffective.

In foreign policy Ford was equally lacking in presidential leadership. He maintained Nixon's initiatives toward détente by asking Henry Kissinger to stay on as secretary of state, a position he had held since 1973. Ford met with Soviet leaders hoping to hammer out the details of a SALT II (Strategic Arms Limitation Talks) agreement, but he made little progress. Ford and Kissinger also continued Nixon's policy of increasing American support for the shah of Iran, ignoring the bitter opposition and anti-Western sentiment that the shah's policy of rapid modernization was provoking among Iran's growing Muslim fundamentalist population.

After the abuses of the Nixon era, Ford's genial style and candor were refreshing, but he failed to convey the assurance and competence needed in a time of mounting economic and international problems. "Gerald Ford is an awfully nice man who isn't up to the presidency," *The New Republic* concluded, and voters agreed.

Jimmy Carter: The Outsider as President

Only in the skewed political atmosphere of post-Watergate America could the Democrats have chosen their 1976 nominee, James E. Carter Jr. "Jimmy Who?" the media scoffed about this engineer and former entrepreneur in agricultural commodities from Plains, Georgia, popularly portrayed as a peanut farmer. But they soon changed their tune. Avoiding issues and controversy, Carter played up his role as a Washington outsider, pledging to restore morality to government. "I will never lie to you," he piously told voters. President Ford staved off a conservative challenge from Governor Ronald Reagan of California; then he dumped his moderate vice-president, Nelson Rockefeller, in favor of the more conservative Senator Robert J. Dole of Kansas. Carter chose as his running mate Senator Walter F. Mondale of Minnesota, who had ties to the traditional Democratic constituencies of labor, liberals, blacks, and big-city machines. Carter won the election with 50 percent of the popular vote to Ford's 48 percent.

Carter immediately tried to set a different tone for his administration. On Inauguration Day he renounced formal wear in favor of a business suit; instead of riding in a limousine, he and his wife, Rosalynn, walked from the Capitol to the White House. Throughout his term he relied heavily on symbolic gestures—staying in the homes of ordinary citizens, holding town meetings, and dressing in an informal cardigan sweater for fireside chats to the nation. But Carter's homespun approach soon wore thin as people looked for substance behind the symbols.

Ultimately Carter failed to develop an effective style of domestic leadership, a task made more difficult by the post-Watergate climate of skepticism and apathy. His outsider strategy distanced him from traditional sources of power in Washington, and he did little to heal the breach. After three years in office, Carter's chief domestic aide, Hamilton Jordan, still had not introduced himself to Thomas ("Tip") O'Neill, the Speaker of the House of Representatives and the most powerful Democrat on Capitol Hill. Shying away from established Democratic leaders, Carter turned to advisors and friends who had worked with him in Georgia, none of whom had Washington experience. When his budget director, Bert Lance, was questioned about financial irregularities at his Atlanta bank, the case undercut Carter's pledges to restore integrity and morality to the government.

Inflation was Carter's major domestic challenge. When he took office, the nation was still recovering from the severe 1975–1976 recession. Carter called for increased government spending and lower taxes, but when those actions provoked renewed inflation, he called for spending cuts and a delay in the tax reductions. This zigzag fiscal policy eroded both business

and consumer confidence. Unemployment hovered between 6 and 7 percent, and inflation rose from 6.5 percent in 1977 to 13.4 percent in 1980 (see Figure 30.2). To counter inflation, the Federal Reserve Board repeatedly raised interest rates; in 1980 they topped 20 percent, a historic high. A deep recession finally broke the inflationary spiral in 1982, a year after Carter left office.

The Carter administration expanded the federal bureaucracy in some cases while limiting its reach in others. Carter created the separate cabinet-level departments of energy and education and approved new environmental protection measures, such as a $1.6 billion "Superfund" to clean up chemical pollution sites. Through an executive order in 1978, he set aside 56 million acres in Alaska as national park and forest lands. But Carter also reformed the civil service system to streamline the federal bureaucracy, and he presided over the deregulation of the airline, trucking, and railroad industries. With deregulation, prices often dropped, but the resulting cutthroat competition drove many firms out of business and encouraged corporate consolidation. The president also unsuccessfully supported gradual decontrol of oil and natural gas prices as a spur to domestic production and conservation.

Overall, Carter's attempt to provide leadership during the energy crisis failed. He called efforts for energy conservation "the moral equivalent of war" (borrowing a phrase from the nineteenth-century philosopher William James). The media, unable to find the substance behind the rhetoric, reduced the phrase to "MEOW." In early 1979 a revolution in Iran spurred higher oil prices, and gas lines again reminded Americans of their dependence on foreign oil. That summer Carter's approval rating dropped to 26 percent, lower than Richard Nixon's at the height of the Watergate scandal.

Foreign Policy and Diplomacy. Jimmy Carter's commitment to human rights was the centerpiece of his new direction in foreign affairs. He criticized the suppression of dissent in the Soviet Union and withdrew economic and military aid from Argentina, Uruguay, Ethiopia, and other countries that violated human rights. He also established an Office of Human Rights within the State department. Unable to change the abusive policies of the Philippines, South Korea, South Africa, and other longtime U.S. allies, he did manage to raise public awareness of human rights, making it an issue that future administrations would have to address.

In Latin America, Carter's most important contribution was the resolution of the lingering dispute over control of the Panama Canal. In a treaty signed on September 7, 1977, the United States agreed to turn over control of the canal to Panama on December 31, 1999. In return, the United States retained the right to send its ships through the canal in case of war, even though

A Framework for Peace
President Jimmy Carter's greatest foreign-policy achievement was the personal diplomacy he exerted to persuade President Anwar Sadat of Egypt (left) and Prime Minister Menachem Begin of Israel (right) to sign a peace treaty in 1978. The signing of the Camp David accords marked an important first step in constructing a framework for peace in the Middle East.
Jimmy Carter Presidential Library.

the canal itself would be declared neutral territory. Despite conservatives' outcry that the United States was giving away more than it got, the Senate narrowly approved the treaty.

Although Carter had campaigned to free the United States from its "inordinate fear of Communism," relations with the Soviet Union soon became tense, largely because of problems surrounding arms limitation talks. Soviet leader Leonid Brezhnev signed SALT II in 1979, but hopes for Senate ratification of the arms control treaty collapsed when the Soviet Union invaded Afghanistan in December. In retaliation for this aggression, which Carter viewed as a threat to Middle Eastern oil supplies, the United States curtailed grain sales to the USSR and boycotted the 1980 summer Olympic Games in Moscow. (The Soviets returned the gesture by boycotting the 1984 summer games in Los Angeles.) When Carter left office in 1981, relations with the Soviet Union were worse than they had been since the 1960s.

President Carter achieved both his most stunning success and his greatest failure in the Middle East. Relations between Egypt and Israel had remained tense since the 1973 Yom Kippur War. In 1978 President Carter helped to break the stalemate by inviting Israel's prime minister, Menachem Begin, and Egyptian president Anwar Sadat to Camp David, the presidential retreat in Maryland. Two weeks of discussions and Carter's promise of significant additional foreign aid to Egypt persuaded Sadat and Begin to agree on a "framework for peace." The framework outlined in the Camp David peace accords included Egypt's recognition of Israel's right to exist and Israel's return of the Sinai peninsula, which it had occupied since 1967. The transfer of Sinai territory took place from 1979 to 1982.

The Iranian Hostage Crisis. Dramatically less successful was U.S. policy toward Iran. Ever since the CIA had helped install Muhammad Reza Pahlavi on the throne in 1953, the United States had counted on Iran as a faithful ally in the troubled Middle East. The shah was a major customer for American arms, using "petrodollars" from the sale of oil to the United States to purchase close to $20 billion worth of weapons between 1972 and 1979. Visiting Iran in late 1977, President Carter declared it "an island of stability in one of the more troubled areas of the world." Overlooking the repressive tactics of Iran's CIA-trained secret police, SAVAK, Carter followed the lead of previous Cold War policy makers for whom access to oil reserves and the shah's consistently anticommunist stance outweighed all other considerations.

Early in 1979, however, a revolution led by a fundamentalist Muslim leader, Ayatollah Ruhollah Khomeini, overthrew the shah's government and drove him into exile. The United States had ignored warning signs that the shah's efforts to westernize Iran had offended fundamentalist Islamic leaders; the CIA had also downplayed the extent to which hatred of the United States had helped coalesce opposition to the shah. In late October 1979 the Carter administration made a controversial decision to admit the deposed shah, who was suffering from incurable cancer, into the United States for medical treatment. Iran's new leaders had warned that such an action would provoke retaliation, but Henry Kissinger and other foreign policy leaders argued that the United States should assist the shah, both for humanitarian reasons and in return for his years of support for American policy. In response, on November 4, 1979, fundamentalist Muslim students under Khomeini's direction seized the U.S. Embassy in Teheran, taking American hostages in a flagrant violation of the principle of diplomatic immunity. The hostage takers demanded that the shah be returned to Iran for trial and punishment, but the United States refused. Instead President Carter suspended arms sales to Iran, froze Iranian assets in American banks, and

American Hostages in Iran
Images of blindfolded, handcuffed American hostages seized
by Iranian militants at the American embassy in Teheran in
November 1979 shocked the nation and created a foreign-
policy crisis that eventually cost Jimmy Carter the presidency.
Mingam/Liaison.

threatened to deport Iranian students in the United
States. Fifty-two hostages remained in captivity.

For the next fourteen months the Iranian hostage
crisis paralyzed the presidency of Jimmy Carter. Night
after night humiliating pictures of blindfolded hostages
appeared on television newscasts. (Media-conscious
Iranian students printed their anti-American placards
in English.) The late-night television news program
Nightline, featuring the journalist Ted Koppel, originated as "America Held Hostage," a nightly update on
the news from Iran that provided an unexpected way
for ABC to compete with Johnny Carson's *Tonight
Show*. The extensive media coverage and Carter's insistence that the hostages' safe return was his top priority
enhanced their value to their captors, but he could do
little to win their release until the Iranian government
was willing to negotiate. An attempt to mount a military rescue of the hostages failed miserably in April
1980, six months into the crisis, because of helicopter
equipment failures in the desert. Secretary of State
Cyrus Vance, who had not been informed about the rescue attempt, resigned in protest, claiming that it had
further endangered the lives of the hostages. The
abortive rescue mission reinforced the view of Carter as
bumbling and ineffective.

The Reagan Revolution

With Carter embroiled in the hostage crisis on the eve
of the 1980 presidential election, the Republicans

gained momentum by nominating former California
governor Ronald Reagan. Born in Tampico, Illinois, in
1911, Reagan won a modest reputation as a Hollywood
actor in the late 1930s and early 1940s. As president of
the Screen Actors Guild in the early 1950s, he was
deeply affected by the anticommunist crusade in Hollywood, which hastened his political metamorphosis
from New Deal Democrat to conservative Republican.
After endorsing Barry Goldwater in 1964, Reagan
entered politics, serving as governor of California from
1967 to 1975. After losing a bid for the presidency in
1976, Reagan secured the nomination easily in 1980,
choosing former CIA director George Bush as his running mate.

In the final months of the campaign, Carter took on
an embattled and defensive tone while Reagan
remained upbeat and decisive. Exploiting the hostage
issue, Reagan called the Iranians "barbarians" and
"common criminals" and hinted that he would take
strong action to win the hostages' return. At the same
time, Reagan effectively appealed to the politics of
resentment that flourished during the lean years of the
1970s. In a televised debate between the candidates,
Reagan emphasized the economic plight of working-
and middle-class Americans when he posed the rhetorical question, "Are you better off today than you were
four years ago?" Battered by inflation, unemployment,
and income stagnation, many viewers answered no.

In November, Reagan won in a landslide, with
51 percent of the popular vote to Carter's 41 percent
(Map 30.3). Riding his coattails, the Republicans won
control of the Senate for the first time since 1954,
although the Democrats maintained their hold on the
House. Voter turnout, however, was at its lowest level
since the 1920s; only 53 percent of those eligible went
to the polls, and many poor and working-class voters
stayed away. Nevertheless, the election confirmed the
growth in the power of the Republican Party since
Richard Nixon's victory in 1968.

Superior financial resources and a realignment of
the electorate contributed to the Republican resurgence of the 1970s. The political action committees that
had proliferated under the Fair Campaign Practices Act
of 1974 collected large sums for both parties, but particularly for the Republicans. While the Democratic
Party saw its key constituency—organized labor—
dwindle, the GOP's financial superiority enabled it to
make sophisticated and effective use of television and
direct mail to reach voters directly. This aggressive out-
reach helped bring about a realignment of the electorate. The core of the Republican Party that elected
Ronald Reagan remained the upper-middle-class white
Protestant voters who supported balanced budgets, disliked government activism, feared crime and communism, and believed in a strong national defense. Those
values had been the essence of postwar conservatism.
But now new groups gravitated toward the Republican

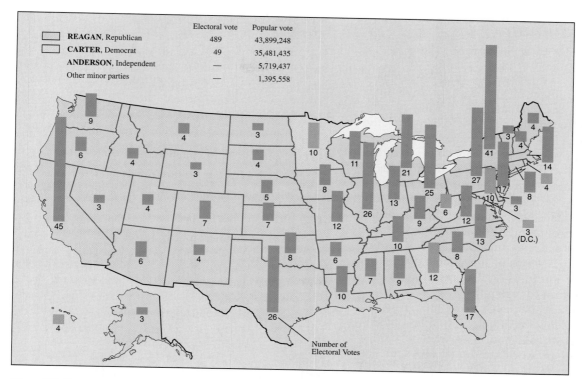

	Electoral vote	Popular vote
REAGAN, Republican	489	43,899,248
CARTER, Democrat	49	35,481,435
ANDERSON, Independent	—	5,719,437
Other minor parties	—	1,395,558

Number of Electoral Votes

MAP 30.3
The Election of 1980
Ronald Reagan defeated Democratic incumbent Jimmy Carter, winning all but six states and the District of Columbia. Winning 51 percent of the popular vote, Reagan cut deeply into the traditional Democratic coalition by wooing many southern whites, urban ethnics, and blue-collar workers. Republicans also won control of the Senate for the first time since 1954.

vision: southern whites disaffected by big government and black civil rights gains; urban ethnics who had moved to the suburbs; blue-collar workers, especially Catholics; young voters who identified themselves as conservatives; and voters in the West who had become increasingly unhappy with Jimmy Carter's policies on the environment and energy development. With the wooing of these "Reagan Democrats," the Republican Party made deep inroads into Democratic territory, eroding that party's traditional coalition of southerners, blacks, laborers, and urban ethnics.

Perhaps the most significant constituency in the Republican Party was the New Right, whose emphasis on traditional values and fundamentalist Christian morality dovetailed well with conservative Republican ideology. In 1980 New Right concerns formed the basis for the party's platform, which called for a constitutional ban on abortion, voluntary prayer in the public schools, and a mandatory death penalty for certain crimes. The Republicans also demanded an end to court-mandated busing and, for the first time in forty years, opposed the Equal Rights Amendment. A key factor in the 1980 election, the emergence of the New Right contributed to the conservative rebirth of the Republican Party under Ronald Reagan.

On January 20, 1981, at the exact moment when Carter turned over the presidency to Reagan, the Iranian government released the American hostages. After 444 days of captivity, the hostages returned home to an ecstatic patriotic welcome, a reflection of the public's frustration over their long ordeal. While most Americans continued to maintain that "We're Number One," the hostage crisis in Iran came to symbolize the loss of America's power to control world affairs. Its psychological impact was magnified because it came at the end of the decade that had witnessed Watergate, the American defeat in Vietnam, and the OPEC embargo.

To a great extent this decline in influence was magnified by the unusual predominance the United States had enjoyed after World War II, an advantage that could not realistically last forever. The return to economic and political power by Japan and Western Europe, the control of vital oil resources by Middle Eastern countries, and the industrialization of some Third World nations had widened the cast of international actors. Still, many Americans were unable to accept anything less than the economic and political supremacy of the postwar years. Ronald Reagan rode their frustrations and their hopes to victory in 1980.

Summary

★

With his election to the presidency in 1968, Richard Nixon became a harbinger of more conservative times in American social and political life. During his five years in the White House Nixon sought to trim back the welfare state through federal revenue sharing, cutbacks in Great Society antipoverty programs, and a reduced commitment to civil rights. But Nixon did not shrink from the use of executive power; he implemented wage and price controls to fight inflation, periodically impounded federal funds, and expanded the role of the government in environmental and consumer affairs. Nixon's plans, however, were cut short after his administration took part in a series of illegal acts during his campaign for reelection in 1972. The resulting Watergate scandal forced him to resign in 1974.

For much of the decade the United States struggled with economic problems, including high inflation, skyrocketing energy costs, stagnation of income, and a diminished position in world trade. A series of gas shortages during the Arab oil embargo of 1973–1974 and the Iranian revolution in 1979 had a devastating impact on American society and caused many people to question the country's voracious pattern of energy consumption.

Although many Americans became cynical about politics after Watergate and Vietnam, some continued to pursue the unfinished social agendas of the 1960s. Most notably, the environmental and women's movements showed dynamic growth and activism at the grass-roots level. Movements for consumer protection, gay and lesbian rights, and racial equality also continued to make modest gains. By the late 1970s, however, a new, more conservative social mood—based in part on the resurgence of evangelical Christianity—limited further progress on issues such as abortion rights, the Equal Rights Amendment, gay and lesbian rights, busing, and affirmative action.

On the national level ineffective political leadership by Gerald Ford led to his defeat in 1976 by Jimmy Carter of Georgia, who campaigned as a Washington outsider. Taking a high moral tone, Carter made human rights a priority of his administration and helped negotiate the Camp David peace accords between Egypt and Israel in 1978. But his own inexperience, mounting economic problems, and growing troubles abroad plagued his administration. The end of the decade was dominated by the Iranian hostage crisis, as Islamic fundamentalists held fifty-two hostages at the U.S. embassy in Teheran for 444 days. The hostage crisis virtually paralyzed Carter's presidency, helping Ronald Reagan win election in 1980.

TIMELINE

1968	Richard Nixon elected president
1970	Earth Day first observed
	Environmental Protection Agency established
1971	Pentagon Papers published
	Nixon suspends Bretton Woods system
	Swann v. Charlotte-Mecklenburg institutes busing
1972	Revenue sharing begins
	Watergate break-in; Nixon reelected
	Congress passes Equal Rights Amendment
1973	Spiro Agnew resigns; Gerald Ford appointed vice-president
	Roe v. Wade legalizes abortion
1973–1974	Arab oil embargo; gas shortages
1974	Nixon resigns; Ford becomes president and pardons Nixon
1974–1975	Busing controversy in Boston
1975–1976	Recession
1976	Jimmy Carter elected president
1978	Carter brokers Camp David accords
	Bakke v. University of California limits affirmative action
	Love Canal crisis begins
1979	Second oil crisis
	Three Mile Island nuclear accident
	Hostages seized at American embassy in Teheran, Iran
	USSR invades Afghanistan
1980	"Superfund" created to clean up chemical pollution
	Ronald Reagan elected president

Suggested Readings

───────────── ★ ─────────────

A definitive scholarly history of the 1970s has yet to be written. Peter N. Carroll's popular history, *It Seemed Like Nothing Happened* (1982), provides a general overview of the period, as do Paul Boyer's chapters on the 1970s in *Promises to Keep* (1995).

The Nixon Years

Jonathan Schell, *The Time of Illusion* (1976), offers an insightful discussion of the Nixon administration. Herbert Parmet's *Richard Nixon and His America* (1990) and Stephen Ambrose's three-volume *Nixon* (1987, 1991) are two of many biographies of a complex political leader. Kim McQuaid, *The Anxious Years: America in the Vietnam-Watergate Era* (1989), is an overview of the Nixon era. See also Garry Wills, *Nixon Agonistes* (rev. ed., 1990), and Nixon's own recollections in *RN: The Memoirs of Richard Nixon* (1978).

Stanley Kutler, *The Wars of Watergate* (1990); Anthony Lukas, *Nightmare: The Underside of the Nixon Years* (1976); and Theodore H. White, *Breach of Faith* (1975), are comprehensive accounts of the Watergate scandal. Also of interest are the books by the *Washington Post* journalists who broke the story, Carl Bernstein and Bob Woodward: *All the President's Men* (1974) and *The Final Days* (1976). Stanley Kutler, *Abuse of Power: The New Nixon Tapes* (1997), is a collection of transcripts from the White House tapes relating to Watergate and other Nixon-era scandals.

The Economic Downturn

Barry Commoner, *The Closing Circle* (1971) and *The Poverty of Power* (1976), and Robert Heilbroner, *An Inquiry into the Human Prospect* (1974), cogently assess the origins of the energy crisis and the prospects for the future. See also Lester C. Thurow, *The Zero-Sum Society* (1980), and Robert Stobaugh and Daniel Yergin, *Energy Future* (1980). Daniel Yergin, *The Prize* (1991), and John M. Blair, *The Control of Oil* (1976), treat OPEC developments.

General introductions to the economic developments of the decade are Barry Bluestone and Bennett Harrison, *The Deindustrialization of America* (1982); Richard J. Barnet and Ronald E. Muller, *Global Reach* (1974); Richard J. Barnet, *The Lean Years* (1980); John P. Hoerr, *And the Wolf Finally Came: The Decline of the Steel Industry* (1988); Robert Calleo, *The Imperious Economy* (1982); and Gardner Means et al., *The Roots of Inflation* (1975).

Reform and Reaction in the 1970s

Tom Wolfe gave the decade its name in "The Me Decade and the Third Great Awakening," *New York Magazine* (August 23, 1976). Influential books include Christopher Lasch, *The Culture of Narcissism* (1978), and Gail Sheehy, *Passages* (1976).

For a general overview of the environmental movement, see Samuel P. Hays, *Beauty, Health, and Permanence: Environmental Politics in the United States, 1955–1985* (1987). Roderick Nash provides a history of environmental ethics in *The Rights of Nature* (1989). Books that were influential in shaping public awareness of ecological issues include Rachel Carson, *Silent Spring* (1962); Paul R. Ehrlich, *The Population Bomb* (1968); Frances Moore Lappé, *Diet for a Small Planet* (1971); and Philip Slater, *Earthwalk* (1974). Lois Marie Gibbs describes her experience with the Love Canal crisis in *Love Canal: My Story* (1982). Charles McCarry chronicles Ralph Nader's crusade for consumer protection in *Citizen Nader* (1972).

On women and feminism in the 1970s, see Alice Echols, *Daring to Be Bad* (1989); Susan M. Hartmann, *From Margin to Mainstream: American Women and Politics Since 1960* (1989); and Winifred D. Wandersee, *On the Move: American Women in the 1970s* (1988). Donald G. Mathews and Jane S. De Hart analyze the struggle over the ERA in *Sex, Gender, and the Politics of ERA* (1990), and Carol Felsenthal examines the life of the ERA opponent Phyllis Schlafly in *The Sweetheart of the Silent Majority* (1981). David Garrow, *Liberty and Sexuality: The Right to Privacy and the Making of* Roe v. Wade (1994), is an in-depth examination of the 1973 abortion decision. On the public abortion debate, see Faye Ginsberg, *Contested Lives* (1989), and Kristen Luker, *Abortion and the Politics of Motherhood* (1984).

Leigh W. Rutledge surveys the gay and lesbian movement in *The Gay Decades: From Stonewall to the Present* (1992). Thomas Byrne Edsall with Mary D. Edsall, *Chain Reaction: The Impact of Race, Rights and Taxes on American Politics* (1991), examines some of the divisive social issues of the 1970s. J. Anthony Lukas, *Common Ground* (1985), tells the story of the Boston busing crisis through the biographies of three families. Paul Moreno, *From Direct Action to Affirmative Action* (1997); Robert J. Weiss, *We Want Jobs* (1997); and Lydia Chavez, *The Color Bind* (1998), treat the controversial topic of affirmative action.

Alan Crawford, *Thunder on the Right* (1980), and Peter Steinfels, *The Neo-Conservatives* (1979), survey the new conservatism. John Woodridge, *The Evangelicals* (1975), analyzes the rise of evangelical religion, and Quentin J. Schultze looks at evangelicals' use of the media in *Televangelism and American Culture* (1991). On the political role of the Christian right, see Michael Liensch, *Redeeming America: Piety and Politics in the New Christian Right* (1993).

From Ford to Reagan

John R. Greene examines the Ford administration in *The Presidency of Gerald R. Ford* (1995), as do James Cannon, *Time and Chance: Gerald Ford's Appointment with History* (1993), and Richard Reeves, *A Ford, Not a Lincoln* (1975).

Peter G. Bourne, *Jimmy Carter* (1997), is a comprehensive biography. Generally unfavorable portraits of the Carter presidency are found in Burton Kaufman, *The Presidency of James Earl Carter Jr.* (1993); Robert Shogan, *Promises to Keep* (1977); Haynes Johnson, *In the Absence of Power* (1980); and Clark Mollenhoff, *The President Who Failed* (1980). See also Erwin Hargrove, *Jimmy Carter as President* (1989); Charles Jones, *The Trusteeship Presidency* (1988); and Jimmy Carter's presidential memoirs, *Keeping Faith* (rev. ed., 1995). James Fallows, *National Defense* (1981), provides an incisive overview of defense developments. See also A. Glenn Mower Jr., *Human Rights and American Foreign Policy: The Carter and Reagan Experiences* (1987). Gary Sick, *All Fall Down: America's Tragic Encounter with Iran* (1986), provides an account of the Iranian hostage crisis, and Jack Germond, *Blue Smoke and Mirrors* (1981), examines the presidential election of 1980.

A New Domestic and World Order, *1981–1996*

O N NOVEMBER 9, 1989, millions of television viewers worldwide watched jubilant Germans swarm through the Berlin Wall after the East German government lifted all restrictions on passage between the eastern and western sectors of the city. The Berlin Wall, which had divided the city since 1961, was the foremost symbol of communist repression and the Cold War division of Europe. Over the years more than four hundred East Germans had lost their lives trying to escape to the freedom of the other side. Now East and West Berliners, young and old, danced and mingled on what remained of the structure. When the Berlin Wall came down, it brought communism's grip over Eastern Europe down with it. Soon the Soviet Union would fall to the forces of change. In 1956 Soviet premier Nikita Khrushchev had told the United States, "We will bury you." Now the tombstone read, "The Soviet Union, 1917–1991."

Just as Americans had been drawn into a web of shared national experience in the 1920s, globalization linked Americans with the rest of the world in the 1980s and 1990s. Political choices made in Washington had international economic implications, but so did decisions made in Tokyo, Beijing, Bonn, and Brussels, as the United States increasingly shared power and influence with other nations in an interconnected global economy. Paradoxically, with the collapse of the Soviet Union, the United States achieved military dominance as the world's only remaining superpower. During the Persian Gulf crisis of 1990–1991 President George Bush called for a "new world order . . . in which nations recognize the shared responsibility for freedom and injustice."

The Wall Comes Tumbling Down
The destruction of the Berlin Wall in November 1989 symbolized the end of the Cold War.
Alexandra Avakian/Woodfin Camp & Associates.

VANITY FAIR

JUNE 1985

$2.00

THE REAGAN STOMP

THEY COULD HAVE DANCED ALL NIGHT

THE SOCIAL SWIM:
William F. Buckley, Jr.
Peter Duchin
& Brooke Hayward
Ann Getty
Mortimer's

Festive Times at the Reagan White House
Since Ronald and Nancy Reagan were both former actors, perhaps they thought of Fred Astaire and Ginger Rogers (see p. 783) when they struck this pose at a White House state dinner in May 1985. Some former White House staffers now suspect that Reagan was already showing signs of early Alzheimer's disease by that point.
Photo by Harry Benson. Cover courtesy VANITY FAIR. © 1985 by Condé-Nast Publications, Inc.

As the United States struggled to redefine its role in the post–Cold War world, it faced critical challenges at home. Americans grappled with racial, ethnic, and cultural conflict; fears about the economy; and a growing disenchantment with the failure of political leaders to solve many of the nation's pressing problems. But the most far-reaching debate was over the role of the federal government in public life. The rise of the state, one of the most important developments in twentieth-century American history, was slowed and even partially reversed by Ronald Reagan's election in 1980, the presidency of George Bush, and the election of a Republican Congress in 1994. New Deal liberalism and an activist federal government were in retreat, despite the Democratic capture of the White House in 1992. In his 1996 State of the Union address, President Clinton acknowledged this new domestic order by declaring, "The era of big government is over."

The Reagan-Bush Years, 1981–1993

★

George Bush's one term as president often seems indistinguishable from the two terms of his predecessor Ronald Reagan, in part because Bush followed the basic policies of the previous administration. But Bush was also overshadowed because Reagan, though not a particularly capable president, possessed extraordinary charisma. First elected at sixty-nine, he was the oldest person ever to serve as president, yet he conveyed a sense of physical vigor. By capitalizing on his skills as an actor and a public speaker, winning the support of the emerging New Right within the Republican Party, and appealing to core American values such as family, liberty, and economic freedom, Reagan became one of the most popular presidents of the twentieth century.

Reaganomics

Since the New Deal programs of the 1930s, Americans had generally assumed that federal action could best solve the nation's social and economic problems. The election of Ronald Reagan called into question almost half a century of activism. "Government is not the solution to our problem," he declared. "Government is the problem."

Reagan's first priority was to reshape the nation's fiscal and tax policies. The term *Reaganomics* came to stand for the tax cuts and domestic budget reductions enacted in 1981 and 1982 and the controversial supply-side economic theory that lay behind them. According to this theory, high taxes siphoned capital that would otherwise be invested, stimulating economic growth. Tax cuts therefore would promote investment, causing an economic expansion that would increase tax revenues. Together with cuts in government spending, especially on entitlement programs, tax cuts would also shrink the federal budget deficit. Critics charged that conservative Republicans deliberately cut taxes to force reductions in federal funding for the social programs that they abhorred.

The first part of this economic policy—tax cuts—was enacted in the Economic Recovery Tax Act of 1981, arguably the most significant legislation of the Reagan years. This across-the-board tax cut reduced basic personal income tax rates 25 percent over three years and introduced the indexation of tax brackets, which kept tax rates constant when incomes rose solely because of inflation. The reductions were supposed to be linked to drastic cutbacks in federal expenditures. But while cuts were made in food stamps, unemployment compensation, and welfare programs such as Aid to Families with

Dependent Children (AFDC), congressional resistance kept intact the Medicare and Social Security programs, which consumed a far greater proportion of the budget.

All the money saved from the cuts in government spending—and far more—was plowed into a five-year, $1.2 trillion defense buildup. This huge increase fulfilled Reagan's campaign pledge to "make America Number One again." The B-1 bomber, which Carter had canceled, was resurrected, and the development of a new missile system, the MX, was begun. Reagan's most ambitious, and controversial, weapons plan was the 1983 Strategic Defense Initiative (SDI), popularly known as "Star Wars" from the movie of that name. SDI would be a satellite and laser shield to detect and intercept incoming missiles. Reagan supporters claimed that SDI would render nuclear war obsolete, but scientists doubted its feasibility.

Another basic tenet of Reaganomics was that many federal regulations impeded growth and productivity because of the high cost of compliance. The administration moved to abolish or reduce federal regulation of the workplace, health care, consumer protection, and the environment. Much of the responsibility, and the cost, of those activities was transferred to the states.

Meanwhile, the Federal Reserve Board chose to combat inflation, which had been high since the mid–1970s, with *monetary policy*—that is, setting interest rates and controlling the amount of money in circulation to stimulate or slow the economy as needed. By raising the interest rate for corporate borrowers, the Federal Reserve reduced inflation from 12.4 percent in 1980 to 4 percent in 1982. Unfortunately, the Fed's tightening of the money supply also brought on the "Reagan Recession" of 1981–1982, which threw some 10 million Americans out of work. The recession bottomed out in early 1983, however, and the economy began to grow. For the rest of the decade inflation stayed low, aided by a worldwide drop in energy costs. Despite limited growth of the gross national product, the Reagan administration presided over the longest peacetime economic expansion in American history to date.

If all had gone according to the administration's plan, the budget should have been balanced by 1984, but that did not happen. The increased revenue from economic growth promised by supply-side economics fell far short of expectations. Furthermore, despite what seemed like wrenching cuts in federal programs, the drop in revenues from the tax cuts was far steeper than the amount pruned from the budget, mainly because of the military buildup. Federal deficits began to balloon alarmingly.

Reagan's Second Term

During the 1984 presidential campaign, Reagan ran on the theme "It's Morning in America," suggesting that a new day of prosperity and pride was dawning. The Democrats nominated Walter Mondale, Carter's vice-president and a former Minnesota senator, to run against Ronald Reagan. With strong ties to labor unions, minority groups, and party leaders, Mondale epitomized the New Deal coalition. To appeal to women voters, he selected Representative Geraldine Ferraro of New York as his running mate, the first woman on a major party ticket. Reagan won a landslide victory, carrying the entire country except Minnesota and the District of Columbia. He did especially well among young (eighteen- to twenty-one-year-old) voters, receiving 62 percent of their support.

After a string of administrations that had ended in discord (Johnson and Vietnam), disgrace (Nixon and Watergate), or frustration (Carter and Iran), many Americans responded warmly to Reagan's confident leadership. He became known as the "Great Communicator" because of his ability to establish a rapport with the American people through the medium of television. Reagan's enormous personal popularity brought to mind that of Dwight Eisenhower in the 1950s. Also like Eisenhower's, his coattails were short: Democrats maintained control of the House and picked up two seats in the Senate; they would regain control of the Senate in 1986.

The Iran-Contra Affair. A major scandal marred Reagan's second term. In 1986 news leaked out that the administration had negotiated an arms-for-hostages deal with the revolutionary government of Iran, the same government Reagan had denounced during the 1980 hostage crisis. In an attempt to gain Iran's help in freeing American hostages held by pro-Iranian forces in Lebanon, the United States had covertly sold arms to Iran. Some of the profits generated by the arms sales were diverted by the Central Intelligence Agency as military aid to the Contras, counterrevolutionaries in Nicaragua, whom the administration supported over the popularly elected communist regime of the Sandinistas.

The covert diversion of funds, an action both illegal and unconstitutional, was the brainstorm of Marine Lieutenant Colonel Oliver North, a National Security Council aide at the time. After the American press picked up the story, North shredded hundreds of documents but missed a key memo that linked the White House to the plan. Congress investigated the mounting scandal in 1986 and 1987, but White House officials testifed that the president knew nothing about the diversion. Ronald Reagan's defense remained simple and consistent: "I don't remember."

The scandal bore many similarities to Watergate, including the possibility that the president had acted illegally and unconstitutionally, but this time there were no significant calls for impeachment. Early in Reagan's administration, one of his critics had coined the phrase "Teflon presidency" to describe Reagan—bad news didn't stick; it just rolled off. Reagan weathered "Iran-Contragate," but the scandal did weaken his presidency.

Reagan Legacies. The president proposed no bold domestic policy initiatives in his last two years in office. Reagan had come into office promising to dismantle an intrusive federal bureaucracy, reduce federal entitlement programs, and give free-market forces greater scope in the economy. During his two terms Reagan reordered the priorities of the federal government but failed to reduce its size or scope. Although spending for most poverty programs was cut, Social Security and other entitlement programs remained untouched. Despite Reagan's failure to achieve his goals, his spending cuts and antigovernment rhetoric shaped the terms of political debate for the rest of the century.

One of Reagan's most significant legacies was his conservative judicial appointments, the area where the New Right had the greatest impact on his administration. In 1981 he nominated Sandra Day O'Connor to the Supreme Court, the first woman ever to serve, and in his second term he appointed two more justices, Antonin Scalia and Anthony Kennedy. Justice William Rehnquist, a noted conservative appointed by Nixon, was elevated to Chief Justice in 1986. Under Rehnquist's leadership the Court, often by a 5-to-4 mar-

Patriotism and Politics
At a confetti parade for the 1988 Summer Olympic team held at Disneyland, California, in September 1988, Republican presidential candidate George Bush and his wife Barbara bask in the glow of America's success.
Cynthia Johnson. © TIME Magazine.

gin, chipped away at the Warren Court's legacy in decisions on individual liberties, affirmative action, and the rights of criminal defendants.

Ironically, for a president who had promised to balance the budget by 1984, Reagan's largest legacy was the national debt, which tripled during his two terms from the combined effects of increased military spending, tax reductions for high-income taxpayers, and Congress's refusal to approve deep cuts in domestic programs (Figure 31.1). In 1989 the national debt stood at $2.8 trillion, more than $11,000 for every American citizen.

The nation was also running an annual deficit in its trade with other nations. Exports had been falling since the 1970s, when American products began to encounter increasing competition in world markets. In the early 1980s the high exchange rate for dollars made U.S. goods more expensive for foreign buyers and imports more affordable for Americans. The budget and trade deficits contributed to a major shift in 1985: for the first time since 1915 the United States was a debtor rather than a creditor nation. Since then, with phenomenal speed, the United States has accumulated the world's largest foreign debt.

Another Barrier Falls
In 1981 Sandra Day O'Connor (shown here with Chief Justice Warren Burger) became the first woman appointed to the Supreme Court. In 1993 she was joined by Ruth Bader Ginsburg.
Fred Ward/Black Star.

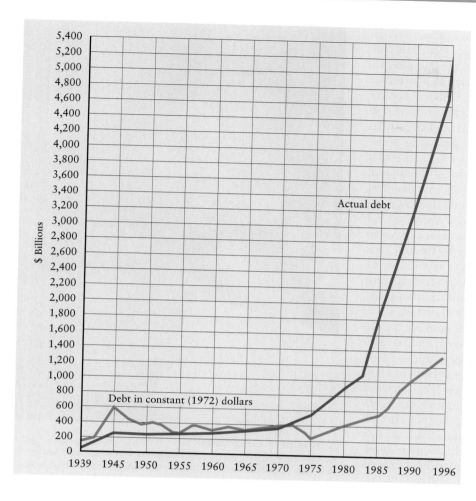

$ Billions

Debt in constant (1972) dollars

Actual debt

1939 1945 1950 1955 1960 1965 1970 1975 1980 1985 1990 1996

FIGURE 31.1
***The Escalating Federal Debt,
1939–1996***
The federal debt, which soared during
World War II, remained fairly stable
until the huge annual deficits of the
1980s. Deficits remained high in the
1990s, but political pressure to balance
the budget promised reductions in the
national debt.
Source: U.S. Statistical Abstract, 1997.

The Bush Presidency

George Herbert Walker Bush was a loyal vice-president
but did not share all of Reagan's conservative views.
Bush won the Republican nomination in 1988 by beating back challenges from Senate minority leader
Robert Dole, television evangelist Pat Robertson, and
congressional representative Jack Kemp. Bush's choice
for vice-president, young conservative Indiana senator
Dan Quayle, who had used family connections to avoid
service in Vietnam, added little to the ticket. In the
Democratic primaries, the contest was between Governor Michael Dukakis of Massachusetts and the charismatic civil rights leader Jesse Jackson, whose populist
Rainbow Coalition embraced the diversity of Democratic constituencies. Dukakis, a somewhat bland figure
known for a technocratic approach to state government, received the party's nomination and chose Senator Lloyd Bentsen of Texas as his running mate.

The 1988 campaign had a harsh cast to it, with negative commercials and televised "sound bites" replacing
meaningful discussion of the issues. The sound bite
"Read My Lips: No New Taxes," drawn from Bush's
acceptance speech at the Republican convention,
became that party's campaign mantra. In a television

ad featuring a mug shot of Willie Horton, a black man
convicted of murder who had killed again while on
parole from a Massachusetts prison, Republicans pan-
dered to voters' racist fears and implied that Dukakis
was soft on crime. Forced on the defensive, Dukakis
failed to mount an effective counterattack. Bush carried thirty-eight states, winning the popular vote
53.4 percent to 45.6 percent.

Domestic and Economic Policy. A key issue during
Bush's four years as president was the economy. His campaign promise of a "kinder, gentler administration" was
doomed by his predecessor's economic policies, especially the budget deficit, which had peaked at $221 billion
in 1986 before leveling off. The Gramm-Rudman Balanced Budget Act, passed in 1985, had mandated automatic cuts if budget targets were not met in 1991. Facing
the prospect of a halt in nonessential government services and the layoff of thousands of government employees, Congress froze annual outlays for discretionary
spending and initiated one of the largest tax increases in
history. Bush's failure to keep his "no new taxes" promise
earned him the undying enmity of Republican conservatives, who saw it as a betrayal of Reaganomics, and

dramatically hurt his chances for reelection in 1992. In the long run, however, the 1990 budget deal laid the groundwork for the balanced budgets of the late 1990s.

Changing federal spending priorities had a direct impact on state and local governments. Under Reagan's New Federalism, states and localities had been forced to take over some federal programs entirely and cope with cuts in federal grants for many others, including housing, education, transportation, public works, and social services. Federal-state programs such as Medicaid, whose costs soared in the 1970s and 1980s as a result of inflation and higher demand, accounted for increasingly large parts of state budgets, as did spending for welfare, education, and prisons. State and local governments could balance their budgets only by finding new sources of revenue (thus risking taxpayer revolts) or by reducing spending and services. Fiscal conditions were especially bad in the Northeast, but California and several midwestern states also faced severe shortfalls.

A recession that began in 1990 further eroded state and local tax revenues. Incomes decreased, and poverty increased sharply. In 1991 unemployment approached 7 percent nationwide; state and local governments laid off workers to save money even as they faced greater demands for social services and unemployment compensation. Industrial and white-collar layoffs spread, and in many American families someone had already lost a job or feared that a layoff might happen soon. Recovery was slowed by the massive federal debt, overburdened state and local governments, and decreasing consumer confidence.

The Savings and Loan Crisis.   Another drag on the economy was the collapse of the savings and loan industry. The scandal had its roots in decisions made during the Reagan administration, but its full impact was felt only after Bush took office.

Savings and loan associations (S & Ls), also called "thrifts," invested depositors' savings in home mortgages. Since 1934 deposits in S & Ls had been insured by the Federal Savings and Loan Insurance Corporation (FSLIC). After S & Ls complained in 1982 that high inflation and soaring interest rates were reducing their profits, Reagan's deregulation program permitted them to invest in commercial real estate and businesses. The real-estate market boomed for most of the 1980s, so the loans and investments were profitable. But when construction and the oil boom in the Southwest slowed and the stock market tumbled sharply in 1987, savings and loan associations' losses mounted, and the value of their assets plummeted. Some S & Ls were taken over by commercial banks, but many simply went bankrupt, forcing the federal government to make good its guarantee to depositors. To recoup some of the massive losses, the Bush administration set up a temporary agency in 1989 to sell the remaining assets—primarily defaulted real estate. It took the Resolution Trust Cor-

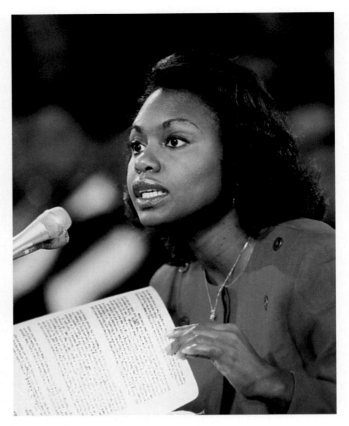

A Woman of Conscience
Accusations by University of Oklahoma law professor Anita Hill that Supreme Court nominee Clarence Thomas had sexually harassed her sparked fierce debate. Many felt that had there been more women in the Senate, Hill's charges would have been treated more seriously. After the 1992 election, women's representation did in fact increase to six women in the Senate and forty-seven in the House of Representatives.
Markel/Gamma Liaison.

poration six years to clean up the mess, at a total cost to American taxpayers of $150 billion.

Supreme Court Conservatism.   During the Bush administration, the Supreme Court continued to move away from liberal activism toward a more conservative stance, especially on the issue of abortion. The 1989 *Webster v. Reproductive Health Services* decision permitted states to restrict abortion, and the next year, in *Rust v. Sullivan*, the Court upheld a federal regulation barring personnel at federally funded health clinics from discussing abortion with their clients. In 1992, in *Planned Parenthood v. Casey*, the Court upheld a Pennsylvania law mandating informed consent and a twenty-four-hour waiting period before an abortion could be performed. But the justices also reaffirmed the "essential holding" of *Roe v. Wade:* women had a constitutional right to abortion.

In 1990 David Souter, a little known federal judge from New Hampshire who appealed to Bush because he had not taken a stand on abortion, easily won confirmation to the Supreme Court. But the next year a major controversy erupted over Bush's nomination of Clarence Thomas, a black conservative with little judicial experience. Just as Thomas's confirmation hearings were drawing to a close, a former colleague, Anita Hill, testified publicly that Thomas had sexually harassed her in the early 1980s. After widely watched (and widely debated) televised testimony by both Thomas and Hill before the all-male Senate Judiciary Committee, the Senate confirmed Thomas by a narrow margin. In the wake of the hearings, national polls confirmed the pervasiveness of sexual harassment on the job: four out of ten women said they had been the object of unwanted sexual advances from men in the workplace.

Foreign Relations under Reagan and Bush

★

The collapse of détente late in the Carter administration, after the Soviet Union's invasion of Afghanistan, underlay Ronald Reagan's confrontational approach toward the Soviet Union and inspired the major defense buildup that occurred during his first term. Backed by Republican hard-liners, and determined to reduce communist influence in developing nations, Reagan articulated some of the harshest anti-Soviet rhetoric since the 1950s. In 1983 he went so far as to call the Soviet Union an "evil empire." The collapse of the Soviet Union in 1991 removed that nation as a credible threat, but new post–Cold War challenges quickly appeared.

Third World Interventions and a Soviet Thaw

Despite Reagan's rhetoric, not all of his international problems involved U.S.-Soviet confrontations. In 1983, after Israel invaded Lebanon, anti-Israeli Muslim fundamentalists bombed the U.S. Embassy in Beirut. A second bombing killed 239 U.S. Marine peacekeepers barracked in the city. Around the world, terrorist assassins struck down Prime Minister Indira Gandhi in India and President Anwar Sadat in Egypt. But it was airplane hijackings and countless terrorist incidents in the Middle East that led Reagan to order air strikes against one highly visible source of terrorism, Muammar Khadafy of Libya.

The administration reserved its most concerted attention for Central America, however. Halting what was seen as the spread of communism in that region became practically an obsession. In El Salvador it supported a repressive right-wing regime that was fighting against leftists. In 1983 Reagan ordered U.S. Marines to

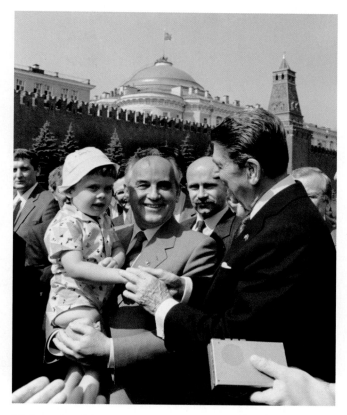

Sightseeing in Moscow
Just five years after calling the Soviet Union an "evil empire," Ronald Reagan poses for a photo with Soviet premier Mikhail Gorbachev in front of Moscow's St. Basil Cathedral in May 1988. The incongruity of consummate cold warrior Ronald Reagan in Red Square was on a par with the sight of Richard Nixon strolling along the Great Wall of China in 1972.
Joe Marquette.

invade the tiny Caribbean island of Grenada, claiming that its Cuban-supported communist regime posed a threat to other states in the region.

Reagan's top priority, however, was to overthrow the communist-led Sandinista government in Nicaragua. In 1981 the United States suspended aid to Nicaragua, charging that the Sandinistas, along with Cuba and the Soviet Union, were supplying arms to the rebels in El Salvador, which the Sandinistas denied. At the same time, the CIA began to provide extensive covert support to Nicaragua's opposition forces, known as the Contras, whom Reagan called "freedom fighters." Wary of the assumption of unconstitutional powers by the executive branch, Congress responded in 1984 by passing the Boland Amendment, which banned the CIA or any other intelligence agency from providing military support to the Contras—a provision violated in the Iran-Contra affair, the greatest crisis of Reagan's presidency.

Surprisingly, given Reagan's rhetoric, his second term brought a reduction in tension with the Soviet Union. In 1985 Reagan met the new Soviet premier, Mikhail Gorbachev, in Geneva in the first superpower

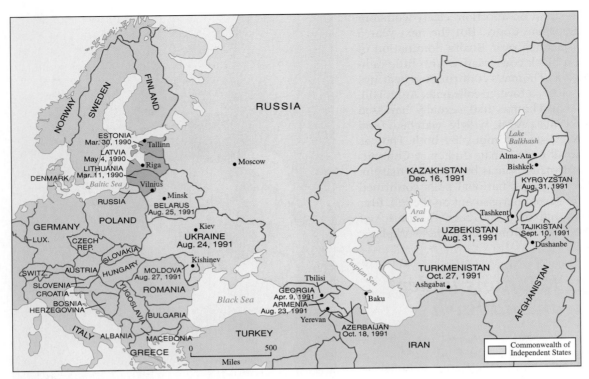

MAP 31.1

The Collapse of Communism in Eastern Europe and the Soviet Union
The end of the Soviet empire in Eastern Europe and the collapse of communism in the
Soviet Union itself dramatically changed the borders of Europe and Central Asia. West
and East Germany reunited, while the nations of Czechoslovakia and Yugoslavia, created
by the 1919 Versailles treaty, divided into smaller states. The old Soviet Union produced
fifteen new countries, of which eleven remained loosely bound in the Commonwealth of
Independent States (CIS).

summit meeting since 1979. They met again the following year in Reykjavik, Iceland. In December 1987
Reagan and Gorbachev agreed at a Washington summit
to eliminate all intermediate-range missiles based in
Europe. The agreement marked the first time an existing
category of weapons was scrapped, and it was the most
significant postwar disarmament decision since the 1972
SALT I agreement. Although a fourth summit in Moscow
in April 1988 produced no further cuts in nuclear arms,
the sight of the two first families attending the Bolshoi
Ballet together and strolling amiably in Red Square
demonstrated the new cordial relationship between the
former rivals. When the Soviets announced soon afterward that they were withdrawing from Afghanistan,
prospects for cooperation appeared to be even brighter.

The End of the Cold War

For years American policy makers had warned about the
"domino" effect of countries falling to communism. Now
the domino effect was unexpectedly working in the opposite direction. In 1989 the grip of communism on Eastern
Europe loosened and then let go completely in a series of

mostly nonviolent "velvet revolutions" (the phrase came
from Czech leader Vaclav Havel) that climaxed in the
destruction of the Berlin Wall in November. Soon the
Soviet Union itself succumbed to the forces of change.

The background for those dramatic upheavals lay in
changes set in motion by the Soviet leader Mikhail Gorbachev after 1985. His policies of *glasnost* (openness)
and *perestroika* (economic restructuring) signaled a willingness to tolerate significant changes in the Soviet bloc
and in Soviet relationships with the rest of the world.
But the Soviet leader, always more popular outside his
country than at home, found it easier to call for the dismantling of the old system than to build something new.

On August 19, 1991, alarmed Soviet military leaders seized Gorbachev and attempted unsuccessfully to
oust him. The failure of the coup broke the grip of the
Communist Party over the Soviet Union. Lithuania had
declared its independence in March 1990, and now the
Baltic republics of Latvia and Estonia followed suit. In
December the Union of Soviet Socialist Republics formally dissolved itself to make way for the eleven-
member Commonwealth of Independent States (CIS)
(Map 31.1). Gorbachev resigned, and the charismatic

reform leader Boris Yeltsin, president of the new state of Russia—the largest and most populous republic—became the preeminent leader in the region.

The suddenness of the collapse of the Soviet Union and the end of the Cold War stunned America and the rest of the world. For more than forty years the United States had been locked in an ideological battle with its archenemy, the Soviet Union. American citizens had endured fear of nuclear annihilation, anticommunist witch-hunts, and secret radiation experiments. During the Cold War the United States spent some $4 trillion on nuclear weapons alone. Republicans claimed that Reagan's military buildup had caused the Soviet Union to collapse, but George Kennan—the only original architect of containment still alive—disagreed: "Nobody—no country, no party, no person—'won' the cold war." According to Kennan (and many other observers), both sides paid a heavy price.

The director of the Central Intelligence Agency summed up the dilemma of forging a post–Cold War foreign policy: "We have slain a large dragon, but we live now in a jungle filled with a bewildering variety of poisonous snakes. And in many ways, the dragon was easier to keep track of." Instead of superpower confrontations, violence often arose from regional conflicts over ethnicity, religion, and nationalism, such as in Bosnia, the former Yugoslavia, after 1991. As the only military superpower, the United States was often asked to wield its still enormous influence in the void left by the collapse of communism. Far from receding as the Cold War ended, American military and political leadership seemed even more necessary in the new world order.

War in the Persian Gulf, 1990–1991

The first new challenge arose in the Middle East. On August 2, 1990, Iraq invaded Kuwait. Saddam Hussein's brutal conquest of his oil-rich neighbor took American policy makers by surprise (see Voices from Abroad, "Saddam Hussein: Calling for a Holy War against the United States," p. 1014). President Bush orchestrated broad international support for a series of United Nations Security Council resolutions condemning Iraq, calling for its withdrawal from Kuwait, and imposing an embargo and trade sanctions. The United Nations was finally working the way its Dumbarton Oaks planners had hoped, in large part because superpower tensions had abated with the end of the Cold War.

When Saddam Hussein showed no signs of complying with the resolutions, Bush prodded the United Nations to create a legal framework for an international military offensive against the man he repeatedly called "the butcher of Baghdad." In November the Security Council voted to use force if Iraq did not withdraw from Kuwait by January 15. In early January, Congress debated whether to give sanctions more time

Women at War
Women played key and visible roles in the Persian Gulf War, comprising approximately 10 percent of the American troops. Increasing numbers of women are choosing military careers, despite widespread reports of sexual harassment and other forms of discrimination.
Luc Delahaye/SIPA Press.

to work, and then, in a 52-to-48 vote, the Senate authorized military action. On January 16, President Bush announced to the nation that "the liberation of Kuwait has begun."

The American commitment of 540,000 troops matched the number at the height of the Vietnam War in 1968. But this was a new, all-volunteer military that included thousands of reservists called up from civilian jobs. Blacks and members of other minorities, many attracted to military service by benefits such as education and health care, made up a third of the force. Women, accounting for approximately 10 percent of the troops, were a far greater presence than in Vietnam, although they served in support, not direct combat, positions.

The forty-two-day war was a resounding success for the coalition forces, which, as in the Korean War, were predominantly American. In a series of well-orchestrated briefings, General Colin Powell, chairman of the Joint Chiefs of Staff, and the commanding general, H. Norman Schwarzkopf, projected a confident new image for the post-Vietnam military. The air-land strategy of "Operation Desert Storm" began with a month of air strikes to crush communications, destroy armaments, and pummel the morale of the Iraqi troops, followed by a ground offensive against Iraqi troops in Kuwait and southern Iraq. The ground phase

VOICES FROM ABROAD

SADDAM HUSSEIN

Calling for a Holy War against the United States

————★————

After Iraq invaded Kuwait in August 1990, President Saddam Hussein of Iraq justified the action in the language of Jihad, Muslim holy war. Hussein's call for a holy war against the United States suggested the ways in which Islamic fundamentalism had become part of the larger political discourse of the Arab world, particularly in political relations with Western nations.

This great crisis started on the 2d of August, between the faithful rulers and presidents of these nations—the unjust rulers who have abused everything that is noble and holy until they are now standing in a position which enables the devil to manipulate them. This is the great crisis of this age in this great part of the world where the material side of life has surpassed the spiritual one and the moral one. . . . This is the war of right against wrong and is a crisis between Allah's teachings and the devil.

Allah the Almighty has made his choice—the choice for the fighters and the strugglers who are in favor of principles, God has chosen the arena for this crisis to be the Arab World, and has put the Arabs in a progressive position in which the Iraqis are among the foremost. And to confirm once more the meaning that God taught us ever since the first light of faith and belief, which is that the arena of the Arab world is the arena of the first belief and

Arabs have always been an example and a model for belief and faith in God Almighty and are the ones who are worthy of true happiness.

It is now your turn, Arabs, to save all humanity and not just save yourselves, and to show the principles and meanings of the message of Islam, of which you are all believers and of which you are all leaders.

It is now your turn to save humanity from the unjust powers who are corrupt and exploit us and are so proud of their positions, and these are led by the United States of America. . . .

For, as we know out of a story from the Holy Koran, the rulers, the corrupt rulers, have always been ousted by their people for it is a right on all of us to carry out the holy jihad, the holy war of Islam, to liberate the holy shrines of Islam. While the ruler of Saudi Arabia called himself the custodian of the two holy shrines, while in fact he is an agent, for he has given away his land to the foreigners.

We call upon all Arabs, each according to his potentials and capabilities within the teachings of Allah and according to the Muslim holy war of jihad, to fight this U.S. presence of non-believers and to fight the stance taken by the Arab agents who have followed these foreigners. And we hail the people of Saudi Arabia who are being fooled by their rulers, as well as the people of dear Egypt, as well as all the people of the Arab nations who are not of the same position as their leaders, and they believe in their pride and their sovereignty over their land. We call on them to revolt against their traitors, their rulers, and to fight foreign presence in the holy lands. And we support them, and more important, that God is with them.

Source: New York Times, September 6, 1990, A19.

---

of the war was launched on February 23; within days thousands of Iraqi troops fled or surrendered, and the fighting quickly ended (Map 31.2). Saddam Hussein remained firmly in power, however, with his arsenal of weapons of mass destruction intact, despite his promise to remove all biological, chemical, and nuclear arms and allow United Nations inspectors to verify their destruction.

The rapid success of the ground war and relief at the amazingly low number of U.S. casualties (145 Americans killed in action, a stark contrast to the high Iraqi civilian and military casualties) produced a euphoric reaction at home. For many, the stellar performance of American troops banished the ghost of Vietnam, the antimilitary malaise resulting from that prolonged, inconclusive, and divisive war. "By God,

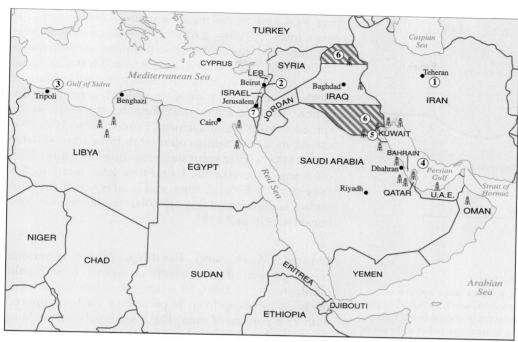

1. Teheran hostage taking, Nov.1979–Jan.1981
2. 241 U.S. peacekeeping troops die in bombing, Oct. 1983.
3. U.S. air strikes, Mar.–Apr. 1986.
4. U.S. Navy shoots down Iranian airliner, July 1988.
5. Operation Desert Storm (Gulf War) Jan.-Feb. 1991.
6. U.S. declares "no-fly zones" in northern and southern Iraq, 1992.
7. U.S. brokers Israeli-Palestinian peace treaty, May 1994.

 Oil fields

MAP 31.2

U.S. Involvement in the Middle East, 1980–1994

The United States has long played an active role in the Middle East, pursuing the twin goals of protecting Israel's security and ensuring a reliable supply of low-cost oil from the Persian Gulf states. By far the largest intervention came in 1991, when, under United Nations auspices, President Bush sent 540,000 American troops to liberate Kuwait from Iraq. The United States also played a major role in the 1994 agreement allowing for Palestinian self-rule in the Gaza Strip and parts of the West Bank.

we've kicked the Vietnam Syndrome once and for all," gloated George Bush. The president's approval rating shot up precipitously, but it declined almost as quickly when the continuing recession showed that the easy victory had masked the country's serious economic problems. One consumer observed, "The country is feeling good about the war, I'm feeling good about it, but I still can't afford a new car."

Uncertain Times

★

Opinion polls taken in the early 1990s showed that Americans were deeply concerned about the future— their own and their children's. Americans were also concerned about crime in the streets, terrorism from abroad, increases in poverty and homelessness, the decline of the inner cities, illegal immigration, the environment, the failure of public schools, the unresolved abortion issue, and AIDS. But above all they worried about their own economic security and

whether they would be able to keep their jobs in an era of global competition. These fears persisted despite the fact, which became increasingly clear as the 1990s progressed, that the U.S. economy remained the strongest in the world.

The Economy

Slow growth in productivity and growing inequality in income distribution were the most salient economic trends in the 1980s and 1990s. From the late nineteenth century through World War II, productivity grew at an average of about 1.8 percent per year, enough to double living standards every forty years. From 1945 to 1973 productivity grew 2.8 percent annually, allowing the standard of living to double in one generation. In the quarter-century since 1973, however, productivity increased less than 1 percent annually, barely enough to double the standard of living in eighty years.

Along with slowed productivity went stagnating real income (Figure 31.2). Adjusted for inflation, the wages of the typical, or median, family basically stayed the same. In 1991 the typical family's real income was

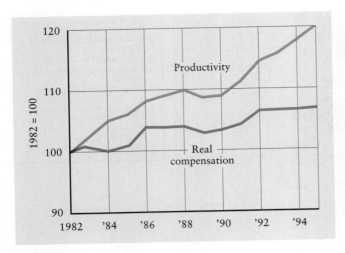

FIGURE 31.2
Productivity and Wages, 1982–1995
Usually as productivity increases, so does labor's share of national income. In the 1990s, however, workers failed to reap the rewards of the increased productivity shown here. Labor's relative loss in real compensation in turn contributed to a rise in corporate profits.
Source: New York Times, January 2, 1996, C20. Copyright © 1996 by The New York Times Co. Reprinted by permission.

ing jobs kept shrinking. For many—one-fifth of the work force in 1994—part-time or temporary work was the only work available (these positions are sometimes called "McJobs," a reference to jobs at McDonald's and other fast-food outlets). Moreover, in the 1980s and 1990s the downsizing trend, in which companies deliberately shed permanent workers to cut wage costs, spread to middle management. From 1980 to 1995 IBM shrank its mostly white-collar work force from 400,000 to 220,000, a 45 percent decrease. Although most laid-off managers eventually found new jobs, many took a large pay cut. Federal, state, and local governments also scaled back, eliminating 454,000 public service jobs between 1979 and 1993.

Women, Work, and Families. These economic trends put even more pressure on women to seek paid employment. In 1996, 59.1 percent of women were in the labor force (up from 38 percent in 1962), compared with 75.8 percent of men. The traditional nuclear family of employed father, homemaker wife, and children was found in less than 15 percent of U.S. households. Married working women and single or divorced working women with children continued to bear the major share of household and child-care responsibilities. For working parents with children, family schedules were often as intricate as time-and-motion studies.

While business leaders and the media often focused on the breakthroughs made by women near the top of the corporate ladder, one of every five working women still held a clerical or secretarial job—the same proportion as in 1950. Women's pay lagged behind men's, and the gap was especially wide for black and Latino women. Yet women continued to make inroads in male-dominated fields. Among all workers under age thirty-five, women accounted for one in three doctors, four in ten mail carriers, and a majority of purchasing agents.

only 5 percent higher than it had been in 1973, and that increase was achieved mainly because Americans were working more hours and because multiple members of a household were employed.

At the same time that wage stagnation was squeezing the middle class, economic inequality increased: the rich got richer, the poor got poorer, and the middle class shrank. By 1996 the United States was the most economically stratified industrial nation in the world. Instead of the broadly based prosperity of the immediate postwar years, statistics from the Congressional Budget Office showed that the richest 1 percent of American families reaped most of the gains of Reaganomics. This trend continued in the 1990s: in 1996, according to a *Business Week* study, the pay of top executives was 209 times that of a factory employee, a pay gap double what it had been five years earlier. Even relatively well-advantaged Americans felt a sense of diminished expectations. Earlier generations had aspired to doing better than their parents financially; now many young adults wondered whether they could achieve even a modest middle-class life-style.

These diminished expectations stemmed in part from changes in the job market. By the end of the twentieth century, the average employee could typically expect to make several job or career shifts over the course of a lifetime. Following an established pattern, the number of minimum-wage service jobs continued to grow, while the number of union-protected manufactur-

Corporate Strategies. Another major cause of diminished economic expectations in the 1980s and early 1990s was the widespread fear that American corporations were no longer competitive in the global marketplace. Americans viewed with alarm the economic success of Germany and Japan, the growing U.S. trade deficit, and the infusion of foreign investment money into the United States. In order to compete, American corporations adopted new technologies, including microelectronics, biotechnology (see New Technology, "The Biotech Revolution," pp. 1018–1019), computers, and robots, and by the mid-1990s they saw their former competitiveness begin to return. For example, Bethlehem Steel, which invested $6 billion to modernize its operations between 1989 and 1997, doubled its productivity.

Other firms retooled their corporate vision. In 1980–1981 Ford Motor Company lost $2.5 billion, despite laying off 150,000 workers. In the face of this desperate situation, Ford shifted its focus from maximizing output to improving quality and consumer satisfaction, making assembly-line workers more involved in the company and its products by giving them more responsibility. The popular Ford Taurus, introduced in 1986, typified the new focus on quality.

While management struggled to improve productivity, the labor movement—hurt by downsizing, foreign competition, fear of layoffs, government hostility during the Reagan-Bush years, and its own failure to organize unskilled workers—continued to decline. The number of union members dropped from 20 million in 1978 to 16.3 million in 1996, representing only 14.5 percent of the labor force. Although union membership was more than one-third female and one-fifth black, union leadership remained overwhelmingly white and male.

An Increasingly Pluralistic Society

The 1990 census counted 246.9 million Americans, an increase of over 22 million people since the 1980 census. In 1996, the United States had a population of 265.5 million people, one-fourth of whom claimed African, Asian, Hispanic, or American Indian ancestry. The main reason for the growth in population was increased immigration, especially from Latin America and Asia (Maps 31.3 and 31.4). In 1994, 8.7 percent of the U.S. population was foreign-born, almost double the 4.8 percent of 1970 and the highest proportion since World War II. This level, however, was still far below its modern historic high of 14.7 percent in 1910, after the great tide of early twentieth-century immigration.

In the 1980s over 7 million immigrants entered the country, accounting for more than a third of the population growth in that decade. LAX and JFK, the Los Angeles and New York international airports, were the main points of entry, replacing Ellis Island, which, after decades of abandonment and decay, was turned into a museum and tourist attraction. The first major immigration legislation since 1965, the 1986 Immigration Reform and Control Act (Simpson-Mazzoli Act), attempted to establish a fair entry process. It also granted legal status to some illegal aliens, primarily Mexicans and other Latinos, who had entered the United States before 1982. Revisions to the law in 1990 expanded the quota of immigrants to 700,000 per year and gave priority to skilled workers and relatives of current residents.

Hispanic Immigration. Much of the new immigration came from Latin America and the Caribbean. In 1950 there were 4 million Hispanics in the United States; in 1996 the number was 28.3 million. The terms *Hispanic* and *Latino*, which include Spanish-speaking people from Mexico, Cuba, Puerto Rico, El Salvador,

and other Latin American countries, refer to a variety of distinctive heritages. Hispanics are the second largest minority group after blacks and the second fastest growing after Asians. Western states such as California, Texas, and New Mexico, which border Mexico, originally contained the most immigrants, but in the postwar period new arrivals from Puerto Rico and Central and South America increasingly settled on the East Coast. Latinos now live in urban areas throughout the country, making up more than one-tenth of the populations of Florida and New York, for example.

Asian Americans. Asia was the other major source of immigrants. This migration, which increased almost 108 percent from 1980 to 1990, consisted mainly of people from China, the Philippines, Vietnam, Laos, Cambodia, Korea, India, and Pakistan. Chinese Americans are still the dominant Asian group in the United States, followed by Filipinos. In 1990 California had more Asian Americans—almost 10 percent of the population—than did any other state.

Some of this immigration was traceable to upheavals in Southeast Asia. More than 700,000 Indochinese refugees entered the country in the decade after American involvement in Vietnam ended in 1975. The first arrivals were highly educated people, who, after a few years, generally achieved economic success. Many of the later refugees came with less education

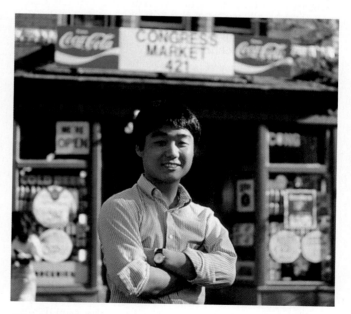

New Immigrants
In the 1980s many Korean immigrants got their start by opening small grocery stores in urban neighborhoods. Their success sometimes led to conflicts with other racial groups, such as blacks and Hispanics, who were often their customers as well as competitors.
Kay Chernush/The Image Bank.

The Biotech Revolution

★

W AS ZACHARY TAYLOR poisoned? Did Abraham Lincoln have a rare disease called Marfan's syndrome? Were Tzar Nicholas II and his family executed during the Bolshevik Revolution in 1918? Was the Vietnam serviceman buried in Arlington Cemetery's Tomb of the Unknowns really Air Force Lieutenant Michael Blassie? Recent advances in DNA testing, part of the dramatic growth in biotechnology in the 1980s and 1990s, mean that these historical questions, plus a host of contemporary ones, can be answered. With promises of breakthroughs in medicine (gene therapy and cancer research), the environment (genetically altered microorganisms for pollution cleanup), and agriculture (genetically engineered foods), biotechnology offers the possibility not just to understand but also to manipulate the processes of life.

The essence of biotechnology is exploiting genes, a process revolutionized by the 1953 discovery of DNA by scientists James Watson and Francis Crick. DNA (deoxyribonucleic acid) is the molecule that carries the genetic blueprint of all living things; genes are DNA chains made up of hundreds or some-

Cracking the Genetic Code
A researcher enters DNA sequences into a computer as part of the effort to map the human genome.
© J. Griffin/The Image Works.

and fewer skills and struggled for a foothold. When the Cambodian population in the former textile town of Lowell, Massachusetts, increased from 3,500 in 1985 to 20,000 just three years later, the school system struggled to find bilingual teachers fluent in Khmer, the Cambodian language.

The new immigrants' impact on the social, economic, and cultural landscape of the country has been tremendous. In many places they have created thriving ethnic communities, such as Little Saigon in Orange County, California; Little Havana in Miami; and Koreatown in Los Angeles. Tens of thousands of Soviet Jews fleeing religious and political persecution in the 1980s

created Little Odessa in Brooklyn, New York. Ethnic restaurants and shops have sprung up across the country, and at least three hundred specialized periodicals serve immigrant readers. But demographers noted another pattern in major metropolitan areas with heavy immigration: for every immigrant who moved in, a native-born (usually white) person left.

Anti-Immigrant Sentiment.   Ethnic and racial diversity, always a source of conflict in American culture, became a defining theme of the 1990s as new immigrants often became scapegoats for all that was wrong in the United States. Even though economists gener-times thousands of simple molecules. Like finger-prints, no two people (other than identical twins) have the same genetic characteristics. Once DNA's structure was understood, it became theoretically possible to isolate the genetic codes that control everything from hair color to height to inherited diseases and certain cancers. In the 1980s laboratory advances such as PCR (polymerase chain reaction, polymerase being the enzyme that triggers the replication of DNA) made it possible to take a single fragment of DNA and copy it infinitely. In the past, DNA samples had often been too meager to work with. One immediate result of PCR was the introduction of the most sensitive test yet for the AIDS virus.

One of the earliest applications of DNA research was in criminal justice cases. From blood, saliva, semen, or hair samples, it became possible to show whether the genetic profile of a suspect matched the DNA information gathered at the crime scene. By 1995, DNA testing had been used in more than twenty-four thousand criminal cases. Some of its most dramatic results proved the innocence of individuals convicted before this technology was available; DNA testing established that their genetic makeup was so markedly different from the surviving evidence that they could not possibly have committed the crimes for which they were imprisoned. Even so, as the 1995 murder trial and acquittal of former football star O.J. Simpson showed, DNA testing remained controversial. Simpson's defense team was able to raise doubts about possible contamination of Simpson's blood samples by faulty laboratory procedures and to counter seemingly overwhelming DNA-based medical evidence that linked bloodstains on Simpson's socks, gloves, and car to the victims.

DNA testing was just one of many promising medical and scientific discoveries to emerge in the 1980s and 1990s. Biotech companies such as Genentech, Amgen, and Biogen pioneered in finding practical—and potentially profitable—applications for the new technology, making biotech companies hot tickets for investors. Nowhere was the promise of this research more evident than in medical technology, where biotechnology became the driving force in the creation of genetically engineered drugs and vaccines, the identification of specific genes that cause cystic fibrosis and sickle-cell anemia, and the transplantation of either healthy or genetically altered cells to treat cancer. But initial excitement palled as companies found it difficult to translate this new understanding of the cell's nucleus into products that could actually be shown in clinical trials to benefit humans. So volatile has the biotech business been that one analyst called it "free fall" rather than free enterprise—bungee jumping without the bungee.

One of the most ambitious projects undertaken to date is the Human Genome Project, launched in 1988 with the goal of deciphering the entire human genetic code (the entirety of the DNA in an organism is called its genome). If completed as planned early in the twenty-first century, this genetic blueprint would serve a purpose not unlike the periodic table of elements, the basis for twentieth-century research in chemistry. Given that there are approximately 3 billion nucleic acid base pairs in just one set of human chromosomes, the success of this project is intricately linked to the expanding capacities of modern computers. Biochemistry, medical research, and computer science are increasingly intertwined as earlier technological revolutions spawn new ones.

ally believe that immigrants give more than they take, providing a fresh source of predominantly youthful and highly motivated workers who take jobs that are not wanted by other people or move into new jobs in the growing service sector, many American-born workers still feared that immigrants would adversely affect their job prospects in a time of diminished economic opportunity. Immigrants, both legal and illegal, provided inviting targets when budgetary crises on the state and local levels mandated cutbacks (see American Voices, "Cuauhtémoc Menendez: The Undocumented Worker," p. 1022). Polls showed strong public support for denying government assistance to all

immigrants, regardless of their legal status, on the unproven assumption that immigrants were lured here by generous public services.

The most dramatic challenges to immigrants have emerged on the state level. In the 1980s California absorbed far more immigrants than any other state: more than a third of its growth in that decade came from foreign immigration. In 1994 California voters (including a majority of Hispanic voters) overwhelmingly approved a ballot initiative provocatively called "Save Our State," also known as Proposition 187. This initiative barred undocumented aliens from public schools, nonemergency care at public health clinics,

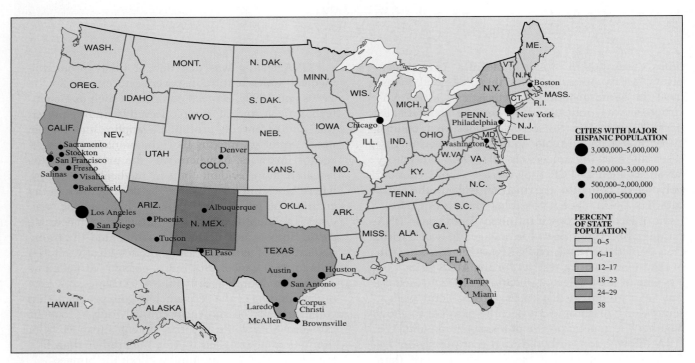

MAP 31.3
Hispanic American Population, 1990
The Hispanic population of the United States is concentrated in California, New York, Texas, Florida, and Illinois, mainly in urban areas. Demographers predict that Hispanic Americans will overtake African Americans as the largest minority group early in the twenty-first century and that by the year 2050 non-Hispanic whites will constitute only about half of the U.S. population.

and all other state social services. It also required law enforcement officers, school administrators, and social workers to report suspected illegal immigrants to the federal Immigration and Naturalization Service. Though opponents challenged the constitutionality of the ballot referendum, anti-immigrant feeling soon spread to other parts of the country.

The Plight of Urban America. One by-product of this increased immigration was that black Americans constituted a comparatively smaller percentage of the minority population in 1990 than they had earlier in the century. (Black immigration from the Caribbean and Africa has been too small to affect this trend.) Demographers predict that Latinos will outnumber blacks in the U.S. population early in the twenty-first century. Although a 1997 National Academy of Sciences report found that "some black workers have lost their jobs to immigrants," for the most part African Americans were not adversely affected by the new immigration. But economic necessity and entrenched segregation patterns forced urban blacks and new immigrants to fight for space in decaying, crime-ridden ghettos, where unemployment rates sometimes

hit 60 percent and overcrowded and underfunded inner city schools struggled to provide a proper education.

In the 1980s the historical tide of black migration to the cities that had begun before World War I started to recede. Southern blacks who learned about the poor job prospects were less likely to seek new lives in urban areas; quite the contrary, almost anyone who could leave was moving out of the inner cities, usually for a more stable urban neighborhood or the suburbs. In Los Angeles, as Asians and Latinos moved in, middle-class blacks moved out, usually to neighboring counties such as Riverside, San Bernardino, and Ventura. Some blacks even made a reverse migration back to the South. Compared with the crime-ridden and dilapidated housing projects in Chicago or South-Central Los Angeles, the post–civil rights South seemed attractive. Atlanta was one of the most popular destinations.

In April 1992 the frustration and anger of impoverished urban Americans erupted in five days of riots in Los Angeles, the worst civil disorder since the 1960s. The violence took sixty lives and caused $850 million in damage. The rioting was set off by the acquittal on all but one charge of four white Los Angeles police officers accused of using excessive force while arresting a black

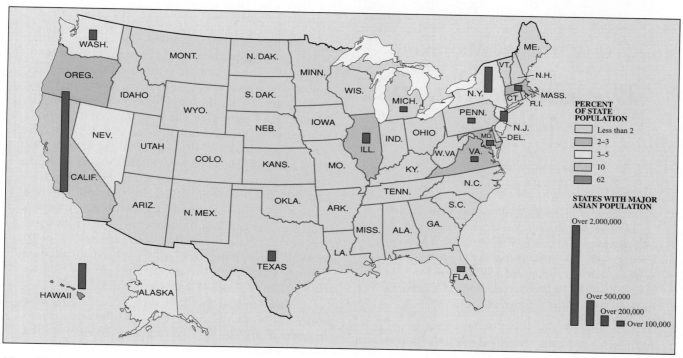

MAP 31.4
Asian American Population, 1990
In 1990 Asian Americans made up just under 3 percent of the total U.S. population. Asian population is concentrated on the East and West coasts, especially in California, and in major cities.

motorist, Rodney King, on March 3, 1991. The predominantly white jury was not swayed by a graphic 81-second amateur video of the arrest that showed the officers kicking, clubbing, and beating King. The video, shown repeatedly on television, brought renewed attention to the issue of police brutality and the harassment of minorities. Three of the officers were later convicted on federal charges of violating King's civil rights.

The Los Angeles riots exposed the cleavages in urban neighborhoods. Trapped in the nation's inner cities, many blacks resented recent immigrants who were struggling to get ahead—and often succeeding. As a result some blacks targeted Korean-owned stores for arson and looting. Latinos also felt frustrated about high unemployment and crowded housing conditions. According to the Los Angeles Police Department, Latinos accounted for more than half of those arrested and a third of those killed during the rioting.

The Debate over Affirmative Action. One of the ways federal and state governments had tried to help blacks and Latinos was through the establishment of affirmative action programs in government hiring, contracts, and university admissions. From the inception of affirmative action programs in 1965 and their extension to women in 1967, many Americans, often white men, had viewed

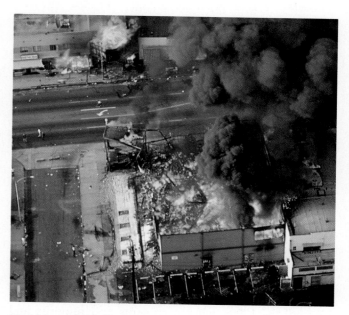

To Live and Die in L.A.
The images from South-Central Los Angeles in the wake of the 1992 riots looked eerily similar to those from Watts in 1965. The underlying causes of both riots were similar as well—police brutality, racism, and frustration about lack of jobs and opportunity.
Sylvie Kreiss/Liaison.

Cuauhtémoc Menendez

The Undocumented Worker

──────★──────

In this oral history, Cuauhtémoc Menendez, an immigrant construction worker, reflects on the controversial issue of undocumented Mexican workers—an issue that helped feed anti-immigrant sentiment in the 1980s and 1990s. After working for ten years in the United States, Menendez returned to Guadalajara, Mexico, for good.

In the United States, to get rid of all the illegals, you don't need a border or the Immigration. Simply, if there is no work, what would the illegals do there? Really, I don't see the reason to form groups and lines at the border like in the thirties. The United States is an advanced industrial society, the same in the city as it is in the agricultural areas. It's logical that there is the need for workers. For the United States it is a great advantage, because Mexican labor is very cheap. The illegal produces his product much cheaper, and they can sell it cheaper to the American people. In this sense the illegal helps the United States.

He also helps Mexico. All of the *mojados* bring money back. We don't take money out of Mexico. Those of us who work in the United States help our country more than the rich who send their Mexican money out. We support our country.

Normally the Mexican who goes to the United States goes to work in jobs that many Americans don't want. In the first place, it's hard work. I'm not going to say that they can't do the work, but they don't want to work for the same price as the Mexican. It's clear that there is this contradiction, this antipathy toward the Mexican who is there illegally. They look at the *mojados* as scabs. The Chicanos and Mexican-Americans look at us from this perspective because they think we are the reason they don't have jobs. But it's not true. We are there at the convenience of the owners and bosses who want cheap labor, cheaper than they can get there. It isn't our fault. We have the necessity to work. I don't think it's a sin to subsist in another country that offers the opportunity to live a little better than is possible for us in Mexico.

Some Americans think they are going to take away our work, but it isn't certain, because it's an important factor to the economy of the United States. What I want to say is that I didn't take work away from any North American. What happened was, there was a competition for the work. I'm not saying I was better, but I worked harder, and they paid for the work. My boss always accepted me because my work was good; he knew it was good. I worked faster and harder. For this my work was accepted. You know, an American boss doesn't pay someone for his good looks, no matter where you're from, nor for friendships or *compadrazgo*. It's for the skill. If a Mexican can demonstrate that he's a good worker, they will pay him.

───────────

Source: Marilyn P. Davis, *Mexican Voices, American Dreams: An Oral History of Mexican Immigration to the United States* (New York: Henry Holt, 1990), 410–411.

them as unfair and discriminatory. Some, like Allen Bakke, even took their cases to court (see Chapter 30). But affirmative action remained official government policy until the 1990s, when arguments over minority and immigrant rights as well as the shrinking economy and white resentment fueled a renewed debate on the issue.

The impact of affirmative action was most evident in college admissions. The University of California system had undertaken one of the most far-reaching plans. As late as 1984 whites had made up about two-thirds of the undergraduate student body. In 1994, as a result of the implementation of affirmative action, students at the Berkeley campus were 39 percent Asian, 32 percent white, 14 percent Latino, 6 percent black, and 1 percent native American (8 percent of the students did not identify their race). In 1996 California voters banned consideration of race, ethnicity, or gender in college admissions, public employment, and contracting. The next year the number of blacks admitted to Berkeley dropped 57 percent, and admissions of Hispanics declined 40 percent. Minority enrollments dropped in the rest of the California system as well, though not to the same extreme.

Culture Wars

One reason affirmative action became a political issue in the 1990s was that many—including prominent conservatives like George F. Will, William Bennett, and Patrick Buchanan—saw it as a threat to core American values. Linking affirmative action with multiculturalism—the attempt to represent the diversity of American society and its peoples—critics feared that all this counting by race, gender, sexual preference, and age would lead to the fragmentation of American society. Attempts to revise American history textbooks along multicultural lines were especially contentious, as were efforts by Stanford and other universities to revise college curricula to include non-European cultures in the study of Western civilization.

Culture wars broke out on other fronts as well. Conservatives in Congress led an effort to eliminate federal funding for the arts, humanities, and public television, arguing that the federal government should not be in the business of supporting works that many found offensive or antithetical to traditional American values. The National Endowments for the Arts and the Humanities survived, but with drastically reduced budgets. Conservatives also took aim at the speech codes that many colleges adopted to ban racist or sexist comments from everyday language.

Backlash against Feminism. The women's movement also became a target of conservative critics. In the widely read *Backlash: The Undeclared War on American Women* (1991), journalist Susan Faludi described a powerful reaction against the gains American women had won in the 1960s and 1970s. Spearheaded by New Right leaders, the media, and organizations such as Concerned Women for America, an increasing number of conservatives held the women's movement responsible for every ill afflicting modern women—from infertility to eating disorders to rising divorce rates. Yet polls showed strong support for many feminist demands, such as pay equity, increased access to jobs, reproductive rights, and more equitable sharing of household and child-care responsibilities.

Feminism was also weakened by racial and generational fault lines. Despite the attempts of prominent feminist organizations such as the National Organization for Women (NOW) to focus on racial and ethnic differences among women, African Americans and other women of color often felt themselves to be tokens in a predominantly white movement. Many young women felt that the movement had become too obsessed with women as passive victims (of date rape, discrimination, sexual harassment, the media's beauty myth, and so forth) rather than offering women models of empowerment. But other young women, influenced by women's studies programs and the explosion of feminist scholarship, forged a third wave of feminism in the 1990s (see American Voices, "Laurie Ouellette: A Third-Wave Feminist," p. 1024).

The deep national divide over abortion, one of the main issues associated with feminism, continued to polarize the country. In the 1980s and 1990s harassment and violence toward those who sought or provided abortion became increasingly common. In 1994 four workers were killed, including two receptionists at Boston clinics. Although only a fraction of anti-abortion activists supported such extreme acts, disruptive confrontational tactics made it more dangerous for women to exercise their legal right to an abortion. In May 1994 Congress passed the Freedom of Access to Clinic Entrances Act (FACE), which imposed federal fines and prison terms on those who used physical obstruction or intimidation to interfere with access to reproductive health services.

Gays and American Society. Gay rights was another field of battle. Gay activists used their political clout in more than a hundred communities across the country to win civil rights legislation protecting gay men and lesbians from discrimination in public housing, education, real estate, public accommodations, and employment. Certain cities, including New York City, Washington, D.C., and San Francisco, allowed same-sex couples to register as domestic partners.

To conservatives, especially the Christian Right and its sympathizers in Congress, a gay life-style was an affront to traditional family values. Pat Robertson, Jesse Helms, and others denounced civil rights protections for gays as undeserved "special rights." Such tactics helped antigay forces win a 1992 Colorado referendum to add a state constitutional amendment barring local jurisdictions from passing laws protecting gays and lesbians from discrimination. The U.S. Supreme Court overturned the Colorado provision in 1996, but this decision had little or no effect on the rising incidence of antigay harassment and violence. Twenty-five years after Stonewall, gay people were more visible in American society but were not universally accepted.

A grim backdrop to gay men's struggles against discrimination was the AIDS epidemic. Physicians first recognized acquired immune deficiency syndrome (AIDS) in 1981, and its cause was identified as the human immunodeficiency virus (HIV). At first little government funding was directed toward AIDS research or treatment; critics charged that this lack of attention reflected society's antipathy toward gay men, the earliest victims of the disease in the United States. The 1985 death from AIDS of Rock Hudson, a film star who had hidden his sexual orientation to maintain his Hollywood career, finally broke through the barrier of public apathy. But AIDS began to gain public attention only when it became clear that heterosexuals, such as hemophiliacs and others who received the virus through blood transfusions, were affected as well. A galvanizing moment was the 1991

Laurie Ouellette

A Third-Wave Feminist

———————★———————

Born in 1966 and educated at the University of Minnesota, Laurie Ouellette represents the generation of women who benefited from the changes set in motion by the revival of feminism but who are confused about what feminism means. She calls on the movement to broaden its vision.

As a member of the first generation of women to benefit from the gains of the '70s women's movement without participating in its struggles, I grew up on the sidelines of feminism—too young to take part in those moments, debates, and events that would define the women's movement but old enough to experience firsthand the societal changes it had wrought.

Ironically, it is due to the modest success of feminism that many young women like myself were raised with an illusion of equality. Like most women my age, I never really thought much about feminism while I was growing up. Looking back, though, I believe it has always influenced me. Growing up with divorced parents, especially a father who was ambivalent about parental responsibilities, probably has much to do with this fact. I was only five when my parents separated in 1971, and I couldn't possibly have imagined or understood the ERA marches or the triumphal result of *Roe v. Wade* that would make history in just a few short years. Certainly I couldn't have defined the word *feminism*. Still, watching my mother struggle emotionally and financially as a single parent made the concept of gender injustice painfully clear. . . .

It was at the University of Minnesota that I first took an interest in feminist classics like *The Feminine Mystique*, *Sisterhood Is Powerful*, and *Sexual Politics*. They expressed the anger of an earlier generation that simultaneously captivated me and excluded me. Reading them so long after the excitement of their publication made my own consciousness-raising seem anticlimactic. Like many of my white middle-class friends, I believed that we wouldn't have to worry about issues like discrimination, oppression, and getting stuck in the housewife role. We wondered why we should join forces with a battle for women's equality that the media repeatedly declared was already "won."

My experiences after college made me think again about feminism. A public television internship where I was expected to perform menial secretarial tasks while my male (and, I might add, less experienced) co-interns worked on interesting and challenging projects shocked me into realizing the difficulties facing women in the workplace. Likewise, living in an inner-city neighborhood and being involved in community issues there showed me the dire need for feminism in the lives of the poor women, elderly women, and women of color who were my neighbors. Watching these women, many of them single mothers, struggle daily to find shelter, child care, and food made me realize that they had not been touched at all by the women's movement gains of the '70s. . . .

My 24-year-old sister stands out as an example of other routes that feminism must move toward. Whereas I have focused my energies on attending graduate school and working toward a professional career, she has chosen to forfeit similar plans, for now, in favor of marrying young, moving to the country, and raising a family. Does she signify a regression into the homemaker role of the 1950s? On the contrary. For her, issues such as getting midwifery legalized and insured, providing information about breast-feeding to rural mothers, countering the male-dominated medical establishment by using and recommending natural and alternative healing methods, and raising her own daughter with positive gender esteem are central to a feminist agenda.

Only by recognizing and helping to provide choices—both lifestyle and reproductive—for women of all races, economic levels, and ages, as well as supporting all women in their struggles to make those choices, will the women of my generation, the first to be raised in the shadow of feminism and witness its successes and failures, be able to build a successful third wave of the feminist movement.

Source: Laurie Ouellette, "Our Turn Now: Reflections of a 26-Year-Old Feminist," *Utne Reader* (July–August 1992), 118–120.

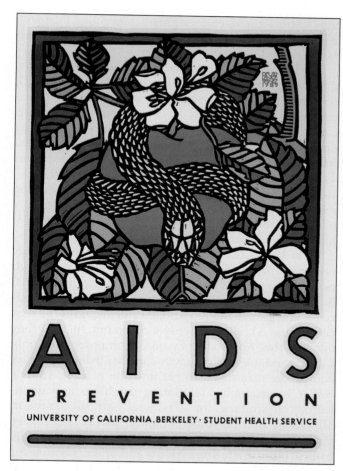

AIDS Awareness
This poster by David Lance Goines uses the image of the Garden of Eden to warn of the dangers of AIDS. By 1985, the year this poster appeared, 12,500 Americans had already died of AIDS, and the country began to confront the epidemic's human and medical costs.
David Lance Goines.

The Environmental Movement at Twenty-five

On April 26, 1995, when Americans came together for the twenty-fifth anniversary of Earth Day, they had much to celebrate. The nation's rivers and waterways were cleaner; air pollution had been reduced by a third; and lead emissions from fuel, a cause of retardation in children, had been cut by an astounding 98 percent. The bald eagle and the California condor had come back from the brink of extinction. More than six thousand communities across the country had recycling programs. Activists realized there was still much to be done, however. Despite efforts to reduce urban smog, two of five Americans lived in areas with unhealthy air. Many rivers and lakes were still unsafe for fishing and swimming. One of four Americans lived within four miles of a toxic waste dump, and this trend, which activists termed *environmental racism*, disproportionally affected lower-income communities.

In addition to addressing problems in their own communities, Americans were becoming increasingly aware that the environment required action not just from the United States but from the global community as a whole. Three pressing environmental problems crossed national boundaries and demanded international action: the depletion of the ozone layer, acid rain, and global warming. An important precedent for international action on environmental issues was set by the 1987 Montreal protocol, in which thirty-four nations agreed to phase out ozone-damaging chlorofluorocarbons (CFCs) by 1999. In June 1992 delegates from 170 countries to the United Nations Earth Summit in Rio de Janeiro adopted a treaty on global warming, and in 1994 the United States joined sixty-three other countries in signing the Basel Convention, which banned the export of hazardous wastes from industrialized to developing countries. In the future, U.S. environmental policy, like so much else of modern life, would operate more and more within an international framework.

Popular Culture and Popular Technology

Image was everything in the 1980s and 1990s, or so commentators said, pointing to the flamboyant rock stars Michael Jackson and Madonna and even to the genial, charismatic President Reagan. One strong influence on popular culture was MTV, which premiered in 1981. With its creative choreography, flashy colors, and rapid cuts, it seemed a perfect fit to the short attention span of a TV generation raised on programs such as *Sesame Street*. The MTV style soon showed up in mainstream media and even political campaigns, which adapted the 30-second sound bites common on television news

announcement by basketball great Earvin ("Magic") Johnson that he was HIV-positive. Since the mid-1980s, however, AIDS cases had been increasing among heterosexuals, especially intravenous drug users and their sex partners, as well as bisexuals. At the end of the twentieth century, women constituted the group with the fastest growing incidence of HIV infection in the United States. Some people lived for years symptom-free while being HIV-positive, and new treatment strategies using "cocktails" of several powerful drugs were leading to cautious optimism about controlling the disease, although scientists warned that the drugs were not effective for between 30 and 50 percent of patients. To date, more Americans have died of AIDS than were killed in the Korean and Vietnam Wars combined.

Be Kind to Your Mother (Earth)
This poster, created by Jennifer Morla to commemorate the twenty-fifth anniversary of Earth Day in 1995, urges people to celebrate the event by "making everyday [sic] Earth Day." Simple things that ordinary citizens can do to save the earth include stopping junk mail, recycling cans and bottles, carpooling, taking shorter showers, and recharging batteries rather than throwing them away.
© 1995 Morla Design, San Francisco.

shows to their own purposes. The national newspaper *USA Today*, which debuted in 1982, also adapted the style, featuring eye-catching graphics, color photographs, and short, easy-to-read articles. Soon more staid newspapers followed suit.

New technology, especially satellite transmission and live "minicam" broadcasting, reshaped the television industry. Also new was the increased availability of cable channels. By the mid-1990s viewers could choose from over a hundred channels, including upstarts such as Ted Turner's all-news CNN (Cable News Network), the ESPN all-sports channel, and the Fox network, which were all challenging the three major networks for viewers and profits. Media, com-

munications, and entertainment were big business, increasingly drawn into global financial networks, markets, and mergers.

Technology also reshaped the home. The 1980s saw the introduction of videocassette recorders (VCRs), compact disc (CD) players, cellular phones, and inexpensive fax machines. By 1995 eight out of ten American households had a VCR. At first Hollywood feared decreasing box-office admissions, but it soon found that VCRs created a large new market for recent films as well as for vintage movies. Video was everywhere—stores, elevators, airplanes, tennis courts, operating rooms. With the introduction of camcorders, the family photo album could be supplemented by a video of a high school graduation, a marriage, or a birth.

But it was the personal computer (PC) that truly revolutionized home and office. The big breakthrough came from Apple Computer. Two young hobbyists, Steve Jobs and Steve Wozniak, operating from a bedroom and garage in Palo Alto, California, built the first easy-to-use, small, inexpensive computer. In 1977 they offered the Apple II personal computer for only $1,195, and it was a runaway success. Belatedly, other companies scrambled to get into the market. IBM, a leader in producing tabulating machines and mainframe computers for business and government, offered its first personal computer in 1981. Software companies such as Microsoft and Lotus grew rapidly by providing operating systems and other software for this expanding market (see American Lives, "Bill Gates: Microsoft's Leader in the Computer Revolution," pp. 1028–1029). In January 1983 *Time* magazine broke with fifty-five years of tradition by naming the personal computer its "machine of the year." In 1995, 37 percent of American households had at least one personal computer.

The impact of the personal computer on business was nearly universal. More than any other technological advance, the computer created the modern electronic office. Even the smallest business could keep all its records, do all its correspondence and billing, and run its own direct-mail advertising campaigns on a single desktop machine. The very concept of the office was changing as a new category of telecommuters were able to work at home by means of computer, modem, electronic mail, and fax machine.

Today new technologies utilizing fiber optics, microwave relays, and satellites can transmit massive quantities of information to and from almost any place on earth, and even in outer space, via the *information superhighway*, or Internet. By 1996, 40 million people in the United States alone used the Internet, and experts predicted that by the year 2000 more than 250 million people in over 170 countries would have access to cyberspace—that place behind the computer screen that you can't see but you know is there.

Honey, Where's the Remote?
How many channels can you watch? How many websites can you visit? In the 1990s
Americans began to complain of information overload. This image of a person viewing
500 cable TV stations simultaneously was created by photographer Louis Psihoyos for
an article on technology that appeared in *National Geographic.*
© 1995 Louis Psihoyos-Matrix.

The Internet had Cold War roots, originating in a 1969 effort by the Pentagon to create a communications network that could survive a nuclear war. The Pentagon gave up control of the Internet in 1984, and the subsequent rapid spread of personal computers, modems, and networked computing made the Internet attractive (some would say addictive) to average citizens and commercial enterprises. At first the Internet was used mainly by scientists and other professionals to communicate with their peers through electronic mail (e-mail); then the arrival of the World Wide Web in 1991 enhanced its commercial possibilities. The Web allowed companies, organizations, political campaigns, and even the White House to create their own websites of visual and textual information for consumers to click on to at their discretion. Businesses and entrepreneurs began to use the Internet to sell their products and services, leading critics to fear that the Net would become a big shopping mall. But many economists and business analysts thought that cyberspace would be one of the driving forces for economic growth in the twenty-first century.

Theoretically available to all, at the close of the twentieth century cyberspace was still mostly available to those who could afford it, and the gap between information haves and have-nots was wide and getting wider. In 1995 only 10 percent of American households (generally those with incomes above $50,000) had the computers, modems, telephone connections, and gateway software necessary to participate in this revolution. According to a 1993 Census Bureau study, the gap was racial as well as economic: 37.5 percent of whites had computers at home, work, or school, compared with 25 percent of blacks and 22 percent of Hispanics. Who was going to get on the information superhighway and who was going to be left by the wayside was one of the most troubling issues for the twenty-first century. Critics warned against "information apartheid" or "electronic redlining" (the latter term derived from the banking practice of refusing loans to people in low-income areas).

Popular writers Alvin and Heidi Toffler used the term *Third Wave* for the new computing and telecommunications technologies and predicted that they would transform the global economy as dramatically as did the first wave (the agricultural revolution) and the second (the Industrial Revolution). The Tofflers suggested that if the wave of the future is indeed information, individuals who are not highly educated and computer-literate will find themselves greatly disadvantaged as they try to compete in the twenty-first-century workplace.

Bill Gates: Microsoft's Leader in the Computer Revolution

———————★———————

IN THE ELEVENTH grade Bill Gates told a friend that he would be a millionaire by the time he was thirty. When Gates went to Harvard two years later, he revised his prediction downward to twenty-five. He was being far too modest. At the age of thirty-one Bill Gates became the youngest self-made billionaire ever. In 1992 *Forbes* magazine named him the richest person in America. What was the source of all this wealth? Microsoft Corporation, whose software runs on nine of every ten personal computers sold in the United States. Microsoft is the most successful start-up company in the history of American business.

This is no Horatio Alger, rags-to-riches story. William Henry Gates III was born into a wealthy Seattle family on October 28, 1955. His father, William Gates Jr., is a successful corporate lawyer and former president of the Washington State Bar Association; his mother, Mary, was a prominent United Way volunteer who also served as a regent of the University of Washington. Gates attended the exclusive Lakeside School, one of the first schools in the country to offer students computer access, thanks to a time-sharing arrangement paid for by the school's mothers' club. The eighth-grader was hooked. Another Lakeside classmate and computer whiz was tenth-grader Paul Allen, who joined Gates in 1972 to found a company called Traf-O-Data, which counted vehicles at busy intersections by using a rudimentary computer device. In 1975 these two former classmates founded Microsoft. Allen was twenty-one; Gates, who would soon drop out of Harvard, all of nineteen.

Gates looked even younger. When Miriam Lubow became Microsoft's office manager in 1977, she was appalled when some "kid" whipped by her desk into the office of "Mr. Gates" and began playing with the computer terminal. That kid was Bill Gates. In the early days of Microsoft, Gates was too young to rent a car or have a drink with prospective clients on a business trip. His smudged glasses and unkempt hair became trademarks. But looks can be deceiving, as competitors have found out ever since.

In certain ways Gates and Allen were classic hackers—nerdy, mathematically inclined, and fascinated by the possibilities for computation (and mischief) that early computers provided. But most hackers saw computers as a hobby or a game. Back then the thought of owning one's own computer seemed as far-fetched as owning a nuclear submarine. But right from the start Gates and Allen saw commercial possibilities in the new field, long before the personal computer revolution of the 1980s. They anticipated that there would be money to be made writing, and especially marketing, software for the new machines. Microsoft's domination has resulted less from developing innovative products than from anticipating trends in the industry, getting products quickly into the marketplace, and then using its market share to bludgeon the competition. The phenomenal success of products such as MS-DOS and Windows was due as much to Microsoft's relentless marketing barrage as to any inherent technological superiority of its products. One Microsoft veteran described the corporate strategy in this way: "See where everybody's headed then catch up and go past them."

In the early days Microsoft was more like a college dorm than the billion-dollar business it later became. The "Microkids" were barely out of their teens, and some were still in high school. Nobody kept regular hours (in fact, the walls lacked clocks), and they existed on junk food, rock music, and free Coke, a tradition that Microsoft still maintains. A married employee was an oddity, and almost all the programmers were men. Parking slots were unnumbered as a way to reward early arrivals. Gates's competitive and confrontational managerial style set the tone: "That's the stupidest thing I ever heard" was a frequently heard comment.

Gates literally could not sit still, and Seattle-based Microsoft continued to grow at a fantastic rate. Gates had once thought it might employ 20 people; by 1982, Microsoft had 200 employees and sales of $32 million. In 1985, when the company went public, Gates, Allen (who had left the company in

1983 after a bout with Hodgkin's disease), and many Microsoft employees became overnight millionaires. Allen later cashed in some of his stock to buy the Portland Trailblazers. Gates used some of his personal wealth to build a $53 million house on Lake Washington outside Seattle, whose property taxes alone (estimated at $620,000 in 1998) would buy a luxury home in most U.S. cities. The house is a series of interconnected pavilions set deep into a hillside, with its own salmon estuary, a twenty-car subterranean garage, a trampoline room, and video "walls" in every room to display changing electronic images of art (for which Gates has bought the rights from major museums). "Working for Bill, you design for change," said the architect. That sums up Gates's approach to business as well.

The next step for Gates and Microsoft was onto the information superhighway. Internet commerce is projected to generate $180 billion of business a year by the beginning of the twenty-first century, and Gates wants Microsoft to be part of that connection. But if Microsoft is able to use its market share to force consumers to use its applications and links to the World Wide Web rather than competitors' browsers, thereby controlling access to the information, entertainment, shopping, real estate, and travel services that the Web provides, its dominance will increase even more. When the Justice department took Microsoft to court in 1998 for violating the antitrust laws, Gates brashly replied that he was simply giving consumers what they wanted. The fact that Attorney General Janet Reno did not even use a personal computer seemed to confirm Microsoft's view that the Department of Justice was out of touch with the importance of computers to modern life.

Friends note Bill Gates's "extraordinary bandwidth"—that is, the amount of information he can absorb—but it is his insights into business rather than technology that set Gates apart. His entrepreneurial streak would have made Henry Ford or John D. Rockefeller proud. The future, however, comes quickly in the computer field, and Gates keenly worries about being left behind in the next stage of the revolution: "It's a little scary that as computer technology has moved ahead there's never been a leader from one era who was also a leader in the next." He takes this as a warning and a challenge: "I want to defy historical tradition."

"Software is cool," Gates told CNN's Larry King to explain the hoopla surrounding the release of Microsoft's Windows 95. To the computer crowd, cool is the opposite of random, which means out of it, wrong, or inane. No one, especially not his competitors, has ever accused Bill Gates of being random.

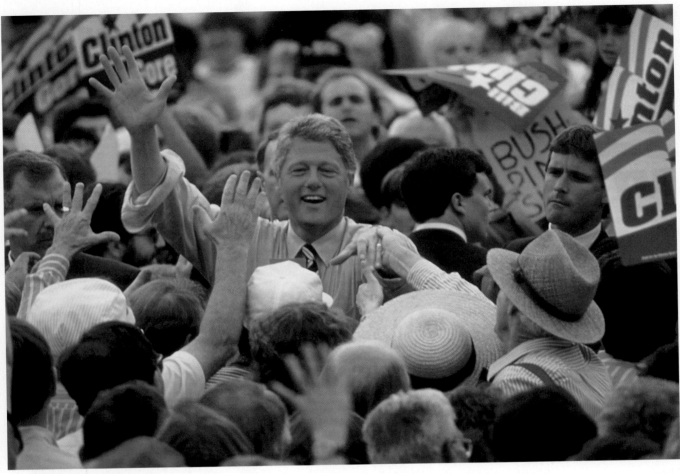

Passing the Torch to a New Generation
Baby boomer Bill Clinton, shown here campaigning in 1992, and his running mate Al
Gore billed themselves as representing a "new generation of leadership." Born in 1946
and 1948, respectively, they came of age in the turbulent 1960s. Vietnam, not World
War II or Korea, was the war that defined their generation.
Ira Wyman/Sygma.

Restructuring the Domestic Order: Public Life, 1992–1996

★

To make progress on the environment, on the faltering
economy, and on the deep social cleavages surrounding race, gender, and sexual orientation, Americans
needed forceful leadership. But the strong showing of
independent candidate Ross Perot and low voter
turnout in the 1992 presidential election signaled deep
dissatisfaction with the American political system. As
if using a remote control device, Americans were click-
ing off politics as usual. After sixty years of supporting
federal activism to combat social ills, the Democratic
Party found that its core ideology was out of step with
a country more concerned with cutting taxes, scaling
back government, and balancing the budget. As
Democrats abandoned many of their long-held liberal
beliefs, the Republican Party moved even farther to the
right. Looming over all their political debates was the
federal deficit.

Clinton's First Term

With the end of the Cold War, domestic affairs
returned to their normal place at the center of American politics. As the campaign for the 1992 presidential election got under way, the economy was the
overriding issue because the recession that had

begun in 1990 showed no signs of abating. Bush easily won renomination, overwhelming his lone opponent, the conservative columnist Pat Buchanan. To solidify the support of the New Right, Vice-President Dan Quayle spoke out strongly for "family values" and other conservative social agendas. Bush responded to criticism that he lacked a vision for domestic affairs by blaming the Democratic Congress for thwarting his initiatives.

Bill Clinton, the longtime governor of Arkansas, one of the nation's poorest states, emerged as the Democratic front-runner. He survived charges of marital infidelity and draft dodging and questions about a dubious Arkansas real-estate deal dubbed "Whitewater" to win the Democratic nomination. For his running mate he chose Al Gore, a second-term senator from Tennessee, widely known for his environmental best seller, *Earth in the Balance*. At age forty-four, Gore was a year and a half younger than Clinton, making them the first baby-boom national ticket.

In the middle of the primary season, the Texas billionaire H. Ross Perot capitalized on voters' desire for change by announcing on CNN's "Larry King Live" that he would run as an independent candidate. Although Perot dropped out of the race on the last day of the Democratic convention, he reentered it less than five weeks before the election, adding a well-financed wild card in an unusual election year.

The Democrats mounted an aggressive, effective campaign that focused on Clinton's plans to solve domestic problems, especially education, health care, and the economy. Gore added expertise on defense and environmental issues. Bush was hurt by the weak economy, his continued focus on foreign over domestic policy, and especially his reneging on the "no new taxes" pledge. On election day Clinton received 43 percent of the popular vote to Bush's 38 percent and Perot's 19 percent (Map 31.5). Although Perot did not win a single state, his popular vote was the highest for an independent candidate since Theodore Roosevelt in 1912. The Democrats retained control of both houses of Congress, ending twelve years of divided government. But the narrowness of Clinton's victory and the public's perception that he waffled on the issues did not bode well for his ability to lead the country.

Early Administrative and Legislative Record. As William Jefferson Clinton was sworn into office in January 1993, the liberals who had supported him hoped that a Democratic presidency could erase the Reagan-Bush legacy and oversee the creation of a new democratic social agenda. At first, Clinton seemed to fulfill that promise. In 1993 he nominated the liberal Ruth Bader Ginsburg for a seat on the Supreme Court. The president also appointed Janet Reno as attorney general, the first woman to hold that post. Other trailblazing cabinet appointments included Secretary of Health and Human Services Donna E. Shalala and, in Clinton's second term, Secretary of State Madeleine K. Albright. Clinton chose an African American, Ron Brown, as secretary of commerce, and two Latinos, Henry Cisneros and Frederico Peña, to head the Department of Housing and Urban Development (HUD) and the Department of Transportation, respectively.

Clinton's early legislative record was mixed. In early 1993 he signed into law the Family and Medical Leave Act, twice vetoed by Bush. It provided workers with up to twelve weeks of unpaid leave to tend to a newborn or an adopted child or a family medical emergency. In May, Congress passed the so-called motor-voter bill, which required states to allow citizens to register to vote when they applied for or renewed a driver's license. But when Clinton tried to implement his campaign promise to lift the ban on gays serving in the armed forces, he ran into such fierce opposition that he backed off. His compromise policy of "don't ask, don't tell, don't pursue" satisfied no one, and the bungled handling of this emotionally charged issue called into question his willingness to stand firm on issues of principle.

By the time Clinton took office, the economy had pulled out of the 1990 recession, so he was able to focus on other economic issues, especially the opening of foreign markets to U.S. goods. In 1992 President Bush had signed the North American Free Trade Agreement (NAFTA), in which the United States, Canada, and Mexico agreed to create a free-trade zone covering all of North America, the largest such zone in the world. Strongly supported by the business community, NAFTA was bitterly opposed by labor unions worried about losing jobs to lower-paid Mexican workers, and by environmentalists concerned about weak enforcement of antipollution laws south of the border. Nonetheless, with Clinton's support, Congress narrowly passed NAFTA in November 1993.

Another major development in international trade was the revision in 1994 of the General Agreement on Tariffs and Trade (GATT), the treaty governing most international trade that was part of the Bretton Woods system created at the end of World War II (see Chapter 28). This new round of revisions, the eighth since the 1940s, cut tariffs on many manufactured products and for the first time established regulations protecting intellectual property such as patents, copyrights, and trademarks for software, entertainment, and pharmaceuticals. The U.S. Senate ratified the treaty in December 1994.

With the recession over but crime rates on the rise, crime replaced the economy as a major concern among voters. In 1993, despite the opposition of the National

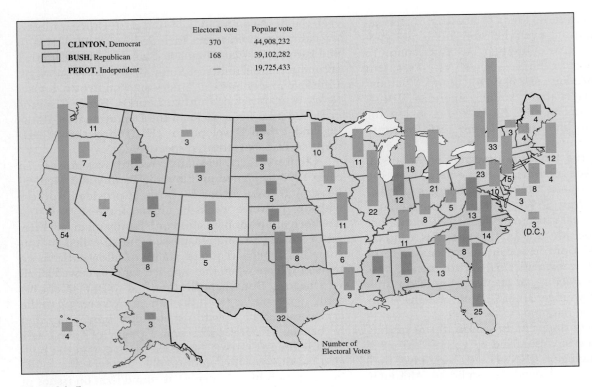

MAP 31.5
The Election of 1992
The first national election since the end of the Cold War was dominated by concern over
the economy. The first-ever all-southerner Democratic ticket of Bill Clinton and Al Gore
won broad support across the country, cutting into Republican strongholds in the South
and West. The independent candidate, H. Ross Perot, won no electoral votes but polled
an impressive 19 percent of the popular vote.

Rifle Association, Congress passed the Brady Handgun
Violence Prevention Act, named for James Brady, the
White House press secretary who was crippled in a
1981 attempted assassination of President Reagan. A
much more wide-ranging piece of legislation was the
Omnibus Violent Crime Control and Prevention Act
(1994), which authorized $30.2 billion for stepped-up
law enforcement, crime prevention, and prison construction and administration. The act also expanded
the death penalty to more than fifty federal crimes and
banned the sale and possession of certain kinds of
assault weapons. One result was a dramatic increase in
the federal and state prison population, from 774,000
in 1990 to almost 1.2 million in 1996. The U.S. incar-
ceration rate was six to ten times higher than the rate
in most industrial nations, and only Russia had a larger
share of its citizens behind bars.

Health Care Reform.   Responding to the deep anxieties Americans had about their economic security and
despite his slender electoral mandate, Clinton staked
his political fortunes on his campaign promise of uni-

versal health care. Though the United States spent
more on health care than any other country ($843 bil-
lion in 1992, up 9.5 percent from the year before), it
remained the only major industrialized country not to
provide national health insurance. Spiraling medical
costs (double the rate of inflation since 1970), rising
premiums, and the large number of Americans without
health insurance (one-sixth of the population in 1992)
had brought the health care system to a crisis.

The president chose his wife, Hillary Rodham
Clinton, to head the task force that would draft the legislation, a controversial move since no first lady had
ever played such a formal role in policy making. The
resulting proposal was based on the idea of managed
competition: market forces, not the government, would
control health care costs and expand citizens' access to
health care. But even this mild form of social engineering ran into intense opposition from the well-financed
pharmaceutical and insurance industries. In August
1994 the Senate failed to act on the plan, and by September congressional leaders admitted that health
care reform was dead.

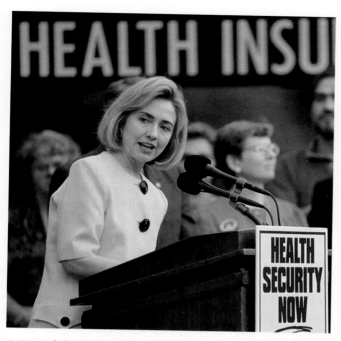

A Forceful and Controversial First Lady
Drawing inspiration from Eleanor Roosevelt, Hillary Rodham Clinton hoped the country would be ready for a first lady who could play a role in shaping health care policy. It wasn't.
Robert Trippet/SIPA Press.

While the political system dithered, private market forces were already transforming the nation's medical system, replacing the traditional "fee for service" system with managed care plans that limited consumers' choice of doctors and treatments to cut costs. Medical care was rapidly becoming the domain of Wall Street and big business, and growing numbers of Americans joined health maintenance organizations (HMOs) or looser "preferred provider" networks. While managed care succeeded in curbing the cost of health care premiums, private sector initiatives did nothing to help the unemployed and workers without health insurance, whose numbers continued to grow. An estimated 43.4 million Americans had no health insurance in 1995, over 17 percent of the population under the age of sixty-five, and experts predicted that these statistics would climb.

Post–Cold War Foreign Policy. One reason why health care reform failed was that President Clinton was never able to devote his full attention to building a consensus for the plan and shepherding it through Congress. In October 1993, for example, just after he had announced the plan, twelve American soldiers were killed on a United Nations peacekeeping mission in Somalia. Then Clinton had to turn his attention to divisive issues such as the closely contested NAFTA vote, Haiti, and the worsening situation in Bosnia. This patchwork approach to foreign policy added to the perception of Clinton as vacillating, indecisive, and lacking a central vision. Not until 1996 did Clinton's foreign policy team begin to articulate a clear policy on when the United States should intervene in crises overseas.

In the former Soviet Union the increasing unpopularity of Russian president Boris Yeltsin's efforts to bring about fundamental market reforms and the mounting evidence of rampant corruption made American leaders less optimistic about the emergence of democracy in Russia. Yeltsin's harsh repression of dissent in the breakaway region of Chechnya strained the already difficult relationship with the United States.

Nothing seemed more intractable than the problems engulfing the former state of Yugoslavia, which typified the localized conflicts based on ethnicity, religion, and nationality that increasingly replaced the superpower conflicts of the Cold War era. In what military analysts call "postmodern" or "future" wars, there is no distinction between armies and people—anybody who gets in the way gets killed. Unlike the Persian Gulf War, these conflicts do not rely on highly sophisticated technology and massive armies but still can be incredibly destructive.

The roots of the Bosnian conflict went back at least as far as the outbreak of World War I, but the immediate backdrop was the breakup of the state of Yugoslavia in 1991 into five independent states in the wake of the collapse of communism in Eastern Europe (see Map 31.1). The province of Bosnia and Herzegovina, made up largely of Muslims and committed to a multiethnic (Serb, Croat, and Muslim) state, had declared its independence in 1992. But Bosnian Serbs, supported financially and militarily by what remained of Yugoslavia, formed their own breakaway state and began a siege of Sarajevo, the Bosnian capital, which was the site of the 1984 Winter Olympics. In the countryside the Serbs launched a ruthless campaign of "ethnic cleansing," driving Bosnian Muslims and Croats from their homes and into concentration camps or shooting them in mass executions. More than 250,000 people were killed or reported missing after war broke out in April 1992.

After three years of unsuccessful efforts by the European powers to stop the carnage, the world's only superpower, the United States, exercised some leadership—backed by military force—to end the worst conflict in Europe since World War II. In November 1995 Secretary of State Warren Christopher and chief negotiator Richard Holbrooke brokered the Dayton Peace Accords, which ended the war at least temporarily. To implement the peace, the United States sent troops to

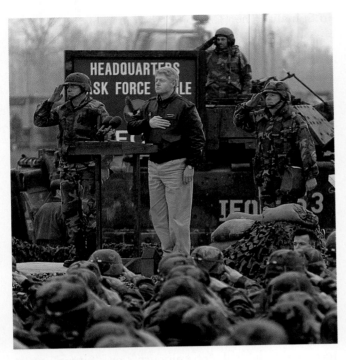

Clinton in Bosnia
In his role as commander in chief, President Clinton visited Bosnia in January 1996 to show his support for the peacekeeping mission. Here he salutes American troops in the Bosnian town of Tuzla.
Peterson/Gamma Liaison.

Bosnia as part of a NATO-led force, although a major goal of American policy—a viable and unified Bosnia—remained unfulfilled.

At the same time, the end of Cold War superpower rivalry presented unexpected opportunities to resolve other longstanding regional, ethnic, and religious conflicts. In Haiti, the threat of a U.S. invasion in October 1993 led to the restoration of the exiled president, Jean-Bertrand Aristide, who had been ousted by a military coup in 1991. In South Africa, the end of the fifty-year policy of racial separation was capped in May 1994 by the election of Nelson Mandela, who had spent twenty-seven years in prison for challenging apartheid, as the country's first black president. And in a move that was seen as a symbolic end to the American experience in Vietnam, the United States established diplomatic relations with Hanoi in July 1995, two decades after the fall of Saigon.

With the end of the Cold War, many citizens had hoped for a peace dividend, redirecting money from defense to domestic programs. But America's global responsibilities had not declined. Given the new budget-cutting consciousness in Washington, the Department of Defense entered a period of retrench-

ment. By closing military bases around the country, cutting total personnel by 20 percent from 1900 to 1994, and making cutbacks in research and development for new weapons systems, the post–Cold War defense budget leveled off at around $250 billion, down from a peak in 1989 of $346 billion (in 1994 dollars). This small peace dividend was swallowed up by the huge deficit.

Scandals and Independent Counsels. In June 1994 President Clinton signed a little-noticed piece of legislation that reauthorized the independent counsel statute, which had lapsed in late 1992. The law, which applied to approximately seventy top Washington officials, gave the attorney general the authority to request a three-judge court to appoint an independent counsel if there were "reasonable grounds" to believe investigation of official misconduct was warranted. A legacy of Watergate originally passed in 1978, the law was intended to remove the potential for conflict of interest that would arise if the attorney general investigated members of the administration of which he or she was a member. It replaced special prosecutors, who had been part of the Justice department and (as Archibald Cox found out in 1973) subject to firing, with independent counsels, who could not be fired and who were given unlimited budgets and time to complete their investigations.

Five weeks after Clinton reactivated the law and at the request of Attorney General Janet Reno, a panel of federal judges named Kenneth Starr to investigate a set of allegations involving the defunct Whitewater Development Corporation and a bankrupt S & L called Madison Guaranty in Arkansas with which Bill and Hillary Clinton had been involved. In the initial stage of his Whitewater investigations Starr produced three convictions and ten guilty pleas, some from Clinton's close associates. The independent counsel statute, however, empowered the independent counsel to pursue "related matters," and Starr's case steadily widened into a probe that included investigating the 1993 suicide of a White House aide and former Arkansas colleague of the Clintons named Vincent Foster, staff firings at the White House travel office, and finally, four years and $40 million later, allegations that President Clinton had a sexual affair with a White House intern named Monica Lewinsky.

President Clinton was not the only member of his administration to be the target of an independent counsel. In 1994 agriculture secretary Mike Espy was investigated for accepting illegal gratuities. In 1995 independent counsels looked into charges that HUD Secretary Henry Cisneros had made false statements during confirmation, and into Commerce Secretary Ron Brown's personal finances. Later, independent counsels were appointed to investigate allegations surrounding Interior Secretary Bruce Babbitt and Labor Secretary Alexis Herman.

Despite the good intentions of the original statute, the breadth of its scope (one Justice department insider called it an "unguided missile"), its vulnerability to partisan politics, and the fact that the vast majority of its investigations ended without the filing of any criminal charges led many to question its usefulness. Instead of increasing public trust, the independent counsel statute tended to encourage citizens' cynicism with government, an unfortunate side effect in already cynical times.

"The Era of Big Government Is Over"

The 1994 midterm election produced one of the most significant sea changes in recent political history—the culmination of the shift that had begun with Ronald Reagan's election in 1980. Republicans gained 52 seats in the House, giving them control for the first time in forty years; they also retook the Senate for the first time since 1986. In the House the centerpiece of the new Republican majority was the "Contract with America," a list of legislation that Newt Gingrich of Georgia, the new Speaker, vowed would be voted on in the first one hundred days of the session. The contract included constitutional amendments to balance the budget and term limits for congressional office; $245 billion in tax cuts for individuals and incentives for small businesses; cuts in welfare and other entitlement programs; anticrime initiatives; and cutbacks in federal regulations. Initially portrayed as ideological revolutionaries determined to shake Congress to its core, the members of the GOP "Class of '94" became more pragmatic as they settled into Congress. Said Mississippi congressman Roger Wicker, "I didn't come to Washington to burn all the buildings down."

Balancing the Budget. A balanced budget and reducing the national debt, key Republican goals, were endorsed by many Democrats as well. Both practical and political considerations made these difficult to achieve, especially since the Republicans also wanted to cut taxes. Interest on the debt had to be paid. Defense spending in the post–Cold War world had declined only slightly. That left Medicare and Medicaid, Social Security, and all other government programs as targets for savings. Since Social Security was considered untouchable, Congress looked to health care and discretionary spending for savings.

Despite the failure of Clinton's health care reform bill, by 1995 wide public agreement supported the notion that it was essential to bring health care costs under control. Medicare, signed into law by President Johnson in 1965, had cost almost $160 billion in 1994, almost 10 percent of the entire federal budget. As new medical technologies proliferated and the number of elderly people increased, expenses were rising at a rate of 10 percent a year. In the fall of 1995 Congress passed a budget cutting $270 billion from projected spending on Medicare and $170 billion from Medicaid over seven years. Other savings came from cuts in various discretionary programs, including education and the environment.

Clinton accepted Congress's resolve to balance the budget in seven years but, vowing to protect the nation from an "extremist" Congress, vetoed the budget itself. In the standoff that followed, nonessential departments of the government were forced to shut down twice for lack of funds, but polls showed that a majority of Americans held Congress, not the president, responsible. The budget that Clinton finally signed in April 1996 left Medicare and Social Security intact, though it did meet the Republicans' goal of cutting $23 billion in discretionary spending. In 1997 Clinton and congressional leaders announced a historic balanced budget agreement, and in January 1998, aided by a strong economy swelling the U.S. Treasury, Clinton submitted the first balanced budget in nearly thirty years.

Welfare Reform. Since the Reagan Era, the long-accepted argument that the federal government had an obligation to the poor was supplanted by rhetoric about cost-effectiveness, personal responsibility, and turning programs over to the states. Although Clinton promised in the 1992 campaign to "end welfare as we know it," serious debate on the issue did not begin until the Republicans took over Congress in 1995. Welfare, a joint federal-state program, represented a fairly small part of the budget, but to Republicans it was the prime example of misguided government priorities. The benefits of the main welfare program, AFDC, were far from generous: the average annual welfare payment to families (including food stamps) was $7,740, well below the 1995 poverty line of $12,188. In the 1990s both Democratic and Republican statehouses adopted various financial incentives to try to change welfare beneficiaries' behavior, including setting time limits, imposing work requirements, and denying benefits for additional children born to women on AFDC.

In August 1996, after vetoing two Republican-authored bills, President Clinton signed into law the Personal Responsibility and Work Opportunity Act, mandating a historic overhaul of federal entitlements. The law ended the federal guarantee of cash assistance to poor children by abolishing AFDC, required most adult recipients to find work within two years, set a five-

A Bipartisan Balanced Budget
On August 5, 1997, a smiling President Clinton signs the balanced budget bill, surrounded by congressional leaders including House Speaker Newt Gingrich of Georgia (second from right) and House Budget Committee chairman John Kasich of Ohio (far right). Also looking on with satisfaction is Vice-President Al Gore, who already had hopes for the presidency in 2000.
Ron Edmonds/Wide World Photos, Inc.

year limit on payments to any family, and gave states wide discretion in running their welfare programs.

The 1996 Election. The Republican takeover of Congress had one unintended consequence—it united the usually fractious Democrats behind Bill Clinton. Unopposed in the primaries, Clinton was able to burnish his image as a moderate "New Democrat." His political fortunes were aided by the unpopularity of the Republican Congress since the government shutdowns.

He also benefited from the strong state of the economy. Economic indicators released shortly before election day showed that the "misery index"—a combination of the unemployment rate and inflation—was the lowest it had been in twenty-seven years.

In the Republican primaries, voters flirted with conservative commentator Pat Buchanan and magazine publisher Steve Forbes before settling on Senate Majority Leader Bob Dole of Kansas as their presidential candidate. Dole was acceptable to both conserva-

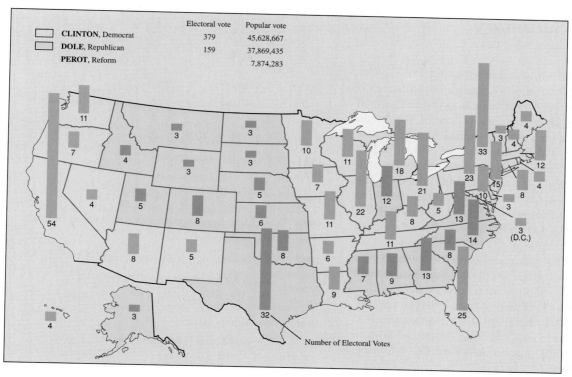

MAP 31.6
The Election of 1996
Clinton and Gore broadened their electoral base from 1992, picking up traditional
Republican strongholds like Florida and dominating all regions of the country except the
South and the Great Plains. But with Republicans still in control of both houses of
Congress, Clinton faced uncertain prospects in his second term.

tive and moderate wings of the party, though his detached campaign style failed to generate much enthusiasm. He made a 15 percent across-the-board tax cut the centerpiece of his campaign, and selected former representative Jack Kemp, a leading proponent of supply-side economics, as his running mate.

Americans seemed to make up their minds early about the candidates, so the campaign was rather lackluster. Clinton emphasized his success in reducing the budget deficit, raising the minimum wage to $5.15 an hour, and reforming welfare, and he took credit for the 10 million new jobs created during his first term. In November, Clinton became the first Democratic president since Franklin Roosevelt to win reelection (Map 31.6). However, voter turnout was the lowest since Calvin Coolidge won in 1924. Despite fears of Democratic coattails, Republicans retained control of the House of Representatives and increased their majority in the Senate; they also maintained control of the majority of statehouses. The main lesson of the election

was voters' endorsement of the status quo of divided government, with the hope that cooperation, rather than gridlock and paralysis, would characterize the final years of the twentieth century.

The period from 1981 to 1996 brought enormous changes to the United States: the end of the four-decade Cold War; a dramatic rethinking of the role of the state in modern American life; the ongoing globalization of political and economic life; and growing diversity in American culture and public life. Those fifteen years seemed likely to be as important a period of realignment as the 1930s and 1940s, when the New Deal state was formed and the United States took on its global responsibilities in World War II and its aftermath. The period was certainly as dramatic as the 1890s, when the country completed the process of industrialization, absorbed a huge wave of immigrants, and secured an overseas empire. But given all the challenges the nation faced at home and abroad, it was too soon to declare an end to the activist American state.

Summary

★

In the 1980s and 1990s a new domestic and world order shaped American life. Ronald Reagan's administration advocated a smaller role for the federal government in domestic programs and the restoration of American prestige abroad through a massive military buildup. The term *Reaganomics* stood for tax cuts and budget reductions enacted in 1981 and 1982. Reagan's economic policies, notably deregulation and tax cuts, added to the concentration of wealth in the 1980s. Reagan remained enormously popular throughout his two terms but left large budget deficits to his successor, Vice-President George Bush.

The most important change during the Bush administration was the end of the Cold War, which had been the guiding principle of American foreign policy since the end of World War II. The dramatic collapse of communism in the Soviet Union in 1991 further complicated the old truisms. The post–Cold War future seemed to promise a fragile world peace that would be vulnerable to regional and ethnic conflicts but in which the United States, as the world's only remaining superpower, would still play the dominant leadership role. The United States also played a leading role in an increasingly global economy but no longer dominated the world economy as it had done during the Pax Americana of the immediate postwar world.

American society in the 1980s and 1990s continued to turn inward to address its own needs. Increased immigration, notably from Latin America and Asia, changed the demographic balance of many areas, especially the cities, and the strains of an increasingly diverse society were reflected in debates over affirmative action and multiculturalism. Slow productivity growth, wage stagnation, and growing inequality in income were the major domestic economic trends. Meanwhile, American businesses struggled to compete in an increasingly competitive global marketplace. The information superhighway and cyberspace pointed to a high-tech future.

Soon after the Democrats regained the White House with the election of Bill Clinton in 1992, the Republican landslide of 1994 reshaped politics dramatically by emphasizing a balanced budget, tax cuts, and shrinking the federal government by turning programs over to the states. In January 1996 even President Clinton admitted, "The era of big government is over." In August he signed a welfare reform bill that ended the federal guarantee of cash assistance to the poor. Clinton won reelection to a second term, but continued Republican control of Congress suggested that the long-term trend of federal activism had been slowed, if not reversed.

TIMELINE

1981	Economic Recovery Tax Act
	Sandra Day O'Connor nominated to Supreme Court
	Beginning of AIDS epidemic
1981–1983	Recession
1983	Star Wars proposed
1984	Geraldine Ferraro becomes first woman on major party ticket
1985	Gramm-Rudman Balanced Budget Act
	United States becomes a debtor nation
	Mikhail Gorbachev takes power in USSR
1986	Iran-Contra affair
	Simpson-Mazzoli Immigration Act
1987	Montreal environmental protocol
1988	George Bush elected president
1989	Savings and loan crisis
	Political revolutions in Eastern Europe
	Webster v. Reproductive Health Services
1990–1991	Persian Gulf crisis
1990–1992	Recession
1991	Dissolution of Soviet Union ends Cold War
	Clarence Thomas–Anita Hill hearings
1992	Los Angeles riots
	Earth Summit at Rio de Janeiro
	Bill Clinton elected president
1993	Family and Medical Leave Act
	NAFTA ratified
1994	Omnibus Violent Crime Control and Prevention Act
	Health care reform fails
	Republicans gain control of Congress
1995	United States establishes diplomatic relations with Vietnam
	Twenty-fifth anniversary of Earth Day
	U.S. troops enforce peace in Bosnia
1996	Personal Responsibility and Work Opportunity Act
	Clinton reelected

Suggested Readings

Few historians have turned their attention to the period after 1980, leaving the field to journalists, economists, and political scientists. The Bureau of the Census offers a fine introduction to the period in its *Statistical Abstract of the United States* (117th ed., 1997). Essays on important issues are available in the *Congressional Quarterly Researcher*.

The Reagan-Bush Years, 1981–1993

Haynes Johnson, *Sleepwalking through History* (1991), provides an excellent overview of America in the Reagan years. See also Michael Rogin, *Ronald Reagan: The Movie* (1987); Lou Cannon, *President Reagan: A Role of a Lifetime* (1991); Michael Schaller, *Reckoning with Reagan: America and Its President in the 1980s* (1992); and Peggy Noonan, *What I Saw at the Revolution* (1990).

On Reaganomics, George Gilder's *Wealth and Poverty* (1981) represents the views held by many in the Reagan administration, but David Stockman's memoir, *The Triumph of Politics* (1986), is more revealing. See also Benjamin Friedman, *Day of Reckoning: The Consequences of American Economic Policy under Reagan and After* (1988).

On the Bush administration, see James A. Baker, *The Politics of Diplomacy* (1995), and Stephen R. Graubard, *Mr. Bush's War: Adventures in the Politics of Illusion* (1992). On politics, see E. J. Dionne, *Why Americans Hate Politics* (1992); William Greider, *Who Will Tell the People?* (1992); and Kevin Phillips, *The Politics of Rich and Poor: Wealth and the American Electorate in the Reagan Aftermath* (1990).

Foreign Relations under Reagan and Bush

For foreign policy, Stephen Ambrose and Douglas Brinkley, *Rise to Globalism* (8th ed., 1997), provide a comprehensive overview of the Reagan and Bush years. The Iran-Contra scandal is covered in Jane Hunter et al., *The Iran-Contra Connection* (1987). Good introductions to U.S. foreign relations with Central and South America include Walter LaFeber, *Inevitable Revolutions* (1984), and Thomas Carothers, *In the Name of Democracy: U.S. Policy toward Latin America in the Reagan Years* (1991).

The emergence of a new world order has provoked commentary from economists, journalists, and historians, including Paul Kennedy, *The Rise and Fall of the Great Powers* (1987); Joseph Nye, *Bound to Lead: The Changing Nature of American Power* (1990); Robert Kuttner, *The End of Laissez Faire* (1991); and Henry R. Nau, *The Myth of America's Decline* (1990). See also Michael Beschloss and Strobe Talbott, *At the Highest Levels: The Inside Story of the End of the Cold War* (1994), and Michael J. Hugan, ed., *The End of the Cold War: Its Meanings and Implications* (1992).

Uncertain Times

Paul Krugman, *Peddling Prosperity: Economic Sense and Nonsense in the Age of Diminished Expectations* (1994), and Jeffrey Madrick, *The End of Affluence* (1995), provide overviews of economic trends since the 1970s. Lester C. Thurow offers an insightful analysis of the world economic changes accompanying the collapse of communism in *The Future of Capitalism* (1996). For overviews of U.S. competitiveness in the global marketplace, see Daniel Yergin and Joseph Stanislaw, *The Commanding Heights* (1998); Hedrick Smith, *Rethinking America* (1995); and Robert B. Reich, *The Work of Nations: Preparing Ourselves for 21st Century Capitalism* (1991). Books that address the growing inequality in American life include William J. Wilson, *The Truly Disadvantaged* (1987); Nicholas Lemann, *The Promised Land* (1989); and Andrew Hacker, *Two Nations: Black and White, Separate, Hostile, Unequal* (1992).

On women, work, and families, see Hilda Scott, *Working Your Way to the Bottom: The Feminization of Poverty* (1985), and Arlie Hochschild, *The Second Shift: Working Parents and the Revolution at Home* (1989). For feminism and its critics, see Susan Faludi, *Backlash: The Undeclared War on American Women* (1991). Toni Morrison, ed., *Race-ing Justice, En-gendering Power* (1992), covers the Clarence Thomas–Anita Hill hearings.

David Reimers, *Still the Golden Door* (2nd ed., 1992), covers immigration policy in the postwar period. Roberto Suro, *Strangers among Us* (1998), shows how Latino immigration is transforming America. Ronald Takaki, *Strangers from a Different Shore* (1989), covers Asian Americans. On race and politics in California since 1978, see Peter Schrag, *Paradise Lost* (1998).

Randy Shilts, *And the Band Played On: Politics, People, and the AIDS Epidemic* (1987), is a controversial critique of inaction in the early years of the AIDS epidemic. Allan Bloom, *The Closing of the American Mind* (1987), and E. D. Hirsch Jr., *Cultural Literacy* (1988), deal with issues of curriculum, learning, and literacy. Lawrence W. Levine, *The Opening of the American Mind* (1996), challenges many of their assumptions. For differing views on affirmative action, see Stephen L. Carter, *Reflections of an Affirmative Action Baby* (1991), and Gertrude Ezorsky, *Racism and Justice: The Case for Affirmative Action* (1991). Gregg Easterbrook provides a general overview of the environment in *A Moment on the Earth* (1995). Daniel Yergin, *The Prize* (1991), chronicles how oil dominates modern life, with both economic and environmental consequences.

For the story of Bill Gates and Microsoft, see Steven Manes, *Gates* (1993), and James Wallace, *Hard Drive* (1992). Also of interest is Joshua Quittner and Michelle Slatalla, *Speeding the Net: The Inside Story of Netscape and How It Challenged Microsoft* (1998). For biotechnology, see Robert Cook-Deegan, *The Gene Wars* (1994); Arthur Kornberg, *The Golden Helix: Inside Biotech Ventures* (1996); and Eric S. Grace, *Biotechnology Unzipped* (1997).

Restructuring the Domestic Order: Public Life, 1992–1996

For an excellent overview of the Clinton administration's first year, see Elizabeth Drew, *Finding His Voice* (1994). Other sources include Bob Woodward, *The Agenda* (1994), and Roger Morris, *Partners in Power: The Clintons and Their America* (1996). James B. Stewart, *Blood Sport: The President and His Adversaries* (1996), analyzes Whitewater. Richard Holbrooke, *To End a War* (1998), provides a compelling insider's account of the Dayton peace talks on Bosnia. William Greider, *Fortress America* (1998), examines the American military in the post–Cold War era. On the Republican agenda, see Newt Gingrich, *To Renew America* (1995). See also Dan Balz and Ronald Brownstein, *Storming the Gates: Protest Politics and the Republican Revival* (1996), and Ralph Reed, *Active Faith: How Christians Are Changing the Soul of American Politics* (1996).

Epilogue

★

America and the World at 2000:
How Historians Interpret Contemporary Events and Their Legacy for the Future

IT IS THE year 2000. Here, courtesy of one of those catchy communications that circulate on the Internet from time to time, are some verbal snapshots of what a person born in 1980—for example, a college student reading this textbook—remembers about the events of the past twenty years. (If you were born before 1980, be forewarned that this will make you feel old, perhaps very old.)

- You have never been afraid of nuclear war. To you, "the day after" means a pill, not a movie about the aftermath of nuclear conflagration.
- You were nine years old when the Berlin Wall fell and eleven years old when the former Soviet Union broke up, and therefore you do not remember the Cold War.
- The Vietnam War seems as distant as World War II or the Civil War, and you have only preadolescent memories of the Persian Gulf War.
- You are too young to remember the space shuttle *Challenger* blowing up in 1986 or the Chinese uprising at Tiananmen Square in 1989.
- You have no recollections of the Reagan era and do not know that he was once shot.
- You have always had an answering machine and cable television, and you cannot imagine not having a remote control.
- Your lifetime has always included awareness of AIDS.

Many, but by no means all, of these topics are covered in the last chapter of *America's History*, including the end of the Cold War, new technology, Operation Desert Storm, and the AIDS epidemic. These topics represent a sample of what historians currently think is important to include in a comprehensive survey of late twentieth-century American life. In contrast, the 1981 Reagan assassination attempt, the nuclear freeze movement of the early 1980s, the *Challenger* disaster, and Tiananmen Square didn't make the cut.

Writing history is about making choices, about deciding what to include and what to leave out; and nowhere is this process more difficult than in writing the history of recent events. The key question for future editions of *America's History* is what contemporary events will emerge as truly significant historically (and thus warrant inclusion in a broad synthesis of American history and culture) and what events will be judged mere blips on the historical consciousness (things that seemed all-encompassing at the time but whose long-term significance subsequently paled). What the historian's knowledge can add is some sense from the past about how to think about the present, when all of us are bombarded daily with headlines and breaking stories and when our own memories and reactions to stories and events can cloud or influence our ability to regard them objectively. Today's headlines do not always become tomorrow's history.

In a 1992 interview former president Richard M. Nixon stated bluntly, "In my view, history is never worth reading until it's fifty years old. It takes fifty years before you're able to come back and evaluate a man or a period of time." The mere passage of time does often help participants understand events and place them in a broad historical context. For example, historians know much more about the origins of the Cold War now that documents are surfacing from the former

Soviet Union and other formerly communist states that present their side of the global conflict. Fifty years after the fact, Swiss banks are now coming up with an accounting of what happened to money deposited there by Jews later killed in Hitler's concentration camps.

Yet if textbook writers took Nixon's advice literally, they would end their books just after World War II and the onset of the Cold War. Of course this isn't possible or desirable, and the enormous outpouring of excellent scholarship that informs Part Six of *America's History* demonstrates that it is indeed possible to assess and interpret historically events of the fairly recent past such as the Cold War, the civil rights movement, the growth of suburbia, and the changing contours of the global economy. But the closer the past gets to the present, the harder the task becomes. That does not mean, however, that historians have to cede the recent past, or even contemporary events, to journalists and television analysts.

What follows is an overview of the key areas in modern American life that have been traced throughout this book—politics, society and culture, the economy, and diplomacy—at the historical moment when the twentieth century turns into the twenty-first. Thinking about the range of topics covered reinforces the point that reading a textbook like *America's History* is just the first step toward mastering the history of the enormously complex world we inhabit. Just as in earlier chapters, we examine the larger themes, shifting perspectives, and emerging syntheses in these key areas, but with a more tentative and open-ended perspective. Think of this part of *America's History* as a historical document: how a group of American historians saw the challenges and promises of writing the contemporary history of their society as the year 2000 approached. Look at the choice of issues and mode of analysis to discover how historians gather and evaluate evidence, how they link individual events to larger patterns and themes, and yes, how they are often forced to revise their earlier conclusions or change their minds entirely.

Readers of this last part have an advantage over its authors: you know how certain stories have turned out by 2000, something that historians writing about them in 1999 do not. Maybe fifty years from now you will pass along an old copy of this college textbook to your grandchildren, and future generations, like Richard Nixon said, will be able to tell us how we did.

Politics. Although most recent textbooks seek to replace a "presidential synthesis"—that is, a narrative and analysis structured around specific administrations—with an organization that treats social and cultural history as fully as political developments, it is certainly true that the importance of the office and the power of the president require every textbook to men-

tion all, or almost all, presidential elections. The last chapter of *America's History* ended, for example, with the 1996 election, and the next edition will certainly give a prominent place to the results of the election in 2000. But which accomplishments and failures historians will choose to write about for Bill Clinton's second term is far less clear. In fact, Clinton's impeachment by the House and subsequent trial in the Senate raised the possibility that the popular president, whose approval ratings remained high throughout the crisis, might not even serve out his second term. As journalist R. W. Apple observed, "In the toxic politics of century's end in Washington, the inconceivable has become the commonplace."

The political fallout from President Clinton's affair with White House intern Monica Lewinsky is an excellent example of the difficulties of writing contemporary history when the story is literally unfolding on a day-to-day basis. Indeed, we sympathized with a journalist in the *Washington Post* writing about December 19, 1998, the historic day when the House of Representatives voted two articles of impeachment—obstruction of justice and perjury—against President Clinton: "So this is what history feels like before the historians get hold of it. Before they choose, interpret, compress, highlight and elide. History feels awfully confusing."

As historians, we attempt no assessment here about the nature of the scandal or the political maneuvering surrounding impeachment and the subsequent Senate trial. Instead, we try to step back and think about the implications of the political crisis for the institution of the presidency and the country as a whole. For example, will the presidency be permanently undermined by the impeachment process (Clinton's case was only the second time in America's history that a president was impeached), or will the institution and the country prove as resilient as they did in 1974 in the aftermath of Richard Nixon's resignation to avoid imminent removal from office? Has the historic balance of power between the three branches of government been permanently upset by a partisan Congress pursuing an open-ended investigation of a sitting president of the opposite political party? What will be the effects of the impeachment proceedings on citizens' attitudes toward their elected representatives and the system of government in Washington in general? These are some of the larger questions that will concern historians who evaluate this era in the years to come.

One striking aspect of the political crisis on which historians will no doubt focus is the role that the Internet and cable news (whose extensive coverage spawned the slogan "All Monica, all the time") played in spreading the story. In the past, information about the unfolding story would have filtered through journalistic or congressional sources, or it would have remained secret entirely. Think how different the Watergate

THE CAST
(in order of appearance)

The President	WILLIAM J. CLINTON
The Intern	MONICA S. LEWINSKY
The Secretary	BETTY CURRIE
The President's Wife	HILLARY CLINTON
The Independent Counsel	KENNETH W. STARR
The Intern's Best Friend	LINDA TRIPP
The President's Best Friend	VERNON JORDAN
The President's Lawyer	DAVID E. KENDALL
The Plaintiff	PAULA JONES
The Literary Agent	LUCIANNE GOLDBERG
The Dog	BUDDY
The Chief House Prosecutor	HENRY HYDE
The Vice Preside	

The Impeachment Players
For more than a year the Monica Lewinsky story dominated the news, making household names of major and minor characters. Then, like a movie, it ended. Most Americans seemed relieved that the ordeal was over, telling pollsters that they were ready for Clinton and the country to move on.
Jesse Gordon/The New York Times. Reprinted with permission.

impeachment hearings would have been if ordinary citizens had had direct access in 1974 to the masses of detail and evidence that were available to the public at century's end. The Internet, barely a factor in public life until the mid-1990s, is challenging more traditional sources of news information, such as television or newspapers, as a major purveyor of information about contemporary events. The downside to such instant information is that much of it is circulated with minimal editorial controls or checks, leading to unsubstantiated statements and more than a few rumors. One of the tasks for future historians will be to sift fact from fiction in this proliferation of new sources of information.

Another factor that turned the Clinton-Lewinsky scandal into an even bigger story than it might have been otherwise was the way in which the media has turned the world into a global village: anyone, anywhere in the world, could tune in and watch the story unfolding live. (CNN's on-the-spot coverage of the Persian Gulf War in 1990–1991 was a turning point in such media coverage.) This explosion of information access coincided with what one critic has called the "growing tabloidization of American culture," a frenzy for gossip that has blurred the lines between public and private. What does it say about contemporary American culture that we know more about the intimate details of the president's sexual habits than about nearly anyone else's but our own? These trends, building in the late twentieth century, will be hard to derail in the twenty-first.

Yet it is quite possible that when historians draw up their assessment of the Clinton presidency and the politics of governance in the 1990s, the impeachment scandal, in hindsight, will not be seen as the most serious or important issue of President Clinton's eight years in office. Writing in the heat of the moment robs historians of the ability to step back, gather evidence, and listen to and weigh different viewpoints—essential to the historian's craft. But it is not always necessary to wait fifty years in order to get a better historical perspective on events; sometimes just a few years will do.

A good case in point is the 1994 congressional election, in which Republicans won control of the House of Representatives for the first time in forty years with a campaign organized around an antigovernment theme spelled out in their "Contract with America." When the previous edition of *America's History* was being written, the congressional election had just occurred, and as historians and authors we interpreted the electoral results as a potential watershed in twentieth-century political history, perhaps (although we intentionally fudged a bit here) one that signaled the end of the rise of the state. Four years later, in the wake of the results of the 1998 congressional election in which Democrats picked up five seats in the House (unprecedented for a party in power in an off-year election) instead of losing seats in an anti-Clinton stampede, it was the architect of the 1994 Republican victory, Speaker of the House Newt Gingrich, who resigned, not Bill Clinton. Not a single Washington pundit had predicted this startling turn of events. Suddenly the "Republican revolution" of 1994 looked less like a history-altering turning point than a minor political realignment.

History will always have to take account of these sudden, unexpected turns of events—the election upsets, the assassinations, the natural disasters—that can seem to change the course of history overnight. But historians need not place themselves at the mercy of fast-breaking news; instead, they can attempt to place

Part of the Problem, Part of the Solution
Since Bill Clinton is part of the baby-boom generation that will put pressure on the ailing social security system in the twenty-first century, he has a personal stake in the issue. His political investment is stronger: a successful overhaul of Social Security could be a major legacy of his administration.
Chick Harrity for USN & WR.

events in the broader historical context of the country's national history and promise to revisit their assessment later to see if it has weathered the test of time and evidence. In other cases, historians can draw on their knowledge of the past to identify contemporary issues likely to emerge as defining moments when they write about this period in the future. Please excuse us if the details are a bit hazy as we gaze into our crystal balls.

One such issue is Social Security. Perhaps when we look back at the Clinton years, one of the most important critical markers will be whether the budget surplus that began in 1997 was used to shore up the ailing Social Security system. A driving concern at the close of the century is what will happen when the baby boomers (Americans born between 1945 and 1963) begin to retire and collect Social Security. Current projections show Social Security running short of money to pay all promised benefits by 2032. As a result of these gloomy predictions, many Americans are losing confidence that government pensions, one of the cornerstones of the American welfare state, will actually be available for them when they retire. The historical problem has been identified, but not the solution.

Another political issue that historians will be writing about in the future is health care. As we discussed in the last chapter of *America's History*, Clinton's 1994 plan for reform of the health care system was considered overly sweeping. An incremental, market-driven approach featuring managed care seemed to better suit the needs of the country at the time, with the result that by 1998 almost two-thirds of the population (61%) belonged to some kind of health maintenance organization (HMO). But no sooner had managed care become the predominant method of dispensing health

care than doubts set in. Complaints about restrictions on the kinds of care and services available, often fueled by heart-wrenching stories of patients denied access to potentially lifesaving treatments by their cost-conscious HMOs, became so widespread that health care advocates and politicians proposed a "Patient's Bill of Rights" to expand patient choice and make HMOs accountable for the quality of care provided. Furthermore, managed care had failed to reach the growing proportion of Americans (more than one-sixth of the population) who had no access to health insurance at all.

Another puzzle of contemporary politics that history must address is what happened to the welfare system and its beneficiaries after Congress and the states passed sweeping changes in the 1990s, especially the 1996 federal law placing a five-year lifetime limit on assistance for single mothers and a two-year limit for adults without dependent children. Welfare recipients affected by these changes would theoretically reach the end of their benefits at various points between 1998 and 2001, but welfare rolls were already dropping precipitously before the federal deadlines kicked in. For example, Wisconsin, which had developed an ambitious "workfare" program to get people off welfare, saw its number of cases drop from almost 80,000 in 1994 to just over 10,000 four years later.

Yet there was no consensus on what this drop meant or what had happened to the former welfare recipients. Were they able to use state employment services to develop skills and find jobs, or did they find jobs simply because the economy was booming? What will happen if the economy slows down, becoming unable to absorb all those who want to work and possi-

Proud New Citizens
The many faces of America are
reflected in this group of newly
naturalized citizens in Brooklyn,
New York. Behind each of these
smiles is a story that is part of
America's history at the end of
the twentieth century.
Lynn Johnson.

bly throwing them back on welfare? Is the goal of workfare to help people find jobs in the private sector, or
merely to discourage the poor from applying for public
assistance in the first place? Some answers will emerge
when the time limits are reached; others will take
longer. Only with the completion of substantive studies
of what actually happened to former welfare recipients
will historians have the data to mount an assessment of
the success or failure of attempts, in President Clinton's
words, to "end welfare as we know it." As with Social
Security and health care, this task will be crucial to
understanding the evolution of the commitment of the
state to public welfare, one of the major themes of the
twentieth century.

Society and Culture.   There are no accurate data at
the time this book goes to press to predict the future of
welfare, but there are much more reliable projections
about the changing racial makeup of American society.
The U.S. Census Bureau predicts that in the year 2050
whites will make up 52.7 percent of the American population (down from 75.7% in 1990), with Hispanics
accounting for 21.1 percent, blacks 15 percent, and
Asians 10.1 percent. If any level of intermarriage had
been factored in (studies show Hispanics and Asians
marry outside their racial groups much more often
than do blacks), the projected white "majority" would
probably have slipped to a white "minority." At the
close of the twentieth century, already one out of
twenty-five married couples is interracial, and there are
at least three million children of mixed-race parentage
in the country. (This latter figure does not even include
the millions of Hispanic mestizos, as well as black
Americans who have either European or American

Indian ancestors.) Probably the best known example of
the country's increasingly multi-racial heritage is golfer
Tiger Woods, who likes to call himself a "Cablinasian"
to reflect his multiracial background of Caucasian,
black, native American, and Asian heritages.

It won't be necessary to wait until 2050 for
another demographic milestone: around the year
2005, according to Census Bureau projections, Hispanics will surpass blacks as the country's largest
minority group. This is a development of great historical import. For most of the country's history, racial
issues have been seen literally as "black and white."
The rising numbers of Hispanics and Asians will push
the United States to reframe the American discourse
on race. Whether or not Hispanics and Asians join
forces with blacks will have significant implications
for civil rights organizations and divisive national
issues such as affirmative action. By contrast, if Hispanics and Asians are seen more as "honorary whites"
in a mostly white mixed-race majority, then the historic black-nonblack dichotomy may continue or even
intensify. Americans have often talked about their
society as a melting pot, and the twentieth century
witnessed a broadened acceptance of a wider range of
cultures and skin colors. Deep divisions accompanied
the shift, however, and such acrimony (which died
down temporarily in the late 1990s after flaring up
earlier in the decade) is likely to return periodically in
the next century, especially during periods of economic or social conflict.

The changing nature of the American population is
also having a decided impact on America's religious life.
In a trend that will likely continue into the next century,
mainline (and often liberal) Protestant denominations

Southern Baptists Reach Out
In 1995, as part of their effort to reach
out to African Americans (who currently account for about 500,000 of the
Southern Baptist Convention's 15.5 million members), Southern Baptist leaders officially repudiated racism and
asked for forgiveness for their role in
defending segregation.
Alan S. Weiner/Gamma Liaison.

such as Episcopalians, Methodists, and Presbyterians
have been losing members since their peak during the
baby-boom era in the mid-1960s. The greatest growth
for Protestants since the 1970s has been in the more
conservative Southern Baptist Convention, which
became the largest religious organization in the United
States after the Roman Catholic Church. At the same
time, changes in immigration laws have increased the
ranks of Catholics as well as believers of other faiths,
including larger numbers of American Muslims, Buddhists, and Hindus—religions that had not previously
been well represented in the United States. A multiracial society is also increasingly a multireligious one.

In a trend with wide-reaching implications, some
American-based faiths have become so multinational
that they no longer depend solely on American believers. The most striking example of that trend is the
Church of Jesus Christ of Latter-day Saints, or Mormons. In 1980 three-quarters of Mormonism's 4.6 million believers lived in the United States; by 1997 the
church had 10 million followers, the majority of them
overseas. The Assemblies of God, a pentecostal denomination founded in Arkansas in 1914 whose believers
seek to be filled with the Holy Spirit, also had more followers abroad than in the United States, especially in
Brazil. Reflecting this new complexity of American religious life, one scholar observed, "It's a fun time to be a
student of religion, because there are a lot of interesting changes going on. We don't know where they're
going to end up." That sums up the challenge of writing
the history of contemporary America.

Another contemporary trend worth watching is the
nation's energy use at the turn of the century, a phenomenon that calls into question how significant a
realignment actually occurred as a result of the energy
crisis of the 1970s. By the late 1990s Americans were
using almost as much energy per capita as they had in
1973, wiping out practically all the savings that had
occurred through conservation and efficiency after the
energy crisis. At century's end, Americans consume
more than twice as much energy per person as Europeans or Japanese. (Only Canadians, with a larger percentage of heavy industry and a colder climate,
consume more worldwide.) The short-term reason for
the turnaround is clear: a worldwide decline in oil
prices, which made it cheaper and easier for Americans
to live more energy-intensive life-styles. Two symptoms
of the shift: the growing popularity of sports utility
vehicles, and the trend toward larger, more appliance-
laden houses. To meet these energy needs, the United
States now imports about 50 percent of its oil, up from
35 percent in 1973. Even though energy experts warn
that a tightening of oil supplies and higher prices are
inevitable, few are heeding the message. This change in
mentality also threatens to undercut the international
progress made in the 1980s and 1990s on pressing environmental issues such as global warming, acid rain,
and depletion of the ozone layer.

As befits *America's History*'s overarching interpretation of the twentieth century—globalization—many of
the issues that face the United States at 2000 are global
issues. The environment is one; the AIDS epidemic is

Los Angeles by Night
The vast expanse that is the Los Angeles metropolitan area is especially striking at night, as captured by artist Peter Alexander. Yet think of the vast amounts of energy being consumed by those city lights.
James Corcoran Gallery, Santa Monica, CA.

another. According to a United Nations study conducted in 1997, more than 30 million people worldwide suffered from AIDS or were infected with HIV, the virus that causes AIDS. The problem was especially acute in Africa, where 21 million were infected; in the country of Zimbabwe, the rate was one in four. Rates were lower in Asia, Eastern Europe, and South America, but the disease was spreading there as well. In the United States, by contrast, the number of AIDS deaths dropped from 31,256 in 1995 to 16,685 just two years later, the result of potent—and expensive—drugs that allowed certain infected people to manage their disease. But even after extensive public health campaigns were launched, the number of new infections was not dropping in the United States. The worldwide impact of AIDS puts it on a comparable basis to the Black Death, the bubonic plague epidemic that swept through fourteenth-century Europe and killed 20 million people (one-quarter of Europe's population), and the influenza pandemic of 1918–1919 that killed 20 million people worldwide. With an AIDS vaccine a distant hope, there is no end in sight to this terrible scourge.

According to *USA Today*, 75 percent of Americans believe that another major and deadly disease will appear by 2025. In other ways, however, Americans seem to expect miracles from medical science in the next century. Fueled by consumer demands for health information and a desire to live longer, healthier lives, the news media routinely treat advances in science and medicine as front-page news. When the *New York Times* ran a feature story about a possible breakthrough in cancer research in 1998, hopes soared that cancer might once and for all be conquered. "OUR BEST HOPE" proclaimed one headline, with an accompanying article by a cancer-stricken journalist that stated, "Maybe we don't have to die." Doctors often learn about new drugs and procedures right along with their patients through newspaper accounts and drug company–sponsored advertisements; patients also surf the Internet for information about clinical trials of new treatments or experimental drugs for specific diseases. This democratization of medical knowledge empowers some consumers, but at the cost of inflating hopes about untested drugs and procedures that are years away from marketability. Yet Americans' hope for a cure—for breast cancer, for AIDS, for Alzheimer's disease—continues unabated.

The Economy. Nowhere has it been harder for historians to use the past to make predictions about the future than in the field of economics. Past mistakes can be embarrassing. Here is what the authors of *America's*

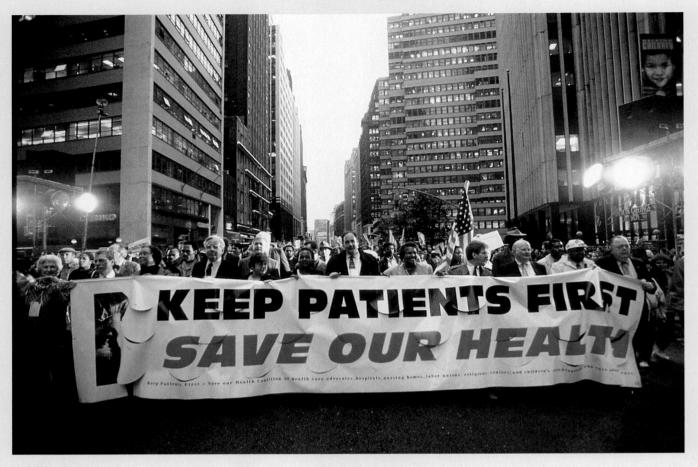

Health Care
Throughout the 1990s, America grappled with how to provide affordable health care
for its citizens. First lady Hillary Rodham Clinton took part in this protest against
Medicare and Medicaid cuts in New York City in 1995.
Stephan Ferry/Gamma Liaison.

History said at the conclusion of the second edition (1993): "The early twenty-first century will likely be most favorable to Pacific Rim and EC [European Community] countries. . . . The strongest individual economies will likely continue to be those of Japan and Germany." By the publication of the third edition (1997) our tone had shifted a bit, with the United States emerging as the dominant player in the new world order but sharing global economic and political influence with Japan, China, Singapore, Hong Kong, and other Pacific Rim countries; Canada and Mexico in North America; and the newly revitalized EC. We concluded, "Temporarily on the sidelines are the nations of the former Soviet Union and Eastern Europe."

At least we were right about Russia: in the summer of 1998 the Russian economy essentially went bankrupt, defaulting on loans and devaluing the ruble. All the other countries mentioned—with the exception of Canada, Mexico, and Germany—were engulfed in a

global economic slowdown that started in 1997. The change in fortunes was especially acute in Asia, where the picture went from miracle to meltdown, with nine of Asia's thirteen major economies either in recession or depression by 1998. Especially hard hit was Japan, the world's second largest economy after the United States and the one country that just a few years earlier had seemed poised to dominate the global economy.

As the world's economic troubles deepened, the new buzzword among politicians and economists was an updated version of the domino theory called *contagion*—the idea that if one country's economy was allowed to implode, it might set in motion an uncontrollable sequence of events around the world. The International Monetary Fund (IMF) and the World Bank, set up in the wake of World War II to ensure financial stability in world markets, responded by making one costly rescue bailout of a shaky economy after another—Thailand, Indonesia, South Korea, and Rus-

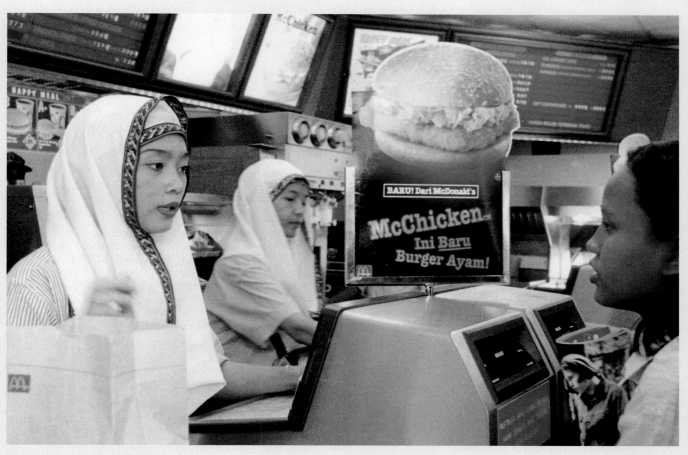

Multinational McChicken
The proliferation of McDonald's franchises worldwide symbolizes the multinational nature of modern economic life. However, reaching new markets often necessitates a certain amount of cultural adaptation, as these McDonald's workers in traditional Muslim dress demonstrate in Jakarta, Indonesia.
Wide World Photos, Inc.

sia. Fears were raised that Brazil, Venezuela, or Mexico might be next.

How could things change so quickly? In 1989 it was widely accepted that Japan was rising and America was declining, or, as the scholar Chalmers Johnson put it, "The cold war is over, and Japan won." Now the opposite appears to be true: the U.S. economy looks strong, almost invincible, and the Asian economies are in serious trouble. One conclusion that seems likely is that when an economy is performing well, as was Japan's in the late 1980s and America's in the late 1990s, it temporarily hides all sorts of problems. As economist Laura D'Andrea Tyson observes, "In prosperous times we overstate the good and understate the bad." One of the most troubling "bad" trends is the growing disparity in wealth and opportunity that characterizes the American economy at the end of the century, with the very rich profiting the most from the recent period of prosperity.

As historians struggle to make sense of the global economic picture, they are hampered not just by the dramatic turn of events in Asia but also by the fact that many economic tenets no longer seem as reliable as they once did. For example, since 1960 a widely accepted economic principle called the Phillips Curve posited that there could be low inflation or low unemployment, but not both. Yet the boom of the 1990s has seen inflation *and* unemployment drop to their lowest levels in generations. Another long-held economic tenet claimed that measures to lower the deficit would act as a drag on the economy, thereby slowing economic growth. Yet in the 1990s the United States has experienced both significant deficit reduction and a period of sustained economic growth. No longer does world economic growth automatically lead to higher oil prices: oil prices have fallen steadily since the early 1980s as a result of new sources of oil flooding the market. In other words, many of the principles and tenets on

Chemical Warfare
The threat of chemical and biological warfare posed new challenges for American security. Here soldiers engage in chemical warfare training at Fort Drum, New York.
© M. Greenlar/The Image Works.

which economists—and historians who rely on those economists—depend seem to have broken down. Perhaps the ups and downs of the past ten years will lead to the emergence of new economic laws, but for now we are all struggling to make sense of a complex and deeply interconnected world economy.

Diplomacy. Just as complicated are the emerging contours of the post–Cold War world. Note that historians are still using the Cold War as the organizing concept for the late twentieth century, even though it ended a decade earlier. Future textbooks will probably recognize the events of 1989–1991 in Eastern Europe and the Soviet Union as *the* defining watershed in the late twentieth century; certainly the years 1945–1991 would provide a logical periodization for Part Six in a future edition of *America's History*. Events since then—the last part of Chapter 31 and this epilogue—would in effect be the opening of a new Part Seven, as yet unnamed and (with apologies to the sports world) with themes and "players" to be announced later.

Despite the end of the Cold War, much of American foreign policy is still directed toward the goals that have shaped much of the twentieth century, such as the desire to contain powerful or potentially powerful nations that might appear as rivals. Thus the United States supported the expansion of NATO to include former Communist bloc members Poland, Hungary, and the Czech Republic as a hedge against a resurgent Russia. As to policy toward China, the world's most populous country, the United States promoted its version of free-market capitalism and democracy at the same time as it worried about China's nuclear capabilities and

human rights violations. Protecting U.S. access to oil reserves worldwide remained a high priority, with the oil-rich Caspian region (wedged between Russia and Iran) emerging as the newest stage for superpower maneuvering.

On the eve of the twenty-first century, terrorism emerged as a central concern of U.S. foreign policy. A series of terrorist attacks, often directed at American citizens or embassies abroad but occasionally at targets in the United States (such as the 1993 bombing of New York City's World Trade Center), heightened America's sense of vulnerability. Even though the number of lives lost was relatively small (98 Americans were killed in foreign terrorist attacks between 1989 and 1998, less than are killed on average each year by lightning), driving the fear was the perception that terrorists pose a continuous, deadly, and invisible threat to American interests and installations throughout the world. Like the Cold War fears of nuclear annihilation that sent schoolchildren ducking and cowering under their desks, no one is ever safe in a world where terrorists reign.

But unlike the Cold War, a period during which the Soviet Union was identified as America's primary enemy, terrorist attacks cannot necessarily be traced to a single state or a single leader. Instead of having a central headquarters like the Kremlin, loose organizations are dispersed throughout many countries. At the end of the twentieth century, the strongest threats to American interests come from militant Islamic sects committed to a messianic vision of the end of Western influence in the Arab world and the ultimate destruction of the United States. Responsibility for attacks is often difficult to pin down—was it Hezbollah, Islamic Jihad, or

Crisis in Kosovo
In 1999 violence broke out in the Yugoslavian province of Kosovo, spearheaded by
Yugoslav president Slobodan Milosevic's attempts to "cleanse" the province of ethnic
Albanians. Here a group of ethnic Albanian refugees weep as they leave their homes in
Kosovo.
Wide World Photos, Inc.

Osama bin Laden's followers?—and bringing terrorists
to international justice is even harder to carry out.
Retaliation can sometimes be effective, but at other
times it simply provokes further terrorism in a war of
attrition.

Although there are few rules or guidelines for a
coming war against terrorism, the world was beginning to feel confident that nuclear proliferation had
been slowed or even halted as the century drew to an
end. Then, in 1998, India and Pakistan each defied
world opinion by testing a nuclear device. In the immediate aftermath of World War II, only the largest and
most advanced countries could realistically hope to
develop nuclear weapons; but fifty years later, the
capacity is spread much more broadly. Until India and
Pakistan conducted their tests, only five countries had
declared nuclear-weapons capability: the United
States, Russia, Britain, France, and China (although
most observers believe that Israel had such capacity as
well). In addition, Iran, Iraq, North Korea, and Libya
were suspected of having secret nuclear-weapons programs. What was especially worrisome about the
Indian and Pakistani tests was that these neighboring
countries had a long history of acrimony in one of the
world's most dangerous regions. While the world
talked gravely about nuclear proliferation, India and

A Hero for Our Jaded Times

Nelson Mandela is that rare contemporary hero whose stature seems destined to be confirmed posthumously by history. In a valedictory address to the United Nations in 1998, Mandela spoke of his long personal journey:

> Born as the First World War came to a close and departing from public life as the world marks half a century of the Universal Declaration of Human Rights, I have reached that part of the long walk when the opportunity is granted, as it should be to all men and women, to retire to some rest and tranquility in the village of my birth.
>
> As I sit in Qunu and grow as ancient as its hills . . . I will continue to hope that Africa's renaissance will strike deep roots and blossom forever, without regard to the changing seasons. . . .
>
> Then would history and the billions throughout the world proclaim that it was right that we dreamed and that we toiled to give life to a workable dream.

Louise Gubb/The Image Works.

Pakistan talked about national pride, national security, and self-defense. This new round of nuclear testing confirms how profoundly the detonation of the atomic bomb in 1945 affected the subsequent history of the world. It may be possible to manage and contain nuclear capacities and to discourage their use, but they will never be halted entirely.

Small countries as well as terrorist organizations realize that they do not require a nuclear bomb to be taken seriously: short-range nuclear missiles, germ warfare, and poison gas can be just as effective, and far cheaper. (This threat is sometimes abbreviated as "NBC"—nuclear, biological, and chemical weapons; or alternatively, weapons of mass destruction.) Much of the basic material and technology is available for purchase on the thriving world arms market, in which countries like the United States, the former states of the Soviet Union, France, and Britain are large dealers. Given this traffic in arms, it is fairly easy for inter-

mediaries in the Middle East and the Third World to buy what they need. It is said that highly destructive Cruise missiles can be bought for approximately $10,000 apiece, making them in some ways the "poor man's nukes." Obviously their potential danger increases when combined with the capacity for chemical and biological warfare. Unlike policing who has and who doesn't have the bomb, the containment of arms proliferation and suspected chemical and biological warfare is an even more complex task, as the United States has discovered in its dealings with Iraq and Saddam Hussein in the aftermath of the 1990–1991 Gulf War.

At the same time, incredibly destructive conflicts that have little to do with high-tech weaponry and everything to do with ethnicity, religion, and territory have flared up periodically in the aftermath of the Cold War and threaten to do so for the foreseeable future. The Balkans especially continue to challenge U.S. pol-

Facing the Millennium
Until the sixteenth century, maps of the world were flat. On the eve of the twenty-first century, our vision of the world is practically infinite.
CORBIS/Randy Faris.

icy makers, NATO leaders, and United Nations peace-keeping forces. Would the Yugoslavian province of Kosovo, which U.S. peace envoy Richard Holbrooke in 1998 called "the most dangerous place in Europe," become the next Bosnia? Or would it be the Yugoslavian republic of Montenegro? Can genocides such as occurred in Bosnia and Rwanda be prevented in the future?

The contemporary world can be a scary place indeed, but there are rays of hope at the end of the twentieth century, especially the possible resolutions of problems that have long defied peaceful solutions: the hope that the 1998 Good Friday accords may finally bring peace to Ireland, that U.S.–Cuban relations might improve in the wake of Pope John Paul II's visit to Cuba in 1998, even that Palestinians and Israelis may work out a mutually acceptable framework for the West Bank. The end of apartheid in South Africa and that country's determination to come to grips with its past is surely one of the twentieth century's most inspiring developments, as are the emergence of democratic countries from the former Soviet satellites in Eastern Europe. Along with globalization and the challenge of forging a post–Cold War foreign policy, these potential breakthroughs are part of the story of America and the world in 2000.

★ ★ ★

As the world counted down the days until the new century, millennial fever gripped the nation. That is, of course, if the world did not shut down because of a computer glitch on January 1, 2000. Despite billions of dollars spent worldwide to upgrade old systems, even computer scientists could not predict whether computers would boot up, whether planes would be able to fly safely, whether the microchip in the coffee machine would perk on that morning. That cup of coffee might be especially necessary after the New Year's Eve celebrations planned to ring in the new century. Never mind that technically the millennium doesn't begin until January 1, 2001.

By the time you read this textbook, the Y2K problem will have turned out to be a huge hoax, a massive disaster, or some of both. You know what happened and we don't, a perfect example of the pitfalls of writing the history of contemporary America and the world. Welcome to the new millennium!

The Declaration of Independence

In Congress, July 4, 1776,
The Unanimous Declaration of the
Thirteen United States of America

When in the Course of human events, it becomes necessary for one people to dissolve the political bands which have connected them with another, and to assume among the Powers of the earth, the separate and equal station to which the Laws of Nature and of Nature's God entitle them, a decent respect to the opinions of mankind requires that they should declare the causes which impel them to the separation.

We hold these truths to be self-evident, that all men are created equal, that they are endowed by their Creator with certain unalienable rights, that among these are Life, Liberty, and the pursuit of Happiness. That to secure these rights, Governments are instituted among Men, deriving their just powers from the consent of the governed. That whenever any Form of Government becomes destructive of these ends, it is the Right of the People to alter or to abolish it, and to institute new Government, laying its foundation on such principles and organizing its powers in such form, as to them shall seem most likely to effect their Safety and Happiness. Prudence, indeed, will dictate that Governments long established should not be changed for light and transient causes; and accordingly all experience hath shown, that mankind are more disposed to suffer, while evils are sufferable, than to right themselves by abolishing the forms to which they are accustomed. But when a long train of abuses and usurpations, pursuing invariably the same Object evinces a design to reduce them under absolute Despotism, it is their right, it is their duty, to throw off such Government, and to provide new Guards for their future security.—Such has been the patient sufferance of these Colonies; and such is now the necessity which constrains them to alter their former Systems of Government. The history of the present King of Great Britain is a history of repeated injuries and usurpations, all having in direct object the establishment of an absolute Tyranny over these States. To prove this, let Facts be submitted to a candid world.

He has refused his Assent to Laws, the most wholesome and necessary for the public good.

He has forbidden his Governors to pass Laws of immediate and pressing importance, unless suspended in their operation till his Assent should be obtained; and, when so suspended, he has utterly neglected to attend to them.

He has refused to pass other Laws for the accommodation of large districts of people, unless those people would relinquish the right of Representation in the Legislature, a right inestimable to them and formidable to tyrants only.

He has called together legislative bodies at places unusual, uncomfortable, and distant from the depository of their public Records, for the sole purpose of fatiguing them into compliance with his measures.

He has dissolved Representative Houses repeatedly, for opposing with manly firmness his invasions on the rights of the people.

He has refused for a long time, after such dissolutions, to cause others to be elected; whereby the Legislative powers, incapable of Annihilation, have returned to the People at large for their exercise; the State remaining in the mean time exposed to all the dangers of invasion from without and convulsions within.

He has endeavoured to prevent the population of these States; for that purpose obstructing the Laws of Naturalization of Foreigners; refusing to pass others to encourage their migrations hither, and raising the conditions of new Appropriations of Lands.

He has obstructed the Administration of Justice, by refusing his Assent to Laws for establishing Judiciary powers.

He has made Judges dependent on his Will alone, for the tenure of their offices, and the amount and payment of their salaries.

He has erected a multitude of New Offices, and sent hither swarms of Officers to harass our People, and eat out their substance.

He has kept among us, in times of peace, Standing Armies without the Consent of our legislature.

He has combined with others to subject us to a jurisdiction foreign to our constitution, and unacknowledged by our laws; giving his Assent to their Acts of pretended Legislation:

For quartering large bodies of armed troops among us:

For protecting them, by a mock Trial, from Punishment for any Murders which they should commit on the Inhabitants of these States:

For cutting off our Trade with all parts of the world:

For imposing taxes on us without our Consent:

For depriving us, in many cases, of the benefits of Trial by jury:

For transporting us beyond Seas to be tried for pretended offences:

For abolishing the free System of English Laws in a neighbouring Province, establishing therein an Arbitrary government, and enlarging its Boundaries so as to render it at once an example and fit instrument for introducing the same absolute rule into these Colonies:

For taking away our Charters, abolishing our most valuable Laws, and altering fundamentally the Forms of our Governments:

For suspending our own Legislatures, and declaring themselves invested with Power to legislate for us in all cases whatsoever.

He has abdicated Government here, by declaring us out of his Protection and waging War against us.

He has plundered our seas, ravaged our Coasts, burnt our towns, and destroyed the lives of our people.

He is at this time transporting large armies of foreign mercenaries to compleat the works of death, desolation, and tyranny, already begun with circumstances of Cruelty & perfidy scarcely paralleled in the most barbarous ages, and totally unworthy the Head of a civilized nation.

He has constrained our fellow Citizens taken Captive on the high Seas to bear Arms against their Country, to become the executioners of their friends and Brethren, or to fall themselves by their Hands.

He has excited domestic insurrections amongst us, and has endeavoured to bring on the inhabitants of our frontiers, the merciless Indian Savages, whose known rule of warfare, is an undistinguished destruction of all ages, sexes, and conditions.

In every stage of these Oppressions We have Petitioned for Redress in the most humble terms: Our repeated Petitions have been answered only by repeated injury. A Prince, whose character is thus marked by every act which may define a Tyrant, is unfit to be the ruler of a free people.

Nor have We been wanting in attention to our British brethren. We have warned them from time to time of attempts by their legislature to extend an unwarrantable jurisdiction over us. We have reminded them of the circumstances of our emigration and settlement here. We have appealed to their native justice and magnanimity, and we have conjured them by the ties of our common kindred to disavow these usurpations, which, would inevitably interrupt our connections and correspondence. They too have been deaf to the voice of justice and of consanguinity. We must, therefore, acquiesce in the necessity, which denounces our Separation, and hold them, as we hold the rest of mankind, Enemies in War, in Peace Friends.

We, therefore, the Representatives of the United States of America, in General Congress, Assembled, appealing to the Supreme Judge of the world for the rectitude of our intentions, do, in the Name, and by Authority of the good People of these Colonies, solemnly publish and declare, That these United Colonies are, and of Right ought to be FREE AND INDEPENDENT STATES; that they are Absolved from all Allegiance to the British Crown, and that all political connection between them and the State of Great Britain, is and ought to be totally dissolved; and that as Free and Independent States, they have full Power to levy War, conclude Peace, contract Alliances, establish Commerce, and to do all other Acts and Things which Independent States may of right do. And for the support of this Declaration, with a firm reliance on the Protection of Divine Providence, we mutually pledge to each other our Lives, our Fortunes, and our sacred Honor.

John Hancock

Button Gwinnett	George Wythe	James Wilson	Josiah Bartlett
Lyman Hall	Richard Henry Lee	Geo. Ross	Wm. Whipple
Geo. Walton	Th. Jefferson	Caesar Rodney	Matthew Thornton
Wm. Hooper	Benja. Harrison	Geo. Read	Saml. Adams
Joseph Hewes	Thos. Nelson, Jr.	Thos. M'Kean	John Adams
John Penn	Francis Lightfoot Lee	Wm. Floyd	Robt. Treat Paine
Edward Rutledge	Carter Braxton	Phil. Livingston	Elbridge Gerry
Thos. Heyward, Junr.	Robt. Morris	Frans. Lewis	Step. Hopkins
Thomas Lynch, Junr.	Benjamin Rush	Lewis Morris	William Ellery
Arthur Middleton	Benja. Franklin	Richd. Stockton	Roger Sherman
Samuel Chase	John Morton	John Witherspoon	Sam'el Huntington
Wm. Paca	Geo. Clymer	Fras. Hopkinson	Wm. Williams
Thos. Stone	Jas. Smith	John Hart	Oliver Wolcott
Charles Carroll of Carrollton	Geo. Taylor	Abra. Clark	

The Articles of Confederation and Perpetual Union

*Agreed to in Congress,
November 15, 1777
Ratified March 1781*

BETWEEN THE STATES OF NEW HAMPSHIRE, MASSACHUSETTS BAY, RHODE ISLAND AND PROVIDENCE PLANTATIONS, CONNECTICUT, NEW YORK, NEW JERSEY, PENNSYLVANIA, DELAWARE, MARYLAND, VIRGINIA, NORTH CAROLINA, SOUTH CAROLINA, GEORGIA.*

Article 1.

The stile of this confederacy shall be "The United States of America."

Article 2.

Each State retains its sovereignty, freedom and independence, and every power, jurisdiction, and right, which is not by this confederation expressly delegated to the United States, in Congress assembled.

Article 3.

The said states hereby severally enter into a firm league of friendship with each other for their common defence, the security of their liberties and their mutual and general welfare; binding themselves to assist each other against all force offered to, or attacks made upon them, or any of them, on account of religion, sovereignty, trade, or any other pretence whatever.

Article 4.

The better to secure and perpetuate mutual friendship and intercourse among the people of the different states in this union, the free inhabitants of each of these states, paupers, vagabonds, and fugitives from justice excepted, shall be entitled to all privileges and immunities of free citizens in the several states; and the people of each State shall have free ingress and regress to and from any other State, and shall enjoy therein all the privileges of trade and commerce, subject to the same duties, impositions, and restrictions, as the inhabitants thereof respectively; provided, that such restrictions shall not extend so far as to prevent the removal of property, imported into any State, to any other State of which the owner is an inhabitant; provided also, that no imposition, duties, or restriction, shall be laid by any State on the property of the United States, or either of them.

If any person guilty of, or charged with treason, felony, or other high misdemeanor in any State, shall flee from justice and be found in any of the United States, he shall, upon demand of the governor or executive power of the State from which he fled, be delivered up and removed to the State having jurisdiction of his offence.

Full faith and credit shall be given in each of these states to the records, acts, and judicial proceedings of the courts and magistrates of every other State.

Article 5.

For the more convenient management of the general interests of the United States, delegates shall be annually appointed, in such manner as the legislature of each State shall direct, to meet in Congress, on the 1st Monday in November in every year, with a power reserved to each State to recal its delegates, or any of them, at any time within the year, and to send others in their stead for the remainder of the year.

No State shall be represented in Congress by less than two, nor by more than seven members; and no person shall be capable of being a delegate for more than three years in any term of six years; nor shall any person, being a delegate, be capable of holding any office under the United States, for which he, or any other for his benefit, receives any salary, fees, or emolument of any kind.

Each State shall maintain its own delegates in a meeting of the states, and while they act as members of the committee of the states.

In determining questions in the United States, in Congress assembled, each State shall have one vote.

Freedom of speech and debate in Congress shall not be impeached or questioned in any court or place out of Congress: and the members of Congress shall be protected in their persons from arrests and imprisonments, during the time of their going to and from, and attendance on Congress, except for treason, felony, or breach of the peace.

*This copy of the final draft of the Articles of Confederation is taken from the *Journals*, 9:907–925, November 15, 1777.

Article 6.

No State, without the consent of the United States, in Congress assembled, shall send any embassy to, or receive any embassy from, or enter into any conference, agreement, alliance, or treaty with any king, prince, or state; nor shall any person, holding any office of profit or trust under the United States, or any of them, accept of any present, emolument, office or title, of any kind whatever, from any king, prince, or foreign state; nor shall the United States, in Congress assembled, or any of them, grant any title of nobility.

No two or more states shall enter into any treaty, confederation, or alliance, whatever, between them, without the consent of the United States, in Congress assembled, specifying accurately the purposes for which the same is to be entered into, and how long it shall continue.

No state shall lay any imposts or duties which may interfere with any stipulations in treaties entered into by the United States, in Congress assembled, with any king, prince, or state, in pursuance of any treaties already proposed by Congress to the courts of France and Spain.

No vessels of war shall be kept up in time of peace by any State, except such number only as shall be deemed necessary by the United States, in Congress assembled, for the defence of such State or its trade; nor shall any body of forces be kept up by any State, in time of peace, except such number only as, in the judgment of the United States, in Congress assembled, shall be deemed requisite to garrison the forts necessary for the defence of such State; but every State shall always keep up a well regulated and disciplined militia, sufficiently armed and accoutred, and shall provide, and constantly have ready for use, in public stores, a due number of field pieces and tents, and a proper quantity of arms, ammunition and camp equipage.

No State shall engage in any war without the consent of the United States, in Congress assembled, unless such State be actually invaded by enemies, or shall have received certain advice of a resolution being formed by some nation of Indians to invade such State, and the danger is so imminent as not to admit of a delay till the United States, in Congress assembled, can be consulted; nor shall any State grant commissions to any ships or vessels of war, nor letters of marque or reprisal, except it be after a declaration of war by the United States, in Congress assembled, and then only against the kingdom or state, and the subjects thereof, against which war has been so declared, and under such regulations as shall be established by the United States, in Congress assembled, unless such State be infested by pirates, in which case vessels of war may be fitted out for that occasion, and kept so long as the danger shall continue, or until the United States, in Congress assembled, shall determine otherwise.

Article 7.

When land forces are raised by any State for the common defence, all officers of or under the rank of colonel, shall be appointed by the legislature of each State respectively, by whom such forces shall be raised, or in such manner as such State shall direct; and all vacancies shall be filled up by the State which first made the appointment.

Article 8.

All charges of war and all other expences, that shall be incurred for the common defence or general welfare, and allowed by the United States, in Congress assembled, shall be defrayed out of a common treasury, which shall be supplied by the several states, in proportion to the value of all land within each State, granted to or surveyed for any person, as such land and the buildings and improvements thereon shall be estimated according to such mode as the United States, in Congress assembled, shall, from time to time, direct and appoint.

The taxes for paying that proportion shall be laid and levied by the authority and direction of the legislatures of the several states, within the time agreed upon by the United States, in Congress assembled.

Article 9.

The United States, in Congress assembled, shall have the sole and exclusive right and power of determining on peace and war, except in the cases mentioned in the 6th article; of sending and receiving ambassadors; entering into treaties and alliances, provided that no treaty of commerce shall be made, whereby the legislative power of the respective states shall be restrained from imposing such imposts and duties on foreigners as their own people are subjected to, or from prohibiting the exportation or importation of any species of goods or commodities whatsoever; of establishing rules for deciding, in all cases, what captures on land or water shall be legal, and in what manner prizes, taken by land or naval forces in the service of the United States, shall be divided or appropriated; of granting letters of marque and reprisal in times of peace; appointing courts for the trial of piracies and felonies committed on the high seas, and establishing courts for receiving and determining, finally, appeals in all cases of captures; provided, that no member of Congress shall be appointed a judge of any of the said courts.

The United States, in Congress assembled, shall also be the last resort on appeal in all disputes and differences now subsisting, or that hereafter may arise between two or more states concerning boundary, jurisdiction or any other cause whatever; which authority shall always be exercised in the manner following: whenever the legislative or executive authority, or lawful agent of any State, in controversy with another, shall present a petition to Congress, stating the matter in question, and praying for a hearing, notice thereof shall be given, by order of Congress, to the legislative or executive authority of the other State in controversy, and a day assigned for the appearance of the parties by their lawful agents, who shall then be directed to appoint, by joint consent, commissioners or judges to constitute a court for hearing and determining the matter in question; but, if they cannot agree,

Congress shall name three persons out of each of the United States, and from the list of such persons each party shall alternately strike out one, the petitioners beginning, until the number shall be reduced to thirteen; and from that number not less than seven, nor more than nine names, as Congress shall direct, shall, in the presence of Congress, be drawn out by lot; and the persons whose names shall be so drawn, or any five of them, shall be commissioners or judges to hear and finally determine the controversy, so always as a major part of the judges who shall hear the cause shall agree in the determination; and if either party shall neglect to attend at the day appointed, without shewing reasons which Congress shall judge sufficient, or, being present, shall refuse to strike, the Congress shall proceed to nominate three persons out of each State, and the secretary of Congress shall strike in behalf of such party absent or refusing; and the judgment and sentence of the court to be appointed, in the manner before prescribed, shall be final and conclusive; and if any of the parties shall refuse to submit to the authority of such court, or to appear or defend their claim or cause, the court shall nevertheless proceed to pronounce sentence or judgment, which shall, in like manner, be final and decisive, the judgment or sentence and other proceedings begin, in either case, transmitted to Congress, and lodged among the acts of Congress for the security of the parties concerned: provided, that every commissioner, before he sits in judgment, shall take an oath, to be administered by one of the judges of the supreme or superior court of the State where the cause shall be tried, "well and truly to hear and determine the matter in question, according to the best of his judgment, without favour, affection, or hope of reward:" provided, also, that no State shall be deprived of territory for the benefit of the United States.

All controversies concerning the private right of soil, claimed under different grants of two or more states, whose jurisdictions, as they may respect such lands and the states which passed such grants, are adjusted, the said grants, or either of them, being at the same time claimed to have originated antecedent to such settlement of jurisdiction, shall, on the petition of either party to the Congress of the United States, be finally determined, as near as may be, in the same manner as is before prescribed for deciding disputes respecting territorial jurisdiction between different states.

The United States, in Congress assembled, shall also have the sole and exclusive right and power of regulating the alloy and value of coin struck by their own authority, or by that of the respective states; fixing the standard of weights and measures throughout the United States; regulating the trade and managing all affairs with the Indians not members of any of the states; provided that the legislative right of any State within its own limits be not infringed or violated; establishing and regulating post offices from one State to another throughout all the United States, and exacting such postage on the papers passing through the same as may be requisite to defray the expences of the said office; appointing all officers of the land forces in the service of the United States, excepting regimental officers; appointing all the officers of the naval forces, and commissioning all officers whatever in the service of the United States; making rules for the government and regulation of the said land and naval forces, and directing their operations.

The United States, in Congress assembled, shall have authority to appoint a committee to sit in the recess of Congress, to be denominated "a Committee of the States," and to consist of one delegate from each State, and to appoint such other committees and civil officers as may be necessary for managing the general affairs of the United States, under their direction; to appoint one of their number to preside; provided that no person be allowed to serve in the office of president more than one year in any term of three years; to ascertain the necessary sums of money to be raised for the service of the United States, and to appropriate and apply the same for defraying the public expences; to borrow money or emit bills on the credit of the United States, transmitting, every half year, to the respective states, an account of the sums of money so borrowed or emitted; to build and equip a navy; to agree upon the number of land forces, and to make requisitions from each State for its quota, in proportion to the number of white inhabitants in such State; which requisitions shall be binding; and thereupon, the legislature of each State shall appoint the regimental officers, raise the men, and cloathe, arm, and equip them in a soldier-like manner, at the expence of the United States; and the officers and men so cloathed, armed, and equipped, shall march to the place appointed and within the time agreed on by the United States, in Congress assembled; but if the United States, in Congress assembled, shall, on consideration of circumstances, judge proper that any State should not raise men, or should raise a smaller number than its quota, and that any other State should raise a greater number of men than the quota thereof, such extra number shall be raised, officered, cloathed, armed, and equipped in the same manner as the quota of such State, unless the legislature of such State shall judge that such extra number cannot be safely spared out of the same, in which case they shall raise, officer, cloathe, arm, and equip as many of such extra number as they judge can be safely spared. And the officers and men so cloathed, armed, and equipped, shall march to the place appointed and within the time agreed on by the United States, in Congress assembled.

The United States, in Congress assembled, shall never engage in a war, nor grant letters of marque and reprisal in time of peace, nor enter into any treaties or alliances, nor coin money, nor regulate the value thereof, nor ascertain the sums and expences necessary for the defence and welfare of the United States, or any of them: nor emit bills, nor borrow money on the credit of the United States, nor appropriate money, nor agree upon the number of vessels of war to be built or purchased, or the number of land or sea forces to be raised, nor appoint a commander in chief of the army or navy, unless nine states assent to the same; nor shall a question on any other point, except for adjourning from day to day, be determined, unless by the votes of a majority of the United States, in Congress assembled.

The Congress of the United States shall have power to adjourn to any time within the year, and to any place within the United States, so that no period of adjournment be for a longer duration than the space of six months, and shall publish the journal of their proceedings monthly, except such parts thereof, relating to treaties, alliances or military operations, as, in their judgment, require secrecy; and the yeas and nays of the delegates of each State on any question shall be entered on the journal, when it is desired by any delegate; and the delegates of a State, or any of them, at his, or their request, shall be furnished with a transcript of the said journal, except such parts as are above excepted, to lay before the legislatures of the several states.

Article 10.

The committee of the states, or any nine of them, shall be authorized to execute, in the recess of Congress, such of the powers of Congress as the United States, in Congress assembled, by the consent of nine states, shall, from time to time, think expedient to vest them with; provided, that no power be delegated to the said committee, for the exercise of which, by the articles of confederation, the voice of nine states, in the Congress of the United States assembled, is requisite.

Article 11.

Canada acceding to this confederation, and joining in the measures of the United States, shall be admitted into and entitled to all the advantages of this union; but no other colony shall be admitted into the same, unless such admission be agreed to by nine states.

Article 12.

All bills of credit emitted, monies borrowed and debts contracted by, or under the authority of Congress before the assembling of the United States, in pursuance of the present confederation, shall be deemed and considered as a charge against the United States, for payment and satisfaction whereof the said United States and the public faith are hereby solemnly pledged.

Article 13.

Every State shall abide by the determinations of the United States, in Congress assembled, on all questions which, by this confederation, are submitted to them. And the articles of this confederation shall be inviolably observed by every State, and the union shall be perpetual; nor shall any alteration at any time hereafter be made in any of them, unless such alteration be agreed to in a Congress of the United States, and be afterwards confirmed by the legislatures of every State.

These articles shall be proposed to the legislatures of all the United States, to be considered, and if approved of by them, they are advised to authorize their delegates to ratify the same in the Congress of the United States; which being done, the same shall become conclusive.

The Constitution of the United States of America

Agreed to by Philadelphia Convention,
September 17, 1787
Implemented March 4, 1789

We the People of the United States, in Order to form a more perfect Union, establish Justice, insure domestic Tranquility, provide for the common defence, promote the general Welfare, and secure the Blessings of Liberty to ourselves and our Posterity, do ordain and establish this Constitution for the United States of America.

Article I

SECTION 1 All legislative Powers herein granted shall be vested in a Congress of the United States, which shall consist of a Senate and a House of Representatives.

SECTION 2 The House of Representatives shall be composed of Members chosen every second Year by the People of the several States, and the Electors in each State shall have the Qualifications requisite for Electors of the most numerous Branch of the State Legislature.

No Person shall be a Representative who shall not have attained to the Age of twenty-five Years, and been seven Years a Citizen of the United States, and who shall not, when elected, be an Inhabitant of that State in which he shall be chosen.

Representatives and direct Taxes shall be apportioned among the several States which may be included within this Union, according to their respective Numbers, *which shall be determined by adding to the whole Number of free Persons, including those bound to Service for a Term of Years, and excluding Indians not taxed, three fifths of all other Persons.** The actual Enumeration shall be made within three Years after the first Meeting of the Congress of the United States, and within every subsequent Term of ten Years, in such Manner as they shall by Law direct. The Number of Representatives shall not exceed one for every thirty Thousand, but each State shall have at Least one Representative; and *until such enumeration shall be made, the State of New Hampshire shall be entitled to chuse three, Massachusetts eight, Rhode Island and Providence Plantations one, Connecticut five, New-York six, New Jersey four, Pennsylvania eight, Delaware one, Maryland six, Virginia ten, North Carolina five, South Carolina five, and Georgia three.*

When vacancies happen in the Representation from any State, the Executive Authority thereof shall issue Writs of Election to fill such Vacancies.

The House of Representatives shall chuse their Speaker and other Officers; and shall have the sole Power of Impeachment.

SECTION 3 The Senate of the United States shall be composed of two Senators from each State, *chosen by the Legislature thereof,*† for six Years; and each Senator shall have one Vote.

Immediately after they shall be assembled in Consequence of the first Election, they shall be divided as equally as may be into three Classes. The Seats of the Senators of the first Class shall be vacated at the Expiration of the second Year, of the second Class at the Expiration of the fourth Year, and of the third Class at the Expiration of the sixth Year, so that one-third may be chosen every second Year; *and if Vacancies happen by Resignation, or otherwise, during the Recess of the Legislature of any State, the Executive thereof may make temporary Appointments until the next Meeting of the Legislature, which shall then fill such Vacancies.*‡

No person shall be a Senator who shall not have attained to the Age of thirty Years, and been nine Years a Citizen of the United States, and who shall not, when elected, be an Inhabitant of that State for which he shall be chosen.

The Vice President of the United States shall be President of the Senate, but shall have no Vote, unless they be equally divided.

The Senate shall chuse their other Officers, and also a President pro tempore, in the absence of the Vice President, or when he shall exercise the Office of President of the United States.

The Senate shall have the sole Power to try all Impeachments. When sitting for that Purpose, they shall be on Oath or Affirmation. When the President of the United States is tried, the Chief Justice shall preside: And no Person shall be convicted without the Concurrence of two thirds of the Members present.

Judgment in Cases of Impeachment shall not extend further than to removal from Office, and disqualification to hold and enjoy any Office of honor, Trust or Profit under the United States: but the Party convicted shall nevertheless be liable and subject to Indictment, Trial, Judgment and Punishment, according to Law.

Note: The Constitution became effective March 4, 1789. Provisions in italics are no longer relevant or have been changed by constitutional amendment.
*Changed by Section 2 of the Fourteenth Amendment.

†Changed by Section 1 of the Seventeenth Amendment.
‡Changed by Clause 2 of the Seventeenth Amendment.

SECTION 4 The Times, Places and Manner of holding Elections for Senators and Representatives, shall be prescribed in each State by the Legislature thereof; but the Congress may at any time by Law make or alter such Regulations, except as to the Places of Chusing Senators.

The Congress shall assemble at least once in every Year, and such Meeting *shall be on the first Monday in December, unless they shall by Law appoint a different Day.**

SECTION 5 Each House shall be the Judge of the Elections, Returns and Qualifications of its own Members, and a Majority of each shall constitute a Quorum to do Business; but a smaller number may adjourn from day to day, and may be authorized to compel the Attendance of absent Members, in such Manner, and under such Penalties, as each House may provide.

Each House may determine the Rules of its Proceedings, punish its Members for disorderly Behavior, and, with the Concurrence of two thirds, expel a Member.

Each House shall keep a Journal of its Proceedings, and from time to time publish the same, excepting such Parts as may in their Judgment require Secrecy; and the Yeas and Nays of the Members of either House on any question shall, at the Desire of one-fifth of those Present, be entered on the Journal.

Neither House, during the Session of Congress, shall, without the Consent of the other, adjourn for more than three days, nor to any other Place than that in which the two Houses shall be sitting.

SECTION 6 The Senators and Representatives shall receive a Compensation for their Services, to be ascertained by Law, and paid out of the Treasury of the United States. They shall in all Cases, except Treason, Felony and Breach of the Peace, be privileged from Arrest during their Attendance at the Session of their respective Houses, and in going to and returning from the same; and for any Speech or Debate in either House, they shall not be questioned in any other Place.

No Senator or Representative shall, during the Time for which he was elected, be appointed to any civil Office under the Authority of the United States, which shall have been created, or the Emoluments whereof shall have been increased, during such time; and no Person holding any Office under the United States, shall be a Member of either House during his Continuance in Office.

SECTION 7 All Bills for raising Revenue shall originate in the House of Representatives; but the Senate may propose or concur with Amendments as on other Bills.

Every Bill which shall have passed the House of Representatives and the Senate, shall, before it becomes a Law, be presented to the President of the United States; If he approve he shall sign it, but if not he shall return it, with his Objections to that House in which it shall have originated, who shall enter the Objections at large on their Journal, and proceed to reconsider it. If after such Reconsideration two thirds of that House shall agree to pass the Bill, it shall be sent, together with the Objections, to the other House, by which it shall likewise be reconsidered, and if approved by two thirds of that House, it shall become a Law. But in all such Cases the Votes of both Houses shall be determined by Yeas and Nays, and the Names of the Persons voting for and against the Bill shall be entered on the Journal of each House respectively. If any Bill shall not be returned by the President within ten Days (Sundays excepted) after it shall have been presented to him, the Same shall be a Law, in like Manner as if he had signed it, unless the Congress by their Adjournment prevent its Return, in which Case it shall not be a Law.

Every Order, Resolution, or Vote to which the Concurrence of the Senate and the House of Representatives may be necessary (except on a question of Adjournment) shall be presented to the President of the United States; and before the Same shall take Effect, shall be approved by him, or being disapproved by him, shall be repassed by two thirds of the Senate and House of Representatives, according to the Rules and Limitations prescribed in the Case of a Bill.

SECTION 8 The Congress shall have Power To lay and collect Taxes, Duties, Imposts and Excises, to pay the Debts and provide for the common Defence and general Welfare of the United States; but all Duties, Imposts and Excises shall be uniform throughout the United States;

To borrow money on the credit of the United States;

To regulate Commerce with foreign Nations, and among the several States, and with the Indian Tribes;

To establish an uniform Rule of Naturalization, and uniform Laws on the subject of Bankruptcies throughout the United States;

To coin Money, regulate the Value thereof, and of foreign Coin, and fix the Standard of Weights and Measures;

To provide for the Punishment of counterfeiting the Securities and current Coin of the United States;

To establish Post Offices and post Roads;

To promote the Progress of Science and useful Arts, by securing for limited Times to Authors and Inventors the exclusive Right to their respective Writings and Discoveries;

To constitute Tribunals inferior to the supreme Court;

To define and punish Piracies and Felonies committed on the high Seas, and Offenses against the Law of Nations;

To declare War, grant Letters of Marque and Reprisal, and make Rules concerning Captures on Land and Water;

To raise and support Armies, but no Appropriation of Money to that Use shall be for a longer Term than two Years;

To provide and maintain a Navy;

To make Rules for the Government and Regulation of the land and naval Forces;

To provide for calling forth the Militia to execute the Laws of the Union, suppress Insurrections and repel Invasions;

To provide for organizing, arming, and disciplining the Militia, and for governing such Part of them as may be employed in the Service of the United States, reserving to the States respectively, the Appointment of the Officers, and the Authority of training the Militia according to the discipline prescribed by Congress;

To exercise exclusive Legislation in all Cases whatsoever, over such District (not exceeding ten Miles square) as may, by Cession of particular States, and the acceptance of Congress, become the Seat of Government of the United States, and to

---

*Changed by Section 2 of the Twentieth Amendment.

exercise like Authority over all Places purchased by the Consent of the Legislature of the State in which the Same shall be, for the Erection of Forts, Magazines, Arsenals, dock-Yards, and other needful Buildings;—And

To make all Laws which shall be necessary and proper for carrying into Execution the foregoing Powers, and all other Powers vested by this Constitution in the Government of the United States, or in any Department or Officer thereof.

SECTION 9 The Migration or Importation of such Persons as any of the States now existing shall think proper to admit, shall not be prohibited by the Congress prior to the Year one thousand eight hundred and eight but a tax or duty may be imposed on such Importation, not exceeding ten dollars for each Person.

The privilege of the Writ of Habeas Corpus shall not be suspended, unless when in Cases of Rebellion or Invasion the public Safety may require it.

No Bill of Attainder or ex post facto Law shall be passed.

*No capitation, or other direct, Tax shall be laid, unless in Proportion to the Census or Enumeration herein before directed to be taken.**

No Tax or Duty shall be laid on Articles exported from any State.

No Preference shall be given by any Regulation of Commerce or Revenue to the Ports of one State over those of another: nor shall Vessels bound to, or from, one State, be obliged to enter, clear, or pay Duties in another.

No Money shall be drawn from the Treasury, but in Consequence of Appropriations made by law; and a regular Statement and Account of the Receipts and Expenditures of all public Money shall be published from time to time.

No Title of Nobility shall be granted by the United States: And no Person holding any Office of Profit or Trust under them, shall, without the Consent of the Congress, accept of any present, Emolument, Office, or Title, of any kind whatever, from any King, Prince, or foreign State.

SECTION 10 No State shall enter into any Treaty, Alliance, or Confederation; grant Letters of Marque and Reprisal; coin Money; emit Bills of Credit; make any Thing but gold and silver Coin a Tender in Payment of Debts; pass any Bill of Attainder, ex post facto Law, or Law impairing the Obligation of Contracts, or grant any Title of Nobility.

No State shall, without the Consent of the Congress, lay any Imposts or Duties on Imports or Exports, except what may be absolutely necessary for executing its inspection Laws: and the net Produce of all Duties and Imposts, laid by any State on Imports or Exports, shall be for the Use of the Treasury of the United States; and all such Laws shall be subject to the Revision and Control of the Congress.

No State shall, without the Consent of the Congress, lay any duty of Tonnage, keep Troops, or Ships of War in time of Peace, enter into any Agreement or Compact with another State, or with a foreign Power, or engage in War, unless actually invaded, or in such imminent Danger as will not admit of delay.

Article II

SECTION 1 The executive Power shall be vested in a President of the United States of America. He shall hold his Office during the Term of four Years, and, together with the Vice President, chosen for the same Term, be elected, as follows:

Each State shall appoint, in such Manner as the Legislature thereof may direct, a Number of Electors, equal to the whole Number of Senators and Representatives to which the State may be entitled in the Congress; but no Senator or Representative, or Person holding an Office of Trust or Profit under the United States, shall be appointed an Elector.

The Electors shall meet in their respective States, and vote by Ballot for two Persons, of whom one at least shall not be an Inhabitant of the same State with themselves. And they shall make a List of all the Persons voted for, and of the Number of Votes for each; which List they shall sign and certify, and transmit sealed to the Seat of the Government of the United States, directed to the President of the Senate. The President of the Senate shall, in the Presence of the Senate and House of Representatives, open all the Certificates, and the Votes shall then be counted. The Person having the greatest Number of Votes shall be the President, if such Number be a Majority of the whole Number of Electors appointed; and if there be more than one who have such Majority, and have an equal Number of Votes, then the House of Representatives shall immediately chuse by Ballot one of them for President; and if no Person have a Majority, then from the five highest on the List the said House shall in like Manner chuse the President. But in chusing the President, the Votes shall be taken by States, the Representation from each State having one Vote; a quorum for this Purpose shall consist of a Member or Members from two thirds of the States, and a Majority of all the States shall be necessary to a Choice. In every Case, after the Choice of the President, the Person having the greatest Number of Votes of the Electors shall be the Vice President. But if there should remain two or more who have equal Votes, the Senate shall chuse from them by Ballot the Vice President.†

The Congress may determine the Time of chusing the Electors, and the Day on which they shall give their Votes; which Day shall be the same throughout the United States.

No Person except a natural born Citizen, or a Citizen of the United States, at the time of the Adoption of this Constitution, shall be eligible to the Office of President; neither shall any Person be eligible to that Office who shall not have attained to the Age of thirty five Years, and been fourteen Years a Resident within the United States.

In Case of the Removal of the President from Office, or of his Death, Resignation, or Inability to discharge the Powers and Duties of the said Office, the same shall devolve on the Vice President, *and the Congress may by Law provide for the Case of Removal, Death, Resignation, or Inability, both of the President and Vice President, declaring what Officer shall then act as President, and such Officer shall act accordingly, until the Disability be removed, or a President shall be elected.‡*

The President shall, at stated Times, receive for his Services a Compensation, which shall neither be increased nor

---

*Changed by the Sixteenth Amendment.

†Superseded by the Twelfth Amendment.
‡Modified by the Twenty-fifth Amendment.

diminished during the Period for which he shall have been elected, and he shall not receive within that Period any other Emolument from the United States, or any of them.

Before he enter on the Execution of his Office, he shall take the following Oath or Affirmation:—"I do solemnly swear (or affirm) that I will faithfully execute the Office of President of the United States, and will to the best of my Ability, preserve, protect and defend the Constitution of the United States."

SECTION 2 The President shall be Commander in Chief of the Army and Navy of the United States, and of the Militia of the several States, when called into the actual Service of the United States; he may require the Opinion, in writing, of the principal Officer in each of the executive Departments, upon any Subject relating to the Duties of their respective Offices, and he shall have Power to Grant Reprieves and Pardons for Offences against the United States, except in Cases of Impeachment.

He shall have Power, by and with the Advice and Consent of the Senate, to make Treaties, provided two thirds of the Senators present concur; and he shall nominate, and by and with the Advice and Consent of the Senate, shall appoint Ambassadors, other public Ministers and Consuls, Judges of the supreme Court, and all other Officers of the United States, whose Appointments are not herein otherwise provided for, and which shall be established by Law: but the Congress may by Law vest the Appointment of such inferior Officers, as they think proper, in the President alone, in the Courts of Law, or in the Heads of Departments.

The President shall have Power to fill up all Vacancies that may happen during the Recess of the Senate, by granting Commissions which shall expire at the End of their next Session.

SECTION 3 He shall from time to time give to the Congress Information of the State of the Union, and recommend to their Consideration such Measures as he shall judge necessary and expedient; he may, on extraordinary Occasions, convene both Houses, or either of them, and in Case of Disagreement between them, with Respect to the Time of Adjournment, he may adjourn them to such Time as he shall think proper; he shall receive Ambassadors and other public Ministers; he shall take Care that the Laws be faithfully executed, and shall Commission all the Officers of the United States.

SECTION 4 The President, Vice President and all civil Officers of the United States, shall be removed from Office on Impeachment for, and Conviction of, Treason, Bribery, or other high Crimes and Misdemeanors.

Article III

SECTION 1 The judicial Power of the United States, shall be vested in one supreme Court, and in such inferior Courts as the Congress may from time to time ordain and establish. The Judges, both of the supreme and inferior Courts, shall hold their Offices during good Behaviour, and shall, at stated Times, receive for their Services a Compensation, which shall not be diminished during their Continuance in Office.

SECTION 2 The judicial Power shall extend to all Cases, in Law and Equity, arising under this Constitution, the Laws of the United States, and Treaties made, or which shall be made, under their Authority;—to all Cases affecting Ambassadors, other public Ministers and Consuls;—to all Cases of admiralty and maritime Jurisdiction;—to Controversies to which the United States shall be a Party;—to Controversies between two or more States;—*between a State and Citizens of another State;**—between Citizens of different States;—between Citizens of the same State claiming Lands under Grants of different States, and between a State, or the Citizens thereof, and foreign States, Citizens or Subjects.

In all Cases affecting Ambassadors, other public Ministers and Consuls, and those in which a State shall be Party, the supreme Court shall have original Jurisdiction. In all the other Cases before mentioned, the supreme Court shall have appellate Jurisdiction, both as to Law and Fact, with such Exceptions, and under such Regulations as the Congress shall make.

The trial of all Crimes, except in Cases of Impeachment, shall be by Jury; and such Trial shall be held in the State where said Crimes shall have been committed; but when not committed within any State, the Trial shall be at such Place or Places as the Congress may by Law have directed.

SECTION 3 Treason against the United States, shall consist only in levying War against them, or in adhering to their Enemies, giving them Aid and Comfort. No Person shall be convicted of Treason unless on the Testimony of two Witnesses to the same overt Act, or on Confession in open Court.

The Congress shall have Power to declare the Punishment of Treason, but no Attainder of Treason shall work Corruption of Blood, or Forefeiture except during the Life of the Person attainted.

Article IV

SECTION 1 Full Faith and Credit shall be given in each State to the public Acts, Records, and judicial Proceedings of every other State. And the Congress may by general Laws prescribe the Manner in which such Acts, Records, and Proceedings shall be proved, and the Effect thereof.

SECTION 2 The Citizens of each State shall be entitled to all Privileges and Immunities of Citizens in the several States.

A Person charged in any State with Treason, Felony, or other Crime, who shall flee from Justice, and be found in another State, shall on demand of the executive Authority of the State from which he fled, be delivered up, to be removed to the State having Jurisdiction of the Crime.

No Person held to Service or Labour in one State, under the Laws thereof, escaping into another, shall, in Consequence of any Law or Regulation therein, be discharged from such Service or Labour, but shall be delivered up on Claim of the Party to whom such Service or Labour may be due.†

---

*Restricted by the Eleventh Amendment.
†Superseded by the Thirteenth Amendment.

SECTION 3 New States may be admitted by the Congress into this Union; but no new State shall be formed or erected within the Jurisdiction of any other State; nor any State be formed by the Junction of two or more States, or parts of States, without the Consent of the Legislatures of the States concerned as well as of the Congress.

The Congress shall have Power to dispose of and make all needful Rules and Regulations respecting the Territory or other Property belonging to the United States; and nothing in this Constitution shall be so construed as to Prejudice any Claims of the United States, or of any particular State.

SECTION 4 The United States shall guarantee to every State in this Union a Republican Form of Government, and shall protect each of them against Invasion; and on Application of the Legislature, or of the Executive (when the Legislature cannot be convened) against domestic Violence.

Article V

The Congress, whenever two thirds of both Houses shall deem it necessary, shall propose Amendments to this Constitution, or, on the Application of the Legislatures of two thirds of the several States, shall call a Convention for proposing Amendments, which, in either Case, shall be valid to all Intents and Purposes, as Part of this Constitution, when ratified by the Legislatures of three fourths of the several States, or by Conventions in three fourths thereof, as the one or the other Mode of Ratification may be proposed by the Congress; Provided that no Amendment which may be made prior to the Year One thousand eight hundred and eight shall in any Manner affect the first and fourth Clauses in the Ninth Section of the first Article; and that no State, without its Consent, shall be deprived of its equal Suffrage in the Senate.

Article VI

All Debts contracted and Engagements entered into, before the Adoption of this Constitution, shall be as valid against the United States under this Constitution, as under the Confederation.

This Constitution, and the Laws of the United States which shall be made in Pursuance thereof; and all Treaties made, or which shall be made, under the Authority of the United States, shall be the supreme Law of the Land; and the Judges in every State shall be bound thereby, any Thing in the Constitution or Laws of any State to the Contrary notwithstanding.

The Senators and Representatives before mentioned, and the Members of the several State Legislatures, and all executive and judicial Officers, both of the United States and of the several States, shall be bound by Oath or Affirmation, to support this Constitution; but no religious Test shall ever be required as a Qualification to any Office or public Trust under the United States.

Article VII

The Ratification of the Conventions of nine States shall be sufficient for the Establishment of this Constitution between the States so ratifying the Same.

Done in Convention by the Unanimous Consent of the States present the Seventeenth Day of September in the Year of our Lord one thousand seven hundred and Eighty seven and of the Independence of the United States of America the Twelfth. In Witness whereof We have hereunto subscribed our Names.

Go. Washington
President and deputy from Virginia

New Hampshire
John Langdon
Nicholas Gilman

Massachusetts
Nathaniel Gorham
Rufus King

Connecticut
Wm. Saml. Johnson
Roger Sherman

New York
Alexander Hamilton

New Jersey
Wil. Livingston
David Brearley
Wm. Paterson
Jona. Dayton

Pennsylvania
B. Franklin
Thomas Mifflin
Robt. Morris
Geo. Clymer
Thos. FitzSimons
Jared Ingersoll
James Wilson
Gouv. Morris

Delaware
Geo. Read
Gunning Bedford jun
John Dickinson
Richard Bassett
Jaco. Broom

Maryland
James McHenry
Dan. of St. Thos. Jenifer
Danl. Carroll

Virginia
John Blair
James Madison, Jr.

North Carolina
Wm. Blount
Richd. Dobbs Spaight
Hu Williamson

South Carolina
J. Rutledge
Charles Cotesworth Pinckney
Pierce Butler

Georgia
William Few
Abr. Baldwin

Amendments to the Constitution with Annotations
(Including the Six Unratified Amendments)

In their effort to gain Antifederalists' support for the Constitution, Federalists frequently pointed to the inclusion of Article 5, which provides an orderly method of amending the Constitution. In contrast, the Articles of Confederation, which were universally recognized as seriously flawed, offered no means of amendment. For their part, Antifederalists argued that the amendment process was so "intricate" that one might as easily roll "sixes an hundred times in succession" as change the Constitution.

The system for amendment laid out in the Constitution requires that two-thirds of both houses of Congress agree to a proposed amendment, which must then be ratified by three-quarters of the legislatures of the states. Alternatively, an amendment may be proposed by a convention called by the legislatures of two-thirds of the states. Since 1789, members of Congress have proposed thousands of amendments. Besides the seventeen amendments added since 1791, only the six "unratified" ones included here were approved by two-thirds of both houses but not ratified by the states.

Among the many amendments that never made it out of Congress have been proposals to declare dueling, divorce, and interracial marriage unconstitutional as well as proposals to establish a national university, to acknowledge the sovereignty of Jesus Christ, and to prohibit any person from possessing wealth in excess of $10 million.*

Among the issues facing Americans today that might lead to constitutional amendment are efforts to balance the federal budget, to limit the number of terms elected officials may serve, to limit access to or prohibit abortion, to establish English as the official language of the United States, and to prohibit flag burning. None of these proposed amendments has yet garnered enough support in Congress to be sent to the states for ratification.

Although the first ten amendments to the Constitution are commonly known as the Bill of Rights, only Amendments 1–8 actually provide guarantees of individual rights. Amendments 9 and 10 deal with the structure of power within the constitutional system. The Bill of Rights was promised to appease Antifederalists who refused to ratify the Constitution without guarantees of individual liberties and limitations to federal power. After studying more than two hundred amendments recommended by the ratifying conventions of the states, Federalist James Madison presented a list of seventeen to Congress, which used Madison's list as the foundation for the twelve amendments that were sent to the states for ratification. Ten of the twelve were adopted in 1791. The first on the list of twelve, known as the Reapportionment Amendment, was never adopted (see p. D-15). The second proposed amendment was adopted in 1992 as Amendment 27 (see p. D-23).

Amendment I [1791]†

Congress shall make no law respecting an establishment of religion, or prohibiting the free exercise thereof; or abridging the freedom of speech, or of the press; or the right of the people peaceably to assemble, and to petition the government for a redress of grievances.

★ ★ ★

The First Amendment is a potent symbol for many Americans. Most are well aware of their rights to free speech, freedom of the press, and freedom of religion and their rights to assemble and to petition, even if they cannot cite the exact words of this amendment.

The First Amendment guarantee of freedom of religion has two clauses: the "free exercise clause," which allows individuals to practice or not practice any religion, and the "establishment clause," which prevents the federal government from discriminating against or favoring any particular religion. This clause was designed to create what Thomas Jefferson referred to as "a wall of separation between church and state." In the 1960s, the Supreme Court ruled that the First Amendment prohibits prayer and Bible reading in public schools.

Although the rights to free speech and freedom of the press are established in the First Amendment, it was not until the twentieth century that the Supreme Court began to explore the full meaning of these guarantees. In 1919, the Court ruled in Schenck v. United States *that the government could suppress free expression only where it could cite a "clear and present danger." In a decision that continues to raise controversies, the Court ruled in 1990, in* Texas v. Johnson, *that flag burning is a form of symbolic speech protected by the First Amendment.*

*Richard B. Bernstein, *Amending America* (New York: Times Books, 1993), 177–181.

†The dates in brackets indicate when the amendment was ratified.

Amendment II [1791]

A well-regulated militia being necessary to the security of a free State, the right of the people to keep and bear arms shall not be infringed.

★ ★ ★

Fear of a standing army under the control of a hostile government made the Second Amendment an important part of the Bill of Rights. Advocates of gun ownership claim that the amendment prevents the government from regulating firearms. Proponents of gun control argue that the amendment is designed only to protect the right of the states to maintain militia units.

In 1939, the Supreme Court ruled in United States v. Miller *that the Second Amendment did not protect the right of an individual to own a sawed-off shotgun, which it argued was not ordinary militia equipment. Since then, the Supreme Court has refused to hear Second Amendment cases, whereas lower courts have upheld firearm regulations. Several justices currently on the bench seem to favor a narrow interpretation of the Second Amendment, which would allow gun control legislation. The controversy over the impact of the Second Amendment on gun owners and gun control legislation will certainly continue.*

Amendment III [1791]

No soldier shall, in time of peace, be quartered in any house without the consent of the owner, nor in time of war, but in a manner to be prescribed by law.

★ ★ ★

The Third Amendment was extremely important to the framers of the Constitution, but today it is nearly forgotten. American colonists were especially outraged that they were forced to quarter British troops in the years before and during the American Revolution. The philosophy of the Third Amendment has been viewed by some justices and scholars as the foundation of the modern constitutional right to privacy.

Amendment IV [1791]

The right of the people to be secure in their persons, houses, papers, and effects, against unreasonable searches and seizures, shall not be violated, and no warrants shall issue but upon probable cause, supported by oath or affirmation, and particularly describing the place to be searched, and the persons or things to be seized.

★ ★ ★

In the years before the Revolution, the houses, barns, stores, and warehouses of American colonists were ransacked by British authorities under "writs of assistance" or general warrants. The British, thus empowered, searched for seditious material or smuggled goods that could then be used as evidence against colonists who were charged with a crime only after the items were found.

The first part of the Fourth Amendment protects citizens from "unreasonable" searches and seizures. The Supreme Court has interpreted this protection as well as the words search *and* seizure *in different ways at different times. At one time, the Court did not recognize electronic eavesdropping as a form of search and seizure, although it does today. At times, an "unreasonable" search has been almost any search carried out without a warrant, but in the two decades before 1969 the Court sometimes sanctioned warrantless searches that it considered reasonable based on "the total atmosphere of the case."*

The second part of the Fourth Amendment defines the procedure for issuing a search warrant and states the requirement of "probable cause," which is generally viewed as evidence indicating that a suspect has committed an offense.

The Fourth Amendment has been controversial because the Court has sometimes excluded evidence that has been seized in violation of constitutional standards. The justification is that excluding such evidence deters violations of the amendment, but doing so may allow a guilty person to escape punishment.

Amendment V [1791]

No person shall be held to answer for a capital, or otherwise infamous crime, unless on a presentment or indictment of a grand jury, except in cases arising in the land or naval forces, or in the militia, when in actual service in time of war or public danger; nor shall any person be subject for the same offence to be twice put in jeopardy of life or limb; nor shall be compelled in any criminal case to be a witness against himself, nor be deprived of life, liberty, or property, without due process of law; nor shall private property be taken for public use without just compensation.

★ ★ ★

The Fifth Amendment protects people against government authority in the prosecution of criminal offenses. It prohibits the state, first, from charging a person with a serious crime without a grand jury hearing to decide whether there is sufficient evidence to support the charge and, second, from charging a person with the same crime twice. The best-known aspect of the Fifth Amendment is that it prevents a person from being "compelled . . . to be a witness against himself." The last clause, the "takings clause," limits the power of the government to seize property.

Although invoking the Fifth Amendment is popularly viewed as a confession of guilt, a person may be innocent yet still fear prosecution. For example, during the Cold War era of the late 1940s and 1950s, many people who had participated in legal activities that were associated with the Communist Party claimed the Fifth Amendment privilege rather than testify before the House Un-American Activities Committee because the mood of the times cast those activities in a negative light. Because "taking the Fifth" was viewed as an admission of guilt, those people often lost their jobs or became unemployable. Nonetheless, the right to protect oneself against self-incrimination plays an important role in guarding against the collective power of the state.

Amendment VI [1791]

In all criminal prosecutions, the accused shall enjoy the right to a speedy and public trial, by an impartial jury of the State and district wherein the crime shall have been committed, which district shall have been previously ascertained by law, and to be informed of the nature and cause of the accusation; to be confronted with the witnesses against him; to have compulsory process for obtaining witnesses in his favor, and to have the assistance of counsel for his defence.

The original Constitution put few limits on the government's power to investigate, prosecute, and punish crime. This process was of great concern to the early Americans, however, and of the twenty-eight rights specified in the first eight amendments, fifteen have to do with it. Seven rights are specified in the Sixth Amendment. These include the right to a speedy trial, a public trial, a jury trial, a notice of accusation, confrontation by opposing witnesses, testimony by favorable witnesses, and the assistance of counsel.

Amendment VII [1791]

In suits at common law, where the value in controversy shall exceed twenty dollars, the right of trial by jury shall be preserved, and no fact tried by a jury shall be otherwise reexamined in any court of the United States, than according to the rules of the common law.

This amendment guarantees people the same right to a trial by jury as was guaranteed by English common law in 1791. Under common law, in civil trials (those involving money damages) the role of the judge was to settle questions of law and that of the jury was to settle questions of fact. The amendment does not specify the size of the jury or its role in a trial, however. The Supreme Court has generally held that those issues be determined by English common law of 1791, which stated that a jury consists of twelve people, that a trial must be conducted before a judge who instructs the jury on the law and advises it on facts, and that a verdict must be unanimous.

Amendment VIII [1791]

Excessive bail shall not be required, nor excessive fines imposed, nor cruel and unusual punishments inflicted.

The language used to guarantee the three rights in this amendment was inspired by the English Bill of Rights of 1689. The Supreme Court has not had a lot to say about "excessive fines." In recent years it has agreed that despite the provision against "excessive bail," persons who are believed to be dangerous to others can be held without bail even before they have been convicted.

Although opponents of the death penalty have not succeeded in using the Eighth Amendment to achieve the end of

capital punishment, the clause regarding "cruel and unusual punishments" has been used to prohibit capital punishment in certain cases.*

Amendment IX [1791]

The enumeration in the Constitution, of certain rights, shall not be construed to deny or disparage others retained by the people.

Some Federalists feared that inclusion of the Bill of Rights in the Constitution would allow later generations of interpreters to claim that the people had surrendered any rights not specifically enumerated there. To guard against this, Madison added language that became the Ninth Amendment. Interest in this heretofore largely ignored amendment revived in 1965 when it was used in a concurring opinion in Griswold v. Connecticut *(1965). While Justice William O. Douglas called on the Third Amendment to support the right to privacy in deciding that case, Justice Arthur Goldberg, in the concurring opinion, argued that the right to privacy regarding contraception was an unenumerated right that was protected by the Ninth Amendment.*

In 1980, the Court ruled that the right of the press to attend a public trial was protected by the Ninth Amendment. Although some scholars argue that modern judges cannot identify the unenumerated rights that the framers were trying to protect, others argue that the Ninth Amendment should be read as providing a constitutional "presumption of liberty" that allows people to act in any way that does not violate the rights of others.

Amendment X [1791]

The powers not delegated to the United States by the Constitution, nor prohibited by it to the States, are reserved to the States respectively, or to the people.

The Antifederalists were especially eager to see a "reserved powers clause" explicitly guaranteeing the states control over their internal affairs. Not surprisingly, the Tenth Amendment has been a frequent battleground in the struggle over states' rights and federal supremacy. Prior to the Civil War, the Jeffersonian Republican Party and Jacksonian Democrats invoked the Tenth Amendment to prohibit the federal government from making decisions about whether people in individual states could own slaves. The Tenth Amendment was virtually suspended during Reconstruction following the Civil War. In 1883, however, the Supreme Court declared the Civil Rights Act of 1875 unconstitutional on the grounds that it violated the Tenth Amendment. Business interests also called on the amendment to block efforts at federal regulation.

The Court was inconsistent over the next several decades as it attempted to resolve the tension between the restrictions of the Tenth Amendment and the powers the Constitution granted to Congress to regulate interstate commerce and levy taxes. The

Court upheld the Pure Food and Drug Act (1906), the Meat Inspection Acts (1906 and 1907), and the White Slave Traffic Act (1910), all of which affected the states, but it struck down an act prohibiting interstate shipment of goods produced through child labor. Between 1934 and 1935, a number of New Deal programs created by Franklin D. Roosevelt were declared unconstitutional on the grounds that they violated the Tenth Amendment. As Roosevelt appointees changed the composition of the Court, the Tenth Amendment was declared to have no substantive meaning. Generally, the amendment is held to protect the rights of states to regulate internal matters such as local government, education, commerce, labor, and business, as well as matters involving families such as marriage, divorce, and inheritance within the state.

Unratified Amendment

Reapportionment Amendment (proposed by Congress September 25, 1789, along with the Bill of Rights)

After the first enumeration required by the first article of the Constitution, there shall be one Representative for every thirty thousand, until the number shall amount to one hundred, after which the proportion shall be so regulated by Congress, that there shall be not less than one hundred Representatives, nor less than one Representative for every forty thousand persons, until the number of Representatives shall amount to two hundred; after which the proportion shall be so regulated by Congress, that there shall not be less than two hundred Representatives, nor more than one Representative for every fifty thousand persons.

★ ★ ★

If the Reapportionment Amendment had passed and remained in effect, the House of Representatives today would have more than 5,000 members rather than 435 to reflect the current U.S. population.

Amendment XI [1798]

The judicial power of the United States shall not be construed to extend to any suit in law or equity, commenced or prosecuted against one of the United States by citizens of another State, or by citizens or subjects of any foreign state.

★ ★ ★

In 1793, the Supreme Court ruled in favor of Alexander Chisholm, executor of the estate of a deceased South Carolina merchant. Chisholm was suing the state of Georgia because the merchant had never been paid for provisions he had supplied during the Revolution. Many regarded this Court decision as an error that violated the intent of the Constitution.

Antifederalists and many other Americans feared a powerful federal court system because they worried that it would become like the British courts of this period, which were accountable only to the monarch. Furthermore, Chisholm v. Georgia prompted a series of suits against state governments by creditors and suppliers who had made loans during the war.

In addition, state legislators and Congress feared that the shaky economies of the new states, as well as the country as a whole, would be destroyed, especially if Loyalists who had fled to other countries sought reimbursement for land and property that had been seized. The day after the Supreme Court announced its decision, a resolution proposing the Eleventh Amendment, which overturned the decision in Chisholm v. Georgia, *was introduced in the U.S. Senate.*

Amendment XII [1804]

The electors shall meet in their respective States, and vote by ballot for President and Vice-President, one of whom, at least, shall not be an inhabitant of the same State with themselves; they shall name in their ballots the person voted for as President, and in distinct ballots the person voted for as Vice-President, and they shall make distinct lists of all persons voted for as President, and of all persons voted for as Vice-President, and of the number of votes for each, which lists they shall sign and certify, and transmit sealed to the seat of government of the United States, directed to the President of the Senate;—the President of the Senate shall, in the presence of the Senate and House of Representatives, open all the certificates and the votes shall then be counted;—the person having the greatest number of votes for President shall be the President, if such number be a majority of the whole number of electors appointed; and if no person have such majority, then from the persons having the highest numbers not exceeding three on the list of those voted for as President, the House of Representatives shall choose immediately, by ballot, the President. But in choosing the President, the votes shall be taken by States, the representation from each State having one vote; a quorum for this purpose shall consist of a member or members from two-thirds of the States, and a majority of all the States shall be necessary to a choice. And if the House of Representatives shall not choose a President whenever the right of choice shall devolve upon them, before *the fourth day of March* next following, then the Vice-President shall act as President, as in the case of the death or other constitutional disability of the President.

The person having the greatest number of votes as Vice-President shall be the Vice-President, if such number be a majority of the whole number of electors appointed; and if no person have a majority, then from the two highest numbers on the list the Senate shall choose the Vice-President; a quorum for the purpose shall consist of two-thirds of the whole number of Senators, and a majority of the whole number shall be necessary to a choice. But no person constitutionally ineligible to the office of President shall be eligible to that of Vice-President of the United States.

★ ★ ★

The framers of the Constitution disliked political parties and assumed that none would ever form. Under the original system, electors chosen by the states would each vote for two candidates. The candidate who won the most votes would become president, and the person who won the second-highest number of votes would become vice-president. Rivalries between Federalists and Republicans led to the formation of political parties, however, even before George Washington had left office. In 1796, Federalist John Adams was chosen as president, and his great rival, Thomas Jefferson (whose party was called the Republican Party), became his vice-president. In 1800, all the electors cast their two votes as one of two party blocs. Jefferson and his fellow Republican nominee, Aaron Burr, were tied with seventy-three votes each. The contest went to the House of Representatives, which finally elected Jefferson after thirty-six ballots. The Twelfth Amendment prevents these problems by requiring electors to vote separately for the president and vice-president.

Unratified Amendment

Titles of Nobility Amendment (proposed by Congress May 1, 1810)

If any citizen of the United States shall accept, claim, receive or retain any title of nobility or honor or shall, without the consent of Congress, accept and retain any present, pension, office or emolument of any kind whatever, from any emperor, king, prince or foreign power, such person shall cease to be a citizen of the United States, and shall be incapable of holding any office of trust or profit under them, or either of them.

★ ★ ★

This amendment would have extended Article 1, section 9, clause 8 of the Constitution, which prevents the awarding of titles by the United States and the acceptance of such awards from foreign powers without congressional consent. Historians speculate that general nervousness about the power of the Emperor Napoleon, who was at that time extending France's empire throughout Europe, may have prompted the proposal. Though it fell one vote short of ratification, Congress and the American people thought the proposal had been ratified, and it was included in many nineteenth-century editions of the Constitution.

The Civil War and Reconstruction Amendments (Thirteenth, Fourteenth, and Fifteenth Amendments)

In the four months between the election of Abraham Lincoln and his inauguration, more than two hundred proposed constitutional amendments were presented to Congress as part of a desperate attempt to hold the rapidly dissolving Union together. Most of these were efforts to appease the southern states by protecting the right to own slaves or by disfranchising African Americans through constitutional amendment. None were able to win the votes required from Congress to send them to the states. Ultimately, the Corwin Amendment seemed to be the only hope for preserving the Union by amending the Constitution.

The northern victors in the Civil War tried to restructure the Constitution just as the war had restructured the nation. Yet they were often divided in their goals. Some wanted to end slavery; others hoped for social and economic equality regardless of race; others hoped that extending the power of the ballot box to former slaves would help create a new political order. The debates over the Thirteenth, Fourteenth, and Fif-

teenth Amendments were bitter. Few of those who fought for these changes were satisfied with the amendments themselves; fewer still were satisfied with their interpretation. Although the amendments put an end to the legal status of slavery, it was nearly a hundred years after the amendments' passage before most of the descendants of former slaves could begin to experience the economic, social, and political equality the amendments were intended to provide.

Unratified Amendment

Corwin Amendment (proposed by Congress March 2, 1861)

No amendment shall be made to the Constitution which will authorize or give to Congress the power to abolish or interfere, within any State, with the domestic institutions thereof, including that of persons held to labor or service by the laws of said State.

★ ★ ★

Following the election of Abraham Lincoln, Congress scrambled to try to prevent the secession of the slaveholding states. House member Thomas Corwin of Ohio proposed the "unamendable" amendment in the hope that by protecting slavery where it existed, Congress would keep the southern states in the Union. Lincoln indicated his support for the proposed amendment in his first inaugural address. Only Ohio and Maryland ratified the Corwin Amendment before it was forgotten.

Amendment XIII [1865]

SECTION 1 Neither slavery nor involuntary servitude, except as a punishment for crime whereof the party shall have been duly convicted, shall exist within the United States, or any place subject to their jurisdiction.

SECTION 2 Congress shall have power to enforce this article by appropriate legislation.

★ ★ ★

Because the Emancipation Proclamation of 1863 abolished slavery only in the parts of the Confederacy still in rebellion, Republicans proposed a Thirteenth Amendment that would extend abolition to the entire South. In February 1865, when the proposal was approved by the House, the gallery of the House was newly opened to black Americans who had a chance at last to see their government at work. Passage of the proposal was greeted by wild cheers from the gallery as well as tears on the House floor, where congressional representatives openly embraced one another.

The problem of ratification remained, however. The Union position was that the Confederate states were part of the country of thirty-six states. Therefore, twenty-seven states were needed to ratify the amendment. When Kentucky and Delaware rejected it, backers realized that without approval from at least four former Confederate states, the amendment would fail. Lincoln's successor, President Andrew Johnson, made ratification of the Thirteenth Amendment a condition for southern states to rejoin the Union. Under those terms, all the former Confederate states except Mississippi accepted the Thirteenth Amendment, and by the end of 1865 the amendment had become part of the Constitution and slavery had been prohibited in the United States.

Amendment XIV [1868]

SECTION 1 All persons born or naturalized in the United States, and subject to the jurisdiction thereof, are citizens of the United States and of the State wherein they reside. No State shall make or enforce any law which shall abridge the privileges or immunities of citizens of the United States; nor shall any State deprive any person of life, liberty, or property, without due process of law; nor deny to any person within its jurisdiction the equal protection of the laws.

SECTION 2 Representatives shall be appointed among the several States according to their respective numbers, counting the whole number of persons in each State, excluding Indians not taxed. But when the right to vote at any election for the choice of electors for President and Vice-President of the United States, Representatives in Congress, the executive and judicial officers of a State, or the members of the legislature thereof, is denied to any of the male inhabitants of such State, being twenty-one years of age and citizens of the United States, or in any way abridged, except for participation in rebellion, or other crime, the basis of representation therein shall be reduced in the proportion which the number of such male citizens shall bear to the whole number of male citizens twenty-one years of age in such State.

SECTION 3 No person shall be a Senator or Representative in Congress, or Elector of President and Vice-President, or hold any office, civil or military, under the United States, or under any State, who, having previously taken an oath, as a member of Congress, or as an officer of the United States, or as a member of any State legislature, or as an executive or judicial officer of any State, to support the Constitution of the United States, shall have engaged in insurrection or rebellion against the same, or given aid or comfort to the enemies thereof. Congress may, by a vote of two-thirds of each house, remove such disability.

SECTION 4 The validity of the public debt of the United States, authorized by law, including debts incurred for payment of pensions and bounties for services in suppressing insurrection or rebellion, shall not be questioned. But neither the United States nor any State shall assume or pay any debt or obligation incurred in aid of insurrection or rebellion against the United States, or any claim for the loss or emancipation of any slave; but all such debts, obligations, and claims shall be held illegal and void.

SECTION 5 The Congress shall have power to enforce, by appropriate legislation, the provisions of this article.

★ ★ ★

Without Lincoln's leadership in the reconstruction of the nation following the Civil War, it soon became clear that the Thirteenth Amendment needed additional constitutional support. Less than a year after Lincoln's assassination, Andrew Johnson was ready to bring the former Confederate states back into the Union with few changes in their governments or politics. Anxious Republicans drafted the Fourteenth Amendment to prevent that from happening. The most important provisions of this complex amendment made all native-born or naturalized persons American citizens and prohibited states from abridging the "privileges or immunities" of citizens; depriving them of "life, liberty, or property, without due process of law"; and denying them "equal protection of the laws." In essence, it made all former slaves citizens and protected the rights of all citizens against violation by their own state governments.

As occurred in the case of the Thirteenth Amendment, former Confederate states were forced to ratify the amendment as a condition of representation in the House and the Senate. The intentions of the Fourteenth Amendment, and how those intentions should be enforced, have been the most debated point of constitutional history. The terms due process and equal protection have been especially troublesome. Was the amendment designed to outlaw racial segregation? Or was the goal simply to prevent the leaders of the rebellious South from gaining political power?

The framers of the Fourteenth Amendment hoped section 2 would produce black voters who would increase the power of the Republican Party. The federal government, however, never used its power to punish states for denying blacks their right to vote. Although the Fourteenth Amendment had an immediate impact in giving black Americans citizenship, it did nothing to protect blacks from the vengeance of whites once Reconstruction ended. In the late nineteenth and early twentieth centuries, section 1 of the Fourteenth Amendment was often used to protect business interests and strike down laws protecting workers on the grounds that the rights of "persons," that is, corporations, were protected by "due process." More recently, the Fourteenth Amendment has been used to justify school desegregation and affirmative action programs, as well as to dismantle such programs.

Amendment XV [1870]

SECTION 1 The right of citizens of the United States to vote shall not be denied or abridged by the United States or by any State on account of race, color, or previous condition of servitude.

SECTION 2 The Congress shall have power to enforce this article by appropriate legislation.

★ ★ ★

The Fifteenth Amendment was the last major piece of Reconstruction legislation. Although earlier Reconstruction acts had already required black suffrage in the South, the Fifteenth Amendment extended black voting rights to the entire nation. Some Republicans felt morally obligated to do away with the double standard between North and South because many northern states had stubbornly refused to enfranchise blacks.

Others believed that the freedman's ballot required the extra protection of a constitutional amendment to shield it from white counterattack. But partisan advantage also played an important role in the amendment's passage, because Republicans hoped that by giving the ballot to northern blacks, they could lessen their party's political vulnerability.

Many women's rights advocates had fought for the amendment. They had felt betrayed by the inclusion of the word male *in section 2 of the Fourteenth Amendment and were further angered when the proposed Fifteenth Amendment failed to prohibit denial of the right to vote on the grounds of sex as well as "race, color, or previous condition of servitude." In this amendment, for the first time, the federal government claimed the power to regulate the franchise, or vote. It was also the first time the Constitution placed limits on the power of the states to regulate access to the franchise. Although ratified in 1870, however, the amendment was not enforced until the twentieth century.*

The Progressive Amendments (Sixteenth–Nineteenth Amendments)

No amendments were added to the Constitution between the Civil War and the Progressive Era. America was changing, however, in fundamental ways. The rapid industrialization of the United States after the Civil War led to many social and economic problems. Hundreds of amendments were proposed, but none received enough support in Congress to be sent to the states. Some scholars believe that regional differences and rivalries were so strong during this period that it was almost impossible to gain a consensus on a constitutional amendment. During the Progressive Era, however, the Constitution was amended four times in seven years.

Amendment XVI [1913]

The Congress shall have power to lay and collect taxes on incomes, from whatever source derived, without apportionment among the several States, and without regard to any census or enumeration.

★ ★ ★

Until passage of the Sixteenth Amendment, most of the money used to run the federal government came from customs duties and taxes on specific items, such as liquor. During the Civil War, the federal government taxed incomes as an emergency measure. Pressure to enact an income tax came from those who were concerned about the growing gap between rich and poor in the United States. The Populist Party began campaigning for a graduated income tax in 1892, and support continued to grow. By 1909 thirty-three proposed income tax amendments had been presented in Congress, but lobbying by corporate and other special interests had defeated them all. In June 1909 the growing pressure for an income tax, which had been endorsed by Presidents Roosevelt and Taft, finally pushed an amendment through the Senate. The required thirty-six states had ratified the amendment by February 1913.

Amendment XVII [1913]

SECTION 1 The Senate of the United States shall be composed of two Senators from each State, elected by the people thereof, for six years; and each Senator shall have one vote. The electors in each State shall have the qualifications requisite for electors of [voters for] the most numerous branch of the State legislatures.

SECTION 2 When vacancies happen in the representation of any State in the Senate, the executive authority of such State shall issue writs of election to fill such vacancies: Provided, that the Legislature of any State may empower the executive thereof to make temporary appointments until the people fill the vacancies by election as the Legislature may direct.

SECTION 3 This amendment shall not be so construed as to affect the election or term of any Senator chosen before it becomes valid as part of the Constitution.

★ ★ ★

The framers of the Constitution saw the members of the House as the representatives of the people and the members of the Senate as the representatives of the states. Originally senators were to be chosen by the state legislators. According to reform advocates, however, the growth of private industry and transportation conglomerates during the late nineteenth century had created a network of corruption in which wealth and power were exchanged for influence and votes in the Senate. Senator Nelson Aldrich, who represented Rhode Island in this period, for example, was known as "the senator from Standard Oil" because of his open support of special business interests.

Efforts to amend the Constitution to allow direct election of senators had begun in 1826, but because any proposal had to be approved by the Senate, reform seemed impossible. Progressives tried to gain influence in the Senate by instituting party caucuses and primary elections, which gave citizens the chance to express their choice of a senator who could then be officially elected by the state legislature. By 1910 fourteen of the country's thirty senators received popular votes through a state primary before the state legislature made its selection. Despairing of getting a proposal through the Senate, supporters of a direct-election amendment had begun in 1893 to seek a convention of representatives from two-thirds of the states to propose an amendment that could then be ratified. By 1905 thirty-one of forty-five states had endorsed such an amendment. Finally, in 1911, despite extraordinary opposition, a proposed amendment passed the Senate; by 1913 it had been ratified.

Amendment XVIII [1919; repealed 1933 by Amendment XXI]

SECTION 1 After one year from the ratification of this article the manufacture, sale, or transportation of intoxicating liquors within, the importation thereof into, or the exportation thereof from the United States and all territory subject to the jurisdiction thereof, for beverage purposes, is hereby prohibited.

SECTION 2 The Congress and the several States shall have concurrent power to enforce this article by appropriate legislation.

SECTION 3 This article shall be inoperative unless it shall have been ratified as an amendment to the Constitution by the legislatures of the several States, as provided by the Constitution, within seven years from the date of the submission thereof to the States by the Congress.

★ ★ ★

The Prohibition Party, formed in 1869, began calling for a constitutional amendment to outlaw alcoholic beverages in 1872. A prohibition amendment was first proposed in the Senate in 1876 and was revived eighteen times before 1913. Between 1913 and 1919, another thirty-nine attempts were made to prohibit liquor in the United States through a constitutional amendment. Prohibition became a key element of the Progressive agenda as reformers linked alcohol and drunkenness to numerous social problems, including the corruption of immigrant voters. Whereas opponents of such an amendment argued that it was undemocratic, supporters claimed that their efforts had widespread public support. The admission of twelve "dry" western states to the Union in the early twentieth century and the spirit of sacrifice during World War I laid the groundwork for passage and ratification of the Eighteenth Amendment in 1919. Opponents added a time limit to the amendment in the hope that they could thereby block ratification, but this effort failed. (See also Amendment XXI.)

Amendment XIX [1920]

SECTION 1 The right of citizens of the United States to vote shall not be denied or abridged by the United States or by any State on account of sex.

SECTION 2 Congress shall have the power to enforce this article by appropriate legislation.

★ ★ ★

Advocates of women's rights tried and failed to link woman suffrage to the Fourteenth and Fifteenth Amendments. Nonetheless, the effort for woman suffrage continued. Between 1878 and 1912, at least one and sometimes as many as four proposed amendments were introduced in Congress each year to grant women the right to vote. Although over time women won very limited voting rights in some states, at both the state and federal levels opposition to an amendment for woman suffrage remained very strong. President Woodrow Wilson and other officials felt that the federal government should not interfere with the power of the states in this matter. And many people were concerned that giving women the vote would result in their abandoning traditional gender roles. In 1919, following a protracted and often bitter campaign of protest in which women went on hunger strikes and chained themselves to fences, an amendment was introduced with the backing of President Wilson. It narrowly passed the Senate (after efforts to limit the suffrage to white women failed) and was adopted in 1920 after Tennessee became the thirty-sixth state to ratify it.

Unratified Amendment

Child Labor Amendment
(proposed by Congress June 2, 1924)

SECTION 1 The Congress shall have power to limit, regulate, and prohibit the labor of persons under eighteen years of age.

SECTION 2 The power of the several States is unimpaired by this article except that the operation of State laws shall be suspended to the extent necessary to give effect to legislation enacted by Congress.

★ ★ ★

Throughout the late nineteenth and early twentieth centuries, alarm over the condition of child workers grew. Opponents of child labor argued that children worked in dangerous and unhealthy conditions, that they took jobs from adult workers, that they depressed wages in certain industries, and that states that allowed child labor had an economic advantage over those that did not. Defenders of child labor claimed that children provided needed income in many families, that working at a young age helped to develop character, and that the effort to prohibit the practice constituted an invasion of family privacy.

In 1916, Congress passed a law that made it illegal to sell through interstate commerce goods made by children. The Supreme Court, however, ruled that the law violated the limits on the power of Congress to regulate interstate commerce. Congress then tried to penalize industries that used child labor by taxing such goods. This measure was also thrown out by the courts. In response, reformers set out to amend the Constitution. The proposed amendment was ratified by twenty-eight states, but by 1925 thirteen states had rejected it. Passage of the Fair Labor Standards Act in 1938, which was upheld by the Supreme Court in 1941, made the amendment irrelevant.

Amendment XX [1933]

SECTION 1 The terms of the President and Vice-President shall end at noon on the twentieth day of January, and the terms of Senators and Representatives at noon on the third day of January, of the years in which such terms would have ended if this article had not been ratified; and the terms of their successors shall then began.

SECTION 2 The Congress shall assemble at least once in every year, and such meeting shall begin at noon on the third day of January, unless they shall by law appoint a different day.

SECTION 3 If, at the time fixed for the beginning of the term of the President, the President-elect shall have died, the Vice-President-elect shall become President. If a President shall not have been chosen before the time fixed for the beginning of his term, or if the President-elect shall have failed to qualify, then the Vice-President-elect shall act as President until a President shall have qualified; and the Congress may by law provide for the case wherein neither a President-elect nor a Vice-President-elect shall have qualified, declaring who shall then act as President, or the manner in which one who is to act shall be selected, and such person shall act accordingly until a President or Vice-President shall have qualified.

SECTION 4 The Congress may by law provide for the case of the death of any of the persons from whom the House of Representatives may choose a President whenever the right of choice shall have devolved upon them, and for the case of the death of any of the persons from whom the Senate may choose a Vice-President whenever the right of choice shall have devolved upon them.

SECTION 5 Sections 1 and 2 shall take effect on the 15th day of October following the ratification of this article.

SECTION 6 This article shall be inoperative unless it shall have been ratified as an amendment to the Constitution by the Legislatures of three-fourths of the several States within seven years from the date of its submission.

Until 1933, presidents took office on March 4. Because elections are held in early November and electoral votes are counted in mid-December, this meant that more than three months passed between the time a new president was elected and when he took office. Moving the inauguration to January shortened the transition period and allowed Congress to begin its term closer to the time of the president's inauguration. Although this seems like a minor change, an amendment was required because the Constitution specifies terms of office. This amendment also deals with questions of succession in the event that a president- or vice-president-elect dies before assuming office. Section 3 also clarifies a method for resolving a deadlock in the electoral college.

Amendment XXI [1933]

SECTION 1 The eighteenth article of amendment to the Constitution of the United States is hereby repealed.

SECTION 2 The transportation or importation into any State, Territory, or Possession of the United States for delivery or use therein of intoxicating liquors, in violation of the laws thereof, is hereby prohibited.

SECTION 3 This article shall be inoperative unless it shall have been ratified as an amendment to the Constitution by conventions in the several States, as provided in the Constitution, within seven years from the date of the submission thereof to the States by the Congress.

★ ★ ★

Widespread violation of the Volstead Act, the law enacted to enforce prohibition, made the United States a nation of lawbreakers. Prohibition caused more problems than it solved by encouraging crime, bribery, and corruption. Further, a coalition of liquor and beer manufacturers, personal liberty advocates, and constitutional scholars joined forces to challenge the amendment. By 1929 thirty proposed repeal amendments had

been introduced in Congress, and the Democratic Party made repeal part of its platform in the 1932 presidential campaign. The Twenty-first Amendment was proposed in February 1933 and ratified less than a year later. The failure of the effort to enforce prohibition through a constitutional amendment has often been cited by opponents of subsequent efforts to shape public virtue and private morality.

Amendment XXII [1951]

SECTION 1 No person shall be elected to the office of the President more than twice, and no person who has held the office of President, or acted as President, for more than two years of a term to which some other person was elected President shall be elected to the office of President more than once. But this article shall not apply to any person holding the office of President when this Article was proposed by the Congress, and shall not prevent any person who may be holding the office of President, or acting as President, during the term within which this Article becomes operative from holding the office of President or acting as President during the remainder of such term.

SECTION 2 This article shall be inoperative unless it shall have been ratified as an amendment to the Constitution by the legislatures of three-fourths of the several States within seven years from the date of its submission to the States by the Congress.

★ ★ ★

George Washington's refusal to seek a third term of office set a precedent that stood until 1912, when former president Theodore Roosevelt sought, without success, another term as an independent candidate. Democrat Franklin Roosevelt was the only president to seek and win a fourth term, though he did so amid great controversy. Roosevelt died in April 1945, a few months after the beginning of his fourth term. In 1946 Republicans won control of the House and the Senate, and early in 1947 a proposal for an amendment to limit future presidents to two four-year terms was offered to the states for ratification. Democratic critics of the Twenty-second Amendment charged that it was a partisan posthumous jab at Roosevelt.

Since the Twenty-second Amendment was adopted, however, the only presidents who might have been able to seek a third term, had it not existed, were Republicans Dwight Eisenhower and Ronald Reagan. Since 1826, Congress has entertained 160 proposed amendments to limit the president to one six-year term. Such amendments have been backed by fifteen presidents, including Gerald Ford and Jimmy Carter.

Amendment XXIII [1961]

SECTION 1 The District constituting the seat of Government of the United States shall appoint in such manner as the Congress may direct: A number of electors of President and Vice-President equal to the whole number of Senators and Representatives in Congress to which the District would be entitled if it were a State, but in no event more than the least populous State; they shall be in addition to those appointed by the States, but they shall be considered for the purposes of the election of President and Vice-President, to be electors appointed by a State; and they shall meet in the District and perform such duties as provided by the twelfth article of amendment.

SECTION 2 The Congress shall have the power to enforce this article by appropriate legislation.

★ ★ ★

When Washington, D.C., was established as a federal district, no one expected that a significant number of people would make it their permanent and primary residence. A proposal to allow citizens of the district to vote in presidential elections was approved by Congress in June 1960 and was ratified on March 29, 1961.

Amendment XXIV [1964]

SECTION 1 The right of citizens of the United States to vote in any primary or other election for President or Vice-President, for electors for President or Vice-President, or for Senator or Representative in Congress, shall not be denied or abridged by the United States or any State by reason of failure to pay any poll tax or other tax.

SECTION 2 The Congress shall have the power to enforce this article by appropriate legislation.

★ ★ ★

In the colonial and Revolutionary eras, financial independence was seen as necessary to political independence, and the poll tax was used as a requirement for voting. By the twentieth century, however, the poll tax was used mostly to bar poor people, especially southern blacks, from voting. Although conservatives complained that the amendment interfered with states' rights, liberals thought that the amendment did not go far enough because it barred the poll tax only in national elections and not in state or local elections. The amendment was ratified in 1964, however, and two years later the Supreme Court ruled that poll taxes in state and local elections also violated the equal protection clause of the Fourteenth Amendment.

Amendment XXV [1967]

SECTION 1 In case of the removal of the President from office or of his death or resignation, the Vice-President shall become President.

SECTION 2 Whenever there is a vacancy in the office of the Vice-President, the President shall nominate a Vice-President who shall take office upon confirmation by a majority vote of both Houses of Congress.

SECTION 3 Whenever the President transmits to the President pro tempore of the Senate and the Speaker of the House of Representatives his written declaration that he is unable to

discharge the powers and duties of his office, and until he transmits to them a written declaration to the contrary, such powers and duties shall be discharged by the Vice-President as Acting President.

SECTION 4 Whenever the Vice-President and a majority of either the principal officers of the executive departments or of such other body as Congress may by law provide, transmit to the President pro tempore of the Senate and the Speaker of the House of Representatives their written declaration that the President is unable to discharge the powers and duties of his office, the Vice-President shall immediately assume the powers and duties of the office as Acting President.

Thereafter, when the President transmits to the President pro tempore of the Senate and the Speaker of the House of Representatives his written declaration that no inability exists, he shall resume the powers and duties of his office unless the Vice-President and a majority of either the principal officers of the executive department[s] or of such other body as Congress may by law provide, transmit within four days to the President pro tempore of the Senate and the Speaker of the House of Representatives their written declaration that the President is unable to discharge the powers and duties of his office. Thereupon Congress shall decide the issue, assembling within forty-eight hours for that purpose if not in session. If the Congress, within twenty-one days after receipt of the latter written declaration, or, if Congress is not in session, within twenty-one days after Congress is required to assemble, determines by two-thirds vote of both Houses that the President is unable to discharge the powers and duties of his office, the Vice-President shall continue to discharge the same as Acting President; otherwise, the President shall resume the powers and duties of his office.

★ ★ ★

The framers of the Constitution established the office of vice-president because someone was needed to preside over the Senate. The first president to die in office was William Henry Harrison, in 1841. Vice-President John Tyler had himself sworn in as president, setting a precedent that was followed when seven later presidents died in office. The assassination of President James A. Garfield in 1881 posed a new problem, however. After he was shot, the president was incapacitated for two months before he died; he was unable to lead the country, and his vice-president, Chester A. Arthur, was unable to assume leadership. Efforts to resolve questions of succession in the event of a presidential disability thus began with the death of Garfield.

In 1963 the assassination of President John F. Kennedy galvanized Congress to action. Vice-President Lyndon Johnson was a chain smoker with a history of heart trouble. According to the 1947 Presidential Succession Act, the two men who stood in line to succeed him were the seventy-two-year-old Speaker of the House and the eighty-six-year-old president of the Senate. There were serious concerns that any of these men might become incapacitated while serving as chief executive. The first time the Twenty-fifth Amendment was used, however, was not in the case of presidential death or illness, but during the Watergate crisis. When Vice-President Spiro T. Agnew was forced to resign following allegations of bribery and tax violations, President Richard M. Nixon appointed House Minority

Leader Gerald R. Ford vice-president. Ford became president following Nixon's resignation eight months later and named Nelson A. Rockefeller as his vice-president. Thus, for more than two years, the two highest offices in the country were held by people who had not been elected to them.

Amendment XXVI [1971]

SECTION 1 The right of citizens of the United States, who are eighteen years of age or older, to vote shall not be denied or abridged by the United States or by any State on account of age.

SECTION 2 The Congress shall have power to enforce this article by appropriate legislation.

★ ★ ★

Efforts to lower the voting age from twenty-one to eighteen began during World War II. Recognizing that those who were old enough to fight a war should have some say in the government policies that involved them in the war, Presidents Eisenhower, Johnson, and Nixon endorsed the idea. In 1970, the combined pressure of the antiwar movement and the demographic pressure of the baby-boom generation led to a Voting Rights Act lowering the voting age in federal, state, and local elections.

In Oregon v. Mitchell *(1970), the state of Oregon challenged the right of Congress to determine the age at which people could vote in state or local elections. The Supreme Court agreed with Oregon. Because the Voting Rights Act was ruled unconstitutional, the Constitution had to be amended to allow passage of a law that would lower the voting age. The amendment was ratified in a little more than three months, making it the most rapidly ratified amendment in U.S. history.*

Unratified Amendment

Equal Rights Amendment (proposed by Congress March 22, 1972; seven-year deadline for ratification extended, June 30, 1982)

SECTION 1 Equality of rights under the law shall not be denied or abridged by the United States or by any State on account of sex.

SECTION 2 The Congress shall have the power to enforce, by appropriate legislation, the provisions of this article.

SECTION 3 This amendment shall take effect two years after the date of ratification.

★ ★ ★

In 1923, soon after women had won the right to vote, Alice Paul, a leading activist in the woman suffrage movement, proposed an amendment requiring equal treatment of men and women. Opponents of the proposal argued that such an amendment would invalidate laws that protected women and would make women subject to the military draft. After the 1964 Civil Rights Act was adopted, protective workplace legislation was removed anyway.

The renewal of the women's movement, as a byproduct of the civil rights and antiwar movements, led to a revival of the Equal Rights Amendment (ERA) in Congress. Disagreements over language held up congressional passage of the proposed amendment, but on March 22, 1972, the Senate approved the ERA by a vote of eighty-four to eight, and it was sent to the states. Six states ratified the amendment within two days, and by the middle of 1973 the amendment seemed well on its way to adoption, with thirty of the needed thirty-eight states having ratified it. In the mid-1970s, however, a powerful "Stop ERA" campaign developed. The campaign portrayed the ERA as a threat to "family values" and traditional relationships between men and women. Although thirty-five states ratified the ERA, five of those state legislatures voted to rescind ratification, and the amendment was never adopted.

Unratified Amendment

D.C. Statehood Amendment (proposed by Congress August 22, 1978)

SECTION 1 For purposes of representation in the Congress, election of the President and Vice President, and article V of this Constitution, the District constituting the seat of government of the United States shall be treated as though it were a State.

SECTION 2 The exercise of the rights and powers conferred under this article shall be by the people of the District constituting the seat of government, and as shall be provided by Congress.

SECTION 3 The twenty-third article of amendment to the Constitution of the United States is hereby repealed.

SECTION 4 This article shall be inoperative, unless it shall have been ratified as an amendment to the Constitution by the legislatures of three-fourths of the several states within seven years from the date of its submission.

★ ★ ★

The 1961 ratification of the Twenty-third Amendment, giving residents of the District of Columbia the right to vote for a president and vice-president, inspired an effort to give residents of the district full voting rights. In 1966, President Lyndon Johnson appointed a mayor and city council; in 1971, D.C. residents were allowed to name a nonvoting delegate to the House; and in 1981, residents were allowed to elect the mayor and city council. Congress retained the right to overrule laws that might affect commuters, the height of federal buildings, and selection of judges and prosecutors. The district's nonvoting delegate to Congress, Walter Fauntroy, lobbied fiercely for a congressional amendment granting statehood to the district. In 1978 a proposed amendment was approved and sent to the states. A number of states quickly ratified the amendment, but, like the ERA, the D.C. Statehood Amendment ran into trouble. Opponents argued that section 2 created a separate category of "nominal" statehood. They argued that the federal district should be eliminated and that the territory should be reabsorbed into the state of Maryland. Although these theoretical arguments were strong, some scholars believe that racist attitudes toward the predominantly black population of the city also constituted a factor leading to the defeat of the amendment.

Amendment XXVII [1992]

No law, varying the compensation for the services of the Senators and Representatives, shall take effect, until an election of Representatives shall have intervened.

★ ★ ★

Whereas the Twenty-sixth Amendment was the most rapidly ratified amendment in U.S. history, the Twenty-seventh Amendment had the longest journey to ratification. First proposed by James Madison in 1789 as part of the package that included the Bill of Rights, this amendment had been ratified by only six states by 1791. In 1873, however, it was ratified by Ohio to protest a massive retroactive salary increase by the federal government. Unlike later proposed amendments, this one came with no time limit on ratification. In the early 1980s, Gregory D. Watson, a University of Texas economics major, discovered the "lost" amendment and began a single-handed campaign to get state legislators to introduce it for ratification. In 1983 it was accepted by Maine. In 1984 it passed the Colorado legislature. Ratifications trickled in slowly until May 1992, when Michigan and New Jersey became the thirty-eighth and thirty-ninth states, respectively, to ratify. This amendment prevents members of Congress from raising their own salaries without giving voters a chance to vote them out of office before they can benefit from the raises.

★

The American Nation

Admission of States into the Union

State	Date of Admission	State	Date of Admission	State	Date of Admission
1. Delaware	December 7, 1787	18. Louisiana	April 30, 1812	35. West Virginia	June 20, 1863
2. Pennsylvania	December 12, 1787	19. Indiana	December 11, 1816	36. Nevada	October 31, 1864
3. New Jersey	December 18, 1787	20. Mississippi	December 10, 1817	37. Nebraska	March 1, 1867
4. Georgia	January 2, 1788	21. Illinois	December 3, 1818	38. Colorado	August 1, 1876
5. Connecticut	January 9, 1788	22. Alabama	December 14, 1819	39. North Dakota	November 2, 1889
6. Massachusetts	February 6, 1788	23. Maine	March 15, 1820	40. South Dakota	November 2, 1889
7. Maryland	April 28, 1788	24. Missouri	August 10, 1821	41. Montana	November 8, 1889
8. South Carolina	May 23, 1788	25. Arkansas	June 15, 1836	42. Washington	November 11, 1889
9. New Hampshire	June 21, 1788	26. Michigan	January 26, 1837	43. Idaho	July 3, 1890
10. Virginia	June 25, 1788	27. Florida	March 3, 1845	44. Wyoming	July 10, 1890
11. New York	July 26, 1788	28. Texas	December 29, 1845	45. Utah	January 4, 1896
12. North Carolina	November 21, 1789	29. Iowa	December 28, 1846	46. Oklahoma	November 16, 1907
13. Rhode Island	May 29, 1790	30. Wisconsin	May 29, 1848	47. New Mexico	January 6, 1912
14. Vermont	March 4, 1791	31. California	September 9, 1850	48. Arizona	February 14, 1912
15. Kentucky	June 1, 1792	32. Minnesota	May 11, 1858	49. Alaska	January 3, 1959
16. Tennessee	June 1, 1796	33. Oregon	February 14, 1859	50. Hawaii	August 21, 1959
17. Ohio	March 1, 1803	34. Kansas	January 29, 1861		

Territorial Expansion

Territory	Date Acquired	Square Miles	How Acquired
Original states and territories	1783	888,685	Treaty of Paris
Louisiana Purchase	1803	827,192	Purchased from France
Florida	1819	72,003	Adams-Onís Treaty
Texas	1845	390,143	Annexation of independent country
Oregon	1846	285,580	Oregon Boundary Treaty
Mexican cession	1848	529,017	Treaty of Guadalupe Hidalgo
Gadsden Purchase	1853	29,640	Purchased from Mexico
Midway Islands	1867	2	Annexation of uninhabited islands
Alaska	1867	589,757	Purchased from Russia
Hawaii	1898	6,450	Annexation of independent country
Wake Island	1898	3	Annexation of uninhabited island
Puerto Rico	1899	3,435	Treaty of Paris
Guam	1899	212	Treaty of Paris
The Philippines	1899–1946	115,600	Treaty of Paris; granted independence
American Samoa	1900	76	Treaty with Germany and Great Britain
Panama Canal Zone	1904–1978	553	Hay–Bunau-Varilla Treaty
U.S. Virgin Islands	1917	133	Purchased from Denmark
Trust Territory of the Pacific Islands*	1947	717	United Nations Trusteeship

*A number of these islands have recently been granted independence: Federated States of Micronesia, 1990; Marshall Islands, 1991; Palau, 1994.

Presidential Elections

Year	Candidates	Parties	Percentage of Popular Vote	Electoral Vote	Percentage of Voter Participation
1789	**George Washington**	No party designations	*	69	
	John Adams[†]			34	
	Other candidates			35	
1792	**George Washington**	No party designations		132	
	John Adams			77	
	George Clinton			50	
	Other candidates			5	
1796	**John Adams**	Federalist		71	
	Thomas Jefferson	Democratic-Republican		68	
	Thomas Pinckney	Federalist		59	
	Aaron Burr	Democratic-Republican		30	
	Other candidates			48	
1800	**Thomas Jefferson**	Democratic-Republican		73	
	Aaron Burr	Democratic-Republican		73	
	John Adams	Federalist		65	
	Charles C. Pinckney	Federalist		64	
	John Jay	Federalist		1	
1804	**Thomas Jefferson**	Democratic-Republican		162	
	Charles C. Pinckney	Federalist		14	
1808	**James Madison**	Democratic-Republican		122	
	Charles C. Pinckney	Federalist		47	
	George Clinton	Democratic-Republican		6	
1812	**James Madison**	Democratic-Republican		128	
	De Witt Clinton	Federalist		89	
1816	**James Monroe**	Democratic-Republican		183	
	Rufus King	Federalist		34	
1820	**James Monroe**	Democratic-Republican		231	
	John Quincy Adams	Independent Republican		1	
1824	**John Quincy Adams**	Democratic-Republican	30.5	84	26.9
	Andrew Jackson	Democratic-Republican	43.1	99	
	Henry Clay	Democratic-Republican	13.2	37	
	William H. Crawford	Democratic-Republican	13.1	41	
1828	**Andrew Jackson**	Democratic	56.0	178	57.6
	John Quincy Adams	National Republican	44.0	83	
1832	**Andrew Jackson**	Democratic	54.5	219	55.4
	Henry Clay	National Republican	37.5	49	
	William Wirt	Anti-Masonic	8.0	7	
	John Floyd	Democratic	‡	11	
1836	**Martin Van Buren**	Democratic	50.9	170	57.8
	William H. Harrison	Whig		73	
	Hugh L. White	Whig		26	
	Daniel Webster	Whig	49.1	14	
	W. P. Mangum	Whig		11	
1840	**William H. Harrison**	Whig	53.1	234	80.2
	Martin Van Buren	Democratic	46.9	60	

*Prior to 1824, most presidential electors were chosen by state legislators rather than by popular vote.
[†]Before the Twelfth Amendment was passed in 1804, the electoral college voted for two presidential candidates; the runner-up became vice-president.
‡Percentages below 2.5 have been omitted. Hence the percentage of popular vote might not total 100 percent.

Year	Candidates	Parties	Percentage of Popular Vote	Electoral Vote	Percentage of Voter Participation
1844	**James K. Polk**	Democratic	49.6	170	78.9
	Henry Clay	Whig	48.1	105	
	James G. Birney	Liberty	2.3		
1848	**Zachary Taylor**	Whig	47.4	163	72.7
	Lewis Cass	Democratic	42.5	127	
	Martin Van Buren	Free Soil	10.1		
1852	**Franklin Pierce**	Democratic	50.9	254	69.6
	Winfield Scott	Whig	44.1	42	
	John P. Hale	Free Soil	5.0		
1856	**James Buchanan**	Democratic	45.3	174	78.9
	John C. Frémont	Republican	33.1	114	
	Millard Fillmore	American	21.6	8	
1860	**Abraham Lincoln**	Republican	39.8	180	81.2
	Stephen A. Douglas	Democratic	29.5	12	
	John C. Breckinridge	Democratic	18.1	72	
	John Bell	Constitutional Union	12.6	39	
1864	**Abraham Lincoln**	Republican	55.0	212	73.8
	George B. McClellan	Democratic	45.0	21	
1868	**Ulysses S. Grant**	Republican	52.7	214	78.1
	Horatio Seymour	Democratic	47.3	80	
1872	**Ulysses S. Grant**	Republican	55.6	286	71.3
	Horace Greeley	Democratic	43.9		
1876	**Rutherford B. Hayes**	Republican	48.0	185	81.8
	Samuel J. Tilden	Democratic	51.0	184	
1880	**James A. Garfield**	Republican	48.5	214	79.4
	Winfield S. Hancock	Democratic	48.1	155	
	James B. Weaver	Greenback-Labor	3.4		
1884	**Grover Cleveland**	Democratic	48.5	219	77.5
	James G. Blaine	Republican	48.2	182	
1888	**Benjamin Harrison**	Republican	47.9	233	79.3
	Grover Cleveland	Democratic	48.6	168	
1892	**Grover Cleveland**	Democratic	46.1	277	74.7
	Benjamin Harrison	Republican	43.0	145	
	James B. Weaver	People's	8.5	22	
1896	**William McKinley**	Republican	51.1	271	79.3
	William J. Bryan	Democratic	47.7	176	
1900	**William McKinley**	Republican	51.7	292	73.2
	William J. Bryan	Democratic; Populist	45.5	155	
1904	**Theodore Roosevelt**	Republican	57.4	336	65.2
	Alton B. Parker	Democratic	37.6	140	
	Eugene V. Debs	Socialist	3.0		
1908	**William H. Taft**	Republican	51.6	321	65.4
	William J. Bryan	Democratic	43.1	162	
	Eugene V. Debs	Socialist	2.8		
1912	**Woodrow Wilson**	Democratic	41.9	435	58.8
	Theodore Roosevelt	Progressive	27.4	88	
	William H. Taft	Republican	23.2	8	
	Eugene V. Debs	Socialist	6.0		

Year	Candidates	Parties	Percentage of Popular Vote	Electoral Vote	Percentage of Voter Participation
1916	**Woodrow Wilson**	Democratic	49.4	277	61.6
	Charles E. Hughes	Republican	46.2	254	
	A. L. Benson	Socialist	3.2		
1920	**Warren G. Harding**	Republican	60.4	404	49.2
	James M. Cox	Democratic	34.2	127	
	Eugene V. Debs	Socialist	3.4		
1924	**Calvin Coolidge**	Republican	54.0	382	48.9
	John W. Davis	Democratic	28.8	136	
	Robert M. La Follette	Progressive	16.6	13	
1928	**Herbert C. Hoover**	Republican	58.2	444	56.9
	Alfred E. Smith	Democratic	40.9	87	
1932	**Franklin D. Roosevelt**	Democratic	57.4	472	56.9
	Herbert C. Hoover	Republican	39.7	59	
1936	**Franklin D. Roosevelt**	Democratic	60.8	523	61.0
	Alfred M. Landon	Republican	36.5	8	
1940	**Franklin D. Roosevelt**	Democratic	54.8	449	62.5
	Wendell L. Willkie	Republican	44.8	82	
1944	**Franklin D. Roosevelt**	Democratic	53.5	432	55.9
	Thomas E. Dewey	Republican	46.0	99	
1948	**Harry S Truman**	Democratic	49.6	303	53.0
	Thomas E. Dewey	Republican	45.1	189	
1952	**Dwight D. Eisenhower**	Republican	55.1	442	63.3
	Adlai E. Stevenson	Democratic	44.4	89	
1956	**Dwight D. Eisenhower**	Republican	57.6	457	60.6
	Adlai E. Stevenson	Democratic	42.1	73	
1960	**John F. Kennedy**	Democratic	49.7	303	64.0
	Richard M. Nixon	Republican	49.5	219	
1964	**Lyndon B. Johnson**	Democratic	61.1	486	61.7
	Barry M. Goldwater	Republican	38.5	52	
1968	**Richard M. Nixon**	Republican	43.4	301	60.6
	Hubert H. Humphrey	Democratic	42.7	191	
	George C. Wallace	American Independent	13.5	46	
1972	**Richard M. Nixon**	Republican	60.7	520	55.5
	George S. McGovern	Democratic	37.5	17	
1976	**Jimmy Carter**	Democratic	50.1	297	54.3
	Gerald R. Ford	Republican	48.0	240	
1980	**Ronald W. Reagan**	Republican	50.7	489	53.0
	Jimmy Carter	Democratic	41.0	49	
	John B. Anderson	Independent	6.6	0	
1984	**Ronald W. Reagan**	Republican	58.4	525	52.9
	Walter F. Mondale	Democratic	41.6	13	
1988	**George H. W. Bush**	Republican	53.4	426	50.3
	Michael Dukakis	Democratic	45.6	111*	
1992	**Bill Clinton**	Democratic	43.7	370	55.1
	George H. W. Bush	Republican	38.0	168	
	H. Ross Perot	Independent	19.0	0	
1996	**Bill Clinton**	Democratic	49	379	49.0
	Robert J. Dole	Republican	41	159	
	H. Ross Perot	Reform	8	0	

*One Dukakis elector cast a vote for Lloyd Bentsen.

Supreme Court Justices

Name	Terms of Service	Appointed by	Name	Terms of Service	Appointed by
John Jay*, N.Y.	1789–1795	Washington	Joseph McKenna, Cal.	1898–1925	McKinley
James Wilson, Pa.	1789–1798	Washington	Oliver W. Holmes, Mass.	1902–1932	T. Roosevelt
John Rutledge, S.C.	1790–1791	Washington	William R. Day, Ohio	1903–1922	T. Roosevelt
William Cushing, Mass.	1790–1810	Washington	William H. Moody, Mass.	1906–1910	T. Roosevelt
John Blair, Va.	1790–1796	Washington	Horace H. Lurton, Tenn.	1910–1914	Taft
James Iredell, N.C.	1790–1799	Washington	Charles E. Hughes, N.Y.	1910–1916	Taft
Thomas Johnson, Md.	1792–1793	Washington	**Edward D. White,** La.	1910–1921	Taft
William Paterson, N.J.	1793–1806	Washington	Willis Van Devanter, Wy.	1911–1937	Taft
John Rutledge, S.C.	1795	Washington	Joseph R. Lamar, Ga.	1911–1916	Taft
Samuel Chase, Md.	1796–1811	Washington	Mahlon Pitney, N.J.	1912–1922	Taft
Oliver Ellsworth, Conn.	1796–1800	Washington	James C. McReynolds, Tenn.	1914–1941	Wilson
Bushrod Washington, Va.	1799–1829	J. Adams	Louis D. Brandeis, Mass.	1916–1939	Wilson
Alfred Moore, N.C.	1800–1804	J. Adams	John H. Clarke, Ohio	1916–1922	Wilson
John Marshall, Va.	1801–1835	J. Adams	**William H. Taft,** Conn.	1921–1930	Harding
William Johnson, S.C.	1804–1834	Jefferson	George Sutherland, Utah	1922–1938	Harding
Brockholst Livingston, N.Y.	1807–1823	Jefferson	Pierce Butler, Minn.	1923–1939	Harding
Thomas Todd, Ky.	1807–1826	Jefferson	Edward T. Sanford, Tenn.	1923–1930	Harding
Gabriel Duvall, Md.	1811–1835	Madison	Harlan F. Stone, N.Y.	1925–1941	Coolidge
Joseph Story, Mass.	1812–1845	Madison	**Charles E. Hughes,** N.Y.	1930–1941	Hoover
Smith Thompson, N.Y.	1823–1843	Monroe	Owen J. Roberts, Pa.	1930–1945	Hoover
Robert Trimble, Ky.	1826–1828	J. Q. Adams	Benjamin N. Cardozo, N.Y.	1932–1938	Hoover
John McLean, Ohio	1830–1861	Jackson	Hugo L. Black, Ala.	1937–1971	F. Roosevelt
Henry Baldwin, Pa.	1830–1844	Jackson	Stanley F. Reed, Ky.	1938–1957	F. Roosevelt
James M. Wayne, Ga.	1835–1867	Jackson	Felix Frankfurter, Mass.	1939–1962	F. Roosevelt
Roger B. Taney, Md.	1836–1864	Jackson	William O. Douglas, Conn.	1939–1975	F. Roosevelt
Philip P. Barbour, Va.	1836–1841	Jackson	Frank Murphy, Mich.	1940–1949	F. Roosevelt
John Cartron, Tenn.	1837–1865	Van Buren	**Harlan F. Stone,** N.Y.	1941–1946	F. Roosevelt
John McKinley, Ala.	1838–1852	Van Buren	James R. Byrnes, S.C.	1941–1942	F. Roosevelt
Peter V. Daniel, Va.	1842–1860	Van Buren	Robert H. Jackson, N.Y.	1941–1954	F. Roosevelt
Samuel Nelson, N.Y.	1845–1872	Tyler	Wiley B. Rutledge, Iowa	1943–1949	F. Roosevelt
Levi Woodbury, N.H.	1845–1851	Polk	Harold H. Burton, Ohio	1945–1958	Truman
Robert C. Grier, Pa.	1846–1870	Polk	**Frederick M. Vinson,** Ky.	1946–1953	Truman
Benjamin R. Curtis, Mass.	1851–1857	Fillmore	Tom C. Clark, Texas	1949–1967	Truman
John A. Campbell, Ala.	1853–1861	Pierce	Sherman Minton, Ind.	1949–1956	Truman
Nathan Clifford, Me.	1858–1881	Buchanan	**Earl Warren,** Cal.	1953–1969	Eisenhower
Noah H. Swayne, Ohio	1862–1881	Lincoln	John Marshall Harlan, N.Y.	1955–1971	Eisenhower
Samuel F. Miller, Iowa	1862–1890	Lincoln	William J. Brennan Jr., N.J.	1956–1990	Eisenhower
David Davis, Ill.	1862–1877	Lincoln	Charles E. Whittaker, Mo.	1957–1962	Eisenhower
Stephen J. Field, Cal.	1863–1897	Lincoln	Potter Stewart, Ohio	1958–1981	Eisenhower
Salmon P. Chase, Ohio	1864–1873	Lincoln	Bryon R. White, Colo.	1962–1993	Kennedy
William Strong, Pa.	1870–1880	Grant	Arthur J. Goldberg, Ill.	1962–1965	Kennedy
Joseph P. Bradley, N.J.	1870–1892	Grant	Abe Fortas, Tenn.	1965–1969	Johnson
Ward Hunt, N.Y.	1873–1882	Grant	Thurgood Marshall, Md.	1967–1991	Johnson
Morrison R. Waite, Ohio	1874–1888	Grant	**Warren E. Burger,** Minn.	1969–1986	Nixon
John M. Harlan, Ky.	1877–1911	Hayes	Harry A. Blackmun, Minn.	1970–1994	Nixon
William B. Woods, Ga.	1881–1887	Hayes	Lewis F. Powell Jr., Va.	1971–1987	Nixon
Stanley Matthews, Ohio	1881–1889	Garfield	William H. Rehnquist, Ariz.	1971–1986	Nixon
Horace Gray, Mass.	1882–1902	Arthur	John Paul Stevens, Ill.	1975–	Ford
Samuel Blatchford, N.Y.	1882–1893	Arthur	Sandra Day O'Connor, Ariz.	1981–	Reagan
Lucius Q. C. Lamar, Miss.	1888–1893	Cleveland	**William H. Rehnquist,** Ariz.	1986–	Reagan
Melville W. Fuller, Ill.	1888–1910	Cleveland	Antonin Scalia, Va.	1986–	Reagan
David J. Brewer, Kan.	1890–1910	B. Harrison	Anthony M. Kennedy, Cal.	1988–	Reagan
Henry B. Brown, Mich.	1891–1906	B. Harrison	David H. Souter, N.H.	1990–	Bush
George Shiras Jr., Pa.	1892–1903	B. Harrison	Clarence Thomas, Ga.	1991–	Bush
Howell E. Jackson, Tenn.	1893–1895	B. Harrison	Ruth Bader Ginsburg, N.Y.	1993–	Clinton
Edward D. White, La.	1894–1910	Cleveland	Stephen G. Breyer, Mass.	1994–	Clinton
Rufus W. Peckham, N.Y.	1896–1909	Cleveland			

*Chief Justices are printed in bold type.

The American People: A Demographic Survey

A Demographic Profile of the American People

Year	Life Expectancy from Birth		Average Age at First Marriage		Number of Children Under 5 (per 1,000 Women Aged 20–44)	Percentage of Women in Paid Employment	Percentage of Paid Workers Who Are Women
	White	Black	Men	Women			
1820					1,295	6.2	7.3
1830					1,145	6.4	7.4
1840					1,085	8.4	9.6
1850					923	10.1	10.8
1860					929	9.7	10.2
1870					839	13.7	14.8
1880					822	14.7	15.2
1890			26.1	22.0	716	18.2	17.0
1900	47.6	33.0	25.9	21.9	688	21.2	18.1
1910	50.3	35.6	25.1	21.6	643	24.8	20.0
1920	54.9	45.3	24.6	21.2	604	23.9	20.4
1930	61.4	48.1	24.3	21.3	511	24.4	21.9
1940	64.2	53.1	24.3	21.5	429	25.4	24.6
1950	69.1	60.8	22.8	20.3	589	29.1	27.8
1960	70.6	63.6	22.8	20.3	737	34.8	32.3
1970	71.7	65.3	22.5	20.6	530	43.3	38.0
1980	74.4	68.1	24.7	22.0	440	51.5	42.6
1990	76.2	71.4	26.1	23.9	377	57.4	45.2
1996	76.8	71.9	26.3	24.3	339	59.8	46.1

Source: Historical Statistics of the United States, Colonial Times to 1970 (1975); Statistical Abstract of the United States, 1998.

American Population

Year	Population	Percentage Increase	Year	Population	Percentage Increase
1610	350	—	1810	7,239,881	36.4
1620	2,300	557.1	1820	9,638,453	33.1
1630	4,600	100.0	1830	12,866,020	33.5
1640	26,600	478.3	1840	17,069,453	32.7
1650	50,400	90.8	1850	23,191,876	35.9
1660	75,100	49.0	1860	31,443,321	35.6
1670	111,900	49.0	1870	39,818,449	26.6
1680	151,500	35.4	1880	50,155,783	26.0
1690	210,400	38.9	1890	62,947,714	25.5
1700	250,900	19.2	1900	75,994,575	20.7
1710	331,700	32.2	1910	91,972,266	21.0
1720	466,200	40.5	1920	105,710,620	14.9
1730	629,400	35.0	1930	122,775,046	16.1
1740	905,600	43.9	1940	131,669,275	7.2
1750	1,170,800	29.3	1950	150,697,361	14.5
1760	1,593,600	36.1	1960	179,323,175	19.0
1770	2,148,100	34.8	1970	203,235,298	13.3
1780	2,780,400	29.4	1980	226,545,805	11.5
1790	3,929,214	41.3	1990	248,709,873	9.8
1800	5,308,483	35.1	1997	267,901,000	7.7

Note: These figures largely ignore the native American population. Census takers never made any effort to count the native American population that lived outside their political jurisdictions and compiled only casual and incomplete enumerations of those living within their jurisdictions until 1890. In that year the federal government attempted a full count of the Indian population: the Census found 125,719 Indians in 1890, compared with only 12,543 in 1870 and 33,985 in 1880.

Source: Historical Statistics of the United States, Colonial Times to 1970 (1975); Statistical Abstract of the United States, 1998.

White/Nonwhite Population

Urban/Rural Population

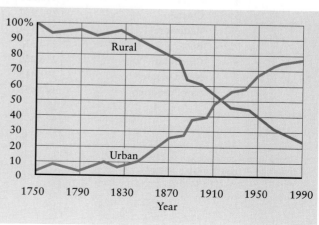

The Ten Largest Cities by Population, 1700–1990

		City	Population			City	Population
1700	1.	Boston	6,700	1910	1.	New York	4,766,883
	2.	New York	4,937*		2.	Chicago	2,185,283
	3.	Philadelphia	4,400†		3.	Philadelphia	1,549,008
1790	1.	Philadelphia	42,520		4.	St. Louis	687,029
	2.	New York	33,131		5.	Boston	670,585
	3.	Boston	18,038		6.	Cleveland	560,663
	4.	Charleston, S.C.	16,359		7.	Baltimore	558,485
	5.	Baltimore	13,503		8.	Pittsburgh	533,905
	6.	Salem, Mass.	7,921		9.	Detroit	465,766
	7.	Newport, R.I.	6,716		10.	Buffalo	423,715
	8.	Providence, R.I.	6,380	1930	1.	New York	6,930,446
	9.	Marblehead, Mass.	5,661		2.	Chicago	3,376,438
	10.	Portsmouth, N.H.	4,720		3.	Philadelphia	1,950,961
1830	1.	New York	197,112		4.	Detroit	1,568,662
	2.	Philadelphia	161,410		5.	Los Angeles	1,238,048
	3.	Baltimore	80,620		6.	Cleveland	900,429
	4.	Boston	61,392		7.	St. Louis	821,960
	5.	Charleston, S.C.	30,289		8.	Baltimore	804,874
	6.	New Orleans	29,737		9.	Boston	781,188
	7.	Cincinnati	24,831		10.	Pittsburgh	669,817
	8.	Albany, N.Y.	24,209	1950	1.	New York	7,891,957
	9.	Brooklyn, N.Y.	20,535		2.	Chicago	3,620,962
	10.	Washington, D.C.	18,826		3.	Philadelphia	2,071,605
1850	1.	New York	515,547		4.	Los Angeles	1,970,358
	2.	Philadelphia	340,045		5.	Detroit	1,849,568
	3.	Baltimore	169,054		6.	Baltimore	949,708
	4.	Boston	136,881		7.	Cleveland	914,808
	5.	New Orleans	116,375		8.	St. Louis	856,796
	6.	Cincinnati	115,435		9.	Washington, D.C.	802,178
	7.	Brooklyn, N.Y.	96,838		10.	Boston	801,444
	8.	St. Louis	77,860	1970	1.	New York	7,895,563
	9.	Albany, N.Y.	50,763		2.	Chicago	3,369,357
	10.	Pittsburgh	46,601		3.	Los Angeles	2,811,801
1870	1.	New York	942,292		4.	Philadelphia	1,949,996
	2.	Philadelphia	674,022		5.	Detroit	1,514,063
	3.	Brooklyn, N.Y.	419,921‡		6.	Houston	1,233,535
	4.	St. Louis	310,864		7.	Baltimore	905,787
	5.	Chicago	298,977		8.	Dallas	844,401
	6.	Baltimore	267,354		9.	Washington, D.C.	756,668
	7.	Boston	250,526		10.	Cleveland	750,879
	8.	Cincinnati	216,239	1990	1.	New York	7,322,564
	9.	New Orleans	191,418		2.	Los Angeles	3,485,398
	10.	San Francisco	149,473		3.	Chicago	2,783,726
					4.	Houston	1,630,553
					5.	Philadelphia	1,585,577
					6.	San Diego	1,110,549
					7.	Detroit	1,027,974
					8.	Dallas	1,006,877
					9.	Phoenix	983,403
					10.	San Antonio	935,933

*Figure from a census taken in 1698.
†Philadelphia figures include suburbs.
‡Annexed to New York in 1898.
Source: U.S. Census data.

Immigration by Decade

Year	Number	Percentage of Total Population	Year	Number	Percentage of Total Population
1821–1830	151,824	1.6	1921–1930	4,107,209	3.9
1831–1840	599,125	4.6	1931–1940	528,431	0.4
1841–1850	1,713,251	10.0	1941–1950	1,035,039	0.7
1851–1860	2,598,214	11.2	1951–1960	2,515,479	1.6
1861–1870	2,314,824	7.4	1961–1970	3,321,677	1.8
1871–1880	2,812,191	7.1	1971–1980	4,493,000	2.2
1881–1890	5,246,613	10.5	1981–1990	7,338,000	3.0
1891–1900	3,687,546	5.8	1991–1996	6,146,300	2.3
1901–1910	8,795,386	11.6	Total	29,485,135	
1911–1920	5,735,811	6.2			
Total	33,654,785		1821–1996		
			Grand Total	63,139,920	

Source: U.S. Bureau of the Census, *Historical Statistics of the United States, Colonial Times to 1970* (1975), part 1, 105–106; *Statistical Abstract of the United States, 1998.*

Regional Origins

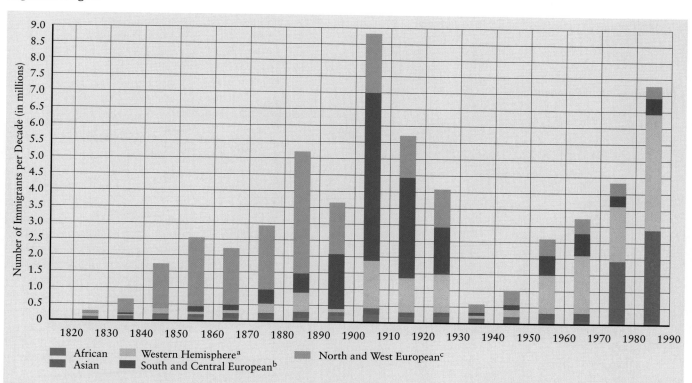

■ African ■ Western Hemisphere[a] ■ North and West European[c]
■ Asian ■ South and Central European[b]

[a] Canada and all countries in South America and Central America.

[b] Italy, Spain, Portugal, Greece, Germany (Austria included, 1938–1945), Poland, Czechoslovakia (since 1920), Yugoslavia (since 1920), Hungary (since 1861), Austria (since 1861, except 1938–1945), former USSR (excludes Asian USSR between 1931 and 1963), Latvia, Estonia, Lithuania, Finland, Romania, Bulgaria, Turkey (in Europe), and other European countries not classified elsewhere.

[c] Great Britain, Ireland, Norway, Sweden, Denmark, Iceland, Netherlands, Belgium, Luxembourg, Switzerland, France.

Source: Stephan Thernstrom, ed., *Harvard Encyclopedia of American Ethnic Groups* (1980), 480; U.S. Bureau of the Census, *Statistical Abstract of the United States, 1991.*

The Labor Force (Thousands of Workers)

Year	Agriculture	Mining	Manufacturing	Construction	Trade	Other	Total
1810	1,950	11	75	—	—	294	2,330
1840	3,570	32	500	290	350	918	5,660
1850	4,520	102	1,200	410	530	1,488	8,250
1860	5,880	176	1,530	520	890	2,114	11,110
1870	6,790	180	2,470	780	1,310	1,400	12,930
1880	8,920	280	3,290	900	1,930	2,070	17,390
1890	9,960	440	4,390	1,510	2,960	4,060	23,320
1900	11,680	637	5,895	1,665	3,970	5,223	29,070
1910	11,770	1,068	8,332	1,949	5,320	9,041	37,480
1920	10,790	1,180	11,190	1,233	5,845	11,372	41,610
1930	10,560	1,009	9,884	1,988	8,122	17,267	48,830
1940	9,575	925	11,309	1,876	9,328	23,277	56,290
1950	7,870	901	15,648	3,029	12,152	25,870	65,470
1960	5,970	709	17,145	3,640	14,051	32,545	74,060
1970	3,463	516	20,746	4,818	15,008	34,127	78,678
1980	3,364	979	21,942	6,215	20,191	46,612	99,303
1990	3,223	724	21,346	7,764	24,622	60,849	117,914
1997	3,399	634	20,835	8,302	26,777	69,611	129,558

Source: Historical Statistics of the United States, Colonial Times to 1970 (1975), 139; Statistical Abstract of the United States, 1998, table 675.

Changing Labor Patterns

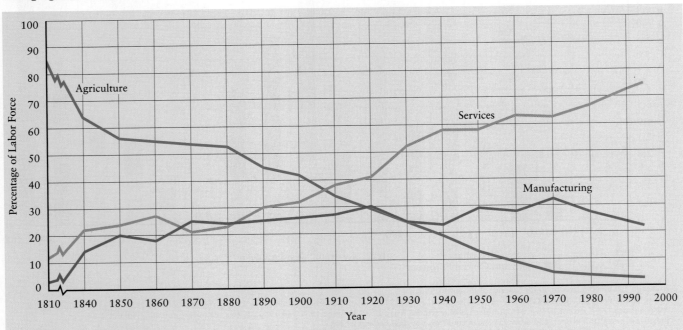

Source: Historical Statistics of the United States, Colonial Times to 1970 (1975), 139; Statistical Abstract of the United States, 1998, table 675.

Birth Rate, 1820–2000

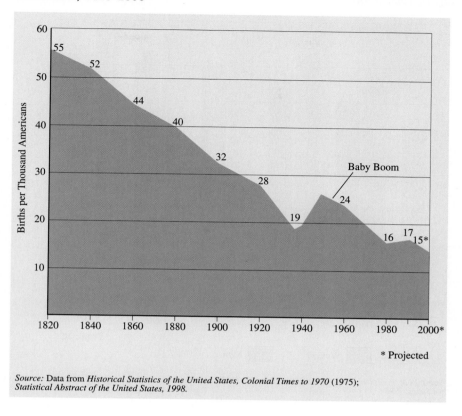

Source: Data from *Historical Statistics of the United States, Colonial Times to 1970* (1975); *Statistical Abstract of the United States, 1998.*

Death Rate, 1900–2000

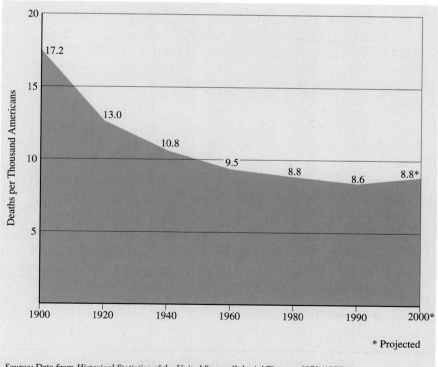

Source: Data from *Historical Statistics of the United States, Colonial Times to 1970* (1975); *Statistical Abstract of the United States, 1998.*

Life Expectancy (at birth), 1900–2000

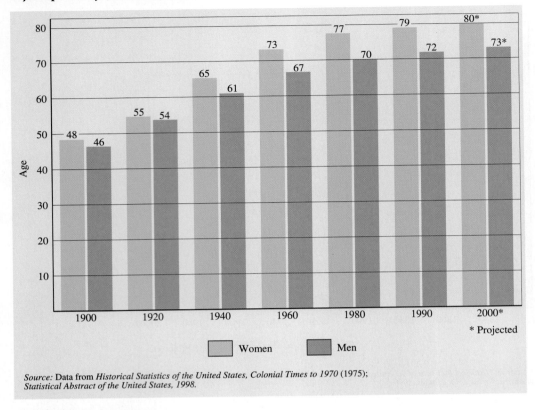

Source: Data from *Historical Statistics of the United States, Colonial Times to 1970* (1975); *Statistical Abstract of the United States, 1998.*

The Aging of the U.S. Population, 1850–1997

Source: *Historical Statistics of the United States, Colonial Times to 1970* (1975); *Statistical Abstract of the United States, 1998.*

The American Government and Economy

The Growth of the Federal Government

| Year | Employees (millions) | | Receipts and Outlays ($ millions) | |
	Civilian	Military	Receipts	Outlays
1900	0.23	0.12	567	521
1910	0.38	0.13	676	694
1920	0.65	0.34	6,649	6,358
1930	0.61	0.25	4,058	3,320
1940	1.04	0.45	6,900	9,600
1950	1.96	1.46	40,900	43,100
1960	2.38	2.47	92,500	92,200
1970	3.00	3.06	193,700	196,600
1980	2.99	2.05	517,112	590,920
1990	3.13	2.07	1,031,321	1,252,705
1997	2.78	1.43	1,579,292	1,601,235

Source: Statistical Profile of the United States, 1900–1980; Statistical Abstract of the United States, 1998.

Gross National Product, 1840–1990

Note: GNP values have not been adjusted for inflation or deflation. GNP is plotted here on a logarithmic scale.
Source: Statistical Abstract of the United States, 1995.

GNP per Capita, 1840–1990

Note: GNP values have not been adjusted for inflation or deflation. GNP is plotted here on a logarithmic scale.

Main Sectors of the U.S. Economy: 1849, 1899, 1950, 1990

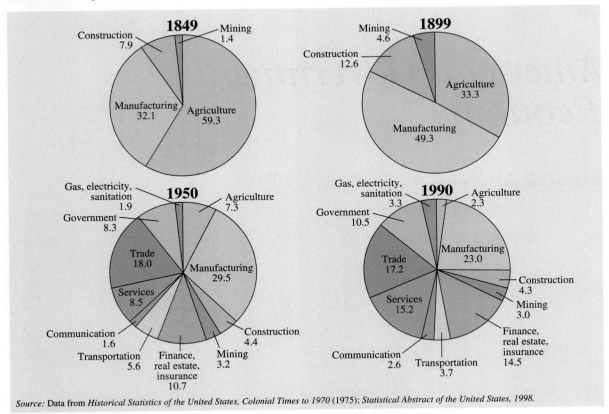

Source: Data from *Historical Statistics of the United States, Colonial Times to 1970* (1975); *Statistical Abstract of the United States, 1998.*

This index estimates how consumer prices changed on the average over ten-year intervals. Such estimates are highly uncertain, particularly when they are used to make comparisons over long periods of time.

To convert £ (pounds Sterling, until 1770) or $ (U.S. dollars, beginning in 1780) from any date in the past to the equivalent in 1990 dollars, multiply the historical price by the appropriate conversion multiplier. For example, £10 Sterling in 1730 would equal about $867 in 1990 (£10 × 86.7 = $867), or $10 in 1870 would equal about $99 in 1990 ($10 × 9.9 = $99). Then add another 20 percent to account for the rise in prices between 1990 and 1997.

Consumer Price Index and Conversion Table

Year	Price Index (1860 = 100)	Conversion Multiplier
1700	130	53.3
1710	100	69.3
1720	76	91.3
1730	80	86.7
1740	66	105.1
1750	84	82.6
1760	96	72.3
1770	100	69.3
1780	165	9.5
1790	148	10.6
1800	151	10.4
1810	148	10.6
1820	141	11.1
1830	111	14.1
1840	104	15.1
1850	94	16.6
1860	100	15.6
1870	157	9.9
1880	123	12.7
1890	109	14.3
1900	101	15.5
1910	114	13.7
1920	240	6.5
1930	200	7.8
1940	168	9.3
1950	288	5.4
1960	354	4.4
1970	464	3.4
1980	985	1.6
1990	1563	1.0
1997	1950	0.8

Source: Adapted from John J. McCusker, "How Much Is That in Real Money? A Historical Price Index for Use as a Deflator of Money Value in the Economy of the United States," *Proceedings of the American Antiquarian Society*, vol. 101, pt. 2 (1991), 297–390; *Statistical Abstract of the United States*, 1998, table 772.

Internet Resources

The Internet has been a useful place for scholars to communicate and publish information in recent years. Electronic discussion lists, electronic journals, and primary texts are among the resources available for historians on the Internet. The following sources are good places to find historical information. You can also search for information on the World Wide Web using any of a number of search engines. However, bear in mind that there is no board of editors screening Internet sites for accuracy or usefulness, and the search engines generally rely on free-text searches rather than subject headings. Be critical of all of your sources, particularly those found on the Internet.

American Memory: Historical Collection from the National Digital Library Program. <http://rs6.loc.gov/amhome.html> An Internet site that features digitized primary source materials from the Library of Congress, among them African American pamphlets, Civil War photographs, documents from the Continental Congress and the Constitutional Convention of 1774–1790, materials on woman suffrage, and oral histories.

Decisions of the U.S. Supreme Court. <http://supct.law.cornell.edu/supct/#historic> This database can be used to search for information on various Supreme Court cases. Although the site primarily covers cases that occurred after 1990, there is information on some earlier historic cases. The justices' opinions, as originally written, are also included.

Directory of Scholarly and Professional Electronic Conferences. <http://n2h2.com/KOVAKS/> A good place to find out what electronic conversations are going on in a scholarly discipline. Includes a good search facility and instructions on how to connect to e-mail discussion lists, newsgroups, and interactive chat sites with academic content. Once identified, these conferences are good places to raise questions, find out what controversies are currently stirring the profession, and even find out about grants and jobs.

Douglass Archives of American Public Addresses. <http://douglass.speech.nwu.edu/> An electronic archive of American speeches and documents by a variety of people from Jane Addams to Jonathan Edwards to Theodore Roosevelt.

Historical Text Archive. <http://www.msstate.edu/Archives/History> A Web interface for the oldest and largest Internet site for historical documents. Includes sections on native American, African American, and U.S. history, in which can be found texts of the Declaration of Independence, the U.S. Constitution, the Constitution of Iroquois Nations, World War II surrender documents, photograph collections, and a great deal more. These can be used online or saved as files.

History Links from Yahoo. <http://www.yahoo.com/Humanities/History/> A categorically arranged and frequently updated site list for all types of history. Some of the sources are more useful than others, but this can be a helpful gateway to some good information.

Index of Civil War Information. <http://www.cwc.lsu.edu/cwc/civlink.html> Compiled by the United States Civil War Center, this index lists everything from diaries to historic battlefields to reenactments.

Index of Native American Resources on the Internet. <http://hanksville.phast.umass.edu/misc/Naresources.html> A vast index of native American resources organized by category. Within the history category, links are organized under subcategories: oral history, written history, geographical areas, timelines, and photographs and photographic archives. A central place to come in the search for information on native American history.

Index of Resources for Historians. <http://kuhttp.cc.ukans.edu/history/index.html> A vast list of more than 1,700 links to sites of interest to historians, arranged alphabetically by general topic. Some links are to sources for general reference information, but most are on historical topics. A good place to start an exploration of Internet resources.

Internet Archives of Texts and Documents. <http://history.hanover.edu/texts.html> As stated on its home page, the purpose of this site is to make primary sources available to students and faculty. Arranged chronologically, geographically, and by subject, the site lists speeches, reports, and other primary-document links. It also includes some secondary sources on each subject.

Internet Resources for Students of Afro-American History. <http://www.libraries.rutgers.edu/rulib/socsci/hist/afrores.html> A good place to begin research on topics in African American history. The site is indexed and linked to a wide variety of sources, including primary documents, text collections, and archival sources on African American history. Individual documents such as slave narratives and petitions; the Fugitive Slave Acts; and speeches by W. E. B. Du Bois, Booker T. Washington, and Martin Luther King Jr. are categorized by century.

The Martin Luther King Jr. Papers Project. <http://www.stanford.edu/group/King/> Organized by Stanford University, this site gives information about Martin Luther King Jr. and offers some of his writings.

Native Web. <http://www.nativeweb.org> One of the best organized and most accessible sites available on native American issues, *Native Web* combines an events calendar and message board with history, statistics, a list of news sources, archives, new and updated related sites each week, and documents. The text is indexed and can be searched by subject, nation, and geographic region.

Perry-Castañeda Library Map Collection. <http://www.lib.utexas.edu/Libs/PCL/MAP_collection.html> The University of

Texas at Austin Library has put over seven hundred U.S. maps on the Web for viewing by students and professors alike.

Smithsonian Institution. <http://www.si.edu> Organized by subject, such as military history or Hispanic/Latino American resources, this site offers selected links to sites hosted by Smithsonian Institution museums and organizations. Content includes graphics of museum pieces and relevant textual information, book suggestions, maps, and links.

United States History Index. <http://www.ukans.edu/~usa/index.html> Maintained by a history professor and arranged by subject, such as women's history, labor history, and agricultural history, this index provides links to a variety of other sites. Although the list is extensive, it does not include a synopsis of each site, which makes finding specific information a time-consuming process.

United States History Resources by Period. <http://www.cms.ccsd.k12.co.us/SONY/Intrecs/byperiod.html> This list of links to a variety of history sites is arranged chronologically and updated periodically.

United States Holocaust Museum. <http://www.ushmm.org/learn.html> This site contains information about the Holocaust Museum in Washington, D.C., as well as information on the Holocaust in general, and it lists links to related sites.

Women's History Resources. <http://www.mcps.k12.md.us/curriculum/socialstd/Women_Bookmarks.html> An extensive listing of women's history sources available on the Internet. The site indexes resources on subjects as diverse as woman suffrage, women in the workplace, and celebrated women writers. Some of the links are to equally vast indexes, providing an overwhelming wealth of information.

Credits

Chapter 2

"A Franciscan Reflects on Spain's Policies in New Mexico." Excerpt from pages 692–695 in *Don Juan de Onate, Colonizer of New Mexico, 1595–1628*, Part II, by G. P. Hammond and Agapito Rey. Reprinted by permission of University of New Mexico Press.

"Mary Rowlandson: A Captivity Narrative." Excerpt from *Original Narratives of Early American History, Narratives of Indian Wars, 1675–1699*, vol. 14, edited by C. H. Lincoln. Barnes and Noble, 1952. Courtesy of the publisher.

Chapter 4

"Nathan Cole: The Power of a Preacher." Excerpt from pages 67–71 in *The Great Awakening: Documents on the Revival of Religion, 1740–1745* by Richard Bushman. Copyright © 1989 by Richard Bushman. Reprinted by permission of University of North Carolina Press.

"Charles Woodmason: Social Chaos on the Carolina Frontier." Excerpt from pages 16–18, 41–46, in *The Carolina Backcountry on the Eve of the Revolution* by Charles Woodmason and edited by Richard Hooker. Copyright © 1953 by Richard Hooker. Reprinted by permission of University of North Carolina Press.

"Gottlieb Mittelberger: The Perils of Migration." Excerpt from *Journey to Pennsylvania* by Gottlieb Mittelberger, edited and translated by Oscar Handlin. Copyright © 1960 by the President and Fellows of Harvard College. Reprinted by permission of the publisher, Harvard University Press and Oscar Handlin.

Chapter 5

"Josiah Quincy Jr: The Threat of Mob Rule." Excerpt from pages 61–63 in *Colonies to Nation: A Documented History of the American Revolution* edited by Jack P. Greene. Copyright © 1967 by Jack P. Greene. Reprinted by permission of the publisher.

"To the Associators of the City of Philadelphia." Letter to The Library Company of Philadelphia from *Pennsylvania History*, volume 52 (October 1985). Courtesy of The Library Company of Philadelphia.

"A British View of Lexington and Concord." As stated by Lieutenant Colonel Franklin Smith in *Proceedings of the Massachusetts Historical Society 14* (1875–1876): 350ff. Courtesy Massachusetts Historical Society.

Chapter 6

"On Jefferson and Natural Rights." From Benjamin Banneker's letter to Thomas Jefferson in 1791, as it appears on pages 102–105 in *Founding the Republic: A Documentary History* by John J. Patrick, editor. Copyright © 1995 by John J. Patrick.

Reprinted with permission of Greenwood Publishing Group, Inc., Westport, CT.

Chapter 7

"Abigail and John Adams: The Status of Women." From pages 1, 94, 370, 382–383, 402–403 in *The Adams Family Correspondence* by L. H. Butterfield, editor. Copyright © 1963 by the Massachusetts Historical Society. Reprinted by permission of the publisher, Harvard University Press.

"Change in the Wealth of Elected Officials." Adapted from "Government by the People: The American Revolution and the Democratization of the Legislatures" by Jackson Turner Main. Published in *William and Mary Quarterly* 3rd series, vol. 23, 1966. Reprinted by permission.

Chapter 8

"Chief Shabonne: The Battle of Tippecanoe, 1811." Excerpt from pages 355–359 in *Indiana Magazine of History*, December 1921, Wesley Whickar, editor. Reprinted by permission of the Indiana Historical Society.

"Alexis de Tocqueville: Law and Lawyers in the United States." Excerpt from pages 283–290 in *Democracy in America* by Alexis de Tocqueville. Copyright © 1945 and renewed 1973 by Alfred A. Knopf, Inc. Reprinted by permission of the publisher.

Chapter 9

"Jacob Stroyer: A Child Learns the Meaning of Slavery." Excerpt from pages 71–72 in *Ordinary Americans: U.S. History Through the Eyes of Everyday People* by Linda R. Monk, editor. Copyright © 1994 Close Up Foundation, Alexandria, Virginia. Reprinted with permission.

"Eliza Southgate: The Dilemmas of Womanhood." Excerpt from page 285 in *Sources of the American Social Tradition* edited by David J. Rothman and Sheila M. Rothman. Copyright © 1975 by David J. Rothman. Reprinted by permission of BasicBooks, a division of HarperCollins Publishers, Inc.

Table 9.1: "Number of Lawyers in Three Selected States, to 1820." Adapted from p. 49 in *Law in the New Republic: Private Law and the Public Estate* by George Dargo. Copyright © 1980 by George Dargo. Reprinted by permission of The McGraw-Hill Companies.

Table 9.2: "African Slaves Imported into North America by Ethnicity, 1775–1809." Adapted from table A.6 in "From Slaves, Convicts, and Servants to Free Passengers: The Transformation of Immigration in the Era of the American Revolution," as published in the *Journal of American History* 85 (June 1998). Reprinted with permission.

Excerpt from pages 27–29 in *"Smoked Yankees" and the Struggle for Empire, 1898–1902* by Willard B. Gatewood. Copyright © 1987 by the Board of Trustees of the University of Arkansas. Reprinted by permission of the University of Arkansas Press.

Chapter 22

"Frederick A. Pottle: Mustard Gas." Excerpt from pages 117–118 in *Stretchers: The Story of a Hospital on the Western Front* by Frederick A. Pottle. Copyright © 1929 by Frederick A. Pottle. Reprinted by permission of Yale University Press.

Chapter 27

"Mark Goodson: Red Hunting on the Quiz Shows; or, What's My Party Line?" Excerpt from pages 320–324 in *Memories of the American Inquisition: An Oral History* by Griffin Fariello. Copyright © 1995 by Griffin Fariello. Reprinted by permission of W.W. Norton & Company, Inc.

"Isaac Nelson: Atomic Witness." Excerpt from pages 133–135 in *American Ground Zero: The Secret Nuclear War* by Carole Gallagher. Copyright © 1993 Carole Gallagher. Reprinted by permission of the author.

"Jean Monnet: Truman's Generous Proposal." Excerpt from pages 264–265 in *Memoirs* by Jean Monnet, translated by Richard Mayne. Translation copyright © 1978 by Doubleday, a division of Bantam Doubleday Dell Publishing Group, Inc. Used by permission of Doubleday, a division of Random House, Inc.

Chapter 28

"Joy Wilner: A Fifties Housewife." Excerpt from pages 103–104 in *The Fifties: An Oral History* by Brett Harvey, editor. Copyright © 1993 by Brett Harvey. Reprinted by permission of HarperCollins Publishers, Inc.

"Ann Moody: 'We Would Like to Be Served.'" Excerpt from pages 264–267 in *Coming of Age in Mississippi* by Anne Moody. Copyright © 1968 by Anne Moody. Used by permission of Doubleday, a division of Random House, Inc.

"Hanoch Bartov: 'Everyone Has a Car.'" Excerpt from *Arbaah Israelim Vekhol America (Four Israelis and the Whole of America)* by Hanoch Bartov. © Hanoch Bartov, Acum House, Israel. Reprinted by permission of the author and Acum House.

Chapter 29

"Mary Crow Dog: The Trail of Broken Treaties." Excerpt from pages 86–91 in *Lakota Woman* by Mary Crow Dog and Richard Erdos. Copyright © 1990 by Mary Crow Dog and Richard Erdos. Reprinted by permission of Grove Atlantic, Inc.

"Dave Cline: A Vietnam Vet Remembers." Excerpt from pages 135–141 in *Winter Soldiers: An Oral History of the Vietnam Veterans against the War* by Richard Stacewicz. Copyright © 1997 by Richard Stacewicz. Reprinted by permission of Macmillan, a division of Simon & Schuster.

"Che Guevara: Vietnam and the World Freedom Struggle." Excerpt from pages 144–159 of *Ernesto Che Guevara Speaks: Selected Speeches & Writings.* Copyright © Pathfinder Press. Reprinted by permission.

Chapter 30

"Phyllis Ellison: Busing in Boston." Excerpt from pages 600, 610, 612–613 in *Voices of Freedom: An Oral History of the Civil Rights Movement from the 1950s through the 1980s* by Henry Hampton and Steve Fayer. Copyright © 1990 by Blackside, Inc. Used by permission of Bantam Books, a division of Bantam Doubleday Dell Publishing Group, Inc.

"Watergate and Due Process." Excerpt from *The London Times*, Editorial, June 5, 1973, page 17. © Times Newspapers Limited, London, 1973. Reprinted by permission of News International Syndication.

"David Kopay: The Real Score: A Gay Athlete Comes Out." Excerpt from *The David Kopay Story: An Extraordinary Self-Revelation* by David Kopay & Perry D. Young. Copyright © 1988 by David Kopay & Perry D. Young. Reprinted by permission of Donald I. Fine, an imprint of Dutton/Plume, a division of Penguin Putnam, Inc.

Chapter 31

"Saddam Hussein: Calling for a Holy War against the United States." From *The New York Times*, September 6, 1990, page A19. Copyright © 1990 by The New York Times Company. Reprinted by permission.

"Cuauhtemoc Menendez: The Undocumented Worker." Excerpt from pages 410–411 in *Mexican Voices, American Dreams: An Oral History of Mexican Immigration to the United States* by Marilyn P. Davis. Copyright © 1990 by Marilyn P. Davis. Reprinted by permission of Henry Holt & Company, Inc.

Figure 31.2: "Productivity and Wages, 1982–1995." From *The New York Times*, January 2, 1996, page C20. Copyright © 1996 by The New York Times Company. Reprinted by permission.

Index

Stanley, Ann Lee (Mother Ann), 308, 385
Stanton, Edwin M., 486
Stanton, Elizabeth Cady, 392, 393, 396, 397*i*, 488
Staple Act of 1663, 74*t*
Starr, Ellen Gates, 645
Starr, Kenneth, 1034
Star Wars, defense initiative, 1007
state governments
    and commonwealth system, 270–271, 328
    democratic evolution of, 348
    labor laws, 648
    Populist view, 588
    Progressive Era reform, 644–645, 648*t*, 649, 650–651
    takeover of federal programs, 1010, 1035
    voting rights for women, 649, 650*m*
states and federal government
    Continental Congress issue, 222–224, 226
    due process clause, 580
    and economic development, 270–272
    interstate commerce, 275, 330, 537
    and Jackson presidency, 356–358
    Kentucky and Virginia Resolutions, 240
    McCulloch v. Maryland, 274–275
    state-chartered banks, 267, 274, 357–360
    transportation projects, 328, 352
States' Rights Party, 881
steamboats, 330
steam power
    steam engines, 544
    technology powered by, 316–317
    war ships, 678–679
steam turbine, 544
Stearns, Sarah Ripley, 108
steel
    Homestead strike, 569
    manufacturing of, 542–543, 738*i*
    uses of, 543
Steel Workers Organizing Committee (SWOC), 813, 813*i*
Steffens, Lincoln, 642
Stein, Gertrude, 762, 763
Steinbeck, John, 783, 788, 824
Steinem, Gloria, 990
Stephens, Alexander, 445, 470
Stephenson, David, 760
Steuben, General von, 191
Stevens, Thaddeus, 430, 459, 485
Stevens, Wallace, 764
Stevenson, Adlai E., 881, 888
Stewart, Jimmy, 847
Stewart, Maria W., 392
Stiles, Ezra, 141, 211
Stimson, Henry, 834, 838, 861
Stinkards, 10
stint, 560
stock
    railroad corporations, 546, 547
    of trusts, 659
stock exchange, New York, 332
stock market crash. *See also* Great Depression

of 1893, 585–587
of 1929, 772–774
of 1987, 1010
Stockton, Robert F., 417
stockyards, 551, 552
Stoddard, Solomon, 126
Stone, Lucy, 392, 398, 488
Stone, Samuel, 281
Stono rebellion, 95
STOP ERA organization, 991–992
Stowe, Harriet Beecher, 391, 393, 426
Strategic Air Command, 893
Strategic Arms Limitations Treaty (SALT I), 967
Strategic Arms Limitations Treaty (SALT II), 999
Strategic Defense Initiative (SDI), 1007
streetcars, 610
streptomycin, 913
strikes, 569–570
    agricultural, 790
    antistrike tactics of employers, 567
    federal intervention, 569–570, 571, 659, 796
    federal regulation, 639
    first strikes, 326
    grape pickers, 958
    Homestead strike, 569
    miners, 571
    post–World War I, 731–732
    post–World War II, 880–881
    Pullman strike, 569–570, 639
    railroad workers, 541
    World War II era, 843
strip mining, 822
Stroyer, Jacob, 297
Stuart, Gilbert, 223*i*
Student Non-Violent Coordinating Committee (SNCC), 927
Students for a Democratic Society (SDS), 950, 951
Student Strike against War, 782
Stuyvesant, Peter, 48
submarine, U-boat, 708, 710
suburbs
    and African Americans, 906–907
    automobiles and growth of, 748, 757, 908
    industrial parks, 910
    middle class, 631–632
    post–World War II boom, 906–907
    social class divisions, 631–632
    wealthy, 629, 920
subway, 611, 613
Suez Canal, 673, 894–895
suffrage. *See* voting rights; women's movement
sugar
    Cuba, 695
    European demand for, 82
    Hawaii, 673*i*
    plantations, 82–83, 86–87
    refineries, 96
    World War II rationing, 849
Sugar Act of 1764, 149–150
    modification of, 157
Sukarno, Achmed, 894

Sullivan, Louis, 612
Sullivan, Tim, 620
    biographical information, 622–623
Sumner, Charles, 407, 459, 485, 499
Sumner, William Graham, 579
Sun Also Rises, The (Hemingway), 763
Sun Belt
    post–World War II boom, 907–908, 984
    states of, 907
Sun Dance, 510
Sunday, Billy, 624, 761
Superfund, 998
Superman, 784
supermarkets, 746
supernatural
    African beliefs, 82
    native American beliefs, 67
    Puritan belief in, 61–62, 121–122
supply-side economics, Reagan era, 1006–1007
Supreme Court
    abortion decisions, 977, 990, 1010
    Bush appointments, 1010–1011
    Clinton appointment, 1031
    creation of, 230
    on due process, 580
    judicial review, 274
    Nixon appointments, 977
    packing, during New Deal, 811
    Progressive Era labor decisions, 648*t*
    Reagan appointments, 1008
    on separate but equal, 598
    women on, 1008, 1008*i*
Surveyors of the Woods, 153
Susquehanna Company, 137
Susquehannock Indians, 55
Sutter, John A., 421
Swann v. Charlotte-Mecklenburg Board of Education, 977
Swedish, 515, 616
Swift & Co., 552, 743
Swift, Gustavus F., 551–552
Swisshelm, Jane, 453
syndicalism, meaning of, 571
Syngman Rhee, 877
Syria, 982

tabloids, 751
Taft, Robert A., 878, 888
Taft, William Howard (1857–1930), 726
    anti–civil rights position, 655
    and election of 1908, 663
    as president, 663–664, 695, 697, 699
Taft-Hartley Act, 881, 883, 884
Taino Indians, 22
Taiwan, 876, 967
Tallender, Lydia, 287
Tallmadge, James, 292
Talleyrand, Charles, 239
Tammany Hall, 582, 620, 622
Taney, Roger B., 355
    as Chief Justice, 364–365, 433
    as secretary of Treasury, 360
tangible property, meaning of, 334
Tanner, Henry O., 763
Tappan, Arthur, 340, 400, 402
Tappan, Lewis, 340, 400, 402, 403

Political divisions as of September 1999